43RD EDITION

KOVELS'
Antiques &
Collectibles
PRICE GUIDE 2011

BLACK DOG
& LEVENTHAL
PUBLISHERS
NEW YORK

SEP 10

CH/
cont

Published by
Black Dog & Leventhal Publishers, Inc.
151 W. 19th Street
New York, NY 10011

Distributed by
Workman Publishing Company
225 Varick Street
New York, NY 10014

Designed by Sheila Hart Design, Inc.
Manufactured in the United States of America

ISBN-13: 978-1-57912-853-1
Library of Congress Cataloging-in-Publication Data is available on file at
the offices of the publisher.

Paperback
b d f h g e c a

Front cover photographs, from top to bottom:
Furniture, cupboard, corner, painted pine;
Lamp, electric, Wilkinson;
Toy, robot, Robert the Robot
On the spine: Tiffany silver, sauceboat, floral repousse
Back cover photographs, from top to bottom:
A. Walter, vase, misty landscape;
Gaudy Dutch, plate, single rose;
Advertising, mirror, Liberty Mills, peacock

Authors' photographs © Molly Nook (top) and Alex Montes de Oca (bottom)

BOOKS BY RALPH AND TERRY KOVEL

American Country Furniture, 1780–1875

A Directory of American Silver, Pewter, and Silver Plate

Kovels' Advertising Collectibles Price List

Kovels' American Antiques 1750–1900

Kovels' American Art Pottery

Kovels' American Collectibles 1900–2000

Kovels' American Silver Marks, 1650 to the Present

Kovels' Antiques & Collectibles Fix-It Source Book

Kovels' Antiques & Collectibles Price Guide

Kovels' Bid, Buy, and Sell Online

Kovels' Book of Antique Labels

Kovels' Bottles Price List

Kovels' Collector's Guide to American Art Pottery

Kovels' Collectors' Guide to Limited Editions

Kovels' Collectors' Source Book

Kovels' Depression Glass & Dinnerware Price List

Kovels' Dictionary of Marks—Pottery and Porcelain, 1650 to 1850

Kovels' Guide to Selling, Buying, and Fixing Your Antiques and Collectibles

Kovels' Guide to Selling Your Antiques & Collectibles

Kovels' Illustrated Price Guide to Royal Doulton

Kovels' Know Your Antiques

Kovels' Know Your Collectibles

Kovels' New Dictionary of Marks—Pottery and Porcelain, 1850 to the Present

Kovels' Organizer for Collectors

Kovels' Price Guide for Collector Plates, Figurines, Paperweights, and Other Limited Edition Items

Kovels' Quick Tips: 799 Helpful Hints on How to Care for Your Collectibles

Kovels' Yellow Pages: A Resource Guide for Collectors

The Label Made Me Buy It: From Aunt Jemima to Zonkers—The Best-Dressed Boxes,
Bottles, and Cans from the Past

INTRODUCTION

This is the forty-third year *Kovels' Antiques & Collectibles Price Guide* has been published. Many things have changed over the past few years. The ongoing worldwide recession is still affecting the value of stocks, real estate—and antiques. The absence of eBay as a live online auction platform as of January 1, 2009, created new opportunities for auction galleries, shop owners, and online sites that hoped to replace the live buy-and-sell market of eBay. Most large auctions are now held online and on land in real time, so anyone in any country in the world can bid. Final prices are showing that the average auction ends with many unsold lots, but the auction makes enough money to stay in business. Prices for items offered by individuals on eBay have dropped; it is said that only about one-third of the collectibles offered are actually sold. Prices have gone up for some things that have international appeal and down for other things, like Hummel and Royal Doulton figurines and "country furniture" with peeling paint. Through it all, the malls, shows, and shops have experienced a slower economy and lower prices than they could get four years ago. But we have talked to collectors and dealers, and most agree that "good stuff sells" and that well-run shows, shops, and sales are doing "okay." Usable furniture in good condition and "smalls" are selling as well as the best of every type of antique or collectible. And auction prices are closer to retail than they were before because of the large, new, worldwide pool of bidders.

Kovels' Antiques and Collectibles Price Guide 2011 still has the same reliable content, plus two generations of collectors editing the content. The book has 2,600 color photographs, 42,000 prices, and dozens of added facts of interest and tips about care. Each photograph is shown with a complete caption that includes the price. The book has color tabs and color-coded paragraphs that make it easy to find the listings you want. And it has a modern, readable typestyle. There are about 775 categories with introductory paragraphs that include company history. We make some changes in the paragraphs every year to indicate new owners or new distributors or new information about production dates. And, as always, all of the antiques and collectibles priced here were offered for sale during the past year, most of them in the American market.

READ THIS FIRST

This is a book for the collector. We check prices, visit shops, shows, and flea markets, read hundreds of publications and catalogs, check Internet sales and other online services, and decide which antiques and collectibles are of most interest to most collectors. We concentrate on the average pieces in any category. Sometimes high-priced items are included so you will realize that rarities are very valuable.

Examples of furniture, silver, Tiffany, art pottery, and some other items may sell for more than $40,000; we list a few. Most listed pieces cost less than $10,000. The highest price in this book is $422,500 for a Tiffany laburnum lamp with a leaded glass shade and a bronze base. The lowest price is 15 cents for a milk bottle cap labeled H.F. Morrill Milk & Cream Dairy. Made in about 1950, it was only 1 ⅝ inches in diameter. The smallest item in the book is a ¼-inch mother-of-pearl button for $7. The biggest is a piece of furniture, a walnut wall unit by Edgar Britton, decorated with animals and trees that is 12 x 16 feet. It sold for $14,640.

We also include the weird and the wonderful. This year we list a 3-foot-long brass safety pin for $94. A brass Victorian "skirt lifter" shaped like a hand is priced $285. A blown glass "lacemaker's lamp" with cork and pewter burners sold for $281. A vintage wooden coffin with a hole in it so the head could be viewed, 12 x 52 inches, sold for only $75. We wondered about a sign, 40 x 22 inches, that sold for $468. It read "Dr. Weaver's Heave Cure does it." Another strange object is a "squirter," a bisque bust of a naughty girl lactating. The 2 ½ x 1-inch figure made in Germany in about 1900 sold for $55. A 1795 pewter commode shaped like a Pilgrim hat, 7 ½ inches, sold for $411.

There is an aqua bottle that held poisonous embalming fluid. The label said "National Casket Company." Price? Only $50. We wonder who bought the brass knuckles listed this year. The 4 x 3-inch piece with sharp points sold for $690.

Collecting is alive and well. Although the national economic outlook is still gloomy, the prices of antiques and collectibles are "behaving" normally. Some dealers tell us that serious collectors seem to have missed collecting and are returning to shop at local auctions, shows, flea markets, and garage sales. The high end of the art market also seems to be attracting more interest, although even there it is only the very best pieces that are bringing record prices. Over the years, we have seen the rise and fall (or sometimes the fall and rise) of Victorian, oak, Mid-Century Modern, and shabby country furniture, bottles, trivets, Hummels, collector plates, plastic, majolica, Royal Doulton, pressed glass, milk glass, and Depression glass. But through it all, informed collectors and dealers made good buys and profitable sales.

When we started collecting, we were young and antiques dealers and buyers were "old" (in their late fifties and sixties). By 1967, the year our first price book was published, there was a new group of dealers—free-spirited independent entrepreneurs who were willing to gamble on their own talent and taste. Books that explained or priced antiques were not readily available, so collectors depended on dealers. Today the older dealers have retired, younger (under forty years old) dealers are appearing at shows and online, and everyone has access to information on the Internet and in price guides like this one.

There are still bargains to be had, but most are in newer categories like modernist jewelry and twentieth-century studio pottery. Big is "big." Small sets of figurines or plates are out. But large-scale accent pieces with colors and lines that blend in with modern furnishings—pieces like huge crocks, floor vases, centerpieces, and garden statuary—attract decorators and those with large homes. Anything from clothes and glass to ceramics and furniture that was in the newest style in the 1950s to 1990s is hot. Pieces representing a theme (American Indian, African, Asian, Western, or rustic) all have special buyers. And some old standbys, like toy cars, mechanical banks, and war and political memorabilia are going up in price because they are attracting new buyers. Of major interest today are antique guns and ammunition. Several major collections of toys and mechanical banks were auctioned this year, and prices were high because these early collections were in better-than-average condition. Art pottery and costume jewelry are probably the most popular items we see selling at shows. Hummel and Royal Doulton figurines and sets of old Limoges dishes are the most difficult to sell. Quality sells high—even with the uncertain economy, it retains its value.

This book seems to have gotten younger over the past forty-three years. Most items in our original book were made before 1860. Today we list pieces made as recently as 2000, and there is great interest in furniture, glass, and ceramics made since 1950.

The book is about 750 pages long and crammed full of prices and photographs. We try to have a balanced format—not too many glass, pottery, or collectible items; furniture from the eighteenth through the twentieth centuries; and not too many items that sell for over $5,000. We list a few very expensive pieces so you will realize that a great paperweight may cost $9,000 but an average one only $25. Nearly all the prices are from the American market for the American market. Few European sales are reported. We take the editorial privilege of not including prices we think result from "auction fever." There is a computer-generated index. Use it often. It includes categories and much more. For example, there is a category for Celluloid. Most celluloid will be there, but a toy made of celluloid will be listed under Toy and also indexed under Celluloid. There are also cross-references in the listings and in the paragraphs. But some searching must be done. For example, Barbie dolls are in the Doll category; there is no Barbie category. And when you look at "doll, Barbie," you see a note that Barbie is under "doll, Mattel, Barbie" because most dolls are listed by maker. Where possible, we list the maker at the beginning of an entry, and the size and age at the end.

All photographs and prices are new. Antiques and collectibles pictured are items that were offered for sale or sold for the amount listed in 2009-10. Wherever we had extra space on a page, we filled it with new tips about care of collections and other useful information. Don't discard this book. Old Kovels' price guides should be saved for future reference and for tax, estate, and appraisal information.

The prices in this book are reports of the general antiques market. Every price in the book is new. We do not estimate or "update" prices. Prices are either realized prices from auctions or completed sales or they're asking prices; a buyer may have negotiated an asking price to a lower selling price. But no price is an estimate. We do not pay dealers, collectors, or experts to estimate prices. Experience has shown us that estimated prices are usually high or low, but rarely an accurate report. If the price is from an auction, it includes the buyer's premium if one was charged; but like all the prices, it does not include sales tax. If a price range is given, at least two identical items were offered for sale at different prices. Price ranges are found only in categories like Pressed Glass, where identical items can be identified. Some prices in *Kovels' Antiques & Collectibles Price Guide* may seem high and some may seem low because of regional variations, but each price is one you could have paid for the object somewhere in the United States. Some Internet-only shop and auction prices, carefully edited, are included, but we find prices there can be misleading. Because so many non-collectors sell online but know little about the objects they are describing, there are often inaccuracies in the descriptions.

If you are selling your collection, do not expect to get retail value unless you are a dealer. Wholesale prices for antiques are usually 50 percent of retail prices. The antiques dealer must make a profit or go out of business. Internet auction prices are less predictable—because of an international audience and "auction fever," prices can be higher or lower than retail.

RECORD PRICES

CLOCKS & WATCHES

Howard & Davis clock/drum-top clock: $161,000 for a Howard & Davis astronomical regulator clock in a walnut case with crotch mahogany veneers, 16-in. silvered dial signed "Howard & Davis Makers Boston," c.1853, 92 ½ in. h. x 21 ½ in. w. x 14 in. d.

Patek Philippe Calibre 89 pocket watch: $5,053,360 for the Patek Philippe Calibre 89 pocket watch, the world's most complicated timepiece, 18K yellow gold, with 33 complications, weighing 2.5 lbs., made in 2001 to honor the 150th anniversary of the Swiss watchmaker.

Patek Philippe wristwatch ref. 3939: $684,000 for a Patek Philippe minute-repeating platinum wristwatch, reference No. 3939 with 2 black enamel dials and fitted box with certificate of origin.

Patek Philippe wristwatch ref. 5016P: $780,000 for a Patek Philippe platinum wristwatch, reference No. 5016P, with black dial and second silvered dial, one-minute tourbillon regulator, perpetual calendar, and moon phases, in a fitted wooden box with certificate of origin.

FURNITURE

Front and back bar: $302,500 for a Brunswick, Balke & Collender Co. mahogany front and back bar with hand-carved life-size nude supports, beveled mirrors, and matching liquor cabinet with adjustable shelves and zinc-like base, c.1893, 11 ft. h. x 24 ft. w.

Regional form: $120,750 for a c.1820 walnut Swisegood corner cupboard made in Davidson County, North Carolina, with rope-carved quarter columns, original brasses, and bracket feet; original blue paint can be seen under the orange and red painted surface, 96 ½ in. h. x 50 in. w. x 25 ¼ in. d.

GLASS

California Clubhouse Whiskey bottle: $30,240 for a "California Clubhouse Pure Bourbon imported only by Jno Morrison 316 Sac. St. S.F." western fifth, medium chocolate amber, embossed, monogrammed center, c.1872-74.

Eagle-Cornucopia flask, GII-69: $44,850 for an Eagle-Cornucopia flask, GII-69, yellow with an olive tone, sheared mouth, pontil scar, blown in Pittsburgh, c.1830, half-pint.

"Firecracker Flask," GI-14: $100,620 for the General Washington and bust, T.W.D., and eagle portrait flask, GI-14, by Kensington Glass Works, Philadelphia, deep sapphire blue with inward-rolled mouth and pontil scar, 1820-1840, pint. This bottle is referred to as the "firecracker flask" because the names "John Adams" and "Thomas Jefferson" and the year "1776" are embossed on the medial ridge of the flask. The two Founding Fathers both died on July 4, 1826, 50 years after the founding of the country.

"Peach" label-under-glass back-bar bottle: $10,200 for a deep amber back-bar bottle with "Peach" label under glass, stopper.

The following bottles were sold for record prices by Norman C. Heckler & Company, Woodstock Valley, Connecticut, at a March 2010 auction:

13-star flag flask, GX-28: $35,100 for a 13-star flag embossed historical flask, GX-28, marked "Granite Glass Works, Stoddard, N.H.," yellow olive, 1860-70, half pint.

Benjamin Franklin–T.W. Dyott, M.D., flask, GI-94: $23,400 for a Benjamin Franklin bust and T.W. Dyott, M.D., bust portrait flask, GI-94, by Kensington Glass Works, Philadelphia, medium tobacco amber with puce tone, 1820-40, pint.

Benjamin Franklin–Wheeling Glass Works flask, GI-98: $37,440 for a Benjamin Franklin bust, Wheeling Glass Works, and Dyott bust portrait flask, GI-98, olive yellow, pint.

Double eagle flask in pale to light puce, GII-30: $9,945 for a double eagle flask, GII-30, eggshell thin glass, pale to light puce, Louisville Glass Works, Kentucky, 1840-50, half-pint.

Double eagle flask, GII-25: $14,040 for a double eagle flask, GII-25, Kentucky Glass Works, Louisville, brilliant medium olive yellow, 1840-60, pint.

Eagle medallion flask, GII-8: $64,350 for an eagle medallion historical flask, GII-8, with sheared mouth and pontil scar, brilliant olive yellow, 1820-40, pint.

General Jackson, B. & M., eagle portrait flask, GI-67: $11,115 for a General Jackson bust, B. & M., and eagle portrait flask, GI-67, attributed to Baker & Martin Manufacturers, Perryopolis (Pittsburgh), clear, 1820-40, pint.

General Jackson-J.R. Laird SC. Pitt. eagle portrait flask, GI-66: $12,870 for a General Jackson bust, J.R. Laird. SC. Pitt. and eagle portrait flask, GI-66, by John Robinson Manufacturers, Pittsburgh, colorless with a hint of violet, 1820-40, pint.

George Washington eagle portrait flask, GI-1: $16,380 for a George Washington bust and eagle portrait flask, GI-1, Pittsburgh District, blue-green, 1820-40, pint.

Isabella Glass Works flask, GXIII-55: $16,380 for an Isabella Glass Works, anchor, and glass factory flask, GXIII-55, New Brooklyn, New Jersey, medium blue green, 1840-60, quart.

Masonic "1829" eagle flask, GIV-22: $19,890 for a Masonic "1829" eagle historical flask, GIV-22, by New England Glass Bottle Company, Boston, amber tint, 1820-30, pint.

Washington flask, GI-8: $30,420 for a G.G. Washington bust–Pittsburgh eagle F.L. portrait flask, GI-8, deep green aqua marine, 1820-40, pint.

Washington–sheaf of wheat portrait flask, GI-59: $17,550 for a Washington and sheaf of wheat portrait flask, GI-59, by Dyottville Glass Works, Philadelphia, yellowish olive, 1840-60, half-pint.

Zanesville and eagle cornucopia flask, GII-18: $11,700 for a Zanesville and eagle cornucopia flask, GII-18, embossed, yellow green, 1830-50, half-pint.

Dr. Wright's Tonic Bitters bottle: $14,040 for a Dr. Wright's Tonic Bitters and Invigorating Cordial bitters bottle, square with beveled corners, yellow with olive tone, 1845-60, 10 in.

St. Nicholas Stomach Bitters bottle: $9,360 for a figural St. Nicholas Stomach Bitters–Imported by Gentry & Otis, NY, bitters bottle, wedge form, deep honey amber, 1845-60, 9 in.

Wheeler's Berlin Bitters: $11,700 for a Wheeler's Berlin figural bitters bottle, Baltimore, open pontil, applied sloping collar, brilliant yellowish grass green, 1840-60, 9 ⅜ in.

American sealed wine bottle: $26,910 for an American sealed wine bottle, embossed initials JH, free-blown, Mt. Vernon Glass Co., deep clear green, 1810-20, 7 ⅞ x 3 ⅝ in.

Medicine or Utility bottle: $6,435 for a medicine or utility bottle made by Pitkin Glass Works, Manchester, Connecticut, octagonal, light yellow olive, 1783-1830, 7 ⅞ in.

R. Flanagan's Mineral Water bottle: $11,115 for a ten-pin-form R. Flanagan's Double Pressure Mineral Water Philadelphia soda water bottle, brilliant whittled yellow green, 1840-60, half-pint, 7 ⅜ in.

Free blown creamer: $4,680 for a free blown creamer, golden amber, New Jersey, Type 1 lily pad decoration, solid ear handle, flared tooled mouth, pour spout, matching ball stopper, 1840-60, 4 x 5 ¾ in.

Pattern molded creamer: $15,210 for a pattern molded creamer, 24 ribs swirled right, Zanesville, Ohio, ear handle, green aquamarine, 1820-40, 4 x 2 ⅞ in.

Pattern molded covered sugar bowl: $8,190 for a pattern molded covered sugar bowl, 18-rib construction, brilliant cobalt blue, 5 ½ x 4 ¾ in.

Free blown trumpet form vase: $5,265 for a free blown trumpet-form vase, tooled knop pedestal, tooled rim, golden amber with a red tone, 1820-40, 5 ¼ x 3 ¼ in.

LAMPS & LIGHTING

Tiffany Elaborate Peony lamp: $1,538,500 for a Tiffany Studios Elaborate Peony leaded glass lamp with adjustable bronze base, stamped Tiffany Studios New York 1903, c.1915, 29 ½ in. h. x 22 ¼ in. dia.

MISCELLANEOUS

Delaware license plate: $675,000 for Delaware license plate, No. 6.

Lower Mississippi River map: $315,999 for a 1858 map of the lower Mississippi River, known as Norman's Chart, after the name of the publisher, hand-colored, Marie Adrien Persac (b. France 1823, d. Manchac, La., 1873) drew the original, 61 x 31 in.

Michigan carver's work: $100,000 for an Oscar Peterson (1887-1951) fish carving mounted on an 11-x-57-in. wooden plaque, carved and painted, c.1920.

Persian ivory box: $471,529 for an ivory box, cover with central medallion in shape of Star of Paradise and cabochon ruby on top and inside, etched wavy patterns of gold and black alloy, and turquoise insets, mid-19th century, 1 ¼ x 6 ¾ x 3 ½ in. Surpassed later the same year: $3,672,490 (£2,393,250) for the same ivory box.

Saloon doors: $77,000 for a set of solid mahogany swinging saloon doors, with applied carvings, refinished 25 years ago with beveled glass incorporated in the panels, from a saloon in Milwaukee, 78 in. h. x 96 in. w.

Superior Horserace gambling machine: $45,000 for a 5-cent Superior Horserace slot machine with keys, countertop.

Van Cleef & Arpels Ballerina brooch: $422,500 for the diamond, ruby, and emerald Ballerina brooch by Van Cleef & Arpels, depicting Maria Camargo, arabesque pose, inverted pear-shaped diamond face, circular-cut diamond bodice, rose-cut diamond full-skirted tutu, headband and costume decorated with circular-cut rubies and emeralds, mounted in platinum, 1942.

Jukebox at auction: $120,750 for a 1940 Gabel Kuro jukebox, nicknamed "the last jukebox," plays 78 rpm records, Art Deco style.

Wurlitzer jukebox: $77,625 for an unrestored 1936 Model 35 Wurlitzer jukebox, plays 78 rpm records, prototype that never went to production, 142 in. h. x 113 in. w. x 61 in. d.

MOVIE & CELEBRITY

The Black Cat movie poster: $334,600 for the Style B one-sheet movie poster for the 1934 Universal movie, The Black Cat, lithographed red, black, and white, starring Boris Karloff and Bela Lugosi, their first collaboration.

James Bond 007 Dr. No movie poster: $7,800 for the James Bond 007 one-sheet movie poster for the film Dr. No, starring Sean Connery as James Bond and Ursula Andress as Honey Ryder, released by United Artists in 1962.

Josephine Baker in Prinsesse Tam-Tam movie poster: $9,000 for the Svend Koppel 1935 French movie poster Prinsesse Tam-Tam, starring Josephine Baker as the lead character, 33 ½ x 24 ¼ in.

PAINTINGS & PRINTS

Any work of art sold at auction: $106,482,500 for Pablo Picasso's oil-on-canvas painting of his mistress, Nude, Green Leaves, and Bust, signed "Picasso XXXII" at the upper right, 63 ¾ x 51 ¼ in.

Audubon print: $82,250 for the John James Audubon print, "Blue Crane or Heron," No. 62, Plate CCCVII from Birds of America, hand-colored engraving, Havell edition, matted and framed, elephant folio paper watermarked "J. Whatman/1836," sheet 25 ½ x 36 ¼ in.

Frank Frazetta's paperback cover painting: $1,000,000 for Frank Frazetta's 1967 paperback cover painting for Lancer Books' Conan the Conqueror, picturing Conan wearing armor in "berserker" rage on an armored horse.

Ruscha print at auction: $170,000 for the Edward Ruscha 1966 print, "Standard Station," an iconic 1960s-style Standard Oil gas station, bright red, orange and blue, dated and numbered 33/50, signed in pencil, sheet 25 ⅝ x 40 in.

PAPER

Choubrac, Alfred, poster: $3,360 for the Alfred Choubrac poster, "Nectar Bourguignon," Paris, 1891, 60 x 39 in.

Dartmouth Carnival poster: $7,200 for the 1936 Dartmouth Winter Carnival poster by Dwight Clark Shepler, picturing a skier on a snowy mountain along with carnival information, 37 ¾ x 24 in.

Flash Comics No. 1: $450,000 for DC Comics 1940 issue of Flash Comics No. 1 introducing the "Fastest Man Alive," The Flash, shown on the cover stopping a bullet with his bare hand, graded by CGC as Near Mint Plus, 9.6. The comic went on sale November 10, 1939.

The Incredible Hulk No. 1 comic book: $125,475 for a copy of The Incredible Hulk No. 1 Silver Age Marvel comic, 1962.

Jourdain, Roger, poster: $12,000 for the Roger Jourdain poster, "Aerodrome de Vichy," Paris, 1909, with images of a Wright-Ariel biplane and a Voisin biplane to promote a 1909 air show in Vichy.

Mucha poster "Lefèvre-Utile/Sarah Bernhardt": $7,800 for the 1904 Alphonse Mucha poster "Lefèvre-Utile/Sarah Bernhardt."

POTTERY & PORCELAIN

Press-molded bottle: $100,000 for a press-molded turtle bottle, from the communal village of Salem, North Carolina, with stylized markings on a glossy green-glazed back, impressed feet & tail, c.1805, 9 x 6 in.

Roseville Futura "tank" vase: $11,657 for a Roseville Futura "tank" vase in orange and blue mottled glaze, early 20th century, 10 x 9 in. In 2008, a Roseville Futura "tank" vase in blue to ivory shaded glaze, 10 x 9 in., auctioned for $22,800.

TEXTILES

Single sampler: $465,750 for an 18th-century Boston schoolgirl sampler, silk on linen, numbers and alphabets, pheasant at the top in a flower and vine border, central panel with spotted black dog, buck against tree, large turkey, apple tree, strawberries, and "Betsey Bentley, Her Sampler In The 13 Year Of Her Age," sewn in 1781.

TOYS, DOLLS & GAMES

Mama Katzenjammer bank: $54,675 for the Mama Katzenjammer bank by Kenton Hardware, Ohio, Mama Katz holding her little boys Hans & Fritz, insert coin and Mama rolls her eyes upward, cast iron, c.1905.

Marklin live-steam fire truck: $149,500 for a Marklin live-steam fire truck, hand-painted open frame with exposed boiler and intricate gear work, made in Germany, c.1912, 18 in. l.

North Pole bank: $42,525 for the original first casting North Pole bank by J. & E. Stevens Co., Cromwell, Connecticut, depicting Admiral Robert E. Peary's race to the North Pole in 1909, push the flag down, insert a coin and press forward, flag pops up, cast iron and brass, c.1910.

Panorama bank: $26,730 for the mechanical Panorama bank by J. & E. Stevens, insert coin in roof slot and the picture wheel advances in the window, cast iron, wood and lithographed paper, c.1876.

Picture Gallery bank: $54,675 for the Picture Gallery bank by Shepard Hardware, with two distinct functions: the owner can save money inside, and it taught the alphabet to children, three windows on the front with a dial that rotates images, cast iron, c.1885.

Royal Circus Calliope wagon: $23,085 for a Hubley Royal Circus Calliope, embossed body with interior bells, cast organ pipes, painted blue, gold trim, two black horses, red and gold spoke wheels, driver and organ player, in original box, 1920s, 16 in.

Target Robot: $52,900 for the multi-action tinplate Target Robot, one of the "Gang of Five" robots made by Masudaya in the late 1950s and early 1960s, battery operated, with tin shooting pistol and two rubber-tipped darts, original box and shooting accessories in original sealed bag, 15 in.

WEAPONS

Lugar firearm: $494,500 for the rare 1907 U.S. Test Trials .45 ACP semiautomatic pistol, Serial No. 2.

A NOTE TO COLLECTORS

You already know this is a great overall price guide for antiques and collectibles. Each entry is current, every photograph is new, and all prices are accurate.

There is another Kovel publication designed to keep you up-to-the-minute in the world of collecting. Things change quickly. Important sales produce new record prices. Fakes appear. Rarities are discovered. To keep up with developments, you can read *Kovels on Antiques and Collectibles*, our monthly newsletter. It is now available by subscription in two forms: a print edition that is mailed and a digital edition available on our website, www.Kovels.com. Both have the identical current information and are filled with color photographs—about forty per issue—which are so useful for collectors. The newsletter reports prices, trends, auction results, Internet sales, and other news for collectors as it happens.

Join the community of collectors at www.Kovels.com to keep up on more in the buy-sell world of antiques. Register; there is no charge for most of the information on the site, including our directory of services for collectors and dealers and thousands of searchable prices. Other information, including an illustrated listing of pottery and porcelain marks and makers and another of silver marks and makers, is available for a fee.

HOW TO USE THIS BOOK

There are a few rules for using this book. Each listing is arranged in the following manner: CATEGORY (such as Pressed Glass), OBJECT (such as vase), DESCRIPTION (as much information as possible about size, age, color, and pattern). Some types of glass, pottery, and silver are exceptions to this rule. These are listed CATEGORY, PATTERN, OBJECT, DESCRIPTION. All items are presumed to be in good condition and undamaged, unless otherwise noted. In most sections, if a maker's name is easily recognized, like Gustav Stickley, we include it near the beginning of the entry. If the maker is obscure, the name may be at the end.

Many of the general glass entries are in special categories: Glass-Art, Glass-Blown, Glass-Bohemian, Glass-Contemporary, Glass-Midcentury, and Glass-Venetian. Major glass factories are listed under factory names. Well-known types of glass, such as Cut, Pressed, Depression, Carnival, etc., can be found in their own categories. You will find silver flatware in either Silver Flatware Plated or Silver Flatware Sterling. There is also a section for Silver Plate, which includes coffeepots, trays, and other plated pieces. Most solid or sterling silver is listed by country, so look for Silver-American, Silver-Danish, Silver-English, etc. Silver jewelry is listed under Jewelry. Most pottery and porcelain is listed by factory name, such as Weller; by item, such as Calendar Plate; in sections like Dinnerware or Kitchen; or in a special section, such as Pottery-Art, Pottery-Contemporary, Pottery-Midcentury, etc.

Sometimes we make arbitrary decisions. Fishing has its own category, but hunting is part of the larger category called Sports. We have omitted most guns except toys. It is not legal to sell weapons without a special license, so guns are not part of the general antiques market. Airguns, BB guns, rocket guns, and others are listed in the Toy section. Everything is listed according to the computer alphabetizing system. This means words such as "Mt." are alphabetized as "M-T," not as "M-O-U-N-T." All numerals are before all letters; thus "2" comes before "A."

We also made several editorial decisions. A butter dish is a "butter." A salt dish is called a "salt" to differentiate it from a saltshaker. It is always "sugar and creamer," never "creamer and sugar." Political collectors often refer to "pinbacks," the round celluloid or tin pins decorated with candidates' names and faces. We use the word "button" instead of "pinback." The word "button" is also used when referring to fasteners on clothing. Where one dimension is given, it is the height; or if the object is round, the dimension is the diameter. The height of a picture is listed before width. Glass is clear unless a color is indicated.

Entries are listed alphabetically, but idiosyncrasies of language remain. There is some confusion caused by words with more than one meaning, like iron (the metal) and iron (the pressing tool) or enamel (granite ware) and enamel (painted decoration on glass) and enamel (ground glass heated on metal to make an ashtray or a sign or a piece of jewelry). We have indexed these so the appropriate pieces are listed together.

Some antiques terms, such as "Sheffield" or "Pratt," also have two meanings. Read the paragraph headings to know the meaning used. All category headings are based on the language of the average person, and we use terms like "mud figures" even if not technically correct.

This book does not include price listings for fine art paintings, antiquities, stamps, coins, or most types of books. *Big Little Books* and similar children's books are included. Comic books are listed only in special categories like Superman, but original comic art and cels are listed in their own categories.

Prices for items pictured can be found in the appropriate category. Look for the matching entry with the abbreviation "illus." The picture will be nearby.

Because of the computer, the book can be produced quickly. The last entries are added in June; the book is available in August. But human help finds prices and checks accuracy. We read everything at least three times, sometimes more. We edit more than 50,000 entries down to the approximately 42,000 entries found here. We correct spelling, remove incorrect data, write category paragraphs, and decide on new categories. We proofread copy and prices many times, but there will always be some misspelled words and other errors. Information in the paragraphs is updated each year.

Prices are reported from all parts of the United States, Canada, and Europe, converted to U.S. dollars at the time of the sale. The average rate of exchange between June 2009 and June 2010 was $1 U.S. to about $1.15 Canadian, €.78 (Euro), and £.68 (British Pound). Prices are from auctions, shops, Internet sales, and shows. Every price is checked for accuracy, but we are not responsible for errors.

We cannot answer your letters asking for price information, but please write if you have any requests for categories to be included in future editions or any corrections to the paragraphs or prices. You may find the answers to your questions at Kovels.com.

When you see us at shows and flea markets, please stop and say hello. Don't be surprised if we ask for your suggestions. You can write to us at P.O. Box 22192-K, Beachwood, OH 44122, or visit us on our website, www.Kovels.com.

TERRY KOVEL AND KIM KOVEL
July 2010

ACKNOWLEDGMENTS

The world of antiques and collectibles is filled with people who have answered our every request for help. Dealers, auction houses and shops have given advice and opinions, sent pictures and prices, and made suggestions for changes. Special thanks to all of them: Alderfer Auction Co., Allard Auctions, Aspire Auctions, Auction Team (Köln) Breker, Be-hold, Belhorn Auction Services, Bertoia Auctions, Bonhams & Butterfields, Brown Auction Services, Brunk Auctions, Cincinnati Art Galleries, Collect.com, Conestoga Auction Co., Copake Auction, Cottone Auctions, Cowan's Auctions, Cripple Creek Auctions, CRN Auctions, DuMouchelles, Early American History Auctions, Early Auction Co., Eastbourne Auction, Eldred's Auction, Fairfield Auction, Fellows & Sons Auctioneers, Fontaine's Auction Gallery, Fox Auctions, Freeman's Auctioneers, Garth's Auction, Gary Kirsner Auctions, Glass Works Auctions, Hake's Americana & Collectibles, Heritage Auction Galleries, Ivey-Selkirk Auctioneers, Jackson's International Auctioneers, James D. Julia Auctioneers, Jeffrey S. Evans, L.H. Selman, Lang's Sporting Collectables, Legendary Auctions, Leland Little Auctions, Leslie Hindman Auctioneers, Los Angeles Modern Auctions, Martin J. Donnelly Antique Tools, McMaster Harris Auction Co., Michaan's Auctions, Morphy Auctions, Neal Auction Co., New Orleans Auction Galleries, Noel Barrett Antiques & Auctions, Norman C. Heckler & Co., Northeast Auctions, Pook & Pook, Rachel Davis Fine Arts, Rago Arts and Auction Center, Randy Inman Actions, Replacements Ltd., Richard Opfer Auctioneering, Rich Penn Auctions, Ruby Lane, Showplace Antique Center, Showtime Auction Services, Skinner, Sloans & Kenyon, Sotheby's, Stair Galleries, Stein Auction Co., Strawser Auctions, Tear Drop Memories, Theriault's, Tom Harris Auctions, Treadway Toomey Galleries, Trocadero, William Morford Auctions, Willis Henry Auctions, and Woody Auction Co.

To the others who knowingly or unknowingly contributed to this book we say "thank you": Aberdeen Auctions, Aleph-Bet Books, Alex Cooper Auctioneers, Alistair Crawford, American Bottle Auctions, American Cut Glass Association, American Political Items Collectors, Anderson Auctions, Antique Bottle & Glass Collector, Antique Fan Collectors Association, Antique Place, Antiquing Online, Auction Gallery of the Palm Beaches, Austin Auction Co., B.S. Slosberg Auctioneers, Barrett Antiques, BBR Auctions, Bill Hood & Sons Auctions, Bob Courtney Auctions, Bottles & Extras, Breweriana.com, Burley Auction Group, C. Downing Auctions, Cairns Antiques, Carlton Antique Toys, Case Antiques Auctions, Charles Gilbert Toys, Christie's, Circle M Auctions, Clars Auction Gallery, Cody Old West Show & Auction, Collection Liquidators Auction Service, Crocker Farm, Crosstie Glass, Crown Jewels of the Wire, Cyr Auction Gallery, Dallas Auction Gallery, Dan Ripley's Antique Helper, Dennis Auction Service, Depew Auction Gallery, Dirk Soulis Auctions, Doyle New York, East Dennis Antiques, Faganarms, Farm & Dairy, Fenton Art Glass Collectors, FloBlue Shoppe, Frank & Grace Zuest, Frank & Mary Ann Brandt, Frank's Antiques & Auctions, Gasoline Alley Antiques, Gibson Girl Memories, Gisela Luce, Glass Cupboard, Glass Discoveries, Green Valley Auctions, Grey Flannel Auctions, Guernsey's, Halls Fine Art, Harlowe-Powell Auction Gallery, Heisey Collectors of America, Hewlett's Antique Auctions, Hi & Lo Modern, Hollywood Poster Auction, Homestead Auctions, Hoosier Peddler, Howard Peirce Auctions, J. Greenstein & Co., JK Galleries, Joy Luke Auctioneers, Just Art Pottery, Kaminski Auctions, Ken Farmer Auctions, Keystone Toy Trader, Last Moving Picture Co., Leonard Auction, Lilly Auction & Gallery, Live Free or Die Antique Tool Auctions, Lloyd Ralston Toys, Love's Auctioneers, Manion's International Auction House, Martine's Antiques, Matthews Auctions, McCoy Lovers' NMXpress, McCulloh's Antiques & Collectibles, McMillan Bros., McMurray Antiques & Auctions, Metropolitan Galleries, Michael Ivankovich Antiques & Auction Co., Midwest Auction Galleries, Modfather.com, Monsen & Baer, Mother Druckers, Music City Auction, National Association of Aladdin Lamp Collectors, National Association of Breweriana Advertising, National Association of Milk Bottle Collectors, National Toothpick Holder Collector's Society, Nicole Maleine Antiques, O.J. Club, O'Gallerie, Old Barn Auction, Old Toy Shop, Old

Toy Soldier Auction, Page Button Auctions, Paper & Advertising Collectors' Marketplace, Past Tyme Pleasures, PBA Galleries, Pewter Collectors Club of America, Philip Weiss Auctions, Phoebus Auction Gallery, Pole Top Discoveries, Political Bandwagon, Potteries Specialists Auctions, Quinn & Waverly Auction Galleries, R.O. Schmitt Fine Arts, Reagan-Watson Auctions, Red Wing Collectors Society, Rex Stark Americana, Richard D. Hatch & Associates, Robert Edward Auctions, Ron Rhodes, RSL Auction Co., Russ Cochran's Comic Art Auction, San Rafael Auction Gallery, Savoia's Auction, Schmidt's Antiques, Seeck Auctions, Serious Toyz, Silver Magazine, Simmons & Co. Auctioneers, Smith House Toys & Auction Co., Sollo Rago Modern Auctions, Southern Folk Pottery Collectors Society, Southern Liquidators, Stanton's Auctioneers, Stephenson's, Stephen Bennett Auctions, Steve Butler, Susanin's Auctions, Swann Auction Galleries, Tea Leaf Club International, Team's Tiffany Treasures, Ted Kromer, The Internet Antique Shop, Thomas C. Campbell Maine Antiques, Thomaston Place Auction Galleries, Timeless Treasures, Toy Shop, Trader Fred's Toys of Yore, Treasures of Yesterday, Vera Battemarco, Vicki & Bruce Waasdorp, Victorian Casino Antique Auction, Vintage Jewelry, Vintage Treasures, W. Yoder Auction, William J. Jenack Auctioneers, and Yankee Toys.

Our publisher, Black Dog & Leventhal, and its president, J.P. Leventhal, have continued to suggest and implement improvements to this book. We are excited to announce that for the first time it will be available as an ebook as well as in printed form. There have also been improvements in design and technology that add to the speed of production and the ease of use. Thanks to J.P. Leventhal and Lisa Tenaglia, our editor, and their staff: True Sims, production director; Judy Courtade, Courtney Cullinan, and Maureen Winter, sales; and Camille March and Allison Frascatore, publicity. Mary Flower, Georgia S. Maas, and Robin Perlow did the job of copyediting and proofreading the entire book and found the tiniest of errors.

Thanks to Sheila Hart and her assistant, Mike Levay, who put all the prices, photographs, and paragraphs together and created the look and layout of *Kovels' Antiques & Collectibles Price Guide 2011*.

The details and hard work required to record prices, assemble photos and information, check accuracy and spelling, and solve many other problems are all done by our Kovel staff. We thank Carmie Amata, Lisa Bell, Grace DeFrancisco, Marcia Goldberg, Katie Karrick, Karen Kneisley, Kim Kovel, Liz Lillis, Mary Ellen Malone, Tina McBean, Renee McRitchie, Nancy Saada, Julie Seaman, June Smith, and Cherrie Smrekar. Photographs came from many sources, and they were all sized and digitally enhanced by our photo editorl Janet Dodrill, and her staff, Pat Kilkenny and Carolyn K. Lewis. Additional photos were taken by Miranda Orbach and Cloe Eiber. Gay Hunter, our in-house editor, always worries the most about the book. She kept detailed records and made sure all of us were on track and on schedule. She read and reviewed pages of prices, corrected our spelling errors, and handled computer problems. Together we updated paragraph information when a company closed or was purchased. Thanks to all of them. We have what we are sure is our best book ever. We know that the book is possible only because of the group effort, even though it is our names that appear on the cover.

A. WALTER made pate-de-verre glass under contract at the Daum glassworks from 1908 to 1914. He decorated pottery during his early years in his studio in Sevres, where he also developed his formula for pale, translucent pate-de-verre. He started his own firm in Nancy, France, in 1919. Pieces made before 1914 are signed *Daum, Nancy* with a cross. After 1919 the signature is *A. Walter Nancy*.

Bowl, Black Moth On Top, Yellow, 3-Sided, c.1920, 6 ½ In.	3600.00
Bowl, Henri Berge, Beetle, Molded On Body, Orange, Brown, c.1920, 11 In.	8365.00
Bowl, Slithering Snake On Top, Light To Dark Green, Impressed, c.1920, 4 ⅝ x 7 In.	2450.00
Bowl, Wreath Of Hawthorn Berries, Leaves, Mottled, Cobalt Blue, Bubbles, 2 ⅛ x 3 ¾ In.	1380.00
Dish, Figural, Snake, Cream To Amber, 7 In.	1610.00
Dish, Gecko, Impressed, A. Walter Nancy, Berge, S.C., c.1920, 7 In.	2700.00
Dish, Oval, Crayfish, Signed, 6 ¾ In.	2728.00
Dish, Scarab, Signed, 3 ¾ x 2 In. .... *illus*	1093.00
Dish, Spade Shape, Bumblebee, Signed, 4 In.	3200.00
Figurine, Bird, Blue Shaded To Blue Green, Signed, 3 ½ x 4 In.	915.00
Figurine, Bird, Crouching, Yellow, 3 ¾ In.	1438.00
Figurine, Bird, Green, Signed, 1920s, 4 x 3 ½ In.	1200.00
Figurine, Bird, Looking Up, Beak Open, Tree Branch, Leaves, Cones, 4 ¼ In.	3400.00
Figurine, Goose, Rectangular Base, c.1920, 4 ⅝ In.	2800.00
Figurine, Sleeping Woman, Signed, c.1910, 2 ¾ x 5 ⅝ In.	4920.00
Figurine, Woman, Flowing Robe, Dancing, Yellow, Cream Head, Mottled Green Foot, 8 ½ In.	2875.00
Fish, Blue Body, Green Head, Riding Waves, Luminaire, 8 ¼ x 4 x 6 ¾ In.	10350.00
Paperweight, Frog, Signed, A. Walter Nancy, c.1920, 3 In. .... 2100.00 to 2800.00
Paperweight, Mussels, On Rock, Signed, 1 ¾ In.	2880.00
Paperweight, Seashell, In Dish, Brown, Blue, Impressed, A. Walter Nancy, 2 ½ x 4 In.	2500.00
Paperweight, Shell, Brown, Blue, White Base, Seafoam, c.1920, 3 In.	3500.00
Paperweight, Snail, Brown, Yellow, Red, Green, Black, Signed, A. Walter Nancy, 2 ½ In.	2500.00
Tray, Lobster, Black, Brown, Signed, A. Walter Nancy, Berge, c.1920, 5 x 6 In. .... 2500.00 to 3500.00
Tray, Lobster, Full-Bodied, Mottled Green To Frost Ground, Triangle Shape, Signed, 6 In.	1610.00
Tray, Scarab, Blue, Black, Red, Signed, 5 In. .... *illus*	2530.00
Vase, 3 Beetles, Long Feelers, Thick Flared Stem, Signed, 6 ¼ In.	4600.00
Vase, Leaves & Berries, Signed, M. Corrette, 4 x 8 ½ In. .... *illus*	3000.00
Vase, Misty Landscape Through Trees, Signed, 11 In. .... *illus*	1150.00

ABC plates, or children's alphabet plates, were most popular from 1780 to 1860, but are still being made. The letters on the plate were meant as teaching aids for children learning to read. The plates were made of pottery, porcelain, metal, or glass. Mugs and other items were also made with alphabet decorations.

Plate, Boys, With Kites, 7 ½ In.	120.00
Plate, Bucolic Landscape, Mulberry, 6 ¾ In.	62.00
Plate, Children, Beehive, Poem, Raised Rim	95.00
Plate, Deer, Lion, Stork, 6 In., 3 Piece	184.00
Plate, Duck, This Little Duck Is Out Of Luck, East Liverpool, 8 In.	28.00
Plate, Fox & Goose, England, 8 In.	168.00
Plate, Fox Hunt, Hunter, Hounds, Fox, White Ground, Blue Transfer, 7 ¼ In.	165.00
Plate, Gathering Cotton, Raised Rim	75.00
Plate, Independence Hall, Philadelphia, Scenic Transfer, 7 In.	28.00
Plate, Juvenile Companions, Jump Tom Jump, Pearlware, 1840s	108.00
Plate, Kite, Hunt, Rowboat, Staffordshire, 1800s, 6 & 7 In., 3 Piece	122.00
Plate, Little Red Riding Hood, Raised Rim, 7 ½ In.	92.00
Plate, Newspaper Boy, 7 ¼ In.	156.00
Plate, Peacock, On Fence, Transfer, Embossed, 7 In.	73.00
Plate, The Walk, Equestrian, 19th Century, 7 ⅞ In.	75.00
Plate, Traditional & Signing Alphabet, 2 Dressed Bunnies, Aynsley China, 8 ¼ In. ...	440.00

ABINGDON POTTERY was established in 1908 by Raymond E. Bidwell as the Abingdon Sanitary Manufacturing Company. The company started making art pottery in 1934. The factory ceased production of art pottery in 1950.

Bowl, Candleholders, Shell Shape, Green Gloss Glaze, 15 & 4 ¼ In., 3 Piece	59.00
Bowl, Pink Matte Glaze, 9 In.	17.00
Cookie Jar, Humpty Dumpty, Marked, 11 In.	82.00
Cookie Jar, Mammy, Holding Flowers, c.1940, 9 ¼ In.	189.00
Cookie Jar, Witch, Cat Finial, Round, Impressed, Stamped, 11 ⅜ In.	715.00
Flowerpot, Morning Glory, Ribbed, Lafleu, 4 In.	17.00

A. Walter, Dish, Scarab, Signed, 3 ¾ x 2 In. $1093.00

A. Walter, Tray, Scarab, Blue, Black, Red, Signed, 5 In. $2530.00

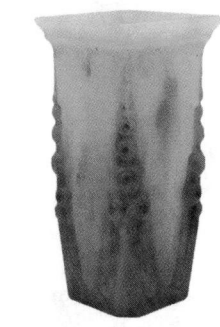

A. Walter, Vase, Leaves & Berries, Signed, M. Corrette, 4 x 8 ½ In. $3000.00

A. Walter, Vase, Misty Landscape Through Trees, Signed, 11 In. $1150.00

Abingdon Pottery, Vase,
Mexican Man, Resting Against Cactus,
Marked, No. 616, 6 ½ In.
$29.00

Adams, Cup & Saucer,
Farmers Arms, Tools, Farmer's Prayer,
Staffordshire, 7 ¾ In.
$264.00

Advertising, Box, Day's Soap,
Paper Label, c.1870, 18 In.
$88.00

Advertising, Box, Elk Oats, Picture,
Cardboard, Krenning-Schlapp Grocers,
St. Louis, 9 ½ x 5 ½ In.
$550.00

Vase, Art Deco, White, Flared Rim, Angular Handles, Marked, 9 ½ In.	29.00
Vase, Blue Flying Bird, White Ground, Footed, Marked, 7 ¼ x 7 In.	40.00
Vase, Blue Gloss Glaze, Base To Center Loop Handles, Signed, 10 ¾ In.	17.00
Vase, Blue Wave, Foil Label, Marked, 10 ¾ x 11 ½ In.	29.00
Vase, Flowers, Green, Silver Overlay, Handles, Marked, 9 ¾ In.	55.00
Vase, Gray, Marked, 8 ¾ In.	12.00
Vase, Leaves, Turquoise Gloss Glaze, Marked, 9 In.	29.00
Vase, Mexican Man, Resting Against Cactus, Marked, No. 616, 6 ½ In. ....*illus*	29.00
Vase, Scroll, Beige Gloss Glaze, Marked, 8 In.	46.00
Wall Pocket, Fern Leaf, Green, Stamped, 9 In.	98.00

ADAMS china was made by William Adams and Sons of Staffordshire, England. The firm was founded in 1769 and became part of the Wedgwood Group in 1966. The name *Adams* appeared on various items through 1998. All types of tablewares and useful wares were made. Other pieces of Adams may be found listed under Flow Blue and Tea Leaf Ironstone.

Bowl, Cries Of London, Brown Border, 9 In., 4 Piece	85.00
Bowl, Cries Of London, Scarlet Strawberries, Brown Border, 9 In.	35.00
Cup & Saucer, Chusan, Birds & Blossoms	17.00
Cup & Saucer, Farmers Arms, Tools, Farmer's Prayer, Staffordshire, 7 ¾ In. ....*illus*	264.00
Cup, Breakfast, Cries Of London, 3 ¾ In.	10.00
Gravy Boat, Attached Underplate, Chusan	75.00
Pitcher, Adams' Rose Style Flower, Multicolored Leaf, Flowers, Bulbous, Handle, 8 ½ In.	396.00
Pitcher, Cries Of London, 5 In.	48.00
Pitcher, Ironstone, White, Angular Handle, 1950s, 5 ¾ x 3 ¾ In.	20.00
Plate, Adams' Rose, Red, Blue, Green Spatter, Scalloped Edge, 9 ¼ In.	249.00
Plate, Audubon, American Flamingo, Trillium Border, c.1968	90.00
Plate, Audubon, Cedar Waxwing, Trillium Border, Transfer, c.1968	65.00
Plate, Audubon, Pileated Woodpecker, Trillium Border, c.1968	70.00
Plate, Bread & Butter, Chusan, Birds & Blossoms, 6 ¼ In.	8.00
Plate, Dinner, Chusan, 10 ¼ In.	25.00
Plate, Historical, Landing Of Columbus, Transfer, Blue & White, 11 In.	125.00
Plate, Luncheon, Pink Rose, Blue & Yellow Pansies, Swansea, 9 ¼ In.	24.00
Plate, Raised Rim, Pinecones, Acorns, Leaves, Titan Ware, Brown Transfer, 10 ¾ In.	50.00
Plate, Shanghai, Flow Blue, c.1870, 10 In.	135.00
Plate, Venetian Scenery, Swans, Vignette Border, Flow Blue, 9 In.	132.00
Sugar, Cover, Blue & White, Staffordshire, c.1830, 6 x 8 In.	35.00

ADVERTISING containers and products sold in the old country store are now all collectibles. These stores, with the crackers in a barrel and a potbellied stove, are a symbol of an earlier, less hectic time. Listed here are many of the advertising items. Other similar pieces may be found under the product name, such as Planters Peanuts. We have tried to list items in the logical places, so enameled tin dishes will be found under Graniteware, paper items in the Paper category, etc. Store fixtures, cases, signs, and other items that have no advertising as part of the decoration are listed in the Store category. The early Dr Pepper logo included a period after "Dr," but it was dropped in 1950. We list all Dr Pepper items without a period so they alphabetize together. For more prices, go to kovels.com.

Ashtray, Burns Extra Special-Sheer Perfection From Drybroughs, Round, 6 In.	8.00
Ashtray, El Witto Cigar, Cast Iron, Match, Cigar Cutter, 5 Cent, 5 ½ x 11 ½ In.	283.00
Ashtray, Hadees Heater, Woman, Soldier, 2-Sided, Cast Iron, Hotternell, 5 x 3 ¾ In.	48.00
Ashtray, H.E. Wogan's Drug Stores, Skillet, Cast Iron, 1971	40.00
Ashtray, McEwans Export, Ceramic, Round, 6 In.	5.00
Ashtray, Philip Morris, Bellhop, Painted, Cast Iron, 1927, 33 In.	495.00
Ashtray, Players No. 3, Virginia Cigarettes, Round, 5 ½ In.	8.00
Ashtray, T.B. Woods Sons Co. Molding Line 1975, Cast Iron	35.00 to 45.00
Ashtray, Youngers Tartan Bitter, Logo, Ceramic, Round, 6 In.	12.00
Bag Holder, Goddard Peck Grocer Co., Wood, Bags, Fan Form, 15 x 16 x 8 In.	720.00
Banner, Chesterfield Cigarette, 30 x 62 In.	83.00
Banner, Circus, Women Wrestling, Canvas, Painted, c.1980, 54 x 74 In.	469.00
Banner, Dr Pepper, King Of Beers, Paper, 13 x 40 In.	440.00
Banner, Electra Circus Sideshow, Canvas, Painted, 1988, 67 x 47 In.	341.00
Banner, Eveready Spotlight, 300 Foot Range, Man, Woman, Flashlights	300.00
Banner, King Pin Tobacco, Hey You, Chew King Pin, Man, 1920s, 29 x 62 In.	88.00
Banner, Velvet Ice Cream, Russ Bros., Serve It, 29 x 55 In.	110.00
Barrel, Rochester Root Beer, Oak, Nickel Hoops, 5 Cent Decals, c.1900, 26 In.	330.00
Bean Pot, Pooley Lumber Co., Greene, Iowa, 2 Tone, Brown, Handles, Pottery, 6 In.	95.00
Bench, Red Goose School Shoes, 3 Seats, Atlantic & Pacific Shoe, Wood, 36 x 62 In.	285.00

Bin, Jersey Coffee, Wood, Stenciled, 100 Lb., 32 x 22 ½ x 17 In.	480.00
Bin, John Sexton & Co., Teas, Coffees & Spices, Tin, 16 x 11 ½ x 11 In.	135.00
Bin, Luxury Coffee, Wood, Red, Stenciled, 100 Lb., 32 x 21 ½ x 16 In.	680.00
Blackboard, Orange Crush, 5 Cent, Crushy, Bottle Graphics, 27 x 19 ½ In.	390.00
Blackboard, Whistle Soda Pop, Multicolored Graphics, c.1948, 27 x 19 ½ In.	480.00
Blanket, Horse, Wells Fargo & Co., Yellow, Red & Blue Stripes, 80 In.	4600.00
Booklet, Dr. Haines Golden Specific For Drunkeness Liquor Habit, c.1885, 5 x 7 In.	72.00
Bookmark, Comfort Soap, Gold, Purple, Green, 7 x 2 In.	34.00
Books may be included in the Paper category.	
Bootjack, Gun Shape, Cast Iron, Our 3S Shoe The Best, Phila., 8 In.	395.00
Bottle Openers are listed in their own category.	
Bottle Topper, Cherry Blossoms, Girl, Boy, Die Cut, Tin, 2-Sided, Paper Label, 1921, 7 x 11 In..	1400.00
Bottle Topper, Red Wing Grape Juice, Boy, Girl, Green, Red, 16 x 11 In.	240.00
Bottles are listed in their own category.	
Box, Albers Flapjack Flour, Hotcakes Of The West, Cardboard, 4 ¼ x 2 ¾ x 1 ½ In.	132.00
Box, Commonwealth Toilet Paper, Paper, Lithograph, 7 x 5 In.	47.00
Box, Cremor Pills, H.I. True, MD, McConnelsville, Ohio, Oval, Wood, Wrapper, 2 In.	83.00
Box, Dana's Sarsaparilla, Guaranteed To Absolutely Cure Disease, Wood, 11 x 9 In.	72.00
Box, Day's Soap, Paper Label, c.1870, 18 In. ....*illus*	88.00
Box, Dr. Daniels' Wind Colic Drops, Screw Top, 2 Square Bottles, Wrap Labels, 3 In...............	11.00
Box, Dr. John Bull's Round Worm Lozenges, Women, Children, 50 Cents A Box, 3 x 2 In.	220.00
Box, Dr. Shores Catarrh Cure, Salt Lake City, Utah, $2.00 A Box, 1 ⅝ x 2 ½ In.	330.00
Box, Elk Oats, Picture, Cardboard, Krenning-Schlapp Grocers, St. Louis, 9 ½ x 5 ½ In. ...*illus*	550.00
Box, Gum, Card, Man From U.N.C.L.E., MGM, c.1965, 3 ¾ x 8 In.	278.00
Box, Honeycomb, Chitty Chitty Bang Bang, Glidrose Productions, c.1969, 13 ½ x 20 In.	158.00
Box, Hoosier Poet Jar Rings, Red Lipped, Cardboard, 1 Doz., 3 ⅛ x 3 ⅛ x 1 ¼ In.	253.00
Box, Ivory Soap, Procter & Gamble, 17 In. ....*illus*	59.00
Box, Jantzen Bathing Suit, Man, Child & 2 Ladies, Empty, 1920s, 14 x 11 In. ...	129.00
Box, Long Chew, Giraffe, Clark Bros. Chewing Co., Pittsburg, 9 x 5 In.	385.00
Box, Nabisco Rice Honey, Rin-Tin-Tin, Frontier Hero Medal, Fort Scene, 1950s, 13 x 17 In.	127.00
Box, Oatmeal, Chest-O-Silver Instant Oats, Treasure Chest, Cardboard, Cylindrical, 9 x 5 In.	231.00
Box, Oatmeal, Happy Home Rolled Oats, House, Cardboard, Cylindrical, St. Louis, Mo., 10 x 5 In. ..	66.00
Box, Oatmeal, Vanity Rolled Oats, Peacock, Kickbusch Grocery, Cylindrical, Cardboard, 9 ½ x 5 In.	358.00
Box, Oatmeal, White Villa Rolled Oats, House, Landscape, Cardboard, Cylindrical, 3 Lbs., 10 x 5 In. .	633.00
Box, Recipe, Van Camp's, Pork & Beans, Aluminum, Multicolored, c.1986, 3 ½ x 5 ¼ In.	16.00
Box, Rice Krispies Cereal, Dilly Dally Mask On Box, 1953, 9 ½ In.	400.00
Box, Shoeshine, Wooden, Ask For Whittacker's Polishes, Pat. Nov. 28, 1898, 14 x 13 In.	65.00
Box, Wheaties, All American Tackle George Maddox, 1934 On Front, 3 x 6 x 8 In.	450.00
Box, Williams Improved Police Foot Powder, Cardboard, Majestic Drug Co., Round, 5 In.	176.00
Box, see also Box category.	
Bracket, Iron, Gray Paint, James Weathervane Co., 8 ½ x 12 In.	135.00
Broom Holder, Wilbur's Cocoa, Cherub, Tin Lithograph, 6 ¾ x 2 ½ In.	176.00
Brush, Clothing, Ames Sword Company, Chicopee, Mass., 6 In.	24.00
Cabinet, Diamond Dyes, Fairy, Multiple Scenes, 31 In. ....*illus*	1112.00
Cabinet, Diamond Dyes, Governess, Oak, Tin, Embossed, 30 x 22 ½ In.	590.00
Cabinet, Diamond Dyes, Washer Woman, 30 In. ....*illus*	2633.00
Cabinet, Dr. Daniels', Veterinary Medicines, Oak, Printed Handle, Label, 1890s, 13 x 7 In.	365.00
Cabinet, Goff's Braid, Wood, 2 Drawers, 17 x 8 In.	121.00
Cabinet, Humphreys' Veterinary, 3-D Horse Head, 21 x 10 x 34 In.	4025.00
Cabinet, Humphreys' Specifics, Homeopathic, Tin Lithograph, Wood, 28 x 21 In. ....*illus*	5820.00
Cabinet, Putnam Dyes, Wood, Tin Lithograph, c.1910, 21 x 10 In.	332.00
Cabinet, Spool, Clark's, O.N.T., Oak, 4 Drawers, Late 1800s, 11 ½ x 22 x 16 In.	200.00
Cabinet, Spool, Clark's, O.N.T., Oak, Leather Top, 4 Drawers, 15 x 30 x 20 ½ In.	175.00
Cabinet, Spool, Clark's Mile End, 2 Drawers, Cherry, 7 ¼ x 22 ¾ In.	115.00
Cabinet, Spool, Corticelli Silk, 20 Drawers, 32 x 36 ½ x 17 In.	1050.00
Cabinet, Spool, Corticelli Silk, Oak, 9 Drawers, 26 ½ x 21 x 19 ½ In.	1520.00
Cabinet, Spool, Corticelli Silk & Twist, Oak, 10 Glass Front Drawers, 35 ½ x 21 x 19 In.	288.00
Cabinet, Spool, Merrick's, Oak, Round, Revolving Inside, Glass Windows, 20 In.	1180.00
Cabinet, Spool, O.N.T., Oak, Etched Insert Panels, 6 Drawers, 22 x 28 In.	413.00
Cabinet, Spool, Richardson, Silk, 16 Drawers, 39 x 28 x 17 In.	440.00
Cabinet, Spool, Royal Society, 12 Shelves, Wood, 35 ¾ x 18 ½ x 20 In.	250.00
Cabinet, Spool, Willimantic, Oak, 4 Drawers, c.1890, 14 ½ x 31 x 23 ½ In.	260.00
Cabinet, Spool, Willimantic, Mahogany, 6 Drawers, Logo Panel On Side, 21 x 24 In.	679.00
Cabinet, Sun Garter Belt, Oak, Curved Glass Front, c.1902, 7 ¾ x 11 In.	575.00
Cabinet, Waterman's Fountain Ideal Pens, Oak, Glass, Marked, 17 x 17 x 9 In.	862.00
Calendars are listed in their own category.	

Advertising, Box, Ivory Soap, Procter & Gamble, 17 In. $59.00

Advertising, Cabinet, Diamond Dyes, Fairy, Multiple Scenes, 31 In. $1112.00

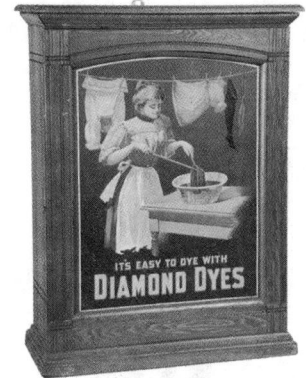

Advertising, Cabinet, Diamond Dyes, Washer Woman, 30 In. $2633.00

Advertising, Cabinet, Humphreys' Specifics, Homeopathic, Tin Lithograph, Wood, 28 x 21 In. $5820.00

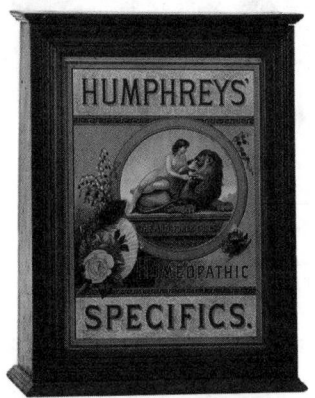

Advertising, Cooler, Nichol Kola, 31 x 22 x 34 In. $234.00

Advertising, Dispenser, Lash's Syrup, Milk Glass Base, Depression Glass Top, 1940s, 13 In. $176.00

Mail Pouch Ads on Barns
Mail Pouch tobacco used signs painted on barns as huge ads from the beginning of the twentieth century until the 1990s.

Calling Card, Adams Express Company, Orange, Yellow, 2-Sided, 13 ½ x 20 In.	275.00
Calling Card, Wells Fargo & Co. Express, Red, Black, 4-Sided, 19 In.	1420.00
Can, Bowey's Hot Chocolate, Hinged Lid, Aluminum, 8 ½ In.	192.00
Can, Donald Duck Popcorn, Donald In Chef's Hat Reading Cookbook, 1950, 6 In.	175.00
Can, Home Run Cigar, Baseball Scene, Tin Lithograph, 6 x 5 In.	1600.00
Can, Jim Dandy Cleanser, Company's Trademark Character, Dated 1911, 3 x 7 In.	385.00
Can, London Bank Cigars, Factory, Tin Lithograph, 1909 Tax Stamp, 6 x 4 In.	145.00
Can, Negrohead Oysters, 6 Oz., 3 In.	118.00
Can, Shelter Island Oyster, Friction Cover, Greenport, N.Y., ¼ Gal., 4 ¼ In.	140.00
Can, Yellow Cab Cigar, Orange Ground, Black & Orange Cab, Driver, 5 ½ In.	1090.00
Canisters, see introductory paragraph to Tins in this category.	
Cards are listed in the Card category.	
Case, Display, Robeson's Shuredge Knives, Oak, Shaped Gallery, Glass Door, 35 x 22 In.	325.00
Case, Sauers Extract, Wood, Glass, 28 ½ x 16 ½ x 12 ½ In.	440.00
Case, Star Kraft, Slant Front, 7 Metal Compartments, Wood, Glass, 14 x 63 x 22 In.	110.00
Case, Utica Drop Forge & Tool, 5 Drawers, American Art Works, 14 x 18 x 9 In.	275.00
Chair, Berry's 80 Years Of Good Furniture, Wood, Turned Spindles, 18 x 10 In.	58.00
Chair, Piedmont Cigarette, Folding, Porcelain Signs, Blue, White, 30 x 16 In.	240.00
Chair, RCA Victor, Chrome Frame, Vinyl Upholstery, Plastic Arm, 1950s, 33 x 21 x 25 In.	420.00
Chair, RCA Victor, Tubular Steel, Vinyl Seat & Back, 2 Arms, 33 In.	738.00
Change Receiver, Pointer's Cigar, 5 Cent Cigar, Dogs, Blue, White, Glass, 1 ¾ x 6 ¾ In.	1200.00
Change Receiver, see also Tip Tray in this category.	
Checkerboard, Banner Lye, 12 x 12 In.	60.00
Cigar Cutter, A.B. Smith & Co., Cast Iron, Lever Action, 8 ¼ x 6 In.	396.00
Cigar Cutter, Betsy Ross, Cast Iron, A.S. Valentine & Son, 7 ½ x 6 In.	750.00
Cigar Cutter, Black Beauty, Horse Head On Handle, Iron, Black Paint, 10 In.	120.00
Cigar Cutter, Country Gentleman 5 Cent, Lever Action, Chrome, 3 ½ x 3 x 4 ½ In.	181.00
Cigar Cutter, Cressman's Counsellor 5 Cent Cigar, Cast Iron, Windup	203.00
Cigar Cutter, Dutch Masters, Oak Base, Silver Frame, Stamped Brunhoff Mfg., 5 x 8 In.	300.00
Cigar Cutter, El Praco, Slant Front Cardboard, 8 ¾ x 9 ¼ x 10 In.	113.00
Cigar Cutter, General Electric, Figural, Cast Bronze, Steel Door, 1899, 4 ¼ x 4 ½ In.	357.00
Cigar Cutter, Lord Gloster Cigars, Man, 1920-30, 8 x 5 ½ x 5 ½ In.	275.00
Cigar Cutter, New Currency Tobacco, Lombard Co., 4 ½ x 8 In.	303.00
Cigar Cutter, Odd Or Even, Trade Stimulator, Cast Iron, White Metal, 4 x 6 In.	1200.00
Cigar Cutter, Peter Schuyler, 10 Cent Cigar, Reverse Painted Top, 4 ½ x 8 ¼ x 7 In.	226.00
Cigar Cutter, Peter Schuyler, Get Back Of A, Painted, 4 ½ x 8 ¼ x 6 ½ In.	240.00
Cigar Cutter, Smokettes Cigars, Trade Stimulator, Powell, Smith & Co., 1890, 7 x 6 In.	1200.00
Cigar Cutter, Spear Head Tobacco, P.J. Sorg Co., Embossed, Rogers Iron Corp., 16 ¾ In.	250.00
Cigar Lighter, La Palina, Electric, Woman, Palm Trees, 14 ½ In.	825.00
Clicker, Weather Bird Shoes, Image Of Bird, Yellow Ground, 1940s, 1 x 1 ½ In.	30.00
Clocks are listed in their own category.	
Clown, Coney Island Roller Coaster, Ziz, Celluloid, Die Cut, Multicolored, 2 ½ In.	569.00
Coaster, Stork Brewing Co., Schleisingerville, Wis.	350.00
Compass, Round, Lando, Manufacturing Optician, Bring Your Work To Us, 1 ¾ In. ....*illus*	165.00
Cooler, Nichol Kola, 31 x 22 x 34 In. ....*illus*	234.00
Counter Card, Ayer's Sarsaparilla, Girl, Red Hair, Blue Dress, Text On Back, Cardboard, 6 x 9 In.	264.00
Counter Card, Dent's Toothache Gum Stops Toothaches, A Swell Affair, Cardboard, 7 x 10 In.	523.00
Counter Card, Peck's Headache Powders Will Cure, Child's Head, Cardboard, Frame, 11 x 16 In.	209.00
Crayon Set, Pad & Eraser, Dr Pepper, 1982, Unopened	30.00
Cup & Saucer, Reddy Kilowatt, Ceramic, Syracuse China, 1950s	45.00
Cup, Tastee Freeze, Elf, 3 ½ In.	35.00
Cuspidor, Old Coon Cigars, Blue & White, Lava Ware, Graniteware, 2 Piece	325.00
Decal, Plumb Hand Tools, Philadelphia, Pennsylvania	121.00
Dispenser, Alka-Seltzer, Counter, 6 ½ x 5 ½ In.	220.00
Dispenser, Bromo-Seltzer, Cobalt Blue, Stand, Emerson Drug Co., July 5, 1910	138.00
Dispenser, Buckeye Root Beer, 5 Cent, Satyr Border, 14 x 7 ½ In.	1600.00
Dispenser, Buckeye Root Beer, Black, White Letters, Horseshoe Pump, Knob, c.1918	488.00
Dispenser, Drink Mo-Pep, White Barrel, 13 ¾ x 8 In.	695.00
Dispenser, Eskimo Pie, Tin Lithograph, Cast Metal Eskimo Feet & Base, Thermos, 16 In.	189.00
Dispenser, Fowler's Cherry Smash, Always Drink, 14 ½ x 9 In.	1750.00
Dispenser, Fowler's Cherry Smash, Always Drink, 5 Cent, 13 ½ x 9 ½ In.	1800.00
Dispenser, Fowler's Root Beer, The Best, 5 Cent, 14 ½ x 9 ½ In.	1000.00
Dispenser, Grape Crush, Amethyst, Barrel Form, 13 ¾ x 6 ½ In.	550.00
Dispenser, Grapefruitola, Ceramic, Plunger Cap, F.M. Williams, c.1913, 15 In.	40800.00
Dispenser, Green River, Glass Center, Metal Base, Original Jug, 1910, 17 In.	310.00
Dispenser, Hires Root Beer, Ceramic, Painted, Original Pump, 14 In.	620.00

Dispenser, Hires Root Beer, White, Red, Hourglass Form, 14 ½ In.	220.00
Dispenser, Howels Cherry-Julep, 5 Cents, Pump, c.1920	4400.00
Dispenser, Ice Cream Cone, Pikes Peak, Enjoy Lots Of Ice Cream, Metal, 20 x 13 In.	115.00
Dispenser, Lash's Dixie Dew, Glass, Pedestal Base, Spigot, c.1900, 16 In.	743.00
Dispenser, Lash's Orangeade, From Sun Ripened Fruit, Orange Finial, Spout, 22 x 16 In.	366.00
Dispenser, Lash's Syrup, Milk Glass Base, Depression Glass Top, 1940s, 13 In. .... *illus*	176.00
Dispenser, Malted Grape-Nuts, Chocolate Flavored, Yellow, 15 In.	690.00
Dispenser, Mansfield's Pepsin Gum, 5 Cent Coin Mechanism, c.1900, 12 In.	570.00
Dispenser, Mission Grapefruit, Black Base, Lid, Spigot, c.1900, 14 In.	352.00
Dispenser, Mission Orange, Painted, Metal, Spigot, 28 x 16 In.	1080.00
Dispenser, Mission Orange, Yellow, Black, 1920-30, 28 In.	330.00
Dispenser, Mission Orangeade, Orange Slices On Top, Spigot, Footed, 15 ½ In.	1121.00
Dispenser, Mission Rickey Lime, Lime Slices On Top, Spigot, Footed, 15 ½ In.	880.00
Dispenser, Orange-Crush, Black Glass Base, Frosted Globe, Metal Lid, c.1910, 17 In.	525.00
Dispenser, Orange-Crush, Mailbox Form, 2-Sided Porcelain Marquee, 17 x 10 x 5 ½ In.	920.00
Dispenser, Peterson's Flavor Roasted Nuts, Glass, Wood, 14 ½ x 24 x 9 In.	248.00
Dispenser, Pulver Chewing Gum, 1 Cent, Red, Enamel, Glass, Slot, Labels, 9 x 21 In.	690.00
Dispenser, Steamro, Spicy Red Hots Hot Dog, White, Red, 13 ½ x 20 ½ x 12 ¾ In.	165.00
Dispenser, Ward's Grape-Crush, Grapes, Amethyst Glass, 15 In.	1100.00
Dispenser, Ward's, Lemon-Crush, Lemon, 12 x 11 In.	1000.00
Dispenser, Ward's Lemon-Crush, Ceramic, 13 ½ In.	1300.00
Dispenser, Ward's Lime-Crush, Ceramic, 13 ½ In.	3800.00
Dispenser, Ward's, Orange-Crush, Orange, 14 x 9 In.	1000.00
Dispenser, Ward's Orange-Crush Syrup, Figural, Ceramic, Ball Style Pump, c.1910, 14 ½ In. .	2500.00
Display, 7Up, Man, Soda Case, 1950, 12 In.	53.00
Display, A.P.W. Tissues, Children, Dollhouse, 2 Piece Folding Cardboard, 12 x 10 In.	468.00
Display, Ardenter Mustard, Dean's Patent, Label, Wood, 16 ¼ x 22 ⅝ x 11 In.	385.00
Display, Becker's Avio Helmet, Face, Helmet, Goggles, Chalkware, 16 x 7 x 6 In.	1950.00
Display, Beechnut Gum, Tin Lithograph, Foldover Marquee, 15 In.	213.00
Display, Beringer Jewelry Store, Man, Woman Swinging, Flower, Dog, Automaton, 13 x 25 In.	4100.00
Display, Boot, Plaster, Wall Mount, 18 x 9 In.	110.00
Display, Bowtie, Par Bow For Perfection, Revolving, Wood, 23 ½ x 6 ½ In.	135.00
Display, California Syrup Of Figs, For Healthy Children, Cardboard, 35 x 21 In.	469.00
Display, Calox Tooth Powder, Your 32 Teeth Are 32 Reasons, Mirrored Glass, 12 x 7 x 4 In.	385.00
Display, Carborundum Razor Strop Dressing, Man, Shaving, Tin Lithograph, 9 x 13 In.	935.00
Display, Chalkboard, Better Buy Blitz, Incised, c.1951, 9 x 9 ½ In.	195.00
Display, Chase & Sanborn's Teas & Coffees, White, Tin, Pat June 16, 1908, 33 x 16 x 9 In.	440.00
Display, Children's Hickory Garters, Children, Umbrella, Wood, 19 x 13 In.	743.00
Display, Coconut Oil Shampoo, Cardboard, 11 Starlets Of The Era, 1930s, 37 x 44 In.	60.00
Display, Colburn's Bag Blue, Wood, Paper Label, 14 x 11 ¾ x 11 ¾ In.	469.00
Display, Columbian Pure Manila Rope, Tape Marked, Wood, Painted, 16 x 11 In.	83.00
Display, Country Gentlemen Tobacco, 12 Cloth Pouches, Cardboard, 9 x 8 x 5 In.	143.00
Display, Cow-Ease, Spray Your Team Free, Keeps Flies Off, Metal, Wood, 34 ¼ In.	2420.00
Display, Dandy Catnip Mouse, Make Kitty Happy, Mouse In Top Hat, Electric, 34 x 26 x 12 In.	1480.00
Display, Diamond Dyes, Woman Using Dye On Clothes, Metal, Glass, 2-Sided, 30 x 11 In.	1265.00
Display, Double Cola, Woman, In Canoe, Lily Pads, Trifold, Cardboard, 24 x 101 In.	900.00
Display, Eveready Flashlight, Red, Blue, Metal, 19 x 7 x 8 In.	44.00
Display, Fad-A-Way Gum Ball, American Chicle, Hinged, c.1910, 7 x 4 In.	2640.00
Display, Folding Rule, J. Rabone & Sons, England, Boxwood, c.1930, 8-Ft. Open	4180.00
Display, Freihofer's Cake, Metal, Glass, 2 Shelves, 28 x 15 x 17 In. .... *illus*	263.00
Display, General Electric Iron, You Can Put Your Confidence In, 1960s .... *illus*	176.00
Display, Gibson Music Strings, Art Deco Architectural Shape, Yellow, Blue, Wood, 14 x 22 In.	468.00
Display, He's Got Moxie, 5 Cents, Boy Ball Player, Die Cut Cardboard, Easel Back, 13 x 9 In. ..	743.00
Display, Heinz Pickle, Pickle Shape, Papier-Mache, Brown, Pink, 20 x 5 ½ In.	2640.00
Display, Heinz Tomato Head, Top Hat, Monocle, Red, Black, White, Composition, 5 ½ x 3 In.	440.00
Display, Hickman's Silver Birch Chewing Gum, Bird, 20 Packages, Box, c.1920s, 5 x 4 In.	523.00
Display, Hood Rubber Canvas Footwear, Man, Flag, Red, Die Cut Tin Lithograph, 14 x 14 In.	2430.00
Display, Ingersoll Watches, Tin, Slanted Glass Front, Wood, c.1920s, 5 ½ x 12 ½ In.	380.00
Display, J. & P. Coats', Rack, Metal, 24 Compartment, 14 ¼ x 13 ¼ x 7 In.	65.00
Display, Jar, Planter's Fishbowl, Lid, Clear, Red, Brown Label, 13 x 10 In.	385.00
Display, Lamb's Knit Sweater, Figural, Lamb, Papier-Mache, Plaster, Paint, 15 x 17 In.	908.00
Display, Lenox Soap, Stand-Up, 64 In. .... *illus*	234.00
Display, Life Savers, Product Rack, Tin Lithograph, Multicolored, 9 ½ x 13 In.	853.00
Display, Lucky Strike Cigarette, 3-D, Die Cut, 4-Fold, Cardboard	6325.00
Display, Lucky Strike, Swimmer, Tennis Player, Diver, Pitcher, Die Cut, Quad-Fold, 40 x 75 In.	6100.00
Display, Lucky Strike, The Cream Of The Crop, Cardboard, Window, c.1915-20, 46 x 34 In. ...	1155.00

Advertising, Display, Freihofer's Cake, Metal, Glass, 2 Shelves, 28 x 15 x 17 In. $263.00

A

Advertising, Display,
General Electric Iron,
You Can Put Your Confidence In,
1960s
$176.00

Advertising, Display, Lenox Soap,
Stand-Up, 64 In.
$234.00

Advertising, Display, Red Goose,
Golden Egg, Plastic, Electric, 31 x 29 In.
$468.00

Display, Merkle's Blu-J Broom, Embossed, Tin Panels, Steel, 34 ¾ x 23 x 10 ½ In. 1200.00
Display, National Mazda Lamps, Tin, 11 Lights, 19 x 28 x 6 In. 820.00
Display, Noxaboil, Internal Remedy, Cardboard, Flip Top Lid, 3 ½ x 6 In. 1980.00
Display, Perfumer, Richard Hudnut, Electric, 3-Rib Panels, 9 x 21 In. 1456.00
Display, Philip Morris, Factory Scene, Mechanical, 41 x 50 x 23 In. 1750.00
Display, Pon-Tam-Pon, Improved Method Of Local Medication For Women, Contents, 4 x 7 ⅜ In. .. 1100.00
Display, RCA Radiotron, Look'N The Book, Man Reading, Cardboard, c.1920, 12 ¾ x 13 In. .. 715.00
Display, RCA Radiotron, Tubes Tested Free, Reverse Glass, Metal, Light-Up, 6 x 11 x 4 In. 530.00
Display, Red Dot, Truly Different, 5 Cent, Boxes, Cutout Cigar, Cardboard, 38 x 16 In. 168.00
Display, Red Goose, Golden Egg, Plastic, Electric, 31 x 29 In. ....*illus* 468.00
Display, Rice's Seed, Tin Lithograph, Wood Table, 55 x 24 x 22 In. 395.00
Display, Ruppert Beer-Ale, Foam Scraper Holder, Glass, Bakelite Base, 6 ½ x 4 ¾ In. 358.00
Display, Safe-T-Cup Ice Cream Cones, Ice Cream Cone, Figural, Papier-Mache, 21 In. 121.00
Display, Screwdriver, Wood, 42 In. 220.00
Display, Smith Bros. Cough Drops, Black, Red, Boxes, 9 ¾ x 4 x 4 In. 520.00
Display, Smith Brothers Cough Drops, Tin Lithograph, Black, Red, 11 x 4 In. 2970.00
Display, Standard Licorice Lozenges, Glass, Tin, Hinged Lid, Chinese Figures, 5 x 7 In. 303.00
Display, Star Pepsin Chewing Gum, 2 Packages 5 Cents, Tin Lithograph, 11 x 9 In. 200.00
Display, Sunbeam Bread, Girl, Cardboard, Stand-Up Bread Box, 1950s, 40 x 27 In. ....*illus* 205.00
Display, Sunset Soap Dyes, 20 Slots, Wood, 7 ¾ x 14 x 18 In. 135.00
Display, Trunk, Honey Tolu Chewing Gum, Dome Top Interior Label, 11 x 12 In. 154.00
Display, Uncle John's Syrup, Die Cut, Cardboard, Karle Litho Co., 16 ¾ x 12 In. 36.00
Display, Vidor Batteries, Robot, For Super Power, Super Life, Cardboard, 14 x 9 In. 112.00
Display, Whistle Soda, Elf Pushing Cart With Bottle, Cardboard, Die Cut, Glass, 8 ½ x 8 In. ... 175.00
Display, Winchester, Cowboy, On White Horse, Die Cut, Cardboard, 36 x 80 In. 4600.00
Display, Window, Red Wing Grape Juice, Indian, Field, Die Cut, Cardboard, 35 ½ x 70 In. 240.00
Dolls are listed in their own category.
Door Pull, Land O' Lakes, Sweet Cream Butter, White, Embossed, Tin, Brass, 1940, 18 ½ x 3 In. .. 40.00
Door Pull, Major's Cement, Mends Everything, Blue, White, Oval, Porcelain, 3 ¾ x 2 ½ In. ... 495.00
Door Push, Braun's Town Talk Bread, Yellow, Red, Blue, Tin, T-Shape 60.00
Door Push, Bunny Bread, Mom Be A Honey, Yellow, Red, Tin, 12 x 4 In. 330.00
Door Push, Crescent Flour, Push & Try A Snack, Blue, White, Embossed, Tin Litho, 10 x 3 In. .. 2035.00
Door Push, Dr Pepper, Drink A Bite To Eat, Metal, c.1940, 4 x 8 In. 325.00
Door Push, Grain Belt, 2-Sided, Adjustable, 34 In. 85.00
Door Push, Hoffman Bicycles, Please Close Door, Best In The World, Embossed, Tin, 9 x 3 In. 522.00
Door Push, Orange Crush, Come In, Orange, Black, Embossed, Tin Lithograph, c.1920, 12 x 3 In. . 469.00
Door Push, Purity Bread, Tin, 5 x 30 In. 135.00
Door Push, Smoke Blue Bell, Beveled Glass, 2 x 6 In. 212.00
Door Push, Wise Potato Chips, Did You Buy Wise?, Embossed, Tin Lithograph, 6 ⅝ x 3 ¼ In. .. 1925.00
Door Push-Pull Bar, Orange-Crush, Feel Fresh, Painted, Tin, 6 x 3 In., 2 Piece 2000.00
Door Push-Pull Bar, Salada Tea, Porcelain, 1930s, 3 x 31 ½ In. 127.00
Door Screen, Colonial Is Good Bread, 84 x 42 In. 66.00
Doorstop, Quaker Rolled White Oats, Yellow, Blue, White, Tin, 5 ¼ x 3 ¾ In. 295.00
Dose Glass, Laird & Dines, Arizona, 1 In. 530.00
Drinking Glass, Canada Dry, 1939, Show Trylon, Perisphere, 3 Cents, Set Of 6 .... 635.00
Dustpan, Treasure Line Of Stoves & Ranges, Tin Lithograph, D. Moore & Co., 6 x 9 In. 100.00
Fans are listed in their own category.
Figure, Dog, RCA, Nipper, Black Ears, Collar, Plaster, 14 ½ In. 66.00
Figure, Dog, RCA, Nipper, Brown Ears, Vinyl, 17 ½ In. 66.00
Figure, Dog, RCA, Nipper, Brown Eyes, Black Collar, Papier-Mache, 11 ½ In. 121.00
Figure, Dog, RCA, Nipper, Plaster, 9 ½ In. 88.00
Figure, Dog, RCA, Nipper, Plaster, 15 In. 780.00
Figure, Dog, RCA, Nipper, Plaster, 19 ½ In. 396.00
Figure, Dog, RCA, Nipper, Studded Collar, Paper Label, Painted, Papier-Mache, 36 x 26 x 16 In. .. 863.00
Figure, Dog, RCA, Nipper, Vinyl, 36 In. 413.00
Figure, Dog, RCA, Nipper, White, Black, Chalkware, 14 ½ In. 175.00
Figure, Dog, RCA, Nipper, Yesterday Once Again, Huntington Beach, California, Cement, 12 In. . 28.00
Figure, Dog, RCA, Old King Cole Displays, 11 In. 150.00
Figure, Eskie, Man In Suit & Topcoat, Esquire Magazine Mascot, 24 ½ In. 366.00
Figure, Hills Bros. Coffee, Man Drinking Coffee, Yellow, White, Plaster, 18 ½ In. 500.00
Figure, Jockey, Jimmy Wink Winkfield, Admiral Cigarette, 1901, 2 ½ In. 50.00
Figure, Mr. Peanut, Papier-Mache, Stand-Up, Old King Cole Company, c.1920, 13 x 7 In. 1100.00
Figure, Nipper & Chipper, RCA, Happy Holidays, Dakin, Box 50.00
Figure, RCA Radiotron, Maxfield Parrish Style, Wood, Painted, 1930s, 15 ½ In. 690.00
Figure, Red Goose Shoes, Goose, Chalkware, 11 ½ In. 145.00
Figure, Ziz The Clown, Celluloid, Coney Island Roller Coaster, Red Body, 1800s, 3 In. 575.00

Flask, Green River Whiskey, Leather Covered, Shot Glass Lid, 2 Pt. ....*illus*		110.00
Flue Dampener, Round Oaks, Indian, Embossed, Cast Iron, 6 ½ x 4 ½ In.		301.00
Flyswatter, W.L. McCulloh, Frick, Ferguson Tractors, Implements		18.00
Globe, Optician, Milk Glass, Painted, 2-Sided, Electric, Brass Hanger, 12 In. ....*illus*		878.00
Globe, Pensupreme Ice Cream, Light-Up, Green, Red, White, 17 x 16 In., 3 Piece		7040.00
Handkerchief, Harley-Davidson, Too Tough To Die, Eagle, Emblem, 14 ½ x 15 In.		140.00
Hot Plate, Lydia Pinkham's, Pot Metal, 5 x 5 In.		121.00
Humidor, Bromo-Seltzer, Interior Label, Wood, 4 ½ x 10 ½ x 5 ¾ In.		30.00
Ink Blotter, Old Colony Insurance Co.		4.00
Inkwell, Stephanie Biscuits, Mouse Eating Cookies, Insert, Lead Alloy, 5 x 2 In.		263.00
Jar, Bull's Head Mustard, Pat Applied For, Milk Glass, c.1875, 4 ¼ In.		79.00
Jar, Chicos Spanish Peanuts, 3-Sided Base, Glass, Tin Lid, 12 x 8 In.		550.00
Jar, Faultless Wonder Nipples, Nipple Lid, 13 x 6 In.		5300.00
Jar, Honey-Moon Tobacco, Will Not Bite The Tongue, Paper Label, 5 ¼ x 5 x 5 In.		550.00
Jar, Noggle's Orangeade Syrup, Lug, Metal Cap, 11 In.		209.00
Jar, Piedmont Candy, Lexington, N.C., 13 x 10 In.		118.00
Jar, Ramon's Brownie Pills, Tins, Contents Paper Wrapped, 8 x 6 In.		176.00
Jar, W & S Cough Drop, Pressed Glass, 7 ½ x 8 ¼ In.		145.00
Jar, Welch's Jelly, Howdy Doody & Friends, 1953		44.00
Keg, Powder, Texas Rifle Oriental Powder Mill, Wood, Red Paint, Label, Indian, 9 x 6 In.		489.00
Key Chain, Flashlight, Reddy Kilowatt, Plastic, Flip-Open, 1950s, 3 In.		30.00
Kit, Our Gang, Activities, Morton Salt Premium, 1937, 7 ¼ x 9 ¾ In.		173.00
Label, Cigar, National Sportsman, Embossed, 24K Gold, Hunting & Fishing Scene, 9 x 7 In. ..		67.00
Label, Food, Old Sleepy Eye Milling Co., Strong Bakers, Indian Chief, Vilmanns Bros., 16 In. .		50.00
Label, Tobacco, Crusader, Watson & McGill, Petersburg, Va., 14 ¼ x 7 In.		35.00
Label, Tobacco, Diana, Bow & Arrow, 11 x 7 In.		30.00
Label, Tobacco, Golden Eagle, T.C. Williams Co., 10 ½ x 10 ¼ In.		123.00
Label, Tobacco, Kohinoor Man, David Dunlop, Petersburg, Va., 13 ½ x 6 ½ In.		60.00
Label, Tobacco, Nosegay, Woman Holding Flower Basket, American Tobacco Co., 13 x 7 In. ...		60.00
Label, Tobacco, Old Sport Dog In Suit, 11 x 10 ¾ In.		250.00
Lamps are listed in the Lamp category.		
Light Bulb, Victory Glow, Standard Socket, V With Lightning Bolt In Center, 1940s, 4 In.		310.00
Lunch Box, Dixie Kid Cut Plug, Black Child, Nall & Williams. Co., 4 x 8 x 5 In. ...	385.00 to	715.00
Lunch Box, Pedro Smoking Tobacco, Cut Plug, Yellow, Red, 4 ½ x 8 x 5 ¼ In.		495.00
Lunch Box, Winner Cut Plug, Smoke & Chew, Race Car Scene, 4 ¼ x 7 ⅞ In.		632.00
Lunch Boxes are also listed in their own category.		
Lunch Pail, Winner Cut Plug, Indy Style Race Cars, Handle, 4 x 5 x 7 ¾ In. ....*illus*		410.00
Manual, Advertising Strategy, Phillips Petroleum Company, 1930s......................		118.00
Marquee, Meat Hook, J.E. Smith's Sons, Bull, Cast Iron, Embossed, Painted, 1880s, 15 x 8 In. .		240.00
Meat Grinder, Cast Iron, Crank, Wood Handle, James L. Haven & Co., Pat. Jan. 22, 1867		12.00
Menu Board, Budweiser Light, Plastic, Light-Up, 33 ¼ x 13 ¾ In.		50.00
Menu Board, Dad's Root Beer, Unbelievable, 27 ½ x 19 ½ In.		118.00
Menu Board, Heinz Soups, 2 Minute Service, Have A Bowl 15 Cents, Wood, 13 x 26 ¾ In.		56.00
Menu Board, Orange Crush, Vintage Painted-Label Bottle, Tin, Cardboard, 24 x 36 In.		443.00

Advertising mirrors of all sizes are listed here. Pocket mirrors range in size from 1 ½ to 5 inches in diameter. Most of these mirrors were given away as advertising promotions and include the name of the company in the design.

Mirror, Bob & Jake's Good For 5 Cents In Trade, Celluloid, Pocket, 1 ¾ In.	744.00
Mirror, Bradford Wholesale Furniture Mfg., Stork, Baby, Celluloid, Oval, 2 ¾ x 1 ¾ In.	605.00
Mirror, Buckwalter Stove, Pocket, Oval, Enameled Range, Tin Lithograph, 2 ¾ x 1 ¾ In.	88.00
Mirror, Dr. Daniels Dog & Puppy Bread, Celluloid, G.A. Quimby, 2 ½ In.	180.00
Mirror, Egg Baking Powder, Child Holding Product, Red, Blue, White, Pocket, 2 In.	468.00
Mirror, Falls City Brewing Co., Whitehead & Hoag, Celluloid, Nov. 1906, 1 ¾ x 2 ¾ In. ...*illus*	234.00
Mirror, F.C. Krug Cigars, Compliments Of Sports Cigar Store, Oval, Celluloid, 2 ¾ x 2 In.	240.00
Mirror, Grapette Soda, Bottle, 10 x 7 In.	110.00
Mirror, Grapette Soda, Thirsty Or Not, 11 x 7 In.	110.00
Mirror, Have You A Victrola In Your Home, Nipper Dog, Victrola, Celluloid, Victor, 3 x 2 In. ...	132.00
Mirror, His Master's Voice, 16 x 20 In.	72.00
Mirror, King Arthur Flour, Knight, Horse, 2 In.	132.00
Mirror, Liberty Mills, Peacock, Celluloid, 1 ¾ x 2 ¾ In. ....*illus*	351.00
Mirror, Long's California Maraschino Cherries, Yellow Ground, Pocket, 1 ¾ x ⅜ In.	160.00
Mirror, Mahlon N. Haines, Show Wizard, Photo, Blue, White, Celluloid, 2 ¼ In.	11.00
Mirror, Nature's Remedy Better Than Pills For Liver Ills, Happy Face, Blue, Celluloid, 2 In. ...	110.00
Mirror, Queen Quality Shoes, Woman Wearing Hat, 1 ¾ x 2 ¾ In.	68.00
Mirror, Seager Engine Works, Olds Engine, Celluloid, 2 ½ In. Diam......................	176.00

Advertising, Display, Sunbeam Bread, Girl, Cardboard, Stand-Up Bread Box, 1950s, 40 x 27 In.
$205.00

Advertising, Flask, Green River Whiskey, Leather Covered, Shot Glass Lid, 2 Pt.
$110.00

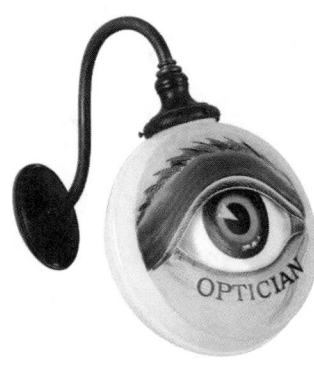

Advertising, Globe, Optician, Milk Glass, Painted, 2-Sided, Electric, Brass Hanger, 12 In.
$878.00

ADVERTISING

Advertising, Lunch Pail,
Winner Cut Plug, Indy Style Race Cars,
Handle, 4 x 5 x 7 ¾ In.
$410.00

Advertising, Mirror,
Falls City Brewing Co., Whitehead & Hoag,
Celluloid, Nov. 1906, 1 ¾ x 2 ¾ In.
$234.00

Advertising, Mirror, Liberty Mills,
Peacock, Celluloid, 1 ¾ x 2 ¾ In.
$351.00

Advertising, Mug, Hires, Ugly Kid,
Bib, 4 ⅜ x 4 ¾ In.
$59.00

Mirror, Security Life Insurance, Celluloid, Lithograph, Pocket, 1 ¾ x 2 ¾ In.	45.00
Mirror, Skeezix Shoes, Outgrown Before Outworn, 12 Months, Celluloid, 2 ½ In. Diam.	75.00
Mirror, Snow Shoe, Man With Dog, Celluloid, Oval, 2 ¾ x 1 ¾ In.	30.00
Mirror, Stutz-Ideal Motor Car Co., Indianapolis, Ind., 2 ½ In. Diam.	165.00
Mirror, Sunlight Soap, For Dainty Clothes, Woman Hanging Laundry, Celluloid, 2 ¼ In.	550.00
Mirror, Traveler's Insurance, Locomotive, Celluloid, Oval, 2 ⅝ In.	138.00
Mirror, W. Jones Brewing Co., Barrel, Granite State, Celluloid, 1 ¾ x 2 ¾ In.	176.00
Mirror, Willow Brothel, Woman, Good For 10 Cents, Lebanon, Pa., Celluloid, 2 ¼ In. Diam.	240.00
Mirror, Woolseys Marine & Yacht Paint, Special Red, Green, Celluloid, 2 ¾ x 1 ¾ In.	165.00
Mug, Arrow Beer, Stoneware, Decal, Globe Brewing Co., Balto. Md., 10 ½ In.	30.00
Mug, Beer, Ayinger-Bier-Spezialitaten, Glass, Bavaria, ⅓ Liter	6.00
Mug, Beer, Becks Logo, Embossed, 5 In.	8.00
Mug, Dove Brand Ginger Ale, Porcelain, Tan, Brown, Transfer, Branch Handle, 5 In.	20.00
Mug, Heineken, Red Windmill Logo, Glass, 6 ½ In.	8.00
Mug, Hires, Ugly Kid, Bib, 4 ⅜ x 4 ¾ In. .....*illus*	59.00
Mug, Shaving, Pond's White Areca Nut Tooth Paste, Porcelain, Transfer, Portmerion, 4 In.	12.00
Nail Bag, Mercersburg Builders Supply Co.	10.00
Pack, Long Tom Smoking Tobacco, Cloth Label, Contents, 1 ¼ Oz., 4 ¾ x 1 ½ In.	529.00
Package, Cycle Cigarettes, Bike Riders, Liggett & Myers, 2 ¾ x 2 In.	154.00
Package, Lipstick Tissue, Kleenex, Broadmoor Colorado Hotel, Contents, Parrish, 3 x 2 In.	112.00
Package, Mr. Wiggle, Gelatin Dessert, Solid Hollow Vinyl, General Foods, 1968	225.00
Package, Sample, Blue Car Tobacco, Blue Paper, New York, c.1909, 4 x 2 In.	170.00
Package, Wood's Hog Cholera Food, Pigs Eating, Wood Food Company, 5 x 6 In.	231.00
Pail, Big Sister Peanut Butter, Producers Co., Witch On Broom, Tin, 3 ½ x 3 ¾ In. .....*illus*	819.00
Pail, Bluhill Coffee, Blue, White, Bail Handle, 5 Lb.	190.00
Pail, Calumet Lard, Pure Leaf Lard, Indian, Tin Litho, Handle, G.H. Hammond Co., 6 x 5 ¾ In.	1595.00
Pail, Clark's Peanut Butter, Wilderness Scene, Tin, Handle, Lid, Can Co., Canada, 3 x 4 In.	1404.00
Pail, Dinner Party, Coffee, Red, White, Bail Handle, 5 Lb.	140.00
Pail, Fi-Na-St Peanut Butter, Tin, Lid, Handle, First National Stores Inc., 3 ¾ x 3 ¾ In.	527.00
Pail, Garland Blend Coffee, Blue, White, Bail Handle, 5 Lb.	275.00
Pail, Giant Salted Peanuts, Circus Images, Tin Litho, Handle, Superior Peanut Co., 3 x 4 In.	580.00
Pail, Happy Kids Peanut Butter, W.B. Roddenberry, Paper Label, Tin, 3 ½ x 4 In. .....*illus*	527.00
Pail, Morris Supreme Peanut Butter, Children At Seashore, 3 x 3 ½ In.	550.00
Pail, Mount Cross Coffee, Red, White, Blue, Bail Handle, 5 Lb.	195.00
Pail, Old Reliable Peanut Butter, Children Playing, Handle, 1 Lb., 3 ¾ x 3 ¼ In.	550.00
Pail, Penny Post Cut Plug Tobacco, Red, 4 ½ x 7 In.	212.00
Pail, Red Riding Hood Candy, Nursery Rhyme Story, Handle, 2 ¾ x 2 ⅞ In.	253.00
Pail, School Days Peanut Butter, Tin, Handle, Lid, United Fig & Date Co., 3 ½ x 4 In.	995.00
Pail, Wizard Of Oz Peanut Butter, Dorothy, Bail Handle, 2 Lb.	44.00
Pails are also listed in the Lunch Box category.	
Patch, Chas. H. Sixeas Motor Transit, Mercersburg, 8 ½ x 13 ½ In.	18.00
Pennant, None Such Pancake Flour, Blue, Yellow, Felt, c.1910, 27 ½ In.	85.00
Pennant, Summit Dress Shirts, Trademark Man Buttoning, Blue, White, 25 x 11 In.	132.00
Pin, 7th Annual Reunion Baer Family, Kutztown Park, Aug. 4, 1906, Celluloid, 2 ¼ In.	147.00
Pin, 7Up, Zorro, Orange Z, Black Horse, Rider, Lithograph, ⅞ In.	13.00
Pin, Baltimore Orioles, I'm A Bird Watcher At WBAL-TV 11, Orange, Black, Celluloid, 1 ¾ In.	31.00
Pin, Buffalo Bill, England Tour, 1903-1907, 1 ⅜ In.	459.00
Pin, Buitoni Foods Corp., Joe DiMaggio Club, Tin Lithograph, 1950s, 1 ½ In. .....*illus*	633.00
Pin, Chiquita, Cuban Midget, Woman, Evening Dress, Multicolored, 2 ⅛ In.	115.00
Pin, Christmas Greetings From Sears, Santa, Holly, Spencer Back Paper, ⅞ In.	58.00
Pin, Cinderella Stoves & Ranges Never Fail, Whitehead & Hoag Back Paper, ⅞ In.	30.00
Pin, Fleischmann's Yeast, Horse & Delivery Wagon, In Snow, 1900-12, 1 ¾ In.	177.00
Pin, Fly Wein Air Alaska, Goose Wearing Flying Cap & Goggles, Celluloid, 1 ¼ In.	73.00
Pin, George Washington Soda, Whitehead & Hoag, 1 ¼ In.	99.00
Pin, Gimme H-O Oats For Breakfast, Celluloid, 1 ¼ In.	17.00
Pin, Gold Dust Washing Powder, Black Babies In Tub, 1896, 1 In.	62.00
Pin, Hoffman's Rice Starch, Whitehead & Hoag Back Paper, ⅞ In.	13.00
Pin, Iowa Association Southern California, Corn, Celluloid, 1 ¾ In.	45.00
Pin, Knute Rockne All American, Pudlin, Back Paper, Celluloid, Warner Bros., ⅞ In.	43.00
Pin, Kodak, You Press The Button, We Do The Rest, Color, c.1896, ⅞ In.	115.00
Pin, Kukla, Fran & Ollie, Photo Of Fran Allison, 1950s, 1 ⅛ In.	75.00
Pin, Mannings Nylon Hosiery, Sheer But Sure, Posed Woman, Raised Skirt, 1940s, 4 In.	115.00
Pin, Milk Button, Graphic, Baby Drinking Milk, Quality Milk None Better, 1 ¼ In.	115.00
Pin, Only Trotting Steer In The World, Photo, Steer Harnessed To Sulky, 2 ⅛ In.	177.00
Pin, Pollyanna Club, Be Glad, Boston Badge, Back Paper, Celluloid, ⅞ In.	10.00
Pin, Roper Snow Suits, For Boys & Girls, Color, Bastian, c.1910, 1 ¼ In.	601.00

Pin, Satan-Et The Drink With A Wink, Winking Devil, 1910-20, ⅞ In.	139.00
Pin, Toys Galore At The Penny Store, Santa Claus, Toys, Philadelphia Badge, ⅞ In.	58.00
Pin, UPS, Go Big Brown, Derby Winner, Rider In Silks, Brown, White, 2 ¼ In.	9.00
Pin, Velie Brand, Carriages, Saddles, Automobiles, Airplanes, Kansas, c.1900	233.00
Pin, Webster City Carnival, We Meet At Webster City, Woman, Clown, Whitehead & Hoag, 1899, 1 ¾ In.	85.00
Pitcher, Friends Oats, Girl Holding Box & Sign, Gilt Trim, Porcelain, 2 ¾ x 1 ¾ In.	440.00
Pitcher, Henderson's Wild Cherry Beverage, Glass, Embossed, Shaped Rim, 8 ½ In.	71.00
Plaque, Arrowsharp Axes-Knives, 5 x 14 In.	106.00
Plaque, Beaver Underwear, Bronze, 7 ½ x 12 In.	189.00
Plaque, Chippewa Iron Works, Albany, N.Y., 9 ½ x 22 In.	307.00
Plaque, Donnely Brick Co., Cameo, Terra-Cotta, Early 20th Century, 6 x 8 In.	403.00
Plaque, Tri-State Antique, Porcelain, 6 In.	175.00
Plate, Abbottmaid Ice Cream, 6th Anniversary, c.1920, 6 ½ In.	250.00
Plate, Calvert, Clear Heads Choose, Owl, 10 In., 12 Piece	30.00
Platter, Robert Burns Cigar, 10 Cent, Tin, 24 In. Diam.	660.00
Pot Lid, X. Bazin, Purified Charcoal Tooth Paste, White Glazed Pottery, c.1860, 3 ¾ x 2 ⅜ In. *illus*	173.00
Pot Scraper, Fairmont Creamery, Tin, Red Ground, 3 x 2 ¼ In.	450.00
Pot Scraper, Junket Powder Milk Desserts, White, Red, Black, 3 ¼ x 2 ½ In.	550.00
Pot Scraper, Mardi-Gras Teas & Coffees, Chas. W. Shonk, Tin, 6 ½ x 9 ¼ In. *illus*	322.00
Pot Scraper, Sharples Cream Separators, 1909, 2 ¼ x 3 In.	395.00
Pot Scraper, Snow King, Sam W. Weidler Co. *illus*	410.00
Pouch, Quadroon Tobacco, Cloth, Image Of Woman With Fan, 1883 Tax, 4 ½ x 3 In.	770.00
Pouch, Tobacco, Victory Smoking Tobacco, Indian On Horse, Cloth, Paper Label, 4 x 2 ½ In.	385.00
Printer's Plate, Chesterfield Cigarettes, Fred MacMurray, 1949, 8 x 10 In.	30.00
Printer's Plate, Chesterfield Cigarettes, Janis Carter, 1949, 8 x 10 In.	30.00
Printer's Plate, Chesterfield Cigarettes, Kirk Douglas, 1950, 6 x 10 In.	30.00
Rack, Fairmaid Is Good Bread, Wire, 3 ½ x 96 In.	55.00
Rack, Greyhound, Depot Timetable, c.1940	700.00
Rack, Greyhound, Map Of Depot, c.1940	395.00
Rack, Merkle's Blu-J Brooms, 34 ¾ x 23 ½ x 12 In.	385.00
Rack, Smoke, Moxie, Butler, Tray, Paint, Wood, Moxie Soda Co., 32 x 7 In.	440.00
Rack, Wrigley's Chewing Gum, Metal, 5 Slots, 4 ½ x 17 ¼ In.	77.00
Rattle, Heinz Baby Food, Hard Plastic, Baby Blue & Pink, 1950s	13.00
Regulator, Pratt's Poultry Tonic & Appetizer, Sealed Package, 4 x 8 In.	61.00
Ring, Nabisco, Ted Williams, Brass, Plastic, Adjustable, c.1948, 1 In. *illus*	140.00
Ring, Popsicle Premium, Cowboy Boot, Red & White, 3-D, Plastic, 1951	65.00
Ring, Smith Brothers Cough Drops, Western Saddle, Order Form, c.1951, 5 x 7 In.	115.00
Roaster, Butter-Kist Toasted Peanut, Stand, 24 x 28 x 18 In.	440.00
Salt & Pepper Shakers are listed in their own category.	
Scales are listed in their own category.	
Scoop, Nabisco Grain Co., Wood, 28 ½ x 11 ½ x 5 ½ In.	330.00
Sign, 4th Liberty Loan, Sweep Them Out Of France, German Soldiers, Cardboard, 12 x 22 In.	255.00
Sign, 7Up, The Uncola, Stylized Sunrise, Peter Max, Enameled Metal, Flange, 24 In.	118.00
Sign, 7Up, Tin, 1954, 13 x 43 In.	277.00
Sign, 7Up, Your Fresh Up, Hand Holding Bottle, Tin, Iron, Sidewalk, 2-Sided, 33 x 20 In.	760.00
Sign, A. Fisher Brewing Co., Paper Lithograph, 20 x 16 In.	1382.00
Sign, ABC Washers & Ironers, E.J.J. Gobrecht, Wooden, Half Circle, c.1910, 56 In.	527.00
Sign, Abbott & Costello, Jack In The Bean Stalk Brand Carrots, 17 x 22 In.	115.00
Sign, Acme Beer On Draught, 5 Cent, Army & Navy Bar, Reverse Glass, c.1910, 42 x 22 In.	1600.00
Sign, Amen, Wood, White Paint, Applied Molding, Black Letters, c.1890, 14 x 32 In.	356.00
Sign, American Beach, Fla., Negro Ocean Playground, Marlin, Woman, Iron, 4 x 12 In.	99.00
Sign, American Central Insurance Co., Tin, Wood, 1853, 15 x 23 ½ In.	13.00
Sign, American Lever Cuff & Collar Button Co., Metal Bands, c.1884, 29 x 12 In. *illus*	1872.00
Sign, American Powder Company, Cardboard, Stone Lithograph, Duck, Frame, 26 x 20 In.	2875.00
Sign, American Radiator, Twin Girls Keeping Warm By Radiator, Paper, 21 ½ x 19 ¾ In.	357.00
Sign, Amos 'n' Andy Candy, Fresh Air Taxi Cab, Die Cut, c.1930, 11 x 5 ⅝ In.	173.00
Sign, Anheuser-Busch Brewing, Custer's Last Fight, Print, Canvas, Frame, 1896, 38 x 48 In.	2468.00
Sign, Antiques, Neon, Green Letters, Metal Frame, 1940s, 9 x 36 In.	575.00
Sign, Aqua Crystal, For Sale Here, Eyeglasses, Reverse Glass, Oak Frame, 5 ¼ x 15 ¼ In.	1265.00
Sign, Armour's Extract Of Beef, Trademark Child Cowboy, Paper Lithograph, 57 x 42 In.	1870.00
Sign, Ashbury Bar, H. Gerken, Jackson, On Draught Lager, Green, Reverse Glass, 1910, 44 x 22 In.	24000.00
Sign, Atkinson's Pecks Bad Boy Co., Anemic Horse, 19 ½ x 27 In.	1250.00
Sign, Atlantic Ale-Beer, Man Holding Tray, Yellow, Green, Black, Porcelain, Convex, 38 In.	950.00
Sign, A.W. Stevens & Sons Mfg., Threshers, Engines, Buhr Mills, Paper, Frame, 21 x 27 In.	1500.00
Sign, Ayer's Cherry Pectoral Patent Medicine, St., Nick, Boxes, Sleigh, Die Cut Cardboard, 13 x 7 In.	743.00
Sign, Ayer's Hair Vigor, Restores Gray Hair, Woman, Paper, Frame, 16 ½ x 13 ½ In.	1350.00
Sign, Ayrshire Cattle, Orange, Blue, White, Embossed, Tin, 19 ½ x 28 In.	500.00

Advertising, Pail, Big Sister Peanut Butter, Producers Co., Witch On Broom, Tin, 3 ½ x 3 ¾ In.
$819.00

Advertising, Pail, Happy Kids Peanut Butter, W.B. Roddenberry, Paper Label, Tin, 3 ½ x 4 In.
$527.00

Advertising, Pin, Buitoni Foods Corp., Joe DiMaggio Club, Tin Lithograph, 1950s, 1 ½ In.
$633.00

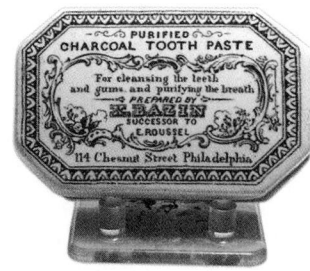

Advertising, Pot Lid, X. Bazin, Purified Charcoal Tooth Paste, White Glazed Pottery, c.1860, 3 ¾ x 2 ⅜ In.
$173.00

Advertising, Pot Scraper, Mardi-Gras Teas & Coffees, Chas. W. Shonk, Tin, 6 ½ x 9 ¼ In.
$322.00

Advertising, Pot Scraper, Snow King, Sam W. Weidler Co.
$410.00

Advertising, Ring, Nabisco, Ted Williams, Brass, Plastic, Adjustable, c.1948, 1 In.
$140.00

Sign, Baby Label Bread, Victorian Children, Cardboard, Embossed, Die Cut, 8 x 7 In.	187.00
Sign, Baker's Cocoa, Woman With Tray, Pure, Delicious, Nutritious, Tin Litho, Frame, 22 x 17 In.	1165.00
Sign, Ball's Health Preserving Corsets, Woman, Dog, Cardboard, 14 x 11 In.	1320.00
Sign, Ballantine Beer, Celebrating Thanksgiving, Die Cut, Easel Back, 22 x 25 In.	59.00
Sign, Barber Trade, Wood, Razor Shape, Paint, c.1890, 29 In.	385.00
Sign, Barq's Root Beer, Red, Black, Yellow, Porcelain, Flange, 2-Sided, 14 x 21 ¾ In.	275.00
Sign, Bartholomay Brewing Co., Trademark Girl, Brewery, Die Cut, Stand-Up, 8 x 4 In.	264.00
Sign, Bartles Bonded Oils & Greases, Attendant Image, Tin Lithograph, 10 x 28 In.	3630.00
Sign, Beacon Blankets, Pueblo Marriage, Die Cut, c.1940, 59 x 29 In.	1650.00
Sign, Beech-Nut Chewing Tobacco, Porcelain, 30 x 46 In.	236.00
Sign, Beech-Nut Gum, Hello, Have You Had Your Gum Today?, Cardboard, 16 x 44 In.	330.00
Sign, Blackstone Cigar, Watt & Bond, Blue, Yellow, Embossed, Porcelain, 12 x 36 In.	240.00
Sign, Blatz, Milwaukee's Finest Beer, Draft-Brewed, White, Red Lettering, Metal, Plastic, Lighted	23.00
Sign, Bloodhound Chew, Dog, Text, Tin, c.1945, 18 x 28 In.	224.00
Sign, Blue Ribbon Bourbon, Farm Scene, Oil On Canvas, Frame, 29 x 39 In.	275.00
Sign, Blue Ridge Bus, Santa, Cutout Cardboard, 1950s, 26 x 36 In.	281.00
Sign, Bond Bread, Porcelain, 15 x 18 In.	225.00
Sign, Bond Bread, The Vitamin-D, Yellow, Green, Red, Embossed, Porcelain, 14 x 19 In.	198.00
Sign, Boot, Shoemaker Trade, Tin, 2-Sided, Paint, c.1885, 14 x 20 In.	444.00
Sign, Borden's, Double Dutch Chocolate, Tin, 12 x 24 In.	325.00
Sign, Borden's, Elsie The Cow, No Wording, Yellow, Brown, White, Tin, 17 ½ x 17 ½ In.	110.00
Sign, Borden's, Elsie The Cow, Yellow, White, Blue Ground, Metal, 23 ½ In. Diam.	305.00
Sign, Borden's Ice Cream, Candy, Sodas, Blue, Red, White, Porcelain, 47 x 59 In.	1400.00
Sign, Borden's Ice Cream, Elsie The Cow, Painted, Steel, Flange, 15 x 24 In.	480.00
Sign, Boston Globe, Man, Top Hat, Globe Stomach, Tin Lithograph, 18 x 11 In.	743.00
Sign, BPS Hardware Paint, Blue, Red, White, Porcelain, 2-Sided, 14 x 28 In.	275.00
Sign, Brahmans Build Beef, Bull In Oval, Multicolored, 23 ¾ x 23 ¼ In.	79.00
Sign, Brilliant White Safety Oil, Cardboard, Frame, c.1800, 16 ¾ x 20 In.	33.00
Sign, Bucking Bronco Roundup Coal, Yellow, Red, Black, Tin, 13 ½ x 19 ¾ In.	495.00
Sign, Bud's Barber Shop, 2-Sided, Black Letters, White Ground, Frame, 27 x 28 ¾ In.	45.00
Sign, Budweiser, Girl, White Cap, Holding Bottle & Glass, Tin Lithograph, 38 x 26 In.	1062.00
Sign, Budweiser, Red, White, Anheuser-Busch In Bottles, Reverse Glass, 6 x 15 In.	1450.00
Sign, Budweiser, Red, White, Neon Over Porcelain, 36 x 72 x 5 ½ In.	3850.00
Sign, Budweiser, Woman, Red Dress, Holding Bottle, Cardboard, 1907, 33 x 18 In.	48.00
Sign, Budweiser, Woman, Red Dress, Paper, Frame, 1907, 38 ¾ x 23 ½ In.	560.00
Sign, Buffalo Brewing, Bohemian, Woman, Gold Leaf Frame, 32 In.	12000.00
Sign, Buick, Valve-In-Head, Authorized Service, 2-Sided, Porcelain, 42 In.	3300.00
Sign, Bull Durham New Size 5 Cents, String Hung, Die Cut, Bull, Brown, Green, 13 x 11 In.	1650.00
Sign, Burgie, Concave Glass & Bottle, Wooden, Pastel Colors, c.1958, 21 In.	50.00
Sign, Butter Krust Bread, Red, White, Blue, Tin, 5 x 27 In.	110.00
Sign, Butter-Nut Bread, Tin, Enameled, 28 x 12 In.	67.00
Sign, Butterine, Girl Riding Calf, Capitol City Dairy Co., Celluloid, 10 x 14 In.	1600.00
Sign, Campbell's, Vegetable Soup, Curved, Porcelain, c.1920s, 12 ½ x 22 In.	3651.00
Sign, Canada Dry Spur Soda, 2 Bathing Beauties, Cardboard Die Cut, 11 x 9 In.	231.00
Sign, Candy Store Trade, Woman, Carved, Weathered Multicolored Paint, 23 x 10 ½ In.	652.00
Sign, Carhartt's, Pants, Overalls & Gloves, Die Cut, Tin, 2-Sided, Flange, 18 ½ x 18 In.	2750.00
Sign, Carmona Lawn Fertiliser, We Sell It, Makes Turf, Lawn Sports, Tin Litho, 13 x 19 In.	605.00
Sign, Case Threshing Machine Co., Steam Tractor, Tin Lithographed, 18 x 12 In.	1207.00
Sign, Case Threshing Machine Co., Tin, Eagle On Globe, Embossed, 19 ¼ x 27 In.	2012.00
Sign, Catignani's Ice Cream, Deluxe Aristocrat Of Creams, Tin Flange, 14 x 16 In.	153.00
Sign, C.F. & I. Coals, Sold Here, Men, Colorado Fuel & Iron Co., Porcelain, 16 x 22 In.	578.00
Sign, Charles Harvey, Justice Of The Peace, Tin, Sand, 2-Sided, 14 ½ x 26 In.	780.00
Sign, Charles The Great, Cigar Box, Gran Fabrica De Tobacos, Tin, 13 x 19 In.	495.00
Sign, Chas. Goodall & Sons Playing Cards, Hand Holding Cards, Die Cut, Cardboard, 8 x 6 In.	1375.00
Sign, Cheatham's Chill Tonic, Free-Form Poison, Cardboard, 8 x 12 In.	176.00
Sign, Chew Mail Pouch Tobacco, Hand Holding Pouch, Steel, 2-Sided, 8 x 11 ½ In.	510.00
Sign, Chief Paints, Indian, Headdress, Tin, 2-Sided, 24 x 18 In.	360.00
Sign, Chromolithograph, Illinois Watch Co., Lincoln, Canvas, c.1913, 14 x 11 In. ....*illus*	118.00
Sign, Cigarettes, White Letters, Maroon Ground, Chrome, Plastic, 2 ⅝ x 22 ⅞ In.	49.00
Sign, Cigars & Tobacco, Man Smoking Pipe, Prosperous Merchant, Paper, 24 ½ x 18 In.	7300.00
Sign, Cigars, Neon, Wood, 16 x 46 x 7 ½ In.	580.00
Sign, Clement's Bottling Co., 3 Clown Drinkers, Paper Lithograph, Frame, 30 x 24 In.	385.00
Sign, Climax Plug Tobacco, Blue, Red, White, Porcelain, 15 x 15 In.	200.00
Sign, Coats & Clark, Cat Congress, Paper, Marked, Frame, c.1900, 18 x 25 In.	743.00
Sign, Coldwell Lawn Mowers, Horse Pulling Mower, Linen-Backed, 1920s, 22 x 28 In.	375.00
Sign, Columbia Records, Mother, Children, Phonograph, Cardboard	1870.00

Sign, Conestoga Hotel, 2-Sided, Stenciled, Wooden, Pa., 1800s, 27 x 40 ½ In. 761.00
Sign, Continental Fire Insurance Co., Indian Camp, Paper, Frame, 1895, 26 x 31 In. 9200.00
Sign, Cook's Paints, Porcelain, 24 x 36 In. 177.00
Sign, Cooks Beer, Black Maid & Butler, Tin Over Cardboard, 13 x 21 In. 450.00
Sign, Coors Beer, Adolf Coors Golden Brewery, Red-Haired Woman, Colorado, 38 x 30 In. 2200.00
Sign, Corticelli Spool Silk, Paper, Frame, c.1912, 21 x 29 In. ....*illus* 1521.00
Sign, Cowhide Brand Overalls & Pants, Cow, Blue, Yellow, 2-Sided, Flange, Tin, 10 x 12 In. 200.00
Sign, Crab, Jersey Blue Claw, Gautier, Lepuis 1847, Wood, 41 x 58 In. 4600.00
Sign, Crane's Philadelphia Ice Cream, Best After All, Girl, Die Cut, Cardboard, Easel, 14 x 8 In. ... 495.00
Sign, Crane's Philadelphia Ice Cream, Standard For 25 Years, Die Cut, Cardboard, 14 x 8 In. 330.00
Sign, Cream Of Wheat, Earhart's Last Flight 950.00
Sign, Crimps Cigarettes, Liggett & Myers, Drunk Woman Smoking, Paper, 18 x 24 In. 1870.00
Sign, Cuban Cousin Cigar, Woman, 5 Cent, Linen, 18 x 35 ¼ In. 240.00
Sign, Cyclone Fence, Red, White, Blue, Porcelain, Portland, 4 ½ x 13 ½ In. 24.00
Sign, Daisy Air Rifles, Happy Daisy Boy, 21 x 14 In. 7250.00
Sign, Dandro Solvent, Hand Holding Ointment, Tin Lithograph, Cardboard, 9 x 13 In. 345.00
Sign, Daniel Cigar, They Will Not Bite, Daniel, Lion's Den, Marshalltown Grocery, Tin, 10 x 13 In. ... 500.00
Sign, Del-Monte Food Products, Green Red, Yellow Logo, Porcelain, 20 x 24 In. 230.00
Sign, Deppen Beer, Shipping Crate, Glass, 1930s, 25 ¼ x 13 ¼ x 5 In. 1870.00
Sign, Derby Pipe Slices Tobacco, Horse, 10 ¾ x 14 In. 200.00
Sign, Devlish Good Cigars, Tin, Embossed, Chain Hanger, 14 x 10 In. ....*illus* 193.00
Sign, Diamond Dyes, Busy Day In Dollville, Beveled Tin Over Cardboard, Frame, 11 x 17 In. . 3190.00
Sign, Dickinson Pine Tree Seed, 99 ½ Percent Pure, Tin, Self-Framed, 13 x 37 ½ In. 610.00
Sign, Dixon's Stove Polish, Magician Girl Cleaning, Cardboard Lithograph, 8 x 12 In. 2750.00
Sign, Dobbs Hats, Brass, Raised Letters & Border, Painted Ground, 3 x 10 In. 36.00
Sign, Dolly Madison Ice Cream, Deliciously Different, Wood, Frame, 1920s, 9 x 15 In. 60.00
Sign, Dolly Madison Ice Cream, Wood, Die Cut, Josias Mfg., 14 ½ x 36 In. ....*illus* 176.00
Sign, Dr. D. Jayne's Ague Mixture, Chills, Fevers, Etc, Reverse Glass, Frame, 11 x 5 In. 578.00
Sign, Dr. Daniels' Vet Wonder Worker, Banner, Frame, 16 x 28 In. 231.00
Sign, Dr Pepper, 10 2 4, Red, White, Porcelain, 10 In. Diam. 140.00
Sign, Dr Pepper, Cardboard, 1940s, 15 x 25 In. 248.00
Sign, Dr Pepper, Drink, Red, White, Porcelain, 8 x 24 In. 88.00
Sign, Dr Pepper, Good For Life, Raised Logo, Porcelain, c.1940, 10 ½ x 26 ½ In. 365.00
Sign, Dr Pepper, Take Home A Carton, Embossed, Tin, 27 x 19 In. 485.00
Sign, Dr Pepper, Thank You Call Again, Paper Lithograph, c.1940, 8 ¾ x 11 ½ In. 275.00
Sign, Dr. Weave's Heave Cure Does It, Canvas, Fairport, New York, 40 x 22 In. 468.00
Sign, Dr. Willis A. Myers & Co., Veterinary Medicines, Supplies, Cardboard, 21 x 8 In. 154.00
Sign, Dress, Cloak Maker's Trade, Applied Molding, Paint, Gilt, c.1895, 16 x 30 In. 296.00
Sign, Drink Budweiser, Red, White, Porcelain, 2-Sided, 36 x 65 In. 1750.00
Sign, Drink City Club Beer, Metal, Bottle Graphics, Schmidt Brewing Co., St. Paul, 40 x 14 In. .. 240.00
Sign, Drink Squirt, It Quenches Quicker, Yellow Red, Metal, c.1947, 32 x 56 In. 210.00
Sign, Drink Sterling, Tin Over Cardboard, 6 x 15 In. 239.00
Sign, Drink Sun Crest, It's The Best, Blue, Orange, Die Cut, Tin, Flange, 2-Sided, 13 ½ x 18 In. 480.00
Sign, Drugs, Black, Light-Up, 2-Sided, 17 ½ x 50 x 8 In. 770.00
Sign, Duke & Sons Tobacco, Cameo Cigarettes, Woman, White Hair, Frame, 23 x 10 ⅞ In. 1650.00
Sign, Dura-Products, JC Soda, Reverse On Glass, c.1940, 9 x 12 In. 800.00
Sign, E-A-Co. Flour, Cardboard, Tin, Frame, 14 x 14 In. 47.00
Sign, Eagle Mower & Reaper, Eagle, Farmers, Paper, Frame, 27 x 21 In. 2850.00
Sign, Eagle Optometrist, Eagle, Glasses In Beak, Eyeglasses, Painted, Wood, 1880s, 30 x 54 In. ... 6700.00
Sign, Edgeworth Tobacco, Ready Rub, No Bite, Beveled, Crystoglass, Whitehead & Hoag, 6 x 11 In. .. 280.00
Sign, Eley Grand Prix Cartridges, Shotgun Shell, 2-Sided, Painted, Metal, Flange, 123 x 22 x 2 In. .. 385.00
Sign, Ellis Tiger Co., Fishing Tackle That's Fit For Fishing, Embossed, Tin Litho, 11 ¾ x 35 ⅝ In. . 615.00
Sign, Elm's Hotel, Cutout Leaf Panel, 2-Sided, Wood, Iron, Mass., c.1900, 40 x 40 In. 1067.00
Sign, Eureka Stock Food, Great Flesh Producer, 3 Skating Girls, Paper Lithograph, 25 x 20 In. ... 413.00
Sign, Eveready Batteries & Flashlights, Eveready Man, Green, Red, Porcelain, 40 x 18 In. 350.00
Sign, Eyes Tested At Frost's, Optometrist's Office, Woman, Pince Nez, 20 x 28 In. 275.00
Sign, Falstaff Beer, Hare'm Scare'm, Cardboard, Frame, 29 ¼ x 42 ½ In. 110.00
Sign, Falstaff Beer, Hunter Climbing Under Fence, Cardboard, Self-Framed, 32 x 27 In. 99.00
Sign, Favorite Chewing Tobacco, Ralph Houck, Nellie Fox, Tin Litho, 1950s, 10 x 60 In. 275.00
Sign, Favorite Stoves & Ranges, We Guarantee, Porcelain, Flange, 24 ½ x 18 In. 1500.00
Sign, Fels-Naptha, 2-Sided, Tin, 7 x 14 In. 59.00
Sign, Ferguson Tractor & Implement, Blue, White, Porcelain, 38 x 60 In. 720.00
Sign, Fern Glen Rye, Black Man, With Watermelon, Tin, Self-Framed, 33 x 22 ½ In. 4500.00
Sign, Ferry Seeds, Jack & The Beanstalk Plant, Jack Holding Shovel, Parrish, c.1923, 25 x 20 In. .. 1595.00
Sign, Fitch's Standard Heart Chewing Gum, Victorian Woman, Die Cut Card Stock, 12 x 8 In. 440.00
Sign, Five Roses Flour, Trademark Indian, Wheat Sheaves, 8-Sided, Tin Litho, 14 x 14 In. 798.00

Advertising, Sign,
American Lever Cuff & Collar Button Co.,
Metal Bands, c.1884, 29 x 12 In.
$1872.00

Advertising, Sign, Chromolithograph,
Illinois Watch Co., Lincoln, Canvas,
c.1913, 14 x 11 In.
$118.00

Advertising, Sign, Corticelli Spool Silk,
Paper, Frame, c.1912, 21 x 29 In.
$1521.00

Advertising, Sign, Devlish Good Cigars,
Tin, Embossed, Chain Hanger, 14 x 10 In.
$193.00

Advertising, Sign,
Dolly Madison Ice Cream, Wood,
Die Cut, Josias Mfg., 14 ½ x 36 In.
$176.00

Advertising, Sign, Hires R-J Root Beer,
Girl, So Good With Food, Paper,
c.1945, 34 x 58 In.
$173.00

Advertising, Sign, Hot Ball Tobacco,
Canvas, 8 ¾ x 23 ¼ In.
$949.00

Store Signs

Some old store signs were
lithographed directly on
tin and made to look like a
picture with a wooden frame.
The Grape-Nuts sign picturing a girl and her St. Bernard
is one of the best known
examples.

Sign, Flexible Curried Leather, Tin, 17 x 22 In.	295.00
Sign, Four Roses Whiskey, Tin Lithograph, c.1900, 32 x 46 In.	767.00
Sign, Francisco Auto Heaters, Tin, Self-Framed, c.1920, 18 x 40 In.	1325.00 to 1400.00
Sign, Frazer Axle Grease, Horse Drawn Cart, Broken Wheel, Cardboard, Frame, 32 x 33 In.	725.00
Sign, Free Land Overalls, Union Made Guaranteed, Purple, Red, White, Porcelain, 10 x 30 In.	475.00
Sign, Free Land Overalls, Worlds Highest Standard, Red, White, Blue, Porcelain, 10 x 30 In.	580.00
Sign, Fresh Eggs For Sale, Chicken, Wood, 2-Sided, c.1925, 24 x 30 ½ In.	805.00
Sign, Frostie Old Fashion Root Beer, Tin, Embossed, Parker Metal, 1940s, 23 x 36 In.	230.00
Sign, Gambrinus Quality Pale Beer, Tin, 11 x 12 ¾ In.	273.00
Sign, Gammell & Kimble Velvet Ice Cream, Green, White, Steel, Enamel, 17 x 17 In.	82.00
Sign, Genesee Brewing Co., Factory Scene, Reverse Glass, Frame, 30 x 40 In.	3100.00
Sign, Gold Medal Hosiery, Man Seated, Woman Behind Counter, Cardboard, Fold-Out, 9 x 13 ¾ In.	469.00
Sign, Golden Orangeade, Delicious, 5 Cents, Gold, Black, Red, Rolled Corner Edge, 5 ¾ x 9 ¾ In.	550.00
Sign, Golden Quality Ice Cream, Groceries, Yellow, Blue, Tin, 43 ½ x 60 In.	770.00
Sign, Gollam's Lebanon Ice Cream, Metal, 26 x 11 ¼ In.	90.00
Sign, Goo-Goo Candy, Boy Eating, Tin, 24 x 33 In.	83.00
Sign, Grand Prize Lager Beer, Finest In The South, Red, Green, Porcelain, 38 ½ x 58 In.	1100.00
Sign, Granger Pipe Tobacco, Victor Lawson, Cutout, Cardboard, 46 ½ x 23 In.	25.00
Sign, Gray Dunn & Co's Biscuits, Frame, 29 ½ x 38 In.	180.00
Sign, Green River Whiskey, Black Man, Horse, Tin, 24 In.	575.00
Sign, Greyhound Package Express, White, Light Blue, Flange, 18 x 28 In.	385.00
Sign, Greyhound, Red, White, Blue, Porcelain, 2-Sided, 24 x 48 In.	175.00
Sign, Greyhound, Ticket Office, Greyhound Lines, 2-Sided, Porcelain, 1920s, 25 x 30 In.	10000.00
Sign, Guinness & Lobster, Slate Board, Hand Painted, 30 x 42 In.	3300.00
Sign, Gunther's Candies, Springtime, Tin Lithograph, Self-Framed, 28 ½ x 22 ½ In.	440.00
Sign, H. Clausen & Son Lager Beer, 18 ¾ x 29 ½ In.	300.00
Sign, Hail Insurance, Chas. W. Bert, Jr., Greencastle, 20 x 13 ¾ In.	145.00
Sign, Hancock, Cock O' The Walk, Globe Body, Rooster Graphic, 15 In.	7979.00
Sign, Hanger, J.P. Alley's Hambone 5 Cent Cigars, Cardboard, 2-Sided	40.00
Sign, Hannons-Sons Barbers, Straight Razor, Painted, Wood, 39 In. Closed	510.00
Sign, Harp, Yellow Ground, Green & Blue, Board, 52 x 32 In.	2500.00
Sign, Harry J. Ainscow, Undertaker, Wood, Ogee Molding, c.1875, 26 x 39 x 4 In.	705.00
Sign, Hartford Insurance, Elk, Brass, Blackened, Frame, 19 ¾ x 19 ¾ In.	69.00
Sign, Harvard Brewing Co., Lowell, Mass., Woman, 24 x 36 In.	8.00
Sign, Heinz 57, Chili Sauce, Taste Is The Test, Steak, Corn, Cardboard, 13 ¾ x 23 In.	112.00
Sign, Heinz 57, Mince Meat, One Of Heinz Holiday Desserts, Pie, Can, Jar, Cardboard, 14 x 23 In.	168.00
Sign, Heinz Peanut Butter, Delicious, Sandwiches, Jar, Cardboard, 12 ½ x 22 ½ In.	112.00
Sign, Heinz Vinegars, You Can Be Sure Of Them, 3 Bottles, Cardboard, 12 x 22 In.	168.00
Sign, Heinz's Dusseldorfer Mustard, Cruet Form, Tin Lid, 5 In.	240.00
Sign, Hendler's Ice Cream, Black, Yellow, Checkerboard, Steel, Enamel, 18 In. Diam.	142.00
Sign, Hereford Assoc., Cow, Rolling Ridge Ranch, Porcelain, 2-Sided, 47 x 60 In.	2750.00
Sign, H.G. Hill Stores, Nashville, Tenn. Grocery, Wood Frame, 18 ½ x 30 ½ In.	142.00
Sign, Hills Bros. Coffee, 1935, 31 x 52 In.	175.00
Sign, Hires R-J Root Beer, Girl, So Good With Food, Paper, c.1945, 34 x 58 In. *illus*	173.00
Sign, Hires Root Beer, Courteous Service, Painted, Wood, 10 x 40 In.	176.00
Sign, Hires Root Beer, Drink, 2 Women, Tin, Self-Framed, Oval, 20 x 24 In.	1210.00
Sign, Hires Root Beer, Tin, Embossed, Vertical Bottle, 1960s, 8 x 35 ½ In.	127.00
Sign, Hires Root Beer, Ugly Kid & Mug, Oval, Self-Framed, 1907, 20 x 24 In.	1010.00
Sign, Hires Root Beer, Woman, Holding Glass, Hires R-J Root Beer, c.1940, 34 x 58 In.	250.00
Sign, Holland Vaporaire Heating, Yellow, Blue, Porcelain, 24 x 36 In.	110.00
Sign, Holsum Bread, Red, White, Blue, Tin, 5 ½ x 27 In.	77.00
Sign, Hood's Ice Cream Cone, Cow, Tin, Frame, 23 x 31 In.	340.00
Sign, Hostetter's Stomach, Reverse On Glass, St. George, Horse, Black, Gold, Frame, 24 x 29 In.	1380.00
Sign, Hot Ball Tobacco, Canvas, 8 ¾ x 23 ¼ In. *illus*	949.00
Sign, Hudson Terraplane Authorized Service, Red, Porcelain, 2-Sided, 42 In. Diam.	1980.00
Sign, Hudson's Soap, Porcelain, 14 x 19 In.	130.00
Sign, Humble, Red, White, Black, Porcelain, 2-Sided, Oval, 27 ½ x 52 In.	2200.00
Sign, Humphrey's Homeopathic Remedies, Nude, Lion, Cardboard, c.1910, 14 x 18 In.	150.00
Sign, Hyco Smoking Tobacco, Indian, C.R. Ayers, Paper, Frame, 12 ¼ x 15 ¼ In.	852.00
Sign, Ice Cream Cone, 5 Cent, Painted, Copper, Hanging Bracket, 13 ¼ In.	990.00
Sign, Ice Cream Cone, Yellow, Pink, Green, Milk Glass, Light-Up, George Jones, Co., 12 x 5 ½ In.	1000.00
Sign, Idaho Brewing Co., Waterfall, Boise City, Embossed, Tin, 27 ½ x 19 ¾ In.	8200.00
Sign, Illinois Farm Supply, Tin, 10 x 14 In.	40.00
Sign, Imperial Club Cigar, Best For The Money, Tin, Embossed, 9 ⅞ x 13 ¾ In.	143.00
Sign, Index Room, 126, Finger Pointing, Black, Gold, Wood, 24 In.	495.00
Sign, Information, Pine, Black Letters, White Border, c.1910, 7 x 45 In.	296.00

Sign, Inner-Southern Insurance, Kentucky Building, Calendar, Tin Litho, 19 x 13 In.	132.00
Sign, Interlux Marine Paint, The Smartest Boat In The Fleet, Porcelain, c.1940, 14 x 24 In. ..	4485.00
Sign, International Hand Numbering Machine, $5.00, Tin Over Cardboard, 9 x 6 In.	330.00
Sign, International Stock Food, Veterinary Feed, Paper Lithograph, Red, 30 x 22 In.	523.00
Sign, Interwoven Socks, Leyendecker Santa, Socks, Multicolored, Cloth, 47 x 29 In.	633.00
Sign, Ironbrew, We Serve Ironbrew In Bottles Ice Cold, Blake Slee Bros., c.1940, 9 x 12 In.	800.00
Sign, Irving Mason Jewelers, Wood, 13 ¼ x 35 ½ In.	170.00
Sign, Ivory Soap, Cardboard, c.1933, 11 x 21 In.	41.00
Sign, Ivory Soap, Cherub, Soap Bar, Die Cut Cardboard, 11 x 6 In.	303.00
Sign, I.W. Harper Whiskey, Here's Happy Days, Hunting Cabin Scene, Frame, 28 x 22 In.	1300.00
Sign, I.W. Harper Whiskey, Indian Woman, Chromolithograph, Frame, 29 x 14 In.	633.00
Sign, Jack Sprat Food Store, Jack In Center, Painted, Aluminum, 12 ¼ x 11 In.	140.00
Sign, Jack Sprat Foods, Blue Letters, Yellow Ground, Wood, 16 x 139 In.	275.00
Sign, Jacuzzi Pumps, Jensen Pump & Well Service, Yellow, Red Blue, Tin, 34 x 58 In.	82.00
Sign, Japp's Hair Rejuvenator, Restores Gray Hair Instantly, Men, Women, Tin, 9 x 13 In.	115.00
Sign, Jell-O, Mickey Mantle Baseball Card In Every Box, 1962, 27 x 33 In.	7275.00
Sign, John Bardenheier Wine & Liquor Co., Old Couple, Tin, Self-Framed, Oval, 19 ½ x 23 In.	1800.00
Sign, John Deere, Deer, In Buckled Belt, Cast Iron, Black Paint, Wall Mount, 1847, 18 x 11 In.	275.00
Sign, John Deere, Green, Yellow, Rounded Corners, 42 ½ x 59 In.	440.00
Sign, John Deere Implements, Porcelain, 3 x 9 Ft.	5500.00
Sign, John Gahan, Roi-Tan Cigars, Reverse Painted Glass, 60 ¼ x 29 ¾ In.	1540.00
Sign, John Meehan, Dayton, Ohio, Large Headed Grocer, Cardboard Die Cut, Frame, 12 x 13 In.	275.00
Sign, Joseph Arthur's Blue Jeans, Chromolithograph, Frame, 31 x 46 In.	823.00
Sign, Jung Brewing Co., Irmal, Tin, 19 x 15 In.	1000.00
Sign, Kayo Chocolate, Tops In Taste, Man, Derby Hat, Bottle, Red, Black, Metal, 14 x 27 In.	330.00
Sign, Keil, Charlestown, N.H., Key Form, Keys Made, Painted, Wood, 27 ½ x 12 In.	96.00
Sign, Kellogg's Boy Scout, First Call For Breakfast, Paper, 26 x 31 ¾ In.	520.00
Sign, Kellogg's Campfire Girl, Ready To Serve, Paper, 26 x 21 ¾ In.	520.00
Sign, Kelly Duplex Grinding Mill, Paper Litho, Metal Bands, 24 x 18 In. ....*illus*	546.00
Sign, Kemps Balsam, For That Cough, Girl, With Spoon, 2-Sided, Die Cut, Cardboard, 15 x 10 In.	176.00
Sign, Kline's Best Flour, Baseball Pictures, History Data, 1839-1939, Paper, 28 x 21 In.	187.00
Sign, Ko-Ko Tulu Chewing Gum, Turbaned Woman, Cardboard Lithograph, 10 x 6 In.	853.00
Sign, Kodak, Developing, Printing, Enlarging, 2-Sided, Enamel, 17 x 17 In.	145.00
Sign, Kodak, Enamel 2-Sided, Die Cut, 17 x 17 In.	145.00
Sign, Kodak, Orange, Red, Blue, Black, 2-Sided, Porcelain, 12 x 30 In.	522.00
Sign, Kodak, Take A Kodak With You, Girl, Boy With Luggage, Cardboard, c.1920, 33 x 25 In. .	198.00
Sign, Kodak, Verichrome Safety Film, V 620, Yellow, Red, Black, 2-Sided, Porcelain, 13 x 24 In.	380.00
Sign, Kool Cigarettes, Blond Woman, Green Halter Dress, Japan, 1950s, 14 ½ x 19 ¼ In.	62.00
Sign, Kreso Dip No. 1, Protects All Livestock From Parasites & Disease, Tin, 23 x 12 In.	88.00
Sign, La Flor De Carvalho Havana Cigars, Tin, Frame, 15 x 21 In.	176.00
Sign, Learn With R.A.C Reg, Porcelain, Stick Figure, 7 ½ x 12 In.	112.00
Sign, Lee Union-Alls, For Comfort, Economy, Safety, 2 Men, Grommets, Porcelain, 11 x 30 In.	1792.00
Sign, Lee Whizit Overalls & Union-Alls, Man, Embossed, Die Cut, Stand-Up, 8 In.	85.00
Sign, Lemmy Lemonade, Lemonade Drink, 19 x 14 In.	345.00
Sign, Lessive Phenix Soap, Woman Doing Laundry, Paper, Frame, France, 63 x 42 In.	117.00
Sign, Lewis 66 Whiskey, Woman, Floral Bonnet, Tin, 17 ½ In.	240.00
Sign, Lincoln Highway, Coast To Coast, Truly A Cigar, Red, Blue, Cardboard, 10 x 30 In.	360.00
Sign, Linen Rub-No-More, Uncut, Late 1800s, 38 x 42 In. ....*illus*	1872.00
Sign, Lipton's Tea, Green, Red, Cream, 2-Sided, Flange, 9 x 18 In.	165.00
Sign, Lipton's Teas, Famous The World Over, Women, Blue, Yellow, Cardboard, 22 x 14 In.	240.00
Sign, Liverpool & London, Globe Insurance Co., Red, Reverse Painted, Frame, 15 x 43 In.	75.00
Sign, L.L. Brown Paper Co., Linen Ledger & Record Papers, 2-Sided, 24 x 144 In.	1287.00
Sign, Log Cabin Tobacco, Smoke Log Cabin, Cowboy, Paper, Frame, 26 ½ x 22 In.	1210.00
Sign, Lone Star Beer, Indian On Horse, Buffalo, Tin Lithograph, Self-Framed, 14 In.	1300.00
Sign, Lone Star Beer, Lightning Bolt, Blue, White, Porcelain, Oval, 33 x 56 In.	770.00
Sign, Lone Star Beer, Multicolored, Scroll, Electric, 7 x 24 x 6 ½ In.	330.00
Sign, Long Wharf Chandlery, Ships Instruments, Painted, Wood, 26 x 37 In.	400.00
Sign, Lucky Strike Cigarette, Bill Tilden, 10 ½ x 22 In.	245.00
Sign, Lucky Strike Do You Inhale, Romantic Man, Woman, Paper Litho, 15 x 25 In.	358.00
Sign, Luro Dyes, Woman, Red, Blue Cloths, French Text, Tin Litho, c.1920, 12 x 10 In.	132.00
Sign, Luxury Cigarette, Woman Holding Cigarette Pack, Frame, 24 x 16 In.	120.00
Sign, Lynes Perfume, Lady Luxury, Die Cut Cardboard, Easel Back, 13 ½ x 11 ½ In.	42.00
Sign, Ma's Cola, Tin, c.1945, 12 x 28 In.	94.00
Sign, Magic Washer, The Chinese Must Go, Uncle Sam, Frame, c.1890, 32 x 25 In.	5850.00
Sign, Magic Yeast, Child, With Wand, Baked Goods, Paper, Frame, 1906, 26 ½ x 20 In.	79.00
Sign, Mandeville & King Flower Seeds, Garden Scene, Paper Lithograph, 32 x 22 In.	495.00

A

Advertising, Sign,
Kelly Duplex Grinding Mill, Paper Litho,
Metal Bands, 24 x 18 In.
$546.00

Advertising Collectible "Firsts"

Cigarette cards: In 1885 Allen and Ginter of Richmond, Virginia, issued ten cigarettes in a box plus a picture card for five cents. These eventually inspired baseball cards.

Paper advertising fans: Paper fans were made starting in the eighteenth century. A Crystal Palace exhibition in New York in 1853 used advertising fans.

Paper napkins: The first paper napkins, which were plain tissue paper squares, were introduced at the Chicago World's Fair in 1893. The first printed paper napkin appeared in 1898.

U.S. advertising wall calendar: An 1863 calendar advertising medicine for John L. Hunnewell of Boston, Massachusetts, was the earliest.

Paper bags: Paper bags appeared in Europe in the seventeenth century and in the United States in the nineteenth century. In 1852 Frances Wolle of Bethlehem, Pennsylvania, invented a machine that made bags. By 1884 the Union Bag & Paper Company was making brown bags with flat bottoms and pleated sides. Advertising was soon printed on the bags.

Advertising, Sign, Linen Rub-No-More, Uncut, Late 1800s, 38 x 42 In. $1872.00

Advertising, Sign, Natural Chilean Soda, Black Farmer, Yassuh Uncle Natchez, 2-Sided, Metal, 15 x 22 In. $234.00

Sign, Marine Gasoline, Speedboat, Blue, White, Porcelain, 48 x 30 In.	3400.00
Sign, Mary A. Swain Dress & Cloak, Black Paint, Pine, c.1890, 14 x 48 In.	356.00
Sign, Master Big Loaf, Rally Big, Really Good, Red, White, Blue	130.00
Sign, Mayo's Plug, Smoking Cock O' The Walk, Rooster, Porcelain, 13 x 6 ½ In.	1945.00
Sign, Maytag, Washer, Die Cut Tin, 1930s, 48 x 72 In.	413.00
Sign, McColl-Frontenac, Red Indian Products, 1946, 18 x 21 In.	3750.00
Sign, McCormick Painter & Grainer, Painted, Wood, 15 x 81 In.	3600.00
Sign, Meadville Pure Rye Whiskey, Angel On Heart, Tin, Frame, 43 ½ x 33 ½ In.	14000.00
Sign, Meckumfat, Sussex Ground Oats, Barnyard Scene, c.1920	358.00
Sign, Meek & Sons Reel, Brown Flock Cardstock, Raised Embossed Lettering, 8 x 4 ½ In.	900.00
Sign, Mercury, Fishermen, Mercy Outboard Motor, Cardboard, Frame, 31 x 24 In.	106.00
Sign, Midshipman, Man, Sailor Suit, Wide Brim Hat, Wood, England, 1920s, 36 x 27 In.	1500.00
Sign, Miller & Mosack, Beck's Beer, Eagle Rolling Keg, Flags, Wood, 38 x 96 In.	10625.00
Sign, Miller Bock Beer, Special Brew, Girl Riding Goat, Paper Litho, 23 x 18 In.	797.00
Sign, Minneapolis Expo, Flag, Sailor Suited Girl, Die Cut Cardboard Lithograph, 1890, 12 x 9 In.	715.00
Sign, Minnequa Coffee, Trademark Indian, Orange, Yellow, Tin Lithograph, 6 x 5 In.	495.00
Sign, Mirror, Thompson's Coca Wine, Invaluable For Invalids, Barrow & Furness, 19 x 8 In.	523.00
Sign, Model Ranges & Stoves, Reverse Glass, Inlay Letters, 1892, 17 x 27 In.	1700.00
Sign, Model Smoking Tobacco, Did You Say 10 Cents?, Red, White, Tin, 11 x 34 In.	150.00
Sign, Model Tobacco, Cigar Store Indian Pose, Die Cut, Easel Back, Multicolored, 22 x 8 In.	385.00
Sign, Mohawk Beverage Co., Arched Panel, 2-Sided, Gilt, Green, Tin, c.1900, 16 x 48 In.	356.00
Sign, Moon Spots, 5 Cent Cigar, Blue, Brown, Papier-Mache, Oval, 36 x 34 In.	2200.00
Sign, Morton's Salt, It Pours, Blue, White, Tin, 9 ¾ x 27 ¾ In.	60.00
Sign, Mother's Best Flour, Red, White, Blue, Light-Up, Convex Glass, Chain, 17 In. Diam.	1210.00
Sign, Moxie Soda, Woman Sipping Soda, Tin Lithograph Die Cut, Round, 6 In.	770.00
Sign, Mt. Vernon Pure Rye Whiskey, Bottle, Cup, Matches, Frame, 20 ½ x 16 In.	500.00
Sign, Mundell's Mechanical Solar Tip Shoes, Puppet Theater, Heavy Paper, c.1890, 7 x 7 In.	209.00
Sign, Murad, Turkish Cigarette, 15 Cent, Woman, 2-Sided, Flange, Porcelain, 20 x 12 In.	600.00
Sign, Nabisco Biscuit Co., Uneeda Bakers, O-So-Gud Pretzels, Cardboard, Frame, 14 x 24 In.	742.00
Sign, Nash Trucks, Truck, Red, Paper, 38 x 24 In.	460.00
Sign, National Roasted Coffee, Flag, Coffee Can, Multicolored, Cardboard, 14 x 11 In.	1540.00
Sign, Natural Chilean Soda, Black Farmer, Yassuh Uncle Natchez, 2-Sided, Metal, 15 x 22 In. *illus*	234.00
Sign, Neon, Bud, Anheuser-Busch, 19 In.	30.00
Sign, New Idea Dealership, 1955, 33 x 72 In.	150.00
Sign, New Kineo Ranges, Victorian Girl, Toy Stove, Paper Lithograph, Frame, 22 x 18 In.	209.00
Sign, Nichol Kola, Tin, 1940s, 8 x 24 In.	70.00
Sign, No Trespassing, Florida Power & Light Co., Porcelain, 1926, 15 x 11 In.	89.00
Sign, Noerenberg Brewer, Wet, Dry Downtown, Scenes, Paper Litho, Frame, 22 x 34 In.	908.00
Sign, Northwestern Fire & Marine Insurance, Mahogany, Gold Paint, Frame, 20 x 28 In.	46.00
Sign, NuGrape Soda, Bottle Shape, Embossed, Enamel, Tin, Die Cut, 5 x 17 In.	88.00
Sign, NuGrape Soda, Die Cut Cardboard, c.1925, 16 x 22 In.	70.00
Sign, Oaklite Laundry Compound, Tin, Spinner, c.1909, 10 ½ x 7 In.	24.00
Sign, Office Trade, W.A. Hutchinson's Office, Gilt, Blue Border, Pine, c.1890, 13 x 43 In.	593.00
Sign, Old Dutch Cleanser, Pan Scrubbed, Cleanser Can, Tin, Cardboard, 16 x 11 In.	660.00
Sign, Old Havana Cigars, Young Girl, Tin Lithograph, Round, 13 ½ In.	364.00
Sign, Old Reliable Brand Fresh Oysters, Slogan, Lord-Mott Co., Tin, Embossed, 9 x 13 In.	1650.00
Sign, Old Reliable Coffee, Abe Lincoln, Coffee Cup, Russian Man, Frame, 12 x 22 In.	853.00
Sign, Oliver Chilled Plows, Wood Sand, Late 1800s, 12 ½ x 96 In.	8200.00
Sign, Olympia Bock Beer, Pilsen Brewing Co., Rams, Woman, Barrel, Paper, Frame, 35 x 26 In.	480.00
Sign, Orange Crush, Bottle, Come In Drink Orange Crush, 12 x 3 In.	305.00
Sign, Orange Crush, Orange, Blue, Porcelain, Self-Framed, 47 x 94 In.	1000.00
Sign, Orange Crush, Slogan, Blond Girl, Bottle, Cardboard, 1950, 12 x 16 In.	59.00
Sign, OshKosh B'Gosh Overalls, Uncle Sam, Tin, Frame, Pat May 14, 1912, 14 x 30 In.	590.00
Sign, Owbridge's Lung Tonic, Lithograph, William Mellor, Frame, c.1890, 25 x 19 ½ In.	300.00
Sign, Oxydol, Tin, c.1927, 10 ¼ x 6 ¼ In.	59.00
Sign, Oyster Creek Inn, Arrow Shape, Oak Panel, Painted, c.1950, 8 x 72 In.	326.00
Sign, Pa-Poose Root Beer, Indians, Settlers, Multicolored, Tin Lithograph, 13 x 39 In.	3850.00
Sign, Pabst, Good Old Time Flavor, 12 x 24 In.	6.00
Sign, Padlock, Key, Movable Keeper, Tin, Iron, Salmon Paint, Late 1800s, 13 In. *illus*	940.00
Sign, Pangburn's Candies, Polly Says, Patt's Drugstore, Reverse Painted Glass, 59 x 25 In.	770.00
Sign, Parker Brothers, Self-Framed, Wood Base Mount, 7 x 26 In.	7543.00
Sign, Passing Show Cigarettes, Porcelain On Steel, c.1900, 16 ½ x 9 ½ In.	235.00
Sign, Pawnbroker, 3 Gold Balls On Chains, 19th Century, 10 In. Diam. Ea.	854.00
Sign, Peaches, Cherries, Strawberries, Asparagus, Wood, Black Letters, c.1950, 5 x 23 In., 4 Piece	296.00
Sign, Pearl Lager Beer, Red, White, Neon, 17 x 19 ½ In.	675.00
Sign, Pears' Soap, Cardboard, 16 ¼ x 12 ¼ In.	24.00

Sign, Penn Leather Co., Dependable Oak, Pelt Form, Red, Yellow, 32 x 26 In. 275.00
Sign, Pensupreme Ice Cream, 3 Inserts, Enamel, 20 x 11 In. 60.00
Sign, Persil Soap, Girl Ironing, Paper, Linen Backed, Frame, Continental, 38 x 53 In. 351.00
Sign, Pet Milk, Oval Bubble, Tin, 1961, 30 x 36 In. 354.00
Sign, Peter Lorillard Plug Tobacco, Women, Cardboard, Frame, 14 x 9 In. 495.00
Sign, Phil. Schneider Brewing Co., Woman, Man, Holding Glass, Self-Framed, 20 x 24 In. 795.00
Sign, Philip Morris, Call For, Red, Yellow, Tin, 23 x 41 ½ In. 153.00
Sign, Philip Morris, Cardboard, Stand-Up, 64 In. ....*illus* 205.00
Sign, Picaninny Freeze Ice Cream, Black Boy Eating Watermelon, Cardboard, 1922, 9 x 12 In. 88.00
Sign, Piedmont Cigarettes, Announcement Board, Tin Lithograph, Wood Frame, c.1920, 2 x 3 In. 300.00
Sign, Piedmont Cigarettes, Blue, White, Porcelain, Self-Framed, 9 x 18 In. 240.00
Sign, Pig, I Make Squire's Pure Food Products, Tin, Lithograph, Oval, 18 ½ In. 236.00
Sign, Pillsbury, Color, Lithograph, 11 x 17 In. 70.00
Sign, Pipe, Chesterfield, Die Cut, String Hung, 24 x 12 In. 176.00
Sign, Player Cigarettes, Player's Please, Reverse On Glass, Oval, 14 ¼ x 24 ½ In. 99.00
Sign, Pocket Watch, Hearne & Smith, Cast Zinc, Painted, Gilt, 27 In. 1050.00
Sign, Poll-Parrot Shoes, 2-Sided, Die Cut, Tin, 3 ¼ x 4 In. ....*illus* 322.00
Sign, Poll-Parrot Shoes, Neon, Die Cut Porcelain, Parrot On New Can, 38 x 19 ½ In. 1020.00
Sign, Produits A La Croix, French Laundry Brand, Cardboard, Easel Back, 15 ½ x 10 In. 24.00
Sign, Promotional, Ingram-Richardson Co., Large Waterfall, Beaver Falls, Penn., 13 x 8 In. . 1045.00
Sign, Queen Quality Beer, Shipping Crate, Glass, Banner, Bottle, 25 x 13 x 5 In. 2640.00
Sign, R & R Syrup Of White Pine Tar, Woman, Smelling Flower, Cardboard, 15 x 10 In. 469.00
Sign, Raleigh, Bicycle, Embossed, Tin, 14 x 11 In. 11.00
Sign, RCA, His Master's Voice, Porcelain On Steel, 26 In. 795.00
Sign, Reach Baseball Equipment, Keep Up Your Game, Die Cut, Cardboard, Easel Back, 10 x 8 In. 962.00
Sign, Reach For Bunny Bread, Rolled Edge, Red Ground, White Letters, 28 x 3 In. 55.00
Sign, Record & Hooker, Poplar, Sanded Paint, Signed Derby, 8 x 38 In. 176.00
Sign, Record, RCA Victor, Masonite, Lithograph, Round, 47 In. 236.00
Sign, Red Goose Shoes, Red, White, Neon Over Porcelain, 36 x 20 x 7 In. 1630.00
Sign, Red Hook Ale, 1980s, 18 x 25 In. 12.00
Sign, Red Indian Tobacco, 5 Cents, Indian, Bow & Arrow, Paper Litho, Frame, 31 x 25 In. 1650.00
Sign, Red Indian Tobacco, Must Have It, 2 Oz., 5 Cents, Paper Litho, Frame, 33 x 27 ½ In. 1210.00
Sign, Red Man Cigar Leaf Tobacco, Fresh, Wax Wrapped, Red, Yellow 50.00
Sign, Red Rock Cola, Sold Here, Ice Cold, Yellow, Red, Embossed, Tin, 28 x 20 In. 410.00
Sign, Red Top Flour, Child On Box, Red, White, Black, Porcelain, c.1920s 2290.00
Sign, Reddy Kilowatt, Cardboard, Black Ground, 1930s, 8 x 13 In. 205.00
Sign, Reid's Flower Seeds, Black Man, Spider, Cats, Paper Lithograph, 15 x 12 In. 330.00
Sign, Robin Starch, Porcelain, 2 Boys In Suits Sitting On White Tablecloth, 36 x 24 In. 702.00
Sign, Rold Gold, Ice Cream Cone Form, Concrete, Painted, 25 x 10 In. 780.00
Sign, Royal Baking Powder, Butter & Eggs, Price Wheel, Tin Lithograph, 9 x 13 ¼ In. 2200.00
Sign, Ruff 1909 Greetings, Tin, 14 x 14 In. 623.00
Sign, R.W. Bell & Co., Favorite Soap, Black Woman, White Woman, Buffalo, Tin, 22 x 16 In. .. 1872.00
Sign, S. Hyde Co., Ales, Wines, Liquors, Cigars, Black, Gold Paint, 1800s, 61 x 40 In. 452.00
Sign, S. Kattar Shoes, Tennis Player, Cardboard, Humble, Texas, Frame, 15 x 9 ¾ In. 99.00
Sign, Saloon, Toby Mug, Arrow, Painted Tin, Iron Hangers, Wood Frame, 1900s, 23 x 26 In. .. 690.00
Sign, Sanitized Rest Rooms, 2-Sided, Porcelain, 18 x 24 In. 106.00
Sign, Santa Fe Trail System, Bus Depot, 2-Sided, Porcelain, 1920-30, 26 x 23 In. 7150.00
Sign, Savon Rectifie Soap, Paper, Linen Backed, Frame, Continental, 52 x 33 In. 322.00
Sign, Sawyer & Massey Threshers & Engines, Paper, Frame, 27 x 20 In. 1450.00
Sign, Saxoleine, Petrole De Surete, Lithograph, Chetet, France, Art Deco Frame, 48 x 32 In. .....*illus* 805.00
Sign, Scheidt's Valley Forge Bock Beer, Paper Lithograph, 30 x 19 ¼ In. 316.00
Sign, Schlitz, 26 ¼ x 18 ¼ In. 532.00
Sign, Schuttler Wagon Co., Covered Wagons, Through Ute Pass, Paper, Frame, 27 x 33 In. 2970.00
Sign, Schwinn, Bicycle, Embossed, 22 In. 17.00
Sign, Schwinn, Bicycle, Embossed, Oval, 18 x 7 ¾ In. 22.00
Sign, Schwinn, Paramount, Bicycle, Embossed, 20 x 15 In. 6.00
Sign, Sears Service Station, Porcelain, New York, 1930s, 61 x 92 In. 590.00
Sign, Seilheimer's Pale Dry Ginger Ale, Cream, Red, Blue, Porcelain, Wood Mount, 10 x 10 In. 468.00
Sign, Selz Shoes, Flapper In Evening Dress, Paper Lithograph, Christy, Frame, 32 x 12 In. 633.00
Sign, Seneca Cameras & Supplies, Indian Maiden, Die Cut, Tin, Flange, 18 x 14 In. 6700.00
Sign, Seneca Cameras, It Pays To Visit, Indian Girl, Yellow, Red, Tin Lithograph, 11 x 36 In. .. 1210.00
Sign, Sensation Cut Plug Tobacco, Greek Man, Dog, Frame, 17 x 22 In. 165.00
Sign, S.H. Siekerman & Co., International Harvester Machines & Implements, 9 ½ x 84 In. .. 400.00
Sign, Sherwin Williams Paints, Cover The Earth, Painted, Porcelain, 3-D, 36 ½ x 24 In. 550.00
Sign, Sherwin Williams Paints, Cover The Earth, Yellow, Red, Green, 3 Dimensional, 36 x 18 In. 840.00
Sign, Sherwin Williams Paints, Painted, Tin, Marked, MM-57R, 34 x 70 In. 140.00

Advertising, Sign, Padlock, Key, Movable Keeper, Tin, Iron, Salmon Paint, Late 1800s, 13 In. $940.00

Advertising, Sign, Philip Morris, Cardboard, Stand-Up, 64 In. $205.00

Advertising, Sign, Poll-Parrot Shoes, 2-Sided, Die Cut, Tin, 3 ¼ x 4 In. $322.00

Advertising, Sign, Saxoleine, Petrole De Surete, Lithograph, Chetet, France, Art Deco Frame, 48 x 32 In. $805.00

Advertising, Sign, Star Bottling Works, Tin, 36 x 11 In. $88.00

Advertising, Sign, Washboard, Deep River Store, 87 x 44 ½ In. $644.00

Sign, Shredded Wheat Biscuit, All Day Food, Indians, Niagara Falls, Glass, 17 x 17 In.	2420.00
Sign, Simon Pure, Old Abbey Ale, Easel Back, 1960s	18.00
Sign, Simpson Springs Beverages, Red, Green, Tin, Embossed, 19 ½ x 14 In.	275.00
Sign, Sir Walter Raleigh, Now 44 Percent Fresher, Pouch Packed, Tin, 24 x 16 In.	38.00
Sign, Smith's Green Mountain Renovator, Mirror, Round, Woman, Blowing Hair, 2 In.	413.00
Sign, Snider's Catsup, Bottle, Die Cut, Tin, 6-Sided, 17 x 11 ¼ In.	1970.00
Sign, Soapine Did It, Whale, Men Scrubbing, Black, White, Die Cut, Cardboard, 19 x 6 In.	440.00
Sign, Soapine Soap, Kendall Mfg. Co., Dirt Killer, Paper Litho, 1880s, 30 x 38 In.	17250.00
Sign, South Farview Broom Works, Painted, Wood, 13 ½ x 70 ½ In.	380.00
Sign, Southern Select, Script, Green, Neon, 6 ½ x 35 In.	770.00
Sign, Sportsman's Lodge, Rustic Cabin Rentals, Dog, Painted, Wood, 20 x 48 In.	85.00
Sign, Squeeze Soft Drink, Between Bites, Man, Boy Fishing, Dog, Cardboard, 19 x 15 In.	200.00
Sign, Squibb Milk Of Magnesia, Girl, 29 Cent, Cardboard, Standing, 46 x 24 In.	70.00
Sign, Squirrel Peanut, Cardboard, Die Cut Squirrel Carries Bag Of Peanuts, 30 In.	230.00
Sign, Squirt Beverage, Bathing Beauty, Bottle, Cardboard, 1947, 28 x 37 In.	70.00
Sign, Standard Shirts, Tin Lithograph, Victorian Ladies, Skinny Dipping Men, 29 x 21 In.	5175.00
Sign, Star Bottling Works, Tin, 36 x 11 In. ....*illus*	88.00
Sign, Star Soap, Cardboard, Die Cut, 2-Sided, Children Sitting On Swing, 5 x 9 In.	632.00
Sign, Steinfels Seife, German Laundry Brand, Porcelain, 17 ½ x 11 ¾ In.	53.00
Sign, Stetson Hats, Brown, Tin, Frame, 6 ¼ x 8 ¼ In.	175.00
Sign, Stroehmann Sunbeam Bread, Original Packing, 36 x 72 In.	295.00
Sign, Stroh's Beer, Welcome Aboard, Bell Shape, Plastic, Lighted, 17 ½ x 12 ½ In.	28.00
Sign, Studebaker Farm Wagon, Green Wagon, Embossed, Tin, Self-Framed, 32 x 26 In.	1000.00
Sign, Stull Hybrids, Man Smoking, Crossed Ears Of Corn, Steel, 25 x 20 In.	175.00
Sign, Subrikups Plumbing, We Sell 'Em, Celluloid Over Tin Over Cardboard, 9 x 13 In.	440.00
Sign, Sun Crest, Porcelain, Flange, 2-Sided, 11 ¾ x 18 ½ In.	165.00
Sign, Sunbeam Bread, For Safety Sake, Wood, 2-Sided, 48 x 36 In.	250.00
Sign, Sunbeam Bread, Girl, Red, Yellow, Pressed Steel, 47 ½ x 47 ½ In.	300.00
Sign, Sunbeam Bread, Trademark Girl Eating Bread, Metal Lithograph, c.1955, 12 x 30 In. ..	358.00
Sign, Sundrymen, Green, Reverse Painted Glass, 13 ¾ x 68 ¾ In.	140.00
Sign, Sunshine Beer, 3 Triple Crown Winners, Paper, Frame, 27 x 34 In.	295.00
Sign, Sunshine Coffee, Girl Holding Umbrella, Blue, White, Enterprise Co., 5 ¾ x 4 ¼ In.	253.00
Sign, Superb Ink Pad, Leading Pad, Always Reliable, Tin Lithograph, Frame, 10 x 14 In.	143.00
Sign, Superflame, No Smoke, No Odor, See It Burn, Red, White, Steel, 14 x 30 In.	50.00
Sign, Superflame, Fuel-Saver, Reverse Painted Glass, Curved, 12 x 6 In.	60.00
Sign, Sweet Caporal Cigarettes, Clown, Red, White, Paper Lithograph, 32 x 22 In.	825.00
Sign, Sweet Caporal Cigarettes, Please Shut Door, Woman, Cardboard, Die Cut, 14 x 5 In.	330.00
Sign, Sweet Caporal Cigarettes, Woman & Putti In Blue Hat, Paper, 36 ½ x 20 In.	700.00
Sign, Sweet-Orr Overalls, Union Made, Men Pulling On Pants, Porcelain, 14 x 20 In.	6800.00
Sign, Swift's Ice Cream, Pints 20 Cents, Quarts 35 Cents, Painted, Wood, 85 ½ x 26 In.	330.00
Sign, Swift's Ice Cream, We Serve, Blue, White, Porcelain, 2-Sided, 18 x 24 In.	220.00
Sign, Tavern, Black Horse, E. Griffiths, Oval, Blue, White, England, c.1885, 33 x 52 In.	690.00
Sign, The Bath Tub, Wood, Multicolored, 16 ¾ x 21 ¾ In.	40.00
Sign, The Black Shells, Falcon Taking Duck, 1920s, 20 x 30 ¼ In.	12768.00
Sign, The Centlivre Tonic, Nurse, Glass, Cardboard, Fort Wayne Indiana, 28 x 19 In.	523.00
Sign, Tipper's Veterinary, 3 Tips, Bull, Paper, 43 x 32 In.	255.00
Sign, Tobacco, Grand Cut Plug, Victorian Woman, Low-Cut Dress, Frame, c.1900, 14 x 10 In. .	150.00
Sign, Toy Town Tavern, Tin, Wood Molding, Paint, Mass., c.1915, 20 x 28 In.	385.00
Sign, Turf & Sport Digest, Woman Reading Book, February, Painted On Board, Frame, 24 x 18 In.	84.00
Sign, Tuxedo Club 10 Cent Cigar, Beveled, Tin, Chain Hanger, 9 ½ x 13 ½ In.	60.00
Sign, Twitchell, Champlin & Co.'s Standard Neuralgic Anodyne, Cardboard, 5 x 7 In.	121.00
Sign, Two Friends, Cigars, Woman, Dog, Die Cut Cardboard, 2-Sided, String Hanger, 7 In.	198
Sign, Two Joes Co., Clothiers, Hatters, Gents Furnishers, Woman, 15 ½ x 10 In.	175.00
Sign, Tygert-Allen Fertilizer, Office, 2 Chestnut St., Buildings, Boats, Paper, Frame, 25 x 31 In.	252.00
Sign, UMC, Bull's Eye Cartridges, Bull's Head, Die Cut, Tin, Flange, 25 x 18 In. ...... 3050.00 to 4068.00
Sign, Uneeda Biscuit, Yellow Slicker Boy, Paper Lithograph, Nabisco, Frame, 25 x 19 In.	303.00
Sign, Union Bar, Hotel & Restaurant Employees, Yellow, Tin Lithograph, 6 x 11 In.	115.00
Sign, US Ammunition, Self-Framed, Tin, 22 ¼ x 28 ¼ In.	2260.00
Sign, U.S. Government Inspected Choice Top Sirloin, Red, White, Blue, Wooden.....................	395.00
Sign, U.S. Rubber, Blue, Yellow, White, Porcelain, 2-Sided, 24 In. Diam...........................	550.00
Sign, Use Dr. David Robert's Healing Powder, 25 Cents, Orange, Cardboard, 22 x 6 In.	330.00
Sign, Utility & Atlas Numbering Machines, Tin Over Cardboard, 6 ¾ x 9 ¾ In.	198.00
Sign, Valley Gold Ice Cream, Red, White, Neon, 24 x 68 x 9 In.	1100.00
Sign, Van Dyck Cigar, Man, Frame, 33 ½ x 22 ½ In.	60.00
Sign, Van Heusen Shirts, Give Your Neck A Break, Frame, 1950s, 36 x 24 In.	112.00
Sign, Vaseline Capsicum For Colds, Smiling Ill Boy, Multicolored, Printer's Proof, 16 x 24 In.	330.00

Sign, Velvet Pipe Tobacco, Blue, Red, White, Porcelain, 12 x 39 In.	240.00
Sign, Vernor's Ginger Ale, Trademark Man, Barrel, Tin, Cardboard, Easel Back, 9 x 7 In.	2420.00
Sign, Victor, Nipper, His Master's Voice, Styrofoam Frame	28.00
Sign, Wagar's Ice Cream, Famous For Quality, Black, Yellow, Tin, 28 x 20 In.	83.00
Sign, Walter A. Wood Harvesting Machines, Blue, White, 2-Sided, Frame, 13 ½ x 31 In.	232.00
Sign, Ward's Ice Cream, Season's Greetings, Wreath Shape, 15 In.	19.00
Sign, Ward's Lemon Crush, Multicolored, Metal, Self-Framed, 9 x 6 ¼ In.	1140.00
Sign, Ward's Orange Crush, Ice Cold, Sold Here, Tin, Flange, 9 x 11 In.	920.00
Sign, Warren's Paints, 2-Sided, Die Cut, Nashville, Tenn., 24 x 26 In.	384.00
Sign, Warrior Mower Co., Indian, Horse Drawn Farm Machinery, Paper, Frame, 27 x 33 In.	3100.00
Sign, Washboard, Deep River Store, 87 x 44 ½ In. ....*illus*	644.00
Sign, We Dispense, Pharmaceutical & Biological Products Of Parke-Davis, Glass, 25 x 14 In.	413.00
Sign, We Sell Kodak Film, Steel, Painted, 2-Sided, Red, Yellow, 1960s, 18 x 24 In.	115.00
Sign, Wedding Bell Chocolates, St. Nick, Sleeping Girls, Cardboard, Die Cut, 15 x 14 ¾ In.	440.00
Sign, Weinbergers Ingersoll Watches, Yellow, Blue, Cardboard, 21 x 25 In.	33.00
Sign, Wells Fargo & Co. Express, 2-Sided, Card Stock, Navy, Black, Red, White, 14 x 14 In.	470.00
Sign, Wells Fargo & Co. Express, Yellow Letters, Wood, 2-Sided, 11 x 72 In.	1250.00
Sign, Wesco, Big W, Jet Logo, Porcelain, 48 In.	4125.00
Sign, Westchester Fire Insurance Company, Reverse On Glass, Frame, 1837, 12 x 28 In.	46.00
Sign, Western Shade Cloth Co., Factories, H.M. Pettit, Frame, c.1915, 40 x 75 In.	180.00
Sign, Western Wear, Directory, Wood, Painted, Tombstone Shape, 44 In.	12.00
Sign, Western Winchester, Winter Rabbit, 40 x 26 In.	60.00
Sign, Westinghouse Generators, Black, Orange, White, Tin, Embossed, 24 x 22 ½ In.	98.00
Sign, Whistle Golden Orange, Thirsty?, Pegs, Wood, 8 x 35 In.	105.00
Sign, Whistle Orange, Thirsty?, Just Whistle, Blue, Red, Yellow, Beveled, Tin, 30 x 26 In.	720.00
Sign, Whistle Soda, Just Whistle, Morning, Noon, Night, Tin, Embossed, 1938, 13 x 27 In.	330.00
Sign, Whistle Soda, Thirsty?, Certified Pure, Tin, 2-Sided, Flange, 12 x 12 In.	145.00
Sign, Whistle Soda, Thirsty?, Just Whistle, Wholesome, Delicious, Porcelain, 7 x 20 In.	990.00
Sign, Whistle Soda, Thirsty?, Yellow, Red, Tin, 32 x 56 In.	145.00
Sign, Whistle, Thirsty?, Just Whistle, Tin, Embossed, Self-Framed, 1948, 18 ½ x 55 In.	720.00
Sign, White House Coffee, Tin Lithograph, Die Cut Flange, 14 x 9 In.	3520.00
Sign, White House Coffee, Trademark Can, Red, White, Cardboard, 14 x 10 In.	440.00
Sign, White Label Cigars, Favorite Everywhere, 5 Cents, Tin, Embossed, 10 x 11 In.	154.00
Sign, White Rose Oats, 3 Victorian Girls, Cardboard Die Cut, Stand-Up, 9 x 7 In.	198.00
Sign, White's Excelsior Chewing Gum, Girl, Baby, Carriage, Die Cut, Cardboard, 7 x 8 In.	220.00
Sign, Who's Your Clothier, Go To J. Limpert, Owl Holding Ad, Metal, Paint, 36 ½ x 12 In.	440.00
Sign, Wilcox Jewelers, Pocket Watch Shape, Cast Iron, Tin, Painted, 23 x 16 In.	825.00
Sign, Wildroot, Embossed Metal, A-M Sign Co., 13 ½ x 39 ½ In.	480.00
Sign, William Conways Pure Wood Ash Soap, Red, Gold, Black, Tin, 1878, 10 x 14 In.	385.00
Sign, Willis Benson Meats & Vegetables, Boy, Vegetables, Die Cut, Paper Lithograph	220.00
Sign, Winchester Leader, Case Insert, Grouse, Bullets, Die Cut, c.1920, 7 ⅜ x 12 In.	5270.00
Sign, Winchester Leader, Shell For Nitro Powders, Brass Embossed, 9 ¾ x 13 ½ In.	2500.00
Sign, Winchester Repeating Arms, Double-W, Hunters, Animals, Cardboard, 40 x 78 In.	16156.00
Sign, Wm. Cameron & Bros. Tobacco, Lithograph, Frame, Petersburg, Va., 13 x 19 In.	130.00
Sign, Woolsey Marine Paints, Serving At Sea Since 1853, Porcelain, 34 x 22 In.	625.00
Sign, Worden's Ice Cream Bricks, Red, White, Porcelain, 30 x 20 In.	275.00
Sign, World's Greatest Flyer, 5 Cent Cigar, Blue, White, Paper, Frame, 14 x 26 In.	240.00
Sign, Wright's Indian Vegetable Pills, Cures All Bilious Complaints, E. Ferrett, 16 x 23 In.	2310.00
Sign, Wrigley's P.K. Gum, In The Evening, By The Moonlight, Paper, Frame, 15 x 25 In.	290.00
Sign, Wrigley's Spearmint, Cat, Chewing Gum, Black, Red, Gray, Shepard, 11 x 21 In.	275.00
Sign, Wrigley's Spearmint Chewing Gum, Girl With Gum, Cardboard, 1920s, 25 x 17 In.	175.00
Sign, Yankee Tennis Racket Co., 2 Racquets, Blue, White, Porcelain, Frame, 20 x 39 In.	1100.00
Sign, Yellowstone Whiskey, Woman, Reverse Glass, Copper Flash Frame, 14 ¼ In.	1100.00
Sign, Your Kidneys Need Dr. Pierce's Anuric, Walk Good & Strong, Paper, 8 x 45 In.	1155.00
Soap Holder, Garland Stoves & Ranges, Red, Yellow, Black, 5 x 4 In.	260.00
Soap Holder, Remember Troy Laundry Soap, Wire, 5 x 5 In.	209.00
Soap, Dog, Medicated Lister's, Dog Picture, Paper Wrap, Johnson & Johnson, 2 x 3 In.	143.00
Spinner, Lady's Leg, Bal-Tabarin, Paris, France, Die Cut, Tin Lithograph, 3 In.	120.00
Spinning Top, Geo. D. Fisher Optical Co., Celluloid, Parisian Novelty Co., 1 ¼ In.	125.00
Stamp, Tombstone & Patagonia Arizona Territory Stagecoach, Rubber, Wood Handle, 3 In.	4994.00
Step Plate, F.W. Woolworth, Cast Bronze, 3 ⅛ x 23 ½ In.	205.00
Stove Pipe Flapper, Dieters' Foundry, Cast Iron, 6 In.	12.00
Strawberry, Jersey Creme, Pressed Glass, Tin Lid, 4 ½ x 10 x 5 In.	720.00
Stringholder, 7Up, You Proudly Serve, Green, Red, White, Tin, 2-Sided, 16 x 12 ½ In.	275.00
Stringholder, Bay State Liquid Paints, Pilgrim, Tin Lithograph, Chain, 20 x 20 In.	1375.00
Stringholder, Bean Hole Beans, Die Cut, Tin, 13 x 12 ½ In.	950.00

Advertising, Tin, Alright Tobacco, Joh Wilh Von Eicken Co., Pocket, Vertical, 4 ¼ x 3 In.
$88.00

Advertising, Tin, Bambino Smoking Tobacco, Silhouette Ball Player, Round, 5 ¼ In.
$234.00

Advertising, Tin, Biscuit, Barcelona, Child Eating, Boy & Girl In Car, 6 ½ x 7 x 6 In.
$936.00

Advertising, Tin, Boots Baby Powder, Graphics, 2 ⅝ x 4 ¼ In.
$819.00

Advertising, Tin, Campfire Coffee, Blue Ribbon Products Co., San Francisco, 5 x 8 In. $995.00

Advertising, Tin, Jack Rabbit Candy, Diamond Pattern, Yellow, Red, 5 Lbs., 5 ½ x 8 ½ In. $234.00

Advertising, Tin, Krout's Baking Powder, Flag, Eagle, Cardboard, Paper Label, 3 x 6 In. $1170.00

Advertising, Tin, Log Cabin Syrup, Colored Paper Label, Towle & McCormick Co., 6 x 4 In. $1045.00

Stringholder, Dutch Boy, Anchor White Lead, Boy, 26 x 14 In.	480.00
Stringholder, Jason Soap, Figural, Kettle, Cast Iron, 4 ½ x 5 In.	132.00
Stringholder, Jaxon Soap, Kettle Form, 3-Footed, Cast Iron, Wire Bail Handle, 4 ½ x 5 In.	12.00
Stringholder, SSS For The Blood, Kettle Form, Cast Iron, 4 ½ In.	120.00
Stringholder, Van Vleet Mansfield Drug Co, Memphis, Glass, 5 x 6 In.	231.00
Sugar Cubes, Jack Dempsey's Broadway Restaurant, Dempsey Boxing, 6 Piece	66.00
Thermometers are listed in their own category.	
Tie Bar, Straight Arrow, Mailer, Patch, Nabisco Premiums, 1949-50, 2 ¾ In.	115.00

Advertising tin cans or canisters were first used commercially in the United States in 1819 and were called tins. Today the word *tin* is used by most collectors to describe many types of containers, including food tins, biscuit boxes, roly poly tobacco containers, gunpowder cans, talcum powder sprinkle-top cans, cigarette flat-fifty tins, and more. Beer Cans are listed in their own category. Things made of undecorated tin are listed under Tinware.

Tin, 3 Feathers Tobacco, Plug Cut, Choice Granulated, 4 x 3 ¼ x 1 In.	412.00
Tin, A & P Baking Powder, Paper Lithograph Label, Embossed Lid, 7 In.	41.00
Tin, Abbott's Menthol Plaster, Cures Nervous Disorders, Severs Aches, Round, Mass, 6 In.	50.00
Tin, After Glow Coffee, Marshalltown, IA, Red, Bail Handle, 4 Lb.	95.00
Tin, Air Float Talc, Tin Lithograph, 5 x 3 In.	66.00
Tin, Alright Tobacco, Joh Wilh Von Eicken Co., Pocket, Vertical, 4 ¼ x 3 In. ....*illus*	88.00
Tin, Apache Trail Cigar, Indian On Horse, Coast To Coast, 50 Count, 5 ⅝ x 6 x 4 In.	1870.00
Tin, Aristocrat Condom, Tin Lithograph, Trademark Parrot, Black, Multicolored, Round, 2 In.	413.00
Tin, Association Cut Plug Tobacco, Green, Red, Tin Lithograph, 3 x 5 In.	660.00
Tin, Bagleys Game Cut Tobacco, Birds, Flowers, 7 ⅜ x 11 ½ x 8 In.	660.00
Tin, Bambino Smoking Tobacco, Silhouette Ball Player, Round, 5 ¼ In. ....*illus*	234.00
Tin, B.F. Gravely & Sons Pipe Tobacco, Turbaned Man Holding Poster, 4 x 3 In.	798.00
Tin, Biddles Cough Drops, Tin Lithograph, Green, Black, 7 ¼ x 8 ¾ In.	1155.00
Tin, Biscuit, Barcelona, Child Eating, Boy & Girl In Car, 6 ½ x 7 x 6 In. ....*illus*	936.00
Tin, Biscuit, Bus, Driver, Land's End, Passengers, Ticket Collector, Roof Lifts, 7 ½ In.	5175.00
Tin, Biscuit, Car, Autorail, Grenoble, Roof Lifts, Embossed, Brun, c.1935, 19 ½ In.	288.00
Tin, Biscuit, Dining Car Passengers, LMS, England, 9 In.	2875.00
Tin, Biscuit, MacFarlane, Lang, Delivery Truck, Driver, Roof Lifts, England, c.1920, 7 ½ In.	4600.00
Tin, Biscuit, Mackintosh Toffee De Luxe, Enclosed Cab, Red, Removable Lid, England, c.1925	4313.00
Tin, Biscuit, McVittie & Price, British Military Scenes, 5 ½ In.	50.00
Tin, Biscuit, Racing, Gondola Biscuits, Car, Red, Gray, Graphics, Disc Wheels, 18 In.	1725.00
Tin, Biscuit, Wickerwork Biscuit, Basket Shape, Tin Lithograph, c.1904, 6 x 6 In.	242.00
Tin, Blenown Tobacco Mixture, Brown, Yellow, Tin Lithograph, 4 x 4 In.	358.00
Tin, Blue Ribbon Coffee, Bower & Bartlett, Boston, c.1885, 17 x 19 ¼ In.	702.00
Tin, Boots Baby Powder, Graphics, 2 ⅝ x 4 ¼ In. ....*illus*	819.00
Tin, Borden's Malted Milk, Eagle Brand, Has No Equal, 10 In.	41.00
Tin, Buffalo Brand Peanut Butter, Red, Black, Gold, 9 ¼ x 8 ¼ In.	150.00
Tin, Bulldog Cut Plug, De Luxe, Blue, Gold, Red, Green, Unopened, Pocket	825.00
Tin, Bulldog Insect Powder, Orange, Blue, Green, Tin Lithograph, 8 x 3 In.	187.00
Tin, Bunte Marshmallows, Child, Factory Scene, Tin Lithograph, 5 Lb., 5 ⅜ x 12 ⅝ In.	440.00
Tin, Cadette Tooth Powder, Figural Soldier, Red, White, Tin Lithograph, 7 x 2 In.	468.00
Tin, Campbell Brand Coffee, Arabic Scene, Yellow, Red, Bail Handle, Bloomingoton, Ill., 4 Lb.	50.00
Tin, Campfire Coffee, Blue Ribbon Products Co., San Francisco, 5 x 8 In. ....*illus*	995.00
Tin, Cannon's Tobacco, Irish Sliced Plug Flake, Blend, Aromatic, 3 x 3 ⅜ x 1 In.	121.00
Tin, Cardui Wash Antiseptic, 50 Cents, Chattanooga Medicine Co., 2 x 3 ⅛ In.	770.00
Tin, Cash Meat Market, Lard, 3 Little Pigs, Handle, Melbourne, Ia., 2 ⅞ In.	188.00
Tin, Checkers Tobacco, Weisert Bros., 4 ½ x 3 x ⅞ In.	495.00
Tin, Chocolate Cream Coffee, Steel Cut, Western Grocers, Paper Label, Oval, 6 ½ In.	115.00
Tin, Cloverine Talcum Powder, Woman's Face, Oval, Wilson Chemical Co, 5 x 3 In.	77.00
Tin, Coffee, Luzianne Coffee & Chicory, Handle, 2 Lb.	195.00
Tin, College Town Spices, Always A Treat, 1 ½ Oz., 2 ¾ x 2 ½ In.	385.00
Tin, Colonial Coffee, Cover, Thomas Co., York, Pa., 1930s, 1 Lb., 4 ½ x 6 In.	115.00
Tin, Colonial Coffee, Gold Luster, Thomas Co., York, Pa., 1930, 1 Lb.	130.00
Tin, Comfort Powder, Nurse Holding Can, c.1890, 4 x 2 ½ In.	440.00
Tin, Continental Cubes Tobacco, George Washington, 3 ¾ x 3 ¼ In.	632.00
Tin, Coronet, Condom, Yellow, Brown, Tin Lithograph, Killian Mfg. Co., 2 x 2 In.	633.00
Tin, Dentogen Tooth Powder, Round, Brighton Chemical Co, 4 In.	83.00
Tin, Dixie Jumbo Salted Peanuts, Red, Yellow, 10 Lb., 11 ½ x 8 ½ In.	480.00
Tin, Dixie Queen Tobacco, Plug Cut, Woman, Embossed, Paper Label, Handle, 6 x 4 ¾ In.	660.00
Tin, Donald Duck, Goyer Coffee Co., Early 1950s, Lb., 3 ½ x 5 In.	266.00
Tin, Dr. Belding Tooth Powder, Woman's Face, Yellow, Tin Lithograph, 5 x 3 In.	425.00
Tin, Dr. Daniels' Hoof Grower & Softner Price 50 Cents, 3 x 2 ½ In.	83.00

Tin, Dr. Jermyn Royal Imperial Pennyroyal Female Pills, Red, Chicago, 2 ¾ x 2 In.	198.00
Tin, Dr. Matchette's Indian Tobacco Treatment For All Tobacco Habits, Round, 2 ¾ In.	413.00
Tin, Dr. Sayman's Toilet Talcum Powder, Man's Head, Cardboard, Cylindrical, 5 x 2 In.	61.00
Tin, Dr. Tucker's Cough Drops, 2 ¼ x 3 ½ In.	825.00
Tin, Drug-Pack Condom, Mortar, Pestle, Black, White, Tin Lithograph, 2 x 2 In.	121.00
Tin, Drury's Vinco Plasters, Conquering Remedy, Hinged Lid, Cleveland Ohio, 4 x 2 In.	242.00
Tin, Dusenberry's Moth Destroyer, Extra Strength, Yellow, Black, 6 ½ x 4 ½ In.	253.00
Tin, Eagle Brand Coffee, George Buell & Co., 1 Lb.	30.00
Tin, Falk Tobacco Co., Humidor Lid, Turquoise, Rectangular, Richmond, 5 ½ x 7 In.	330.00
Tin, Forest & Stream Tobacco, Men In Canoe Fishing, Canada, 4 ¼ x 3 In.	632.00
Tin, Four Roses Tobacco, 4 Pink Roses, Nall & William, 5 x 3 In. 495.00 to 580.00	
Tin, Glove Kid Peanut Butter, 10 Lb.	22.00
Tin, Gold Bond Tobacco, Blue Ribbon, Tin Lithograph, 3 ½ x 3 In.	522.00
Tin, Gold Star Condom, Black, Gold, Tin Lithograph, 2 x 2 In.	660.00
Tin, Grosvenor & Richards Antiseptic Gauze, Somers Bros, Pat. 1879, 5 ½ x 3 ½ In.	66.00
Tin, Guide Pipe & Cigarette Tobacco, Your Way To Better Smoking, 4 ¼ x 3 x ⅞ In.	242.00
Tin, Handsome Dan Tobacco, Yale Dog, Hinged Lid, L.L. Stoddard, 5 x 6 ½ x 2 ½ In.	358.00
Tin, Honey Moon Tobacco, Rum-Flavored, Man On Moon, Woman In Space, 4 x 3 In.	635.00
Tin, Improved Peaches Condom, Cream, Black, Red, 1 ¾ x 3 In.	550.00
Tin, International Stock Food, 3 Feeds For 1 Cent, Stock Food Tonic, 9 ¾ x 8 x 7 In.	550.00
Tin, Iodoformal Antiseptic Surgical Dressing Powder, Round, Wm. R. Warner Co., 2 In.	121.00
Tin, Jack Rabbit Candy, Diamond Pattern, Yellow, Red, 5 Lbs., 5 ½ x 8 ½ In. ....*illus*	234.00
Tin, Jack Sprat Peanut Butter, 10 Lb.	180.00
Tin, Jack Sprat Peanut Butter, 25 Lb., 8 ½ x 6 ½ In.	260.00
Tin, Jack Sprat Peanut Butter, Handle, 12 Oz., 3 x 3 ⅝ In.	405.00
Tin, Jack Sprat White Syrup, Paper Label, Handle, 10 Lb., 7 ½ In.	79.00
Tin, Jayne's Asthma Remedy, Jayne's Drug Co., Boston, Mass, 4 x 3 In.	176.00
Tin, Jayne's Expectorant Tablets, Opium 1 Grain To Oz., 1 ⅞ x 2 ⅞ In.	187.00
Tin, Johnson's Peacemaker Coffee, Log Cabin, 1915, 25 x 24 x 18 In.	467.00
Tin, Krout's Baking Powder, Flag, Eagle, Cardboard, Paper Label, 3 x 6 In. ....*illus*	1170.00
Tin, Listerine Talcum Powder, Lambert Pharmmacal Co., St. Louis, 4 In.	72.00
Tin, Listerine Tooth Powder, Oval, Cream, Black Lettering, 2 In.	165.00
Tin, Log Cabin Syrup, Colored Paper Label, Towle & McCormick Co., 6 x 4 In. ....*illus*	1045.00
Tin, Log Cabin Syrup, Frontier Inn, Log Cabin, People, Horses, 6 ½ x 6 ½ x 4 In.	121.00
Tin, Loving Cup Tobacco, Cup, Red, Yellow, Tin Lithograph, 4 ½ x 3 In.	1210.00
Tin, Lunch Box, Dixie Kid, Black Baby, Tin, 3 ¾ x 7 ¾ In.	240.00
Tin, Lunch Box, Dixie Kid, Girl, Straw Hat, Nall & Williams, 3 ¾ x 7 ¾ In.	510.00
Tin, Lutteds S.P. Cough Drop, Log Cabin Form, 7 x 8 x 5 ½ In.	390.00
Tin, McHie's Canadian Club Tobacco Mixture, Yellow, Blue, Red, Tin Lithograph, 5 x 3 In.	935.00
Tin, Mentholatum, Japanese Woman, Fan, 1 ½ In. Diam.	209.00
Tin, Michigan Mixture Tobacco, Yellow, Blue, Rounded Corners, Tin Lithograph, 3 x 4 In.	44.00
Tin, Minty's Calla Lilly Talcum, Palmer's Ltd., Montreal, 1 ½ x 2 ½ x 4 ¾ In. ....*illus*	1112.00
Tin, Monopol Smoking Tobacco, London Club, 2 ½ x 4 ½ x 3 ¼ In.	88.00
Tin, Moshier Bros. Spices, Gilt Edge, Hinged Lid, 11 x 7 ½ x 7 ½ In. .... 880.00 to 1320.00	
Tin, Mother's Mustard Plasters, First Aid For The Household, Hinged Lid, 5 x 4 In.	50.00
Tin, Mother's Remedies Co.'s Ideal Borated Talcum Powder, Round Canister, 4 In.	66.00
Tin, Mrs. Brookes Guest Coffee, Woman, Key Wind, 1 Lb., 4 x 5 ⅛ In.	385.00
Tin, Newly Wed Candy, Chocolate Bon-Bons, Comic Strip Characters, 5 x 5 ½ In.	302.00
Tin, Nonsuch Harness Oil Dressing, Horse Head, Canada, 5 In. Diam.	187.00
Tin, North Pole Smoking Tobacco, North Pole Scene, Hinged Lid, Handle, 6 x 4 In.	770.00
Tin, Orrison Cigar Co., Cigar, Indian Graphics, Heekin Can Co., c.1919, 5 ½ x 6 In.	400.00
Tin, Pal Tooth Powder, Police Your Teeth, Wood Head Cap, Lordent Co., 5 In.	468.00
Tin, Palmy Day Tobacco, Green, Tin Lithograph, Utica, N.Y., 5 x 4 In.	253.00
Tin, Par After Shave Powder, Golfer, Nyal Co., 5 ⅝ x 2 ¼ In.	275.00
Tin, Patrol, Condom, Airplanes Aloft, Wilson-Robinson Co., Boston, Mass.	936.00
Tin, Pedro Cut Plug Smoking Tobacco, Yellow, Red, 6 ½ x 5 In.	845.00
Tin, Pennsylvania Oil, Tin Litho, Lawn Mower, Supple Hardware Co., 5 x 2 In. ....*illus*	303.00
Tin, Peter Pan Peanut Butter, Yellow, Black, No Lid, 25 Lb., 10 x 10 In.	25.00
Tin, Peter Rabbit Candy, Nursery Rhyme Story, Handle, Lovell & Covel, 2 ¾ x 2 ⅞ In.	209.00
Tin, Planters House Coffee, Steel Cut, Building, Red, White, Blue, Hanley & Kinsella Co., 1 Lb.	242.00
Tin, Post Office Tobacco Mixture, Building, E.G. Steane Co., Tin Lithograph, 5 x 3 ½ In.	688.00
Tin, Prim Genuine 5 Cent Aspirin, 30 Containers, Metal Caps, Chicago, 3 ¾ x 8 In.	715.00
Tin, Prince Albert Tobacco, Crimp Cut, Packed For Panama Railroad Co., Red, 4 x 3 x 1 In. ..	99.00
Tin, Puritan Talcum Powder, Baby With Banner, Round, 4 In.	33.00
Tin, Quinine Sulfate, Animals Hauling Materials, 5 Oz., 6 x 3 ⅜ In.	138.00
Tin, Red Cross, Antiseptic Foot Powder, Foot, Oval, Providence, R.I., 4 ½ In.	83.00

Advertising, Tin,
Minty's Calla Lilly Talcum, Palmer's Ltd.,
Montreal, 1 ½ x 2 ½ x 4 ¾ In.
$1112.00

Advertising, Tin, Pennsylvania Oil,
Tin Litho, Lawn Mower,
Supple Hardware Co., 5 x 2 In.
$303.00

Advertising, Tin,
Sunflower Steel Cut Coffee,
Dulland Mercantile, Sunflower,
3 ¾ x 5 ¼ In.
$1287.00

Advertising, Tin, Three Knights,
Condom, Black, Gray Graphics,
Goodwear Rubber Co., N.Y.
$88.00

Advertising, Tin, Turkey Coffee,
A.J. Kasper Co., 3-Pound,
5 ½ x 10 ¾ In.
$995.00

Advertising, Tin,
Yacht Club Smoking Tobacco,
Pocket, Vertical, 4 ½ x 3 In.
$702.00

Advertising, Tin, Yankee Boy Tobacco,
Scott & Dylan Co., Detroit, Pocket,
Vertical, 3 ½ x 4 In.
$761.00

Advertising, Tip Tray, Apollinaris,
Chas. W. Shonk Co.,
Signed, Phil May, 4 ⅛ x 6 In.
$59.00

Tin, Regal Smoking Tobacco, Cube Cut, Embossed, Foldover Lid, Canada, 4 x 3 ½ In.	522.00
Tin, Rexall Antiseptic Tooth Powder, Oval, Smiling Woman, 5 In.	330.00
Tin, Rexall Orderlies, Image Of Woman, Boy Soldier, United Drug Co., Boston., 3 In.	72.00
Tin, Rolled Nu-Tips Condoms, Tin Lithograph, Red, 2 x 2 In.	523.00
Tin, Roly Poly, Dixie Queen Cut Plug, Dutchman, 1912, 6 ½ In.	480.00
Tin, Roly Poly, Dixie Queen Cut Plug, Mammy, 1912, 6 ½ In.	480.00
Tin, Roly Poly, Dixie Queen Cut Plug, Man Smoking Pipe, 1912, 6 ½ In.	330.00
Tin, Roly Poly, Dixie Queen Cut Plug, Storekeeper, 1912, 6 ½ In.	120.00
Tin, Roly Poly, Man From Scotland Yard, Mammy, 1912, 6 ½ In.	120.00
Tin, Roly Poly, Mayo's, Tobacco, Dutchman, Yellow Shirt, Red Scarf, 7 In.	315.00
Tin, Roly Poly, U.S. Marine Cut Plug, Singing Waiter, 1912, 6 ½ In.	200.00
Tin, Royal Albert Cigarette, Tobacco, Tole, Signed, Japanned Black, c.1920	48.00
Tin, Scissors Cut Plug Tobacco, Scissors, Yellow Green Red, Tin Lithograph, 5 x 3 In.	468.00
Tin, Scotch Gall Remedy, For Man & Beast, Marshall Oil Co., Lithograph, 4 Oz., 3 ½ In.	275.00
Tin, Scott's Blood Tablets, Woman's Half Portrait, Bellefontaine, Ohio, 3 x 2 In.	88.00
Tin, Seal Of North Carolina Tobacco, Man, Woman, 6 ¼ x 4 ⅞ In.	42.00
Tin, Sheridan Veterinary Condition Powder, General On Horse, Paper Label, 5 x 4 In.	385.00
Tin, Snow Maid Scourer, Makes Dirt Fly, Girl Shoveling Snow, Paper Label, Contents, 5 x 3 In.	468.00
Tin, Society Brand Salted Peanuts, Orange, Blue, 10 Lb., 9 ¾ x 8 ¼ In.	400.00
Tin, Squirrel Brand, Salted Peanuts, Yellow, Red, 10 Lb, 10 x 8 In.	338.00
Tin, Strong Heart Coffee, Charles Hewitt & Sons, Indian, 1 Lb., 5 ¾ x 4 ¼ In.	522.00
Tin, Sunflower Steel Cut Coffee, Dulland Mercantile, Sunflower, 3 ¾ x 5 ¼ In. ....*illus*	1287.00
Tin, Surburg High Grade Tobacco, Woman's Face, Green, Tin Lithograph, 3 x 5 In.	242.00
Tin, Sure Shot Chewing Tobacco, It Touches The Spot, Indian Shooting Arrow, 8 x 15 x 10 In.	825.00
Tin, Sutherlands Pile Prescriptions, Green, Black, Cylindrical, 4 x 1 ½ In.	209.00
Tin, Sweet Bye & Bye Talcum Powder, Tappan Perfumers Co., 5 x 3 x 1 ½ In.	385.00
Tin, Sweet Cuba Chewing Tobacco, Yellow, Red, Slant Lid, 14 x 18 x 12 ½ In.	930.00
Tin, Three Cadets Condom, Red, Yellow, Black, Tin Lithograph, 1930s, 2 x 1 In.	242.00
Tin, Three Knights, Condom, Black, Gray Graphics, Goodwear Rubber Co., N.Y. ......*illus*	88.00
Tin, Three States Tobacco Mixture, Oval, 2 ¾ x 5 In.	209.00
Tin, Tiger Chewing Tobacco, Bright, Sweet, Tiger, 15 Cents, Lorillard Co., 2 ⅞ x 3 In.	412.00
Tin, Tobacco, Nigger Hair Smoking Tobacco, Brown Pail, B. Leidersdorf Co., 7 x 5 ½ In.	1020.00
Tin, Toilet Tripolio Cleanser, Woman Cleaning Sink, 5 ½ x 2 ½ In.	209.00
Tin, Tostadas Corn Chips, 1940s, 4 ½ In.	19.00
Tin, Turkey Coffee, A.J. Kasper Co., 3 Lb., 5 ½ x 10 ¾ In. ....*illus*	995.00
Tin, Union Leader Cut Plug Tobacco, Milk Can, Red, Gold, 9 x 5 In.	220.00 to 408.00
Tin, Urethral Bougies, Medicated, Grape Capsule Co., 1 ¼ x 6 ⅝ In.	523.00
Tin, U.S. Marine Tobacco Flake Cut, Tin Lithograph, Red, Yellow, Blue, 4 x 3 In.	358.00
Tin, Veteran Brand, Brewster-Gordon & Co., 1 Lb.	195.00
Tin, Voigt Milling, Flour, Gilt, Black Rooster, Red Striping, Slanted Hinged Cover, 20 x 12 In.	70.00
Tin, Watkins Talcum Powder, Man, Woman, Formal Attire, Lithograph, 6 x 3 In.	154.00
Tin, Wellington Tobacco London Mixture, Yellow, Tin Lithograph, 5 x 3 In.	176.00
Tin, White Hands Soap Tin, Black Man Washing Hands White, Tin Lithograph, 5 x 2 In.	209.00
Tin, Yacht Club Smoking Tobacco, Pocket, Vertical, 4 ½ x 3 In. ......*illus*	702.00
Tin, Yankee Boy Tobacco, Scott & Dylan Co., Detroit, Pocket, Vertical, 3 ½ x 4 In. .....*illus*	761.00
Tin, Yellow Cab Cigar, Takes The Right Of Way, 50 Count, c.1920s, 5 ⅝ x 5 ⅜ In.	962.00

Advertising tip trays are decorated metal trays less than 5 inches in diameter. They were placed on the table or counter to hold either the bill or the coins that were left as a tip. Change receivers could be made of glass, plastic, or metal. They were kept on the counter near the cash register and held the money passed back and forth by the cashier. Related items may be listed in the Advertising category under Change Receiver.

Tip Tray, Apollinaris, Chas. W. Shonk Co., Signed, Phil May, 4 ⅛ x 6 In. ....*illus*	59.00
Tip Tray, Bevo Soft Drink, Horses Pulling Stagecoach, 6 ½ x 4 ½ In.	167.00
Tip Tray, Big Jo Flour, Best Flour On Earth, Wabasha Roller Mill, 4 ¼ In.	156.00
Tip Tray, Compliments Greening Big Nurseries, Monroe, Mich., Art Deco Girl, 1906	55.00
Tip Tray, DeLaval Cream Separators, Woman, Boy, Tin Lithograph, May 14, 4 ¼ In.	230.00
Tip Tray, Deppen Brewing Co., Extra Pale, Stag, Tin Lithograph, 1930s, 4 ¼ In.	330.00
Tip Tray, Dr. A.C. Daniels, Horse & Cattle Medicines, 3 White Horses, 4 In.	521.00
Tip Tray, Drink King Cola, Royal Drink, Girl, Bouquet, Lithograph, c.1908, 4 In.	138.00
Tip Tray, E. Myers & Son Cigar, Royal Token, 10 Cent, Cedar River, Tin, 4 In. Diam.	85.00
Tip Tray, Fairy Soap, Girl With Bouquet, Seated On Soap, Tin Lithograph, 4 In. Diam.	70.00
Tip Tray, Franklin Life Insurance, Benjamin Franklin, Gold Tone, Springfield, 4 ¼ In.	98.00
Tip Tray, Globe-Wernicke, Man, Woman, Stacked Bookcase, Houlton Furniture, 4 In.	118.00
Tip Tray, Have Some Junket, Girl Eating Ice Cream, Round, 4 ¼ In.	156.00
Tip Tray, Hintz Foundation, 4 ¼ In.	56.00

Tip Tray, Hyroler Whiskey, Man In Tuxedo, Louis J, Adler & Co., Tin, 4 ⅛ In. Diam.	115.00
Tip Tray, Jenney Aero Gasoline, H.D. Beach & Co., 4 ⅛ In. ....*illus*	146.00
Tip Tray, Kemp & Burpee Success Manure Spreader, Horse Drawn, 3 ⅜ x 4 ¾ In.	235.00
Tip Tray, Laxol Castor Oil, Chas. W. Shonk Co., Chicago, 4 ⅛ In. ....*illus*	146.00
Tip Tray, Lieber's Gold Medal Beer, St. Louis World's Fair, Red, Yellow, 1904, 5 In.	77.00
Tip Tray, Los Angeles Brewing Co., Home Of East Side Beer, Building, Tin Litho, 5 In. Diam....	412.00
Tip Tray, Magnus Beck Brewing Co., Buffalo's Best, Beck's, Eagle, Tin, 4 ⅛ In. Diam.	240.00
Tip Tray, Marshalltown Gates Cigar, Children, Dog, Tin Lithograph, 5 x 3 ⅜ In.	150.00
Tip Tray, Mokaine Liqueur, Man & Parrot At Table, Tin Lithograph, France, 4 ⅞ x 3 In.	150.00
Tip Tray, New England Furniture & Carpet, Priscilla, Maid, Tin, 4 ¼ In. Diam.	35.00
Tip Tray, Quandt's Famous Beer & Ales, Tin Lithograph, Round, 4 ¼ In.	79.00
Tip Tray, Rockford Watches, Woman, Blue Dress, Tree, Tin Lithograph, 4 ⅞ x 3 In.	95.00
Tip Tray, S & H Green Trading Stamps, Woman Profile, Tin Lithograph, Shonk, 4 ¼ In.	189.00
Tip Tray, Schmauss Garden & Cafe, Diners, Bar Scene, Orchestra, 4 In.	100.00
Tip Tray, See, Hear, Speak No Evil, Kaufman & Strauss Co., N.Y., 4 ¼ In. ....*illus*	410.00
Tip Tray, The Hintz Fountain Pen, Geo. Hintz Stationery, Reading, Pa., 4 ¼ In.	56.00
Tip Tray, Woman, Holding Cup, Green, Gold, 6 In.	360.00
Tobacco Cutter, Betsy Ross, A. S. Valentine & Son, Cast Iron, 8 ¾ x 8 ½ In.	605.00
Tobacco Cutter, La Confession Cigar, 6 ¾ x 8 In.	550.00
Tobacco Cutter, Master Mason, Embossed, Painted, Cast Iron, 6 ¾ x 19 x 4 ½ In.	77.00
Tobacco Cutter, RJR Tobacco Co., Brown's Mule, Enterprise, No. 5837, Cast Iron, 7 x 19 In. .	73.00
Tray, Angeles Brewing & Malting Co., Griselda, 1907, 13 ¼ In. Diam......................	360.00
Tray, Anheuser-Busch Brewing Ass'n., St. Louis, Factory, Tin Lithograph, 19 In.	189.00
Tray, Banquet Ice Cream, Banana Split, 13 ¼ In. Diam.	92.00
Tray, Blatz, The Star Milwaukee Beer, 13 In. Diam.	2900.00
Tray, Blue Wing Whiskey, 2 Birds, Oval, 16 ½ x 13 ½ In.	800.00
Tray, Buffalo Brewing Co., Bohemian Lager, Sacramento, Indian On Horse, 4 In.	1064.00
Tray, Buffalo Brewing Co., Bohemian, Woman, Black Hair, Round, 13 In.	3250.00
Tray, Clysmic Table Water, Woman Holding Bottle, Deer, Tin, Oval, 6 x 4 In.	155.00
Tray, Cream City Brewing Co., Milwaukee, 13 In. Diam...................................	900.00
Tray, Cunningham's Ice Cream, Factory Behind The Product, Oval, 18 ½ x 15 In.	275.00
Tray, Edelweiss Beer, Smiling Woman, Schoenhofen Brewery, Round, c.1913, 13 In.	231.00
Tray, Ever Welcome Beer, People, Party, Cherubs, Terre Haute Brewing Co., Tin, Oval, 15 x 12 In.	440.00
Tray, Fayette Ice Cream Co., Woman On Phone, 13 In. Diam................................	250.00
Tray, Golden Ribbon Beer, Cowgirl On Horse, Tin, Round, 13 ¼ In.	4500.00
Tray, Hanley's, Peerless Ale, Providence, R.I., Porcelain, Round, 12 In.	41.00
Tray, Home Brewing Co., Adeline, Oval, 16 x 12 ½ In.	145.00
Tray, J. Gordino Jeweler, Victorian Women Serving Tea, Oval, California, Tin, 14 x 17 In.	523.00
Tray, J. Leisy Brewing Co., Cleveland, Factory Scene, Oval, 13 ½ x 16 ½ In.	1250.00
Tray, Jung Beer, Milwaukee, Carl Friese & Co., 13 In. Diam..............................	250.00
Tray, Juntz Remmler Co., Chicago Restaurant, Image Of Building, 4 x 6 In.	212.00
Tray, Lykens Brewing Co., Cream Top, Woman, Horse, Oval, 17 x 14 In.	450.00
Tray, Marrow's Ice Cream, 13 ¼ In.	185.00
Tray, McAvoys Malt-Marrow, Beats 'Em All, Boy, Dog, Tin, 1899, 12 In. Diam.	495.00
Tray, Miller Beer, High Life, Woman On Crescent Moon, Holding Beer Up, 12 In. Diam...........	44.00
Tray, Monticello Whiskey, Hunters, Horses, Dogs, Tin, Oval, 4 ⅜ x 6 ⅛ In.	98.00
Tray, Moxie Soda, Violets, Purple, Green, Tin Lithograph, Round, 6 In.	495.00
Tray, Nittanus Chiefs Cigars, 6 Indian Chiefs, Dog, Embossed, Celluloid, 7 x 7 In.	1485.00
Tray, Orange Julep, Bathing Suit Girl, Tin Lithograph, 13 x 10 ½ In.	210.00
Tray, Pabst, Milwaukee, 13 In. Diam.	1700.00
Tray, Pearl Beer, Keg & Bottle, Texas Own, San Antonio, Texas, 10 ¾ x 13 ½ In.	190.00
Tray, Pepper & Co. Whiskey Born With The Republic, Fife Corps, Tin Lithograph, 12 In.	154.00
Tray, Peter Schuyler Perfecto Cigars, Man, Colonial Outfit, Tin, 6 In. Diam.	105.00
Tray, Purity, Erie Brewing Co., Kaufman & Strauss, Woman, Tiger, 13 In. ....*illus*	176.00
Tray, Purity Ice Cream, Boy & Girl, Peace & Plenty, c.1915, 13 In. Diam..................	140.00
Tray, Purity Ice Cream, York, Pa., Woman & Polar Bear, 10 ½ x 13 ½ In.	195.00
Tray, Queen Quality, Deppen Brewing, Stag, Tin Lithograph, Round, 1930s, 12 ¼ In.	198.00
Tray, Rainier Beer, Girl With Bear, Tin, 13 In. Diam....................................	330.00
Tray, Rainier Beer, Woman On Horse, Tin, Round, 13 In.	825.00
Tray, Roland Rye Whiskey, The Dice Throwers, C.A. Feisst & Co., 12 x 17 In.	616.00
Tray, Schlitz, The Beer That Made Milwaukee Famous, Round, 13 In. Diam.	250.00
Tray, Sears, Roebuck & Co., Chicago, Tin Lithograph, Factory Scene, 6 ¼ x 4 ¼ In.	123.00
Tray, Tip, see Tip Trays in this category.	
Tray, Treasure Line Stoves, Woman Cooking, D. Moore Co., 4 x 7 ½ In.	188.00
Tray, Tri-State Ice Cream, Mother Serving Children, 10 ½ x 13 ¼ In. ....*illus*	468.00
Tray, Union Beer, Monks, Beer Pitcher, Bread, Tin Lithograph, Tarr, Penn., 12 In.	1430.00

Advertising, Tip Tray,
Jenney Aero Gasoline,
H.D. Beach & Co., 4 ⅛ In.
$146.00

Advertising, Tip Tray, Laxol Castor Oil,
Chas. W. Shonk Co., Chicago, 4 ⅛ In.
$146.00

Advertising, Tip Tray, See, Hear,
Speak No Evil, Kaufman & Strauss Co.,
N.Y., 4 ¼ In.
$410.00

Advertising, Tray, Purity,
Erie Brewing Co., Kaufman & Strauss,
Woman, Tiger, 13 In.
$176.00

Advertising, Tray, Tri-State Ice Cream, Mother Serving Children, 10 ½ x 13 ¼ In. $468.00

Agata, Pitcher, Wild Rose, Amber & Purple Stain, c.1887, 7 ½ In. $1553.00

Akro Agate, Cup & Saucer, Concentric Ring, Cobalt Blue, 1 ¼ x 2 ¾ In. $28.00

Akro Agate, Planter, Jonquil, Embossed, Orange, Yellow & White Slag, c.1970, 5 ¼ x 3 In. $25.00

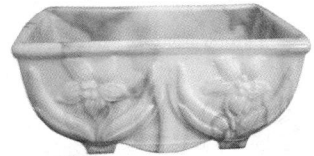

Tray, Utah Brau Beer, Woman, 12 In. Diam.		450.00
Tray, West End Brewing Co., Woman, Stars & Stripes Dress, 13 In. Diam.		900.00
Tray, Wielands Extra Pale Lager, Indian Woman, Tin, Round, 13 In.		510.00
Tray, Wielands Extra Pale Lager, Woman, Dog, Oval, 13 In.		2305.00
Tray, York Sanitary Milk Co., Purity Ice Cream, Bottle, Metal, 13 ¼ In. Diam.		115.00
Tray, Zang's Ice Cream, Chinese Boy, Lantern, Yama Yama, 13 ½ x 10 ½ In.		49.00
Tray, Zipp's Cherri-O, Bird, Drinking From Glass, c.1920, 12 In.		625.00
Tray, Zipp's Cherri-O, Tin Lithograph, H.D. Beach Co., c.1915, 12 In.		600.00
Vial, Dent's Toothache Gum, Paper Wrap, C.S. Dent & Co., 2 In.		50.00
Viewer, Stereo, Kis-Me Gum, 3 Kis-Me Photo Cards, American Chickle, 1 x 4 In.		825.00

AGATA glass was made by Joseph Locke of the New England Glass Company of Cambridge, Massachusetts, after 1885. A metallic stain was applied to New England Peachblow, which the company called Wild Rose, and the mottled design characteristic of agata appeared. There are a few known items made of opaque green with the mottled finish.

Bowl, Centerpiece, Plum, Pink, Burgundy, White, Scalloped Rim, 12 x 3 In.		36.00
Bowl, Crimped Fluted Rim, Pontil, 2 ½ x 5 In.		520.00
Bowl, Swan, Cornucopia Style, Triangular, Green, Red, White, Plum, 1950s, 14 x 10 In.		38.00
Bride's Bowl, Iridescent Plum, Crimped Ruffled Rim, 12 x 3 ¾ In.		45.00
Creamer, Glossy, Tricornered Rim, New England, Maude Feld Paper Label, 4 ½ In.		431.00
Cruet, Bulbous, New England, 5 ½ In.		1093.00
Cruet, Green Opaque, Oval, Stopper, New England, 5 ½ In.		748.00
Cruet, Tricornered Rim, Bulbous, Applied Handle, Stopper, 5 ½ In.		690.00
Pitcher, Purple, Gold Stain, Oval, New England, 6 In.		748.00
Pitcher, Wild Rose, Amber & Purple Stain, c.1887, 7 ½ In.	*illus*	1553.00
Spooner, Cylinder, Crimped Ruffled Rim, Pink To Rose, New England, 5 In.		403.00
Sugar, Creamer, Green Opaque, Lacy Overlay To Neck, New England, 4 In.		1150.00

AKRO AGATE glass was founded in Akron, Ohio, in 1911, and moved to Clarksburg, West Virginia, in 1914. The company made marbles and toys. In the 1930s it began making other products, including vases, lamps, flowerpots, candlesticks, and children's dishes, Most of the glass is marked with a crow flying through the letter A. The company was sold to Clarksburg Glass Co. in 1951. Akro Agate marbles are listed in this book in the Marble category.

Ashtray, Ox Blood, White, 4 ¾ In.		26.00
Cup & Saucer, Concentric Ring, Cobalt Blue, 1 ¼ x 2 ¾ In.	*illus*	28.00
Cup & Saucer, Demitasse, Blue, White, 2 x 4 ¼ In., 4 Piece		32.00
Cup & Saucer, Stacked Disc, Interior Panel, Cobalt Blue		33.00
Cup & Saucer, Stacked Disc, Interior Panel, Transparent Green		25.00
Cup & Saucer, Stippled Band, Transparent Green		30.00
Cup, Concentric Ring, Transparent Blue		65.00
Cup, Interior Panel, Green, 1 ¼ In.		15.00
Dish, Condiment, Green, White, Oblong, Marked USA, 3 x 2 ½ In.		15.00
Incense Burner, Dragon Head, Urn Form, Natural Color, Rings, Wood Base, 11 x 9 x 7 In.		690.00
Pitcher, Stippled Band, Transparent Topaz		42.00
Planter, Jonquil, Embossed, Orange, Yellow & White Slag, c.1970, 5 ¼ x 3 In.	*illus*	25.00
Plate, Concentric Ring, Green, 4 ¼ In.		10.00
Plate, Interior Panels, Maroon, White, 3 ⅜ In.		12.00
Plate, Stacked Disc, Interior Panel, Cobalt Blue, 4 ¼ In.		9.50
Plate, Stacked Disc, Interior Panel, Transparent Green, 3 ³⁄₁₆ In.		6.50
Pot, Stacked Disc, Blue, White, 5 x 5 ½ In.		24.00
Powder Jar, Colonial Lady, White Opaque, 1940s, 6 ¼ x 4 In.		45.00
Powder Jar, Orange, Cream, Ribbed, Beaded Cover, Footed, 1940s, 2 ¼ In.		24.00
Saucer, Blue, Octagonal, 4 ¼ In.		16.00
Sugar, Stacked Disc, Interior Panel, Cobalt Blue, 1 ⅜ In.		30.00
Tea Set, Interior Panel, Play-Time, Transparent Green, Box, 3 ⁵⁄₁₆-In. Plates	*illus*	107.00
Tea Set, Interior Panel, Teal Blue, Box, Child's, 8 Piece		125.00
Tea Set, Play-Time, Jade, Trans-Optic, Stippled Band, Box, 14 Piece		245.00
Tea Set, Stippled Band, Transparent Green, Child's, 26 Piece		300.00
Tea Set, Stippled Band, Transparent Topaz, 16 Piece		375.00
Teapot, Lid, Interior Panels, Maroon, White, 2 ⅜ x 3 In.		59.00
Teapot, Open, Stacked Disc, Interior Panel, Cobalt Blue		25.00
Toothpick, Vogue Mercantile, Blue, 2 ½ x 3 In.		20.00
Tumbler, Octagonal, Yellow, 2 In.		20.00
Vase, Green, White, Embossed Flower, Relief Leaves, Footed, 4 ¼ x 4 ¾ In.		16.00
Vase, Lily, White, Green, Opaque, Marked USA, 3 x 4 ¼ In.		10.00

Vase, Urn Shape, Caramel, Butterscotch, Footed, 3 ¼ x 2 ½ In.	20.00
Water Set, Stippled Band, Transparent Green, Pitcher 2 ⅞ In., 6 Cups, 7 Piece	145.00

ALABASTER is a very soft form of gypsum, a stone that resembles marble. It was often carved into vases or statues in Victorian times. There are alabaster carvings being made even today.

Beaker, Ale, Turned From 1 Piece, Brass Rim, Engraved Initials, England, c.1760	285.00
Bowl, Centerpiece, Grapevine Border, Stylized Shell Base, 13 ½ x 17 In.	115.00
Bust, Bashful Child, Timido, Signed, U. Hiaccini, 9 In.	92.00
Bust, Christ, Carved, Milky White, Gray Base, c.1900, 8 ½ In.	180.00
Bust, Girl, Smiling, Early 1900s, 6 In.	92.00
Bust, Maid, Renaissance Dress, Lace Collar, Braids, Carved Flowers Base, c.1890, 19 In.	356.00
Bust, Venus, Ribbons In Hair, Socle Base, 19th Century, 14 ¾ In.	415.00
Bust, Woman, Signed, A. Michelotti, Italy, Early 20th Century, 13 x 9 ½ In. ....*illus*	585.00
Bust, Woman, Smiling, In Feathered Cap, Illuminated, Art Deco, Italy, c.1925, 21 ½ In.	415.00
Bust, Young Woman In A Lace Hat, Signed, Fini C., Italy, c.1900, 8 x 15 In.	147.00
Candlestick, Ewer Shape, Spiral Column, 2 Pierced Top Handles, Brown, Black, 72 In., Pair..	4313.00
Column, Ball Tapered, Brass Section, Square Top & Base, 19th Century, 41 In.	900.00
Figurine, Eagle, Perched On Branch, Gray & White, Glass Eyes, Italy, 18 x 6 In., Pair.	531.00
Figurine, Madonna, Standing, Flowing Robes, Painted Accents, Shell & Scroll Base, 18 In.	948.00
Group, Couple, Flirting, Girl Holding Flowers, Boy Touching Skirt, Italy, 34 In.	4266.00
Group, Putto Wrestling With Cupid, Italy, 19th Century, 9 ¾ In.	265.00
Group, Young Shepherdess, Goat, Carved, Italy, c.1900, 16 In.	450.00
Jar, Cover, Carved Swags, Tassels, Bands, Cylindrical, Domed Cover, Neoclassical, 10 In.	316.00
Lamp, Electric, Domed Shade, 3 Parrots, Art Deco, c.1935, 27 ½ In.	1896.00
Lamp, Electric, Urn Shape, Classical, White Stone, Reeded Pedestal, 40 ½ In.	259.00
Lamp, Electric, Waves, Reclining Woman, Oyster Shell, 19 ½ x 21 In.	4600.00
Lamp, Electric, Young Woman, Standing, Italy, 36 In. ....*illus*	300.00
Pedestal, Canted Corners, Ring Turned, Fluted Stem, Octagonal Base, 40 x 11 In.	300.00
Pedestal, Columnal, Twister Center Band, Hexagonal Base, 5 Sections, 41 In.	440.00
Pedestal, Round, Turned, Square Top, Renaissance Style, 37 x 12 In.	720.00
Pedestal, Square Top, Clipped Corners, Fluted, Stepped Octagonal Base, c.1905, 11 x 29 In. ..	237.00
Pedestal, Square Top, Column Support, Swag, Ring, Bronze, c.1900, 41 x 12 In.	690.00
Sculpture, Abstract, Rotates, Base, 18 x 10 x 6 In.	115.00
Sculpture, Boy, Tree Trunk, Eagle, American Banner Shield, Brown, 10 x 22 In.	690.00
Sculpture, Indian Woman, Holding Bag, Signed, Evelyn Fredericks, 25 x 8 x 6 In.	690.00
Sculpture, Indian Woman, Wrapped In Robe, Signed, Doug Hyde, 13 x 5 ½ x 4 ½ In.	575.00
Sculpture, Maiden Pouring Water Into Well, 3-Footed Base, Carved, Signed, A. Giorgi, 24 In.	840.00
Tray, Carved, Bronze & Champleve Enamel Figural Mounts, c.1900, 16 In.	240.00
Urn, Turned, Oval, 3 Handles, 7 In.	165.00

ALUMINUM was more expensive than gold or silver until the 1850s. Chemists learned how to refine bauxite to get aluminum. Jewelry and other small objects were made of the valuable metal until 1914, when an inexpensive smelting process was invented. The aluminum collected today dates from the 1930s through the 1950s. Hand-hammered pieces are the most popular.

Bowl, Biomorphic Shape, Brushed, Hammered, Signed, Bruce Fox, 1950s, 11 x 3 In.	175.00
Bowl, Leaf Shape, Handles, Arthur Court, 1970s, 28 x 10 In.	115.00
Bowl, Wheat Pattern, Ring Handles, Cover, 7 In.	65.00
Box, Oriental Style, Green, Gold, Silver Handle, Textured, Scrolled Base, 1940s, 7 x 4 In.	57.00
Candelabrum, 2-Light, Nambe, 9 ¼ In., Pair	65.00
Candelabrum, 5-Arm, Sculptural, Donald Drumm, 1970s, 19 x 17 In. ....*illus*	780.00
Casserole, Cover, Hammered, Pressed, Fruit Design, Nasco, Italy, 8 ⅜ x 4 ½ In.	25.00
Coaster Set, Gold, Radiant Leaf Shape, Ray J. Walther Co., 4 In., 8 Piece	15.00
Cocktail Shaker, Red Top, Scalloped Ridges, 10 ½ In.	12.00
Coffeepot, Favo Drip De Lux Aluminumware, West Bend	25.00
Figurine, Billiken, Holding Diaper, Painted, 5 In.	240.00
Glove Box, Composite, Green Leatherette Cover, 1920s, 11 ½ x 4 ¼ In.	45.00
Ice Bucket, Flower Handles, Flower Knob, Monogram, 7 ½ x 7 In.	27.00
Ice Bucket, Hammered, Triangle Shape Handles, Italy, 8 x 7 ½ In.	22.00
Ice Bucket, Sea Lion, Arthur Court, Hinged Head, Tail, Stamped, 23 x 16 In. ....*illus*	4800.00
Megaphone, 3 Telescoping Pieces, Geometric Design, c.1860, 4 x 32 In.	118.00
Mobile, Snowflake, Box, Aarikka Toy, Finland, 39 x 11 ½ In.	50.00
Model, Thunderchief F-105, Republic Aviation, M.M. Verkuyl, Holland, c.1958, 16 x 9 In.	575.00
Platter, Fish, Arthur Court, Green Stone, Stamped, 1975, 12 ½ x 24 In. ....*illus*	150.00
Print, Talking Birds, Inuit, Kenojuk Ashevak, Canada, 19 x 14 ½ In.	495.00

A

Akro Agate, Tea Set, Interior Panel, Play-Time, Transparent Green, Box, 3 ⁵⁄₁₆-In. Plates
$107.00

Alabaster, Bust, Woman, Signed, A. Michelotti, Italy, Early 20th Century, 13 x 9 ½ In.
$585.00

Alabaster, Lamp, Electric, Young Woman, Standing, Italy, 36 In.
$300.00

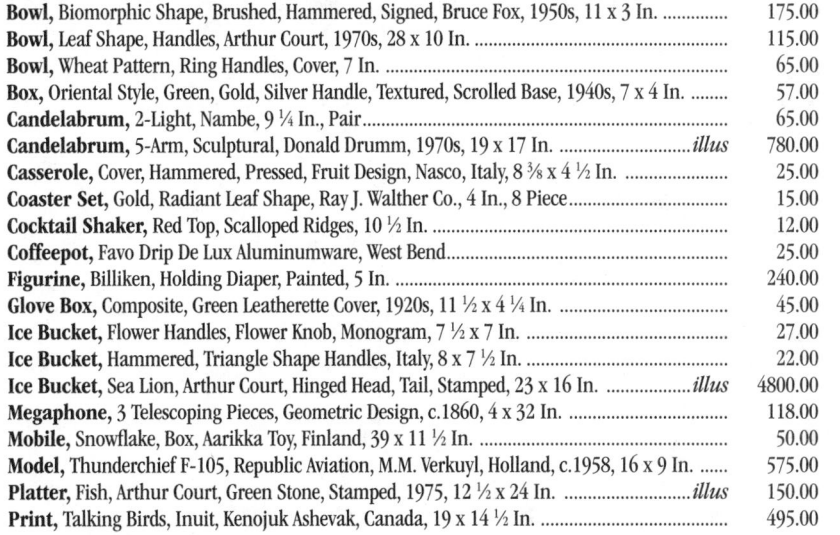

Aluminum, Candelabrum, 5-Arm, Sculptural, Donald Drumm, 1970s, 19 x 17 In.
$780.00

Aluminum, Ice Bucket, Sea Lion, Arthur Court, Hinged Head, Tail, Stamped, 23 x 16 In.
$4800.00

Aluminum, Platter, Fish, Arthur Court, Green Stone, Stamped, 1975, 12 ½ x 24 In.
$150.00

Aluminum, Sculpture, Owl, Glass Bead Eyes, Wood Base, Signed Curtis Jere, c.1970, 11 ½ In.
$780.00

Sculpture, 2 Vertical Projections At Top, Slate Base, Incised, James Myford, 1975, 48 x 66 In. .	900.00
Sculpture, Owl, Glass Bead Eyes, Wood Base, Signed Curtis Jere, c.1970, 11 ½ In. ....*illus*	780.00
Silent Butler, With Cobalt Cambridge Insert, Farber Brothers, 3 x 5 ½ In.	195.00
Token, Good For 25 Cents In Trade, Signed, Wm. Herdman...	10.00
Tray, Cake Server, Butterscotch & Black Handle, Farber Bros., 1940s, 10 ½ In.	64.00
Tray, Fish Shape, Jade Eye, Arthur Court, Cast, 12 x 6 ½ In.	45.00
Tray, Goldtone, 3 Rearing Horses, Handles, Round, 14 In.	100.00
Tray, Wrought, Hammered, Etched, Farberware, 14 In.	12.00

AMBER, *see Jewelry category.*

AMBER GLASS is the name of any glassware with the proper yellow-brown shading. It was a popular color just after the Civil War and many pressed glass pieces were made of amber glass. Depression glass of the 1930s–50s was also made in shades of amber glass. Other pieces may be found in the Depression Glass, Pressed Glass, and other glass categories. All types are being reproduced.

Basket, Inverted Ends, Split Handle, 4 ½ x 5 In.	14.00
Bottle, Swan Stopper, Blown, Enameled Birds, Flowers, Signed, 13 In.	212.00
Candy Dish, Cover, Panel, Indiana Glass Co., 7 x 5 In.	39.00
Chip & Dip, Art Deco, Gold Trim, Starburst Pattern, 12 In., 2 Piece	100.00
Compote, Square, Button & Daisy, 7 In.	10.00
Cordial Set, Decal Transfer, Yellow & Pink Flowers, Lubiana, Italy, 7 Piece	37.00
Creamer, Deep Amber, Applied Handle, c.1830, 3 ¼ In.	323.00
Decanter, Blown, Embossed Grapes, 8-In. Stopper, Rainbow Glass, 1960s, 14 x 4 In.	35.00
Flask, Broken Swirled Ribs, Zanesville, Ohio, c.1825, 8 ½ In.	471.00
Goblet, Thumbprint, 9 ½ In.	20.00
Knob, Flower Shape, Beaded Ends, 3 x 1 ½ In., 4 Piece	295.00
Pan, Folded Rim, Midwest, c.1820, 4 ¼ x 8 In. ....*illus*	1872.00
Pitcher, Painted Flowers, Applied Handle, Ruffled Edge, 9 x 5 ½ In.	54.00
Platter, Center Star, Thumbprint, 11 ¾ In.	24.00
Shoe, Embossed, Bow, 2 ¼ x 4 ½ In.	12.00
Slipper, Daisy & Button, Hanging Match Holder, 6 ¼ In.	335.00
Syrup, Swirl, Metal Hinged Lid..	40.00
Turkey, On Nest, 5 In.	21.00
Vase, Art Deco, Ziggurat, Pyramidal Shape, Frosted, 3 Vases, Chrome Base, 8 In.	100.00
Vase, Blown, Threaded Exterior, Spherical, 3 In.	9.00
Vase, Painted Leaves, Shouldered, Applied Blue Glass Ruffled Rim & 4 Feet, 13 In.	207.00
Vase, Pressed, Relief Grapes, Leaves, Footed, 10 In.	35.00
Vase, Sunflower Shape, Ruffled Rim, 4 ¾ x 2 ½ x 6 ½ In.	25.00
Vase, White Enameled Figure, 18th Century Clothing, 12 ½ In., Pair.....................................	153.00

AMBERETTE *pieces are listed in the Pressed Glass category under the pattern name Amberette.*

AMBERINA, a two-toned glassware, was originally made from 1883 to about 1900. It was patented by Joseph Locke of the New England Glass Company, but was also made by other companies and is still being made. The glass shades from red to amber. Similar pieces of glass may be found in the Baccarat, Libbey, Plated Amberina, and other categories. Glass shaded from blue to amber is called *Blue Amberina* or *Bluerina*.

Beaker, Diamond Optic, Flared Rim, Pour Spout, Pontil, c.1875, 3 ⅝ In.	145.00
Bowl, Diamond-Quilted, Scalloped Rim, 8 ½ In.	978.00
Bowl, Inverted Thumbprint, Ruffled Edge, c.1870, 2 x 5 ½ In.	266.00
Butter, Covered, Thumbprint, White Flowers, Gold Tracery, 8 In.	518.00
Claret, Rib Optic, Pontil, c.1875, 4 ½ In.	53.00
Compote, Moon & Stars, L.E. Smith Glass Co., c.1967, 4 x 6 In.	35.00
Compote, Optic Diamond, 7 In.	690.00
Creamer, Hobnail, Applied Handle, Pontil, c.1875, 4 ⅝ In.	118.00
Cruet, Inverted Coin Spot, Tricorn Rim, Bluerina, Faceted Stopper....................................	173.00
Finger Bowl, Underplate, Ruffled Rim, 7 In.	403.00
Flask, Bulbous, Tricornered, Amber Rigaree Collar, New England, 9 In.	748.00
Flask, Wine, Footed, Optic Ribs, Multicolored Flowers, Twisted Acorn Stopper, 14 In.	345.00
Pitcher, Crackle Glass, 6 In.	45.00
Pitcher, Ribbed, 11 In.	194.00
Syrup, Coin Spot, Oval, Metal Collar, Handle, New England, 6 In.	662.00
Syrup, Inverted Thumbprint, Silver Plated Lid, Handle, c.1900, 6 In. ....*illus*	489.00
Syrup, Thumbprint, Pewter Lid & Handle, Mt. Washington, 5 In.	546.00
Toothpick, Diamond-Quilted, Tricornered, New England, 2 In.	160.00

Tumbler, Diamond, 3 ¾ In., 8 Piece		173.00
Tumbler, Reddish Purple Shaded To Yellow, 4 In.	*illus*	1495.00
Tureen, Cover, Ruby To Amber, Crosshatch Ground, Irregular Finial, 15 In.		288.00
Vase, Bowling Pin Shape, Applied Swirled Neck, 5 ½ In.		50.00
Vase, Bulbous, Pinched Sides, Tricornered Rim, Rigaree Collar, 6 ½ In.		633.00
Vase, Celery, Inverted Thumbprint, Waist, Scalloped Rim, c.1875, 7 In.		132.00
Vase, Jack-In-The-Pulpit, Footed, Oval, Optic Diamond, 3 Amber Rigaree Feet, 6 In.		160.00
Vase, Lily, 7 In.		196.00
Vase, Matching Pedestal, Flowers, Enameled, Scalloped, Flared Rim, Gold, Red, c.1900, 29 In.		2632.00
Vase, Reverse, Carafe Shape, Coin Spot Pattern, Ma-Su-No-Ke Collar, 8 ½ In.		115.00
Vase, Reverse, Oval, Diamond Quilted, Ruffled Rim, 5 In.		86.00
Vase, Trumpet Shape, Tricornered Rim, 14 In.		546.00

AMERICAN DINNERWARE, *see Dinnerware.*

AMERICAN ENCAUSTIC TILING COMPANY was founded in Zanesville, Ohio, in 1875. The company planned to make a variety of tiles to compete with the English tiles that were selling in the United States for use in fireplaces and other architectural designs. The first glazed tiles were made in 1880, embossed tiles in 1881, faience tiles in the 1920s. The firm closed in 1935 and reopened in 1937 as the Shawnee Pottery.

Ashtray, Heart Shape, Blue Glaze, Marked AE, 3 ½ x 3 ¼ In.		55.00
Dish, Eagle, Spread Wings, Green Glaze, c.1920, 7 ½ x 5 ¾ x 4 ½ In.		300.00
Dish, Heart Shape, Blue Glaze, 1920s, 3 ½ x 3 ¼ In.		55.00
Inkwell, 2 Pen Rests, 2 Wells, Covers, Logo, Blue High Glaze, 6 x 5 In.		325.00
Inkwell, Blue Glaze, Pen Rest, 2 Wells, c.1940, 6 x 5 In.		95.00
Tile, 2 Dutch Boys, Yellow, Blue, Green, Brown, Glazed, c.1940, 4 ¼ x 4 ¼ In.		35.00
Tile, Abstract Scroll, Brown, Yellow, White, Orange, 6 x 6 In.		95.00
Tile, Aesop's Fables, Man That Pleased None, Walter Crane, c.1930, 6 x 6 In.		150.00
Tile, Bird, Oak Leaves, Green, Brown, Beige, c.1940, 4 x 4 In.		35.00
Tile, Bird On Branch, Oak Leaves, Pastel Glaze, c.1940, 4 ⅛ x 4 ⅛ In.		35.00
Tile, Cattail, Lime Green, Vertical, c.1880, 6 x 6 In., 3 Piece		130.00
Tile, Classical Woman Playing Musical Instrument, Green, Frame, 18 x 6 In., Pair		1700.00
Tile, Deer, Art Deco, Silver Glaze, c.1920, 4 ¼ x 4 ¼ In.		140.00
Tile, Faience, Blue, Gold Mottled Glaze, c.1830, 4 ⅜ x 4 ⅜ In., 4 Piece		48.00
Tile, Horse, Art Deco, Silver Glaze, Cranberry Red, c.1920, 4 ¼ x 4 ¼ In.		160.00
Tile, Leaf, Black Ground, Gold Semimatte Glaze, 3 x 3 In.		55.00
Tile, Man On Horse, Art Deco, Silver Glaze, Black, Red, c.1920, 4 ¼ x 4 ¼ In.		160.00
Tile, Man On Horse, Art Deco, Yellow, Green, Brown, Black, c.1920, 4 ½ x 4 ½ In.		160.00
Tile, Man, Woman, Mottled White & Brown, Frame, 17 ¾ x 6 In., Pair		976.00
Tile, Nursery Rhyme, Boaster, Walter Crane, July 31 1926, 6 x 6 In.		170.00
Tile, Portrait, Man & Woman, Relief, Brown Glaze, c.1890, 8 x 8 In., Pair		575.00
Tile, Portrait, Woman, Blue, 1890s, 6 x 6 In.		225.00
Tile, Warrior Profile, Rose, Frame, 6 x 6 In., Pair	*illus*	263.00
Tile, Windmill, Yellow, Blue, Green, Matte & Gloss Glazes, c.1940, 4 ¼ x 4 ¼ In.		35.00
Trivet, Arts & Crafts, Stylized Flower, Multicolored, Copper, 1920s, 6 ½ x 6 ½ In.		135.00
Trivet, Fortune & The Boy, Walter Crane, 6 x 6 In.		65.00
Trivet, White Ground, Green Design, Copper, 1920s, 6 ½ x 6 ½ In.		135.00

AMETHYST GLASS is any of the many glasswares made in the dark purple color of the gemstone amethyst. Included in this category are many pieces made in the nineteenth and twentieth centuries. Very dark pieces are called *black amethyst* and are listed under that heading.

Ashtray, Crimped, Rolled Rim, 2 ½ x 4 ¾ In.		14.00
Box, Lid, Hinged, Round, White Enamel Blossom, Gold Trim, 3 ½ In.		225.00
Condiment, Pattern Molded, Stopper, Early 19th Century, 6 ¼ In.		770.00
Creamer, 16 Ribs, Heavy Striations, Footed, c.1820, 4 ¼ In.		1025.00
Decanter Set, Bowling Pin Shape, Teardrop Stopper, 4 Tumblers, Italy		125.00
Flower Frog, Candleholder, Oval Bowl, Base, 1950s, 6 ½ x 5 In.		75.00
Goblet, Clear Ball Stem, 6 ¼ x 3 ¾ In.		7.50
Goblet, Florentine Diamond, 1880s		55.00
Jewelry Box, Lid, Hinged, White Rose Enamel, Black Ground, Round, 4 x 3 ½ In.		50.00
Perfume Bottle, Art Deco Style, 13 x 9 In.	*illus*	322.00
Pitcher, Barrel Shape, Tooled Rim, Threaded Rim, Footed, Pontil, c.1805, 4 ½ In.		840.00
Pitcher, Hobnail, 9 x 5 In.		69.00
Pitcher, Ribbed, Applied Handle, 3-Part Mold, 6 ½ x 6 ½ In.		24.00
Punch Set, Sterling Silver Overlay, 13 x 10-In. Bowl, 16-In. Tray, 11 Cups		1840.00
Toothpick, Holly Band, 2 ¼ x 2 ¾ In.		19.00

Amber Glass, Pan, Folded Rim, Midwest, c.1820, 4 ¼ x 8 In. $1872.00

Amberina, Syrup, Inverted Thumbprint, Silver Plated Lid, Handle, c.1900, 6 In. $489.00

Amberina, Tumbler, Reddish Purple Shaded To Yellow, 4 In. $1495.00

American Encaustic, Tile, Warrior Profile, Rose, Frame, 6 x 6 In., Pair $263.00

A

Amethyst Glass, Perfume Bottle, Art Deco Style, 13 x 9 In. $322.00

Animal Trophy, Buffalo Head, 2-Tone Brown Hair, 48 x 26 In. $495.00

Animal Trophy, Crocodile, Pelt, Head, Teeth, 95 x 38 In. $2832.00

TIP

Never bend or roll an animation cel. It might crack.

Animal Trophy, Elephant Foot, Footstool, Wood Top, c.1950, 18 In. $450.00

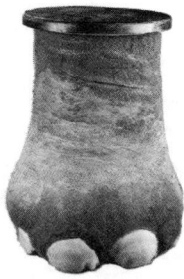

Tumbler, Enamel Flowers, Gold Rim, 4 In., 4 Piece	45.00
Vase, Bubbled Prunts, Bulbous, Tapered Neck, Rolled Rim, 10 In.	276.00
Vase, Campana Shape, Scalloped, Wreaths, Ormolu Mounted, 1860s, Pair	12900.00
Vase, Shaded, Flared Rim, Pedestal, 10 ½ In.	60.00
Vase, Urn Shape, Cover, Georgian, 18th Century, 8 x 3 ½ In.	595.00

AMPHORA *pieces are listed in the Teplitz category.*

ANDIRONS *and related fireplace items are included in the Fireplace category.*

ANIMAL TROPHIES, such as stuffed animals, rugs made of animal skins, and other similar collectibles made from animal, fish, or bird parts, are listed in this category. Collectors should be aware of the endangered species laws that make it illegal to buy and sell some of these items. Any eagle feathers, many types of pelts or rugs (such as leopard), ivory, and many forms of tortoiseshell can be confiscated by the government. Related trophies may be found in the Fishing category. Ivory items may be found in the Scrimshaw or Ivory categories.

African Gazelle Head, c.1975, 33 x 10 x 18 In.	127.00
African Gray Hornbills, Pair, On Forked Branch, Wood Slab Base, 15 x 24 In.	780.00
Antler Rack & Skull, England, Early 1900s, 42 x 35 In.	550.00
Bedspread, Asian White Yak, 9 Ft. 7 In. x 8 Ft. 4 In.	950.00
Buffalo Head, 2-Tone Brown Hair, 48 x 26 In. ....*illus*	495.00
Clark's Grebe, Perched On Log, Craning Neck, Taxidermy, 18 ¾ x 22 ½ In.	450.00
Crocodile, Pelt, Head, Teeth, 95 x 38 In. ....*illus*	2832.00
Deer Antlers, On Plaque, England, Late 1800s, 26 ½ x 32 In.	725.00
Deer Head, Mounted, 3-Point Horns, 23 In.	100.00
Elephant Foot, Footstool, Wood Top, c.1950, 18 In. ....*illus*	450.00
Eurasian Bittern, On Log, 18 x 19 ½ In.	450.00
Kangaroo Skin, Australian, Wool Felt Back, 71 x 42 In.	48.00
Peacock, Mounted On Branch, 20 x 59 In., Pair	2645.00
Rug, Bear Skin, 6 Ft. 5 In. x 5 Ft. 10 In.	805.00
Rug, Jaguar, Bound Backing, Taxidermied Eyes, Front Claws, 90 x 23 In.	2160.00
Rug, Leopard, Tanzania, Full Head, Wool Felt Backing, Display Board, c.1950, 94 x 61 In.	3120.00
Rug, Mountain Lion, Felted, 1940s, 90 x 60 In.	575.00
Rug, Polar Bear, Full Skin, Head, Claws, Wool Felt Backing, c.1975, 100 x 89 In.	2640.00
Rug, Zebra Skin, Backed With Leather, 9 Ft. 7 In. x 6 Ft. 2 In.	1380.00
Salmon, Carved Plaque, Brass Plate, Malloch, Perth, Scotland, 1933, 48 In.	10620.00
Skull, Cape Buffalo, Curled Horns, c.1950, 41 x 30 In.	127.00

ANIMATION ART collectibles include cels that are painted drawings on celluloid needed to make animated cartoons shown in movie theaters or on TV. Hundreds of cels were made, then photographed in sequence to make a cartoon showing moving figures. Early examples made by the Walt Disney Studios are popular with collectors today. Original sketches used by the artists are also listed here. Modern animated cartoons are made using computer-generated pictures. Some of these are being produced as cels to be sold to collectors. Other cartoon art is listed in Comic Art and Disneyana.

Cel, 101 Dalmations, Sgt. Tibbs, Great Dane, Mat, 1961, 9 x 12 In., 2 Piece	230.00
Cel, Bullwinkle, Dancing, Setup, Mat, Frame, Acetate Sheet, Jay Ward Prod., 10 x 13 In.	209.00
Cel, Donald Duck, Mat, Frame, 9 x 6 In.	550.00
Cel, Fantasia, Pastoral Symphony, Pegasus Babies, Courvoisier, 10 ½ x 14 In.	974.00
Cel, Ferdinand The Bull, Sniffing Flowers, Courvoisier, 1938, 9 x 9 ½ In.	1504.00
Cel, Flintstones, Pebbles & Bambam, 1960s	1250.00
Cel, Jetsons, George & Astro, Hanna-Barbera, Frame, 12 ½ x 8 ½ In.	300.00
Cel, Jungle Book, Baloo, Mat, Frame, 13 ¼ x 17 ¼ In.	316.00
Cel, Jungle Book, Mowgli & 2 Beatles-Like Vultures, Frame, 1967, 17 x 21 In.	433.00
Cel, Jungle Book, Ziggy The Vulture, Mat, 17 ½ x 13 ½ In. ....*illus*	538.00
Cel, Mickey Mouse, Black & White, Landscape, Disney Studios, 19 ¼ x 21 ½ In.	1265.00
Cel, Mr. Magoo, Black Wood Frame, c.1970, 4 In.	240.00
Cel, Oliver & Company, Dodger & Francis, Mat, c.1988, 17 ½ x 13 ½ In. ....*illus*	323.00
Cel, Pink Panther, Snow Shark, MGM, TV Series, Mat, Frame, 10 x 7 In.	150.00
Cel, Pluto, Put-Put Troubles, Disney Studios, c.1940, 16 ½ x 19 In.	475.00
Cel, Snow White, Singing, Double Mat, Frame, 1938, 11 x 12 In.	1837.00
Cel, Sylvester & Son, Warner Bros., Limited Edition, Mat, Frame, 12 x 10 In. ....*illus*	439.00
Cel, Tasmanian Devil, Whirlwind Tantrum, Signed, Frame, 17 ¾ x 19 ¾ In.	345.00
Model Sheet, Ugly Duckling, Silly Symphony, c.1937, 12 ½ x 10 In.	95.00
Storyboard, Nightmare Before Christmas, Jack Skellington, 5 ½ x 8 In.	224.00

ANNA POTTERY was started in Anna, Illinois, in 1859 by Cornwall and Wallace Kirkpatrick. They made many types of utilitarian wares, bricks, drain tiles, and giftware. The most collectible pieces made by the pottery are the pig-shaped bottles and jugs with special inscriptions, applied animals, and figures. The pottery closed in 1894.

Anna Pottery

Bottle, Pig, Incised, Arkansas Railroad, Stagecoach, River Routes, 1876, 6 ¾ In.	9400.00
Bottle, Pig, Incised Map Of Midwest..	4945.00

ARABIA began producing ceramics in 1874. The pottery was established in Helsinki, Finland, by Rörstrand, a Swedish pottery that wanted to export porcelain, earthenware, and other pottery from Finland to Russia. Most of the early workers at Arabia were Swedish. Arabia started producing its own models of tiled stoves, vases, and tableware c.1900. Rörstrand sold its interest in Arabia in 1916. By the late 1930s, Arabia was the largest producer of porcelain in Europe. Most of its products were exported. A line of stoneware was introduced in the 1960s. Arabia worked in cooperation with Rörstrand from 1975 to 1977. Arabia was bought by Hackman Group in 1990 and Hackman was bought by Iittala Group in 2004. Arabia is now a brand owned by Iittala Group.

ARABIA FINLAND

Casserole, Kosmos, Cover, Green, Brown, Black Stripe, c.1970, 2 Qt., 7 ½ x 5 ½ In.	50.00
Charger, Apple, Brown, Black, Earthenware, c.1980, 13 In.	100.00
Charger, Cobalt Blue, Green, Black Glazes, Signed, Toini Muona, c.1961, 17 ¼ In.	2800.00
Creamer, White, Green Laurel, 3 ⅜ In.	10.00
Figurine, Zebra, Black Matte Stripes, White Porcelain, Kaasinen, c.1963, 5 ¾ x 6 In.	220.00
Pitcher, Brown, Intaglio Leaf Design, 7 In.	100.00
Pitcher, Cat, Cream Ground, Green, Blue, Kaj Franck, c.1960, 8 x 6 In.	85.00
Pitcher, White Ground, Tan & Green Vertical Leaf Patterns, Narrow Neck, 7 ½ In.	250.00
Plate, Annual, Fisherman, Big Fish, c.1985	100.00
Plate, Annual, Hiker, Woman With Flowers, Kalevala, Raija Liisa, c.1977, 8 In.	135.00
Plate, Annual, Planter Sowing Seeds, Kalevala, c.1976, 8 In.	300.00
Plate, Annual, Skier, Reindeer, Kalevala, Raija Liisa, c.1978, 8 In.	135.00
Plate, Dinner, Meri, Blue, 10 ¼ In.	35.00
Plate, Iridescent, Blue Dove, Flowers, Oval, Kaipiainen, 8 ½ x 7 ½ In.	250.00
Platter, Rosmarin, Earth Tones, Ulla Procope, 1960s, 13 In.	70.00
Trivet, Valencia, Cobalt Blue Flower, White, Heart Shape Handle, Ulla Procope, 8 ½ x 6 ½ In. .	95.00
Vase, Iridescent Luster Glaze, Blue, Gray, Tan, Mark, 1932-1949, 5 x 6 In.	120.00
Vase, MOD, White Matte Glaze, Oval, Porcelain, Finland, 7 x 4 ½ & 5 x 2 ¾ In., 2 Piece..........	75.00
Vase, Narrow Opening, Blue Ground, Pink & Green Flowers, 4 x 7 In.	95.00

ARCHITECTURAL antiques include a variety of collectibles, usually very large, that have been removed from buildings. Hardware, backbars, doors, paneling, and even old bathtubs are now wanted by collectors. Pieces of the Victorian, Art Nouveau, and Art Deco styles are in greatest demand.

Altar, Side, Walnut, Gothic Style, Columns, 1800s, 37 x 24 x 37 In.	900.00
Applique, Renaissance, Wood, Winged Angels, Coat Of Arms, Italy, 41 x 15 In.	470.00
Backbar, Flame Mahogany, Carved, Drawers, Door, Mirror, Berninghaus, c.1899, 86 x 50 In. .	9000.00
Backbar, Soda Fountain, Quartersawn Oak, Mirror, c.1900, 9 x 9 ½ Ft..........................	1500.00
Basin, Well, Dolphins, Shells, Twyford-Hanley Mark, c.1910, 22 x 18 In. ....*illus*	470.00
Bracket, Mantel, Wood, 21 ½ x 11 ¾ In., Pair...	150.00
Bracket, Wall, Oak, Gothic, Openwork, Scrolls, 24 x 39 x 13 In.	179.00
Chain Lock, Security Door, Bronze, Silver Plated, Bundled Reed Border, 3 x ½ In., 2 Piece	80.00
Column, Giltwood, Baroque, Corinthian Capitals, Spirals, Grape Vines, 6 ½ In., Pair	2056.00
Column, Pedestal, Corinthian, Rose Marble, Brass Capital, Rotating Top, 43 x 13 In., Pair	1495.00
Column, Poplar, Block Base, Fluted, Ring Turned Standards, Gilt, Red Stain, 94 In., 4 Piece ..	646.00
Column, Limestone, Stepped Square Base, Octagonal Shafts, Gothic, 19 ½ In., Pair	201.00
Column, Marble, Veined, Michel Roux-Spitz, c.1930, 59 x 9 x 10 In., Pair.....................	3585.00
Corbel, Carved Scroll, Leaves, White Paint, 1800, 12 ½ x 5 In., Pair	1541.00
Corbel, Wood, Rococo, 2 Winged Putto, Paint, Parcel Gilt, Austria-Germany, c.1775, 20 In. ...	1080.00
Cornice, Window, Pressed Brass, Swag & Tassel, Acorn Clusters, 6 ½ x 54 In., Pair.............	176.00
Door Handle, Brass, Art Deco, Leaf Pattern, France, c.1930, 6 x 1 In., 4 Piece..............	35.00
Door Handle, Brass, Cast, Slotted Backplate, c.1920, 1 ¾ x 4 In., Pair	28.00
Door Handle, Brass, Woman's Leg Shape, Late 19th Century, 3 ½ x 2 In.	159.00
Door Handle, Bronze, Dolphin, Cast, 5 In.	253.00
Door Handle, Bronze, Figural Critters, Thumb Latch, Patina, 15 ½ x 3 In., Pair	300.00
Door Handle, Bronze, Geometric & Stylized Design, Patina, Corbin, 2 ¾ x 9 ¼ In., Pair........	175.00
Door Handle, Bronze, Twist Rod, Shaped Plate, 15 x 3 ¼ In., Pair	200.00
Door Handle, Crystal Knob, Brass Frame, 5 In.	100.00
Door Handle, Pewter, Cast, Draped Acanthus, c.1870, 2 ½ x 5 ½ In., 6 Piece	156.00

Animation Art, Cel, Jungle Book, Ziggy The Vulture, Mat, 17 ½ x 13 ½ In. $538.00

Animation Art, Cel, Oliver & Company, Dodger & Francis, Mat, c.1988, 17 ½ x 13 ½ In. $323.00

Animation Art, Cel, Sylvester & Son, Warner Bros., Limited Edition, Mat, Frame, 12 x 10 In. $439.00

Architecture, Basin, Well, Dolphins, Shells, Twyford-Hanley Mark, c.1910, 22 x 18 In. $470.00

Architecture, Door Panel, Wood, Relief Carved, Crest, Fruit, Strapwork, Mask, Griffins, 24 x 22 In. $178.00

Architecture, Doorknocker, Cast Iron, Parrot, On Branch, Hubley, 4 ⅝ x 2 ⅞ In. $88.00

Architecture, Finial, Zinc, Flame Shape, England, 17 x 7 ½ In., Pair $735.00

TIP

A stained glass window is probably more stable than it looks. Small cracks in the glass, even a bowed window, are usually not a problem. Cracked solder joints between pieces of glass should be repaired.

Door Hinge, Bronze, Basket Weave, Hopkins & Dickenson, c.1883, 5 x 5 In., Pair	175.00
Door Hinge, Bronze, Windsor Pattern, Reading, 6 x 6 In., Pair	225.00
Door Latch, Thumbpiece, Wrought Iron, 20 In.	385.00
Door Panel, Oak, Carved, Cherubs, Scrolling, 21 x 62 In., Pair	720.00
Door Panel, Scrolls, Flowers, Green Paint, Gilt, Italy, c.1700, 20 x 90 In., Pair	2478.00
Door Panel, Wood, Relief Carved, Crest, Fruit, Strapwork, Mask, Griffins, 24 x 22 In. ......*illus*	178.00
Door Plate, Bronze, Double Key Hole, Geometric, Stylized Designs, 7 x 2 In.	110.00
Door Plate, Bronze, Geometric, Triangular, Mallory Wheeler	146.00
Door Plate, Bronze, Leaf Cutouts, Spiral Rosette, Corbin, c.1890, 10 ½ x 2 ¾ In.	125.00
Door Plate, Bronze, Number Plate, Letter Slot, Late 1870s, 16 x 5 ½ In.	63.00
Door Plate, Bronze, Shaped, Vining, Norwalk, c.1875, 3 x 9 In.	295.00
Door Plate, Bronze, Women, Men, Nautical Design, 12 x 3 In., Pair	98.00
Door Plate, Gabled Top, Stork, Chalice, Swing Cover, Anchor, 9 ½ x 3 In.	518.00
Door Plate, Geisha Girl, Cast, 8 ½ x 2 ½ In.	144.00
Door Plate, Keyhole Bluebird, Russell & Erwin, 10 ½ x 2 ½ In.	460.00
Door Pull, Cast Iron, Pocket, Aesthetic, Nashua, 8 x 3 In.	12.00
Door Pull, Cast, Neo-Grec, Embossed, Scrolling, Vining, 1870s, 14 ¾ x 2 ½ In.	63.00
Door Set, Elevator, Wood, Glass, Flowers, Red, White Paint, France, 27 x 92 In., 3 Piece	472.00
Door, Armoire, Pine, Louis XVI, Provincial, Shaped Raised Panels, Late 1700s, 67 x 48 In.	823.00
Door, Carved Wood, Iron, 3 Panels, Male, Female Figures, Metal Stand, 69 x 20 ½ In.	1320.00
Door, Pine, Thick Boards, Painted Folk Scene, House, Hill, Trees, c.1830, 67 x 32 In.	823.00
Doorbell Pull, Multicolored, Footed Shank, Threaded Extension, 1860s, 2 In.	196.00
Doorbell Pull, Plate, Mallory Wheeler, c.1880, 5 ½ x 4 In.	69.00
Doorbell Pull, Recessed, Stylized Design, Quatrefoil, Corbin, 1880s, 1 ¼ In.	52.00
Doorbell, Twist Handle, Bronze, Marked Turn, Round Shaft, 3 In.	70.00
Doorbell, Woman, Nude, Push Nipple, Brass, 1890s, 4 x 3 In.	5000.00
Doorknob, Agrillo Glass, Swirl Pattern, Rosette, Mounted, Mallory Wheeler	75.00
Doorknob, Alloy, Lead, Deep Casting, Rosette, Brown Wash	69.00
Doorknob, Antebellum Woman, Footed Shank, Jahn, Phila., 1870s	259.00
Doorknob, Black Glass, Tapered Shank, Dish Top	40.00
Doorknob, Bronze, Hexagonal, Flower Design, Corbin, 2 ¼ In., Pair	180.00
Doorknob, Bronze, Round, Decorated Shank, 2 ¼ In.	35.00
Doorknob, Bronze, Warrior, Russell & Erwin, 1870s, 7 x 3 ½ In.	147.00
Doorknob, Carnival Glass, Mushroom, Tapered Shank, 1900s	52.00
Doorknob, Cast Bronze, Compression, Russell & Erwin	204.00
Doorknob, Cast Bronze, Neo-Grec, Sunken Center, Early 1870s	29.00
Doorknob, Cast, Emblem Seal, City Of New Orleans	115.00
Doorknob, Cast, Metallic Art Works	259.00
Doorknob, Cobalt Blue Glass, Silver Plate Shank, Early 1900s	69.00
Doorknob, Compass Rose, Russell & Erwin	29.00
Doorknob, Cut Glass, Tapered Brass Shank	12.00
Doorknob, Drum Style, Entry Plate, Swinging Key Cover, Rosette, 7 x 2 ¼ In.	200.00
Doorknob, Lion's Head, Bronze, Hopkins & Dickenson, 1870s	70.00
Doorknob, Lion's Head, Rosette, Footed Shank, 1860s	228.00
Doorknob, Opalescent Cut To Clear, Merurcy Glass Center, Pointed Flower, Circles, 1890s	36.00
Doorknob, Passage, Anthemion, Scrolling	85.00
Doorknob, Passage, Fox Head, Scrolling, Brown Patina, Reading	65.00
Doorknob, Passage, Pinwheel, Geometric Design, M.W.	90.00
Doorknob, Passage, Scroll Design, Hexagon, Hopkins & Dickenson, c.1879	220.00
Doorknob, Porcelain, Multicolor Mottled, Iron Handle, 1860s	10.00
Doorknob, Porcelain, Painted, Pink Rose, Iron Shank	29.00
Doorknob, Rosette, French Design, Fleur-De-Lis, Diapered Field, Russell & Erwin, 1860s	86.00
Doorknob, Torches, Wreath, Ribbon, Beaded Border, Oval, 3 In.	85.00
Doorknocker, Brass, Anchor, Shield, 8 x 6 In.	205.00
Doorknocker, Bronze, Medusa Head, 7 x 5 ½ In.	85.00
Doorknocker, Bronze, Renaissance, Grotesque Mask, Mouth Knocker, c.1875, 10 In., Pair	300.00
Doorknocker, Cast Iron, Cardinal, Berry Branch, Red, Oval, 5 x 3 In.	175.00
Doorknocker, Cast Iron, Flower Basket, White, Yellow, Red, Blue Bow, Oval, Hubley, 3 ½ In.	86.00
Doorknocker, Cast Iron, Lion's Head Mask, Verdigris Finish	150.00
Doorknocker, Cast Iron, Lower Basket, Pink, Blue, White, Yellow, Hubley, 4 x 2 In.	30.00
Doorknocker, Cast Iron, Parrot, Looking Backward, Blue, Yellow, Green, Oval, 5 x 9 In.	55.00
Doorknocker, Cast Iron, Parrot, On Branch, Hubley, 4 ⅝ x 2 ⅞ In. ......*illus*	88.00
Doorknocker, Cast Iron, Ship, Yellow, White, Red, Green, Oval, Hubley, 3 ½ In.	60.00
Doorknocker, Iron, Mixed Flowers, Basket, Black, Multicolored, Hubley, 2 x 4 In.	117.00
Doorknocker, Iron, Mixed Flowers, Basket, Pastels, Hubley, 2 x 4 In.	29.00
Doorknocker, Iron, Snowy Owl, White, Green, Yellow, Hubley, 5 x 3 In.	176.00
Doorknocker, Iron, Woodpecker, Brown, Black, Red, Hubley, 4 x 3 In.	88.00

Doorknocker, Wrought Iron, Double Dragon, 11 ½ In.	550.00
Entry Plate, Keyhole Single, Cast, Cut Form, Early 1870s..............................	127.00
Finial, Beechwood, Vase Shape, Carved, Green, Parcel Gilt, Flowers, 14 ½ In., Pair	960.00
Finial, Cast Iron, Pineapple, 9 ½ In., Pair	110.00
Finial, Copper, Applied Leaves, Sphere, Tapered Spire, Cone Terminal, Patina, 34 ½ In.	525.00
Finial, Copper, Roof, Applied Leaves, Square, Tapered, Central Sphere, Patina, 34 ½ In.	510.00
Finial, Eagle, Iron, Spherical Plinth, Reticulated Feathers, c.1875, 22 ¼ In., Pair	805.00
Finial, Oak, Square, 14 In.	250.00
Finial, Pole, Carved Wood, Gilt, Palmettes, Fleur-De-Lis, Italy, 12 x 5 In., Pair	600.00
Finial, Zinc, Flame Shape, England, 17 x 7 ½ In., Pair............................illus	735.00
Finial, Zinc, Roof Top, Spire, 26 x 6 In.	700.00
Fireboard, Pine, Pegged Beadboard, Faux Painted Red Brick Fireplace, c.1820, 30 x 41 In. ...	4740.00
Fireplace Surround, Georgian Pine, Stepped, Acanthus, Masks, Swags, 60 x 74 In.	1955.00
Fireplace Surround, Mantel, Eastlake, Turned Spindles, Carved, Beveled Mirror, 80 x 60 In. ..	600.00
Fireplace Surround, Marble, Rococo Revival, Serpentine Shelf, Arched, 47 x 72 In.	2040.00
Fireplace Surround, Marble, Rouge, Rosette Corners, Fluted, France, 19th Century, 43 x 51 x 11 In.	440.00
Fireplace Surround, Marble, White, Ormolu Mounts, 44 x 60 x 19 In.	1230.00
Fireplace Surround, Scrubbed Pine, Stepped, Panels, Carved Cornucopia, Jabots, 54 x 72 In.	1554.00
Fretwork, Oak, Stick & Ball, Molded Edges, Late 19th Century, 17 x 60 In.	165.00
Gargoyle, Stone, Grant Bldg., Atlanta, Ga., 8 ½ x 12 x 8 In. ....illus	173.00
Gate, Scrolled Leaves, Latticework, Flower Panels, Cast Iron, 114 x 157 ½ In., Pair............	2500.00
Gate, Wrought Iron, Antelopes, Stands, c.1920, 82 x 73 x 10 ½ In., Pair	42700.00
Gate, Wrought Iron, Grapevine, Twisted, Scrolled, 47 x 32 In.	484.00
Grill, Wrought Iron, Scrolls & Arrows, 40 x 15 In.	203.00
Hinge, Bronze, Stork, Steeple Finials, Polished, Russell & Erwin, 4 x 4 In.	167.00
Hinge, Cast Iron, Steeple Finial, Sargent, 4 x 4 In., Pair......................................	23.00
Hook, Chandelier, Cast Iron, Marine Creature Shape, 3 ¾ x 3 ½ In.	29.00
Keyhole Escutcheon, Bluebird Knob, Plate, Swing Cover, 3 x 1 ¼ In.	86.00
Keyhole Escutcheon, Porcelain, Swing Cover, 1860s, 3 ¾ x 2 In.	12.00
Keyhole Escutcheon, Swing Cover, Bronze, 1870s, 2 ¾ x 3 ¼ In.	29.00
Latch, Door, Iron, Tooled Design, Penn., 1832, 13 ½ In.	382.00
Lavabo, Zinc, Bombe, Tapered Lid, Ring Handle, Applied Leaf, Continental, 1700s, 19 In.	485.00
Louver, Oval, Center Disc, Fanned Rays, Weathered Patina, 67 In.	2500.00
Mantel, Cast Iron, Faux Marble, Serpentine Top, Scrolled Terminals, 37 x 42 x 18 In.	276.00
Mantel, Marble, Cast Iron Surround, Flower, Sprays, 75 x 35 x 15 ¾ In.	4994.00
Mantel, Marble, Neoclassical Style, White, Urns, Garland, Carved, 48 x 59 x 12 In.	1750.00
Mantel, Marble, Serpentine Top, Shell & Acanthus Carved Beast, c.1875, 51 x 71 In.	1997.00
Mantel, Oak, Neoclassical, Ebonized, Gilt, Dentil, Lion Mask, Griffin Supports, 1920s, 80 x 71 In.	795.00
Mantel, Oak, Prairie School, Raised Beveled Panels, 64 x 77 In. ....illus	600.00
Mantel, Pine, Applied Columns, Mustard, Brown Grain, c.1810, 48 x 56 In. ....illus	235.00
Mantel, Pine, Federal, Flowers, Gilt, Carved, Early 19th Century, 56 x 62 In.	840.00
Mantel, Poplar, Side Columns, Beaded Decoration, Late 1800s, 48 x 60 x 13 In.	71.00
Mantel, Walnut, Arts & Crafts, c.1895, 47 x 62 x 11 In.	600.00
Mantel, Walnut, Regency, Serpentine Top, Scalloped, Pilasters, c.1700, 44 x 58 x 25 In.	2937.00
Mantel, Wood, Carved, 2 Columns, Holly Berry Design, X In Center, Victorian, 53 x 63 In.	316.00
Mantel, Wood, Federal Style, Blue Paint, Projecting Corners, Pilasters, Late 1800s, 57 x 80 In. .	529.00
Mantel, Wood, Molded Cornice, Dentiled Molding, Garlands, Bellflowers, 1900s, 57 x 73 In. ..	570.00
Mantel, Wood, Mustard Paint, 19th Century, 54 x 65 In.	110.00
Mantel, Yellow Pine, Blue Paint, Georgia, c.1800, 67 x 79 In.	805.00
Medallion, Ceiling, Stucco, Louis XVI Style, Acanthus, Ribbons, c.1900, 20 In.	550.00
Model, Swan House, Roof Lifts Off, Winding Staircase, 29 x 71 x 52 In.	2850.00
Mount, Bronze, Oak Leaf, Acorns, England, 26 x 6 ½ In., Pair	147.00
Ornament, Giltwood, Restauration, Carved, Leaf Sprays, Flowerhead, 13 ½ x 9 ⅜ In.	420.00
Ornament, Oak, Bow Crest, Fruit & Flower Garland, England, c.1775, 43 x 14 In., Pair.........	2880.00
Overmantel Mirror, Beaux Arts, Pedimented Crest, Gothic Shelves, 78 x 66 In.	705.00
Overmantel Mirror, Federal, 3 Sections, Mahogany, Gilt Flame Finial, c.1876, 32 x 48 In. ...	230.00
Overmantel Mirror, Gilt Wood, Classical, Paired Cluster Column, c.1910, 25 x 62 In.	235.00
Overmantel Mirror, Giltwood, Arched Crest, Stepped Sidelights, Continental, 48 x 60 In.	633.00
Overmantel Mirror, Giltwood, Carved, Flower Cartouche, Scrolling Ribbon, 72 x 59 In.	863.00
Overmantel Mirror, Giltwood, Classical Revival, Egg & Dart Cornice, 30 x 64 In.	529.00
Overmantel Mirror, Giltwood, Crest, Carved Supports, Sphinx Ends, c.1885, 66 x 78 In.	705.00
Overmantel Mirror, Giltwood, Divided Panes, Classical Frieze, 54 In.	5800.00
Overmantel Mirror, Giltwood, Georgian, Pagoda Crested, Scrolling Leaf Frame, 43 x 69 In.	1912.00
Overmantel Mirror, Giltwood, Plaster, Louis XVI, Sunflower, Leaves, 69 x 45 In.	3360.00
Overmantel Mirror, Giltwood, Scrolling Frame, Fruit, Shell Crest, Oval, 60 x 64 In. ....illus	2728.00
Overmantel Mirror, Gothic Style, Giltwood, 3 Arched Panels, Pilasters, 36 x 50 In.	403.00
Overmantel Mirror, Limed Pine, Leaves, Branches, Ireland, c.1850, 55 x 63 In.	1175.00

Architecture, Gargoyle, Stone,
Grant Bldg., Atlanta, Ga., 8 ½ x 12 x 8 In.
$173.00

Architecture, Mantel, Oak,
Prairie School, Raised Beveled Panels,
64 x 77 In.
$600.00

Architecture, Mantel, Pine,
Applied Columns, Mustard, Brown Grain,
c.1810, 48 x 56 In.
$235.00

Architecture, Overmantel Mirror,
Giltwood, Scrolling Frame, Fruit,
Shell Crest, Oval, 60 x 64 In.
$2728.00

Arequipa, Vase, Squeezebag, Enameled, White Glaze, Blue & Green Ground, 6 x 3 ½ In.
$4200.00

Arita, Vase, Bottle Shape, Enameled, Chrysanthemums, Quince, Kakiemon Style, c.1900, 11 ½ In.
$570.00

William Morris

William Morris (1834–96), British designer, writer, and artist, was the leader of the Arts & Crafts movement in England. He preached a return to medieval traditions of craftsmanship. In 1861 he and some associates started Morris, Marshall, Faulkner & Company, a store in London. It changed its name to Morris and Company and operated from 1874 to 1940. The company designed and made home furnishings ranging from textiles and wallpaper to furniture and stained glass. Morris and his ideas inspired the Arts & Crafts movement in the United States.

Overmantel Mirror, Pine, 3 Sections, Gilt & Black Painted Turnings, 20 x 50 In.	129.00
Overmantel Mirror, Walnut, Victorian, Arched Top, 46 x 44 In.	120.00
Panel, Boiserie, Carved, Louis XVI Style, Painted, Floral Garland, 79 x 16 In., Pair	3360.00
Panel, Carved Oak, Fowl, Berry Branches, c.1900, 15 x 47 In.	390.00
Panel, Carved Walnut, Whimsical Mask, Italy, c.1900, 15 x 11 In., Pair	420.00
Panel, Pietra, Gray Variegated Marble, Dura, Green, Inlaid Compass Star, 47 x 47 In.	235.00
Panel, Walnut, Carved Grapes, Vines, Shield, Latin Text, 52 x 20 In.	920.00
Pedestal, Column Shape, Leaf Molding, Lion, Terra-Cotta, 41 ½ In.	316.00
Pedestal, Ebonized, Gilt, Rectangular, Inlaid, Flowers, Butterflies, c.1890, 15 x 28 In.	470.00
Pedestal, Rouge Marble, Brass Capitals, Square Base, 13 x 47 In.	518.00
Pediment, Pine, Sunburst, Alligatored Paint, Carved, c.1870, 72 x 33 In.	1850.00
Pediment, Pineapple Finial, White Paint, 23 x 74 In.	95.00
Pilaster, Oak, Carved, Fluted, Painted, c.1800, 81 x 6 ½ In., Pair	460.00
Railing, Wrought Iron, White, Footed, Rose Ironworks, 75 In.	1000.00
Roman Bath, Variegated Marble, Paw Feet, 19th Century, 4 x 11 In.	1292.00
Sash Lift, Bronze, Twist Handle, Yale, c.1890, 7 ¼ x 2 ¼ In.	35.00
Screens are listed in the Fireplace and Furniture categories.	
Scroll, Rococo, Central Shell, c.1900, 15 ½ x 51 In.	288.00
Shutter Stop, Figural, Woman, Cast Iron, France, 2 ½ x 2 ¾ In.	23.00
Spire, Molded Copper, Cut Leaf Design, Applied Crest, c.1895, 52 x14 In.	575.00
Stair Riser, Cast Iron, Chicago Stock Exchange, L. Sullivan, c.1893, 43 ½ x 13 In.	3360.00
Staircase, Library, Gothic Revival, Oak, Lion Newel Top, Mid 1800s, 62 x 80 x 34 In.	3720.00
Staircase, Spiral, Metal, Chrome, Space Age, Red Steps, c.1970, 12 Ft.	7350.00
Stand, Oak, Brass Hardware, Footed, Grillwork, Hinged Door, c.1910, 40 x 19 In.	720.00
Street Sign, Blue & White, No. 79, France, 19th Century, 6 x 9 In.	17.00
Tabernacle, Oak, Bronze Door, Embossed Cross, Carved Gothic Arch, c.1920, 27 x 13 In.	270.00
Thumb Latch, Wrought Iron, Pointed Terminals, New England, 18th Century, 15 In.	59.00
Tieback, Pressed Glass, Opalescent, Rosette Shape, Sandwich, c.1870, 3 ¼ x 4 In., 6 Piece	173.00
Valence, Fruitwood, Gesso, Bough Of Laurel Shape, Center Tie, Carved, c.1890, 38 In.	593.00
Window Ornament, Wreath Design, Cornucopia, Cast Iron, France, 1800s, 48 x 44 In., Pair	690.00

APPLE PEELERS *are listed in the Kitchen category under Peeler, Apple.*

AREQUIPA POTTERY was produced from 1911 to 1918 by the patients of the Arequipa Sanatorium in Marin County, north of San Francisco. The patients were trained by Frederick Hurten Rhead, who had worked at the Roseville Pottery.

Vase, Squeezebag, Enameled, White Glaze, Blue & Green Ground, 6 x 3 ½ In. *illus*	4200.00

ARGY-ROUSSEAU, *see G. Argy-Rousseau category.*

ARITA is a port in Japan. Porcelain was made there from about 1616. Many types of decorations were used, including the popular Imari designs, which are listed under Imari in this book.

Box, Cover, Flowers, Blue & White, Footed, c.1925, 5 x 4 In.	385.00
Box, Egg Shape, Pine Trees, Wisteria, Bamboo, Cranes, Fukagawa, c.1880, 7 ½ x 5 x 4 ½ In.	695.00
Charger, Flowers, Bamboo, Blue & White, c.1790, 12 ½ In.	565.00
Charger, Flowers, Bird, Blue & White, 19th Century, 16 ¼ In.	450.00
Charger, Landscape, Lakeside, Mountains, Blue, White, Scalloped Rim, Keyfret Band, 18 ¼ In.	498.00
Charger, Mountains, Landscape, Stream, Blue, White, 19th Century, 21 In.	275.00
Charger, Pair Of Rabbits, Molded, Daffodils, Blue & White, 1868-1912, 16 ⅝ In.	351.00
Charger, Transfer, Flower Basket, 3 Fan Reserves, Blue & White, 19th Century, 12 ¼ In.	285.00
Ewer, Globular, Waisted Neck, Lop Handle, Blue Underglaze, Late 17th Century, 8 ½ In.	2500.00
Plate, Fukagawa, Ephemeral Flower, Gold Highlights, Rim, Raised Base, 5 In.	65.00
Plate, Ko, Blue Underglaze, Pastoral Landscape, 18th Century, 9 ½ In.	700.00
Sugar, Flower & Leaf Design, Blue & White, c.1900, 3 x 5 In.	125.00
Vase, Bottle Shape, Enameled, Chrysanthemums, Quince, Kakiemon Style, c.1900, 11 ½ In. ...*illus*	570.00
Vase, Geisha, Samurai, Raised Panels, Flower & Vine, Blue & White, Square Mouth, c.1900, 9 In.	175.00
Vase, Hand Painted Flowers, Hand Turned, 19th Century, 5 x 3 ½ In.	150.00

ART DECO, or Art Moderne, a style started at the Paris Exposition of 1925, is characterized by linear, geometric designs. All types of furniture and decorative arts, jewelry, book bindings, and even games were designed in this style. Additional items may be found in the Furniture category or in various glass and pottery categories, etc.

Coffee Set, Cocktail Shape, Farber Bros., Krome-Kraft, 5 Piece	293.00
Dish, Jester, Cover, Black Amethyst, Silver Cap & Border, c.1925, 4 ½ In.	106.00

Figurine, Le Soir & Le Matin, White Metal, Black Plastic Base, England, Pair	23.00
Planter, Bronzed Metal, Removal Insert, 17 x 8 In.	58.00

ART GLASS, *see Glass-Art category.*

ART POTTERY *see Pottery-Art category.*

ARTHUR OSBORNE *plaques are found in the Ivorex category.*

ARTS & CRAFTS was a design style popular in American decorative arts from 1894 to 1923. In the 1970s collectors began to rediscover Mission furniture, art pottery, metalwork, linens, and light fixtures from this period. The interest has continued. Today everything from this era is collectible, including jewelry, graphics, and silverware. Additional items may be found in the Furniture category and other categories.

Charger, 8-Sided, Pewter Plated Metal, Repousse, Moths, Roses, Spider Webs, Marked, 15 In.	60.00
Humidor, Copper & Antler, 1915-20, 4 x 14 In.	1528.00
Lamp, Open Wicker Shade, 24 ½ x 22 In.	244.00
Mirror, Round, Wrought Iron Leaf & Scroll Frame, 17 x 24 In.	118.00
Vase, Stylized Flower, Hand Painted, Reverse Tapered Shape, 4 x 10 In.	150.00

AURENE glass was made by Frederick Carder of New York about 1904. It is an iridescent gold, blue, green, or red glass, usually marked *Aurene* or *Steuben*.

Ashtray, Blue, 3 Opened Cigarette Rests, Steuben, 4 ½ In.	288.00
Basket, Gold Calcite, Curved Handle, Pigtail Prunts, Steuben, 8 ½ In.	460.00
Basket, Gold, Oval, Fold Handle Basket, Swirled Prunts, Steuben, 9 In.	800.00
Bowl Set, Gold, Iridescence, Steuben, 6 In., 6 Piece	345.00
Bowl, Blue, Calcite, Blue Interior, Green Overtones, Steuben, 11 In.	400.00
Bowl, Blue, Footed, Steuben, 9 In.	510.00
Bowl, Blue Iridescence, Purple Interior, Pinched Rim, Steuben, 10 In.	690.00
Bowl, Blue Iridescent, Flared Rim, Cone Shape, Steuben, 3 x 6 In.	356.00
Bowl, Blue, Oval, Inverted Rim, Steuben, 5 In.	200.00
Bowl, Blue, Round, Low, Folded Rim, Calcite, Steuben, 12 In.	850.00
Bowl, Gold, Calcite, 10 In.	300.00
Bowl, Gold, Calcite, Footed Oval, Steuben, 9 In.	250.00
Bowl, Gold Interior, Calcite Exterior, Steuben, 10 x 3 In.	295.00
Bowl, Gold, Iridescent, 3 Handles, Inscribed, Steuben, 5 x 9 In.	1700.00
Bowl, Gold, Oval, Inverted Rim, Steuben, 6 In.	125.00
Bowl, Wide Ruffled Border, Blue To Purple, Steuben, 6 In.	431.00
Candlestick, Blue, Footed Twist Stem, Amethyst Overtones, Steuben, 12 In., Pair	3450.00
Candlestick, Blue Twist Stem, Mirror Finish, Signed, Steuben, 10 In.	700.00
Candlestick, Gold Prunts, Squatty Baluster, Signed, F. Carder, 3 ¾ In., Pair	978.00
Candlestick, Gold, Stretched Mushroom Top, Purple, Red Iridescence, Steuben, 6 In., Pair	767.00
Candlestick, Gold, Twist Stem, Mirror Finish, Signed, Steuben, 10 In.	550.00
Candlestick, Green Ground, Heart, Vine Platinum Overlay, Gold Interior, Steuben, 10 In.	2242.00
Compote, Blue, Calcite, Ribbed Interior, 7 In.	500.00
Compote, Blue, Flared, Star Lily Pad Ribbed Foot, Signed, Steuben, 12 In.	1610.00
Compote, Blue, Scalloped Edge, Ribbed Stem, Steuben, 3 ½ x 8 In.	863.00
Compote, Gold, Cupped Waffle Design Base, Steuben, 3 x 5 In.	403.00
Compote, Gold, Ruffled, Swirled Body, Raised Base, Steuben, 7 x 4 In.	375.00
Compote, Gold, Twisted Bulbous Stem, Applied Prunts, 6 ¼ In. ....*illus*	863.00
Cruet, Gold, Bulbous, Matching Stopper, Signed, Steuben, 7 ½ In.	1610.00
Cruet, Gooseneck Spout, Gold, 5 In.	1800.00
Cup, Barrel Shape, Gold, 2 x 2 ½ In.	230.00
Darner, Blue, Snap Handle, 6 ½ In.	325.00
Finger Bowl, Underplate, Gold, Scalloped Onion Rim, Signed, Steuben, 6 In.	300.00
Flower Frog, Gold, 2 Tiers, Steuben, 1 ¼ In.	58.00
Goblet, Gold, Green Pulled Swags, Ruffled Rim, Signed, Steuben, 7 ½ In.	4025.00
Goblet, Gold, Iridescent, Marked, Steuben, 2 ¾ x 6 In.	230.00
Goblet, Gold, Tulip Form, Steuben, 6 ¼ x 4 ¼ In.	195.00
Lamp, Gold, Pink & Purple Highlights, Ribbed Body, Shade, 10 ½ In. ....*illus*	3277.00
Nut Dish, Gold, Fluted Globular Shape, Pink Iridescence, Steuben, 2 Piece	207.00
Perfume Bottle, Cone Shape, Teardrop Stopper, Steuben, 7 In.	300.00
Perfume Bottle, Footed, Blue, Teardrop Stopper, 8 In.	805.00
Perfume Bottle, Gold, Iridescent, Finial Stopper, Steuben, 8 In.	575.00
Perfume Bottle, Gold, Melon Ribbed, Teardrop Stopper, Signed, Steuben, 5 In.	500.00

Aurene, Compote, Gold, Twisted Bulbous Stem, Applied Prunts, 6 ¼ In.
$863.00

Aurene, Lamp, Gold, Pink & Purple Highlights, Ribbed Body, Shade, 10 ½ In.
$3277.00

Aurene, Vase, Gold, Green Heart & Vine, Applied White Millefiori Canes, Signed, 5 ¾ In.
$5175.00

Aurene, Vase, Heart, Vine, Applied Collar, Tyrian, Signed, Steuben, 12 ½ In.
$10925.00

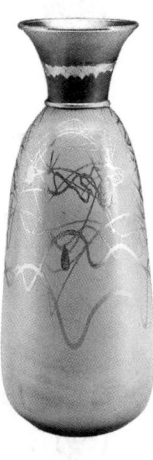

TIP
Valuable glass should not be washed in a dishwasher.

Perfume Bottle, Teardrop Stopper, Melon Ribbed, Steuben, 5 In.	475.00
Salt, Blue, Footed, Steuben, 2 ¼ In.	403.00
Salt, Ribbed Body, Ruffled Rim, Signed, Steuben, 3 In.	200.00
Shade, Gold, Double Bulbous, Steuben, Signed, 5 In.	115.00
Sherbet, Under Plate, Blue, Calcite, 6 In.	288.00
Underplate, Yellow, Gold Highlights, Steuben, 6 In.	60.00
Urn, Cover, Chalice Form, Footed, Gold, Crown Finial, Signed, Steuben, c.1920, 11 In.	720.00
Vase, 4 Peacock Eyes, Gold Pulled Feathers, Ivory Ground, Stepped Shoulder, Steuben, 10 In.	11500.00
Vase, Acid Gold, Stem Prunts, Pink, Purple, Blue Highlights, Steuben, 10 In.	1150.00
Vase, Blue, 3 Egyptian Style Handles, Bulbous, Signed, Steuben, 6 x 6 ¾ In.	4313.00
Vase, Blue, 3 Handles, Footed, Iridescent, Steuben, 6 In.	1610.00
Vase, Blue Body, Purple Stem Ribbing, Steuben, 6 x 8 In.	748.00
Vase, Blue, Flared Rim, Art Glass, Steuben, 8 In.	1007.00
Vase, Blue Interior, Scalloped Rim, Calcite Exterior, Steuben, 6 x 10 In.	489.00
Vase, Blue, Oval, Pink & Gold Highlights, Wrought Iron Frame, Steuben, 15 ¾ In.	705.00
Vase, Blue, Purple, Green, Steuben, 8 In.	1150.00
Vase, Blue, Ribs, Relaxed Scalloped Rim, Signed, Steuben, 5 ½ In.	546.00
Vase, Blue Scalloped Rim, Corset Tapered, Steuben, 7 In.	1093.00
Vase, Blue, Shouldered, Flared Rim, Steuben, 9 In.	1500.00
Vase, Blue, Shouldered, Round, Signed, Steuben, c.1920, 12 ¼ In.	1320.00
Vase, Blue, Squat, Rolled Rim, 3 Looped Handles, Steuben, 8 In.	1400.00
Vase, Blue, Stump, Yellow To Green Iridescent, Steuben, 5 ¾ In.	978.00
Vase, Blue, Trumpet Shape, Optic Ribs, Signed, Steuben, 5 In.	525.00
Vase, Blue, Trumpet Shape, Pedestal Foot, Steuben, 6 In.	403.00
Vase, Blue, Vertical Ribs, Flared Scalloped Rim, Signed, Steuben, 5 ½ In.	460.00
Vase, Blue, White Threads, Gold Hearts, Green Highlights, Bulbous, Steuben, 6 In.	5750.00
Vase, Calcite, Blue, Corset Shape, Spreading Ruffled Rim, Steuben, 4 ½ In.	300.00
Vase, Finger, Blue, Flattened Body, 4 Flower Openings, Steuben, 10 In.	1600.00
Vase, Flaring Ribbed, Ruffle Rim, Green & Blue Iridescence, 5 ¼ In.	329.00
Vase, Gold, Applied Metal Handle, Flower, Basket Shape, Steuben, 7 ½ x 12 In.	1080.00
Vase, Gold, Concave Body, Cylinder Neck, Signed, 6 In.	325.00
Vase, Gold, Flared Ribbed, Round Rim, 5 ½ In.	500.00
Vase, Gold, Green Heart & Vine, Applied White Millefiori Canes, Signed, 5 ¾ In. ....*illus*	5175.00
Vase, Gold, Green Hearts, Vines, White, Yellow, Millefiori, Bulbous, Signed, 5 In.	3738.00
Vase, Gold, Green Hooked Feathers, Purple Highlights, Steuben, Signed, 2 ½ In.	2530.00
Vase, Gold, Hooked Feather, Alabaster, Squatty Shape, Signed, Steuben, 2 In.	1438.00
Vase, Gold, Iridescent, Blue & Pink Highlights, Tapered, Steuben, c.1925, 7 ⅛ In.	411.00
Vase, Gold, Iridescent, Ribs, 4 ¼ In.	300.00
Vase, Gold Oval, 4-Fold Rim, Steuben, Signed, 2 ½ In.	375.00
Vase, Gold, Pinched Sides, 4-Fold Rim, Signed, Steuben, 3 In.	460.00
Vase, Gold, Pinched Sides, Bottle Shape, 6 In.	550.00
Vase, Gold, Ribs, Scalloped Rim, Trumpet Shape, Signed, Steuben, 10 In.	1725.00
Vase, Gold, Silver Pulled Feathers, 4 Green Eyes, Double Bulbous Shape, Steuben, 8 In.	6900.00
Vase, Gold, Stump, 3 Prongs, Gold Iridescent, Paper Label, Steuben, 6 ½ In.	863.00
Vase, Gold, Stump, Blue, Purple Iridescent, Steuben, 6 ¼ In.	1495.00
Vase, Gold, Stump, Gold Iridescence, Pink, Blue, Steuben, 6 In.	345.00
Vase, Gold, Trunk, 3 Prongs, Steuben, 6 In.	1093.00
Vase, Gold, Urn Shape, Optic, Ribbed Foot, Steuben, 7 In.	750.00
Vase, Green Vines, White Millefiori, Gold Ground, Oval, Ruffled Rim, Footed, Steuben, 7 In.	4715.00
Vase, Heart, Vine, Applied Collar, Tyrian, Signed, Steuben, 12 ½ In. ....*illus*	10925.00
Vase, Jack-In-The-Pulpit, Fluted, Gold, Blue, Rim, Orange, Green Stem, Steuben, 6 In.	1725.00
Vase, Jack-In-The-Pulpit, Pink, Purple, Stretched Face, Gold Stem, Blue Tints, Steuben, 10 In.	2070.00
Vase, Millefiori, Gold, Blue Finish, White Hearts, Vines, Applied Purple Foot, Steuben, 8 In.	6900.00
Vase, Morning Glory, Blue, Ribbed Amethyst, Steuben, 5 ½ In.	633.00
Vase, Red, Optic Ribs, Gold Hearts, Vines, Rim, Cylinder Shape, Steuben, 7 In.	11500.00
Vase, Ribbed, Pontil, Marked, Steuben, c.1900, 4 ½ x 4 ¼ In.	298.00
Vase, Urn, Optic Diamond Pattern, Gold, Steuben, 5 In.	500.00

AUTO parts and accessories are collectors' items today. Gas pump globes and license plates are part of this specialty. Prices are determined by age, rarity, and condition. Signs and packaging related to automobiles may also be found in the Advertising category. Lalique hood ornaments will be listed in the Lalique category.

Ad, Magazine, General Motors, Fisher, 1944, 10 ½ x 13 ¾ In.	4.00
Ad, Magazine, Saturday Evening Post, Texaco, August 1944, 10 ½ x 13 ¾ In.	4.00
Ad, Magazine, Saturday Evening Post, World War II, International Truck, 1943	4.00

Air Pump, Balance Inflation, Red, Eco Tireflator, Mich., 49 ½ In.	810.00
Ashtray, Dash, Chevy, 1955	25.00
Badge, Stag Motor Oil, Deer, Embossed, Inlaid Cloisonne, Enamel, Porcelain, 1 ⅝ x 2 In.	850.00
Bottle, Motor Oil, Texaco, Star Logo, Embossed	226.00
Bottle, Oil, Shell-Penn Motor Oil, Embossed, c.1917, 14 ½ In., 6 Piece	210.00
Can, Grease, Wadhams, Metal, 1 Lb.	130.00
Can, Husky Motor Oil, Frisky Dog, Orange Ground, Metal, Full, Qt.	2090.00
Can, Iroquois Motor Oil, Pennsylvania, Red, Yellow, Tin Lithograph, 1 Qt., 5 ½ x 4 In.	408.00
Can, May-Flower Motor Oil, Red, Blue, Yellow, 2 Gal., 11 ¾ In.	130.00
Can, Motor Oil, Pure Quill, Squatty, Warren Oil, 1 Gal.	11.30
Can, Motor Oil, Route 66 Premium, Metal, Rectangular, 2 Gal.	226.00
Can, Motor Oil, Wadhams Big W, Metal, Rectangular, 2 ½ Gal.	294.00
Carburetor, Brass, Single Barrel, Schebler, Indianapolis, c.1907, 6 ½ In.	300.00
Clock, Brass Marker, 6 Volt, Round, 3 In.	72.00
Clock, Dash, Ford, 1957	10.00
Clock, Mobil Gas, Pegasus, Red, Light-Up, Glass, American Time Corp., 14 ½ In. Diam.	590.00
Clock, Pennzoil, Pam, Glass Face, Bubble Glass Cover, 15 In.	360.00
Clock, Skelly Motor Oil, Brown, Red, Blue, White, Glass, Pam Clock Co., 15 ⅜ x 15 ⅜ In.	198.00
Display, Anco Windshield Blades & Arms, Metal, Countertop, 16 x 15 x 14 In.	68.00
Display, Hoods Tires, Man Holding Sign, Flag, Outdoor Parking, 2-Sided, Tin Litho, 48 x 15 In.	5170.00
Display, Mobile Oil 6 Bottle Island, Shield Shape Sign	395.00
Display, Sunoco Blue, Sunoco Gas Globe, Metal Frame, Blue, Yellow, 12 x 16 In.	187.00
Display, Trico Windshield Wiper, 40 x 14 x 14 In.	56.00
Gas Pump Globe, Browder Special Gasoline, 13 ½ In.	452.00
Gas Pump Globe, Buick Sales Service, Black, White, Plastic Body, Glass Lenses, 16 In.	360.00
Gas Pump Globe, Clark, Capco Globe Body, 13 ½ In.	181.00
Gas Pump Globe, Conoco Red, Plastic Body, 16 In.	306.00
Gas Pump Globe, Crown Gasoline, White Milk Glass, Light-Up, 18 x 17 In.	540.00
Gas Pump Globe, D-X Boron, White, Red, Yellow, Black, Plastic Body, Glass Lenses, 16 In.	240.00
Gas Pump Globe, D-X Lubricating Gasoline, Plastic Body, 16 In.	300.00
Gas Pump Globe, Kanotex, Orange Body, Ripple Finish, Reverse Painted, 16 x 13 ½ In.	1380.00
Gas Pump Globe, Liberty Gasoline, Statue Of Liberty, 15 In.	734.00
Gas Pump Globe, Magnolia Gasoline, Plastic Body, Glass Lenses, White, Red, Green, c.1983, 17 In.	480.00
Gas Pump Globe, Phillips 66, Decal, Oval	226.00
Gas Pump Globe, Pure Oil Company, White, Blue, 3-Piece Glass Body, Lenses, 17 x 15 In.	540.00
Gas Pump Globe, Sinclair H-C Gasoline, 13 ½ In.	311.00
Gas Pump Globe, Southwest Oil Company Kerosene, Capco Globe, 13 ½ In.	311.00
Gas Pump Globe, Standard Oil, Milk Glass Crown, Red Paint, Metal Flange, 17 x 16 In. *illus*	193.00
Gas Pump Globe, Standard Oil Of Indiana, Flame Shape, Plastic	395.00
Gas Pump Globe, Standard Oil Of Indiana, White Crown	124.00
Gas Pump, Guarantee Fry, Gravity Fed, Glass Cylinder, Brass Nozzle, Plastic Body, 1915, 5 Gal., 10 Ft.	3600.00
Gas Pump, Shell, Milk Glass Globe, Electrified	738.00
Gas Pump, Skelly Supreme, Red, White, Blue, 2-Sided, Opaque, 17 In.	354.00
Gas Pump, Standard Oil, Crown, Gold, Opaque Glass, 17 In.	295.00
Generator, Brass, Acetylene, 12 In.	1680.00
Grill, Chevy, 1955	150.00
Headlamp, Brass, Powell & Hammer, England, 12 x 8 ¼ In.	420.00
Hood Ornament, 1951-55 Nash, Art Deco Woman, Chrome, 11 In.	110.00
Hood Ornament, Chrome, Chevy, 1955	45.00
Hood Ornament, Eagle, Soaring, Bronze, c.1920, 14 In.	420.00
Hood Ornament, Rolls-Royce, Flying Lady, Nickel Plated Bronze, 1930s, 5 In.	999.00
Hood Ornament, Rolls-Royce, Winged Woman, Radiator Cap, Nickel Plated, 7 In.	300.00
Hood Ornament, Swan, Outstretched Wings, Silvered Metal	41.00
Hood Ornament, Winged Flight, Dart Engineering, Model V801, Blue Glass, 3 ½ x 9 In.	360.00
Horn, Brass, Electric, Klaxonet, Lovell McConell Mfg., Model 696, c.1899, 4 x 5 In.	240.00
Horn, Brass, Flexible Coil, Bracket, Marked Cicca Marque Depgsee, Paris, 5 x 53 In.	180.00
Horn, Brass, Omni, Single Twist, 10 In.	120.00
Lamp, Brass, Kerosene Burners, Iron Brackets, 20th Century, 10 ½ In., Pair	56.00
Lamp, Side, Brass, Gray & Davis, Model 934, Beveled Glass, Red Jewel, 13 In.	240.00
License Plate Attachment, War Worker, Cleveland Towmotor Co., Beige, Black, Red, 4 x 11 In.	290.00
License Plate, Delaware, 1944	53.00
License Plate, Michigan, 1913, Green, White, 4 ½ x 12 In., Pair	480.00
License Plate, Rhode Island, c.1941, White, Black Numbers, 10 ¾ x 6 In.	25.00
License Plate, Tractor, Pennsylvania, c.1916, Orange, Black Letters, E1792, 16 ½ x 6 In.	135.00
License Plate, West Virginia, 1973, Orange With Blue Letters	8.00
Measuring Tool, Cast Iron, Morris Brothers, 5 Gal. Increments	23.00

Auto, Gas Pump Globe, Standard Oil, Milk Glass Crown, Red Paint, Metal Flange, 17 x 16 In. $193.00

A

Auto, Tote, Atlas Battery Service, Porcelain Over Metal, 15 x 13 In. $138.00

Mirror, Socony Motor Gasoline, Standard Oil, 3 ½ In. Diam.	130.00
Model Airplane, Wings Of Texaco, Northrop Gamma, Box, 1932, 12 Piece	90.00
Model Airplane, Wings Of Texaco, Stearman Biplanes, Box, 1931, 10 Piece	84.00
Oil Bottle Spout, Wadhams, Embossed	40.00
Oil Can, Drab Green, Chain Attached Lid, 1940s, 5 x 2 ¾ In.	13.00
Pin, Esso, Merry Christmas, Santa Claus, Red, White, Gray, Celluloid, 1940, 1 ¼ In.	55.00
Pin, Now A Cadillac For Only $1345, Red, White, Celluloid, ⅞ In.	17.00
Pump Topper, Phillips 66, Gasoline That Won The West, Cowboy, Indian, 16 x 15 In.	250.00
Racer, Dirt Track, No. 2, Little Red Deuce, Aluminum Body, 221 CID 85 Flathead V8, 1937	13200.00
Radio, Tucker, Box, c.1948, 5 ½ x 9 ½ & 10 x 12 In.	1500.00
Radio, Tucker, Buttons, Motorola, No. 102954, Box, c.1948, 10 x 12 In.	1800.00
Sign, AAA Emergency Service, Red, White, Blue, Oval, Porcelain, 2-Sided, 24 ½ x 35 ½ In.	330.00
Sign, Ace High Motor Oil, Roadster Speeding, Country Road, Wood Frame, 48 x 96 In.	23100.00
Sign, Approved Chrysler Service, Blue, Red, Yellow, Die Cut Porcelain, 32 x 30 In.	1150.00
Sign, Armstrong Tires, Red, Yellow, Embossed, Tin, 1948, 18 x 48 In.	275.00
Sign, B.F. Goodrich Tires, Blue, White, Porcelain, 2-Sided, 26 x 60 In.	550.00
Sign, Buick Authorized Service, Valve In Head, 2-Sided, Porcelain, 42 In. Diam.	8800.00
Sign, Champlin Gasoline, Red, White, Blue, Porcelain, 2-Sided, 30 In. Diam.	660.00
Sign, Champlin HI-V-I Motor Oil, Red, Yellow, Porcelain, 2-Sided, 20 x 32 In.	330.00 to 360.00
Sign, Chevrolet Genuine Parts, Neon, 26 In.	330.00
Sign, Chevrolet Service, 2-Sided, Rotates, Neon, Porcelain, Enamel, Blue, Gold, 130 x 32 In.	3900.00
Sign, Chevrolet Superior Service, Neon, Blue, Yellow, White, Porcelain, 2-Sided, 42 x 48 In.	20900.00
Sign, Chevrolet Used Cars, 2-Sided, Blue, White Letters, Light-Up, 28 x 42 In.	7040.00
Sign, Chicago Automotive Club Bonded Service, 2-Sided, Porcelain, 44 x 36 In.	480.00
Sign, Chrysler, Plymouth, Neon, 15 In.	330.00
Sign, Clipper Gas, Porcelain, 18 x 30 In.	195.00
Sign, Conoco Gasoline, Soldier Image, Porcelain, 2-Sided, 26 In.	5500.00
Sign, Conoco Nth Motor Oil, Tin, 2-Sided, 36 x 31 ½ In.	135.00
Sign, Corduroy Tires, Man, Blowing Horn, Factory Fresh, 2-Sided, Tin, 27 ½ x 19 ½ In.	275.00
Sign, Curb, Stop Here For Mobiloil, Gargoyle Logo, Iron Base, 2-Sided, 23 In.	621.00
Sign, Dodge-Plymouth, Dependable Service With Dodge Trucks, 2-Sided, Porcelain	4620.00
Sign, Enco Gasoline, Porcelain, 1957, 60 x 83 In.	295.00
Sign, Essex Super Six, Blue, Milk Glass Letters, Tin, 46 x 78 x 5 In.	1320.00
Sign, Federal Tires, Blue, White, Porcelain, 2-Sided, Flange, 20 x 25 In.	220.00
Sign, Fire-Chief Gasoline, 100 Percent Anti-Knock, No Extra Price, Red, Black, Canvas, 30 x 17 In.	70.00
Sign, Firestone, Ground Grip Farm Tires, Orange, Blue, White, Porcelain, Frame, 23 ½ x 74 In.	350.00
Sign, Firestone, Red, White, Metal, 71 x 15 ½ In.	145.00
Sign, Fisk Tires, Yellow, Blue, Tin, 73 x 19 In.	660.00
Sign, Ford, Blue, White, Oval, 2-Sided, 22 ½ x 33 In.	920.00
Sign, Ford V-8 Genuine Parts, Porcelain, 2-Sided, Die Cut, 36 x 28 In.	6600.00
Sign, Gasoline Motor Oils, Red Indian, Porcelain, 60 In.	5500.00
Sign, Globe Gasoline, Red, White, Blue, Porcelain, 2-Sided, 42 In. Diam.	770.00
Sign, GMC Trucks, Neon, Porcelain, 2-Sided, 45 x 72 In.	14850.00
Sign, Gold Medal Oils, Best For The North, Green, Yellow, Porcelain, 2-Sided, 30 In.	46000.00
Sign, Goodrich Tires Batteries, Blue, Green, Red, Porcelain, 78 x 18 In.	500.00
Sign, Goodyear Tires, Blue, Yellow, Porcelain, 24 x 66 In.	275.00
Sign, Gulf Gasoline, Porcelain, 1966, 72 In.	212.00
Sign, Gulf, Orange, Blue, Porcelain, 2-Sided, 30 In. Diam.	385.00
Sign, Hudson Regular, Octane Gas, Red, White, Black, Porcelain, 25 ½ In. Diam.	360.00
Sign, Iroquois Auto Insurance, Indian, Red, Yellow, Porcelain, 47 x 36 In.	1050.00
Sign, Leak-Proof Rings, Bell Attached, Steel, 19 ¾ x 28 In.	360.00
Sign, Michelin, Bildeum Holding Tire, 26 x 26 In.	282.00
Sign, Mobil Gas Station, Round, 24 In.	195.00
Sign, Mobil Oil, Pegasus, Red, Enamel, Die Cut, 30 x 36 In.	469.00
Sign, Mobil Oil, Pegasus, Red, Facing Left, Porcelain, 70 x 92 In.	2200.00
Sign, Mobil Oil, Pegasus, Red, Facing Right, Porcelain, 70 x 92 In.	1200.00
Sign, Mobil Oil, Pegasus, Red, Porcelain, Neon, Rotates, 2-Sided, 72 x 90 x 17 In.	6000.00
Sign, Mobil Service Chart For Cars 1955-62, Cardboard, 42 x 26 In.	23.00
Sign, Mobilgas Mobiloil For Top Performance, Pegasus, 48 x 30 In.	124.00
Sign, Mobilgas, Pegasus, 2-Sided, Porcelain, French Canadian, 38 x 39 In.	472.00
Sign, Mobiloil, Pegasus, Shield Shape, 8 x 8 In.	508.00
Sign, New Idea Farm Equipment, 1955, 33 x 72 In.	150.00
Sign, Oilzum Motor Oil, Text, Man In Oval, Tin, Wood Frame, Graded 9.75, 1948	4510.00
Sign, Oldsmobile, Cadillac, Blue, White, Neon, Porcelain, 2-Sided, 14 Ft.	20000.00
Sign, Oldsmobile GM Hydra-Matic Drive, Neon, 2-Sided, Porcelain, 35 x 102 In.	17050.00
Sign, Oldsmobile Service, Crest Logo, Porcelain, 2-Sided, 42 In.	5170.00

Sign, Phillips 66 Gasoline, Porcelain, 1958, 70 x 70 In.	295.00
Sign, Quaker State Motor Oil, Green, White, Porcelain, 2-Sided, 29 x 26 ½ In.	390.00
Sign, Quaker State Motor Oil, Self-Framed, 36 x 60 In.	90.00
Sign, Quiet, Avoid Any Unnecessary Horn Blowing, White, Black, Oval, 1920s, 12 ½ x 22 In. ..	50.00
Sign, Red Crown Gasoline, Red, White, Blue, Porcelain, 2-Sided, 41 In. Diam......	880.00
Sign, Richlube Motor Oil, Blue, Yellow, Porcelain, 24 In. Diam.	1800.00
Sign, Road, Curve, Arrow, Cast Iron, 24 x 24 In.	102.00
Sign, Rolls-Royce, RR, Wood Over Tin, 50 x 26 In.	440.00
Sign, RPM Motor Oil, 100 Percent Paraffin Base, Red, White, Porcelain, 2-Sided, 28 In. Diam.	500.00
Sign, Seiberling, America's Finest Tires, Red, White, Porcelain, 24 ½ x 72 In.	280.00
Sign, Shell, Huiles Pour Moteurs, Yellow, Red, Black, Porcelain, 3-Sided, 20 ½ x 30 ½ In.	360.00
Sign, Sinclair Gas Ahead, Tin, Wood, 58 x 58 In.	271.00
Sign, Sinclair Opaline Motor Oil, Green, Red, White, Porcelain, 20 x 48 ½ In.	1200.00
Sign, Sinclair Pennsylvania Motor Oil, Red, White, Green, Porcelain, 60 x 15 In.	295.00
Sign, Socony, Pegasus, Shield Shape, c.1935, 47 x 47 In.	508.00
Sign, Standard Gasoline, Porcelain, 2-Sided, 60 x 82 In.	342.00
Sign, Standard Oil, Porcelain, 48 x 96 In.	248.00
Sign, Star Cars, Authorized Service Durant Motors, Green, Blue, Porcelain, 2-Sided, 24 x 36 In.	1300.00
Sign, Star Motor Gasoline, Tin, 12 In.	189.00
Sign, Sterling Gasoline, Ethyl, Yellow, Blue, White, Porcelain, Oval, 8 ¾ x 11 ¼ In.	360.00
Sign, Sunoco, Distilled Oil, Blue, Yellow, Porcelain, Flange, 2-Sided, 18 x 25 In.	440.00
Sign, Supreme Motor Oil, Gulf Refining, Orange, Blue, White, Porcelain, Flange, 18 x 22 In. .	440.00
Sign, Texaco, Clean Clear Golden Motor Oil, Porcelain, 30 In.	450.00
Sign, Texaco, Diesel Chief, c.1963, 18 x 12 In.	243.00
Sign, Texaco Farm Lubricants, Sold Here, Green, Red, White, Porcelain, 1946, 30 x 42 In.	550.00
Sign, Texaco Fire Chief Gasoline, Hat, Red, White, Porcelain, 1956, 18 x 12 In.	165.00
Sign, Texaco Fire Chief Gasoline, Helmet, Curved, c.1940, 18 x 12 In.	85.00
Sign, Texaco Motor Oil, Free Crankcase Service, Porcelain, 30 x 30 In.	880.00
Sign, Texaco Motor Oil, Lubester, Red, White, Green, Black, White, Porcelain, 2-Sided, 5 ½ x 5 In.	198.00
Sign, Texaco Motor Oil, Tin, 11 x 21 In.	224.00
Sign, Texaco, No Smoking, 4 x 23 In.	113.00
Sign, Texaco, Sky Chief Supreme With Petrox, c.1960, 15 x 10 In.	96.00
Sign, Union 76 Gasoline, Orange, Blue, White, Porcelain, 11 ¾ In. Diam......	78.00
Sign, Union 76 Triton Motor Oil, Red, White, Porcelain, 2-Sided, 30 In. Diam.	495.00
Sign, U.S. Tires, Orange, Blue, White, Porcelain, 72 x 18 In.	500.00
Sign, Vacuum Cup Tires, Victorian Woman, Evening Dress, Paper Lithograph, 44 x 15 In.	1980.00
Sign, Valvoline Motor Oil, Blue, White, Porcelain, Flange, 2-Sided, 14 x 20 In.	275.00
Sign, Western Auto Wrecking, Tin Reflector, 14 x 20 In.	250.00
Sign, Wheeler's Service Station, Wood, 2-Sided, Signed, MacAllister, 22 x 49 In.	141.00
Siren, Police Car, 6 Volt, Chrome Plated, Federal Enterprises, 8 x 6 In.	360.00
Speed Indicator, Lintner & Sporborg, Gloversville, New York, Pistol Type, Pat. Dec. 31, 1889.	660.00
Speedometer, Brass, Glass Face, Jones, N.Y., c.1908, 3 In.	180.00
Stop Light, 4-Way Intersection, Yellow, 44 x 28 In.	290.00
Tote, Atlas Battery Service, Porcelain Over Metal, 15 x 13 In. ....*illus*	138.00
Traffic Light, Electric, 56 In.	59.00
Traffic Light, Metal Case, Black Paint, 3 Colored Glass Lenses, Eagle Signal Corp., 32 x 12 x 13 In. *illus*	173.00
Tray, Goodyear, Metal, Embossed, Name, Winged Foot, 1920s, 3 ½ x 5 ½ In.	144.00
Trunk, 1932 Packard, Leather, Nickel Plated Hardware, Leather Straps, Handles, 1930s, 22 x 36 In.	900.00
Watch & Fob, Golden Shell Oil, Inlaid Cloisonne Enamel, 1 ⅝-In. Watch, 1 ¼-In. Fob	715.00
Window, Rear, Chevy, 1955	300.00

Auto, Traffic Light, Metal Case, Black Paint, 3 Colored Glass Lenses, Eagle Signal Corp., 32 x 12 x 13 In. **$173.00**

Road Maps
The first automobile road maps were printed in 1914.

AUTUMN LEAF pattern china was made for the Jewel Tea Company beginning in 1933. Hall China Company of East Liverpool, Ohio, Crooksville China Company of Crooksville, Ohio, Harker Potteries of Chester, West Virginia, and Paden City Pottery, Paden City, West Virginia, made dishes with this design. Autumn Leaf has remained popular and was made by Hall China Company until 1978. Some other pieces in the Autumn Leaf pattern are still being made. For more prices, go to kovels.com.

Bean Pot, Lid, Handles, Box, 2 Qt......	99.00
Bowl, 5 ½ In.	9.00
Bowl, 6 In.	15.00
Bowl, 7 ½ In.	42.00
Bowl, 8 ½ In., 8 Piece	66.00
Bowl, Fruit, 5 ½ In.	11.95
Bowl, Vegetable, Oval, 10 ⅜ In.	15.00
Bowl, Vegetable, Ruffled, 9 In.	110.00
Butter, Cover, Lb., 4 x 9 ⅝ x 5 ½ In.	237.00 to 600.00

Autumn Leaf, Gravy Boat
$75.00

Autumn Leaf, Mixing Bowl Set,
Nesting, 3 Piece
$85.00

Azalea, Salt & Pepper
$23.00

Azalea, Snack Set, 2 Piece
$19.00

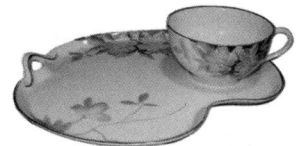

Cake Plate, 9 ½ In.	20.00
Cake Stand, Brass Foot, Box, 3 ½ x 9 In.	275.00
Casserole, 1 ¼ Qt.	25.00
Casserole, 3 x 7 In.	30.00
Clock	340.00
Coffeepot, Aluminum Insert, Stamped	75.00
Coffeepot, Double	187.00
Coffeepot, Electric	400.00
Creamer	15.00
Cup & Saucer	5.00
Custard Cup, 2 ⅛ In.	5.00
Gravy Boat	*illus* 75.00
Marmalade, Underplate, 6 ⅛ In.	30.00
Mixing Bowl Set, Nesting, 3 Piece	*illus* 85.00
Mixing Bowl, 3 ½ x 6 ¼ In.	24.00
Mixing Bowl, 4 x 7 ½ In.	35.00
Mixing Bowl, 5 x 9 In.	45.00
Pie Bird, 5 x 2 In.	30.00
Pitcher, 5 ½ In.	68.00
Pitcher, Ball, 9 x 8 In.	70.00
Pitcher, Ball, Ice Lip, Tumbler, Frosted, 7 & 5 ½ In., 7 Piece	88.00
Pitcher, China Specialties, Child's, 2 ¼ In.	40.00
Pitcher, Ice Lip, 3 ¼ In.	40.00
Plate, Bread & Butter, 6 ⅛ In.	5.00
Plate, Dinner, 9 In.	20.00
Plate, Dinner, 10 In., 8 Piece	61.00
Plate, Salad, 7 In.	11.95
Reamer, China Specialties, Child's, 1 x 3 In.	50.00
Rolling Pin, China Specialties, 15 In.	66.00
Salt & Pepper, 1 ¾ In.	30.00
Saucepan, 6 x 13 ¾ In.	100.00
Saucer, 6 In.	6.00 to 9.95
Serving Bowl, 9 In.	18.00
Soup, Dish, Rim, 8 ½ In.	12.00
Sugar, Cover	5.00
Teapot, Aladdin, China Specialties, 2 ¾ x 4 ½ In.	38.00
Teapot, Newport, Box, 7 ½ In.	110.00
Vase, 5 ¾ In.	230.00

AVON *bottles are listed in the Bottle category under Avon.*

AZALEA dinnerware was made for Larkin Company customers from 1918 to 1941. Larkin, the soap company, was in Buffalo, New York. The dishes were made by Noritake China Company of Japan. Each piece of the white china was decorated with pink azaleas.

Bowl, Fruit, 7 ⅞ In.	280.00
Bowl, Fruit, Ladle, 4 ½ In.	24.00
Bowl, Oatmeal, 5 ¾ In.	20.00
Bowl, Soup, Coupe, 7 ½ In.	26.00
Bowl, Vegetable, Handles, Round, 10 In.	40.00
Bowl, Vegetable, Oval, 9 ⅜ In.	40.00
Bowl, Vegetable, Round, 10 In.	34.00
Bowl, Vegetable, Round, Cover, Finial	250.00
Butter Chip	59.00
Cake Plate, 12 In.	35.00
Cake Plate, Handles, 9 ¾ In.	36.00
Casserole, Cover, 10 In.	50.00
Celery Dish, 12 ½ In.	30.00
Creamer, Berry, Pitcher Shape, 5 ½ In.	74.00
Creamer, Individual, 2 ⅝ In.	230.00
Creamer, Underplate	25.00
Cup & Saucer	22.00
Cup & Saucer, Demitasse	99.00
Gravy Boat, Attached Underplate	40.00 to 45.00
Mayonnaise Set, Bowl, Underplate, Ladle	40.00
Pitcher, 28 Oz., 5 ¾ In.	140.00
Plate, Bread & Butter, 6 ½ In.	10.00

Plate, Dinner, 9 ⅞ In.	25.00
Plate, Lemon, 5 ½ In.	33.00
Plate, Lunch, 8 ½ In.	12.00 to 16.00
Plate, Salad, 7 ½ In.	5.00 to 15.00
Platter, 10 In.	95.00
Platter, 14 In.	55.00
Platter, Oval, 10 ¼ In.	180.00
Relish, 8 ¼ In.	18.00
Relish, Oval, 8 ¼ In.	20.00
Salt & Pepper ....*illus*	23.00
Saucer	8.00
Snack Set, 2 Piece ....*illus*	19.00
Sugar & Creamer	135.00
Sugar Shaker, 6 ½ In.	137.00
Sugar, Cover	20.00
Sugar, Cover, 2 Handles	25.00
Teapot, Cover	160.00
Toothpick	70.00 to 74.00
Vase, Bud, 5 ¾ In.	210.00

BACCARAT glass was made in France by La Compagnie des Cristalleries de Baccarat, located 150 miles from Paris. The factory was started in 1765. The firm went bankrupt and began operating again about 1822. Cane and millefiori paperweights were made during the 1845 to 1880 period. The firm is still working near Paris making paperweights and glasswares.

Bowl, Etched Rose, Geometric, 8 In.	323.00
Bowl, Flower Form, Lobes, Signed, 3 ½ x 9 ¾ In.	94.00
Bucket, Champagne, Clear, Horizontal Graduated Ribs, 8 In.	978.00
Candlestick, Clear, Sawtooth Edge, Round Foot, 10 In., Pair	205.00
Candlestick, Twisted, Clear, Flared Base & Rim, Marked, 9 In., Pair	86.00
Centerpiece, Ruby, Clear, 8 x 8 In.	1112.00
Champagne Set, 9 ¼ In., 13 Piece	1030.00
Decanter Set, Cranberry, 5 Piece	351.00
Decanter, Baluster, Etched, Ball Stopper, 15 x 4 In.	82.00
Decanter, Flattened, Green To Clear, Hobstar, Stopper, c.1907, 17 In.	863.00
Decanter, Ship's Style, Arched Panels, Flattened Stopper, 8 In.	148.00
Decanter, Sterling Silver Scotch Label, Faceted Stopper, Paneled, 20th Century, 9 ¼ In.	180.00
Dish, Frog At Pond, 7 In.	34.00
Figurine, 4 Dolphins, 6 ¼ In.	418.00
Figurine, Cat, Seated, 11 ½ x 8 x 5 In.	500.00
Figurine, Dolphin, Clear, 4 x 5 In.	110.00
Figurine, Nautilus Shell, Marked, Box, 4 ¾ In.	140.00
Figurine, Number 1, Marked, 10 ½ x 4 ½ In.	230.00
Figurine, Porcupine, Clear, 5 In.	147.00
Figurine, Sphinx, With Snake, 4 ¼ x 5 ½ In.	125.00
Lamp, Hurricane, Etched, Prisms, Signed, 20 ¾ In., Pair	1750.00
Paperweight, Blue, Bird, Acid Etched, Signed, c.1989, 3 ¼ In.	340.00
Paperweight, Bouquet, Flat, Leafy Stems, Cruciform, Faceted, Millefiori, 3 ½ In. ....*illus*	13800.00
Paperweight, Clear, Star Shape, 4 ½ x 4 ¾ In.	47.00
Paperweight, Concentric, Millefiori, Translucent Blue Ground, Red, White, Yellow, 2 ¾ In. ...	250.00
Paperweight, Dogrose, Bold Red Flower, Green Leaves, Base Cut With Star, 3 In.	1500.00
Paperweight, Elephant, Clear, 2 ¾ x 3 In.	45.00
Paperweight, Fish, Frosted, Cast, Etched Insignia, 5 ½ x 2 x 2 ¼ In. ....*illus*	127.00
Paperweight, Forget-Me-Nots, White, Red, Bouquet, Yellow, Blue, Flowers, 3 In.	14000.00
Paperweight, Ladybug & Flowers, White, Red, Green Ground, No. 70/300, 1976	240.00
Paperweight, Millefiori, Butterfly, Garland, Marbled Wings, Star Cut Ground, 3 In. ....*illus*	9775.00
Paperweight, Millefiori, Canes, White Muslin Ground, 2 ¾ In.	1450.00
Paperweight, Pansy, Garland, Millefiori Border, White Ground, 2 ¹¹⁄₁₆ In.	2400.00
Paperweight, Stars & Geometric, Canes, Pink, Marked, 1848, 1 ⅛ x 2 ½ In.	290.00
Paperweight, Sulphide, George Washington, Cameo, 1954, 2 ⅝ In.	275.00
Paperweight, Sulphide, Patrick Henry, Faceted, Signed, J. Coy	85.00
Paperweight, Sulphide, Pope, Faceted, Inscribed, A. David, Paris, 1966	75.00
Paperweight, Sulphide, Thomas Paine, Clear, Blue, Faceted, Signed, J. Coy, 1975	85.00
Paperweight, Trefoils On Muslin, Bold Garlands, Red, White, Gray, Black, 3 In.	7500.00
Scent Bottle, Stopper, Shell Shape, Gilt Edge, Box, E. Arden, 6 ½ x 5 ½ In.	1200.00
Tumbler, Etna, Acid Stamp, Late 20th Century, 3 ¾ In., 4 Piece	71.00
Vase, Clear, Swirled, Ribbed, 10 In.	201.00

Baccarat, Paperweight, Bouquet, Flat, Leafy Stems, Cruciform, Faceted, Millefiori, 3 ½ In.
$13800.00

Baccarat, Paperweight, Fish, Frosted, Cast, Etched Insignia, 5 ½ x 2 x 2 ¼ In.
$127.00

Baccarat, Paperweight, Millefiori, Butterfly, Garland, Marbled Wings, Star Cut Ground, 3 In.
$9775.00

Badge, Police, Reagan Inauguration, F.P.S., Brass, Enamel, Blackington, 1985, 2 ¾ In.
$144.00

Bank, Apple, Cast Iron, Painted, Kyser & Rex, M 1621, 3 x 5 ¼ In.
$1872.00

Bank, Billiken, On Throne, Cast Iron, A.C. Williams, M 81, 6 ½ In.
$59.00

Vase, Diva, 4 ½ x 17 In.	527.00
Vase, Faceted, Corset Shape, Paper Label, 8 In.	70.00
Vase, Flattened Flared Rim, Hexagonal Base, Marked, 9 ½ x 7 In.	259.00
Vase, Flight To Love, Bronze Birds Feeding On Grapes, Marked, 12 In.	2935.00
Vase, Flowers, Cobalt Blue Cut To Clear & Frosty, Footed, Etched, Cameo, 10 In.	660.00
Vase, Green & Crimson, Leafy Flowers, Branches, Urn Form, Cameo, Signed, 1900s, 10 In.	1020.00
Vase, Stepped Spiral, 9 In.	896.00
Vase, Tornado, Clear, 15 In.	995.00

BADGES have been used since before the Civil War. Collectors search for examples of all types, including law enforcement and company identification badges. Well-known prison or law enforcement badges are most desirable. Most are made of nickel or brass. Many recent reproductions have been made.

9th Lancers, Queen Victoria Crown, Crossed Lances, Banner, Brass	34.00
American Protective League Secret Service, Pressed Metal, July 27, 1917	285.00
Chauffeur, Illinois, Licensed, C-Clasp, c.1930, 1 ¼ x 1 In.	110.00
Chauffeur, Minnesota, Licensed, No. 4390, Pin Back, c.1926	30.00
Civil Air Patrol Glider, Wing Shape, World War II	24.00
Deputy Sheriff, Norfolk, Va., 5-Point Star	47.00
Fall 1938 Sucony Vacuum, Employee Uniform Red, Blue, 2 x 2 In.	88.00
Fireman, Asst. Fire Chief, 3 Relief Fire Horns, Gold Tone, Montgomery, Ala., 1890s, 2 In. Diam.	75.00
Fireman, Commissioner, New York Fire Dept., Gold, Sunburst Shape, Red Enamel	177.00
Guard, Elmira Reformatory, No. 115-S	24.00
Hat, Co-Operative Bus Co., Shield Shape, Metal, 2 ¼ x 1 ½ In.	35.00
International Police Pistol Tournament, Police Pistol Range, Bronze, Teaneck, N.J., 12 x 13 In.	100.00
London Scottish, 14th County Of London, White Metal, Lion, Cross, Strike Sure, Thistles	27.00
Massachusetts Grange Patrons Of Husbandry, Ribbon, Ashfield, c.1890	31.00
Military, Hackney Regt., 10th County Of London, Brass, c.1916	26.00
Northumberland Fusiliers, Motto On Grenade, Quo Fatis Vocant, Bi-Metal	23.00
Onondaga County Defense Committee, Shield Shape, Seated Eagle, World War II	35.00
Paddington Rifles, White Metal, 10th County Of London Regt., Stamped Gaunts, c.1916	26.00
Patrolman, Civil Defense, Baltimore, Shield Shape, Perched Eagle, World War II	24.00
Police Detective, Lapel Pin, Initials M.B., Blue Enameling, Gold Tone, New York City, ¾ x ⅝ In.	20.00
Police, Massachusetts State Police Officer, Shield Shape, Gold, Blue	41.00
Police, Pittston, Penn., Shield Shape, Nickel, c.1900, 2 ½ x 2 ½ In.	328.00
Police, Reagan Inauguration, F.P.S., Brass, Enamel, Blackington, 1985, 2 ¾ In. ......*illus*	144.00
Post Office Rifles, 8th City Of London, White Metal, Wreath, Maltese Cross, Stamped Gaunts	40.00
Presentation, Hercules Powder Company, Christmas 1916, 2 ¼ x 2 ¼ In.	475.00
Queens Royal Irish Hussars, Bi-Metal, Erin Harp, Belt, Motto Mente Et Manu, c.1955	26.00
Reynolds Metal Co., Protection Division, Sergeant, Whitehead & Hoag, N.J., 2 ¼ x 2 In.	175.00
Rough Riders, City Of London Yeomanry, Brass, Round, Armorial Center, Motto	29.00
Taxi Driver, Boston Red Cab Co., Metal, Cloisonne Enamel, 2 ¼ x 4 ⅛ In.	357.00
Technical Observer, Wing Shape, World War II	83.00
United Steelworkers, Convention Delegate, Chicago, Ribbon, Name Tag, c.1968	31.00
U.S. Coast Guard, Cutterman, Clutch Back Closure, 2 ½ In.	5.00
U.S. Navy, Master At Arms, Shield Shape, Marked U.S. Govt.	47.00
U.S. Navy, Officer, Hat, Sterling Silver, Gold, Eagle, Shield, 1 ¼ In.	45.00
Wells Fargo Services, Silver Tone, Blue Enamel, 2 ¾ x 2 ½ In.	7.50
Westmorland & Cumberland Yeomanry, Brass, c.1914	24.00
Yorkshire Hussars, Yeomanry, Rose, Prince Of Wales Feathers, Bi-Metal	24.00

BANKS of metal have been made since 1868. There are still banks, mechanical banks, and registering banks (those that show the total money deposited on the face of the bank). Many old iron or tin banks have been reproduced since the 1950s in iron or plastic. Some old reproductions marked *Book of Knowledge, John Wright,* or *Capron* may be listed. Pottery, glass, and plastic banks are also listed here. Mickey Mouse and other Disneyana banks are listed in Disneyana. We have added the M numbers based on *The Penny Bank Book: Collecting Still Banks* by Andy and Susan Moore and the R numbers based on *Coin Banks by Banthrico* by James L. Redwine.

A Little Doe, In Glass Bubble, Cardboard, Wood, 6 In.	115.00
Andy Gump, On Stump, Reading Paper, Cast Iron, Arcade, M 217, 4 ⅜ In.	1100.00
Apple, Cast Iron, Painted, Kyser & Rex, M 1621, 3 x 5 ¼ In. ......*illus*	1872.00
Apple, Pottery, Coin Slot, 2 ½ In.	102.00
Aunt Jemima, Blue Dress, Red Scarf, White Apron, Cast Iron, A.C. Williams, M 168, 5 ¾ In.	150.00
Automat Dispensing, Tin Lithograph, Glass Back, Stollwerck, 6 ¼ In.	115.00
Bank Building, Crown With Tower, Painted, Red, Black, Iron, M 1230, 3 ³⁄₁₆ In.	3000.00

Bank Building, Double Door, Iron, Silver Paint, A.C. Williams, c.1905-20, M 1125, 5 x 4 In. .	78.00
Bank Building, Eagle, With Ball On Top, Cast Iron, M 1133, 10 ⅛ In.	1870.00
Bank Building, First Federal Savings & Loan, Greenville, S.C., Banthrico, R 595, 1950s, 6 In. .	79.00
Bank Building, Globe Savings Fund, 1888, Iron, Green, Copper, Red Paint, M 1199, 7 ⅛ In. . .	4850.00
Bank Building, Home Savings, Cast Iron, 10 ¼ In.	480.00
Bank Building, Jarmulowsky, Double Your Money Where It Is Safe, J. & E. Stevens, M 1086, 8 x 5 In.	5750.00
Bank Building, Michigan Avenue National, Gold, Black Paint, Lead, 5 ⁷⁄₁₆ In.	900.00
Bank Building, Painted, Iron, Crown, Red, Yellow, Green, J. & E. Stevens, M 1225, 5 In.	500.00
Bank Building, Painted, Yellow, Red, Blue, Cast Iron, 2 x 2 x 3 In.	675.00
Barrel, White City, Cast Iron, Nickel Plated, Nicol, c.1893, M 916, 5 In.	147.00
Baseball Player, Cast Iron, Painted, Gold, Red, A.C. Williams, M 18, 5 ¾ In.	292.00
Baseball, On 3 Bats, American & National, Cast Iron, Nickel Plated, Hubley, M 1608, 5 ¼ In.	2100.00
Basset Hound, Flying A Logo On Collar, Plastic	124.00
Bear, Standing, Cast Iron, Painted, John Harper, M 710, 6 ⅛ In.	82.00
Bear, With Honey Pot, Seated, Cast Iron, Painted, Hubley, M 717, 6 ½ In.	184.00
Beehive, Williams & Co., Chicago Cast Iron, Rotating Top, c.1875, 7 x 7 x 7 In.	413.00
Beehive, Wooden, Lehnware, 3 ⅜ In.	143.00
Beggar Boy, Help The Crippled Children Of Wisconsin, Cast Iron, 6 ⅞ In.	120.00
Billiken, On Throne, Cast Iron, A.C. Williams, M 81, 6 ½ In. ....*illus*	59.00
Billy Bounce, Iron, Painted, Hubley, c.1906, M 15, 4 ¹¹⁄₁₆ In.	415.00
Billy Can, Iron, Painted, c.1910, M 79, 5 ⅛ In.	795.00
Billy Possom, Cast Iron, Painted, J. & M. Harper, M 563, 3 In.	4000.00
Black Man, Give Me A Penny, Cast Iron, Hubley, M 166, 5 ½ In. .... 650.00 to 720.00
Boat, Battleship Kentucky, White, Green, Cast Iron, J. & E. Stevens, M 1439, 6 In.	1750.00
Boat, Battleship Oregon, Cast Iron, Gold Paint, J. & E. Stevens, M 1450, 4 x 5 In.	380.00
Boat, Battleship Oregon, Cast Iron, J. & E. Stevens, M 1450, 3 ⅞ In.	275.00
Boat, Battleship Oregon, Cast Iron, J. & E. Stevens, M 1452, 4 ⅞ In.	340.00
Boat, Lifeboat, Royal National Lifeboat Institution, Tin, Painted, Key, M 1466, 4 ½ x 14 In.	370.00
Boy, 2 Faces, Cast Iron, A.C. Williams, M 84, 3 ¼ In.	44.00
Buffalo, Cast Iron, Gold Paint, A.C. Williams, M 560, 3 In.	110.00
Buffalo, Movable Head & Tail, Cast Iron, c.1900, M 558, 5 ¾ x 9 ½ In.	644.00
Bugs Bunny, Leaning On Barrel, White Metal, Coin Slot On Barrel, Moss, 1940s, M 270, 5 ½ In.	145.00
Building, Castle, Cast Iron, Japanned, Kyser & Rex, c.1882, M 954, 3 In.	58.00
Building, Church, Cast Iron, Gray, Gold, Spire, 9 ¾ In.	690.00
Building, Eiffel Tower, Cast Iron, Sydenham & McOustra, England, c. 1908, 8 ¾ In.	144.00
Building, Equitable, White Metal, Banthrico, R 576, 5 ⅛ In.	120.00
Building, Gladiator On Cupola, Iron, Painted Red, Yellow Steps, Continental, 9 ½ In.	230.00
Building, House, Beverly State Savings, Save For A Home, Bankers Thrift, Tin, M 1018, 3 x 4 In. .	165.00
Building, Independence Hall, Centennial, Bronze Finish, Bell, Enterprise, Semimechanical, 9 ½ In.	316.00
Building, Independence Hall Tower, Cast Iron, Enterprise, M 1202, 9 ½ In.	292.00
Building, Masonic Temple, Brass, M 1061, 6 In.	2100.00
Building, Pagoda, Cast Iron, Green, Curved Steps, Pedestal Feet, England, c.1889, M 1153, 5 In.	58.00
Building, People's Savings, 4 Coin Slots, Embossed Shingle Roof, Nickel Finish, 10 ¾ In.	748.00
Building, Pottery, Chimney, Coin Slot, Brown Glaze, 1888, 5 ½ In.	259.00
Building, Skyscraper, 6 Posts, A.C. Williams, M 1241, 6 ½ In.	88.00
Building, Skyscraper, Cast Iron, Overall Gold, Coin Slot, A.C. Williams, M 1240, 5 ⅝ In.	173.00
Building, Strauss National Painted, Lead, 5 ⅛ In.	35.00
Building, Tower, Japanned, Bronze, Red, Combo Lock Door, Maroon Roof, Kyser & Rex, 7 In.	489.00
Building, Tower, Windows, 3 Levels, Cast Iron, Embossed Top, Grey Iron Casting, 7 In.	1955.00
Building, Travel & Transportation, Lead, 3 ¼ In.	120.00
Building, World's Fair, Century Of Progress, Cast Iron, Embossed, Arcade, 1934, M 1064, 4 ½ x 7 In.	1380.00
Camel, Gold Paint, Brown Saddle, Red Trim, Cast Iron, 7 ¼ In.	280.00
Camel, Gray, Brown, Gold, Red Paint, Cast Iron, 4 ¾ In.	105.00
Canister, Earthenware, Spinach Green, Brown, 4 ¼ In.	88.00
Canned Foods Week, March 3-10, National Canners Assoc., Tin Lithograph, 4 ½ x 3 ½ In. ..	24.00
Cannon, Green, Red Wheels, Cast Iron, Hubley, 1914, M 1425, 3 In.	1510.00
Car, Cab, Driver, Brown, White, Black, Cast Iron, 4 ¼ In.	1820.00
Car, Cab, Driver, Yellow Cab Co., Park 1345, Orange, Black, Cast Iron, 4 ¼ In.	2100.00
Car, Cab, Flat Top, Green, Black, Driver, Cowl Lights, Cast Wheels, Spare, Arcade, 8 In.	14373.00
Car, Ford, Model T, Touring Car, Back, Cast Iron, Arcade, M 1483, 4 x 6 ⁵⁄₁₆ In.	220.00
Car, Sedan, Silvered Lead, Slot On Roof, Key Lock Trap, Germany, 4 ⅜ In.	1265.00
Car, Yellow Cab, Cast Iron, Arcade, 8 In. .... 489.00 to 825.00
Car, Yellow Cab, Cast Iron, Painted, Arcade, M 1489, 4 ¼ x 7 ⅞ In. ....*illus*	1404.00
Car, Yellow Cab, Cast Iron, Steel Wheels, Painted, Orange, Black, Arcade, c.1921, M 1482, 8 In.	1020.00
Cash Register, Junior Cash, Cast Iron, Gold Paint, J. & E. Stevens, M 930, 4 ¼ In.	180.00
Cat, Brass Colored Metal, Ben Seibel, Raymor-Jenfred, 11 In.	205.00

Bank, Car, Yellow Cab, Cast Iron,
Painted, Arcade, M 1489, 4 ¼ x 7 ⅞ In.
$1404.00

Bank, Chest Of Drawers, Empire,
Earthenware, Scroddleware, 3 x 4 In.
$162.00

Bank, Harold Lloyd, Safety Last!,
Movie Premium, Tin Lithograph,
c.1923, 2 ¼ In.
$205.00

Bank, Mechanical, Bulldog, Standing,
Tail Moves, Cast Iron, Copper Flashing,
H.L. Judd
$468.00

TIP
*Never repaint an old
bank. It lowers the
resale value.*

Bank, Mechanical, Butting Goat,
Cast Iron, H.L. Judd
$468.00

Bank, Mechanical, Calamity,
Football Players, Iron, Painted,
J. & E. Stevens, 7 ½ x 6 In.
$6435.00

Bank, Mechanical, Dog On Turntable,
Cast Iron, H.L. Judd
$4388.00

Cat, Bust, In Nightcap, Ceramic, White, Pink, Green, Blue, 3 ¾ In.	240.00
Cat, White, Walking On Red Brick Wall, Iron, Painted, 8 ½ In.	495.00
Chest Of Drawers, Empire, Earthenware, Scroddleware, 3 x 4 In. ....*illus*	162.00
Chicken Feed, Chicken, In Glass Bubble, Cardboard, Wood, 6 In.	105.00
Chicken, Blue, Seagrove Pottery, 10 ½ In.	90.00
Children Playing, Alphabet Rim On Lid, Oval, Tin, 2 ¾ x 4 x 1 ¾ In.	130.00
City, Cast Iron, Kenton, 5 In.	66.00
Coin Deposit, Grey Iron Casting, c.1903, 6 ¾ x 5 ¼ x 4 ½ In.	275.00
Conoco Station Attendant, Green, White, Black, Plastic, Figural, Dayton Oil Co., 5 In.	44.00
Cottage, Tin Lithograph, George W. Brown, M 1035, 6 ⅜ In.	198.00
Covered Bridge, Cast Iron, Red, Tan, John Wright, c.1960, M 1195, 2 ½ x 6 ⅛ In.	125.00
Cow, Cast Iron, Painted, A.C. Williams, c.1920, M 553, 3 ¼ x 5 In.	130.00 to 200.00
Cupola, White, Blue Trim, Red Windows, Stenciled Roof, Metal, 4 ¼ In.	2875.00
Cylindrical, Wooden, Treenware Type, Removable Base, 3 ¾ In.	55.00
Devil, 2-Faces, Cast Iron, Red, Black, A.C. Williams, M 31, 4 ¼ In.	1050.00
Dog, Basset Hound, Seated, Cast Iron, Painted, 7 ¼ In.	330.00
Dog, Boston Bull Terrier, Seated, Cast Iron, Gray, White, M 413, 4 ⅜ In.	210.00
Dog, Boston Bulldog, Seated, Cast Iron, Painted, Hubley, M 396, 4 ½ In.	190.00
Dog, Bulldog, Black, Cast Iron, Arcade, M 403, 2 ¼ In.	485.00
Dog, By Barrel, Candy Container, Glass, 3 ⅛ In.	65.00
Dog, Fido, Cast Iron, Black, White, Red, Collar, Hubley, Pre 1940, M 417, 5 In.	225.00
Dog, Fido On Pillow, Iron, Painted, Hubley, c.1920, M 443, 7 ⅜ In.	410.00
Dog, Pack Dog, Cast Iron, Painted, 7 ½ In.	70.00
Dog, Puppo, On Cushion, Black, White, Cast Iron, Hubley, M 442, 5 ⅝ In.	480.00
Dog, Spaniel, Iron, White, Brown, Trap, Key, Hubley, M 418, 3 ¾ In.	285.00
Dresser, Cast Iron, Blue Drawers, White Top, Red Frame, White Knobs, J. & E. Stevens, 6 ¼ In.	690.00
Drum, American Bald Eagle, Miss Liberty 2 ¾ x 3 In.	65.00
Duck, On Tub, Save For A Rainy Day, Cast Iron, Painted, Hubley, 1930s, M 616, 5 ½ In.	150.00
Duck, Round, Cast Iron, Yellow, Red, Black, Kenton, M 619, 4 In.	605.00
Duckling, Spread Wings, Cast Iron, White, Yellow, Green, Hubley, M 624, 4 ¾ In.	188.00
Elephant, Cast Iron, Gray, Red Blanket, Kenton, M 487, 3 ⅛ In.	1430.00
Elephant, Howdah, Cast Iron, Painted, A.C. Williams, c.1910-30, M 474, 5 x 6 ⅜ In.	47.00
Elephant, On Wheels, Cast Iron, A.C. Williams, 1920, M 446, 4 ⅛ In.	450.00
Elephant, Seated, Cast Iron, Polka Dot Shirt, Yellow Hat, Blue Pants, Hubley, M 462, 3 ⅞ In.	167.00
Elmer Fudd, Cast Metal, Hunting Outfit, Shotgun, By Tree, Moss, 1940s, M 308, 6 In.	225.00
Finial, Iron, Bronze Painted, Kyser & Rex Co., c.1887, M 1158, 5 ¾ In.	230.00
Foxy Grandpa, Cast Iron, Painted, Hubley, M 320, 5 ½ In.	140.00
Gas Pump, Cast Iron, Blue, Gold, Cast Iron, Arcade, 6 In.	310.00
Gas Pump, Cast Iron, Red, Gold, Cast Iron, Arcade, 4 ¾ In.	315.00
Gas Pump, Cast Iron, Red, Gold, Cast Iron, Arcade, 5 ¾ In.	140.00
Gas Pump, Cast Iron, Red, Gold Trim, Dial, Cast Iron, Arcade, 5 ¾ In.	546.00
General Sheridan, On Horse, Cast Iron, Painted, Arcade, M 50, 6 In.	285.00
Get Rich Quick, Tin, Red, Yellow, Black, Marx, 3 ½ x 2 ½ In.	25.00
Girl, On Chamber Pot, Ceramic, White, Blue, Peach, 3 ¾ In.	140.00
Give Me A Penny, Man, Hands On Hips, Painted, Cast Iron, Hubley, M 166, 5 ½ In.	220.00
Globe, Universal Stoves & Ranges, Tin, Spins, Save Your Money, Cribben & Sexton Co., M 787, 4 In.	1125.00
Golliwog, Standing, Iron, Red Pants, Painted, John Harper, M 85, 6 In.	200.00
Hall Clock, Brown Paint, Cast Iron, Hubley, M 1535, 5 ⅞ In.	610.00
Hansel & Gretel, Cottage, Child At Door, Father Chasing Witch, Denmark, 4 x 4 ½ In.	748.00
Happifats On Drum, Glass, Candy Container, Painted, M 302, 4 ½ In.	65.00
Harold Lloyd, Safety Last!, Movie Premium, Tin Lithograph, c.1923, 2 ¼ In. ....*illus*	205.00
Heatrola, Red, Gold Paint, Cast Iron, Tin, 4 ½ In.	95.00
Hen On Nest, Stoneware, 3 ½ In.	66.00
Hen, Chick, Cast Iron, 9 ⅞ In.	660.00
Horse, On Tub, Iron, Black, Red Saddle, A.C. Williams	340.00
Icebox, Save For Ice, White, Footed, Cast Iron, Tin, Arcade, M 1337, 4 ¼ In.	950.00
Indian, With Tomahawk, Iron, Painted, Hubley, M 228, 5 ⅞ In.	153.00 to 265.00
John Golliwog, Man, Dress Suit, Cast Brass, England, c.1920, 6 In.	95.00
Jug, Fieldman Pottstown Store, Die Cut, 4 ½ In.	316.00
Keyless Safety Deposit, Fleur-De-Lis, Shields, Keyless Lock Co., Indianapolis, 6 x 4 In.	92.00
Lennie Lennox, Composition, Painted, 1949, 7 ½ In.	105.00
Lennie Lennox, Lennox Aire-Flo Heating, Composition, Painted, 1952, 8 ¾ In.	105.00
Liberty Bell, Cast Iron, Grey Iron Casting, M 782, 3 ⅞ In.	30.00
Lion, On Tub, Cast Iron, Gold Paint, A.C. Williams, M 746, 5 ⅜ In.	70.00
Lion, Standing, Cast Iron, Painted, 9 In.	153.00
Lion, Tail Right, Cast Iron, A.C. Williams, M 754, 4 In.	33.00

B

Mailbox, U.S. Mail, Eagle, Letters, Pull Down, Green, Gold, Cast Iron, Kenton, M 852, 3 ⅝ In.	60.00
Mailbox, U.S. Mail, Eagle, Pull Down, Nickeled, Cast Iron, Hubley, M 855, 4 In.	79.00
Mailbox, U.S. Mail, Hanging, Iron, Green, Gold, A.C. Williams, M 856, 5 ⅛ In.	200.00
Mailbox, U.S. Mail, Platform, Cast Iron, Japanned, Black, Coin Slot, Trapdoor, 1800s, M 858, 7 ¼ In.	978.00
Mammy, Red Dress, White Apron, Cast Iron, Hubley, M 176, 5 ¼ In.	150.00
Mammy, With Spoon, Cast Iron	71.00
Man, On Stump, Smoking Pipe, Black Coat, Yellow Knickers, Ceramic, Borgfeldt, 13 ¼ In.	72.00
Marconi Savings, Painted, White Metal, 2 ⅜ In.	185.00
Mary & Lamb, Cast Iron, Painted, M 164, 4 ⅜ In.	485.00
Mascot, On Baseball, Red Cap, Yellow Jacket, Cast Iron, Hubley, M 3, 5 ¹³⁄₁₆ In.	1500.00

Mechanical banks were first made about 1870. Any bank with moving parts is considered mechanical. The metal banks made before World War I are the most desirable. Copies and new designs of mechanical banks have been made in metal or plastic since the 1920s. The condition of the paint on the old banks is important. Worn paint can lower a price by 90 percent. This year there were several auctions of mechanical banks in excellent condition that sold for very high prices. Other examples of the same banks with poor paint and missing parts sold for very low prices. Listed here are the high and low prices seen during the year.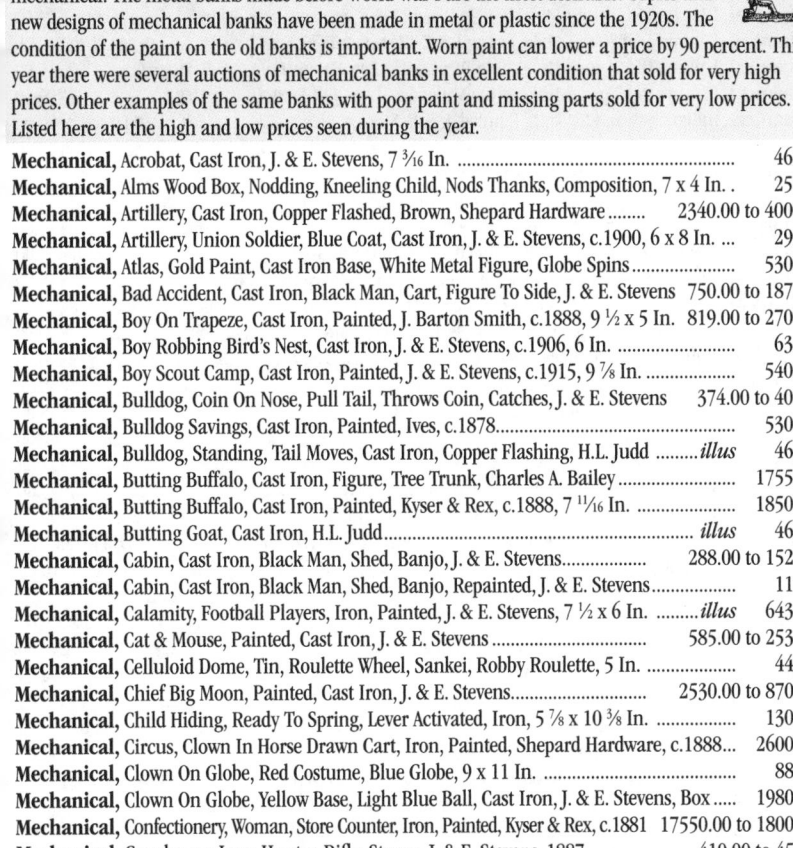

Mechanical, Acrobat, Cast Iron, J. & E. Stevens, 7 ³⁄₁₆ In.	468.00
Mechanical, Alms Wood Box, Nodding, Kneeling Child, Nods Thanks, Composition, 7 x 4 In.	259.00
Mechanical, Artillery, Cast Iron, Copper Flashed, Brown, Shepard Hardware	2340.00 to 4000.00
Mechanical, Artillery, Union Soldier, Blue Coat, Cast Iron, J. & E. Stevens, c.1900, 6 x 8 In.	294.00
Mechanical, Atlas, Gold Paint, Cast Iron Base, White Metal Figure, Globe Spins	5300.00
Mechanical, Bad Accident, Cast Iron, Black Man, Cart, Figure To Side, J. & E. Stevens	750.00 to 1872.00
Mechanical, Boy On Trapeze, Cast Iron, Painted, J. Barton Smith, c.1888, 9 ½ x 5 In.	819.00 to 2700.00
Mechanical, Boy Robbing Bird's Nest, Cast Iron, J. & E. Stevens, c.1906, 6 In.	633.00
Mechanical, Boy Scout Camp, Cast Iron, Painted, J. & E. Stevens, c.1915, 9 ⅞ In.	5400.00
Mechanical, Bulldog, Coin On Nose, Pull Tail, Throws Coin, Catches, J. & E. Stevens	374.00 to 403.00
Mechanical, Bulldog Savings, Cast Iron, Painted, Ives, c.1878	5300.00
Mechanical, Bulldog, Standing, Tail Moves, Cast Iron, Copper Flashing, H.L. Judd *illus*	468.00
Mechanical, Butting Buffalo, Cast Iron, Figure, Tree Trunk, Charles A. Bailey	17550.00
Mechanical, Butting Buffalo, Cast Iron, Painted, Kyser & Rex, c.1888, 7 ¹¹⁄₁₆ In.	18500.00
Mechanical, Butting Goat, Cast Iron, H.L. Judd *illus*	468.00
Mechanical, Cabin, Cast Iron, Black Man, Shed, Banjo, J. & E. Stevens	288.00 to 1521.00
Mechanical, Cabin, Cast Iron, Black Man, Shed, Banjo, Repainted, J. & E. Stevens	117.00
Mechanical, Calamity, Football Players, Iron, Painted, J. & E. Stevens, 7 ½ x 6 In. *illus*	6435.00
Mechanical, Cat & Mouse, Painted, Cast Iron, J. & E. Stevens	585.00 to 2530.00
Mechanical, Celluloid Dome, Tin, Roulette Wheel, Sankei, Robby Roulette, 5 In.	446.00
Mechanical, Chief Big Moon, Painted, Cast Iron, J. & E. Stevens	2530.00 to 8700.00
Mechanical, Child Hiding, Ready To Spring, Lever Activated, Iron, 5 ⅞ x 10 ⅜ In.	1304.00
Mechanical, Circus, Clown In Horse Drawn Cart, Iron, Painted, Shepard Hardware, c.1888	26000.00
Mechanical, Clown On Globe, Red Costume, Blue Globe, 9 x 11 In.	889.00
Mechanical, Clown On Globe, Yellow Base, Light Blue Ball, Cast Iron, J. & E. Stevens, Box	19800.00
Mechanical, Confectionery, Woman, Store Counter, Iron, Painted, Kyser & Rex, c.1881	17550.00 to 18000.00
Mechanical, Creedmoor, Iron, Hunter, Rifle, Stump, J. & E. Stevens, 1887	410.00 to 450.00
Mechanical, Darktown Battery, Black Players, Iron, J. & E. Stevens, c.1888, 10 In.	1000.00 to 2250.00
Mechanical, Darktown Battery, Iron, Wooden Box Stand, J. & E. Stevens, c.1888, 7 x 9 ¾ In.	14100.00
Mechanical, Dentist, Patient, Exam, Cast Iron, Black, Red, Yellow, J. & E. Stevens	21600.00
Mechanical, Dinah, Coin To Mouth, Eyes Roll, Iron, Painted, John Harper	230.00 to 535.00
Mechanical, Dog On Turntable, Cast Iron, H.L. Judd *illus*	4388.00
Mechanical, Dog On Turntable, Penny, Comes Out Door, Iron, Painted, H.L. Judd, c. 1870	1287.00 to 1410.00
Mechanical, Dog, Tray, Cast Iron, Painted, Kyser & Rex, c.1880	3218.00
Mechanical, Eagle & Eaglets, Iron, Gray Base, J. & E. Stevens, c.1883	400.00 to 4800.00
Mechanical, Elephant & 3 Clowns, Iron, Elephant, J. & E. Stevens, c.1882	3850.00 to 8190.00
Mechanical, Elephant, 3 Stars, Black, Cast Iron	290.00
Mechanical, Elephant, Howdah, Man Pops Out, Iron & Wood, Enterprise.	485.00
Mechanical, Elephant, On Drum, Painted, Tin, Chein, 5 In.	65.00
Mechanical, Elephant, Pull Tail, Iron, Gray, Painted, Hubley	550.00
Mechanical, Elephant, Pull Tail, Iron, White, Painted, Hubley	450.00 to 1800.00
Mechanical, Ferris Wheel, Cast Iron, Figures, Wheel, Added Base, Red, Black, Hubley, c.1950.	4972.00
Mechanical, Ferris Wheel, Cast Iron, Painted, Hubley, c.1950	5125.00
Mechanical, Flying Saucer, Die Cast, Decal, Duro Mold Mfg., 1956, 4 In.	147.00
Mechanical, Frog, On Rock, Cast Iron, Painted, Kilgore	870.00
Mechanical, Frog, On Round Base, Lattice, J. & E. Stevens, 1880s, 4 ¼ In.	3185.00
Mechanical, Frog, On Round Base, Lattice, Lavender, Cast Iron, J. & E. Stevens, 7 ⅝ In.	330.00
Mechanical, Frogs, 2, Cast Iron, J. & E. Stevens, 9 In.	2690.00

Bank, Mechanical, Girl Skipping Rope, Cast Iron, Painted, J. & E. Stevens
$32760.00

Bank, Mechanical, Hall's Liliput, Cast Iron, J. & E. Stevens
$761.00

Bank, Mechanical, Pay Phone, Insert Coin, Bell Rings, J. & E. Stevens
$410.00

Bank, Mechanical, Penny Pineapple, Cast Iron, 50th Anniversary, July 4th 1960 $234.00

Bank, Mechanical, Trick Dog, Cast Iron, Shepard Hardware, 9 x 7 ½ In. $468.00

TIP

To clean lithographed tin banks, try using Sani Wax and 0000-grade steel wool, but use with extreme caution.

Mechanical, General Butler, Cast Iron, Painted, Caricature, Frog's Body, J. & E. Stevens, 6 ½ In.	1500.00
Mechanical, Girl Skipping Rope, Cast Iron, Painted, J. & E. Stevens ....*illus*	32760.00
Mechanical, Hall's Excelsior, Cast Iron, Orange, White, Painted, J. & E. Stevens.....................	322.00
Mechanical, Hall's Excelsior, Cast Iron, Tan, Orange, Blue, Painted, J. & E. Stevens...............	1112.00
Mechanical, Hall's Excelsior, Cast Iron, Yellow, Red, J. & E. Stevens..........................	360.00
Mechanical, Hall's Liliput, Cast Iron, J. & E. Stevens ....*illus*	761.00
Mechanical, Hen & Chick, Cast Iron, Brown Hen, Yellow Chick, J. & E. Stevens.....	6435.00 to 6500.00
Mechanical, Hen & Chick, Cast Iron, White Hen, Early Repaint, J. & E. Stevens......	1112.00
Mechanical, Hold The Fort, 5-Hole, Cannon, Flag, Cast Iron, Painted	2200.00
Mechanical, Hold The Fort, 7-Hole, Cannon, Flag, Cast Iron	5300.00
Mechanical, Hoop-La, Clown, Dog, Barrel, Cast Iron, Multicolored, John Harper	1112.00
Mechanical, Horse Race, Cast Iron, J. & E. Stevens	878.00
Mechanical, Humpty Dumpty, Cast Iron, Shepard Hardware, 7 ½ In.	495.00 to 2000.00
Mechanical, I Always Did 'Spise A Mule, Boy On Bench, J. & E. Stevens, 1897, 10 In.	415.00 to 527.00
Mechanical, I Always Did 'Spise A Mule, Jockey, J. & E. Stevens, c.1879, 8 x 11 x 3 In.	240.00 to 247.00
Mechanical, I Always Did 'Spise A Mule, Mule Turns, Kicks Boy, Throws Coin, J. & E. Stevens......	2415.00
Mechanical, I Always Did 'Spise A Mule, White Mule, Cast Iron, J. & E. Stevens, c.1920	1750.00
Mechanical, Indian & Bear, Cast Iron, Painted, J. & E. Stevens........................	2400.00 to 8400.00
Mechanical, Joe Socko, Boxers, Tin, Painted	175.00
Mechanical, Jolly Nigger, Cast Iron, J. & E. Stevens.................................	410.00
Mechanical, Jolly Nigger, Eyes Roll, Boater Hat, Aluminum, Painted, 7 In.	196.00
Mechanical, Jolly Nigger, High Hat, John Harper.....................................	143.00
Mechanical, Jonah & The Whale, Iron, Painted, Shepard Hardware	403.00 to 855.00
Mechanical, Leap Frog, Iron, 2 Boys, Tree, Fence, Painted, Shepard Hardware	936.00
Mechanical, Leap Frog, Iron, 2 Boys, Tree, Fence, Painted, Shepard Hardware, Box	8400.00
Mechanical, Light Of Asia, Elephant, On Wheels, Cast Iron, Painted, J. & E. Stevens................	3600.00
Mechanical, Lighthouse, Red, Black, Cast Iron, Painted	2400.00
Mechanical, Lion & 2 Monkeys, Cast Iron, Painted, Kyser & Rex	615.00
Mechanical, Magic Bank Building, Cashier, Cast Iron, J. & E Stevens, c.1875, 6 ¾ x 4 ¼ In. ..	558.00
Mechanical, Magic Cashier, Cast Iron, J. & E. Stevens..	1200.00
Mechanical, Magician Cast Iron, J. & E. Stevens, c.1901, 8 x 6 ¾ In.	403.00
Mechanical, Mammy & Child, Cast Iron, Kyser & Rex, c.1884	9945.00
Mechanical, Mammy & Child, Yellow Dress, Cast Iron, Kyser & Rex, c.1884....................	11200.00
Mechanical, Mason, Brick Wall, 2 Men, Red, Black Paint, Shepard Hardware.......	995.00 to 4400.00
Mechanical, Milking Cow, Fence, Tail, Kicking Leg, Cast Iron, J. & E. Stevens.....................	1210.00
Mechanical, Minstrel With Tray, Head, Brown, Black, Yellow, Red, Tin, Saalheimer & Strauss	520.00
Mechanical, Monkey & Coconut, Cast Iron, Brown Base, J. & E. Stevens, c.1886 ...	1155.00 to 2106.00
Mechanical, Monkey & Parrot, Tin, Painted, Saalheimer & Strauss...........................	240.00
Mechanical, Monkey, Zoo Scenes On Base, Tin Lithograph, 6 ¼ In.	66.00
Mechanical, Moon Ship, White Metal, Alan Shepard 1961 Flight, 10 ¾ In.	96.00
Mechanical, Mule Entering Barn, Cast Iron, J. & E. Stevens..................................	403.00 to 840.00
Mechanical, Negro Face, Rolling Eyes, Metal	68.00
Mechanical, New Bank, Black, Red, Cast Iron, Painted, J. & E. Stevens	1287.00 to 1320.00
Mechanical, Novelty, Building, Red Roof, Door Opens, Teller, Iron, J. & E. Stevens, 6 ¾ In.	356.00
Mechanical, Organ Grinder, Dancing Bear, 3 Men, House, Multicolored, Kyser & Rex	1521.00 to 2020.00
Mechanical, Organ, Bells Ring, Monkey Deposits From Tambourine, Tips Hat, Kyser & Rex...	6038.00
Mechanical, Organ, Boy & Girl, Cast Iron, Painted, Kyser & Rex	1310.00
Mechanical, Organ, Cat & Dog, Cast Iron, Painted, Kyser & Rex	503.00 to 605.00
Mechanical, Organ, Cat & Dog, With Monkey, Cast Iron, Painted, Kyser & Rex, c.1882, 9 ½ x 5 In. .	1150.00
Mechanical, Organ, Monkey, Yellow Pants, Hat, Iron, Painted, Kyser & Rex...........	819.00 to 840.00
Mechanical, Organ, Painted, Cast Iron, Kyser & Rex, c.1882, 5 ¼ In.	460.00
Mechanical, Owl, Painted Cast Iron, 1875, 7 ½ In.	178.00
Mechanical, Owl, Slot In Book, Cast Iron, Painted, Kilgore, c.1926	200.00
Mechanical, Owl, Turns Head, Iron, Brown, Yellow Eyes, Gold, Paint, J. & E. Stevens.	294.00 to 900.00
Mechanical, Owl, Turns Head, White, Yellow Eyes, Cast Iron, J. & E. Stevens	8775.00 to 9000.00
Mechanical, Paddy & Pig, Coin In Paddy's Mouth, Iron, J. & E. Stevens, 8 In.	1150.00 to 1375.00
Mechanical, Panorama, Cast Iron, White Building, Painted Mural, J. & E. Stevens	21645.00
Mechanical, Patronize The Blind Man, Cast Iron, Painted, J. & E. Stevens, 2/19/1878, 9 In. ..	1469.00
Mechanical, Pay Phone, Insert Coin, Bell Rings, J. & E. Stevens ....*illus*	410.00
Mechanical, Pelican, Food In Mouth, Cast Iron, Trenton Lock & Hardware	1010.00
Mechanical, Penny Pineapple, Cast Iron, 50th Anniversary, July 4th 1960 ....*illus*	234.00
Mechanical, Pig In High Chair, Cast Iron, J. & E. Stevens, c.1900, 6 In.	705.00
Mechanical, Professor Pug Frog's Bicycle Great Feat, Iron, J. & E. Stevens, c.1880..................	3300.00
Mechanical, Punch & Judy, Cast Iron, Shepard Hardware, 1884...............	1175.00 to 4800.00
Mechanical, Rabbit, Standing, Movable Ears, Cast Iron, Lockwood	100.00 to 678.00
Mechanical, Reclining Chinaman, Cast Iron, Painted, J. & E. Stevens	10200.00
Mechanical, Rooster, Cast Iron, Painted, Kyser & Rex, c.1880..	410.00

Mechanical, Satellite, Metal, Shepard, Grissom, Glenn, Carpenter, Shirra, Duro Mold Mfg., 8 In.	65.00
Mechanical, Speaking Dog, Girl, Iron, Maroon Base, Shepard Hardware, c.1885, 7 x 7 In.	267.00 to 1404.00
Mechanical, Speaking Dog, Opens, Closes Mouth, Wags Tail, Girl, Shepard Hardware	259.00
Mechanical, Springing Cat, Cast Iron, Wood Base, Gold Mounts, Charles Bailey...	17550 to 18500.00
Mechanical, Squirrel & Tree Stump, Iron, Painted, Mechanical Novelty Works, c.1881	7605.55 to 7700.00
Mechanical, Stump Speaker, Iron, Painted, Shepard Hardware, c.1886, 10 In.	748.00 to 8900.00
Mechanical, Tammany, Brown Pants, Dark Blue Coat, Coin Trap, J. & E. Stevens, 4 ⅜ In.	237.00
Mechanical, Tammany, Brown Suit, Yellow Shirt, Iron, J. & E. Stevens, 1873, 6 x 5 In.	173.00 to 400.00
Mechanical, Tammany, Cast Iron, Painted, Box, J. & E. Stevens................	3000.00
Mechanical, Teddy & The Bear, Teddy Roosevelt, J. & E. Stevens, 1941	1550.00
Mechanical, Toad On Stump, Green, Brown, Cast Iron, J. & E. Stevens, c.1886.................	3850.00
Mechanical, Trenton Trust, 75th Anniversary, Painted, Cast Iron................	710.00
Mechanical, Trick Dog, 6-Part Base Variation, Yellow Clown, Cast Iron, Shepard Hardware ...	468.00
Mechanical, Trick Dog, Black Face Clown, Cast Iron, Hubley................	850.00
Mechanical, Trick Dog, Cast Iron, Shepard Hardware, 9 x 7 ½ In. ....*illus*	468.00
Mechanical, Trick Dog, Jumps Through Hoop, Deposits Coin In Barrel, Iron, Shepard Hardware	690.00
Mechanical, Trick Pony, Deposits Coin In Manger, Shepard Hardware, c.1885......	489.00 to 1150.00
Mechanical, Turtle, Cast Iron, Painted, Black, Red, Blue Trim, Kilgore...	65520.00 to 67600.00
Mechanical, Uncle Sam, Satchel, Walking Stick, Red, White, Blue, Shepard Hardware	920.00 to 2950.00
Mechanical, Uncle Tom, With Star, Cast Iron, Painted, Kyser & Rex, c.1882.........	468.00 to 480.00
Mechanical, Vending, Pinball, Tin Lithograph, Glass View Front, Pinball Slots, Children, 6 ½ In.	230.00
Mechanical, Vending, Red Riding Hood, Rhymes, Tin, Stollwerck, Germany, 6 In.	403.00 to 3450.00
Mechanical, Vending, Tin, Glass Window, Pull-Out Tray, Children, Hartwig & Vogel, 5 In.	173.00
Mechanical, William Tell, Cast Iron, Painted, J. & E. Stevens, c.1896	330.00 to 1420.00
Mechanical, Zoo, Cast Iron, Painted, Kyser & Rex................	1420.00
Money Bag, 100,000, Cast Iron, Painted, M 1262, 3 ⅜ In.	130.00
Monkey, Standing, With Tray, Painted, Ceramic, Marked, Borgfeldt, 13 ¾ In.	105.00
Moo-La, Cow, In Glass Bubble, Cardboard, Wood, 6 In.	175.00
Mrs. Simms Lucky Jumbo, Syrup, Glass................	40.00
Officer Cadet, Cast Iron, Painted, Hubley, M 8, 6 In. ....*illus*	322.00
Old King Cole, Book Shape, Tin Lithograph, Mohawk Metal Co., 1919, 4 x 3 In.	75.00
Orange, Pottery, Coin Slot, 2 ¾ In.	113.00
Oriental Children, With Plum, Ceramic, Painted, 3 ¾ In.	65.00
Owl, Be Wise, Save Money, Gold, Red, White Paint, Cast Iron, A.C. Williams, 5 In.	238.00
Owl, Gray, White, Yellow Eyes, Cast Iron, Vindex, c.1930, 4 ¼ In.	265.00
Parrot, On Stump, Cast Iron, Painted, M 668, 6 ¼ In.	350.00
Pelican, White, Orange Beak, Cast Iron, Hubley, c.1930, M 679, 4 ¾ In.	1560.00
Pet Milk, Carton Shape, Circus Animals, 1955, 2 ⅞ x 3 ½ In.	80.00
Piano, Wood, Hinged Keyboard, 5 x 7 ¾ In.	66.00
Piano, Wood, Top Lifts, Closed Keyboard, Continental, 6 In.	690.00
Pig, In Satchel, Pink, Green, Porcelain, Germany, 3 ½ In.	87.00
Pig, Laughing, Light Blue, Pink, Cast Iron, Hubley, M 640, 2 ½ In......	350.00
Pig, Seated, Cast Iron, A.C. Williams, M 582, 2 ⅞ In.	33.00
Pin Money, Bowler, In Glass Bubble, Cardboard, Wood, 6 In.	175.00
Policeman, Every Copper Helps, Cast Iron, Painted, Chamberlain & Hill, M 72, 6 In.	600.00
Porky Pig, Red Jacket, Blue Cap, Base, Cast Iron, Hubley, c.1930, M 264, 6 In.	298.00
Rabbit, Brown, White, Cast Iron, Hubley, M 570, 4 ½ In.	175.00
Radio, G.E., Footed, Cast Iron, Arcade, c.1932, M 822, 3 ⅞ In.	95.00
Radio, Templeton, Red, Footed, Cast Iron, Tin, Kenton, c.1930, M 826, 4 ⁵⁄₁₆ In.	360.00
Radio, Wood, 1930-40s, 6 ⅜ In.	55.00
Refrigerator, Majestic, Green, Cast Iron & Sheet Metal, Ardace, c.1932, M 1332, 4 ½ In.	350.00
Register, Beehive, Dime, Cast Iron, c.1891, 6 ⁷⁄₁₆ x 5 ⅜ In. ....*illus*	117.00
Register, Keep 'Em Flying, Dime, Tin, 2 ½ In.	290.00
Register, Keep 'Em Rolling, Dime, Tin, 2 ½ In.	240.00
Register, Keep 'Em Sailing, Dime, Tin, 2 ½ In.	240.00
Register, Nursery Rhyme, Little Folks Cash, Painted, Tin Lithograph, 3 x 3 ¾ In.	82.00
Register, Phoenix, H & H Registering Savings, Pat. June 12, 1888, Cast Iron, 4 x 5 In., Dime..	140.00
Register, Trunk, H & H Registering Savings Bank, Registering Window, 1888, Iron, 4 x 5 In., Dime..	29.00
Reindeer, Green, Cast Iron, M 736, 6 ¼ In.	155.00
Rex Water Heater, Tin Lithograph, 7 ¾ In.	60.00
Rocking Horse, White, Red, Yellow, SBCCA, Cast Iron, M 1593, 5 ⅝ In.	350.00
Royal Gelatin, Figural, King Royal, Slot In Back Of Head, 1950s, 10 In.	115.00
Safe, American Home Deposit, Painted, Cast Iron, Tin, 5 ¼ In.	95.00
Safe, Cast Iron, Wood Drawers, c.1875, 8 ¼ In.	120.00
Safe, Combination, Cast Iron, Wheels, Painted, Daisy Design, 12 ¾ x 10 x 16 ½ In.	3450.00
Safe, Dog, Man, Eagle On Top, Combination Lock, Cast Iron, Tin, Steel, 3 ¾ x 3 x 2 ¾ In.	56.00
Safe, Flowers, Openwork, Green Paint, Cast Iron, Key Lock, 4 x 2 ⅞ x 2 ⅞ In.	118.00

Bank, Officer Cadet, Cast Iron, Painted, Hubley, M 8, 6 In.
$322.00

Bank, Register, Beehive, Dime, Cast Iron, c.1891, 6 ⁷⁄₁₆ x 5 ⅜ In.
$117.00

Bank, Uncle Sam, Glass, Screw Top, 3 ½ In.
$644.00

Barber, Chair, Koken, Green Porcelain, Dark Green Upholstery, 47 x 29 In. $330.00

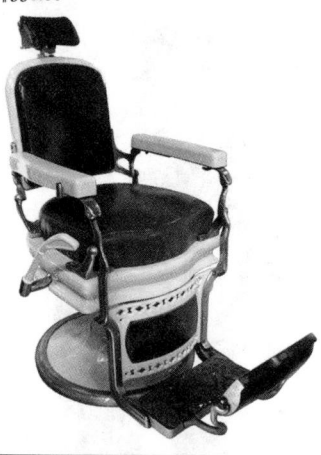

Barber, Chair, Pedal Car Style, Flame Decoration, Adjustable, Child's, 44 x 24 In. $825.00

Barber, Pole, Painted, Red, White, Blue, Iron Attachments, c.1900, 57 In. $441.00

Safe, Horse Heads, Combination Lock, Cast Iron, Nickel Plated, Kenton, 5 x 4 x 3 In.	92.00
Safe, Ideal, Cast Iron, 6 ½ In.	77.00
Safe, Merry-Go-Round, Cast Iron, Painted, c.1880, 5 x 4 In.	410.00
Safe, Moon, Star, Leaf, Combination Lock, Cast Iron, Nickel Plated, 4 x 3 x 3 In.	69.00
Safe, Mrs. O'Leary, SBCCA Convention, Cast Iron, 2003, 4 ½ In.	45.00
Safe, P.A. Stern Clothier, One Price, Cast Iron, Regent Mfg., Chicago, 4 x 2 ⅝ x 2 ¾ In.	2600.00
Safe, Policeman, Holding Billyclub, Cast Iron, Painted, J.M. Harper, M 162, 5 ¼ In.	1750.00
Safe, Roller Safe, Roller Skaters, Key Lock, Cast Iron, Kyser & Rex, c.1882, M 880, 4 x 3 x 2 ¾ In.	205.00
Safe, Santa Claus With Pack, White, Red, Gold, Cast Iron, Harper, M 63, 4 ⅛ In.	2700.00
Safe, Security, Red, Black, Cast Iron, M 889, 4 ½ In.	110.00
Sailor, Standing, Saluting, White, Blue, Peach, Cast Iron, Hubley, c.1905, M 29, 5 ⅝ In.	310.00
Satchel, Bronze Over Cast Iron, Handle, Embossed Plaque, M 1268, 3 ⅜ x 5 ¾ In.	575.00
Save For The Day He Returns, Military Men, In Glass Bubble, Cardboard, Wood, 6 In.	175.00
Save For Your Sunny Suds, Record Player, Brass, Footed, M 824, 4 ½ In.	60.00
Sewing Machine, Singer, Black, Brown, Tin, M 1369, 5 ⅛ In.	310.00
Sharecropper, Black, Red, Gold Paint, Cast Iron, A.C. Williams, M 173, 5 ½ In.	145.00
Sinclair Gas Pump, Tin, 4 In.	55.00
Skookum The Indian, Glass	350.00
Speedy Alka Seltzer, Vinyl, Painted, 1960s, 5 ½ In.	115.00
Steamboat, Wheels, Cast Iron, Painted, M 1458, 7 ½ In.	180.00
Stop Sign, Nickel Plated, Cast Iron, Dent, c.1920s, M 1481, 5 ⅝ In.	863.00
Sundial, Embossed Top, Stand, Iron, Overall Gold, Arcade, M 1549, 4 ⁵⁄₁₆ In.	690.00
Time Safe, Iron, Painted, E.M.Roche, M 895, 7 ⅛ In.	1025.00
Turbojet, Tin Lithograph, Spring Loaded Coin Launcher, West Germany, c.1960, 7 ½ In.	157.00
Turkey, Iron, Painted, A.C. Williams, M 585, 4 ¼ In.	395.00
Turkey, Iron, Painted, A.C. Williams, M 587, 3 ½ In.	59.00 to 72.00
Uncle Sam, Glass, Screw Top, 3 ½ In. *illus*	644.00
Windmill, Brass, M 1191, 8 In.	205.00
Woman, On Chicken Coop, Ceramic, Borgfeldt, 9 ⅞ In.	72.00
Zentral Sparkasse, Sheet Metal, Copper Plate, Plunger, Key, Germany, 5 ⅛ In.	44.00

BARBER collectibles range from the popular red and white striped pole that used to be found in front of every shop to the small scissors and tools of the trade. Barber chairs are wanted, especially the older models with elaborate iron trim.

Backbar Base, Oak, 4 Drawers, Marble Top, 38 x 78 x 24 In.	255.00
Chair, Berninghaus, Flame Mahogany, Carved Shells, Spindles, Lions' Heads, c.1899, 42 x 25 In.	9600.00
Chair, Berninghaus, Hercules, Quartersawn Oak, Green Leather Upholstery, c.1903, 43 x 23 In. .	3000.00
Chair, Booster Seat, Adjustable Sides, Child's, 7 x 27 In.	420.00
Chair, Buick Pedal Car, Koch-Chicago, Green Body, Leather Upholstery, c.1926, Child's, 52 x 23 In.	6000.00
Chair, Child's, Fluted White Porcelain, Red Leather Upholstery, 1920, 44 x 19 In.	2520.00
Chair, Harley-Davidson, Chrome Plated, Black Leather Upholstery, Patches, 1920s, 39 x 24 In.	4200.00
Chair, Horse, Plastic, Galaxy, 41 ½ In.	770.00
Chair, Horse's Head, Yellow Frame, Red Leather Seat, Child's, 46 x 21 In.	915.00
Chair, Kern, Quartersawn Oak, Leather, Metal, 4-Footed, Late 1800s	4256.00
Chair, Kline, White Porcelain, Black Tufted Leather Upholstery, c.1912, 42 x 24 In.	840.00
Chair, Koken, Green Porcelain, Dark Green Upholstery, 47 x 29 In. *illus*	330.00
Chair, Koken, Horse's Head, Brown, Blue, White, Porcelain, Wood, 44 ¾ x 20 x 31 In.	3100.00
Chair, Koken, Hydraulic, Leather Seat, Back, Cast Iron, Porcelain, 42 In.	57.00
Chair, Koken, Mahogany, Red Velvet Upholstery, Headrest, c.1880, 43 x 27 In., 2 Piece	660.00
Chair, Koken, Quartersawn Oak, Round Seat, Back, Blue Leather Upholstery, c.1908, 43 x 24 In. .	4800.00
Chair, Koken, White, Black, Salesman's Sample, 16 ¼ x 14 In.	11500.00
Chair, Mahogany, Tufted Leather, Carved Seashells, Spindles, Lions' Heads, c.1899	8000.00
Chair, Oak, Button Tufted Leather Upholstery, Nickel Plated Trim, c.1908, 43 x 24 In.	4000.00
Chair, Pedal Car Style, Flame Decoration, Adjustable, Child's, 44 x 24 In. *illus*	825.00
Coat Rack, Koken, Wood, Shelf, Fluted White Porcelain Base, 10 Hooks, 1920s, 88 In.	3000.00
Counter, Display Case, Oak, 16 x 15 x 10 In.	240.00
Finger Bowl, Red Stars, Stripes, Opalescent Cranberry, Smooth Base, c.1900, 2 ¾ In.	518.00
Mirror, Shaving, Red & White Candy-Striped Enameled Stand, 2-Sided	30.00
Pole, Brass Column, Finials, Cast Iron, Electric, James Barker, c.1911, 81 x 12 In.	6600.00
Pole, Harley-Davidson, Wall Mount, Orange, Black, Fluted Bottom, Koken, 1928, 34 x 9 In.	1200.00
Pole, Painted, Red, White, Blue, Iron Attachments, c.1900, 57 In. *illus*	441.00
Pole, Porcelain, Red, White, Leaded Slag Glass, Electric, Wall Mount, Koken, c.1920, 33 In.	515.00
Pole, Porcelain, White & Blue, Wall Mount, Kline, c.1914, 42 x 11 In.	900.00
Pole, Red, White, Blue, Revolves, Gold Top, Windup, Atwater, Chicago, Cyclo, 84 x 20 In.	9000.00
Pole, Red, White, Blue, Wall Mounted, c.1920, 49 x 11 In.	345.00
Pole, Walnut, Hanging Slot, Painted, c.1900, 55 In. *illus*	823.00

Pole, Wood, Black, White, Gilt Acorn Finial, Iron Brackets, 36 In., Pair	2370.00
Pole, Wood, Red & White, Ball Finial, 23 In.	220.00
Pole, Wood, Red & White, Gold Finial, 62 ¾ In.	330.00
Pole, Wood, Red & White Spiral, Black Stepped Base, Acorn Finial, Turned, 69 x 5 In.	605.00
Pole, Wood, Red & White Stripes, Blue, Gold, Ball Top & Bottom, 19th Century, 44 In.	840.00
Pole, Wood, Red, Blue, Gilt, Turned, Acorn Finial, Wood Stand, 36 In.	326.00
Pole, Wood, Red, White, Blue, Ball Finial, 48 In.	165.00
Pole, Wood, Red, White, Blue, Ball Finial, 78 ¼ In.	372.00
Pole, Wood, Red, White, Blue, Gold Ball, c.1860-1910, 74 In.	440.00
Pole, Wood, Red, White, Blue, Spiral, Painted, 31 ½ In.	195.00
Pole, Wood, Red, White, Blue, Turned, Painted, 1800s, 44 In.	840.00
Pole, Wrought Iron, Wood, 41 In.	565.00
Pole, Zinc, Red, White, Removable Wood Finial, c.1860, 58 In.	1528.00
Rack, Shaving Mug, Mahogany, 6 Rows, 24 Slots, 38 x 26 ¾ In.	138.00
Rack, Shaving Mug, Mission-Style, Grain Paint, 5 Rows, 20 Slots, 33 ¼ x 24 ½ In.	146.00
Rack, Shaving Mug, Oak, 5 Rows, 10 Slots, 38 ½ x 43 In.	146.00
Rack, Shaving Mug, Walnut, 5 Rows, 25 Slots, 33 ½ x 29 ¼ In.	118.00
Shaving Brush, Butterscotch, Bakelite, Stand, Signed, Ever-Ready, 4 In.	95.00
Shaving Kit, Celluloid, Horsehair Brush, Porcelain Mustache Cup, Enameled Box................	315.00
Sign, Barber Shop, Red, White, Blue, Porcelain, Curved, 24 x 16 In.	250.00
Sign, Barber Shop, Stripes, Porcelain, Flange, William Marvy Sign Co., 12 x 24 In.	200.00
Sign, Straight Razor, Black, Gold Paint, Thos. Parry Mark, c.1880, 68 In.	2938.00
Sink, Victorian, Walnut Cabinet, White Marble Top, Faucet, 1880s, 34 x 24 x 24 In.	3900.00
Steamer, Hot Towel, Vulcan, 57 x 20 In.	330.00

BAROMETERS are used to forecast the weather. Antique barometers with elaborate wooden cases and brass trim are the most desirable. Mercury column barometers are also popular with collectors. It is difficult to find someone to repair a broken one, so be sure your barometer is in working condition.

Admiral Fitzroy, Storm, Glass, Carved, Victorian, Oak, Round Dial, Tubes, 1800s, 47 In.	649.00
Aneroid, C-Scroll, Rocaille, Swagged Tablet, Carved, Gilt, 38 x 17 In.	115.00
Aneroid, Renaissance Revival, Oak, Carved, Porcelain Dial, 19th Century, 36 In.	450.00
Aneroid, Rope Carved, Wood, 19th Century, 8 In. Diam.	115.00
Aneroid, Wood, Beveled Glass, Gischard, Germany, c.1920, 5 In.	45.00
Angle, Walnut, Inverted L-Shape, Thomas Cotterell, George I, 34 x 29 In.	9150.00
Banjo, Bestendig, Art Nouveau, Mahogany, 22 ½ In.	175.00
Banjo, F. Karn, Ampthill, Mahogany, Hygrometer, Spirit Level, c.1840, 42 In.	169.00
Banjo, G. Copini, Shoreditch, Clock, Thermometer, Hygrometer, Spirit Level, c.1860, 43 In. ...	394.00
Banjo, M. Pius Drescher, Rosewood, Victorian, 36 In.	230.00
Banjo, Mahogany Inlay, Lione & Co., England, 38 In.	138.00
Banjo, Pendant Base, Inlaid, England, 19th Century, 43 x 12 In. ....*illus*	299.00
Banjo, Thermometer, Hygrometer, Silvered Scale, c.1860, 38 In.	242.00
Banjo, Thermometer, L. Cerlett, Mahogany, 19th Century, 39 In.	240.00
Banjo, Thermometer, Regency, Mahogany, Inlaid, 3 Urn Finials, 2 Dials, Adamson, 46 In.	805.00
Bernasconi, Merthry, Mahogany Wheel, Swan Neck Pediment, Hygrometer, c.1830, 40 In.	353.00
Brass, Coles, Germany, 9 In. Diam.	60.00
Chaillou, Black Forest, Carved, Boar's Head, Game Birds, Enameled, 1800s, 28 In. ....*illus*	403.00
Chelsea, Holosteric, Silver Dial, Brass, 10 In. Diam.	460.00
G. Schliavetti, Mahogany, Inlaid Flowers, Shells, Silvered Faces, England, c.1825, 28 In.	206.00
George III, Mahogany Inlaid Pinstripe, Scrolled Arch, c.1800, 44 In.	360.00
Mahogany, Thermometer, Hygrometer, Wheel, c.1830, 38 In.	1093.00
Marine, Brass, Fortin, Gimbals, England, c.1900, 36 In.	353.00
Marine, Mahogany, Gimbals, Brass, c.1900, 36 In.	1116.00
Nautical, Napoleon III, Giltwood, Carved, Shell, 45 x 5 ½ In.	1560.00
Pini & Co., Figure 8 Shape, London, 38 In.	472.00
Pocket, Brass, Leather Case, Round, England, c.1890, 3 In.	375.00
Regency, Mahogany, Wheel, Swan Neck, Brass Finial, c.1830, 51 x 14 ⅜ In.	1792.00
Stick, Casella & Tagliabue, Mahogany, Inscribed, London, c.1800, 37 ½ In.	1170.00
Stick, CG Gibbard, Brass, Walnut Tall Case, Marked, 40 In.	1035.00
Stick, D.L. Lent, Mahogany, Metal Face, Applied Molding, Rochester, Late 1800s, 36 ¼ In.	470.00
Stick, Jn. Russell, Mahogany, Fluted Column, Brass Capital, Falkirk, c.1800, 41 In.	11162.00
Stick, Mahogany, Bone Scale, Sliding Vernier, Wood Leather, 37 In.	770.00
Stick, Mahogany, Broken Arch Pediment, Silver Face, England, c.1820, 38 ½ In.	805.00
Stick, Mahogany, Crest, Brass Finial, Silver Dial, Long Waist, 1800s, 39 In.	649.00
Stick, Mahogany, Ivory, Mercury, Huddleston, Boston, 36 In.	1438.00
Stick, Thermometer, Hygrometer, Mahogany, Swan Neck Pediment, Mirror, 44 x 12 In.	1058.00

Barber, Pole, Walnut, Hanging Slot, Painted, c.1900, 55 In.
$823.00

Barometer, Banjo, Pendant Base, Inlaid, England, 19th Century, 43 x 12 In.
$299.00

As always, the edited listings in *Kovels' Antiques & Collectibles Price Guide 2011* aren't available on any website, but readers should visit Kovels.com for information on trends, tips, reproductions, marks, old prices, and more!

Barometer, Chaillou, Black Forest, Carved, Boar's Head, Game Birds, Enameled, 1800s, 28 In. $403.00

Basket, Cheese, Splint, Hexagonal Holes, 6 ¼ x 20 ½ In. $232.00

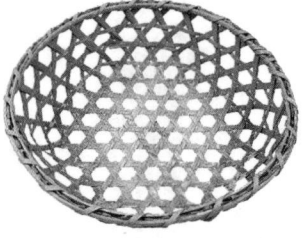

TIP

Splint baskets should have an occasional light shower. Shake off the excess water. Dry the basket in a shady spot.

Stick, Thermometer, Milk Glass Plate, Enamel Dial, Early 1900s, 38 In.	441.00
Thermometer, Clock, Hygrometer, Chelsea, Mahogany, Inlay, 1900s, 38 ½ In.	475.00
Thermometer, French Empire Style, Beechwood, Centigrade, c.1810, 52 x 6 In.	1050.00
Thermometer, Louis XVI Style, Musical, Instrument, Gilt, 46 x 19 In.	996.00
Thermometer, R. Field, Mahogany, Scroll Pediment, Brass Finial, England, 1800s, 41 In.	212.00
Thermometer, Rosewood, Mother-Of-Pearl Inlay, Spade Form Crest, 40 ½ x 12 ½ In.	480.00
Thermometer, Stick, Benjamin Pike & Sons, Rosewood, Arch, Engraved, c.1890, 36 In.	3555.00
Thermometer, Stick, Gothic, Walnut, Carved, Finials, B. Pike & Son, c.1850, 47 x 8 In.	3819.00
Thermometer, Stick, Mahogany, Arched Crest, Sliding Vernier, C, Wilder, c.1860, 37 In.	563.00
Thermometer, Timby's, Rosewood, 2 Oval Glasses, Patent, Nov. 3, 1857, 4 x 40 In.	460.00
Wheel, Mahogany, Broken Arch Pediment, String Inlay, Early 1800s, 37 ¾ In.	264.00
Wheel, Selva, Mahogany Veneer, Inlaid, Pediment, Medallions, Early 1800s, 38 ½ In.	646.00
Wood, Carved Scrolls, Painted, Baroque, Italy, c.1930, 36 In.	614.00

BASALT is a special type of ceramic invented by Josiah Wedgwood in the eighteenth century. It is a fine-grained, unglazed stoneware. Some pieces are listed in that section. The most common type is black, but many other colors were made. It was made by many factories. Some pieces are listed in the Wedgwood section.

Cup & Saucer, Basket Weave, Black, Pair	45.00
Jug, Sacrifice Figures, Rope Handle, Black, c.1891, 6 x 4 ¾ In.	750.00
Pitcher, Black, Rope Handle, c.1930, 4 x 5 In.	95.00
Plate, Mother & Child, Black, Urn, Early 20th Century, 6 ¼ In.	100.00
Teapot, Pear Shape, Figural Finial, Seated Woman, Widow Of Zerepath, Black, c.1840, 5 ½ In.	350.00
Vase, Jar Shape, Concentric Circles, Black, c.1928, 4 ¼ x 5 In.	175.00

BASEBALL *collectibles are in the Sports category, except for baseball cards, which are listed under Baseball in the Card category.*

BASKETS of all types are popular with collectors. American Indian, Japanese, African, Shaker, and many other kinds of baskets can be found. Of course, baskets are still being made, so the collector must learn to tell the age and style of the basket to determine the value.

Arschbacke, Butte, Oak, Splint, Loop Handles, Lattice, 3 ½ x 4 ¼ x 4 In.	57.00
Arschbacke, Oak Splint, Loop Handle, Brown Patina, 7 x 9 x 7 In.	28.00
Bentwood, Overlapping Seams, Swing Handle, Blue Paint, c.1890, 7 In.	911.00
Buttocks, Splint, Fixed Loop Handle, 12 ½ x 14 x 12 In.	55.00
Buttocks, Splint, Oak, Carved Bentwood Handle, Braided Design, 9 x 9 In.	44.00
Buttocks, Splint, Oak, Oval, Carved Bentwood Handle & Rim, 9 x 12 x 11 In.	66.00
Buttocks, Splint, Oak, Wide Handle, Band, Early 20th Century, 9 ½ x 10 In.	55.00
Cheese, Splint, Hexagonal Holes, 6 ¼ x 20 ½ In. ....*illus*	232.00
Comb, Decorated, Maine, 11 x 10 x 4 In.	375.00
Egg, Hickory, Splint, Carved Handle, c.1900, 11 In.	72.00
Field, Splint, Ash, Taconic, Double Wrapped, Strap Handle, 13 x 17 In.	175.00
Field, Splint, Cone Shape, Open Hand Grips, Brown Patina, 14 ½ x 12 In.	209.00
Field, Splint, Oak, Convex Bottom, Swing Handle, Brown Patina, 8 ½ In.	192.00
Field, Splint, Oak, Loop Handle, Patina, 11 x 13 In.	68.00
Field, Splint, Oak, Round, Conical Interior Bottom, Carved Bentwood Handle, 14 x 21 In.	110.00
Field, Splint, Oak, Round, Woven, Hand Grips, 10 ½ x 22 In.	45.00
Fish, Splint Reed, 16 ¾ In.	35.00
Gathering, Bentwood Handles, Green Paint, c.1890, 13 x 19 In. ....*illus*	411.00
Gathering, Splint, Carved Upright Handle, Oval, Painted, c.1890, 12 ½ In.	652.00
Gathering, Splint, Oak, Handles, 19th Century, 14 ¼ x 20 ¾ In.	150.00
Gathering, Splint, Oak, Orange, Red, Natural, Signed, Lillian Thompson, 11 x 8 ½ In.	44.00
Gathering, Splint, Oak, Vegetable, Handle, 3 Bands, 12 x 15 x 25 In.	165.00
Gathering, Splint, Rectangular, Bentwood Handles, 8 ½ x 19 ¼ In.	88.00
Gathering, Splint, White, Oval, Open Hand Grips, 7 ½ x 28 ¼ x 18 ¼ In.	66.00
Hamper, Heywood-Wakefield, Wicker, Cover, Green Bands, Ring Handles, 1920s, 28 x 20 In.	374.00
Intricate Handles, Japan, 15 x 10 In.	780.00
Market, Splint, Fixed Loop Handle, Brown Patina, 14 ½ x 13 ½ x 14 ½ In.	44.00
Market, Splint, Oak, God's Eyes Attachment, Carved & Bentwood Handle, 11 x 17 x 11 In.	358.00
Market, Splint, Oak, Stained.Bentwood Handle, 11 x 14 ½ x 11 In.	100.00
Mounted On Stand, Mortise & Pin Construction, Carved Legs, Painted, c.1900, 25 x 28 x 15 In.	206.00
Nantucket, Carved Heart Staves, Woven Loops, 1910, 3 ½ x 7 ½ In.	17400.00
Nantucket, Lightship, Swing Handle, 8 Incised Rings, Turned Wood Base, Signed, 6 x 9 In.	875.00
Nantucket, Lightship, Swing Handle, Turned Wood, Incised Rings, Patina, Signed, 6 x 9 In.	275.00
Nantucket, Oval, Lightship, Swing Handle, Wood Base, Brass Pin, 11 In.	2632.00

Nantucket, Purse, Friendship, Oval, Woven Cane, Hinged, Sailboats, 1965, 5 x 9 ½ In.	2015.00
Nantucket, Purse, Woven Cane, Splint, Ivory Seagull, Walnut Plaque, 1975, 10 ⅜ x 10 ⅝ In.	474.00
Nantucket, Purse, Woven Cane, Splint, Swing Handle, Ivory Seal, 7 ⅛ x 9 ¼ In.	1659.00
Nantucket, Round, Brass Pins, Freeman, 6 ⅜ In.	863.00
Nantucket, Swing Handle, Bird Carving On Lid, Signed, Formose Rey, 1974, 10 ½ x 10 x 8 In.	3300.00
Nantucket, Swing Handle, Nut Brown, Engraved Plaque, A.D. Williams, 1918, 5 x 5 ½ In.	36800.00
Oval, Twisted Handle, 13 x 25 In.	47.00
Paper, Paper Cord, Mary Merkell Hess, Campana, Signed, 23 ¼ x 23 ½ In.	2440.00
Papyrus, Red, Yellow, Blue, Natural, Roll Rim, Cord Style Handles, 14 ¾ x 15 In.	33.00
Picnic, Splint, Double Hinged Cover, Fixed Handle, 12 x 10 ½ x 10 ¼ In.	66.00
Regency, Black, Gold Pen, Brushwork, Swing Handle, England, 3 ½ x 8 ½ x 5 ¼ In.	720.00
Round, Wood, Cover, Carved, Double Handles, Gilt Decoration, Chinese, 18 x 13 In.	35.00
Splint, 2 Carved Side, Handles, Woven, Twilled Medial Band, Oblong, 6 ½ x 12 ½ In.	148.00
Splint, Ash, Bentwood Handle, 2 x 17 x 10 In.	100.00
Splint, Ash, Handle, Oval, 19th Century, 12 x 16 In.	120.00
Splint, Ash, Woven, Market, Swing Handles, 8 x 14 x 19 In.	68.00
Splint, Bentwood Handle, Blue Paint, c.1900, 9 ½ In.	441.00
Splint, Blue Paint, Copper Rivets, 15 In.	790.00
Splint, Carved Swing Handle, Black Paint, c.1880, 9 ½ In.	830.00
Splint, Carved Swing Handle, Green Paint, 1800s, 18 In.	2489.00
Splint, Carved Swing Handle, Mustard Paint, Round, c.1890, 10 ½ x 16 In.	593.00
Splint, Cone Shape, Fixed Loop Handle, Brown Patina, 19 ½ x 6 x 4 ¼ In.	66.00
Splint, Cover, Green, Handles, New England, c.1900, 21 ½ In.	178.00
Splint, Cover, Overall Projections, Red, Yellow, Green, Black Paint, Round, 7 x 10 In.	237.00
Splint, Cover, Yellow, Deep Blue, Early 20th Century, 11 x 14 In. ....illus	82.00
Splint, God's-Eyes Weave, Loop Handle, Twisted Straw Banding, 4 ½ x 7 x 5 ½ In.	339.00
Splint, Green Paint, Fixed Loop Handle, 4 x 3 ½ In.	187.00
Splint, Oak, 100 Ribs, Handle, Shelton Baskets, North Carolina, c.1915, 6 ½ x 5 ¾ In.	5500.00
Splint, Oak, Bentwood Handle, Sled-Runner Base, White Paint, 17 In.	690.00
Splint, Oak, Corn, Stave Construction, Double Loop Handles, 16 x 19 In.	198.00
Splint, Oak, Fixed Loop Handle, 4 ½ x 5 x 4 ½ In.	34.00
Splint, Oak, Fixed Loop Handle, Honey Brown Patina, 19th Century, 2 ½ x 3 ¼ x 3 In.	593.00
Splint, Oak, Handles, White Paint, Late 19th Century, 16 x 31 In.	265.00
Splint, Oak, Notched Bentwood Handle, Round Rim, Square Base, 8 ¼ x 7 ¼ x 7 In.	28.00
Splint, Oak, Oval, 20th Century, 13 x 15 x 12 ½ In.	316.00
Splint, Oak, Ribbed, Oval, Dome Bottom, Open Weave Handles, Bentwood Rim, 5 ¾ x 19 x 15 In.	132.00
Splint, Oak, Split Ribs, Weavers, Shaped Hickory Rim, Oval, 10 x 37 x 29 In. ....illus	288.00
Splint, Pine, Oval, Painted, Double Lids, Hinged, Flat Board Bottom, 17 In.	1265.00
Splint, Rattan, Copper Rivets, Carved Wood Swing Handles, c.1890, 10 In.	948.00
Splint, Rectangular, Red, Black Painted Rim, Carved Upright Handles, 1800s, 10 x 17 In.	889.00
Splint, Red, White, Blue, Fixed Loop Handle, 13 x 13 x 12 ½ In.	2090.00
Splint, Round, Domed Center, Carved Wood Handle, Yellow, Red Paint, c.1890, 8 x 12 In.	1541.00
Splint, Round Over Square, Upright Handle, Red Paint, 1800s, 4 ½ In.	1007.00
Splint, Round, Wood Base, 36 Wood Pegs, Fastener, Carved Handles, 1800s, 4 In.	533.00
Splint, Swing Handle, Cone Shape, 2 Bentwood Handle Supports, 14 In.	55.00
Splint, Wide Fixed Handle, Brown Patina, 6 x 6 In. ....illus	377.00
Splint, Wide Loop Handle, Brown Patina, 2 x 2 ¼ x 2 In.	468.00
Splint, Wide Loop Handle, Brown Patina, 6 x 6 In.	358.00
Split Weave, Wood Backing, White Paint, Galvanized Insert, France, 21 x 18 In.	450.00
Storage, Splint, Oak, Brown Patina, 15 x 24 x 35 In.	158.00
Straw, Coiled, Round, Open Weave Handles, 6 ½ x 18 ½ In.	16.00
Taconic, Swing Handle, 19th Century, 13 In. Diam.	110.00
Twig, Painted, Red, Blue, 11 ½ x 22 ½ In.	147.00
Wastebasket, River Cane, Rowena Bradley, Diamond Pattern, Qualla, 1981 15 x 14 In.	863.00

Basket, Gathering, Bentwood Handles, Green Paint, c.1890, 13 x 19 In. $411.00

Basket, Splint, Cover, Yellow, Deep Blue, Early 20th Century, 11 x 14 In. $82.00

Basket, Splint, Oak, Split Ribs, Weavers, Shaped Hickory Rim, Oval, 10 x 37 x 29 In. $288.00

Basket, Splint, Wide Fixed Handle, Brown Patina, 6 x 6 In. $377.00

BATCHELDER products are made from California clay. Ernest Batchelder established a tile studio in Pasadena, California, in 1909. He went into partnership with Frederick Brown in 1912 and the company became Batchelder and Brown. In 1920 he built a larger factory with a new partner. The Batchelder-Wilson Company made all types of architectural tiles, garden pots, and bookends. The plant closed in 1932. In 1936 Batchelder opened Batchelder Ceramics, also in Pasadena, and made bowls, vases, and earthenware pots. He retired in 1951 and died in 1957. Pieces are marked *Batchelder Pasadena* or *Batchelder Los Angeles*.

BATCHELDER
LOS ANGELES

Tile, 3 Checkered Flowers, Urn, Tan Matte Glaze, Blue Engobe, c.1920, 5 ¾ x 5 ¾ In.	180.00
Tile, Dog & Tree, Brown & Blue Matte Glaze, c.1920, 5 ¾ x 5 ¾ In.	355.00
Tile, Flower & Buds, Diamond, Brown & Blue Matte Glaze, c.1920, 3 ¾ x 3 ¾ In.	95.00
Tile, Geometric, Patina, Glazed, 1920s, 1 ¾ x 1 ¾ In.	20.00

Batman, Comic Book, No. 42, 3-D, 1953 Reprint, 3-D Glasses, c.1966, 8 ½ x 11 In. $316.00

Batman, Toy, Batmobile, Bump & Go Action, Battery Operated, AHI Inc., Box, c.1972, 11 ½ In. $459.00

Bauer, Cal-Art, Candlestick, 3-Light, Matte $71.00

Bauer, Ring, Mixing Bowl, Yellow, No. 36, 2 ¾ x 5 ⅜ In. $16.00

Tile, Landscape, Trees, Rolling Hills, Brown & Blue Matte Glaze, 3 ¾ x 3 ¾ In.	125.00
Tile, Mythical Bird, Gray To Beige Matte Glaze, Blue Engobe, Frame, c.1920, 5 ⅞ x 5 ⅞ In.	365.00
Tile, Patina, Brown, Glaze, 1920s, 1 ¾ x 1 ¾ In.	20.00
Tile, Reticulated Grill, Butterfat Glaze, 1930s, 9 x 9 In.	450.00

BATMAN and Robin are characters from a comic strip by Bob Kane that started in 1939. In 1966, the characters became part of a popular television series. There have been radio and movie serials that featured the pair. The first full-length movie was made in 1989.

Book, Batwoman, Kathy Kane & The Boy Wonder, You Truly Are A Boy Wonder, 1950s, 8 Pages	115.00
Comic Book, Batman Fighting Klan Knight, 1989, 10 ¼ In., 55 Pages	34.00
Comic Book, No. 42, 3-D, 1953 Reprint, 3-D Glasses, c.1966, 8 ½ x 11 In. ....*illus*	316.00
Comic Book, No. 119	230.00
Comic Book, No. 135	1380.00
Comic Book, No. 142	167.00
Lobby Card, Robin, New Adventures, Serial, Tunnel Of Terror, c.1949, 11 x 14 In.	209.00
Pin, I Am A Batman Crimefighter, Batman, Robin, Crimefighters, 1 ⅜ In.	17.00
Poster, Movie, Robin, Batman Leaping Toward Villain, 14 x 21 ½ In.	202.00
Puppet, Vinyl, Ideal, Box, 1966	225.00
Toy, Batball, Rack Card, Gravity Defying, National Latex Products, c.1966, 4 x 7 ½ In.	253.00
Toy, Batmobile, Blue, Yellow, Silver Decals, BZ RTR, c.1966, 7 ¾ In.	748.00
Toy, Batmobile, Bump & Go Action, Battery Operated, AHI Inc., Box, c.1972, 11 ½ In. .....*illus*	459.00
Toy, Shooting Range, Encased Arcade, B-B Gun, Marx, Box, c.1966, 8 x 21 ½ In.	345.00

BATTERSEA enamels, which are enamels painted on copper, were made in the Battersea district of London from about 1750 to 1756. Many similar enamels are mistakenly called Battersea.

Candlestick, Flowers, Gilt, 18th Century, 10 ¾ In., Pair	385.00
Pill Box, Motto On Lid, Wish Of An Englishman, Enamel, Blue Wreath, c.1800, 2 In.	2750.00
Pill Box, Peach Form, White, Red, Pink, Enamel, 18th Century, 1 ¾ x 1 ½ In.	1600.00

BAUER pottery is a California-made ware. J.A. Bauer bought Paducah Pottery in Paducah, Kentucky, in 1885. He moved the pottery to Los Angeles, California, in 1909. The company made art pottery after 1912 and dinnerwares marked *Bauer* in 1930. The factory went out of business in 1962. See also the Russel Wright category.

Cal-Art, Candlestick, 3-Light, Matte ....*illus*	71.00
Monterey Moderne, Casserole, Cover, 1 ½ Qt.	30.00
Ring, Mixing Bowl, Yellow, No. 36, 2 ¾ x 5 ⅜ In. ....*illus*	16.00

BAVARIA is a region in Europe where many types of porcelain were made. In the nineteenth century, the mark often included the word *Bavaria*. After 1871, the words *Bavaria, Germany*, were used. Listed here are pieces that include the name *Bavaria* in some form, but major porcelain makers, such as Rosenthal, are listed in their own categories.

Bowl, Dresden Wreaths, Reticulated, Scalloped Rim, Schumann, 12 x 8 ½ In.	64.00
Cake Plate, Violets, Leaves, Vines, Gold Accents, 10 In.	129.00
Centerpiece, 4 Cherubs Supporting Dish, Applied Flowers, Leaves, 5 x 9 In.	263.00
Charger, Dresden Flowers, Reticulated Border, Scalloped, Schumann, 1918-29, 11 ⅜ In.	125.00
Container, Milk, Condensed, Lid, Flowers, Gilt, Blue, Handles, 5 ½ In.	41.00
Container, Milk, Condensed, Lid, Pink Roses, White Ground, Gilt, Handles, 5 ½ In.	24.00
Cup & Saucer, Cream Soup, Double Handles, Pink Roses, Gilt Rim, Marked, c.1902	30.00
Cup & Saucer, Demitasse, Roses, Daises, Gilt Trim, 2 ¼ x 2 ½ & 4 ½ In.	15.00
Cup & Saucer, Dessert Plate, White Ground, Roses, Gilt Trim, 2 ⅜ x 4 & 5 ⅝ In.	25.00
Cup & Saucer, Roses, Blue & Red, Gold, White Ground, 1945-49	27.00
Dresser Box, Figural, Woman With Dog, Dressel Kister, 5 ½ In.	450.00
Hair Receiver, Red Rose, Painted, Green & Cream, Scalloped Rim, 4 In.	25.00
Pitcher, Roses, Leaves, Ruffled Edge, Gold Rim, 4 ¼ x 5 ¾ In.	25.00
Plate, Cobalt Blue, Scalloped Edges, Transfer, Gold, White Handles, 1800s, 10 x 11 In.	75.00
Plate, Yolanda, Pink Roses, Gold Trim, Leaves, Edelstein, c.1934, 6 In.	28.00
Salt, Flowers, Gold Trim, c.1920, 3 ¾ In.	35.00
Salt, Lusterware, Gold Trim, Handles, Signed, 2 ½ In.	7.00
Salt, Round, White, Mint Green, Gold Scrolls, 3 Footed, 1 x 1 ¾ In.	10.00
Serving Dish, Flowers, Pink, Yellow & Blue, Gold Rim, Handles, 10 ½ In.	42.00
Serving Dish, Pink Roses Wreaths, Green Linked Chain, Marked, 2 ¼ x 10 In.	15.00
Shaker, Dogwood, Blue Ground, Painted, Marked, Victorian	33.00
Sugar, Cover, Autumn, Colored Leaves, Gold Trim	45.00

BEADED BAGS *are included in the Purse category.*

BEATLES collectors search for any items picturing the four members of the famous music group or any of their recordings. Because these items are so new, the condition is very important and top prices are paid only for items in mint condition. The Beatles first appeared on American network television in 1964. The group disbanded in 1971. Ringo Starr and Paul McCartney are still performing. John Lennon died in 1980. George Harrison died in 2001.

Album Cover, Christmas, Fan Club Release, 1970	434.00
Album Cover, Mono LP, Germany, 1964	299.00
Album Cover, Wedding Album, John Lennon, 1969	299.00
Album Cover, White Album, Sealed, 1968	1195.00
Beach Hat, Cotton, Portraits, Signatures, Blue & White, Red & White, Medium, 7 x 9 In., Pair	158.00
Button, John Lennon, Yellow Submarine, Red, Green, Blue, Black, 3 In.	28.00
Button, The 4 Portraits, Gray, White, Celluloid, 3 In.	42.00
Button, The 4 Portraits, Names, Black, White, Red, Celluloid, 3 In.	31.00
Button, Yesterday & Today, Banned Album Cover, 4 Singers, Butchered Dolls, 2 ⅛ In.	72.00
Disk-Go-Case, Plastic, Holds 45-RPM Records, Charter Industries, c.1966, 7 x 8 In. ......*illus*	313.00
Doll Set, John, Paul, George, Ringo, Seltaeb, NEMS Ltd., 1964, 4 Piece	183.00
Handbill, Empire Theatre, Liverpool, 1963	1434.00
Handbill, Heswall Jazz Club, Liverpool, 1962	1912.00
Handbill, Odeon Concert, Leeds, England, 1960s	1963.00
Kaboodle Kit, Tan, Facsimile Signatures, Vinyl, Standard Plastic, c.1964 ......*illus*	380.00
Lithograph, John Lennon, This Is My Story Both Humble & True, Taste, Signed, 10 ¾ x 14 ¾ In.	470.00
Lunch Box, John, Paul, George, Ringo, Metal, Thermos, NEMS Lid, 1965	295.00
Magazine, Beatle Mania, Color Photos, No. 1, 50 Cent	55.00
Ornament Trio, Glass, Painted, Portraits, Glitter Jackets, 1964, 3 ½ In.	379.00
Pennant, Caricatured Images, Felt, Orange, Black, American Flag Co., c.1964, 30 In.	230.00
Record, Magical Tours, 33 RPM, 1968	17.70
Record, Yesterday & Today, 33 RPM, 1966	65.00
Street Sign, Abbey Road, Westminster, England	5976.00
Ticket, Concert, Japan, Unused, 1966	956.00
Ticket, Concert, Shea Stadium, 8/23/66	448.00
Ticket, Concert, Suffolk Downs, Boston, 8/18/66, Framed With Beverage Cup, Lips	236.00
Tin, With The Beatles, Talcum Powder, Lithograph, Plastic Dispenser, Margo Of Mayfair, c.1964, 7 ½ In.	403.00
Tour Book, Paul McCartney, 1989	765.00
Toy, Guitar, John, Paul, George, Ringo, Logo, Plastic, Selcol, England, 23 In.	590.00
Wall Hanging, Facsimile Signatures, Guitar & Drum Border, Linen, 20 x 30 In. ......*illus*	115.00

BEEHIVE, Austria, or Beehive, Vienna, are terms used in English-speaking countries to refer to the many types of decorated porcelain bearing a mark that looks like a beehive. The mark is actually a shield, viewed upside down. It was first used in 1744 by the Royal Porcelain Manufactory of Vienna. The firm made what collectors call Royal Vienna porcelains until it closed in 1864. Many other German, Austrian, and Japanese factories have reproduced Royal Vienna wares, complete with the original shield or beehive mark. This listing includes the expensive, original Royal Vienna porcelains and many other types of beehive porcelain. The Royal Vienna pieces include that name in the description.

Bowl, Venus Spielt Mi Game, Blue, Gilt, Scalloped Rim, Handles, Royal Vienna, c. 1890, 11 x 6 In.	2400.00
Bowl, Yellow, Red, Wild Flowers, Gold Border, Medallion Scenes, Royal Vienna, 10 ¼ In. *illus*	100.00
Box, Woman's Portrait, Cobalt Blue, Gold Highlights, Mark, Royal Vienna, 6 In.	230.00
Case, Portrait, Emilene, Gilt Handles, Foot, Royal Vienna, 14 ½ In.	915.00
Charger, Roman Garden Scene, Gilt, Swirling Leaf, Royal Vienna, 16 ½ In.	1495.00
Ewer, Undertray, Scenic, Paris & Helen, Beehive Mark, Royal Vienna, 8 x 7 ¼ In.	219.00
Figurine, Boy, Sled, Multicolored, Royal Vienna, c.1900, 5 ¾ In.	176.00
Figurine, Woman, Flowers, Goose, Grapes, Rococo Base, Royal Vienna, 5 ¾ In. ......*illus*	121.00
Lamp, Urn Shape, Scenic, Diana, Young Lovers, Royal Vienna, Early 20th Century, 19 In., Pair	1035.00
Pitcher, Chintz, Flowers, Yellow Ground, Elongated Spout, Royal Vienna, 7 x 5 In.	106.00
Pitcher, Woman, Putti Oval Portrait, Red Porcelain, Gold Scrolling, Mark, Royal Vienna, 10 In.	978.00
Plaque, 3 Fates, Painted, Pierced Gold Frame, Oval, Marked, Royal Vienna, 9 x 12 In.	2300.00
Plate, Amicitia, Cast Bronze, Flower Reticulated Holder, Royal Vienna, 14 ½ In.	110.00
Plate, Echo, Woman, In White Gown, Frame, Blue, Brown, Royal Vienna, 9 ½ In.	1380.00
Plate, Flora, Raised Gold Border, Blue Beehive Mark, Signed, Wagner, 9 ½ In.	1320.00
Plate, Gold, 8 ¼ In., Pair	1150.00
Plate, Hophen, Woman, In Dress, Ivy In Hair, Frame, Royal Vienna, 9 ½ In.	1495.00
Plate, Loreley Lingner, Raised Gold Border, Blue Beehive Mark, Royal Vienna, 9 ½ In.	1320.00
Plate, Maiden, Partially Nude, Horse, Shield Mark, Blue Underglaze, 9 ¼ In.	495.00

Beatles, Disk-Go-Case, Plastic, Holds 45-RPM Records, Charter Industries, c.1966, 7 x 8 In. $313.00

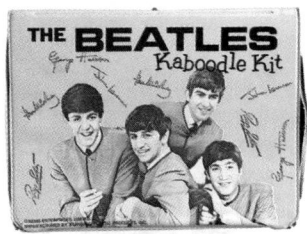

Beatles, Kaboodle Kit, Tan, Facsimile Signatures, Vinyl, Standard Plastic, c.1964 $380.00

Beatles, Wall Hanging, Facsimile Signatures, Guitar & Drum Border, Linen, 20 x 30 In. $115.00

Beehive, Bowl, Yellow, Red, **Wild Flowers**, Gold Border, Medallion Scenes, Royal Vienna, 10 ¼ In. $100.00

Beehive, Figurine, Woman, Flowers, Goose, Grapes, Rococo Base, Royal Vienna, 5 ¾ In.
$121.00

Bell, School, Iron, Yoke, Wood Stand, Stamped, C.P. & F. Bough & Co., c.1886, 27 x 30 In.
$531.00

TIP

To "uncrush" a beer can, fill it up to the top with dried split peas. Just drop them in the hole, then add water to the top. Let stand and add water again an hour later. In about three hours the swelling peas will push all the dents from the can. Remove the peas or they may keep swelling and crack the can at a weak spot. This works only if the top is on.

Plate, Marie Antoinette, In White Gown, Frame, Royal Vienna, 9 ½ In.	1380.00
Plate, Venus Und Amor, Classical Figures, Portrait Border, Gold Rim, Royal Vienna, 10 In.	732.00
Plate, Woman, Holding Violin, Blue & Gilt Border, Scrolling Leaves, Signed, Wagner, 9 ½ In.	700.00
Plate, Woman, Pink Dress, Man, Harp, Child, Landscape, Gold Flower Border, Royal Vienna, 8 ½ In.	60.00
Stein, Courting Scene, Gold Trim, Chartreuse, Eagle Finial, Marked, Royal Vienna, 3 ⅜ In.	1150.00
Stein, Friar Eating, Gold Rim, Blue Beehive Mark, Royal Vienna, 5 ½ In.	1220.00
Tray, Maiden, Playing Harp, Cobalt Blue, Gilt, Oval, Handles, Crown & Shield Mark, 12 In.	1950.00
Urn, 3 Gleaners, Cobalt Blue, Gilt Flowers, Handles, 22 ½ In.	395.00
Urn, Gilt Metal Mounts, Watteau Style Landscape, Royal Vienna, Early 1900s, 12 x 12 ½ In.	403.00
Urn, Lid, Portrait, Woman, Lyre, Purple Glaze, Gold Garlands, Handles, Royal Vienna, 12 In.	1610.00
Urn, Tankard, Mythological Scene, Jupiter, Gallisto, Jewels, Gilt, Shield Mark, 6 In.	2240.00
Urn, Woman, Cobalt Blue, Gilt, Royal Vienna, c.1900, 27 In.	835.00
Urn, Women, Seated, Blue, Gilt, Painted Vienna, Royal Vienna, 12 In.	468.00
Vase, Hoffnung & Liebling, Women Reaching Up, Siscameo, Gold, Blue Royal Vienna, 9 In., Pair	1287.00
Vase, Innocenze, Woman, Portrait, Dark Brown, Gold, Royal Vienna, 5 ¼ In.	650.00

BEER BOTTLES *are listed in the Bottle category under Beer.*

BEER CANS are a twentieth-century idea. Beer was sold in kegs or returnable bottles until 1934. The first patent for a can was issued to the American Can Company in September of that year; and Gotfried Kruger Brewing Company, Newark, New Jersey, was the first to use the can. The cone-top can was first made in 1935, the aluminum pop-top in 1962. Collectors should look for cans in good condition, with no dents or rust. Serious collectors prefer cans that have been opened from the bottom.

Apollo, Cone Top, American Brewing, White, Red, Black, Gold	3601.00
Blatz, Heileman Brewing, Milwaukee, Pull Tab, 12 Oz.	2.50
Boddingtons Pub Ale, Strangeways Brewery, Manchester, England, Pull Tab, 16 Oz.	2.95
Buckeye Sparkling Dry Beer, Cone Top, Buckeye Brewing Co. Toledo, Ohio, 1950s, 6 In.	65.00
Buckeye, Cone Top, Sparkling, Red, White, 1950s, 6 In.	65.00
Cold Spring, Cold Spring Brewery, Minnesota, 12 Oz.	2.50
Croft Cream Ale, Cone Top, Green, Yellow	3550.00
Erlangers Pilsner Beer, Cone Top, Green, Yellow, Red	6100.00
Gem State	280.00
Generic Light Beer, Falstaff Brewery, 12 Oz.	2.53
Genesee, Pull Tab, c.1970	6.00
Grain Belt Special, Cone Top, Red, Orange, Gold, 1940s, 6 In.	40.00
Heineken, Blue Can, Imported, Holland, Pull Tab, 12 Oz.	2.50
Ind Coope, Flat Top, Long Life, Beer, Steel, Imported	5.00
J.R. Beer, Dallas TV Show Character, Pearl Brewing Co., San Antonio, Texas, 1980	5.00
Kingsbury Near Beer, Heileman's Famous, Pull Tab, 12 Oz.	2.50
Kool Beer, Grace Bros. Brewing, Blue, Santa Rosa, Ca.	5000.00
Kuebler Bock Beer	1625.00
Olde Frothingslosh Fatima Yechburgh, Pull Tab, Pittsburgh Brewing Co., 12 Oz.	4.95
Pig's Eye Pilsner Beer, Minnesota Brewing Co., Contents	4.95
Pilsener Club Beer, Pearl Breweries, Pull Tab, 12 Oz.	2.54
Premium Grain Belt, Cone Top, Minneapolis Brewing Co., Minneapolis, Minn.	120.00
Schmidt Beer, Lassie & Flock Of Sheep Scene, Jacob Schmidt, St. Paul, Minn., 12 Oz.	10.00
Steinlager, White, Red, Turquoise, Pull Tab, Wellington, New Zealand, 12 Oz.	2.50

BELL collectors collect all types of bells. Favorites include glass bells, figural bells, school bells, and cowbells. Bells have been made of porcelain, china, or metal through the centuries.

Brass, Cast Iron Frame, Striker Ball, 4-Legs, Brass Stand, 12 x 12 x 21 In.	600.00
Brass, Religious Figures, F.E., 6 ½ x 5 ¾ In.	49.00
Brass, Woman, Austria, c.1918, 3 In.	646.00
Brass, Woman, Victorian Style Coat, Muff, Hat, Clapper Legs, 5 ¼ In.	295.00
Brass, Woman, Victorian Style Dress, Bonnet, Clapper Legs, 3 In.	140.00
Brass, Wood Handle, 11 ¼ x 7 ¼ In.	88.00
Bronze, Ashanti, Slaver's, Oval, Banded, c.1850, 4 ⅜ In.	145.00
Bronze, Plantation, Marked, Clapper, 1879, 16 x 16 In.	881.00
Cut Glass, Strawberry Diamond, Crosscut Diamond & Fan, Cut Knob, 4 ½ In.	275.00
Iron, Macaw, Green, Red, Hubley, 5 x 2 ⅜ In.	60.00
Iron, On Brass, Macaw, Green, Yellow, Blue, Gold, Hubley, 5 x 2 ⅜ In.	23.00
Iron, Plantation, Bell Pull, 19th Century, Marked, 31 x 36 In.	2350.00
Iron, Plantation, Yoke, Mid 1800s, 15 x 16 In.	295.00
Metal, Turtle, Black, Brown, 5 ½ In.	290.00

School, Iron, Yoke, Wood Stand, Stamped, C.P. & F. Bough & Co., c.1886, 27 x 30 In. ......*illus* 531.00
Sleigh, 41 Brass Bells, Leather Strap, c.1910, 79 In. ....*illus* 127.00
Steel Alloy, Plantation, Yoke, Cradle, C.S. Bell Co., Hillsboro, Ohio, Late 1800s, 20 In. 588.00
Turtle, Clockwork, Windup, Germany, c.1875, 6 In. 323.00

BELLEEK china was made in Ireland, other European countries, and the United States. The glaze is creamy yellow and appears wet. The first Belleek was made in 1857. All pieces listed here are Irish Belleek. The mark changed through the years. The first mark, black, dates from 1863 to 1890. The second mark, black, dates from 1891 to 1926 and includes the words *Co. Fermanagh, Ireland*. The third mark, black, dates from 1926 to 1946 and has the words *Deanta in Eirinn*. The fourth mark, same as the third mark but green, dates from 1946 to 1955. The fifth mark (second green mark) dates from 1955 to 1965 and has an R in a circle added in the upper right. The sixth mark (third green mark) dates from 1965 to 1981 and the words *Co. Fermanagh* have been omitted. The seventh mark, gold, was used from 1981 to 1992 and omits the words *Deanta in Eirinn*. The eighth mark, used from 1993 to 1996, is similar to the second mark but is printed in blue. The ninth mark, blue, includes the words *Est. 1857* and the words *Co. Fermanagh Ireland* are omitted. The tenth mark, black, is similar to the ninth mark but includes the words *Millennium 2000* and *Ireland*. It was used only in 2000. The eleventh mark, similar to the millennium mark but green, was introduced in 2001 and will be used until 2010, according to the company. The word *Belleek* is now used only on the pieces made in Ireland even though earlier pieces from other countries were sometimes marked *Belleek*. These early pieces are listed by manufacturer, such as Ceramic Art Co., Haviland, Lenox, Ott & Brewer, and Willets.

Bowl, Roses, Mums, White, Scalloped Rim, Footed, Signed, 10 In. 1495.00
Bust, Clytie, 1st Black Mark, 12 In. 1400.00
Bust, Woman, Head Tilted Right, Ivory Glaze, 3rd Green Mark, 11 In. 210.00
Butter, Cottage Cover, Signed, Green Mark, 4 ½ x 6 ½ In. ....*illus* 100.00
Ewer, Applied Flowers, Handle, Signed, 9 In. 350.00
Figurine, Classical Robed Woman, Green Mark, 14 ¾ In., Pair 468.00
Jardiniere, Cherubs, Reeds, Water Creatures, 3-Footed, 1st Black Mark, 10 x 8 In. 1300.00
Loving Cup, Blackberries, Gilt, 3 Handles, 7 x 6 In. 325.00
Pitcher, Apples, Hand Painted, 6 x 9 In. 215.00
Tea Set, Shamrock, 6 Cups & Saucers, Teapot, Cake, Sugar & Creamer, 16 Piece 132.00
Teapot, Echinus, Pink Coral, Ivory Glaze, 2nd Black Print Mark, 5 In. 365.00
Teapot, Neptune, Pink, Ivory Glaze, 1st Black Print Mark, 4 ½ In. 121.00
Vase, Flowers, Shamrocks, Scalloped Rim, 9 In. 77.00
Vase, Flowers, Silver Overlay, Bulbous, Marked, Eva Cordery, c.1900, 11 In. 531.00
Vase, White, Lily Shape, Entwined Lizard, Black Mark, 9 In. 999.00

BENNINGTON ware was the product of two factories working in Bennington, Vermont. Both the Norton Company and the Lyman Fenton Company were out of business by 1896. The wares include brown and yellow mottled pottery, Parian, scroddled ware, stoneware, graniteware, yellowware, and Staffordshire-type vases. The name is also a generic term for mottled brownware of the type made in Bennington.

Bank, Bird, Yellow, Green, 19th Century 275.00
Bowl, Flared Sides, Glazed, 3 ¼ x 8 ⅝ In. 49.00
Creamer, Cow Shape, Mocha Spatter, 19th Century, 7 x 5 ½ In. 485.00
Crock, Cobalt Blue Flower, Edward & Luman P. Norton, 1858-81, 1 ½ Gal., 7 x 8 In. 229.00
Crock, Cover, Potbelly, Applied Handles, 1800s, 1 ½ Gal., 11 ¾ In. 450.00
Flask, Book, Departed Spirits, Yellowware, Mottled, Flint Enamel, 5 ¾ x 4 ¾ In. 441.00
Flask, Book, Ladies Companion, Runny Glaze, Mid 1800s, 7 ¾ x 6 In. ....*illus* 633.00
Jug, Blue, Leaves, Stoneware, Impressed, E. Norton & Co., 19th Century, 10 ½ In. 85.00
Jug, Stoneware, Small Mouth, Late 1800s, 5 Gal. 697.00
Milk Pan, Irregular Shape, 19th Century, 11 In. 80.00
Mold, Turk's Head, 9 ⅛ x 3 ½ In. 35.00
Pitcher, Paneled, Flint Enamel, Impressed Mark, 1849-58, 12 ¼ In. 235.00
Pitcher, Penguin Shape, Brown Glaze, Green Highlights, 8 x 3 ½ In. 75.00
Pitcher, Spatter, Yellow Stoneware, Scroll Lip, 7 ½ x 4 In. 60.00
Sculpture, Face, Metal Pedestal Base, David Gil, 21 x 12 In. 350.00
Trivet, Wood Dowel Handles, Mottled Glaze, 12 x 8 In. 50.00
Umbrella Stand, Cobalt Blue, Brown Glaze Over Yellow, 1840-50, 22 ¼ x 10 In. 400.00

BERLIN, a German porcelain factory, was started in 1751 by Wilhelm Kaspar Wegely. In 1763, the factory was taken over by Frederick the Great and became the Royal Berlin Porcelain Manufactory. It is still in operation today. Pieces have been marked in a variety of ways.

Basket, Reticulated, Hand Painted, 18th Century, 3 ¼ x 4 ¼ In. 350.00

Bell, Sleigh, 41 Brass Bells, Leather Strap, c.1910, 79 In. $127.00

Belleek, Butter, Cottage Cover, Signed, Green Mark, 4 ½ x 6 ½ In. $100.00

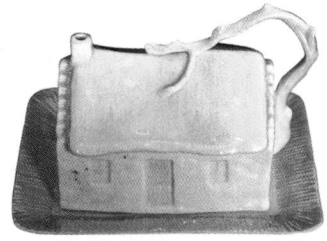

Bennington, Flask, Book, Ladies Companion, Runny Glaze, Mid 1800s, 7 ¾ x 6 In. $633.00

Belleek Baskets
Irish Belleek collectors can date the "woven" baskets and bowls by looking closely at the strands of clay in the basket's weave. Each strip in the weave is made of several strands of clay. Baskets woven with clay made of four strands date from about 1900. Fewer strands were used on newer baskets. Look at the bottom of a bowl or basket and count the strands.

Betty Boop, Figure, Composition, Jointed, Green Dress, Fleischer Studios, 12 In. $527.00

Betty Boop, Figure, Jointed, Paper Lithograph, Cardboard, Wood Base, c.1935, 9 ½ In. $88.00

Betty Boop, Placecard Holder, Celluloid, Die Cut House, Rat, Japan, 1930s, 2 In. $285.00

Dessert Set, Cup, Saucer, Plate, Crest, Wide Gold Rim, Marked, Schedel Bavaria, 7 ¾ & 5 ¾ In.	24.00
Pill Box, Round, Shell Shape Lid, Enameled Flowers Inside Lid, Blue Mark, 2 In.	173.00
Plaque, Gypsy Woman, Mandolin, Scrolled Gesso Frame, Stamped, 5 x 11 In.	633.00
Plaque, Queen Louisa Of Prussia, Descending Steps, Incised 433, Gilt Frame, 18 x 23 In.	4250.00
Plaque, Woman, Seminude, Profile, Gesso Frame, Shadowbox, Epanouissement Asti, 13 x 12 In.	1100.00
Sugar, Dome Lid, Blue & White, Transferware, Mid 1800s, 6 x 4 In.	200.00
Tureen, Men, At Table, Cover, Bacchus Finial, c.1880, 13 x 10 ⅜ In.	2530.00

BESWICK started making earthenware in Staffordshire, England, in 1936. The company is now part of Royal Doulton Tableware, Ltd. Figurines of animals, especially dogs and horses, Beatrix Potter animals, and other wares are still being made.

Figurine, Bald Eagle, No. 1018, 7 ½ x 8 ½ In.	41.00
Figurine, Boar, Wall Champion Boy 53rd, 1987-89, 2 ¾ In.	74.00
Figurine, Bulldog, Gloss, No. 965, 1987-89, 5 ½ In.	513.00
Figurine, Cat, Laughing, No. 2101, 3 In.	58.00
Figurine, Cheetah, Standing, No. 3009, 5 In.	107.00
Figurine, Dairy Shorthorn Cow, No. 1510, 4 ¾ In.	494.00
Figurine, Grey Stallion, No. 1772, 8 In.	74.00
Figurine, Guernsey Bull, No. 1451, 4 ¾ In.	132.00
Figurine, Hackney Horse, Black, Gloss, No. 1361, 7 ¾ In.	99.00
Figurine, Horse, Spirit Of Peace, No. 2916, 4 ¾ In.	82.00
Figurine, Kingfisher, Luster Glaze, No. 2371, 5 In.	313.00
Figurine, Pheasant, No. 849, 6 x 10 In., Pair	293.00
Figurine, Staffordshire, Bull Terrier, Dark Brindle, No. 1982A, 5 x 6 In.	412.00
Figurine, Stallion, Brown, White Socks, No. 1772, 11 x 15 In.	400.00
Figurine, Susan, BP 3B, Beatrix Potter, Box, 1983-89, 4 ¼ In.	198.00
Figurine, Swish Tail Horse, Palomino, No. 1182, 1970-82, 8 ¾ In.	96.00
Figurine, Tom Kitten, BP 2, Beatrix Potter, 3 ½ In.	58.00
Figurine, Wigeon, No. 1526, 1940-59, 3 ½ In.	115.00
Plate, Christmas In England, Relief, c.1972, 8 In.	75.00
Toby Jug, Midshipman, No. 1112, 5 ¼ In.	164.00

BETTY BOOP, the cartoon figure, first appeared on the screen in 1931. Her face was modeled after the famous singer Helen Kane and her body after Mae West. In 1935, a comic strip was started. Her dog was named Bimbo. Although the Betty Boop cartoons ended by 1938, there was a revival of interest in the Betty Boop image in the 1980s and new pieces are being made.

Booklet, Movie Cartoon Lessons, Color, 1930s, 9 x 12 In., 32 Pages	173.00
Doll Sewing Pattern, Uncut, 18-In. Doll, Black, Red, White, King Features, c.1969	11.00
Doll, Composition Head, Wood Body, Green Dress, Cameo, 1932, 12 In.	672.00
Figure, Composition, Jointed, Green Dress, Fleischer Studios, 12 In. ....*illus*	527.00
Figure, Jointed, Paper Lithograph, Cardboard, Wood Base, c.1935, 9 ½ In. ....*illus*	88.00
Figurine Set, Playing Instruments, Bisque, Painted, Japan, Mid 1930s, 3 ¼ In., 4 Piece	288.00
Figurine, Composition, Painted, Fleischer Studios, c.1931, 14 In.	1450.00
Pin Set, Betty & Bimbo, Metal, Woolco Card, 1960s	250.00
Placecard Holder, Celluloid, Die Cut House, Rat, Japan, 1930s, 2 In. ....*illus*	285.00
Salt & Pepper, Bimbo, White Glaze, Black, Red, 1930s, 2 ½ In.	65.00
Stringholder, Chalkware, Painted, c.1950, 7 ½ In.	350.00
Wristwatch, Antiqued Gold Case, Faux Reptile Band, Pin, Fossil, Limited Edition, 1994	125.00
Wristwatch, Portrait, 18K Gold Plated, Leather Snap Case, Woman's, c.1992	173.00

BICYCLES were invented in 1839. The first manufactured bicycle was made in 1861. Special ladies' bicycles were made after 1874. The modern safety bicycle was not produced until 1885. Collectors search for all types of bicycles and tricycles. Bicycle-related items are also listed here.

3 Wheeler, Steel Tubular Frame, Spoke Wheels, Rubber Tires, Velvet Seat, 1880s, 33 x 49 In.	540.00
Acme Mfg., Stormer, Convertible, Female, Male, 2 Handlebars, Wheel Bells, 1899	605.00
Barnes, Tandem, White Flyer, Convertible Seats, White, 1890s	345.00
Boneshaker, Boy's, Wood, Metal, c.1869, 30 In.	1320.00
Boneshaker, Hanlon Type, 1865, 36-In. Front Wheel	3875.00
Boneshaker, No. 1210, Steel, Leather Seat, Black, Cleveland, Ohio, 1970s, 48-In. Front Wheel, 52 In.	1020.00
Boneshaker, Saddle, Spool Pedals, Wood Grips, c.1800, 31-In. Front Wheel, 26-In. Rear Wheel	3520.00
Box, Tire, Wooden, c.1900, 18 x 7 ½, 4 ¼ In.	66.00
Butler Adams, Octagonal Handlebars, Leather Grips, Pedals, Rims, Saddle, 1896	1018.00
Circus Clown, Wood, Painted Red, White, Blue, Cast Iron Stand, Georgia, c.1900, 40 x 27 In.	356.00
Colson, Firestone Cruiser, Woman's, Cream, Leather Saddle Seat, Lamp, c.1945, 26 In. ....*illus*	999.00

Columbia, Model F9T, Girl's, Dashboard Clock, Speedometer, Maroon, Cream, c.1941, 26 In. .	540.00
Columbia, Spring Fork, Boy's, Cushion Tire Safety, Pilot Lamp, 1893.....................................	2900.00
Crown, Pneumatic Safety, Wood Steering Wheel, c.1898...	2200.00
Cyclometer, Mounting Bracket, Dial, c.1893, 2 x 2 ¼ In.	358.00
Elgin, Black Hawk, Boy's, Maroon, c.1933, 26 In.	960.00
Elgin, Bluebird Deluxe, c.1938	4510.00
Elliot, Hickory, Hard Tire Safety, 1891...	4510.00
Harley-Davidson, Special, Boy's, Green, Pinstripe, Wood Wheels, Leather Seat, c.1917, 26 In.	1700.00
High Wheel, Crypto, 1893, 36 In.	6050.00
High Wheel, Iron Frame, Spoked Wheel, Rubber Tires, c.1900, 59 In.	660.00
High Wheel, Leather Seat, Ratchet Pedals, Steel, c.1894, 44-In. Front Wheel........................	4000.00
Huffman-Dayton, Twin-Flex, Blue, Gray, c.1939, 26 In.	1800.00
Indian, Child's, 16 In.	5000.00
Monarch, Silver King 26X, Boy's, c.1940, 26 In.	1080.00
Monark, Whitewall Tires, Saddle, Chrome, c.1950	715.00
Murray, Western Flyer X-53, 1950s	440.00
Open Mouth Snake Shape Seat, Green, Black, Red Paint, Stand, c.1890, 45 x 65 In.	690.00
Ornament, Front Fender, Hiawatha, 3 ¾ x 2 In.	99.00
Peugeot, Racer, 10-Speed, Saddle, Handlebars, c.1970...	143.00
Pope, Columbia Shaft Drive, c.1897...	990.00
Quadracycle, Murray, Steel, Belt Drive, Bent Tube Frame, Black Seat, 26 x 32 In.	210.00
Quadracycle, Tandem, Child's..	83.00
Racing, Men's, Wooden Spoke Wheels, Leather Seat, Blue Paint, 1890s, 26 In.	1440.00
Repair Kit, 2 Military Cyclists, Tin Lithograph, Germany, c.1913, 3 ¼ x 2 ¼ x 1 In.	88.00
Rex, 3-Wheel Inline, c.1897, 2 28-In. Wheels, 1 16-In. Wheel	13200.00
Roadmaster, Luxury Liner, Boy's, Red & Black, 1953, 26 In.	600.00
Rollfast, Roy Rogers, Boy's, Tan, c.1952, 24 In.	6000.00
Schwinn, Apple Krate Sting-Ray, Red With White Lettering, 1970, 56 x 42 In.	450.00
Schwinn, B6, Boy's, Blue, Cream, c.1952, 26 In.	1080.00
Schwinn, Gray Ghost, Boy's, Silver, c.1971, 20 In.	1680.00
Schwinn, Panther, Girl's, Saddle, Headlight Key Locking Spring Fork, 1951	660.00
Schwinn, Panther, Green, Decals, Omaha 1954 License Plate, Headlight, 26 In. .. 1200.00 to 2040.00	
Schwinn, Phantom, Black, Chrome, Light, Leather Seat, Headlight	880.00
Schwinn, Stingray Apple Krate 5, 5-Speed, Red, Chrome Fenders, Handlebars, c.1971, 41 In. ..*illus*	705.00
Scooter, Adult, Skate, Adjustable Steering	28.00
Scooter, Kick 'N Go, Red Flower	28.00
Sears Roebuck, Boy's, Red, Black, c.1958, 26 In.	720.00
Seat, Child's, Sheet Metal, c.1900	28.00
Singer, Xtraordinary, Nickel Finish, 1886, 50-In. Front Wheel.....................................	19800.00
Speedwell Racing Trainer, Boy's, Red, White, Blue, Wood Grips, c.1928, 26 In.	540.00
Sportster, Roadmaster, Harley-Davidson, Red, Black, Battery Powered, Boy's, c.1994, 20 In. .	420.00
Stand, 2-Rail, Cast Iron .... 55.00 to 77.00	
Stand, Cast Iron, Footed, 20 In.	211.00
Tandem, Fongers, Black, Front Drum Brakes, 26 In.	420.00
Tire Pump, Schwinn Typhoon, Oak Handle, Wood Box, Brass Horn, Bulb, 28 In.	210.00
Tricycle, Aluminum, Springer Seat, Hard Rubber Tires, Twister Handlebars, 26 x 32 In.	150.00
Tricycle, American National Co., Sidecar, Red, Yellow, Rubber Tires, c.1920, 30 In.	400.00
Tricycle, Boneshaker, Wood Spoke Wheels, Iron Frame, 1800s, 26-In. Front Wheel.................	10950.00
Tricycle, Steel, Red, Gray, Closed Wheels, Hard Rubber Tires, 25 x 32 In.	180.00
Victor, Light Roadster, 1888, 52 In.	5225.00
Victor, Roadster, c.1886, 51 In.	9900.00
Victor, Split Frame, Spring Fork, Pneumatic Safety Tires, c.1889, 30-In. Wheels..................	5775.00
Whizzer Sportsman, Boy's, Green, c.1950, 26 In.	4500.00

BING & GRONDAHL is a famous Danish factory making fine porcelains from 1853 to the present. Underglaze blue decoration was started in 1886. The annual Christmas plate series was introduced in 1895. Dinnerwares, stoneware, and figurines are still being made today. The firm has used the initials B & G and a stylized castle as part of the mark since 1898. The company became part of Royal Copenhagen in 1987.

Bell, Christmas, 1981, Christmas Peace, 3 In.	16.00
Centerpiece, Scrollwork, Lily Pad Stem, Blue Heron Supports, c.1955, 20 In.	6900.00
Figurine, Boy, Holding Dog, No. 1747	75.00
Figurine, Boy, Kissing Girl, No. 2162, 6 In.	96.00
Figurine, Dog, Cocker Spaniel, 3 ¼ x 4 In.	39.00
Figurine, Dog, Springer Spaniel, 6 ½ x 8 ½ In.	299.00

Bicycle, Colson, Firestone Cruiser, Woman's, Cream, Leather Saddle Seat, Lamp, c.1945, 26 In.
$999.00

Bicycle, Schwinn, Stingray Apple Krate 5, 5-Speed, Red, Chrome Fenders, Handlebars, c.1971, 41 In.
$705.00

Bing & Grondahl
When Bing & Grondahl became part of Royal Copenhagen in 1987, some Bing & Grondahl dinnerware, figurines, and vases were discontinued; some remained in production but were marked with the Royal Copenhagen mark. The Bing & Grondahl name was used only on commemorative and annual pieces and a few overglaze-decorated figurines.

Birdcage, Metal, Wire, Gothic Revival, Multicolored, 3 Gables, Trays, 50 x 45 In. $430.00

Birdcage, Pine, Wire Bars, Door Latches, Drawer, Grain Painted, Late 1800s, 9 x 11 In. $235.00

TIP

Don't dry your china and crystal with a cloth that has been laundered with fabric softener. The softener may leave a film.

Bisque, Figurine, Cherub, Sitting On Shell, Karl Schneider, 7 ½ x 8 ½ In. $127.00

Figurine, First Kiss, Youthful Boldness, No. 2162, 8 In.	84.00
Figurine, Pad About, No. 1757, 8 In.	30.00
Figurine, People, Little Hunter, 6 In.	150.00
Figurine, Sandman, Boy With Umbrella, 7 ¼ x 3 ¼ In.	88.00
Gravy Boat, Seagull, Seahorse Handles, 8 ¼ In.	135.00
Plate, Chandelier, Cross, 7 In.	120.00
Plate, Children's Day, 1988, Wash Day	45.00
Plate, Christmas, 1899, Crows Enjoying Christmas	1400.00
Plate, Christmas, 1900, Bell, 7 In.	300.00
Plate, Christmas, 1901, 3 Wisemen, 7 In.	131.00
Plate, Christmas, 1904, 2 Trees, 7 In.	110.00
Plate, Christmas, 1906, Sleighing To Church On Christmas Eve, 7 In.	110.00
Plate, Christmas, 1917, Christmas Boat	89.00
Plate, Christmas, 1927, Skating Couple	85.00
Plate, Christmas, 1964, Fir Tree & Hare	45.00
Plate, Mother's Day, 1969, Dog With Puppies, 9 In.	35.00
Plate, Mother's Day, 1997, Goose & Goslings	120.00
Vase, Landscape, Windmill, Marked, 9 ¾ In.	29.00
Vase, Sea Gull, Blue Ground, Gold Trim, 8 ½ x 4 ½ In.	150.00

BINOCULARS of all types are wanted by collectors. Those made in the eighteenth and nineteenth centuries are favored by serious collectors. The small, attractive binoculars called opera glasses are listed in their own category.

Artillerie, Hensoldt, Brown Leather Case, Adjustable Strap, 1940s, 8 x 24 In.	225.00
Begelow Bennard, Leather Case, Silk Lined, Early 1900s, 3 ¼ x 4 ¼ In.	275.00
C.F. Foth, 8x, Leather Cover, Germany, 4 ½ x 5 ¼ In.	60.00
Chevalier, Painted Silver, Bird Designs, Central Focus, c.1870	290.00
Hercules, 6x13, Leather Case, Occupied Japan, 1940s, 3 ½ In.	69.00
Leitz Wetzlar, 8x60, Black, Painted, Leather Case, 8 x 8 ½ In.	47.00
Max Balbreck, Porro Prism, Black Enamel, Steel, Pouch, 2 ¼ x 2 ⅝ In.	175.00
Silvered Brass, Engraved, C.W. Dixey, 19th Century, 5 In.	118.00
Sportiere, Embossed, Black Japanned Brass, Leather Wraps, Early 1900s, 4 ¼ x 4 ½ In.	35.00
Sportiere, Military, U.S. Calvary, Day & Night, Leather Case, 1870s	299.00
Swift, Skipper, 7x50, No. 789, Trilar 7x RLE 764, Case	86.00
Verdi, Military, Paris, 7 ¼ x 5 ½ In.	95.00
Yachting, Brass, Polished, LeMaire, Paris, Early 20th Century, 5 x 8 In.	115.00

BIRDCAGES are collected for use as homes for pet birds and as decorative objects of folk art. Elaborate wooden cages of the past centuries can still be found. The brass or wicker cages of the 1930s are popular with bird owners.

Beehive Style, Detachable Base, Seed Screen, Water Cups, Hendryx, 1870s	185.00
Brass, 3-Footed Base, 19 x 40 In.	59.00
Brass, Art Deco, Greek Key Acid Etched, Glass Seed Guard, 15 x 12 In.	400.00
Brass, Craftsman Style, Removable Bottom, Slide-Out Tray, Hendryx, 15 x 13 In.	600.00
Brass, Hammered, Painted Seed Guard, Stand	900.00
Metal, Shaped Cast Iron Stand, Plastic Food Containers, 63 In.	155.00
Metal, Wire, Gothic Revival, Multicolored, 3 Gables, Trays, 50 x 45 In. ....*illus*	430.00
Pine, Wire Bars, Door Latches, Drawer, Grain Painted, Late 1800s, 9 x 11 In. ....*illus*	235.00
Pine, Wire Bars, Wood Crest, Lift Door, Wood Bird, c.1910, 17 x 11 In.	323.00
Thermoplastic, Celluloid, Clear, Decorative Designs, 14 ¾ x 9 x 12 ¾ In.	325.00
Victorian, Painted, Finials, Applied Scrolling, 3 Doors, Square Stand, 61 x 18 In.	660.00
Walnut, Brass, Cathedral Shape, 3 Spires, Victorian, 49 x 21 In.	325.00
Wicker, Fernery, Weave, Cane Pattern, Latticework Panels, 1920s, 63 x 36 In.	1450.00
Wire, Painted White, Green, Victorian, c.1880, 21 x 16 In.	475.00
Wood, Wire Dome, 34 ¾ x 14 x 9 In.	33.00
Wood, Wire, Edwardian, Philadelphia Row House Style, Multicolored, c.1910, 21 x 20 In.	2500.00
Wood, Wire, Gothic Revival Church Style, Patina, Victorian, 23 x 19 In.	2500.00
Wood, Wire, Green, Columns, Peaked Roof, c.1890, 17 ¼ x 15 In.	322.00

BISQUE is an unglazed baked porcelain. Finished bisque has a slightly sandy texture with a dull finish. Some of it may be decorated with various colors. Bisque gained favor during the late Victorian era when thousands of bisque figurines were made. It is still being made. Additional bisque items may be listed under the factory name.

Bust, Boy, Blue Striped Shirt, Victorian, 11 ½ In.	65.00

Bust, Boy, Brown Hair, Flower Shirt, Victorian, 9 In.		52.00
Bust, George Washington, Cylindrical Plinth, 14 In.		255.00
Bust, George Washington, Marked, G. Washington, 10 ½ In.		180.00
Bust, Naughty Girl, Lactating Squirter, Victorian, Incised, No. 1503, Germany, c.1900, 2 ½ x 1 In.		55.00
Decanter, Grape Bunch Shape, Green Gloss Glaze, Germany, 6 ½ x 5 In., Pair		68.00
Figurine, Athena & Nemean Lion, 12 ½ In.		215.00
Figurine, Boy & Girl, Boy In Sailor Suit, Girl Holding Gun, Japan, 1940s, 3 ¾ In., Pair		35.00
Figurine, Boy, In Clown Suit, Painted, Germany, c.1920, 11 x 4 ⅝ In.		60.00
Figurine, Boy On Hobby Horse, Painted, c.1970, 10 In.		28.00
Figurine, Cherub, Sitting On Shell, Karl Schneider, 7 ½ x 8 ½ In.	*illus*	127.00
Figurine, Colonial Boy, Blue, White, Gold Accents, c.1945, 6 x 2 ½ In.		55.00
Figurine, Dutch Boy, Blue Hat, Pants, White Shirts, Yoke, 4 In.		12.00
Figurine, Fancy Gentleman, 17 ½ In.		75.00
Figurine, Frozen Charlotte, Cape, Painted, Germany, 4 In.		24.00
Figurine, George & Martha Washington, Molded Head & Feet, Painted Features, 16 In., Pair		60.00
Figurine, Harold Lloyd, Painted, Incised, 3511, Germany, 4 ⅞ In.		55.00
Figurine, Japanese Girl, Top Bun, Yellow Kimono, Holding Fan, 4 In.		10.00
Figurine, Portrait Bust, Man, Woman, England, 1800s, 14 ½ x 10 In.		585.00
Figurine, Rose, Pink, Green Leaves, Label, Napoleon, Italy, 5 x 3 ½ In.		12.00
Flower, Magnolia, 5 x 11 In.		59.00
Group, Girl, Dog, c.1930, 15 x 10 In.		146.00
Mustard Pot, Duck, In Basket, Duck Head Spoon, 19th Century, 4 ½ x 5 In.		145.00
Pin Tray, 2 Indians, Kiffhook & Tsi Lora, Gold Bead Edge, Germany, 5 ⅝ x 5 ⅝ In.		30.00
Planter, Draped Woman, Resting In Lilies, Austria, c.1900, 11 x 16 In.		644.00
Plaque, Amorous Couple, Sitting On Branches, Continental, 20th Century, 7 ½ In.		45.00
Vase, Boy & Girl, Embracing, Tree Stump, Painted, Gloss Glaze, American Bisque		48.00
Vase, Victorian Girl, Standing By Petal From Vase, Blue, White, 6 In.		56.00

Black, Figurine,
Child Looking In Outhouse,
Child Inside, Bisque, 2 ½ x 2 In.
$58.00

BLACK memorabilia has become an important area of collecting since the 1970s. The best material dates from past centuries, but many recent items are also of interest. F & F is the mark used on plastic made by Fiedler & Fiedler Mold & Die Works, Inc. in the 1930s and 1940s. Objects that picture a black person may also be listed in this book under Advertising, Sign; Bank; Bottle Opener; Cookie Jar; Doll; Salt & Pepper; Sheet Music; Toy; etc.

Andirons, Men, Formal Dress, Crouched, Billet Bars, Cast Iron, 1800s, 16 In.		201.00
Ashtray, Butler, Holding Tray, Cigarette & Match Box Holder, Painted, Iron, 34 In.		1110.00
Ashtray, Waiter, Red Coat, Black Pants, Holding Tray, Cast Iron, 33 In.		340.00
Automaton, Fishing Tackle, Boy, Holding Fishing Rod, Fish, 35 x 13 x 14 In.		4950.00
Baby, Bisque, Jointed Arms, Legs, Hair Tufts, Ribbons, Painted Face, Occupied Japan, 4 In.		75.00
Bag, Clothespin, Large Mouth Mammy, Muslin, Embroidered, Hanger, 17 In.		162.00
Bellman Holding Pole, Wood, 48 In.		142.00
Book, Child's, Ten Little Niggers, McLoughlin Co., 1894		502.00
Box, Recipe, Aunt Jemima, Red, Fosta Products, 3 ¾ x 5 ½ In.	178.00 to	145.00
Card Holder, Butler, Man, Red Coat, Tails, Brass Tray, Paint, Cast Iron, 43 x 8 In.		633.00
Card Holder, Man, Holding Tray, Painted, Cast Iron, Late 1800s, 9 ¼ In.		1350.00
Cards, Amos 'n' Andy, Heavy Cardstock, 4 Scenes From Radio Show, Arcade, 5 ¼ In.		55.00
Charm, Gambler's, Man, Dice, Chain, Bakelite, 1930s, 2 In.		35.00
Cocktail Pick Set, Stick Men, Wood Holder, Round, Plastic, Stainless Steel, 3 ¾ In., 10 Piece		125.00
Condiment Set, 3 Natives, Leaf Holder, Salt, Pepper, Mustard, Spoon, Japan, 1950s		60.00
Cookie Jars are listed in the Cookie Jar category.		
Cup, 2 Girls Riding Scooter, Golliwog Doll, 14K Yellow Gold Trim, c.1920, 2 ¼ In.		50.00
Doll, Aunt Jemima, Climbing, Lithograph, Die Cut Cardboard, David Milling Co., 15 x 6 In.		1200.00
Doll, Automaton, Man, Nodder, Windup, Key, 22 ¼ In.		2607.00
Doll, Belindy, Button Eyes, Watermelon Smile, Red & White Dress, Bolland, 15 In.		1035.00
Doll, Bisque, Open Mouth, Red Lips, Teeth, Glass Eyes, Composition, 11 ½ In.		267.00
Doll, Bisque Socket Head, Composition, Caracul Wig, Jointed, Child, Recknagel, 19 In.		3081.00
Doll, Bisque Socket Head, Side Glancing Eyes, Pierced Nostrils, Ears, Brass Rings, 7 In.		326.00
Doll, Cloth, Needle Stitched Features, Cotton Dress, Underclothes, Late 19th Century, 7 In.		593.00
Doll, Cloth, Papier-Mache Head, Bellows Pressed, Jaw Moves, Squeeze, 13 ½ In.		1495.00
Doll, Cloth, Weighted Bottle Base, Faded Costume, Cotton, 1800s, 15 In.		509.00
Doll, Composition, Glass Eyes, Hand Painted, Boot, Cloth Dress, 9 ¼ In.		690.00
Doll, Composition, Shoulder Head, Side Glancing Eyes, Black Pigtails, G. Drayton, 1924, 13 In.		448.00
Doll, Jackie Robinson, Dodgers Uniform, Composition, Jointed, Allied Grand, 13 In.		1008.00
Doll, Mammy, Porcupine Quill Fingernails, Original Clothes, 19th Century, 14 In.		510.00
Doll, Mammy, White Baby, Composition, Head, Painted, Cotton Dress, T. Sarg, c.1935, 18 In.		1120.00
Doll, Peterkin, Composition Head, Side Part, Closed Mouth, Horsman, c.1929, 13 In.		560.00

BLACK

Black, Figurine, Eating Watermelon, On Cotton Bale, Bisque, Germany, 4 x 4 In.
$86.00

Black, Head, Smoking Cigar, Wood, Carved, Label, Cigar, 3 Cents, 14 x 16 In.
$552.00

Black, Poster, Military, Colored Man Is No Slacker, E.G. Renesch, c.1918, 16 x 12 In.
$529.00

Drawing, Slavery, Kneeling Slave, Text, Ink, Frame, 4 x 6 In.	975.00
Figurine Set, Swing Band, Musicians, Iron, Blue White, Hubley, 2 ½ x 2 In., 6 Piece	527.00
Figurine, Boy Shining Shoes, Man, Wrought Iron, Cloth, France, 1930, 11 ½ In.	80.00
Figurine, Child Looking In Outhouse, Child Inside, Bisque, 2 ½ x 2 In. *illus*	58.00
Figurine, Child On Toilet, You R Next, White, 3 ¾ In.	33.00
Figurine, Eating Watermelon, On Cotton Bale, Bisque, Germany, 4 x 4 In. *illus*	86.00
Figurine, Jockey, Melon Between Legs, 1902 Farmers' Outing, Bisque, Austria, 4 In.	176.00
Figurine, Man Playing Banjo, Terra-Cotta, 19th Century, 8 ¼ In.	305.00
Figurine, Man's Face, Egg, More Chicken, Milk Glass, J. Murphy & Co., c.1920, 4 In.	184.00 to 212.00
Figurine, Uncle Tom & Eva, Pottery, Painted, Staffordshire, 8 In.	118.00
Flyer, The Negro Races, A Sociological Study, Jerome Dowd, 4 Pages, c.1920	14.00
Game, Ball Toss, Dodger, Head Peers Through Canvas Backdrop, 10 ½ In.	288.00
Game, Bowling, Balls, Paperboard, 5 Faces, Mouths Open, Spears Games, 1928	425.00
Game, Pickaninny Bowling, 5 Balls, Black Faces, Mouths Open, Box, 15 x 11 In.	395.00
Game, Pinball, Sleepy Men, Wood, Glass, Metal, Northwest Products, 1920s, 17 In.	90.00
Game, Target, Jolly Darkie, Box, 16 x 8 In.	450.00
Grocery List, I's Gotta Get, Mammy, Yellow Ground, Red, 1920s, 10 ½ x 6 ¼ In.	99.00
Head, Smoking Cigar, Wood, Carved, Label, Cigar, 3 Cents, 14 x 16 In. *illus*	552.00
Humidor, Man's Head, Smoking Cigarillo, Austria, 1890s, 8 ½ In.	361.00
Humidor, Man's Head, Tyrolean Cap, Austria, 1890s, 8 In.	356.00
Humidor, Sailor, Pineapple, Dewey's Black Shipmen On Olympia, Porcelain, Austria, 1900s, 7 In.	333.00
Laundry Bag, Mammy Cover, c.1900	173.00
Mortgage Deed, Plantation & Slaves, William McKenzie Parker, S.C., c.1859, 16 x 10 ½ In.	184.00
Mug, Man, Figural Bust, Hat, Stoneware, c.1850, 5 In.	337.00
Nodder, Man, Waistcoat, Vest, Spring Mounted, Composition, Hand Painted, Germany, c.1897, 6 In.	100.00
Nutcracker, Man's Head, Nightcap, Wood, Hand Painted, Germany, 1900s, 10 ½ In.	237.00
Ornament, Girl, With Umbrella, Spun Cotton, Crepe Paper Dress, Wide Hat, 5 In.	230.00
Ornament, Man, Cotton, Wearing Paper Top Hat, Paper Pants, Red Lips, 5 ½ In.	115.00
Pedestal, Blackamoor, Handstand, Tambourine Shape Table On Feet, Painted Wood, 37 In.	1380.00
Pin, Wattle Day League, Celluloid, Multicolored, c.1918, 1 ¼ In.	71.00
Pitcher, Syrup, Black Woman, Hands On Spout, White, Blue Stripe Body, Mammy Line, c.1938	230.00
Poster, Military, Colored Man Is No Slacker, E.G. Renesch, c.1918, 16 x 12 In. *illus*	529.00
Poster, Movie, Negro Soldier, U.S. Films Inc., c.1944, 40 x 60 In.	7768.00
Poster, Uncle Tom's Cabin, Robert Kemp, 3 Sheet, Moody Bros., No. 27072, 89 x 42 In.	3300.00
Puppet, Minstrel, Grinning, Top Hat, 9 In.	248.00
Puzzle, Dexterity, Embossed, Child Sitting On Pillow, Eating Watermelon, Round	307.00
Puzzle, Dexterity, Embossed, Man, Tie, Top Hat, Googly Eyes, Mirror Back, Marked D.R.G.M.	319.00
Rattle, Baby, Indian Headdress, Guitar, Ball Hangs From Ring, Japan, 1920s, 7 In.	121.00
Sign, Aunt Jemima Pancake Flour, Aunt Jemima, Die Cut, Cardboard, 17 x 8 ¼ In.	1100.00
Sign, Aunt Jemima, Pancake Flour, Perfect Pancakes Every Time, Cardboard, 1918, 12 x 22 In.	280.00
Sign, Drinking Fountain, Segregation, Cast Iron, Montgomery, Ala., July 14, 1931, 4 ¾ x 11 In.	7638.00
Skittle Set, Musical Troupe, Hand Painted, Wood Base, 8 ½ In., 9 Piece	690.00
Slave Collar Restraint, Hand Forged Iron, Hinge, 3-Pronged Spikes, 6 x 6 In.	7344.00
Slave Collar Restraint, Wrought Iron, Hinge, Lock, 10 Spikes, 2 x 7 In.	4230.00
Slave Leg Irons, Iron, 19th Century	351.00
Slave Receipt, Harriet Ann, 30 Yrs, 200, 1840, Peter Causey, Delaware, 15 x 13 In.	590.00
Smilin' Sam, Checkered Shirt, Hat, Opens & Closes Mouth, Easel Back, Frame, 25 x 21 x 5 In.	3600.00
Snuffbox, Oval, Man's Face On Cover, 3 In.	50.00
Spice Set, Aunt Jemima, Red, White, Plastic, 6 Spice Jars, Rack, F & F, Lustro-Ware, 4 x 13 In.	295.00
Statue, Seminude, Creole, Blue Head Wrap & Dress, Chalkware, Early 1900s, 23 x 14 In.	540.00
Statue, Woman, Carrying Tray On Shoulder, Wood, Carved, 3-Griffin Base, c.1880, 47 In.	2950.00
Sugar & Creamer, Uncle Mose & Aunt Jemima, Yellow, Red, White, F & F, 3 ¾ x 2 In.	70.00
Syrup, Aunt Jemima, Red, White, F & F Mold & Die, 5 ⅜ x 3 ¼ In.	68.00
Tea Towel, Man Flipping Pancakes, Kitchen Utensil Border, 1940-50, 27 x 15 In.	21.00
Tobacco Jar, Cover, Boy, Open Mouth, Bisque, Multicolored, 5 ½ x 4 ½ x 5 In. *illus*	92.00
Tobacco Tin, Nigger Hair, Bail Handle, c.1878, 7 In. *illus*	819.00
Tray, Ballerina, Full Dress, Wooden Feet, Taps, Drum, Tin Lithograph, Ives, 1874, 9 ¾ In.	173.00
Watermelon, Cardboard, Lithograph Face, Celluloid Baby Inside, 4 x 2 & 3 ¼ In. *illus*	150.00

BLACK AMETHYST glass appears black until it is held to the light, then a dark purple can be seen. It has been made in many factories from 1860 to the present.

Ashtray, Chase, Brass Slide Top, 3 ⅜ x 2 ¾ x 1 ¾ In.	19.00
Bowl, Oval, Footed, Shaped Edge, 12 ½ x 8 ¼ In.	95.00
Compote, White Enamel Flowers, Ruffled Rim, Blown, c.1880, 6 ½ x 3 In.	45.00
Cracker Jar, Cover, Tab Handles, 6 ½ x 5 In.	155.00

B

Tidbit, Center Handle, 8-Sided, 11 x 5 In.	35.00
Tip Tray, 8 ⅝ x 7 ½ In.	65.00
Vase, Loving Cup Shape, L.E. Smith, 6 In.	25.00
Vase, Ruffled Rim, 6 ¼ In.	13.00
Vase, Tapered, Ruffled Rim, 21 In.	61.00

BLENKO GLASS COMPANY is the 1930s successor to several glassworks founded by William John Blenko in Milton, West Virginia. In 1933, his son, William H. Blenko Sr., took charge. The company made tablewares and vases in classical shapes. In the late 1940s it hired talented designers and made innovative pieces. The company made a line of reproductions for Colonial Williamsburg. It is still in business and is best known today for its decorative wares and stained glass.

Bottle, Azure Blue, Crackled, Tapered, 18 In.	165.00
Bottle, Cobalt, Square Base, Raised Dot Side, Hank Adams, 14 In.	175.00
Bottle, Olive, Flat Top, No. 6937, Joel Myers, c.1969, 22 In.	450.00
Candlestick, Surf Green, No. 990A, c.1970, 3 In., Pair	25.00
Canister, Tangerine, Cork Lid, No. 7227LM, c.1972, 10 ¼ In.	60.00
Decanter, Blue, Bulbous, Narrow Neck, Stopper, No. 657LL, c.1965, 23 x 10 In.	500.00
Decanter, Blue Crackle, Ground Stopper, Wayne Husted, c.1956, 11 ½ In.	75.00
Decanter, Blue, No. 6029, Wayne Husted, 26 In.	400.00
Decanter, Blue, Shouldered, Flattened Body, Flanged Neck, 1956, 11 x 8 In.	150.00
Decanter, Blue, Shouldered, Flattened Body, No. 566, Husted, c.1956, 10 x 8 In.	265.00
Decanter, Blue, Stopper, Somerso Inclusion, No. 7222, c.1972, 20 ½ In.	450.00
Decanter, Charisma, Ruby Swirl, No. 7225X, 13 ¾ x 10 ¾ In.	900.00
Decanter, Genie, Amethyst, Rainbow Stopper, 18 x 8 In.	250.00
Decanter, Genie, Blue, No. 5815, Wayne Husted, 1958, 29 ½ In.	500.00
Decanter, Honey Crackle, No. 6826, Myers, c.1968, 18 In.	155.00
Decanter, Jonquil Yellow, No. 6123, Wayne Husted, c.1961, 29 ½ In.	775.00
Decanter, Rose, No. 6310, c.1963, 12 ½ x 10 In.	250.00
Decanter, Tangerine, Ribbed Optic, Stopper, No. 6954, 27 In.	400.00
Decanter, Turquoise, No. 564, Wayne Husted, c.1956, 17 ½ In.	255.00
Decanter, Wheat, No. 6948, Joel Myers, c.1971, 20 ½ In.	155.00
Flask, Yellow, Flared Rim, Flintcraft, 12 x 9 ¾ In.	185.00
Lamp Base, Jonquil Yellow, No. 6123LL, 37 In.	250.00
Pitcher, Amberina, Hand Blown, Applied Clear Handle, 10 ¾ x 7 ½ In.	36.00
Rose Bowl, No. 625L, c.1962, 14 In.	65.00
Vase, Azure Blue, Textured, Hank Adams, 18 In.	85.00
Vase, Blenko Blue, Free-Form Top, No. 7223, Nickerson, 25 In.	165.00
Vase, Blenko Blue, Indented, No. 921M, Winslow Anderson, c.1950, 10 In.	85.00
Vase, Blue, Bulbous Bottle Shape, Indented, No. 647, Joel Myers, 1964, 17 In.	250.00
Vase, Clear, Wiggle, 16 ½ x 9 ½ In., 2 Piece	135.00
Vase, Emerald Green, 1980s, 11 x 7 ½ In.	40.00
Vase, Peacock, Flat Top, Joel Myers, c.1964, 16 ½ In.	300.00
Vase, Tangerine, Amberina, Rough Ribbed, No.6223, 1962, 12 In.	185.00
Vase, Tangerine, Charisma, No. 7221, John Nickerson, c.1972, 17 ¾ In.	145.00

BLOWN GLASS, *see Glass-Blown category.*

BLUE GLASS, *see Cobalt Blue category.*

BLUE ONION, *see Onion category.*

BLUE WILLOW, *see Willow category.*

BOCH FRERES factory was founded in 1841 in La Louviere in eastern Belgium. The wares resemble the work of Villeroy & Boch. The factory is still in business.

Box, Geometric Blue Enamel, Crackled Glaze, Gilt Bronze, c.1940, 5 ½ x 4 In.	225.00
Dish, Cover, Blue & Purple Flower Rim, Marked, 5 ½ x 4 In.	25.00
Dish, Cover, Blue & Purple Flower Rim, Marked, 9 ¾ x 3 ½ In.	35.00
Jardiniere, Antelope, Marked, Charles Catteau, c.1926, 10 ½ In.	5900.00
Plate, Snow Landscape, 19th Century, Marked, 10 In.	45.00
Tile, Water Lily, Art Nouveau, Cream, Green, Gold, Marked, c.1905, 6 x 6 In.	145.00
Tray, Asian Horsemen, Burnt Orange, Apricot, Black, Marked, 14 x 9 ½ In.	229.00
Vase, Art Deco, Abstract, Bands, Scrolling, Pink, Lavender, Purple, 3 ¼ x 4 In., Pair	3950.00
Vase, Art Deco, Deer, Crackle Ground, Cobalt Blue, Turquoise, c.1920, 9 x 8 In. ....*illus*	760.00
Vase, Art Deco, Stylized Flower, Blue, Yellow, Aqua Enamel, 6 ¼ In.	125.00
Vase, Art Nouveau, Baluster Shape, Red, Brown, Ivy Leaves, Berries, Flowers, 10 ½ x 7 In.	600.00

Black, Tobacco Jar, Cover, Boy, Open Mouth, Bisque, Multicolored, 5 ½ x 4 ½ x 5 In.
$92.00

Black, Tobacco Tin, Nigger Hair, Bail Handle, c.1878, 7 In.
$819.00

Black, Watermelon, Cardboard, Lithograph Face, Celluloid Baby Inside, 4 x 2 & 3 ¼ In.
$150.00

Boch Freres, Vase, Art Deco, Deer, Crackle Ground, Cobalt Blue, Turquoise, c.1920, 9 x 8 In.
$760.00

Boehm, Barn Owl, Spread Wings, Signed, Dated June 6, 1975, 20 x 26 In. **$738.00**

Boehm, Crested Flycatcher, Sweet Gum Tree, Mark, 18 ¾ In. **$575.00**

Boehm, Magnolia Grandiflora, Butterfly, Stamped, Signed, 6 ¼ In. **$299.00**

Boehm, Prula Warblers, Stamped, Signed, 15 ¾ In. **$388.00**

Vase, Flowers, Blue, Green, White, Glazed Stoneware, Ch. Catteau, c.1930, 14 In., Pair	2032.00
Vase, Flowers, Vertical Stripes, Catteau, 17 ⅜ In.	374.00
Vase, Pairs Of Birds On Branches, Fruit Bands, Stepped Form, Keramis, c.1939, 14 In.	2032.00
Vase, Shorebirds, Red Clay Ground, Ivory Birds, Flowers, Keramis, c.1930, 13 ¼ In.	1434.00

BOEHM is the collector's name for the porcelains of Edward Marshall Boehm. In 1953 the Osso China Company was reorganized as Edward Marshall Boehm, Inc. The company is still working in England and New Jersey. In the early days of the factory, dishes were made, but the elaborate and lifelike bird figurines are the best-known ware. Edward Marshall Boehm, the founder, died in 1969, but the firm has continued to design and produce porcelain. Today, the firm makes both limited and unlimited editions of figurines and plates.

Baby Blue Jay, 4 ¾ In.	88.00
Barn Owl, Spread Wings, Signed, Dated June 6, 1975, 20 x 26 In. .... *illus*	738.00
Black Capped Chickadee, Holly Branch, 8 ¾ In.	259.00
Black-Throated Blue Warblers, Flower, Leaves	198.00
Blue Grosbeak, 11 In.	210.00
Bluebirds, 12 In.	999.00
Calliope Hummingbird, With Hibiscus	145.00
Cardinal, 8 ½ x 5 ½ x 4 ½ In.	176.00
Catbird, 15 ¼ In.	400.00
Cedar Waxwing, Male, Female, Pair	940.00
Chick, Hatching, 14 ¼ In.	230.00
Crested Flycatcher, Sweet Gum Tree, Mark, 18 ¾ In. ....*illus*	575.00
Downy Woodpecker, 13 ¼ In.	588.00
Flicker, Branch, Woodland Creatures, 13 In.	940.00
Giraffe, 14 ¼ x 7 ¾ In.	353.00
Hooded Mergansers, Pink Flowers, 10 ¾ In.	269.00
Hummingbird, On Cactus, 8 In.	198.00
Hummingbirds, Tree Trunk, 25 ½ In.	657.00
Hunter, Standing Horse, 14 ½ x 14 ½ In.	439.00
Magnolia Grandiflora, Butterfly, Stamped, Signed, 6 ¼ In. ....*illus*	299.00
Marsh Harrier With Water Lilies, Yellow Blossoms, 26 x 20 In.	850.00
Mockingbird, Male, Female, 12 ¾ & 11 ⅜ In., Pair	705.00
Mountain Bluebirds, Flowers, 12 x 16 In.	400.00
Orchard Orioles, 10 ⅝ In.	470.00
Orchid, Hummingbird, 27 ½ In.	2702.00
Orchid, Pink	82.00
Percheron, Prancing, 1950, 8 ¼ x 12 In.	4270.00
Pink Peony, 7 x 21 x 12 In.	1404.00
Prothonotary Warbler, 6 ½ In.	150.00
Prula Warblers, Stamped, Signed, 15 ¾ In. ....*illus*	388.00
Raccoons, On Tree, 12 In.	310.00
Roadrunner & Lizard, 13 ½ In.	764.00
Robin In Nest, 10 x 10 In.	351.00
Ruffed Grouse, Male, Female, 11 ¼ x 8 In., Pair	470.00
Towhee On Stump, Mushrooms, Fungus, 7 ½ In.	495.00
Tufted Titmouse, 13 ¼ In.	470.00
Varied Buntings, Red Flowers, Green Leaves, 23 In.	418.00
Western Bluebird, 17 ⅝ x 19 ½ In.	1920.00
White-Throated Sparrow, 9 ¼ In.	198.00

BOOKENDS have probably been used since books became inexpensive. Early libraries kept books in cupboards, not on open shelves. By the 1870s bookends appeared, especially homemade fret-carved wooden examples. Most bookends listed in this book date from the twentieth century. Bookends are also listed in other categories by manufacturer or material. All bookends listed here are pairs.

2 Children, Playing, Bronze, Signed, E. Barrett Parsons, 1913, 6 x 6 ½ In.	2300.00
Adam & Eve, Caramel Glaze, California Clay Products, c.1928, 6 x 7 In.	316.00
Antelope Heads, Curved Horns, Metal, Patinate, Square Base, 14 x 4 In.	115.00
Asian Man, Seated, Woman, Orientalist, Bronze, Austria, c.1900, 4 x 8 In.	936.00
Beethoven, At Piano, Bronze, Variegated Black Marble Base, J.B. Hirsch, 6 x 6 In.	69.00
Birds, Bronze, Ivory Beaks, Signed, B. Ntman, 9 ½ In. ....*illus*	3803.00
Boy & Girl Carrying Books, Carved, Relief, Brown Patina, Franz Ziegler, 6 ¾ x 4 In.	240.00
Cathedral Of Rheims, Facade, Iron	75.00
Children At Gate, Cast Iron, Hubley, Signed, G.G.D., 5 ⅜ x 4 In. ....*illus*	59.00
Chippendale Chair Back, Openwork Splat, Iron, Painted, Bradley & Hubbard, c.1920	150.00

B

Covered Wagon, Team Of Horses, Cast Iron, Signed, Hubley, No. 375, 3 ¾ x 6 ¾ In. ......*illus*	59.00
Crescent, Chrome, Brass, Bakelite, 4 ½ x 3 ¾ x 3 In.	149.00
Dancing Couple, Bronze, John Held Jr., Bronze	1200.00
Deco Lady Heads, Bronze Finish, Frankart, 6 ¾ In.	245.00
Dog Head, Wagging Tongue, Bronze, 8 ½ In.	218.00
Dog, Bull Terrier, Seated, Silver Plate, Marble, L-Shape, 7 x 6 ¾ In.	201.00
Dog, German Shepherd, Standing, Arched Plaque, Bronze, Bradley & Hubbard, 6 x 5 In.	115.00
Dog, Greyhound, Art Deco, Cast Iron, Brass Patina, 1930s, 5 In.	144.00
Dog, Setter, Black & White, Green Base, Cast Iron, Hubley, No. 363, 5 x 8 In. ....*illus*	146.00
Dogs, Looking Through Gate, Bronze, 5 ½ x 5 In. ....*illus*	75.00
Dutch Boy & Girl, Kissing, Painted, Cast Iron, Hubley, 4 ¾ In. ....55.00 to 175.00	
End Of The Trail, Figural, After James Earle Fraser Statue, Cast Iron	150.00
Female Nudes, Art Deco, Bronze, 8 In.	410.00
Fireplace, Kettle, Cast Iron, Painted, 6 ½ x 2 ¼ x 6 In.	110.00
Flower Basket, Mixed Flowers, Multicolored, Cast Iron, Marked, Bradley & Hubbard, 5 ⅝ In. ..	275.00
Flowers, Basket, Cast Iron, Bradley & Hubbard, 5 ⅝ x 5 In. ......*illus*	293.00
Frog, Playing Banjo, Pottery, Painted, 4 ½ x 3 ½ In.	25.00
Gazelle, Silver Plate, Franz Hagenauer, Austria, 4 x 5 In.	1440.00
General Motors Building, Cast Iron, Detroit Headquarters, Blue Finish	350.00
General Motors Building, Cast, Patinate	350.00
General Motors Building, Detroit Headquarters, Cast Iron, Blue Finish	350.00
Grand Old Man, Alonzo Stagg, Cast Bronze, Western Foundry Co., 6 ¾ x 6 In.	120.00
Green Soapstone, Oriental Carved, 6 x 5 In.	205.00
Grouse, High Tail Feathers, Bronze, Marble Base, C. Rischman, 7 In.	480.00
Gymnast, Nude Male, Bronze, Mark, c.1930, 7 ½ In.	558.00
Hiawatha, Quote, Shaped Plaque, Image Of Hiawatha, Iron, 1920s	175.00
Horse, Carved, Alabaster, Italy, 20th Century, 7 x 8 ½ In.	118.00
Horse, Prancing, Cast Iron, Stepped & Scrolled Base, Greenlees, Glasgow, 11 x 11 In.	288.00
Huckleberry Finn, Paddlewheel Boat, Metal, Patinate, Painted, Embossed, 7 ¾ In.	295.00
John Alden & Priscilla, Cast Iron, Bradley & Hubbard	90.00
Knight, In Archway, Holding Shield, Crest Of Griffin With Prey In Claws, 7 ⅝ In.	144.00
Laddie Boy Dog, Figural, Cast Iron, Painted, 5 ¾ In.	495.00
Leaf Design, Copper, Jarvie, Thomas Maher, 5 x 4 ½ x 5 In.	1020.00
Libbiloo, Nickel-Plated Metal, Russel Wright, c.1930, 6 x 7 In.	9000.00
Liberty Bell, Proclaim Liberty, Pass & Stow, Cast Iron, Bronze Finish, Philad., 1753, 5 In.	145.00
Lily Pads, Cattails, Gilt Bronze, Art Nouveau, Signed, McClelland-Barclay, 4 ½ x 4 In.	295.00
Lion, Bronze, 7 x 4 In.	45.00
Man On Mule, Bronze, Heinrich W. Hirschler, Austria, c.1900, 5 x 6 In.	702.00
Man, Holding Books, Bronze, Marble Base, 7 In. ......*illus*	88.00
Masonic Temple Door, Column Sides, Bronze, Painted, Armor Bronze, 1920s	475.00
Nude Males, Penseur, 5 ½ In.	45.00
Owl, Bronze, Sculptured, Brutalist, 1960s, 5 x 3 ½ In.	280.00
Punch & Judy, Figural, Cast Iron, Painted, 12 ½ x 8 ¾ In.	173.00
Raggedy Ann & Andy, Cast Iron, P.F. Volland & Co., c.1931, 6 In. ......*illus*	1872.00
Robert E. Lee, Bust, Bronze	95.00
Scholars, Reading, Middle Eastern, Bronze, Ronson, c.1920	85.00
Schoolboy, Scottie Dog, Full Figure, Painted, Cast Iron, Hubley, 5 ¼ x 2 ½ In.	55.00
Shakespeare Shrine, Iron, Bradley & Hubbard, c.1925	250.00
Shakespeare, Portrait, Relief, Shaped Plaque, Bradley & Hubbard, 1920s	125.00
Shell, Brass Plated	30.00
Ship, Cast Iron, Japanned Brass Patina, Marked, Bradley & Hubbard, 6 ¼ In.	125.00
Ship, Galleon, Iron, 1920s	65.00
Ship, Sailing, Art & Crafts Style, Painted, 5 ¾ x 3 ½ x 5 ½ In.	100.00
Ship, Sailing, Painted, Invincible, Armor Bronze, 1930s	150.00
Stagecoach, Iron, Painted, Nuydea, England, 7 ½ x 6 x 1 ¼ In., Pair	265.00
Sunbonnet Girl, Cast Iron, Marked, National Fdry, 6 x 3 In.	58.00
Temple Of Saturn, Columns, Iron, Bradley & Hubbard, 1920s	225.00
Tribal Figure, Bust, Feathers, Art Deco, Marble, White, Gold, Black Base, 6 ½ In.	259.00
Wirehaired & Scottish Terriers, On Stump, Painted, Cast Iron, Hubley, 5 x 5 ⅜ In.	200.00
Wood, Ceramic Tile Insets, Metal Base, Marshall Studios, Martz, 19 ¼ In.	135.00
Wood, Metal, Stringed Guitar, Marked	75.00

Bookends, Birds, Bronze, Ivory Beaks, Signed, B. Ntman, 9 ½ In.
$3803.00

Bookends, Children At Gate, Cast Iron, Hubley, Signed, G.G.D., 5 ⅜ x 4 In.
$59.00

Bookends, Covered Wagon, Team Of Horses, Cast Iron, Signed, Hubley, No. 375, 3 ¾ x 6 ¾ In.
$59.00

Bookends, Dog, Setter, Black & White, Green Base, Cast Iron, Hubley, No. 363, 5 x 8 In.
$146.00

BOOKMARKS were originally made of parchment, cloth, or leather. Soon woven silk ribbon, thin cardboard, celluloid, wood, silver, tortoiseshell, and metals were used. Examples made before 1850 are scarce, but there are many to be found dating before 1920.

Banded Agate, Acorn, 2 Leaves, Gold Tone Metal, 5 In.	220.00

TIP
Always remove a book from the shelf to dust. All sides need cleaning.

B

Bookends, Dogs, Looking Through Gate,
Bronze, 5 ½ x 5 In.
$75.00

Bookends, Flowers, Basket, Cast Iron,
Bradley & Hubbard, 5 ⅝ x 5 In.
$293.00

Bookends, Man, Holding Books, Bronze,
Marble Base, 7 In.
$88.00

Bookends, Raggedy Ann & Andy,
Cast Iron, P.F. Volland & Co., c.1931, 6 In.
$1872.00

Barber Bottles

The era of barber bottles
came to an end when the
Pure Food and Drug Act of
1906 regulated the use of
alcohol-based substances in
refillable containers. Barbers
stopped using them in their
shops, but some bottles were
made until the 1920s for
home use.

Celluloid, Totem Pole, Pacific Coast Steamship Co., Calif., Wash., Alaska, 5 ¼ In.	50.00
Portrait, Robert Burns, Victorian Style Frame, 4 ¼ In.	149.00
Punchwork, Challis, Hand Sewn, Crown, Crucifix, Alphabet, 4 ½ x 2 In.	65.00
Punchwork, Green Satin Ribbon, Hand Sewn, Brown Cross, 4 ⅛ x 2 ⅛ In.	20.00
Scrimshaw, Piano Key, Ram's Head	10.00
Sterling Silver, Banner Shape, Italy, 2 ¼ x ¾ In.	38.00
Sterling Silver, Dragonfly, 2 ¼ x 1 ¼ In.	30.00
Sterling Silver, Hickory Dickory Dock, Clock & Mouse, 3 ⅝ x ⅞ In.	20.00
Wood, Man, Double Sided, Hand Painted	20.00

BOSSONS character wall masks (heads), plaques, figurines, and other decorative pieces **BOSSONS** were made by W.H. Bossons, Limited, of Congleton, England. The company was founded in 1946 and closed in 1996. Dates shown are the date the item was introduced.

Wall Figure, Peon, 1963, 15 ½ In.	275.00
Wall Figure, Raccoon In Tree, 12 ¼ In.	65.00
Wall Figure, Woodpecker & Babies, Tree, c.1968, 12 x 5 ¼ In.	75.00
Wall Mask, Abdhul, 7 ½ In.	135.00
Wall Mask, Betsy Trotwood, c.1982, 6 In.	120.00
Wall Mask, Bretonne Lady, c.1982, 7 In.	185.00
Wall Mask, Chef, c.1969, 6 ¼ In.	110.00
Wall Mask, Eskimo, 8 In.	200.00
Wall Mask, Himalayan Man, c.1966, 6 In.	70.00
Wall Mask, Saracen, 1960, 7 In.	165.00
Wall Mask, Sarah Gamp, c.1982, 6 In.	120.00
Wall Mask, Sardinian, c.1967, 6 In.	85.00
Wall Mask, Sir Henry Morgan, 8 x 8 In.	175.00
Wall Plaque, Koala, 10 In.	110.00
Wall Plaque, Old English Cottage, c.1948, 14 In.	175.00

BOSTON & SANDWICH CO. *pieces may be found in the Sandwich Glass category.*

BOTTLE collecting has become a major American hobby. There are several general categories of bottles, such as historic flasks, bitters, household, and figural. ABM means the bottle was made by an automatic bottle machine after 1903. Pyro is the shortened form of the word *pyroglaze,* an enameled lettering used on bottles after the mid-1930s. This form of decoration is also called ACL or applied color label. For more prices, go to kovels.com.

Avon started in 1886 as the California Perfume Company. It was not until 1929 that the name **Avon** Avon was used. In 1939, it became Avon Products, Inc. Avon has made many figural bottles filled with cosmetic products. Ceramic, plastic, and glass bottles were made in limited editions.

Avon, Alaskan Moose Aftershave, 1974, 6 Oz.	14.00
Avon, Decanter, Windjammer Aftershave Town Pump, Black Glass, 1968, 6 Oz.	13.00
Barber, Ayer's Hair Vigor, Peacock Blue, 6 In.	59.00
Barber, Bay Rum, White, Painted Flowers, Smooth Base, 9 In.	101.00
Barber, Blue Opalescent, Jigsaw Pattern, Round, 7 ¼ In.	595.00
Barber, Blue Opalescent, Swirls, Round, 9 In.	550.00
Barber, Cobalt Blue, Lady's Leg, White Enamel, Boy Playing Tennis	239.00
Barber, Cobalt Blue, Lady's Leg, White Enamel, Girl & Boy Playing Tennis, 7 In.	595.00
Barber, Cobalt Blue, Mary Gregory Girl Tennis Player, Tooled Mouth, Pontil, 1885-1925, 8 In.	115.00
Barber, Cobalt Blue, Ribbed, White, Orange Enamel Flowers, Corset Waist, c.1900, 7 ½ In. *illus*	138.00
Barber, Cologne, Sparrows, Flowers, Porcelain Spout, 8 ¾ In.	146.00
Barber, Cranberry Opalescent, Jigsaw Pattern, Square, 8 In.	675.00
Barber, Cranberry Opalescent, Windows, Bulbous, Pontil, Hobbs, Brockunier, c.1900, 7 In.	529.00
Barber, Grass Green, Swirled Ribs, White Enamel Flowers, Open Pontil, 8 In.	59.00
Barber, Green, Ribs, Mary Gregory Girl, White Enamel, Tooled Mouth, Pontil, 1885-1925, 8 In.	184.00
Barber, Jade, Green, Enameled Flowers, 6 ¾ In.	67.00
Barber, Milk Glass, Water, Cabin In The Woods, Wintertime, Metal Cap, 10 In.	420.00
Barber, Multicolored Enameled Fern, Clear, Tooled Mouth, 1885-1925, 10 ⅞ In.	316.00
Barber, Purple Amethyst, Frosted, Gold Flower, Ribs, Rolled Lip, Pontil, 1885-1925, 7 ¾ In.	161.00
Barber, Purple Amethyst, Gilt, Rolled Lip, Pontil, c.1900, 8 ⅛ In.	316.00
Barber, Purple Amethyst, Ribs, White Enameled Windmill, Rolled Lip, Pontil, 1885-1925, 7 ¾ In.	207.00
Barber, Sapphire Blue, Coin Spot, Melon Sides, Tooled Mouth, c.1900, 7 ⅛ In.	265.00
Barber, Spanish Lace, Opalescent Cranberry, Square, Tooled Mouth, c.1900, 8 ½ In. *illus*	242.00
Barber, Toilet Water, Cobalt Blue, 3-Piece Mold, Rolled Lip, Pontil, Stopper, 1815-35, 6 ⅛ In.	230.00
Barber, Toilet Water, Purple Cobalt Blue, 3-Piece Mold, Tooled, Lip, Stopper, 1835, 5 ⅜ In.	403.00

B

Barber, Turquoise Blue, Opalescent, Swirled Stripes, Rolled Lip, c.1900, 9 ⅛ In.	184.00
Barber, Yellow Green, Bell Shape, Ribs, Mary Gregory Girl, Tooled Mouth, Pontil, c.1885, 8 ⅛ In.	127.00
Beer, Bismarck Bottling Works, Dakota, Slug Plate, Amber, 11 ½ In.	3200.00
Beer, Chas. R. Puckhaber, Fresno, Amber, Crown Top, Qt.	90.00
Beer, Columbia Weiss Beer B'wy., St. Louis, Mo., Green, Wire Bail, Porcelain Stopper, c.1880, 9 In.	146.00
Beer, E. Tousley Cronk's, Cobalt Blue, 12-Sided, Smooth Base, 1855-65, 10 In.	3136.00
Beer, Grasser Brewing, Toledo, Dark Amber, Blob Top, Qt.	30.00
Beer, G.W. Hoxie's Premium, Blue Green, Cylindrical, U.S.A., 1855-65, 6 ¾ In.	213.00
Beer, Muskegon Brewing Co., Blob Top, c.1880s, 5 ½ In.	200.00
Beer, Patent, Olive Amber, Double Ring Collar, Iron Pontil, c.1863, Pt.	35.00
Beer, Property Of Chas. R. Puckhaber Beers, Fresno, Cal., Amber, Crown Top, Split	157.00
Beer, Property Of Fredericksburg Brewery, San Jose, Cal., Monogram, Red Amber, Qt.	336.00
Beer, Theodore Lutge & Co., San Jose, Cal., Not To Be Sold, Green, Applied Top, Qt.	190.00
Beer, Wm. Pfeiffer, Lime Green, Monogram, Blob Top	50.00
Bininger, A.M. & Co., Amber, Applied Double Collar, Handle, 1860-70, 8 In.	633.00
Bininger, A.M. & Co., Yellow Olive Green, Applied Double Collar, Handle, c.1860, 8 In.	4025.00
Bininger, Clock, Regulator, Golden Amber, Applied Double Collar, Pontil, 5 ¾ In.	863.00
Bininger, Old Kentucky, Barrel, Amber, Applied Collar, Pontil, 8 In.	420.00
Bininger, Old Kentucky, Reserve Bourbon, Golden Amber, 1849, 9 ½ In.	339.00
Bitters, American Life, Log Cabin, Amber, Smooth Base, P.E. Iler, Tiffin, Ohio, c.1870, 9 In. ...	805.00
Bitters, American Life, P.E. Iler, Omaha, Neb., Amber, Cabin, c.1870, 9 ⅛ In. ....illus	29900.00
Bitters, Baker's Orange Grove, Amber, Roped Corners, Applied Collar	476.00
Bitters, Baker's Orange Grove, Amber, Tapered Collar Mouth, Labels, c.1875, 9 ½ In. .....illus	805.00
Bitters, Baker's Orange Grove, Golden Amber, Olive Tone, Square, Domed Shoulders, 9 In. ...	1344.00
Bitters, Baker's Orange Grove, Golden Yellow Amber, Roped Corners, Applied Mouth, 1865, 9 ⅝ In.	489.00
Bitters, Barrel, Amber, Applied Mouth, Iron Pontil, 9 In.	308.00
Bitters, Barrel, Cherry Puce, Applied Mouth, 1855-70, 10 In.	431.00
Bitters, Barrel, Cobalt Blue	560.00
Bitters, Big Bill Best, Tooled Lip, 11 ½ In.	350.00
Bitters, Bourbon Whiskey, Light Yellow, Embossed, Applied Mouth	10640.00
Bitters, Bowe's Cascara, Embossed, Tooled Lip, 9 ½ In.	336.00
Bitters, Brown's Celebrated Indian Herb, Indian Queen, Golden Amber, 12 ⅜ In.	978.00
Bitters, Brown's Celebrated Indian Herb, Indian Queen, Feb. 11 1868, Rolled Lip, Cork 364.00 to 896.00	
Bitters, Brown's Celebrated Indian Herb, Patented Feb 11 1868, Deep Amber, Rolled Lip, 12 In.	952.00
Bitters, Brown's Celebrated Indian Herb, Patented Feb 11 1868, Indian Queen, Amber, 12 In. ...	840.00
Bitters, Brown's Celebrated Indian Herb, Yellow Amber, c.1865, 12 ⅜ In. ....illus	1035.00
Bitters, Brown's Celebrated Indian Root, Indian Queen, Patented 1867, Rolled Lip	1008.00
Bitters, Brown's Indian Queen, Pat. Feb. 11, 1868, Yellow Amber, Rolled Lip, 12 ¼ In.	1008.00
Bitters, Bryant's Stomach, Lady's Leg, Emerald Green, Applied Top	4032.00
Bitters, Cabin, Amber, Roped Corners, Applied Tapered Collar, c.1875, 10 In.	392.00
Bitters, Cabin, Roped Corners, Amber, Sloping Collar, c.1855, 10 In.	532.00
Bitters, Caldwell's Herb, Great Tonic, Amber, Applied Mouth, Iron Pontil, c.1865, 12 ½ In.	207.00
Bitters, Celery Nervine, Label, 8 ¼ In.	35.00
Bitters, Clark's Sherry Wine, Aqua, 9 ⅓ In.	178.00
Bitters, Clarke's Vegetable Sherry Wine, Mass, Aqua, Pebbly Finish, c.1850, 11 ½ In.	403.00
Bitters, Colleton, Aqua, Applied Mouth, Open Pontil, 1840-60, 6 ½ In.	374.00
Bitters, Doctor Fisch's, Patented 1866, Fish, Golden Yellow Amber, Applied Mouth, 11 ¾ In. ..	748.00
Bitters, Doctor Fisch's, Patented 1866, Fish, Root Beer Amber, Applied Mouth, 11 ¾ In.	489.00
Bitters, Dr. A.W. Coleman's Antidyspeptic & Tonic, Green, Applied Top, Iron Pontil, 9 ¼ In.	3808.00
Bitters, Dr. Ball's Vegetable Stomachic, Green Aqua, Applied Mouth, Pontil, c.1840-60, 6 ¾ In.	546.00
Bitters, Dr. Ball's Vegetable Stomachic, Northboro, Mass., Aqua, Open Pontil, c.1860, 6 ⅞ In. .	345.00
Bitters, Dr. Birmingham's Antibillious Blood Purifying, Blue Green, c.1885, 9 In. ....illus	2645.00
Bitters, Dr. Bishop's Wahoo, New Haven, Conn., Yellow Amber, c.1870, 10 ⅛ In. ....illus	690.00
Bitters, Dr. Carey's Original Mandrake, Aqua, 12-Sided, 6 ½ In.	130.00
Bitters, Dr. C.W. Roback's Stomach, Amber, Barrel, Applied Mouth, Pontil, c.1860, 9 ¾ In.	748.00
Bitters, Dr. C.W. Roback's Stomach, Cincinnati, O., Golden Amber, 9 ¼ In.	299.00
Bitters, Dr. C.W. Roback's Stomach, Cincinnati, Ohio, Barrel, Golden Amber, c.1860, 9 ¾ In. . .	863.00
Bitters, Dr. C.W. Roback's Stomach, Medium Amber, Applied Mouth, 9 ¾ In.	280.00
Bitters, Dr. C.W. Roback's Stomach, Tobacco Amber, Barrel, Applied Mouth, c.1865, 9 ⅛ In. ..	276.00
Bitters, Dr. Fisch's, W.H. Ware, Fish, Patented 1866, Amber, Drippy Top	448.00
Bitters, Dr. Fisch's, W.H. Ware, Fish, Patented 1866, Yellow Green, Applied Mouth	2240.00
Bitters, Dr. Flint's Quaker, Aqua, Beveled Corners, Square Collar, 9 ¼ In.	2760.00
Bitters, Dr. Henley's Wild Grape Root, Aqua, Tooled Top, Pontil	4256.00
Bitters, Dr. Henley's Wild Grape Root IXL, Olive Green, c.1875, 12 In. ....illus	4025.00
Bitters, Dr. J. Hostetter's Stomach, Amber Yellow Green, Applied Top	616.00
Bitters, Dr. J. Hostetter's Stomach, Golden Amber, Square, Beveled Corners, Sloping Collar, 9 ¾ In.	4600.00

Bottle, Barber, Cobalt Blue, Ribbed, White, Orange Enamel Flowers, Corset Waist, c.1900, 7 ½ In. $138.00

Bottle, Barber, Spanish Lace, Opalescent Cranberry, Square, Tooled Mouth, c.1900, 8 ½ In. $242.00

Bottle, Bitters, American Life, P.E. Iler, Omaha, Neb., Amber, Cabin, c.1870, 9 ⅛ In. $29900.00

As always, the edited listings in *Kovels' Price Guides* aren't available on any website, but readers should visit Kovels.com for information on trends, tips, reproductions, marks, old prices, and more!

Bottle, Bitters, Baker's Orange Grove,
Amber, Tapered Collar Mouth, Labels,
c.1875, 9 ½ In.
$805.00

Bottle, Bitters,
Brown's Celebrated Indian Herb,
Yellow Amber, c.1865, 12 ⅜ In.
$1035.00

Bottle, Bitters,
Dr. Birmingham's Antibillious Blood
Purifying, Blue Green, c.1885, 9 In.
$2645.00

Bottle, Bitters, Dr. Bishop's Wahoo,
New Haven, Conn., Yellow Amber,
c.1870, 10 ⅛ In.
$690.00

Bitters, Dr. J. Hostetter's Stomach, Yellow Green, Applied Drippy Top	448.00
Bitters, Dr. Lamot's Botanic, Amber, Inset Panels, Applied Mouth, 8 ½ In.	235.00
Bitters, Dr. Langley's Root & Herb, 99 Union St. Boston, Aqua, 8 ¼ In.	199.00
Bitters, Dr. Langley's Root & Herb, 99 Union St., Boston, Open Pontil, 9 In.	119.00
Bitters, Dr. Lowe's Celebrated Stomach & Nerve Tonic, Roped Neck, 7Up Green, 9 ½ In.	560.00
Bitters, Dr. Manly Hardy's Genuine Jaundice, Aqua, Applied Mouth, Pontil, c.1840, 7 ⅛ In.	403.00
Bitters, Dr. Michael Cox's, 3 Birds, Amber, Tooled Mouth, 1880-95, 10 ⅛ In.	863.00
Bitters, Dr. Soule's Hop, 1872, Ginger Ale Yellow, Bubbles, 9 ¾ In.	259.00
Bitters, Dr. Soule's Hop, Tobacco Green, Applied Top	392.00
Bitters, Dr. Soule's Hop, Yellow Butterscotch, Applied Top	146.00
Bitters, Dr. Stephen Jewett's Celebrated Health Restoring, Aqua, Applied Top, Pontil, 7 ¼ In.	672.00
Bitters, Dr. Stephen Jewett's Celebrated Health Restoring, Aqua, Pontil, 7 ¼ In.	315.00 to 431.00
Bitters, Dr. Stephen Jewett's, Rindge, N.H., Green Aqua, Open Pontil, c.1850, 7 ¼ In.	242.00
Bitters, Dr. Von Hopf's Curacoa, Square, Tooled Top	90.00
Bitters, Dr. Wood's Sarsaparilla & Wild Cherry, Green Aqua, Applied Mouth, Pontil, 8 ⅞ In.	489.00
Bitters, Drake's 1860 Plantation, Patented 1862, Cabin, Yellow	479.00
Bitters, Drake's Plantation, 4 Log, Golden Amber, 1860	336.00
Bitters, Drake's Plantation, 4 Log, Lemon Yellow, 1860	784.00
Bitters, Drake's, Plantation, 6 Log, Cabin, Applied Sloping Collar, 1860, 9 ⅝ In.	1456.00
Bitters, Drake's Plantation, 6 Log, Golden Yellow Olive, c.1860, 9 ¾ In.	460.00
Bitters, Drake's Plantation, 6 Log, Medium Copper, c.1860, 10 In.	345.00
Bitters, Drake's Plantation, 6 Log, Medium Puce, Applied Mouth, 1862-75, 10 In.	374.00
Bitters, Drake's Plantation, 6 Log, Puce, 1860	280.00
Bitters, Drake's Plantation, 6 Log, Red Orange	179.00
Bitters, Drake's Plantation, 6 Log, Shaded Strawberry Puce, Applied Collar, 9 ⅝ In.	1035.00
Bitters, Drake's Plantation, 6 Log, Yellow, Green, Sloping Collar, 9 ¾ In.	3738.00
Bitters, Drake's Plantation, Cherry Puce, Applied Mouth, 1862-75, 10 In.	431.00
Bitters, Embossed, Cherry Tree, H.P. Herb, Wild Cherry, Roped Corners	7840.00
Bitters, F. Brown Sarsaparilla & Tomato, Boston, Aqua, Applied Double Collar, c.1840, 9 In.	345.00
Bitters, Fish, W.H. Ware, Patent 1865, Yellow Amber, Applied Mouth, 11 ½ In. ....*illus*	690.00
Bitters, Fish, W.H. Ware, Patent 1866, Amber, Smooth Base, Applied Mouth, 11 ½ In.	489.00
Bitters, Fish, W.H. Ware, Patent 1866, Chocolate Amber	448.00
Bitters, Fish, W.H. Ware, Patent 1866, Tobacco Amber, Applied Mouth, 11 ⅝ In.	4025.00
Bitters, G.C. Segur's Golden Seal, Aqua, Applied Mouth, Open Pontil, 1840-60, 8 ⅜ In.	1093.00
Bitters, Germania, Seated Woman, Milk Glass, Label, Applied Mouth, 9 ½ In.	5152.00
Bitters, Greeley's Bourbon, Barrel, Copper Puce, Applied Square Collar, c.1865, 9 In.	616.00
Bitters, Greeley's Bourbon, Barrel, Puce, Applied Mouth, c.1860, 9 ¼ In.	690.00
Bitters, Greeley's Bourbon, Barrel, Salmon Puce, Applied Mouth, c.1860, 9 ⅜ In.	863.00
Bitters, Greeley's Bourbon, Barrel, Smoky Copper Puce, Applied Mouth, 9 ¼ In.	403.00
Bitters, Greeley's Bourbon, Barrel, Smoky Olive Topaz, Applied Mouth, c.1870, 9 ⅜ In.	1725.00
Bitters, Greeley's Bourbon, Barrel, Smoky Olive Yellow, Square Collar Mouth, 9 ⅛ In.	2300.00
Bitters, Greeley's Bourbon, Barrel, Smoky Pink Topaz, Applied Mouth, 9 ¼ In.	863.00
Bitters, Greeley's Bourbon, Light Purple, Applied Square Collar	560.00
Bitters, Greeley's Bourbon Whiskey, Barrel, Strawberry Puce, c.1865, 9 ⅜ In. ....*illus*	460.00
Bitters, Hall's, Barrel, Amber, Applied Square Collar, 1842	179.00
Bitters, Hall's, Barrel, Golden Amber, Applied Mouth, c.1865, 9 ⅛ In.	316.00
Bitters, Hartwig Kantorowicz, Milk Glass, Applied Top	224.00
Bitters, Hentz's Curative, Aqua, Square, 9 ⅝ In.	89.00
Bitters, Highland Bitters & Scotch Tonic, Barrel, Red Amber, Applied Mouth, c.1870, 9 ⅝ In.	1380.00
Bitters, Holtzermann's Patent Stomach, Cabin, Amber, Applied Mouth	2240.00
Bitters, Holtzermann's Patent Stomach, Cabin, Orange Amber, 9 ¾ In.	295.00
Bitters, Holtzermann's Patent Stomach, Cabin, Yellow Amber, 1867-75, 9 ½ In.	4480.00
Bitters, Holtzermann's Patent Stomach, Cabin, Yellow Amber, 9 In.	4480.00
Bitters, Holtzermann's Patent, Stomach, Yellow Amber, Collar Mouth, c.1870, 9 ⅝ In. ...*illus*	1840.00
Bitters, Hop Tonic, Semi-Cabin, Amber, Tooled Top	112.00
Bitters, H.P. Herb Wild Cherry, Cabin, Cherry Tree, Green, Tooled Lip	7840.00
Bitters, H.P. Herb Wild Cherry, Embossed Tree, Light Amber, Tooled Top	560.00
Bitters, Hutchings Dyspepsia, Blue Aqua, Applied Mouth, Iron Pontil, c.1840, 8 ½ In.	426.00
Bitters, Indian Vegetable & Sarsaparilla, Aqua, Applied Mouth, Open Pontil, c.1840, 8 In.	978.00
Bitters, Isham's Stomach, Tobacco Amber	728.00
Bitters, Jackson's Aromatic Life, Olive Green, Smooth Base, c.1860, 9 In.	6330.00
Bitters, James W. Price Aromatic Stomach, Yellow Amber, c.1875, 8 ⅞ In.	138.00
Bitters, John Moffat, Phoenix, Olive Green, Applied Collar, c.1850, 5 ¾ In. ....*illus*	748.00
Bitters, John W. Steele's Niagara Star, Embossed Bird, Amber, Applied Mouth	476.00
Bitters, John W. Steele's Niagara Star, Semi-Cabin, Golden Amber, c.1870, 10 ¼ In.	1035.00
Bitters, Johnson's Indian Dyspeptic, Aqua, Applied Mouth, Open Pontil, 1840-60, 6 ½ In.	431.00

Bitters, Johnson's Indian Dyspeptic, Teal, Applied Mouth, Pontil, 6 ½ In.	364.00
Bitters, Jones Universal Stomach, Golden Amber, Applied Mouth, Labels, 1875-85, 9 ⅛ In.	1265.00
Bitters, Kaiser Wilhelm Co., Ladies Leg Neck, Squat, 10 In.	69.00
Bitters, Kelly's Old Cabin, Patented 1863, Amber, Applied Drippy Top	2464.00
Bitters, Kelly's Old Cabin, Patented 1863, Amber, Applied Top	2240.00
Bitters, Kelly's Old Cabin, Patented 1863, Olive Yellow Amber, Applied Mouth, c.1865-75, 9 ⅛ In.	6900.00
Bitters, Kimball's Jaundice, Amber, Rectangular, Beveled, Stoddard Glass Works, Pontil, c.1846, 7 In.	1400.00
Bitters, Kimball's Jaundice, Olive Amber, Beveled Corners, 1846-60, 6 ⅞ In.	1400.00
Bitters, Lacour's Sarsapariphere, Green, Applied Top	1904.00
Bitters, Lash's, Natural Tonic Laxative, Contents, Amber, Square, Paper Label, 4 ¾ In.	440.00
Bitters, Lash's, Natural Tonic Laxative, Contents, Amber, Square, Paper Label, 9 ½ In.	130.00
Bitters, Lediard's Celebrated Stomach, Teal, Double Sloping Collar, Iron Pontil, 10 In.	5376.00
Bitters, Lyman's Dandelion, Bangor, Me., Aqua, Rectangular, Embossed, 10 ½ In.	170.00
Bitters, National, Ear Of Corn, Claret, Drippy, Applied Top, 1867	5152.00
Bitters, National, Ear Of Corn, Patent 1867, Amber, 12 ½ In.	5500.00
Bitters, National, Ear Of Corn, Patent 1867, Blue Aqua, Applied Mouth, 12 ½ In.	9200.00
Bitters, National, Ear Of Corn, Patent 1867, Deep Strawberry Puce, 12 ½ In.	3640.00
Bitters, National, Ear Of Corn, Patent 1867, Golden Amber, Applied Mouth, 12 ⅝ In.	403.00
Bitters, National, Ear Of Corn, Patent 1867, Maroon, U.S.A., c.1867, 12 ½ In.	3640.00
Bitters, National, Ear Of Corn, Yellow Green, Drippy, Applied Top, 1867	4032.00
Bitters, Old Homestead Wild Cherry, Cabin, Amber, c.1870, 9 ⅝ In.	431.00
Bitters, Old Homestead Wild Cherry, Cabin, Medium Amber, Applied Top	364.00
Bitters, Old Homestead Wild Cherry, Cabin, Yellow Green, Applied Top	2688.00
Bitters, Old Homestead Wild Cherry, Cabin, Yellow Olive, c.1870, 9 ¾ In.	4888.00
Bitters, Old Sachem & Wigwam Tonic, Barrel, Lemon Yellow, Square Collar, 9 ½ In.	8625.00
Bitters, Old Sachem & Wigwam Tonic, Barrel, Olive Amber, Applied Mouth, 1860-70, 9 ½ In.	748.00
Bitters, Old Sachem & Wigwam Tonic, Barrel, Orange Amber, Applied Mouth, 1860-75, 9 ¼ In.	345.00
Bitters, Old Sachem & Wigwam Tonic, Barrel, Puce, Applied Mouth, 1860-80, 9 In.	1957.00
Bitters, Old Sachem Bitters & Wigwam Tonic, Barrel, Medium Golden Amber	448.00
Bitters, Old Sachem Bitters & Wigwam Tonic, Barrel, Orange Amber, Applied Square Collar	672.00
Bitters, Old Sachem Wigwam Tonic, Barrel, Amber, 9 ½ In.	885.00
Bitters, Original Pocahontas, Y. Ferguson, Barrel, Aqua, Applied Mouth	4928.00
Bitters, Peruvian, W. & K., Monogram, Applied Top	168.00
Bitters, Pineapple, Amber, Smooth Base, Drippy, Applied Mouth, 8 ⅞ In.	258.00
Bitters, Pineapple, Medium Amber	336.00
Bitters, Pineapple, Olive Green	4928.00
Bitters, Pineapple, Orange Amber, 9 In.	195.00
Bitters, Pineapple, W & Co., N.Y., Yellow Amber, Open Pontil, c.1865, 8 ½ In. ...illus	316.00
Bitters, Pineapple, Yellow, Slug Plate, Tubular Pontil	1232.00
Bitters, Polo Club Stomach, Amber, 9 ¼ In.	175.00
Bitters, Professor Geo. J. Byrne, Patented 1870, Red Amber, Embossed, 10 ¾ In.	3163.00
Bitters, Sanborn's Kidney & Liver Vegetable Laxative, Amber, 10 In.	180.00
Bitters, Scheetz, Celebrated Bitter Cordial, Strawberry Puce, c.1870, 9 ½ In.	2070.00
Bitters, Schroeder's, Amber, Tooled Lip, 1885-95, 8 ¼ In.	690.00
Bitters, Semi-Cabin, Unembossed, Tobacco Amber	123.00
Bitters, Simon's Centennial, Bust Of George Washington, Aqua, 1876, 10 ¼ In. ...illus	1265.00
Bitters, Simon's Centennial, Bust Of George Washington, Aqua, Olive Striation, Applied Mouth, 10 In.	1035.00
Bitters, Solomons' Strengthening & Invigorating, Cobalt Blue, c.1875, 9 ¾ In. ...illus	1840.00
Bitters, Southern Aromatic Cock Tail, J. Grossman, New Orleans, Amber, Long Neck, Tooled Lip	6160.00
Bitters, Stomach, Olive Amber, Square, Beveled Corners, Applied Tapered Collar, c.1870, 9 In.	252.00
Bitters, Suffolk, Philbrook & Tucker, Boston, Pig, Orange Amber, 10 ½ In.	1099.00
Bitters, Suffolk, Philbrook & Tucker, Pig, Yellow Amber, Applied Mouth, c.1870, 10 ⅛ In. illus	978.00
Bitters, Wallace's Tonic Stomach, Chicago, Amber, Pebbly, Smooth Base, c.1885, 9 In.	207.00
Bitters, Wallace's Tonic Stomach, Chicago, Geo. Powell & Co., Amber, Square, Applied Top	202.00
Bitters, Warner's Safe Tonic, Amber, Tooled Lip, 7 ½ In.	840.00
Bitters, West India Stomach, St. Louis, Amber, 9 In.	120.00
Bitters, W.F. Severa Stomach, Tooled Top	56.00
Bitters, William Allen's Congress, Blue Green, Recessed Panels, Smooth Base, c.1870, 10 ¼ In.	2875.00
Black Glass, Cylindrical, Olive Yellow, Seal, Sloping Collar, Pontil, Qt.	1150.00
Black Glass, Dip Mold, Open Pontil, 1780-1820, 10 In.	39.00
Black Glass, Dutch Onion, Horsehoof, Olive Amber, Holland, c.1735, 7 ¾ In. ...illus	138.00
Black Glass, Dutch Onion, Yellow Olive, Applied String Lip, 7 ½ x 5 ½ In.	161.00
Black Glass, Mallet, Olive Amber, Applied Lip, England, c.1745, 8 x 5 ½ In. ...illus	196.00
Black Glass, Mallet, Olive Amber, Sheared Mouth, Applied String Lip, Pontil, 9 x 5 In.	1495.00
Black Glass, Mallet, Olive Amber, Tooled Mouth, Applied String Lip, Kick-Up, Pontil, 1745, 8 In.	288.00
Black Glass, Mallet, Olive Green, Applied String Lip, England, c.1760, 7 ⅛ x 4 ¾ In.	489.00

Bottle, Bitters,
Dr. Henley's Wild Grape Root IXL,
Olive Green, c.1875, 12 In.
$4025.00

Bottle, Bitters, Fish, W.H. Ware,
Patent 1865, Yellow Amber,
Applied Mouth, 11 ½ In.
$690.00

Bottle, Bitters,
Greeley's Bourbon Whiskey, Barrel,
Strawberry Puce, c.1865, 9 ⅜ In.
$460.00

Bottle, Bitters, Holtzermann's Patent,
Stomach, Yellow Amber, Collar Mouth,
c.1870, 9 ⅝ In.
$1840.00

Bottle, Bitters, John Moffat,
Phoenix, Olive Green, Applied Collar,
c.1850, 5 ¾ In.
$748.00

Bottle, Bitters, Pineapple, W & Co., N.Y.,
Yellow Amber, Open Pontil,
c.1865, 8 ½ In.
$316.00

Bottle, Bitters, Simon's Centennial,
Bust Of George Washington, Aqua,
1876, 10 ¼ In.
$1265.00

Bottle, Bitters,
Solomons' Strengthening & Invigorating,
Cobalt Blue, c.1875, 9 ¾ In.
$1840.00

Black Glass, Mallet, Olive Green, Sheared Mouth, Applied String Lip, 1750-65, 7 ½ x 4 ⅜ In.	431.00
Black Glass, Mallet, Olive Green, Sheared Mouth, String Lip, Pontil, c.1730, 8 In.	258.00
Black Glass, Onion, Emerald Green, Sheared Mouth, Applied String Lip, 1720-40, 6 ⅝ x 5 ⅞ In.	184.00
Black Glass, Onion, Olive Green, Applied String Lip, Germany, 7 x 5 ¾ In. ....*illus*	104.00
Black Glass, Onion, Olive Green, String Lip, Domed Base, c.1710, 5 ¼ In.	476.00
Black Glass, Onion, Yellow Olive Green, Sheared Mouth, Applied String Lip, Pontil, c.1720, 7 x 6 In. .	161.00
Black Glass, Square, Rounded Corners, Sheared & Tooled Mouth, Pontil, c.1780, 11 In.	316.00
Black Glass, Utility, Square, Olive Green, Sheared & Tooled Mouth, c.1775, 8 ⅛ In. ....*illus*	748.00
Black Glass, Wine, Olive Amber, Rolled Lip, Seal, Squat, Pontil, 9 x 5 In.	2300.00
Black Glass, Wine, Olive Amber, Seal, 3-Piece Mold, Applied Mouth, Pontil, c.1790, 10 x 4 In.	345.00
Black Glass, Wine, Olive Amber, Seal, 3-Piece Mold, Double Collar, c.1831, 11 ½ In.	345.00
Black Glass, Wine, Olive Amber, Seal, Double Collar, 1830-50, 10 ¾ In.	316.00
Black Glass, Wine, Olive Amber, Sheared, Mouth, Applied String Lip, Seal, c.1777, 10 ⅜ In. ..	1380.00
Black Glass, Wine, Olive Green, Seal, 3-Piece Mold, Applied Mouth, Pontil, c.1789, 9 ⅜ x 4 ⅜ In.	546.00
Black Glass, Wine, Olive Green, Seal, 3-Piece Mold, Double Collar, c.1831, 11 ½ In.	374.00
Black Glass, Wine, Olive Yellow, Seal, Horsehoof, Applied Lip, Sheared Mouth, c.1800, 8 x 7 In.	374.00
Black Glass, Wine, Yellow Olive Amber, Seal, 3-Piece Mold, Tooled Mouth, Applied Lip, 8 ¾ In.	978.00
Black Glass, Wine, Yellow Olive Amber, Seal, Tooled Mouth, Applied Lip, Pontil, c.1815, 10 ½ In.	403.00
Black Glass, Wine, Yellow Olive Green, Seal, Sheared Mouth, Applied Lip, Flowerpot, 8 ⅞ In.	1265.00
Black Glass, Wine, Yellow Olive Green, Sheared Mouth, Applied String Lip, 1800-21, 21 In. ...	374.00
Blown, Amber, Shouldered, Outward Rolled Lip, Pontil, 4 ¾ In.	395.00
Blown, Chestnut, Amber, Long Neck, Applied Lip, Pontil, c.1800, 8 ¾ In.	269.00
Blown, Chestnut, Emerald Green, Applied Mouth, Open Pontil, c.1790, 5 ¼ In. ....*illus*	345.00
Blown, Chestnut, Olive Yellow, Laid On Ring, Pontil, 1780-1820, 5 ¼ In.	336.00
Blown, Globular, 24 Vertical Ribs, Aqua, Sheared Mouth, Applied Ring Lip, Pontil, c.1820, 7 ½ In. .	168.00
Blown, Globular, Green Aqua, 3-Piece Mold, Rolled Mouth, Pontil, 7 ⅛ In.	3738.00
Coca-Cola bottles are listed in the Coca-Cola category.	
Cologne, 6-Sided, Powder Blue Milk Glass, Corset Waist, 1860-80....................	230.00
Cologne, 12-Sided, Cobalt Blue, Sloping Shoulder, Rolled Lip, 1860-80, 7 ⅜ In.	253.00
Cologne, 12-Sided, Opalescent Turquoise, Tooled Mouth, 1860-80, 5 ¾ In.	316.00
Cologne, 12-Sided, Purple Amethyst, Tooled Lip, c.1870, 10 ¾ In.	633.00
Cologne, 12-Sided, Sapphire Blue, Tooled Mouth, 1860-80, 7 ½ In.	178.00
Cologne, 16 Ribs, Swirled To Left, Blue, Flared Lip, Pontil, 5 ½ In.	270.00
Cologne, Blue, Corset Waist, 4 ¾ In.	364.00
Cologne, Cobalt Blue, Tooled Mouth, Faceted Stopper, 1865-80, 9 In.	633.00
Cologne, Elephant Shape, Open Pontil, Flared Lip, c.1860, 5 In. ....*illus*	288.00
Cologne, Milk Glass, Dancing Indian, Tool Flared Out Lip, Pontil, 1830-60, 4 ⅞ In.	2645.00
Cologne, Palmetto & Acanthus, Cobalt Blue, Open Pontil, Rolled Lip, c.1860, 5 ½ In. ....*illus*	1265.00
Cologne, Pink Amethyst, Outward Rolled Lip, Pontil, 1830-60, 6 ¾ In.	4025.00
Cologne, Rose, Emerald Green, Lobed, Sheared Mouth, Pontil, c.1850, 2 ½ In.	1680.00
Cologne, Scroll, Flower Heads, Aqua, Rolled Lip, Pontil, c.1850, 5 In.	106.00
Cologne, Scrolled Acanthus, Blue, Rolled Lip, Pontil, Corset Waist, c.1850, 5 ½ In.	1568.00
Cologne, Shell Ribs, Scalloped Edge, Rolled Lip, Pontil, 3 ½ In.	275.00
Cologne, Stiegel Type, Blown, Flowers, Multicolored, German Text, Pewter Collar, 6 ½ In.	68.00
Cologne, Thousand Eye, Square, Stopper, c.1891, 6 ¾ In.	45.00
Cordial, Charles London, Olive Green, Applied Collar, c.1860, 9 ⅜ In. ....*illus*	863.00
Cordial, Dr. Bates Pineapple Cordial, Embossed Pineapple, Blue Aqua, 9 In.	795.00
Cordial, L.Q.C. Wishart's Pine Tree, Patent 1859, Tree, Blue Green, 10 In.	202.00
Cordial, L.Q.C. Wishart's Pine Tree Tar, Phila., Patent 1859, Blue Green, 8 ½ In.	129.00
Cordial, L.Q.C. Wishart's Pine Tree Tar, Yellow Olive, c.1865, 9 ⅜ In. ....*illus*	863.00
Cosmetic, A.A. Snyder, Indian Hair Restorer, Cobalt Blue, Square Mouth, c.1865, 8 ¾ In.	2645.00
Cosmetic, Ayer's Hair Vigor, Peacock Blue, 6 In.	48.00
Cosmetic, B.F. Fish's Hair Restorative, Blue Aqua, 7 ½ In.	504.00
Cosmetic, C.A.P. Mason, Alpine Hair Balm, Providence, R.I., Green, Applied Lip, 6 ¾ In.	3800.00
Cosmetic, C.A.P. Mason, Alpine Hair Balm, Yellow Olive Green, Double Ring Mouth, 6 ⅞ In. .	4313.00
Cosmetic, Church's Circassian Hair Restorer, Grape Amethyst, Applied Mouth, c.1865, 7 ⅝ In.	1035.00
Cosmetic, Dodge Brothers Melanine Hair Tonic, Case Gin Shape, Applied Top, 7 ½ In.	616.00
Cosmetic, Dodge Brothers Melanine Hair Tonic, Puce, Shaded, Double Collar, 7 ½ In.	1456.00
Cosmetic, Dr. Leon's Electric Hair Renewer, Amethyst, Tooled Top, 7 ¼ In.	1008.00
Cosmetic, Dr. Tebbetts' Physiological Hair Regenerator, Burgundy Amethyst, 7 ⅝ In.	336.00
Cosmetic, Dr. Tebbetts' Physiological Hair Regenerator, Grape Amethyst, c.1865, 7 ⅜ In.	403.00
Cosmetic, Dr. Tebbetts' Physiological Hair Regenerator, Pink Amethyst, c.1865, 7 ⅝ In.	316.00
Cosmetic, Dr. Tebbetts' Physiological Hair Regenerator, Topaz, c.1865, 7 ⅝ In.	2185.00
Cosmetic, Fish's Infallible Hair Restorative, Cobalt Blue, Applied Mouth, 1863	360.00
Cosmetic, Jerome's Hair Color Restorer, Green, Flared Lip, Open Pontil, 6 ¼ In.	4032.00
Cosmetic, J.L. Giofray & Co. Hair Renovator, Amber, Square Mouth, c.1865, 8 In.	2760.00

Cosmetic, J.R. Tilton, Great Hair Producer, Sapphire Blue, 6 ¾ In.	364.00
Cosmetic, Ko Ko For The Hair, Embossed On Both Sides, Teal Green	70.00
Cosmetic, L. Miller's Hair Invigorator, Aqua, Oval, Open Pontil, 5 In.	89.00
Cosmetic, M.A. Reaves, Great Electric Hair Tonic, Blue, Tooled Lip, 6 ½ In.	280.00
Cosmetic, Mrs. Mason's Old English Hair Tonic, Box, 7 In.	231.00
Cosmetic, Mrs. S.A. Allen's World's Hair Balsam, Aqua, Bimal, 6 ½ In.	29.00
Cosmetic, Mrs. S.A. Allen's World's Hair Restorer, Dark Purple, Panels, Rolled Lip	308.00
Cosmetic, Mrs. S.A. Allen's World's Hair Restorer, Pink Amethyst, Double Collar, c.1865, 7 ¼ In.	345.00
Cosmetic, Professor Mott's Magic Hair Invigorator, Aqua, Open Pontil, c.1850, 6 ⅜ In.	253.00
Cosmetic, Renovo For The Hair, Grape Amethyst, Oval, Applied Double Collar, c.1860, 7 ⅞ In.	5463.00
Cosmetic, Sandell's Hair Restorer, Pink Amethyst, 1880-90, 6 ⅛ In.	518.00
Cosmetic, Sarsaparilla, John Bull Extract, Louisville, Ky., Aqua, Rectangular, c.1845, 8 ¾ In. .	476.00
Cosmetic, St. Clair's Hair Lotion, Cobalt Blue, Panels, Tooled Lip, 8 In.	504.00
Cosmetic, St. Clair's Hair Lotion, Tooled Lip, 7 ⅝ In.	146.00
Cosmetic, Swedish Hair Creator, Barrel, Opalescent Milk Glass, Tooled Mouth, c.1865, 3 ⅛ In.	316.00
Cosmetic, W.C. Montgomery's Hair Restorer, Apricot Puce, Double Collar, 7 ⅝ In.	863.00
Cosmetic, W.C. Montgomery's Hair Restorer, Strawberry Puce, Double Collar, 7 ¾ In.	805.00
Cure, Alexander's Catarrh & Asthma Cure, Otto O. Hoffman, Amber, 4 ½ In.	95.00
Cure, Alexander's Sure Cure For Malaria, Amber, 8 In.	125.00
Cure, Bird's Lung Cure, Aqua, Oval, 2 ⅞ In.	50.00
Cure, Bradycrotine, A Sure Cure For All Headaches, 4 In.	35.00
Cure, Carramon, Great Cough Cure, Aqua, Round, 4 ⅝ In.	80.00
Cure, Clear, Wilbur's Pink Eye Cure, Horse, Owner, 6 In.	55.00
Cure, Collian Opium Habit Cure, Dr. S.B. Collins, Round, 8 In.	140.00
Cure, Criswell's Bromo-Pepsin Cures Headaches, Amber, Round, 2 ½ In.	17.00
Cure, DeWitt's Colic & Cholera, Chicago, Rectangular, Aqua, 4 ⅛ In.	25.00
Cure, Dr. Brooks Anti Malarial Tonic, Chill & Fever Cure, Rectangular, 5 In.	40.00
Cure, Dr. Dornsife's Favorite Cough Cure, Aqua, Rectangular, 6 ½ In.	100.00
Cure, Dr. Hale's Household Cough Cure, Aqua, Rectangular, 4 ⅞ In.	50.00
Cure, Dr. Kline's Fit Cure & Great Nerve Restorer, Aqua, Rectangular, 8 ⅛ In.	160.00
Cure, Dr. L. Burdick's Kidney Cure, Amber, Rectangular, 7 ⅝ In.	75.00
Cure, Edward's Cornish Cough Cure, Aqua, Rectangular, 5 ⅛ In.	100.00
Cure, Elepizone, Certain Cure For Fits & Epilepsy, Dr. H.G. Root, Aqua, Square Collar	134.00
Cure, Elepizone, Safe Cure For Fits & Epilepsy, H.G. Root, London, Aqua, Round, 7 ⅝ In.	150.00
Cure, Emerson's Sarsaparilla, 3-Bottles Guaranteed To Cure, Oval, 8 ⅛ In.	110.00
Cure, Fitch's, Dandruff Cure, 6 ½ In.	22.00
Cure, Gilbert's Cure For Cholera Infantum, Rectangular, 5 ¾ In.	8.00
Cure, Hague's Kure-A-Kof, Lincoln, Aqua, Rectangular, 4 ⅞ In.	50.00
Cure, Hamilton's Medicines Cure, 7-Pointed Star, Aqua, Rectangular, 8 ¾ In.	250.00
Cure, Hires Cough Cure, Aqua, Square, 4 ½ In.	29.00
Cure, Hite's Pain Cure For Man & Animals, Aqua, Rectangular, 6 ⅛ In.	60.00
Cure, H.K.B. Safe Cure For The Heart, Kidney, & Bladder, Rectangular, 8 ⅞ In.	200.00
Cure, Holmes Sure Cure Mouth Wash, Oval, Flat Panel, 6 ¼ In.	130.00
Cure, Mrs. Bush Specific Cure For Burns & Scalds, Round, 5 ¾ In.	80.00
Cure, Peters P.A.C. Rheumatism Cure, Script, Rectangular, 6 In.	100.00
Cure, Warner's Safe Kidney & Liver Cure, Amber, Oval, 9 ¼ In.	65.00
Cure, Warner's Safe Kidney & Liver, Dark Amber, Embossed, 9 ½ In.	35.00
Cure, Warner's Safe, 4 City, Yellow Apricot, Blob Top..	299.00
Cure, Warner's Safe, Golden Amber, Oval, Applied Collar, 10 ¾ In.	1093.00
Cure, Warner's Safe, London, Golden Amber, Applied Lip, Pt.	179.00
Cure, Warner's Safe, Yellow Amber, Oval, 4 ⅝ In.	1150.00
Cure, Wickes' Arctic Flower, Cures Coughs, Aqua, Rectangular, 5 ⅞ In.	190.00
Cure, Wm. Radam's Microbe Killer, Cures All Diseases, Embossed Man, Skeleton, Amber........	90.00
Cure, Wm. Radam's Microbe Killer, Cures All Diseases, Red Amber, Square, 10 In.	179.00
Cure, Wonder Cure For Epilepsy, Aqua, Rectangular, 5 In.	100.00
Cure, Woods' Great Peppermint Cure For Coughs & Colds, Sapphire, Rectangular, 5 ⅝ In.	8.00
Decanter, Barrel Shape, Yellow Green, 3-Piece Mold, Flared Mouth, Pontil, 1820-30, Pt.........	4720.00
Decanter, Blown, Clear, 3-Piece Mold, Tooled Lip, Pinwheel Stopper, 1815-35, 2 ⅞ In.	460.00
Decanter, Blown, Olive Amber, 3-Piece Mold, Tooled Lip, Keene, N.H., c.1835, 7 In. ....*illus*	575.00
Decanter, Blown, Olive Green, 3-Piece Mold, Applied Collar, Keene, c.1835, 7 ½ In. ....*illus*	3450.00
Decanter, Blown, Olive Green, 3-Piece Mold, Applied Double Collar, 1815-35, 10 In.	4600.00
Decanter, Cone, Black Glass, Open Pontil, 10 In.	336.00
Decanter, Excelsior, Bar Lip, McKee Glass, Late 1860s, 9 ½ In.	110.00
Decanter, Olive, Amber, 3 Piece-Mold, Sheared Lip, Pontil, Keene Glassworks, 1820-40...........	616.00
Decanter, Pineapple, Yellow Green, 3-Piece Mold, Sloping Collar, Pontil, 7 ¾ In.	4600.00
Demijohn, Blown, Amber, 3-Piece Mold, Applied Lip, 5 x 11 ½ In.	35.00

Bottle, Bitters, Suffolk, Philbrook & Tucker, Pig, Yellow Amber, Applied Mouth, c.1870, 10 ⅛ In. $978.00

Bottle, Black Glass, Dutch Onion, Horsehoof, Olive Amber, Holland, c.1735, 7 ¾ In. $138.00

Bottle, Black Glass, Mallet, Olive Amber, Applied Lip, England, c.1745, 8 x 5 ½ In. $196.00

Bottle, Black Glass, Onion, Olive Green, Applied String Lip, Germany, 7 x 5 ¾ In. $104.00

BOTTLE

Bottle, Black Glass, Utility, Square, Olive Green, Sheared & Tooled Mouth, c.1775, 8 ⅛ In.
$748.00

Bottle, Blown, Chestnut, Emerald Green, Applied Mouth, Open Pontil, c.1790, 5 ¼ In.
$345.00

Bottle, Cologne, Elephant Shape, Open Pontil, Flared Lip, c.1860, 5 In.
$288.00

Bottle, Cologne, Palmetto & Acanthus, Cobalt Blue, Open Pontil, Rolled Lip, c.1860, 5 ½ In.
$1265.00

Bottle, Cordial, Charles London, Olive Green, Applied Collar, c.1860, 9 ⅜ In.
$863.00

Bottle, Cordial, L.Q.C. Wishart's Pine Tree Tar, Yellow Olive, c.1865, 9 ⅜ In.
$863.00

Bottle, Decanter, Blown, Olive Amber, 3-Piece Mold, Tooled Lip, Keene, N.H., c.1835, 7 In.
$575.00

Bottle, Decanter, Blown, Olive Green, 3-Piece Mold, Applied Collar, Keene, c.1835, 7 ½ In.
$3450.00

Bottle, Demijohn, Bread Loaf Shape, Blue Green, Applied Mouth, c.1870, 8 ¾ x 9 ½ x 6 In.
$863.00

Bottle, Figural, Coachman, Van Dunck's, Genever, Strawberry Puce, c.1875, 8 ⅞ In.
$460.00

Bottle, Figural, Horse's Hoof, Mackay's Hoof Ointment, Tooled Mouth, c.1900, 5 ½ In.
$748.00

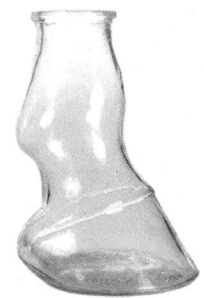

Bottle, Figural, Pineapple, Amber, Applied Mouth, c.1870, 9 In.
$207.00

Demijohn, Blue Green, Applied Mouth, Pontil, 1850-75, 20 ¼ x 8 ⅝ In.	345.00
Demijohn, Bread Loaf Shape, Blue Green, Applied Mouth, c.1870, 8 ¾ x 9 ½ x 6 In. ...... *illus*	863.00
Demijohn, Bread Loaf Shape, Dip Mold, Green Amber, Sloping Collar, Pontil	505.00
Demijohn, Emerald Green, Applied Mouth, Iron Pontil, 1850-65, 9 ¼ In.	265.00
Demijohn, Emerald Green, Oval, Open Pontil, 1840-60, 3 Gal., 19 In.	159.00
Demijohn, Flattened Apple Shape, Basket, Handles, Applied Collar, c.1860, 8 In.	364.00
Demijohn, Green, Flattened Heart Shape, Tapered Collar, c.1865, 18 In.	182.00
Demijohn, Kidney Shape, Blue Green, Iron Pontil, Qt.	59.00
Demijohn, Olive Green, Cylindrical, Dip Mold, Applied Lip, Pontil, c.1800, 12 In.	728.00
Demijohn, Olive Yellow Amber, Applied Mouth, 1790-1820, 14 x 6 In.	219.00
Demijohn, Olive, Yellow, Cylindrical, Square Collar, Pontil, c.1840, 21 In.	241.00
Demijohn, Olive Yellow, Deep Kick-Up, Applied Mouth, 11 In.	280.00
Demijohn, Orange Amber, 4-Piece Mold, Cylindrical, 2 Gal., 17 ½ In.	119.00
Demijohn, Orange Amber, Squat, Stoddard Type, Squat, 1860-70, ½ Gal, 12 In.	39.00
Demijohn, Sapphire Blue, Applied Mouth, Iron Pontil, 1850-65, Qt., 9 ½ In.	748.00
Figural, Book, Departed Spirits G, Mottled Flint, Enameled, Bennington, Flask, 5 ½ In.	560.00
Figural, Clam, Cobalt Blue, Flask, Ground Lip, Metal Screw Cap, 1885-1910, 5 ¼ In.	920.00
Figural, Coachman Stoneware, Bennington, 1840-60, 10 ½ In.	784.00
Figural, Coachman, Van Dunck's, Genever, Strawberry Puce, c.1875, 8 ⅞ In. .... *illus*	460.00
Figural, Flamenco Dancer, Brandy Anejo, Painted, Tiered Skirt, 12 ¼ In.	41.00
Figural, Horse's Hoof, Mackay's Hoof Ointment, Tooled Mouth, c.1900, 5 ½ In. .... *illus*	748.00
Figural, Japanese Mikado, Amber, Tooled Lip, Label, 1885-1900, 4 ¾ In.	288.00
Figural, Monument, Admiral Lord Nelson Stopper, Amethyst, 20 In.	199.00
Figural, Pig, Glass, 10 ½ x 19 In.	82.00
Figural, Pineapple, Amber, Applied Mouth, c.1870, 9 In. .... *illus*	207.00
Figural, Tombstone, Aqua, Sloping Collar, Tubular Pontil, 1820-40, 8 ¼ In.	3163.00
Figural, Turkey, Amber, Metal Cap, 4 ½ In.	69.00
Figural, Violin, Cobalt Blue, 8 In.	30.00
Figural, Wheel, Woman, On Safety Bicycle	50.00
Figural, Whiskbroom, Clear, Pocket, ½ Pt.	19.00
Figural, Woman Holding Fan, Long Dress, Woman's Head Stopper, Embossed, 13 In.	89.00
Flask, 10 Diamond, Yellow Green, Sheared Mouth, Pontil, Pocket, 5 ½ In.	5175.00
Flask, 16 Ribs, 20 Diamonds, Lavender, Coin Shape, Sheared Mouth, Pontil, 6 ⅛ In.	1265.00
Flask, 16 Ribs, Swirled To Left, Sapphire Blue, Coin Shape, Sheared Mouth, Pocket, 6 ⅜ x 5 In.	2645.00
Flask, 20 Ribs, Amethyst, Teardrop, Sheared Mouth, Pontil, Pocket, 1820-40, 6 ½ In.	690.00
Flask, 20 Ribs, Golden Honey Amber, Teardrop, Sheared Mouth, Pontil, 6 ⅝ In.	460.00
Flask, 20 Ribs, Olive Yellow, Sheared Mouth, Pontil, 6 In.	1232.00
Flask, 24 Ribs, Swirled To Left, Amber, Flattened, Sheared Lip, Pocket, 4 ½ In.	190.00
Flask, 24 Ribs, Vertical, Amber, Flattened, Sheared Mouth, Pontil, c.1820, 4 ⅝ In.	364.00
Flask, 30 Ribs, Swirled, Aqua, Flattened, Globular, c.1820, 9 In. .... *illus*	219.00
Flask, Adams & Jefferson, July 4, 1775, Aqua, Pontil, Sheared, Tooled Mouth, Pontil, 1825-35, Pt.	1265.00
Flask, Addison Hills, Olive Green, Oval, Double Collar, c.1850, 9 ¼ In. .... *illus*	575.00
Flask, Amber, Anchor, Embossed, Strap Side, ½ Pt.	48.00
Flask, Ambrosial, B.M. & E.A.W. & Co., Amber, Chestnut, Handle, c.1860, 9 In. .... *illus*	288.00
Flask, Anchor & Phoenix, Resurgam, Olive Yellow, c.1865, Pt. .... *illus*	4600.00
Flask, Beehive, Blue Aqua, Applied Collar, Pontil, c.1830, Qt.	69.00
Flask, Benjamin Franklin, Aqua, Open Pontil, c.1825, Qt.	633.00
Flask, Benjamin Franklin, Aqua, Open Pontil, c.1830, Pt.	374.00
Flask, Blue, Flared Lip, Pontil, Pocket, c.1860, 5 ½ In.	112.00
Flask, Byron & Scott, Yellow Amber, Sheared Lip, c.1830, ½ Pt. .... *illus*	403.00
Flask, Chestnut, 18 Ribs, Aqua, Applied Handle, Tooled Lip, Open Pontil, 1815, 5 ¾ In.	1380.00
Flask, Chestnut, Nailsea, Blue Aqua, White Splotch, Sheared Mouth, Pontil, c.1810, 8 ⅝ In. ..	403.00
Flask, Chestnut, Olive Green, Outward Rolled Lip, Pontil, 1780-1800, 9 ½ In.	374.00
Flask, Chestnut, Vertical Ribs, Amber, Pontil, 1815-35, 4 ¾ In.	280.00
Flask, Chestnut, Yellow Olive, Applied Mouth, Pontil, 1783-1820, 10 ½ In.	616.00
Flask, Chestnut, Yellow Olive Green, Outward Rolled Mouth, Pontil, 1780-90, 11 ⅜ In.	1495.00
Flask, Clasped Hands & Eagle, Olive Yellow, Applied Mouth, c.1860, Qt.	5463.00
Flask, Coffin, Red Amber, Keystone With Wreath, Embossed, Pt.	48.00
Flask, Columbia, Eagle, Embossed, Sheared Mouth, Pontil, Pt.	952.00
Flask, Concentric Ring Eagle, Green, Tooled Lip, c.1830, Qt.	1610.00
Flask, Corn For The World, Baltimore Monument, Amber, Double Collar, Qt.	7840.00
Flask, Corn For The World, Cornflower Blue, Applied Mouth, 1860-70, Qt.	633.00
Flask, Corn For The World, Ice Blue, Applied Double Collar, c.1865, Qt.	374.00
Flask, Corn For The World, Monument, Baltimore, Peacock Blue, 1860-70	4250.00
Flask, Corn For The World, Teal, Applied Mouth, c.1860-70, Qt.	4888.00
Flask, Cornucopia & Urn, Blue Green, Open Pontil, c.1845, Pt.	1035.00

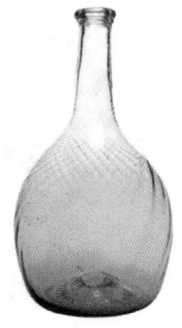

Bottle, Flask, 30 Ribs, Swirled, Aqua,
Flattened, Globular, c.1820, 9 In.
$219.00

Bottle, Flask, Addison Hills, Olive Green,
Oval, Double Collar, c.1850, 9 ¼ In.
$575.00

Bottle, Flask, Ambrosial,
B.M. & E.A.W. & Co., Amber, Chestnut,
Handle, c.1860, 9 In.
$288.00

Bottle, Flask, Anchor & Phoenix,
Resurgam, Olive Yellow, c.1865, Pt.
$4600.00

B

Bottle, Flask, Byron & Scott,
Yellow Amber, Sheared Lip, c.1830, ½ Pt.
$403.00

Bottle, Flask, Double Eagle, Louisville,
Amber, Tooled Lip, c.1835, Qt.
$4888.00

Bottle, Flask, Eagle & Flag, Grass Green,
Calabash, Applied Sloping Collar, c.1860
$345.00

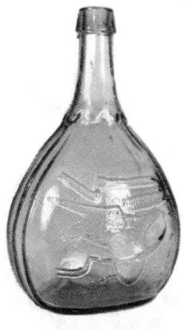

Bottle, Flask, Eagle & Louisville,
Golden Amber, Applied Mouth,
c.1845, ½ Pt.
$2070.00

Flask, Cornucopia & Urn, Blue Green, Sheared Mouth, Pontil, 1825-35, ½ Pt.	518.00
Flask, Cornucopia & Urn, Olive Green, Pontil, ½ Pt.	146.00
Flask, Cornucopia & Urn, Olive Green, Pt.	168.00
Flask, Cornucopia & Urn, Olive Yellow Amber, Sheared Mouth, Pontil, ½ Pt.	134.00
Flask, Cornucopia & Urn, Yellow Amber, Olive Tone, Sheared Mouth, Pontil, 1825-35, ½ Pt.	374.00
Flask, Cornucopia, Olive Green, Sheared Lip, Tubular Pontil	224.00
Flask, Cranberry Opalescent White Swirl, c.1870, 7 x 5 In.	207.00
Flask, Cut Glass, Heart Shape, Sterling Silver Lid, 5 x 3 ½ In.	175.00
Flask, Double Eagle, Amber, Applied Mouth, Qt.	336.00
Flask, Double Eagle, Amber, Bubbles, Applied Band, Smooth Base, Pittsburg, Pa.	728.00
Flask, Double Eagle, Louisville, Amber, Tooled Lip, c.1835, Qt. *illus*	4888.00
Flask, Double Eagle, Olive Amber, Sheared Lip, Pontil, ½ Pt.	269.00
Flask, Double Eagle, Olive Amber, Sheared Lip, Pontil, 1825-35, Pt.	546.00
Flask, Eagle & Anchor, Blue Green, Sheared Mouth, Tubular Pontil, Pt.	2185.00
Flask, Eagle & Banner, Calabash, Green, Sloping Collar, Pontil, c.1855, Qt.	269.00
Flask, Eagle & Coffin, Aqua, Tooled Lip, Open Pontil, 1825-35, ½ Pt.	690.00
Flask, Eagle & Cornucopia, Sheared, Rolled Lip, Pontil, c.1830, ½ Pt.	840.00
Flask, Eagle & Flag, Grass Green, Calabash, Applied Sloping Collar, c.1860 *illus*	345.00
Flask, Eagle & Flag, Tobacco Green With Striations, Sheared Mouth, Pontil, Pt.	14560.00
Flask, Eagle & Grapes, Green Aqua, Ribs, Sheared Mouth, Pontil, Qt.	190.00
Flask, Eagle & Louisville, Golden Amber, Applied Mouth, c.1845, ½ Pt. *illus*	2070.00
Flask, Eagle & Morning Glory, Aqua, Midwestern Glass House, c.1840, Pt. *illus*	863.00
Flask, Eagle & Sheaf Of Rye, Green, Aqua, Sheared Mouth, Pontil, Pt.	2645.00
Flask, Eagle & Shield, Green, Pt.	308.00
Flask, Eagle & Shield, Yellow Amber, Applied Double Collar, 1870-80, ½ Pt.	160.00 to 184.00
Flask, Eagle & Shield, Yellow Olive, Applied Double Collar, 1870-80, ½ Pt.	500.00
Flask, Eagle & Sunburst, Vertical Ribs, Blue Aqua, Pontil, Tooled Lip, 1835-45, Pt.	2760.00
Flask, Eagle & Willington, Olive Green, Applied Double Collar, 1855-70, ½ Pt.	345.00
Flask, Eagle & Willington, Tobacco Amber, Applied Mouth, 1855-70, Pt.	345.00
Flask, Eagle, Aqua, Round Collar, Iron Pontil, c.1855, Pt.	118.00
Flask, Eagle, Calabash, 7-Up Green, Applied Lip, Iron Pontil, Qt.	280.00
Flask, Enameled, Blue, Multicolored Flowers, Chamfered Corners, Pewter Collar, c.1800, 6 In.	364.00
Flask, Figural, Book, Porcelain, Gin, Painted Street Scene, 7 x 5 In.	77.00
Flask, Flora Temple, Horse, Strawberry Puce, Applied Mouth, Handle, 1859-65, Pt.	518.00
Flask, For Pike's Peak, Pale Aqua, Applied Band, Qt.	504.00
Flask, Free-Blown, Teal, Applied Sterling Silver Top, Pontil, c.1870, Qt.	99.00
Flask, German Spirits, Multicolored Enamel, Blacksmith Tools, Chestnut, 6 ⅝ In. *illus*	207.00
Flask, Granite Glass Co., Stoddard, N.H., Amber, Pontil, Pt.	450.00
Flask, Granite Glass Co., Stoddard, N.H., Blood Amber, Pt.	550.00
Flask, Granite Glass Co., Stoddard, N.H., Orange Amber, Double Collar, Pt.	840.00
Flask, Hunter & Fisherman, Calabash, Golden Amber, Iron Pontil, Qt.	280.00
Flask, Hunter & Stag, Blue, Applied Mouth, Pontil, ½ Pt.	179.00
Flask, Jas. Tharp's Sons, Wines & Liquors, Orange, Strap Side, ½ Pt.	48.00
Flask, Jenny Lind & Glasshouse, Calabash, Aqua, Qt.	99.00
Flask, Jenny Lind & Glasshouse, Calabash, Sapphire Blue, Iron Pontil, 1865	3250.00
Flask, John Ferguson A.B.C., Coffin, ½ Pt.	1008.00
Flask, Kossuth & Frigate, Calabash, Aqua, 1855-60, Qt.	275.00
Flask, Kossuth & Tree, Amber, Applied Double Collar, 1855-65	750.00
Flask, Kossuth & Tree, Calabash, Blue Aqua, Applied Mouth, 1855-60	316.00
Flask, Kossuth & Tree, Calabash, Blue Green, Iron Pontil, Qt.	79.00 to 119.00
Flask, Lafayette & Clinton, Yellow Amber, c.1830, Pt. *illus*	1495.00
Flask, Lafayette, Pale Aqua, Open Pontil, c.1822, Pt.	748.00
Flask, Liberty Eagle, Olive Green, Applied Double Collar, c.1860, Pt.	2070.00
Flask, Liberty Eagle, Olive Green, Tooled Lip, c.1860, Pt.	374.00
Flask, Lowell Railroad & Eagle, Horse Pulling Cart, Moss Green, 1825-35, ½ Pt.	750.00
Flask, Masonic & Eagle, Light Green, Tooled Lip, Pontil, Pt.	952.00
Flask, Masonic & Eagle, Olive Amber, Sheared Mouth, Pontil, Pt.	308.00
Flask, Masonic & Eagle, Olive Green, Tooled Lip, c.1815-25, Pt.	431.00
Flask, Masonic & Eagle, Yellow Amber, Sheared, Tooled Lip, Open Pontil, 1815-25, Pt.	374.00
Flask, Masonic & Eagle, Yellow Green, Sheared Mouth, Pontil, Pt.	4600.00
Flask, Masonic, Keene Marlboro Street Glassworks, Olive, Sheared Mouth, Pontil, c.1825, Pt.	364.00
Flask, N. Wood, Blue Aqua, Open Pontil, Applied Tapered Collar, c.1850, 7 ½ In.	150.00
Flask, Oval, Strawberry Puce, Copper Tone, Applied Mouth & Handle, c.1870, 7 ¾ In.	374.00
Flask, Peacock Blue Green, Applied Sterling Silver Top, Pontil, Qt.	89.00
Flask, Pitkin Type, 20 Ribs, Swirled To Right, Emerald Green, Tooled Lip, 1810, 5 ¾ In.	748.00
Flask, Pitkin Type, 24 Ribs, Swirled To Left, Cross Ribbing, Sheared Mouth, Lip, Pontil, 6 ¾ In.	728.00

Flask, Pitkin Type, 30 Ribs, Swirled To Left, Yellow Olive, Sheared Mouth, Pontil, 1783-1840, 4 ⅞ In.	1090.00
Flask, Pitkin Type, 32 Ribs, Swirled To Right, Sheared Mouth Pontil, 6 ¼ In.	168.00
Flask, Pitkin Type, 36 Ribs, 36 Swirled To Left, Flattened Oval, Pontil, c.1800, 5 In.	952.00
Flask, Pitkin Type, 36 Ribs, Swirled To Left, Olive Green, Yellow Tone, Sheared Mouth, Pontil, 7 In.	4150.00
Flask, Pitkin Type, 36 Ribs, Swirled To Right, Yellow Amber, Tooled Lip, Pontil, 5 ¾ In.	805.00
Flask, Pitkin Type, Broken Ribs, Swirled, Olive Amber, Half Post Neck, c.1825, 5 In.	411.00
Flask, Pitkin Type, Broken Ribs, Swirled, Pale Green, Half Post Neck, c.1830, 7 In.	294.00
Flask, Pitkin Type, Ribs, Swirled, Olive Green, 6 In.	975.00
Flask, Republican Gratitude, Lafayette, Aqua, Kensington Glass Works, 1825-35 ....illus	460.00
Flask, S. Roherer Liquors, Amber, Strap Side, Qt.	129.00
Flask, Scroll, Amber, Applied Mouth, Iron Pontil, 1845-55, Pt.	489.00
Flask, Scroll, Amber, Pontil, 1845-60, Pt., 6 ⅞ In.	560.00
Flask, Scroll, Amber, Pontil, 1845-60, Qt., 9 In.	1904.00
Flask, Scroll, Amber, Sheared Mouth, Iron Pontil, Pt.	672.00
Flask, Scroll, Apple Green, Tooled Lip, Pontil, c.1860, Gal. ....illus	4025.00
Flask, Scroll, Aqua, Sheared Mouth, Iron Pontil, Pt.	280.00
Flask, Scroll, Aqua, Sheared Mouth, Rectangular Iron Pontil, Qt.	336.00
Flask, Scroll, Blue Aqua, Corset Shape, Tooled Lip, c.1850, Pt. ....illus	920.00
Flask, Scroll, Blue Aqua, Pontil, Pt., 6 ⅞ In.	84.00
Flask, Scroll, Cobalt Blue, Pontil, 1845-60, Pt., 6 ¾ In.	3360.00
Flask, Scroll, Fleur-De-Lis, Yellow Green, Inward Rolled Lip, c.1850, ½ Pt. ....illus	2185.00
Flask, Scroll, Light Electric Blue, Applied Double Collar, Iron Pontil, 1845-60	4125.00
Flask, Scroll, Moonstone, Pink Tint, Pontil, 1845-60, 9 In.	1904.00
Flask, Scroll, Sapphire Blue, Applied Lip, Graphite Pontil, Pt.	4032.00
Flask, Scroll, Tobacco Amber, Pontil, 1845-55, ½ Pt.	850.00
Flask, Scroll, Tobacco Olive Amber, Sheared Mouth, Pontil, 1845-55, Pt.	1265.00
Flask, Scroll, Yellow Olive, Open Pontil, 1850, ½ Pt.	3738.00
Flask, Sheaf Of Grain & Star, Calabash, Blue Aqua, Open Pontil, Qt.	99.00
Flask, Sheaf Of Grain & Tree, Calabash, Aqua, Double Open Pontil, Qt.	129.00
Flask, Sheaf Of Grain & Tree, Calabash, Open Pontil, Qt.	109.00
Flask, Sheaf Of Grain, Aqua, Applied Lip, Pontil, 1850-60, Pt.	748.00
Flask, Sheaf Of Grain, Aqua, Embossed, Pt.	140.00
Flask, Sheaf Of Grain, Aqua, Olive, Tooled Mouth, Open Pontil, 1850-60, ½ Pt.	1380.00
Flask, Sheaf Of Grain, Blue Aqua, Pt.	119.00
Flask, Sheaf Of Grain, Green Aqua, Tooled Lip, c.1830, Pt.	12650.00
Flask, Silver Overlay, Gorham, 4 ½ x 3 ¾ In.	280.00
Flask, Stoddard Type, Olive Yellow Amber, Squat, Double Collar, IMAL, Pt.	39.00
Flask, Success To The Railroad, Aqua, Sheared Mouth, Pontil, Pt.	1008.00
Flask, Success To The Railroad, Blue Aqua, Sheared, Tooled, Open Pontil, 1835-45, Pt.	863.00
Flask, Success To The Railroad, Horse Pulling Cart, Olive, Sheared Mouth, Pontil, c.1836, Pt.	420.00
Flask, Success To The Railroad, Lime Green, Sheared Mouth, Open Pontil, Pt.	392.00
Flask, Success To The Railroad, Olive Green, Keene, c.1830, Pt. ....illus	431.00
Flask, Success To The Railroad, Olive Green, Tooled Lip, Open Pontil, 1830, Pt.	518.00
Flask, Success To The Railroad, Yellow Amber, 1825-35, Pt.	110000.00
Flask, Success To The Railroad, Yellow Amber Olive, Tooled Lip, Pontil, 1825-35, Pt.	1265.00
Flask, Success To The Railroad, Yellow Amber, Tooled Lip, Open Pontil, c.1830, Pt.	489.00
Flask, Summer & Winter, Aqua, Applied Collar, Pt.	123.00
Flask, Summer & Winter, Tree, Bird, Aqua, Pt.	109.00
Flask, Summer & Winter, Tree With Leaves, Bird, Tree Without Leaves, Pt.	129.00
Flask, Sunburst, Blue Green, Pontil, Sheared & Tooled Mouth, c.1825-35, ½ Pt. ....illus	374.00
Flask, Sunburst, Deep Amber, Sheared Mouth, Pontil, c.1825, ½ Pt.	2576.00
Flask, Sunburst, Golden Olive, Pontil Scar, 1815-30, ½ Pt.	1400.00
Flask, Sunburst, Moss Green, Pontil, 1815-30, 5 ⅝ In.	1792.00
Flask, Sunburst, Moss Green, Pontil, New England, 1815-30, ½ Pt.	1792.00
Flask, Sunburst, Olive Green, Elliptical, Tooled Lip, 1825, ½ Pt. ....illus	4888.00
Flask, Sunburst, Olive, Marlboro Street Glass Works, Pontil, 1815-30, ½ Pt.	896.00
Flask, Sunburst, Olive, Pontil, New England, 1815-30, ½ Pt.	1400.00
Flask, Sunburst, Olive Yellow, Sheared Mouth, Pontil, Pt.	2530.00
Flask, Sunburst, Olive Yellow, Tooled Lip, Pontil, 1815-25, ½ Pt.	978.00
Flask, Sunburst, Shaded Copper Puce, ½ Pt.	11200.00
Flask, Sunburst, Teal, Sheared Lip, 7 In.	308.00
Flask, Sunburst, Yellow Olive Amber, Tooled Lip, Open Pontil, c.1835, Pt.	748.00
Flask, Sunburst, Yellow Olive, Tooled Lip, Pontil, 1815-35, ½ Pt.	850.00
Flask, Traveler's Companion & Sheaf Of Grain, Red Amber, Qt.	308.00
Flask, Traveler's Companion & Star, Amber, Applied Collar, Iron Pontil, c.1860, ½ Pt.	575.00
Flask, Union, Clasped Hands & Eagle, Banner, E. Wormser & Co., Glass Works, c.1860	21850.00

Bottle, Flask, Eagle & Morning Glory, Aqua, Midwestern Glass House, c.1840, Pt.
$863.00

Bottle, Flask, German Spirits, Multicolored Enamel, Blacksmith Tools, Chestnut, 6 ⅝ In.
$207.00

Bottle, Flask, Lafayette & Clinton, Yellow Amber, c.1830, Pt.
$1495.00

Bottle, Flask, Republican Gratitude, Lafayette, Aqua, Kensington Glass Works, 1825-35
$460.00

Bottle, Flask, Scroll, Apple Green, Tooled Lip, Pontil, c.1860, Gal. $4025.00

Bottle, Flask, Scroll, Blue Aqua, Corset Shape, Tooled Lip, c.1850, Pt. $920.00

Bottle, Flask, Scroll, Fleur-De-Lis, Yellow Green, Inward Rolled Lip, c.1850, ½ Pt. $2185.00

Bottle, Flask, Success To The Railroad, Olive Green, Keene, c.1830, Pt. $431.00

Flask, Union, Clasped Hands & Eagle, Blue Green, Applied Collar, c.1865, Qt. ....*illus*	21850.00
Flask, Union, Clasped Hands & Eagle, Calabash, Amber, Applied Double Collar, Iron Pontil, c.1860, Qt..	575.00
Flask, Union, Clasped Hands & Eagle, Olive Yellow, Applied Collar, 1855-70, Qt.	748.00
Flask, Union, Clasped Hands & Eagle, Yellow Green, Applied Collar, 1860-70, Qt.	1840.00
Flask, Union, Clasped Hands, Amber, Applied Ring, c.1865, Pt.	489.00
Flask, Union, Clasped Hands, Blue Aqua, Applied Ring, c.1865, Qt.	518.00
Flask, Union, Clasped Hands, Yellow Amber, Applied Ringed Collar, c.1865, Pt........	633.00
Flask, Union, Clasped Hands, Yellow Green, Applied Collar, c.1860, ½ Pt.	230.00
Flask, Union, Clasped Hands, Yellow Green, Applied Ring, c.1860, ½ Pt.	690.00
Flask, Union, Clasped Hands, Yellow Olive Amber, Applied Ring, c.1860, Qt.	690.00
Flask, Washington & Clay, Blue Green, Sheared Mouth, Pontil, Qt.	2645.00
Flask, Washington & Eagle, Adams, Jefferson, Pt.	1100.00
Flask, Washington & Frigate, Amber, Applied Double Collar, Pontil, Pt.	5463.00
Flask, Washington & Jackson, Green, Pontil, 7 In.	245.00
Flask, Washington & Jackson, Olive Amber, Sheared Mouth, c.1850, 6 ¾ In.	235.00
Flask, Washington & Jackson, Yellow Amber, Coventry Glass Works, Conn., c.1830 ....*illus*	805.00
Flask, Washington & Monument, Aqua, Sheared Mouth, Pontil, Qt., c.1830	151.00
Flask, Washington & Monument, Green, Shaded, Rolled Lip, Pontil, Pt.	8400.00
Flask, Washington & Taylor, 1850-55	1400.00
Flask, Washington & Taylor, Aqua, Pt.	119.00
Flask, Washington & Taylor, Medium To Deep Amber, Sheared Mouth, Pontil, Pt.	10080.00
Flask, Washington & Taylor, Never Surrenders, Light Green, Sheared Mouth, Qt.	616.00
Flask, Washington & Taylor, Never Surrenders, Teal Blue, Sheared Mouth, Open Pontil, Qt.....	896.00
Flask, Washington & Taylor, Teal, Sheared Mouth, Pt.	123.00
Flask, Washington & Taylor, Yellow, Green, Applied Double Collar, 1850-55, Qt.	1610.00
Flask, Washington, Bridgeton, New Jersey, Aqua, Tooled Lip, c.1830 ....*illus*	316.00
Flask, Wheeling Glass Works, Franklin, Aqua, Sheared Mouth, Pontil, Pt., c.1830	3584.00
Flask, Zanesville, 24 Ribs, Amber, Chestnut, Midwestern Grandfather, c.1820, 7 ¾ In. .....*illus*	690.00
Flask, Zanesville, Golden To Orange Amber, Sheared Mouth, Pontil, c.1830, Pt.	1232.00
Food, Black Glass, Yellow Olive Green, Iron Pontil, c.1770, 8 x 3 ¾ In.	288.00
Food, Blueberry Preserve, Olive Yellow, Fluted Shoulders, Double Collar, 11 ⅛ In.	2185.00
Food, Dorlon & Shaffer Pickled Oysters, Aqua, Glass Lid, Metal Clamp, 6 ¾ In.	560.00
Food, Gold Medal Maple Syrup, Hopkins Patent 1871, Barrel Shape, Blue Aqua, 8 ¾ In.	195.00
Food, Maple Sap & Boiled Cider Vinegar, East Rindge, N.H., Blue, Tooled Lip, Qt.	392.00
Food, McCormick & Co., Manufacturing Chemists, Baltimore, Red Label, 3-Sided, Aqua, 4 ½ In.	280.00
Food, Storage, Pink Amethyst, Ribs, Flared Out Rim, Pontil, 1780-90, 11 In.	633.00
Food, T.A. Bryan & Co., Perfection Tomato Sauce, Baltimore, Md., Gold Amber, 8 ½ In.	199.00
Food, Wm. Underwood & Co., 18-Sided, Blue Green, Sloping Collar, Label, 7 ¼ In.	3450.00
Fruit Jar, A. Stone & Co., Philada, Light Aqua, 6 ¼ In.	1512.00
Fruit Jar, Air-Tight, Dark Aqua, Iron Pontil, Wax Seal Groove, 7 ¼ In.	1680.00
Fruit Jar, Aqua, Barrel, Applied Wax Seal Groove, Kick-Up, Iron Pontil, Qt., 7 ¼ In.	1680.00
Fruit Jar, Aqua, Glass Lid, Brass Clamp, ½ Gal., 9 ⅝ In.	235.00
Fruit Jar, Aqua, Straight-Sided, ½ Gal., 8 ½ In.	1064.00
Fruit Jar, Ball, 3-L Loop, Yellow Green, Striations, Zinc Screw Lid, c.1830 ....*illus*	316.00
Fruit Jar, Beaver, Beaver Chewing Log, Amber, 7 ¼ In., Qt.	1904.00
Fruit Jar, Bennett's, Patent Feb 6th 1866, Aqua, Qt., 8 In.	672.00
Fruit Jar, Blue Aqua, Embossed, Ground Lip, Metal Closure, 8 In.	3920.00
Fruit Jar, Cadiz, Patd 1883, Light Green, ½ Gal., 9 In.	1176.00
Fruit Jar, Canadian Queen, Pt.	557.00
Fruit Jar, C.K. Halle, 121 Water St. Cleveland Oh, Aqua, Kline Stopper, Qt., 8 ¾ In.	157.00
Fruit Jar, Commodore, Aqua, Embossed, Metal Closure, Qt., 8 ½ In.	1008.00
Fruit Jar, Fruit-Keeper, Aqua, Lid, Metal Clamp, Qt.	48.00
Fruit Jar, Gem, Aqua, Hourglass, Qt.	40.00
Fruit Jar, Gilberds Improved, Aqua, Glass Lid, Wire Clamp, 9 ¼ In., ½ Gal.	246.00
Fruit Jar, Hartell's, Pat. Oct. 19 1858, Aqua, Pt., 5 ⅝ In.	235.00
Fruit Jar, Jersey, Pat. June 12th 1866, Aqua, Glass Lid, Metal Band, Qt., 7 ⅞ In.	448.00
Fruit Jar, J.M. Lewins Pat. U.S. & Canada, Aqua, 8 ⅝ In., Qt.	2016.00
Fruit Jar, Joshua Wright, Philada., Aqua, Barrel, 10 ⅜ In.	335.00
Fruit Jar, Keeffer's No. 1., Aqua, 8 In., Qt.	1008.00
Fruit Jar, Lafayette, Embossed Profile, Glass Stopper, 3-Piece Closure, Qt., 7 ¾ In.	812.00
Fruit Jar, Lafayette, Script, Aqua, Cylindrical, Sheared Mouth, Glass & Metal Stopper, 1885-95, Pt.	5000.00
Fruit Jar, Mason's CFJCo Improved, Yellow Amber, Milk Glass Lid, ½ Gal.	179.00
Fruit Jar, Mason's Pat'd Feb 5 1867, Stoneware, Black Transfer, Zinc Screw Lid, 1899, Qt.......	161.00
Fruit Jar, Mason's Pat'd Feb 5 1867, Stoneware, Blue Transfer, Zinc Screw Lid, 1899, Gal.......	345.00
Fruit Jar, Mason's Patent Nov. 30th, 1858, Amber, Ground Lip, Seal, Qt.	246.00
Fruit Jar, Mason's Patent Nov 30th 1858, Aqua, ½ Gal., 8 ⅞ In.	1456.00

B

Fruit Jar, Mason's Patent Nov. 30th 1858, Aqua, Milk Glass Liner, Lid, Gal., 12 ¼ In.	1568.00
Fruit Jar, Mason's Patent Nov 30th 1858, Aqua, Zinc Screw Lid, c.1880, Midget	316.00
Fruit Jar, Mason's Patent Nov 30th 1858, Blue Aqua, Ground Lip, c.1875, Gal.	575.00
Fruit Jar, Mason's Patent Nov 30th 1858, Cross, Amber, Qt.	202.00
Fruit Jar, Mason's Patent Nov 30th 1858, Green, ABM, Rubber Seal, ½ Gal.	560.00
Fruit Jar, Mason's Patent Nov 30th 1858, Squat, Zinc Lid, Qt., 6 ½ In.	952.00
Fruit Jar, Mason's Patent Nov 30th, 1858, Yellow Amber, Ground Lip, Pt. ....illus	1610.00
Fruit Jar, McCully & Co., Dark Aqua, Tin Lid, 7 ¾ In, Qt.	756.00
Fruit Jar, Middleby Jr. Inc., Clear, Aqua Lid, ½ Gal.	20.00
Fruit Jar, Ohio, S.S. Made By Ohio Fruit Jar Co., Patented March 1876, Qt.	1625.00
Fruit Jar, Peerless, Pat. Feb, 13 1863, Aqua, Glass Lid, Iron Yoke, Qt., 8 ½ In.	235.00
Fruit Jar, Petal Jar, Blue Aqua, Applied Wax Sealer, Iron Pontil	190.00
Fruit Jar, Petal Jar, Deep Green, Applied Top, Iron Pontil	896.00
Fruit Jar, Potter & Bodine's Air-Tight, Patented, April 13th 1858, Barrel, Aqua, ½ Gal. ....illus	920.00
Fruit Jar, Potter & Bodine's Air-Tight, Philada, 8 ½ In.	1064.00
Fruit Jar, Potter & Bodine's Air-Tight, Philada, Aqua, 7 ⅛ In.	896.00
Fruit Jar, Safety Valve, Patd May 21 1895, Greek Key, Yellow Green, Metal Clamp, c.1895, ½ Gal.	370.00
Fruit Jar, Scranton Jar, Aqua, Qt., 8 ¼ In.	1624.00
Fruit Jar, Star, Pat'd Feb 5 1867, Aqua, Embossed Circles, Zinc Screw Lid, c.1867, Qt.	115.00
Fruit Jar, Sure Seal In Circle, Blue, Embossed, Qt., 7 ⅜ In.	280.00
Fruit Jar, Swayzee's Improved Mason, Yellow Green, Smooth Lip, Shoulder Seal, c.1903, Qt.	45.00
Fruit Jar, Trademark Lightning, Clear, ½ Gal.	56.00
Fruit Jar, Trademark Lightning, Putnam 10 On Base, Cornflower Blue, Qt.	146.00
Fruit Jar, Trademark Lightning, Putnam 17 On Base, Yellow Green, Qt.	274.00
Fruit Jar, Trademark Lightning, Putnam 193 On Base, Light Apple Green, Qt.	258.00
Fruit Jar, Trademark Lightning, Putnam On Base, Medium Amber, Ground Lip, ½ Gal.	90.00
Fruit Jar, Trademark Lightning, Putnam On Base, Olive Green, ½ Gal. .... 1120.00 to 3808.00	
Fruit Jar, Trademark Lightning, Smooth Lip, Qt.	336.00
Fruit Jar, Valve Jar Co., Philadelphia, Aqua, Glass Lid, Wire Coil Clamp, 7 ¾ In., Qt.	280.00
Fruit Jar, Victory 1, Apple Green, Original Closure, Qt.	1456.00
Fruit Jar, Victory, Pacific Glassworks, S.F., Aqua, Qt.	246.00
Fruit Jar, Whitmore's Patent, Rochester, N.Y., Aqua, Qt., 8 ⅞ In.	146.00
Gin, Juniper Leaf, Odore Netter, Golden Amber, Case, 1860-80, 10 In.	69.00
Gin, London Jockey Club House, Horse & Rider, Case, Teal Blue, 9 ¼ In.	2464.00
Gin, Olive Green, Square, Tooled Lip, 1760-90, 15 ⅞ In.	1035.00
Gin, Olive Green, Tubular Pontil, 9 ½ In.	168.00
Gin, Seahorse Brand, Pollen & Zoon Rotterdam Distillers, Etched Horse, Handle, 9 In.	134.00
Ginger Beer, Penny Farthing Rider, c.1885, ½ Pt., 8 ¼ In.	165.00
Household, Race & Sheldon Magic Boot Polish, Emerald Green, c.1850, 5 ½ In. ....illus	3163.00
Ink, 6-Sided, Blue Aqua, Rolled Lip, Open Pontil, 1840-60, 2 ¾ In.	518.00
Ink, 12-Sided, Blue Green, Inward Rolled Lip, Open Pontil, 1840-60, 2 In.	460.00
Ink, 12-Sided, Blue Green, Open Pontil, 1 ⅞ In.	139.00
Ink, 12-Sided, Forest Green, 3 Embossed Panels, Square Collar, Pontil, Pt.	5175.00
Ink, B.A. Fahnestock & Co., Blue Aqua, Open Pontil, Rolled Lip, c.1850, 2 ⅜ In.	575.00
Ink, Bertinguiot, Sapphire Blue, Sheared Mouth, Pontil, 1845-60, 2 ¾ In.	2128.00
Ink, Bertinguoit, Round, Olive Amber, Open Pontil	119.00
Ink, Blown, Golden Yellow, 2 ⅞ x 1 ¾ In.	364.00
Ink, Boss Patent, 6-Sided, Aqua, Inward Rolled Lip, Pontil, 2 ⅝ In.	679.00
Ink, Carter's, Cathedral, Cobalt Blue, 9 ¾ In.	360.00
Ink, Carter's, Cathedral, Cobalt Blue, Label, 11 In.	168.00
Ink, Carter's, Cathedral, Cobalt Blue, Original Cap, 3 In.	275.00
Ink, Carter's, Cathedral, Cobalt Blue, Original Cap, 6 ¼ In.	550.00
Ink, Carter's, Cathedral, Cobalt Blue, Original Cap, 8 In.	523.00
Ink, Carter's, Clear, Original Top, 7 ½ In.	358.00
Ink, Carter's, Cobalt Blue, Round, Metal Pour Top, Label, 7 ½ In.	65.00
Ink, Carter's, Green, 9 ¾ In.	10.00
Ink, Commercial Ink, Teal, Barrel, Double Pour Spout, 5 ¼ In., Pair	952.00
Ink, Cone, Aqua, 3 Rows Of Dots, Ribs, 1 ¾ In.	258.00
Ink, Cone, Blue Green, Rolled Lip, Open Pontil, 1840-60, 2 ⅝ In.	288.00
Ink, Cone, Cobalt Blue, 2 In.	39.00
Ink, Davids & Black, New York, Green, Applied Pour Spout, Pontil, Master, 9 ½ In.	235.00
Ink, Davids, Electro Chemical Writing Fluid, Cobalt Blue, Original Cap, 32 Oz., 9 In.	198.00
Ink, Davids, Turtle, Teal, Sheared Mouth, 2 ½ In.	476.00
Ink, Drape, Green, Applied Double Rolled Collar, Pontil, Label, 3 ⅞ x 2 ¾ In.	5152.00
Ink, E. Waters, Troy, N.Y., Light Green, Fluted Shoulders, Applied Square Collar, Pontil, 5 ½ In.	1075.00
Ink, Farley's, 8-Sided, Amber, Octagonal, Open Pontil, c.1842, 1 ⅞ In.	644.00

Bottle, Flask, Sunburst, Blue Green, Pontil, Sheared & Tooled Mouth, c.1825-35, ½ Pt.
$374.00

Bottle, Flask, Sunburst, Olive Green, Elliptical, Tooled Lip, 1825, ½ Pt.
$4888.00

Bottle, Flask, Union, Clasped Hands & Eagle, Blue Green, Applied Collar, c.1865, Qt.
$21850.00

Bottle, Flask, Washington & Jackson, Yellow Amber, Coventry Glass Works, Conn., c.1830
$805.00

Bottle, Flask, Washington, Bridgeton, New Jersey, Aqua, Tooled Lip, c.1830
$316.00

Bottle, Flask, Zanesville, 24 Ribs, Amber, Chestnut, Midwestern Grandfather, c.1820, 7 ¾ In.
$690.00

Bottle, Fruit Jar, Ball, 3-L Loop, Yellow Green, Striations, Zinc Screw Lid, c.1830
$316.00

Bottle, Fruit Jar, Mason's Patent Nov 30th, 1858, Yellow Amber, Ground Lip, Pt.
$1610.00

Ink, Farley's, 8-Sided, Olive Green, Flared Lip, Pontil, 3 ½ In.	420.00
Ink, Gaylord's Superior, Olive Green, Flared Lip, Open Pontil, 1840-60, 5 ¾ In.	2760.00
Ink, Geometric, Clear, Tooled Funnel Mouth, Pontil, Boston & Sandwich Glass Works, 2 ⅛ In.	1265.00
Ink, Geometric, Olive Amber, Tooled Disc Mouth, Pontil, Mt. Vernon Glass Works, 1 ¾ In.	374.00
Ink, Geometric, Olive Green, Tooled Disc Mouth, Pontil, Keene Glass Works, 2 In.	178.00
Ink, Geometric, Sapphire Blue, Disc Mouth, Mt. Vernon Glass Works, c.1835, 2 In. ....*illus*	5175.00
Ink, Gross & Robinson's, American Writing Fluid, Aqua, Applied Mouth, Pontil, 3 ⅞ In.	460.00
Ink, Harrison's Columbian, 6-Sided, Emerald Green, Inward Rolled Mouth, Pontil, 1 ½ In.	1330.00
Ink, Harrison's Columbian, 8-Sided, Aqua, 2 In.	134.00
Ink, Harrison's Columbian, 8-Sided, Green Aqua, 2 In.	336.00
Ink, Harrison's Columbian, 8-Sided, Sapphire Blue, 2 In.	3808.00
Ink, Harrison's Columbian, 12-Sided, Aqua, Applied Flared Collar, Pontil, 9 In.	1500.00
Ink, Harrison's Columbian, 12-Sided, Aqua, Applied Flared Mouth, Pontil, Paper Label, 4 ⅞ In.	540.00
Ink, Harrison's Columbian, 12-Sided, Green Aqua, Applied Mouth, Iron Pontil, c.1840-60, 7 ½ In. .	978.00
Ink, Harrison's Columbian, 12-Sided, Yellow Green, Applied Flared Collar, Pontil, 4 ½ In.	510.00
Ink, Harrison's Columbian, Blue, Applied Mouth, Open Pontil, 4 In.	1232.00
Ink, Harrison's Columbian, Blue, Rolled Lip, Pontil, 2 ⅛ In.	840.00
Ink, Harrison's Columbian, Cobalt Blue, Applied Mouth, c.1850, 7 ⅛ In. ....*illus*	2760.00
Ink, Harrison's Columbian, Cobalt Blue, Cylindrical, Applied Flared Mouth, Pontil, 4 ⅝ In. ...	1120.00
Ink, Harrison's Columbian, Cobalt Blue, Square Collar, Tubular Pontil, 6 ⅞ In.	2645.00
Ink, Harrison's Columbian, Green, Applied Top, 5 ¾ In.	616.00
Ink, Harrison's Columbian, Olive Yellow Green, Rolled Lip, Pontil, 1 ½ x 2 In.	2688.00
Ink, H.C. Hotchkiss Lyons, Tooled Top, Cobalt Blue, Master	134.00
Ink, Heath's Indelible, 8-Sided, Blue Green, Applied Mouth, Open Pontil, 1840-60, 4 ⅛ In.	2645.00
Ink, Hover, Phila., 8-Sided, Umbrella, Aqua, Rolled Lip, Open Pontil	420.00
Ink, Hover, Phila., Olive Green, Flared Lip, Open Pontil, c.1850, 6 In. ....*illus*	230.00
Ink, Hover, Phila., Umbrella, 8-Sided, Green, Open Pontil, c.1845-55, 2 ½ In.	1792.00
Ink, Jones' Empire, 12-Sided, Embossed Panels, Olive Yellow, Green, Pontil, 5 ⅞ x 3 ⅛ In.	5175.00
Ink, J.S. Dunham, 8-Sided, Umbrella, Green, Open Pontil, c.1845-55, 2 ¾ In.	2016.00
Ink, J.S. Dunham, 12-Sided, Aqua, Inward Rolled Mouth, Pontil, 1840-60, 2 ¼ In.	490.00
Ink, Laughlin's & Bushfield, 8-Sided, Blue Aqua, Applied Mouth, Wheeling, c.1850, 3 In. ....*illus*	230.00
Ink, L.H. Thomas, Cone Shape, Aqua, Tooled Lip	67.00
Ink, P & J Arnold's, London, England, Stoneware, Denby Pottery, 7 ½ In.	15.00
Ink, P & J Arnold's, Ledger Red, Embossed, Paper Label, Original Top, 4 ½ In.	145.00
Ink, P & J Arnold's, Writing Fluid, Embossed, Paper Label, Clear, Original Top, 5 ½ In.	1322.00
Ink, P & J Arnold's, Writing Fluid, Embossed, Paper Label, Clear, Original Top, 9 In.	210.00
Ink, Pitkin Type, 36 Ribs, Swirled To Left, Olive Green, Tooled Disc Mouth, 1790-1810	1380.00
Ink, Sanford's Fountain Pen, Embossed, Pamphlet, Box, 2 Oz., 2 ¾ In.	198.00
Ink, S.O. Dunbar, Umbrella, Taunton, Rolled Lip, Pontil, 2 ½ In.	180.00
Ink, Stafford's, Cylindrical, Cobalt Blue, Pour Spout, Label, ½ Contents, 9 ½ In.	85.00
Ink, Stafford's, Umbrella, Cobalt Blue, Pour Spout, Label, ½ Contents, 9 ½ In.	25.00
Ink, Stickwell & Co., 8-Sided, Umbrella, Aqua, Bulbous Knop, Sheared Lip	112.00
Ink, Teakettle, 4-Sided, Amethyst, Beveled Corners, 2 x 3 ½ In.	728.00
Ink, Teakettle, 8 Concave Panels, Ribs, Sapphire Blue, Sheared & Ground Lip, Brass Cap, 2 In.	403.00
Ink, Teakettle, 8-Sided, Golden Amber, Metal Closure, Chain, Pontil, 3 x 3 In.	364.00
Ink, Teakettle, 8-Sided, Green, Burst Lip, Double Font, 3 ½ x 3 ½ In.	784.00
Ink, Teakettle, 8-Sided, Violet Blue, Gold Design, Brass Closure, 2 ¾ x 3 ¾ In.	616.00
Ink, Teakettle, 8-Sided, Yellow, Bulbous Top, Brass Cap, 2 In.	952.00
Ink, Teakettle, 10-Sided, Opalescent Milk Glass, Embossed Flowers, Enameled, c.1895, 3 In. *illus*	575.00
Ink, Teakettle, Barrel, Amethyst, 2 In.	890.00
Ink, Teakettle, Barrel, Turquoise, Gold Paint, Brass Cap	1560.00
Ink, Teakettle, Blue Clambroth, 2 ½ In.	475.00
Ink, Teakettle, Cobalt Blue, Brass Cap, 2 x 4 ½ In.	280.00
Ink, Teakettle, Cobalt Blue, Ground Lip, Neck Ring, 1875-90, 1 ⅞ In.	635.00
Ink, Teakettle, Double Font, Green, Burst Lip, 3 ½ x 3 ½ In.	785.00
Ink, Teakettle, Opalescent Lime Green, 2 ⅞ x 3 ½ In.	365.00
Ink, Teakettle, Opaque Green, Melon Ribbed, Sheared Lip, 1875-90, 2 ¾ In.	195.00
Ink, Teakettle, Turquoise, Ground Lip, 1880, 2 ⅝ In. ....*illus*	748.00
Ink, Umbrella, 8 Sided, Cobalt Blue, Applied Mouth, 1855-65, 2 ⅝ In.	1035.00
Ink, Umbrella, 8-Sided, Blue Green, Hinged Cap	395.00
Ink, Umbrella, 8-Sided, Blue Green, Inward Rolled Mouth, Pontil, c.1850, 2 ½ x 2 ⅛ In.	2125.00
Ink, Umbrella, 8-Sided, Cobalt Blue, Sheared Mouth, Pontil, 2 ½ In.	1955.00
Ink, Umbrella, 8-Sided, Olive Green, Tooled Lip, Open Pontil, 2 ¾ In.	368.00
Ink, Umbrella, 8-Sided, Sapphire Blue, Tooled Mouth, 1860-80, 2 ⅝ In.	589.00
Ink, Umbrella, 8-Sided, Teal, Rolled Lip, Open Pontil, 2 ⅝ In.	190.00
Ink, Umbrella, Blue, Green, Open Pontil, 2 ½ In.	89.00

Bottle, Fruit Jar,
Potter & Bodine's Air-Tight, Patented,
April 13th 1858, Barrel, Aqua, ½ Gal.
$920.00

Bottle, Household,
Race & Sheldon Magic Boot Polish,
Emerald Green, c.1850, 5 ½ In.
$3163.00

Bottle, Ink, Geometric, Sapphire Blue,
Disc Mouth, Mt. Vernon Glass Works,
c.1835, 2 In.
$5175.00

Bottle, Ink, Harrison's Columbian,
Cobalt Blue, Applied Mouth, c.1850, 7 ⅛ In.
$2760.00

Bottle, Ink, Hover, Phila., Olive Green,
Flared Lip, Open Pontil, c.1850, 6 In.
$230.00

Bottle, Ink, Laughlin's & Bushfield, 8-Sided,
Blue Aqua, Applied Mouth, Wheeling,
c.1850, 3 In.
$230.00

Bottle, Ink, Teakettle, 10-Sided,
Opalescent Milk Glass, Embossed Flowers,
Enameled, c.1895, 3 In.
$575.00

Bottle, Ink, Teakettle, Turquoise, Ground Lip,
1880, 2 ⅝ In.
$748.00

Bottle, Ink, Vertu Bordeaux,
Encre De La Grande, Pink Amethyst,
Rolled Lip, c.1860, 2 In.
$230.00

Bottle, Ink, W.E. Bonney, Barrel, Aqua,
Applied Mouth, Tooled Spout, c.1860, 7 ¼ In.
$345.00

TIP
*Commercial false teeth
cleaners are good to use
to remove scum from
the inside of old glass
bottles.*

Bottle, Medicine, B.M. Keeney,
Honey Balm, Aqua, Applied Mouth,
c.1850, 5 ⅜ In.
$253.00

Bottle, Medicine,
C. Brinkerhoff's Health Restorative,
Olive Green, c.1850, 7 ⅝ In.
$978.00

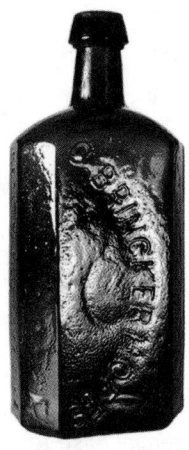

Ink, Umbrella, Ice Blue, Rolled Lip, Pontil, 2 ¾ In.	100.00
Ink, Umbrella, Mossy Green, Rolled Lip, Pontil, 2 ½ In.	420.00
Ink, Vertu Bordeaux, Encre De La Grande, Pink Amethyst, Rolled Lip, c.1860, 2 In. ......*illus*	230.00
Ink, Warrens Congress, 8-Sided, Medium Olive, Open Pontil, 1840-60, 3 In.	2576.00
Ink, Warrens Congress, 8-Sided, Olive Green, Inward Rolled Lip, Open Pontil, 1840-60, 2 ⅞ In.	2185.00
Ink, Warrens Congress, 8-Sided, Olive, Open Pontil, c.1840, 3 In.	2576.00
Ink, W.E. Bonney, Barrel, Aqua, Applied Mouth, Tooled Spout, c.1860, 7 ¼ In. ....*illus*	345.00
Medicine, 8-Sided, Golden Yellow Amber, Sheared Lip, Applied Mouth, Pontil, c.1825, 6 In. ...	1380.00
Medicine, Abbeys Effervescent Salt, Shakespeare, Square, Contents, Pamphlet, Box, 3 ½ In. ..	248.00
Medicine, Allen's Dyspeptic, Aqua, Rectangular, 6 In.	225.00
Medicine, Apothecary Case, 16 Hand Blown Bottles, Glass Stoppers, Mortar & Pestle, 8 ¾ x 10 ½ In.	1116.00
Medicine, Apothecary, Clear, Cylindrical, Footed, Stopper, 16 In.	330.00
Medicine, Apothecary, Clear, Cylindrical, Footed, Stopper, 20 In.	330.00
Medicine, Apothecary, Clear, Cylindrical, Footed, Stopper, 24 In.	330.00
Medicine, Apothecary, Clear, Oval, Footed, Pointed Stopper, 26 In.	385.00
Medicine, Apothecary, Clear, Panels, Footed, Stopper, 10 In.	385.00
Medicine, Apothecary, Clear, Round, Footed, Stopper, 15 In.	275.00
Medicine, Apothecary, Flower Sprays, Multicolored, Stopper, 12 x 3 ¼ In., Pair	60.00
Medicine, Atlas Aconic Oil, Atlas Medicine Co., Box, Henderson, N.C., 5 ½ In.	39.00
Medicine, Avery C. Smith, Druggist, St. Albans, Vt., 5 ¼ In.	10.00
Medicine, Balsam Of Honey, Aqua, Round, Open Pontil, 3 In.	59.00
Medicine, Barker's Antiseptic Dental Wash, Milk Glass, Stopper, F.A. Baker Co., 4 ½ In.	176.00
Medicine, Barrett's Mandrake Embrocation, Green, Flared Lip, 5 ¼ In.	146.00
Medicine, Bartine's Lotion, Blue Green, Beveled Corners, Sloping Collar, 6 In.	1725.00
Medicine, Beaver Oil Compound, Aqua Green, 5 In.	20.00
Medicine, Black Glass, Olive Green, Applied Mouth, England, c.1800, 6 ¼ In.	518.00
Medicine, B.M. Keeney, Honey Balm, Aqua, Applied Mouth, c.1850, 5 ⅜ In. ....*illus*	253.00
Medicine, Brandons Diarrhea Remedy, Box, 5 In.	165.00
Medicine, C. Brinkerhoff's Health Restorative, Olive Green, c.1850, 7 ⅝ In. ....*illus*	978.00
Medicine, C. Heimstreet & Co., Troy, N.Y., Cobalt Blue, Double Collar, 6 ¾ In.	224.00
Medicine, Carbon's Medicated Gin, Clear, Square, 10 In.	29.00
Medicine, Cod Liver Oil, Fish, Amber, Original Eli Lily Label, 9 ¾ In.	35.00
Medicine, Curo Mineral Springs Co., South Omaha, Neb., Aqua, Round, 6 ⅜ In.	25.00
Medicine, Cuticura Treatment For Affections Of The Skin & Neck, Aqua, Square, 6 Oz.	13.00
Medicine, Davis' Vegetable Painkiller, Aqua, Open Pontil, 5 In.	48.00
Medicine, Dickey Pioneer, Chemist, S.F., 1850, Cobalt Blue, Squared Lip	90.00
Medicine, Dickey Pioneer, Chemist, S.F., 1850, Embossed Mortar & Pestle, Light Blue	101.00
Medicine, Dickey Pioneer, Creme De Lis, Amber, Embossed, 1850, 5 ½ In.	143.00
Medicine, Doct. Robt. B. Folger's, Aqua, c.1850, 7 ⅜ In.	276.00
Medicine, Dr. A. Boschee's German Syrup, Aqua, 6 ½ In.	9.00
Medicine, Dr. A.E. Flint's Heart Remedy, Tobacco Amber, Tooled Top, 7 ½ In.	123.00
Medicine, Dr. Browder's Compound Syrup Of Indian Turnip, Aqua, Applied Lip, Pontil	392.00
Medicine, Dr. C. Grattan's Diphtheria Remedy, Aqua Green, Recessed, Applied Lip, 7 In.	476.00
Medicine, Dr. C.W. Roback's Scandinavian Blood Purifier, Aqua, Applied Lip	280.00
Medicine, Dr. Guysott's Yellow Dock, Aqua, 9 In.	89.00
Medicine, Dr. Hartshorn's, Olive Amber, Oval, Squared Mouth, 6 ⅛ In.	1265.00
Medicine, Dr. James Cannabis Indica, Craddock & Co., Proprietors, Embossed, Aqua, Oval, 8 In.	248.00
Medicine, Dr. Jayne's Vermifuge Tonic, Philada., Aqua Blue, Flared Lip, Open Pontil, 5 In.	420.00
Medicine, Dr. Kaiser's German Elixir, Toledo, O., Aqua Green, Indented Panels, 6 ¾ In.	308.00
Medicine, Dr. Kline's Great Nerve Restorer, Aqua, Embossed, $2.00, 8 ½ In.	154.00
Medicine, Dr. Larookah's Indian Vegetable Pulmonic Syrup, Aqua	88.00
Medicine, Dr. Miles' Blood Purifier, Embossed, Contents, Booklet, Box, $1.00, 8 ¼ In.	187.00
Medicine, Dr. Morse's Invigorating, Pale Aqua, Oval, Open Pontil, 1850, 7 ½ In.	127.00
Medicine, Dr. S. Fitch, Aqua, Oval, 6 ½ In.	70.00
Medicine, Dr. S.A. Weaver's Canker & Salt Rheum Syrup, Blue, Oval, Hinged, 9 In.	69.00
Medicine, Dr. S.F. Stowe's Ambrosial Nectar, Applied Band, Amber, Embossed, c.1866	123.00
Medicine, Dr. Simmons Squaw Vine Compound, Strictly Vegetable, Indian, 9 In.	121.00
Medicine, Dr. Steelling's Pulmonary Syrup, Blue Aqua, Applied Mouth, Pontil, c.1840, 5 ¾ In.	178.00
Medicine, Dr. Tobias Venetian Horse Liniment, New York, Aqua, 8-Sided, Open Pontil, 6 In. ..	69.00
Medicine, Dr. Wistar's Balsam Of Wild Cherry, Aqua, 8-Sided, 6 ½ In.	90.00
Medicine, Friedenwald's Buchugin For Kidney & Liver Troubles, 8-Sided, Green, 10 In.	695.00
Medicine, G.W. Merchant, Chemist, Lockport N.Y., Emerald Green, 5 ⅝ In.	239.00
Medicine, Gargling Oil, Lockport, N.Y., A Liniment For Man Or Beast, Green, 5 ½ In.	88.00
Medicine, Gargling Oil, Lockport, N.Y., Green, 5 In.	39.00
Medicine, George W. Carpenter, Genuine Preparations, Aqua, c.1850, 6 ⅛ In. ....*illus*	127.00
Medicine, Greensfelder & Laupheimer Druggists, Baltimore, Md., Amber, 10 Panels, 8 ¾ In. .	65.00

Medicine, Hall's Balsam For The Lungs, 9 Cottage Place, N.Y., Sapphire Blue, 7 ¾ In.	728.00
Medicine, Hall's Balsam For The Lungs, Medium Blue Green, 7 ¼ In.	39.00
Medicine, Haskin's Nervine, Great Nerve Tonic, Binghamton, N.Y, Aqua, Box, 8 ½ In.	88.00
Medicine, Healy & Bigelow's, Indian Sagwa, Embossed Indian Chief, Aqua, 8 In.	39.00
Medicine, Hexagonal, Strawberry Puce, Indented Panels, Sloping Shoulder, c.1865, 9 ⅜ In. . .	7840.00
Medicine, Hutty & Dickinson Druggists, 5 ¼ In.	125.00
Medicine, Indian Sanative For Salt Rheum, Blue Aqua, Rolled Lip, c.1850, 4 ⅞ In.	431.00
Medicine, J.J. McLaughlin, Yellow Copper, Blob Mouth, Mortar & Pestle, c.1860, 6 ¼ In.	633.00
Medicine, John Hart & Co., Heart Shape, Amber, Applied Double Collar, c.1875, 7 In.	615.00
Medicine, Laudanum, Open Pontil, Label, c.1820, 6 ½ In.	69.00
Medicine, Lediard's Morning Call, Olive Green, Applied Mouth, c.1865, 9 ⅞ In. ....*illus*	431.00
Medicine, Life Plant, Eagle, Amber, Oval, 8 In.	48.00
Medicine, Log Cabin Cough & Consumption Remedy, Amber, Tooled Mouth, c.1887, 8 ⅞ In.	316.00
Medicine, Log Cabin Extract, Amber, Tooled Mouth, Box, 1887-95, 6 ⅜ In.	489.00
Medicine, Log Cabin Hops & Buchu Remedy, Amber, Applied Mouth, 1887-95, 9 ⅞ In.	431.00
Medicine, Log Cabin Scalpine, Chocolate Amber, Applied Mouth, 1887-95, 8 ⅞ In.	2185.00
Medicine, Lyon's Powder, Olive Green, Rolled Lip, Open Pontil, c.1835, 4 ⅜ In.	460.00
Medicine, M.B. Robert's Vegetable Embrocation, Aqua, 5 In.	69.00
Medicine, M.B. Robert's Vegetable Embrocation, Cobalt Blue, 5 In.	79.00
Medicine, Melvin & Badger Apothecaries, White Wash Lotion, Cobalt Blue, c.1890, 5 ⅛ In.	207.00
Medicine, Nerve & Bone Liniment, Green, Shaded, Round, Rolled Lip, Open Pontil, 4 In.	308.00
Medicine, N.Y. Medical University, Cobalt Blue, 7 In.	89.00
Medicine, O'Neill's Catholicon, Aqua, Applied Collar Mouth, Open Pontil, c.1850, 8 ½ In.	3163.00
Medicine, Old Indian Liver & Kidney Tonic, Paper Label, 5 ½ x 2 x 1 ¼ In.	385.00
Medicine, Olive Green, Sheared, Tooled Lip, Pontil, 1780-90, 4 x 2 ¼ In.	219.00
Medicine, O.O. Woodman, Vicksburg, Mississippi, Aqua, Open Pontil, c.1855, 6 ¾ In.	518.00
Medicine, Peptenzyme, Reed & Carnick, Jersey City, N.J., Cobalt Blue, 8 ½ In.	66.00
Medicine, Perrine's Apple Ginger, Embossed Apple, Golden Tobacco...........................	308.00
Medicine, Planters Cuban Relief, For Internal & External Pains, 1 Oz., 6 ¼ In.	154.00
Medicine, Podophyllin, Teal Green, Cork, 3 ½ In.	99.00
Medicine, Pratt's Abolition Oil, For Abolishing Pain, Aqua Green, Flared Lip, 6 ¼ In.	476.00
Medicine, Pratt's New Life, McBoyle & Co., San Francisco, Honey Amber, 7 ¾ In.	532.00
Medicine, Rev. T. Hill's Vegetable Remedy, Aqua, 5 In.	6.00
Medicine, Rev. W. Clarke's European Cough Remedy, Aqua, Open Pontil, c.1850, 7 ½ In.	431.00
Medicine, Rohrer's Expectoral Wild Cherry Tonic, Lancaster, Pa., Orange Amber, Iron Pontil	499.00
Medicine, Rohrer's Expectoral, Yellow Amber, Applied Double Collar, Pontil, c.1860, 10 ¾ In. ..	518.00
Medicine, Rohrer's Wild Cherry Tonic, Lancaster, Penn...	336.00
Medicine, Sagine For Diseases Of The Skin & Mucous Membrane, Columbus, Ohio, Clear, 6 ¾ In.	28.00
Medicine, Samaritan's Nervine, Ice Blue Aqua, Bearded Man, 8 In.	39.00
Medicine, Sanford's Cholera & Diarrhea Mixture, Baltimore, Clear, Box, 6 In.	50.00
Medicine, Schenck's Seaweed Tonic, Aqua, 8 ½ In.	12.00 to 20.00
Medicine, Selden's Wigwam Liniment, Blue Aqua, Oval, Open Pontil, c.1850, 9 ¼ In.	978.00
Medicine, Seymour's Compound, Green Aqua, Beveled Corners, Sloping Collar, 9 ⅝ In.	2530.00
Medicine, Simmon's Liver Regulator, J.H. Zeilin & Co., St. Louis, Clear, Box, 7 In.	154.00
Medicine, S.O. Richardson's Jaundice Bitters, Aqua	78.00
Medicine, Swaim's Panacea, Aqua, Round	70.00
Medicine, Swaim's Panacea, Green Aqua, Applied Collar, Open Pontil, c.1850, 7 ⅞ In.	633.00
Medicine, Swaim's Panacea, Green, Striations, Vertical Panels, Sloping Collar	168.00
Medicine, Swaim's Panacea, Philada., Aqua, Panels, 8 In.	39.00
Medicine, Swaim's Panacea, Philada., Emerald Green, c.1850, 8 In. ....*illus*	575.00
Medicine, Taylor's Pain Annihilating Liniment, Oil Of Life, Aqua, Oval, Open Pontil, 7 In.	159.00
Medicine, True Worm Elixir For Horses, Amber, 8 ½ In.	80.00
Medicine, U.S.A. Hosp. Dept., Chartreuse Green, Applied Double Collar, 8 ⅞ In.	2760.00
Medicine, U.S.A. Hosp. Dept., Green, Applied Top, Label..	1120.00
Medicine, U.S.A. Hosp. Dept., Olive Green, Applied Collar, 9 In.	840.00
Medicine, U.S.A. Hosp. Dept., Yellow Amber, Applied Collar, 9 In.	728.00
Medicine, U.S.A. Hosp. Dept., Yellow Amber, Applied Double Collar, Qt., 9 In.	346.00
Medicine, U.S.A. Hosp. Dept., Yellow Citron, Applied Collar, 9 In.	532.00
Medicine, Vaughn's Vegetable Lithontriptic Mixture, Aqua, Square, 1855-65, 6 ⅛ In.	364.00
Medicine, Vaughn's Vegetable Lithontriptic Mixture, Buffalo, Aqua, Arched Panels.............	336.00
Medicine, Vaughn's Vegetable Lithontriptic Mixture, Ice Blue, Beveled Corners, 8 In.	863.00
Medicine, W. Mentiplay & Sons, Reliable Remedies, Green, Square, 9 ¼ In.	364.00
Medicine, Warner's Safe, Orange Amber, Oval, Applied Double Collar Mouth, 9 ½ In.	805.00
Medicine, Warner's Safe Remedies, Rochester, N.Y., Amber, Cork Top, Box, Seal, 9 In.	468.00
Medicine, Warner's Safe Remedies, Rochester, N.Y., Amber, Cork Top, ½ Pt., 7 In.	198.00
Medicine, Warner's Safe Rheumatic Remedy, Sciatica, Lumbago, Gout, Embossed, 12 ½ Oz., 9 In.	132.00

Bottle, Medicine, George W. Carpenter, Genuine Preparations, Aqua, c.1850, 6 ⅛ In. **$127.00**

The Free 1960s Flasks

Lestoil is a liquid cleaner originally made by Adell Chemical Co. of Holyoke, Mass., a company founded in 1943. The product was very successful. In 1963 and 1964, Lestoil was sold in special bottles shaped like early American flasks. There were three designs that closely resembled the old originals. Five molds were used and flasks had numbers on the bottom. The bottles came in four colors: deep purple, deep blue, deep green, and amber. Some bottles had random streaks of color created when the machines changed from one glass color to another. There were light-colored bottles and even clear color-less flasks. They had plastic stoppers. Each full bottle sold for about 65 cents. Probably more than a million flasks were made. An empty Lestoil flask sells for about $10 today.

BOTTLE

Bottle, Medicine,
Lediard's Morning Call, Olive Green,
Applied Mouth, c.1865, 9 ⅞ In.
$431.00

Bottle, Medicine, Swaim's Panacea,
Philada., Emerald Green, c.1850, 8 In.
$575.00

Bottle, Mineral Water,
Congress & Empire Spring Co.,
Emerald Green, c.1870, Pt.
$345.00

Medicine, Warner's Safe, Yellow Topaz, Oval, Applied Collar, 11 In.	1035.00
Medicine, Whittemore's Vegetable Syrup For Dairrhoea, Aqua, Open Pontil, c.1855, 5 ⅜ In.	460.00
Medicine, Wisdom's Robertine, Cobalt Blue, Rectangular, 5 In.	79.00
Milk, Annapolis Dairy Products Co., Embossed, Cream Top, Pt.	16.00
Milk, Annie Oakley, Coleman Milk, 8 ½ In.	35.00
Milk, Antietam Dairy, Waynesboro, Pa., Qt.	18.00
Milk, Aristocrat Dairy, Baltimore, Phone La-3000, Baby Face, Square, Qt.	75.00
Milk, Arter's Dairy, Waynesbroro, Pa., Pt.	16.00
Milk, Arthur's Dairy, Waynesboro, Pa., ½ Pt.	18.00
Milk, Barati Dairy, Broughton, Pa., Embossed, Qt.	12.00
Milk, Begley Bros., Quaker Dairy, W. Springfield, Ma., Clear, Qt.	18.00
Milk, Biltmore Dairy Farms, The South's Finest Dairy, Asheville, N.C.	476.00
Milk, Blais Dairy Farm, Lewiston, Maine, Cow, Orange & Black Pyro, Tall, Round, Qt.	70.00
Milk, Borden's, Embossed Script, ½ Pt.	6.00
Milk, Brandt's Dairy, Old King Cole, Orange ACL, Pt.	125.00
Milk, Brown's Dairy, Fairfield, Pa., Embossed, Qt.	95.00
Milk, Cambridge Dairy Co., Cambridge, O., Orange & Black Pyro, Tall, Round Pt.	25.00
Milk, Cambridge Dairy Co., Cambridge, O., Orange & Black Pyro, Tall, Round, Qt.	65.00
Milk, Cedar Grove Dairy, Slinger, Wis., Embossed, Round, Qt.	58.00
Milk, Cedar Grove Dairy, Slinger, Wis., Picture, Red Pyro, Round, Qt.	72.00
Milk, Cedar Lane Farm, Swansea, Mass., Orange, Cows, Dairy Farm, Pt.	45.00
Milk, Charles Tift Pasteurized Milk, Key West, Fla., Cross Pattern, Pt.	408.00
Milk, Cherry Lane Dairy, Chambersburg, Pa.	35.00
Milk, Cloverleaf Blue Ribbon Farms, Stockton, Calif., Orange Pyro, Round, Cream Top	45.00
Milk, Colorado State, ACL, Round, Qt.	225.00
Milk, Consumers Dairy, Beloit, Wis., Embossed, Round, ½ Pt.	33.00
Milk, Cox Dairy, Cow Kicking, Matador, Charging Bull, Orange, Green ACL, Round, Qt.	95.00
Milk, Cream Top, Carlsbad Cavern, N. Mexico, Embossed, Pyro, Qt.	375.00
Milk, Creamer, Bancroft, Family Treat, Red ACL, Square	35.00
Milk, Creamer, Byrne Dairy, Mighty Fine, Black ACL, Round	40.00
Milk, Creamer, Diffines Dairy, Niagara Falls, Round The Clock Restaurant, Red ACL, Round	40.00
Milk, Creamer, Dolly Madison, LaCrosse, Wis., ACL, Round	42.00
Milk, Creamer, Olbrych's, Amsterdam, N.Y., Red ACL, Square	35.00
Milk, Creamer, Producer's Dairy, Illinois, Orange ACL, Round	45.00
Milk, Creamer, Quality Dairy, None Better, Red ACL, Round	28.00
Milk, Creamer, Rose Lawn Milk, Both Sides, Maroon ACL, Square	35.00
Milk, Creamer, Sullivan Dairy, Sullivan, Ill., ACL, Square	38.00
Milk, Creamer, Sunset Dairy, Stolen From Tucson, Ariz., Yellow ACL, Round	35.00
Milk, Creamer, Toddle House, 2 Cooks, White ACL, Round, 2 Oz.	35.00
Milk, Creamer, Valley Bell, Laboratory Controlled Products, Maroon ACL, Round	35.00
Milk, Curt's Dairy, Nekoosa, Wis., ACL, Square, Pt.	35.00
Milk, Dairy Distributors, Inc., Milwaukee, Wis., Black ACL, Round, Qt.	57.00
Milk, Dairy, L. Vincent, Danville, Pa., Cop Top, Tall, ACL, Round, Qt.	344.00
Milk, Dairylea Milk, Hoppy's Favorite Milk, Black ACL, Square	50.00
Milk, Daisy Dell Farm Dairy, Pasteurized Guernsey Milk, Springfield, Missouri, Red, Qt.	40.00
Milk, Dellinger Dairy Farm, Jeffersonville, Ind., Medal, Herd, Standing Cow, Black, Gold, Qt.	60.00
Milk, Drink Producers Pasteurized Milk, Greenville, Texas, Red, Qt.	60.00
Milk, Eden Plains Dairy Farms, Hagerstown, Md., Qt.	40.00
Milk, Edgewood, 4-Sided, ACL, Square, Qt.	15.00
Milk, Elm Place, Wheaton, Ill., Embossed, Round, ½ Pt.	42.00
Milk, Ernest Brooks, Covington, Pa., Red ACL, Round, 1936, Qt.	25.00
Milk, Fairview Farm Dairy, Dixon, Ill., Brown ACL, Square, Qt.	38.00
Milk, Farmers Fairfield Dairy Co., Pt.	45.00
Milk, Fillmore Farms, Historic Bennington, Green Letters, Embossed, Pt.	615.00
Milk, Flanders Dairy, Red ACL, Baby Holding Bottle, Round, ½ Pt.	65.00
Milk, Fox's Guernsey Dairy, Waukesh, Wis., Orange ACL, Round, ½ Pt.	33.00
Milk, Frey's Farm Dairy, Falling Spring Road, Chambersburg, Pa., ½ Gal.	16.00
Milk, Freyes Dairy Inc., Leominster, Mass., Orange ACL, Double Baby Top, Square, Qt.	95.00
Milk, G.A. Harrris & Son Raw Milk, Cardboard Cap, A. Harris, Gladevill, Tenn., Pt.	18.00
Milk, Gem City Dairy, Baraboo, Wis., Cottage Cheese, Round, Embossed	28.00
Milk, Geo. T. Chambers, Providence, R.I., Round, Embossed CY, Qt.	15.00
Milk, Gold Creek Farms, Medice Bros., Apollo, Pa., Baby Face, Qt.	250.00
Milk, Golden Bell Dairy, Embossed, Cow, Bell, Round, ½ Pt.	45.00
Milk, Golden Harvest Dairy, Milwaukee, Wisc., Green ACL, Round, ½ Pt.	35.00
Milk, Goyon Creamery, Palo Alto, Calif., War Bonds For Victory, Uncle Sam Holds Milk, Orange, Qt.	65.00
Milk, Grant Patten Milk Co., Chattanooga, Tenn., Round Embossed Tree, Cow, Pt.	15.00

Milk, Greencastle Sanitary Dairy, Greencastle, Pa., Qt.	25.00
Milk, Greenleaf Dairy, Cop The Cream, Green ACL, Square, Qt.	85.00
Milk, H, J. Culler, Inc., Milk Transportation, McConnellsburg, Pa., 1944, Qt.	16.00
Milk, Hawthorn Mellody Dairy, Chicago, Ill., Red ACL, Square, ½ Gal.	38.00
Milk, Heiss & Sons Dairy, Rochelle Park, N.J., Bottled On Our Farm, Orange, Qt.	39.00
Milk, Hershey's Chocolate Milk, ACL, ½ Pt.	10.00
Milk, Hillcrest Dairy, Bentleyville, Pa., Cow, Orange, Thatcher Glass, Qt.	49.00
Milk, Hillcrest Dairy, Better Baby Milk, Americus, Ga., Pt.	20.00
Milk, Hillside Dairy, Huntington, Sta., L.I., Yellow, Silo, Dairy, Qt.	29.00
Milk, Hoffman Minick, Cream Top, Pat. March 3rd 1925, Qt.	18.00
Milk, Hogan's Dairy, Hudson Falls, N.Y., Clear, Qt.	8.00 to 12.00
Milk, Hoile's Dairy, Embossed, Round, ½ Pt.	35.00
Milk, Homestead Dairy, Hot Springs, Va., Green	40.00
Milk, Homestead Dairy, Salisbury, Md., Orange	30.00
Milk, Hull's Dairy, Waynesboro, Pa., Qt.	18.00
Milk, Inch's Dairy, Selinsgrove Pa., Tall, ACL, Round, Qt.	550.00
Milk, Indian Ladder Farms, Altamont, N.Y., Indian Head, Ladder, ACL	5.00
Milk, Isaly's Milk, Baby Face, Red ACL, Square, Qt.	75.00
Milk, James W.K. Arper, Mercersburg, Pa., Qt.	150.00
Milk, Jersey Farm Dairy, Embossed, Round, Qt.	35.00
Milk, Kentucky Acres Dairy, Buy War Bonds, 10 Percent, Orange ACL, Round	75.00
Milk, Kilbourn Co-Op Cream, Wisconsin Dells, Pasteurized Products, Black,	55.00
Milk, King's Dairy, Hartville, S.C., Consult Your Doctor Annually, Green ACL, Round, Qt.	59.00
Milk, Land O' Lakes Dairy, Oconomowoc, Wis., Red ACL, Round, ½ Pt.	33.00
Milk, Locust Grove Farm, Marshallton, Del., Farm, Cow, Yellow	75.00
Milk, Maple Farm Dairy, Boy, Holding 2 Bottles Of Milk, Black ACL, Qt.	55.00
Milk, Maple Leaf Dairy, Lake Geneva, Wis., Red, Green ACL, Round, ½ Pt.	33.00
Milk, Markel's Glen Rock, Pa., Embossed, Pt.	12.00
Milk, McConnellsburg Dairy, McConnellsburg, Pa., Pt.	38.00
Milk, McConnellsburg Dairy, McConnellsburg, Pa., Qt.	38.00
Milk, Meadow Brook Farm Dairy, Cow, Baby, From Farmer To Customer, Orange, Qt.	49.00
Milk, Meadow Gold Dairy, Cream Top, Round, Qt.	39.00
Milk, Merritt's Farm Dairy, Bridgeport, Ct., Embossed, Round, Qt.	10.00
Milk, Meyer Bros. Dairy, Arlington Heights, Ill., ½ Gal.	39.00
Milk, Miller's Dairy, Elizabeth, Pa., Tall, ACL, Round, Qt.	85.00
Milk, Mountain Dairy, Mansfield, Ct., 125th Anniversary	15.00
Milk, Muenchow Dairy, Playtime, Mealtime, Any Time, Alphabet Blocks, Duraglas, ½ Gal.	20.00
Milk, N.E. Oliver, Oriskey Falls, N.Y., Drink Oliver's Milk, Be A Winner, ½ Pt.	20.00
Milk, Natural Milk, Cow's Head, Maroon, Orange ACL, Round, Qt.	75.00
Milk, Nelson Dairy, Wikhorn, Wisc., Round, Embossed, ½ Pt.	95.00
Milk, New Haven Dairy, Embossed Script, Round, Qt.	12.00
Milk, New Holstein Creamery, Orange ACL, Square, Qt.	35.00
Milk, Oaks Dairy, Green ACL, Round, ½ Pt.	30.00
Milk, Oaks Dairy, Ripon, Wis., Baby, ACL, Round, Qt.	64.00
Milk, Old Tavern Farm, Portland, Maine, Red & Black Pyro, Tall, Round Qt.	75.00
Milk, Onatru Farm Goat Milk, Ridgefield, Conn., Green ACL, Qt.	60.00
Milk, Orchard Farm Dairy, Dallas, Pa., Red ACL, Cream Top	80.00
Milk, Otto Milk Company, Pittsburgh, Pa., Cream Top, Round, Embossed, Qt.	15.00
Milk, Palmerton Sanitary Dairy, Embossed, ½ Pt.	12.00
Milk, Penn-Creek Farm Dairy, Greencastle, Pa., RR 3, Gal.	25.00
Milk, Pet Milk Co, Orange ACL, Round, ½ Pt.	33.00
Milk, Piche's Dairy, No. Smithfield, R.I., Embossed, Pt.	12.00
Milk, Pine State Dairy, Bangor, Maine, Baby Face Top, Green ACL, Square, Qt.	80.00
Milk, Pitstick Dairy, Ottawa, Ill., ACL, Square, ½ Gal.	30.00
Milk, Pitstick Dairy, Ottawa, Ill., ACL, Square, Qt.	43.00
Milk, Pleasant View Dairy, Sherman, N.Y., Red, Barn, Truck, House, Direct To You, Qt.	65.00
Milk, Portage Creamery Assn., Indian Carrying Canoe, Portage, Wisc., Red ACL, Square, ½ Pt.	10.00
Milk, Preston Dairy, Woman Running, Vitamins, Minerals, Duraglas, ½ Gal.	18.00
Milk, Pure Milk Assn., A Farmers Cooperative, Red ACL, Square, Chicago, Ill., Pt.	30.00
Milk, Purity Dairy, Mother & Child Vita Rich Mineral Soft Curd Milk, ½ Gal.	18.00
Milk, Quality Guernsey Dairy, Beaver Dam, Wis., Cream Top, Orange ACL, Square, Qt.	62.00
Milk, Quary, Embassy Dairy Inc., Washington, D.C., Baby Face, Qt.	88.00
Milk, R.G. Miller & Sons, Store, Sealtest Emblem, ACL, Round.	15.00
Milk, Rathbun Farms, Finest Under The Sun, Dutch Boy & Girl Drinking Milk, ACL, Gal.	75.00
Milk, Readings Dairy, Jersey Shore, Penn., Tall, ACL, Round, Qt.	100.00
Milk, Reeder Bros. Dairy, Shippensburg, Pa., Pt.	35.00

Bottle, Mineral Water, J. Schweppe, Genuine Superior Aerated Waters, Green, Torpedo, 8 ¾ In.
$207.00

Bottle, Mineral Water, Luke Beard, Emerald Green, 10-Pin, c.1860, 7 ¼ In.
$230.00

Bottle, Mineral Water, Tweddle's Celebrated, New York, Blue Green, c.1850, 7 ⅝ In.
$242.00

Bottle, Mineral Water,
W. Heiss Jr.'s Superior, Cobalt Blue,
c.1850, 7 ¼ In.
$6900.00

Bottle, Poison, Cobalt Blue, Coffin,
Embossed Skull & Crossbones, DP,
c.1910, 3 In.
$748.00

Bottle, Poison,
Lattice & Diamond, Cobalt Blue,
Tooled Mouth, c.1900, 9 ⅛ In.
$316.00

Bottle, Sarsaparilla,
Dr. Guysott's Yellow Dock, Aqua,
Applied Mouth, c.1850, 10 ¼ In.
$518.00

Milk, Reymer's Dairy, Harford, Wis., ACL, Square, ½ Pt.	35.00
Milk, Rhode Island College, Squat, ACL, Qt.	130.00
Milk, Ritchey Dairy, Martinsburg, Pa., Pt.	8.00
Milk, Robert H. Shoap, Shippensburg, Pa, Qt.	45.00
Milk, Russell's Dairy Farms, North Freedom, Wis., Red ACL, Round, Qt.	69.00
Milk, Sauquoit Valley Dairy, Utica, New York, Embossed Indian Head, Ribbed, Round, Pt.	25.00
Milk, Shades Dairy, Santa Fe, New Mexico, Cow's Head, Maroon, Qt.	65.00
Milk, Shively's Milk, Chambersburg, Pa., Qt.	16.00
Milk, Spicklers Dairy, Elizabethtown, Pa., Embossed, 5 ½ In.	20.00
Milk, Spinney Run Farms, Embossed, Round, ½ Pt	38.00
Milk, Starland Dairies, Savannah, Ga., Brown, Round, Embossed Star, Starland Dairies	24.00
Milk, Steward's, The Best Milk, Thermopolis, Wy., Black	40.00
Milk, Strickler's Vita-Min, Huntington, Pa., Amber, Qt.	30.00
Milk, Strohm's Dairy, Shippensburg, Pa., Qt.	35.00
Milk, Sunshine Dairy, Orange ACL, Baby Top, Square, Qt.	70.00
Milk, Superior Dairy, Martinsburg, W.Va., Pt.	16.00
Milk, Sweet Clover Dairy, Roosevelt, L.I., Orange ACL, Baby Face Top, Square, Qt.	75.00
Milk, Torrington Creamery, Torrington, Ct., Embossed, ½ Pt.	10.00
Milk, Union Dairy Farms, Freeport, Ill., Square, Red Pyro, ½ Gal.	39.00
Milk, Upland Farm Of Barrington, RI., Builds Em Healthy, Cow's Head, 2 Children, Orange	25.00
Milk, Urbandale Guernsey Dairy, Elkhorn, Wis., Orange & Black Pyro, Tall, Round Qt.	70.00
Milk, Waynesboro Sanitary Dairy Milk Plant, Waynesboro, Pa, Qt.	45.00
Milk, W.B. Brown & Sons, Orange ACL, Double Baby Face Top, Square, Qt.	95.00
Milk, Weeden's Dairy, Sheboygan, Wisc., Brown ACL, Round, ½ Pt.	30.00
Milk, Wehr's Dairy, Mifflinburg, Pa., Cow, Our Blue Ribbon Winner, Orange, Black, Qt.	75.00
Milk, White's Dairy Farm, Red & Yellow ACL, Baby Face Top, Square, Qt.	85.00
Milk, Willow Farms Dairy, LaGrange, Ill., Round, Embossed, ½ Pt.	27.00
Milk, Willow Farms Dairy, Westminster, Md., Pt.	18.00
Milk, Winkler & Warren Dairy, Burlington, Wis., Round, Embossed, Pt.	48.00
Milk, Workmans Dairy, Saxton, Pa., Orange, Yellow, Brown & Green Sides, Qt.	16.00
Milk, Wrightwood Dairy, For Freedom Buy War Bonds, Eagle, Red ACL, Round, Qt.	175.00
Mineral Water, Alburgh A Springs, Vt., Yellow Amber, Applied Double Collar, c.1870, Qt.	345.00
Mineral Water, Azule Seltzer Springs, Bear, Teal Green, Blob Top	168.00
Mineral Water, Bremenkampf & Regli, Eureka, Nev., Aqua, 1878-85, Blob Top	476.00
Mineral Water, Chapman's Mineral Spring, Embossed Indian Bust, Crown Top, Qt.	48.00
Mineral Water, Cheltenham Natural Aperient Water, Olive Green, Gin Shape, Qt.	89.00
Mineral Water, Clarke & White, Olive Green, Pt., 7 ⅝ In.	69.00
Mineral Water, Congress & Empire Spring Co., Deep Blue Green, Pt.	50.00
Mineral Water, Congress & Empire Spring Co., Emerald Green, c.1870, Pt. .....*illus*	345.00
Mineral Water, Congress & Empire Spring Co., Olive Green, Applied Double Collar, c.1865, Pt.	1610.00
Mineral Water, Congress & Empire Spring Co., Olive Yellow, Qt.	295.00
Mineral Water, Congress & Empire Spring Co., Saratoga, N.Y., Olive Yellow, c.1865, Qt., 9 ⅝ In.	112.00
Mineral Water, Congress Spring Co., Green, 10 In.	20.00
Mineral Water, Coventry, Hamilton, Aqua, c.1892, 9 ¼ In.	165.00
Mineral Water, Croft's Swiss Milk Cocoa, Aqua, Wire Closure, Oval, c.1885-95, Pt.	104.00
Mineral Water, D.A. Knowlton, Saratoga, N.Y., Olive Green, Pt.	125.00
Mineral Water, Emmerson Coddswollop, Penny Farthing Racer, Aqua, Clear, c.1885	77.00
Mineral Water, Excelsior Spring, Saratoga Type, Lime Green	325.00
Mineral Water, Gardner & Landon, Yellow Olive Green, Applied Double Collar, c.1855, Qt.	2070.00
Mineral Water, Gettysburg Katalysine Water, Yellow, Green, c.1870, Qt., 9 ½ In.	489.00
Mineral Water, Geyser Springs, Saratoga Springs, Aqua, 9 ½ In.	20.00 to 55.00
Mineral Water, Ghirardelli's Branch, Oakland, Deep Cobalt Blue, Blob Top, 7 ½ In.	476.00
Mineral Water, G.W. Weston & Co., Saratoga, N.Y., Olive Green, Qt.	150.00
Mineral Water, Hathorn Spring, Saratoga, N.Y., Orange Amber, Qt.	105.00
Mineral Water, Hathorn Spring, Saratoga, N.Y., Yellow Olive, 1869-85, Pt., 7 ¼ In.	101.00
Mineral Water, Highrock Congress Spring, Olive Amber, Applied Mouth, 1865-75, Pt.	920.00
Mineral Water, J. Schweppe, Genuine Superior Aerated Waters, Green, Torpedo, 8 ¾ In. ..*illus*	207.00
Mineral Water, John S. Baker, Teal, 8-Sided, Blob Top, Iron Pontil, 7 ¼ In.	308.00
Mineral Water, Luke Beard, Emerald Green, 10-Pin, c.1860, 7 ¼ In. .....*illus*	230.00
Mineral Water, Lynch & Clarke, Yellow Olive, Pt.	258.00
Mineral Water, Massena Spring, Clear, Tooled Mouth, 1875-85, Qt.	460.00
Mineral Water, Massena Spring, Teal Blue, Applied Double Collar, c.1870-80, Qt.	184.00 to 299.00
Mineral Water, Middletown Healing Springs, Grays & Clark, Green, Double Collar, c.1865, Qt.	863.00
Mineral Water, Middletown Healing Springs, Nature's Remedy, Green, Double Collar, c.1865, Qt.	230.00
Mineral Water, Mt. Tamalpais Natural, San Rafael, Cal., Light Aqua, Blob Top	1120.00
Mineral Water, Napa Soda, Natural Mineral Water, Green, Embossed, 1861-73	364.00

Mineral Water, Pacific Congress Springs, Running Deer, Saratoga, Calif., Yellow Green, Pt....	1232.00
Mineral Water, Pavilion & United States Spring Co., Blue Green, Applied Double Collar, 1865, Qt.	3450.00
Mineral Water, Quaker Springs, I.W. Meader & Co., Blue Aqua, Applied Double Collar, 1865, Qt.	978.00
Mineral Water, S. Moore Superior Mineral Water Philada., Blue Green, Blob Top, Squat, Iron Pontil	199.00
Mineral Water, Saratoga Spring, Amber, Applied Double Collar, 1865-75, Qt.	161.00
Mineral Water, Saratoga Vichy Spouting, Aqua, Pt., 7 In.	48.00
Mineral Water, Saratoga Vichy Water, Light Amber, Qt..	88.00
Mineral Water, Saxlehner's Bitterquelle-Hunyadi Janos, Olive Green, Cylindrical, c.1880, 9 In. .	35.00
Mineral Water, Summit, J.H., Teal Green, Blob Top..	280.00
Mineral Water, Thompson's Premium, Union Soda Works, San Francisco, Green, Torpedo ...	476.00
Mineral Water, Tweddle's Celebrated, New York, Blue Green, c.1850, 7 ⅝ In. ....*illus*	242.00
Mineral Water, W. Heiss Jr.'s Superior, Cobalt Blue, c.1850, 7 ¼ In. ....*illus*	6900.00
Mineral Water, Wm. A. Carpenter's, Hudson, N.Y., Green, 8-Sided, Blob Top, 1845-55, 7 In. ...	420.00
Pepper Sauce, Cathedral, 4-Sided, Green, c.1860, 8 ½ In.	224.00
Pepper Sauce, Cathedral, 4-Sided, Light Green, 1860-70, 8 ½ In.	224.00
Pepper Sauce, Cathedral, 6-Sided, Blue Green, Applied Double Collar, Open Pontil, 8 ⅝ In. .	265.00
Pepper Sauce, Cathedral, Aqua, Pontil, c.1850, 9 ¾ In.	168.00
Pepper Sauce, Cathedral, Blue, Aqua, 4 Windows, 8 In.	79.00
Pepper Sauce, Cathedral, Blue, Aqua, 8 In.	69.00
Pepper Sauce, Cathedral, Blue Aqua, Applied Double Collar, 1855-70, 10 ⅛ In.	265.00
Pepper Sauce, Cathedral, Blue Aqua, Applied Double Collar, Pontil, 1840-60, 10 In.	403.00
Pepper Sauce, Cathedral, Blue Green, Applied Double Collar, Open Pontil, 1840-60, 8 ⅞ In. .	431.00
Pepper Sauce, Cathedral, Green, Applied Double Collar, Open Pontil, 10 In.	168.00
Pepper Sauce, E.R. Durkee, Spiral, Aqua, 8 In.	25.00
Pepper Sauce, Rosekrans & Ovens, Aqua, Applied Mouth, Iron Pontil, 1840-60, 9 ⅛ In.	374.00
Pepper Sauce, Wells Miller & Provost, New York, Green, 8-Sided, Applied Top, Pontil	336.00
Perfume Bottles are listed in their own category.	
Pickle, Bengal, Mixed, Tooled Top, Label, 11 In.	45.00
Pickle, Cathedral, 4-Sided, Aqua, 11 ½ In.	185.00
Pickle, Cathedral, 6-Sided, Apple Green, Rolled Collar, 1860-90, 13 In.	616.00
Pickle, Cathedral, 6-Sided, Aqua, 13 ¼ In.	335.00
Pickle, Cathedral, 6-Sided, Aqua, Outward Rolled Lip, Yarnall Bros., 12 ⅞ In.	863.00
Pickle, Cathedral, Aqua, Outward Rolled Lip, Pontil, c.1855, 9 ¼ In.	286.00
Pickle, Cathedral, Aqua, Rolled Lip, Iron Pontil, 1845-60, 11 ½ In.	690.00
Pickle, Cathedral, Blue Aqua, Applied Mouth, 1855-70, 9 ¼ In.	316.00
Pickle, Cathedral, Teal, Rolled Lip, Pt., 8 ¾ In.	2016.00
Pickle, Flower Design, Paneled, Aqua, Embossed Rose & Leaf, 12 ¾ In.	250.00
Pickle, J. McCollick & Co., Blue Aqua, Rolled Lip, 1845-60, 11 ¼ In.	316.00
Pickle, Seville Packing Co., New York, Yellow Green, Embossed Crown, 8 In.	39.00
Pickle, Wells Miller & Provost, Blue Aqua, Applied Mouth, Iron Pontil, 1845-60, 11 ½ In.	460.00
Pickle, W.K. Lewis & Co., Blue Aqua, Applied Mouth, Iron Pontil, 1845-60, 10 ¾ In.	374.00
Pickle, W.M. & P., Apple Green, Applied Mouth, 3-Piece Mold, 1845-60, 10 ¾ In.	178.00
Pickle, W.M. & P., Blue Aqua, Applied Mouth, Iron Pontil, 1840-60, 6 In.	127.00
Pickle, Wm. Underwood & Co., Aqua, Rolled Lip, Pontil, 1845-60, 11 ¼ In.	316.00
Pickle, Wm. Underwood & Co., Blue Aqua, Applied Mouth, Open Pontil, 1840-60, 8 ¾ In.	633.00
Pickle, Wm. Underwood & Co., Blue Aqua, Rolled Lip, Iron Pontil, 1845-60, 11 ⅜ In.	748.00
Poison, 3-Sided, Ribbed Corners, Amber, Parke Davis, 2 ¾ In.	15.00
Poison, Bowman's Drug Store, Cobalt Blue, 6-Sided, Tooled Lip, c.1890, 5 In.	364.00
Poison, Cobalt Blue, 3 Panels, Horizontal Ribs, 2 ¾ In.	15.00
Poison, Cobalt Blue, 6-Sided, Ribs, 7 In.	12.00
Poison, Cobalt Blue, Coffin, Embossed Skull & Crossbones, DP, c.1910, 3 In. ....*illus*	748.00
Poison, Cobalt Blue, Quilted, 5 In.	25.00
Poison, Coffin, Tooled Lip, 3 ½ In.	90.00
Poison, Embalming Fluid, National Casket Co., Aqua, Qt.	50.00
Poison, Embossed, Not To Be Taken, Cobalt Blue, 6-Sided, Ribs, 7 In.	40.00
Poison, Embossed, Not To Be Taken, Embossed, Ribs, 7 ¾ In.	40.00
Poison, F. & E. Bailey & Co., Cobalt Blue, Hexagonal, Square Collar, 6 ¼ In.	316.00
Poison, F.A. Thompson & Co., Detroit, Coffin, Amber, Embossed, 3 ¼ In.	799.00
Poison, Figural, Skull, Cobalt Blue, Crossbones, Tooled Mouth, c.1900, 4 In. .... 863.00 to 1495.00
Poison, Figural, Skull, Embossed Poison, Cobalt Blue, Cylindrical Neck, Tooled Lip, 4 ¼ In. ..	2016.00
Poison, H.K. Mulford Co., Chemists, Skull & Crossbones, Amber, c.1890, 3 ¼ In.	633.00
Poison, Lattice & Diamond, Cobalt Blue, Tooled Mouth, c.1900, 9 ⅛ In. ....*illus*	316.00
Poison, Lobilia Extract, Skull & Crossbones, Amber, White & Red Label, 4 ½ In.	25.00
Poison, Mercury Oxycyanide, Max Wocher & Son, Coffin, Tooled Mouth, 1880-1900, 5 In.	1120.00
Poison, Norwich, Coffin, Cobalt Blue, Diamond Hobnails, Tooled Lip, c.1890, 7 ½ In.	1400.00
Poison, Owl Drug Co., 1-Wing Owl On Mortar & Pestle, Cobalt Blue, Tooled Lip, 9 ½ In.	952.00

Bottle, Sarsaparilla, Dr. Townsend's,
Olive Green, Applied Mouth,
c.1850, 9 ⅝ In.
$403.00

Bottle, Sarsaparilla,
Dr. Wilcox's Compound Extract,
Blue Green, c.1850, 9 ¼ In.
$4888.00

Bottle, Seal, ICC, Black Glass,
Olive Green, Holland, c.1790,
10 ¼ x 3 ¾ In.
$690.00

TIP
*A dating tip for bottle
collectors: The words
"Federal Law forbids
sale or re-use of this
bottle" were used on
liquor bottles from
1933 to 1964.*

Bottle, Snuff, Agate, Blue Lace, Lavender, Carved, Birds, Pink Quartz Stopper, 3 x 2 ⅝ In. $529.00

Bottle, Snuff, De Voe's, Eagle, Red Amber, Zinc Screw Band, Cohansey Glass Mfg., c.1910 $242.00

Bottle, Snuff, Flask Shape, Blue & White, Carved Coral Top, 3 ½ In. $253.00

Bottle, Snuff, Glass, Reverse Painted, Horses, Landscape, Malachite Stopper, 2 ⅝ In. $1104.00

Poison, Owl Drug Co., Owl On Mortar & Pestle, Cobalt Blue, 3-Sided, Square Collar, 7 ¾ In. .	345.00
Poison, Owl Drug Co., Owl On Mortar & Pestle, Dark Cobalt Blue, 3 ¼ In.	84.00
Poison, Owl Drug Co., Owl On Mortar & Pestle, Dark Cobalt Blue, 9 In.	756.00
Poison, Rochester Germicide Embalming Fluid, Square, Hangs Upside Down, c.1920, 8 ½ In.	100.00
Poison, S. & D., Golden Amber, Skull & Crossbones, Tooled Mouth, 1890-1910, 4 ⅝ In.	374.00
Sarsaparilla, A.D. & C. Co.'s Best, Aqua, Tooled Mouth, c.1880, 9 ½ In.	104.00
Sarsaparilla, Bristol's Genuine, New York, Blue Aqua, 10 In.	89.00
Sarsaparilla, Cantrell's Compound, Aqua, Applied Mouth, Open Pontil, c.1840, 6 In.	1035.00
Sarsaparilla, Catlins For The Blood, St. Louis, Amber, Tooled Mouth, 1880-95, 7 ⅞ In.	184.00
Sarsaparilla, Colburn's Root, Bark & Herb, Aqua, Tooled Mouth, 1880-95, 9 In.	178.00
Sarsaparilla, Crescent Drug Co., Blue Aqua, Tooled Mouth, 9 In.	242.00
Sarsaparilla, Dalton's Sarsaparilla & Nerve Tonic, Belfast, Maine, Aqua, Contents, Label, 9 In.	44.00
Sarsaparilla, Dana's, Claremont, N.H., Aqua, Tooled Mouth, 1880-95, 7 ⅞ In.	345.00
Sarsaparilla, Dr. Bailey's, Apple Green, Square, Applied Lip, c.1865, 9 In.	379.00
Sarsaparilla, Dr. Clarke's, Olive Green, Tooled Mouth, 1880-95, 8 ½ In.	138.00
Sarsaparilla, Dr. Guysott's Compound Extract Of Yellow Dock, Blue Aqua, Oval, 10 ¼ In.	219.00
Sarsaparilla, Dr. Guysott's Compound Extract Of Yellow Dock, Blue Aqua, Pontil, 9 ⅜ In.	575.00
Sarsaparilla, Dr. Guysott's Yellow Dock, Aqua, Applied Mouth, c.1850, 10 ¼ In. ....*illus*	518.00
Sarsaparilla, Dr. James, Clear, Tooled Mouth, 1889-95, 9 ¼ In.	104.00
Sarsaparilla, Dr. Jarman's, Blue Aqua, Tooled Mouth, 1880-95, 9 ½ In.	178.00
Sarsaparilla, Dr. Townsend's, Albany, N.Y., Emerald Blue Green, 9 ½ In.	299.00
Sarsaparilla, Dr. Townsend's, Albany, N.Y., Green, Square, Iron Pontil, 1840-55, 9 ½ In.	728.00
Sarsaparilla, Dr. Townsend's, Albany, N.Y., Light To Dark Amber, Sloping Collar	840.00
Sarsaparilla, Dr. Townsend's, Albany, N.Y., Shaded Green, Sloping Collar	336.00
Sarsaparilla, Dr. Townsend's, Albany, Yellow Amber, Square, Applied Mouth, Pontil, 1846-60, 9 ¼ In.	3375.00
Sarsaparilla, Dr. Townsend's, Emerald Green, Applied Mouth, Iron Pontil, c.1850, 9 ⅝ In.	575.00
Sarsaparilla, Dr. Townsend's, Olive Green, Applied Mouth, c.1850, 9 ⅝ In. ....*illus*	403.00
Sarsaparilla, Dr. Townsend's, Square, Beveled Corners, Amber, Smooth Base, c.1855, 9 ¾ In.	1904.00
Sarsaparilla, Dr. Townsend's, Square, Beveled Corners, Green, Sloping Mouth, Pontil, c.1850, 9 In.	728.00
Sarsaparilla, Dr. Wilcox's Compound Extract, Blue Green, c.1850, 9 ¼ In. ....*illus*	4888.00
Sarsaparilla, Foley's, Amber, Rectangular, 9 ½ In.	59.00 to 68.00
Sarsaparilla, Georges, Comstock & BR, N.Y., Aqua, Applied Mouth, c.1865, 9 ½ In.	178.00
Sarsaparilla, Gleason's Sarsaparilla & Lemon Mineral Water, Blue, Pontil, 8-Sided, Sloping Collar	1008.00
Sarsaparilla, Graefenberg Co., Blue Aqua, Applied Mouth, Open Pontil, 1840-60, 7 In.	219.00
Sarsaparilla, Gray's, Montrose, Pa., Blue Aqua, Tooled Mouth, 1880-95, 8 ⅝ In.	178.00
Sarsaparilla, Hall's, Aqua, 9 ¼ In.	85.00
Sarsaparilla, Hall's, San Francisco, Aqua	100.00
Sarsaparilla, Hall's, San Francisco, Cornflower Blue	50.00
Sarsaparilla, Hart's, Aqua, Tooled Mouth, 1880-95, 9 In.	374.00
Sarsaparilla, Honduras, Wing & Joel, Aqua, Tooled Mouth, 1880-95, 9 ⅝ In.	178.00
Sarsaparilla, Hurd's, Aqua, Applied Mouth, Open Pontil, 1840-95, 9 ⅜ In.	1150.00
Sarsaparilla, Indian, J.J. Mack & Co., Blue Aqua, Tooled Mouth, 1880-95, 9 ¼ In.	316.00
Sarsaparilla, J. Calegaris Compound Extract, Blue Aqua, Panels, Tooled Mouth, 9 In.	127.00
Sarsaparilla, John Bull Extract, Aqua, Rectangular, Iron Pontil, 1845-60, 8 ¾ In.	476.00
Sarsaparilla, John Bull Extract, Blue, Applied Mouth, Iron Pontil, c.1840, 9 ⅜ In.	345.00
Sarsaparilla, Kennedy's Sarsaparilla & Celery Compound, Aqua, Tooled Mouth, 1880-95, 9 ⅝ In.	230.00
Sarsaparilla, Old Dr. J. Townsend's, N.Y, Applied Collar, Iron Pontil, 1845-60, 9 ½ In.	179.00
Sarsaparilla, Rush's Sarsaparilla & Iron, Aqua, 8 In.	29.00
Sarsaparilla, Sands' Genuine, Blue Aqua, Applied Double Collar, Iron Pontil, c.1850, 10 In.	489.00
Sarsaparilla, Skoda's Discovery Concentrated Extract, Belfast, Maine, Amber, Box, 1892-93, 9 In.	358.00
Sarsaparilla, Warner's Log Cabin, 3 Embossed Panels, Yellow Amber, Blob Top, 9 In.	970.00
Scent, Oval, 12 Ribs, Applied Round Foot, Pontil, Screw Cap, c.1860, 2 ¼ In.	633.00
Seal, Black Glass, Lion, Ship's Mast, Olive Green, Cylinfrical, Kick-Up, c.1800, 10 ⅛ In.	190.00
Seal, Boar Coronet, Black Glass, Green, Cylindrical, String Lip, c.1800, 11 ⅝ In.	308.00
Seal, D. Clerkson, 1738, Mallet, Olive Yellow, String Lip, 9 ¾ x 6 ¼ In.	4025.00
Seal, G. Forester, Wine, Black Glass, Olive Green, Applied Mouth, 14 ⅜ In.	1456.00
Seal, ICC, Black Glass, Olive Green, Holland, c.1790, 10 ¼ x 3 ¾ In. ....*illus*	690.00
Seal, Sidney Breese, 1765, Cylindrical, Yellow, Olive Sheared, String Lip, Pontil, Magnum, 11 In.	18800.00
Seltzer, Azule, Seltzer Springs, Bear, Walking, Blob Top, Aqua, c.1885	200.00
Seltzer, Joplin, Mo., Coca-Cola Bottling Co.	336.00
Seltzer, Truckee Soda Works, Clear, Painted Letters, Stopper	672.00
Seltzer, Wieland Bottling Works, Reno, Nev.	224.00
Snuff, Agate, Blue Lace, Lavender, Carved, Birds, Pink Quartz Stopper, 3 x 2 ⅝ In. ....*illus*	529.00
Snuff, Agate, Marquette, Flattened Oval, Lion & Ring Handles, Chinese, 19th Century	418.00
Snuff, Carnelian, Metal Cap, Turquoise & Emerald Beads, 3 ½ In.	288.00
Snuff, De Voe's, Eagle, Red Amber, Zinc Screw Band, Cohansey Glass Mfg., c.1910 ....*illus*	242.00

Snuff, Dragon, Orange, Cylindrical, Porcelain, Jade Stopper, 1800s, 3 ⅜ x 1 In. 820.00

Snuff, Flask Shape, Blue & White, Carved Coral Top, 3 ½ In. ....*illus* 253.00

Snuff, Glass, Reverse Painted, Horses, Landscape, Malachite Stopper, 2 ⅝ In. ....*illus* 1104.00

Snuff, Glass, Yellow Amber, Rectangular, Sheared Lip, Open Pontil, c.1795, 5 ¾ In. 403.00

Snuff, Horn, Etched Forest Scene, Chinese Characters, 3 In. 58.00

Snuff, Ivory, Figural, Scholar Holding Book, Staff, Gold, Stone Set, Late 19th Century, 3 ⅜ In. 2726.00

Snuff, Ivory, Figurine, Boy, Smiling, Gourd On Head Stopper, Chinese, 1800s, 3 ½ In. 316.00

Snuff, Ivory, King & Queen, Carved, Painted, 3 ⅛ In., Pair ....*illus* 190.00

Snuff, Jasper, Red & Brown, Stepped Panel Sides, Jade Stopper, 2 ¾ In. 173.00

Snuff, Peking Glass, Characters, Faceted Stopper, 5 ½ In. 173.00

Snuff, Peking Glass, Elephant Shape, Mustard Yellow, Teak Stand, Early 1900s, 4 ¼ x 2 ½ In. 390.00

Snuff, Porcelain, Enamel, Multicolored, Gold Trim, Chinese, 3 ¼ In. 353.00

Snuff, Red Coral, Fish Shape, Carved, Ivory Cap, Spoon, Cork Stopper, 4 In. 708.00

Snuff, Whale's Tooth, Applied Metal Cover, Cap, 4 In. 388.00

Soda, A. Hain & Son, Lebanon, Pa., Emerald Green, Squat, Double Collar 79.00

Soda, A.W. Cudworth & Co., San Francisco, Aqua, Slug Plate, 1856-61 .... 168.00

Soda, A.W. Schrader, Scranton, Pa., Aqua, Blob Top, Stopper, 7 In. 39.00

Soda, B.A. Gottleib, Richmond, Va., Blue Aqua, Squat, Blob Top 129.00

Soda, Bay City Soda Water Co. S.F., Sapphire Blue, Blob, Squat 499.00

Soda, Bay City Soda Water Co. S.F., Star, Blue, Blob Top, 7 ¼ In. 146.00

Soda, Bay City Soda Water Co., Star, Embossed, Medium Blue, 1871-80 .... 146.00

Soda, Benicia, B.J. McGee, Green, Blob Top, 1869-75 .... 672.00

Soda, Blue Lick Water Co., Ky., Amber, Rounded Shoulder, Sloping Collar 364.00

Soda, C & K Eagle Works, Sac City, Sapphire Blue, Blob Top, 7 ½ In. 190.00

Soda, C.A. Reiners & Co., San Francisco, Moon & Stars, Aqua, 1873-75 .... 336.00

Soda, Cherry Smash Syrup, Reverse Label, Metal Cap, 12 In. 35.00

Soda, Christian Heller Jr. Bottler, Bridgeton, N.J., Citron, Blob Top, 9 In. 48.00

Soda, City Ice & Bottling Wks, Georgetown, Texas, Green, Shouldered, Hutchinson 476.00

Soda, Clark Bros., Cyclists, Winged Wheel, Aqua, c.1895, 8 In. 61.00

Soda, Columbia Soda Works, Seated Liberty, Blue Aqua, 1879-81 .... 258.00

Soda, Cottle Post & Co., Teal, Eagle, Spread Wings, 1877-87 .... 308.00

Soda, Crystal Soda Water Co., Patented Nov. 12 1872, Aqua, Flared Skirt, Blob Top 420.00

Soda, Crystal Soda Water Co., Patented Nov. 12 1872, Blue, Flared Skirt, Blob Top 190.00

Soda, Dr. Bates Trademark National Tonic Beer Centennial 1876, Red Amber, 8 In. 499.00

Soda, D.S. Co., San Francisco, Blue, Slug Plate, Blob Top 896.00

Soda, D.S. Co., San Francisco, Electric Blue, Embossed, 1861-64 .... 420.00

Soda, E. Duffy & Son, Blue Green, Squat, Slug Plate, Double Collar, 7 In. 59.00

Soda, E. Higgins, Oroville, Teal, Blob Top 213.00

Soda, Eagle Works, Philada, Squat, Emerald Green, Iron Pontil, c.1855, 7 ¼ In. 316.00

Soda, Eastern Cider Co., Amber, Blob Top 420.00

Soda, E.L. Billing's, Sac City, Geyser Soda, Lime Green, Blob Top 448.00

Soda, El Dorado, Green, Blob Top, 7 ¼ In. 364.00

Soda, Embossed Cross, Green, 1850s 784.00

Soda, Emerson's Ginger Mint Julep, Backbar, Cap, 1910-15 .... 495.00

Soda, Empire Soda Works, D & M, San Francisco, Sapphire Blue, Blob Top, 7 ¼ In. 560.00

Soda, Empire Soda Works, San Francisco, Light Green Aqua, Embossed, 1861-71 .... 392.00

Soda, Empire Soda Works, San Francisco, Teal Green, Blob Top, 7 ¼ In. 67.00

Soda, Empire Soda Works, Vallejo, Embossed Bird, Light Green, Blob Top, 7 ¼ In. 246.00

Soda, F.B.C., Teal, Squat, 7 In. 59.00

Soda, F.M., Modesto, Teal Green, Blob Top, c.1875 .... 504.00

Soda, G.G. Merced, Teal, Blob Top 420.00

Soda, Ghiradelli's Branch Oakland, Deep Blue, Blob Top, 1863-69 .... 560.00

Soda, Golden Gate, Blue, Slugged Name, Graphite Pontil, 1850s-60s 1120.00

Soda, Golden Gate, Teal Green, Drippy, Slug Plate, Blob Top, Pontil, 7 ½ In. 202.00

Soda, G.P. Morrill, Green, Blob Top, 7 ½ In. 336.00

Soda, Hoffman & Joseph, Albany, Ogn., Lion, Light Teal, Blob Top 101.00

Soda, Hollister Soda Works, A. Mans, Deep Teal, Blob Top, 7 ¼ In. 235.00

Soda, Hughes, Pittston, Pa., Teal Blue Green, Squat, Double Collar 179.00

Soda, H.W. Stoll, Los Angeles Soda & Mineral Water Factory, Aqua, Blob Top 258.00

Soda, J. & A. Dearborn, New York, Deep Blue, Embossed 190.00

Soda, J. Boardman, N.Y., Sapphire Blue 157.00

Soda, J. Schweppe & Co. Aerated Waters, Aqua Green, Torpedo, Tooled Top 179.00

Soda, J.A. Heilman Lebanon, Pa., Aqua, Blob Top, Lightning Stopper, Squat, 6 In. 48.00

Soda, J.T. Brown, Chemist, Blue Green, Torpedo, Blob Top, Metal Stand, c.1855, 8 ¾ In. 489.00

Soda, J.T. Brown, Chemist, Boston, Teal, Torpedo, Blob Top, c.1855, 9 ⅛ In. 460.00

Soda, J.T. Nusbaum & Brothers, N. Weissport, California, Green, Pontil 213.00

Bottle, Snuff, Ivory, King & Queen, Carved, Painted, 3 ⅛ In., Pair
$190.00

Bottle, Soda, S. Smith, Auburn, N.Y., Cobalt Blue, 10-Pin, c.1860, 8 ¼ In.
$546.00

Bottle, Soda, Southwick & Tupper, Cobalt Blue, 10-Sided, c.1860, 7 ⅜ In.
$633.00

Bottle, Spirits, Cobalt Blue, Enameled Flowers, Pewter Neckband, Germany, c.1800, 6 ½ In.
$978.00

Syrup, Lemon Life, Best What Gives, Label Under Glass, John Graf Co., c.1925, 11 ¾ In.
$219.00

Bottle, Target Ball, Bogardus, Olive Green, Rough Sheared Mouth, c.1877, 2 ¾ In.
$489.00

Bottle, Target Ball, Charlottenburg, Glasshutten, Dr. A. Frank, Olive Yellow, Germany, c.1910, 2 ⅝ In.
$431.00

Bottle, Target Ball, Diamond, Yellow Green, Czechoslovakia, 1880-1915, 2 ⅝ In.
$374.00

Soda, Keach Balt., Emerald Green, Torpedo, Applied Tapered Collar, 8 ⅞ In.	633.00
Soda, Keach Balt., Yellow Topaz, Torpedo, Applied Collar, c.1860, 9 In.	1035.00
Soda, L. Keoning, Tamaqua, Pa., Aqua Blob Top, Squat, Kick-Up, 7 In.	79.00
Soda, Lancaster XXX Glass Works, Green, Graphite Pontil	190.00
Soda, Los Angeles Soda Works, Trade Star Mark, Star On Base, Hutchinson	60.00
Soda, Luke Beard, Blue Green, Ten Pin, Pontil, c.1855, 7 In.	374.00
Soda, Moriarity & Carroll, Registered, Waterbury, Conn., Amber, Hutchinson	336.00
Soda, Owen Casey, Eagle Soda Works, Sapphire Blue, Blob Top, 7 In.	213.00
Soda, Pacific Congress Water, San Francisco, Leaping Deer, Green, Sloping Collar	728.00
Soda, Robinson Wilson & Legallee, 192 Sudbury St., Boston, Deep Green, 6 ¾ In.	168.00
Soda, Rushton & Aspinwall, Olive Amber, Ten Pin, Applied Mouth, c.1815-25 7 In.	1380.00
Soda, S. Smith, Auburn, N.Y., Cobalt Blue, Ten Pin, c.1860, 8 ¼ In. ....*illus*	546.00
Soda, San Luis Obispo Soda Water Works, Embossed, Blue Aqua, Crown Top, 1874-1882	336.00
Soda, San Rafael Soda Works, Green Aqua, 1880s	2688.00
Soda, Sloper & Frost, Cobalt Blue, Iron Pontil, Blob Top, 7 ⅝ In.	123.00
Soda, Smile, Aqua, Embossed, c.1920, Gal., 19 x 5 ½ In.	187.00
Soda, Southwick & Tupper, Cobalt Blue, 10-Sided, c.1860, 7 ⅜ In. ....*illus*	633.00
Soda, Tahoe Soda Springs, Aqua Green, Blob Top, 7 ¼ In.	616.00
Soda, Thos. Maher, Blue Green Squat, 6 In.	79.00
Soda, T.W. Gillett, New Haven, Blue, 8-Sided, Iron Pontil, 1845-55, 7 ½ In.	644.00
Soda, Victoria Extra Dry Ginger Ale, Green, Embossed On Both Sides, 6 ½ Oz.	80.00
Soda, Victoria Extra Dry Ginger Ale, Green Glass, Embossed, 6 ½ Oz.	50.00
Soda, Victoria Extra Dry Ginger Ale, Queen Wearing Crown, Green, Embossed, 6 ½ Oz.	50.00
Soda, Vin Fix, Buffalo Bill, Pawnee Bill, 20th Century, 12 In.	210.00
Soda, Waring Webster & Co., New York, Cobalt Blue, 8-Sided	784.00
Soda, W.H. Burt, San Francisco, Green, 1852	728.00
Soda, Wm. Russell, Baltimore, Blue Green, Blob Top, Iron Pontil, c.1860, 7 ⅛ In.	219.00
Soda, W.P. Knicker-Bocker Soda Water, N.Y., Cobalt Blue, 12-Sided, Iron Pontil, 1848	395.00
Soda, W.S. Kinch & Co., Cobalt Blue, Blob Top.c.1875, 8 ⅛ In.	403.00
Spirits, Cobalt Blue, Enameled Flowers, Pewter Neckband, Germany, c.1800, 6 ½ In. .....*illus*	978.00
Syrup, Lemon Life, Best What Gives, Label Under Glass, John Graf Co., c.1925, 11 ¾ In. ...*illus*	219.00
Syrup, Tango-La, Fountain, Label Under Glass, Red, White, Black, 11 x 3 In.	253.00
Target Ball, Bogardus, Olive Green, Rough Sheared Mouth, c.1877, 2 ¾ In. ....*illus*	489.00
Target Ball, Charlottenburg, Glasshutten, Dr. A. Frank, Olive Yellow, Germany, c.1910, 2 ⅝ In. ......*illus*	431.00
Target Ball, Charlottenburg, Glasshutten, Yellow, Diamond, Embossed, Sheared Mouth, c.1885, 2 In. ..	196.00
Target Ball, Diamond, Yellow Green, Czechoslovakia, 1880-1915, 2 ⅝ In. ....*illus*	374.00
Target Ball, N.B. Glass Works, Perth, Sapphire Blue, Sheared Mouth, 1880-1900, 2 ¾ In.	207.00
Target Ball, Van Cutsem A St. Quentin, Diamond, Cobalt Blue, Banded, 2 ½ In.	148.00
Tonic, Clemen's Indian, Geo. W. House, Embossed Indian, Green, Label	896.00
Tonic, Mull's Grape, Rock Island, Ill., Amber, Tooled Lip, Pt.	123.00
Tonic, Rohrer's Expectoral Wild Cherry, Lancaster, Pa., Orange Amber, Iron Pontil	539.00
Whiskey, 26 Ribs, Amber, Applied Double Collar, Pontil, c.1855-75, 9 ¾ In.	184.00
Whiskey, AAA Old Valley, Embossed Cross, Letters, Amber, Flask, Pt.	896.00
Whiskey, Ambrosial, Amber, Applied Mouth, Handle, Seal, Chestnut, Pontil, 1860-70, 9 In.	403.00
Whiskey, Arlington M.A. Lindberg Prop., Amber, Pumpkinseed, Bakersfield, Cal., ½ Pt.	3136.00
Whiskey, Backbar, C. & K. Bourbon, Casey & Kavanaugh, Sacramento, Cal., Amber,	1232.00
Whiskey, Backbar, Castle, F. Chevalier & Co., Ferns, Decanter, Squat,	179.00
Whiskey, Backbar, Crown Of Baltimore, Yellow Crown, White Lettering, Enamel, Pt.	195.00
Whiskey, Backbar, Manhattan Club Pure Rye, Clover, Shot Glass Stopper,	157.00
Whiskey, Backbar, Old Continental, White Enamel, Cannon, Tooled Mouth, c.1890, 6 ⅜ In. ..	518.00
Whiskey, Backbar, Old Jefferson County, Enamel Writing, Fluted Stopper, 1900s	308.00
Whiskey, Backbar, Scotch, Cobalt Blue, Fluted Panels, Silver Overlay, Tooled Mouth, 1885, 11 In.	230.00
Whiskey, Bourbon, Horizontal Ribs	10640.00
Whiskey, Brandy, Flowers, Etched, Enamel Label, 11 ¼ In.	120.00
Whiskey, Brooklyn Glass Works, Yellow Amber, 3-Piece Mold, Applied Double Collar, 11 ½ In.	374.00
Whiskey, Brown Forman, Brown, Ribs, Enamel, Stopper, 10 ½ In.	125.00
Whiskey, California, 1866, 2 Barrels, Yellow Amber, Applied Mouth, 1870-80, 12 ¼ In.	748.00
Whiskey, Cartan, McCarthy & Co., San Francisco, Monogram, Amber, Fifth	420.00
Whiskey, Casper's, Made By Honest North Carolina People, Cobalt Blue, c.1885, 12 In.	863.00
Whiskey, Casper's, Made By Honest North Carolina People, Cobalt Blue, c.1900, 12 In. ..*illus*	460.00
Whiskey, Chestnut Grove, C.W., Amber, Flask, Applied Mouth, Handle, c.1870, 9 In.	242.00
Whiskey, Chestnut Grove, Red Amber, Applied Mouth, Handle, Pontil, 1855-70, 8 ⅞ In.	207.00
Whiskey, Choice Old, Cabinet, Ky. Bourbon, Crown, Amber, Applied Sloping Collar, Fifth	1792.00
Whiskey, C.O. Blakes Rye & Bour Whisky, Clear, 2 Barrels, Cylinder, 12 In.	29.00
Whiskey, D. Sachs & Sons, Orange Amber, Squat, Embossed, Qt.	69.00

Whiskey, E.G. Booz's Old Cabin, Amber, Cabin, Applied Top	....	3136.00
Whiskey, E.G. Booz's Old Cabin, Golden Amber, Sloping Collar, 7 ½ In.	....	1150.00
Whiskey, E.G. Booz's Old Cabin, Orange Amber, Applied Mouth, c.1865, 7 ⅞ In.	*illus*	2875.00
Whiskey, E.G. Booz's Old Cabin, Yellow Green, Cabin	....	39.00
Whiskey, F. Chevalier & Co., San Francisco, Whiskey Merchants, Light Yellow Amber, Neck Ring, Qt.		392.00
Whiskey, Figural, Grape Cluster, Amber, Applied Mouth, Iron Pontil, 1855-60, 9 ¾ In.	....	1380.00
Whiskey, Fleckenstein & Mayer, Portland, Oregon, Amber, Pt.		1064.00
Whiskey, Foust's Old Rye, Factory Buildings, Amber, 1890-1900, 11 In.	....	79.00
Whiskey, G.O. Blake's, Bourbon Co., Ky., Adams Taylor & Co., 2 Barrels, Amber, Sixth		952.00
Whiskey, G.O. Blake's Bourbon Co., Yellow Amber, Barrel, Tooled Mouth, 1885-1900, 10 ⅝ In.		375.00
Whiskey, Griffith Hyatt & Co., Copper Amber, Applied Mouth, Handle, Pontil, c.1860, 7 ⅜ In.		805.00
Whiskey, Hildebrandt, Posner & Co., S.F., Monogram, Clear, Pumpkinseed, ½ Pt.	....	202.00
Whiskey, Hopatkong, J.C. Hess & Co., Phila., Blue, 12-Sided Base, Ring Mouth		2128.00
Whiskey, Jesse Moore & Co., Louisville, Ky., Old Bourbon & Rye, Antlers, Olive Amber, Fifth	....	532.00
Whiskey, Jesse Moore Old Bourbon, Amber, Flask, Double Ring Mouth, Pt.	....	3808.00
Whiskey, Jesse Moore-Hunt Co., San Francisco., Antlers, Deep Amber, Fifth	....	1064.00
Whiskey, J.F. Cutter, Extra Old Bourbon, Star & Shield, Applied Top, 1870s		952.00
Whiskey, J.H. Cutter, Extra Old Bourbon, Star In Shield, Olive Amber, Fifth		2240.00
Whiskey, J.H. Cutter, Old Bourbon, A.P. Hotaling, Amber, Fifth		840.00
Whiskey, J.H. Cutter, Old Bourbon, E. Martin & Co., Amber, Flask, Rolled Rim, Pt.	....	5376.00
Whiskey, J.H. Cutter, Old Bourbon, E. Martin & Co., Crown In Middle, Amber, Tooled Top	......	784.00
Whiskey, J.H. Cutter, Old Bourbon, E. Martin & Co., Crown On Shoulder, Amber, Applied Top .		1008.00
Whiskey, J.W. Peters, Dog, Yellow, Green, Case, 8 In.	....	48.00
Whiskey, Keswick Rye Whiskey, W.O. Ferguson, Cleveland, Oh., Label, 7 x 4 ¾ In.	*illus*	25.00
Whiskey, Keystone Malt Whiskey, Orange, Amber, Oval, Applied Top, 1860-70, 10 In.		48.00
Whiskey, Label Under Glass, Drink Moonshine, Makes You Happy, W.T. Co., Amber, c.1910, 11 In.	*illus*	575.00
Whiskey, Mammoth Cave, Pinched, Enamel Label, 6 ½ In.	....	265.00
Whiskey, McHenry, 1812, Orange Amber, Square, 10 In.		39.00
Whiskey, Merry Christmas, Happy New Year, Bird, Branch, Label Under Glass, Flask, 5 x 4 In.		605.00
Whiskey, Miller's Extra, E. Martin & Co., Old Bourbon, Shield, Amber, Fifth		8960.00
Whiskey, Miller's Extra, E. Martin & Co., Old Bourbon, Yellow Olive Amber, Flask, Pt.	....	2016.00
Whiskey, Minnehaha Martindale & Johnston, Indian Woman, Pottery, Jug, c.1885, 7 In.	......	633.00
Whiskey, Mirror, James Lertora, Santa Maria, Cal., Amber, Tooled Top, Screw Threads, Fifth ..		392.00
Whiskey, Mist Of The Morning, S.M Barnett & Co., Barrel, Amber, Rings		308.00
Whiskey, Mist Of The Morning, S.M. Barnett & Co., Barrel, Applied Sloping Collar		392.00
Whiskey, Nabob, Amber, High Kick-Up, Neck Ring, Tooled Top		235.00
Whiskey, Old Bourbon Castle, Applied Top, Amber, Embossed		420.00
Whiskey, Old Castle, Chevalier's, Amber, Tooled Top, Fifth		213.00
Whiskey, Old Fitzgerald, Bighorn, Decanter, 12 ½ In.		14.00
Whiskey, Old Fitzgerald Prime Wildlife, Kentucky Bourbon, 1960, 12 In.		18.00
Whiskey, Patent, Salmon Puce, Cylindrical, 3-Piece Mold, Applied Double Collar, c.1855, 11 ¼ In. ..		345.00
Whiskey, Perrine's, Ginger, Figural, Apple, Cabin, Amber, Roped Corners, Applied Mouth, c.1875, 10 In.		431.00
Whiskey, Phoenix Old Bourbon, Alfs & Brune, Phoenix, Amber, Tooled Top, Fifth		364.00
Whiskey, Phoenix Old Bourbon, Embossed, Medium Amber, Tooled Top		101.00
Whiskey, Pink Amethyst, Rings, Applied Top Hat Mouth, 1860-70, 9 ⅝ In.	....	575.00
Whiskey, Pure Malt Whiskey, Root Beer Amber, Applied Mouth, Handle, c.1860, 8 ¾ In.	....	1035.00
Whiskey, Pure Rye, Pennsylvania Club, Vines, Silver Overlay, 11 In.		110.00
Whiskey, R.B. Cutter, Louisville, Ky., Chocolate Amber, Applied Mouth, Handle, 1855-65, 8 ⅝ In.		546.00
Whiskey, R.C. Ridgway & Co., Phila., Lady's Leg, Puce To Pink, Square Collar, Iron Pontil, 10 ¾ In.		3163.00
Whiskey, Roehling & Schultz, Semi-Cabin, Tooled Top		308.00
Whiskey, Smokine, Cabin, Amber, Tooled Top, 7 In.	....	224.00
Whiskey, Spruance Stanley & Co., Horseshoe, Red Amber, Applied Top, Late 1880s	....	258.00
Whiskey, Star, New York, W.B. Crowell, Seal, Ribs, Spout, Handle, Pontil		123.00
Whiskey, Star, New York, W.B. Crowell, Yellow Amber, Cone, Handle, Applied Spout, Pontil	......	269.00
Whiskey, Star Wine Co., Los Angeles, Megaphone, Amber, 13 In.		476.00
Whiskey, Theodore Netter, Barrel, Cobalt Blue, Embossed, 5 ⅞ In.		448.00
Whiskey, Turner Brothers, Barrel, Olive, Yellow Amber, Applied Mouth, 1865-75, 10 ⅛ In.	.....	1035.00
Whiskey, Udolpho Wolfe's Schiedam Aromatic Schnapps, Backward S, Yellow Olive, Pontil	....	190.00
Whiskey, Udolpho Wolfe's Schiedam Aromatic Schnapps, Tobacco Amber, 1855-65, 8 In.	......	79.00
Whiskey, Udolpho Wolfe's Schiedam Aromatic Schnapps, Yellow, Olive Amber, 8 In.	....	79.00
Whiskey, Very Old Corn, From Casper, Winston, N.C., Stopper, Handle, Flask, c.1900, 7 ¼ In. .		316.00
Whiskey, Vidvard & Sheehan, Olive Yellow, Applied Mouth, Spout, Handle, c.1865, 9 ¾ In.		6900.00
Whiskey, Wharton's Chestnut Grove, Amber, Tooled Mouth, Spout, Handle, c.1865, 10 In.		920.00
Whiskey, Whitney Glass Works, Emerald Green, Cylindrical, Applied Double Collar, c.1855, 10 ⅞ In.		316.00
Whiskey, Wm. H. Spears & Co., Old Pioneer, Bear, A. Fenkhausen Sole Agents, Applied Collar, Clear		476.00

Bottle, Whiskey, Casper's, Made By Honest North Carolina People, Cobalt Blue, c.1900, 12 In. $460.00

Bottle, Whiskey, E.G. Booz's Old Cabin, Orange Amber, Applied Mouth, c.1865, 7 ⅞ In. $2875.00

Bottle, Whiskey, Keswick Rye Whiskey, W.O. Ferguson, Cleveland, Oh., Label, 7 x 4 ¾ In. $25.00

Bottle, Whiskey, Label Under Glass, Drink Moonshine, Makes You Happy, W.T. Co., Amber, c.1910, 11 In. $575.00

BOTTLE

Bottle, Wine, Onion, Olive Green, Applied String Lip, Open Pontil, c.1750, 7 x 5 ½ In. $345.00

Bottle Opener, Clown, Wall Mount, Cast Iron, Wilton Products, 4 x 4 In. $59.00

Bottle Opener, Cowboy, Cactus, Cast Iron, Hollow Blow Mold, John Wright, 4 ⅝ In. $88.00

Bottle Opener, Mule, Brown, Open Mouth, Cast Iron, 3 ½ In. $125.00

Whiskey, Wm. H. Spears & Co., Old Pioneer, Bear, Amber, Applied Sloping Collar, Fifth	2016.00
Whiskey, Wolters Bros. & Co., 115 & 117 Front St., S.F., Amber, Shaded, Fifth	392.00
Whiskey, Young's Y.P.M., Diagonal Banner, Yellow Amber, Cylindrical	56.00
Wine, A. Werner & Co., Extra Dry, Champagne, Teal, Applied Band, Tooled Lip, 1883, Miniature	112.00
Wine, Emerald Green, Tooled Lip, Tester, 8 ¼ x 1 ¼ In.	12.00
Wine, J.V.H., Forest Lawn, Dark Green, Freeblown, Applied Top, Pontil	246.00
Wine, Mallet, Dark Green, Applied Mouth, Kick-Up, Pontil, 1730s, 8 In.	190.00
Wine, Onion, Olive Green, Applied String Lip, Open Pontil, c.1750, 7 x 5 ½ In. ....*illus*	345.00
Zanesville, 24 Swirled Ribs, Amber, Early 1800s, 7 In.	881.00

BOTTLE CAPS for milk bottles are the printed cardboard caps used since the 1920s. Crown caps, used after 1892 on soda bottles, are also popular collectibles. Unusual mottoes, graphics, and caps from bottlers that are out of business bring the highest prices.

Anchorlok, Cork Lined, For Home Bottling, Box Of 12	6.00
Anselmo Dairy Farm, Porterville, California, Pasturized Chocolate Drink	10.00
H.F. Morrill Milk & Cream Dairy, c.1950, 1 ⅝ In.	0.15
Hoopingarner Dairy, Here's Your Milk, Service Phone 37 3-F, Cardboard	1.50
Jersey Parlor Dairy, Whitman Monument, 1 ⅝ In.	0.30
Mahelona Hospital, Kapaa, Kauai, Hawaii, Pasturized Milk	15.00
Mapleview Farm Dairy, Pasteurized Whipping Cream, Moscow, Pa.	10.00
Markley College Dairy, Buttermilk, Turlock, Calif.	10.00
Pure Fresh Milk, Cow, Pull Tab, c.1930, 1 ⅝ In.	0.20
Rushmore Milk, Pasteurized Chocolate Drink, Mt. Rushmore, Custer, S.D., No. 3B	50.00
Simpson's Dairy, Fresno, Cal., Grade A Raw Milk, Cardboard	10.00

BOTTLE OPENERS are needed to open many bottles. As soon as the commercial bottle was invented, the opener to be used with the new types of closures became a necessity. Many types of bottle openers can be found, most dating from the twentieth century. Collectors prize advertising and comic openers.

Beanie Bert, Cast Iron, Marked, Winter Weekend, L & L Favors	945.00
Bear Head, Wall Mount, Cast Iron, John Wright Company, 3 ¾ x 3 ⅛ In.	275.00 to 293.00
Beer Drinker, Cast Iron, 5 ⅜ In.	264.00
Beer Drinker, Cast Iron, Wall Mount, Sprenger Brewing Co., Pa., 6 In.	177.00
Black Man, Smiling, Red, Pink, White, Black, Wilton, 4 ⅛ x 3 ½ In.	340.00
Black Man, Wall Mount, Cast Iron, Wilton, 4 ⅛ x 3 ½ In.	351.00
Cast Iron, Mexican Cactus, Souvenir Of New Mexico, Wilton Products	542.00
Clown, Wall Mount, Cast Iron, Wilton Products, 4 x 4 In. ....*illus*	59.00
Cockatoo, Cast Iron, John Wright Company, 3 ¼ x 2 ⅞ In.	146.00
Cockatoo, Red, Yellow, Blue, Green, Cast Iron, John Wright Co., 3 ¼ x 2 ⅞ In.	140.00
Cowboy, Cactus, Cast Iron, Hollow Blow Mold, John Wright, 4 ⅝ In. ....*illus*	88.00
Cowboy, Cast Iron, Painted, Hot Springs, Ark., 5 In.	250.00
Crawfish, Cast Iron, 3 ½ In.	45.00
Dinky Dan, Class Of 52, Blue, White, Red, Green, Cast Iron, Signed, Phil. Gadzik, 4 x 2 In.	60.00
Elephant, Cast Iron, John Wright, 5 In.	160.00
Elephant Head, Gray, Metal, Scott Prod., Newark, N.J., c.1950, 5 ½ x 4 ½ In.	52.00
Fish Shape, Teak, HAJ, Denmark, 3 ½ x 1 ¾ In.	45.00
Golden Pheasant, Cast Iron, John Wright Company, 2 ¼ x 3 ⅞ In.	117.00
Handy Hans, Holding Paddle, Pi Kappa Alpha, Red Shirt, Cast Iron, L & L Favors, 4 x 2 In.	120.00
Hanging Drunk, Cast Iron, 5 In.	50.00
Hires Root Beer, Metal, Lithograph, c.1905-15, 3 ¼ In.	76.00
Horse Tail, Cast Iron, Wilton Products, Marked, WO 36, Box, 5 ⅛ In.	188.00
Horse's Rear, Brown, White, Black, Metal, Scott Products, N.J., c.1950, 3 x 5 x 2 In.	55.00
Mexican Cactus, Souvenir Of Albuquerque, New Mexico, Cast Iron, Wilton Products	540.00
Mule, Brown, Open Mouth, Cast Iron, 3 ½ In. ....*illus*	125.00
Mule, Figural, Cast Iron, Paint, 3 ½ In.	125.00
Palm Tree, Cast Iron, Wilton Products, 5 In.	58.00 to 62.00
Palm Tree, Drunk, Iron, Multicolored, 4 In. ....*illus*	70.00
Palm Tree, Green, 2 Red Flowers, Cast Iron, Wilton, 4 x 2 ⅝ In.	60.00
Parrots On Perch, Cast Iron, 4 ¾ In.	50.00
Pheasant, Gold, Red, Blue, Green, Cast Iron, John Wright Co., 2 ¼ x 3 ⅞ In.	120.00
Pheasant Head, Green, Yellow, Red, Cast Metal, Rubal, N.Y., c.1950, 4 x 4 ½ In.	55.00
Seahorse, Cast Iron, 4 In.	95.00
Skunk, Cast Iron, 2 ¼ In.	45.00
Souvenir, Cowboy, Drunk, Cactus, Painted, Cast Iron, Phoenix, John Wright Co., 4 x 3 In.	145.00

Stainless Steel, Silver Plate, Cohr Co., Denmark 65.00

BOXES of all kinds are collected. They were made of thin strips of inlaid wood, metal, tortoiseshell, embroidery, or other material. Additional boxes may be listed in other sections, such as Advertising, Battersea, Ivory, Shaker, Tinware, and various Porcelain categories. Tea Caddies are listed in their own category.

Accessory, Inlaid, Art Deco, Dancing Figure, Hinged Lid, Silver Handles, 10 x 20 x 13 In.	179.00
Anglo-Indian, Brass Mounted, Mother-Of-Pearl Inlaid Mahogany, Cube Shape, 3 x 3 In.	210.00
Apple Shape, Turned Fruitwood, Brass Hinge & Escutcheon, 19th Century, 4 ¾ In.	1495.00
Art Nouveau, Silver Plate, Gilt Wash, Leaves, Fabric Lined Interior, c.1900, 3 x 8 x 11 In.	176.00
Ballot, Wood, Stone Balls, Early 20th Century...	60.00
Band, Lid, Oval, Finger Lap Joints, Opposing Lid Latches, Signed, 4 x 6 x 3 ½ In.	358.00
Band, Lid, Wallpaper, Castle Garden, Blue Ground, Oblong, c.1825, 11 x 16 In.	705.00
Band, Pasteboard & Wallpaper, Oval, Leaf Stripe, Green, Ivory, Brown, c.1875, 10 ½ x 14 In. .	235.00
Band, Softwood, Green Painted, Single Finger, Tacked Joints, 2 ¾ x 5 ½ In.	385.00
Band, Soldier, Holding Walking Staff, Shaker Style, Oval, Finger Joints, Brass Tacks, 4 x 9 ⅞ In.	165.00
Band, Wallpaper, Building, Swags, Roses, Blue Ground, Oblong, 12 x 18 In.	588.00
Band, Wallpaper, Figures, Palm Trees, Blue Ground, 19th Century, 13 x 17 In.	700.00
Band, Wallpaper, Flowers, Oval, 19th Century, 13 ¼ x 22 ¼ In.	700.00
Band, Wallpaper, Mahogany, Turkey, Stonington, Conn., Mid 1800s, 7 ¾ x 4 ½ In.	382.00
Band, Wallpaper, N.Y.C. Firemen, Yellow Ground, H. Branes & Co., c.1835, 12 x 22 In.	411.00
Basswood, Faux Rosewood Graining, Stencil Eagle, Flowers, Lock, c.1830, 7 x 17 ½ In.	936.00
Basswood, Painted, Sponge Design, Lock, New England, c.1825, 7 x 17 ½ In. ...... 1053.00 to 1080.00	
Basswood, Painted, Sponged Surface, Lock, New England, c.1835, 5 ¾ x 10 In.	351.00
Bentwood, Ash, Round, Lid, Heart, Evan, Flowers, Bird, Painted, 1800s, 9 In.	118.00
Bentwood, Pine, Tulip, Dot, Laced, Pinned, Salmon Ground, Painted, 5 x 16 In.	374.00
Bentwood, Wallpaper, Late 1800s, 9 ½ x 14 ¾ In.	60.00
Bible, Oak, Wrought Iron Hinges, Carving, England, c.1800, 12 x 27 ½ x 15 ½ In.	176.00
Bible, Poplar, Red Painted Designs, Carved Books Lid, c.1890, 11 x 16 In.	235.00
Bible, Queen Anne, Walnut, Inlaid Initials AC, Pennsylvania, c.1750, 9 x 20 In.	1170.00
Bird Shape, Carved, Folk Art, Hinged Lid, Painted Black, 4 x 13 In.	329.00
Blanket, Pine, Stenciled Fruit & Flowers, Black Ground, Till, c.1850, 5 x 9 x 5 In.	470.00
Blanket, Wood, Handles, Worn, Bucks County, Penn., c.1800, 19 x 31 In.	52.00
Book, Decorated, Painted, Simulated Leather, Wood Grain, Flowers, Late 1800s, 12 x 3 In.	270.00
Brass, Dragon, Jade Pendant, Bat, Ruyi, Chinese, 19th Century, 5 x 3 ¾ In.	179.00
Brass, Gothic Style, High Relief, Religious Scenes, Hinged Lid, Marked, Germany, 3 ½ x 8 ½ In.	118.00
Brass, Hinged Lid, Chase, 1930s, 2 ½ x 5 ¾ x 4 ¾ In.	5490.00
Brass, Hinged Lid, Heyno Focken, Stamped, c.1930s, 3 x 11 x 3 ½ In.	732.00
Brass, Stacked, Copper Lid, Stamped, Otar, 1920s, 4 ¼ x 5 In.	3172.00
Brass, Woman, Wide Brimmed Straw Hat, Victorian, Gilt, Painted, Round, Signed, 3 ½ In.	950.00
Bride's, Bentwood, Flowers, Multicolored, Salmon Ground, 19th Century, 7 ¾ x 10 ¾ x 17 In.	235.00
Bride's, Bentwood, Flowers, Painted, Red Ground, Overlapping Seams, c.1850, 8 x 11 x 17 In. .illus	441.00
Bride's, Bentwood, Laced Joints, Multicolored, Flower, Leaves, Oval, 6 x 17 x 10 In.	440.00
Bride's, Bentwood, Tulips, Flowers, Multicolored, Oval, Laced Joints, 6 ¾ x 16 ¼ x 10 ¼ In. ...	605.00
Bride's, Bentwood, Tulips, Multicolored, Blue Ground, Oval, Laced Seams, 1800s, 7 x 17 In. ..	558.00
Bronze, Boulle, Portraits, Ivory, France, 19th Century, 3 x 8 ¾ x 5 In.	575.00
Bronze, Hinged Lid, Medallion, Raised Panel, Embossed Scrolls, Footed, Early 1900s, 3 ¾ x 11 In.	130.00
Bronze, Ivory, Lid, Stone Inlaid Border, Figures Playing Instruments Panels, Blue, Gold, 11 In.	5975.00
Bronzed Metal, Patina, Wood Liner, Oscar Bach Style, Arts & Crafts, 5 ½ x 2 In.	120.00
Camphorwood, Whales, Painted, Leather Bound, Nailhead Trim, Early 1800s, 16 ½ x 36 In.	1400.00
Candle, Cherry, Slide Lid, Dovetailed, Molded Edge, Hanging, 16 x 6 ¼ x 3 In.	212.00
Candle, Chippendale, Walnut, Slant Lid, Tea Nail Construction, Shaped Top, c.1800, 20 In. ...	236.00
Candle, Grain Paint, Hanging, 19th Century, 15 In.	193.00
Candle, Oak, Stylized Stars, Painted, Scrubbed, 4 ¾ x 11 x 5 In.	316.00
Candle, Pine, Double, Painted Red, Square Nails, Hanging, Mid 1800s, 19 x 10 ½ In. ......illus	1175.00
Candle, Pine, Drawer, Lollipop Top, 19th Century	450.00
Candle, Red Paint, 2 Carved Finger Indentations, c.1820, 4 ½ x 10 In.	996.00
Candle, Tiger Maple, Slide Lid, Dovetailed, 1800s, 16 In.	325.00
Candy, Lid, Flowers, Leaves, Porcelain, Painted, Gilt Borders, c.1890, 3 ½ x 4 In.	240.00
Candy, Napoleon III, Porcelain, Painted, Bouquet, Purple Frame, Gilt, c.1900, 2 x 5 x 4 In.	245.00
Carved, Ivory, Japan, Dragons, Oval, Lid, Finial, 19th Century, 3 ½ x 4 x 3 ½ In.	920.00
Carved, Leaf & Berry, Stylized Designs, Lock, Key, Cincinnati Art, 10 ½ x 7 ½ In. ....illus	600.00
Casket, Glass, Green Cut To Clear, Diamond Pattern, Gilt Oak Leaf, Acorn Band, 6 x 7 In. ..illus	1116.00
Cassone Chest, Walnut, Carved, Paw Feet, Italy, 13 x 21 In.	1528.00
Cheese, Salmon Paint, 19th Century, 17 In. Diam..	385.00

Bottle Opener, Palm Tree, Drunk, Iron, Multicolored, 4 In. $70.00

Box, Bride's, Bentwood, Flowers, Painted, Red Ground, Overlapping Seams, c.1850, 8 x 11 x 17 In. $441.00

Box, Candle, Pine, Double, Painted Red, Square Nails, Hanging, Mid 1800s, 19 x 10 ½ In. $1175.00

Box, Carved, Leaf & Berry, Stylized Designs, Lock, Key, Cincinnati Art, 10 ½ x 7 ½ In. $600.00

Box, Casket, Glass, Green Cut To Clear, Diamond Pattern, Gilt Oak Leaf, Acorn Band, 6 x 7 In. $1116.00

Box, Cutlery, Arts & Crafts, Chip Carved, Sunbursts, Diamonds, Early 1900s, 6 ½ x 12 In. $173.00

Box, Dresser, Slant Front, Pine, Painted, Scalloped Backsplash, Tulips, Pa., 1800s, 7 ¼ x 11 ½ In. $2574.00

Box, Hat, Wallpaper, Federal, Grand Canal, Oblong, c.1810, 18 x 14 In. $489.00

Chest, Laque Burgautte, Geometric, Hinged Door, Fitted Interior, Handle, Lacquer, Japan, 2 ½ x 3 In. ...	236.00
Cigar, Hammered Copper, Cedar Lining, Gustav Stickley, Signed, 4 ½ x 7 ½ x 6 In.	1200.00
Cigar, Painted Toothpicks, Stars, U.S. Of A, Carved Bird, 1945, 2 ½ x 9 ¼ x 6 ½ In.	264.00
Cigarette, Cast Metal, Cork Lined Compartments, Teak Inlaid Strips, Curved Edges, 9 x 4 In. ...	65.00
Coffer, Oak, Wrought Iron Hardware, Double Eagle Escutcheon, 1700s, 3 ½ x 7 In.	470.00
Coffer, Wood, Carved, Domed, 2 Drawers, Gold Maki, Abalone, Bronze, Lacquer, 1600s, 16 x 25 In.	2990.00
Copper, Hinged Lid, Chase, 1930s, 2 ½ x 5 ¾ x 3 ¼ In.	3538.00
Copper, Stylized Designs, Enamel, Footed, Patina, Arts Craft Shop, 6 x 2 ¼ In.	390.00
Cricket, Lid, Rooster, Flowers, Trees, Painted, Carved, Wood, 3 In., Pair.	1800.00
Crystal, Enamel, Austria, c.1880, 2 In.	88.00
Curly Maple, Dovetailed, Iron Lock, Bail Handles, 1800s, 15 ½ x 24 x 15 In.	480.00
Curly Maple, Poplar, Lift Out Tray, Lock, Inscribed, T.S. Probasco, Oct., 27, 1875, 5 x 12 In. ..	264.00
Cutlery, Arts & Crafts, Chip Carved, Sunbursts, Diamonds, Early 1900s, 6 ½ x 12 In. ......*illus*	173.00
Cutlery, Pine, 2 Sections, Cutout Handle, 19th Century, 14 x 9 In.	50.00
Cutlery, Pine, Painted, Sloping Sides, Divider, Pierced Grip, c.1825, 5 x 13 x 7 In.	977.00
Cutlery, Pine, Turned Handle, 2 Sections, 19th Century, 14 x 9 In.	53.00
Cutlery, Poplar, Dovetailed, Grain Paint, Center Handle, c.1825, 9 x 18 In.	147.00
Cutlery, Softwood, Slanted Sides, Scalloped Cutouts, 11 ¼ In.	45.00
Cutlery, Wood, Black Paint, Cutout Heart Handle, New York, 1800s, 6 x 15 In.	148.00
Cutlery, Wood, Leaf & Fruit Decoration, Red, Yellow, Green, Heart Cutout Handle, 1700s, 12 x 8 In.	7605.00
Decanter Set, Rosewood, Inlaid, Tray, Fold-Out Sides, Turned Feet, 4 Amber Bottles, 10 x 13 In.	633.00
Decoupage Lid, Family Comforting Old Man, Red, Green, Yellow, Black, Painted, 12 x 8 x 4 ½ In.	2900.00
Deed, Regency, Mahogany Inlay, Square, Hinged Lid, Lion's Head Pulls, Turned Legs, 21 In. ..	748.00
Deed, Slant Lid, Iron Strap Hardware, Arts & Crafts, 18 x 13 In.	180.00
Desk, Mahogany, Slant Lid, Fitted Interior Drawers, 1800s, 9 x 16 In.	1304.00
Desk, Maple, Pine, Slant Lid, Wrought Iron Hinges, Latch, Fitted Interior, 1700s, 11 x 20 In. .	2252.00
Desk, Shaker, Pine, Red Paint, Slant Lid, Arched Back, Fitted Interior, 16 x 28 In.	819.00
Desk, Traveling, Mahogany, Brass, 1800s, 9 x 16 ½ In.	201.00
Document, American Federal, Inlaid Mahogany, Scalloped Apron, 1800s, 10 x 18 In.	1245.00
Document, Cherry, Yellow Pine, Dovetailed Case, Lift Lid, Drawer, Pin Locks, 7 ½ x 10 In.	353.00
Document, Dome Lid, Giltwood, Carved Fans, Figures, Urns, Angel Masks, Italy, 1800s, 11 x 12 In.	4740.00
Document, Dome Lid, Wood, Red & Black Paint, 2 Interior Drawers, Dovetailed, 1800s, 13 In.	365.00
Document, Jacobean, Oak, Marquetry, Paneled, Chip Carved Corners, Ogee Base, 9 x 27 In. .	2133.00
Document, Lid, Stenciled Swag, Red Paint, Tassel, Wire Bail, 1800s, 4 x 4 ½ In.	1185.00
Document, Oak, Kneeling Angels, Renaissance Style, Carved, Wrought Iron, 1800s, 12 x 7 x 5 In.	270.00
Document, Pine, Applied Molding, Red, Black Paint, Brass Lid Handle, c.1830, 6 x 13 In.	264.00
Document, Pine, Nails, Wrought Iron Hardware, c.1800, 10 ¾ x 19 x 10 In.	176.00
Document, Pine, Red Paint, Oshawa, Ontario, c.1840, 8 x 10 ½ In.	797.00
Document, Tooled Leather, Bail Handle, Brass Corners, 9 x 19 x 13 In.	2116.00
Document, Walnut, Hinged, Bird's-Eye Maple Border, Key, 19th Century, 6 ½ x 12 ¾ x 9 In. ..	460.00
Document, Walnut, Molded Lid, Pierced Brass Escutcheon, Late 1700s, 11 x 8 In.	470.00
Document, Yellow, Black, Crosshatched Design, Turned Feet, Wood, 9 x 16 x 9 ½ In.	550.00
Dome Lid, Burl, Ivory & Brass Applique, 6 x 8 x 4 ½ In.	260.00
Dome Lid, Eagle, Lion, Repousse Brass Covered, Hinged, 21 x 28 In.	58.00
Dome Lid, Flower Basket, Birds, Leaves, Flowers, Continental, 19th Century, 12 x 25 ½ In.	300.00
Dome Lid, Multicolored Paint, 1800s, 10 x 16 ½ In.	296.00
Dome Lid, Pine, Dovetailed, Iron Hardware, c.1850, 10 ⅞ x 24 x 12 ½ In.	352.00
Dome Lid, Pine, Flowers, Basket, Wire Handle, Lock, Green, Yellow Borders, Paint, c.1830, 7 x 18 In.	504.00
Dome Lid, Pine, Flowers, Green Ground, 1800s, 4 x 6 In.	118.00
Dome Lid, Pine, Mahogany Grain Paint, c.1810, 12 x 27 In.	119.00
Dome Lid, Pine, Punched Tin, Heart Panel, Inscription, 1700s, 13 x 25 In.	59.00
Dome Lid, Pine, Wire Hinged Lid, Red Paint, Brass Bail, c.1800s, 4 x 12 In.	385.00
Dome Lid, Stylized Flowers, Red, White, Blue Ground, Compass Artist, 1820s, 7 ¾ x 13 In.	15600.00
Dome Lid, Stylized Flowers, Red, White, Blue Ground, Compass Artist, Early 1800s, 11 x 13 In.	50200.00
Dome Lid, Woodflowers, Birds, Cut Nail, Painted, France, 19th Century, 10 ¾ x 15 x 11 In. ...	259.00
Dresser, Crotch Mahogany, Inlay, Satinwood Band, Drawer, Shield Escutcheon, George III, 7 x 11 x 7 In.	240.00
Dresser, Flowers, Bun Shape, Porcelain, c.1900, 4 x 8 ¼ In.	201.00
Dresser, Girl, Seated, With Horn, Cymbals, Porcelain, Continental, 9 In.	82.00
Dresser, Glass, Boy With Net, Girl With Basket, Turquoise, 2 x 8 x 2 ⅝ In.	118.00
Dresser, Hardwood, Carved, Brass Mounted, Gentleman's, Drop Down Mirror, Chinese, 7 ¼ x 9 In. ..	276.00
Dresser, Pine, Paint, Pink Paper Lining, Carved, BH. 1794, 8 ½ x 4 In.	550.00
Dresser, Pine, Painted, Inscribed, Edward W. Norton, Limington, Maine, 4 ¾ x 11 ¾ In.	200.00
Dresser, Pine, Slant Lid, Tulips, Hearts, Painted, Scalloped Backsplash, 1800s, 7 x 11 In.	2600.00
Dresser, Rosewood Veneer, Lift Lid, Mother-Of-Pearl Inset, Drawer, Bottles, Containers, 12 x 9 In.	288.00
Dresser, Slant Front, Pine, Painted, Scalloped Backsplash, Tulips, Pa., 1800s, 7 ¼ x 11 ½ In. ...*illus*	2574.00
Dresser, Woman, Hand Painted, Porcelain Lid, Gilt Metal Sides, Oval, 5 ½ In.	805.00

Ebony, Oak, Craftwork Inlaid Parquetry, Hinged, Mirror Lid, Fitted Interior, c.1850, 6 x 9 In.	764.00
Enamel, Red Roses, Black Swirls, Lid, Steinschonau, Round, Clear Glass, 5 In.	180.00
Flowers, Black, Cartouche Shape, Bombe Sides, Blue, 14K, Gold, 1 x 3 In.	4140.00
Flowers, Yellow, Blue, Lilac, Orange, Enamel, c.1800, 3 x 2 In.	345.00
Glass, Cover, Scarabs, Leaves, Frosted, Saumont, France, Round, 20th Century, 3 ½ In.	39.00
Glove, Napoleon III, Ribbon, Flowers, Acanthus, Mythological Scene, Silver Plated, c.1870, 5 x 13 In.	890.00
Hat, Wallpaper, Federal, Grand Canal, Oblong, c.1810, 18 x 14 In. ......*illus*	489.00
Hat, Wallpaper, Rounded Corners, Pennsylvania, c.1835, 10 x 14 In.	585.00
Hat, Wallpaper, State House, Whig Newspaper Lining, Chambersburg, c.1835, 13 x 16 In. *illus*	2106.00
Heat, Tin, Officer's Military Hat, Brass Officers Plaque, Marlborough Devonport, c.1860, 9 x 19 In.	950.00
Hinged Lid, Sheffield Plate, Mahogany Lined, 9 x 8 x 6 In.	410.00
Hinged Lid, Woman, Bench, Garden, Landscape, Enamel, Oval, Interior Designs, 1 x 2 ½ In.	575.00
Hinged Lid, Wood, Silver Overlay, Green Enamel, Rectangular Plate, Ottaviani, 2 x 5 In.	150.00
Incense, Flower Heads, Gold, Gray Hiramaki-E, Gold Ground, Japan, 19th Century, 2 ½ In.	418.00
Inlaid Craftwork, c.1880, 5 x 12 In.	588.00
Ivory Inlay, Tortoiseshell, Victorian, Mid 19th Century, 3 x 4 ½ In.	1708.00
Jewelry, 14K Yellow Gold, Hinged, Woven Pattern, Neiman Marcus, 5 x 3 In.	3884.00
Jewelry, Brass, Stippled, Fleur-De-Lis, Scrolls, Newcomb College, c.1910, 3 x 6 In. .... illus	3120.00
Jewelry, Burl Walnut Veneer, Trunk Shape, Brass Mounts, Continental, 6 ¼ x 8 ¾ In.	184.00
Jewelry, Cherry, Sculpted, Laminated, Wendell Castle, 1978, 8 x 12 In.	5100.00
Jewelry, Court Scene Plaques, Stand, Copper, Brass, Malachite, Velvet Lined, c.1890, 39 x 24 In.	3851.00
Jewelry, Dome Lid, Flowers, Swags, Cornucopia, Tassels, Gilt, Brass Mounted, Lined, 6 x 8 x 11 In.	510.00
Jewelry, English Walnut, Geometric Inlay, England, 5 ¾ x 10 ⅞ x 7 ⅞ In.	81.00
Jewelry, Flowers, Hunt Scene, 3 Tiers, Marble Inset, Frieze, Pietre Dura, Italy, 10 In.	518.00
Jewelry, Hinged Lid, Wrought Iron, Lock, Mahogany, Inlay, Octagonal, Bone Inlay, 1800s, 8 ¾ In.	474.00
Jewelry, Love's Lesson, Honey Blond Wood, Pen Work, Polished, 7 In.	1200.00
Jewelry, Mahogany, Ormolu, Mirror, Fitted Drawers, Swing Doors, Ogee Bracket Feet, 56 x 26 In.	1003.00
Jewelry, Rootwood, Naturalistic Shape, 2 Sections, 2 Lids, 3 ½ x 21 In.	460.00
Jewelry, Rosewood, Hinged Lid, Interior, Drawer, Glass, Silver Bottles, Jars, Tools, Mirror, 13 x 7 In.	345.00
Jewelry, Rosewood, Veneer, 4 Drawers, Victorian, 14 x 14 ¾ x 9 ½ In.	329.00
Jewelry, Satinwood, Mirror, Nailhead, Ivory Satin, Biedermeier, c.1825, 7 x 3 In.	420.00
Jewelry, Silver, Hammered, Scrolling, Cabochons, Anderson, 4 x 8 ¼ x 4 ½ In. ....*illus*	3900.00
Jewelry, Wood, Half-Circle, Hinged Lid, 8 Sections, Monogram, Charles Rohlfs, 1900, 10 x 1 ½ In.	1800.00
Kindling, Lift Lid, Animals, People, Flowers, Leaf, Brass, Copper Over Wood, 20 ¾ x 26 x 16 In.	90.00
Knife, Federal, Figured Fruitwood, Barber Pole Inlay, Canted Lid, c.1800, 15 x 10 In. .....*illus*	1093.00
Knife, Hepplewhite, Mahogany Inlay, Shell Design, Serpentine Lid, c.1775, 14 x 8 In.	448.00
Knife, Mahogany, Hinged Lid, Dividers, Georgian, 1800s, 14 ½ x 8 ¾ x 10 ¼ In., Pair	1725.00
Knife, Mahogany, Inlaid Insert, Serpentine Case, Early 1800s, 15 ½ x 8 In.	610.00
Knife, Mahogany, Pine, Serpentine Front, Flame Grain, c.1810, 14 ½ x 9 In., Pair	1763.00
Knife, Mahogany, Slant Lid, Shaped Sides, England, c.1800, 14 x 9 x 10 In., Pair	2074.00
Knife, Mahogany, Urn Shape Finials, Stringing, Banding, George III Style, 28 In., Pair ..*illus*	2645.00
Knife, Oak, Black Stenciled Design, James Gibbs, Batavia, N.Y., 4 ¾ x 13 ¼ x 7 ⅜ In.	100.00
Knife, Pine, Cutout Handle, Yellow Paint, c.1859, 5 x 14 In.	235.00
Knife, Regency, Mahogany, Urn Shape, Fitted Interior, Gilt Pinecone Finial, 1900s, 24 ½ In. ..*illus*	269.00
Knife, Satinwood, Mahogany Inlay, Slant Front Lid, Fitted Interior, George III, 15 x 9 In., Pair	1175.00
Knife, Satinwood, Mahogany Inlay, Slant Lid, Fitted Interior, c.1850, 9 x 14 In.	1175.00
Knife, Shagreen, Paper & Velvet Fitted Interior, Brass, c.1760, 13 ½ x 8 ¼ In., Pair	1998.00
Knife, Thomas Sheraton, Mahogany, Slant Front, Rope Twist Marquetry, Georgian, 13 x 7 ¼ In.	2640.00
Lacquer, Barn Scene, Rectangular, Painted, Russia, 2 x 8 In.	117.00
Lacquer, Domestic Scene, Oval, Shell Lid, Painted, Russia, 2 x 6 x 4 In.	146.00
Lacquer, Flowering Branch, Butterfly, Red, Gold, Sharkskin Lined, Japan, 1 ¾ x 8 x 4 ¾ In.	60.00
Lacquer, Mother-Of-Pearl Inlay, Papier-Mache Over Wood, Korea, 4 x 10 x 10 In.	47.00
Lacquer, Red, Gilt, Applied Carved Ivory Dragons, Japan, 6 x 11 In.	212.00
Lacquer, Woman, Carrying Child On Back, Painted, Rectangular, Russia, 2 x 6 x 4 In.	234.00
Lap Desk, Inlaid Bands, Slanted Surface, Fitted Interior, Turnbridgeware, 1883, 6 x 12 x 9 In.	269.00
Lap Desk, Kingwood, Inlaid Slant Front, Cartouche, Hinged Lid, Compartments, 5 x 14 x 11 In.	239.00
Leather, Dome Lid, Embossed, Eagle Design On Lid, 18th Century, 8 ¼ x 12 ¾ In.	210.00
Letter Holder, Mahogany, Inlay, 4 Notched Slots, Early 1900s	225.00
Letter, Casket Shape, Hinged Lid, Inlaid, Divided Interior, Victorian, Silver Stringing, 6 x 8 ½ In.	546.00
Lid, Rooster, Art Deco, Enamel, Cloisonne Style, 1 ⅝ x 3 ⅞ x 3 ⅛ In.	480.00
Liqueur Case, Calamander Wood, Brass, Cut Glass Decanters, Tumblers, 1800s, 10 ¾ x 9 ½ In.	1830.00
Mahogany, Band Inlay Lid, Lift Out Round Tray, Handle, England, 1800s, 7 ½ x 8 In.	288.00
Mahogany, Hinged Lid, Compartments, Well, Leather, 19th Century, 5 x 12 x 8 In.	345.00
Mahogany, Hinged Lid, String Inlay, Corner Fluted Pilasters, George III, 25 x 14 ½ x 11 In.	390.00
Mahogany, Octagonal, Inlaid, Maitland Smith, 10 x 8 In.	59.00
Mahogany, Regency, Inlays, Lion Head Ring Handles, Paw Feet, Stand, c.1900, 32 x 17 In.	173.00

Box, Hat, Wallpaper, State House, Whig Newspaper Lining, Chambersburg, c.1835, 13 x 16 In.
$2106.00

Box, Jewelry, Brass, Stippled, Fleur-De-Lis, Scrolls, Newcomb College, c.1910, 3 x 6 In.
$3120.00

Box, Jewelry, Silver, Hammered, Scrolling, Cabochons, Anderson, 4 x 8 ¼ x 4 ½ In.
$3900.00

Box, Knife, Federal, Figured Fruitwood, Barber Pole Inlay, Canted Lid, c.1800, 15 x 10 In.
$1093.00

Box, Knife, Mahogany,
Urn Shape Finials, Stringing, Banding,
George III Style, 28 In., Pair
$2645.00

Box, Knife, Regency, Mahogany,
Urn Shape, Fitted Interior,
Gilt Pinecone Finial, 1900s, 24 ½ In.
$269.00

Box, Tea, Quillwork, Paneled, Inlay, Gilt,
Monogram, Late 1700s, 5 ¾ x 7 ¼ In.
$2415.00

Mahogany, Rosewood, Bird's-Eye Maple, Stars, Geometric, Ball Feet, New England, 7 ½ x 12 In.	1450.00
Malachite, Gilt Brass, Hinged Lid, Black Slate Interior, France, 3 x 11 ¾ In.	1320.00
Map, Basswood, Yellow & Orange Paint, c.1830, 5 ¼ x 30 ¼ In.	1750.00
Map, Hinged Lid, Painted, Port De Maho, Enamel, 19th Century, 1 ¼ x 2 ½ x 2 In.	86.00
Maple, Figured Cherry, Snipe Hinges, Hasp, T-Head Nails, c.1800, 10 ½ x 6 ¼ x 5 ¼ In.	2400.00
Maple, Square Nails, Applied Molding, Blue, White, Lock, Paint, c.1850, 6 x 13 In.	588.00
Marquetry, Victorian, Boulle, Cedar Lined Divided Interior, Mid 19th Century, 3 ½ x 10 ¾ In.	1220.00
Marriage, Pine, Slide Lid, Carved, Initials, JR & RB, 1820s, 9 In.	175.00
Milliner, Oval, Ebonized Lid, Wood Stand, Stencil, Richard Williams, England, c.1860, 24 x 19 In.	1350.00
Mixed Hardwood, Lovebirds, Veneer, Inlaid, Dovetailed Case, 12 ¾ x 7 In.	235.00
Molded Lid, Bootjack Ends, 6-Board, Blue Paint, New England, c.1810, 27 x 49 In.	504.00
Money Chest, Colonial, Iron Lock, Ecuador, 10 ½ x 15 In.	2100.00
Money, Monkey Head Form, Gray Matte, White, 2 ¼ In.	60.00
Nantucket, Sweetheart, Sailors, Heart Shape, Wood, Rattan, Hinged Lid, Lined, 6 x 10 In.	468.00
Necessaire, Regency, Inlaid Fans, Shells, Banded, Hinged Lid, Mirror, Fitted Interior, 7 x 9 In.	633.00
Necessaire, Rosewood, Grain Paint, Tray, Brushes, Inkwells, S. Mordan, 1851, 14 x 16 x 7 In.	1150.00
Necessaire, Walnut, Piano Shape, Brass Bosses, Ebonized Legs, Implements, Music, 6 x 11 In.	1150.00
Oak, Pine, Hinged Lid, 3 Drawers, England, c.1850, 8 x 18 In.	235.00
Pantry, Bentwood, Blue, Green Paint, Round, Overlapping Seams, Iron Tacks, 4 x 9 In.	383.00
Pantry, Bentwood, Blue Paint, Round, Lapped Seams, Iron Tacks, 19th Century, 4 ½ x 8 ½ In.	499.00
Pantry, Bentwood, Flowers, Red, Yellow, Oval, Iron Tacks, Black Ground, c.1850, 4 x 9 In.	911.00
Pantry, Bentwood, Green Paint, 1830, 6 In.	145.00
Pantry, Bentwood, Mustard Paint, Oval, Lapped Seams, Steel Tacks, 4 ½ x 10 ¾ In.	558.00
Pantry, Bentwood, Red Paint, Stamped, CA Andrews, c.1820, 12 ½ In.	185.00
Pantry, Green Paint, Lid, Lapped Seam, Oval, 1800s, 4 x 13 In.	652.00
Pantry, Mustard Paint, Round, 8 ¾ In.	110.00
Pantry, Old Blue Paint, Marked, W. Moor, 6 x 10 ½ In.	560.00
Pantry, Pine, Ash, Red Paint, Lapped Seam, Oval, 1800s, 8 x 14 In.	385.00
Pantry, Red Paint, Lid, Lapped Seam, Oval, 1800s, 4 x 8 In.	474.00
Pantry, Red Paint, Lid, Lapped Seam, Round, 1800s, 29 x 17 In.	533.00
Pantry, Wood, Mustard Paint, Lapped Seam, Round, 8 ¾ In.	106.00
Papier-Mache, Dome Lid, Mythical Figures, Dogs, Gilt, Round, c.1875, 7 x 9 ½ In.	345.00
Pen, Ribbon Bouquets, Rectangular, Fumibako, Japan, 19th Century, 10 ½ In.	568.00
Pencil, Felix The Cat, Painted, Stenciled, Slide Opening, 1920s, 8 ⅝ In.	148.00
Pill, Crab Shape, 14k Yellow Gold, Oval, Hinged Locking Lid, 2 In.	840.00
Pill, Enamel, Copper, Purple, Maiden, Blue Dress, Oval, France, 3 ¼ In.	460.00
Pill, Flower Basket, Scrolls, 8-Sided, Chatelaine, 14K Gold, Finger Ring, 1 ¼-In. Box	360.00
Pill, Gilt Metal, Napoleon Medallion, Oval, Signed, Kirk, 2 In.	288.00
Pine, Blue Paint, 6-Board, Wire Hinge Handle, c.1835, 4 x 11 In.	652.00
Pine, Dovetailed, Hinged Lift Lid, Green Paint, c.1830, 16 x 29 In.	237.00
Pine, Flowers, Dovetailed, Stamped, Sawtooth Border, Lock & Hasp, c.1875, 5 ½ x 12 x 7 In.	499.00
Pine, Hinged Lid, Circles, Red, Blue, Black, Yellow, Paint, c.1910, 15 x 11 In.	711.00
Pine, Lid, Blue Paint, c.1850, 8 x 18 In.	176.00
Pine, Lid, Merganser Drake, Salesman Sample, 1985, 6 ¼ x 10 x 6 In.	33.00
Pine, Slide Lid, Pinned Construction, Flowers, Multicolored, 19th Century, 5 x 7 x 13 In.	323.00
Pine, Slide Lid, Rococo Carving, Blue Gray Paint, Stark County, Ohio, Mid 1800s, 4 x 9 ¼ In.	1763.00
Pipe, Fruitwood, Top Cutout, Drawer, Wall Mount, c.1810, 19 In.	2530.00
Pipe, Pine, Carved Flower, Painted, Pegged & Cut Nail, Dovetailed Drawer, c.1800, 20 In.	201.00
Pipe, Pine, Pierced Whale's Tail Shaped Backboard, Brown Paint, c.1800, 21 x 6 In.	1304.00
Pipe, Softwood, Drawer, Nails, C.F. Hopf, 18 ½ In.	55.00
Pipe, Tiger Maple, Dovetailed Drawer, 18th Century, 18 ¼ In.	9480.00
Poplar, Fruit Basket, Lyre, Griffins, Painted, Gilt, c.1840, 11 ½ x 6 ¾ In.	1645.00
Poplar, Fruit, Leaves, Painted Red, Gilt, 19th Century, 4 ½ x 12 ½ In.	441.00
Poplar, Slide Lid, Nailed, Painted, Lock, Key, 1829, 3 ½ x 5 ½ In.	176.00
Poplar, Stags, Birds, Trees, Painted, Cartouche, Canted Corners, Cut Nail, 1800s, 5 x 11 x 7 In.	518.00
Poplar, Woman, Eagle, Banner, Smoked Border, Gilt Trim, Dovetailed, Footed, 19th Century, 4 x 11 In.	705.00
Porcelain, Painted, Divided, Wood Scrolled Base, Chinese, 2 x 8 x 4 In.	322.00
Powder, Pink Quartz, Gilt Metal, Gold Figure Base, c.1920, 6 ½ In.	351.00
Puzzle, Wood, Carved, Tulips, Vines, Letters, Numbers, Pennsylvania Dutch, HB, 1808	4956.00
Quillwork, Inlaid, Fitted Interior, 19th Century, 4 ⅛ x 10 ¾ In.	235.00
Regency, Ivory, Black Penwork, Chinoiserie, Octagonal, Paper Lined, 9 Compartments, 2 ½ x 11 In.	900.00
Ring, Porcelain, Man, Woman, Seated, Hand Painted, c.1900, 2 In.	47.00
Salt, Painted, Yellow, Green, Red, Hanging, Carved, Late 1800s, 15 x 11 ½ In.	705.00
Salt, Poplar, Hinged Lid, Stained, Scalloped Backsplash, Shoe Feet, Pa., 9 ¾ x 10 ½ In.	819.00
Seed, Bentwood, Blue Paint, Harvard Type Fingers, Copper Tacks, 19th Century, 1 ¼ x 2 In.	352.00
Sevres Style, Fan Shape, Mother With Children, Hinged Lids, Sprays, c.1900, 5 x 12 x 7 In.	8625.00
Shaving, Flowers, Engraved, Silver, Rosewood Veneer Lid, Hinged Mirror Inside, 4 x 7 ½ x 11 In.	80.00

Shaving, Wood, Hinged Lid, Mirror Inside, 4 ¼ x 8 x 11 ¼ In.	55.00
Shoe Shine, Lift Lid, Blue Paint, c.1890, 15 x 14 In.	356.00
Slide Lid, Tulips, Multicolored Paint, Northern Europe, 1800s, 8 x 9 In.	533.00
Softwood, Slide Lid, Foltz & Boyer, 1979, 5 ⅛ x 7 ⅝ x 6 ⅛ In.	44.00
Spinach Jade, Lid, Hardwood Stand, c.1900, 2 ½ x 5 ½ x 3 ¾ In.	546.00
Spirits, Mahogany, Brass Inlay, 1820s, 18 x 18 x 18 In.	184.00
Stamp, Bronze, Jarvie, George G. Elmslie, 4 x 2 x 2 In.	1440.00
Stationary, Flowers, Multicolored, Kashmiri, Lacquer, Dome Lid, Interior Compartments, 6 x 10 In.	240.00
Stationary, Mahogany, Satinwood, Inlaid, Geometric, England, 3 ⅜ x 12 ¼ x 8 In.	153.00
Stick, Walnut, Top Door, Paneled, Patina, England, 19 ½ x 34 In.	2850.00
Storage, Basswood, Painted, Smoke Sign, New England, c.1835, 12 ¾ x 29 ¾ In. ...	527.00
Storage, Dome Lid, Pine, Flowers, Painted, Scroll Border, Dovetailed, c.1800, 9 x 23 x 11 In. .	805.00
Storage, Elm, Hinged Lid, Dovetailed, Raised Painted Goldfish, Flowers, c.1900, 12 x 18 In. ..	115.00
Storage, Maple, Figured, Lift Lid, Side Handle, c.1800, 4 ¾ x 19 In.	495.00
Storage, Trunk, Plaid, Brass Bound, Leather Trim, Great Britain, c.1950, 24 x 18 In., Pair	700.00
Storage, Wood, Pineapple & Strawberry, Painted Green, Signed, Jean Dewey, 28 x 37 In.	595.00
Strong, Iron, Swing Handle, Brass, Black Paint, c.1825, 4 x 8 In.	415.00
Strong, Pine, Overhang Lid, Handmade Lock, Green, Blue Paint, 1800s, 14 x 29 In.	294.00
Sugar, Orange Over Yellow Graining, Dovetailed, Scandinavia, 19th Century, 8 x 12 ¾ In.	176.00
Tantalus, Gothic Revival, Coromandel, Brass Scrolls & Strapwork, Tiffany & Co., 14 In.	1778.00
Tantalus, Oak Frame, Center Handle, Shield Escutcheon, 3 Glass Bottles, Faceted Stoppers, 12 In.	207.00
Tantalus, Oak, Silver Plate Fittings, 2 Cut Glass Bottles, Falstaff, England, 6 In.	242.00
Tea, Burlwood, Barber Pole Inlays, Brass Knob, Trace Of Original Foil, England, 1800s, 5 x 6 In.	546.00
Tea, Chinoiserie, Papier-Mache, Black Gilt, Mother-Of-Pearl, Abalone Inlay, Figure, 5 x 9 In. .	670.00
Tea, Chinoiserie, Papier-Mache, Black Lacquer, Mother-Of-Pearl Inlay, 4 ¾ x 9 ½ In.	720.00
Tea, Mahogany, Boat Shape, Concave Top, Flower Inlay, c.1805, 6 x 7 In.	978.00
Tea, Quillwork, Paneled, Inlay, Gilt, Monogram, Late 1700s, 5 ¾ x 7 ¼ In. ....*illus*	2415.00
Till, Mahogany, O'Brien's Self-Closing Till, Liverpool, Marked, 19th Century, 7 ½ x 10 x 18 In.	160.00
Tin, Black, Circles, Diamonds On Lid, Oval, Marked, NBD, Scandinavia, 1860, 3 x 7 x 4 In.	456.00
Tin, Blue, Circles, Diamonds On Lid, Oval, Marked, M.J-D, Scandinavia, 1795, 6 x 17 x 10 In.	520.00
Tin, Light Blue, Gilt Borders, Brass Swing Handles, John Cane, London, c.1820, 9 x 20 In.	267.00
Tinder, Brass, Hinged Lid, Oval, Flint Striker, Flint, England, c.1720..........................	235.00
Tobacco, Brass, Cityscape Of Amsterdam, Engraved, c.1750	410.00
Tobacco, Brass, Combination Lock, England, 3 Dials, c.1810..............................	350.00
Tobacco, Brass, Cow, Hourglass, Instruments, Skeleton, Oval, Dutch, 18th Century, 4 ¾ In. ...	470.00
Tobacco, Brass, Engraved, Round, 19th Century	425.00
Tobacco, Brass, Slide Lid, Engraved, A. Smith, Esq., Dutch, 1700s, 3 ¼ In. ....*illus*	708.00
Tobacco, Honor, Brass, Ball Feet, Press Button To Drop Coin, c.1800, 7 x 9 ½ In. ....*illus*	1380.00
Tobacco, Horn, Silver Inlay, Engraved, c.1720	265.00
Tobacco, Rosewood, Silver Mounts, Applied Cutwork Vignette, Louis Philippe, 3 ¼ x 1 ¾ In. .	72.00
Tortoiseshell & Ivory, Wood, Flower, Scroll Borders, Iron Hinges, Anglo-Indian, 1800s, 4 x 11 In. ...	2070.00
Tortoiseshell, 19th Century, 5 ½ x 12 x 6 In.	3965.00
Tortoiseshell, Hinged, Rounded Edge, Victorian, 19th Century, 1 ½ x 9 ½ x 2 ¼ In.	489.00
Tortoiseshell, Mahogany, 9 Sections, Lift-Out Tray, 4 x 12 ¼ x 8 In.	1725.00
Traveling, Wood, Stamp Decorated Oilcloth, Leather Trim, Brass Tacks & Handle, c.1820, 7 x 15 In.	176.00
Trinket, Cornelian, Guilloche Enamel, Gilt Metal Top, Sapphire Cabochon, 5 x 4 ½ In.	2070.00
Trinket, Mahogany, Brown Graining, Yellow Ground, Brass Hinge, Fabric Interior, c.1810, 6 x 3 In.	1650.00
Trinket, Mahogany Veneer, Oval Plaque, Inlaid Mother-Of-Pearl, Hinged Lid, 4 ½ x 9 ¼ x 5 ½ In.	5036.00
Trinket, Romantic Couple, Blue Ground, Bombe Case, c.1900, 4 x 8 x 6 ½ In.	662.00
Trinket, Satinwood, Ebony, Flattened Feet, Ebony Purling, Hinged Lid, 1800s, 7 ¾ x 13 ⅝ In.	489.00
Trinket, Tulips, Initials, Christian Prenzer, Bucher, Berks County, c.1800, 3 x 10 In. ....*illus*	5616.00
Trinket, Turned From Single Piece Of Wood, Painted, c.1850, 2 ¾ x 1 ½ In.	650.00
Turtle Shape, Clock, Brass, Enameled Landscapes, Dragon Head, Claw Feet, 1800s, 8 x 4 In. .*illus*	5288.00
Utility, Poplar, Dovetailed, Cutout Handle, Divided, Arched Center, 4 ½ x 14 ½ In.	55.00
Vanity, Campaign Style, Mahogany, Brass Mounts, Glass Containers, Plateau, 6 x 12 In.	120.00
Wall, Fishtail Back, Painted, Chamfered Edge, c.1820, 13 ½ x 8 ¼ x 6 ½ In.	3200.00
Wall, Pine, Red Paint, 1800s, 8 x 11 In.	700.00
Wall, Softwood, Cutout Heart, Hinged Lid, Dovetailed, 2 Drawers, 11 x 15 ½ x 8 In.	2310.00
Wall, Softwood, Gray, Rectangular, Scalloped, Hanging Holes, Bird, Star, 11 ¼ x 24 x 8 In.	66.00
Wall, Walnut, Slant Lid, Dovetailed, Scrolled Hanger, Drawer, 11 ¼ x 12 x 8 ½ In.	632.00
Walnut, Lift Lid, Dovetailed Case, Bun Feet, Lock, Pennsylvania, c.1760, 12 ½ x 20 ½ In.	995.00
Wood, Carved, Chinese, 10 ¾ x 6 ¾ x 3 ½ In.	86.00
Wood, Dome Lid, Blue Paint, 4 ½ x 8 ½ In.	118.00
Wood, Free Edge Top, Carved, Robert Whitley, 5 x 10 ½ In.	510.00
Wood, Lid, Turned Legs, Stenciled, P. Bell, Red Paint, Iron Handles, c.1850, 17 x 15 In.	353.00
Wood, Lift Top, Carved Flowers, Trees, Fluted Edges, Multicolored, Spain, 1800s, 11 x 23 In. ...	115.00

Box, Tobacco, Brass, Slide Lid, Engraved, A. Smith, Esq., Dutch, 1700s, 3 ¼ In. $708.00

Box, Tobacco, Honor, Brass, Ball Feet, Press Button To Drop Coin, c.1800, 7 x 9 ½ In. $1380.00

Box, Trinket, Tulips, Initials, Christian Prenzer, Bucher, Berks County, c.1800, 3 x 10 In. $5616.00

Box, Turtle Shape, Clock, Brass, Enameled Landscapes, Dragon Head, Claw Feet, 1800s, 8 x 4 In. $5288.00

Bradley & Hubbard, Lamp, 3-Light, Bronze Baluster Shaft, Hexagonal Slag Shade, 20 x 24 In. $1507.00

Bradley & Hubbard, Lamp, 3-Light, Flowers, Bulbous, 3-Footed, Circular Platform, 14 x 16 In. $1610.00

Bradley & Hubbard, Lamp, Owl Base, Slag Glass, Metal Filigree, 11 In. $995.00

Bradley & Hubbard, Letter Rack, Brass, Filigree, Scrolling, Marked, c.1900, 13 x 16 In. $205.00

Wood, Parquetry Inlay, Star, Interior Tray, Hinged Lid, 4 Bun Feet, 4 ¾ x 12 x 9 ¾ In.	418.00
Wood, Round, Inscribed Lid, Crossed Anchors, Hope, c.1800, 2 x 4 In.	106.00
Work, Regency, Mahogany, Brass Inlay, Ebony, Hinged Lid, Divided Tray, Drawer, c.1815, 12 x 8 In.	1350.00
Work, Regency, Tortoiseshell, Silver, Abalone Bird, Moire Interior.c.1820, 13 x 9 In.	2726.00
Work, Tunbridge, Interior Compartments, Castle Design, 10 ½ In.	2250.00
Work, Wood, Book Form, Straw, Inlay, Escutcheon On Pages, 3 x 15 x 11 In.	12.00
Writing, Anglo-Indian, Rosewood, Brass Bound, Handles, Hinged Lid, 7 ½ x 16 In.	201.00
Writing, Brass, Inlaid, Calamander, Leather, Instrument Wells, 19th Century, 8 x 20 x 11 In.	1410.00
Writing, Mahogany, Scrolling Brass Inlay, Medallion, Hinged, c.1875, 7 x 19 x 10 In.	288.00

BOY SCOUT collectibles include any material related to scouting, including patches, manuals, and uniforms. The Boy Scout movement in the United States started in 1910. The first Jamboree was held in 1937. Girl Scout items are listed under their own heading.

Backpack, Canvas, Printed, B.S.A. Logo, Loops & Eyelets, Leather Straps	55.00
Bank, Boy Scout, Holding Pole, Cast Iron, Brown Paint, A.C. Williams, c.1915, 6 In.	153.00
Belt Buckle, Brass, Emblem, 1 ½ x 2 ¼ In.	40.00
Book, The Boy Scouts With Red Cross, 1915	8.00
Booklet, Rope Knowledge For Scouts, 1933	20.00
Card Holder, Membership, Paper, Boys Life Magazine Ad, c.1941	20.00
Coin, Boy Scout Jamboree, Aluminum, 1969, 1 ½ In.	15.00
Compass, Original Box, England	25.00
Cufflinks, Emblem, Gold Tone, ¾ x ½ In.	15.00
Handbook, 50th Anniversary, Norman Rockwell Cover Art, 6th Ed., c.1959, 478 Pages	45.00
Humidor, Be Prepared, Ceramic, 5 ½ In.	225.00
Hymn Folder, Camp Service, Religious Songs, c.1960, 5 ½ x 8 ½ In., 8 Pages	5.00
Manual, Scouting For Rural Boy's, For Leaders, 1938	35.00
Neckerchief Slide, Brass, Blue Enamel, 1 ½ x 1 ⅛ In.	12.00
Neckerchief Slide, Silver Plate, 1950s	5.95
Neckerchief, Gold & Navy, 1950s	25.00
Paperweight, Glass, Blue, Yellow, Gentile Glass Co., 1980s, 3 x 3 ½ In.	95.00
Patch, Boy Scout Honor Unit, 1957, 10 In.	75.00
Plaque, Honor Award, Shield Shape, Oath, 33 Award Symbols, Carved, Painted, 36 x 34 In.	3081.00
Pocket Watch, Shock Proof, Emblem, Ingersoll, 1930s, 1 ¾ In.	173.00
Postcard, McDonald's Salutes Scouting, 1967 World Jamboree Logo	8.00
Ribbons, National Recognition, 1956	52.00
Ring, Eagle Scout, 10K Gold, Notification Letter, Rope Knots, Insignia, c.1942, Size 9	228.00
Sheath, Western Knife Official Leather, 1950s	75.00
Songbook, National Council, Soft Cover, c.1956, 118 Pages	16.00
Token, Colorado Springs Boy Scout Jamboree, 1960	10.00
Wristwatch, Directional Sign Hands, Be Prepared, Ingersoll, Tag, Box, c.1934, 1 ¼ In.	844.00

BRADLEY & HUBBARD is a name found on many metal objects. Walter Hubbard and his brother-in-law, Nathaniel Lyman Bradley, started making cast iron clocks, tables, frames, andirons, lamps, chandeliers, sconces, and sewing birds in 1854 in Meriden, Connecticut. The company became Bradley & Hubbard Manufacturing Company in 1875. Charles Parker Company bought the firm in 1940. Their lamps are especially prized by collectors.

Andirons, Dolphin, Brass, Iron Fire Dogs, Early 1900s, 13 ½ x 21 In.	2450.00
Andirons, Urn Shape, Square Base, Ball Footed, 14 ½ x 5 ¾ In.	495.00
Blotter, Pen Tray, Brass, Marked, 1920s, 6 x 3 & 10 ½ x 3 In.	49.00
Candlestick, Palm Leaf Design, Bronze, Patina, 22 ½ x 8 In.	725.00
Figurine, 3 Kittens On Tray, Cold Painted, 5 x 7 In.	118.00
File Holder, Scrolls, Metal, Footed, 12 x 10 ½ x 4 ½ In.	225.00
Inkwell, Double, Stamp Drawer, Pen Holder, Brass, 10 ½ x 5 ¾ In.	350.00
Inkwell, Jumping Deer, Letter Rack, Gilt, Iron, c.1900, 9 In.	180.00
Lamp, 3-Light, Bronze Baluster Shaft, Hexagonal Slag Shade, 20 x 24 In. .....*illus*	1507.00
Lamp, 3-Light, Flowers, Bulbous, 3-Footed, Circular Platform, 14 x 16 In. .....*illus*	1610.00
Lamp, 8-Sided Base, Leaves & Berries, Spelter, Caramel Slag Glass, 21 ½ In.	2100.00
Lamp, Banquet, Fruit, Lattice Ground, Puffy Shade, 27 In.	315.00
Lamp, Brown & White Glass Shade With Gold Leaf, Bronze, Electric, 1920s, 23 In.	460.00
Lamp, Cased Opaque To Iridized Amber Mushroom Shade, c.1920, 16 In.	822.00
Lamp, Cast Metal, Tapered Column, Glass Painted Shade, 22 x 14 In.	350.00
Lamp, Flowers, Incised Metal Base, Leaded Glass Shade, Signed, 15 x 20 In.	1920.00
Lamp, Frogskin Patina On Metal, Hexagonal Shade, 18 In.	485.00
Lamp, Hanging, 8-Panels, Stylized Flower, Octagonal, Tapered, 20 x 20 x 40 In.	1680.00
Lamp, Hanging, Leaded Glass Shade, Metal Overlay, Chain, Signed, 18 x 16 In.	2640.00

Lamp, Kerosene, Bronzed Metal, Marble Base, Ball Shade, Electrified, 8 x 32 In.	86.00
Lamp, Kerosene, Urn, Green, Red, Marked, 16 ¾ In.	118.00
Lamp, Nude Women, Oval Crest, Garlands, Slag Glass, Metal, c.1910, 14 x 10 In.	1250.00
Lamp, Oil, 3-Headed Elephant, Gold Wreaths, Bow Ties, Signed, 14 x 27 In.	2400.00
Lamp, Oil, Pierced, Embossed, Scrolls, Marked, c.1890, 20 x 12 ½ In.	295.00
Lamp, Owl Base, Slag Glass, Metal Filigree, 11 In. ....*illus*	995.00
Letter Rack, Brass, Filigree, Scrolling, Marked, c.1900, 13 x 16 In. ....*illus*	205.00
Match Holder, Beetle, Cast Iron, Hinged Lid, Sticker, 3 ½ In.	118.00
Plaque, Woman, With Cape, Holly Berry Garland, Relief, Round, 8 In.	650.00
Sconce, Cast Brass, Baroque Style, Dark Patina, c.1900, 18 In., Pair	440.00
Stand, Smoking, Cast Metal, Ashtray, Match Holder, c.1900, 29 In.	150.00
Teapot, Heater Base, Copper, Wood Handle, Cast Iron Base, Pat. 1896, 14 In.	110.00

BRASS has been used for decorative pieces and useful tablewares since ancient times. It is an alloy of copper, zinc, and other metals. Additional brass items may be found under Bell, Candlestick, Tool, or Trivet.

Arch, Gilt, Japanese Style, 11 x 10 In.	88.00
Ashtray, Hand Beaten, Atomic Style, Italy, 1950s, 10 ¼ x 7 ½ In.	65.00
Bed Warmer, Copper Bottom, 1800s, 40 In.	117.00
Bed Warmer, Embossed, Turned Wood Handle, England, c.1830, 43 In.	176.00
Bed Warmer, Engraved Lid, Turned Wood Handle, 19th Century, 43 In.	176.00
Bed Warmer, Flower, Etched, Pierced, Mahogany Handle	77.00
Bed Warmer, Flowers, Goat, Turned Wood Handle, 43 ½ In.	460.00
Bed Warmer, Flowers, Wood Handle, Early 19th Century, 36 ½ In.	85.00
Bed Warmer, Pan, Engraved Flowers, Turned Handle, 43 In.	118.00
Bed Warmer, Sunburst Flower, Hinged Lid, Wood Handle, 44 ½ In.	79.00
Biscuit Barrel, Repousse Flowers, Scalloped Base Rim, England, c.1820, 9 ¼ x 7 In. .....*illus*	176.00
Bowl, Fruit, Napoleon III, Reticulated, Paris Porcelain Floral Plaques, 1 ½ x 15 ½ x 11 In. ...	1200.00
Bowl, Hammered, Flared, 4 x 15 In.	55.00
Box, Copper, Stacked Rectangles, Stamped OTAR, USA, c.1920, 4 ¼ x 5 In. ....*illus*	3120.00
Box, Lid, Imperium Britannicum, Christmas 1914, 5 In.	205.00
Box, Liquor, Heart, Flowers, Iron Strapwork, 8 Bottles, Hinged, P. Tracy, c.1800, 10 x 15 In. ...	1380.00
Box, Rolled, 6-Sided, Hinged, 3 ¾ x 2 ½ x 2 ½ In.	18.00
Brazier, Lift Out Bowl, Urn Pedestal, Round Base, Wood Mount, Tab Handles, 26 x 29 In.	115.00
Bucket, Hand Hammered, 17 x 20 In.	351.00
Bucket, No. 12, Market H.W. Hayden's, Pat. Dates Dec. 18, 1851 & 1870	70.00
Bucket, Spun, Handle, Signed, Hiriam Haydon, Waterbury, Conn., 19th Century, 6 x 10 In. ...	60.00
Bucket, Wrought Iron Swing Handle, Pa., c.1800, 12 x 20 ½ In.	115.00
Buckle, Moose Head, Blank Banner, Maple Leaves, Patina, 3 ½ x 2 ½ In.	60.00
Cachepot, Urn Shape, Column Support, Hammered, 17 In.	23.00
Candle Lamp, Candle, Pierced Metal Shade, Beaded Fringe, c.1890, 17 In., Pair	59.00
Candleholder, Drip Tray, Flared Base, 4 ½ x 4 ¾ In.	339.00
Candleholder, Handle, Copper Cup, W.A.S. Benson, 6 x 3 In., Pair	230.00
Candleholder, Repousse Pattern, Poppy Pods, Keswick School, Marked, 6 x 2 ½ In., Pair......	540.00
Card Press, Repousse, Scrolls, c.1870, 6 ¼ In.	350.00
Case, Document, Copper, Cylindrical, Brass Cap, 14 ½ In.	115.00
Casket, Hinged Mirror Lid, Silk, Lion's Masks, Roses, Splayed Tubular Legs, c.1875, 31 x 17 x 17 In.	4406.00
Charger, Hammered, Fully Rigged Galleon, Rope Design, Mid 1900s, 34 In.	358.00
Cigar Cutter, Match Box Holder, Scrolls, Woman On Stairs, Man On Bench, Cast, 4 ½ x 7 ¼ In.	110.00
Cigar Cutter, Padlock Form, Marked, DBGM1623984, Germany, 4 ¼ x 2 ⅜ In.	105.00
Cigar Holder, Victorian, Child Finial, Footed, 9 ½ In.	280.00
Cocktail Shaker Set, Engraved, Flowers, Leaves, 3 Sections, 4 ½-In. Goblets, 8 In., 5 Piece ...	185.00
Copper, Ashtray, Black Genie, Germany, 4 ½ In.	129.00
Cuspidor, Arcade Manufacturing, Freeport, Ill., 8 In. ....*illus*	29.00
Desk Set, Burl Walnut, Mother-Of-Pearl, Silver Inlay, c.1900, 5 Piece............................	309.00
Desk Stand, Victorian, Postage Scale, Pen Rest, Inkwells, Ball Feet, Late 19th Century, 10 In.	504.00
Figurine, Pig, Hammered, Mahogany Base, 17 ½ x 30 x 3 ½ In.	764.00
Figurine, Savage Sporting Arms, Stevens, 4 ½ x 2 ¼ x 6 In.	142.00
Frame, Art Nouveau, Tooled Design, Ivory Face, Patina, 4 ½ x 5 In. ....*illus*	660.00
Frame, Burled Wood Inlay, Cattails, Water, Insects, Arts & Crafts, 5 ¼ x 5 ½ In.	480.00
Girandole, 5 Holders, Scroll Arms, Applied Flowers, Leaves, Multi-Tiered, 3-Footed, 17 In., Pair	121.00
Girandole, 5-Light, Gilt, Scrolled Arms, Fleur-De-Lis, Coffin Prisms, Marble Base, 21 x 19 In.	353.00
Hook, Elk's Head, Antlers, 7 x 9 In.	50.00
Horn, Fishmongers, Duck Bill Mouth Piece, 14 x 4 In.	42.00
Incense Burner, Foo Dog Finial, Handles, 1800s, 16 x 19 In.	293.00

Brass, Biscuit Barrel, Repousse Flowers, Scalloped Base Rim, England, c.1820, 9 ¼ x 7 In. $176.00

Brass, Box, Copper, Stacked Rectangles, Stamped OTAR, USA, c.1920, 4 ¼ x 5 In. $3120.00

Brass, Cuspidor, Arcade Manufacturing, Freeport, Ill., 8 In. $29.00

Brass, Frame, Art Nouveau, Tooled Design, Ivory Face, Patina, 4 ½ x 5 In. $660.00

Brass, Pitcher, Normandie, Revere Copper & Brass, Chrome Plate, Peter Muller-Munk, c.1935, 10 In. $1440.00

Brass, Samovar, Undertray, Hammered Bowl, Russia, 18 ½ In. $186.00

Bride's Bowl, Apricot Cased, New Amsterdam Silver Plated Frame, 11 ½ In. $175.00

Bride's Bowl, Cranberry, Etched Flowers, Silver Plated Reticulated Frame, 8 In. $58.00

Jar, Silvered Patinated Overlay, Orange Knob, Lid, P. Haustein, WMF, c.1929, 10 In.	4780.00
Jug, Cider, Dovetailed, England, Gal.	265.00
Nutcracker, Pipe Tamper, England, c.1740	195.00
Pail, Wrought Iron Swing Handle, 19th Century, 11 x 17 In.	120.00
Pen Rest, Art Nouveau, Gilt, c.1900, 9 ⅜ x 3 In.	85.00
Pitcher, Hammered, Incised Circle, Lines, Stamped, Hayno Focken, Germany, 19 x 9 In.	1440.00
Pitcher, Normandie, Revere Copper & Brass, Chrome Plate, Peter Muller-Munk, c.1935, 10 In. ....*illus*	1440.00
Planter, Hammered, Pyramids, Sphinx, Squat, Shouldered, Stand-Up Neck, 9 x 12 In.	41.00
Plaque, Arcade Foundry, 1927, 3 x 5 In.	225.00
Plaque, Indian Profile, Brown Patina, 10 In.	250.00
Plaque, Nude Woman, Art Deco, 1920s, 14 ½ x 8 In., Pair	175.00
Plateau, Silvered, Sculpted Leaf & Bell Flower Rim, Lion's Head Feet, c.1875, 16 In.	240.00
Podium, Figural Eagle, Sphere, Column, Platform Base, 4-Lion Feet, 21 x 60 In.	2530.00
Safety Pin, 3 Ft.	94.00
Samovar, Undertray, Hammered Bowl, Russia, 18 ½ In. ....*illus*	186.00
Samovar, Urn Form, Swivel Side Handles, Marked, Tula, Petersburg, Russia, 1800s, 27 ¼ In.	600.00
Shoehorn, Curved Handle, England, c.1770	150.00
Stand, Bible, Gorham, c.1920, 12 x 18 In.	140.00
Stand, Bible, Pierced, Engraved Design, Marked, Gorham, Special, 12 In.	210.00
Teakettle, Spirit, Engraved Rosewood Handle, Warming Stand, c.1860, 12 x 9 ½ In.	795.00
Tray, Cockerel Handle, Grasoli, West Germany, 1950s, 13 x 7 ½ In.	35.00
Tray, Tea, Chippendale, English, c.1790, 18 x 14 ½ In.	325.00
Tussy Mussy Posy Holder, Gilt, 5 ¼ In.	795.00
Valet, Man's, 20th Century, 58 In.	60.00
Wall Pocket, Opposing Doves, Scalloped Pocket, 19th Century, 6 x 16 ½ In.	71.00
Weight, Cherub, Jewels, Lapis Lazuli Ground, Victorian, 6 In.	88.00
Whistle, Street Car, Stone Mountain To Atlanta Car, 22 x 3 In.	390.00

BRASTOFF, *see Sascha Brastoff category.*

BREAD PLATE, *see various silver categories, porcelain factories, and pressed glass patterns.*

BRIDE'S BOWLS OR BASKETS were usually one-of-a-kind novelties made in American and European glass factories. They were especially popular about 1880 when the decorated basket was often given as a wedding gift. Cut glass baskets were popular after 1890. All bride's bowls lost favor about 1905. Bride's bowls and baskets may also be found in other glass sections. Check the index at the back of the book.

Apricot Cased, New Amsterdam Silver Plated Frame, 11 ½ In. ....*illus*	175.00
Blown, Spatterware, Footed, England, c.1900, 9 ½ x 11 In.	550.00
Blue Satin, Diamond Quilted, Square, Silver Plated Frame, 9 x 7 ½ In.	125.00
Brass, Pierced, Movable Handle, 5 x 7 ½ In.	75.00
Chartreuse, Diamond Quilted, Mother-Of-Pearl Design, Pheasant, Butterfly, 5 x 12 In.	259.00
Cranberry, Etched Flowers, Silver Plated Reticulated Frame, 8 In. ....*illus*	58.00
Glossy, Square Shape, Crimped Rim, Pontil, Derby Stand, Wings, c.1875, 9 ½ In.	198.00
Griffin, Flowers, Silver Plated Frame, 10 ½ x 9 ½ In.	150.00
Jack-In-The-Pulpit, Enameled Flowers, Silver Plated Base, Meriden, 13 ½ x 13 In.	1050.00
Lavender Cased, Flowers, Ruffled, Silver Plated Frame, 9 ½ x 10 In. ....*illus*	175.00
Mother-Of-Pearl, Blue, Acid Finish, Diamond Quilted, Victorian, 13 In.	1250.00
Opaline Cased, Silver Plate, Painted, Pink Fitted, Handle, Pairpoint, c.1890, 12 In. ....*illus*	106.00
Orange, Amber Ruffled Rim, Applied Handle, c.1920, 10 x 8 x 7 In.	110.00
Pink Cased, Bird, Ruffled Edge, Enamel, Silver Plate, 6 ½ x 10 In.	75.00
Pink Cased, Flowers, Leaves, Enamel, Resilvered Frame, Victorian, 8 ½ x 9 In.	895.00
Pink Cased, Ruffled, Square, Embossed Woman's Head, Silver Plate, Frame, 10 ½ In.	100.00
Pink, Ruffled Rim, Electroplated Frame, c.1870, 12 x 12 In.	263.00
Pink, White, Ruffled, Benedict Silver Plated Frame, 11 x 11 In.	175.00
Pink, White, Satin, Enamel, Frosted Thorn Handle, Art Glass, 8 x 10 ½ In.	75.00
Rainbow Glass, Crimped Ruffled Rim, 8 In.	125.00
Silver, Engraved, Square, 12 x 9 ½ x 4 ⅝ In.	295.00
Silver, Oval, Flared Rim, Flowers, Leaves, Swing Handle, Germany, c.1925, 12 x 11 In.	780.00
White Cased, Pink Bowl, Enameled Flowers, Chariot, Silver Plated, Meriden, 10 ½ x 17 ½ In.	8500.00
White Cased, Rose, Flowers, Ruffled Edge, Silver Plate, Van Bergh Silverplate Co.	640.00
Yellow, Flowers, Enamel, Pink Interior, Satin Case, Victorian, 10 ½ In.	720.00

BRISTOL glass was made in Bristol, England, after the 1700s. The Bristol glass most often seen today is a Victorian, lightweight opaque glass that is often blue. Some of the glass was decorated with enamels.

Lamp, Bohemian, Monarch On Shade, Aqua Twisted Stem & Base, 19th Century, 17 ¼ In.	625.00
Lamp, Green, Gold Highlights & Prisms, 26 In.	30.00
Pitcher, Blue, Hobnail, Ruffled Collar Rim, Spout, Green Handle, 10 x 8 In.	295.00
Urn, Birds, Flowers, Aqua, Gilt, Enamel, 19th Century, 18 ½ In.	675.00
Urn, Black, Enameled Flowers, Square Foot, c.1870, 11 In., Pair	1521.00
Urn, Cover, Opaline, Cornucopias, Baluster, Painted, c.1775, 11 ¾ x 5 In.	1250.00
Urn, Flowers, Black Crystal, Square Foot, c.1870, 11 In., Pair	1690.00
Vanity Set, Blue, White Flowers, Gold, Jar, 2 Cologne Bottles, 8 & 6 In., 3 Piece	75.00
Vase, Banjo Form, Oval Reserve, Cherubs, Blue, Green, c.1870, 15 In.	118.00
Vase, Blue, Enameled Flowers, c.1875, 7 ½ In., Pair	47.00
Vase, Blue, Frosted & Enameled, Prunus Blossoms, Oval, c.1900, 10 In.	448.00
Vase, Clambroth, Flowers, Leaves, Insects, Painted, 10 ¼ x 4 ¾ In.	110.00
Vase, Dragon, Painted, Cream Ground, Gold Detail, c.1900, 8 x 3 ¼ In.	100.00
Vase, Flowers, Pink, Yellow, Gray, White Glass, Gilt, Late 1800s, 10 ¼ In., Pair	62.00
Vase, Flowers, Shaded Orange To Peach, Painted, Late 1800s, 9 ⅜ x 5 ½ In.	495.00
Vase, Landscape, Dark Shaded To Light Green, Painted, 9 In., Pair	85.00
Vase, Lilies, Lavender, White, Footed, 7 ½ x 2 ½ In.	140.00
Vase, Opalescent Yellow, Blue Plums, Leaves, Butterflies, 7 x 5 In.	145.00
Vase, Oriental Flowers, Multicolored, 8 ½ In.	600.00
Vase, Pink, Blue & White Flowers, Urn Shape, Stylized Tulip Neck, Footed, 15 In., Pair	201.00
Vase, White Lilies, Green Leaves, Rose Ground, 1800s, 11 x 5 In., Pair	176.00
Vase, White, Scenic, Birds, Flowers, c.1870, 14 ½ In.	70.00

BRITANNIA, *see Pewter category.*

BRONZE is an alloy of copper, tin, and other metals. It is used to make figurines, lamps, and other decorative objects. Bronze lamps are listed in the Lamp category. Pieces listed here date from the eighteenth, nineteenth, and twentieth centuries.

Ashtray, Nude Woman, Kneeling, Alabaster Tray, Marked, Austria, 4 ¾ x 3 ¾ x 3 ½ In.	395.00
Basin, Animal Shape, Footed, 12 ½ In.	1528.00
Basin, Squat, Flared Rim, Handles, 3-Footed, 10 ½ x 35 In.	863.00
Book Slide, Egyptian Revival, Pyramid, Sphinx Ends, Gilt, England, c.1920, 5 x 13 In.	470.00
Bowl, Flat Rim, Lion Handles, Signed, Chinese, 3 ¾ x 9 ½ In.	500.00
Bowl, Lily Pad, Japan, 3 x 8 In.	117.00
Bowl, Overlapping Leaves, Scalloped Rim, Footed, Gilt, 2 x 4 ¾ In.	413.00
Bowl, Ritual, Mythical Beast, Horns, Round Body, 3-Footed, Square Handles, Chinese, 8 In. ..	840.00
Bowl, Zodiac, Figures, Animals, Cast, Japan, 4 ¼ x 6 In.	450.00
Bracket, Peacock, Flowers, Cast, 14 ½ x 13 ½ In., Pair	295.00
Bust, Athena, Patinate, Orange Stepped Marble Base, 23 x 8 In.	460.00
Bust, Child, Onyx Pedestal, 4 In.	515.00
Bust, Colombo, Renzo, Napoleon, Brown Patina, c.1885, 22 x 15 In. ....*illus*	1955.00
Bust, Dutch Girl, Wearing Traditional Cap, 18 ½ x 12 x 7 In.	620.00
Bust, Fordtay, A., Arabian Man, Signed, Paris, 24 In.	825.00
Bust, Morris, Paul, Abraham Lincoln, Signed, 1907, 23 In.	3231.00
Bust, Muller, H., Abraham Lincoln, Mark, Austria, 4 ¾ In.	250.00
Bust, Muller, H., Shakespeare, Carved Marble Base, Inscribed, 18 ½ In.	1800.00
Bust, Officer, Marble Pedestal, Raised Square Plinth, France, 12 ¾ In.	504.00
Bust, Rimbez, Zacharie, Armide, Silver & Gold Patina, Signed, 24 ¾ In.	3480.00
Bust, Roman Head, Verdigris, Square Marble Base, 19 x 38 In.	3105.00
Bust, Woman, Tanagra, Art Deco, c.1900, 13 ½ x 24 ½ In.	1320.00
Candleholder, Regency, Gilt, Sphinx, Black Marble Base, 8 ¾ x 4 ¼ x 2 ½ In., Pair	2350.00
Cannon, Signal, Touch Hole, Movable Carriage, Early 20th Century, 4 ½ x 9 In.	235.00
Casket, Jewel, Renaissance Revival, Gilt, France, Mid 19th Century, 4 ¼ x 7 ¼ In.	1037.00
Censer, Dragons, Butterfly Mount Handle, Round, Open Wood Lid, Japan, 1900s, 11 In.	316.00
Censer, Drum Form, Lion Masks, 3-Footed, 6-Character Reign Mark, Chinese, 5 ¾ In.	725.00
Censer, Footed, Handles, Chinese, 20th Century, 4 ¼ In.	478.00
Censer, Gilt, Pagoda Shape, Paw Feet, Openwork Designs, Chinese, 41 x 26 x 17 In.	173.00
Charger, Romantic Garden Scene, Shepherd & Maiden, Sculpted, Signed, France, 1800s, 21 In.	330.00
Compote, Marble, Handles, France, 1800s, 10 x 10 In.	351.00
Decanter, Wine, Ritual, Wide Cylinder, 3 Legs, Incised Design, Spout, Handle, Chinese, 10 In.	600.00
Dish, Card, Woman, On Pedestal, Between Trays, Figural, Austria, c.1890, 17 x 7 ¾ x 9 ¾ In.	1800.00
Dish, Lily Pad, Vine Pedestal, 3 ¾ x 6 In.	300.00
Dish, Woman's Profile, Wearing Big Hat, Incised, 3 ½ x 2 ⅝ In.	23.00
Dresser Set, Gilt, Guilloche, Enamel, Painted Portraits, France, Mirror 11 x 4 In., 8 Piece	1715.00
Electrolier, Newel Post, Black Marble Base, c.1900, 35 x 18 In.	1410.00
Encrier, Double Swan, 1st Empire Style, Gilt, Footed, Elliptical, Covered Inkwells, 3 ⅝ x 6 In.	1200.00

Bride's Bowl, Lavender Cased, Flowers, Ruffled, Silver Plated Frame, 9 ½ x 10 In.
$175.00

Bride's Bowl, Opaline Cased, Silver Plate, Painted, Pink Fitted, Handle, Pairpoint, c.1890, 12 In.
$106.00

Bronze, Bust, Colombo, Renzo, Napoleon, Brown Patina, c.1885, 22 x 15 In.
$1955.00

Bronze, Figurine, Bertrand, S., Young Woman, Coat, Brimmed Hat, Ivory, Art Deco, 6 In.
$702.00

Bronze, Figurine, Poodle, Pierrot Hat, Brown Patina, Marble Base, Signed, 8 In. $133.00

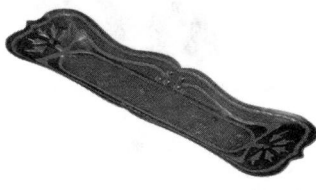

Bronze, Pen Tray, Arts & Crafts, Multicolored Enamel, Patina, Impressed Mark, 19 x 3 In. $210.00

Bronze, Sculpture, Bergman, Arab, Holding Towel, Nude Woman, Rug Base, Nam Greb, 7 x 8 In. $2000.00

Bronze, Sculpture, Botinelly, Louis, Nude, Infants, Plinth Base, Art Deco, 14 ½ x 24 In. $2530.00

Epergne, Art Nouveau, Crystal, Leaf Base, Standing Figure, 8 x 4 In.	88.00
Ewer, Amber Glass Insert, Scrolled Handle, Mask, Footed, 19th Century, 19 ½ In.	124.00
Ewer, Gothic Style, Cast, Hand Chased, 12 In.	58.00
Figurine, Bertrand, S., Young Woman, Coat, Brimmed Hat, Ivory, Art Deco, 6 In. *illus*	702.00
Figurine, Poodle, Pierrot Hat, Brown Patina, Marble Base, Signed, 8 In. *illus*	133.00
Fountain, Man, Classical, Scantily Clad, Wearing Helmet, Seated, Black Patina, 20 In.	474.00
Frame, Flowers, Basket, Rococo, Filigree, 2-Tier Base, Gold, 9 x 15 In., Pair	575.00
Garniture, Neo-Grec Scenes, Handles, Black Shades, Barbedienne, Paris, c.1880, 29 In., Pair..	3600.00
Guard Lion, Gilt Mane, Green Patina, Burma, 28 x 20 In., Pair	1800.00
Hook, Dragon Shape, c.1880, 6 x 4 In.	90.00
Hook, Greek Goddess Bust, Figural, Mounting Screw, c.1860, 6 x 4 ½ In.	110.00
Hook, Serpent, Nickel Plated, 2 Mounting Holes, c.1900, 7 ½ x 2 ⅛ In.	120.00
Incense Burner, 3 Cabriole Legs, Monster Head Top, Handles, Bulbous, Chinese, 8 ½ x 7 ½ In. ..	360.00
Incense Burner, 10 Climbing Dragons, 4 Legs, Reticulated Cover, Dragon Handles, Chinese, 20 In.	1150.00
Incense Burner, Applied Animal, Flower Finial, Handles, Chinese, 15 In., Pair	690.00
Incense Burner, Chinese, c.1930, 6 ¾ x 6 ¼ In.	294.00
Incense Burner, Dome Cover, Foo Dog, Masques, Dragons, Bulbous Base, Chinese, 9 x 7 ¾ In.	150.00
Incense Burner, Dragons, Monster Legs, Cover, Bulbous, Relief Cast, 17 ½ In., Pair	1020.00
Incense Burner, Fierce Dragons, Melon Body, Reticulated Cover, Dragon Head Legs, Chinese, 22 In.	1840.00
Incense Burner, Hotei, With Bag, Japan, 19th Century, 6 ¼ x 7 In.	294.00
Incense Burner, Mythological Figure, Carved, Chinese, 3 x 4 In., Pair	439.00
Jar, Holy Water, Tibet, 11 x 7 In.	293.00
Jardiniere, Birds, Branches, Incised, Lobed, Deep Red-Brown Patina, 9 x 11 ½ In.	360.00
Jardiniere, Lacquer, Cover, Black, Applied Flowers, Scrolls, France, c.1820, 9 x 19 In.	1170.00
Jardiniere, Louis XVI Style, Wreath Handles, Footed, France, 10 x 26 x 10 ½ In.	810.00
Jardiniere, Mask Head, Empire Style, Pedestal Foot, Black Marble Base, 11 ¾ In., Pair	896.00
Latch, Icebox, Dragon, Swing Handle, 5 x 2 ½ In.	80.00
Lavabo, Twin Spouts, Stylized Dog Heads, Brass Handle, Swivel Ring, Germany, c.1700, 12 In.	540.00
Letter Holder, Oriental Style, 2 Crystal Inkwells, Faceted Stoppers, c.1900, 8 x 10 ½ In.	351.00
Letter Holder, Sterling Silver Accents, Marked, Pat., Aug. 27, 1912, 6 x 2 x 4 ¼ In.	350.00
Liquor Service, Napoleon III, Gilt, Paneled Glass, Decanters, Cordials, 17 x 16 In.	7320.00
Medallion, Garnets, Commemorative, Napoleon As Consul Of France, c.1803, 2 In.	588.00
Mirror, Bust, Woman, Pearl Necklace, Beaded Edge, Case, Impressed, Erte, 1985, 11 In.	440.00
Mirror, D'Artage, Hand, Leaf & Scrolling Frame, Signed, Barbedienne, Paris	150.00
Mirror, Oriental Nature Scene, Lotus Tree, Cranes, Turtle, c.1900, 9 ½ x 13 ¾ In.	106.00
Mirror, Round, Vertical Rim, Chinese, 4 ⅛ In.	120.00
Mold, Casting Buckshot, 18th Century	225.00
Pen Tray, Arts & Crafts, Multicolored Enamel, Patina, Impressed Mark, 19 x 3 In. *illus*	210.00
Pen Tray, Pheasant In Landscape, Molded, Early 20th Century, 8 ⅛ In.	29.00
Planter, Figures, Classical Style, Basket Top, Paw Feet, 36 ½ x 20 In.	1093.00
Plaque, Crest, Falcon, 3 Crowns, 18 ½ x 21 In.	600.00
Plaque, Expulsion Of Adam & Eve, Cast In Relief, Round, c.1900, 9 ½ In.	660.00
Plaque, Figures, Harvesting Wheat, Marked, c.1900, 13 ½ In.	150.00
Plaque, Memorial, Relief, Angel Receiving Soul Into Heaven, France, 1800s, 20 x 12 In.	480.00
Plaque, Nymph & Satyr, Brown Patina, Signed, Early 20th Century, 19 ¾ x 22 ¼ In.	1495.00
Plaque, Philipp, Karl, Peaceful Melody, Man Playing Violin, Signed, 10 ½ x 11 In.	330.00
Plaque, Portrait, Theodore Roosevelt, Relief, 7 x 4 ¾ In.	288.00
Plaque, Water Maiden Pouring Water From Urn, 35 ¾ x 9 ¾ In.	1304.00
Plaque, Youth, Wearing Animal Pelt & Ivy Wreath, Classical, Oval, Relief, 16 x 14 In.	115.00
Plateau, Rococo, Mirror, Shells, Scrolls, 8-Sided, Handles, France, c.1925, 21 x 26 In.	1440.00
Pricket, Silvered, Regency Style, Rope Twist, Triangular Base, Paw Feet, 69 x 11 x 11 In.	915.00
Putti, Holding Tambourine, Playing Pipe, 9 ⅝ x 3 ¼ In.	3240.00
Roundel, Declaration Of Independence Congress, 4th July 1776, Cast Relief, Frame, 8 In.	288.00
Screen, Table, Gothic Revival, Telescoping, Columnar Standard, Arches, Gilt, 23 ½ In.	411.00
Sculpture, Alligator, 16 x 72 x 23 In.	1035.00
Sculpture, Andre, Maid, Holding Casket, Medieval Dress, Ivory Face, Hands, Marble Base, c.1900, 15 In.	1541.00
Sculpture, Arab Boys, Sitting, Studying Book, Cold Painted, Vienna, 2 x 2 In.	444.00
Sculpture, Archer, On Raised Base, Drawn Bow, Marble Plinth, 22 ¾ In.	1778.00
Sculpture, Arrotino, Grand Tour, Crouching Figure, Honing Knife, Early 20th Century, 5 ½ x 3 ¼ In.	118.00
Sculpture, Arson, Alphonse-Alexander, Rabbit, Babies, Metal Base, France, 4 ⅝ x 4 ½ In.	940.00
Sculpture, Athena, Seated, Stringing Her Bow, 19th Century, 19 In.	288.00
Sculpture, Bacchante, Faun, Black Patination, Italy, 19th Century, 12 ¾ In.	1126.00
Sculpture, Ballerina, Arabesque Pose, Onyx & Slate Stepped Base, 21 ½ In.	201.00
Sculpture, Ballerina, Naughty, Doing Splits, 4 ½ In.	295.00
Sculpture, Bamboo, Russia, France, 1892-1900, 22 ¼ In.	3510.00
Sculpture, Barreau, Auguste Marie, Young Woman, Grecian Dress, Gilt, Patina, Signed, 24 ½ In.	7250.00
Sculpture, Barye, A., Lion, Paw On Hissing Snake, Oval Stepped Pink Marble Base, 11 x 10 In.	354.00

Sculpture, Bear, Walking, 11 ½ x 20 In.		575.00
Sculpture, Bergman, Arab, Holding Towel, Nude Woman, Rug Base, Nam Greb, 7 x 8 In. ..*illus*		2000.00
Sculpture, Bofill, A., Egyptian Man, Water Vessel On Back, Red Cold Painted Cap, 24 In.		2844.00
Sculpture, Bonheur, Horse, Arabian Stallion, On Stepped Oval Base, 6 ¾ In.		1304.00
Sculpture, Bonheur, I.J., Bull, Standing, France, c.1885, 7 x 10 In.		575.00
Sculpture, Bonheur, I.J., Bull, Walking, Rocky Outcrop Base, 12 x 14 In.		3200.00
Sculpture, Bonheur, Isidore, Horse & Jockey, Le Grand Jockey, c.1900, 41 x 40 In.		10800.00
Sculpture, Bonheur, Rosa, Bull, Resting, Taureau Couche Stamp, c.1850, 6 x 11 In.		920.00
Sculpture, Botinelly, Louis, Nude, Infants, Plinth Base, Art Deco, 14 ½ x 24 In. .....*illus*		2530.00
Sculpture, Boys, Playing Musical Instruments, Cold Painted, Vienna, 2 x 3 In.		711.00
Sculpture, Breitner, Joseph, St. George On Rearing Horse, Slaying Dragon, Signed, 25 In.		2489.00
Sculpture, Bruchon, E., Charity, Woman & Child, Patina, Incised Base, 23 ¾ In.		2400.00
Sculpture, Buddha, Chiangsaen Style, Dore, Wood Base, 7 ½ In.		2420.00
Sculpture, Buddha, Dhyanasana, Korea, 15 In.		4422.00
Sculpture, Buddha, Seated, 10 x 8 In.		409.00
Sculpture, Buddha, Seated, Asia, 8 ¾ In.		239.00
Sculpture, Buddhist Deity, Hand Raised In Blessing, Rose, Flaming Mandoria, Chinese, 6 ½ In.		450.00
Sculpture, Bull, Patinate, After Pierre Jules Mene, 1900s, 9 x 14 ½ x 5 ¾ In. ....*illus*		767.00
Sculpture, Bulldog, Wearing Harness, Patina, 19 ½ x 28 x 10 ½ In., Pair		840.00
Sculpture, Burlini, Alfredo, Free-Form Black Lucite Base, 2-Parts, 1976, 22 In.		480.00
Sculpture, Calvet, Gregoire, Ballerina, Seated, Holding Calling Card Tray, Dore, Signed, 6 ½ In.		1495.00
Sculpture, Camolera, P., Majestic Stag, Patina, Marble Base, Inscribed, 20 ½ In.		1200.00
Sculpture, Caravan, Oxen, Wagon, South America, 10 x 41 ½ x 9 In.		323.00
Sculpture, Cartier, T., Elk, 10-Point Stag, Signed, Patina, 17 x 18 In.		1035.00
Sculpture, Cartier, Thomas F., Alsatian Licking His Paw, Patina, Inscribed, 5 x 7 In.		780.00
Sculpture, Cat, Conducting, Music Stand, Cold Painted, Vienna, 2 ⅛ In. ....*illus*		115.00
Sculpture, Cats, 2 At Sewing Machine, Vienna, 2 ⅜ In.		275.00
Sculpture, Cats, 2 Seated On Moon Like Canoe, Vienna, 3 In.		330.00
Sculpture, Cats, Depicting Hunter, Wearing Jacket, Rifle, Haversack, Basket Of Kittens, 3 ½ & ¾ In.		2233.00
Sculpture, Chapu, Henri Michel Antoine, Joan Of Arc, Sitting, Inscribed, c.1850, 17 In.		1560.00
Sculpture, Cheyenne, Indian, Horse, Brown Patina, Signed, Marked, Heikka Foundry, 1983, 21 In.		708.00
Sculpture, Child, Lying Down, Kissing Bird, Onyx Base, 3 x 3 x 4 In.		59.00
Sculpture, Child, Song Bird On Shoulder, Slate Base, France, 20th Century, 19 In.		590.00
Sculpture, Children Playing, France, 16 ¼ x 11 ½ In.		359.00
Sculpture, Chiparus, Actress, Ivory, Marble & Onyx Base, Signed, Etling Mark		3700.00
Sculpture, Chiparus, Anastasia, Ivory, Marble & Onyx Base, Signed, Foundry Mark, 16 In.		4600.00
Sculpture, Chiparus, Book Lady, Ivory, Marble & Onyx Base, Patina, Signed, Foundry Mark, 20 In.		2650.00
Sculpture, Chiparus, Creed, Ivory, Marble & Onyx Base, Signed, Foundry Mark, 16 In.		2950.00
Sculpture, Chiparus, Dolly Sisters, Ivory, Marble & Onyx Base, Signed, Etling Mark, 19 x 11 x 5 In.		2850.00
Sculpture, Chiparus, Pajama Lady, Ivory, Marble & Onyx Base, Signed, Etling Mark		4700.00
Sculpture, Chiparus, Starfish, Ivory, Marble & Onyx Base, Patina, Signed, Foundry Mark, 25 In.		3700.00
Sculpture, Chiparus, Tender Promises, Ivory, Marble & Onyx Base, Signed, Foundry Mark, 15 x 31 In.		5895.00
Sculpture, Christie, Keith, El Segundo On Horse Back, Oak Base, c.1940, 19 x 18 x 8 In.		3600.00
Sculpture, Classical Woman Adjusting Tunic, Gilt Metal Foot, Lamp Base, 20 ½ In.		593.00
Sculpture, Conte, Pino, Head, Young Woman, Wood Base, Signed, 12 In.		1320.00
Sculpture, Crayfish, Cold Painted, Vienna, 7 In.		711.00
Sculpture, Crushed Fedora, Continental, Late 19th Century, 6 x 2 ¼ In.		385.00
Sculpture, Cupid, Psyche, Original Patina, Marble Pedestal, 110 x 33 x 40 In.		4994.00
Sculpture, D'Ambrosi, Dodge City Steer, Signed, 1978, 16 x 23 x 14 In.		4200.00
Sculpture, Dancer, Holding Parrot, Raised Arm, c.1920, 16 ½ In.		56.00
Sculpture, Debut, Marcel, Man, Middle East, Rifle, Water Jugs, Red Paint On Turban, Shoes, 17 In.		531.00
Sculpture, Deer, Stylized Shape, Benin, Africa, 8 x 13 In.		118.00
Sculpture, Defense Du Sol, Man Holding Spear, Knife, Axe On Ground, 40 x 13 ¼ x 20 In.		5875.00
Sculpture, Deity, Turquoise Mounts, Nepal, 6 ½ In.		1750.00
Sculpture, Dewitt, Horse, Running, Neck Stretched Forward, 20th Century, 6 ¼ x 10 In.		588.00
Sculpture, Dog, Greyhound, Marble Stand, Brown Patina, Marble Base, 6 ¼ In.		385.00
Sculpture, Dog, Greyhound, Oval Base, Brown Patination, Marble Stand, Italy, 9 In.		948.00
Sculpture, Dog, Hound, Seated, Vienna, 20th Century, 6 ¼ In.		296.00
Sculpture, Dog, Mastiff, Lunging On Rear Legs, Mouth Open, Oval Base, 24 In.		1896.00
Sculpture, Dog, Retriever, Mounted, Stepped Oval Base, Dark Brown Patina, 9 In.		385.00
Sculpture, Dog, Whippet, Seated, 31 ½ x 13 In.		1292.00
Sculpture, Dog, Whippet, Stepping Over Lily Stem, 20th Century, 16 ¼ x 21 In.		2607.00
Sculpture, Dore, A., Buddha, Seated, 11 ½ In.		15340.00
Sculpture, Elephant, Ivory, Trunk Up, Japan, 14 x 19 In.		995.00
Sculpture, Elephant, Ivory Tusks, 20th Century, 12 In.		300.00
Sculpture, Elephant, Trunk Raised, Marked, 20th Century, Japan, 8 In.		24.00
Sculpture, Elephant, Standing On Top Of One Another, Wood Base, 14 In.		976.00

Bronze, Sculpture, Bull, Patinate, After Pierre Jules Mene, 1900s, 9 x 14 ½ x 5 ¾ In. $767.00

Bronze, Sculpture, Cat, Conducting, Music Stand, Cold Painted, Vienna, 2 ⅛ In. $115.00

Bronze, Sculpture, Goodnight, Veryl, Plowing Snow, Moose, Inscribed, c.1975, 12 x 18 In. $1800.00

Bronze, Sculpture, Kirmse, Marguerite, Scottish Terrier, Crouching, Gorham, 2 x 3 ½ In. $978.00

Bronze, Sculpture, Liberich, N., Resting Bear, Brown Patina, Inscribed, 8 In. $4800.00

Bronze, Sculpture, Pilet, L., Athena, Sphinx On Helmet, Marble Base, Signed, 12 x 10 ½ In. $483.00

Bronze, Sculpture, Profillet, Anne-Marie, Pheasant, Art Deco, c.1930, 19 x 28 In. $360.00

Bronze, Sculpture, Sandoz, Edouard Marcel, Rabbit, Patina, Signed, Swiss, c.1920, 2 x 4 In. $1898.00

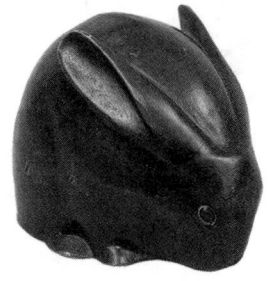

Sculpture, Eliqut, Child In Basket, Mechanical, 5 ½ x 5 ½ In.	144.00
Sculpture, End Of The Trail, Man, On Horse, 30 In.	761.00
Sculpture, Erte, Heat, Woman, In Tree, 17 ¾ In.	3510.00
Sculpture, Erte, Mystic, Woman, Holding Mirror, 14 ¾ In.	3510.00
Sculpture, Erte, Triumph, Woman, Arms Above Head, 21 ¾ In.	3510.00
Sculpture, Evans, R., Eve, Nude Holding Fruit, Green Brown Patina, Inscribed, Stamped, 32 In.	5040.00
Sculpture, Falcon, Dark Patina, Asia, 8 x 9 ¼ In.	4888.00
Sculpture, Fiedler, Suzann, I Got Legs, Mare & Foal, Wood Base, 1900s, 9 x 13 x 10 In.	978.00
Sculpture, Fiedler, Taking The Plunge, Mare & Foal, Marble Base, 1900s, 11 x 12 x 12 In.	431.00
Sculpture, Fiedler, Winter's Orphans, 3 Horses Standing Together, Wood Base, 1900s, 13 In.	403.00
Sculpture, Fillini, Scharaid, Nude Athlete, Raised Arms, Brown Patina, 2 x 9 In.	354.00
Sculpture, Fiot, M., Dog, German Shepherd, Seated, Incised, Signed, Early 1900s, 9 ½ In.	450.00
Sculpture, Foo Dog, Chinese, 6 x 6 In., Pair	460.00
Sculpture, Foo Dogs, Sitting On Haunches, Brocade Ball, Cub, Wood Base, Chinese, 8 In.	2160.00
Sculpture, Fratin, Christopher, Stag, Standing, Reclining Doe, Signed, c.1850, 5 ½ In.	585.00
Sculpture, Fremiet, E., Warrior, Female, Horse, Gilt, Green Marble Base, France, 23 ½ In.	2714.00
Sculpture, Gallo, Ignacio, Woman With Greyhound, Silver & Gold Patina, Inscribed, 25 In.	1800.00
Sculpture, Ganesha, India, 6 In.	239.00
Sculpture, Gazelle, Gilt, Diamond Set Head Ornament, Crystal Horns, Lapis Base, 9 ½ x 9 ½ In.	3105.00
Sculpture, Geefs, Guillaume, Artist, Brush, Bruxelles, 1842, 6 ½ x 14 ½ In.	920.00
Sculpture, Gerson, F., Indian Chief, Fur Headdress, Bull Horns, Feathers, Patina, 7 ½ x 10 In.	863.00
Sculpture, Geschutz, Dog, Bulldog, Vienna, Signed, 3 In.	410.00
Sculpture, Girl, Leaning On Fence, Marble Base, 6 ½ In.	89.00
Sculpture, Girl, Seated On Wall, Goat, 39 ½ In.	2034.00
Sculpture, Girl, With Goat, Black Marble Base, Marked, 21 ½ In.	358.00
Sculpture, Gladiator, Stepped Ebonized Wood Plinth, c.1950, 10 In.	295.00
Sculpture, Gloria Victus, Parcel Gilt, Patinate, Early 1900s, 41 ½ x 22 In.	5490.00
Sculpture, Goat, Head Turned, 4 In.	1750.00
Sculpture, Goodnight, Veryl, Plowing Snow, Moose, Inscribed, c.1975, 12 x 18 In. ......*illus*	1800.00
Sculpture, Gory, A., Child, On Table, Signed, 9 In.	535.00
Sculpture, Grappling Wrestlers, Lutteurs De Florence, Brown Patina, Square Yellow Base, 6 In.	443.00
Sculpture, Grosse Berliner-Kunst Ausstellung, Archer, Bow, Arrow, 11 x 21 In.	1150.00
Sculpture, Guanyin, Seated, Holding Cup, Flower, Chinese, 19th Century, 11 In.	1380.00
Sculpture, Hagenauer, African Boy, Seated, Nude, Encircled Mark, WHW, Wein, 1930s, 3 ⅜ In.	646.00
Sculpture, Hagenauer, Heron, Impressed, 1 x 2 In.	300.00
Sculpture, Hagenauer, Indian Men, Canoe, 6 ½ x 2 ½ In.	480.00
Sculpture, Hagenauer, Karl, Tennis Player, Stamped, c.1930, 7 In.	1075.00
Sculpture, Hartwig, Cleo, Ram, On Stone Sculpted Base, Signed, c.1945, 6 ½ x 5 ¾ In.	300.00
Sculpture, Head Of Poseidon Of Cape Artemision, 16 In.	1093.00
Sculpture, Head Of Zeus, Patinate, Black Marble Base, 17 ½ In.	299.00
Sculpture, Herbert, Gary, Indian Standing, Marble Base, Signed, 16 In.	705.00
Sculpture, Horse Head, Gold Patina, Wood Mount, 12 x 9 In.	144.00
Sculpture, Horse, Equestrian, Standing, c.1860, 24 x 30 In.	863.00
Sculpture, Horse, Marwari Stallion, Standing, Cold Painted, 9 x 10 ½ In.	956.00
Sculpture, Hounds, 2 Fighting Over Stick, Cold-Painted, Vienna, 2 x 5 In.	173.00
Sculpture, Jere, Curtis, Wall, Sea Gulls, Steel, Signed, 1968, 20 x 58 x 8 In.	1464.00
Sculpture, Jockey On Horseback, Plinth, c.1975, 34 ½ x 40 In.	1150.00
Sculpture, Joire, Jean, Seated German Shepherd, Alert Pose, Signed, c.1900, 22 In.	3120.00
Sculpture, Kauba, C., Whimsical, Boys Fishing, Crab On Finger, Signed, Marble Base, 7 ¼ In., Pair	1080.00
Sculpture, Kelsey, Greg, Get Off My Back, c.1975, 33 x 16 In.	1955.00
Sculpture, King Arthur, Wearing Armor, Inscribed, 1800s, 11 ½ In.	660.00
Sculpture, Kirmse, Marguerite, Scottish Terrier, Crouching, Gorham, 2 x 3 ½ In. ....*illus*	978.00
Sculpture, Kocharzik, Warrior, Romanesque, Sword, Helmet, Onyx Base, Signed, 3 x 8 In.	531.00
Sculpture, Korbel, Mario J., Nude Woman, Stamped, 3 x 8 ¾ In.	510.00
Sculpture, La Porteuse De Paniers, Marble Base, c.1834, 26 x 13 x 13 In.	2160.00
Sculpture, Laborers, 2 Seated, Standing, Shaking Hands, 32 x 19 ¾ x 9 ½ In.	5036.00
Sculpture, Lanceray, Yevgeny A., Cossack Couple On Horseback, Dark Patina, Russia, c.1800s, 15 In.	1860.00
Sculpture, Lanceray, Yevgeny A., Cossack On Horseback, Cap, Winter Coat, Russia, 8 ¾ In.	1380.00
Sculpture, Laplanch, A., Dog, German Shepherd, Lying Down, Flat Base, 3 ¼ x 6 ¼ In.	106.00
Sculpture, Le Verrier, Squirrel, Nut, Signed, 5 In.	300.00
Sculpture, Leduc, A., Boys, Climbing On Horse, France, 26 ¾ x 25 x 10 ½ In.	7050.00
Sculpture, Lenordez, P., Horse, Equestrian, Gold Patina, c.1890, 12 x 15 In.	1495.00
Sculpture, Lentelli, L., Centerpiece With Archer, Green Brown Patina, Signed Base, 23 In.	7800.00
Sculpture, Leonard, Lambert, Fox, Bird, Oval Base, Stamped, 8 ½ In.	385.00
Sculpture, Leopard, On Tree Limb, 34 x 36 In.	1287.00
Sculpture, Levasseur, Henri Louis, Sower, Man, Sowing Seeds, Signed, 31 In.	1554.00
Sculpture, Levasseur, H.L., Femme De France, Signed, 21 In.	1006.00

B

Sculpture, Liberich, N., Resting Bear, Brown Patina, Inscribed, 8 In. ....*illus*	4800.00
Sculpture, Lion, Carved Wood Base, Signed, Japan, 12 x 23 In.	940.00
Sculpture, Lion Crushing Serpent, Brown Patina, Oval Base, Marble Stand, 6 ¼ In.	504.00
Sculpture, Lion, Freestanding, Hollow, Molded, Applied Dark Patina, c.1900, 45 In., Pair......	3055.00
Sculpture, Lorenzo De Medici, In Armor, Seated, Tiger Head Helmet, Late 1800s, 18 In.	1750.00
Sculpture, Magician, Loose Robes, Tunic, Peaked Hat, Holding Vase, Cast, Chinese, 13 In.	480.00
Sculpture, Maiden & Ram, Round Plinth, 20th Century, 19 ½ In.	172.00
Sculpture, Maitreya, Seated On Lotus Throne, Lotus Stems Trailing, 1800s, 12 ¾ In.	9430.00
Sculpture, Makonika, Horse, Grazing, Signed, 16 x 9 ½ In.	863.00
Sculpture, Man, Boy On Shoulders, Standing On Seahorses, Kunst Foundry, 38 In.	5463.00
Sculpture, Man, Holding Books, Writing Tablet, Square Base, Brown Patina, c.1895, 7 In.	148.00
Sculpture, Man, Nude, Reclining, Reading To Stork, 17 ¾ In.	2607.00
Sculpture, Man, On Horse, Napoleonic Clothing, Cobblestone Base, Late 1700s, 19 x 20 In. ..	460.00
Sculpture, Man, Wearing Robe, Turban, Holding Bird, Parrot On Perch, Painted, Vienna, 4 In.	2015.00
Sculpture, Man, With Fez, Brewing Coffee On Fire, Vienna, 7 ¾ In.	153.00
Sculpture, Man, With Sword, Gilt, Ivory Hand Head, Marble Base, 8 In.	593.00
Sculpture, Masson, C., Tigers Fighting, Ibex Kill, 17 x 13 In.	1208.00
Sculpture, Marioton, Claudius, Gypsy, Woman, Standing, Tambourine, France, c.1890, 17 In.	940.00
Sculpture, Martel, Jan & Joel, Jazz Musician, c.1928, 1 ½ In.	2390.00
Sculpture, Mene, Jules, Horse, Stallion, On Rectangular Base, 5 ¼ In.	107.00
Sculpture, Mene, P.J., Mare & Foal, France, Late 19th Century, 12 In.	1220.00
Sculpture, Mercury, Fortuna, Marble Base, 19 In., Pair..	431.00
Sculpture, Moigniez, J., Eagle, On Branch, Marble Base, Signed, France, 1835-94, 30 ¾ In. ..	805.00
Sculpture, Moigniez, J., Horse, Bridle Bits, Saddle, Oval Base, 15 x 12 In.	633.00
Sculpture, Moigniez, J., Pheasant, Walking On Naturalistic Outcrop, Oak Leaves, 13 In.	711.00
Sculpture, Monk, Standing On Lotus Plinth, Chinese, 20th Century, 14 In.	299.00
Sculpture, Monks, Hands Clasped, Kneeling On Lotus Flowers, Thai, 19th Century, 13 In.	345.00
Sculpture, Moreau, A., Boy, Holding Branch, 2 Birds, Marble Base, France, 1834-1917, 31 In.	805.00
Sculpture, Moreau, A., Nude Woman, Robe, Shell, Brown Patina, Signed, 6 ½ x 11 In.	748.00
Sculpture, Moreau, A., Seated Woman, Robe Putto, Marble Base, Patina, 25 x 15 In.	1725.00
Sculpture, Moreau, August, Toddler, Diaper, Soldier Hat, c.1910, 20 ½ In.	558.00
Sculpture, Moreau, Hippolyte F., Young Fishergirl, Patina, Inscribed Base, 20 ¾ In.	3840.00
Sculpture, Moreau, Tiny, 24 x 12 x 10 In.	650.00
Sculpture, Morlon, Alexandre, Best Friends, Nude Woman Sitting, Goat, Inscribed, 14 ¼ In. .	1440.00
Sculpture, Musical Putti, Cavorting, Silvered, Wood Pedestals, 59 x 13 x 19 In., 2 Piece	5875.00
Sculpture, Mythical Lion, Raised Paw, Incense Holder, Turned Heads, 9 ¼ x 7 ½ In., Pair......	600.00
Sculpture, Mythological Figure, Continental, 5 x 11 ½ In.	450.00
Sculpture, Native American, Kneeling, Peering At Tracks, Brown Patina, c.1920, 16 ¼ In.	2370.00
Sculpture, Native American, Sundial, Brown Patina, Round Marble Base, 7 ½ In.	384.00
Sculpture, Nude Woman, Bather, Seated, 2 Lovebirds, 18 ¼ In.	2370.00
Sculpture, Nude Woman, Bather, Standing Among Bulrushes, 21 ¾ In.	2726.00
Sculpture, Ostrich, Arab Boy, Vienna, 3 In.	400.00
Sculpture, Paillet, Charles, Dog, German Shepherd, Reclining, Slab Base, France, 12 In.	1708.00
Sculpture, Parks, Bob, Horse Trader, Base, No. 10/28, c.1992, 16 x 25 x 9 In.	748.00
Sculpture, Pautrot, Ferdinand, Pheasant, Mounted, Patina, Inscribed, 13 ½ In.	889.00
Sculpture, Peddler, Arab Man, Table, Goods, Cold Paint, Vienna, c.1920, 7 ½ x 5 In.	1410.00
Sculpture, Peinte, Henri, Man Stringing Bow, Saredon, Inscribed, Stamped, c.1900, 16 In. ...	1200.00
Sculpture, Pheasant, Cold Painted, Gold, Red, Green, Stamped, Vienna, 28 x 12 In.	1725.00
Sculpture, Picault, Pegasus, 21 In.	950.00
Sculpture, Pilet, L., Athena, Sphinx On Helmet, Marble Base, Signed, 12x 10 ½ In. ....*illus*	483.00
Sculpture, Poertzel, Aristocrat, Ivory, Marble & Onyx Base, Signed, Foundry Mark, 17 In.	6200.00
Sculpture, Potter, Dish, Kiln, Stamped, Tiffany, New York, 11 x 18 In.	2358.00
Sculpture, Powell, Ace, Takin' The Kinks Out, Wood Base, 17 In.	2585.00
Sculpture, Predier, J., Erato, Pedestal, Lyre, Gold Finish, Signed, 1848, 9 ½ x 19 ½ In.	1725.00
Sculpture, Preiss, Golf Lady, Ivory, Marble & Onyx Base, Patina, Signed, Foundry Mark, 12 ½ In.	2520.00
Sculpture, Profillet, Anne-Marie, Pheasant, Art Deco, c.1930, 19 x 28 In. ....*illus*	360.00
Sculpture, Putti, With Paintbrush, Palette, c.1900, 10 ¾ In.	440.00
Sculpture, Putto, On Marble Seat, Playing Tambourine, Green Marble Base, France, 8 x 5 x 4 In.	823.00
Sculpture, Putto, Reclining, Leaning On Mound Of Wheat, France, 8 x 11 ¼ x 4 ½ In.	1058.00
Sculpture, Putto, Seated On Seaweed Rock, Fishing Net, Holding Clamshell, c.1900, 13 In. ...	460.00
Sculpture, Rat, Napoleon III, Among Oak, Ivy Leaves, 2 ¾ x 6 ½ x 4 In.	780.00
Sculpture, Rattlesnake, Brown Patina, 23 In.	384.00
Sculpture, Rhinoceros, Black Marble Base, 20th Century, 10 ¼ x 17 In.	1645.00
Sculpture, Rumsey, Charles, Seated Pan, Playing Instrument, Gilt, Signed, 20 ¼ In.	4800.00
Sculpture, Russian Peasant, Horse, Cart, Patinate, Late 20th Century, 15 x 39 x 14 In.	1998.00
Sculpture, Sandoz, Edouard Marcel, Rabbit, Patina, Signed, Swiss, c.1920, 2 x 4 In. ......*illus*	1898.00
Sculpture, Sanford, E.F., Dog, Great Dane, Lying Down, Brown Patina, Signed, 1913, 5 ¼ x 9 In.	1320.00

Bronze, Sculpture, Semard, Marie-Louis, Exotic Bird, Gilt Detail, Signed, 1900s, 10 In. $2400.00

Bronze, Sculpture, Sheep, Grazing, After Rosa Bonheur, Mid 1800s, 5 ¼ x 7 ¾ x 3 ⅜ In. $375.00

BRONZE

Brownie, Candy Mold, Dude, Lead, Hinged, 1890s, 5 In. $115.00

Brownie, Figure, Policeman, Cast Metal, Painted, c.1900, 2 ¾ In. $115.00

Brush Pottery, Figurine, Frog, Marked, 10 x 6 In. $115.00

Sculpture, Saste, J., Pan & Billy Goat, Green Marble Base, Signed, 8 ½ x 9 ½ x 4 ¾ In.	190.00
Sculpture, Scriver, Bob, Buffalo Bill, 1976, 26 In.	4500.00
Sculpture, Semard, Marie-Louis, Exotic Bird, Gilt Detail, Signed, 1900s, 10 In. *illus*	2400.00
Sculpture, Sheep, Grazing, After Rosa Bonheur, Mid 1800s, 5 ¼ x 7 ¾ x 3 ⅜ In. *illus*	375.00
Sculpture, Shiva, Dancing On Lotus Plinth, India, 19 ½ In.	359.00
Sculpture, Sphinx, Painted Terra-Cotta, Pharaonic Beards, Continental, 25 x 45 In., Pair	4406.00
Sculpture, Spider, Vienna, c.1920, 1 ¾ x 4 ½ In.	495.00
Sculpture, Spirit Of Ecstasy, After Charles Sykes, Brown Patina, Marble Base, 21 ¼ x 11 ¾ In.	259.00
Sculpture, Standing Gentleman, Hand In Pocket, Holding Hat, c.1900, 17 ½ In.	840.00
Sculpture, Stylized Lady, Dog On Leash, Oak Plinth, 8 In.	90.00
Sculpture, Taylor, R., Eagle, Abstract, Titled Eagle's Watch, Patinated, Marble Base, 15 In.	633.00
Sculpture, The Fencing Lesson, Marble Base, 19th Century, 31 x 17 x 14 In.	3062.00
Sculpture, Tiger, Stepped Base, Barbedienne, Stamped, 10 ⅝ In.	1896.00
Sculpture, Tiger, Striding, Roaring, Brown Patina, Glass Eyes, Wood Plinth Base, 13 x 31 In.	1150.00
Sculpture, Tigers, Attacking Bull, c.1900, 10 x 17 In.	1770.00
Sculpture, Tigers, Attacking Elephant, Variegated Patina, c.1900, 7 x 11 In.	1298.00
Sculpture, Titze, Jester, Female, Art Deco, Ivory Face, Signed, 8 In.	420.00
Sculpture, Valiqar, Man, Discus Thrower, Classical Style, Round Base, Signed, 22 ½ In.	1708.00
Sculpture, Vaquero, On Horse, Raised Marble Base, Mexico, 1936, 12 ¾ In.	948.00
Sculpture, Vidal, L., Bull, Standing, Head Lowered, Naturalistic, 13 x 18 In.	2489.00
Sculpture, Waholi, Nude Philosopher, Pointing, Signed, 10 x 27 In.	920.00
Sculpture, Warrior, Holding Sword & Shield, 20th Century, 15 x 6 In.	82.00
Sculpture, Warrior, Wearing Armor, Helmet, Fighting Stance, Marble Plinth, Japan, 19 ½ In.	235.00
Sculpture, Warrior, Wounded, Bugles, Sword, Brown Patina, 17 ½ x 9 ½ In.	690.00
Sculpture, Waterfowl, Gold Patina, France, c.1880, 8 x 7 In.	558.00
Sculpture, Woman, Draped, Looking Right, Brown Patina, 24 In.	649.00
Sculpture, Woman, Holding Lyre, Cupid, Holding Triangle, Signed, France, 1865, 16 ¾ In.	2844.00
Sculpture, Woman, With Tambourine, Patina, Square Wood Base, c.1858, 48 x 15 In.	10980.00
Sculpture, Women, Gathering Flowers, Patina, Green Marble Plinth, 28 In.	948.00
Sculpture, Yamagata, Pipe Man, Striped Pants, Red Tie, Marble Base, Signed, 17 x 10 x 8 In.	480.00
Sculpture, Youth, Seated, Bird On Knee, Oval Base, Marble Stand, France, 19th Century, 10 In.	593.00
Sculpture, Zach, B., Woman, With Sword, Gilt Body, Green Hat, Shorts, 1935, 29 x 12 In.	5700.00
Sign, Confessions 5:00-7:00 Daily, 2 ½ x 7 ¼ In.	89.00
Sign, For Use Of Patients Only, 3 x 10 In.	47.00
Tazza, Center Portrait Medallion, Scrolled Leaf Shape Handles, Continental, 7 ¼ x 7 ½ In.	161.00
Tray, Bust Of Bacchus, Cherubs, Wrestling, Flower Garlands, Ball Feet, 18 ¼ x 12 In.	326.00
Tray, Hurley, Spider & Web, 5 In.	633.00
Tray, Pen, Enameled Design, Patina, Marked, Art Crafts Shop, 10 x 3 In.	210.00
Urn, Campagna, Gilt, Classical Figural Frieze, Leaf, Egg & Dart Band, Marble Plinth, 9 ⅝ In.	235.00
Urn, Charles X, Dore, Handles, Ram's Head, 8 ½ x 4 ½ x 3 In., Pair	2350.00
Urn, Cover, Flower Festoons, Lion Masks, Rings, Brown Patina, 18 In.	593.00
Urn, Dancing Satyrs, Putti, Pedestal, Empire Style, 13 ¼ In.	1195.00
Urn, Embossed, Maitland Smith, 13 x 19 In., Pair	761.00
Urn, Gilt, 2 Handles, Leaves, Berries, Roman Procession Band, Black Slate Base, 11 ½ In.	385.00
Urn, Inverted Bell Form, Twisted Dragon Stem, Rockwork Base, Waves, c.1900, 24 In.	1600.00
Urn, Onyx, Bulbous, Gilt Bronze Fittings, Scrolled Handles, Lion's Masks, Early 1800s, 19 In.	1350.00
Vase, Art Deco, Brown, Green, Handles, 9 ½ In.	89.00
Vase, Arts & Crafts, Bulbous, Inverted Rim, c.1900, 4 ½ x 4 ¼ In.	365.00
Vase, Bud, Moreal, August, Cupids, 8 ½ In.	1404.00
Vase, Champleve, Arts & Crafts, Oak Leaves, Vines, Enamel, 8 ¾ x 3 ⅛ In.	160.00
Vase, Champleve, Multicolored, Chinese, 10 x 13 In.	176.00
Vase, Cockerels, Branches, Flowers, Metal Inlays, Japan, 1900s, 8 In., Pair	633.00
Vase, Dragon, Relief, Pear Shape, Trumpet Mouth, 1800s, 13 In.	58.00
Vase, Flower Arranger, Gilt, Flower Frog, 3 Rooster Feet, 2 Sections, Japan, 10 ½ x 11 ¾ In.	540.00
Vase, Flowers, Animals, Silver, Gold, Inlay, Phoenix Handles, Japan, 1890s, 14 In., Pair	800.00
Vase, Louchet, Woman, Nude, Bulrushes, Art Nouveau, Marked, Paris, 10 In.	2500.00
Vase, Korschann, Charles, Woman, Leaves, Round, Flared Base, Signed, 16 x 5 ½ In.	2520.00
Vase, Prunus Branches, Gold & Black, Brown Patina, Tapered, Cherry Stem Handles, 12 In., Pair	1778.00
Vase, Samurai Helmet, Shishi, Scrolls, Patina, Japan, 21 In.	4800.00
Vase, Serpentine Dragons, Birds, Bulbous, Tubular Body, 24 In., Pair	1500.00
Vase, Sorensen, Carl, Green, Textured, Brass Bands, 6 ½ In.	58.00
Vase, Spiders, Webs, Silver & Copper Bamboo Plants, Marked, c.1930, 13 ⅛ In., Pair	384.00
Wall Hanger, Adam & Eve, Garden Of Eden, Snake Hook, c.1900, 7 ½ x 9 ¼ In.	176.00

BROWNIES were first drawn in 1883 by Palmer Cox. They are characterized by large round eyes, downturned mouths, and skinny legs. Toys, books, dinnerware, and other objects were made with the Brownies as part of the design.

Bottle, Figural, Majolica, 7 In.	35.00
Candlestick, Sailor, Figural, Majolica, 9 In.	141.00
Candlestick, Uncle Sam, Figural, Majolica, 9 In.	250.00
Candy Mold, Dude, Lead, Hinged, 1890s, 5 In.	*illus* 115.00
Croquet Wicket, Cast Iron, Painted, Signed, G. Freihofer, 16 x 7 ¾ In., Pair	1025.00
Figure, Policeman, Cast Metal, Painted, c.1900, 2 ¾ In.	*illus* 115.00
Humidor, Sailor's Head, Defender On Hat Rim, Majolica, 6 ¼ In.	169.00
Match Holder, Brownie, Resting On Stump, Schafer & Vader, 1880s, 7 ¼ In.	240.00

BRUSH POTTERY was started in 1925. George Brush first worked in 1901 in Zanesville, Ohio. He started his own pottery in 1907, but it burned to the ground soon after. In 1909 he became manager of the J.W. McCoy Pottery. In 1911, Brush and J.W. McCoy formed the Brush-McCoy Pottery Co. After a series of name changes, the company became The Brush Pottery in 1925. It closed in 1982. Old Brush was marked with impressed letters or a palette-shaped mark. Some new pieces are being marked in raised letters or with a raised mark. Collectors favor the figural cookie jars made by this company. Because there was a company named Brush-McCoy, there is great confusion between Brush and Nelson McCoy pieces. See McCoy category for more information.

Ashtray, Double Frog, Open Mouths, Marked, 42, 2 ⅞ x 7 In.	48.00
Bowl, Zuniart, Off-White Ground, Blue, Green Design, 1923-28, 8 ¼ x 2 ½ In.	450.00
Candleholder, Amaryllis, Majolica Glaze, 3 ½ x 3 ¾ In.	25.00
Cookie Jar, Crock, Embossed Cookies, Pink, Bat Finial	41.00
Cookie Jar, Davy Crockett, c.1956, 10 ½ In.	458.00
Cookie Jar, Formal Pig, Marked, W-7, U.S.A., 11 In.	114.00
Cookie Jar, Granny, Holding Rolling Pin, Plaid Skirt, 1956	80.00
Cookie Jar, Hippo, Monkey On Back, 1961	300.00
Cookie Jar, Humpty Dumpty, Marked, 9 ⅞ In.	66.00
Cookie Jar, Old Shoe, Shoe-Shaped House, 1959	72.00
Cookie Jar, Rabbit Chef, Blue Scarf, Chef Hat, Impressed, W25 Brush, U.S.A., 14 In.	44.00
Cookie Jar, Teddy Bear, Feet Together, 1940s, 11 In.	180.00 to 189.00
Figurine, Frog, Marked, 10 x 6 In.	*illus* 115.00
Figurine, Owl, Stylized, Yellow, c.1968, 6 ¾ x 4 ¾ In.	36.00
Flower Frog, Fish Shape, Green Gloss Glaze, c.1915, 4 x 3 In.	61.00
Flowerpot, Saucer, Olive Green, Wood Grain Design, 5 ½ x 5 ¾ In.	20.00
Jardiniere, Grapes, Green, Blue, Purple Glaze, 8 ⅜ x 10 In.	95.00
Jardiniere, Lion's Head, Green, Brown Glaze, 8 ¾ x 9 ½ In.	155.00
Jardiniere, Roses & Satyr, Brown Glaze, 9 x 10 In.	135.00
Match Holder, Striker, Kolor-Kraft, Dark Maroon, Ribbed, 1930s, 6 ¼ In.	250.00
Planter, Swan, Yellow, 5 ¼ x 6 In.	17.00
Planter, Textured Basket Weave, Green Gloss Glaze, 4 ¼ x 7 x 5 ½ In.	18.00
Vase, Acanthus, White Glaze, Leaves, Ringed Collar, 8 ½ In.	31.00
Vase, Marbleized Aqua Glaze, Handles, 5 ½ x 8 ½ In.	27.00
Vase, Onyx, Ginger Jar, 1920s, 6 ¼ In.	45.00

BRUSH-MCCOY, *See Brush category and related pieces in McCoy category.*

BUCK ROGERS was the first American science fiction comic strip. It started in 1929 and continued until 1967. Buck has also appeared in comic books, movies, and, in the 1980s, a television series. Any memorabilia connected with the character Buck Rogers is collectible.

Button, 25th Century Acousticon Jr., Buck & Wilma, Multicolored, c.1937, 2 ¼ In.	3061.00
Helmet, Cloth, Ear Flaps, Snap Closures, Celluloid Ear Guards, c.1935	173.00
Toy, Car, Police Patrol, Striped Wings, Nose, Siren, Clockwork, Marx, Box, 1927, 12 In.	1725.00
Toy, Comet Socker, Ball Paddle, Morton's Salt, Lee-Tex, Die Cut, Cardboard, c.1935, 5 x 8 ½ In.	575.00
Toy, Daisy Atomic Pistol, Buck Rogers 25th Century, 10 In.	195.00
Toy, Pistol, Atomic, U-235, Gold, Pressed Steel, Emits Pop, Daisy Mfg., Box, 9 ½ In.	690.00
Toy, Pistol, Futuristic, Pressed Steel, Molded Sight, Daisy Mfg., 9 ½ In.	115.00
Toy, Rocket Ship, Green, Yellow, Black, Tin Lithograph, Clockwork, Marx, 12 In.	2588.00
Toy, Rocket Ship, Tin Lithograph, Windup, Insert, Box, Marx, c.1935, 12 In.	*illus* 1521.00
Toy, Sonic Ray Gun, Black, Yellow, Red, Battery Operated, Box, 1952, 7 ½ In.	285.00
Toy, Water Pistol, Liquid Helium, Steel Lithograph, Daisy, 1936, 7 ¼ In.	288.00 to 601.00

BUFFALO POTTERY was made in Buffalo, New York, after 1902. The company was established by the Larkin Company, famous manufacturers of soap. The wares are marked with a picture of a buffalo and the date of manufacture. Deldare ware is the most famous pottery made at the factory. It has either a khaki-colored or green background with hand-painted transfer designs.

Buck Rogers, Toy, Rocket Ship, Tin Lithograph, Windup, Insert, Box, Marx, c.1935, 12 In.
$1521.00

Buffalo Pottery Deldare, Bowl, Ye Village Street, A. Delaney, c.1909, 3 ¼ x 7 ⅝ In.
$236.00

Buffalo Pottery Deldare, Teapot, Breaking Cover, Marked HB, c.1908, 4 ½ In.
$443.00

Buffalo Potter Deldare, Vase, Rouge Ware, Fallowfield Hunt, Breaking Cover, Marked, 8 In.
$288.00

Burmese Glass, Bride's Basket,
Trifold Ruffled Rim Bowl, Silver Plate,
Mt. Washington, 9 In.
$1610.00

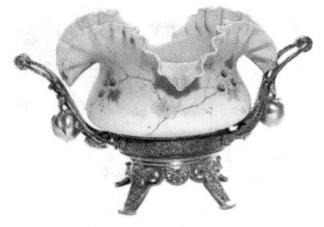

Burmese Glass, Ewer,
Pink Shaded To Yellow,
Swirling Flower Bands, Applied Handle,
10 x 8 In.
$4600.00

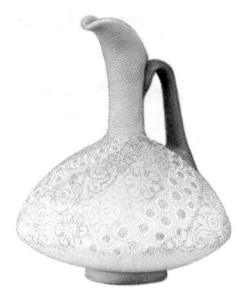

Burmese Glass, Vase,
Multicolored Flowers, Bulbous,
Cylindrical Neck, Mt. Washington,
9 ½ x 5 ½ In.
$546.00

Buster Brown, Beanbag Toss,
Buster & Tige, Lithograph,
Paper On Wood, c.1900, 10 x 24 In.
$99.00

BUFFALO POTTERY

Butter Tub, Pink Roses, Leaves, Blue Ground, Gold Handles, 5 ⅛ x 2 ½ In.	40.00
Canister, Cover, Sugar, Medallion, Roses, Blue Print Band, Gold Accents, 8 ¼ In.	60.00
Pitcher, Buffalo Hunt, c.1905	425.00
Pitcher, Cinderella, Transfer, Hand Tinted, c.1906, 11 ½ x 17 In.	286.00
Pitcher, Gloriana, Female Nymphs In Garden, Flowers, Foxes, Marked, 9 ⅛ In.	295.00
Pitcher, Rip Van Winkle, c.1906, 6 ½ In.	350.00
Pitcher, Robin Hood, c.1907, 8 ½ In.	325.00
Pitcher, Roosevelt Bears, Sepia Transfer, 7 ⅞ In.	1490.00
Plate, Dinner, Pink Flowers, Gold Trim, Scalloped Edge, c.1920, 9 ½ In.	15.00
Plate, Wild Ducks & Wild Game, Teal, Scalloped Edge, c.1907, 9 In.	55.00
Tankard, Maritime Theme, Ships, Sailors, Lighthouse, Flow Blue, Marked, 9 In.	175.00

BUFFALO POTTERY DELDARE

Bowl, Fallowfield Hunt, Signed, 1909, 9 In.	375.00
Bowl, Fallowfield Hunt, The Death, Interior Scene, A. Stiner, 3 ¾ x 9 In.	236.00
Bowl, Village Tavern, c.1924, 3 ¾ x 9 In.	425.00
Bowl, Ye Village Street, A. Delaney, c.1909, 3 ¼ x 7 ⅝ In. ....*illus*	236.00
Bowl, Ye Village Tavern, Marked, 1908, 9 In.	280.00
Candlestick, Village Scene, Signed, 1909, 9 ½ x 5 In.	450.00
Charger, An Evening At Ye Lion Inn, Marked, 13 ¾ In.	1900.00
Charger, Fallowfield Hunt, Breakfast At The 3 Pigeons, c.1908, 12 In.	495.00
Humidor, Dome Cover, Ye Lion Inn, 8-Sided, Scenic, Marked, 1909, 6 ¾ In.	190.00
Humidor, Dr. Syntax Returned Home, Emerald, 1911, 7 ½ In.	280.00
Mug, Dr. Syntax Again Filled Up His Glass, Marked, 1911, 5 ¼ In.	410.00
Pitcher, Fallowfield Hunt, Breaking Cover, Marked, 1909, 8 ¾ In.	99.00
Pitcher, Vicar Of Wakefield, 8-Sided, c.1908, 9 In.	650.00
Plaque, An Evening At Ye Lion Inn, Signed, 1908, 13 ½ In.	236.00
Plate, At Ye Lion In, Signed, J. Gerhardt, c.1908, 6 ¼ In.	110.00
Plate, Dr. Syntax Observing Man Wooing Susan, Emerald, Marked, 10 In.	345.00
Plate, Dr. Syntax Star Gazing, Signed, M. Gerhardt, c.1911, 9 ½ In.	600.00
Plate, Fallowfield Hunt, The Death, c.1909, 8 ¼ In.	125.00
Plate, Ye Olden Times, 9 ½ In.	60.00
Plate, Ye Village Street, Marked, 7 ⅜ In.	166.00
Teapot, Breaking Cover, Marked HB, c.1908, 4 ½ In. ....*illus*	443.00
Vase, Rouge Ware, Fallowfield Hunt, Breaking Cover, Marked, 8 In. ....*illus*	288.00

BUNNYKINS, *see Royal Doulton category.*

BURMESE GLASS was developed by Frederick Shirley at the Mt. Washington Glass Works in New Bedford, Massachusetts, in 1885. It is a two-toned glass, shading from peach to yellow. Some pieces have a pattern mold design. A few Burmese pieces were decorated with pictures or applied glass flowers of colored Burmese glass. Other factories made similar glass also called Burmese. Related items may be listed in the Fenton category, the Gundersen category, and under Webb Burmese.

Berry Bowl, Ruffled Edge, 4 ½ x 1 In.	150.00
Bowl, 3 Serpentine Legs, Ivy Leaves, Vine, 3 x 3 ½ In.	748.00
Bowl, Trifold Ruffled Rim, Shading Yellow To Pink, Striped, Mt. Washington, 9 In.	575.00
Bride's Basket, 2 Ruffled Bowls, Silver Plated Holder, Pairpoint, 20 x 19 In.	8000.00
Bride's Basket, Trifold Ruffled Rim Bowl, Silver Plate, Mt. Washington, 9 In. ....*illus*	1610.00
Compote, Bulging Stem, Ruffled Rim, Saucer Foot, Glossy, 4 ½ x 7 In., Pair	403.00
Creamer, Cone Shape, Crimped Rim, Applied Handles, Mt. Washington, 5 ½ In.	403.00
Cruet, Ribbed, Stopper, Applied Handle, Mt. Washington, 6 ½ In., Pair	489.00
Ewer, Pink Shaded To Yellow, Swirling Flower Bands, Applied Handle, 10 x 8 In. ....*illus*	4600.00
Finger Bowl, Tooled Rectangular Rim, Pontil, Mt. Washington, c.1875, 2 x 2 x 5 In.	79.00
Lamp, Scalloped Rim Shade, Footed, Embossed Baluster Stand, Mt. Washington, 7 & 9 ½ In.	2645.00
Pitcher, Applied Green Vine, Leaves & Reeded Handle, Ruffled Edge, 9 ¼ In.	230.00
Pitcher, Tankard, Enameled Ivy, Green, Brown, Handle, 9 In.	3738.00
Shade, Scalloped Rim, Bell Shape, Mt. Washington Satin Finish, 5 In.	115.00
Sugar & Creamer, Applied Reed Handles	800.00
Sugar & Creamer, Teardrop & Dot, Beaded, Enamel	2600.00
Toothpick, Enameled Chrysanthemums, Bulbous, Square Mouth, 2 ¾ In.	403.00
Toothpick, Enameled Mums, Yellow, White, Tricornered, 2 In.	272.00
Toothpick, Glossy, Mt. Washington	259.00
Toothpick, Green, Pink, Blue Flowers, Mt. Washington, 2 ½ In.	295.00
Toothpick, Hat Shape, Enamel Flowers, Barrel Shape, Mt. Washington	288.00
Toothpick, Hat Shape, White Flowers, Mt. Washington	546.00

Vase, Berry & Leaf, 2 ½ x 3 ¼ In.	230.00
Vase, Bulbous, Crimped Rim, 3 ¼ In.	115.00
Vase, Bulbous, Enameled Gold Swirls, Leaves, Mt. Washington, 12 In.	1380.00
Vase, Bulbous, Long Neck, Daisies, Leaves, Mt. Washington, 5 ¼ x 7 In.	518.00
Vase, Bulbous, Narrow Neck, Mt. Washington, 12 In.	230.00
Vase, Bulbous, Tricornered Ruffled Edge, Footed, 12 ½ In.	403.00
Vase, Daisies, Enamel, Oval, Footed, Folded Rim, Mt. Washington, c.1890, 13 In.	1175.00
Vase, Double Gourd, 6 ¾ In.	421.00
Vase, Egyptian Bottle Form, Elongated Scroll Handles, 12 In.	572.00
Vase, Glossy, Scalloped Rim, Footed, 10 ¼ In.	385.00
Vase, Gourd, 4 Enameled Swallows, Gold Beaded Rim, 8 In.	4690.00
Vase, Lavender Flowers, Leaves, Acid Finish, 3 In., Pair	288.00
Vase, Multicolored Flowers, Bulbous, Cylindrical Neck, Mt. Washington, 9 ½ x 5 ½ In. ...illus	546.00
Vase, Oval, Trifold Inverted Rim, 3 Reeded Feet, Raspberry Pontil, Mt. Washington, 7 In.	253.00
Vase, Pink, Yellow, Enameled Flower, Leaves, Berries, Matte Finish, Mt. Washington, 12 In.	690.00
Vase, Stick Neck, Bulbous Base, Pink Rose, Mt. Washington, 6 In.	700.00
Vase, Tooled Rim, Pinched Neck, Pontil, c.1875, 2 ½ x 3 ¼ In.	79.00
Vase, Trumpet, Scalloped Rim, 10 In.	345.00
Vase, Urn Form, Handles, Metal Rod, Ruffled Foot, Stopper, 4-Part, 14 In.	395.00
Vase, Yellow, Orange, White Flowers, Pink, Yellow Ground, Oval, Mt. Washington, 4 ½ In.	518.00

BUSTER BROWN, the comic strip, first appeared in color in 1902. Buster and his dog, Tige, remained a popular comic and soon became even more famous as the emblem for a shoe company, a textile firm, and other companies. The strip was discontinued in 1920. Buster Brown sponsored a radio show from 1943 to 1955 and a TV show from 1950 to 1956. The Buster Brown characters are still used by Brown Shoe Company, Buster Brown Apparel, Inc., and Gateway Hosiery.

Balloon Blowerhead, Painted, Fiber Glass, 1960s, 21 x 24 In.	308.00
Bank, Buster Brown & Tige, Cast Iron, Painted, A.C. Williams, 6 In.	95.00
Bank, Buster Brown & Tige, Gold, Red, Cream, Iron, A.C. Williams, 5 In.	120.00 to 182.00
Bank, Buster Brown & Tige, Horseshoe, Gold, Black, Cast Iron, Arcade, 5 x 4 In.	190.00 to 336.00
Beanbag Toss, Buster & Tige, Lithograph, Paper On Wood, c.1900, 10 x 24 In. ...illus	99.00
Button, Red Shirt, Tige Facing Left, Ehrman, c. 1908, 1 ¼ In. ...illus	115.00
Camera, Ansco, No. 2A, Wood, Leather, Black, Box, 1920s, 6 ¼ x 5 ¼ In.	30.00
Clicker, Hosiery, Tin, 1 x 1 ¼ In.	20.00
Finger Puppet, Mask, Die Cut, Multicolored, 8 ½ In.	13.00
Magic Pad, Plastic, Cardboard, Red Wood Stylus, 8 ¼ x 5 ¼ In.	20.00
Mirror, Buster Brown Vacation Days Carnival, Celluloid, 2 ¼ In.	24.00
Pin, Buster Brown Shoes, Green Ground, Early 1900s, 1 ½ In.	285.00
Rattle, Pacifier, Mother-Of-Pearl, Sterling, Engraved, 1 ¼ x 3 ¼ In. ...illus	234.00
Sign, Golden Sheaf Bakery, Buster Brown Bread, Embossed, 1920s, 20 x 28 In.	1165.00
Toy, Buster & Tige, Rocking, Tin, Windup, Face Each Other, Gunthermann, 9 In.	1265.00
Toy, Rocking Wonder Horse, Painted, Decals, 1950s	550.00
Toy, Roly Poly, Weighted Base, Painted, 2 ¼ In.	85.00

BUTTER MOLDS *are listed in the Kitchen category under Mold, Butter.*

BUTTON collecting has been popular since the nineteenth century. Buttons have been known throughout the centuries, and there are millions of styles. Gold, silver, or precious stones were used for the best buttons, but most were made of natural materials, like bone or shell, or from inexpensive metals. Only a few types are listed for comparison.

Antler, Carved, Doe, 1 ¾ In.	125.00
Bakelite, Pear, Large	25.00
Brass, Figural, Bowling Pins & Ball, Patina, ¾ In.	10.00
Brass, Scroll & Fleur-De-Lis, Turquoise, 18th Century, 1 ½ In.	65.00
Celluloid, Stylized Peacock, Extra Large	130.00
Chained Crown, Stag, Standing, Escutcheon On Pearl, Large	660.00
Collar, Removable, 6 Small Crystals Around Big Crystal, Gold Filled Fastener, 1800s	19.00
Collar, Removable, Diamond Solitaire, 10K Yellow Gold, Curlicue Fastener, Late 1800s	39.00
Cover, Sterling Silver, Flower, 1 In., Pair	59.00
Cuff, Continental Soldier's Uniform, Cast Pewter, c.1775, ⅞ In.	492.00
Czechoslovakian Glass, Painted, Glass Loop, Card, 1920s, ¾ In., 5 Piece	21.00
Enamel, Bamboo, Gin-Bari, Medium	120.00
Enamel, Bird, Grape Leaf, Gold Filled, Victorian, ¾ In.	38.00
Enamel, Floral Gin-Bari, Medium	120.00

Buster Brown, Button, Red Shirt, Tige Facing Left, Ehrman, c.1908, 1 ¼ In. $115.00

Buster Brown, Rattle, Pacifier, Mother-Of-Pearl, Sterling, Engraved, 1 ¼ x 3 ¼ In. $234.00

Buttonhook, Celluloid, Breakfast Cheer Coffee, 3 x 6 ½ In. $117.00

BUTTON

Calendar,1891,
Great Rock Island Route,
Train Passengers, Cardboard, 14 x 22 In.
$2200.00

Calendar,1930, Orange Julep,
It's Julep Time, Frame, 12 ½ x 26 ½ In.
$234.00

Calendar,1937, Penn. Railroad,
Multicolored Graphic, Dec. Page,
28 x 29 In.
$59.00

Enamel, Flowers, Pastes, Large	110.00
Enamel, Flowers, Pink & Blue Flowers, France, 1 In.	85.00
Horn, Carved, Geometrics, 4 Holes, 1 ½ In.	18.00
Hosiery, Tin, 1 x 1 ¾ In.	20.00
Ivory, Bird, Flowers, Leaves, Carved, 4-Way Self Shank, 1920s, 1 In.	60.00
Ivory, French Diplomat, 18th Century, Large	1100.00
Ivory, Man In 16th Century Costume, Medium	100.00
Jewel, Ray Art Glass Cabochon, Riveted Cut Steel, 1 ½ In.	55.00
Lacquer, Silver, Zodiac, Russia, 12 Piece	130.00
Liverpool, Dog, Transfer, Medium	330.00
Metal, German Man, Riding Sled Downhill, Marked, Heil Rodl, 1 ¼ In.	50.00
Mother-Of-Pearl, ¼ In.	7.00
Mother-Of-Pearl, Discs, Blue-Green Enamel Border, Silver, Liberty & Co., 6 Piece	366.00
Mother-Of-Pearl, Fish, Carved, ¾ x ½ In.	10.00
Paperweight, Flowers, Charles Kazium	340.00
Plastic, Basket Form, Fruit, Hand Painted, 1 x ⅞ In.	7.00
Porcelain, Man With Flowers, Set In Silver, High Dome, Extra Large	1320.00
Satsuma, Woman In Kimono, Arranging Flowers, Extra Large	550.00
Sterling Silver, Woman's Profile, Art Nouveau, c.1900, 1 In.	75.00
Transfer-On-Porcelain, Classical Profile, Purple Ground, Cobalt Blue, Pair	230.00
Victorian, Roses, White Field, Blue Ground, Parrot Tulip, Hand Painted, 13 ⅛ In., 4 Piece	35.00

BUTTONHOOKS have been a popular collectible in England for many years but are now gaining the attention of American collectors. The buttonhooks were made to help fasten the many buttons of the old-fashioned high-button shoes and other items of apparel.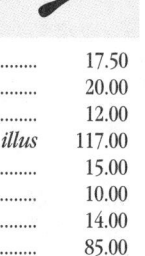

Bakelite Handle, 4 ¾ In.	17.50
Bone Handle, 4 ¾ In.	20.00
Celluloid Handle, Steel, Made In USA, 1890-1910, 8 In.	12.00
Celluloid, Breakfast Cheer Coffee, 3 x 6 ½ In. ....*illus*	117.00
Celluloid, Scalloped Shape, Ivory Color, c.1900, 6 ½ In.	15.00
Celluloid, Steel Hook, Ivory Color	10.00
Edwardian, Dark Wood Handle, Early 1900s, 7 In.	14.00
Folding, Steel, George B Mallory Taxi-Auto-Livery, Telephone 92-J	85.00
Folding, Steel, Open Loop Handle, c.1800, 2 ¾ In.	17.00
French Ivory, Metal, 7 ¾ In.	7.50
Ivory Handle, Metal Hook, France, 6 ½ In.	8.50
Robert Peschke, Flat Loop Top, 5 ⅛ In.	12.50
Silver Plate, Wrapped Top, Ornate Openwork, 7 In.	28.00
Silver, Raised Flowers, Art Nouveau, 7 In.	25.00
Sterling Silver, Edwardian, Marked, C. & N., Hallmark, Birmingham 1906	80.00
Sterling Silver, Embossed, Dove, Old Man Face, Hallmark, WJM Lion, 8 ¾ In.	190.00
Sterling Silver, Garland & Bow, Mark, Birks Sterling, 8 ¼ In.	220.00
Sterling Silver, Repousse, Hallmark, Anchor, 4 ½ In.	125.00
Sterling Silver, Tiffany & Co., Art Nouveau, Monogram, Signed, 7 ½ In.	290.00
Victorian, Ebony Handle, Signed, 8 In.	95.00

BYBEE POTTERY of Bybee, Kentucky, was started by Webster Cornelison. The company claims it started in 1809, although sales records were not kept until 1845. The pottery is still operated by members of the sixth generation of the Cornelison family. The handmade stoneware pottery is sold at the factory. Various marks were used, including the name Bybee, the name Cornelison, or the initials BB. Not all pieces are marked. A mark shaped like the state of Kentucky with the words "Genuine Bybee" and similar marks were used by a different company, Bybee Pottery Company of Lexington, Kentucky. It was a distributor of various pottery lines from 1922 to 1929.

Bank, Pig, Standing, Gray, Glossy, 5 ⅝ In.	16.00
Pitcher, Rebecca, Blue, Handles, 15 ½ x 9 In.	50.00

CALENDARS made to hang on the wall or to be displayed on a desk top have been popular since the last quarter of the nineteenth century. Many were printed with advertising as part of the artwork and were given away as premiums. Calendars with guns, gunpowder, or Coca-Cola advertising are most prized.

1891, Great Rock Island Route, Train Passengers, Cardboard, 14 x 22 In. ....*illus*	2200.00
1891, Pure Rye Whiskey, Pinup, Lithographed Cardboard, December, 19 x 10 In.	600.00
1891-92, Simmon's Iron Cordial, King Of Tonics, Sept. To Sept., 6 x 9 In.	66.00
1896, Bartholomay Brew Co., Lady Holding Glass, Full Pad, Frame, 46 ½ x 36 ¼ In.	2750.00

1900, Laflin & Rand Powder Co., Great Elk Picture, 4 x 6 In.	364.00
1901, Dr. Daniels' Veterinary Medicines, Women, Horse, Dog, Paper, Metal, 15 x 20 In.	990.00
1901, Dr. Daniels' Veterinary Medicines, Woman & Gentleman, 20 x 14 In.	390.00
1901, Laflin & Rand Powder Co., American Warrior, Soldiers, Indian, Frame, 20 x 26 In.	425.00
1902, Laflin & Rand Powder Co., It's Infallible, 3 Men, 24 x 16 In.	1750.00
1902, Light Of The Home, Child's Portrait, Paper, Lithograph, Frame, 13 x 9 ½ In.	30.00
1905, 4 Girls, 4 Seasons, Frame, 29 x 10 In.	240.00
1905, Youth's Companion Magazine, Girl With Flowers, Trifold, Cardboard, 11 x 20 In.	110.00
1906, Libby, McNeill & Libby, Corned Beef, Girl, In Straw Hat, Frame	187.00
1906, Mutual Life Insurance, Indian, First American, Full Pad, 22 x 14 In.	285.00
1907, DuPont Powder Co., Dog, Pointer, Black & White, 20 ½ x 30 In.	480.00
1907, Frank Coe-Mortimer Fertilizers, Farmer, Man In Car, Frame, 16 x 12 In.	1100.00
1907, Morton & Taylor, Victorian Woman, Asti, Calendar Pad, Athens, Ga., 21 x 15 In.	120.00
1910, California Perfume Co., Image Of Woman In Bonnet, 12 x 9 In.	635.00
1910, California Perfume Co, Woman With Red Hair, Green Hat, 12 x 9 In.	635.00
1910, DuPont, Thomas Jefferson & General Du Pont, Tin On Cardboard, 19 x 29 In.	1210.00
1910, Hood's, Girl, Pink Bow In Hair, Frame, 13 x 12 In.	142.00
1911, April, Man, Horse, Whitehead & Hoag, Cardboard, 4 ½ x 10 ½ In.	32.00
1913, O.H. Woodward, Gen. Hardware, Woman, Die Cut, Embossed, Frame, 14 x 20	202.00
1914, Cardoza Bros. Bakers, Cowgirl On Horse, Embossed, Die Cut, 22 ½ x 11 In.	825.00
1914, Pabst, Extract, Victorian Lady, Orange Dress, 37 x 10 In.	250.00
1916, DeLaval Cream Separators, Boy, Girl On Counter, Frame, 16 x 28 In.	374.00
1916, Red Wing Advertising Co., Indian, Metal Bands, December Page Only, 32 x 16 In.	385.00
1918, Italo-American Bread Co., Baker, Woman, Children, James V. Cardi, 22 x 15 In.	90.00
1925, DeLaval Cream Separators & Milkers	3480.00
1925, DeLaval Cream Separators & Milkers, Equipment, 52 x 21 In.	3480.00
1926, Cassels Clothing Store, Christy Girl, 37 In.	375.00
1927, General Electric, Bathing Beauty, Pool, Cardboard Lithograph, Hayden, 21 x 10 In.	468.00
1930, Dallas Top Shop & Body Works, Rose O'Kildare, Full Calendar Pad, 47 x 24 In.	180.00
1930, Orange Julep, It's Julep Time, Frame, 12 ½ x 26 ½ In. ....*illus*	234.00
1933, Anheuser-Busch Yeast, Surprising The Camp, Metal Bands, 21 x 14 In.	240.00
1937, Penn. Railroad, Multicolored Graphic, Dec. Page, 28 x 29 In. ....*illus*	59.00
1939, Great Northern Railway, Full Pad, Frame, 39 x 21 In.	132.00
1939, Orange Crush, John Epping Bottling Works, Girl, Peddle Car, Glass, Frame, 36 x 18 In.	300.00
1940, 7Up, Pinup Girl Art, Pad	35.00
1942, Kelly Tires, Woman, In Swimsuit, Green Car, Full Pad, 33 ½ x 16 In.	115.00
1944, Howe Fur Co., Caught With Camera, Copper's Mill, Maine, Frame, 22 x 17 ½ In.	83.00
1944, Pharr, Texas, Woman, Sitting On Wall, Horse, Full Pad, 22 x 17 ½ In.	68.00
1947, Corn Bell Veterinary Medicines, Baby, Wagon, Comical Pigs, Frame, 24 x 17 In.	550.00
1947, Mutual Benefit Life Insurance Co., Evening Landscape, 33 x 16 In.	285.00
1952, Royal Crown Cola, Loretta Young, 13 Month, 11 ½ x 24 In. ....*illus*	115.00
1952, Simonds Saw & Steel Company, Fitchburg, Massachusetts	38.00
1954, Gilmor Liquors, Marilyn Monroe, Golden Dreams, 12 x 18 ½ In.	115.00
1954, Pinup, Gil Elvgren, Roofing Company Ad, Metal Binding, 11 x 23 In. ....*illus*	86.00
1956, Frosty Root Beer, Winter Scene, Frosty Figures, Frame, 15 x 27 In.	173.00
1956, Victor Gaskets, Woman, Eating Lunch, Eastern Auto Supply, Full Pad, 33 x 16 In.	95.00
1957, Marilyn Monroe, Golden Dreams, Peek-A-Boo, Wintersville, Oh., 16 x 9 In.	70.00
1958, Amboy Milk, Cowgirl & Horse, Metal Frame, 34 x 16 In.	36.00
1958, G.L. Pine, Mercersburg	35.00

CALENDAR PLATES were popular in the United States as advertising giveaways from 1906 to 1929. Since then, a few plates have been made every year. A calendar and the name of a store, a picture of flowers, a girl, or a scene were featured on the plate.

1908, Flower Spray Border, Dresden, 8 In.	35.00
1909, Garvanza Meat Market & Grocery, R. Stuart, Homer Laughlin, 10 In.	19.00
1909, Red Lake Fall, Minn., Gold Mark	50.00
1909, Santa Claus, In Car, Toys, Transfer, H.C. Kase, Elysburg, Pa., 7 ⅜ In.	75.00
1910, 2 Cherubs Striking A Bell	20.00
1910, Compliments Of Peter Wolf, General Merchandise, 7 ¼ In.	125.00
1911, Flatbush Trust Company, Brooklyn, N.Y., Dresden	70.00
1911, Globe Jewelry Company, Butte, Montana, World Clock Border, 22K Gold Trim	35.00
1915, Panama Canal, D. Trozzo Company, Pittsburgh, Pa.	45.00
1915, Smith & Hurley, Milford, Del.	18.00
1920, Great World War, Muskegon Heights Furn. Co., Michigan, 8 ¼ In.	35.00
1953, 4 Seasons, Gold On Blue, Homer Laughlin, Jubilee Series, 10 In.	5.00
1957, Months Around Central Scene, Mint Green, 10 In.	10.00
1959, Holland Scene, Blue, Taylor, Smith & Taylor, 9 ¼ In.	10.00

Calendar, 1952, Royal Crown Cola, Loretta Young, 13 Month, 11 ½ x 24 In. $115.00

Calendar, 1954, Pinup, Gil Elvgren, Roofing Company Ad, Metal Binding, 11 x 23 In. $86.00

C

Cambridge Glass, Ball, Jug, Cobalt Blue, Chrome, Farber Brothers, 6 ¾ x 3 ¼ In.
$60.00

Cambridge Glass, Caprice, Wine, Moonlight Blue, 3 Oz.
$75.00

Cambridge Glass, Crown Tuscan, Compote, Mermaid & Shell, Garden Flowers, Gold Highlights, 9 x 12 ½ In.
$546.00

1962, Finke Monument Co., Wentzville, Sabina Line Advertising, 9 In.		10.00
1964, Gold Calendar Center, Seasonal Activities Border, 10 ¼ In.		10.00
1965, Black Printing, White Ground, Pink Flower, Gold Trim, 9 ¾ In.		15.00
1966, 4 Sports, Red & White, 9 In.		18.00
1969, Green, Rimmed Version, Currier & Ives, Royal China, 10 In.		30.00
1972, Zodiac, Gold & White, 10 In.		10.00
1977, God Bless America, Spencer Gifts, Japan, 9 In.		7.50
1977, God Bless Our House Throughout 1977, Brown Transferware, Meakin, 9 ⅛ In.		15.00
1979, Fair Store 90th Anniversary Year, Binghamton, N.Y.		6.00
1980, Home Of The Free, White, Red & Blue Print, Spencer Gifts, Japan		10.00
1983, Zodiac, Blue, Royal Staffordshire, God Bless This House		25.00
1986, Blue, Currier & Ives, Royal China, 10 In.		40.00

CAMARK POTTERY started out as Camden Art Tile and Pottery Company in Camden, Arkansas. Jack Carnes founded the firm in 1926 in association with John Lessell, Stephen Sebaugh, and the Camden Chamber of Commerce. Many types of glazes and wares were made. The company was bought by Mary Daniel in the early 1960s. Production ended in 1983.

Flower Frog, Blue & White Stipple, Triangle, 4 ⅜ In.		50.00
Pitcher, Blue, Parrot Handle, 6 ½ In.		250.00
Vase, Aqua Gloss Glaze, Ringed Base, Ruffled Edge, 5 ⅜ x 6 ¼ In.		50.00
Vase, Arts & Crafts, Drab Green Over Mustard Drip Glaze, Paper Label, 7 ½ In.		425.00
Vase, Azurite Blue, Bulbous, c.1960, 4 ¾ x 4 ¾ In.		60.00
Vase, Blue Gloss Glaze, Squat, Handles, 5 ⅝ x 8 In.		198.00
Vase, Blue Stipple, Triangle Shape, Footed, Foil Label, 2 ½ x 3 ⅜ In.		50.00
Vase, Fan, Frosted Green Glaze, Impressed Mark, 5 ¾ x 7 ⅜ In.		65.00
Vase, Green Gloss Glaze, Flute Leaf Shape, 10 ¼ x 7 In.		18.00
Vase, Green Matte Glaze, 6 x 4 In.		115.00
Vase, Maroon, Tapered, Rippled Handles, Footed, Foil Label, Impressed Mark, 5 ⅝ In.		40.00
Vase, Maroon, Wheel Thrown, Ring Base, Pinched Rim, 5 In.		60.00
Vase, Orange Drip, Over Green, Vertical Leaf, Scalloped Edge, 8 In.		100.00
Vase, White Matte Glaze, Ringed Base, Handles, c.1931, 5 In.		70.00
Vase, White Matte Glaze, Tapered, Twisted, Square Mouth, 9 x 3 ¾ In.		35.00
Vase, Yellow Gloss Glaze, Tapered, Twisted, Square Mouth, 12 ½ x 5 ½ In.		65.00

CAMBRIDGE GLASS COMPANY was founded in 1901 in Cambridge, Ohio. The company closed in 1954, reopened briefly, and closed again in 1958. The firm made all types of glass. Its early wares included heavy pressed glass with the mark *Near Cut*. Later wares included Crown Tuscan, etched stemware, and clear and colored glass. The firm used a *C* in a triangle mark after 1920.

Azurite, Candy Dish, Cover, Pedestal, 11 In.		295.00
Azurite, Compote, 6 ½ In.		75.00
Azurite, Console, Low, 12 In.		78.00
Ball, Jug, Cobalt Blue, Chrome, Farber Brothers, 6 ¾ x 3 ¼ In.	*illus*	60.00
Candlelight, Plate, Luncheon, 8 ½ In.		35.00
Caprice, Candlestick, 3-Light, 6 ¼ x 10 In., Pair		96.00
Caprice, Candlestick, 3-Light, Cascading, 6 ½ x 6 ½ In., Pair		55.00
Caprice, Cigarette Set, Moonlight Blue, Triangular, 5 Piece		185.00
Caprice, Oil Cruet, Stopper, Moonlight Blue, 4 ¾ In.		65.00
Caprice, Relish, 2 Sections, Moonlight Blue, 6 ½ In.		68.00
Caprice, Salt & Pepper, Tray, 5 ¾ In.		95.00
Caprice, Wine, Moonlight Blue, 3 Oz.	*illus*	75.00
Chantilly Etch, Compote, Sterling Foot, c.1936, 6 x 6 ¾ In.		135.00
Chantilly, Champagne, 6 Oz.		30.00
Cleo, Cigarette Jar, Cover, Pink, No. 617, 4 In.		395.00
Colonial, Toothpick, Clear, 2 x 2 In.		13.00
Crown Tuscan, Compote, Mermaid & Shell, Garden Flowers, Gold Highlights, 9 x 12 ½ In.	*illus*	546.00
Crown Tuscan, Compote, Pink, Flowers, Ship, Marked, 9 ¼ x 5 ¼ In.	*illus*	195.00
Decagon, Cup & Saucer, Moonlight Blue		22.00
Decagon, Plate, Luncheon, Amber, 8 In.		12.00
Decagon, Plate, Luncheon, Green, 8 In.		16.00
Decagon, Sandwich Server, Center Handle, Amber, 10 ½ x 5 In.	*illus*	49.00
Decanter, Barrel Shape, Ring Handle, Platinum Trim, 4 Barrel Shape Glasses, 5 Piece		525.00
Diane, Relish, 5 Sections, 1 Long & 4 Small Sections, 12 In.		65.00
Diane, Vase, Globe Shape, 3 ½ In.		95.00
Georgian, Tumbler, Amberina, Ruby To Amber, 4 In., 14 Piece		230.00
Iced Tea Set, Green, Windows Border, Etched, Wicker Carrier, 7 Piece		96.00

Cambridge Glass, Crown Tuscan, Compote, Pink, Flowers, Ship, Marked, 9 ¼ x 5 ¼ In.
$195.00

Cambridge Glass, Decagon, Sandwich Server, Center Handle, Amber, 10 ½ x 5 In.
$49.00

Cambridge Glass, Majestic, Candy Dish, Lid, Green, 3-Footed, Marked, c.1920, 6 ½ In.
$120.00

Cambridge Glass, Nude, Compote, Carmen Red Bowl, Concentric Loops, 8 ½ x 6 ½ In.
$350.00

Cambridge Glass, Portia, Bowl, Divided, Tally Ho Blank, Sterling Silver Rim, Wallace, 6 ½ x 3 In.
$56.00

Cambridge Glass, Swan, Black, 12 x 7 x 6 In.
$500.00

Cambridge Glass, Valencia, Mayonnaise, Underplate, Handles, Footed, 7 ½ x 3 ¼ & 8 ¼ In.
$50.00

Cameo Glass, Vase, Enamel, Plums, Currants, Leaves, Etched Leaves, Jules Barbe, 8 ½ In.
$24725.00

Cameo Glass, Vase,
Panoramic Lake View, Swans, Vining,
Plum Over Opal Blue, Signed, 5 ⅝ In.
$748.00

Cameo Glass, Vase, Vines,
Orange Fuchsia Blossoms, Iridized,
Swirl Ribbing, Scalloped, Pantin, 5 In.
$403.00

Cameo Glass, Vase,
White Opal Over Russet Cut, Tall Neck,
Stevens & Williams, 12 In.
$6000.00

Candelabrum, 2-Light, Sterling Silver,
Amorphic, Anton Michelsen, Denmark,
5 In., Pair
$682.00

Majestic, Candy Dish, Lid, Green, 3-Footed, Marked, c.1920, 6 ½ In. ....*illus*	120.00
No. 1191, Salt Cellar, Clear, c.1915, 1 ¾ In.	8.00
Nude, Compote, Carmen Red Bowl, Concentric Loops, 8 ½ x 6 ½ In. ....*illus*	350.00
Portia, Bowl, Divided, Tally Ho Blank, Sterling Silver Rim, Wallace, 6 ½ x 3 In. ....*illus*	56.00
Rose Point, Relish, Handles, 3 Sections, Footed, 10 In.	65.00
Roselyn, Dish, Mayonnaise, Underplate, 3 Piece................	85.00
Swan, Black, 12 x 7 x 6 In. ....*illus*	500.00
Swan, Punch Bowl, 12 Cups	2100.00
Tally-Ho, Salt, Handle	10.00
Valencia, Mayonnaise, Underplate, Handles, Footed, 7 ½ x 3 ¼ & 8 ¼ In. ....*illus*	50.00
Wheat Sheaf, Punch Bowl, Serrated Edge Points, c.1905, 3 ½ x 4 ⅜ In.	35.00
Wildflower, Candy Dish, Cover, Footed, 1940, 8 ½ x 5 ¼ In.	225.00
Wildflower, Goblet, 11 Oz., 8 ½ In.	40.00

CAMEO GLASS was made in much the same manner as a cameo in jewelry. Parts of the top layer of glass were cut away to reveal a different colored glass beneath. The most famous cameo glass was made during the nineteenth century. Signed cameo glass pieces are listed under the glasswork's name, such as Daum or Galle.

Bowl, Canoe Shape, Trumpet Flowers, Leafy Vine, Yellow, 1 ½ x 12 In.	1035.00
Bowl, Red Frosted, Flower, Branches, Trifold Rim, England, 5 In.	400.00
Lamp Base, Bulbous Prussian Blue Body, Woodsy Woodbine Vine, 3 ¾ In.	805.00
Lamp, Cylinder Shade, Flowers, Red, White, Yellow, Footed, Bulbous, Metal, England, 9 In.	5512.00
Lamp, Fairy, Matching Shade, Base, White Flowers, Citron Ground, 5 x 5 In.	4025.00
Lamp, White Ivy, Butterfly, Purple Ground Shade, Matching Base, 7 ½ In.	17250.00
Mug, St. Louis, Cranberry Glass, Flowers, Scrolls, Textured Matte, 3 Gold Carved Handles, 7 In.	460.00
Perfume Bottle, Blue Body, Base, White Blue Jasmine, Hinged Silver Dome, 5 ½ In.	920.00
Perfume Bottle, White Flower, Cranberry Ground, Silver Top, Laydown, Box, Mappin, 5 In. .	4888.00
Perfume Bottle, White Flowers, Cranberry Ground, Silver Screw Top, Laydown, Eng., 3 In. ..	1150.00
Pitcher, Birds, Red, White Cameo, Bulbous, Leaves, Applied Clear Handle, 6 ½ x 8 In.	63.00
Potpourri Keeper, Brass Filigree Top, Shaped Glass Body, Brown Over Yellow, 7 In., Pair.......	115.00
Sconce, 3-Light, Gilt Bronze, Mahogany, L. Majorelle, c.1900, 17 x 25 x 15 In.	16250.00
Sconce, Cylinder, Textured Yellow Flowers, Stems, Embossed Brass Cherub, St. Louis, 24 In. ..	400.00
Sconce, Wrought Iron, Oak Applied Leaves, Carvings, 1900, 18 In., Pair................	8963.00
Vase, Amber Ground, Red Leaf, Flowers, 5 x 11 In.	176.00
Vase, Blue Ground, White Flower Wreath, Rose, Passion Flower, Dentil Border, 10 In.	3335.00
Vase, Bottle Shape, Frosted, Green Leaves, Art Nouveau, France, Signed, c.1900, 3 x 6 In.	263.00
Vase, Bottle Shape, Yellow, Red Flowers, Signed, C. Pantin, 6 ½ In.	300.00
Vase, Bud, Deep Red, Flower Vines, Early 20th Century, 3 x 3 In.	150.00
Vase, Cinnamon Red, Leafy Stalk, Foxglove Blossoms, Butterfly, Drilled For Lamp, 9 ¾ In.	978.00
Vase, Cylinder, Frosted Amethyst, Stemmed Flowers, Gilt, Icicle Border, Burgun Schverer, 9 In.	1750.00
Vase, Cylinder Shape, Opal, Red, Yellow Leaves, Weis, Signed, 1 ½ In.	300.00
Vase, Enamel, Pale Green Shaded To Salmon, Woodland Design, Signed, 3 ¼ In.	400.00
Vase, Enamel, Plums, Currants, Leaves, Etched Leaves, Jules Barbe, 8 ½ In. ....*illus*	24725.00
Vase, Flower, Leaf, White, Cranberry, 3 ¼ In.	460.00
Vase, Frosted Blue, White Leaves, Cinched Neck, Pinwheel Flowers, England, 9 ½ In.	4313.00
Vase, Frosted White, Cascading Rainbow Wisteria, Bottle Form, Signed, Weis, c.1910, 9 In.	480.00
Vase, Orange, Green Flowers, Vines, Rose Ground, Arsall, Germany, 5 In.	230.00
Vase, Orange, Red, Green Blossoms, Yellow Opaque Ground, Cylindrical, c.1920, 13 ¾ In.	568.00
Vase, Panoramic Lake View, Swans, Vining, Plum Over Opal Blue, Signed, 5 ⅝ In. ....*illus*	748.00
Vase, Prussian Blue, Berries, Leafy Branch, Ribbed, Marked, 9 ¼ In.	1380.00
Vase, Purple, White Bell Flower, Bulbous, Signed, Poelatte Nancy, 9 ½ In.	1035.00
Vase, Rainbow, Scalloped Trim, Ruffled Edge, Interior Design Blackberries, Leaves, 2 ½ x 5 In.	690.00
Vase, Red, Cascading White Vines, Neck Leaf Border, Bulbous Stick Shape, England, 4 In.	633.00
Vase, Scalloped Rim, Swirled, Vines, Fuchsia, Pantin, 5 In.	403.00
Vase, Tapered Cylinder Shape, Everted Rim, Plum, Gilt, Round Pedestal Base, France, 4 In. ...	275.00
Vase, Vines, Orange Fuchsia Blossoms, Iridized, Swirl Ribbing, Scalloped, Pantin, 5 In. .*illus*	403.00
Vase, White Opal Over Russet Cut, Tall Neck, Stevens & Williams, 12 In. ....*illus*	6000.00
Vase, Yellow, Cream, Pink, Stems, Round, Signed, Burgun, Schverer, 3 ¼ In.	4035.00

CAMPAIGN *memorabilia are listed in the Political category.*

CAMPBELL KIDS were first used as part of an advertisement for the Campbell Soup Company in 1904. The kids were created by Grace Drayton, a popular illustrator of the day. The kids were used in magazine and newspaper ads until about 1951. They were presented again in 1966; and in 1983, they were redesigned with a slimmer, more contemporary appearance.

Bookends, Dolly & Bobby, Cast Iron, 4 In.	50.00

Doll, Puggy, Composition, Socket Head, Sculpted Hair, Suit, American Character, c.1930, 12 In. ... 448.00
Sign, Tomato Soup, Porcelain, Curved, c.1920-30, 12 x 22 ½ In. 2290.00

CANDELABRUM refers to a candleholder with more than one arm to hold many candles; a candlestick is designed to hold one candle. The eccentricity of the English language makes the plural of candelabrum into candelabra.

2-Light, Brass, Faceted Cut Glass Finial, Amethyst Drop Prisms, France, c.1885, 16 In. 429.00
2-Light, Brass, Faceted Cut Glass Finial, Molded Glass Body, Amethyst Drops, 16 In., Pair 429.00
2-Light, Brass, Open Roses, Gilt, Porcelain, Baluster, Chinese, 19th Century, 11 In., Pair........ 660.00
2-Light, Bronze Dore, Louis XVI, Dancing Satyrs Holding Cups, c.1890, 9 ½ In. 474.00
2-Light, Bronze, Winged Woman, Standing On Ball, Figural, Late 1800s, 14 In., Pair 485.00
2-Light, Figural Scenes, Stone, Black Wrought Iron Stand, 50 In., Pair............................... 191.00
2-Light, Pewter, Stylized Figure, Flared Base, Joseph Maria Olbrich, c.1901, 14 ¼ In., Pair 7170.00
2-Light, Pottery, Teal, Stylized Face, Spread Foot Is Neck, Bjorn Wiinblad, c.1950, 8 In. 450.00
2-Light, Sheffield Silver, Matthew Boulton, c.1700s, 15 x 19 In., Pair 527.00
2-Light, Silver, Reeded, Scroll, Flowers, Jones & Schofield, 1776, 16 ½ In, Pair................... 40000.00
2-Light, Silver, Scroll Arms, Center Flame Finial, Elkington & Co., England, 1940, 18 In. 2070.00
2-Light, Sterling Silver, Amorphic, Anton Michelsen, Denmark, 5 In., Pair ....*illus* 682.00
3-Light, Brass, Bronze Flower Scroll Arms, Prisms, c.1850, 17 x 17 In. 900.00
3-Light, Bronze, Egret Finial, Lion Head, Claw Feet, Chains, Dore, 10 ½ x 34 In., Pair............ 2300.00
3-Light, Bronze, Green Patina, Signed, E.T. Hurley, 1918, 10 x 15 In. 900.00
3-Light, Bronze Patinated Brass, Louis XVI, Gilt, Marble, Putto, 1910, 23 x 9 ½ In., Pair....... *illus* 2640.00
3-Light, Figural Flowers, Birds, Bronze, Porcelain, 15 x 15 x 7 In. 510.00
3-Light, French Empire Revival, Gilt Bronze, Egyptian Figure, 16 In., Pair ....*illus* 1440.00
3-Light, Gilt Brass, Sconce, Neoclassical, France, 18 In., Pair.. 212.00
3-Light, Gilt Bronze, Louis Philippe, Figural, Winged Putti, c.1850, 18 In., Pair 1175.00
3-Light, Gilt Bronze, Ormolu, Marble, Obelisk Stem, c.1850, 21 ¼ In. 206.00
3-Light, Glass, Flowers, Leaf Branches, Multicolored, 22 ½ x 12 In., Pair........................... 2360.00
3-Light, Patinated, Gilt Bronze, Avian Finials, Scrolling Arms, France, c.1870, 23 ½ In., Pair ... 1058.00
3-Light, Silver, Fisher, 7 x 12 In., Pair.. 293.00
3-Light, Silver, George II Style, Baluster, Cavetto Canted, 9 ¼ x 10 ¼ In., Pair 840.00
3-Light, Silver Plate, Circular Leaf Border, Old Sheffield, 21 ½ In. 215.00
3-Light, Silver Plate, Ellis-Barker, Sheffield, c.1920, 18 In. 380.00
3-Light, Silver Plate, Footed, Rogers, 13 In., Pair... 65.00
3-Light, Silver Plate, Hammered Cup Support, Fluted Stem, J. Despres, 8 x 10 In., Pair 4800.00
3-Light, Silver Plate, Navette Shape, Run Shape Candlecups, Reeded, c.1900, 18 In. 528.00
3-Light, Silver Plate, Reeded Scrolled Arms, Georgian, Sheffield, 19 ½ In., Pair 2350.00
3-Light, Silver Plate, Removable Cups, Impressed Mark, Sheffield, 1800s, 21 In., Pair............ 413.00
3-Light, Silver Plate, Sheffield, Finials, Mid 19th Century, Roberts Smith & Co., 21 In., Pair... 610.00
3-Light, Silver Plate, Trumpet Shape, Stepped Foot, Scrolling Arms, 1800s, 18 x 15 In., Pair... 732.00
3-Light, Silver Plated Arms, Stepped Glass Post, Square Slate Base, 28 In., Pair.................... 518.00
3-Light, Silver, Urns, Rams' Heads, Gadroon, Flame Finial, France, 19 ½ In., Pair................. 1952.00
3-Light, Sterling Silver, Cartier, N.Y., 13 In. 1750.00
4-Light, Boy, Cornucopia, 4 Branches, Cups, Flower Base, Von Schierholz, 1900s, 18 In, Pair .. 118.00
4-Light, Boy, Cornucopia Vase, Applied Flowers, Von Schierholtz, 1900s, 15 In., Pair 177.00
4-Light, Bronze, 5-Flower Bobeche, Marble Stem, Base, 8 x 23 In., Pair 920.00
4-Light, Gilt Brass, Cut Glass, Pendant Jewels, Shades, Restauration, 28 x 16 In., Pair............ 1680.00
4-Light, Gilt Bronze, George III Style, Scrolled Arms, 19 ½ In., Pair 657.00
4-Light, Iron, Cloverleaf Shape, Dansk, Denmark, 3 ½ x 2 ½ In., Pair 85.00
4-Light, Porcelain, Bronze, Signed, Laurant, France, 18 x 10 In., Pair 702.00
4-Light, Sconce, Bow Shape, Porcelain Oval Romantic Plaque, France, Gilt, 1900s, 30 In. 212.00
4-Light, Silver, 3 Scroll Arms, Reeded, Acanthus, M. Boulton, England, 26 In., Pair 2185.00
5-Light, Brass, Scroll Design, Art Nouveau, Prisms, 3-Footed, 17 ¼ In., Pair...................... 720.00
5-Light, Brass, Tommy Parzinger, Bobeches, Dorlyn Silversmiths, 9 ½ x 9 ½ In., Pair 840.00
5-Light, Bronze, Cherub, Stem, c.1900, 23 In. 1053.00
5-Light, Bronze, Gilt, Leaves, Cast Scrolls, Pierced Tripod Base, France, 20 In., Pair.............. 175.00
5-Light, Bronze, Louis XVI Style, Garlands, Paneled Base, Tapered Feet, 25 In. 338.00
5-Light, Bronze, Patinated, Classical, Crest Urn Shape Cup, Scroll Arms, 26 ½ x 8 ½ In., Pair .. 1998.00
5-Light, Bronze, Putto Stems, Ornate, France, 1800s, 20 In., Pair 805.00
5-Light, Bronze, Urn Form, Acanthus Finial, Raised Fluted Base, c.1890s, 20 x 9 ½ In., Pair..... 720.00
5-Light, Gilded Bronze, Urn Crest Cup, Leaf Cups, Square Plinth, c.1865, 9 x 27 In, Pair........ 1998.00
5-Light, Girandole, Cast Brass, Native American Figure, Prisms, Marble Base, 20 In., Pair 403.00
5-Light, Malachite, Bronze Mounts, 24 ½ In., Pair.. 2970.00
5-Light, Silver, 4 Arms, Octagonal Stepped Base, Tane, Mexico, 16 x 15 In. 1093.00
5-Light, Silver, Renaissance, Reed & Barton, 16 x 16 In., Pair 2925.00
5-Light, Silver, Scrolled, Stepped, Square Base, 16 x 12 In. 1380.00

Candelabrum, 3-Light, Bronze Patinated Brass, Louis XVI, Gilt, Marble, Putto, 1910, 23 x 9 ½ In., Pair $2640.00

As always, the edited listings in *Kovels' Antiques & Collectibles Price Guide 2011* aren't available on any website, but readers should visit Kovels.com for information on trends, tips, reproductions, marks, old prices, and more!

Candelabrum, 3-Light,
French Empire Revival, Gilt Bronze,
Egyptian Figure,16 In., Pair
$1440.00

Candlestick, Brass, Tapered Shape,
Scalloped Base, Mid 1700s, 10 ⅝ In., Pair
$374.00

Candlestick, Bronze, Faun,
Standing On Tortoise, Greek Urn Cup,
Marked, Christophle, 8 ¼ In., Pair
$822.00

Candlestick, Bronze, Figural, Genie,
Holding Bowl, Star Shape Flower,
Art Deco, 10 In.
$483.00

5-Light, Sterling Silver, Ornate, Gilt, Gorham, 17 ½ In.	4313.00
6-Light, Bronze, Patinated, Louis XVI, Parcel Gilt, Tripod Base, Hoof Feet, 30 x 14 In., Pair	6710.00
6-Light, Bronze, Slate, Scrolling Arms, Urn Form Supports, Fluted Base, Aesthetic, 28 In., Pair	413.00
6-Light, Gilded Column, Tripod, Paw Feet, 1800s, 24 ½ In., Pair	1416.00
6-Light, Parcel Gilt Bronze, Renaissance Revival, Alabaster, 3-Part Stem, 25 ⅜ In., Pair	1659.00
6-Light, Silver Plate, Marked, Sabattini, Italy, c.1970, 14 x 11 In.	385.00
7-Light, Brass, Oak, Gothic Revival, Figures, Angels, Tracery, Gilt, 74 In., Pair	2500.00
7-Light, Bronze, Classical Maiden, Putti, Figural, Marble Socle, c.1890, 33 ½ In., Pair	3120.00
7-Light, Bronze Dore, Baroque, Putto Holding Floral Festoon, 22 In., Pair	2760.00
7-Light, Bronze, Gilt, Trifid & Quatrefoil Scroll Work, Tripod Base, Late 1800s, 30 In.	250.00
7-Light, Cast Brass, Applied Opaline Glass Flowers, 19th Century, 39 ½ In., Pair	750.00
7-Light, Cast Iron, Center Pole, Arms Rotate, Jens Quistgaard, Dansk, Denmark, 18 ½ In.	95.00
7-Light, Gilt Bronze, Chinese Urn Shape, Elephant Head Handles, 37 x 15 In., Pair	4880.00
7-Light, Gilt Bronze, Scrolled Acanthine Arms, Putti, Marble Socle, Napoleon III, 34 In., Pair	3120.00
7-Light, Gilt Bronze, White Marble, Flower Swags, Louis XV/XVI Style, 28 In.	889.00
7-Light, Gilt Metal, Flowerheads, Leafy Branches, Continental, 38 ½ In.	179.00
7-Light, Parcel Gilt, Patinated Bronze, Spiral Turned Standard, Napoleon III, 33 In., Pair	1830.00
7-Light, Silver Plate, Medallions, Reed, Ribbon, England, Late 19th Century, 27 x 18 x 7 In.	748.00
8-Light, Bronze Cherub, Parcel Gilt Torch Arms, Scrolls, Louis XV, 28 In., Pair	10073.00
8-Light, Cast Iron, Trumpet Shape, Dansk IHQ, Denmark, 7 In.	125.00
9-Light, Bronze Dore, Cherub Holding Urn, Festoons, Fruit, Louis XVI, 34 In., Pair	12650.00
10-Light, Figural, Carved, Blackamoor, Holding Cornucopia, Electric, c.1900, 80 In., Pair	4994.00
10-Light, Kneeling Putto Stem, Gold Putti, Leaf Base, Picard, 17 x 32 In., Pair	9200.00
Brass, Urn, Tree Shape, White Flowers, France, 1800s, 23 In., Pair	146.00
Bronze, Women, Holding Candles, 25 x 9 In., Pair	201.00
Iron, Round, 8 Cups, Dansk IBR, Denmark, 7 ½ In.	85.00
Silver Plate, Pairpoint, Late 19th Century, 21 x 12 In.	705.00
Sterling Silver, English Rose, Weighted, 2 Sections, Fisher, c.1920, 17 x 14 ½ In.	165.00

CANDLESTICKS were made of brass, pewter, glass, sterling silver, plated silver, and all types of pottery and porcelain. The earliest candlesticks, dating from the sixteenth century, held the candle on a pricket (sharp pointed spike). These lost favor because in times of strife the large church candlesticks with prickets became formidable weapons, so the socket was mandated. Candlesticks changed in style through the centuries, and designs range from Classical to Rococo to Art Nouveau to Art Deco.

Aluminum, Dome Shape, Nambe, 3 x 1 In.	35.00
Antler, Boar Tusk, Presentation Inscription, Germany, c.1878, 14 ½ In., Pair	2160.00
Art Glass, Yellow Cased, Blue Base, Rim, 9 ¼ In., Pair	86.00
Bisque, Dolphin, Gilt Plinth, Signed, Italy, 9 In., Pair	360.00
Brass, Baluster Shaft, Mid-Drip Pan, Scandinavia, c.1690, 6 ½ In.	830.00
Brass, Beehive, 7 ¼ In., Pair	81.00
Brass, Beehive, Push-Up, 19th Century, 10 In., Pair	70.00
Brass, Counterweight, 6 x 11 In.	94.00
Brass, Empire, 9 ¾ In., Pair	183.00
Brass, Jessie Preston, Signed, Anderson Foundry Mark, 13 In., Pair	4200.00
Brass, Lion's & Ram's Heads, Wound Ivy Stem, Grapes, 3 Lion's Feet, 12 ¼ In., Pair	118.00
Brass, Mahogany, Fluted Stop, Turned Base, Brass Nozzle, England, c.1760, 15 In.	1116.00
Brass, Petal Base, England, c.1750, 8 In.	225.00
Brass, Petal Base, Scalloped Sockets, England, c.1750, 7 ½ In.	499.00
Brass, Pricket, 19th Century, 45 x 9 ½ In.	110.00
Brass, Queen Anne, Cut Corner Base, 18th Century, 11 In., Pair	92.00
Brass, Sheraton, Square Base, Early 19th Century, 9 In., Pair	148.00
Brass, Square, Raised Paw Feet, c.1725, 7 In.	294.00
Brass, Tapered Shape, Scalloped Base, Mid 1700s, 10 ⅝ In., Pair ....*illus*	374.00
Brass, Tavern Stick, Bell Ring, England, c.1840, 13 x 5 In., Pair	1850.00
Brass, Trifid Shape Handle, c.1720.	285.00
Brass, Tulip Shape Nozzle, Twist Shaft On Ball & Bell Base, 1840, 5 ¾ In., Pair	430.00
Bronze, Baluster, Octagonal Base, England, 12 In., Pair	153.00
Bronze, Faun, Standing On Tortoise, Greek Urn Cup, Marked, Christophle, 8 ¼ In., Pair .*illus*	822.00
Bronze, Figural, Genie, Holding Bowl, Star Shape Flower, Art Deco, 10 In. .....*illus*	483.00
Bronze, Gilt, Gothic, Scrolled Crowns, Stems, Spires, Hexagonal Base, 24 ½ In., Pair	375.00
Bronze, Gilt, Gothic, Trifid Crown, Carved Stem, Hexagonal Base, 1800s, 20 In.	112.00
Bronze, Jarviel, Epsilon Model, Removable Bobeche, Signed, 1906, 6 x 3 In.	780.00
Bronze, Joan Of Arc, Figural, Gilt, Late 1800s, 11 In., Pair	60.00
Bronze, Male, Female, Classical Style, 19th Century, 16 In., Pair	2223.00
Bronze, Man & Woman Holding Candlestick, Victorian, 11 ½ In.	485.00

Bronze, Neoclassical, Nudes, Upraised Hands, Tambourine, Openwork Feet, 1900s, 11 In.	119.00
Bronze, Ostrich Leg Shape, 23 ½ In., Pair..	722.00
Bronze, Patinated, Parcel Gilt, Louis Philippe, Paw Feet, Mid 1800s, 13 ½ In., Pair.......... *illus*	1560.00
Bronze, Patinated Spelter, Knight In Armor, Parcel Gilt, Germany, 16 x 5 In., Pair .... *illus*	1020.00
Bronze, Regency, Ormolu, Classical Woman, Crossed Arms, Fluted Pedestals, 11 ¾ In., Pair...	3290.00
Bronze, Renaissance Revival, Polished, Cascades, Scrolling, France, Mid 1800s, 22 In., Pair ..	1410.00
Bronze, Renaissance Style, Lion's Head Feet, Swirling Baluster, Continental, 23 ¾ In.	299.00
Bronze, Rowfant, Standing Beaver, William McVey, c.1976, 9 In.	546.00
Bronze, Snake, Art Nouveau, Signed, 7 ½ In.	120.00
Chamber, Silver, Reeded Thistle, Gadroon Rim, Loop, Shell Handle, Snuffer, Denmark, 1831, 3 ⅜ In. .	326.00
Chrome Plated Metal, Red Plastic, Stacking, Nagel, 3 ½ x 3 ½ In.	275.00
Chrome, Flute Shape, Germany, 5 In., Pair..	45.00
Cloisonne, Pricket, Lotus Flower, Turquoise Ground, Signed Lao Tien Li Chith, 18 In., Pair ...	1778.00
Copper, Delta Model, Patina, Jarvie, Signed, 6 x 14 In., Pair...	1080.00
Extinguisher, Silver, Rectangular, England, c.1811, 6 In.	397.00
Gilt Socket, Verdigris Seated Sphinx Stem, Alabaster, Marble Base, c.1875, 9 In., Pair...........	1200.00
Gilt, Sculpted Poppies, Art Nouveau, Marked, c.1900, 9 ½ In., Pair	120.00
Giltwood, Scrolled Brass Arm, Mirror, Italy, 27 x 15 In., Pair..	2115.00
Giltwood, Urn, Crackle Paint, Flower Bobeche, Wrought Iron Scroll Handle, Pair, 32 In., Pair .	1680.00
Glass, Blown, Amethyst, c.1920, 11 In., Pair..	293.00
Iron, S-Shape Base, Brass Ring Separator, Jens Quistgaard, Dansk, 4 ¼ x 4 ½ In.	115.00
Iron, Sticking Tommy, Forged, Hat Hook, 8 ½ In.	110.00
Jade, Green, Swirled, Ribbed, Alabaster Wafer Connector, 10 In., Pair..............................	800.00
Leather Wrapped Brass Handle, Flat Copper Plate, Carl Aubock, 6 ½ x 3 ¼ In.	540.00
Mahogany, Cut Crystal Hurricane Shade, 25 x 4 In.	47.00
Metal, Black, Brad Nichols, 1998, 6 x 18 In., Pair...	88.00
Metal, Pricket, Parcel Gilt, Painted, 31 In., Pair..	900.00
Oak, Carved Cherub, Holding Water Pitcher Holder, 6 ½ x 26 In., Pair	2185.00
Pewter, Removable Bobeches, Fuller & Smith, Poquonock Bridge, Conn., c.1850, 8 ¾ In.	411.00
Porcelain, Cupid, Cornucopia Vase, Flower Cup, Applied Roses, Schierhotz, Plaue, Germany, 1900s, 9 In.	118.00
Porcelain, Figural, Griffon, Gilt Wings, Green Base, Flowers, 7 In., Pair.............................	4313.00
Porcelain, Figural, Shepherd, Shepherdess, Scrolled Base, Samson Style, c.1920, 11 In.	296.00
Porcelain, Gilt Metal, Blue Ground, Stem Figures, Flowers, Painted, France, 1800s, 9 In., Pair	177.00
Rock Crystal, Tapered Shafts, Molded Round Base, 10 x 3 ½ In., Pair ....*illus*	1315.00
Sawtooth Iron Trammel, Adjustable, Drip Tray, 2 Push-Up Holders, 27 In.	935.00
Silver Plate, Adams Style, Sheffield, 12 In., Pair	288.00
Silver Plate, Baluster Form, Square Base, Embossed Flowers, 8 ¼ In., Pair.........................	55.00
Silver Plate, Column Stem, Marble Base, Drum Shade, France, 23 In., Pair.........................	1080.00
Silver Plate, Extendable, England, c.1900, 12 ½ To 19 In., Pair	105.00
Silver Plate, Fluted Baluster Stem, Stepped Base, Scrolling, Mappin & Webb, c.1890, 9 In., Pair *illus*	173.00
Silver Plate, Fluted Column, Square Rams' Heads & Swag Base, 12 In.	403.00
Silver Plate, Fluted, Rounded Square Stepped Base, Mappin & Webb, 9 In., Pair...............	173.00
Silver Plate, Sheffield, George III, Embossed Scrolls, Drip Guards, c.1800, 10 In., Pair	236.00
Silver Plate, Spiral, 12 Taper Holes, France BV, Dansk Designs..	115.00
Silver Plate, Square Stepped Base, Rounded Scrolled Corners, Elkington, 5 In., Pair	35.00
Silver Plate, Tapered, Dome Base, Bowl Drip Plate, Marked WMF, c.1910, 9 In., Pair ....*illus*	173.00
Silver Plate, Telescoping, Tapered Column, Gadroon Border, 8 To 10 In., Pair...................	115.00
Silver Rock Crystal, 8-Sided Base, 3 Silver Ball Feet, Italy 12 ½ In., Pair........................	2280.00
Silver, 4-Footed, Lions Heads On Each Foot, Austria, 1900s, 13 x 5 ½ In., Pair...................	787.00
Silver, Acanthus Leaf & Flowers, Sheffield, John Watson, William IV, 9 ¼ In., Pair	1265.00
Silver, Arts & Crafts, Tapered, Rivets, Square Base, Sheffield, 1906, 9 x 4 In.	1955.00
Silver, Baluster, 4-Footed, Continental, c.1900, 11 ½ In., Pair...	179.00
Silver, Bead Base, Cup Trim, Gorham, 3 In., Pair...	89.00
Silver, Beta Model, Verdigris Patina, Scoop Bobeche, Jarvie, 5 ½ x 12 ½ In., Pair	4800.00
Silver, Birks, Canada, 12 x 4 ¼ In., 4 Piece...	308.00
Silver, Chased Flower Rims, Bamboo, Engraved, 1900s, 4 ⅝ x 2 ⅝ In., Pair ....*illus*	638.00
Silver, Club Shape Plate, Scroll Handle, Marked, c.1873, 1 ⅝ x 4 ¾ In. ....*illus*	368.00
Silver, Engraved Flowers, Domed Foot, Leafy Scrolls, 14 In., Pair......................................	518.00
Silver, Gilt, Carved, Wood, Scrolled Tripod Base, 1800s, 34 In.	441.00
Silver, Lines, H. Bushnell, 10 In., Pair..	125.00
Silver, Louis XVI Style, Towle, c.1920, 10 ½ In., Pair...	405.00
Silver, Prestner, 5 In., Pair	205.00
Silver, Ribbed Stem, Mueck-Cary Co., c.1950, 11 In., Pair..	94.00
Silver, Rococo Revival, Inverted Baluster Stem, Germany, c.1900, 13 x 6 In., Pair ....*illus*	720.00
Silver, Square Base, Baluster Form, 9 ½ In.	1567.00
Silver, Tapered, Ellis J. Greenberg, c.1908, 7 x 4 In., Pair ....*illus*	420.00

Candlestick, Bronze, Patinated, Parcel Gilt, Louis Philippe, Paw Feet, Mid 1800s, 13 ½ In., Pair
$1560.00

Candlestick, Bronze, Patinated Spelter, Knight In Armor, Parcel Gilt, Germany, 16 x 5 In., Pair
$1020.00

> **TIP**
> *Keep your keys on a pull apart chain so the house keys and car keys can be separated when you leave the car in a parking lot.*

CANDLESTICK

Candlestick, Rock Crystal, Tapered Shafts, Molded Round Base, 10 x 3 ½ In., Pair
$1315.00

Candlestick, Silver, Chased Flower Rims, Bamboo, Engraved, 1900s, 4 ⅝ x 2 ⅝ In., Pair
$638.00

Candlestick, Silver, Club Shape Plate, Scroll Handle, Marked, c.1873, 1 ⅝ x 4 ¾ In.
$368.00

Candlestick, Silver Plate, Fluted Baluster Stem, Stepped Base, Scrolling, Mappin & Webb, c.1890, 9 In., Pair
$173.00

Candlestick, Silver Plate, Tapered, Dome Base, Bowl Drip Plate, Marked WMF, c.1910, 9 In., Pair
$173.00

Candlestick, Silver, Rococo Revival, Inverted Baluster Stem, Germany, c.1900, 13 x 6 In., Pair
$720.00

Candlestick, Silver, Tapered, Ellis J. Greenberg, c.1908, 7 x 4 In., Pair
$420.00

Teak, Turned, Brass Candle Holder Insert, Denmark, 4 ¾ In.	45.00
Tin, Hog Scraper, 19th Century, 18 ½ In., Pair	561.00
Tole, Hog Scraper, 19th Century, 7 ½ In.	50.00
Walnut, Brass 2 Block Cups, Geometric, 11 ½ In., Pair	135.00
Wood, Carved, Circular Top, Brass Drip Pan, Triangular Stem, Tripod, Italy, 39 In.	450.00
Wood, Carved, Tin Bobeches, Italy, 1700s, 21 In., Pair	805.00
Wrought Iron, Spiral, Wood Base, 18th Century, 8 x 3 ½ In.	339.00

CANDLEWICK *items may be listed in the Imperial Glass and Pressed Glass categories.*

CANDY CONTAINERS have been popular since the late Victorian era. Collectors have long favored the glass containers, but now all types, including tin and papier-mache, are collected. Probably the earliest glass container sold commercially was the Liberty Bell made in 1876 for sale at the Centennial Exposition. Thousands of designs were made until the cost became too high in the 1960s. By the late 1970s, reproductions were being made and sold without the candy. Containers listed here are glass unless otherwise described. A Belsnickle is a nineteenth-century figure of Father Christmas. Some candy containers may be listed in Toy or in other categories.

Airplane, Spirit Of St. Louis, Green Glass, Tin Wings, Westmoreland Glass Co., c.1927	605.00
Amos 'n' Andy, Victory Car, Glass, Painted, 4 ½ In. ....*illus*	468.00
Auto, 4 Doors, Maroon Body Paint, Silver Wheel Paint, West Bros. Co., 4 In.	1430.00
Automobile, Open Air, Glass, Metal Wheels, Roof ....*illus*	117.00
Barney Google, Next To Bank, Glass, Green Lid	680.00
Baseball Player, Mustache, Holding Ball, Original Clothes, Cloth, 9 ½ In.	2128.00
Baseball, West Germany, 1960s, 2 ¾ In.	30.00
Basketball, Roundtree Co., 4 In.	30.00
Battleship On Waves, Glass	77.00
Bell, Gold, Painted, Pressed Paper, US Zone Germany, 4 ⅝ x 3 ½ In.	11.00
Bell, Painted, Pressed Paper, US Zone Germany, 4 ¾ x 3 ½ In.	23.00
Belsnickle, Applied Mica, Ribbon Belt, 16 ½ In. ....*illus*	4600.00
Belsnickle, Carries Sheep, Rabbit Fur Beard, Red Robe, 14 In.	288.00
Billiken, Painted, Milk Glass	113.00
Black Cat, In Orange Pumpkin, Composition, Marked, Germany, 5 ½ In.	675.00
Black Cat, Winking, Seated, Gold Collar	8200.00
Box, Beautiful Woman, Yellow Daisy Border, Paper Lithograph, 13 x 16 ½ In.	295.00
Boy, Pulling Pumpkin House, Composition, 4 In. ....*illus*	234.00
Bucket, Luden's Victor Mixture, Wood, Label, 10 In. ....*illus*	29.00
Buddy Bank, Tin, Glass, Marx, 4 ¼ In.	695.00
Building, Walgreens, Painted, Tin	70.00
Bulldog, Brown Paint, Silver Collar, Round Base	56.00
Car, Race, Image Of Driver, Tin Lithograph, Top Panel, c.1920s, 6 ½ In.	1955.00
Car, V.G. Co. Airflow, Silver Paint	498.00
Carousel, Red Top, Black Base, Tin Lithograph	140.00
Carpet Bag, Roosters, Yellow Bead, Strap Handle, 3 ¼ In.	173.00
Carpet Sweeper, Baby Sweeper, Painted, Tin, Twisted Wire Handle	600.00
Cat, Black, Cardboard, Slide, Marked, Germany, 5 ¾ In.	500.00
Cat, Black Velvet, Papier-Mache, Glass Eyes, Wood Legs, Germany, 10 In.	4035.00
Cat, Coming Out Of Jack-O'-Lantern, 4 In.	565.00
Choir Girl, Glass, Cork Top	33.00
Clown, On Rocking Horse, Painted, Glass, Tin Closure, Contents, 3 ½ x 4 ¼ In.	108.00
Dirigible, Los Angeles, Painted, Tin	113.00
Dog, Bulldog, Seated, Black, Glass, Tin Closure, Marked, Avor, ¾ Oz., 4 ⅛ In.	48.00 to 72.00
Dog, Cannon, Magnificent Quick Firer, Painted, Tin	113.00
Don't Park Here, Painted, Glass, Contents	280.00
Donkey, Emerging From Egg, 4 ½ In.	410.00
Duck, Long Neck, Painted, Composition, Marked, Germany, c.1920, 5 ¾ x 2 ½ In.	55.00
Duck, Papier-Mache, Removable Head, 9 ½ In.	60.00
Easter Bunny, Standing, Basket On Back, Papier-Mache, 14 In.	236.00
Felix The Cat, Black Paint, Glass Pedestal Base	4350.00
Felix The Cat, Embossed Name, Inverted Tub Base, c.1924, 3 ¼ In.	4675.00
Fire Engine, Little Boiler No. 1, Dark Blue, Glass	113.00
Fish, Brown, Yellow, Glass Eyes, Painted, Papier-Mache, Composition, c.1920, 10 x 3 In.	85.00
Flossie Fisher's Chair, Painted, Tin	480.00
Gas Pump, Embossed, Gas 23 Cents Today, c.1927	313.00
Globe, On Stand, Glass, Black Metal Base	700.00
Golf Club, Glass	175.00

Candy Container, Amos 'n' Andy, Victory Car, Glass, Painted, 4 ½ In. $468.00

Candy Container, Automobile, Open Air, Glass, Metal Wheels, Roof $117.00

Candy Container, Belsnickle, Applied Mica, Ribbon Belt, 16 ½ In. $4600.00

Candy Container, Boy, Pulling Pumpkin House, Composition, 4 In. $234.00

Candy Container, Bucket, Luden's Victor Mixture, Wood, Label, 10 In. $29.00

Candy Container, Rabbit, Cloth Covered, Orange Glass Eyes, Painted, Fur Tail, Basket, 8 In. $259.00

Candy Container, Sheep, Bell, Wood, Composition, Glass Eyes, 6 x 4 In. $322.00

Candy Container, Tune In Radio, Glass $117.00

Gray Cat Head, Also A Toothpick Holder, Ceramic, 3 In.	117.00
Hen, On Nest, Painted, Pressed Paper, FN Burt, 1924, 7 x 6 ½ In.	30.00
Horn, Musical Clarinet, No. 515A	230.00
Horse Head, Cart, 3 Wheels, Painted, Glass, Marked, Avor., Oz., 2 ¾ x 4 ½ In.	92.00
Hot Doggie, Brown Paint, Glass	600.00
Ice Cream Freezer, Turning Crank, Wire Handle, Dresden, 2 ½ In.	115.00
Jackie Coogan, Painted, Glass	725.00
Jockey, Black, On Pig, Hand Painted, Composition, Nodder, Glass Eyes, 6 ¾ In.	144.00
Jug, Snake, Curls Around Handle, Stoneware, Dresden, 3 In.	75.00
Kangaroo, Clear Glass, Metal Closure	3850.00
Kangaroo, Glass, Tin Lid Base	3950.00
Lamp, Flower Shade, Souvenir Of Boston, Mass., Glass, Ribbed Interior, Contents	275.00
Liberty Bell, Blue, Glass, Bail Handle	56.00
Locomotive, John Bell, Cotton In Smokestack, Dresden, 2 ¾ In.	2588.00
Man, Black, Hand Painted, Red Tails, Blue Top Hat, Head Separates, 5 ⅞ In.	92.00
Man, Stuck In Eggshell, Nodder, 6 ¼ In.	345.00
Monkey Head, Pressed Paper, Painted, 5 ¾ x 4 ½ In.	55.00
Opera Glasses, Plain Panels, Ruby Stain	195.00
Owl, Brown, Black, White Paint, Glass, Tin Closure, 4 ½ In.	190.00
Parrot, Glass Eyes, Painted, Paper Pulp, c.1930, 12 ½ x 4 In.	65.00
Pencil, Baby Jumbo, Glass, Paper Label, Contents	92.00
Penknife, Glass, Tin Lid, Germany	465.00
PEZ, Alpine Man, 1972 Olympics, Munich, Red Stem	1725.00
PEZ, Bozo The Clown, Die Cut Stem, 1960s	86.00
PEZ, Bullwinkle, Brown Stem, Yellow Antlers	259.00
PEZ, Daniel Boone, Green Stem	144.00
PEZ, Frankenstein, Black Stem, White Face, Red Scar	173.00
PEZ, Green Hornet, Gray Hat, Green Mask	460.00
PEZ, Hippo, 1970s	863.00
PEZ, Santa Claus, Full-Bodied, Red Outfit, Black Boots, White Bears, 1950s, 4 In.	110.00
PEZ, Space Gun Shooter, Black, Instruction Sheet, 1950s	316.00
PEZ, Spaceman, Cocoa Marsh Variation, 1950s	115.00
PEZ, Uncle Sam, Stars & Stripes Hat, Blue Stem	86.00
Planetarium, Glass	250.00
Platypus, Hugging Tree, Glass	246.00
Policeman's Nightstick, No. 2, Glass, Tin	35.00
Puck, Sitting In Chair, Glass	13.00
Pumpkin Man, In Uniform, Nodder, Composition, Round Box, Germany, 8 ¼ In.	850.00
Pumpkin Man, Painted Composition, Marked, Nov. 2, 1922, Germany	760.00
Pumpkin Man, Pressed Cardboard, Composition, Bottom Plug, Germany, 5 In.	375.00
Pumpkin, Green, Papier-Mache, Bail Handle, 2 ¼ In.	275.00
Rabbit Clown, Head Lifts, Composition, Painted, 7 ½ In.	443.00
Rabbit Family, 3 Rabbits On Base, Victory Glass Co., 1920s, 3 ½ In.	1595.00
Rabbit Family, Glass, Gold Paint	1650.00
Rabbit, Brown Flocked Body, Glass Eyes, Carrot In Backpack, 1920s, 6 In.	145.00
Rabbit, Cloth Covered, Orange Glass Eyes, Painted, Fur Tail, Basket, 8 In. ......*illus*	259.00
Rabbit, Composition, Cardboard, Painted, Elongated Ears With Springs, 7 In.	118.00
Rabbit, In Egg, Painted, Composition, Marked, Germany, 5 ¼ x 2 ¼ In.	30.00
Rabbit, Painted, Paper Pulp, Glass Eyes, Marked, Drake Process, 10 ½ x 8 In.	18.00
Rabbit, Playing Baseball, Opens At Head, Papier-Mache, Germany, 1890s, 8 In.	1035.00
Rabbit, Pushing Chick, In Shell Cart, Painted, Glass	256.00
Rabbit, Seated, Glass, Aluminum Ears	788.00
Rabbit, Standing, With Basket In Right Arm, Glass, Tin Closure, 4 ½ In.	48.00
Rabbit, With Basket, Sitting On Dome, Tin Screw-On Closure, Gold Paint	1100.00
Radio, Raised Lettering, Tune In, Dials, Speakers, Glass, Victory, Pa., 1930s, 3 In.	125.00
Radio, Tune In, Speaker Horn On Top, Glass, Marked, VC, J'Ne't, Pa., 4 ½ In.	62.00
Remember The Maine, Glass, 3 ½ x 7 In.	72.00
Rocking Horse, Glass	410.00
Rooster, Crowing, Painted, Glass	300.00
Rooster, Painted, Cardboard, Marked, Germany, 4 ¼ x 3 In.	30.00
Safe, Bank Penny Trust Co., Glass, Slotted Tin Roof, 3 x 2 x 2 In.	48.00
Santa Claus, Arms In Sleeves, Painted, Glass, Tin Closure, Avor, 4 In.	35.00
Santa Claus, At Chimney, Painted, Glass, Tin Closure, Marked, VC, U.S.A., 5 In.	82.00
Santa Claus, Brush Tree, Sled, Painted, Composition, 6 ¾ x 3 In.	36.00
Santa Claus, Glass, Cloetta	1025.00
Santa Claus, Holding Tree, Red Coat, Tan Pants, Germany, 23 In.	2355.00

C

Santa Claus, In Boot, Painted, Pressed Paper, 1950s, 7 ¼ x 4 In.	28.00
Santa Claus, In Chimney, Painted, Pressed Paper, 1950, 6 x 3 In.	28.00
Santa Claus, Plastic Head, Glass, Millstein Co., 5 ⅝ In.	42.00
Santa Claus, Wearing Mohair Coat, Germany, c.1895, 17 In.	3995.00
Sheep, Bell, Wood, Composition, Glass Eyes, 6 x 4 In. ......illus	322.00
Sitting Cat, Slid Composition, 4 In.	292.00
Skull & Owl, Painted Composition, Germany, 7 ½ In.	2635.00
Snowman, Nodder, Candy Cane, Pressed Cardboard, US Zone Germany, 7 ½ In.	28.00
Soldier, With Sword, Painted, Glass, Tin	690.00
Stork, White, Green, Painted, Pressed Paper, Germany, 8 ⅛ x 4 ¾ In.	33.00
Streamline Motor Bus, Glass, Clear, 5 In.	22.00
Suitcase, Bears, Milk Glass, Bail Handle	65.00
Swiss Chalet, Window Inserts, Dresden, 1 ½ In.	345.00
Table, Ruby Flashed Top, Glass	1025.00
Telephone, Bell & Receiver, Redlick's Cork Top, Glass	460.00
Top Form, Glass, Wood Spinner Handle, c.1940, 3 ⅞ x 1 ⅞ In.	50.00
Top, Glass, Red Paint, Wood Winder	95.00
Truck, Express, White, Red, Glass, Tin	580.00
Truck, Gasoline, Glass	295.00
Tune In Radio, Glass ......illus	117.00
Turkey, Black, Red, Green, Pressed Paper Pulp, ACTO, 1930s, 6 ¾ x 4 In.	18.00
Turkey, Glass, Tin Closure, 3 ⅝ In.	85.00
Turkey, Oven Roaster, Painted, Germany, 1910, 7 x 5 ¾ In.	195.00
Turkey, Painted, Pressed Paper Pulp, ACTO, 1930s, 7 x 5 ¾ In.	25.00
Turkey, Roasted, Thanksgiving, Papier-Mache, Composition, Painted, Germany, 14 In. ......illus	263.00
Turkey, Thanksgiving, Papier-Mache, Composition, Germany, c.1935, 12 In. ......illus	2106.00
Uncle Sam, Right Arm Reaching For Sword, Painted, Glass, Tin Lid, 4 In.	105.00
Well, Ye Olde Oaken Bucket, Bail Handle, Wood, Painted	36.00
Wicker Picnic Basket, Double Handles, Hinged Lid, Braided Trim, 2 ½ In.	978.00
Witch, Black Cat, Composition, Remove Head To Open, Germany, c.1920, 4 In.	675.00
Witch, In Rocket, Plastic, Orange, Black Wheels, 8 In.	895.00
Witch, On Motorcycle, Plastic, Pumpkin, Orange, Green, Black, 7 In.	695.00
Witch, Riding Black Cat, Composition Cat With Glass Eyes, 9 ¾ In.	2925.00
Witch, With Spring Arms, Solid Composition, 7 ¼ In.	585.00

CANES and walking sticks were used by every well-dressed man in the nineteenth century, but by World War I the style had changed. Today canes are used by few but the infirm. Collectors prize old canes made with special features, like hidden swords, whiskey flasks, or risqué pictures seen through peepholes. Examples with solid gold heads or made from exotic materials are among the higher-priced canes. See also Scrimshaw.

14K Gold, L-Form Handle, Stamped Diamond Designs, Knotty Wood, Marked, 34 In.	80.00
Bone, Straight Handle, Inscribed Dragon, Ironwood Shaft, Mother-Of-Pearl Dot Inlays, 34 ¾ In.	88.00
Briarwood, Ivory, Horse & Jockey Heads, 1860-80, 35 In.	1763.00
Cloisonne, Stylized Flowers, Bamboo Shaft, Metal Ferrule, 36 In.	55.00
Ebony Shaft, Horn Handle, Silver End, Engraved Geo. W. Moon, Wigan, England, 45 In.	7050.00
Ebony, Ivory, Gold Band, Oval Shaft, Initials J.L.S., 36 In.	695.00
Gesso Over Wood, Dagger, England, Late 1800s, 35 ½ In.	55.00
Horn, Ringed Black, Ivory Handle, Citron Orange, Bakelite Ferrule, Continental, 39 In.	246.00
Horn, Stacked Fish Vertebrae Shaft, 36 ¾ In.	99.00
Ivory Handle, Dog Head, 3 ½ In.	230.00
Ivory, Human Head, Horn & Ivory Collar, Wood Shaft, 34 ¼ In.	88.00
Mahogany, Soldier Head Handle, Ivory, Metal Helmet, White Metal Ferrule, 34 In.	172.00
Narwhal Tusk, Baleen Rings, Ebony Tip, 38 In.	1725.00
Reptile Skin, Spiral Carved Burl Wood, 14K Gold Collar, Horn Ferrule, 36 In.	154.00
Rosewood, Ivory Head, Band Signed, A.G. Lucas, Lowell Mass., 34 ½ In.	138.00
Scepter, Woman's Figure, Tribal, Wood, Carved, Mother-Of-Pearl, Africa, 40 In. ......illus	1725.00
Silver, Atlas Shape, Man Carrying Sphere On Back, Metal Collar & Ferrule, Hallmarks, 39 In.	209.00
Snake, Coiled, Cottonwood, Painted, c.1900, 34 In.	382.00
Snake, Painted, Nail Eyes, Disc Shape Handle, c.1900, 38 In.	470.00
Sterling Silver, Horse's Head, Rosewood, Marked, Buccellati, 36 ½ In. ......illus	1208.00
Surgeon's Gadgets, Wood Head, Brass Anchor, Crown, Brass Cylinder, Scalpels, Syringe, 38 In.	750.00
Sword, Silver Handle, Raised Flowers, Metal Ferrule, 41 ½ In.	176.00
Telescope Handle, 2-Part Hardwood & Brass Shaft, Thos J. Evans, London, 36 In.	275.00
Walking Stick, Beechwood, Human Hand, Fingers, Fingernails Clutching Handle, 37 In.	88.00
Walking Stick, Brass, Dragon Handle, Middle Eastern, 35 In.	45.00
Walking Stick, Cedar, Carved Florets, Winding Snake, Brass Caps, 38 In.	110.00

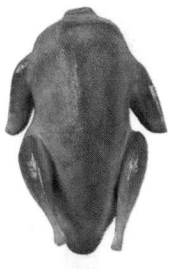
Candy Container, Turkey, Roasted, Thanksgiving, Papier-Mache, Composition, Painted, Germany, 14 In. $263.00

Candy Container, Turkey, Thanksgiving, Papier-Mache, Composition, Germany, c.1935, 12 In. $2106.00

Cane, Scepter, Woman's Figure, Tribal, Wood, Carved, Mother-Of-Pearl, Africa, 40 In. $1725.00

Cane, Sterling Silver, Horse's Head, Rosewood, Marked Buccellati, 36 ½ In. $1208.00

Cane, Walking Stick, Hardwood, Monkey's Head, Glass Eyes, Ebony, Early 1900s, 35 ½ In. $240.00

Cane, Walking Stick, Sterling Silver Handle, Chased, Ebony, Engraved H, 31 In. $230.00

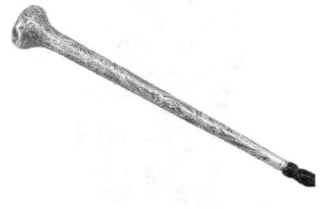

Cane, Walking Stick, Wood, Dog's Head, Copper, Brass, Detachable Handle, Marked, 36 In. $495.00

Capo-di-Monte

Don't be confused by the porcelains sold today under the name "Capodimonte." Capodimonte Ltd., the British company using that name, is not related to the famous Capo-di-Monte porcelain of Italy.

Walking Stick, Ebony, Carved Hardwood, Monkey's Head Grip, Glass Eyes, Continental, 35 ½ In.	240.00
Walking Stick, Exotic Fruitwood, Carved, 19th Century, 35 In.	60.00
Walking Stick, Fruitwood, Ivory & Bone Inlaid, c.1900, 37 In.	180.00
Walking Stick, Hardwood, Carved Root, Boxer Dog Head Grip, Glass Eyes, Continental, 30 In.	150.00
Walking Stick, Hardwood, Carved Root, Boxer Dog Head Grip, Glass Eyes, Continental, 35 ¼ In.	300.00
Walking Stick, Hardwood, Human Face, Bird-Like Body, Shaved Bark, 19th Century, 38 In.	88.00
Walking Stick, Hardwood, Monkey's Head, Glass Eyes, Ebony, Early 1900s, 35 ½ In. *illus*	240.00
Walking Stick, Hardwood, Winding Snake, Diamond Shape Head, Eyes, Ball, 37 In.	154.00
Walking Stick, Ivory, Elephant, Carved, 36 ½ In.	410.00
Walking Stick, Sterling Silver Handle, Chased, Ebony, Engraved H, 31 In. *illus*	230.00
Walking Stick, Sweet Gum Wood, Deer Head, Varnished, c.1988, 38 In.	55.00
Walking Stick, Totem, 2 Balls, Bear, Indian Warrior, Man, Indian Chief, Headdress, 51 In.	88.00
Walking Stick, Walnut, Camera Tripod, Engraved, Made In Germany, c.1900, 36 In.	362.00
Walking Stick, Wood, African American Carved Face, Maple, c.19th Century, 35 In.	99.00
Walking Stick, Wood, Carved, Burr Grip, Female Head, Headdress, 18th Century, 33 ¾ In.	86.00
Walking Stick, Wood, Carved, Leg, Shoe Handle, 1800s, 32 In.	57.00
Walking Stick, Wood, Carved Lizard, Snake, Nails Used As Eyes, Intertwined Limb, 39 In.	132.00
Walking Stick, Wood, Carved, Stars, Crosses, Shields, Folk Art, c.1850, 34 ½ In.	1150.00
Walking Stick, Wood, Dog's Head, Copper, Brass, Detachable Handle, Marked, 36 In. *illus*	495.00
Walking Stick, Wood, Human Face, Lizard On Branch, Geometric, Leaves, Grass, 40 In.	77.00
Walking Stick, Wood, Root Snake Shape, Black Paint, c.1900, 35 In.	59.00
Walking Stick, Yew Wood, Handle, Silly Faces, Fox, Hounds, c.1740	395.00
Whalebone, Ivory, Tortoiseshell, Presentation, Masonic Symbol Inlaid Knob, c.1870	1760.00
Woman's Leg, High Button Shoe, Garter Below Knee, Brass, Wood Shaft, Metal Ferrule, 33 In.	595.00
Wood, Animals, Flowers, Carved, Opens To Fishing Rod, 35 In.	410.00
Wood, Carved Head Handle, Bead Eyes, c.1900, 35 In.	382.00
Wood, Carved, Ivory Dog Head, 34 In.	138.00
Wood, Carved, Jockey Head, Painted, 36 In.	138.00
Wood, Gentleman's Head, Long Beard, Carved, 1800s, 36 In.	117.00
Wood, Leg Form, Carved, Fruit & Natural Wood, 35 ½ In.	55.00
Zebra Wood, Dog Head, Gouged Spiral Shaft, Mother-Of-Pearl Inlays, 36 In.	44.00

CANTON CHINA is blue-and-white ware made near the city of Canton, in China, from about 1785 to 1895. It is hand decorated with Chinese scenes. Canton is part of the group of porcelains known today as Chinese Export Porcelain.

Bowl, Harbor Scene, Fishing Boats, Scalloped Rim, 10 & 8 & 7 In., 3 Piece	1035.00
Bowl, House, River, Cut Corner, Late 19th Century, 10 In.	633.00
Bowl, Vegetable, Cover, Nut Finial, 4 ½ x 8 ½ x 7 In.	289.00
Candlestick, 6 ½ In., Pair	526.00
Dish, Leaves, Handle, 12 ½ In.	960.00
Ewer, Leaf Design, Mid 19th Century, 12 ½ In.	2013.00
Planter, House, Landscape, 11 ¼ x 19 ½ In.	195.00
Platter, City Scene, 8-Sided, Cut Corner, 17 x 13 ¾ In.	920.00
Punch Bowl, Famille Rose, Figure & Bird Panels, Auspicious Symbol, 5 x 11 ½ In.	499.00
Sauce Bowl, Fish Shape, 5 ¼ In.	225.00
Teapot, Wire Handle, 8-Sided Lid, 18th Century, 10 x 11 In.	360.00

CAPO-DI-MONTE porcelain was first made in Naples, Italy, from 1743 to 1759. The factory moved near Madrid, Spain, reopened in 1771, and worked to 1821. Since that time, the Doccia factory of Italy acquired the molds and is using the crown and N mark. Societa Ceramica Richard is a modern-day firm often referred to as Ginori or Capo-di-Monte. This company also uses the crown and N mark.

Box, Hinged, Embossed Cherubs, Interior Flowers, Signed, 2 x 3 In.	100.00
Charger, Coat Of Arms, Crown Crest, Red Shield, Flower, Gilt Borders, 2 ⅞ x 16 In.	345.00
Cigarette Carousel, Dome Top, Boys, Winged Figure, Instrument, Gilt Metal, 1900s, 13 In.	165.00
Cup, Cartouche, Children, Gold Rim & Handle, Mid 20th Century, 3 x 5 In., 12 Piece	95.00
Ewer, Putti, Riding Seahorse, Dolphins, Satyr Handle, Late 19th Century, 14 ½ In.	460.00
Figurine, Dancing Couple, Rustic Attire, c.1920, 9 In.	234.00
Figurine, Flower Seller, Marked, 9 ¼ In.	60.00
Figurine, Gentleman, Caricature, Rococo Details, Glazed, 3 ¾ In. *illus*	161.00
Figurine, Maestro, Hand Painted, 5 ¾ In.	48.00
Group, Lady Entertaining Man At Table, c.1900, 7 ½ x 8 In.	169.00
Jewelry Box, Decorated, Toilet Of Venus, Marine Deities, Oval, 13 In. *illus*	1093.00
Plaque, 17th Century Battle, Holland, Cavalry, Swords, Pistols, c.1890, 5 x 9 In.	450.00
Plaque, Chamfered Corners, Mythological Scene, Frame, c.1900, 22 x 22 ½ In.	920.00

Plaque, Mythological Female Figures, Lions, Frame, 12 ¾ x 16 ¾ In.		671.00
Plate, Display, Relief Scene, Bathing & Erotic, 12-Portrait Rim, Gilt, Frame, 1900s, 9 In.		148.00
Tea Set, Flowers, Allover Cartouches, Heavy Gold Trim, Mid 20th Century, 21 Piece		177.00
Tin, Cover, Nymphs, Cupids, Satyrs, Handle, 14 x 7 In.		146.00
Urn, Figures, Landscape, Relief, Gilt, Handles, 9 ½ x 11 In.		175.00
Urn, Putti, Reeds, Pink, Green, Italy, c.1900, 14 x 7 In., Pair		353.00

CAPTAIN MARVEL was introduced in February 1940 in Whiz comic books. An orphan named Billy Batson met the wizard, Shazam, and whenever he said the magic word he was transformed into a superhero. A movie serial was released in 1940. The comic was discontinued in 1954. A second Captain Marvel appeared in 1966, a third in 1967. Only the original was transformed by shouting "Shazam."

Book, Punch-Out, Unpunched, 1940s, 11 ¾ x 8 ½ In.		288.00
E.Z. Code Finder, Graphic, Blue, Red, White, Premium, Fawcett Comics, 4 In.		230.00
Magic Dime Saver, Figure Flying, Blue Back, Tin Lithograph, Fawcett, c.1948, 2 ½ In.	120.00 to	201.00
Membership Card, Magic, Lift-Up Flap, Fawcett Publications, 1940s, 2 ½ x 3 ¾ In.		115.00
School Bag, Canvas, Vinyl, Lining, Pouch Straps, Fawcett, c.1947, 11 x 14 In.	*illus*	822.00
Tie, Synthetic, Black Ground, Silk Screened Design, Fawcett, Child's, 1940s, 42 In.		316.00
Wristwatch, Cardboard Insert, Price Tag, Box, c.1948, 6 ½ In.	*illus*	410.00
Wristwatch, Chromed Metal Case, Green Band, Figure Holding Jet, Box, 3 ¾ x 6 In.		460.00

CAPTAIN MIDNIGHT began as a network radio show in September 1940. The first comic book appeared in July 1941. Captain Midnight was really the aviator Captain Albright, who was to defeat the Nazis. A movie serial was made in 1942 and a comic strip was published for a short time. The comic book version of Captain Midnight ended his career in 1948. Radio premiums are the prized collector memorabilia today.

Badge, Flight Wings, Mysto-Magic, Weather Forecasting, Skelly Oil, c.1939, 2 In.		48.00
Decoder, Secret Squadron, Captain Photo		175.00
Ring, Marine Corps, Story Folder, Ovaltine Premium, 3 ¼ x 5 ½ In.		223.00
Spy-Scope, Metal, Black, Orange Lens Holders, Ovaltine Premium, 5 x 3 ½ In.		168.00

CARAMEL SLAG, *see Imperial Glass category.*

CARDS listed here include advertising cards (often called trade cards), baseball cards, playing cards, and others. Color photographs were rare in the nineteenth century, so companies gave away colorful cards with pictures of children, flowers, products, or related scenes that promoted the company name. These were often collected and stored in albums. Baseball cards also date from the nineteenth century, when they were used by tobacco companies as giveaways. Gum cards were started in 1933, but it was not until after World War II that the bubble gum cards favored today were produced. Today over 1,000 cards are issued each year by the gum companies. Related items may be found in the Christmas, Halloween, Movie, Paper, and Postcard categories.

Advertising, Dunham's Cocoanut, 4 ½ x 2 ¾ In.	*illus*	10.00
Advertising, Frank Miller Crown's Dressing, Ladies & Children's Shoes, Victorian Shoe		11.00
Advertising, Pallas Patroness Of Art, Theatrical, Late 19th Century		6.00
Advertising, Phenyo-Caffeine, For Headache, 4 ½ x 2 ¾ In.	*illus*	20.00
Baseball, Babe Ruth, American Caramel, Full Uniform, 1922		2232.00
Baseball, Babe Ruth, American Caramel, Lancaster, Pa., E120, 1922		488.00
Baseball, Babe Ruth, Goudey, No. 149, 1933	*illus*	1673.00
Baseball, Charlie Bennett, Old Judge Cigarettes, Cabinet, 1888		3294.00
Baseball, Christy Mathewson, Cracker Jack, No. 88, 1915		41125.00
Baseball, Cy Young, Briggs, 1909-10		3422.00
Baseball, Cy Young, Croft's Cocoa, 1909		1175.00
Baseball, Eddie Plank, Philadelphia Caramel, 1909		1762.00
Baseball, Harry Stovey, Dog's Head & Old Judge Cigarettes, 1889		5185.00
Baseball, Honus Wagner, Tip Top Bread, Pittsburgh Pirates, 1910	*illus*	219225.00
Baseball, Jack Clements, Old Judge Cigarettes, 1888		1220.00
Baseball, Jackie Robinson, Throwing, Low Pop, Bond Bread, 1947		2963.00
Baseball, Jim Mutrie, Old Judge Cigarettes, 1889		2318.00
Baseball, Joe Jackson, American Caramel, 1909		23500.00
Baseball, Joe Jackson, National Game, 1913		1762.00
Baseball, Lou Gehrig, U.S. Caramel, No. 26, 1932		8225.00
Baseball, Mickey Mantle, Topps, No. 150, 1958	*illus*	896.00
Baseball, Napoleon Lajoie, Goudey, No. 106, 1933		26400.00
Baseball, Ty Cobb, Green Background, 1909		2350.00

Capo-di-Monte, Figurine, Gentleman, Caricature, Rococo Details, Glazed, 3 ¾ In.
$161.00

Capo-di-Monte, Jewelry Box, Decorated, Toilet Of Venus, Marine Deities, Oval, 13 In.
$1093.00

Captain Marvel, School Bag, Canvas, Vinyl, Lining, Pouch Straps, Fawcett, c.1947, 11 x 14 In.
$822.00

Captain Marvel, Wristwatch, Cardboard Insert, Price Tag, Box, c.1948, 6 ½ In.
$410.00

Card, Advertising, Dunham's Cocoanut, 4 ½ x 2 ¾ In.
$10.00

Card, Advertising, Phenyo-Caffeine, For Headache, 4 ½ x 2 ¾ In.
$20.00

Card, Baseball, Babe Ruth, Goudey, No. 149, 1933
$1673.00

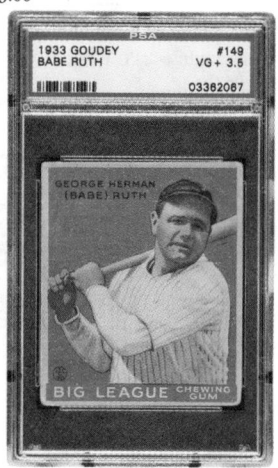

Card, Baseball, Honus Wagner, Tip Top Bread, Pittsburgh Pirates, 1910
$219225.00

Card, Baseball, Mickey Mantle, Topps, No. 150, 1958
$896.00

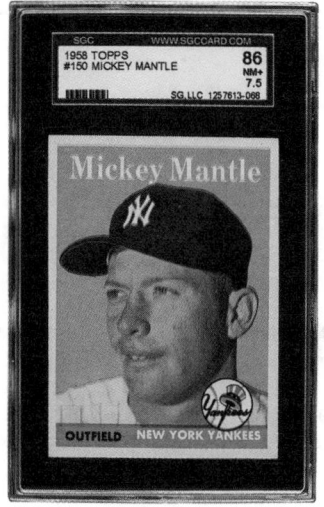

Card, Baseball, Wrapper, 1930s Orbit Tattoo, Goudey, National Chicle, Play Ball, 4 Piece
$356.00

Card, Boxing, Frank Klaus, Dixie Queen, T223, 1910
$657.00

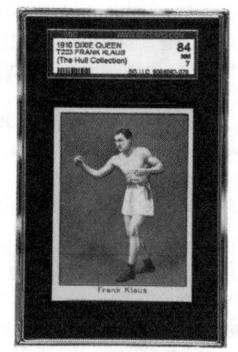

Card, Football, Jim Brown, Topps, No. 62, 1958
$1912.00

Card, Golf, Bobby Jones, Lambert, Who's Who In Sports, 1926
$717.00

Card, Greeting, Birthday, Puffy, Pansies, Printed Satin, Russ Craft, Box
$8.00

Baseball, Will Kid Gleason, Old Judge Cigarettes, 1889	3294.00
Baseball, Wrapper, 1930s Orbit Tattoo, Goudey, National Chicle, Play Ball, 4 Piece ....*illus*	356.00
Boxing, Frank Klaus, Dixie Queen, T223, 1910 ....*illus*	657.00
Football, Jim Brown, Topps, No. 62, 1958 ....*illus*	1912.00
Golf, Bobby Jones, Lambert, Who's Who In Sports, 1926 ....*illus*	717.00
Greeting, Birthday, Girl, Arm Moves, Lifts Lid On Basket, Embossed, Mechanical, Germany, 1908	6.00
Greeting, Birthday, Puffy, Pansies, Printed Satin, Russ Craft, Box ....*illus*	8.00
Greeting, Bon Voyage, 1950s, 6 ½ x 4 ½ In. ....*illus*	5.00
Greeting, Valentine, Banjo, Silk Ruffle, Coarse Paper Lace, Box, Early 1900s, 13 In. ....*illus*	88.00
Greeting, Valentine, Cutout, Cherubs, Hearts, Tulips, Watercolor, Ink, Frame, 1764, 12 x 14 In.	529.00
Greeting, Valentine, Gulliver's Travels, Mechanical, 4 Scenes, c.1939, 4 ⅝ To 5 ¼ In.	144.00
Greeting, Valentine, Heart Shape, Ribbon, Woman's Head, Gold Foil, 1800s, 6 x 6 In.	4148.00
Greeting, Valentine, Love's Offering To You, Embossed, Gold, 6 ¼ In. ....*illus*	10.00
Greeting, Valentine, Paper, Watercolor, Pinprick, Painted Wood Frame, Pa., Dec., 1837, 13 ½ In.	711.00
Greeting, Valentine, Seaplane, 3 Girls, Flower Frame, Crepe Paper, Honeycomb, 11 ¼ In.	58.00
Greeting, Valentine, To My Valentine, Girl, Honeycomb, Early 1900s................................	6.00
Greeting, Valentine, Zeppelin, Child, Waves U.S.A., Honeycomb Body, 15 In.	201.00
Gum, Pack, Zorro, Gai-Graded, Unopened, Topps, Wax Pack, 1958	253.00
Gum, Zorro, Color Photos, Text Back, Topps, 2 ½ x 3 ½ In., 88 Piece	158.00
Hockey, Bobby Orr, Topps, No. 35, 1966-67 ....*illus*	1076.00
Playing, Marilyn Monroe, Tom Kelly Nude Photograph, Deck............................	130.00
Playing, Steamboat, U.S. Playing Co., Ohio, c.1900, Deck..............................	41.00

CARDER, *See Aurene and Steuben categories.*

CARLSBAD is a mark found on china made by several factories in Germany, Austria, and Bavaria. Many pieces were exported to the United States. Most of the pieces available today were made after 1891.

Vase, Transfer, Nymphs, Flowers, Cherubs, Signed Carl Larson, Austria, Early 1900s, 14 ¼ In.	71.00

CARLTON WARE was made at the Carlton Works of Stoke-on-Trent, England, beginning about 1890. The firm traded as Wiltshaw & Robinson until 1957. It was renamed Carlton Ware Ltd. in 1958. The company went bankrupt in 1995, but the name is still in use.

Dish, Leaf, Green, 5 x 4 In.	10.00
Figurine, Golly Band, Piano Player	48.00
Ginger Jar, Cover, Spider Web, Cobalt Blue Ground, Early 1900s, 16 In.	375.00
Vase, Rouge Royal, Cylinder, Swirling Gilt Design, 12 ½ In.	48.00

CARNIVAL GLASS was an inexpensive, iridescent pressed glass made from about 1907 to about 1925. More than 1,000 different patterns are known. Carnival glass is currently being reproduced. Additional pieces may be found in the Northwood category.

Acorn Burrs & Bark pattern is listed here as Acorn Burrs.	
Acorn Burrs, Tumbler, Purple	85.00
Acorn, Bowl, Aqua, Butterscotch Overlay, Iridescent, 7 ½ x 2 ½ In. ....*illus*	95.00
Amaryllis pattern is listed here as Tiger Lily.	
American Beauty Roses pattern is listed here as Wreath Of Roses.	
Apple Blossom Twigs, Bowl, Banana Boat Shape, Peach Opal	175.00
Apple Blossom Twigs, Bowl, Peach Opalescent, Ruffled, Edge........................	85.00
Apple Blossom Twigs, Plate, Peach Opalescent, 9 In.	275.00
Apple Tree, Tumbler, Marigold..	57.00
April Showers, Vase, Amethyst, 12 In.	30.00
April Showers, Vase, Blue, Peacock Tail Interior, 10 ¾ In.	135.00
April Showers, Vase, Green, 10 ½ In.	30.00
April Showers, Vase, Marigold, 10 ½ In.	67.00
April Showers, Vase, Peacock Tail Interior, Green, Squat, 6 In.	70.00
April Showers, Vase, Squat, Blue...	45.00
April Showers, Vase, White, 7 In.	1435.00
Argonaut Shell pattern is listed here as Nautilus.	
Asters, Compote, Marigold, Stemmed	50.00
Atlantic City Elks, Plate, Blue, 7 In.	450.00
Aurora Pearls, Bowl, Ruffled Edge, Moonstone Iridescence, Painted Flowers, 11 ½ In.	950.00
Australian Butterfly Bush, Compote, Purple, Ruffled Edge........................	300.00
Autumn Acorns, Bowl, Marigold, Ruffled Edge......................................	67.00
Banded Medallion & Teardrop pattern is listed here as Beaded Bull's-Eye.	
Basketweave, Basket, Open Edge, Ruffled Edge, Aqua	20.00

Card, Greeting, Bon Voyage, 1950s, 6 ½ x 4 ½ In. $5.00

Card, Greeting, Valentine, Banjo, Silk Ruffle, Coarse Paper Lace, Box, Early 1900s, 13 In. $88.00

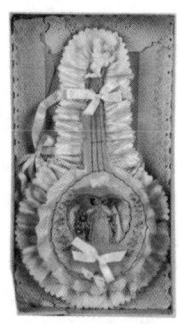

Card, Greeting, Valentine, Love's Offering To You, Embossed, Gold, 6 ¼ In. $10.00

Card, Hockey, Bobby Orr, Topps, No. 35, 1966-67 $1076.00

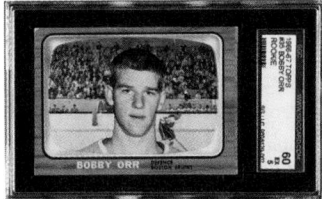

C

Carnival Glass, Acorn, Bowl, Aqua, Butterscotch Overlay, Iridescent, 7 ½ x 2 ½ In. $95.00

Carnival Glass Sets
Some carnival glass patterns were made in full sets that include bowls, plates, and accessories in numerous sizes. Other patterns were for novelties made in only one shape.

Basketweave, Basket, Red, Open Edge	50.00
Battenburg Lace No. 1 pattern is listed here as Hearts & Flowers.	
Battenburg Lace No. 3 pattern is listed here as Fanciful.	
Beaded Acanthus, Pitcher, Milk, Marigold	50.00
Beaded Bull's-Eye, Vase, Purple, 7 ½ In.	110.00
Beaded Bulls-Eye, Vase, Marigold, 7 ½ In.	95.00
Beaded Medallion & Teardrop pattern is listed here as Beaded Bull's-Eye.	
Beaded Shell, Mug, Blue	165.00
Beads & Flowers, Plate, Peach Opal, 6 In.	20.00
Bells & Beads, Sauce, Peach Opalescent, Ruffled Edge	5.00
Berry & Leaf, Vase, Squat, Jack-In-The-Pulpit, Marigold	22.00
Big Fish, Bowl, Amethyst, 3-In-1 Edge	795.00
Big Fish, Bowl, Marigold	1100.00
Birds & Cherries, Bonbon, Card Tray Shape, Amethyst	45.00
Birds & Cherries, Bonbon, Card Tray Shape, Green	115.00
Birds & Cherries, Compote, Amethyst	95.00
Birds On Bough pattern is listed here as Birds & Cherries.	
Blackberry Wreath, Sauce, Amethyst	85.00
Blackberry Wreath, Sauce, Green	60.00
Blossomtime, Compote, Purple, Ruffled Edge	175.00
Blueberry, Tumbler, Blue	40.00
Boggy Bayou, Vase, Marigold, 5 In.	23.00
Broken Arches, Punch Set, Purple, 8 Piece	750.00
Butterfly & Berry, Berry Bowl, Blue, Footed, Master	65.00
Butterfly & Berry, Butter, Marigold	45.00
Butterfly & Berry, Vase, Blue, 8 ½ In.	25.00
Butterfly & Berry, Vase, Marigold, 9 In.	20.00
Butterfly & Berry, Whimsy, Leaves, Blue	1500.00
Butterfly & Fern, Water Set, Blue, 5 Piece	200.00
Butterfly & Grape pattern is listed here as Butterfly & Berry.	
Butterfly & Plume pattern is listed here as Butterfly & Fern.	
Butterfly & Stippled Rays pattern is listed here as Butterfly.	
Butterfly & Tulip, Bowl, Purple, Square	2200.00
Butterfly, Bonbon, Purple, Ribbed Back	190.00
Cactus Leaf Rays pattern is listed here as Leaf Rays.	
Carolina Dogwood, Bowl, Ruffled Edge, Milk Glass	33.00
Caroline, Bowl, Crimped Edge, Square, Peach Opal	25.00
Cherries & Mums pattern is listed here as Mikado.	
Cherry, Bowl, Cherries, Leaves, Footed, Amethyst, 4 x 8 In.	360.00
Christmas Cactus pattern is listed here as Thistle.	
Christmas Rose & Poppy pattern is listed here as Six Petals.	
Chrysanthemum Wreath pattern is listed here as Ten Mums.	
Chrysanthemum, Chop Plate, Marigold	450.00
Chrysanthemum, Chop Plate, Purple, Qt.	3000.00
Coin Dot, Bowl, Red, Round, Deep, 9 In.	825.00
Coin Dot, Bowl, Red, Ruffled Edge, 9 In.	675.00
Concave Flute, Vase, Peach Opalescent, 10 In.	115.00
Concord, Bowl, Green, Ruffled Edge, 9 In.	675.00
Corinth, Vase, Aqua, 9 In.	25.00
Corinth, Vase, Peach Opalescent, Pinched In, 6 In.	28.00
Corinth, Vase, Pinched, Peach Opal, 6 In.	27.00
Corn, Bottle, Smoke	265.00
Cosmos & Cane, Rose Bowl, Honey Amber	305.00
Cosmos, Bowl, 9 ½ In.	35.00
Cosmos, Bowl, Amethyst, Ruffled Edge, 10 In.	35.00
Crab Claw, Water Set, Marigold, 7 Piece	85.00
Cut Flowers, Vase, Marigold	105.00
Dahlia, Berry Set, White, 5 Piece	125.00
Dahlia, Creamer, White, Footed, 6 ¼ x 4 ½ x 4 In.	24.00
Daisy & Drape, Vase, Turned In, Marigold	200.00
Daisy Band & Drape pattern is listed here as Daisy & Drape.	
Daisy Cut, Bell, Marigold	85.00
Daisy Wreath, Bowl, Blue Opalescent, Ruffled Edge	290.00
Daisy Wreath, Bowl, Ruffled Edge, Blue Opal, 9 In.	115.00
Diamond & Bows, Vase, Green, Paneled, 8 In.	17.00
Diamond & Column, Vase, Amethyst, 14 In.	12.00

Diamond & Column, Vase, Marigold, 5 ½ In. 18.00
Diamond & Column, Vase, Marigold, 15 In. 15.00
Diamond & Column, Vase, Squat, Marigold, 5 ½ In. 17.00
Diamond & Sunburst, Bottle, Wine, Purple 55.00
Diamond Lace, Pitcher, Water, Purple 140.00 to 180.00
Diamond Lace, Water Set, Amethyst, 9 Tumblers, Pitcher, 4 ⅛ In. 88.00
Diamond Point, Vase, Purple, 10 In. 25.00
Diamond Point, Vase, Squat, Marigold, 7 In. 15.00
Dogwood Spray, Bowl, Peach Opalescent, Ruffled Edge, Footed 25.00
Dogwood, Bowl, Amethyst, Sawtooth Edge, c.1920, 5 ¾ x 2 1/14 In. 55.00
Double Stem Rose, Bowl, Dome, Ruffled Edge, Footed, Peach Opalescent 25.00
Dragon & Lotus, Bowl, Blue, Ruffled Edge 200.00
Dragon & Lotus, Bowl, Ice Cream, Amber, Iridescence, 8 ¼ In. *illus* 150.00
Dragon & Lotus, Bowl, Lime Green, Ruffled Edge 1300.00
Dragon & Lotus, Bowl, Marigold, Spatula Footed, c.1920, 8 ½ x 2 ¾ In. 90.00
Dragon & Lotus, Bowl, Ruffled Edge, Marigold 50.00
Dragon & Strawberry, Tumbler, Square, Blue 287.00
Drapery, Rose Bowl, Ice Blue, 4 In. 150.00
Drapery, Vase, Emerald Green, Variant, 8 ½ In. 295.00
Drapery, Vase, Sapphire, 8 In. 300.00
Egyptian Band pattern is listed here as Round-Up.
Embroidered Mums, Bowl, Aqua Opalescence 2000.00
Embroidered Mums, Bowl, Blue, Ruffled Edge, 9 In. 325.00
Embroidered Mums, Bowl, Ruffled Edge, Ribbed Back, Blue 315.00
Embroidered Mums, Bowl, Ruffled Edge, Ribbed Back, Purple 250.00
Enameled Daisy & Little Flowers, Water Set, Blue, 5 Piece 240.00
Estate, Vase, Smoke 45.00
Fan & Arch pattern is listed here as Persian Garden.
Fanciful, Plate, Marigold, 9 In. 45.00
Fantasy pattern is listed here as Question Marks.
Farmyard, Bowl, Purple, Ruffled Edge, 8 In. 4000.00
Fashion, Pitcher, Water, Purple 950.00
Feather & Hobstar pattern is listed here as Inverted Feather.
Featherstitch, Bowl, Blue 322.00
Field Rose pattern is listed here as Rambler Rose.
Field Thistle, Plate, Marigold, 6 In. 115.00
Fishnet, Epergne, Peach Opal 400.00
Fishscale & Beads, Banana Boat, Peach Opalescent 25.00
Fishscale & Beads, Bowl, Ruffled Edge, Peach Opal, 5 In. 15.00
Fishscale & Beads, Plate, Marigold, 6 In. 85.00
Florentine, Candlestick, Ice Green, 10 In. 120.00
Florentine, Candlestick, Lavender, 10 In. 15.00
Florentine, Candlestick, Marigold, 10 In. 15.00
Florentine, Candlestick, Purple, 10 In. 55.00
Florentine, Candlestick, Russet, 8 ½ In. 35.00
Flower Pot pattern is listed here as Butterfly & Tulip.
Flute & Cane, Pitcher, Milk, Squat, Marigold 60.00
Four Flowers, Banana Boat, Ruffled Edge, Peach Opalescent 165.00
Four Flowers, Bowl, Peach Opalescent, Ruffled Edge, 10 In. 50.00
Four Pillars, Vase, Aqua Opal, 11 In. 200.00
Four Pillars, Vase, Olive Green, 10 In. 17.00
Four Seventy Four, Punch Set, Marigold, 14 Piece 145.00
Freefold, Vase, Marigold, 12 In. 10.00
Fruit Basket, Bonbon, Amethyst, Stemmed 2100.00
Garden Path, Bowl, Purple, Ruffled Edge, 10 In. 1100.00
Good Luck, Bowl, Amethyst, Piecrust Edge, 8 ¾ In. 210.00
Good Luck, Bowl, Basketweave Exterior, Marigold, 8 ¾ In. 150.00
Good Luck, Bowl, Basketweave, Marigold, 8 ¾ In. 150.00
Good Luck, Bowl, Blue, Piecrust Edge, 8 ¾ In. 240.00
Good Luck, Bowl, Green, Ruffled Edge 525.00
Good Luck, Bowl, Ice Blue, Ruffled Edge 1600.00
Good Luck, Bowl, Marigold, Ribbed Back 110.00
Grape & Cable, Biscuit Jar, 2 Handles, Cover, Marigold 185.00
Grape & Cable, Biscuit Jar, Purple 95.00
Grape & Cable, Bonbon, Green, Handles, 6 In. 70.00
Grape & Cable, Bonbon, Purple, Handles, 6 In. 75.00

Carnival Glass, Dragon & Lotus, Bowl, Ice Cream, Amber, Iridescence, 8 ¼ In.
$150.00

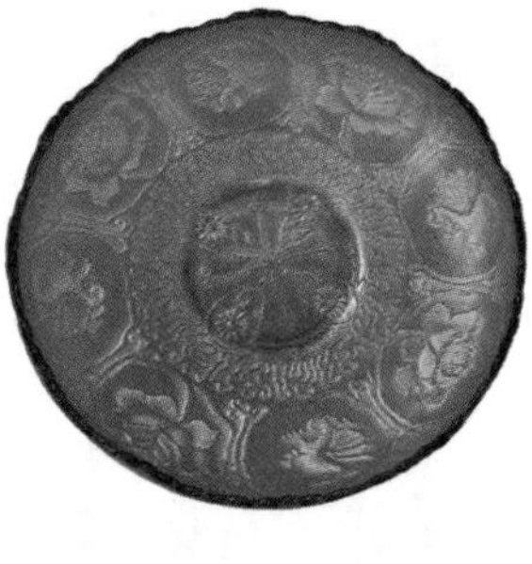

Carnival Glass, Heart & Vine, Bowl, Piecrust Edge, Blue, 8 In.
$120.00

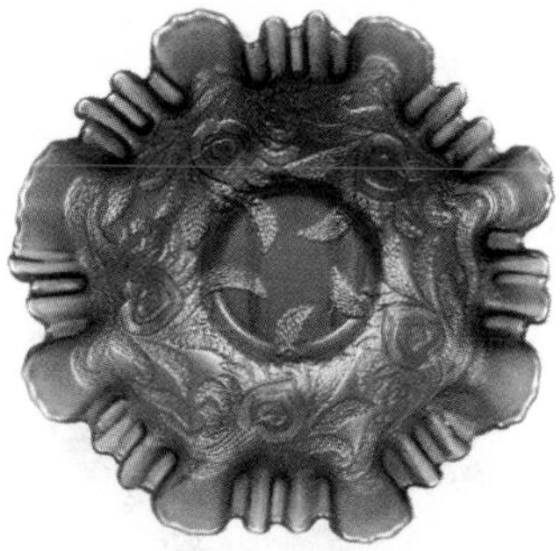

Carnival Glass, Inverted Feather, Biscuit Jar, Handles, 6 ½ x 8 ½ In.
$75.00

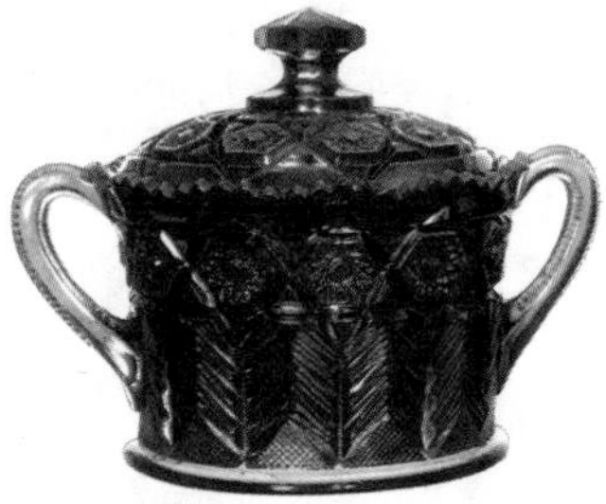

How Was Carnival Glass Made?

An iridescent finish is added to molded glass to make carnival glass. The glass, usually colored, is pressed in the mold, then removed. Additional shaping may be done by hand. Then the piece is sprayed with a coating of liquid metallic salts to create the iridescent finish.

Carnival Glass, Lacy Dewdrop, Water Pitcher, Pearlized Milk Glass, 7 ¾ In. **$160.00**

Carnival Glass, Leaf Chain, Plate, Beaded Berry Exterior, 9 ¼ x 1 ½ In. **$180.00**

Grape & Cable, Bottle, Cologne, Green	275.00
Grape & Cable, Bottle, Cologne, Purple	155.00
Grape & Cable, Hatpin Holder, Green	185.00
Grape & Cable, Pin Tray, Purple	170.00
Grape & Cable, Pitcher, Green, 8 In.	525.00
Grape & Cable, Pitcher, Water, Purple, Northwood, 8 In.	250.00
Grape & Cable, Plate, Basketweave Exterior, Amethyst, 9 In.	90.00
Grape & Cable, Plate, Handgrip, Purple, 8 In.	55.00
Grape & Cable, Plate, Plain Back, Purple, 9 In.	95.00
Grape & Cable, Plate, Purple, 6 In.	100.00
Grape & Cable, Punch Bowl Set, Purple Iridescence, Bowl, 12 Cups, 14 x 16 In.	900.00
Grape & Cable, Sweetmeat, Purple	185.00
Grape Delight pattern is listed here as Vintage.	
Grape Leaves, Bowl, Green, Tricornered, Blue Iridescence Over Bowl	9000.00
Grape Wreath, Sauce, Amethyst, Crimped Edge, Ruffled Edge	175.00
Grape Wreath, Sauce, Marigold	80.00
Grapevine Lattice, Tumbler, White	110.00
Hanging Cherries, Bowl, Amethyst, Hobnail Back, Ruffled Edge, 10 In.	725.00
Hanging Cherries, Sauce, Green, Ruffled Edge	45.00
Hanging Cherries, Table Set, Green, 4 Piece	1600.00
Hattie, Chop Plate, Green	135.00
Hattie, Chop Plate, Marigold	475.00
Heart & Vine, Bowl, Blue, 3 In 3 Edge, c.1912, 8 x 3 In.	85.00
Heart & Vine, Bowl, Piecrust Edge, Blue, 8 In. *illus*	120.00
Heart & Vine, Plate, Blue, 9 In.	230.00
Hearts & Flowers, Bowl, Aqua, Ruffled Edge, Ribbed	525.00
Hearts & Flowers, Bowl, Ice Blue, Ribbed	195.00
Hearts & Flowers, Bowl, Ice Blue, Ruffled Edge, Ribbed	105.00
Hearts & Flowers, Compote, White, 6 x 7 In, Pair	125.00
Hearts & Flowers, Compote, White, Ruffled Edge	70.00
Heavy Grape, Chop Plate, Green	65.00
Heavy Grape, Chop Plate, Marigold	45.00
Heavy Grape, Plate, Purple, 8 In.	280.00
Heavy Web, Bowl, Round, Peach Opal, 11 In.	475.00
Heron & Rushes pattern is listed here as Stork & Rushes.	
Hobnail pattern is listed in this book as its own category.	
Hobstar & Cut Triangles, Bowl, Amethyst, Ruffled Edge	15.00
Hobstar & Cut Triangles, Bowl, Rose, Amethyst	7.50
Hobstar & Feather, Punch Bowl Set, Fleur-De-Lis Interior, Marigold, 12 Cups, 12 x 16 In.	1800.00
Hobstar, Biscuit Jar, Marigold	20.00
Holly & Berry, Bowl, Ruffled Edge, Peach Opal, 7 In.	20.00
Holly, Bonbon, c.1911	30.00
Holly, Bowl, Marigold, Ruffled Edge	25.00
Holly, Plate, Blue, 9 In.	120.00
Holly, Plate, Marigold, 9 In.	85.00 to 110.00
Holly, Plate, White, 9 In.	150.00
Holly Spray pattern is listed here as Holly Sprig.	
Holly Sprig, Card Tray, Bonbon Shape, Amethyst	85.00
Holly Sprig, Card Tray, Bonbon Shape, Green	35.00
Homestead, Chop Plate, Purple	1300.00
Honeycomb Collar pattern is listed here as Fishscale & Beads.	
Illinois Solders & Sailors, Plate, Blue, 7 In.	300.00 to 450.00
Imperial Grape, Bowl, Purple, Ruffled Edge	150.00
Imperial Grape, Bowl, Smoke, Ruffled Edge, Low	225.00
Imperial Grape, Water Set, Purple, 6 Piece	250.00
Intaglio pattern is listed here as Hobstar & Feather.	
Interior Of Cherries & Mums pattern is listed here as Mikado.	
Inverted Feather, Biscuit Jar, Handles, 6 ½ x 8 ½ In. *illus*	75.00
Iris, Goblet, Buttermilk, Amethyst	65.00
Iris, Goblet, Buttermilk, Green	70.00
Jacob's Ladder, Rose Bowl, Marigold	45.00
Kittens, Bowl, 4 Sides Folded Up, Iridescent, c.1918, 4 x 2 In.	113.00
Kittens, Sauce Bowl, Marigold, Ruffled Edge	80.00
Kittens, Saucer, Marigold, 4 ½ In.	70.00
Knotted Beads, Vase, Marigold, Crimped Edge, 8 ½ In.	40.00
Knotted Beads, Vase, Marigold, Crimped Edge, 10 In.	15.00

Kokomo, Rose Bowl, Footed, Marigold 10.00
Labelle Poppy pattern is listed here as Poppy Show.
Labelle Rose pattern is listed here as Rose Show.
Lacy Dewdrop, Water Pitcher, Pearlized Milk Glass, 7 ¾ In. ....*illus* 160.00
Lattice & Grape, Water Set, Blue, 7 Piece.. 350.00
Lattice & Points, Vase, Hat Shape, Purple, Ruffled Edge, 4 In. 307.00
Leaf & Beads, Rose Bowl, Footed, Scalloped Rim, Aqua Opal 170.00
Leaf & Beads, Rose Bowl, Footed, Scalloped Rim, Purple 65.00
Leaf Chain, Bowl, Ruffled Edge, Blue 50.00
Leaf Chain, Plate, Beaded Berry Exterior, 9 ¼ x 1 ½ In. ....*illus* 180.00
Leaf Chain, Plate, Green, 9 In. 85.00
Leaf Medallion pattern is listed here as Leaf Chain.
Leaf Rays, Nappy, Handle, Peach, Opalescent, Daisy, Ray Exterior........................ 35.00
Lined Lattice, Vase, Marigold, 9 In. 35.00
Lined Lattice, Vase, Purple, Squat, 6 In. 289.00
Little Flowers, Plate, Marigold, 4-Sided, 6 In. 170.00
Little Flowers, Sauce, Ruffled Edge, Aqua... 95.00
Little Stars, Bowl, Green, 7 In. 105.00
Long Hobstar, Bowl, Marigold, Ruffled Edge, 10 In. 23.00
Long Hobstar, Bowl, Purple, Ruffled Edge, 10 In. 23.00
Loop & Column pattern is listed here as Pulled Loop.
Looped Petals pattern is listed here as Scales.
Lotus & Grape, Bowl, Powder Blue, Round, Footed, 7 In. 55.00
Lotus & Grape, Plate, Blue, 9 In. 1300.00
Lotus & Grape, Sauce, Footed, Blue, Round 40.00
Lustre Rose, Bowl, Purple, Ruffled Edge, 10 In. 285.00
Lustre Rose, Pitcher, Water, Purple 675.00
Mae West, Candlestick, Red 165.00
Magnolia & Poinsettia pattern is listed here as Water Lily.
Maine Coast pattern is listed here as Seacoast.
Many Fruits, Punch Set, Purple, 7 Piece... 500.00
Maple Leaf, Table Set, Blue, 4 Piece.. 105.00
Maple Leaf, Table Set, Purple, 4 Piece.. 125.00
Mary Ann, Loving Cup, 3 Handles, Marigold.. 375.00
Mary Ann, Vase, Marigold 20.00
Mary Ann, Vase, Purple 105.00
Maryland pattern is listed here as Rustic.
Melinda pattern is listed here as Wishbone.
Memphis, Berry Bowl, Purple, Master.. 65.00
Memphis, Berry Set, Marigold, 5 Piece 180.00
Memphis, Punch Bowl, Marigold... 425.00
Memphis, Punch Set, Ice Blue, 7 Piece... 900.00
Memphis, Punch Set, Purple, 8 Piece.. 400.00
Mikado, Compote, Lavender, Ruffled Edge 425.00
Milady, Powder Jar, Covered, Marigold... 20.00
Miniature Morning Glory, Vase, Marigold, 7 In. 12.00
Mitered Ovals, Vase, Amethyst 7100.00
Morning Glory, Vase, Funeral, Marigold, 16 In. 170.00
Multi Fruit & Flowers pattern is listed here as Many Fruits.
Mums & Greek Key pattern is listed here as Embroidered Mums.
Nautilus, Sugar, Whimsy, Peach Opal... 45.00
Nesting Swan, Bowl, Amethyst, 9 ¾ In. 150.00
Nesting Swan, Bowl, Amethyst, Millersburg, 9 ¾ In. ....*illus* 150.00
Nesting Swan, Bowl, Amethyst, Round 3200.00
Oak Leaf & Acorn pattern is listed here as Acorn.
Ohio Star, Toothpick, Clear, Handles, Millersburg Glass, 2 x 2 In. 125.00
Old Fashion Flag pattern is listed here as Iris.
Open Rose, Plate, Amber, 9 In. 45.00
Orange Tree, Berry Bowl, 4-Footed Marigold, 1911, 5 ½ In. 32.00
Orange Tree, Bowl, Blue, 3-Footed, 5 ¾ x 10 In. ....*illus* 150.00
Orange Tree, Compote, Powder Blue, Ruffled Edge 25.00
Orange Tree, Hatpin Holder, Blue .... 105.00 to 135.00
Orange Tree, Loving Cup, Blue... 210.00
Orange Tree, Loving Cup, Green 165.00
Orange Tree, Loving Cup, Marigold 115.00
Orange Tree, Mug, Marigold, Iridescent, 1900s, 3 ½ x 3 ¼ In. 100.00

Carnival Glass, Nesting Swan, Bowl, Amethyst, Millersburg, 9 ¾ In. $150.00

Carnival Glass, Orange Tree, Bowl, Blue, 3-Footed, 5 ¾ x 10 In. $150.00

Carnival Glass, Peacock & Grape, Bowl, Marigold, 8 ¼ x 2 ½ In. $70.00

Carnival Glass, Peacock, Bowl, Ruffled Edge, Blue, 9 In. $300.00

Carnival Glass, Ribbon Tie, Bowl, Amethyst, 8 ½ In. $115.00

> **TIP**
> To clean carnival glass, try using a mixture of ½ cup ammonia and ⅛ cup white vinegar.

Carousel, Rooster, Wood, Painted, Herschell-Spillman, c.1915 $3218.00

Orange Tree, Plate, Blue, 9 In.	300.00
Orange Tree, Plate, Marigold, 9 In.	275.00
Orange Tree, Punch Set, White, 8 Piece	525.00
Orange Tree, Table Set, Marigold, 4 Piece	150.00
Palm Beach, Plate, Amethyst, Gold Back, 7 In.	200.00
Paneled Bachelor Buttons pattern is listed here as Milady.	
Paneled Diamond & Bow, Vase, Blue, 6 In.	23.00
Pansy, Bowl, Ruffled Edge, Purple	180.00
Pansy, Dish, Pickle, Marigold	10.00
Pansy, Nappy, Marigold, Handle	5.00
Panther, Sauce, Aqua, Ruffled Edge, Footed	190.00
Peach & Pear, Berry Bowl, Banana Boat, Marigold	15.00
Peach, Tumbler, Blue	50.00
Peacock & Grape, Bowl, Green	300.00
Peacock & Grape, Bowl, Green Ruffled Edge, Footed	55.00
Peacock & Grape, Bowl, Marigold, 8 ¼ x 2 ½ In. ....*illus*	70.00
Peacock & Grape, Plate, Marigold, 9 In.	600.00 to 800.00
Peacock & Urn, Bowl, Amethyst, 9 In.	108.00
Peacock & Urn, Creamer, Sugar, White	160.00
Peacock At The Fountain, Fruit Bowl, 3-Footed, Purple	450.00
Peacock At The Fountain, Water Pitcher, Purple, Northwood, 8 ½ In.	250.00
Peacock At Urn, Bowl, Ruffled, Blue, 8 In.	125.00
Peacock At Urn, Bowl, Ruffled, Marigold, 6 In.	55.00
Peacock At Urn, Plate, Blue, 9 In.	325.00 to 900.00
Peacock, Bowl, Amethyst, Piecrust Edge, 8 ¾ In.	330.00
Peacock, Bowl, Marigold, 8 ¾ In.	120.00
Peacock, Bowl, Master, Amethyst	1700.00
Peacock, Bowl, Master, Green	575.00
Peacock, Bowl, Piecrust Edge, Amethyst, Northwood, 9 In.	350.00
Peacock, Bowl, Ruffled Edge, Blue, 9 In. ....*illus*	300.00
Peacock, Bowl, Ruffled Edge, Ribbed Back, Aqua Opal, Slag	575.00
Peacock, Plate, Amethyst, 9 In.	325.00
Peacock, Plate, Ice Green, 9 In.	210.00
Peacock, Plate, Marigold, 9 In.	200.00
Peacock, Plate, Ribbed Back, Marigold, 9 In.	250.00
Pearly Dots, Compote, Peach Opalescent, Ruffled Edge	40.00
Persian Garden, Bowl, Fruit, Marigold, Round	130.00
Persian Garden, Bowl, White, C Shape, 11 In.	115.00
Persian Garden, Bowl, White, Master	205.00
Persian Garden, Plate, Marigold, 6 In.	20.00
Persian Garden, Plate, White, Pearls, 6 ⅞ In.	40.00
Persian Medallion, Hair Receiver, Marigold	15.00
Persian Medallion, Sauce, Marigold, 4 Sides Up	15.00
Petal & Fan, Plate, Peach Opalescent, Crimped, 6 In.	45.00
Petal & Fan, Plate, Purple, Crimped, 6 In.	145.00
Petal & Fan, Sauce, Crimped, Purple	125.00
Pine Cone Wreath pattern is listed here as Pine Cone.	
Pine Cone, Plate, Green, 6 In.	55.00
Pine Cone, Saucer, Amethyst, 6 In.	75.00
Pine Cone, Saucer, Blue, 6 In.	150.00
Pineapple & Fan, Bottle, Wine, Marigold	105.00
Pineapple & Fan, Wine Set, Marigold, 8 Piece	265.00
Plume Panels, Vase, Blue, 11 In.	32.00
Plume Panels, Vase, Green, 11 In.	50.00
Pond Lily, Card Tray, Bonbon Shape, White	40.00
Pony Rosette pattern is listed here as Pony.	
Pony, Bowl, Marigold, Ruffled Edge	55.00
Poppy Scroll pattern is listed here as Poppy.	
Poppy Show, Bowl, Ice Blue, Ruffled Edge	800.00
Poppy Show, Bowl, Marigold, Ruffled Edge	70.00
Poppy Show, Plate, Blue, 9 In.	1200.00
Poppy Show, Plate, Ice Blue, 9 In.	900.00
Poppy, Compote, Marigold, Salver Shaped	1050.00
Pulled Loop, Vase, Squat, Purple, 5 In.	275.00
Question Marks, Plate, Peach Opalescent, Crimped Edge	40.00

C

C

Question Marks, Plate, Purple, Footed	295.00
Raindrops, Bowl, Dome, Footed, Ruffled Edge, Peach Opal................	45.00
Raindrops, Bowl, Peach Opalescent, Ruffled Edge	40.00
Rambler Rose, Tumbler, Blue	30.00
Raspberry, Pitcher, Milk, Marigold	75.00
Raspberry, Pitcher, Water, Marigold	80.00
Raspberry, Pitcher, Water, Purple	175.00
Raspberry, Tumbler, Green	25.00
Rays & Ribbons, Bowl, Vaseline, Crimped Edge, Ruffled Edge	1550.00
Ribbed, Vase, Jack-In-The-Pulpit, Marigold, 9 ½ In.	33.00
Ribbon Tie, Bowl, Amethyst, 8 ½ In. ....*illus*	115.00
Ribbon Tie, Bowl, Ruffled Edge, Green...	40.00
Ripple, Vase, Funeral, Marigold, 15 In.	135.00
Ripple, Vase, Purple, 17 In.	1300.00
Rose & Ruffles pattern is listed here as Open Rose.	
Rose Bowl, Purple..	55.00
Rose Show, Bowl, Purple, Ruffled Edge...	275.00
Rose Show, Plate, Blue, 9 In.	400.00
Rose Show, Plate, Lime Green, 9 In.	600.00
Rose Show, Plate, Marigold, 9 In.	600.00
Rose Tree, Bowl, Blue, Ruffled Edge, 10 In.	1000.00
Roses & Loops pattern is listed here as Double Stem Rose.	
Rosette & Prisms pattern is listed here as Rosette.	
Rosette, Bowl, Purple, Ruffled Edge...	329.00
Round-Up, Bowl, Ruffled Edge, Peach Opal...................................	120.00
Rustic, Vase, Funeral, Marigold, 18 In.	600.00
Rustic, Vase, Squat, White, 7 In.	35.00
Sailboat & Windmill pattern is listed here as Sailboats.	
Sailboats, Bowl, Ruffles, Stipples, Curves, Marigold, c.1911, 6 In. ...	30.00
Scales, Bowl, Marigold, Ruffled Edge...	55.00
Scroll-Cable pattern is listed here as Estate.	
Seacoast, Pin Tray, Amethyst..	1200.00
Shell & Sand, Bowl, Round, Marigold...	10.00
Shell & Wild Rose pattern is listed here as Wild Rose.	
Six Petals, Bowl, Peach Opalescent, Ruffled Edge	15.00
Ski Star, Bowl, Peach Opalescent, Dome, Footed	30.00
Ski Star, Bowl, Peach Opalescent, Ruffled Edge............................	105.00
Ski Star, Sauce, Peach Opalescent, Tricornered, Crimped Edge........	30.00
Ski Star, Sauce, Ruffled Edge, Peach Opal	10.00
Smooth Rays, Bowl, Ruffled Edge, Jeweled Heart Back, Peach Opal, 10 In. ...	25.00
Stag & Holly, Bowl, Ice Cream, Footed, Lime Green, Marigold Iridescence............	120.00
Stag & Holly, Bowl, Marigold, Footed, 10 In.	85.00
Stag & Holly, Bowl, Marigold, Ice Cream Shape, 10 ¼ In.	80.00
Stag & Holly, Bowl, Ruffled Edge, Blue..	115.00
Stag & Holly, Chop Plate, Marigold	525.00
Stag & Holly, Dish, Green, Scalloped Rim, 10 In.	140.00
Stag & Holly, Plate, Marigold, Footed, 9 In.	65.00
Starfish, Bonbon, Peach Opalescent..	55.00
Stippled Clematis pattern is listed here as Little Stars.	
Stippled Diamond & Flower pattern is listed here as Little Flowers.	
Stippled Leaf & Beads pattern is listed here as Leaf & Beads.	
Stippled Posy & Pods pattern is listed here as Four Flowers.	
Stippled Rays, Bonbon, Olive Green	25.00
Stippled Ribbons & Rays pattern is listed here as Rays & Ribbons.	
Stippled Singing Birds, Mug, Marigold	45.00
Stippled Three Fruits, Bowl, Ruffled Edge, Ribbed Back, Marigold........	65.00
Stork & Rushes, Tumbler, Cobalt Blue, Iridescent, c.1912, 4 x 3 In.	60.00
Stork & Rushes, Water Set, Blue, 5 Piece......................................	425.00
Strawberry Wreath, Bowl, Green, 10 In.	300.00
Strawberry, Plate, Purple, 9 In.	165.00
Stream Of Hearts, Compote, Crimped Edge, Ruffled Edge, Marigold......	35.00
Sunflower & Diamond, Vase, Marigold, 9 In.	35.00
Sunflower, Bowl, Green, Ruffled Edge, Footed	318.00
Sunflower, Bowl, Ice Blue, Ruffled Edge, Footed	700.00
Target, Vase, Purple, 9 ½ In.	20.00

> **TIP**
> *American carousel figures are more heavily carved on the right side because they went around counterclockwise. The left side is more ornate for European carousel figures because the carousel turned the other way. American figures sell for more money.*

Carousel, Zebra, Carved, Painted, c.1900, 43 In. $8775.00

Carriage, Horse, Leather Upholstery, 3 Iron Wheels, Victorian, 57 In. $682.00

Cash Register, National, Model 126-2-X, Chrome, 17 ½ x 13 x 15 In. $138.00

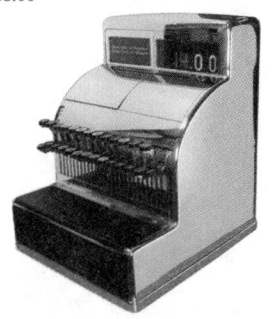

Cash Register, National, Model 313, Brass, 17 In. $468.00

Cash Register, National, Model 445, Brass, Wood, Hand Crank, 20 x 16 ½ In. $410.00

Cash Register, National, Model 452, Brass, Oak Base, 23 x 26 x 17 In. $518.00

Target, Vase, Squat, Peach Opal, 6 In.	45.00
Target, Vase, White, Squat, 6 ½ In.	30.00
Teardrops pattern is listed here as Raindrops.	
Ten Mums, Bowl, Blue, Ruffled Edge	265.00
Thistle, Bowl, Ruffled Edge, Amethyst	274.00
Three Fruits, Bowl, Purple, Ruffled Edge	60.00
Three Fruits, Plate, Amethyst, 9 ½ In.	210.00
Three Fruits, Plate, Green, 9 In.	160.00
Three Fruits, Plate, Marigold, 9 In.	55.00
Three Fruits, Plate, Purple, 9 In.	105.00 to 125.00
Tiger Lily, Water Set, Green, 6 Piece	175.00
Tree Trunk, Vase, Green, 12 ½ In.	240.00
Tree Trunk, Vase, Ice Blue, 11 In.	325.00
Tree Trunk, Vase, Marigold, 6 ½ In.	40.00
Tree Trunk, Vase, Purple, 9 In.	40.00
Tree Trunk, Vase, Purple, 10 In.	70.00
Tree Trunk, Vase, Squat, Green, 6 In.	15.00
Tree Trunk, Vase, Squat, Marigold, 6 ½ In.	40.00
Vintage, Bowl, Aqua Opalescent, Ruffled Edge, 9 In.	240.00
Vintage, Bowl, Blue, Hobnail Back, 10 In.	5700.00
Vintage, Bowl, Ruffled Edge, Marigold, 10 In.	15.00
Vintage, Fernery, Blue	20.00
Vintage, Plate, Blue, 7 In.	105.00
Vintage, Rose Bowl, Purple	55.00
Water Lily, Pitcher, Water, Marigold	250.00
Wild Grapes pattern is listed here as Grape Leaves.	
Wild Rose, Syrup, Marigold, 6 In.	403.00
Windmill Medallion pattern is listed here as Windmill.	
Windmill, Dish, Pickle	95.00
Windmill, Pitcher, Milk, Green	50.00 to 80.00
Windmill, Water Set, Marigold, 7 Piece	85.00
Wishbone & Spades, Plate, Purple, 6 In.	145.00 to 294.00
Wishbone, Bowl, Marigold, 3-Footed, Northwood, 7 ½ In.	100.00
Wishbone, Bowl, Purple, Ruffled Edge, Footed	85.00
Wishbone, Bowl, Smoke, 10 In.	225.00
Wreath Of Roses, Bonbon, 2 Handles, c.1910	78.00
Zipper Stitch, Wine, Marigold	55.00

CAROUSEL or merry-go-round figures were first carved in the United States in 1867 by Gustav Dentzel. Collectors discovered the charm of the hand-carved figures in the 1970s, and they were soon classed as folk art. Most desirable are the figures other than horses, such as pigs, camels, lions, or dogs. A jumper is a figure that was made to move up and down on a pole; a stander was placed in a stationary position.

Band Organ, Wurlitzer, Style 153, Coin-Operated, White Enamel, Scroll Work, 7 x 8 Ft.	33000.00
Bear, Carved, Mexico, c.1935, 38 In.	523.00
Bear, On Hind Legs, Wood & Composition, Painted, Brass Pole Mount, Wood Base, 32 In.	295.00
Black Pole, County Fair Style, Paint, Herschell-Spillman, 1800s, 50 x 48 In.	528.00
Dog, St. Bernard, Herschell-Spillman, Blue & White Blanket, 40 x 55 In.	6000.00
Giraffe, Wood, Painted, Glass Eyes, Dentzel, 77 x 48 In.	5400.00
Giraffe, Wood, Painted, Glass Eyes, Jewels, Orange & Green Saddle, 67 x 42 In.	8400.00
Goat, Raised Front Legs, Painted, Tasseled Blanket, C.I.D. Looff Co., N.Y., 66 x 63 In.	53125.00
Horse, Brown, Green, Black, Yellow, Metal, 42 In.	293.00
Horse, Jumper, Carved, Painted, Gold Stand, Herschell-Spillman Company, c.1915, 73 x 55 In.	1659.00
Horse, Jumper, Outside, Painted Wood, 1915-25, 62 In.	3173.00
Horse, Jumper, Outside Row, Beige, Parker, c.1900, 46 In.	1175.00
Horse, Jumper, Wood, 2-Tone Brown, Blue & Orange Saddle, Allan Herschell, 38 x 48 In.	600.00
Horse, Jumper, Wood, Carved, Painted, Glass Eyes, Chicago, 1906, 36 x 46 In.	2150.00
Horse, Jumper, Wood, Gray, Orange & Blue Saddle, Allan Herschell, 36 x 48 In.	840.00
Horse, Leaping, Cast Aluminum, Painted, Coca-Cola Base, 54 In.	71.00
Horse, Metal, Prancer, Painted, Brown, Green, Black, Yellow, 42 In.	175.00
Horse, Prancer, Black, Pink Saddle, Metal Stand, A. Herschell, New York, c.1920, 62 In.	3173.00
Horse, Prancer, Carved, Harness Glass Jewel, Paint, Leather, Iron, Glass Eye, Stand, c.1903, 54 In.	5629.00
Horse, Prancer, Inner Row Glass Eyes, Paint, Dentzel, Philadelphia, c.1900, 53 x 61 In.	3680.00
Horse, Prancer, White, Pink Saddle, Metal Stand, Spillman, N.Y., c.1920, 50 In.	1763.00
Horse, Prancer, Wood, Carved, Painted, Applied Tail, Leather Bridle & Stirrups	1135.00

Horse, Raised Front Legs, Tossed Head, Carved, Painted, Hair Tail, Charles Looff, 58 x 59 In.	4000.00
Horse, Rising On Rear Legs, White, Gray Mane, Hair Tail, Rhode Island, 19th Century, 47 x 11 In.	9500.00
Horse, Zebra Stripe Repaint, Iron Bit, c.1900, 39 x 65 In.	940.00
Lion, Running, Wood, Carved, Painted, c.1880-1910, 53 In.	925.00
Pig, Running, Wood, Painted, Blue Neck Ribbon, Herschell-Spillman, 43 x 46 In.	4800.00
Rabbit, Prancer, White, Red Saddle, G. Baynol, France, c.1899, 40 x 60 In.	940.00
Road Runner, Wood, Painted, Hinged Neck, Herschell-Spillman, 43 x 46 In.	2280.00
Rooster, Wood, Painted, Herschell-Spillman, c.1915 ....*illus*	3218.00
Rounding Board, Western Scene, Wood, Gessom, c.1910, 40 x 103 ½ In.	690.00
Squirrel, Wood, Carved, Painted, Iron Mount, 32 x 36 In.	767.00
Zebra, Carved, Painted, c.1900, 43 In. ....*illus*	8775.00

CARRIAGE means several things, so this category lists baby carriages, buggies for adults, horse-drawn sleighs, and even strollers. Doll-sized carriages are listed in the Toy category.

Baby Buggy, Black, Green, Red, Folding Chair, 1800s, 43 x 23 In.	146.00
Baby Buggy, Stick & Ball Frame, Steel Suspension, Spoke Wheels, Umbrella Holder, 36 x 55 In.	420.00
Baby Buggy, Wicker, Cloth Lined, Detachable Roof, Windshield, c.1908, 46 ½ In.	5463.00
Baby Buggy, Wicker, Green, Steel Suspension, Spoke Wheels, Rubber Tires, 36 x 39 In.	120.00
Baby Buggy, Wicker, Wood Frame, Spoke Wheels, Steel Suspension, Fringe Top, 48 x 23 In.	330.00
Baby Buggy, Wicker, Wood Handle, Padded Seat, Steel Frame, Spoke Wheels, 22 x 52 In.	180.00
Carriage, Horse, Leather Upholstery, 3 Iron Wheels, Victorian, 57 In. ....*illus*	682.00
Pram, Wicker, Scrolls, 19th Century, 24 x 26 x 12 In.	120.00

CASH REGISTERS were invented in 1884 because an eye on the cash was a necessity in stores of the nineteenth century, too. John and James Ritty invented a large model that resembled a clock and kept a record of the dollars and cents exchanged in the store. John Patterson improved the cash register with a paper roll to record the money. By the early 1900s, elaborate brass registers were made. More modern types were made after 1920.

Audit, No. 7, Nickel Plated, 20 x 9 ¾ x 16 ¾ In.	275.00
Burroughs, Art Deco, Black	110.00
Model 313, Nickel-Plated Brass, Early 20th Century, 17 In.	397.00
National, Brass, Oak, Amount Purchased, 20 x 8 ½ x 15 In.	595.00
National, Model 38, Nickel Finish	265.00
National, Model 50, Brass, 17 x 10 In.	2420.00
National, Model 126-2-X, Chrome, 17 ½ x 13 x 15 In. ....*illus*	138.00
National, Model 138, Copper, Art Nouveau Top Sign, c.1900	269.00
National, Model 216, Candy Store, Copper Over Brass, Marquee, 21 In.	797.00
National, Model 313, Brass & Nickel, Later Plated With 24K Gold, 1913	3300.00
National, Model 313, Brass, 17 In. ....*illus*	468.00
National, Model 313, Marble Shelf	570.00
National, Model 313, Swag, Flowers, Brass, Marble, 21 x 9 ½ In.	767.00
National, Model 317, Receipt Writer, H.E. Sweeney, c.1910, 17 x 12 x 16 In.	960.00
National, Model 332, Key, 79 x 17 x 15 In.	175.00
National, Model 333, Brass Plated, Milk Glass Coin Shelf, Oak Stand, 18 x 22 x 16 In.	633.00
National, Model 349, Nickel Plated, Marble Coin Shelf, Oak Stand, c.1909, 17 x 22 In.	460.00
National, Model 349-2, Side-By-Side, From Plaza Hotel, 24 x 27 x 16 In.	1200.00
National, Model 416, Crank, Receipt Writer, 21 x 20 ½ In.	1020.00
National, Model 442, Nickel Finish, Oak Base, 22 ½ x 20 In.	470.00
National, Model 445, Brass, Wood, Hand Crank, 20 x 16 ½ In. ....*illus*	410.00
National, Model 452, Brass, Oak Base, 23 x 26 x 17 In. ....*illus*	518.00
National, Model 452, Nickel Finish, Oak Base, 26 ½ x 23 ½ In.	590.00
Nickel Finish, Michigan, 17 x 10 x 17 In.	136.00
Wood, Metal Face, Patent February 4, 1890, 19 x 16 x 16 In.	5175.00

CASTOR JARS for pickles are glass jars about six inches in height, held in special metal holders. They became a popular dinner table accessory about 1890. Each jar had a top that was usually silver or silver plate. The frame, also of a silver metal, had a handle that arched above the jar and a hook that held a pair of tongs. By 1900, the pickle castor was out of fashion. Many examples found today have reproduced glass jars in old holders. Additional pickle castors may be found in the various Glass categories.

Pickle, Amber Dugan Block, Bird Head, Tong, Holder	395.00
Pickle, Amber, Beaded Dart, Frame	475.00
Pickle, Amber, Beaded Dart, Wilcox Frame	450.00

Castor Jar, Pickle, Blue, Star & Bar, Meriden Silver Plated Frame, 12 In.
$260.00

Castor Jar, Pickle, Cranberry, Coin Spot, Enameled, Silver Plated Frame, 10 ½ In.
$375.00

Castor Jar, Pickle, Cranberry, Enameled Flowers, Derby Silver Plated Frame, 9 In.
$475.00

Castor Jar, Pickle, Pressed Diamond Variant, Vaseline, Silver Plated Frame, Tongs, 11 x 4 In.
$173.00

Castor Jar, Pickle, Vaseline Diamond, Wilcox Silver Plated Frame, Mechanical, 12 In.
$550.00

Castor Set, 4 Bottles, King's Crown, Ruby Stained, Metal Handle, 9 ½ x 6 ¼ In.
$316.00

Castor Set, 5 Bottles, Cranberry Glass, Wilcox Silver Plated Frame, 14 In.
$200.00

Castor Set, 6 Bottles, Engraved Flowers, Silver Plate, Middletown, 18 In.
$100.00

Pickle, Amber, Daisy & Button	500.00
Pickle, Aqua Pattern, Brooklyn Silverplate Co.	750.00
Pickle, Barrel Shape, Clear, Reed & Barton	225.00
Pickle, Blown Glass, White Cased Glass, Blue, Insert, Lattice, Satin, Frame, Tongs	695.00
Pickle, Blue Diamond, Silver Plate Tray Frame, Meriden, 10 ½ In.	275.00
Pickle, Blue Opalescent Coin Spot, Wheeton Frame, Tongs	995.00
Pickle, Blue Opalescent Daisy, Fern	850.00
Pickle, Blue Pattern, Brooklyn Silverplate Co.	725.00
Pickle, Blue, Star & Bar, Meriden Silver Plated Frame, 12 In. ....*illus*	260.00
Pickle, Cobalt, Gilt, Flowers, Forbes Silver Co., Tongs, c.1875, 9 In.	112.00
Pickle, Cranberry, Coin Spot, Enameled, Silver Plated Frame, 10 ½ In. ....*illus*	375.00
Pickle, Cranberry, Daisy & Fern, Tongs	625.00
Pickle, Cranberry, Enameled Flowers, Derby Silver Plated Frame, 9 In. ....*illus*	475.00
Pickle, Cranberry, Melon Rib, Enameled, Silver Plated Frame, Animals, 12 In.	650.00
Pickle, Cranberry, Paneled Sprig, Tongs, Wilcox Silver Plate Co.	725.00
Pickle, Cranberry, Royal Mfg. Co.	675.00
Pickle, Cranberry, Silver Plated Frame, 12 ½ In.	265.00
Pickle, Cranberry, Victorian, Thumbprint, Silver Plated Frame	795.00
Pickle, Diamond & Fan, Silver Frame, Tongs	385.00
Pickle, Diamond Mirror, Fostoria Glass Co., c.1880	325.00
Pickle, Dugan Block, Tongs	550.00
Pickle, Flower Paneled Cane, Clear	485.00
Pickle, Frosted Panels, 3 Herrings, Fork, Meriden Silver Plate Co.	325.00
Pickle, Frosted, Pressed Glass, Pickle Barrel Shape, Vines, Flowers, Vine Handles	385.00
Pickle, Hand Painted Enameled Flowers, Reed & Barton	550.00
Pickle, Light Purple, Flowers, Victorian Frame, Meriden Silver Plate, 8 ½ x 4 x 4 ½ In.	72.00
Pickle, Opalescent Seaweed	125.00
Pickle, Paneled Button, Footed	350.00
Pickle, Pressed Diamond Variant, Vaseline, Silver Plated Frame, Tongs, 11 x 4 In. ....*illus*	173.00
Pickle, Red, Buttons & Bows, Silver Metal Stand, Tongs, 4-Footed, 13 In.	88.00
Pickle, Stepped Diamond Point, Boston & Sandwich Glass Co.	285.00
Pickle, Stork, Tongs, Meriden	385.00
Pickle, Strawberry, Fan	425.00
Pickle, Tongs, Adelphi Silverplate Co.	185.00
Pickle, Tongs, Fork Holders	365.00
Pickle, Vaseline Diamond, Wilcox Silver Plated Frame, Mechanical, 12 In. ....*illus*	550.00
Pickle, Waffle, Button, Pickle Shaped Frame, Fork, Rogers, Smith & Co.	295.00
Pickle, Zipper Insert, Tongs	285.00
Pickle, Zipper, Tongs	350.00

CASTOR SETS holding just salt and pepper castors were used in the seventeenth century. The sugar castor, mustard pot, spice dredger (shaker), bottles for vinegar and oil, and other spice holders became popular by the eighteenth century. These sets were usually made of sterling silver. The American Victorian castor set, the type most collected today, was made of silver plated Britannia metal. Colored glass bottles were introduced after the Civil War. The sets were out of fashion by World War I. Be careful when buying sets with colored bottles; many are reproductions. Other castor sets may be listed in various porcelain and glass categories in this book.

2 Bottles, Diamond Quilted Panels, Silver Plated Stand, Lucius Hart Mfg. Co.10 ¼ x 9 x 3 In.	120.00
2 Oval Shakers, Mustard, Red Flowers, Original Caddy, 7 In.	25.00
3 Bottles, 2 Blue Shakers, Mustard, Dithridge, Bulging Teardrop, Original Caddy, 8 In.	135.00
4 Bottles, Crystal Stand, Wire Holder, 8 ¾ In.	225.00
4 Bottles, King's Crown, Ruby Stained, Glass Frame, Metal Handle, 9 ½ x 6 ¼ In.	316.00
4 Bottles, King's Crown, Ruby Stained, Metal Handle, 9 ½ x 6 ¼ In. ....*illus*	316.00
4 Bottles, Silver, Oval Basket, Putti, Etched, Frosted Scrolls, Figural Finials, Germany, 10 ½ In.	657.00
5 Bottles, Cranberry Glass, Wilcox Silver Plated Frame, 14 In. ....*illus*	200.00
5 Bottles, Pedestal, Pairpoint Frame, Flowers, Birds, Crystal, Silver Plate, Signed, 18 In.	250.00
6 Bottles, Cranberry, Reverse Thumbprint, Silver Plate, Homan Silver Co.	120.00
6 Bottles, Engraved Flowers, Silver Plate, Middletown, 18 In. ....*illus*	100.00
6 Bottles, Honeycomb, Webster Silver Plated Frame, Crane, Leaves, Cut Stoppers, 17 x 7 ¼ In.	81.00
6 Bottles, Red Bohemian Glass, Silver Plated Holder, Victorian	111.00
Silver Plate, Engraved Flowers, 6 Inserts, 17 ½ In.	70.00
Silver Plate, Oval, Openwork, Scroll Feet, Thomas Bradbury & Sons, Sheffield, 9 x 6 In.	115.00
Square, Gadroon Border, 8 Cut Bottles, Matthew Boulton, Sheffield, 1794, 8 x 9 In.	1035.00

CATALOGS *are listed in the Paper category.*

CAUGHLEY porcelain was made in England from 1772 to 1814. Caughley porcelains are very similar in appearance to those made at the Worcester factory. See the Salopian category for related items.

Dish, Asparagus, Blue, White, Fisherman, c.1787, 3 x 3 In.	80.00
Dish, Leaf Shape, Blue Flowers, Vines, Butterflies, Crescent Mark, c.1790, 14 x 10 In. ....*illus*	322.00
Plate, Flowers, Cone, Blue, White, Scalloped Rim, c.1780, 9 ¾ In.	125.00
Teapot, Fence Pattern, Blue, White, Flower Finial, c.1780, 5 ½ x 6 ½ In.	100.00

CAULDON Limited worked in Staffordshire, Great Britain, and went through many name changes. John Ridgway made porcelain at Cauldon Place, Hanley, until 1855. The firm of John Ridgway, Bates and Co. of Cauldon Place worked from 1856 to 1859. It became Bates, Brown-Westhead, Moore and Co. from 1859 to 1862. Brown-Westhead, Moore and Co. worked from 1862 to 1904. About 1890, this firm started using the words *Cauldon* or *Cauldon Ware* as part of the mark. Cauldon Ltd. worked from 1905 to 1920, Cauldon Potteries from 1920 to 1962. Related items may be found in the Indian Tree category.

Bowl, Multicolored, Flowers, Leaves, Gold Trim, 8-Sided, 6 ½ In.	60.00
Cup & Saucer, Birds, Flowers, Teal, Violet, Brown, Marked..............................	12.00
Cup & Saucer, Pink Roses, Blue & Gold Trim, c.1900	10.00
Eggcup, Pink Roses, Blue Violets, Gilt Trim, Marked, 3 ¾ In.	21.00
Pitcher, Brown Leaf Branches, Blue Outline, Ribbed, Handle, c.1940, 10 ½ In.	85.00
Plate, Bird, Tanager, Leaves, Berries, Marked, 9 In.	25.00
Plate, Dinner, Flowers, Scrolling Pale Yellow Rim Border, Beaded, 10 ¾ In.	45.00
Plate, Flowers, Imari Style, Iron Red, Gold Trim, Blue Feathers, Gold Crosshatching, 9 In.	82.00
Plate, Gold Shield, Gold & Black Border, 10 In.	100.00
Plate, Greek Key Design Border, Gold & Red, White Ground, 8 ¾ In.	35.00
Plate, Pansies, Yellow & Purple, Scalloped Rim, Raised Scalloped Border, 11 In.	30.00
Platter, Flowers, Scrolls, Multicolored, Blue Rim, Oval, c.1910, 21 In.	220.00
Tray, Arcadian Chariot Scene, Blue & White Transfer, 9 ¾ In.	49.00
Tureen, Cover, Underplate, Chintz, Flowers, Butterflies, c.1916, 8 x 6 In.	150.00
Vase, Flowers, Coral, Pink, Green, Folded Top, Marked, 5 ½ In.	24.00

CELADON is the name of a velvet-textured green-gray glaze used by Chinese, Japanese, Korean, and other factories. The name refers both to the glaze and to pieces covered with the glaze. It is still being made.

Basin, Relief Dragon, Incised Waves, Lotus Leaves, Flared, Scalloped Rim, 3 x 13 In.	1150.00
Bottle, Wine, Flowers, Relief, Handles, 6 ¾ In.	250.00
Bowl, Chinese, 5 x 8 In.	263.00
Bowl, Gray, Brown Crackling, 1800s, 3 x 6 In.	575.00
Bowl, Lotus, Cone Shape, Jade Glaze, 6 ¾ In.	210.00
Bowl, Medallion, Cresting Wave, Scrolling Lotus, Chinese, 5 ½ x 12 ¼ In.	3360.00
Box, Cover, Inlaid, Fish, Korea, 5 In.	2510.00
Brush Pot, Porcelain, Incised Scrolls, Chinese, 6 x 7 In.	585.00
Censer, Pinched Waist, Flared, 3-Footed, Chinese, 5 In.	1793.00
Dish, Flower, Medallion, Radiating Ribs, 10 ⅝ In.	720.00
Dish, Scalloped Rim, Craquelure Design, Chinese, 20th Century, 1 ¾ x 4 ½ In.	529.00
Jar, Applied 4 Frog Handles, White Flower Head, Korea, 3 ⅛ In.	1076.00
Teapot, Enamel, Gilt Decorated, Flowering, Branches, Bamboo Shape Handle, Finial, 5 ¾ In. ...	24.00
Vase, Amphora, Molded Flower, Plantain Leaf, Dragon Head Handles, 16 In.	359.00
Vase, Cylindrical, Bulbous Knop, Flared Rim, 22 x 11 In.	3450.00
Vase, Double Gourd, Blue Seal, Chinese, 13 In.	777.00
Vase, Double Gourd, White Enamel Branches, Blossoms, Marked, 5 ⅛ In., Pair.......................	24.00
Vase, Flower Stems, Willow, Bottle Shape, Korea, 12 In.	288.00
Vase, Incised, Birds, Bamboo, Chinese, c.1900, 11 x 5 ¾ In.	382.00
Vase, Incised, Deer Under Pine Tree, Water, Crane, Bulbous, Rolled Rim, Footed, 8 In.	1495.00
Vase, Ormolu Mounted, Oval, Rococo Mount, 18 In., Pair	1035.00
Vase, Raised Rings, Ovoid, Footed, Elongated Floral Neck, Chinese, 5 ½ In.	575.00
Vase, Relief Painted Prunus Branches, Baluster, Flared, Hardwood Stand, Chinese, 17 In.	4888.00
Vase, Relief Rondels, Incised Cloud Ground, Bottle Shape, Petal Tip Band, 8 ¾ In.	460.00
Vase, Shaped Handles, Wood Scrolled Base, Chinese, 4 Piece	64.00

CELS *are listed in this book in the Animation Art category.*

Caughley, Dish, Leaf Shape, Blue Flowers, Vines, Butterflies, Crescent Mark, c.1790, 14 x 10 In. $322.00

Celluloid, Photo Album, Courting Scene, Woman On Sofa, Man With Bouquet, 11 x 9 In. $100.00

Chalkware, Figurine, Cat, Seated, Painted, Black, Red, Gold, 19th Century, 7 ½ In. $9945.00

Chalkware, Figurine, Stag, Lying Down, Pennsylvania, 19th Century, 5 In. $410.00

Charlie Chaplin, Toy, Walker, Composition, Metal, Label, Ferguson Novelty Co., c.1920, 9 ½ In.
$176.00

Charlie McCarthy, Alarm Clock, Painted, Mouth Moves, Metal, Gilbert Clock Corp., Box, 4 In.
$2223.00

Charlie McCarthy, Toy, Drummer Boy, Marx, c.1938, 8 In.
$1064.00

Charlie Chaplin, Toy, Walker, Tin Lithograph, Windup, Cast Iron Feet, B & R, Box, c.1915, 8 ½ In.
$8190.00

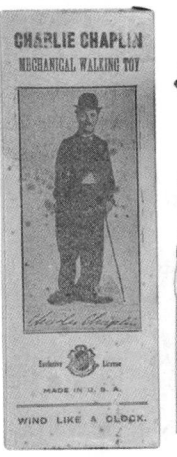

Charlie McCarthy, Toy, Mortimer Snerd, Private Car, Marx, c.1939, 17 In.
$1792.00

TIP
Dust your antiques regularly but carefully. Dust leads to mold growth and attracts insects.

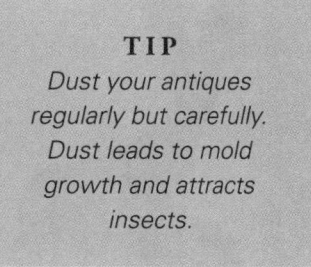

CELLULOID is a trademark for a plastic developed in 1868 by John W. Hyatt. Celluloid Manufacturing Company, the Celluloid Novelty Company, Celluloid Fancy Goods Company, and American Xylonite Company all used celluloid to make jewelry, games, sewing equipment, false teeth, and piano keys. The name *celluloid* was often used to identify any similar plastic. Celluloid toys are listed under Toy.

Bobby Pin Holder, Hinged Lid, Pearlized, 3 ⅞ In.	12.50
Crumber Set, Blue, Cream & Pale Yellow, Pink Flowers, 2 Piece	17.50
Cuticle Tool, Ivory Color Handle, Steel Blade, c.1900, 4 In.	5.50
Hand Mirror, Magnified On Other Side, Creamy Ivory Color, 13 ½ In.	18.00
Nail Buffer, Amber & Gold, Black & Gold Painted Design, 6 ¼ In.	2.00
Nail Cleaner, Green & Butterscotch Handle, Pearlized, 1930s, 5 In.	6.50
Photo Album, Courting Scene, Woman On Sofa, Man With Bouquet, 11 x 9 In. ......*illus*	100.00
Shoehorn, Hole For Hanging, 1940s, 6 In.	7.95

CERAMIC ARTS STUDIO was founded about 1940 in Madison, Wisconsin, by Lawrence Rabbett and Ruben Sand. Their most popular products were expensive molded figurines. The pottery closed in 1955. Do not confuse these products with those of the Ceramic Art Co. of Trenton, New Jersey.

Figurine, Fawn, Marked, 2 ¾ x 3 ¾ In.	45.00
Figurine, Girl, Playing Drum, Blue Skirt, White & Blue Dots, 4 ¼ In.	75.00
Figurine, Victorian Couple, Dog, Incised, Gay 90, Marked, 6 ½ In., Pair	85.00
Vase, Head, Lotus, Manchu, Marked, 7 ¾ & 7 ¼ In., Pair	250.00

CHALKWARE is really plaster of Paris decorated with watercolors. One type was molded from Staffordshire and other porcelain models and painted and sold as inexpensive decorations in the nineteenth century. This type is very valuable today. Figures of plaster, made from about 1910 to 1940 for use as prizes at carnivals, are also known as chalkware. Kewpie dolls made of chalkware will be found in their own category.

Ashtray, Dog, Herbie, Painted, 6 ¾ x 4 ¾ In.	30.00
Bank, Apple Shape, Stem & 2 Leaves, Painted, Early 20th Century, 4 x 4 ½ In.	70.00
Bank, Peach Form, Multicolored, Vertical Slot, 3 ¼ In.	248.00
Bank, Still, Apple Form, Multicolored, 3 ½ In.	132.00
Bust, Comical Face, c.1850, 3 ¼ In.	29.00
Bust, Esther Anne Hunt, Painted, 7 In.	165.00
Compote, Fruit, c.1850, 14 In.	1997.00
Figurine, Bird, On Nest, Yellow, Red, c.1875, 3 In.	345.00
Figurine, Cat, Seated, Painted, Black, Red, Gold, 19th Century, 7 ½ In. ....*illus*	9945.00
Figurine, Dog, Boston Terrier, Black, Red Collar, Blue Dots, Marked, Aug., 1937, 17 In.	230.00
Figurine, Dog, Poodle, Seated, Multicolored, 5 ½ In., Pair	132.00
Figurine, Dog, Poodle, Seated, Painted, 5 In., Pair	88.00
Figurine, Dog, Poodle, Standing, Painted, Red, Brown, c.1850, 8 In.	235.00
Figurine, Dog, Spaniel, White, Brown, Black, Early 1900s, 11 In.	35.00
Figurine, George Washington, On Horse, 14 In.	30.00
Figurine, Girl, Kneeling, Praying, Painted, c.1890, 13 ¾ In.	497.00
Figurine, Horse, Carnival, Multicolored, Silver Glitter, c.1940, 11 x 8 In.	45.00
Figurine, Lovebirds, c.1850, 3 ½ In.	352.00
Figurine, Rooster, Molded, Hollow, Multicolored, 8 ¼ In.	303.00
Figurine, Rooster, On Base, Glass Eyes, Molded, Hollow, 15 ½ In.	77.00
Figurine, Sheep, Lamb, Reclining, White, Pink Ears, Late 1800s, 6 x 9 In.	323.00
Figurine, Squirrel, Eating Nuts, c.1850, 5 ½ In.	317.00
Figurine, Stag, Lying Down, Pennsylvania, 19th Century, 5 In. ....*illus*	410.00
Fruit Basket, c.1875, 8 In.	153.00
Garniture, Fruit Basket, Multicolored, Penn., Late 1800s, 10 ¾ In.	382.00
Garniture, Fruit, Multicolored, Pedestal Base, c.1870, 14 In.	236.00
Watch Hutch, George Washington Figure, Columns, Arch, c.1880, 12 In.	411.00

CHARLIE CHAPLIN, the famous comedian, actor, and filmmaker, lived from 1889 to 1977. He made his first movie in 1913. He did the movie *The Tramp* in 1915. The character of the Tramp has remained famous, and in the 1980s appeared in a series of television commercials for computers. Dolls, candy containers, and all sorts of memorabilia with the image of Charlie's Tramp are collected. Pieces are being made even today.

Button, Charlie Chaplin Is Here, Economy Novelty Co., Blue On White, ⅞ In.	236.00
Candy Container, Charlie Chaplin, Next To Barrel, Painted, Borgfeldt	105.00

Charlie McCarthy, Toy, Mortimer Snerd, Walker, Tin Lithograph, Marx, Box, c.1939, 8 ½ In.
$878.00

Charlie McCarthy, Toy, Walker, Tin Lithograph, Marx, Box, c.1939, 8 ½ In.
$878.00

Charlie McCarthy, Tumbler Set, Box, Die Cut, Cardboard Insert, c.1938, 10 x 11 ½ In., 8 Piece
$410.00

Chelsea, Figurine, Bocage, Woman With Mandolin, Bagpipe Player, Late 1700s, 10 ½ In., Pair
$1755.00

Chinese Export, Basket, Fitzhugh, Blue, Painted Pagoda, Basket Shape, c.1812, 9 ½ In.
$5625.00

Chinese Export, Bowl, Monteith, Bombe Shape, Enameled Flowers, Oval, 8 x 13 In.
$2040.00

Chinese Export, Brush Holder, Famille Noire, Flowers, 6 In.
$896.00

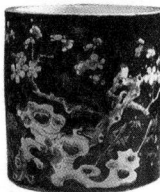

Chocolate Mold, Little Tramp, Metal, Trays, 1920s, 8 ¾ In., 6 Piece	168.00
Handkerchief, Glove, Box, Little Tramp Design, 1920s, 6 x 3 ½ x 2 In.	143.00
Match Safe, Little Tramp, Charlie Salutes, Out For Revenge, c.1918, 2 ⅝ x 3 ½ x 3 In.	543.00
Toy, Composition, Squeeze Bellows, Squeaks, c.1920, 7 ½ In.	205.00
Toy, Dancing, Paper, String, Envelope, Instruction, 1930s, 6 x 9 ½ In.	142.00
Toy, Dancing, Wood, Jointed, Control Strings, 1920s, 11 ¾ In.	183.00
Toy, Tin Lithograph, Windup, DRGM Germany, c.1920, 6 ¾ In.	2632.00
Toy, Walker, Composition, Metal, Label, Ferguson Novelty Co., c.1920, 9 ½ In. ......*illus*	176.00
Toy, Walker, Tin Lithograph, Windup, Cast Iron Feet, B & R, Box, c.1915, 8 ½ In. ......*illus*	8190.00
Toy, Windup, Composition, Metal, Ferguson Co., 1918, 9 ¼ In.	351.00
Toy, Windup, Tin Lithograph, INGAP Italy, c.1920, 7 ½ In.	2925.00
Wristwatch, Cadeaux, Little Tramp, Cane 2nd Hand, Velvet Band, Plastic Case, 1972	144.00

CHARLIE MCCARTHY was the ventriloquist's dummy used by Edgar Bergen from the 1930s. He was famous for his work in radio, movies, and television. The act was retired in the 1970s.

Alarm Clock, Painted, Mouth Moves, Metal, Gilbert Clock Corp., Box, 4 In. ......*illus*	2223.00
Dancer, Wood Jointed, Marks Bros., Box, c.1938, 1 ½ x 5 ¼ x 20 In.	288.00
Doll, Effanbee, Composition, Button, Box, Late 1930s, 20 In.	748.00
Doll, Sportsman, Composition Head, Double Breasted Jacket, 1930s, 15 In.	1035.00
Game, Radio Party, Chase & Sanborn Premium, Board, 1938	40.00
Puppet, Hand, Composition Head, Cloth Body, Tuxedo, Box, 1938, 11 In.	293.00
Radio, Majestic, Brown Case, Bakelite, Charlie Figure, c.1940, 6 x 7 In.	1495.00
Spoon, Marked, Duchess Silver Plate, 6 In.	18.00
Toy, Benzene Buggy, Head Moves, Tin Lithograph, Windup, Marx, c.1938, 8 In.	448.00
Toy, Buggy, Windup, Marx, Box, 1930s	850.00
Toy, Celluloid, Mouth, Chin Moves, Windup, Box, 1930s, 7 In.	485.00
Toy, Crazy Car, Tin, Windup, Marx, 8 In.	110.00
Toy, Drummer Boy, Marx, c.1938, 8 In. ......*illus*	1064.00
Toy, Mortimer Snerd, Private Car, Marx, c.1939, 17 In. ......*illus*	1792.00
Toy, Mortimer Snerd, Walker, Tin Lithography, Marx, Box, c.1939, 8 ½ In. ......*illus*	878.00
Toy, Walker, Tin Lithograph, Marx, Box, c.1939, 8 ½ In. ......*illus*	878.00
Tumbler Set, Box, Die Cut, Cardboard Insert, c.1938, 10 x 11 ½ In., 8 Piece ......*illus*	410.00

CHELSEA porcelain was made in the Chelsea area of London from about 1745 to 1769. Some pieces made from 1770 to 1784 are called Chelsea Derby and may include the letter *D* for *Derby* in the mark. Ceramic designs were borrowed from the Meissen models of the day. Pieces were made of soft paste. The gold anchor was used as the mark, but it has been copied by many other factories. Recent copies of Chelsea have been made from the original molds. Do not confuse Chelsea porcelain with Chelsea Grape, a white pottery with luster grape decoration.

Figurine, Bocage, Woman With Mandolin, Bagpipe Player, Late 1700s, 10 ½ In., Pair ....*illus*	1755.00
Figurine, Boy & Girl, 18th Century French Provincial Dress, Converted To Lamp, 22 In., Pair	105.00

CHINESE EXPORT porcelain comprises all the many kinds of porcelain made in China for export to America and Europe in the eighteenth, nineteenth, and twentieth centuries. Other pieces may be listed in this book under Canton, Celadon, Nanking, Rose Canton, Rose Mandarin, and Rose Medallion.

Basket, Fitzhugh, Blue, Painted Pagoda, Basket Shape, c.1812, 9 ½ In. ......*illus*	5625.00
Bottle, Blue & White, Bulbous, Tapered, c.1600, 10 ½ In.	956.00
Bottle, Water, Cover, Green Vines, Blue Design, c.1800, 14 x 8 In.	625.00
Bough Pot, Gilt, Landscape Panels, Octagonal Base, 19th Century, 9 ½ x 7 ¾ In., Pair	5795.00
Bowl, 3-Color Glaze, 12 In.	896.00
Bowl, Blue & White, 3 ⅛ x 8 ⅞ In.	3510.00
Bowl, Blue & White, 4 ½ x 11 ¾ In.	441.00
Bowl, Blue & White, Dragons Chasing Flaming Pearl Of Wisdom, 4 In.	1554.00
Bowl, Blue & White, Figural & Flower Panels, River Bank, Wood Stand, 6 x 13 In.	4575.00
Bowl, Blue & White, Fitzhugh, Gilt, Fruits, Flowers, 1800s, 16 In.	805.00
Bowl, Blue & White, Gold Interior, Footed, 4 ½ x 10 ½ In.	1265.00
Bowl, Blue & White, Mythical Animal, Seated In Landscape, Palm Tree, 15 In.	1912.00
Bowl, Blue & White, Peonies, Birds, Rocks, Prunus Border, Wood Stand, 6 x 15 In.	978.00
Bowl, Blue & White, Persian Designs, Vines, Flared, Ring Foot, Wood Base, 6 x 13 In.	690.00
Bowl, Buildings, Trees, Bridge, Man Fishing, Ring Foot, 4 x 8 In.	575.00
Bowl, Burgundy Exterior, Blue Interior, Applied Projections, 4 x 10 In.	462.00
Bowl, Famille Rose, Flowers, Bird, Carved Stand, 4 x 12 ⅝ x 7 ½ In.	463.00

Bowl, Famille Rose, Ruffled Rim, Gilt, Oval, Flowers, Footed, c.1820, 3 x 10 x 7 In.	345.00
Bowl, Famille Rose, Stand, 8 x 16 ½ In.	2420.00
Bowl, Famille Verte, Butterfly, Flowers, Garden, Blue Ground, Lotus Petal, 11 ½ In.	900.00
Bowl, Famille Verte, Landscape, Dragon Panels, Red, Gilt, Lotus Ground, 1800s, 15 In.	1150.00
Bowl, Fish, Leaves, Iron Red, Green, Flared, Late 1800s, 12 In.	717.00
Bowl, Fox Hunting, Scrolling Gilt Border, c.1775, 11 ⅜ In.	3680.00
Bowl, Fretted Edge, Coastal Scene, Boats, Villages, Starbursts, 1700s, 10 ¼ In.	215.00
Bowl, Girl With 2 Suitors, Dog, Birdcage, Swag Border, 18th Century, 9 In.	590.00
Bowl, Lotus Petal Form Rim, Flowering Branches, Stand, 9 ⅜ In.	388.00
Bowl, Monteith, Bombe Shape, Enameled Flowers, Oval, 8 x 13 In. ....*illus*	2040.00
Bowl, Mythical Figures, Turquoise Interior, 6 ¾ In.	146.00
Bowl, Peach Bloom, 6 Characters, 19th Century, 5 In.	239.00
Bowl, Scenic, Flower Border, 3 ¾ x 8 ¼ In.	5270.00
Bowl, Temmoku Glaze, Red, Black, Brown, 2 x 5 In.	460.00
Bowl, Yellow, Blue Flowers, 2 ½ x 6 In.	235.00
Brush Holder, Blue & White, Boats On River, 20th Century, 7 ½ In.	3585.00
Brush Holder, Famille Noire, Flowers, 6 In. ....*illus*	896.00
Brushpot, Blue & White, Figures, 7 ¼ x 7 ¼ In.	235.00
Brushpot, Blue, Figures, 6 ½ x 8 In.	764.00
Brushpot, Green Glaze, Cylindrical, Reticulated Sides, 4 ¾ In.	366.00
Brushpot, Incised Leaves, Blue, White, 7 x 7 In.	819.00
Canister, Canton, Armorial, De Wendt Arms, c.1750, 4 ½ In. ....*illus*	15000.00
Censer, Ding Shape, White Glaze, Dragons, Silver Plated Dome Lid.1800s, 8 In.	4600.00
Censer, Wood Lid, Mottled Gray, Flambe, Tripod, Handles To Rim, c.1800, 6 x 7 In.	1610.00
Charger, Blue & White, 3 Friends Of Winter, Butterflies, Plants, Octagonal, 13 ¼ In.	540.00
Charger, Blue & White, Buildings, 15 ⅜ In.	1434.00
Charger, Blue & White, Mountains Rising From Lake, Pavilions, Figures, 14 ½ In.	330.00
Charger, Famille Rose, 4 Ships, Figures, Cargo, Cliffside Landscape, Building, 15 In.	1440.00
Charger, Multicolored, Deer Beneath Pine Tree, Cranes, Garden, 15 ⅛ In.	480.00
Charger, Phoenix Birds, Leaves, Scalloped Edge, Blue & White, 12 ¼ In.	96.00
Chocolate Pot, Pistol Grip Handle, Doe Top, Figures, Landscape, 8 ¼ In.	747.00
Coffeepot, Silver, 3 Panels, Battle Scenes, Cast Bamboo Handle & Spout, 7 ¼ In.	2808.00
Creamer, Famille Rose, Village, Bird, Flowers, Leaves, 4 ½ In.	303.00
Cup & Cover, Pot-De-Creme, Blue & White, Bombe Shape, Strap Handle, 3 ½ In., 6 Piece	510.00
Cup & Saucer, Blue & White, Women, Flowers, Child, 4 Panels, Peaches, 4 In.	120.00
Cup & Saucer, Gilt, Blue Flowers, 1760-1810, 3 x 6 ½ In., 28 Piece........................	177.00
Dish, Bands Of Flowers & Ribbons, Light Blue Ground, 18th Century, 8 In.	657.00
Dish, Black Decoration, Moss Green, Gilding, Classical Scene, Scrollwork Border, 9 ¼ In.	510.00
Dish, Blue & White, Bird, On Lotus, Panels Of Flowers, Fish Scale Ground, 15 ½ In.	960.00
Dish, Blue & White, Medallions, Women, Garden Setting, Fruit, 6 Characters, 8 ⅛ In., Pair	720.00
Dish, Blue & White, Spray Of Peonies, 3 Flower Sprays Groups On Rim, 9 ⅛ In.	84.00
Dish, Blue, Red Underglaze, Gilt, Flowering Plum Trees, Bananas, Bamboo, Imari, 9 ¼ In. ...	84.00
Dish, Cover, Famille Rose, Oval, 1800s, 7 x 15 In.	690.00
Dish, Famille Rose, Flower Bouquet, Ribbon, Scattered Flowers, 8 ⅝ In.	180.00
Dish, Famille Rose, Flowers, Pheasant, Gilt Rim, Oval, 1800s, 12 x 14 In.	390.00
Dish, Famille Rose, Fruit & Flower Arrangements, c.1729, 10 ½ In., Pair.	705.00
Dish, Famille Rose, Lobed Corners, Lobed Corners, Fruit, Flowers, c.1800, 9 x 9 x 2 In.	805.00
Dish, Figures In Pavilion, Water, Oval, Lobed Border, 10 In., Pair....................	1093.00
Dish, Moss Green, Gilding, Classical Scene, 3 Reclining, Standing Figures, 9 ¼ In.	1140.00
Dish, Painted, Pastel Butterflies, 19th Century, 1 ¾ x 7 In., Pair....................	259.00
Dish, Underglaze, Enamel, Blue, Chrysanthemum, Brocade Border, 9 In.	300.00
Ewer, Red & Blue Flowers, White Ground, Ormolu Mounts, 18th Century, 5 ¾ In.	1075.00
Figurine, Famille Rose, Boy, Sitting, Holding Jui Scepter, 6 In.	299.00
Figurine, Famille Rose, Immortal, Standing, Dragon Robe, 1800s, 10 In. ....*illus*	418.00
Figurine, Famille Rose, Man Holding Child, 23 In.	717.00
Figurine, Famille Verte, Buddhist Lions, Multicolored, 14 In., Pair......................	120.00
Figurine, Foo Dog, Male, Female, Brocade Ball, Club, Multicolored Glaze, 9 ½ In., Pair........	270.00
Figurine, Guanyin, Many-Armed Form, On Lotus Throne, Blanc-De-Chine, 13 In.	633.00
Figurine, Parrot, Molded, Rockwork Base, Multicolored Enamel, 7 ¾ In., Pair ....*illus*	1080.00
Figurine, Parrot, Perched On Rock, Green, Pierce Carved Wood Base, c.1925, 10 In., Pair	374.00
Figurine, Stag, Brown, 14 x 10 In.	82.00
Figurine, Stag, Reclining, Enameled, Detachable Antlers, c.1775, 8 In. ....*illus*	62500.00
Flask, Flattened, Moon, Stylized Dragon Handles, Enamel, 12 ½ In. ....*illus*	960.00
Footbath, Flowers, Blue & White, Round, Deep, 9 ¼ x 24 ⅞ In., Pair..................	1035.00
Footbath, Oval, Handles, Blue, Birds, Flowers, Yellow Ground, 1900s, 7 x 16 x 10 In.	316.00
Fruit Cooler, Flowers, 10 x 10 In.	70.00

Chinese Export, Canister, Canton, Armorial, De Wendt Arms, c.1750, 4 ½ In.
$15000.00

Chinese Export, Figurine, Famille Rose, Immortal, Standing, Dragon Robe, 1800s, 10 In.
$418.00

Chinese Export, Figurine, Parrot, Molded, Rockwork Base, Multicolored Enamel, 7 ¾ In., Pair
$1080.00

Chinese Export, Figurine, Stag, Reclining, Enameled, Detachable Antlers, c.1775, 8 In.
$62500.00

Chinese Export, Flask, Flattened, Moon, Stylized Dragon Handles, Enamel, 12 ½ In.
$960.00

Chinese Export, Jar, Cover, Famille Rose, Flowers, Buddhist Symbols, 19th Century, 17 In.
$1076.00

Chinese Export, Jar, Famille Verte, Paper Label, 1800s, 7 In.
$1150.00

Ginger Jar, Blue & White, 6 ¼ x 5 ½ In. 351.00
Ginger Jar, Blue & White, Oval, Panels, Antiques, Buddhist Emblems, 6 In., Pair 840.00
Ginger Jar, Bulbous, Apple Green, Carved Wood Cover, Stand, c.1850, 11 ½ In. 720.00
Ginger Jar, Cover, Famille Verte, Panels, Figures, Antiques, Blue Underglaze, 10 ½ In. 330.00
Ginger Jar, Cover, Figures, Multicolored, Cobalt Blue Ground, Late 1800s, 13 ½ In. 345.00
Jar, Blue & White, 3 Quatrefoil Scenes, Paper Label, c.1800, 8 In. 575.00
Jar, Blue & White, Riverscape, 5 In. 329.00
Jar, Bulbous Urn Shape, Blue White, 1700s, 14 ½ x 10 ½ In. 431.00
Jar, Cover, Blue, White, Flowers, Furniture, c.1900, 12 x 10 In., Pair 1150.00
Jar, Cover, Famille Noire, Round, Trees, Birds, Label, 10 In. 748.00
Jar, Cover, Famille Rose, Flowers, Buddhist Symbols, 19th Century, 17 In. *illus* 1076.00
Jar, Cover, Famille Rose, Octagonal Baluster Shape, 8 Shaped Panels, Flowers, 27 In. 5040.00
Jar, Dragons, Buddhist Symbols, Multicolored, Chinese, 1800s, 8 In., Pair 4830.00
Jar, Famille Rose, Flat Cover, Knop Finial, Oval, Applied Loop Handles, 10 ½ x 9 ½ In. 230.00
Jar, Famille Verte, Paper Label, 1800s, 7 In. *illus* 1150.00
Jar, Sang De Boeuf, Strawberry Glaze, White Interior, 1800s, 7 ½ In. 1035.00
Jar, Sang De Bouef Glaze, Blue Flecks, Bulbous, Wood Covers, 9 In., Pair 345.00
Jar, Squash Vine, Green Ocher, Blue, Speckled White Ground, Rolled Rim, 34 x 32 In. 460.00
Jar, Umbrella, Scenic, Tree, 23 x 9 In. 59.00
Lamp, Famille Rose, Gods, Gilt Text, Mazarin Blue, Shade, c.1925, 35 In. 900.00
Marriage Lantern, Famille Rose, Hexagonal, Pierced, Painted, Flowers, 2 Sections, 10 In. 359.00
Mug, Famille Rose, Armorial, Turquoise Chicken Skin, Straight-Sided, 18th Century, 5 In. 448.00
Mug, Famille Rose, Double Strap Handle, Flower Border, Figures, Birds, Fruit, 1800s, 4 In. 330.00
Mug, Reeded Handle, Applied Leaves, Gilt Diaper, Flower Border, 5 In. 1067.00
Pitcher, Water, Blue & White, Bulbous, Elongated Flared Neck, Spout, 7 ¼ In. 1434.00
Pitcher, Water, Blue & White, Elongated & Flared Neck, Gold Rim & Spout, 9 ¾ In. 777.00
Planter, Teakwood Stand, Flowers, 13 x 14 ¼ In. 176.00
Plaque, Blue Flowers, Grass, White Ground, Pierced & Carved Wood Frame, 14 x 14 In. 259.00
Plate, Armorial, Brown Fitzhugh, 7 ⅞ In. 29250.00
Plate, Armorial, Gilt Border, Flower Sprays, Payne Crest, c.1732, 8 ¾ In. 633.00
Plate, Armorial, Gilt Spearhead Border, Coat Of Arms, 18th Century, 9 ⅛ In. 978.00
Plate, Blue & White, Copper Red, Flowers, Barbed Rim, 8 In. 896.00
Plate, Blue & White, Fish, Flowers, Scalloped Rim, 9 ¼ In., Pair 657.00
Plate, Blue & White, Kraak, Medallion, Songbird, Peonies, Asters, 11 ¾ In., Pair 840.00
Plate, Blue, Iron Red Underglaze, Gnarled Flowering Plum Branch, Leaf Border, 9 ⅜ In. 84.00
Plate, Central Peonies, Bamboo, Scalloped Rim, Vines, 18th Century, 9 In., Pair 288.00
Plate, Dinner, Rain Cloud Edge, Temple, Pagoda, Blue & White, 1700s, 10 ⅛ In. 135.00
Plate, Famille Rose, Armorial, Scalloped, Bouquet, Fleur-De-Lis Border, 9 In., 18 Piece 3840.00
Plate, Famille Rose, Flower Sprays, Octagonal, Pendants, 8 ½ In. 60.00
Plate, Famille Rose, Gilded, Shield, Flower Wreaths, Garlands, Octagonal, 9 ½ In., Pair 510.00
Plate, Famille Rose, Gilt Enamels, Stag, Kneeling, 3 Flower Bouquets, 9 ¼ In. 780.00
Plate, Famille Rose, Goat's Head, Fleur-De-Lis, Gilt Garlands, 9 In. 1080.00
Plate, Famille Rose, Lake Scene, Fenced Garden, Bamboo, Chrysanthemums, 9 In., Pair 510.00
Plate, Famille Rose, Lotus, Crane, Butterfly, Mandarin Duck, 8 In. 299.00
Plate, Famille Verte, Basket Of Flowers, Asters, Fall Flower Bouquets, 8 ½ In. 480.00
Plate, Famille Verte, Basket, Reserve Panels, Flowers, Green Cracked Ice, 9 In. 450.00
Plate, Fitzhugh, Orange, Green, c.1820, 9 ¾ In. *illus* 16250.00
Plate, Goddess Holding Spear, Octagonal, Fruit & Vine Border, c.1745, 8 ½ In. 2185.00
Plate, Reticulated, Basket Weave, Flowers, c.1765, 9 ¼ In. 288.00
Plate, Sepia Swags, 18th Century, 9 ¾ In., 6 Piece 441.00
Plate, Soup, Central Flower, 3 Wheat Clusters, c.1810, 9 ¾ In. 6552.00
Platter, Armorial, Border, Shells, Flowers, Birds, Chamfered Corners, c.1760, 17 x 14 In. 2415.00
Platter, Armorial, Knight's Helmet Crest, Puce & Gilt Swags, Oval, 25 In. 6900.00
Platter, Blue & White, Double Wall, Waterside Pavilions, 3 ¼ x 15 ½ x 10 ¾ In. 316.00
Platter, Blue & White, Lakeside Pavilion, Boatman, 9 ¼ x 11 ½ In. 180.00
Platter, Famille Rose, European Scene, 2 Landscape, Crest Of Cat, 12 x 16 ⅛ In. 240.00
Platter, Famille Rose, Flowers, Leaves, Birds, Village, 10 ⅜ x 13 ¼ In. 187.00
Platter, Famille Rose, Oval, Orange Fitzhugh, Flower, Animal Roundel, 12 ⅝ In., Pair 1410.00
Platter, Famille Rose, Rectangular, Chamfered Corners, Flowers, 14 ½ x 11 ¼ In. 144.00
Platter, Famille Rose, Rose & Leaf Center, Scalloped Edge, Orange Peel Back, 13 ¾ x 10 ¾ In. 633.00
Platter, Flared Rim, Chamfered Corners, Fitzhugh, c.1800, 2 ½ x 14 ¼ x 10 ½ In. 230.00
Platter, Gilt Rim, Orange Fitzhugh, Oval, Early 19th Century, 12 x 14 ¾ In. 705.00
Platter, Travelers In Courtyard, Horse, c.1850, 11 ¼ x 8 ¾ In. 862.00
Punch Bowl, 2 Cartouches, Men In Outdoors, Merrymakers, Flower Sprays, 5 x 12 In. 3380.00
Punch Bowl, Famille Rose Center, Flower Border, c.1800, 4 ¾ x 11 ½ In. 1610.00

Punch Bowl, Famille Rose, Crossed Cornucopia, Flower Garland Border, 10 In.	518.00
Punch Bowl, Famille Rose, Dancing Children, Women, Plants, 4 ¾ x 10 ½ In.	420.00
Punch Bowl, Famille Rose, Floral Band Border, Gilt, Late 1700s, 6 x 14 In.	1220.00
Punch Bowl, Famille Rose, Flowers, Figures In Garden Pavilion, 4 ¾ In.	900.00
Punch Bowl, Famille Rose, Peacock On Rockwork, Tree, Peony, 14 ⅛ In.	1080.00
Punch Bowl, Hunting Scene, Gold Trim, Panels, c.1775, 15 ¾ In.	10350.00
Punch Bowl, Mythological Scene, Goddess In Chariot, Flowers, 7 x 15 In.	4888.00
Punch Bowl, Ship, Garden Pavilion, Figures, Birds, 6 x 14 In.	2185.00
Rose Bowl, Famille Rose, Octagonal, Late 19th Century, 2 ½ x 8 ¼ In.	81.00
Saucer, Blue & White, Foo Dog, Piecrust Border, Peonies, Coffee Ground, 23 In., Pair	360.00
Saucer, Famille Rose, Fitzhugh Border, Underglaze Blue, 9 ½ In.	1440.00
Saucer, Famille Rose, Trellis Border, River Scene, c.1750, 11 In.	288.00
Saucer, Famille Verte, Peonies, Butterflies, Double Footed Base, 13 ½ In.	2400.00
Serving Dish, Lotus Shape, Blue, Green, Pink Blossom, 7 In.	264.00
Strainer, Liner, 18 ½ x 16 In.	1380.00
Tea Bowl, Villages On Island, Pagodas, Hatched Bands, Blue On White, 1700s, 3 ⅝ In.	65.00
Teapot, Blue & White, 5 x 7 ¾ In.	106.00
Teapot, Blue & White, Fruit Clusters, Leaf Border, Carved Handle, 1800s, 6 ½ In.	115.00
Teapot, Blue Flowers, Lobed Melon, Silver Mount, Blue, Iron Red, Gilt, 3 ½ In.	210.00
Teapot, Cover, Figural, Landscape Panels, Puce Ground, Brocade Ground, 5 In.	480.00
Teapot, Famille Rose, Bird, Butterfly, Flowers, Leaves, Cylinder, Goose Neck, 6 ½ In.	132.00
Teapot, Pomegranate Finial, Sloped Shoulders, Cylinder Body, Court Scene, c.1820, 6 In.	374.00
Teapot, Raised Plantain Leaves, Squat, Pottery, Marked Huang Yonglin, 6 In.	1016.00
Tray, Famille Rose, Rectangular, Figures, 19th Century, 7 ¾ In.	150.00
Tureen, Cover, Blue Fitzhugh, Oval, 1800s, 9 In.	474.00
Tureen, Cut Corner, Footed, Blue & White, Boar's Head Handles, 8 x 14 x 9 In.	1035.00
Tureen, Famille Rose, Flowers, Footed, Handles, Lid, Gilt Mushroom Finial, Underplate, 9 x 12 In.	1438.00
Tureen, Flowers, Red Birds, Blue Handles & Finial, 9 ½ x 14 ½ x 9 In.	478.00
Urn, Blue & White, Double Handles, 16 x 8 In.	146.00
Urn, Cover, Multicolored, Flowers, c.1950, 36 x 18 In.	176.00
Urn, Famille Rose, Oval, Domed Cover, 1800s, 17 In.	92.00
Urn, Handles, Pierced, Onion Finial, Blue, Gold, Wreaths, Sprays, Plinth, c.1850, 17 In., Pair.	9487.00
Urn, Palace, Porcelain, Baluster Shape, Landscape Cartouche, Flowers, Insects, 7 ½ In.	230.00
Vase, 4 Cartouches, Buddhist Emblems, Dragon Bands, Dragon Handles, 13 ¼ In.	2390.00
Vase, Amphora, Green Glazed, Dragon Form Handles, 20 In.	203.00
Vase, Baluster, Flowers, Birds, Blue, Rust, White Ground, 44 x 19 In., Pair	436.00
Vase, Baluster, Trumpet Neck, Red Glaze, Paper Label, c.1900, 9 In.	1955.00
Vase, Beaker, Blue & White, Baluster Shape, Tapered Cylinder, Splayed Foot, 9 ½ In.	450.00
Vase, Black, 15 In.	411.00
Vase, Black Mirror, Bottle Shape, Cafe Au Lait Rim, c.1800, 15 In.	1725.00
Vase, Blue & White, 10 In.	1293.00
Vase, Blue & White, 2 Dragons, Chasing Flaming Pearl Of Wisdom, 22 ½ In.	299.00
Vase, Blue & White, 2 Medallions, Riverscape, Figures, Bulbous Middle, 15 In.	1076.00
Vase, Blue & White, 6 Panels, Flowering Plants, Rockwork, Baluster Form, 10 In.	510.00
Vase, Blue & White, Baluster, Pinched Neck, Figures, Characters, 9 ½ In.	350.00
Vase, Blue & White, Buddhist Emblems, Clouds, 6 In.	657.00
Vase, Blue & White, c.1875, 16 In.	1293.00
Vase, Blue & White, Coastal Village, Mountains, 20th Century, 20 In.	690.00
Vase, Blue & White, Dragon, 11 ½ In.	179.00
Vase, Blue & White, Elongated Neck, Garlic Mouth, Children, Woman, Oval, 12 In.	1673.00
Vase, Blue & White, Flowers, Plantain Leaves, Bulbous, Flared Neck, Qianlong, 6 In.	1673.00
Vase, Blue & White, Garlic Mouth, Elephant Handles, Clouds, Dignitaries, Horses, 9 ½ In.	2510.00
Vase, Blue & White, Mirror Image, Men In Garden, Dragon Form Handles, 23 ½ In.	489.00
Vase, Blue Ground, Elephant Masks, Butterfly, 8 x 10 In.	351.00
Vase, Blue, Crackle Glaze, 10 ½ In., Pair.	118.00
Vase, Blue, Tapered, Signed, 2 ½ x 5 In., Pair	144.00
Vase, Blush White, Fluted Body, Neck, Scalloped Mouth, Dragon Form Handles, 7 ½ In.	179.00
Vase, Bottle Shape, Blue, Famille Rose, Flowers, Long Neck, Gilded Lip, 10 ⅜ x 6 ¾ In.	1410.00
Vase, Bottle Shape, Famille Jaune, Enameled Fruits, Flowers, Cartouches, 25 In., Pair	353.00
Vase, Bottle, Flambe, Runny Purple Glaze, Mark, c.1800, 8 In.	978.00
Vase, Bulbous, Baluster, Ducks, Lotus, 17 In., Pair	871.00
Vase, Bulbous, Blue & White, Peaches On Branches, 9 ¾ In.	478.00
Vase, Ceramic, Flared Rim, Yellow Birds In Trees, White Ground, 13 ¼ In.	12.00
Vase, Cover, Famille Rose, Hexagonal, Foo Dog Finial, Panels, Figural Scenes, 21 In., Pair	8100.00
Vase, Double Gourd Shape, Scrolls, Symbols, Flowers, Blue, White, c.1900, 7 In.	1955.00

Chinese Export, Plate, Fitzhugh, Orange, Green, c.1820, 9 ¾ In. $16250.00

Chinese Export, Vase, Famille Rose, Scenic, With Figures, Handles, 19th Century, 16 ¾ In. $388.00

C

Chinese Export, Watch Holder, Cover, Famille Rose, Lobed, Painted, Applied Detail, c.1770, 8 ½ In. $5000.00

Vase, Famille Noire, Prunus Trees, Birds, Baluster, Wood Lid & Stand, 18 In.	920.00
Vase, Famille Noire, Tapered Square, Eight Treasure Symbols, Green, Black, 1800s, 21 In.	1725.00
Vase, Famille Rose, Baluster, Buddhist Lions, Dragons, Officials, c.1900, 14 In., Pair	1840.00
Vase, Famille Rose, Bird, Flowers, Elephant Form Handles, 16 In.	717.00
Vase, Famille Rose, Bronze Mounted, Baluster Shape, 19th Century, 28 In.	4700.00
Vase, Famille Rose, Enamel, Garden Scene, Mythological Figures, 18 ½ In.	1320.00
Vase, Famille Rose, Enamel Women, Children, 8 Treasures, Bats, Early 1900s, 15 ¾ In.	288.00
Vase, Famille Rose, Flowers, Rocks, Garden, c.1800, 11 In.	2760.00
Vase, Famille Rose, Hundred Boys Decoration, Molded Dragon Neck, Lions, 36 In.	518.00
Vase, Famille Rose, Panels, Birds, Flowers, Flared Rim, c.1930, 16 In., Pair	660.00
Vase, Famille Rose, Scenic, With Figures, Handles, 19th Century, 16 ¾ In. .... *illus*	388.00
Vase, Famille Rose, Spherical, Narrow Neck, Flower Scene, 1700s, 9 ¾ In.	1035.00
Vase, Famille Rose, Woman, Child, Courtyard, Symbols, Blue Mark, 1900s, 9 In., Pair	1380.00
Vase, Famille Verte, Birds, Flowers, Rocks, Marked, 1800s, 23 In.	575.00
Vase, Famille Verte, Elongated Neck, Tapered Square, Blooming Branches, Birds, 9 ½ In.	115.00
Vase, Famille Verte, Fish, Shaped Cartouches, Blue Ground, 19th Century, 14 In.	388.00
Vase, Famille Verte, Judge, On Table, Clerk, Holding Tablet, 10 ¼ In.	960.00
Vase, Famille Verte, Man On Horse, Attendants, Bulbous, Flared Neck, 9 ¾ In.	657.00
Vase, Figural Scene, Porcelain, Blue, White, 13 x 7 In.	878.00
Vase, Figures, Garden, Blue, Famille Rose Enamels, Celadon Ground, Metal Mounts, 14 In.	900.00
Vase, Flambe, Trumpet Neck, Red, Purple Glaze, Paper Label, Takemoto, c.1800, 7 In.	431.00
Vase, Flared, Scalloped Rim, Shaped Body, Dragons, Landscape, 33 ½ x 15 In.	288.00
Vase, Flowers, Children, Blue, White, Signed, 14 x 8 In.	644.00
Vase, Irises, Basket Weave, Blue & White, Hirado Style, Wood Stands, 1800s, 12 In., Pair	1150.00
Vase, Landscape In Reserve, Birds, Mountain Pagoda, Gold Scroll Handles, 8 In.	1534.00
Vase, Mallet, Blue Phoenixes, Red, Gold Accents, Label, 1800s, 8 In.	11500.00
Vase, Millefleur, Turquoise Interior, 10 In., Pair	878.00
Vase, Mountain Scene, Red Dragon Handles, Bulbous, Tapered Neck, 18 x 13 In.	1062.00
Vase, Oval, Elongated Neck, Everted Mouth, Peach Bloom & Gray, c.1700, 8 ¼ In.	418.00
Vase, Oxblood Glaze, 14 In.	1659.00
Vase, Peach Bloom, Copper Red, 10 ½ In.	478.00
Vase, Robin's-Egg Blue, Oval Base, Elephant Handles, Mottled Glaze, c.1800, 5 In.	2070.00
Vase, Sang De Boeuf Glaze, White Rim, c.1800, 12 In.	6900.00
Vase, Sang De Bouef, c.1900, 16 x 9 In.	644.00
Vase, Shield, Bird, Flower, Geometric, Marked, 12 In.	115.00
Vase, Stick Neck, Woman, Child, 9 ½ In.	441.00
Vase, Trees, Blue & White, Applied White Serpent, Flared Flattened Rim, 12 In., Pair	488.00
Vase, White Blossoms, Cobalt Ground, Gourd Shape, Long Neck, Wood Stand, 17 In.	183.00
Vase, White Flowers, Cobalt Ground, Double Gourd Shape, 19 In.	1098.00
Vase, White Ground, Dragon, 3 Men Fighting, 5 x 10 In.	527.00
Vase, Yellow Ground, White Enameled Flowers & Birds, Flared Rim, 6 ¾ In., Pair	183.00
Warming Dish, Courtyard, Figures, Dragons, Flower Rims, 11 In.	356.00
Watch Holder, Cover, Famille Rose, Lobed, Painted, Applied Detail, c.1770, 8 ½ In. .... *illus*	5000.00
Watch Holder, Cover, Painted Enamel Flowers, Birds, Flowers, c.1870, 8 x 5 In. .... *illus*	3408.00

CHINTZ is the name of a group of china patterns featuring an overall design of flowers and leaves. The design became popular with English makers about 1928. A few pieces are still being made. The best known are designs by Royal Winton, James Kent Ltd., Crown Ducal, and Shelley. Crown Ducal and Shelley are listed in their own sections.

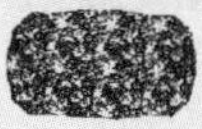

Beeston, Bowl, Pink & Yellow Roses, Black Ground, Royal Winton, 1920s, 5 In.	39.00
Bermuda, Cake Plate, Shaped Edge, Tab Handles, Myott & Sons, England, 10 x 11 In.	98.00
Black Crocus, Lamp, Vase Shape, Handles, Royal Winton, 26 In.	2295.00
Brama, Biscuit Jar, Cover, Midwinter, England, c.1940	228.00
Calico, Plate, Blue & White, Burleigh, Staffordshire, 6 In.	8.00
Chelsea Rose, Plate, Square, Scalloped Corners, Rosina, 8 In.	40.00
Du Barry, Plate, Round, James Kent, 8 ½ In.	36.00
Du Barry, Plate, Square, Cut Corners, James Kent, 5 ¾ In.	25.00
Du Barry, Teapot, James Kent, Individual, 4 In.	199.00
Du Barry, Vase, Cover, James Kent	47.00
Du Barry, Washbowl Set, James Kent, 7 ¼ In., 2 Piece	167.00
Hazel, Bud Vase, Footed, Narrow Neck, Flared Rim, Royal Winton, 5 In.	320.00
Lilies, Cup & Saucer, Taylor & Kent	78.00
Marigold, Candy Dish, Square, Ruffled & Crimped Rim, 5 In.	65.00
Marina, Plate, Lord Nelson, 5 ¾ In.	35.00
Marina, Sugar & Creamer, Lord Nelson	145.00

Melody, Plate, Royal Crown, 9 In.	237.00
Mille Fleurs, Dish, James Kent, Shaped Rim, 6 ½ x 5 In.	25.00
Pekin, Plate, Dinner, Royal Winton, 10 ½ In.	23.00
Rosalie, Coffeepot, Empire, England, 8 In.	125.00
Rosalynde, Cup & Saucer, James Kent..	49.00
Rosalynde, Plate, Round, James Kent, 9 ½ In.	45.00
Rose Teapot Set, Stacking, Sugar, Creamer, Basin, Lefton	250.00
Rosina, Cup & Saucer	94.00

CHOCOLATE GLASS, sometimes mistakenly called caramel slag, was made by the Indiana Tumbler and Goblet Company of Greentown, Indiana, from 1900 to 1903. It was also made at other National Glass Company factories. Fenton Art Glass Co. made chocolate glass from about 1907 to 1915. More recent pieces have been made by Imperial and others.

Cactus, Butter, Cover, Pedestal, Wafer Construction, Greentown, c.1900, 8 In.	264.00
Cactus, Compote, Cover, Greentown, 9 ½ In.	173.00
Cactus, Tumbler, Greentown, 4 In., 6 Piece	96.00
Dewey, Butter, Dome Cover, ¼ Lb., Greentown, Indiana, 4 ⅜ x 5 In. ....*illus*	69.00
Feather, Pitcher, Early 1900s, 8 ⅛ x 4 ¼ In.	863.00
Feather, Pitcher, Milk, c.1925, 8 ⅛ In.	991.00
Fish, Dish, Fish In Big Fish Mouth, Greentown, 4 ½ x 7 In.	160.00
Leaf Bracket, Cruet, Dewey Stopper, Greentown, 5 ¼ x 3 In. ....*illus*	92.00
Rabbit, Dish, Cover, Basket Base, Greentown, 4 ¼ x 5 ½ In.	480.00
Rabbit, Dish, Cover, Greentown, c.1900, 4 ¼ x 4 ¼ x 5 ½ In.	264.00
Racing Deer, Pitcher, Scalloped Rim, Applied Handle, Greentown, 9 x 4 In.	345.00
Scalloped Edge, Pitcher, Footed, 9 In.	205.00
Squirrel, Pitcher, Indiana Tumbler & Goblet Co., c.1900, 9 x 4 ¾ In. .... 374.00 to 428.00	
Squirrel, Pitcher, Water, Pedestal, Greentown, 10 ½ In.	325.00
Wild Rose & Bowknot, Cruet, McKee, 7 In.	259.00

CHRISTMAS collectibles include not only Christmas trees and ornaments listed below, but also Santa Claus figures, special dishes, and even games and wrapping paper. A Belsnickle is a nineteenth-century figure of Father Christmas. A kugel is an early, heavy ornament made of thick blown glass, lined with zinc or lead, and often covered with colored wax. Christmas cards are listed in this section under Greeting Card. Christmas collectibles may also be listed in the Candy Container category. Christmas trees are listed in the section that follows.

Advertising Card, Santa & Simplex Typewriter, Diecut, 1920s, 5 x 2 ½ In.	40.00
Belsnickle, Brown Coat, Chalkware, 10 In. ....*illus*	5175.00
Belsnickle, Papier-Mache, Composition, Blue Coat, Mica Snow, Feather Tree, c.1910, 8 In.	1600.00
Belsnickle, Papier-Mache, Composition, Gold Coat, Flecks, Holds Switch, c.1910, 10 In.	1400.00
Belsnickle, Papier-Mache, Composition, White Coat, Mica Snow, Blue Switch, c.1910, 9 ¾ In.	1200.00
Book, Kris Kringle's, Poems, Peter, Paul & Brother, Buffalo, N.Y., 1881	30.00
Book, Treasure Chest Of Christmas Songs & Carols, Treasure Chest Publications, 1936..........	58.00
Box, Hinged, Bell Shape, Flowers, Frosted, Enamel, 3 ½ In.	25.00
Button, Santa Claus Club, Porteous, Celluloid, Mitchell & Braun, Portland, Me., 1 ¼ In.	30.00
Button, Santa Claus, Montreal, Canada, Celluloid, 1 ¼ In.	19.00
Button, Santa, Look For Me At The May Co., Bastian Paper, c.1907, 1 ½ In.	173.00
Button, Santa, Strawbridge & Clothier Toy Store, Giving Presents To WW I Soldier, 1 ¼ In. ...	190.00
Button, Santa, Volunteers Of America, I Helped, 1 In.	8.50
Candy Containers are listed in the Candy Container category.	
Creche, Man, Moor, Standing, Carved, Painted, Stuffed Body, Dressed, 1800s, 6 x 14 In.	1649.00
Display, Santa Claus, Composition, Cloth, Cardboard Legs, Body, Germany, 32 In.	489.00
Display, Santa Claus, Deer, Church, Trees, Mica Snow, Musical, Silent Night, 7 x 12 In. ....*illus*	633.00
Display, Santa's Workshop, Mechanical, 36 x 84 In.	1035.00
Doorstop, Santa Claus, Waving Left Hand, Painted, Cast Iron, Signed, Hubley, 12 In.	150.00
Figure, Angel, Wax, Dresden Accents, Spun Glass Wings, Lace, 12 In. ....*illus*	316.00
Figure, Creche, 1 Of 3 Kings, Composite, Multicolored, Silk, Paper, Sequins, Stand, 13 In. .....*illus*	380.00
Figurine, Santa Claus, Painted, Chalkware, c.1900	75.00
Figurine, Santa, Ice Skating, Cold Paint, Bisque, Marked, Japan, 1 ⅝ In. ....*illus*	20.00
Match Holder, Santa, St. Nick, Tree, Child, Tin Lithograph, 9 x 4 In.	4620.00
Mold, Cake, Santa Claus, Embossed, Hey Kiddies, Iron, 12 In.	405.00
Mold, Chocolate, Father Christmas, Tin, Long Coat, Lantern, Kutzcher Co., Germany, 1920s, 8 In. ..	285.00
Mold, Ice Cream, Christmas Tree, Pewter, Hinged, 5 In.	250.00
Music Box, Santa Claus, White Gloss Glaze, Berman & Anderson	55.00
Nativity Set, Figures, Animals, c.1890, 10 In., 8 Piece...........................	410.00
Nodder, Santa, Clockwork, Hooded Coat, Fir Sprig, Basket, Key, Germany, 29 In. ....*illus*	4830.00

C

Chinese Export, Watch Holder, Cover, Painted Enamel Flowers, Birds, Flowers, c.1870, 8 x 5 In.
$3408.00

Chocolate Glass, Dewey, Butter, Dome Cover, ¼ Lb., Greentown, Indiana, 4 ⅜ x 5 In.
$69.00

Chocolate Glass, Leaf Bracket, Cruet, Dewey Stopper, Greentown, 5 ¼ x 3 In.
$92.00

Holiday Collectibles
Save New Year's noisemakers and other things marked with a year. Lithographed tin or plastic is best, but unusual paper hats and other decorations are OK. Collectors already hunt for anything related to Christmas, Halloween, Thanksgiving, and the Fourth of July. New Year's Eve should be next on the holiday list.

Christmas, Belsnickle, Brown Coat, Chalkware, 10 In.
$5175.00

Christmas, Display, Santa Claus, Deer, Church, Trees, Mica Snow, Musical, Silent Night, 7 x 12 In.
$633.00

Christmas, Figure, Angel, Wax, Dresden Accents, Spun Glass Wings, Lace, 12 In.
$316.00

Christmas, Figure, Creche, 1 Of 3 Kings, Composite, Multicolored, Silk, Paper, Sequins, Stand, 13 In.
$380.00

Christmas, Nodder, Santa, Clockwork, Hooded Coat, Fir Sprig, Basket, Key, Germany, 29 In.
$4830.00

Christmas, Toy, Santa Claus, Composition Face, Pull, Marked, Germany, 8 In.
$585.00

Christmas, Toy, Santa Claus, Roly Poly, Schoenhut, Label, 11 In.
$1989.00

Christmas, Toy, Santa Claus, Walker, Celluloid, Tin, Windup, Occupied Japan, 1940s, 6 In.
$173.00

Christmas, Toy, Santa's Sleigh, Reindeer, Painted, Cast Iron, Hubley, 16 In.
$819.00

Christmas Tree, Light Set, 8 Cartoon Characters, Glass, Box, Japan, 1930s, 4 ¾ x 6 ½ In.
$310.00

CHRISTMAS TREE

Pencil Sharpener, Santa Claus, Celluloid, Japan, 1930s, 2 ½ In.	295.00

Plates that are limited edition are listed in the Collector Plate category or in the correct factory listing.

Puzzle, Santa Claus, Trimming Christmas Tree, Whitman, 1957	32.00
Rattle, Santa Claus, Standing, Holding Gift Basket, Toy Sack, Marked, 5 ½ In.	165.00
Salt & Pepper, Boy & Girl, Red & Green Clothes, Avon, c.1983	12.00
Santa Claus, Coming Out Of Chimney, Signed, 1980s, 15 x 8 ½ In.	99.00
Santa Claus, Father Frost, Holding Staff, Bag Of Flowers, Papier-Mache, Cloth, Russia, 28 In.	288.00
Santa Claus, Papier-Mache Mold, Robe, Sack, Hardwood, c.1900, 40 ½ In.	3055.00
Santa Claus, Toy Bag, Stepping Into Chimney, Die Cut, Shoenman Bro's., Phila., 13 In.	565.00
Santa Claus, White Coat, Red Sash, Tree, Cane, Papier-Mache, Painted, c.1900, 17 In.	468.00
Sticker, Merry Christmas, Happy New Year, Wells Fargo & Co. Express, 3 ¼ x 5 ½ In.	120.00
Stocking, Angel & Santa, White Thread Mesh, Tinsel Hanger, Paper, c.1910, 12 In.	60.00
Tin, Santa Claus, Girl Holding School Slate, Pocket, 1910, 1 ⅞ x ⅞ In.	139.00
Toy, Santa Claus, Composition Face, Pull, Marked, Germany, 8 In. ....illus	585.00
Toy, Santa Claus, Nodder, Glass Eyes, Rabbit Fur Hair, Composition Face, Key Windup, 24 In.	585.00
Toy, Santa Claus, On Handcar, Tin Lithograph, Battery Operated, Japan, Box, 1960s, 8 x 10 In.	158.00
Toy, Santa Claus, On Sleigh, Tin, Windup, Japan, 1950s, 8 In.	95.00
Toy, Santa Claus, Roly Poly, Painted, Pressed Paper, 1950, 8 x 4 In.	60.00
Toy, Santa Claus, Roly Poly, Papier-Mache, Painted, Egg Shape, Schoenhut, 9 In.	384.00
Toy, Santa Claus, Roly Poly, Schoenhut, Label, 11 In. ....illus	1989.00
Toy, Santa Claus, Roly-Poly, Toy Sack, Celluloid, 3 ¼ In.	225.00
Toy, Santa Claus, Sleigh, 2 Reindeer, Bells, Tin, Windup, Strauss, 12 In.	610.00
Toy, Santa Claus, Sleigh, Reindeer, White, Red, Gold, Painted, Cast Iron, Hubley, 15 In.	1080.00
Toy, Santa Claus, Walker, Celluloid, Tin, Windup, Occupied Japan, 1940s, 6 In. ....illus	173.00
Toy, Santa's Sleigh, Reindeer, Painted, Cast Iron, Hubley, 16 In. ....illus	819.00

CHRISTMAS TREES made of feathers and Christmas tree decorations of all types are popular with collectors. The first decorated Christmas tree in America is claimed by many states, including Pennsylvania (1747), Massachusetts (1832), Illinois (1833), Ohio (1838), and Iowa (1845). The first glass ornaments were imported from Germany about 1860. Dresden ornaments were made about 135 years ago of paper and tinsel. Manufacturers in the United States were making ornaments in the early 1870s. Electric lights were first used on a Christmas tree in 1882. Character light bulbs became popular in the 1920s, bubble lights in the 1940s, twinkle bulbs in the 1950s, plastic bulbs by 1955. In this book a Christmas light is a holder for a candle used on the tree. Other forms of lighting include light bulbs. Other Christmas collectibles are listed in the preceding section.

Aluminum, Feather, Iridescent, Mercury Glass Balls, 5 Rows, 15 In.	35.00
Aluminum, Green, Stand, Box, 78 In.	198.00
Aluminum, Pompom Ends, Stand, Box, Sleeves, 48 In.	97.00
Feather, Berries On Branches, Painted, Poinsettias, Wood Base, Germany	268.00
Feather, Dyed, Wire Base, Ornaments, Stencil Painted Box, c.1920, 46 In.	529.00
Feather, Yellow Green Tipped Branches, Red Berries, Germany, 31 In.	675.00
Light Bulb, Santa Claus, Holding Tree, Hand Painted, Japan, 1930s, 8 ½ x 3 ¼ In.	32.00
Light Set, 8 Cartoon Characters, Glass, Box, Japan, 1930s, 4 ¾ x 6 ½ In. ....illus	310.00
Light Set, Mickey Mouse, Bell Shape, Plastic, Noma, Box, 2 ¼ x 16 In.	80.00
Light, Diamond Quilt, Milk Glass, Brock, France, 3 ¾ In.	125.00
Light, Thousand Eye, Amber Glass, 3 ¾ In.	185.00
Ornament, 2 Angels, Paper Scrap, Tinsel Hanger, 9 ½ x 6 In.	65.00
Ornament, Beatles, Reflective Bodies, Glitter Jackets, c.1964, 6 ¼ In., 3 Piece	295.00
Ornament, Bull Moose, Dresden, Germany, c.1910, 2 In.	135.00
Ornament, Claus & Co. Railroad, Trestle Stand, Engine, Gift Car, Caboose, Hallmark, 1991	35.00
Ornament, Clown, 4 Faces, Blown Glass, Painted, Gold, Red Hats, 2 ½ x 3 In. ....illus	345.00
Ornament, Devil's Head, Neck, Glass, Painted, c.1950	125.00
Ornament, Kugel, Green, Metal Cap, Hanging Hook, Germany, 8 In. ....illus	197.00
Ornament, Lantern, Santa Head, Papier-Mache, Paper Insert Eyes, Mouth, Red Hat, Mica, 5 In. illus	460.00
Ornament, Pinecone, 5 Frosted Colors, Occupied Japan, 1945-54, 2 In., 10 Piece	126.00
Ornament, Rabbit, Holding Large Carrot, Matt, Silver & Gold Color, Germany, 3 ½ In.	55.00
Ornament, Silver Star, 3-Piece Train Set, Locomotive, Luggage Car & Dome Car, Hallmark	15.00
Ornament, Snoopy, Carrying Tree, United Features, 1958, 3 x 2 ½ In.	25.00
Ornament, Stippled Border, Beaded Candle Scene, Mercury Glass, Japan, 1950s, 2 ½ In.	29.00
Ornament, Stylized Child, Mercury Glass, Painted, Czechoslovakia, Box, 3 In.	12.00
Ornament, Tree Bulb, Log Cabin, Cardboard, U.S.A., 3 ½ In.	25.00
Ornament, Victorian Man & Lady, Chromolithograph Paper, 6 In.	65.00
Stand, 3 Legs, Locking Jaws, North Bros. Mfg. Co., Philadelphia, Pa.	115.00
Stand, Musical, Turns, Figures Dance, Tin, Wood, Iron, 12 Tunes, 14 x 10 In. ....illus	2185.00

CHRISTMAS TREE

Christmas Tree, Ornament, Clown, 4 Faces, Blown Glass, Painted, Gold, Red Hats, 2 ½ x 3 In.
$345.00

Christmas Tree, Ornament, Kugel, Green, Metal Cap, Hanging Hook, Germany, 8 In.
$197.00

Christmas Tree, Ornament, Lantern, Santa Head, Papier-Mache, Paper Insert Eyes, Mouth, Red Hat, Mica, 5 In.
$460.00

Christmas Tree, Stand, Musical, Turns, Figures Dance, Tin, Wood, Iron, 12 Tunes, 14 x 10 In.
$2185.00

C

Chrome, Compote, Art Deco, Amethyst Glass, Nude Figural Stem, Farber Bros., 7 ⅝ x 5 ½ In. $132.00

Cigar Store Figure, Indian, Maiden, Holding Cigars, Pine, Painted, 20th Century, 75 In. $2409.00

Cinnabar, Smoke Set, Carved, Buddha Center, 2 Holders, 3 x 8 ½ In. $110.00

Civil War, Pouch, Leather, U.S. Brass Buckle, 9 x 6 In. $410.00

CHROME items in the Art Deco style became popular in the 1930s. Collectors are most interested in high-style pieces made by the Connecticut firms of Chase Brass & Copper Co. and Manning-Bowman & Co.

Ashtray, Cowboy Hat, Griswold	1800.00
Compote, Art Deco, Amethyst Glass, Nude Figural Stem, Farber Bros., 7 ⅝ x 5 ½ In. ....*illus*	132.00
Flask, Double, Screw Cap, Tin Lined, Germany, 7 ½ In., 13 Oz.	85.00
Tray, Art Deco, Red & Black Handles, Footed, 15 x 5 ¾ In.	175.00
Tray, Art Deco, Red Bakelite Handles, Footed, 7 ¼ x 8 In.	109.00
Tray, Cutout Edge, Farber Brothers, c.1940, 15 In.	25.00
Yarn Holder, Bakelite, Manning Bowman, Mid 1900s	125.00

CIGAR STORE FIGURES of carved wood or cast iron were used as advertisements in front of the Victorian cigar store. The carved figures are now collected as folk art. They range in size from counter type, about three feet, to over eight feet high.

Indian, Brave, Folded Hands, Loin Cloth, Wood, Old Paint, 66 In.	293.00
Indian, Chief, Full Headdress, Red Cloak, On Mountain Lion, Painted, Zinc, 1890s, 71 In.	5750.00
Indian, Full Headdress, Carved, Painted, Arm Raised, Tapered Square Base, 1900s, 46 ½ In.	4200.00
Indian, Full Headdress, Carved, Painted, Ax, Fur, Attributed To Thomas Brooks, Wheels, 86 In.	36750.00
Indian, Full Headdress, Carved, Painted, Holding Leaves, Attributed To Samuel Robb, 66 In.	23100.00
Indian, Full Headdress, Tunic, Leggings, Carved, Painted, c.1890, 70 x 20 In.	4444.00
Indian, Mahogany, Painted, 75 ½ x 22 In.	6500.00
Indian, Maiden, Holding Cigars, Pine, Painted, 20th Century, 75 In. ....*illus*	2409.00
Indian, Princess, Wood, c.1880, 72 In.	8050.00
Jack, Bell Hop, Holding Cigar Box, Humidor, Carved, Wood, Jim Smock, 45 x 19 In.	840.00
Punch, Wood, Carved, Painted, 20th Century, 61 x 16 x 11 In.	550.00
Scotsman, Kilt, Sporin, Wood, Carved, Painted, c.1930s, 71 In.	3422.00
Scottish Highlander, Wood, Carved, Painted, c.1900, 28 In.	1896.00
Woman, Wood, Columbia, 56 In.	17600.00

CINNABAR is a vermilion or red lacquer. Pieces are made with tens to hundreds of thicknesses of the lacquer that is later carved. Most cinnabar was made in the Orient.

Bowl, Pumpkin, Cover, 3 ½ x 6 x 6 In.	30.00
Box, Cover, Figures, Chinese, 4 In. Square	167.00
Box, Cover, Landscape, Figures, Round, Chinese, 7 In.	3105.00
Box, Dome Lid, 5 Birds, 5 Human Symbols, Carved, Relief, 19th Century, 6 x 12 In.	6300.00
Box, Flower, 4 In.	55.00
Box, Lid, Equestrian Scene, 7 In. Diam.	1400.00
Box, Lid, Scrolling Leaves, Figures, Qing Reign Mark, 5 ½ In.	400.00
Brushpot, Carved, Relief Pagoda Scene, Straight Sides, 5 ½ x 4 ¾ In.	472.00
Jar, Gourd Shape, Lid, 6 In.	175.00
Smoke Set, Carved, Buddha Center, 2 Holders, 3 x 8 ½ In. ....*illus*	110.00

CIVIL WAR mementos are important collectors' items. Most of the pieces are military items used from 1861 to 1865. Be sure to avoid any explosive munitions.

Bayonet, 58 Cal., Scabbard	185.00
Button, Confederate Officer, Eagle, Stars, Brass, Coat Size, Pair	1116.00
Cane, Confederate, Hand Carved, Snake On Base, Camp Chase Prisoner Of War, 31 In.	1763.00
Canteen, Drum Style, Copper, Dovetail, 8 ½ x 2 ¾ In.	475.00
Cap, Forage, Model 1858, Blue Wool, Leather Visor	3408.00
Cap, Forage, Union, Blue Wool, Leather Visor, 6-In. Crown	3408.00
Chart, Signal Flags, Hooker's, Chancellorsville, Hand Drawn, Frame, 7 ½ x 9 ½ In.	529.00
Coat, General, New York State	5500.00
Decoy, Soldier, Wrought Iron, Metal Platform, c.1865, 30 x 75 In.	1120.00
Drum, H. Laurence Company B Vt. 3rd	6325.00
Field Surgeon's Kit, Mahogany, Brass Mounts, 3-Tier Case, Gutta Percha Handles, 16 x 6 ¼ In.	1440.00
Glasses, Sniper, Leather Case	80.00
Holster, Colt Revolver, Black Bridle Leather, 3 Brass Rivets, Army Contractor J. Davy & Co.	588.00
Knife, Confederate, Spear Point Blade, Shaped Wood Handle	705.00
Medical Kit, Amputation Tools, Leather Hardcase, 3 Piece	329.00
Photograph, Albumen Print, Infantry Officer, Frame, 12 ¾ x 9 ½ In.	147.00
Plate, Centennial, Robert E. Lee, 1807-70, 10 In.	24.00
Pouch, Leather, Stamped US 0120 Dept., Metal Container, 9 x 6 In.	263.00

Pouch, Leather, U.S. Brass Buckle, 9 x 6 In. ....*illus*   410.00
Stand, Walnut, 3-Sided, Canvas, Cannons, Text, Guns, GAR Ill Post 283, c.1890, 32 x 36 In. ..   705.00
Sword, Officer's, Phrygian Helmet Pommel, Wood Grip, c.1865, 36 ¼ In. 805.00

CKAW, *see Dedham category.*

CLARICE CLIFF was a designer who worked in several English factories, including A.J. Wilkinson Ltd., Wilkinson's Royal Staffordshire Pottery, Newport Pottery, and Foley Pottery after the 1920s. She is best known for her brightly colored Art Deco designs, including the Bizarre line. She died in 1972. Reproductions have been made by Wedgwood.

Biarritz, Plate, Rectangular, No. 4, 6 ½ x 5 ½ In. ....*illus*   68.00
Bizarre, Dish, Gollywog, Cream Ground, Pink Pants, Blue Shirt, Orange Jabot, 8 In. 1750.00
Bizarre, Pitcher, 11 ¾ In. 104.00
Crocus, Jug, Egg Shape, Cream Ground, Yellow Border, Handles, c.1939, 11 ¾ In. 232.00
Rodanthe, Bizarre, Coffee Set, c.1934, 7-In. Coffeepot, 5 Piece..................................   415.00
Rodanthe, Bizarre, Vase, 3-Footed, 9 In. ....*illus*   1500.00
Summerhouse, Bizarre, Plate, Wedgwood, 8 In. 29.00
Tonquin, Sauceboat, Underplate, Royal Staffordshire..   35.00

CLEWELL ware was made in limited quantities by Charles Walter Clewell of Canton, Ohio, from 1902 to 1955. Pottery was covered with a thin coating of bronze, then treated to make the bronze turn different colors. Pieces covered with copper, brass, or silver were also made. Mr. Clewell's secret formula for blue patinated bronze was burned when he died in 1965.

Vase, Copper Clad, Applied Fish, Sponge, Incised, 5 ½ In. 288.00
Vase, Copper Clad, Bulbous, Green, Maroon Mottled Patina, 4 x 5 In. 510.00
Vase, Copper Clad, Flared, Bulbous Bottom, 4 x 8 ½ In. 460.00
Vase, Copper Clad, Pinched Bottom, 5 x 4 ½ In. 431.00
Vase, Copper Clad, Pinched Neck, Ruffled Rim, 6 In. 439.00
Vase, Copper Clad, Shouldered, Marked, 3 x 4 In. 173.00

CLOCKS of all types have always been popular with collectors. The eighteenth-century tall case, or grandfather's, clock was designed to house a works with a long pendulum. The name on the clock is usually the maker but sometimes it is a merchant or other craftsman. In 1816, Eli Terry patented a new, smaller works for a clock, and the case became smaller. The clock could be kept on a shelf instead of on the floor. By 1840, coiled springs were used and even smaller clocks were made. Battery-powered electric clocks were made in the 1870s. A garniture set can include a clock and other objects displayed on a mantel.

Advertising, 7Up, Get Teal Action, Metal Case, Molded Plastic Dial, c.1960, 16 x 16 In. 240.00
Advertising, A & W Root Beer, Bubble, Light-Up, c.1940-50..   1265.00
Advertising, Autolite Sta-Ful Battery, Light-Up, 18 In. 339.00
Advertising, Baird, Diamond Black Leather Oil, Tin, Wood, c.1897, 29 x 18 In. ....*illus*   1989.00
Advertising, Borden's Milk & Cream, Blue, Plastic, Aluminum, Light-Up, 12 x 18 ½ In. 110.00
Advertising, Boston Laundry Starch, Oak, Tin Front, Baird Clock Co., c.1920, 33 In. 1521.00
Advertising, Calumet Baking Soda, Calendar Regulator, Oak Case, c.1910, 36 x 16 ½ In. 1020.00
Advertising, Coles Jewelers, Pocket Watch Shape, Oak Case, Seth Thomas, c.1900, 28 x 23 In. ..   540.00
Advertising, Crosley, Radios, Time For Crosley, Contemporary, Steel Case, Blue Neon, 18 x 18 In.   420.00
Advertising, Dr Pepper, Drink, Red, White, Yellow Circles, 4-Sided, 21 ¾ In. 130.00
Advertising, Dr Pepper, Roman Numerals, 5-Sided, 38 x 20 In. 350.00
Advertising, Ever-Ready Safety Razor, Lathered Man Smiling, Roman Numerals, Painted......   810.00
Advertising, Frostie Root Beer, Cuckoo, Simulated Wood, Plastic, 1970s, 10 x 19 In. 173.00
Advertising, Frostie Root Beer, Light-Up, 18 ¾ x 13 ¼ In. 153.00
Advertising, Gas-Oil, Light-Up, 26 ½ x 23 x 5 In. 360.00
Advertising, Gilbert Clock Co., Store, Regulator, c.1910, 19 x 39 In. 325.00
Advertising, Gold Seal Ice Cream, Time To Buy, Plastic, Aluminum, 10 x 25 ½ In. 25.00
Advertising, Grand Prize Beer, Enjoy, Light-Up, 14 x 12 ½ In. 145.00
Advertising, Greenleaf Ice Cream, Model SQ-212, No. 7484, 12 x 12 In. 60.00
Advertising, John Deere, Green, Yellow, White, Light-Up, 16 x 16 In. 195.00
Advertising, John R. Dickey's Eye Water, Baird Clock Co., c.1894, 30 ½ In. 1955.00
Advertising, Katy Flyer Cigars, Train Engine, Copper Flashed, Cast Iron, Golden Novelty, 14 x 15 In.   6250.00
Advertising, Kendall Oil, 2000 Mile Oil, Electric, Rotating Second Hand, Black, Chrome, 21 ½ In.   523.00
Advertising, Monarch Finer Foods, Lion, Telechron Inc., 14 ½ In. Diam. 140.00
Advertising, Old Mr. Boston, Fine Liquors, White, Blue, Bottle Form, Metal, c.1920, 22 In. 385.00
Advertising, Pearl Beer, Bottle Of Lager Beer Please, Neon, 8-Sided, 18 ¼ In. 795.00
Advertising, Royal Crown Soda, Metal Rim, Electric, 15 In. ....*illus*   263.00
Advertising, Sauer's Extract, Regulator, Birch, Reverse Painted Glass, New Haven, c.1900, 42 x 15 In.   3750.00

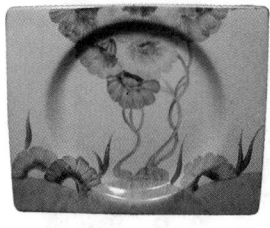

Clarice Cliff, Biarritz, Plate, Rectangular, No. 4, 6 ½ x 5 ½ In. $68.00

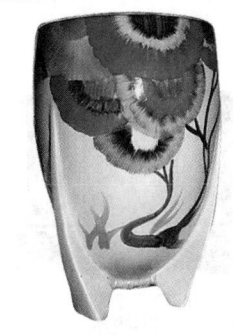

Clarice Cliff, Rodanthe, Bizarre, Vase, 3-Footed, 9 In. $1500.00

Clock, Advertising, Baird, Diamond Black Leather Oil, Tin, Wood, c.1897, 29 x 18 In. $1989.00

Clock, Advertising, Royal Crown Soda, Metal Rim, Electric, 15 In. $263.00

Clock, Advertising, Tru-Pals Shoes, For Comfort Wear, Electric, c.1940, 15 ½ x 15 ½ In. $263.00

Clock, Ansonia, Shelf, Architectural, Open Escapement, Key Wind, 12 ¼ x 16 In. $115.00

Clock, Banjo, New Haven, Reverse Painted Tablet, Mt. Vernon, Mid 1900s, 41 In. $240.00

Advertising, Seagram's, Blended Whiskey, Horses, 15 x 15 In.	120.00
Advertising, Simmons Liver Regulator Patent Medicine, Horseshoe Shape, Brass, 6 x 5 ½ In.	358.00
Advertising, Squirt, Drink With The Happy Taste, Boy, Bottle, Pam, c.1960, 15 x 15 In.	195.00
Advertising, St. Charles Evaporated Milk, Figural, Cow With Clock In Body, 8 ¾ In.	425.00
Advertising, Thirsty Just Whistle, Elf, Soda, Red, Blue, Masonite, Wood, 24 x 24 In.	3190.00
Advertising, Tru-Pals Shoes, For Comfort Wear, Electric, c.1940, 15 ½ x 15 ½ In. ....*illus*	263.00
Advertising, Zonweiss Tooth Powder, Girl Brushing Teeth, Round, Footed, 4 ¼ In.	1430.00
Ansonia, Clarence, Gingerbread, Oak, 8-Day, Gong Striking Movement, 22 ½ In.	165.00
Ansonia, Figural, Soldier, Metal, Iron Base, 8-Day, Open Escapement, c.1890, 22 In.	1150.00
Ansonia, Gallery, Walnut, Round, 8-Day, Pendulum, c.1890, 23 ½ In.	478.00
Ansonia, Novelty, Mirror, 30-Hour, Rear Wind, c.1885, 14 ¼ In.	242.00
Ansonia, Porcelain, Open Escapement, c.1900, 11 ½ In.	431.00
Ansonia, Regulator, 4-Glass Crystal, 8-Day, c.1904, 14 In.	288.00
Ansonia, Regulator, Crystal, Spelter, Urn, Open Escapement, Time & Strike, 16 In.	427.00
Ansonia, Shelf, Amiens, Louis XIV Style, Enameled Iron, c.1894	475.00
Ansonia, Shelf, Architectural, Brass, Marble, Key, 10 ¾ x 12 ¾ In.	141.00
Ansonia, Shelf, Architectural, Open Escapement, Key Wind, 12 ¼ x 16 In. ....*illus*	115.00
Ansonia, Shelf, Gilt Iron, Painted Porcelain Scene, Urn Finial, 1900-20, 15 x 8 In.	176.00
Ansonia, Shelf, Monarch, Crystal Palace Series, 8-Day Time & Strike, Cast Bezel, c.1880, 24 ½ In.	450.00
Ansonia, Shelf, No. 1, Flanking Statues, 2-Jar Pendulum, Wood Pedestal, 18 ½ In.	504.00
Ansonia, Shelf, Oak, 8-Day, Gong, c.1901, 16 ½ In.	115.00
Ansonia, Shelf, Porcelain, 8-Day, Gong, Flowers, c.1910, 12 In.	546.00
Ansonia, Shelf, Rococo Revival, Enameled Gilt, Porcelain, 1800s, 11 In.	180.00
Ansonia, Shelf, Rosewood, Porcelain Face, Outside Escapement, Half & Hour Strike, c.1900	185.00
Ansonia, Shelf, Shakespeare, Seated Spelter Figure, Gilt Dial, Open Escapement, c.1890, 14 In.	390.00
Ansonia, Shelf, Thebes, Art Nouveau, Cast Iron, Pewter, Porcelain Dial, c.1911, 11 ¼ In.	107.00
Ansonia, Trinket, Porcelain, 8-Day Time & Strike, Paper Dial, Sky Blue, c.1910, 11 In.	56.00
Ansonia, Wall, General, Oak, 8-Day, 2-Weight, c.1915, 68 In.	2233.00
Ansonia, Wall, Kobe, Walnut, Maple, Rosettes, Mosaic, 8-Day, Strike, c.1901, 18 In.	144.00
Ansonia, Wall, Queen Elizabeth, Oak, 8-Day, c.1901, 37 In.	288.00
Ansonia, Walnut, Columns, 8-Day Time & Strike, Drop Finials, c.1874, 26 In.	315.00
Art Deco, Annular, Brass, Embossed, 3 x 5 ½ In.	760.00
Art Deco, Chromed Metal, Clear Round Face, Painted Metallic Roman Numerals, 6 ¼ x 10 In.	86.00
Art Deco, Silver Frame, Blue Enamel, Wood Back, 5 x 3 In.	450.00
Art Deco, Westminster Chimes, Mahogany, Beveled Glass, 27 x 16 ½ In.	360.00
Art Deco, Wood Case, Ceramic Girl, Kneeling, Green Matte Glaze, 9 ½ x 5 ¼ In.	115.00
Art Nouveau, 3-Panel Screen Shape, 3 French Women, Gold, Porcelain Crest, 5 x 4 In.	853.00
Atkins, Shelf, London Mantel, Chronometer, Rosewood, 2 Gilt Columns, Glass, Painted, c.1865, 17 In.	6518.00
Atkins, Shelf, London Mantel, Chronometer, Rosewood, 2 Gilt Columns, Gold Dog, c.1860, 17 In.	2370.00
Atkins, Shelf, Rosewood, Blue Ground, Transfer Decorated, Door, 30-Day Fusee, c.1860, 18 In.	1185.00
Austrian, Picture, Grand Sonnerie, Pull Wind, Clock On Church Tower, c.1840, 34 x 25 In.	4313.00
Banjo, 8-Day, Strike, Germany, c.1920, 38 In.	288.00
Banjo, Aaron Willard, Mahogany, Boston Massacre, Patriotic Symbols Panels, 41 In.	2585.00
Banjo, Aaron Willard, Mahogany, Carved Lyre, 40 In.	2875.00
Banjo, Attleboro Clock Co., Mahogany, 8-Day, Weight Driven, c.1850, 33 In.	506.00
Banjo, Chelsea Clock Co., Cast Brass Eagle Finial, Painted Metal Dial, 32 In.	711.00
Banjo, Daniel Pratt & Sons, Grain Painted, Roman Numerals, Weight Driven, 19th Century	330.00
Banjo, E. Howard, 8-Day, Bicentennial, Throat Glass, Mahogany, c.1976, 40 In.	2300.00
Banjo, E. Howard, No. 5, Cherry Wood, Weight Driven, 8-Day, 28 ½ x 12 x 3 ¾ In.	896.00
Banjo, E. Howard, No. 5, Rosewood, 2 Reverse Painted Glass Panels, Roman Numerals, 38 In.	2400.00
Banjo, Elmer O., Stennes, Tablets, Mt. Vernon, Geo. Washington, c.1962, 41 In.	3375.00
Banjo, Federal, Eglomise Glass Panel, Gilded, Gilded Finial, Brass Bezel, c.1815, 43 x 10 In.	1150.00
Banjo, Federal, Eglomise Throat & Panel, Painted Dial, 35 In.	403.00
Banjo, Federal, Mahogany, Brass, Woman Harpist, Reverse Painted Tablets, c.1825, 32 ¾ In.	1057.00
Banjo, Federal, Mahogany, Eglomise Panel, c.1810, 41 x 10 In.	936.00
Banjo, Foster, Campos, Mahogany, Cross Banded, 8-Day, c.1985, 40 In.	3565.00
Banjo, Foster Campos, Mahogany, Reverse Painted Glass, George Washington, c.1975	1422.00
Banjo, Howard & Davis, No. 1, Grained Fruitwood Case, Meter Pendulum, c.1842, 50 In.	4500.00
Banjo, Ingraham, Mahogany, Treasure Island Panel, Brass Eagle Finial, 38 In.	198.00
Banjo, Mahogany, Brass Dials, Red Ground, Carved, Black Border, Gilt, Boston, c.1830, 41 In.	5036.00
Banjo, Mahogany, Reverse Painted Constitution Tablet, Weight Driven, c.1890, 36 In.	235.00
Banjo, Mahogany, Reverse Painted Glass Tablet, 8-Day Movement, 1800s, 33 ½ In.	500.00
Banjo, Mahogany, Thermometer & Barometer Attachments, c.1875, 28 In.	236.00
Banjo, New Haven, 8-Day, Strike, Spring Movement, c.1928, 40 In.	127.00
Banjo, New Haven, 30-Day, Spring, Eagle, c.1925, 41 In.	190.00
Banjo, New Haven, Reverse Painted Tablet, Mt. Vernon, Mid 1900s, 41 In. ....*illus*	240.00

Banjo, New Haven, Reverse Painted Tablet Of Mt. Vernon, c.1950, 41 In.	240.00
Banjo, Sessions, Nautical Scene Panel, 42 x 12 ½ In. ....*illus*	275.00
Banjo, Waltham, Mahogany, Cast Eagle Finial, Convex Glass, Reverse Painted, 40 In.	844.00
Banjo, Waltham, Mahogany, Gilt, Lever Movement, 8-Day, c.1928, 21 In.	633.00
Banjo, Waltham, Mahogany, Reverse Painted Tablets, 8-Day, 40 In.	1422.00
Banjo, Waltham, Mahogany, Weights, Eagle Finial, 1813 Naval Battle Panel, 10 x 41 In.	920.00
Banjo, Waterbury, Mahogany, Brass, Multicolored Enamel Patriotic Symbols, c.1890, 10 x 33 In.	702.00
Banjo, Wood, Weight Driven, Pennsylvania, 28 In.	531.00
Birge & Fuller, Shelf, Federal, Gilt, 19th Century, 33 ½ x 15 ½ In.	175.00
Birge & Fuller, Steeple, Mahogany, Wagon Spring, Ball Feet, 13 ½ x 27 ½ In.	4888.00
Birge & Mallory, Shelf, Triple Decker, Gilt Eagle, Columns, Painted House Scene, 28 In.	593.00
Black Forest, Cuckoo, 1-Day, 7 Leaves, Bird, Germany, c.1910, 17 In.	104.00
Black Forest, Cuckoo, Deer Head, Rifles, Game, Horn, Oak Leaf, Music Box Tunes, 61 ½ In. .	2250.00
Black Forest, Cuckoo, Maple Leaf Pattern, 5 Leaves, Bird, 30-Hour, Strike, Germany, c.1920, 17 In.	121.00
Black Forest, Cuckoo, Wood Case & Weight, Carved Bird, 14 x 9 x 8 In.	575.00
Boardman, Chauncey, Shelf, Mahogany Veneer, Half Column, Splat, 30-Hour, c.1830, 35 In.	115.00
Bodet, Exterior, Roman Numerals, Plexiglas, Iron, 50 In.	2850.00
Bosch, Honig & Cie, Shelf, Delft, Tall Case Form, Windmill, Boats, Flowers, Utrecht, 15 ½ In.	620.00
Boucheron, Travel, Art Deco, Silver, Enamel, 2 ½ x 2 ½ In.	1986.00
Bracket, Ebonized Pearwood, Brass Inlaid, 3-Fusee, Ball Feet, c.1850, 26 In.	2185.00
Bracket, Neuchatel Style, Painted Red, Flowers, 8-Day, Time & Bell Strike, c.1975, 11 ¼ In. ..	90.00
Bronze, Enamel, Pink, Blue, Oval, Marble Base, Footed, Gubelin, Lucerne, c.1920, 6 x 6 In. ....*illus*	748.00
Brown, J.C., Mahogany, Beehive, Full Ripple, 8-Day, Time, Strike, Alarm, Spring, c.1860, 19 In.	575.00
Brown, J.C., Mahogany, Flowers, Ripple Steeple, 30-Hour, Time & Strike, c.1848, 16 In.	4725.00
Brown, J.C., Rosewood, Beehive, Ripple Front, Spring Driven, Painted, Signed, 1890, 10 x 19 In.	2128.00
Brown, J.C., Shelf, Gothic, Rosewood, Rounded, 4 Columns, Brass Pendulum, 12 x 20 In.	4313.00
Campos, Foster, Girandole, Weight Driven, 8-Day, Aurora Tablets, c.1999, 44 In.	4600.00
Carriage, Benetfink & Co., England	850.00
Carriage, Brass, Beveled Glass, Bail Handle, Repeater, T. Martin & Co., Late 1800s, 6 ½ x 3 ½ In.	920.00
Carriage, Brass, Beveled Glass, Bailey, Banks & Biddle, 19th Century, 6 In.	450.00
Carriage, Brass, Corniche Case, Strike, Alarm, Repeater, France, c.1900, 6 ½ In.	357.00
Carriage, Brass, England, c.1890, 7 x 10 ¾ In.	351.00
Carriage, Champleve Enamel, Brass, L. Epee, 8 x 4 In. ....*illus*	649.00
Carriage, Cylindrical, Alarm, Case, c.1900, 5 ½ In.	81.00
Carriage, Drum Shape, Brass Case, 6 Pillars, Porcelain Dial, c.1886, 4 ¼ x 6 In.	2025.00
Carriage, French Movement, Shreve & Co., 6 x 3 x 2 ½ In.	133.00
Carriage, Gilt Metal, Embossed Egyptian Figures, Scrolls, 3 In.	173.00
Carriage, Music Box, Silver Plate, Germany, c.1930, 6 x 5 ¼ In.	29.00
Carriage, Oval Glass Case, Gilt Brass Mount, Champleve Enamel, Urn Pediment, 15 In.	3105.00
Cartier, Desk, Art Deco, Chrome, Square, Square Dial, Wood Mount, Leather Fitted Box, 4 In.	259.00
Chelsea Clock Co., Boudoir, Red Brass, Doric, 5 In.	259.00
Chelsea Clock Co., Carriage, Copper & Brass, Enameled Dial, Signed, Boston, 4 ½ In.	468.00
Chelsea Clock Co., Shelf, Yacht Wheel, 8-Day, Model L Movement, c.1926, 14 In.	1495.00
Cottage Form, 3 Stories, 3-Leg, Twig Stand, Marked Camp Jack Ponds, 41 ¼ x 14 In.	605.00
Deniere, Shelf, Rouge, Marble, France, 15 In.	2875.00
Desk, Cottage, 1-Day, Calendar, Brass, Rear Wind, Key, c.1895, 7 In.	155.00
Desk, Plexiglas, Chrome, Pendulum, Windup, Key	200.00
Downes, Ephraim, Mahogany, House, Pillar & Scroll, For George Mitchell, Bristol, Conn., 31 In.	805.00
Edwards, William, Bracket, George III, Walnut, Arched, 8-Day, Fusee, London, 23 In.	1896.00
Empire Style, Portico, Marble, Ormolu Trim, Pendulum, 30-Day, c.1860, 24 In.	719.00
Empire, Annular, Bronze, Wood, Missing Works, 20 In.	2925.00
Empire, Figural, Putto In Chariot Pulled By Hound, Wheel Dial, Bronze Dore, France, 7 In. ..	896.00
Empire, Wood, Finials, Reverse Painted Panel, House, Tree, Gold Claw Feet, 27 ½ In.	177.00
Enamel Dial, Gilt Metal, Glass Case, 15 Jewel, Switzerland, 9 ¼ x 8 ¼ x 6 ½ In. .. 384.00 to 590.00	
Ever Ready, Chronos, Cylindrical Case, Windup, 5 In.	135.00
Federal, Mahogany, Eagle Finial, Ship Battle Tablet, New England, c.1810, 31 ½ In.	1007.00
Figural, Ax Shape, I Can Not Tell A Lie, c.1900, 8 x 6 In. ....*illus*	113.00
Figural, Bell, Brass Case, Relief Molding, Inset Porcelain, Late 19th Century, 7 ¾ In.	127.00
Figural, Cherub Holding Ball, Kimoto Dragon Hands, France, c.1880, 12 ½ In.	2070.00
Figural, Elephant, Trunk Holding Armature, Brass Pendulum, 10 ¾ x 9 ½ x 7 In.	294.00
Figural, Empire State Building, 30-Hour, Cast Metal, Dressler, c.1930, 5 In.	35.00
Figural, Fireman Holding Child, Ladder, Spelter, 8-Day, c.1912, 17 ½ In.	460.00
Figural, Kit Kat, Tail Pendulum, Black, Allied Mfg., Co., 15 In.	48.00
Figural, Lighthouse, Brass Case, Platform Cylinder Movement, Porcelain Dial, c.1890, 18 ½ In.	1969.00
Figural, Pocket Watch, 39-Hour, Rear Wind, c.1910, 10 In.	357.00
Figural, Sea Gull, Art Deco, Bell Strike Movement, Bronzed Ball, France, c.1935, 23 In.	805.00

Clock, Banjo, Sessions, Nautical Scene Panel, 42 x 12 ½ In. $275.00

Clock, Bronze, Enamel, Pink, Blue, Oval, Marble Base, Footed, Gubelin, Lucerne, c.1920, 6 x 6 In. $748.00

Clock, Carriage, Champleve Enamel, Brass, L. Epee, 8 x 4 In. $649.00

Clock, Figural, Ax Shape, I Can Not Tell A Lie, c.1900, 8 x 6 In.
$113.00

Clock, Gilbert, Egyptian, No. 63, Oak, Pressed Tulip Design, Label, 24 x 16 In.
$125.00

Clock, Gilbert, Shelf, Brass Face, Cobalt Blue Case, Flower Highlights, Scrolled Rim
$290.00

Clock, Herman Miller, Ball, Brass, Painted Wood Balls, Key Wind, George Nelson, 13 In.
$210.00

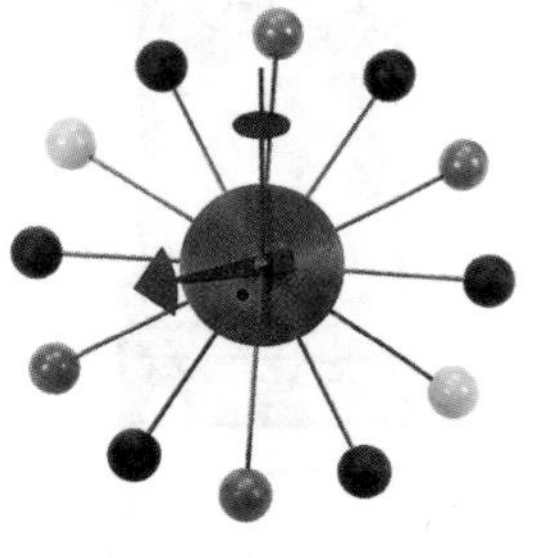

Figural, Shmoo, Pink Plastic, Graphic Box, c.1948, 4 1/12 x 8 ½ x 2 ½ In.	326.00
Figural, Statue, Globe On Head, Second Hand, c.1900, 28 ½ In.	1438.00
Figural, Victorian Girl, Holding Cast Spelter, 17 ½ x 6 In.	300.00
Forestville Mfg. Co., Shelf, Mahogany Veneer, 8-Day, Gong, c.1850, 31 In.	207.00
Forestville Mfg. Co., Shelf, Steeple, Mahogany Ripple, 30-Hour, Strike, c.1848, 16 In.	3335.00
French, 4 Marble Columns, Putti In Chariot On Top, Time & Strike, 19th Century, 22 In.	1098.00
French, Bronze Dore, Scrolls, Putti, 18 x 25 In.	2223.00
French, Garniture Set, Neoclassical, Gilt Bronze Mount, Marble, 2 Urns, 19 ½ & 20 ½ In.	3660.00
French, Gravity, Brass, Glass Dial, Compound Pendulum, 1-Day, c.1920, 10 In.	403.00
French, Portico, Marble, White, Glass Dome, Black Base, 19th Century, 19 ¼ In.	720.00
General Electric, Art Deco, Black, Gold Accents, Model No. 3H172, 6 ½ x 5 ½ In.	58.00
General Electric, Higgins, Black Numbers, Red Hands, 1960s, 7 ¾ In.	550.00
German, White Orb Shape, Black Conical Base, Black Face, Alarm, 1970s, 8 ¾ In.	125.00
Gilbert, Egyptian, No. 63, Oak, Pressed Tulip Design, Label, 24 x 16 In. *illus*	125.00
Gilbert, Gingerbread, Walnut, 8-Day, 24 ¼ In.	160.00
Gilbert, Regulator, Defender, Oak Case, 50 x 18 In.	450.00
Gilbert, Regulator, Railroad Station, c.1900	141.00
Gilbert, Shelf, Brass Face, Cobalt Blue Case, Flower Highlights, Scrolled Rim *illus*	290.00
Gilbert, Shelf, Porcelain, Floral, 8-Day, Time & Gong Strike, c.1898, 9 ½ In.	158.00
Gilbert, Wood, Green Stenciled Paint, Hands, 8-Day, c.1935, 17 In.	68.00
Gilt Brass, Champleve Enamel, Women In Wraps, Ship Pendulum, Urn, Key Wind, 18 In.	518.00
Gothic, Mahogany, 8-Day, Strike, Alarm, Key Lock, c.1848, 20 In.	288.00
Gubelin, Ormolu, Marble, Pink Guilloche Enamel, Time & Strike, Swiss, c.1920, 7 ½ In.	1800.00
Gubelin, Pink Marble, Cherubs, 8-Day, 7 x 6 In.	1112.00
Guilmet, Mystery, Figural, 8-Day, Marble Dial, Brass, Pendulum Swings, c.1880, 25 In.	3738.00
Gustav Becker, Mahogany, Silvered Dial, Bronze Movement, Chimes, c.1900, 13 In.	270.00
Gustav Becker, Regulator, Vienna, Domed Pediment, Carved Flowers, Columns, 54 In.	920.00
Gustav Becker, Shelf, Mahogany, Domed, Double Column Pilasters, Gold & Silvered Dial, 17 In.	295.00
Gustavsberg Sundell, Wall, Battery, 8 ¼ In.	600.00
Haddon Products, Home Sweet Home, Night-Light, Animated, c.1945, 7 ½ In.	107.00 to 200.00
Hatch, Regulator, Mahogany, Waisted Case, 8-Day, Weight Driven, c.1840, 31 In.	1013.00
Herman Miller, Ball, Brass, Painted Wood Balls, Key Wind, George Nelson, 13 In. *illus*	210.00
Herman Miller, Maidou Burl Case, Metal Banded Trim, Gilbert Rohde, c.1933, 13 x 7 In. *illus*	1680.00
Herman Miller, Meridian Series, Walnut, Hexagonal, Electric, 14 In.	250.00
Herschede, Shelf, Gothic, Mahogany, Brass Ball Finials, Quarter Column Pilasters, 14 ¾ In.	94.00
Herter Brothers, Shelf, Carved, Marble Dial, Brass Roman Numbers, Signed J.B.D., 19 x 20 In.	7188.00
Howard & Davis, Mahogany, 70-Beat Pendulum, Cylindrical Weight, c.1970, 60 In.	460.00
Howard & Davis, Regulator, No. 3, Mahogany, Reverse Painted Tablets, c.1860, 38 ¼ In.	1778.00
Howard Miller, Desk, Pedestal, Battery, Movado, 5 ½ In.	200.00
Howard Miller, Museum, Quartz, Nathan George Horwitt, West Germany, c.1940, 5 ½ x 4 ¾ In.	125.00
Howard Miller, Pretzel, Enameled Steel, Birch, No. 4774, George Nelson, 17 In. *illus*	1080.00
Howard, E. & Co., Regulator, No. 58, Cherry, Meter Pendulum, 8-Day, Weight Driven, c.1890, 64 In.	6188.00
Howard, E., Wall, No. 8, Robed Woman Holds Pendulum, Gilt, Marble Base, 15 x 37 In.	18400.00
Imhof, Carriage, White Agate, Swiss Movement, 4 ½ x 3 x 1 ¼ In.	22.00
Imperial, Shelf, Buffalo Bill, 8-Day, Half-Hour Strike, Cathedral Gong	1800.00
Ingraham, E. & Co., Shelf, Rounded Gothic, 8-Day, Time & Gong Strike, c.1930, 13 In.	124.00
Ingraham, E. & Co., Spanish American War, 8-Day, Commemorative, 1899, 23 In.	440.00
Ingraham, E., Grecian Mosaic, Walnut, 8-Day, Time & Strike, Alarm, c.1870, 15 In.	450.00
Ingraham, E., Oak, Calendar, 8-Day, c.1907, 36 In.	236.00
Ingraham, E., Oak, Calendar, Roman Numerals, 36 ½ x 16 In.	360.00
Ingraham, E., Regulator, Oak, Calendar, 8-Day, Spring Driven, c.1907, 36 In.	316.00
Ingraham, E., School, Long Drop, c.1911	115.00
Ingraham, E., Shelf, Domino, 8-Day, Time, Strike, Alarm, Finials, Black Finish, c.1886, 16 In.	176.00
Ingraham, E., Shelf, Oak, 30-Hour, Strike, Alarm, c.1880, 15 In.	115.00
Ingraham, E., Wall, Gingerbread, Oak, 8-Day, Thermometer, Level, Bell Strike Alarm, 28 ½ In.	248.00
Ingraham, E., Wall, Gingerbread, Walnut, 8-Day, Bell Strike, Thermometer, 29 In.	275.00
Ingraham, E., Wall, Oak, 8-Day, Gong, Pendulum, c.1896, 37 In.	460.00
Ingraham, E., Wall, Reflector, Figure 8, 8-Day, Gong, Spring, c.1880, 29 In.	115.00
Ingram, Oak, Carved, Torch Designs, Stenciled Gold Leaf Designs, Glass Door, c.1890, 15 x 22 In.	82.00
Jacob Petit, Shelf, Porcelain, Scrolled, Gold Trim, 8-Day Chime, Curled Feet, 16 x 11 In.	708.00
Jaeger-LeCoultre, Atmos, Glass, Brass, 9 x 6 ½ In.	525.00
Jaeger-LeCoultre, Travel, Leather, Opens Into Stand, Marked, Hermes, 4 ½ x 2 ½ In.	411.00
Jahresuhrenfabrik, Model 218, Art Nouveau, Cherry Case, Brass Decoration, c.1905, 12 ¼ In.	1800.00
Japy Freres, Brass, Flamingo, Serpent, Pendulum, Marked, 15 ½ x 4 ¾ In. *illus*	2400.00
Japy Freres, Figural, Flamingo, Bronze, Serpent, Dragonfly Pendulum, c.1858, 15 x 4 x 9 In.	2400.00
Japy Freres, Garniture, Porcelain, Ormolu Mounts, 2 Urns, France, c.1890, 22 In., 25 In.	308.00

Japy Freres, Porcelain, 8-Day, Flowers, Royal Bonn, c.1895, 10 ½ In.	196.00
Japy Freres, Regulator, Jeweled, Champleve Enameled Bronze, Paste Gems, c.1900, 13 In. ...*illus*	2880.00
Japy Freres, Shelf, Barley Twist Columns, Gilt Capitals, c.1875, 22 In.	518.00
Japy Freres, Shelf, Black Marble, Bronze Statuary, Writing Instruments, c.1880, 3 ½ In.	415.00
Japy Freres, Shelf, Bronze, Porcelain, 2-Train, Half-Hour Strike, Cupid, Shooting Arrow, 16 In.	593.00
Japy Freres, Shelf, Louis XVI, Gilt Metal, Porcelain, Paw Feet, P.H. Mourey 63, 13 x 14 In.	206.00
Japy Freres, Shelf, Oval Case, 8-Day, Strike Crystal, 2-Vial Pendulum, c.1910, 9 ¾ In.	161.00
Japy Freres, Shelf, Plaquettes, Romantic Figures, c.1870, 8 ½ In.	3450.00
Jerome, Chauncey, School, Mahogany Veneer, Fusee, c.1850, 21 In.	633.00
Jeune, Morbier, 8-Day, Time & Strike, Crown Wheel, Paris, c.1840	394.00
J.J. Beals & Co., Cottage, Rosewood, Paint Decorated Tablet, Gilt, 12 In.	1778.00
Junghans, Elephant, Swinger, Wooden Base, c.1910, 11 In.	1265.00
Junghans, Leaded, Beveled Door, c.1910, 25 x 10 In.	206.00
Junghans, Monkey, Eyes & Jaw Move, c.1915, 9 ½ In.	920.00
Junghans, Swinger, Walnut Veneer, 8-Day, Gong, Germany, c.1905, 32 In.	219.00
Junghans, Wall, Gothic, Walnut, Carved, Spires, Tracery, Columns, 8-Day, 55 In.	1125.00
KEM Weber, Cyclometer Digital, Silver Plate, Lucite, Lawson Metal Plaque, 13 x 3 ¾ In. ......*illus*	480.00
KEM Weber, Model P40, Brass, Metal Plaque, 14 ¼ x 3 ½ In.	450.00
Kenmore, Art Deco, Faux Marble, Spin Start, Calendar, Electric, c.1930...........................	299.00
Kienzle, Art Deco, Round, Brass, Copper Casing, Cobalt Blue Glass, Zodiac Signs, 12 In.	1800.00
Kroeber, F., Shelf, Porcelain, Flowers, 8-Day, Strike, c.1898, 12 In.	230.00
Kroeber, F., Shelf, Walnut, Balustrade, Walnut, 8-Day, c.1875, 16 ½ In.	92.00
Kroeber, F., Winged Cherub Pendulum, Paper Dial, 8-Day, c.1882, 18 In.	1495.00
Lantern, Wall Brackets, Driving Weights, Brass, Japan, c.1800, 22 In.	6900.00
LeCoultre, Atmos, Perpetual Motion, Brass, Glass Panels, Revolving Pendulum, 9 In.	423.00
LeCoultre, Shelf, Brass, Encased, 9 x 9 x 7 In.	520.00
LeCoultre, Shelf, Marina Atmos, Beveled Glass, Black, Gold Ship Designs, 7 x 9 In.	1093.00
Louis Philippe, Shelf, Cathedral, Gilt Bronze, Plinth Base, Tracery, 14 x 7 In.	518.00
Lux, Cat, Moving Eyes, Tail Pendulum, c.1948, 7 ½ In.	51.00
Lux, Dixie Boy, Animated, Pendulette, 30-Hour, c.1935, 9 In.	267.00
Lux, Grandma & Grandpa, Fireplace, Alarm, c.1935, 5 In.	173.00
Manross, Prichard & Co., Mahogany, 30-Hour Brass Works, 2-Weight, c.1842, 26 In.	68.00
Marti & Cie, Shelf, Classical Female Bust, Gilt Bronze, France, c.1889, 14 x 8 In.	323.00
Marti & Cie, Wall, Brass, Porcelain Dial, c.1890, 27 In.	338.00
Marti, Shelf, Gilt Bronze, Birds, Flowers, Round Enamel Dial, Blue, White Enamel Plaques, 16 In.	384.00
Marti, Shelf, Porcelain, 2-Train, Half-Hour Striking, 4 Seasons, Cherubs, France, 20 ⅜ In.	1007.00
Mathieu, Empire Style, Portico, Black Marble, Ormolu, Bell Strike, c.1830, 22 ½ In.	1575.00
Meissen, Shelf, 4 Columns, Cherubs, Flowers, Cobalt, c.1890, 18 In.	2726.00
Meissen, Shelf, Balloon Case, Urn, Flowers, 4 Seasons, Putti, Loving Couple, Gilt, c.1890, 9 x 17 In. .	8295.00
Miracle, Spinner Hand, Good Any Time, Plastic, Metal, Light-Up, 11 ¼ x 13 ¼ x 5 ½ In.	110.00
Moreau, Winged Victory Statue, Painted White Metal, Onyx Base, 30 In.	732.00
Movado, Ermeto, Moon Phase, Calendar, Night Stand Arm, Leather, Key Ring, 17 Jewels, 1940s	956.00
Mystery, Figural, Robed Maiden, Chain Swinger, Roman Numerals, Jeweled Pallet, 8 x 29 In. ..	6613.00
Napoleon III, Ebonized Wood, Brass & Mother-Of-Pearl Inlay, Chimes, c.1870, 19 x 19 x 5 In. .	710.00
Napoleon III, Gilt Bronze, Bracket, Mask, Reticulated Base, France, c.1900, 21 In. ....*illus*	450.00
National Time Recorder Co., Wood, Painted, Aquinas St., London, S.E.1, 35 x 26 x 20 In. ...	600.00
New Haven, Art Moderne, Mahogany Case, Bird's-Eye Maple, Westminster Chime, c.1929, 19 In.	984.00
New Haven, Columbia, 30-Day Regulator, Cherry, c.1892, 46 In.	499.00
New Haven, Regulator, Walnut, 8-Day, Spring, c.1880, 33 In.	259.00
New Haven, Shelf, Abbey, Gothic Arch, Mahogany, 8-Day, Westminster Chime, c.1929, 15 ½ In.	135.00
New Haven, Shelf, Acrobatic Skeleton, Theater Style Case, 8-Day, c.1905, 19 ½ In.	1688.00
New Haven, Trouville, Art Nouveau, Gilt Spelter, 30-Hour, c.1913, 12 In.	281.00
New Haven, Wall, Hardwood, 8-Day, Brass Movement, Spring Driven, c.1917, 42 In.	316.00
New Haven, Walnut, 2-Key Wind, Roman Numerals, Late 19th Century, 22 x 14 In.	94.00
Norton, Eardley, Bracket, George III, Mahogany, Ormolu, Fusee, 10 Musical Bells, 17 In.	10665.00
Oldfield, Shelf, Ormolu, 8-Day, Gong, Brass, Columns, Lady Bust, c.1895	460.00
Oswald, Daschund, Rotating Eye, Molded Composition Case, Germany, c.1955, 5 In.	478.00
Parrot Freres, Shelf, Louis XV Style, Gilt Bronze, Figural, Putto, Garland, 25 x 17 In.	4575.00
Picture, Time & Strike Movement, Painted Village Scene, c.1850, 33 x 40 In. ....*illus*	1955.00
Raingo Freres, Louis XV Style, Bronze, Pierced, Arched, Warrior Cherubs, Paris, 40 In.	11850.00
Raymor, Wall, Marble, Aluminum Face, Battery, Germany, 12 x 12 In.	300.00
Regulator, Jeweler's Colonial Pinwheel, Paper Dial, Gridiron Pendulum, H.J. Hoffman, 94 In.	6900.00
Regulator, Victorian, Venetian, Porcelain Dial, Roman Numerals....................................	226.00
Regulator, Vienna, Walnut Case, Arched Carved Crest, Ebonized, Grand Sonnerie Strike, 51 In. .	675.00
Regulator, Walnut, 2-Weight, Pendulum, Contoured Crest, 3 Finials, Side Spindles, 50 x 17 In. .	205.00
Regulator, Walnut, Carved, Brass Dial, 4 Column Front, Drop Finials, 39 x 17 In.	300.00

Clock, Herman Miller,
Maidou Burl Case, Metal Banded Trim,
Gilbert Rohde, c.1933, 13 x 7 In.
$1680.00

Clock, Howard Miller, Pretzel,
Enameled Steel, Birch, No. 4774,
George Nelson, 17 In.
$1080.00

Clock, Japy Freres, Brass, Flamingo,
Serpent, Pendulum, Marked,
15 ½ x 4 ¾ In.
$2400.00

Clock, Japy Freres, Regulator, Jeweled,
Champleve Enameled Bronze, Paste
Gems, c.1900, 13 In.
$2880.00

Clock, KEM Weber, Cyclometer Digital, Silver Plate, Lucite, Lawson Metal Plaque, 13 x 3 ¾ In.
$480.00

Clock, Napoleon III, Gilt Bronze, Bracket, Mask, Reticulated Base, France, c.1900, 21 In.
$450.00

Clock, Picture, Time & Strike Movement, Painted Village Scene, c.1850, 33 x 40 In.
$1955.00

Clock, Seth Thomas, Shelf, Celluloid, Marbleized Veneer, Bronzed Decoration, c.1900, 14 In.
$120.00

Rococo, Shelf, Porcelain, White & Gilt Scrolled Case, Flowers, Gold Trim, 12 x 8 In.	259.00
Round, White, Black Hour Markers, Red Second Hand, Marble Carving, Wall, Italy, 1950s.13 In.	150.00
School, Mahogany, Carved Accents, Pendulum, c.1870, 23 In.	518.00
Sessions, Shelf, Ramona, Mission Oak, 8-Day, Time & Strike, c.1908, 31 In.	208.00
Sessions, Steeple, Mahogany, Pointed Finials, c.1900, 16 x 8 In.	70.00
Seth Thomas, Art Deco, Wood Case, Electric	55.00
Seth Thomas, Art Nouveau, Regulator, 4-Glass Crystal, White Metal, 8-Day, Gong, c.1910, 15 In.	253.00
Seth Thomas, Cottage, Floral Tablet, Time & Strike, Alarm, 1-Day, c.1875, 14 In.	68.00
Seth Thomas, Cottage, Mahogany, Round Top, 1-Day, Time & Strike, c.1886, 9 In.	56.00
Seth Thomas, Empire Style, Weight Driven, Half Post, 32 x 19 In.	136.00
Seth Thomas, Gingerbread, Oak, 8-Day, Cup Bell Strike Alarm, Lion's Mask, 24 ¼ In.	132.00
Seth Thomas, Lobby, Carved Oak, Round Dial, Roman Numerals, c.1910, 22 ½ x 19 In.	425.00
Seth Thomas, Mahogany, Calendar, Double Dial, Pat. 1875 & 1876, 25 In.	720.00
Seth Thomas, Metal Case, Brass Drum Top, Spelter Base, 8-Day, Time & Strike, Electric, c.1910, 10 In.	135.00
Seth Thomas, Peace Cruise, Oak, Black Stone Highlights, White Stencil, c.1909, 23 x 15 In. .	150.00
Seth Thomas, Pillar & Scroll, Mahogany, Painted Face, House Glass Panel, c.1810, 32 In.	705.00
Seth Thomas, Pillar, Wood, Painted Flower Panel, c.1840, 33 x 18 In.	205.00
Seth Thomas, Regulator, No. 5, Mahogany, 8-Day, Weight, c.1885, 50 In.	6756.00
Seth Thomas, Regulator, No. 17, Walnut, Glazed Door, Zinc Dial, c.1885, 8-Day, 66 In.	3437.00
Seth Thomas, Shelf, Calendar, 8-Day, Weight Driven, c.1865, 30 ½ In.	588.00
Seth Thomas, Shelf, Celluloid, Marbleized Veneer, Bronzed Decoration, c.1900, 14 In. ....*illus*	120.00
Seth Thomas, Shelf, Figural, Classical Women Reading Book, Spelter, Late 1800s, 20 In. *illus*	480.00
Seth Thomas, Shelf, Mahogany, 8-Day, 4-Bell, 5 Hammers, c.1913, 18 In.	518.00
Seth Thomas, Shelf, Mahogany, 8-Day, Time & Strike, c.1870, 16 x 10 ¾ In.	595.00
Seth Thomas, Shelf, Mahogany, Arched Body, Front Door, Gilt, 8-Day, 17 ½ In.	94.00
Seth Thomas, Shelf, Regulator, Crystal, Gilt Bronze, 20th Century, 12 In.	324.00
Seth Thomas, Shelf, Rosewood, 8-Day, Bell Strike, c.1880, 16 In.	127.00
Seth Thomas, Shelf, Shell Column & Cornice, 8-Day, 2-Weight, Time & Gong Strike, c.1870, 33 In.	225.00
Seth Thomas, Wall, Queen Anne, Regulator, Ebonized, Gilt Trim, c.1890, 36 In.	420.00
Seth Thomas, Wall, Regulator, No. 2, Oak, 8-Day, Weight Driven, c.1889, 36 In.	1035.00
Seth Thomas, Wall, Regulator, Oak, 8-Sided, Short Drop, Time Only, Key, 12-In. Dial.	88.00
Seth Thomas, Walnut, Cupped Bells, Cathedral Gong, Nickeled Bezel, c.1890, 46 In.	8165.00
Seth Thomas, Walnut, Gingerbread, Gong Striking Movement, 18 ¼ In.	177.00
Seth Thomas, Walnut, No. 10, Calendar, 23 x 37 In.	4600.00
Shelf, 3-Face, Thermometer, Aneroid Barometer, Champleve Rotating Base, 14 ½ In.	6400.00
Shelf, Animated, French Style, Girl Swinging, Marble, German Works, 20 x 10 In. ....*illus*	850.00
Shelf, Architectonic, Bronze, Electric, Scrolling Reticulated Framework, c.1900, 27 x 30 In. ..	2937.00
Shelf, Art Deco, Enamel, Engine Turned, Purple, Green, Jade Phoenix, Plinth Base, 9 x 15 In.	1304.00
Shelf, Art Deco, Green Onyx, Octagonal Case, Balls, Rectangular Base, 10 x 11 ½ x 3 In.	143.00
Shelf, Art Deco, Onyx, Electric, c.1940, 9 x 14 In.	176.00
Shelf, Athena Holding Parcel Gilt Shield, Patinated Bronze, Marble, 1800s, 71 x 33 In. ....*illus*	4800.00
Shelf, Beveled Glass, Gold Face, 12 In.	177.00
Shelf, Biedermeier, Fruitwood, 30-Hour, Time & Strike, Paw Feet, Gold Leaves, c.1800, 14 In..	353.00
Shelf, Black Forest, Carved Pheasants, Leaves, France, Late 19th Century, 33 x 24 In.	2074.00
Shelf, Black Walnut, Columns, 8-Day, Strike, Spring, c.1880, 24 ½ In.	403.00
Shelf, Brass Pedestal, Alabaster Base, Face Swivels, 8-Day, Swiss, 5 ¾ In.	395.00
Shelf, Bronze Dore, Boulle Bracket, Black, Putti Mounts, Signed Robert, Paris, 1800s, 13 x 44 In.	3510.00
Shelf, Bronze Dore, Marble, Carved Ivory, Continental Woman, Book, France, 11 x 13 In.	7897.00
Shelf, Calendar, Moon Phase, Black Marble, France, c.1890, 16 In.	3910.00
Shelf, Cut Crystal, Eagle Feet, Bronze, c.1800s, 16 x 9 x 6 In.	1057.00
Shelf, Cut Crystal, Engine-Turned Dial, 8-Day, c.1880, 22 In.	16800.00
Shelf, Edwardian, Mahogany, Fruitwood, Harewood Inlay, Half-Hour Strike, 2-Train, 16 x 13 x 8 In.	415.00
Shelf, Eli Terry, Mahogany, Pillar & Scroll, Door, Painted Dial & Tablet, c.1825, 29 x 16 In. ...	489.00
Shelf, Empire Revival, 2-Train, ½ Striking, Flowers, Swans, France, 1800s, 18 ⅝ In.	1007.00
Shelf, Empire Style, Mahogany, Gilt Metal Urn, Scrolls, Bun Feet, 14 x 8 In.	269.00
Shelf, Empire Style, Musician, Playing Flute, Mandolin, Enamel Dial, 15 x 12 x 3 In.	1315.00
Shelf, Empire, Carved Wood, Door, Building Scene, Eagle Crest, 17 x 33 In.	748.00
Shelf, Figural, Babe Ruth, Bust, 2 Baseballs, Bronze Finish, Wood Base, 1948, 10 ½ x 13 In. .	1300.00
Shelf, Figural, Cherub, Holding Dove, Bronze, Onyx, Inset Porcelain Numerals, 16 x 9 In.	330.00
Shelf, Figural, Girl, Rocks, Bronze, Gilt, Slate, Scrolled Case, 2-Train Movement, c.1900, 25 In.	711.00
Shelf, Figural, Man Holding Paper, Bronze Dore, France, 19th Century, 20 x 15 x 5 ½ In.	1530.00
Shelf, Forestville Mfg. Co., Eagle, Spread Wings, Gilt, Tortoiseshell Columns, 1870s, 29 ½ In.	960.00
Shelf, Forestville Mfg. Co., Triple Decker, Gilt Basket, Columns, House Scene, Multicolored, 30 In.	1067.00
Shelf, George III, Mahogany, Dome Top, Roman Numerals, Scale Fret Sides, Handle, 16 x 11 x 6 In.	1195.00
Shelf, George III Style, Mahogany, Dome Top, Brass Handle, Finials, 11 ½ In.	239.00
Shelf, Gilt Brass, Enamel, Coraline, Dome Top, Finial, Lion's Head Mounts, c.1880, 3 ¾ x 8 ¼ In.	1035.00

Shelf, Gilt Bronze, Sevres Style Scenic Panels, Signed, France, 1855, 15 x 7 ½ In. ....*illus*	805.00
Shelf, Iron Front, Tropical Birds, Flowers, 21 x 16 In.	150.00
Shelf, L. & J.G. Stickley, Brass Dial, 22 x 16 x 8 In.	8540.00
Shelf, Louis Philippe, Figural, Astronomer Gazes At Stars, Gilt Bronze, 19 x 15 x 4 ½ In.	2938.00
Shelf, Louis XVI, Classical Vase Shape, Gilt, Patinated, Pineapple Finials, Fluted Case, 15 x 5 In.	1175.00
Shelf, Louis XVI Style, Gilt Bronze, Apollo & Nymph, Red Marble Arch, Paw Feet, 28 In.	5629.00
Shelf, Louis XVI Style, Parian & Gilt Bronze, Scenes, Cupid, Embossed, 1800s, 16 In.	660.00
Shelf, Mahogany, 2-Fusee, Bell Strike, Bracket, Halifax Moon, Calendar, c.1860, 25 In.	1380.00
Shelf, Mahogany, Gilt Bronze Mounted, Portico Shape, Mid 1800s, 17 ½ x 10 In.	600.00
Shelf, Mahogany Veneer, Pilasters, Corinthian Capitals, Fruit Bowl Splat, c.1830, 31 In.	4140.00
Shelf, Mahogany Veneer, Pillar & Scroll, 30-Hour, Strike, 2-Weight, c.1825, 28 In.	1150.00
Shelf, Marble Inlay, Porcelain Dial, Fluted Pilasters, Scrolls, 19th Century, 18 ½ x 15 In.	588.00
Shelf, Napoleon III, Bronze, Marble, Maiden Leaning On Globe, c.1875, 15 x 22 x 6 In.	1195.00
Shelf, Napoleon III, Man Driving Chariot, Horses, Gilt Bronze, 17 ½ x 17 ½ x 6 In.	4406.00
Shelf, Neoclassical, Black, Iron, Brass Dial, W. Barnes, c.1866, 11 x 14 In. ....*illus*	86.00
Shelf, Onyx, Bronze, Gong Movement, Plinth Base, Mercury Bust Finial, 21 x 14 x 7 In.	705.00
Shelf, Onyx, Parcel Gilt, Plinth, Eagle, Lyre Finials, Sunburst Pendulum, Brass Feet, 15 x 9 In.	690.00
Shelf, Porcelain, Giltwood, Tazza Top, Flowers, Gilt Mounts, Paris, c.1840, 7 x 15 In.	1175.00
Shelf, Porcelain, Pink, White, Gilt, 8-Day, France, c.1900, 9 In.	81.00
Shelf, Regulator, Crystal, Bronze Dore Columns, Urn Finial, France, c.1900, 17 In.	976.00
Shelf, Rococo, Bronze, Putto, Classical Face, Marble Stand, Gilt, 1800s, 47 x 28 In.	5463.00
Shelf, Rococo, Ormolu, Sitting Putti, France, c.1860, 24 ½ In.	4313.00
Shelf, Rococo Style, Alabaster, Striking Bell Movement, Carved, Vines, Octagonal, 20 x 8 In. ..	529.00
Shelf, Rosewood, Bird, Flower, Mother-Of-Pearl Inlay, Metal Handle, France, 9 x 6 ¼ x 4 ½ In.	403.00
Shelf, Royal Blue Guilloche Over Silver, Rear Wind, Swiss, c.1935, 3 ¼ In.	2070.00
Shelf, Skeleton, Porcelain Dials, Glass Dome, Continental, 1900s, 23 x 17 x 12 In.	2390.00
Shelf, Tudric Pewter, Enamel Face, 4 x 8 In.	1200.00
Shelf, Victorian, Black Onyx, Applied Gilt Trim, Carved Wood, Round Pediment, 15 In.	248.00
Shelf, Wall Bracket, Bronze, Black, Applied Angel Mounts, France, 1800s, 17 x 44 In.	4880.00
Shelf, Walnut, Cherry, Mahogany, Pillar & Scroll, Tin, Painted Winter Scene, Pa., 30 x 17 In. ..	8519.00
Shelf, Woman's Portrait, Yellow, Blue, Green, Red Enamel, Brass Mounts, 8 ½ In.	460.00
Skeleton, Brass, Marble Base, c.1900, 15 x 11 In.	410.00
Skeleton, Fusee, Cable Drive, Fretted & Silvered Dial, Glass Dome, c.1890, 15 In.	1495.00
Southern Clock Co., Ogee, Shelf, Door, Painted Dial, Reverse Painted Tablet, 26 x 15 In.	115.00
Steeple, Gothic, Carved, Germany, c.1890, 39 In.	263.00
Steeple, Gothic, Veneer, 1-Day Fusee, c.1850, 19 In.	173.00
Stowell, Abel, Victorious Archer, Gilt Bronze, Marble, 8-Day, c.1890, 15 In.	1705.00
Sunbeam, Art Deco, White Onyx, 1930s, 8 x 6 ½ In.	135.00
Swinging Arm, Geisha Girl, 3-Day, Japan, c.1925, 13 In.	385.00
Swiss, Guilloche, Metal Dore, Ivory Face, Painted, Bailey, Banks & Biddle, c.1900, 5 ¼ In.	295.00
Tall Case, A. Edwards Ashby, No. 29, Pine, 30-Hour, Signed, c.1820, 81 In.	1675.00
Tall Case, Art Deco, Chromed Metal, Finial Top, Electric, 18 ¾ In.	1534.00
Tall Case, Arts & Crafts, Leaded Glass, Carvings, 75 x 23 x 16 ¾ In.	2928.00
Tall Case, Banjo Shape, Round Hood, Drop Front Door, Sweden, Mid 1800s, 77 x 22 In.	4560.00
Tall Case, Benjamin Simpson, 30-Hour, Time & Hour Strike, Engraved Dial, c.1770, 89 x 19 In.	1410.00
Tall Case, Cherry, 8-Day, Boston Enamel, Dial, Signed, Matthais Fruh, c.1810, 94 In.	1998.00
Tall Case, Cherry, Mahogany Veneer, Poplar, Early 1800s, 94 ½ x 20 x 11 In.	6076.00
Tall Case, Cherry, Poplar, Mother-Of-Pearl, Heart & Flower Vase Inlay, 94 ½ x 20 x 11 In.	9012.00
Tall Case, Chippendale, Ship, Naval Symbols, Brass Dial, John Harper, c.1790, 91 x 20 In.	8510.00
Tall Case, Chippendale, Scroll Top, Carved Roses, Moon, Globes, Gilt, c.1790, 94 x 20 In.	13035.00
Tall Case, Colonial Clock Co., Overhanging Top, Corbel Supports, Glass, 17 x 85 In.	5400.00
Tall Case, Cooper, Federal, Cherry, Swan's Neck Crest, Spread Wing Eagle Inlay, 1820s, 95 ½ In.	9000.00
Tall Case, Country, Mahogany, Engraved Brass Dial, Calendar, Bell Strike, c.1765, 82 x 17 In. ..	6900.00
Tall Case, Custer, Cherry, Broken Arch Bonnet, 8-Day Movement, Signed, c.1835, 94 In.	7700.00
Tall Case, Daniel Oyster, Federal, Walnut, Castle Top, Eagle Inlay, 8-Day, Reading, Pa., 100 In.	11115.00
Tall Case, Edgar, 8-Day, Weight Driven, Time, Strike Brass Movement, England, 89 x 22 x 10 In.	2500.00
Tall Case, Elm, Inlaid Mahogany, Arch Door, Scrolling Broken Arch, c.1800, 88 x 19 In.	1553.00
Tall Case, Empire, Mahogany, Roman Numerals, 8-Day, Time & Strike, Brass Pendulum, 77 ½ In.	3081.00
Tall Case, F. Garrick, Mahogany, Rolled Hood, Painted Dial, Stranraer, Scotland, c.1820, 80 In.	1062.00
Tall Case, Federal, Cherry, Painted Iron Dial, Glazed Door, c.1800, 91 In.	2963.00
Tall Case, Federal, Cherry Wood, Pine, Bonnet, Brass Finials, Painted Face, c.1800, 91 x 18 In.	2400.00
Tall Case, Foucry, Pine, Iron Frame, Prayer Repeat Movement, Toulouse, c.1840, 97 In.	675.00
Tall Case, Frederic Wingate, Fox, Goose, Full Column Bonnet, Maine, 1806, 19 x 92 In.	19550.00
Tall Case, French Provincial, Morbier, Fruitwood, Arched Bonnet, 8-Day, 104 x 22 In.	1150.00
Tall Case, French Provincial, Walnut, Paneled Door, Time & Strike, 94 x 17 x 11 In.	580.00
Tall Case, Frick, Sheraton, Cherry, Mahogany, Painted Moon Phases, Shells, Pa., c.1825, 93 In.	7050.00

Clock, Seth Thomas, Shelf, Figural, Classical Women Reading Book, **Spelter,** Late 1800s, 20 In.
$480.00

Clock, Shelf, Animated, French Style, Girl Swinging, Marble, German **Works,** 20 x 10 In.
$850.00

Clock, Shelf, Athena Holding **Parcel** Gilt Shield, Patinated Bronze, **Marble,** 1800s, 71 x 33 In.
$4800.00

Clock, Shelf, Gilt Bronze,
Sevres Style Scenic Panels, Signed,
France, 1855, 15 x 7 ½ In.
$805.00

Clock, Shelf, Neoclassical, Black, Iron,
Brass Dial, W. Barnes, c.1866, 11 x 14 In.
$86.00

Clock, Tall Case, Georgian, Chinoiserie,
Painted, Arched Gilded Hood, 1700s,
92 x 19 In.
$3346.00

Tall Case, George IV, Mahogany, Inlaid, Carved, Scallop-Top Door, c.1830, 87 ½ x 20 x 10 ½ In.	1410.00
Tall Case, Georgian, Chinoiserie, Painted, Arched Gilded Hood, 1700s, 92 x 19 In. ....*illus*	3346.00
Tall Case, Georgian, Mahogany, Arched Bonnet, Tombstone Glazed Door, c.1800, 84 x 20 In.	920.00
Tall Case, Georgian, Mahogany, Broken Arch Bonnet, Brass Finial, Shaped Door, c.1820, 92 x 21 In.	1955.00
Tall Case, Georgian, Walnut, Arched Door, Brass, Steel Face, 2-Train Movement, c.1740, 86 ½ In.	3437.00
Tall Case, Griffith Owen, Broken Arch Pediment, Carved Rosettes, Turned Pillars, 8-Day, 1802	11400.00
Tall Case, H. Cook, Cherry, 30-Hour, Birdcage Movement, Marked, Medina, 1800s, 92 In.	1420.00
Tall Case, Hepplewhite, Cherry, Pine, Poplar, Fretwork Crest, Bracket Feet, c.1820, 93 x 18 x 10 In.	1292.00
Tall Case, Herschede Hall Co., Mahogany, Arched, 2-Weight, 5-Chime, Cincinnati, 83 In.	518.00
Tall Case, Herschede, Mahogany, 9-Tube, Moon Dial, Early 1900s, 93 x 29 x 18 In.	5100.00
Tall Case, J. Owen's, Mahogany, Broken Arch Pediment, Perth, 87 x 21 In. ....*illus*	2300.00
Tall Case, J.E. Caldwell & Co., Mahogany, Glass Door, Moon Phases, Philadelphia, 96 In.	1062.00
Tall Case, James Reynolds, Rosewood, Roman Numerals, Signed, England, c.1850, 79 x 17 In.	600.00
Tall Case, John Barr, Queen Anne, Walnut, Blind Fretwork, 8-Day, Brass, Glasgow, c.1760, 91 In.	7020.00
Tall Case, John Wilder, Fret Top, Brass Finials, Columns, Painted Iron Dial, c.1810, 91 In.	30810.00
Tall Case, Kienzle, Oak, Mahogany Veneers, Chain Drive, Early 1900s, 74 In.	265.00
Tall Case, Le Couve A Napoleonville, Enamel Dial, Painted Pink Flowers, Key Wind, 93 In.	708.00
Tall Case, Louis XVI, Walnut, Provincial, Carved, Molded Crest, Bell Shape Case, 102 x 21 In.	1800.00
Tall Case, Mahogany, 6-Tube, Moon Dial, Germany, Early 1900s, 93 x 23 x 16 In.	3600.00
Tall Case, Mahogany, Inlaid, Stringing, Urn, 3 Brass Orb Finials, 30-Day, England, 92 In.	915.00
Tall Case, Mahogany, Inlaid, Swan's Neck Crest, Arched Door, 2-Train Movement, 92 In.	3851.00
Tall Case, Morbier, Pine, Shaped Case, Glazed Doors, Weight-Driven Movement, Signed, 89 x 20 In.	1840.00
Tall Case, Morbier, Walnut Veneer, 2-Weight, Cast Brass Sunburst Pendulum, c.1745, 91 In. .	225.00
Tall Case, O. Hopkins, Cherry, Broken Arch Pediment, Painted Wood Face, Litchfield, c.1820, 86 In.	2468.00
Tall Case, Organ, George III, Walnut, Arched Hood, Scrolled Fret, 8-Day Movement, 108 In. ..	18300.00
Tall Case, Parkinson & Frodsham, Mahogany, Pineapple Finials, 8 Bells, 88 x 20 ½ x 12 ¼ In. ..	11321.00
Tall Case, Peter Faichney, 8-Day, 2-Weight, Tombstone Door, Reeded Columns, England, c.1790, 88 In.	2875.00
Tall Case, Ridgeway, Pendulum, 3-Weight, 72 In.	148.00
Tall Case, Riley Whiting, Grain Painted, 30-Hour, c.1825, 80 In.	506.00
Tall Case, Shaker Style, Poplar, Square Top & Dial, 72 In.	259.00
Tall Case, Sheraton, Cherry, Mahogany Inlay, 3 Finials, Moon Phases, Ships, Castles, c.1820, 98 In.	3173.00
Tall Case, Sheraton, Mahogany, Brass Urn Finial, Dial Door, 8-Day, Time & Strike, Ireland, 89 ½ In.	1541.00
Tall Case, Silas Hoadley, Cherry, Masonic Symbols, 30-Hour, Time & Strike, Plymouth, 88 In.	1315.00
Tall Case, Silas Hoadley, Pine, 8-Day, Wooden Works, 89 In.	633.00
Tall Case, Stickley Bros., Oak, 80 x 26 x 15 In.	5185.00
Tall Case, Thomas Browne, 8-Day, Time & Strike, Mahogany, Arched Top, Late 1700s, 86 x 19 In.	3290.00
Tall Case, Thomas Wagstaff, Walnut, 8-Day, 5-Pillar Movement, 90 ½ In.	4740.00
Tall Case, Tiffany & Co., Louis XVI, Mahogany, Bronze Mount, 3-Train Movement, 91 In.	3555.00
Tall Case, Tiger Maple, Broken Arch Pediment, Sailing Ship, Dial, c.1830, 91 x 21 In.	5060.00
Tall Case, Walter Durfee, Oak, Broken Arch Bonnet, 9-Tube, Columns, Finials, 25 x 101 In. ..	15125.00
Tall Case, Waltham, 5-Tube Movement, Rolling Moon, Quarter Chime, 80 In.	2645.00
Tall Case, Waterbury, Arts & Crafts, Oak, Glass Door, Arched Aprons, Beveled Overhang, 22 x 76 In.	690.00
Tall Case, Wood, Federal, Birch, Pierced Fret Top, 3 Finials, Columns, c.1815, 91 In.	8295.00
Telechron, Wall, Ceramic, White Matte Glaze, Electric, 12 In.	145.00
Terry & Sons, Box, Mahogany, Cherry, Funereal Scene, Painted Face, Mass., c.1830, 22 In. ...	7703.00
Terry & Sons, Pillar & Scroll, 30-Hour, Wooden Works, c.1825, 32 In.	1208.00
Terry Clock Co., 30-Hour Time & Strike, Iron Case, Waterbury, Conn., c.1875, 8 ½ In.	56.00
Terry Clock Co., Cottage, 1-Day, Spring, c.1870, 12 In.	92.00
Terry, Eli & Samuel, Mahogany, Pillar & Scroll, Brass Urn Finials, Country Scene, c.1824, 31 In.	2726.00
Tiffany clocks that are part of desk sets made by Louis Comfort Tiffany are listed in the Tiffany Category. Clocks sold by the store Tiffany & Co. are listed here.	
Tiffany & Co., Brass, 8-Day Movement, 3 ¼ x 4 ¾ In.	60.00
Tiffany & Co., Desk, Pyramid Shape, Silver, Engraved, 4 x 3 ¼ x 3 In.	680.00
Tiffany & Co., Mirror, 8-Day, Round Goldtone Dial, c.1920, 36 In.	253.00
Tiffany & Co., Oak, Weight Driven, Pallets, Pendulum, c.1890, 63 In.	978.00
Tiffany & Co., Shelf, Classical Style, Marble, c.1900, 13 x 10 x 6 In.	2340.00
Tiffany & Co., Shelf, Flower Inlay, Marble, Blue, White, Aesthetic Movement, Signed, 11 x 10 In. ..	730.00
Tiffany & Co., Shelf, Green Marble, Stepped Form, Round Inset Face, 8 ¾ x 11 In.	177.00
Tiffany & Co., Travel Alarm, Brass Case, Turn Cover To Show Dial, Cloth Bag, Swiss, c.1970, 2 ¼ In.	214.00
Tiffany & Co., Travel, Sterling Silver Case, Monogram, Signed, 2 ½ x 3 In.	345.00
U.S. Clock Co., Regulator, Astronomical, Style D, Silvered Dial, 33 x 87 x 12 In.	9200.00
Victorian, Gingerbread, Oak, Reverse Painted, Pressed Design, 24 In.	108.00
Vincent & Cie, Bracket, Louis XV Style, Boulle Marquetry, Sunburst Pendulum, c.1855, 34 In.	976.00
Wag-On-Wall, Porcelain Dial, Brass Pendulum, Ornate Repousse Molded Face, 51 In.	210.00
Wag-On-Wall, Pressed Metal, 2-Train, Chimes, 19th Century, 19 x 14 In.	999.00
Wag-On-Wall, Wooden, 8-Day, 2-Weight, Gong, Steel Arbors, c.1870, 16 In.	230.00
Wall, American Renaissance Revival, Carved Mahogany, Finials, Weights, 17 x 53 In.	585.00

Wall, American Renaissance Revival, Wood, Finials, c.1890, 16 x 60 In.	936.00
Wall, Brass, 8-Day Time, Strike Movement, Bust, Finials, France, c.1900, 36 x 11 ½ In.	353.00
Wall, Chippendale, Mahogany, Silvered Dial, Carved Fruiting Vine, 8 ½ In.	711.00
Wall, Frame Style, Scalloped Grained Wood, Mosaic Inlay, France, 1800s, 24 In.	240.00
Wall, Inlaid, Rolling Pin Bottom, 8-Day, c.1875, 36 In.	299.00
Wall, Louis XVI Style, Barometer, Gilt Bronze, Putto, Dolphins, Festoons, 31 x 15 In.	7625.00
Wall, Louis XVI Style, Ormolu, 8-Day, Bell Strike, c.1860, 20 ½ In.	489.00
Wall, Napoleon, 8-Sided, Blue Enamel, Marble, Wood, Red Boulle, Moon Pendulum, 26 x 25 In.	1800.00
Wall, Rococo, Walnut, Figural Parrot Crest, Bee, Cat, Gilt, Bronze Mount, Italy, c.1870	1200.00
Wall, Rosewood, Mother-Of-Pearl Inlay, 8-Sided, Painted Family Scene, England, c.1820, 32 x 20 In.	144.00
Wall, Spring, Keyhole Door, 8-Day, Germany, c.1890, 41 In.	391.00
Wall, Walnut, Porcelain Dial, Brass Frame, c.1850, 60 x 19 x 10 In.	5581.00
Walnut, Mahogany, Carved Pediment, Turned Columns, Drop Finial, Austria, 1800s, 54 x 18 In.	410.00
Waltham, Desk, Bronze, 8-Day, Car Clock Movement, Gilt Dial, c.1935, 10 In.	104.00
Waltham, Desk, Mahogany, 8-Day, Jeweled Car Clock Movement, c.1930, 11 In.	104.00
Water, Painted Oak Base, Brass Dial, Engraved Brass Plates, Cylinder, Basin, 17 x 5 ½ In.	83.00
Waterbury, Bahia, Mosaic, Walnut, Ash, Figure 8, 8-Day, Time & Strike, c.1915, 22 In.	703.00
Waterbury, Gallery, Maple, Round, 8-Day, Spring, c.1893, 25 In.	546.00
Waterbury, School, Regulator, Oak, c.1906, 32 In.	92.00
Waterbury, Shelf, Black Case, Brass Dial, 11 In.	215.00
Waterbury, Shelf, Enameled Iron, Open Escapement, Waisted Oval, Arched Top, c.1900, 9 ¾ In.	330.00
Waterbury, Shelf, Iron Case, Alarm, 8-Day, Bell Strike, c.1860, 13 In.	368.00
Waterbury, Walnut, Gingerbread, 8-Day, Alarm, 23 ¼ In.	187.00
Welch, Spring & Co., Drop Calendar, Rosewood Veneer Case, Zinc Dial, c.1874-79, 30 In.	4740.00
Westclox, Art Deco, Pink Tinted Glass, Chrome Columns, Base, LaSallie, Ill., 1932, 6 x 5 In. ..	360.00
Westclox, Ball Shape, Glowing Dial, Manual Wind, Alarm, c.1970.........................	80.00
Westclox, Early Bird, Rocking Robin Catching Worm, Red Painted Case, c.1933, 5 In.	163.00
Whistler, Wood, Painted, Man, Hat, Leaning On Post, Head Moves, KenD, 15 x 7 In. ....*illus*	575.00
Willard, A., Shelf, Walnut, Weight Driven, Eagle Finial, Country Scene Panel, Painted, 13 x 32 In.	16100.00
Worle, Johann, Wall, Mahogany, 30-Day Calendar Movement, 9-Light, c.1830, 37 In.	5750.00

CLOISONNE enamel was developed during the tenth century. A glass enamel was applied between small ribbons of metal on a metal base. Most cloisonne is Chinese or Japanese. Pieces marked *China* are twentieth-century examples.

Beaker, Scrolled Flower Overlay, Silver Gilt, Textured, Russia, c.1890, 2 x 2 In.	956.00
Beaker, Scrolling Leaves, Flowers, Gilt, Fitted Case, Moscow, Marked, c.1910, 1 ¾ In.	1320.00
Belt Buckle, Scrolls, 2-Piece Design, St. Petersburg, Marked, c.1890, 3 In.	360.00
Bowl, Black Ground, Meandering Peony, Green Fish Scale Banding, 3 ¼ x 8 ½ In.	59.00
Bowl, Dragon Design, Black Ground, Chinese, 2 ¾ In.	40.00
Bowl, Flowers, Blue, Red, Brass Rim, 3 ¼ x 8 ⅝ In.	236.00
Bowl, Pink & Yellow Peonies, Green Leaves, Black Ground, Chinese	29.00
Bowl, Yellow, Green Leaves, Pink Flowers, Wood Pedestal, Chinese, 15 In., Pair	293.00
Box, Butterfly Shape, 4 ½ x 14 ¾ In.	75.00
Box, Cover, Cylindrical Shape, Multicolored Floral, 5 ½ In.	35.00
Box, Cover, Pear Shape, Brown Twig, Green Leaves, 1960s, 4 In.	30.00
Box, Cover, Round, Brick Body, Multicolored Flowers, Lions, 3-Footed, 6 In.	345.00
Box, Cover, Yellow, Blue, Green, Pink Flowers, Wood Stand, c.1950, 10 In.	59.00
Box, Round, Bird, Flowers, Turquoise Scrolling Cloud Ground, Early 1900s, 1 ¾ x 5 In.	106.00
Box, Vermeil, Japan, 2 x 6 x 4 In.	177.00
Charger, Bird On Cherry Blossom Branch, Blue Ground, Brass Rim, Japan, 12 In.	266.00
Charger, Blue Ground, Multicolored Flowers, Butterflies, Teak Wood Stand, 20 In.	500.00
Charger, Flower Border, 2 Cranes Center, Blue, Gray, Chinese, 1800s, 12 In.	205.00
Charger, Pink Peony Blossoms, Leaves, Blue Ground, Brass Base, Japan, 12 In.	148.00
Cigarette Case, Beaded Border, Scrolling Leaves, Moscow, c.1890, 3 ¼ In.	960.00
Figurine, Crane, Manchurian, Twig In Beak, Lotus, Mound Base, Multicolored, 13 In., Pair...	288.00
Figurine, Crane, Multicolored, Chinese, 7 In.	59.00
Figurine, Peacock, Multicolored, Circular Stepped Base, 70 x 22 x 20 In., Pair	7050.00
Ginger Jar, Cover, Teal Ground, Floral, 7 In.	173.00
Ginger Jar, Multicolored Flowers, Autumn Colors, Chinese, 7 ¼ In.	83.00
Jar, Cover, Bulbous, Flowers, Green Ground, Chinese, 8 ½ In.	40.00
Jar, Cover, Dragons Chasing Flaming Pearl Of Wisdom, Round, Blue Ground, 45 In.	777.00
Jar, Koi, Blue Latticed Ground, Bulbous, Domed Cover, 19th Century, Japan, 4 ¼ In.	325.00
Jardiniere, Flower Border, Bulbous, Mums, Birds, Butterflies, c.1900, 12 x 15 In.	354.00
Jardiniere, Flowering Tree, Blossoms, Blue Ground, Hardstone, Chinese, 25 In., Pair	1075.00
Jardiniere, Multicolored, Chinese, 19th Century, 6 ½ x 9 In.	205.00
Jardiniere, Squat, Round, Pedestal, Mask & Veil Handle, 14 x 22 In.	288.00

Clock, Tall Case, J. Owen's, Mahogany, Broken Arch Pediment, Perth, 87 x 21 In. $2300.00

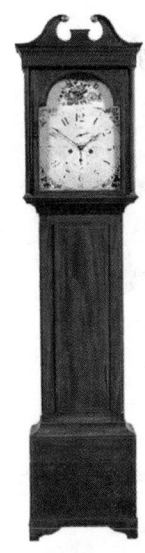

Clock, Whistler, Wood, Painted, Man, Hat, Leaning On Post, Head Moves, KenD, 15 x 7 In. $575.00

Cloisonne, Spoon, Caviar, Silver, Scrolling, Strapwork, Twist Handle, Russia, c.1896, 6 ¾ In. $1200.00

Cloisonne, Teapot, Cover, Cylindrical, Enameled, Figures, Flowers, 1913, 5 In. $150.00

Clothing, Belt, Soda Pop Tops, Lavender, Metallic Cord, Plastic Beads, 1990s, 42 ½ In. $40.00

Clothing, Costume, Painted, Cotton, Mask, Carved Wood, 12 Small Masks, 55 x 21 & 15 x 8 In. $1978.00

Kovsh, Cup, Silver, Flowers, Cream Ground, Hook Handle, Moscow, Marked, c.1900, 4 ¾ In. ..	4200.00
Pill Box, Flowers, Turquoise Beading, Hinged Lid, Marked, Moscow, Klingert, 1899, 2 In.	1320.00
Plate, Bird Perched At Well, Mica Flecks, Scalloped Rim, Japan, c.1900, 12 In.	767.00
Salt, Chair, Scrolling Leaves, Beaded Border, Hinged Seat, Gilded Interior, Moscow, c.1900, 3 In.	3000.00
Salt, Master, Beaded Rim, Scrolls, Cyrillic Letters, 3-Footed, Russia, c.1970, 3 ½ In.	330.00
Salt, Silver Gilt, Gilded Interior, Russia, 2 In., Pair	720.00
Snuffbox, Fitted Lid, Peacock Design, Round, 3-Footed, Japan, 1 x 2 In.	118.00
Spoon, Berry, Scalloped Bowl, Blue, Red, Turquoise, Flat Handle, Klingert, 1894, 6 In.	900.00
Spoon, Caviar, Silver, Scrolling, Strapwork, Twist Handle, Russia, c.1896, 6 ¾ In. ....*illus*	1200.00
Spoon, Salt, Flowers, Scrolls, Cream Ground, Eagle Handle, M. Semenova, Russia, 1896, 3 In.	2440.00
Spoon, Serving, Silver, Almond Shaped Bowl, Twist Handle, Stamped, Russia, 7 ½ In.	720.00
Spoon, Twist Handle, Blue, Turquoise, Marked, Moscow, c.1900, 7 ½ In.	720.00
Sugar Scoop, Silver, Stippled Gilt Ground, Flat Handle, Cyrillic Marked, G.K., Russia, 5 In. ...	780.00
Tea Glass Holder, Flowers, Leafy, Stippled Gilt, Beaded Band, Handle, Moscow, c.1900, 3 ¾ In.	4200.00
Tea Set, Demitasse, Flowers, Multicolored, Black Ground, Green Interior, 7 Piece..................	535.00
Teapot, Cover, Cylindrical, Enameled, Figures, Flowers, 1913, 5 In. ....*illus*	150.00
Teapot, Cylindrical, Dome Lid, Sloping Shoulders, Flames, Kylin, Enameled, c.1913, 5 ¼ In. ..	150.00
Teaspoon, Silver, Russian Style, 1900s, 4 ½ In., 4 Piece..	240.00
Tray, Flowers In Urn On Stand, Well, Cartouche Shape, Japan, 12 In.	531.00
Tray, Pond Scene, Birds, Flowers, Fish, Chinese, 7 x 10 In.	196.00
Urn, Bronze, Handles, Wood Base, Chinese, 8 Piece	205.00
Vase, Bird, Butterfly, Flowers, Double Gourd Reserves, Bird Shape Handles, Chinese, 12 ¾ In.	239.00
Vase, Bird, Butterfly Medallion, Brown Ground, Baluster, Japan, 1800s, 3 In., Pair..............	295.00
Vase, Birds, Flowers, Red, Blue Interior, Chinese, 1800s, 9 ¾ x 5 1/12 In., Pair....................	173.00
Vase, Blue, Green, Birds, Flowers, Stand, Chinese, 17 x 6 In., Pair....................................	1380.00
Vase, Blue, Orange, Flowers, Gold Rim, Wood Stand, Chinese, 1960, 3 In., Pair..................	117.00
Vase, Cherry Blossoms, Celadon, Shells, Characters, Gilt, Pear Shape, Japan, c.1900, 78 In., Pair	518.00
Vase, Dragon & Bird, Cobalt Blue Ground, Bulbous, Elongated Neck, Chinese, 12 ¼ In.	230.00
Vase, Dragon, Blue Ground, Metal Rim, Stick Neck, Oval, c.1800, 5 In.	220.00
Vase, Finches & Prunus, Red Ground, Cone Shape, Wood Stand, c.1900, 47 In.	345.00
Vase, Flower Heads, Leafy Vines, Turquoise Ground, Bulbous, 3 Cabriole Legs, c.1700, 9 x 7 In.	295.00
Vase, Flowers In Relief, Powder Blue Ground, 12 In.	118.00
Vase, Flowers, Multicolored, White Ground, Baluster, 20th Century, 24 ¾ In.	138.00
Vase, Flying Bluebirds, Flowers, Gray Green Ground, Blue & White Flared Rim, Footed, 12 In., Pair	1150.00
Vase, Geometric & Scroll Design, Multicolored, Chinese, 9 In.	70.00
Vase, Geometric Design, Red & Blue, Green Ground, Urn Shape, Foo Dog Handles, 12 In.	115.00
Vase, Gin-Bari, Rose Branch, Red Foil Ground, Embossed Bird, Metal Bands, 8 ½ In.	106.00
Vase, Gold, Purple, Black Stand, Chinese, 7 x 4 ½ In., Pair..	293.00
Vase, Green, Urn Shape, Chinese, 10 x 5 In., Pair..	146.00
Vase, Hexagonal, Japan, 7 ¼ In., Pair...	585.00
Vase, Mountain Landscape, Pale Blue Ground, Metal Mounts, Japan, 1900s, 7 In.	189.00
Vase, Multicolored Flowers, Baluster, 8 In.	29.00
Vase, Multicolored Flowers, Birds, Blue Ground, Flared Lip, Chinese, 1800s, 7 x 4 In.	293.00
Vase, Openwork, Lotus Scrolls, Green, Blue, Bordered, 15 In.	660.00
Vase, Red, Silver, Japan, 12 In.	468.00
Vase, Roses, Hollyhocks, Blue Ground, Pink, White, Birds, Butterflies, Chinese, 12 In.	47.00
Vase, Scalloped Rim, Chinese, c.1900, 9 In.	147.00

CLOTHING of all types is listed in this category. Dresses, hats, shoes, underwear, and more are found here. Other textiles are to be found in the Coverlet, Movie, Quilt, Textile, and World War I and II categories.

Apron, Bibbed, Little Flowers, Pink Trim, Dark Ground, 2 Side Pockets, Cotton, Size 18	12.00
Armor, Suit, Burnished Steel, Sword, Cloth, Wood Base, Toledo, Spain, 1920s, 75 x 32 In.	3600.00
Armor, Suit, Segments, Interior Fabric, Incised Sword, Wood Base, 1800s, 74 x 22 In.	1998.00
Belt, Aluminum, Gold Tone, Interlocking Loop Links, Chain Tassel, 1970s, 35 In.	14.00
Belt, Leather, Black, Gold Dome Nail Heads, Buckle, Celine, 42 x 2 In.	100.00
Belt, Soda Pop Tops, Lavender, Metallic Cord, Plastic Beads, 1990s, 42 ½ In. ....*illus*	40.00
Bishop's Miter, Embroidered, Silk Lining, Tassels, Episcopal Coat Of Arms, 1800s, 17 In.	240.00
Bodice, Broderie Anglaise, Bias Cut, Linen Shoulder Buttons, White, c.1900	125.00
Boots, Cowboy, Mule Ear, Texas Star Stitching, Heels, 1880s, 19 ½ In.	2415.00
Boots, Leather, High Button, Black, Victorian, Size Small	125.00
Boots, Riding, Child's, Pennsylvania.	225.00
Boots, Riding, Leather, Burgundy, Side Zippers, Salvatore Ferragamo, Size 8AAA...................	495.00
Boots, Suede, Red, Ankle Height, Red Laces, Calvin Klein, Size 8N	75.00
Cap, Jackie Coogan, Kid Jackie, Brown Wool, Leather Brim, Fur Flaps, 1920s.........................	145.00

C

Cape, Raccoon, Bleached, Feathered, 1960s	650.00
Chaps, Angora, Carved Flowers, C.P. Shipley Saddlery, Early 1900s	1265.00
Coat, Blue Fox, Blue Lining, ¾ Sleeves, Woman's, Full Length, 44 In.	345.00
Coat, Blue Silk, Embroidered, Medallions, Pavilion, Deer, Boat, Peonies, Chinese, 41 ½ In.	388.00
Coat, Chinchilla, Gray, 3 Pelts, Cowl Collar, Size 6/8	3840.00
Coat, Leopard, Gaylon, Ardmore, Matching Pill Box Hat, Size Medium	734.00
Coat, Lunarine Mink, Sable Collar, Mink Belt, Rhinestone Buckle, Neiman Marcus, 44 In.	1035.00
Coat, Mink, Black, Swing, 2 Pocket, Lengthwise Pelts, Lined, Menstadter Furs, Size 10	4220.00
Coat, Mink, Light Gray Tones, J.L. Hudson Label, ¾ Length, c.1980	263.00
Coat, Mink, Velvet Lining, Vertical Pelts, Oscar De La Renta, c.1975, Size 10-12	1560.00
Coat, Ocelot, Double Breasted, Long Sleeves, Lapel Collar, Paris, c.1950, Size 6-8	1800.00
Coat, Satin Brocade, Flowers, ¾ Sleeves, 1950s, Medium	193.00
Coat, Silk Brocade, Faux Buttonholes, Matching Mini Dress, Gustave Tassell, 1960s	633.00
Coat, Silk, Satin, Peking Stitch, Flowers, Black Ground, Fur Trim & Lining, Chinese, 44 In. ...	227.00
Coat, Swing, Blue Wool, Burgundy Velvet Collar, Christian Dior, 1952, Size 40 Bust	450.00
Coat, Wool, Velvet Collar, ¾ Sleeves, Christian Dior, 1952, 40 In.	518.00
Costume, Cockney, Suit Jacket, Tam, Tie, Pearly Buttons, Stand, England, 1900s, 68 In.	1541.00
Costume, Painted, Cotton, Mask, Carved Wood, 12 Small Masks, 55 x 21 & 15 x 8 In. ....*illus*	1978.00
Costume, Parade, Uncle Sam, Cane, Top Hat, Woven Cotton, Red, White, Blue, Stand, 21 x 76 In.	2963.00
Dress, Brocade Stitched, Beige, Open Neck, Self Belt, Designer Original, Scarab Club, c.1881 .	23.00
Dress, Chiffon, Beaded, Chrysanthemum Pattern, Scalloped Hem, Embroidered, 45 In. Long.	1265.00
Dress, Cocktail, Bolero, Silk, Starburst Trim, Rodriquez, 1980s, Size 6-8 ....*illus*	1224.00
Dress, Communion, Lace, Center Daisy Placket, White, Glass Frame, 48 In.	71.00
Dress, Cotton, Back Zipper, Belt, Matching A-Line Coat, c.1962, 31 In.	50.00
Dress, Cotton, Tucked Bodice, Back Buttons, Ruffled Train, Mid 20th Century	978.00
Dress, Crepe, Black, Keyhole Blouse, Bias Cut Skirt, Ossie Clark, 1960s, Small	1185.00
Dress, Crepe, Net Lace, Dolman Sleeve, Camisole, Back Zipper, Irene, c.1945, 43-In. Skirt	230.00
Dress, Ecru Lace, Silk Lining, Flower Shoulder Trim, Crocheted Cap, c.1920, 40 x 18 In.	224.00
Dress, Evening, Silk, Paisley, Russet, Carolyne Roehm, c.1970, Size 6	360.00
Dress, Satin, Strapless, Back Zipper, Underskirt, Velveteen Dots & Flowers, c.1980	184.00
Dress, Silk, Abstract Print, Spread Collar, Lined, Pauline Trigere, 1970s, 41 In.	69.00
Dress, Silk, Boned Bodice, Pleated, V-Front, Side Zipper, Madame Gres, 38 In.	5750.00
Dress, Silk Brocade, Floral, Side Pockets, Train, Shrug, Cape, Pauline Trigere, 1960s, 41-In. Skirt	288.00
Dress, Souper, After Andy Warhol, Campbell Soup Cans, Cotton, Screenprint, c.1965, 39 x 23 In.	2450.00
Dress, Tuxedo, Black, Satin Lapel, Rive Gauche, Yves Saint Laurent, Size 38	600.00
Dress, Velvet, Boned Bodice, Silk Lining, Oleg Cassini, c.1950, 44-In. Skirt Length	920.00
Dress, Wool, A Line, Empire Waist, Attached Belt, Bill Blass, 1960s, Size 12, 39 ½ In.	173.00
Dress, Wool Gabardine, Navy Blue, White Collar, Yves Saint Laurent, c.1969, Medium	925.00
Gloves, Embroidered, Leather, Silk, Hearts, Flourishes, Red, Blue, Late 1800s, 7 In.	59.00
Gloves, Hide, Beaded, Multicolored Flowers, Leaves, 1900s, 15 In.	259.00
Handkerchief, Tillie The Toiler, King Features, c.1921, 19 x 19 ½ In. ....*illus*	115.00
Hat, Fox, Brown, 1960s	150.00
Hat, Mandarin, Red Silk, Fur Trim, Embroidered Ruyi, Streamers, Chinese, Child's, 8 ½ In. ..	1020.00
Jacket, Leather, Orange, Zipper, Long Sleeves, Lined, Chanel Label, 1970, Size 4	510.00
Mittens, Hand Knit, Cotton, Red & Brown Mixed, c.1910, 9 ¾ In.	65.00
Muff, Aqua Satin, Ecru Lace, Celluloid Insert, 9 x 9 In.	165.00
Nightgown, Victorian, White Cotton, Pin Tucking On Bust, Button Down Front, 1890s	60.00
Obi, Cream Silk Brocade, Metallic Threads, Fans, Flowers, Japan, 154 ½ x 24 ¾ In.	120.00
Overblouse, Floral Beaded Netting, Victorian, Size Small	110.00
Play Clothes, Yankiboy, Big 4 Baseball 525, Hat, Pants, Belt, Jersey, Box	100.00
Robe, Silk, Blue, 9 Dragons, Clouds, Emblems, Waves, Rocks, Metallic Thread, Chinese, 58 In.	9775.00
Robe, Silk, Deep Pink, Flower Embroidery, 53 In.	275.00
Robe, Silk, Red, Embroidered, Chinese, 39 In.	117.00
Scarf, Le Carnaval De Venise, Venetian Scenes, Harlequins, Revelers, Hermes .... 237.00 to 444.00	
Scarf, Polyester, Hand Rolled Edge, Red, White, Blue, Italy, 54 x 11 In.	23.00
Scarf, Rabbit Fur, White, Clip On, 27 x 3 ½ In.	45.00
Scarf, Silk, Bar Pattern, Gold, Blue, White, Vertical Gold Chains, Celine, Paris, 35 x 34 In.	100.00
Scarf, Silk, Beige, Brown, Cream, Diagonal Center Feather Design, Cesare Piccini, 32 In.	150.00
Scarf, Silk, Brown, Gold, Flower Garden Design, Tiffany & Co., Italy, 36 x 36 In.	79.00
Scarf, Silk, Brown, Rust Gray, Cream, Hand Rolled Edge, Halston, 30 x 30 In.	11.00
Scarf, Silk, Burgundy, Gold Wheel Design, Caty Latham, Hermes, 35 x 35 In.	179.00
Scarf, Silk, Horse & Carriage, Black, Red, Tan, Celine, Paris, 34 In.	100.00
Scarf, Silk, Multicolored, Hermes	207.00
Scarf, Silk, Red Ground, Gold & Green Flowers, Chanel, Paris	75.00
Scarf, Silk Twill, Navy, Brides De Gala, Hermes, 35 x 35 In.	169.00
Scarf, Silk, Twill, Navy, Green, Red, Vue Du Carosse De LaGalere La Reale, Hermes, 35 x 35 In.	192.00

TIP

If a zipper is stuck on a vintage dress or old suitcase, try rubbing soap or a candle on the zipper teeth. It may help.

Clothing, Dress, Cocktail, Bolero, Silk, Starburst Trim, Rodriquez, 1980s, Size 6-8
$1224.00

Clothing, Handkerchief, Tillie The Toiler, King Features, c.1921, 19 x 19 ½ In.
$115.00

TIP

Rust stains from old pins or hooks and eyes may come out with lemon juice.

Clothing, Shawl, Paisley, Blue, Orange, Red, Wool, Fringe, c.1880, 59 x 120 In. $324.00

Cluthra, Vase, Green, Bubbling, Steuben, 10 In. $805.00

Cluthra, Vase, Pink & White Cascading Bubbles, Flared, Mark, Steuben, 6 ½ x 8 In. $840.00

Shawl, Cashmere, Paisley Border, Black Center Panel, c.1900, 11 Ft. 2 In. x 5 Ft. 2 In.	115.00
Shawl, Paisley, Blue, Orange, Red, Wool, Fringe, c.1880, 59 x 120 In. ....*illus*	324.00
Shawl, Paisley, Purple Fringe, 66 x 68 In.	51.00
Shirt, Cotton, Psychedelic Flowers, Paisley, Tag, Vera, Size 16	75.00
Shirt, Deer Hide, Bib Front, Scalloped Collar & Pockets, Fringe, 1870-80	2588.00
Shoe Buckles, Silver, Hallmarks, Engraved Initials, c.1720, Pair	225.00
Shoes, Alligator, Buckles, Mr. Herbert, 2-In. Heel, Size 9N	89.00
Shoes, High Top, String, Victorian, 10 ½ x 10 In.	55.00
Shoes, Patent Leather, Hermes, Men's, Size 7	495.00
Skirt, Fragment, Pleated, Gold Dragon, Phoenix, Blue, Cotton, Silk, Chinese, c.1800, 42 x 64 In.	1495.00
Skirt, Wedding, Pleated Silk, Embroidered, Framed Under Glass, Chinese, 1880, 46 x 29 In. ..	525.00
Sneakers, Converse, Lou Brock, Red Canvas, 1974, Size 3 ½, 9 ½ In.	115.00
Spurs, Engraved Steel, Tooled Leather Straps, Mexico, c.1920, 5 In.	118.00
Stole, Suede Silk, Rose Scallop, Italy, Giorgio Armani, 90 x 18 In.	169.00
Suit, Blouse, Brown Velvet, Gold Silk, Beading, Carlo Ferrini, Woman's, 1960s	300.00
Suit, Lord Fauntleroy, Blue Velvet, Silk Shirt, Butterfly Fabric, Lined, Boy's, 1900, Small	125.00
Suit, Minstrel, Felt Hat, Vest, Tambourine Jingles, Green, Black, White, Stand, c.1930, 72 In. ..	2726.00
Suit, Undertaker's Burial Suit, Cotton, Silk, Wooden Display Box, New York, 1900s, 37 x 19 In.	1304.00
Surcoat, Silk, Embroidered, Sprays, Butterflies, In Shadowbox, Chinese, 53 ½ x 41 ½ In.	1440.00
Sweater, Cashmere, Black, Geometric Trim, Red, Cream, Pringle Of Scotland, 1950s, Small...	175.00
Sweater, Flowers, Swirls, Pink, Yellow, Cotton, Pucci, Woman's, Size 12	148.00
Top Hat, Velvet, Buckram Interior, Light Brown, c.1820..	350.00
Vest, Fox, Dyed Royal Blue, Chevron, Suede Trim, Bayshore Furriers, Size Small.....................	900.00

CLUTHRA glass is a two-layered glass with small bubbles and powdered glass trapped between the layers. The Steuben Glass Works of Corning, New York, first made it in 1920. Victor Durand of Kimball Glass Company in Vineland, New Jersey, made a similar glass from about 1925. Durand's pieces are listed in the Durand category. Related items are listed in the Steuben category.

Basket, White, Cylindrical, Heavy Lip Wrap, Steuben, 10 ½ In.	550.00
Bowl, Powder, Rose Pink Lid, Creamy White Base, Crystal Finial, Bubbles, Steuben..................	460.00
Jar, Cover, Waisted, White Mottled Opaque Glass, Pamona Green Cover, Steuben, 5 ½ x 5 In. .	288.00
Vase, Amethyst, Steuben, 8 In.	1100.00
Vase, Black To White Shading, Cinched Neck, Signed, Steuben, 8 In.	1093.00
Vase, Cylindrical, Blue & White, Clear Foot, Steuben, 9 ¾ In.	316.00
Vase, Green, Bubbling, Steuben, 10 In. ....*illus*	805.00
Vase, Mottled White, Green, Yellow, Ruby Ground, Steuben, 8 ¼ In.	489.00
Vase, Orange, White, Crystal Foot, Kimball, 8 ½ In.	230.00
Vase, Pink & White Cascading Bubbles, Flared, Mark, Steuben, 6 ½ x 8 In. ....*illus*	840.00
Vase, Pomona Green, Steuben, 8 In.	230.00
Vase, Shouldered, Mottled Light Green, Steuben, 10 In.	805.00
Vase, Shouldered, Pale Blue, Steuben, 8 In.	978.00
Vase, Squat, Pink, Fleur-De-Lis, Steuben, 4 ½ In.	518.00
Vase, White, Bubbles, Steuben, 8 In.	431.00
Vase, White, M-Shaped Opalescent Handles, Signed, Steuben, 10 ½ In.	863.00

COALBROOKDALE was made by the Coalport porcelain factory of England during the Victorian period. Pieces are decorated with floral encrustations.

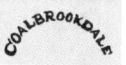

Umbrella Stand, Open Top, Ferns & Vine Design, Drip Pan, 19th Century, 22 x 10 In.	480.00

COALPORT ware has been made by the Coalport Porcelain Works of England from 1795 to the present time. Early pieces were unmarked. About 1810–25 the pieces were marked with the name *Coalport* in various forms. Later pieces also had the name *John Rose* in the mark. The crown mark has been used with variations since 1881. The date 1750 is printed in some marks, but it is not the date the factory started. Some pieces are listed in Indian Tree.

Bough Pot, Sarcophagus, Flowers, Man, Dog, 3 Cups, Mask Handles, c.1825, 6 x 10 In.	956.00
Bowl, Oval, Molded Feet, Gilt Rim, Hand Painted, England, c.1810, 11 x 8 In.	177.00
Cachepot, Scenic, Gold Trim, Paneled, Stand, c.1800, 4 In.	630.00
Cup & Saucer, Demitasse, Turquoise Jewelling, Gold Ground, Landscapes, c.1912, 3 ½ In.	652.00
Figurine, Ascot Lady, Box........................	66.00
Figurine, Basil Brush, 4 ¼ In.	49.00
Figurine, Romeo & Juliet, 10 ½ In.	89.00
Jug, Cabbage Leaf, 1800s, 7 ½ In.	690.00
Loving Cup, Woman's Portrait, Oval, Handles, Signed, F.N. Sutton, 9 ½ In.	400.00
Plate, Bread & Butter, Medallion, Paneled Border, Flower Reserve, 12 Piece, 6 ¾ In.	191.00

Platter, Green, Gilt Swirl, 1893 Chicago Exposition Issue, 12 x 9 ¼ In.	.....	69.00
Vase, Cornucopia Form, Cobalt Blue, Gilt, Applied Flowers, Leaves, 1800s, 5 In., Pair	.....	83.00

COBALT BLUE glass was made using oxide of cobalt. The characteristic bright dark blue identifies it for the collector. Most cobalt glass found today was made after the Civil War. There was renewed interest in the dark blue glass in the late 1930s and dinnerwares were made.

Compote, White Enamel Lace, Blown, Round Foot, 8 ¼ x 8 ¾ In.	.....	83.00
Cruet, 16 Ribs, Applied Hollow Handle, Stopper, Pa., 8 ½ In.	.....	1800.00
Decanter, Silver Plate, 10 In., Pair	.....	69.00
Decanter, Whiskey, Silver Overlay, Crystal Stopper	.....	120.00
Jug, Claret, Silver Mounted, Hinged, Ewer Shape Spout, C-Scroll Handle, Bulbous, 10 In.	.....	81.00
Sugar, Cover, Conical Finial, Flared Foot, Flint, 6 ¾ In.	.....	720.00
Vase, Barbell Stems, Ruffled Tooled Rim, Blown, Late 18th Century, 8 ½ In., Pair	.....	825.00
Wig Stand, Woman's Head, Formed, 11 ¼ In.	.....	80.00

COCA-COLA was first served in 1886 in Atlanta, Georgia. It was advertised through signs, newspaper ads, coupons, bottles, trays, calendars, and even lamps and clocks. Collectors want anything with the word *Coca-Cola*, including a few rare products, like gum wrappers and cigar bands. The famous trademark was patented in 1893, the *Coke* mark in 1945. Many modern items and reproductions are being made.

Ashtray, Coke Bottle Under Lampshade Top, Match Pull, Bakelite, c.1930, 7 ½ In.	.....	850.00
Ashtray, Gerry, Drink Coca-Cola, Green Glaze, Decoware, No. 200, 10 ¾ x 7 ¾ In.	.....	24.00
Ashtray, Ruby Glass, Diamond, Spade, Heart & Club, 1950s, 7 x 7 In., Set Of 4	.....	460.00
Barrel, Wood, Round, Label On Top, 34 In.	*illus*	176.00
Bingo Set, Box Has Silhouette Of Girl Drinking, 1930s, 8 x 14 ½ In.	.....	115.00
Bottle Carrier, Aluminum, Raised Lettering, 1950s, 8 ¼ x 5 ¼ In.	.....	130.00
Bottle Case, Holds 12 Bottles, 50 Cents, Cardboard, Morris Paper Mills, 20 x 18 In.	.....	35.00
Bottle Opener, Drink Coca-Cola, Wall, Starr-X Brown Co., USA	.....	36.00
Bottle, Amber, Circle Arrow, Lexington, Tenn.	.....	94.00
Bottle, Amber, Paper Label, New York, 1905, 7 ½ In.	*illus*	59.00
Bottle, Large Script, Coca-Cola Wyanokee Brand, Qt.	.....	55.00
Bottle, Seltzer, Salinas, Calif., Not To Be Sold	.....	364.00
Bottle, Seltzer, Santa Maria, Frosted Band	.....	392.00
Bottle, Syrup, Delicious & Refreshing, 5 Cents Per Glass, Enameled, Cap, c.1900	.....	2360.00
Bowl, 3 Bottle Feet, Pewter, Brunhoft Mfg. Co., 4 ¼ x 8 ¼ In.	.....	169.00
Bowl, Green, 6-Sided, Embossed, 1930s, 10 ¼ In.	*illus*	468.00
Calendar, 1918, 2 Girls At Beach, 31 ¼ x 13 In.	*illus*	1725.00
Calendar, 1920, Golfer Girl, 27 ½ x 12 In.	.....	3400.00
Calendar, 1923, Girl Drinking, Full Pad, 25 x 12 In.	.....	360.00
Calendar, 1926, Girl With Tennis Racket, 18 ½ x 10 In.	.....	901.00
Calendar, 1927, Girl With Flower Bouquet, C.J. Redmond, 12 ⅞ x 6 ⅞ In.	.....	691.00
Calendar, 1936, 50th Anniversary, Girl, Boat, Fisherman Holding Bottle, Frame, 10 x 18 ½ In.	.....	625.00
Carrier, Picnic, Red, Cardboard, Gardner Board & Carton Co., Ohio, 10 x 15 x 6 In.	.....	32.00
Carrier, Wood, Wing Emblems, Yellow, Red, 6-Pack, c.1930s, 7 ⅜ x 8 x 5 ½ In.	.....	58.00
Cigarette Case, Frosted Glass, Embossed, 1936, 2 Piece	.....	425.00
Clock, Drink Coca-Cola In Bottles, 64 ½ x 27 In.	.....	220.00
Clock, Drink Coca-Cola In Bottles, Wood Frame, 1939, 16 x 16 In.	.....	185.00
Clock, Drink Sessions, Bakelite, Metal Face, Convex Glass, Electric, 16 ½ In.	.....	480.00
Clock, Light-Up, Electric, 110v, c.1950, 9 In.	.....	252.00
Clock, Regulator, Burl, 18 ¼ x 9 x 4 In.	.....	495.00
Coffee Cup, Pottery, White, Red & Black Lettering, Rim, 1930s, 2 ½ In.	*illus*	585.00
Cooler, Airline, Red, 12 x 18 x 6 ½ In.	.....	340.00
Cooler, Drink Coca-Cola In Bottles, Vinyl, Metal Opener & Handles, c.1950s, 17 x 14 In.	.....	115.00
Cooler, Junior, 34 x 25 x 18 In.	.....	580.00
Cooler, Picnic, c.1950, 18 x 9 x 14 In.	.....	201.00
Cooler, Picnic, Drink Coca-Cola In Bottles, Red, White, Insert Tray, 1950s, 12 x 17 In.	.....	291.00
Cooler, Westinghouse Junior, Embossed Letter, Holds 51 Bottles, 1940s, 25 x 34 In.	.....	805.00
Cribbage & Dice Set, Red, White, 4 Wood Dice, 11 ¾ x 10 ⅜ In.	.....	60.00
Display, Thirst Asks Nothing More, Aluminum Deco Trim, Ay Displays, 1938, 39 In.	.....	920.00
Door Push, Drink Coca Cola, Delicious & Refreshing, 5 Cents, Aluminum, c.1905, 3 x 8 In.	.....	955.00
Festoon, Colonial Figures, Masonite, Wood, Tin, 11 ½ x 85 In.	.....	87.00
Festoon, Nautical Island Theme, Die Cut, Metal, Wood, 1930s, 22 Piece	.....	4070.00
Gas Pump Globe, Red, White, Plastic Body, Glass Lenses, c.1982, 16 In.	.....	420.00
Glass Holder, Logo, Silver, c.1900, 2 ½ In.	.....	140.00

Coca-Cola, Barrel, Wood, Round, Label On Top, 34 In.
$176.00

Coca-Cola, Bottle, Amber, Paper Label, New York, 1905, 7 ½ In.
$59.00

Coca-Cola, Bowl, Green, 6-Sided, Embossed, 1930s, 10 ¼ In.
$468.00

Popular Brands
Some brands are more popular with collectors than others. Coca-Cola, McDonald's restaurants, and M&Ms are tops. Others are Planters Peanuts, Anheuser-Busch, Budweiser, Kentucky Fried Chicken, and soft drinks like Pepsi-Cola, Moxie, and Hires Root Beer.

C

Coca-Cola, Calendar, 1918,
2 Girls At Beach, 31 ¼ x 13 In.
$1725.00

Coca-Cola, Coffee Cup, Pottery,
White, Red & Black Lettering, Rim,
1930s, 2 ½ In.
$585.00

Globe, Frosted Glass, Tassel, c.1930	3200.00
Globe, Green Pinstripe, Milk, Frosted Glass, c.1930, 12 In.	800.00
Kickplate, Drink Coca-Cola, Fountain Service, Porcelain, c.1950, 12 x 28 In.	550.00
Kickplate, Embossed, Tin, 1933, 11 x 34 In.	625.00
Kickplate, Fountain Service, Porcelain, 1950s	1650.00
Lamp, Hanging, Leaded Glass Shade, Flat Panels, 14 x 16 In.	600.00
Lamp, Hanging, Leaded Glass, White, Green, Brown, 13 x 16 In.	920.00
Machine, Cavalier C-51, Holds 51 Bottles, 10-Cent, 1950s, 25 x 65 x 21 In.	1265.00
Menu Board, Drink Coca-Cola, Special Today, Embossed, Tin, Coshocton, Ohio, 1937, 27 x 19 In.	410.00
Music Box, Cooler Style, Plastic, Metal, Windup, 1950s, 1 ¾ x 2 ¾ x 2 ¼ In.	115.00
Plate, Bottle & Glass, c.1930, 8 In.	1675.00
Plate, Bottle, Glass Of Coke, Knowles China, 1931, 7 ¼ In.	500.00
Plate, Coca-Cola, Good With Food, Scalloped Edge, Wellsville, 1940s, 7 In.	1485.00
Postcard, Soda Fountain, Welch's Grape Juice Bottles, 3 ½ x 5 ½ In.	275.00
Rack Topper, Take Home A Carton, Steel, Marked, St. Thomas Metal Signs, 1939, 16 x 12 In.	55.00
Radio, Bottle, 1930s, 24 In.	4695.00
Radio, Cooler Style, 1950s, 10 x 12 In.	420.00
Radio, Maharlika, Airline Cooler Form, c.1950	1590.00
Sign, 2-Sided, Die Cut, Tin, Triangle, Iron Bracket, 1936, 28 x 36 In.	1365.00
Sign, 50th Anniversary, 2 Women, 1886-1936, Cardboard, 50th Anniversary, Frame, 1936, 50 x 30 In.	2500.00
Sign, 50th Anniversary, 2 Women In Bathing Suits, Cardboard, 1930s, 30 x 30 In.	3750.00
Sign, Accepted Home Refreshment, Couple By Fireside, Frame, 1940s, 27 ½ x 56 ½ In.	480.00
Sign, Arrow, Ice Cold Coca-Cola, Christmas Bottle, Red, Green, White, Masonite, 28 x 23 In.	718.00
Sign, Arrow Through Cooler, Kay, 32 In.	850.00
Sign, Be Really Refreshed, Cardboard, 2-Sided, Winter, Summer, Frame, 1950s, 20 x 36 In.	420.00
Sign, Bottle, Green, Brown, Tin Lithograph, Marked, AM 1-52, c.1950, 16 ¾ x 5 ½ In.	38.00
Sign, Bottle, In Sun, Flange, 2-Sided, Die Cut Filigree, 24 x 20 ½ In.	193.00
Sign, Bottle, Red, Tin, String Hanger, c.1950, 9 In. Diam.	85.00
Sign, Bottle, Sprite Kid, Red, Yellow, White, Brown, Tin Lithograph, c.1947, 12 ¾ In. Diam.	825.00
Sign, Button, Coca-Cola, Bottle, Red, Brown, White, 36 In.	385.00
Sign, Clown, Ice Skater, Pause, Frame, 1950, 16 x 27 In.	1650.00
Sign, Coca-Cola, 2-Sided, Light-Up, Rotates, Plastic, Metal, c.1950	1600.00
Sign, Coca-Cola Dispenser, Cup, Red, White, Green, Porcelain, 2-Sided, 28 x 27 In.	1300.00
Sign, Coca-Cola, State Flowers Festoon, Woman, Slogan, Cardboard, Die Cut, 1950s, 7 In.	59.00
Sign, Coke, Bottle, Porcelain, Die Cut, c.1940-50, 16 ½ x 5 In.	328.00
Sign, Coke Bottle, Red Ground, Enamel, On Metal, Round, c.1950, 24 In.	780.00
Sign, Coke Time, Join The Friendly Circle, Cardboard, 1955, 27 ½ x 56 ½ In.	480.00
Sign, Coca-Cola, Delicious & Refreshing, Red, Yellow, Green Border, Porcelain, 1930, 34 x 60 In.	1100.00
Sign, Coca-Cola, Santa, Elves, A Merry Christmas Calls For Coke, Cardboard, 32 x 49 In.	29.00
Sign, Coca-Cola, Santa, Toys, They Remembered Me, Cutout Cardboard, 1942, 18 In.	88.00
Sign, Delicatessen, Bottle, Ice Cold, Refreshes You, Tin, 1968, 32 x 55 ½ In.	198.00
Sign, Delicious, Pole Topper, 24 x 24 In.	130.00
Sign, Drink Coca-Cola, Coca-Cola, Bottle, 18 x 53 ¾ In.	165.00
Sign, Drink Coca-Cola, Bottle, Flange, Tin, 1946, 21 x 24 In.	401.00
Sign, Drink Coca-Cola, Bottle, Ice Cold, Embossed, Tin, Coshocton, Ohio, 1937, 27 x 19 In.	715.00
Sign, Drink Coca-Cola, Button, Red, Tin, 16 In.	195.00
Sign, Drink Coca-Cola, Cardboard Die Cut, Woman, Swimsuit, Bottle, c.1940, 26 x 19 In.	990.00
Sign, Drink Coca-Cola, Christmas Bottle, Yellow, Red, Wood, Metal, 3-Sided, 20 x 19 ¼ In.	1150.00
Sign, Drink Coca-Cola, Embossed, Tin, Marked, Dasco, 1933, 5 ⅞ x 17 ¾ In.	400.00
Sign, Drink Coca-Cola, Fountain Service, Porcelain, c.1930	2225.00
Sign, Drink Coca-Cola, Ice Cold, Bottle, Embossed, Tin Lithograph, c.1937, 19 x 27 In.	577.00
Sign, Drink Coca-Cola, Jones Drug, Painted, Porcelain, 2-Sided, 1941, 59 x 66 In.	6600.00
Sign, Drink Coca-Cola, Lunch With Us, Light-Up, Brunhoff, 14 x 12 x 5 In.	12000.00
Sign, Drink Coca-Cola, Porcelain, 1960s, 22 x 16 In.	89.00
Sign, Drink Coca-Cola, Red, White, Porcelain, 46 x 96 In.	500.00
Sign, Drink Coca-Cola, Red, White, Tin, 1960s, 5 x 12 In., Pair	410.00
Sign, Drink Coca-Cola, Seated Girl, Holding Glass, 1970s, 23 x 33 In.	10.00
Sign, Drink Coca-Cola, Woman, Man, Cardboard, 1944, 30 x 50 In.	224.00
Sign, Drink Coca-Cola, Woman, With Bottle, Painted, Tin, Frame, 1941, 21 x 56 In.	85.00
Sign, Enjoy Coca-Cola, Red, Plastic, Aluminum Frame, Marked, AM119, 34 x 68 In.	79.00
Sign, Extra Bright Refreshment, Woman, Umbrella, Paper, Cardboard, 1955, 27 x 56 In.	73.00
Sign, Fishtail Logos, 6-Pack, Big King Size, Tin, Iron, Sidewalk, 2-Sided, 32 x 20 In.	315.00
Sign, Fishtail, Bottle, Painted, Tin, 1960-63, 18 x 54 In.	75.00
Sign, Fishtail, Drink Coca-Cola, 1962, 37 x 57 ½ In.	495.00
Sign, Fishtail, Ice Cold Coca-Cola, Bottle, Tin, 19 ¾ x 27 ¾ In.	205.00
Sign, Flange, Bottle In Sun, 2-Sided, Die Cut Filigree, 24 x 20 ½ In.	193.00

Sign, Fountain Service, Shield, Red, Green, Yellow, Die Cut, 2-Sided, 1936, 23 x 25 ½ In.	2320.00
Sign, Girl, Groceries, 2-Sided, Cardboard, 1950, 16 x 27 In.	950.00
Sign, Girl In Lounge Chair, Paper, Frame, 1942	770.00
Sign, Girl On Beach, Silhouette, Frame, 1951	990.00
Sign, Grocery, Bottle, Ice Cold, Refreshes You, Tin, 1960s, 32 x 56 ½ In.	295.00
Sign, Hanging, Drink Coca-Cola, Trademark Boy, Cooler, Arrow, Masonite, c.1940, 30 x 12 In.	1870.00
Sign, Have A Coke Now, Bottle, 2-Sided, Cardboard, 1951, 16 x 27 In.	375.00
Sign, Home Hospitality, 3 People Singing, 1951, 30 x 50 In.	700.00
Sign, Home Refreshment, Take Some Home Today, 2-Sided, Cardboard, 1950, 16 x 27 In.	950.00
Sign, Ice Cold Coca-Cola Sold Here, Embossed, Tin, 1933, 19 ½ In.	651.00
Sign, Ice Cold Coca-Cola Sold Here, Embossed, Tin, Coshocton, Ohio, 1933, 19 ¾ In. Diam.	970.00
Sign, Ice Cold, Coke Bottle, 2-Sided, Die Cut, Flange, 1951, 18 x 22 In.	600.00
Sign, Iced Coca-Cola Here, Red, Yellow, Flange, Porcelain, 2-Sided, 20 x 18 In.	1800.00
Sign, James Brown, Easel Back, Aluminum Frame, 1970s, 18 x 30 In.	70.00
Sign, Light-Up, 16 x 18 In.	94.00
Sign, Lunch & Soda, Porcelain, c.1950, 18 x 30 In.	1126.00
Sign, Man Offering Woman Bottle, Tin, 37 x 58 In.	660.00
Sign, Men, Women, In Car, Drinking Coca-Cola, Cardboard, 1939, 27 x 16 In.	920.00
Sign, Neon, 10 x 23 In.	136.00
Sign, Pause, Drink Coca-Cola, Bottle, Tin, Marked, W.F.R., 35 ½ x 71 In.	660.00
Sign, Pause That Refreshes, Cardboard, Frame, 1947, 25 x 39 In.	200.00
Sign, Picnic Scene, Take Coke A Long, Frame, c.1950	1760.00
Sign, Please Pay Cashier, Coca-Cola, Glass, Hanging, Plastic, Metal Trim, 1948, 18 x 13 In.	777.00
Sign, Please Pay Cashier, Coca-Cola, Light-Up, 9 x 19 ½ x 3 In.	560.00
Sign, Quick Service, Coca-Cola, Tin, Wood, 10 ¼ x 37 In.	1200.00
Sign, Really Refreshes, Tin, 18 x 40 In.	153.00
Sign, Refreshing New Feeling, 2-Sided, Flange, October, 1961	400.00
Sign, Santa Claus, Train, Helicopter, Stock Up For The Holidays, Cardboard, 32 x 66 In.	145.00
Sign, School Crossing Guard, Policeman, Metal, Cast Iron Base, Feb. 1959, 63 x 30 In.	3975.00
Sign, School Girl, Slow School Zone, Steel, Metal, 2-Sided, Die Cut, c.1940, 53 x 16 In.	4950.00
Sign, Sign Of Good Taste, 2-Sided, Flange, February, 1959, 15 x 18 In.	400.00
Sign, Coca-Cola, Slogan, Red, White, Green Border, 1930, 24 x 60 Porcelain, 34 x 60 In.	1170.00
Sign, Spinner, Red, Yellow, Green, White, Top Of Vending, 1950s, 6 x 14 ½ In.	1100.00
Sign, Street Crossing Guard, Slow School Zone, Die Cut, Tin, 2-Sided, 62 ½ x 30 In.	2500.00
Sign, Take A Case Home Today, 24-Pack, Big King Size, Tin, Iron, 2-Sided, 32 x 20 In.	315.00
Sign, Take Home A Carton, Big King Size, Frame, 1961, 20 x 28 In.	2700.00
Sign, They All Want Coca-Cola, Cardboard, 1941, 20 x 36 In.	660.00
Sign, Things Go Better With Coke, Bottle, Tin, 53 ½ x 17 ¾ In.	440.00
Sign, Woman, In Canoe, Delicious & Refreshing, Cardboard, Signed, Elvgren, 27 x 56 In.	150.00
Sign, Yes, Swimmer Girl, Cardboard, 1945, 27 ½ x 56 ½ In.	660.00
Stringholder, Take Home Coca-Cola In Cartons, 6-Pack, Red, Yellow, Tin, 2-Sided, 16 x 12 In.	960.00
Stringholder, Take Home Coca-Cola In Cartons, Red, White, Tin, 2-Sided, 16 x 12 ½ In.	360.00
Thermometer, 2 Bottles, Drink Coca-Cola, Tin, 1941, 16 x 7 In.	105.00
Thermometer, Bottle, Ask For It Ice Cold, Embossed, Tin, 17 ¼ x 5 In.	375.00
Thermometer, Bottle Shape, Green, Brown, Tin Lithograph, c.1950, 17 In.	78.00
Thermometer, Christmas Bottle, Embossed, Tin, 17 x 5 In.	240.00
Thermometer, Coca-Cola Bottle, Christmas Bottle, 16 ¾ x 4 ⅞ In.	245.00
Thermometer, Coca-Cola Bottle Shape, Tin, 1950s, 17 In.	75.00
Thermometer, Drink Coca-Cola, Coca-Cola In Bottles, Aluminum, Domed Glass, 1950s, 12 In. Diam.	153.00
Thermometer, Drink Coca-Cola, Ijskoud, Bottle, Porcelain, Belgium, 1938, 21 x 7 ½ In.	3850.00
Thermometer, Drink Coca-Cola, Sign Of Good Taste, Red, White, c.1950, 8 x 30 In.	575.00
Thermometer, Gold Bottle, Red Ground, Tin, 1936, 16 x 6 In.	205.00
Thermometer, Woman Drinking From Bottle, Tin Lithograph, 1939, 16 In.	115.00
Tip Tray, 1900, Hilda, Drink Coca-Cola, Refreshing, Delicious, 5 ½ In. Diam.	523.00
Tip Tray, 1906, Juanita, Delicious, Refreshing, White Dress, 4 In. Diam.	475.00
Tip Tray, 1909, Exhibition Girl, Oval, 6 ¼ x 4 ½ In. .... *illus*	1170.00
Tip Tray, 1910, Coca-Cola Girl, 6 ⅛ x 4 ⅜ In.	155.00 to 250.00
Tip Tray, 1914, Betty, Drink Coca-Cola, Passaic Metal Ware Co., 6 x 4 ¾ In.	115.00 to 239.00
Tip Tray, 1916, Elaine, Basket Of Flowers, Oval, 6 x 4 ¼ In.	92.00 to 190.00
Tip Tray, 1920, Golfer Girl, Yellow Dress, Oval, 6 ¼ x 4 ½ In.	150.00 to 550.00
Toy, Car, Tin Friction, Japan, 1962, 10 In.	275.00
Toy, Dispenser, Bottle Inside, Pull Lever, Plastic, 4 Bottles, 3 Glasses, 11 In.	175.00
Toy, Truck, Allen Haddock, Metal, Battery Operated, Yellow, Cream, Box, 12 ½ In.	210.00
Toy, Truck, Bottles, Metalcraft	350.00
Toy, Truck, Delivery, Cast Aluminum, Pressed Steel, Bottle Cases, c.1963, 13 In.	1840.00
Toy, Truck, Red, Yellow, Rubber Tires, Highlights, Bottles, Metalcraft, 11 ½ In.	460.00
Toy, Truck, Yellow, Red, Steel, Buddy L, 15 In.	59.00

Coca-Cola, Tip Tray, 1909,
Exhibition Girl, Oval, 6 ¼ x 4 ½ In.
$1170.00

Coca-Cola, Tray, 1908, Topless Girl,
12 ¼ In.
$9360.00

TIP
*Most Coca-Cola trays
had green or brown
borders in the 1920s,
red borders in
the 1930s.*

Coca-Cola, Vending Machine, Venco V39, 10 Cent, 39 Bottles, 1949, 27 x 16 x 58 In. $460.00

Coffee Mill, Enterprise, No. 12, 2 Wheels, Cast Iron, Red, Eagle Finial, 39 In. $1112.00

Coin-Operated Machine, Arcade, Donkey-Kong, 2 Players, Seated Version, 29 x 34 x 23 In. $138.00

Toy, Truck, Yellow, White, Battery Operated, Sanyo, Box, c.1950, 12 ½ In.	450.00
Trash Can, Domed Top, Metal, Red, Bottle In Hand Decal, 36 x 15 In.	250.00
Tray, 1900, Hilda Clark, At Table, Coke Glass, 9 ¼ In.	7000.00
Tray, 1907, Relieves Fatigue, Oval, 13 ¼ x 10 ⅞ In.	718.00
Tray, 1908, Topless Girl, 12 ¼ In.	*illus* 9360.00
Tray, 1909, Exhibition Girl, H.D. Beach Co., 12 ⅞ x 10 ¾ In.	468.00
Tray, 1914, Betty, Tin Lithograph, 13 x 10 ½ In.	248.00 to 270.00
Tray, 1916, Elaine, Tin Lithograph, 19 x 8 ½ In.	275.00
Tray, 1920, Golfer Girl, Holding Glass, 13 ¼ x 10 ¼ In.	440.00 to 475.00
Tray, 1921, Autumn Girl, Holding Glass, 13 ¼ x 10 ¼ In.	520.00 to 531.00
Tray, 1923, Flapper Girl, 13 ¼ x 10 ¼ In.	205.00
Tray, 1924, Smiling Girl, 13 ¼ x 10 ¼ In.	550.00
Tray, 1925, Party Girl, American Art Works, 13 ¼ x 10 ¼ In.	275.00
Tray, 1926, Golfing Couple, American Art Works, 13 ¼ x 10 ½ In.	550.00 to 600.00
Tray, 1927, Curb Service, Tindeco, 10 ¼ x 13 ¼ In.	385.00 to 400.00
Tray, 1927, Soda Jerk, Fountain Sales, American Art Works, 13 x 10 ½ In.	90.00
Tray, 1929, Girl In Yellow Bathing Suit, American Art Works, 13 ¼ x 10 ½ In.	420.00
Tray, 1930, Telephone Girl, American Art Works, 13 ¼ x 10 ½ In.	170.00
Tray, 1931, Barefoot Boy, Norman Rockwell, American Art Works, 13 x 10 ½ In.	275.00 to 300.00
Tray, 1932, Girl In Bathing Suit, American Art Works, 13 x 10 ½ In.	180.00
Tray, 1933, Frances Dee, American Art Works, Tin Lithograph, 13 ¼ x 10 ½ In.	660.00 to 700.00
Tray, 1934, Johnny Weismuller & Maureen O'Sullivan, American Art Works, 10 ½ x 13 In.	138.00
Tray, 1935, Madge Evans, American Art Works, 13 ¼ x 10 ½ In.	190.00
Tray, 1936, Hostess, American Art Works, 13 ¼ x 10 ½ In.	195.00 to 200.00
Tray, 1937, Running Girl, American Art Works, 13 ¼ x 10 ½ In.	420.00
Tray, 1938, Girl In Yellow Hat, American Art Works, 13 ¼ x 10 ½ In.	170.00 to 195.00
Tray, 1939, Springboard Girl, American Art Works, Sundblom, 13 x 10 ½ In.	120.00 to 195.00
Tray, 1940, Sailor Girl, American Art Works, 10 ½ x 13 ¼ In.	245.00 to 330.00
Tray, 1941, Skater Girl, Girl Seated On Log, American Art Works, 13 ¼ x 10 ½ In.	121.00
Tray, 1942, 2 Girls At Car, American Art Works, 13 ¼ x 10 ½ In.	180.00 to 295.00
Tray, 1950, Menu Girl, Holding Bottle, American Art Works, 13 x 10 ½ In.	142.00
Tray, 1961, Pansy Garden, 13 ¾ x 10 ¼ In.	45.00
Vending Machine, Red Metal, 54 In.	118.00
Vending Machine, Venco V39, 10 Cent, 39 Bottles, 1949, 27 x 16 x 58 In.	*illus* 460.00
Vending Machine, Vendo 44, Enjoy A Coke, White, Red, 58 x 24 In.	1650.00
Vending Machine, Vendo A238 5k, Drink Coca-Cola In Bottles, Red, 36 x 24 In.	900.00
Vending Machine, Vendo, V-23, Spin Top, Manual, Key, 37 x 24 x 21 In.	880.00
Vending Machine, White, Colored Drinking Fountains, 10 Cent, c.1954, 52 x 26 In.	1600.00

COFFEE MILLS are also called coffee grinders, although there is a difference in the way each grinds the coffee. Large floor-standing or counter-model coffee mills were used in the nineteenth-century country store. Small home mills were first made about 1894. They lost favor by the 1930s. The renewed interest in fresh-ground coffee has produced many modern electric mills and hand mills and grinders. Reproductions of the old styles are being made.

Arcade, Crystal, No. 3, Cast Iron, Wall Mount, 18 ½ In.	45.00 to 70.00
Arcade, Crystal, No. 4, Cast Iron, Marked, No. 40, Wall Mount, 12 ¾ In.	57.00
Arcade, No. 3, Glass, Wall Mount, 11 ½ In.	49.00
Cast Iron Handle, Wood, Drawer, 19th Century, 6 In.	35.00
Cast Iron, Woodruff & Edwards Co., Illinois, c.1880, 28 ½ In.	444.00
Douwe Egberts Koffie, Pottery, Iron, Wood, Wall Mount, Glass Measure, 13 In.	118.00
Elgin, Red, Tin Oval Pan, Cast Brass Eagle Finial, Woodruff & Edwards Co., 26 In.	380.00
Enterprise, 2 Wheels, Cast Iron, Drawer, Salmon Paint, Pat. 1873, 12 ½ x 10 ½ In.	1150.00
Enterprise, 2 Wheels, Wooden Hand Grip, Cast Iron, Drawer, 12 ¾ In.	605.00
Enterprise, Black, Red, Eagle Finial, Drawer, 2 Wheels, 25 In.	199.00
Enterprise, No. 1, Cast Iron, Black Paint, Flower Design, Hinged Cover, 12 ¾ x 10 In.	175.00
Enterprise, No. 2, Red, Stenciled, July 12, 1898, 12 ½ In.	1450.00
Enterprise, No. 4, Red, Gold, Eagle Finial, Drawer, Stenciled, 21 In.	2750.00
Enterprise, No. 7, 2 Wheels, Cast Iron, Wooden Hand Grip, Red, Blue, Drawer, 21 ½ In.	495.00
Enterprise, No. 12, 2 Wheels, Cast Iron, Red, Eagle Finial, 39 In.	*illus* 1112.00
Grand Union Tea Co., Red, Cast Iron, Wood Base	605.00
National Specialty Co., No. 5, 2 Wheels, Wood Handles, Cast Iron, Steel, 20 In.	1180.00
New London, Side Mount, Increase Wilson Patent, Early 1800s, 8 ½ x 6 ½ In.	195.00
Pe. Be., Dutch Scene, Pottery Canister, Iron, Wood, Wall Mount, Glass Measure, 15 In.	24.00
Rev-O-Noc, Cast Iron, Glass Canister, Tin Lid, Red Paint, Handle, Wall Mount, 16 In.	68.00
Softwood, Dovetailed, Drawer, Brass Pull, Pewter Fill Cup, Iron Grinder, 9 x 10 x 6 In.	605.00

Star, No. 10, Nickel Plated Hopper, 33 In.	450.00
Swift Mill, No. 15, Red, Stenciled, Lane Brothers, Pat. 1875, 29 ½ In.	2300.00
Universal, No. 20, Black, Drawer, Landers, Frary & Clark, 8 ½ x 14 In.	2650.00
Universal, No. 20, Black, Eagle Finial, Drawer, Stenciled, Landers, Frary & Clark, 14 In.	605.00

COIN SPOT is a glass pattern that was named by collectors for the spots resembling coins, which are part of the glass. Colored, clear, and opalescent glass was made with the spots. Many companies used the design in the 1870–90 period. It is so popular that reproductions are still being made.

Pitcher, Water, Blue Opalescent, Pressed Leaf Handle, Star Crimp, c.1900, 8 ½ In.	118.00
Pitcher, Water, Star Crimp, Cranberry, Clear Handle, c.1900, 8 ½ In.	171.00
Sugar Shaker, 9 Panels, Cranberry Opalescent, Lid, c.1900, 4 ¾ In.	563.00
Sugar Shaker, Tapered, Canary Opalescent, Lid, Hobbs, Brockunier, c.1875, 5 ¼ In.	171.00
Syrup, 9 Panels, Cranberry Opalescent, Clear Handle, Lid, c.1875, 6 In.	1150.00
Syrup, Bulbous, Blue Opalescent, Handle, Lid, c.1900, 6 ¼ In.	171.00

COIN-OPERATED MACHINES of all types are collected. The vending machine is an ancient invention dating back to 200 B.C., when holy water was dispensed in a coin-operated vase. Smokers in seventeenth-century England could buy tobacco from a coin-operated box. It was not until after the Civil War that the technology made modern coin-operated games and vending machines plentiful. Slot machines, arcade games, and dispensers are all collected.

Alka-Seltzer, Be Wise Alkasize, Pedestal, 15 In.	504.00
Arcade, Challenger Shooting, 10 Shots For 1 Cent, 1941, 15 x 9 x 23 In.	275.00
Arcade, Clown, Wood, Cast Iron, Marque, 33 x 20 x 10 ½ In.	1430.00
Arcade, Dancing Dolls, Porcelain, Philco TV Cabinet, Music, 10 Cent, 34 x 32 In.	180.00
Arcade, Donkey-Kong, 2 Players, Seated Version, 29 x 34 x 23 In. ....*illus*	138.00
Arcade, Game, Thomas Novelties Peerless Products, Key, 21 x 9 ¼ In.	690.00
Arcade, Ms. Pac Man, 25 Cent, 88 x 25 In.	1440.00
Arcade, Target Shooter, 5 Shots, 1 Cent, Wooden Cases, ABT Mfg., 26 x 18 In.	144.00
Arcade, US Marshal, Shooting Game, 5 Cent, 53 x 15 x 33 In. ....*illus*	1053.00
Cail-O-Scope, Peep Show, Stereo Cards, Wood, Crank Handle, 72 x 22 x 19 In.	4600.00
Dispenser, Cards, Postage Stamps, Metal, Painted, Shipman Mfg., 26 In.	59.00
Dispenser, Match, San Telmo Havana Cigars, Cigar, Cutter, Cast Iron, 5 x 6 ½ x 8 In.	509.00
Drop Card, Accidents Will Happen, Pine Cabinet, Electric, 10 Cent, 57 x 23 In.	960.00
Foot Massager, A Treat For Your Feet, 25 Cent, 56 x 10 In.	600.00
Fortune Teller, Gambling Wheel, 5 Cent	5000.00
Gambling Wheel, Animal Designs, Tin, Lithograph, 17 In.	115.00
Game, Bowling, Win Cigars, Wood Cabinet, Glass Top, Bowling Pins, 21 In.	288.00
Gum, Baseball, 1 Cent, Wood Case, Speckled Paint, 14 In. ....*illus*	575.00
Gum, Pulver Chewing Gum, Blue Case, Key, 20 ¼ x 8 ½ In.	1955.00
Gum, Yellow Kid, Clockwork, Pulver, Porcelain, Wood, c.1920, 10 x 6 x 24 In.	3680.00
Gumball, 1 Cent, Cast Iron Base, Globe, Round, c.1900, 16 In.	323.00
Gumball, Acorn, 1 Cent, Painted Metal, Glass Globe, 17 In.	65.00
Gumball, Acorn, 5 Cent, Light Blue, 14 ½ x 6 ½ x 7 In.	66.00
Gumball, Ford, Glass Globe, Nickel Plated, 1 Cent, 15 In.	40.00
Gumball, Indoor Striker Ball, Pacific Manufacturing, Key, 1930, 19 x 9 ½ In.	1150.00
Gumball, Victor, 1 Cent, Wood, Metal, 15 x 7 ½ In.	150.00
Horse, Leather Saddle, Penny Or Peso, Chain Model 102, Shahin, Mexico, c.1940	2495.00
Mutoscope, Caught By His Wife, 10 Cent, Wood Cabinet, 59 x 16 In.	660.00
Mutoscope, Charlie Chaplin, Birch Cabinet, 25 Cent, Electric, 53 x 21 In.	1000.00
Mutoscope, Digger, 5 Cent, Oak Case, c.1930, 38 x 21 ½ In.	2590.00
Mutoscope, Joe Louis Vs. Max Schmeling Fight, Birch, 25 Cent, 53 In.	780.00
Mutoscope, Tom Mix, Miracle Rides, Oak Cabinet, 25 Cent, Electric, 53 In.	1020.00
Pinball, Major League, Pacific Amusement, 1920s, 40 x 48 x 24 In.	690.00
Pinball, Play-Boy, Wood, Glass, Spring Shot Ball, 28 In.	531.00
Pinball, Rose Bowl, Wood Legs, Chicago Coin, c.1937, 67 x 22 In.	480.00
Pinball, Slug Fest, Baseball Card Dispenser, William's, c.1991	480.00
Play Football, 5 Cent, Pine, Chester Pollard, 73 x 46 x 20 In.	3100.00
Sculptoscope, Whiting's Travel System, Nickel Plated, Box, 1913, 15 x 11 In.	950.00
Sculptoscope, Whiting's, 1 Cent, Red, American Novelty, 15 x 7 ½ In.	1200.00
Skill, Kicker Catcher, Stand, Iron Coca-Cola Base, 25 Cent, 52 x 14 In.	660.00
Skill, Whiz Ball, 1 Cent, 18 x 8 In.	633.00
Slot, Bangtails Horse Racing, Evans, 1939, 45 x 37 ½ x 26 ¼ In.	1320.00
Slot, Bell, Mills Operator, 1922, 21 x 14 x 14 In.	900.00
Slot, Jennings, Chief, Tic-Tac-Toe, 10 Cent, Chrome, Wood, 27 x 15 x 15 In.	1000.00

Coin-Operated Machine, Arcade, US Marshal, Shooting Game, 5 Cent, 53 x 15 x 33 In. $1053.00

Coin-Operated Machine, Gum, Baseball, 1 Cent, Wood Case, Speckled Paint, 14 In. $575.00

Coin-Operated Machine, Slot, Jennings, Little Duke, 1 Cent, Art Deco, Keys, 26 In. $1521.00

COIN-OPERATED MACHINE

Coin-Operated Machine,
Trade Stimulator, Fairest Wheel,
14 x 22 In.
$605.00

Coin-Operated Machine, Trade
Stimulator, Reel 21, Cast Aluminum,
1930s, 11 ½ x 11 In.
$575.00

Coin-Operated Machine,
Trade Stimulator, Spiral Penny,
20th Century Novelty Co.,
c.1906, 11 x 17 In.
$1921.00

Coin-Operated Machine,
War Game Mermaid, Iron,
Automatic Sports Co., c.1912, 24 x 76 In.
$192500.00

Slot, Jennings, Dutch Boy & Girl, 5 Cent, 1920s, 25 x 15 In.	1200.00
Slot, Jennings, Dutch Girl, Boy, Skill Stop, 5 Cent	1150.00
Slot, Jennings, Little Duke, 1 Cent, Art Deco, Keys, 26 In. *illus*	1521.00
Slot, Jennings, Tri-Plex, 5, 10, 25 Cent, 1930	3163.00
Slot, Mills, 5 Cent, Side Vendor, 1930	2875.00
Slot, Mills, 50 Cent, Black Cherry, Half Top, 1946, 27 x 15 In.	2588.00
Slot, Mills, 777, High Top, 5 Cent, Hand Loaded Jackpot, 1948, 27 In.	1265.00
Slot, Mills, Baseball, 5 Cent, Aluminum, Lithograph, 16 x 16 x 27 In.	4600.00
Slot, Mills, Black Cherry, Half Top, 10 Cent, c.1930-50, 26 In.	862.00
Slot, Mills, Bursting Cherry, 1 Cent, Oak Cabinet, Aluminum, Mid 1930s, 17 x 17 x 34 In.	1150.00
Slot, Mills, Caille, Silent Sphinx, 5 Cent, Mechanical Clock	1093.00
Slot, Mills, Diamond Front, 10 Cent, Black Paint, Chrome, 1940s, 16 x 16 x 24 In.	978.00
Slot, Mills, Lion Front, Wolf's Head, 5 Cent, Oak Cabinet, 1930s, 17 x 17 x 34 In.	1438.00
Slot, Mills, Oak Case, 25 Cent, c.1899, 66 x 27 In.	17000.00
Slot, Mills, Operator's Bell, Cast Iron, 5 Cent	3738.00
Slot, Mills, Silent Mystery, 5 Cent, c.1933, 26 x 16 In.	1320.00
Slot, O.D. Jennings, Chinese, Light-Up, 5 Cent, Chrome, Aluminum, 20 x 17 x 60 In.	1725.00
Slot, Ohio Superior Confection, Play Buffalo Nickels Only, 21 x 12 ½ x 14 In.	1700.00
Slot, Owl, Lithographed Orange, Black, Blue, Oak Cabinet	10005.00
Slot, Silver King, 5 Cent, Side Vendor, 1915-29, Cast Iron	1093.00
Slot, Watling Blue Seal, 5 Cent	978.00
Slot, Watling, Front Rol-A-Top, 5 Cent	2587.00
Slot, Watling, Treasury, 5 Cent	1265.00
Stamp, U.S. Postage, 1 Cent, Oak, Aluminum, Mirror, 21 x 10 x 8 In.	5000.00
Stamp, U.S. Postage, 10 Cent, Red, White, Blue, 20 x 8 x 4 ¼ In.	50.00
Symphonion Music Automaton, Walnut, Oak Case, Muse Panel, 27 x 20 In.	3105.00
Trade Stimulator, Cigar Store, Oak Case, Paper Dial, Griswold, 16 ½ x 15 In.	1200.00
Trade Stimulator, Cigarette, Ball Gum, Aluminum, Art Deco Style, 1930s, 9 x 9 x 12 In.	403.00
Trade Stimulator, Daval Fortune Gum, Key, 1932, 11 x 8 In.	575.00
Trade Stimulator, Fairest Wheel, 14 x 22 In. *illus*	605.00
Trade Stimulator, Mills, 25 Cent, Puritan Bell, Key, 1926, 14 ½ x 9 ¼ In.	517.00
Trade Stimulator, Nickel Plated, Cast Iron, Elk Mills Novelty Co., 19 x 13 In.	3500.00
Trade Stimulator, Play Poker, Game Of Skill, 1930s	275.00
Trade Stimulator, Reel 21, Cast Aluminum, 1930s, 11 ½ x 11 In. *illus*	575.00
Trade Stimulator, Slot, American Eagle, 5 Cent, Key, 11 x 8 x 9 In.	250.00
Trade Stimulator, Spiral Penny, 20th Century Novelty Co., c.1906, 11 x 17 In. *illus*	1921.00
U.S. Marshall Target Game, 5 Cent, c.1960, 53 x 14 In.	300.00
Vending, Baseball, Cards, 2 Tiers, 1950s, 57 x 12 In.	830.00
Vending, Candy Bar, 1 Cent, Little Aristocrat, Rex American Candy Co., 1920, 16 x 13 In.	201.00
Vending, Chewing Gum, Colgan's Taffy Tolu, 1 Cent, National Vending, 1905	3600.00
Vending, Cigarette, 15 Cent, Advance Machine Co., 1930	517.00
Vending, Deluxe Hot Nuts, Challenger, Tropical Trading, 1947, 54 In.	316.00
Vending, Dixie Cup, Wall Dispenser, 1 Cent, Dixie Mfg., Decal, 1920, 32 ½ In.	402.00
Vending, Fresh Hot Nuts, 3 Sections, 5 Cent, Key, 22 x 16 ½ x 6 In.	440.00
Vending, Fresh Nuts, 3 Separate Containers, Metal Arcade, 14 x 21 In.	146.00
Vending, Hershey Chocolate, 5 Cent, Advance Machine Co., Key, 1920s, 33 ½ In.	632.00
Vending, Hershey's Candy Bar, 5 Cents, Brown, White, Dispenser, 18 x 9 In.	448.00
Vending, Jennings, Golf Ball, 25 Cent, 1937	5200.00
Vending, Peanut, Challenger, Tropical Trading, Keys, 1947, 21 ½ x 17 In.	460.00
Vending, Peanut, Columbus Vendor, Model A, 2 Barrel Locks, Key, 16 x 8 In.	345.00
Vending, Peanut, Master, Penny, Key, 16 x 6 In.	632.00
Vending, Peanuts, Smilin' Sam From Alabam, Painted, 13 ½ In.	550.00
Vending, Pepsin Gum, Chocolate, Peanuts, Key, 36 x 8 ¾ In.	2588.00
Vending, Perfume, Bull, Take The Bull By The Horn, Metal, Toronto, 5 x 5 In.	5925.00
Vending, Perfume, Bull's Head, Cast Iron, Continental Novelty Co., Buffalo, N.Y., c.1904	8500.00
Vending, Perfume, Whiffs Of Fragrance, Aluminum Casting, Cherubs, Garlands, 14 x 17 x 10 In.	9200.00
Vending, Roth's Pansy Gum, Fortune, Love Letter, Key, 1900s, 18 ½ x 6 In.	4887.00
Vending, Simpson Convertible Vendor, Cast Iron, Nickel Plated, c.1927, 13 In.	450.00
War Game Mermaid, Iron, Automatic Sports Co., c.1912, 24 x 76 In. *illus*	192500.00

COMIC ART, or cartoon art, is a relatively new field of collecting. Original art for comic strips, magazine covers, and even printed strips are collected. The first daily comic strip was printed in 1907. The paintings on celluloid used for movie cartoons are listed in this book under Animation Art.

Cover Art, Batman, No. 55, Dick Sprang, Mixed Media, Matt, Frame, c.1990, 22 x 27 In.	2875.00
Cover Art, Black Cat Mystic, No. 58, Jack Kirby, Joe Simon, 1956, 12 x 17 ½ In.	2390.00
Cover Art, Casper, The Friendly Ghost, Raindrops Keep Falling, No. 19, 1954, 7 x 10 In.	1195.00

Cover Art, Daredevil, Man Without Fear, F. Miller, K. Janson, Marvel, 1981, 12 x 17 14 In.	3227.00
Cover Art, Dick Tracy, Assume The Position, No. 101, Harvey, 1956, 11 x 11 In.	796.00
Cover Art, Dick Tracy, Traffic Stop, No. 108, Harvey, 1957, 12 x 11 In.	538.00
Cover Art, Ghostly Tales, No. 102, Charlton, 1973, 12 ½ x 18 ½ In.	2868.00
Cover Art, House Of Mystery, I Vampire, No. 315, 9 ¾ x 15 In.	1673.00
Cover Art, Richie Rich Millions, No. 6, Warren Kremer, 1963, 7 x 10 In.	335.00
Cover Art, Richie Rich Millions, No. 7, Warren Kremer, 7 x 10 In.	448.00
Cover Art, Richie Rich Millions, No. 9, Warren Kremer, 7 x 11 In.	2868.00
Cover Art, Richie Rich Millions, No. 24, Warren Kremer, 7 x 10 ¼ In.	837.00
Cover Art, Richie Rich, No. 57, Warren Kremer, 7 x 10 ½ In.	896.00
Cover Art, The Warlords, No. 31, Mike Grell, 1980, 10 x 15 In.	3107.00
Cover Art, Vampierlla, No. 2, Michael W. Kaluta, 1992, 16 x 21 In.	5676.00
Cover, All Star Squadron, No. 49, Mike Harris, Tony DeZuniga, 1985	478.00
Drawing, Bear On Tree Stump, Chopped Trees, C.K. Berryman, c.1932, 7 ½ x 5 ½ In. ...... illus	329.00
Drawing, Donald Duck, Long Billed, Orphan's Benefit, c.1934, 9 ½ x 12 In.	345.00
Drawing, Donald Duck, Self Control, Pencil, c.1938, 10 x 12 In.	316.00
Drawing, Horace Horsecollar, Camping Out, c.1934, 9 ½ x 12 In.	316.00
Drawing, Mickey & Minnie Mouse, 2-Gun Mickey, Color, 9 ½ x 12 In., 2 Piece	546.00
Drawing, Mickey Mouse, Fantasia, Sorcerer's Apprentice, 1940, 12 x 15 ½ In.	403.00
Panel, Uncle Scrooge, Carl Barks, Pen & Ink, No. 63, 4 Panel, 1966, Frame, 19 x 25 In.	5750.00
Strip, Sunday, Li'l Abner, Apr. 9 1950, 11 Panel Story, Al Capp, 19 ½ x 22 ½ In.	633.00
Strip, Sunday, Sears Roebuck & Co., Toyland, 1939, 13 x 10 ½ In.	338.00

COMMEMORATIVE items have been made to honor members of royalty and those of great national fame. World's Fairs and important historical events are also remembered with commemorative pieces. Related collectibles are listed in the Coronation and World's Fair categories.

Button, Confederate Reunion, Case Machine Co., Louisville, Ky., 1905, 1 ¾ In.	221.00
Button, Confederate Veterans Reunion, Little Rock, c.1928, 1 ¼ In.	115.00
Cup, Kentucky Derby, Glass, 1953	66.00
Cup, Young Prince Charles, Bone China, Marcus Adams, Paragon, c.1950, 3 x 2 ¾ In.	30.00
Flask, Society Of Illustrators, 20 Engraved Signatures, Sterling Silver, 1928, Qt.	425.00
Magazine, Sports Illustrated, Muhammad Ali, Joe Frazier, Signed, 1971, 8 ¼ x 11 In.	173.00
Pin, Amelia Earhart, Photo, Aviator's Helmet, 1st Lady To Cross Atlantic, c.1932, 1 ¼ In.	555.00
Pin, Great Lakes Steamship, Color, Yea, Photo, Billowing Smoke, c.1912, 1 ¾ In.	127.00
Plaque, Lusitania, Reverse On Glass, Blue, Black, Red, 9 x 9 In.	30.00
Plate, Admiral Dewey, Spanish American War, c.1899, 5 ½ In.	27.00
Plate, Remember The Maine, Burford, 9 In.	33.00
Plate, St. Augustine, Old City Gate, Blue Transfer, 8 ¾ In.	90.00
Plate, U.S. Maine, Multicolored, Transfer Print, Edwin Bennett Pottery, c.1898	110.00
Program, Olympics, Stockholm, Track & Field, Jim Thorpe, c.1912, 10 x 12 In., 16 Pages	115.00
Tile, State Sunday School Convention, Zanesville, American Encaustic, c.1915, 2 In.	130.00
Trivet, Kansas City Centennial 1850-1950, Cast Aluminum, Triangular, Handle, 9 ¼ In.	25.00

COMPACTS hold face powder. A woman did not powder her face in public until after World War I. By 1920, the beauty parlor, permanent waves, and cosmetics had become acceptable. A few companies sold cake face powder in a box with a mirror and a pad or puff. Soon the compact was designed by jewelers and made of gold, silver, and precious materials. Cosmetic companies began to sell powder in attractive compacts of less valuable metal or plastic. Collectors today search for Art Deco designs, commemorative compacts from World's Fairs or political events, and unusual examples. Many were made with companion lipsticks and other fittings.

18K Gold, Square, Allover Honeycomb Pattern, Italy, 3 In.	3538.00
Art Deco Style, Sterling Silver, Enamel, Green & Cream, Gold Rim, 2 ¼ In.	125.00
Birks Sterling, Sterling Silver, Carved Flowers, 2 ½ x 2 ½ In.	95.00
Boucheron, Silver, Gold Leaping Fish, Stylized Waves, Fitted Case, London, c.1930	1098.00
Cartier, Flowers, Emeralds, Sapphires, Rubies, Full Cut Diamond, Mirror, 18K Gold	2963.00
Cigarette Case, Faberge, 14K Yellow Gold, Sapphire, Early 1900s, 2 ½ x 3 ½ In. ...... illus	4388.00
Evans, Guilloche Enamel, White Ground, Rose, Leaves, Black Reverse, 1950s, 2 ¼ x 2 ¼ In.	78.00
Gold, Platinum, Peridot, Mirror, Puff, 14K, 2 x 2 ½ In.	1763.00
K&G Co., Dance, Goldtone, Basket Shape, Silvertone Wreath, Pearl, Mirror, Puff, 2 x 1 ½ In.	110.00
Kaycraft, Mother-Of-Pearl, Mirror, Powder, Lipstick, 4 ¼ x 3 ¼ In.	99.00
Lucretia Vanderbilt, Silver, Enamel, Butterfly, Good Luck Symbols, 2 x 3 In.	85.00
Minadiere, Attached Lipstick, 14K Yellow Gold, Victorian, Mark, 6 ½ In.	1650.00
Mother-Of-Pearl, Abalone, Checkerboard Design, Powder, Mirror, 2 ½ x 3 In.	125.00
Saks Fifth Avenue, Sterling Silver, Engraved Design, Monogram, Round, Puff, c.1940, 4 In.	59.00
Silver Gilt, Shaded Enamel, Couple Courting, Mirror, c.1900, 3 In.	590.00
Silver, Enameled Urn, Mauve, Round, c.1920, 2 In.	160.00

Comic Art, Drawing, Bear On Tree Stump, Chopped Trees, C.K. Berryman, c.1932, 7 ½ x 5 ½ In. $329.00

Compact, Cigarette Case, Faberge, 14K Yellow Gold, Sapphire, Early 1900s, 2 ½ x 3 ½ In. $4388.00

Compact, Sterling Silver, Scrolling, Gold Washed, Initials, 4 x 4 In. $92.00

TIP

To display your compacts and other small collectibles, make metal drapery-hook stands. Bend the hooks to look like little easels.

Consolidated, Lamp, Parrot,
Early 20th Century, 13 In.
$450.00

Consolidated, Vase, Ruba Rombic,
Green Opalescent, Reuben Haley,
R. Lalique Mark, 4 ½ x 6 In.
$600.00

TIP

*A small chip in a
glass goblet or vase
can be ground off by
a glass-repair expert,
but there is little
that can be done
for cracks.*

Silver, Melon Eaters, Glaze Enamel Painted Scene, Engraved, Inlaid, 3 ⅛ 3 ⅛ In.	230.00
Sterling Silver, Scrolling, Gold Washed, Initials, 4 x 4 In. ....*illus*	92.00
Stratton, Enamel, Painted Roses, Round, Pill Box, Rectangular, 1950s	110.00
Tortoiseshell Vanity, Mirror, Comb, Canted Corners, 4 ¾ x 3 ½ x 1 ¼ In.	365.00
Vanity Case, Chain, Mirror, Powder & Rouge Sections, Engraved, c.1914, 3 ½ x 2 ½ In.	130.00
Volupte, Hand Shape, Goldtone Metal, Burnished, Powder Puff, Mirror, 4 ½ In.	295.00
Whiting & Davis, Delysia, Vanity Bag, Silvertone Mesh, Flowers, Rouge, Powder, Mirror, 4 In.	855.00
Woman, Flowing Brown Hair, Floral Chasing, Silver, Enamel, Continental 800	440.00
Woven Design, 14K Gold, 8-Sided, Chain	1350.00

CONSOLIDATED LAMP AND GLASS COMPANY of Coraopolis, Pennsylvania, was founded in 1894. The company made lamps, tablewares, and art glass. Collectors are particularly interested in the wares made after 1925, including black satin glass, Cosmos (listed in its own category in this book), Martele (which resembled Lalique), Ruba Rombic (1928–32 Art Deco line), and colored glasswares. Some Consolidated pieces are very similar to those made by the Phoenix Glass Company. The colors are sometimes different. Consolidated made Martele glass in blue, crystal, green, pink, white, or custard glass with added fired-on color or a satin finish. The company closed for the final time in 1967.

Bowl, Catalonian, Green, 8 ½ In.	40.00
Bowl, Line 700, French Crystal, 12 In.	550.00
Bowl, Olives, French Crystal, c.1928, 8 In.	225.00
Bowl, Swallows, Green, 9 In.	295.00
Box, Lovebird, Clear, Green Wash, Cover, c.1925, 3 ¼ x 4 ⅞ x 8 ¾ In.	118.00
Candlestick, Catalonian, Green	35.00
Candlestick, Line 700, French Crystal, Pair	395.00
Creamer, Tri, Catalonian, Emerald Green	65.00
Jug, Tri, Catalonian, Emerald Green, 20 Oz., 6 ½ In.	150.00
Lamp, Bittersweet, Martele Line, Milk Glass, Orange Berries, Leaves, 1920s, 13 In.	225.00
Lamp, Kerosene, Custard Glass, Brass Openwork Base	375.00
Lamp, Parrot, Early 20th Century, 13 In. ....*illus*	450.00
Pitcher, Crisscross, Opalescent Cranberry, 9 In.	2013.00
Plate, Dancing Nymphs, White, 1928, 8 ¼ In.	165.00
Plate, Dinner, Line 700, French Crystal, 10 In.	250.00
Relish, Ruba Rombic, Divided, Smokey Topaz	875.00
Salt & Pepper, Shell Overlapping, Pink Cased, c.1894	110.00
Salt, Santa Maria, Columbus Ship, c.1938, 3 x 2 In.	15.00
Sugar, Catalonian, Jade Green	65.00
Sugar, Cover, Finial, Bulging Loop Design, Blue, c.1890, 5 ½ In.	115.00
Sugar Shaker, Cone, Opaque Green, Lid, c.1875, 5 ¼ In.	79.00
Sugar Shaker, Melligo, Amber, Lid, c.1875, 4 ¾ In.	79.00
Sugar Shaker, Melligo, Opaque White, Lid, c.1875, 4 ¾ In.	79.00
Syrup, Cosmos, White, Pink Stain, Multicolored Flowers, Lid, c.1900, 6 ¼ In.	118.00
Syrup, Cranberry, Crisscross, 6 In.	1668.00
Syrup, Cranberry, Guttate Pattern, 7 In.	259.00
Tumbler, Catalonian, Jade Green, Footed, 10 Oz.	48.00
Tumbler, Dancing Nymphs, Pink Satin, Footed, 5 ½ In.	265.00
Vase, Bulbous, Tan, Pink Dancing Nudes, Cream Ground, 12 In.	510.00
Vase, Bulbous, White Dancing Nudes, Blue Ground, 12 In.	450.00
Vase, Catalonian, Flared, Green, 5 ½ In.	45.00
Vase, Catalonian, Pinch, Emerald Green, Spanish Knobs, 6 In.	175.00
Vase, Catalonian, Spanish Knobs, Honey, 6 ½ In.	150.00
Vase, Catalonian, Sweet Pea, 4 ½ In.	165.00
Vase, Chrysanthemum, Clear, Purple Stain, c.1925, 12 ¼ In.	118.00
Vase, Fan, Catalonian, Pink, Spanish Knobs, 6 In.	165.00
Vase, Opaque White, Green, Brown, Globular, Frosted, c.1925, 6 ⅞ x 2 ½ In.	79.00
Vase, Pillow, Catalonian, Jade Green, 6 In.	110.00
Vase, Pinch, Catalonian, Honey, 4-Hole, 6 In.	285.00
Vase, Pine Cone, Blue Crystal Satin, c.1928, 6 ½ In.	350.00
Vase, Ruba Rombic, Green Opalescent, Reuben Haley, R. Lalique Mark, 4 ½ x 6 In. ......*illus*	600.00
Vase, Tri, Catalonian, Emerald Green, 4 In.	65.00

CONTEMPORARY GLASS, *see Glass-Contemporary.*

COOKBOOKS are collected for various reasons. Some are wanted for the recipes, some for investment, and some as examples of advertising. Cookbooks and recipe pamphlets are included in this category.

American Women's Bicentennial Cook Book, 1776-1976, 6 x 8 In.	20.00

C

Cookie Jar, Blackboard, Little Girl, American Bisque, Marked, ABC Block Label, 13 In.
$130.00

Cookie Jar, Elsie The Cow, Pottery Guild Of America, 1940s, 11 ½ In.
$267.00

Cookie Jar, Flintstones, Dino, Property Of Fred Flintstone, Marked USA, 13 In.
$189.00

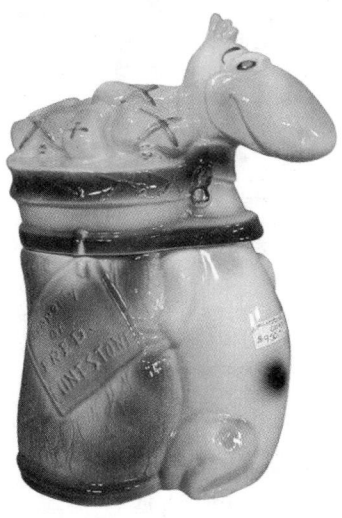

Cookie Jar, Humpty Dumpty, Red Brick, Regal, Marked 707, 12 In.
$130.00

Cookie Jar, Rocket Ship, Cookies Out Of This World, American Bisque, 1950s, 8 x 12 In.
$127.00

Cookie Jar, Yogi Bear, Better Than Average Cookies, American Bisque, 1960s, 13 ¼ In.
$259.00

Copeland, Figurine, Corinna, Seated, Scroll & Pen, Lyre, Signed, 1800s, 21 ¾ In.
$748.00

Copeland, Pitcher, Chicago, Blue & White, Historical Scenes, Parian, Frank E. Burley, 8 ¼ In.
$224.00

Copper, Bowl, Cover, Hammered, Applied Strap & Rivet Handle, Roycroft, 3 ½ x 5 In.
$201.00

Bon Appetit Appetizers, Hardcover, 1982, 120 Pages	10.00
Plate Of Toasts, By Edwin Osgood Grover, 64 Pages Of Toasts, Dated 1912, 5 ¾ x 4 ¾ In.	13.00
Tabasco Sauce, 1979, 37 Pages	13.00
The Art Of Cookery, Made Plain & Easy, By Hannah Glasse, London, 1774	395.00

COOKIE JARS with brightly painted designs or amusing figural shapes became popular in the mid-1930s. Many companies made them and collectors search for cookie jars either by design or by maker's name. Listed here are examples by the less common makers. Major factories are listed under their own names in other categories of the book, such as Abingdon, Brush, Hull, McCoy, Metlox, Red Wing, and Shawnee. See also the Disneyana category.

Aluminum, Textured, Black Plastic Cover, Kromex, 1960s, 8 x 7 In.	22.00
Aunt Jemima, Red Dress, F & F, 11 ½ In.	62.00 to 195.00
Barn, Red Roof, Marked, Regal, 9 In.	65.00
Big Bird, Seated, Holding Cookie Jar, Marked California Originals, 1977, 14 In.	55.00
Black Mammy, Marubonware, Painted, Basket Handle, Mark, Japan, 7 ¼ In.	695.00
Blackboard, Little Girl, American Bisque, Marked, ABC Block Label, 13 In. ....*illus*	130.00
Boy At Churn, Regal, 12 In.	58.00
Car, Convertible, Green, Beige Seats, Appleman, 1977, 16 In.	425.00
Car, Polka Dots, Red Bow, No. 131A, Marked, American Bisque, 12 In.	25.00
Cookie Clown, Derby Hat, Blue, Pink, Brown, American Bisque, 11 In.	150.00
Elsie The Cow, Pottery Guild Of America, 1940s, 11 ½ In. ....*illus*	267.00
Flintstones, Dino, Property Of Fred Flintstone, Marked USA, 13 In. ....*illus*	189.00
Flintstones, Fred Playing Golf, Dino Finial, Marked, Hanna-Barbera, 1962, 14 ½ In.	238.00
Flintstones, Rubbles, Barney In Doorway, Bird Finial, Painted, Marked, U.S.A., 9 ½ In.	95.00
Flintstones, Rubbles, House, Betty, Bird Handle, American Bisque, 10 In.	122.00
Free Parking For Cookies, Cardinal Co., 5 In.	48.00
Goldilocks, Mouse, Blue, Yellow, Red, Regal, 12 In.	118.00
Guard Shack, Guard In Doorway, Black, White, Blue, Yellow, No. 743, U.S.A., 11 In.	48.00
Hen, Chick Finial, Cream, Brown, Black, Apco, 7 ½ In.	32.00
Humpty Dumpty, Red Brick, Regal, Marked 707, 12 In. ....*illus*	130.00
Jack In The Box, American Bisque, 1950s	75.00
Lil' Miss Muffet, Flowers, Gold Trim, Incised, Regal China, 705, 11 In.	348.00
Mammy, Black, Red Dress, White Apron, Brayton Laguna, 13 In.	108.00
Mammy, Yellow, Brown, Green Polka Dot Apron, N.S. Co., 9 ½ In.	178.00 to 188.00
Pig, Pig Finial, Japan, 1979	20.00
Pig, Polka Dots, Red Bow, Marked, American Bisque, 13 In.	12.00
Puss-N-Boots, Fish On Hat, Tan Glaze, Regal, 9 ½ In.	88.00
Rocket Ship, Cookies Out Of This World, American Bisque, 1950s, 8 x 12 In. ....*illus*	127.00
Rooster, Gold Letters, Pottery Guild, 13 In.	47.00
Turquoise, Heavy Gold Stripes, Acme Craftware USA	55.00
Yogi Bear, Better Than Average Cookies, American Bisque, 1960s, 13 ¼ In. ....*illus*	259.00

COORS ware was made by the Coors Porcelain Company of Golden, Colorado, a company founded with the help of the Coors Brewing Company. Its founder, John Herold, started the Herold China and Pottery Company in 1910. The company name was changed in 1920, when Herold left. Dishes were made from the turn of the century. Coors stopped making nonessential wares at the start of World War II. After the war, the pottery made ovenware, teapots, vases, and a general line of pottery, but no dinnerware—except for special orders. The company is still in business making industrial porcelain. For more prices, go to kovels.com.

COORS U.S.A.

Plate, Dessert, Rosebud, Yellow, 7 ⅛ In.	12.00
Plate, Luncheon, Rosebud, Blue, 9 ¼ In.	32.00
Plate, Luncheon, Rosebud, Orange, 9 ¼ In.	32.00

COPELAND pieces listed here are those that have a mark including the word *Copeland* used between 1847 and 1976. Marks include *Copeland Spode* and *Copeland & Garrett*. See also Copeland Spode and Royal Worcester.

Bust, Queen Victoria, Marble Pedestal, Parian, W. Theed, 1874, 12 In.	350.00
Cake Plate, Blue Willow, Transfer, Gilt Rim, Round, Fluted Pedestal, c.1881, 6 ½ x 17 ½ In.	950.00
Figurine, Corinna, Seated, Scroll & Pen, Lyre, Signed, 1800s, 21 ¾ In. ....*illus*	748.00
Figurine, Napoleon, Parian, Seated In Defeat, W. Theed, c.1873, 12 In.	652.00
Pitcher, Chicago, Blue & White, Historical Scenes, Parian, Frank E. Burley, 8 ¼ In. ....*illus*	224.00
Plate, Little John Decoys Sheriff, Robin Hood Series, Blue & White Transfer, 9 ¼ In.	145.00
Plate, Shakespeare, Sir Andrew, Sir Toby, Clown, Blue & White Transfer, 10 ½ In.	185.00
Tile, Temple Of Diana At Ephesus, Green Transfer, Round, c.1900, 6 ¼ In.	90.00

COPELAND SPODE appears on some pieces of nineteenth-century English porcelain. Josiah Spode established a pottery at Stoke-on-Trent, England, in 1770. In 1833, the firm was purchased by William Copeland and Thomas Garrett and the mark was changed. In 1847, Copeland became the sole owner and the mark changed again. W.T. Copeland & Sons continued until a 1976 merger when it became Royal Worcester Spode. The company was bought by the Portmeirion Group in 2009. Pieces are listed in this book under the name that appears in the mark. Copeland Spode, Copeland, and Royal Worcester have separate listings.

Pitcher, Copeland Spode Tower, Blue & White, 19th Century, 10 In.	266.00
Plate, Crest In Cartouche, Flower Cartouche Border, Red Ground, 10 In., 12 Piece	207.00
Tureen, Underplate, Blue & White, Gilt Highlight Scroll Handles, 6 x 7 ½ In.	88.00

COPPER has been used to make utilitarian items, such as teakettles and cooking pans, since the days of the early American colonists. Copper became a popular metal with the Arts & Crafts makers of the early 1900s, and decorative pieces, like desk sets, were made. Other pieces of copper may be found in Arts & Crafts, Bradley & Hubbard, Kitchen, Roycroft, and other categories.

Ale Flagon, Repousse, Dutch, Marked, 1752	395.00
Basin, Cooking, Rolled Lip, Handles, France, Early 1900s, 14 x 17 In.	140.00
Bed Warmer, Birds, Pierced & Tooled, Turned Wood Handle, 46 ½ In.	110.00
Bed Warmer, Brass, Engraved, Maple Handle, 1850s, 43 In.	90.00
Bed Warmer, Eagle, Spread Wings, Brass, Turned Wood Handle, 1713, 40 In.	275.00
Bed Warmer, Wood Handle, 19th Century, 35 ½ x 10 ½ In.	117.00
Blotter, Hammered, Raised Diamond Form, AKW Monogram, 25 x 39 In.	45.00
Bowl, Cover, Hammered, Applied Strap & Rivet Handle, Roycroft, 3 ½ x 5 In. ....*illus*	201.00
Bowl, Gilded, Hammered, Flared, Flower Shape, 4 x 14 ¾ In.	1800.00
Bowl, Hammered, Ball Feet, J. Heichlinger, Germany, Marked, 10 x 3 In.	450.00
Bowl, Hammered, Flower Shape, Marie Zimmermann, Stamped, 7 ½ x 11 ¼ In.	2318.00
Bowl, Hammered, Patina, Kalo, 7 x 3 In.	270.00
Bowl, Petal, Black, Hand Beaten Base, Rebajes, 1960s, 3 x 4 ¼ In.	155.00
Bowl, Shaped Paneled Sides, Craftsman Studios, 5 x 8 In.	35.00
Box, Hammered, Round, Enamel Lid, Flowers, Signed, H.E. Potter, Cleveland, 3 ½ In.	2400.00
Box, Hinged, Wood Lining, Nekrassoff, 1940s, 5 ½ x 3 ½ In.	115.00
Box, Variegated Green & White Enamel, Wood Lining, Nekrassoff, c.1930, 5 ½ x 3 ½ In.	165.00
Bucket, Coal, Repousse Oval, Adjustable Handle, G. Stickley, Signed, 13 x 14 x 24 In.	6600.00
Bucket, Coal, Wrought Iron, Impressed Mark, G. Stickley, c.1905, 24 ⅞ In.	12500.00
Bucket, Handmade, Wrought Iron Handle, c.1880, 12 x 18 In.	94.00
Can, Hinged Cover, Oil Filler, Light House Style Form, Applied Handle, Spout, 5 ¾ x 8 ½ In. ...	88.00
Cauldron, Flared, Wrought Iron Handles, Continental, 12 ¼ x 19 ½ In.	240.00
Centerpiece, Hammered, Flower Shape, Frans Gyllenberg, 3 ½ x 10 ¼ In.	1952.00
Chafing Dish, Cover, Brass, Silver, Oak, 3 Hinged Burner, Pan, Liner, 11 ½ x 20 ½ In.	1830.00
Chafing Dish, Hammered, 4 Antler Feet, Handles On Lid, Round Oak Platform, c.1905, 11 ½ In.	1150.00
Chafing Dish, Stand, Hammered, Wood Base, Lid, Terra-Cotta Dish, Gustav Stickley, 16 x 14 In. *illus*	1800.00
Chamber Pot, Dovetailed, Flat Lip, Handle, Ireland, c.1800	250.00
Chamberstick, Bobeche, Gustav Stickley, Marked, 9 ½ x 7 In., Pair	960.00
Chamberstick, Hammered, Scenic Enamel Tile, Square Base, 5 ½ x 8 In.	633.00
Charger, Daffodils, Leaves, Hand Hammered, Arts & Crafts, 12 In.	219.00
Charger, Hammered, Rectangular, Benedict, 22 x 11 ½ In.	580.00
Charger, Leaf, Curled Stem, Triple Circle, Rebajes, c.1950, 16 In.	240.00
Charger, Pods, G. Stickley, 19 ½ In.	19520.00
Chocolate Pot, Acorn Finial, Joseph Heinrich, Paris, New York, 19th Century, 8 ¼ In.	70.00
Coffeepot, Cover, Hinged, Goose Neck, Side Spout, Applied Handle, Mushroom Finial, 12 In. .	110.00
Compote, Red & White, Footed, Nekrassoff, c.1940, 6 x 2 ¼ In.	87.00
Copper Luster items are listed in the Luster category.	
Dish, 3 Applied Wrought Iron Feet, Marked, Gustav Stickley, 4 x 9 In.	1440.00
Dish, Square, Enamel, Ball Feet, Green & White Interior, Nekrassoff, 6 x 3 ⅜ In.	125.00
Door Pull, Comedie Dell'Arte, Gio Ponti, c.1955, 9 x 5 In., Pair	717.00
Flagon, Hammered, Tooled Medallions, Handles, Footed, Patina, Mark, WMF, 10 x 9 In. .... *illus*	210.00
Foot Warmer, Hammered, Brass, Bail Ring Handle, Oval, 10 ¼ x 4 ⅛ In.	57.00
Glue Pot, Double Boiler, Brass Handle, Marked, Size 2 ½, 4 In.	55.00
Glue Pot, Double Boiler, Iron Handle, 6 In.	160.00
Humidor, Deer Antler Supports, Albert Berry Mark, c.1920, 4 x 14 In.	1528.00
Jardiniere, Hammered, Benedict, 9 ¾ x 14 ¼ In.	1342.00
Jardiniere, Hammered, Patina, Stickley Bros.	1464.00
Jardiniere, Pedestal, Hammered, Stickley Bros. 28 x 17 In.	2196.00
Jardiniere, Urn, Gadrooned, Satyr Mask Handles, Lion's Paw Feet, 11 x 15 In.	224.00
Kettle, Apple Butter, Dovetailed, Handles, 19 ½ In. Diam.	200.00

Copper, Chafing Dish, Stand, Hammered, Wood Base, Lid, Terra-Cotta Dish, Gustav Stickley, 16 x 14 In. $1800.00

Copper, Flagon, Hammered, Tooled Medallions, Handles, Footed, Patina, Mark, WMF, 10 x 9 In. $210.00

Copper, Kettle, Rolled Rim, Iron Swing Handle, Dovetailed, c.1850, 13 x 22 In. $644.00

Copper, Plaque, Embossed, Stylized Pods, Open Center, Gustav Stickley, 19 ¾ In. $18000.00

COPPER

Copper, Sculpture, Maple Leaf Branch, Signed, Curtis Jere, c.1972, 52 x 34 In. $120.00

Copper, Still, Spherical, Elongated Spout, Dovetailed, Riveted, 2 Sections, Stamped, 1700s, 35 In. $2530.00

Copper, Vase, Hammered, Applied Flowers, Birds, Mixed Metals, Scrolled Feet, Gorham, c.1883, 10 In. $2480.00

Copper, Watering Can, Elliptical, Tubular Handle, Early 1900s, 14 x 23 In. $420.00

Kettle, Apple Butter, Swing Handle, 19th Century, 18 x 27 ½ In.	170.00
Kettle, Apple Butter, Wrought Iron Swing Handle, c.1880, 16 ½ x 26 ½ In.	600.00
Kettle, Dovetailed, Iron Bail Handle, Lid, 17 x 26 In.	230.00
Kettle, Dovetailed, Swing Handle, Brass Finial, Stamped, Adam Wolf, 1800s, 11 In.	323.00
Kettle, Large Loop Handle, Stamped Harbeson 5, c.1800, 11 ¾ In.	1170.00
Kettle, Rolled Rim, Iron Swing Handle, Dovetailed, c.1850, 13 x 22 In. ....*illus*	644.00
Kettle, Sheet Iron Swing Handle, Dovetailed Shoulder, Bottom, 9 x 7 ½ In.	3335.00
Kettle, Swing Handle, Stamped MBM, 1800s, 6 ½ In.	411.00
Kettle, Swing Handle, Stamped McIntosh, c.1825, 7 In.	470.00
Mask, Pierced Face, Black Metal Stand, Sierra Leone, c.1950, 16 x 8 In.	2400.00
Mirror, Hanging, Hammered, Scottish Arts & Crafts, 21 x 28 ¾ In.	854.00
Molds are listed in the Kitchen category.	
Mug, Nautical Scenes Enamel, Gilt, 1800s, 5 In.	353.00
Mug, Strap Handle, Blue Enamel, Nekrassoff, 4 ⅛ x 3 ¾ In.	115.00
Pitcher, Hammered, Bronze Rabbit Handle, Stitched Silver Detail, 10 x 10 In.	2684.00
Plaque, Embossed, Stylized Pods, Open Center, Gustav Stickley, 19 ¾ In. ....*illus*	18000.00
Plaque, Hammered, Repousse Design, Round, Patina, Signed, G. Stickley No. 347, 23 In.	3900.00
Plate, Enamel, Multicolored, Drooly Swirls, Black, Blue Underside, G. Hildenbran, 8 ¼ In.	88.00
Plate, Enamel, Red, Drooling, Black, Blue Underside, Copper Bottom, G. Hildenbran, 11 In.	88.00
Plate, Hammered, 3 Sections, Arts & Crafts, 12 In.	11.00
Plate, Hammered, Patina, Benedict Studios, Marked, 12 In., 4 Piece	90.00
Pot, Apple Butter, 19 In.	177.00
Pot, Apple Butter, Handle, 25 In.	207.00
Pot, Bent Wire Handles, 10 x 28 In.	105.00
Salver, Repousse, Scalloped Rim, Medieval Sporting Scene, c.1800s, 18 In.	180.00
Sculpture, Bird, Bulbous Pink Breast, Arts & Crafts, France, Signed, 9 x 12 In., Pair	6275.00
Sculpture, Maple Leaf Branch, Signed, Curtis Jere, c.1972, 52 x 34 In. ....*illus*	120.00
Shoe, Pouring Spout, Soldered, Folded Rims, Applied Handle, 5 x 14 ¼ x 5 ½ In.	165.00
Spoon, Nut, Hammered, Patina, Jarvie, Marked, 2 ¾ x 9 ½ In.	210.00
Still, Spherical, Elongated Spout, Dovetailed, Riveted, 2 Sections, Stamped, 1700s, 35 In. ....*illus*	2530.00
Teakettle, Dovetail, Swing Handle, Gooseneck Spout, Brass Finial, 18th Century, 6 ½ In.	593.00
Teakettle, Gooseneck Spout, Shaped Handle Tabs, Swing Shaped Handle, Arched Lid, 11 In.	468.00
Teakettle, Gooseneck Spout, Swing Handle, Early 19th Century, 12 In.	220.00
Teakettle, Lid, Gooseneck Spout, Brass Handle, Knop, Dovetailed, 13 x 14 In.	147.00
Teakettle, Lid, Squat Form, Swing Handle, Dovetailed, c.1800, 13 In.	118.00
Teapot, Hinged Lid, Brass Gooseneck Spout, Finial, Wood Handle, Lighthouse Shape, 7 ½ In.	113.00
Teapot, Trivet, Oval, 4 Iron Feet, Upright Handle, 1800s, England, 8 x 10 In.	212.00
Teapot, Wood, Brass, Arts & Crafts, Signed, WMF, 7 ½ In.	48.00
Tray, Card, Tooled Organic Design, Patina, Round, Jarvie, 6 In.	960.00
Tray, Hammered, Impressed, Gustav Stickley, 12 x 18 In.	1680.00
Tray, Primitive Hunters, Prey, Incised Relief, Rectangular, Rhodesia	45.00
Tray, Tooled, Swans, Leaves, Patina, Square, Marked, Art Crafts Shop, 5 ¼ In.	150.00
Trough Light, Linolite, I.P. Frink, 5 x 48 x 6 ½ In.	83.00
Vase, Applied Brass, Bird & Flowers, Bulbous, Japan, 6 In.	173.00
Vase, Cloisonne, Blue, Copper Scene Inserts, Handles, Chinese, 12 In.	936.00
Vase, Conical, Hammered, Patina, Arts & Crafts, c.1910, 7 In.	295.00
Vase, Enamel, Colonial Man, Red Coat, Hat, Cane, Platinum Flowers, Leaves, Signed, Vile, 5 In.	230.00
Vase, Hammered, Applied Flowers, Birds, Mixed Metals, Scrolled Feet, Gorham, c.1883, 10 In. ..*illus*	2480.00
Vase, Hammered, Flared, Patina, G. Stickley, 6 ½ x 10 ½ In.	3600.00
Vase, Hammered, Flower Shape, Painted Patina, Marie Zimmermann, 6 ¼ x 16 ¼ In.	2806.00
Vase, Hammered, Shouldered, Applied Brass Eucalyptus Branch, Jauchen's, 10 In.	288.00
Vase, Ribbed, Parcel Gilt Hammered, Wiener Werkstatte, 11 ½ x 6 ½ In.	18300.00
Vase, Verdigris Patina, Flared, Marie Zimmermann, 9 ¾ x 10 In.	1586.00
Watering Can, Elliptical, Tubular Handle, Early 1900s, 14 x 23 In. ....*illus*	420.00
Weather Vane, Golfer, Full Body Figure With Clubs, Embossed Features, 1930s, 25 x 25 In.	1422.00

CORALENE glass was made by firing many small colored beads on the outside of glassware. It was made in many patterns in the United States and Europe in the 1880s. Reproductions are made today. Coralene-decorated Japanese pottery is listed in the Japanese Coralene category.

Bottle, Barber, Blue, Opalescent, White Seaweed Design, 7 x 4 In.	288.00
Dresser Bottle, Blue To White Satin, Stopper, 6 ½ In.	99.00
Tumbler, Leaf & Berry, Applied Gold Honey Amber, 4 ¾ In.	35.00
Vase, Blue Bird, Branches, Leaves, Tulip Cut Rim, 10 In.	250.00
Vase, Cherry Blossoms, Frosted White Ground, 9 In.	195.00
Vase, Seaweed, Cream & Yellow, Webb Glass Co., 1880s, 7 ½ In.	347.00

Vase, Seaweed, Shaded Pink To White, 1880s, 5 ¼ In.	27.00
Vase, Turquoise Satin, Bulbous, Flowers, Leaves, 8 In.	89.00

CORDEY CHINA COMPANY was founded by Boleslaw Cybis in 1942 in Trenton, New Jersey. The firm produced gift shop items. In 1969 it was acquired by the Lightron Corp. and operated as the Schiller Cordey Co., manufacturers of lamps. About 1950 Boleslaw Cybis began making Cybis porcelains, which are listed in their own category in this book.

Duck, Mallard, 14 In., Pair	495.00
Figurine, Gentleman, 11 In.	57.00
Vase, Rose, Bud, Leaves, 12 ¼ x 6 ½ In.	85.00

CORKSCREWS have been needed since the first bottle was sealed with a cork, probably in the seventeenth century. Today collectors search for the early, unusual patented examples or the figural corkscrews of recent years.

Bakelite, Mottled Brown & Tan, 3 ¾ x 5 In.	19.00
Bone, Bird Perched On Stump, Japan, 5 In.	177.00
Bone, Man, Open Mouth, Vampire Teeth, 4 Knobs, 8 In.	282.00
Boxwood, Marked, France, 9 ¼ In.	10.00
Double Handle, Wood, 7 In.	38.00
Fat Man, Bowler Hat, Chubby Body, Anri, 2 Piece	45.00
Golf Ball, Plastic, 4 ¼ In.	7.50
Horn Handle, 5 In.	35.00
Ivory Handle, Cast Iron Shank, 5 In.	225.00
Manneken Pis, Whimsical, Brass, 2 ½ In.	18.00
Maple, Germany, 1950s, 5 In.	16.00
New Orleans Souvenir, Jeweled, 4 In.	9.00
Silver Plated, Vivianna Torun Bulow-Hube, Dansk, 1980s, 8 ½ x 3 In.	125.00
Sterling Silver, Stag Point Handle, 6 ¾ In.	125.00
Turned Handle, Green, 4 x 3 ¾ In.	23.00

CORONATION souvenirs have been made since the 1800s. Pottery, glass, tin, silver, and paper objects with a picture of the monarchs and date have been sold at many coronations. The pieces that mention King Edward VIII, the king who was never crowned, are not rare; collectors should be sure to check values before buying. Related pieces are found in the Commemorative category.

Badge, King Edward VII & Queen Alexandra, Pinback, c.1902, 1 ¼ In.	87.00
Beaker, Czar Alexander III, Impressed Imperial 2 Headed Eagle, Ceramic, 1883, 4 In.	960.00
Beaker, King Edward VII, Queen Alexandra, c.1902, 4 ¼ In.	110.00
Cruet, Queen Elizabeth II, Amber, Numbered, June 2, 1955	125.00
Jug, King George V & Queen Mary, Green Transfer, c.1911	125.00
Jug, Queen Victoria, Gold Jubilee, Purple Transfer, 1887, 7 ½ In.	325.00
Pitcher, Queen Elizabeth, Westminster Abbey, June 2, 1953, Royal Doulton, 6 In.	92.00
Plate, King Edward VII, Lattice, c.1902, 8 ½ In.	125.00
Scarf, Czar Nicholas II, Linen, Stamped Edge, c.1896, 27 ¾ x 28 In.	2160.00
Tin, King Edward VIII, 12-Sided, 7 In.	55.00
Tin, King George V & Queen Mary, Barringer Wallis, Rectangular, c.1911	85.00
Tray, King George V & Queen Mary, Portraits, Floral Border, MZ Austria, 9 x 6 In.	182.00
Vase, Queen Mary, White, Portrait, Porcelain, 2 Handles, 2 In.	12.00

COSMOS is a pressed milk glass pattern with colored flowers made from 1894 to 1915 by the Consolidated Lamp and Glass Company. Tablewares and lamps were made in this pattern. A few pieces were also made of clear glass with painted decorations. Other glass patterns are listed under Consolidated Lamp and also in various glass categories. In later years, Cosmos was also made by the Westmoreland Glass Company.

Butter, 6 x 8 In.	70.00
Butter, Cover, Milk Glass, c.1890, 6 x 8 In. .... *illus*	70.00

COVERLETS were made of linen or wool during the nineteenth century. Most of the coverlets date from 1800 to the 1880s. There was a revival of hand weaving in the 1920s and new coverlets, especially geometric patterns, were made. The earliest coverlets were made on narrow looms, so two woven strips were joined together and a seam can be found. The weave structures of coverlets can include summer and winter, double weave, overshot, and others. Jacquard coverlets have elaborate pictorial patterns that are made on a special loom or with the use of a special attachment. Quilts are listed in this book in their own category.

Double Weave, Natural & Red Wool, Reads E Pluribus Unum, 1851, 95 x 82 In.	1035.00

Cosmos, Butter, Cover, Milk Glass, c.1890, 6 x 8 In.
$70.00

Coverlet, Jacquard, Blue, Green, Red, Cream, Inscribed Adam Wolf, Penn., c.1835, 95 x 77 In.
$527.00

Coverlet, Jacquard, Peafowl, Turkeys, Rust, Indigo, Wool, Cotton, Mid 1800s, 76 x 90 In.
$470.00

Coverlet, Jacquard, Red, Blue, Green, Inscribed Henry Oberly, Womelsdorf, Penn., c.1850, 74 x 90 In.
$439.00

C

Cowan Pottery, Figurine, Groundhog, Rowfant Club, Black Over Green Matte Glaze, Frank Wilcox, 9 ⅛ In.
$863.00

Cowan Pottery, Vase, Egyptian Blue, Footed, Impressed Mark, 8 ⅝ In.
$46.00

Cowan Pottery, Vase, Oriental Red, Impressed Mark, 4 ⅝ In.
$115.00

Cranberry Glass, Pitcher, Water, Tumblers, Opalescent Coin Spot, 9-In. Pitcher, 7 Piece
$325.00

Jacquard, Blue, Green, Red, Cream, Inscribed Adam Wolf, Penn., c.1835, 95 x 77 In. ....*illus*	527.00
Jacquard, Blue, White, Signed, Delhi, N.Y., 1837, 100 x 76 In.	1320.00
Jacquard, Double Weave, Center Seam, Navy Blue, Natural, Cotton, c.1864, 87 x 76 In.	294.00
Jacquard, Double Weave, Red Wool, Natural Cotton, Inscribed, Sybil Duncan, 89 x 75 In.	2040.00
Jacquard, Eagle Border, Blue, White, Sunburst & Lily, S. Day, Orleans, 1840, 92 x 77 In.	120.00
Jacquard, Floral & Geometrics, Fringe, Wiand, Allentown, 1843, 91 x 74 In.	231.00
Jacquard, Flower Blocks, Red, Green, Cream, Wool, Cotton, L. Metz, 1842, 88 x 105 In.	235.00
Jacquard, Flower Medallions, Stars, Eagles, Deer, Monkeys, Wool, Cotton, 1832, 77 x 90 In. ..	587.00
Jacquard, Flowers, Blue, White, Flower Border, 1821, 85 x 81 In.	189.00
Jacquard, Flowers, Blue, White, Flower Border, House Corners, Marked, 1844, 85 x 71 In.	620.00
Jacquard, Flowers, Eagle Border, Blue, Red, Black, Marked, Samuel Hicks, 95 x 67 In.	520.00
Jacquard, Flowers, Peacock Corner Blocks, Red, Blue, Green, c.1850, 94 x 77 In.	545.00
Jacquard, Made By Wm. Ney, Meyerstown, Lebanon Co., Pa, c.1850, 85 x 83 In.	176.00
Jacquard, Ovals, Flowers, Wool, Cotton, Red, Green, 2 Panels, J. Sherman, 1858, 74 x 84 In. .	294.00
Jacquard, Peafowl, Turkeys, Rust, Indigo, Wool, Cotton, Mid 1800s, 76 x 90 In. ....*illus*	470.00
Jacquard, Red, Blue, Green, Flowers, Bird, Wool, Cotton, 86 x 74 In.	162.00
Jacquard, Red, Blue, Green, Geometric, John Smith, Pennsylvania, Patent 1836, 92 x 81 In. .	588.00
Jacquard, Red, Blue, Green, Inscribed Henry Oberly, Womelsdorf, Penn., c.1850, 74 x 90 In. ...*illus*	439.00
Jacquard, Red, Blue, Green, Wool, Natural Cotton, Geometric, 80 x 102 In.	288.00
Jacquard, Red, Blue, White, Flowers, Geometric, Emanuel Meily, Lebanon, 1842, 95 x 84 In. .	385.00
Jacquard, Red, Tan & Green, Ohio In Corner, Wool & Cotton, 1846, 75 x 83 In.	350.00
Jacquard, Single Weave, Eagle, Bird, Flowers, Blue, Salmon, Beige, Fringe, G. Rottman, 77 x 62 In. .	495.00
Jacquard, Wool & Cotton, Red, White & Blue, Double Rose, Flower Field, 1850, 95 x 77 In. ...	363.00
Overshot, Governors Garden Pattern, Wool, Blue & Natural, Fringe, 1810, 95 x 66 In.	325.00
Overshot, Lover's Knot, Wool & Linen, Green, Mauve, Brown, 3 Panels, 1800s, 90 x 71 In.	259.00
Overshot, Snail Tail & Cat's Paw, Wool, Cotton, Blue, White, 3 Panels, Georgia, 1800s, 98 x 82 In.	115.00
Overshot, Wool, Linen, Woven Date, Initials, 2 Piece, c.1817, 72 x 91 In.	764.00
Shaker, Dark, Light Gray Squares, 3-Panel, Wool, 70 x 90 In.	235.00

COWAN POTTERY made art pottery and wares for florists. Guy Cowan made pottery in Rocky River, Ohio, a suburb of Cleveland, from 1913 to 1931. A stylized mark with the word *Cowan* was used on most pieces. A commercial, mass-produced line was marked *Lakeware*. Collectors today search for the Art Deco pieces by Guy Cowan, Viktor Schreckengost, Waylande Gregory, or Thelma Frazier Winter.

Bookends, Pouter Pigeon, October Crystalline Glaze, Gold, 4 ½ In.	1093.00
Figurine, Groundhog, Rowfant Club, Black Over Green Matte Glaze, Frank Wilcox, 9 ⅛ In. ....*illus*	863.00
Figurine, Repose, Half Draped Woman, Ivory Glaze, Impressed, 6 ½ In.	345.00
Lamp, Blue Green Swirl Design Ball, Marked, 21 ½ In.	260.00
Plate, Sea Plate, Undersea Flora, Fauna, Blue, White, Mother-Of-Pearl Glaze, 11 ¼ In.	518.00
Vase, Baluster Shape, Raised Mottled Oak Leaves, Acorns, Blue Delphinium Glaze, Marked.....	173.00
Vase, Delphinium, Marked, 7 In.	29.00
Vase, Egyptian Blue, Footed, Impressed Mark, 8 ⅝ In. ....*illus*	46.00
Vase, Informal Decoration, Maple Leaves, Yellow, Brown, c.1930, 6 In.	575.00
Vase, Oriental Red, Impressed Mark, 4 ⅝ In. ....*illus*	115.00

CRACKER JACK, the molasses-flavored popcorn mixture, was first made in 1896 in Chicago, Illinois. A prize was added to each box in 1912. Collectors search for the old boxes, toys, and advertising materials. Many of the toys are unmarked.

Mirror, Sailor Jack & Bingo, Rueckheim Bros. & Eckstein, Pocket, 2 ¾ In.	253.00
Postcard, Address & Message Space, Bears, Copyright 1907, 3 x 5 ½ In., Set Of 18................	638.00
Toy, Baseball Catcher, Standing Position, Yellow, Norsco, 1950s, 2 In.	14.00
Toy, Horse-Drawn Delivery Wagon, White Metal, 1900s, 1 ¾ In.	185.00
Toy, Toonerville Trolley, Tin Lithograph, Germany, 1 ¾ In.	200.00

CRACKLE GLASS was originally made by the Venetians, but most of the ware found today dates from the 1800s. The glass was heated, cooled, and refired so that many small lines appeared inside the glass. It was made in many factories in the United States and Europe.

Basket, Green, Kanawha, 4 x 4 x 3 In.	25.00
Candy Jar, Iridescent Body, Smokey Blue Finial Top & Base, 8 ¼ x 4 In.	70.00
Pitcher, Applied Coil Cranberry Snake, Gold Enamel, 1896, 12 ½ In.	695.00

CRANBERRY GLASS is an almost transparent yellow-red glass. It resembles the color of cranberry juice. The glass has been made in Europe and America since the Civil War. It is still being made, and reproductions can fool the unwary. Related glass items may be listed in other categories, such as Northwood, Rubina Verde, etc.

Bowl, Fluted Rim, Signed, 9 x 14 ½ In.	120.00

C

Bowl, Hobnail, Scalloped Rim, Hobbs, Brockunier, 10 In.	75.00
Bowl, Oval, Folded Out & Flattened Rim, c.1900, 17 x 12 In.	148.00
Bowl, Straight-Sided, Ruffled Custard Glass Rim, c.1880, 3 ¾ x 10 In.	177.00
Box, Hinged Lid, Flowers, Enamel, 3 ½ In.	125.00
Carafe, White & Blue Enamel Flowers, Flared Flattened Rim, c.1875, 7 In.	106.00
Decanter, Cut Panels, 12 ¾ In.	275.00
Decanter, Frosted, Gilt, 10 In.	105.00
Dish, Rectangular, Rounded Ruffled Corners, Enamel Ribbon, Flowers, 10 x 7 In.	177.00
Epergne, 4-Trumpet Vases, Brass Center Mount, Round, Scalloped Base, 19 x 10 In.	546.00
Jar, Inverted Thumbprint Flower Pattern, Lid, Silver Plated Collar, Bail Handle, 5 In.	316.00
Jewelry Box, White Enamel Flowers, Round, 4 ¾ In.	175.00
Lamp, Hobnail, Prisms, Brass Base, Victorian, 13 In.	100.00
Lamp, Kerosene, Opalescent Swirl, Sheldon Font, 6 In.	250.00
Lamp, Luster Prisms, c.1910, 13 In., Pair	468.00
Lampshade, Blown, Etched Decoration, Brass Wall Mount, 20th Century, 12 In., Pair	115.00
Lampshade, Light, Hobnail, 8 ½ x 9 In.	100.00
Pitcher, Claret, Clear Handle, Foot, Stopper, c.1870, 15 In.	82.00
Pitcher, Opalescent Hobnail, 5 ½ In.	56.00
Pitcher, Scalloped, Applied Loop Handle, Cylindrical, 9 ¼ In.	99.00
Pitcher, Shaded To Clear, Etched Fern & Heron, Clear Reeded Handle, 9 ½ In.	295.00
Pitcher, Stripe, Ring Neck, Opalescent, Handle, c.1900, 9 ¼ In.	554.00
Pitcher, Tumbler, Enamel Flowers, Ruffled Edge, c.1870, 10 In., 7 Piece	263.00
Pitcher, Tumbler, Inverted Thumbprint, Clear Handle, Fluted Rim, 9 & 4 In., 7 Piece	105.00
Pitcher, Vertical Stripes, Ruffled Rim, Applied Handle, Opalescent, 9 In.	518.00
Pitcher, Water, Diamond Quilted, Ruffled Rim, 9 In.	44.00
Pitcher, Water, Tumblers, Opalescent Coin Spot, 9-In. Pitcher, 7 Piece ....*illus*	325.00
Punch Bowl, Inverted Raindrop, Amber Shaded, Enamel Flowers, 14 x 9 In.	502.00
Sconce, Purple, Clear, Flared Rims, Textured, Engraved, Barbini, 14 x 6 ¾ x 9 In., Pair	330.00
Sugar Shaker, Ribbed Opal Lattice, Lid, c.1875, 4 ¾ In.	264.00
Syrup, Lid, Clear Applied Handle, 6 ½ In. ....*illus*	489.00
Syrup, Metal Lid, Coin Spot, Applied Handle, Opalescent, Northwood Glass, 6 In.	1035.00
Syrup, Reverse Swirl, Clear Handle, Lid, c.1875, 6 ¾ In.	463.00
Syrup, Squat, Clear Handle, Lid, c.1900, 3 ½ In.	171.00
Syrup, Swirl, Lid, c.1875, 6 ¼ In.	357.00
Syrup, Waisted, Rib Optic, Gilt, Clear Handle, c.1900, 7 In.	185.00
Tumbler, Coin Spot, Opalescent, 1890s	65.00
Tumbler, Windows Swirl, Opalescent, Hobbs, Brockunier & Co., c.1875, 3 ¾ In.	330.00
Vase, Coin Spot, Ruffled Rim, Mid 20th Century, 6 In.	47.00
Vase, Fluted, Scalloped Rim, Clear Stem, Base, Victorian, 12 In.	234.00
Vase, Lily Form, Applied Rigaree Vine & Petals, Clear Foot, 10 ½ In.	207.00
Vase, Opalescent, Hobnail, Ruffled Rim, 7 ½ x 9 In.	71.00
Vase, Swirl, 8 x 6 In.	33.00
Vase, Thorn, Branching, Clear Feet, 6 ½ In.	160.00
Vase, Thumbprint, Ruffled & Ribbed Rim, c.1875, 8 In.	22.00
Vase, White Overlay, Painted Multicolored Flowers, Fired Gold Highlights, 8 In.	70.00
Water Set, Pink Enameled Iris, Applied Handle, 3 Tumblers, 12-In. Pitcher	155.00

CREAMWARE, or queensware, was developed by Josiah Wedgwood about 1765. It is a cream-colored earthenware that has been copied by many factories. Similar wares may be listed under Pearlware and Wedgwood.

Bowl, Lady Washington, Sailor's Farewell, Sailor's Return, Black Transfer, c.1786, 11 ¾ In.	8775.00
Cup & Saucer, Portrait, Man & Woman, Initials KV & NL, Early 1800s, 2 ¼ In. ....*illus*	761.00
Flask, Lead Glaze, Round, Impressed Birds, Green, Brown Glazes, Staffordshire, 1700s, 5 In.	178.00
Inkstand, Enameled Band Of Grapes, Sawtooth Band, Pierced Lid, Plinth Base, 4 In.	403.00
Jelly Mold Core, Cover, Octagonal, Enameled Fruit, Flowers, Pierced Stand, 13 In.	5629.00
Jelly Mold Core, Dome Shape, Fluted Sides, Enameled Fruit, Flowers, Staffordshire, 8 In.	770.00
Mug, Flower, Bud, Leaf, Straight-Sided, Applied Loop Handle, Child's, 2 ½ In.	113.00
Pitcher, American Ship, Putting Off, Oval Reserve, United States Seal, 5 ¾ In.	1541.00
Pitcher, Double Strap Handle, Mounts, Beaded Borders, Iron Red, Blue Flowers, c.1790, 8 In.	288.00
Pitcher, Portrait, General Jacob Brown, Niagara, 5 ¼ In.	2100.00
Plate, Blue & White, Feather Edge, England, 18th Century	325.00
Plate, Cottage, Tree, Landscape, Octagonal, Soft Paste, 8 ¾ In.	275.00
Plate, John Turne, Overglaze Enamel, Biblical Scene, Mid 1700s, 10 In.	270.00
Plate, Lead Glazed, Scalloped, Gray, Yellow, Green, Staffordshire, c.1750, 9 In.	119.00

Cranberry Glass, Syrup, Lid,
Clear Applied Handle, 6 ½ In.
$489.00

Creamware, Cup & Saucer, Portrait,
Man & Woman, Initials KV & NL,
Early 1800s, 2 ¼ In.
$761.00

Crown Derby, Vase, Cover, Aesthetic,
Ruby Ground, Birds, Flowers, Handles,
c.1886, 13 x 4 ⅜ In.
$840.00

Crown Milano, Vase, Swirled,
Quad-Ra-Fold Rim, Paper Label, 6 ½ In.
$978.00

As always, the edited listings in *Kovels'*
Antiques & Collectibles Price Guide
2011 aren't available on any website,
but readers should visit Kovels.com for
information on trends, tips, reproductions,
marks, old prices, and more!

Cruet, Art Glass, Green, Coralene Overlay, Stopper, 7 In. $150.00

Cruet, Cobalt Blue Glass, 16 Rib, Applied Hollow Handle, Stopper, Pittsburgh, 8 ½ In. $1872.00

Cruet, Glass Set, 4 Bottles, Silver Plate, Scroll Handle, Deykin & Harris, Edwardian, 5 x 5 ½ In., 4 Piece $300.00

Cup Plate, Amethyst, Rope Rim, c.1845, 3 In. $1725.00

Sugar & Creamer, Profile Of Columbia & Eagle Shield, Green Bands, Castleton	230.00
Tankard, Commodore Decatur, 19th Century, 5 ¾ In.	2252.00
Teapot, Cover, Doubled Handle, Black Transfer, Multicolored Design, c.1785, 4 ½ In.	237.00
Teapot, Cover, Entwined Handle, Flowers, Aurora, Chariot, Sun, Staffordshire, c.1775, 6 In.	2252.00
Teapot, Cover, Melon Design, Crabstock Handle, Spout, Green, Yellow Stripes, Staffordshire, 3 In.	5925.00
Teapot, Cover, Multicolored, Flowers, Leaf Molded Handle, Spout, Staffordshire, c.1770, 5 In.	296.00
Teapot, Cover, Tortoiseshell Glaze, Bird Finial, Applied Grapevines, Paw Feet, 1700s, 4 In.	504.00

CROWN DERBY is the name given to porcelain made in Derby, England, from the 1770s to 1935. Pieces are marked with a crown and the letter *D* or the word *Derby*. The earliest pieces were made by the original Derby factory, while later pieces were made by the King Street Partnerships (1848–1935) or the Derby Crown Porcelain Co. (1876–90). Derby Crown Porcelain Co. became Royal Crown Derby Co. Ltd. in 1890. It is now part of Royal Doulton Tableware Ltd.

Bowl, Cartouche Shape, Scalloped Borders, Asian Landscape, c.1830, 12 In., Pair	690.00
Lamp, Urn Shape, Landscape Panel, Near Edinburgh, Snake Handles, Gilt Scrolls, 15 In.	178.00
Vase, Bulbous, Long Neck, Goffered Rim, Gilded, Oriental Flowers, c.1886, 6 x 3 In.	270.00
Vase, Cover, Aesthetic, Ruby Ground, Birds, Flowers, Handles, c.1886, 13 x 4 ⅜ In. .... *illus*	840.00
Vase, Garniture, Oriental Flowers, Ringed Neck, Gilded, 1889, 7 ½ x 4 ¼ In., Pair	900.00

CROWN DUCAL is the name used on some pieces of porcelain made by A.G. Richardson and Co., Ltd., of Tunstall and Cobridge, England. The name has been used since 1916.

Plate, Dragon Design, Green, Yellow, Red, Charlotte Rhead, Mark, 13 In.	120.00
Plate, Tulip, Freesia, Enamel, Yellow Ground, 12 Piece	250.00
Tea For 2 Set, Ascot, 1930s, 8 Piece	244.00

CROWN MILANO glass was made by the Mt. Washington Glass Works about 1890. It had a plain biscuit color with a satin finish. It was decorated with flowers and often had large gold scrolls.

Biscuit Jar, Cover, Bale, Peach, Gold Oak Leaf, Acorn, Cream, Melon Ribbed, 5 In.	1035.00
Biscuit Jar, Enameled Acorns, Leaves, Orange, Yellow, Satin Glass, 5 ½ x 7 ½ In.	201.00
Biscuit Jar, Green Ground, Flower, Leaves, Multicolored, Signed, 6 x 6 ½ In.	575.00
Breakfast Set, Flowering Orchid Cactus, Syrup & Jam Jar, Lids, 5 ⅝ In., 4 In., 2 Piece	690.00
Dish, Sweetmeat, Fiddlehead Ferns, Raised, Gold, Butterfly Finial, Lid, 5 ¼ In.	575.00
Ewer, Gold Mums, Cream, Oval, Rope Twist Handle, 10 In.	2530.00
Jardiniere, Oak Leaves, Cream Ground, Oval, Marked, Mt. Washington, 9 In.	633.00
Lamp Base, Kerosene Style Base, Birds In Flight, Gold Sun, Stars, Bulbous, 11 In.	460.00
Lamp, Ducks, Flying, Gold Scrolling Rim, Foot, Reeded Handles, Cylindrical, 12 ½ In.	3680.00
Pitcher, Flat, Woman Under Tree, Dog, Blue, White, Wreath, Coiled Handle, 8 x 9 ½ In.	863.00
Syrup, Wild Rose, Silver Spout, Bulbous Ovals, 3 ¾ In.	715.00
Vase, Blue Ground, Flowers, Scrolled, Cut Gold Handles, Signed, 9 ½ In.	3910.00
Vase, Bulbous, Ruffled Rim, Swirled, Flowers, Yellow, Pink, Blue, Signed, 7 In.	431.00
Vase, Goldfish, Trumpeted Neck, Coralline, Seaweed & Shells, Enamel, 10 ½ In.	6900.00
Vase, Melon Ribs, 3-Fold Rim, Yellow, Leaves, Acorns, 9 In.	2013.00
Vase, Stick, Flower Medallion, Gold Lattice Neck, Foot, Opal Gloss, 6 In.	2300.00
Vase, Swirled, Quad-Ra-Fold Rim, Paper Label, 6 ½ In. .... *illus*	978.00
Vase, Thistles, Geometric Border, Applied Glass Handles, Gold Trim, 14 In.	1553.00

CROWN TUSCAN *pattern is included in the Cambridge glass category.*

CRUETS of glass or porcelain were made to hold vinegar, oil, and other condiments. They were especially popular during Victorian times and have been made in a variety of styles since the eighteenth century. Additional cruets may be found in the Castor Set category and also in various glass categories.

Art Glass, Green, Coralene Overlay, Stopper, 7 In. .... *illus*	150.00
Cobalt Blue Glass, 16 Rib, Applied Hollow Handle, Stopper, Pittsburgh, 8 ½ In. .... *illus*	1872.00
Glass Set, 4 Bottles, Silver Plate, Scroll Handle, Deykin & Harris, Edwardian, 5 x 5 ½ In., 4 Piece *illus*	300.00
Glass Set, Cut Glass, 4 Bottles, Silver Mounts, Gadroon Border, Claw Feet, George III, c.1815	1035.00
Glass, Double, Silver Plate Overlay, Scrollwork, Spread Foot, 8 In.	71.00
Pottery, Impromptu, Bridal White, Oil & Vinegar, Iroquois, Ben Diebel, 6 ½ In.	50.00
Pressed Glass, Diamond Ridge, Stopper, Clear, Duncan & Sons, c.1901, 5 ¼ In.	29.00
Pressed Glass, Feather, Stopper, c.1896	65.00

CT GERMANY was first part of a mark used by a company in Altwasser, Germany, in 1845. The initials stand for C. Tielsch, a partner in the firm. The Hutschenreuther firm took over the company in 1918 and continued to use the *CT*.

Bowl, Flowers, Light Green, Handles, 13 ½ In.	210.00
Coffeepot, Flowers, Handle, Gold	1295.00

CUP PLATES are small glass or china plates that held the cup while a diner of the mid-nineteenth century drank coffee or tea from the saucer. The most famous cup plates were made of glass at the Boston and Sandwich factory located in Sandwich, Massachusetts. There have been many new glass cup plates made in recent years for sale to gift shops or collectors of limited editions. These are similar to the old plates but can be recognized as new.

2 Hearts, Pierced By Arrow, Light Blue, Scalloped Edge, 3 ⅜ In.	15.00
Amethyst, Rope Rim, c.1845, 3 In. ....*illus*	1725.00
Bilton's, English Town Scene, Gold Accents, England, 6 ½ In.	20.00
Castle Garden Battery, Wood, c.1825, 3 ⅝ In.	250.00
Egg In The Sand, Pressed Glass, 3 ⁷⁄₁₆ In.	16.00
Fleur-De-Lis, Eagle, Flowers, Scalloped Edge, 3 ⅜ In.	40.00
Ironstone, White, 10-Sided, Molded Edge, J Wedgwood China, 1842, 4 ⅛ In.	50.00
Mount Repose, Bisland, 1824, 3 ⁷⁄₁₆ In.	16.00
Napoleon Bust Center, Scalloped Edge, 3 ⁵⁄₁₆ In.	275.00
Olive Green, 8 Serrated Scallops, c.1845, 3 ½ In. ....*illus*	115.00
Rope Rim, c.1850, 3 In. ....*illus*	104.00
Royal Copenhagen, Frigate Julen 1864, 5 In.	15.00
Staffordshire, English Garden Scene, Flower Border, Transferware, 1850s	40.00
Staffordshire, Figures In Boat, Blue & White, Podmore, Walker & Co., 4 In.	109.00
Staffordshire, Flowers, Red, Blue, Green, Embossed, 1800s, 4 ⅛ In.	55.00

CURRIER & IVES made the famous American lithographs marked with their name from 1857 to 1907. The mark used on the print included the street address in New York City, and it is possible to date the year of the original issue from this information. Earlier prints were made by N. Currier and use that name from 1835 to 1847. Many reprints of the Currier or Currier & Ives prints have been made. Some collectors buy the insurance calendars that were based on the old prints. The words *large, small,* or *medium folio* refer to size. The original print sizes were very small (up to about 7 x 9 in.), small (8.8 x 12.8 in.), medium (9 x 14 in. to 14 x 20 in.), and large (larger than 14 x 20 in.). Other sizes are probably later copies. Other prints by Currier & Ives may be listed in the Card category under Advertising and in the Sheet Music category. Currier & Ives dinnerware patterns may be found in the Adams or Dinnerware categories.

American Choice Fruits, Lithograph, Hand Colored, Frame, c.1869, 17 x 24 In.	1680.00
American Farmyard, Evening, Colored, Curly Maple Frame, c.1850, 24 ¾ x 31 ¾ In.	2233.00
Battle Of Pittsburg, Stone Lithograph, Frame	400.00
Celebrated Mare Flora Temple, Lithograph, Frame, c.1860, 17 x 23 In.	705.00
City Of Chicago, Lithograph, c.1892, 22 ½ x 32 ⅜ In.	3738.00
City Of New York, Hand Colored, 58 Keyed Landmarks, Frame, 1884, 28 x 40 In.	7703.00
City Of New York, Lithograph, c.1856, 20 x 29 In.	1840.00
Crack Trotter, Coming Around, Little Off, Lithograph, c.1880, 13 x 16 ½ In., Pair	411.00
Darktown Bicycle Race, A Sudden Halt, Frame, 11 ½ x 15 ½ In.	395.00
Darktown Sports, A Grand Spurt, Frame, 1885, 11 ½ x 15 ½ In.	550.00
Famous Trotter Majolica, Colored Lithograph, Frame, c.1884, 25 x 33 In. ....*illus*	470.00
Fruit & Flowers, Lithograph, Frances F. Palmer, Maple Frame, 1863, 11 x 15 In.	705.00
Home On The Mississippi, Lithograph, Frame, 10 ⅛ x 14 In.	470.00
Hyde Park, Hand Colored, Frame, 16 x 19 In.	150.00
Jockey's Dream, Stable Scene, Lithograph, Frame, 12 ¾ x 15 In.	294.00
Kentucky Cavalry At Buena Vista, Lithograph, Hand Colored, N. Currier, Frame, c.1847, 10 x 14 In.	176.00
Last Ditch Of The Chivalry Or President In Petticoats, Frame, 13 x 17 ¹⁵⁄₁₆ In.	235.00
Last Shot, Lithograph, Frame, c.1950, 24 ¼ x 34 ½ In. ....*illus*	764.00
Lexington, Great Monarch Of The Turf & Sire Of Racers, Lithograph, 13 x 15 ½ In.	764.00
Liberty Enlightening The World, 30 ½ x 25 ½ In.	700.00
Life Of A Fireman, Frame, 19th Century, 17 x 26 In.	113.00
Life Of A Fireman, Oak Frame, 29 x 37 In.	950.00
Loss Of U.S.M. Steamship Arctic, Frame, 13 x 9 In.	190.00
Majr Genl William S. Rosecrans, Lithograph, Frame, c.1863, 14 x 9 ½ In. ....*illus*	353.00
May Morning, American Country Life, Lithograph, N. Currier, Frame, 27 x 33 In.	1058.00
Midnight Race On The Mississippi, 1860, 18 ½ x 27 In.	3840.00

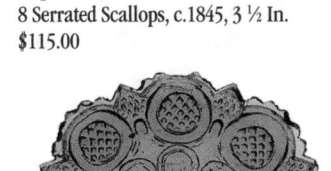

Cup Plate, Olive Green, 8 Serrated Scallops, c.1845, 3 ½ In.
$115.00

Cup Plate, Rope Rim, c.1850, 3 In.
$104.00

Currier & Ives, Famous Trotter Majolica, Colored Lithograph, Frame, c.1884, 25 x 33 In.
$470.00

Currier & Ives, Last Shot, Lithograph, Frame, c.1950, 24 ¼ x 34 ½ In.
$764.00

Currier & Ives,
Majr Genl William S. Rosecrans,
Lithograph, Frame, c.1863, 14 x 9 ½ In.
$353.00

Currier & Ives,
Trotting Gelding Frank With J.O. Nay,
No. 6174, c.1884, 30 x 19 In.
$529.00

Custard Glass, Berry Bowl, Master,
Chrysanthemum Sprig, Opaque Blue,
Blue Stain, Gilt, 5 x 10 ½ In.
$127.00

Cut Glass, Biscuit Jar, Brilliant Cut,
Sterling Lid, Repousse, Leaf Border,
Redlich & Co., 7 x 6 In.
$293.00

Midnight Race On The Mississippi, Natchez, Eclipse, 1860, 22 x 30 In.	3437.00
Mill-Stream, Lithograph, Gilt Frame, 14 x 17 ¾ In.	204.00
New York Yacht Club Regatta, Hand Colored, Frame, 1869, 24 x 34 In.	10073.00
Preparing For Market, Child & Toy, Lithograph, N. Currier, Frame, 24 x 31 In.	1410.00
Presidents Of The United States, Zachary Taylor, People's Choice, 12th President	179.00
Scoring, Coming Up For The Word, Lithograph, Frame, 24 x 32 ¼ In.	1410.00
Star Spangled Banner, Hand Colored, 16 x 12 In.	296.00
Summer Evening, American Country Life, N. Currier, Frame, 21 x 27 In.	1410.00
Tom Bowling, Horse Race, Lithograph, Signed, Frame, 13 ½ x 17 ½ In.	294.00
Trotting Cracks On The Snow, Lithograph, Frame, 18 ⅞ x 31 ½ In.	2585.00
Trotting Gelding Frank With J.O. Nay, No. 6174, c.1884, 30 x 19 In. ....*illus*	529.00
Trotting On The Road, Swill Against Swell, Lithograph, Frame, c.1873, 10 ¼ x 14 In.	529.00
U.S. Steam Frigate, Niagara, Frame, 9 ½ x 13 ½ In.	260.00

CUSTARD GLASS is a slightly yellow opaque glass. It was made in England in the 1880s and was first made in the United States in the 1890s. It has been reproduced. Additional pieces may be found in the Cambridge, Fenton, Heisey, and Northwood categories. Custard glass is called *Ivorina Verde* by Heisey and other companies.

Berry Bowl, Master, Chrysanthemum Sprig, Opaque Blue, Blue Stain, Gilt, 5 x 10 ½ In. ......*illus*	127.00
Decanter, Matching Stopper, Pinched Sides, 8 ½ In.	30.00
Maize is its own category in this book.	
Preserve Jar, Hobnail, White, Blue Footed, Cover, Bail Handle, 19th Century, 5 In.	47.00
Vase, Enameled Flowers, Amber Handles, 19th Century, 8 In.	94.00

CUT GLASS has been made since ancient times, but the large majority of the pieces now for sale date from the American brilliant period of glass design, 1880 to 1905. These pieces have elaborate geometric designs with a deep miter cut. Modern cut glass with a similar appearance is being made in England, Ireland, Poland, and the Czech and Slovak republics. Chips and scratches are often difficult to notice but lower the value dramatically. A signature on the glass adds significantly to the value. Other cut glass pieces are listed under factory names, like Hawkes, Libbey, and Sinclaire.

Basket, Flowers, Applied Twisted Handle, c.1900, 16 ¾ In.	147.00
Basket, Hobstar, Prism & Star Burst, Double Notched Handle, Ray Base, 13 x 9 ½ In.	400.00
Basket, Sterling Handle, Hobstar Center, Reticulated Sterling Rim, 4 In.	30.00
Berry Bowl, Ellsmere Pattern, Silver Rim, Black, Starr & Frost, American Brilliant, 4 x 11 In.	540.00
Berry Bowl, Emerald Pattern, Maple City Glass Co., American Brilliant, c.1925, 8 In.	240.00
Berry Bowl, Hobstar & Harvard Cross, American Brilliant, Quaker City, c.1905, 9 In.	120.00
Berry Bowl, King George Pattern, Sawtooth Rim, Hobstars, Nailheads, Fry, c.1910, 3 x 8 In. .	360.00
Biscuit Jar, Brilliant Cut, Sterling Lid, Repousse, Leaf Border, Redlich & Co., 7 x 6 In. ...*illus*	293.00
Biscuit Jar, Cranberry, Diamond & Fan, Metal Lid, 5 ½ x 6 ½ In.	288.00
Bonbon, Hobstar, Fan & Prism, Loop Handle, 3 Sections, 10 x 6 In.	1595.00
Bottle, Spirit, Square, White Brass Cap, Cork Stopper, Holland, c.1825, 7 ½ In., Pair	180.00
Bowl, 4-Sided, Strawberries, Diamonds, 7 x 2 ½ In.	29.00
Bowl, Banana Shape, Hobstar Cluster, 4 ½ x 11 ½ In.	50.00
Bowl, Bowler Hat Shape, 2 ½ x 7 In.	395.00
Bowl, Centerpiece, Navette Form, Square, Lozenge Shape Foot, 8 ½ x 8 x 13 ½ In.	720.00
Bowl, Circular Pinwheel, Tusk, Cane, 8 In.	150.00
Bowl, Cover, Hobstar, Strawberry Diamond & Fan, 2 Handles, American Brilliant, 8 In.	75.00
Bowl, Crested Bird Shape, Stem, Red Stand, Parcel Gilt, Engraved, Germany, c.1925, 10 x 11 In.	4320.00
Bowl, Diamond & Crosshatch Buttons, c.1900, 9 In.	324.00
Bowl, Expanding Star, American Brilliant, 3 ½ x 8 In.	90.00
Bowl, Fruit, Harvard Pattern, Graduated, Round, J. Hoare, c.1895, 4 x 11 ½ In.	240.00
Bowl, Fruit, North Star Pattern, Hawkes, American Brilliant, 4 ¾ x 10 In.	330.00
Bowl, Grapefruit, Dorflinger Kalana Lily, Etched, Engraved Flowers, 5 x 5 In. ....*illus*	115.00
Bowl, Hobstar Border, Clear Gothic Columns With Cane Fields, 4 ¼ x 8 ½ In.	80.00
Bowl, Hobstar Center, Harvard, 4 x 8 In.	10.00
Bowl, Hobstar Center, Harvard Style Body, 3 ¾ x 8 In.	175.00
Bowl, Hobstar, Arch, Nailhead Diamond & Star, Pitkin & Brooks, American Brilliant, 4 x 9 In.	70.00
Bowl, Hobstar, Cane & Fan, American Brilliant, 3 ½ x 8 In.	70.00
Bowl, Hobstar, Clark, Round, Signed, 8 x 4 In.	58.00
Bowl, Hobstar, Diamond, Oval, Signed J. Hoare, 10 x 7 ½ x 3 In.	403.00
Bowl, Hobstar, Flared, Pinwheel & Strawberry Diamond, 3 ¼ x 9 In.	50.00
Bowl, Hobstar, Hexagonal, Cane, Nailhead Diamond & Fan Motif, 9 In.	75.00
Bowl, Hobstar, Maple Leaf, Snowflakes, Scalloped Rim, T.B. Clark & Company, 4 x 9 In.	115.00
Bowl, Hobstar, Stepped & Crosshatch, Marked, c.1900, 9 ½ In.	324.00
Bowl, Hobstar, Strawberry Diamond, 8 In.	80.00

Bowl, Hobstar, Strawberry Diamond, J. Hoare, American Brilliant, 4 x 8 In. 275.00
Bowl, Hobstar, Strawberry Diamond, Shooting Star, Prism, Fan, American Brilliant, 4 x 9 In. 950.00
Bowl, Hobstar, Triple Miter, Notched Fan & Strawberry Diamond, 4 x 8 In. 150.00
Bowl, Hobstar, Vertical Zipper, Sterling Band, Cross Mark, American Brilliant, 5 x 9 ½ In. ..*illus* 435.00
Bowl, Hobstar, Vesica & Cane, Double Notched Handles, 8 In. 100.00
Bowl, Hobstar, Vesica & Fan, American Brilliant, 3 ½ x 8 In. 125.00
Bowl, Hobstar, Vesica, Strawberry Diamond, Cane & Fan, American Brilliant, 9 In. 50.00
Bowl, Hobstar, Vertical Zipper, Flared Top, Sterling, Scroll, Flowers, 4 ⅝ x 9 ½ In. 413.00
Bowl, Intaglio, Flowers & Wrath Design, Footed, 4 x 14 ¾ In. 330.00
Bowl, Napoleon's Hat, Carolyn, Hoare, 13 ½ In. 1150.00
Bowl, Nordica, Blackmer, 9 In. 1795.00
Bowl, Oval, Windsor Pattern, Dorflinger, 11 x 10 In. 1600.00
Bowl, Pattern No. 9091, J. Hoare, 7 ¼ In. 295.00
Bowl, Pedestal, Hobstar, 2 Double Notched, Handles, Cane, Nailhead, Diamond & Fan, 6 x 9 In. 450.00
Bowl, Pedestal, Hobstar Base, Flashed Star, File & Prism Highlights, 4 ½ x 7 In., Pair............ 175.00
Bowl, Pineapple & Hobstar, Scalloped & Notched Edge, American Brilliant, 4 x 9 In. 148.00
Bowl, Propeller Pattern, Marshall Field, 8 In. 125.00
Bowl, Punch, On Stand, Cut With Hobstars, Hobnail, Crosshatched, Matching Base, 12 ½ In. ... 650.00
Bowl, Rosebud, 8 ¼ In. 100.00
Bowl, Royal, Hunt, American Brilliant, c.1905, 4 ¾ x 10 In. 300.00
Bowl, Russian, Hobstar Cut Buttons, Ray Center, Square, 3 ½ x 8 ¼ In. 125.00
Bowl, Russian, Scalloped Rim, 4 x 7 x 10 In. 117.00
Bowl, Russian, Scalloped Rim, Bull's-Eye, 4 x 10 In. 146.00
Bowl, Salad, Wheat, J. Hoare, 6 x 13 In., 2 Piece 10000.00
Bowl, Scallop & Point Rim, American Brilliant, c.1910, 4 x 8 In. ....*illus* 138.00
Bowl, Sterling Reticulated Edge, Crosscut Diamond, Block & Hobstar, 3 x 11 In. 250.00
Bowl, Tulip, Low Gravic, 9 In. 250.00
Bowl, Windsor, Straus, 8 ¼ In. 475.00
Box, Glove, Hobstar, Strawberry Diamond Bars, 3 ½ x 10 ½ In. 425.00
Bread Tray, Folded, Hobstar, Block & Fan, 11 ½ In. 75.00
Butter, Cover, Hobstar, Cane, Star & Fan, 5 x 7 ¼ In. 50.00
Butter, Cover, Hobstar, Strawberry Diamond & Fan, American Brilliant, 7 x 9 ½ In. 300.00
Butter, Hobstar, Cane, Vesica, Nailhead Diamond & Strawberry Diamond, Cover, 5 x 8 In. 100.00
Butter, Hobstar Cluster Pattern, Cover, 7 x 10 In. 225.00
Butter, Hobstars With Russian, Cover, Faceted Cut Final, 4 ½ x 8 In. 125.00
Cake Stand, Hobstar, Vesica, Prism & Fan Motif, Scalloped Base, 8 x 9 In. 290.00
Cake Stand, Nassau, 3-Footed, J. Hoare, 10 In. 375.00
Candelabrum, 5-Light, Hobstar, Cane, Prism & Fan, 20 In., Pair 13000.00
Candlestick, Hobstar & Twist Prism, Air Stem, Hobstar Base, 10 ½ In., Pair 1950.00
Candlestick, Hobstar Base, Teardrop, Notched Stem, Clear Blank, 11 In., Pair...................... 600.00
Candlestick, White Opalescent Ribbed Stem, Green Base, Dorflinger, 9 ¾ In., Pair................. 374.00
Carafe, Water, Hobstar & Strawberry Diamond, 9 In. 350.00
Carafe, Water, Hobstar, Strawberry Diamond & Fan, Corset Shape, American Brilliant, 8 In. . 50.00
Celery Dish, Boat Shape, Hobstar, Strawberry Diamond & Fan, 13 ¼ In. 70.00
Celery Dish, Hobstar & Fan, American Brilliant, 20 ½ In. 60.00
Celery Dish, Hobstar, Strawberry Diamond & Fan, Boat Shaped, 13 ¼ In. 15.00
Celery Dish, Sultana, Dorflinger, Long Leaf, 16 In. 675.00
Celery Tray, Folded, Geometric Cut Strawberry Ends, Nailhead Diamond & Fan Trim, 11 In. ... 50.00
Celery Tray, Folded, Geometric Strawberry Ends, Nailhead Diamond, Fan Highlights, 11 x 4 In. 50.00
Celery Tray, Folded, Wedgmere Pattern, Libbey, 11 ½ x 4 In. 325.00
Celery Tray, Kimberly, Folded, 11 ¾ In. 70.00
Centerpiece, Oval Bowl, Diamond, Oval Design, Gilt Metal Foot, Stand, 1900s, 6 x 19 In. 283.00
Centerpiece, Regency, Bronze Mounted, Serpent Handles, Molded Plinth, 7 ½ x 10 ¾ In. 411.00
Champagne Bucket, Pinwheel, 10 x 10 In. 59.00
Champagne, Flute, St. Louis, Diamond Point & Star Pattern, 20th Century, 7 ½ In., 9 Piece .. 115.00
Champagne, Monarch Pattern, Notched Stem, Ray Base, 4 ⅜ In. 225.00
Champagne, Wheat, J. Hoare, 4 ¾ In. 225.00
Cheese Dish, Marlboro, Dorflinger, 7 x 9 In. 600.00
Cheese Dome, Plate, Hobstar, Strawberry Diamond, Nailhead, Brilliant, c.1880, 7 x 8 ¾ In. . 360.00
Compote, Button & Daisy, Sawtooth Rim, Faceted Ball Square Base, 7 x 14 In. 290.00
Compote, Clear, Sawtooth, Hexagonal Pedestal, Circular, 10 x 10 ⅜ In. 45.00
Compote, Cover, Blown Bowl, Pressed Foot, Fluted, Diamond Band, Early 1800s, 13 In. 5288.00
Compote, Cover, Bull's-Eye, Double Teardrop Stem, 11 ½ In. 500.00
Compote, Crosshatch Stem, Sawtooth Edge, Hob Stars, 10 In. 489.00
Compote, El Tova Pattern, Round, Reverse Cut Hobstar Base, Clark Glass Co, c.1910, 8 x 6 In. 120.00

Cut Glass, Bowl, Grapefruit, Dorflinger Kalana Lily, Etched, Engraved Flowers, 5 x 5 In.
$115.00

Cut Glass, Bowl, Hobstar, Vertical Zipper, Sterling Band, Cross Mark, American Brilliant, 5 x 9 ½ In.
$435.00

Cut Glass, Bowl, Scallop & Point Rim, American Brilliant, c.1910, 4 x 8 In.
$138.00

Cut Glass, Decanter, Panel Neck, Stopper, Eggington, American Brilliant, c.1910, 12 ¼ In.
$299.00

Cut Glass, Ewer, Overlay, Punty, Footed, Cobalt Blue, Urn Shape, Strap Handle, 10 x 3 ⅜ In.
$345.00

Cut Glass, Goblet, Double Overlay, Windows, Green Cut To White To Amber, Cut Stem, 6 In.
$575.00

Cut Glass, Goblet, Free-Blown, Engraved, Military Reserves, Continental, 8 x 4 In.
$633.00

Cut Glass, Goblet, Ruby Stained, Engraved, Panel Cut Bowl, Baluster Stem, Foot, 6 ½ In.
$81.00

Compote, Flaring Form, Etched Daisies & Leaves, 8 In.	230.00
Compote, Hobstar & Fan, Notched Stem, American Brilliant, 8 x 5 ¾ In.	50.00
Compote, Hobstar, 2 Sections, 8 x 9 In.	1295.00
Compote, Hobstar, Cane, Fluted Stem, Optic Beading, Scalloped Base, 6 x 10 In.	115.00
Compote, Hobstar, Cane, Teardrop Stem, 7 x 6 In.	175.00
Compote, Hobstar, Nailhead Diamond & Cane, Petticoat Base, 6 ½ x 8 In.	10.00
Compote, Hobstar, Prism & Strawberry Diamond, Teardrop Stem, 9 ¼ x 7 ¼ In.	30.00
Compote, Hobstar, Strawberry Diamond & Fan, Twist Stem, American Brilliant, 8 x 6 In.	60.00
Compote, Hobstar, Strawberry Diamond, Hollow Stem, Hobstar Scalloped Base, 8 x 9 In.	150.00
Compote, Hobstar, Teardrop Stem, American Brilliant, 7 ¾ x 6 ½ In.	50.00
Compote, Open, Diamond Point, Wafer Construction, 10 ¼ x 10 ⅜ In.	104.00
Compote, Petticoat Base, Pinwheel, Hobstar & Fan, 5 x 6 In.	30.00
Compote, Regency, Faceted Bowl, Scrolled Rim, 7 ½ x 9 In.	71.00
Creamer, Hobstar, Silver Plate Top, Cover, Handle, 4 In.	46.00
Decanter, Bell Shape, Sterling Silver Repousse Stopper, Molded Poppies, 10 ¼ x 5 In., 3 Piece	823.00
Decanter, Crosscut Diamond, Fan, Handle, American Brilliant, 11 In.	125.00
Decanter, Ewer, Trumpet Shape, Silver Mounted, Shaped Spout, Scrolling Arm, 15 In.	316.00
Decanter, Green To Clear, Rococo & Intaglio Flowers, Stopper, 7 ¼ In.	3800.00
Decanter, Harvard With Strawberry Diamond, Double Notched Handle, Hobstar Base, 9 In.	70.00
Decanter, Hobstar & Fan, Double Notched Handle, Oval, 9 In.	100.00
Decanter, Hobstar, Nailhead Diamond & Star, Triple Ring Neck, Embossed Silver Stopper, 13 In.	400.00
Decanter, Hobstar, Strawberry Diamond & Fan, Cut Stopper, 6 ½ In.	150.00
Decanter, Hobstar, Strawberry Diamond, Triple Notched Snake Handle	75.00
Decanter, Long Spout, Bent Neck, Grape Design, Hammered Pewter Stopper, 11 x 11 In.	316.00
Decanter, Marlboro, Dorflinger, Cut Stopper, 7 ½ In.	1900.00
Decanter, Panel Neck, Stopper, Eggington, American Brilliant, c.1910, 12 ¼ In. ....*illus*	299.00
Decanter, Parisian, Strap Handle, Hob Diamond, Stopper, Dorflinger, 8 In., Pair	650.00
Decanter, Ship's, Hobstar & Fans, Tapered, Notched Handle, 10 In.	144.00
Decanter, Stopper, Clear, 12 ¼ x 5 In.	47.00
Decanter, Stopper, Sterling, Vertical Zipper, 13 ½ In.	154.00
Decanter, Tantalus, Quartersawn Oak Base, Betjemann's Patent, 11 ½ x 14 In., 3 Piece	275.00
Dish, Hobstar & Cane, Spade Shape, 5 ½ In.	75.00
Dish, Lemon, Vintage, 7 ½ In.	275.00
Dresser Box, Hobstar & File, Hinged, 3 x 6 ½ In.	550.00
Dresser Box, Hobstar & Reed Flutes, Mirror, c.1900, 8 ¼ In.	324.00
Epergne, Prism, Fluted, C.F. Monroe, 31 x 9 In.	18750.00
Ewer, Overlay, Punty, Footed, Cobalt Blue, Urn Shape, Strap Handle, 10 x 3 ⅜ In. ....*illus*	345.00
Goblet, Double Overlay, Windows, Green Cut To White To Amber, Cut Stem, 6 In. ....*illus*	575.00
Goblet, Free-Blown, Engraved, Military Reserves, Continental, 8 x 4 In. ....*illus*	633.00
Goblet, Pink Over White, Clear Hollow Stem, Footed, 1800s, 9 ¼ In.	120.00
Goblet, Ruby Stained, Engraved, Panel Cut Bowl, Baluster Stem, Foot, 6 ½ In. ....*illus*	81.00
Goblet, Wine, Fan & Diamond, 4 ½ In., 6 Piece	115.00
Humidor, Marlboro, Dorflinger, Cut Lid, Sterling Collar, 8 x 6 ½ In.	1600.00
Humidor, Nevada, Pairpoint, 9 ¾ In.	975.00
Humidor, Plymouth, Meriden, 9 In.	450.00
Ice Cream Tray, Cluster, 18 x 10 ¼ In.	1150.00
Ice Tub, Hobstar, Arched Hobnail, Engraved Rosettes, Tab Handles, 5 ½ In.	75.00
Jar, Hobstar, Flashed Crossed Bar & Fan, Lid, 8 ½ In.	150.00
Jewelry Box, Brass Lid & Bottom Mounts, France, 4 x 4 ¼ x 3 ¼ In.	219.00
Jewelry Box, Hinged, Flashed Hobstar Lid, 5 In.	75.00
Jewelry Box, Hinged, Hobstar & Fan, 4 x 10 In.	750.00
Jewelry Box, Hinged, Oval, Crossed Bar & Fan, 6 ½ In.	75.00
Jug, Claret, Handle, Crisscross, Stopper, 19th Century, 18 ½ In.	420.00
Knife, Ice Cream, Crosscut Diamond Handle, Dorflinger, 13 In.	1550.00
Knife Rest, Geometric Cut Design, 3 ¾ In.	40.00
Knife Rest, Hobstar & Prism, American Brilliant, 5 In.	25.00
Knife Rest, Hobstar & Prism, Honeycomb Cut Stem, 5 In.	100.00
Knife Rest, Prism, 4 ½ In.	40.00
Lamp, Hobstar & Prism, 13 In.	300.00
Lamp, Kerosene, Russian Cut, Star Buttons, 16 ½ In.	2100.00
Lamp, Mushroom, India, 2-Arms, Acorn Pulls, J.D. Bergen, 24 x 12 In., Pair	6800.00
Lamp, Mushroom Shade, Harvard, Cone Shape, 17 In.	719.00
Lamp, Oil, Russian, 2 Handles, Silver Plate Double Burner, Globe, 16 In.	5800.00
Nappy, Curled, Handle, Gotham, J. Hoare, 6 ¾ In.	75.00
Nappy, Hobstar, 3-Footed, 5 ¼ In.	40.00

Nappy, Royal, Handle, 6 In.	50.00
Obelisk, Beveled, Silvered, Wooden Paw Feet, Panels, 35 ¼ x 7 ½ x 7 ½ In., Pair	1680.00
Pitcher, Block Motif, 10 In.	125.00
Pitcher, Bulls-Eye Cut Body, Scalloped Edge, Crook Handle, Dorflinger, c.1870, 10 x 6 In.	180.00
Pitcher, Butterfly, Notched Handle, Brilliant, Mortenson, 6 In.	210.00
Pitcher, Cider, Flashed Pinwheels, Fans, 6 In.	92.00
Pitcher, Cross Hatched Diamond & Star Band, Barrel, 18th Century, 6 ¾ In.	150.00
Pitcher, Engraved Man & Woman Riding Horses, Triple Notched Handle, 12 In.	455.00
Pitcher, Handle, Star Designs, Notches, 13 In.	173.00
Pitcher, Hobstar, Strawberry, Diamond & Fan, American Brilliant, 11 In.	125.00
Pitcher, Hobstar, Strawberry, Diamond, Zipper & Fan, Handle, American Brilliant, 13 ¼ In.	125.00
Pitcher, Large & Small Hobstars, Cross Hatching, Cut Base, c.1900, 14 In.	413.00
Pitcher, Lozenge & Fan, Step Cut Lip, 19th Century, 8 ¼ In.	240.00
Pitcher, Water, Pinwheel & Cane, 2 Notched Handle, American Brilliant, 9 In.	90.00
Plate, Hobstar Border, Split Leaf Design, 7 In.	175.00
Plate, Rose Diamond, Meriden, 9 In.	4900.00
Punch Bowl, Chester, Dorflinger, 12 x 14 In., 2 Piece	3400.00
Punch Bowl, Mary, Rose Shape, Hobstars, Leaves, Stand, Anderson, 9 x 12 In.	690.00
Punch Cup, Russian, Ray Base, Pedestal, 3 ½ In., 12 Piece	150.00
Punch Set, Dorflinger, c.1920, 11 x 14-In. Bowl, 24 Piece	6710.00
Punch Set, Whirling Star, 14 Piece	550.00
Salt, Boat Shape, Stepped Diamond Base, Intaglio, 3 x 4 In., 4 Piece	58.00
Sandwich Server, Greek Key, Meriden, 10 In.	990.00
Scent Bottle, Dressing Table, Enameled Silver Cover, Stylized Blossoms, 5 ½ In., Pair	854.00
Spoon Holder, 3-Handles, Flared Sterling Collar, Shreve, Crump & Low, 4 In.	345.00
Stringholder, Prism Cut, Reticulated Sterling Top, 3 ½ In.	500.00
Sugar & Creamer, Pedestal, Hobstar & Fan, Faceted Cut Teardrop Stem	275.00
Sugar Shaker, Hobstar, File, Prism, Fan, Egg Shaped, Silver Plate Top, 4 ¼ In.	75.00
Talcum Bottle, Blue, Oval, Latticework Cutting, Octagons, c.1890, 5 x 1 ¾ In.	165.00
Tankard, Cane, Step Cut Handle, 12 ½ In.	350.00
Tankard, Propeller, Double Notched Handle, Ray Base, Marshall Field, 15 In.	300.00
Tray, Calve, Triple Miter Trellis, Scalloped Edge, Signed Egginton, 14 ½ In.	28950.00
Tray, Climax, Round, Empire, 14 In.	1800.00
Tray, Hobstar, Cranberry To Clear, Pinwheel & Geometric, Round, 12 In.	550.00
Tray, Hobstar, Crosscut Diamond, Fan, Round, 12 In.	225.00
Tray, Hobstar, File & Fan, 14 x 8 In.	175.00
Tray, Hobstar, Pinwheel & Geometric, Cranberry Cut To Clear, 12 In.	550.00
Tray, Ice Cream, Cane Bars With Prism & Strawberry Diamond, 17 x 10 In.	550.00
Tray, Ice Cream, Diamond Shape, Overall Harvard Cut, 16 ½ x 10 In.	230.00
Tray, Ice Cream, Old Irish, 15 ½ x 9 ½ In.	600.00
Tray, Round, Climax, 13 In.	1800.00
Tray, Triple Lobed, Acorns, Leaves, 10 x 1 ½ In.	460.00
Tumbler, Water, Russian With Star Cut Buttons, 6 ⅜ In., 12 Piece	225.00
Tumbler, Whiskey, Hobstars, Crosscut Diamond, 2 ½ In., 8 Piece	115.00
Urn, Chestnut, Engraved, Swags, Husk Band, Trumpet Foot, Anglo-Irish, c.1820, 7 ½ In.	441.00
Vase, Alhambra, Pinched Waist, Toothed Rim, Meriden, 24 x 8 In.	14950.00
Vase, Allover Hobstar, Crosshatch & Hobnail, Flared Base, c.1900, 14 In.	206.00
Vase, Cane, Cylindrical, Silver Rim, 6 ¼ In., Pair	100.00
Vase, Diamond Point Cutting, Pendant Prisms, Rolled Rim, c.1900, 9 ¾ In.	383.00
Vase, Engraved, Bird Of Paradise, 16 In.	125.00
Vase, Forest Green, Optic Cylinder, Polished Pontil, Dorflinger, 13 ½ In.	50.00
Vase, Hobstar & Fan, Beaded Flute, Footed, Bell Base, c.1900, 12 In.	265.00
Vase, Hobstar & Fan, Sweet Pea, 6 In.	50.00
Vase, Hobstar Cluster & Fan Highlights, Pinched Waist, Vertical Pinwheels, 16 In.	550.00
Vase, Hobstar, Cane, Strawberry Diamond, Zipper & Fan, Pinched Waist, American Brilliant, 10 In.	175.00
Vase, Hobstar, Fan Design, Dorflinger, 6 x 5 ½ In.	201.00
Vase, Hobstar, Nailheads, Sunray Pattern Base, American Brilliant, c.1920, 12 x 5 In.	241.00
Vase, Hobstar, Strawberry, Diamond & Fan, Bowling Pin Shape, 13 ¾ In.	150.00
Vase, Hobstar, Swirl Feather & Star, 17 ½ In.	400.00
Vase, Hobstar, Thumbprints, Beaded Flutes, Footed, Star Cut Base, c.1900, 14 ¼ In.	472.00
Vase, Hobstar, Vesica & Starburst, Step Cut Neck, Ray Base, 20 ½ In.	800.00
Vase, Hobstar, With Prism Cut Body & Fan, Oval, 8 ½ In.	70.00
Vase, Hobstar, With Strawberry Diamond & Fan, Notched Handles, American Brilliant, 12 In.	500.00
Vase, Intaglio Cut, Amber To Clear, Cupids Playing Instruments, 12 ½ In.	288.00
Vase, Lavender To Clear, Stylized Design, Dorflinger, 13 In.	546.00

Cut Velvet , Vase, Diamond Quilted, Satin, Cased Pink, Crimped & Tooled Rim, Late 1800s, 9 In. **$92.00**

Cybis, Figurine, Camille, Hand Mirror, Flowers, 14 In. **$176.00**

TIP
Do you have a large exposed window? Put up glass shelves and fill them with inexpensive, colorful bottles. A burglar would have to break all of it, with accompanying noise, to get in.

Czechoslovakia Glass, Flask, Perfume, Nude Profile, Art Deco, Ingrid, Malachite, 6 x 3 In.
$276.00

Czechoslovakia Glass, Vase, Green Trumpet Shape, Red Spot Finish, Black Snake, 8 In.
$35.00

Czechoslovakia Pottery, Vase, Curved Handles, Mottled Matte Glaze, Multicolored, 6 x 6 ½ In.
$98.00

D'Argental, Vase, Harbor Scene, Gondolas, Red, Amethyst, Marked, Early 1900s, 12 In.
$944.00

Vase, Strawberry Diamond, Cornucopia Shape, Pedestal, Flashed Star, 9 ¾ x 10 In.	1800.00
Vase, Tazza, Harvard, 24-Point Hobstar Base, 11 ½ In.	150.00
Vase, Tiffany Pattern, Corset, Dorflinger, 13 ¾ In.	1400.00
Vase, Trumpet, Emerald Green To Clear, 16 In.	500.00
Vase, Trumpet, Flowers, Leaves, Footed	24.00
Vase, Trumpet, Hobstar, Cane & Strawberry Diamond, Sterling Rim, Scalloped Base, 10 In.	150.00
Vase, Trumpet, Thistle, Cut Base, 14 In.	50.00
Vase, Urn Shape, Square Base, Italy, c.1900, 14 ½ In., Pair	201.00
Wine, Parisian, Blue To Clear, Dorflinger, 4 ½ In.	4100.00
Wine, Parisian, Gold To Clear, Dorflinger, 4 ½ In.	4000.00
Wine, Rhine, Hobstar Foot, Amethyst, Clear, 9 In.	175.00

CUT VELVET is a special type of art glass, made with two layers of blown glass, that shows a raised pattern. It usually had an acid finish or a texture like velvet. It was made by many glass factories during the late Victorian years.

Vase, Diamond Quilted, Satin, Cased Pink, Crimped & Tooled Rim, Late 1800s, 9 In. ......*illus*	92.00

CYBIS porcelain is a twentieth-century product. Boleslaw Cybis came to the United States from Poland in 1939. He started making porcelains in Long Island, New York, in 1940. He moved to Trenton, New Jersey, in 1942 as one of the founders of Cordey China Co. and started his own company, Cybis Porcelains about 1950. The firm is still working. See also Cordey.

CYBIS

Figurine, Camille, Hand Mirror, Flowers, 14 In. ......*illus*	176.00
Figurine, Carmen, Red Skirt, 15 In.	234.00
Figurine, Ducklings, Bisque, Pastels, 5 x 6 In.	117.00
Figurine, Kneeling Native American, 12 In.	351.00
Figurine, Melissa, Wearing Cloak, Holding Rabbit, Bisque, 10 In.	105.00
Figurine, Portia, Lavender, No. 411, c.1975, Bisque, 14 In.	205.00

CZECHOSLOVAKIA is a popular term with collectors. The name, first used as a mark after the country was formed in 1918, appears on glass and porcelain and other decorative items. Although Czechoslovakia split into Slovakia and the Czech Republic on January 1, 1993, the name continues to be used in some trademarks.

CZECHOSLOVAKIA GLASS

Basket, Handle, Raised Figures, Malachite, 5 ½ x 5 ¾ x 5 In.	45.00
Bowl, Footed, Pink To Purple Ground, Blue, Platinum, Signed, ¾ x 8 In.	58.00
Dresser Jar, Cover, Nudes, Flowing Fabric, Malachite, 1920s, 3 ¾ x 2 In.	175.00
Flask, Perfume, Nude Profile, Art Deco, Ingrid, Malachite, 6 x 3 In. ......*illus*	276.00
Perfume Bottle, Green, Mythological Figure, Incised, Woman Stopper, Frosted, 6 ¾ In.	270.00
Perfume Bottle, Jeweled Lid, Molded Flowers, Malachite, 2 ½ x 1 ½ In.	65.00
Perfume Bottle, Pyramid Shape, Cut Diamond & Fan, Long Square Stopper, 6 ⅜ In., Pair	71.00
Perfume, Atomizer, Square, Footed, Malachite, 5 x 3 ⅜ In.	165.00
Trinket Box, Leaves, Malachite, 4 x 1 ¾ In.	35.00
Vase, Bulbous Base, Green Glass, Blue Lines, c.1904, 3 ½ x 6 In.	210.00
Vase, Clear, Frosted Etching, Leaves, Flower, Globe, c.1910, 7 ½ In.	130.00
Vase, Cut Crystal, 6 x 12 In.	176.00
Vase, Figures, Maidens, Birds, Grapes, Flowers, Malachite, 10 x 6 In.	695.00
Vase, Green Trumpet Shape, Red Spot Finish, Black Snake, 8 In. ......*illus*	35.00

CZECHOSLOVAKIA POTTERY

Candleholder, Flowing Design, Octagon Base, Signed, 2 ½ x 4 ½ In., Pair	45.00
Figurine, Flower Frog Nymph, White, Green, c.1940, 5 x 6 In.	58.00
Plate, Painted, Multicolored Flowers, Fruit, Blue Spatter Rim, 7 ½ In.	40.00
Vase, Curved Handles, Mottled Matte Glaze, Multicolored, 6 x 6 ½ In. ......*illus*	98.00

D'ARGENTAL is a mark used in France by the Compagnie des Cristalleries de St. Louis. The firm made multilayered, acid-cut cameo glass in the late nineteenth and twentieth centuries. D'Argental is the French name for the city of Munzthal, home of the glassworks. Later the company made enameled etched glass.

Bonbon, Circular, Trailing Flowers, Yellow To Amethyst Ground, c.1900, 5 x 6 ¾ In.	2151.00
Bowl, Royal Blue & Claret, Clematis Vines, Signed, 6 ¼ In.	780.00
Vase, Amber, Red Roses, Squat, Signed, 5 In.	518.00
Vase, Camphor, Sienna, Red, Trees, Castle, Hill, Signed, 10 In.	1495.00
Vase, Flowers, Leaves, Red, Yellow Ground, 14 In.	1200.00

C

Vase, Harbor Scene, Gondolas, Red, Amethyst, Marked, Early 1900s, 12 In. ....*illus*	944.00
Vase, Nautical Scene, Red Ships, Yellow Rose Sky, Signed, 3 ½ In.	1438.00
Vase, Oval, Frosted, Green, Purple Iris, Ginkgo Leaves, Blossoms, Signed, 8 In.	1200.00
Vase, Pink & Purple Flowers, Ivory Ground, Bulbous, 11 ¾ In.	920.00
Vase, Purple Morning Glory, Tan To Brown Ground, Signed, 6 In.	345.00
Vase, Stick, Citron, Umber Pinecone Branches, Signed, 1900s, 9 In.	1440.00

DANIEL BOONE, a pre–Revolutionary War folk hero, was a surveyor, trapper, and frontiersman. A television series, which ran from 1964 to 1970, was based on his life and starred Fess Parker. All types of Daniel Boone memorabilia are collected.

Autolite, Woodland Whistle, TV Show, 6 In.	99.00
Jigsaw Puzzle, Wilderness Scout, Fess Parker As Daniel, Jaymar	45.00
Lunch Box, Fess Parker, Metal, Thermos..	115.00
Ring, Plastic With Color Insert, Cereal Premium, 1950s	25.00
Slate, Fess Parker Super Magic Slate, TV Show, Saalfield, 1964	85.00
Toy, Inflatable Indian Canoe, Indian Head Attached, Multiple Products, 1965	49.00

DAUM, a glassworks in Nancy, France, was started by Jean Daum in 1875. The company, now called *Cristalleries de Nancy*, is still working. The *Daum Nancy* mark has been used in many variations. The name of the city and the artist are usually both included. The term *martele* is used to describe applied decorations that are carved or etched in the cameo process.

Basket, Flowers, Stems, Leaves, Enameled, Red, Purple, Arching Handle, Cameo, 7 ¼ In.	920.00
Bottle, Flowers, Enameled, Cylindrical, Signed, Daum Nancy, Cross Of Lorraine, 3 In.	480.00
Bottle, Red Enamel Flowers, Green, Pink, Frosted Body, Up, Down Silver Caps, Cameo, 6 In. ...	748.00
Bowl, Art Deco, Black Foot, Graduated Gray Arch Pattern, 9 In.	234.00
Bowl, Berries, Leaves, Quatrefoil Design, Mottled White & Yellow Ground, Signed, 2 ¾ x 6 In.	1320.00
Bowl, Centerpiece, Swans, Mottled Blue Ground, Trees, Handles, Diamond Shape, 4 ¾ x 13 In.	10925.00
Bowl, Flower Form, Apple Green, Wheel Engraved, 3 ⅜ x 6 ½ In.	115.00
Bowl, Flowers, Leaves, Mottled White, Yellow, Apricot, Siennas, Green, Cameo, 2 ¾ x 4 ½ In. ..	1668.00
Bowl, Multicolored Flowers, Blue Ground, Mottled Base, Pinched Shape, Signed, 3 x 6 In.	1265.00
Bowl, Mushrooms, Green, Orange, Brown, Mottled, Diamond Shape, 11 x 8 x 5 ½ In.	4775.00
Bowl, Orange, Yellow Mottled Ground, Winter Snow Scene, Cameo, Signed Cross Of Lorraine, 6 In.	3750.00
Box, Cover, Edelweiss Flowers, White, Green, Gilding, Enamel, Cameo, Signed, 3 x 6 In.	3680.00
Box, Cover, Enameled, Thistle, Pink Shaded To Yellow To Clear, Cameo, 3 x 2 In. ....*illus*	3738.00
Box, Cover, Peacock Feathers, Padded Sapphire Eyes, Green Stems, Cameo, 5 x 6 In.	6325.00
Case, Snow, Woods, Sky, Brown, White, Orange, 4 ¾ In.	2415.00
Clock, Crystal, 3 Applied Green Frogs, 7 x 10 In.	1053.00
Ewer, Clear Frosted White Enamel Designs, Gilt, Stopper, Signed, 8 In.	1840.00
Figurine, Bird, Clear Glass, Arched 4-Sided Base, 8 In.	173.00
Figurine, Dragon, Amber, Yellow, 8 x 9 In.	819.00
Figurine, Horse, Amber, Turquoise, Swirls, Clear Base, Signed, Limited Edition, 6 x 7 In.	920.00
Figurine, Stag, Blue, Gilt Border On Base, Crystal, 5 x 5 In.	176.00
Inkwell, Brown Lake Scene, Yellow Glass, Lid, Signed, 5 In.	1495.00
Jar, Cover, Textured & Enameled, Coastal Village, Windmill, Ships, Signed, 3 In.	1380.00
Lamp Base, Enameled Black Sailboats, Trees, Birds, White Frosted Ground, Signed, 10 In.	575.00
Lamp Shade, Egg Shape, 2-Tone Orange, Mottled, 6 ½ In. ....:	230.00
Lamp, Baluster Stem, Mottled Green, Vine, Grapes, Mushroom Shade, Yellow, Signed, 25 x 12 In.	3500.00
Lamp, Flowers, Leaves, Mottled Yellow Ground, 4 Metal Support, Arms, 15 ¼ In.	4025.00
Lamp, Mottled Pink, Vertical Striping, Round Shade, 3 Metal Support Arms, 19 In.	8050.00
Night-Light, Grapes & Leaves, Wrought Iron Frame, Signed, 6 ½ In. ....*illus*	1437.00
Perfume Bottle, Flip Lid, Metal, Textured Green Flowers, Gold Leaf, Cameo Glass, Signed, 4 In.	550.00
Perfume Bottle, Flower, Apple Green, White Ground, Carved, Laydown, 5 ½ In.	2875.00
Pitcher, Green Flowers, Amethyst Ground, Cameo, Lid, 8 ¼ In.	1150.00
Pitcher, Red, Textured Gray, Gold Berries, Black Vines, Gold Trim, Signed, 2 ¾ In.	1150.00
Salt Bucket, Winter Scene, Enameled Trees, Snow, Mottled Orange Ground, 1 ¾ x 1 ¼ In.	1725.00
Sculpture, Animal, Pate-De-Verre, Amber, 5 ½ x 10 In.	1140.00
Stickpin, Papillion, Crystal, 3 In., Pair	146.00
Toothpick, Winter Scene, Signed, 2 In.	2700.00
Tray, Black, Gray, Enamel Dutch Harbor Scene, White Opalescence, Signed, 9 x 2 ½ In.	1003.00
Tumbler Set, Green, Gold Acid Etched Flowers, Signed, 1 ⅞ In., 4	1380.00
Tumbler, Green, Flower, Gold Highlights, Cameo, Signed, Daum Nancy, 3 ¼ In.	360.00
Tumbler, Winter Scene, Meadow, Mottled Yellow, Barrel Form, Signed, Cameo, Signed, 5 In. ..	2040.00
Tumbler, Winter Scene, Snow, Trees, Windmills, White, Blue, Peach Brown, Signed, 5 In.	2875.00
Vase, 3 Colors, Corset Shape, Nighttime Tree & Lake Scene, Cameo, Signed, 16 In.	3750.00
Vase, 3 Colors, Lake Scene, Cameo, Signed, 13 ¾ In.	3700.00

Daum, Box, Cover, Enameled, Thistle, Pink Shaded To Yellow To Clear, Cameo, 3 x 2 In. $3738.00

Daum, Night-Light, Grapes & Leaves, Wrought Iron Frame, Signed, 6 ½ In. $1437.00

Daum, Vase, Footed, Mold Blown, Saffron Glass, Gold Foil, Wrought Iron, Louis Marjorelle, 6 ½ In. $1725.00

TIP

Spray a glass flower vase with nonstick cooking spray. It will keep the water from staining the glass.

Daum, Vase, Silver Base, Flying Swallows, Sunrise, Enameled, Blue Cameo, Signed, 3 ¼ In. $1035.00

Daum, Vase, Snow Covered Trees, Orange Ground, Signed, 4 ¾ In. $2415.00

Daum, Vase, Spring Scene, Tree, Landscape, Frosted Ground, Flattened Pillow, Signed, 5 In. $5015.00

D

TIP

To test the age of an engraving on glass, place a white handkerchief on the inside. If the engraving is old, the lines will usually show up darker than the rest of the glass. A new engraving has a bright, powder-like surface.

Vase, Applied Snail, Leaves, Vines, Grapes, Mottled Ground, Cameo, 4 ¾ In.	6900.00
Vase, Berluze, Oval, Thin Cylindrical Neck, Blue, Green, Etched, Signed, c.1920, 18 In.	705.00
Vase, Berries, Blue Mottled Green, Amethyst, Chartreuse, Yellow Leaves, Cameo, Signed, 17 In.	4313.00
Vase, Black, Dutch Windmill, Harbor Scene, Gray Frosted Ground, 2 In.	590.00
Vase, Black, Peach, Green Tree Scene, Gray Mottled Ground, Bulbous, Signed, 1 ½ In.	354.00
Vase, Blue, Carved, 3 Birds, Sun, Enameled, Silver Footed Base, Cameo, 3 In.	1035.00
Vase, Bottle Shape, Ruby, Amber, Lake Scene, Gold Enamel, Cameo, Signed, 2 In.	1025.00
Vase, Bud, Cameo, Signed, 4 ¼ In.	600.00
Vase, Bulbous, Carved Blue Flowers, Green Leaves, Mottled Orange Ground, Cameo, Signed, 4 In.	805.00
Vase, Bulbous Stick Shape, Mottled Yellow, Purple, Vitrified Fall Leaves, Cameo, Signed, 14 In.	2000.00
Vase, Burgundy, Iridescent Flowers, Purple Stems, Bulbous, Padded Foot, Martele, Signed, 6 In.	4025.00
Vase, Crocus, Amethyst, Opalescent White, Cameo, Signed, c.1900, 14 In.	3840.00
Vase, Cut Blackberry, Bulbous, Flared Rim, Yellow, Black, Orange, Cameo Cut, 6 ½ In.	920.00
Vase, Cylindrical, Clear Glass, Bubbles, Signed, 7 ½ x 8 In.	144.00
Vase, Cylindrical, Yellow & Rose Design, Crimson & Gray Berries, 16 ½ In.	3000.00
Vase, Dutch Winter Landscape, Pillow Shape, Blue, Yellow Sky, Cameo, Signed, 9 In.	7475.00
Vase, Enamel, Poppies, Leaves, Bulbous, Cameo, Signed, 11 ⅝ In.	805.00
Vase, Etched, Enameled Winter Landscape On Mottled Orange & Yellow Ground, 1910, 4 In.	3200.00
Vase, Fall Scene, Setting Sun, Multicolored, Signed, 8 x 6 In.	8625.00
Vase, Flower, Orange, Red Against Yellow Ground, Cameo, Signed, 5 ½ x 23 ½ In.	4313.00
Vase, Flowering Vines, Metal Base, Ruffled Rim, Cameo, Signed, 2 ½ x 3 ¾ In.	230.00
Vase, Flowers, Leaves, Multicolored, White Opalescent Ground, Handles, 5 ¾ x 8 ½ In.	4600.00
Vase, Flowers, Opalescent Amber, Crimson, Green Leaves, Martele, Footed, Cylindrical, 6 In.	2588.00
Vase, Flowers, Purple, Green Branches, Frosted Glass Shading To Amber, Pillow, Cameo, 5 In.	1150.00
Vase, Flowers, Purple, Iridescence, Martele Ground, Signed, 4 In.	3220.00
Vase, Flowers, Red Flowers, Green Leaves, Yellow Mottled Ground, Cameo, Signed, 12 In.	3105.00
Vase, Flowers, Violet, Enameled, Gold Leaf, Art Nouveau, Cameo, Signed, Late 1800s, 3 x 2 ½ In.	3850.00
Vase, Flowers, Yellow, Crimson, Green Stems, Toothbrush Form, Cameo, Signed, 4 ¾ In.	1495.00
Vase, Footed, Enamel, Bees, Spider Webs, Yellow To Orange Ground, Cameo, 8 ¼ In.	14950.00
Vase, Footed, Enameled Orange Flowers, Green Leaves, Amethyst Ground, 1905, 6 In.	2160.00
Vase, Footed, Free-Form Triangular Shape, Skyline, Bats, Cameo, Signed, 10 In.	6325.00
Vase, Footed, Martele, Bulbous Stick, Red, Stemmed Green Flowers, Silver Rim, Cameo, Signed, 8 In.	2000.00
Vase, Footed, Mold Blown, Saffron Glass, Gold Foil, Wrought Iron, Louis Marjorelle, 6 ½ In. ...*illus*	1725.00
Vase, Golden Blossoms, Mottled Yellow & Purple Frosted Ground, Square, 4 ½ x 2 In.	1920.00
Vase, Green Body, Applied Cobalt Blue Leaves, Spiral Neck, Art Deco, Signed, 6 In.	633.00
Vase, Green, Gilt Lion, Base, Rim, Acid Etched, Cameo, Signed, 11 ½ In.	863.00
Vase, Iris, Pate-De-Verre, Yellow & Purple, Inscribed, c.1970, 11 ⅛ In.	822.00
Vase, Ivory Money Plant, Mottled Orange, Yellow, Green, Pedestal, Cameo, Signed, 14 In.	2243.00
Vase, Lake Scene, Frosted Orange, White, Cylindrical, Bulb Rim, Foot, Cameo, 13 ½ In.	1265.00
Vase, Landscape, Green, Silver, Cameo, Signed, c.1900, 12 In.	1645.00
Vase, Maroon Poppies, Rays, Sun, Stems, Leaves, Opalescent White Martele, Cameo, Signed, 8 In.	3968.00
Vase, Martele, Cameo, Pink Ground, Green Leaves, Berries, Handles, c.1900, 8 In.	9560.00
Vase, Mottled Pink, Red Wheel Carved Orchid, 2 Buds, Engraved, 7 In.	6325.00
Vase, Mushroom Pattern, Mottled Yellow, Orange, Green, Pillow Shape, Cameo, c.1900, 5 In.	4320.00
Vase, Opalescent White, Dutch Windmills, Ship, Oval, Signed, 1 ¾ In.	489.00
Vase, Orange, Art Deco, Cameo Glass, 16 x 11 ½ In.	3660.00
Vase, Orange Berries, Green Leaves, Mottled Peach, Green, Purple, Tumbler Shape, 3 ¼ In.	1955.00
Vase, Orchid, Pate-De-Verre, Blue, Clear & Purple, Pierced Rim, Inscribed, c.1965, 12 ¼ In.	1293.00
Vase, Orchids, Spider Webs, White To Purple, Overlaid & Cut, Enamel, Cameo, c.1900, 5 ⅝ In.	1998.00
Vase, Padded Yellow, Orange Jonquils, Frosted Peach, Purple, Green Foot, Incised, 6 In.	6037.00
Vase, Pillow, Fuchsia, Purple, Burgundy, Green Leaves, Brown Stems, Mottled White, 4 ½ In.	3450.00
Vase, Pink Cosmos Flowers, Wheel Carved Green Leaves, Opalescent, Signed, 12 In.	5750.00
Vase, Poppies, Enameled, Multicolored, Clear Ground, Leaf Patterns, Signed, 12 x 4 ½ In.	9760.00
Vase, Prunus, Engraved, Applied Cameo, c.1900, 10 In.	8125.00
Vase, Purple Flowers, White, Green Base, Pedestal Shape, Enamel, Cameo, Signed, 8 In.	2530.00
Vase, Purple Iris, Gold Trim, Gray Mottled Ground, Acid Etched, 4 Sides, Cameo, Signed, 7 In.	403.00
Vase, Purple Poppy Flowers, Gilt Details, Rectangular Shape, Cameo, Signed, 7 In.	604.00
Vase, Rain Scene, Gourd Shape, Etched, 7 ¾ x 4 ¼ In.	9760.00
Vase, Rectangle, Cut, Enamel Yellow Orchids, Green Stem, Signed 5 x 2 In.	1380.00
Vase, Rectangular, Cut & Enameled Orchids, Yellow & Green, Signed, 5 In.	1380.00
Vase, Red Flowers, Green Leaves, Lemon Ground, Purple Foot, Fold Rim, Cameo, Signed, 4 In.	1438.00
Vase, Red Flowers, Green Leaves, Mottled Opal, Amber, 11 ½ In.	4140.00
Vase, Rose, Pink, Light Green To Medium Green, Pedestal Foot, 11 ¾ In.	2070.00
Vase, Sailing Ships, Mottled Yellow, Pillow Form, Cameo, Signed, 5 In.	1610.00
Vase, Silver Base, Flying Swallows, Sunrise, Enameled, Blue Cameo, Signed, 3 ¼ In. ...*illus*	1035.00
Vase, Snow Covered Trees, Orange Ground, Signed, 4 ¾ In. ...*illus*	2415.00
Vase, Spring Scene, Tree, Landscape, Frosted Ground, Flattened Pillow, Signed, 5 In. ...*illus*	5015.00
Vase, Storks In Flight, Marsh Landscape, Lily Pads, Gold Flowers, 3 Frosted Handles, 6 In.	6325.00

Vase, Stylized Flowers & Leaves, Orange Overlay, c.1922, 6 ¾ In.	489.00
Vase, Swan, Lake, Marsh, Pillow Shape, Peach, Yellow, White, Enamel, Signed, 4 ½ In.	10350.00
Vase, Tricornered, Padded Narcissus, Yellow, White, Gold, Green Base, Cameo, Signed, 14 x 8 In.	9200.00
Vase, Tumbler, Dutch Snow Scene, Mottled Blue Glass, Yellow, White, Signed, 2 In.	1495.00
Vase, Tumbler, Flowers, Leaves, Multicolored, Mottled Ground, Enamel, Cameo, Signed, 5 In.	2013.00
Vase, Tumbler, Mottled Blue, Mountain Lake Scene, Trees, Forest Shoreline, Cameo, Signed, 2 ½ In.	1208.00
Vase, Tumbler, Purple Violets, Green Stems, Frosted Mottled Ground, Enamel, Cameo, 5 In.	2875.00
Vase, Wheat, Enamel, Gilt, Black, Purple, Ivory, Marked, Cross Of Lorraine, 1890s, 11 ¼ In.	9560.00
Vase, Wheel Carved Flowers, Leaves, Purple, Yellow, Pink Mottled Frosted Ground, 13 In.	6900.00
Vase, White, Blue, Brown, Dutch Snow Scene, Cylinder, Slender, Mottled, Blue Ground, 10 In.	8050.00
Vase, White, Pink, Yellow & Purple, Croix De Lorraine, 1905, 7 In.	6430.00
Vase, Winter Scene, Trees, Snow, Yellow, Brown Ground, Cameo, Signed, 12 In.	9200.00
Vase, Winter Scene, Trees, Snow, Yellow, Orange Earthen Hued Ground, Cylindrical, 9 ½ In.	7475.00
Vase, Winter, Trees, Snow Patches, White, Brown, Orange, Yellow, Signed, 7 In.	4888.00
Vase, Yellow, Dark Blue Base, Mottled, Signed, Rectangular, c.1920, 5 In.	795.00
Vase, Yellow, Green, Acid Textured Clear Ground, Flared, Cameo, Signed, 1895, 7 In.	431.00
Vase, Yellow Panels, Ice Chipped Finish, Ball Shape, c.1910, 4 In.	745.00

DAVENPORT pottery and porcelain were made at the Davenport factory in Longport, Staffordshire, England, from 1793 to 1887. Earthenwares, creamwares, porcelains, ironstone, and other ceramics were made. Most of the pieces are marked with a form of the word *Davenport*.

DAVENPORT LONGPORT STAFFORDSHRE.

Biscuit Jar, Silver Plated Cover, Cobalt Blue, Rust, Gold Gilding, Imari Style, c.1875, 6 x 4 In.	350.00
Compote, Daffodils, c.1850, 9 x 3 In.	62.00
Cup & Saucer, 3 Chinese Musicians, Dog, Flowers	160.00
Jug, Hydra Handle, Iron Red, Salmon, Cobalt Blue, Gilding, Marked, 4 ½ In.	450.00
Pitcher, White, Ironstone, Late 1800s, 7 ½ In.	40.00
Plate, Chinese Pastime, Children Playing, Red & White, Staffordshire, 1840, 7 ½ In.	215.00
Plate, Flowers, Chinese Style, Blue Underglaze, Enamels, Marked, c.1815, 6 In.	62.00
Plate, Poinsett's Defense, Man On Balcony, American Flag, 7 In.	375.00

DAVY CROCKETT, the American frontiersman, was born in 1786 and died in 1836. The historical character gained new fame in 1954 when the Walt Disney television show ran a series of episodes featuring Fess Parker as Davy Crockett. Coonskin caps and buckskins became popular and hundreds of different Davy Crockett items were made.

Badge, Indian Scout, Brass, 2 Crossed Muskets, Powder Horn In Center	25.00
Badge, Scout, Silver Pot Metal, 2 Crossed Muskets, Red Lettering	29.00
Car Seat, Padded Vinyl, Repeat Images, Stuffed Vinyl Horsehead, Reins, 2 ½ x 5 ½ In.	230.00
Cookie Jar, Full-Bodied, Marked, Brush, 10 In.	89.00
Cookie Jar, Head, Marked, McCoy, 10 In.	125.00
Cookie Jar, Marked, C. Miller, 55-140B, Cold Painted, Regal, 11 In. ...*illus*	118.00
Doll, Hard Plastic, Hat & Pouch, 8 In.	225.00
Flashlight, Gun Charms, Store Display Card, Holds 12, Boxes, Bantam-Lite, 9 ½ x 15 In.	355.00
Game, Adventure Trails, Larry's Toy Products, Pa., Box, 1955, 16 x 8 In.	115.00
Guitar, Marbleized Chocolate Brown, Plastic, Reliable Plastic, 1956, 20 In.	250.00
Lamp, Figural, Graphic Shade, Gold Paint, Box, Remco Mfg., c.1955, 5 x 5 x 15 In.	254.00
Lamp, Figural, Premco Co., 1954, 14 In.	225.00
Lunch Box, Davy Fighting Indian, Metal, Thermos, 1955	99.00
Lunch Box, Frontier, Green Plastic, Red Handle, Latches, Art illustration, 1950s, 5 x 9 x 7 In.	221.00
Mug, Davy Crockett In Brown, Fire-King, Anchor Hocking	28.00
Mug, Rifle Handle, Full-Bodied, Marked, McCoy, 10 In.	125.00
Pin, Davy Crockett Indian Fighter, Kneeling, Rifle, Coonskin Cap, Yellow Ground, ⅞ In.	23.00
Pocket Knife, Fess Parker As Davy, 3 In.	90.00
Puzzle, Davy With Powder Horn & Pistol, Whitman, 1955, 15 x 15 In.	60.00
Sheet Music, Ballad Of Davy Crockett, Wonderland Music, Davy On Cover, 16 Pages, 1955	58.00
Statue, Coonskin Cap, Musket, Powder Horn, Fringe Buckskin, 15 ½ In.	183.00
Toy Chest, Padded Lid Seat, Hinged, Pennant Corp, c.1955, 15 x 30 x 15 In. ...*illus*	115.00
Wallet, Brown, Vinyl, Portrait, Frontier Hero, Coin Snap	17.00
Wristwatch, Powder Horn Whistle, Waterproof, Box, 7 ¾ x 3 In.	150.00

DE VEZ was a signature used on cameo glass after 1910. E. S. Monot founded the glass company near Paris in 1851. The company changed names many times. Mt. Joye, another glass by this factory, is listed in its own category.

Vase, Arabian Skyline, Purple Palm Trees, Pink Mountains, Signed, c.1920, 8 In.	840.00
Vase, Blue & Green, Lady, Island Castle, Quadrafold Bird Beak Rim, Signed, 9 ¼ In.	840.00

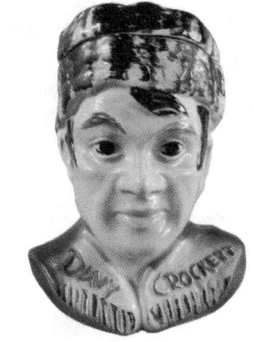

Davy Crockett, Cookie Jar, Marked, C. Miller, 55-140B, Cold Painted, Regal, 11 In.
$118.00

Davy Crockett, Toy Chest, Padded Lid Seat, Hinged, Pennant Corp, c.1955, 15 x 30 x 15 In.
$115.00

De Vez, Vase, Maiden Portrait, Lake Scene, Signed, 8 In.
$920.00

Decoy, Blue-Winged Teal Drake & Hen, Des Allemandes, Ski Roger, Pair
$717.00

Decoy, Canvasback, Carved, Painted, Karl Smeltzer, High Rock, Penn., 15 ½ In. $263.00

Decoy, Eider Drake, Hardwood, Painted, Stenciled WB, Early 1900s, 22 ½ In. $353.00

Decoy, Goose, York County, Penn., Susquehanna River, Early 1900s, Ralph Gipe, 24 ½ In. $527.00

Decoy, Sea Gull, Hollow Body, Relief Carved Wings, Early 20th Century, 22 ½ In. $1112.00

Decoy, Shorebird, Yellow Legs, Hurley Conklin, 20th Century, 14 ¼ In. $234.00

Vase, Blue, Green Winter Village Scene, Lake, Sleds, Cylinder Shape, Signed, 7 ½ In.	633.00
Vase, Green Glass, Squirrel, Tree, Lake Mountains, Cylinder, Signed, 19 ½ In.	1840.00
Vase, Maiden Portrait, Lake Scene, Signed, 8 In. *illus*	920.00
Vase, Mountain, Trees, Lake Scene, Green, Pink & Yellow, Signed, 10 In.	1000.00
Vase, River Scene, Tree, Golden Yellow & Orange Ground, Carved, Oval, 20th Century, 6 ⅞ x 4 In.	930.00
Vase, Yellow, Lake Scene, Sailing Ships, Squat, Oval, Signed, 5 In.	425.00
Vase, Yellow, Red Mountain, Lake Scene, Boater, Signed, 5 In.	500.00

DECORATED TUMBLERS have been made by Anchor Hocking, Federal, Hazel Atlas, Libbey, and other companies since the 1930s, when the pyroglaze process of printing was introduced. The barware and other glasses feature drinking jokes, characters, or decorative geometric patterns. Swankyswigs are listed in their own category. Decorated tumblers may also be listed in Advertising, Coca-Cola, Pepsi-Cola, and many other categories.

Bass Since 1777, Red Triangle Logo, 6 In., 14 Oz.	7.00
Carlsberg, Green Letters, Crown, Gold Rim, Flared Pilsner, 8 In.	10.00
Carlsberg, Red Letters, Crown, Dimpled Base, 5 ¾ In.	9.00
Guinness-Draught, Irish Harp Logo, 6 ¼ In., Pt.	7.00
Haake-Beck, Crossed Anchor Logo, Footed, 6 ¾ In.	7.00
Newcastle Brown Ale, 6 ¼ In., Pt.	7.00
Pilsner Urquell, Crest, Gold Rim, 9 In.	10.00
Schweppes, Logo, Etched, Panels, Fluted, 1983, 6 In.	10.00

DECOYS are carved or turned wooden copies of birds, fish, or animals. The decoy was placed in the water or propped on the shore to lure flying birds to the pond for hunters. Some decoys are handmade; some are commercial products. Today there is a group of artists making modern decoys for display, not for use in a pond. Many sell for high prices.

Black-Bellied Plover, Carved, Painted, Stamped, William J. Mackey Jr., c.1910, 10 In.	1521.00
Blue-Winged Teal Drake & Hen, Des Allemandes, Ski Roger, Pair *illus*	717.00
Blue-Winged Teal Drake, Carved, Painted, A. Elmer Crowell, c.1922, 4 In.	1404.00
Bluebill Drake, Brass Tack Eyes, Incised Feathers, Ontario, 16 In.	173.00
Bluebill Drake, Glass Eyes, Painted, High Metal Keel, Wisconsin, 14 In.	173.00
Bluebill, Carved Wing & Tail Feathers, Glass Eyes, 20th Century, 13 ½ In.	294.00
Bluebill, Painted, Glass Eyes, Mason, 14 In.	201.00
Bufflehead, Black, White, Gray Speckled, Glass Eyes, 6 x 8 ½ In.	489.00
Canada Goose, Painted Slat Body, Carved, c.1920, 45 In.	350.00
Canvasback Drake, Carved, Painted, Applied Head, Glass Eyes, Mason Decoy Co., 6 ½ x 15 In.	132.00
Canvasback Drake, Combed Back Feathers, Wood, Raoul Pilon, Quebec, 16 In.	106.00
Canvasback Drake, Painted, Ward Brothers, Crisfield, Maryland, c.1930, 7 x 16 In.	6250.00
Canvasback, Carved, Painted, Karl Smeltzer, High Rock, Penn., 15 ½ In. *illus*	263.00
Canvasback, Glass Eyes, Painted Feathers, Branded Mark, Reeves, Ontario, 15 In.	173.00
Duck Drake, Wood, Multicolored Paint, Log Base, Tony Chiado, c.1930, 11 In.	353.00
Duck, Black, Ben Schmidt, Stamped Feathers, Raised Wing Tips, Detroit, Mich., c.1940, 17 In.	295.00
Eider Drake, Hardwood, Painted, Stenciled WB, Early 1900s, 22 ½ In. *illus*	353.00
Fish, Chautauqua Lake, Leather Tail, Bulbous Tack Eyes, Carved, Painted, c.1900, 6 ½ In.	283.00
Fish, Double Headed, Copper, Charlie Slecta, Wayzata, Minn., 1930s, 9 x 9 In.	354.00
Fish, Musk, Dellunge, Glass Eyes, Wood, 20th Century, 18 In.	470.00
Fish, Perch, Painted Eye, 6 Tin Fins, George Aho, Elk Lake, Mich., July, 1986	118.00
Fish, Pike, Carved, Painted, Applied Tin Fins, Tack Eyes, Line Attachments, Weight, 8 ¼ In.	121.00
Fish, Pike, John Fairfield, 1989, 10 ½ In.	173.00
Fish, Tin Tail, Red Paint, 4 Tin Fins, Bead Eyes, Wooden Silver Colored Body, Beads, Sequins, 1950s	70.00
Fish, Trout, Brown, Carved, Painted, Applied Tin Fins, Weighted, On Pedestal, 8 ¼ In.	99.00
Frog, Wood Body, Rubber Legs, Red, White Belly, Bud Stewart, 5 ½ In.	106.00
Goldeneye Drake, Working, Carved, Painted, Glass Eyes, Lead Weight, 6 ½ x 13 In.	33.00
Goose, Long Neck, Painted, Carved, Signed, G. Mirando	85.00
Goose, York County, Penn., Susquehanna River, Early 1900s, Ralph Gipe, 24 ½ In. *illus*	527.00
Horned Owl, Carved, Metal Hanger, Shotgun Casing Eyes, Block Base, Casey Edwards, 1970s, 19 In.	248.00
Mallard Drake, Carved, Painted, Mason Decoy Factory, Michigan, c.1905, 18 In.	760.00
Mallard Drake, Herter's, Wood, Rough Finish, Painted, 17 In.	205.00
Mallard Drake, Signed, Tom Taber, 15 In.	115.00
Mallard, Glass Bead Eyes, Wood, Dodge Decoy Factory, Detroit, Michigan, c.1895, 15 In.	646.00
Mallard, Glass Eyes, Painted, George Red Weir, 7 ½ x 19 In.	294.00
Merganser Hen, Working, Applied Head, Glass Eyes, Lead Weight, 6 ½ x 16 ½ In.	176.00
Merganser, Ridged Head & Wings, c.1925, 8 ½ x 18 In.	1150.00
Owl, Wood, Carved, Painted, Glass Eyes, Base, 20 In.	47.00
Owl, Wood, Carved, Painted, Slats, Steel & Leather Mounts, Hanging, 27 In.	2070.00

D

Pintail Drake, Signed, Tom Taber, 16 In.	115.00
Quail, Metal, Hollow Body, Hand Painted, Internal Squeaker, 9 ½ In.	130.00
Red-Breasted Merganser, Incised Eyes & Bill, Mortised Head, G.R. Guey, 1940, 7 x 18 In.	2130.00
Ruddy Trunstone, Carved, Painted, Carved Eye Grooves, c.1905, 8 In.	527.00
Sea Gull, Hollow Body, Relief Carved Wings, Early 20th Century, 22 ½ In. .... *illus*	1112.00
Shorebird, Inserted Eyes, Long Bill, 5 ½ x 14 In.	2300.00
Shorebird, Wood, Glass Eyes, Painted, Wood Stand, Late 20th Century, 14 In.	118.00
Shorebird, Yellow Legs, Carved, Painted, Tack Eyes, Stand, 19th Century, 9 ½ & 9 ⅝ In., Pair.	8888.00
Shorebird, Yellow Legs, Hurley Conklin, 20th Century, 14 ¼ In. .... *illus*	234.00
Snow Goose, Wood, 17 x 11 x 8 In.	55.00
Snowy Owl, Carved Body, Glass Eyes, Stamped B.B.D., Back Bay Decoys, 1900s, 16 In.	121.00
Swan, Carved, Painted, Harpers Island, N.C., 9 x 30 In.	92.00
Swan, Wood, White Paint, 32 x 34 In.	220.00
Wood Duck, Black, White Paint, R. Madison, Mitchell, Maryland, 1948, 24 In.	206.00
Wood Duck, Carved, Painted, c.1930, 6 x 6 x 15 In.	70.00

DEDHAM POTTERY was started in 1895. Chelsea Keramic Art Works was established in 1872 in Chelsea, Massachusetts, by members of the Robertson family. The factory closed in 1889 and was reorganized as the Chelsea Pottery U.S. in 1891. The firm used the marks *CKAW* and *CPUS*. It became the Dedham Pottery of Dedham, Massachusetts. The factory closed in 1943. It was famous for its crackleware dishes, which picture blue outlines of animals, flowers, and other natural motifs. Pottery by Chelsea Keramic Art Works and Dedham Pottery is listed here.

4 Stylized Buds, Plate, Flower Center, Marked, 6 In.	360.00
Ashtray, Nude Carrying Yoke, 4 ⅝ In.	1508.00
Birds In Potted Orange Tree, Plate, Impressed, 1895, 8 ½ In.	257.00
Crab, Plate, Waves, Marked, 5 ⅞ In.	295.00
Duck, Plate, Marked, 8 ½ In.	115.00
Flower, Plate, Stylized, Blue & Gray Crackle Glaze, 6 In. ....*illus*	360.00
Grape, Charger, Marked, 12 In.	390.00
Iris, Plate, 8 ½ In.	186.00
Lotus Petal, Bowl, Marked, 5 ⅛ In.	162.00
Magnolia, Plate, 7 ⅜ In.	158.00
Magnolia, Plate, Marked, 10 In.	190.00
Mushroom, Plate, Blue On White Crackle Ground, Marked, 10 In. ....*illus*	360.00
Mushroom, Plate, Marked, 10 In.	360.00
Pineapple, Plate, Blue, White, Crackle Glaze, 8 ⅝ In.	207.00
Polar Bear, Plate, Marked, 8 ¼ In.	378.00
Pond Lily, Plate, Marked, 10 In.	115.00
Poppy, Plate, Marked, 8 ½ In.	400.00
Rabbit, Bowl, 2 ⅝ x 4 ⅞ In.	35.00
Rabbit, Bowl, Marked, 2 ½ x 6 In.	395.00
Rabbit, Mixing Bowl, Blue Stamp, 4 x 9 In.	115.00
Rabbit, Mug, Blue Stamp, 4 ¼ In.	219.00
Rabbit, Salt & Pepper, Bulbous, Blue Stamp, 2 ⅝ In.	142.00
Snowtree, Plate, Marked, 10 ¼ In.	420.00
Turkey, Plate, Blue On White Crackle Ground, Marked, 10 In.....................*illus*	360.00
Turkey, Plate, Marked, 10 In.	360.00
Vase, Landscape, Shouldered, Crackleware, Hugh Robertson, 7 ¾ x 5 ½ In.	1098.00
Vase, Mirrored Oxblood Glaze, Green Streaks, Hugh Robertson, 6 ¼ x 5 In.	3172.00
Vase, Mirrored Oxblood Glaze, Hugh Robertson, 5 ¼ x 3 In.	1830.00

DELATTE glass is a French cameo glass made by Andre Delatte. It was first made in Nancy, France, in 1921. Lighting fixtures and opaque glassware in imitation of Bohemian opaline were made. There were many French cameo glassmakers, so be sure to look in other appropriate categories.

Vase, Blue Grass & Flowers, White Ground, Bulbous, Squat, Flared Rim, 5 ½ In.	549.00

DELDARE, *see Buffalo Pottery Deldare.*

DELFT is a tin-glazed pottery that has been made since the seventeenth century. Delft was made in England in the eighteenth century. It is decorated with blue on white or with colored decorations. Most of the pieces sold today were made after 1891, and the name *Holland* usually appears with the Delft factory marks. The word *Delft* appears alone on some inexpensive twentieth- and twenty-first-century pottery from Asia and Germany that is also listed here.

Bowl, 2 Branch Handles, Bulbous, Crimped Flaring Rim, Landscape, Cherub, c.1850, 4 x 9 In.	402.00
Box, Hinged Metal Cover, Frame, Flower, Leaf Border, Couple Playing, Landscape, 5 ¼ In.	356.00

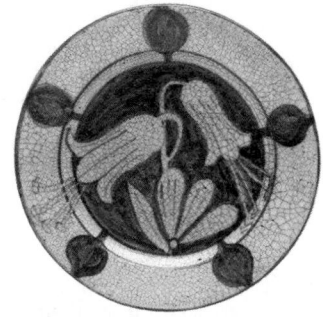

Dedham Pottery, Flower, Plate, Stylized, Blue & Gray Crackle Glaze, 6 In.
$360.00

Dedham Pottery, Mushroom, Plate, Blue On White Crackle Ground, Marked, 10 In.
$360.00

Dedham Pottery, Turkey, Plate, Blue On White Crackle Ground, Marked, 10 In.
$360.00

Delft, Caudle Cup, Cover, Chinese Pavilions, Blue, White, Handles, Mid 1800s, 4 ½ x 4 ¾ In.
$72.00

Delft, Flower Brick, Cobalt Blue, 12 Holes, 18th Century, 3 ¾ x 6 ¼ x 2 ⅝ In. $920.00

Delft, Jar, Cover, Flower Vase, Scroll, Leaves, Flowers, Marked, Dutch, 1700s, 13 In., Pair $1003.00

Delft, Jug, Puzzle, Earthenware, Pierced Heart, 3 Spouts, Verse, c.1730, 7 In. $2938.00

Delft, Vase, Cover, Chinese Style, Octagonal, Paneled, Foo Dog Finial, Marked, 23 x 10 ¼ In. $900.00

Canister, Blue & White, Flowers, Octagonal, 4 ⅞ In.	563.00
Castor, Sugar, Blue & White, 18th Century, 7 In.	295.00
Caudle Cup, Cover, Chinese Pavilions, Blue, White, Handles, Mid 1800s, 4 ½ x 4 ¾ In. ....*illus*	72.00
Figurine, Woman In Rocking Basket Bed, 18th Century Dress, Painted Coverlet, 4 x 6 In.	748.00
Flower Brick, Cobalt Blue, 12 Holes, 18th Century, 3 ¾ x 6 ¼ x 2 ⅝ In. ....*illus*	920.00
Ginger Jar, Lid, Lion & Crest Finials, 15 x 7 In., Pair	960.00
Jar, Cover, Flower Vase, Scroll, Leaves, Flowers, Marked, Dutch, 1700s, 13 In., Pair ....*illus*	1003.00
Jar, Cover, Houses, Trees, Blue, White, Panels, Ribs, Baluster, Foo Dog Finial, Marked, AL, 15 In., Pair	465.00
Jar, Domed Cover, Figure & Landscape Cartouches, Ovoid, Relief Notches, 16 In., Pair	1150.00
Jar, Domed Cover, Vase Of Flowers, Scrolls, Leaves, Stylized Axe Mark, 13 In., Pair	978.00
Jug, Puzzle, Earthenware, Pierced Heart, 3 Spouts, Verse, c.1730, 7 In. ....*illus*	2938.00
Mug, Buildings, Tower, Applied Handle, Pewter Hinged Lid, Shell Finger Grip, c.1750, 7 In.	805.00
Punch Bowl, Peony Sprays, Blue & White, 4 Lobed Panels, c.1750, 10 In.	1425.00
Tile, Blue & White, Figural, Boats, Seaside House, Peasant Woman, Boy, Dutch, 6 Piece, 7 x 7 In.	240.00
Tile, Stallion, Black Wood Frame, 6 Piece, 12 x 17 In.	1007.00
Tureen, Cover, Grape Cluster Form, Manganese Glaze, Green Leaf Knop & Finial, 6 In.	2070.00
Urn, Blue & White, Baluster Shape, Chinoiserie Figural Landscape, 1700s, 11 ½ In.	345.00
Urn, Cover, Final, Blue & White, Dutch, Signed, 17 In.	263.00
Vase, Blue & White, Basket Of Flowers, Bird Finial, Leaf Border, Octagonal, 18th Century, 14 ½ In.	415.00
Vase, Cover, Chinese Style, Octagonal, Paneled, Foo Dog Finial, Marked, 23 x 10 ¼ In. ....*illus*	900.00
Vase, Cylindrical, Turquoise Glaze, Black Geometric Designs, Marked, 9 In.	259.00
Wine Bottle, Round, 1646, 7 ¼ In.	4148.00

DENTAL cabinets, chairs, equipment, and other related items are listed here. Other objects may be found in the Medical category.

Cabinet, Eastlake, Walnut, Marble, 2 Tiers Gallery, Mirror, Doors, Fitted Interior, 33 x 70 In.	3163.00
Cabinet, Oak, Glass Doors, Fitted Interior, Drawers, Doors, American Cabinet Co., 28 x 66 In.	5175.00
Cabinet, Pine, 30 Stacked Drawers, Enamel Pull Knobs, c.1850, 53 ½ In.	644.00
Key, Wrought Iron, Locking Mechanism, 5 ¼ In.	275.00
Key, Wrought Iron, Ring Handle, Single Claw, Early 1800s, 4 ¾ In.	150.00
Key, Wrought Iron, Studded, Single Claw, 5 In.	150.00
Scaler Set, Ivory Handles, Mahogany Case, 7 Piece	420.00
Sign, Keep The Happy Smile, Elf Character, Wood, Die Cut, 32 x 46 In.	118.00

DENVER is part of the mark on an American art pottery. William Long of Steubenville, Ohio, founded the Lonhuda Pottery Company in 1892. In 1900 he moved to Denver, Colorado, and organized the Denver China and Pottery Company. This pottery, which used the mark Denver, worked until 1905 when Long moved to New Jersey and founded the Clifton Pottery. Long also worked for Weller Pottery, Roseville Pottery, and American Encaustic Tiling Company. Do not confuse this pottery with the Denver White Pottery, which worked from 1894 to 1955 in Denver.

DENVER
C T &
P Co

Vase, Blue,White Embossed Design, Tapered, Marked, 3 x 4 In. ....*illus*	180.00

DEPRESSION GLASS is an inexpensive glass that was manufactured in large quantities during the 1920s and early 1930s. It was made in many colors and patterns by dozens of factories in the United States. Most patterns were also made in clear glass, which the factories called *crystal.* If no color is listed here, it is clear. The name *Depression glass* is a modern one and also refers to machine-made glass of the 1940s through 1970s. For more prices, go to kovels.com. Sets missing a few pieces can be completed through the help of one of the many matching services listed on our website.

Adam, Bowl, Cover, Pink, 9 In.	80.00
Adam, Bowl, Pink, 7 ¾ In.	30.00
Adam, Bowl, Pink, 8 In. ....*illus*	25.00
Adam, Bowl, Vegetable, Oval, Green	36.00
Adam, Butter, Cover, Pink	95.00
Adam, Cake Plate, Pink	30.00
Adam, Candlestick, Pink, Pair	77.00
Adam, Grill Plate, Divided, Green	22.00
Adam, Pitcher, Pink, 8 In.	72.00
Adam, Plate, Bread & Butter, Pink, 6 In.	10.00
Adam, Plate, Salad, Square, Pink, 7 ¾ In.	19.00
Adam, Relish, 2 Sections, Pink, 8 In.	30.00
Adam, Sherbet, Pink, 6 In., 8 Piece	44.00
Adam's Rib, Compote, Oval, Pink	18.00
Alice, Saucer, Jade-Ite	8.00
American Sweetheart, Berry Bowl, Pink, 3 ¾ In.	75.00

D

American Sweetheart, Bowl, Oval, Pink, 10 ¾ x 8 ¼ In.	70.00
American Sweetheart, Chop Plate, Monax, 10 ½ In.	20.00
American Sweetheart, Plate, Luncheon, Monax, 9 ⅛ In.	12.00
American Sweetheart, Soup, Cream, Handles, Pink, 4 ½ In.	82.00

Apple Blossom pattern is listed here as Dogwood.

Aramis, Tumbler, Cobalt Blue, c.1936, 12 Oz., 5 In.	20.00
Aunt Polly, Berry Bowl, Blue, 4 In.	12.00
Aunt Polly, Bowl, Fruit, Blue, 8 In.	40.00
Aunt Polly, Dish, Pickle, Oval, 2 Handles, Green, 7 ¼ In.	20.00
Aunt Polly, Plate, Bread & Butter, Blue, 6 ⅛ In.	10.00
Aunt Polly, Vase, Blue, 6 ½ In.	52.00
Aurora, Bowl, Cereal, Pink, 5 ⅜ In.	10.00
Aurora, Creamer, Ritz Blue .... *illus*	6.00
Aurora, Tumbler, Ritz Blue, 9 Oz., 4 ¾ In.	20.00
Avocado, Sugar & Creamer, Green, 4 ¾ In. & 3 ⅝ In.	90.00

Ballerina pattern is listed here as Cameo.

Bamboo Optic, Console, Rolled Edge, Pink, 13 ½ In.	95.00
Bamboo Optic, Creamer, Green...	10.00
Bamboo Optic, Plate, Luncheon, Pink, 8 In.	6.00
Bamboo Optic, Plate, Salad, Octagonal, Pink, 7 In.	6.00

Banded Rib pattern is listed here as Coronation.

Basket pattern is listed here as No. 615.

Beaded Block, Bowl, 7 In.	20.00
Beaded Block, Bowl, Cupped, 5 ½ In.	24.00
Beaded Block, Bowl, Oval, 8 ½ In.	24.00
Beaded Block, Bowl, Round, 5 ½ In.	24.00
Beaded Block, Candy Dish, Cover, Pear Shape, Amber......................	423.00
Beaded Block, Creamer...	12.00
Beaded Block, Soup, Cream, Blue Opalescent	90.00
Beaded Block, Vase, Pink, 6 In.	20.00

Block pattern is listed here as Block Optic.

Block Optic, Bowl, Cereal, Green, 5 ½ In.	12.00
Block Optic, Bowl, Green, 4 ¼ In.	7.75
Block Optic, Creamer, Green, 4 ¼ In.	14.00
Block Optic, Cup & Saucer, Green	15.00
Block Optic, Goblet, Water, 9 Oz., 5 ¾ In.	15.00
Block Optic, Pitcher, Green, 54 Oz., 8 ½ In.	65.00
Block Optic, Plate, Dinner, Green, 9 In.	30.00
Block Optic, Plate, Dinner, Yellow, 9 In.	45.00
Block Optic, Plate, Salad, Green, 8 In.	7.00
Block Optic, Plate, Salad, Yellow, 8 ¼ In.	6.00
Block Optic, Plate, Sandwich, 10 ¼ In.	12.00
Block Optic, Sherbet, Footed, 3 ½ In.	8.00
Block Optic, Sherbet, Green .... *illus*	8.00
Block Optic, Sugar, Handles, Green, 4 ¼ In.	12.50
Block Optic, Sugar, Pink, Tall	13.00

Bouquet & Lattice pattern is listed here as Normandie.

Bowknot, Cup, Green..	10.00
Bowknot, Sherbet, Footed, Green, 2 x 3 ¾ In.	20.00
Bubble, Bowl, Cereal, Forest Green, 5 ¼ In.	8.00
Bubble, Bowl, Fruit, 4 ¼ In.	4.00
Bubble, Bowl, Fruit, Red, 4 ½ In.	10.00
Bubble, Bowl, Vegetable, Marigold Iridescent, 8 ¼ In.	16.00
Bubble, Creamer, Forest Green	18.00
Bubble, Cup & Saucer, Green	11.00
Bubble, Cup & Saucer, Sapphire Blue..	6.50 to 9.00
Bubble, Plate, Dinner, Green	25.00
Bubble, Plate, Dinner, Red, 9 ⅜ In.	25.00
Bubble, Serving Bowl, Forest Green, 8 ½ In.	18.00
Bubble, Sherbet, Ruby, 3 ½ In. .... *illus*	12.00
Bubble, Soup, Dish, Sapphire Blue, 7 ¾ In.	16.00
Bubble, Tumbler, Cocktail, Desert Gold	10.00
Bubble, Tumbler, Juice, Desert Gold..	12.00
Bubble, Tumbler, Juice, Forest Green, 4 ⅝ In.	12.50

Bullseye pattern is listed here as Bubble.

Buttons & Bows pattern is listed here as Holiday.

Cabbage Rose pattern is listed here as Sharon.

D

Denver, Vase, Blue, White Embossed Design, Tapered, Marked, 3 x 4 In. $180.00

Depression Glass, Adam, Bowl, Pink, 8 In. $25.00

Depression Glass, Aurora, Creamer, Ritz Blue $6.00

Depression Glass, Block Optic, Sherbet, Green $8.00

TIP

Use a Depression glass or plastic knife to cut lettuce. The lettuce won't turn brown.

Depression Glass, Bubble, Sherbet, Ruby, 3 ½ In. $12.00

Depression Glass, Cameo, Relish, 3 Sections, Green, 7 ½ In. $20.00

Depression Glass, Cherry Blossom, Pitcher, Pink, 6 ¾ In. $55.00

Depression Glass, Fire-King, Batter Bowl, Jade-Ite, 9 ½ In. $55.00

Depression Glass, Fire-King, Mixing Bowl, Splashproof, Turquoise, Graduated, 6 ¾ & 7 ½ & 8 ½ In., 3 Piece $125.00

Cameo, Bowl, Dessert, 4 ½ In.	7.00
Cameo, Bowl, Vegetable, Green	35.00
Cameo, Bowl, Vegetable, Green, Oval, 10 In.	30.00
Cameo, Cake Plate, 3-Footed, Green, 10 In.	40.00
Cameo, Console, Green, 3-Footed, 11 In.	85.00
Cameo, Cookie Jar, Cover, Green	60.00
Cameo, Goblet, Water, Green, 6 In.	65.00
Cameo, Grill Plate, Yellow	12.00
Cameo, Plate, Dinner, Yellow	12.00
Cameo, Plate, Salad, 7 In.	5.00
Cameo, Relish, 3 Sections, Green, 7 ½ In. ....*illus*	20.00
Cameo, Sherbet, Green, 3 ¼ In.	15.00
Candlewick pattern is listed in the Imperial Glass category.	
Cape Cod pattern is listed in the Imperial Glass category.	
Caprice pattern is included in the Cambridge Glass category.	
Charm, Bowl, Fruit, Forest Green, 4 ¾ In.	8.00
Charm, Bowl, Royal Ruby, 4 ¾ In.	7.00
Charm, Creamer, Forest Green	7.00
Charm, Cup & Saucer, Forest Green	8.00 to 9.00
Charm, Plate, Dinner, Azurite, 9 ¼ In.	23.00
Charm, Plate, Salad, Azurite, 6 ½ In.	10.00
Charm, Sugar & Creamer, Forest Green	16.00
Cherry Blossom, Berry Bowl, Large, Pink, 8 ⅜ In.	50.00
Cherry Blossom, Bowl, 2 Handles, Delphite, 9 ½ In.	25.00
Cherry Blossom, Bowl, Green, Oval, 9 x 6 ¾ In.	50.00
Cherry Blossom, Bowl, Pink, Oval, 9 x 6 ¾ In.	50.00
Cherry Blossom, Cake Plate, Footed, Pink, 10 ¼ In.	35.00
Cherry Blossom, Cup & Saucer, Pink, 14 Piece	94.00
Cherry Blossom, Cup, Delphite	18.00
Cherry Blossom, Pitcher, Pink, 6 ¾ In. ....*illus*	55.00
Cherry Blossom, Pitcher, Scalloped Base, Green, 6 ¾ In.	75.00
Cherry Blossom, Plate, Dinner, Pink, 9 In.	16.00
Cherry Blossom, Sherbet, Footed, Green	20.00
Cherry Blossom, Soup, Dish, Flat, Green, 7 ¾ In.	105.00
Cherry Blossom, Sugar & Creamer, Cover, Pink	60.00
Cherry Blossom, Sugar, Cover Only, Green	25.00
Cherry Blossom, Sugar, Cover, Pink, 4 ⅜ In.	34.00
Cherry Blossom, Tray, 2 Handles, Round, Pink, 10 ½ In.	32.00
Cherry Blossom, Tumbler, Footed, Delphite, 4 Oz., 3 ¾ In.	24.00
Cherry Blossom, Tumbler, Iced Tea, Footed, Pink	48.00
Cherry Blossom, Tumbler, Juice, Footed, Pink, 3 ⅝ In.	18.00
Cherry Blossom, Tumbler, Round Base, Pink, 4 ⅜ In.	38.00
Cherry, Tumbler, Flat, Green, 9 Oz.	24.00
Cherry, Tumbler, Scalloped, Green, 8 Oz.	39.00
Cherryberry, Sugar, Cover Only, Green	40.00
Chevron, Pitcher, Milk, Blue, 4 ¼ In.	24.00
Chinex Classic, Bowl, Cereal, Castle Decal, Blue Trim, 5 ¾ In.	18.00
Chinex Classic, Cake Plate, Flower Decal, 12 ⅛ In.	12.00
Chinex Classic, Sherbet, Castle Decal, Blue Trim, 4 ½ In.	25.00
Chinex Classic, Soup, Dish, Castle Decal, Blue Trim, 7 ½ In.	35.00
Christmas Candy, Sugar, Teal	29.00
Cloverleaf, Plate, Luncheon, Pink, 8 In.	10.00
Cloverleaf, Sherbet, Black, Footed, 3 In.	20.00
Cloverleaf, Sherbet, Green, Footed, 3 In.	10.00
Cloverleaf, Tumbler, Green, 4 In.	95.00
Coin Spot, Pitcher, Amber, 32 Oz.	25.00
Colonial Block, Creamer, Pink	15.00
Colonial Block, Powder Jar, Cover, Green, Footed	40.00
Colonial Block, Sugar, Cover, Pink	25.00
Colonial Fluted, Berry Bowl, Green, 7 ½ In.	20.00
Colonial Fluted, Bowl, Cereal, Green, 6 In.	18.00
Colonial Fluted, Cup & Saucer, Green	10.00
Colonial Fluted, Plate, Luncheon, Green 8 In.	9.00
Colonial, Berry Bowl, Green, 4 ½ In.	20.00
Colonial, Butter, Cover, Green	60.00
Colonial, Cup, Green	12.50
Colonial, Pitcher, 68 Oz., 7 ¾ In.	35.00
Colonial, Plate, Luncheon, Green, 8 ½ In.	6.00

Colonial, Plate, Luncheon, Pink, 8 ½ In.	12.00
Colonial, Sherbet, Pink, 3 ⅞ In.	12.00
Columbia, Bowl, Cereal, 5 In.	18.00
Columbia, Bowl, Ruffled, 10 ½ In.	20.00
Columbia, Butter, Dome Cover, 6-In. Square	20.00
Columbia, Plate, Bread & Butter, 6 In.	3.00
Columbia, Plate, Salad, 8 ½ In.	20.00
Coronation, Berry Bowl, Royal Ruby, 8 In.	20.00
Coronation, Bowl, Royal Ruby, 6 ½ In.	20.00
Cremax, Cup & Saucer, Bluebell	12.00
Cremax, Sugar, Bluebell	10.00
Daisy & Button, Tray, Round, 12 In.	45.00
Daisy pattern is listed here as No. 620.	
Dancing Girl pattern is listed here as Cameo.	
Diamond pattern is listed here as Miss America.	
Diamond Block, Sugar & Creamer, Green...	26.00
Diamond Quilted, Cup & Saucer	12.00
Diamond Quilted, Cup, Pink	8.00
Diana, Bowl, Cereal, Pink, 5 In.	7.00
Diana, Coaster Set, Pink, 3 ³⁄₁₆ In., 4 Piece	40.00
Diana, Cup, After Dinner, 2 In.	25.00
Diana, Sandwich Server, Amber, 11 ½ In.	15.00
Dogwood, Cake Plate, Pink, 13 In.	61.00
Dogwood, Grill Plate, Divided, Pink, 10 ½ In.	21.00
Dogwood, Pitcher, Pink, 80 Oz., 8 In.	228.00
Dogwood, Plate, Dinner, Pink, 9 ¼ In.	30.00
Dogwood, Salver, Pink, 12 In.	35.00
Dogwood, Saucer, Pink	14.00
Dogwood, Sherbet, Low Footed, Pink...	33.00
Dogwood, Tray, 2 Tiers, Pink	44.00
Doric & Pansy, Berry Bowl, Green, 8 In.	28.00
Doric, Berry Bowl, Pink, 8 ¼ In.	25.00
Doric, Butter, Cover, Round, Pink...	44.00
Doric, Cake Plate, Footed, Green, 10 In.	16.00
Doric, Candy Dish, 3 Sections, Pink, 6 ¾ In.	15.00
Doric, Candy Jar, Open, Green	23.00
Doric, Goblet, Footed, Pink, 5 In., Pair...	11.00
Doric, Sugar, Cover, Green	30.00
Doric, Tumbler, Footed, Pink, 5 In., 5 Piece....................................	110.00
Driftwood, Pitcher, Peacock Blue, 8 In.	57.00
Driftwood, Tumbler, Juice, Daphine Blue, 4 ⅛ In.	14.25
Dutch Rose pattern is listed here as Rosemary.	
Fine Rib pattern is listed here as Homespun.	
Fire-King, Batter Bowl, Jade-Ite, 9 ½ In. ....*illus*	55.00
Fire-King, Bowl, Chili, Jade-Ite, 5 In.	13.00
Fire-King, Bowl, Fruit, Jade-Ite, 4 ⅞ In.	14.00
Fire-King, Bowl, Maple Leaf, Tab Handle, Jade-Ite, 5 ½ In.	25.00
Fire-King, Casserole, Anchor Hocking, 11 x 7 ½ In.	8.00
Fire-King, Cup & Saucer, Forest Green	6.00
Fire-King, Cup & Saucer, Primrose...	5.00
Fire-King, Grease Jar, Tulip Lid, Ivory..	40.00
Fire-King, Jug, Ball, Tangerine...	72.00
Fire-King, Mixing Bowl Set, Swirl, Jade-Ite, 6 In., 7 In., 8 In., 9 In., 4 Piece	180.00
Fire-King, Mixing Bowl, Beaded Edge, Ivory, 4 ⅞ In.	15.00
Fire-King, Mixing Bowl, Red	28.00
Fire-King, Mixing Bowl, Splash Proof, Turquoise Blue, 2 Qt.........	45.00
Fire-King, Mixing Bowl, Splashproof, Turquoise, Graduated, 6 ¾ & 7 ½ & 8 ½ In., 3 Piece ....*illus*	125.00
Fire-King, Mixing Bowl, Swirl, Ivory, 8 In.	18.00
Fire-King, Mixing Bowl, Tulip, 3 Qt.	30.00
Fire-King, Mug, Restaurant, Jade-Ite	19.00
Fire-King, Mug, Turquoise Blue, 8 Oz.	18.00
Fire-King, Pitcher, Forest Green, 86 Oz..	48.00
Fire-King, Pitcher, Milk, Jade-Ite...	105.00
Fire-King, Plate, Lotus, Jade-Ite, 8 ¼ In. ....*illus*	16.00
Fire-King, Punch Set, 12 Punch Cups, Forest Green, 10-In. Bowl ..	85.00
Fire-King, Punch Set, 12 Punch Cups, Royal Ruby, 10-In. Bowl.....	115.00
Fire-King, Snack Set, Leaf & Blossom, Forest Green, 8-In. Plate, 4-In. Bowl	36.00
Fire-King, Sugar & Creamer, Cover, Primrose..................................	20.00

Depression Glass, Fire-King, Plate, Lotus, Jade-Ite, 8 ¼ In.
$16.00

Depression Glass, Floragold, Pitcher, Ice Lip, 64 Oz.
$45.00

Depression Glass, Floral, Butter, Cover, Pink
$90.00

Depression Glass, Florentine No. 2, Candy Dish, Cover, Yellow, 5 ½ In.
$275.00

DEPRESSION GLASS

Depression Glass, Georgian, Butter, Cover, Green
$115.00

Depression Glass, Homespun, Butter, Cover, Pink
$80.00

Depression Glass, Madrid, Pitcher, Amber, 36 Oz., 5 ¾ In.
$35.00

Depression Glass, Moderntone, Soup, Cream, Amethyst, Handles
$12.00

Depression Glass, Moderntone, Sugar, Platonite, Fired-On Green
$14.00

Fire-King, Sugar & Creamer, Flat, Royal Ruby	24.00
Fire-King, Sugar & Creamer, Footed, Royal Ruby	24.00
Fire-King, Tumbler, Roly Poly, Royal Ruby, 5 In.	8.00
Fire-King, Vase, Ball, Ivy, Royal Ruby, 6 In.	20.00
Fire-King, Vase, Bud, Ruffled, Royal Ruby, 3 In.	5.00
Fire-King, Vase, Deco Style, Jade-Ite, 5 ½ In.	22.00
Flat Diamond pattern is listed in the Imperial Glass category.	
Floragold, Berry Bowl, Square, 4 ½ In.	8.00
Floragold, Pitcher, Ice Lip, 64 Oz. ....*illus*	45.00
Floragold, Salt & Pepper, Iridescent	60.00
Floragold, Sugar & Creamer	36.00
Floral & Diamond Band, Sherbet, Green	7.00
Floral, Bowl, Vegetable, Cover, Pink, 8 In.	45.00
Floral, Butter, Cover, Pink ....*illus*	90.00
Floral, Butter, Cover, Poinsettia, Pink	90.00
Floral, Candy Dish, Pink	42.00
Floral, Candy Dish, Poinsettia, Pink, 4 ⅜ In.	40.00
Floral, Candy Jar, Cover, Pink	40.00
Floral, Cup & Saucer, Green	23.00
Floral, Pitcher, Lemonade, Pink, 48 Oz.	413.00
Floral, Pitcher, Lemonade, Pink, 48 Oz., 10 ¼ In.	342.00
Floral, Pitcher, Poinsettia, Pink, 7 ¾ In.	40.00
Floral, Plate, Dinner, Pink, 9 In.	15.00
Floral, Tray, Poinsettia, Pink, Square, 6 ½ In.	33.00
Floral, Tumbler, Footed, Pink, 9 Oz., 5 ¼ In.	54.00
Floral, Tumbler, Juice, Poinsettia, Pink, 4 In.	28.00
Floral, Tumbler, Water, Pink, 4 ¾ In.	20.00
Florentine No. 1, Creamer, Ruffled, Pink	45.00
Florentine No. 1, Cup & Saucer, Pink	17.50
Florentine No. 1, Plate, Dinner, Pink, 10 In.	30.00
Florentine No. 1, Sherbet, Pink, 3 In.	9.00
Florentine No. 1, Sugar & Creamer, Ruffled	20.00
Florentine No. 2, Berry Bowl, Green, 4 ½ In.	17.50
Florentine No. 2, Berry Bowl, Yellow, 8 In.	40.00
Florentine No. 2, Bowl, Cereal, Yellow, 6 In.	41.00
Florentine No. 2, Bowl, Cover, Yellow, 9 In.	90.00
Florentine No. 2, Butter, Cover, Round, Green	72.00
Florentine No. 2, Butter, Cover, Round, Yellow	88.00
Florentine No. 2, Candlestick, Yellow, 2 ¾ In., Pair	67.00
Florentine No. 2, Candy Dish, Cover, Yellow, 5 ½ In. ....*illus*	275.00
Florentine No. 2, Creamer, Green, 3 ⅜ In.	12.50
Florentine No. 2, Cup & Saucer, Green	12.50
Florentine No. 2, Grill Plate, Yellow	20.00
Florentine No. 2, Pitcher, Tumbler, Footed, Yellow, 7 & 5 In., 5 Piece	99.00
Florentine No. 2, Plate, Dinner, Yellow, 10 In., 8 Piece	121.00
Florentine No. 2, Plate, Dinner, Yellow, 9 ⅞ In.	15.00
Florentine No. 2, Plate, Salad, Yellow, 8 ½ In., 8 Piece	70.00
Florentine No. 2, Platter, Yellow, 11 In.	24.00
Florentine No. 2, Salt & Pepper, Green	43.00
Florentine No. 2, Sherbet, Yellow	10.00
Florentine No. 2, Soup, Cream, Green	17.00
Florentine No. 2, Tray, Sugar & Creamer, Salt & Pepper, Round, Yellow	105.00
Florentine No. 2, Tumbler, Juice, Flat, Yellow, 3 ½ In.	26.00
Florentine No. 2, Tumbler, Juice, Footed, Yellow, 5 Oz., 4 In.	15.00
Flower Rim pattern is listed here as Vitrock.	
Fruits, Cup & Saucer, Green	15.00
Georgian, Butter, Cover, Green ....*illus*	115.00
Georgian, Sugar, Cover, Green, 3 In.	40.00
Georgian, Sugar, Cover, Green, 4 ¾ In.	50.00
Georgian, Tumbler, Juice, Red, 2 Oz.	6.00
Golden Shell, Bowl, Vegetable, 9 In.	10.00
Golden Shell, Cup & Saucer	8.00
Golden Shell, Plate, Dinner, 9 ⅛ In.	12.00
Golden Shell, Soup, Dish, 6 ¼ In.	9.00
Grape, Tumbler, Iced Tea, Pink, 11 Oz., 4 ⅞ In.	10.00
Grape, Tumbler, Water, Pink, 9 Oz., 4 ½ In.	8.00
Hairpin pattern is listed here as Newport.	
Harp, Cake Stand, 9 In.	35.00

Hex Optic pattern is listed here as Hexagon Optic.
Hexagon Optic, Candy Dish, Iridescent Marigold, Ruffled, 1900, 6 ¾ In. 100.00
Holiday, Butter, Cover, Pink 55.00
Holiday, Sherbet, Pink 9.00
Holiday, Tumbler, Juice, Iridescent, 4 In. 25.00
Homespun, Butter, Cover Only, Pink, 4 ¾ In. 35.00
Homespun, Butter, Cover, Pink ....*illus* 80.00
Homespun, Cup, Pink 8.00
Homespun, Sherbet, Pink, 2 ⅜ In. 18.00
Honeycomb pattern is listed here as Hexagon Optic.
Horizontal Ribbed pattern is listed here as Manhattan.
Horseshoe pattern is listed here as No. 612.
Iris & Herringbone pattern is listed here as Iris.
Iris, Butter, Cover 30.00
Iris, Cup & Saucer 19.50
Iris, Nut Set, Flowers, Bowl, Nutcracker, 6 Picks, 12 In. 145.00
Iris, Plate, Dinner, 9 In. 38.00
Iris, Sugar & Creamer, Cover 35.00
Jane-Ray, Soup, Dish, Jade-Ite, 7 ⅝ In. 26.00
Jane-Ray, Sugar, Lid Only, Jade-Ite 35.00
Kings Crown, Compote, Ruby Flashed, 7 x 7 In. 55.00
Knife & Fork pattern is listed here as Colonial.
Lace Edge pattern is listed here as Old Colony. There is also a pattern called Lace Edge listed in the Imperial Glass category.
Line 300 pattern is listed in the Paden City category as Peacock & Wild Rose.
Lorain pattern is listed here as No. 615.
Louisa pattern is listed here as Floragold.
Lovebirds pattern is listed here as Georgian.
Madrid, Cookie Jar, Cover Only, Amber 28.00
Madrid, Creamer 50.00
Madrid, Cup, Amber 5.00
Madrid, Cup, Blue 16.00
Madrid, Pitcher, Amber, 36 Oz., 5 ¾ In. ....*illus* 35.00
Madrid, Plate, Amber, 9 In., 14 Piece 28.00
Madrid, Plate, Luncheon, Blue, 9 In. 20.00
Madrid, Plate, Salad, Amber, 7 ½ In. 7.75
Madrid, Sherbet, Amber, 2 ⅜ In. 12.50
Madrid, Sherbet, Blue, 2 ⅞ In. 17.50
Madrid, Soup, Cream, Amber 16.00
Madrid, Sugar, Cover, Amber .... 35.00 to 52.00
Madrid, Tumbler, Footed, Amber, 5 5/16 In. 34.00
Madrid, Tumbler, Juice, Amber, 5 Oz., 3 ¾ In. 14.50
Manhattan, Candlestick, 4 5/16-In. Square, 1 ⅜ In., Pair 18.00
Manhattan, Compote, 5 ¾ In. 47.00
Manhattan, Pitcher, Juice, 24 Oz. 34.00
Manhattan, Sherbet, 3 ¾ In. 13.00
Manhattan, Sugar & Creamer 15.00
Manhattan, Sugar, Oval, Pink 15.00
Manhattan, Tumbler, Pink, 10 Oz., 5 3/16 In. 25.00
Mayfair Federal, Bowl, Blue, 2 ½ x 11 ⅝ In. 85.00
Mayfair Federal, Bowl, Low, Pink, 11 ¾ In. 59.00
Mayfair Federal, Butter, Cover, Blue 309.00
Mayfair Federal, Celery Dish, Divided, Blue, 10 In. 62.00
Mayfair Federal, Cup & Saucer, Blue 70.00
Mayfair Federal, Decanter, Stopper, Pink, 10 ¾ In. 190.00
Mayfair Federal, Goblet, Water, Blue, 9 Oz. 280.00
Mayfair Federal, Plate, Dinner, Pink, 9 ½ In. 53.00
Mayfair Federal, Plate, Luncheon, 8 ⅜ In. 25.00
Mayfair Federal, Plate, Luncheon, Blue, 8 ¼ In. .... 40.00 to 50.00
Mayfair Federal, Plate, Sherbet, Round, Pink, 6 ¾ In. 14.00
Mayfair Federal, Platter, Oval, Handles, Pink, 13 ¾ In. 32.00
Mayfair Federal, Sherbet, Pink, 3 3/16 In. 15.00
Mayfair Federal, Soup, Cream, Pink, 9 ½ In. 60.00
Mayfair Federal, Sugar, Blue 80.00
Mayfair Federal, Sugar, Footed, Pink 29.00
Mayfair Federal, Tumbler, Water, Pink, 9 Oz., 4 In. 38.00
Mayfair Open Rose, Bowl, Fruit, Scalloped Rim, Blue 110.00
Mayfair Open Rose, Bowl, Vegetable, Blue, 10 In. 88.00

Depression Glass, Moroccan Amethyst, Cup & Saucer
$15.00

Depression Glass, New Century, Pitcher, Amethyst, 9 In.
$50.00

Depression Glass, Ovide, Sugar & Creamer, Fired-On Terra-Cotta
$10.00

Depression Glass, Oyster & Pearl, Candlestick, Vitrock, Fired-On Green, 2 ½ In.
$20.00

Depression Glass, Patrician, Plate, Dinner, Amber, 11 In.
$23.00

D

Depression Glass, Ribbon, Candy Dish, Cover, Green
$25.00

Depression Glass, Royal Lace, Candlestick, Pink, Pair
$145.00

Depression Glass, Sandwich Indiana, Butter, Cover
$25.00

Depression Glass, Sharon, Soup, Cream, Pink, Handles
$50.00

Depression Glass, Soreno, Creamer, Avocado Green
$8.00

Mayfair Open Rose, Cake Plate, Blue, 10 In.	55.00
Mayfair Open Rose, Pitcher, Blue, 80 Oz., 8 ½ In.	219.00
Mayfair Open Rose, Saltshaker, Blue	66.00
Miss America, Berry Bowl, 6 ¼ In.	9.00
Miss America, Berry Bowl, Green, 4 ½ In.	32.00
Miss America, Bowl, 4 ½ In.	20.00
Miss America, Bowl, Inverted Rim, Pink, 8 In.	165.00
Miss America, Bowl, Vegetable, Oval, Pink, 10 In.	38.00
Miss America, Candy Dish, Lid, Pink, 11 ½ In.	157.00
Miss America, Cup	7.00
Miss America, Cup & Saucer	9.00
Miss America, Goblet, Water, Pink, 5 ½ In.	14.00
Miss America, Pitcher, Ice Lip, Pink, 8 ½ In.	232.00
Miss America, Plate, Dinner, 10 ¼ In.	25.00
Miss America, Plate, Grill, Pink, 10 ¼ In.	17.00
Moderntone, Cup & Saucer, Cobalt Blue	11.50
Moderntone, Plate, Salad, Cobalt Blue, 6 ¾ In.	8.50
Moderntone, Platter, Cobalt Blue, 12 x 9 ½ In.	100.00
Moderntone, Salt & Pepper, Cobalt Blue	20.00
Moderntone, Sherbet, Cobalt Blue, 3 In.	11.50
Moderntone, Soup, Cream, Amethyst, Handles ....*illus*	12.00
Moderntone, Soup, Dish, Cobalt Blue	18.50
Moderntone, Sugar, Platonite, Fired-On Green ....*illus*	14.00
Moderntone, Tumbler, Green, Hazel Atlas, 7 Piece	155.00
Moondrops pattern is listed in the New Martinsville category.	
Moroccan Amethyst, Candy Jar, Cover, Tall	25.00
Moroccan Amethyst, Cup & Saucer ....*illus*	15.00
Moroccan Amethyst, Vase, Ruffled	25.00
New Century, Pitcher, Amethyst, 9 In. ....*illus*	50.00
Newport, Sugar, Amethyst	14.00
Newport, Tumbler, Amethyst	22.00
No. 601 pattern is listed here as Avocado.	
No. 610, Bowl, Green, 8 ½ In.	62.00
No. 612, Bowl, Cereal, Yellow, 6 ½ In.	40.00
No. 612, Grill Plate, Divided, Green, 10 ⅜ In.	65.00 to 85.00
No. 612, Tumbler, Footed, Green, 9 Oz.	30.00
No. 615, Creamer, Yellow, 4 ⅝ In.	25.00
No. 615, Plate, Bread & Butter, Yellow, 5 ½ In.	11.50
No. 615, Plate, Dinner, Yellow, 10 ¼ In.	90.00
No. 615, Plate, Salad, 7 ¾ In.	12.50
No. 615, Plate, Salad, Yellow, 7 ¾ In.	14.00
No. 615, Platter, Oval, Yellow, 11 ⅜ In.	50.00
No. 615, Saucer, Yellow	4.50
No. 615, Sherbet, Yellow, 3 ⅛ In.	27.00
No. 615, Tumbler, Footed, Yellow, 4 ¾ In.	40.00
No. 615, Tumbler, Yellow, 9 Oz., 4 ¾ In.	30.00
No. 618, Plate, Dinner, 9 ⅜ In.	15.00
No. 618, Tumbler, 4 ¼ In.	22.00
No. 620, Berry Bowl, Amber, 4 ¾ In.	6.00
No. 620, Bowl, Amber, 9 ⅜ In.	16.00
No. 620, Cake Plate, Amber, 11 ½ In.	12.50
No. 620, Platter, Amber, 10 ¾ In.	12.50
No. 620, Sugar, Open, Handles, Amber	7.00
Normandie, Grill Plate, Divided, Iridescent, 11 In.	12.00
Normandie, Plate, Salad, Pink, 7 ¾ In.	13.50
Old Cafe, Plate, Dinner, Pink, 9 ¾ In.	68.00
Old Colony, Candlestick, Pink, Pair	465.00
Old Colony, Sherbet, Pink	107.00
Old Florentine pattern is listed here as Florentine No. 1.	
Open Lace pattern is listed here as Old Colony.	
Open Rose pattern is listed here as Mayfair Open Rose.	
Ovide, Sugar & Creamer, Fired-On Terra-Cotta ....*illus*	10.00
Oyster & Pearl, Candlestick, Vitrock, Fired-On Green, 2 ½ In. ....*illus*	20.00
Oyster & Pearl, Dish, Handle, White & Green, 5 ¼ In.	15.00
Park Avenue, Ashtray	10.00
Park Avenue, Cup	5.00
Parrot pattern is listed here as Sylvan.	
Patrician, Bowl, Oval, Amber, 10 In.	28.00

Patrician, Bowl, Vegetable, Oval, Amber	30.00
Patrician, Cup & Saucer, Amber	16.00
Patrician, Plate, Dinner, Amber, 11 In. ....*illus*	23.00
Patrician, Saucer, Amber	8.00
Patrician, Tumbler, Amber, 9 Oz., 4 ½ In.	30.00
Peacock & Wild Rose pattern is listed in the Paden City category.	
Petal Swirl pattern is listed here as Swirl.	
Petalware, Bowl, Cereal, Pink, 5 ¾ In.	16.00
Petalware, Plate, Dinner, Florette, Monax, 9 In.	18.00
Petalware, Plate, Dinner, Monax, 9 In.	10.00
Petalware, Plate, Serving, Monax, 12 In.	30.00
Petalware, Saucer, Cremex	2.00
Petalware, Sherbet, Footed, Monax, 2 x 4 ¼ In.	20.00
Petalware, Soup, Cream, Monax	12.50
Petalware, Sugar & Creamer, Florette, Monax..................................	20.00
Pillar Optic, Cup & Saucer..	4.00
Pillar Optic, Plate, Luncheon, 8 In.	12.00
Pillar Optic, Tumbler, Water, Pink, 4 In.	14.50
Pillar Optic, Whiskey, Pink, 1 ½ Oz., 1 ⁵⁄₁₆ In.	10.00
Pineapple & Floral pattern is listed here as No. 618.	
Pinwheel pattern is listed here as Sierra.	
Pioneer, Bowl, Handles, Green, 9 In.	38.00
Pioneer, Plate, Salad, Pink, 8 In.	14.00
Poinsettia pattern is listed here as Floral.	
Poppy No. 1 pattern is listed here as Florentine No. 1.	
Poppy No. 2 pattern is listed here as Florentine No. 2.	
Pretty Polly Dinner Set, Pink, Child's, 14 Piece	200.00
Pretty Polly Party Dishes, see also the related pattern Doric & Pansy.	
Princess, Bowl, Cereal, Green, 5 In.	38.00
Princess, Bowl, Green, 9 In.	48.00
Princess, Coaster, Green	62.00
Princess, Plate, Sherbet, Yellow, 5 ½ In.	4.00
Princess, Vase, Deco Shape, Green, 8 In.	45.00
Prismatic Line pattern is listed here as Queen Mary.	
Provincial pattern is listed here as Bubble.	
Pyramid pattern is listed here as No. 610.	
Queen Mary, Bowl, Pink, 6 ¼ In.	24.00
Queen Mary, Sugar, Oval	6.00
Radiance pattern is listed in the New Martinsville category.	
Rainbow, Tumbler, Fired-On Green, 10 Oz., 4 ½ In.	12.00
Rainbow, Tumbler, Fired-On Tangerine, 10 Oz., 4 ½ In.	10.00
Ribbon, Candy Dish, Cover, Green ....*illus*	25.00
Rope pattern is listed here as Colonial Fluted.	
Rosemary, Plate, Dinner, Amber, 9 ½ In.	10.00
Roxana, Bowl, Cereal, Yellow, 6 In.	22.00
Royal Lace, Candlestick, Pink, Pair ....*illus*	145.00
Royal Lace, Cup & Saucer, Cobalt Blue..	43.00
Royal Lace, Cup & Saucer, Pink...	23.00
Royal Lace, Cup, Pink	16.00
Royal Lace, Plate, Bread & Butter, Cobalt Blue, 6 In.	16.00
Royal Lace, Plate, Luncheon, Cobalt Blue, 8 ⅜ In.	40.00
Royal Lace, Platter, Oval, Cobalt Blue, 9 ¾ In.	75.00
Royal Lace, Soup, Cream, Pink	29.00
Royal Lace, Tumbler, Green, 5 In., 4 Piece......................................	116.00
Royal Lace, Tumbler, Juice, Cobalt Blue, 5 Oz., 3 ½ In.	50.00
Royal Lace, Tumbler, Pink, 9 Oz.	18.00
Royal Lace, Tumbler, Water, Cobalt Blue, 9 Oz., 4 ⅜ In.	43.00
Royal Lace, Tumbler, Water, Pink, 9 Oz., 4 ¼ In.	25.00
Royal Ruby, Bowl, Classic Rachael, Oval, 12 In.	88.00
Royal Ruby, Bowl, Scalloped, 5 ¼ In.	20.00
Royal Ruby, Cup & Saucer..	7.50
Royal Ruby, Sugar & Creamer..	15.00
Sailboat pattern is listed here as Sportsman Series.	
Sandwich Anchor Hocking, Bowl, Pink, 8 ¼ In.	28.00
Sandwich Anchor Hocking, Bowl, Vegetable	12.00
Sandwich Anchor Hocking, Custard Cup, Green, 2 ⅜ In.	5.00
Sandwich Anchor Hocking, Pitcher, 8 ½ In.	70.00

Depression Glass, Spiral, Jam Jar, Notched Cover, Green, 6 In.
$48.00

Depression Glass, Sunflower, Cake Plate, Green, 3-Footed, 9 ¾ In.
$18.00

Depression Glass, Tea Room, Dish, Banana Split, Green
$105.00

Depression Glass, Wexford, Plate, Hexagonal, 7 ¾ In.
$12.00

As always, the edited listings in *Kovels' Antiques & Collectibles Price Guide 2011* aren't available on any website, but readers should visit Kovels.com for information on trends, tips, reproductions, marks, old prices, and more!

Depression Glass, Wheat, Creamer
$10.00

Depression Glass, Windsor,
Cup & Saucer
$20.00

Derby, Cup & Saucer, George III,
Van Dyke Rim, Patera Banding,
c.1800, 2 ¾ x 5 ¼ In.
$54.00

Derby, Figurine, 4 Continents, America,
Europe, Africa, Asia, 1800s, 10 ½ In.,
4 Piece
$5060.00

Sandwich Anchor Hocking, Plate, Custard Line, Forest Green, 4 ½ In.	6.00
Sandwich Anchor Hocking, Plate, Dinner, Forest Green, 9 In.	125.00
Sandwich Anchor Hocking, Sugar, Open, Handles, Forest Green	45.00
Sandwich Anchor Hocking, Tumbler, Juice, Forest Green	8.00
Sandwich Anchor Hocking, Tumbler, Juice, Green, 3 ½ In.	7.00
Sandwich Anchor Hocking, Tumbler, Water, Green, 3 ⅞ In.	8.00
Sandwich Indiana, Butter, Cover ....*illus*	25.00
Saxon pattern is listed here as Coronation.	
Sharon, Berry Bowl, Cabbage Rose, Green, 8 ⅜ In.	38.00
Sharon, Bowl, Cereal, Cabbage Rose, Green, 6 In.	25.00
Sharon, Butter, Amber	12.00
Sharon, Butter, Amber, Cover	45.00
Sharon, Butter, Green, Cover	75.00 to 90.00
Sharon, Butter, Pink, Cover	38.00
Sharon, Cheese Dish, Amber, Cover	214.00
Sharon, Creamer, Green, 3 ½ In.	20.00
Sharon, Cup & Saucer, Pink	16.00
Sharon, Plate, Pink, 9 In.	33.00
Sharon, Plate, Salad, Amber, 7 ½ In.	9.00
Sharon, Soup, Cream, Pink, Handles ....*illus*	50.00
Sharon, Sugar, Cover, Green, 4 ⅞ In.	55.00
Sharon, Tumbler, 9 Oz.	25.00
Sharon, Tumbler, Iced Tea, Pink, 6 ½ In.	52.00
Sharon, Tumbler, Pink, 5 ¼ In.	48.00
Sierra, Cup & Saucer, Pink	28.00
Sierra, Plate, Dinner, Pink, 9 In.	18.00 to 30.00
Sierra, Platter, Oval, Pink, 11 In.	60.00
Sierra, Sandwich Server, Handles, Pink, 10 ¼ In.	25.00
Soreno, Butter, Cover, Green	10.00
Soreno, Creamer, Avocado Green ....*illus*	8.00
Spiral, Jam Jar, Notched Cover, Green, 6 In. ....*illus*	48.00
Spoke pattern is listed here as Patrician.	
Sportsman Series, Cocktail Set, Shaker, Ice Pail, Tumblers, Cobalt Blue, Windmill, 6 Piece	325.00
Sportsman Series, Ice Bucket, Cobalt Blue, Sailboats	100.00
Sportsman Series, Tumbler, Iced Tea, Cobalt Blue, Sailboats, 10 ½ Oz., 4 ⅞ In.	14.00
Sportsman Series, Tumbler, Old Fashion, Cobalt Blue, Sailboats, 8 Oz.	20.00
Sportsman Series, Tumbler, Water, Cobalt Blue, Sailboats, 9 Oz., 4 ⅝ In.	15.00
Stars & Bars, Bowl, Sawtooth Edge, 8 x 2 ½ In.	18.00
Strawberry, Berry Bowl, Pink	12.00
Strawberry, Sugar, Open, Pink, Large	45.00
Sunburst, Tray, Oval, 8 ¾ In.	16.00
Sunflower, Cake Plate, Green, 3-Footed, 9 ¾ In. ....*illus*	18.00
Swan, Bowl, 2 Handles, 12 In.	55.00
Swirl, Berry Bowl, Delphite, 5 ½ In.	14.50
Swirl, Bowl, Fruit, Azurite, 4 ⅞ In.	9.00
Swirl, Bowl, Salad, Ultramarine, 9 In.	25.00
Swirl, Creamer, Delphite, 3 In.	12.00
Swirl, Creamer, Ultramarine	10.00 to 16.00
Swirl, Cup & Saucer, Ultramarine	12.50
Swirl, Plate, Bread & Butter, Delphite, 6 ½ In.	6.50
Swirl, Plate, Dessert, Delphite, 6 ½ In.	8.00
Swirl, Plate, Dinner, Ivory, 9 ⅛ In.	8.00
Swirl, Soup, Dish, Lug, Tab Handles, Ultramarine	50.00
Swirl, Sugar & Creamer, Delphite, 3 In. & 3 ⅛ In.	30.00
Swirl, Sugar, Handles, Delphite, 3 In.	12.00
Swirl, Sugar, Handles, Ultramarine	16.00
Sylvan, Berry Bowl, Green, 5 In.	40.00
Sylvan, Butter, Cover, Green	292.00
Sylvan, Plate, Salad, Green, 7 ⅜ In.	45.00
Sylvan, Plate, Sherbet, Green, 5 ¾ In.	23.00
Sylvan, Salt & Pepper, Green	204.00
Sylvan, Sugar & Creamer, Green	72.00
Sylvan, Tumbler, Green, 5 ¾ In., Pair	226.00
Tea Room, Dish, Banana Split, Green ....*illus*	105.00
Tea Room, Tumbler, Footed, Pink, 8 Oz.	35.00
Tulip, Ice Tub, Green, 4 ¾ In.	47.00
Vertical Ribbed pattern is listed here as Queen Mary.	

Vitrock, Vase, 5 In.	16.00
Waffle pattern is listed here as Waterford.	
Waterford, Berry Bowl, 8 ¼ In.	10.00
Waterford, Berry Bowl, Pink, 8 ¼ In.	33.00
Waterford, Cake Plate, Handles, Pink	20.00
Waterford, Cup	10.00
Waterford, Goblet, Footed, 5 ¼ In.	18.00
Waterford, Plate, Salad, 7 In.	8.00
Waterford, Saucer, Pink	5.00
Waterford, Sherbet	4.75
Wexford, Plate, Hexagonal, 7 ¾ In. ....*illus*	12.00
Wheat, Creamer ....*illus*	10.00
Wheat, Custard Cup, Milk White, 6 Oz.	4.00
Wheat, Saucer, 5 ¾ In.	1.00
White Ship pattern is listed here as Sportsman Series.	
Wild Rose pattern is listed here as Dogwood.	
Windmill pattern is listed here as Sportsman Series.	
Windsor Diamond pattern is listed here as Windsor.	
Windsor, Console, Pink, 12 ½ In.	140.00
Windsor, Cup & Saucer ....*illus*	20.00
Windsor, Pitcher, Milk, 5 In.	15.00
Windsor, Pitcher, Pink, 6 ½ In.	45.00
Windsor, Tumbler, Green, 4 In., 9 Oz.	30.00

DERBY has been marked on porcelain made in the city of Derby, England, since about 1748. The original Derby factory closed in 1848, but others opened there and continued to produce quality porcelain. The Crown Derby mark began appearing on Derby wares in the 1770s.

Cup & Saucer, George III, Van Dyke Rim, Patera Banding, c.1800, 2 ¾ x 5 ¼ In. ....*illus*	54.00
Figurine, 4 Continents, America, Europe, Africa, Asia, 1800s, 10 ½ In., 4 Piece ....*illus*	5060.00
Platter, Flower Bouquets, Gilt, Oval, Marked, c.1800, 17 ¾ In.	259.00

DICK TRACY, the comic strip, started in 1931. Tracy was also the hero of movies from 1937 to 1947 and again in 1990, and starred in a radio series in the 1940s and a television series in the 1950s. Memorabilia from all these activities are collected.

Button, Dick Tracy Detective, Celluloid, 1 ¼ In.	46.00
G-Man Gun, Sparking, Windup, Flint, Revolving Bullet Chamber, c.1930, 23 In.	306.00
Game, Crimestopper Club Kit, 1961	65.00
Magic Kit, Ultraviolet Black Light, Invisible Ink, Pen, Magic Cloth, 9 ¼ x 12 ¼ x 2 In.	230.00
Mask, Die Cut Paper, Handi-Tape, Einson-Freeman, F.A. Syn., 1933, 7 ½ x 10 ¾ In.	259.00
Model Detective Revolver, Clicker, Painted Image On Grip, c.1940, 9 In.	672.00
Paint Book, Black & White Pictures, Whitman, c.1935, 11 x 14 In. ....*illus*	253.00
Sculpture, Unaccountable, Wood, Gold Plate, Head On Globe, Stepped Base, Clifford, 1959, 28 x 12 In.	85188.00
Toy, Car, Dick Tracy Police Dept., Plastic, Friction, Decal, Marx, Box, 1950s, 10 In.	190.00
Toy, Squad Car, Green, Tin, Windup, Battery Operated Light, Marx, 6 ½ In.	66.00
Toy, Squad Car, No. 1, Green, Tin Lithograph, Windup, Marked, F.A. Synd., Marx, 7 In.	92.00
Toy, Squad Car, Remote Control, Battery Operated, Linemar, Box, 5 ¾ x 9 In. ....*illus*	380.00
Toy, Squad Car, Remote Control, Linemar, Painted Tin, F.A. Syn., c.1949, 8 ½ In.	173.00
Water Pistol, Pressed Steel, Colt 1911, Tracy Decal & Signature On Grip, c.1930, 6 ¾ In.	287.00
Wrist Radio, 2-Way, Electronic, Remco, 9 ½ x 13 x 2 ½ In.	278.00
Wristwatch, Moving Gun, Box, Insert, New Haven Watch Co., c.1951, 6 In. ....*illus*	878.00

DICKENS WARE *pieces are listed in the Royal Doulton and Weller categories.*

DINNERWARE used in the United States from the 1930s through the 1950s is listed here. Most was made in potteries in southern Ohio, West Virginia, and California. A few patterns were made in Japan, England, and other countries. Dishes were sold in gift shops and department stores, or were given away as premiums. Many of these patterns are listed in this book in their own categories, such as Autumn Leaf, Azalea, Coors, Fiesta, Franciscan, Hall, Harker, Harlequin, Red Wing, Riviera, Russel Wright, Vernon Kilns, Watt, and Willow. For more prices, go to kovels.com. Sets missing a few pieces can be completed through the help of one of the many matching services listed on our website, www.kovels.com.

Abingdon, Sugar, Cover, Skyline Shape, Blue Ridge	18.00
Acapulco, Bowl, Cereal, Salem China, 6 ¾ In.	12.00
Acapulco, Chop Plate, Tab Handles, Salem China, 13 ¼ In.	45.00
Acapulco, Plate, Dinner, Salem China, 10 In.	9.00

Dick Tracy, Paint Book, Black & White Pictures, Whitman, c.1935, 11 x 14 In.
$253.00

Dick Tracy, Toy, Squad Car, Remote Control, Battery Operated, Linemar, Box, 5 ¾ x 9 In.
$380.00

Dick Tracy, Wristwatch, Moving Gun, Box, Insert, New Haven Watch Co., c.1951, 6 In.
$878.00

Dinnerware, Ballerina, Bowl, Vegetable, Flowers, Tab Handles, Universal Potteries, 10 ½ In.
$12.00

Dinnerware, Boutonniere, Sugar, Taylor, Smith & Taylor
$8.00

Dinnerware, Bucks County, Plate, Dinner, Yellow, Royal China, 10 In.
$9.00

Dinnerware, Calico Fruit, Grease Jar, Cover, Universal Potteries, 4 ¾ x 6 In.
$30.00

Apple Blossom, Plate, Sugar, Cover, Edwin Knowles	28.00
Apple Trio, Bowl, Fruit, Blue Ridge, 5 ⅜ In.	12.00
Apple Trio, Cup, Blue Ridge	18.00
Apple Trio, Plate, Bread & Butter, Blue Ridge, 6 ¼ In.	11.00
Athena, Bowl, Vegetable, Cover, Johnson Brothers	65.00
Athena, Plate, Luncheon, Johnson Brothers, 9 In.	12.00
Athena, Platter, Johnson Brothers, 13 ¾ In.	35.00
Athena, Soup, Coupe, Johnson Brothers, 7 ⅜ In.	12.00
Autumn Apple, Cup, Blue Ridge	8.00
Autumn Apple, Plate, Salad, Blue Ridge, 7 ¼ In.	14.00
Autumn Apple, Sugar, Cover, Blue Ridge	25.00
Autumn Berry, Plate, Dinner, Blue Ridge, 9 ¼ In.	17.00
Autumn Gold, Bowl, Vegetable, Round, Homer Laughlin, 8 In.	20.00
Autumn Harvest, Bowl, Vegetable, Taylor, Smith & Taylor, 8 ¼ In.	19.00
Autumn Harvest, Cup & Saucer, Taylor, Smith & Taylor	10.00
Autumn Harvest, Plate, Bread & Butter, Taylor, Smith & Taylor, 6 ¾ In.	6.00
Autumn Harvest, Plate, Dinner, Taylor, Smith & Taylor, 10 ¼ In.	12.00
Autumn Leaf, Coffeepot, Hall	250.00
Autumn Rose, Plate, Dinner, 10 ¼ In., 8 Piece	77.00
Autumn Rose, Platter, Oval, 13 ½ In., 5 Piece	77.00
Autumn, Bowl, Vegetable, Edwin Knowles, 9 In.	18.00
Autumn, Plate, Dinner, Edwin Knowles, 9 ⅝ In.	12.00
Autumn, Platter, Edwin Knowles, 14 In.	25.00
Autumn, Salt & Pepper, Edwin Knowles	18.00
Ballerina Mist, Bowl, Cereal, Tab Handles, Universal Potteries	12.00
Ballerina Mist, Gravy Boat, Liner, No Decal, Universal Potteries	28.00
Ballerina Moss Rose, Bowl, Fruit, Platinum Trim, Universal Potteries	8.00
Ballerina Moss Rose, Plate, Dinner, Platinum Trim, Universal Potteries, 10 In.	15.00
Ballerina Wheat, Cup & Saucer, Universal Potteries	12.00
Ballerina Wheat, Plate, Luncheon, Universal Potteries, 9 ¼ In.	12.00
Ballerina, Bowl, Fruit, Forest Green, Universal Potteries, 5 ⅜ In.	7.00
Ballerina, Bowl, Vegetable, Flowers, Tab Handles, Universal Potteries, 10 ½ In. ....*illus*	12.00
Ballerina, Cup & Saucer, Forest Green, Universal Potteries	10.00
Ballerina, Plate, Bread & Butter, Forest Green, Universal Potteries, 6 ¼ In.	3.00
Beaded Apple, Cup, Blue Ridge	15.00
Beaded Apple, Plate, Dinner, Blue Ridge, 10 ¼ In.	16.00
Big Apple, Bowl, Fruit, Blue Ridge, 5 ¼ In.	10.00
Big Apple, Creamer, Blue Ridge	15.00
Big Apple, Plate, Dinner, Blue Ridge, 9 ⅞ In.	21.00
Bittersweet, Casserole, Cover, Universal Potteries	45.00
Blue Bonnet, Bowl, Fruit, Taylor, Smith & Taylor, 5 ¼ In.	8.00
Blue Bonnet, Bowl, Vegetable, Cover, Taylor, Smith & Taylor	65.00
Blue Bonnet, Cup & Saucer, Taylor, Smith & Taylor	12.00
Blue Bonnet, Platter, Taylor, Smith & Taylor, 13 ½ In.	35.00
Blue Meadow, Plate, Salad, Royal China, 7 In.	6.00
Blue Rose, Berry Bowl, Crooksville	8.00
Blue Rose, Bowl, Cereal, Crooksville	12.00
Blue Rose, Plate, Bread & Butter, Crooksville, 6 In.	8.00
Blue Twig, Plate, Bread & Butter, Taylor, Smith & Taylor, 6 ⅝ In.	6.00
Boutonniere, Bowl, Fruit, Taylor, Smith & Taylor, 5 ¼ In.	5.00
Boutonniere, Creamer, Taylor, Smith & Taylor	10.00
Boutonniere, Cup & Saucer, Taylor, Smith & Taylor	8.00
Boutonniere, Plate, Bread & Butter, Taylor, Smith & Taylor, 6 ¾ In.	4.00
Boutonniere, Plate, Dinner, Taylor, Smith & Taylor, 10 ¼ In.	7.00
Boutonniere, Sugar, Taylor, Smith & Taylor ....*illus*	8.00
Bow Knot, Bowl, Vegetable, Colonial Shape, Blue Ridge, 9 In.	20.00
Bramble, Creamer, Blue Ridge	7.00
Bramble, Cup & Saucer, Blue Ridge	12.00
Bramble, Plate, Dinner, Blue Ridge, 10 ½ In.	12.00
Bridal Bouquet, Bowl, Fruit, Salem China, 5 ½ In.	8.00
Bridal Bouquet, Plate, Bread & Butter, Salem China, 6 ⅜ In.	8.00
Bucks County, Plate, Dinner, Yellow, Royal China, 10 In. ....*illus*	9.00
Buttercup, Plate, Bread & Butter, Edwin Knowles, 6 In.	8.00
Buttons & Beaux, Cup & Saucer, Harmony House	12.00
Buttons & Beaux, Gravy Boat, Harmony House	24.00
Calico Fruit, Grease Jar, Cover, Universal Potteries, 4 ¾ x 6 In. ....*illus*	30.00
Camellia, Berry Bowl, Johnson Brothers	10.00

Camellia, Plate, Bread & Butter, Johnson Brothers, 6 ¼ In.		10.00
Cape Cod, Bowl, Vegetable, Cover, W.S. George		38.00
Carol's Roses, Platter, Blue Ridge, 11 ⅞ In.		65.00
Cascade, Bowl, Fruit, Harmony House, 5 ⅝ In.		10.00
Cascade, Cup & Saucer, Harmony House		12.00
Cascade, Plate, Dinner, Harmony House, 10 ⅝ In.		22.00
Cascade, Plate, Salad, Harmony House, 7 ⅝ In.		12.00
Cascade, Soup, Coupe, Harmony House, 7 ⅝ In.		12.00
Cheerio, Chop Plate, Blue Ridge, 12 ½ In.		24.00
Chintz, Candy Dish, Cover, Blue Ridge, 6 In.		125.00
Chintz, Plate, Bread & Butter, Blue Ridge, 6 ¼ In.		8.00
Chintz, Plate, Dinner, Blue Ridge, 10 In.		12.00
Chrysanthemum, Plate, Salad, Blue Ridge, 7 ⅛ In.		12.00
Chrysanthemum, Plate, Salad, Fitz & Floyd, 7 ¾ In.		18.00
Coaching Scene, Bowl, Vegetable, Round, Blue, Johnson Brothers, 8 ⅜ In.		28.00
Coaching Scene, Plate, Dessert, Pink, Johnson Brothers, 6 ⅞ In.		9.00
Coaching Scene, Plate, Dinner, Blue, Johnson Brothers, 9 ⅞ In.		15.00
Coaching Scene, Platter, Pink, Johnson Brothers, 12 In.		28.00
Colonial Couple, Plate, Bread & Butter, Salem China, 6 ¼ In.		8.00
Colonial Couple, Plate, Dinner, Salem China, 10 In.		15.00
Colonial Couple, Plate, Salad, W.S. George, 7 ¼ In.		12.00
Colonial Couple, Soup, Coupe, W.S. George, 7 ¾ In.		15.00
Colonial Gold, Plate, Dinner, George & Martha Washington Dancing, Royal China, 9 ⅞ In.		12.00
Colonial Homestead, Plate, Dinner, Royal Dinner, 10 In.	*illus*	8.00
Commodore, Bowl, Vegetable, Oval, Salem China, 9 ½ In.		32.00
Commodore, Platter, Salem China, 12 ⅛ In.		35.00
Country Charm, Cup, Straight Sides, Royal China		5.00
Country Charm, Plate, Dinner, Royal China, 10 In.		10.00
Country Charm, Plate, Salad, Royal China, 7 ¼ In.		6.00
Country Charm, Soup, Dish, Royal China, 6 ¾ In.		5.00
Country Fair, Plate, Salad, Grapes, Blue Ridge, 8 ½ In.		12.00
Country Fair, Plate, Salad, Peaches, Blue Ridge, 8 ½ In.		12.00
Country Road, Bowl, Fruit, Blue Ridge, 5 ¼ In.		8.00
Country Road, Creamer, Blue Ridge		14.00
Country Road, Cup & Saucer, Blue Ridge		12.00
Country Road, Plate, Dinner, Blue Ridge, 10 ⅜ In.		21.00
Crab Apple, Bowl, Blue Ridge, 7 In.		21.00
Crab Apple, Plate, Dinner, Blue Ridge, 10 ¼ In.		25.00
Crab Apple, Sugar, Handles, Blue Ridge		10.00
Currier & Ives, Teapot, Blue, Royal China	*illus*	95.00
Dairy Maid, Bowl, Fruit, Crooksville, 5 ⅜ In.		11.00
Dairy Maid, Cup & Saucer, Crooksville		21.00
Dairy Maid, Plate, Bread & Butter, Crooksville, 6 In.		10.00
Dairy Maid, Plate, Dinner, Crooksville, 10 ¼ In.		15.00
Dazzle, Plate, Bread & Butter, Blue Ridge, 6 In.		8.00
Delta Daisy, Bowl, Fruit, Blue Ridge		9.00
Delta Daisy, Cup & Saucer, Blue Ridge		12.00
Delta Daisy, Plate, Dinner, Blue Ridge, 10 ¼ In.		16.00
Delta Daisy, Plate, Salad, Blue Ridge		10.00
Delta Daisy, Soup, Dish, Blue Ridge		10.00
Diana, Bowl, Cereal, Harmony House, 6 ⅛ In.		4.00
Diana, Plate, Salad, Harmony House, 7 ⅝ In.		4.00
Dogwood, Coffeepot, Salem China		48.00
Dogwood, Creamer, Salem China		26.00
Dogwood, Gravy Boat, Homer Laughlin		8.00
Dogwood, Plate, Luncheon, Salem China, 9 In.		12.00
Dogwood, Plate, Salad, Harmony House, 7 ½ In.		12.00
Dogwood, Sugar, Homer Laughlin		9.50
Dutch Petit Point, Plate, Luncheon, Salem China, 9 In.		12.00
Dutch Petit Point, Sugar, Open, Salem China		12.00
Early American, Bowl, Fruit, Universal Potteries		8.00
Early American, Creamer, Universal Potteries		22.00
Early American, Plate, Luncheon, Universal Potteries, 9 In.		12.00
Early American, Sugar, Cover, Universal Potteries		28.00
Eggshell Nautilus, Plate, Bread & Butter, Homer Laughlin, 6 In.		3.00
Eggshell Nautilus, Plate, Dinner, Homer Laughlin, 10 In.		5.00
Eggshell Nautilus, Platter, Homer Laughlin, 11 ½ In.		12.00

Dinnerware, Colonial Homestead, Plate, Dinner, Royal Dinner, 10 In. $8.00

Dinnerware, Currier & Ives, Teapot, Blue, Royal China $95.00

Dinnerware, English Abbey, Creamer, Taylor, Smith & Taylor, 4 ¼ In. $29.00

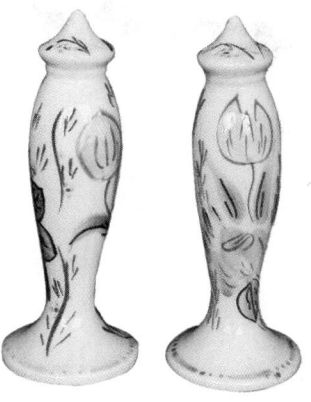

Dinnerware, Fancy, Salt & Pepper, Blue Ridge, 5 ⅜ In. $32.00

Dinnerware, Fruit & Flowers,
Sugar, Cover, Republic, Homer Laughlin
$16.00

Dinnerware, Green Plaid, Sugar &
Creamer, Blue Ridge
$36.00

Dinnerware, Jaderose, Creamer,
Cavalier Eggshell, Homer Laughlin, 4 In.
$8.00

Dinnerware, Lady Greenbriar,
Sugar & Creamer, Homer Laughlin
$52.00

Enchanted Garden, Cup & Saucer, Johnson Brothers	8.00
Enchanted Garden, Plate, Bread & Butter, Johnson Brothers, 6 ⅜ In.	8.00
Enchanted Garden, Plate, Dinner, Johnson Brothers, 10 ⅛ In.	18.00
Encore, Bowl, Vegetable, Round, Johnson Brothers, 8 ¼ In.	26.00
Encore, Creamer, Johnson Brothers	26.00
Encore, Plate, Dinner, Johnson Brothers, 9 ⅞ In.	15.00
Encore, Sugar, Cover, Johnson Brothers	32.00
English Abbey, Creamer, Taylor, Smith & Taylor, 4 ¼ In. ....*illus*	29.00
English Village, Bowl, Vegetable, Cover, Salem China	75.00
English Village, Cup & Saucer, Salem China	15.00
English Village, Plate, Dinner, Salem China, 9 ⅞ In.	18.00
Fair Oaks, Plate, Bread & Butter, Royal China, 6 ⅜ In.	6.00
Fair Oaks, Saucer, Royal China	3.00
Falling Leaves, Cup, Blue Ridge	5.00
Falling Leaves, Gravy Boat, Blue Ridge	35.00
Falling Leaves, Plate, Dinner, Royal China, 10 ¼ In.	8.00
Falling Leaves, Platter, Royal China, 13 ⅛ In.	8.00
Falling Leaves, Saucer, Blue Ridge	5.00
Family Affair, Bowl, Fruit, Steubenville, 5 ⅜ In.	7.00
Family Affair, Plate, Bread & Butter, Steubenville, 6 ¼ In.	6.00
Fancy, Salt & Pepper, Blue Ridge, 5 ⅜ In. ....*illus*	32.00
Fantasy, Cup & Saucer, Edwin Knowles	12.00
Fantasy, Plate, Bread & Butter, Edwin Knowles, 6 ¼ In.	6.00
Fantasy, Plate, Dinner, Edwin Knowles, 10 ¼ In.	12.00
Flair, Berry Bowl, Harmony House, 5 ½ In.	8.00
Flair, Bowl, Vegetable, Oval, Harmony House, 10 ⅛ In.	35.00
Flair, Creamer, Harmony House	26.00
Flair, Plate, Dinner, Harmony House, 10 ¼ In.	15.00
Flair, Sugar, Cover, Harmony House	35.00
Flower Chain, Bowl, Vegetable, Cover, Edwin Knowles, 10 In.	79.00
Forest Fruit, Plate, Bread & Butter, Blue Ridge, 6 ¼ In.	6.00
Forest Fruit, Plate, Dinner, Blue Ridge, 10 ¼ In.	15.00
Frageria, Plate, Dinner, Blue Ridge, 10 ¼ In.	14.00
Friendly Village, Bowl, Cereal, Johnson Brothers, 6 ⅛ In.	15.00
Friendly Village, Bowl, Vegetable, Round, Johnson Brothers, 8 ¼ In.	35.00
Friendly Village, Cup & Saucer, Flat, Johnson Brothers	12.00
Friendly Village, Plate, Dinner, Johnson Brothers, 10 ½ In.	15.00
Fruit & Flowers, Sugar, Cover, Republic, Homer Laughlin ....*illus*	16.00
Fruit Sampler, Cup & Saucer, Johnson Brothers	15.00
Fruit Sampler, Plate, Dinner, Johnson Brothers, 10 In.	20.00
Game Birds, Mug, Partridge, Johnson Brothers	25.00
Gardenia, Plate, Dinner, Syracuse China, 9 ⅞ In.	24.00
Georgette, Plate, Luncheon, W.S. George, 9 ⅜ In.	15.00
Gingham Garden, Chop Plate, Round, Royal China, 11 ½ In.	28.00
Golden Heron, Mug, Fitz & Floyd, 4 In.	42.00
Golden Heron, Plate, Dinner, Fitz & Floyd, 10 ¼ In.	35.00
Golden Wheat, Bowl, Fruit, Edwin Knowles, 6 In.	6.00
Golden Wheat, Cup & Saucer, Edwin Knowles	12.00
Golden Wheat, Plate, Dinner, Edwin Knowles, 10 In.	12.00
Golden Willow, Cup & Saucer, Crooksville	9.00
Golden Willow, Plate, Bread & Butter, Crooksville, 6 In.	7.00
Granite, Bowl, Vegetable, Taylor, Smith & Taylor, 9 In.	10.00
Grapevine, Bowl, Fruit, Edwin Knowles, 5 ⅝ In.	8.00
Grapevine, Plate, Dinner, Edwin Knowles, 10 ¼ In.	12.00
Grapevine, Platter, Edwin Knowles, 12 ⅝ In.	28.00
Green Briar, Bowl, Fruit, Blue Ridge, 5 ⅜ In.	10.00
Green Briar, Plate, Bread & Butter, Blue Ridge, 6 ¼ In.	7.00
Green Briar, Plate, Dinner, Blue Ridge, 9 ⅜ In.	16.00
Green Plaid, Sugar & Creamer, Blue Ridge ....*illus*	36.00
Harvest Time, Cup & Saucer, Ben Seibel, Iroquois	8.00
Harvest Time, Cup & Saucer, Johnson Brothers	15.00
Harvest Time, Plate, Bread & Butter, Ben Seibel, Iroquois, 6 ½ In.	4.00
Harvest Time, Plate, Dinner, Ben Seibel, Iroquois, 10 ¼ In.	15.00
Harvest, Berry Bowl, Salem China	8.00
Harvest, Bowl, Vegetable, Divided, John B. Taylor, 10 ¾ In.	62.00
Harvest, Creamer, John B. Taylor	15.00
Harvest, Cup & Saucer, John B. Taylor	12.00

Harvest, Gravy Boat, Freeform, Salem China	35.00
Harvest, Plate, Dinner, John B. Taylor, 10 ⅛ In.	25.00
Harvest, Plate, Dinner, Salem China, 10 In.	12.00
Harvest, Plate, Salad, John B. Taylor, 7 ⅞ In.	21.00
Harvest, Sugar, Cover, John B. Taylor	17.00
Hawaiian Fruit, Creamer, Blue Ridge	15.00
Hawaiian Fruit, Cup & Saucer, Blue Ridge	15.00
Hawaiian Fruit, Plate, Dinner, Blue Ridge, 10 ½ In.	22.00
Hawaiian Fruit, Platter, Oval, Blue Ridge, 14 In.	40.00
Heritage, Coffeepot, Cover, Johnson Brothers	48.00
Heritage, Creamer, Johnson Brothers	18.00
Heritage, Sugar, Cover, Johnson Brothers	26.00
Hibiscus, Cup & Saucer, Salem China	17.00
Hibiscus, Plate, Bread & Butter, Salem China	6.00
His Majesty, Soup, Dish, Johnson Brothers, 8 ⅝ In.	10.00
His Majesty, Tidbit, 2 Tiers, Johnson Brothers	42.00
Holiday, Plate, Salad, Montgomery Ward, 7 ⅝ In.	12.00
Holland, Bowl, Cereal, Johnson Brothers, 6 ½ In.	12.00
Holland, Plate, Dessert, Johnson Brothers, 7 In.	15.00
Holland, Sugar, Cover, Johnson Brothers	30.00
Honey Hen, Creamer, Harmony House	22.00
Honey Hen, Plate, Bread & Butter, Harmony House, 7 In.	6.00
Honey Hen, Sugar, Cover, Harmony House	25.00
Honolulu Cherries, Plate, Salad, Blue Ridge, 8 ¼ In.	12.00
Informal, Coffeepot, Bombay Green, Iroquois, Ben Seibel	100.00
Iva-Lure, Bowl, Vegetable, Crooksville, 8 ½ In.	26.00
Iva-Lure, Cup & Saucer, Crooksville	15.00
Iva-Lure, Gravy Boat, Stand, Crooksville, 9 ½ x 5 ¼ In.	48.00
Iva-Lure, Plate, Salad, Crooksville, 8 In.	12.00
Jaderose, Creamer, Cavalier Eggshell, Homer Laughlin, 4 In. ....*illus*	8.00
Janet, Bowl, Vegetable, Oval, Harmony House, 10 ⅜ In.	35.00
Janet, Plate, Bread & Butter, Harmony House, 6 In.	8.00
Janet, Plate, Dinner, Harmony House, 10 In.	15.00
Janet, Platter, Harmony House, 14 In.	48.00
Jubilee, Plate, Dinner, Peach, Salem China, 10 In.	12.00
Jubilee, Saucer, Peach, Salem China	3.00
Karen Rose, Plate, Dinner, Johnson Brothers, 10 In.	15.00
Kate, Creamer, Blue Ridge	14.00
Kate, Cup & Saucer, Blue Ridge	21.00
Kate, Plate, Salad, Blue Ridge, 8 ¼ In.	21.00
Lady Greenbriar, Sugar & Creamer, Homer Laughlin ....*illus*	52.00
Lazy Daisy, Bowl, Cereal, Taylor, Smith & Taylor, 7 ⅜ In.	8.00
Lazy Daisy, Bowl, Vegetable, Informal, Iroquois, Ben Seibel, 10 In.	20.00
Lazy Daisy, Butter, Cover, Round, Informal, Iroquois, Ben Seibel	65.00
Lazy Daisy, Casserole, Cover, Taylor, Smith & Taylor, 2 Qt.	75.00
Lazy Daisy, Coffeepot, Cover, Taylor, Smith & Taylor, 8 ½ In.	65.00
Lazy Daisy, Creamer, Ben Seibel, Iroquois	12.00
Lazy Daisy, Plate, Bread & Butter, Taylor, Smith & Taylor, 7 In.	6.00
Lazy Daisy, Plate, Dinner, Taylor, Smith & Taylor, 10 ⅝ In.	12.00
Lazy Daisy, Sugar & Creamer, Cover, Taylor, Smith & Taylor	32.00
Leaf Dance, Plate, Bread & Butter, Edwin Knowles, 6 In.	8.00
Luray, Creamer, Pastel Green, Taylor, Smith & Taylor	18.00
Luray, Creamer, Yellow, Taylor, Smith & Taylor, 2 ½ In.	12.00
Luray, Gravy Boat, Attached Underplate, Yellow, Taylor, Smith & Taylor	25.00
Luray, Plate, Dessert, Pastel Green, Taylor, Smith & Taylor, 7 ⅜ In.	10.00
Luray, Teapot, Windsor Blue, Taylor, Smith & Taylor ....*illus*	185.00
Mad Hatter, Teapot, Hat Is Lid, Handle Is Stack Of Cups, Regal China, 1951, 8 In.	750.00
Mandarin, Berry Bowl, Salem China	6.00
Mandarin, Plate, Bread & Butter, 6 In.	6.00
Mandarin, Plate, Dinner, Salem China, 10 In.	12.00
Maple Leaf, Cup & Saucer, Salem China	10.00
Maple Leaf, Plate, Salad, Salem China, 8 In.	8.00
Marble, Plate, Dinner, Taylor, Smith & Taylor, 10 In.	15.00
Marble, Platter, Taylor, Smith & Taylor, 13 ½ In.	21.00
Margarita, Plate, Dinner, Royal China, 10 ¼ In.	9.00
Margarita, Plate, Salad, Royal China, 7 ¼ In.	6.00
Melody Lane, Cup & Saucer, Salem China	12.00

Dinnerware, Luray, Teapot, Windsor Blue, Taylor, Smith & Taylor
$185.00

Dinnerware, Milady, Pitcher, No. 1, Blue Ridge
$145.00

Dinnerware, Paper Rose, Bowl, Vegetable, Blue Ridge, 9 ¼ In.
$14.00

Dinnerware, Pompom, Pitcher, Impromptu, Iroquois, 12 In.
$20.00

D

Dinnerware, Priscilla, Teapot, Homer Laughlin
$59.00

Dinnerware, Quaker Apple, Bowl, Cereal, Blue Ridge, 6 In.
$7.00

Dinnerware, Saxon, Chocolate Pot, Regal, Homer Laughlin
$47.00

Dinnerware, Sheraton, Platter, Harmony House, 12 In.
$40.00

Melody Lane, Gravy Boat, Salem China	28.00
Melody Lane, Sugar, Cover, Salem China	26.00
Memory Lane, Creamer, Royal China	16.00
Memory Lane, Cup & Saucer, Royal China	10.00
Milady, Pitcher, No. 1, Blue Ridge ......*illus*	145.00
Milano, Cup & Saucer, Edwin Knowles	12.00
Milano, Plate, Bread & Butter, Edwin Knowles, 6 In.	6.00
Milano, Plate, Dinner, Edwin Knowles, 10 In.	12.00
Mirror Image, Bowl, Fruit, Blue Ridge	7.00
Morning Glory, Bowl, Cereal, Johnson Brothers	12.00
Morning Glory, Sugar, Cover, Johnson Brothers	28.00
Morning Glory, Teapot, Johnson Brothers	35.00
Mountain Ivy, Cup, Blue Ridge	15.00
Navajo, Plate, Dinner, Royal China, 10 1/8 In.	8.00
Norma, Plate, Salad, Blue Ridge, 7 1/8 In.	12.00
Normandy, Bowl, Fruit, Edwin Knowles	8.00
Normandy, Saucer	4.00
North Star, Berry Bowl, Salem China, 5 3/8 In.	8.00
North Star, Plate, Luncheon, Salem China, 9 1/4 In.	12.00
North Star, Soup, Dish, Salem China	12.00
Old Chelsea, Bowl, Vegetable, Oval, Johnson Brothers, 8 3/4 In.	45.00
Old Chelsea, Platter, Johnson Brothers, 13 1/2 In.	48.00
Old Chelsea, Soup, Dish, Square, Johnson Brothers, 7 In.	18.00
Old Chelsea, Sugar, Cover, Johnson Brothers	38.00
Old Curiosity Shop, Cake Plate, Tab Handles, Royal China, 10 In.	30.00
Old Curiosity Shop, Cup & Saucer, Royal China	10.00
Old Curiosity Shop, Soup, Dish, Flat Rim, Royal China, 8 1/4 In.	10.00
Old Ivory, Plate, Salad, Syracuse China, 7 1/8 In.	15.00
Old Mill, Plate, Bread & Butter, Johnson Brothers, 6 1/4 In.	10.00
Paper Rose, Bowl, Vegetable, Blue Ridge, 9 1/4 In. ......*illus*	14.00
Parrot-In-Ring, Plate, Salad, Fitz & Floyd, 7 1/2 In.	21.00
Pebbleford, Plate, Bread & Butter, Sunburst Yellow, Taylor, Smith & Taylor, 6 In.	3.00
Pebbleford, Plate, Dinner, Sand, Taylor, Smith & Taylor, 10 1/4 In.	10.00
Pebbleford, Plate, Dinner, Turquoise, Taylor, Smith & Taylor, 10 1/4 In.	9.00
Penthouse, Chop Plate, Edwin Knowles	45.00
Petit Point House, Bowl, Cereal, Crooksville	12.00
Petit Point House, Plate, Bread & Butter, Crooksville, 6 In.	8.00
Petit Point House, Plate, Luncheon, Crooksville, 9 In.	15.00
Petit Point House, Plate, Salad, Crooksville, 7 In.	12.00
Pink Crocus, Cup & Saucer, Crooksville	12.00
Pink Crocus, Plate, Bread & Butter, Crooksville, 6 In.	8.00
Pink Crocus, Plate, Luncheon, Crooksville, 9 1/4 In.	12.00
Pink Crocus, Saucer, Crooksville	4.00
Pink Dogwood, Plate, Bread & Butter, Edwin Knowles, 6 In.	8.00
Pink Dogwood, Plate, Dinner, Edwin Knowles, 10 In.	12.00
Platinum Garland, Bowl, Vegetable, Divided, Harmony House, 11 In.	78.00
Platinum Garland, Bowl, Vegetable, Oval, Harmony House, 11 In.	38.00
Platinum Garland, Creamer, Harmony House	22.00
Platinum Garland, Gravy Boat, Underplate, Harmony House	45.00
Platinum Garland, Sugar, Cover, Harmony House	28.00
Poinsettia, Bowl, Vegetable, Blue Ridge, 10 1/2 In.	40.00
Poinsettia, Cup, Blue Ridge	10.00
Poinsettia, Plate, Salad, Blue Ridge, 7 1/4 In.	12.00
Poinsettia, Platter, Blue Ridge, 15 3/4 In.	80.00
Pompom, Pitcher, Impromptu, Iroquois, 12 In. ......*illus*	20.00
Primrose, Cup & Saucer, Salem China	15.00
Primrose, Gravy Boat, Salem China	50.00
Primrose, Plate, Bread & Butter, Salem China, 6 1/4 In.	8.00
Priscilla, Teapot, Homer Laughlin ......*illus*	59.00
Pristine, Plate, Dinner, Blue Ridge, 10 1/4 In.	14.00
Provincial, Coffeepot, Cover, Johnson Brothers	65.00
Provincial, Creamer, Johnson Brothers	18.00
Provincial, Sugar, Cover, Johnson Brothers	26.00
Pyramids, Cup & Saucer, Ben Seibel, Iroquois	9.00
Pyramids, Pitcher, Water, Impromptu, Ben Seibel, Iroquois	80.00
Quaker Apple, Bowl, Cereal, Blue Ridge, 6 In. ......*illus*	7.00
Quaker Apple, Plate, Bread & Butter, Blue Ridge, 6 1/8 In.	10.00

Queen's Rose, Cup & Saucer, Royal China	12.00
Queen's Rose, Plate, Bread & Butter, Royal China, 6 ⅜ In.	6.00
Queen's Rose, Plate, Dinner, Royal China, 10 ½ In.	12.00
Red Apple, Plate, Dinner, Blue Ridge, 10 ¼ In.	15.00
Rehobeth, Plate, Salad, Blue Ridge	12.00
Renaissance, Plate, Bread & Butter, Black Band, Fitz & Floyd, 6 ⅜ In.	12.00
Renaissance, Plate, Bread & Butter, Green Band, Fitz & Floyd, 6 ⅝ In.	12.00
Revere, Cup & Saucer, Johnson Brothers	12.00
Ridge Daisy, Bowl, Fruit, Blue Ridge, 5 ⅜ In.	8.00
Ridge Daisy, Eggcup, Blue Ridge	20.00
Ridge Daisy, Sugar & Creamer, Blue Ridge	50.00
Rondelet, Cup, Taupe, Fitz & Floyd	18.00
Rondelet, Plate, Salad, Peach, Fitz & Floyd, 7 ½ In.	12.00
Rose Chintz, Bowl, Cereal, Square, Johnson Brothers, 6 ¼ In.	12.00
Rose Chintz, Plate, Bread & Butter, Johnson Brothers, 6 ¼ In.	8.00
Rose Chintz, Plate, Dinner, Johnson Brothers, 9 ¾ In.	15.00
Rosette, Refrigerator Set, Cover, Universal Potteries, 5 In., 6 In., 7 In., 6 Piece	90.00
Rustic Plaid, Butter, Cover, Blue Ridge	20.00
Rustic Plaid, Creamer, Blue Ridge	21.00
Rustic Plaid, Cup & Saucer, Blue Ridge	16.00
Rustic Plaid, Plate, Bread & Butter, Blue Ridge, 6 ½ In.	5.00
Sarasota, Bowl, Blue Ridge, 8 In.	21.00
Saxon, Chocolate Pot, Regal, Homer Laughlin ....*illus*	47.00
Serenade, Teapot, Salem China	75.00
Shasta Pine, Plate, Dinner, Royal China, 10 In.	11.00
Shasta Pine, Soup, Dish, Royal China, 7 In.	12.00
Sheraton, Platter, Harmony House, 12 In. ....*illus*	40.00
Silhouette, Coaster, Crooksville	7.00
Silhouette, Mug, Crooksville	41.00
Silhouette, Teapot, Crooksville, c.1936, 8 Cup	128.00
Silver Elegance, Plate, Salad, Salem China, 7 In.	12.00
Skytone, Bowl, Vegetable, Homer Laughlin	35.00
Skytone, Cup & Saucer, Homer Laughlin	12.00
Skytone, Plate, Bread & Butter, Homer Laughlin, 6 ⅛ In.	8.00
Skytone, Plate, Dinner, Homer Laughlin, 10 In.	12.00
Skytone, Saucer, Homer Laughlin, 6 ¼ In.	5.00
Snowhite Regency, Cup & Saucer, Johnson Brothers	12.00
Snowhite, Plate, Salad, Johnson Brothers, 8 In.	8.00
Snowhite, Serving Bowl, Johnson Brothers, 8 ½ In.	32.00
Southern Bell, Cup & Saucer, Apple Blossom Decal, Crooksville	12.00
Southern Bell, Saucer, Apple Blossom Decal, Crooksville	4.00
Southern Dogwood, Cup & Saucer, Blue Ridge	12.00
Southern Dogwood, Plate, Luncheon, Blue Ridge, 9 ½ In.	12.00
Southern Dogwood, Platter, Blue Ridge, 11 ¾ In.	18.00
Southern Dogwood, Sugar, Cover, Blue Ridge	26.00
Spray, Bowl, Fruit, Blue Ridge	12.00
Spray, Cup & Saucer, Blue Ridge	13.00
Spring Hill Tulip, Bowl, Vegetable, Oval, Blue Ridge, 9 ⅜ In.	22.00
Spring Morning, Coffeepot, Johnson Brothers	55.00
Star Glow, Bowl, Vegetable, Royal China	28.00
Star Glow, Cake Plate, Tab Handles, Round, Royal China, 10 ½ In.	28.00
Star Glow, Plate, Dinner, Royal China, 10 In.	12.00
Star Glow, Platter, Royal China, 13 In.	28.00
Starfire, Cake Plate, Tab Handles, Harmony House, 13 In. ....*illus*	29.00
Starlight, Bowl, Vegetable, Oval, Salem China, 9 ⅜ In.	22.00
Starlight, Plate, Salad, Salem China, 7 ¼ In.	12.00
Starlight, Soup, Dish, Salem China	12.00
Strawberry Fair, Berry Bowl, Johnson Brothers	15.00
Strawberry Fair, Saucer, Johnson Brothers	8.00
Summer Chintz, Bowl, Cereal, Square, Johnson Brothers, 6 ⅛ In.	10.00
Summer Chintz, Bowl, Fruit, Johnson Brothers, 6 ⅜ In.	6.00
Summer Chintz, Cup & Saucer, Johnson Brothers	10.00
Sunlight, Cup & Saucer, Edwin Knowles	12.00
Sunlight, Plate, Dinner, Edwin Knowles, 10 In.	12.00
Sunlight, Soup, Dish, Edwin Knowles	12.00
Sweet Pea, Plate, Salad, Blue Ridge, 7 ⅛ In.	12.00
Sweetie Pie, Bowl, Fruit, Blue Ridge	4.00

Dinnerware, Starfire, Cake Plate, Tab Handles, Harmony House, 13 In. $29.00

Dinnerware, Wood Hue, Casserole, Cover, Taylor, Smith & Taylor, 10 ¼ In. $25.00

Dionne Quintuplets, Dolls, Composition, Painted Hair, Face, 5-Person Scooter, Box, 7 In.
$2576.00

Dirk Van Erp, Bookends, Copper, Pierced, Stylized Poppies, 5 x 6 In.
$1440.00

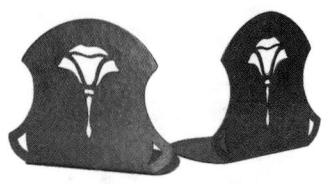

Disneyana, Ashtray, Mickey Mouse, Standing Near Floor Lamp, Metal, Germany, 6 In.
$1686.00

Sweetie Pie, Cup & Saucer, Blue Ridge	20.00
Symphony, Plate, Luncheon, Pink, Harmony House, 9 ¼ In.	7.50
Tahiti Flower, Creamer, Edwin Knowles	22.00
Tahiti Flower, Gravy Boat, Stand, Edwin Knowles	48.00
Tahiti Flower, Plate, Salad, Edwin Knowles	8.00
Tahiti Flower, Platter, Edwin Knowles, 15 ½ In.	55.00
Talisman, Cake Plate, Tab Handles, Salem China, 12 ¾ In.	28.00
Talisman, Sugar, Cover, Salem China	26.00
Tick Tack, Plate, Dinner, Blue Ridge, 9 In.	25.00
Trend, Gravy Boat, Attached Underplate, Steubenville	15.00
Trotter, Plate, Dinner, Crooksville, 10 In.	22.00
Tulip Time, Butter	35.00
Tulip Time, Plate, Luncheon, Salem China, 9 ¼ In.	12.00
Tulip Time, Salt & Pepper	28.00
Tulip Time, Saucer, Blue Ridge	5.00
Twelve Days Of Christmas, Plate, Lords Leaping, Johnson Brothers, 8 ¾ In.	15.00
Versatile, Soup, Dish, Taylor, Smith & Taylor, 6 ⅝ In.	10.00
Vintage, Berry Bowl, Salem China, 5 ⅝ In.	10.00
Vintage, Plate, Bread & Butter, John B. Taylor, 6 ⅛ In.	11.00
Vintage, Plate, Dinner, Salem China, 10 In.	32.00
Vintage, Platter, Salem China, 13 ⅝ In.	45.00
Vintage, Saucer, John B. Taylor	8.00
Virginia Rose, Cup & Saucer, Homer Laughlin	7.50
Virginia Rose, Plate, Dinner, Homer Laughlin, 9 ½ In.	6.00
Virginia Rose, Platter, Homer Laughlin, 13 In.	16.00
Virginia Rose, Serving Bowl, Homer Laughlin, 9 ½ In.	12.00
Vogue, Cup & Saucer, Johnson Brothers	20.00
Wheat, Bowl, Fruit, Taylor, Smith & Taylor, 5 ¼ In.	5.00
Wheat, Bowl, Vegetable, Oval, Taylor, Smith & Taylor, 8 ½ In.	18.00
Wheat, Plate, Bread & Butter, Taylor, Smith & Taylor, 6 ¼ In.	3.00
Wheat, Plate, Dinner, Taylor, Smith & Taylor, 10 ⅛ In.	8.00
Wheat, Plate, Salad, Taylor, Smith & Taylor, 8 ¼ In.	5.00
Wheat, Platter, Oval, Taylor, Smith & Taylor, 13 ½ In.	15.00
Wheat, Sugar & Creamer, Taylor, Smith & Taylor	21.00
Whirligig, Plate, Dinner, Blue Ridge, 10 ½ In.	20.00
Wild Strawberry, Plate, Dinner, Blue Ridge, 10 ¼ In.	12.00
Wild Strawberry, Saucer, Blue Ridge	3.00
Willow, Cup & Saucer, Washington Pottery	14.50
Windblown, Bowl, Cereal, Tab Handle, Crooksville, 6 ¾ In.	15.00
Windblown, Creamer, Crooksville	28.00
Windblown, Cup & Saucer, Crooksville	15.00
Windblown, Cup & Saucer, Salem China	15.00
Windblown, Plate, Bread & Butter, Salem China, 6 In.	8.00
Windblown, Plate, Dinner, Crooksville, 10 In.	15.00
Windblown, Plate, Salad, Crooksville, 7 ¼ In.	12.00
Windblown, Platter, Tab Handles, Crooksville, 13 ½ In.	38.00
Windblown, Sugar, Cover, Crooksville	35.00
Windsor Flowers, Plate, Bread & Butter, Johnson Brothers, 6 ⅜ In.	10.00
Windsor Flowers, Plate, Dinner, Johnson Brothers	22.00
Windsor Flowers, Platter, Johnson Brothers, 14 In.	55.00
Windsor Flowers, Sugar, Cover, Johnson Brothers	129.00
Wood Hue, Casserole, Cover, Taylor, Smith & Taylor, 10 ¼ In. ....*illus*	25.00
Woodfield, Snack Plate, Coral, 9 In.	10.00
Woodfield, Snack Plate, Dove Gray, Steubenville, 9 In.	10.00
Woodfield, Snack Set, Fawn, Steubenville, 9 In.	15.00
Woodfield, Snack Set, Tropic, Steubenville, 9 In.	15.00
Yellow Nocturne, Platter, Blue Ridge, 11 ⅞ In.	25.00
Yorktown, Cup & Saucer, Salem China	12.00

DIONNE QUINTUPLETS were born in Canada on May 28, 1934. The publicity about their birth and their special status as wards of the Canadian government made them famous throughout the world. Visitors could watch the girls play; reporters interviewed the girls and the staff. Thousands of special dolls and souvenirs were made picturing the quints at different ages. Emilie died in 1954, Marie in 1970, Yvonne in 2001. Annette and Cecile still live in Canada.

Clock, Baby Faces, Names, Cast Zinc, Painted, Lux, 4 ¾ x 3 ⅞ In.	95.00
Doll, Annette, Composition, Jointed, Madame Alexander, 11 ½ In.	145.00

Doll, Emilie, Teddy Bear, Madame Alexander, Composition, Box, c.1935, 16 In.	1053.00
Dolls, Composition, Jointed, 3-Wheel Cart, Madame Alexander, 6 Piece....................................	520.00
Dolls, Composition, Jointed, Madame Alexander, 7 ¾ In., 6 Piece	520.00
Dolls, Composition, Painted Hair, Face, 5-Person Scooter, Box, 7 In. ....*illus*	2576.00
Dolls, Composition Socket Head, Side-Glancing Eyes, Bed, Alexander, c.1935, 7 In.	952.00
Dolls, Toddlers, Madame Alexander, Composition, Molded Hair, c.1935, 11 In.	468.00
Radio, Gray, Stewart Warner, 7 ¾ In., 6 Piece	520.00
Sign, Musterole, Cardboard, Photos, 1940s, 21 x 22 In.	115.00

DIRK VAN ERP was born in 1860 and died in 1933. He opened his own studio in 1908 in Oakland, California. He moved his studio to San Francisco in 1909 and the studio remained under the direction of his son until 1977. Van Erp made hammered copper accessories, including vases, desk sets, bookends, candlesticks, jardinieres, and trays, but he is best known for his lamps. The hammered copper lamps often had shades with mica panels.

Bookends, Copper, Pierced, Stylized Poppies, 5 x 6 In. ....*illus*	1440.00
Lamp, Boudoir, Copper, Hammered, 4-Panel Mica Shade, Patina, Marked, 11 x 12 In.	9000.00
Lamp, Copper, Hammered, 2-Light, Mica Shade, Windmill Stamp, 20 ½ x 16 ¾ In.	9150.00
Lamp, Copper, Hammered, Bean Pot, 3-Light, Mica Shade, Windmill Stamp, 20 x 20 In.	12200.00
Lamp, Copper, Hammered, Bean Pot, 4-Panel Mica Shade, Flowers, Windmill, 12 x 11 In.	9760.00
Lamp, Copper, Hammered, Mica Shade, Panel, Pull Chain, Windmill Stamp, 15 x 11 ¼ In.	7320.00
Lamp, Copper, Hammered, Pierced, Mica Shade, Windmill Stamp, 64 x 24 ¼ In.	19520.00
Lamp, Copper, Hammered, Trumpet, 3-Light, Mica Shade, Windmill, 22 x 19 In.	7320.00
Porringer, Sterling Silver, Hammered, 2 Handles, Cutout Design, Marked, 7 ¾ In.	600.00
Vase, Copper, Hammered, Flared Shape, Signed, 6 x 7 ½ In.	1320.00
Vase, Copper, Hammered, Fluted, 13 ¼ x 8 In.	2318.00
Vase, Copper, Hammered, Red Patina, Urn Shape, 11 ¾ x 7 In.	4270.00
Vase, Copper, Hammered, Shouldered, Red Warty, 5 ¾ x 5 In.	1952.00
Vase, Copper, Hammered, Shouldered, Red Warty, 6 ½ x 4 ¾ In.	2440.00
Vase, Copper, Hammered, Tapered, Patina, 8 x 4 ½ In.	1320.00
Vase, Copper, Hand Wrought, Warty, Stamped, c.1911-14, 8 ⅜ x 10 ¾ In.	53125.00

DISNEYANA is a collectors' term. Walt Disney and his company introduced many comic characters to the world. Collectors search for examples of the work of the Disney Studios and the many commercial products modeled after his characters, including Mickey Mouse and Donald Duck, and recent films, like *Beauty and the Beast* and *The Little Mermaid*.

Ashtray, Donald Duck, Double, Lusterware, Marked, 1936, 7 ⅞ x 4 ¼ In.	165.00
Ashtray, Mickey Mouse, Painted, Black, White, Composition, 1930s, 3 ⅛ In.	203.00
Ashtray, Mickey Mouse, Standing Near Floor Lamp, Metal, Germany, 6 In. ....*illus*	1686.00
Bank, Donald Duck, Book Shape, Metal, Pearson-Paige Jewsbury Co., 1950s, 3 x 4 ½ In.	209.00
Bank, Donald Duck, Dime, Register, Lookie What I Saved, Tin Litho, 1939, 2 ½ x 2 ½ In.	285.00
Bank, Donald Duck, Right Hand On Stomach, Painted, Cast Iron, 8 ¾ In.	118.00
Bank, Donald Duck, With Coins, Painted, White Metal, 6 ½ In.	150.00
Bank, Mickey & Minnie Mouse, House Shape, S.A. Gulliver, France, 2 ½ x 5 ¼ In.	195.00
Bank, Mickey Mouse, Beehive Shape, Tin Lithograph, Germany, 2 ½ x 3 In. ....*illus*	430.00
Bank, Mickey Mouse, Bronze, Painted, France, 1930s, 8 In.	475.00
Bank, Mickey Mouse, Post Office, Minnie, Pluto, Tin, Cylindrical, Happynak, 6 In.	100.00
Bank, Mickey Mouse, Suitcase, Metal, Carrying Handle, Travel Sticker, 1935, 2 ½ In.	440.00
Bank, Mickey Mouse, Suitcase, Painted, Metal, Automatic Recording Safe Co., 4 x 2 ½ In.	443.00
Bank, Mickey Mouse, Waving, Painted, Iron, 9 x 6 x 4 In.	140.00
Bank, Snow White & The Seven Dwarfs, Dime Register, Tin, 2 ½ In.	70.00
Bicycle, Donald Duck, Boy's, Shelby, Head Mounted In Front, Marked, c.1949, 60 x 34 In.	7020.00
Bicycle, Donald Duck, Girl's, Blue, Yellow, Shelby Cycle Co., 1949..............................	675.00
Big Little Set, Mickey Mouse, Display Card, Book, Crayons, c.1936, 8 ¼ x 8 ½ In.	1990.00
Book, Mickey Mouse, Ye Olden Days, Pop Up, Blue Ribbon Press, c.1934, 4 x 5 In.	230.00
Book, Snow White & Seven Dwarfs, Masks, Whitman, c.1938, 10 ½ x 10 ¾ In., 8 Pages............	348.00
Bowl, Warming, Donald Duck, 3 Sections, Patriot China, c.1938, 7 ¾ In.	95.00
Button, Donald Duck, Wanna Fight, Portrait, c.1935..	654.00
Button, Mickey Mouse, Chums, Red, Black, Gold Rim, 1 In.	85.00
Button, Mickey Mouse Club, Black & White, Fox Hollywdy Theatre, 1 ¼ In.	230.00
Button, Mickey Mouse, Running, Arms Extended, Multicolored, 1930s, 1 In.	153.00
Card Holder, Mickey Mouse, Celluloid, 1930s, 1 ¾ In.	195.00
Cel, see Animation Art category.	
Cereal Box, Pinocchio, Post Toasties, Homeward Bound, Tomart, c.1941, 9 ¼ x 12 In.	184.00
Charm Bracelet, Mickey Mouse, Brass Link Chain, Enamel, Alice, Box, c.1935	115.00
Christmas Card, Studio, Mickey Mouse Clubhouse, 1956, Calendar, 7 x 7 ¼ In.	152.00

Disneyana, Bank, Mickey Mouse, Beehive Shape, Tin Lithograph, Germany, 2 ½ x 3 In. $430.00

Disneyana, Doll, Pinocchio, Composition, Painted Wood, Jointed, Ideal, c.1940, 19 In. $560.00

TIP

You can cover up a small chip in an enamel or even a piece of porcelain with a bit of colored nail polish. It comes in almost every color now.

Disneyana, Doll, Pinocchio, Jointed, Ideal, 19 In.
$468.00

Disneyana, Figurine, Donald Duck, Golfer, Painted, Zaccagnini, c.1947, 5 x 6 x 9 In.
$2247.00

TIP

Don't let plastic toys or dishes touch each other. Different types of plastic may react to each other and be damaged.

Christmas Card, Studio, Mickey Mouse In Santa Suit, 1948, Calendar, 7 ¼ x 8 In.	115.00
Clock, Mickey & Minnie Mouse, Chrome, Tin, Al Horen, Ingersoll, 1960s, 5 ½ In.	350.00
Clock, Mickey Mouse, Alarm, Copper, Square, Model No. 0175, Electric	148.00
Cookie Jar, Cinderella, Flower Wreath Mark, 11 In.	62.00
Cup, Pinocchio, Carrying Buckets, Puppet Became A Real Little Boy, 1940, 4 ⅜ In.	115.00
Dish Set, Mickey Mouse Fireman, Mug, Bowl, Plate, Divided Dish, Salem China Co.	917.00
Dog, Lady & The Tramp, Schuco, 1955, 9 ½ In.	295.00
Doll, Ariel The Little Mermaid, Head Turns, Jointed Arms, Tyco, 9 ½ In.	30.00
Doll, Dopey, Blue Hat, Purple Coat, Knickerbockers, 1938	230.00
Doll, Mickey Mouse, Walking, Straw Hat, Movable Head, 2 Sections, Britain, 2 ½ In.	748.00
Doll, Minnie Mouse, Green Hat, Movable Head, 2 Sections, Britain, 2 ½ In.	748.00
Doll, Pinocchio, Composition Head, Jointed Wood Body, Walt Disney, Ideal, c.1940, 7 In.	168.00
Doll, Pinocchio, Composition, Painted Wood, Jointed, Ideal, c.1940, 19 In. ....*illus*	560.00
Doll, Pinocchio, Composition, Painted Wood, Label, Freundlich, c.1940, 17 In.	280.00
Doll, Pinocchio, Jointed, Hard Plastic, Composition, Felt, Cloth, 13 In.	98.00
Doll, Pinocchio, Jointed, Ideal, 19 In. ....*illus*	468.00
Doll, Snow White & Seven Dwarfs, Composition, Jointed, Knickerbocker, Box, c.1937, 8 Piece..	2910.00
Doll, Tweedledee & Tweedledum, Cloth, Felt, Signed, Mary Peterson, 20 ½ In.	790.00
Doorstop, Donald Duck, Holds STOP & ENTER Sign, 8 ½ In.	173.00
Egg Timer, Snow White, Doc, White China, 3 ½ In.	144.00
Figurine Set, 3 Little Pigs, Painted, Bisque, Box, 3 ½ In.	200.00
Figurine Set, Snow White & Seven Dwarfs, Painted, Bisque, Box, 12 ¾ In.	165.00
Figurine, Donald Duck, Bisque, 1 ¾ In.	65.00
Figurine, Donald Duck, Chef, Multicolored, Black Ground, Stoneware, WDP, 10 In.	60.00
Figurine, Donald Duck, Crawling, Celluloid, Prewar, Box, c.1935, 9 ¾ In.	1952.00
Figurine, Donald Duck, Golfer, Painted, Zaccagnini, c.1947, 5 x 6 x 9 In. ....*illus*	2247.00
Figurine, Dumbo, Messenger Stock, Multicolored, Vernon Kilns, c.1941, 4 ½ x 9 In.	3704.00
Figurine, Dwarf, Happy, Rubber Seiberling, Orange Jacket, Marked, Marked, 1940s, 5 ¾ In. ...	95.00
Figurine, Elmer, Elephant, Silly Symphonies, Celluloid, c.1933, 5 In.	88.00
Figurine, Ferdinand The Bull, Multicolored, Brayton Laguna, 4 ½ x 3 ¾ In.	288.00
Figurine, Maleficent, Porcelain, Hagen-Renaker, c.1959, 2 ½ x 3 In.	1107.00
Figurine, Mickey Mouse, Baseball Player, Bat, Painted, Bisque, Incised, 3 ⅜ In.	50.00
Figurine, Mickey Mouse, Baseball Player, Catcher, Painted, Bisque, Incised, 3 ¼ In.	55.00
Figurine, Mickey Mouse, Baseball Player, Glove & Ball, Painted, Bisque, Incised, 3 ½ In.	60.00
Figurine, Mickey Mouse, Bisque, Made In Japan, 4 ¼ x 2 ¼ In.	15.00
Figurine, Mickey Mouse, Celluloid, Japan, c.1935, 7 ¼ In.	149.00
Figurine, Mickey Mouse, Riding Pluto, Bisque, Japan, 1930s, 3 In.	125.00
Figurine, Mickey Mouse, Saxophone, Bulbous Head, Painted, Bisque, Incised, 3 ⅜ In.	60.00
Figurine, Minnie Mouse, Bisque, Made In Japan, 4 ¼ x 2 ¼ In.	15.00
Figurine, Minnie Mouse, Celluloid, Japan, c.1935, 5 ¾ In.	77.00
Figurine, Nubian Centaurette, Holding Flowers, Fantasia, Vernon Kilns, 1940, 8 In.	673.00
Figurine, Pinocchio, Holding Apple, Schoolbook Over Shoulder, Brayton Laguna, 1940, 5 ¾ In.	336.00
Figurine, Pluto, Sniffing, Painted, Porcelain, Marked, Zaccagnini, W45, c.1950, 12 In.	570.00
Figurine, Sleepy, Brown Jacket, Marked, Rubber Seiberling, 1940s, 5 ¼ In.	95.00
Figurine, Sprite, Fantasia, No. 10, Vernon Kilns, c.1940, 4 ½ In.	275.00
Figurine, Wolf, Pinocchio, Glazed, Marked W.D.P., 3 In.	28.00
Game, Donald Duck Quoits, Donald Bull's-Eye Target, Chad Valley, 1940s	172.00
Game, Donald Duck, Target, Bean Bag Party Game, Parker Brothers, 1939	172.00
Game, Mickey Mouse, Target Marksman Baseball, Square, 18 x 18 In.	345.00
Globe, Tin Lithograph, Disney, Characters, 1950s, 10 In.	144.00
Handkerchief, Snow White & 7 Dwarfs, White, Red Border, Cotton, c.1938, 8 ½ x 9 In. ....*illus*	50.00
Ice Cream Cup, Lid, Mickey Mouse, Southern Dairies, Wax Paper, 1930s, 2 x 2 ¾ In.	190.00
Lamp, Mickey & Minnie Mouse, Pluto, Shade, Battery Operated, Metal Base, 8 In.	454.00
Letter Opener, Sword, Metal, Walt Disney World Florida, 6 ⅛ In.	30.00
Lunch Box, Disney Characters, Firefighters, Dome, Thermos, Aladdin	220.00
Lunch Box, School Bus, Mickey Mouse, Characters In Windows, Tin, Aladdin, 9 In.	30.00
Marionette, Mickey Mouse, Hestwood Marionette Studio, Box, 1933, 12 In.	863.00
Marionette, Minnie Mouse, Composition, Wood, Velveteen Arms, 1933, 12 In.	863.00
Match Holder, Ashtray, Mickey Mouse, Bulbous Head, Painted, Chalkware, 1930s, 6 ¼ In.	85.00
Match Holder, Mickey Mouse, Painted, Lead, Germany, 3 ⅝ x 3 ½ In.	120.00
Mechanical Pencil, Fountain Pen, Mickey Mouse, Inkograph Co., c.1935, 5 ¼ In., Pair	127.00
Mug, Mickey & Minnie Mouse, Dancing In Window, Paragon, 1933, 3 ¾ In.	1478.00
Napkin Ring, Donald Duck, Plastic Catalin, 1930s, 2 ¾ In., Pair	143.00
Nodder, Donald Duck, Limited Edition, Box, 8 In.	80.00
Nodder, Mickey Mouse, Thinker, Limited Edition, Box, 8 In.	80.00
Pail, Donald Duck, At Beach, Nephews, Tug-O-War, Tin Lithograph, c.1939, 4 ¼ In.	370.00

Pail, Mickey's Band, Mickey, Horace, Goofy, Pluto, Tin Lithograph, Ohio Art, 1930s, 5 ¾ In.	345.00
Pencil Box, Mickey Mouse Form, Die Cut, Cardboard, Dixon, 1930s, 8 ¼ In.	683.00
Pencil Sharpener, Donald Duck, Bakelite, Red, Paper Sticker, 8-Sided	75.00
Pencil Sharpener, Pluto, Round, Red, Bakelite, Paper Sticker	75.00
Pin, Mickey Mouse, With Umbrella, Die Cut Enamel, Brass, 1930s, 1 In.	285.00
Pitcher, Donald Duck, Incised, 6 ¼ In.	75.00
Planter, Bambi, Tree Stump, Incised, 7 x 7 ¼ In.	65.00
Planter, Donald Duck, Painted, Porcelain, Fence, Grass, Mid 1930s, 5 ½ In.	345.00
Plaque, Dumbo, Circus Tent, Child, Wash Tub, 1951, 4 Piece	19.00
Pocket Knife, Mickey Mouse, Pluto, Hunting Scene, Metal Grip, c.1932, 3 ⅜ x 2 ¼ In.	575.00
Poster, Alice In Wonderland, Caterpillar, White Rabbit, Animated, c.1959, 36 x 54 In.	6916.00
Poster, Song Of The South, Br'er Fox & Br'er Rabbit, 14 x 36 In.	173.00
Press Kit, Mickey & Minnie Mouse, Model Sheet, King Features, Mat, 1930s, 16 x 17 In.	6958.00
Puppet, Donald Duck, Molded Vinyl Head, Cloth Body, 1950s..	99.50
Puppet, Dopey, Pointed Red Hat, Open Mouth, Brown Shirt, Label, 1960s..........................	30.00
Puppet, Jiminy Cricket, Molded Vinyl Head, Blue Top Hat, Gund, 1950s............................	75.00
Puppet, Pongo, 101 Dalmatians, Black Ears, Gund, 1960s	85.00
Puppet, Shaggy Dog, The Shaggy Dog Movie, Gund, 1960s	85.00
Purse, Mickey Mouse, Plays Guitar, Minnie, Pluto Sings, Metal, 2 ¼ x 2 ¼ In.	834.00
Radio, Mickey Mouse, Wood Lacquer, Corner Disney, Emerson, 1930s, 7 x 7 In.	748.00
Salt & Pepper, Mickey & Minnie Mouse, White, Red, Black, Paint, Leeds, 1935, 3 ¼ In.	75.00
Sieve, Mickey Mouse, Tin Lithograph, Handle, Ohio Art, 8 x 2 In.	230.00
Sign, Donald Duck Soft Drinks, Tin, Celluloid, String, Hanger 9 In.	209.00
Stickers, Fabric, Disney, Cartoon Characters, Press Iron, 1946, 7 x 1 ¾ In., Pair	35.00
Storyboard, Sleeping Beauty, Charcoal, Eyvind Earle, 6 x 13 ½ In.	765.00
Straws, Donald Duck, Sunshine, Super Long, Unopened Box, 100 Straws..............................	14.00
Tea Set, Donald Duck, Picnic Scenes, Tin Lithograph, Ohio Art, c.1938, 22 Piece....................	627.00
Tea Set, Snow White & Seven Dwarfs, Wadeheather, 1938, 10 Piece.......................................	435.00
Tie Rack, Mickey Mouse, Wood, 8 ¾ In.	140.00
Toothbrush Holder, 3 Little Pigs, Bisque, Incised, No. 5336, Made In Japan, c.1950, 3 ½ In. ..	195.00
Toothbrush Holder, Donald Duck, Blue Jacket..	325.00
Toothbrush Holder, Donald Duck, Double...	350.00
Toothbrush Holder, Mickey & Minnie Mouse, Cold Paint, Bisque, 2 Holes, Japan, 4 ½ In.	150.00
Toothbrush Holder, Mickey Mouse, Bisque, 6 In. .... 225.00 to 245.00	
Toothbrush Holder, Minnie Mouse, Standing, Trash Can, Bisque, 1930s, 4 ½ In.	552.00
Toy, Donald Duck, Acrobat, Plastic, Metal, Windup, Linemar, Box, 1950s, 12 ¼ In.	210.00
Toy, Donald Duck, Beak Opens, Closes, Windup, Schuco, Box	475.00
Toy, Donald Duck, Carousel, Celluloid, Tin, Windup, Borgfeldt, Box, 10 ½ In.	3278.00
Toy, Donald Duck, Dipsy Car, Nodder, Tin, Windup, Marx .... 180.00 to 350.00	
Toy, Donald Duck, Driver, Pluto In Back, Blue Convertible, Rubber, Sun Rubber Co., 6 In.	58.00
Toy, Donald Duck, Drum Major Cart, Pull Toy, Fisher-Price, No. 400-500, 10 x 10 ¼ In.	195.00
Toy, Donald Duck, Drum Major Cart, Pull Toy, Fisher-Price, No. 550-463, 10 x 12 In.	240.00
Toy, Donald Duck, Duet, Goofy, Tin Lithograph, Windup, Marx, 1946, 10 In.	220.00
Toy, Donald Duck, Duet, Windup, Marx, Box, 1940s..	890.00
Toy, Donald Duck, Flowers On Cart, Pull-Toy, Fisher-Price, No. 605, 8 x 10 In.	130.00
Toy, Donald Duck, Huey, Tin Windup, Linemar, Box, 5 ¼ In.	750.00
Toy, Donald Duck, Jack-In-Box, Celluloid, 1930s...	425.00
Toy, Donald Duck, Nodder, Celluloid, Windup, Lead Pendulum, Metal Base, 1930s, 6 In.	785.00
Toy, Donald Duck, Nodder, Dipsy Car, Windup, Marx	350.00
Toy, Donald Duck, On Rocking Horse, Plastic, WindupUp, Illco	15.00
Toy, Donald Duck, On Tricycle, Tin, Celluloid, Windup, Linemar, 4 x 3 ½ In.	125.00
Toy, Donald Duck, Playing Xylophone, Pull Toy, Fisher-Price, No. 177, 13 x 11 In.	198.00
Toy, Donald Duck, Railcar, Pluto, Doghouse, Tin, Composition, Windup, Lionel, Box, 10 In. ...	910.00
Toy, Donald Duck, Riding Pluto, Rocker, Celluloid, Windup, Prewar, Japan, 8 In. .... *illus*	878.00
Toy, Donald Duck, Tin, Plastic Beak, Arms, Legs, Windup, Germany, Schuco, 6 In. ....*illus*	468.00
Toy, Donald Duck, Tricycle, Long Billed, Alps Toys, c.1940..	650.00
Toy, Donald Duck, Tricycle, Tin, Windup, 1930s	575.00
Toy, Donald Duck, Xylophone, Arms Move, Fisher-Price, No. 185, c.1938, 14 In. ....*illus*	205.00
Toy, Dopey, Walker, Eyes Move, Tin Lithograph, Windup, Marx, 1938, 8 In.	170.00
Toy, Dopey, Walker, Tin Lithograph, Windup, Wells Brimtoy, 5 ⅛ In.	115.00
Toy, Drum, Mickey & Minnie Mouse, Tin Lithograph, Donald Duck, Rope Strap, 10 x 5 ½ In. .	880.00
Toy, Dumbo, Flips Backwards, Marx, 1941	385.00
Toy, Ferdinand & Matador, Tin, Windup, Marx, Box, 7 In. .... *illus*	527.00
Toy, Fishing Kit, Mickey & Minnie Mouse, In Rowboat, Metal, Hinged, 4 ½ x 7 ½ In.	440.00
Toy, Goofy, Cyclist, Rubber Ears, Linemar, Japan, Box, 1950s, 7 In. ....*illus*	1170.00
Toy, Goofy, Gardener, Tin Lithograph, Windup, Marx, c.1935, 8 In. ....*illus*	336.00

Disneyana, Handkerchief,
Snow White & 7 Dwarfs, White,
Red Border, Cotton, c.1938, 8 ½ x 9 In.
$50.00

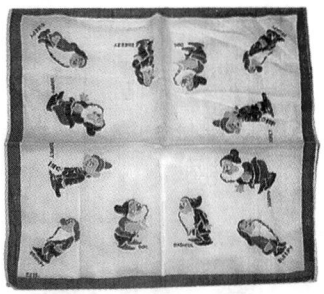

Disneyana, Toy, Donald Duck,
Riding Pluto, Rocker, Celluloid,
Windup, Prewar, Japan, 8 In.
$878.00

Disneyana, Toy, Donald Duck, Tin,
Plastic Beak, Arms, Legs, Windup,
Germany, Schuco, 6 In.
$468.00

Disneyana, Toy, Donald Duck, Xylophone, Arms Move, Fisher Price, No. 185, c.1938, 14 In.
$205.00

Disneyana, Toy, Ferdinand & Matador, Tin, Windup, Marx, Box, 7 In.
$527.00

Disneyana, Toy, Goofy, Cyclist, Rubber Ears, Linemar, Japan, Box, 1950s, 7 In.
$1170.00

Toy, Goofy, Turns In Circles, Tail Spins, Windup, Linemar	295.00
Toy, Jiminy Cricket, Hops, Windup, Umbrella, Linemar, 1950s, 5 ¼ In.	474.00
Toy, Jiminy Cricket, Walker, Ramp, 1960s	50.00
Toy, Mickey & Minnie Mouse, Acrobats, Celluloid, Windup, Nifty Toy, Box, 14 In.	950.00
Toy, Mickey & Minnie Mouse, Handcar, Tin, 8 Tracks, Composition, Lionel, 8 In.	1404.00
Toy, Mickey & Minnie Mouse, Handcar, Tin, Celluloid, Red, Yellow, 1930s, 5 x 7 ¼ In.	330.00
Toy, Mickey & Minnie Mouse, Handcar, Tin, Composition, Windup, Lionel, Box, 8 In.	1320.00
Toy, Mickey & Minnie Mouse, Handcar, Track, Metal, Wood, Lionel, 1930s, 7 ½ x 5 ½ In.	558.00
Toy, Mickey & Minnie Mouse, Trapeze, Celluloid, Windup, c.1936, 14 ½ In.	368.00
Toy, Mickey Mouse & Donald Duck, Handcar, Tin, Composition, Windup, Wells, 7 In.	395.00
Toy, Mickey Mouse, Acrobat, Celluloid, Moves, Windup, Box, 1930, 4 In.	650.00 to 750.00
Toy, Mickey Mouse, Acrobat, Trapeze, Celluloid, Prewar Japan, Borgfeldt, Box, 10 ½ In.	610.00
Toy, Mickey Mouse, Choo-Choo, Bell Rings, Pull Toy, Fisher-Price, No. 485, 7 x 8 ½ In.	48.00
Toy, Mickey Mouse, Cowboy, On Horse, Wood, Celluloid, Label, Japan, Prewar, 8 ½ x 5 ½ In. *illus*	527.00
Toy, Mickey Mouse, Cowboy, On Pluto, Celluloid, Wood Rocking Base, Pre War, 8 In.	8775.00
Toy, Mickey Mouse, Dipsy Car, Nodder, Tin, Windup, Linemar, Box, 6 In. *illus*	468.00
Toy, Mickey Mouse, Donald Duck, Handcar, Windup, Paperboard Toy Town, Box	1450.00
Toy, Mickey Mouse, Driver, Tin Lithograph, Windup, Built-In Key, 1950s, 6 ½ In.	173.00
Toy, Mickey Mouse, Fire Truck, Donald Duck, Hard Rubber, Sun Rubber Co., 6 ½ In.	38.00
Toy, Mickey Mouse, Flashlight, Minnie Mouse, Pluto, Tin Lithograph, 6 In. *illus*	585.00
Toy, Mickey Mouse, Handcar, Donald Duck, Pluto, Tin, Composition, Wells, c.1935, 7 In.	410.00
Toy, Mickey Mouse, Handcar, Santa Claus, Tin, Composition, Windup, Lionel, Box, 10 In.	1450.00
Toy, Mickey Mouse, Happy New Year, Pipe Cleaner, Spun Cotton, Germany, 3 ½ In.	40.00
Toy, Mickey Mouse, In Car, Tin, Plastic, Windup, Marx	650.00
Toy, Mickey Mouse, Pram, Babies, Pluto, Tin Lithograph, 8 In. *illus*	2106.00
Toy, Mickey Mouse, Santa Car, Pressed Steel, Composition, Pride Lines Ltd., 6 x 11 ½ In.	540.00
Toy, Mickey Mouse, Sparkler, Die Cut, Tin Lithograph, Chein, 5 ½ In.	144.00
Toy, Mickey Mouse, Sparkler, In Litho, Die Cut, Chein, 5 ½ In.	144.00
Toy, Mickey Mouse, Tail, Spins, Windup, Linemar, Box, 5 In.	410.00
Toy, Mickey Mouse, Top, Plays Tuba, Minnie, Pluto, Big Bad Wolf, 3 Little Pigs, Tin, 10 x 11 In.	201.00
Toy, Mickey Mouse, Washing Machine, Washing Scenes, Electric, 1930s	350.00
Toy, Mickey Mouse, Xylophone Player, Plastic, Tin, Windup, Box, 1950s, 12 x 10 In.	260.00
Toy, Mickey Mouse, Xylophone Player, Plastic, Tin, Windup, Marx, W.D.P., 12 x 10 In.	175.00
Toy, Mickey Mouse, Xylophone, Songbook, No. 135, Tudor Metal Products, Box, 12 In.	140.00
Toy, Minnie Mouse, Celluloid, Acrobat, Windup, Box, 1930, 4 In.	650.00 to 750.00
Toy, Minnie Mouse, Rocking Chair, Knitting, Windup, Linemar, Box	650.00
Toy, Pinocchio, Carrying Buckets, Tin Lithograph, Windup, Walker, c.1939, 8 ½ In.	230.00
Toy, Pinocchio, Donkey, Rings Bell, Pull Toy, Wood, No. 494, Fisher-Price, 1939, 9 In.	170.00
Toy, Pinocchio, Eyes Move, Windup, Walker, Marx, 1939	350.00
Toy, Pinocchio, Rookie Pilot, Tin Lithograph, Windup, Marx, 7 In.	360.00
Toy, Pinocchio, Walker, Eyes Move, Marx, 1939	350.00
Toy, Pinocchio, Walker, Tin, Windup, Marx, 1939, 8 ½ In.	406.00
Toy, Pinocchio, Wobbles, Eyes Move, Tin Lithograph, Windup, Marx, 8 ¼ In.	138.00
Toy, Pinocchio, Wood, Jointed, Ideal, 7 In., Box	280.00 to 385.00
Toy, Pluto, Acrobat, On Wire, Plastic, Windup, Gym Toys, Linemar, Box	385.00
Toy, Pluto, Cart, Friction, Marx, Box, 7 x 6 In. *illus*	205.00
Toy, Pluto, Pull-Toy, Wood, Silkscreen, Cardboard Ears, Balantyne Mfg., 1940s, 12 x 8 ½ In.	201.00
Toy, Pluto, Tail Spins, Windup, Nodder, Linemar	295.00
Toy, Pluto, The Pup, Painted Wood, Felt Ears, c.1930, 6 ½ In.	296.00
Toy, Pluto, Tricycle, Tin, Celluloid, Windup, Linemar, Box, 3 ¾ In.	395.00 to 595.00
Toy, Pluto, Tricycle, Tin, Windup, Bell Ringer, Celluloid, Linemar, Box	395.00
Toy, Pluto, Watch Me Roll Over, Tin, Windup, Marx, 1939, 9 In.	112.00
Toy, Pluto, Windup, Marx, 1939, Box	485.00
Toy, Tractor, Mickey Mouse, Rubber, Sun, 5 In.	275.00
Toy, Zorro, Horse, Accessories, Marx, Box, c.1958, 7 ½ & 9 In.	380.00
Tumbler, Horace Horsecollar, Marked, c.1938, 4 ¾ x 6 ¾ In.	75.00
Vase, Fantasia, Milkweed Ballet, Nutcracker Suite, Blue Ground, Porcelain, Wade, 1940s, 8 In.	115.00
Vase, Goddess Diana, Fantasia, Vernon Kilns, Porcelain, Blue, c.1940, 10 In.	690.00
Waffle Maker, Dumbo, Disneyland, Electric, 1960s, 7 ½ x 16 In.	115.00
Watch, Mickey Mouse, Animated Hands, No. 5 Below Mickey, Ingersoll, Box, c.1937	543.00
Watch, Pocket, Mickey Mouse, Fob, Ingersoll, 1930s	495.00
Wristwatch, Mickey Mouse, Animated, Metal Band, Ingersoll, Box, 1930s	650.00
Wristwatch, Mickey Mouse, Hands Point, Metal, Yellow Vinyl Band, Italy, 1960s	172.00
Wristwatch, Mickey Mouse, Leather Band, Ingersoll, Box, c.1935	260.00
Wristwatch, Mickey Mouse, Leather Band, Paperwork, Box, c.1935	350.00
Wristwatch, Mickey Mouse, Metal Band, Ingersoll, Box, c.1933	360.00

Disneyana, Toy, Goofy, Gardener, Tin Lithograph, Windup, Marx, c.1935, 8 In. $336.00

Disneyana, Toy, Mickey Mouse, Cowboy, On Horse, Wood, Celluloid, Label, Japan, Prewar, 8 ½ x 5 ½ In. $527.00

Disneyana, Toy, Mickey Mouse, Flashlight, Minnie Mouse, Pluto, Tin Lithograph, 6 In. $585.00

TIP
To clean terminals on batteries, use a standard pencil eraser.

Disneyana, Toy, Mickey Mouse, Pram, Babies, Pluto, Tin Lithograph, 8 In. $2106.00

Disneyana, Toy, Pluto, Cart, Friction, Marx, Box, 7 x 6 In. $205.00

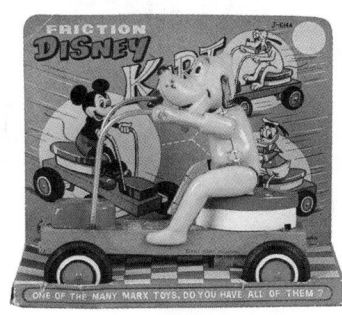

Disneyana, Toy, Mickey Mouse, Dipsy Car, Nodder, Tin, Windup, Linemar, Box, 6 In. $468.00

TIP

Early Raggedy Ann dolls by Georgene Novelties Company have wool wigs. By the mid 1940s the wigs were made of cotton.

Doll, Advertising, Buddy Lee, Googly Eyes, Bandanna, Denim Shirt, Overalls, Cap, c.1922, 13 In.
$336.00

Doll, A.M., Just Me, Bisque Socket Head, Blond Mohair Wig, Closed Pouty Mouth, c.1928, 9 In.
$784.00

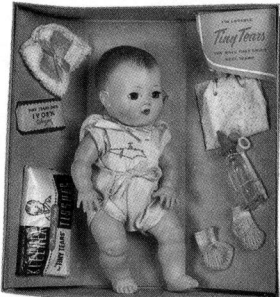

Doll, American Character, Tiny Tears, Plastic Head, Original Presentation Box, 1950, 11 In.
$448.00

Wristwatch, Mickey Mouse, Pink Cheeks, 2nd Version, England, Box	350.00
Wristwatch, Mickey Mouse, Silvered Metal Case, Celluloid Dial, Ingersoll, 1 ¼ In.	716.00
Wristwatch Set, Minnie Mouse, Figurine, Pink Outfit, Ingersoll, U.S. Time, 1958	465.00

DOCTOR, see Dental and Medical categories.

DOLL entries are listed by marks printed or incised on the doll, if possible. If there are no marks, the doll is listed by the name of the subject or country or maker. Notice that Barbie is listed under Mattel. G.I. Joe figures are listed in the Toy section. Eskimo dolls are listed in the Eskimo section and Indian dolls are listed in the Indian section. Doll clothes and accessories are listed at the end of this section. The twentieth-century clothes listed here are in mint condition.

77 Football Hero, Composition, Flanged Neck, Painted Face, Muslin Body, c.1930, 27 In.	224.00
Advertising, Anty Drudge, Cloth, Stuffed, Fels Naptha Soap, 6 ½ x 11 In.	45.00
Advertising, Buddy Lee, Googly Eyes, Bandanna, Denim Shirt, Overalls, Cap, c.1922, 13 In. ...*illus*	336.00
Advertising, Buddy Lee, Philgas, Hard Plastic, Gray Uniform, Hat, 12 ½ In.	236.00
Advertising, Buddy Lee, Train, Allied Van Lines, U.S. 1, Dark Green Uniform, Hat, 12 ½ In.	236.00
Advertising, Cuheb Tobacco Co., Flapper, Composition Socket Head, Jointed, Cigarette, 25 In.	448.00
Advertising, Fels Naptha Soap, Cloth, Sewn Together, 6 ½ x 11 In.	45.00
Advertising, Hamburglar, McDonald's, Cloth, 16 In.	30.00
Advertising, Hotel Essex, Googly Eyed, Bellman Blue Cap & Hat, 1930s, 22 In.	135.00
Advertising, Hotpoint Devil Man, Decal On Chest, Posable Arms & Legs, Cameo, 1930s, 15 In.	1050.00
Advertising, Lee Jeans, Buddy Lee, Plastic Body, Jointed, Painted, Jeans, Hat, Shirt, c.1950, 13 In.	224.00
Advertising, Lennie Lennox, Linen, Uncut, 11 ¾ x 18 ¼ In.	95.00
Alexander dolls are listed in this category under Madame Alexander.	
A.M., 323, Sleep Eyes, Glass Googly, Closed Mouth, Mohair Wig, 5-Piece Composition, 9 In.	862.00
A.M., 341, Sterling Doll Co., Dream Baby, Bisque, Closed Mouth, Glass Eyes, Composition, 14 In.	83.00
A.M., 390, Bisque Head, Sleep Eyes, Open Mouth, Teeth, Jointed Composition Body, c.1900, 34 In.	351.00
A.M., 971, Bisque Head, Open Mouth, Teeth, Glass Eyes, Blond Mohair, Composition, Boy, 13 In.	267.00
A.M., 1894, Bisque Head, Open Mouth, 4 Teeth, Painted Lashes, Brows, Sleep Eyes, Jointed, 23 ½ In.	230.00
A.M., 3200, Bisque Shoulder Head, Open Mouth, Teeth, Glass Eyes, Human Hair, 19 In.	86.00
A.M., Bisque Head, Sleep Eyes, Open Mouth, Teeth, Cloth Body, Bisque Hands, 16 In.	120.00
A.M., Bisque Shoulder Head, Glass Eyes, Mohair, Jointed Kid Body, Limbs, Bisque Hands, 22 In.	178.00
A.M., Florodora, Bisque Shoulder Head, Mohair, Gusseted Kid Body, Limbs, Bisque Hands, Box, 12 In.	89.00
A.M., Just Me, Bisque Socket Head, Blond Mohair Wig, Closed Pouty Mouth, c.1928, 9 In. ...*illus*	784.00
American Character, Sally, Composition Swivel Head, Sculpted Hair, Muslin Torso, c.1935, 21 In.	336.00
American Character, Sweet Sue, Plastic, Socket Head, Saran Wig, Walker, Cotton Dress, c.1952, 20 In.	1064.00
American Character, Sweet Sue Sophisticate, Vinyl, Socket Head, Rooted Hair, Walker, c.1958, 20 In.	448.00
American Character, Tiny Tears, Plastic Head, Original Presentation Box, 1950, 11 In. ...*illus*	448.00
American Character, Toni, Vinyl, Socket Head, Rooted Hair, Sleep Eyes, Walker, c.1958, 20 In.	280.00
American Character, Toni, Vinyl, Socket Head, Rooted Saran Hair, Nylon Dress, Walker, c.1957, 20 In.	336.00
Armand Marseille dolls are listed in this category under A.M.	
Arranbee, Nancy Lee, Composition, Original Ice Skating Costume, c.1949, 11 In. ...*illus*	224.00
Arranbee, Nanette, Composition, Brown Sleep Eyes, Mohair Wig, Dress, Hat, c.1940, 13 In.	672.00
Arranbee, Plastic, Blue Sleep Eyes, Floral Dress, Organdy Sleeves, Straw Hat, c.1959, 21 In.	336.00
Automaton, Bird, Red, Moving Wings, Gilt, Brass Scrollwork Case, c.1950, 2 x 4 In. ...*illus*	1064.00
Automaton, Bisque Head & Hands, Blond Hair, Wood Body, Black & Gold Velvet Dress, 15 In.	885.00
Automaton, Boy, With Pig, Composition, Wire Attached To Pig, Clockwork, 11 x 12 ½ In.	920.00
Automaton, Captain & Tennille, Clothing, Hat, Mego, 12 ½ In., Pair	80.00
Automaton, Clown, Ladder, Papier-Mache, Glass Eyes, Windup, France, 1800s, 24 In. ...*illus*	4388.00
Automaton, Clown, Plays Violin, Bisque Head, Hands, Dressed, Clockwork, Key Wind, 14 In.	7475.00
Automaton, Mephistopheles, Under Dome, Bisque Flange Head, Hands, Paperweight Eyes, 4 In.	2370.00
Automaton, Pianist, Bisque Head, Turns, Rises, Emits Sound, Lever, 7 ¾ x 7 In.	2300.00
Automaton, Rabbit, Fur, Holding Basket, Noisemaker, Wood Stand, Label, Vichy, 14 In. ...*illus*	546.00
Automaton, Waltzing Couple, Bisque Socket Heads, Glass Eyes, Mohair, Musical, France, 13 In.	4740.00
Averill, Baby Snookums, Composition, Open Mouth, Teeth, Madame Hendren, Cloth, 1928, 14 In.	250.00
Averill, Bonnie Babe, Bisque Head, Painted Hair, Sleep Eyes, Teeth, Cloth Body, c.1926, 11 In.	468.00
Barbie dolls are listed in this category under Mattel.	
Bisque Head, 3 Faces, Rotating, Sleeping, Smiling, Crying, Glass Eyes, Cloth, Composition, 14 In.	460.00
Bisque Head, Painted Eyes, Closed Mouth, Molded Hair, Kid Body, 18 In.	230.00
Bisque Shoulder Head, Limbs, Molded Headband, Cloth Body, Painted Boots, 9 In.	296.00
Bisque Shoulder Head, Sausage Curls, Cloth Body, Porcelain Legs, Arms, 7 In.	948.00
Bisque Shoulder Head, Upswept Molded Hair, Painted Eyes, Cloth & Kid Body, 18 In.	489.00
Bisque, Baby, Molded Clothes, Bonnet, In Oval Basket, c.1890, 3 ½ In.	178.00
Black dolls are also included in the Black category.	
Boy Scout, Composition, Socket Head, Glass Eyes, Jointed Arms, c.1915, 14 ½ In.	652.00
Bru Jne, 11, Closed Mouth, Molded Tongue, Paperweight Eyes, Silk Lashes, Bebe, 24 ½ In.	3105.00

Bru Jne, Bisque Head, Blue Paperweight Eyes, Moon & Crescent Mark, Bebe, 16 In.	14950.00
Bru Jne, Bisque Head, Eye Shadow, Amber Paperweight Eyes, Leather Shoes, Bebe, 10 In.	16100.00
Bru Jne, Bisque Head, Paperweight Eyes, Closed Mouth, Jointed, Composition, Walker, Bebe, 22 In.	3738.00
Bru Jne, Fashion, Wood Body, Articulated, Bisque, Paperweight Eyes, Mohair Wig, Cotton Dress, 14 In. .	6613.00
Buddy Lee, Train Engineer, Hard Plastic, Union Made Uniform, Lee, Hat, 12 ½ In.	170.00
Bye-Lo, Fly-Lo, Composition Head, Sleep Eyes, Cloth Body, Wings, G. Putnam, c.1925, 13 In. ..	392.00
Cameo Doll Co., Little Annie Rooney, Composition, Side-Glancing Eyes, J. Kallus, c.1926, 17 In.	1232.00
Chase, Mr. Micawber, Stockinet Head, Painted Features, Brush, Stroked Hair, Limbs, 15 ½ In.	4740.00
China Head, Legs, Painted Eyes, Closed Mouth, Molded Collar, Cloth Body, Bisque Hands, 18 In.	46.00
China Shoulder Head, Flat Topped Hair, Painted Eyes, Muslin Body, China Limbs, 19 ½ In. .	237.00
China Shoulder Head, Glass Eyes, Molded Hair, Cloth Body, Kid Hands, c.1870s, 23 In.	1422.00
Cloth, Addams Family, Morticia, Wednesday, Aboriginals, Linen, Stuffed Body, 56 & 19 In.	4888.00
Cloth, Boob McNut, Copyright, The Star Co., 1923, 34 In.	100.00
Cloth, Kid, Body, Hands, Brown Striped Dress, Stand, 1885, 16 In.	889.00
Cloth, Moravian, Painted Facial Features, Hair, Cotton Dress, Apron, c.1900, 18 In.	5925.00
Cloth, Moravian, Polly Heckewelder, Hand-Painted Features, Cotton Dress, c.1900, 17 In.	1900.00
Cloth, Moravian, Woman & Baby, Stitched Features, Peru, Columbian, 12 In.	60.00
Cloth, Sepia Features, Blue Accent, 2-Piece Suit, 1880, 12 In.	695.00
Cloth, Socket Head, Painted Eyes, Hair, 5-Piece Bent Limb, Spring Joints, U.s.a., 15 In.	119.00
Cloth, Wool Yarn Hair, Kid Hands, Blue Dress, Shoes, c.1890, 25 In.	830.00
Coconut, Painted Face, Woven Hat, Lei, Hawaii, 8 ½ In.	195.00
Cradleboard, Indian, Nez Perce, Beaded, 10 x 27 In.	1610.00
Dollhouse, Bisque Shoulder Head, Arms & Legs, Molded Hair, Cloth Body, Germany, c.1900, 6 In.	770.00
Dollhouse, Bisque Shoulder Head, Butcher, Cloth Body, Molded, c.1900, 7 ¼ In.	1304.00
Dollhouse, Bisque Shoulder Head, Cloth Body, Dresden Paper Trim, Germany, c.1900, 8 In. ..	1067.00
Dollhouse, Bisque Shoulder Head, Molded Hair, Mustache, Cloth Body, Germany, c.1900, 5 ¾ In. .	711.00
Dollhouse, Bisque Shoulder Head, Soldier, Cloth Body, Dresden Paper Trim, Germany, c.1900, 7 In.	1422.00
Dollhouse, Bisque Shoulder Head, Soldier, Cloth Body, Germany, c.1900, 8 ¼ In.	593.00
Dollhouse, Bisque Socket Head, Peg Strung Body, Jointed, Germany, c.1890, 3 ½ In.	119.00
Dollhouse, Bisque Swivel Head, Glass Eyes, Mohair, Cloth Body, Bisque Arms, 2 ¾ In.	593.00
Dollhouse, Buffalo Bill, Bisque Shoulder Head, Cloth Body, c.1900, 7 ½ In.	2015.00
Door Of Hope, Amah, Child On Back, Carved Head, Hands, 10 ½ In.	2070.00
Door Of Hope, Mourner, Male, Carved Head, Hands, 11 ½ In.	863.00
Door Of Hope, Policeman, Carved Face, Wooden Hands, Blue Uniform, White Hat, 11 ½ In. ..	2875.00
Door Of Hope, Priest, Charcoal & Blue Cotton Outfit, Mitt Hands, 12 In.	1610.00
Door Of Hope, Young Girl, Long Hair, Mitt Hands, Silk Dress, Bonnet, 8 ½ In.	2875.00
Door Of Hope, Youth, Painted Hair, Silk Clothes, 9 ¼ In. ....*illus*	2300.00
Dressel, Uncle Sam, Bisque Head, Composition, Wood, c.1896, 10 In. ....*illus*	878.00
Effanbee, Anne Shirley, Composition, Sleep Eyes, Human Hair, Check Dress, c.1935, 22 In.	395.00
Effanbee, Baby, Black, Muslin Body, Painted Eyes, Face, White Gown, c.1925, 13 In.	504.00
Effanbee, Baby Grumpy, Composition, Painted Face, Googly, c.1915, 14 In.	336.00
Effanbee, Baby Tinyette, Patsy Ann, Composition, Sleep Eyes, Human Wig, Dress, c.1932, 19 In.	560.00
Effanbee, George & Martha Washington, Patsyette, Composition, c.1936, 10 In., Pair .... *illus*	392.00
Effanbee, Hat, Plastic, Sleep Eyes, Closed Mouth, Green Corduroy Coat, Dress, 1950s, 14 In. ..	336.00
Effanbee, Lucille Ball, I Love Lucy Show, Cloth, Cotton Filled, 1953, 28 In.	460.00
Effanbee, Patsy Lou, Composition, Brown Sleep Eyes, Mohair Wig, Yellow Dress, 22 In.	560.00
Effanbee, Patsy Lou, Composition, Socket Head, Sculpted Bob Hair, Dress, c.1930, 22 In.	280.00
Effanbee, Skippy, Aviator, Composition, Original Outfit, Goggles, c.1938, 14 In. ....*illus*	1344.00
Fashion, Bisque Swivel Head, Closed Mouth, Paperweight Eyes, Mohair, Gusseted Kid, Baby, 17 In.	474.00
Fashion, Cork Pate, Swivel Neck, Paperweight Eyes, Closed Mouth, Mohair, France, 14 In.	1265.00
Fashion, Porcelain Flange Head, Shoulder Plate, Painted Features, Kid Body, 14 In.	3851.00
French, Bisque Swivel Head, Shoulder Plate, Closed Mouth, Paperweight Eyes, No. 4, 13 In. ...	900.00
Gaultier, Fashion, Bisque Head, Paperweight Eyes, Closed Mouth, Poupee Peau, c.1870, 22 In.	2633.00
Gaultier, Pressed Bisque Socket Head, Milliner-Type Body, Kid, Wood Limbs, 7 ¼ In.	770.00
Gebruder Heubach, 8315, Boy, Bisque Socket Head, Human Hair, Jointed Composition, c.1910, 16 In.	3437.00
Gebruder Heubach dolls may also be listed in this category under Heubach.	
Gebruder Kuhnlenz, Bisque Socket Head, Glass Eyes, Human Hair, Jointed Composition, Child, 23 In.	1778.00
German, Bisque Flange Head, Glass Eyes, Open Mouth, Wood, Bells, Crank, Child, c.1900, 12 In.	431.00
German, Bisque Head, Closed Mouth, Paperweight Eyes, Jointed Composition, Wood, c.1880, 24 In.	760.00
German, Bisque Head, Glass Eyes, Teeth, Brown Wig, Jointed, Composition, c.1910, 30 In.	410.00
German, Bisque Head, Red Mohair Wig, Glass Eyes, Closed Mouth, c.1880, 14 In.	410.00
German, Boy, Bisque Shoulder Head, Sleep Eyes, Cloth, Composition Limbs, c.1900, 1 ½ In. ..	267.00
German, Papier-Mache Shoulder Head & Limbs, Human Hair, Braids, Kid Body, c.1850, 25 In. .	3851.00
German, Porcelain Shoulder Head & Limbs, Bun, Cloth Body, c.1850, 14 ½ In.	4148.00
German, Porcelain Shoulder Head & Limbs, Coiled Bun, Cloth Body, c.1850, 25 In.	5333.00
German, Porcelain Shoulder Head & Limbs, Jointed Wood Body, c.1860, 8 ½ In.	5036.00

D

Doll, Arranbee, Nancy Lee, Composition,
Original Ice Skating Costume,
c.1949, 11 In.
$224.00

Doll, Automaton, Bird, Red,
Moving Wings, Gilt,
Brass Scrollwork Case, c.1950, 2 x 4 In.
$1064.00

Doll, Automaton, Clown, Ladder,
Papier-Mache, Glass Eyes, Windup,
France, 1800s, 24 In.
$4388.00

Doll, Automaton, Rabbit, Fur, Holding Basket, Noisemaker, Wood Stand, Label, Vichy, 14 In.
$546.00

Doll, Door Of Hope, Youth, Painted Hair, Silk Clothes, 9 ¼ In.
$2300.00

Doll, Dressel, Uncle Sam, Bisque Head, Composition, Wood, c.1896, 10 In.
$878.00

Doll, Effanbee, George & Martha Washington, Patsyette, Composition, c.1936, 10 In., Pair
$392.00

German, Soldier, Bisque Head, Glass Eyes, Teeth, Candy Box Body, Sword, c.1900, 8 In.	819.00
G.I. Joe figures are listed in the Toy category.	
Goldberger, Dolly Parton, Posable, White Hoop Earrings, Red High Heels, 1970s, 11 In.	45.00
Goldberger, Miss Charming, Composition, Brown Sleep Eyes, Dress, Fur Coat, Hat, c.1935, 19 In.	728.00
Goodyear, Rubber Shoulder Head, Curls, Pupilless Eyes, Cloth Body, Kid Arms, c.1860, 12 In.	593.00
Googly Eyes, Composition Face, Cloth Head, Mohair, 5-Piece Cloth Body, 1920s, 12 In.	805.00
Half Dolls are listed in the Pincushion Doll category.	
Hardwerck, Bisque, Human Hair Wig, Brown Glass Sleep Eyes, Ball Jointed, Composition, 41 In.	4313.00
Head, Waltzing, Celluloid, Wire Frame, Whirls, Clockwork, Lehmann, Germany, 1900s, 9 In.	4025.00
Heddi, Stroller, Plastic, Blue Sleep Eyes, Walker, Dress, Belle & Toy Co., c.1950, 20 In.	392.00
Heubach, See also Gebruder Heubach.	
Heubach, 6969, Boy, Composition, Mohair Wig, Pouty Mouth, Germany, c.1910, 17 In.	644.00
Heubach, Bisque Head, Molded, Painted Hair, Intaglio Eyes, Laughing, Kid Body, c.1910, 18 In.	293.00
Heubach, Bisque Shoulder Head, Blond, Intaglio Eyes, Oilcloth Body, 18 ½ In.	415.00
Heubach, Boy, Bisque Socket Head, Black, Side Glancing Eyes, 5 Piece Body, Heubach, 10 In.	130 4.00
Heubach, Girl, Black, Bisque Socket Head, Dark Brown, Intaglio Eyes, 5-Piece Body, 9 In.	1126.00
Horsman, Baby Dimples, Composition Head, Sculpted Hair, Muslin Body, c.1927, 18 In. ..*illus*	448.00
Horsman, Composition, Flanged Neck, Painted Hair, Muslin Dress, Baby, Box, c.1940, 23 In.	504.00
Horsman, Patty Duke, Play Telephone, Star Pin, 1965, 8 ¾ In.	360.00
Ideal, Betsy Wetsy, Sculpted Hair, Sleep Eyes, Latex Body, Original Trunk, 1950, 13 In. ...*illus*	840.00
Ideal, Saucy Walker, Plastic Head, Brunette, Blue Sleep Eyes, Open Mouth, 1952.14 In.	315.00
Ideal, Toni, Plastic, Blond Wig, Sleep Eyes, Beauty Accessories, Box, c.1950, 14 In.	322.00
Ideal, Toni, Plastic, Nylon Blond Wig, Pink, Gold, Blue Dress, c.1950, 21 In.	224.00
Indian dolls are listed in the Indian category.	
Jacob, Porcelain Shoulder Head, Painted Eyes, Bun, Cloth Body, Kid Arms, France, 19 In.	3200.00
Joel Ellis, Wood, Carved Head, Hair, Painted Eyes, Jointed, 12 ¼ In.	385.00
Jumeau, 10, Cork Pate, Dandy Human Hair, Open Mouth, Composition Body, 23 In.	1380.00
Jumeau, 16, Bisque Head, Open Mouth, Paperweight Eyes, Ball-Jointed, Sailor Outfit, 35 In.	3738.00
Jumeau, Bisque Head, Blond Mohair, Threaded Glass Eyes, Ball-Jointed, Bebe, c.1880, 17 ½ In.	3450.00
Jumeau, Bisque Head, Mohair Wig, Paperweight Eyes, Ball-Jointed, Bebe, 1880s, 21 ½ In. ....*illus*	10350.00
Jumeau, Bisque Head, Paperweight Eyes, Closed Mouth, Pierced Earrings, Mohair, Bebe, 18 ½ In.	2645.00
Jumeau, Hair Wig, Closed Mouth, Jointed Wood & Composition Body, Bebe, 25 ½ In.	1035.00
K * R, 112, Scottish Boy, Bisque Socket Head, Mohair, Jointed Composition, Kilt, Hat, 16 ½ In.	9480.00
K * R, 114, Gretchen, Bisque Socket Head, Mohair, Jointed Composition, Child, 20 ½ In.	4740.00
K * R, 117/76, Bisque Socket Head, Sleep Eyes, Mohair, Jointed Composition, 28 In.	8888.00
K * R, Bisque Head, Flirty Eyes, Open Mouth, Mohair Wig, Composition Jointed Body, c.1900, 18 In.	760.00
K * R, Bisque Head, Glass Sleep Eyes, Open Mouth, 5-Piece Composition, Toddler, 8 In.	444.00
K * R, Gretchen, Bisque Head, Intaglio Eyes, Human Hair, Jointed, Composition, c.1909, 12 In.	889.00
Kamkins, Cloth, Mohair, Blue Eyes, Cloth, Jointed, Dutch Costume, Wooden Shoes, Boy, c.1930, 19 In.	2133.00
Kestner, 128, Bisque, Glass Eyes, Plaster Pate, Jointed, Composition, Shoulder Joint, 17 ½ In.	1422.00
Kestner, 154, Bisque Shoulder Head, Open Mouth, Teeth, Glass Eyes, Mohair, Jointed, 16 In.	178.00
Kestner, 167, Bisque Head, Sleep Eyes, Open Mouth, Teeth, Pull Strings, Fur Cape, Muff, c.1900, 16 In.	644.00
Kestner, 168, Bisque Head, Open Mouth, Teeth, Glass Eyes, Mohair, Jointed, Composition, 18 In.	356.00
Kestner, 211, Bisque, Open-Close Mouth, Glass Eyes, Mohair, Jointed Composition, 11 In.	592.00
Kestner, 211, Bisque, Open-Close Mouth, Tongue, Glass Eyes, Plaster Pate, Mohair, Baby, 10 In.	296.00
Kestner, Bisque Head, Breastplate, Arms, Open Mouth, Sleep Eyes, Mohair, Jointed, Kid Body, 26 In.	239.00
Kestner, Bisque Head, Glass Eyes, Open Mouth, Composition, Jointed, Scottish Dress, 17 In.	173.00
Kestner, Bisque Head, Glass Sleep Eyes, Closed Mouth, Blond Mohair, Box, 19 In.	2015.00
Kestner, Bisque Head, Shoulder Plate, Arms, Sleep Eyes, Open Mouth, Kid, Gusseted Knees, 32 In.	203.00
Kestner, Bisque, Girl, Closed Mouth, Glass Eyes, Blond Mohair, Jointed, 5 ¾ In.	1007.00
Kestner, Bisque, Socket Neck, Kid Lined, Glass Eyes, Blond Mohair, Jointed, Bent Elbows, 7 In.	1896.00
Kestner, Gibson Girl, Bisque Shoulder Head, Sleep Eyes, Jointed Leather Body, c.1910, 20 In.	1035.00
Kewpie dolls are listed in the Kewpie category.	
Knickerbocker, Dagwood, Composition, Socket Head, Black Suit, Slippers, c.1940, 14 In.	1680.00
Knickerbocker, Little Lulu, Oilcloth Face, Saturday Evening Post Promotion, 12 In. ....*illus*	234.00
K.P.M., Porcelain Shoulder Head, Dome Head With Holes, Human Hair, Braids, Cloth, Leather, 17 In.	5333.00
Larry Harmon, Laurel & Hardy, Vinyl Head & Hands, Cloth Clothing, 1978, 13 In., Pair	139.00
Lenci, Boy, Felt, Inset Hair, Painted Brown Eyes, Blue, White Cotton Suit, c.1920, 22 In.	409.00
Lenci, Boy, Felt Swivel Head & Body, Pouty Face, Jointed, 300 Series, 17 In. ....*illus*	1380.00
Lenci, Girl, Felt, Left Glancing Eyes, Mohair Bob, Swivel-Jointed, Stitched Fingers, 13 In.	563.00
Lenci, Puss In Boots, Fur-Covered Velveteen, Red Velvet Jacket, Boots, 1930s, 20 In.	575.00
Libby, I Dream Of Jeannie, Vinyl Head & Arms, Hollow Plastic Body, Sleep Eyes, 1966, 20 In.	265.00
L.W. Co., Bisque, Box, Label, Scrappy, 2 Dolls, Dog, Doghouse, Japan, 1 ¾ To 3 ½ In., 4 Piece ..*illus*	173.00
Madame Alexander, Alexanderkins, Plastic, Closed Mouth, Dress, Flowers, Hat, 1953, 8 In.	1456.00
Madame Alexander, Alice In Wonderland, Cloth, Googly Blue Eyes, Painted, c.1933, 20 In.	784.00
Madame Alexander, Alice In Wonderland, Plastic, Sleep Eyes, Dress, Suitcase, c.1950, 15 In.	504.00

Madame Alexander, Babs, Skating, All Plastic, Blue Satin Feather-Trim Costume, c.1950, 21 In.	1456.00
Madame Alexander, Bobby Q & Susie Q, Matching Yellow, Blue Outfits, c.1939, 13 In., Pair...	672.00
Madame Alexander, Bride, Hard Plastic, Socket Head, Sleep Eyes, c.1950, 18 In.	935.00
Madame Alexander, Cissy, Plastic, Sleep Eyes, Cocktail Dress, Hat, Cape, Box, c.1956, 20 In.	784.00
Madame Alexander, Cissy, Plastic, Sleep Eyes, Dress, Earrings, c.1957, 20 In.	952.00
Madame Alexander, Cissy, Sleep Eyes, Jointed, No. 2135, Box, 1956, 20 In. ....illus	1120.00
Madame Alexander, Elise Ballerina, Plastic, Jointed, Sleep Eyes, Gold Net Tutu, Tiara, c.1959, 15 In.	616.00
Madame Alexander, Flora McFlimsey Of Madison Square, Composition, Cotton Dress, c.1938, 15 In.	224.00
Madame Alexander, Jane Withers, Composition, Human Hair, c.1935, 12 In. ....illus	952.00
Madame Alexander, Jo, Little Women, Plastic, Sleep Eyes, Red Hair, Box, c.1950, 14 In.	293.00
Madame Alexander, Kate Greenaway, Composition, Blond Mohair Wig, c.1935, 15 In. ....illus	1008.00
Madame Alexander, Leslie, Brown Complexion, Sleep Eyes, Hair, Dress, 1965, 18 In.	168.00
Madame Alexander, Little Women Set, Cloth, Hand Painted Faces, Mohair Wig, c.1934, 16 In., 4 Piece.	3136.00
Madame Alexander, Madeline, Vinyl Socket Head, Blue Sleep Eyes, Plastic Body, c.1960, 15 In.	392.00
Madame Alexander, Margaret O'Brien, Brown Mohair Wig, Jointed, Tagged Outfit, 21 In.	414.00
Madame Alexander, Margaret O'Brien, Composition, Green Sleep Eyes, c.1946, 18 In.	1064.00
Madame Alexander, Margaret O'Brien, Composition, Sleep Eyes, Brown Wig, 1946, 14 In.	1725.00
Madame Alexander, Margaret Rose, Hard Plastic, Mohair Wig, Blue Gown, c.1950, 14 In.	2464.00
Madame Alexander, Margaret, Bride, Hard Plastic, Ivory Satin Gown, 1950, 18 In. ....illus	616.00
Madame Alexander, Mary Martin, Plastic, Socket Head, Brown Sleep Eyes, Sailor Suit, c.1950, 14 In.	588.00
Madame Alexander, McGuffe, Ana, Plastic, Braids, Purple Velvet Coat, Hat, Label, Box, 1948, 15 In..	1680.00
Madame Alexander, Meg, Little Women, Plastic, Sleep Eyes, Blond, Box, c.1950	292.00
Madame Alexander, Quizkin, Plastic, Sleep Eyes, Pink Polka Dot Suit, 1953, 8 In.	308.00
Madame Alexander, Scarlett O'Hara, Composition, Original Dress, c.1939, 15 In. ....illus	252.00
Madame Alexander, Scarlett O'Hara, Composition, Sleep Eyes, Brown Human Hair, 17 In.	1145.00
Madame Alexander, Sweet Violet, Plastic, Sleep Eyes, Ball-Jointed, Blue Taffeta Dress, c.1954, 18 In.	784.00
Madame Alexander, Wendy, At Home, Sleep Eyes, Walker, No. 544, 1956, 8 In. ....illus	308.00
Madame Alexander, Wendy, Goes Ice Skating, Plastic, Walker, Skirt, Hat, Skates, c.1956, 8 In.	308.00
Madame Alexander, Wendy, Loves To Waltz, Blond Wig, Sleep Eyes, Walker, c.1955, 8 In.	605.00
Madame Alexander, Wendy, Takes Her Dog For A Walk, Plastic, Blue Dress, 1955, 8 In.	420.00
Madame Alexander, Wendykins Bride, Plastic, Bent Knee, Gown, Veil, Flowers, c.1960, 8 In.	336.00
Maggie Bessie, Cloth, Oil Painted Face, Painted Brown Hair, Moravian, 1918, 13 ½ In.	15795.00
Matchbox, Christie Brinkley, Change-Around Fashion Portfolio, Beauty Secrets, 1989, 11 In.	16.00
Mattel, Barbie, Guinevere, Blond, Medieval Purple Dress, Hat, Box, c.1964, 11 In.	784.00
Mattel, Barbie, No. 2, Commuter Set Ensemble, No. 916, 1960, 11 In. ....illus	2912.00
Mattel, Barbie, No. 3, Blond Ponytail, Black & White Swimsuit, Red Hair, 1960, 11 In.	560.00
Mattel, Barbie, No. 4, Brunette, Accessories, Box, Promo Albums, No. 850, c.1960, 11 ½ In.	221.00
Mattel, Barbie, No. 5, Blond Ponytail, Black & White Striped Swimsuit, Box, 1961	201.00
Mattel, Barbie, No. 6, Blond Ponytail, Tan, Red Swimsuit, Blue Eyes, 1962, 11 In.	336.00
Mattel, Barbie, No. 6, Red Ponytail, Garden Party Dress, Gloves, Box, 1961, 11 In.	840.00
Mattel, Barbie, Sparkling Pink Gift Set, Red Bubble Cut, Model 1011, 1964, 11 In............. illus	1232.00
Mattel, Barbie, Wedding Gift Set, Brunette Bubble Cut, Box, Model 1017, 1964 ....illus	1904.00
Motherau, Metal Body, Jointed, Paperweight Eyes, Skin Wig, Bebe, 15 ½ In.	12650.00
Nancy Ann Storybook, Muffie, Plastic, Blond Wig, Pink Dress, Hat, Muffie Handbag, 1950s, 7 In.	650.00
Norah Wellings, TSS Tuscania Sailor, Fabric, Molded Face & Hands, 1920s, 12 In.	65.00
Paper dolls are listed in their own category.	
Papier-Mache Shoulder Head, Closed Mouth, Painted Eyes, Upturned Chin, c.1840, 20 ¼ In.	3200.00
Papier-Mache Shoulder Head, Hair Wig, Leather Body, France, 1870s, 18 In.	575.00
Papier-Mache Shoulder Head, Human Hair, Curls, Kid Body, Carved Wood Limbs, 14 In.	2489.00
Papier-Mache Shoulder Head, Human Hair, Glass Eyes, 8 Teeth, Kid Body, France, c.1840, 21 In.	889.00
Papier-Mache Shoulder Head, Human Hair, Glass Eyes, Kid Body, Wood Limbs, 10 ½ In.	1659.00
Papier-Mache Shoulder Head, Man, Center Part, Kid Body, Wood Limbs, Germany, c.1850, 16 In.	1067.00
Papier-Mache Shoulder Head, Painted Features, Kid Body, Wood Limbs, Man, 14 In.	3851.00
Papier-Mache Shoulder Head, Painted Hair, Curly, Braids, Kid Body, Carved Wood Limbs, 23 In.	3555.00
Papier-Mache Shoulder Head, Sausage Curls, Pupilless Eyes, Cloth Body, Kid Hands, 29 In.	2015.00
Papier-Mache, Milliner's Model, Painted Face, Wood Limbs, Clothes, Germany, 1850, 15 In. ..	652.00
Pincushion dolls are listed in their own category.	
Porcelain Shoulder Head, Woman, With Bun, Blue Eyes, Cloth Body, Porcelain Limbs, 19 In.	6518.00
Puppet, 3 Stooges, Soft Vinyl Head, Cloth Body, 1960s, 9 In., 3 Piece	201.00
Puppet, Archie Andrews, Molded Vinyl Body, Ideal, 1973	139.50
Puppet, Archie, Vinyl Head & Body, Copyrighted By Archie Comics, Ideal, 1973	140.00
Puppet, Bob Hope, Vinyl Molded Head, Cloth Body, 1940s	150.00
Puppet, Bob Hope, Vinyl, Rubber Molded Head, Cloth Body, 1940s	149.50
Puppet, Captain America, Molded Vinyl, Imperial Toy, Box, 1978	55.00
Puppet, Casper, Vinyl Head, Cloth Body, Gund, Window Box, 1950s, 10 In.	221.00
Puppet, Charley Horse, Shari Lewis Show, Vinyl Head, Stocking Body, Tarcher Pro., 1960	45.00

Doll, Effanbee, Skippy, Aviator, Composition, Original Outfit, Goggles, c.1938, 14 In. $1344.00

Doll, Horsman, Baby Dimples, Composition Head, Sculpted Hair, Muslin Body, c.1927, 18 In. $448.00

Doll, Ideal, Betsy Wetsy, Sculpted Hair, Sleep Eyes, Latex Body, Original Trunk, 1950, 13 In.
$840.00

Doll, Jumeau, Bisque Head, Mohair Wig, Paperweight Eyes, Ball-Jointed, Bebe, 1880s, 21 ½ In.
$10350.00

Doll, Knickerbocker, Little Lulu, Oilcloth Face, Saturday Evening Post Promotion, 12 In.
$234.00

TIP

Don't wash, set, comb, or change the original hair on a vinyl doll. It lowers the value. Clean the dust from a doll's wig by blowing it with a hair dryer set on low or cool.

Puppet, Dean Martin & Jerry Lewis, Both Faces On 1 Body, Vinyl, 1950s	225.00
Puppet, Dennis The Menace, Large Head With Spectacles, Bowtie, Hall Syndicate	75.00
Puppet, Dennis The Menace, Soft Vinyl Head, Cloth Body, c.1958, 8 ½ To 10 In., 6 Piece	25.00
Puppet, Droop-A-Long Coyote, Molded Vinyl Head, Printed Cloth Body, Ideal, 1960s	100.00
Puppet, Emmett Kelly As Willie The Clown, Baby Barry Toy Co., 1950s	120.00
Puppet, Fat Albert, Molded Vinyl Head, Printed Body, Ideal, 1973	175.00
Puppet, Gabby Hayes, Rubber Head, White Beard, Blue Hat, Cloth, JVZ, 1949	200.00
Puppet, George Jetson, Molded Vinyl Head, Knickerbocker, 1963	130.00
Puppet, Grimace, Vinyl Head, 1993	45.00
Puppet, Hamburglar, Molded Vinyl Head, Black Hat & Mask, Artwork Tie, 1993	40.00
Puppet, Heckle, Full-Bodied, Vinyl Head, Fuzzy Cloth Body, Rushton Star Creation, 1950	75.00
Puppet, Hotpoint Devil, Vinyl Head, Cloth Body, Hotpoint Logo On Chest, 1950s	250.00
Puppet, Judy Jetson, Molded Vinyl Head, Green & Orange Outfit, Knickerbocker, 1963	150.00
Puppet, Lambchop, The Shari Lewis Show, Vinyl Head, Stocking Body, 1960	20.00
Puppet, Little Audrey, Vinyl Head, Cloth Body, Satin Bow, Gund, Window Box, 1950s, 10 In.	291.00
Puppet, Little Iodine, Molded Vinyl Head, Cloth Body, 1950s	100.00
Puppet, Mammy Yokum, Molded Head, Stuffed Body, Baby Barry Toy Co., 1957	125.00
Puppet, McDonald's, Ronald McDonald, Hamburgler, Grimace, Box, Early 1990s, 12 In., 3 Piece	115.00
Puppet, Mister Rogers' Neighborhood, Vinyl, Fabric, Dakin, c.1988, 7 To 9 In., 6 Piece	443.00
Puppet, Mother Goose, Babes In Toyland, Gund, 1960s	99.50
Puppet, Nestles, Red Hair & Red Body, Round Bugged Out Eyes, Felt Hands, 1950s	150.00
Puppet, Our Miss Brooks, Googly Eyes, Vinyl Head, Loews, 1950s	150.00
Puppet, Pebbles Flintstone, Vinyl Head, Cloth Body, Turquoise Material, Ideal, 1966	95.00
Puppet, President Jimmy Carter, Cloth Body, Vinyl Head, I Am Jimmy Button, 1970s	60.00
Puppet, Reddy Griffin, Devil, Griffin Fuel Co., 1953	185.00
Puppet, Rory Calhoun, The Texan, Vinyl Head, 1960s	195.00
Puppet, Smokey Bear, Molded Head, Cloth Body, Ideal, 1959	185.00
Puppet, Smokey Bear, Molded Head, Printed Cloth Body, Ideal, 1959	185.00
Puppet, Soupy Sales, Vinyl Head, Cloth Body, Soupy Sez Lets Do The Mouse, Gund, 1965	225.00
Puppet, Sylvester Cat, Vinyl Head, Warner Bros., 1969	15.00
Puppet, Wilma Flintstone, Vinyl Head, Cloth Body, Germany, 1960s	75.00
Puppet, Woody Woodpecker, Talking, Orange Felt Comb, Mattel, 1960s	80.00
Remco, Dave Clark, Vinyl Head, Rooted Hair, Plastic Body, 1964, 5 In.	105.00
Roberta Doll Co., Roberta Ann, Plastic, Blue Sleep Eyes, Open Mouth, Blond, 1950s, 14 In.	90.00
Rohmer, Fashion, Porcelain Flange Swivel Head, Shoulder Plate, Sheepskin Wig, Kid, 17 ½ In.	5629.00
S & H dolls are listed here as Simon & Halbig.	
Schoenhut, Carved Hair, Braids, Intaglio Eyes, Jointed Body, Steel Sprung, 14 ½ In.	575.00
Schoenhut, Miss Dolly, Wood, Painted Eyes, Blond Wig, 21 In.	118.00
Schoenhut, Wood, Barney Google, Spark Plug, Blanket, Box, King Features, 1922, 9 In.	1053.00
Schoenhut, Wood, Pouty, Brown Intaglio Eyes, Mohair Wig, Jointed, c.1913, 14 In.	748.00
Schoenhut, Wood, Pouty, Intaglio Eyes, Jointed Spring Body, Carved Hair, 16 ½ In.	345.00
S.F.B.J., 301, Bisque Head, Open Mouth, Teeth, Weighted Eyes, Wig, Jointed Composition, 15 ½ In.	415.00
S.F.B.J., Bisque Head, Blond Wig, Composition Body, Green Suit, France, Toddler, c.1910, 23 In.	761.00
S.F.B.J., Poulbot, Bisque Head, Paperweight Eyes, Jointed, Composition Body, Marked, 14 In.	3163.00
Shirley Temple dolls are included in the Shirley Temple category.	
Simon & Halbig, 122, Bisque Head, Sleep Eyes, Open Mouth, 2 Teeth, Wood, Composition, 11 In.	144.00
Simon & Halbig, 126, Bisque Head, Trembling Tongue, Glass Eyes, 5-Piece Composition, 18 ½ In.	415.00
Simon & Halbig, 151, Bisque Socket Head, Mohair, Jointed, Composition, Boy, c.1910, 25 In.	5036.00
Simon & Halbig, 939, Bisque Socket Head, Paperweight Eyes, Jointed Composition, Child, 26 In.	2963.00
Simon & Halbig, Bisque Shoulder Head, Glass Eyes, Cloth Body, c.1880, 10 In.	533.00
Simon & Halbig, Bisque Socket Head, Composition, Sleep Eyes, Curly Wig, Jointed, 20 In.	5036.00
Simon & Halbig, Bisque Socket Head, Jointed Wood & Composition Body, Paperweight Eyes, 17 In.	1035.00
Simon & Halbig, Bisque Socket Head, Arms, Set Eyes, Open Mouth, Jointed, Composition, 26 In.	179.00
Simon & Halbig, Eleanor, Blue Wool Nun's Habit, Rosary, Blue Glass Eyes, Marked, 24 In.	400.00
Simon & Halbig, Googly, Clockwork Eye, Open Mouth, Jointed Body, Blond, Child, 30 In.	1265.00
Simon & Halbig, Sleep Eyes, Open Mouth, Composition, Arms, Legs, 20 In.	143.00
Steiff, Captain, From Katzenjammer Kids, Arms & Head Swivel, Felt & Cloth, 1910, 15 In.	3500.00
Steiner, Bisque, Blue Paperweight Eyes, Hair Wig, Bebe, 23 In. *illus*	4600.00
Steiner, Bisque Head, Extended Upper Lip, Paperweight Eyes, Mohair Wig, Bebe, 20 In.	3163.00
Steiner, Bisque Head, Paperweight Eyes, Wood, Composition, Jointed, Phenix, Bebe, 1890s, 22 In.	3450.00
Steiner, Bisque, Paperweight Eyes, Walker, Mama Papa Bellows, Bebe, 24 In.	3162.00
Swaine & Co., Molded Painted Hair, Intaglio Eyes, Closed Mouth, Composition, Baby, c.1910, 13 In.	351.00
Topsyturvy, Canvas, Printed Faces, Checkered Dress, 12 In.	165.00
Toy, Cat In The Hat, Dr. Seuss, Plush Fabric, Felt Hat, Random House, 1960s, 23 In.	150.00
Toy, Felix The Cat, Composition, Name On Chest, Original Tail, 1920s, 13 In.	345.00
Toy, Jeep, Popeye's Dog, Composition Head, Wood, Jointed, King Features 1935, 6 In.	1100.00

Doll, Lenci, Boy, Felt Swivel Head & Body, Pouty Face, Jointed, 300 Series, 17 In. $1380.00

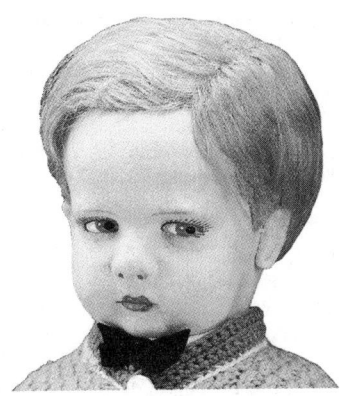

Doll, L.W. Co., Bisque, Box, Label, Scrappy, 2 Dolls, Dog, Doghouse, Japan, 1 ¾ To 3 ½ In., 4 Piece $173.00

Doll, Madame Alexander, Cissy, Sleep Eyes, Jointed, No. 2135, Box, 1956, 20 In. $1120.00

Doll, Madame Alexander, Jane Withers, Composition, Human Hair, c.1935, 12 In. $952.00

Doll, Madame Alexander, Kate Greenaway, Composition, Blond Mohair Wig, c.1935, 15 In. $1008.00

Doll, Madame Alexander, Margaret, Bride, Hard Plastic, Ivory Satin Gown, 1950, 18 In. $616.00

Doll, Madame Alexander, Scarlett O'Hara, Composition, Original Dress, c.1939, 15 In. $252.00

Doll, Madame Alexander, Wendy, At Home, Sleep Eyes, Walker, No. 544, 1956, 8 In. $308.00

Doll, Mattel, Barbie, No. 2, Commuter Set Ensemble, No. 916, 1960, 11 In. $2912.00

Doll, Mattel, Barbie, Sparkling Pink Gift Set, Red Bubble Cut, Model 1011, 1964, 11 In. $1232.00

Doll, Mattel, Barbie, Wedding Gift Set, Brunette Bubble Cut, Box, Model 1017, 1964 $1904.00

Doll, Steiner, Bisque, Blue Paperweight Eyes, Hair Wig, Bebe, 23 In. $4600.00

Trixie Toy, Mugsy & Marcie, Cloth, Painted Imp Features, Clothes, Labels, 16 In., Pair	560.00
Uneeda, Rita Hayworth As Carmen, Composition, Socket Head, Blue Eyes, Red Wig, 1948, 15 In.	650.00
Unis, Bisque Head, Brown, Open Mouth, Brown Glass Eyes, Jointed, 10 In.	144.00
Ventriloquist Dummy Head, Carved Wood, Black Stand, c.1850, 12 x 6 In.	770.00
Ventriloquist Dummy, Carved, Velvet, High Button Leather Shoes, c.1890, 32 In.	2607.00
Vogue, Ginny, 2-Piece Green Beach Wear, Shoes, Eyeglasses, Non Walking, 1952, 8 In.	280.00
Vogue, Ginny, Crib Crowd Baby, Brown Sleep Eyes, Organdy Dress, 1950s, 7 In.	1415.00
Vogue, Ginny, Kay, Kindergarten Series, Blue Sleep Eyes, Red Organdy Dress, 1953, 8 In.	280.00
Vogue, Ginny, Rose Satin Party Dress, Black Velvet, Sleep Eyes, Purse, c.1953, 8 In.	250.00
Vogue, Ginny, Ski Bunny, Straight Legged Walker, Pink & Gray Outfit, Skis, Poles, 7 ½ In.	165.00
Vogue, Ginny, Straight Legged Walker, Blue & White Pinafore, Red Undergarment, Hat, 7 ½ In.	165.00
Vogue, Ginny's Pup, Terrier, Plaid Coat, Marked, 3 ½ In.	225.00
Vogue, Plastic, Closed Mouth, Short Red Hair, Pants, Hat, 1951, 8 In.	280.00
Wax Over Composition, Shoulder Head, Closed Mouth, Glass Eyes, Mohair, 16 ½ In.	474.00
Wax, Peddler Woman In Glass Dome, Carrying Basket With Wares, Painted Features, 10 ¼ In.	2133.00
Wood, Carved Pine, Jointed, 19th Century, 20 In.	2726.00
Wood, Carved, Woman, Seated, Holding Needlework, Knitting, Lever Operated, c.1840, 6 ¼ In.	2963.00
Wood, Queen Anne Type, Pupilless Eyes, Closed Mouth, Mortise Joints, Cloth Arms, 10 ¾ In.	593.00
Wood, Yellow Pine, Gesso, Horsehair, Painted Details, Jointed, Red Polka Dot Dress, 1800s, 23 In.	2185.00

DOLL CLOTHES

Barbie, Apron, What's Cookin', Blue, 1964-65	20.00
Barbie, Barbie-Q, Dress, Apron, Chef Hat, Shoes, Knife, Spatula, Rolling Pin, Potholder, 1959-62.	50.00
Barbie, Cheerleader, Sweater, Red Skirt, Pompons, Sneakers, Socks, Megaphone, No. 876	85.00
Barbie, Crisp 'n Cool, Blouse, Ascot, Skirt, No. 1604, 1964	65.00
Barbie, It's Cold Outside, Coat, Belt, Hat, Hanger, No. 0819, 1964-66	65.00
Barbie, Peachy Fleecy, Coat, Belt, Hat, Gloves, Purse, Shoes, No. 915, 1959-61	75.00
Barbie, Raincoat, Belt, Hat, Umbrella, Boots, No. 949, 1963	42.00
Dress, Jacket, Bustle Back Skirt, Machine Stitched, Tan, Beige, Wool, Silk	178.00
Francie, Green & Navy Striped Dress, Belt, Hat, Scarf, Shoes, No. 1452, 1970	85.00
Jacket, 2-Tier Skirt, Undergarments, Leather Shoes	237.00
Ken, Tuxedo, Jacket, Pants, Shirt, No. 787, 1961-65	25.00
Masquerade, Black & Yellow Outfit, Pompons, Shoes, Nylons, Mask, Invitation, No. 944	75.00

DONALD DUCK *items are included in the Disneyana category.*

DOORSTOPS have been made in all types of designs. The vast majority of the doorstops sold today are cast iron and were made from about 1890 to 1930. Most of them are shaped like people, animals, flowers, or ships. Reproductions and newly designed examples are sold in gift shops.

3 Geese, Walking, Cast Iron, Hubley, Marked, Fred Everett, 8 ¼ x 6 ¼ In.	263.00
3 Iris Flowers, Leaves, Painted, Cast Iron, 11 In.	200.00
Aunt Jemima, Cast Iron, Hollow Casting, Classic Pose, Hubley, 8 ½ x 4 ½ In.	345.00
Aunt Jemima, White Apron, Blue Sash, Hands On Hips, Cast Iron, Littco, 13 ¼ x 8 In.	288.00
Baby Cop, Red Gloves, Painted, Cast Iron, c.1950, 10 ½ In.	237.00
Baby, Nude, Right Arm Reaching Up, Painted, Cast Iron, Studroz, Elba Rd., 17 In.	5300.00
Bell Hop, Red Jacket, White Pants, Cast Iron, 8 ⅞ In.	100.00
Black Boy, Holds Pipe, Holds Leg By Ankle, Sits On Inverted Cast Iron Basket, 5 x 7 ¼ In.	201.00
Bobby Blake, With Teddy Bear, Cast Iron, Grace Drayton, Hubley, 1930s, 9 ½ In.	295.00 to 350.00
Brass, Scrolling Leaf Bracket Design, Handle Top, Late 19th Century, 13 ¼ x 9 ½ In.	69.00
Bullfrog, Green, Cast Iron, Full Figure, Hubley, 7 x 7 In.	175.00
Caddy, Hold Golf Bag With Clubs, Painted, Orange Jacket, Green, Brown Garments, 6 x 8 In.	633.00
Cape Cod Cottage, Painted, Shingled Roof, Flowers, Picket Fence, Hubley, 7 ¾ x 5 ¾ In.	288.00
Cape Cod Cottage, Thatched Roof, Picket Fence, Flowers, Vines, 7 ⅜ x 4 ⅞ In.	3105.00
Cat, Arched Back, Black Paint, Cast Iron, 10 In.	220.00
Cat, Black Cast Iron, 10 ½ x 8 In.	70.00
Cat, Black, Sleeping, Painted, Cast Iron, 13 In.	800.00
Cat, Fireside, Bell On Neck, Green Eyes, Pink Ear Tips, 5 ⅝ x 10 In.	115.00
Cat, On Rug, Brown, Green, Cast Iron, National Foundry, 2 ⅞ x 6 ⅞ In.	300.00
Cat, Persian, Seated, Cast Iron, Hubley, 9 In.	79.00
Cat, Seated, Full Figure, Hubley, Cast Iron, 9 In.	95.00
Cat, Seated, Gold Paint, Cast Iron, 6 ⅞ In.	72.00
Cat, Sleeping, Tail Curled To Side, Ribbon, Hollow, Japanned, National Foundry, 9 ½ x 6 In.	201.00
Cat, White, Arched Back, Full Figure, Cast Iron, Iron Art, 10 ¼ x 7 ⅞ In.	140.00
Cat, White, Gray, Seated, Sleeping, Full Figure, Cast Iron, Hubley, 8 x 5 ½ In.	250.00
Cat, White, Seated, Head Tilted, Full Figure, Cast Iron, Hubley, 10 x 3 ¾ In.	82.00

> **TIP**
>
> To clean a Barbie doll's arms and legs use a cotton swab soaked in acetone. Do not use on the vinyl body or face. Clean these with rubbing alcohol.

Cat, White, Seated, Marble Eyes, Base, Cast Iron, 12 ¾ x 7 ¾ In.	330.00
Charleston Dancers, Cast Iron, Hubley, Signed, Fish, 8 ¾ x 5 ¼ In.	263.00
Charleston Dancers, Cast Iron, Hubley, Signed, Fish, 9 x 5 ⅜ In.	3300.00
Chrysanthemums, White Wicker Basket, Cast Iron, Marked, Pat. Nov 23, 1926, 9 x 7 In.	185.00
Civil War Soldier, Full, Cast Iron, 7 ¼ In.	250.00
Clown, Painted, Red Suit, White Ruff, Black Hat, Shoes, Cast Iron, 4 ¼ x 10 ¼ In.	1200.00
Clown, Red Outfit, Blue Hat, White Collar, 2-Sided, Cast Iron, Hubley, 10 ½ x 4 ½ In.	450.00
Clown, Ruffled Collar, Cuffs, Oversized Shoes, Sarah Symonds, Cast Iron, 11 ½ x 5 ¾ In. *illus*	468.00
Cockatoo, Full Figure, Cast Iron, 12 In.	160.00
Cockatoo, On Perch, Polly, Cast Iron, Hubley, 8 ½ x 5 ¼ In.	145.00
Cottage, Ann Hathaway, Thatched Roof, Flowers, 2-Piece Casting, Cast Iron, Hubley, 6 ½ x 8 In.	565.00
Cottage, Brown Roof, Arched Door, Flowers, Painted, Cast Iron, Hubley, 5 ¾ x 7 ½ In.	195.00
Cottage, Cape Cod, Dark Roof, Cast Iron, Hubley, 5 ½ x 7 ¾ In.	303.00
Cottage, Cape Cod, Gray Roof, Flowers, Cast Iron, Hubley, 5 ½ x 7 ¼ In.	120.00
Country Doctor, Medical Bag, Broad Brim Hat, Cast Iron, Painted, 6 ½ In.	500.00
Covered Wagon, Painted, Cast Iron, Creations Co., c.1930, 7 ½ x 11 In.	60.00
Covered Wagon, Team Of Horses, Painted, Cast Iron, Signed, Hubley, 5 ¼ x 10 In.	120.00
Dapper Dan, Painted, Cast Iron, Hubley, 7 ⅝ x 4 ⅜ In.	275.00
Dog, Airedale Terrier, Cast Iron, Painted, Brown & White, 3 ½ In.	95.00
Dog, Basset Hound, Pup, Seated, Brown, White, Full Figure, Cast Iron, 7 ⅛ x 7 ¼ In.	1700.00
Dog, Basset Hound, Seated, Full Figure, Brown, Painted, Cast Iron, 7 x 7 In.	1755.00
Dog, Beagle, Pup, Seated, Brown, White, Full Figure, Cast Iron, 7 ½ x 5 ⅜ In.	890.00
Dog, Bloodhound, Cast Iron, Black, Tan, Wrinkled Face, Drooping Ears, 6 x 6 ½ In.	201.00
Dog, Boston Bull, Cast Iron, Multicolored, 10 ½ In.	104.00
Dog, Boston Terrier, Black, White, Cast Iron, Hubley, c.1930, 10 In.	285.00
Dog, Boston Terrier, Black, White, Red Collar, Cast Iron, 4 ⅛ x 4 ¼ In.	72.00
Dog, Boston Terrier, Black, White, Red Collar, Full Figure, Cast Iron, Hubley, 10 ½ In.	115.00
Dog, Boston Terrier, Brown, White, Looking Left, Front Leg, Full Figure, Cast Iron, 10 x 8 ¾ In.	425.00
Dog, Boston Terrier, Looking Over Right Leg, Painted, Iron, 10 ¼ x 11 x 5 ½ In. ..... 95.00 to 225.00	
Dog, Bulldog, Cobalt Blue, Red Leather Collar, Glass Eyes, Summit Glass Co., c.1950, 6 In.	118.00
Dog, Bulldog, Opaque White, Red Leather Collar, Glass Eyes, Summit Glass Co., c.1950, 6 In. .	118.00
Dog, Cocker Spaniel, Black, White, Full Figure, Cast Iron, Hubley, 7 x 11 In.	55.00
Dog, Doberman Pinscher, Standing, Full Figure, Hubley, No. 306, 7 ⅞ x 7 ⅝ In.	995.00
Dog, Fox Terrier, Full Figure, Facing Left, White, Black, Painted, Cast Iron, Hubley, 9 x 9 In. ...	351.00
Dog, French Bulldog, Seated, Black, White, Cast Iron, Hubley, 8 x 7 In.	55.00
Dog, French Bulldog, Sitting, Red Collar, Ears Stand At Alert, 7 ⅝ x 6 ¾ In.	201.00
Dog, German Shepherd, Black, Cast Iron, 6 ¼ In.	69.00
Dog, German Shepherd, Brown, Full Figure, Cast Iron, Hubley, 11 x 14 In.	145.00
Dog, German Shepherd, Gold Paint, Cast Iron, Hubley, 9 ⅞ x 13 ½ In.	82.00
Dog, Pekingese, Brown, Black, Full Figure, Cast Iron, Hubley, 9 ¾ x 14 In.	1989.00
Dog, Pointer, Black, White, Cast Iron, Hubley, 8 ⅝ x 15 In.	198.00
Dog, Pointer, Brown, Black, Green, Cast Iron, Marked, Hubley, 5 x 10 ½ In.	340.00
Dog, Russian Wolfhound, White, Gray, Full Figure, Cast Iron, Hubley, 8 x 11 ¾ In.	165.00
Dog, Scottie, Cast Iron, 5 ½ x 9 In.	81.00
Dog, Scottie, Double, Cast Iron, Incised, 9 x 6 In.	165.00
Dog, Scottie, Sitting, Cast Iron, Full Figure, 5 x 6 In. ....*illus*	176.00
Dog, Scottie, White Paint, Full Figure, Cast Iron, Hubley, 9 x 11 In.	145.00
Dog, Sealyham, White, Red Collar, Cast Iron, Full Figure, Hubley, 9 x 14 In. .... 1778.00 to 2500.00	
Dog, Springer Spaniel, White, Black, Full Figure, Cast Iron, Hubley, 8 ⅞ x 15 ½ In.	92.00
Dog, St. Bernard, Recumbent, Painted, Cast Iron, Hubley, 3 ½ x 10 ½ In.	3600.00
Dog, Terrier Pup, Drooped Ears, Black, White, Red Collar, Cast Iron, 4 ½ x 6 ¼ In.	78.00
Dog, Terrier Pup, Seated, Black, White, Red Collar, Cast Iron, 4 ⅛ x 5 ¾ In.	72.00
Dog, Terrier, Seated, Cast Iron, Multicolored, 5 In.	115.00
Dog, Wirehaired Terrier, Painted, Cast Iron, Full Figure, Hubley, 10 x 11 In.	175.00
Dolly Dimple, Yellow Dress, Blue Bonnet, Cast Iron, Hubley, Drayton, 7 ½ In.	200.00
Dolly, Hubley, Cast Iron, 9 ¼ In.	20.00
Dolphin, Black Painted, Cast Iron, c.1920, 12 In.	1007.00
Drum Major, Full Figure, Cast Iron, 12 ½ In.	100.00
Duck, Top Hat, Duck Strolls Along, Wings Held High, Cast Iron, 4 ¼ x 7 ¾ In.	489.00
Duck, Yellow, Orange, Green, Cast Iron, Hubley, 5 ½ In.	165.00
Ducks, Brown Female, Gray Drake, Original Paint, 7 x 8 ½ In.	374.00
Dutch Children, Kissing, Cast Iron, 8 ½ x 9 In.	144.00
Elephant, Gold Paint, Red Blanket, Marked, Bradley & Hubbard, 10 x 11 ¾ In.	278.00
Elephant, Trunk Up, Painted, Cast Iron, Figural, 11 In.	175.00
Flamingo, Reeds, Pink, Green, Painted, Cast Iron, Hubley, 4 x 10 ½ In.	468.00
Flower Basket, Cast Iron, Hubley, 9 ¾ x 5 ½ In.	138.00

D

Doorstop, Clown, Ruffled Collar, Cuffs, Oversized Shoes, Sarah Symonds, Cast Iron, 11 ½ x 5 ¾ In. $468.00

Doorstop, Dog, Scottie, Sitting, Cast Iron, Full Figure, 5 x 6 In. $176.00

Doorstop, French Girl, Cast Iron, Hubley, 9 x 5 ½ In. $117.00

Doorstop, Lilies Of The Valley, Cast Iron, Hubley, 10 ½ x 7 ½ In. $293.00

Doorstop, Lyre, Copper Electroplate On Iron, Hubley, 9 ⅝ x 5 ⅞ In. $59.00

Doorstop, Penguin, Top Hat, Tux, Full Figure, Cast Iron, Hubley, 10 ½ x 3 ¾ In. $761.00

Doorstop, Poppies, Cast Iron, Hubley, 10 ⅝ x 7 ⅞ In. $293.00

Flower Basket, Dahlias, Multicolored, Cast Iron, Hubley, 9 ½ x 7 In.	110.00
Flower Basket, In Oval, Cast Iron, Painted, 5 ¾ x 7 ½ In.	110.00
Flower Basket, Lily-Of-The-Valley, Multicolored, Pink Bow, Iron, Hubley, 10 ½ x 7 In.	220.00
Flower Basket, Marigolds, Yellow, Blue, Pink, Green, Cast Iron, Hubley, 7 ¾ x 8 In.	85.00
Flower Basket, Poppies, Snapdragons, Red, Blue, Pink, Cast Iron, Hubley, 7 ½ x 7 In.	130.00
Flower Basket, Roses, Daisies, Multicolored, Cast Iron, Hubley, 7 In.	80.00
Flower Basket, Roses, Multicolored, Blue Bow, Cast Iron, Hubley, 11 x 8 In.	165.00
Flower Basket, Wild Roses, Multicolored, Yellow Bow, Cast Iron, Hubley, 7 x 7 In.	110.00 to 220.00
Flower Bowl, Zinnias, Red, Yellow, Pink, Blue & Gray Bowl, Cast Iron, Hubley, 7 x 7 In.	285.00
Flower Oval, Carry Handle, Cast Iron, Bradley & Hubbard, Marked B&H, 7 ½ In.	175.00
Flower Seller, Painted, Cast Iron, 10 In.	354.00
Flower Urn, Narcissus, Yellow, Pink, White, Green, Cast Iron, Hubley, 7 x 6 ¾ In.	135.00
Flower Vase, Cosmos, Pink, White, Green, Cast Iron, Hubley, 17 ¾ x 10 ¼ In.	620.00
Flower Vase, Gladiolas, Pink, Yellow, White, Cast Iron, Hubley, 10 x 8 In.	165.00
Flower Vase, Primrose, Pink, White, Green, Cast Iron, Hubley, 7 ⅜ x 6 ¼ In.	295.00
Flower Vase, Roses, Pink, Slant Vase, Cast Iron, Hubley, 10 ⅛ x 8 In.	55.00
Flowerpot, Poppies, Red, Clay Pot Design, Cast Iron, Hubley, 7 In.	30.00
Flowers, Cosmos, Vase, Pastels, Painted, Cast Iron, Hubley, 18 x 10 In.	644.00
Flowers, Mixed, Multicolored, Painted Cast Iron, Hubley, 6 In.	88.00
Flowers, Poppies, Snapdragons, Multicolored, Painted, Cast Iron, Hubley, 7 ½ x 7 In.	146.00
Flowers, Tulip Pot, National, Cast Iron, 8 ¾ In.	220.00
Football Player, Cast Iron, 11 ¼ x 6 In.	16500.00
French Girl, Cast Iron, Hubley, 9 x 5 ½ In. ....*illus*	117.00
Fruit Bowl, Flowers, Painted, Cast Iron, Hubley, 7 x 7 In.	120.00
Gamecock, Painted, Full Figure, Cast Iron, Hubley, 7 ½ x 7 In.	250.00
Geisha, Playing Instrument, On Cushion, Painted, Cast Iron, Hubley, 7 ⅝ x 6 ¼ In.	120.00
George Washington, Cast Iron, Painted, 1920s, 7 In.	350.00
George Washington, Gold Paint, Cast Iron, 8 ½ In.	79.00
Giraffe, In Vine, Painted, Full Figure, Cast Iron, No. 425, Hubley, U.S.A., 10 ½ x 6 In.	240.00
Girl, Kicking Flowers, Blue, White Dress, 9 ¾ x 6 ¾ In.	173.00
Gnome With Keys, Full Figure, Cast Iron, 10 In.	65.00
Gnome, Left Arm Bent, Painted, Cast Iron, 10 ⅞ In.	175.00
Golfer, Overhead Swing, A Difficult Lie, Painted, Cast Iron, Hubley, 10 x 7 In.	385.00
Golfer, Putting, Painted, Cast Iron, Hubley, Marked, 8 ⅜ x 7 ⅛ In.	140.00
Heron, Painted, Cast Iron, 7 ½ In.	600.00 to 649.00
Horse, Black, White, Cast Iron, Hubley, 10 ½ x 12 ¼ In.	236.00
Horse, Brown & Natural Colors, Cast Iron, Hubley, 7 ¾ In.	50.00
Horse, Full Figure, Brown, Painted, Cast Iron, Hubley, 10 ½ In.	351.00
Horse, Jumping Fence, Cast Iron, Painted, Eastern Specialty Co., c.1920, 8 In.	1600.00
Horse, Percheron, Cast Iron, Hubley, 7 ¾ In.	234.00
Horses, Thoroughbred Mare & Foal, Brown, Full Figure, Cast Iron, Hubley, 6 x 7 In.	135.00
Huck Finn, Blue Overalls, Yellow Straw Hat, Iron, Littco, 1920s, 9 x 12 In.	630.00 to 1200.00
Huck Finn, Rumpled Collar, Fish Pole, Bradley & Hubbard, 5 ½ x 9 ¾ In.	489.00
Indian Head, Red, Black Hair, Yellow, Cast Brass, Signed, West, 5 ⅝ x 7 ⅜ In.	185.00
Jonquils, Leaning Forward, Yellow, Orange, Green, Cast Iron, Hubley, 7 ⅜ In.	250.00
Jungle Boy, In Leopard Skin Pelt, Kneeling, Outstretched, 12 ¾ x 12 In.	748.00
Kitten, Perched, Stand, Marble Eyes, White, Painted, Cast Iron, 12 ¾ x 7 ¾ In.	351.00
Kitten, Twins, Black, Brown, Blue, Yellow, Cast Iron, Hubley, Drayton, 7 x 5 ¼ In.	710.00 to 760.00
Kitten, With Bow, Full Figure, Cast Iron, 4 ¾ In.	50.00
Kittens, In High Top Shoe, Cast Iron, 9 In.	200.00
Lighthouse, White, Teal, Yellow, Black, Cast Iron, 1920, 8 ¼ In.	750.00
Lilies Of The Valley, Cast Iron, Hubley, 10 ½ x 7 ½ In. ....*illus*	293.00
Little Red Riding Hood, Wolf, Basket, Cast Iron, Creation Co., 1930, 4 ⅞ x 8 ¾ In.	489.00
Lyre, Copper Electroplate On Iron, Hubley, 9 ⅝ x 5 ⅞ In. ....*illus*	59.00
Major Domo, Hubley, Cast Iron, 8 ½ In.	70.00
Mammy, Blue Dress, White Apron, Full Figure, Cast Iron, Hubley, 9 ½ In.	160.00
Mammy, Hands On Hips, Red Dress, Painted, Cast Iron, Hubley, 12 In.	468.00
Mammy, Red Dress, White Apron, Blue Bandanna, Full Figure, Cast Iron, Hubley, 12 In.	160.00
Mary Quite Contrary, Holding Watering Can, Rake, Flowers, Cast Iron, 15 ¼ In.	1170.00
Monkey, Crouching, Full Figure, Screw-On Tail, Brown, Painted, Cast Iron, 5 x 9 In.	205.00
Monkey, On Barrel, Green, Yellow, Cast Iron, Inscribed, 1930, 8 ½ In.	119.00
Monkey, Seated, Painted, Full Figure, Cast Iron, Hubley, 8 ⅞ x 4 ⅝ In.	200.00
Narcissus, Pastel Yellow, Painted, Cast Iron, Hubley, 6 ¾ x 7 In.	146.00
Olive Picker, Orange, Brown, Green, Painted, Cast Iron, Hubley, 8 x 7 ½ In.	644.00
Owl, Cast Iron, Bradley & Hubbard, 15 ⅝ In.	1159.00

Owl, On Stump, Holly Berries, Brass Finish, Cast Iron, Hubley, 10 x 4 ½ In.		234.00
Parrot, On Round Stand, Multicolored Paint, Cast Iron, 12 In.		118.00
Parrot, Red, Green, Yellow, Black, Cast Iron, 8 In.		72.00
Peacock, By Urn, On Fence, Painted, Cast Iron, Hubley, 7 ⅝ x 4 ¼ In.		140.00
Peacock, Male, Full Plumage, Cast Iron, 5 ¾ x 6 ¼ In.		201.00
Penguin, Top Hat, Tux, Full Figure, Cast Iron, Hubley, 10 ½ x 3 ¾ In.	*illus*	761.00
Peter Rabbit, Eating Carrot, Painted, Cast Iron, G. G. Drayton, Hubley, 9 ⅜ x 5 In.		300.00
Pheasant, Head Turned, Painted, Iron, Hubley, Marked, Everett, 8 ½ x 7 ½ In.		565.00 to 644.00
Pilgrim, John Alden, Cast Iron, c.1930, 7 In.		295.00
Poinsettia, Cast Iron, 8 ¾ In.		220.00
Poppies, Cast Iron, Hubley, 10 ⅝ x 7 ⅞ In.	*illus*	293.00
Punch, Seated, Multicolored Paint, Cast Iron, England, 12 x 9 In.		300.00
Rabbit, By Fence, Cast Iron, Albany, 6 ¾ In.		130.00
Rabbit, By Fence, Cast Iron, Painted, Albany Foundry, 7 ¼ x 6 ¼ In.		795.00
Rabbit, Cast Iron, Hubley, 12 x 11 ½ In.		1250.00
Rabbit, Cottontail, Facing Forward, Full Figure, Cast Iron, 9 x 8 ½ In.	*illus*	4025.00
Rabbit, Eating Carrot, Hubley, Cast Iron, 8 ¼ In.		120.00
Rabbit, Sitting Up, Bull Figure, Black, Cast Iron, 7 In.		80.00
Rabbit, Standing, Full Figure, Cast Iron, 9 In.		55.00
Rabbit, Upright, Bradley & Hubbard, Cast Iron, 15 In.		60.00
Rabbit, With Top, Hat, Albany, Cast Iron, 10 In.		15.00
Raggedy Ann, Multicolored, Paint, Cast Iron, 9 ½ In.		58.00
Ram, Cast Iron, 7 In.		384.00
Rooster, Full Figure, Cast Iron, 9 ½ In.		190.00
Rooster, On Ground, Flowers, Leaves, Full Figure, Painted, Cast Iron, Early 1900s, 13 In.		510.00
Royal Mail Coach, Iron, England, c.1900, 7 x 12 In.		826.00
Sailor, Old Salt, Hands In Pocket, Rain Coat, White Pants, Black Hat, Cast Iron, Hubley, 8 In.		350.00
Ship, 4-Masts, Cast Brass, 19th Century, 6 In.		50.00
Ship, Anchor, Black, Green, Blue, Cast Iron, Painted, Bronze, Bradley & Hubbard, 11 ¼ In.		575.00
Ship, Brass, 19th Century, 6 In.		53.00
Ship, Sailing, Blue Nose, Cast Iron, Painted, Canada, 1920s, 6 ¼ In.		750.00
Ship, Schooner, 3-Masted, Cast Iron, Painted, Marked, Greenblatt Studio, Copyright 1925, 12 In.		205.00
Skunk, Raised Back Toes, Upturned Tail, Cast Iron, Hollow, 8 x 6 In.		345.00
Soldier, Flower In Gun, Cast Iron, Painted, 12 ⅞ x 7 ⅛ In.	*illus*	527.00
Southern Belle, Blue Dress, Holding Hat, Flowers, Cast Iron, National Foundry, 11 In.		169.00
Southern Belle, Yellow Dress, Holding Flowers, Cast Iron, National Foundry, 6 ½ In.		169.00
Squirrel, Eating Nut, Cast Iron, 11 In.		700.00
Squirrel, Eating Nut, On Log, Painted, Cast Iron, 11 x 9 ½ In.		365.00
Squirrel, Nut, Gray, Brown, Painted, Cast Iron, Hubley, 6 x 9 ½ In.		117.00
Squirrel, Seated, Holding Nut, Blue, Brown, Full Figure, Cast Iron, Hubley, 9 ½ x 6 In.		120.00
Stagecoach, 2 Horses, Beach Lake, Pa., Painted, Cast Iron, 7 In.		175.00
Stagecoach, Green, Red, Orange, Cast Iron, Creations Co., 1930, 7 ⅜ x 8 ½ In.		92.00
Stork, Full Figure, White, Painted, Cast Iron, Hubley, 7 x 12 In.		1170.00
Stork, Green, Blue, Red, Cast Iron, Hubley, 5 ½ In.		300.00
Stork, White, Red, Black, Full Figure, Cast Iron, Hubley, 12 ¼ x 7 In.		1100.00
Sunbonnet Baby, Red Polka Dot Dress, Paint, Cast Iron, 6 In.		326.00
Sunrise Design, Enamel, Green, Cast Iron, 5 ¾ x 5 ½ In.		77.00
Swallows, On Berry Branches, Painted, Cast Iron, 8 ½ x 7 ½ In.		720.00
Swan, Swimming, Black Neck, Feather Tips, Yellow Beak, Orange Feet, 5 ½ x 7 ⅜ In.		201.00
Swan, White, Blue, Pink, Painted, Cast Iron, Embossed Manley, c.1910, 8 x 9 In.		474.00
Swan, White Paint, Feathers Accented, Cast Iron, Spencer, 13 ½ x 8 In.		2350.00
Topsy, Black Girl, Blue Checked Dress, Painted, Cast Iron, Hubley, 3 x 6 In.		263.00
Trellis, Yellow Finch, Cast Iron, Painted, H.L. Judd, c.1930, 6 ⅝ x 5 ½ In.		450.00
Windmill, Cast Iron, A.M. Greenblatt Studios, 9 x 11 ¾ In.		633.00
Windmill, Cast Iron, National Fdry., 7 x 6 In.		58.00
Woman, Blue Hoop Dress, Bonnet, Cast Iron, Hubley, 7 ¾ x 4 In.		275.00
Woman, In Hoop Skirt, Holds Fan, 6 x 9 ½ In.		230.00
Woman, Nude, Seated, Green, Full Figure, Cast Iron, Signed, Hubley, 8 ½ x 3 ½ In.		30.00
Woman, Painted, Green & Brown Dress, Yellow Bonnet, Blue Bow, Cast Iron, 5 ½ In.		250.00

DORCHESTER POTTERY was founded by George Henderson in 1895 in Dorchester, Massachusetts. At first, the firm made utilitarian stoneware, but collectors are most interested in the line of decorated blue and white pottery that Dorchester made from 1940 until it went out of business in 1979.

DORCHESTER
POTTERY WORKS
BOSTON, MASS.

Pot, Lid, Blue & White, Fruit, Marked, 3 ¼ In.	125.00

D

Doorstop, Rabbit, Cottontail, Facing Forward, Full Figure, Cast Iron, 9 x 8 ½ In. $4025.00

Doorstop, Soldier, Flower In Gun, Cast Iron, Painted, 12 ⅞ x 7 ⅛ In. $527.00

Doulton, Vase, Jessica, Flow Blue, Gold Highlights, Burslem, 23 ¼ In. $850.00

Doulton, Vase, Monkeys, Cobalt Blue, Brown Gloss Glaze, Lambeth, c.1881, 18 ½ x 11 In. $9945.00

Doulton, Vase, Sheep, Meadow, Leaf Border, Lambeth, c.1880, 13 ¾ In. $920.00

Dresden, Figurine, Bat Flying, Painted, Gold, Red Highlights, Veined Wings, 4 In. $2588.00

Dresden, Figurine, Stork, Painted, White, Black, Orange Legs, Bill, 4 In. $345.00

Dresden, Group, 18th-Century Concert Performers & Dancers, 19 In. $1240.00

DOULTON pottery and porcelain were made by Doulton and Co. of Burslem, England, after 1882. The name *Royal Doulton* appeared on the company's wares after 1902. Other pottery by Doulton is listed under Royal Doulton.

Bowl, Footed, Imari Style Flowers, Cobalt Blue, Gilt, Pottery, 4 x 9 In.	89.00
Bowl, Painted, Molded Handles, 4 ½ x 10 ½ x 7 ½ In.	82.00
Ewer, Blue Flower, Gold, Burslem, c.1890, 8 ¾ In.	380.00
Humidor, Verse, When All Things Were Made, Ridged Lines, Lid, Lambeth, 6 ½ In.	220.00
Jardiniere, Flowers, Branches, Green, Gilt, Lacework, Reticulated, Slaters Patent, Lambeth, 7 ¼ In.	260.00
Jardiniere, Flowers, Molded, Yellow, Blue, Brown, Impressed, Lambeth, 7 ¾ In.	80.00
Jardiniere, Yellow Flowers, Blue Leaves, Yellow Ground, Lambeth, 7 In.	188.00
Jug, Medieval Figures, Flowers, Chevron Border, Brown, Cream, Buff, Lambeth, 1895, 10 In.	175.00
Mug, Hunt & Garden Scene, Brown, 2-Tone, Lambeth, 1883-86, 5 ¼ In.	99.00
Pepper Pot, Ye Olde Cheshire Cheese 1667, Brown, 2-Tone, Lambeth, 1877, 4 ½ x 2 ½ In.	99.00
Pitcher, Cameo Portraits, Enamel, Verse, Oval, Lambeth, PP & Boo, 1879, 6 x 4 In.	750.00
Pitcher, Christopher Columbus, Relief, Salt Glaze, Colombian Expo, Lambeth, 1893, 6 ⅝ In.	199.00
Pitcher, Cider, Lid, Silver Ring, Hunter, Hound, Stag, Lambeth, 1890s, 8 ½ In.	168.00
Pitcher, Drinking Scenes, Hounds, Horsemen, Deer, Brown, 2-Tone, Lambeth, 1890, 7 In.	85.00
Pitcher, Medallions, Verse, Oval, Lambeth, c.1891, 7 ¼ In.	175.00
Plaque, Gloaming, Water Landscape At Dusk, Noke & Hopkins, Frame, c.1902, 12 x 5 In.	3355.00
Plate, Chase, Wounded Stag, White, Cobalt Blue Trim, Burslem, 10 In.	70.00
Plate, Red Ground Borders, Gold Scrolled Leaves, Castle Landscapes, 12 Piece, 10 ⅜ In.	3851.00
Platter, Turkey, Flow Blue, Tom Turkey, Floral Border, Late 1800s, 22 x 18 In.	588.00
Salad Serving Set, Aesthetic, Central Spiral Twist, Hammered Silver, Lambeth, 1880, 11 ½ In., 2 Piece.	1850.00
Salt, Hounds, Man Drinking, Raised Design, Brown, Lambeth, 2 In.	35.00
Syrup Pitcher, Flow Blue, Gold Flowers, Metal Hinged Lid, Burslem, c.1902, 6 In.	425.00
Tankard, Hunt & Garden Scene, Salt Glaze, Lambeth, 5 ½ x 4 ½ In.	84.00
Vase, Blue Ground, Gold, Long Neck, Lambeth, 10 In., Pair	234.00
Vase, Blue, Iris, Yellow, Glaze, 1875 Mark, 21 x 9 ½ In.	159.00
Vase, Flowers, White, Green, Gold Ground, Blue, Marked, Slater, 7 In.	150.00
Vase, Jessica, Flow Blue, Gold Highlights, Burslem, 23 ¼ In. ....*illus*	850.00
Vase, Lady Hamilton Oval Portrait, Red Ground, Gilt, Handles, 7 In.	460.00
Vase, Monkeys, Cobalt Blue, Brown Gloss Glaze, Lambeth, c.1881, 18 ½ x 11 In. ....*illus*	9945.00
Vase, Painted, Venetian Scene, Panoramic, Gold Trim, 7 ½ In.	184.00
Vase, Red, Yellow Mums, Gold, Shouldered, Burslem, 4 ½ In.	115.00
Vase, Sheep, Meadow, Leaf Border, Lambeth, c.1880, 13 ¾ In ....*illus*	920.00
Wine Vessel, Strainer, Flow Blue, Gold Flowers, Burslem, Late 1800s, 11 ½ In.	695.00

DRESDEN china is any china made in the town of Dresden, Germany. The most famous factory in Dresden is the Meissen factory. Figurines of eighteenth-century ladies and gentlemen, animal groups, or cherubs and other mythological subjects were popular. One special type of figurine was made with skirts of porcelain-dipped lace. Do not make the mistake of thinking that all pieces marked *Dresden* are from the Meissen factory. The Meissen pieces usually have crossed swords marks, and are listed under Meissen. Some recent porcelain from Ireland, called *Irish Dresden,* is not included in this book.

Bowl, Reticulated, Baluster Shaft, Cherubs, Flowers, Scroll Feet, c.1900, 14 In.	546.00
Candelabrum, 4-Light, 15 In.	59.00
Candelabrum, 4-Light, Applied Flowers, Trees, Figures, White Flower Underglaze, c.1905, 19 In., Pair...	326.00
Clock, Shelf, Applied Flowers, Putti, White Ground, Gilt, Schierholtz, 1900s, 13 x 14 In.	200.00
Compote, Musical Figures, Reticulated, Applied Flowers, Tree, Marked, 12 x 9 ½ In.	185.00
Cup & Saucer, Bakers Cocoa, Woman, Gilt Handle	395.00
Cup & Saucer, Classical Scene, 6 Figures, Green Ground	225.00
Dog, Pug, Brown & White, Relief Gilt Balls On Collar, Early 1900s, 9 In., Pair	2875.00
Figurine, Bat, Flying, Painted, Gold, Red Highlights, Veined Wings, 4 In. ....*illus*	2588.00
Figurine, Chinese Man Playing Lute, Enameled Flowers, Brocade, Early 1900s, 7 In.	136.00
Figurine, Dog, Pug, Brown & White, Gold Trim, 7 In.	748.00
Figurine, Flamenco Dancer, 10 In.	84.00
Figurine, King, Portly, Shield, Sword, Gilt, Germany, c.1820, 16 ½ In.	3450.00
Figurine, Lace Lady With Fan, Glass Dome, Reine Handarbeit, Crown Over D Mark, 6 In.	83.00
Figurine, Parrot On Tree Stump, Multicolored Plumage, 18 In.	385.00
Figurine, Stork, Painted, White, Black, Orange Legs, Bill, 4 In. ....*illus*	345.00
Figurine, Tailor Astride Goat, 12 In.	538.00
Group, 18th-Century Concert Performers & Dancers, 19 In. ....*illus*	1240.00
Lamp, Lithophane Panels, Pierced, 4 Colonial Figures On Base	266.00
Lamp, Owl Shape, Tree Trunk, Naturalistic Fern Base, Glass Eyes, Frosted Shade, 13 In.	1185.00
Nodder, Chinese Man, Woman, Seated, Porcelain, Multicolored, 20th Century, 7 In., Pair	173.00

Plate, Flowers, Floral Wreath & Swag Border, Gold Trim, 10 ¾ In.	227.00
Stein, Old Testament Scene, Spies, Grapes, Tin, Glazed, Polychrome, Pewter Lid, 7 In.	1304.00
Urn, Cover, Classic Shape, Handles, Mask Terminals, Pedestal Base, Marked, c.1920, 10 In.	71.00
Urn, Landscape, Yellow Ground, Goat Masks, Reticulated Cover, Pinecone Knop, 1910, 16 In., Pair	990.00
Vase, Flowers, Enamel, Gilt, Mask Handles, 6 In., Pair..	550.00

DUNCAN & MILLER is a term used by collectors when referring to glass made by the George A. Duncan and Sons Company or the Duncan and Miller Glass Company. These companies worked from 1893 to 1955, when the use of the name *Duncan* was discontinued and the firm became part of the United States Glass Company. Early patterns may be listed under Pressed Glass.

Bagware, Salt, Canary Yellow, Heavy Paneled, Fine Cut, 1 ¼ x 1 In.	22.00
Button Panels, Toothpick, c.1903, 2 ½ x 1 ⅞ In.	33.00
Canterbury, Tumbler, Copen Blue, 9 Oz., 4 ½ In.	32.00
Canterbury, Tumbler, Pink Opalescent, 12 Oz., 5 ½ In.	45.00
Duck, Ashtray, Pipe Rest, c.1935, 8 x 5 ½ In.	24.00
Festive, Bowl, Salad, Honey, 9 ½ In.	175.00
Festive, Creamer, Honey	75.00
Festive, Gravy Boat, Ladle, Honey...	300.00
First Love, Goblet, Water, Terrance, 10 Oz., 6 ¾ In.	32.00
Hobnail, Powder Jar, Green, 4 x 5 In. ....*illus*	65.00
Lily Of The Valley, Goblet, Ice Tea, 1955, 7 In.	32.00
Polished Mirrors, Toothpick, 6 Panels, Pentagonal Base	28.00
Sandwich, Epergne, Sawtooth Edge, Vase, Crimped Rim, 12-In. Tray, 2 Piece ....*illus*	195.00
Sandwich, Oil Cruet, Stopper, 5 ¼ In.	45.00
Sandwich, Sugar & Creamer, Tray..	48.00
Shell & Tassel, Mug, Cobalt Blue, c.1881, 3 ½ x 3 In.	225.00
Snowflake, Salt, Square, c.1890, 1 ½ In.	6.00
Sylvan, Swan, Yellow Opalescent, 5 ½ In. ....*illus*	165.00

DURAND art glass was made from 1924 to 1931. The Vineland Flint Glass Works was established by Victor Durand and Victor Durand Jr. in 1897. In 1924 Martin Bach Jr. and other artisans from the Quezal glassworks joined them at the Vineland, New Jersey, plant to make Durand art glass. They called their gold iridescent glass Gold Luster.

Bowl, Rose, Blue Luster Ground, Coil Pattern, Applied Glass Foot, 5 ¼ In.	1380.00
Candlestick, Blue Luster, White Coil, Purple Iridescence, 7 In.	1380.00
Candlestick, Spanish Yellow, Green Rim, 1926, 6 In., Pair	350.00 to 475.00
Compote, Cobalt Blue Over Crystal, Pulled Peacock Feathers, 4 x 10 In.	690.00
Ginger Jar, Lid, Transparent Glass Finial, Vertical Ribbing, Panels, 9 In.	9775.00
Jar, Temple, Cover, Amber Rosette, White Ground, Crisscross Gold Threads, Green, Gold Leaves, 7 In. ...	518.00
Lamp Base, Green Heart & Vine, Orange Ground, 16 In.	410.00
Lamp, Iridescent Gold Shade, Pulled Feathers, Allover Gold Threads, Metal Stand, 19 In., Pair.	920.00
Lampshade, Gold Glass, Dome Shape, Applied Threading, 13 In.	345.00
Vase, Amber & Red Textured Glass, Inverted Neck, Shouldered, 5 ½ In.	288.00
Vase, Amethyst, Optical Ribbing, Spool Stem, Disc Base, 15 ½ In.	518.00
Vase, Blue, Green Leaves, Entangled Vines, Iridescent 2-Tone Gold Luster, 8 In.	748.00
Vase, Blue, Green Luster, Overall Threading, Bulbous, Flared Rim, Signed, 8 In.	546.00
Vase, Blue Iridescent, Flared, Footed, 4 ½ x 12 In.	600.00
Vase, Blue Iridescent, Magenta & Gold Neck, Marked, 8 ½ In.	460.00
Vase, Blue Luster, Cylindrical, Shouldered, Turned In Scalloped Rim, White Coil, 7 In. ....*illus*	978.00
Vase, Blue Luster, Flaring, Trumpet Form, Bulbous, 9 ½ In.	518.00
Vase, Blue Luster, Shouldered, Gold Highlights, Signed, 7 In.	425.00
Vase, Blue Luster, Shouldered, Overall White Hearts, Vines, Signed, 6 In.	950.00
Vase, Cobalt Blue, Pulled Feather, Shouldered, Flared Rim, 7 In.	259.00
Vase, Gold & Orange Iridescent, Green Leaves & Vines, Broad Shape, Signed, 6 x 9 ½ In.	1440.00
Vase, Gold Iridescent, Baluster, Flared Rim, 9 In.	397.00
Vase, Gold Iridescent, Bulbous, Blue Heart & Vines, 6 ¾ In. ....*illus*	776.00
Vase, Gold Luster, 4-Tiered Beehive Form, 9 In.	115.00
Vase, Gold Luster, Baluster, Everted Rim, Signed V. Durand, 4 ½ In.	316.00
Vase, Gold Luster, Marigold, Green Heart & Vine, Squat, Signed, 6 In.	345.00
Vase, Gold Luster, Red Hues, Bulbous, Signed, 8 In.	863.00
Vase, Heart & Clinging Vine, Blue Luster, 8 ½ In.	1870.00
Vase, Iridescent Blue, Gold, Overall Gold Threading, Pulled White Feathers, Shouldered, 9 In.	1700.00
Vase, Iridescent Blue Ground, White Leaves, Carmel Tips, 7 ½ In.	978.00
Vase, Iridescent Gold Body, Green Random Coil, Blue Highlights, 7 In.	1050.00
Vase, King Tut, Gold Iridescent, Bulbous, Green, Signed, 7 In.	900.00

Duncan & Miller, Hobnail, Powder Jar, Green, 4 x 5 In.
$65.00

Duncan & Miller, Sandwich, Epergne, Sawtooth Edge, Vase, Crimped Rim, 12-In. Tray, 2 Piece
$195.00

Duncan & Miller, Sylvan, Swan, Yellow Opalescent, 5 ½ In.
$165.00

Durand, Vase, Blue Luster, Cylindrical, Shouldered, Turned In Scalloped Rim, White Coil, 7 In.
$978.00

Durand, Vase, Gold Iridescent, Bulbous, Blue
Heart & Vines, 6 ¾ In.
$776.00

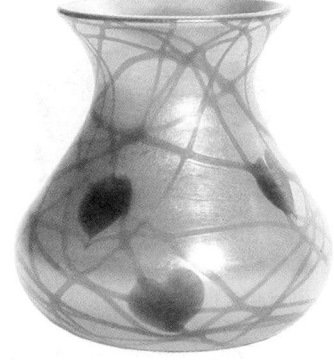

Durand, Vase, King Tut, Opalescent,
Gold & Blue Hooked Feathers,
Signed, 10 In.
$2358.00

Elvis Presley, Scarf, Facsimile Signature, Silk,
c.1956, 28 ½ x 31 ½ In.
$115.00

Elvis Presley, Tile, Black & White,
Gold Accents, Ceramic, c.1956, 6 x 6 In.
$345.00

Enamel, Beaker, Cloisonne, Silver Gilt,
Scrolling, Strapwork, Flowers, Russia,
c.1887, 3 In.
$1200.00

Enamel, Bowl, Brazier Shape, Gilded,
Champleve, Bronze, Engraved Glass,
c.1875, 17 x 13 In.
$1200.00

Enamel, Cigarette Box,
Commedia Dell'Arte, Banjo, Gilt,
Wood, Thelma Frazer, 2 x 7 In.
$81.00

Enamel, Dish, Abstract, Multicolored, Copper,
Inscribed, Denslous Fairmont Hotel, 10 In.
$150.00

Enamel, Dish, Flared Rim,
Stenciled Design, Green, White,
Signed, Edward Winter, 10 In.
$58.00

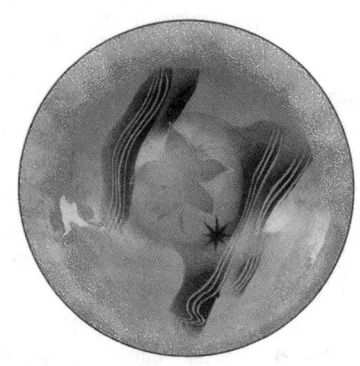

Enamel, Dish, White,
Multicolored Flowers, Signed, 7 In.
$11.00

Vase, King Tut, Gold Luster, Cylinder Shape, Signed 10 In.	1300.00
Vase, King Tut, Green Iridescent, Shouldered, Gold, Signed, 9 In.	1900.00
Vase, King Tut, Iridescent Blue Globe, Carmel Highlight, Gold Foot, 5 ¼ In.	920.00
Vase, King Tut, Iridescent Gold Luster, Green, Shouldered, Signed, 7 ½ In.	1000.00
Vase, King Tut, Iridescent Wave Lines, Blue, Green, Flared, Ruffled Rim, 6 ½ In.	1400.00
Vase, King Tut, Opal, Iridescent Gold, Blue, Gold Interior, Bulbous, Flared, 6 ½ In.	1000.00
Vase, King Tut, Opalescent, Gold & Blue Hooked Feathers, Signed, 10 In. ....illus	2358.00
Vase, Leaves, Vines, Iridescent Blue, Cone Shape, Flared Rim, 8 ⅜ In.	889.00
Vase, Moorish Crackle, White, Royal Blue Overlay, 8 ½ In.	288.00
Vase, Opal, Blue Coil Design, Pinched Waist, 10 ½ In.	900.00
Vase, Opal Body, Everted Rim, Blue, Green Iridescent Coil Design, Oval, 10 In., Pair	1800.00
Vase, Opal, Gold, Footed, Trumpet Form, Allover Gold, Green Hearts, Gold Vines, Signed, 12 In.	1035.00
Vase, Red, Opal Crackle Panels, Iridescent Gold Lava, Signed, 8 ½ In.	2760.00
Vase, Red, Translucent, Gold, White Pulled Feather Design, 8 ½ In.	950.00
Vase, Tapered, Flared Rim, Blue Iridescent Coil, Dark Ground, Gold Interior, Oval, 7 In.	1600.00
Vase, White Heart, Vine, Blue Luster, Oval Shouldered Form, Signed, 9 ¼ In., Pair	2472.00
Vase, Yellow Luster, Bulbous, Cut Leaves, Branches, No. 1700, 7 In.	225.00

ELVIS PRESLEY, the well-known singer, lived from 1935 to 1977. He became famous by 1956. Elvis appeared on television, starred in twenty-seven movies, and performed in Las Vegas. Memorabilia from any of the Presley shows, his records, and even memorials made after his death are collected.

Guitar, Acoustic, c.1962	26290.00
Love Ya' Fuchsia Lipstick, Metal Tube, Signature, 1956, 2 ¼ In.	145.00
Menu, International Hotel Las Vegas, 1969	598.00
Photo, By Mirror, 1957, 11 x 14 In.	359.00
Photo, Looking Out Window, Black & White, Warwick Hotel, 1957, 11 x 14 In.	335.00
Poster, Frankie & Johnny, Frame, 1966, 23 x 29 In.	118.00
Poster, Hotel, Summer Festival, Hilton, 1975, 35 x 35 In.	1195.00
Ring, Turquoise, Opalescent Stone, Sterling, 1970s	6572.00
Scarf, Facsimile Signature, Silk, c.1956, 28 ½ x 31 ½ In. ....illus	115.00
Sheet Music, I Want You, I Need You, I Love You, Blue Cover	88.00
Sheet Music, Too Much, Frame	22.00
Tile, Black & White, Gold Accents, Ceramic, c.1956, 6 x 6 In. ....illus	345.00

ENAMELS listed here are made of glass particles and other materials heated and fused to metal. In the eighteenth and nineteenth centuries, workmen from Russia, France, England, and other countries made small boxes and table pieces of enamel on metal. One form of English enamel is called *Battersea* and is listed under that name. There was a revival of interest in enameling in the 1930s and a new style evolved. There is now renewed interest in the artistic enameled plaques, vases, ashtrays, and jewelry. Enamels made since the 1930s are usually on copper or steel, although silver was often used for jewelry. Graniteware is a separate category, and enameled metal kitchen pieces may be included in the Kitchen category.

Ashtray, Blue Green, Linear Pattern, Bovano, Marked	55.00
Beaker, Blood Cup, Coronation, Tsar Nicholas II, Russia, 1896, 4 ¼ In.	480.00
Beaker, Cloisonne, Silver Gilt, Scrolling, Strapwork, Flowers, Russia, c.1887, 3 In. ....illus	1200.00
Beaker, Spiraling Ribbons Of Various Patterns, Gilt Silver, Footed, A. Kuzmichev, Russia, 5 In.	4270.00
Bowl, Blue Green, Abstract, 1960, 8 ½ x 6 In.	100.00
Bowl, Brazier Shape, Gilded, Champleve, Bronze, Engraved Glass, c.1875, 17 x 13 In. ....illus	1200.00
Bowl, Gold Green Base, Kareka, Rounded Triangle, 6 ½ x 1 ½ In.	45.00
Bowl, Textured, Chartreuse, Turquoise, Cobalt, Black Interior, Vallenti, Italy, 6 ½ In.	95.00
Bowl, Textured, Chartreuse, Turquoise, Cobalt, Black Interior, Vallenti, Italy, 8 ½ In.	135.00
Cigarette Box, Commedia Dell'Arte, Banjo, Gilt, Wood, Thelma Frazer, 2 x 7 In. ....illus	81.00
Compote, Red, Gold Flowers, Doves, Semi-Nude Figure, Copper Stem, Vienna, 5 ½ In.	776.00
Cup, Textured, Chartreuse, Turquoise, Cobalt, Black Interior, Vallenti, Italy, 4 In.	45.00
Dish, Abstract, Multicolored, Copper, Inscribed, Denslous Fairmont Hotel, 10 In. ....illus	150.00
Dish, Copper, Abstract Bird, Rebajes, 6 x 6 In.	145.00
Dish, Flared Rim, Stenciled Design, Green, White, Signed, Edward Winter, 10 In. ....illus	58.00
Dish, Flowers, Blue, Edward Winter, Signed, 6 ½ In.	115.00
Dish, Paella, Open, Red Koben Style, 13 In.	95.00
Dish, Swordfish Shaped, Valleau, Signed, 5 ½ In., Pair	95.00
Dish, White, Multicolored Flowers, Signed, 7 In. ....illus	11.00
Egg, Faberge Style, Gilt Metal, Blue, Festoons, Swags, Necklace, 3 In.	263.00
Egg, Faberge Style, Gilt Metal, Red, Scrolling, Pedestal Base, 3 ½ In.	351.00
Ginger Jar, Cover, Cloisonne, Wood Base, Chinese, 11 x 7 In.	35.00

Enamel, Plate, Gold Ground, Green Leaves, Annemarie Davidson, Sierra Madre, Calif., 8 x 8 In. $65.00

Enamel, Vase, Flowers, Burgundy Ground, Oval, Limoges, Signed Camille F'aure, 7 In. $1150.00

Enamel, Vase, Woman, In Woodlands, Copper, Signed, Louit, France, 4 In. $351.00

E

ES Germany, Bowl, Portrait, Spring Scene, Prov SXE Backstamp, 9 In. $270.00

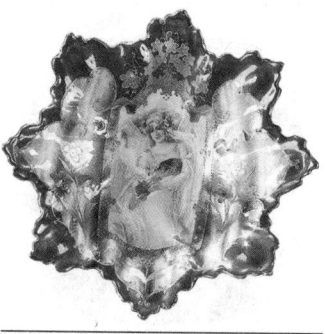

Eskimo, Purse, Sealskin, Embroidered, Carved Bone Seal Effigy Button, c.1900, 4 x 5 ½ In. $300.00

Faience, Plate, Moravian Provincial, Guitarist, Holiday Dress, Fern & Flower Border, 12 In. $108.00

Plaque, Aristocratic Woman, Gilt Frame, 19th Century, 8 ¾ x 6 ¾ In.	1600.00
Plaque, Copper, Farrier Shoeing Horse Scene, Frame, Continental, c.1920, 10 x 7 In.	236.00
Plaque, Sorrowful Madonna At Base Of Cross, Limoges, 19th Century, 5 In.	360.00
Plaque, Zeus, Burning City, Metal Frame, c.1800, 4 ⅜ x 3 ⅝ In.	633.00
Plate, Copper, Amber, White Dots, 6 In.	65.00
Plate, Copper, Yellow, Sierra Madre, California, 8 In.	85.00
Plate, Gold Ground, Green Leaves, Annemarie Davidson, Sierra Madre, Calif., 8 x 8 In. ......*illus*	65.00
Pot, Casserole, Open, Red Koben Style, 10 x 13 In.	100.00
Powder Jar, Silver, Champleve, Scrolls, Cyrillic Monogram, Garnets, Russia, 3 In.	5490.00
Tea Caddy Spoon, Silver, Red, Blue, White Flowers, Russia, 1908-17	207.00
Tray, Gold Green, Teal & Orange Blob Decoration, Bovano, 8 ½ x 8 ½ In.	40.00
Vase, Bamboo, Translucent Red, Granulated Ground, Baluster, Silver Foil Rim, Japan, 10 In. .	1180.00
Vase, Bulbous Body, Pearl To Citron, Flowers, France, 4 In.	60.00
Vase, Cylindrical, Red Orange, Vallenti, Italy, 11 x 4 In.	225.00
Vase, Flowers, Burgundy Ground, Oval, Limoges, Signed Camille Faure, 7 In. ....*illus*	1150.00
Vase, Gentleman, With Spectacles, Limoges, 4 In.	600.00
Vase, Portrait, Woman, Landscape, Limoges, c.1900, 4 ¾ In.	368.00
Vase, Stylized Flowers, Leaves, Red, Green, Gold Ground, Copper, Camille Faure, 8 ½ In.	5900.00
Vase, Stylized Leaves, Ovoid, Impressed Mark, WMF, Cherub, 6 In.	35.00
Vase, Sweet Peas, Multicolored, Oval, Signed, Faure, Limoges, c.1950, 6 In.	1850.00
Vase, Woman, In Woodlands, Copper, Signed Louit, France, 4 In. ....*illus*	351.00
Vase, Woman, Landscape, 2-Sided, Gilt, Footed, Limoges, c.1900, 4 ¾ In.	360.00
Vase, Woman, Long Brown Hair, Reclining, Flowers, Pink, Limoges, 18th Century, 4 ½ In.	710.00
Vase, Yellow Ground, Multicolored, Ruffled Edge, Footed, Stevens & Williams, 13 In.	263.00

ERPHILA is a mark found on Czechoslovakian and other pottery and porcelain made after 1920. This mark was used on items imported by Ebeling & Reuss, Philadelphia, a giftware firm that is still operating in Pennsylvania. The mark is a combination of the letters *E* and *R* (Ebeling & Reuss) and the first letters of the city, Phila(delphia). Many whimsical figural pitchers and creamers, figurines, platters, and other giftwares carry this mark.

Cake Plate, Floral Garlands, Bouquets, Gold Trim, Marked, Germany, 11 ¼ In.	36.00
Figurine, Dog, Japanese Spaniel, Sitting, Black & White, Marked, Germany, 4 x 4 ½ In.	65.00
Figurine, Scarf Dancer, Nude Woman On Water, Stamped, Germany, c.1925, 7 In.	125.00
Grou, 2 Pheasants, Bisque, 24K Gold Trim, Marked Germany, c.1886	49.00
Pitcher, Cover, Orange, Czechoslovakia, c.1925, 9 In.	70.00
Pitcher, Girl, Holding Flowers, Green Hat, c.1930, 6 In.	50.00
Pitcher, Goat, Red, Black, Yellow, Marked, Czechoslovakia, 8 ½ In.	795.00
Pitcher, Granny, White Dress, Orange Polka Dots, Orange Hat, Marked, Germany, 6 In.	8.00
Pitcher, Lime Green Ribbed Body, Cat Handle, Black Ears, Marked, Germany, 7 ½ In.	195.00
Pitcher, Toucan, Red, Black, Yellow, Czechoslovakia, 9 ¼ In.	486.00
Teapot, Pig, Gold Paper Label, Impressed AK722, Germany, 7 ½ In.	215.00

ES GERMANY porcelain was made at the factory of Erdmann Schlegelmilch from 1861 to 1937 in Suhl, Germany. The porcelain, marked *ES Germany* or *ES Suhl*, was sold decorated or undecorated. Other pieces were made at a factory in Saxony, Prussia, and are marked *ES Prussia*. Reinhold Schlegelmilch made the famous wares marked *RS Germany*.

Bowl, Portrait, Spring Scene, Prov SXE Backstamp, 9 In. ....*illus*	270.00
Cake Plate, Cobalt Blue, Yellow Rose, 2 Handles, Prov Saxe, 11 In.	50.00

ESKIMO artifacts of all types are collected. Carvings of whale or walrus teeth are listed under Scrimshaw. Baskets are in the Basket category. All other types of Eskimo art are listed here. In Canada and some other areas, the term *Inuit* is used instead of Eskimo.

Bag, Soft Bladder, Embroidered, Flowers, Drawstring, 7 ⅜ In.	248.00
Basket, Cover, Coiled Bands, V-Shaped Designs, Bulbous, 7 In.	403.00
Basket, Multicolored, Bird & Butterfly Forms, Lid, c.1950, 12 x 11 In.	431.00
Box, Cigar, Wood, Greenland, Ivory Decoration, 3 x 6 ¾ In.	3525.00
Cribbage Board, Ivory, Seal Supports, Otter Tail Plug, c.1975, 2 x 19 x 3 In.	1035.00
Cribbage Board, Walrus Tusk, 16 ¼ In.	529.00
Figure Set, Rachel, Seal Hunter, Kunuk, C. Alan Johnson, 1962, 3 Piece	715.00
Figure, Eskimo & Seal In Kayak, 13 x 4 In., 3 Piece	402.00
Figure, Eskimo Pulling Seal, 7 In.	546.00
Figure, Frog Crouching, Knife & Pan In Hands, Inuit, 2 ¾ x 5 In.	226.00
Figure, Hunter, Stone, Inuit, 5 X 5 x 4 In.	232.00
Figure, Inuit, Eskimo On Polar Bear, Adrel Vasseka, 10 x 11 In.	761.00
Figure, Inuit, Walrus Bone, Eskimos In Kayak, Signed, Ken Heindel, 5 x 11 In.	468.00

Figure, Man Wrestling Polar Bear, Soapstone, Carved, 11 x 9 In.	748.00
Figure, Mother Pulling Swaddled Child, Soapstone, Carved, 9 ¼ In.	460.00
Figure, Rapa-Nui, Easter Island, Whalebone, 19th Century, 10 ¾ In.	820.00
Figure, Walrus, Reclining, Inuit, 5 In.	96.00
Figure, Walrus, Stone, Carved, Signed, Bekoalook, 3 ½ x 5 ½ In.	24.00
Mask, Ingalik, Grouse Dance, Wood, Carved, Painted, Early 20th Century	600.00
Pipe, Ivory, Bering Sea, Flared Bowl, 4-Faced Figure, Whales, Loons, c.1875, 15 In.	11162.00
Purse, Sealskin, Embroidered, Carved Bone Seal Effigy Button, c.1900, 4 x 5 ½ In. .... *illus*	300.00
Snowshoes, Bentwood Frame, Leather Harness, Woven Sinew Decking, c.1900s, 30 In., Pair ..	118.00

FABERGE was a firm of jewelers and goldsmiths founded in St. Petersburg, Russia, in 1842, by Gustav Faberge. Peter Carl Faberge, his son, was jeweler to the Russian Imperial Court from about 1870 to 1917. The rare Imperial Easter eggs, jewelry, and decorative items are very expensive today. **ФАБЕРЖЕ КФ**

Beaker, Leaf Scroll, Enameled, Gold Washed, Beaded Leaves, Oak Case, 1908-17, 2 ¼ In., Pair.	4740.00
Bowl, Copper, Double-Headed Eagle, War 1914 In Cyrillic, Faberge, 4 ¼ In.	4200.00
Case, Jewelers, Green Leather, Hinged Lid, Chamois Interior, Stamped Faberge, 15 x 10 In.	3600.00
Clock, Carriage, Gold Wash Silver, Green Enamel, Diamond Encrusted, Eagle Mounts, 4 x 3 x 2 In.	5100.00
Dish, Cut Glass, Silver Rim, Reeded, Ribbons, Oak Fitted Case, 10 ¼ In.	9775.00
Letter Opener, Gold On Silver, Enamel, Diamond Encrusted, Elephant Head Handle, 9 ¾ In.	1450.00
Spoon, Gold Wash, Silver, Twist Handle, Flowers, Leaves	690.00

FAIENCE refers to tin-glazed earthenware, especially the wares made in France, Germany, and Scandinavia. It is also correct to say that faience is the same as majolica or Delft, although usually the term refers only to the tin-glazed pottery of the three regions mentioned.

Bowl, Man Carrying Sword, Cross & Shovel, Je Suis Las De Les Porter, France, 10 In.	115.00
Charger, Floral, Banded, Multicolored, Purple, Yellow, Green, 18th Century, 11 ¾ In.	235.00
Charger, Fruit Basket Center, Husk & Leaf Serpentine Border, 13 In.	173.00
Charger, Scalloped Rim, Painted, Pastoral Landscape, Country Figures, 1800s, 14 In.	104.00
Ewer, Flowers, Gilt, Blue, Gold Handles, Mark, New York, c.1885, 12 In.	575.00
Jar, Bow-Knotted Floral Pendants, Blue & White, Domed Cover, Basket Weave, 10 In., Pair	144.00
Jar, Tin Glazed, Jesus, Lamb, Cross, Blue, Yellow, c.1750, 11 In.	8813.00
Jardinere, Globular, Blue, Green, Tan Crane, Passion Flower, J. Vieillard & Co., 12 x 17 In.	978.00
Jug, Figural, Potbellied Man, Medieval Costume, Yellow Clogs, Handle, 12 In.	374.00
Plaque, Portrait, Woman, Ruffles, Hat With Ostrich Feathers, Coraline Ground, France, 20 In.	889.00
Plate, Moravian Provincial, Guitarist, Holiday Dress, Fern & Flower Border, 12 In. ....*illus*	108.00
Salt, 2-Sided Women, Holding Bowls, Blue, Red, Gilt, Late 1800s, 7 In.	110.00
Tureen, Soup, Painted, Geometric, Flowers, Leaves, Rouen, c.1920, 12 ½ x 21 In.	754.00
Urn, Cover, Tuscan, Yellow, Cream Glaze, Twist Handles, Scrolled Acanthus, 23 x 16 ½ In.	235.00
Urn, Tuscan, Yellow, Cream, Applied Swag, 16 ¼ x 13 In.	276.00
Urn, Twin Female Mask Handles, Applied Swags, Flowers, Painted, Square Foot, 9 In.	186.00
Vase, Painted Flowers, Green Ground, Squat, Egg Shape, Angular Handles, France, 5 x 9 In. ..	296.00

FAIRINGS are small souvenir boxes and figurines that were sold at country fairs during the nineteenth century. Most were made in Germany. Reproductions of fairings are being made, especially of the famous *Twelve Months after Marriage* series.

Box, Child With Cross, Reclining, Pink Blanket, Bisque, 2 ¼ x 3 In.	78.00
Figurine, Pink Pig, Wheeling His Own Baby, On Carriage, Germany, 3 ½ In.	59.00
Figurine, Woman Up On The Bed, Man Crawling, A Mouse, A Mouse, 3 x 3 ½ In.	55.00
Trinket Box, Dresser, Mirror, Molded Binoculars, Pipe, Book, Telescope, Victorian, 3 x 4 In.	75.00
Trinket Box, Gentleman's Bureau, Pocket Watch, Signet Ring, Cologne Bottles	125.00
Trinket Box, Homing Pigeon, 2 ½ x 2 ¾ In.	95.00
Trinket Box, Young Woman Sitting In Wicker Hamper, 3 ¼ In.	175.00

FAIRYLAND LUSTER *pieces are included in the Wedgwood category.*

FAMILLE ROSE, *see Chinese Export category.*

FANS have been used for cooling since the days of the ancients. By the eighteenth century, the fan was an accessory for the lady of fashion and very elaborate and expensive fans were made. Sticks were made of ivory or wood, set with jewels or carved. The fans were made of painted silk or paper. Inexpensive paper fans printed with advertising were giveaways in the late nineteenth and early twentieth centuries. Electric fans were introduced in 1882.

Bamboo, Painted, Courting Couple, Musician, Rose, Picture Box Frame, 16 ½ In. ....*illus*	153.00
Court Scene, Figures, Painted, Mother-Of-Pearl, Gold Inlay, Frame, Early 1800s, 20 x 12 In. .	121.00

Fan, Bamboo, Painted, Courting Couple, Musician, Rose, Picture Box Frame, 16 ½ In. $153.00

Fan, Electric, Westinghouse, Brass Mounted, 16 In. $230.00

Fan, Ivory, 16 Sticks, Carved, Wheat Sheaves, Morning Glories, Leaves, 1800s, 9 ½ In. $360.00

Fan, Ivory, Hand Painted, Social Gathering Scene, Castle Ruins, Vernis Martin, 1700s, 8 x 14 In. $1150.00

Fenton, Aqua Crest, Vase, Ruffled Edge, Milk Glass Base, Iridescence, 7 In. $75.00

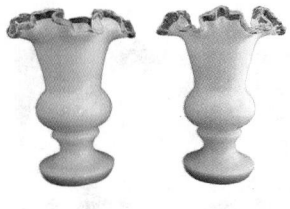

Fenton, Bubble Optic, Pitcher, Honey Amber Overlay, 70 Oz., 8 ¾ x 8 In. $175.00

Fenton Art Glass, Burmese, Vase, Coral Pink Flowers, Yellow Ground, Ruffled Rim, 5 x 7 In. $95.00

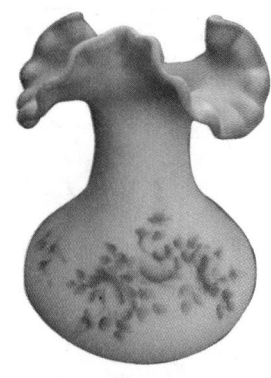

Fenton, Chevron, Vase, Rose, Signed Minnie Cooper, 1940s, 8 x 5 ¾ In. $120.00

Electric, Brass Mounted, Brass Cage, 4 Blades, Westinghouse, 16 In.	230.00
Electric, Emerson, 3-Speed, 4 12 In.-Brass Blades, 17 ½ In.	300.00
Electric, Emerson, Silver Swan, 18 In.	81.00
Electric, Emerson Type, No. 27666, 6 Brass Blades, Black Enamel Stands, 3-Speed, 19 x 13 In.	190.00
Electric, General Electric, Brass, 4 Blades, 13 In.	20.00
Electric, General Electric, Brass, 6 Blades, 13 In.	65.00
Electric, General Electric, Residential, 6 Brass Blades, 3-Speed, Oscillates, 20 ¼ x 17 ½ In.	165.00
Electric, Marelli Partners, 4 Brass Blades, No. 3154652, Italy, 18 ½ x 12 ½ In.	290.00
Electric, Robbins & Myers, Brass, 4 Blades, 13 In.	20.00
Electric, Westinghouse, Brass Mounted, 16 In. ....*illus*	230.00
Fly, Cast Iron Base, Brown & Gold Paint, Horizontal Fabric Paddles, 1880s, 30 x 50 In.	3720.00
Ivory, 16 Sticks, Carved, Wheat Sheaves, Morning Glories, Leaves, 1800s, 9 ½ In. .....*illus*	360.00
Ivory, Classical Figures, Birds, Animals, Cherubs, Painted, c.1885, 9 In.	237.00
Ivory, Hand Painted, Social Gathering Scene, Castle Ruins, Vernis Martin, 1700s, 8 x 14 In. *illus*	1150.00
Ivory, White Feathers, Asian Figures, Flowers, Fruit, Peacock Feather Caps, Chinese, 15 x 23 In.	144.00
Mother-Of-Pearl, Hand Painted, Courting Scene, Gold Handle, Lace, Gold Beading, Tiffany, 8 In.	201.00
Mother-Of-Pearl, Paper, Painted, Maiden Fishing In Stream, Gold Trim, France, 33 In.	179.00
Mother-Of-Pearl, Women, Landscape, Hand Painted, Victorian, 11 In.	88.00
Papier-Mache, Flowers, Black, Mother-Of-Pearl, Cutout Rim, Handle, 19th Century, 16 ½ In., Pair	333.00
Punkah, Ceiling, Walnut & Cherrywood, Trapezoidal, Arched Top, Fitted Stand, 1800s, 69 x 32 In.	420.00
Sleepy Eye Flour, Indian, Die Cut, Cardboard, 13 ⅝ x 6 In.	275.00
Zig Zag Confections, Honeycomb Tissue Paper, Premium, D.L. Clark, 17 ½ x 6 ¾ In.	35.00

FAST FOOD COLLECTIBLES *may be included in several categories, such as Advertising, Coca-Cola, Toy, etc.*

FEDERZEICHNUNG, *see Loetz category.*

FENTON ART GLASS COMPANY, founded in Martins Ferry, Ohio, by Frank L. Fenton, is now located in Williamstown, West Virginia. It is noted for early carnival glass produced between 1907 and 1920. Some of these pieces are listed in the Carnival Glass category. Many other types of glass were also made. The pottery closed in 2007.

American Craftsman, Plate, Madonna With Sleeping Child, 10 In.	50.00
Aqua Crest, Basket, Handle, 5 In.	70.00
Aqua Crest, Bowl, c.1941, 7 In.	19.00
Aqua Crest, Vase, Footed, Ruffled Edge, 4 In.	15.00
Aqua Crest, Vase, Footed, Ruffled Edge, 6 In.	47.00
Aqua Crest, Vase, Ruffled Edge, Milk Glass Base, Iridescence, 7 In. ....*illus*	75.00
Blackberry Spray, Bowl, Hat Shape, Marigold, Iridescent, 1908	40.00
Blue Burmese, Vase, Hobnail, 3 In.	50.00
Blue Burmese, Vase, Rose Edge Top, 5 In.	60.00
Bubble Optic, Pitcher, Honey Amber Overlay, 70 Oz., 8 ¾ x 8 In. ....*illus*	175.00
Burmese, Vase, Coral Pink Flowers, Yellow Ground, Ruffled Rim, 5 x 7 In. ....*illus*	95.00
Burmese, Vase, Floral Breeze, 13 In.	150.00
Burmese, Vase, Glossy, Sample, 4 In.	65.00
Burmese, Vase, Jack-In-The-Pulpit, Hand Painted, C. Evans, 10 In.	80.00
Burmese, Vase, Tricolor, 7 In.	45.00
Butterfly & Berry, Bowl, Footed, Golden, c.1911-25, 5 In.	35.00
Butterfly & Berry, Tumbler, Panels, Dark Blue, Iridescent, c.1920, 4 x 2 ¾ In.	65.00
Candlestick, Gold Crest, Cornucopia Shape	37.00
Cattail & Water Lily, Pitcher, Water, Chocolate Glass, 9 In.	3508.00
Chevron, Vase, Rose, Signed, Minnie Cooper, 1940s, 8 x 5 ¾ In. ....*illus*	120.00
Coin Dot, Creamer, Blue Opalescent	46.00
Coin Dot, Lamp, Blue Opalescent	135.00
Coin Dot, Lamp, Electric, Butterscotch Opalescent, Brass, 17 ½ In.	225.00
Coin Dot, Plate, Topaz Opalescent, Ruffled Edge, c.1959-61, 6 In.	100.00
Coin Dot, Rose Bowl, Topaz Opalescent, 4 In.	85.00
Coin Dot, Vase, Blue Iridescent, Bulbous, 8 ½ In.	85.00
Coin Dot, Vase, Cranberry Opalescent, 2 Handles, 8 In.	250.00
Coin Dot, Vase, Cranberry Opalescent, Crimped, Pinched, 6 In. ....*illus*	85.00
Coin Dot, Vase, Cranberry Opalescent, Lampshade Shape, 6 x 7 In.	185.00
Coin Dot, Vase, Lime Green Opalescent, Ruffled Edge, c.1953, 8 In.	125.00
Coin Dot, Vase, Topaz, c.1960, 7 ½ In.	125.00
Coin Dot, Vase, Topaz Opalescent, Ruffled Edge, c.1960, 8 In.	200.00
Coin Dot, Water Set, Cranberry Opalescent, Ice Lip, 6 Ball Shaped Tumblers, 1940s	515.00
Coinspot, Lemonade, Green Opalescent	40.00

Coinspot, Pitcher, Water, Opalescent...	155.00
Cruet, Dragonfly, Flowers, Iridized Vaseline Opalescent, Teardrop Stopper, T. Kelley, 6 ¾ In. ...	83.00
Cut & Cable, Bowl, Rose, White Satin Finish, Levay Glass, c.1980, 4 In.	45.00
Daisy & Button, Hat, Blue Opalescent, 5 In.	22.00
Daisy & Button, Shoe, Milk Glass, Signed	5.00
Daisy & Fern, Barber Bottle, Stopper, Cranberry Opalescent	375.00
Diamond Optic, Vase, Ruby Overlay, Double Crimped Top, 7 ½ In. ....*illus*	35.00
Dogwood, Bell, Blue Cameo	45.00
Egg, Apple Tree Design, Blue, Gold, 3 ¾ In.	42.00
Egg, Gold Butterfly, Sea Green, Flowers, White, Purple, Green, Signed, Label, 3 ¾ In.	45.00
Egg, No. 5145, Roses On Custard, Pink, Blue Flowers, Green Leaves, Gold, c.1997, 3 ¾ In.	45.00
Egg, No. 5146, French Opal Dragon Fly, Floral, Gold Accents, c.1998........................	55.00
Emerald Crest, Compote, Ruffled Edge, c.1948-53	45.00
Epergne, 5-Lily, 14 In.	235.00
Figurine, Alley Cat, Purple Iridescent, 10 ½ In. ....*illus*	73.00
Figurine, Frog, Purple, White Satin, Blue..	25.00
Figurine, Heart Throb Bear Cub, Clear, c.1990, 3 ½ In.	48.00
Flower Bowl, Elephant, Opaque Black, c.1925, 6 ¾ x 8 ¾ In.	330.00
Georgian, Sherbet, Ruby, 6 Oz., 4 ⅜ In.	18.00
Grape & Cable, Bowl, Fruit, Persian Medallion, Blue......................................	105.00
Grape & Cable, Bowl, Fruit, Persian Medallion, Green.....................................	215.00
Hearts & Flowers, Bowl, 12 Ruffles, Rayed, Domed Foot, 4 x 10 In.	100.00
Historic America, Wine, Fort Dearborn, c.1937, 4 ½ In., Pair	80.00
Hobnail, Basket, Blue Opalescent, 4 ½ In.	40.00
Hobnail, Basket, Blue, Oval, Handle, 7 In.	52.00
Hobnail, Basket, Cranberry, Opalescent, 10 In.	75.00
Hobnail, Bowl, Footed, Milk Glass, 7 x 11 ¼ In.	55.00
Hobnail, Bowl, Plum Opalescent, Ruffled Rim, c.1960, 5 ½ In.	34.00
Hobnail, Candy Dish, Milk Glass, Handle, Signed	12.00
Hobnail, Cruet, Oil, Cranberry Opalescent, Original Stopper.............................	185.00
Hobnail, Cruet, Stopper, French Opalescent..	75.00
Hobnail, Dresser Set, Blue Opalescent, Powder Dish With Lid, 2 Perfumes, Stoppers.............	115.00
Hobnail, Jug, Cranberry Opalescent, 80 Oz.	350.00
Hobnail, Perfume, French Opalescent, Stopper, 4 ½ In.	30.00
Hobnail, Rose Bowl, Egg Shape, Amber, 3 Toes, 4 ¾ x 3 In. ....*illus*	15.00
Hobnail, Salt & Pepper, Cranberry Opalescent, c.1945....................................	100.00
Hobnail, Sugar & Creamer, Covered Mustard, Blue Opalescent..........................	45.00
Hobnail, Toothpick, Green Opalescent, 2 x 2 ½ In.	15.00
Hobnail, Tumbler, Various Colors, 4 In., 8 Piece	115.00
Hobnail, Vase, Amberina, 3 ⅞ In.	18.00
Hobnail, Vase, Blue Opalescent, Ruffled Edge, 5 In.	55.00
Hobnail, Vase, Bud, Green Opalescent, c.1960, 8 In.	37.00
Hobnail, Vase, Fan Shape, Vaseline, 9 In.	145.00
Hobnail, Vase, Fan, Topaz Opalescent, 9 In.	145.00
Hobnail, Vase, Milk Glass, 11 In.	55.00
Hobnail, Vase, Springtime Green, Flared & Rolled Edge, 1977, 5 In.	12.00
Hobnail, Water Set, Blue Opalescent, 80 Oz. Jug, 8 Tumblers............................	500.00
Lamp, Pancake, Acid Cut Back, Pink, Allover Flower Pattern, 1931......................	450.00
Lampshade, Cranberry, Opalescent, 5 In.	55.00
Mandarin Red, Candlestick, Single Lite, 4 ⅜ x 3 ¼ In.	85.00
Ming, Vase, c.1936, 11 ½ x 7 ½ In. ....*illus*	95.00
Olde Virginia, Nut Dish, c.1970, 3 ½ x 4 ½ In.	20.00
Olde Virginia, Vase, Milk Glass, 14 ½ In.	25.00
Orange Tree, Creamer, Blue, 6 x 3 In.	32.00
Panels, Vase, Ice Green, 12 In.	40.00
Peach Crest, Basket, Handle, 5 In.	60.00
Peach Crest, Basket, Ruffled Edge, Handle, 1941-67, 7 In.	42.00 to 72.00
Peach Crest, Candlestick, c.1941-67, 5 In., Pair	87.00
Peach Crest, Hat, 4 In.	35.00
Peach Crest, Pitcher, Ruffled Rim, Ivy, 9 In.	125.00
Peach Crest, Vase, 1941-67, 5 In.	28.00
Peach Crest, Vase, Footed, Ribbed, 9 In.	110.00
Peach Crest, Vase, Gourd Shape, Ribbed, 6 In.	25.00
Pink Chiffon, Basket, White, Pink Flowers, Twisted Handles, Signed Raddish, 4 ½ x 3 In.	55.00
Poppy, Vase, Lime Sherbet Satin, 7 In.	35.00
Ribs, Optic, Vase, Blue, Signed On Bottom, 11 In.	35.00

Fenton, Coin Dot, Vase, Cranberry Opalescent, Crimped, Pinched, 6 In. $85.00

Fenton, Diamond Optic, Vase, Ruby Overlay, Double Crimped Top, 7 ½ In. $35.00

Fenton, Figurine, Alley Cat, Purple Iridescent, 10 ½ In. $73.00

F

Fenton, Hobnail, Rose Bowl,
Egg Shape, Amber, 3 Toes, 4 ¾ x 3 In.
$15.00

Fenton, Ming, Vase, c.1936,
11 ½ x 7 ½ In.
$95.00

Fenton, Stretch Glass, Tumble-Up,
Celeste Blue, Optic Rib, Iridescent,
Cobalt Handle, 7 & 3 ⅝ In., 2 Piece
$217.00

Rosalene, Vase, 3-Footed, Grapes	50.00
Rosalene, Vase, White Flowers, Hummingbird, 9 ½ In.	125.00
Rose, Basket, Handle, 7 In.	75.00
Rose, Jug, c.1940, 9 In.	70.00
Silver Crest, Basket, Hat, White Handle, 1924, 3 ½ In.	45.00
Silver Crest, Cake Stand, 5 x 13 In.	50.00
Silver Crest, Candy Dish, Footed, Cover, Finial, 9 ½ x 6 ¾ In.	80.00
Silver Crest, Vase, 4 In.	30.00
Silver Crest, Vase, 12 ¾ In.	55.00
Silver Crest, Vase, Long Neck, Ruffled Edge, 7 In.	18.00
Stag & Holly, Bowl, Pink, 10 ¾ In.	44.00
Stippled Rays, Bowl, Green, Ruffled, Collar Base, 9 ½ x 2 ¾ In.	55.00
Stretch Glass, Basket, Pink, Pedestal, 10 ½ In.	30.00
Stretch Glass, Tumble-Up, Celeste Blue, Optic Rib, Iridescent, Cobalt Handle, 7 & 3 ⅝ In., 2 Piece *illus*	217.00
Swan, Salt, Ice Green, Frosty Iridescence, Spoon, 1900s, 3 ¾ x 2 ¾ In.	35.00
Thin Rib, Vase, Blue, 16 In.	40.00
Thin Rib, Vase, Marigold, 15 In.	15.00
Thumbprint, Bowl, Cranberry, Footed, Crimped Rim, 6 ½ In.	40.00
Vasa Murrhina, Basket, Rose Aventurine, 7 In. *illus*	125.00
Vase, Fan Shape, Cobalt Glass, Red, Yellow Mosaic, Overall Blue Threading, 9 In.	2000.00
Water Lily, Candy Box, Rosalene	75.00
Water Set, Red Pitcher, 4 Glasses With Embossed Flowers	225.00

FIESTA, the colorful dinnerware, was introduced in 1936 by the Homer Laughlin China Co., redesigned in 1969, and withdrawn in 1973. It was reissued again in 1986 in different colors and is still being made. New colors, including some that are similar to old colors, are introduced regularly. The simple design was characterized by a band of concentric circles beginning at the rim. Cups had full-circle handles until 1969, when partial-circle handles were made. Harlequin and Riviera were related wares. For more prices, go to kovels.com.

Chartreuse, Bowl, Dessert, 6 In.	35.00
Chartreuse, Casserole, Cover	95.00
Chartreuse, Plate, Dinner, 10 In.	65.00
Chartreuse, Platter, 12 ¾ In.	75.00
Chartreuse, Saucer	5.00
Chartreuse, Soup, Cream	28.00
Cobalt Blue, Carafe	155.00
Cobalt Blue, Chop Plate, 13 In.	25.00
Cobalt Blue, Coffeepot, Cover	250.00
Cobalt Blue, Creamer, Ring Handle	25.00
Cobalt Blue, Mixing Bowl, No. 4	200.00
Cobalt Blue, Nappy, 8 ½ In.	46.00
Cobalt Blue, Pitcher, Disk	15.00
Cobalt Blue, Plate, Bread & Butter, 6 ¼ In.	7.00
Cobalt Blue, Plate, Dinner, 10 In.	35.00
Cobalt Blue, Serving Bowl, 8 ½ In.	5.00
Cobalt Blue, Sugar	10.00
Cobalt Blue, Teapot, 6 Cup	40.00
Cobalt Blue, Tray, Figure 8	90.00
Cobalt Blue, Tray, Relish, 5 Sections	276.00
Forest Green, Bowl, Fruit, 4 ¾ In.	40.00
Forest Green, Nappy	32.00
Forest Green, Pitcher, Disk	149.00
Forest Green, Soup, Dish	55.00
Gray, Bowl, Cereal, 6 ¼ In.	45.00
Gray, Plate, Dinner, 10 In.	55.00
Gray, Platter, Oval, 12 ½ In.	62.00
Gray, Saucer	5.00
Gray, Soup, Dish	30.00 to 55.00
Green, Vase, 8 In.	650.00
Ivory, Bowl, Cereal, 6 ¼ In.	45.00
Ivory, Calendar Plate, 1954, Signed Back, 10 ¼ In.	90.00
Ivory, Candlestick, Bulb, Pair	140.00
Ivory, Mixing Bowl, No. 4	55.00
Ivory, Mug, Tom & Jerry	60.00
Ivory, Plate, 3 Compartments, 10 ⅜ In.	30.00

Ivory, Plate, Dessert, 7 In.	10.00
Ivory, Platter, 12 ½ In.	43.00
Ivory, Sauceboat	45.00
Ivory, Tumbler, Juice, 3 ½ In.	28.00
Ivory, Tumbler, Water, 4 ½ In.	70.00
Ivory, Vase, 8 In.	45.00
Ivory, Vase, 12 In.	2500.00
Light Green, Bowl, Oatmeal, 6 In.	35.00
Light Green, Carafe	81.00
Light Green, Creamer, Ring Handle	22.00 to 26.00
Light Green, Jug, 2 Pt.	80.00
Light Green, Mixing Bowl, No. 2	92.00
Light Green, Plate, Bread & Butter, 7 ½ In.	8.00 to 9.00
Light Green, Utility, Tray, 10 ½ In.	12.00
Light Green, Vase, 8 In.	595.00
Medium Green, Bowl, Salad, 11 ½ In.	76.00
Medium Green, Cup & Saucer	38.00
Medium Green, Mug	115.00
Medium Green, Plate, Bread & Butter, 6 ⅜ In.	21.00
Medium Green, Salt & Pepper, Ball Shape	175.00
Medium Green, Vase, Bud, 6 ½ In.	68.00
Old Ivory, Chop Plate, 13 In.	18.00
Red, Carafe	250.00
Red, Casserole, Cover Only, 8 In.	22.00
Red, Creamer, Stick Handle, 4 ⅝ In.	25.00
Red, Kitchen Kraft, Cake Server, 9 ½ In.	190.00
Red, Mixing Bowl, No. 4	1100.00
Red, Pitcher, Disk	150.00
Red, Pitcher, Ice, Lip, 6 ½ In.	165.00
Red, Syrup, Drip Cut Lid, 5 ¾ In.	450.00
Red, Tumbler, Juice, 3 ½ In.	65.00
Red, Tumbler, Water, 4 ½ In.	70.00 to 75.00
Rose, Bowl, Cereal, 6 ¼ In.	47.00
Rose, Bowl, Soup, Cream	66.00
Rose, Butter, Cover	10.00
Rose, Creamer	49.00
Rose, Mug, Tom & Jerry	60.00
Rose, Plate, Deep, 8 In.	60.00
Rose, Plate, Dinner, 10 In.	65.00
Rose, Plate, Salad, 7 ½ In.	7.99
Rose, Platter, 12 ½ In.	45.00
Rose, Saucer	5.00 to 10.00
Rose, Soup, Dish	12.00
Rose, Tumbler, Juice, 3 ½ In.	35.00
Turquoise, Ashtray, 5 ½ In.	75.00
Turquoise, Candleholder, Tripod, Pair	625.00
Turquoise, Carafe	150.00
Turquoise, Casserole, Cover, 9 ¾ In.	75.00 to 80.00
Turquoise, Chop Plate, 11 ¾ In.	12.50
Turquoise, Coffeepot	17.50
Turquoise, Mug	30.00
Turquoise, Nappy, 8 ½ In.	25.00
Turquoise, Pitcher, Disk	36.00
Turquoise, Salt & Pepper, Ball Shape	22.00
Turquoise, Soup, Dish	28.00
Turquoise, Teapot, Cover, 6 Cup	160.00
Yellow, Bowl, Casserole	135.00
Yellow, Candleholder, Bulb, 4 In.	50.00
Yellow, Carafe	185.00
Yellow, Coffeepot, Cover	195.00
Yellow, Cup	25.00
Yellow, Cup & Saucer	10.00
Yellow, Mixing Bowl, No. 6	184.00
Yellow, Pitcher, Ice, Ball Shape	115.00
Yellow, Pitcher, Juice	40.00
Yellow, Pitcher, Juice, Disk	60.00

Fenton, Vasa Murrhina, Basket, Rose Aventurine, 7 In. $125.00

Findlay Onyx, Sugar, Cover, Ivory Onyx, Platinum Flowers, Gilt, 5 ¾ x 4 In. $46.00

TIP
New security idea: Have one of the neighbors park a second car in your driveway. Your house will look occupied and the car will be seen coming and going.

Firefighting, Bucket, Tub, Red Leather,
Painted 1, Handle, 11 ½ In., Pair
$4125.00

Firefighting, Fire Mark, F.A.,
Embossed Snake, Cast Iron, 11 In.
$29.00

Firefighting, Fire Mark,
Fireman's Assoc., Philadelphia, Iron,
Oval, F.A., Hydrant, 7 ½ x 12 In.
$116.00

Firefighting, Grenade,
California Fire Extinguisher,
Walking Bear, Amber, c.1900, 6 ½ In.
$6900.00

Yellow, Plate, 3 Compartments, 10 ⅜ In.	30.00
Yellow, Plate, Deep, 8 ⅜ In.	16.00
Yellow, Plate, Dinner, 10 In.	21.00
Yellow, Plate, Salad, 7 ¼ In.	8.00
Yellow, Sugar, Ring Handle	30.00
Yellow, Teapot, 6 Cup.	65.00
Yellow, Tumbler, Water, 4 ½ In.	30.00 to 80.00
Yellow, Utility Tray.	65.00

FINCH, *see Kay Finch category.*

FINDLAY ONYX AND FLORADINE are two similar types of glass made by Dalzell, Gilmore and Leighton Co. of Findlay, Ohio, about 1889. Onyx is a patented yellowish white opaque glass with raised silver daisy decorations. A few rare pieces were made of rose, amber, orange, or purple glass. Floradine is made of cranberry-colored glass with an opalescent white raised floral pattern and a satin finish. The same molds were used for both types of glass.

Butter, Cover, Opal Glass, Silver Inclusions, 6 In.	805.00
Butter, Floradine, Opalescent Finial, 6 In.	4370.00
Creamer, Opal, Silver Inclusions, Opalescent Handle, 4 ½ In.	311.00
Pitcher, Bulbous, Ivory Opalescent, Molded Silver Flowers, Leaves, Handles, 4 ½ In.	144.00
Pitcher, Bulbous, Pink, Opalescent Molded Purple Flowers & Leaves, 4 ½ In.	863.00
Pitcher, Cream, Floradine, Opalescent, 4 ½ In.	1035.00
Pitcher, Syrup, Opal Glass, Silver Detail, Metal Spout, Handle, 7 ½ In.	518.00
Salt, Amber, Pale Cranberry Inclusions, Opal, Cased, 3 In.	5864.00
Saltshaker, Opal Glass, Silver Inclusions, 3 In.	431.00
Sugar Shaker, Floradine, Metal Lid, 5 ½ In.	17250.00
Sugar Shaker, Pearlized Ground, Flowers, Leaves, Gray Tones, 5 ¼ In.	500.00
Sugar, Cover, Ivory Onyx, Platinum Flowers, Gilt, 5 ¾ x 4 In. ....*illus*	46.00
Sugar, Opal Glass, Silver Details, 6 In.	431.00
Toothpick, Bulbous, Opaline Glass, Silver Flowers, Cinched, Scalloped Rim	316.00
Toothpick, Floradine, Bulbous, Ruby Red, White Flowers, Cinched, Scalloped Rim	1955.00
Tumbler, Barrel Shape, Amber, Cranberry Inclusions, 3 ½ In.	3565.00
Tumbler, Silver Inclusions, Opal Glass, 3 ½ In.	920.00

FIREFIGHTING equipment of all types is wanted, from fire marks to uniforms to toy fire trucks. It is said that every little boy wanted to be a fireman or a train engineer 75 years ago and the collectors today reflect this interest.

Bucket, Leather, Franklin Fire Society, Charlestown-Protection In Danger, c.1800	9500.00
Bucket, Leather, Gold Paint, Hand In Oval, Ribbons, Isaac Hinckley, 1797, 13 In., Pair	21250.00
Bucket, Leather Handle, Black Paint, c.1796, 13 In.	830.00
Bucket, Leather, Handle, Green Paint, Yellow Letters, R.I.W. Pleasant St., 14 x 7 In.	330.00
Bucket, Leather, Multicolored, Red Winged Heart, Assistance, Dated 1803, 12 ½ In.	2010.00
Bucket, Leather, Painted, Inscribed J. Kimmel No. 12, 1800s, 12 ¾ In.	1404.00
Bucket, Leather, Painted, Maine No. 54, Green, Handle, 12 In.	863.00
Bucket, Leather, Red, Yellow Initials J.R.M., England, Late 1800s, 13 x 9 ¾ In.	550.00
Bucket, Leather, Scrolled Banner, Black Paint, S. Holman, 13 In.	148.00
Bucket, Leather, W. Bird, Painted, Swing Handle, 13 In.	95.00
Bucket, Tub, Red Leather, Painted 1, Handle, 11 ½ In., Pair ....*illus*	4125.00
Bucket, Waggoner Sanatory, Red, Tin, Handle, No Lid, Pat. Feb. 5, 1905	500.00
Fire Mark, F.A., Embossed Snake, Cast Iron, 11 In. ....*illus*	29.00
Fire Mark, F.A., Hose Wrapped Hydrant, Cast Iron, Deep Relief, c.1830	575.00
Fire Mark, Fireman's Assoc., Philadelphia, Iron, Oval, F.A., Hydrant, 7 ½ x 12 In. ....*illus*	116.00
Fire Mark, Lumbermen's Insurance Co., Green Paint, Cast Iron, 11 ½ x 11 ½ In.	66.00
Fire Mark, Shield Form, Sheep, On Rock, Banner, Green, Gilt, Wood, F Y, 1800s, 21 x 23 In.	485.00
Grenade, Amber, Diamond, Spherical, Monogram, c.1890, 7 ¼ In.	476.00
Grenade, Babcock's Hand, Amber, Ground Lip, American LaFrance, c.1880-1900, 7 ⅜ In.	2760.00
Grenade, Babcock's Hand, Cobalt Blue, Ground Lip, c.1880-1900, 7 ½ In.	2185.00
Grenade, California Fire Extinguisher, Walking Bear, Amber, c.1900, 6 ½ In. ....*illus*	6900.00
Grenade, Harden, Star, Cobalt Blue, Vertical Ribs, Embossed, Sealed, Contents, 6 ½ In.	92.00
Grenade, Harden, Star, Cork, Contents, Blue Green, 7 In., Pt.	235.00
Grenade, Harden's Hand, Aqua, Ribs, Embossed Star, Contents, 6 ½ In.	162.00
Grenade, Harden's Hand, Star, Cobalt Blue, Ribs, Embossed, Sealed, Contents, 6 ½ In.	195.00
Grenade, Hayward's Hand, Fire Extinguisher, Cobalt Blue, Tooled Lip, c.1900, 5 ¾ In. ....*illus*	316.00
Grenade, Hayward's Hand, Golden Yellow Amber, Tooled Mouth, c.1880-1900, 4 ¼ In.	325.00
Grenade, Hayward's Hand, Golden Yellow, Cork, Contents, Patent Aug 8 1871, 6 ¼ In.	258.00

Grenade, Hayward's, Cobalt Blue, Flat Panel, Tooled Lip, Contents, 1873-95, 6 In. ....*illus*	242.00
Grenade, Spong & Cos, Hand Fire, Extinguishing Tube, Grass Green, Label, c.1900, 13 In. ....*illus*	546.00
Helmet, Brass, Crest, Sapeurs Pompiers, Lachapelle, France, 8 x 11 x 10 In.	1600.00
Horn, Red, Tole, 20th Century, 26 In.	230.00
Lantern, Fire Engine, Dietz, King, Marked, American LaFrance Fire Engine Co., 14 ½ In.	120.00
Lightning Rod Pendant, Cobalt Blue, Metal Hanger, Screw-On Cap, c.1890, 4 ½ In.	115.00
Parade Ax, Carved, Painted, 1800s, 49 ½ In.	510.00
Parade Hat, Applied Fire Hydrant, Figure, Black Letters, Red, Gilt Paint, c.1880, 6 x 14 In.	2370.00
Parade Horn, Silver Plated, 19th Century, 17 ½ In. ....*illus*	995.00
Station Alarm, Brass, Glass Panels, Lever, Gamewell Co. Patent, 20th Century, 8 ¾ In.	394.00
Trumpet, Presentation, Silver Plated, Flower & Scroll Decoration, Louisiana, 19 In.	1150.00

FIREPLACES were used to cook food and to heat the American home in past centuries. Many types of tools and equipment were used. Andirons held the logs in place, firebacks reflected the heat into the room, and tongs were used to move either fuel or food. Many types of spits and roasting jacks were made and may be listed in the Kitchen category.

Andirons, Arts & Crafts, Owl Shape, Cast Iron, Glass Eyes, c.1900, 14 x 8 ½ In.	650.00
Andirons, Bell Metal, Ball Finial, Ring Turned Column, Ball & Claw Feet, c.1800, 18 In.	840.00
Andirons, Brass, Acorn Finials, Baluster Posts, Double Feet, c.1920, 23 In.	259.00
Andirons, Brass, Acorn Top, Spurred Arch Supports, Penny Feet, c.1800, 20 ½ In.	1035.00
Andirons, Brass, Art Deco, Spade Shape, 10 x 7 x 5 In.	350.00
Andirons, Brass, Arts & Crafts, Sunflower Shape, Reeded Ball, Paw Feet, Tools, 21 ½ In.	1058.00
Andirons, Brass, Ball Finial, Arched Feet, Iron Supports, 9 ¾ In.	68.00
Andirons, Brass, Ball Top, Finial Log Stops, Iron Supports, 17 In.	309.00
Andirons, Brass, Baluster Posts, Spur Arches, Ball Feet, England, 1800s, 18 In.	259.00
Andirons, Brass, Bell Metal, Federal, Lemon Tops, Square Base, Swags, Tassels, c.1800, 12 x 20 In.	948.00
Andirons, Brass, Chippendale Style, Urn & Flame Finials, Ball & Claw Feet, 33 In. ....*illus*	235.00
Andirons, Brass, Classical, Baluster Shafts, Octagonal Plinths, Early 1900s, 22 In. ....*illus*	288.00
Andirons, Brass, Column Form, Arts & Crafts, 11 ½ x 23 ½ x 18 In.	330.00
Andirons, Brass, Corinthian Column, Ball Finial, Stepped Base, 30 ½ x 9 ½ x 20 In.	460.00
Andirons, Brass, Faceted & Ball Spire Top, Spur & Ball Legs, 18 ½ In.	403.00
Andirons, Brass, Federal, Acorn Finial, Octagonal Standard, Scrolled Legs, c.1800, 20 ½ In. ..	1265.00
Andirons, Brass, Federal, Ball Finial, 19th Century, 15 In.	150.00
Andirons, Brass, Federal, Bellflower Swag, Engraved Urn, Rope Twist, c.1790, 30 In.	10530.00
Andirons, Brass, Federal, Branded T. Wittingham, New York, c.1795, 22 ¾ In.	1800.00
Andirons, Brass, Federal, Double Lemon Top, c.1810, 19 ¼ In.	770.00
Andirons, Brass, Federal, Faceted Lemon Top, Slipper Feet, J. Davis, c.1810, 21 ½ In.	1521.00
Andirons, Brass, Federal, Lemon Shape Finial, Spurred Supports, Ball Feet, Early 1800s, 27 In.	610.00
Andirons, Brass, Federal, Lemon Shape Finials, Match Log Stops, c.1800, 18 In.	235.00
Andirons, Brass, Federal, Paneled Lemon Finials, Spur Arches, c.1800, 17 In.	230.00
Andirons, Brass, Federal, Urn Finial, Engraved, Vine Shaft, Ball & Claw Feet, c.1790, 27 In. ...	25740.00
Andirons, Brass, Federal, Urn, Squared, Tapered, Engraved, Arched Foot, c.1800, 25 In.	20000.00
Andirons, Brass, Federal, Urn Top, Cylindrical Shafts, Pad Feet, c.1810, 22 ½ In.	527.00
Andirons, Brass, Federal, Wrought Iron, Urn Finials, Initials JC, 20 In.	351.00
Andirons, Brass, Finials, Iron Spit Hooks, Penny Feet, 18th Century, 25 ½ In.	558.00
Andirons, Brass, Georgian, Turned, Shaped Shaft, Spurred Legs, Ball Feet, 22 In.	323.00
Andirons, Brass, Iron Ball Top, Square Plinth Shaft, Log Stops, Boston, c.1830, 18 x 9 In.	385.00
Andirons, Brass, Iron, Federal, Lemon Top, Cabriole Legs, c.1800, 19 x 10 In.	770.00
Andirons, Brass, Iron, Octagonal Finial, Ring Turned Shaft, Arched Legs, Ball Feet, 22 In.	518.00
Andirons, Brass, Iron, Steeple Top, Beaded Belted Balls, 20 ⅛ x 9 ¾ x 26 ½ In.	711.00
Andirons, Brass, Knife Blade, Urn Form, Arched Tripod, 1780s, 19 In.	715.00
Andirons, Brass, Late Classical, Ribbed, Faceted Finials, Plinth, 18 x 12 In.	420.00
Andirons, Brass, Lemon Drop, 18 ¼ In.	205.00
Andirons, Brass, Ornate Dragon Uprights, 20 x 14 In.	5700.00
Andirons, Brass, Regency, Ball & Spire, Shaped Iron Legs, c.1820, 14 x 6 In.	926.00
Andirons, Brass, Ring-Turned Shafts, Spurred Cabriole Legs, Ball Feet, c.1840, 16 ½ x 17 In. ..	875.00
Andirons, Brass, Seamed, Pointed Slipper Feet, Wrought Iron Billets, c.1830, 11 In.	235.00
Andirons, Brass, Slipper Feet, Cannonball Finial, Log Stop, c.1820, 15 In.	176.00
Andirons, Brass, Urn Finials, 36 ½ In., Pair..	403.00
Andirons, Brass, Urn Finials, Ball Claw Feet, c.1790, 27 In.	1528.00
Andirons, Brass, Urn Finials, Spiraling Vine, Flowers, Ball & Claw Feet, c.1790, 27 ½ In.	25000.00
Andirons, Brass, Wreath Finial, France, 23 x 18 In.	259.00
Andirons, Bronze, Cat, Wheat, Mice, Janes Fuller, Roman Bronze Works, 19 In. ....*illus*	2728.00
Andirons, Bronze, Cupid & Snake, Cast Iron Base, Victorian, England, c.1900, 15 ¾ In.	360.00
Andirons, Bronze, Firedogs, Louis XVI Style, Flame Finials, c.1850...............................	378.00

Firefighting, Grenade, Hayward's Hand, Fire Extinguisher, Cobalt Blue, Tooled Lip, c.1900, 5 ¾ In.
$316.00

Firefighting, Grenade, Hayward's, Cobalt Blue, Flat Panel, Tooled Lip, Contents, 1873-95, 6 In.
$242.00

Firefighting, Grenade, Spong & Cos, Hand Fire, Extinguishing Tube, Grass Green, Label, c.1900, 13 In.
$546.00

Firefighting, Parade Horn, Silver Plated, 19th Century, 17 ½ In.
$995.00

Fireplace, Andirons, Brass, Chippendale Style, Urn & Flame Finials, Ball & Claw Feet, 33 In. $235.00

Fireplace, Andirons, Brass, Classical, Baluster Shafts, Octagonal Plinths, Early 1900s, 22 In. $288.00

Fireplace, Andirons, Bronze, Cat, Wheat, Mice, Janes Fuller, Roman Bronze Works, 19 In. $2728.00

Fireplace, Andirons, Cast Iron, George Washington, Holding Book, Flat Relief, 1800s, 19 ½ In. $323.00

Andirons, Bronze, Renaissance Style, Man Supporting Urn, Flame Finial, 40 ½ x 19 ½ In.	4583.00
Andirons, Cast Iron, African-American Men, Striped Shirt, Bowtie, Rolled-Up Sleeves, 20 In. .	715.00
Andirons, Cast Iron, Anchor, Joined By Chain, 18 x 13 x 16 In.	641.00
Andirons, Cast Iron, Arts & Crafts, Curule Finial, Scrolled Feet, 24 ½ x 23 ½ x 12 ½ In.	92.00
Andirons, Cast Iron, Arts & Crafts, Hammered, 12 x 19 x 15 In.	210.00
Andirons, Cast Iron, Arts & Crafts, Sunflower Shape, Reeded Ball, Baluster, England, 21 ½ In.	1058.00
Andirons, Cast Iron, Baseball Players, Pitcher, Batter, 1920s, 19 In.	3616.00
Andirons, Cast Iron, Black Man & Woman, Drop-In Billet Bars, 16 ½ In.	345.00
Andirons, Cast Iron, Brass, Donald Deskey, Embossed Bennett, 20 x 9 x 18 ½ In.	4800.00
Andirons, Cast Iron, Brass, Donald Deskey, Stamped Bennett, 1950s, 19 ½ In.	510.00
Andirons, Cast Iron, Deer, Figural, Forged, 8 x 17 In.	358.00
Andirons, Cast Iron, George Washington, Holding Book, Flat Relief, 1800s, 19 ½ In. ....*illus*	323.00
Andirons, Cast Iron, George Washington, Standing, Uniform, Round Billet Bars, 1800s, 16 x 23 In.	288.00
Andirons, Cast Iron, Intertwined Snakes, Arched Ball Feet, 1800s, 16 ¾ x 14 ⅜ In. ....*illus*	374.00
Andirons, Cast Iron, Pine Tree, Martin Pat. Applied For, c.1900, 20 x 11 In.	830.00
Andirons, Cast Iron, Shield Form, Acanthus Leaves, Adams Style, Dore, 27 x 7 x 26 In.	820.00
Andirons, Cast Iron, Soldier, Hessian, c.1885, 20 x 10 In.	148.00
Andirons, Cast Iron, Stylized Flame Design, Raymond Subes, 16 x 9 In., Pair	6600.00
Andirons, Iron, Dog's Head, Loop Design, 21 x 10 x 18 In.	450.00
Andirons, Iron, G. Stickley, 20 ½ x 12 x 24 In.	6100.00
Andirons, Iron, George Nelson, X-Shape, Howard Miller, 8 ¼ x 15 x 13 In. ....*illus*	840.00
Andirons, Iron, George Washington, Plinth, Drapery, Star, Gilt, Removable Rests, Mid 1800s, 20 In.	460.00
Andirons, Wrought Iron, Arts & Crafts, Curled, Twisted, 12 x 24 In.	450.00
Andirons, Wrought Iron, Arts & Crafts, Faceted Finial, Column Base, 11 x 23 In.	300.00
Andirons, Wrought Iron, Arts & Crafts, Griffin Design, Twisted, Curled 12 x 22 x 25 In.	600.00
Andirons, Wrought Iron, Arts & Crafts, Ring, Curled Base, Twisted Stem, Ball Finial, 12 x 25 In.	330.00
Andirons, Wrought Iron, Arts & Crafts, Twisted, Curled, 13 x 24 In.	360.00
Andirons, Wrought Iron, Faceted Finials, Fleur-De-Lis, 1800s, 48 In.	470.00
Andirons, Wrought Iron, Firedogs, 21 In.	2200.00
Andirons, Wrought Iron, Flower Decorated Baluster Stem, Lion's Mask, Scrolling Feet, 1800s, 31 In.	1265.00
Andirons, Wrought Iron, Folk Art, Stars, 20th Century, 36 x 25 x 29 In.	358.00
Andirons, Wrought Iron, Gothic Revival, Spiral, Cup Finials, 32 x 25 x 12 In.	480.00
Andirons, Wrought Iron, Oil Field Drill Bits, Scroll Feet, 1900s, 14 x 17 In.	294.00
Andirons, Wrought Iron, Sailboats In Full Sail, Sheet Metal Sails, 26 In.	1098.00
Andirons, Wrought Iron, Shield Shape, Pierced Brass Boxes, Late 1800s, 31 x 20 In.	127.00
Andirons, Wrought Iron, Stylized Flowers, Verdigris Patina, Prairie School, 8 x 28 x 20 In.	900.00
Andirons, Wrought Iron, William Wallace Denslow, c.1905, 19 ½ x 13 x 26 ¼ In.	40625.00
Bellows, Blacksmith, Wood, Leather, Stand, France, c.1880, 25 x 43 x 63 In.	2800.00
Bellows, Leather, Stenciled, Painted Fruit, Brass Nozzle, 1800s, 17 ½ In. ....*illus*	235.00
Bellows, Painted, Teardrop Form, Leather & Tack Construction, Stencil, 18 x 7 ½ In.	88.00
Bellows, Turtleback, Stenciled Flowers, Yellow Ground, Brass Nozzle, Leather, 17 In.	235.00
Bellows, Wood, Leather, England, Early 1900s, 18 ½ In.	140.00
Bellows, Wood, Painted, Ivory Ground, Flowers, Leather, England, Late 1900s, 19 ¼ In.	250.00
Bellows, Wood, Painted, Leather, Brass Nozzle, England, Early 1900s, 15 In.	140.00
Bucket, Peat, George III, Mahogany, Brass Straps, Liner, Handles, Oval, c.1900, 12 In.	593.00
Chenet, Andirons, Brass, Acorn Finials, Late 19th Century, 9 x 13 ½ x 3 In.	60.00
Chenet, Andirons, Brass, Lion & Shield Shape, 17 ½ x 11 In.	32.00
Chenet, Andirons, Brass, Lion, Resting, Stepped Base, 1800s, 10 x 12 In.	518.00
Chenet, Andirons, Bronze, Louis XV, Sphinx, Reclining, Rectangular Base, Tapered Feet, 12 In.	2370.00
Chenet, Andirons, Bronze, Neoclassical, Acanthus, Hoof Supports, France, 12 ½ x 11 x 19 In.	1410.00
Chenet, Andirons, Cast Brass, Griffin, 20 In.	790.00
Chenet, Andirons, Cast Iron, Figural, Griffins, Holding Rings & Chains, J.L. Mott, 16 ½ x 42 In.	764.00
Chenet, Andirons, Louis XV Style, Bronze, Cherub, Scroll Base, Stamped, Bouhon, 1800s, 12 x 11 In.	720.00
Coal Grate, Cast Iron, Georgian, Silvered Bronze, Late 18th Century	717.00
Coal Grate, Steel, Brass, Open Box, Columnar Supports, Fluted Legs, 26 ½ x 39 x 21 In.	3346.00
Coal Scuttle, Art Nouveau, Inlaid Leaves, Brass Shovel, 12 x 13 x 18 In. ....*illus*	310.00
Coal Scuttle, Brass, Copper, Urn & Scroll, England, c.1900, 15 ½ x 11 x 18 In. ....*illus*	259.00
Coal Scuttle, Brass, Oval, Removable Liner, Paw Feet, England, 1900s, 16 x 17 In.	374.00
Coal Scuttle, Copper, Iron, Handle, D Monogram, 15 x 28 In.	1440.00
Coal Scuttle, Flowers, Black Ground, Footed, Stamped, G.D.W. Mfg. Co., 26 x 12 ¼ In.	115.00
Coal Scuttle, Mahogany, Flower Inlay, 18 In.	110.00
Coal Scuttle, Metal, Hinged Lid, Ball Finial, Handles, c.1910, England, 15 x 18 In.	148.00
Coal Scuttle, Oak, Carved, Rectangular Case, Brass Handles, Lift-Up Sloping Face, 16 x 14 In.	86.00
Coal Scuttle, Pressed Brass, Handle, Wall Mount, Scenic, Continental, Late 1800s, 2 Piece......	176.00
Coal Scuttle, Stand, Edwardian, Embossed Copper, Brass Helmet Shape, Ebonized, 22 ¼ In. ..	732.00
Crane, Hand Wrought, Wall Mount, Brackets, 44 In.	88.00

Fireplace, Andirons, Cast Iron,
Intertwined Snakes, Arched Ball Feet,
1800s, 16 ¾ x 14 ⅜ In.
$374.00

Fireplace, Andirons, Iron, George Nelson,
X-Shape, Howard Miller, 8 ¼ x 15 x 13 In.
$840.00

Fireplace, Bellows, Leather, Stenciled,
Painted Fruit, Brass Nozzle, 1800s, 17 ½ In.
$235.00

Fireplace, Coal Scuttle, Art Nouveau,
Inlaid Leaves, Brass Shovel, 12 x 13 x 18 In.
$310.00

Fireplace, Coal Scuttle, Brass, Copper,
Urn & Scroll, England, c.1900,
15 ½ x 11 x 18 In.
$259.00

Fireplace, Fender, Federal, Brass,
Engraved Urn, c.1810
$345.00

Fireplace, Screen, Arts & Crafts, Mesh,
Iron Frame, Applied Mixed Metal Decoration,
50 x 47 In.
$1920.00

Fireplace, Screen, Pole, William IV, Adjustable,
Needlework, 1800s, 65 x 15 In.
$259.00

Fireplace, Tool Set, Brass, Copper,
3 Leg Stand, Sailing Ship, 16 x 47 In.,
4 Piece
$510.00

TIP
To clean small pieces
of iron, try soaking them
in white vinegar for
24 to 48 hours.

FIREPLACE

Fischer, Jardiniere, Rothschild Bird, Butterflies, Gilt Lion's Paw Feet, Herend, 7 x 6 In., Pair
$989.00

Fischer, Tureen, Soup, Cover, Rothschild Bird, Flowers, Lemon Finial, Herend, 9 ½ x 12 ½ In.
$1035.00

Fischer, Tureen, Soup, Cover, Underplate, Bird, Handles, Bird Finial, 1700s, 12 x 16 In.
$2040.00

Fischer, Tureen, Underplate, Ladle, Queen Victoria, Flowers, Lemon Finial, Gilt, Herend, 11 x 8 In.
$598.00

Fender, Brass, Openwork, Flowers, Paw Feet, Iron Rim, 10 x 46 In.	460.00
Fender, Brass, Openwork, Leaf, Flower Design, Rope Edge, 5 Paw Feet, England, 1800s, 11 x 51 In.	633.00
Fender, Brass, Openwork, Serpentine, Paw Feet, Iron Floor, England, 1800s, 12 x 49 In.	920.00
Fender, Brass, Pierced, Iron Floor, 1800s, 9 x 52 In.	144.00
Fender, Brass, Pierced, Paw Feet, 11 x 57 In.	201.00
Fender, Brass, Spirals, Flame Finials, Reeded Columns, Festoons, Continental, 13 x 62 In.	443.00
Fender, Brass, Wire, Ball Finials, George III, c.1800, 15 x 63 In.	825.00
Fender, Brass, Wire, D-Shape, Crosshatched Top Rail, Howard & Morse, NYC, 12 x 40 In.	850.00
Fender, Brass, Wire, Folding, Rail, Scroll Ornament, c.1820, 24 x 38 In.	1126.00
Fender, Brass, Wire, Scroll, Lemon Top Finials, Early 19th Century, 13 x 53 x 15 In.	1380.00
Fender, Brass, Wirework, Rail, Geometric Design, c.1820, 7 x 28 In.	356.00
Fender, Brass, Wirework, Serpentine, 3-Ball Finials, Scrolls, 16 ¼ x 54 ¼ x 14 ¼ In.	830.00
Fender, Brass, Wirework, Wavy Line, Scrolls, c.1800, 10 x 57 In.	326.00
Fender, Federal Brass, D-Shape, Faceted Beehive Finials, Claw Feet, c.1800, 14 x 47 In.	690.00
Fender, Federal, Brass, Engraved Urn, c.1810 ....*illus*	345.00
Fender, Pierced, High Ends, Brass, France, 23 x 18 In.	288.00
Fender, Regency, Brass, Reticulated, Early 19th Century, 7 ½ x 41 ½ In.	195.00
Fender, Scrolls, Finials, Wrought Iron, 1900s, 10 x 45 In.	115.00
Fender, Wire, D-Shape, 19th Century, 12 x 44 ½ x 14 In.	345.00
Fireback, Arched Top, Crown, Shield, Unicorn, Colonial Williamsburg, 24 x 21 In.	184.00
Fireback, Baroque Design, Iron, Winchester, Va., c.1692, 27 x 24 ¾ In.	3500.00
Fireback, Cast Iron, Indian Princess, Bow & Arrow, Dogs, Scroll, Drapery Beadwork, 35 x 35 In.	1265.00
Fireback, Cast Iron, Renaissance, Stage Hunt, 31 x 39 In.	823.00
Fireback, Fleur-De-Lis Design, Cast Iron, France, 1613, 10 x 28 ½ In.	225.00
Firedogs, Brass, England, 8 x 10 In.	176.00
Firehouse, Fan Crest, Ram Heads, Swags, Brass Front, Acorn Finials, Flowers, Urns, 26 x 29 In.	236.00
Grate, Federal Style, Brass, Iron, Pierced Front Rail, Finials, Figural Back Plate, 1800s, 25 x 34 In.	2242.00
Mantel is listed in the Architectural category.	
Screen, 3-Fold, Iron Frames, Wire Mesh Panels, Peacock, Scrollwork, 36 x 34 ½ In.	338.00
Screen, Aesthetic, Mahogany, Trestle Support, Needlework Image, 42 x 29 In.	500.00
Screen, Arts & Crafts, Mesh, Iron Frame, Applied Mixed Metal Decoration, 50 x 47 In. ....*illus*	1920.00
Screen, Bamboo, Textile Crest Panel, Top Handles, St. John's College, Oxford, 42 x 24 In.	165.00
Screen, Brass, Central Medallion, Goddess, Putti, Early 20th Century, 46 In.	695.00
Screen, Brass, Fan Shape, Scalloped, 6-Sided Base, c.1920, France, 28 x 28 In.	106.00
Screen, Brass, Hammered, Family In Kitchen, Footed, 26 x 28 x 10 In.	165.00
Screen, Brass, Jewels, Paw Feet, Tube Frame, Impressed Flowers, Leaves, 36 x 24 In.	3450.00
Screen, Classical, Floral Needlework, Mahogany, Cast Brass Trim, 32 x 24 In.	184.00
Screen, Copper, Hammered Arts & Crafts Symbols, Sinewy Shaped Iron Frame, 30 x 20 In.	259.00
Screen, Empire Revival, Arched, Painted, Gilt Bronze Masks, Anthemion, 41 In.	415.00
Screen, Fan Shape, Openwork, Figures, Scalloped, Collapsible, 34 In.	177.00
Screen, George III, Brass, Wire, Folding, c.1790, 30 x 54 In.	1560.00
Screen, George III, Multicolored, Shield Form, Oval Panel, Quill, Splayed Legs, 57 x 13 ½ In.	900.00
Screen, Gilt Bronze, Leaf Frame, Shell Crest, Masque Pendant, 28 x 35 In.	764.00
Screen, Gilt, Wrought Iron, Scrolls, Woman, Edgar Brandts, c.1925, 33 x 31 x 12 In.	25000.00
Screen, Leather, Mahogany Trestle Frame, Painted Basket Of Flowers, Swags, 36 In.	59.00
Screen, Louis XV, Gilt Wood, Trestle Support, Needlework Scene, c.1910, 35 x 36 In.	294.00
Screen, Louis XV Style, Brass, Wreath & Torch Crest, Allover Leaves, 27 x 27 In.	142.00
Screen, Louis XV, Walnut, Carved C-Scrolls, Tapestry Inset, Satyr With Pipe, 39 ½ x 24 In.	1896.00
Screen, Louis XVI Creme Peinte, Oval Insert, Molded, Flowers, 1700s, 24 x 39 In.	490.00
Screen, Louis XVI, Off-White, Rosette Corners, Floral Cartouche, Aubusson Panel, 39 x 24 In.	490.00
Screen, Louis XVI Style, Patinated Bronze, Shield Shape, Torchere Crest, Finials, 31 x 29 In.	240.00
Screen, Mahogany, Bronze Mounted, Gilt Wood Bust Finials, France, 1800s, 40 x 26 In.	236.00
Screen, Multicolored Shield, Adjustable, Acorn Finial, c.1810, 57 x 11 In.	176.00
Screen, Needlepoint Scene, Carved Frame, Contoured Crest, Spindle Supports, 39 x 29 In.	585.00
Screen, Papier-Mache, Gilt Border, Twist Carved Base, Snake Feet, 1830s, 53 x 19 In.	823.00
Screen, Peacock Fan, Victorian, Stained Glass, Wrought Iron, 33 ½ x 47 In.	270.00
Screen, Pewter, Copper, Parchment, Inlaid Walnut, Bugatti, c.1900, 37 x 39 x 12 In.	20315.00
Screen, Pole, Mahogany, Beadwork, Gothic Arch, Brass Pole, 19th Century, 70 In.	881.00
Screen, Pole, Mahogany, Silkwork Flowers, Acorn Finial, Cabriole Legs, c.1775, 57 In.	891.00
Screen, Pole, Needlepoint, Flowers, 41 x 25 In.	70.00
Screen, Pole, Regency, Federal, Mahogany, Needlework, 8-Sided Frame, 1820s, 48 In.	1500.00
Screen, Pole, Regency Style, Mahogany, Shield Form, Needlework, c.1890, 56 x 13 In., Pair	465.00
Screen, Pole, William IV, Adjustable, Needlework, 1800s, 65 x 15 In. ....*illus*	259.00
Screen, Regency Style, Rosewood, Paint, Turned Stem, Bronze Mounted, Bird, Flowers, 49 In.	470.00
Screen, Rococo, Rosewood, Petit Point, Flower Carved Frame, Arched Legs, 50 x 28 x 20 In.	858.00
Screen, Rosewood, Pedestal, Claw Feet, Felt Floral Panel, Frame, 25 x 54 x 18 In.	805.00

Screen, Victorian, Brass, Diamond Beveled Glass, Ball & Claw Feet, 39 x 32 In.	560.00
Screen, Victorian, Needlepoint, Flowers, Grapes, 52 x 34 In.	250.00
Screen, Victorian, Rosewood, Figures, Grapevine, Tambourine, Needlework, 59 x 32 In.	710.00
Screen, Wire Mesh, Brass Frame & Handles, 3 Sections, Arts & Crafts, 55 x 30 In.	390.00
Screen, Wood, Marquetry, Shield Form, Glass Panel, Dutch, Mid 1800s, 35 x 21 x 12 In.	360.00
Screen, Wrought Iron, 3-Panel, Fleur-De-Lis Hinges, 35 x 55 In.	215.00

Screens are also listed in the Architectural and Furniture categories.

Tool Holder, Dog, White, Collar, Tassels, On Footstool, Victorian, 24 ¾ x 16 ½ In.	725.00
Tool Rest, Brass, Balusters, Lateral Rod, 4-Footed Base, 6 ½ x 8 ¼ In., Pair.......................	22.00
Tool Rest, Brass, Seated Lion, Stepped Base, Ring Handle, 1800s, 18 In., Pair	690.00
Tool Set, Arts & Crafts, Metal, Curled, Brushed, Stand, Twisted, 12 ½ x 35 In., 4 Piece..........	210.00
Tool Set, Brass, Copper, 3 Leg Stand, Sailing Ship, 16 x 47 In., 4 Piece ....*illus*	510.00
Tool Set, Bronze, Ship, Oscar Bach	495.00
Tool Set, Cast Iron, Brass, Donald Deskey, 3 Piece, 33 x 11 ½ x 7 In.	840.00
Tool Set, Charles II Style, Brass, Candelabra, Lion, Shield, Tongs, Shovel, Poker, 55 x 17 x 13 In.	478.00
Tool Set, Owl Finial, Cast Iron, Shovel, Poker, Tongs, Stand, c.1900, 26 & 27 In., 4 Piece	695.00
Tool Set, Shovel, Fork, Tongs, Poker, Wrought Iron, Serpent Design Base, 13 x 33 In.	1200.00
Tool Stand, Brass, Lions On Haunches, 14 ¼ x 8 ¾ In., Pair..	323.00
Trammel, Heart Finials, Wrought Iron, c.1800, 53 ½ In.	237.00
Trammel, Iron, Brass, Pencil Clip, Finial, Pair	66.00
Trammel, Wrought Iron, c.1820, 23 In.	646.00

FISCHER porcelain was made in Herend, Hungary, by Moritz Fischer. The factory was founded in 1839 and continued working into the twentieth century. The wares are sometimes referred to as Herend porcelain.

Basket, Chinese Bouquet Rust, Herend, 1 ¾ x 6 In., Pair..	69.00
Coffeepot, Cover, Rothschild Bird, Herend, 8 x 14 ½ In.	431.00
Dish, Shell, Rothschild Bird Blue, Herend, 9 In., Pair..	978.00
Ewer, Arabian Design, Applied Flowers, Beaded Handle, 13 ½ In.	236.00
Figurine, Bunny, Seated, Blue, Fishscale, Gilt, Herend, 3 ½ In.	130.00
Figurine, Cat, Seated, Blue, Gilt, Marked, Herend, 3 ½ In.	95.00
Figurine, Equestrian, Lippinzaner Being Led By Hussar, Herend, 8 In.	135.00
Figurine, Koala Bears, Hugging, Black On White Fishnet, Gold Noses, 4 ½ In.	118.00
Figurine, Seal, Red, Multicolored Feet, Gilt, Herend, 7 x 7 ½ In.	200.00
Jar, Cover, Chinese Bouquet Rust, Herend, 6 ¼ x 6 In.	69.00
Jardiniere, Rothschild, Bird, Butterflies, Gilt Lion's Paw Feet, Herend, 7 x 6 In., Pair ....*illus*	989.00
Lamp, Fruits & Flowers, Herend, 15 In.	403.00
Leopard, Growling, Black, White, Gilt, Herend, 18 In.	1500.00
Placecard Holder, Dolphin, Red, Brown, Gilt, Marked, Herend, 3 In., 12 Piece	950.00
Planter, Bird, Multicolored, Black Head Feathers, 9 x 16 x 6 In.	515.00
Plate, Salad, Crescent, Rothschild Bird Blue, Herend, 7 ¼ In., 8 Piece	489.00
Platter, Rothschild Bird, Herend, 13 ½ In.	230.00
Tureen, Soup, Cover, Rothschild Bird, Flowers, Lemon Finial, Herend, 9 ½ x 12 ½ In. ....*illus*	1035.00
Tureen, Soup, Cover, Underplate, Bird, Handles, Bird Finial, 1700s, 12 x 16 In. ....*illus*	2040.00
Tureen, Soup, Yellow Dynasty, Herend, 11 x 14 In.	614.00
Tureen, Underplate, Ladle, Queen Victoria, Flowers, Lemon Finial, Gilt, Herend, 11 x 8 In. ....*illus*	598.00
Vase, Flowers, Butterflies, Leaf Border, Herend, 12 ½ In.	395.00
Vase, Vines, Birds, Flowers, Green, Red, Yellow, Herend, 16 x 7 In.	266.00

FISHING reels of brass or nickel were made in the United States by 1810. Bamboo fly rods were sold by 1860, often marked with the maker's name. Lures made of metal, or metal and wood, were made in the nineteenth century. Plastic lures were made by the 1930s. All fishing material is collected today and even equipment of the past thirty years is of interest if in good condition with original box.

Bag, Hardy Brothers, Canvas, Top Hole, Front Netting, Leather Trim, 16 In.	41.00
Banner, Penn Reels Best For Sport Fishing, Cloth, 4 Different Reels, 1960s, 22 x 33 In.	115.00
Catalog, Edward Vom Hofe, 34th Edition, 1931, 171 Pages...	189.00
Catalog, Heddon, Bait, Color illustrations, 1937, 40 Pages...	106.00
Catalog, Orvis, Rods, Reels, Hooks, Lines, Accessories, No. 16, c.1888, 56 Pages...................	649.00
Creel, French Weave, Leather Trim, 14 x 7 x 10 ½ In.	236.00
Creel, Turtle, Trademark, Woven Checkered Cane, Hemp Cord Bottom, Colo., 16 x 7 ½ x 8 In.	2596.00
Creel, Willow, Woven, Wire Side Strap Holders, Brass Latch, Logo, 1930s, 8 x 15 In. ....*illus*	236.00
Float, Glass, Emerald Green, Mold Blown, Net Wrapped, c.1920, 37 x 11 In.	475.00
Fly Chest, Orvis, Wood, Limited Edition, No. 198, 3 Salmon Flies, 14 x 11 x 2 ½ In.	65.00
Fly Vise, Thomas, No. 1, Adjustable, Ball Socket, Abercrombie & Fitch, c.1949...................*illus*	189.00
Fly, Red Tail, Alex Rogan, c.1947, 2 In.	35.00

Fishing, Creel, Willow, Woven, Wire Side Strap Holders, Brass Latch, Logo, 1930s, 8 x 15 In.
$236.00

Fishing, Fly Vise, Thomas, No. 1, Adjustable, Ball Socket, Abercrombie & Fitch, c.1949
$189.00

Fishing, Line Dryer, Mahogany, 7 Spindles, Foil Label, Abercrombie & Fitch, 8 ½ In.
$590.00

Fishing, Lure, Buel, Musky, Spinner, Pearl Spoon, Trebled Fly, Box Swivel, Wire Leader, 3 ½ In.
$384.00

F

Fishing, Lure, Outing, Pikey Getum
Minnow, 1920s, 3 ⅝ In.
$159.00

Fishing, Lure, Shakespeare, Spinner,
Rotary Head, Wood, Yellow Spots, Box,
c.1904, 3 In.
$142.00

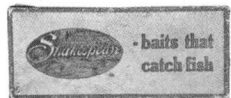

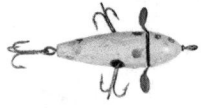

Fishing, Minnow Bucket, Tin, Platform
Base, Hinged Top
$106.00

Fishing, Reel, Pflueger, Trout, Progress,
Gun Metal Finish, Amber Grasp,
Bulldog Mark, Box, 60 Yd.
$354.00

Hook Display, Kingfisher, Salesman's Sample, 6 10 x 5 ½ In. Boards	59.00
Line Dryer, Mahogany, 7 Spindles, Foil Label, Abercrombie & Fitch, 8 ½ In. .... *illus*	590.00
Line Winder, Hardy, Stamped, 14 In.	59.00
Lure, Buel, Musky, Spinner, Pearl Spoon, Trebled Fly, Box Swivel, Wire Leader, 3 ½ In. ..... *illus*	384.00
Lure, Carrie Stevens, Streamer Fly, Gray Ghost, 2 ¾ x 3 ¾ In.	425.00
Lure, Delany Spinner, No. 8, Dimpled Edge, Feathered Treble Hook, Box Swivel, Coubourg, Ont.	283.00
Lure, Gruber Glowurm Fish, Yellow, Green Stripes, Medical Lake, Wash., c.1920	271.00
Lure, Harkauf, Minnow, Wood Body, Painted Eyes, Trailing Treble Hook, Box, 2 ½ In.	2950.00
Lure, Heddon, Underwater Minnow, No. 150, Glass Eyes, L-Rig Hardware	189.00
Lure, Hosmer, Mechanical Froggie, Green, White Belly, Red Trim, Box, 1930s, 5 In.	4838.00
Lure, Macatawa Bait Co., Musky Frog, Black Lake Angler's Association, Box, 12 ½ In.	201.00
Lure, Outing, Pikey Getum Minnow, 1920s, 3 ⅝ In. .... *illus*	159.00
Lure, Pardee, Minnow, Yellow Glass Eyes, Silver, Kent, Ohio, c.1900, 3 ⅞ In.	8732.00
Lure, Shakespeare, Revolution, Mickey Mouse Propellers, Round Tail, Aluminum, c.1902	165.00
Lure, Shakespeare, Spinner, Rotary Head, Wood, Yellow Spots, Box, c.1904, 3 In. ..... *illus*	142.00
Lure, Winchester, Multi Wobbler, White Body, Green Stripe, Red Eye Shadow	153.00
Lure, Winchester, Underwater Minnow, 3 Hooks, Red, Glass Eyes, Front Spinner	153.00
Lure, Winchester, Underwater Minnow, Green To Gold, Front Spinner, Box	212.00
Minnow Bucket, Bowed Sides, Flat Top, Galvanized Metal, Green Paint, Footed, 23 In.	201.00
Minnow Bucket, Tin, Platform Base, Hinged Top .... *illus*	106.00
Minnow Bucket, Torpedo Shape, Sheet Iron, Soldered Seams, Platform Base, 6 ½ x 18 In.	153.00
Minnow Trap, Double Funnel, Glass, Applied Top Ring, 11 In.	472.00
Minnow Trap, Glass, Square, 7 x 7 x 13 ½ In.	2419.00
Minnow Trap, Ground Lip, Checotah, Okla., 10 ½ In.	202.00
Net, Folding, Hardy Bros Bamboo Shaft Handle, Brass, Chrome, 53 In.	118.00
Net, Landing, Winchester, Flexible Metal, Cloth Netting, Bamboo Handle, Logo, 51 In.	153.00
Reel, Bellinger Saracione, Trout, Arne Mason, Case, 2 ¾ In.	844.00
Reel, Conroy Nickel Silver Bay, Rosewood, New York City, c.1865	1320.00
Reel, Edward Vom Hofe, Salmon, Tobique, Silver, Rubber, 3 In.	7080.00
Reel, Edward Vom Hofe, Trolling, Pat. May 20, '02, 5 x 4 ¼ In.	575.00
Reel, Edward Vom Hofe, Trout, Perfection, 3 ½ In.	7021.00
Reel, Edward Vom Hofe, Trout, Perfection 360, Model 360, Size ¹⁄0, Germany, 3 ⅛ In.	4720.00
Reel, Everol, Big Game, Gold Anodized, Italy	142.00
Reel, Farlow, Ebonite, Brass Winding Plate, London, 2 ½ In.	201.00
Reel, Fin-Nor, Fly Salt Water, Direct Drive, 3 ⅝ x 1 ½ In.	236.00
Reel, Fin-Nor, Fly, Wedding Cake, Gold Anodized Finish, Right Hand, 3 In.	767.00
Reel, Hardy, Fly Salmon, Spare Spool, 3 ½ In.	153.00
Reel, Orvis, Fly, Click Housing Cap, Nickel Plating, 1874 Patent, 2 ¾ In.	336.00
Reel, Pflueger, Trout, Progress, Gunmetal Finish, Amber Grasp, Bulldog Mark, Box, 60 Yd. *illus*	354.00
Rod, Gallas, Trout, Parabolic, 93, 7 Ft. 9 In.	885.00
Rod, Hardy, Palakona, Western Style, Bag, Plain Tube, 8 Ft.	189.00
Rod, Heddon Trout, DeLuxe Peerless, Heavy, 9 ½ Ft.	201.00
Rod, Leonard, Salmon, 2 Handles, Tip Sack & Tube, Canvas Sack, 13 Ft.	118.00
Rod, Leonard, Trout, Model 50, Pinched Snake Guides, Bag, 8 Ft.	1265.00
Rod, Orvis, Trout Wes Jordan, Heavy, Chrome Guides, Western Style Handle, 8 ½ Ft.	177.00
Rod, Pettengill Side Mount Reel, 1887 & 1889 Patents, 7 Ft., 4 In.	266.00
Rod, Thomas, Trout, Special, 8 Ft.	443.00
Rod, Winchester, Casting, Split Bamboo, 2 Sections, 5 Ft.	59.00
Rod, Wm. Read & Sons, Trolling, Kennebago, Maine, 11 Ft.	83.00
Rod, Young, Trout, Perfectionist, 7 Ft.	4484.00
Tackle Box, Shakespeare, Domed Compartment, Lift Out Drawer, Black, Brass Handle, Logo	47.00
Tackle Box, Winchester, Tin, Green, Gold Trim, Cork Lined, 12 ½ x 6 x 5 In.	177.00

FLAGS *are included in the Textile category.*

FLASH GORDON appeared in the Sunday comics in 1934. The daily strip started in 1940. The hero was also in comic books from 1930 to 1970, in books from 1936, in movies from 1938, on the radio in the 1930s and 1940s, and on television from 1953 to 1954. All sorts of memorabilia are collected, but the ray guns and rocket ships are the most popular.

Pistol, Ray Gun, Red, Silver, 10 In.	115.00
Pistol, Ray Gun, Tin Lithograph, Pull Trigger, Clicking Sound, Box, 10 In.	431.00
Pistol, Repeater, Tin Lithograph, Clicking Sound, Flash Graphics, Box, 10 In.	546.00
Pistol, Signal, Pressed Steel, Red, Green, Emits Sound, Marx, Box, 7 In.	978.00
Toy, Ship, Rocket Fighter, Tin Lithograph, Clockwork, Marx, Box, 12 In.	863.00 to 994.00
Water Pistol, Marx, Box, 7 ¾ In. .... *illus*	351.00

FLORENCE CERAMICS were made in Pasadena, California, from World War II to 1977. Florence Ward created many colorful figurines, boxes, candleholders, and other items for the gift shop trade. Each piece was marked with an ink stamp that included the name *Florence Ceramics Co.* The company was sold in 1964 and although the name remained the same, the products were very different. Mugs, cups, and trays were made.

Figurine, Marie Antoinette, Painted, Gilt Dress, 10 In., Pair 115.00

FLOW BLUE was made in England and other countries about 1830 to 1900. The dishes were printed with designs using a cobalt blue coloring. The color flowed from the design to the white body so that the finished piece has a smeared blue design. The dishes were usually made of ironstone china. More Flow Blue may be found under the name of the manufacturer.

Bone Dish, Touraine, Half Moon Shape, Marked, 6 ½ In., 7 Piece	121.00
Bowl & Pitcher, Poppy, Johnson Brothers, 11 ½ & 16 ½ In.	236.00
Bowl, U.S.S. Maine, Gold Rim, Oval, 13 In.	118.00
Bread Tray, Scenic, Castle & Boat, Gold Highlights, 14 ½ In.	275.00
Casserole, Clover, Cover, 7 x 3 ¾ In.	145.00
Casserole, Cover, Fishing Scene, James Edward, 8-Sided, 7 ½ x 10 In.	200.00
Chamber Pot, Art Nouveau Style, Flowers, Handles	70.00
Charger, Pekin, Albert E. Jones, 11 ¾ In.	44.00
Coffeepot, Brush Stroke, Cobalt Blue Foliates, Ironstone, c.1850, 12 ½ In.	510.00
Coffeepot, Pagoda Bells, Paneled, T. Phillips, 9 ½ In. ....*illus*	132.00
Creamer, Kyber, Paneled, J. Meir & Son, 5 ½ In. ....*illus*	88.00
Gravy Boat, Nonpareil, 4 ¼ x 8 In. ....*illus*	50.00
Jug, Toby, Twig Handle, Glaze Crazing, c.1800, 5 ½ x 6 In.	200.00
Plate, Barratt's Chapel, Fredica Delaware, 9 ½ In.	148.00
Plate, Hindustan, Paneled, Maddock, 9 ¾ In. ....*illus*	46.00
Plate, Lugano, Gold Trim, 9 ½ In.	66.00
Plate, Manilla, Marked P.W. & Co., 9 ½ In.	110.00
Plate, Oregon, T.J. & J. Mayer, 10 ½ In.	44.00
Plate, Pelew, Marked, Ironstone, E. Challinor, 9 ½ In.	145.00
Plate, Roseville, Marked, John Maddock, 9 ½ In.	110.00
Plate, Scalloped Border, Arch Rock, Wheelock, England, 10 In.	117.00
Plate, Scinde, c.1840, 10 ½ In.	25.00
Plate, Washington's Headquarters At Valley Forge, 9 ⅞ In.	120.00
Platter, Arcadia, Marked, 15 x 20 ⅝ In.	154.00
Platter, Formosa, W. Ridgway, 11 In. ....*illus*	162.00
Platter, Kyber, Adams & Co., 10 In. ....*illus*	99.00
Platter, Nonpareil, Scalloped Edge, Burgess & Leigh, 13 ½ In.	44.00
Platter, Scinde, c.1840, 16 In.	225.00
Platter, Sobraon, Temple, Landscape, Staffordshire, c.1840, 16 ¼ x 12 ½ In.	205.00
Slop Jar, Cover, Handles, 13 In.	225.00
Sugar & Creamer, Covered Sugar, Marked, 5 ¾-In. Sugar, 5 ¼-In. Creamer............	165.00
Teapot, Floral, Incised E, 8 ¾ In.	695.00
Teapot, Touraine, Marked, 6 ¾ In.	143.00
Vase, Flowers, Gold Sponge Detail, 7 ⅝ In.	106.00
Vase, Roses, Pierced Edges, Gold Wreath Draped Handles, 4-Footed, 5 ¼ In.	153.00
Warming Plate, Chinese Pattern, Tin Base, Brass Cap, Wire Loop Handles, 10 ½ In.	66.00

FLYING PHOENIX, *see Phoenix Bird category.*

FOLK ART is also listed in many categories of this book under the actual name of the object. See categories such as Box, Cigar Store Figure, Paper, Weather Vane, Wooden, etc.

Bird Tree, 9 Birds, Painted, Bentwood Tree, Pedestal, Signed Ludwig, 20 In.	495.00
Bird Tree, 11 Birds, Fenced Platform Base, Carved, Painted, c.1910, 36 In.	1053.00
Bird Tree, 15 Birds, Pine, Carved, Painted, Turned Bedpost, David Ludwig, 21 ½ In. ...	1540.00
Bird Tree, Wood, 3 Birds, Rooster, On Bentwood Twig Tree, 21 ½ In.	124.00
Bird Tree, Wood, 4 Carved, Multicolored Roosters, Bentwood Tree, 18 In.	385.00
Bird Tree, Wood, 6 Multicolored Birds, Bentwood Twig Tree, Signed, Strawser, 1985, 15 In.	170.00
Bird Tree, Wood, 12 Painted Birds, On Bentwood Twig, Turned, Block Base, 45 In.	158.00
Boat, Model, Mixed Wood, Glass Windows, Propeller, Anchor, Paint, c.1950.13 x 27 In.	499.00
Bottle, Sand Picture, Multicolored, Paddlewheeler, Calling Card, A. Clemens, c.1888, 8 ⅝ In..	17775.00
Bottle, Sand Picture, Sailing Ships, Blown Glass, Footed, Geometric Design, Nosegay, 1892, 7 ¼ In.	15725.00
Busk, Geometrics, Flowers, Sealing Wax Inlays, Wood, Signed LC, 1845, 14 In.	382.00

Flash Gordon, Water Pistol, Marx, Box, 7 ¾ In.
$351.00

F

Flow Blue, Coffeepot, Pagoda Bells, Paneled, T. Phillips, 9 ½ In.
$132.00

Flow Blue, Creamer, Kyber, Paneled, J. Meir & Son, 5 ½ In.
$88.00

Flow Blue, Gravy Boat, Nonpareil, 4 ¼ x 8 In.
$50.00

Flow Blue, Plate, Hindustan, Paneled, Maddock, 9 ¾ In.
$46.00

Flow Blue, Platter, Formosa, W. Ridgway, 11 In.
$162.00

Flow Blue, Platter, Kyber, Adams & Co., 10 In.
$99.00

Folk Art, Sweetheart Bears, Holding Heart, Patchwork, Button Eyes, 1880s
$75.00

Bust, Man, Wavy Hair, Cast Iron, Old Paint, 1900s, 23 x 13 In.	13035.00
Canada Goose, Glass Eye, Paint, c.1930, 21x 40 In.	705.00
Canister, Lid, Metal, Painted Scene, Black Family, Cooking, c.1910, 5 x 6 ¼ In.	117.00
Coffee Tin, Tole, Homemade From Coffee Can, Drip Grind, Key On Bottom, Black, 5 x 4 In.	25.00
Container, Ice Cream, Cover, Metal, Mustard Ground, Red & White Houses, Jean Dewey, 21 In.	225.00
Dancing Man, Pine, Jointed, Paint Traces, c.1890, 11 In.	118.00
Dancing Man, Wood, Carved, Jointed, Painted Features, Red, Paint Body, c.1890, 10 In.	441.00
Dice, Painted, White, Black, Wood, 7 ½ In.	748.00
Doll, Woman, Cloak, Bonnet, Cotton Batting, Newspaper Core, Stitched, 12 In.	119.00
Dovecote, Shingled Roof, 10 Bird Openings, Worn White Paint, 1900s, 54 x 16 In.	805.00
Eagle, Spread Wings, Yellow, Brown, Wilhelm Schimmel, 10 ¼ x 13 ¼ In.	3600.00
Eaglet, Black, Yellow Red, Wood, Carved, Wilhelm Schimmel, 4 In.	5200.00
Eaglet, Green, Red Wings, Wilhelm Schimmel, 3 ½ In.	5000.00
Eaglet, Painted, Wilhelm Schimmel, 9 In.	25740.00
Frame, Chip-Carved Pyramids, 18 In.	370.00
Gourd, American Flag, U.S.A., Painted, B.F. Perkins, Marked, 1995, 11 In.	115.00
Gourd, Carved, Figural Scenes, Japan, 19th Century, 2 ¼ In., 3 Piece	71.00
Head, Mechanical, Movable Features, Plywood, Paint, E.E. Baun, 1938, 19 x 9 In.	4444.00
Horse, Softwood, Brown Paint, Leather Mane, Tail, c.1905, 12 x 14 In.	823.00
Indian, Seated, Headdress, Bearclaw Necklace, Sandstone, Signed, E. Reed, c.1950, 32 In.	941.00
Jewelry Case, Matchstick, Heart Shape Top With Photo, c.1930, 14 In.	83.00
Man On Stump, Carved From Single Tree Branch, 20th Century, 18 ¾ In.	235.00
Mermaid, Wood, Carved, Painted, Arms Behind Head, 49 x 17 x 7 In.	500.00
Oil Can, Metal, Mustard, Strawberry & Pineapple, Signed, Jean Dewey, 19 ½ In.	225.00
Owl, Carved, Painted, Stand, 30 In.	3450.00
Paddle, Geometrics, Masks, Multicolored, Carved, Wood, Early 1900s, 45 In.	60.00
Panel, Angel, Outstretched Arms, 2 Girls, Flowers, Relief Carved, Painted, 15 x 11 In.	173.00
Pen Wipe, Dog, Poodle, Black, Figural, Looped Wool, Stocking Face, Bead Eyes, 3 ¼ x 5 In.	40.00
Penguin, Emperor, Tack Eyes, Applied Feet, Flippers, Wood, C. Hart, Mass., c.1935, 5 In.	1659.00
Penguin, Emperor, Tack Eyes, Applied Feet, Flippers, Wood, C. Hart, Mass., c.1935, 7 In.	2252.00
Picture, Cutout, Metal, Painted, Iwo Jima Flag Raising, Frame, World War II, 11 x 15 In.	275.00
Pipe, Horse Shape, Stone, Pewter, Stand, c.1950, 5 x 8 In.	2844.00
Rooster, Black, Yellow, Red, Green Ground, Wilhelm Schimmel, 3 ¾ In.	5200.00
Rooster, Carved, Painted, 22 In.	750.00
Rooster, Yellow, Black, Red, Signed, Lonnie & Twyla Money, 30 In.	1265.00
Rooster, Yellow, Black Streaks, Red, Wilhelm Schimmel, 6 ¼ In.	18000.00
Scarecrow, Wood, Jointed Arms & Hips, Carved Toes, Fingers, Face, Cloth, Stand, 41 In.	4600.00
Seal, Lid On Back, Glass Eyes, Carved, Wood, Green, Black Paint, 25 x 94 x 24 In.	13800.00
Snake, Root, Painted, Red, White, Black, 76 In.	316.00
Squirrel, Eating Nut, Red, Gold, Green, Wilhelm Schimmel, 1817-18, 4 In.	26000.00
Statue Of Liberty, Wood, Carved, Early 1900s, 25 x 8 In.	600.00
Sweetheart Bears, Holding Heart, Patchwork, Button Eyes, 1880s *illus*	75.00
Tiger, Black & White Stripe, Green Ground, Wood, Wilhelm Schimmel, 4 ¼ x 7 ¼ In.	84000.00
Tower, Wood, Whimsy, Open Cages, Painted, c.1900, 19 ½ In.	59.00
Toy, Soldiers, Musicians, Prisoner-Of-War Carved, Ivory, Windup, Box Stand, 6 In.	3393.00
Turkey, Carved, Painted, Glass Eyes, Wood Plinth, c.1975, 27 x 29 In.	1150.00
Uncle Sam, Painted, Red, White, Blue, Jointed Arms, Wood, Carved, 61 In.	518.00
Vase, Textured, Turned Olivewood, Marked, Phil Pratt, 8 x 7 In.	145.00
Whirligig, Baseball Player, Wood, Carved, Painted, Green Mound, Signed, D&BS, 1979, 14 ½ In.	102.00
Whirligig, Car, Driver, Passenger, Pink, White & Red Paint, 1930s, 32 In.	358.00
Whirligig, Carved Man, Iron Hat, Holding Apple & Walking Stick, Windmill, 1920s, 18 In.	5300.00
Whirligig, Doughboy, Painted, Flag Propellers, 31 In.	1860.00
Whirligig, Farmer, Wood, Carved, Yellow Hat, Overalls, Pitchfork Hands, Picket Fence, 11 ½ In.	45.00
Whirligig, Horse & Rider, Wood, Metal, Painted	359.00
Whirligig, Indian, In Canoe, Carved Wood, Multicolored, 20th Century, 11 x 15 In.	382.00
Whirligig, Indian, In Canoe, Red, White, Green, 10 x 18 In.	495.00
Whirligig, Mammy, Doing Laundry, Man Smoking Pipe, Tin, c.1920s, 17 x 18 In.	820.00
Whirligig, Mammy, Doing Laundry, Wood, Stand, 20 x 26 In. *illus*	263.00
Whirligig, Man, 2-Sided, Hat, Wood, Painted, 15 ½ In.	468.00
Whirligig, Man, Movable Arms, Wood, Carved, Painted, 5 ½ x 27 In.	390.00
Whirligig, Man, Wearing Cap, Wood, Tin, 20th Century, 34 In.	499.00
Whirligig, Sailor, Carved Wood, Multicolor, Tin Feet, Pease & Ceely, Nantucket, 16 ½ In.	441.00
Whirligig, Sailor, Painted, Nantucket, Early 1900s, 10 ½ In.	85.00
Whirligig, Soldier, Wood, Multicolored, Iron Tack Eyes, Buttons, 21 In.	2252.00
Whirligig, Washerwoman, Scrubbing, Washboard, Bird, Wood, c.1950, 15 x 25 In.	415.00
Whirligig, Windmill, Wood, Metal, Mounting Pole, c.1900, 30 In.	176.00

Whirligig, Woman, White, Hat, Ruffled Brown Dress, Carved, Wood, Early 1900s, 21 In.	385.00
Whirligig, Woman, Working Churn, Dasher Up & Down, Wire, Nails, 23 In.	201.00
Whirligig, Wood, Red, Green Paint, 50 x 72 In.	920.00

FOOT WARMERS solved the problem of cold feet in past generations. Some warmers held charcoal, others held hot water. Pottery, tin, and soapstone were the favored materials to conduct the heat. The warmer was kept under the feet, then the legs and feet were tucked into a blanket, providing welcome warmth in a cold carriage or church.

Brass, Hot Water, Carpet Covering, c.1910, 26 ½ x 8 In.	125.00
Brass, Punched Holes, Case Form, Swivel Handle, La Frileuse, France, 7 ½ In.	195.00
Cherry, Pierced, Cut Nail Construction, Sheet Iron Inner Box, 8 x 10 x 7 In.	595.00
Cherry, Square Nails, Brass Bail Handle, c.1800	350.00
Cherry, Steel Bail Handle, Pa., 19th Century, 6 ¾ x 9 ½ In. ....*illus*	540.00
Copper, Patina, Oval, Squat, Shaped Bail Handle, Rein Kupfer, Germany, 10 ½ x 7 In.	85.00
Hardwood, Sheet Metal Liner, Turned Posts, 1800s, 8 x 11 In.	264.00
Henderson Foot Warmer, Pottery, Ivory Glaze, Bottle Shape, Side Stopper, Chain, 11 In.	200.00
Metal, Cylindrical, Needlepoint Cover, Drawer, Ring Handles, Clark Heater No. 3D, 11 In.	70.00
Oak, Carved, Wrought Iron Bail Handle, Frisian, c.1800, 6 ¾ In. ....*illus*	330.00
Oak, Chip Carved Geometrics & Leaves, Hinged Door, 8 x 9 ¾ x 8 ½ In.	395.00
Stoneware, Bottle Shape, 3 Lobes, Laydown, Threaded Stopper, England, 11 x 6 In.	20.00
Stoneware, Brown Glaze, 3 Rounded Sides, Stopper, 12 In.	140.00
Stoneware, Tan, Arched Shape, Brown Handled Stopper, Lorinan, Belfast, 11 x 4 In.	50.00
Tin, Geometric, Walnut Mortises, Wire Bail Handle, 6 ½ x 9 ⅝ In.	143.00
Tin, Punched, Heart Design, Cherry, Mortised Posts, Wire Bail Handle, 5 ¾ x 7 ½ In.	411.00
Tole, Tin, Punched, Stenciled Flowers, 5 x 7 x 7 In.	150.00
Wood, Turned Spindle Frame, Hinged, Punched Tin Box, 8 x 8 x 6 In.	195.00
Wood, Turned Spindle Frame, Punched Tin Panels, Hearts, Wire Bail Handle, 9 x 8 In.	245.00

FOOTBALL *collectibles may be found in the Card and the Sports categories.*

FOSTORIA glass was made in Fostoria, Ohio, from 1887 to 1891. The factory was moved to Moundsville, West Virginia, and most of the glass seen in shops today is a twentieth-century product. The company was sold in 1983; new items will be easily identifiable, according to the new owner, Lancaster Colony Corporation. Additional Fostoria items may be listed in the Milk Glass category.

American, Bonbon, Footed, 2 ¼ x 7 In.	30.00
American, Creamer, Tea, 3 In. ....*illus*	25.00
American, Toothpick, Clear, c.1915, 2 x 1 In.	28.00
Animal, Duck, Mama, Cobalt Blue, 4 In.	36.00
Atlanta, Cake Stand, Square Lion, Pressed Glass, 5 ¾ x 9 In. ....*illus*	196.00
Baroque, Relish, 3 Sections, Topaz, 10 In.	62.00
Berry, Sugar & Creamer, Milk Glass, 3 ⅝ In. & 2 ⅞ In.	40.00
Brazilian, Syrup, Cover, Emerald Green, c.1925, 6 ½ In.	456.00
Brocade, Sandwich Server, Grape, Azure, Center Handle, 11 ½ In. ....*illus*	89.00
Chintz, Sugar	15.00
Coin, Cigarette Urn, Amber, 3 ¼ In. ....*illus*	45.00
Colony, Dish, Mayonnaise, Spoon, 5 ½ In.	37.00
Colony, Goblet, 9 Oz.	20.00
Colony, Lustres, 1938, 6 In.	195.00
Crown Collection, Candy Jar, Cover, Pedestal, Hapsburg, Ruby, 9 ½ In.	145.00
Diadem, Candy Jar, Cover, Ebony, c.1932	80.00
Fairfax, Bowl, 2 Handles, Topaz, 8 ½ In.	60.00
Fairfax, Cup & Saucer, Footed, Azure Blue	25.00
Fairfax, Cup & Saucer, Green	16.00
Hapsburg Crown, Candy Box, Cover, Topaz, c.1962, 5 ¾ In.	78.00
Heirloom, Bowl, Blue Opalescent, 5 In. ....*illus*	34.00
Heirloom, Bowl, Blue, White, Ribbed, Round, 11 In.	51.00
Hermitage, Mustard, Cover	15.00
Horizon, Bowl, Cereal, Cinnamon, 6 In.	26.00
Horizon, Cup & Saucer, Cinnamon, c.1955	24.00
Horizon, Plate, Dinner, Cinnamon, 10 In.	32.00
Jamestown, Goblet, Blue, 9 Oz., 5 ⅞ In.	26.00
Jamestown, Pitcher, Pink, 48 Oz., 7 ⁵⁄₁₆ In.	200.00
Jamestown, Salt & Pepper, Green	85.00
Jamestown, Tumbler, Iced Tea, Blue, 11 Oz., 6 In.	28.00

Folk Art, Whirligig, Mammy, Doing Laundry, Wood, Stand, 20 x 26 In. $263.00

Foot Warmer, Cherry, Steel Bail Handle, Pa., 19th Century, 6 ¾ x 9 ½ In. $540.00

Foot Warmer, Oak, Carved, Wrought Iron Bail Handle, Frisian, c.1800, 6 ¾ In. $330.00

Fostoria, American, Creamer, Tea, 3 In. $25.00

Fostoria, Atlanta, Cake Stand, Square Lion, Pressed Glass, 5 ¾ x 9 In. $196.00

Fostoria, Brocade, Sandwich Server, Grape, Azure, Center Handle, 11 ½ In. $89.00

Fostoria, Coin, Cigarette Urn, Amber, 3 ¼ In. $45.00

June, Candy Dish, Fold Up Sides, Tab Handles, 2 ½ x 7 x 5 ½ In.	25.00
June, Celery Dish, 11 ½ In.	34.00
June, Cup & Saucer	30.00
Kashmir, Bonbon, Blue, Handles, 6 ¾ In. ....*illus*	25.00
Lafayette, Plate, Salad, Wisteria, 7 ¼ In.	45.00
Lamp, Electric, Spider Web, Flowers, Milk Glass, Umbrella Shade, c.1900, 5 In. Base	66.00
Lido, Plate, Salad, 7 In.	18.00
Lotus, Vase, George Sakier, Fluted Black Glass, 6 ¼ To 12 ¾ In., 3 Piece ....*illus*	900.00
Mayfair, Relish, Green, 5 Sections, 13 x 9 In. ....*illus*	34.00
Meadow Rose, Sherbet, Tall, 6 Oz., 5 ⅝ In.	32.00
Navarre, Cordial, Stem, 3 ⅞ In.	95.00
Navarre, Tumbler, Juice, 4 ⅝ In.	30.00
Nut Dish, Amber, Paneled, Folded, c.1930, 1 x 2 In.	19.00
Priscilla, Custard, Handle, Blue, c.1928	38.00
Priscilla, Syrup, Emerald Green, Gilt, c.1900, 6 ¼ In.	198.00
Tut, Vase, 2 Handles, Amber, 6 ½ In.	95.00
Versailles, Finger Bowl, Yellow, Blown, 4 ½ In.	42.00
Vesper, Compote, Azure, 6 x 7 In. ....*illus*	41.00
Vulcan, Salt, Clear, 2 In.	12.00
Willow, Sugar & Creamer, Raleigh Blanks, 3 In.	40.00

FOVAL, *see Fry category.*

FRAMES *are included in the Furniture category under Frame.*

FRANCISCAN is a trademark that appears on pottery. Gladding, McBean and Company started in 1875. The company grew and acquired other potteries. It made sewer pipes, floor tiles, dinnerwares, and art pottery with a variety of trademarks. In 1934, dinnerware and art pottery were sold under the name *Franciscan Ware*. The company made china and cream-colored, decorated earthenware. Desert Rose, Apple, El Patio, and Coronado were best-sellers. The company became Interpace Corporation and in 1979 was purchased by Josiah Wedgwood & Sons. The plant was closed in 1984, but a few of the patterns are still being made. For more prices, go to kovels.com.

Apple, Ashtray, 9 In.	64.00
Apple, Bowl, Cereal, 6 In.	14.00
Apple, Bowl, Fruit, 5 ¼ In.	10.00
Apple, Bowl, Salad, 10 ¼ In.	75.00
Apple, Bowl, Vegetable, Cover, 1 ½ Qt.	55.00
Apple, Butter, Cover, ¼ Lb.	45.00
Apple, Casserole, Cover, Individual, 4 In.	42.00
Apple, Chop Plate, 12 In.	34.00
Apple, Compote, 8 x 4 In.	65.00
Apple, Creamer, 3 ¼ In.	12.00
Apple, Creamer, Individual, 2 ¾ In.	22.00
Apple, Cup & Saucer	64.00
Apple, Eggcup, 1 ¾ In.	27.00
Apple, Gravy Boat, Attached Underplate	35.00
Apple, Plate, Bread & Butter, 6 In.	10.00
Apple, Plate, Dinner, 10 ⅝ In.	21.00
Apple, Relish, 3 Sections, Handles, 11 x 9 ½ In.	41.00
Apple, Saucer	5.00
Apple, Sugar & Creamer	25.00
Autumn, Ashtray, Individual, 4 ¾ In.	4.50
Autumn, Bowl, Cereal, 7 ⅜ In.	14.00
Autumn, Bowl, Fruit, 5 ⅛ In.	6.00
Autumn, Bowl, Vegetable, Divided, 1¾ In.	16.00
Autumn, Creamer, 3 ¼ In.	12.00 to 15.00
Autumn, Cup	8.00
Autumn, Cup & Saucer	12.00
Autumn, Mug, 5 ¼ In.	25.00
Autumn, Plate, Bread & Butter, 6 ½ In.	6.00 to 7.00
Autumn, Plate, Dinner, 10 ½ In.	15.00
Autumn, Platter, 13 ¾ In.	21.00
Autumn, Salt & Pepper	28.00
Autumn, Sugar	12.00
Autumn, Sugar, Lid	22.00

Beverly, Coffeepot, Cover	110.00
Beverly, Creamer	45.00
Beverly, Cup & Saucer, After Dinner	21.00
Beverly, Sugar, Cover	65.00
Blueberry, Bowl, Fruit, 5 ¼ In.	10.00
Blueberry, Cup	8.00
Bountiful, Cup & Saucer	11.00
Bountiful, Plate, Dinner, 10 ¾ In.	35.00
Bouquet, Cup & Saucer	15.00
Bouquet, Plate, Bread & Butter, 6 ¾ In.	8.00
Bouquet, Plate, Dinner, 10 ½ In.	15.00
Cafe Royal, Bowl, Cereal, 6 In.	8.00
Cafe Royal, Butter, Cover	45.00
Cafe Royal, Compote, 6 In.	82.00
Cafe Royal, Creamer	18.00
Cameo, Cup & Saucer	17.00
Cameo, Plate, Bread & Butter, 6 ⅜ In.	12.00
Cameo, Plate, Salad, 8 ½ In.	17.00
Coronado, Bowl, Vegetable, Coral, Gloss, 10 ½ In.	20.00
Coronado, Bowl, Vegetable, Turquoise, Gloss, 7 ¾ In.	18.00
Coronado, Chop Plate, Ivory, Matte, 11 ¾ In.	20.00
Coronado, Chop Plate, Yellow, Matte, 11 ¾ In.	20.00
Coronado, Creamer, Ivory, Matte	15.00
Coronado, Cup & Saucer, Coral, Gloss	10.00
Coronado, Plate, Bread & Butter, Coral, Gloss, 6 ¼ In.	4.00
Coronado, Plate, Bread & Butter, Turquoise, Gloss, 6 ¼ In.	5.00
Coronado, Plate, Luncheon, Coral, Gloss, 9 ½ In.	8.00
Coronado, Plate, Luncheon, Yellow, Gloss, 9 ¼ In.	10.00
Coronado, Plate, Turquoise, Gloss, 8 In.	7.00
Coronado, Teapot, Coral Gloss	35.00
Daisy, Creamer, 3 ¼ In.	14.00
Daisy, Plate, Bread & Butter, 6 ½ In.	5.00
Del Mar, Bowl, Fruit, 5 In.	10.00
Del Mar, Bowl, Vegetable, Divided, 10 In.	17.00
Del Rio, Plate, Dinner, 10 ½ In.	15.00
Desert Rose, Bowl, Cereal, 5 ¼ In.	10.00
Desert Rose, Bowl, Fruit, 5 ¼ In.	10.00
Desert Rose, Creamer	13.00
Desert Rose, Cup & Saucer	7.00 to 15.00
Desert Rose, Cup ....*illus*	10.00
Desert Rose, Gravy Boat, Attached Underplate	37.00
Desert Rose, Grill Plate, 11 In.	70.00
Desert Rose, Plate, Bread & Butter, 6 ⅜ In.	6.00
Desert Rose, Plate, Dinner, 9 ½ In.	10.00
Desert Rose, Plate, Dinner, 10 ⅝ In.	18.00
Desert Rose, Plate, Salad, Crescent, 8 In.	25.00
Desert Rose, Platter, 14 ¼ In.	32.00
Desert Rose, Sugar, Cover	21.00
Dogwood, Bowl, Fruit, 6 ¼ In.	12.00
Dogwood, Plate, Dinner, 10 ¾ In.	15.00
Duet, Creamer	12.00
Duet, Gravy Boat, Attached Underplate	35.00
Duet, Plate, Dinner, 10 ¾ In.	12.00
Duet, Plate, Salad, Crescent, 9 ½ In.	16.00
El Patio, Bowl, Vegetable, Oval, Coral, Matte, 9 ⅛ In.	26.00
El Patio, Plate, Bread & Butter, Coral, Matte, 6 ½ In.	4.00
El Patio, Plate, Dinner, Flame Orange, 10 ½ In.	21.00
El Patio, Plate, Dinner, Gray, Matte, 10 ½ In.	15.00
El Patio, Plate, Dinner, Turquoise Gloss, 10 ½ In.	21.00
El Patio, Saucer, Coral, Gloss	3.00
Fern Dell, Bread Tray, 18 In.	25.00
Fresh Fruit, Bowl, Cereal, 6 In.	12.00
Fresh Fruit, Butter, Cover	95.00
Gingersnap, Plate, Salad, 8 ¾ In.	7.00
Gingersnap, Serving Bowl, 9 ½ In.	35.00
Hacienda, Creamer, Gold	16.00

Fostoria, Heirloom, Bowl,
Blue Opalescent, 5 In.
$34.00

Fostoria, Kashmir, Bonbon,
Blue, Handles, 6 ¾ In.
$25.00

Fostoria, Lotus, Vase, George Sakier,
Fluted Black Glass, 6 ¼ To 12 ¾ In.,
3 Piece
$900.00

Fostoria, Mayfair, Relish, Green,
5 Sections, 13 x 9 In.
$34.00

F

Fostoria, Vesper, Compote, Azure,
6 x 7 In.
$41.00

Franciscan, Desert Rose, Cup
$10.00

Franciscan, Meadow Rose, Cup, Yellow
$5.00

Franciscan, October, Creamer, 4 ¼ In.
$10.00

Madeira

Madeira is the name of both a shape and a pattern of earthenware dishes. The pattern is dark brown with an overall center design of pale yellow lines forming flowers and scrolls. It was introduced in 1967.

Hacienda, Creamer, Green		16.00
Hacienda, Cup & Saucer, Gold		10.00
Hacienda, Gravy Boat, Attached Underplate, Gold		28.00
Hacienda, Plate, Bread & Butter, Green, 6 ⅝ In.		6.00
Hacienda, Plate, Dinner, Gold, 10 ¾ In.		12.00
Hacienda, Plate, Dinner, Green, 10 ¾ In.		12.00
Hacienda, Plate, Salad, Gold, 8 ⅜ In.		8.00
Heritage, Bowl, Fruit, 5 In.		15.00
Heritage, Coffeepot		45.00
Heritage, Creamer		12.00
Heritage, Cup & Saucer		7.00
Indian Summer, Casserole, Cover.		33.00
Indian Summer, Creamer		12.00
Indian Summer, Platter, 13 In.		19.00
Ivy, Casserole, Cover, 7 In.		110.00
Ivy, Chop Plate, 14 In.		82.00
Ivy, Tidbit, 3 Tiers		85.00
Jamocha, Cup & Saucer, Footed		9.00
Madeira, Plate, Bread & Butter, 6 ¾ In.		8.00
Madeira, Saucer, 3 In.		3.00
Maytime, Bowl, Fruit, 5 In.		20.00
Maytime, Bowl, Soup, 6 ¼ In.		25.00
Maytime, Plate, Dinner, 10 ⅛ In.		15.00
Meadow Rose, Cup, Yellow	*illus*	5.00
Moondance, Bowl, Soup, 6 ¼ In.		12.00
Moondance, Bowl, Vegetable, 7 ½ In.		21.00
Moondance, Cup & Saucer		10.00
Moondance, Plate, Dinner, 10 ½ In.		13.00
Moondance, Platter, Oval, 13 ½ In.		31.00
October, Creamer, 4 ¼ In.	*illus*	10.00
Pickwick, Butter, Cover		21.00
Pickwick, Plate, Dinner, 10 ⅜ In.		10.50
Poppy, Butter, Cover		16.00
Poppy, Plate, Bread & Butter, 6 ¼ In.		10.00
Radiance, Creamer		14.00
Radiance, Sugar, Cover		28.00
Rosette, Bowl, Cereal, 6 ⅛ In.		8.00
Rosette, Platter, Oval, 13 In.		60.00
Rossmore, Plate, Salad, 8 ⅜ In.		12.00
Spice, Platter, 16 ½ In.		30.00
Starburst, Egg Cup		125.00
Terra-Cotta, Gravy Boat, Attached Underplate		35.00
Terra-Cotta, Plate, Bread & Butter, 6 ¼ In.		8.00
Terra-Cotta, Plate, Salad, 8 ⅜ In.		10.00
Tulip Time, Creamer, 4 ¼ In.	*illus*	10.00
Tulip Time, Platter, 14 In.		35.00
Winsome, Creamer		10.00

FRANCISWARE is the name of a glassware made by Hobbs, Brockunier and Company of Wheeling, West Virginia, in the 1880s. It is a clear or frosted hobnail or swirl pattern glass with an amber-stained rim. Some pieces were made by a pressed glass method, others were mold blown.

Pitcher, Milk, Hobnail, 6 In.	125.00
Sugar Shaker, Swirl, Clear Frosted, Amber Stain, Lid, Hobbs, Brockunier, c.1875, 5 ¼ In.	224.00

FRANKART INC., New York, New York, mass-produced nude *dancing lady* lamps, ashtrays, and other decorative Art Deco items in the 1920s and 1930s. They were made of white lead composition and spray-painted. *Frankart Inc.* and the patent number and year were stamped on the base.

Bookend, Dog, Cocker Spaniel, Metal, c.1934, 5 ⅞ x 7 ¼ In.	35.00
Bookends, Nude Dancers, Arched Back, Copper Paint, Cast Metal, 1920s	195.00
Bookends, Nude Playing Peek-A-Boo, Art Deco, 8 In.	700.00
Cardholder, Dog, Scottie, Standing, Art Deco, 4 ½ x 4 ½ In.	95.00
Doorstop, Nude Woman, Reclining, White Paint Over Red, Cast Iron, 7 x 4 In.	295.00
Figurine, Nude, Dancing, Black, Signed, 1922	250.00

Figurine, Nude, Kneeling, Holding Ashtray Overhead, Bronze Brown, 9 In.	250.00
Figurine, Nude, Standing, Holding Ashtray Overhead, Painted Metal, 25 ½ In.	400.00
Lamp, Jockey, On Horse, Signed, 17 x 8 In.	350.00
Lamp, Nude Woman, Standing On Glass Globe, Green Glass, Art Deco, 15 In.	375.00
Plaque, Nude Archer, Bronze, Art Nouveau, Marked, 1930, 8 x 8 In.	145.00

FRANKOMA POTTERY was originally known as The Frank Potteries when John F. Frank opened shop in 1933. The factory is now working in Sapulpa, Oklahoma. Early wares were made from a light cream-colored clay from Ada, Oklahoma, but in 1956 the company switched to a red clay from Sapulpa. The firm made dinnerwares, utilitarian and decorative kitchenwares, figurines, flowerpots, and limited edition and commemorative pieces. John Frank died in 1973 and his daughter, Joniece, inherited the business. Frankoma went bankrupt in 1990. The pottery operated under various owners for a few years and was bought by Joe Ragosta in 2008.

Ashtray, Arrowhead, Turquoise, 7 In.	18.00
Ashtray, Plainsman, Brown Satin, 12 ½ x 7 In. ....*illus*	15.00
Butter, Cover, Gracetone, Orbit Gray, ¼ Lb.	26.00
Creamer, Wagon Wheel, Prairie Green ....*illus*	21.00
Cup & Saucer, Lazybones, Blue	22.00
Decanter, Stopper, Cream & Brown, Joniece Frank, 12 ¼ In. ....*illus*	14.00
Dish, Leaf Shape, Desert Gold, 4 ⅜ In.	15.00
Figurine, Coyote Pup, Prairie Green, 7 ¾ In.	15.00
Plate, Bread & Butter, Lazybones, Blue, 7 ¼ In.	8.00

FRATERNAL objects that are related to the many different fraternal organizations in the United States are listed in this category. The Elks, Masons, Odd Fellows, and others are included. Also included are service organizations, like the American Legion, Kiwanis, and Lions Club. Furniture is listed in the Furniture category. Shaving mugs decorated with fraternal crests are included in the Shaving Mug category.

American Legion, Gasoline Globe, Glass Body, Lenses, 18 x 16 In., 3 Piece	270.00
American Order Of United Workmen, Paperweight, Emblems, Round, c.1868, 3 In.	59.00
B.P.O.E., Flask, Elk, Clock Face, Stoneware, Rheingold Beer, c.1912, 5 x 3 In. ....*illus*	104.00
Eastern Star, Paperweight, North Dakota School Of Mines, Cranberry, 5-Sided, 2 x 1 ¼ In. ...	140.00
Elks, Bowl, Ruffled Edge, Carnival Glass, Blue, Detroit, 1910	525.00
Elks, Bowl, Ruffled Edge, Carnival Glass, Green, Detroit, 1910	575.00
Elks, Stickpin, 14K Yellow Gold, 2 ⅞ In.	105.00
Elks, Tile, Elk Emblem, Hexagonal, White, Unglazed, Mosaic Tile Co., 1950s, 2 ¼ In.	65.00
International Order Of Good Templars, Badge, Gilt, Silk Ribbon, c.1900, 6 ¾ In.	20.00
Jewish Independent Order Brith Abraham, Badge, Grand Masters, 1930s ....*illus*	197.00
Knights Of Columbus, Sword, Engraved, George H. Bissman, Scabbard, Enameled, c.1890, 33 ½ In.	59.00
Knights Templar, Medal, Ribbon, Raised Relief, Hexagonal, 1900s, 2 ¼ In.	155.00
Knights Templar, Medallion, Tri-Annual Louisville Cyrene Commandery, c.1901, 2 ½ In.	125.00
Knights Templar, Plate, Duquesne Commandery, Pittsburgh, c.1899, 5 ½ In.	28.00
Knights Templar, Sword, Engraved, Scabbard, Albert Sargent, Ames Sword Co., 34 In.	83.00
Lions Club, Paperweight, Pottery, Press Molded, Signed, c.1953, 1 ½ x ⅜ In.	160.00
Loyal Order Of Moose, Pin, Moose Figure, Red, Enamel, Gold Plated, FCH, 1 ½ x ½ In.	20.00
Masonic, Apron, Sun, Moon, Star, Compass, White Ground, Trowel & Mallet, 1789............	1380.00
Masonic, Ashtray, Ceramic, Emblem, Blue & Gold, White Ground, c.1954, 6 ¼ x 6 ¼ In.	18.00
Masonic, Certificate, Master Mason, Ribbon, Seal, Vellum, Frame, New York, 1809, 10 x 11 In.	178.00
Masonic, Chair, Oak, Back Carved Symbols, Turned Legs, Dark Patina, 49 In., Pair...............	382.00
Masonic, Flask, Embossed Eagle, Shepard & Co., Red Amber To Orange Amber, Pontil, 6 ¾ In.	1344.00
Masonic, Kerchief, Song Lyrics, Attic Fire, Printed Emblems, Red, Linen, Frame, c.1817, 21 x 23 In.	390.00
Masonic, Membership Certificate, Sheepskin, Grand Lodge Of Quebec, c.1879, 20 x 16 In. *illus*	110.00
Masonic, Pendant, Gold, Enamel, 8-Sided, ⅝ In.	30.00
Masonic, Plaque, Wall, Pine, Symbols, Letter G, Shield Shape, Red, White, Blue, Gold, 34 x 29 In.	2133.00
Masonic, Ring, 10K Gold, Red Stone, Georgia, 1785...	128.00
Masonic, Rug, Hooked, Compass & Angle Center, Sword & Crescent Star Corners, 35 x 25 In.	154.00
Masonic, Sword, Sheath, White Handle, Horstman, Philadelphia	89.00
Masonic, Walking Stick, Maple, Carved, Symbols, Inscribed C.H. Henson, 37 ½ In.	356.00
Masonic, Walking Stick, Wood, Carved Symbols, c.1890, 34 In.	323.00
Masonic, Wall Shelf, Walnut, Pierced, Carved Symbols, 18 x 11 In.	474.00
Masonic, Watch Fob, Grand Lodge Of England, Silver, Enamel, Presentation, 1923, 1 ¼ In. ...	165.00
Masonic, Watch Fob, Hikock, Silver, Nickel Chain, 5 ¾-In. Chain, 1 ⅛ In.	55.00
Masonic, Watch Key, Gold Filled, Engraved Symbols, Devices, 2 In.	205.00
Masonic, Watch, Dudley No. 2, Flip Back, White Gold Filled, Arabic, 19 Jewels, Pocket, c.1932.	2270.00
Masonic, Watch, Dudley No. 3, Flip Back, Gold Filled, 19 Jewels, Pocket, 1940s	3884.00

F

Franciscan, Tulip Time, Creamer, 4 ¼ In.
$10.00

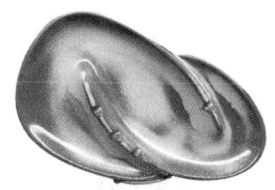

Frankoma Pottery, Ashtray, Plainsman, Brown Satin, 12 ½ x 7 In.
$15.00

Frankoma Pottery, Creamer, Wagon Wheel, Prairie Green
$21.00

Moondance

Moondance is decorated with what looks like a spiral of ink blots in gray to dark blue. There is also a dark blue band. The fine china pattern was first made in 1972 as part of the Madeira line.

Frankoma Pottery, Decanter, Stopper, Cream & Brown, Joniece Frank, 12 ¼ In. $14.00

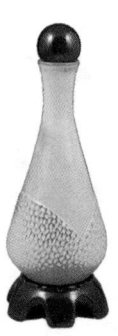

Fraternal, B.P.O.E., Flask, Elk, Clock Face, Stoneware, Rheingold Beer, c.1912, 5 x 3 In. $104.00

Fraternal, Jewish Independent Order Brith Abraham, Badge, Grand Masters, 1930s $197.00

Fraternal, Masonic, Membership Certificate, Sheepskin, Grand Lodge Of Quebec, c.1879, 20 x 16 In. $110.00

Masonic, Watch, Elgin, Blue Lodge, Custom Dial, Major Symbols, Gold Filled, c.1924	299.00
Masonic, Watch, Mathey Tissot, Sterling Silver, Triangular, 19 Jewels, Nylon Weave, c.1950	956.00
Masonic, Watch, Waltham, Triangular, Chain Link Bezel, 17 Jewel, Leather, 1960s	597.00
Medallion, Knights Templar, Ribbon, Early 1900s, 2 ¼ In.	155.00
Odd Fellows, Ark Of Covenant, Wood, 3 Rings, Carving, Red, Gold Paint, c.1900, 54 In.	494.00
Odd Fellows, Badge, Montana, 7 ¼ In.	22.00
Odd Fellows, Ceremonial Staff, Heart & Hand, Wood, Carved, Gilt, Red, Stand, 1800s, 75 In.	1659.00
Odd Fellows, Costume, Jonathan Coat, Emblems, Embroidered Velvet, c.1900, 36 In.	588.00
Odd Fellows, Emblem, Pick Ax, Shovel, Wood, Painted, c.1900, 35 & 39 In.	235.00
Odd Fellows, Horn Of Plenty, Wood, Painted, Black, Gilt, c.1900, 9 ½ x 12 In.	323.00
Odd Fellows, Hourglass, Wood, Lathe Turned, Emblem, c.1900, 7 In.	353.00
Odd Fellows, Mask, Man's Head, Black Hair, Beard, Papier-Mache, 20 x 12 In. ....*illus*	75.00
Odd Fellows, Peephole Cover, Figural, Sliding, 3-Link Chain, FLT, Cast Iron, 1900s, 7 x 4 In.	140.00
Odd Fellows, Print, Lithograph, Currier & Kellogg, Hand Colored, 1800s, 11 x 15 ¼ In., 2 Piece	176.00
Odd Fellows, Quiver, Arrows, Wood, Carved, Painted Salmon, Gilt, Black, c.1900, 30 In.	1058.00
Odd Fellows, Staff, Arrow Finial, Entwined Snake, Carved, Painted, c.1900, 63 In.	294.00
Odd Fellows, Stage Front, Wood, Arch, Red, Gold Paint, Scalloped Crest, Early 1900, 108 x 120 In.	353.00
Odd Fellows, Tablets, I-X Roman Numerals, Yellow Stand, c.1900, 20 ½ In.	323.00
Odd Fellows, Trivet, Iron, 4 Posts, Signed, Wilton, 5 ¼ x 7 ¾ In.	22.00
Rotary, Medallion, Zanesville, White Unglazed Tile, c.1940, 2 ⅜ In.	40.00
Shriner, Cup, Demitasse, Homer Laughlin	2.00
Shriner, Tile, Crescent Moon, Sword, Star, Blue, Gold, Wheeling Tile Co., 1940, 4 ¼ x 4 ¼ In.	85.00
Woodmen Of The World, Merit Badge, c.1910, 1 ¼ x 3 ⅛ In.	45.00

FRY GLASS was made by the H.C. Fry Glass Company of Rochester, Pennsylvania. The company, founded in 1901, first made cut glass and other types of fine glasswares. In 1922 it patented a heat-resistant glass called Pearl Ovenglass. For two years, 1926–1927, the company made Fry Foval, an opal ware decorated with colored trim. Reproductions of this glass have been made. Depression glass patterns made by Fry may be listed in the Depression Glass category. Some pieces of cut glass may also be included in the Cut Glass category.

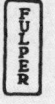

FRY GLASS

Bowl, Scalloped, Thistle, Marked, 7 In.	70.00
Clear Glass, Bubbles, Green Threading, Bowl, 2 Candlesticks, 14 In., 3 Piece	150.00
Pot, Hot Water, Cover, Cylindrical Form, White Pour Spout, Jade Green Handle, 12 Oz.	220.00
Sugar & Creamer, Clear Ground, Purple Handles, 4 In.	69.00

FRY FOVAL

Bowl, Centerpiece, Opal, Jade Green Stem, Flared Out Rim, 6 ¼ x 10 In.	480.00
Bowl, Fruit, Opal, Delft Blue Rim & Foot, c.1922, 5 ½ x 9 ½ In.	360.00
Candlestick, Opal, Jade Green Threading, 12 In.	275.00
Goblet, Opal, Jade Green Stem, 5 ¾ In.	90.00
Perfume Bottle, Opal, Cone Shape, Blue Stopper, 7 ¾ In.	480.00
Perfume Bottle, Opal, Tapered, Jade Green Stopper Flattened Foot & Stopper, 8 In.	240.00
Perfume Bottle, Opal, Teardrop Shape, Delft Blue Foot, Atomizer, 7 ½ In.	350.00
Vase, Opal, Transparent Blue Handles, Scalloped Folded In Rim, 2 ½ In.	24.00

FULPER POTTERY COMPANY was incorporated in 1899 in Flemington, New Jersey. It made art pottery from 1909 to 1929. The firm had been making bottles, jugs, and housewares from 1805. Doll heads were made about 1928. The firm became Stangl Pottery in 1929. Stangl Pottery is listed in its own category in this book.

Basket, Handle, Moss Green To Rose Flambe Glaze, Marked, 6 ½ x 9 In.	225.00
Bookends, Art Deco, Brown, Tan, Gold Mottled Glaze, 6 x ⅝ In.	300.00
Bowl, Blue & Green Flambe Glaze, Marked, 2 x 5 ½ In.	84.00
Bowl, Scalloped Rim, Blue Crystalline Glaze, Marked, 6 ¾ x 11 ½ In.	175.00
Bowl, Vaz-Bowl, Brown Matte Glaze, Blue Green Flambe Gloss Glaze Interior, Footed ....*illus*	518.00
Figurine, Black Cat, On Rooftop, 15 ½ x 17 ½ In.	9150.00
Figurine, Egyptian Princess, Standing On Scarab Flower Frog, 7 ½ In.	995.00
Flower Frog, Scarab, Blue Matte Glaze, 3 ¼ x 2 ⅜ In.	115.00
Jar, Copper Dust Glaze, Strap Handle, 11 ¾ In.	863.00
Jardiniere, Green Drip Glaze, Early 20th Century, 9 x 11 In.	6325.00
Jug, 3-Sided, Brown & Blue Flambe, Silver Overlay, Ship Design, 5 ¾ x 10 In.	115.00
Jug, Frothy, Gold Crystalline Glaze, 12 x 8 In.	1830.00
Jug, Zinc, Albany Slip Interior, Bird Decoration, Gal.	75.00
Pitcher, Mottled Green Glaze, c.1927, 4 ½ In.	138.00
Vase, Blue & Green Glaze, Spherical, 8 x 10 ¾ In.	840.00
Vase, Blue & Green, Streaks, Footed, Signed, c.1915, 11 ¾ In.	203.00
Vase, Blue Streaky Glaze, Baluster, Flared Rim, Footed, c.1915, 11 ¾ In.	207.00

Vase, Brown, Green Glaze, Shouldered, 3 ½ x 4 ½ In.	420.00
Vase, Bulbous, 3 Handles, Turquoise & Green Glaze, Marked, 7 ¾ x 6 In.	345.00
Vase, Bulbous, Mottled Green Matte Glaze, Mark, c.1920, 7 In.	546.00
Vase, Bulbous, Side Handles, Green-Brown Glaze, Signed, Early 20th Century, 7 ½ In.	150.00
Vase, Chinese Blue Flambe, Copper Dust Crystalline, 12 x 8 ¾ In.	1220.00
Vase, Chinese Blue Flambe, Crystalline Glaze, 12 x 11 ½ In.	1830.00
Vase, Chinese Blue, Fluted, Marked, 10 ½ In.	20.00
Vase, Cucumber Crystalline Glaze, Double Handle, 6 x 4 ¾ In.	360.00
Vase, Drip Glaze, Shaded Blue & Green, Stand, Early 1900s, 16 ¼ In. ....*illus*	2880.00
Vase, Frothy Chinese Blue Flambe, Matte Red, 7 ¾ x 7 ½ In.	580.00
Vase, Frothy Glaze, Cat's-Eye Flambe, 12 x 9 In.	976.00
Vase, Germanic, Brown Mottled Matte Glaze, Light Brown Band, 12 ⅜ In. ....*illus*	3450.00
Vase, Germanic, Light Brown, Blue Crystalline Glaze, Stamp, 12 In.	2530.00
Vase, Gourd Shape, Green, Brown & Tan Flambe, Marked, 5 x 13 In.	173.00
Vase, Green, Oval, Angular Handles, Ribbed, Floor, 10 x 22 In.	585.00
Vase, Leopard Skin Crystalline Glaze, Baluster, 15 ½ x 7 In.	2562.00
Vase, Long Neck, Flemington Green Glaze, 1909, 5 In.	230.00
Vase, Mirror Black Crystalline Glaze, 2 Handles, Bulbous, 8 x 6 In.	450.00
Vase, Mirror Black Glaze, 2 Handles, Signed, 7 ½ x 9 ½ In.	420.00
Vase, Pink, Blue, Green Flambe Glaze, 2 Handles, 6 x 4 ¼ In.	210.00
Vase, Ring Handles, Flambe Glaze, Marked, 7 x 13 In.	374.00
Vase, Stepped Shoulders, Square Handles, Green, Blue Flambe Glaze, Stamp, 6 x 10 In.	633.00
Vase, Tapered, Vertical Ridges, Blue To Rose, 8 ½ x 6 In.	402.00
Vase, Turquoise, Mustard Glaze, Incised Racetrack Mark, c.1915, 12 ½ In.	470.00
Vase, Violet, Brown, Grass Green Drip Glaze, Long Neck, 20th Century, 15 ¼ In.	1680.00
Vase, Yellow Amber Glaze, 2 Handles, 7 x 7 In.	225.00

FURNITURE of all types is listed in this category. Examples dating from the seventeenth century to the 1970s are included. Prices for furniture vary in different parts of the country. Oak furniture is most expensive in the West; large pieces over eight feet high are sold for the most money in the South, where high ceilings are found in the old homes. Condition is very important when determining prices. These are NOT average prices but rather reports of unique sales. If the description includes the word *style*, the piece resembles the old furniture style but was made at a later time. It is not a period piece. Garden furniture is listed in the Garden Furnishings category. Related items may be found in the Architectural, Brass, and Store categories.

Armchairs are listed under Chair in this category.

Armoire, Aesthetic Revival, Rosewood, Pediment, Oak Leaf Panel, Colonnettes, Mirror, 108 x 51 In.	881.00
Armoire, Art Deco, Zebrawood, 2 Doors, Shelves, Bun Feet, 70 ⅝ x 55 x 17 ¾ In.	2640.00
Armoire, Art Nouveau, Walnut, Burl, Kingwood, Austria, 78 x 47 x 18 In.	450.00
Armoire, Bookcase, Fruitwood, Walnut, Applied Leaves, Austria, c.1900, 84 x 68 In.	960.00
Armoire, Directoire Style, Provincial, Oak, 2 Doors, Diamond Grill Panels, 83 x 59 x 23 In. ...	2160.00
Armoire, Edwardian, Mahogany, Dentil Molded Cornice, 2 Doors, Plinth Base, 78 In.	711.00
Armoire, Empire, Flame Walnut Veneer, Step Back, 3 Paneled Doors, Inlaid, c.1810, 88 x 67 In.	5260.00
Armoire, Ezio Ravi, Red Lacquer, Parchment, Gilt, c.1935, 72 x 92 x 24 In.	5676.00
Armoire, Federal, Flame Mahogany, Arched Frieze, 2 2-Panel Doors, 83 x 57 In.	1840.00
Armoire, French Provincial, Cherry, Paneled Doors, 64 ½ x 23 In.	239.00
Armoire, French Provincial, Elm, Paneled Doors, Shelves, 1800s, 87 x 59 x 26 In.	1007.00
Armoire, French Provincial, Oak, Carved, Doors, Panels, Block Feet, 78 x 60 x 20 ½ In.	2400.00
Armoire, French Provincial, Oak, Paneled Doors, Carved Moldings, 102 x 60 x 27 In.	3525.00
Armoire, French Provincial, Walnut, 2 Shaped Panel Doors, 19th Century, 71 x 49 In.	397.00
Armoire, French Provincial, Walnut, Arch, Shaped Doors, Fitted Interior, 1700s, 57 x 95 In. ..	2006.00
Armoire, French Provincial, Walnut, Carved, Domed Cornice, Paneled Door, 79 x 38 In.	2415.00
Armoire, French Provincial, Walnut, Mirror, Carved Crest, c.1900, 95 x 50 x 24 In.	480.00
Armoire, Fruitwood, Inlaid, Recessed Panel Door, Shelves, 73 ¾ x 44 x 21 In.	1554.00
Armoire, Louis Philippe, Pine, 4 Double Paneled Doors, Painted, c.1830, 85 x 98 In.	3880.00
Armoire, Louis XV Style, Crest, Flower Frieze, Shaped Panel Doors, 1900s, 55 x 88 In.	1062.00
Armoire, Louis XV Style, Oak, Provincial, Bleached, 2 Doors, Panel, Drawers, 78 x 63 x 24 In.	2400.00
Armoire, Louis XV Style, Pine, Triple Paneled Recessed Doors, c.1780, 86 x 69 In.	3010.00
Armoire, Louis XV Style, Walnut, Molded Cornice, Paneled Doors, France, c.1760, 86 x 59 In.	6480.00
Armoire, Louis XV Style, Walnut, Panels, Leaf Covered Frieze, 2 Doors, 97 x 66 x 28 In.	6900.00
Armoire, Louis XV, Cherry, Oak, Floral Marquetry, 2 Doors, Carved, Molded, c.1790, 96 x 59 In.	2200.00
Armoire, Louis XV, Fruitwood, Arched, Carved Baskets, Shaped Glazed Panel Doors, 79 In.	1016.00
Armoire, Louis XV, Fruitwood, Carved, Stepped Cornice, Scalloped Doors, 92 x 69 x 26 In.	1838.00
Armoire, Louis XV, Molded Cornice, Carved Frieze, Flower Basket, Panel Doors, 90 x 51 In.	2233.00
Armoire, Louis XVI Style, Mahogany, Mirror Doors, Brass Eagle, H. Dasson, 1893, 96 x 54 In. ..	1955.00

Fraternal, Odd Fellows, Mask, Man's Head, Black Hair, Beard, Papier-Mache, 20 x 12 In.
$75.00

Fulper Pottery, Bowl, Vaz-Bowl, Brown Matte Glaze, Blue Green Flambe Gloss Glaze Interior, Footed
$518.00

Fulper Pottery, Vase, Drip Glaze, Shaded Blue & Green, Stand, Early 1900s, 16 ¼ In.
$2880.00

Fulper Pottery, Vase, Germanic, Brown Mottled Matte Glaze, Light Brown Band, 12 ⅜ In.
$3450.00

Furniture, Bed, Federal, Mahogany, Reeded Posts, Carved Headboard, 1800s, 89 x 57 In.
$1298.00

Furniture, Bed, Four-Poster, Curly Maple, Cannonball, Rope, 1820-25, 60 x 54 In.
$1175.00

Furniture, Bed, Four-Poster, George III, Mahogany, Carved, Scrolled, Early 1800s, 95 x 68 In.
$1180.00

Armoire, Louis XVI, Mahogany, Ormolu Mounted, Molded Crown, Mirrored Doors, 97 x 57 In.	1100.00
Armoire, Louis XVI, Walnut, Oak, Carved, Arched Crest, Paneled Door, France, c.1780, 95 x 58 In.	6250.00
Armoire, Mahogany, Dentil Molded Cornice, Satinwood Inlay, Paneled Doors, 52 x 22 In.	805.00
Armoire, Mahogany, Flame Grain, 2 Doors, 3 Inside Shelves, 4 Bracket Feet, 74 x 49 In.	1464.00
Armoire, Mahogany, Mirror, Drawer, Carved, Shell, Leaf, Griffin, Claw Feet, 42 x 69 In.	2588.00
Armoire, Neoclassical, Mahogany, 2 Panel Doors, Fitted Interior, Gilt Bronze, c.1825, 96 x 68 In.	8400.00
Armoire, Neoclassical, Walnut, Recessed Panels, Scrolled Leaf & Lattice, Drawers, 78 x 50 In.	840.00
Armoire, Pine, 2 Doors, Molded Cornice, Bun Feet, Continental, 84 x 66 x 22 In.	2400.00
Armoire, Pine, Finger Mold Carving, Herringbone Panels, Continental, 1700s, 76 x 54 x 22 In.	2400.00
Armoire, Pine, Painted, Flowers, Base Molding, Bun Feet, c.1700, 72 x 60 x 20 In.	538.00
Armoire, Pine, Unfinished, Austria, Late 19th Century, 73 x 46 x 19 ¾ In.	270.00
Armoire, Renaissance Revival, Walnut, Arched Cornice, Frieze, Drawers, Doors, c.1800, 100 x 58 In.	1292.00
Armoire, Rococo, Rosewood, Arched Crest, Bracket Stiles, Arched Doors, 108 x 63 In.	6463.00
Armoire, Rococo, Rosewood, Broken Arch, Finial, Mirror Doors, 2 Drawers, c.1875, 99 x 62 In.	2640.00
Armoire, Rococo, Rosewood, Carved, Mirror Door, Plinth Drawer, 99 x 47 In.	3231.00
Armoire, Rococo, Rosewood, Plinth Drawer, Carved Crest, New Orleans, 1800s, 99 x 47 In.	3231.00
Armoire, Rosewood, Oak, Leaf Carved Pediment, Mirror Door, Drawer, Columns, 51 x 108 In.	881.00
Armoire, Rosewood, Turned Feet, Austria, c.1900, 74 x 50 x 18 ½ In.	900.00
Armoire, Victorian, Walnut, 2 Doors, Racetrack Rim, 79 x 55 In.	458.00
Armoire, Walnut, 2 Panel Doors, Drawer, Ball & Claw, Spain, 1800s, 85 x 57 x 25 In.	600.00
Armoire, Walnut, Door, Recessed Panel, Shelves, Shaped Apron, 75 x 42 ½ x 16 In.	418.00
Armoire, Walnut, Pickled Finish, Mustard Accents, 2 Doors, Footed, Italy, 1700s, 80 x 58 x 20 In.	800.00
Armoire, Walnut, Stepped Cornice, Drawers, Shelves, Ball Feet, c.1850, 86 x 61 x 24 In.	1645.00
Bar Cart, Ico & Louisa Parisi, Birch, Glass, Brass, 26 ¾ x 33 x 20 ½ In.	2806.00
Bar Cart, McCobb, Metal, Glass Lower Shelf, Wood Top, Calvin, c.1952, 30 x 16 In., Pair	980.00
Bar, Oak, Hammered Copper Top, Base, Hinged Doors, Shelves, Drawers, 60 x 27 x 43 In.	230.00
Barstool, Norman Cherner, Vinyl Seat & Back, Metal Footrest, Plycraft, 1963, 17 x 44 In.	300.00
Bed Steps, Georgian, Mahogany, 2 Open Steps, Reeded Edges, Cabriole Legs, 19 x 9 In.	881.00
Bed Steps, Mahogany, 3 Step, Leather Treads, Compartment, Turned Legs, c.1875, 26 x 27 In.	460.00
Bed Steps, Victorian, Mahogany, Needlepoint, Hinged Treads, 1800s, 30 In.	1080.00
Bed Steps, William IV, Mahogany, 3 Steps, 2 Lift Tops, Leather Treads, c.1840, 27 x 33 In.	960.00
Bed Steps, William IV, Mahogany, Lift Tops, Tooled Leather Treads, c.1840, 26 x 19 In.	764.00
Bed, Bamboo, Fretwork, France, c.1890, 77 ½ x 57 In.	8500.00
Bed, Brass, Rounded Head & Footboard, 5 Vertical Rails, Full, 58 x 56 In.	117.00
Bed, Cannonball, Cherry, Burl Headboard, c.1830, Queen, 72 ½ x 45 In.	6400.00
Bed, Cannonball, Cherry, Footboard Quilt Rack, Davis Cabinet Co., 58 x 82 x 44 In.	89.00
Bed, Cannonball, Curly Maple, Shaped Headboard, 53 x 83 In.	353.00
Bed, Cannonball, Tulipwood, Ram's Ear Headboard, Turned Rail, c.1830, Queen, 61 ½ In.	4200.00
Bed, Canopy, Federal, Mahogany, Carved Rails, Paneled Headboard, c.1840, 94 x 68 In.	2468.00
Bed, Canopy, Federal, Maple, Turned Urn Posts, Reeding, Brass Rosettes, 83 x 80 In.	353.00
Bed, Canopy, George III, Mahogany, Rosette Center Fabric, Carved Columns, 1900s, 88 x 60 In.	1175.00
Bed, Carved Wood Headrest, Incised Designs, Senufo Tribe, Ivory Coast, 25 x 94 In.	1020.00
Bed, Cherry, Pine, Bamboo Turning, France, Late 1800s, 46 In.	3800.00
Bed, Directoire Style, Mahogany, Pedimented Paneled Headboard, 79 x 41 In.	235.00
Bed, Eastlake, Headboard & Footboard, Rails, Carved Shield, 75 In. & 36 In.	138.00
Bed, Eastlake, Walnut, Carved, Arched Headboard, c.1875, 85 x 61 In.	173.00
Bed, Faux Bamboo, Pine, Pierced Spindle Rail Gallery, c.1880, 52 x 74 In.	930.00
Bed, Federal, Mahogany, Reeded Posts, Carved Headboard, 1800s, 89 x 57 In. ....*illus*	1298.00
Bed, Four-Poster, Curly Maple, Cannonball, Rope, 1820-25, 60 x 54 In. ....*illus*	1175.00
Bed, Four-Poster, Curly Maple, Scrolled Headboard, 1860s, 49 x 51 In.	940.00
Bed, Four-Poster, Federal, Mahogany, Carved Pineapple Finials, 97 x 22 ½ In.	17500.00
Bed, Four-Poster, Federal, Mahogany, Reeded Columns, Urns, Spade Feet, 68 x 83 In.	4482.00
Bed, Four-Poster, Federal, Mahogany, Reeded, Tapered, Carved Leaves, 89 x 53 In.	1265.00
Bed, Four-Poster, Federal, Mahogany, Spreading Capitals, Tobacco Leaf Carving, 99 x 73 In. ..	3290.00
Bed, Four-Poster, George III, Mahogany, Carved, Scrolled, Early 1800s, 95 x 68 In. ....*illus*	1180.00
Bed, Four-Poster, Louis XVI, Gilt, Carved, Leaf Cresting, Silk Damask Drape, 60 x 65 In.	2540.00
Bed, Four-Poster, Mahogany, Overhead Framing, Carved Eagle Relief, Phila., c.1885, 87 x 58 In.	1989.00
Bed, Four-Poster, Neoclassical, Cherry, Shaped Headboard, Ball Finials, 49 x 77 In., Pair	1058.00
Bed, Four-Poster, Neoclassical, Mahogany, Chamfered Posts, Scrolled Headboard, c.1830.........	2400.00
Bed, Four-Poster, Neoclassical, Mahogany, Spirals, Scrolled Paneled Headboard, 96 x 78 In. ...	4994.00
Bed, Four-Poster, Pineapple Carved, Brass Inlaid Headboard, Paw Feet, c.1835, 89 x 66 In.	1175.00
Bed, Four-Poster, Softwood, Acorn Finials, c.1800, 47 x 55 In.	646.00
Bed, Four-Poster, Softwood, Rosewood Graining, Rails, c.1830, 77 x 50 ½ In.	118.00
Bed, French Provincial, Oak, Scrolled Head & Footboard, Turned Columns, c.1900, 57 x 74 In.	580.00
Bed, French, Walnut, Carved, Shaped Headboard, Channeled Rails, Scroll Feet, Twin, 68 x 38 In.	1150.00
Bed, G. Stickley, No. 924, Double Rail, 10 Vertical Slats, 46 x 80 x 50 In.	1320.00

Bed, G. Stickley, Paneled, Inverted V Top, Decal, Double, 50 x 59 In. ....*illus* 3240.00
Bed, Gothic Revival, Arched Headboard, Ball Finials, Spindle Rails, c.1850, Child's, 35 x 53 In. 705.00
Bed, Half-Tester, Renaissance Revival, Rosewood, Canopy, Crest, 134 x 90 In. ....*illus* 5040.00
Bed, Half-Tester, Rococo, Mahogany, Turreted Stiles, Finials, c.1850, 120 x 61 x 79 In. 9694.00
Bed, Half-Tester, Rococo, Rosewood, Serpentine, Finials, Oval Corners, Mid 1800s, 114 x 80 In. 6900.00
Bed, Half-Tester, Rococo, Walnut, Carved Crest, Finials, Paneled Headboard, 81 x 128 In. 3231.00
Bed, Half-Tester, Rococo, Walnut, Carved Crest, Paneled Headboard, Finials, 128 x 81 In. 3231.00
Bed, Half-Tester, Rosewood, Canopy, Broken-Arch, Leaf & Shell Cartouche, c.1875, 134 x 62 x 81 In. 5040.00
Bed, L. & J.G. Stickley, No. 84, 5 Vertical Slats, Tapered Post, Signed, 44 x 81 x 54 In. 1680.00
Bed, Louis XV Style, Limewood, Covered Headboard, c.1880, Twin, 40 x 77 In., Pair 1980.00
Bed, Louis XV Style, Tufted Headboard, Carved, Gilt Surround, Twin, 49 x 41 x 78 In., Pair 575.00
Bed, Louis XVI, Beech, Cane, Painted, Double, 62 x 77 In. ....*illus* 1920.00
Bed, Louis XVI Style, Cane Head & Footboards, Gilt, Label, 61 x 56 In. ....*illus* 3910.00
Bed, Louis XVI Style, Limewood, Demilune Headboard, Volutes, c.1890, 55 x 75 In. 1220.00
Bed, Louis XVI Style, Parcel Gilt, Ribboned Wreath, Garland Drape, 48 x 78 x 43 In. 568.00
Bed, Mahogany, Paneled Headboard, Carved Posts, Brass Feet, 78 x 96 In. 4994.00
Bed, Mahogany, Paneled Headboard, Leaf, Fruit, Brass Ball Feet, c.1810, 74 x 97 In. 6168.00
Bed, Mahogany, Reeded Swag & Tassel, c.1900, Twin. 3250.00
Bed, Maple, Acorn & Ring Top, Twin, 54 In., Pair 5200.00
Bed, Maple, Pine, Rope, Painted, Molded Frame, 1800s, 30 x 45 In. ....*illus* 316.00
Bed, Maple, Pine, Scrolled Headboard, Turned Post, Acorn Finials, c.1830, 38 x 45 In. 593.00
Bed, Maple, Tulip Top, Octagonal, Crested Headboard, Molded Edge, c.1840, 72 ½ In. 7200.00
Bed, Mustard, Brown Paint, Headboard, Ball Finials, Turned Posts, Rope, 39 ½ x 51 ½ x 76 In. 495.00
Bed, Neoclassical, Mahogany, Carved Crest, Shaped Headboard, c.1810, 97 x 74 In. 6169.00
Bed, Neoclassical, Satinwood Veneer, Shaped Headboard, Twin 418.00
Bed, O. Borsani, Mahogany, Tufted Cream Silk, Head & Footboards, Queen, 38 x 70 In. 1220.00
Bed, Old Hickory, Twig, Woven Splint, Full, 57 x 80 x 34 In. 600.00
Bed, Opium, Lacquered, Scrolled Vines, Flower Heads, Chinese, 91 x 86 x 58 In. 3346.00
Bed, Pine, Maple, Shaped Headboard, Powder Blue, New England, c.1830, 49 x 73 In. 1067.00
Bed, Prairie School, Spindle Head & Foot Boards, Full Corbels, Queen, 72 x 89 x 44 In. 1020.00
Bed, Renaissance Revival, Herter Bros., Ebonized, Inlaid, c.1872, 84 x 72 x 71 In. 326000.00
Bed, Shaker, Butternut, Pine, Arched Headboard, Rope, c.1860, 27 x 19 In. 705.00
Bed, Shaker, Maple, Pine, Arched Headboard, Wood, Iron Wheels, N.Y., c.1840, 30 x 65 In. 410.00
Bed, Shaker, Mixed Wood, Green Pine, Curved Headboard, N.Y., 1830, 21 x 76 In. 410.00
Bed, Sleigh, Charles X, Mahogany Inlay, Scrolling Head & Footboards, 42 x 75 In. 588.00
Bed, Sleigh, Empire, Mahogany, c.1880, Double. 4125.00
Bed, Sleigh, Empire Style, Flame Mahogany, Stamped, Jacox Bros., 38 x 56 ½ x 85 In. 410.00
Bed, Sleigh, Empire, Tiger Maple, c.1850, Double 3600.00
Bed, Sleigh, Mahogany, Flower & Urn Inlays, Ball & Claw, 43 x 61 In. 575.00
Bed, Sleigh, Mahogany, Ormolu Brass, c.1880, 45 ½ x 76 In. 8500.00
Bed, Slender Lemon Top, Age Green Paint, Twin, 48 In., Pair 2400.00
Bed, Victorian, Walnut, Arched Headboard, Recessed Burled Panels, 1800s, 57 x 75 In. 360.00
Bed, Walnut, Arch Crest Head, Oval Panel Footboard, Leaf Carvings, c.1875, 86 x 54 In. 720.00
Bed, Walnut, Kingswood, Inlay, Urn, Flower & Bow, Early 19th Century, 50 In. 546.00
Bed, Wrought Iron, Scrolling Crest, Flower Accents, c.1875, 61 x 36 x 82 In. 720.00
Bedroom Set, Aesthetic Revival, Walnut, Bed, Armoire, Dresser, Washstand, c.1880 38775.00
Bedroom Set, Burled Walnut, Mitchell & Rammelsburg, 3 Piece ....*illus* 6000.00
Bedroom Set, Eastlake, Chest, Dresser, Marble Top, Carved, Mirror, Hat Box, Queen Bed 7188.00
Bedroom Set, Empire, Mahogany, Headboard, Footboard, Rails, 2 Dressers, Mirror, c.1830 316.00
Bedroom Set, Gothic Revival, Walnut, Gilt Incised, Bed, Dresser, Commode, c.1880 10575.00
Bedroom Set, Renaissance Revival, Walnut, Bed, Dresser, Washstand, Arched, Carved, 1800s . 3173.00
Bench, Art Deco, Iron, Winged Griffin, 20 ½ x 25 ½ x 11 ½ In. 92.00
Bench, Arts & Crafts, Spindle Back, Leather Seat, 45 x 39 In. 6609.00
Bench, Baroque, Pine, Red Paint, Green Traces, c.1800, 45 x 45 In. 1725.00
Bench, Bootjack, Yellow Pine, Southern, 1800s, 13 ½ x 29 In. 863.00
Bench, Brass, Leather, Upholstered, Brass Supports, 25 x 57 x 19 In. 575.00
Bench, Bronze, Hide, 19 x 48 x 24 In. 2318.00
Bench, Bucket, Pine, 2 Shelves, Cutout Feet, 19th Century, 34 x 49 In. 1200.00
Bench, Bucket, Softwood, Green Paint, Splash Back, Shaped Shelf, 37 x 30 ½ x 12 In. 1540.00
Bench, Bucket, Southern Pine, Green Paint, 22 x 60 x 13 In. 403.00
Bench, Carved, Central Shield, Acanthus Leaf, Plank Seat, Spain, c.1920, 42 x 52 In. 390.00
Bench, Corner, Wood, Arms, Continental, 1800s, 42 x 58 In. 460.00
Bench, Crescent Shape, Concave Back, Vertical Planks, Rolled Arms, England, 1800s, 42 x 61 In. 472.00
Bench, Curule, Scrolled Seat, X Shape Supports, Ball Feet, 19 x 31 ½ In. 470.00
Bench, Deacon's, Scalloped Crest Rail, Spindles, Green Paint, New England, 1800s, 35 x 75 In. 235.00
Bench, Empire Style, Mahogany, Parcel Gilt, Silk Seat, Ram's Head Handholds, 21 ½ x 32 In. 474.00

Furniture, Bed, G. Stickley, Paneled, Inverted V Top, Decal, Double, 50 x 59 In.
$3240.00

Furniture, Bed, Half-Tester, Renaissance Revival, Rosewood, Canopy, Crest, 134 x 90 In.
$5040.00

Furniture, Bed, Louis XVI, Beech, Cane, Painted, Double, 62 x 77 In.
$1920.00

Furniture, Bed, Louis XVI Style, Cane Head & Footboards, Gilt, Label, 61 x 56 In.
$3910.00

F

Furniture, Bed, Maple, Pine, Rope, Painted, Molded Frame, 1800s, 30 x 45 In. $316.00

Furniture, Bedroom Set, Burled Walnut, Mitchell & Rammelsburg, 3 Piece $6000.00

Furniture, Bench, Hepplewhite, Mahogany, Rolled Arms, Upholstered, 1800s, 26 x 39 In. $748.00

Furniture, Bench, Mammy's, Windsor, Cherry, Black Paint, Rocker, 1800s, 28 x 48 In. $431.00

Bench, Folk Art, Rural Farm Scenes, Carved Relief Livestock, c.1975, 47 x 40 In.	236.00
Bench, French Provincial, Painted, Carved, Green Upholstered Pad Seat, Pair	600.00
Bench, French Rococo Revival, Carved Apron & Legs, Upholstered, 45 x 20 x 19 In.	200.00
Bench, Fruitwood, Upholstered Back, Rush Seat, Rounded Arms, Seat Rail, 1700s, 39 x 68 In.	1410.00
Bench, G. Nelson, Platform, Birch Slat Top, Ebonized Legs, Herman Miller, 72 x 18 In.	1080.00
Bench, G. Nelson, Platform, Herman Miller, c.1948, 14 x 19 In.	858.00
Bench, George III Style, Mahogany, Serpentine Apron, Upholstered, 47 In.	593.00
Bench, Georgian Style, Mahogany, Carved, Upholstered, Overstuffed Seat, Cabriole Legs	538.00
Bench, Gilt, Carved, Cherub Corners, X-Stretcher, Upholstered Pad Seat, Italy, Square	1800.00
Bench, Gothic Revival, Oak, Turreted Top, Lift Seat, 3 Front Panels, 53 x 47 x 19 In.	1320.00
Bench, Gothic Revival, Walnut, Paneled, Tracery, Crest, Monk's Head Arms, 61 x 46 In.	1495.00
Bench, Hall, Lifetime, Cube Lift Seat, Paper Label, 36 x 50 x 20 In.	2160.00
Bench, Hassock, Upholstered, Moire Taffeta, Rope Trim, Tassels, 19 x 18 In., Pair	90.00
Bench, Hepplewhite, Mahogany, Rolled Arms, Upholstered, 1800s, 26 x 39 In. ....*illus*	748.00
Bench, Hugh Acton, Slat, Suspended Beam, Birmingham, Mich., 1954, 14 x 108 x 20 In.	3300.00
Bench, Iron, Tufted Leather Back, 53 x 42 x 21 In.	175.00
Bench, L. & J.G. Stickley, 3 Horizontal Back Rails, Cushion, Corbel Supports, 53 x 37 In.	660.00
Bench, Louis Philippe, Walnut, Brown Leather, Nail Trim, Turned Legs, c.1830, 44 x 147 In.	2180.00
Bench, Louis XV, Beech, Painted, Gilt Gesso, Serpentine Rail, 19 x 79 In.	1045.00
Bench, Louis XV, Fruitwood, Needlepoint Top, Carved, Rectangular, 19 x 39 In.	823.00
Bench, Louis XVI, Multicolored, Pierced Leaf, Acorn Carved Frieze, Teardrop Accent, 20 x 44 In.	1560.00
Bench, Louis XVI, Oak, Velvet Upholstery, 6 Legs, c.1780, 20 x 111 ½ x 16 ½ In.	700.00
Bench, Mammy's, Windsor, Cherry, Black Paint, Rocker, 1800s, 28 x 48 In. .... *illus*	431.00
Bench, McCobb, Planner Group, Maple, Low, Tapered Legs, Winchendon, 48 x 9 In.	90.00
Bench, Milo Baughman, Glenn Of California, c.1950, 11 ½ x 18 x 81 In.	1225.00
Bench, Mucki, Jacaranda, Sergio Radrigues, c.1958, 11 x 60 x 23 In.	8125.00
Bench, Neoclassical, Parcel Gilt, Concave, Carved Scrolls, Square Legs, c.1920, 18 x 42 In.	1020.00
Bench, Oak, Carved Arches, Turned Legs, England, 19th Century, 36 x 11 ½ x 19 In.	253.00
Bench, Oak, Plank Top, 3 Shaped Supports, Continental, 19 x 7 ¼ In.	720.00
Bench, Oscar Bach, Brass, Iron, Ship Design Base, Flower Supports, Seat Cushion, 56 x 24 In.	840.00
Bench, Piano, Arts & Crafts, Stretcher, Key & Tenon, Vertical Slat Sides, 38 x 16 x 20 In.	420.00
Bench, Pine, Bootjack Ends, Gray Paint, c.1850, 18 x 72 In.	294.00
Bench, Pine, Carved Tulips & Sunbursts, 19th Century, 18 ½ x 42 In.	176.00
Bench, Pine, Painted, Stenciled, Shaped Crest, Spindles, Plank Seat, 34 x 71 x 24 In.	2400.00
Bench, Pine, Splayed Legs, c.1800, 18 x 62 ½ x 10 ¾ In.	264.00
Bench, Plank, Triangle Seat, Vertical Slats, Splayed Legs, 32 x 72 In.	1178.00
Bench, Renaissance Revival, Walnut, Molded Top Rail, Guilloche Border, 1880s, 39 x 75 In.	2585.00
Bench, Robsjohn-Gibbings, Mahogany, Upholstered Seat, 35 x 15 ½ In. ....*illus*	1200.00
Bench, Rococo, Padded Top, Shaped Frieze, Lattice Design, Flowers, Scrolls, 18 x 45 In.	900.00
Bench, Salmon Paint, 3 Bookjack Legs, 18 ½ x 120 In.	275.00
Bench, Shaker, Walnut, Union Village, Ohio, 19th Century, 15 x 78 In.	118.00
Bench, Shaped Crest, Spindled Splat, Scroll Arms, Plank Seat, Indigo Paint, 33 x 66 In.	1762.00
Bench, Shaped Crest, Spindles, Scroll Arms, Blue Paint, c.1850, 33 x 66 In.	1763.00
Bench, Softwood, Beaded Skirt, Shaped Cutout Legs, 19 x 49 x 11 In.	215.00
Bench, Steelcase, Tufted Tan Leather Cushion, Chrome Frame, 1960s, 49 x 17 In.	660.00
Bench, Stickley Bros., No. 3574, 2 Horizontal Slat Back, Slab Seat, 38 x 18 x 32 In.	1020.00
Bench, Stitched Panels, Leather Top, Tapered Base, Block Feet, 18 ½ x 66 x 26 ½ In.	470.00
Bench, Turned Feet, Scroll Arms, Paneled Back, 1800s, 18 x 36 In.	118.00
Bench, Victorian, Walnut, Upholstered, Scalloped Detail, 1800s, 16 x 42 In.	144.00
Bench, Walnut, George Nakashima, c.1962, 32 x 60 x 18 In. ....*illus*	37500.00
Bench, Walnut, Needlepoint Seat, Flowers, French Feet, 23 x 16 In.	59.00
Bench, Walnut, Rectangular, Round Stretchers & Legs, Chinese, c.1880, 22 x 80 In.	239.00
Bench, Walnut, Trumpet Turned Legs, Carved Stretcher, Upholstered, c.1900, 19 x 39 In.	777.00
Bench, Walter Lamb, Metal Frame, Plastic, Medium, Brown Jordan, c.1950, 22 x 66 In.	597.00
Bench, Window, Duncan Phyfe, Mahogany, Slip Seat, N.Y., c.1810, 29 x 46 In. ....*illus*	3540.00
Bench, Window, Satinwood, Carved Anthemion, Scroll, Italy, 1800s, 16 x 64 x 24 In.	3220.00
Bench, Windsor, Bamboo, Turned, Pa., 19th Century, Child's, 20 x 33 In.	520.00
Bench, Windsor, Continuous Knuckle Arms, Overlap Bow Crests, 40 x 72 In.	705.00
Bench, Windsor, Poplar, Plank Seat, Fruit Stencil, Green, Yellow Paint, 1800s, 33 x 78 In.	978.00
Bench, Windsor, Tablet Back, Plank Seat, Black Paint, Arms, 8 Legs, 32 x 113 In.	1175.00
Bench, Wood, Blue Paint, Double Skirt, Cutout Feet, 6 ¾ x 24 x 6 ¾ In.	158.00
Bench, Work, Head & Tail Vises, Drawers, c.1875	550.00
Bench, Wrought Iron, Scrolls, Leopard Print Upholstery, Gilt, 19 x 36 x 14 In.	240.00
Bench, Yellow Pine, White Cedar, Log Shape, Spoke Legs, Georgia, c.1850, 64 x 16 In.	1035.00
Bidet, Louis XV, Walnut, Carved, Padded Hinged Lift Seat, Pot Chamber, 37 x 20 x 16 In.	418.00
Book Slide, Egyptian Revival, Gilt Bronze, Pyramid, Sphinx, c.1920, 5 ¼ x 23 ¾ In.	470.00

F

Bookcase, Art Deco, Wood, 84 x 45 In.	431.00
Bookcase, Arts & Crafts, 12-Pane Doors, Signed, Decal, Ridenour, 48 x 12 x 57 In. ....*illus*	2040.00
Bookcase, Bentwood, Metal Caps, Peaked Supports, Dark Finish, Vienna, c.1900.70 x 45 In. ..	1793.00
Bookcase, Biedermeier, 2 Doors, Drawer, Oval Mirror, Late 1800s, 65 x 31 x 14 In.	670.00
Bookcase, Biedermeier, Ebonized & Mother-Of-Pearl Inlaid Wreaths, Glazed, 72 In., Pair	1150.00
Bookcase, Biedermeier, Fruitwood, 2 Glazed & Paneled Doors, 64 x 43 In.	345.00
Bookcase, Biedermeier, Walnut, Marble Top, Drawer, Paneled Doors, 61 x 42 x 15 ¼ In.	705.00
Bookcase, Bureau, Chippendale, Mahogany, Astragal Glazed Doors, 87 x 44 In.	1150.00
Bookcase, Burled Walnut, Pine, Veneers, Divided Interior, England, c.1835, 75 x 60 In.	999.00
Bookcase, Chippendale, Mahogany, Glazed Doors, Dentil Cornice, 75 x 36 In.	161.00
Bookcase, Chippendale, Mahogany, Upper Glazed Doors, Lower Desk, 1800s, 94 x 46 In.	690.00
Bookcase, Crotch Walnut Veneer, Beveled Glass Door, Drawers, c.1820, 85 x 41 In.	2840.00
Bookcase, Desk, Slant Front, 3 Drawers, Fitted Interior, 42 x 91 In.	856.00
Bookcase, Eastlake, Walnut, 2 Arched Glass Doors, Drawers, Carved, Incised, 66 x 79 In.	3393.00
Bookcase, Edwardian, Fruitwood, Harewood, Mahogany, Inlaid, Drawers, 67 x 27 x 19 In.	1185.00
Bookcase, Edwardian, Mahogany, String Inlay, Breakfront Case, 51 x 48 x 14 In.	598.00
Bookcase, Empire, Bronze Face, Acanthus Mounts, 2 Glass Panel Doors, 44 x 62 In.	840.00
Bookcase, Empire, Mahogany, Stepped Back, Doors, Shelves, 71 ¾ x 49 ½ x 22 ½ In.	299.00
Bookcase, Federal Style, Mahogany, Breakfront, 4 Glazed Doors, 84 x 76 x 15 ¾ In.	896.00
Bookcase, Federal Style, Walnut, 4 Shelves, 20th Century, 48 x 36 x 13 In.	280.00
Bookcase, G. Stickley, No. 700, Glass Door, Shelves, 58 x 36 x 14 In.	6710.00
Bookcase, G. Stickley, No. 703, Ellis Glass Doors, Overhanging Top, Arched Apron, 48 x 54 In.	12650.00
Bookcase, G. Stickley, Oak, Open Gallery, 2 Glass Doors, Label, 56 x 43 In.	3105.00
Bookcase, George III, Mahogany, Arched Panels, Bracket Feet, 82 ½ x 48 x 18 In.	2160.00
Bookcase, George IV, Rosewood, Brass Inlay, Lotus Carved Crest, Column Stiles, 36 x 33 In. ..	2987.00
Bookcase, Georgian, Mahogany, 2 Glazed Doors, Drawer, 2 Paneled Doors, c.1760, 88 x 44 In.	1645.00
Bookcase, Georgian, Mahogany, Adjustable Open Shelves, Single Door, 71 x 28 x 11 In.	325.00
Bookcase, Georgian, Mahogany, Paned Upper Doors, 4 Panel Doors, c.1820, 88 x 45 In.	2645.00
Bookcase, Georgian, Pierced, Scrolled Pediment, Glazed Doors, c.1910, 102 x 55 In.	3525.00
Bookcase, Georgian Style, Yew, Cove Molded Crown, Ogee Feet, Doors, c.1900, 83 x 36 In.	896.00
Bookcase, Globe-Wernicke, Oak, Stacked, 4 Sections, 62 ½ In.	585.00
Bookcase, Globe-Wernicke, Oak, Stacked, 5 Sections, 75 In.	565.00
Bookcase, Gothic Revival, Oak, 2 Glazed Doors, 2 Panel Doors, Arches, c.1875, 99 x 45 In.	2160.00
Bookcase, Hepplewhite, Mahogany, Inlay, Dental Molded Crown, Glazed Doors, 41 x 79 In. ...	563.00
Bookcase, Jacobean Revival, Oak, 2 Doors, Beveled Glass, Stretcher Base, 71 x 43 In.	510.00
Bookcase, L. & J.G. Stickley, 2 Doors, Gallery Top, 3 Shelves, 56 ½ x 52 ½ x 12 In.	6600.00
Bookcase, L. & J.G. Stickley, No. 645, 2 Doors, 24 Panes, 3 Shelves, 55 ½ x 50 x 12 In.	7930.00
Bookcase, Library, George III, Mahogany, Glazed Doors, Arched Mullions, 97 x 49 In.	3437.00
Bookcase, Limbert, Door, Spade Cutouts, Tapered Top, Label, 47 x 16 ½ x 11 ½ In.	4500.00
Bookcase, Limbert, No. 355, Door, 6 Panes, Copper Hardware, 3 Inside Shelves, 33 x 48 In.	6000.00
Bookcase, Lou Hodges, Desk, Drop Front, Doug Blume, c.1979, 78 x 95 In.	1164.00
Bookcase, Louis Philippe, Burl Mahogany, 2 Doors, Drawer, c.1860, 84 x 41 x 19 In.	1500.00
Bookcase, Louis XV Style, Walnut, Center Niche, Shelves, Glass Doors, c.1900, 63 x 61 In.	2420.00
Bookcase, Louis XVI Style, Walnut, Gilt Metal, Glazed Panel Doors, 59 x 34 ½ x 13 ¼ In.	1076.00
Bookcase, Mahogany, 3 Mullion Doors, Carved Pilasters, Paw Feet, c.1900, 54 x 73 In.	1080.00
Bookcase, Mahogany, Carved, 2 Glass Doors, Bracket Feet, England, 40 x 46 x 14 In.	889.00
Bookcase, Mahogany, Mullion Doors, Drawers, Scrolls, c.1825, 93 x 54 In.	5520.00
Bookcase, Mahogany, Top Rail, Mullion Doors, 66 x 67 In.	2185.00
Bookcase, Marquetry Vitrine, Column Supports, Drawer, Plinth, c.1800, 66 x 34 x 17 In.	1135.00
Bookcase, Napoleon III, Faux Bamboo, Pine, Beveled Glass Door, c.1870, 92 x 40 In.	2440.00
Bookcase, Napoleon III, Parquetry, Bronze Mounted, Breakfront Case, 94 x 74 In.	4116.00
Bookcase, Neoclassical, Fruitwood, Carved, Desk, Slant Front, Drawers, 67 x 25 x 17 ½ In.	3055.00
Bookcase, Neoclassical Style, Fruitwood, Fluted Feet, 85 x 55 x 20 In.	299.00
Bookcase, Oak, 5 Sections, Scroll Panel Base, c.1900, 57 x 34 x 12 In.	540.00
Bookcase, Oak, Bead Molded Cornice, Glazed Doors, Adjustable Shelves, c.1900, 62 x 46 In. ..	705.00
Bookcase, Oak, Stacking, 5 Drawers, Scalloped Base, c.1900, 66 x 34 x 12 In.	780.00
Bookcase, Overhung Pediment, 2 Glazed Doors, Ball & Claw, England, 1800s, 52 x 66 In.	826.00
Bookcase, Regency Style, Mahogany, Burl Walnut, Round, Adjustable Shelves, 35 x 24 In.	431.00
Bookcase, Renaissance Revival, Burl Walnut, Glazed Doors, 100 x 50 x 22 In.	1800.00
Bookcase, Renaissance Revival, Walnut, 2 Glass Doors, Columns, Incised, 51 x 60 In.	748.00
Bookcase, Renaissance Revival, Walnut, Corner, Arched Cornice, Doors, c.1870, 82 x 38 In. ...	1469.00
Bookcase, Revolving, Edwardian, Painted, 2 Round Tiers, Drum Table, Drawers, 56 x 32 In. .	633.00
Bookcase, Revolving, Mahogany, 3 Tiers, Late 19th Century, 44 ½ x 20 x 20 In.	200.00
Bookcase, Revolving, Regency, Mahogany, 4 Tiers, Drawers, 19th Century, 62 x 31 In.	6169.00
Bookcase, R.J. Horner, Oak, 2 Doors, Carved Griffins, Flowers, 2 Drawers, 53 x 66 In.	6038.00
Bookcase, Scrubbed Pine, Carved Double Arched Frieze, Panel Sides, 94 x 71 x 25 ¼ In.	657.00

F

Furniture, Bench, Robsjohn-Gibbings, Mahogany, Upholstered Seat, 35 x 15 ½ In.
$1200.00

Furniture, Bench, Walnut, George Nakashima, c.1962, 32 x 60 x 18 In.
$37500.00

Furniture, Bench, Window, Duncan Phyfe, Mahogany, Slip Seat, N.Y., c.1810, 29 x 46 In.
$3540.00

Furniture, Bookcase, Arts & Crafts, 12-Pane Doors, Signed, Decal, Ridenour, 48 x 12 x 57 In.
$2040.00

Furniture, Breakfront,
Chippendale Style, Inlaid Walnut Veneer,
1900s, 94 x 76 In.
$2760.00

Furniture, Breakfront, Hepplewhite,
Mahogany, Veneers, Cornice, 1800s,
90 x 89 In.
$6900.00

Furniture, Buffet, Louis XV Style,
Multicolored, Garland, Carved Frieze,
93 x 54 In.
$2640.00

Bookcase, Sliding Glass Door, Slant Front Doors, 4 Drawers, Continental, 1800s, 57 x 64 In. .	2124.00
Bookcase, Stained, Plank Construction, Back Brace, Bookjack Sides, 1700s, 37 x 35 x 10 In. .	209.00
Bookcase, Walnut, Burl, Open, Lobed Corners, Split Columns, Black Lacquer, 39 x 29 In.	978.00
Bookcase, Walnut, Dovetail Sides, 4 Shelves, 44 x 36 In.	3900.00
Bookcase, Walnut, Flared Cornice, Glazed, Paneled Doors, Drawer, c.1825, 93 x 50 In.	2400.00
Bookcase, Walnut, Pine, Beveled Glass Doors, Austria, 19th Century, 71 x 60 In.	690.00
Bookcase, Walnut, Pine, Waterfall, Molded Crown, Tiered Shelves, 1800s, 81 x 49 In.	518.00
Bookcase, Walnut, Stand, Cove Molding, Arch Tracery Door, Drawer, c.1850, 92 x 39 In.	1440.00
Bookcase, William IV, Mahogany, 2 Glass Doors, Acanthus Supports, 96 x 46 x 16 In.	3000.00
Bookrack, G. Stickley, Cut-Out Handles, Paper Lapel, 31 x 32 x 10 In.	1952.00
Bookrack, G. Stickley, Revolving, Leather Lined, Lazy Susan Base, 10 x 12 In.	1830.00
Bookstand, Gilt Gesso, Shield, Scrolls, Birds, Painted Accents, C-Scroll Base, Italy, 1800s, 11 x 15 In.	889.00
Bookstand, Napoleon III, Walnut, Gilt, Moorish Arches, Rose Windows, c.1870, 27 x 13 In.	890.00
Bookstand, Revolving, Beaux-Arts Style, Black Walnut, Mahogany, Inlay, c.1900, 66 ½ In.	2813.00
Bookstand, Revolving, Edwardian, Fruitwood, Line & Fan Inlay, 2 Tiers, 33 x 18 x 18 In.	288.00
Bottle Board, George III, Mahogany, Bowfront, Fitted Drawer, England, c.1800, 43 x 67 In.	2115.00
Box, Log, Shaker, Pine, Open Front, Sloped Sides, Arched Base, c.1810, 36 x 26 In.	1053.00
Bracket, Baroque Style, Wood, Winged Angel, Leaf Swag, Pineapple Pendant, 10 x 9 In., Pair .	178.00
Bracket, Calcutta Marble, Seashells, Coral, Nickel, Italy, 15 x 12 x 6 In., Pair	3120.00
Bracket, Corner, Lacquer, Gilt, Carved, Flower Basket, Scalloped Skirt, 15 x 27 In., Pair	1175.00
Bracket, Mahogany, Shaped Shelves, Turned Supports, Mirror, c.1870, 26 x 12 In., Pair	259.00
Bracket, Napoleon III, Walnut, Serpentine Gadrooned Top, Acanthus, c.1860, 15 x 14 In.	1534.00
Bracket, Neoclassical, Gilt, Carved, Winged Angels, Garlands, c.1800, 19 x 19 In., Pair	8500.00
Bracket, Walnut, Mustard Paint, Late 1800s, 8 ½ x 19 x 5 In.	470.00
Bracket, Wood, Carved Eagle, Cannons, Flags, Dove, Good Luck, 20 ½ x 10 In.	294.00
Bracket, Wood, Gilt, Carved, Continental, c.1890, Pair	3850.00
Brandy Board, Irish Chippendale, Mahogany, Carved, Backsplash, Early 1900s, 38 x 43 In. ..	690.00
Breakfront, Art Nouveau, Walnut, Carved, Marble Inset Top, 92 x 43 x 23 In.	2100.00
Breakfront, Chippendale, Mahogany, Inlaid Glazed Doors, Lower Doors, 1700s, 106 x 58 In. .	4370.00
Breakfront, Chippendale Style, Inlaid Walnut Veneer, 1900s, 94 x 76 In. ....*illus*	2760.00
Breakfront, Edwardian, Mahogany, Broken Swan's Neck Pediment, 97 x 57 In.	900.00
Breakfront, George I, Yellow Lacquer, Broken Arch, Plinth, c.1900, 87 x 73 x 13 In.	478.00
Breakfront, George III, Figured Mahogany, Inlaid, Glazed Diamond Doors, 98 x 72 In.	3680.00
Breakfront, Georgian, Mahogany, Fret Carved Broken Arch, Glazed Doors, 106 x 62 In.	6335.00
Breakfront, Gothic Revival, Walnut, 2 Doors, Mercier Freres, Paris, 109 x 39 x 19 In.	4790.00
Breakfront, Hepplewhite, Mahogany, Painted, Glazed Doors, 85 x 47 In.	863.00
Breakfront, Hepplewhite, Mahogany, Veneers, Cornice, 1800s, 90 x 89 In. .... *illus*	6900.00
Breakfront, Lane, White Laminate Doors, Steeples, Oak Drawers, Lights, 1960s, 71 x 76 In. ..	120.00
Breakfront, Mahogany, 4 Glazed Doors, 4 Paneled Doors, Arched Muntins, 84 x 79 In.	767.00
Breakfront, Mahogany, Geometric Glazed Doors, Shelves, Paneled Doors, 76 x 84 In.	805.00
Breakfront, Mahogany, Serpentine, Crested Top, Dutch, c.1890, 88 x 60 x 20 In.	1970.00
Breakfront, Renaissance Revival, Burl Walnut, Carved, Glazed Doors, 82 x 77 In.	4406.00
Breakfront, Renaissance Revival, Walnut, Arched Doors, Fitted Interior, Carvings, 77 x 85 In.	4543.00
Breakfront, Rococo Revival, Carved, Rocaille Crest, 4 Shaped Glass Panel Doors, 104 In.	1195.00
Breakfront, William IV, Rosewood, 6 Doors, c.1840, 89 x 84 x 17 In.	4100.00
Buffet, Burl Walnut, Inset Glass Top, Carved Giltwood Mirror, Italy, 1930s, 94 x 97 In.	1688.00
Buffet, Cherry, Carved, 2 Drawers, 2 Paneled Doors, Steel Escutcheons, 29 x 53 In.	3055.00
Buffet, Directoire Style, Mahogany, Granite Top, Straight Doors, c.1850, 36 x 51 In.	1840.00
Buffet, Empire, Mahogany, Gilt Bronze, Drawer, Doors, Urn Mount, 38 ½ x 43 x 19 ¾ In.	4700.00
Buffet, Flemish Renaissance Revival, Oak, Angel's Heads, c.1650, 50 x 62 In.	3790.00
Buffet, French Provincial, Cherry, 2 Drawers, 2 Paneled Doors, 39 x 53 In.	3055.00
Buffet, French Provincial, Fruitwood, Carved, 2 Doors, Drawers, 92 ½ x 61 x 27 In.	4935.00
Buffet, French Provincial, Oak, 2 Drawers, Cupboard Door, 42 ½ x 45 x 20 In.	1680.00
Buffet, French Provincial, Oak, 3 Drawers, 2 Cupboard Doors, 34 x 48 In.	1020.00
Buffet, French Provincial, Oak, Carved, Spindled Doors, Plate Shelf, Scroll Feet, 89 x 59 In. ...	2820.00
Buffet, French Renaissance Revival, Oak, Carved, Step Front, c.1870, 100 x 87 In.	12690.00
Buffet, Gothic Style, Oak, Carved, Drawers, Iron Handles, Paneled Doors, c.1930, 45 x 87 In. .	2580.00
Buffet, Herter Bros., Renaissance Revival, Walnut, Carved, Inlay, c.1872, 106 x 70 In.	194000.00
Buffet, Louis XIII Style, Walnut, Carved, Faux Drawers, Paneled Doors, c.1630, 39 x 62 In.	3290.00
Buffet, Louis XV, Cherry, Painted, Paneled Doors, c.1920, 38 x 37 In.	1720.00
Buffet, Louis XV Style, Fruitwood, 2 Drawers, Doors, Shelves, 86 x 56 x 24 In.	4580.00
Buffet, Louis XV Style, Fruitwood, Frieze Drawer, Panel Door, 37 x 27 x 19 In.	359.00
Buffet, Louis XV Style, Multicolored, Garland, Carved Frieze, 93 x 54 In. ....*illus*	2640.00
Buffet, Louis XV Style, Provincial, Painted, Drawers, Paneled Doors, c.1900, 41 x 89 In.	2580.00
Buffet, Louis XV Style, Provincial, Pine, Cupboard Doors, Panel Inset, 44 x 54 x 20 In.	1680.00
Buffet, Louis XV Style, Walnut, Banded, Doors, Drawer, c.1825, 38 x 55 x 24 In.	3600.00

Buffet, Louis XV Style, Walnut, Marble, 3 Drawer Frieze, Paneled Doors, c.1880, 44 x 67 In. ...	2750.00
Buffet, Louis XV, Fruitwood, Hinged, Fitted Top, Shaped Paneled Doors, c.1850, 42 x 53 In.	5760.00
Buffet, Louis XV, Fruitwood, Mixed Woods, 2 Drawers, 2 Doors, Carved, c.1790, 39 x 50 In.	253.00
Buffet, Louis XV, Fruitwood, Spindle Doors, Medial Drawer, Paneled, 87 x 51 In.	2056.00
Buffet, Louis XV, Oak, 4 Open Top Shelves, Lower Doors, Drawers, c.1840, 88 x 56 In.	2280.00
Buffet, Louis XV, Oak, Pegged Top, Drawers, Sunflower, Vines, c.1775, 36 x 67 x 21 In.	2115.00
Buffet, Louis XV, Provincial, Cherry, 2 Drawers, 2 Doors, Scroll Feet, 42 x 49 In.	2000.00
Buffet, Louis XV, Provincial, Pine, 2 Drawers, 2 Carved Doors, Shaped Skirt, 1800s, 41 x 51 In.	748.00
Buffet, Louis XV, Walnut, Mixed Woods, 2 Drawers, 2 Doors, Carved, c.1800, 40 x 51 In.	1610.00
Buffet, Louis XVI Style, Mahogany Veneer, Marble Top, Drawer, Doors, c.1890, 41 x 62 In.	2580.00
Buffet, Louis XVI, Gilt Bronze Mounted, Marble Top, 3 Drawers, 4 Doors, 43 x 80 In.	5288.00
Buffet, Mahogany, Poplar, Pine, 3 Drawers, 3 Doors, New Orleans, c.1820, 56 x 66 In.	3220.00
Buffet, Mirror, Carved Column Back, Doors, Drawers, 75 x 60 In.	489.00
Buffet, Neoclassical, Mahogany, Backsplash, Side Galleries, c.1835, 53 x 70 In.	920.00
Buffet, Oak, Lion's Head Frieze, Step Back, Carved, Glass Doors, c.1870, 95 x 57 In.	3120.00
Buffet, Overhanging Pediment, Pierced Frieze, 5 Display Shelves, 44 x 72 In.	767.00
Buffet, Renaissance Revival, Fruitwood, Carved, Mirror, Marble Top, 69 x 47 In.	478.00
Buffet, Renaissance Revival, Oak, Carved Panel Doors, 83 ½ x 55 x 25 ¼ In.	478.00
Buffet, Renaissance Revival, Oak, Ogee Molded Frieze Drawers, Lion's Masques, 40 x 51 In. ...	2640.00
Buffet, Renaissance Revival, Walnut, Mirror Top, Drawers, 3 Door Base, 79 x 61 x 24 In.	388.00
Buffet, Sheraton, Mahogany, Bowfront, 5 Drawers, James Shoolbred & Co., 36 x 40 In. ....*illus*	3186.00
Buffet, Spanish Renaissance Revival, Oak, Niches, Paneled Doors, c.1890, 75 x 85 In.	3120.00
Buffet, Walnut, 2 Doors, France, c.1850, 37 x 42 x 20 In.	1970.00
Bureau Bookcase, George III Style, Mahogany, Carved, Astragal Glazed Doors, 68 x 37 In.	920.00
Bureau, Cherry, Mahogany, Drawers, Scroll Mirror Supports, Carvings, c.1860, 65 x 49 In.	780.00
Bureau, Dressing, Mahogany, Glove Drawers, Marble Top, Mirror, Man's, 91 x 40 ½ x 22 In. ..	2056.00
Bureau, Dutch Elm, Ogee Molded Case, Fall Board, 3 Drawers, Early 1800s, 44 x 46 In.	575.00
Bureau, Eastlake, Walnut, Marble Top, Molded Sides, Mirror, 3 Paneled Drawers, 84 x 42 In. .	184.00
Bureau, English Hepplewhite Style, Mahogany, Bowfront, 4 Drawers, 43 x 46 In.	4200.00
Bureau, Federal, Birch, Mahogany, Shaped, Cutout Skirt, Inlay, c.1800, 36 x 38 In.	1067.00
Bureau, Federal, Mahogany, 4 Drawers, Cutout Feet, Stringing, c.1810, 32 x 28 In., Child's....	7110.00
Bureau, George III, Mahogany, Slant Front, Fitted Interior, 4 Graduated Drawers, 42 x 41 In.	1410.00
Bureau, George III, Mahogany, Slant Front, Hinged, Fitted Interior, 4 Drawers, 41 x 42 In.	805.00
Bureau, Georgian, Mahogany, Slant Front, Fitted Interior, Prospect Door, 45 x 23 In.	920.00
Bureau, Louis XV Style, Walnut, Burgundy Gilt Tooled, Leather, Drawer, 31 x 48 x 26 In.	777.00
Bureau, Mahogany, Bombe, 3 Drawers, Pilasters, Leather, Fitted Interior, France, 44 x 55 In. .	708.00
Bureau, Mahogany, Slant Front, Serpentine, 3 Drawers, Dutch, 1800s, 32 ½ x 44 In.	2115.00
Bureau, Oak, Ash, Slant Front, Fitted Interior, Drawers, Pigeonholes, 38 x 30 In.	173.00
Bureau, Sheraton, Tiger Maple, Cherry, Gallery, Finials, Turned Columns, c.1820, 61 x 43 In.	823.00
Bureau-On-Stand, Queen Anne, Mahogany, Fallboard, Fitted Interior, Drawers, 39 x 32 In. ..	259.00
Cabinet, Art Deco, Chrome, Glass, Arched Top, Drawers, Cabriole Legs, c.1930, 41 x 39 In.	861.00
Cabinet, Art Deco, Walnut, Carved Crest, Glass Doors, Lower Drawer, c.1920, 54 x 38 In.	59.00
Cabinet, Art Nouveau, Desk, Drop Front, Oak, 4 Shelves, Glass Door, c.1910, 71 x 41 In.	468.00
Cabinet, Art Nouveau, Mahogany, Stained Glass, Round Mirror Crest, 54 x 20 x 15 In.	322.00
Cabinet, Asian Design, 2 Doors, Interior Shelves, Brass Pulls, Green, 34 x 60 In.	4500.00
Cabinet, Baroque Style, Elm, Mortise & Tenon, Plank Top, 2 Drawers, Door, 40 x 46 In.	411.00
Cabinet, Biedermeier, Birch Burl Inlay, Oval, Door, Shelf Interior, Gilt Metal, 57 x 25 In., Pair	1093.00
Cabinet, Biedermeier, Fruitwood, Ebonized, Parcel Gilt, Glazed Doors, 79 x 57 In. ....*illus*	7200.00
Cabinet, Biedermeier, Walnut, Glass Door, 2 Shelves, 1800s, 70 x 30 In.	1955.00
Cabinet, Biedermeier, Walnut, Pyramid Crest, 2 Glazed Doors, Drawers, 73 x 42 x 21 In.	2400.00
Cabinet, Boule, Ormolu Mounted, Ebonized Wood, 44 x 33 In.	460.00
Cabinet, Carved Crest, 2 Glass Pane Doors, 3 Drawers, Dutch, Late 1700s, 36 x 31 In.	3800.00
Cabinet, Cherry, Pine, Paneled Door, Shelves, 30 ¼ x 23 x 9 In.	173.00
Cabinet, China, Arts & Crafts, 2 Doors, Leaded Glass Panels, Green Glass, 44 x 59 In.	1440.00
Cabinet, China, Arts & Crafts, 2 Glass Doors, 3 Shelves, 43 x 14 ½ x 54 ½ In.	1020.00
Cabinet, China, L. & J.G. Stickley, No. 746, Glass Doors, Copper Pulls, 44 x 67 In.	2013.00
Cabinet, China, Mahogany, Curved Glass Doors, 61 x 42 In.	748.00
Cabinet, China, Oak, Bowfront, 4 Shelves, 20th Century, 54 x 38 In.	69.00
Cabinet, China, Oak, Bowfront, 4 Shelves, Scroll Feet, 59 x 35 In.	150.00
Cabinet, China, Oak, Carved, Maiden, Man, Claw Feet, Glass, 4 Shelves, 55 x 72 In.	5578.00
Cabinet, China, Oak, Curved Side Glass, Mirrored Top, 72 x 39 x 12 In.	480.00
Cabinet, China, Oak, Glass Doors, Claw Feet, Shelves, Lock, 70 x 44 x 18 In.	1300.00
Cabinet, China, R.J. Horner, Mahogany, Beveled Glass, 71 x 48 x 21 In.	1300.00
Cabinet, China, Tiger Oak, Carved, Curved Glass Door, Glass Shelves, 71 x 46 In.	805.00
Cabinet, China, Victorian, Curved Beveled Glass, Claw Feet, c.1900, 69 x 36 In.	540.00
Cabinet, Chinoiserie, Gothic Glazed Doors, Black Ground, Painted, England, 50 x 62 In.	1763.00

F

Furniture, Buffet, Sheraton, Mahogany, Bowfront, 5 Drawers, James Shoolbred & Co., 36 x 40 In. $3186.00

Furniture, Cabinet, Biedermeier, Fruitwood, Ebonized, Parcel Gilt, Glazed Doors, 79 x 57 In. $7200.00

Furniture, Cabinet, French Provincial, Oak, Marble, Beveled Glass Doors, Early 1900s, 83 x 61 In. $840.00

FURNITURE

Furniture, Cabinet, Hanging, Evans,
Patinated Copper, c.1960, 60 x 49 In.
$50000.00

Furniture, Cabinet, Hat Chest,
Paneled, Lockplate, Fish Handles,
Chinese, 62 x 39 In.
$110500.00

Furniture, Cabinet, James Mont,
Lacquered, Gilt, Multicolored, Grillwork,
78 x 80 x 21 In.
$3416.00

Cabinet, Chippendale, Mahogany, Inlaid, Shelves, 39 x 55 ½ x 18 ¾ In.	10350.00
Cabinet, Corner, Bowed Top, Fitted Doors, Continental, c.1825, 34 x 28 In., Pair	1080.00
Cabinet, Corner, Bowfront, Japanned, Butterfly Hinges, Doors, 36 x 23 x 15 In.	1673.00
Cabinet, Corner, Cherry, 2 Sections, 12-Pane Door Over Paneled Door, 85 x 44 In.	1035.00
Cabinet, Corner, Chippendale, Mahogany, 2 Glazed Doors, Gothic Muntins, 93 x 46 In.	3450.00
Cabinet, Corner, Chippendale Style, Mahogany, Broken Arch, Rosette Terminals, 94 x 44 In.	3231.00
Cabinet, Corner, Ethan Allen, English Oak, Leaded Glass Door, Paneled Door, 73 x 27 In.	230.00
Cabinet, Corner, Federal, 1 Over 1 Door, Post Feet, Bucks County, Pa., 77 x 41 In.	1076.00
Cabinet, Corner, Federal, Mahogany, Arched Glazed Door, Paneled Door, 2 Sections, 82 In.	3245.00
Cabinet, Corner, Federal, Walnut, 2 Over 4 Doors, Fluted Pilasters, 91 ¾ x 53 x 36 ¾ In.	1554.00
Cabinet, Corner, Fruitwood, Chamfered Leg, Medial Shelf, Stand, 74 x 28 ¾ x 14 ¾ In.	359.00
Cabinet, Corner, Fruitwood, Parquetry, Glazed Doors, Silk Lined, 75 ½ x 37 x 21 In.	474.00
Cabinet, Corner, Georgian Style, Mahogany, Crossband, Glass Doors, 73 ¾ x 39 ½ x 21 In.	296.00
Cabinet, Corner, Hanging, Chinoiserie, Black Lacquer, Gilt, England, 1800s, 23 x 42 In.	472.00
Cabinet, Corner, Hanging, Eastlake, Walnut, Spindled Gallery, Mirrored Door, 34 x 14 In.	86.00
Cabinet, Corner, Hanging, Inlaid Mahogany, Broken-Arch Pediment, Brass Finial, 47 x 31 In.	489.00
Cabinet, Corner, Hanging, Oak, Glass Doors, Continental, 19th Century, 42 x 30 x 19 In.	500.00
Cabinet, Corner, Inlays, Glass Door, Shelves, Ormolu Mounts, France, 1900s, 62 x 22 In.	345.00
Cabinet, Corner, Louis XVI Style, Pine, 3 Shelves, c.1900, 73 x 35 In., Pair	2420.00
Cabinet, Corner, Low Gallery Surround, Panel Door, Shaped Apron, 1800s, 51 x 38 In.	885.00
Cabinet, Corner, Mexican Folk Art, Angel Gabriel, Iron Handle, 75 x 32 x 20 In.	540.00
Cabinet, Corner, Oak, Domed Cornice, Slant Front, Drawers, Doors, c.1800, 79 x 36 In.	2400.00
Cabinet, Corner, Pine, Recessed Paneled Doors, Painted, c.1890, 36 x 36 In.	1280.00
Cabinet, Corner, Red Wash, 12-Pane Door Over Single Panel Door, 87 x 43 x 22 In.	6100.00
Cabinet, Cornish, Painted, Open Upper Shelving, Paneled Lower Doors, c.1760, 78 x 70 In.	6800.00
Cabinet, Display, Aesthetic Revival, Rosewood, Marquetry, Mirror Backed, c.1885, 42 x 60 In.	1955.00
Cabinet, Display, Bombe, Vernis Martin, Painted, 39 x 26 x 17 In.	1100.00
Cabinet, Display, Bowfront, Curved Glass Sides, Cabriole Legs, 67 x 29 x 15 In.	450.00
Cabinet, Display, Chinese Chippendale, Mahogany, Glazed Door, Pierce Carved, 31 x 20 In.	201.00
Cabinet, Display, Chinese, Rosewood, Glazed Doors, Geometric, 73 x 27 ½ x 13 In., Pair	4080.00
Cabinet, Display, Damascus Style, Mixed Wood, Glazed Doors, 87 x 46 In., Pair	1380.00
Cabinet, Display, English Walnut, Dentil Molding, Glass Panel Doors, c.1870, 83 x 48 In.	518.00
Cabinet, Display, Glazed Shelves, Drawers, Doors, Insects, Flowers, Dutch, 1900s, 38 x 83 In.	1185.00
Cabinet, Display, Louis XVI, Off-White Paint, Oval, Brass Ormolu Trim, Gallery, 30 x 16 ½ In.	575.00
Cabinet, Display, Louis XVI Style, Chinoiserie, Gallery Shelf, Fluted Columns, 49 x 26 In.	403.00
Cabinet, Display, Oak, 3 Shelves, 66 x 42 In.	413.00
Cabinet, Display, Painted, Wood Doors, 2 Over 1 Drawer, 34 x 77 In.	999.00
Cabinet, Display, Walnut, Glazed Doors, Shelves, Drawers, Dutch, 90 x 50 x 13 ½ In.	660.00
Cabinet, Dutch, Bombe, 3 Drawers, Glass Doors, Ball & Claw, 85 x 59 In.	3800.00
Cabinet, E. Gaillard, Mahogany, Burl Walnut, Gilt Bronze, c.1910, 78 x 81 x 19 In.	74500.00
Cabinet, Ebonized Wood, Gilt Inlay, Fluted Columns, 3 Glazed Doors, France, 40 x 72 In.	1035.00
Cabinet, Edwardian, Mahogany, Dentil Molded Crown, Glazed Doors, c.1900, 86 x 64 In.	2990.00
Cabinet, Edwardian, Satinwood, 3 Parts, Glazed Door, Glass Shelves, c.1910, 69 x 65 In.	1880.00
Cabinet, Elm, 4 Drawers, 2 Doors, Brass Mounts, Rectangular, 38 x 21 x 15 ½ In.	269.00
Cabinet, Empire, Fruitwood, Bowfront, Drawers, Columns, Inlay, Continental, c.1850, 36 x 42 In.	533.00
Cabinet, Empire, Gilt Bronze, Mahogany, Molded Cornice, Egyptian Pilasters, 83 x 60 In.	2644.00
Cabinet, Filing, Oak, Frame & Panel Construction, 4 Vertical Drawers, 1900s, 52 x 17 ½ In.	259.00
Cabinet, Filing, Poplar, 8 Drawers, Painted Stylized Flowers & Leaves, 39 x 19 In., Pair	478.00
Cabinet, Flemish Baroque, Ebonized, Bone, Plaque Figures, Trees, Beast Feet, 20 x 25 In.	2844.00
Cabinet, Florence Knoll, Walnut Case, 3 Drawers, Metal Pulls, 36 x 30 In.	1440.00
Cabinet, French Provincial, Door, 2 Interior Shelves, Paneled Sides, c.1800, 21 x 30 In.	705.00
Cabinet, French Provincial, Oak, Brass Mounted, Drawers, Doors, 2 Sections, 40 x 51 x 20 In.	415.00
Cabinet, French Provincial, Oak, Marble, Beveled Glass Doors, Early 1900s, 83 x 61 In. .... *illus*	840.00
Cabinet, French Provincial, Walnut, Carved, Paneled Doors, 92 x 33 x 19 In.	206.00
Cabinet, G. Nakashima, Elm, Sliding Door, 4 Walnut Drawers, 2 Shelves, Widdicomb, 84 x 32 In.	5700.00
Cabinet, G. Nakashima, Walnut, 2 Sliding Doors, 3 Inside Drawers, 1956, 32 x 72 In.	12000.00
Cabinet, G. Nakashima, Walnut, Pandanus Cloth, Slide Doors, c.1967, 28 x 73 In.	18750.00
Cabinet, G. Nelson, Thin Edge, Herman Miller, c.1955, 31 x 34 In.	2450.00
Cabinet, George III, Inlaid Mahogany, Serpentine Crossbanded Top, 36 x 47 In.	4230.00
Cabinet, Gothic Revival, Oak, 2 Doors, Bracket Feet, Continental, c.1875, 30 x 30 x 17 In.	1440.00
Cabinet, Gothic Revival, Oak, Leaded Glass, Arched, Flemish, 1800s, 121 x 62 In.	3163.00
Cabinet, Gun, Green Paint, Pheasants, Ducks, Geese, England, c.1840, 63 x 23 x 14 In.	1000.00
Cabinet, Gun, Oak, Carved Crest, Glass Doors, Game Carvings, Drawer, 41 x 87 In.	2013.00
Cabinet, Hanging, Evans, Patinated Copper, c.1960, 60 x 49 In. ....*illus*	50000.00
Cabinet, Hanging, Federal, Mahogany, Curved & Beveled Glass Door, Mirror, 24 x 36 In.	1093.00
Cabinet, Hanging, Gothic Style, Oak, Glass Door, Twisted Column, 56 x 55 In.	425.00

Cabinet, Hanging, Pine, Arched Panel Door, Molded Crest, Base, c.1875, 27 x 27 In.	382.00
Cabinet, Hanging, Rosewood, Fitted Interior, 38 x 27 x 10 In.	356.00
Cabinet, Hardwood, Brass Mounted, Burl, Lacquer, 4 Drawers, Korea, 1800s, 61 x 42 In.	881.00
Cabinet, Hat Chest, Paneled, Lockplate, Fish Handles, Chinese, 62 x 39 In. ....*illus*	110500.00
Cabinet, Herter Brothers, Renaissance Revival, Ebonized, Gilt, c.1872, 82 x 62 In.	230.00
Cabinet, Italian Baroque, Figured Walnut, Door, Inlaid Crest, 2 Drawers, 41 x 39 In.	3680.00
Cabinet, Italian Neoclassical, Pedestal Form, Painted Cartouche, 37 x 16 In., Pair	1840.00
Cabinet, Italian Renaissance Revival, Oak, Recessed Paneled Doors, c.1890, 59 x 51 In.	2420.00
Cabinet, Italian Renaissance Revival, Walnut, Trapezoid Top, Doors, 29 x 29 ½ x 14 In.	1659.00
Cabinet, J. Hoffmann, Parcel Ebonized Mahogany, Birch, Oval, c.1901, 74 x 48 In.	2390.00
Cabinet, James Mont, 2 Doors, Embossed Panels, Black, Stromberg Carlson, 35 x 40 In.	720.00
Cabinet, James Mont, Lacquered, Gilt, Multicolored, Grillwork, 78 x 80 x 21 In. ....*illus*	3416.00
Cabinet, Jewelry, Bird's-Eye Maple Veneer, Mirrored Panel Doors, 24 x 14 x 6 In.	538.00
Cabinet, Kingwood, Gilt Bronze, Marquetry, Durand, c.1880, 60 x 46 In. ....*illus*	9375.00
Cabinet, L. & J.G. Stickley, No. 727, 9-Pane Glass Door & 3 Glass Side Panels, 34 x 54 In.	4200.00
Cabinet, Lacquered, Black, 2 Doors, 3 Over 2 Drawers, Chinese, 40 x 36 x 18 In.	209.00
Cabinet, Lacquered, Black, Red, Pavilion, Landscape, Chinese, 64 x 45 x 20 In. .	568.00
Cabinet, Lacquered, Doors, Fitted Interior, Moon Hardware, Chinese, 1800s, 33 x 28 In., Pair .	2640.00
Cabinet, Library, Italian Renaissance Revival, Walnut, Fruitwood Inlay, Penwork, 69 x 62 In.	2726.00
Cabinet, Library, Oak, 12 Over 6 Large Drawers, Casters, Keystone, c.1920, 52 x 21 In.	410.00
Cabinet, Louis XV Style, Beech, Marble Top, Serpentine, Door, Drawer, 36 x 24 x 16 In.	148.00
Cabinet, Louis XV Style, Gilt, Marble Top, Door, Warrior Scene, 39 x 36 In.	2640.00
Cabinet, Louis XV Style, Oak, Bleached, Domed, Molded, Doors, Shelves, 98 x 45 x 21 In.	3840.00
Cabinet, Louis XV Style, Walnut, Shaped, Molded Crown, Hand Carved, 68 x 24 x 91 In.	4500.00
Cabinet, Louis XVI, Kingwood Parquetry, Chinoiserie, Drop Fronts, c.1780, 10 x 20 In.	2350.00
Cabinet, Louis XVI, Oak, Egg & Dart Cornice, Scalloped, Carved Flowers, c.1775, 95 x 50 In. ..	8519.00
Cabinet, Louis XVI Style, Ebony Top, Mirror, String Work, c.1890, 40 x 35 x 16 In.	360.00
Cabinet, Louis XVI Style, Mahogany, Gilt Bronze, D-Shape, c.1880, 44 x 65 In. ....*illus*	20000.00
Cabinet, Louis XVI Style, Mahogany, Parquetry, Bronze, Marble Top, 1900, 44 x 59 In.	1680.00
Cabinet, Louis XVI Style, Marble Top, Drawer, Doors, Shelves, c.1890, 51 x 53 In. ....*illus*	944.00
Cabinet, Louis XVI, Walnut, Marble Top, Ormolu, Drawer, Mesh Panel Door, 32 x 27 In., Pair .	546.00
Cabinet, Mahogany, Burl, Gilt Bronze, Gaillard, c.1910, 78 x 81 In. ....*illus*	74500.00
Cabinet, Mahogany, Marquetry, Glazed Doors, Panels, Shelves, 77 x 37 ½ x 14 In.	2233.00
Cabinet, Mahogany, Mirrored, Carved, Drop Front, 2 Lower Doors, Chinese, 46 x 38 In.	374.00
Cabinet, Marcel Kammerer, Bentwood, Door, Open Sides, G. Thonet, c.1905, 33 x 23 In.	3107.00
Cabinet, Ming Style, Hardwood, Red Lacquer, Paneled Doors, 73 x 41 In.	235.00
Cabinet, Mixed Wood, Fruit, 2 Doors, Parquetry, Vertical Bands, 22 x 18 In.	1955.00
Cabinet, Multicolored, Shaped Faux Marble Top, Paneled Door, 34 x 43 In., Pair	4320.00
Cabinet, Music, Hepplewhite, Corner, Painted, Interior Shelves, 1800s, 31 x 23 In. ....*illus*	805.00
Cabinet, Music, Renaissance Revival, Herter Bros., Rosewood, Maple, Gilt, c.1872, 44 x 60 In.	85400.00
Cabinet, Neoclassical, Mahogany, Glazed Door, Brass Banding, Russia, 43 x 27 In.	1440.00
Cabinet, Neoclassical, Oak, Bowfront, Carved, Glass Panels, Mirror, 67 x 44 In. ....*illus*	1410.00
Cabinet, Oak, 4 Shelves, Scroll Feet, American, 20th Century, 59 x 35 x 13 In.	150.00
Cabinet, Oak, Bowfront, Carved Flowers, Convex Glass Doors, Mirror Inside, 1800s, 51 x 71 In.	1534.00
Cabinet, Oak, Bowfront Glass, Carved Cornice, 3 Shelves, Paw Feet, c.1900, 67 x 46 In.	826.00
Cabinet, Oak, Curved Glass Doors, Glass Shelves, Carved, c.1890, 62 x 41 In.	575.00
Cabinet, Oak, Frieze Pediment, Glazed Doors, Carved Ram Heads, Fruit, Festoons, 70 x 84 In.	2124.00
Cabinet, Open Bin, Bead Trim Panel Doors, 2 Short Drawers, 1800s, 50 x 83 In.	1033.00
Cabinet, Orange Paint, Overhanging Top, Paneled Doors, Chinese, 19th Century, 26 x 36 In. .	750.00
Cabinet, P. Evans, Cityscape, Chrome, Brass Square, 4 Doors, 4 Interior Shelves, 1970s, 72 x 18 In.	2160.00
Cabinet, Persimmon Wood, 4 Drawers, Doors, Bracket Feet, Korea, 21 x 36 In.	306.00
Cabinet, Pewter, Mahogany, Hinged Storage Base, 16-Pane Upper Doors, Paint, 57 x 85 In.	590.00
Cabinet, Pine, 7 Drawers, Brass Pulls, Footed, 20th Century, 50 ½ x 18 x 12 In.	170.00
Cabinet, Pine, Framed Glass Doors, Shelves, 2 Drawers, Scroll Feet, c.1900, 60 x 43 In.	410.00
Cabinet, Pine, Painted, Stenciled, Molded Cornice, Paneled Doors, Drawers, 76 x 43 In.	796.00
Cabinet, Provincial, Carved, Stepped Cornice, Glazed Door, 2 Shelves, Early 1800s, 30 x 21 In.	705.00
Cabinet, Provincial Empire, Fruitwood, Recessed Paneled Cupboard Door, 34 x 30 In.	1320.00
Cabinet, Quartersawn Oak, 2 Paneled Doors, Marble Top, 1940s, 23 ½ x 22 In.	132.00
Cabinet, Record, Quartersawn Oak Veneer, Player Inset, 33 x 22 In.	250.00
Cabinet, Red Lacquer, 2 Decorated Doors, 2 Interior Drawers, Chinese, 17 ½ x 12 In.	219.00
Cabinet, Red Lacquer, Sandalwood, 2 Doors, 2 Shelves, Chinese, 47 x 30 In., Pair	896.00
Cabinet, Regency, Gilt Metal, Black, Parcel Gilt, Drawers, 34 x 45 In. ....*illus*	7500.00
Cabinet, Regency Style, Mahogany, 4 Drawers, Lattice Work Doors................................	230.00
Cabinet, Renaissance Revival, Ebonized, Parcel Gilt, Porcelain Portrait, 46 x 55 x 20 In.	5333.00
Cabinet, Renaissance Revival, Oak, Bowfront, Glass Sides, Mirror, c.1910, 67 x 48 In. ....*illus*	1763.00
Cabinet, Renaissance Revival, Rosewood Inlay, Ebonized, Parcel Gilt, 44 x 40 In.	1304.00

Furniture, Cabinet, Kingwood, Gilt Bronze, Marquetry, Durand, c.1880, 60 x 46 In. $9375.00

Furniture, Cabinet, Louis XVI Style, Mahogany, Gilt Bronze, D-Shape, c.1880, 44 x 65 In. $20000.00

Furniture, Cabinet, Louis XVI Style, Marble Top, Drawer, Doors, Shelves, c.1890, 51 x 53 In. $944.00

Furniture, Cabinet, Mahogany, Burl, Gilt Bronze, Gaillard, c.1910, 78 x 81 In. $74500.00

Furniture, Cabinet, Music, Hepplewhite, Corner, Painted, Interior Shelves, 1800s, 31 x 23 In. $805.00

Furniture, Cabinet, Neoclassical, Oak, Bowfront, Carved, Glass Panels, Mirror, 67 x 44 In. $1410.00

Furniture, Cabinet, Regency, Gilt Metal, Black, Parcel Gilt, Drawers, 34 x 45 In. $7500.00

Borax

"Borax" is the slang name for very cheap furniture. It originally referred to cheap, poorly made but flashy furniture made for the bottom of the market during the Depression. It was often made of inexpensive gum or poplar wood with a printed veneer pattern. The term is still used today.

Cabinet, Renaissance Revival, Walnut, Burled, Backsplash, Doors, c.1870, 56 x 72 x 24 In.	1837.00
Cabinet, Renaissance Revival, Walnut, Doors, Knight, Panel Doors, c.1890, 61 x 46 In.	2185.00
Cabinet, Renaissance Revival, Walnut, Wrought Iron, Grill Door, Drawer, Italy, 41 x 36 x 16 In.	1778.00
Cabinet, Risom, Walnut, Lift Up Tambour Door, 54 x 32 In.	600.00
Cabinet, Rococo Style, Pine, Paned Glazed Doors, Bun Feet, 30 x 80 In.	619.00
Cabinet, Saarinen & Swanson, Birch, 4 Drawers, Johnson Furniture, 1940s, 36 x 30 In.	600.00
Cabinet, Saarinen & Swanson, Birch, 4 Drawers, Metal Pulls, 1940s, 48 x 30 In.	780.00
Cabinet, Sewing, Shaker, Pine, Painted, Dovetailed Construction, 3 Drawers, Iron Pulls, 28 x 29 In.	1770.00
Cabinet, Sheet Music, Carved R, Rohlfs, 20 x 36 x 11 ½ In.	10980.00
Cabinet, Side, Louis XV, Cherry, Carved, 2 Glazed Doors, 66 x 49 x 16 In.	711.00
Cabinet, Smoking, Art & Crafts, Open Shelf, Lower Door, 15 x 28 In.	420.00
Cabinet, Smoking, Door, Cutouts, Slag Glass, Side Pipe Stand, 18 x 28 In.	270.00
Cabinet, Spanish Colonial, Paneled Doors, 3 Drawers, 57 x 42 In.	1952.00
Cabinet, Specimen, Federal, Swan's Neck Crest, 2 Doors, 8 Drawers, 19 x 17 In.	575.00
Cabinet, Spice, Federal, Door, 4 Drawers, Turned Feet, c.1830, 15 x 11 In.	748.00
Cabinet, Spice, Mahogany, Crossband Doors, Fitted Interior, Bun Feet, c.1760, 17 x 17 In.	1175.00
Cabinet, Spice, Red Stain, 20 Drawers, Painted, Turned Pulls, 30 x 31 x 9 In.	690.00
Cabinet, Spice, Serpentine Gallery Top, 24 Drawers, Bracket Feet, 18 x 16 In.	269.00
Cabinet, Spice, Wood, Drawers, Tin Liners, Porcelain Handles, 15 x 7 ½ In.	44.00
Cabinet, Stained Glass Door, Oak, Carved, Molded Cornice, Twist Columns, c.1800, 98 In.	3800.00
Cabinet, Step Back, Burl Walnut, Cartouche-Shaped Glass Panel Doors, Dutch, 94 x 68 In.	4063.00
Cabinet, Storage, Black Lacquer, Staggered Shelves, Drawers, Doors, Gilt, 44 x 34 In.	316.00
Cabinet, Table Top, Chippendale, Poplar, Yellow Pine, Arch, Southern, c.1790, 22 x 18 In.	690.00
Cabinet, Tubular Chrome Frame, Drawers, Metal Pulls, Rougier, Canada, 24 x 21 In., Pair.....	960.00
Cabinet, Victorian, Mahogany, Flat Molded Cornice, Glass Doors, Sidelights, 1800s, 71 x 49 In.	259.00
Cabinet, Victorian, Mahogany, Walnut, Drawers, Paneled Door, Turned Columns...................	150.00
Cabinet, Walnut, 5 Drawers, Metal Frame, Florence Knoll, 26 x 37 In.	720.00
Cabinet, Walnut, Arched Cornice, Glazed Doors, Drawer, Panel Doors, 36 x 75 In.	2350.00
Cabinet, Walnut, Burled, Frieze Drawers, Doors, Apron, Cabriole Legs, 33 x 42 x 20 In.	388.00
Cabinet, Walnut, Enameled Gilt Chinoiserie, c.1920, 74 x 46 In.	325.00
Cabinet, Walnut, Fruitwood Inlay, Marble Top, Serpentine Front, 3 Mirrored Doors, 48 In.	948.00
Cabinet, Walnut Inlay, Arched Cornice, Glazed Doors, Drawer, 75 x 36 In.	2350.00
Cabinet, Walnut, Paneled Cupboard Doors, Carved Classical Urns, 70 x 48 In.	345.00
Cabinet, Widdicomb, Walnut, 3 Drawers, Carved Pulls, Metal Legs, 35 x 32 In.	330.00
Cabinet, Widdicomb, Walnut, Bleached, 2 Doors, Grass Cloth Front, 41 x 37 In., Pair.............	240.00
Cabinet, Wine, Pine, Slats, 3 Shelves, Casters, c.1875, 47 x 34 x 15 In.	480.00
Cabinet, Wine, Victorian, Oak, Double-Paneled Door, Pomegranate Backsplash, 1870, 57 In. ...	2495.00
Cabinet, Wormley, Mahogany, Bleached, Sliding Doors, Drawers, Dunbar, c.1940, 49 x 31 In. ...	660.00
Cabinet-On-Stand, Fruitwood, Paneled, 2 Doors, 6 Leg Stand, 67 x 35 x 18 In.	448.00
Cabinet-On-Stand, George III Style, Fruitwood, Harewood, Doors, 84 x 47 x 15 In.	2963.00
Cabinet-On-Stand, Renaissance Revival, Walnut, Figural Carved, 77 x 46 x 20 In.	7768.00
Cabinet-On-Stand, Spanish Baroque, Ivory, Tortoiseshell, 9 Drawers, Door, 55 x 44 In.	7110.00
Candlestand, Birch, 8-Sided Top, Tripod Base, Georgia, Mulberry, c.1830, 22 x 28 In.	8280.00
Candlestand, Birch, Tilt Top, Turned Stem, Tripod Base, c.1800, 28 x 20 In.	1150.00
Candlestand, Cherry Inlay, Octagonal Top, 3-Footed, c.1810, 29 ½ x 20 In.	1095.00
Candlestand, Cherry, Round, Vase, Ring Turned, 3-Footed, Red Stain, c.1810, 28 x 19 In.	593.00
Candlestand, Cherry, Screw Top, 3-Footed, Connecticut River Valley, 1800s, 27 x 16 x 16 In. ..	2100.00
Candlestand, Cherry, Tilt Top, Dish Top, Birdcage, Turned Pedestal, c.1780, 29 x 21 In.	411.00
Candlestand, Chippendale, Cherry, Round Top, Tripod Base, Snake Feet, 26 x 13 In.	440.00
Candlestand, Chippendale, Mahogany, Tilt Top, Open Fretwork Gallery, c.1760, 29 x 24 In. ...	1650.00
Candlestand, Curly Maple, Poplar, Oval Corners, Ring-Turned Shaft, Scroll Legs, 28 x 17 In. .	235.00
Candlestand, Curly Maple, Square, Oval Corners, Urn Shaft, 1800s, 28 x 17 In.	764.00
Candlestand, Federal Style, Mahogany, Shaped Top, Shell Inlay, 3 Spider Legs, 29 In.	310.00
Candlestand, Federal Style, Walnut, Tripod, Urn Pedestal, c.1850, 29 x 21 In.	303.00
Candlestand, Federal, Burl, Round Top, Metal Support, 3 Legs, 24 x 28 In.	58.00
Candlestand, Federal, Cherry, Pine, Round Top, 3-Footed, 1820, 29 x 17 In.	265.00
Candlestand, Federal, Cherry, Rectangular Top, 3-Footed, 29 ¼ x 16 ½ In.	240.00
Candlestand, Federal, Cherry, Spider Legs, c.1800, 26 ½ x 15 ½ x 15 In.	264.00
Candlestand, Federal, Cherry, Square Top, Tripod Base, c.1810, 28 x 17 ½ In.	480.00
Candlestand, Federal, Cherry, Square Top, Turned Post, New Eng., c.1800, 27 x 17 In.	356.00
Candlestand, Federal, Cherry, Tilt Top, Square, Tripod, 30 x 31 In.	385.00
Candlestand, Federal, Cherry, Tray Top, Herringbone Inlays, Tripod Base, c.1820, 29 x 19 In.	889.00
Candlestand, Federal, Mahogany, Round Top, Spade Feet, 1700s, 28 x 21 In.	240.00
Candlestand, Federal, Mahogany, Tilt Top, Cut Corners, c.1810, 27 x 24 In. ....*illus*	382.00
Candlestand, Federal, Mahogany, Tilt Top, Oval, Tripod Base, Spade Feet, 29 x 24 In.	715.00
Candlestand, Federal, Tiger Maple, Drawer, Scalloped Skirt, c.1810, 27 x 17 In. ....*illus*	3540.00

Candlestand, Federal, Tiger Maple, Tilt, Inset Corners, Spider Leg Tripod, c.1800, 28 x 21 x 17 In. .	632.00
Candlestand, Federal, Tiger Maple, Shaped Tilt Top, 1800s, 27 x 24 In. .... *illus*	1003.00
Candlestand, George III, Mahogany, Oval, Turned Stem, Angular Tripod Base, 32 In.	770.00
Candlestand, George III, Mahogany, Twisted Baluster Stem, Snake Feet, 25 x 14 In.	431.00
Candlestand, George III, Oak, Round Top, Vase Shape Stem, Slipper Feet, 27 x 20 In.	411.00
Candlestand, Georgian, Mahogany, Dish Top, Turned Stem, Arched Arms, 30 x 17 In.	470.00
Candlestand, Georgian, Oak, Beech, Dish Top, Tripod Base, England, 1800s, 18 x 27 In.	805.00
Candlestand, Hepplewhite, Mahogany, Applied Molding, Tripod Base, c.1775, 15 x 15 x 25 In.	411.00
Candlestand, Mahogany, Adjustable, Oblong, 2 Cups, Telescopic Support, Tripod Base, 48 In.	325.00
Candlestand, Mahogany, Cherry, Crossed Shoe Base, New England, 1800s, 52 In.	1638.00
Candlestand, Mahogany, Round Top, Turned Stem, Tripod Base, c.1795, 27 x 18 In.	403.00
Candlestand, Mahogany, Shell Center, Veneer Tilt Top, c.1800, 30 x 22 In.	4148.00
Candlestand, Mahogany, Square Top, Turned Shaft, Central Drop, Cutout Legs, 24 x 20 In. ...	176.00
Candlestand, Mahogany, Tilt Top, Pedestal, Tripod Base, Slipper Feet, Eng., 1800s, 27 x 16 In.	354.00
Candlestand, Mahogany, Tilt Top, Urn Shaft, 3 Pad Feet, Snake Legs, 27 ½ x 18 ¾ In.	2185.00
Candlestand, Oval Top, Baluster-Turned Shaft, Tripod Base, c.1800, 27 x 17 x 12 In.	646.00
Candlestand, Peter Ompir, Painted, Green Ground, Mustard Highlights, Fruit, 22 ½ x 15 In. .	995.00
Candlestand, Pine, Tilt Top, Round, Baluster Shaft, Snake Feet, c.1800, 26 ½ x 18 In.	470.00
Candlestand, Queen Anne, Mahogany, Round Top, Pedestal, 27 x 17 In.	345.00
Candlestand, Queen Anne, Mahogany, Tilt Top, Tripod, Phila., c.1750, 27 x 23 In.	12500.00
Candlestand, Queen Anne, Maple, Tilt Top, Serpentine Edge, Urn, c.1750, 27 x 20 x 20 In.	690.00
Candlestand, Renaissance Revival, Inlaid Top, Bird Carved Tripod Base, c.1875, 29 In.	561.00
Candlestand, Shaker, Butternut, Round Top, Tripod Feet, Brown Stain, Watervliet, c.1825, 24 In.	2925.00
Candlestand, Shaker, Drying, Birch, Maple, 4-Arm, Snake Legs, Mass., c.1840, 26 x 35 In.	1287.00
Candlestand, Shaker, Drying, Walnut, Slide Lid Box, Arms, Holes, N.Y., c.1845, 34 x 35 In.	293.00
Candlestand, Shaker, Maple, Cherry, Spider Legs, 19th Century, 27 x 21 x 19 In.	2800.00
Candlestand, Shaker, Pine, Adjustable, Round, c.1790, 33 x 20 In.	2340.00
Candlestand, Tiger Maple, Oval Top, 3-Footed, 27 x 19 x 16 In.	1700.00
Candlestand, Tiger Maple, Tilt Top, 3-Footed, N.Y., 26 ½ x 23 x 20 In.	1695.00
Candlestand, Turned, Carved Post, Brown Paint, New England, c.1820, 24 x 17 In.	326.00
Candlestand, Walnut, 16 Facet Top, Baluster Maple Support, Tripod Base, 1800s, 27 x 22 In. .	633.00
Candlestand, Walnut, Oval Top, 19th Century, 28 ¼ x 25 ¾ x 17 In.	175.00
Candlestand, Walnut, Round Top, Baluster, Oak Legs, Snake Feet, c.1800, 29 In.	380.00
Candlestand, Walnut, Tilt Top, Round, c.1900, 26 x 19 In.	140.00
Candlestand, William & Mary, Maple, Blue Paint, Baluster Support, c.1725, 25 x 15 In. *illus*	3540.00
Candlestand, William & Mary, Maple, Cherry, Turned Support, 26 x 18 In. ....*illus*	2360.00
Candlestand, Windsor, Mixed Woods, Tilt Top, Round, 8-Sided Pillar, Tripod, Painted, 27 x 18 In.	470.00
Candlestand, Wood, Red Paint, Spider Legs, 1800s, 28 x 17 x 18 In.	396.00
Candlestand, Wrought Iron, Tripod Base, Accordion Arm, 19th Century, 43 In.	1087.00
Canterbury, George III, Mahogany, Oak, c.1800, 21 x 18 In.	1528.00
Canterbury, Mahogany, Drawer, 3 Slots, 19th Century, 19 x 22 x 12 In.	600.00
Canterbury, Mahogany, Drawer, Brass Pulls & Casters, c.1810, 20 x 17 x 13 In.	1200.00
Canterbury, Regency Style, Mahogany, Finials, Reticulated Dividers, Drawer, 20 x 19 In.	764.00
Canterbury, Sheraton, Mahogany, Spindled Gallery, Drawer, Brass Pulls, 18 x 23 In.	1725.00
Canterbury, Victorian Style, Mahogany, Spindles, Turned Feet, 18 x 18 In.	173.00
Canterbury, Walnut, Oval, 3 Sections, Spindles, Casters, c.1880, 20 x 22 x 15 In.	237.00
Canterbury, William IV, Carved Rosewood, Laurel Wreath, Drawers, 1830, 22 x 20 In.	1460.00
Canterbury, William IV, Laurel Wreath, Spindles, Drawer, c.1830, 22 x 20 x 15 In.	1792.00
Cart, Bar, Aldo Tura, 2 Shelves, Goat Skin Cover, Bottle Storage, Casters, Italy, 34 x 30 In.	540.00
Cart, Ingvard Jensen, Teak, 6 Shelves, Casters, Denmark, 24 x 25 In.	150.00
Case, Bottle, Divided Interior, Bracket Feet, Holds 36 Bottles, c.1890, 13 x 34 x 15 In.	230.00
Cassone, Italian Renaissance Revival, Walnut, Carved Battle Scene, Ball Feet, 24 x 59 In.	474.00
Cellarette, Arts & Crafts, Storage, Door, Applied X, Pullout Shelf, 16 x 16 x 44 In.	480.00
Cellarette, Cherry, Figured Inlays, Hinged Top, Divided Interior, Ky., c.1805, 23 x 19 In.	19550.00
Cellarette, Chippendale, Walnut, Molded Lid, Tapered Square Legs, 32 x 22 x 17 In.	2990.00
Cellarette, Coffin Shape, Mahogany, Lid, S-Scroll Carved Feet, c.1830, 23 x 23 x 17 In., Pair...	3290.00
Cellarette, Federal, Mahogany, Veneers, Inlays, Casters, c.1820, 27 x 23 In.	8050.00
Cellarette, George III, Brass Bound, Mahogany, Octagonal Lid, 33 x 20 x 20 In.	1159.00
Cellarette, George III, Mahogany, Brass Bands, Lift Top, Lined, Hexagonal, 28 x 18 x 16 In. ...	3000.00
Cellarette, George III, Mahogany, Brass Bands, Metal Liner, c.1775, 27 x 22 x 16 In.	1920.00
Cellarette, George III, Mahogany, Sarcophagus, Lion Masque, Ring Handles, 23 x 26 x 19 In. ..	1075.00
Cellarette, Hinged Lid, Regency Style, Mahogany, Divided, Brass Handles, 24 x 23 x 18 In.	2415.00
Cellarette, Mahogany, Pedestal, Drawer, Racks, c.1790, 43 x 19 x 18 In., Pair...................	4406.00
Cellarette, Mahogany, Sarcophagus, Tapered Rectangle, 18 x 25 In.	1298.00
Cellarette, Regency, Mahogany, 6-Sided, Hinged Lid, 3 Square Legs, 26 x 19 x 16 In.	460.00
Cellarette, Regency, Mahogany, Brass, 6-Sided, Divided, Lead Lining, Square Legs, 19 x 26 In. .	652.00

F

Furniture, Cabinet,
Renaissance Revival, Oak, Bowfront,
Glass Sides, Mirror, c.1910, 67 x 48 In.
$1763.00

Furniture, Candlestand, Federal,
Mahogany, Tilt Top, Cut Corners, c.1810,
27 x 24 In.
$382.00

Furniture, Candlestand, Federal,
Tiger Maple, Drawer, Scalloped Skirt,
c.1810, 27 x 17 In.
$3540.00

FURNITURE

Furniture, Candlestand, Federal, Tiger Maple, Shaped Tilt Top, 1800s, 27 x 24 In.
$1003.00

Furniture, Candlestand, William & Mary, Maple, Blue Paint, Baluster Support, c.1725, 25 x 15 In.
$3540.00

Furniture, Candlestand, William & Mary, Maple, Cherry, Turned Support, 26 x 18 In.
$2360.00

Cellarette, Regency, Mahogany, Ebonized, Inlaid, Sarcophagus, Paw Feet, 22 x 25 In.	863.00
Cellarette, Stand, Hepplewhite Style, Mahogany, Inlays, Pullout Slide, 1900s, 40 x 18 In.	2530.00
Cellarette, Stickley Bros., No. 7626, Applied Hammered Copper, Doors, 24 x 15 x 33 In.	1560.00
Cellarette, Walnut, Bottle Case, Inlaid Escutcheons, Turned Legs, 1800s, 38 x 20 x 17 In.	12650.00
Cellarette, William IV, Mahogany, Sarcophagus, Metal Lining, Paw Feet, 21 x 31 In.	2400.00
Cellarette, William IV, Mahogany, Stepped, Beveled, Chamfered Corners, c.1800, 21 x 28 In.	2937.00
Cellarette, William IV, Oak, Coffin Shape, Stepped, Grapes, Leaves, c.1850, 24 x 31 x 23 In.	4112.00
Chair Set, Art Deco, Jacquard Style Fabric, c.1930, 32 x 18 x 19 In., 8	2360.00
Chair Set, Arts & Crafts, Oak, Upholstered, H-Back, c.1912, 39 ¼ In., 6	1126.00
Chair Set, Arts & Crafts, Walnut, 3 Horizontal Slats, Cane Seat, Brass Caps, 6	3200.00
Chair Set, Bamboo Turnings, Gilt Stencil Flowers, Red, Black, c.1815, 33 x 18 In., 6	2963.00
Chair Set, Biedermeier, Birch, Crest Rail, Shaped Back, Overupholstered Seat, c.1835, 35 In., 5	1293.00
Chair Set, Biedermeier, Cherry, Carved, Scrolled Back, Dolphin Splat, Slip Seat, 38 In., 4	230.00
Chair Set, Borge Mogensen, Oak, Arms, Buckled Leather Sling Seats, 27 x 33 In., 4	4800.00
Chair Set, Carolean, English Oak, Crown Centered Crest, Barley Twist Upright, 48 In., 6	3600.00
Chair Set, Chinese Chippendale, Mahogany, C-Scroll Crest, Pierced Splat, 39 In., 4	633.00
Chair Set, Chinese Chippendale, Yellow Lacquer, Pierced Lattice Back, 30 x 20 In., 4	431.00
Chair Set, Chippendale, Mahogany, Acanthus Crest Rail, Pierced Splat, 2 Armchairs, 6	1265.00
Chair Set, Chippendale, Mahogany, Carved, Scrolled Splat, 2 Armchairs, 39 In., 8	863.00
Chair Set, Chippendale Style, Carved Crest, Solid Splat, Slip Seat, Early 1900s, 41 In., 8 *illus*	2832.00
Chair Set, Chippendale Style, Mahogany, Overupholstered, Carved, 2 Armchairs, 10	2489.00
Chair Set, Chippendale Style, Splat Back, Chinese Symbol, Upholstered, Armchair, 42 In., 8	575.00
Chair Set, Dining, Aalto, Birch, Round Seat, Curved Backrest, Artek, 15 x 31 In., 4	840.00
Chair Set, Dining, Arne Jacobsen, Ebonized Laminate, Steel Legs, 30 x 20 In., 8	720.00
Chair Set, Dining, Shaker, Blue Paint, Woven Rush Seats, 7	2760.00
Chair Set, Eames, La Fonda, Herman Miller, c.1961, 29 x 25 In., 6	1286.00
Chair Set, Eliel Saarinen, Birch Frames, Black, White Upholstery, 1930s, 19 x 33 In., 4	270.00
Chair Set, Fauteuil, Empire, Mahogany, Gilt Bronze Mounted, Griffin Legs, 41 In., 4	12810.00
Chair Set, Fauteuil, Louis XV, Painted, Carved, Upholstered, Curved Back, Armchairs, c.1790, 4	854.00
Chair Set, Faux Bamboo, Latticework Frame, Padded Seat, 2 Armchairs, 36 ½ In., 6	978.00
Chair Set, Flared Seat, Painted Designs, Green, Yellow, Mass., c.1820, 18 x 33 In., 7	711.00
Chair Set, French Provincial, Green Paint, 2 Rows Of Spindles, Rush Seat, c.1950, 37 In., 6	708.00
Chair Set, G. Nakashima, Walnut, Hickory Spindles, 19 x 16 ½ x 35 ½ In., 4	9000.00
Chair Set, G. Stickley, No. 354 ½, V Back, 5 Vertical Slats, Leather Seat, 36 In., 8	9600.00
Chair Set, George III, Mahogany, 3 Vertical Cluster Splats, Reeded, Padded Seat, Open Arms, 4	3422.00
Chair Set, George III Style, Mahogany, Arched Crest Rail, Pierced Splat, 2 Armchairs, 8	3525.00
Chair Set, George III Style, Mahogany, Pierced Splat, Overupholstered, 2 Armchairs, 19 In., 6	1422.00
Chair Set, Georgian, Mahogany, Pierced Backs, Scrolling, Carvings, Ball & Claw, 1900s, 8	2360.00
Chair Set, Gondola, Neoclassical, Mahogany, Ached Rounded Crests, Vase Splat, c.1830, 6	1645.00
Chair Set, J. Hoffmann, Beech, Curved Back, Upholstered, Bentwood Supports, 30 In., 4	2040.00
Chair Set, Jacobean, Oak, Ebonized, Carved Panels, Strapwork, 2 Armchairs, c.1912, 19 In., 12	1896.00
Chair Set, Louis XIV, Fruitwood, Pierced Splat, Shell & Leaf Carved Crest, 1800s, 4	823.00
Chair Set, Louis XVI Style, Gilt, Velvet Upholstery, Nail Head Trim, Open Arms, 4	702.00
Chair Set, Louis XVI Style, Multicolored, Cane Back, Leaf Carved Frieze, 35 In., 6	3120.00
Chair Set, Louis XVI, Wood, Painted, Suede Upholstery, Padded, 36 x 19 x 17 In., 6	2629.00
Chair Set, Mackintosh, Bedroom, Oak, Ebonized, Ladder-Type Back, Upholstered Seat, 55 In., 4	1560.00
Chair Set, Mahogany, Carved, Wave Crest, Scrolled Ribbons, Latticework Splat, 42 In., 4	805.00
Chair Set, Mahogany, Curved Crest, Shieldback, Kittinger Biggs, 2 Armchairs, 38 In., 8	2124.00
Chair Set, Mahogany, Scalloped Crest, Pierced Splat, Slip Seat, Square Legs, c.1775, 6	3744.00
Chair Set, Meeks, Rococo Revival, Pierced Crest, Upholstered Seat & Back, 41 In., 4	3290.00
Chair Set, Mies Van Der Rohe, Brno, Steel Cantilevered Frame, Upholstered, Knoll, 32 In., 4	600.00
Chair Set, Neoclassical, Mahogany, Balloon Back, Parcel Gilt, Upholstered, 36 In., 6	8100.00
Chair Set, Neoclassical, Mahogany, Carved Crest, Volute Ears, Reed Splat, 6	900.00
Chair Set, Neoclassical, Tiger Maple, Cane Seat, Shaped Crest, Vase Shape Splat, 35 In., 6	1333.00
Chair Set, Niels Vodder, Teak, Black Leather, 2 Armchairs, 32 x 27 x 23 In., 6	4270.00
Chair Set, Old Hickory, Woven Splint, Rocker, Footstool, 2 Armchairs	1320.00
Chair Set, P. Fabricius, J. Kastholm, Steel Frame, Black Leather, Casters, 44 x 29 In., 3	7200.00
Chair Set, Queen Anne Style, Curly Maple, Vase Splat, Rush Seat, 1900, 40 In., 6	1055.00
Chair Set, Queen Anne Style, Maple, Yoke Crest Rail, Rush Seat, 1930s, 6	1055.00
Chair Set, Queen Anne, Windsor, Bow Back, Continuous Arm, 42 In., 8	1016.00
Chair Set, Red, Black Grain Painted, Striping, Flowers, Marked, c.1850, 34 In., 4 *illus*	499.00
Chair Set, Regency, Inlaid Tablet Back, Upholstered Seat, 2 Armchairs, c.1820, 33 In., 8	1763.00
Chair Set, Regency, Mahogany, Arched Back Rail, Upholstered Seat, Saber Legs, 33 ½ In., 6	230.00
Chair Set, Regency, Mahogany, Prince Of Wales Splat, Cane Seat, 2 Armchairs, 12	2940.00
Chair Set, Regency, Mahogany, Shield Shaped, Open Splat, Overupholstered, 4 Armchairs, 6	830.00
Chair Set, Renaissance Revival, Beech, Painted, Rectangular Crest, c.1900, 44 In., 6	2067.00

F

Chair Set, Shaker, Ladder Back, Cherry, Tape Seat, New Lebanon, c.1840, 41 In., 6	9500.00
Chair Set, Sheraton, Cherry, Cane Seat, Cartouche Shape Back, Tapered Legs, Cushion, 37 In., 4.	403.00
Chair Set, Sheraton, Rosewood, Carved, Cane, 4 Armchairs, 32 ½ x 17 In., 7	3318.00
Chair Set, Spindles, Rush Seat, 1 Armchair, England, Mid 1800s, 43 In., 8 ....*illus*	2760.00
Chair Set, Stacking, Arne Jacobsen, No. 3103, Molded Teak, Black Enamel, F. Hansen, 16 x 31 In., 6	840.00
Chair Set, Stacking, Fritz Hansen, Teak, Molded Black Enamel Legs, Denmark, c.1966, 16 x 31 In., 8	1560.00
Chair Set, Stickley Bros., 3 Vertical Slats, Leather Seat, 35 In., 6	1800.00
Chair Set, Victorian, Mahogany, Violin Back Frame, Upholstered Cushions, 4	146.00
Chair Set, W. Platner, Nickel Plated, Wire Base, White Upholstery, Knoll, 1977, 27 x 30 In., 6 ..	5100.00
Chair Set, Walnut, Curved Crest Rail, Horizontal Splat, Cane Seat, Saber Legs, c.1900, 4	59.00
Chair Set, Walnut, High Cane-Panel Back, Cushion Seat, Century Furniture, c.1940, 6	59.00
Chair Set, Wegner, Shell, Wood, Fritz Hansen, c.1948, 28 x 27 In., 3	5513.00
Chair Set, Wicker, Painted White, Ottoman, Nautical Design Cushions, Early 1900s, 4	230.00
Chair Set, Windsor, Bow Back, Saddle Seats, Bulbous, Splayed Legs, 36 In., 4	825.00
Chair Set, Windsor, Fanback, Oak, Ash, Saddle Seat, New England, c.1800, 40 x 18 In., 6	3851.00
Chair Set, Wormley, Mahogany, Curved Backs, Cream Upholstery, Dunbar, 1950s, 33 In., 6	720.00
Chair, 3 Spindles, Green Paint, Straight Rail, Painted Flowers, 15 x 10 In., Child's	460.00
Chair, A. Dubreuil, Spine, Bent Steel, Green Enamel Finish, 32 x 29 In.	4500.00
Chair, A. Girard, Black, White Wool, Aluminum Legs, Herman Miller, 27 x 40 In.	1800.00
Chair, Aalto, Birch C-Shape Arms, Upholstered Seat, Back Cushions, Artek, 29 x 28 In.	1020.00
Chair, Aalto, Laminated Birch, c.1933-35, 31 x 14 ¾ In.	143.00
Chair, Aalto, No. 15, Laminated Birch, Finmar, c.1929-30, 27 x 18 ½ x 21 In.	2629.00
Chair, Aalto, No. 21, Laminated Birch, 1931-32, 28 x 19 In., Pair	2390.00
Chair, Aalto, No. 69, Laminated Birch, 29 x 16 x 18 In.	96.00
Chair, Adirondack Twig, Hoop Back, Downswept Ribbon Arms, Black Paint, 42 x 30 In.	115.00
Chair, Andre Groult, Gilt, Blue, Orange, Lacquered, 39 x 17 x 20 In.	657.00
Chair, Anglo-Indian, Hardwood, Tiered, Pierce Carved Back, 1800s, 36 ¾ In.	115.00
Chair, Arne Jacobsen, No. 3316, Chromium Plated Metal, Leather, c.1962, 40 ½ In.	22500.00
Chair, Arne Jacobsen, Pot, No. 3318, Label, Fritz Hansen, c.1959, 28 x 28 In.	490.00
Chair, Arrow Back, Black, Gold Paint Designs, Rush Seat, New York, c.1800, 34 In.	382.00
Chair, Art Deco, Asymmetrical Fanback, Channeled, Purple Upholstery, Pair	600.00
Chair, Art Deco, Curved, Metal Tubular Frame, Enameled Seat & Back, 32 x 20 In., Pair	316.00
Chair, Art Deco, Wood, Painted Black, Round Seat & Back, Oval Cutout, 34 ¾ In.	175.00
Chair, Arts & Crafts, 3 Vertical Arm Slats, Upholstered Seat & Back, 39 In., Pair	300.00
Chair, Arts & Crafts, Back Slats, Loose Cushion, Arms, 29 x 42 In.	90.00
Chair, Arts & Crafts, Beech, Morris Style, Arms, England, c.1935, Pair	705.00
Chair, Arts & Crafts, Morris, Oak, Leather, Adjustable Back, c.1912, 38 ½ x 30 x 37 ¾ In.	1778.00
Chair, Asparagus, Lisa Lombardi, Signed, c.1984, 65 x 15 x 27 In.	2450.00
Chair, B. Mathsson, Beech Frame, Black Cotton Webbing, Sweden, 1959, 19 x 33 In., Pair	1320.00
Chair, Ballroom, Rococo, Rosewood, Faux Bois, Scroll Splat, Upholstery, 1800s	82.00
Chair, Banister Back, Turned, Arched, Molded Crest, Splint Seat, Paint, 16 x 43 In.	326.00
Chair, Banister, Shaped Crest, Ribbed Slats, Rush Seat, Black Paint, Arms, 17 x 45 In.	676.00
Chair, Barcelona, Mies Van Der Rohe, Black Leather, Steel, X Base, Knoll, 30 x 30 In., Pair	3600.00
Chair, Baroque, Arch Top Rail, Tapestry Seat & Back, Block, Turned Legs, 1800s, 26 x 46 In. ..	826.00
Chair, Baroque Style, Beech, Mixed Woods, Carved, 56 ½ x 27 ½ x 25 In.	805.00
Chair, Baroque Style, Ebonized Barley Twist, Cane Seat & Back, Carved, Arms, 46 x 25 x 22 In. .	209.00
Chair, Baroque Style, Elm, Carved Figural, Overupholstered Seat, Arms, 49 x 25 x 25 In.	239.00
Chair, Baroque Style, Mahogany, Arching Crest, Loose Cushion, 55 x 36 x 22 In.	359.00
Chair, Baroque Style, Oak, Bird, Leaves, Fruit, Scrolled Armrests, Upholstered, 19 In., Pair	356.00
Chair, Baroque Style, Walnut, Mixed Woods, Lyre Form, Tapestry, Arms, 60 ½ x 30 In.	920.00
Chair, Barrel, Velvet Upholstery, Gilt Carved Legs, Robert Counturier, 28 x 32 In.	3900.00
Chair, Bentwood Rail, Foot, Cushion, J. Van Koet, Towle & Drexel, 29 x 27 In., Pair	863.00
Chair, Bergere, Empire, Mahogany, Bronze Mounted, Paneled Rail, Closed Arms, 37 x 34 In., Pair	2233.00
Chair, Bergere, Fruitwood, Carved, Carved Rail, Loose Cushion, Closed Arms, 36 x 27 In.	299.00
Chair, Bergere, Louis XV, Beech, Flower Carved Frame, Cabriole Legs, Closed Arms, 1800s	237.00
Chair, Bergere, Louis XV, Fruitwood, Carved, Arched Crest, Closed Arms, Rectangular Seat	940.00
Chair, Bergere, Louis XV, Fruitwood, Flower Crest, Upholstered, Closed Arms, c.1880, 39 In.	360.00
Chair, Bergere, Louis XV Style, Walnut, Upholstered, Gout Stool, Closed Arms, 19 In., Pair	593.00
Chair, Bergere, Louis XVI, Barrel Backrest, Round Fluted Legs, Closed Arms, Painted, 18 In., Pair.	1067.00
Chair, Bergere, Louis XVI, Carved Ribbons, Flowers, Reeded Legs, Closed Arms, 27 x 42 In.	590.00
Chair, Bergere, Louis XVI Style, Gilt, Upholstered, Closed Arms, 33 x 21 In.	1725.00
Chair, Bergere, Napoleon III, Fruitwood, Paneled Crest, Acorn Finials, Closed Arms, 37 In., Pair.	3840.00
Chair, Bergere, Neoclassical, Silk Upholstery, Closed Arms, 1800s, 39 x 26 In., Pair	3220.00
Chair, Bergere, Orielle, Louis XV, Multicolored, Domed, Floral Crest, Closed Arms, 38 In., Pair.	3360.00
Chair, Bergere, Regency, Mahogany, Carved, Padded Arms, Leather Cushion, Closed Arms, c.1820	3055.00
Chair, Bergere, Regency, Mahogany, Upholstered, Closed Arms, Pair	2644.00

Furniture, Chair Set, Chippendale Style, Carved Crest, Solid Splat, Slip Seat, Early 1900s, 41 In., 8
$2832.00

Furniture, Chair Set, Red, Black Grain Painted, Striping, Flowers, Marked, c.1850, 34 In., 4
$499.00

Furniture, Chair Set, Spindles, Rush Seat, 1 Armchair, England, Mid 1800s, 43 In., 8
$2760.00

F

Furniture, Chair, Biedermeier, Figured Walnut Veneer, Balloon Back, Vienna, c.1820, 36 In., Pair $881.00

Furniture, Chair, Charles II, Oak, Carved, Cane Seat & Back, 1800s, 55 x 27 In. $478.00

Furniture, Chair, Chippendale Style, Carved, Needlepoint Upholstery, Open Arms, 1900s, 41 x 30 In. $2318.00

Chair, Bergere, Wing, Scrolls, Arch Top, Closed Arms, France, 1800s, 32 x 42 In.	1416.00
Chair, Bertoia, Lounge, Diamond, Yellow, Black Metal, Freeform, 29 In.	248.00
Chair, Biedermeier, D-Form Seat, Saber Front Legs, Curving Crest Rails, 32 x 19 x 15 In.	657.00
Chair, Biedermeier, Figured Walnut Veneer, Balloon Back, Vienna, c.1820, 36 In., Pair ....*illus*	881.00
Chair, Biedermeier, Fruitwood, Arched, Pierced Crest, Upholstered, c.1900, 36 x 20 In.	575.00
Chair, Biedermeier, Fruitwood, Slip Seat, Curved Side Rails, Saber Legs, Pair	120.00
Chair, Biedermeier, Inlaid Fruitwood Ebonized Maple, Birch Panel, c.1830, 18 ½ In.	237.00
Chair, Birch, Molded Shape, Black Leather Seat, Back, Thonet, Arms, 24 x 34 In.	90.00
Chair, Birdcage Back, Bamboo Turnings, Windsor, 1830, Pine & Ash, 33 In.	250.00
Chair, Black Forest, Walnut, Carved, Cane Seat, Arms, Swiss, c.1880, 40 x 25 In.	6500.00
Chair, Bleached Walnut, Carved Arms, Stretcher Base, Late 1800s	1250.00
Chair, Blue Leather, Brass Tacks, Wood Base, Arms, Parzinger, 28 x 24 In.	10200.00
Chair, Brown Leather, Scrolled, Fluted Frame, Nickel Accents, Arms, Paul Kiss, 31 x 25 In.	1800.00
Chair, Bugatti, Ebonized, Copper, Pewter, Walnut, c.1905, 47 x 16 x 16 In., Pair	16730.00
Chair, C. Pollock, Leather Sling Seat, Coated Armrests, Steel Frame, Knoll, 25 x 28 In., Pair	900.00
Chair, Campaign, Victorian, Mahogany, Folding, Slung Seat & Back, Brass Tack, 35 ½ In.	1800.00
Chair, Campeachy, Walnut, Leather Upholstery, Padded, Bamboo, 38 x 23 x 32 In.	388.00
Chair, Captain's, Oak, Cane Seat, Curved Armrests, Spindle Seat Back, Legs, Stretcher, c.1920	70.00
Chair, Carlo Di Carli, Lounge, Upholstered, Singer, c.1951, 30 x 31 x 25 In., Pair	2205.00
Chair, Carnival, Walnut, Arched Shell Carved Crest, Pierced Back, Italy, 1800s, Pair	840.00
Chair, Carved Figural Bust Crests, Cabriole Legs, 1800s, 37 In.	177.00
Chair, Carved Quartersawn Oak, North Wind Face Crest, Early 1900, 35 x 24 In.	995.00
Chair, Carved, Spiral Turned Legs, Silk Upholstery, France, 1800s, 39 x 20 x 21 In.	288.00
Chair, Charles II, Oak, Carved, Cane Seat & Back, 1800s, 55 x 27 In. ....*illus*	478.00
Chair, Chinese Chippendale, Mahogany, Padded Back, Outscrolled Arms, 39 In.	546.00
Chair, Chippendale Style, Carved, Needlepoint Upholstery, Open Arms, 1900s, 41 x 30 In. *illus*	2318.00
Chair, Chippendale Style, Cherry, Upholstered, Fretwork Legs, Stretcher, Arms, 38 x 31 In.	177.00
Chair, Chippendale Style, Mahogany, Carved, Scroll Arms, Slip Seat, 19th Century, 18 In.	178.00
Chair, Chippendale Style, Pierced & Carved Splat, Slip Seat, England, c.1900, 38 In., Pair	823.00
Chair, Chippendale, Arms, Upholstered Slip Seat, Carved & Pierced Splat, 1700s, 40 In.	1050.00
Chair, Chippendale, Beaded Scroll Crest, Cabriole Legs, Philadelphia, c.1760, 18 x 39 In.	3200.00
Chair, Chippendale, Boston, Carved Shell Crest, Solid Splat, 1700s, 38 x 22 In.	31050.00
Chair, Chippendale, Carved Ears, Knuckles, Shell Carved Crest, Trapezoid Seat, c.1975, 39 In.	499.00
Chair, Chippendale, Ladder Back, Pierced Slats, Beaded Legs, New Eng., c.1790, 18 x 38 In.	474.00
Chair, Chippendale, Mahogany, Ball & Claw, Carved Knees, c.1900	69.00
Chair, Chippendale, Mahogany, Carved Crest, Gothic Tracery, England, c.1790, 39 x 23 In.	403.00
Chair, Chippendale, Mahogany, Carved Crest, Pierced Splat, c.1780, 17 ½ x 37 ½ In.	411.00
Chair, Chippendale, Mahogany, Carved Crest, Slip Seat, Delaware Valley, c.1775, Pair	1170.00
Chair, Chippendale, Mahogany, Carved, Pierced Back, Upholstered Seat, 1800s, 39 x 23 In.	92.00
Chair, Chippendale, Mahogany, Carved, Serpentine Crest, Owl Splat, c.1775, 37 In.	5400.00
Chair, Chippendale, Mahogany, Pierced, Carved Top Rail, Back, Upholstered Seat, Pair	127.00
Chair, Chippendale, Mahogany, Serpentine Crest, Vase Splat, Thistle Openwork, 37 In.	478.00
Chair, Chippendale, Mahogany, Shaped Crest, Scrolled Ears, Intertwined Splat, 1700s	529.00
Chair, Chippendale, Mahogany, Shaped Crest, Upholstered, Open Arms, Philadelphia, 41 In.	6250.00
Chair, Chippendale, Mahogany, Slip Seat, Shaped Crest, Carved Shell, Philadelphia, 1700s, 40 In.	1293.00
Chair, Chippendale, Mahogany, Upholstered, Carved Seat Rail, Pair	3819.00
Chair, Chippendale, Maple, Pierced Owl Splat, Rolled Ears, Ball Feet, 1780-90, Pair	850.00
Chair, Chippendale, Shaped Splat, Ball & Claw, Early 20th Century	50.00
Chair, Chippendale, Walnut, Arched Backrest, Shaped Arms, N.C., c.1790, 27 x 25 In.	18400.00
Chair, Chippendale, Walnut, Drop Seat, Openwork Splat, 37 x 21 In.	550.00
Chair, Chippendale, Walnut, Slip Seat, Beaker Shape Splat, H-Stretcher, 1770-90	3200.00
Chair, Chippendale, Wing, Serpentine Top, Padded Back, Upholstery, c.1900	2800.00
Chair, Club, Art Deco, Green Leather Upholstery, 34 x 32 In., Pair	2040.00
Chair, Club, Art Deco, Original Upholstery, Cap D'Afrique Club, Paris, c.1925, 27 x 27 In.	600.00
Chair, Club, Juan Montoya, Upholstery, Wood Frame, 42 x 33 In., Pair	1440.00
Chair, Club, Karl Springer, c.1975, 31 x 30 x 29 In., Pair	4080.00
Chair, Club, Leather, Barrel Back, Splayed Tapered Feet, c.1930, 38 In.	500.00
Chair, Club, Leather, Scrolled Tufted Back, Arms, Turned Legs, Late 1800s, Pair	4700.00
Chair, Coconut, G. Nelson, Knoll Cato Fabric, White Steel Shell, Steel Base, 1960s, 31 In.	3240.00
Chair, Continuous Bow, Windsor, Pine, Peaked Comb, Arms, Rhode Island, 1800s, 50 In.	6756.00
Chair, Corner, Arts & Crafts, Curved Crest, 10 Straight & Bowed Spindles, Rush Seat, 29 In.	115.00
Chair, Corner, Chinese Chippendale, Walnut, Dome Crest, Lattice Splat, 46 x 20 In., Pair	2645.00
Chair, Corner, Chinese, Rosewood, Carved Panels, Marble Inset, c.1900, 34 In., Pair	690.00
Chair, Corner, Chippendale, Mahogany, 18th Century, 31 ½ x 29 x 26 ½ In.	748.00
Chair, Corner, Chippendale, Mahogany, Cabriole Legs, Paw Feet, Ireland, 1700, 34 x 26 x 26 In.	1150.00
Chair, Corner, Chippendale, Tiger Maple, Sycamore, Birch, 30 ¾ x 16 ½ In.	6518.00

Chair, Corner, George II, Mahogany, Solid Splat, Serpentine Slip Seat, Pad Feet, c.1750	1521.00
Chair, Corner, George III, Mahogany, Openwork Splat, Slip Seat, Marlboro Legs, 17 In.	711.00
Chair, Corner, Georgian, Oak, Carved, Shaped Crest Rail, Serpent Head Terminals	294.00
Chair, Corner, Georgian Style, Mahogany, Overupholstered Seat, Shaped Crest	269.00
Chair, Corner, Mahogany, Carved Crest Rail, Pierced Splat, Ball & Claw, c.1770	15210.00
Chair, Corner, Mahogany, Carved Frame, Ball & Claw, 30 x 27 x 28 In.	275.00
Chair, Corner, Mahogany, Carved, Needlepoint, Pierced Splat, Cabriole Legs, c.1900, 32 x 34 In.	240.00
Chair, Corner, Mahogany, Crest Rail, Pierced Splat, Ball & Claw Front, c.1770	15000.00
Chair, Corner, Mahogany, Double Latticework Splat, Slip Seat, Continuous Arm, 32 x 30 In. ...	316.00
Chair, Corner, Mahogany, Tapestry Upholstery, Outscrolled Arms, Double Splat, 31 x 19 In.	345.00
Chair, Corner, Oak, Horizontal Slats, Turned Posts, Reed Woven Seat, England, 1800s, 29 ½ In.	176.00
Chair, Corner, Photographer's, Gilt Faux Bamboo, Needlepoint Seat, 30 x 17 In.	86.00
Chair, Corner, Victorian, Walnut, Needlepoint Seat, Velvet Trim, Arms, 24 x 29 In.	95.00
Chair, Corner, Walnut, Triangular Seat, Open Back Support, Arms, 36 In.	89.00
Chair, Corona, Erik Jorgensen, Upholstered, 1961, 36 ½ x 34 x 31 In.	4800.00
Chair, Council Craftsman, Cherry, Upholstered, Gilt Trim, Scroll Crest, Arms, 35 In.	165.00
Chair, D. Borsani, Lounge, Leather, Metal, Black, Adjustable Frame, Tenco, 80 In.	10200.00
Chair, Desk, Oak, Pattern Crest, Turned Spindles, Arms, Swivel ....*illus*	80.00
Chair, Directoire, Beech, Urn Crest Rail, Cane, Turned Legs, Arms, c.1890, 37 In., Pair	2010.00
Chair, Directoire Style, Iron, Steel, Rope & Tassel Back, Arms, c.1910, 33 x 27 In. ....*illus*	575.00
Chair, Dressing, Shaker, Tiger Birch, 2 Rod Back, Tape Seat, N.Y., c.1880, 18 x 28 In.	468.00
Chair, Eames, Birch, Postman's Bag, Leather, 1950s, 22 x 23 In.	3500.00
Chair, Eames, DAX-I, Tubular Legs, Yellow Vinyl, 1958, 31 ¾ x 25 In., Pair	384.00
Chair, Eames, Fiberglass, Birch, Enameled Metal Wire, c.1953, 31 In.	625.00
Chair, Eames, LCW, Molded Walnut Plywood Seat, Calf Hide, Herman Miller, 1950s, 27 In.	2880.00
Chair, Eames, Lounge, Metal, Vinyl, Aluminum Group, Herman Miller, 22 x 35 In., Pair	480.00
Chair, Eames, Lounge, Ottoman, Rosewood, Metal, Leather, Herman Miller, 33 x 33 In.	2040.00
Chair, Eames, Molded, Rosewood, Leather, Flared Arms, Swivel, Ottoman, Herman Miller.......	2875.00
Chair, Eames, Zenith, Shell, Rope Edge, Zinc Legs, Label, Herman Miller, 29 In.	720.00
Chair, Edwardian, Satinwood, Painted, Parcel Gilt, Overupholstered, Scene, 18 ½ In.	237.00
Chair, Eero Aarnio, Molded Shape, Cream, Black Wool Upholstery, Arms, 27 x 26 In., Pair.......	2400.00
Chair, Egg, Arne Jacobsen, Leather, Aluminum Base, F. Hansen, 42 x 34 In.	5700.00
Chair, Egyptian Revival, Carved, Inlay, Figural Back, Wing Arms, Hoof Feet, c.1920 ....*illus*	3540.00
Chair, Egyptian Revival, Carved, Male Figure Back, Wing Arms, Hoof Feet, Upholstered, c.1900	3231.00
Chair, Empire Style, Mahogany, Inlaid, Griffin Supports, Arms, c.1900, 30 x 24 In. ....*illus*	240.00
Chair, English Oak, Square, Paneled Back, Carved, Scroll Arms, 39 In.	191.00
Chair, Erwin & Estelle Lavern, Clear, Acrylic, Knit Cushion, 24 x 30 In.	1200.00
Chair, Exotic Woods, Barrel Shape, Marquetry, Mother-Of-Pearl, Upholstered, 1800s...............	345.00
Chair, F. Gehry, Cardboard, Masonite Trim, Double-S Base, Easy Edges, 16 x 34 In., Pair.........	1560.00
Chair, F. Gehry, Cross Check, Ribbon Design, Metal Strips, Impressed, Knoll, Arms, 1993, 28 x 34 In.	960.00
Chair, F. Porsche, Aluminum Frame, Leather, Adjustable, Interprofil, W. Germany, 1984, 29 x 47 In.	6000.00
Chair, Fauteuil, Charles X Style, Mahogany, Carved, Square, Padded Seat, Arms, Pair.............	1175.00
Chair, Fauteuil, Directoire, Fruitwood, Carved, Upholstered, c.1780, Pair.............................	1410.00
Chair, Fauteuil, Directoire, Fruitwood, Padded Back, Arms, Bowed Seat Rail, 18th Century......	705.00
Chair, Fauteuil, Directoire, Fruitwood, Padded Seat & Back, Scroll Arms, Carved, Late 1700s, Pair	1410.00
Chair, Fauteuil, French Provincial, Carved Shell Crest, Carving, Upholstery, 26 x 42 In.	531.00
Chair, Fauteuil, Louis XIV, Fruitwood, Needlework, Pad Seat, Scroll Arms, c.1880, 42 In.	1320.00
Chair, Fauteuil, Louis XIV Style, Walnut, Carved, Needlepoint Upholstery, 45 In.	529.00
Chair, Fauteuil, Louis XV, Cane Seat & Back, Carved Flower Crest, Apron, Arms, c.1875, 37 In.	600.00
Chair, Fauteuil, Louis XV, Carved Beech, Arched Crest, Padded Armrest, Mid 1700s, Pair	1586.00
Chair, Fauteuil, Louis XV, Multicolored, Padded Shaped Back, Arms, Cabriole Legs, 36 In., Pair	2040.00
Chair, Fauteuil, Louis XV, Painted Gray, Shaped Back, Padded Arms, Scrolling, c.1790	610.00
Chair, Fauteuil, Louis XV, Provincial, Fruitwood, Cane Seat & Back, Padded Arms, 36 In., Pair	1800.00
Chair, Fauteuil, Louis XV, Provincial, Walnut, Cane Cartouche, Scroll Arms, c.1790.................	976.00
Chair, Fauteuil, Louis XV, Provincial, Walnut, Shaped Back, Padded Arms, c.1790	854.00
Chair, Fauteuil, Louis XV Style, Giltwood, Cartouche, Padded Back, Flower Crest, 40 In., Pair..	230.00
Chair, Fauteuil, Louis XV Style, Giltwood, Carved, Painted, Arched Back, Padded Arms, 1800s, Pair	2115.00
Chair, Fauteuil, Louis XVI, Provincial, Beech, Arched Back, Flared Seat, Late 1700s.................	793.00
Chair, Fauteuil, Louis XVI, Shieldback, Rosettes, Suede Padding, Reeded Legs, 28 x 29 In.	531.00
Chair, Fauteuil, Louis XVI Style, Fruitwood, Medallion Back, Padded, 39 x 23 x 19 In., Pair.....	388.00
Chair, Fauteuil, Louis XVI Style, Mahogany, Carved, Needlepoint Upholstery, 45 In.	529.00
Chair, Fauteuil, Provincial Continental, Painted, Barrel Shape Slatted Back, Padded Seat, 35 In., Pair	2400.00
Chair, Fauteuil, Regency, Fruitwood, Cane Back, Flower Crest, Pad Seat, Arms, c.1890, 47 In. .	1140.00
Chair, Fauteuil, Regency Style, Fruitwood, Upholstered, Open Scroll Arms, 45 In.	3600.00
Chair, Fauteuil, Restauration, Mahogany, Padded Seat & Back, Molded Frame, 37 In., Pair.....	1140.00
Chair, Fauteuil, Rococo Style, Hardwood, Mother-Of-Peal, Inlaid Silver, Syria, Pair	4113.00

Furniture, Chair, Desk, Oak, Pattern Crest, Turned Spindles, Arms, Swivel
$80.00

Furniture, Chair, Directoire Style, Iron, Steel, Rope & Tassel Back, Arms, c.1910, 33 x 27 In.
$575.00

Furniture, Chair, Egyptian Revival, Carved, Inlay, Figural Back, Wing Arms, Hoof Feet, c.1920
$3540.00

Furniture, Chair, Empire Style, Mahogany, Inlaid, Griffin Supports, Arms, c.1900, 30 x 24 In. $240.00

Furniture, Chair, Federal, Mahogany, Slip Seat, Virginia, c.1810, 38 x 20 In. $690.00

Furniture, Chair, Franco Albini, Bamboo, Reed, V. Bonacin, Italy, 36 x 32 In., Pair $1680.00

> **TIP**
> *Natural, unpainted wicker is more valuable than painted wicker, so do not paint a natural piece. It will lower the value.*

Chair, Fauteuil, Walnut, Arched Square Back, Shaped Arms, Stretchers, France, 1800s, 43 In., Pair	1125.00
Chair, Federal, 3 Spindles, Mahogany, Straight Crest, Open Arms, c.1805, 33 In., Pair	12500.00
Chair, Federal, Inlaid Mahogany, Lolling, Upholstered, Arms, Serpentine Crest, c.1800	10800.00
Chair, Federal, Inlaid Mahogany, Serpentine Crest, Scroll Arms, c.1800	2031.00
Chair, Federal, Mahogany, Slip Seat, Virginia, c.1810, 38 x 20 In. ......*illus*	690.00
Chair, Federal, Shield, Open Back, Upholstered Seat, Massachusetts, c.1899, 18 x 39 In.	353.00
Chair, Federal Style, Mahogany, Carved Back & Legs, c.1900, 37 In.	144.00
Chair, Finn Juhl, Easy Chair, No. 53, Rosewood, Upholstered, Arms, Niels Vodder, 29 In., Pair	4200.00
Chair, Finn Juhl, Leather Upholstery, Rosewood, Arms, France & Sons, 32 x 27 In., Pair	900.00
Chair, Finn Juhl, Teak, Tan Leather Seat, Backrest, 32 x 27 In.	1680.00
Chair, Flemish Baroque Style, Scroll Arms & Legs, Overupholstered, 18 x 22 In.	593.00
Chair, Flemish Style, Walnut, Tapestry Upholstery, Downswept Arms, 1800s, 46 x 20 In., Pair	3220.00
Chair, Flower Carved Splat, Arms, Chinese, 47 x 24 In., Pair	518.00
Chair, Folke Ohlsson, Sculpted Shape, Wood Frame, Upholstery, Dux, Denmark, 34 x 35 In.	960.00
Chair, Franco Albini, Bamboo, Reed, V. Bonacin, Italy, 36 x 32 In., Pair ......*illus*	1680.00
Chair, Frank Lloyd Wright, Cypress, c.1939, 28 In.	7500.00
Chair, Frankl, Curve, Wood, Casters, Frankl Studio, c.1940, 28 x 18 In.	1593.00
Chair, French Provincial, Beech, Arched Back, Scroll Arms, 45 In., Pair	173.00
Chair, French Style, Walnut, Carved Arms, Legs, Applied Gild, Arms, 44 x 29 x 26 In., Pair	1121.00
Chair, Fretwork, Carved Arms & Legs, Leather, 19th Century, 39 In.	800.00
Chair, G. Nakashima, Walnut, Hickory Spindles, 35 x 20 In.	3900.00
Chair, G. Offredi, Leather, Metal Base, Cantilevered Arms, Saporiti, 30 x 35 In.	960.00
Chair, G. Rietveld, Beech, Plywood Frame, Red, Blue, Cassina, 34 x 26 In.	660.00
Chair, G. Rietveld, Zigzag Stoel, Elm, Brass, 1934, 29 ½ In.	25000.00
Chair, G. Stickley, Leather Seat & Back, 37 x 26 ½ x 19 In.	3172.00
Chair, G. Stickley, Morris, Spring Seat, Loose Cushion, Upholstered, 38 ½ x 27 ½ x 34 In.	3000.00
Chair, G. Stickley, No. 310, Rush Seat, Corbel Supports, Arms, 25 x 36 In.	270.00
Chair, G. Stickley, No. 336, Morris, Corbel Supports, Leather, Bow Arm, 30 x 36 x 40 In.	7200.00
Chair, G. Stickley, No. 350A, 3 Vertical Slats, Corbel Supports, Arms, 27 x 23 x 38 In.	660.00
Chair, G. Stickley, No. 355A, Upholstery, Brass Tacks, Decal, Arms, 1904, 37 In.	17500.00
Chair, G. Stickley, No. 367, Spindle Arm Supports, Morris, Seat, 27 x 37 In.	4800.00
Chair, G. Stickley, No. 369, Morris, Drop Arm, 5-Slat Adjustable Back, 32 x 41 In.	9200.00
Chair, G. Stickley, No. 369, Morris, Spring Seat, Spindled, Velvet Upholstered, 39 ½ x 33 In.	7930.00
Chair, G. Stickley, No. 384, H Back, Spindles, Leather Cushion, 19 x 17 x 46 In.	2280.00
Chair, G. Stickley, No. 1291A, Horizontal Slat, Leather, 22 x 19 x 42 In.	1440.00
Chair, G. Stickley, No. 2342, Morris, 5 Vertical Slats, Leather Cushions, Signed, 31 x 39 In.	9600.00
Chair, G. Stickley, Oak, Pewter Inlay, Leather Cushion, c.1880	6250.00
Chair, G. Stickley, Reclining, No. 336, Cushions, Arms, 39 x 30 In.	1770.00
Chair, Geometric Carved Crests, Shield Form, Padded Backs, Seats, 1800s, 40 In., Pair	295.00
Chair, George II, Walnut, Carved, Waved Crest, Latticework Splat, Scalloped Rails, Arms, 38 In.	225.00
Chair, George III, Mahogany, Carved, Rectangular, Padded, Cabriole Legs, c.1775	3525.00
Chair, George III, Mahogany, Domed Crest, Padded, Square Legs, Arms, 19th Century, 37 In.	420.00
Chair, George III, Mahogany, Domed Crest, Pierced Splat, Padded, Square Legs, 37 In., Pair	420.00
Chair, George III, Mahogany, Padded Back, Slip Seat, Claw Feet, S-Curved Arms, 42 In., Pair	3910.00
Chair, George III, Mahogany, Pierced Splat, Slip Seat, Open Arms, 1700s, 39 In. ......*illus*	403.00
Chair, George III, Mahogany, Rolling Top Rail, Square Legs, England, 22 x 37 In., Pair	148.00
Chair, George III, Mahogany, Scrolled Reeded Arms, Upholstered Seat, 1800s	529.00
Chair, George III, Mahogany, Shaped Crest, Leaf Carved, 37 In., Pair	600.00
Chair, George III, Mahogany, Shaped Crest Rail, Upholstered, Curved Armrests, 39 x 24 In.	4650.00
Chair, George III, Mahogany, Slatted Back, Bellflower Carving, Padded Seat, 34 In.	120.00
Chair, George III, Mahogany, Yoked Crest, Pierced Splat, Mythological Animals, 42 x 20 In.	2300.00
Chair, George III Style, Mahogany, Carved, Swags, Sheaves Of Wheat, Pair	2703.00
Chair, George III Style, Mahogany, Domed Back, Brass Tacks, Square Legs, 1930, 46 In.	2280.00
Chair, George III Style, Mahogany, Needlepoint, Open Arms	474.00
Chair, George III Style, Mahogany, Padded Back, Arms, Seat, 1900s, 39 In., Pair ......*illus*	1440.00
Chair, George III Style, Mahogany, Yoke Crest, Lattice Splat, Serpentine Seat, 39 x 20 In.	805.00
Chair, Georgian, Mahogany, Carved, Yoked Crest, Reticulated Splat, Claw Feet, 1900s, 37 In., Pair.	748.00
Chair, Georgian, Mahogany, Crest, Openwork Splat, England, c.1745, Seat 18 In., Pair	948.00
Chair, Georgian, Mahogany, Leaf Carved, Trapezoid Slip Seat, c.1750, 18 x 20 x 15 In., Pair	948.00
Chair, Georgian Style, Mahogany, Carved, Padded, Paw Feet, Upholstered, Pair	8519.00
Chair, Georgian Style, Serpentine Back, Padded Downswept Arms, 36 x 25 In.	288.00
Chair, Georgian Style, Walnut, Needlepoint Upholstered, Slip Seat, Open Arm	593.00
Chair, Gondola, Restauration, Mahogany, Carved, Scroll Crest Rail, Blocked Rosettes	646.00
Chair, Gossip, Wicker, Victorian, Rolled Back, Curved Arms, Upholstered, 49 x 36 In.	920.00
Chair, Gothic Revival, Open, Pierced Back, Velvet Upholstered, Arms, 1880s, 53 x 23 In.	230.00
Chair, Gothic Revival, Rosewood, Pointed Arch Crest, Pierced Tracery, 52 In., Pair	1955.00

Chair, Gothic Revival, Walnut, Needlework Upholstery, Arched Rail Crest	69.00
Chair, Gothic Revival, Walnut, Sphinx & Lion's Heads, c.1900, 40 In. ....*illus*	840.00
Chair, Gothic Revival, Walnut, Velvet Upholstery, Late 19th Century, 58 x 27 In.	950.00
Chair, Gothic Style, Walnut, Mask, Lion Arm Grips, France, 1800s, 48 x 24 In., Pair......	489.00
Chair, Grandpa Beaver, Corrugated Cardboard, Frank Gehry, c.1986, 33 In. ....*illus*	5000.00
Chair, H. Bertoia, Diamond, Chrome Wire, Knoll, 33 x 30 In., Pair	1080.00
Chair, H. Meister, Learning Her Lie, Painted, Cut Steel, Split Seat, Signed, 1984, 38 In., Pair	600.00
Chair, Hardwood, Bamboo Carving, Flowers, Dragon, Pierced Back, Arms, Asia, 43 x 22 In.	354.00
Chair, Heart Cone, V. Panton, 35 x 39 In.	1620.00
Chair, Hepplewhite, Mahogany, Ash, Shieldback, Phila., c.1800, 39 x 22 In. ....*illus*	690.00
Chair, Hepplewhite, Mahogany, Shield Shape Back, Carved, Pierced Splat, Pair..........	104.00
Chair, Heritage Henredon, Upholstered, Taliesan Edge, 33 x 35 x 28 In.	2160.00
Chair, High Back, Dan Johnson Studios, Gazelle, Cane, 1957, 37 x 34 In.	9600.00
Chair, High Back Frame, Carved, Shells, Acanthus, Upholstered, 1800s, 52 x 19 In.	460.00
Chair, High Banister Back, Turned Rungs, Rush Seat, Paint, Morris, c.1730, 36 In. ...	26450.00
Chair, Horn, Canvas, Nail Head Decoration, c.1920, 41 x 36 In.	900.00
Chair, Inlaid Back Slat, Seat, No. 320, Shop Of The Crafters, 43 ½ In.	840.00
Chair, Irish Chippendale, Mahogany, Carved, Molded Crest, Latticework Splat, Arms, 42 In., Pair .	690.00
Chair, Irish Chippendale, Walnut, Carved, Lobed Crest, Shaped Splat, 40 x 20 In.	3105.00
Chair, Iron, Steel, Poplar, Center Spring, Velvet Upholstery, c.1853, 42 In.	705.00
Chair, J. Adnet, Lounge, Stitched Leather, Brass, 31 ¾ x 32 ½ In., Pair....................	19520.00
Chair, J. Hoffmann, Barrel Shape, Sycamore Laminate, Butternut Leather, c.1905, 32 x 28 In.	4780.00
Chair, J. Pollard, Lounge, Leather Cushion, Folded Chrome Frame, Matteograssi, Italy, c.1987 ..	2520.00
Chair, Jacobean, Oak, Joined, Panel Back, Scroll Arms, Molded Legs, 1600s	306.00
Chair, Jacobean, Oak Wainscot, Floral Carved Back, Figural, Plank Seat, 45 In.	805.00
Chair, Jacobean Style, Mahogany, Carved Shells, Leaves, Putti, Scroll Arms	356.00
Chair, Jelliffe, Mahogany, Inlaid Medallion, Carved Busts, c.1900	518.00
Chair, Jelliffe, Walnut, Carved Crest Rail, Roundels, Lady Liberty Supports, 44 In., Pair...........	885.00
Chair, J.M. Young, Morris, 5 Slats, Cushion	3800.00
Chair, Jose Caldas, Wood Frame, Leather Seat, Back, Moveis Artisticos Z, Brazil, 1950s, 29 In. .	420.00
Chair, Juan Montoya, Mahogany, Leather, Arms, 35 x 24 In., Pair.............................	1680.00
Chair, Juan Montoya, Mahogany, Leather Upholstery, Arms, 36 x 22 In., Pair	2520.00
Chair, Kem Weber, Airline, Birch, Leather, Steel, 1934 Design, c.1990, 25 x 31 In.	1800.00
Chair, Klismos, Mixed Wood, Decorated, Tablet Top, Cane Seat, c.1830, 32 In., Pair	441.00
Chair, Klismos, Tablet Crest, Stenciled, Cane, Baltimore, c.1820, 32 In., Pair ....*illus*	441.00
Chair, Koloman, Bentwood, Arms, c.1900-05, 35 x 25 In., Pair.................................	1673.00
Chair, L. & J.G. Stickley, No. 427, Fixed Back, 4 Vertical Side Slats, Bow Arm, Brown, 31 x 39 In.	2588.00
Chair, L. & J.G. Stickley, No. 428, 4 Slats, Leather Cushions, 30 x 30 In.	4200.00
Chair, L. & J.G. Stickley, No. 471, Morris, 6 Side Slats, Cushions, 32 x 36 x 40 ½ In.	2160.00
Chair, L. & J.G. Stickley, No. 471, Morris, Drop-In Spring Seat, Leather, 40 x 32 x 35 In.	3050.00
Chair, L. & J.G. Stickley, No. 766, 3 Horizontal Slats, Arms, 26 x 37 In.	480.00
Chair, Ladder Back, 3 Slats, Painted, Down-Sloping Arms, Woven Seat, 41 x 27 In.	7480.00
Chair, Ladder Back, 3 Slats, Rush Seat, Salmon, Black, Vermont, c.1800...................	1600.00
Chair, Ladder Back, 4 Shaped Slats, Oak Split Seat, Painted, Georgia, 1800s, 37 x 20 In.	403.00
Chair, Ladder Back, 4 Shaped Slats, Painted, Delaware Valley, c.1800 ....*illus*	380.00
Chair, Ladder Back, 5 Arched Slats, Turned, c.1750, 42 In.	474.00
Chair, Ladder Back, 5 Slats, Rush Seat, Club Shape Legs, 1800s, 40 In.	130.00
Chair, Ladder Back, Black Lacquer, Cane Seat, Italy, 52 In., Pair.............................	120.00
Chair, Ladder Back, Maple, Paper Rush Seat, Red Paint, Scroll Arms, c.1830, 40 In.	264.00
Chair, Ladder Back, Mixed Woods, 3 Slats, Blue Paint, Rush Seat, 38 In.	118.00
Chair, Ladder Back, Mixed Woods, 4 Slats, Disc Arm Posts, Dark Paint, Rush Seat, c.1790.......	264.00
Chair, Ladder Back, Mixed Woods, Arched Slats, Turned Finials, Scroll Arms, c.1800, 45 In.	206.00
Chair, Leaf Carved Seat & Back Frame, Slip Seat, Anglo-Indian, 38 In.	288.00
Chair, Lifetime, No. 569, Morris, Slat Sides, Adjustable Back, Red Cushions, 31 x 37 In.	2013.00
Chair, Limbert, 3 Vertical Slats, Curved Slatted Seat, Shoefoot Base, Arms, 28 x 34 In.	420.00
Chair, Limbert, No. 841, Morris, Slat Back & Sides, Leather Cushions, 33 x 37 In.	2880.00
Chair, Lina Bo Bardi, Folding, Wood, Wide Slats, Barauna, 33 x 18 In.	1320.00
Chair, Lobby, 3-Section Unit, Upholstered, 1980s, 33 x 74 In.	30.00
Chair, Lolling, Federal, Mahogany, Maple, Carved, Upholstered, c.1815, 42 In.	881.00
Chair, Louis Sognot, Desk, Swivel, Walnut, Nickel, Leather, c.1930, 33 x 30 In.	1912.00
Chair, Louis XIV, Beech, Upholstered, Shepherd's Crook Arms, 44 x 27 In.	633.00
Chair, Louis XIV, Oak, Carved, Acanthus & Bellflower Scroll Arms, Upholstered, Pair...............	940.00
Chair, Louis XV Style, Fruitwood, Flower Head Carved Crest, Overupholstered Seat, 36 x 24 In.	191.00
Chair, Louis XV Style, Needlework Upholstered Seat, Back, Padded Arms, Carved	150.00
Chair, Louis XV Style, Parlor, Carved, Striped Upholstery, Open Arms, 24 ½ In., Pair...............	115.00
Chair, Louis XV Style, Square Back, Upholstered, Continental, 1900s, Pair.................	652.00

Furniture, Chair, George III Style, Mahogany, Padded Back, Arms, Seat, 1900s, 39 In., Pair
$1440.00

Furniture, Chair, George III, Mahogany, Pierced Splat, Slip Seat, Open Arms, 1700s, 39 In.
$403.00

F

Furniture, Chair, Gothic Revival, Walnut, Sphinx & Lion's Heads, c.1900, 40 In.
$840.00

Furniture, Chair, Grandpa Beaver, Corrugated Cardboard, Frank Gehry, c.1986, 33 In.
$5000.00

Furniture, Chair, Hepplewhite, Mahogany, Ash, Shieldback, Phila., c.1800, 39 x 22 In.
$690.00

Furniture, Chair, Klismos, Tablet Crest, Stenciled, Cane, Baltimore, c.1820, 32 In., Pair
$441.00

Chair, Louis XV Style, Walnut, Carved, Upholstered, 36 x 21 ¾ In., Pair	239.00
Chair, Louis XV, Domed Padded Back, Scrolling Leaf Crest, Padded Seat, 40 In., Pair	360.00
Chair, Louis XV, Flower Carved Crest, Tufted Upholstery, 37 In.	236.00
Chair, Louis XV, Gilt, Serpentine Seat, Velvet Upholstery, Late 1700s, 17 x 42 In.	671.00
Chair, Louis XV, Mahogany, Kingwood, Round Top, Inlaid Band, Ormolu Wreaths, 29 x 20 In.	900.00
Chair, Louis XV, Oak, Flower Carved Crest, Apron, Legs, Upholstery, c.1890, 37 In.	570.00
Chair, Louis XV, Walnut, Shieldback, Carved Crest, Cane Seat & Back, Cresson, 40 In., Pair	470.00
Chair, Louis XVI Style, Beech, Carved, Shield Shape Back, 35 x 24 In., Pair ....*illus*	944.00
Chair, Louis XVI Style, Beech, Medallion Back, Carved, Upholstered, Arms, 38 In., Pair	2236.00
Chair, Louis XVI Style, Carved, Gilt Wood, Leaf, Bellflower, c.1890, 39 x 25 In., Pair	547.00
Chair, Louis XVI Style, Gilt, Padded Back, Arms, Fluted Legs, 29 In., Child's	1140.00
Chair, Louis XVI Style, Gilt, Padded, Scrolling Arms, Leaf Carved Legs, 39 In., Pair	2400.00
Chair, Louis XVI Style, Striped Upholstery, Gold Paint, France, 35 In.	374.00
Chair, Louis XVI, Beech, Painted, Cartouche Crest Rail, Turned Legs, Stretchers, 36 In., Pair	434.00
Chair, Louis XVI, Carved, Needlepoint Chair, Bead & Channel Frame, Padded Arms, 34 In., Pair	575.00
Chair, Louis XVI, Fruitwood, Cane, Carved, Cartouche Shape Back, Inturned Arms, 37 In.	173.00
Chair, Louis XVI, Multicolored, Padded Round Crest, Spindled Splats, 37 In., Pair	1560.00
Chair, Louis XVI, Padded Seat & Back, Arms, Tapered Legs, c.1875, 35 In.	2160.00
Chair, Louis XVI, Walnut, Carved, Overupholstered, Leaf Carved, Scroll Arms, 18 x 22 In.	2489.00
Chair, Lounge, Eileen Gray, Black Metal Frame, Leather Cushions, 39 x 23 In.	2880.00
Chair, Lucite, 1 Piece, Molded, 16 x 35 In., Pair	240.00
Chair, Lucite Seat, Vinyl Seat Cushion, Aluminum Base, Casters, 17 x 33 In.	90.00
Chair, M. Young, Tapered Mahogany Legs, Upholstery, 32 x 31 In., Pair	840.00
Chair, Mahogany, Arch Back, Scrolls, Round Pad Feet, Arms, England, c.1730, 27 x 39 In.	1770.00
Chair, Mahogany, Carved Crest, Pierced Back, Upholstered, Arms, Virginia, c.1790, 51 x 32 In.	4830.00
Chair, Mahogany, Carved Crest Rail, Splat, Silk Upholstery, Boston, c.1820, Pair	1293.00
Chair, Mahogany, Carved Winged Griffin, Upholstery, Pad Arms, 25 x 35 In.	3163.00
Chair, Mahogany, Flower Carved, Swan's Head Stiles, Tufted Back, Padded Arms, Pair	1880.00
Chair, Mahogany, High Back, Tufted Leather, Arms, 1900s, 42 In., Pair	805.00
Chair, Mahogany, High Back, Turned Stiles, Splats, Rush Seat, c.1890, 49 In., Pair	956.00
Chair, Mahogany, Lattice Back, Square Legs, Arms, c.1800 ....*illus*	2574.00
Chair, Mahogany, Marquetry, Twisted Columns, Arms, 50 x 24 x 19 In.	460.00
Chair, Mahogany, Ribbon, Curved Supports, Round, 2 Leaves, France, 30 x 45 In.	1440.00
Chair, Mahogany, Shaped Splat, Eagle Arms, Lion's Mask Legs, 19 x 22 In.	1541.00
Chair, Mahogany, Tall Rounded Back, Scrolled Supports, Upholstered, c.1850, 44 In.	940.00
Chair, Maple, Ash, Banister Back, Vase, Ring Turnings, 17 x 43 In.	652.00
Chair, Maple, Ash, Slat Back, Turned, Arms, c.1730, 16 x 42 In.	474.00
Chair, Maple, Banister Back, Splint Seat, Painted, New England, 1700s, 17 x 43 In.	504.00
Chair, Maple, Pine, Banister Back, Molded Slats, Turned Stretcher, Late 1800s, 34 In.	120.00
Chair, Marc Newson, Lounge, Bucky, Free-Form, Velvet, 23 x 40 In.	1560.00
Chair, Marc Newson, Lounge, Embryo Shape, Neoprene Cushion, Steel Legs, 30 x 33 In.	3480.00
Chair, Marcel Breuer, Lounge, Bent Plywood, Leather Cushion, 33 x 26 In.	2280.00
Chair, Marquetry, Shaped Crest Rail, Pierced Splat, Cabriole Legs, Hoof Feet, 1800s, Pair	1880.00
Chair, Meeks, Carved, Laminate, Upholstered, Cabriole Legs, c.1860, 38 ½ In.	780.00
Chair, Memento Mori, Seated Human Skeleton Shape, Saddle Seat, Stretchers, White Paint	1175.00
Chair, Michel Dufet, Beech, Upholstered, c.1925-30, 35 x 30 x 24 ½ In.	1554.00
Chair, Mies Van Der Rohe, Barcelona, Leather, Tufted Cushions, Knoll, 1974, 30 In., Pair	3480.00
Chair, Mies Van Der Rohe, Chrome Frame, Leather Cushion, 30 x 30 In.	2640.00
Chair, Mies Van Der Rohe, MR, Tubular Chromed Steel, Leather, Knoll, 21 x 32 In., Pair ....*illus*	900.00
Chair, Milo Baughman, Square Tubular Chrome, Upholstered, Thayer-Coggin, 1976, 23 x 30 In., Pair	240.00
Chair, Nakashima, Lounge, Cone Shape, Signed, c.1974, 34 ½ x 34 ½ In.	11638.00
Chair, Nakashima Style, Oak, Arched Crest, 6 Flat Splats, Low Arms, 1989, 41 x 23 In.	167.00
Chair, Napoleon III, Gilt, Bronze Mounted, Ebonized, Padded Back, Scroll Arms, 1800s	353.00
Chair, Napoleon III Style, Beech, Upholstered, Low Seat, c.1880, 29 x 22 In.	780.00
Chair, Neoclassical, Cherry, Arched Crest, Leather Upholstery, Volute Arms, c.1830	3408.00
Chair, Neoclassical, Mahogany, Anthemion Carved Crest Rail, Silk Upholstery, Pair	1293.00
Chair, Neoclassical, Mahogany, Arched, Leaf Carved Crest, Padded Scroll Arms, c.1850	470.00
Chair, Neoclassical, Oval Back, Scroll Arms, Compass Seat, Green Paint, Arms, c.1890, 19 In.	830.00
Chair, Neoclassical Style, Mahogany, Garland, Carved, Gadrooned Urn, 37 x 23 x 20 In.	329.00
Chair, Neoclassical, Walnut, Trapezoid, Scroll Arms, Molded Seat, Italy, Arms, 17 ½ In.	178.00
Chair, Nutting, Ladder Back, Rush Seat, Signed, 49 In.	193.00
Chair, Nutting, Maple, Chestnut, Slat Back, c.1950, 41 x 18 In.	296.00
Chair, Ole Wanscher, Lounge, Sculpted Teak, France & Sons, Denmark, 27 x 28 In.	570.00
Chair, Otto Wagner, Bent Beech, Cutouts, Saddle Seat, J. & J. Kohn, 31 In., Pair	1560.00
Chair, Ottoman, Arts & Crafts, Oak, Carved Arms, Frame, Leather, c.1900, 32 x 35 In.	2875.00
Chair, Ottoman, Eero Saarinen, Womb, Knoll, c.1947, 35 x 39 & 17 x 25 In.	2328.00

Chair, Ottoman, G. Nelson, Coconut, Herman Miller, c.1955, 32 x 40 x 33 In.	2450.00
Chair, Ottoman, I. Lappalainen, Leather, Aluminum, Adjustable Seat, Asko, Finland, 30 x 28 In.	720.00
Chair, Ottoman, Parzinger, c.1960, 39 x 26 & 17 x 24 In.	2756.00
Chair, Overman, Lounge, Swivel, Egg Shape, Aluminum, Vinyl Upholstery, Cushion, 28 x 35 In., Pair	90.00
Chair, P. Evans, Patinated Copper, Enameled Steel Base, Cube, 28 ½ x 30 x 30 In.	1464.00
Chair, Paul Laszlo, Bleached Mahogany, Cane Seat & Back, 29 x 32 In.	3480.00
Chair, Paul Rudolph, Tubular Chrome, Acrylic, Casters, Shepherd, Arms, 30 x 28 In.	6600.00
Chair, Paulin, Lounge, Cowhide, Nickel-Plated Steel Rod Base, Artifort, 30 x 26 In.	7638.00
Chair, Paulin, Ribbon, No. 582, Tiger Stretch Upholstery, Jack Lenor, 27 x 39 x 31 In. ......*illus*	7320.00
Chair, Percival Lafer, Lounge, Ottoman, Metal, Vinyl Cushion, Standing, c.1970, 33 x 29 In., Pair	919.00
Chair, Pierre Chareau, No. MF 172, Walnut, Upholstered, Arms, c.1924, 25 In.	68500.00
Chair, Pine, Turned, Sloping Arms, Button Feet, Stenciled, c.1825, 21 In., Child's	499.00
Chair, Plantation, Louisiana Walnut, Scrolled Back, Leather Seat, 19th Century	2985.00
Chair, Planter's, Caribbean Hardwood, Cane, Arched Crest Rail, Scroll Arms, 1800s	1410.00
Chair, Planter's, Pine, Canvas Cover, Long Tapered Arms, Ring-Turned Legs	823.00
Chair, Porter's, Louis XVI Style, Gilt, Paneled, Domed Hood, Wreath Crest, 62 In.	3360.00
Chair, Potty, Captain Style, Painted, 8 Turned Spindles, Cape Cod, 1800s, 11 x 17 In.	450.00
Chair, Prayer, Leaf Carved, Hoof Feet, Velvet Upholstery, France, 1800s, 30 x 24 In.	345.00
Chair, Queen Anne Style, Wing, Oak Leather, Domed Back, Rolled Arms, c.1850, 43 In., Pair	1680.00
Chair, Queen Anne, 6 Spindles, Yew, Arms, Saddle Seat	1210.00
Chair, Queen Anne, Baluster Turned Stiles & Legs, Finials, 18th Century, 41 In.	176.00
Chair, Queen Anne, Chinese, Walnut, Pillow Crest Rails, Cabriole Legs, c.1740, 40 In., Pair	823.00
Chair, Queen Anne, Elm, Marquetry Splat, Flowers, Carved, Scalloped, c.1710, 44 In., Pair	2280.00
Chair, Queen Anne, Hardwood, Duck Feet, Rush Seat, Shaped Splat, c.1790, 41 In.	411.00
Chair, Queen Anne, Ladder Back, 4 Slats, Rush Seat, Arms, Turned Stretcher, 1750	560.00
Chair, Queen Anne, Mahogany, Flared Back, Shaped Crest, Slip Seat, 1740-60	720.00
Chair, Queen Anne, Maple, Carved, Spanish Foot, 1750, 41 x 17 In.	207.00
Chair, Queen Anne, Maple, Oxbow Crest, Vase Splat, Rush Seat, Arms, c.1740	146.00
Chair, Queen Anne, Maple, Rush Seat, Yoked Crest, Vase Splat, c.1760, 43 In.	144.00
Chair, Queen Anne, Maple, Scroll Arms, Paper Rush Seat, Vase Splat, Arms, c.1750, 17 x 41 In.	206.00
Chair, Queen Anne, Maple, Vase Shape Splat, Turned Front Stretcher, Rush Seat, 41 In., Pair	382.00
Chair, Queen Anne, Oak, Solid Seat, Spanish Feet, c.1800, 37 x 19 In., Pair	546.00
Chair, Queen Anne, Painted, Woven Seat, Arms, 45 x 16 In.	850.00
Chair, Queen Anne, Rush Seat, Turned Legs, Front Stretcher, Pad Feet, 18th Century, 39 In.	1500.00
Chair, Queen Anne, Walnut, Carved, Volute Crest, Vase Shape Splat, Scroll Arms, Pair	1528.00
Chair, Queen Anne, Walnut, Compass Seat, Upholstered, c.1775, 16 x 39 In.	1880.00
Chair, Queen Anne, Walnut, Sack Back	875.00
Chair, Queen Anne, Walnut, Scroll Back, Acanthus Legs, Ball & Claw, Arms, c.1800, 37 In.	354.00
Chair, Queen Anne, Walnut, Shaped Crest Rail, Cabriole Legs, Arms, 1700s	881.00
Chair, Queen Anne, Walnut, Shaped Crest Rail, Splat, Upholstered Slip Seat, c.1740, 39 In.	2650.00
Chair, Queen Anne, Walnut, Shaped Crest Rail, Vase Splat, Crook Arms, 1700s	881.00
Chair, Queen Anne, Walnut, Shell Crest, Shaped Splat, Compass Seat, Boston, c.1750, 37 In.	10625.00
Chair, Queen Anne, Walnut, Vase Splat, Cabriole Legs	119.00
Chair, Queen Anne, Walnut, Yoke Crest, Vase Shape Splat, Slip Seat, c.1760	3000.00
Chair, Regency, Black Lacquer, Chinoiserie Landscape, Curved Splat, Scrolling Arms, 33 In.	489.00
Chair, Regency, Faux Bamboo, Painted, Chinoiserie, Spindle Arms, Rush Seat, c.1820, Pair	705.00
Chair, Regency, Flower Crest, Diamond Splats, Cane Seat, Arms, Painted, c.1900, 34 In., Pair	2400.00
Chair, Regency, Hinged Seat, Steps, Tooled Leather Inset, c.1815, 34 x 25 In.	1998.00
Chair, Regency, Mahogany, Cane, Reeded, Casters, England, 38 x 28 In., Pair	4830.00
Chair, Regency, Parcel Gilt, Pierced Crest, Splats, Pad Seat, Arms, c.1825, 34 In., Pair	600.00
Chair, Regency Style, Mahogany, Shaped Crest Rail, Arched Splat, Upholstered Seat, 1800s	470.00
Chair, Regency Style, Walnut, Upholstered Slip Seat, Late 1800s, 33 In., Pair	58.00
Chair, Regency, Upholstered, Mahogany, Urn & Ring-Turned Arms, 1850, 35 In.	880.00
Chair, Relax, Oak, Velvet Upholstery, Arms, Jean Royere, c.1950, 41 In., Pair	43750.00
Chair, Renaissance Revival, Burl Walnut, Carved, Incised Shaped Back, Mid 1800s	47.00
Chair, Renaissance Revival, Herter Bros., Walnut, Crest, Swags, Arms, c.1872, 54 In., Pair	42700.00
Chair, Renaissance Revival, Walnut, Padded Horseshoe Shape Crest Rail, Acanthus Splat, 1800s	3300.00
Chair, Rocker, is listed under Rocker in this category.	
Chair, Rococo, Laminated Rosewood, Carved, Belter, Mid 1800s, Pair	2350.00
Chair, Rococo Revival, Mahogany, Upholstered, Cabriole Legs, Arm, 30 ¾ In.	300.00
Chair, Rococo, Rosewood, Carved, Laminated, Grape & Flower, Cornucopia, c.1850, 38 In.	3819.00
Chair, Rococo, Rosewood, Carved Pierced Scrolled Crest, Upholstered, 1845, N.Y., 42 In.	206.00
Chair, Rococo, Serpentine, Carved, Laminated, Upholstered, c.1850, Pair	2350.00
Chair, Rococo, Walnut, Needlepoint Seat & Back, c.1870, 43 x 26 In.	413.00
Chair, Rohlfs, Mahogany, Carved Sign Of The Saw, c.1898, 52 ¾ In.	62500.00
Chair, Rolling Top Rails, Solid Back, Drop-In Seat, England, 1700s, 22 x 38 In., Pair	443.00
Chair, Ron Arad, Stainless Steel, Curved Shape, 31 x 38 In.	19200.00

Furniture, Chair, Ladder Back, 4 Shaped Slats, Painted, Delaware Valley, c.1800
$380.00

Furniture, Chair, Louis XVI Style, Beech, Carved, Shield Shape Back, 35 x 24 In., Pair
$944.00

Furniture, Chair, Mahogany, Lattice Back, Square Legs, Arms, c.1800
$2574.00

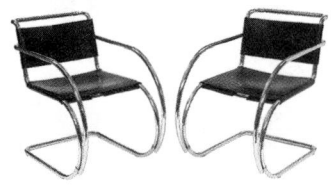

Furniture, Chair, Mies Van Der Rohe, MR, Tubular Chromed Steel, Leather, Knoll, 21 x 32 In., Pair
$900.00

Furniture, Chair, Paulin, Ribbon, No. 582, Tiger Stretch Upholstery, Jack Lenor, 27 x 39 x 31 In. $7320.00

Furniture, Chair, Sheraton, Mahogany, Upholstered, c.1800, 34 x 24 In. $374.00

Furniture, Chair, Sheraton Style, Mahogany, Upholstered Seat, Inlay, Late 1800s, 35 x 20 In. $403.00

Chair, Rosewood, Carved, Arched Cushion Back, Flower Finial, Upholstered Seat, c.1825, 48 In.	420.00
Chair, Rosewood, Carved, Black Upholstery, Arms, Belter, c.1855, 36 In., Pair	1175.00
Chair, Rosewood, Carved Splat, Bats, Peaches, Arms, Chinese, 39 x 24 In., Pair	1140.00
Chair, Rosewood, Marble, Mother-Of-Pearl, Carved, Arms, Chinese, 38 x 26 In.	300.00
Chair, Rosewood, Pierced Fretwork, Inlaid Blossoms, Gilt, Turned Legs, c.1875, 33 In.	587.00
Chair, Ross Bellah, Carl Anderson, Rattan, Upholstered Cushions, c.1941, 29 x 27 In., Pair	613.00
Chair, Ross Littell, Lounge, Woven Black Leather Straps, Steel Frame, 30 x 26 In., Pair	3900.00
Chair, Roycroft, 3 Horizontal Slats, Leather Seat, Nail Heads, Name On Front, 17 ½ x 37 In., Pair	6000.00
Chair, Ruhlmann, Ebony Macassar, Nickel Plated Bronze, Arms, c.1925, 37 In., Pair	40625.00
Chair, Safari, Arne Norell, Beech, Leather Sling Seat & Arms, Sweden, 26 x 30 ½ In.	330.00
Chair, Savonarola, Carved, Masks, Shaped Legs, Italy, 19th Century	325.00
Chair, Savonarola, Oak, Leather, Paw Feet, Christopher Columbus, 1900s, 38 ¾ In.	546.00
Chair, Scarpa, Lauriana, Leather Upholstery, Tufted Buttons, B&B Italia, 40 x 34 In., Pair	1200.00
Chair, Scoop, Milo Baughman, Upholstered, c.1954, 29 x 26 x 26 In., Pair	3000.00
Chair, Shaker, Birch, 2 Slats, Varnish, Cane Seat, Tilters, Enfield, c.1840, 38 In.	1405.00
Chair, Shaker, Birch, 3 Arched Slats, Cane Seat, Varnish, N.H., c.1840, 42 In.	819.00
Chair, Shaker, Birch, Pine, Low Spindles, 4 Tapered Legs, Canterbury, c.1840, 18 x 24 In.	1814.00
Chair, Shaker, Birch, Tall Finials, Cane Seat, Tilters, Enfield, c.1840, 41 In.	4680.00
Chair, Shaker, Cherry, Cane Seat, 2 Stamp, Harvard, c.1835, 38 In., Pair	2633.00
Chair, Shaker, Ladder Back, Rush Seat, Black Paint, Turned Finials, 19th Century	106.00
Chair, Shaker, Ladder Back, Woven Seat, 19th Century	310.00
Chair, Shaker, Maple, 2 Shaped Crested Slats, Oak Splint Seat, Ohio, 17 ½ x 28 In.	293.00
Chair, Shaker, Maple, 3 Beveled Slats, Rush Seat, Watervliet, N.Y., c.1830, 41 In.	468.00
Chair, Shaker, Maple, 3 Slats, Walnut Finish, Red, Khaki Tape Seat, 33 ½ In.	1287.00
Chair, Shaker, Maple, 4 Slats, Walnut Finish, Tan Seat, Arms, Mt. Lebanon, c.1930, 46 In.	1287.00
Chair, Shaker, Maple, Birch, 3 Slats, Black Ash Splint Seat, Label, N.Y., c.1840, 39 In.	468.00
Chair, Shaker, Maple, Painted, Tape Seat, Mt. Lebanon, N.Y., c.1830, 37 In.	2925.00
Chair, Shaker, Maple, Red, Black Tape, Mushroom Caps, N.Y., c.1890, 15 x 34 In.	644.00
Chair, Shaker, Maple, Stuffed Horsehair, Turned Posts, Walnut Stain, Mass., c.1850, 12 x 12 In.	234.00
Chair, Shaker, Revolving, Maple, 3 Sets Of 4 Stretchers, c.1850, 45 In.	3218.00
Chair, Shaker, Tiger Maple, 3 Beveled Slats, Cane Seat, Harvard, c.1830, 42 In.	2633.00
Chair, Shaker, Tiger Maple, 3 Slats, Walnut Varnish, Rush Seat, Harvard, c.1840, 42 In.	1287.00
Chair, Shaker, Tiger Maple, Yellow, Black Tape Seat, Walnut Varnish, Mt. Lebanon, 34 In.	702.00
Chair, Sheraton, Beech, Cane Seat, Cross Back, Multicolored, Arms, Eng., c.1800, 33 x 21 In., Pair	1610.00
Chair, Sheraton, Mahogany, Upholstered, c.1800, 34 x 24 In. *illus*	374.00
Chair, Sheraton Style, Mahogany, Upholstered Seat, Inlay, Late 1800s, 35 x 20 In. *illus*	403.00
Chair, Slat Back, Hickory, Turned Finials, Oak Split Seat, Virginia, 1700s, 47 x 25 In. *illus*	5520.00
Chair, Slat Back, Rush Seat, Blue Paint, Arms, c.1800, 6 x 13 In., Child's	207.00
Chair, Slat Back, Splint Seat, Arms, Red Paint, 1700s, 43 In.	267.00
Chair, Slat Back, Splint Seat, Turned Finials, Supports, Arms, 43 In.	711.00
Chair, Sleigh, Velvet Upholstery, Walnut, Steel Frame, 37 x 24 In.	900.00
Chair, Sling, H. Probber Inc., c.1968, 27 ½ x 29 x 30 In., Pair	2400.00
Chair, Slipper, Belter, Rosewood, Carved, Pierced Back, Needlepoint Seat, 39 In.	2900.00
Chair, Slipper, Mahogany, Tufted Balloon Back, Upholstered, 1800s, 39 x 25 In. *illus*	442.00
Chair, Slipper, Mask Carved Back, Griffins, Scrolls, Upholstery, Italy, c.1890, 27 x 26 In.	863.00
Chair, Slipper, Renaissance Revival, Walnut, Padded, Upholstery, 29 x 28 x 20 In., Child's	418.00
Chair, Slipper, Rococo Revival, Mahogany, Medallion Back, Upholstered, 39 x 22 x 21 In.	179.00
Chair, Slipper, Rococo, Rosewood, Flower Crest, Pierced Back, Upholstery, 1850s, 37 In.	144.00
Chair, Slipper, Rococo Style, Carved, Masks, Griffins, Painted, Gold Detail, 27 x 26 In. *illus*	944.00
Chair, Slipper, Victorian, Carved Flower Crest, Upholstered, Arms, 45 ½ In., Pair	248.00
Chair, Slipper, White Paint, Carved Openwork Chinoiserie, Seat Cushion, 28 In.	748.00
Chair, Slipper, Wormley, Mahogany, Upholstered, Dunbar, 1950s, 26 x 31 In., Pair	1080.00
Chair, Slipper, Wormley, Mahogany, Upholstered, Dunbar, 27 x 29 In., Pair	960.00
Chair, Smoking, Walnut, Padded Crest, Pierced, Carved Pipes, Tobacco, Cigars, Italy	411.00
Chair, Southern Baroque, Maple, Baluster Turned Legs, Splat Back, 1700s, 41 x 23 In.	1380.00
Chair, Spanish Baroque, Beech, Walnut, Turned Spindles & Legs, 33 x 18 In., Pair	230.00
Chair, Spindle Back, Plank Seat, Yellow Flower, Stripe, 28 In., Child's	198.00
Chair, Stickley & Brandt Co., Arch Support Under Arms	2562.00
Chair, Stickley & Brandt Co., Tenon Construction, Arms, 32 x 22 In. *illus*	510.00
Chair, Stickley, 4 Slats, Arch Top, Arms, Stickley In Box Signature, 27 x 37 In.	690.00
Chair, Stickley Bros., Morris, Leather Cushions, 34 x 37 In.	2640.00
Chair, Stickley Bros., Morris, Pierced Back Crest, Cushion Seat, 33 x 38 In. *illus*	1920.00
Chair, Stool, Louis XVI Style, Padded Back, Carved Frame, 1800s, 41 In., 2 Piece *illus*	1680.00
Chair, Studio, G. Nakashima, Cone Shape, Walnut, Ash Vertical Spindles, 1900s, Pair	4600.00
Chair, Swan, Arne Jacobsen, Leather, Swivel Aluminum Base, F. Hansen, 34 x 29 In.	900.00
Chair, Swan, Arne Jacobsen, Upholstered, Aluminum Base, F. Hansen, 30 x 30 In., Pair	1200.00

Chair, T. Wirkkala, Birch, Teak, Steel Legs, Laminated, Bent, Nikke, 32 x 20 In.	1560.00
Chair, Tank, Aalto, Birch Laminate Frame, Wool Upholstery, Arms, Artek, 28 x 29 In.	3000.00
Chair, Tavern, 17 Spindles, Maple, Ash, Horseshoe Shape Rail, Splayed Legs, 27 x 28 In.	575.00
Chair, Teak, Carved Back, Arms, 1800s, Chinese, 40 x 24 In., Pair	978.00
Chair, Theo Ruth, Folding, Upholstered, Wood Frame, Artifort, 32 x 20 In., Pair	1800.00
Chair, Throne, Hardwood, Clouds, Sea Ivory Landscape, Multicolored, Chinese, 42 In., Pair	1688.00
Chair, Throne, Lacquered, Landscape, Calligraphy, Foo Dog Finials, Chinese, 34 x 36 In.	2640.00
Chair, Throne, Moorish, Carved, Inlay, Shells, Geometric Patterns, Bracketed Legs, Pair	2115.00
Chair, Throne, Rococo Revival, Carved, Acanthus Back, Leather Seat, Italy, c.1900, 56 In.	570.00
Chair, Tub, Art Deco, Mahogany, Domed Back, Downswept Arms, Cushion, 32 In., Pair	1920.00
Chair, Tub, Empire Style, Mahogany, Ormolu Mounted, Padded Back, Sides, 33 In. *illus*	780.00
Chair, Tub, George III Style, Mahogany, Continuous Back & Arm, Shaped Seat, 33 In., Pair	1093.00
Chair, Tub, Robsjohn-Gibbings, Rounded Frame, Widdicomb, 1952, 25 x 30 In., Pair	3720.00
Chair, Tube, Walter Lamb, Thick, Metal Frame, Plastic, Brown Jordan, c.1950, 34 x 22 In.	2450.00
Chair, Uldum Mobelfabrik, Rosewood, Beige Wool Seat, 30 x 20 In., Pair	3600.00
Chair, V. Kagan, Lounge, Lucite Arms, Upholstery, Brass, 1970s, 30 x 30 In., Pair	1560.00
Chair, V. Kagan, Lounge, Velvet Upholstery, Brass Casters, 31 x 30 In.	3120.00
Chair, V. Kagan, Lounge, Wool Upholstery, Rosewood Swivel Base, 32 x 27 In.	1200.00
Chair, V. Kagan, Upholstery, Walnut Feet, 31 x 30 In.	1320.00
Chair, V. Panton, Plastic, Injection-Molded, Stamped, Herman Miller, 19 x 33 In. *illus*	330.00
Chair, V. Panton, Steel, Cone Base, Upholstery, Plus-Linje, c.1960, 33 In., Pair	2880.00
Chair, Velvet Upholstery, Ebonized Wood Feet, 30 ½ x 36 In., Pair	1560.00
Chair, Venetian Rococo, Walnut, Scrolled Lyre Back, Painted, Scrolled Legs, 39 In., Pair	460.00
Chair, Victorian, Mahogany, Concave Rail, Serpentine Seat, Upholstered, 35 ¾ In., Pair	240.00
Chair, Victorian, Mahogany, Gondola Shape, Needlepoint Slip Seat, c.1890, 33 In.	58.00
Chair, Victorian, Mahogany, Spindle Back, Tapestry Upholstery, c.1890, 39 x 51 In.	1020.00
Chair, Victorian, Mahogany, Upholstered, Backscrolled Back, Arms, Cushion, 34 In.	1080.00
Chair, Victorian, Rosewood, Carved Stag Hunt, Oak Leaves, Acorns, Upholstered, Arms	4740.00
Chair, Victorian, Walnut, Folding, Turned Spindles, Flowered Needlepoint Seat	50.00
Chair, Victorian, Wax Flowers, Gilt Metal, Leaves, Birds, Mirrors, Velvet Seat, 19 x 16 In.	118.00
Chair, W. Platner, Lounge, Wool Upholstery, Wire Base, Knoll, 43 x 40 In., Pair	2760.00
Chair, W. Platner, Metalwork, Bronze Finish, Knoll, 28 ¾ x 26 In.	400.00
Chair, Walnut, Carved, Cartouche Shape Back, Cane Insert, Serpentine Seat, 36 In., Pair	518.00
Chair, Walnut, Carved Gilt Arms, Upholstered, c.1800	1645.00
Chair, Walnut, Carved, Upholstered, Hand Holds, Padded Arms, 33 x 24 In.	191.00
Chair, Walnut, Chippendale, Shell Crest, Scrolls, Slip Seat, Arms, Phila., c.1765, 40 In.	2015.00
Chair, Walnut, Woven Rush Seat, Contoured Splat, Turned Legs, Stretchers, c.1900	105.00
Chair, Weaver's, Shaker, 2 Back Slats, Rush Seat, Union Village, Ohio, c.1840, 25 x 40 In.	1116.00
Chair, Weaver's, Shaker, Footstool, Slat Back, Maple, Arms, Woven Rush Seat, 40 & 6 ½ x 12 In.	705.00
Chair, Weaver's, Union Village Shaker, Ohio, c.1840, 25 In.	1116.00
Chair, Wedding, Lacquer, Gold Trim, Drawer, Molded Figural Splat, 31 In.	295.00
Chair, Wegner, Folding, Oak, Cane, c.1960, 30 In.	12500.00
Chair, Wegner, Teak, Cane, Denmark, 30 ½ x 24 ½ In.	118.00
Chair, Wegner, Teak, Cushion, Arms, Fritz Hansen, Chinese, 1986, 32 x 22 In., Pair	7800.00
Chair, Wegner, Teak, Woven Seats, Arms, Carl Hansen, Denmark, 28 x 27 In., Pair	7200.00
Chair, Wegner, The Chair, Teak, Vinyl Seat, Branded Johannes Hansen, 30 In., Pair	2040.00
Chair, White Streaked Oak, Chrome, Arms, 26 x 28 In.	360.00
Chair, Wicker, Bar Harbor Style, Painted, 1930s, 22 In., Child's	150.00
Chair, Wicker Seat & Back, Black Ebonized Tripod Frame, 34 x 24 In.	1920.00
Chair, Wilhelm, Bamboo Frame, Striped Upholstery, Open Arms, 36 x 29 In.	1200.00
Chair, William & Mary, Banister Back, Maple, Finials, Arms, 46 In.	999.00
Chair, William & Mary, Banister Back, Split Spindle Slats, Rush Seat, 44 In.	2250.00
Chair, William & Mary, Banister Back, Walnut, Plank Seat, Scroll Crest, Arms, c.1730	5000.00
Chair, William & Mary, Hardwood, Painted, Spindle Turned Crest Rail, Arms, 24 In.	201.00
Chair, William & Mary, Mahogany, Shaped, Carved Arch Crest, Arms, 1800s, 57 In., Pair	588.00
Chair, William & Mary, Oak Wainscot, Plank Seat, Stretchers, Shaped Arms, 48 x 27 In.	431.00
Chair, William IV, Mahogany, Carved, Padded, Tufted, Upholstery, 43 In.	1680.00
Chair, William IV, Mahogany, Carved, Saddle Seat, Scrolled Ears, c.1835	3525.00
Chair, William IV, Mahogany, Carved, Tufted Leather Seat & Back, Adjustable, Arms, c.1875, 41 In.	1200.00
Chair, Windsor, 9 Spindles, Bamboo Turnings, Stepped Crest Rail, 33 ½ In.	90.00
Chair, Windsor, 9 Spindles, Continuous Arm, 19th Century, 36 In.	895.00
Chair, Windsor, Bamboo, Grapevine Crest, Green Paint, New England, c.1820, 35 In., Pair	237.00
Chair, Windsor, Birdcage, Bamboo Turnings, Raking Back, Label, Boston, c.1810, 34 In.	385.00
Chair, Windsor, Bow Back, 8 Spindles, Ebonized, Saddle Seat, Arms, c.1800, 36 ½ In.	401.00
Chair, Windsor, Bow Back, 9 Spindles, Bamboo Turnings, Scroll Arms, Pa., c.1815	12600.00
Chair, Windsor, Bow Back, Brown Paint, Arms, c.1820, 16 ½ x 33 ½ In.	267.00

Furniture, Chair, Slat Back, Hickory, Turned Finials, Oak Split Seat, Virginia, 1700s, 47 x 25 In.
$5520.00

Furniture, Chair, Slipper, Mahogany, Tufted Balloon Back, Upholstered, 1800s, 39 x 25 In.
$442.00

Furniture, Chair, Slipper, Rococo Style, Carved, Masks, Griffins, Painted, Gold Detail, 27 x 26 In.
$944.00

Furniture, Chair, Stickley & Brandt Co., Tenon Construction, Arms, 32 x 22 In. $510.00

F

Furniture, Chair, Stickley Bros., Morris, Pierced Back Crest, Cushion Seat, 33 x 38 In. $1920.00

Furniture, Chair, Stool, Louis XVI Style, Padded Back, Carved Frame, 1800s, 41 In., 2 Piece $1680.00

Dining Chairs

The experts say a dining chair seat should be 18 inches from the floor so your feet will touch the floor and your knees will miss the tabletop. The seat should be 16 inches deep, not as deep as a sofa. The seat and back should support the spine and the small of the back so you are comfortable even if not leaning back.

Chair, Windsor, Bow Back, Spindles, Shaped Seat, Bamboo Legs, 1800s, 38 In.	118.00
Chair, Windsor, Brace Back, Brown Paint, Arms, c.1800, 18 x 36 In.	235.00
Chair, Windsor, Brace Back, Carved Ears, Knuckle Arms, Nantucket, c.1790, 38 In.	4720.00
Chair, Windsor, Brace Back, Nutting, Mixed Wood, Baluster Legs, 37 ½ In.	235.00 to 529.00
Chair, Windsor, Comb Back, 4 Spindles, Rolling Top Rail, Saddle Seat, c.1790, 44 x 27 In.	501.00
Chair, Windsor, Comb Back, 7 Spindles, Saddle Seat, Bobbin Stretchers, Late 1700s	5200.00
Chair, Windsor, Comb Back, 9 Spindles, Alligatored Black Paint, 42 In.	660.00
Chair, Windsor, Comb Back, 9 Spindles, Continuous Arm, H-Stretcher, 43 x 28 In.	6900.00
Chair, Windsor, Comb Back, Arms, Philadelphia, c.1760 ....*illus*	1521.00
Chair, Windsor, Comb Back, Nutting, Softwood, No. 309, Label, 43 In.	460.00
Chair, Windsor, Comb Back, Scrolled Crest, 43 x 26 In. ....*illus*	1265.00
Chair, Windsor, Fanback, Arms, Old Refinish, New England, c.1790, 44 In.	1304.00
Chair, Windsor, Fanback, Ash, Pine, Maple, New England, c.1790, 36 In.	415.00
Chair, Windsor, Fanback, Painted, Connecticut, c.1780, 35 In., Pair	823.00
Chair, Windsor, Fanback, Serpentine Handholds, Raked Legs, c.1775, 37 In.	1292.00
Chair, Windsor, Fanback, Spindles, Shaped Crest, Hartford, Conn., c.1780	944.00
Chair, Windsor, Green Paint, Arms, Signed, J. Beal, 19th Century, 38 In., Pair	265.00
Chair, Windsor, Hoop Back, Maple, Ash, Continuous Knuckle Arms, E. Tracy, Lisbon, Conn.	2655.00
Chair, Windsor, Hoop Back, Oak, Spindles, Pierced Splat, Shaped Arms, 34 In.	201.00
Chair, Windsor, Hoop Back, Pierced Splat, Wraparound Armrests, England, 46 x 25 In. ....*illus*	266.00
Chair, Windsor, Hoop Back, Yew, Spindles, Pierced Splat, Splayed Legs, Arms, 45 In.	470.00
Chair, Windsor, Nutting, Straight Back, Stamp Mark, 39 In.	240.00
Chair, Windsor, Sack Back, 7 Spindles, Black Over Blue Paint, Arms, c.1790, 39 ½ In.	950.00
Chair, Windsor, Sack Back, 7 Spindles, Continuous Arm, T.C. Hayward, 38 x 28 In.	1265.00
Chair, Windsor, Sack Back, Arms, c.1780, 38 In.	235.00
Chair, Windsor, Sack Back, Arms, New York, c.1770, 37 In.	294.00
Chair, Windsor, Sack Back, Ash, Maple, New England, c.1790, 17 x 38 In.	1126.00
Chair, Windsor, Sack Back, Black Paint, 36 In.	303.00
Chair, Windsor, Sack Back, Carved Knuckles, Oval Saddle, Arms, 38 x 16 ½ In.	550.00
Chair, Windsor, Sack Back, Carved Knuckles, Splayed Legs, Lancaster Co., Pa., 36 In.	412.00
Chair, Windsor, Sack Back, Carved Seat, Splayed Legs, Turned Arms, 16 x 36 In.	1304.00
Chair, Windsor, Sack Back, Dark Brown Over Green, Arms, 18 x 38 In.	470.00
Chair, Windsor, Sack Back, Knuckle Arms, Philadelphia, c.1770, 17 x 36 In.	411.00
Chair, Windsor, Sack Back, Metal, Black Paint, Canton, Ohio, Early 1900s, 36 In.	705.00
Chair, Windsor, Sack Back, Nutting, Extended Comb, Carved Knuckles, c.1925, 49 x 18 In.	1410.00
Chair, Windsor, Sack Back, Tapered Spindles, Saddle Seat, c.1800, 36 In.	295.00
Chair, Windsor, Sack Back, Writing Arm, Saddle Seat, Black, New England, c.1785, 40 x 17 In.	2370.00
Chair, Windsor, Shaped Crest Rail, Plank Seat, Turned Legs, Arms, 42 In. ....*illus*	502.00
Chair, Windsor, Spindle Back, Bentwood, Maple, Woven Seat, 1800s, 29 x 20 In. ....*illus*	201.00
Chair, Windsor, Spindle Back, Mixed Woods, Painted, Arms, Phila., c.1790, 38 x 25 In., Pair	2415.00
Chair, Windsor, Spindles, Turned Supports, Shield Shaped Seat, Arms, c.1800, 35 ½ In.	1057.00
Chair, Windsor, Writing Arm, Drawer, D-Shape Seat, 17 x 45 In.	367.00
Chair, Windsor, Yellow Ocher Paint, Arms, c.1830, 34 In.	7469.00
Chair, Wing, Arch Top Rail, Wing Sides, Pad Feet, Scroll Arms, England, 34 x 45 In.	472.00
Chair, Wing, Fruitwood, Shaped Bead & Channel Frame, Ram's Head Handrests, 46 x 20 In.	230.00
Chair, Wing, George II, Mahogany, Straight Top Rail, Upholstered, 1800s, 29 x 44 In.	767.00
Chair, Wing, Georgian, Leather Upholstery, Brass Tacks & Casters, 44 x 35 In.	748.00
Chair, Wing, Georgian, Mahogany, Upholstery, Carved Legs, 1800s, 45 In.	353.00
Chair, Wing, Hans Wagner, Canted Open Arms, Teak Handrests, Dowel Legs, c.1975, 39 In.	3360.00
Chair, Wing, J. Hoffmann, No. 666, Beech, Leather, c.1905, 47 x 29 x 29 In.	3884.00
Chair, Wing, Leather, Brass Tacks, Square Legs, Arms, 42 In.	489.00
Chair, Wing, Leather Upholstered, Brass Tacks, Mahogany, 44 x 31 x 27 In., Pair	1840.00
Chair, Wing, Louis XV, Walnut, Carved, Scrolled, Padded Arms, Cabriole Legs, 15 In., Child's	2015.00
Chair, Wing, Mahogany, Top Nailed Leather, Serpentine Back, Claw Feet, 43 x 22 In.	2300.00
Chair, Wing, Mahogany, Upholstery, Scroll Arms, c.1940, 42 x 29 In.	117.00
Chair, Wing, Queen Anne Style, Arched Back, Upholstery, Pad Feet, Ireland, 52 x 36 In.	920.00
Chair, Wing, Queen Anne Style, Mahogany, Cabriole Legs, Pad Feet, Upholstery, 50 In.	1560.00
Chair, Wood, Arts & Crafts, Barley Twist Design, Carved Back Shield, 25 x 48 In.	240.00
Chair, Wood, Carved Tiger Head Arms, Paw Feet, Upholstery, Chinese, 36 x 28 In.	2760.00
Chair, Wood, Heavily Carved Back, Arms, Chinese, 1800s, 41 ¾ x 23 In.	4600.00
Chair, Wood, Ornate Carved Back, Arms, Chinese, 34 x 25 In.	374.00
Chair, Wood, Pierced Slats, Tacks, Leather Upholstery, Arms, 36 ¾ In.	74.00
Chair, Wormley, Lounge, Mahogany, Cane Seat & Back, Adjustable, 27 x 27 ½ In.	3360.00
Chair, Wormley, Lounge, No. 5499, Dunbar, c.1955, 28 x 32 In., Pair	1470.00
Chair, Wormley, White Upholstery, Flared Mahogany Legs, Dunbar, 26 x 28 In.	120.00
Chair-Table, 3-Board Top, Wood, Red Paint, 40 ½ x 48 In.	4295.00

Chair-Table, Monk's, Pine, Plank Top, Hinged Seat, Bootjack Sides, Trestle Base, 33 x 60 In. ..		717.00
Chair-Table, Pine, Ash, Peg Construction, Scrub Surface, 1800s, 27 x 48 In.		999.00
Chair-Table, Pine, Lift Lid Base, Old Paint, Pa., 1800s, 30 x 36 In.		1058.00
Chair-Table, Pine, Red Paint, Black Chair Base, 20th Century, 29 x 29 In.		120.00
Chair-Table, Pine, Tilt Top, Blue, Green Paint, Cutout Support, Hinged Seat, 28 x 41 ½ In.		1210.00
Chaise Longue, Aalto, Bentwood, Cross Woven Webbing, c.1930s, 20 x 72 x 24 In.		4780.00
Chaise Longue, B. Mathsson, Pernilla, Molded Beech, Marked, Sweden, 64 In.		1020.00
Chaise Longue, French Rococo, Walnut, Scrolled Back, Arms, Scalloped Apron, Late 1800s, 71 In.		1688.00
Chaise Longue, Juan Montoya, Leather, Brass Tacks, Wood, Carved Feet, 30 x 76 In.		3120.00
Chaise Longue, Kem Weber, Nickel Plated Metal, Upholstered, 74 x 29 In.		5000.00
Chaise Longue, Louis Philippe, Mahogany, Barrel Back, Spiral Arm, Bowed Seat, c.1800		717.00
Chaise Longue, Louis XVI Style, Upholstery, Ribbed Back, Arms, c.1840, 64 In.		805.00
Chaise Longue, Mahogany, Crest Pierced, Anthemion, Carved Arms, c.1800, 33 x 88 x 27 In.		2400.00
Chaise Longue, Rattan, Adjustable Back, Flat Raised Arms, 36 x 30 x 71 In., Pair..................		1464.00
Chaise Longue, Restauration, Mahogany, Pierced, Carved Splat, Single Arm, 33 x 88 In. *illus*		2400.00
Chaise Longue, V. Kagan, Erica, Velour Upholstery, Lucite Base, 60 x 35 In.		1800.00
Chaise Longue, Walter Lamb, Metal Frame, Plastic, Brown Jordan, c.1950, 33 x 69 In., Pair ..		6738.00
Chaise Rocker, Cabreuva, Fabric, Cane, Joaquim Tenreiro, c.1947, 32 x 63 In.		50000.00
Chamberstand, Corner, Federal, Mahogany, Shelf, Drawers, c.1835, 41 x 16 In.		356.00
Chest, 6-Board, Overhanging Hinged Lid, Red Paint, Miniature, Pa., 1800s, 11 x 13 In.		1778.00
Chest, Antonio Cierio, Wood, 8 Long Drawers, B & B Italia, c.1983, 28 x 71 In.		2450.00
Chest, Bachelor's, Chippendale, Mahogany, 4 Drawers, Bracket Feet, Britain, 1700s, 33 x 37 x 18 In.		3000.00
Chest, Bachelor's, George I, Walnut Veneers, Pullout Slide, 5 Drawers, 30 x 32 x 19 In.		4370.00
Chest, Bachelor's, George III, Chippendale, Mahogany, 4 Graduated Drawers, 33 ½ x 34 In. ...		1725.00
Chest, Bachelor's, George III, Mahogany, 4 Drawers, Bracket Feet, c.1780, 32 x 34 In.		2223.00
Chest, Bachelor's, George III, Mahogany, Slide, 3 Drawers, Bracket Feet, c.1810, 32 x 34 In. ...		1175.00
Chest, Bachelor's, Georgian Style, Yew, Mahogany, Molded Top, 4 Drawers, 33 x 34 In., Pair....		1125.00
Chest, Bachelor's, Mahogany, Slide, 3 Drawers, England, c.1910, 21 x 24 In.		920.00
Chest, Baroque, Walnut, Crossband, 3 Drawers, Bowfront, Shaped Feet, France, 32 x 42 x 23 In.		2489.00
Chest, Baroque, Walnut, Crossband, 3 Drawers, France, 31 x 42 x 22 In.		2489.00
Chest, Biedermeier, Fruitwood, Marble Top, 3 Drawers, Inlaid Diamond, 32 x 38 In.		415.00
Chest, Biedermeier, Rosewood, Drawer, Black Lacquered Columns, 32 x 35 In.		863.00
Chest, Birch, Bowfront, 3 Drawers, Scalloped Skirt, Turned Feet, Scotland, 47 x 48 In.		1150.00
Chest, Black Forest, Carved Woman, Basket Lid, Velvet Interior, Shell Carvings, 24 x 24 In.		4600.00
Chest, Blanket, 2 Drawer, Till Box, Bracket Feet, c.1840		265.00
Chest, Blanket, Baroque, Fruitwood Parquetry, Medallions, Germany, 19 x 68 x 23 In.		504.00
Chest, Blanket, Blue Paint, Bootjack Base, 19th Century, 22 x 47 x 17 In.		396.00
Chest, Blanket, British Campaign, Camphorwood, Brass Mounts, c.1850, 17 x 36 In.		652.00
Chest, Blanket, Cherry, 2 Lower Drawers, Hinged Lid, 19th Century, 25 x 49 x 23 In.		531.00
Chest, Blanket, Cherry, Pine, Apron, New England, c.1800, 34 x 41 In. ....*illus*		823.00
Chest, Blanket, Chippendale, Curly Walnut, Drawers, Interior Till Lid, Pa., c.1780, 31 x 56 In.		940.00
Chest, Blanket, Chippendale, Walnut, 2 Drawers, Bracket Feet, Pa., 28 ¾ x 50 In.		1404.00
Chest, Blanket, Chippendale, Walnut, Hinged Top, North Carolina, c.1800, 20 x 40 In.		345.00
Chest, Blanket, Chippendale, Walnut, Poplar, 6-Board, Applied Molding, c.1810, 54 x 26 In. ...		2233.00
Chest, Blanket, Curly Maple, Poplar, Inlaid Flower, D. Richard Dunlap, Ohio, 1900s, 8 x 15 In.		705.00
Chest, Blanket, Dovetail Case, Interior Till, Black, Red Paint, c.1880, 25 x 46 In.		353.00
Chest, Blanket, Drawer, Turned Legs, Red, Mustard Paint, Miniature, 14 x 16 In.		460.00
Chest, Blanket, Drawers, Lid Till, Bear Trap Lock, Strap Hinges, c.1800, 50 x 22 In.		499.00
Chest, Blanket, Elm, Carved, Wrought Iron Hardware, 1718, 20 x 44 x 18 In.		1304.00
Chest, Blanket, Federal, Dovetailed, Molded Edge Hinged Lid, Pad Feet, 26 x 51 In.		448.00
Chest, Blanket, Gothic Revival, Walnut, Tracery Panels, Bracket Feet, 23 ½ x 63 In.		235.00
Chest, Blanket, Hepplewhite, Pine, Old Red Wash, Dovetailed, 19th Century, 27 x 49 In.		515.00
Chest, Blanket, Hepplewhite, Walnut, Adam & Eve Fraktur, Dovetailed, Hinged, 29 x 52 In.		1100.00
Chest, Blanket, Hinged Top, Drawer, Painted, Fruit & Leaves, Jean Dewey, 34 x 32 In.		695.00
Chest, Blanket, Hinged Top, Flower, Geometric Carving, Paint, Continental, 25 x 43 In.		266.00
Chest, Blanket, Hinged Top, Mitered Edge, Ball Feet, c.1800, 20 x 38 x 18 In.		179.00
Chest, Blanket, Inlaid Birds, Branches, D. Richard Dunlap, Ohio, 1900s, 8 x 14 In.		734.00
Chest, Blanket, Jacobean, Oak, Carved Relief Figures, Arcaded Panels, Bun Feet, 37 In.		1067.00
Chest, Blanket, Oak, Chip-Carved Arches, Bootjack Ends, 18th Century, 23 x 40 x 16 In.		732.00
Chest, Blanket, Oak, Lift Top, Low Drawer, c.1820, 39 x 40 In.		690.00
Chest, Blanket, Paneled Lid, Walnut, Carved, 22 x 44 x 22 In.		657.00
Chest, Blanket, Pine, 3 Drawers, Straight Bracket Feet, Pa., 1790, 28 x 50 In.		505.00
Chest, Blanket, Pine, 6-Board, Dovetail Corners, Bracket Feet, 24 x 47 x 17 In.		324.00
Chest, Blanket, Pine, 6-Board, Vinegar Graining, c.1850, 20 x 42 In.		353.00
Chest, Blanket, Pine, Blue Paint, Interior Till, 1800s, 21 x 38 In.		1087.00
Chest, Blanket, Pine, Blue Paint, Tapered Feet, Iron Butt Hinges, 20 x 72 x 17 In.		505.00

Furniture, Chair, Tub, Empire Style, Mahogany, Ormolu Mounted, Padded Back, Sides, 33 In. $780.00

F

Furniture, Chair, V. Panton, Plastic, Injection-Molded, Stamped, Herman Miller, 19 x 33 In. $330.00

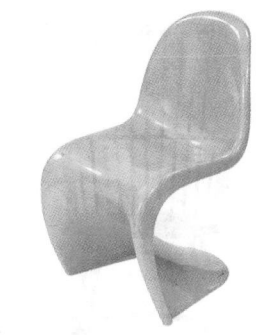

Furniture, Chair, Windsor, Comb Back, Arms, Philadelphia, c.1760 $1521.00

Furniture, Chair, Windsor, Comb Back, Scrolled Crest, 43 x 26 In. $1265.00

Furniture, Chair, Windsor, Hoop Back, Pierced Splat, Wraparound Armrests, England, 46 x 25 In.
$266.00

Furniture, Chair, Windsor, Shaped Crest Rail, Plank Seat, Turned Legs, Arms, 42 In.
$502.00

Furniture, Chair, Windsor, Spindle Back, Bentwood, Maple, Woven Seat, 1800s, 29 x 20 In.
$201.00

Chest, Blanket, Pine, Bracket Feet, Pa., c.1800, 26 x 54 In.	198.00
Chest, Blanket, Pine, Dovetailed Case, Ogee Bracket Feet, Painted, 1852, 26 x 20 In.	646.00
Chest, Blanket, Pine, Dovetailed, Molded Edge, Turned Feet, Till, 22 x 43 In.	239.00
Chest, Blanket, Pine, Grain Painted, Paneled Sides, 4 Turned Feet, 27 x 43 x 20 In.	915.00
Chest, Blanket, Pine, Hearts, Flowers, Red Ground, Drawers, Pa., Inscribed, 1808, 30 x 51 In.	8813.00
Chest, Blanket, Pine, Hinged Lid, Interior Till, Drawers, Block Feet, Early 1800s, 21 x 41 In.	173.00
Chest, Blanket, Pine, Hinged Lid, Till, Moldings, Blue Paint, c.1800, 25 x 40 In.	3105.00
Chest, Blanket, Pine, Interior Lid, Till, Yellow Initials W.W.D., Blue Paint, 15 x 41 In.	411.00
Chest, Blanket, Pine, Interior Till, Iron Straps, Blue & Red Paint, c.1850, 17 x 46 In.	499.00
Chest, Blanket, Pine, Interior Till, Red, Black Paint Design, Cutout Feet, c.1835, 25 x 44 In.	646.00
Chest, Blanket, Pine, Interior Till, Red Varnish, 26 x 42 In.	558.00
Chest, Blanket, Pine, Interior Till, Turned Feet, Red Paint, c.1850, 20 x 29 In.	323.00
Chest, Blanket, Pine, Interior Till, Yellow Paint, 23 x 44 In.	499.00
Chest, Blanket, Pine, Lift Top, 2 Drawers, 40 x 40 x 17 ½ In.	300.00
Chest, Blanket, Pine, Molding, Turned Feet, Blue Paint, c.1810, 22 x 35 In.	999.00
Chest, Blanket, Pine, Old Red Stain, Drawer, c.1750, 36 ¼ In.	2596.00
Chest, Blanket, Pine, Painted, Leaves, Wrought Iron Handles, Bun Feet, Bavaria, 18 x 45 In.	296.00
Chest, Blanket, Pine, Painted, Nesting Diamonds, Rectangles, Shaped Feet, 20 x 35 In.	144.00
Chest, Blanket, Pine, Poplar, Grain Painted, Till, Turned Feet, 1830-40, 25 x 49 In. .... *illus*	500.00
Chest, Blanket, Pine, Poplar, Turned Feet, Paneled Case, c.1850, 24 x 37 x 18 In.	382.00
Chest, Blanket, Pine, Red & Black Grain, Ball Feet, 19th Century, 23 x 44 In.	1210.00
Chest, Blanket, Pine, Red Paint, Drawer, Hinged Lid, Shaped Feet, c.1750, 36 In.	2655.00
Chest, Blanket, Pine, Red Paint, Snipe Hinges, Arched Feet, c.1740, 22 x 30 x 12 In.	2242.00
Chest, Blanket, Pine, Yellow, Cutout Feet, New England, c.1790, 32 x 36 In.	800.00
Chest, Blanket, Poplar, Grain Paint, Jacob Werrey, German Twp., 1890, 24 x 44 In.	8200.00
Chest, Blanket, Poplar, Interior Till, Bracket Base, Red, Black Paint, c.1830, 27 x 44 In.	294.00
Chest, Blanket, Poplar, Interior Till, Flower, Brown, Lancaster Co., c.1885, 25 x 44 In.	353.00
Chest, Blanket, Poplar, Lift Top, Candle Box, Decorated, 1800s, 27 x 40 In. .... *illus*	633.00
Chest, Blanket, Poplar, Painted, Pa., 19th Century, 22 ½ x 36 In.	175.00
Chest, Blanket, Poplar, Pine, Till, Blue Paint, Black Molding, Early 1800s, 13 ¾ x 30 In.	499.00
Chest, Blanket, Poplar, Red Paint, Paneled, 2 Drawers, Turned Feet, c.1850, 30 x 45 In.	499.00
Chest, Blanket, Poplar, Till, Lid, Brown Flame Grain, Turned Feet, Pa., 1800s, 27 x 50 In.	264.00
Chest, Blanket, Poplar, Till, Lid, Red Flame Grain, Gold Stencils, 1800s, 23 x 38 In.	940.00
Chest, Blanket, Red Paint, Molded Lid, Drawer, Bracket Feet, 29 ½ x 38 x 18 ½ In.	605.00
Chest, Blanket, Rohlfs, Wrought Copper, Pullout Trays, Drawer, 1903, 49 x 26 In.	32940.00
Chest, Blanket, Shaker, Cherry, Lift Top, 2 Drawers, 19th Century, 41 x 43 In.	2800.00
Chest, Blanket, Shaker, Hinged Lid, 2 Lower Drawers, Harvard, 44 x 43 In.	1652.00
Chest, Blanket, Shaker, Mixed Woods, Hinged Top, 2 Drawers, N.H., c.1840, 38 x 41 In.	2633.00
Chest, Blanket, Shaker, Pine, Breadboard Lid, Canted Feet, Green, Red Paint, c.1840, 23 x 45 In.	878.00
Chest, Blanket, Shaker, Pine, Drawers, Dovetailed, Mt. Lebanon, N.Y., c.1830, 31 x 42 In.	39780.00
Chest, Blanket, Shaker, Pine, Lift Top, Tills, Arch Molding, 6 Drawers, c.1840, 44 x 48 In.	2633.00
Chest, Blanket, Shaker, Pine, Red Paint, 6-Board, Footed, 25 x 43 ½ x 18 ½ In.	1100.00
Chest, Blanket, Sheraton, Molded Lid, Split Lip Dovetailed Drawers, 29 x 43 x 22 In.	254.00
Chest, Blanket, Softwood, Mustard, Brown Swirl, Grain, 23 x 43 x 19 In.	1100.00
Chest, Blanket, Softwood, Red, Basket, Melons, Flowers, Leaf Stenciled, 26 x 48 x 21 In.	9350.00
Chest, Blanket, Sponge Decorated, 2 Drawer, Bookjack Ends, c.1825, 43 x 43 x 20 In.	805.00
Chest, Blanket, Tree Of Life, Geometric, Molded Lid, Bracket Feet, 22 x 52 x 22 In.	770.00
Chest, Blanket, Walnut, 2 Drawers, Strap Hinges, Bracket Feet, 27 x 49 x 19 In.	915.00
Chest, Blanket, Walnut, Pine, 6-Board Case, Turned Feet, c.1825, 28 x 50 In.	470.00
Chest, Blanket, William & Mary, Pine, Lift Lid, Paneled Case, 2 Drawers, c.1730, 44 x 38 In.	4680.00
Chest, Blanket, Wood, Grain Paint, Pa., 19th Century, 24 x 41 In.	175.00
Chest, Blanket, Wooden, Painted, Jacob Stobler, Pennsylvania, 1856, 43 x 26 x 20 In.	1287.00
Chest, Blanket, Yellow Pine, 2 Drawers, Painted, Georgia, c.1825, 28 x 44 In.	6900.00
Chest, Blanket, Yellow Pine, Butt Hinges, Fitted Interior, Georgia, c.1800, 25 x 50 In.	546.00
Chest, Blanket, Yellow Pine, Hinged Top, Fitted Interior, Drawers, Georgia, c.1820, 33 x 43 In.	1840.00
Chest, Blanket, Yellow Pine, Shaped Skirt, Hinged Top, Painted, Georgia, c.1810, 43 x 47 In.	920.00
Chest, Bombay, 3 Drawers, Burled, 36 x 47 In.	325.00
Chest, Bombe, Marquetry & Pencil Inlay, Bronze Ormolu Mounts, 2 Doors, 64 x 40 In.	307.00
Chest, Bookcase, Walnut, Poplar, Doors, 4 Drawers, Grain Painted, c.1875, 85 x 42 In.	617.00
Chest, Bowfront, Federal, Mahogany, Figured Veneers, 1900s, 36 x 40 In.	1380.00
Chest, Bowfront, Federal, Mahogany, Inlaid, Stepped Drawers, New Eng., c.1800, 38 x 43 In.	859.00
Chest, Bowfront, Federal, Mahogany, Inlay, 4 Drawers, Flare Feet, c.1800, 34 x 40 In.	474.00
Chest, Bowfront, Federal, Mahogany, Molded Top, 4 Drawers, Boston, c.1807, 32 x 41 In.	3318.00
Chest, Bowfront, Hepplewhite, Elm, Pine, 3 Drawers, England, 1800s, 35 x 35 In.	1265.00
Chest, Bowfront, Hepplewhite, Mahogany, 4 Drawers, England, c.1790, 37 x 40 In.	2115.00

FURNITURE

Chest, Bowfront, Hepplewhite, Mahogany, 6 Drawers, Brass Pulls, Eng., 1800s, 41 x 47 In.	1495.00
Chest, Bowfront, Hepplewhite, Mahogany, Pine, Drawers, String Inlay, c.1800, 38 x 41 In.	1058.00
Chest, Bowfront, Inlaid, Satinwood Banding, 5 Drawers, Scotland, 48 x 45 In.	1380.00
Chest, Bowfront, Mahogany, 2 Over 3 Drawers, c.1860, 46 x 41 In.	3800.00
Chest, Bowfront, Mahogany, 2 Short & 3 Long Drawers, England, 1800s, 34 x 42 In.	738.00
Chest, Bowfront, Mahogany Inlay, Shaped Top, 2 Over 3 Drawers, 40 x 40 In.	1150.00
Chest, Bowfront, Mahogany, Pine, 4 Drawers, c.1800, 41 x 47 In.	705.00
Chest, Bowfront, Mahogany, Poplar, Pine, Drawers, Veneer, Reeded, c.1820, 42 x 43 In.	353.00
Chest, Bowfront, Mahogany, Satinwood Bands, 4 Drawers, Brass, Eng., 1800s, 36 x 39 In.	738.00
Chest, Bowfront, Mahogany, Shaped Top, 2 Short, 3 Long Drawers, 43 x 44 In.	1150.00
Chest, Bowfront, Mahogany, Tiger Maple Panels, Burl Ash Bands, 4 Drawers, c.1815	2645.00
Chest, Bowfront, Maple, Ivory Escutcheons, c.1805, 38 x 40 In.	9375.00
Chest, Bowfront, Sheraton, Poplar, 4 Drawers, Reeded, Turned Legs, c.1820, 41 x 42 In.	1610.00
Chest, Brass, Carved, Drawer, Zanzibar, Late 1700s, 27 ½ x 43 In.	2400.00
Chest, Burl Walnut, 12 Drawers, Barley Twist Frame, Maitland-Smith, 60 x 39 x 19 In.	1100.00
Chest, Butler's, Empire, Mahogany, Cherry, Drawer, 2 Doors, 45 x 45 In.	420.00
Chest, Butler's, George III, Mahogany, Drop Front Drawer, Cupboard, 41 x 54 In.	7200.00
Chest, Butler's, Oak, Paneled Doors, Inside Drawers, Silver Drawer, c.1910, 61 x 37 In.	330.00
Chest, Butternut, Painted, 5 Drawers, 19th Century, 37 x 35 In.	531.00
Chest, Campaign, 2 Sections, 4 Drawers, Brass Handles, 35 x 29 x 16 In.	1220.00
Chest, Campaign, 3 Sections, 7 Drawers, Brass Handles, Baker Furniture, 53 x 46 x 24 In.	1586.00
Chest, Campaign, Brass Mounts, England, c.1850, 22 x 38 In.	415.00
Chest, Campaign, Camphor, Brass Mounted, Handles, 1800s, 20 x 22 In. ....illus	1035.00
Chest, Campaign, Camphorwood, 3 Long Drawers, Bun Feet, England, c.1850, 37 x 42 In.	1896.00
Chest, Campaign, Mahogany, 2 Case, 5 Drawers, England, 1800s, 40 x 42 In.	1840.00
Chest, Campaign, Mahogany, Molded Gallery, Drawers, c.1850, 40 x 36 In.	3105.00
Chest, Campaign, Mahogany, Pine, Brass Hardware, Mid 1800s, 43 x 42 In.	5500.00
Chest, Campaign, Mahogany, Veneer, Pine, Drop Front, Brass Hardware, 42 x 40 In.	5900.00
Chest, Campaign, Teak, 2 Over 3 Drawers, Late 19th Century, 46 x 41 In.	3800.00
Chest, Campaign, Teak, Stacking, Brass, Britain, 19th Century, 38 x 30 x 17 In.	1200.00
Chest, Camphor Seaman, Brass Corners, Iron Handles, c.1850, 16 x 39 x 19 In.	345.00
Chest, Cassone, Baroque Style, Walnut, Carved, Putti, Cherub, 26 x 73 x 22 In.	956.00
Chest, Cedar, Mahogany, Overhang Hinged Lid, Casters, c.1940, 19 x 40 In.	146.00
Chest, Charles II, Oak, Molded Top, Frame & Panel Case, Drawers, 36 x 36 In.	633.00
Chest, Cherry, 4 Drawers, Ogee Bracket Feet, Late 1700s, 36 x 39 x 20 In.	1100.00
Chest, Cherry, 4 Graduated Drawers, String Inlay, French Feet, c.1820, 36 x 42 x 22 In.	671.00
Chest, Cherry, 8 Drawers, Footed, Ethan Allen, 34 ½ x 55 In.	240.00
Chest, Cherry, Corbels, 4 Long Drawers, Bun Feet, c.1900, 51 x 42 In.	230.00
Chest, Cherry, Drawers, Cock-Beaded Molding, Pulls, c.1790, 65 x 45 In.	12925.00
Chest, Cherry, Maple, Drawers, Shaped Skirt, French Feet, 19th Century, 35 x 16 In.	805.00
Chest, Cherry, Outset Drawer, 3 Recessed Drawers, Columns, c.1825, 49 x 41 In.	294.00
Chest, Cherry, Tiger Maple, 4 Drawers, Paneled Sides, 46 x 46 ½ x 20 In.	1130.00
Chest, Chestnut, Daffodils, Pyrography Panel, 18 x 30 x 17 In.	3172.00
Chest, Chippendale Style, Mahogany, Inlay, Banded, Bracket Feet, 1800s, 33 x 44 x 20 In.	345.00
Chest, Chippendale Style, Walnut, Burled Walnut Top, Scalloped Drawer, 35 x 44 x 22 In.	1265.00
Chest, Chippendale, Birch, 4 Drawers, Cock-Beaded, Bracket Feet, c.1780, 32 x 34 In.	2640.00
Chest, Chippendale, Birch, 4 Drawers, Serpentine Front, Mass., 35 x 40 In.	1955.00
Chest, Chippendale, Cherry, 4 Drawers, Fluted Chamfered Columns, Pa., c.1785, 37 x 39 In.	936.00
Chest, Chippendale, Cherry, 4 Drawers, Footed, Late 18th Century, 33 x 36 In.	395.00
Chest, Chippendale, Cherry, 4 Drawers, Molded Top, Bracket Feet, c.1775, 32 x 32 In.	15405.00
Chest, Chippendale, Cherry, 6 Drawers, Dovetailed, Connecticut River Valley, 52 x 41 In.	2840.00
Chest, Chippendale, Cherry, Bonnet Top, Fan, Bracket Feet, Conn., c.1780, 55 x 39 In.	6250.00
Chest, Chippendale, Cherry, Molded Cornice, Graduated Drawers, New England, 53 x 36 In.	4148.00
Chest, Chippendale, Cherry, Pine, Reverse Serpentine, c.1780, 36 x 39 In.	5288.00
Chest, Chippendale, Fruitwood, 3 Drawers, Reddish Finish, c.1780, 37 ¾ In.	510.00
Chest, Chippendale, Mahogany, 4 Drawers, Serpentine, Boston, c.1770, 30 x 35 In.	10000.00
Chest, Chippendale, Mahogany, 4 Drawers, Serpentine Top, c.1790, 38 x 46 In.	2880.00
Chest, Chippendale, Mahogany, Drawers, Blind Pediment, Eng., c.1800, 72 x 45 In.	1955.00
Chest, Chippendale, Mahogany, Lift Top, 2 Drawers, Brass Fittings, Ireland, 37 x 52 In.	805.00
Chest, Chippendale, Mahogany, Oxbow, 3 Drawers, Serpentine Top, Bracket Feet, 31 x 38 In.	6000.00
Chest, Chippendale, Mahogany, Oxbow, 4 Drawers, Ball & Claw, 1770, 34 In.	12000.00
Chest, Chippendale, Maple, 5 Drawers, Tray Top, 51 ½ x 36 x 18 ½ In.	2200.00
Chest, Chippendale, Maple, 6 Drawers, Late 18th Century, 55 x 38 In.	4600.00
Chest, Chippendale, Maple, 7 Drawers, Molded Edge, 55 x 38 x 17 In.	2585.00
Chest, Chippendale, Maple, New England, c.1790, 57 x 36 In.	3200.00
Chest, Chippendale, Pine, 3 Drawers, 3 Fake Drawers, Lift Top, Bracket Feet, c.1790, 53 x 37 In.	889.00

Furniture, Chaise Longue, Restauration, Mahogany, Pierced, Carved Splat, Single Arm, 33 x 88 In.
$2400.00

Furniture, Chest, Blanket, Cherry, Pine, Apron, New England, c.1800, 34 x 41 In.
$823.00

Furniture, Chest, Blanket, Pine, Poplar, Grain Painted, Till, Turned Feet, 1830-40, 25 x 49 In.
$500.00

Furniture, Chest, Blanket, Poplar, Lift Top, Candle Box, Decorated, 1800s, 27 x 40 In.
$633.00

Furniture, Chest, Campaign, Camphor, Brass Mounted, Handles, 1800s, 20 x 22 In.
$1035.00

Furniture, Chest, Chippendale, Walnut, Yellow Pine, Drawers, N.C., c.1800, 60 x 42 In.
$7820.00

Furniture, Chest, Dower, Painted, Hearts, Stars, Drawers, Inscribed, Pa., c.1809, 30 x 48 In.
$22230.00

Furniture, Chest, Federal, Cherry, Inlay, Dovetailed Drawers, c.1810, 39 x 40 In.
$1840.00

Chest, Chippendale, Pine, 3 Drawers, Thumb-Molded, New England, 1700s, 52 x 36 In.		593.00
Chest, Chippendale, Softwood, Red Paint, 3 Over 2 Drawers, 47 x 44 x 20 In.		1430.00
Chest, Chippendale, Tiger Maple, 4 Drawers, Bail Handles, 34 x 36 x 19 In.		747.00
Chest, Chippendale, Tiger Maple, 4 Drawers, Molded Top, 34 ¼ In.		1400.00
Chest, Chippendale, Walnut, 4 Drawers, c.1770, 36 ½ x 40 In.		810.00
Chest, Chippendale, Walnut, 4 Drawers, Ogee Bracket Feet, c.1760-80, 33 ½ x 37 In.		4800.00
Chest, Chippendale, Walnut, 4 Drawers, Ogee Bracket Feet, c.1760-80, 40 x 41 In.		3200.00
Chest, Chippendale, Walnut, 4 Drawers, Serpentine Front, Inlay, c.1780, 34 x 36 In.		8400.00
Chest, Chippendale, Walnut, 4 Graduated Drawers, Bracket Feet, c.1775, 36 x 40 x 20 In.		793.00
Chest, Chippendale, Walnut, 7 Drawers, Fluted Columns, c.1770, 54 x 39 In.		2340.00
Chest, Chippendale, Walnut, 8 Drawers, Ogee Bracket Feet, 1760-80, 64 x 39 In.		8400.00
Chest, Chippendale, Walnut, 9 Drawers, 59 x 37 ½ In.		800.00
Chest, Chippendale, Walnut, 9 Drawers, Ogee Bracket Feet, 66 ½ x 42 In.		1292.00
Chest, Chippendale, Walnut, Poplar, Broken Pediment, c.1780, 93 x 42 In.		4406.00
Chest, Chippendale, Walnut, Poplar, Yellow Pine, 5 Drawers, Scallops, c.1800, 44 x 21 In.		6900.00
Chest, Chippendale, Walnut, Yellow Pine, Drawers, N.C., c.1800, 60 x 42 In.	*illus*	7820.00
Chest, Chippendale, Walnut, Yellow Pine, Lift Top, Scalloped Skirt, 1700s, 10 x 18 In.		3220.00
Chest, Chippendale, Yellow Pine, Lift Top, Panels, Grain Paint, N.C., c.1820, 21 x 37 In.		2760.00
Chest, Chippendale, Yellow Pine, Molded Top, Open Interior, c.1790, 22 x 50 In.		1495.00
Chest, Colonial Revival, Mahogany, Line Strung, Hidden Frieze Drawer, 69 x 39 In.		3120.00
Chest, Curly Maple, Gallery, 6 Drawers, Mid-Atlantic, c.1820, 51 x 40 In.		823.00
Chest, Document, Oak, 13 Drawers, 60 x 23 x 21 In.		695.00
Chest, Dower, Blue Paint, 19th Century, 26 x 48 In.		240.00
Chest, Dower, Oak, Paneled, Post Feet, Iron Hardware, 27 x 51 In.		299.00
Chest, Dower, Painted, Breadboard Ends, Hinged Lid, Stencil, Urferin, 1795, 52 In.		896.00
Chest, Dower, Painted, Hearts, Stars, Drawers, Inscribed, Pa., c.1809, 30 x 48 In.	*illus*	22230.00
Chest, Dower, Painted, Scrolling Tulips, Pennsylvania, c.1800, 26 x 48 In.		2596.00
Chest, Dower, Panels, Tulips, Iron Strap Hinges, 21 x 50 x 24 In.		468.00
Chest, Dower, Pine, Paint Designs, Wrought Iron, Handles, Pennsylvania, 1700s, 22 x 44 In.		353.00
Chest, Dower, Softwood, Stipple Paint, Molded Lid, Strap Hinges, 30 x 52 x 24 In.		1430.00
Chest, Dower, Walnut, Sulphur Inlaid Cartouche, Inscribed, Lancaster County, 20 x 50 In.		1053.00
Chest, Dressing, Edwardian, Satinwood, Painted, Sliding Shelf, 3 Drawers, 50 In.		948.00
Chest, Dressing, Louis XIV Style, Brass, Faux Tortoiseshell, Figures, Animals, 1900s, 33 x 47 In.		7703.00
Chest, Eastlake, Maple, 4 Drawers, 36 x 39 In.		546.00
Chest, Edwardian, Satinwood, Bowfront, 5 Drawers, Early 1900s, 39 x 39 In.		805.00
Chest, Empire, 3 Drawers, Fan Inlay, Curved Pilaster, Gold Stencil, c.1850, 25 x 20 In.		8519.00
Chest, Empire, Mahogany, 2-Drawer Gallery Top, Rope Twist Columns, Paw Feet, 42 In.		443.00
Chest, Empire, Mahogany, 4 Drawers, Turned Legs, 40 x 43 x 20 ½ In.		660.00
Chest, Empire, Mahogany, Drawers, Carved Columnar Post, Backsplash, 51 x 43 x 20 In.		239.00
Chest, Empire, Mahogany, Inlays, New England, c.1850, 22 x 17 In.		441.00
Chest, Empire, Mahogany, Walnut, Pine, Shaped Back, 12 x 14 In.		176.00
Chest, Empire Style, Butternut, Mahogany, Rope Carved Edge, 1840, 19 x 20 x 7 In., Child's		2700.00
Chest, Empire, Walnut, 6 Drawers, Columns, Pad Feet, c.1850, 49 x 45 In.		130.00
Chest, Faux Bamboo, Painted, 2 Over 3 Drawers, Turned Feet, 43 x 39 x 20 In.		546.00
Chest, Faux Bamboo, Pine, Carrara Marble, 3 Drawers, c.1890, 11 x 12 In.		740.00
Chest, Federal, 4 Drawers, Banded, Inlaid Maple, Shaped Skirt, New Eng., c.1800, 39 x 42 In.		1093.00
Chest, Federal, 4 Drawers, Shield, Star Inlays, Cornucopia Brass Hardware, 37 x 39 In.		2185.00
Chest, Federal, Birch, Inlaid Cherry, Bowfront, 37 x 40 ¾ In.		10000.00
Chest, Federal, Cherry, 4 Drawers, Bracket Feet, Southern, 1800s, 40 x 41 In.		374.00
Chest, Federal, Cherry, 4 Drawers, Late 19th Century, 40 ½ x 42 In.		275.00
Chest, Federal, Cherry, 4 Graduated Drawers, Ogee Feet, 38 x 85 x 19 In.		568.00
Chest, Federal, Cherry, Inlay, Dovetailed Drawers, c.1810, 39 x 40 In.	*illus*	1840.00
Chest, Federal, Cherry, Mahogany, 4 Drawers, Pine Inlays, New Eng., c.1810, 38 x 38 In.		690.00
Chest, Federal, Cherry, Mahogany, Bowfront, Cock-Beaded, c.1800, 37 x 42 In.		1440.00
Chest, Federal, Cherry, Maple, 4 Drawers, Inlaid, Carved, New Eng., c.1800, 37 x 42 In.		583.00
Chest, Federal, Curly Maple, 4 Drawers, 19th Century, 37 x 43 x 21 In.		1810.00
Chest, Federal, Double, Cherry, Pine, Reeded Edge Top, 8 Drawers, 48 x 79 In.		9400.00
Chest, Federal, Flame Crotch Mahogany, Marble Top, c.1820, 38 x 40 x 18 In.		7800.00
Chest, Federal, Mahogany, 4 Drawers, Footed, Early 1800s, 33 x 36 ½ In.		405.00
Chest, Federal, Mahogany, 4 Drawers, Inlay, Reeded Posts, Valance Skirt, c.1800, 37 x 42 In.		1304.00
Chest, Federal Mahogany, 4 Graduated Drawers, Bracket Feet, Virginia, 1800, 38 x 43 In.		1955.00
Chest, Federal, Mahogany, 6 Drawers, Ivory Escutcheons, c.1800, 52 x 41 x 19 In.		8812.00
Chest, Federal, Mahogany, Bowfront, 4 Graduated Drawers, Cock-Beaded, 43 In.		2813.00
Chest, Federal, Mahogany, Bowfront, Oval Brasses, French Feet, c.1810, 38 x 40 x 21 In.		915.00
Chest, Federal, Mahogany, Cherry, String Inlays, New England, c.1800, 36 x 39 In.		859.00
Chest, Federal, Mahogany, Drawers, String Inlay, Scalloped Skirt, c.1800, 12 x 13 x 6 In.		1175.00

Chest, Federal, Mahogany, Line Strung, 4 Graduated Drawers, c.1800, 35 x 39 In. ....*illus*	2880.00
Chest, Federal, Maple, 4 Drawers, 3 Recessed, Bracket Feet, 35 x 42 In.	649.00
Chest, Federal, Mixed Woods, 4 Drawers, Inlaid Initials, c.1840, 42 x 40 In.	1380.00
Chest, Federal Style, Mahogany, 4 Drawers, 40 x 43 ¼ x 20 ⅝ In.	748.00
Chest, Federal, Tiger Maple, Bowfront, 43 ¼ In.	4750.00
Chest, Federal, Walnut, 4 Graduated Drawers, Inlay, Shaped Skirt, c.1830, 42 x 41 In.	330.00
Chest, Federal, Walnut, Pine, 4 Drawers, Shaped Skirt, c.1820, 17 x 15 In.	6565.00
Chest, Federal, Walnut, Pine, 7 Drawers, Inlay, Southern, c.1820, 42 x 41 In.	9780.00
Chest, French Empire Style, Mahogany Veneer, Marble, Brass, 3 Drawers, c.1810, 34 x 46 In. .	2960.00
Chest, G. Stickley, 2 Over 3 Drawers, Paneled Sides, 42 x 36 x 20 In.	6600.00
Chest, G. Stickley, No. 622, 2 Over 4 Drawers, Dark Brown, 41 x 51 In.	4600.00
Chest, G. Stickley, No. 627, Oak, 2 Short Over 4 Long Drawers, 53 x 40 In.	11400.00
Chest, George I, Burl, Double, 6 Drawers, Engraved Brasses, Bun Feet, 35 x 66 x 24 In.	8050.00
Chest, George III, Mahogany, 2 Short Over 3 Graduated Long Drawers, 35 x 37 In.	2280.00
Chest, George III, Mahogany, 4 Drawers, Cock-Beaded, Serpentine Front, 33 x 39 In.	6600.00
Chest, George III, Mahogany, 5 Drawers, Bracket Feet, 40 x 40 x 21 In.	1200.00
Chest, George III, Mahogany, 5 Drawers, Inlaid Crossband, Columns, c.1770, 33 x 36 In.	474.00
Chest, George III, Mahogany, 5 Drawers, Quarter Fan Inlay, Fluted Pilaster, 33 x 43 x 21 In. ..	1400.00
Chest, George III, Mahogany, 5 Drawers, Satinwood Bands, England, 1800s, 43 x 46 In.	518.00
Chest, George III, Mahogany, Bowfront, 2 Over 2 Drawers, Cock-Beaded, 35 x 34 x 19 In.	717.00
Chest, George III, Mahogany, Bowfront, 4 Graduated Drawers, Early 1800s, 32 x 30 In.	366.00
Chest, George III, Mahogany, Bowfront, 6 Drawers, Late 1700s, 37 x 46 In.	360.00
Chest, George III, Mahogany, Double Banded, 4 Drawers, 1800s, 38 x 39 In. ....*illus*	1140.00
Chest, George III, Mahogany, Dressing Slide, 1700s, 30 x 33 In.	2468.00
Chest, George III, Mahogany Inlay, 5 Drawers, Ogee Bracket Feet, 1800s, 41 x 50 In.	823.00
Chest, George III, Mahogany, Pullout Slide, 4 Graduated Drawers, England, c.1790, 34 x 37 In. .	1380.00
Chest, George III, Mahogany, Serpentine, 3 Drawers, Fluted Stiles, Bracket Feet, 30 x 39 In. ...	575.00
Chest, George III, Mahogany, Serpentine, 4 Graduated Drawers, c.1800, 41 x 45 In.	2530.00
Chest, George III, Oak, Mahogany Veneers, 5 Drawers, Bracket Feet, 39 x 36 x 19 In.	1300.00
Chest, George III, Pine, Banded Rectangular Top, 4 Drawers, Bracket Feet, 34 x 23 In.	1080.00
Chest, George III Style, Burl, Oak, 2 Short Drawers, 3 Long, 35 x 41 x 19 In.	2280.00
Chest, George III Style, Mahogany, 2 Short Drawers, 3 Drawers, 36 x 34 x 19 In.	1200.00
Chest, George III Style, Mahogany, Bowfront, French Feet, c.1875, 34 x 35 x 22 In.	1035.00
Chest, George III Style, Pine, 4 Drawers, Bracket Feet, Late 1800s, 33 x 22 x 18 In.	990.00
Chest, George III Style, Walnut, Mahogany, Banded, 4 Drawers, Bracket Feet, 24 x 16 In., Pair .	1680.00
Chest, George III, Walnut Inlay, 3 Over 3 Graduated Drawers, Fluted Corners, 67 x 45 In.	2400.00
Chest, Georgian, Burl Walnut, 6 Drawers, Herringbone Inlay, Bracket Feet, 1720s, 40 x 32 In. .	1860.00
Chest, Georgian, Mahogany, Bowfront, 2 Short Over 3 Graduated Drawers, 37 x 42 In.	1293.00
Chest, Georgian, Mahogany, Quarter Patera Inlay, 2 Over 3 Drawers, Ireland, 33 x 34 In.	657.00
Chest, Georgian, Oak, Burled Walnut Veneer, 4 Drawers, Eng., 18th Century, 39 x 42 In.	403.00
Chest, Georgian, Walnut, 2 Over 3 Drawers, Beaded Edge, 42 x 18 x 37 In.	837.00
Chest, German Baroque, 3 Drawers, Applied Husk Swags, Bun Feet, c.1720, 36 x 51 In.	2196.00
Chest, Gothic Revival, Oak, Carved Tracery Panels, Hinged Lid, Stile Feet, 25 x 53 In.	403.00
Chest, Grain Painted, Footed, 19th Century, 23 x 36 In.	150.00
Chest, Grain Painted, Pine, 4 Drawers, New England, c.1800, 46 x 41 In.	529.00
Chest, Hepplewhite, 3 Drawers, c.1790, 11 x 12 In.	411.00
Chest, Hepplewhite, Blue Paint, 4 Drawers, French Feet, 19th Century, 39 x 41 x 21 In.	1065.00
Chest, Hepplewhite, Cherry, 4 Drawers, Scalloped Apron, French Feet, 37 x 42 x 21 In.	960.00
Chest, Hepplewhite, Cherry, 4 Drawers, Scalloped Skirt, 37 x 38 x 17 In.	452.00
Chest, Hepplewhite, Cherry, Drawers, String Inlay, French Feet, c.1800, 36 x 45 In.	587.00
Chest, Hepplewhite, Cherry, Scalloped Aprons, Dovetailed, French Feet, c.1810, 37 x 41 x 20 In.	441.00
Chest, Hepplewhite, Cock-Beaded, French Feet, String Inlays, 4 Drawers, 1700s, 33 x 43 In.	805.00
Chest, Hepplewhite, Curly Maple, Maple, Pine, Bowfront, 4 Drawers, Shaped Feet, 41 x 37 In. .	1763.00
Chest, Hepplewhite, Curly Maple, Poplar, 4 Graduated Drawers, Ohio, 1900, 38 x 39 In.	353.00
Chest, Hepplewhite, Mahogany, 4 Drawers, French Feet, England, c.1830, 30 x 25 In.	860.00
Chest, Hepplewhite, Mahogany, 4 Graduated Cock-Beaded Drawers, c.1810, 36 x 43 In.	1116.00
Chest, Hepplewhite, Mahogany, 5 Drawer, Banded, Inlaid Top, England, 1800s, 41 x 40 In.	575.00
Chest, Hepplewhite, Mahogany, 5 Drawers, Bracket Feet, England, 1800s, 44 x 40 In.	1035.00
Chest, Hepplewhite, Mahogany, Bowfront, 4 Drawers, J. & T. Seymour, 38 In.	5900.00
Chest, Hepplewhite, Mahogany, Line Inlays, Shaped Skirt, 5 Drawers, Eng., 1800s, 39 x 43 In. .	1380.00
Chest, Hepplewhite, Mahogany, Oak, Pine, 43 ¾ x 51 ½ x 9 ¾ In.	4140.00
Chest, Hepplewhite, Mahogany Veneer, Graduated Drawers, c.1815, 35 x 43 In. ....*illus*	764.00
Chest, Hepplewhite, Red & Black Grain Painted, Birch, Pine, Backsplash, c.1820s, 14 x 14 In. .	499.00
Chest, Italian Baroque, Walnut, Inlaid, 3 Paneled Drawers, 38 x 40 In.	1380.00
Chest, Jacobean, Oak, Geometric Paneled Drawers, 33 ½ x 37 ¼ x 22 ¾ In.	948.00
Chest, Jacobean Style, Oak, 3 Graduated Drawers, Bracket Feet, England, 38 x 37 x 21 In.	504.00

Furniture, Chest, Federal, Mahogany, Line Strung, 4 Graduated Drawers, c.1800, 35 x 39 In. $2880.00

Furniture, Chest, George III, Mahogany, Double Banded, 4 Drawers, 1800s, 38 x 39 In. $1140.00

Furniture, Chest, Hepplewhite, Mahogany Veneer, Graduated Drawers, c.1815, 35 x 43 In. $764.00

Furniture, Chest, Lift Top, Yellow Pine, Rosehead Nail Construction, N.C., c.1740, 22 x 42 In. $1265.00

Furniture, Chest, Pine, Drawers, Sienna Paint, 1700s, 39 x 26 In. $2832.00

Furniture, Chest, Queen Anne, Cherry, Pine, Molded Cornice, 5 Over 3 Drawers, c.1740, 72 x 38 In. $3055.00

Furniture, Chest, Silver, Mahogany, Lift Top, Drawers, Doors, Chinese, 1900s, 30 x 22 In. $531.00

Furniture, Chest, Stepped Panels, Carved Rosettes, Bronze, Belgium, 32 x 24 In. $707.00

Chest, Kittinger, Chippendale Style, Paneled Sides, 3 Over 2 Drawers, Bracket Feet, 32 x 53 In.	2074.00
Chest, Lift Top, Walnut, Yellow Pine, Panel Front, Back, Sides, Open Interior, 1800s, 15 x 38 In.	316.00
Chest, Lift Top, White Pine, Drawer, Blue, Cream Paint, 1800s, 28 x 49 In.	1265.00
Chest, Lift Top, Yellow Pine, Paneled, Shaped Feet, Brown Paint, c.1810, 29 x 48 In.	978.00
Chest, Lift Top, Yellow Pine, Poplar, Scalloped Skirt, Green Paint, 24 x 42 ¾ x 19 In.	1093.00
Chest, Lift Top, Yellow Pine, Rosehead Nail Construction, N.C., c.1740, 22 x 42 In. ....*illus*	1265.00
Chest, Lingerie, Arts & Crafts, Swivel Mirror, 2 Doors Over, 4 Drawers, Narrow, 23 x 67 In.	1020.00
Chest, Lingerie, Louis XV, Kingwood, Inlay, Coffered Serpentine Top, 7 Drawers, 63 x 30 In.	575.00
Chest, Louis XV, Cherry, Hinged Top, Wells, Drawers, Writing Slide, 28 x 23 x 16 In.	296.00
Chest, Louis XV Style, Multicolored, Faux Marble, 3 Drawers, Cabriole Feet, 36 x 49 In.	4320.00
Chest, Louis XVI Style, Fruitwood, 5 Drawers, Fluted Pilasters, 45 x 25 x 15 In.	329.00
Chest, Mahogany, 2 Over 3 Drawers, Bracket Feet, 1850s, 41 x 43 x 20 In.	1025.00
Chest, Mahogany, 3 Drawers, Bracket Feet, England, c.1900s, 12 ½ In.	230.00
Chest, Mahogany, 4 Beaded Drawers, 3 Lower Drawers, Inlay, England, 1800s, 47 x 71 In.	1062.00
Chest, Mahogany, 4 Graduated Drawers, Brass Pulls, French Feet, c.1820, 48 x 45 In.	519.00
Chest, Mahogany, 6 Drawers, Wood Inlays, Brass Pulls, England, c.1820, 46 x 48 In.	1380.00
Chest, Mahogany, 7 Drawers, Bracket Feet, 40 x 49 x 20 In.	300.00
Chest, Mahogany, 7 Drawers, Turned Feet, Paneled, 45 x 42 x 21 In.	179.00
Chest, Mahogany, Beaded Molding, Ball Feet, Scissor Hinges, c.1815, 31 x 26 x 19 In.	2937.00
Chest, Mahogany, Block Front, Thumb-Molded Top, 4 Drawers, c.1770, 32 x 31 ½ In.	49140.00
Chest, Mahogany, Breakfront Top, Lower Drawers, Twist Turnings, c.1880, 48 x 48 In.	546.00
Chest, Mahogany, Carved, Applied Column, Leaf Shape Corbel, 6 Drawers, 62 x 50 In.	345.00
Chest, Mahogany, Frieze Drawer Over Recessed Drawers, Glass Knobs, 1800s, 42 x 44 In.	531.00
Chest, Mahogany, Ogee Molded Drawers, 3 Long Drawers, Scrolling Corbels, 46 x 52 In.	460.00
Chest, Mahogany, Poplar, Serpentine Front, 4 Graduated Drawers, Virginia, 38 x 42 In.	4140.00
Chest, Mahogany, Sandwich Glass Pulls, Scrolled Legs, Hanky Drawers, c.1850, 42 x 41 In.	265.00
Chest, Mahogany, Serpentine, Ogee Molded Frieze Drawer, 5 Drawers, Scotland, 50 x 51 In.	633.00
Chest, Map, 9 Map Drawers, 28 x 20 In.	184.00
Chest, Maple, 6-Board, Molded Top, Cutout Ends, New England, c.1790, 25 x 41 In.	533.00
Chest, Maple, Pine, Red Paint, New England, c.1790, 57 x 36 In.	1422.00
Chest, Marriage, Drop Front, Needlepoint, Barley Twist Legs, Bun Feet, 53 x 33 In.	1920.00
Chest, Meeks, Mahogany, 5 Drawers, Serpentine, French Feet, 40 x 40 In.	2350.00
Chest, Mixed Woods, 4 Drawers, Bracket Feet, W.H. Rutland, Beaded Frame, 33 x 41 In.	1175.00
Chest, Mule, Cherry, 3 Drawers, Lift Top, Tapered Legs, Mid 19th Century, 35 x 37 x 19 In.	1370.00
Chest, Mule, Chippendale, Pine, Faux & Real Drawers, Painted, c.1808, 45 x 44 In.	1410.00
Chest, Mule, Mixed Woods, 2 Drawers, Old Red Paint, New Eng., c.1740, 39 x 43 In.	489.00
Chest, Mule, Oak, Lift Top Paneled Front, 2 Drawers, 26 x 55 In.	403.00
Chest, Mule, Pine, 2 Drawers, Black Over Yellow Paint, 19th Century, 37 x 42 In.	4935.00
Chest, Mule, Pine, Drawer, Lift Lid, Green Paint, New England, c.1830, 38 x 38 In.	764.00
Chest, Mule, White Pine, Blanket Chest, 2 Drawers, Grain Paint, c.1800, 38 x 44 In.	764.00
Chest, Neoclassical, Cherry, Outset Drawer Over 3 Graduated, Early 1800s, 49 x 41 In.	294.00
Chest, Neoclassical, Mahogany Veneer, Inset Mirror, 7 Drawers, c.1810, 21 x 19 In.	411.00
Chest, Oak, 3 Drawers, Bracket Feet, England, 42 x 38 In.	288.00
Chest, Oak, Carved Panel Front, England, c.1720, 23 x 27 In., Child's	690.00
Chest, Oak, Drawer, Wrought Iron Hinges, Eng., 1700s, 14 x 22 In.	1528.00
Chest, Oak, Gray, Marble Top, Grain Mahogany, Drawers, France, 1800s, 30 x 30 In.	558.00
Chest, Oak, Lift Top, Dovetailed, Candle Box, Bracket Feet, England, 12 x 26 x 15 In.	403.00
Chest, Oak, Maple, Cedar, 2 Drawers, Panels, Plymouth, Mass., c.1690, 32 x 53 In.	50000.00
Chest, Oak, Pine, Painted, Drawer, c.1670-1700, 30 ¾ x 43 x 20 In.	7110.00
Chest, Oak, Walnut, Paneled Sides & Top, Inlay, 18th Century, 30 x 56 In.	3978.00
Chest, Oak, Walnut, Poplar, 2 Drawers, Tiered Edge, 8 ¾ x 8 In., Child's	275.00
Chest, Oak, Wrought Iron Handles, Carved, Molding, Ball Feet, c.1800, 22 x 55 x 23 In.	203.00
Chest, Oriental, Carved Scenic Panels, c.1975, 40 x 24 x 21 In.	147.00
Chest, P. Evans, Polished Chrome, 3 Drawers, Tiled Design, 26 x 36 In.	2040.00
Chest, Painted, Shaped Case, 4 Long Drawers, Gilt Highlights, c.1780, 40 x 51 In.	3525.00
Chest, Painted, Trees, Horse, Rider, Tombstone Panels, Berks County, Pa., c.1790, 24 x 48 In.	7020.00
Chest, Papelera, Walnut, Multicolored, Balustrade Gallery, Geometric Inlay, 30 x 44 In.	3819.00
Chest, Pine, 2 Drawers, Hinged Lift Top, Cutout Feet, Painted, c.1750, 44 x 36 In.	5925.00
Chest, Pine, 3 Drawers, White Paint, 19th Century, 35 x 41 In.	220.00
Chest, Pine, 4 Drawers, Turned Pulls, Painted, New Hampshire, c.1820, 40 x 30 In.	1007.00
Chest, Pine, 6-Board, Bracket Feet, Blue Paint, New England, c.1820, 20 x 36 In.	770.00
Chest, Pine, 6-Board, Lift Top, Till, Cutout Base, Grain Paint, Mass., c.1820, 22 x 39 In.	356.00
Chest, Pine, Banded, Fluted Frieze, Drawers, Paneled, Bracket Feet, c.1875, 42 x 41 x 21 In.	1560.00
Chest, Pine, Carved, Curved Reeded Frieze, New England, c.1790, 39 x 39 In.	593.00
Chest, Pine, Drawers, Sienna Paint, 1700s, 39 x 26 In. ....*illus*	2832.00
Chest, Pine, Lift Top, 2 Drawers, Cutout Base, Red Paint, c.1750, 43 x 38 In.	889.00

Chest, Pine, Original Lock, Handles, Grain Painted, 1800s, 11 x 27 In. 264.00
Chest, Pine, Painted, 4 Drawers, Salmon, Potato Stamp, Pa., 50 x 40 In. 5850.00
Chest, Pine, Painted White, 3 Drawers, 19th Century, 35 x 41 In. 207.00
Chest, Poplar, 2 Over 3 Graduated Drawers, Turned Columns, 1800s, 14 x 14 In. 575.00
Chest, Poplar, 6 Drawers, Half Columns, Painted, Red Yellow Grain, 1850s, 47 x 23 In. 293.00
Chest, Poplar, Blue Paint, Lift Top, Tang Hinges, 1 Drawer, 1848, 14 x 15 In. 1150.00
Chest, Poplar, Molded Edge Top, 5 Graduated Drawers, Bracket Feet, c.1800, 49 x 43 In. 690.00
Chest, Poplar, Yellow Pine, Shaped Splash, 4 Drawers, Inlay, Georgia, 1800s, 46 x 40 In. 1035.00
Chest, Queen Anne, Bonnet Top, Curly Walnut, Pinecone Finial, c.1750, 87 x 44 In. 15275.00
Chest, Queen Anne, Cherry, Pine, Molded Cornice, 5 Over 3 Drawers, c.1740, 72 x 38 In. ....illus 3055.00
Chest, Queen Anne, Flat Top, Walnut Veneer Curly Maple, c.1740, 69 x 40 In. 10575.00
Chest, Queen Anne, Maple, 6 Drawers, Cabriole Legs, Mass., c.1800, 58 x 37 In. 2015.00
Chest, Queen Anne, Maple, Figured, 8 Drawers, High Legs, 1761, 68 x 39 In. 12500.00
Chest, Queen Anne, Pine, Lift Lid, Raised Panel Case, Drawer, N.Y., c.1760, 40 x 41 In. 4914.00
Chest, Queen Anne Style, Tiger Maple, Graduated Drawers, Reeded, 37 x 42 x 22 In. 777.00
Chest, Queen Anne, Sycamore, Applied Beaded Facade, c.1750, 37 x 41 In. 948.00
Chest, Queen Anne, Tiger Maple, c.1790, 70 ½ x 38 In. 2607.00
Chest, Queen Anne, Tiger Maple, Molded Cornice, Valanced Skirt, c.1760, 74 x 39 In. 5036.00
Chest, Queen Anne, Walnut, 2 Over 1 Drawer, Cabriole Legs, Pad Feet, 30 x 43 x 19 In. 356.00
Chest, Queen Anne, Walnut, 4 Drawers, Herringbone Banded, 30 x 38 In. 3840.00
Chest, Queen Anne, Walnut, 6 Drawers, Molded Top, Bracket Feet, c.1750, 49 x 39 In. 1880.00
Chest, Queen Anne, Walnut Veneer, Maple, Drawers, Cabriole Legs, 39 x 20 ¾ In. 5925.00
Chest, Rectangular Top, 3 Long Drawers, Turned Front Feet, 1800s, England, 41 x 43 In. 413.00
Chest, Renaissance Revival, Oak, Carved Trellis, Hinged Top, 8 Drawers, c.1900, 35 x 58 In. ... 711.00
Chest, Renaissance Revival, Ornate Carving, 3 Drawers, Figural Pulls, 38 x 32 In. 1020.00
Chest, Renaissance Revival, Rosewood, Marble Top, 4 Drawers, Carving, 1800s, 40 x 48 In. 1293.00
Chest, Renaissance Revival, Walnut, 8 Drawers, Plinth Base, 60 x 48 x 21 In. 1500.00
Chest, Robsjohn-Gibbings, 3 Drawers, Rounded Trim, Widdicomb, 19 x 31 In., Pair.............. 390.00
Chest, Rococo Revival, Burl Walnut, Bombe Case, Drawers, 35 x 56 x 25 In. 3851.00
Chest, Salem, Mahogany, Tiered Drawers, Pineapple Columns, Carvings, c.1890, 52 x 46 In. ... 518.00
Chest, Satinwood, Overhanging Top, 3 Drawers, Curved Skirt, England, c.1880, 31 x 37 In. 800.00
Chest, Sewing, Victorian, Walnut, 8 Drawers, Brass Handles, Drawers, 41 x 30 x 21 In. 598.00
Chest, Shaker, Butternut, Poplar, 4 Drawers, Porcelain Pulls, Painted, c.1850, 29 x 29 In. 1989.00
Chest, Shaker, Cherry, 6 Drawers, Dovetailed, 36 x 75 In. 1050.00
Chest, Shaker, Pine, 6 Drawers, Dovetailed, Beading, Iron Pulls, 62 x 37 In. 950.00
Chest, Shaker, Pine, Poplar, 3 Drawers, Red Stain, Canted Feet, Conn., c.1850, 37 x 42 In. 2633.00
Chest, Shaker, Pine, Poplar, 3 Drawers, Shaped Back, Brown, c.1850, 31 x 39 In. 936.00
Chest, Shaker, Pine, Till, Bootjack Ends, Dark Stain, 19 x 34 In. 644.00
Chest, Sheraton, Bowfront, 4 Drawers, Turned Stiles, c.1800, 36 x 44 x 24 In. 1750.00
Chest, Sheraton, Cherry, 4 Drawers, Footed, 19th Century, 45 x 41 In. 145.00
Chest, Sheraton, Figured Cherry, Tambour Doors, 3 Drawers, 1800s, 20 x 17 In. 1410.00
Chest, Sheraton, Mahogany, 4 Drawers, Scalloped Apron, Turned Legs, 42 x 39 x 19 In. 600.00
Chest, Sheraton, Mahogany, 5 Drawers, Ogee Bracket Feet, 40 x 45 In. 575.00
Chest, Sheraton, Mahogany, Bowfront, 4 Cock-Beaded Drawers, c.1820, 40 x 41 In. 1116.00
Chest, Sheraton, Mahogany, Bowfront, 4 Drawers, Reeded Stiles, c.1820, 39 x 42 In. 940.00
Chest, Sheraton, Mahogany, Bowfront, 4 Drawers, c.1800, 40 x 41 x 21 In. 1100.00
Chest, Sheraton, Mahogany, Bowfront, 4 Drawers, c.1820, 38 x 42 In. 2800.00
Chest, Sheraton, Mahogany, Bowfront, Inlay, 4 Drawers, Columns, Eng., c.1810, 42 x 44 In. 4100.00
Chest, Sheraton, Mahogany, Line Inlay, 4 Drawers, Ring-Turned Feet, c.1825, 36 x 42 In. 1420.00
Chest, Sheraton, Mahogany, Scalloped Back, Drawers, Turned Legs, 52 x 43 In. 805.00
Chest, Sheraton, Sugar, Cherry, Poplar, Breadboard Lid, 1800s, 31 x 22 In. 705.00
Chest, Sheraton, Walnut, 4 Drawers, Footed, Pa., c.1870, 39 x 40 In. 395.00
Chest, Sheraton, Walnut, Poplar, 6 Drawers, Shaped Skirt, Pa., c.1830, 45 x 41 In. 764.00
Chest, Silver, Mahogany, Lift Top, Drawers, Doors, Chinese, 1900s, 30 x 22 In. ....illus 531.00
Chest, Softwood, Salmon Grain Paint, Interior Till, Dovetailed, Jaw Lock, c.1810, 29 x 52 In. . 825.00
Chest, Spice, Chippendale, Walnut, Door, Ogee Bracket Feet, c.1770, 24 x 17 In. 8900.00
Chest, Spice, Rosewood, Geometrics, Brass Mounts, Portugal, 18th Century, 30 x 54 In. 810.00
Chest, Stepped Panels, Carved Rosettes, Bronze, Belgium, 32 x 24 In. ....illus 707.00
Chest, Storage, Pine, 2-Paneled Case, Lift Lid, Tapered Feet, 1800s, 35 x 26 In. 176.00
Chest, Sugar, Cherry, Drawer, Divided Interior, Hinged Lid, Tennessee, 29 x 27 x 18 In. 2300.00
Chest, Sugar, Cherry, Hinged Lid, Drawer, Divided Interior, Tenn., 1800s, 36 x 32 In. 1265.00
Chest, Sugar, Cherry, Hinged Top, Escutcheon, Tenn., 1800s, 35 x 31 In. ....illus 1380.00
Chest, Sugar, Cherry, Poplar, Lift Top, Fitted Interior, Lower Shelf, Drawers, c.1830, 31 x 32 In. 1175.00
Chest, Sugar, Cherry, Poplar, Yellow Pine, Hinged Top, Tenn., 1800s, 29 x 27 In. ....illus 2360.00
Chest, Sugar, Poplar, Yellow Pine, Hinged, Fitted, Panels, Stain, Georgia, c.1850, 29 x 30 In. ... 13800.00
Chest, Sugar, Sheraton, 3 Drawers, Turned Legs, 20th Century, 31 x 31 x 18 In. 235.00

Furniture, Chest, Sugar, Cherry,
Hinged Top, Escutcheon, Tenn., 1800s,
35 x 31 In.
$1380.00

F

Furniture, Chest, Sugar, Cherry, Poplar,
Yellow Pine, Hinged Top, Tenn., 1800s,
29 x 27 In.
$2360.00

Furniture, Chest, Sugar, Sheraton,
Cherry, Poplar, Lift Top, Kentucky,
c.1815, 37 x 40 In.
$3525.00

TIP
As a general rule, the drawer bottom of an eighteenth-century chest was made of two or three pieces of wood; the Victorian drawer bottom was made from a single piece. The Victorian bottom was often screwed in place.

Furniture, Chest, Sugar, Walnut, Paneled Top, Inlay, False Drawers, 16 x 16 In.
$4012.00

Furniture, Chest, Wormley, Mr. & Mrs., Mahogany, Plywood, Dunbar, 49 x 38 In.
$1020.00

Furniture, Chest-On-Chest, Chippendale, Mahogany, Secretary Drawer, c.1800, 79 x 43 In.
$2300.00

Chest, Sugar, Sheraton, Cherry, Poplar, Divided Interior, Turned Legs, c.1830, 29 x 29 In.	1528.00
Chest, Sugar, Sheraton, Cherry, Poplar, Lift Top, Kentucky, c.1815, 37 x 40 In. .... *illus*	3525.00
Chest, Sugar, Sheraton, Cherry, Yellow Pine, Drawer, Turned Legs, c.1830, 33 x 36 In.	1880.00
Chest, Sugar, Sheraton, Walnut, 2 Parts, Drawers, 29 x 31 x 19 In.	3051.00
Chest, Sugar, Walnut, Hinged Lid, Drawer, Piedmont, N.C., 32 x 25 x 17 In.	9775.00
Chest, Sugar, Walnut, Paneled Top, Inlay, False Drawers, 16 x 16 In. .... *illus*	4012.00
Chest, Tiger Maple, 5 Drawers, New England, c.1790, 46 x 38 In.	2760.00
Chest, Tiger Maple, 5 Drawers, Patina, c.1785, 45 x 36 In.	3437.00
Chest, Tiger Maple, Drawers, Columnar Support, Bail Feet, c.1800, 43 x 39 x 22 In.	568.00
Chest, Victorian, Mahogany, 2 Over 4 Drawers, Scotland, 19th Century, 51 x 45 x 23 In.	650.00
Chest, Victorian, Mahogany, 4 Drawers, Contoured Backsplash, Inlay, c.1900, 47 x 42 x 21 In.	351.00
Chest, Walnut, 2 Over 3 Graduated Drawers, Inlaid Herringbone Skirt, 39 x 39 In.	2530.00
Chest, Walnut, 4 Drawers, 2 Half Column Pilasters, Short Legs, 1800s, 43 x 47 In.	177.00
Chest, Walnut, 4 Drawers, Bench Made, 1900s, 24 x 22 In.	235.00
Chest, Walnut, 4 Graduating Drawers, Dovetailed, c.1850, 36 x 40 x 20 In.	472.00
Chest, Walnut, Banded, Rectangular, 4 Drawers, 31 x 31 x 17 In.	2280.00
Chest, Walnut, Figured, Pennsylvania, c.1790, 67 x 38 In.	13900.00
Chest, Walnut, Graduated Drawers, Columns, Ogee Bracket Feet, c.1770, 35 x 35 x 20 In.	8125.00
Chest, Walnut, Hinged Lids, 8 Drawers, Breakfronted Crown, 58 ¾ x 24 x 16 In.	657.00
Chest, Walnut, Marble Top, 9 Drawers, Flower & Leaf Inlay, Footed, Italy, 1910, 32 x 88 In.	1600.00
Chest, Walnut, Pine, 4 Graduated Drawers, Reeded Stiles, Flared Feet, c.1840, 43 x 42 In.	499.00
Chest, Walnut, Pine, Red, Brown Stain, 6 Drawers, No Pulls, Georgia, c.1830, 39 x 48 In.	3450.00
Chest, Walnut, Yellow Pine, 3 Graduated Drawers, Wooden Pulls, c.1830, 45 x 42 x 21 In.	805.00
Chest, William & Mary, Burl Walnut, 2 Over 3 Drawers, Crossband Top, Bun Feet, c.1720	4000.00
Chest, William & Mary, Pine, 4 Drawers, Bun Feet, Red Wash, c.1820, 36 x 38 In.	3408.00
Chest, William & Mary, Walnut Inlay, Laburnum, Oyster Veneer, Drawers, 31 x 37 x 23 In.	7703.00
Chest, Work, Shaker, Pine, Drawer, Square Legs, Red Paint, N.H., c.1840, 30 x 37 In.	2925.00
Chest, Work, Shaker, Walnut, Poplar, Drop Front, Drawer Interior, Top Handle, N.H., c.1865, 15 x 16 In..	1287.00
Chest, Wormley, 4 Drawers, Dunbar, c.1952, 33 x 34 x 19 In.	2450.00
Chest, Wormley, Mr. & Mrs., Mahogany, Plywood, Dunbar, 49 x 38 In. .... *illus*	1020.00
Chest, Wormley, Walnut, Brass, Pulls, Dunbar, 34 x 38 x 18 In.	1200.00
Chest, Yellow Pine, Lift Top, Interior Till, Red Paint, Georgia, c.1840, 24 x 49 In.	13800.00
Chest, Yellow Pine, Paint, Blue, Green, Lift Top, Hinged, Turned Feet, 25 x 36 In.	518.00
Chest, Yellow Pine, Poplar, 4 Drawers, Grain Painted, North Carolina, 1800s, 45 x 44 In.	1495.00
Chest, Zebra Hide, Base Molding, Bun Feet, Hinged Lid, 18 x 48 In.	1380.00
Chest-On-Chest, Baroque Style, Red Japanned, Doors, Drawers, Dutch, 98 x 72 x 25 In.	3081.00
Chest-On-Chest, Chippendale, Cherry, Bonnet Top, 10 Drawers, Connecticut, 86 x 42 In.	13750.00
Chest-On-Chest, Chippendale, Mahogany, 2-Case, 6 Over 3 Drawers, 72 x 44 In.	3105.00
Chest-On-Chest, Chippendale, Mahogany, Greek Key Cornice, England, 1700s, 70 x 42 In.	1610.00
Chest-On-Chest, Chippendale, Mahogany, Secretary Drawer, c.1800, 79 x 43 In. ....*illus*	2300.00
Chest-On-Chest, Chippendale, Tiger Maple, 9 Drawers, c.1790, 75 x 39 In.	6992.00
Chest-On-Chest, Chippendale, Walnut, 57 ¼ x 37 ¼ In.	14500.00
Chest-On-Chest, Federal, 10 Drawers, Finials, Shaped Bonnet, 83 x 36 In.	10000.00
Chest-On-Chest, George III, 6 Drawers, Writing Slide, 3 Drawers, 74 x 45 x 22 In.	8400.00
Chest-On-Chest, George III, Drop Front, Mahogany, Gadroon Crest, c.1775, 74 x 43 x 21 In. .	3120.00
Chest-On-Chest, George III, Japanned, Dentil Cornice, Painted Landscapes, 74 x 43 In.	2074.00
Chest-On-Chest, George III, Mahogany, 5 Drawers, 72 x 43 x 22 In.	1778.00
Chest-On-Chest, George III, Mahogany, 6 Drawers, Molded Cornice, 69 x 44 In.	2056.00
Chest-On-Chest, George III, Mahogany, 8 Drawers, c.1840, 75 x 44 x 24 In.	3670.00
Chest-On-Chest, George III, Mahogany, Flat Top, 2 Short Over 6 Long Drawers, 68 x 43 In. ...	1180.00
Chest-On-Chest, George III, Mahogany, Flat Top, 2 Short Over 6 Long Drawers, 78 x 44 In. ...	1770.00
Chest-On-Chest, George III, Mahogany, Fretwork Frieze, 9 Drawers, c.1790, 44 x 69 In.	2056.00
Chest-On-Chest, George III, Mahogany, Oak, Drawers, 70 x 40 x 19 In.	1800.00
Chest-On-Chest, Georgian, Drop Down Desk, Cubbyholes, 73 x 44 In.	5400.00
Chest-On-Chest, Georgian, Mahogany, 2 Sections, Shaped Skirt, French Feet, 72 x 46 In.	1955.00
Chest-On-Chest, Georgian Style, Mahogany, 8 Drawers, 73 x 41 x 20 In.	670.00
Chest-On-Chest, Mahogany, Bonnet Top, Rosettes, Spread Winged Eagle Finial, 88 x 47 In. ..	3220.00
Chest-On-Chest, Oak, 8 Drawers, 4 False Drawers, England, 80 x 41 In.	978.00
Chest-On-Chest, Queen Anne, Mahogany, Bonnet Top, 10 Drawers, 89 x 43 In.	5750.00
Chest-On-Chest, Walnut, Cornice, Reeded Corners, 3 Short, 3 Long Drawers, 73 x 43 In.	4700.00
Chest-On-Frame, Colonial Revival, Rosewood, 7 Drawers, Barley Twist Legs, Portugal, 28 x 23 In.	3200.00
Chest-On-Frame, Flame Mahogany, Drawer, Square Tapered Legs, 40 x 21 In.	1090.00
Chest-On-Frame, George II, Burl Walnut, Molded Cornice, 5 Drawers, 60 x 45 In.	1037.00
Chest-On-Frame, George III, Mahogany, Molded Crown, 6 Drawers, c.1800, 71 x 44 In.	2070.00
Chest-On-Frame, Georgian, Mahogany, Dentil Molded Cornice, Fretwork, Drawers, 69 x 44 In.	863.00
Chest-On-Frame, Jacobean Style, Oak, 5 Drawers, Panels, 47 x 30 ½ x 20 In.	359.00

Chest-On-Frame, Mahogany, Dome Top, Musical Designs, Painted, c.1900, 23 x 16 x 12 In. ..	538.00
Chest-On-Frame, Queen Anne, Inlaid Walnut, 6 Drawers, 1700s, 65 x 45 In.	3231.00
Chiffonier, Regency, Rosewood, Inlaid Brass, Pierced Shelf, Mirrored, 45 x 36 x 17 In.	2938.00
Chiffonier, Regency, Rosewood, Marquetry, Mirror, Door, 19th Century, 57 x 25 x 13 In.	1175.00
Chifforobe, Mahogany, 2 Door Wardrobe, 8 Drawers, Mirror, c.1910, 57 x 54 x 22 In. ....*illus*	823.00
China Press, Cover Molded Cornice, 2 Paneled Doors, 2 Drawers, 90 x 41 In.	7050.00
China Press, Federal, Walnut, Glazed Doors, 2 Paneled Doors, Virginia, 87 x 41 In.	2300.00
China Press, Federal, Walnut, Poplar, Paneled, Glazed Doors, Va., 87 x 41 In. ....*illus*	2360.00
Cistern, George III Style, Mahogany, Oval, Double Brass Banding, c.1900, 8 x 25 In.	1140.00
Coat Rack, Bentwood, England, Late 1800s, 84 x 35 In.	1650.00
Coat Rack, Brass, Round Swivel Rack, Hooks, Tubular Stem, Arched Supports, c.1875, 80 ½ In.	235.00
Coat Rack, Eames, Metal, 6 Rods, Wood Sphere, 70 ½ In.	260.00
Coat Rack, J. Adnet, Leather Over Metal, 5 Hooks, Bamboo Ends, France, 28 x 4 ½ In.	2400.00
Coat Rack, S. Werner, Chromed Steel, 8 Branches, Plastic Pegs, Fritz Hansen, c.1971, 26 x 76 In.	360.00
Coffer, Baroque, Elm, Chestnut, Hinged, Carved Panels, 17th Century, 27 x 73 x 23 In.	518.00
Coffer, George III, Mahogany, Hinged, Drawer, Brass Handles, 14 ¾ x 21 ½ x 12 ½ In.	577.00
Coffer, Gothic Revival, Carved, Burl Walnut, Stepped Lid, 7 x 11 ¾ In.	294.00
Coffer, Louis XV Style, Fruitwood, Hinged Lid, Paneled Sides, 28 x 74 In.	4230.00
Coffer, Walnut, Griffins, Carved, Crest, Claw Feet, Continental, 13 ½ x 24 In.	505.00
Commode, Aesthetic Revival, Burl Walnut, Carved, Marble Top, Drawer, c.1870, 18 x 32 In. ...	2350.00
Commode, Aesthetic Revival, Burl Walnut, Marble Top, Paneled Compartment, 32 x 18 In. ...	2350.00
Commode, Art Deco, Oak, Parchment, Marble, Gilt Bronze, France, 1935, 32 x 37 x 18 In.	8760.00
Commode, Art Deco, Walnut, Demilune, 3 Drawers, Splayed Legs, 44 x 42 x 21 In.	1200.00
Commode, Bedside, Mahogany, Blocked Corners, 4 Drawers, 33 x 16 In., Pair	1103.00
Commode, Bedside, Sheraton, Mahogany, Bowfront, Drawer, Chamber Pot, 1800, 34 In.	1840.00
Commode, Biedermeier, Mixed Woods, 2 Doors, 2 Drawers, Moldings, 1800s, 40 x 52 In.	1380.00
Commode, Bombe Case, Drawers, Cabriole Legs, c.1900, 29 x 35 x 19 In.	2640.00
Commode, Bombe, Louis XV Style, Kingwood, Marble Top, Drawers, 32 x 46 x 19 In.	388.00
Commode, Bombe, Louis XV Style, Kingwood, Marquetry, Serpentine, Marble Top, 34 x 37 In. ..	259.00
Commode, Bombe, Louis XV Style, Medallion, Drawers, Marble Top, c.1930, 35 x 47 In.	960.00
Commode, Bombe, Louis XVI Style, Marble Top, 35 x 50 x 23 In.	956.00
Commode, Bombe, Marble Top, Inlay, Bronze Ormolu, France, 1820s, 37 x 47 x 21 In.	2600.00
Commode, Bombe, Painted Scenes, Flowers, 3 Drawers, Venetian, 30 x 28 In. .... *illus*	1416.00
Commode, Bombe, Red Lacquer, Gilt Chinoiserie, Marble Top, 34 x 49 In.	2645.00
Commode, Bombe, Regency, Ebonized, Marble, Gilt, Oriental Landscapes, 34 x 50 In. ....*illus*	4800.00
Commode, Bombe, Walnut, Molded Edge, 4 Drawers, 32 x 50 In.	5280.00
Commode, Burled Walnut, Molded Cornice Top, Shaped Apron, Block Feet, 40 x 51 In.	1140.00
Commode, Charles X, Fruitwood, Black, White Veined Marble Top, Frieze Drawer, 37 x 48 In. ...	4255.00
Commode, Chippendale, Mahogany, Pullout Drawer, Tambour Door, Eng., c.1790, 30 x 21 In. ...	518.00
Commode, Chippendale Style, Shaped Gallery, Tambour Doors, Chamber Pot, 31 x 24 In. *illus*	826.00
Commode, Demilune, George III, Mahogany, D-Form Top, Doors, Drawer, c.1800, 35 x 36 In. ..	388.00
Commode, Dutch Neoclassical, Mahogany, Rosewood, Kingwood, Marble, 37 x 45 In.	4080.00
Commode, Eastlake Style, Ebonized, Marble Top, Paneled Drawers, 34 x 39 x 18 In.	388.00
Commode, Empire, Fruitwood, Marble Top, 4 Long Drawers, 37 x 50 In.	3360.00
Commode, Empire, Mahogany, Marble Top, 3 Drawers, 35 x 51 In.	3120.00
Commode, Federal, Mahogany, Corner, Blue & White Bowl, 3 Drawers, c.1815, 38 x 26 x 15 In. ..	413.00
Commode, French Provincial, Molded Top, Paneled Sides, Paneled Doors, 36 x 48 In.	115.00
Commode, Fruitwood, Plank Top, Bow Center, Drawers, Shaped Apron, c.1750, 33 x 47 In.	6300.00
Commode, George III, Mahogany, Gallery, Pierced Handles, Shelf, Drawer, 31 x 22 x 18 In.	420.00
Commode, George III, Mahogany, Pierced Handles, Cupboard, Drawer, 30 x 21 x 17 In.	510.00
Commode, George III, Mahogany, Scalloped Gallery, Inlaid Doors, 29 x 20 In., Pair	2468.00
Commode, Italian Neoclassical, Kingwood, Marquetry, Frieze Drawer, 36 x 51 In.	2629.00
Commode, Japanned, Painted, Scenic, Maitland Smith, 32 x 29 ½ In. .... *illus*	234.00
Commode, Kingwood, Marquetry, Marble, 3 Drawers, Flowers, Geometric Designs, 37 x 46 In. .	575.00
Commode, Kingwood, Rosewood, Ebony Inlays, 2 Over 2 Drawers, 30 x 36 x 19 In.	1912.00
Commode, Louis Philippe, Mahogany, Marble Top, 4 Drawers, Bun Feet, 36 x 51 In.	1150.00
Commode, Louis Philippe, Rosewood, Cylinder, Gres De Ste. Anne Marble Top, 29 x 15 In.	705.00
Commode, Louis XV, Bronze Mounted, Parquetry, Serpentine Marble Top, 32 x 25 In., Pair.....	1528.00
Commode, Louis XV, Fruitwood, Gallery Top, Shaped Skirt, Cabriole Legs, 30 x 16 In.	441.00
Commode, Louis XV, Fruitwood, Serpentine Molded Top, Raised Panel Drawers, 50 x 25 In. ...	470.00
Commode, Louis XV, Fruitwood, Serpentine Top, Molded Drawers, 38 x 50 In.	3995.00
Commode, Louis XV, Kingwood, Marble, Frieze, Drawers, Musical Trophies, c.1900, 34 x 25 In. .	840.00
Commode, Louis XV, Kingwood, Marble Top, 3 Drawers, Banding, Inlays, 35 x 43 In.	2400.00
Commode, Louis XV, Kingwood, Serpentine, Marble Top, 3 Drawers, c.1810, 35 x 52 In.	1725.00
Commode, Louis XV, Painted, Green, Roses, Angels, Scrolls, Bombe, 30 x 28 x 14 In.	800.00
Commode, Louis XV, Provincial, Cherry, Serpentine Front, Chinoiserie Pulls, 35 x 48 In.	2745.00

F

Furniture, Chifforobe, Mahogany, 2 Door Wardrobe, 8 Drawers, Mirror, c.1910, 57 x 54 x 22 In. $823.00

Furniture, China Press, Federal, Walnut, Poplar, Paneled, Glazed Doors, Va., 87 x 41 In. $2360.00

Furniture, Commode, Bombe, Painted Scenes, Flowers, 3 Drawers, Venetian, 30 x 28 In. $1416.00

Furniture, Commode, Bombe, Regency, Ebonized, Marble, Gilt, Oriental Landscapes, 34 x 50 In. $4800.00

Furniture, Commode, Chippendale Style, Shaped Gallery, Tambour Doors, Chamber Pot, 31 x 24 In. $826.00

Furniture, Commode, Japanned, Painted, Scenic, Maitland Smith, 32 x 29 ½ In. $234.00

Commode, Louis XV Provincial, Walnut, Bronze Mounts, Serpentine Front, 32 x 51 In.	3081.00
Commode, Louis XV Style, Marble Top, 2 Drawers, Cabriole Legs, 31 x 30 x 16 In.	269.00
Commode, Louis XV Style, Marble Top, Brass Mounts, 39 x 15 In., Pair ....*illus*	690.00
Commode, Louis XV Style, Parquetry, Marble Top, 2 Drawers, 29 ¾ x 23 x 13 ¾ In.	478.00
Commode, Louis XV, Tulipwood, Gilt Bronze Mounted, Marble Top, 34 x 21 In.	732.00
Commode, Louis XV, Walnut, 3 Drawers, Bronze Pulls, 35 x 49 x 23 In.	4266.00
Commode, Louis XV, Walnut, Marble Top, Scalloped Front, 4 Drawers, c.1790, 38 x 51 In.	8100.00
Commode, Louis XV, Walnut, Serpentine Top, Scroll Floral Carved, c.1810, 38 x 49 In.	4700.00
Commode, Louis XVI, Elm, 2 Drawers, Fluted Fronts & Legs, 30 x 38 In.	2070.00
Commode, Louis XVI, Fruitwood, Carved, Serpentine, Molded Top, 33 x 45 In.	2585.00
Commode, Louis XVI, Fruitwood, Marble Top, 3 Paneled Drawers, 35 x 48 x 21 In.	2115.00
Commode, Louis XVI, Mahogany, Brass Mounted, Marble Top, c.1800, 35 x 48 In.	1220.00
Commode, Louis XVI, Mahogany, Marble Top, 3 Drawers, Herringbone Inlay, 35 x 20 In.	3840.00
Commode, Louis XVI Style, Fruitwood, Drawers, Stop Fluted Uprights, c.1875, 31 x 19 x 13 In.	1200.00
Commode, Louis XVI Style, Marble Top Inlaid, 2 Drawers, 29 ½ x 24 x 13 ½ In.	418.00
Commode, Louis XVI Style, Marble Top, Marquetry, Drawer, Door, c.1900, 34 x 23 In. ....*illus*	767.00
Commode, Louis XVI Style, Marble Top, Marquetry, Drawers, Panels, 33 x 32 In. ....*illus*	826.00
Commode, Mirror, Eastlake, Walnut, Shelf, 3 Drawers, Door, 70 x 30 In.	300.00
Commode, Mounted Parquetry, Serpentine Marble Top, Drawers, 1800s, 32 x 25 In., Pair	1528.00
Commode, Napoleon III, Parquetry, Marquetry, Bronze Mounted, Marble Top, 44 x 64 In.	2115.00
Commode, Neoclassical, 3 Drawers, Tapered Legs, Italy, 35 ¾ x 45 ¾ x 20 In.	837.00
Commode, Neoclassical, Fruitwood, Shield Escutcheons, Square Legs, c.1800, 31 x 23 In.	747.00
Commode, Neoclassical, Multicolored, Faux Marble Top, 3 Long Drawers, 37 x 49 In.	4800.00
Commode, Neoclassical, Multicolored, Flowers, Urn, Splayed Legs, c.1850, 39 x 54 x 24 In.	3360.00
Commode, Neoclassical, Walnut Inlay, 4 Drawers, Italy, 37 ½ x 27 x 13 ¾ In.	2271.00
Commode, Neoclassical, Walnut Inlay, Fleur De Peche Marble Top, Italy, c.1790, Pair	2440.00
Commode, Petit, Louis XVI, D-Shape Marble Top, Drawer, Door, Marquetry, 34 x 23 In.	748.00
Commode, Pine, Blue Paint, Drawer, Recessed Paneled Door, c.1850, 30 x 25 In.	889.00
Commode, Regency, Mahogany, Gallery, Pierced Handles, Doors, Drawer, 32 x 20 In. ....*illus*	540.00
Commode, Regency, Mahogany, Leather Top, Hinged Lid, Pullout Step, 19 x 19 In.	259.00
Commode, Renaissance Revival, Rosewood, Carved, Leaf Edge, Drawer, Cupboard, 31 x 21 In.	900.00
Commode, Renaissance Revival, Walnut, Burled, Marble Top, Sevres Plaque, c.1870, 30 x 18 In.	3307.00
Commode, Renaissance Revival, Walnut, Ebonized, Marble Top, Anthemion Carving, 30 x 22 In.	529.00
Commode, Rococo Style, Painted, Gilt, Shaped Marble Top, 3 Drawers, Italy, 30 x 28 In., Pair	1410.00
Commode, Scalloped Marble Top, 3 Cameo Scenes, Bronze Mounts, c.1900, 44 x 37 In.	295.00
Commode, Stand, George III, Mahogany, Molded Top, Shelf, Drawer Front, 33 x 23 In.	294.00
Commode, Venetian Rococo, Cream To Green Paint, Serpentine Doors, Scrolls, 38 x 43 In.	2760.00
Commode, Venetian Style, 3 Long Drawers, Painted, Scrolling Acanthus, 36 x 49 In.	960.00
Commode, Victorian, Marble Top, Backsplash, Drawer, Turned Legs, 38 x 31 In. ....*illus*	270.00
Commode, Walnut, Baltic, Banded, Burled Panels, Drawers, Bracket Feet, c.1775, 30 x 44 In.	2640.00
Commode, Walnut, Burled, Crossbanded, Drawers, Scalloped, Slipper Feet, c.1850, 31 x 27 In.	587.00
Commode, Walnut, Fluted Apron & Pilasters, Drawers, Ring-Turned Feet, c.1775, 32 x 44 x 20 In.	1150.00
Counter, Shaker, Drop Leaf, Pine, Drawers, New Lebanon, N.Y., c.1840, 29 x 46 In.	5850.00
Cradle, Canoe Shape, Wood Slats, Gilt Flowers, Wheels, Ford Johnson & Co., 1876, 26 In.	440.00
Cradle, Chippendale, Cherry, Hooded, 19th Century, 40 In.	120.00
Cradle, Chippendale, Cutout Handles, Mahogany, c.1770	165.00
Cradle, Curly Maple, Shaped Ends, Heart Cutouts, Scroll Rockers, c.1850, 37 In.	118.00
Cradle, Field, Boat Shape, Gray Paint, Wood, Iron Wheels, 30 x 45 x 24 In.	195.00
Cradle, Hooded, Grain Painted, New England, c.1810, 33 x 41 In.	30.00
Cradle, Maple, Grain Painted, Flowers, 18th Century, 34 x 23 In.	148.00
Cradle, Pine, Dark Stain, Spindled Crest Rail, c.1900, 23 x 43 In.	35.00
Cradle, Pine, Poplar, Painted, Gilt, Bridges, Lake, House, Mid 1800s, 16 In.	206.00
Cradle, Pine, Red Paint, Hooded, Pa., 19th Century, 38 In.	135.00
Cradle, Poplar, Heart Cutouts, c.1790, 41 In.	190.00
Cradle, Walnut, Turned Spindles, Shaped Rockers, Victorian, 26 x 26 In.	58.00
Credenza, Arne Vodder, Teak, 6 Drawers, 2 Sliding Doors, 31 x 72 In.	1320.00
Credenza, Drawers, Florence Knoll, 1961, 25 ½ x 74 ½ x 17 ¾ In.	2640.00
Credenza, Neoclassical, Walnut, Drop Front, Dragons, Columns, Italy, 1800s, 58 x 65 In.	1100.00
Credenza, P. Evans, Black, Laminate Top, 6 Lobed Steel Base, 37 x 118 In.	20400.00
Credenza, Pottier & Stymus, Walnut, Rosewood, Flowers, Inlay, 59 x 39 x 19 In.	2930.00
Credenza, Renaissance Revival, Maple, Rosewood, Satinwood, c.1890, 48 x 72 x 23 In.	10950.00
Credenza, Serpentine, Curved Doors, 10 Swing-Out Drawers, Marble Top, Paul Follot	3000.00
Credenza, Wall Hanging, Walnut, 2 Bifold Doors, Red Interior, Phillip L. Powell, 17 x 36 In.	8400.00
Credenza, Wirkkala Style, Kipp Stewart, c.1960, 30 x 67 x 17 In.	1225.00
Crib, French Directoire, Painted, Peaked Head, Footboard, Spindles, 34 x 20 In.	115.00
Crib, Tiger Maple, Turned Finials, Spindle Sides, Casters, c.1850, 28 x 18 x 38 In.	70.00

F

Crib, Victorian, Walnut, Turned Finials, Arched Headboard, 41 x 50 x 30 In.	28.00
Crib, Walnut, Shaped Crests, Turned Spindles, Victorian, 40 x 27 x 47 In. ....*illus*	117.00
Cupboard, Ash, Poplar, Upper Panes, Lower Drawers, Doors, Painted, c.1850, 84 x 51 In.	1998.00
Cupboard, Blue Paint, Paneled Door, Interior Shelves, 48 x 30 x 19 In.	1495.00
Cupboard, Bonnetiere, Biedermeier, Elm Veneer, Scrolled Cornice, Doors, c.1820, 67 x 43 In.	3650.00
Cupboard, Bonnetiere, Fruitwood, Apron, Molded Edge, Escutcheon, c.1700, 73 x 31 x 21 In.	597.00
Cupboard, Bonnetiere, Louis XIII, Poplar, Chestnut, Cornice, Paneled Door, c.1800, 78 x 43 In.	2580.00
Cupboard, Bonnetiere, Louis XIII Style, Walnut, Burl Elm, Shaped Door, 87 x 44 x 30 In.	388.00
Cupboard, Bonnetiere, Louis XIV Style, Oak, Cornice, Paneled Doors, c.1710, 73 x 42 In.	2280.00
Cupboard, Bonnetiere, Louis XV Style, Cherry, 2 Cupboards, Doors, Drawer, 91 x 38 x 25 In. ..	2760.00
Cupboard, Bucket Bench, Double Paneled Doors, Shelves, 51 x 27 x 19 ½ In.	550.00
Cupboard, Cherry, Dovetailed Case, 4-Pane Door, Drawer, J.L. Treharn, c.1975, 28 x 28 In.	382.00
Cupboard, Cherry, Flared Cornice, French Feet, c.1875, 72 x 37 x 18 In.	1527.00
Cupboard, Cherry, Overhang Pediment, Carved Frieze, 4 Doors, 2 Drawers, 1800s, 76 x 61 In.	1180.00
Cupboard, Chimney, Cherry, Poplar, 4-Panel Door, Yellow Grained, c.1850, 75 x 32 In.	1175.00
Cupboard, Chimney, Pine, Raised Panel Door, 19th Century, 73 x 27 x 20 In.	963.00
Cupboard, Chippendale, Walnut, 2 Sections, 4 Doors, 3 Drawers, 1780, 87 x 66 In.	6500.00
Cupboard, Chippendale, Walnut, Paneled Doors, N.C., 73 x 39 In. ......*illus*	1610.00
Cupboard, Continental, Pine, Mustard Paint, 3 Shelves, 2 Doors, 2 Sections, 76 x 56 x 21 In. .	2070.00
Cupboard, Corner, 4 Paneled Doors, Interior, Grain Paint, Georgia, c.1850, 47 x 46 In.	11500.00
Cupboard, Corner, Cherry, Maple, 2 Pane Doors, 2 Drawers, c.1840, 47 x 22 In.	2468.00
Cupboard, Corner, Cherry, Poplar, 12-Pane Door, Applied Turnings, Ohio, Mid 1800s, 85 x 43 In.	940.00
Cupboard, Corner, Chippendale, Pine, Green Paneled Doors, Interior Shelves, 81 x 51 In.	3910.00
Cupboard, Corner, Chippendale Style, Mahogany, 2 Sections, Footed, c.1900, 95 x 41 In.	1320.00
Cupboard, Corner, Chippendale, Walnut, 2 Glazed Doors, 2 Paneled Doors, c.1800, 41 x 22 In.	1150.00
Cupboard, Corner, Chippendale, Walnut, Pane Doors, Pierced Cornice, 1800s, 89 x 61 x 29 In.	2185.00
Cupboard, Corner, Chippendale, Walnut, Pine, Scroll Pediment, c.1800, 108 x 53 In.	8050.00
Cupboard, Corner, Chippendale, Yellow Pine, Walnut, Paneled, Southern, c.1800, 87 x 50 In.	1265.00
Cupboard, Corner, Curly Maple, Poplar, Glass Pane Doors, Drawers, c.1850, 82 x 55 In.	588.00
Cupboard, Corner, Federal, Cherry, Arched, Paneled Doors, 91 x 54 x 30 In.	6780.00
Cupboard, Corner, Federal, Walnut, 8-Pane Glazed Doors, Paneled Doors, 84 x 50 x 30 In.	1074.00
Cupboard, Corner, Hanging, Pine, Ocher Grain Paint, Mid 1800s, 33 x 27 ½ In.	1100.00
Cupboard, Corner, Hanging, Queen Anne, Tombstone Panel Door, Painted, 43 x 32 In.	1528.00
Cupboard, Corner, Hanging, Scalloped, Shelf, Biblical Scenes, Painted, 1800s, 43 x 26 x 17 In.	857.00
Cupboard, Corner, Louis XV, Tulipwood, Serpentine Front, Bracket Feet, 28 x 30 In.	1464.00
Cupboard, Corner, Louis XVI, Kingwood, Purplewood, Marble Top, c.1800, 33 x 27 In., Pair....	610.00
Cupboard, Corner, Neoclassical, Mahogany, Bowed Marble Top, Paneled Door, 36 x 24 In., Pair	1440.00
Cupboard, Corner, Oak, Swing-Out Drawer, Door, c.1915, 24 x 21 In.	250.00
Cupboard, Corner, Painted, Geometric Mullions, Carved Cornice, Shelves, 76 x 38 In.	2820.00
Cupboard, Corner, Painted, Pine, Mixed Wood, 2 Sections, c.1815, 98 x 63 In. ......*illus*	17550.00
Cupboard, Corner, Paneled, Walnut, Shaped Skirt & Feet, c.1800, 81 x 48 x 22 In.	1093.00
Cupboard, Corner, Pine, Beaded Front, 3 Serpentine Shelves, Door, Red Stain, 80 x 34 In.	7110.00
Cupboard, Corner, Pine, Painted Blue, Arched, 3 Shelves, 1700s, 79 x 44 In.	2350.00
Cupboard, Corner, Pine, Painted, Scalloped Shelves, New England, 79 x 37 In.	6264.00
Cupboard, Corner, Pine, Paneled Door, 3 Drawers, 9-Light Door, c.1845, 82 x 40 In.	720.00
Cupboard, Corner, Pine, Poplar, Arch Glass Doors, Drawers, Panel Doors, 1800s, 91 x 60 In. ..	1763.00
Cupboard, Corner, Poplar, 4 Paneled Doors, Shaped Skirt, Red Wash, c.1855, 79 x 45 In.	2350.00
Cupboard, Corner, Poplar, Pine, Panes, Lower Drawers, Door, Grained, 1800s, 40 x 21 In.	36425.00
Cupboard, Corner, Poplar, Red & Yellow Grain Paint, 3 Drawers, 2 Doors, 87 x 44 In.	5500.00
Cupboard, Corner, Softwood, 2 Lattice Doors Over Paneled Doors, 22 x 16 x 9 ½ In.	330.00
Cupboard, Corner, Softwood, Green Paint, Barrel Back, Door, Panels, Open, 81 x 46 x 20 In. .	2200.00
Cupboard, Corner, Step Back, Yellow Paint Over Green, c.1840, 97 x 47 In.	3485.00
Cupboard, Corner, Walnut, 4 Doors, 19th Century, 79 ½ x 43 ½ In.	500.00
Cupboard, Corner, Walnut, 20 Panes, 3 Drawers, 2 Doors, 2 Sections, c.1780, 99 x 56 In.	6000.00
Cupboard, Corner, Walnut, Blind Door, 2 Over 2 Doors, Blue Interior, Chester Co., Pa., 82 In.	2860.00
Cupboard, Corner, Walnut, Broken-Arch, Glazed & Paneled Doors, Georgia, 102 x 52 In.	9200.00
Cupboard, Corner, Walnut, Poplar, 6-Pane Doors, Indiana, Mid 1800s, 86 x 51 In.	1410.00
Cupboard, Corner, Wood, Pane Doors, Paneled Doors, Drawers, Grain Paint, Pa., c.1850, 80 x 62 In. .	4465.00
Cupboard, Corner, Yellow Pine, 4 Paneled Doors, Fitted Interior, Georgia, c.1800, 84 x 27 In.	4830.00
Cupboard, Corner, Yellow Pine, 4 Paneled Doors, Fitted Interior, Georgia, c.1810, 46 x 85 In.	2300.00
Cupboard, Corner, Yellow Pine, Carved, Painted, c.1800, 88 x 39 In. ......*illus*	2340.00
Cupboard, Court, Oak, 4 Door Base, Lattice Panel, 2 Door Top, England, c.1700, 65 x 48 In. ..	480.00
Cupboard, Curly Maple, Pine, 2 Pane Doors, Lower Shelf, Cutout Edge, 1850, 35 x 35 In.	1763.00
Cupboard, Curly Maple, Pine, 2 Sections, Pie Shelf, Doors, Drawers, Doors, 1900s, 88 x 61 In.	1175.00
Cupboard, Drawer, Door, Beaded, Plate Grooves, c.1800	2467.00
Cupboard, Ecclesiastical, Italian Renaissance Revival, Walnut, Carved Mask, 48 x 23 x 16 In. .	1778.00

Furniture, Commode, Louis XV Style, Marble Top, Brass Mounts, 39 x 15 In., Pair
$690.00

Furniture, Commode, Louis XVI Style, Marble Top, Marquetry, Drawer, Door, c.1900, 34 x 23 In.
$767.00

Furniture, Commode, Louis XVI Style, Marble Top, Marquetry, Drawers, Panels, 33 x 32 In.
$826.00

Furniture, Commode, Regency, Mahogany, Gallery, Pierced Handles, Doors, Drawer, 32 x 20 In.
$540.00

Furniture, Commode, Victorian, Marble Top, Backsplash, Drawer, Turned Legs, 38 x 31 In.
$270.00

Furniture, Crib, Walnut, Shaped Crests, Turned Spindles, Victorian, 40 x 27 x 47 In.
$117.00

Furniture, Cupboard, Chippendale, Walnut, Paneled Doors, N.C., 73 x 39 In.
$1610.00

Cupboard, Empire, Pine, Painted, Red & Orange Swirl, 1800s, 20 ¾ x 24 In. .... *illus*	761.00
Cupboard, English Oak, Raised Panel Doors, 2 Short Over 3 Long Drawers, 75 x 48 In.	575.00
Cupboard, Federal, Cherry, 2 Sections, Glazed Doors, Shelves, 83 x 72 x 21 ½ In.	3955.00
Cupboard, Flower, Leaves, 2 Mirrored Doors, Drawers, Tramp Art, 18 x 8 7 In.	770.00
Cupboard, Gallery, Drawer, 2 Doors, Fitted Interior, Painted, Washburn, Ill., c.1830, 67 x 37 In.	4444.00
Cupboard, Gothic Panel Doors, Inset Sink, Zinc, Blue Paint, c.1800s, 30 x 70 In.	395.00
Cupboard, Grain Paint, Design, Upper, Lower Doors, 81 x 38 In.	3495.00
Cupboard, Grain Painted, 2 6-Pane Doors, 2 Paneled Doors, Pennsylvania Dutch, 82 x 58 In.	6710.00
Cupboard, Hanging, Chippendale, Pine, 2 Arched Doors, Stepped Cornice, Georgia, 63 x 40 In.	3680.00
Cupboard, Hanging, Mahogany, Pine, Dentil Molding, 2 Doors, 46 x 30 x 20 In.	770.00
Cupboard, Hanging, Mixed Wood, Glazed Door, Shelves, 35 x 20 x 8 In.	170.00
Cupboard, Hanging, Pine, Ebonized Detail, D. Richard Dunlap, Ohio, 1900s, 39 x 15 In.	353.00
Cupboard, Hanging, Pine, Original Paint, c.1840, 54 x 32 In.	5727.00
Cupboard, Hanging, Pine, Pediment, 2 Glass Doors, Cutout Detail, c.1850, 38 x 31 In.	382.00
Cupboard, Hanging, Pine, Poplar, Glass Door, Pa., Early 1800s, 30 x 24 In. ....*illus*	644.00
Cupboard, Hanging, Pine, Scalloped, Shelf, Door, Paint, Corner, 1800s, 30 x 20 x 13 In.	499.00
Cupboard, Hanging, Shaker, Butternut, 19th Century, 22 x 12 ¾ In.	200.00
Cupboard, Jelly, 6 Punched Tin Panels, Wood, 47 ½ x 42 x 15 ¾ In.	550.00
Cupboard, Jelly, Blue Paint, Door, Cock-Beaded, c.1820, 47 x 31 In.	1304.00
Cupboard, Jelly, Dovetailed Splashguard, Drawers, Doors, c.1800, 50 x 44 x 17 In.	4312.00
Cupboard, Jelly, Pine, Door, Yellow Paint, Fitted Interior, 56 x 36 In.	1659.00
Cupboard, Jelly, Pine, Doors, Fitted Shelves, Gray Paint, c.1790, 63 x 53 In.	823.00
Cupboard, Jelly, Pine, Painted, 2 Drawers, Paneled Door, Georgia, 48 x 51 In.	1610.00
Cupboard, Jelly, Pine, Poplar, 4 Drawers, 2 Doors, Shelves, 48 x 43 x 20 ½ In.	863.00
Cupboard, Jelly, Poplar, Painted, Dovetailed, Backsplash, 2 Drawers, 2 Doors, 51 x 44 In.	1300.00
Cupboard, Jelly, Red Paint, 2 Doors, 20th Century, 65 x 35 ½ In.	265.00
Cupboard, Jelly, Softwood, Painted, Stenciled, 2 Drawers, Paneled Doors, 49 x 43 x 21 In.	413.00
Cupboard, Jelly, Wood, Grain Paint, 2 Drawers, 2 Doors, Arched Panel, c.1850, 53 x 42 In.	300.00
Cupboard, Jelly, Yellow Pine, Drawer, Arched Door, Shelf, Nailed, Georgia, 1800s, 57 x 43 In. .	4830.00
Cupboard, Linen, Walnut Veneer, Marquetry, 13 Drawers, Twist Legs, c.1910, 69 x 47 In.	633.00
Cupboard, Louis XV Style, Oak, Provincial, Drawer, Door, Splayed Feet, 57 x 23 x 14 In.	1100.00
Cupboard, Mahogany, Inlays, Bowfront, 2 Doors, England, 1800s, 44 x 32 In.	575.00
Cupboard, Mahogany, Stepped, Molded Cornice, Ogee Shape Door, Scotland, 80 x 25 In., Pair.	1150.00
Cupboard, Milk, Softwood, 2 Double Paneled Doors, Shelves, 48 x 42 x 17 ¾ In.	2373.00
Cupboard, Milk, Softwood, Door, Pie Board End Door, Box Hinges, Shelves, 41 x 25 x 14 In. ..	880.00
Cupboard, Molded Cornice, 4 Hinge Doors, Recessed Panels, Salmon Paint, c.1825, 75 x 36 In.	2370.00
Cupboard, Open Shelves, Hand Forged Nails, 72 x 72 In.	4200.00
Cupboard, Pennsylvania Dutch, Walnut, Molded Cornice, 6-Pane Doors, 1800s, 85 x 49 In. ...	2350.00
Cupboard, Pewter, Pine, 2 Plate Rails, Open Base, Scroll Edge, Red Finish, 69 x 59 In.	3525.00
Cupboard, Pewter, Pine, 3 Plate Rail Shelves, Double Door Base, c.1820, 65 x 40 In.	705.00
Cupboard, Pewter, Walnut, 2 Paneled Doors, Upper Shelves, Pewter Rails, c.1800, 81 x 53 In.	2300.00
Cupboard, Pine, 2 Drawers, 2 Doors, Gallery, Red Finish, Label, c.1862, 44 x 20 In.	1880.00
Cupboard, Pine, 2 Raised Panel Doors, 2 Drawers, Red Paint, c.1830, 76 x 49 In.	1821.00
Cupboard, Pine, 2-Paneled Door, 2 Interior Shelves, Ivory Paint, Flame Grain, c.1850, 42 x 21 In.	646.00
Cupboard, Pine, Board, Batten Door, Open Top Shelf, Blue Paint, c.1850, 66 x 31 In.	2115.00
Cupboard, Pine, Domed Top, Scroll Carving, Paneled Doors, Bombe Base, Multicolored, 69 x 59 In.	4080.00
Cupboard, Pine, Door, Wrought Iron Hinges, Pa., c.1750, 43 x 45 In.	323.00
Cupboard, Pine, Dovetailed Case, Door, Drawer, Painted, 19th Century, 12 x 12 x 10 In.	705.00
Cupboard, Pine, Hinged Upper, Over Drawer, Door, Brown Over Cream Paint, 47 x 30 In.	1528.00
Cupboard, Pine, Paneled Door, Interior Shelves, Turned Feet, Red Paint, 1800s, 58 x 18 In. ...	646.00
Cupboard, Pine, Paneled Doors, Shelves, Paint, 82 x 43 x 22 In.	3450.00
Cupboard, Pine, Picture Frame Molding, Paneled Doors, 18th Century, 82 x 44 In.	750.00
Cupboard, Pine, Red, Green Paint, Iron Door Catches, Hinges, 77 x 53 x 19 In.	575.00
Cupboard, Pine, Step Back, 2 Glass Panel Doors Over 2 Frieze Drawers, 87 x 52 In.	767.00
Cupboard, Pine, Step Back, Crown Molding, 4 Shelves, Wales, 1900s, 82 x 65 In. ....*illus*	359.00
Cupboard, Pine, Stripped, 2 Paneled Doors, Late 1800s, 36 x 41 x 10 ½ In.	150.00
Cupboard, Pine, Top Gallery, Shelf, Drawer, c.1850, 53 x 26 ¾ x 17 ½ In.	441.00
Cupboard, Poplar, 1 Piece, 4 Paneled Doors, Dark Brown Paint, 1800s, 78 x 49 In.	235.00
Cupboard, Poplar, 2 Drawers, 2 Doors, Gallery, Grain Painted, 1800s, 39 x 44 In.	294.00
Cupboard, Poplar, Angled Cornice, Paneled Door, Cutout Feet, Red Paint, 64 x 40 In.	1116.00
Cupboard, Poplar, Arched, Gothic Door, Base Molding, Spoon Slots, Corner, c.1800, 91 x 48 In.	4406.00
Cupboard, Poplar, Chestnut, 4-Pane Doors Over 2 Doors, Painted, Licking County, 80 x 51 In.	411.00
Cupboard, Poplar, Diamond Panels, Doors, Drawers, Blue Paint, Ohio, c.1850, 90 x 64 In.	4700.00
Cupboard, Provincial, Fruitwood, 2 Upper, Lower Doors, Veneers, Drawers, 1800s, 90 x 56 In.	1725.00
Cupboard, Provincial, Louis XV, Oak, Fluted Drawer, Door, Panel, 1910, 57 x 24 In. ....*illus*	1080.00
Cupboard, Provincial, Pine, Tiered Shelf Risers, Floral Pediment, Austria, Late 1800s, 74 x 40 In.	518.00

F

Furniture, Cupboard, Corner, Painted, Pine, Mixed Wood, 2 Sections, c.1815, 98 x 63 In. $17550.00

Furniture, Cupboard, Corner, Yellow Pine, Carved, Painted, c.1800, 88 x 39 In. $2340.00

F

Furniture, Cupboard, Empire, Pine, Painted, Red & Orange Swirl, 1800s, 20 ¾ x 24 In. $761.00

Furniture, Cupboard, Pine, Step Back, Crown Molding, 4 Shelves, Wales, 1900s, 82 x 65 In. $359.00

Furniture, Cupboard, Provincial, Louis XV, Oak, Fluted Drawer, Door, Panel, 1910, 57 x 24 In. $1080.00

Furniture, Cupboard, Hanging, Pine, Poplar, Glass Door, Pa., Early 1800s, 30 x 24 In. $644.00

Rustic Furniture

Furniture made with antlers was in style in the last half of the 1800s for use in hunting lodges and rustic retreats. Out of favor by the 1930s, it came back into fashion in the 1990s and prices went up.

Furniture, Cupboard, Step Back, Painted, Peter Hunt, 76 x 24 In. $1872.00

Furniture, Daybed, Chippendale, Maple, Oak, Oxbow Crest, Ropes, 37 x 24 In. $748.00

Furniture, Daybed, Empire, Fruitwood, Paneled, Caryatid Column, Ormolu Paw Feet, 35 x 77 In. $1800.00

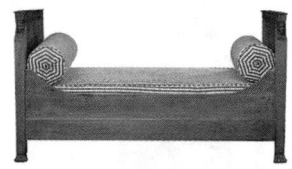

Furniture, Daybed, Louis XVI, Painted, Rope Carved Crest, Fluted Columns, 28 x 69 In. $3600.00

Cupboard, Red Stain, Plank Top, Arching Bookjack Sides & Front, c.1800, 54 x 42 x 17 In.	418.00
Cupboard, Renaissance Revival, Mahogany, Domed Door, Drawer, 60 x 18 x 44 In.	478.00
Cupboard, Renaissance Revival, Oak, Open Shelf, Carved Doors, Iron Hinges, c.1890, 75 x 66 In.	575.00
Cupboard, Shaker, Built-In, Poplar, Pine, Blind Paneled Door, Brown Paint, c.1830, 83 x 47 In.	882.00
Cupboard, Shaker, Cherry, Poplar, 2 Paneled Doors, Drawers, Bracket Feet, c.1850, 84 x 48 In.	11163.00
Cupboard, Shaker, Chest, Pine, 6 Drawers, Yellow Paint, New Hampshire, c.1840, 79 x 38 In.	5036.00
Cupboard, Shaker, Chimney, Pine, Painted, Raised Panels, Pegged, N.Y., 1800s, 74 x 20 In.	266.00
Cupboard, Shaker, Pine, Panel Doors, Interior Shelves, Orange Stain, c.1840, 48 x 42 In.	6143.00
Cupboard, Shelves, Lower Pie Safe, Punched Tin Panels, Mustard Paint, c.1840, 77 x 50 In. ..	14500.00
Cupboard, Sheraton, Cherry, Blind Door, Step Back, Drawers, 85 x 46 x 23 In.	1356.00
Cupboard, Softwood, Mustard Grain Paint, 6 Pane Doors, Pie Shelf, 82 x 56 x 22 In.	2420.00
Cupboard, Stand, Georgian, Bowfront, 2 Interior Shelves, England, c.1800, 70 x 26 In.	1293.00
Cupboard, Step Back, Cherry, Glazed Doors, Over 2 Frieze Drawers, Panel Doors, 80 x 45 In. .	885.00
Cupboard, Step Back, Cherry, Pine, 2 Pane Doors, 2 Paneled Doors, 2 Drawers, c.1850, 89 x 46 In.	1293.00
Cupboard, Step Back, Green Paint, Door, 3 Shelves, 19th Century, 81 x 39 x 13 In.	961.00
Cupboard, Step Back, Oak, Glazed, Paneled Doors, Drawers, 37 x 26 x 12 In.	283.00
Cupboard, Step Back, Painted, Peter Hunt, 76 x 24 In. ....*illus*	1872.00
Cupboard, Step Back, Pine, 10 Drawers, Open Top, 4 Shelves, Lower Doors, N.Y., c.1850, 78 x 62 In.	5640.00
Cupboard, Step Back, Pine, 2 Pane Doors, 2 Drawers, 2 Paneled Doors, Ohio, c.1830, 88 x 51 In.	823.00
Cupboard, Step Back, Pine, Blue Paint, 2 Doors Over Single Plank Door, 76 x 38 In.	1265.00
Cupboard, Step Back, Pine, Blue Paint, c.1885, 22 x 16 In., Child's............................	563.00
Cupboard, Step Back, Pine, Shelves, Plate Guards, 2 Doors, Wood Latch, 75 x 47 In.	345.00
Cupboard, Step Back, Pine, Paneled Doors, Red Paint, New England, c.1830, 75 x 59 In.	5925.00
Cupboard, Step Back, Poplar, Painted, Open Shelves, Paneled Doors, 75 x 42 In.	1880.00
Cupboard, Step Back, Softwood, 3 Shelves, Panel Door, Red Paint, 72 x 26 ½ x 13 ½ In.	2373.00
Cupboard, Step Back, Walnut, Cornice, Turned Feet, Plate Rail, 1842, 87 x 71 x 21 In.	7500.00
Cupboard, Step Back, Walnut, Poplar, 2 Upper, 2 Lower Doors, c.1850, 77 x 47 In.	1557.00
Cupboard, Utility, Shaker, Pine, Panel Door, 4 Interior Shelves, Red Grain, Mass., c.1855, 56 x 36 In.	1463.00
Cupboard, Wall, Hinged Door, Fitted Interior, 2 Red Flowers, Green, White, c.1910, 26 x 13 In.	267.00
Cupboard, Wall, Mixed Woods, Large Cornice, Tan Paint, c.1800, 81 x 73 In.	12338.00
Cupboard, Wall, Pine, Door, Paneled, Red Paint, New England, c.1830, 18 x 24 In.	1778.00
Cupboard, Wall, Red, Blue Paint, Frame & Panel Door, Molded Cornice, 26 x 23 x 11 In.	505.00
Cupboard, Wall, Tiger Maple, Painted, 19th Century, 54 x 13 In.	649.00
Cupboard, Walnut, 4 Caryatids, 3 Bronze Knobs, Panels, Italy, 50 x 105 In.	5581.00
Cupboard, Walnut, Chestnut, Poplar, 2 Doors, 2 Drawers, c.1890, 87 x 51 In.	588.00
Cupboard, Walnut, Open Top, Cutout Sides, Applied Molding, Paint Traces, 82 x 43 In.	764.00
Cupboard, Walnut, Paneled Door, H Hinges, Turned Ball Feet, 23 x 20 x 12 In.	413.00
Cupboard, Welsh, 2 Upper Shelves, Gothic Cornice, 3 Drawers, Dark Patina, c.1800, 74 x 20 In.	2760.00
Cupboard, Wood, Double Paneled, Dark Blue, c.1840, 50 x 62 In.	1975.00
Cupboard, Wood, Red Stain, Corner, 2 Sections, Pa., 19th Century, 76 x 42 In.	400.00
Daybed, Biedermeier, Walnut, S-Scroll Ends, Fitted Cushion, Block Feet, 1830, 91 In.	1425.00
Daybed, Black Frame, Silk Upholstery, Parzinger, 29 x 62 In.	7800.00
Daybed, Blue Paint, Maple & Pine, Peaked Headboard, Turned Legs, 1850, 33 x 27 In.	530.00
Daybed, Chippendale, Maple, Oak, Oxbow Crest, Ropes, 37 x 24 In. ....*illus*	748.00
Daybed, Directoire Style, Walnut, Classical Cassolette, Velvet, c.1920, 28 x 75 In.	1280.00
Daybed, Empire, Fruitwood, Paneled, Caryatid Column, Ormolu Paw Feet, 35 x 77 In. ....*illus*	1800.00
Daybed, Empire, Mahogany, Gilt Bronze, c.1820, 42 x 73 ½ x 47 In.	1560.00
Daybed, G. Nelson, No. 5088, Backrest, For Herman Miller, 1947, 70 x 33 In.	1800.00
Daybed, Kem Weber, Tubular Chromed Metal, Vinyl Cushion, 22 x 75 x 29 In.	1652.00
Daybed, Laminate, Bentwood Back Support, Legs, Trim, 1960s, 113 x 26 In.	450.00
Daybed, Louis XV Style, Beech, Serpentine Frame, Leaf Carved, Velvet, 78 In.	830.00
Daybed, Louis XVI, Painted, Rope Carved Crest, Fluted Columns, 28 x 69 In. ....*illus*	3600.00
Daybed, Louis XVI Style, Walnut, Spindle Rail Gallery, Fluted Columns, c.1880, 53 x 78 In.	2320.00
Daybed, Mahogany, Marquetry, Domed Foot, Headboard, Onion Finials, 34 x 45 x 79 In., Pair..	4080.00
Daybed, Mahogany, Spiral Acanthus-Carved & Ring-Turned Rails, 1840, 32 x 74 In.	3815.00
Daybed, Mies Van Der Rohe, Tufted Leather, Ramin Wood, Steel Frame, Knoll, 78 x 40 In.	4200.00
Daybed, Queen Anne, Maple, Carved, Arched Crest, Splat, Canvas Seat, 62 In.	2600.00
Daybed, Rounded Arms, Bracket Feet, Upholstered, 35 x 71 x 26 In.	350.00
Daybed, Softwood, Shaped Feet & Back, Square Nail Construction, 19th Century, 31 x 68 In. .	470.00
Daybed, William & Mary, Cane, Black Paint, 42 x 21 x 62 In.	863.00
Daybed, William & Mary, Maple, Arched Crest, Banister Back, Rush Seat, c.1740......................	2106.00
Daybed, William & Mary, Maple, Old Green Paint, 1735, 39 ½ x 69 In.	4400.00
Daybed, Wood, Velour Upholstery, Metal Tag, Chase Chair, 1960s, 38 x 69 In. ....*illus*	660.00
Deck Lounge, Maple, Adjustable, Cane Seat, Front & Back, c.1890.............................	130.00
Desk, Abatante, Drawer, Rosewood Inlays, Flowers, Filigree, Pad Foot Rest, Lady's, 25 x 52 In. ..	1150.00
Desk, Aesthetic Revival, Lady's, Ebonized, Gilt, Gallery Top, Leather Inset, Geo. C. Flint, 28 x 21 In. .	450.00

Desk, Arts & Crafts, Tiger Oak, 7 Drawers, Kneehole, Patinated Metal Hardware, 30 x 48 In. ... 657.00
Desk, Baroque Style, Burl, Pine, Veneers, Slant Front, Italy, Late 1800s, 34 x 20 x 13 ½ In. 356.00
Desk, Baroque, Walnut, Mixed Woods, Drawers, Locks, Handles, Spain, 28 x 42 x 15 In. 7475.00
Desk, Biedermeier, Ash, Mahogany, Cylinder Bureau, Mirrored Door, c.1830, 75 x 44 In. 3680.00
Desk, Biedermeier, Marble Top, 2 Mirror Arch Doors, Panel Door, 62 x 35 In. 3600.00
Desk, Birch, Double Pedestal, 4 Drawers, Norm Cherner, 30 x 60 In. 900.00
Desk, Bombe, Drop Front, Ebonized Wood, Ormolu Trim, Bronze Gallery, 34 ½ x 29 In. 690.00
Desk, Bookcase, Venetian Rococo Style, Painted, Shelves, Fall Front, 85 x 33 In. ....*illus* 2185.00
Desk, Bureau Marzarin, Louis XIV Style, Horn, Brass, Gallery, Drawers, 1800s, 32 x 36 In. *illus* 881.00
Desk, Butler's, Federal, Figured Mahogany, Fan Inlay, Drawers, Cubbyholes, 45 x 47 In. 1955.00
Desk, Butler's, Hepplewhite, Mahogany, Fitted Compartment, 3 Drawers, 45 x 45 In. 575.00
Desk, Butler's, William IV, Mahogany, Molded Gallery, Handles, c.1800, 32 x 30 In. 499.00
Desk, Cabinet, Carved & Burled Walnut, Crest, Letter Slot, Moore, c.1880, 61 x 35 x 27 In. 6900.00
Desk, Cabinet, Carved, Walnut, Oak, Elm Burl, Center Hinge, c.1880, Moore, 51 x 36 x 21 In. . . 5865.00
Desk, Caddy, Roll Top, Drawer, Calendar Mechanism, Inkwell, 12 x 9 ½ In. 345.00
Desk, Captain's, Walnut, Porcelain Insets, Hinged Top, 3 Drawers, Inscribed, 1874, 37 x 35 In. .. 2360.00
Desk, Carlton House, Edwardian, Mahogany, String Inlay, Tapered Legs, 30 x 54 In. 1067.00
Desk, Carlton House, Edwardian, Satinwood, Drawers, Leather, Gilt Edges, c.1900, 38 x 48 In. ... 3081.00
Desk, Carlton House, Mahogany, 8 Drawers, Cubbyholes, Brass Gallery, c.1930, 39 x 50 In. 1586.00
Desk, Carved, Incised Oak, Bronze Gallery, Wooton Co., c.1880, 56 x 36 x 29 In. 9200.00
Desk, Chair, Mirror, Aesthetic Revival, Faux Bamboo, Burled Wood, Cane Seat, 42 x 38 In. *illus* 817.00
Desk, Chair, Wicker, Woven, Painted White, Oak Top, c.1930, 39 x 31 In. ....*illus* 210.00
Desk, Chalet, Drop Front, G. Stickley, No. 505, Oak, Interior Letter Racks, 1902, 46 In. 1410.00
Desk, Chippendale, Curly Maple, Pine, 11 Drawers, Cutout Bracket Feet, 1900s, 79 x 41 In. 2350.00
Desk, Chippendale, Drop Front, Mahogany, Carved, Fluted, 3 Drawers, 41 x 20 x 20 In. 920.00
Desk, Chippendale, Drop Front, Maple, Fitted Interior, 4 Drawers, 40 x 37 In. 2360.00
Desk, Chippendale, Ribbon Grain Mahogany, Serpentine Top, 7 Drawers, c.1860, 30 In. 4200.00
Desk, Chippendale, Slant Front, Cherry, 4 Drawers, 18th Century, 41 x 36 In. 385.00
Desk, Chippendale, Slant Front, Cherry, Drawers, Pigeonholes, 42 ½ x 36 x 19 ½ In. 474.00
Desk, Chippendale, Slant Front, Cherry, Fitted Interior, 4 Drawers, c.1790, 41 x 36 In. 822.50
Desk, Chippendale, Slant Front, Curly Maple, 41 x 37 ½ x 18 ½ In. 908.00
Desk, Chippendale, Slant Front, Mahogany, 4 Drawers, Ball & Claw, Columns, 1800s 575.00
Desk, Chippendale, Slant Front, Mahogany, 4 Drawers, England, 1700s, 40 x 38 In. 1150.00
Desk, Chippendale, Slant Front, Mahogany, Carved, 1777, 44 x 42 x 22 In. 3200.00
Desk, Chippendale, Slant Front, Maple, Pine, Fitted Interior, 4 Drawers, c.1880, 43 x 30 In. 617.00
Desk, Chippendale, Slant Front, Mixed Woods, Drawers, Fitted Interior, c.1780, 42 x 48 In. 2350.00
Desk, Chippendale, Slant Front, Oak, Batwing Brass, England, 1700s, 41 x 37 In. 748.00
Desk, Chippendale, Slant Front, Tiger Maple, 4 Drawers, Stepped Interior, c.1785, 42 x 37 In. .. 2489.00
Desk, Chippendale, Slant Front, Tiger Maple, Cherry, 4 Drawers, c.1790, 41 x 38 In. 2070.00
Desk, Chippendale, Slant Front, Walnut, 4 Drawers, 44 x 44 x 20 In. 550.00
Desk, Chippendale, Slant Front, Walnut, 4 Drawers, Upper Doors, Shelves, 1700s, 92 x 39 In. . . 2990.00
Desk, Chippendale, Slant Front, Walnut, Drawers, Compartments, 43 x 41 x 22 ½ In. 1896.00
Desk, Chippendale, Slant Front, Walnut, Shell Carved, Bracket Feet, 39 x 21 x 33 In. 1056.00
Desk, Chippendale, Slant Front, Walnut, Veneers, Upper Panel Doors, 1700s, 82 x 41 In. 4370.00
Desk, Clerk's, Pine Top, Lift Lid, Fitted Interior, Inkwell Cutout, Gallery, c.1850, 42 x 23 In. 499.00
Desk, Danish Modern, Teak, 2 Pedestals, 4 Drawers, Tapered Legs, 30 x 59 In. 167.00
Desk, Davenport, Burled Walnut, Carved, Lift Top, Victorian, c.1830, 35 x 29 In. 12500.00
Desk, Davenport, Edwardian, Banded Mahogany, Leather Inset, 4 Drawers, 1890s, 33 In. 486.00
Desk, Davenport, Mahogany, Veneers, Fitted Top Case, 4 Side Drawers, c.1880, 34 x 21 In. 470.00
Desk, Davenport, Slant Front, Burl Walnut, Drawer, England, 32 x 23 x 24 In. 800.00
Desk, Davenport, Slant Front, Mahogany Veneer, Felt Lid, Interior Drawers, 1800s, 34 x 21 In. . . 345.00
Desk, Davenport, Walnut, Spindles, Victorian, 35 x 25 ½ x 25 In. 375.00
Desk, Display Cabinet, Oak, Carved, Lion's Head, Scrollwork, Mirror, Shelves, 74 x 40 In. 500.00
Desk, Drop Front, Birch, Poplar, Pine, James Gheen, N.C., c.1805, 42 x 39 In. ....*illus* 3910.00
Desk, Drop Front, Carved Crest, Burled, Fitted Interior, Drawers, Wooton, 41 x 73 In. 7475.00
Desk, Drop Front, Dovetailed, Steel Panel Doors, Ivory Columns, Gilt, Spain, 25 x 41 In. 16500.00
Desk, Drop Front, Mahogany, Doors, Drawer, Carved Gilt Pediment, c.1890, 30 x 16 In. 805.00
Desk, Drop Front, Pine, Upper Glazed Doors, Interior Shelves, 73 In. 165.00
Desk, Eames, Esu, Metal Frame, Yellow, Blue, Red Panels, Herman Miller, c.1951, 30 x 46 x 28 In. . . 3675.00
Desk, Empire, Base, Mahogany, Flat Front, 2 Drawers, Wood Knobs, Bun Feet, 37 x 32 In. 230.00
Desk, Escritoire, Rosewood, Mirror, Drawers, Tiered, Carved, c.1850, 54 In. 12338.00
Desk, Executive, G. Nelson, By Herman Miller, Walnut, Rectangular Writing Top, 83 In. 2760.00
Desk, Federal, Cherry, Birch, Inlaid, 2 Parts, 2 Doors, Fitted Interior, Drawers, c.1815, 40 x 40 In. 2963.00
Desk, Federal, Cherry, Tambour, 2 Doors, 2 Drawers, Reeded Stiles, 1815, 50 x 58 In. 5000.00
Desk, Federal, Mahogany, Upper Gothic Arch Doors, Lower Drawers, c.1890, 67 x 39 In. 518.00
Desk, Federal, Slant Front, Mahogany Inlay, Drawers, Cubbyholes, 45 x 42 x 22 In. 6325.00

Furniture, Daybed, Wood, Velour Upholstery, Metal Tag, Chase Chair, 1960s, 38 x 69 In. $660.00

F

Furniture, Desk, Bookcase, Venetian Rococo Style, Painted, Shelves, Fall Front, 85 x 33 In. $2185.00

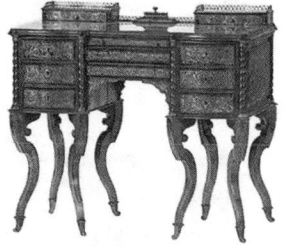

Furniture, Desk, Bureau Marzarin, Louis XIV Style, Horn, Brass, Gallery, Drawers, 1800s, 32 x 36 In. $881.00

Fake Carving

A faker will often carve an extra design on the lid of a desk or the leg of a table to add to the value.

Furniture, Desk, Chair, Mirror, Aesthetic Revival, Faux Bamboo, Burled Wood, Cane Seat, 42 x 38 In. $817.00

Furniture, Desk, Chair, Wicker, Woven, Painted White, Oak Top, c.1930, 39 x 31 In. $210.00

Furniture, Desk, Drop Front, Birch, Poplar, Pine, James Gheen, N.C., c.1805, 42 x 39 In. $3910.00

Furniture, Desk, G. Stickley, Drop Front, Lady's, No. 706, Copper Hinges, 30 x 44 In. $5700.00

Desk, Federal Style, Mahogany Inlay, Tambour, 2 Drawers, c.1930, 43 ½ x 35 x 18 In.	480.00
Desk, Federal Style, Mahogany, String Inlay, Tambour, Fold-Out, 2 Drawers, 41 x 28 In.	490.00
Desk, Flemish Style, Marquetry, Bonnet Top, Shaped Doors, Bombe Base, Flowers, 88 x 51 In.	2820.00
Desk, Frame, Stepped, Fitted Interior, Cock-Beaded Legs, Drawer, Painted, 1700s, 37 x 37 In. .	1126.00
Desk, French Empire, Roll Top, Cherry, 2 Drawers, Fitted Drawer, Bracket Feet, c.1890, 10 x 12 In.	474.00
Desk, French Style, Coulle, Simulated Shell & Brass Inlay, 3 Drawer, 32 x 57 In.	460.00
Desk, French Style, Half-Circle, Carved, Chair, c.1920, 30 x 63 x 32 In.	518.00
Desk, G. Nakashima, Walnut, Crossed Legs, Free-Form Top, 1978, 29 x 69 x 45 In.	53125.00
Desk, G. Stickley, 3 Drawers, Spindled, 29 ¼ x 78 x 32 ½ In.	7320.00
Desk, G. Stickley, 6 Drawers, Gallery, Paneled Sides, 36 x 60 x 32 In.	12200.00
Desk, G. Stickley, 9 Drawers, Mortised, Chamfered, 30 ½ x 63 x 30 In.	3538.00
Desk, G. Stickley, Blind Drawers, Red Decal, 29 x 36 x 23 ½ In.	2196.00
Desk, G. Stickley, Drop Front, Lady's, No. 706, Copper Hinges, 30 x 44 In. .... *illus*	5700.00
Desk, G. Stickley, Drop Front, No. 518, Panels, Strap Hinges, 26 x 11 x 52 In.	5700.00
Desk, G. Stickley, No. 708, Letter Racks, 2 Drawers, Shelf, Signed, 40 x 22 x 36 In.	2160.00
Desk, George II, Chippendale, Mahogany, Oak, Kneehole, Brass Pulls, 1700s, 31 x 32 In.	1035.00
Desk, George III, Mahogany, ¾ Gallery, Drawers, Banded, Hinged, c.1775, 40 x 24 x 17 In.	1800.00
Desk, George III, Mahogany, Double Pedestal, Drawers, 19th Century, 29 x 59 x 31 In.	1195.00
Desk, George III, Mahogany, Inset Leather Writing Surface, 3 Drawers, Pedestals, 30 x 54 In. .	720.00
Desk, George III, Pedestal, Mahogany, Leather, 3 Drawers, c.1850, 30 x 60 In.	2056.00
Desk, George III, Slant Front, Mahogany, Drawers, Pigeonholes, Flared Feet, 40 x 39 x 50 In. .	239.00
Desk, George III, Slant Front, Mahogany, Fitted Interior, Drawers, 1700s, 44 x 42 In.	1998.00
Desk, George III, Slant Front, Mahogany, Glass Doors, Leather, Drawers, c.1775, 47 x 87 In. ...	4148.00
Desk, George III, Slant Front, Mahogany, Pine, Late 18th Century, 42 x 37 x 23 In.	690.00
Desk, George III, Slant Front, Mahogany, Stepped Interior Drawers, Cubbies, 45 x 42 In.	1998.00
Desk, George III, Slant Front, Satinwood, Fruitwood Mahogany, Inlaid, 39 ½ x 30 x 17 In.	2963.00
Desk, George III Style, Mahogany, 2 Drawers, 6 Cock-Beaded Drawers, 30 x 45 x 23 In.	178.00
Desk, George III Style, Mahogany, Yew, Kidney Form, 30 x 60 x 27 In.	448.00
Desk, Georgian, Slant Front, Mahogany, 1700s, 41 x 34 In.	5800.00
Desk, Georgian, Slant Front, Mahogany, 4 Drawers, Britain, 19th Century, 43 x 21 x 43 ½ In. ..	1900.00
Desk, Georgian Style, Slant Front, Mahogany, Herringbone Inlay, 4 Drawers, 1870s, 40 x 31 In.	495.00
Desk, Gerald McCabe, Walnut, 3 Drawer, Tree Trunk Leg, Branch Handles, 30 x 85 In.	3105.00
Desk, Gothic Revival, Walnut, Paneled, Carved Skirt, 2 Drawers, Trestle, 31 x 56 In.	1495.00
Desk, Hepplewhite, Cherry, Poplar, 3 Drawers, Fitted Interior, 44 x 31 In.	235.00
Desk, Hepplewhite, Mahogany, Kneehole, 30 ¼ In.	3800.00
Desk, Hepplewhite, Mahogany, Tambour Top, 3 Drawers, Inlays, 1800s, 46 x 36 In.	2990.00
Desk, Hepplewhite, Slant Front, Prospect Door, Drawers, Pigeonholes, 42 x 38 x 20 ½ In.	904.00
Desk, Hepplewhite, Slant Front, Walnut, Hidden Section, Bookend Drawers, 47 x 36 In.	1540.00
Desk, H.P. Hansen, Teak, Storage, Locking Door, Drawers, Raised Lid, Denmark, 60 x 29 x 28 In.	660.00
Desk, Iberian Baroque, Walnut, Hinged Top, Trestle Base, Carved Designs, 1700s, 32 x 46 In. .	830.00
Desk, Ico Parisi, Wood Top, Black Metal, Steel Frame, Mim Roma, 29 x 82 In.	3000.00
Desk, Invalid, Shaker, Pine, Cherry, Cutout Top, Hinged Adjustable Legs, c.1850, 10 x 24 In. ...	527.00
Desk, Kittinger, Regency, Paneled, 5 Drawers, Gilt Tooled Leather, Reeded Edge, 30 x 54 In.	359.00
Desk, L. & J.G. Stickley, Drop Front, No. 374, Ash, Chamfered, 36 x 14 x 47 In.	1080.00
Desk, L. & J.G. Stickley, No. 512, Rectangular, Drawer, Bookshelves, 40 x 26 ½ x 30 In.	2160.00
Desk, Limbert, Drop Front, No. 713, 3 Drawers, Copper Strap Hardware	2640.00
Desk, Limbert, Oak, 2 Drawers, Shelf, Chair, c.1912, 29 x 36 x 47 ¾ x 32 In.	1007.00
Desk, Louis XV Style, Walnut, Bronze, Clock, 7 Drawers, Leather, 31 x 20 ½ x 48 In.	563.00
Desk, Louis XV, Drop Front, Fitted Pigeonhole Interior, Gilt Hardware, 44 x 21 x 34 In.	500.00
Desk, Louis XV, Drop Front, Kingwood, Upper Frieze Drawer, Drawers, Mounts, 54 x 36 In.	1200.00
Desk, Louis XV, Lady's, Kingwood, Tulipwood, Slant Front, 3 Drawers, 38 x 38 In.	1464.00
Desk, Louis XVI, Drop Front, Oak, Fitted Front, 3 Frieze Carved Drawers, c.1890, 45 x 53 In. ...	2280.00
Desk, Mahogany, 11 Drawers, Leather Top, Turned Legs, France, 1850s, 40 x 50 In.	495.00
Desk, Mahogany, Drawers, Oriental Designs, Carved Knees, Square Legs, c.1850, 31 x 48 In. ..	1320.00
Desk, Mahogany, Inlay, Center Door, Tambour Doors, Pigeonholes, c.1810, 45 x 36 In.	1150.00
Desk, Mahogany, Oak, Ebony Inlays, 5 Drawers Knee Cutout, Gallery, Ireland, 1800s, 32 x 37 In.	1058.00
Desk, Maple Veneer, Kidney Shape, Trefoil Front, Art Deco, 29 x 84 x 58 In.	826.00
Desk, McCobb, Mahogany, Connoisseur Collection, Calvin, 42 x 35 In. .... *illus*	1200.00
Desk, Molesworth, 3-Panel Screen, Leather Covered Pine, c.1945, 48 x 28 & 59 x 70 In. ...*illus*	1920.00
Desk, Oak, Grained & Carved, Beveled Mirror, Fitted Interior, c.1880, 67 x 30 x 15 In.	1610.00
Desk, Oak, Mill, Paneled Sides, 5 Drawers, 30 Cubbyholes, 55 x 78 x 37 In.	366.00
Desk, Oak, Raised Panels, Glass Surface, Felt, c.1910, 32 x 63 x 35 In.	575.00
Desk, On Chest, Mahogany, Paneled Fall Board, Fitted Interior, 3 Drawers, 59 x 36 In.	575.00
Desk, Partners, Edwardian, Slant Front, Oak, Lift Top, Drawers, c.1900, 30 x 57 In.	940.00
Desk, Partners, French Provincial, Leather Top, Ormolu, Inlay, Drawer, 1800s, 60 x 29 In.	7800.00
Desk, Partners, George III, Mahogany, 9 Drawers, Leather Top, 52 x 40 In.	720.00

Desk, Partners, George III, Mahogany, Tooled Leather Insert, Drawers, Fretwork, 32 x 61 In. .. 1093.00
Desk, Partners, Mahogany, Inset Leather, Pullout Slide, c.1900, 32 x 58 In. ....*illus* 1920.00
Desk, Partners, Mother-Of-Pearl Inlay, Carved Women Corners, Paw Feet, 35 x 55 In. 2124.00
Desk, Partners, R.J. Horner, Mahogany, Winged Griffin, 2 Sets Of 2 Drawers, 56 x 31 In. 3450.00
Desk, Partners, R.J. Horner, Oak, Legs, Lion's Head, Hairy Feet, Drawers, Carved, 59 x 30 In. ... 11500.00
Desk, Pine, 2 Drawers, Lift Top, Fitted Interior, New England, c.1790, 43 x 32 In. 948.00
Desk, Pine, Kneehole, Brown Paint, Top Over Drawer Cases, New England, 1800s, 28 x 55 In. 711.00
Desk, Plantation, Slant Front, Yellow Pine, Red Paint, 2 Doors, Drawer, 83 x 37 In. 19550.00
Desk, Plantation, Slant Front, Yellow Pine, Top Arch, Open Shelves, Paint, 1800s, 83 x 36 In. .. 1380.00
Desk, Plantation, Softwood, Reeded Cornice, Paneled Doors, Pigeonholes, 77 x 39 x 22 ½ In. .. 339.00
Desk, Plantation, Walnut, Yellow Pine, Bookcase, 2 Doors, Turned Legs, Southern, c.1830, 71 x 48 In. .. 1175.00
Desk, Postmaster's, Burl Walnut, Barrel Front, 50 Drawers, 45 Letter Slots, Pat., 1878, 42 x 62 In. .. 3900.00
Desk, Queen Anne, Drop Front, Birch, Fitted Interior, Cabriole Legs, c.1765, 43 x 34 In. 1422.00
Desk, Queen Anne, Drop Front, Mahogany, Breadboard Ends, Rosettes, c.1700, 41 x 33 In. 657.00
Desk, Queen Anne, Slant Front, Burl Walnut, Fitted, High Cabriole Legs, 39 x 25 In. 598.00
Desk, Queen Anne, Slant Front, Maple, 3 Drawers, Conn. River Valley, c.1740, 39 x 36 In. 2938.00
Desk, Queen Anne, Slant Front, Oak, Drawers, Pigeonholes, Pad Feet, 38 x 31 x 20 In. 1304.00
Desk, R. Loewy, Wood Laminate, 2 Drawers, Door, Sliding Trays, Doubinsky Freres, France, 61 x 31 In. .. 1200.00
Desk, Regency, Rosewood, Hinged Writing Surface, Lined, 44 x 30 x 17 ¾ In. 4148.00
Desk, Regency Style, Rosewood, Turner Stretcher, Drawers, c.1900, 29 x 34 In. ....*illus* 410.00
Desk, Renaissance Revival, Roll Top, Burled Walnut, Tambour Door, Leather, 47 x 60 In. 3360.00
Desk, Renaissance Revival, Slant Front, Carved Walnut, c.1870, 64 x 30 x 17 In. 690.00
Desk, Retractable, Elm Veneer, Double Doors, Reading Lamp, c.1954, 32 x 45 In. 940.00
Desk, R.J. Horner, Drop Front, North Wind, Griffin, Lion Carvings, 3 Drawers, 45 x 43 In. 6325.00
Desk, Rococo, Slant Front, Fruitwood, Inlays, 3 Drawers, Leaf Mounts, Continental, 21 x 41 In. .. 593.00
Desk, Rococo Style, Slant Front, Flowers, Drawers, Apron, Cabriole Legs, 40 x 34 x 17 In. 657.00
Desk, Roll Top, Quartersawn Oak, Raised Panels, 9 Drawers, 45 x 50 x 30 In. 900.00
Desk, Roll Top, Quartersawn Oak, W.D. Allison Co., 45 ½ x 60 x 26 In. 925.00
Desk, Roll Top, S Roll, Quartersawn Oak, Carved, Fitted Interior, c.1890, 50 x 61 x 35 In. 2300.00
Desk, Roll Top, Walnut, Kneehole, Cylinder, 8 Drawers, c.1890, 53 x 50 x 31 In. 2120.00
Desk, Roll Top, Walnut, Pine, Bowed File Drawers, Fitted Interiors, c.1950, 51 x 72 In. 1645.00
Desk, Rustic, Pine, Folding Writing Area, Lift Top, Niche, Drawer, c.1850, 36 x 35 In., Child's .. 1280.00
Desk, School, Oak, Wrought Iron, Hinged, Inkwells, Shelf, Drawer, 38 x 30 In. 176.00
Desk, Schoolmaster's, Pine, 2 Tiers Pigeonholes, 2 Drawers, 1800s, 39 x 26 In. 705.00
Desk, Schoolmaster's, Slant Front, Poplar, Painted, Pa., 19th Century, 47 ½ x 35 ¾ In. 175.00
Desk, Schoolmaster's, Slant Front, Walnut, Turned Spindle Gallery, Tapered Legs, 41 x 26 In. .. 230.00
Desk, Secretary, Maple, Cherry, Carved, Paw Feet, New England, 53 x 35 In. 2500.00
Desk, Shaker, 2 Drawer Rows, 2 Lower Drawers, N.Y., c.1865, 42 x 32 In. 10530.00
Desk, Shaker, School, Double Slant Front, Trestle Base, Enfield, c.1825, 30 x 50 In. 1872.00
Desk, Shaker, Seed-Shop, Butternut, Pine, Cherry, Orren Haskins, 1838, 31 x 25 x 22 In. 43875.00
Desk, Shaker, Slant Front, Cherry, 19th Century, 8 ½ x 19 In. 495.00
Desk, Shaker, Slant Front, Cherry, Pine, Turned Legs, Brass Pulls, 31 x 24 In. 35100.00
Desk, Shaker, Slant Front, Pine, Lower Panel Door, Interior Shelf, Brass, c.1850, 46 x 36 In. ... 1989.00
Desk, Shaker, Slant Front, Poplar, Fitted Interior, c.1900, 35 x 38 In. 499.00
Desk, Sheraton, Slant Front, Mahogany, 4 Drawers, 8 Inside Drawers, Pa., c.1810, 45 x 40 In. . 1140.00
Desk, Sheraton Style, Bench Made, Mahogany, Center Drawer, Small Side Drawers, 32 x 41 In. . 230.00
Desk, Slant Front, Birch, Yellow Pine, Open Interior, Brown Paint, 1800s, 31 x 29 In., Child's.. 288.00
Desk, Slant Front, Cherry, 4 Drawers, 18th Century, 44 x 39 x 19 In. 1075.00
Desk, Slant Front, Cherry, Fitted Interior, Drawers, Pigeonholes, 4 Drawers, 41 x 44 In. 748.00
Desk, Slant Front, Cherry, Table Top, 19th Century, 8 ½ x 19 In. 531.00
Desk, Slant Front, Lady's, Dutch Marquetry, Interior Slide, Drawers, Late 1800s....................... 900.00
Desk, Slant Front, Maple, Cherry, Fitted Interior, Painted, New Hampshire, c.1820, 45 x 41 In. . 3318.00
Desk, Slant Front, Maple, Fitted Interior, Brown Stain, Mass., c.1790, 43 x 39 In. 6518.00
Desk, Slant Front, Oak, 4 Drawers, Fitted Interior, 1800s, 42 x 37 In. 863.00
Desk, Slant Front, Pine, 2 Nailed Drawers, Fitted Interior, Paint Traces, c.1850, 13 x 10 In. 382.00
Desk, Slant Front, Step Back, Scrubbed Pine, 2 Paneled Doors, 2 Over 3 Drawers, 73 In. 896.00
Desk, Slant Front, Tiger Maple, 4 Drawers, Fitted Interior, Carved Columns, 43 x 43 In. 764.00
Desk, Slant Front, Tiger Maple, 4 Lower Drawers, 42 ½ x 37 In. 4600.00
Desk, Slant Front, Tiger Maple, Pine, Poplar, Drawers, Maine, 1700s, 41 x 38 In. .... *illus* 3860.00
Desk, Slant Front, Walnut Veneer, Pigeonholes, Bun Feet, c.1750, 40 x 35 In. 6462.00
Desk, Slant Front, Wood, Painted, Pigeonholes, Mickey Mouse, 25 x 9 x 15 In., Child's............ 356.00
Desk, Stand, Mixed Woods, Line Inlay, Banding, Divided Compartments, 29 x 18 In. 646.00
Desk, Table Top, Pine, Dovetailed, Drawers, c.1850, 13 ⅜ x 25 ½ x 20 In. 323.00
Desk, Table Top, Pine, Dovetailed, Shelves, Cubbyholes, Painted, 12 x 23 x 18 In. 288.00
Desk, Table Top, Slant Front, Chestnut, Drawers, Wrought Iron Hinges, Lock, 12 x 26 x 17 In. . 158.00
Desk, Teak, Fitted Interior, Lift-Out Boxes, Brass Handles, 15 x 10 In. 585.00

Furniture, Desk, McCobb, Mahogany, Connoisseur Collection, Calvin, 42 x 35 In.
$1200.00

Furniture, Desk, Molesworth, 3-Panel Screen, Leather Covered Pine, c.1945, 48 x 28 & 59 x 70 In.
$1920.00

Furniture, Desk, Partners, Mahogany, Inset Leather, Pullout Slide, c.1900, 32 x 58 In.
$1920.00

Furniture, Desk, Regency Style, Rosewood, Turner Stretcher, Drawers, c.1900, 29 x 34 In.
$410.00

Furniture, Desk, Slant Front, Tiger Maple, Pine, Poplar, Drawers, Maine, 1700s, 41 x 38 In. **$3860.00**

Furniture, Desk-Bookcase, Plantation, Yellow Pine, Poplar, Maple, Doors, Southern, 65 x 44 In. **$708.00**

Furniture, Desk-Bookcase, William & Mary Style, Arched Top, Doors, Drawers, 89 x 43 In. **$1534.00**

Desk, Tiger Maple, Poplar, Recessed Panel, Fitted Interior, c.1825, 40 x 60 In.	948.00
Desk, Torben Strangard, Teak, 3 Drawers, Raised Back Edge, Brass, Denmark, 1960s, 48 x 29 In.	270.00
Desk, Travel, Pine, Hinged Front, Fitted, Washington Portrait, Painted, 1812, 10 x 22 In.	3450.00
Desk, Victorian, Burled Walnut, Marble Top, 1880s, 31 x 36 In.	201.00
Desk, Victorian, Drop Front, Carved Detail, Legs, Stretcher, 36 x 15 x 44 In.	86.00
Desk, Victorian Style, Mahogany, Ovolu Corners, Leather Inset, Columns, 29 x 76 x 49 In.	3450.00
Desk, Victorian, Walnut, Brass Mounted, Domed Top, Flared Sides, 10 5/8 x 6 3/4 In.	296.00
Desk, Walnut, Flip Top, Apron Drawer, Octagonal Legs, c.1800, 60 x 37 x 13 In.	836.00
Desk, William & Mary, Upper Arch Doors, Fitted Drop Front, Drawers, c.1890, 27 x 43 In.	1495.00
Desk, Wooton, Renaissance Revival, Figured Walnut, Indiana, c.1880, 72 x 42 x 28 In.	20000.00
Desk, Wooton, Rotary, Oak, Cardboard Drawers, Brass Pulls, 31 x 60 In.	575.00
Desk, Wormley, Mahogany, Bleached, Double Pedestal, 8 Drawers, Dunbar, 1940s, 44 x 30 In.	270.00
Desk, Wormley, Mahogany, Rosewood, Tambour Doors, c.1960s, 35 x 75 x 28 1/4 In.	5185.00
Desk-Bookcase, Federal, Mahogany, Tapered Legs, Eagle Finial, N.Y., c.1810, 77 x 33 In.	5000.00
Desk-Bookcase, Plantation, Yellow Pine, Poplar, Maple, Doors, Southern, 65 x 44 In. ....*illus*	708.00
Desk-Bookcase, William & Mary Style, Arched Top, Doors, Drawers, 89 x 43 In. ....*illus*	1534.00
Dining Set, G. Nelson, Walnut, Gateleg Table, 6 Chairs, Herman Miller, 30 x 65 Table	720.00
Dining Set, Hans Olsen, Teak, Vinyl Upholstery, F. Rojle, Table, 4 Chairs, 1960s, 42 x 29 In. *illus*	900.00
Dining Set, Lucite Base, Chrome, Glass Top, 4 Lucite Chairs, Patent Leather Seat, c.1960, 5 Piece	1895.00
Dining Set, Oak, Table, Round, Claw Feet, 5 Chairs, Cane Bottom, Pressed Back, 48 In.	500.00
Dining Set, Pecan Finish, 4 Upholstered Chairs, 2 Leather Armchairs, Aico Monte Carlo	1035.00
Dining Set, Wicker, Glass Top Table, Tea Cart, Dessert Stand, 4 Chairs	588.00
Dresser, Aalto, Birch Plywood, Divided Drawer, Velvet Lined, 30 x 40 x 18 In.	3965.00
Dresser, Aesthetic Revival, Burled Walnut, Pediment, Cove Molded Cornice, 96 x 60 In.	2115.00
Dresser, Aesthetic Revival, Faux Bamboo, Cone Finials, Fretwork, 3 Drawers, Mirror, 78 x 45 In. .	1680.00
Dresser, American Empire, Walnut, 3 Drawers, Wooden Knobs, Bracket Feet, 34 x 39 In.	227.00
Dresser, Bird's-Eye Maple, Kneehole, Splashboard, Drawers, England, 33 x 47 x 20 In.	593.00
Dresser, Borge Mogensen, Teak, 6 Drawers, P. Dineson, 34 x 59 In.	1320.00
Dresser, Cherry, 3 Drawer, Davis Cabinet Company, 40 x 48 In.	325.00
Dresser, Cherry, Mirror, 5 Drawers, 2 Hat Boxes, Davis Cabinet Company, 48 x 78 In.	266.00
Dresser, Dog Kennel, English Oak, Blue Green Panels, Cup Hooks, c.1800, 86 x 70 In.	16500.00
Dresser, Eastlake, Walnut, Drop Center, Carved, Architectural Frame, Beveled Mirror, 86 x 53 In.	173.00
Dresser, Empire, Birch, Mahogany, c.1845, 47 1/2 x 40 1/2 In. ....*illus*	420.00
Dresser, Faux Bamboo, Mirror, Fretwork, Finials, 3 Drawers, 44 x 78 In.	1680.00
Dresser, French Provincial, Oak, Molded Cornice, Spindle Doors, Shelf, Panel Doors, 1800s, 59 x 89 In.	2820.00
Dresser, George III Style, Pine, Scalloped Frieze, Plate Racks, Drawers, Doors, 73 x 51 x 17 In.	705.00
Dresser, H. Probber, Walnut, Light & Dark Stained, Double	480.00
Dresser, L. & J.G. Stickley, 4 Drawers, Mirror, 67 1/2 x 42 x 21 In.	854.00
Dresser, L. & J.G. Stickley, 4 Over 2 Drawers, Cast Copper Pulls, 36 x 65 x 22 In.	1037.00
Dresser, McHugh, 2 Over 5 Drawers, Geo. C. Flint Co. Tag, 32 x 59 In. ....*illus*	1140.00
Dresser, Oak, 3 Open Shelves, Turned Uprights, Fluted Frieze, Cupboard Door, 78 x 59 In.	1320.00
Dresser, Pewter, 2 Sections, 3 Shelves, Spoon Shelf, Black, New Eng., c.1800, 74 x 14 In.	2607.00
Dresser, Pine, Molded Cornice, Plate Shelves, 6 Drawers, 2 Doors, 80 x 61 In.	2585.00
Dresser, Pine, Plate Rack Shelves, Lower Cupboard, 87 x 59 In.	527.00
Dresser, Renaissance Revival, Herter Bros., Mirror, Inlaid, c.1872, 108 x 60 x 24 In.	103700.00
Dresser, Rococo, Walnut, Shield Shape Mirror, Marble Top, Candle Shelves, 86 x 44 In.	2056.00
Dresser, Rosewood, Marble, Mirror, Carved Flowers, Drawers, 2 Scroll Supports, Ohio, 41 x 79 In.	531.00
Dresser, Stickley & Brandt Co., Mirror, 6 Drawers, Hammered Copper Strap, 66 x 48 x 22 In. .	11590.00
Dresser, Stickley & Brandt Co., Peaked Rail Top, 6 Drawers, 40 1/2 x 50 1/2 In.	2640.00
Dresser, Victorian, Burled Walnut, Marble Top, Mirror, 50 x 22 x 31 In.	201.00
Dresser, Victorian, Oak, Inlay, Hanky Drawers, 1800s, 17 x 43 x 34 In.	110.00
Dresser, Victorian, Pine, 2 Stacks Of 3 Drawers, Center Door, 39 x 64 In.	805.00
Dresser, Victorian, Pine, Multicolored Flowers, Hanky Boxes, Mirror, c.1880, 79 x 38 In.	295.00
Dresser, Victorian, Walnut, 4 Drawers, Carved Crest, Marble Top, 96 x 45 x 19 In.	270.00
Dresser, Victorian, Walnut, Marble, Incised Leaves, Rosettes, 1800s, 84 x 48 In. ....*illus*	1560.00
Dresser, Victorian, Walnut, Mirror, Carved Crest, Contoured Supports, 2 Drawers, 88 x 34 In.	146.00
Dresser, Victorian, Walnut, White Marble Top, 3 Drawers, 44 In.	295.00
Dresser, Walnut, Mirror, Arch Crest, Drawers, Carvings, Marble, c.1875, 96 x 55 In.	660.00
Dresser, Walnut, Step Drawer, 4 Drawer, 1800s, 43 x 22 x 44 In.	2500.00
Dresser, Welsh, George II, Oak, Plate Rack, 3 Drawers Across, Rolling Apron, 41 x 83 In.	3540.00
Dresser, Welsh, George III, Oak Inlay, Crossbanded Top, 3 Drawers, Snake Feet, 32 x 83 In.	2233.00
Dresser, Welsh, George III, Pine, Cornice, Frieze, Plate Shelves, Scalloped Supports, 80 x 61 In.	1410.00
Dresser, Welsh, Oak, Canted Crown, Decorated Frieze, Shelves, Mid 1800s, 86 x 69 In.	663.00
Dresser, Welsh, Oak, Pewter, Cup Hooks, Shelves, Drawers, 76 1/2 x 56 x 16 In.	1541.00
Dresser, Welsh, Oak, Rack, Pine, Mahogany, Bone Detail, 1800s, 85 x 69 In. ....*illus*	4600.00
Dresser, Welsh, Pine, 2 Drawers, Turned Legs, England, c.1800, 34 x 50 In.	1955.00

Dresser, Welsh, Plate Rack, Drawers, England, 1800s, 69 x 57 In. *illus* 1298.00
Dresser, Wormley, Mahogany, Bleached, 7 Drawers, Cutout Pulls, Leather, Dunbar, c.1940, 46 x 31 In. 600.00
Dry Sink, Bucket Shelf, Scrolled Backsplash, Cutouts, Bench, Old Paint, c.1820, 36 x 55 In. 2726.00
Dry Sink, Pine, 19th Century, 34 ½ x 39 In. 250.00
Dry Sink, Pine, Dovetailed Gallery Frame, Drawers, Turned Feet, 18th Century, 32 x 56 x 22 In. 896.00
Dry Sink, Pine, Painted, Shelf, Zinc, Drawers, Doors, 1890, 46 x 40 In. *illus* 1755.00
Dry Sink, Pine, Plank Top, Doors, Shelves, England, 38 x 45 x 22 In. 590.00
Dry Sink, Pine, Recessed Top, 30 x 32 x 19 In. 105.00
Dry Sink, Pine, Rounded Backsplash, 2 Doors, Late 1800s, 37 x 49 In. 176.00
Dry Sink, Pine, Yellow Sponge Painted, Door, 30 ½ x 26 In. 845.00
Dry Sink, Poplar, 8 Stepped Drawers, 2 Hinged Doors, Tombstone Panels, 1886 9480.00
Dry Sink, Poplar, Drawer, 2 Doors, 19th Century, 36 x 44 In. 402.00
Dry Sink, Poplar, Painted, Door, Cutout Feet, Yellow Paint, 34 x 36 In. 3055.00
Dry Sink, Poplar, Red Paint, 2 Doors, Cutout Feet, 39 x 50 x 22 ½ In. 605.00
Dry Sink, Raised Drawer, Paneled Doors, 33 x 48 x 19 In. 189.00
Dry Sink, Shaped Sides, Cutouts, Hinged Doors, Raised Panels, Painted, c.1820, 39 x 40 In. 1659.00
Dry Sink, Softwood, Hinged Lid, Red Paint, Paneled Doors, 35 x 38 x 20 In. 770.00
Dry Sink, Softwood, Red Paint, Open Well, Splash Back, 2 Paneled Doors, 35 x 42 x 17 In. 3080.00
Dry Sink, Southern Pine, 3 Drawers, 2 Paneled Doors, 49 x 49 x 22 In. 2825.00
Dry Sink, Walnut, Dovetailed Drawer, 2 Double Paneled Doors, Pa., 36 x 52 x 20 In. 154.00
Dumbwaiter, Chippendale, Mahogany, 3 Tiers, Tripod Base, c.1700, 43 x 24 In. 1093.00
Dumbwaiter, George III, Mahogany, 3 Tiers, Dish Edge, Tripod Base, 44 In. 474.00
Dumbwaiter, George III, Mahogany, 3 Tiers, Piecrust Borders, Revolving, c.1750, 46 x 22 In. 2900.00
Dumbwaiter, George III, Mahogany, 3 Tiers, Tripod Base, Pad Feet, 1780s, 43 ¾ In. 605.00
Dumbwaiter, Georgian, Mahogany, 3 Tiers, Raised Edges, Tripod, Snake Feet, 43 x 25 In. 1076.00
Dumbwaiter, Mahogany, 2 Tiers, Ring-Turned Standard, Paw Feet, c.1820, 36 x 20 In. 1135.00
Dumbwaiter, Mahogany, 3 Tiers, Birdcage Support, Tripod Base, Eng., 1700, 23 x 45 In. 1180.00
Dumbwaiter, Mahogany, 3 Tiers, Shaped Gallery, Reeded Supports, Urn Feet, c.1850, 47 x 36 In. 1057.00
Dumbwaiter, Mahogany, 3 Tiers, Spiral Baluster Supports, Tripod Base, 44 x 23 In. *illus* 1912.00
Dumbwaiter, Regency, Egyptian Revival, Mahogany, Acorn Finial, England, 56 x 32 In. 1830.00
Dumbwaiter, Regency, Mahogany, Brass Standard, Galleries, Inlay, c.1810 *illus* 805.00
Dumbwaiter, Regency Style, Mahogany, 2 Tiers, Drop-Leaf Top, Pedestal, c.1900, 36 x 24 In. 120.00
Easel, Ebonized, Neo-Grec Gilt, Scroll Pediment, Incised Stiles, Adjustable, c.1870, 70 x 27 In. 836.00
Easel, Iron, Adjustable, Scroll Legs, Impressed Paul Kiss, Table Top Style, c.1925, 16 ¾ In. 1528.00
Easel, Table Top, Gilt, Late 19th Century, 21 ¾ x 8 ¾ x 9 In. 582.00
Easel, Victorian, Walnut, Inlaid Ebony, Gold Highlights, 84 In. 1350.00
Etagere, American Rococo Revival, Rosewood, Carved, Serpentine Frame, c.1860, 113 In. 27255.00
Etagere, Directoire Style, 3 Tiers, Metal, Brass, Multicolored, Beading, Scrolling, 39 x 13 x 13 In. 780.00
Etagere, Ebonized, Asymmetrical, Shell, Ivory Inlay, 1800s, 64 x 34 In. *illus* 1315.00
Etagere, Hardwood, Divided Stepped Sections, Chinese, 20th Century, 18 x 14 ¾ In. 149.00
Etagere, Louis XVI Style, Tulipwood, Inlay, Marble Top, Late 1800s, 48 x 21 In., Pair 854.00
Etagere, Mahogany, Beveled Mirrors, Tiered Shelves, Curved Glass, c.1900, 68 x 35 x 16 In. 420.00
Etagere, Regency, Mahogany, 3 Tiers, Turned Supports, Drawer, c.1800, 58 x 18 x 18 In. 1265.00
Etagere, Regency, Mahogany, 5 Tiers, Drawer, Urn Form Spindles, c.1800, 61 x 18 x 18 In. 2012.00
Etagere, Regency, Mahogany, Turned Uprights, Finials, Brass Ferrules, c.1800, 45 x 20 x 17 In. 1195.00
Etagere, Regency Style, Mahogany, Molded Top, Drawer, 4 Gallery Shelves, 48 x 19 In. 546.00
Etagere, Renaissance Revival, Walnut, Marble, Carved Crest, Mirror, Shelves, 1800s, 54 x 91 In. 2475.00
Etagere, Rococo, Rosewood, 3 Tiers, Mirror, Marble Top, Drawer, Doors, Carvings, c.1875, 76 x 49 In. 920.00
Etagere, Rococo, Rosewood, Carved Crest, Mirrors, Shelves, Cabinet, c.1875, 105 x 56 In. 3840.00
Etagere, Rococo, Walnut, 5 Shaped Shelves, Rose Pink Marble, 95 x 59 In. 3800.00
Etagere, Rococo, Walnut, Mirror, Marble Base, Arched, Carved Crest, Shelves, c.1875, 93 x 54 In. 2400.00
Etagere, Rosewood, Carvings, 2 Mirrors, Lower Oval Mirror Door, Shelves, Drawer, 60 x 81 In. 4025.00
Etagere, Rosewood, Marble Top, 2 Mirror Shelves, Ornate Carvings, 62 x 28 In. 2300.00
Etagere, Victorian, Walnut, 5 Graduated Shaped Shelves, Openwork, c.1860, 65 In. 207.00
Etagere, Victorian, Walnut, 6 Graduated Tiers, Turned Supports, 53 x 33 In. 144.00
Etagere, Victorian, Walnut, Scalloped Carved Supports, Graduating Backsplashes, 60 x 26 In. 147.00
Etagere, Walnut, Marquetry, Galle, Signed, 44 x 29 In. *illus* 20000.00
Etagere, Wood, Carved, 2 Doors, Chinese, 80 x 40 In. 11500.00
Fainting Couch, Art Nouveau, Mahogany, Upholstered, Carved, 5-Footed, 58 In. 1200.00
Footstool, Animal Shape, Kotobuki, 1954, 12 x 19 ¾ x 17 ½ In. 600.00
Footstool, Arts & Crafts, Oak, Leather, c.1911, 8 x 12 ½ In. 130.00
Footstool, G. Stickley, Spindles, Beige Leather, Faceted Tacks, 15 x 20 x 16 In. 900.00
Footstool, George II, Walnut, Burl, Needlepoint Slip Seat, Oval Rails, Mid 1800s, 17 x 21 In. 259.00
Footstool, George II, Walnut, Carved, Cabriole Legs, Shell Carved Knees, c.1900, 18 x 24 In. 230.00
Footstool, George III, Chippendale, Mahogany, Slip Seat, Stretcher, c.1790, 18 x 19 In. 270.00
Footstool, George III, Mahogany, Needlepoint, Cabriole Legs, Pad Feet, c.1800, 18 x 23 In. 460.00

Furniture, Dining Set, Hans Olsen, Teak, Vinyl Upholstery, F. Rojle, Table, 4 Chairs, 1960s, 42 x 29 In.
$900.00

Furniture, Dresser, Empire, Birch, Mahogany, c.1845, 47 ½ x 40 ½ In.
$420.00

Furniture, Dresser, McHugh, 2 Over 5 Drawers, Geo. C. Flint Co. Tag, 32 x 59 In.
$1140.00

Hang-Ups

Plain wooden dressing-table mirrors with handles have a new use. Decorators are hanging groups of the mirrors in powder rooms, partly as decoration and partly to be used as mirrors. Dealers at shows find the mirrors are selling again.

FURNITURE

Furniture, Dresser, Victorian, Walnut, Marble, Incised Leaves, Rosettes, 1800s, 84 x 48 In.
$1560.00

Furniture, Dresser, Welsh, Oak, Rack, Pine, Mahogany, Bone Detail, 1800s, 85 x 69 In.
$4600.00

Furniture, Dresser, Welsh, Plate Rack, Drawers, England, 1800s, 69 x 57 In.
$1298.00

Furniture, Dry Sink, Pine, Painted, Shelf, Zinc, Drawers, Doors, 1890, 46 x 40 In.
$1755.00

Furniture, Dumbwaiter, Mahogany, 3 Tiers, Spiral Baluster Supports, Tripod Base, 44 x 23 In.
$1912.00

Furniture, Dumbwaiter, Regency, Mahogany, Brass Standard, Galleries, Inlay, c.1810
$805.00

Furniture, Etagere, Ebonized, Asymmetrical, Shell, Ivory Inlay, 1800s, 64 x 34 In.
$1315.00

Furniture, Etagere, Walnut, Marquetry, Galle, Signed, 44 x 29 In.
$20000.00

Footstool, George III Style, Walnut, Needlepoint, Cabriole Legs, c.1850, 19 x 19 x 15 In.	374.00
Footstool, Georgian, Walnut, Cabriole Legs, Block Turned Stretchers, 19th Century, 17 x 19 In.	441.00
Footstool, Hardwood, Cutout Apron, Mortised Feet, 19th Century, 7 x 12 x 7 In.	235.00
Footstool, Limbert, No. 224, Leather Top, Arched Rails, 18 x 12 x 12 In.	240.00
Footstool, Louis XVI, Giltwood, Upholstered, Compartment, Scroll Arms, France, 4 x 14 In.	330.00
Footstool, Louis XVI Style, Fruitwood, Needlepoint Seat, 6 Legs, c.1900	110.00
Footstool, Louis XVI Style, Oval, Wood Base, Upholstered, Fluted Legs, 15 x 7 In. ....*illus*	368.00
Footstool, Mahogany, Carved, Slip Seat, Plain Rails, Cabriole Legs, c.1880, 20 x 21 In.	2185.00
Footstool, Mahogany, Figured Skirt, U-Scroll Supports, Nailhead Trim, c.1820, 15 x 19 x 19 In.	427.00
Footstool, Mahogany, Leather, Upholstered Cushions, Molded Frame, c.1840, 6 x 12 In.	323.00
Footstool, Mahogany, Scroll Arms & Feet, Rosewood Terminal, c.1825, 10 x 18 x 10 In.	294.00
Footstool, Needlepoint, Deer Hoof Legs, 13 x 24 x 14 In.	345.00
Footstool, Neoclassical, Mahogany, Needlepoint, Curule Base, Turned Stretcher, 15 x 18 In. ...	411.00
Footstool, Neoclassical, Upholstered Seat, Scroll Supports, Feet, Stretcher, 15 x 20 In., Pair	1293.00
Footstool, Ornate Carved Feet, Red Upholstery, 8 ½ x 16 In.	259.00
Footstool, Polar, Mortised, Splayed Legs, Drawer, c.1850, 8 x 16 x 7 In.	646.00
Footstool, Regency, Cane Seat, Settee Style, c.1850, 14 x 22 In.	176.00
Footstool, Regency, Rosewood, Scrolled Ends, Carved Leaf Tips, Brass Mounts, 11 x 18 In.	711.00
Footstool, Rococo, Rosewood, Carved, Serpentine Upholstered Seat, Mid 1800s, 14 x 19 In.	423.00
Footstool, Shaker, Splint Seat, Union Village, Ohio, 19th Century, 11 x 14 In.	646.00
Footstool, Victorian, Carved, Upholstered Top, England, Early 1800s, 7 ¼ x 12 ½ In.	395.00
Footstool, Victorian, Cast Iron, Upholstered, Filigree Skirt, c.1890, 9 x 15 x 11 In.	58.00
Footstool, Victorian, Cast Iron, Upholstered, Filigree Skirt, c.1890, 8 x 14 x 18 In.	75.00
Footstool, Walnut, Carved, Serpentine Rails, Pad Feet, Late 1800s, 19 x 17 In.	978.00
Footstool, Walnut, Flower & Leaf Carved, Upholstered Seat, 14 x 19 In.	288.00
Footstool, Walnut, Scrolled Feet, 11 ¼ x 17 x 11 ½ In.	66.00
Footstool, Walnut, Tenons, Scalloped Skirt, Early 1800s, 8 x 19 In. ....*illus*	230.00
Footstool, William & Mary, Flame Stitch Upholstery Seat, Carved, Turned Frame, 18 x 18 In. .	489.00
Footstool, Windsor, Splayed Legs, Black, Yellow Striping, Paint, Oval, c.1800, 5 ½ x 12 In.	326.00
Frame, Arts & Crafts, Mahogany, Carved Twig & Leaves, c.1910, 40 x 30 In.	499.00
Frame, Bird's-Eye Maple Veneer, Pine, Reverse Ogee, c.1850, 21 x 25 In.	395.00
Frame, Figural, Mixed Metal, Jeweled Sickle, Rake, Applied Flowers, 1800s, 11 In. ....*illus*	270.00
Frame, Giltwood, Cove Molded, Carved, c.1860, 27 ⅜ x 35 In., Pair	881.00
Frame, Gold Leaf, Mid 19th Century, 21 x 25 In.	450.00
Frame, Poplar, Pine, Applied, Split Columns, Corner Rosettes, Gilt, c.1850, 15 x 19 In.	117.00
Frame, Repousse Peacock, Round, Bronzed Metal, Impressed, Patina, 9 ½ In.	420.00
Frame, Scandinavian Neoclassical, Giltwood, Carved, Laurel Garland, 1800s, 42 x 29 In.	1200.00
Frame, Shadowbox, Art Deco, Blue Mirror Background, Mahogany, Shelves, 1930s	175.00
Frame, Softwood, Chip Carved, Easel Back, c.1900, 12 x 8 In. ....*illus*	294.00
Frame, Tiger Maple, Cross Lap, Cherry Bull's Eye Bosses, 19th Century, 15 ½ x 11 ½ In.	345.00
Frame, Wood, Newcomb-Cacklin, 30 x 25 In.	760.00
Frame, Wood, Painted Flowers, 6 ½ x 10 In.	180.00
Glider, Old Hickory, Woven Seat, Back, Branch Frame, c.1937, 37 x 82 In. ....*illus*	6600.00
Glider, Porch, Oak, Horizontal Slats, Solid Armrests, Mechanical Pedestal, c.1900, 35 x 48 In.	604.00
Hall Rack, Edgar Brandt, Art Deco, Iron, 90 In.	330.00
Hall Rack, Empire, Mahogany, Mid 19th Century, 90 ½ x 38 In. ....*illus*	1053.00
Hall Rack, Gothic Revival, Oak, Iron Hooks, Umbrella Rack, Germany, c.1890, 94 x 44 In.	3900.00
Hall Rack, Victorian, Oak, Bench, Carved, Crest, Mirror, Hooks, c.1890, 84 x 43 x 17 In.	960.00
Hall Rack, Victorian, Walnut, Marble Top, Broken-Arch, Late 1800s, 98 x 54 x 18 In.	1650.00
Hall Seat, Oak, Beveled Mirror, Coat Hooks, 77 x 26 x 14 In.	725.00
Hall Seat, Oak, Carved Panels, Arms, Victorian, 39 x 46 In. ....*illus*	644.00
Hall Seat, Provincial, Turned Columns, 2-Door Cabinet, Mirror, Austria, c.1900, 82 x 39 In. ..	345.00
Hall Seat, Renaissance Revival, Carved, Scrolled, Nude Caryatids, Italy, c.1890, 47 In.	2160.00
Hall Seat, Victorian, Walnut, 2 Drawers, Animal Head Arms, Upholstered, 97 x 45 In.	660.00
Hall Stand, Art Deco, Oak, Beveled Mirror, c.1930, 82 x 24 x 9 In.	600.00
Hall Stand, Art Nouveau, Beech, Round Mirror, Scrolled Hangers, c.1900, 70 x 28 In.	1280.00
Hall Stand, Burl Walnut, Carved Crest, Mirror, Marble, Drawer, Drip Pans, c.1890, 49 x 85 In. .	411.00
Hall Stand, Burl Walnut, Spindled Crest, Pendant Brackets, Marble Top, Late 1800s, 85 x 49 In.	411.00
Hall Stand, Empire, Mahogany, Recessed Mirror Back, Plank Seat, Drawer, Post Feet, 77 In. ..	227.00
Hall Stand, Hardwood, Inlays, Mirror, Ebony Parcel, Morocco, c.1890, 103 x 50 In.	1041.00
Hall Stand, Hardwood, Parcel Ebonized, Bone Inlaid Tiles, Moorish Arch, Morocco, 103 x 50 In.	1041.00
Hall Stand, Neoclassical Revival, Oak, Castellated End Finials, Hinged Seat, 1800s, 85 x 50 In.	705.00
Hall Stand, Oak, Griffins, Acanthus Leaves, Mirror, Glove Box, Umbrella Holder, 81 x 50 In. ..	600.00
Hall Stand, R.J. Horner, Mahogany, Creature Carved Mirror, Arms, 67 x 98 In.	13800.00
Hall Stand, Victorian, Oak, Carved, Shaped Back Panel, Beveled Mirror, Hinged Bench, 79 x 28 In.	144.00
Hall Stand, Victorian, Walnut, Central Mirror, Cane Holder, Scalloped Supports, 83 x 25 In. ..	265.00
Hall Tree, Gothic Revival, Iron, Twist Frame, Quatrefoil Cutouts, Spain, 1800s, 71 x 43 x 12 In. .	360.00

Furniture, Footstool, Louis XVI Style, Oval, Wood Base, Upholstered, Fluted Legs, 15 x 7 In. $368.00

Furniture, Footstool, Walnut, Tenons, Scalloped Skirt, Early 1800s, 8 x 19 In. $230.00

Furniture, Frame, Figural, Mixed Metal, Jeweled Sickle, Rake, Applied Flowers, 1800s, 11 In. $270.00

TIP
Don't retouch gold leaf picture frames or other gold trim with anything but real gold leaf.

F

Furniture, Frame, Softwood, Chip Carved, Easel Back, c.1900, 12 x 8 In. $294.00

Furniture, Glider, Old Hickory, Woven Seat, Back, Branch Frame, c.1937, 37 x 82 In. $6600.00

Furniture, Hall Rack, Empire, Mahogany, Mid 19th Century, 90 ½ x 38 In. $1053.00

Hall Tree, Louis XIII Style, Walnut, Turned Spindles, 8 Wood Hangers, c.1890, 76 x 46 In.	1650.00
Hall Tree, Mahogany, 4 Scrolling Arms, Hanging Pegs, Umbrella Corral, 1800s, 91 In.	590.00
Hall Tree, Quartersawn Oak, Leaves, Scrolls, Flowers, 19th Century, 90 x 49 x 17 In.	600.00
Hall Tree, Victorian, Cast Iron, Gothic Arches, Umbrella Rests, Drip Pans, White Paint, 71 x 28 In.	1920.00
Hall Tree, Victorian, Walnut, Rosettes, Drawer, Marble Top, Umbrella Holder, 83 x 35 In.	680.00
Hat Rack, Drocco & Mello, Cactus Gufram, 1960s, 66 x 29 x 27 In.	3600.00
Hat Rack, Steer Horn, Montana, c.1875, 13 x 19 In.	127.00
Hat Rack, Wrought Iron, Vine & Leaf Form, Painted, 20th Century, 77 x 45 x 31 In.	230.00
Headboard, G. Nakashima, Walnut, 2 Sliding Storage Doors, 1955, 36 x 12 x 56 In.	1920.00
Headboard, G. Nakashima, Walnut, Cane, 41 x 126 In.	708.00
Headboard, Pierre Cardin, Laminate, White, Metal Trim, Lift Top Light, 1970s, 80 x 28 In.	210.00
Headboard, Salterini, Iron, Scrolled Ribbon, 38 x 41 ½ x ½ In., Pair	915.00
Headboard, Smoked, Reverse Gilt, Tufted Panel, Italy, 59 x 78 ¼ In.	1955.00
Highboy, Maple, 8 Drawers, Shaped Apron, Cabriole Legs, 1800s, 62 x 39 In.	4720.00
Highboy, Queen Anne, 8 Drawers, Footed, 65 x 42 x 20 In.	7063.00
Highboy, Queen Anne, Cherry, Poplar, Upper Map Drawer, Mass., c.1750, 72 x 36 In.	2350.00
Highboy, Queen Anne, Mahogany, Bonnet Top, 3 Over 5 Over 3 Drawers, 82 In.	227.00
Highboy, Queen Anne, Maple, 9 Drawers, Cabriole Legs, Pad Feet, 73 x 41 x 21 In.	9600.00
Highboy, Queen Anne, Walnut, Maple, 2 Sections, Pad Feet, c.1750, 60 x 40 In. *illus*	8260.00
Highboy, Queen Anne, Walnut Veneer, Oak, 6 Drawers, Baker Furniture, 60 x 40 In.	288.00
Highchair, Oak, Spindle Back, Lift-Over Tray, Early 20th Century, 42 x 16 In.	117.00
Highchair, Rod Back, Early 19th Century, 33 ¾ In.	125.00
Highchair, Stroller, Pressed Back Design, Cane Seat, Victorian, 37 x 18 x 28 In. *illus*	270.00
Highchair, Windsor, Comb Back, Carved Ears, Saddle Seat, Green Paint, 39 In.	198.00
Hoosier Cabinet, Fir, Shelves, Ventilation Openings, 101 x 73 x 25 In.	1695.00
Hoosier Cabinet, Wood, 2 Drawers, 4 Doors, Sellers, Elwood, Ill., 50 x 25 x 20 In., Child's	1330.00
Humidor, Burl Veneer, Fitted Interior, Sliding Trays, Brass Inlays, Bun Feet, 8 ½ x 9 In.	764.00
Humidor, Mahogany, Inlaid, Round, Mechanical Lid, White Spot, Faceted, 9 ¼ x 7 ¾ In.	201.00
Huntboard, Birch, Yellow Pine, 2 Drawers, Applied Dentil Moldings, 1800s, 44 x 54 In.	5520.00
Huntboard, Pine, Blue Paint, Cut Nail Construction, Drawer, Southern, 47 x 44 In.	2530.00
Huntboard, Poplar, Yellow Pine, Shaped Back, 2 Drawers, Turned Legs, c.1800, 47 x 52 In.	5520.00
Huntboard, River Birch, Inlay, 2 Center Doors, 2 Drawers, Georgia, c.1830, 48 x 60 In.	29900.00
Huntboard, Shaped Back, 2 Drawers, Brown Paint, Green Star, Stripe, c.1875, 48 x 50 In.	17260.00
Huntboard, Softwood, Blue Paint, Beaded Black Board, Skirt, 2 Drawers, 42 x 78 x 18 In.	3850.00
Huntboard, Tiger Maple, Yellow Pine, Cherry, 4 Drawers, Georgia, 1800s, 41 x 46 In.	6330.00
Huntboard, Walnut, Dovetailed Drawers, Turned Legs & Feet, 1800s, 41 x 48 x 20 ¾ In.	4830.00
Huntboard, Yellow Pine, 2-Board Top, Dovetailed Drawers, 1820s, 54 x 55 In.	5980.00
Huntboard, Yellow Pine, Beveled Drawer, Tall Legs, Red Paint, Georgia, c.1870, 44 x 65 In.	5750.00
Huntboard, Yellow Pine, Drawer, Cut Nail Construction, Georgia, c.1875, 25 x 42 In., Child's	5750.00
Hutch, Baroque Style, Pine, 4 Shelves, Door, Pilasters, 74 ½ x 30 x 14 In.	178.00
Hutch, Corner, Pine, Cherry, 12 Panes, Raised Panel Doors, 92 ½ In.	1416.00
Hutch, Pine, Pegged Board Over Bench Base, Arched Ends, c.1800, 29 x 39 x 73 In.	1880.00
Hutch, Trestle Foot, Red Paint, 1800s, 63 x 39 In.	711.00
Kas, 2 Doors, Drawer, Raised Panels, 3 Shelves, Removable Feet, N.J., 1700s, 78 x 55 In.	4025.00
Kas, Chippendale, Walnut, Scrolled Pediment, Carved, 5 Drawers, c.1790, 101 x 67 In.	8225.00
Kneeler, Prie-Dieu, Napoleon III, Walnut, Serpentine, Carved, Needlepoint, c.1870, 34 x 19 In.	936.00
Ladder, Folding, Oak, 6 Rungs, Leather, Brass Outside Rails, England, Open 81 In.	649.00
Lap Desk, Burl, Brass Bound, Stand, Early 1800s, 6 ¼ x 19 ¼ In.	1586.00
Lap Desk, Burled Walnut, Brass Bound, Stand, Early 19th Century, 7 ¾ x 20 ¼ In.	2440.00
Lap Desk, English Walnut, Fruitwood, Dividers, Drawers, Peasant Scenes, 7 ½ x 17 ¾ x 12 In.	460.00
Lap Desk, Federal, Satinwood, Inlaid Shells, Leaves, Brass Ball Handles, 6 x 12 In.	294.00
Lap Desk, Georgian, Mahogany, Tambour, 2 Drawers, Well, c.1800, 10 ½ x 9 In.	625.00
Lap Desk, Mahogany, Brass Bound, 1800s, 8 x 20 In.	201.00
Lap Desk, Mahogany, Brass, Drawer, Rolling Cover, Fitted Interior, England, 1800s, 9 x 18 In.	325.00
Lap Desk, Regency, Rosewood, Leather Inset Writing Surface, Storage, 23 x 20 x 11 In.	900.00
Lap Desk, Roll Top, Asian Hardwoods, Brass Bound, c.1830, 9 x 19 x 15 In.	267.00
Lap Desk, Rosewood, Brass Inlay & Handles, Fitted Interior, Stand, 22 x 16 x 9 In.	460.00
Lap Desk, Rosewood, Brass Inlay, Covered Fitted Interior, Ink Bottle, England, 1800s, 5 x 18 In.	472.00
Lap Desk, Rosewood, Leather, Divided Compartments, Mahogany Stand, c.1860, 20 x 20 In.	441.00
Lap Desk, Rosewood, Leather Liner, Stand, England, 19th Century, 24 x 21 x 10 ¾ In.	2200.00
Lap Desk, Slant Front, Mahogany, 19th Century, 13 ½ x 23 ½ x 13 ¾ In.	36.00
Lap Desk, Victorian, Burl, Brass Bands, Morocco Writing Surface, Wells, 18 x 11 x 7 In.	178.00
Lap Desk, Victorian, Mahogany, Campaign Style, Brass Bound, 7 ¼ x 22 In.	720.00
Lap Desk, Victorian, Rosewood, Brass Bound, Stand, c.1859, 7 x 10 In.	1098.00
Lap Desk, Walnut, Brass Bound, Mid 19th Century, 18 x 20 ½ x 10 ½ In.	529.00
Lap Desk, Walnut, Brass, Fitted Interior, Stand, England, 1800s, 6 x 16 In.	266.00

Lap Desk, Walnut, Brass, Lined Writing Surface, Fitted Interior, England, 7 x 17 In.	354.00
Lap Desk, Walnut, Brass Mounted, Stretcher Base Stand, England, 7 x 28 In.	374.00
Lectern, Georgian, Mahogany, Adjustable, Candle Slides, Tripod Base, England, 1700s, 29 x 24 In.	1800.00
Lectern, Rococo Style, Walnut, Carved, Tripod Base, 52 x 24 In.	351.00
Lectern, Rosewood, 3 Tiers, Flip Top, Slots, Scroll Feet, France, 1800s, 46 x 26 x 24 In.	625.00
Library Ladder, English Oak, Simulated Bamboo, Graduated, 11 Rungs, 117 In.	450.00
Library Ladder, Pine, 6 Steps, Upright Grip, Stretcher Base, 19th Century, 68 x 36 x 18 In.	294.00
Library Ladder, Pine, Applied Iron Medallions, Folding, England, 1900, 38 x 22 x 47 In.	690.00
Library Ladder, Teak, 4 Steps, Piano Hinge, 34 ½ x 17 x 21 ¼ In.	478.00
Library Steps, Baroque, Pine, 5 Steps, Scalloped Ends, Molded Banister, 78 x 31 In.	863.00
Library Steps, Brass Mounted, Turned Rails, Post, England, 52 x 22 In.	940.00
Library Steps, English Style, Oak, c.1920, 60 x 24 In. ....*illus*	936.00
Library Steps, Pine, Old Paint, 4 Steps, England, 62 In.	236.00
Library Steps, Pine, Walnut, 4 Steps, Pegged, Arched & Pierced Rises, Italy, 37 x 27 In.	2185.00
Library Steps, Regency Style, Mahogany, Bamboo Turned Handrail, 4 Steps, 65 x 21 In.	633.00
Library Steps, Regency, Tooled Leather Step Tops, Hinged Top Compartment, England..........	840.00
Library Steps, Wood, Patina, 3 Steps, c.1890, 36 In.	410.00
Linen Press, Chippendale, Mahogany, 2 Doors, 5 Slides, 3 Drawers, 86 x 50 In.	1725.00
Linen Press, Elm, Pine, 2 Over 3 Drawers, England, 1820s, 73 x 39 x 20 In.	605.00
Linen Press, George III, Mahogany, Molded Cornice, Applied Molding, 72 x 53 In.	2300.00
Linen Press, George III, Mahogany, Molded Cornice, Brass Inlay, 3 Drawers, 75 x 45 In.	1725.00
Linen Press, George III, Mahogany, Molded Cornice, Paneled Doors, 1790, 72 x 48 In. ....*illus*	1920.00
Linen Press, George III Style, Mahogany, 2 Doors, Inlaid Ovals, 4 Drawers, 83 x 49 In.	4025.00
Linen Press, Georgian, Inlaid Mahogany, Broken-Arch Pediment, Inlaid Tablet, 91 x 55 In.	4140.00
Linen Press, Jackson, Walnut, Poplar, 2 Parts, Blind Doors, 4 Drawers, Kentucky, 1830, 82 x 40 In.	1058.00
Linen Press, Mahogany, Paneled Doors, Bracket Feet, 19th Century, 80 x 53 x 22 In.	1610.00
Linen Press, Oak, Doors, Drawers, 72 ½ x 54 ¼ x 25 In.	590.00
Linen Press, Oak, Scrolling Backboard, Cupboard Doors, Drawers, 10 ¾ x 7 ⅝ In.	35.00
Linen Press, Pine, Mixed Woods, Lower Drawers, Grain Painted, c.1890, 80 x 48 In.	1840.00
Linen Press, Regency, Mahogany, Boxwood Inlay, Paneled Doors, Drawers, 83 x 49 x 21 In. ..	5875.00
Linen Press, Regency, Mahogany, Paneled Doors, Shelves, Drawers, c.1820, 84 x 48 x 21 In. ..	889.00
Love Seat, Barrel Back, Garland & Rosette Carved Crest, Upholstered, Early 20th Century.......	720.00
Love Seat, French Provincial, Walnut, Carved Leafy Crest, Shell Carved Skirt, Knees, 49 In. ...	207.00
Love Seat, L. & J.G. Stickley, Slat Back, Drop-In Spring Seat, 37 x 53 In. ....*illus*	1560.00
Love Seat, Queen Anne Style, Oxbow Frame, Needlework Upholstery, Stretchers, 52 In.	374.00
Love Seat, Rococo Revival, Mahogany, Serpentine, Upholstered, Loose Cushion, 34 x 56 x 32 In.	657.00
Love Seat, Sheraton Style, Mahogany Inlay, Carved, Hickory Chair Co., 33 x 53 In.	403.00
Love Seat, Side Chair, Wicker, Long Skirt, Heywood-Wakefield Co., 40 x 42 In., 3 Piece	780.00
Love Seat, T. Coggin, Armless, Blue Wool Upholstery, Steel Legs, 48 x 24 In., Pair	60.00
Love Seat, Victorian, Walnut, Rose Carved Crest, Medallion Back, Blue Silk Brocade, 59 In. ...	863.00
Lowboy, Chippendale, Mahogany, 4 Drawers, Ball & Claw, 31 ½ x 32 ½ In.	6000.00
Lowboy, Chippendale, Mahogany, Carved, Molded Edge, Drawers, 32 x 33 In. ....*illus*	5850.00
Lowboy, George I, Burl Walnut, Shaped Skirt, 3 Drawers, Cabriole Legs, 28 x 29 In.	1912.00
Lowboy, George III Style, Elm, Top Banded, 3 Over 3 Over 3 Drawers, 29 x 29 In.	1320.00
Lowboy, George III, Walnut, Central Drawer, Square Legs, Rectangular, 28 x 30 x 18 In.	1020.00
Lowboy, Georgian Style, Mahogany, 4 Drawers, Cabriole Legs, Shell Carved Knees, 29 x 30 In.	269.00
Lowboy, Mahogany, 1 Drawer Over 3, Fluted Columns, Kittinger Co., c.1966, 32 x 38 In.	1150.00
Lowboy, Queen Anne Style, Mahogany, Rectangular, Shaped Frieze, Drawers, 27 x 3 x 19 In. ..	360.00
Lowboy, Queen Anne Style, Walnut, 3 Drawers, 30 ½ x 35 In.	360.00
Lowboy, Queen Anne, 1 Drawer Over 3 Drawers, 18th Century..	6215.00
Lowboy, Queen Anne, Elm, Mixed Wood, 3 Drawers, Turned Legs, England, c.1800, 28 x 30 In.	748.00
Lowboy, Queen Anne, Walnut, 1 Drawer Over 3 Drawers, 30 x 35 x 20 In.	6215.00
Lowboy, Queen Anne, Walnut, 3 Drawers, Molded Top, Inverted Corners, 1740, 33 ½ In.	3300.00
Lowboy, Sheraton, Mahogany, 5 Drawers, 31 ½ x 36 x 21 ½ In.	450.00
Mirror, 4 Birds, Bicolored, Italy, c.1960, 31 x 27 ½ In.	227.00
Mirror, Adam, Mahogany, Painted, Swags, Flowers, Courting Couple, c.1790, 24 x 19 In.	3500.00
Mirror, Adam Style, Carved, Giltwood, Oval, England, 1800s, 40 x 21 In. ....*illus*	1840.00
Mirror, Adam Style, Wood, Oval, Carved, Green & Gold Paint, Urn & Flower Crest, 45 In.	288.00
Mirror, Art Deco, Ebonized Wood, Octagonal, Multiple Bevels, 1930s, 45 x 34 In.	2160.00
Mirror, Art Deco, Ivory, Shield Form, Label, A. Gason, c.1925, 30 x 21 In.	1116.00
Mirror, Art Deco, Square, Walnut Frame, Off-White Leather Trim, Gold Detail, 44 x 44 In.	120.00
Mirror, Art Nouveau, Wrought Iron, Bronze Patina, Raised Flowers & Butterflies, 15 x 24 In. .	420.00
Mirror, Arts & Crafts, Cherry, Inlaid Corners, Tenon & Key, Plinth Edge, 38 x 46 In.	280.00
Mirror, Baluster, Cornice Top, Acorn Pendants, Rosettes, Reverse Painted, c.1825, 40 x 24 In. ..*illus*	294.00
Mirror, Baroque, Giltwood, Rectangular, Scrolled Acanthus Leaves, 1800s, 48 x 60 In., Pair......	7703.00
Mirror, Baroque Style, Carved Wooden Frame, Giltwood, Italy, 24 ½ In.	169.00

Furniture, Hall Seat, Oak, Carved Panels, Arms, Victorian, 39 x 46 In.
$644.00

F

Furniture, Highboy, Queen Anne, Walnut, Maple, 2 Sections, Pad Feet, c.1750, 60 x 40 In.
$8260.00

Furniture, Highchair, Stroller, Pressed Back Design, Cane Seat, Victorian, 37 x 18 x 28 In.
$270.00

Furniture, Library Steps, English Style, Oak, c.1920, 60 x 24 In.
$936.00

Furniture, Linen Press, George III, Mahogany, Molded Cornice, Paneled Doors, 1790, 72 x 48 In.
$1920.00

Furniture, Love Seat, L. & J.G. Stickley, Slat Back, Drop-In Spring Seat, 37 x 53 In.
$1560.00

Mirror, Baroque Style, Ebony & Brass Mount, Ribbon Border, 32 x 27 In.	830.00
Mirror, Baroque Style, Painted Composition, Openwork Scrolls & Flowers, 40 x 33 In.	518.00
Mirror, Baroque Style, Reverse Painted, Shell Form Fan, Birds, Figure, Spain, 45 x 23 In.	633.00
Mirror, Beech, Painted, Parcel Gilt, Giltwood Crest Rail, Scrolled Cartouche, 72 x 59 In.	1200.00
Mirror, Biedermeier, Triptych, Flat Top, Plain Frieze, Gold Reed Pilasters, 1800s, 32 x 48 In.	649.00
Mirror, Black Forest, Walnut, Arched, 27 x 19 In.	403.00
Mirror, Brass, Art Nouveau, Shield Shape, Sinuous Scrolling Stems, Ivory Tusk, 13 In.	770.00
Mirror, Brass, Bronze Dore, Pediment Scrolls, c.1900, 21 x 13 In., Pair	345.00
Mirror, Brass, Scroll Frame, Pediment, Easel Back, Footed, 18 x 12 In.	176.00
Mirror, Bronze, Round, Molded Central Pierced Cord Knob, Chinese, Tang Dynasty, 3 In.	165.00
Mirror, Bull's-Eye, Giltwood, Acanthus Sprays, Beading, Carved, c.1830, 42 In.	3900.00
Mirror, Bull's-Eye, Girandole, Giltwood, Beaded, Eagle On Top, 32 x 23 ¾ In.	1098.00
Mirror, Bull's-Eye, Wood, Gesso, Flower Crest, Giltwood, c.1850, 30 x 20 In.	529.00
Mirror, Cast Iron, Pointed Arches, Demilune Shape, 23 x 44 In.	575.00
Mirror, Champleve, Bronze Cherub Supports, Easel Back, France, c.1880, 13 ½ In. .... *illus*	1093.00
Mirror, Cheval, Bamboo Maple, Beveled, Turned Supports, Finials, 1800s, 75 x 35 In.	940.00
Mirror, Cheval, Cherry, Carved Stylized Urn & Vine, 66 x 22 In.	288.00
Mirror, Cheval, Empire Style, Mahogany, Shaped Crest, Splayed Legs, c.1900, 77 x 32 In.	900.00
Mirror, Cheval, Neoclassical Style, Oval, Spiraling Feather, Animal Form Feet, 69 x 35 In.	767.00
Mirror, Cheval, Regency, Mahogany, Ebonized, Acorn Finials, Outswept Legs, 73 x 30 In.	4113.00
Mirror, Cheval, Regency, Mahogany Veneer, Brass Cap, Candle Sconces, 63 x 24 In.	588.00
Mirror, Chinese Chippendale, Red Paint, Pagoda Crest, Openwork, 63 x 31 In. ....*illus*	866.00
Mirror, Chippendale Style, Carved, Multiple Panels, Elaborate Frame, 1800s, 69 x 36 In.	2124.00
Mirror, Chippendale Style, Figured Maple, Shaped Crest & Apron, 55 x 24 In.	690.00
Mirror, Chippendale Style, Giltwood, Scroll Pediment, Tassels & Drapes, c.1800, 41 x 24 In.	94.00
Mirror, Chippendale Style, Mahogany, 19th Century, 27 ½ x 15 In.	235.00
Mirror, Chippendale Style, Mahogany, Scrolled Crest, Base & Ears, 1800s, 30 x 19 In.	115.00
Mirror, Chippendale, Giltwood, Acanthus & Leaf Carved, Italy, 1900s, 52 x 36 In.	748.00
Mirror, Chippendale, Giltwood, Carved, Acanthus Crest, c.1850, 22 x 46 In.	2350.00
Mirror, Chippendale, Giltwood, Pagoda & Phoenix Pediment, 54 x 33 In.	920.00
Mirror, Chippendale, Leaves, Flower Heads, Spread Wing Phoenix, c.1775, 61 x 27 In.	2419.00
Mirror, Chippendale, Mahogany, Carved Shell & Leaf Crest, c.1775, 38 x 20 In.	805.00
Mirror, Chippendale, Mahogany, Giltwood, Gesso, Late 18th Century, 36 x 15 In.	2963.00
Mirror, Chippendale, Mahogany, Giltwood, Gesso, New England, c.1800, 35 x 17 In.	119.00
Mirror, Chippendale, Mahogany, Giltwood, Phoenix Bird, 51 x 24 ½ In.	385.00
Mirror, Chippendale, Mahogany, Giltwood, Phoenix Crest, Flower, Filigree Trim, 25 x 42 In.	345.00
Mirror, Chippendale, Mahogany, Giltwood, Plum Crest, Scrolling Crown, Beveled, 1900s, 46 x 28 In.	269.00
Mirror, Chippendale, Mahogany, Parcel Gilt, Late 18th Century, 32 ¾ x 18 In.	403.00
Mirror, Chippendale, Mahogany, Pine, Openwork Crest, Giltwood Phoenix, c.1790, 32 x 18 In.	627.00
Mirror, Chippendale, Mahogany, Scrolled Crest, Pendant, Molded Frame, 29 x 13 In.	1080.00
Mirror, Chippendale, Shield's Station, Grainger County, Tenn., c.1900, 24 x 11 In.	690.00
Mirror, Chippendale, Walnut, Giltwood, Gesso, England, 18th Century, 39 x 19 In.	711.00
Mirror, Composite, Giltwood Detail, Scrolling, Rosettes, Urn, 47 x 21 In.	329.00
Mirror, Contemporary, Argente, Canted Frame, 44 x 31 ½ In.	360.00
Mirror, Continental, Giltwood, Leaf Carved Crest, Applied Scrolls, 1900s, 53 x 19 In., Pair	805.00
Mirror, Courting, Molded, Shaped, Reverse Painted Crest, Mirror Accents, 16 x 10 In.	411.00
Mirror, Courting, Reverse Painted Glass Panels, Flowers, Crest, c.1790, 13 x 9 In.	385.00
Mirror, Courting, Wood, Reverse Painted, Geometric, Flowers, Leaves, c.1790, 18 x 13 In.	563.00
Mirror, Curly Maple, Glass, Wrought Iron, Arched, Carved Crest, c.1790, 7 x 5 In.	4113.00
Mirror, Curtis Jere, Aviator Glasses Shape, 13 x 30 In.	3955.00
Mirror, Directoire Style, Sunburst, Giltwood, Carved, 2 Tiers, Italy, c.1925, 26 In.	660.00
Mirror, Directoire, Wood, Paneled Rails, Ionic Columns, Stylized Flowers, 63 x 41 In.	1320.00
Mirror, Dressing, Black Forest, Walnut, Carved Dolphin, Easel, 29 x 15 ¾ In.	296.00
Mirror, Dressing, Bronze, Reticulated Scrolls & Roses, c.1975, 16 In.	48.00
Mirror, Dressing, Georgian, Inlaid Mahogany, Oval, Shaped Supports, c.1800, 30 x 16 In.	259.00
Mirror, Dressing, Giltwood, Eagles, Star, Flower, Iron, Gold, Green, Black, c.1850, 19 x 10 In.	178.00
Mirror, Dressing, Hardwood, Molded Frame, Meander Border, Shaped Supports, 30 x 20 In., Pair.	106.00
Mirror, Dressing, Hepplewhite, Mahogany, Shield Shape, 2 Drawer Stand, 23 ½ In.	593.00
Mirror, Dressing, Mahogany, Cherry Posts, Trestle, 23 x 15 ½ x 9 ¼ In.	58.00
Mirror, Dressing, Mahogany, Serpentine Crest, Bowfront Base, 3 Drawers, Ogee Feet, 21 In.	593.00
Mirror, Dressing, Walnut, Inlaid Geometric Design, Caddy, Platform Base, 9 x 16 In.	88.00
Mirror, E. Sottsass, Memphis, Adjustable, Sparkled Metal, Chrome, 23 x 19 In. ....*illus*	720.00
Mirror, Ebonized Wood, Rippled Design, Rectangular, 39 x 32 In.	403.00
Mirror, Faceted Green Border, Arching Crest, Divided Beveled Plate, c.1900, 46 x 27 In.	215.00
Mirror, Federal Style, Girandole, Carved, Giltwood, Eagle, Scrolled Drop, c.1900, 40 x 23 In.	1265.00
Mirror, Federal, 3 Parts, Beveled Edge, Shells, c.1800, 27 x 56 In.	382.00

Mirror, Federal, Carved Giltwood, Convex, Eagle, Streamer, c.1890, 35 x 26 In.	1150.00
Mirror, Federal, Giltwood, Convex, Eagle Holding Oak Leaves, Molded Frame, 36 x 28 In.	748.00
Mirror, Federal, Giltwood, Gesso, Molded Cornice, Basket, Columns, Mass., c.1815, 28 x 17 In.	385.00
Mirror, Federal, Giltwood, Gesso, Molded Cornucopia, Flower Cornice, c.1815, 23 x 35 In.	474.00
Mirror, Federal, Giltwood, Reverse Painted Panel, Early 1800s, 48 x 29 In. ....*illus*	288.00
Mirror, Federal, Mahogany, Carved, Dental Pediment, 2 Sections, 19th Century, 36 In.	177.00
Mirror, Federal, Mahogany, Floral Carved Frieze, Reeded Pilasters, c.1820, 55 x 26 In.	497.00
Mirror, Federal, Mahogany, Reverse Painted Church, c.1825, 17 ½ x 11 In.	295.00
Mirror, Federal, Mahogany, Reverse Painted Ship, Flag, c.1820, 47 x 25 In.	294.00
Mirror, Federal, Mahogany, Reverse Painted, Silvered Urn, Leaves & Vine, c.1825, 42 x 21 In.	176.00
Mirror, Federal, Mahogany, Reverse Painted Tablet, Mt. Vernon, Reeded Stiles, 1810, 35 x 16 In.	265.00
Mirror, Federal, Wood, Giltwood, Gesso, Urn & Shell Crest, Flower Garland, c.1900, 32 x 19 In.	179.00
Mirror, Florentine Style, Giltwood, Openwork Shells, Scrolls & Leaves, Oval, 13 In.	403.00
Mirror, French Provincial, Multicolored, Rectangular, Flower Basket Crest, 25 x 13 In.	330.00
Mirror, G. Stickley, Copper Hooks, Marked, 28 x 42 ½ In.	2520.00
Mirror, George II, Giltwood, Arched Crest, Scrolled Brass Arm, Mid 1700s, 20 In., Pair	4406.00
Mirror, George II, Giltwood, Carved, Feathered Crest, Scrolls, Flower Vines, 50 x 27 In.	1528.00
Mirror, George II, Giltwood, Carved, Girandole, Candlearms, c.1750, 38 x 29 In., Pair	1102.00
Mirror, George II, Giltwood, Carved Shell, Leaves, Scrolled Sides, 46 x 33 In.	1840.00
Mirror, George II, Giltwood, Pagoda Crest, Openwork Scrolling, 19th Century, 48 x 26 ¾ In.	807.00
Mirror, George II Style, Giltwood, Bird, Garland, Scrolling Leaf, 62 x 32 x 3 In.	418.00
Mirror, George III, Giltwood, Carved Acanthus Leaves, C-Scrolls, 34 x 19 In.	1067.00
Mirror, George III, Giltwood, Carved, Eagle, 51 x 27 In.	1989.00
Mirror, George III, Giltwood, Hoho Bird Crest, Vines, Scrolls, Carved, c.1760, 22 In., Pair	28440.00
Mirror, George III, Mahogany, Inlay, Urn Finials, 15 ½ x 17 ½ In.	88.00
Mirror, George III Style, Giltwood, Openwork, Acanthus, Scrolls, 47 x 26 In.	1067.00
Mirror, George III Style, Mahogany, Bull's-Eye Border, 11 ½ In. Diam.	295.00
Mirror, George III Style, Mahogany, Giltwood, Eagle, Seashell, Beveled, 43 x 27 In.	270.00
Mirror, Georgian Style, Carved, Painted, Crown Shield, Floral Crest Pediment, 93 x 49 In.	575.00
Mirror, Georgian Style, Giltwood, Bird Crest, 52 ¼ x 30 In.	508.00
Mirror, Georgian Style, Giltwood, Cartouche Form, Vase Crest, Scrolls, Leaves, 56 x 30 In.	300.00
Mirror, Georgian Style, Giltwood, Scrolling Crest, Gadrooned Border, Oval, 42 In.	300.00
Mirror, Gilt Metal, Sunburst, Beveled Glass Plate, Interlacing Rays, c.1950, 52 In.	1140.00
Mirror, Giltwood, Burled, Late 1800s, 36 x 33 In.	750.00
Mirror, Giltwood, Carved Acanthus Leaves Corners, 40 ¾ x 63 In.	2937.00
Mirror, Giltwood, Carved, Divided Plate, Griffins, Leaves, Beading, Swag, c.1790, 33 x 64 In.	6168.00
Mirror, Giltwood, Carved Frame, Flowers, Seashell, Italy, c.1800, 37 In.	323.00
Mirror, Giltwood, Carved, Molded Frame, Berries, Flowers, Scrolls, Reeds, 41 x 36 In.	646.00
Mirror, Giltwood, Carved Pediment, Leaf & Figural Designs, Continental, 60 x 41 In., Pair	920.00
Mirror, Giltwood, Carved, Scenic, Immortals, Round, Cabriole Feet, Stand, Chinese, 27 ¾ In.	180.00
Mirror, Giltwood, Convex, 2 3-Light Sconces, Eagle, Swags, Reeded Frame Liner, 50 x 53 In.	385.00
Mirror, Giltwood, Convex, Parcel Ebonized, Eagle, Reeded Rim, 44 x 22 ½ In.	1440.00
Mirror, Giltwood, Corner Rosettes, Carved, England, 18th Century, 31 ½ x 26 ½ In.	1850.00
Mirror, Giltwood, Gesso, Painted, Lion Carved Pediment, Scrolling Leaves, Italy, 50 x 36 In.	230.00
Mirror, Giltwood, Gesso, Reverse Painted Tablet, c.1815, 38 x 20 In.	237.00
Mirror, Giltwood, Half Round Baluster, Rosette Blocked Corners, 26 x 39 ½ In.	720.00
Mirror, Giltwood, Molded Frame, Berry & Flower Corners, Scrollwork, 41 x 36 In.	646.00
Mirror, Giltwood, Ornate Carved Frame, c.1950, 56 x 32 In.	662.00
Mirror, Giltwood, Reverse Painted, Engagement Of Lake Erie Tablet, c.1815, 42 x 22 In.	1410.00
Mirror, Giltwood, Reverse Painted, Turned, 2 Sections, Landscape Scene, 24 x 12 In.	225.00
Mirror, Giltwood, Sailing Ship, Reverse Painted, Red Flower Border, 31 x 19 In.	823.00
Mirror, Giltwood, Swags, Bellflowers, Green Paint, c.1840, 107 x 45 In.	5500.00
Mirror, Giltwood, Turned Pilaster Frame, Flower Carved Corners, c.1875, 61 ½ x 27 In.	480.00
Mirror, Girandole, Carved, Giltwood, Laurel Wreath Frame, Eagle, c.1800, 26 x 15 In.	587.00
Mirror, Gold Leaf, Hand Carved, Pierced Ribbon, Bow, Leaf Pediment, Italy, 10 x 7 ½ In.	690.00
Mirror, Gothic Revival, Oak, Crocketed Spire Crest, Quatrefoil Panel, c.1800, 63 x 33 In.	2350.00
Mirror, Gothic Style, Fruitwood, Molded Arched, Curved Mullions, 39 ½ x 19 ½ In.	115.00
Mirror, Grotto Style, Shells, Barnacles, Driftwood, 48 x 30 In.	2040.00
Mirror, Hammered Copper, Silver Wash, Enameled, Landscapes, 26 x 18 In.	3172.00
Mirror, Hatchet Shape, Beveled, Stand, 1900s, 14 x 16 In.	296.00
Mirror, Hunting Scenes, Man, Woman, Madonna, Child, Persia, 1850, 11 x 7 In.	4140.00
Mirror, Italian Baroque, Giltwood, Carved Scrolls, Rectangular, 55 x 43 In.	1035.00
Mirror, Italian Neoclassical, Giltwood, Urn Crest, Leaves, Pendant, Lion Paws, c.1890, 47 In.	2552.00
Mirror, Italian Rococo, Giltwood, Carved, Reticulated Openwork, Acanthus, c.1900, 78 In.	4800.00
Mirror, Ivory, Bone, Carved, Shield Shape, Lion Mounted Crest, Oval, 22 x 20 In.	2585.00
Mirror, LaVerne, Patinated Bronze, c.1960s, 47 ⅝ x 35 ¾ In.	8750.00

Furniture, Lowboy, Chippendale, Mahogany, Carved, Molded Edge, Drawers, 32 x 33 In.
$5850.00

F

Furniture, Mirror, Adam Style, Carved, Giltwood, Oval, England, 1800s, 40 x 21 In.
$1840.00

Furniture, Mirror, Baluster, Cornice Top, Acorn Pendants, Rosettes, Reverse Painted, c.1825, 40 x 24 In.
$294.00

TIP

Early (eighteenth-century) glass is thinner than later glass. Early mirrors reflect a darker image than new mirrors.

Furniture, Mirror, Champleve, Bronze Cherub Supports, Easel Back, France, c.1880, 13 ½ in. $1093.00

Furniture, Mirror, Chinese Chippendale, Red Paint, Pagoda Crest, Openwork, 63 x 31 In. $866.00

Furniture, Mirror, E. Sottsass, Memphis, Adjustable, Sparkled Metal, Chrome, 23 x 19 In. $720.00

Mirror, Lime Wood, Giltwood, Pierced Carved Cartouche, c.1900, 22 x 13 In.	1280.00
Mirror, Line Vautrin, Gribiche, Synthetic Resin Frame, Incised, France, c.1955, 7 In.	23750.00
Mirror, Line Vautrin, Synthetic Resin Frame, Mirrored Glass Facets, c.1960, 6 In.	21250.00
Mirror, Louis Philippe Style, Painted Frame, Red, Rounded Corners, c.1830, 30 x 21 In.	806.00
Mirror, Louis XV Style, Giltwood, Carved, Floral Cresting, 28 x 18 In.	660.00
Mirror, Louis XVI, Giltwood, Leaf Carved, 60 ¾ x 30 ½ In.	2032.00
Mirror, Louis XVI, Giltwood, Ribbon Pediment, Floral Swags, 58 x 48 In.	1150.00
Mirror, Louis XVI Style, Giltwood, Torchere, Laurel, Olive Branch Crest, 59 x 27 ½ In.	4080.00
Mirror, Louis XVI Style, Oval, Pierce Carved Cartouche, Ribbon, Beaded, c.1900, 30 x 23 In.	1150.00
Mirror, Mahogany, Broken Arch, Giltwood, Scrolling, Late 1800s, 40 ¾ In.	650.00
Mirror, Mahogany, Reverse Painted Landscape, Cutout Lyres, Abalone, c.1845, 42 x 22 In.	206.00
Mirror, Marquetry, 2 Panels, Square Tapered Legs, c.1875, 67 x 42 In.	2880.00
Mirror, Molded Ribbon & Beaded Frame, Reeded Ebonized Slip, Convex, Eagle, 41 x 26 In.	2357.00
Mirror, Molded, Scrolling Crest, Etched Mirrored Pieces, c.1875, 53 x 34 In.	2160.00
Mirror, Napoleon III, Black Forest, Pierced, Carved, Acanthus, Leaves, c.1870, 54 x 36 In.	2480.00
Mirror, Napoleon III, Giltwood, Cenotaph Shape, Scrolled Crest, 57 x 30 In.	1920.00
Mirror, Napoleon III, Giltwood, Porcelain Plaque, Flower Swags, Carved Frame, 52 x 34 In.	2400.00
Mirror, Neoclassical, Giltwood, Arched Crest, Urn, Leaf Swags, Leaves, Bracket Base, 51 x 27 In.	1293.00
Mirror, Neoclassical, Giltwood, Beading, Ogee Molding, 1800s, 31 x 59 In.	1007.00
Mirror, Neoclassical, Giltwood, Carved Vines, Beading, Italy, c.1899, 27 x 34 In.	588.00
Mirror, Neoclassical, Giltwood, Divided, Leaf & Bead Swagged Urn, Griffins, 64 x 33 In.	6169.00
Mirror, Neoclassical, Giltwood, Flower Basket, Torches, Green Paint, Italy, c.1800, 17 x 31 In.	593.00
Mirror, Neoclassical, Giltwood, Projecting Cornice, Columns, 35 x 17 In.	940.00
Mirror, Neoclassical, Giltwood, Raised Grapevines, Beaded Molding, Early 1800s, 34 x 27 In.	588.00
Mirror, Neoclassical, Giltwood, Reverse Painted, Divided, Landscape Frieze, American, 17 x 35 In.	940.00
Mirror, Neoclassical, Giltwood, Swag & Urn Crest, Griffins, Pendant Finial, c.1925, 74 x 26 In.	1080.00
Mirror, Neoclassical, Girandole, Giltwood, Round, Rope Twist, Eagle, Oak Leaves, 56 x 45 In.	9375.00
Mirror, Neoclassical, Pine, Ormolu Mounts, Pediment, Beaded Trim, c.1840, 20 x 10 In.	323.00
Mirror, Neoclassical Style, Giltwood, Arched, Rope Twist, Urn Crest, 50 x 26 In.	418.00
Mirror, Oak Leaf Cluster Frame, Scalloped Leaf Border, 19th Century, 38 x 33 In.	499.00
Mirror, P. Evans, Burl, Brass, Cityscape, Signed, 36 x 20 In.	2196.00
Mirror, Pier, Adam, Giltwood, Urn, Leaf Crest, Rectangular, England, c.1800, 73 x 31 In.	863.00
Mirror, Pier, Federal, Giltwood, Carved, Arch Frieze, Pendant Acorns, Roses, c.1825, 42 x 72 In.	1528.00
Mirror, Pier, Giltwood, Carved, 2 Divided Plates, c.1850, 62 x 35 In.	705.00
Mirror, Pier, Giltwood, Carved, Arched, Molded Cornice, Oval Cartouche, 48 x 79 In.	374.00
Mirror, Pier, Giltwood, Carved, Divided Plate, New York, c.1810, 59 x 34 In.	3231.00
Mirror, Pier, Giltwood, Leaf, Flower, Reverse Painted Panel, c.1830, 58 x 36 In.	2185.00
Mirror, Pier, Louis XV, Giltwood, Oil On Canvas, Winged Putti, Flowers, 1900s, 76 x 45 In.	2070.00
Mirror, Pier, Louis XVI, Arched Crown, Applied Swag & Garland, Inset Picture, c.1910, 65 x 28 In.	353.00
Mirror, Pier, Louis XVI, Giltwood, Carved Rosettes, Ribbons, Swags, Beading, 1900s, 45 x 61 In.	711.00
Mirror, Pier, Louis XVI, Relief Medallion, Putti, Garland, Fluted Sides, 63 x 37 In.	460.00
Mirror, Pier, Louis XVI Style, Gilt Ribbon Twist & Floral Swags, 64 x 20 In., Pair	1725.00
Mirror, Pier, Louis XVI Style, Pine, Recessed Panel, Garlands, Ribbon, c.1880, 95 x 48 In.	3880.00
Mirror, Pier, Mahogany, Giltwood Capitals, Columns, Black, Gold Cornice, 1800s, 62 x 36 In.	920.00
Mirror, Pier, Mahogany, Giltwood, Reverse Painted Panel, Stencils, Columns, 1800s, 14 x 26 In.	142.00
Mirror, Pier, Mahogany, Scrolled Pediment, Plinth, Molded Edge Base, c.1850, 60 x 25 In.	358.00
Mirror, Pier, Neoclassical, Giltwood, Molded Cornice, Acorn Pendants, Recessed Frieze, 59 x 34 In.	3231.00
Mirror, Pier, Oil Painting, Livestock, Landscape, Urn Crest, Vines, France, 1700s, 61 x 42 In.	5605.00
Mirror, Pier, Parcel Gilt, Divided, Frieze, Carved Swags, Rosettes, c.1800, 60 x 35 In.	3055.00
Mirror, Pier, Queen Anne, Leaf, Scroll Crest, Molded Shaped Rim, Brown Finish, 54 x 20 In.	2850.00
Mirror, Pier, Regency, Beech, Parcel Giltwood, Painted, Diana, France, 91 x 51 In.	2880.00
Mirror, Pier, Regency Style, Fruitwood, Flowers, Urn, Parrot, Egg & Dart, c.1875, 71 x 57 In.	3120.00
Mirror, Pier, Reverse Painted, Fruit & Leafy Panel, Half Pilaster Frame, 25 x 13 In.	177.00
Mirror, Pier, Rococo, Giltwood, Scroll, Cabochon Crest, Strapwork Terminals, 60 x 33 In.	646.00
Mirror, Pier, Rococo Revival, Giltwood, Scrolls, Flowers, 87 x 35 In.	1150.00
Mirror, Pier, Silverwood, Carved, Scrolling Leaf Surround, Gadroon Fillet, 72 x 36 In.	230.00
Mirror, Pier, Victorian, Walnut, Beveled Glass, 94 x 37 In.	400.00
Mirror, Pine, Eagle, Ball Drops, Rope Twists, c.1800, 25 x 17 In.	411.00
Mirror, Pine, Giltwood, Applied Rope Twist, Half Turnings, Shell On Crest, 42 x 25 In.	176.00
Mirror, Pine, Molded, Giltwood Fillet, Rectangular, 1800s, 21 ¾ x 15 In.	69.00
Mirror, Queen Anne, Mahogany, Giltwood, Pierced Shell Crest, c.1700, 43 x 17 In.	18800.00
Mirror, Queen Anne, Oyster Veneer, Parcel Gilt, Arched, Beveled, c.1730, 70 ½ x 27 In.	4140.00
Mirror, Queen Anne, Walnut Veneer, Parcel Gilt, Carved, Early 1700s, 35 x 14 In. *illus*	748.00
Mirror, Regency, Carved Eagle Crest, Reeded, Concave, Ball Accents, c.1800, 24 x 20 In.	2040.00
Mirror, Regency, Giltwood, c.1820, 28 x 37 In.	529.00
Mirror, Regency, Giltwood, Carved, c.1840, 37 x 28 In.	529.00

Mirror, Regency, Giltwood Carved, Convex, Eagle, Reed Frame, c.1800s, 46 x 26 In.	3050.00
Mirror, Regency, Giltwood, Convex, Intertwined Dolphins, Spiral Rim, Round, 42 x 31 In.	1080.00
Mirror, Regency, Giltwood, Convex, Leaf & Eagle Crest, Candlearms, c.1825, 43 x 23 In.	2880.00
Mirror, Regency, Giltwood, Convex, Molded Frame, Carved Leaf Pendant, 46 x 28 In.	3360.00
Mirror, Regency, Giltwood, Convex, Rondels, Applied Ball Accents, 18 ½ In.	780.00
Mirror, Regency, Giltwood, Ebonized Reeded Slip Border, Candlearms, c.1800-25, 19 In.	900.00
Mirror, Regency Style, Giltwood, Carved, Fruit Festoon, Leaf Scale, France, 71 x 53 ½ x 7 In. .	2937.00
Mirror, Regency Style, Reverse Painted, Part Ebonized, 3 Parts, Shelf, 32 x 60 ¾ In.	1422.00
Mirror, Renaissance Revival, Walnut, Flat Molded Cornice, Gadrooned Frieze, c.1880, 59 x 38 In.	1530.00
Mirror, Renaissance Revival, Wood, Carved, Leaves, Beveled, Late 1800s, 52 x 42 In.	400.00
Mirror, Revolving, Scroll Supports, Serpentine Fronted Base, 1800s, 22 x 28 In.	89.00
Mirror, Ring-Turned Half Columns, Leaf Carved Corners, c.1900, 35 x 45 In.	717.00
Mirror, Rococo, Giltwood, Acanthus, Reticulated, 19th Century, 49 x 52 In.	2700.00
Mirror, Rococo, Giltwood, C-Scroll, Flower Basket Crest, Italy, 1700s, 20 x 32 In.	830.00
Mirror, Rococo, Giltwood, Oval, Scrolls, Flowers, Italy, c.1800, 15 x 23 In., Pair	472.00
Mirror, Rococo, Giltwood, Pierced, Carved, Gesso, 20th Century, 44 x 39 In.	764.00
Mirror, Rococo Revival, Giltwood, Carved Scrolls, c.1890, 25 ½ x 35 ½ In.	652.00
Mirror, Rococo Revival, Giltwood, Gesso, Swirling Leaves, Flowers, Oval, 27 x 20 In.	518.00
Mirror, Rococo Style, Giltwood, Flowers, Leaves, Composition Ornaments, 42 x 30 In.	288.00
Mirror, Rococo Style, Giltwood, Scrolling Leaf, Continental, 42 ¼ x 26 In.	359.00
Mirror, Rococo Style, Lime Wood, Acanthus Leaves, Flowers, c.1900, 40 x 21 In.	1450.00
Mirror, Rococo Style, Silvered, Leaf & Flower Pierced Crest, Scalloped, 47 x 33 In.	940.00
Mirror, Rohde, Wood Frame, Leatherette, Square, Herman Miller, 1940s, 27 In.	30.00
Mirror, Rosewood, Grained, 10 ½ In.	100.00
Mirror, Round, Spherules In Cavetto, Lion Passant, Candle Sockets, c.1810, 37 x 28 In.	6572.00
Mirror, Roycroft, Board, Frame, Chain, 50 x 30 In.	3120.00
Mirror, Shaving, Federal, Acorn Finial Uprights, Bowfront Base, Drawers, 180os	176.00
Mirror, Shaving, Federal, Mahogany, Shield Shape Glass, Drawers, c.1800, 22 x 8 In. ....*illus*	441.00
Mirror, Shaving, Federal, Serpentine Drawer, Bracket Feet, c.1800, 23 x 13 ½ In.	840.00
Mirror, Shaving, Hepplewhite, Mahogany, Drawer, Ivory, Swivel, c.1800, 28 x 24 In.	173.00
Mirror, Shaving, Mahogany, Pine, Bowfront, 3 Drawers, Bone Detail, Acorn Finials, 22 x 23 In.	147.00
Mirror, Shaving, Mahogany, Poplar, 3 Drawers, Posts, Flame Grain Paint, c.1850, 22 x 17 In.	411.00
Mirror, Shaving, Mahogany Veneer, Pine, Bowfront, 3 Drawers, Acorn Finials, 22 x 22 In.	176.00
Mirror, Shaving, Maple, 3 Drawers, Oval, Early 1900s, 23 x 19 ½ In.	60.00
Mirror, Shaving, Victorian, Mahogany, Scrolled Supports, c.1840, 31 x 27 In.	323.00
Mirror, Sheraton, Giltwood, Landscape, 2 Sections, Reverse Painted, 35 x 15 ½ In.	110.00
Mirror, Softwood, Molded Frame, Red Paint, 1800s, 13 x 10 In.	294.00
Mirror, Spanish Baroque, Shield Form, Leather & Brass Mounts, 33 x 24 In.	288.00
Mirror, Stand, Carved, Ebonized Hand Detail, Brass, Stamped, Franz Hagenauer, Austria, 13 x 22 In.	1560.00
Mirror, Sunburst, Carved & Silvered Wood, Italy, 28 ¾ In.	1020.00
Mirror, Sunburst, Carved, Giltwood, Convex, 36 x 24 In.	881.00
Mirror, Sunburst, Convex, Composite, Reeded, Italy, 9 In.	360.00
Mirror, Sunburst, Wrought Iron, Blackened, Parcel Giltwood, Drapery, 54 x 30 In.	2160.00
Mirror, Tabernacle, Neoclassical, Giltwood, Drop Acorn Pendants, 1830s, 35 x 21 In.	1058.00
Mirror, Teak, Brass Inlay, Vines, Erhard & Sohne, Austria, c.1905, 9 x 7 In. ....*illus*	472.00
Mirror, Venetian, Giltwood, Carved Scrolls & Leaves, 19th Century, 34 x 26 In.	915.00
Mirror, Venetian Rococo, Giltwood, Carved Shells, Scrolls, Red Paint, Mask, 31 In., Pair........	1725.00
Mirror, Venetian Rococo, Giltwood Rocaille, Cartouche Form, White, Flowers, 44 x 29 In.	633.00
Mirror, Victorian, Walnut, Half Round Spindles, Turned Sphere Crest, 30 x 28 In.	117.00
Mirror, Victorian, Walnut, Round, Turned, Hooks, Swing-Out Arms, 16 In.	169.00
Mirror, Victorian, Woman's Head In Crown, Divided Plate, Gold, c.1850, 61 In.	5940.00
Mirror, Walnut, Thick Stepped Sides, Octagonal, Dutch, 17th Century, 20 x 20 In.	805.00
Mirror, Wood, Dark Red Paint, 19th Century, 6 ½ x 5 ¼ In.	425.00
Mirror, Wood, Gesso Crest, Flower Vase, Beadwork, Multicolored, 40 x 21 ½ In.	518.00
Ottoman, Clover Shape, Blue & Yellow Upholstery, Fringe, 34 x 19 In.	450.00
Ottoman, Olive Green Leather, Nailhead Trim, Upturned Ends, 20 x 49 ½ In.	3200.00
Ottoman, Painted, Tufted Fabric Top, Brown Velveteen, England, 17 x 27 ½ In., Pair..............	2600.00
Overmantel Mirror, see Architectural category.	
Panel, Red Lacquer, Birds On Branches, 41 ½ x 11 In., Pair...	627.00
Parlor Set, Mahogany, Griffins, Carved, Chair, Rocker, Bench, S. Karpen Bros.	1600.00
Parlor Set, Neo-Grec, Marquetry, Upholstered, Sofa, Armchair, 3 Side Chairs, c.1880..............	2400.00
Parlor Set, Renaissance Revival, Walnut, Burl, Sofa, 2 Chairs, Medallion Crest......................	1045.00
Parlor Set, Rococo, Laminated Rosewood, Sofa, Armchair, 3 Side Chairs, Serpentine	3840.00
Parlor Set, Rosewood, Carved Crests, Cabriole Legs, Settee, 3 Side Chairs, 1800s	1180.00
Parlor Set, Walnut, Triple Back Sofa, Shaped Seat Rail, Scrolled Arms......................................	420.00
Pedestal, Adam Style, Mixed Wood, Carved, Tripod Base, 1900s, 44 x 17 In. ....*illus*	144.00

Furniture, Mirror, Federal, Giltwood, Reverse Painted Panel, Early 1800s, 48 x 29 In.
$288.00

Furniture, Mirror, Queen Anne, Walnut Veneer, Parcel Gilt, Carved, Early 1700s, 35 x 14 In.
$748.00

Furniture, Mirror, Shaving, Federal, Mahogany, Shield Shape Glass, Drawers, c.1800, 22 x 8 In.
$441.00

Furniture, Mirror, Teak, Brass Inlay, Vines, Erhard & Sohne, Austria, c.1905, 9 x 7 In.
$472.00

Furniture, Pedestal, Adam Style, Mixed Wood, Carved, Tripod Base, 1900s, 44 x 17 In.
$144.00

Furniture, Pedestal, Napoleon III, Carved, Gilt Gesso, Lion's Masks, Late 1800s, 40 x 10 ½ In.
$600.00

Furniture, Pedestal, Neoclassical, Mahogany Veneer, Fluted Capital, Paneled Column, 48 x 15 In.
$1003.00

Pedestal, Aesthetic Revival, Ebonized, Gilt Incised, Inlaid Butterflies, Vines, 1800s, 28 x 15 In.	470.00
Pedestal, Aesthetic Revival, Mahogany, Ebonized, Inverted Plinth, Incised, c.1880, 40 x 15 In.	764.00
Pedestal, Base Molding, Octagonal Plinth, c.1875, 47 In.	1020.00
Pedestal, Biedermeier, Burl, Square, Stepped Base, 1940s, 47 x 16 ½ In.	1035.00
Pedestal, Biedermeier, Fruitwood, Mahogany, Bronze Mounted, Toupee Feet, 38 x 11 In.	148.00
Pedestal, Biedermeier, Lyre Shape Supports, Round Top, 33 x 17 In.	316.00
Pedestal, Bugatti, Mahogany, Exotic Wood, Pewter, Copper, c.1900, 54 x 15 x 17 ½ In.	14340.00
Pedestal, Carved, Warrior, Holding Shield, Glass Eyes, Ivory Teeth, 1800s, 32 In.	2150.00
Pedestal, Continental, Wood, Parcel Gilt, Painted Landscape, Porcelain Center, 39 ⅓ In.	80.00
Pedestal, Edwardian, Mahogany, Inlaid, Drawer, Paneled Door, 42 x 18 x 20 In.	2585.00
Pedestal, Gothic Revival, Mahogany, Ebonized Marble Top, Arched Base, Door, 37 In.	1659.00
Pedestal, Gothic Revival, Oak, Paneled Stem, Column, Painted, Gilt, Jewels, 32 x 8 In.	256.00
Pedestal, Herter Brothers, Renaissance Revival, Walnut, Carved, Flamingos, c.1865, 43 In.	30500.00
Pedestal, Hunzinger, Mahogany, Rope Pierced Pedestal, Metal Lion's Heads, 37 x 16 In.	1700.00
Pedestal, Italian Neoclassical Style, Gilt & White Stippled Paint, 36 x 9 In.	115.00
Pedestal, Italian Style, Carved, Putti, Valance, Scrolling Paw Foot Base	330.00
Pedestal, L. & J.G. Stickley, No. 27, Reverse Tapered Column, Square Top, 18 x 36 In.	1725.00 to 2013.00
Pedestal, Limbert, No. 245, 2 Shelves, Label, 12 x 12 x 36 In.	1800.00
Pedestal, Louis XIV, Giltwood, Round Top, Gadrooned Edge, Fluted Standard, 59 x 19 In.	900.00
Pedestal, Louis XV Style, Flower Marquetry, Rose To Ivory Marble, 45 x 17 x 9 In.	690.00
Pedestal, Louis XVI Style, Satinwood, Tapered, Painted Design, Bronze Feet, 1800s, 47 In., Pair	1080.00
Pedestal, Louis XVI, Tulipwood, Marble Top, Panels, Ormolu, Tapered, 58 x 21 In.	6518.00
Pedestal, Lucite, White, Cylindrical, 42 x 14 In.	58.00
Pedestal, Mahogany, Reeded, Carved, Square Base, 39 In.	350.00
Pedestal, Mahogany, Reeded Column Base, c.1880, 48 In.	395.00
Pedestal, Marble, Gray, White, Bronze Mounted, 45 x 10 In.	119.00
Pedestal, Marble Top, Ebonized, Ormolu, Round, Gilt Metal Festoons, 42 ½ In.	560.00
Pedestal, Maroon Marble, Round, 36 ½ x 14 In.	201.00
Pedestal, Mirrored Panels, Plinth, Silver Gilt, Shell Decoration, 30 x 18 x 18 In.	345.00
Pedestal, Molded Top, Paneled Sides, 1800s, 23 x 35 In.	177.00
Pedestal, Napoleon III, Carved, Gilt Gesso, Lion's Masks, Late 1800s, 40 x 10 ½ In. *illus*	600.00
Pedestal, Neoclassical, Mahogany Veneer, Fluted Capital, Paneled Column, 48 x 15 In. *illus*	1003.00
Pedestal, Neoclassical Style, Fruitwood, Tapered, Inlaid Marble Panels, 45 ½ x 13 x 13 In.	440.00
Pedestal, Neoclassical Style, Mahogany, 3 Reeded Supports, Animal Form Feet, 41 In.	443.00
Pedestal, Neoclassical Style, Mahogany, Brass Mount, Fluted Stem, 42 ¼ x 10 In.	237.00
Pedestal, Oak, Carved Dragon, Platform Base, 25 x 43 In.	5463.00
Pedestal, Oak, Carved Stem, Fluting, Leaves, 20th Century, 50 ½ In.	356.00
Pedestal, Porcelain, Brass Mounted, Octagonal Top, Trefoil Column & Base, 46 x 16 In.	345.00
Pedestal, Porcelain, Pierced Center Medallion, Leaves, Hexagonal, Chinese, 1800s, 31 In.	444.00
Pedestal, Renaissance Revival, Walnut, Bronze, Revolving Marble Top, c.1873, 42 x 29 In.	10980.00
Pedestal, Rosewood, Herter Bros., Carved Columns, Inlaid Flowers, Urns, 41 x 18 In. *illus*	6325.00
Pedestal, Teak, Tree Root Carved, 4 Platforms, Korea, c.1965, 49 x 35 In.	176.00
Pedestal, Victorian, Oak, Round Top, Bottom, Scrolled Base, c.1900, 37 x 17 In.	117.00
Pedestal, Victorian, Oak, Turned & Fluted Baluster Column, 36 x 13 In.	120.00
Pedestal, Walnut, Carved Griffin Stem, Mother-Of-Pearl Apron, Base Inlay, 16 x 47 In.	5750.00
Pedestal, Walnut, Carved Griffins, 3 Shell Feet, 15 x 49 In., Pair	5178.00
Pedestal, Walnut, Corinthian Scroll, Fluted Column, Stepped Base, 33 x 11 In., Pair	439.00
Pedestal, Walnut, Nude Woman Support, Octagonal Top, Scalloped Apron, 14 x 14 In.	470.00
Pedestal, William IV, Mahogany, Wine Drawers, Downward Taper, c.1830, 43 x 19 In., Pair	1725.00
Pedestal, Wood, Carved, Gilt, Round Molded Top, Laurel Swags, Cherub, 55 x 16 In., Pair	633.00
Pie Safe, Bright Blue Paint, 2 Panels, 19th Century, 45 x 31 x 18 In.	735.00
Pie Safe, Butternut, Star Pierced Tin Panels, Painted White, 52 x 38 In. *illus*	1955.00
Pie Safe, Cherry, Gallery Top, 2 Doors, Turned Legs, Tennessee, c.1860, 64 x 45 In.	1645.00
Pie Safe, Cherry, Geometric Tins On Doors, c.1850, 44 ½ x 54 x 18 In.	4230.00
Pie Safe, Green, Ocher Paint, Door, Shelves, 38 ½ x 22 ½ In.	1035.00
Pie Safe, Green Paint, Punched Tin Panels, 2 Doors, Drawer, 1900s, 54 x 36 In.	420.00
Pie Safe, Hanging, Poplar, Pine, Geometric Tins, Red Wash, 1800s, 34 x 30 In.	588.00
Pie Safe, Hanging, Tin, Pinwheel Punched Designs, 1800s, 35 x 39 In.	588.00
Pie Safe, Pine, 6 Sides, Screened Windows, Lazy Susan, Shaped Legs, Georgia, 68 x 37 In.	2990.00
Pie Safe, Pine, Painted, 2 Doors, Punched Tin Panels, Shelves, Georgia, 1800s, 64 x 46 In.	6440.00
Pie Safe, Pine, Poplar Drawers, 3 Drawers, 2 Doors, Punched Tin Panels, 60 x 56 In.	518.00
Pie Safe, Plank Top, Painted, Pierced Tin Panels, Square Post Legs, c.1800, 43 x 55 x 17 In.	3824.00
Pie Safe, Poplar, 2 Doors, Punched Tin, Masonic Symbols, Flowers, 1859, 59 x 42 x 17 In.	748.00
Pie Safe, Poplar, Cherry, Gallery, Drawer, Punched Star Tin Doors, c.1850, 58 x 43 In.	764.00
Pie Safe, Red Paint, Yellow Rays, Mid-Atlantic, 43 ½ x 55 In.	1528.00
Pie Safe, Softwood, 8 Punched Tin Panels, Drawer, Wood Knobs, 56 x 32 x 15 In.	961.00

Pie Safe, Splash Back, 2 Drawers, 50 x 41 x 20 In.	509.00
Pie Safe, Walnut, 2 Doors, 2 Drawers, Stars & Hearts Punched Tin, 53 x 41 In.	458.00
Pie Safe, Walnut, Poplar, Blue-Gray Paint, Punched Tin Panels, 2 Drawers, 1850s, 49 x 44 In.	1025.00
Pie Safe, Walnut, Poplar, Punched Tin, 4 Doors, Drawers, Ohio, c.1867, 75 x 41 In.	1763.00
Pie Safe, Walnut, Punched Tin Panels, Fitted Interior, North Carolina, c.1900, 50 x 40 In.	575.00
Pie Safe, Wood, Copper Screen, Turned Legs, 19th Century, 41 x 31 x 16 In.	226.00
Pie Safe, Wood, Polychrome, Screened Panels & Doors, c.1800, 25 In.	90.00
Pie Safe, Yellow Pine, Painted, Punched Tin Panels, Georgia, 1800s, 65 x 46 In. ....*illus*	6440.00
Pie Safe, Yellow Pine, Tin Hearts, Compass Star Designs, White Interior, 1800s, 55 x 47 In.	2300.00
Planter, Arts & Crafts, Slatted Bucket, Triangular Shelf, 12 x 27 In. ....*illus*	120.00
Planter, Hardstone Inlay, Bird, Flowers, Openwork Rim, 33 x 24 x 15 In.	366.00
Plinth, Pine, Carved Relief, Cherub Supports Top, Tapered Shaft, Italy, 43 x 15 In.	748.00
Rack, Baking, 3 Shelves, Scroll Top, Wrought Iron, Brass Trim, 84 x 72 x 18 In.	165.00
Rack, Baking, Brass, Iron, 3 Shelves, Scroll & Wheat Crest, France, c.1890, 79 x 41 x 20 In.	1820.00
Rack, Baking, Brass, Iron, Corner, 3 Shelves, Late 19th Century, 83 ½ x 25 ½ x 22 In.	580.00
Rack, Baking, Brass, Iron, Oak Shelves, 51 x 30 In.	210.00
Rack, Baking, Brass, Iron, Scrolls, Flowers, Wheat Stalks, 3 Shelves, Bin, France, 87 x 93 In. ..	1770.00
Rack, Bread, French Provincial, Fruitwood, Serpentine Crest, Door, Spindles, 32 x 34 In.	717.00
Rack, Bread, Walnut, 2 Tiers, Frieze, Turned Legs, Shaped Skirt, France, 1780, 34 x 39 x 19 In. .	2100.00
Rack, Candle Drying, Wood, Carved, 8 Arms, Crossed Shoe Base, 1800s, 41 x 35 In.	920.00
Rack, Drying, 6 Racks, Old White Paint, 58 ¾ x 60 In.	120.00
Rack, Hanging, 6 Folding Arms, 1800s, 6 ¼ x 71 ¾ In.	497.00
Rack, Magazine, Arts & Crafts, Woven Willow, 22 x 13 x 26 In.	210.00
Rack, Magazine, Beech, Blond, Folding, Plywood Slats, Dowel Bars, Nevco, 17 ½ x 19 ½ In. ...	75.00
Rack, Magazine, Ceramic Ashtray, Metal Frame, Wheels, 1950s, 24 x 19 In.	95.00
Rack, Magazine, Mahogany, Dividers, Cutouts, Lakeside Craftshop, 16 ½ x 14 x 35 In.	510.00
Rack, Magazine, Wood, Brass, 12 x 14 x 5 In.	25.00
Rack, Magazine, Wormley, Sap Grain Walnut, Birch, Signed, Label, Dunbar, 25 x 28 In. ....*illus*	6100.00
Rack, Paper, G. Stickley, No. 551, Slatted Canted Top, 2 Lower Shelves, Signed, 30 x 40 In.	9600.00
Rack, Plate, G. Stickley, No. 801, Arched Top, Chamfered Back, Signed, Decal, 47 x 28 In.	3240.00
Rack, Plate, Hanging, Wood, 35 x 14 In.	60.00
Rack, Plate, Molded Cornice, Shelves, Spindles Below, Scallops, Ireland, 49 x 76 In.	1410.00
Rack, Plate, Pine, Molded Cornice, Scalloped Molded Sides, Ireland, 49 x 16 In.	1410.00
Rack, Spoon, Original Red Paint, Pinwheel Carving, 7 Slots, 1800s, 24 In.	367.00
Recamier, Neoclassical, Mahogany, Carved, Shaped Back, Paneled Arm, c.1830, 30 x 58 In. ...	600.00
Recamier, Neoclassical, Mahogany, Upholstered, Scrolled Frame, Cornucopia Headrest, 30 x 23 In.	1495.00
Recamier, Regency, Faux Bois, Bolster, Paneled Frieze, Upholstered, 31 x 56 In. ....*illus*	2280.00
Recamier, Soubrier, Louis XVI, Painted, White, Gold, Silk Upholstery, 81 x 32 In.	1150.00
Recliner, Milo Baughman, Elm Frame, Green Vinyl Seat, 1972, 30 x 42 In.	90.00
Rocker, Adirondack, Bentwood, Green Paint, c.1900, 19 In., Child's	247.00
Rocker, Adirondack Twig, Low Rolled Arms, 46 x 24 x 30 In.	546.00
Rocker, Arrow Back, 3 Horizontal Slats, Arms, New England, 43 x 23 In.	86.00
Rocker, Arrow Back, Plank Seat, 1800s.	61.00
Rocker, Arts & Crafts, Leatherette Top, Vertical Slats, Spring Cushion, 29 x 32 x 39 In.	270.00
Rocker, Bamboo, Mixed Woods, Black Paint, Scroll Arms, 34 In.	235.00
Rocker, Boston, Ebonized, Floral Stencil, Gold Outline, Saddle Seat, c.1830, 36 In.	94.00
Rocker, Eames, Molded Fiberglass Shell, Checkerboard, Herman Miller, 1960s, 27 In.	1440.00
Rocker, Eames, RAR, Fiberglass, Molded, Wire, Birch, Herman Miller, 25 x 27 In. ....*illus*	1020.00
Rocker, G. Stickley, 3-Slat Back, Leather Seat, Open Arm, Red, Brown, 26 x 38 In.	690.00
Rocker, G. Stickley, No. 2603, Ladder Back, Leather Cushion, Hip Rail, 25 x 38 In.	1080.00
Rocker, Glider, Victorian, Walnut, Spindle Back, Upholstered Seat, Head Rest, 44 x 23 In.	210.00
Rocker, Harvey Ellis, Oak, Copper, Pewter, Fruitwood Inlay, Cane Seat, c.1903, 39 In.	15000.00
Rocker, Hickory, Mixed Woods, Hide Seat, c.1910, 24 x 20 In., Child's	978.00
Rocker, Hunzinger, Lollipop, Oak, Carved, Leather Seat, Signed	728.00
Rocker, Hunzinger, Platform, Oak, Lollipop, Leather Seat	708.00
Rocker, Iron, Scrolled Brass Frame, Padded Scroll Arms, Tufted Upholstery, 1800s, 40 In.	470.00
Rocker, L. & J.G. Stickley, Slats, Cross Stitched Leather Cushions, 36 x 30 In. ....*illus*	2400.00
Rocker, Limbert, No. 818 ½, Corbel Supports, Leather Cushions, 32 x 36 x 32 In.	4500.00
Rocker, Limbert, No. 842, 5 Vertical Slats, 32 x 38 x 34 In.	4200.00
Rocker, Limbert, No. 1654, Upholstered Seat, Vertical Slats, Arms, 28 x 34 In.	390.00
Rocker, Limbert, Sewing, Slat Back, Cutouts, Ebony Inlay, Raincross Symbol, Signed, 30 In. ..	2400.00
Rocker, Lincoln, Mahogany, Upholstered, Scroll Arms & Legs, 1855, 43 In.	530.00
Rocker, Maple, Ladder Back, Woven Seat, Knobby Finials, 19th Century, 32 In.	199.00
Rocker, Metal Frame, Upholstered, 39 x 29 In., Pair	4200.00
Rocker, Mixed Woods, Curved Back, Buildings Decoupage, Yellow Ground, c.1840, 43 In.	529.00
Rocker, Mixed Woods, Painted, Spinning Wheel Back, Arms, Late 1800s, 38 x 21 In.	499.00

Furniture, Pedestal, Rosewood, Herter Bros., Carved Columns, Inlaid Flowers, Urns, 41 x 18 In. $6325.00

Furniture, Pie Safe, Butternut, Star Pierced Tin Panels, Painted White, 52 x 38 In. $1955.00

Furniture, Pie Safe, Yellow Pine, Painted, Punched Tin Panels, Georgia, 1800s, 65 x 46 In. $6440.00

F

FURNITURE

Furniture, Planter, Arts & Crafts, Slatted Bucket, Triangular Shelf, 12 x 27 In.
$120.00

Furniture, Rack, Magazine, Wormley, Sap Grain Walnut, Birch, Signed, Label, Dunbar, 25 x 28 In.
$6100.00

Furniture, Recamier, Regency, Faux Bois, Bolster, Paneled Frieze, Upholstered, 31 x 56 In.
$2280.00

Furniture, Rocker, Eames, RAR, Fiberglass, Molded, Wire, Birch, Herman Miller, 25 x 27 In.
$1020.00

Rocker, Oak, Ash, Splint Weave Seat, Poplar Rockers	66.00
Rocker, Oak, Corn Husk, Ladder Back, Bevel Posts Edges, Stylized Arms, 28 x 19 x 24 In.	165.00
Rocker, Old Hickory, 7 Spindles, 25 x 31 ½ x 34 ½ In., Pair	540.00
Rocker, Old Hickory, Woven Splint Seat, Back, Bowed Arms, 31 x 36 x 38 In., Pair	2040.00
Rocker, Platform, Upholstered Seat & Back, Padded Arms, c.1910, 41 In. ....*illus*	205.00
Rocker, Platform, Victorian, Walnut, Geometric Carvings, Tufted Back, c.1890, 36 x 32 x 31 In.	400.00
Rocker, Rush Seat, Union Village, Ohio, c.1840, 16 x 44 In.	176.00
Rocker, Rustic, Bent Twig Construction, 23 x 34 x 40 In., Pair ....*illus*	660.00
Rocker, Sam Maloof, Teak, Spindle Back, Arms, 1982, 45 x 26 In.	21850.00
Rocker, Shaker, 2 Wide Slats, Rush Seat, Yellow Rockers, Conn., c.1830, 17 x 41 In.	1053.00
Rocker, Shaker, Ladder Back, 4 Slats, Rush Seat, Blue Wash, Mt. Lebanon, N.Y., c.1890, 16 x 37 In.	235.00
Rocker, Shaker, Ladder Back, Acorn Finials, Woven Tape Seat, 23 ¾ In., Child's	230.00
Rocker, Shaker, Maple, Black, Green Tape Seat & Back, Arms, Dark Stain, N.Y., c.1875, 40 In.	527.00
Rocker, Shaker, Maple, Cane Seat, Arms, Walnut Stain, N.Y., 1875, 13 x 29 In., Child	702.00
Rocker, Shaker, Maple, Cane Seat, Flame Finials, Mass., c.1830, 13 x 28 In., Child's	936.00
Rocker, Shaker, Maple, Dark Stain, Blue, Red Tape Seat, Back, Arms, N.Y., c.1890, 23 In.	2340.00
Rocker, Shaker, Maple, Flame Finials, 4 Slats, White Tape Seat, 16 x 38 In.	234.00
Rocker, Shaker, Maple, Green Tape Seat, Back, Decal, Arms, N.Y., c.1900, 16 x 34 In.	468.00
Rocker, Shaker, Maple, Ladder Back, Shawl Bar, Tape Seat, Pegged Rockers, c.1870, 41 In.	468.00
Rocker, Shaker, Maple, Red, White Tape Seat & Back, Walnut Stain, Arms, N.Y., 1875, 38 In.	527.00
Rocker, Shaker, Maple, Rush Seat, Arms, Dark Stain, Mark, c.1875, 9 x 21 In., Child's	2340.00
Rocker, Shaker, Maple, Shaped Arms, Mushroom Caps, Upholstered, c.1900, 16 ½ x 42 In.	118.00
Rocker, Shaker, Maple, Splint Seat, Green, Red Paint, Arms, N.Y., c.1810, 14 x 42 In.	1755.00
Rocker, Shaker, Maple, Walnut, Shawl Bar, 4 Slats, Rush Seat, N.Y., c.1889, 15 x 41 In.	351.00
Rocker, Shaker, No. 3, 3 Slats, Turned Post & Finial, Tape Seat, Late 19th Century	290.00
Rocker, Shaker, No. 3, 3 Slats, Woven Tape Seat, Late 1800s	320.00
Rocker, Shaker, No. 7, 4 Slats, Mushroom Arm Caps, Tape Seat, 40 ½ In.	650.00
Rocker, Shaker, No. 7, 4 Slats, Mushroom Arm Caps, Tape Seat, Mt. Lebanon, 40 ½ In.	605.00
Rocker, Shaker, No. 7, Shawl Back, Tape Seat, Mt. Lebanon, 19th Century	1062.00
Rocker, Shaker, Tiger Maple, Cherry, Finial Top, Mushroom Arms, 1820, 46 In.	5925.00
Rocker, Skeleton Figure, Seated On Rockers, Upholstered Seat, 1900s, 54 In.	3120.00
Rocker, Stickley Bros., No. 715, 5 Vertical, 3 Side Slats, Leather Cushion, 28 ½ x 39 x 35 In.	1020.00
Rocker, Turned Wood Frame, Woven Seat, Back, Folding, c.1900, 27 x 16 In., Child's	150.00
Rocker, Victorian, Mahogany, Diamond Back, Bailey Twist Turnings, Arms, Late 1800s	2600.00
Rocker, Victorian, Oak, Pine, Leather Seat, Carved Back Crest, Turned Spindles, 37 In.	59.00
Rocker, Walnut, Carved Armrests, Upholstered Floral Wreath, c.1900, 31 x 20 In.	117.00
Rocker, Walnut, Slat Back, Wooden Pin Construction, 36 x 18 In.	360.00
Rocker, Walter Lamb, Metal Frame, Plastic, Brown Jordan, c.1950, 32 x 32 In.	3675.00
Rocker, Wegner, Teak, Wool Upholstered Seat, Slat Back, 32 x 25 In.	1140.00
Rocker, Wicker, Ball & Stick, Scrolling, White Paint, 29 x 24 In., Child's	175.00
Rocker, Wicker, Oval Back, Scroll Supports, Heywood-Wakefield Co., c.1890, 42 In. ....*illus*	7552.00
Rocker, Windsor, Comb Back, Bamboo Turnings, Stenciled Fruit, 43 ½ x 16 ½ In.	220.00
Rocker, Windsor, Comb Back, Poplar, Plank Seat, Black Paint, 1800s, 42 x 18 In.	345.00
Rocker, Windsor, Comb Back, Yellow, Red Flowers, Brown Paint, Arms, 1800s, 40 ½ In.	793.00
Rocker, Windsor, Mixed Woods, Square Back, Shaped Headrest, 1900s, 16 x 42 In.	147.00
Rocker, Wood, White Paint, Crest Signed Floyd, 19th Century, 20 In., Child's	250.00
Room Divider, Nakashima, Wood, Free-Form Top, Finished Back Panels, 24 x 84 In.	36750.00
Schrank, Pine, Knock-Down, Paneled Doors, Painted, Christian Kammerzell, c.1840, 74 x 61 In. *illus*	1763.00
Schrank, Pine, Painted, Molded Cornice, Raised Panels, Drawers, Pa., c.1780, 91 x 67 In. ....*illus*	2574.00
Schrank, Raised Panel Door, 4 Drawers, Green, Blue Paint, 1800s, 72 x 52 In.	999.00
Screen, 2-Panel, Gilt Carved Ivy, Berries, Red Embroidery Inserts, Italy, 73 x 63 In.	2990.00
Screen, 3-Panel, Aesthetic Revival, Flowering Cherry Branches, Block Feet, c.1875, 67 x 84 In.	881.00
Screen, 3-Panel, Art Deco, Leather, Ebony Frame, Embossed Birds, Flowers, 72 x 70 In.	4500.00
Screen, 3-Panel, Arts & Crafts, Burlap Center, Inset Green Glass, Roundels, 58 ½ x 69 In.	540.00
Screen, 3-Panel, Black Lacquer, Painted Court Scene, Chinese, 34 ½ x 39 ¼ In.	269.00
Screen, 3-Panel, Folding, Wood, Autumn Scenes, Leather Trim, Early 1900s, 66 x 53 In.	270.00
Screen, 3-Panel, Gilt, Stenciled Squares, Red & Black, 78 x 46 ¾ In.	978.00
Screen, 3-Panel, Hardwood, Scroll Carved, 3 Spindle Panels, Morocco, 71 x 71 In.	245.00
Screen, 3-Panel, Leather, Hand Painted, Floral Still Life, Early 1900s, 71 ½ x 60 In.	142.00
Screen, 3-Panel, Louis XV, Painted, Gilt, Courting Scenes, Cherubs, Multicolored, c.1900, 50 In.	1896.00
Screen, 3-Panel, Louis XV Style, Gilt, Painted, Carved, 58 x 54 In.	777.00
Screen, 3-Panel, Mirror, 2 Shelves, Ornate Carving, Pickled Wood, France, c.1900, 24 x 65 In.	978.00
Screen, 3-Panel, Oak, Leaded Glass Inserts, Scrolls, Birds & Flowers, 86 x 91 In.	214.00
Screen, 3-Panel, Paper, Hand Painted, Seaside Scene, Stylized Amphora, Bouquet, 68 ½ x 57 In.	167.00
Screen, 3-Panel, Peaceable Kingdom, 70 ¼ x 62 In.	623.00
Screen, 3-Panel, Polychrome, Carved Figural Parrots, Rising Sun, Mexico, 67 x 60 In.	150.00

Screen, 3-Panel, Stagecoach, Pedestrian, Medieval Village, Oil On Canvas, 1800s, 56 x 54 In.	400.00
Screen, 3-Panel, Victorian, Leather, Venice Scene, c.1900, 70 ¼ x 60 In.	489.00
Screen, 3-Panel, Zitan, Embroidered, Pierced, Carved, Birds, Flowers, 52 x 66 In.	2530.00
Screen, 4-Panel, Arts & Crafts, Landscape, Castle Scene, 25 ½ x 74 In.	570.00
Screen, 4-Panel, Birds, Flowers, Inlaid Black Lacquer, Mother-Of-Pearl Bands, 72 x 64 In.	520.00
Screen, 4-Panel, Black Lacquer, Ivory Urns, Figures, Trees, Openwork Border, 72 In.	566.00
Screen, 4-Panel, Black Lacquer, Mother-Of-Pearl Inlay, Flowers, Carved Base, 72 x 72 In.	288.00
Screen, 4-Panel, Canvas, Painted, Barnyard Scene, Dogs, Turkey, 72 x 64 In.	705.00
Screen, 4-Panel, Chinese, Coromandel, Continuous Water Garden Scene, 1700s, 84 x 21 In.	720.00
Screen, 4-Panel, Embroidered, Dragons, Serpents, Japan, c.1800, 74 x 108 In.	2650.00
Screen, 4-Panel, Empire, Wallpaper, Cornucopia, Faux Marble, Early 1800s, 69 x 82 In.	2056.00
Screen, 4-Panel, Gilt, Carved, Upholstered, Tapestry, 67 ½ x 15 ½ In.	1434.00
Screen, 4-Panel, Landscapes, Calligraphic Inscriptions On Reverse, Chinese, 64 x 54 In.	293.00
Screen, 4-Panel, Leather, Flora & Fauna, Mottled Cream Crackled Ground, c.1900, 71 x 72 In.	191.00
Screen, 4-Panel, Leather, Painted, Flowers, Fauna, 71 x 72 In.	209.00
Screen, 4-Panel, Neoclassical Revival, Canvas, Painted Commedia Dell'Arte Figures, 64 In.	2252.00
Screen, 4-Panel, Oriental Designs, 65 x 72 In.	88.00
Screen, 4-Panel, Silk, Painted Landscape, Cottages, Bridge, Figure, 35 x 68 In.	144.00
Screen, 4-Panel, Wood, Oriental Scene, 19th Century, 74 x 74 In.	588.00
Screen, 5-Panel, Wood, Low Relief, Scholars, Landscapes, Flowers, Black Lacquer, 77 x 65 In.	353.00
Screen, 6-Panel, Carved, Multicolored, Scenic, Flowers, Folding, Chinese, 72 x 98 In.	235.00
Screen, 6-Panel, Eames, Rosewood, Molded, Canvas Webbing, 57 x 68 In.	7800.00
Screen, 6-Panel, Lacquer, Birds, Prunus, Silvered Ground, Bamboo, Chinese, 72 x 96 In.	764.00
Screen, 6-Panel, Leather, Black Ground, Painted Chinoiserie, Flower Urn Border, 84 In.	5463.00
Screen, 6-Panel, Tapestry Style, Printed Hunting Scenes, Metal Handles, 66 x 108 In.	345.00
Screen, Chinese, Hardwood Frame, Embroidery, Pierced Carved, Ivory Insets, 27 x 25 In.	316.00
Screen, Coromandel, Lacquer, Black, Text, Carved Palace Scene, Chinese, 1700s, 140 x 96 In.	5629.00
Screen, Eames, FSW-6, Wood, Box, Herman Miller, c.1946, 68-In. Panel	9188.00
Screen, Hepplewhite, Mahogany, Oval, Needlework, Tripod Base, 1810, 48 In. ....*illus*	411.00
Screen, Rosewood, Spiral Twist Frame, Pierced Crest, Needlework Panel, 44 x 31 In.	489.00
Screen, Scholar's, Porcelain, Children, Famille Rose, Stand, Carved, Rosewood, 1800s, 23 In.	940.00
Screen, Table, Hardwood, Ivory, Carved, 2 Farmers, Women, Children, Chinese, 32 x 31 In.	14040.00
Screen, Walnut, Fabric, 2-Sided, Folding, Flowers, Arched Crest, c.1880, 57 x 59 In.	1450.00
Screens are also listed in the Architectural and Fireplace categories.	
Secretary, Biedermeier, Blond, Faux Inlaid, Balloon Case, Drop Front, Paw Feet, 63 In.	3565.00
Secretary, Biedermeier, Drop Front, Ebonized Trim, Fitted, Drawers, 71 In.	4600.00
Secretary, Biedermeier, Drop Front, Mahogany, Fitted, Drawers, 41 x 42 In.	690.00
Secretary, Chinoiserie, Serpentine Waist, Drawers, Gilt Landscape, c.1700, 81 x 50 In.	5581.00
Secretary, Chippendale, Mahogany, Flat Front, Ogee Bracket Base, Broken-Arch Top, 92 x 44 In.	460.00
Secretary, Chippendale Style, Maple, Slant Front, Stiehl Furniture Co., 40 x 32 In.	649.00
Secretary, Chippendale, Tiger Maple, Bird's-Eye Maple, D.A. Dunlap, N.H., c.1985, 82 x 34 In.	21330.00
Secretary, Drop Front, Double Arch, Fitted Interior, Bun Feet, Japanned, 86 In.	6608.00
Secretary, Eastlake, Walnut, Organ Cabinet, Drop Front, c.1885, 72 x 45 In.	118.00
Secretary, Empire, Cherry, Overhang Drawer, Fitted Interior, 3 Lower Drawers, Carving, 44 x 45 In.	470.00
Secretary, Empire, Gray Marble Top, Drop Front, Frieze Door, Drawers, c.1890, 39 x 56 In.	1422.00
Secretary, Federal, Breakfront, c.1800, 82 x 92 In.	9375.00
Secretary, Federal, Mahogany, Diamond Pane Doors, Drawers, Finials, c.1910, 75 x 35 In.	617.00
Secretary, George I, Burl Walnut, 2 Mirrored Doors, Slant Front, 3 Drawers, 81 x 38 In.	4780.00
Secretary, George III, Chippendale, Mahogany, 89 x 45 In. ....*illus*	34375.00
Secretary, George III, Multicolored, Chinoiserie, Double Dome Top, 82 x 38 In.	11400.00
Secretary, George III Style, Burl Walnut, Leather Lined, Cubbyholes, 43 x 26 x 13 In.	960.00
Secretary, George III Style, Mahogany, Slant Front, Leather Writing Surface, 82 x 36 x 18 In.	1560.00
Secretary, Georgian Style, Burl, Walnut, Mixed Veneers, Doors, 87 ½ x 31 x 18 ¼ In.	2070.00
Secretary, Globe-Wernicke, Oak, 4 Sections, Drawer Base, 59 x 34 x 11 In.	840.00
Secretary, Hepplewhite, Mahogany, Maple Veneer, Doors, Drawers, c.1815, 87 x 40 In. .....*illus*	3525.00
Secretary, Louis XV Style, Burl, Marble Top, Drop Front, 50 x 25 x 14 In.	863.00
Secretary, Louis XVI Style, Marquetry, Drop Front, Mirror, Drawers, 59 x 27 ¼ x 18 ½ In.	329.00
Secretary, Mahogany, 2 Glass Upper Doors, Shelves, 4 Lower Drawers, 1800s, 46 In.	3450.00
Secretary, Mahogany, Carved Crest, Hinged Glass Door, Slant Front, c.1930, 74 x 26 In.	234.00
Secretary, Mahogany, Drop Front, 5 Drawers, 18th Century, 45 x 39 x 20 In.	920.00
Secretary, Mahogany, Empire, c.1835, 23 x 15 In.	881.00
Secretary, Neoclassical, Mahogany, Peaked Pediment, Glazed Doors, c.1820, 74 x 38 In.	2820.00
Secretary, Neoclassical, Mahogany, Reeded Mullioned Doors, Glazed Panels, 84 x 46 In.	3360.00
Secretary, Pine, Picket Top, Slant Front Desk, Late 1800s, 76 x 39 x 24 In. ....*illus*	360.00
Secretary, Queen Anne, Burl, Oak, Pine, Mirrored Doors, c.1730, 101 x 40 x 20 ¾ In.	10350.00
Secretary, Queen Anne, Mulberry, Arch Crest, Mirrored Doors, 94 x 38 In.	11590.00

Furniture, Rocker, L. & J.G. Stickley, Slats, Cross Stitched Leather Cushions, 36 x 30 In.
$2400.00

Lloyd Loom
Marshall Lloyd was the inventor of the Lloyd Loom used to make a type of woven wicker furniture. His invention was spurred by the workers who wove wicker at his factory. In 1917 they went on strike, and within five weeks Lloyd had invented a loom that would replace hand-weaving. Almost all wicker furniture today is made using a Lloyd Loom.

Furniture, Rocker, Platform, Upholstered Seat & Back, Padded Arms, c.1910, 41 In.
$205.00

Furniture, Rocker, Rustic, Bent Twig Construction, 23 x 34 x 40 In., Pair
$660.00

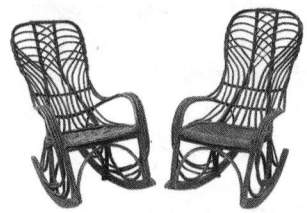

Furniture, Rocker, Wicker, Oval Back, Scroll Supports, Heywood-Wakefield Co., c.1890, 42 In.
$7552.00

Furniture, Schrank, Pine, Knock-Down, Paneled Doors, Painted, Christian Kammerzell, c.1840, 74 x 61 In.
$1763.00

Furniture, Schrank, Pine, Painted, Molded Cornice, Raised Panels, Drawers, Pa., c.1780, 91 x 67 In.
$2574.00

Secretary, Queen Anne Style, 4 Drawers, Bonnet Top, Fitted Interior, 86 x 43 x 24 In.	1464.00
Secretary, Regency, Mahogany, Ebony Inlay, c.1805, 110 x 104 In. ....*illus*	170500.00
Secretary, Regency, Satinwood, Brass Mounted, Ebony, Inlaid, 53 ½ x 42 x 21 In.	8813.00
Secretary, Sheraton, Cherry, 2 6-Pane Doors, 2 Drawers, Ohio, 1850s, 79 ½ x 42 x 27 In.	2350.00
Secretary, Tiger Maple, Cherry, Arched Glass Doors, Stand-Up, 1800s, 86 x 54 In.	2832.00
Secretary, Walnut, Carved Crest, Drop Front, 5 Drawers, Fitted Interior, Germany, 1800s.........	1121.00
Secretary, Walnut, Drop Front, Yellow Pine, Poplar Inlay, Doors, Drawers, 31 x 62 In.	18400.00
Secretary, Walnut, Flip Top, Arched Pediment, 2 Doors Over 3 Drawers, c.1875	944.00
Semainier, Bird's-Eye Maple, Plank Top, Molded Edge, 7 Drawers, 51 ½ x 28 x 18 ¾ In.	448.00
Semainier, Empire, Fruitwood, Ebonized, 7 Drawers, Bracket Feet, Columns, 41 x 22 In.	296.00
Semainier, Empire Style, Mahogany, Marble Top, Maiden Head Mount, 62 x 48 In.	4800.00
Semainier, French Provincial, 7 Drawers, Paneled Sides, Cabriole Legs, 57 x 25 x 15 In.	1434.00
Semainier, Louis XV, Kingwood, Ormolu Mounted, Marble, Early 1900s, 53 x 34 In. ....*illus*	1440.00
Semainier, Louis XV, Marquetry, Metal Fittings, Marble Top, 13 x 52 In. ....*illus*	891.00
Semainier, Louis XV/XVI Style, Tulipwood, Bronze, Marble Top, 7 Drawers, 53 x 24 x 14 In. ...	1422.00
Semainier, Rococo Style, Painted, Gilt, Cabriole Legs, Metal Pulls, Italy, 49 x 26 x 14 In.	598.00
Server, American Empire, Wood, Drawer, Shaped Back, Early 1800s, 37 x 30 x 19 In.	175.00
Server, Arched Carved Back, Ornate, Carved Legs, Continental, c.1800, 33 x 54 In.	575.00
Server, Boehmer, Inlay, Tapered Legs, 39 x 44 x 21 In.	472.00
Server, Cherry, 3 Drawers, France, c.1840, 31 x 73 In.	6500.00
Server, Cherry, Banded & Molded Edge, Drawers, Apron, Cabriole Legs, c.1900, 34 x 73 In.	836.00
Server, Chippendale, Mahogany, Baluster & Urn, Brass Gallery, Drawers, 1980s, 48 x 82 In. ...	2300.00
Server, Empire, Mahogany, Drawer, 2 Doors, Mid 1800s, 37 x 41 In.	268.00
Server, Empire, Mixed Woods, Drawers, Doors, Dovetailed, Columns, c.1875, 51 x 42 In.	969.00
Server, French Provincial, Marble Top, 2 Drawers, Paneled Doors, 41 x 51 In.	345.00
Server, G. Stickley, No. 955, Chestnut, Plate Rail, 2 Half Drawers, Shelf, 59 x 24 x 44 ½ In.	3900.00
Server, George II, Walnut, Burl, Backboard, Drawer, Felt Lined Compartments, 35 x 36 In.	259.00
Server, George III, Inlaid Mahogany, Fluted Frieze, Drawers, 35 x 59 In.	1342.00
Server, Georgian, Mahogany, 6 Legs, England, c.1800, 34 x 66 In.	1763.00
Server, Hepplewhite, Ash, Pine, Line Inlays, c.1800, 35 x 65 In.	2185.00
Server, Hepplewhite Style, Mahogany, Spade Feet, c.1880, 35 x 48 In.	2800.00
Server, L. & J.G. Stickley, 2 Drawers, 2 Doors, Decal, 48 x 36 In.	1140.00
Server, L. & J.G. Stickley, 2 Shelves, Curved Backsplash, Apron, 38 x 40 In. ....*illus*	2040.00
Server, Limbert, No. 402, Mirror, 3 Drawers, Copper Hardware, 54 x 50 In.	3000.00
Server, Limbert, No. 1408, 3 Drawers, Notched Lower Shelf, 42 x 42 In.	1680.00
Server, Louis XV Style, Fluted Panel Doors, Marble Top, 1900s, 40 x 49 In.	210.00
Server, Louis XVI Style, Mahogany, Marble Top, Pierced Brass Gallery, Drawer, 35 x 38 In., Pair	3120.00
Server, Mahogany, Bowfront, Inlaid, Crossbanded, Tapered Legs, Spade Feet, c.1850, 35 x 48 In.	690.00
Server, Mahogany, Carved, 2 Shelves, 2 Door Base, Turned Legs, Caribbean, 1800s ....*illus*	1872.00
Server, Mahogany, Serpentine Base, 2 Drawers, Oval Brass Mount Pulls, c.1930, 36 x 48 In. ...	1800.00
Server, Mirror, 6 Drawers, Brass Pulls, England, 61 x 21 In.	413.00
Server, Napoleon III, Amboyna Burl, Marble, Gilt Bronze, Door, Open Shelf, c.1900, 34 x 54 In.	390.00
Server, Oak, Leaded Glass Doors, Beveled Mirror, Early 1900s, 58 ½ x 44 ½ In.	600.00
Server, Pine, Poplar, Scroll Gallery, Doors, Drawers, Red Flame Graining, c.1835, 49 x 44 In. ..	1175.00
Server, Regency, Mahogany, 3 Tiers, Casters, 19th Century, 45 x 45 In. ....*illus*	1265.00
Server, Regency, Mahogany, 3 Tiers, Gallery, Columnar Supports, 40 x 48 x 16 In.	3465.00
Server, Regency, Mahogany, Marble Top, U-Frame, 2 Drawers, Inlaid Frieze, c.1910, 44 x 47 In.	593.00
Server, Sheraton, Cherry, 3 Drawers, Dovetailed, 35 x 29 In.	360.00
Server, Sheraton, Walnut, Top Gallery, Drawer, Worn Finish, c.1825, 29 x 40 In.	1116.00
Server, Softwood, Dovetailed, 3 Overlapping Drawers, Brass Bails, c.1880, 29 x 68 In.	705.00
Server, Victorian, Oak, Beveled Glass Mirror, Scrolled Door Panels, 56 x 38 x 18 In.	150.00
Server, Victorian, Oak, Shaped Top, 2 Drawers, Turned Legs, 19th Century, 31 ½ x 71 x 27 In. ..	475.00
Server, Yellow Pine, Molded Back, Turned Legs, Drawer, Red, Brown Traces, 1800s, 39 x 42 In.	1380.00
Serving Cart, Mahogany, Gilt Metal, Pierced Gallery, Push Handle, Wheels, c.1950, 29 x 16 In.	1200.00
Serving Cart, Wormley, Mahogany, Inset Textured Glass, 1949, 37 x 29 ½ x 29 ¾ In.	150.00
Settee, Art Deco, Mahogany, Box Shape, Padded Back, Sides, Cushioned Seat, 33 x 84 In.	1560.00
Settee, Barrel, Slats To Floor, Drop-In Spring Leather Seat, Plail Bros., 34 x 46 In. ....*illus*	4200.00
Settee, Biedermeier, Walnut, Shaped Back, Arms, Blue Upholstery, c.1825, 37 x 73 In.	1140.00
Settee, Charles II Style, Oak, Triple Back, Barley Twist Stiles, Openwork, 49 x 65 In.	837.00
Settee, Chippendale, Mahogany, Carved, Shaped Back, Rolled Arms, Yellow Velvet, 32 x 56 In. .	2875.00
Settee, Chippendale, Mahogany, Triple Back, Acanthus Carved Crest Rail, 41 x 81 In.	735.00
Settee, Convertible, Square Back, Ring-Turned Legs, Chinese, c.1825, 37 x 73 x 23 In.	593.00
Settee, Empire Revival, Mahogany, Bronze Mount, Sloped Back, Scroll Arms, 58 In.	1778.00
Settee, Federal, Mahogany, Double Chairback, Reeded Vertical Splats, Arms, 35 x 43 In.	1180.00
Settee, Federal, Mahogany, White Upholstery, Arched Back, c.1800, 34 x 46 In., Pair	31995.00
Settee, Finn Juhl, NV53, Teak, Yellow Fabric Upholstery, Denmark, 19 x 50 ½ In.	1800.00

Settee, French Provincial, Triple Ladder Back, Rush Seat, Painted, 40 x 74 In.	1534.00
Settee, G. Nakashima, Walnut, Cushion Seat, Spindle Back, 1957, 31 x 48 x 31 In.	3240.00
Settee, G. Nakashima, Walnut, Free Edge Seat, Hickory Spindle Back, 33 x 59 In.	7800.00
Settee, G. Nakashima, Walnut, Spindle Back, Seat Cushions, c.1959, 31 x 48 In., Pair	8625.00
Settee, G. Stickley, No. 161, Ladder Back, 4 Slats, Rope Foundation, 51 x 27 x 38 In.	1320.00
Settee, G. Stickley, No. 212, V Back, 12 Vertical Slats, Spring Seat, 47 x 24 x 36 In.	1800.00
Settee, Garouste Bonetti, Koala, Cream Velvet, Cast-Iron Bronzed Legs, 43 x 65 In.	4200.00
Settee, George III, Mahogany, Double Back, Domed, Padded, Early 1800s, 38 x 46 x 19 In.	510.00
Settee, Georgian, Mahogany, Arch Back, Scroll Arms, Upholstered, Shell Carved Cabriole Legs, 56 In.	770.00
Settee, Georgian, Mahogany, Slip Seat, Iron Bracing On Splats, Square Legs, c.1789, 65 In.	1530.00
Settee, Georgian, Triple Back, Arched, Painted Classical Maidens, Multicolored, 60 In.	444.00
Settee, German Rococo Style, Walnut, Leather, Carved, Serpentine Front, 75 In.	2133.00
Settee, Hardwood, Carved, Mother-Of-Pearl Inlay, Paneled Back, Chinese, c.1900, 39 x 72 In.	920.00
Settee, High Back, Black Wool Upholstery, Steel Base, Italy, 36 x 69 In.	7800.00
Settee, Louis XV, Painted Frame, Aubusson Tapestry Upholstery, c.1900, 44 x 79 In.	1680.00
Settee, Louis XV Style, Carved, Armrests, Scrolls, Upholstered, 43 x 70 In.	2832.00
Settee, Louis XV Style, Giltwood, Carved, Aubusson Tapestry Upholstery, 64 In.	2489.00
Settee, Louis XVI, Gilt, Silk Upholstery, Leaf Arm Supports, 16 x 49 In., Pair	948.00
Settee, Louis XVI Style, Beech, Carved, Cream Paint, Padded, Canted, 38 x 50 x 28 In.	1800.00
Settee, Louis XVI Style, Gilt, Velvet Upholstery, Early 1900s, 39 x 51 In. *illus*	920.00
Settee, Louis XVI Style, Mahogany, Shaped Chair Rail, Scalloped Apron, c.1940, 37 x 68 In.	59.00
Settee, Mahogany, Scalloped Crest, Seat Rail, Cabriole Legs, Phila., c.1840, 32 x 42 In.	353.00
Settee, Majorelle, Walnut, Flower Marquetry, Twisted Legs, Upholstered, 46 x 19 x 39 In.	3360.00
Settee, Maple, Faux Bamboo, 4-Chair Back, Crewelwork Upholstery, 32 x 46 In.	940.00
Settee, Mixed Woods, Half Spindle Shape, Scroll Slats, Plank Seat, c.1820, 17 x 35 In.	264.00
Settee, Napoleon III, Louis XV Style, Rosewood, Padded Seat & Back, 37 x 69 x 23 In.	780.00
Settee, Neoclassical, Mahogany, Scalloped Crest, Tufted, Scalloped Seat Rail, c.1840, 32 x 42 In.	353.00
Settee, Neoclassical, Mahogany, Scrolled Crest Rail, Cornucopia Arms, Paw Feet, 33 x 55 In.	823.00
Settee, Neoclassical Style, Painted, Parcel Gilt, Winged Back, Bowed Seat, 39 x 52 ½ x 22 In.	1763.00
Settee, Niels Vodder, Teak, Brass, Velvet Upholstery, Triple Back, c.1950s, 28 ¾ x 73 x 31 In.	2684.00
Settee, Parcel Gilt, Carved, Tripleback, Molded Crest Rail, Vase Shape Splat, 41 x 61 In.	2350.00
Settee, Queen Anne, Vine Scrolled Inlay, Upholstered, Shaped Arms, Early 1900s, 38 x 47 In.	4200.00
Settee, Regency Style, Fruitwood, Padded, Scrolling Arms, Legs, Upholstered, 40 x 51 x 24 In.	3360.00
Settee, Renaissance Revival, Walnut, Triple Back, Turned Legs, c.1870, 45 x 70 x 24 In.	677.00
Settee, Shaker, Cherry, Straight Crest, Spindles, Splayed Legs, 32 x 50 In.	115.00
Settee, Shaped, Red Velvet Upholstery, 34 x 72 In.	3360.00
Settee, Stained Wood, Upholstered, Brass Footcaps, Austria, 30 x 51 In.	1320.00
Settee, Stickley Bros., No. 3574, Cane Back Panels, Sides, Cutout Slat Supports, 65 x 36 In.	2520.00
Settee, Triple Back, Upholstered, Arms, 61 In.	403.00
Settee, Victorian, Mahogany, Contoured, Carved Crest, Swan Motif, Upholstered, 36 x 58 In.	410.00
Settee, Wicker, Bar Harbor Style, White Paint, 1930s, 23 x 28 In., Child's	350.00
Settee, William & Mary, Beech, Walnut, Upholstered, c.1700, 54 ½ x 60 In. *illus*	2760.00
Settee, Windsor, Mixed Woods, Half-Arrow Back, Flowers, 1820-40, 18 x 35 In.	4583.00
Settee, Windsor, Rod Back, Black, c.1820, 77 In.	9360.00
Settee, Wood, Half-Spindle Back, 8-Footed, 19th Century, 33 ½ x 70 In.	140.00
Settle, Arts & Crafts, Ebonized Oak, Back, Side Slats, 83 x 31 ½ In.	1541.00
Settle, Arts & Crafts, Oak, Even Arms, Vertical Slats, Square Posts, c.1912, 36 x 53 In.	1541.00
Settle, Arts & Crafts, Vertical Slats, Leather Cushion, S. Karpen Bros., Signed, 76 x 34 In.	2640.00
Settle, Arts & Crafts, Wide Back Slat, 6 Vertical Arm Slats, Black Paint, 2 Cushions, 86 x 36 In.	2040.00
Settle, G. Stickley, Cube, Spindles, Spring Seat, 29 ½ x 26 x 28 In.	5185.00
Settle, G. Stickley, Cube, Spindles, Spring Seat, 31 ½ x 78 ¼ x 30 In.	7930.00
Settle, G. Stickley, Leather Seat, 36 x 71 ½ x 26 In.	3480.00
Settle, G. Stickley, No. 205, Even Arm, 5 Slats, One Slat Sides, Leather Cushion, 56 x 30 In.	2300.00
Settle, G. Stickley, No. 208, Even Arm, 8 Slats, Leather Cushion, Pillows, 76 x 32 x 29 In.	4800.00
Settle, G. Stickley, No. 222, Even Arm, Pencil Post, Leather Cushion, 36 x 80 x 32 In.	12200.00
Settle, L. & J.G. Stickley, Arched 7-Slat Back, 4 Side Slats, Cushion, Signed, 44 x 38 In.	4200.00
Settle, L. & J.G. Stickley, Crib, Vertical Slats, Black Leather Spring Seat, 39 x 84 x 32 In.	6000.00
Settle, L. & J.G. Stickley, No. 229, Oak, Slat Sides, Back, Leather, 72 x 26 In.	2300.00
Settle, Limbert, Vertical Slats, Back, Sides, Cutout Details, 69 x 26 x 41 In.	2880.00
Settle, Maple, Pine, Cushion, Green Paint, 20th Century, 66 ½ x 48 x 15 ½ In.	382.00
Settle, Oak, Pine, Scrolled Ends, Shaped Seat, c.1800, 60 x 73 In.	999.00
Settle, Pine, Curved Back, Green Paint, c.1820, 31 x 41 In.	852.00
Settle, Pine, Rolled, Paneled Back, Plank Seat, Paint, England, 1800s, 39 x 80 In.	502.00
Settle, Pine, Shaped Sides, Lift Top, Spanish Brown Paint, 23 ½ x 36 In., Child's	1422.00
Settle, Softwood, 4-Board Back, Crescent Cutouts, Hinged Double Seat, 57 x 79 x 19 In.	480.00
Settle, Stickley Bros., Wood, Mother-Of-Pearl, Copper Inlay, Slat Back, Upholstered Seat, 82 x 40 In.	5400.00

Furniture, Screen, Hepplewhite, Mahogany, Oval, Needlework, Tripod Base, 1810, 48 In. $411.00

Furniture, Secretary, George III, Chippendale, Mahogany, 89 x 45 In. $34375.00

Furniture, Secretary, Hepplewhite, Mahogany, Maple Veneer, Doors, Drawers, c.1815, 87 x 40 In. $3525.00

Furniture, Secretary, Pine, Picket Top, Slant Front Desk, Late 1800s, 76 x 39 x 24 In. $360.00

Furniture, Secretary, Regency, Mahogany, Ebony Inlay, c.1805, 110 x 104 In. $170500.00

Furniture, Semainier, Louis XV, Kingwood, Ormolu Mounted, Marble, Early 1900s, 53 x 34 In. $1440.00

Shelf, Black Lacquer, Elm, 4 Shelves, Chinese, 82 x 21 x 16 In., Pair	837.00
Shelf, Bracket, Parcel Gilt, Bianco, Majolica, Parrots, Cut Twigs, 1910s, 10 x 7 ¼ In., Pair	570.00
Shelf, Corner, Pine, Shell, Gesso, Scalloped Sides, c.1850, 28 ½ In.	235.00
Shelf, Corner, Walnut, 5 Shelves, 59 In.	118.00
Shelf, Hanging, 3 Shelves, Shaped Sides, Red Paint, New England, c.1820, 34 x 34 In.	1304.00
Shelf, Hanging, Painted, Scalloped Sides, Green Paint, Pa., 1800s, 33 x 24 In.	1053.00
Shelf, Hanging, Pine, Brown Paint, Applied Molding, Baluster Spacers, c.1880, 19 x 21 In.	533.00
Shelf, Hanging, Pine, Shaped Sides, Green Paint, c.1890, 24 x 19 In.	2133.00
Shelf, Hanging, Queen Anne, Tombstone Back, 4 Shelves, Old Paint, 1700s, 23 x 9 In.	711.00
Shelf, Hanging, Spanish Baroque Style, Walnut, Mixed Wood, c.1910, 29 x 28 In. ....*illus*	575.00
Shelf, Hanging, Victorian, Stick & Ball, Scroll Design, 22 x 25 In. ....*illus*	510.00
Shelf, Hanging, Walnut, 5 Graduated Shelves, Shaped Ends, Mid 19th Century, 58 x 66 In.	1175.00
Shelf, Hardwood, Mother-Of-Pearl Inlay, Reticulated Back, Morocco, 31 x 12 In.	206.00
Shelf, Linen, Pine, Pegged Construction, Late 19th Century, 78 x 65 In.	1175.00
Shelf, Louis Philippe, Pine, c.1830, 27 x 41 x 11 In.	546.00
Shelf, Mahogany, Whale Ends, 4 Shaped Shelves, c.1890, 34 x 17 In.	948.00
Shelf, Nakashima, Hanging, Walnut, Sketch, Signed, c.1981, 6 ½ x 96 In.	11025.00
Shelf, Pine, Scalloped Supports, Dovetailed Drawer, c.1900, 123 x 11 In.	1057.00
Shelf, Poplar, Scalloped Ends, Graduated Shelves, Mortised, c.1800, 35 x 30 In.	822.00
Shelf, Shaker, Butternut, Maple, Dovetailed, 7 x 38 In.	936.00
Shelf, Softwood, Painted, Slotted, Flower, 14 ¾ x 19 In.	22.00
Shelf, Wrought Iron Frame, 5 Oak Shelves, Metamorphic, 60 x 32 In.	660.00
Sideboard, Aesthetic Revival, Mahogany, Gallery Backsplash, Drawers, Doors, c.1900, 54 x 49 In.	450.00
Sideboard, Art Deco, Oak, Marble Top, Carved Cornucopia, Mirror, 41 x 71 x 24 In.	474.00
Sideboard, Arts & Crafts, Oak, Mirrored Back, Drawers, Doors, c.1900, 50 x 54 x 23 In.	345.00
Sideboard, Breakfront, Mahogany, Bowfront, Brass Gallery, Drawers, Scrolling, 54 x 72 In.	978.00
Sideboard, Butternut, 12 Drawers, Door, 19th Century, 45 x 61 ½ In.	285.00
Sideboard, Chinese Provincial, Celadon Lacquer, Double Doors, 3 Drawers, Brass, 36 x 60 In.	2400.00
Sideboard, Chippendale, Mahogany, Serpentine, Shaped Top, Drawers, Doors, 35 x 72 In.	460.00
Sideboard, Corner, Mahogany, Bowfront, 3 Drawers, Tapered Legs, 36 x 59 In.	1554.00
Sideboard, Demilune, Mahogany, Drawer, 2 Doors, Facades, England, 1800s, 36 x 60 In.	2242.00
Sideboard, Eastlake, Walnut, Carved Panels, Beveled Mirrors, 85 x 60 In. ....*illus*	600.00
Sideboard, Edwardian, Mahogany Inlay, Center Drawer, 2 Doors, c.1900, 36 x 30 In.	431.00
Sideboard, Elizabethan, Oak, 2 Carved Doors, Open Interior, England, c.1890, 35 x 52 In.	374.00
Sideboard, Elm, Black Lacquer, Gilt Butterflies, 4 Doors, Shelves, Chinese, 33 x 53 In.	777.00
Sideboard, Empire, Bird's-Eye Maple, Mahogany, Drawers, 1800s, 59 x 52 In. ....*illus*	1840.00
Sideboard, Empire, Mahogany, Drawers, 45 ¾ x 49 x 30 ½ In.	239.00
Sideboard, Federal, Cherry, Poplar, 3 Drawers, Tennessee, 1800s, 42 x 64 In. ....*illus*	7480.00
Sideboard, Federal, Drawers, Cupboard Doors, Brass Knobs, Turned Feet, 42 x 44 In.	944.00
Sideboard, Federal, Mahogany, 2 Side Drawers, Quarter Fans, Inlay, c.1790, 39 x 73 In.	2489.00
Sideboard, Federal, Mahogany, Bellflower Inlay, 39 x 61 In.	1610.00
Sideboard, Federal, Mahogany, Demilune Inlay, Baltimore, c.1805, 38 x 54 In.	12500.00
Sideboard, Federal, Mahogany, Drop Door, Interior Desk, Inlays, Mirrors, c.1810, 32 x 54 In.	3437.00
Sideboard, Federal, Mahogany, Drop Front Drawer, Cubbyholes, 1900s, 46 x 64 x 22 In.	2450.00
Sideboard, Federal, Mahogany, Fan, Flower Inlay, Doors, Drawers, 1900s, 39 x 73 In.	575.00
Sideboard, Federal, Mahogany, Inlay, Bowfront, Drawers, Broken Scroll Backsplash, 53 x 76 In.	3525.00
Sideboard, Federal, Mahogany, Inlay, Shaped Skirt, 3 Over 2 Drawers, c.1800, 37 x 72 In.	4375.00
Sideboard, Federal, Mahogany, Scrolled Gallery, 3 Drawers, 4 Doors, Virginia, 1810, 45 x 61 In.	3220.00
Sideboard, Federal, Mahogany, Inlay, Serpentine Block Front, c.1900, 39 x 70 In.	1763.00
Sideboard, Federal, Mahogany, Veneers, 3 Drawers, 3 Doors, Tapered Legs, 1800s, 41 x 61 In.	518.00
Sideboard, Federal Style, Mahogany, Brass Pull Handles, Cellarettes, 35 x 72 x 21 In.	956.00
Sideboard, Federal, Walnut, Mixed Woods, 10 Drawers, Southern, c.1815, 41 x 85 In.	5980.00
Sideboard, French Provincial, Fruitwood, 2 Door, 2 Drawers, Scrolled Feet, 39 x 52 ½ x 24 In.	593.00
Sideboard, French Renaissance Revival, Walnut, Marble, Gadrooned Drawers, c.1870, 40 x 49 In.	1880.00
Sideboard, G. Nakashima, Walnut, Pandanus Cloth, Signed, 1979, 29 x 90 x 19 In.	20000.00
Sideboard, G. Stickley, No. 800, Drawers, Lower Shelf, Harvey Ellis, 53 x 43 In.	5400.00
Sideboard, G. Stickley, No. 814, Mahogany, Inlay, Copper Hardware, Doors, Drawers, 56 x 48 In.	4500.00
Sideboard, George II, Mahogany, Bowfront, Satinwood String, 3 Drawers, 37 x 72 x 25 In.	2400.00
Sideboard, George III, Mahogany, Hepplewhite Style, Drawer, 2 Doors, Late 1700s, 35 x 66 In.	2350.00
Sideboard, George III, Mahogany, Frieze Drawers, Bowed Center, c.1785, 37 x 75 In.	4444.00
Sideboard, George III, Mahogany, Inlay, Serpentine Top, Drawer, 2 Doors, 39 x 68 x 30 In.	7050.00
Sideboard, Georgia Piedmont, Yellow Pine, 3 Drawers, 3 Doors, Tall Legs, 1800s, 42 x 54 In.	2415.00
Sideboard, Georgian, Mahogany, Drawers, Arched Skirt, Cuffed Legs, c.1800, 36 x 80 In.	1997.00
Sideboard, Georgian Style, Mahogany, Tambour, Spade Feet, c.1875, 35 x 48 x 21 In.	863.00
Sideboard, Georgian, Walnut, Bowfront, Inlay, Cellarettes, 36 x 61 ½ x 27 In.	416.00

Sideboard, Hepplewhite Style, Mahogany, Serpentine, 5 Drawers, 3 Doors, Tapered Legs, 66 In.	550.00
Sideboard, Hepplewhite, Curly Maple, 2 Drawers, 2 Doors, Black Base, 1900s, 38 x 62 In.	294.00
Sideboard, Hepplewhite, Mahogany, Inlay, Brass Gallery, England, c.1890, 52 x 60 In.	1093.00
Sideboard, Hepplewhite, Mahogany, Serpentine, Bellflowers, c.1790, 38 x 58 In.	18212.00
Sideboard, Hepplewhite, Mahogany, Serpentine Front, 6 Tapered Legs, Spade Feet, 66 In.	590.00
Sideboard, Heywood-Wakefield Co., Wood, Blond, 4 Drawers, 2 Doors	341.00
Sideboard, Irish Chippendale, Mahogany, Inlay, Shaped Top, 6 Drawers, 37 x 74 In.	288.00
Sideboard, James Mont, Oak, Orange Lacquer, Gold Wash, c.1954, 32 x 77 In.	1800.00
Sideboard, Jules Bouy, Silvered & Lacquered Wood, 2 Doors, c.1935, 29 ½ x 62 In.	2988.00
Sideboard, L. & J.G. Stickley, 2 Drawers, Cabinets, Plate Rack, 46 x 60 x 22 In.	2160.00
Sideboard, Lifetime, Honey Oak, Doors, Drawers, Arts & Crafts, c.1910, 38 x 50 In.	823.00
Sideboard, Lifetime, No. 5347, 2 Doors, 4 Drawers, Signed, Decal, 66 x 40 In.	3000.00
Sideboard, Limbert, Chestnut, Butterfly Joinery, 2 Drawers, 57 x 51 x 20 In.	6710.00
Sideboard, Limbert, Mirrored Backsplash, 53 x 60 x 23 ½ In.	3660.00
Sideboard, Mahogany, Bowfront, 5 Drawers, Tapered Legs, England, 36 x 54 In.	431.00
Sideboard, Mahogany, Bowfront, Molded Top, Center Drawer, Doors, c.1900, 37 x 60 In.	748.00
Sideboard, Mahogany, Carved Swags, Paneled Doors, Drawer, Lion Mask Pulls, 68 x 83 In.	3680.00
Sideboard, Mahogany, Doors, Drawer, 41 x 63 x 22 In.	8625.00
Sideboard, Mahogany, Inlay, Bowfront, Shaped Top, 3 Drawers, Tapered Legs, 37 x 55 In.	1265.00
Sideboard, Mahogany, Pediment Backsplash, Drawers, Doors, Ball Feet, c.1800, 56 x 74 In. ...	1175.00
Sideboard, Mahogany, Serpentine Front, 6 Drawers, Center Drawer, Patina, c.1800, 37 x 60 In.	2250.00
Sideboard, Mahogany, Serpentine Front, Crossband, 2 Drawers, Doors, 37 x 70 x 25 In.	593.00
Sideboard, Mahogany, Wine Drawers, 1940s, 40 x 78 In.	4900.00
Sideboard, Napoleon III, Directoire Style, Rosewood, Marble Top, Mirror, 3 Drawers, 94 x 54 In.	840.00
Sideboard, Neoclassical, Mahogany, Backsplash, Acorn Finials, Brass Rails, Paw Feet, 52 x 69 In.	3000.00
Sideboard, Neoclassical, Mahogany, Backsplash, Melon & Leaf Finials, Drawers, 65 x 59 In. ..	2056.00
Sideboard, Neoclassical, Mahogany, Drawers, Doors, 4 Carved Pilasters, c.1825, 46 x 73 In. ..	1320.00
Sideboard, Neoclassical, Quartersawn Oak, Cherubs, Lions, Granite Top, 64 x 91 x 25 In.	1450.00
Sideboard, Neoclassical, Walnut, Burl Backsplash, Drawers, Doors, 52 x 59 x 25 In.	633.00
Sideboard, Oak, 3 Drawers, Carved, Ball & Claw, Italy, Early 1900s, 33 x 71 x 23 In.	840.00
Sideboard, Oak, 3 Upper Stacked Drawers, Lower Doors, Claw Feet, 48 In.	266.00
Sideboard, Oak, Acanthus Leaf, Scrolls, Flowers, Windows, 2 Doors, 8 Drawers, 112 In.	900.00
Sideboard, Oak, Animal Carved Crest, Shelves, Drawers, Doors, 83 x 101 In.	14950.00
Sideboard, Oak, Carved, 4-Paneled Doors, Late 1800s, 41 x 95 In.	6800.00
Sideboard, Oak, Game Birds, Dogs, Putti, Lion Carvings, Shelves, Doors, 71 x 91 In.	5923.00
Sideboard, Ole Wanscher, Rosewood, 2 Sliding Tambour Doors, 10 Drawers, 34 x 75 In.	2880.00
Sideboard, Regency Style, Mahogany, Inlay, 3 Drawers, England, 1800s, 36 x 69 x 29 In.	1035.00
Sideboard, Regency, Mahogany, 2 Drawers, Door, England, 1800s, 38 x 69 In.	1265.00
Sideboard, Regency, Mahogany, 3 Drawers, 2 Doors, String Inlay, Scotland, 45 x 88 x 29 In. ..	2400.00
Sideboard, Regency, Mahogany, Bowfront, 3 Drawers, Round Turned Legs, c.1810, 31 x 39 In.	1896.00
Sideboard, Regency, Mahogany, Bowfront, 3 Drawers, Tapered Legs, 32 ⅜ x 36 x 20 In.	1896.00
Sideboard, Regency, Mahogany, Inlay, Bowfront, Sliding Doors, 3 Drawers, c.1810, 43 x 90 In.	6325.00
Sideboard, Regency, Rosewood Veneer, 2-Shelf Top, Turned Brass Supports, Doors, 55 x 37 In.	920.00
Sideboard, Renaissance Revival, Mahogany, Doors, Drawers, Storage, 38 x 23 x 78 In.	717.00
Sideboard, Renaissance Revival, Oak, Geometrics, Leaves, 5 Drawers, 2 Doors, c.1880, 52 x 68 x 25 In.	440.00
Sideboard, Renaissance Revival, Walnut, Arched Carved Crest, Stepped Shelves, 91 x 60 In.	2880.00
Sideboard, Renaissance Revival, Walnut, Burl Walnut, 2 Parts, Mirror, 92 x 65 x 27 In.	2420.00
Sideboard, Renaissance Revival, Walnut, Carved Crest, Paneled Doors, 91 x 60 In. ....*illus*	2880.00
Sideboard, Renaissance Revival, Walnut, Carved, Shelves, Doors, Tiles, c.1800, 86 x 60 In.	3555.00
Sideboard, Renaissance Revival, Walnut, Scalloped Backsplash, Anthemion Cartouche, 91 x 56 In.	1528.00
Sideboard, Roycroft, Mirrored Backsplash, Leaded Glass Doors, Drawers, 54 x 61 x 25 In.	9600.00
Sideboard, Sheraton, Mahogany, Bowfront, 2 Center Drawers, Flanking Drawers, 86 x 75 In. ...	1495.00
Sideboard, Stickley Bros., No. 8338, Plate Rail Over Drawers, Doors, 54 x 22 x 45 In.	1320.00
Sideboard, Stickley Bros., Plate Rail, Linen Drawer, 3 Drawers, 2 Doors, 44 x 48 x 20 In.	2880.00
Sideboard, Walnut, Cherry, 4 Doors, 6-Footed, Backsplash, Carved Sunburst, 54 x 63 x 20 In.	5750.00
Sideboard, Walnut, Poplar, Scroll Backsplash, 6 Drawers, 4 Doors, Tennessee, 1800s, 63 x 71 In.	546.00
Sideboard, Walnut, Scrolls, Marble Top, Thomas Brooks, 92 x 76 x 24 In.	6100.00
Sideboard, William IV, Mahogany, 3 Drawers, 2 Pedestals, 36 x 72 In.	575.00
Sideboard, William IV, Mahogany, Bowfront, Pedestal, Doors, c.1835, 44 x 79 In.	1265.00
Sideboard, Yew Inlay, Bowfront, Frieze, Drawer, Door, Tapered Legs, c.1900, 38 x 61 In.	358.00
Silver Chest, Bird's-Eye Maple, Beveled Lid, Drawer, Fitted Interior, Gorham, c.1890	499.00
Silver Chest, Regency, Drop Front, Mahogany, Drawers, Brass Caps, Casters, 29 x 32 x 15 In. .	660.00
Silver Chest, Renaissance Revival, Beveled Arched Lid, Grotesques, Vines, 17 x 27 In.	353.00
Sofa, A. Girard, Black, White Wool Upholstery, Aluminum Legs, Herman Miller, 26 x 72 In.	2400.00
Sofa, Baku, Bendteen, Modular, Aluminum Clips, Tan, Brown Cushions, Montis, 132 In., 3 Piece	2400.00
Sofa, Belle Epoque, Gilt Decoration, Tufted Back, Turned Legs, Italian, c.1890, 38 x 74 x 27 In.	330.00

Furniture, Semainier, Louis XV, Marquetry, Metal Fittings, Marble Top, 13 x 52 In.
$891.00

Furniture, Server, L. & J.G. Stickley, 2 Shelves, Curved Backsplash, Apron, 38 x 40 In.
$2040.00

Furniture, Server, Mahogany, Carved, 2 Shelves, 2 Door Base, Turned Legs, Caribbean, 1800s
$1872.00

Furniture, Server, Regency, Mahogany, 3 Tiers, Casters, 19th Century, 45 x 45 In.
$1265.00

Furniture, Settee, Barrel, Slats To Floor, Drop-In Spring Leather Seat, Plail Bros., 34 x 46 In. $4200.00

Furniture, Settee, Louis XVI Style, Gilt, Velvet Upholstery, Early 1900s, 39 x 51 In. $920.00

Furniture, Settee, William & Mary, Beech, Walnut, Upholstered, c.1700, 54 ½ x 60 In. $2760.00

Furniture, Shelf, Hanging, Spanish Baroque Style, Walnut, Mixed Wood, c.1910, 29 x 28 In. $575.00

Sofa, Biedermeier, Mahogany, Shaped Crest, Scroll Arms, Splay Feet, Upholstered, 82 In.	1100.00
Sofa, Biedermeier, Walnut, Padded, Mounted Crest, Outscrolled Arms, 36 x 26 x 80 In.	6300.00
Sofa, Camelback, Serpentine Front, Scroll Arms, Molded Legs, 78 In.	3500.00
Sofa, Chesterfield, Edwardian, Mahogany, Leather Upholstered, Tufted, Cushion, 29 x 84 x 35 In.	1920.00
Sofa, Chippendale, Camelback, 8-Leg, Marlboro Legs, 20th Century, 36 x 81 x 22 In.	299.00
Sofa, Chippendale, Camelback, Mahogany, Yellow Upholstery, c.1760, 35 x 80 In.	2133.00
Sofa, Chippendale, Mahogany, Serpentine Back, Scrolled, Square Legs, 1900s, 78 x 21 x 38 In.	587.00
Sofa, Chippendale Style, Camelback, Mahogany, Square Legs, Upholstered	2040.00
Sofa, Chippendale Style, Camelback, Upholstered, Marlboro Legs, 34 x 80 In.	418.00
Sofa, Chippendale Style, Camelback, Upholstered, 82 In.	403.00
Sofa, Eastlake, Walnut, Carved, Paneled Sides, Overstuffed, Lion Masks, c.1885, 79 In.	1067.00
Sofa, Empire, Federal, Mahogany, Upholstered, Claw Feet, 1820s, 32 x 54 x 20 In., Child's	1050.00
Sofa, Empire, Mahogany, Carved, Scrolling Padded Back, Enclosed Bolsters, 39 x 22 In.	460.00
Sofa, Empire, Mahogany, Cornucopia Carved Arms, Paw Feet, 36 x 72 In. ....*illus*	920.00
Sofa, Empire, Mahogany, Green Silk Upholstery, Scroll Arms, Claw Feet, c.1840, 34 x 91 In.	610.00
Sofa, Empire, Mahogany, Upholstered, Rolled Arms, Paw Feet, 34 x 76 x 24 In.	800.00
Sofa, F. Henningsen, Ebony Mahogany, Brass, Leather, c.1930, 29 x 78 x 29 ¾ In.	40625.00
Sofa, Federal Hepplewhite, Green Silk Upholstery, 36 x 78 In.	690.00
Sofa, Federal, Mahogany, Arch Back, Pink Upholstery, Scroll Arms, c.1790, 38 x 87 In.	960.00
Sofa, Federal, Mahogany, Inlay, Arched Crest Rail, Upholstered, Carved Arms, 35 x 74 In.	690.00
Sofa, Federal, Mahogany, Poplar, Reeded Back, Arms, Casters, Baltimore, 36 x 82 In. ...... *illus*	3540.00
Sofa, Federal, Mahogany, Reeded, Curved Arms, Upholstered, 61 x 32 In.	323.00
Sofa, Federal, Reeded Arms, Legs, Veneered Panels, Damask Upholstery, 37 x 79 In.	640.00
Sofa, Frankl, Bamboo, 3 Sections, 6 Band Armrests, 78 ½ x 36 x 30 In.	960.00
Sofa, G. Nelson, Modular, Wedge Back, Loose Cushions, Armless, Herman Miller, 90 x 27 In.	1560.00
Sofa, G. Nelson, Steel Frame, Rubber Sling Seat, Leather Cushions, Herman Miller, 61 x 29 In.	1800.00
Sofa, George III, Mahogany, Arched Backrest, Marlboro Legs, 18th Century, 54 In.	1659.00
Sofa, George III, Mahogany, Camelback, Brass Tacks, Scroll Arms, c.1920, 35 x 84 In.	780.00
Sofa, George III Style, Mahogany, Carved, Cushioned, Cabriole Legs, Ireland, 40 x 87 x 27 In.	2160.00
Sofa, George III Style, Mahogany, Padded Back, Cabriole Legs, Hairy Paw Feet, 1930s, 39 In.	2160.00
Sofa, Grecian, Mahogany, Carved Head, Bolster, 33 ½ x 72 x 22 In.	5400.00
Sofa, Heritage Henredon, Taliesin Edges, White Upholstery, Signed Frank Lloyd Wright, 98 x 27 In.	1440.00
Sofa, Juan Montoya, Linen Upholstery, Tufted Back, Turned Legs, 38 x 88 In.	1560.00
Sofa, L. & J.G. Stickley, No. 285, Even Arm, Back With 7 Slats, Pulls Out To Bed, 79 In.	4500.00
Sofa, Louis XV, Beech, Crest, Padded Seat & Back, Serpentine, c.1750, 17 x 78 In.	1185.00
Sofa, Louis XV Style, Carved, Painted, Bead & Channel Frame, Scrolling Arms, 37 x 30 In.	920.00
Sofa, Louis XV Style, Domed, Shaped Back, Scroll Arms & Toes, Upholstered, c.1900, 37 x 80 In.	1440.00
Sofa, Louis XV Style, Fruitwood, Carved, Serpentine, Loose Cushion, 39 x 80 x 28 In.	538.00
Sofa, Louis XV Style, Fruitwood, Provincial, Padded, Cabriole Legs, 45 x 75 x 31 In.	4080.00
Sofa, Louis XV Style, Gilt, Cushion, Carved Seat Rail, Cabriole Legs, 44 x 72 x 21 ½ In.	388.00
Sofa, Louis XVI Style, Multicolored, Domed, Padded Seat & Back, Outscrolled Arms, 32 x 86 In.	2880.00
Sofa, Mahogany, Gray Upholstery, Leaf Carved Scroll Arms, Crest, Feet, 32 x 84 In.	617.00
Sofa, Mahogany, Molded Back, Apron, Rolled Arms, Brocade Upholstery, c.1825, 37 x 82 In.	2400.00
Sofa, Mahogany, Upholstered, Gadrooned, Brass Spandrels, 30 x 67 x 24 In.	2415.00
Sofa, Marco Zanuso, Metal, Wool Upholstery, c.1954, 33 x 60 x 30 ¾ In.	6250.00
Sofa, Marshmallow, G. Nelson, Steel, Yellow Upholstery, 1956, 55 x 31 In.	7750.00
Sofa, Neoclassical, Mahogany, Carved, Caribbean Islands, 40 ¾ x 22 x 83 In.	1007.00
Sofa, Neoclassical, Mahogany, Carved, Scrolled Crest Rail, Paw Feet, Early 1800s, 35 x 100 In.	2350.00
Sofa, Neoclassical, Mahogany, Inlaid, Carved, Upholstered, c.1804, 36 x 100 In.	2350.00
Sofa, Parlor, Empire, Upholstered, c.1860, 37 x 81 x 25 In.	1990.00
Sofa, Paulin, ABCD, 3 Seats, Fiberglass Frame, Blue & Green Upholstery, 1968, 96 In.	1175.00
Sofa, Renaissance Revival, Walnut, Shaped Frame, Acanthus, Scroll Arms, c.1875, 43 x 79 In.	201.00
Sofa, Robsjohn-Gibbings, Mohair Upholstery, Walnut, Web Frame, 32 x 92 In.	7200.00
Sofa, Rococo, Pierce Carved Crest, Rosewood, Tuthill King, Upholstered, 44 x 68 In.	24400.00
Sofa, Rococo Revival, Rosewood Laminate, Leaf & Scroll Carved, 76 x 52 In. ....*illus*	7800.00
Sofa, Rococo Revival, Walnut, Carved, Scrolled Acanthus Back, Armrests, 40 x 83 x 28 In.	180.00
Sofa, Rococo Revival, Walnut, Carved Serpentine Top, Upholstered, Flared Feet, 38 x 85 In.	227.00
Sofa, Rococo, Rosewood, Laminated, Rosalie With Grapes, Arched Back, c.1850, 39 x 69 In.	3525.00
Sofa, Safari, A. Associati, Fiberglass, Leopard Upholstery, 3 Sections, Poltronova, 1970s, 102 x 24 In.	4500.00
Sofa, Sheraton, Camelback, Mahogany, Silk Upholstery, 6 Legs, 42 x 84 In.	915.00
Sofa, Sheraton, Mahogany, Birch Inlay, Reeded Open Arms, N.H., c.1800, 37 x 72 In. .... *illus*	1175.00
Sofa, Ueli Berger, Channeled, Upholstered, De Sede, 30 x 113 In.	4200.00
Sofa, V. Kagan, Biomorphic Shape, Upholstered, 1 Lucite Leg, 94 x 29 In.	2160.00
Sofa, V. Kagan, Upholstered, Curved, Casters, c.1949, 26 x 136 x 66 In.	28125.00
Sofa, Victorian, 3 Sections, Velvet Upholstery, Rolled Back & Arms, 30 x 107 In.	173.00
Sofa, Victorian, Mahogany, Serpentine, Striped Upholstery, 1800s, 33 x 72 In. ....*illus*	269.00

Sofa, Victorian, Mahogany, Upholstery, Serpentine Crest, 74 x 31 In.	1300.00
Sofa, W. Platner, Metal Base, Orange Boucle Cushion, Knoll, 30 x 67 In.	1800.00
Sofa, Walnut, 3 Medallion Back, Carved, Crests, Scroll Arms, 1800s, 47 x 75 In.	1320.00
Sofa, Wormley, Angled, Upholstered, Dunbar, c.1952, 37 x 82 x 34 In.	2450.00
Sofa, Wormley, Gondola, No. 5719, Walnut Frame, Upholstered, Dunbar, 32 x 112 In.	11950.00
Stand, Adam Style, Painted, Gilt & Cream, Ram's Heads, Tripod Base, Hoof Feet, 48 x 18 In.	863.00
Stand, Antler, Round Pine Top, Gameboard Top, Tripod Antler Stand, c.1930, 29 In.	705.00
Stand, Bamboo, Basket Weave Top, Early 20th Century, 30 x 22 In.	40.00
Stand, Basin, Georgian, Mahogany, 3-Footed, 18th Century, 32 In.	224.00
Stand, Basin, Mahogany, Drawer, Splashboards, Reeded Legs, Shelf, Ireland, 35 x 23 In.	380.00
Stand, Basin, Mahogany, Tripod, Drawers, Kittinger, 32 ½ In. ....*illus*	205.00
Stand, Basin, Sheraton, Tiger Maple, Scalloped Top, Drawer, Turned Legs, c.1820, 43 x 23 In. .*illus*	600.00
Stand, Bible, Italian Baroque, Gilt Gesso, Sloped Front, Carved Flowers, Label, c.1870, 12 x 14 In.	711.00
Stand, Bible, Oak, Barley Twist Stretcher, Early 1900s, 14 In.	72.00
Stand, Bible, Openwork, Scrolling Leaves, Cross, Painted Cherub, 13 x 15 x 4 In.	418.00
Stand, Black Forest, Oak, 2 Drawers, 2 Shelves, Twist Columns, Swiss, c.1900, 39 x 46 In.	720.00
Stand, Black Lacquer, Square, Square Legs, Shaped Stretchers, Chinese, 31 x 15 In., Pair	478.00
Stand, Brass, 2 Tiers, Rococo Decoration, 4 Figural Supports, 19 x 19 In.	81.00
Stand, Brass, Marble Top, Gilt, Shelf, Door, France, 31 ¾ x 15 ¾ x 15 ¾ In., Pair	896.00
Stand, Brass, Variegated Marble Top, Pierced Valances, Lower Glass Shelf, 31 x 12 In.	294.00
Stand, Cast Iron, Marble Top, Scroll Legs, Pierced Top, Shelf, 30 In.	79.00
Stand, Cherry, 2 Drawers, Carving, Horse, Dog, Flowers, Zigzag, c.1840, 28 x 23 In.	3525.00
Stand, Cherry, Drawer, Turned & Squared Legs, Late 1800s, 19 x 19 x 26 In.	325.00
Stand, Cherry, Splayed Legs, 19th Century, 28 ½ x 22 ½ In.	140.00
Stand, Chinese, Rosewood, Scalloped Inset Marble Top, Pierced Frieze, 1800s, 23 x 18 In.	235.00
Stand, Chinese, Teak, Carved, Rouge Marble, Carved Apron, Claw Feet, 18 x 18 In.	288.00
Stand, Chinese, Teak, Stretcher Base, 27 x 10 x 10 In.	23.00
Stand, Corner, Art Deco, Wrought Iron, White Paint, Shells, Scrolls, 84 x 38 In., Pair	978.00
Stand, Country Sheraton, Cherry, Tiger Maple, Drawer, 19th Century, 28 x 20 x 18 In.	826.00
Stand, Display, Rosewood, 2 Shelves, Drawers, Storage, Chinese, 1800s, 32 x 24 x 12 In.	240.00
Stand, Dressing, Mahogany, Shaped Mirror Frame, Tapered Supports, 3 Drawers, 28 x 17 In.	144.00
Stand, Dressing, Mahogany Veneer, Swivel Mirror, 3 Drawers, Acorn Finials, c.1820, 27 x 22 In.	207.00
Stand, Drink, L. & J.G. Stickley, No. 387, Square Top, Lower Stretcher, 16 x 30 In.	1020.00
Stand, Drink, L. & J.G. Stickley, No. 587, Square, Lower Stretcher, 15 x 15 x 28 In.	720.00
Stand, Drink, Stickley Bros., No. 2615, Copper Top, Arched Apron, Splayed, Tapered Legs, 19 x 28 In.	1140.00
Stand, Drop Leaf, Cherry, 2 Drawer, Davis Cabinet Company, 19 x 28 In.	236.00
Stand, Drop Leaf, Maple, 2 Drawers, Early 1800s, 29 x 18 In.	140.00
Stand, Drum, Regency, Satinwood, Oak, Drawer, Flared Legs, Casters, c.1810, 27 x 15 In.	999.00
Stand, Ebonized Wood, Inset Marble, Nubian Figure Support, Paw Feet, 32 x 20 In.	431.00
Stand, Empire, Mahogany, 3 Drawers, Carved Paw Feet, 29 x 25 In.	2400.00
Stand, Empire, Mahogany, Pedestal Base, Curved Drawer Front, c.1850, 29 x 20 In.	1050.00
Stand, Federal, Drawer, Faux Marble, Drawer, Shelf, c.1840, 19 x 29 In.	1896.00
Stand, Federal, Drawer, Yellow Scalloped Borders, Grain Painted, New Eng., c.1810, 28 x 18 In.	1067.00
Stand, Federal, Mahogany, 2 Drawer, Carved, 19th Century, 30 x 16 x 22 In.	410.00
Stand, Federal, Mahogany, Black Paint, N.Y., 19th Century, 29 x 24 In.	110.00
Stand, Federal, Mahogany, Lift Top, Door, Drawer, 30 ½ x 22 x 16 In.	240.00
Stand, Federal, Maple, Beaded Tray Top, Drawer, New England, c.1800, 29 x 19 In.	533.00
Stand, Federal, Tiger Maple, 1 Drawer, Bone Escutcheon, c.1810, 28 ½ x 17 x 16 ⅝ In.	2250.00
Stand, Federal, Tiger Maple, Cherry, Drawer, 26 ½ x 15 ½ x 14 In.	5925.00
Stand, Federal, Walnut, Drawer, Dovetailed, Turned Feet, 28 x 23 x 16 In.	230.00
Stand, Federal, Walnut, Poplar, Drawer, Georgia, 1800s, 30 x 23 In.	1093.00
Stand, Fern, Brass, Marble, Pierced Leaf Borders, Scrolled Legs, c.1880, 31 x 16 In.	235.00
Stand, Fern, Oak, Round Top, Twisted Stem, 4 Ball Feet, 36 x 12 In.	140.00
Stand, Fern, Oak, Wicker, Rattan, Scrolls, Linked Hearts, Beaded Edge, 32 x 16 In.	2233.00
Stand, Fern, Renaissance Revival, Ebonized, Gilt, Buttress Supports, c.1870, 40 x 11 In.	1645.00
Stand, Fern, Rosewood, Carved, Hexagonal Top, Beaded Edge, Marble, c.1890, 25 x 15 In.	300.00
Stand, Fern, Rosewood, Hexagonal Top, Marble Inserts, Pierced Skirt, 6 Legs, 25 In.	881.00
Stand, Fern, Rosewood, Scalloped Marble Top, Paw Feet, Chinese, c.1890, 37 x 16 In.	323.00
Stand, Fern, Victorian, Iron, Ornate Figural Legs, 30 x 15 In.	84.00
Stand, Fern, Walnut, Carved, Gilt, 4-Footed, 19th Century, 33 In.	150.00
Stand, Fern, Walnut, Oval, Heart Design Pedestal, Victorian, 30 In. ....*illus*	400.00
Stand, Florence Knoll, Birch, 3 Drawers, Angled Front, 18 x 29 In.	480.00
Stand, Florence Knoll, Walnut, Laminate Top, Drawer, Shelf, 10 x 18 In., Pair	840.00
Stand, Folio, Herter Brothers, Renaissance Revival, Walnut, Gilt, Carved, c.1972, 48 x 42 In.	85400.00
Stand, Folio, Louis XV Style, Fruitwood, Cane, Cartouche Shape, 34 ½ x 25 x 12 In.	717.00
Stand, Folio, William & Mary Style, Oak, Barley Twist Legs, Cane Panels, 26 In. ....*illus*	764.00

Furniture, Shelf, Hanging, Victorian, Stick & Ball, Scroll Design, 22 x 25 In. $510.00

Furniture, Sideboard, Eastlake, Walnut, Carved Panels, Beveled Mirrors, 85 x 60 In. $600.00

Furniture, Sideboard, Empire, Bird's-Eye Maple, Mahogany, Drawers, 1800s, 59 x 52 In. $1840.00

Furniture, Sideboard, Federal, Cherry, Poplar, 3 Drawers, Tennessee, 1800s, 42 x 64 In. $7480.00

F

FURNITURE

Furniture, Sideboard,
Renaissance Revival, Walnut,
Carved Crest, Paneled Doors, 91 x 60 In.
$2880.00

Furniture, Sofa, Empire, Mahogany,
Cornucopia Carved Arms, Paw Feet,
36 x 72 In.
$920.00

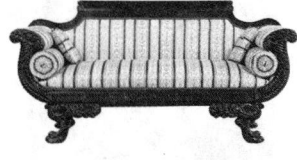

Furniture, Sofa, Federal, Mahogany,
Poplar, Reeded Back, Arms, Casters,
Baltimore, 36 x 82 In.
$3540.00

Furniture, Sofa, Rococo Revival,
Rosewood Laminate,
Leaf & Scroll Carved, 76 x 52 In.
$7800.00

Stand, Fruitwood Butcher Block, Iron Brace Bands, Scalloped Apron, Turned Legs, 32 x 32 In.	529.00
Stand, G. Stickley, Tree Of Life, Square Top, 4 Shelves, Slab Sides, Carved Design, 15 x 44 In. .	1080.00
Stand, George III, Hepplewhite, Drawer, Splayed Legs, Cross Stretcher, 30 x 19 In.	1035.00
Stand, Georgian, Mahogany, ¾ Gallery, Handles, Door, Inlay Band, 30 x 14 In.	382.00
Stand, Globe, McCobb, Paper, On Wood, Brass, c.1955, 37 x 20 In. ....*illus*	1560.00
Stand, Hepplewhite, Cherry, Line Inlay, Drawer, Tapered Legs, c.1805, 27 x 18 In.	470.00
Stand, Hepplewhite, Mahogany, 2 Doors, 19th Century, 29 x 28 x 16 In.	85.00
Stand, Hepplewhite, Mahogany, Tilt Top, Cut Corners, Pedestal, 27 x 26 In. ....*illus*	206.00
Stand, Hepplewhite, Tiger & Bird's-Eye Maple, Drawer, New England	1430.00
Stand, Hepplewhite, Walnut, Drawer, Tapered Legs, c.1850, 26 x 18 x 17 In.	294.00
Stand, Hepplewhite, Walnut, Line Inlay, Drawer, Tapered Legs, c.1805, 29 x 17 In.	353.00
Stand, Herman Miller, Walnut, Aluminum, Medallion, 23 x 19 In., Pair	2196.00
Stand, J. Widdicomb, Bronze Gallery Top, Trefoil Stretcher Shelf, 3 Legs, 29 x 16 In.	620.00
Stand, Lacquered, Red, Painted Flowers, 6-Sided, Chinese, 24 In.	35.00
Stand, Lamp, Cherry, Drawer, Dovetailed, Turned Legs, 19th Century, 26 x 22 x 19 In.	170.00
Stand, Louis Philippe, Pine, Painted, Flowers, Door, Interior Shelf, c.1830, 29 x 17 In.	815.00
Stand, Louis Philippe Style, Burled Walnut, Marble Top, Door, Shelves, 32 x 18 x 14 In.	239.00
Stand, Louis Philippe Style, Oak, Marble Top, Straight Facade, Drawer, Door, c.1830, 31 x 17 In.	890.00
Stand, Louis XV, Round, Fruitwood, Ormolu Mounts, Marquetry, 29 x 20 In.	173.00
Stand, Louis XV Style, Walnut, Red Marble, Leaves, Acanthus, Drawer, Door, c.1880, 34 x 16 In.	765.00
Stand, Louis XV Style, Walnut, Serpentine Marble Top, c.1890, 33 x 16 In.	675.00
Stand, Louis XVI Style, Marble Top, 3 Drawers, Brass Gallery, Ormolu Trim, 30 x 16 In.	374.00
Stand, Magazine, G. Stickley, No. 72 Ellis, Overhanging Top, 3 Shelves, 22 x 42 In.	1840.00
Stand, Magazine, G. Stickley, No. 548, Panel Sides, 4 Shelves, Leather Facing, 15 x 45 In. ..	6600.00
Stand, Magazine, G. Stickley, Tree Of Life, 3 Shelves, 44 x 12 ¾ In.	3965.00
Stand, Magazine, Michigan Chair Co., 4 Shelves, Slat Sides, Key & Tenon, 16 x 33 In.	660.00
Stand, Magazine, Stickley Bros., No. 4702, 3 Shelves, 26 ½ x 13 x 41 ½ In. ....*illus*	720.00
Stand, Mahogany, 2 Cock-Beaded Drawers, Inlays, Reeded Legs, c.1890, 29 x 19 In.	470.00
Stand, Mahogany, 5 Shelves, Cylindrical Supports, France, 41 ½ x 16 x 12 In.	657.00
Stand, Maple, Pine, Drawer, Hepplewhite, Splayed & Tapered Legs, c.1800, 26 x 21 x 31 In.	294.00
Stand, Marble Inlay, Agate, Bronze, Vase Shape Pedestal, 32 x 18 In. ....*illus*	759.00
Stand, McCobb, Metal Legs, Wood, Lower Shelf, Calvin, c.1956, 25 x 20 In., Pair............	1960.00
Stand, Mirror, Gothic Revival, Mahogany, Carved, c.1900, 83 x 48 In. ....*illus*	1320.00
Stand, Music, Burl Walnut, Flower, Inlay, Folio Base, Spindle & Finial Top, 1800s, 46 x 23 In.	1500.00
Stand, Music, G. Stickley, Inlay, Dovetailed, Paneled Base, Decal, 48 x 20 x 17 In. ....*illus*	7800.00
Stand, Music, George III, Mahogany, Adjustable, Arched Legs, Slipper Feet, c.1700, 42 In.	1016.00
Stand, Music, Lyre Top, Metal, 45 In.	28.00
Stand, Music, Stamped, Lambie Co., N.Y., Patd August 11, 1886....................	110.00
Stand, Neoclassical, Cherry, 3 Drawers, Inlaid Shield, Turned Legs, c.1825, 29 x 24 In.	881.00
Stand, Neoclassical, Mahogany, Bird's-Eye Maple Drawer, c.1825, 27 x 20 In.	353.00
Stand, Oak, Poplar, Bootjack Ends, Open Shelves, Gallery Top, c.1870, 34 x 37 In.	323.00
Stand, Parlor, Victorian, Walnut, Marble Top, Rectangular, 29 x 22 ½ x 16 In.	143.00
Stand, Pedestal, Mahogany, Round Marble Top, Contoured Legs, c.1920, 28 x 14 In.	146.00
Stand, Pembroke, Sheraton, Poplar, 2 Drawers, 19th Century, 17 In.	195.00
Stand, Pine, Drawer, Painted, 19th Century, 27 x 17 ½ In.	500.00
Stand, Pine, Oval, Victorian, 28 x 23 In.	265.00
Stand, Pine, Poplar, 3 Drawers, Brass Pulls, Mustard, Brown Stain, Hancock, c.1845, 37 x 27 In.	1170.00
Stand, Pine, Red Paint, Drawer, c.1820, 29 x 17 In.	2963.00
Stand, Plant, 3 Dragon Legs, Claw Foot Base, Cast Iron, 12 x 48 In., Pair...............	2875.00
Stand, Plant, Aesthetic Revival, Carved, Multicolored, Chinoiserie, Sunflower Brackets, 44 x 15 In.	646.00
Stand, Plant, Arts & Crafts, Wrought Iron, Hammered Copper, Patina, 14 ½ x 23 In.	120.00
Stand, Plant, Brass, Embossed, Molded Top, Central Support, 3-Footed, 32 ½ In.	60.00
Stand, Plant, Cast Iron, White Paint, Openwork Scrolls, 4 Graduated Tiers, 38 x 47 In.	1093.00
Stand, Plant, Ebonized Hardwood, Carved Dragons, Marble Inset, 6-Sided Top, 6 Legs, c.1910, 32 In.	533.00
Stand, Plant, G. Stickley, Round Top, Cross Stretcher, 22 x 10 ½ In.	1440.00
Stand, Plant, George III, Reeded Rails, Claw Feet, Wrought Iron, c.1800, 51 x 49 In.	18600.00
Stand, Plant, Hepplewhite Style, Inlaid Mahogany, Round Top, Medial Shelf, 48 ½ x 15 In.	173.00
Stand, Plant, L. & J.G. Stickley, No. 325, Ash, Square Top, Stretcher, 13 ½ x 13 ½ x 22 In.	480.00
Stand, Plant, Louis XIII Style, Oak, Barley Twist Columns, Tripod Base, c.1890, 43 x 15 In.	624.00
Stand, Plant, Louis XV Style, Painted, Carved, Pair..........................	720.00
Stand, Plant, Neoclassical Style, Satinwood, Inlaid, Tapered Legs, Stretcher, 42 x 12 In.	960.00
Stand, Plant, Renaissance Revival, Walnut, Marble Insert, Carved Panels, Legs, 30 In.	1006.00
Stand, Plant, Rosewood, Floating Panel, Indented Apron, Horse-Hoof Feet, 44 x 13 In.	240.00
Stand, Plant, Stickley Bros., Square Top, Splayed Legs, Metal Tag, 14 x 34 In.	330.00
Stand, Plant, Wood, Carved Shaped Legs, Lower Shelf, Chinese, 35 x 14 In.	230.00
Stand, Plant, Wood, Carved, Tripod Base, Black Forest, 34 x 22 ½ In.	710.00

F

Stand, Plate, Chinoiserie, Wood, Gilt, 3 Tiers, Folding, 3 Shelves, 9 x 35 In. ....*illus* 495.00
Stand, Poplar, Red Stain, Stenciled Drawer, Pennsylvania, c.1850, 30 x 21 In. 527.00
Stand, Pot Cupboard, Empire, Mahogany, Marble Top, Cylindrical, 29 x 15 In. 2100.00
Stand, Reading, Oak, Gilt Metal, Pierced, Hinged, 4-Scroll Legs, Casters, 44 In. 280.00
Stand, Reading, Regency, Rosewood, Brass Inlaid, c.1820, 34 x 18 x 13 In. 1645.00
Stand, Red Lacquer, Quatrefoil Top & Stretchers, Painted Figures, Chinese, 31 In., Pair.......... 388.00
Stand, Regency, Bird's-Eye Maple, Inlaid Tray, Gallery, Brass Handles, 20 x 27 In. 490.00
Stand, Renaissance Revival, Brass, Steel, Scrolling Leaves, Circular Top, 33 x 15 In. 770.00
Stand, Renaissance Revival, Herter Bros., Inlaid, Drawer, Cabinet, c.1872, 30 x 18 x 18 In. 5185.00
Stand, Renaissance Revival, Revolving Top, Cast Iron, Lion's Head Legs 240.00
Stand, Rococo Revival, Mahogany, Cylindrical, Drawer, Door, 28 ½ x 17 In. 180.00
Stand, Satinwood, Fruitwood, Marble, Carved, Gilt, Pillar, Tripod Base, c.1840, 29 x 19 In. 3500.00
Stand, Shaker, Birch, Maple, Salmon Paint, Drawer, Pegged, 19th Century, 28 x 23 In. 1500.00
Stand, Shaker, Cherry, Drawer, Tapered Legs, 19th Century, 26 x 18 x 16 In. 800.00
Stand, Shaker, Cherry, Painted, Drawer, 19th Century, 26 x 18 x 18 In. 520.00
Stand, Shaker, Drawer, Red Varnish, Signed S. Munson, N.H., c.1835, 28 x 19 In. 585.00
Stand, Shaker, Maple, Butternut, Candle Drawer, 30 x 23 In. 235.00
Stand, Shaker, Pine, Painted, Scrubbed Top, Canted Legs, 27 x 16 x 17 In. 1000.00
Stand, Shaker, Walnut, Poplar, Drawer, c.1830, 29 x 23 In. 323.00
Stand, Shaving, Empire, Mahogany, Mirror, Tripod, Pedestal, Pad Feet, England, 58 x 16 In. .. 299.00
Stand, Shaving, Federal, Mahogany, Mixed Woods, Hinged Top, Brass, c.1820, 37 x 16 In. 748.00
Stand, Shaving, George III, Oval Mirror, Serpentine Base, 3 Drawers, c.1790, 24 x 17 In. 294.00
Stand, Shaving, Hepplewhite, Mahogany, 2 Drawers, Curved Arms, Oval Mirror, 18 x 8 In. 207.00
Stand, Shaving, Inlaid Mahogany, Serpentine Plate, Beaded Edge, Gilt, c.1700, 21 x 13 x 9 In. . 836.00
Stand, Shaving, Oak, Mirror, Drawer, 64 In. 360.00
Stand, Sheraton, Birch, Mahogany, Pine, Drawer, New England, c.1840, 30 x 22 In. 529.00
Stand, Sheraton, Bird's-Eye Maple, 2 Drawers, Ring-Turned Legs, Ball Feet, c.1840, 31 x 19 x 16 In. 1380.00
Stand, Sheraton, Cherry, 2 Drawers, Brass Casters, 19th Century, 29 x 20 x 17 ½ In. 1150.00
Stand, Sheraton, Cherry, Curly Maple, Poplar, 2 Drawers, Paneled Sides, Turned Legs, 28 x 20 In. 441.00
Stand, Sheraton, Cherry, Drawer, Chamfered, Fluted Legs, Reeded Handles, c.1840, 29 x 19 x 18 In. 460.00
Stand, Sheraton, Cherry, Drop Leaf, 2 Drawers, c.1810 .... 300.00
Stand, Sheraton, Cherry, Maple, 2 Drawers, Pressed Glass Pulls, c.1825, 29 x 19 In. 235.00
Stand, Sheraton, Cherry, Paneled Case, 2 Beaded Drawers, c.1828, 9 x 20 In. 470.00
Stand, Sheraton, Cherry, Walnut, 2 Drawers, Carved Sunbursts, Ohio, c.1830, 30 x 20 In. 1528.00
Stand, Sheraton, Curly Maple, Pine, Turned Legs, Ball Feet, c.1830, 28 ½ x 22 In. 3642.00
Stand, Sheraton, Curly Maple, Turned Legs & Wafers On Feet, Curved Drawer, c.1830, 29 x 22 In. 1880.00
Stand, Sheraton, Mahogany, Reeded Leg, Drop Leaf, 2 Drawers, String Inlay, c.1820, 30 x 16 In. 1250.00
Stand, Sheraton, Mahogany, Turned Rope Legs, Drawers, c.1825, 29 x 18 In. 470.00
Stand, Sheraton, Painted, Drawer, 19th Century, 26 ½ x 19 ¾ In. 120.00
Stand, Sheraton, Smoke, Paint, Hardwood, Drawer, 18 x 16 x 28 In. 12075.00
Stand, Sheraton, Tiger Maple, Bird's-Eye Maple, Drawer, c.1830, 28 x 18 In. 823.00
Stand, Sheraton, Tiger Maple, Drawer, 29 x 19 x 19 In. 396.00
Stand, Shoe Shine, Oak, c.1900, 28 x 23 x 40 In. 819.00
Stand, Smoking, Art Deco, Japanned, Serpentine Top, Landscape, Ashtrays, 16 x 14 In. 176.00
Stand, Smoking, Arts & Crafts, 2 Doors, Pine Side Racks, 14 x 34 In. 840.00
Stand, Smoking, Arts & Crafts, Copper, Wrought Iron, 30 In. 100.00
Stand, Smoking, Arts & Crafts, Oak, Door, Slag Glass, Copper Handle, 28 x 18 In. ....*illus* 588.00
Stand, Smoking, Arts & Crafts, Wrought Iron, Hammered Copper Tray, 12 x 34 In. 180.00
Stand, Smoking, Arts & Crafts, Wrought Iron, Match Holder, Ashtray, Keys, 21 x 8 x 39 In. 420.00
Stand, Smoking, Chestnut, Turned Legs, Recessed Door, Shelf, c.1900, 28 In. 126.00
Stand, Smoking, Flame Mahogany, Lift Lid, Leather, Weiman's Tables, 26 x 14 In. 220.00
Stand, Smoking, Indian, Figural, Cast Iron, Stamped, 38 In. 550.00
Stand, Smoking, Iron, Jadite, 27 In. 140.00
Stand, Smoking, Iron, Tulip Shape, Embossed, Black, Scroll Art Co., Conn., Pat., 1925, 12 x 31 In. 88.00
Stand, Smoking, Oak, Roll Top Desk, c.1910, 10 ½ In. ....*illus* 270.00
Stand, Softwood, Painted, Beaded Skirt, Splayed Legs, Hand Cut Nails, Pa., 29 x 17 x 14 In. ... 770.00
Stand, Somno, G. Stickley, No. 618, Drawer Over Open Shelf, Lower Cabinet, 20 x 34 In. 8400.00
Stand, Syrian Style, Square, Mother-Of-Pearl Inlay, Bone Inlay Feet, Trim............................. 330.00
Stand, Tiger Maple, Drawer, 27 ½ x 16 In. 485.00
Stand, Tiger Maple, Grain Painted Red, Drawer, Ball Feet, Conn., c.1815, 18 x 28 In. 2400.00
Stand, Tilt Top, Mahogany, Oval, Tripod Base, Snake Feet, c.1780, 28 x 22 In. 529.00
Stand, Tilt Top, Mahogany, Piecrust, c.1760, 26 x 18 In. 588.00
Stand, Torchere, Regency, Mahogany, Tripod Base, c.1830, 45 In., Pair. 881.00
Stand, Tray, Inlay, Mahogany, Acanthus, Lunettes, Bellflowers, Brass Handles, 26 x 18 In. 403.00
Stand, Turned Wood Base Mounted With Twigs, Blowing Rock, c.1925, 19 ½ In. 201.00
Stand, Walnut, 2-Board Top, Apron, Ring-Turned Legs, c.1800, 26 x 22 x 17 In. 587.00

Furniture, Sofa, Sheraton, Mahogany, Birch Inlay, Reeded Open Arms, N.H., c.1800, 37 x 72 In.
$1175.00

Furniture, Sofa, Victorian, Mahogany, Serpentine, Striped Upholstery, 1800s, 33 x 72 In.
$269.00

Furniture, Stand, Basin, Mahogany, Tripod, Drawers, Kittinger, 32 ½ In.
$205.00

Furniture, Stand, Basin, Sheraton, Tiger Maple, Scalloped Top, Drawer, Turned Legs, c.1820, 43 x 23 In.
$600.00

F

Furniture, Stand, Fern, Walnut, Oval, Heart Design Pedestal, Victorian, 30 In. $400.00

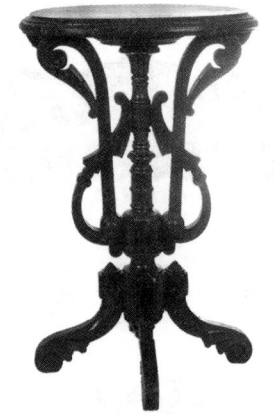

Furniture, Stand, Folio, William & Mary Style, Oak, Barley Twist Legs, Cane Panels, 26 In. $764.00

Stand, Walnut, Carved, Oval Marble Top, Victorian, 30 In.	172.00
Stand, Walnut, Drawer, Penn, c.1790, 28 x 20 In.	711.00
Stand, Walnut, Figural, Heron & Frog, Cattails, Water Lilies, Oval Base, c.1800s, 37 x 18 In.	2232.00
Stand, Wood, Ebonized, Figural Stork Base, Round, 33 x 23 In.	690.00
Stand, Wormley, Mahogany, Bleached, Leather Wrapped, 1950s, 24 x 25 ½ In., Pair	1020.00
Stand, Writing, Mahogany, Pine, Poplar, Pedestal, Drawers, Adjustable, c.1850, 30 x 24 In.	176.00
Stool Set, Chippendale, Padded Arched Back, Marlboro Legs, Stretchers, 42 In., 4 Piece	147.00
Stool Set, Ray Wilkes, Swivel, Chrome, Aluminum, Upholstered, Herman Miller, 18 x 36 In., 4	1800.00
Stool, Aalto, Birch, Low, Upholstered, Laminated, 17 x 13 In., Pair	179.00
Stool, Aalto, Birch, Stamped, Artek, Sweden, 15 x 17 ¼ In. *illus*	210.00
Stool, Aalto, No. Y601, Laminated Birch, Leather, c.1950s, 18 x 18 x 18 In., Pair	1673.00
Stool, Baroque, Walnut, Elongated, Octagonal, Handle, 21 x 15 x 11 In.	948.00
Stool, Baroque, Walnut, Handle, Splayed, Ring-Turned Legs, 18 x 15 x 10 In.	652.00
Stool, Brass, Scrolls, Upholstered, W. H. Howell, Geneva, Ill., 18 x 25 x 13 In.	165.00
Stool, Butterfly, Sori Yanagi, Tendo, c.1955, 15 x 16 ½ In.	1225.00
Stool, Cast Iron, Octagonal, Black, Roundels, Upholstered, 15 x 16 In.	1093.00
Stool, Cherry, Cutout Mortised Feet, Varnish, 1800s, 7 x 13 In.	206.00
Stool, Cornhusks Bottom, Richard Hunter, 1940, 12 x 13 In.	77.00
Stool, Cricket, Pine, Painted, Bookjack Ends, 19th Century, 8 x 17 In.	106.00
Stool, Empire Style, Cerule Form, Gilt, Padded Seat, 20 x 21 x 17 In.	230.00
Stool, Empire Style, Multicolored, Padded, Carved Leaf Accents, 16 x 25 x 17 In.	780.00
Stool, Fledermaus, Bentwood, Painted, Spindles, Padded, J.Hoffmann, 18 In., Pair	920.00
Stool, Flowers, Panels, Lacquer, Gilt, Cutout Base, Japan, c.1900, 31 x 15 In.	300.00
Stool, Franco Albini, Rattan, Vittorio Bonacina, Italy, 24 x 14 In.	510.00
Stool, Frank Lloyd Wright, Cross Base, Upholstered Seat, Heritage Henredon, 18 x 18 In.	1560.00
Stool, G. Nakashima, Plank, Walnut, 3 Legs, 1959, 12 x 22 In.	1200.00
Stool, G. Stickley, No. 395, 7 Spindles On Each Side, Decal, 20 x 16 x 15 In.	1140.00
Stool, Gehry, Easy Edges, 1969-73, 15 x 16 ½ x 14 ½ In.	2450.00
Stool, George I, Walnut, Rectangular, Upholstered Top, Stretcher, c.1715, 18 x 22 In.	1200.00
Stool, George III, Mahogany, Carved, Square Tapered Legs, c.1770, 18 x 22 x 15 In.	3290.00
Stool, George III Style, Mahogany, Shell, Leaf Carved, Paw Feet, 18 x 17 x 25 In., Pair	840.00
Stool, Georgian Style, Mahogany, Carved, Leather, Tufted, Cabriole Legs, 20 x 38 In.	374.00
Stool, Gothic Revival, Oak, Plank Top, Folds, Shields, Ornate Carvings, 20 x 22 In.	148.00
Stool, Handmade, Wooden, 1840s, 5 ½ x 20 In.	58.00
Stool, Hunting, Folding, Hardwood, Hand Forged Metal, England, 19th Century, 31 In.	275.00
Stool, Hunzinger, Walnut, Upholstered, Gilt, Stretcher, 19th Century, 20 x 21 x 12 In.	240.00
Stool, I. Noguchi, No. 85T, Walnut, Chromium Plated Steel, Rocker, c.1955, 11 In.	13750.00
Stool, I. Noguchi, No. 86T, Birch, Chromium Plated, Rocker, c.1954, 17 In.	11250.00
Stool, Iron, Scrolls, Openwork, White Paint, Gilt, Gold Upholstery, 9 x 15 In.	115.00
Stool, Jacobean, Oak, Carved, Plank Top, Blocked Legs, Stretchers, 21 x 17 In.	441.00
Stool, Jacques Quinet, Gray Leather, Tripod Brass Feet, 15 x 15 In.	570.00
Stool, Joint, Oak Carved Skirt, Turned Legs, Molded Top, 23 x 10 x 19 In.	225.00
Stool, Joint, Square Top, Turned Legs, Stretchers, Painted, New Hampshire, 11 x 18 In.	1947.00
Stool, Le Corbusier, Oak, c.1956, 17 x 13 x 10 In.	40625.00
Stool, Louis XV, Beech, Multicolored, Padded Top, Carved Apron, Scrolled Toes, 18 x 22 In.	2040.00
Stool, Louis XV, Needlepoint, Beech, Carved, Upholstered, Cream Paint, c.1910, 9 x 18 In.	267.00
Stool, Louis XV Style, Beech, Carved, Cream Paint, Padded, 18 x 32 x 15 In.	720.00
Stool, Louis XVI Style, Gilt, Carved, Upholstered, 20 x 21 x 17 In.	359.00
Stool, Mahogany, Horsehair, Reeded Curule Base, c.1825, 21 ¾ x 15 ⅜ In.	2074.00
Stool, Mahogany, Leather Upholstery, Brass Nail Heads, 1839	529.00
Stool, Mahogany, Marble, Octagonal, Carved Flowers, Claw Feet, Shelf, Asia, 15 x 18 In.	115.00
Stool, Mahogany, Square Seat Over Oval Support, Square Plinth, c.1835, 18 x 20 x 18 In.	529.00
Stool, Maple, Round Padded Top, 4 Saber Legs, 1800s, 15 ½ x 19 ½ In.	59.00
Stool, Molded Seat, Upholstered, Rounded Aluminum Base, 24 x 22 In.	480.00
Stool, Napoleon III, Rosewood, Serpentine Apron, Upholstered, 15 x 18 x 17 In., Pair	1200.00
Stool, Neoclassical, Upholstered Seat, Ogee Molded Frame, Turned Feet, 14 x 18 In.	705.00
Stool, Nutting, Oval, Splayed Legs, Signed	193.00
Stool, Organ, Empire, Mahogany, Needlepoint, Adjustable, c.1835	120.00
Stool, Organ, Victorian, Walnut Carved, Upholstered, Octagonal, Vine Skirt, 23 In.	121.00
Stool, Organ, Walnut, Carved, Turned Legs, Brass Ball & Claw, c.1880, 19 x 19 In.	234.00
Stool, Piano, George IV, Gilt, Padded, Needlework, 3-Legs, Leaf Carving, 17 x 16 In.	840.00
Stool, Piano, Hunzinger, Mahogany, Basket Weave, Rope Turned Legs, Revolving, c.1890	790.00
Stool, Piano, Oak, Round Cane Seat, Cast-Iron Screw, Out-Turned Legs, 20 x 14 In.	86.00
Stool, Pine, Painted, Tulip & Leaf Design, Black Ground, Splayed Legs, c.1830, 13 x 6 In.	1275.00
Stool, Pine, Turned Leg, Upholstered, 1700s, 17 x 18 ½ In.	267.00
Stool, Queen Anne Style, Walnut, Carved Shells, Bellflowers, Cabriole Legs, 18 x 23 In.	575.00

Stool, Queen Anne, Mahogany, Slip Seat, Scalloped Apron, Pad Feet, c.1740, 20 In.	4000.00
Stool, Queen Anne, Walnut, Cushion, Cabriole Legs, c.1750, 12 x 17 x 15 In.	2340.00
Stool, Regency, Fruitwood, Padded, Ribbon Carved Frieze, Carved, c.1890, 17 x 21 In.	120.00
Stool, Regency, Fruitwood, Padded Seat, Cross Base, c.1880, 17 x 21 In. .....*illus*	120.00
Stool, Regency Style, Fruitwood, Ribbon Frieze, Upholstered, Peg Feet, 17 x 21 In.	112.00
Stool, Renaissance Revival, Walnut, Needlepoint, Turned Legs, Stretcher, c.1880, 17 x 21 In.	936.00
Stool, Restauration, Mahogany, Stepped, Beaded Apron, Bracket Feet, 1880s, 15 x 39 In.	330.00
Stool, Shaker, 2-Step, Pine, Top Tread Cutout, Red Stain, c.1850, 12 x 17 In.	1053.00
Stool, Shaker, Maple, Cherry, Green, Gray Tape, N.Y., c.1880, 16 x 14 In.	351.00
Stool, Shaker, Maple, Green, Khaki Tape Seat, Ebony Finish, N.Y., c.1880, 16 x 14 In.	702.00
Stool, Shaker, Maple, Rush Top, Turned Legs, 8 Stretcher, Varnish, Decal, 16 x 14 In.	468.00
Stool, Shaker, Sister's, Walnut, 2-Step, Arched Sides, c.1850, 9 x 10 In.	1404.00
Stool, Sori Yanagi, Rosewood, Butterfly Shape, 2 Parts, Brass Fittings, 17 x 16 In.	900.00
Stool, Step, Mixed Woods, Paint Layers, Shaped Skirt, Boot Feet, 1800s, 15 x 13 In.	633.00
Stool, Step, Shaker, Walnut, Trestle Feet, Painted Arch Top, c.1870, 19 x 13 In.	117.00
Stool, Step, Victorian, Mahogany, Leather Top Tread, 18 x 14 x 12 In.	652.00
Stool, Stickley, Arts & Crafts, Oak, Quaint Furniture, 15 x 15 x 14 In.	635.00
Stool, Thebe's, Maple, Concave Seat, Turned Legs, 1910-30, 17 ¾ x 15 ¾ In.	325.00
Stool, Walnut, Barley Twist Legs, Upholstered, c.1875	470.00
Stool, Walnut, Ebonized, Gilt, Tufted Brocade Cushion, 18 x 19 x 10 ½ In.	120.00
Stool, Walnut, Scrimshaw Inlays, Cutout Ends, Flowers, 8 x 14 In.	529.00
Stool, Walnut, Swivel, Lady Boot Legs, Bronze, England, c.1900, 21 In.	4100.00
Stool, Wegner, Teak, Gray Wool Upholstery, 16 x 28 In.	1140.00
Stool, William & Mary, Walnut, Tapestry, Barley Twist Legs, 17 x 19 x 18 In.	356.00
Stool, William & Mary, Walnut, Turned Legs, X-Stretcher, c.1870, 18 x 22 In.	975.00
Stool, Windsor, Painted, 19th Century, 7 ½ In.	150.00
Stool, Windsor, Stylized Leaf & Flowers, Original Green Paint, 8 x 12 x 7 ½ In.	1035.00
Stool, Wood, Flattened Mushroom Seat, Red Paint, White Dots, 3 Branch Legs, 7 In.	58.00
Stool, Wood, Splayed Legs, Hand Riveted Legs & Stretchers, c.1915, 22 In.	400.00
Stool, Wood, Zoomorphic Design, Lobi, c.1950, 32 x 42 In.	480.00
Table, 2 Tiers, Lower Shelf, Turned Legs, Casters	199.00
Table, 3 Leaves, Column Pedestal, Carved, Paw Feet, c.1880, 32 x 54 In.	2040.00
Table, Aalto, Birch, Flared Edge, Lower Shelf, c.1931, 20 x 23 In.	3346.00
Table, Acrylic, Cross Shape, Clear, Red, Square Glass Top, 17 x 21 In.	240.00
Table, Adirondack Twig, Rectangular, Trelliswork Sides, Shelf, Splayed Legs, 22 x 20 In.	115.00
Table, Aesthetic Revival, Scorched Bamboo, Lacquer, Birds, Trees, Late 1800s, 32 x 31 In.	374.00
Table, Altar, Hardwood, Beveled Edge, Lozenge Frieze, Chinese, 1800s, 33 x 76 In.	1645.00
Table, Altar, Rosewood, Pierced Ends, Floating Panel, Pendant Tassels, 35 x 60 x 17 In.	720.00
Table, Altar, Walnut, Rectangular, Chinese, 31 x 44 x 10 In.	299.00
Table, Altar, Walnut, Upturned Ends, Reeded Feet, Pierced Fretwork, c.1780, 36 x 89 x 13 In.	3840.00
Table, American Classic, Game, Mahogany, Faceted Pedestal, c.1830, 31 x 36 x 18 In.	2115.00
Table, Anglo Kenyan, Brass Mounted Antelope Horn, Legs, Brass Top, 20 x 13 In. ....*illus*	720.00
Table, Art Deco, Mahogany, 2 Open Shelves, Round, 1900s, 25 x 28 In.	259.00
Table, Art Deco, Marble Top, Iron Base, 33 x 24 In. .....*illus*	817.00
Table, Art Deco, Multicolored, Gilt, Bowed, Ebonized Top, Eagle Base, 31 x 48 x 18 In.	4300.00
Table, Art Deco, Round, Beveled Mirror Top, Inset, Glass Screw Skirt, Bobbin Leg, 30 x 16 In., Pair	196.00
Table, Art Deco, Softwood, Central Panel, Chinese, 31 x 17 ¾ x 17 ¾ In.	1560.00
Table, Art Moderne, Gilt Metal, Glass, Ebonized Glass, Tubular Supports, 24 x 16 In., Pair	540.00
Table, Art Nouveau, Marquetry, Whimsical Insects, France, c.1900, 26 x 16 In.	300.00
Table, Arts & Crafts, 2 Drawers, Vertical Side Slats, 32 x 29 In.	390.00
Table, Arts & Crafts, G. Stickley, Oak, Stretcher Base, Early 1900s, 29 x 48 In.	2703.00
Table, Arts & Crafts, Tile Top, Faux Mosaic Bird, Iron Base, 20 ½ x 20 ½ In. ....*illus*	330.00
Table, Arts & Crafts, Tile Top, Wrought Iron Base, 16 x 10 x 20 In.	306.00
Table, Arts & Crafts, Walnut, Gateleg, Drop Leaf, Beveled Legs, 28 x 30 x 26 In.	474.00
Table, Arts & Crafts, Wood, Cut Corner Top, Splayed Legs, Applied Details, Lower Shelf, 30 x 29 In.	510.00
Table, Baker Furniture, Mahogany, Fan & String Inlay, Cock-Beaded Drawer, 27 x 20 In.	413.00
Table, Baker Furniture, Pembroke, Mahogany, Drawer, Tapered Legs, Brass Caps, 24 x In., Pair	620.00
Table, Baker's, Cast Iron, Marble Top, Gothic Skirt, Acanthus, Scrolled Legs, 31 x 27 In.	3231.00
Table, Baker's, Cast Iron, Marble Top, Scrolled Rosette Base, Stretchers, 1800s, 33 x 48 In.	1763.00
Table, Baker's, Cast Iron, White Marble Top, Casters, France, 19th Century, 39 x 25 In.	1995.00
Table, Baker's, Mahogany, Marble Top, 3 Drawers, 2 Cupboards, 1920s, 48 x 48 x 24 In.	360.00
Table, Bamboo, Painted Top, Jockey, Racehorse, c.1910, 26 x 23 In. .....*illus*	288.00
Table, Bamboo, Round, Swivel Base, Open Storage, Natural Grain Circles, 1960s, 22 x 20 In., Pair	600.00
Table, Baroque, 3 Parts, Metal Band Corners, Iron Supports, Spain, 12 Ft., 3 Piece	6962.00
Table, Baroque, Maple, Fold Leaves, Turned Legs, 33 x 72 In.	978.00
Table, Baroque, Oak, 2-Board, 4 Drawers, Trestle, Stretchers, 18th Century, 33 x 118 In.	3600.00

Furniture, Stand, Globe, McCobb, Paper, On Wood, Brass, c.1955, 37 x 20 In. $1560.00

Furniture, Stand, Hepplewhite, Mahogany, Tilt Top, Cut Corners, Pedestal, 27 x 26 In. $206.00

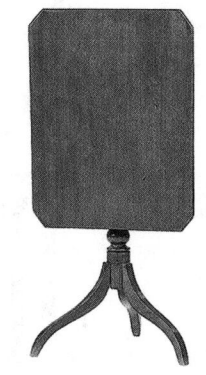

Furniture, Stand, Magazine, Stickley Bros., No. 4702, 3 Shelves, 26 ½ x 13 x 41 ½ In. $720.00

Furniture, Stand, Marble Inlay, Agate, Bronze, Vase Shape Pedestal, 32 x 18 In. $759.00

Furniture, Stand, Mirror, Gothic Revival, Mahogany, Carved, c.1900, 83 x 48 In. $1320.00

Furniture, Stand, Music, G. Stickley, Inlay, Dovetailed, Paneled Base, Decal, 48 x 20 x 17 In. $7800.00

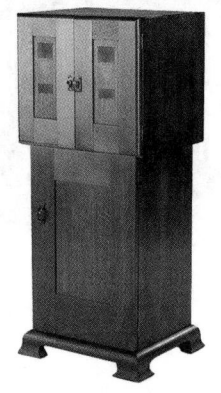

Table, Baroque, Walnut, Box Stretcher, Virginia, c.1730, 23 x 23 In. ....*illus*	1150.00
Table, Baroque, Walnut, Maple, Oak, Gateleg, Red Stain, Virginia, c.1730, 28 x 44 In.	17250.00
Table, Bench, Pine, Lift Top, 19th Century, 30 x 48 x 28 ½ In. ....*illus*	351.00
Table, Beveled Glass Top, Lucite, Chrome Pedestal Base, 18 x 24 In.	1320.00
Table, Biedermeier, Amboyna Inlay, Oval, 2 Frieze Drawers, Shelf Stretcher, 31 x 31 In.	1007.00
Table, Biedermeier, Fruitwood, Amboyna Inlay, Drawers, Angular Legs, 1840, 30 x 31 x 20 In.	415.00
Table, Biedermeier Style, Marble Top, Fruitwood, Acanthus Leaf Carving, 1900s, 29 x 29 In. ...	127.00
Table, Biedermeier, Walnut, Veneered, Drawer, 23 ¾ x 13 ½ In.	356.00
Table, Birch, Tilt Top, Diamond Faceted Pedestal, New Hampshire, 30 In.	995.00
Table, Bird's-Eye Maple, Tilt Top, 3 Cabriole Legs, Snake Feet, c.1900, 28 x 27 In.	633.00
Table, Black Lacquer, 2 Round Tiers, Mother-Of-Pearl Inlay, 3 Scroll Legs, Vietnam, 25 x 26 In.	227.00
Table, Black Lacquer, Papier-Mache, Oval Tilt Top, Scalloped Edge, Gilt, Inlay, c.1870, 27 x 26 In.	403.00
Table, Blackamoor, Walnut, Geometrically Carved, Kneeling Figure, Italy, 1800s, 22 x 12 In. ..	490.00
Table, Bombe, Louis XIV, Fruitwood, Applied Gilt, Green Marble Top, Italy, 1800s, 36 x 66 In. .	2233.00
Table, Bouillotte, Louis XVI Style, Fruitwood, Round Marble Top, 29 x 25 In., Pair.........	1800.00
Table, Brandy Board, George III, Walnut, Bowfront, 1 Over 2 Drawers, 31 x 39 In.	418.00
Table, Brass Plated, Bamboo Frame, Suspended Glass, Handles, Italy, 1950, 24 x 26 x 19 In. ..	330.00
Table, Burled Walnut, Shelf Ends, D-Form, England, 36 x 65 x 17 In.	1793.00
Table, Burled Wood, Carved, Chinese, 13 x 12 x 21 In.	201.00
Table, Butterfly, William & Mary, Drawer, Turned Legs, Painted, New Eng., 1700s, 25 x 29 In. .	2015.00
Table, Butternut, Tray Top, 2 Drawers, Fiery Opalescent Glass Pulls, 24 x 28 x 17 In.	767.00
Table, Cafe, Limbert, Leather Top, Tacks, 29 x 29 ½ In.	5400.00
Table, Card, Chippendale, Mahogany, Drawer, Carved Apron, 1755, 28 x 30 In.	8900.00
Table, Card, Chippendale, Mahogany, Drawer, Marlboro Legs, c.1775, 29 x 35 In.	585.00
Table, Card, Edgar Brandt, Hepplewhite, Demilune, Mahogany, Satinwood Veneer, 30 x 32 In., Pair	431.00
Table, Card, Empire, Mahogany, 19th Century, 29 ¾ x 36 In.	232.00
Table, Card, Empire, Mahogany, Scroll Legs, Shelf, 30 x 45 x 28 In.	90.00
Table, Card, Envelope Folding, Fruitwood, Inlaid, Tapered Legs, 1800s, 29 x 33 x 33 In.	805.00
Table, Card, Federal, Cherry, Mahogany, Bowfront, Inlays, c.1880, 28 x 36 In.	1053.00
Table, Card, Federal, Mahogany, Demilune, 2 Swing Legs, Inlay, Mass., c.1795, 29 x 36 In.	1778.00
Table, Card, Federal, Mahogany, Demilune, Inlay, Tapered Legs, c.1899, 30 x 36 In.	830.00
Table, Card, Federal, Mahogany, Oval Corners, Carved, c.1815, 31 x 36 In. ....*illus*	2340.00
Table, Card, Federal, Mahogany, Shell Inlay, Tapered Legs, Shaped Feet, 28 x 36 In.	920.00
Table, Card, Federal, Mahogany, Stringing, Inlaid Panel Leaves, Square Legs, 29 x 34 In.	5629.00
Table, Card, Federal, Mahogany, Stringing, Inlaid Panels, Leaf Sprigs, Tapered Legs, 30 x 36 In.	1422.00
Table, Card, Federal, Mahogany, Turned, Reeded, String Inlays, 31 x 36 In.	355.00
Table, Card, Federal, Mahogany Veneer, Gatelegs, Foldover, c.1800, 28 x 36 In. ....*illus*	944.00
Table, Card, Federal, Mahogany, Yellow Pine, Bellflower Inlay, Charleston, 28 x 17 In.	2990.00
Table, Card, Federal, Maple, Overhanging Top, New England, c.1810, 29 x 34 In.	700.00
Table, Card, Flame Mahogany, Rosewood Band, Carved Pedestal, c.1840, 39 x 36 In.	12500.00
Table, Card, Flip Top, Chippendale, Mahogany, c.1785, 28 x 35 In.	1200.00
Table, Card, Flip Top, Federal, Inlays, Boston, 29 x 36 In.	8500.00
Table, Card, Flip Top, Federal, Swing Leg, Drawer, Grain Painted, Sample, c.1810, 9 x 11 In. ..	1126.00
Table, Card, Flip Top, Federal, Walnut, Chestnut, Apron, Burl Veneer, 29 x 39 x 19 In.	1150.00
Table, Card, Flip Top, Georgian, Carved, Mahogany, Ribbon & Flower, 29 x 36 In.	863.00
Table, Card, Flip Top, Mahogany, Mixed Woods, Molded Edge, Maryland, c.1780, 30 x 38 In. ..	12650.00
Table, Card, Flip Top, Rosewood, Mahogany, Pine, Turned Legs, 1800s, 30 x 35 In.	411.00
Table, Card, G. Stickley, No. 447, End Drawers, Key & Tenon, c.1902, 30 x 29 In.	6000.00
Table, Card, George III, Inlaid Mahogany, Molded Edge, Serpentine, 1780s, 29 x 37 In.	600.00
Table, Card, Georgian, Walnut, Wells, Frieze Drawer, Shell Carved Apron, 28 x 33 x 16 In.	356.00
Table, Card, Hepplewhite, Cherry, Flip Top, String Inlay, 30 x 35 In. ....*illus*	1175.00
Table, Card, Hepplewhite, Cherry, Oval & Diamonds Satinwood Inlay, 32 x 26 x 17 In.	2825.00
Table, Card, Hepplewhite, Cherry, Poplar, Flip Top, Demilune, Tapered Legs, c.1810, 28 x 35 In.	411.00
Table, Card, Hepplewhite, Mahogany, Inlay Patera, Swing Legs, Britain, Late 1900s, 28 x 36 x 18 In.	920.00
Table, Card, Hepplewhite, Mahogany, Line Inlay, Tapered Legs, 29 x 36 x 17 In.	396.00
Table, Card, Hepplewhite, Mahogany, Satinwood Inlay, Demilune, c.1800.........	2500.00
Table, Card, Mahogany, Carvings, Saber Legs, c.1820, 28 x 37 In.	5520.00
Table, Card, Marquetry, Pedestal, c.1800, 31 x 34 In.	6500.00
Table, Card, Pockets, Yellow Pine, 30 x 24 x 30 In.	107.00
Table, Card, Regency, Boxwood, Inlaid Mahogany, 29 x 35 x 17 In.	296.00
Table, Card, Sheraton, Inlaid Mahogany Serpentine, Reeded Legs, c.1840, 29 x 35 x 18 In.	1150.00
Table, Card, Sheraton, Mahogany, c.1820, 28 ¾ x 36 In.	402.00
Table, Card, Sheraton, Mahogany, Inlaid Maple, Reeded Legs, c.1840, 29 x 35 x 18 In.	1725.00
Table, Card, Sheraton, Mahogany, Reeded Edge, Turned Legs, 29 x 36 x 18 In.	480.00
Table, Card, Sheraton, Mahogany, Satinwood Inlays, Serpentine Shape, Swing Leg, 37 x 30 In.	805.00
Table, Carved, Flip Top, Swivel, Gadrooned Skirt, Paw Feet, c.1830, 29 x 48 In.	353.00

Table, Center, Aesthetic Revival, Octagonal Sunburst Top, Stepped Base, 30 x 35 In.	1495.00
Table, Center, Art Nouveau, Bentwood, Circular Skirt, Arched Legs, 27 x 42 In.	420.00
Table, Center, Baroque Style, Oak, Rectangular, 2 Drawers, Spiral Twist Legs, 29 x 48 In.	288.00
Table, Center, Biedermeier, Walnut, Sunburst Inlay, Drawer, c.1825, 31 x 45 In.	3840.00
Table, Center, Brooks Bros., Walnut, Oval, Pedestal Base, 30 x 48 x 34 In.	320.00
Table, Center, Chippendale, Mahogany, Gadroon Molding, Carved Acanthus, 28 x 45 In.	4600.00
Table, Center, Edwardian, Mixed Wood, Inlaid Musical Symbols, Octagonal, 29 x 37 In.	717.00
Table, Center, Egyptian Revival Rococo, Rosewood, Marble Top, Scalloped Skirt, 31 x 40 In.	3600.00
Table, Center, Empire, Mahogany, Bronze Mounted, Marble Top, France, 29 ½ x 32 In.	770.00
Table, Center, Empire, Marble Top, Scalloped Edge, S-Scroll Supports, c.1840, 28 x 39 In.	323.00
Table, Center, French Restauration, Burl, Figured, Pedestal, Scroll Feet, 30 x 53 In.	1880.00
Table, Center, Grain Painted, Round, Tripod, Curled Feet, Victorian, 28 x 32 In.	259.00
Table, Center, J. Meeks, Neoclassical, Mahogany, Round, Tripod Base, Curled Legs, 27 x 36 In.	4313.00
Table, Center, Limbert, No. 158, Oak, Oval, 29 x 47 ⅝ x 36 In.	18750.00
Table, Center, Louis XIV Style, Mahogany, Caryatids, Carved, X-Stretcher, 31 x 28 In.	529.00
Table, Center, Louis XVI Style, Gilt, Onyx Top, Frieze Carved, 30 x 38 x 25 In.	889.00
Table, Center, Louis XVI Style, Marble, Square Tapered Legs, c.1875, 28 x 38 x 22 In.	5175.00
Table, Center, Maple, Fruitwood Parquetry, S-Scrolls, Medallions, Cabriole Legs, 29 x 39 In.	415.00
Table, Center, Maple, Shaped Top & Stretcher Shelf, Glass Ball Feet, c.1880, 30 x 28 In.	354.00
Table, Center, Marble Top, Ornate Spindles, Carved, 4 Scrolled Legs, Victorian, 29 x 32 In.	840.00
Table, Center, Napoleon II, Ormolu Mounted Mahogany, Exotic Woods, 29 x 52 In.	5040.00
Table, Center, Napoleon III, Brass, Mother-Of-Pearl Inlay, 20 x 53 x 31 In.	717.00
Table, Center, Neoclassical, Mahogany, Round Egyptian Marble Top, Scroll Supports, 32 x 39 In.	4200.00
Table, Center, Neoclassical Style, Bronze, Marble, Game Board, 33 x 36 In.	3525.00
Table, Center, Neoclassical Style, Bronze, Marble Top, Paneled Frieze, 39 x 71 x 26 In.	9800.00
Table, Center, Oak, Golden, Beaded Trim, 8-Sided, Stretcher Board, 29 x 24 In.	175.00
Table, Center, Provincial, Fruitwood, Planked Top, 3 Angled Plank Legs, 29 x 41 In.	780.00
Table, Center, Provincial, Oak, Leather, Rounded, Scalloped Frieze, Shield, c.1850, 31 x 31 x 31 In.	960.00
Table, Center, Regency, Burl Walnut, Sunburst Top, Plinth Base, 30 x 52 In.	1673.00
Table, Center, Regency, Mahogany, Carved Pedestal, Scroll Legs, Ireland, 29 x 46 x 30 In.	2233.00
Table, Center, Renaissance Revival, George Washington, Eagles, Flag, c.1876, 28 x 28 x 19 In.	4880.00
Table, Center, Renaissance Revival, Mahogany, Grotesque Carved Base, 28 x 45 In.	359.00
Table, Center, Renaissance Revival, Walnut, Geometrics, Octagonal, Marquetry, 25 x 23 In.	3081.00
Table, Center, Renaissance Revival, Walnut, Marble, Winged Maidens, c.1850, 29 In.	2400.00
Table, Center, Rococo, Carved, Rosewood, Marble Top, Lion's Head Supports, 31 x 50 In.	4406.00
Table, Center, Rococo, Mahogany, Serpentine Marble Top, Shaped Stretchers, 30 x 38 In.	411.00
Table, Center, Rococo, Rosewood, Rouge Marble Top, Carved Skirt, c.1850, 30 x 44 x 24 In.	1997.00
Table, Center, Rococo, Rosewood, Serpentine Marble Top, Lobed, Scrolled Stretcher, 29 x 40 In.	2468.00
Table, Center, Rosewood, Pedestal Base, 1860-80, 29 x 50 In.	10500.00
Table, Center, Rosewood, Rectangular, Barley Twist Trestle Legs, 28 x 45 x 23 In.	1380.00
Table, Center, Rosewood, Tooled Leather Top, Pedestal Base, c.1820, 41 In.	6800.00
Table, Center, Slab Top, Carved Marble, c.1900, 36 x 76 x 35 In.	12420.00
Table, Center, Spanish Colonial Style, Carved Pine, Splayed Legs, 29 x 47 x 29 ½ In.	1304.00
Table, Center, Victorian, Mahogany, White & Gray Marble Top, Pierced Base, 28 x 31 In.	480.00
Table, Center, Victorian, Walnut, Marble Top, Carved Scrolling, Baluster Standard, 31 x 38 In.	1220.00
Table, Center, Walnut, Ebonized, Gilt, Drawer, Hoof Feet, c.1850, 30 x 51 In.	1762.00
Table, Center, Walnut, Marble Top, Oval, Carved, Filigree Legs, 37 x 29 In.	2243.00
Table, Chair, Cherry, Pine, Hinged Rectangular Top, Penn., c.1820, 28 x 60 In.	1304.00
Table, Chamber, Mahogany, Pine, Drawers, Shelf Stretcher, New York, c.1795, 37 x 35 In.	1528.00
Table, Chan, LaVerne, Pewter, Bronze, Enamel Top, 47 x 18 In. .... *illus*	3795.00
Table, Cherry, Mahogany, Flame Grain Veneer, Rope Turned Legs, c.1875, 31 x 27 In., Pair	823.00
Table, Cherry, Tilt Top, Pedestal Base, Tripod, New England, 27 x 30 In.	1600.00
Table, Cherry, Yellow Pine, Drawer, Stretcher Base, North Carolina, 1700s, 26 x 40 In.	3680.00
Table, Chess, Rosewood, Sandalwood, Inlaid Ivory, Octagonal, Carved Skirt, 30 x 36 x 18 In.	6169.00
Table, Chinese Export, Hardstone, Black Lacquer, c.1950, 20 x 30 In.	59.00
Table, Chinese, Hardwood, Carved, Scalloped Round Top, S-Curve Legs, c.1890, 36 x 14 In.	345.00
Table, Chinese, Hardwood, Frame & Panel Top, 2 Drawers, c.1860, 34 x 36 In.	173.00
Table, Chinese, Rosewood, Carved, Mitered Frame, Pierce Carved Skirt, 24 x 48 In.	173.00
Table, Chinoiserie Incised, Lacquer, Dragons, Clouds, Pierced, 18 x 54 x 28 In.	1195.00
Table, Chippendale, Cherry, Scroll Knees, Tidewater, Virginia, c.1790, 28 x 19 In.	9200.00
Table, Chippendale, Cherry, Tilt Top, Round, 27 x 35 ½ In.	1610.00
Table, Chippendale, Mahogany, Square Legs, Pierced Brackets, Virginia, 1700s, 32 x 48 In.	5060.00
Table, Chippendale, Mahogany, Tilt Top, Birdcage Support, 1700s, England, 27 x 33 In.	489.00
Table, Chippendale, Mahogany, Tilt Top, Buffalo, New York, 1900s, 29 x 35 In.	1528.00
Table, Chippendale, Mahogany, Tilt Top, Dish Top, Tripod Legs, Phila., 30 x 26 In.	3800.00
Table, Chippendale, Mahogany, Tilt Top, Piecrust Edge, 3-Footed, 29 x 27 In.	260.00

F

Furniture, Stand, Plate, Chinoiserie, Wood, Gilt, 3 Tiers, Folding, 3 Shelves, 9 x 35 In.
$495.00

Furniture, Stand, Smoking, Arts & Crafts, Oak, Door, Slag Glass, Copper Handle, 28 x 18 In.
$588.00

Furniture, Stand, Smoking, Oak, Roll Top Desk, c.1910, 10 ½ In.
$270.00

Furniture, Stool, Aalto, Birch, Stamped, Artek, Sweden, 15 x 17 ¼ In.
$210.00

Furniture, Stool, Regency, Fruitwood, Padded Seat, Cross Base, c.1880, 17 x 21 In.
$120.00

Furniture, Table, Anglo Kenyan, Brass Mounted Antelope Horn, Legs, Brass Top, 20 x 13 In.
$720.00

Furniture, Table, Art Deco, Marble Top, Iron Base, 33 x 24 In.
$817.00

Furniture, Table, Arts & Crafts, Tile Top, Faux Mosaic Bird, Iron Base, 20 ½ x 20 ½ In.
$330.00

Table, Chippendale, Mahogany, Tilt Top, Serpentine Top, Ball & Claw, 28 ½ x 32 x 32 In.	900.00
Table, Chippendale Style, 2 Drawers, Maple, Hardwood, Medial Stretchers, 29 x 30 In.	805.00
Table, Chippendale Style, Walnut, Tilt Piecrust Top, Tripod, Paw Feet, 28 x 37 In.	1434.00
Table, Chromium Plated Metal, Tree Trunk Form, Undulating Top, Saendal, 15 x 29 In.	2875.00
Table, Coffee, A. Girard, Glass Top, Steel Base, Herman Miller, 16 x 34 In.	2400.00
Table, Coffee, Art Deco, Blue Mirror Glass Top, U-Shape Base	180.00
Table, Coffee, Beech, Parquetry, Chrome Trim, 15 x 47 x 31 In.	170.00
Table, Coffee, Cassina, Ebonized Side Panels, Stainless Steel Top, Hinged Top, Pedestal	840.00
Table, Coffee, Chinese Chippendale, Mahogany, Serpentine Top, Pierced Gallery, 21 x 39 In. ..	805.00
Table, Coffee, Chinese, Elm, Carved, Panel Top, Pierced Latticework Skirt, 12 x 30 In.	288.00
Table, Coffee, Cini Boeri, Lunario, Cantilevered Glass, Label, Knoll, c.1970, 17 x 44 In.	3675.00
Table, Coffee, Danish Modern, Rosewood, Rectangular, Pullout End Trays, Denmark, 58 x 19 In.	240.00
Table, Coffee, Dunbar, Glass Top Over Stained Walnut Cube Base, 16 x 38 In.	1320.00
Table, Coffee, Dunbar, Shelf, Brass Stretchers, 28 x 48 In.	69.00
Table, Coffee, Edwardian, Satinwood, Recessed Top, Painted Leaves, 17 x 47 In.	173.00
Table, Coffee, F. Knoll, Round, Walnut, Beveled Top Over Square Steel Legs, 42 x 16 In.	900.00
Table, Coffee, Fornasetti, Lithographed Top, Fountain Scene, X-Frame, 18 x 39 In. ....*illus*	2040.00
Table, Coffee, Frankl, Biomorphic Cork Top, Mahogany Legs, Johnson Furniture Co., 38 x 15 In.	3900.00
Table, Coffee, Frankl, Cloud, Mahogany, Cork, Johnson Co., 48 x 15 In. ....*illus*	3600.00
Table, Coffee, Fret Border, Flowers, Black Lacquer, England, c.1920, 22 x 28 In.	720.00
Table, Coffee, G. Mobelfabrik, Teak, Danish Modern, Raised Edges, 9-Slat Shelf, 63 x 17 In.	270.00
Table, Coffee, G. Nakashima, Walnut, 2 Turned Legs, Plank Leg, c.1959, 12 x 45 In.	8510.00
Table, Coffee, G. Nakashima, Walnut, Rosewood, Free-Form Top, c.1985, 15 x 55 x 18 In.	31250.00
Table, Coffee, Hammered Brass Top, Molded Edge, Wood Stretcher Base, c.1960, 14 x 57 In. ...	288.00
Table, Coffee, Hans Von Klier, Free-Form, Glass, 3 Legs, Fiam, Italy, c.1990, 33 x 16 In.	1560.00
Table, Coffee, Heritage Henredon, Mitered Drop Sides, Signed Frank Lloyd Wright, 60 x 14 In. .	1320.00
Table, Coffee, Heritage Henredon, Round Slate Top, Frank Lloyd Wright, 36 x 16 In.	2520.00
Table, Coffee, Inset Tiles, Round, c.1960, 14 ½ x 43 In.	1680.00
Table, Coffee, Juan Montoya, Walnut Top, 2 Drawers, 4 Ebonized Sphere Supports, 18 x 64 In.	3900.00
Table, Coffee, LaVerne, Biomorphic, Bronze, Brass, Acid Etched, 1960s, 47 x 24 In. ....*illus*	4500.00
Table, Coffee, LaVerne, Bronze, Buttressed Legs, Flower, Signed, 17 x 51 x 31 In.	3060.00
Table, Coffee, LaVerne, Patinated Bronze, Pewter, Eternal Forest, c.1970, 16 ½ In.	31250.00
Table, Coffee, Louis XVI, Gilt Metal, Marble Top, Ball Finials, Stretcher, 19 x 35 In.	540.00
Table, Coffee, Louis XVI Style, Gilt Metal, Marble, Square Legs, Top-Shaped Feet, 20 x 44 x 19 In.	1560.00
Table, Coffee, Mahogany, Round, Pierced Frieze, Square Legs, c.1950, 15 x 40 In.	41.00
Table, Coffee, Max Kuehne, Silver Leaf, Flower Design, Lacquer, Enamel, 1935, 58 x 24 In.	5175.00
Table, Coffee, Mixed Wood, Made From Sled, 48 x 29 In.	195.00
Table, Coffee, Modern, Round, Black Enameled Steel Base, Glass Square Cutout Design, 43 x 15 In.	150.00
Table, Coffee, P. Evans, Argente, Glass Top, Zigzag Base, 1971, 17 x 30 In.	15600.00
Table, Coffee, Pace, Chrome, Steel Supports, Glass Top, 52 x 18 In.	480.00
Table, Coffee, Palissandre, Glass, Ico & Luis Parisi, c.1962, 10 x 55 x 29 In.	7500.00
Table, Coffee, Post Modernist, Walnut, 6 Tapered Legs, 1960s, 8 ½ x 138 In.	588.00
Table, Coffee, Poul Kjaerholm, Glass Top, Steel Base, 14 x 34 In.	1320.00
Table, Coffee, Renaissance Revival, Rosewood, Inlaid, Bird's-Eye Maple, c.1870, 17 x 37 x 25 In.	840.00
Table, Coffee, Risom, Birch, Cutout Top, Magazine Rack, 52 x 24 x 18 In.	900.00
Table, Coffee, Robsjohn-Gibbings, Shaped Cherry Top, 3 Steel Legs, Widdicomb, 1952, 71 x 20 In. ..	1440.00
Table, Coffee, Rohde, Cube, Laurel Wood, 3 Open Storage Areas, Herman Miller, 1940s, 32 x 20 In.	3000.00
Table, Coffee, Round, Lower Shelf, Singer & Sons, 1952, 23 x 27 In.	1140.00
Table, Coffee, S. Christian Of Copenhagen, Nickel Top, Incised Design, Italy, 48 x 16 In.	360.00
Table, Coffee, Scandinavian, Walnut Frame, Shaped Glass Top, 51 x 16 In.	510.00
Table, Coffee, Shaped Glass Top, Angled Black Wood Base, Italy, 16 x 51 In.	1200.00
Table, Coffee, Silas Seandel, Burnished, Steel, Glass Top, Signed, 1974, 16 ¾ x 42 In.	1596.00
Table, Coffee, Silas Seandel, Shaped Glass Top, Metal Lily Pad Base, 16 x 42 In.	7800.00
Table, Coffee, Square, Beijing, 14 x 36 In.	1400.00
Table, Coffee, Walnut, 3 Rosewood Tenons, Free-Form Shape, 13 x 46 In.	4800.00
Table, Coffee, Wormley, 2-Tone Mahogany Top, 6 Legs, Brass Stretcher, Dunbar, 66 x 16 In.	360.00
Table, Coffee, Wormley, Angled Shape, Mahogany, Laminate, Dunbar, 1950s, 55 x 20 In.	1200.00
Table, Coffee, Wormley, Mahogany, 1 Drawer, Open Shelf Ends, Dunbar, 56 x 20 In.	360.00
Table, Coffee, Wormley, Olive Burl Base, Round Glass Top, Dunbar, 42 x 17 In.	1080.00
Table, Coffee, Wormley, Round, Mahogany Top, 5 Supports, Leather, Dunbar, 1940s, 34 x 19 In.	510.00
Table, Coffee, Yellow, Black Lithographed Top, Piazza Scene, Fornasetti, Milan, 18 x 39 In.	2040.00
Table, Console, Adam Style, Satinwood, Painted, Demilune, Medallions, Paneled, 30 x 39 In., Pair	1175.00
Table, Console, Art Deco, Burled Walnut, Satinwood, Square Plinth Base, 34 x 42 x 16 In.	448.00
Table, Console, Art Deco, Wrought Iron, Marble, France, c.1930, 33 x 31 ½ x 14 ¾ In.	3750.00
Table, Console, Biedermeier, Fruitwood, Frieze Drawer, Trestle Base, 30 x 40 In.	179.00
Table, Console, Blackamoor Support, Polychrome, Bone Inlaid, Banded Top, Lion's Masks, 36 x 40 In.	3819.00

F

Table, Console, C-Shape Supports, Lacquered Goatskin, Karl Springer, c.1975, 32 x 60 x 15 In.	2400.00
Table, Console, Carved, Scrolled Leaves, Putti, Marble Top, Mirror, Italy, c.1890, 63 x 104 In.	7963.00
Table, Console, Charles X, Mahogany, Bronze Mounted, Marble Top, Drawer, 38 x 51 x 16 In.	3819.00
Table, Console, Chippendale, Mahogany, Frieze Drawers, c.1920, 36 x 61 In., Pair	8400.00
Table, Console, Chippendale Style, Mahogany, Carved, Molded Top, 3 Drawers, 36 x 61 In., Pair.	8400.00
Table, Console, Dutch, Rosewood, Marquetry, Tapered Supports, Block Plinth Base, 36 x 60 In.	2585.00
Table, Console, Eames, Birch, Dowel Legs, Herman Miller, 1950s, 44 x 20 x 30 In.	1560.00
Table, Console, Edgar Brandt, Black Marble Top, Iron Base, Leaves, Scrolls, 35 x 31 In.	7800.00
Table, Console, Federal, Maple, Frieze Drawer, Medial Shelf, Tapered Feet, 1800s, 30 x 37 x 16 In.	538.00
Table, Console, French Provincial, Fruitwood, Long Drawer, Shaped Apron, 1700s, 30 x 53 In.	4115.00
Table, Console, French Provincial, Walnut, Rouge Marble Top, Carved Apron, 1800s, 33 x 53 In.	3231.00
Table, Console, Fruitwood, Drawer, Shaped Apron, France, 30 x 53 In.	4113.00
Table, Console, George III, Satinwood, Classical Frieze, Flowers, Multicolored, c.1805, 31 x 52 In.	1185.00
Table, Console, George III Style, Mahogany, Demilune Top, Blind Fret Carved Frieze, 30 x 54 In.	1800.00
Table, Console, George III Style, Parcel, Gilt, Marble Top, Cherubs, 31 x 34 x 13 In., Pair	1200.00
Table, Console, Georgian, Walnut, Carved, Cabriole Legs, Ball & Claw, 33 x 47 x 20 In.	2350.00
Table, Console, Gilt, Marble Top, Frieze, Egg-And-Dart, Fretwork, 30 x 33 x 18 In., Pair	1200.00
Table, Console, Hepplewhite, Flip Top, Band Inlay, 30 x 35 x 17 In.	285.00
Table, Console, Juan Montoya, Black Patinated Steel, 2 Flared Pedestals, 36 x 60 In.	1800.00
Table, Console, Juan Montoya, Oak, Ebonized, 35 x 58 In.	4800.00
Table, Console, Louis XIV Style, Parcel Gilt, Fruitwood, Bombe, Marble Top, 1800s, 36 x 66 In.	2233.00
Table, Console, Louis XV Style, Giltwood Mirror, Arched Crest, Leaf Swags, 1800s, 126 x 60 In.	1175.00
Table, Console, Louis XV Style, Marble Top, Pierced Guilloche Frieze, c.1875, 37 x 39 x 16 In.	2160.00
Table, Console, Louis XV, Cast Iron, Marble Top, Stretcher, Scrolled Feet, Mid 1800s, 31 x 36 In.	705.00
Table, Console, Louis XV, Gilt, Serpentine Marble Top, Leaf Carved Skirt	353.00
Table, Console, Louis XV, Marble Top, Scrolled Legs, Feet, Italy, 18th Century, 29 x 39 x 18 In.	978.00
Table, Console, Louis XV, Walnut, Scalloped Marble Top, Carved Skirt, Cartouche, 35 x 45 In.	1680.00
Table, Console, Louis XVI Style, Beech, Stucco, Demilune, Marble Top, c.1930, 30 x 92 In.	2990.00
Table, Console, Louis XVI Style, Lime Wood, Demilune, Marble, Carved, c.1870, 36 x 26 In.	2230.00
Table, Console, Louis XVI Style, Parcel Giltwood, Marble Top, Garlands, Swags, 30 x 25 x 13 In.	4080.00
Table, Console, Louis XVI Style, Wood, Painted, Carved, D-Shape, Marble Top, c.1900, 35 x 28 In.	2650.00
Table, Console, Louis XVI, Beech, Painted, Demilune Shelf, Pendant Swags, 24 x 18 In., Pair	2400.00
Table, Console, Louis XVI, Limed Oak, Serpentine Top, Shell Carved Drawer, 40 x 54 In., Pair	470.00
Table, Console, Louis XVI, Mahogany, Brass, Marble Top, Pierced Gallery, c.1780, 37 x 33 In.	978.00
Table, Console, Louis XVI, Mahogany, Demilune, Marble Top, Center Drawer, 31 x 32 In.	732.00
Table, Console, Louis XVI, Mahogany, Marble, Brass, Gallery, Drawers, Shelf, c.1785, 35 x 43 In.	3081.00
Table, Console, Mahogany, Hickory, Crossbanded Top, Drawer, Stretcher, 30 x 51 x 16 In.	320.00
Table, Console, Mahogany, Marble, Carved, Scalloped, Beaded, 1800s, 33 x 36 In.	1200.00
Table, Console, Marquetry, Marble Top, Brass Ormolu Mounts, France, c.1860, 39 x 48 In.	4600.00
Table, Console, Mirror, Giltwood, Openwork Crest, Scrolled Leaves, Putti, Columns, Italy, 104 x 63 In.	7963.00
Table, Console, Mirror, Louis XV, Giltwood, Arched Crest, Ornate Carving, 126 x 60 In.	10577.00
Table, Console, Mirror, Mahogany, Demilune, Marble Top, Bronze Maiden, 1800s, 22 x 90 In.	4113.00
Table, Console, Mother-Of-Pearl Inlay, Ebonized, Lower Gallery Shelf, Syria, 34 x 44 In.	3050.00
Table, Console, Multicolored, Bowed, Faux Marble Top, Tassels, Scroll Support, 40 x 51 In., Pair.	4800.00
Table, Console, Neoclassical, Mahogany, Carved, D-Shape Top, Acanthus Carved Legs, 28 x 48 In.	173.00
Table, Console, Neoclassical, Mahogany, Marble Top, Drawer, Brass Mounts, Pa., c.1830, 44 In.	1995.00
Table, Console, Neoclassical, Mahogany, Serpentine Marble Top, Carving, 33 x 36 In.	1200.00
Table, Console, Neoclassical, Parcel Gilt, Painted, Marble Top, c.1800, 38 x 61 In., Pair	12200.00
Table, Console, Regency, Demilune, Bowfront, Mahogany Inlay, 1810, 31 x 53 In.	431.00
Table, Console, Regency, Oak, Shaped Backsplash, Scalloped Frieze, 1800s, 39 x 42 In.	173.00
Table, Console, Regency Style, Inlaid Walnut, Flip Top, 29 x 36 x 17 ¾ In.	329.00
Table, Console, Restauration, Marble Top, Columns, Gilt Metal Mount, c.1830, 5 x 6 ½ In., Pair	1293.00
Table, Console, Rococo, Gilt, Marble, Apron, Leaf Design, Masques, Swags, c.1800, 37 x 65 In.	8225.00
Table, Console, Tony Duquette, 3 Abalone Inserts, 3 Drawers, Brass Capped Feet, 31 x 72 In.	6600.00
Table, Console, Victorian, Shaped White Marble Top, Carved Legs, Stretcher, 29 x 37 In.	502.00
Table, Console, Wall, V. Kagan Style, Walnut, V-Shape Support, 29 x 48 In.	230.00
Table, Console, Walnut, 2-Board, 3 Drawers, Spindle Stretcher, Spain, 31 x 71 x 19 In.	840.00
Table, Console, William IV, Mahogany, Carved, Frieze Drawer, Twist Turned Legs, 36 x 56 In.	2300.00
Table, Continental, Maiden, Bulbous Standard, Splayed Cabriole Legs, c.1850, 28 x 17 x 13 In.	900.00
Table, Cooper, Thick Rectangular Top, Legs, Continental, 1800s, 16 x 39 In.	1180.00
Table, Cricket, Pegged Construction, 3 Tapered Legs, 29 x 30 x 29 ½ In.	248.00
Table, Curly Maple, Round, Black Stretcher, Turned Legs, Beaded Apron, 1900s, 30 x 48 In.	176.00
Table, D. Deskey, Walnut Veneer Pattern, Shelf, Charak Modern, 26 x 30 In., Pair	1800.00
Table, Danish Modern, Rosewood, Side Compartments, Lovig, Denmark, 18 x 32 In.	144.00
Table, Demilune, Mahogany, Satinwood, Dutch, c.1800, 30 x 29 In.	4200.00
Table, Demilune, Marble Top, 2 Drawers, Cabriole Legs, France, 29 x 27 In.	236.00

Furniture, Table, Bamboo, Painted Top, Jockey, Racehorse, c.1910, 26 x 23 In. $288.00

Furniture, Table, Baroque, Walnut, Box Stretcher, Virginia, c.1730, 23 x 23 In. $1150.00

Furniture, Table, Bench, Pine, Lift Top, 19th Century, 30 x 48 x 28 ½ In. $351.00

Furniture, Table, Card, Federal, Mahogany, Oval Corners, Carved, c.1815, 31 x 36 In. $2340.00

Furniture, Table, Card, Federal, Mahogany Veneer, Gatelegs, Foldover, c.1800, 28 x 36 In.
$944.00

Furniture, Table, Card, Hepplewhite, Cherry, Flip Top, String Inlay, 30 x 35 In.
$1175.00

Furniture, Table, Chan, LaVerne, Pewter, Bronze, Enamel Top, 47 x 18 In.
$3795.00

Furniture, Table, Coffee, Fornasetti, Lithographed Top, Fountain Scene, X-Frame, 18 x 39 In.
$2040.00

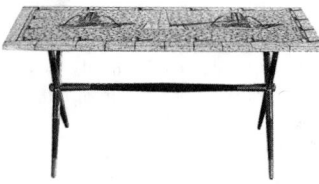

You Get What You Pay For
Be sure you get what you pay for. Many designers created handmade pieces, then had the designs mass-produced. If the furniture was very popular, it was often copied. Copies are worth much less than original works.

Table, Desk, Shaker, Slant Front, Raised Back, Lip, Enfield, c.1850, 7 x 13 In.	2925.00
Table, Deskey Vollmer, Chromium Plated Steel, Vitrolite, 15 x 24 ¾ x 24 ¾ In.	33750.00
Table, Dining, Aalto, No. 83, Laminated Birch, Round, c.1930s, 29 x 48 In.	1434.00
Table, Dining, Arts & Crafts, Oak, Leaves, Tapered Legs, Wood Casters, 76 x 54 x 48 In.	415.00
Table, Dining, Baroque, Pine, Iron Nails, Carved Trestle, Stretcher, Spain, 32 x 140 x 29 In.	2400.00
Table, Dining, British Colonial, Rosewood, Round, Tilt Top, Pedestal, Victorian, 32 x 59 In. ..*illus*	1320.00
Table, Dining, Brooks Bros., Walnut, 5 Leaves, 28 ½ x 48 In.	1000.00
Table, Dining, Brown Jordan, Round, Steel, Glass Top, c.1950, 28 x 42 In.	2400.00
Table, Dining, Chestnut, Carved Orb, Cross, 30 x 131 ½ x 45 In.	2806.00
Table, Dining, Chippendale, Mahogany, 3 Pedestals, Leaves, 18th Century, 29 x 45 x 72 In.	1840.00
Table, Dining, Chippendale, Mahogany, Rococo Carving, 3 Leaves, Cabriole Legs, 30 x 46 In.	1150.00
Table, Dining, Chippendale Style, Rosewood, Painted, Chinese, 2 Leaves, 29 x 67 x 40 In.	633.00
Table, Dining, Christian Liaigre, White Top, Stained Wood Base, 29 x 45 In.	2520.00
Table, Dining, Coggin, Mahogany, Walnut, Rosewood, Ash, Leaves, c.1960, 30 x 72 x 39 In.	1342.00
Table, Dining, Curly Maple Top, Painted Base, Shaped Corners, 2 Leaves, 1900s, 30 x 73 In.	881.00
Table, Dining, Driftwood Base, 5 Logs, Round Glass Top, 42 x 29 In.	240.00
Table, Dining, Drop Leaf, Cherry, 6 Leaves, 5 Legs, Casters, 31 x 57 In. ....*illus*	311.00
Table, Dining, Drop Leaf, Chippendale, Mahogany, Scoop Carved Legs, Ball & Claw, 1700s	1025.00
Table, Dining, Drop Leaf, Chippendale, Oval, Square Molded Legs, 20th Century, 31 x 108 In.	978.00
Table, Dining, Drop Leaf, Directoire, Mahogany, Brass Bound, Oval, c.1800, 30 x 43 In.	11700.00
Table, Dining, Drop Leaf, Empire Style, Mahogany, Platform Base, Turned Feet, 28 x 42 x 19 In.	200.00
Table, Dining, Drop Leaf, Federal, Mahogany, c.1800, 29 ½ x 20 ¼ x 42 In.	300.00
Table, Dining, Drop Leaf, George II, Mahogany, Deep Leaves, Plain Skirt, 28 x 57 In.	1057.00
Table, Dining, Drop Leaf, George II, Mahogany, Tapered Legs, Pad Feet, Mid 1700s, 28 x 57 In.	1058.00
Table, Dining, Drop Leaf, Irish Queen Anne, Cuban Mahogany, Oval Top, Pad Feet, 29 x 48 In.	805.00
Table, Dining, Drop Leaf, Mahogany, 3 Sections, 29 x 115 x 54 In.	6000.00
Table, Dining, Drop Leaf, Mahogany, Early 19th Century, 28 x 88 x 50 In.	1135.00
Table, Dining, Drop Leaf, Mahogany, Round, Turned Tapered Legs, Casters, c.1775, 28 x 56 In.	1410.00
Table, Dining, Drop Leaf, Oval, Spiral Turned Legs, England, 19th Century, 48 x 59 In.	940.00
Table, Dining, Drop Leaf, Queen Anne, Mahogany, Arched Skirt, c.1750, 29 x 48 In.	1175.00
Table, Dining, Drop Leaf, Queen Anne, Mahogany, England, 1700s, 29 x 54 In.	316.00
Table, Dining, Drop Leaf, Queen Anne, Mahogany, Pad Feet, Boston, c.1750, 28 x 42 In.	6875.00
Table, Dining, Drop Leaf, Sheraton, Mahogany, Gateleg, Casters, 29 x 61 x 44 In.	240.00
Table, Dining, Drop Leaf, Sheraton, Maple, Gateleg, Balled Feet, c.1840, 20 x 47 x 62 In.	1265.00
Table, Dining, Drop Leaf, Sheraton, Pine, 19th Century, 29 x 48 x 21 In.	55.00
Table, Dining, Drop Leaf, William & Mary, Maple, Oval Top, Drawer, c.1740, 28 x 41 In.	4800.00
Table, Dining, Edmund Spence, Birch Top, Slide Extensions, Sweden, 91 x 30 In.	120.00
Table, Dining, Empire, Mahogany, Pedestal Base, 5 Leaves, c.1860, 29 x 48 In.	9000.00
Table, Dining, Federal, Mahogany, 3 Pedestals, Banded, Saber Legs, 1900s, 30 x 120 In.	2760.00
Table, Dining, Federal, Mahogany, Inlaid, 2 Sections, New England, c.1805, 29 x 46 x 86 In.	9375.00
Table, Dining, Finn Juhl, Walnut, Oval, Starburst, Leaves, Baker Furniture, 54 x 46 In.	780.00
Table, Dining, Flame Mahogany, Banded, Double Pedestal Base, Paw Feet, Kittinger, 30 x 72 In.	2360.00
Table, Dining, Florence Knoll, Rosewood, Round, Chromed Steel Pedestal, 96 x 54 In.	2880.00
Table, Dining, French Provincial, Louis XV Style, Oak, Serpentine Parquet Top, c.1900, 29 x 58 In.	2120.00
Table, Dining, G. Nakashima, Maple, Round, 3 Keys, 4 Walnut Legs, 28 x 54 In.	4200.00
Table, Dining, G. Nakashima, Trestle, 3 Rosewood Butterfly Keys, 29 x 72 x 37 ½ In.	31720.00
Table, Dining, G. Nakashima, Walnut, Leaves, Splayed Legs, 29 x 60 x 36 In. .... 3600.00 to 4800.00	
Table, Dining, G. Nakashima, Walnut, Rosewood Splayed Legs, 84 In.	8400.00
Table, Dining, G. Nelson, Wood Top, Metal Tubular Legs, Herman Miller, c.1955, 29 x 36 In.	2328.00
Table, Dining, G. Stickley, No. 418, Oak, Round, Octagonal Apron, Splayed Legs, 60 In.	9000.00
Table, Dining, G. Stickley, No. 633, Circular Top, 5 Legs, Signed, Label, 54 x 29 In.	3000.00
Table, Dining, G. Stickley, No. 634, 5 Legs, 3 Leaves, 29 x 54 In.	5490.00
Table, Dining, Garouste & Bonetti, Round, Glass Top, Tapered Walnut Legs, 29 x 71 In.	8400.00
Table, Dining, George III Style, Mahogany, 2 Tripod Pedestal, Pad Feet, 28 x 48 x 72 In.	1422.00
Table, Dining, George III Style, Mahogany, Carved, Cabriole Legs, Ball & Claw, 29 x 63 x 39 In.	940.00
Table, Dining, George III Style, Mahogany, Inlaid, Tilt Top, Turned Stem, c.1800, 30 x 52 x 32 In.	822.00
Table, Dining, George III, Mahogany, 2 Pedestals, Downswept Legs, 3 Leaves, c.1810, 28 x 51 In.	4148.00
Table, Dining, George III, Mahogany, Crossbanded Top, Cabriole Legs, Carved Knees, 30 x 46 In.	489.00
Table, Dining, George III, Walnut, Mahogany Crossband, Stringing, 3 Pedestals, 30 x 114 In.	3437.00
Table, Dining, George IV, Mahogany, Double Pedestal, Reeded Edge, 28 x 45 x 78 In.	2600.00
Table, Dining, Gio Ponti, Mahogany, Round, Singer & Sons, 29 x 38 In.	1800.00
Table, Dining, Gothic Revival, Oak, Overhanging Top, 3 Trestle Base, Cutout Cross, 30 x 108 In.	1380.00
Table, Dining, Louis XIII Style, Oak, Parquet Top, Pullout Leaves, c.1870, 31 x 64 In.	2580.00
Table, Dining, Louis XIII Style, Trestle Base, Pierced Hearts, Stretcher, c.1900, 31 x 82 In.	1580.00
Table, Dining, Louis XV, Elm, Extension, Serpentine Top, Draw Leaves, 29 x 48 In.	802.00
Table, Dining, Louis XV Style, Oak, Draw End, Drawers, Shell Frieze, c.1875, 30 x 48 x 41 In.	1200.00

Table, Dining, Louis XVI, Boxed Florets, Brass, 3 Leaves, 5 Legs, 30 x 72 In.	2640.00
Table, Dining, Louis XVI, Multicolored, Oval Top, Leaf Carving, Stretcher, 30 x 77 In.	2640.00
Table, Dining, Louis XVI Style, Fruitwood, Paneled Frieze, Tapered Legs, Leaves, 29 x 84 In. ...	2880.00
Table, Dining, M. Quarti, Rosewood, Top, Burl Curved Pedestal Base, Leaves, 1930s.................	1440.00
Table, Dining, Mahogany, 2 Tripod Pedestals, Urn Supports, Brass Casters, 1900s, 30 x 67 In. ..	978.00
Table, Dining, Mahogany, Mother-Of-Pearl, Round, 2 Leaves, Birds, Flowers, Chinese, 31 x 46 In.	431.00
Table, Dining, Mahogany, Pedestal, Round, 29 ½ x 54 In.	805.00
Table, Dining, O. Borsani, Cherry Top, Bronze, Splayed Steel Base, 28 ½ x 78 x 48 In.	2440.00
Table, Dining, Oak, Elliptical Top, 2 Demilune Supports, Black Finish, 18 x 118 In.	1200.00
Table, Dining, P. Evans, Burl & Brass Patchwork Base, Glass Top, Signed, 76 x 42 In.	3600.00
Table, Dining, P. Fabricius, J. Kastholm, Round, Gray Marble Top, Steel Base, 19 x 59 In.	5400.00
Table, Dining, Poul Kjaerholm, Teak Top Steel Base, 27 x 40 In.	4800.00
Table, Dining, Regency, Figured Mahogany, 2 Pedestals, Reeded Legs, Paw Feet, 105 In.	1725.00
Table, Dining, Regency, Inlaid Mahogany, Double Pedestal, Leaf, Early 1900s, 30 x 43 In.	1093.00
Table, Dining, Regency, Mahogany, Banded, Saber Legs, Casters, 26 x 67 x 45 In.	2070.00
Table, Dining, Regency, Mahogany, Round, 5 Outer Leaves, 4 Saber Legs, 30 x 60 In.	4600.00
Table, Dining, Regency, Mahogany, Shaped Top, Molding, Fluted Supports, 30 x 86 In.	1528.00
Table, Dining, Regency Style, Mahogany, Crossbanded, Brass Paw Casters, 94 x 29 x 46 In.	2370.00
Table, Dining, Regency, Walnut, Round, Inlaid Star, Parcel Gilt, 3 Dolphin Supports, 48 In. ...	4740.00
Table, Dining, Renaissance Revival, Oak, Parquet Top, Pullout Leaves, Stretcher, c.1900, 29 x 123 In.	2750.00
Table, Dining, Renaissance Revival, Walnut, Round, Thick Scrolled Support, 29 x 46 In.	590.00
Table, Dining, Robsjohn-Gibbings, Mahogany, 18-In. Leaf, 72 x 30 In. ....*illus*	2160.00
Table, Dining, Rosewood, Round Top, Round Arched Base, 4 Legs, c.1950, 48 x 30 In.	560.00
Table, Dining, Silas Seandel, Round Incised Stone Top, Bronze Shaped Base, 28 x 40 In.	6600.00
Table, Dining, Victorian, Carved Oak, Gadroon Edge, Bulbous Legs, 29 x 53 In.	7500.00
Table, Dining, Victorian, Mahogany, Reeded & Turned Legs, Casters, 31 x 43 In.	5800.00
Table, Dining, Victorian, Walnut, Gadrooned Edge, Carved Apron, c.1900, 31 x 54 x 39 In.	1020.00
Table, Dining, Walnut, Marquetry, Satinwood, Split Pedestal, 2 Leaves, 21 x 51 x 91 In.	2300.00
Table, Dining, Waring & Gillow, Mahogany, Demilune Ends, Leaves, 30 x 108 In.	6463.00
Table, Dining, White Marble Top, Round Chrome Steel Base, Directional, 48 x 29 In.	330.00
Table, Dining, William IV, Walnut, Pullout Leg, Demilune Top, c.1875, 30 x 54 x 26 In.	2160.00
Table, Dining, Wormley, Mahogany, 8-Sided, Starburst Inlay, Trim, Dunbar, 68 x 29 In.	660.00
Table, Directoire, Cherry, Octagonal, Black Marble Inset Top, Cabriole Legs, 27 x 28 In.	610.00
Table, Directoire, Mahogany, Tooled Leather Top, Apron Drawer, c.1800, 23 x 25 In.	1410.00
Table, Directoire, Walnut, 2 Drawer Frieze, Brass Handles, c.1800, 30 x 32 In.	1540.00
Table, Drafting, George III, Mahogany, Hinged Top, Drawers, Plinth Base, 1800s, 39 x 50 In. .	6100.00
Table, Dressing, Bird's-Eye Maple, Mirror, Gallery, Drawers, c.1820, 36 x 38 In.	1410.00
Table, Dressing, Chippendale, Mahogany, Drawer, Chamfered Legs, 30 x 30 x 19 In.	717.00
Table, Dressing, Chippendale Style, Mahogany, Fan Carved Drawer, 33 x 33 x 20 In.	403.00
Table, Dressing, Demilune, Scrolled, Cream Paint, Ball Feet, c.1810, 35 x 35 x 18 In.	2300.00
Table, Dressing, Faux Poplar, Mirror, Curved Supports, 3 Drawers, c.1840, 55 x 36 In.	415.00
Table, Dressing, Federal, Cherry, Carved, Mahogany Veneer, 34 ½ x 29 ¾ x 18 ½ In.	5036.00
Table, Dressing, Federal, Mahogany, 2 Hinged Flaps, 2 Drawers, Reeded Legs, 29 x 24 In.	748.00
Table, Dressing, Federal, Mahogany, Ormolu, Cheval Mirror, Hoof Feet, c.1840, 38 x 60 In.	6500.00
Table, Dressing, George II, Walnut, Inlaid, Crossbanded, Chevron Inlaid Top, 29 x 31 In.	2233.00
Table, Dressing, George II, Walnut, Inlaid Drawers, 1700s, 29 x 30 In.	2233.00
Table, Dressing, Georgian, Oak, Molded Top, Drawer, Turned Legs, Stretcher, 28 x 30 In.	764.00
Table, Dressing, Louis XV Style, Kingwood, Divided Top, Mirror, Wells, 28 x 29 ½ x 17 In.	203.00
Table, Dressing, Marble Top, Mahogany, Cheval Mirror, Swan Neck Supports, c.1800, 54 x 32 In.	358.00
Table, Dressing, Neoclassical, Bird's-Eye Maple, Gallery, 2 Short & 1 Long Drawer, 38 x 36 In. .	1410.00
Table, Dressing, Pine, Drawer, Shaped Gallery, Turned Legs, Stenciled Fruit, c.1800, 53 x 32 In.	323.00
Table, Dressing, Queen Anne, Maple, Scalloped, 4 Drawers, Bat Wing Handles, 29 x 32 In.	1150.00
Table, Dressing, Queen Anne, Oak, Drawer, Carved Skirt, Pad Feet, Ireland, 18th Century........	610.00
Table, Dressing, Queen Anne, Oak, Scalloped Skirt, 3 Drawers, Cabriole Legs, 29 x 33 In.	823.00
Table, Dressing, Queen Anne, Walnut, Brass Pulls, Ball & Claw, c.1745, 31 ½ x 31 ¼ In.	6169.00
Table, Dressing, Queen Anne, Walnut, Burl Veneer, Herringbone Edged Drawers, 28 x 21 In. ..	474.00
Table, Dressing, Queen Anne, Walnut, Inlaid Medallion, Carved Shell, 4 Drawers, 31 x 34 In. .	10925.00
Table, Dressing, Regency, Mahogany, Parcel Gilt, Inlaid, Star, Gadrooned Edge, 29 x 60 In.	5629.00
Table, Dressing, Regency, Mahogany, Reeded Edge, Drawers, Kneehole, 29 ½ x 32 ¾ In.	267.00
Table, Dressing, Rococo, Mahogany, Shaped Mirror, Carved, Marble Top, 68 x 45 ½ x 22 In. ...	6169.00
Table, Dressing, Sheraton, Mahogany, Scroll Arms Holding Mirror, 54 x 36 x 17 In.	732.00
Table, Dressing, Victorian, Ebonized, Gilt, Papier-Mache Top, Mother-Of-Pearl Mirror, Tripod	300.00
Table, Dressing, White Paint, Scroll Supports, Mirror, Drawer, Swags, 31 x 38 In.	2585.00
Table, Dressing, William & Mary, Oyster Veneer, c.1700, 28 ½ x 36 ½ x 24 In.	4830.00
Table, Dressing, Wood, Yellow Grain Paint, Splash Back, Drawer, 19th Century, 28 ½ x 30 x 16 In.	204.00
Table, Dressing, Yellow Pine, Drawer, Turned Legs, Scalloped Shelf, Stripped Finish, 30 x 31 In.	316.00

F

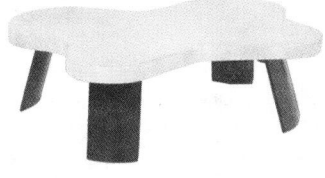

Furniture, Table, Coffee, Frankl, Cloud, Mahogany, Cork, Johnson Co., 48 x 15 In. $3600.00

Furniture, Table, Coffee, LaVerne, Biomorphic, Bronze, Brass, Acid Etched, 1960s, 47 x 24 In. $4500.00

Furniture, Table, Dining, British Colonial, Rosewood, Carved, Round, Tilt Top, Pedestal, Victorian, 32 x 59 In. $1320.00

FURNITURE

Furniture, Table, Dining, Drop Leaf, Cherry, 6 Leaves, 5 Legs, Casters, 31 x 57 In. $311.00

Furniture, Table, Dining, Robsjohn-Gibbings, Mahogany, 18-In. Leaf, 72 x 30 In. $2160.00

Furniture, Table, Drop Leaf, Walnut, Cherry, Butterfly, Stamped Hamlin, 1700s, 26 x 13 In. $3776.00

Table, Dressing, Yellow, White Paint, Scrolled Backboard, Drawers, Stencils, c.1825, 39 x 32 In.	2963.00
Table, Drop Leaf, Chippendale, Cherry, 2 Leaves, Casters, c.1800, 27 x 48 In.	288.00
Table, Drop Leaf, Chippendale, Cherry, 28 x 37 ½ In.	360.00
Table, Drop Leaf, Chippendale, Mahogany, Ball & Claw, 27 x 12 x 36 In.	990.00
Table, Drop Leaf, Chippendale, Mahogany, Rectangular, Salem, Mass., c.1770, 27 x 47 In.	8750.00
Table, Drop Leaf, Country Sheraton, Cherry, Frieze Drawer, 19th Century, 29 x 20 In.	115.00
Table, Drop Leaf, Empire, Mahogany, Rounded Corners, Frieze Drawer, 28 x 39 x 54 In.	1135.00
Table, Drop Leaf, Empire, Mahogany, Shaped Leaves, Carved Legs, c.1845, 29 x 25 In.	235.00
Table, Drop Leaf, Empire Style, Cherry, Square Stem, 41 x 21 x 27 ½ In.	190.00
Table, Drop Leaf, Empire Style, Curly Maple, Shaped Pedestal Base, 4 Ball Feet, 27 x 41 In.	122.00
Table, Drop Leaf, Empire Style, Mahogany, Canted Corners, Reeded Legs, 1870s, 29 x 41 x 45 In.	480.00
Table, Drop Leaf, Federal, Mahogany, 3 Sections, D Ends, c.1890, 30 x 105 In.	2530.00
Table, Drop Leaf, Federal, Walnut, 19th Century, 28 ¼ x 17 ½ x 42 In.	350.00
Table, Drop Leaf, George I, Mahogany, Gateleg, 2 Drawers, 1720, 30 x 60 x 70 In.	19250.00
Table, Drop Leaf, George III, Mahogany, Turned Pedestal, Swept-Down Legs, 28 x 31 In.	1067.00
Table, Drop Leaf, George III, Oak, Baluster Gatelegs, Stretchers, c.1790, 29 x 55 In.	1820.00
Table, Drop Leaf, George III, Walnut, Banded, String Inlay, Frieze Drawers, c.1800, 28 x 41 In.	1075.00
Table, Drop Leaf, Georgian, Mahogany, 3 Graduated Tiers, Molded Edges, Tripod Base, 45 x 24 In.	805.00
Table, Drop Leaf, Georgian, Mahogany, Duck Feet, Swing Legs, England, 1700s, 28 x 44 In.	353.00
Table, Drop Leaf, Georgian, Mahogany, Scalloped Corners, England, c.1750, 29 x 48 In.	1175.00
Table, Drop Leaf, Handkerchief, George III, Mahogany, Plain Frieze, 28 x 28 In.	148.00
Table, Drop Leaf, Hepplewhite, Curly Birch, 6 Legs, New England, c.1820, 28 x 45 In.	556.00
Table, Drop Leaf, Irish Queen Anne, Mahogany, Shaped Skirt, Slipper Feet, 28 x 42 In.	633.00
Table, Drop Leaf, Mahogany, 2 Drawers, Spiral Legs, 29 x 34 ½ x 17 In., Open	325.00
Table, Drop Leaf, Mahogany, Carved Pedestal, Paw Feet, N.Y., c.1820, 28 ½ x 56 ½ In.	489.00
Table, Drop Leaf, Mahogany, Drawer, Diamond Carved & Turned Legs, 29 x 27 In.	2800.00
Table, Drop Leaf, Mahogany, Drawer, Twist Standard, C-Scroll Legs, 29 x 23 In.	366.00
Table, Drop Leaf, Mahogany, Oval, End Drawer, Tapered Legs, Harden, 43 x 33 In.	117.00
Table, Drop Leaf, Mahogany, Pedestal Base, Brass Claw Feet, c.1840, 22 x 25 In.	1450.00
Table, Drop Leaf, Mahogany, Twin Flaps, Frieze Drawer, Chamfered Legs, 1800s, 28 x 36 In.	115.00
Table, Drop Leaf, Neoclassical, Birch, Cherry, Gateleg, Segmented, c.1825, 29 x 47 In.	480.00
Table, Drop Leaf, Neoclassical, Mahogany, Molded Frieze, Drawer, Paw Feet, 30 x 42 In.	1763.00
Table, Drop Leaf, Neoclassical, Mahogany, Wide Pedestal Base, Boston, c.1810, 29 x 61 In.	1035.00
Table, Drop Leaf, Oval Top, Swing Legs, Ball & Claw, England, 68 x 50 In.	360.00
Table, Drop Leaf, Pine, Gateleg, Drawer, Turned Legs, Butterfly Hinges, c.1700	8260.00
Table, Drop Leaf, Queen Anne, Mahogany, 6 Turned Legs, Pad Feet, England, 1700s, 29 x 60 In.	920.00
Table, Drop Leaf, Queen Anne, Mahogany, Round Top, Turned Legs, England, 1700s, 28 x 15 In.	646.00
Table, Drop Leaf, Queen Anne, Maple, Cabriole Legs, c.1750, 27 ½ x 48 In.	1527.00
Table, Drop Leaf, Queen Anne, Oak, Curved Legs, Gatelegs, Spoon Feet, c.1800, 27 x 37 x 13 In.	299.00
Table, Drop Leaf, Queen Anne Style, Mahogany, 30 x 25 x 42 In.	175.00
Table, Drop Leaf, Regency, Mahogany, Frieze Drawers, Bronze Scroll Feet, c.1815, 28 x 36 In.	4406.00
Table, Drop Leaf, Shaker, Birch, Stained, New Hampshire, 29 x 36 x 36 In.	702.00
Table, Drop Leaf, Shaker, Cherry, Tapered Legs, Pegged, 19th Century, 27 x 36 In.	355.00
Table, Drop Leaf, Sheraton, 2 Drawers, White Pulls, 19 x 20 x 27 In.	201.00
Table, Drop Leaf, Sheraton, Mahogany, D-Shape Leaves, Fluted Legs, 28 x 42 In.	201.00
Table, Drop Leaf, Sheraton, Pine, Ash, Square Leaves, Dark Red, c.1850, 28 x 48 In.	617.00
Table, Drop Leaf, Sheraton, Tiger Maple, Cherry, 29 x 20 x 40 In.	2760.00
Table, Drop Leaf, Sheridan, Bird's-Eye Maple, 19th Century, 29 x 42 x 66 In.	605.00
Table, Drop Leaf, Sunderland, Mahogany, String Inlay, Medallion, c.1930, 28 In.	1150.00
Table, Drop Leaf, Sunderland, Neoclassical, Mahogany, Scrolled Legs, 29 x 34 In.	881.00
Table, Drop Leaf, Tailor's, Oak, Brass Yardstick Inset, 2 Frieze Drawers, Eng., c.1900, 30 x 48 In.	443.00
Table, Drop Leaf, Walnut, Cherry, Butterfly, Stamped Hamlin, 1700s, 26 x 13 In. ....*illus*	3776.00
Table, Drop Leaf, Walnut, Oval, Gateleg, Box & Ring-Turned Legs, 19th Century, 1800s, 51 x 56 In.	345.00
Table, Drop Leaf, William & Mary, Gateleg, Oak, Oval Top, Bulbous Turned Base, 28 x 39 In.	546.00
Table, Drop Leaf, William & Mary, Oak, Gateleg, Turned Legs, England, c.1700, 29 x 19 In.	863.00
Table, Drop Leaf, William IV, Mahogany, Oak, Line Inlay, Tapered Legs, 25 x 33 x 18 In.	305.00
Table, Drum, Empire Style, Mahogany, Inset Leather Top, 28 ½ x 42 In.	600.00
Table, Drum, Fruitwood, Round Top, 4 Apron Drawers, Turned Pedestal, 3 Legs, 25 In.	230.00
Table, Drum, George III, Mahogany, Leather Top, 3 Drawers, 3-Footed, 1790s, 30 x 29 In.	330.00
Table, Drum, Mahogany, Inlaid, 2 Frieze Drawers, 3-Sided Plinth Base, 30 x 46 In.	1185.00
Table, Drum, Regency, Leather Top, Mahogany, 4 Working Drawers, 4 Fake, c.1820, 30 In.	1778.00
Table, Drum, Regency, Mahogany, Leather, Drawers, Turned Stem, c.1800, 30 x 41 In.	1778.00
Table, Drum, Regency, Mahogany, Leather Top, 4 Drawers, Tripod Base, 29 ¾ x 38 In.	237.00
Table, Drum, Regency, Mahogany, Leather Top, 4 Frieze Drawers, Saber Legs, 28 x 43 In.	4140.00
Table, Drum, Regency, Mahogany, Leather Top, Alternate Working Drawers, c.1815, 28 x 42 In.	1058.00
Table, Drum, Regency, Rosewood, Inlay, Drawers, 3-Footed, 28 ½ x 26 In.	4600.00

Table, Dunbar, Carved Seashell Pedestal Base, 30 x 32 In.	4800.00
Table, Eames, LTR, Steel, Laminate, Herman Miller, 10 x 15 x 13 In.	144.00
Table, Eastlake, Oak, Parquetry, Geometric, Turtletop, Support Columns, c.1900, 28 x 38 In.	374.00
Table, Eastlake, Walnut, Marble Top, Oval, Contoured Legs, Center Shaft & Finial, 30 x 32 In.	176.00
Table, Edwardian, Mahogany, Inlay, Oval, X-Stretcher, England, c.1900, 29 x 25 In.	1200.00
Table, Edwardian, Satinwood Inlay, 2 Drawers, Casters, c.1910, 28 ½ x 36 x 21 In.	1200.00
Table, Edwardian, Satinwood, Serpentine, Leaf Inlays, Leaf Carved Legs, c.1910, 31 x 43 In., Pair..	948.00
Table, Eero Saarinen, Enameled Aluminum, White Laminate, Round, Spread Foot, 28 x 48 In.	201.00
Table, Eero Saarinen, Walnut, Round, Metal Base, Fused Plastic, Knoll, 16 x 20 In.	420.00
Table, Eileen Gray, Chrome Tubular Frame, Glass Top, Ireland, 20 In.	561.00
Table, Elm, Green Stone, 19th Century, 12 ½ x 32 In.	418.00
Table, Empire, Mahogany, 8 Sides, Pedestal, 9 Scroll Feet, Drawers, 1800s, 30 x 67 In.	1351.00
Table, Empire, Mahogany, Round Marble Top, Column Supports, Shelf, 28 x 28 In.	1680.00
Table, Empire, Mahogany, Round Top, Carved Base, 30 x 48 In.	1200.00
Table, Empire, Parcel Gilt, Ebonized, Round Glass Top, Egyptian Figural Support, 1900s, 24 x 27 In.	230.00
Table, Empire Revival, Round, Gilt Bronze, Marble, Beaded Columns, Tripod Base, 1800s, 48 In.	2040.00
Table, Empire, Round, Marble Top, Base, Stretcher Medallions, Lions, Scrolls, 1900s, 30 x 26 In.	1035.00
Table, Empire, Walnut, Gothic, Tapered Pedestal Apron, 28 x 32 x 31 In.	350.00
Table, Envelope, Empire, Burl Mahogany, Griffin Base, c.1845, 33 x 36 x 36 In.	1400.00
Table, F. Linke, Pink Marble Top, Frieze Drawer, Bronze Dore Garland, 1910, 29 x 21 In.	6195.00
Table, Farm, Cherry, Tapered Legs, Patina, France, 30 x 79 In.	9500.00
Table, Farm, Chestnut, Turned Columns, H-Shape Pediment, c.1890, 30 x 92 In.	2990.00
Table, Farm, Walnut, Pine Top, 2 Drawers, Beaded Skirt, Turned Legs, 30 x 58 x 38 In.	1870.00
Table, Farm, Walnut, Pinned Top, Frieze Drawer, Scalloped Skirt, Pa., 1777, 30 x 59 In.	3660.00
Table, Federal, 3 Sections, Mahogany, Drop Leaf, Inlay, c.1810, 30 x 45 In.	2233.00
Table, Federal, Birch, Walnut, Pine, Inlay, Drawer, Lock, Georgia, c.1835, 29 x 21 In.	1093.00
Table, Federal, Cherry, 3-Board Top, Signed Skirt, North Carolina, 1800s, 26 x 28 In.	431.00
Table, Federal, Cherry, Inlay, Drawer, Turned Legs, 1800s, 29 x 22 In. ....*illus*	708.00
Table, Federal, Cherry, Walnut Legs, 2 Dovetailed Drawers, Georgia, 1800s, 29 x 24 x 17 In. ...	920.00
Table, Federal, Mahogany, Gateleg, Square Edge Top, Drop Leaf, c.1815, 31 x 50 In.	201.00
Table, Federal, Mahogany, Pine, D-Shape, Turned Legs, 1800s, 30 x 51 In.	748.00
Table, Federal, Mahogany, Serpentine, Rope Twist Legs, c.1815, 30 x 37 ¾ In.	1170.00
Table, Federal, Mahogany, Veneers, Pine, Ash, 3 Sections, c.1800, 74 x 60 In.	2300.00
Table, Federal, Tiger Maple, 3 Drawers, 20th Century, 30 x 36 x 19 In.	400.00
Table, Federal, Walnut, Scalloped Skirt, N.C., c.1800, 29 x 36 In. ....*illus*	7670.00
Table, Finn Juhl, Walnut, Tray Top, Free-Form, Baker Furniture, 19 x 63 In.	1200.00
Table, Florence Knoll, Round Walnut Top, Beveled Edge, Brass Base, 48 x 28 In.	240.00
Table, Frank Lloyd Wright, Low Form, Copper Band, Cruciform Base, Copper Band, 54-In. Diam..	1440.00
Table, French Art Moderne, Gilt Metal, Ebonized Glass, 23 x 15 In., Pair	1200.00
Table, French Art Moderne, Gilt Metal, Glass, Tubular Supports, 23 x 15 In., Pair	480.00
Table, French Provincial, Banded, Frieze, Draw Ends, Square Legs, c.1875, 30 x 29 x 62 In.	1440.00
Table, French Provincial, Fruitwood, Shaped Kneehole, 2 Drawers, 30 x 67 In.	1470.00
Table, French Provincial, Walnut Sliding Top, Marble Inset, Cabriole Legs, 26 x 19 In.	184.00
Table, French Restauration, Burl, Round, Veneer Top, Pedestal, Triangular Base, 30 x 53 In. .	1880.00
Table, French Style, Round Marble Top, Ormolu Mounted, Pair	633.00
Table, Frieze Drawer, Reeded Legs, Concave Display Shelf, 29 x 38 In.	207.00
Table, Fruitwood, Tip Top, Ball & Claw, Birdcage Top, Ethan Allen, 20 x 28 In.	115.00
Table, G. Nakashima, Frenchman's Cove, Walnut, c.1965, 48 x 51 x 29 In. ....*illus*	7200.00
Table, G. Nakashima, Slab, Sketch, Signed, c.1981, 28 x 27 In.	5513.00
Table, G. Nakashima, Walnut, Free-Form Edge, 3 Legs, 1959, 13 x 15 In.	2400.00
Table, G. Nakashima, Walnut, Single Board, Turned Legs, c.1959, 21 x 27 ½ In.	2185.00
Table, G. Nakashima, Walnut Wohl, Triangular, 17 x 27 x 21 In.	1464.00
Table, G. Nelson, Attached, Walnut, Drawer, Shelf, Steel Legs, Herman Miller, 17 x 40 In.	240.00
Table, G. Stickley, Leather Top, Drawer, c.1901, 30 x 45 x 44 In.	13420.00
Table, G. Stickley, No. 541, Oak, Copper, Willow, 25 x 24 In.	46875.00
Table, G. Stickley, No. 631, Splayed Legs, Wide Apron, Warren Hile, 78 x 29 In.	2460.00
Table, G. Stickley, Round, Notched Cross Stretcher Base, 2 Leaves, 48 x 30 In.	2880.00
Table, G. Stickley, Stacked Trumpet Stretchers, Finial, c.1902, 28 x 24 In.	6100.00
Table, Game, Bagatelle, Mahogany, Felt Lined Interior, 1800s, 28 x 48 In.	316.00
Table, Game, Black Lacquer, Gilt Figures In Garden, Houses, Lyre Supports, 28 x 24 In.	345.00
Table, Game, Drop Leaf, Victorian, Burl Walnut, Cherry, Drawers, Scrolled Toes, 31 x 29 In. ...	240.00
Table, Game, Eastlake, Walnut, Felt Top, Molded Frame, Drawer, Trestle Base, 31 x 36 In.	144.00
Table, Game, Empire, Mahogany, Flip Top, 4 Curved Saber Legs, 29 x 36 In.	299.00
Table, Game, Empire Revival, Cherry, Triple Top, Brass Mounts, Sliding Leg, 30 x 43 In.	770.00
Table, Game, Empire, Serpentine, Lyre Form Pedestal, Shaped Plinth, Bun Feet, 27 x 34 In.	167.00
Table, Game, Faux Painted Shagreen, Metal Trimmed Legs, Karl Springer, 34 x 29 In.	600.00

F

Furniture, Table, Federal, Cherry, Inlay, Drawer, Turned Legs, 1800s, 29 x 22 In. $708.00

Furniture, Table, Federal, Walnut, Scalloped Skirt, N.C., c.1800, 29 x 36 In. $7670.00

Furniture, Table, G. Nakashima, Frenchman's Cove, Walnut, c.1965, 48 x 51 x 29 In. $7200.00

Furniture, Table, Game, Flip Top, Federal, Mahogany, Panels, Lyre Pedestal, 29 x 35 In. $960.00

Furniture, Table, Game, Flip Top, Marquetry, Tooled Leather, Dutch, 1800s, 29 x 31 In. $2749.00

Furniture, Table, Game, Neoclassical, Walnut, Mahogany, Banding, Swivel Top, 1820s, 28 x 36 In. $1180.00

Furniture, Table, Geometric, Chromed Steel, Inset Glass Top, 1960s, 20 x 13 In. $660.00

Table, Game, Federal, Inlaid Mahogany, Double Gateleg, c.1800, 29 x 36 x 17 In.	805.00
Table, Game, Federal, Mahogany, Casters, c.1800, 29 x 36 In.	431.00
Table, Game, Federal, Mahogany, Turned & Beaded Urn, Pedestal Base, 20 x 35 In.	488.00
Table, Game, Flip Top, Bookmatched Top, Mahogany, Urn Pedestal, c.1825, 30 x 36 In.	353.00
Table, Game, Flip Top, Burl Walnut, Carved Legs, Stretchers, 28 ¾ x 26 ½ x 17 In.	2115.00
Table, Game, Flip Top, Chippendale, Mahogany, Drawer, Carved, Boston, c.1770, 29 x 32 In. ..	74800.00
Table, Game, Flip Top, Chippendale, Mahogany, Drawer, Philadelphia, c.1760, 36 x 15 In.	12250.00
Table, Game, Flip Top, Chippendale, Mahogany, Gateleg, Drawer, England, 1700s, 29 x 35 In.	920.00
Table, Game, Flip Top, Eastlake, Ebonized, Inlaid, Porcelain Plaque, Pottier & Stymus, 1850s.	2100.00
Table, Game, Flip Top, Empire Revival, Mahogany, Paneled Baluster, Pedestal, 30 x 36 In.	270.00
Table, Game, Flip Top, Federal, Mahogany, Panels, Lyre Pedestal, 29 x 35 In. ....*illus*	960.00
Table, Game, Flip Top, Inlay, Signed, Galle, 30 x 18 x 20 In.	2400.00
Table, Game, Flip Top, Louis XV, Rococo, Rosewood, Storage, 30 x 33 x 17 In.	660.00
Table, Game, Flip Top, Louis XV, Serpentine, Tooled Leather Insert, 34 x 39 In.	489.00
Table, Game, Flip Top, Mahogany, Serpentine, Beaded Skirt, Urn, New York, c.1850, 29 x 32 In.	368.00
Table, Game, Flip Top, Marquetry, Dutch, Early 1800s, 30 x 28 x 15 In.	1250.00
Table, Game, Flip Top, Marquetry, Flowers, Dutch, 1800s, 31 x 27 In.	431.00
Table, Game, Flip Top, Marquetry, Tooled Leather, Dutch, 1800s, 29 x 31 In. ....*illus*	2749.00
Table, Game, Flip Top, Neoclassical, Mahogany, Inlay, Swing-Out Legs, c.1800, 29 x 35 x 17 In.	1135.00
Table, Game, Flip Top, Neoclassical, Mahogany, Paneled Skirt, Scrolled Feet, 29 x 36 In.	588.00
Table, Game, Flip Top, Neoclassical, Mahogany, Serpentine, Yoke Support, 1800s, 29 x 32 In. .	368.00
Table, Game, Flip Top, Queen Anne, Mahogany, Drawer, 1700s, 29 x 34 In.	1955.00
Table, Game, Flip Top, Queen Anne, Walnut, Oak, Fitted Interior, England, c.1730, 29 x 32 In.	2875.00
Table, Game, Flip Top, Rococo, Rosewood, Serpentine, Leather Surface, 1800s, 32 x 34 In.	2235.00
Table, Game, Flip Top, Rosewood, Carved Frieze, Turned Column, 4-Footed, 28 x 17 In.	492.00
Table, Game, Flip Top, Secret, Mission Oak, Poker Chip Drawer, 30 In.	177.00
Table, Game, Flip Top, Swivel, George III, Black Lacquer, Japanned, 28 x 31 x 30 In.	1016.00
Table, Game, Flip Top, Swivel, Mahogany, Molded, c.1830, 30 x 36 In., Pair	1998.00
Table, Game, Flip Top, Swivel, Neoclassical, Mahogany, Scroll Feet, c.1830, 30 x 36 In., Pair ...	1998.00
Table, Game, Flip Top, Victorian, Mahogany, Carved Paw Feet, 29 ½ x 35 ½ x 17 ¾ In.	359.00
Table, Game, George II, Mahogany, 3-Fold, Carved Knees, Pad Feet, c.1850, 29 x 34 In.	2820.00
Table, Game, George II, Mahogany, Triple Top, Ball & Claw, 29 x 32 x 16 In.	1185.00
Table, Game, George III, Inlaid Satinwood, Demilune, Felt Interior, 29 x 37 x 19 ½ In.	830.00
Table, Game, George III, Mahogany, Carved, Rectangular Top, 29 x 36 x 17 In.	830.00
Table, Game, George III, Mahogany, Hinged, Baize Lined, 29 x 35 x 17 In.	300.00
Table, Game, George III, Mahogany, Satinwood, Felt Lined, Crossbanded, 29 x 36 x 18 In.	1007.00
Table, Game, George III Style, Inlaid Rosewood, Satinwood, Leather Lined, 29 x 36 x 18 In. ...	575.00
Table, Game, Georgian, Walnut, Felt Lined, Chip Wells, Rectangular Top, 28 x 33 x 16 In.	1304.00
Table, Game, Handkerchief, 4 Leather Inset Triangular Leaves, Shaped Skirt, 30 x 22 x 22 In. ...	305.00
Table, Game, Hepplewhite, Mahogany, Inlaid, Demilune, Tapered Legs, Baltimore, c.1810.......	2655.00
Table, Game, Hepplewhite, Mahogany, Satinwood, Exotic Wood Inlay, Drawer, 30 x 37 In.	403.00
Table, Game, Louis XV, Tulipwood, Inset Leather, Backgammon Board, 1700s, 30 x 25 In.	732.00
Table, Game, Louis XVI, Mahogany, Satinwood, Round, Ormolu Ring Mount, 29 x 19 In.	1680.00
Table, Game, Mahogany, Birch Inlay, Bowfront, Drawer, Swing Leg, 1800s, 30 x 36 In.	288.00
Table, Game, Mahogany, Inlaid Board, 2 Game Drawers, Play Pieces, c.1800, 28 x 29 In.	2875.00
Table, Game, Mahogany, Swivel Top, Carved, c.1825, Pa., 31 x 36 In., Pair	6463.00
Table, Game, Mahogany, Swivel Top, Inset Leather, American, 30 x 36 x 18 In., Pair..............	5875.00
Table, Game, Marble Board Inlay, Carved Base, Flowers, Round, Italy, c.1900, 32 x 28 In.	2070.00
Table, Game, Neoclassical, Walnut, Tiger Maple Banding, Scrolls, Paw Feet, c.1820, 28 x 36 In.	1150.00
Table, Game, Neoclassical, Walnut, Mahogany, Banding, Swivel Top, 1820s, 28 x 36 In. . *illus*	1180.00
Table, Game, Regency, Inlaid Mahogany, Rosewood, Satinwood, 1790, 29 x 36 x 17 In.	148.00
Table, Game, Regency, Rosewood, Brass Inlay & Mounting, Leather, 4 Legs, 29 x 36 x 17 In. ...	1304.00
Table, Game, Regency, Rosewood, Turned Bun Feet, 29 x 36 x 18 ¾ In.	1680.00
Table, Game, Renaissance Revival, Burl, Walnut, Frieze Drawer, 29 x 21 In.	920.00
Table, Game, Renaissance Revival, Mahogany, Carved, Reversible Top, 30 x 24 ¾ x 18 In.	652.00
Table, Game, Rosewood, Carved Apron, Baize Top, Interior Compartments, 30 x 36 In.	1380.00
Table, Game, Rosewood, Ebonized Base, Free-Form Top, Dunbar, 28 x 45 In.	1800.00
Table, Game, Rosewood, Serpentine Front, Swivel Top, X-Stretcher, Urn Finial, c.1840, 30 x 36 In.	322.00
Table, Game, Roulette Wheel, Mirror Top, Castle Club, 1930s, 20 x 31 In.	2100.00
Table, Game, Sewing, Regency, Mahogany, Parquetry, Lift Top, c.1810, 30 x 22 In.	999.00
Table, Game, Sewing, Rosewood, Walnut, Boxwood, Drawer, c.1820, 29 x 19 x 15 In.	595.00
Table, Game, Sheraton, Birch, Mahogany, Cookie Corners, Twisted Legs, 30 In.	502.00
Table, Game, Sheraton, Fruitwood, Demilune, Shaped Apron, Hinged Leaf, 29 x 36 In.	575.00
Table, Gateleg, English Oak, Turned Legs, c.1880, 24 x 22 In.	895.00
Table, Gateleg, George I, Oak, Skirt, Drawer, Box Stretcher, Late 1600s, 28 x 29 In.	5000.00

Table, Gateleg, George II, Walnut, Hinged Top, Shaped Skirt, 19th Century, 30 x 18 In.	748.00
Table, Gateleg, William & Mary, Maple, Skirt, Drawer, Turned Legs, New Eng., c.1720, 27 x 40 ½ In.	7110.00
Table, Gateleg, William & Mary, Oak, Falling Leaf, 27 x 24 ½ In.	823.00
Table, Gateleg, William & Mary Style, Legs Joined By Stretchers, 26 x 27 x 28 In.	366.00
Table, Geometric, Chromed Steel, Inset Glass Top, 1960s, 20 x 13 In. ....*illus*	660.00
Table, George II Style, Painted, Gesso, Scrolls, Shells, Garlands, Cabriole Legs, 31 x 62 In.	8295.00
Table, George II, Tilt Top, 12-Sided Gallery, Rope Twist, Baluster Stem, 29 In.	1304.00
Table, George III, Inlaid Mahogany, Tilt Top, Round Banded Top, Early 1800s, 29 x 42 In.	881.00
Table, George III, Mahogany, Demilune Top, Plain Frieze, Late 1800s, 29 x 48 In.	1080.00
Table, George III, Mahogany, Round Top, Carved, Wheat Sheaves, c.1790, 28 x 28 In.	1955.00
Table, George III, Mahogany, Tilt Top, Piecrust Edge, Leaves, Ball & Claw, 29 x 29 In.	593.00
Table, George III, Mahogany, Tilt Top, Urn Support, England, c.1780, 29 x 53 In.	460.00
Table, George III, Oak, Apron Drawer, Bronze Mounts, Cabriole Legs, c.1790, 23 x 20 In.	705.00
Table, George III, Oak, Carved, Apron Drawer, Bronze Mounts, c.1780, 20 x 23 In.	705.00
Table, George III Style, Japanned, 19th Century, 31 x 37 ½ x 21 In.	764.00
Table, George III Style, Mahogany, ¾ Shape, Pierced, 30 x 23 x 17 In., Pair	960.00
Table, George III, Tilt Top, Spiral Turned Pedestal, Cabriole Legs, 29 x 29 In.	633.00
Table, George III, Yew, Round, Banded, Veneers, Vase Shape, 29 x 60 In.	1920.00
Table, George IV, Mahogany, Demilune, Early 19th Century, 32 x 45 In.	195.00
Table, Georgian, Mahogany, Plain Frieze, Leaves Carved, Ball & Claw, c.1775, 29 x 42 In.	3318.00
Table, Georgian, Satinwood, Crossbanded, Canted Corners, Cuff Feet, 29 x 30 In.	652.00
Table, Georgian Style, Mahogany, Tilt Top, Round Top, 3 Splayed Feet, 27 x 27 In.	300.00
Table, Georgian Style, Mahogany, Tilt Top, Turned Standard, Tripod Base, 27 ¾ x 21 x 28 In. .	275.00
Table, Georgian Style, Tilt Top, Ebonized, Japanned, Landscape, 38 ¼ x 22 ¼ In.	239.00
Table, Georgian Style, Tilt Top, Scalloped, Baluster Standard, Tripod Base, c.1875, 23 In.	115.00
Table, Gilt Bronze, Marble, Faux Bamboo Legs, Round, c.1975, 27 x 20 In.	330.00
Table, Gilt, Marble, Bulbous Legs, Urn Stretcher, Paw Feet, Round, c.1850, 30 x 19 In.	2280.00
Table, Gilt Metal, Smoked Glass, Reeded, Tubular Supports, c.1900, 17 x 21 x 19 In.	330.00
Table, Gothic Revival, Cast Iron, Drawer, 19th Century, 30 x 22 x 25 In.	275.00
Table, Gothic Revival, Oak, Drawer, Stretcher Base, c.1890, 29 x 47 In.	400.00
Table, Gothic Revival, Walnut, Marble Top, Arched Apron, Trestle Base, c.1850, 29 x 36 In.	1320.00
Table, Gothic Revival, Walnut, Pierced Skirt, Twist Supports, Lower Shelf, c.1880, 28 x 29 In. .	2091.00
Table, Guard Room, Spanish Provincial, Fruitwood, Scrolling Iron Supports, 30 x 36 In.	2880.00
Table, Guard Room, Spanish Provincial, Oak, Banded Top, Supports, 30 x 43 In.	1920.00
Table, Hall, Baroque, Walnut, 2 Drawers, Flowers, Stretcher Base, 1690s, 28 x 50 x 22 In.	2200.00
Table, Hall, George III, Mahogany, Chamfered Legs, Fretwork, 32 x 68 In.	770.00
Table, Hall, Jacobean, English Oak, Molded Top, Frieze Drawer, Shelf, c.1900, 40 x 32 In.	422.00
Table, Hardwood, Dreamstone, Bat Carved Skirt, Chinese, Square, 33 x 29 x 29 In.	403.00
Table, Hardwood, Lacquer, Gray Stone Top, Braces, Hoof Legs, Chinese, 1900s, 33 x 71 In.	1150.00
Table, Harvest, Curly Maple, Breadboard Ends, Dovetail Drawer, 30 ¼ x 72 In.	1295.00
Table, Harvest, Drop Leaf, Squared Legs, Leaf, 30 x 53 x 52 In.	366.00
Table, Harvest, Pine, Oak, Scrubbed, Turned Legs, Red Paint, 1700s, 28 x 71 In.	1150.00
Table, Harvest, Pine, Oval, Tapered Black Legs, c.1890, 18 x 42 In.	1095.00
Table, Harvest, Pine, Square Tapered Legs, Plank Top, Drawer, 41 x 132 In.	150.00
Table, Harvest, Yellow Pine, 2 Drawers, Green Paint, Georgia, 1800s, 29 x 90 In.	1093.00
Table, Harvest, Yellow Pine, H-Stretcher, Southern, 1800s, 29 x 74 In.	3220.00
Table, Hepplewhite, Mahogany, Oval, Inlays, 1800s, 29 x 32 In.	374.00
Table, Hepplewhite, Walnut, 2-Board Top, 1800s, 28 x 36 In.	382.00
Table, Hepplewhite, Walnut, Drop Leaf, Tapered Legs, c.1810, 28 x 20 In.	646.00
Table, Heritage Henredon, 6-Sided, Slab Base, Taliesin Edges, Frank Lloyd Wright, 26 x 27 In.	1080.00
Table, Hunt, Kittinger, Mahogany, Drop Leaf, Double Gate Supports, 29 x 79 In. ....*illus*	1121.00
Table, Hunzinger, Mahogany, Barley Twist Legs, Bronze Feet, 34 x 14 x 14 In.	910.00
Table, Hutch, Pine, Trestle Support, Brown Paint, 1700s, 27 x 45 In. ....*illus*	3304.00
Table, Ice Cream, Iron Frame, 4 Swiveling Stools, Glass Vitrine Top, 55 x 55 In.	863.00
Table, Iron, Marble, Urns, Flowers, Birds, Curule Supports, 31 x 48 x 30 In.	3231.00
Table, Italian Baroque, Walnut, Frieze Drawer, Columnar Legs, 1700, 28 x 36 x 37 In.	296.00
Table, Italian Provincial, Walnut, Ebonized Banding, Diamond Panels, 28 x 63 In.	2880.00
Table, Italian Rococo, Beveled Mirror Top, Carved Putti Pedestal Base, 27 x 14 In., Pair	978.00
Table, Italian Walnut, Marquetry, Deer, Drop Leaf, c.1800, 28 x 49 x 19 In.	1435.00
Table, J. Widdicomb, Bronze Dore Inlay, Urn, Women's Faces, Paw Feet, 29 x 32 In.	620.00
Table, Jacobean Revival, Oak, Carved, Splayed Legs, Canted Corners, 24 x 25 x 17 ¾ In.	118.00
Table, Jacobean Style, Oak, Rectangular Top, 2 Draw Leaves, 30 x 59 x 32 In.	474.00
Table, Japanese Wood, Central Dragon, Japan, 20 Century, 15 x 53 x 29 In.	239.00
Table, Jean Royere, Iron, Painted, Glass, Fabric Covered Wood, c.1951, 30 x 35 In.	55000.00
Table, Joe D'Urso, Stainless Steel, Glass, Cube Form, Knoll, 16 x 27 x 27 In.	1840.00
Table, Juan Montoya, Iron, Round Top, Scrolled Feet, 30 x 47 In.	1020.00

Furniture, Table, Hunt, Kittinger, Mahogany, Drop Leaf, Double Gate Supports, 29 x 79 In.
$1121.00

F

Furniture, Table, Hutch, Pine, Trestle Support, Brown Paint, 1700s, 27 x 45 In.
$3304.00

Furniture, Table, Kang, Black Lacquer, Stone Insert, Hoof Legs, Chinese, 17 x 55 In.
$1180.00

Furniture, Table, Library, Mahogany Veneer, Drawers, Stretcher, c.1900, 19 x 54 In. $708.00

Furniture, Table, Library, Renaissance Revival, Carved, Leather Top, Drawers, c.1875, 30 x 48 In. $3408.00

Furniture, Table, Library, Spanish, Walnut, Plank Top, Chip Carved Drawers, 1700s, 32 x 30 In. $5581.00

TIP

Don't ignore signs of "wildlife." Use sprays and exterminators. Moths and carpet beetles eat upholstery and fabrics; termites eat wood; powder post beetles and dry wood termites eat wood.

Table, Kang, Black Lacquer, Stone Insert, Hoof Legs, Chinese, 17 x 55 In. ....*illus*	1180.00
Table, Kang, Black Lacquer, Stone Top, Horse Hoof Legs, Chinese, 1900s, 16 x 65 In.	575.00
Table, Kitchen, Cherry, 3-Board Top, Tapered Square Legs, 28 x 40 In.	546.00
Table, Kitchen, Louis XV, Cherry, Breadboard Top, Cabriole Legs, 20 x 51 x 29 In.	1007.00
Table, Kitchen, Pine, 6-Plank Top, Scrubbed, Rounded Corners, Turned Legs, 30 x 60 In.	1035.00
Table, Kitchen, Yellow Pine, 3-Board Top, Turned Legs, 1800s, 29 x 43 In.	1150.00
Table, Kittinger Georgian, Reed Edge, Triple Supports, Brass Animal Feet, 29 x 46 In.	2478.00
Table, L. & J.G. Stickley, Harvest, Mission Oak Style, Folding Top, Late 1900s, 31 x 72 In.	1180.00
Table, L. & J.G. Stickley, Shelf, Legs Extend Through Top, 19 x 24 In.	1908.00
Table, Lacquer, Red, Gray Stone Top, Hoof Legs, 20th Century, 17 x 51 x 35 In.	920.00
Table, Lacquer, Hoof Feet, Marble Top, 20th Century, Chinese, 31 x 86 x 35 In.	978.00
Table, Lacquered Wood, Metal, Lithograph, Madrepore, Fornasetti, c.1950, 29 In.	6250.00
Table, Laminated Birch, Black Paint, 27 x 39 ½ In.	478.00
Table, Lazy Susan, Yellow Pine, Turning Top, Tapered Legs, 20th Century, 34 x 54 In.	1495.00
Table, Library, Arts & Crafts, Open Design, Stretcher Shelf, Green, 40 x 29 In.	480.00
Table, Library, Arts & Crafts, Rectangular Top, Shoefoot Base, Shelf, 54 x 30 x 30 ½ In.	330.00
Table, Library, Arts & Crafts, Trestle Shape, Slab Sides, Shoefoot Base, 120 x 30 In.	1440.00
Table, Library, Baroque, Walnut, 4 Drawers, Trestle Base, Spain, 1700s, 32 x 65 x 33 In.	650.00
Table, Library, Carved, Oak, Molded Top, Incised, 2 Drawers, Pedestals, 30 x 44 In.	353.00
Table, Library, G. Stickley, No. 655, Spindles, Shelf, 36 x 24 x 29 In.	2160.00
Table, Library, G. Stickley, Oak, Copper Hardware, c.1901, 31 ⅝ x 60 x 35 In.	34375.00
Table, Library, G. Stickley, Red Decal, 29 x 42 x 29 ¾ In.	2318.00
Table, Library, George II Style, Mahogany, Carved, Cabriole Legs, 30 x 60 x 31 In.	657.00
Table, Library, L. & J.G. Stickley, No. 530, Drawer Over Stretcher, 36 x 24 x 29 In.	720.00
Table, Library, Limbert, 2 Drawers, Slatted Sides, 29 x 50 x 36 In.	2040.00
Table, Library, Mahogany, Carved, Lion's Masks, Drawer, Baluster Legs, 32 x 49 In.	1058.00
Table, Library, Mahogany, Carved, Stretcher Shelf, Merklin, N.Y., c.1880, 31 x 42 In.	705.00
Table, Library, Mahogany, Leather, Drawers, Greek Key, Griffins, 1900s, 30 x 68 In.	646.00
Table, Library, Mahogany, Marble Top, Carved, 32 x 72 x 23 In.	825.00
Table, Library, Mahogany Veneer, Drawers, Stretcher, c.1900, 19 x 54 In. ....*illus*	708.00
Table, Library, Regency, Mahogany, Leather, Frieze, 2 Drawers, Splayed Legs, c.1825, 30 x 48 In.	1680.00
Table, Library, Regency, Mahogany, Tooled Leather Top, 2 Drawers, Top-Shaped Feet, 20 x 54 In.	1920.00
Table, Library, Regency Style, Mahogany, Black Leather, Griffin Supports, 30 x 68 In.	646.00
Table, Library, Renaissance Revival, Carved, Leather Top, Drawers, c.1875, 30 x 48 In. ....*illus*	3408.00
Table, Library, Renaissance Revival, Carved Lion, c.1910, 31 x 56 In.	999.00
Table, Library, Renaissance Revival, Walnut, Carved, Embossed Top, 30 x 43 x 28 In.	4406.00
Table, Library, Spanish Colonial, Walnut, Shaped Iron Stretcher Base, 29 x 55 x 18 In.	2562.00
Table, Library, Spanish, Walnut, Plank Top, Chip Carved Drawers, 1700s, 32 x 30 In. ....*illus*	5581.00
Table, Library, Stickley, Quartersawn Top, Drawer, Square Legs, Shelf, 29 x 36 x 24 In.	862.00
Table, Library, Victorian, Burl Walnut, Green Felt Top, Drawer, Carved Stretcher, 29 x 35 In. ..	550.00
Table, Library, Victorian, Oak, Twist Turned Legs, 29 x 48 x 29 In.	150.00
Table, Library, Victorian, Walnut, Poplar, Pine, Baize Top, Drawer, Trestle, c.1860, 30 x 54 In.	805.00
Table, Library, William IV, Mahogany, Leather Top, 2 Drawers, Turned Legs, c.1830, 29 x 36 In.	3819.00
Table, Library, William IV, Mahogany, Trestle Base, Stretcher, c.1835, 29 x 54 In.	1725.00
Table, Library, Winged Creature Supports, Button Feet, Carved Leaf, c.1900, 30 x 50 x 30 In. ..	1093.00
Table, Lifetime, 2 Rounded Drop Leaves, Corbels At Legs, Signed, Puritan, 36 In.	840.00
Table, Lifetime Furniture, Oak, Slab Sides, Grand Rapids, 1910, 29 x 23 In.	345.00
Table, Lift Top, Yellow Pine, Open Interior, Green Blue Paint, Georgia, 1800s, 30 x 32 In.	403.00
Table, Lighted, Applied Leaves, Flowers, Wrought Iron, 3 Legs, Italy, 22 x 20 In.	450.00
Table, Limbert, Cutout Sides, Rounded Top, Shelf, Branded, 30 x 20 In. ....*illus*	4500.00
Table, Limbert, No. 140, Rounded Corners, Square Cutout Sides, 30 x 28 In.	4200.00
Table, Limbert, No. 240, Cutout Shelf, Red Brown Finish, Branded, 20 x 30 In.	2588.00
Table, Limbert, No. 1138, Circular Top, Shelf, Splayed Legs, 30 x 29 In.	1920.00
Table, Limbert, Oval, Cutout Sides, 45 x 30 x 29 In.	3360.00
Table, Limbert, Round, Notched Apron, Corbel Supports, Cross Stretcher Base, 38 x 29 In.	5400.00
Table, Loo, Burl Walnut, Mahogany, Tilt Top, Inlays, Splayed Legs, c.1875, 30 In.	1200.00
Table, Louis XV, Pine, Triangular Wells, Cabriole Legs, Painted, 30 x 41 In.	1175.00
Table, Louis XV Style, Ebonized, Marble Top, Molded Edge, Scalloped Frieze, 27 x 23 In.	900.00
Table, Louis XV Style, Fruitwood, Painted, Marble Top, Pierced Basket, 30 x 21 In.	1380.00
Table, Louis XV Style, Kidney Shape, 2 Tiers, Marble Top, Ormolu, Brass, 27 x 31 In.	2175.00
Table, Louis XV Style, Mahogany, Gilded Bronze, Porcelain Plaques, c.1845, 28 x 17 In. ....*illus*	470.00
Table, Louis XV Style, Oak, Marble, Shell, Flower Carved Frieze, Round, c.1890, 30 x 47 In.	2280.00
Table, Louis XV Style, Pine, Panel Top, Triangular Wells, Cabriole Legs, 30 x 41 In.	1175.00
Table, Louis XV Style, Walnut, Serpentine Top, Cabriole Legs, c.1890, 27 x 28 In.	1490.00
Table, Louis XV, Tulipwood Parquetry, Bronze Mounts, Leather, 3 Drawers, 30 x 61 In.	1778.00
Table, Louis XVI, Mahogany, Marble Top, Kidney Shape, Brass Banding, Lower Shelf, 27 x 23 In.	1320.00

Table, Louis XVI, Mahogany, Trestle Supports, Molded Edge, c.1790, 28 x 36 In.	3050.00
Table, Louis XVI, Multicolored, Flip Top, Demilune, Banding, Laurel Wreath, 32 x 49 In.	1920.00
Table, Louis XVI Style, Console, Gilt, Marble, c.1900, 36 x 17 x 10 In.	720.00
Table, Louis XVI Style, Fruitwood, Bowed Top, Shaped Galley, Drawer, c.1825, 30 x 17 x 12 In.	840.00
Table, Louis XVI Style, Gilt, Marble Top, Ribbon & Leaf Carving, Stretcher, 37 x 57 In.	5040.00
Table, Louis XVI Style, Gilt, Onyx, Shaped Top, Leaf Carving, Fluted Legs, 30 x 32 In.	948.00
Table, Louis XVI Style, Leather Top, Drawers, Tapered Legs, 30 x 49 x 28 In.	1410.00
Table, Louis XVI Style, Mahogany, Marble Top, Brass Gallery, 3 Drawers, 29 x 16 x 12 In.	1320.00
Table, Low, Carved, 2 Apron Drawers, Square Legs, Spain, 18 x 53 In.	1410.00
Table, Low, Embroidered Needlework, Panel, Animals, Flowers, Figures, 25 x 36 x 37 In.	711.00
Table, Low, Giltwood, Leaded Edge, Melon Feet, Christopher Maier, 16 x 36 x 24 In.	3600.00
Table, M. Nakashima, Minguren, Sketch, Signed, c.1980, 13 x 42 x 21 In.	20825.00
Table, Mackintosh Style, Oak, Inlaid Copper, 4 Tiers Of Open Squares, 26 x 29 In.	2300.00
Table, Magazine, Wormley, Walnut, Mahogany, 2 Molded Holders, Dunbar, 25 x 22 In.	900.00
Table, Mahogany, 2 Drop Leaves, Square Legs, England, 1700s, 17 x 28 In.	148.00
Table, Mahogany, 3 Drawers, Turned Support, Carved Legs, Paw Feet, Philadelphia, c.1820, 29 x 23 In.	316.00
Table, Mahogany, Bowfront, Banded, Burl Panels, Tapered Legs, 30 x 33 In.	180.00
Table, Mahogany, Bowfront, Shaped Top, Fitted Drawer, England, c.1885, 31 x 36 In.	690.00
Table, Mahogany, Burl Inlay, Checkerboard, Shapes, Fluted Splayed Legs, 1899, 30 x 15	207.00
Table, Mahogany, Dish Top, Acanthus Spray, Shell Carved, Ireland, 26 x 22 In.	588.00
Table, Mahogany, Drawer, 6 Flared Legs, c.1920, 25 x 22 In.	296.00
Table, Mahogany, Drawer, Ball & Claw, Stretcher, 1920s	110.00
Table, Mahogany, Fluted Turned Legs, Stretchers, 19 x 37 x 21 In.	79.00
Table, Mahogany, Marble Top, Frieze, Panel Door, Scrolls, c.1825, 36 x 34 In.	3360.00
Table, Mahogany, Marble Top, Scroll Supports, New York, c.1835, 30 x 37 In.	1058.00
Table, Mahogany, Mixed Wood Inlays, Oval, 2 Tiers, Emile Galle, c.1900, 30 x 32 In.	1800.00
Table, Mahogany, Octagonal, Legs, Geometric, Middle Eastern, 1800s, 25 x 18 In., Pair	115.00
Table, Mahogany, Pedestal, Flip Top, Oval, Early 20th Century, 25 x 22 In.	70.00
Table, Mahogany, Piecrust Top, Pedestal, Early 1900s, 29 x 23 In.	450.00
Table, Mahogany, Rosewood, Tilt Top, Round, Turned Baluster, Tripod Base, 1800s, 24 x 36 In.	411.00
Table, Mahogany, Round, Egyptian Marble Top, Scroll Supports, Paw Feet, 32 x 39 In.	4200.00
Table, Mahogany, Round, Figural, Painted Cast-Iron Tripod Base, 1900s, 28 x 22 In.	230.00
Table, Mahogany, Round, Inlaid Flowers, Figures, 2 Drawers, Pedestal, c.1910, 30 x 42 In.	1180.00
Table, Mahogany, Round, Pedestal Base, Paw Feet, England	120.00
Table, Mahogany, Round, Shaped Stretcher Plaque, Robert Irwin, 15 x 26 In.	148.00
Table, Mahogany, Tilt Top, Dish Top, Leaf Carved Center, Ireland, 1800s, 22 x 26 In.	588.00
Table, Mahogany, Tilt Top, Reeded & Bulbous Standard, 3-Footed, Late 1800s, 31 x 35 In.	700.00
Table, Mahogany, Tilt Top, Ring-Turned Pedestal, Ebony, Ivory, Burled Maple, 29 x 42 In.	8225.00
Table, Mahogany, Tilt Top, Round, Single Board, Turned Pedestal, 3 Cabriole Legs, 29 x 25 In.	353.00
Table, Mahogany, Tilt Top, Round, Tripod, c.1750, 28 x 22 In.	316.00
Table, Mahogany, Tilt Top, Scalloped Edge, c.1840, 43 x 28 In.	374.00
Table, Majorelle, Mahogany, Bird's-Eye Maple, Parcel Gilt Flowers, 30 x 24 x 22 In.	9760.00
Table, Maple, Single-Board Overhanging Top, Drawer, Button Feet, Connecticut, 1750	1121.00
Table, Marble, Round, Gallery, Tripod Base, 20 In.	186.00
Table, Marble Top, Light Gray, 4 Piece Steel Base, 63 x 29 In.	600.00
Table, Marble Top, Round, Carved & Painted Pineapple Base, 18 x 21 x 21 In.	345.00
Table, Marcel Breuer, Bent Plywood, c.1936, 14 ¾ x 17 ¾ In.	3884.00
Table, Marquetry Top, Drawer, Bronze Mount, France, 31 x 31 x 19 In.	519.00
Table, Maurice Dufrene, Gilt, Carved, Lacquer, Marble Top, c.1925, 30 x 26 In.	1912.00
Table, McCobb, Mahogany, Shelf, Drawer, Connoisseur, 24 x 22 In., Pair	840.00
Table, Mechanical, Mahogany, 3 Rising Shelves, c.1860, 32 x 45 In.	3290.00
Table, Mies Van Der Rohe, Glass Top, Steel Base, 17 x 40 In.	720.00
Table, Milo Baughman, Curved Chrome Base, Glass Top, 44 x 28 In.	480.00
Table, Mirror Paneled Top, 50 In.	174.00
Table, Mixed Woods, Chrysanthemum, Inlay, Stems, Leaves, Shelves, 22 x 31 x 28 In.	2875.00
Table, Mixing, Mahogany, Marble, Ogee Frieze, Scroll Feet, Plinth, c.1835, 35 x 37 x 17 In.	2515.00
Table, Moorish, Mother-Of-Pearl, Bone Inlay, Octagonal, Geometric, 30 x 24 In.	1763.00
Table, Mother-Of-Pearl & Bone Geometric Inlay, Tiered Apron, Hexagonal Top, 32 x 20 In., Pair.	2585.00
Table, Multicolored, Faux Marble Top, Molded Edge, Castellated Frieze, Drop Finials, 38 x 65 In.	3840.00
Table, Napoleon III, Faux Bamboo, Poplar, Drawer, Shaped Legs, c.1860, 28 x 36 In.	1540.00
Table, Neoclassical, Inlaid Walnut, Racetrack Shape, Leaf, Double Pedestals, 29 x 50 In.	1265.00
Table, Neoclassical, Limestone, Wrought Iron, Stretchers, Scrolled Feet, 37 x 50 In.	1200.00
Table, Neoclassical, Mahogany, Flip Top, Swivel, Gadrooned Skirt, 29 x 48 In.	353.00
Table, Neoclassical, Mahogany, Marble Top, Paneled Skirt, Tapered Legs, c.1800s, 30 x 39 In.	3819.00
Table, Neoclassical, Mahogany, Panels, Triangular Base, Paw Feet, c.1830, 29 x 48 In.	4914.00
Table, Neoclassical, Mahogany, Serpentine Marble, Scroll Supports, c.1840, 30 x 37 In.	1058.00

Furniture, Table, Limbert, Cutout Sides, Rounded Top, Shelf, Branded, 30 x 20 In. $4500.00

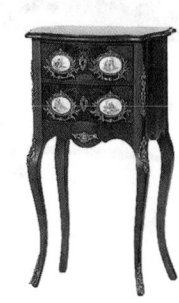

Furniture, Table, Louis XV Style, Mahogany, Gilded Bronze, Porcelain Plaques, c.1845, 28 x 17 In. $470.00

Furniture, Table, Pembroke, George III, Figured Veneer, Inlaid, England, c.1800, 29 x 34 In. $2185.00

Furniture, Table, Pier, Queen Anne, Mahogany, Veneer, Oak, Carved, Ireland, c.1750, 34 x 41 In. $1888.00

Furniture, Table, Pier, Rosewood, Marble Top, Carved Skirt, Victorian, 37 x 59 In.
$1955.00

Furniture, Table, Regency Style, Inlaid Mahogany, Drawers, c.1910, 28 x 32 In.
$546.00

Furniture, Table, Round, French Empire Revival, Gilt Bronze, Malachite, Round Top, 1900s, 36 x 30 In.
$9600.00

Furniture, Table, Sevres Style, Porcelain, Painted Garland, Baluster Pedestal, c.1920, 23 x 15 In.
$633.00

Table, Neoclassical, Mahogany, Tilt Top, Carved, Pedestal, Paw Feet, 18 x 37 In.	840.00
Table, Neoclassical, Restauration, Mahogany, Marble Top, Frieze Drawer, c.1830, 28 x 32 In.	999.00
Table, Neoclassical Style, Round, Marble, Gilt Bronze, Flowers, Butterflies, 32 x 28 In.	7637.00
Table, Nesting, American Modern, Walnut, 5-Sided Top, Reverse Tapered Legs, 24 x 19 In.	180.00
Table, Nesting, Anglo-Indian, Black Lacquer, Mother-Of-Pearl, Stretcher, 19 x 21 In., 3 Piece	259.00
Table, Nesting, English Oak, Scalloped Skirt, Turned Legs, 19 x 22 In.	575.00
Table, Nesting, F. Gehry, Corrugated Cardboard, Slab Sides, Easy Edges, 1970s, 25 x 20 In.	570.00
Table, Nesting, Fruitwood, Inlaid Bird Scene, Paper Label, c.1900, 28 x 23 In., 4 Piece	5079.00
Table, Nesting, G. Nakashima, Walnut, Free-Edge, 3 Legs, 1989, 21 x 19 x 22 In.	3600.00
Table, Nesting, G. Nakashima, Walnut, Triangle Top, 21 x 21 In., 3 Piece	4800.00
Table, Nesting, Japanned, Red, Turned Legs, Stretcher Base, Largest 24 x 19 In., 4 Piece	575.00
Table, Nesting, Mahogany, Inlaid Flower Basket, c.1890, 4 Piece	502.00
Table, Nesting, Mahogany, Marquetry, c.1890, 4 Piece	460.00
Table, Nesting, Mahogany, Splayed Legs, 26 x 18 In., 4 Piece	186.00
Table, Nesting, Papier-Mache, Painted, Lacquered, Gilt, Mother-Of-Pearl, 28 x 15 In., 3 Piece	2900.00
Table, Nesting, Robsjohn-Gibbings, Mahogany, Pickled, Splatter, Widdicomb, 26 x 25 In., 3 Piece	720.00
Table, North African Hardwood, Hexagonal, Banded, Inlaid Star, Frieze, 30 x 26 In.	1560.00
Table, Oscar Bach, Round, Ornate, Tripod Base, Metal, c.1920	8190.00
Table, P. Evans, Copper, Bronze, Pewter Patchwork, Slate Top, Casters, 23 x 30 In.	3965.00
Table, P. Evans, Oval Slate Top, Painted Patchwork Steel Base, Gilt, 39 x 98 In.	13200.00
Table, Papier-Mache, Black, Painted, Cartouche Tray Top, X-Stretcher Base, 20 x 32 In.	209.00
Table, Papier-Mache, Tilt Top, Mother-Of-Pearl Inlay, Scalloped Rim, Tripod Base, 27 In.	340.00
Table, Papier-Mache, Tilt Top, Scalloped Top, Still Life, Continental, 30 x 24 In.	881.00
Table, Pastry, Gothic Style, Granite Top, Acorn Drops, Iron Frieze, 35 x 43 x 22 In.	1725.00
Table, Peachwood, Lacquered, Drawers, Chinese, 19th Century, 31 x 40 x 15 In.	896.00
Table, Pedestal, Glass Top, Corinthian Capital Base, 30 x 40 In.	420.00
Table, Pedestal, Glass Top, Lucite Panels, Rectangular, 29 x 72 x 42 In.	478.00
Table, Pedestal, Mahogany, Frieze, Pillar Support, Stepped Plinth, c.1830, 18 x 34 In.	823.00
Table, Pedestal, Neoclassical, Mahogany, Ogee Molded Frieze, c.1830, 35 x 33 In.	823.00
Table, Pedestal, Regency Style, Mahogany, Inlaid Octagonal, Tripod, 39 x 15 x 19 In.	418.00
Table, Pedestal, Walnut, Mahogany, Marble Top, Beaded Edge Apron, c.1850, 29 x 39 In.	4800.00
Table, Pembroke, Cherry, X-Stretcher, Conn., 19th Century, 28 x 26 In.	780.00
Table, Pembroke, Chippendale, Mahogany, Drawer, 29 x 20 In.	2530.00
Table, Pembroke, Drawer, Doors, Fluted Legs, Block Feet, c.1800s, 29 x 33 x 22 In.	269.00
Table, Pembroke, Federal, Mahogany, Inlaid, Tapered Legs, Newport, R.I., 28 x 19 In.	21250.00
Table, Pembroke, Federal, Mahogany, Oak Gates, String Inlay, Maryland, 29 x 22 In.	575.00
Table, Pembroke, Federal, Mahogany, Pine, Drawer, 2 Leaves, c.1800, 29 x 30 In.	353.00
Table, Pembroke, Federal, Mahogany, Pine, Drawers, Splayed Legs, Paw Feet, 29 x 23 In.	411.00
Table, Pembroke, Federal, Oak, Poplar, Banded Skirt, Tapered Legs, c.1800, 29 x 44 x 36 In.	920.00
Table, Pembroke, Federal Style, Walnut, 30 x 21 x 33 In.	350.00
Table, Pembroke, Federal, Wood Inlays, c.1800, 30 x 25 In.	414.00
Table, Pembroke, George III, Figured Veneer, Inlaid, England, c.1800, 29 x 34 In. *illus*	2185.00
Table, Pembroke, George III, Inlaid Mahogany, Drawer, Late 1700s, 27 x 19 x 30 In.	2620.00
Table, Pembroke, George III, Mahogany, Crossbanded, 28 x 30 x 39 In.	1422.00
Table, Pembroke, George III, Mahogany, Frieze Drawer, 27 x 39 x 23 In.	1434.00
Table, Pembroke, George III, Mahogany, Inlaid Woods, England, c.1790, 29 x 23 In.	1150.00
Table, Pembroke, George III, Mahogany, Oak, Pine, Drawer, Early 1800s, 29 x 30 In.	881.00
Table, Pembroke, George III Style, Drawer, Mahogany, Tapered Legs, 28 x 37 x 31 In.	956.00
Table, Pembroke, George III Style, Mahogany, Inlaid, Crossbanded, 27 x 35 x 30 In.	1778.00
Table, Pembroke, Georgian, Banded Top, Inlays, Drawer, Casters, c.1790, 25 x 31 In.	411.00
Table, Pembroke, Hepplewhite, Cherry, 28 x 35 x 21 In.	185.00
Table, Pembroke, Hepplewhite, Cherry, Drawer, Arched Cross Stretchers, c.1800, 27 x 19 In.	2006.00
Table, Pembroke, Hepplewhite, Cherry, Drawer, X-Stretcher, c.1800, 28 x 28 In.	1850.00
Table, Pembroke, Hepplewhite, Mahogany, Tapered Legs, England, c.1810, 28 x 35 ½ x 23 In.	835.00
Table, Pembroke, Mahogany, 2 Drawers, 1 False, Tapered Legs, Casters, c.1800, 22 x 28 In.	746.00
Table, Pembroke, Mahogany, Drawer, Ring-Turned Legs, 28 x 19 x 21 In.	840.00
Table, Pembroke, Mahogany, Frieze Drawer, Ankle Collars, c.1790, 30 x 31 In.	5290.00
Table, Pembroke, Mahogany, Frieze Drawer, Tapered Legs, 1800s, 28 x 38 x 37 In.	173.00
Table, Pembroke, Mahogany, Inlay, Drawer, Tapered Legs, New York, 19 x 29 In.	1185.00
Table, Pembroke, Mahogany, Oval, Crossbanded, Inlaid Medallion, Drawer, 15 x 29 In.	266.00
Table, Pembroke, Queen Anne, Mahogany, Oak, Round Top, Drawer, 1700s, 29 x 18 In.	823.00
Table, Pembroke, Regency, Mahogany, Oval, Shaped Top, Drawers, 29 x 28 In.	748.00
Table, Pembroke, Regency Style, Mahogany, Frieze, Drawer, c.1875, 28 x 29 x 44 In.	780.00
Table, Pembroke, Walnut, Pine, Banded Inlays, c.1820, 30 x 35 In.	529.00
Table, Petal, Richard Schultz, Knoll, c.1960, 28 x 41 ½ In.	2205.00
Table, Philip Lloyd Powell, Walnut, L Angle Shape, Oval Inlay Top, 14 x 56 In.	1200.00

Table, Piecrust Rim, Spiral Gadrooning, Ball & Claw, 21 In., 9-In. Top	18500.00
Table, Pier, Egyptian Revival, Mahogany, Marble, Supports, c.1850, 35 x 38 x 15 In.	1434.00
Table, Pier, Empire Style, Mahogany, Drawer, Column Front, Applied Bronze, 36 x 43 In.	633.00
Table, Pier, Fruitwood Inlays, Beech, Carved Leaves, c.1790, England, 32 x 45 In., Pair	18400.00
Table, Pier, George III Style, Mahogany, Veneer Inlaid Skirts, 30 x 51 x 24 In.	2530.00
Table, Pier, Gilt, Marble Top, Serpentine, Carved Apron, Knees, Stretcher, Italy, 33 x 45 In.	1265.00
Table, Pier, Lyre Base, Marble, Crotch Mahogany Veneer, c.1850, 36 x 36 In.	6500.00
Table, Pier, Mahogany, Carved Paw Feet, Marble Columns, c.1825, 37 x 41 In.	2938.00
Table, Pier, Mahogany, Marble Top, Cove Molded Skirt, Curved Plinth, c.1815, 29 x 26 In.	1293.00
Table, Pier, Mahogany, Marble Top, Drawer, Scroll Support, c.1820, 26 x 29 In.	1292.00
Table, Pier, Mahogany, Marble Top, Lyre Supports, Scroll Feet, 1830s, 38 x 34 In.	403.00
Table, Pier, Mahogany, Marble Top, Mirror Back, New York, 1830s, 36 x 44 In.	690.00
Table, Pier, Mahogany, Mirror, Marble Top, Carved Painted Caryatids, c.1825, 35 x 41 In.	2233.00
Table, Pier, Mahogany, Mirror, Marble Top, Columns, Paw Feet, c.1825, 37 x 42 In.	2938.00
Table, Pier, Mahogany, Rosewood, Carved, Banded, Marble Top, 40 x 43 x 21 In.	4700.00
Table, Pier, Marble Top, Stencils, Gilt, Mirror, Dolphin Feet, Deming & Buckley, 39 x 44 In.	6250.00
Table, Pier, Neoclassical, Marble, Scroll Ends, c.1825, 36 x 41 In.	1250.00
Table, Pier, Queen Anne, Mahogany, Veneer, Oak, Carved, Ireland, c.1750, 34 x 41 In. ....*illus*	1888.00
Table, Pier, Rosewood, Marble Top, Carved Skirt, Victorian, 37 x 59 In. ....*illus*	1955.00
Table, Pine, 2-Board, Round Top, Splayed Triangle Base, Turned Legs, 33 x 29 In.	259.00
Table, Pine, Maple, Turned Legs, Ball Feet, Red Paint, 29 x 42 In.	889.00
Table, Pine, Oval, Scrubbed Top, Square Stretcher Base, New England, c.1790, 26 x 25 In.	1304.00
Table, Pine, Oval Top, Block Turned Legs, Painted, 1700s, 30 x 52 In.	474.00
Table, Pine, Round, Carved, Gesso, Painted, Marbleized Drum Top, Italy, c.1820, 37 x 17 In.	2820.00
Table, Pine, Round Corners, Frieze, Baluster Turned Legs, 1900s, 30 x 72 x 39 In.	239.00
Table, Pine, Round, Spindle Legs, Ball Feet, 3 Leaves, c.1930, 29 x 108 In.	117.00
Table, Pine, Tall Legs, Green, Yellow Paint, Georgia, 1800s, 32 x 24 In.	978.00
Table, Pine, Taper Leg, Overhanging Top, Red Paint, New England, c.1835, 27 x 25 In.	4145.00
Table, Pine Top, 3-Board, Walnut, Poplar, 2 Drawers, Applied Molding, c.1820, 30 x 54 In.	1175.00
Table, Plain Frieze, 8-Sided Club Shape Legs, H-Stretcher, England, 1800s, 28 x 30 In.	207.00
Table, Poplar, Round Top, Yellow Pine Skirt, Black Paint, Georgia, 1800s, 31 x 33 In.	690.00
Table, Porcelain, Bronze, Sevres Style Top, Flowers, Gold Filigree, Shaped Legs, 29 x 21 In.	690.00
Table, Porcelain, Ormolu, Pierced Gallery, Floral Cartouche, Continental, 27 x 21 In.	345.00
Table, Provincial Louis XV, Fruitwood, Scalloped Apron, Drawer, Cabriole Legs, 28 x 31 In.	2115.00
Table, Provincial Louis XV Style, Cherry, Round, Drawer, Cabriole Legs, 1800s, 30 x 25 In.	1450.00
Table, Provincial, Pine, Painted, Flowers, Geometric, Decorated Frieze, Drawers, 31 x 21 In.	1320.00
Table, Pub, Fruitwood, Oak, Round Top, Square Base, Boot Feet, c.1850, 30 x 46 In.	2160.00
Table, Pub, Iron, Marble, Round, Tapered Base, Flowers, 30 x 24 In., Pair	472.00 to 502.00
Table, Pub, Oak, Barrel Shape, Steel Banding, 28 In.	236.00
Table, Pub, Round Top, 3-Legged Base, Face Medallions, Iron, Paint, 26 x 28 In.	266.00
Table, Queen Anne, Chinoiserie, Dish Top, Scalloped Edge, Figures, Birds, Boat, Gilt, 18 x 26 In.	431.00
Table, Queen Anne, Maple, Oval Top, Straight Turned Legs, New England, 1700s, 27 x 32 In.	593.00
Table, Queen Anne, Maple, Tilt Top, 18th Century, 28 x 29 ½ x 30 In.	725.00
Table, Queen Anne, Oak, Triangle Top, Cock-Beaded Edge, Plain Frieze, England, 27 x 24 In.	325.00
Table, Queen Anne, Tiger Maple, Shaped Top, Curved Skirt, c.1790, 26 x 28 In.	5333.00
Table, Reading, Regency Style, Mahogany, Adjustable, Bun Feet, c.1850, 36 x 19 In.	1100.00
Table, Red Lacquer, 18 x 51 x 31 In.	1554.00
Table, Red Lacquer, Gilt, Black Coastal Village Scene, 1900s, 13 x 39 x 14 In.	201.00
Table, Red Lacquer, Pavilion & Figures, Fretwork Ground, Chinese, 15 x 53 In.	489.00
Table, Refectory, Baroque, Walnut, France, 18th Century, 31 x 91 x 28 In.	5750.00
Table, Refectory, Elizabethan Style, Oak, Urn Shape Supports, 30 x 78 x 33 In.	1304.00
Table, Refectory, English Oak, Breadboard Ends, Molded Skirt, 32 x 71 x 29 In.	2990.00
Table, Refectory, Mahogany, Trestle Supports, Wrought Iron Stretcher, c.1900, 30 x 78 x 33 In.	1960.00
Table, Refectory, Oak, 2-Board Top, 3 Drawers, Stretcher Base, 1700s, 30 x 99 x 32 In.	960.00
Table, Refectory, Oak, 5-Plank Top, X-Supports, France, 17th Century, 30 x 186 x 40 In.	36000.00
Table, Refectory, Oak, Baluster Supports, Trestle Base, 30 x 72 In.	1998.00
Table, Refectory, Oak, Breadboard Ends, Carved Trestle Supports, c.1780, 30 x 84 In.	2600.00
Table, Refectory, Provincial, Oak, Plank Top, Frieze Fitted End Drawer, c.1875, 30 x 31 In.	1800.00
Table, Refectory, Renaissance Revival, Walnut, Carved, 31 x 93 x 31 In.	2468.00
Table, Refectory, Renaissance Revival, Walnut, Carved, Painted, Trestle, 33 x 102 x 38 In.	1422.00
Table, Refectory, Spanish Baroque Style, Walnut, Dentil Frieze, Shaped Legs, 125 In.	1896.00
Table, Refectory, Walnut, Overhanging Top, Raised Panel, Bun Feet, Continental, 31 x 58 In.	2350.00
Table, Refectory, Walnut, Trestle Base, Scrolled Iron Stretcher, 30 x 63 In.	2115.00
Table, Regency, Elm Burl, Mahogany, Rosewood, Tilt Top, Oval, Crossbanded, 31 x 49 In.	863.00
Table, Regency, Mahogany, Drop Leaf, 2 Drawers, Trestle, 28 x 37 x 28 In.	1185.00

Furniture, Table, Sewing, Adam Style, Painted, Swags, Flowers, England, c.1900, 36 x 20 In.
$1150.00

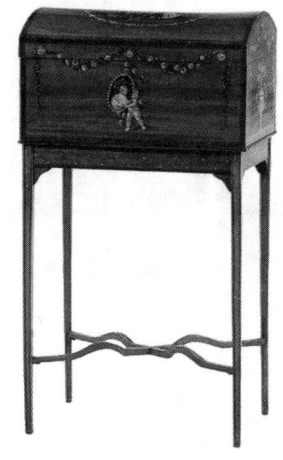

Furniture, Table, Sewing, Edwardian, Mahogany, Hinged Top, Banding, Storage Well, 29 x 19 In.
$540.00

Furniture, Table, Sewing, Tiger Maple, Veneer, Cartouche Shape Top, Drawers, Ohio, 29 x 23 In.
$1725.00

Furniture, Table, Stacking, Giotto Stoppino, Molded Plastic, Kartell, c.1968, 18 x 16 In., 3 Piece $480.00

Furniture, Table, Tavern, Pine, Stretcher Base, Oval Top, Turned Legs, c.1750, 24 x 29 In. $9440.00

Furniture, Table, Tea, Mahogany, Tilt Top, Birdcage, Tripod Base, 1700s, 26 x 32 In. $5192.00

Furniture, Table, Tea, Queen Anne, Birch, Maple, 8-Sided Top, 1700s, 25 x 28 In. $10620.00

Table, Regency, Mahogany, Satinwood Inlay, Turned Stem, 29 x 68 x 48 In.	3318.00
Table, Regency, Mahogany, Scroll Legs, Turned Stretcher, Paw Casters, 29 x 24 In., Pair	1410.00
Table, Regency, Mahogany, Sliding Top, Gameboard, 2 Fitted Drawers, 29 x 48 In.	3851.00
Table, Regency, Mahogany, Tooled Leather Top, 2 Drawers, 1820, 29 x 54 In.	1920.00
Table, Regency, Marble Top, Frieze, Carved Flowers, Fluted Legs, c.1900, 29 x 30 In., Pair	4080.00
Table, Regency, Rosewood, Carved, Round Top, Column Pedestal, 29 x 55 In.	1840.00
Table, Regency, Round, Tooled Leather Top, Pedestal Base, Saber Legs, 29 x 63 In.	3680.00
Table, Regency, Satinwood, Ebony, Inlaid Mahogany, Faux Drawer, 29 x 36 In.	2350.00
Table, Regency Style, Inlaid Mahogany, Drawers, c.1910, 28 x 32 In. ....*illus*	546.00
Table, Regency Style, Mahogany, Brass Marquetry, c.1900, 24 x 30 In.	4600.00
Table, Regency Style, Round, Twist Post Pedestal, Splayed Leg Base	450.00
Table, Regency Style, Silvered Bronze, Ram's Head, Mask, Valance, Signed Elkington	660.00
Table, Renaissance Revival, Burl Walnut, Flower, Inlays, Carved Skirt, Base, Round, 42 x 30 In.	1955.00
Table, Renaissance Revival, Oak, Lion's Heads, Drawer, Dolphin Base, 1890, 30 x 37 In.	840.00
Table, Renaissance Revival, Rosewood, Ebony, Rose, Leaf Inlays, Brass Border, 46 x 30 In.	3738.00
Table, Renaissance Revival, Rosewood, Marble Top, Carved Stretcher, Legs, c.1850, 30 x 33 In.	411.00
Table, Renaissance Revival, Walnut, Marble Top, Paneled Skirt, Fluted Blocks, 33 x 27 In.	173.00
Table, Renaissance Revival, Walnut, Oval, Splayed, Carved Legs, 50 x 30 In.	1725.00
Table, Rent, Mahogany, Round, Veneer Top, 4 Swing Drawers, Carvings, c.1850, 25 x 28 In.	1410.00
Table, Rent, Walnut, Round Top, Octagonal Frieze, Drawers, Stepped Plinth, 31 x 33 In.	529.00
Table, Revolving Drum, Mahogany, Leather Top, Drawers, Baluster Pedestal, c.1800, 25 In.	1075.00
Table, Richard Schultz, Rosewood, Rectangular Top, Steel Legs, Knoll, 76 x 29 In.	1140.00
Table, Ritual, Wood, Carved, Folding, Korea, 19th Century, 17 x 31 In.	588.00
Table, Robsjohn-Gibbings, Mahogany, Low Shelf, Tapered, Flared Legs, Widdicomb, 32 x 20 In.	90.00
Table, Robsjohn-Gibbings, Round, Contrasting Trim, Lower Shelf, 3 Curved Legs, 30 x 20 In.	390.00
Table, Rococo, Carved, Gilt, Marble Top, Skirt, Scrolling Legs, c.1750, 38 x 53 In.	11162.00
Table, Rococo, Glass Gilt Top, Carved, Gilt Apron, Legs, Italy, c.1980, 31 x 36 In.	764.00
Table, Rococo, Mahogany, Serpentine Marble Top, Carved Skirt, Urn, Finial, c.1850, 30 x 38 In.	411.00
Table, Rococo Revival, Mahogany, Cherry, Circular, 1843, 28 ½ x 47 ¾ In.	2040.00
Table, Rococo Revival, Turtle Top, Patriotic Union Shield Medallions, 30 x 33 In.	529.00
Table, Rococo Revival, Walnut, Marble Top, Carved, Shaped, 2 Legs, c.1875, 29 x 44 In., Pair	1200.00
Table, Rococo, Rosewood, Marble, Flower & Shell Carved Skirt, c.1850, 27 x 38 x 26 In.	460.00
Table, Rococo, Rosewood, Marble Top, Carved, Laminated, c.1850, 31 x 50 In.	4406.00
Table, Rococo, Walnut, Shaped Top, Cabriole Legs, Flower, Scroll Carvings, 26 x 33 In.	978.00
Table, Rohde, American Ash Group, No. 4043, Herman Miller, c.1940, 23 x 28 In.	194.00
Table, Rosewood, Carved Flower Apron, Legs, Inset Marble Top, 42 x 30 In.	6325.00
Table, Rosewood, Carved, Onyx Top, Inlaid Greenstone, c.1878, 28 x 44 x 32 In.	97600.00
Table, Rosewood Inset Top, Ornate, Carved Apron, Legs, Chinese, 1800s, 30 x 36 In.	690.00
Table, Rosewood, Marble Top, Scrolled Supports, Scrolled Legs, c.1840, 30 x 46 x 23 In.	4700.00
Table, Rosewood, Tilt Top, Flower Needlework Top, France, 1800s, 30 ½ x 37 ½ In.	690.00
Table, Rosewood, Tilt Top, Matchstick Marquetry, Eagle Emblem, 1975, 32 x 32 x 32 In.	3750.00
Table, Round, Directoire Style, Gilt Bronze, Marble Top, Bamboo, 30 In., Pair	4575.00
Table, Round, French Empire Revival, Gilt Bronze, Malachite, Round Top, 1900s, 36 x 30 In. *..illus*	9600.00
Table, Round, Patinated Bronze, Malachite, Figural Supports, 23 ½ In.	1292.00
Table, Round, Tripod Base, Open Detail Pedestal, Cast Iron, England, c.1870, 29 x 22 In.	2530.00
Table, Round, Wrought Iron, Art Deco, Marble Top, 3-Part Base, Hoof Feet, c.1900, 28 In.	2937.00
Table, Salon, Marble, Carved, Gilt, Geometric Top, Apron, 31 x 50 x 29 In.	5581.00
Table, Sawbuck, Blue, Brown Paint, New England, c.1820, 23 x 28 In.	1778.00
Table, Sawbuck, Pine, 3-Board Top, Breadboards, Gray Paint, c.1850, 29 x 60 In.	1645.00
Table, Sawbuck, Pine, Breadboard Ends, Stretcher Base, Painted, New Eng., 1800s, 21 x 42 In.	2252.00
Table, Scalloped Top, Dolphin Medallion, Marble Base, Pietra Dura, 34 In.	2875.00
Table, Serving, Art Moderne, Silvered Metal, Rosewood Handles, Mirror, 26 x 16 In.	390.00
Table, Serving, George III, Mahogany, Inlaid, Urn, Swags, Drawer, c.1790, 34 x 60 x 28 In.	5581.00
Table, Sevres Style, Porcelain, Painted Garland, Baluster Pedestal, c.1920, 23 x 15 In. ......*illus*	633.00
Table, Sewing, Adam Style, Painted, Swags, Flowers, England, c.1900, 36 x 20 In. ......*illus*	1150.00
Table, Sewing, Arts & Crafts, 2 Drop Leaves, 2 Drawers, 18 x 28 In.	210.00
Table, Sewing, Biedermeier, Walnut Veneer, Drawer, Faceted Stem, Bracket Feet, 24 x 13 In.	296.00
Table, Sewing, Black, Gold Lacquer, Ivory, Serpentine Edge, Dragons, 28 x 25 x 17 In.	3055.00
Table, Sewing, Burl Veneer, Lift Top, Frieze Drawer, 1825, 31 x 22 x 17 In.	2489.00
Table, Sewing, Drop Leaf, 2 Drawers, Turned Legs, 1800s, 23 x 28 In.	354.00
Table, Sewing, Drop Leaf, Empire Revival, Mahogany, Pedestal, Claw Feet, c.1835, 28 x 17 In.	450.00
Table, Sewing, Drop Leaf, Federal, Maple, Pullout Support, Spiral Legs, c.1820, 29 x 29 In.	176.00
Table, Sewing, Drop Leaf, Sheraton, Drawer, Reeded Legs, 28 ½ x 32 In.	1610.00
Table, Sewing, Drop Leaf, Sheraton, Mahogany, 3 Drawers, Bird's-Eye Maple, c.1825, 29 x 18 In.	1552.00
Table, Sewing, Drop Leaf, Sheraton, Walnut, c.1835, 28 ¾ x 18 In.	200.00
Table, Sewing, Edwardian, Mahogany, Hinged Top, Banding, Storage Well, 29 x 19 In. ......*illus*	540.00

Table, Sewing, Empire, Mahogany, Fitted Interior, Drawers, Carved Legs, Shelf, c.1820, 29 x 22 In. .	1115.00
Table, Sewing, Federal, Curly Maple, Checkered Band, 2 Drawers, c.1825, 28 x 20 In.	3960.00
Table, Sewing, Federal, Figured Maple, Frieze Drawer, Tripod Snake Feet, 28 x 15 In.	1150.00
Table, Sewing, French Provincial, Walnut, Serpentine Shape, Cabriole Legs, 1700s, 27 x 23 In.	863.00
Table, Sewing, G. Stickley, No. 630, Drop Side, 2 Drawers, Wood Knobs, Signed, Label, 18 x 28 In.	1560.00
Table, Sewing, Hepplewhite, Mahogany, Ivory Inlay, 8-Sided, Annapolis, c.1805	5605.00
Table, Sewing, Lacquered, Gilt, Court Scenes, Lyre Supports, Chinese, 25 x 22 x 15 In.	1528.00
Table, Sewing, Lift Top, Mahogany, Octagonal Top, Satinwood Line Inlay, 1800s, 31 x 27 In. ...	259.00
Table, Sewing, Mahogany, Satinwood, Ivory Inlay, Cross-Stretcher, Carved Legs, c.1800	5125.00
Table, Sewing, Neoclassical, Mahogany, Poplar, Oak, 2 Drawers, Applied Columns, 30 x 20 In.	2115.00
Table, Sewing, Neoclassical, Rosewood, Grain Painted, Ormolu, Trestle, Baltimore, 30 x 21 In.	31250.00
Table, Sewing, Pine, Painted White, South Carolina..	524.00
Table, Sewing, Regency, Mahogany, 2 Drawers, Turned Legs, England, 1800s, 14 x 27 In.	345.00
Table, Sewing, Regency, Mahogany, Oxbow Front, Drawers, c.1820, 29 x 22 In.	529.00
Table, Sewing, Regency, Rosewood, Drawer, Drop Leaf, Saber Legs, Paw Feet, 1800s, 27 x 24 In. .	3231.00
Table, Sewing, Scrubbed Top, Tapered Legs, Green Paint, David Smith, 1900s, 30 x 60 In.	441.00
Table, Sewing, Shaker, Cherry, 3 Drawers, New Lebanon, N.Y., c.1840, 26 x 31 x 17 In.	58500.00
Table, Sewing, Shaker, Cherry, Drawer, Red Paint, Whitewater, Ohio, c.1840, 28 x 22 In.	761.00
Table, Sewing, Shaker, Drawer, Medial Shelf, Red Varnish, N.H., 1820, 27 x 13 In.	2340.00
Table, Sewing, Shaker, Painted, Drawer, 19th Century, 26 x 18 x 18 In.	561.00
Table, Sewing, Shaker, Pine, Drawer, Turned Legs, Ocher Grain Paint, Mass., c.1845, 24 x 18 In.	585.00
Table, Sewing, Shaker, Pine, Tapered Legs, Beaded Apron, Drawer, c.1890, 30 x 32 In.	499.00
Table, Sewing, Shaker, Pine Top, Maple Skirt, Turned Legs, Red Finish, c.1825, 28 In.	1287.00
Table, Sewing, Shaker, Poplar, Chestnut, 2-Board Top, Brown Varnish, Enfield, c.1840, 33 x 48 In. .	702.00
Table, Sewing, Sheraton, Butternut, 2 Drawers, c.1820, 28 x 24 x 17 In.	715.00
Table, Sewing, Sheraton, Drawer, Spindle Legs, Overhanging Top, New England, 24 x 27 In. ..	288.00
Table, Sewing, Sheraton, Walnut, 3 Drawers, 19th Century, 29 x 29 In.	260.00
Table, Sewing, Tiger Maple, Veneer, Cartouche Shape Top, Drawers, Ohio, 29 x 23 In. ....*illus*	1725.00
Table, Sewing, Victorian, Mahogany, Bracket Supports, Drawer, Bag, Shaped Base, 29 x 18 In.	365.00
Table, Sewing, Walnut, Pine Top, Drawer, Red Paint Traces, c.1825, 30 x 27 In.	588.00
Table, Sewing, Wood, Folding, Carved, Trestle, Stretcher, Spain, Early 1800s, 35 x 76 x 38 In. .	960.00
Table, Sewing, Yellow Pine, 2 Drawers, Grained, Varnished, Tapered Legs, 1800s, 29 x 20 In. ..	489.00
Table, Sewing, Yellow Pine, 2 Drawers, Tapered Fluted Legs, Georgia, 1800s, 22 x 28 In.	2185.00
Table, Shaker, Birch, Pine, Red Stain, Drawer, Turned Legs, Enfield, N.H., c.1835, 27 x 30 In. .	10530.00
Table, Shaker, Cherry, Drop Leaf, Peg Construction, Overhanging Top, 1800s, 27 x 36 In.	384.00
Table, Sheraton, 2 Tiers, 5 Drawers, Stencil Designs, Tall Turned Legs, c.1820, 40 x 35 In.	378.00
Table, Sheraton, Cherry, Tiger Maple, Drawer, 19th Century, 28 x 20 x 18 In.	780.00
Table, Sheraton, Drop Leaf, 6 Legs, c.1840, 30 ½ x 49 In.	600.00
Table, Sheraton, Pine, 3-Board, Turned Legs, Painted, c.1875, 29 x 92 x 35 In.	1645.00
Table, Sheraton, Red Finish, Turned Legs, Wood Casters, c.1840, 29 x 36 In.	558.00
Table, Side, Art Nouveau, Pear Wood, Inlaid Blossoms, 3 Legs, Majorelle Freres, c.1890, 16 In.	660.00
Table, Side, Federal, Walnut, Beaded Frieze Drawer, Tapered Legs, c.1800, 29 x 24 x 17 In.	203.00
Table, Side, Federal, Walnut, Tapered Legs, 19th Century, 26 ½ x 18 x 18 In.	460.00
Table, Side, Florence Knoll, Chrome Legs, Walnut Top	350.00
Table, Side, G. Nakashima, Maple Top, Slatted Shelf, 21 x 36 x 25 ½ In.	1800.00
Table, Side, G. Nakashima, Walnut, Triangle Top, 3 Legs, 21 x 27 In.	2280.00
Table, Side, Grain Painted, Cutout Ends, 3 Scalloped Brackets, c.1835, 30 x 33 In.	770.00
Table, Side, Louis XV, Brass Mounted, Parquet, Book Spine Back, Shelf, 2 Drawers, 34 x 13 In.	1185.00
Table, Side, Louis XV Style, Inlaid Mixed Woods, 3 Leaves, Cabriole Legs, 29 x 19 x 20 In.	388.00
Table, Side, Louis XVI Style, Marble Top, Frieze Drawer, Oval, 29 x 24 x 16 In.	239.00
Table, Side, Mahogany, Leather Slant Front, Drawers, Bracket Feet, c.1900, 32 x 25 x 23 In.	478.00
Table, Side, Oak, Frieze Drawer, Baluster Legs, Block & Ball Feet, c.1850, 30 x 28 x 19 In.	450.00
Table, Side, Oak, Frieze Drawer, Turned Legs, Floor Box Stretcher, England, 1800s, 29 x 32 In.	177.00
Table, Side, Regency, Mahogany, Reeded Edge, Beaded Frieze Drawer, c.1800, 28 x 33 x 19 In.	478.00
Table, Side, Rosewood, Demilune, Carved, Curved, Fretwork, Gourds, Vines, c.1812, 34 x 41 In.	1320.00
Table, Side, Walnut, Shirt, Baluster Turned Legs, Disc Feet, c.1700, 31 x 48 x 24 In.	1645.00
Table, Side, William & Mary, Oak, Paneled Frieze Drawer, Turned Legs, 26 x 28 x 17 In.	831.00
Table, Spanish Baroque, Walnut, Through Tenons, Trestle Base, Stretcher, 28 x 58 In.	3220.00
Table, Spanish, Carved, Plank Top, Apron Drawers, Spain, 18 ½ x 53 ½ In.	1410.00
Table, Spanish Colonial, Walnut, Plank Top, Batten Skirt, Leaf Carved Drawers, 31 x 47 In. ...	2400.00
Table, Square Marble Top, 2 Chrome L-Shape Metal Bases, 1970s, 21 x 17 In., Pair..................	570.00
Table, Stacking, Georgian Style, Mahogany, Inlaid, Strings, Fans, Flower Heads, 4 Piece	119.00
Table, Stacking, Giotto Stoppino, Molded Plastic, Kartell, c.1968, 18 x 16 In., 3 Piece ....*illus*	480.00
Table, Stacking, Tony Paul, Tempo Group, Laminated Plywood, Steel Frame, Ball Feet, 14 x 18 In.	220.00
Table, Stickley Bros., Drawer, Side Vertical Slats, Hammered Hardware, 14 x 30 In.	1800.00
Table, Stickley Bros., Leather, Hexagonal, Tapered Legs, 42 x 42 x 30 In.	2400.00

Furniture, Table, Tea, Queen Anne, Maple, 2-Board Top, Octagonal, 1700s, 27 x 34 In.
$5664.00

Furniture, Table, Tea, Walnut, Baluster, Ring-Turned Legs, Stretcher, c.1850, 27 x 30 In.
$9440.00

Furniture, Table, Tilt Top, Regency Style, Mahogany, Splayed Legs, 28 x 54 In.
$1800.00

Furniture, Table, Tray, Butler's, Regency, Mahogany, Turned Baluster Stand, 1900s, 30 x 40 In.
$359.00

Furniture, Table, Tray, Tole,
Faux Bamboo Stand, 1800s, 22 x 30 In.
$805.00

Furniture, Table, Walnut, Satinwood,
Paneled Cabinet, Austria, c.1880,
59 x 46 In.
$1140.00

Furniture, Table, William & Mary,
Maple, Stretcher, Drawer, c.1725,
28 x 39 In.
$2596.00

Furniture, Table, Work,
Country Sheraton, Cherry,
Tiger Maple Drawer, c.1840
$144.00

Table, Stickley, Oak, Round, Stretcher Shelf, Drawers, Doors, c.1915, 30 x 36 In.	705.00
Table, Stone, Round, Cluster Column Support, Stepped Square Base, 43 In.	1645.00
Table, Surfboard, 3 Tiers, Heywood-Wakefield Co., 22 x 31 In.	70.00
Table, Sycamore, Vellum, Peach Mirror Glass, Brass, c.1950s, 24 x 22 x 14 In.	4183.00
Table, Tavern, Ash, Rectangular, 33 x 38 In.	895.00
Table, Tavern, Blue Over Red Paint, Early 19th Century, 27 x 35 x 25 In.	1300.00
Table, Tavern, French Provincial, Cherry, Serpentine Frieze, 30 x 39 x 23 In.	209.00
Table, Tavern, Hepplewhite, Cherry, Drawer, Breadboard Top, Blue Paint, 29 x 42 In.	705.00
Table, Tavern, Hepplewhite, Drawer, Overhanging Top, 44 x 24 In.	400.00
Table, Tavern, Hepplewhite, Single-Board Top, Drawer, Red Paint	1323.00
Table, Tavern, Hepplewhite Style, Maple, Scrubbed Overhanging Top, 44 x 24-In. Top	443.00
Table, Tavern, Maple, Button Foot, New England, 18th Century, 26 x 31 x 23 In.	1243.00
Table, Tavern, Maple, Pine, Turned Splayed Legs, c.1720, 25 x 29 In.	885.00
Table, Tavern, Maple, Scrubbed Overhanging Top, Drawer, Stretcher Base, c.1730, 29 In.	1121.00
Table, Tavern, Mixed Woods, Gray Paint, 1900s, 27 x 30 In.	411.00
Table, Tavern, Pine, 31 ½ x 76 In.	400.00
Table, Tavern, Pine, Drawer, 28 ¾ x 59 ½ In.	240.00
Table, Tavern, Pine, Drawer, 31 ½ x 76 In.	410.00
Table, Tavern, Pine, Maple, Red Paint, Splayed Marlboro Legs, 26 x 40 In.	2607.00
Table, Tavern, Pine, Stretcher Base, Oval Top, Turned Legs, c.1750, 24 x 29 In. .... *illus*	9440.00
Table, Tavern, Pine Top, Maple Base, Breadboard Ends, Drawer, 25 x 43 x 27 In.	517.50
Table, Tavern, Queen Anne, Cherry, Overhanging Top, Tapered Legs, 26 x 32 x 25 In.	1610.00
Table, Tavern, Queen Anne, Cherry, Shaped Top, Pad Feet, New England, 1700s, 32 x 27 In.	415.00
Table, Tavern, Queen Anne, Drawer, Red Paint, c.1985, 30 x 42 In.	178.00
Table, Tavern, Queen Anne, Oval, 18th Century, 27 x 32 x 25 In.	2825.00
Table, Tavern, Queen Anne, Oval, Arched End Aprons, Tapered Turned Legs, 25 x 27 In.	620.00
Table, Tavern, Queen Anne, Pine, Drawer, Overhanging Top, c.1770, 28 x 31 In.	990.00
Table, Tavern, Queen Anne, Pine, Red Stain, Scrubbed Oval Top, Pad Feet, c.1760, 26 x 38 In.	1528.00
Table, Tavern, Queen Anne, Red Paint, Pad Feet, 28 x 31 x 20 In.	5085.00
Table, Tavern, Queen Anne Style, Walnut, 29 x 44 In.	390.00
Table, Tavern, Queen Anne, Walnut, Poplar, Drawer, Box Stretcher, c.1750, 28 x 50 In.	705.00
Table, Tavern, Scrubbed Pine, Turned Splayed Legs, Scalloped Apron, c.1750, 27 x 30 In.	7000.00
Table, Tavern, Softwood, Stretcher, Pie Board Ends, 26 ½ x 37 ¾ x 25 In.	678.00
Table, Tavern, Stretcher Base, 18th Century, 31 x 22 In.	660.00
Table, Tavern, Tiger Maple, Shaped, Cut Corners, Scalloped Skirt, 27 x 36 x 23 In.	413.00
Table, Tavern, Walnut, 2 Drawers, 20th Century, 29 ½ x 50 x 34 In.	130.00
Table, Tavern, Walnut, 29 x 58 x 35 ¾ In.	515.00
Table, Tavern, Walnut, Drawer, Box Stretcher, 18th Century, 29 x 27 In.	1900.00
Table, Tavern, Walnut, Removable Top, 2 Drawers, Pad Feet, 18th Century, 29 x 40 In.	2400.00
Table, Tavern, Walnut, Scrubbed Top, Blue Painted Base, Square Legs, c.1800, 27 x 51 In.	1150.00
Table, Tavern, William & Mary, Maple, Oval, Aprons, Box Stretcher, 23 x 29 x 23 In.	295.00
Table, Tavern, William & Mary, Oak, Pine, Flat Stretchers, 31 x 60 In.	560.00
Table, Tavern, William & Mary Style, Walnut, 30 x 30 x 28 ½ In.	300.00
Table, Tavern, Windsor, Yellow Paint, Circular Top, Beaded Skirt, 26 x 26 In.	165.00
Table, Tea, Cherry, Tilt Top, Serpentine Molded, 3-Footed, Pad Feet, Hartford, Conn., c.1780	685.00
Table, Tea, Chippendale, Mahogany, Molded Edge, Spiral Support, Tripod Base, 29 x 28 In.	863.00
Table, Tea, Chippendale, Mahogany, Tilt Top, Birdcage, Fluted Standard, c.1770, 27 In.	1872.00
Table, Tea, Chippendale, Mahogany, Tilt Top, Dish, Revolving, Tripod, Snake Feet, 29 x 33 In.	840.00
Table, Tea, Chippendale, Mahogany, Tilt Top, Single Board, Tripod Base, 1700s, 28 x 32 In.	1380.00
Table, Tea, Chippendale, Maple, Tilt Top, Cabriole Legs, c.1775, 26 x 31 In.	1410.00
Table, Tea, Chippendale, Walnut, Tilt Top, Tripod, Pennsylvania, c.1770, 28 x 33 In.	7500.00
Table, Tea, Curly Maple, Cherry, Tilt Top, Turned Base, Tripod Feet, c.1800, 28 x 36 In.	411.00
Table, Tea, G. Stickley, No. 439, Legs Exposed Through Top, Round, 26 In.	4600.00
Table, Tea, G. Stickley, No. 654, Round, Cross Stretchers, Dark Finish, Label, 24 x 29 In.	1610.00
Table, Tea, Georgian, Mahogany, Tilt Top, Shaped Top, Pad Feet, 1700s, 27 x 29 In.	754.00
Table, Tea, Lacquered, Mother-Of-Pearl Inlay, Chinese	81.00
Table, Tea, Mahogany, Fruitwood Flower, Marquetry, c.1900, 31 x 31 x 25 In.	9145.00
Table, Tea, Mahogany, Tilt Top, Birdcage Column, Tripod Base, 1700s, 28 x 34 In.	690.00
Table, Tea, Mahogany, Tilt Top, Birdcage Support, 27 x 26 In.	550.00
Table, Tea, Mahogany, Tilt Top, Birdcage, Tripod Base, 1700s, 26 x 32 In. .... *illus*	5192.00
Table, Tea, Mahogany, Tilt Top, Carved, Shells, Flowers, Slipper Feet, England, 28 x 28 In.	2950.00
Table, Tea, Queen Anne Style, Mahogany, Shaped Skirt, Candle Slides, c.1966, 27 x 29 In.	264.00
Table, Tea, Queen Anne Style, Mahogany, Tilt Top, 3-Footed, 30 x 36 In.	300.00
Table, Tea, Queen Anne, Birch, Maple, 8-Sided Top, 1700s, 25 x 28 In. .... *illus*	10620.00
Table, Tea, Queen Anne, Curly Maple, Shaped Corners, 1900s, 28 x 33 In.	382.00
Table, Tea, Queen Anne, Mahogany, Dish Top, Cabriole Legs, 18th Century, 27 x 31 x 21 In.	2390.00

Table, Tea, Queen Anne, Mahogany, Tilt Top, 3-Plank Top, Tripod Base, 26 x 33 In.	633.00
Table, Tea, Queen Anne, Mahogany, Tilt Top, Late 18th Century, 27 x 31 In.	240.00
Table, Tea, Queen Anne, Maple, 2-Board Top, Octagonal, 1700s, 27 x 34 In. ....*illus*	5664.00
Table, Tea, Queen Anne, Maple, Drop Leaf, Cutout Apron, c.1850, 35 x 36 In.	4148.00
Table, Tea, Queen Anne, Maple, Pine, Oval Top, Splayed Legs, New England, 1700s, 24 x 32 In.	948.00
Table, Tea, Queen Anne, Walnut, Dish Top, Birdcage, Pad Feet, c.1780, 29 x 33 In.	1800.00
Table, Tea, Queen Anne, Walnut, Tilt Top, Birdcage, Cabriole Legs, Pad Feet, c.1770, 27 In.	936.00
Table, Tea, Walnut, Baluster, Ring-Turned Legs, Stretcher, c.1850, 27 x 30 In. ....*illus*	9440.00
Table, Tea, William & Mary, Maple, 24 ½ x 33 ½ x 11 ½ In.	2415.00
Table, Tilt Top, Black Lacquer, Gilt Figures In Garden, Trefoil Base, Paw Feet, 32 x 33 In.	288.00
Table, Tilt Top, Ebonized, Gilt, Flowers, Baluster Pedestal, Tripod Base, 1800s, 29 In.	568.00
Table, Tilt Top, Grain Paint, Birdcage, Center Post, Iron Latch, c.1820, 25 x 25 ½ In.	12500.00
Table, Tilt Top, Inlaid Mother-Of-Pearl, Painted, Castle Landscape, 26 x 42 In.	127.00
Table, Tilt Top, Mahogany, Banner & Pedestal, Floral Edge, Irish, c.1780, 28 x 30 In.	575.00
Table, Tilt Top, Mahogany, Birdcage Support, Tripod Base, England, 1700s, 28 x 33 In.	1534.00
Table, Tilt Top, Mahogany, Round, Carved, Paw Feet, c.1830, 28 x 42 In.	7638.00
Table, Tilt Top, Mahogany, Round, Crossbanded, Ring-Turned Column, 30 x 49 In.	575.00
Table, Tilt Top, Mahogany, Round, Tripod Base, Pad Feet, 1790s, 30 x 31 In.	395.00
Table, Tilt Top, Maple, Scalloped Corner, Cherry Baluster Support, c.1800, 28 x 30 In.	353.00
Table, Tilt Top, Neoclassical, Mahogany, Exotic Inlays, Round, Faceted Stem, Paw Feet, 28 x 47 In.	9560.00
Table, Tilt Top, Neoclassical, Mahogany, Flame Veneer, Figured Apron, Paw Feet, 28 x 42 In. ..	7638.00
Table, Tilt Top, Regency, Mahogany, Carved, Reeded Top, Tapered Stem, Casters, 28 x 62 In. ...	1175.00
Table, Tilt Top, Regency, Mahogany, Gilt, Round, Column Pedestal, 3-Part Base, 29 x 55 In. ...	1800.00
Table, Tilt Top, Regency, Mahogany, Round Top, Column Pedestal, Casters, 30 x 52 In.	1800.00
Table, Tilt Top, Regency Style, Mahogany, Splayed Legs, 28 x 54 In. ....*illus*	1800.00
Table, Tilt Top, Regency Style, Mahogany, Turned Standard, 28 In.	1800.00
Table, Tray, Butler's, Mahogany, 4 Hinged Leaves, Handles, Victorian, 18 x 37 In.	652.00
Table, Tray, Butler's, Mahogany, Brass Handles, Mounts, X-Frame Stand, c.1820, 39 x 28 x 19 In.	575.00
Table, Tray, Butler's, Mahogany, Finger Cutouts, Folding Stand, England, c.1850, 26 x 29 In. .	1500.00
Table, Tray, Butler's, Regency, Mahogany, Turned Baluster Stand, 1900s, 30 x 40 In. ....*illus*	359.00
Table, Tray, Butler's, Faux Bamboo, Tole, Handles, Stenciled Band, 28-In. Tray	377.00
Table, Tray, Butler's, Oak, Full Gallery, Pierced Handles, 19th Century, 33 x 28 In.	259.00
Table, Tray, Butler's, Papier-Mache, Black Lacquer, Raised Edge, Leaves, Butterflies, 20 x 29 In.	1680.00
Table, Tray, Butler's, Red Lacquer, Ormolu Mounted, Flowers, Handles, 21 x 31 In.	230.00
Table, Tray, Butler's, Regency, Tole, Black, Silver, Gold Chinoiserie, Flowers, 14 x 10 In.	1150.00
Table, Tray, Edwardian, Mahogany, Satinwood, Oval, Brass, Bellflower Inlay, Shell, c.1890, 27 x 18 In.	1450.00
Table, Tray, George III Style, Mahogany, 4 Flaps, X-Stretcher, 1900s, 16 x 30 In.	120.00
Table, Tray, Pine, Red Paint, Scrolled Back, Stretchers, c.1820, 30 x 25 In.	889.00
Table, Tray, Rosewood, 3 Folding Trays, Storage Cabinet, Selig, Denmark, 18 x 19 In.	360.00
Table, Tray, Sheraton, Mahogany, 2 Divided Drawers, 1800s, 26 x 21 In.	235.00
Table, Tray, Tole, Faux Bamboo Stand, 1800s, 22 x 30 In. ....*illus*	805.00
Table, Tray, Tole, Faux Bamboo Stand, Tropical Bird, Vines, c.1900, 22 x 25 x 20 In.	748.00
Table, Tray, Venetian Rococo Style, Serpentine Edge, Raised Scroll Toes, c.1900, 18 x 24 x 17 In. .	179.00
Table, Tray, Victorian, Peacock, Flowers, Painted, 1900s, 20 x 29 In.	178.00
Table, Tray, Wendell August, Aluminum, Hammered, Stamped, Engraved, 1937, 24 x 18 In. ...	240.00
Table, Tray, Wood, Oval, 4 Hinges, Hand Grips, Square Legs, c.1900, 28 x 36 In.	118.00
Table, Trestle, Arts & Crafts, Leather Top, Vertical Slat Base Supports, Lower Shelf, 48 x 30 In.	450.00
Table, Trestle, Baroque, Walnut, Frieze Drawer, Spain, 30 x 41 In.	1422.00
Table, Trestle, Baroque, Walnut, Scrolled Legs, Stretchers, Iberia, 30 x 44 x 20 In.	1007.00
Table, Trestle, Pine, Oak, Trestle Supports, Pegged Stretcher, 29 x 77 In.	411.00
Table, Trestle, Renaissance Revival, Walnut, Carved Leaves, Shield, Italy, 26 x 37 x 18 In.	593.00
Table, V. Kagan, Walnut, Free-Form, Brass, Glass Tiles, 15 x 63 ¾ x 32 In.	37500.00
Table, Victorian, Brown, Black Marble Top, Carved, Shaped Legs, Stretcher, 29 x 48 In.	920.00
Table, Victorian, Burl, Tilt Top, Oval, Leaf Carved Support, 4 Legs, 30 x 58 In.	1093.00
Table, Victorian, Burl Walnut, Mahogany, Tilting Oval Top, Turned Vase Shape Base, 30 x 50 In.	1560.00
Table, Victorian, Cast Iron, Wooden Frame, Gray Slate Turtle Top, 27 ¼ In.	81.00
Table, Victorian, Mahogany, Bowfront, Drawer, 31 ¼ x 20 x 19 In.	119.00
Table, Victorian, Mahogany, Brown Marble, Carved Base, 29 x 37 In.	354.00
Table, Victorian, Oval Marble Top, 4 Shaped Legs, 27 ½ x 29 In.	248.00
Table, Victorian, Rosewood, Marble Turtle Top, Brass Casters, 32 x 21 x 29 In.	675.00
Table, Victorian, Tiger Maple, Figured, Carved, England, c.1900, 28 x 32 ¾ x 23 ½ In.	489.00
Table, Victorian, Walnut, Marble Top, 4-Footed, 30 x 15 In.	475.00
Table, Victorian, Walnut, Marble Top, Carved Skirt, 4-Legged Pedestal, 29 x 31 In.	184.00
Table, Victorian, Walnut, Marble Top, Shaped, Carved Stem, Feet, 29 x 29 In.	115.00
Table, Victorian, White Marble Top, Carved, Pedestal, Stretchers, 30 x 30 In.	144.00
Table, Wake, Georgian, Drop Leaf, Plain Skirt, Square Legs, 29 x 56 In.	1293.00

F

Furniture, Table, Writing, Spanish, Walnut, Chip Carved Drawers, Iron Braces, 1600s, 33 x 44 In.
$4115.00

Furniture, Tantalus, Burrwood, Cut Glass Decanters, Chapman's Patent Tag, c.1890, 13 x 10 In.
$210.00

Furniture, Umbrella Stand, Aesthetic Revival, Iron, Cross, Circle, Sunflowers, c.1890, 34 x 24 In.
$540.00

Furniture, Umbrella Stand, Umbrella Stand, Arts & Crafts, Carved, Painted, Pyrographics, 28 ½ In.
$805.00

Furniture, Umbrella Stand, Locking, Cast Iron, Fluted Drip Tray, Ring Handle, c.1860, 40 In. $92.00

Furniture, Vanity, 2 Leatherette Wrapped Drawer Banks, 2 Pedestals, Mirror, 57 x 45 In. $1020.00

The Skyscraper

Paul T. Frankl, the American furniture designer, hired cabinetmakers to make his furniture. Pieces from the 1920s and '30s are rare and high-priced. Skyscraper bookcases can sell for over $50,000. In the late 1930s, he had his designs mass-produced, and these pieces are less expensive. His designs were often copied.

Table, Walnut Inlay, Round, Ebonized, Gilt, Eagle, Shield, Flags, Bulbous Pedestal, c.1876, 28 In.	8225.00
Table, Walnut, 2-Board Top, Round Corners, 2 Drawers, Tapered Legs, 1800s, 29 x 29 In.	354.00
Table, Walnut, Beaded Tilt Top, Angelic Figure & Child, Round, 22 x 31 In.	695.00
Table, Walnut, Black Marble Top, Oblong, Eagle Supports, Carved Legs, Claw Feet, 29 x 29 In.	633.00
Table, Walnut, Carved, 2 Drawers, Shelf, Spain, 27 x 39 x 14 In.	600.00
Table, Walnut, Drawer, Stretcher Base, 27 x 36 In.	259.00
Table, Walnut, Drawer, Turned Legs, Southern, 1800s, 29 x 24 In.	431.00
Table, Walnut, Folding, Round Top, Shaped Stretchers, c.1875, 26 ½ x 23 ½ In.	850.00
Table, Walnut, Frame, Shaped Glass Top, Scandinavia, 24 x 20 In., Pair	450.00
Table, Walnut, Glass Top, Sculptured Legs, Open Framework, 28 x 28 In.	600.00
Table, Walnut, Marble Top, Oval, Carved Eagle Head Supports, Legs, T. Brooks, 37 x 31 In.	1725.00
Table, Walnut, Pietra Dura Marble Inlay, Parrots, 3-Footed, Signed, Rome, 1861, 30 x 33 In.	4000.00
Table, Walnut, Poplar, 2 Drawers, Turned Legs, Pennsylvania, 1800s, 30 x 53 In.	353.00
Table, Walnut, Rough Hewn, 2-Board Top, Trestle Base, Drawer, 30 x 39 ½ x 25 In.	2040.00
Table, Walnut, Round, Ebonized, Gilt Incised, Vase Shape Stem, Disc Feet, c.1875, 29 In.	4700.00
Table, Walnut, Round Top, Gallery Surround, Inset Marble, France, 1800s, 32 x 16 In.	502.00
Table, Walnut, Satinwood, Paneled Cabinet, Austria, c.1880, 59 x 46 In. ....*illus*	1140.00
Table, Walnut, Spanish Colonial, Plank Top, Batten Skirt, Carved Drawers, 31 x 47 In.	2350.00
Table, Walnut, Tilt Top, Round, Marquetry Top, Tripod Base, 29 x 35 In.	1610.00
Table, Walnut, Yellow Pine, Drawer, Ring-Turned Legs, Southern, 30 x 47 In.	3250.00
Table, Water, Yellow Pine, Lower Shelf, Spanish Brown Paint, Georgia, c.1850, 34 x 34 In.	5290.00
Table, White Marble Top, Oval, Carved Mahogany Legs, Apron, 16 x 34 In.	59.00
Table, William & Mary Style, Gateleg, Shaped Top, Stretchers, 26 ¾ x 27 x 28 In.	360.00
Table, William & Mary, Elm, Drawer, Scalloped Skirt, Turned Stretcher, c.1720, 29 x 26 In.	690.00
Table, William & Mary, Maple, Gateleg, Turned Legs, c.1720, 27 x 40 x 47 In.	7110.00
Table, William & Mary, Maple, Stretcher, Drawer, c.1725, 28 x 39 In. ....*illus*	2596.00
Table, William & Mary, Walnut, Inlay, Shaped Skirt & X-Stretcher, 29 x 31 In.	2510.00
Table, William IV, Brass, Inlaid Rosewood, Round Top, Scalloped Skirt, c.1830, 29 x 47 In.	2350.00
Table, William IV, Mahogany, Carved, Serpentine Top, Fluted Frieze, Drawers, 30 x 48 In.	1955.00
Table, William IV, Mahogany, Tilt Top, Round, Gilt Tooled Leather Insert, 1800s, 28 x 48 In.	1495.00
Table, William IV, Rosewood, Round, Mounted Brass Rosettes, Paw Feet, c.1830, 29 x 47 In.	2350.00
Table, Wine, Pine, Circular Hinged Top, Trestle Base, 19th Century, 29 x 42 In.	777.00
Table, Wine, Regency, Mahogany, Crescent Shape, Drop Leaf, Metal, 1800s, 39 x 66 In.	1380.00
Table, Wine, Trestle Base, Round, Tilt Top, 20th Century, 27 x 47 x 47 In.	489.00
Table, Wine, Walnut, Gateleg, Oval Top, Shoe Feet, 1800s, 29 x 52 In.	940.00
Table, Wood, Carved Dragon Legs, Stretcher Shelf, Chinese, 29 x 55 In.	4313.00
Table, Wood, Mother-Of-Pearl Inlay, Shaped Apron, 6 Legs, 19 x 39 In.	657.00
Table, Wood, Painted, Round, Brass Band, 3 Metal Legs, Brass Hooves, 35 x 19 In.	144.00
Table, Work, Country Sheraton, Cherry, Tiger Maple Drawer, c.1840 ....*illus*	144.00
Table, Wormley, Italian Travertine Marble Top, Mahogany Legs, Leather Feet, Dunbar, 28 x 21 In., Pair	1200.00
Table, Wormley, Mahogany, 2 Open Shelves, Dunbar, 24 x 25 In.	330.00
Table, Wormley, Mahogany, Rectangular, Leaves, 1950s, Dunbar, 66 x 30 In.	480.00
Table, Wormley, Mahogany, Stepped, Dunbar, 24 x 25 In.	120.00
Table, Wormley, Wedge, Wood Grain Laminate, Mahogany Legs, Dunbar, 1950s, 21 x 23 In.	270.00
Table, Writing, Caryatid Mounts, 3 Drawers, 5 Drawer Facade, Paw Feet, c.1800, 51 x 58 x 27 In.	1613.00
Table, Writing, Louis Philippe, Bonheur Du Jour, Mirror, Drawers, Leather, c.1800, 45 x 31 In.	1080.00
Table, Writing, Louis XV, Faux Tortoiseshell Top, Bronze, Brass Inlay, 2 Drawers, 30 x 56 In.	830.00
Table, Writing, Louis XV, Flower Brass Mounts, Ebonized Leather Top, 1900s, 30 x 54 In.	1067.00
Table, Writing, Louis XVI, Kingwood, Inset Leather Surface, Drawers, 30 x 40 In.	2640.00
Table, Writing, Louis XVI, Mahogany, Brass Mounted, Marble Gallery Top, 51 x 29 In.	1058.00
Table, Writing, Louis XVI Revival, Tulipwood Inlay, Bronze Gallery, Leather, 30 x 33 In.	1778.00
Table, Writing, Louis XVI Style, Bronze Mounted, Parquetry, Early 1900s, 29 x 43 In.	7930.00
Table, Writing, Louis XVI Style, Mahogany, 4 Drawers, Fluted Legs, 30 x 51 x 27 In.	255.00
Table, Writing, Mahogany, Burled Top, Carved, Drawer, American, 30 x 31 x 18 In.	4406.00
Table, Writing, Mahogany, Gallery Surround, 3 Frieze Drawers, England, 1800s, 34 x 46 In.	797.00
Table, Writing, Mahogany, Inlaid, Drawers, Gilt Lion Mask Pulls, c.1800, 28 x 35 x 18 In.	690.00
Table, Writing, Marquetry, Ormolu, 2 Doors, 2 Drawers, Shelves, Continental, 36 x 45 In.	531.00
Table, Writing, Napoleon III, Mahogany, Bone Inlay, Gilt Brass Mounted, Drawer, 29 x 51 In.	2640.00
Table, Writing, Regency, Mahogany, Inlaid, Upholstered, England, 19th Century, 45 x 22 x 3 In.	240.00
Table, Writing, Regency, Mahogany, Lift Top, Reeded Legs, Banding, Ormolu, c.1825, 35 x 47 In.	2880.00
Table, Writing, Regency, Satinwood, Mahogany, Gilt Tooled Leather, 5 Drawers, 32 x 51 x 28 In.	4740.00
Table, Writing, Satinwood, Tooled Leather, Adjustable, Drawer, 2 Supports, 29 x 19 In.	403.00
Table, Writing, Spanish, Walnut, Chip Carved Drawers, Iron Braces, 1600s, 33 x 44 In. ....*illus*	4115.00
Table, Writing, Victorian, Walnut, Kidney Shape, Slanted Surface, 35 x 48 x 26 In.	1067.00
Table, Writing, Walnut, Marquetry, Folding Top, Interior Compartments, 1800s, 31 x 33 In.	920.00
Table, Yellow Pine, 2-Board Top, Vine, Leaf Design Traces, Brown, Red Paint, 31 x 35 In.	575.00

Table, Yellow Pine, Demilune, Triangular Skirt, Tapered Legs, 1800s, 35 x 33 In.	690.00
Table, Yellow Pine, Nailed, Dovetailed Drawer, Tapered Legs, Painted, c.1950, 29 x 29 In.	1380.00
Table, Yellow Pine, Round, 4-Board Top, Square Skirt, Georgia, 1800s, 29 x 41 In.	575.00
Table, Yew, Double Pedestal, Reeded Tripod Base, Casters, c.1900, 29 x 70 x 44 In.	597.00
Tabouret, Arts & Crafts, Circular Top, Square Apron, Lower Shelf, 16 x 20 In.	240.00
Tabouret, Arts & Crafts, Square Top, Flared Base, 14 x 14 x 18 In.	270.00
Tabouret, Arts & Crafts, Square Top, Shaped Corners, Slab Sides, Vertical Cutouts, Shelf, 12 x 20 In.	420.00
Tabouret, G. Stickley, Mahogany, 20 x 20 In.	4880.00
Tabouret, G. Stickley, Square Top, Apron, 14 x 14 x 20 In.	240.00
Tabouret, L. & J.G. Stickley, No. 558, 8-Sided Top, Arched Cross Stretcher Base, Signed, 15 x 18 In.	1020.00
Tabouret, L. & J.G. Stickley, No. 559, Octagonal, Arched Cross Stretcher, 18 x 18 x 20 In.	1265.00
Tabouret, L. & J.G. Stickley, Oak, Square Top, Cut Corners, Arched Stretchers, Post, 20 x 18 In.	652.00
Tabouret, Limbert, No. 231, Circular Cutouts, Signed, 12 x 12 x 12 In.	1200.00
Tabouret, Mahogany, Arts & Crafts, Octagonal, Slab Legs, Cutout Design, 18 x 19 In.	180.00
Tabouret, Pink Marble, Ornate Carved Apron, Legs, Chinese, 1800s, 23 x 22 In.	1150.00
Tabouret, Pink Marble Top, Carved Apron, Legs, Chinese, 1800s, 19 x 16 In.	575.00
Tabouret, Rosewood Top, Carved Apron, Legs, Chinese, 1800s, 22 x 18 In.	259.00
Tabouret, Stickley Bros., No. 138, Square Top, Mackmurdo Foot, Signed, 14 x 14 x 18 In.	510.00
Tantalus, Burrwood, Cut Glass Decanters, Chapman's Patent Tag, c.1890, 13 x 10 In. ....*illus*	210.00
Tea Cart, Aalto, Birch, Birch Plywood, c.1945, 29 ¾ x 32 x 18 In.	4270.00
Tea Cart, Art Deco, Metal Frame, Wood Shelves, Oval, Casters, 31 x 17 In.	201.00
Tea Cart, Mahogany, Pollard Oak, 2 Tiers, Square Collared, 29 x 47 ½ x 21 In.	1783.00
Teapoy, Regency, Mahogany, Coffin Shape, Pedestal Base, 4 Curled Legs, 30 x 22 In.	460.00
Teapoy, William IV, Rosewood, Sarcophagus Top, Waisted, Lobed Stem, 1800s, 33 x 16 x 14 In.	836.00
Teapoy, William IV, Rosewood, Stepped Top, 2 Lidded Interior Caddies, c.1830, 17 x 15 In.	3850.00
Trolley, Aalto, Birch, Laminated, Wood Wheels, c.1935-36, 21 ½ x 35 x 18 In.	1912.00
Trolley, Edwardian, Mahogany, Brass Mounted, Glazed Doors, Low Shelf, 32 x 28 In.	1175.00
Trolley, Laminated Birch, 30 x 32 x 18 In.	2032.00
Trolley, Victorian, Oak, 3 Shelves, Top-Shaped Feet, Casters, 19th Century, 48 x 54 x 20 ½ In. ..	1080.00
Umbrella Stand, Aesthetic Revival, Iron, Cross, Circle, Sunflowers, c.1890, 34 x 24 In. .....*illus*	540.00
Umbrella Stand, Art Nouveau, Beech, Scrolled, Zinc Pan, c.1930, 26 x 22 In.	806.00
Umbrella Stand, Arts & Crafts, Carved, Painted, Pyrographics, 28 ½ In. ....*illus*	805.00
Umbrella Stand, Bear Above Mirror, Adult Bear Base, Carved, Black Forest, 78 In.	4140.00
Umbrella Stand, Brass, Convex Front, Woman & Boy, Windmill, Ship, c.1875, 34 x 12 In.	201.00
Umbrella Stand, Cast Iron, Duck's Head Finial, White Paint, England, 19th Century, 24 ½ In.	300.00
Umbrella Stand, Eastlake, Wood, Carved Crest, Iron Basin, 38 ½ In.	475.00
Umbrella Stand, Leather, Papier-Mache, Painted, 18 x 9 In.	150.00
Umbrella Stand, Locking, Cast Iron, Fluted Drip Tray, Ring Handle, c.1860, 40 In. ....*illus*	92.00
Umbrella Stand, Oval, Fish, Reeds, Stork, Lavender, Gold Highlights, 23 In.	250.00
Umbrella Stand, Regency Style, Mahogany, 19th Century, 28 x 24 In.	165.00
Umbrella Stand, Victorian, Cast Iron, Cross Inside Circle, Flowers, 34 x 24 x 10 In.	500.00
Urn Stand, Hardwood, Carved, Chinese, 36 x 14 In., Pair..	230.00
Vanity, 2 Leatherette Wrapped Drawer Banks, 2 Pedestals, Mirror, 57 x 45 In. ....*illus*	1020.00
Vanity, Art Deco, Blond Wood, Double Gourd, Drawers, Bench, 61 x 54 x 20 In.	359.00
Vanity, Baroque Style, Walnut, Painted, Carved, Arched Mirror, Side Cupboards, 57 x 53 In. ...	1846.00
Vanity, Leon Jallot, Elm Burl, Amaranthe, Mahogany, c.1925-30, 48 x 47 x 20 In.	3107.00
Vanity, Queen Anne, Lacquer, Beveled Mirror, Slant Lid, Fitted Interior, Chinese, 35 x 16 In. ...	1170.00
Vitrine, Beech, Lined Interior Base, Glazed Lid, Sides, 6 ½ x 18 In.	300.00
Vitrine, Chippendale, Pagoda Shape, 2 Glazed Doors, Lit Mirror Interior, Chinese, 75 x 39 In.	460.00
Vitrine, Curved Glass Door, Gilt Bronze Gallery, Mounts, Lower Shelf, France, 44 x 67 In.	3450.00
Vitrine, Fruitwood, Hinged Glass Top, Lined Compartment, Drawers, France, 28 x 24 In.	881.00
Vitrine, Fruitwood, Lined Compartment, 2 Drawers, France, 1800s, 24 x 28 In.	882.00
Vitrine, Louis XV, Bronze Mounts, Tortoiseshell Veneer, Ornate, 14 In.	4600.00
Vitrine, Louis XV, Gilt, Flower Crest, Curved Glazed Door, Pictorial Panels, 33 x 77 In.	2006.00
Vitrine, Louis XV, Mahogany, Ormolu, Glass Paneled Door, Lower Painted Panel, 68 x 30 In. ..	575.00
Vitrine, Louis XV Style, Gilt Brass Mounted, Vernis Martin Lacquer, 74 x 42 In. ....*illus*	2400.00
Vitrine, Louis XV Style, Heart Shape, Floral Marquetry, Glass Insert, Hinged Lid, c.1900, 29 x 28 In.	1320.00
Vitrine, Louis XV Style, Pierced Shell Pediment, Bombe Base, Gilt, 81 x 32 In.	881.00
Vitrine, Louis XVI, Bronze, Mahogany, Vernis Martin Lacquer, Arched Cornice, Bombe, 74 x 33 In.	2468.00
Vitrine, Louis XVI, Mahogany, Pine, Vernis Martin Lacquer, Putti Scene, c.1890, 55 x 35 In. ...	705.00
Vitrine, Louis XVI Style, Boulle, Black Lacquer, Shaped Top, Beveled Glass Panel, 31 x 29 In. .	230.00
Vitrine, Louis XVI Style, Fruitwood, Carved Crest, Panel Door, 67 x 34 x 14 In.	388.00
Vitrine, Louis XVI Style, Mahogany, Line Inlay, Ormolu Mounts, France, 72 x 44 In. ....*illus*	1053.00
Vitrine, Louis XVI Style, Marble, Paneled Frieze, Turned Tapered Feet, c.1875, 55 x 27 x 12 In.	1725.00

Furniture, Vitrine, Louis XV Style, Gilt Brass Mounted, Vernis Martin Lacquer, 74 x 42 In. $2400.00

Furniture, Vitrine, Louis XVI Style, Mahogany, Line Inlay, Ormolu Mounts, France, 72 x 44 In. $1053.00

Furniture, Wardrobe, Faux Bamboo, Bird's-Eye Maple, Pine, Glazed Doors, c.1900, 86 x 49 In. $944.00

F

Furniture, Washstand, Corner, Hepplewhite, Mahogany, Inlaid, Shelf, 1800s, 43 x 25 In.
$374.00

Furniture, Wastebasket, Lakeside Craftshop, Arts & Crafts, Leather Straps, 12 x 16 In.
$900.00

Vitrine, Louis XVI Style, Multicolored, Fitted Case, 2 Doors, Grill Panel, Block Feet, 63 x 46 In.	1800.00
Vitrine, Mahogany, Bronze Mounts, Vernis Martin Lacquer, Court Life Frieze, c.1890, 32 x 74 In.	2468.00
Vitrine, Napoleon III, Mahogany, Concave Glass & Panels, 67 x 35 x 15 In.	236.00
Vitrine, Rococo Style, Kingwood Veneer, Crest, Serpentine Apron, c.1900, 62 x 22 x 12 In.	329.00
Vitrine, Satinwood, Kidney Shape, Tapered Legs, Stretchers, c.1875, 30 x 24 x 16 In.	690.00
Vitrine, Tabletop, Ash, Glass, Slant Front, 3 Graduated Shelves, Glazed Door, 17 x 15 In.	180.00
Vitrine, Venetian, Baroque Style, Gilt, 2 Cases, Italy, 1800s, 92 x 36 x 16 In.	1955.00
Wall Unit, G. Nelson, CSS, Herman Miller, c.1958, 87 x 97 In.	3308.00
Wall Unit, Walnut, Animals, Trees, Edgar Britton, Signed, 12 x 16 Ft.	14640.00
Wardrobe, Bird's-Eye Maple, Faux Bamboo, Glazed Doors Over Drawer, 85 x 49 In.	920.00
Wardrobe, Brown Over Yellow Paint, Door, Interior Carved Hooks, Ball Feet, 78 x 47 In.	3172.00
Wardrobe, Cherry, Walnut, Grain Paint, Green & Ocher Trim, Star, 1800s, 75 x 48 x 17 In.	9600.00
Wardrobe, Faux Bamboo, Bird's-Eye Maple, Pine, Glazed Doors, c.1900, 86 x 49 In. .... *illus*	944.00
Wardrobe, French Provincial, Oak, Carved, Medallion, Birds, Richardson, England, 83 x 61 In.	900.00
Wardrobe, French Provincial, Pine, Pediment, Mirror, Paneled, Triple, 93 x 78 x 23 In.	510.00
Wardrobe, Louis XV Style, Walnut, Arched, Scrolled Leaves, Mirror, 1800s, 108 x 98 x 22 In.	9000.00
Wardrobe, Mahogany, Carved, Paneled Doors, Drawers, Bulbous Feet, 86 ½ x 60 x 21 ½ In.	1920.00
Wardrobe, Pine, Austria, Late 19th Century, 69 x 50 x 22 In.	120.00
Wardrobe, Pine, Red Paint, Paneled Doors, Stepped Base, Trestle Feet, Pa., 1800s, 49 x 80 In.	267.00
Wardrobe, Thonet Bros., Overhanging Top, Drawer Over 2 Doors, 62 x 30 In.	448.00
Wardrobe, Victorian, Walnut, 2 Doors, 2 Drawers, 53 x 84 In.	708.00
Wardrobe, White Paint, Drawers, Door, 44 x 38 x 16 In.	106.00
Wardrobe, William IV, Mahogany, Arched Frieze, Paneled Cupboard, Drawers, 88 x 79 In.	6000.00
Washstand, Black Paint, Gold Stencil, Scroll Back, Urn, Flowers, Shelf, Drawer, 1800s, 37 x 18 In.	201.00
Washstand, Corner, Hepplewhite, Mahogany, c.1820, 41 x 22 ½ In.	201.00
Washstand, Corner, Hepplewhite, Mahogany, Inlaid, Shelf, 1800s, 43 x 25 In. .... *illus*	374.00
Washstand, Corner, Mahogany, Shaped Backsplash, Inlaid Drawer, Turned Pilasters, 16 x 43 In.	288.00
Washstand, Corner, Regency, Mahogany, Shaped Backsplash, Bow Tiers, 1800s, 42 x 22 In.	403.00
Washstand, Country Sheraton, Cherry, Backsplash, Frieze Drawer, Ring-Turned Legs, 33 x 30 In.	173.00
Washstand, Federal, Mahogany, Arched Backsplash, Drawer, c.1800, 36 x 21 In.	871.00
Washstand, Federal, Maple, Shaped Backsplash, Apron Drawer, Towel Bars, 32 x 22 In.	29.00
Washstand, George III, Inlaid Mahogany, Tall Gallery, Compartments, 44 x 19 In.	353.00
Washstand, George III, Mahogany, Pine, High Gallery, Drawer, Splayed Legs, c.1800, 46 x 24 In.	176.00
Washstand, Georgian, Lower Shelf, Drawer, Basin Cutout, c.1780, 30 In.	450.00
Washstand, Hepplewhite, Cherry, Drawer, 32 x 17 In.	80.00
Washstand, Hepplewhite, Cherry, Shaped Apron, Lover Shelf, Drawer, c.1815, 30 x 16 In.	1058.00
Washstand, Mahogany, 3 Open Holes, Shelf, Drawer, England, 1800s, 23 x 40 In.	236.00
Washstand, Mahogany, Fruitwood Marquetry, Door, Drawer, X-Stretcher, Dutch, 15 In.	533.00
Washstand, Mahogany, Marble Inset, Mirror, Tilts, Drawer, Shelf, 32 x 18 In., Child's	121.00
Washstand, Marquetry, Removable Backboard, 2 Shelves, Fold-Out Top, Drawers, 49 x 18 In.	345.00
Washstand, Orange, Yellow, Fruit, Paint, Scroll Surround, Holes, Shelf, Drawer, 1800s, 17 x 36 In.	295.00
Washstand, Pine, Painted Curly Maple Design, Stand, c.1830, 33 x 19 In.	360.00
Washstand, Regency, Mahogany, Hinged Lid, Mirror, False Drawer Over Drawer, 34 x 18 x 19 In.	520.00
Washstand, Sheraton, Cherry, Mahogany, Cutout Bowl, Doors, 39 x 17 x 18 In.	440.00
Washstand, Sheraton, Grain Painted, Drawer, New England, 1800s, 37 x 18 In.	325.00
Washstand, Sheraton, Maple, Tiger Maple, Bowfront, Backsplash, 38 ½ x 29 x 20 In.	2260.00
Washstand, Sheraton, Pine, Gilt, Grain Painted, c.1820, 33 x 17 In.	294.00
Washstand, Sheraton Style, Mahogany, Marble Top, Turned Legs, Late 1800s, 35 x 36 In.	176.00
Washstand, Sheraton, Tiger Maple, Dovetailed Drawer, Shelf, 36 x 18 x 15 In.	1375.00
Washstand, Victorian, Walnut, Mahogany, Backsplash, Long Drawer Over 2 Doors	201.00
Washstand, Wood Gallery Top, Double, 2 Drawers, Turned Legs, 35 x 41 x 21 In.	519.00
Wastebasket, G. Stickley, No. 94, Slatted, Iron Hoop Frame, Signed, Label, 12 x 14 In.	3000.00
Wastebasket, G. Stickley, No. 94, Slatted, Iron Hoop, Wood, Rivets, 12 x 14 In.	1680.00
Wastebasket, Lakeside Craftshop, Arts & Crafts, Leather Straps, 12 x 16 In. .... *illus*	900.00
Wastebasket, Teak, Cylindrical, Sweden, 18 ½ x 14 In.	106.00
Window Seat, Klismos, U-Shape, Upholstered, Scroll Arms & Legs, 37 x 44 In.	244.00
Window Seat, Louis XV Style, Walnut, Padded Seat, Arms, Upholstered, 26 x 25 x 18 In.	1080.00
Window Seat, Regency, Mahogany, Cushion, Padded Arms, Saber Legs, 33 x 74 x 24 In.	2160.00
Window Seat, Regency, Oak, Turned Handrests, Ring-Turned Legs, Ball Feet, 1800s, 20 x 41 In.	1035.00
Wine Cooler, Georgian Style, Mahogany, Brass Bound, Handles, Cabriole Legs, 27 x 28 x 20 In.	1410.00
Wine Cooler, Georgian Style, Mahogany, Brass Bound, Oval, Handles, Paw Feet, 26 x 28 In.	1434.00
Wine Cooler, Louis XV, Mahogany, Marble Top, Metal Wells, Drawer, Shelf, 23 x 29 In., Pair	2133.00
Wine Cooler, Regency, Mahogany, Octagonal, Splayed Legs, Lion, Ring Mask Handles, 20 x 27 In.	948.00
Wine Cooler, William IV, Mahogany, Canted Top, Tapered Base, Turned Feet, 19 In.	296.00

G. ARGY-ROUSSEAU is the impressed mark used on a variety of objects in the Art Deco style G-ARGY-ROUSSEAU. Gabriel Argy-Rousseau, born in 1885, was a French glass artist. In 1921, he formed a partnership that made pate-de-verre and other glass. He worked until 1952 and died in 1953.

Box, Cornflowers, Purple, Red, Black, Purple Gray Ground, Pate-De-Verre, c.1920, 3 x 3 In.	4700.00
Box, Cover, Flowers, Leaves, Charcoal Ground, Mottled Purple, Green, Blue, 2 ¾ x 5 In.	6037.00
Lamp, 3-Flower Medallions, Blue, Green, Scroll Rows, Frosted Ground, Copper, 22 In.	3163.00
Lamp, Leaf Designs, Orange & Brown, Wrought Iron Base, Pate-De-Verre, 5 x 9 In.	4800.00
Pendant, Butterfly, Pate De Verre, Signed, GAR, 2 ¼ x 2 In. ....*illus*	1150.00
Pendant, Triangle, Mottled Yellow, Green, Green Lizard, Signed, Pate-De-Verre, 2 ½ In.	1495.00
Powder Box, Cover, Hydrangeas, White, Purple Centers, 3 ½ In.	4025.00
Vase, 2 Birds, Trumpet Shape, Amber, Pate-De-Verre, Signed, 1920, 5 In.	3300.00
Vase, Birds, Amber, Flared Shape, Oval Foot, Pate-De-Verre, 5 In.	2588.00
Vase, Embossed Rose, c.1929, 8 ¾ In.	3510.00
Vase, Red Anemones, Mottled Purple, Cream Ground, 6 In.	920.00

GALLE was a designer who made glass, pottery, furniture, and other Art Nouveau items. Emile Galle founded his factory in France in 1874. After Galle's death in 1904, the firm continued to make glass and furniture until 1931. The name *Galle* was used as a mark, but it was often hidden in the design of the object. Galle glass is listed here. Pottery is in the next section. His furniture is listed in the Furniture category.

Bowl, Carved Morning Glory Flowers, Blue, Purple, Yellow, Smoky White, Cameo, 3 x 7 In.	2530.00
Bowl, Flowers, Leaves, Red, Yellow Ground, Cameo, Signed, 4 ½ In.	2200.00
Bowl, Flowers, Orange, Frosted, Clear, Cameo, Scalloped Rim, c.1900, 3 ¾ x 8 In.	1440.00
Bowl, Gold, Tan Bee, Honeycombs, Opalescent Ground, 3-Fold Shape, 2 x 5 In.	1208.00
Bowl, Oval, Frosted Glass, Amber Flowers, Cameo, Signed, 4 ½ In.	375.00
Cologne Bottle, Red Flowers, Leaves, Yellow Ground, Windowpane, Cameo, Signed, 5 In.	374.00
Cordial, Green Textured, Pink Flowers, Gilt Stems, Cameo, Embossed Silver Foot, 3 In.	425.00
Cruet, Topaz, Ribbed Ground, Pedestal Foot, Enameled Flowers, Applied Handle, 9 ¾ In. *illus*	4600.00
Decanter, Enameled Flowers, Pale Amber Ground, Purple Accents, Signed, 9 In.	2415.00
Dish, Purple Enamel Cornflowers, Tan Stems, Smoky Quartz Glass, Crystallerie, Signed, 6 In.	633.00
Lamp, Ferns, Burgundy, Lime Green, Pink Ground, Cameo, 20 x 9 ¾ In.	6600.00
Lamp, Hydrangea, Cameo Glass, Signed, c.1900, 10 ¾ In.	8125.00
Lampshade, Sky Blue, Speckled, 2 Eagles Flying, Cameo, Domed, 6 x 10 In.	4025.00
Perfume Burner, Brown, Green Mottled Ferns, Yellow Ground, Wick, Burner, Cameo, Signed, 9 In.	1150.00
Pitcher, Ceramic, Avian Handle, Blue Enamel, Flying Insect, c.1870, 12 x 6 In. ....*illus*	2640.00
Pitcher, Orchid, Enamel, Signed, c.1900, 12 ½ In.	3125.00
Scent Bottle, Swirling Stopper, Amber Cameo Flowers, Leaves, Stems Silver Foil, 9 In.	14375.00
Vase, 2 Towers, Trees, Bridge, Cut Flowers, Leaves, Green Ground, Cameo, Signed, c.1920, 14 In.	5500.00
Vase, 4-Fold Rim, Pink Bleeding Heart Blossoms, Green Leaves, Blue Sky, Cameo, 8 In.	1380.00
Vase, Amber Daffodils, Leafy Stems, Cameo, Signed, c.1904, 11 In.	1800.00
Vase, Baluster, Flower, Amethyst, Pale Green, Cameo, Signed, c.1900, 6 In.	660.00
Vase, Baluster, Flowers, Raspberry, Yellow, Clear Cameo, c.1900, 6 In.	900.00
Vase, Banjo, Berries, Vine, Yellow Ground, Cameo, Signed, 6 ⅞ In.	748.00
Vase, Banjo, Branches, Berries, Yellow Ground, 5 ½ In.	850.00
Vase, Banjo, Flowers, Vines, Frosted Orange, 6 ½ In.	1265.00
Vase, Banjo, Purple Clematis, Citron, Tan Ground, Cameo, Signed, 5 In.	690.00
Vase, Banjo, Purple, Green Hydrangea, Mottled Ground, Cameo, Signed, 6 ½ In.	863.00
Vase, Beech Leaf & Willow, Olive, Citron, Clear, Tall Neck, Cameo, Signed, c.1875, 23 In.	2640.00
Vase, Blue Enamel, Dragonflies, Flowers, Ribbons, Ribbed Clear, Gold, Cameo, Signed, 6 In.	230.00
Vase, Blue Flowers, Green Leaves, Purple Foot, White Frosted Rim, Cameo, Signed, 11 In.	4602.00
Vase, Boat Shape Top, Oak Leaves, Acorns, Amber, Green, Signed, 6 In.	805.00
Vase, Bottle Shape, Flowers, Yellow, Brown, Footed, Cameo, Signed, 5 ¼ In.	720.00
Vase, Bottle Shape, Red Leafy Vines, Red, Circular Feet, Chartreuse Ground, 16 ¼ In.	2032.00
Vase, Brown, Bulbous, Yellow, Flowers, Leaves, Long Neck, Cameo, Signed, 4 ½ In.	575.00
Vase, Brown Columbine, On Gold To Tan Ground, Cameo, Signed, c.1900, 6 In.	646.00
Vase, Brown Grapevine, Rose, Yellow, Opaque Ground, Cameo, c.1900, 3 ½ In.	568.00
Vase, Brown, Green Leaves, Peach Ground, Dark Foot, Cameo, Signed, 6 In.	805.00
Vase, Brown, Yellow Magnolias, Leaves, Cameo, 3 In.	575.00
Vase, Bud, Flowers, Leaves, Pastel Green, Pink, Frosted, Cameo, Signed, 6 In.	518.00
Vase, Bulbous, Amber, Buds, Leaves, Yellow Ground, Top, Flared Base, Cameo, 19 In.	2875.00
Vase, Bulbous, Amethyst Flowers, Gray To Pink, Smoke Stack, Cameo, Signed, c.1900, 6 ¼ In.	600.00
Vase, Bulbous, Etched Purple Leaves, Chartreuse Opaque Ground, Purple Foot, c.1900, 17 ½ In.	1553.00
Vase, Bulbous, Lilies, Purple, Clear, Cristallerie, Cameo, Signed, 4 ½ x 5 In.	805.00
Vase, Bulbous, Purple Iris, Iridescent Opaque Ground, Cameo, c.1900, 5 ½ In.	568.00
Vase, Bulbous, Raspberries, Leaves, Red, Purple, Orange Ground, Signed, Cameo, 9 ½ In.	7188.00

G. Argy-Rousseau, Pendant, Butterfly, Pate De Verre, Signed, GAR, 2 ¼ x 2 In. **$1150.00**

G

Galle, Cruet, Topaz, Ribbed Ground, Pedestal Foot, Enameled Flowers, Applied Handle, 9 ¾ In. **$4600.00**

GALLE

Galle, Pitcher, Ceramic,
Avian Handle, Blue Enamel,
Flying Insect, c.1870, 12 x 6 In.
$2640.00

Galle, Vase, Lavender,
Green Flowers, Cameo, Signed, 12 ¼ In.
$1534.00

Galle, Vase, Organic Shape,
Wheel Cut, Applied Spider,
Frosted Ground, Footed, Cameo,
3 ½ x 6 In.
$6600.00

Vase, Bulbous, Wisteria, Purple, Green, Peach Ground, Cameo, Signed, 13 In.	1840.00
Vase, Cinnamon, Crimson Berries, Cascading Leaves, Pinched Waist, Cameo, Signed, 11 ½ In.	1495.00
Vase, Crocus, Marquetry Flowers, Purple, Amber, Mauve, Crystal Ground, Signed	34500.00
Vase, Cut Amber Flowers, Leaves, Stem, Blue Ground, Engraved, Signed, 7 x 4 In.	1725.00
Vase, Cut Leaves & Blossoms, Orange Frosted Ground, Pinched Neck, Cameo, Signed, 6 In.	850.00
Vase, Cylindrical, Dual Pointed Rim, Blueberries, Leaves, Cameo, Signed, 8 ½ In.	2000.00
Vase, Cylindrical, Flowers, Leaves, Tapered, Green, Blue, White Ground, Cameo, Signed, 20 ½ In.	1680.00
Vase, Cylindrical, Leaves & Berries On Branch, Chartreuse, Frost Ground, Cameo, 5 ½ In.	546.00
Vase, Cylindrical, Pinched Rim, Wooded Landscape, Ocher, Iridescent To Rose, c.1900, 12 In.	2151.00
Vase, Cylindrical, Royal Blue Pine Trees, Lake, Mountains, Frosted Green Sky, Cameo, Signed, 14 In.	3500.00
Vase, Cylindrical, Tapered, Cut Bellflower, Yellow, Purple, Cameo Cut, 7 In.	748.00
Vase, Cylindrical, Yellow, Frost, Leaves, Wisteria, Cameo, Signed, 10 In.	500.00
Vase, Etched Brown Bird, Mountain Overlay, Pale Blue Ground, Fire Polished, Signed, c.1900, 11 In.	5975.00
Vase, Ferns, Green Tones, Tapered, Cameo, Signed, c.1910, 11 ½ In.	478.00
Vase, Ferns, Green, Yellow, Long Neck, Bulbous Base, Cameo, 3 ½ In.	403.00
Vase, Ferns, Red, Clear, Irregular Form, Cameo, Signed, 5 ½ In.	1320.00
Vase, Flowers, Amethyst, Carved, White Frosted Glass, 5 In.	920.00
Vase, Flowers, Fuchsia, Stems, Leaves, Amber, Yellow, Cream Ground, 8 ¼ In.	4025.00
Vase, Flowers, Ivory Enameled, Purple, Blue, Brown Leaves, Opalescent Green Ground, 9 ¼ In.	2760.00
Vase, Flowers, Leaves, Branches, Green, Baluster, White Ground, Cameo, Signed, 12 ⅛ In.	1410.00
Vase, Flowers, Leaves, Sepia, Cameo, Signed, 3 ⅛ In.	550.00
Vase, Flowers, Purple, Pink Ground, Shouldered, Cameo, Signed, 6 ½ In.	805.00
Vase, Flowers, Red On Off-White Ground, Red Foot, Cameo, Signed, 8 In.	690.00
Vase, Fuchsias, Amethyst, Brown, Yellow Frosted Glass, 3-Sided, Cameo, Signed, 8 ½ In.	4100.00
Vase, Gathered Base, Frosted, Lily Pond, Footed, Cameo, Signed, 12 In.	4600.00
Vase, Globular, Frosted Ground, 2 Handles, Cameo, Signed, 5 In.	1400.00
Vase, Globular, Handles, Dragonfly, Aquatic Plants, Pond, Frosted, Cameo, Signed, 8 In.	3910.00
Vase, Grapevines, Martele Ground, Tapered, Cameo, Signed, 7 ½ x 5 ¾ In.	3000.00
Vase, Gray Violets, Frosted Faded To Light Brown Ground, Cameo, Star, 1904, 9 ¾ x 4 ¾ In.	1100.00
Vase, Green Flowers, Leaves, Pink Ground, Cameo, Signed, 2 In.	374.00
Vase, Green Leaves, Stems, Orange Rim, Long Neck, Cameo, 23 In.	3450.00
Vase, Green Seed Pod, Leaves, Peach, Frosted, Cameo, Signed, 13 In.	1610.00
Vase, Green, White Leaves, Flared Peach Lip, Green Pedestal Foot, Cameo, Signed, 13 In.	1725.00
Vase, Green, Yellow Berries, Leaves, Pink Ground, Cylindrical, Cameo, Signed, 13 In.	1180.00
Vase, Hydrangea, Purple, Green, White, Peach Ground, Side, 1904-16, 12 ⅛ In.	3200.00
Vase, Iridescent Purple Flowers, Yellow Ground, Oval, Signed, c.1920, 4 ¼ In.	657.00
Vase, Iris, Stems, Leaves, Amethyst, Amber, Cameo, 6 ¼ In.	748.00
Vase, Landscape, Amber Trees, Sloping Mountains, Orange, Yellow Frosted Ground, 1900, 14 In.	6325.00
Vase, Landscape, Multicolored, Forked Tree, Footed, Signed, 6 ¾ In.	1725.00
Vase, Landscape, Pink & Green, Overlaid Brown, Cameo, Signed, c.1900, 4 ⅝ In.	470.00
Vase, Lavender, Green Flowers, Cameo, Signed, 12 ¼ In. ....illus	1534.00
Vase, Leaf, Flower, Purple, Blue, Yellow Ground, Cameo, Signed, 4 In.	920.00
Vase, Leaves, Green, Orange, Foliage Pattern, Twisted Neck, Cameo, Signed, c.1920, 6 ¾ In.	1080.00
Vase, Leaves, Hyacinth, Silhouetted, Frosty Ground, Silver Mount, Signed, 13 ¼ In.	2300.00
Vase, Lilac, Green Flowers, Frosted Pink Ground, Cameo, Signed, 9 ½ In.	1265.00
Vase, Maple Seed Pods, Leaves, Frosted 2-Tone, Green, Orange, Signed, 3 ½ In.	518.00
Vase, Morning Glories, Pink & Purple, Sunset Ground, Cameo, Signed, c.1900, 15 ½ In.	1800.00
Vase, Mountain Range, Lake, Mottled Frost, Blue Ground, Cameo, Signed, 5 In.	2300.00
Vase, Orange Flowers, Leaves, Frosted Ground, Cameo, Signed, 4 In.	460.00
Vase, Orange Flowers, Leaves, Mottled Pink, Yellow Frosted Ground, Cameo, Signed, 3 In.	489.00
Vase, Orange Flowers, Peach, Pink Ground, Cameo, Signed, 3 In.	460.00
Vase, Orange Flowers, White Frosted Glass, Dip Top, Cameo, Signed, 4 In.	403.00
Vase, Organic Shape, Wheel Cut, Applied Spider, Frosted Ground, Footed, Cameo, 3 ½ x 6 In. ...illus	6600.00
Vase, Oval, Etched, Purple Flowering Branches, Chartreuse & Iridescent Ground, c.1900, 7 In.	926.00
Vase, Oval, Flaring Rim, Etched Red Flowers, Golden Opaque Ground, c.1900, 6 ½ In.	896.00
Vase, Oval, Footed, Flared Rim, Citron, Blue Wild Roses, Cameo, Signed, 10 In.	3000.00
Vase, Oval, Purple & Green Flowers, Green & Iridescent Opaque Ground, Cameo, c.1900, 3 In.	568.00
Vase, Peach Fuchsia, Amber Leaves, Frosted Ground, Mold Blown, Cameo, Signed, 12 In.	11210.00
Vase, Pilgrim, Vines, Berries, Leaves, Pink, Orange Frosted Glass, Camphor Handles, 4 In.	863.00
Vase, Pillow Shape, Citron, Lake Scene, Brown Trees, Cameo, Signed, 8 ½ In.	1300.00
Vase, Pinched Neck, Footed, Etched, Wooded Landscape, Greens, Browns, c.1900, 23 In.	5975.00
Vase, Pink Flowers, Green Leaves, Frosted To Blue Ground, Footed, Oval, Cameo, 8 x 6 ½ In.	1700.00
Vase, Pink Flowers, Leaves, Bulbous, Short Neck, Signed, 3 In.	633.00
Vase, Poppies, Windowpane, Yellow To Red, Cameo, Signed, 12 ½ In.	4025.00
Vase, Purple Flowers, Leaves, Apricot Ground, Cameo, Signed, 5 In.	575.00
Vase, Purple Hydrangea Blossoms, Green Leaves, Apricot Frost Ground, 10 In.	1265.00

Vase, Purple Hydrangea, Green Leaves, Pale Pink Ground, 13 In.	1265.00
Vase, Purple Leaves, Berries, Pale Green Ground, Cameo, Signed, 4 In.	518.00
Vase, Purple, Orange Leaves, Carved, Frosted, Clear Ground, Maroon Foot, Engraved, 5 In.	9775.00
Vase, Purple Wisteria, Green, Peach Ground, Cameo, Signed, 6 In.	518.00
Vase, Red Berries, Leaves, Frost & Citron Ground, Cameo, Signed, 3 ½ In.	259.00
Vase, Scenic Landscape, Trees, Mountains, Green, Teal, Orange, Signed, c.1900, 12 In.	2988.00
Vase, Seed Pods, Olive Green, Salmon Ground, Cameo, Signed, 4 ¼ In.	489.00
Vase, Squat, Blue & Purple Clematis, Clambroth, Cameo, Signed, 6 ¾ x 9 In.	1610.00
Vase, Squat, Orange Poppies, Iridescent Opaque Ground, Cameo, c.1900, 2 ½ In.	568.00
Vase, Stick, Bulbous, Cascading Oak Leaves, Seed Pods, Peach, Green, Cameo, Signed, 13 ½ In.	1440.00
Vase, Stick, Grapevines, Yellow & Amber Ground, Cameo, Signed, 1925, 5 ¼ In.	600.00
Vase, Stick, Pink Ground, Tall Green Leafy Flowers, Cameo, Signed, 14 In.	1300.00
Vase, Stick, Poppies, Leaves, Orange Ground, Cameo, Signed, 8 ¼ In.	748.00
Vase, Stick, Purple Leaves, Flowers, Vines, Footed, Ruffle Rim, Cameo, Signed, c.1900, 15 In.	1320.00
Vase, Stylized Flowers, Blue, Yellow, Brown, Bottle Form, Cameo, Signed, 7 In.	720.00
Vase, Tan, Brown Flowers, Lavender Ground, High Shoulder, Cameo, Signed, 4 In.	518.00
Vase, Tapered, Cut Leaves & Blossoms, Yellow Frosted Ground, Cameo, 5 ¼ In.	850.00
Vase, Tapered, Leaves, Berries, Shaded Amber, Olive Green Accents, Scalloped Rim, 10 ¾ In.	978.00
Vase, Tapered, Pinched Rim, Cameo Cut Red Leaves, Flowers, Green Ground, Signed, c.1904, 5 x 4 In.	1200.00
Vase, Tapered, Scalloped Rim, Leaves, Berries, Amber, 10 ¾ x 5 In. ....*illus*	1003.00
Vase, Teardrop, Red, Yellow, Crab Apple Branches, Cameo, 11 In.	575.00
Vase, Thistle, Multicolored, Enameled, Clear Ground, Signed, 8 x 5 ½ In.	2280.00
Vase, Thistles, Transparent Green Ground, Cylinder, Padded Round Base, Enamel, Signed, 8 In.	1380.00
Vase, Trees, Valley Lake, Multicolored, Cameo, Signed, 4 ½ In.	1955.00
Vase, Triangular, Flowers, Amethyst, Orange, Cameo, Signed, c.1900, 5 In.	660.00
Vase, Underwater Floral, Orange, Red, Blue, Cream Ground, Cameo, Signed, c.1900, 6 In.	2689.00
Vase, Vines, Squash Blossom, Leaves, Russet, Rum, Satin Peach Ground, Mold Blown, 7 ¼ In.	4600.00
Vase, Wheel Cut Leaves, Applied Spider, Red Web, Frosted, Footed, Signed, Cameo, 3 ½ x 6 In.	660.00
Vase, Wisteria Vines, Purple, Green, 4-Layer Cameo, Signed, 24 ¼ x 9 In.	6600.00
Vase, Yellow & Brown, Overlay, Cut, Poppies, Blossoms, Cameo, Signed, c.1900, 4 ⅜ In.	588.00

GALLE POTTERY was made by Emile Galle, the famous French designer, after 1874. The pieces were marked with the initials *E. G.* impressed, *Em. Galle Faiencerie de Nancy*, or a version of his signature. Galle is best known for his glass, listed above.

Ashtray, Half Moon Form, Frog Playing Mandolin, Stars, Signed, E & G Depose, 4 ½ In.	265.00
Cruet Basket, Faience, Elongated, Handles, 2 Reticulated Baskets, Signed, 2 ¾ x 10 In. ....*illus*	575.00
Oil Lamp, Cylinder, Faience, Gilt Base, Cobalt Blue Ground, Flowers, Grasshopper, 10 In.	920.00
Vase, Insect, Flowers, Leaves, Iridescent, Faience, Signed, 5 ½ In. ....*illus*	518.00

GAME collectors like all types of games. Of special interest are any board games or card games. Transogram and other company names are included in the description when known. Other games may be found listed under Card, Toy, or the name of the character or celebrity featured in the game.

Across The Continent, Tootsie, Board, Box, 11 ½ x 18 In.	75.00
Aeroplane Race, Tin Lithograph, Board, 4 Airplanes, Wolverine, Box, 1922, 11 ½ x 11 ½ In.	288.00
Airport, Hangar, Airplanes, Game Pieces, Cardboard Board, Chart, Liberty, Box, 8 ½ x 11 In.	230.00
Alice In Wonderland, JW Spear & Sons, England, Board, 1973	63.00
Ancient Game Of China, Drawers, Original Box, Milton Bradley, 1923, 8 x 5 In.	70.00
Arcade, Shooting Gallery, Marx, 5 ¾ x 21 ½ In.	50.00
Archie Bunker's, Card Game, Archie, Edith, Meathead & Gloria, Milton Bradley, Cards, 1972	40.00
Auto Race, Tin Board, 2 Marbles, 2 Die Cast Autos, Jeanette Toy Co., 10 ¼ In.	174.00
Baseball, Electric, Model 48-B, Jim Prentice, Box, 13 ¾ x 15 ¾ In.	32.00
Baseball, Home Diamond Co., 1913, 9 ½ x 7 In.	245.00
Baseball, Peg Baseball, Board, Pegs, Dice, Box, Parker Bros., 1915, 12 x 11 x 2 In.	142.00
Baseball, Pinch Hitter, Tin, Cardboard, Marble, Windup, Box, 23 ¾ x 12 ½ In.	80.00
Baseball, Roulette, William Bartholomae, Box, 1929, 9 ¾ x 6 ¾ In.	40.00
Battle Line, Ideal, Board, c.1964, 19 x 9 In.	83.00
Battlestar Galactica, Parker Brothers, Board, 1978	23.00
Bicycle Race, 4 Bisque Head Cyclists, Felt Top, France, 20 x 20 In.	374.00
Bicycle Race, 4 Tin Cyclists, Clockwork, Felt Top, France, c.1900, 18 x 18 In.	2875.00
Billiard, Table Top, Liquid Veneer, Pool Balls, 2 Cues, Lever, 11 x 19 In.	2185.00
Board, Checkers & Backgammon, Inlaid Star, Hinged, Sailor Made, 18 In.	263.00
Board, Checkers & Parcheesi, Sunburst, Zigzag, Inlaid Wood, Canada, 1928, 20 x 14 In.	830.00
Board, Checkers, 2-Sided, Carved, Painted, 1800s, 15 ½ x 15 ¼ In.	1500.00
Board, Checkers, Backgammon, Painted, Square, c.1840, 16 In.	1350.00

Galle, Vase, Tapered,
Scalloped Rim, Leaves, Berries,
Amber, 10 ¾ x 5 In.
$1003.00

Galle Pottery, Cruet Basket,
Faience, Elongated, Handles,
2 Reticulated Baskets, Signed,
2 ¾ x 10 In.
$575.00

Galle Pottery, Vase, Insect,
Flowers, Leaves, Iridescent, Faience,
Signed, 5 ½ In.
$518.00

G

Game, Board, Checkers,
Cards On Reverse, Applied Ends,
Painted, c.1900s, 13 x 19 In.
$3055.00

Game, Board, Checkers, Painted,
Gold, Black, Red, Late 19th Century,
16 x 16 ¼ In.
$527.00

Game, Board, Parcheesi,
Folding, Painted, Orange, White,
19 ¼ x 19 ¼ In.
$556.00

Board, Checkers, Cards On Reverse, Applied Ends, Painted, c.1900s, 13 x 19 In. ....*illus*	3055.00
Board, Checkers, Cherry, Black, Brown, Red Border, c.1900, 11 x 11 In.	176.00
Board, Checkers, Inlaid Tunbridgeware, 8-Sided, Glass Dome Cover, c.1870	1170.00
Board, Checkers, Painted, Gold, Black, Red, Late 19th Century, 16 x 16 ¼ In. ....*illus*	527.00
Board, Checkers, Painted, Red, Black, Green, c.1915, 24 ¼ x 18 In.	234.00
Board, Checkers, Wood, Red, Black Paint, Gilt Game Piece Section, c.1890, 25 x 14 In.	533.00
Board, Chess, Checkers 2-Sided, Wood, c.1900, 10 x 10 In.	795.00
Board, Chess, Pressman, Box, 12 In.	28.00
Board, Close Encounters Of The Third Kind, Parker Brothers, 1978	35.00
Board, Cribbage, Brass, England, 6 Ball Feet, c.1790	110.00
Board, Cribbage, Leather, Logo, Stamped, Fremont Saddlery-Makers-Fremont Neb., 12 In.	275.00
Board, Cribbage, Wood, Mother-Of-Pearl, 1888, 16 In.	120.00
Board, Parcheesi & Checkers, Walnut, Painted, c.1840, 15 ½ x 15 In.	3600.00
Board, Parcheesi, Folding, Painted, Orange, White, 19 ¼ x 19 ¼ In. ....*illus*	556.00
Board, Parcheesi, Pine, Incised Lines, Painted, Red, Yellow, Blue, Green, 18 x 18 In.	588.00
Board, Walnut, 2-Sided, Slide Lid, Red, Yellow, Black Paint, c.1920, 17 x 20 In.	1028.00
Board, Wood Inlay, 20 x 20 In.	144.00
Board, Wood, Painted, Black Checker Squares, Early 20th Century, 17 x 14 ½ In.	350.00
Board, Yellow, Black, Horse Head, Molded Edges, 17 ¾ x 30 In.	452.00
Bowling, Brunswick Candle Pins, Painted, 10 Pins, 3 Balls	175.00
Boy Holding Game Wheel, Multicolored Wheel Interior, Cast Iron, Brass, 1800s, 13 ¾ In.	546.00
Bringing Up Father, Embee Distributing, Board, 1920	30.00
Cage, Chuck-O-Luck, Hour Glass Shape, Nickel, 1920s, 11 In. ....*illus*	28.00
Calling All Cars, Parker Brothers, Board, 1938	35.00
Captain Video, Milton Bradley, Box, 9 ¾ x 19 In.	90.00
Carpet Balls, Ceramic, Multicolored Sponge, Plaid, England, 1875, 3 x 4 In., 4 Piece	176.00
Chess, Burlwood, Ebonized, Hinged Lid, Doors, Fitted Box, Die, Chips, c.1900, 13 x 9 In.	296.00
Chess Set, Ivory, Carved, Box, India, Mid 20th Century, 32 Piece	510.00
Chess Set, Ivory, Carved Soldier Figures, Red, White, Chinese, 30 Piece	354.00
Chinese Checkers, 32 Marbles, Harlequin, Multicolored, c.1860, ¾ In.	11115.00
Chiromagica Wizard, McLoughlin, Sliding Top Lid ....*illus*	585.00
Coin Toss, Frog, Wood Cabinet, Cast Iron Frog, 32 x 16 ½ x 20 ½ In. ....*illus*	460.00
Dexterity Puzzle, Chew Bob's Tobacco, 5 & 10 Cent Plugs, Ballooning, c.1900, 1 ¾ In.	153.00
Dexterity Puzzle, Cowboy Lassos Steer, Hand Held, 3 Small White Balls Roll Into Holes, 1920	70.00
Dexterity Puzzle, Woman With Eyeglasses, Mirrored Back, Mark, D.R.G.M., Germany, 2 ¼ In.	140.00
Dice, 5 Bone Dice, Side Lever, Pocket Watch Form, c.1900, 2 In.	290.00
Donkey Party, 2 Donkeys, Tails, Directions, Box, Stoll & Edwards Co., N.Y., c.1941, 8 x 10 In. ..*illus*	30.00
E.T. The Extra-Terrestrial, Parker Brothers, Board, 1982	17.00
Finance, Parker Brothers, Board, 1936	65.00
Fish Pond, McLoughlin Bros., Box, 1890, 13 x 21 In.	56.00
Football, Tru-Action, Electric, Tudor, Box, 16 ½ x 27 In.	31.00
Fortune Teller, Directions, Milton Bradley, Board, Box, 9 ⅜ In.	40.00
Frank Buck's Bring 'Em Back Alive, All-Fair, Card, 1937, 14 x 20 In.	375.00
Gambling Chips, Markers, Mother-Of-Pearl, Box, Walnut, 13 x 11 In. ....*illus*	1150.00
Game Of Authors, Parker Bros., Deluxe Edition, Board, c.1893, 5 ½ x 4 In.	22.00
Game Of Baseball, McLoughlin Bros., Board, Players, Wood Box, 10 x 17 In.	1073.00
Garrison's Gorillas, Ideal, Board, c.1967, 17 ½ x 9 In.	149.00
G.I. Joe Navy Frogman, Hasbro, Board, 1960s, 17 ½ x 8 ½ In.	55.00
Giant Cootie, Schaper Manufacturing Company, 1949, 12 x 20 In.	115.00
Go To The Head Of The Class, Milton Bradley, Board, 1970s	15.00
Haunted House, Ideal, Board, c.1962, 22 x 19 In.	121.00
Horse Race, Pocket Watch Form, Spins, Enamel Horses, Moko, c.1890, 2 In. Diam. 780.00 to	1150.00
Humpty Dumpty, Ladder Game, Wood, Paper Overlay, c.1910, 3 ½ x 31 ½ In.	386.00
Jigsaw Puzzle, Bugs Bunny, Bugs Driving Thru Drive-Up Bank Window, Whitman, 100 Piece, 1977.	25.00
Jigsaw Puzzle, Fire Engine, Picture Firefighting Scene, McLoughlin, 17 ½ x 25 In.	687.00
Jigsaw Puzzle, Old Woman & Pig, McLoughlin Bros., Box, 1890, 12 ½ x 9 In.	240.00
Jolly Target, Ball Toss Into Mouth Of Black Man, Milton Bradley, Target, 17 In.	402.00
Laramie, Western Images, 4 Cowboy On Horse Markers, Lowell Toy, Board, 1960	240.00
Lucky Lindy, 3 Faces Of Lindy, Mechanic, Pilot, Commander, Card, 53 Cards	75.00
Mahjong, Ivory, Carved Pieces & Dice, Fitted Paneled Box, Sliding Door, 9 ½ x 6 ½ In.	212.00
Marble Shooter, 3 Dog Targets, Cast Iron, Arcade, 29 In.	82.00
Merchant Marine, Lead Ships, Game Board, Spinner, Milton Bradley, Board, Box, 21 In.	83.00
Moon Mullins, Kayo Stealing Turkey, 5 Characters, Milton Bradley, Board, 1927	175.00
Mother Goose, Samuel Lowe, 1941	37.00
Old Maid, McLoughlin Bros., Board, 7 ⅜ x 5 ½ In.	149.00
Our Gang, Tipple Topple Game, Cardboard, Box, All-Fair Inc., c.1930, 9 x 17 ½ In. ....*illus*	452.00

Game, Cage, Chuck-O-Luck, Hour Glass Shape, Nickel, 1920s, 11 In.
$28.00

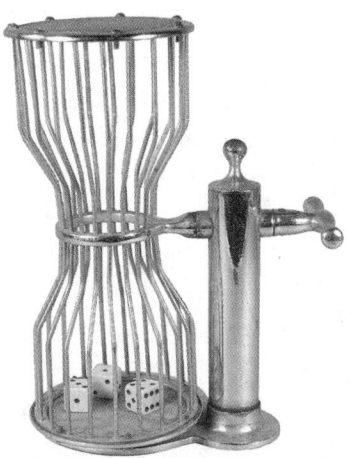

Game, Chiromagica Wizard, McLoughlin, Sliding Top Lid
$585.00

Game, Coin Toss, Frog, Wood Cabinet, Cast Iron Frog, 32 x 16 ½ x 20 ½ In.
$460.00

Game, Donkey Party, 2 Donkeys, Tails, Directions, Box,
Stoll & Edwards Co., N.Y., c.1941, 8 x 10 In.
$30.00

Game, Gambling Chips, Markers, Mother-Of-Pearl, Box, Walnut, 13 x 11 In.
$1150.00

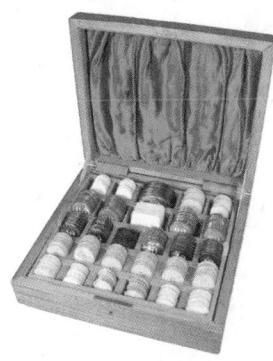

Game, Our Gang, Tipple Topple Game, Cardboard, Box, All-Fair Inc.,
c.1930, 9 x 17 ½ In.
$452.00

Displaying Games

Good idea seen at a picture-frame shop: a game board
mounted in a deep frame. The game pieces are in the
original box Velcroed in place at the back. Hang the board
as a picture, take it off the wall and use the pieces to play
the game. Then store on the wall until the next time.

G

Game, Wonderful Game Of Oz, Playing Pieces, Parker Bros., Board, 20 x 10 In. $525.00

Game, X-Plor U.S. By Airplane, 4 Metal Airplanes, Board, Box, 17 x 9 In. $117.00

Garden, Boot Scraper, Dolphins, Green Man Mask, Iron, Marked 5300 Scrape, 6 x 8 In. $288.00

Outer Limits, Milton Bradley, Board, 1964	335.00
Peanut The Elephant, Children's Hour, Parker Brothers, Box, 1946	50.00
Pin The Tail On The Donkey, Paper, Lithograph, Uncut, 21 x 29 In.	30.00
Playing Cards, Edison Mazda Lamps, Linen, Parrish, Waterfall Cover, Box, c.1930	150.00
Playing Cards, French Aristocracy, Flowers, Mark, Jeu Louis XV, B.P. Grimaud, Deck, Box, 3 ½ In.	195.00
Playing Cards, Pocket Watch Form, Spinner, 2 In. Diam.	285.00
Poker, Chips, Bakelite, Green Holder, Multicolored Chips, 3 ⅓ x 1 ⅜ In.	195.00
Poker, Chips, Clay, Multicolored, Fitted Mahogany Box, Lift-Out Rack, Bail Handle, 1880s	295.00
Poker, Chips, Ivory, $1 & $5, Eagle Motif, 20 Piece	1700.00
Poker, Chips, Mother-Of-Pearl, Dice, Cards, Watch, Robin Hood Derringer Pistol, Case, 2 x 11 x 7 In.	1900.00
Poker, Chips, Mother-Of-Pearl, Dice, Cards, Pocket Watch, 32 Cal. Knuckle Duster, Case, 2 x 12 x 5 In.	2000.00
Poker, Royal Poker Set, Chips, Mother-Of-Pearl, 2 Decks Of Cards, Leather Case, 1910, 2 x 18 x 9 In.	3500.00
Poker, Royal Poker Set, Chips, Nickel, Brass, Copper, Cards, Walnut Case, 1 ½ x 4 x 2 In.	2700.00
Puzzle Package, Metal Puzzles, Box, 10 x 17 In.	11.00
Ring Toss, Black Clown, White Eye Coon, Germany, 1920s, 7 x 5 In.	175.00
Ring Toss, Pressman, Box, 11 x 15 ½ In.	29.00
Robinson Crusoe, Parker Brothers, Card, Copyright 1895, 5 ⅝ x 4 x 1 In.	72.00 to 150.00
Roulette Wheel, Pocket Watch Form, Side Lever Flips To Spin, Marked, Germany, c.1890, 2 In.	310.00
Roulette Wheel, Rocky Mountain Sporting Good Co., Denver, Spindle Mark, 31 ¼ In.	1540.00
Roulette Wheel, Satinwood, Rosewood, Painted Numbers, Signed, Harris & Co., 13 x 31 In.	1050.00
Sandy Andy Across The Channel, Tin, Wolverine, Box, 16 ½ x 16 ½ In.	25.00
Scoreaword, Transogram, Board, Box, 1953, 9 x 17 ½ In.	12.00
Sergeant Preston Of The Yukon, Milton Bradley, Board, 1956	25.00
Shooting Gallery, Red, Yellow, Green, Black, Tin, Wolverine, 17 In.	55.00
Skittles, Turned Hardwood Pins, Green Paint, Multicolored Balls, England, 16 Piece, Early 1900s	72.00
Sledding Slopes, Box Folds To Sled Slope, People At Rail, Table, Germany, 58 In.	4600.00
Solitaire, Marble, The Good Old Game, 32 Swirl Marbles, Germany, Box	295.00
Speedway Set, Track, 8 Die Cast Racers, Roll-Out Game Board, Spinner, Box, 10 x 15 In.	314.00
Spelling Board, Oval, Cardboard Lithograph, Wood Letters, 2-Sided, Richmond, 1940, 13 In.	45.00
Target, Circle, Bird, Star Targets, Spins, Cast Iron, 1940s, 19 In.	200.00
Target, Clown, Red, White, Hand Painted, Die Cut, Sheet Metal, Mechanical, c.1920, 12 Ft.	485.00
Tiddlywinks, 4 Felt Squares, 6 Small Discs, Red, Blue, Yellow & White, Parker Bros., 1897	32.00
Time Tunnel, Sci-Fi TV Series, Pressman Toy Co., 1966, 10 x 15 In.	150.00
Transogram Mr. Novak, Board, 1963	37.00
Twilight Zone, Closed Door Blocking Cards, Cayuga Productions, 1964, 18 x 19 In.	230.00
Twilight Zone, Ideal, Board, c.1964, 19 x 9 In.	286.00
Uncle Wiggily, Parker Brothers, Board, 1979	11.00
Wheel, Carnival, Wood, Painted, Applied Letters & Numbers, 41 In.	106.00
Wheel, Gambling, Domino, 29 In.	110.00
Wheel, Gambling, Red, Yellow, 2-Sided, Stand, 23 ½ In.	220.00
Wonderful Game Of Oz, Playing Pieces, Parker Bros., Board, 20 x 10 In. *illus*	525.00
X-Plor U.S. By Airplane, 4 Metal Airplanes, Board, Box, 17 x 9 In. *illus*	117.00
You Don't Say, Milton Bradley, Board, 1963	24.00

GAME PLATES are plates of any make decorated with pictures of birds, animals, or fish. The game plates usually came in sets consisting of twelve dishes and a serving platter. These sets were most popular during the 1880s.

Birds, Fowl, In Field, Gilt, Scalloped Rim, Limoges, Signed, Puisoyes, c.1920, 9 ½ In.	195.00
Birds, Mallard Ducks, In Flight, Blue Border, Gilt Rim, Limoges, Signed, Mullidy, 9 ½ In.	720.00
Birds, Mallard Drake, In Flight, Yellow, Brown, Limoges, Signed, Thomas, 8 ½ In.	126.00
Birds, Peacock Hen, Pink, Gilt Scalloped Rim, Limoges, Signed, Klingenburg, 1900-10, 9 In.	175.00
Birds, Quail, In Flight, Over Marsh, Limoges, Signed, Thomas, 8 ½ In.	126.00
Birds, Quail, Prairie Ground, Green Grass, Limoges, Signed, Qurog, c.1920, 9 ½ In.	126.00
Fish, Gold Enamel, Ferns, Green Ground, Scalloped Rim, Coiffe Limoges, 9 ¼ In.	185.00
Fox & Hare, Oak Leaves, Acorns, Walnut, Carved, Oval, Black Forest, 22 ½ x 15 In.	995.00

GARDEN FURNISHINGS have been popular for centuries. The stone or metal statues, wire, iron, or rustic furniture, urns and fountains, sundials, and small figurines are included in this category. Many of the metal pieces have been made continuously for years.

Armillary, Neoclassical Style, Iron, Copper, 33 x 16 In.	250.00
Armillary Sphere, Cherub With Arrow, Hour Dial, Brass, 20th Century, 27 x 30 In.	140.00
Bench, Black Paint, Pierced Lobed Panels, Laurel Leaves, Concave Seat, Cast Iron, 43 In.	1840.00
Bench, Cast Iron, Barrow Back, Grapevine Pattern, Dark Green, 32 x 15 In.	325.00
Bench, Fern, Cast Iron, Kramer, Late 19th Century, 33 x 54 x 13 In.	1180.00

Bench, George III, Serpentine Crest Rail, Claw Feet, Painted, Iron, 1800, 43 x 63 In., Pair	17500.00
Bench, George III, Tripartite Back, Concave Seat, Painted, Wrought Iron, 1800, 38 x 61 In.	5600.00
Bench, Marble, Ram's Head Capitals, Fruit, Ribbons, Flowers, Italy, 33 x 79 In.	3540.00
Bench, Openwork Back, Scrolled Legs, Cast Iron, Patented 1891, 36 x 45 In.	550.00
Bench, Openwork, Ferns, Black Paint, Shaped Arms, Wrought Iron, 32 x 51 x 20 In.	1159.00
Bench, Passion Flower, Scrolling Leaves, Vines, Parrot Head Arms, Cast Iron, c.1870, 38 In.	2124.00
Bench, Pierced Leaves, Scrolls, White Paint, Arms, Cast Iron, 1900s, 35 x 44 In.	633.00
Bench, Pierced Medallion Back, Dog, Flowers, Cast Iron, Wooden Seat, 1900s, 31 x 52 In.	240.00
Bench, Scrolls, Leaves, Minerva Crest, White Paint, Cast Iron, c.1920, 33 x 44 In., Pair	1763.00
Bench, Scrolls, Woman Holding Bird Center, Finials, Black, Cast Iron, 34 x 41 In.	195.00
Bench, White Paint, Pierced Urn & Scroll Panels, Rosettes, Trestle Base, Cast Iron, 46 In.	805.00
Bench, Wire, Shaped Back, White Paint, Scrolled Iron Base, Late 1800s, 41 In.	260.00
Birdbath, Black Forest, Walnut, Fountain, Tree Branch Pedestal, Tripod Foot, c.1890, 34 x 21 In.	518.00
Birdbath, Bronze, Fluted Font, Birds, Round Pedestal, Hexagonal Base, 33 x 21 In.	374.00
Birdbath, Marble, Carved, Leaf, Bowl, c.1850, 44 ½ x 19 In.	4800.00
Birdbath, Roses, Fluted Urn Pedestal, 2 Birds, White Paint, Round Base, Cast Iron, 30 x 19 In.	323.00
Birdbath, Victorian, Shell, Perching Birds, Cast Iron, 8 ½ x 15 In.	115.00
Birdhouse, Mailbox Shape, Bird Figure, Painted, Black, Red, Willie Massey, 12 x 11 x 23 In.	201.00
Boot Scraper, 2 Dogs, Iron, 19th Century	145.00
Boot Scraper, Black Shoeshine Boy, Cast Iron, Dolphin Supports, Oval Tray, c.1860, 12 x 10 In.	390.00
Boot Scraper, Dolphins, Green Man Mask, Iron, Marked 5300 Scrape, 6 x 8 In. *illus*	288.00
Boot Scraper, Lyre Shape, Iron, White Marble Chunk Base, 11 ¾ x 9 x 8 In.	230.00
Boot Scraper, Scrolled Shield Shape, Painted Black, Mid 19th Century, 7 x 7 In.	125.00
Chair, Lounge, Wire Seats, High Back, Russell Woodard, 1950s, 25 x 25 x 25, Pair	180.00
Chair, Metal Frame, Spring Base, Wire Mesh, 34 x 22 x 27 In., 3 Piece	180.00
Chair, Rococo Style, White Paint, Scrolls, Wrought Iron, c.1945, 6 Piece	588.00
Chair, Set, Arms, Wire Seats, Green, Integrated Footpads, Table, Russell Woodard, 1950s, 5 Piece	1560.00
Chair, Victorian, Cameo Medallion, Round Seat, Black Paint, Cast Iron, c.1890, Pair	529.00
Chair, Wrought Iron, Painted White, Shepherd & Sheep Design, 6 Piece	518.00
Chaise Longue, Painted, Reclining, Wheels, Iron, Woodward Furniture, 38 x 60 x 29 In.	195.00
Chaise Longue, Vinyl, Mesh, Cast Aluminum, Richard Schultz, Knoll, 34 x 55 x 22 In.	660.00
Cross, Forged Iron, 41 In.	240.00
Door, C-Scrolls, White, Wrought Iron, Victorian, 99 x 24 In., Pair	275.00
Door Set, Softwood, Open Screen Top, Chinese, c.1850, 99 x 23 In., 4 Piece	4320.00
Figure, Artemis Of The Chase, Deer, Cast Iron, 71 ½ x 47 x 24 In.	5288.00
Figure, Boy, Holding Disc To Head, Cast Iron, 32 In.	95.00
Figure, Boy, Playing Lute, Cast Iron, 31 In.	110.00
Figure, Boy, With Conch Shell, Cast Iron, 35 In.	360.00
Figure, Bust, Man, Curly Hair, Cement, 33 In.	175.00
Figure, Bust, Napoleon, Cast Iron, 29 In.	480.00
Figure, Cherub Musician, Painted, Cast Iron, Square Base, 52 x 19 In.	350.00
Figure, Deer, Antlers, Cast Iron, 60 In.	4800.00
Figure, Dog, Bulldog, Cement, 18 In.	360.00
Figure, Dog, Dalmation, Cast Iron, Painted, 41 ½ In., Pair *illus*	1287.00
Figure, Dog, Shepherd, Cast Iron, c.1889, 23 x 25 In.	2370.00
Figure, Dogs, Carrying Basket, Paint Over Concrete, 20 In., Pair	1500.00
Figure, Flower Basket, Cement, 16 In., Pair	175.00
Figure, Fox, Seated, Cement, 24 ½ In.	268.00
Figure, Gargoyle, Cast Iron, 19th Century, 27 ½ In., Pair	1540.00
Figure, Guan Yin, Seated, 2 Hands On Raised Knee, Lotus Base, White Marble, 46 In.	1888.00
Figure, Lion, Reclining, Iron Cast, 19th Century, 13 ½ x 28 x 4 In.	863.00
Figure, Maiden, Hand On Chin, White Paint, Cast Iron, 54 In.	840.00
Figure, Maiden, Hands On Hips, Flowers, Egg & Dart Top Plinth, Cast Iron, 91 ½ In.	1998.00
Figure, Mercury, Lead, Early 20th Century, 32 In.	600.00
Figure, Mermaid, Seated, Iron, 16 In.	354.00
Figure, Muse, Cast Stone, France, c.1900, 48 x 15 In.	840.00
Figure, Musician, Cast Iron, 32 In.	240.00
Figure, Savannah Girl, Holding 2 Bowls, Cement, 45 ½ x 27 In.	165.00 to 280.00
Figure, Temple, Pagoda Shape, Finial, Lobed Base, Plinth, Stone, Late 1800s, 64 x 16 In., Pair	1150.00
Figure, Torchere, Cement, Early 1900s, 34 In.	200.00
Figure, Turtle, Bronze, Signed, Chini, Early 20th Century, 8 ½ x 17 In.	450.00
Figure, Woman, Seminude, Flower Basket, Summer, Pedestal, Concrete, 79 In.	1298.00
Figure, Women, Draped Gown, Jug On Shoulder, Marble, 60 In., Pair	2006.00
Fire Pit, Grill Cover, Stan Hawk, c.1950, 18 x 42 In.	1440.00
Flowerpot, Pedestal, Scrolls, Leaf Design, White Paint, Cement, 51 x 27 In.	1900.00
Fountain, Birdbath, Cherub Pedestal, Lead, Early 20th Century, 27 In. *illus*	441.00

Garden, Figure, Dog, Dalmation, Cast Iron, Painted, 41 ½ In., Pair $1287.00

Garden, Fountain, Birdbath, Cherub Pedestal, Lead, Early 20th Century, 27 In. $441.00

Garden, Fountain, Nymph, Shell Basin, Dolphin Base, Bronze, Verdigris Patina, 62 x 33 In. $6600.00

> **TIP**
> Lead garden sculptures should not be cleaned. The dirt and discoloration add to the beauty of the piece. Lead is so soft that most types of cleaning will harm the finish.

Garden, Garniture, 3-Part, Cast Iron, Octagonal Base, Paneled Center, Tiered, 1950, 43 In.
$600.00

Garden, Gnome, Pine, Painted, Beard, Smiling, Pointed Hat, Tunic, Boots, 1800s
$956.00

Fountain, Boy & Goose, Figural, Zinc, 19th Century, 7 Ft.	7200.00
Fountain, Boy Playing Flute, Sphere With Fish, Bronze, c.1900, 48 x 12 x 16 In.	2151.00
Fountain, Boy, With Snake, Lead, 30 In.	275.00
Fountain, Fairies With Lilies, Bronze, 69 x 34 x 29 In.	5875.00
Fountain, Frog, Piped, Weller Coppertone, 10 In.	3800.00
Fountain, Girl, Bowl On Head, 2 Tiers, Cast Iron, 75 x 34 ½ In.	890.00
Fountain, Glazed, 5 Sections, Terra-Cotta, Stamped, c.1930, 69 In.	4800.00
Fountain, Lead, Late 19th Century, 8 x 69 x 38 In.	840.00
Fountain, Maiden Pouring Water, Lobed Basin, Octagonal Base, Lead, Zinc, c.1955, 63 In.	3819.00
Fountain, Mermaid, Tiered Basins, Continental, Bronze, 117 x 52 In.	3105.00
Fountain, Nymph, Shell Basin, Dolphin Base, Bronze, Verdigris Patina, 62 x 33 In. *illus*	6600.00
Fountain, Oriental Woman, Leafy Hat, 20th Century, Bronze, 40 x 13 x 13 In.	1135.00
Fountain, Putti, On Flower, Frog Finial, Painted, Cast Iron, Mott Iron Works, 101 x 59 In.	21000.00
Fountain, Putti, Seahorses, Dolphin Supports, Round Plinth, Bronze, 62 x 37 In.	5581.00
Fountain, Woman, Standing, Lead, Florentine Craftsman, c.1928, 49 In.	4560.00
Fountainhead, Swan, Lead, Mid 1900s, 13 x 12 In.	375.00
Furniture, Twig, Sassafras, Settee, Armchair, Rocker, Table, Berks Co., c.1910, 4 Piece	2090.00
Garniture, 3-Part, Cast Iron, Octagonal Base, Paneled Center, Tiered, 1950, 43 In. *illus*	600.00
Gate, Leaves, Scrolls, Wrought Iron, c.1900, 71 x 28 ½ In., Pair	890.00
Gate, Louis XV Style, Bars Above Scrollwork, Green Paint, Wrought Iron, 91 x 50 In., Pair	345.00
Gate, Scrolls, Flower Cartouches, Wrought & Sheet Iron, Late 1800s, 90 x 39 In., Pair	345.00
Gazing Ball, Aqua, Children, Horses, Flowers, Birds, Multicolored, Blue, Ground, 11 ½ In.	690.00
Gazing Ball, Mercury, Glass, Attached Stand, 14 x 9 In.	374.00
Gnome, Holding Basket, On Mushroom, Painted, Terra-Cotta, Late 19th Century, 14 In.	360.00
Gnome, Pine, Painted, Beard, Smiling, Pointed Hat, Tunic, Boots, 1800s *illus*	956.00
Hitching Post, Acanthus Reeds, Cast Iron, 19th Century, 65 In., Pair	895.00
Hitching Post, Black Man, On Bale Of Cotton, Painted, Cast Iron, 20th Century, 44 In.	700.00
Hitching Post, Black, Pedestal, J.W. Fiske, New York, Late 1800s, 46 In.	588.00
Hitching Post, Chinaman, Painted, Cast Iron, Marked, Wood Phil, 1890s, 46 In.	2400.00
Hitching Post, Horse Head, Cast Iron, 19th Century, 10 In.	138.00
Hitching Post, Horse Head, Cast Iron, 19th Century, 44 In., Pair	750.00
Hitching Post, Horse Head, Cast Iron, Aaron Wissler, Pa., 19th Century, 68 In., Pair	1065.00
Hitching Post, Horse Head, Cast Iron, Mass., 19th Century, 48 In., Pair	975.00
Hitching Post, Horse Head, Cast Iron, Wm. Adams, Pa., 19th Century, 61 In., Pair	2600.00
Hitching Post, Jockey, Arm Extended, Red Jacket, Yellow Hat, Pants, Cast Metal, 10 In.	78.00
Hitching Post, Jockey, Black Man, Standing, Plinth, Paint, Cast Iron, c.1850, 37 ½ In., Pair	764.00
Hitching Post, Jockey, Black, Pedestal Base, Iron, c.1900, 16 In., Pair	575.00
Hitching Post, Jockey, Green, Yellow, Cast Iron, 19th Century, 69 In., Pair	525.00
Hitching Post, Jockey, Painted, Cast Iron, 20th Century, 47 In.	1200.00
Hitching Post, Jockey, Sign, Hello, Good Bye, Multicolored, 35 ½ In.	102.00
Hitching Post, Napoleon, 2 Rings, Cast Iron, 1800s, 8 In., Pair	550.00
Hitching Post, Stable Boy, Painted, Cast Iron, Marked, Wood Phil, 1890s, 46 In.	2400.00
Hose Reel, Free Standing, Metal, 24 In.	125.00
Jardiniere, Classical, Cast Iron, Late 19th Century, 14 ½ x 27 In.	176.00
Jardiniere, Faux Marble, Gilt, Zinc Liner, Gadrooned Rim, Leaf Carved Pedestal Base, 32 x 31 In.	2350.00
Jardiniere, Lion Handles, Cherubs, Stepped, Round Plinth, Bronze, 30 x 31 In., Pair	2703.00
Jardiniere, Phoenix Birds, Flowers, Bronze, Japan, 14 x 18 In.	335.00
Jardiniere, Slate, Roman Bath Shape, Lion Head Masks, Paw Feet, Marble Base, c.1800, 6 x 14 In.	3231.00
Jardiniere, Tin, Stenciled, Piecrust Edge, Rectangular Insert, Stand, Square Legs, 1900s, 17 x 48 In.	119.00
Lawn Sprinkler, Sprinkling Sam, Clown, Painted, Tin, 34 In.	95.00
Plant Stand, See Furniture, Stand, Plant	
Planter, Bullet Shape, Fiberglass, Pink, Brass Insert, Tripod Mount, 22 x 8 ¾ In.	115.00
Planter, Flower Trellis Relief, Leaf Feet, Painted, Cast Iron, c.1910, 15 x 31 In.	374.00
Planter, Flowers, Leaves, 5 Cup Holders, Painted, 4-Footed, 1920s, 30 x 34 In.	413.00
Planter, Flowers, Purple, Green, Red, Koi Porcelain, Chinese, 20 x 21 In.	205.00
Planter, Footed, Malcolm Leland, Bisque Glaze, Architectural Pottery, c.1951, 20 x 14 In.	720.00
Planter, Gothic Revival, Oak, Turreted Bamboo Corners, Arched Panels, 28 x 33 x 33 In.	2000.00
Planter, Green, 8 Molded Lines, Stoneware, 15 x 16 ½ In., 2 Piece	65.00
Planter, Guhl, Pottery, Hourglass Shape, Swiss, 18 x 19 In., Pair	3000.00
Planter, Lacquer, Cinnabar, 4-Footed, Panels, Flowers, Leaves, Chinese, 4 ¼ x 9 ⅛ x 10 ¼ In.	570.00
Planter, Leaf Design, Composition, Over Concrete, Footed, 29 In., Pair	900.00
Planter, Marilyn Kay Austin, White Glaze, Architectural Pottery, c.1965, 19 x 13 In.	510.00
Planter, Masks, Draped Vines, Footed, Cement, 22 x 31 In.	240.00
Planter, Oval, Training Grate, Cast Iron, 1800s, England, 13 x 25 In.	295.00
Planter, Putti Side Panels, Ram's Head Corners, Lead, Square, 5 ½ x 11 ½ In.	206.00
Planter, Wirework, 3 Tiers, Casters, 70 x 48 In.	198.00

G

Planter, Woven Pattern, Stone, 22 In., 3 Piece	1000.00
Plaque, Woman, With Dog, Art Deco, White Paint, Cement, Round	110.00
Seat, Blue, White, Pierced Coins, Dragons, Water Landscape, Chinese Export, c.1850, 14 x 10 In.	575.00
Seat, Celadon, Pin Flowers, Leaves, Asian, 19 ½ In., Pair	83.00
Seat, Chinese Export, Blue & White, Hexagonal, Pierced Cash Designs, 1800s, 18 ½ x 13 In.	2520.00
Seat, Famille Jaune Yellow, Symbols, Lotus, Scrolling Leaves, Chinese Export, 18 ½ In., Pair ...	150.00
Seat, Famille Rose, Barrel Form, Rose Medallion, Garden Scene, Chinese Export, 18 x 16 In. .	1560.00
Seat, Famille Rose, Pierced Cylinder, Painted, Tobacco Leaf, Chinese Export, 19 x 13 ½ In., Pair	431.00
Seat, Famille Rose, Warriors, Bats, Chinese Export, 13 ½ In.	1434.00
Seat, Flowers, Birds, Cutouts, Multicolored, Chinese Export, 20th Century, 19 In.	83.00
Seat, Ironstone, Flowers, Blue, White, Cutouts, 15 x 13 ½ In.	62.00
Seat, Majolica, White Glaze, Yellow Rope & Tassel Decoration, Tufted Seat, Italy, 17 x 14 In. ...	115.00
Seat, Porcelain, Pink, Green, Scenic, Chinese..	146.00
Settee, Arm Chair, Cast Iron, Fern, Pierced Seats, Splayed Legs, 34 x 52 In., 3 Piece..........	3878.00
Settee, Rococo, Cast Iron, Flower Crest, Reticulated Seat, Leaf Skirt, Cabriole Legs, 36 x 47 x 20 In.	1800.00
Settee, Vintage Pattern, Cast Iron, Leaf Design On Apron, 1870, 31 x 36 In., Pair.............	2115.00
Stand, Fern, Bronze, Brown Marble, 48 x 12 In.	600.00
Stool, Lotus Blossoms, Reticulated Medallions, Wood Base, Chinese, c.1900, 22 In.	24.00
Stool, Pekclaka, Stoneware, Glaze, Claude Conover, 17 x 16 ½ In.	6710.00
Sundial, Brass, Round Plate, 1700s, 6 ½ In.	432.00
Sundial, White, Marble, Brass Mounted Cannon, Magnifying Glass, Iron, Base, 1890s, 32 x 18 In. .	3700.00
Table, 4 Stools, Ceramic, Painted Flower Top, Stan Bitters, c.1960s, 20 x 26 & 12 x 13 In., 5 Piece..	7350.00
Table, Animals, Wrought Iron Base, Tile, Arts & Crafts, Twisted, Curled, 16 X 18 x 13 In.	480.00
Table, Bistro, Cast Iron, Painted, 3 Leg Base, 21 x 20 ½ In., Pair..........................	184.00
Table, Marble Top, Wrought Iron, Black Paint, Copper Border, 3-Footed, c.1950, 29 ½ In.	205.00
Table, Painted, Iron, Glass Top, Woodward Furniture, 17 ½ x 26 In., Pair...................	125.00
Topiary, Cat, Seated, Fake Pine Boughs, Over Metal Frame, 70 In.	3900.00
Topiary, Giraffe, Fake Pine Boughs, Over Metal Frame, 97 In.	4800.00
Topiary, Squirrel, Nibbling, Fake Pine Boughs, Over Metal Frame, 72 In.	695.00
Topiary, Stag, Fake Pine Boughs, Over Metal Frame, 140 x 92 In.	1640.00
Topiary, Swans, Kissing, Fake Pine Boughs, Over Metal Frame, 7 Ft. 6 In. x 11 Ft..............	2400.00
Urn, Campagna, Leaves, Anthemia, Palmettes, Painted, Cast Iron, 21 x 22 In.	345.00
Urn, Cast Iron, 6-Sided Base, Storks, Shells, Lily Pads, White Paint, c.1890, 51 x 41 In., Pair....	2703.00
Urn, Cast Iron, Figural Handles, White Paint, 19th Century, 19 ½ x 30 ½ In., Pair.............	936.00
Urn, Cast Iron, On Stand, Embossed, Kramer Bros. Foundry, Dayton, Ohio, c.1900, 24 In.	180.00
Urn, Cast Iron, Square Base, Column, Lion's Head, Double Ears, White Paint, 28 x 27 In.	294.00
Urn, Classical, Relief Decoration, Iron, Pedestal Base, 20th Century, 36 x 21 In. ....*illus*	920.00
Urn, Classical Style, Figural, Bronze, 71 x 32 In., Pair......................................	2106.00
Urn, Flared Rim, Footed, Iron, 28 ½ In., Pair...	960.00
Urn, Flower Rim, Birds, Cattails, Flowers, Round Base, Cast Iron, Black, 28 x 41 In., Pair.......	2596.00
Urn, Fluted Body, Scrolling Handles, Iron, Pedestal Base, Late 1800s, 53 x 42 In. ....*illus*	780.00
Urn, Leaf Carving, Rolled Rim & Foot, Marble, 17 x 15 In., Pair............................	403.00
Urn, Lid, Reeded Body, Festoons, Square Pedestal, Flowers, Wreath, Cast Iron, 1800s, 40 In.	2065.00
Urn, Metal, Mask Mounts, Garland Swags, Pineapple Finial, Plinth, c.1875, 30 x 14 In., Pair ..	3943.00
Urn, Napoleon III, Ribs, Acanthus Rim, White Paint, Cast Iron, Footed, 25 x 28 In.	2500.00
Urn, Neo-Grec, Egg, Dart Molded Rim, Classical, Handles, Cast Iron, 20 x 25 x 21 In., Pair.....	600.00
Urn, Pedestal, Neoclassical, Masks, Cast Iron, Late 1900s, 63 x 25 In.	1560.00
Urn, Ram's Head Handles, Cast Lead, 19th Century, 11 x 17 In., Pair........................	3500.00
Urn, White Paint, Scroll Handles, Square Base, Cast Iron, 19th Century, 60 x 43 In.	1100.00
Urn, Wirework, Footed, Looped Detail, 1900s, 19 In., Pair..................................	441.00
Watering Can, Copper, Brass, Spherical Body, Ring Foot, Long Spout, 5 ¼ x 18 ½ In.	120.00
Watering Can, Copper, Elliptical, Tubular Handle, Early 1900s, 14 x 8 In.	420.00
Watering Can, Galvanized Metal, England, 2 Gal., 24 In.	45.00
Watering Can, Yellow & White Flowers, Tole, Handle, Long Spout, 1920s, 8 ½-In. Spout	95.00
Wind Chimes, Walter Lamb, Copper, c.1950, 20 ½ In.	3360.00
Windmill Weight, Rooster, Hummer, 10 x 10 In.	395.00
Windmill Weight, Rooster, White, Red, Cast Iron, 17 x 17 In.	1530.00

GAUDY DUTCH pottery was made in England for the American market from about 1810 to 1820. It is a white earthenware with Imari-style decorations of red, blue, green, yellow, and black. Only sixteen patterns of Gaudy Dutch were made: Butterfly, Carnation, Dahlia, Double Rose, Dove, Grape, Leaf, Oyster, Primrose, Single Rose, Strawflower, Sunflower, Urn, War Bonnet, Zinnia, and No Name. Other similar wares are called Gaudy Ironstone and Gaudy Welsh.

Bowl, Sunflower, 3 x 6 In.	330.00
Coffeepot, Double Rose, Gooseneck Spout, Scroll Handle, Impressed, F, 7 In.	1080.00
Cup & Saucer, Butterfly, Vine Border, Handleless	396.00

GAUDY DUTCH

Garden, Urn, Classical,
Relief Decoration, Iron, Pedestal Base,
20th Century, 36 x 21 In.
$920.00

G

Garden, Urn, Fluted Body,
Scrolling Handles, Iron, Pedestal Base,
Late 1800s, 53 x 42 In.
$780.00

TIP
*A garden sculpture
should be mounted
at least 18 inches
above the ground.
It should be cleaned
to keep off moss
and algae.*

Gaudy Dutch, Cup & Saucer, Dove,
19th Century
$351.00

As always, the edited listings in *Kovels'
Antiques & Collectibles Price Guide
2011* aren't available on any website,
but readers should visit Kovels.com for
information on trends, tips, reproductions,
marks, old prices, and more!

Gaudy Dutch, Cup & Saucer, Single Rose, Handleless $220.00

Gaudy Dutch, Plate, Single Rose, 19th Century, 8 In. $117.00

Gaudy Welsh, Mug, Flower, Drape, Swag, Handle, 4 In. $46.00

Gene Autry, Cap Gun, Repeating, Cast Iron, Public Cowboy 1 Promotion, Box, 8 ½ In. $176.00

Cup & Saucer, Dove, 19th Century ....*illus*	351.00
Cup & Saucer, Single Rose, Handleless ....*illus*	220.00
Pitcher, Flowers, Leaves, 8-Sided, Figural Spout, Bearded Man's Head, 6 ¼ In.	489.00
Plate, Single Rose, 19th Century, 8 In. ....*illus*	117.00
Plate, Sunflower, Zigzag Border, 7 ½ In.	339.00
Sugar, Cover, Butterfly, Shell Handles, 5 ½ In.	791.00
Waste Bowl, Urn, 3 x 6 In.	527.00

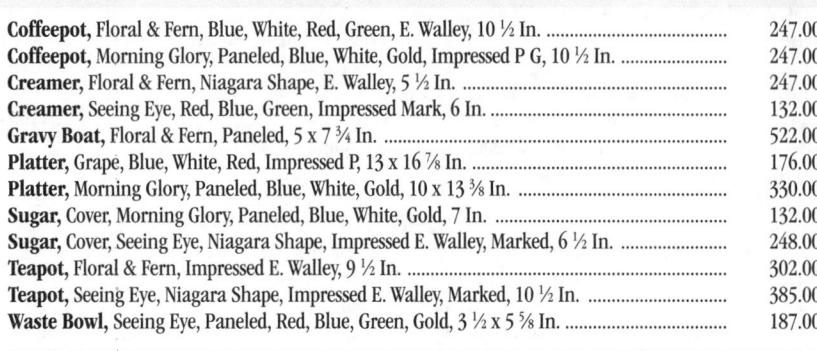

GAUDY IRONSTONE is the collector's name for the ironstone wares with the bright patterns similar to Gaudy Dutch. It was made in England for the American market after 1850. There may be other examples found in the listing for Ironstone or under the name of the ceramic factory.

Coffeepot, Floral & Fern, Blue, White, Red, Green, E. Walley, 10 ½ In.	247.00
Coffeepot, Morning Glory, Paneled, Blue, White, Gold, Impressed P G, 10 ½ In.	247.00
Creamer, Floral & Fern, Niagara Shape, E. Walley, 5 ½ In.	247.00
Creamer, Seeing Eye, Red, Blue, Green, Impressed Mark, 6 In.	132.00
Gravy Boat, Floral & Fern, Paneled, 5 x 7 ¾ In.	522.00
Platter, Grape, Blue, White, Red, Impressed P, 13 x 16 ⅞ In.	176.00
Platter, Morning Glory, Paneled, Blue, White, Gold, 10 x 13 ⅜ In.	330.00
Sugar, Cover, Morning Glory, Paneled, Blue, White, Gold, 7 In.	132.00
Sugar, Cover, Seeing Eye, Niagara Shape, Impressed E. Walley, Marked, 6 ½ In.	248.00
Teapot, Floral & Fern, Impressed E. Walley, 9 ½ In.	302.00
Teapot, Seeing Eye, Niagara Shape, Impressed E. Walley, Marked, 10 ½ In.	385.00
Waste Bowl, Seeing Eye, Paneled, Red, Blue, Green, Gold, 3 ½ x 5 ⅝ In.	187.00

GAUDY WELSH is an Imari-decorated earthenware with red, blue, green, and gold decorations. Most Gaudy Welsh was made in England for the American market. It was made from 1820 to about 1860.

Cake Plate, Columbine, Cobalt Blue Cartouche Border, 2 Handles, 9 ½ In.	120.00
Cup & Saucer, Strawberries, Handleless Cup	50.00
Cup & Saucer, Tulip, Flow Blue, Triangular Swirled Panels, 1830s	80.00
Cup & Saucer, Village, Orange Houses, Spoked Floral Panels, Shaped Handle	135.00
Jug, Flower Basket II, Floral Cartouche, Flow Blue Band, Toed Foot, 5 In.	99.00
Mug, Flower, Drape, Swag, Handle, 4 In. ....*illus*	46.00
Mustard, Flowers, Flow Blue, Orange, Silver Cover & Spoon, 3 ¼ In.	29.00
Pitcher, Bethesda, Flowers, Panels, Bulbous Shaped Rim, Dragon's Head Handle, 6 In.	299.00
Pitcher, Hydra, Flow Blue Flowers, Raised Bulbous Rim, 5 In.	240.00
Pitcher, Swans, Flowers, Flow Blue, 6 Panels, Shaped Rim, Serpent Handle, 7 In.	62.00
Plate, Oyster Pattern, Stylized Flowers, Flow Blue, Orange, Raised Rim, 7 ½ In.	22.00
Teapot, Hotplate, Black Center, Orange, White Design, White, 8 In.	117.00
Teapot, Tulip, Flow Blue, Scalloped Panels, Scalloped Foot, 7 In.	189.00

GEISHA GIRL porcelain was made for export in the late nineteenth century in Japan. It was an inexpensive porcelain often sold in dime stores or used as free premiums. Pieces are sometimes marked with the name of a store. Japanese ladies in kimonos are pictured on the dishes. There are over 125 recorded patterns. Borders of red, blue, green, gold, brown, or several of these colors were used. Modern reproductions are being made.

Vase, Wisteria, 3 ¾ In.	20.00

GENE AUTRY was born in 1907. He began his career as the "Singing Cowboy," in 1928. His first movie appearance was in 1934, his last in 1958. His likeness and that of the Wonder Horse, Champion, were used on toys, books, lunch boxes, and advertisements.

Book, Tell-A-Tale, Gene Autry Goes To The Circus, 1951, Whitman	18.00
Button, Champion, Gene's Horse, Tin, Lithograph, Black & White, 1950s	30.00
Button, Gene Autry & Champ, Yellow Ground, Stanley, Toronto, 1 ¼ In.	75.00
Cap Gun, Cast Iron, Engraved, Red Grips, 1950s, 8 ½ In.	702.00
Cap Gun, Holster, White Handle, Nickel Finish, Kenton, 6 ⅞ In.	135.00
Cap Gun, Junior Model, Kenton, Box, 8 In.	293.00
Cap Gun, Repeating, Cast Iron, Public Cowboy 1 Promotion, Box, 8 ½ In. ....*illus*	176.00
Coloring Book, Oversized, Whitman, 1950	17.00
Gun & Holster Set, Double, 2 Cap Guns & Holster, 11 In.	322.00
Lunch Box, Melody Ranch Scene, Cowhide Print, Universal, Box, 1954	633.00
Paper Doll, Melody Ranch, Merrill, Uncut, c.1950, 13 x 10 ½ In.	115.00
Pin, Gene Autry Photo, Cowboy Hat, ⅞ In.	17.00

Postcard, Gene, Blue Background, Yellow Shirt, Hat, 1940s	15.00
Postcard, Gene Standing By Horse, Color, 1970s	10.00
Puzzle, Gene Standing & Talking To His Horse, Whitman, 1950s	70.00
Ring, Portrait, Aluminum, Silver Luster, Gold Accent, c.1950 ....*illus*	557.00
Sign, Display, Columbia Records, Gene Autry Holds Guitar, Easel Back, 16 x 22 In.	155.00
Suspenders, Dark Maroon, Gene & Champion, Adjustment Clasps, 1950s	45.00
Toy, Dish Set, Dish, 2 Bowls, Mug, Signatures, Knowles China, c.1950, 5 Piece	230.00

GIBSON GIRL black-and-blue decorated plates were made in the early 1900s. Twenty-four different 10 ½-inch plates were made by the Royal Doulton pottery at Lambeth, England. These pictured scenes from the book *A Widow and Her Friends* by Charles Dana Gibson. Another set of twelve 9-inch plates featuring pictures of the heads of Gibson Girls had all-blue decoration. Many other items also pictured the famous Gibson Girl.

Print, Parting Wall, Pen & Ink, Signed, Inscribed, 9 x 13 In.	374.00

GILLINDER pressed glass was first made by William T. Gillinder of Philadelphia in 1863. The company had a working factory on the grounds at the Centennial and made small, marked pieces of glass for sale as souvenirs. They made a variety of decorative glass pieces and tablewares. **GILLINDER**

Bust, Lincoln, Frosted, Embossed, Centennial Exhibition, 6 x 2 ⅝ x 3 ¼ In.	431.00
Paperweight, Ruth The Gleaner, Frosted, Centennial Exhibition, 4 ½ x 2 ⅜ In., 2 Piece	207.00
Shoe, Frosted, Embossed, Silver Plated Stand, Centennial Exhibition, 8 x 4 ¾ In.	259.00
Sugar Shaker, Cover, Melon, Opal, Blue Shading, Multicolored Flowers, 4 ¾ In. ....*illus*	104.00
Sugar Shaker, Cover, Scrolled Rib, Opaque Green, c.1900, 4 ¼ In.	79.00

GIRL SCOUT collectors search for anything pertaining to the Girl Scouts, including uniforms, publications, and old cookie boxes. The Girl Scout movement started in 1912, two years after the Boy Scouts. It began under Juliette Gordon Low of Savannah, Georgia. The first Girl Scout cookies were sold in 1928.

Cup, Collapsible, Aluminum, 2 ½ x 2 ½ In. Open	40.00
Doll, Terri Lee, Plastic Head, Painted Eyes, Original Uniform, 1955, 16 In. ....*illus*	224.00
Game, Trefoil, Wooden People Playing Pieces, Box	85.00
Handbook, Cloth Cover, 510 Pages, 1953, 5 ¾ In.	18.00
Handbook, Junior, 188 Pages, 1986	5.00
Handkerchief, Girl Scout Badges Border Inside Red Border, Cotton, Square, 11 In.	18.00
Key Chain, Eagle, 1970s, ⅞ In.	7.50
Knife, Pocket, Logo, Celluloid Handle, 4 Blades, Kut Master, 1960s	15.00
Lunch Box, Tin, Girl Scout Scenes, Single Handle, 6 x 4 x 3 In.	235.00
Membership Card, Green Cardstock, 1936, 2 ⅛ x 3 ¾ In.	8.99
Mug, Wapsiketa District HAC, Decal, 1982	15.00
Necklace, Emblem, Goldtone, 16-In. Chain	12.95
Photo Album, Girl Scout Logo On Front, Dark Green	2.50
Pin, Columbia River Girl Scout Council, Portland, Oregon, Blue, Green, Yellow, 1987	8.50

GLASS-ART. Art glass means any of the many forms of glassware made during the late nineteenth or early twentieth century. These wares were expensive when they were first made and production was limited. Art glass is not the typical commercial glass that was made in large quantities, and most of the art glass was produced by hand methods. Later twentieth-century glass is listed under Glass-Contemporary, Glass-Midcentury, or Glass-Venetian. Even more art glass may be found in categories such as Burmese, Cameo Glass, Tiffany, and other factory names.

Atomizer, Tapered, Blue Iridescent, 6 ½ In.	201.00
Atomizer, Waisted, Gold Encrusted, Enameled Flowers, 9 ¼ In.	115.00
Bowl, Cover, Clear, Ormolu Rim Mounts, Diamond Bands, Fluted, Lid Finial, 1900s, 10 x 12 In.	237.00
Bowl, J. Hoffmann, Footed, Black, Green Interior, Wiener Werkstatte, c.1924, 6 In.	1793.00
Bowl, Purple, Myra Crystal, Iridescent Gold, Melon Ribs, Footed, WMF, 6 ½ In.	144.00
Bowl, Set, Amber Leaf & Flowers, Hobbs, Master, 7 Berry Bowls, 8 ½ x 3 & 4 x 1 ½ In.	144.00
Bowl, Vertical Orange Striping, Green Ground, Flared Shoulder, 3 x 7 In.	575.00
Bowl, WMF Flared, Green & White Mottled, Ikora, 12 ¾ x 2 ¼ In.	86.00
Box, Cover, Scarabs, Leaves, Frosted, Saumont, France, Round, 20th Century, 3 ½ In.	39.00
Candlestick, Cased Blue, White, Hollow, Denmark, 4 ½ In., Pair	150.00
Compote, Hand Blown, Ridges, Amber, Blue Stem, c.1920, 7 ½ x 8 In.	176.00
Compote, Molded Thumbprints, Mottled, Iridescent, Bronze Base, Grenada, c.1900, 6 x 9 In.	1200.00
Compote, Opaline, Blue, Gold Rim, Scroll Handles, Gold Base, Paw Feet, 5 x 7 In.	431.00
Decanter, Olive, Cased, Clear Stopper, Polished Pontil, 8 In.	145.00
Decanter, Rock Crystal, Flower Design, Stopper, 16 ½ In.	201.00

Gene Autry, Ring, Portrait, Aluminum, Silver Luster, Gold Accent, c.1950
$557.00

G

Gillinder, Sugar Shaker, Cover, Melon, Opal, Blue Shading, Multicolored Flowers, 4 ¾ In.
$104.00

Girl Scout, Doll, Terri Lee, Plastic Head, Painted Eyes, Original Uniform, 1955, 16 In.
$224.00

Glass-Art, Vase, Lithyalin, Enamel Pine Bough, Cones, Agate Marbling, 6-Sided Lip, 3 ⅜ In.
$575.00

Glass-Art, Vase, Trumpet Shape, Footed, Blue & Purple Mottled, Aventurine, Monart, 7 In. $81.00

Glass-Blown, Cuspidor, Olive Green, Flared-Out Rim, Pontil, c.1845, 4 ⅛ x 6 ½ In. $863.00

Glass-Blown, Decanter, Man In The Moon, Ball Stopper, Yellow, Green, Painted, 6 Glasses, c.1900 $690.00

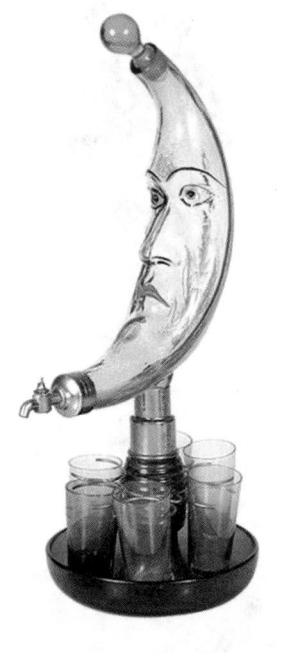

Decanter, Smoky, Flared Stopper, 22 In.	375.00
Decanter, Sterling Silver Mounted, Figure, Riding Burro, Early 20th Century, 9 ¼ In.	46.00
Dish, Cover, Hen On Nest, Opaque Blue, Wheat Stalks, Rope Trim, Bayel Glass, 5 x 4 x 5 In.	374.00
Dish, Rosaline, Apple Shape, Alabaster Leaf Handle, 4 ½ In.	50.00
Figurine, Frog, Acid Etched, Signed Licio Zanetti, 5 In.	485.00
Figurine, Man, Woman, Green Efeso Glass, Gold Highlights, Barovier & Toso, 13 x 7 In., 2 Piece	1440.00
Figurine, Nude Woman, Arms Outstretched, Cloak, Opalescent, France, c.1935, 6 ½ In., 2 Piece	948.00
Figurine, Tulip, Pastel Colors, Spun Glass Leaf, Germany, Early 1900s, 5 In.	264.00
Humidor, Copper Lid, Milk Glass, Painted Landscape, Cigars, Matches, 4 ½ x 6 ½ In.	60.00
Muffineer, Cased Yellow, Pontil, 2-Part Lid, c.1900, 7 ⅛ In.	66.00
Pitcher, Butterscotch To White, Flowers, Applied Clear Handle, Pontil, c.1885, 6 x 4 ½ In.	207.00
Pitcher, Spatter Cream, Tortoiseshell, Brown, Ribbed Swirls, Amber Reeded Handle, c.1890, 9 In.	288.00
Rose Bowl, Swirled, Ribbed, 3 Gilt Feet, Rigaree Waist, Pinched Rim, 6 ½ In.	150.00
Sculpture, Seaform, Dale Chihuly, 8 Piece	7605.00
Sculpture, Woman, Dog, Frosted, Iridescent, Signed Etling, France, 8 x 7 In.	600.00
Sugar Cube Holder, Cover, Cased Spatter Glass, Silver Plated Tongs, Lid, Handle, Mark, 6 ¼ In.	550.00
Sugar Shaker, Reverse Swirl, Vaseline Opalescent, Lid, Buckeye Glass, c.1875, 4 ¾ In.	106.00
Sugar Shaker, Ridge Swirl, Cobalt Blue, Lid, c.1900, 4 ¾ In.	106.00
Syrup, Amber Leaf & Flowers, Pewter Lid, Hobbs, 4 x 6 ½ In., Pair	173.00
Syrup, Block Band, Clear, Flowers, Yellow Stain, Lid, c.1900, 6 ¾ In.	92.00
Syrup, Clear Body, Amber Scrolls, Ruffled Undertray, Geo. Duncan & Sons, Pittsburgh, 6 In.	1380.00
Syrup, Guttate, Pink Cased, Opaque, Applied Clear Handle, Silver Plated, Spout, 6 ¾ In.	375.00
Syrup, Hercules Pillar, Amber, Lid, Hobbs, Brockunier, c.1875, 8 ½ In.	92.00
Syrup, Inside Ribbed, Emerald Green, Pressed Fan Handle, c.1900, 6 ½ In.	79.00
Tankard, Green Ground, 2 Men, Drum, Sword, Enamel Rim Trim, 10 In.	230.00
Vase, Agata, Swirled Black, Yellow, Blue, c.1900, 2 x 6 In.	351.00
Vase, Blue Green, Textured, 10 In.	65.00
Vase, Cased Clear, Turquoise Blue, Flared Top, Basket Weave Sides, 15 In.	135.00
Vase, Clear Iridescent, Ribbed, Right Swirl, Tooled Rim, Pontil, c.1900, 8 In.	26.00
Vase, Cobalt Glass, Silver Mica, Metal Trim, Handles, 7 In.	316.00
Vase, Cylindrical, Amethyst, Geometric Designs, Marked, 6 ½ In.	115.00
Vase, Enameled, Clear To Emerald Green, Leaf Decoration, 10 ¾ In.	33.00
Vase, Flaring & Scalloped Rim, Etched Pears & Leaves, Gold Highlights, 8 x 6 In.	201.00
Vase, Gold, Cream, Green Pulled Design, Platinum Tints, 6 In.	575.00
Vase, Gold, Pink, Green, Purple Iridescence, Cone Shape, Tripod Base, 21 In.	863.00
Vase, Green, Marbleized, 8 ½ In.	105.00
Vase, Green Over White, Cased, Flared, 7 ¼ In., Pair	150.00
Vase, Hand Blown, Scalloped Flared Rim, Mica, Green, 7 In.	94.00
Vase, Hearts, Vines, Orange Iridescent Ground, White Interior, 10 In.	288.00
Vase, Iridescent Pink Swirl, Stick Neck, Bulbous, Cased, 19th Century, 7 In.	395.00
Vase, Iridescent, Yellow Ground, Pulled Purple & Platinum Design, 3 ¼ x 6 ¾ In.	150.00
Vase, Ivory White Ground, Flowers, Blue, Green, Gold, Colonial Ware, 11 ¾ In.	575.00
Vase, Lid, Blue Facets, J. Hoffmann, Wiener Werkstatte, c.1910, 13 In.	1793.00
Vase, Lithyalin, Enamel Pine Bough, Cones, Agate Marbling, 6-Sided Lip, 3 ⅜ In. ....*illus*	575.00
Vase, Monart, Mottled Green & Blue Matte Glass, 7 In.	146.00
Vase, Multicolored Flowers, Green Vines, Iridescent Gold, Baluster, 11 In.	1725.00
Vase, Painted, Multicolored, Green, Flowers, Scrolls, Landscape Reserves, Chinese, 1900s, 6 ¾ x 3 In.	264.00
Vase, Pink, Persian Design, Gold Collar, Glass Beads, 9 In.	316.00
Vase, Purple Iridescent, Reeded, Purple Rim, Kralik, 8 ¼ In.	201.00
Vase, Round, Footed, Cranberry, Molded Gold & Clear Shells, 4 ¾ x 4 ¾ In.	173.00
Vase, Tapered, Cylinder, Swirled, Yellow Mottling, Enameled Stems, Blossoms, Mado Nancy, 12 In.	700.00
Vase, Textured Green, Bulbous, c.1930, 6 ½ In.	352.00
Vase, Trumpet Shape, Footed, Blue & Purple Mottled, Aventurine, Monart, 7 In. ....*illus*	81.00
Vase, Vaseline, Applied Swirl Trim, Feet, Bulbous Base, c.1880, 7 ½ In.	175.00
Vase, Yellow, Pulled Purple, Platinum Design, 3 x 7 In.	210.00
Vessel, Black Round Top, White Bulbous Bottom, Cased, 8 ½ In.	150.00
Wedding Cup, Woman Torso, Cast Bronze, Enameled Green Glass Skirt, Cranberry Top Cup, 9 In.	360.00

GLASS-BLOWN. Blown glass was formed by forcing air through a rod into molten glass. Early glass and some forms of art glass were hand blown. Other types of glass were molded or pressed.

Apothecary Jar, Round Feet, Domed Cover, 19th Century, 17 In., Pair	230.00
Bottle, Clear Olive, Applied Rolled Collar, Pontil, c.1800, 5 ¼ In.	308.00
Bowl, Cobalt, Flared Sides, Folded Rim, 2 x 6 In.	323.00
Bowl, Cobalt, Funnel Foot, Folded Edge, Pittsburgh, c.1820, 3 ¾ In.	470.00
Bowl, Fruit, Laurel Fife, 5 x 14 In.	146.00

G

Bowl, Olive Green, Outward Folded Rim, New England, c.1800, 5 ¼ x 5 ½ In.	960.00
Bowl, Olive Yellow, Outward Rolled Mouth, Cylindrical, Tubular Pontil, 3 ¼ x 5 In.	1610.00
Candlestick, Cylinder Socket, Wide Flange, Flat Round Foot, Penn., c.1850, 9 ½ In.	411.00
Canister, Clear, 2 Applied Base Rings, Cobalt Lid Ring, Wafer Finial, c.1835, 12 x 6 In.	323.00
Canister, Clear, 3 Applied Cobalt Rings, Finial, c.1850, 11 x 4 In.	764.00
Canister, Clear, Applied Cobalt Base, Lid Rings, Wafer Finial, c.1820, 9 x 5 In.	558.00
Celery Vase, 8 Applied Blue Ribs, Baluster Shape Stem, Pontil, c.1860, 10 ¼ In.	8050.00
Celery Vase, Cranberry, 8 Ribs, Gauffered Rim, Double-Knop Stem, Pontil, c.1870, 5 In.	920.00
Celery Vase, Yellow Green, Deep Bowl, 8 Ribs, Baluster Stem, Footed, Pontil, c.1860, 9 ½ In.	805.00
Cologne Bottle, Cut Glass, Sawtooth Base, Stopper, 1800s, 7 ¼ In.	81.00
Compote, Citron, 8 Ribs, Flared Rim, Hourglass Stem, Footed, Pontil, c.1870, 6 In.	2530.00
Compote, Clear, 6-Rib Bowl, Knopped Shaft, Cobalt Blue Undulating Rim, c.1820, 6 x 6 In.	711.00
Compote, Shallow Square Bowl, 8 Ribs, Baluster Stem, Footed, Pontil, c.1860, 7 In.	173.00
Creamer, 3-Piece Mold, Clear Glass, 2-Thumb Ledge, Applied Rib Handle, c.1830, 3 ⅞ In.	403.00
Creamer, 8 Applied Ruby Ribs, Bulbous Body, Pontil, c.1970, 5 ⅜ In.	374.00
Creamer, Amethyst, Bulbous, 10 Ribs, Solid Handle, Pontil, c.1875, 5 ¾ In.	173.00
Creamer, Opaque White, 8 Ribs Swirled Right, Applied Handle, Pontil, c.1860, 5 ⅝ In.	633.00
Cuspidor, Olive Green, Flared-Out Rim, Pontil, c.1845, 4 ⅛ x 6 ½ In. .....*illus*	863.00
Decanter, Acorns, Oak Leaves, Applied Neck, Mouth, Pontil, Late 1700s, 11 ½ In.	80.00
Decanter, Amethyst, Cone Shape, 8 Ribs, Applied Neck Ring, Pontil, c.1860, Qt., 10 ¼ In.	2415.00
Decanter, Blue, Ribbed, Applied Neck Ring, Pontil, Cone Shape, c.1860, Qt., 12 x 5 ¾ In.	3335.00
Decanter, Brown Amber, Tapered Cylinder, Ribbed, Star Cut Base, Stopper, c.1895, Qt., 14 In.	115.00
Decanter, Cobalt Blue, Squat Bell, 10 Ribs, Truncated Neck, Pontil, c.1880, 7 In.	518.00
Decanter, Man In The Moon, Ball Stopper, Yellow, Green, Painted, 6 Glasses, c.1900 .....*illus*	690.00
Decanter, Opaque White, Black Amethyst, Cone Shape, 8 Ribs, Concave Neck, c.1860, Qt., 9 In.	6900.00
Decanter, Plum Purple, Bell Form, Applied Neck, Ribbed, Pontil, Stopper, c.1880, Pt., 10 In.	431.00
Decanter, Ruby In Clear, Corn Form, Cut Ribbed, Flat Top, c.1875, Qt., 11 ¼ In.	403.00
Decanter, Ruby In Clear, Cylindrical, Ribbed, Triple Neck Ring, Flanged Lip, c.1875, Pt., 11 In.	196.00
Decanter, Swirl Design, 19th Century, 8 In., Pair	58.00
Figurine, Bird In Flight, Signed, Mid 20th Century, 16 x 18 In.	234.00
Hurricane Shade, Baluster Shape, Folded Foot Rim, 19th Century, 23 x 8 ½ In.	398.00
Jar, Lid, Cobalt Blue, Baluster, Swirled Ribbed Finial, Folded Base, c.1820, 9 ½ In.	385.00
Jar, Wine, Bellarmine Shape, Green, White Enamel Shield, Text, France, c.1920, 21 ½ In.	330.00
Jug, Deep Amber, Oval, Strap Handle & Rigaree, Folded Flat Collar, Pontil, c.1825, 5 ½ In.	532.00
Jug, Molasses, Cobalt Blue, Bulbous, 8 Ribs, Handle, Pontil, Ball Stopper, c.1855, 9 In.	430.00
Jug, Molasses, Opaque White, 8 Ribs, Applied Handle, Footed, Pontil, c.1860, 7 ½ In.	184.00
Mug, Cobalt Blue, Waisted, 9 Ribs, Applied Handle, Pontil, c.1860, 5 ½ In.	230.00
Nappy, Clear, Folded Rim, Ringed Base, 1 ¼ x 4 In.	77.00
Parade Staff, Red, White & Blue Swirl, 103 In.	500.00
Pitcher, Amber Marbrie, Opalescent White Loops, Dark Amber Foot, Handle, c.1820, 8 ½ In.	2607.00
Pitcher, Cleat, 19th Century, 8 ¼ In.	270.00
Pitcher, Molasses, Amber, 8 Ribs, Applied Neck Ring, Handle, 10 ½ x 3 ¼ In. .....*illus*	1610.00
Pitcher, Pillar Molded, Clambroth, Blue Ribs, Waisted, Handle, 9 x 6 In. .....*illus*	1150.00
Pitcher, Pittsburgh Type, Applied Scroll Hollow Handle, 19th Century, 8 ¾ In.	382.00
Pitcher, Witch's Ball, Blue, White Loop, Whitney Glass Works, c.1850, 9 & 9 ½ In., Pair .....*illus*	28080.00
Plate, Clear, Folded Rim, Ringed Base, Pontil, 6 ½ In.	66.00
Pokal, Clear, Red Stain, Engraved Horse, Lid, Finial, c.1850, 13 In.	1668.00
Rose Bowl, Enameled, White Shaded To Pink, Satin, 5 ½ In.	89.00
Salt, Cobalt Blue, Shallow Bowl, 8 Ribs, Folded Rim, Foot, 3 ¼ x 3 ½ In. .....*illus*	230.00
Salver, Cover, Finial, Hollow Silesian Stem, 3 Basal Rings, Pontil, 1800s, 19 ½ In.	863.00
Shade, Hat Shape, 7 In.	177.00
Sugar & Creamer, Cover, Tapered, 8 Ribs, Handle On Creamer, c.1840, 3 ½ In. & 4 ½ In.	489.00
Sugar, Cover, 16 Ribs, Stem, Tooled, Sapphire Blue, Tooled Rim, Pontil, 1830-60, 5 ⅞ In.	9200.00
Sugar, Domed Cover, Finial, 8 Ribs, Baluster Stem, Footed, Pontil, c.1860, 10 In.	489.00
Tumbler, Clear, Diamond Diaper, Boston & Sandwich Glass Co., c.1830, 5 x 4 In.	176.00
Vase, Amber, Enamel Flowers, Blue Foot, Ruffled Rim, c.1870, 10 In.	129.00
Vase, Applied Black Wrapped Snake, 6 x 10 In.	82.00
Vase, Baluster Stem, White Looped Bowl, Folded Rim, c.1850, 8 x 5 ¼ In. .....*illus*	748.00
Vase, Double Drape Swirls, Cylindrical, Flared Rim, Vertical Panels, 15 In.	201.00
Vase, Lily Pad, Type-1, Aqua, Applied Handles, Crimped Foot, Redford, 6 ¾ In. .....*illus*	1170.00
Vase, Pink, Fired Gold Etched Design, 12 In., Pair	351.00
Vase, Yellow, Bulbous Midsection, Trumpet Neck, Baluster Pedestal Base, Pontil, c.1855, 9 ⅝ In.	168.00
Vase, Yellow Green, Elongated, 8 Ribs, Gauffered Petal Rim, Footed, Pontil, c.1870, 10 In.	748.00
Whimsy, Chain, Amber, Olive, Clear, 1800s, 80 In.	118.00
Witch's Ball, Cobalt Blue, 5 ¼ In., Maple Treen Stand, 3 ¼ In.	382.00
Witch's Ball, Ruby Red, Rough Pontil, 4 In. .....*illus*	288.00

G

Glass-Blown, Pitcher, Molasses, Amber, 8 Ribs, Applied Neck Ring, Handle, 10 ½ x 3 ¼ In.
$1610.00

Glass-Blown, Pitcher, Pillar Molded, Clambroth, Blue Ribs, Waisted, Handle, 9 x 6 In.
$1150.00

Glass-Blown, Pitcher, Witch's Ball, Blue, White Loop, Whitney Glass Works, c.1850, 9 & 9 ½ In., Pair
$28080.00

TIP
Wash art glass in lukewarm water with a little softening agent and some mild dishwashing soap.

Glass-Blown, Salt, Cobalt Blue,
Shallow Bowl, 8 Ribs, Folded Rim,
Foot, 3 ¼ x 3 ½ In.
$230.00

GLASS-BOHEMIAN. Bohemian glass is an ornate overlay or flashed glass made during the Victorian era. It has been reproduced in Bohemia, which is now a part of the Czech Republic. Glass made from 1875 to 1900 is preferred by collectors.

Bottle, Blue, Neck Rings, Gold Flowers, Scrolls, Pointed Stopper, 21 In., Pair	1464.00
Bowl, Berlin, Footed, 4 x 9 In.	30.00
Bowl, Blue Cut To Clear, 7 ½ In.	56.00
Center Vase, Blue Opaque, Butterflies, Flowers, Gilt, 14 In.	420.00
Chalice, Cobalt To Clear, Medieval Harpist Medallion, Signed Carl Pfohl, 13 In.	800.00
Compote, Cranberry Glass, Threaded Surface, Bronze Trim, Handles, c.1900, 16 x 16 In.	1560.00
Compote, Ruby Flashed, Cut Grapevines, Honeycomb Stem, Faceted Foot, 6 x 6 In.	83.00
Decanter, Ruby Flash Cut To Clear, 13 In.	135.00
Decanter, Set, Blue, Gilt Trim, Flowers, Leaves, Stopper, 15 & 5 ⅜ In., 7 Piece	175.00
Decanter, Stopper, Cut Ruby To Clear, 13 x 5 In. ....*illus*	132.00
Dresser Box, Round, Enamel, Gold, Green, 3 x 5 In.	125.00
Ewer, Green Iridescent, Purple Threading, Pallme-Koenig, 3 ½ In. ....*illus*	201.00
Goblet, Cut Crystal, 7 ¼ In., 8 Piece	176.00
Goblet, Rhine, Trumpet Shape, Ruby, Yellow, Clear, Cut Designs, 8 In.	250.00
Goblet, Ruby Cut To Clear Stems, 8 In., 4 Piece	29.00
Jar, Cover, Grapes, Leaves, Ruby Cut To Clear, Footed, 19th Century, 6 ¼ In.	140.00
Perfume Vial, Cobalt Blue, White Overlay, Gilt, Chased Silver, 4 In. ....*illus*	380.00
Pitcher, Berlin, 10 ½ In.	40.00
Pitcher, Water, Oval, Red, Yellow Spots, Vaseline, Wilhelm Kralik, 9 In.	175.00
Placecard Holder, Silver Plate, Cameo Figural Scenes, Flower Shape, 2 In., 12 Piece	374.00
Pokal, Cover, Cranberry, Engraved Animals, Forest Scene, 9 ½ In.	575.00
Punch Set, Art Nouveau, Enamel, Green Shaded To Amethyst, Cover, 7 Cups, 16 In. ......*illus*	1200.00
Salt & Pepper, Diamond Cut, Glass Tops, 6 In.	25.00
Salt & Pepper, Square Shape, Silver Tops, Square Motif, 4 ½ In.	40.00
Vase, 3-Fold Rim, Twisted Middle, Thumbprints, Multicolored, Pallme-Koenig, 13 In.	575.00
Vase, Amethyst, Iridescent, Crackle Finish, Cylinder Shape, Rindskopf, 10 In.	115.00
Vase, Art Nouveau, Blue Iridescent, Wilhelm Kralik, 14 ½ In. ....*illus*	748.00
Vase, Aventurine & Gilt, Enameled Gilt Leaves, c.1920, 16 ½ In.	360.00
Vase, Bud, Free-Form, Camphor, Applied Flower, Leaves, Hosch, 9 In. ....*illus*	259.00
Vase, Bulbous, Winged Cherubs, Scrolling Leaves, c.1875, 12 In.	150.00
Vase, Chrysanthemums, Enamel, Cranberry To Clear, Ruffled Rim, G.P.P., c.1890, 9 ½ In., Pair	385.00
Vase, Corset Shape, Amber Foot, Blue, Green, Gold, Brown Iridescent Drippings, 5 In.	60.00
Vase, Cranberry Cut To Clear, Wheel Ground, Windmill, Deer, Dog, House, Stem, 7 ⅜ In.	47.00
Vase, Craquelle, 3-Fold Rim, Emerald Green, Iridescent Blue, Magenta, Pallme-Koenig, 13 In.	403.00
Vase, Crystal, Flared Scalloped Rim, Gilt Band, Ruckl, 9 x 8 In.	146.00
Vase, Cut To Clear, Trumpet Shape, Bulbous, Moorish Panels, Gold Scrolling, 15 In., Pair	1668.00
Vase, Cylinder, Red Cluthra, Iridescent, Variegated Red Ribbons, Iridescent, Kralik, 9 In.	225.00
Vase, Faceted, Footed, Blue, Josef Hoffman, 9 ½ x 7 In.	960.00
Vase, Flowers, Lavender Cut To Clear, Late 19th Century, 9 In.	295.00
Vase, Grenada, Iridescent, Footed, Green To Red, Inverted Folded Rim, Rindskopf, 10 In.	140.00
Vase, Oval, Shouldered, Translucent Glass, Pink Pulled Feather Design, 5 ½ In.	90.00
Vase, Oval, Textured Amber, Salamander Feet, Drippings, Harrach, 6 In. ....*illus*	690.00
Vase, Portrait, Woman, Bust, Green, Gilt, Footed, Late 1800s, 14 In.	420.00
Vase, Red, Slender Neck, Flared Base, Black Side Prunts, 12 In.	80.00
Vase, Red Tangled Thread Design, Iridescent Ground, Pallme-Koenig, 8 In.	403.00
Vase, Ruby Cut To Clear, Scrolls, Panels, Ground Pontil, Late 1800s, 10 In.	149.00
Vase, Scalloped Rim, Multicolored Birds, Blue Satin, Enamel, Gilt Flowers, 6 In.	125.00
Vase, Shouldered, Green, Multicolored Lily Pond Scene, Dragonflies, Cameo, Mark, 10 In.	1900.00
Vase, Trumpet Form, Flowers, Green Ground, Enamel, Gilt, Late 1800s, 17 ½ In.	200.00
Vase, Tulip Shape, Gold, Cinnabar, Pewter Armatures, Art Nouveau, 12 x 7 In.	1098.00
Vase, Turquoise, Cut To Clear, Tapered, 17 ¼ In.	777.00
Vase, Urn Shape, Blue Satin, Bird, Dogwood, Gilt, Metal, 4-Footed, Harrach, 13 In.	518.00
Water Set, Pitcher, Translucent, Blue Reeded Handle, 3 Tumblers	110.00

Glass-Blown, Vase, Baluster Stem,
White Looped Bowl, Folded Rim,
c.1850, 8 x 5 ¼ In.
$748.00

Glass-Blown, Vase, Lily Pad,
Type-1, Aqua, Applied Handles,
Crimped Foot, Redford, 6 ¾ In.
$1170.00

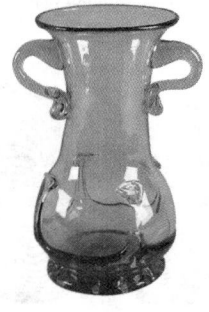

Glass-Blown, Witch's Ball,
Ruby Red, Rough Pontil, 4 In.
$288.00

GLASS-CONTEMPORARY includes pieces by glass artists working after 1970. Many of these pieces are free-form, one-of-a-kind sculptures. Paperweights by contemporary artists are listed in the Paperweight category. Earlier studio glass may be found listed under Glass-Midcentury or Glass-Venetian.

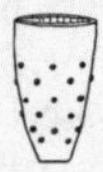

Basket, Blue Macchia, Dale Chihuly, c.1994, 7 In.	3510.00
Bottle, Spiral Wrapped Bend Neck, Antique Green, Don Shepherd, c.1988, 16 In.	175.00
Bowl, Blue, Green Iridescent Feather, Opal Ground, Daniel Lotton, 1995, 7 In.	920.00
Bowl, Blue, Jagged Edge, Toots Zynsky, c.1983, 4 ¾ x 12 In.	5795.00

Glass-Bohemian, Decanter, Stopper,
Cut Ruby To Clear, 13 x 5 In.
$132.00

Glass-Bohemian, Ewer,
Green Iridescent, Purple Threading,
Pallme-Koenig, 3 ½ In.
$201.00

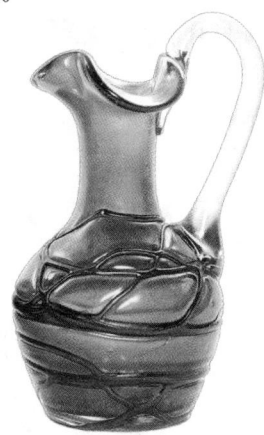

Glass-Bohemian, Perfume Vial,
Cobalt Blue, White Overlay, Gilt,
Chased Silver, 4 In.
$380.00

Glass-Bohemian, Punch Set,
Art Nouveau, Enamel,
Green Shaded To Amethyst, Cover,
7 Cups, 16 In.
$1200.00

Glass-Bohemian, Vase,
Art Nouveau, Blue Iridescent,
Wilhelm Kralik, 14 ½ In.
$748.00

Glass-Bohemian, Vase, Bud,
Free-Form, Camphor, Applied Flower, Leaves,
Hosch, 9 In.
$259.00

Glass-Contemporary, Vase, Oval,
Textured Amber, Salamander Feet, Drippings,
Harrach, 6 In.
$690.00

Glass-Contemporary, Sculpture,
Applied Ornaments, Acrylic Base, Signed, Edris
Eckhardt, c.1964, 9 ½ In.
$150.00

Glass-Contemporary, Sculpture,
Block, Encased Tropical Fish,
Multicolored, 7 x 4 ½ In.
$225.00

G

Glass-Contemporary, Vase, Paperweight, Crystal, Butterflies, Orange, Yellow, Bamboo, Orient & Flume, 11 In.
$920.00

Glass-Contemporary, Vase, Peacock, Cobalt Blue, Amethyst Oil Spot, Textured, Charles Lotton, 11 ⅝ In.
$1495.00

Glass-Midcentury, Console Set, Compote, 2 Candlesticks, Blue Glass, Gold, Wood Stem, Signed
$90.00

TIP

Do not put wire-stemmed artificial flowers in a valuable narrow neck glass vase. The stems will scratch and damage the vase.

G

Bowl, Bluerina, Melon Ribbed Body, Wide Rim, Dominick Labino, 1968, 3 x 8 In.	173.00
Bowl, Caged, Ruby, Flowers, Leaves, Overlayed Trellis, Lotton, 1990, 8 x 11 In.	2070.00
Bowl, Fused Glass Shreds, Green, Blue, White, Black, Toots Zynsky, 6 x 12 In.	6600.00
Bowl, Fused, Purple, Yellow Interior, Toots Zynsky, c.1985, 5 x 12 ¼ In.	6100.00
Bowl, Oval, Amethyst, Red Pulled Feathers, Green Highlights, D. Lotton, 2000, 10 In.	475.00
Compote, Burgundy, Pale Green, Labino, 1971, 4 ½ x 7 In.	288.00
Compote, Variegated Green, Labino, 1968, 5 x 9 In.	259.00
Ewer, Bulbous, Black, Handle, Frosted Blue, Underwater Fish, Signed Ramski, 1995, 8 In.	60.00
Figurine, Dragonfly, Milon Townsend, 4 x 5 In.	94.00
Jar, Teal, Bubble Top, 9 In.	65.00
Sculpture, Applied Ornaments, Acrylic Base, Signed, Edris Eckhardt, c.1964, 9 ½ In. ......*illus*	150.00
Sculpture, Block, Encased Tropical Fish, Multicolored, 7 x 4 ½ In. ......*illus*	225.00
Sculpture, Never Too Close, Vertical Shapes, Polished, L. Boyadjiev, 18 x 12 In.	1150.00
Sculpture, Saturn, White Zanfirico Rod Rings, Lino Tagliapietra, 1990, 24 In.	9000.00
Sculpture, Sea Form, Orange Red, Black Detail, Dale Chihuly, c.1995, 3 ½ x 4 ¾ In.	878.00
Urn, Ribbed, Blue Iridescent, Lundberg Studios, c.1999, 2 ¾ In.	230.00
Vase, 2 Branches, Flower Pods, Moon, Red, R. Satava, 10 In.	460.00
Vase, Adam & Eve, Multicolored, 1987, 9 x 6 In.	3050.00
Vase, Amethyst Oil Spots, Cobalt Glass, Gold Leaves, C. Lotton, 1992, 12 In.	1093.00
Vase, Black, Iridescent Blue Pulled Feather, Signed Peiser, 1974, 4 ½ In.	175.00
Vase, Black, Red, Gourd Shape, Tsuchida Yasuhiko, 1999, 11 ½ x 6 ½ In.	1830.00
Vase, Black Ribbons, Bottle Shape, Tsuchida Yasuhiko, 9 x 5 In.	1586.00
Vase, Blue & Brown Curly Feathers, Iridescent Ground, Vandermark, 1977, 8 ½ In.	127.00
Vase, Blue Feathers, Orange Ground, Iridescent, C. Lotton, 1986	345.00
Vase, Blue Iridescent, Pulled Feather, Orient & Flume, 1981, 8 ½ In.	345.00
Vase, Blue Swirls, White Stars, Evening Star, Lundberg Studios, 2000, 12 In.	300.00
Vase, Blue Translucent, Leaves, Vines, Shouldered, Lotton, 1993, 6 In.	403.00
Vase, Blue, Green Internal Swirl Design, Joel Philip Myers, 8 x 7 In.	1320.00
Vase, Bulbous Bottle, Selenium Red, Black, Iridescent Blue Weave, C. Lotton, 1985, 8 In.	750.00
Vase, Cameo, Grape Leaves, Cranberry, Oval 4-Fold Rim, Kelsey Murphy, 11 In.	575.00
Vase, Christian Landoy, Iridescent Unica, Mottled, Leerdam, 7 x 7 In.	600.00
Vase, Citron, White Pulled Feathers, Plum Iridescence, Orient & Flume, 1977, 8 In.	374.00
Vase, Clear, Amber, Red, Blue, Labino, 1969, 4 x 5 In.	207.00
Vase, Clear, Blue Gray, Cased, Polished Rim, 15 In.	165.00
Vase, Clear, Molded, Red, Green Target, Bud, c.1970, 4 ½ In.	125.00
Vase, Cobalt Blue, Swags, Stick, Labino, 1969, 10 In.	345.00
Vase, Cobalt, Glowing Orb, Tan, Green Leaves, Black Thread, C. Lotton, 1991, 9 In.	1035.00
Vase, Crimson, Blue, Wisteria, Bottle Shape, Charles Lotton, Signed, 1989, 10 ½ In.	540.00
Vase, Double Gourd, Blue Iridescent Swags, Craquelle Ground, Lotton, 1988, 9 In.	575.00
Vase, Double Hook Design, Blue, Gold, White, Iridescent, Orient & Flume, 1975, 7 In.	374.00
Vase, Frosted, 3-Side, Orb Within Cobalt Core, T. Kuhn, 1979, 5 In.	633.00
Vase, Gold, Blue, Opal, Ebony, Designs, Applied Amber Mounts, C. Sorrals, 11 x 13 In.	633.00
Vase, Gold Iridescent, Green Pulled Feathers, Footed, Orient & Flume, 12 In.	288.00
Vase, Gold Iridescent, Trees, Blossoms, Orient & Flume, 6 ½ In.	259.00
Vase, Gold Ruby, White Ferns, Pulled Designs, D. Lotton, 1987, 5 In.	173.00
Vase, Gourd Shape, Combed Feathers, White Tips, Orient & Flume, 1979, 8 In.	207.00
Vase, Green Glass, Red Flowers, Green Stems, Charles Lotton, Cylinder, 1974, 9 ½ In.	863.00
Vase, Green Ground, Green Leaves, Pink Flowers, Charles Lotton, c.1989, 10 In.	819.00
Vase, Hawthorne Trees, Flowers, Blue Iridescent, Orient & Flume, 7 In.	345.00
Vase, Iridescent Amber, Oval, Rolled Rim, Blue, Green Leaf, C. Lotton, 1987, 4 In.	325.00
Vase, Iridescent Blue, King Tut Pattern, Orient & Flume, Signed, 1980, 7 ½ In.	288.00
Vase, Iridescent Blue Vine, Tan Surface, Cypriot Inclusions, D. Lotton, 1991, 6 x 9 In.	1093.00
Vase, Irises, Cobalt Blue, Footed, Orient & Flume, Paper Label, 11 ½ In.	345.00
Vase, Jack-In-The-Pulpit, Orange, Labino, 1969, 7 x 8 In.	230.00
Vase, Jack-In-The-Pulpit, Ribbed, Gold Iridescent, Lundberg, Signed, 1990, 11 In.	360.00
Vase, Lava, Oval, Free-Form, Cut Top, Mottled Pink, Iridescent Blue, Charles Lotton 1998, 8 In.	546.00
Vase, Mandarin Yellow, C. Lotton, 1984, 6 In.	484.00
Vase, Mandarin Yellow, Wrapped Black Vine, C. Lotton, 1993, 7 x 13 In.	1150.00
Vase, Marinot, Mark Matthews, Signed 1985, 11 x 5 In.	1000.00
Vase, Moon, Branches, Flower Pods, Royal Blue Ground, Red Interior, Satava, 6 ½ In.	403.00
Vase, Multi Flora, Blue, 6 Orange Poppies, Green Centers, C. Lotton, 1986, 8 In.	518.00
Vase, Multi Flora, Oval, Amethyst, Blue Flowers, Amber Vines, C. Lotton, 1974, 8 ½ In.	800.00
Vase, Multi Flora, Sunset, Flared & Scalloped Rim, Charles Lotton, 1997, 11 ¾ In.	920.00
Vase, Multicolored, Marbleized, Melon Ribs, Dominick Labino, 1968, 6 ¼ In.	288.00
Vase, Nautilus, Carved, Tsuchida Yasuhiko, 9 x 7 In.	1708.00
Vase, Opal Glass, Blue Hooked Feather, Gold Tip, Signed, Mark Pieser, 4 ½ In.	288.00

Vase, Opal, Red & Blue Swags, Oval, Signed, Daniel Lotton, c.1990, 6 ½ In.	210.00
Vase, Orchid, Flared Rim, Green Ground, Orient & Flume, Paper Label, 9 ¼ In.	374.00
Vase, Organic Shape, Clear, Iridescent, F. Warren, 1981, 8 x 4 In.	350.00
Vase, Oval, Opal To Green Rim, Blue Heart, Vine, C. Lotton, 1979, 8 In.	225.00
Vase, Oval, Shouldered, Iridescent Pulled Tulips, Pink, Green, C. Lotton, Signed, c.1986, 7 In.	441.00
Vase, Pale, Dark Green Pulled Feathers, Swags, Orient & Flume, 8 In.	460.00
Vase, Paperweight, Black Angle Fish, Green Plants, Orient & Flume, 6 ¾ In.	288.00
Vase, Paperweight, Butterflies Over Bamboo, Orient & Flume, 11 In.	920.00
Vase, Paperweight, Cased Primo, Red, Violet Flowers, Leaves, D. Lotton, 1993, 10 In.	546.00
Vase, Paperweight, Crystal, Butterflies, Orange, Yellow, Bamboo, Orient & Flume, 11 In. ....*illus*	920.00
Vase, Paperweight, Kaleidoscope Colors, Dominick Labino, 5 In.	345.00
Vase, Paperweight, Lundberg, Clouds, Landscape, Clear, Green, White, Pink, 1980, 3 In.	288.00
Vase, Paperweight, Reflection, Yellow, Purple Flowers, D. Lotton, 2003, 7 In.	374.00
Vase, Peacock, Cobalt Blue, Amethyst Oil Spot, Textured, Charles Lotton, 11 ⅝ In. ....*illus*	1495.00
Vase, Peacock, Feathers, Cobalt Pulled Eyes, Orange, Yellow, Lotton, 1994, 7 x 13 In.	1955.00
Vase, Peacock, Purple Plumes, Yellow Eyes, Gold Lip, C. Lotton, 1988, 12 In.	1495.00
Vase, Petal Rim, Ribbed Body, Plum, Clear, Green, R. Royal, 1992, 19 x 23 In.	1093.00
Vase, Pink Ground, Fuchsia Orchids, Green Leaves, Purple Base, R. Satava, 1991, 8 In.	431.00
Vase, Pulled Blue Feathers, White Tips, Iridescent, Orient & Flume, 1983, 11 In.	345.00
Vase, Purple Flowers, White Ground, Leaves, Blue Interior, C. Lotton, 1995, 9 In.	374.00
Vase, Rain Forest, Bubbles, Red Heart, Vines, Yellow, Green, Foot, Rick Strini, 13 In.	288.00
Vase, Red Cypriot, Oval, Iridescent Platinum Lava, Charles Lotton, 1989, 5 In.	525.00
Vase, Red Interior, Iridescent Leaves, Vines, Cylinder, Opal Shoulder, C. Lotton, 1974, 9 In.	374.00
Vase, Red, Opal Marbling, Applied Prunts, c.1970, 5 In.	259.00
Vase, Red Swirls, Blue Ground, David Leppla, c.1985, 16 x 6 In.	176.00
Vase, Red, Tooled Prunts, c.1973, 6 ⅝ In.	173.00
Vase, Ringed Base, Blue Threads, Amethyst, Smallhouse, Orient & Flume, 1989, 10 In.	184.00
Vase, Robin's-Egg Blue, 4 Cobalt Blue Birds On Scalloped Rim, Footed, Artemide, 13 In.	150.00
Vase, Ruby, Gold Pulled Feathers, Blue Streaks, Signed, Lundberg, 1982, 8 In.	259.00
Vase, Ruby Red, 4 Iris, Leaves, Green, Blue, R. Satava, 1994, 12 In.	748.00
Vase, Stick, Blue Iridescent, Combed Feathers, Orient & Flume, 1981, 11 In.	230.00
Vase, Studio, Red, Blue Rim, Orange Base, Flared, Monson, Ill., 15 ½ In.	600.00
Vase, Swirl Design In Light & Dark Plum & Gold, Zipper Pattern, Lundberg, 5 ½ In.	374.00
Vase, Swirled Blue, Green Iridescence, Gold Stars, Lundberg, 1999, 11 In.	460.00
Vase, Tangled Gold Threads, Red, Blue Leaves, Opal Ground, C. Lotton, 1974, 9 In.	1650.00
Vase, Translucent, Aqua, Splash Inclusions, Multicolored, Labino, 1974, 6 In.	230.00
Vase, Translucent, Cylinder, Double Carved Flowers, Leaves, J. Lotton, 1998, 16 In.	28.00
Vase, Triangular, Matte Texture, Glossy Trails, Cobalt, B. Cox, 1991, 8 In.	127.00
Vase, Turquoise Blue, White Flower, Silver Vine, C. Lotton, 1973, 6 In.	546.00
Vase, Violet, Gold Iridescent, Zipper Pattern, Lundberg, Signed, 1990, 11 In.	330.00
Vase, White Ground, Black, Blue Iris, Black Interior, R. Satava, 1993, 10 In.	575.00
Vase, Wisteria Moon, Black Glass, Harvest Moon, Branches, R. Satava, 1993, 8 ¼ In.	690.00
Vase, Yellow & Orange Swags, Cranberry Glass, Labino, 1971, 5 In.	345.00
Vase, Yellow, Purple Iris, Green Leaves, Footed, Cylinder, Signed, Orient & Flume, 8 In.	374.00
Vase, Yellow, Red, Swirling Opal Green, Labino, 1972, 5 In.	259.00

GLASS-CUT, *see Cut Glass category.*

GLASS-DEPRESSION, *see Depression Glass category.*

GLASS-MIDCENTURY refers to art glass made from the 1940s to the early 1970s. Some glass factories, such as Baccarat or Orrefors, are listed under their own categories. Earlier glass may be listed in the Glass-Art and Glass-Contemporary categories. Italian glass may be found in Glass-Venetian.

Bottle, Antique Green, Applied Plum Spiral Wrapped Bent Neck, c.1988, 28 ¼ In.	350.00
Bottle, Green, Bulbous, Narrow Lip, Blomberg, Gullaskruf, Sweden, 1963, 6 In.	85.00
Bottle, Green, Bulbous, Narrow Lip, Blomberg, Gullaskruf, Sweden, 1963, 12 In.	310.00
Bottle, Light Green, Blue Applied Handles, Seguso, 6 ½ In.	146.00
Bowl, Clear, Blue & Amethyst Bands, Boat Shape, Etched Dots, 16 x 7 x 4 In.	55.00
Bowl, Deco Style, Purple Interior, Scavo Crusted White Exterior, Rippled, 16 x 4 In.	800.00
Bowl, Fruit, Vaseline, Stretch, Conical Shape, Iridescent, 1940s, 11 ½ x 7 ¼ In.	125.00
Bowl, Olive, Raised Circle Rim, Signed, Hadeland, Norway, 9 ½ In.	225.00
Bowl, Stromberg, Shyttan Crystal, Sweden, c.1950, 4 ¾ x 9 In.	176.00
Cake Stand, Clear, Pukeberg, Sweden, 12 ½ In.	35.00
Candlestick, Mushroom Shape, Scandinavian, 4 x 3 & 2 x 3 ½ In., 2 Piece.............	80.00
Carafe, Viking, Blue, Ole Winther, Kastrup Homegaard, 1970, 9 In.	35.00

G

Glass-Midcentury, Goblet, Cocktail, Bimini, Lime Green Swirls, Horse, Rider, Bubble Stem, 7 ½ In. $69.00

Glass-Midcentury, Plaque, Burning Bush, Layered, Walnut Box, Lit, Edris Eckhardt, 17 x 10 In. $449.00

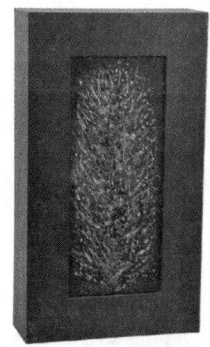

Glass-Midcentury, Sculpture, Multicolored, Fused Tile Mosaic, Higgins, Frame, 7 x 9 In. **$210.00**

Glass-Venetian, Bottle, Internally Decorated, Anzolo Fuga, A.V.E.M., 17 ¼ x 8 ½ In. **$2520.00**

Glass-Venetian, Bottle, Stopper, Blue & Red Plaid, Ercole Barovier, c.1960, 9 In. **$5265.00**

Champagne Bucket, Clear, Handles, Dansk, Romania, 9 x 8 ¼ In.	65.00
Charger, Murano, Black, Off-White, Acid Etched, Yalos Casa, 20 In.	125.00
Compote, Olive, Raised Circle Rim, Signed, Hadeland, Norway, 10 ¾ x 5 ½ In.	375.00
Console Set, Compote, 2 Candlesticks, Blue Glass, Gold, Wood Stem, Signed ....*illus*	90.00
Decanter, Blue, Vertical, Teardrop Stopper, No. 6418, Joel Myers, c.1964, 23 x 8 In.	275.00
Decanter, Horizon Blue, Indiana Handcraft, No. 6534L, c.1965, 19 ½ x 12 In.	325.00
Decanter, Pink Orange, Paolo Venini, Italy, 5 ½ x 5 In.	595.00
Decanter, Tangerine, No. 6029, Wayne Husted, c.1960, 26 In.	525.00
Dish, Delphinium Blue, Gold Circles, Signed, Higgins, 4 ½ In.	75.00
Dish, Geometric, Signed, Michael & Frances Higgins, 11 x 9 ½ In.	125.00
Figurine, Bird, Blue Body, Dark Blue Somerso Insert, Antonio Da Ros, Cenedese, c.1960, 8 In.	500.00
Figurine, Bird, Crystal Body, Somerso Insert, Antonio Da Ros, Cenedese, c.1960, 14 In.	975.00
Figurine, Eskimo, Crystal, Kastrup Holmegaard, 4 ½ To 5 ¼ In., 3 Piece	175.00
Figurine, Rhino, Frosted, Happy, 7 x 4 ¼ In.	45.00
Figurine, Squirrel, Blue, Eating Nut, Josef & Benito Marcolin, FM Ronneby, 1960, 6 ½ In.	65.00
Goblet, Cocktail, Bimini, Lime Green Swirls, Horse, Rider, Bubble Stem, 7 ½ In. ....*illus*	69.00
Gulvase, Cobalt Blue, Kastrup Holmegaard, Denmark, 1962, 10 In.	150.00
Mushroom, Amber, Hand Blown, Murano, 8 x 5 & 6 x 4 In., 2 Piece	350.00
Pitcher, Blue Gray, Pinched Waist, Spout, Blomberg, Gullaskruf, 1950s, 11 In.	75.00
Plaque, Burning Bush, Layered, Walnut Box, Lit, Edris Eckhardt, 17 x 10 In. ....*illus*	449.00
Sculpture, Devil's Pearl, Etched, Timo Sarpaneve, Itala, c.1956, 6 x 6 In.	1225.00
Sculpture, Multicolored, Fused Tile Mosaic, Higgins, Frame, 7 x 9 In. ....*illus*	210.00
Tray, Clear, 6 Sections, Shallow, Pukeberg, 15 ¼ In.	60.00
Vase, Amber, Green, Clear, Bark Texture, Square, Whitefriars, 8 ½ In.	135.00
Vase, Blue, Oval, Engraved, Kaj Franck, Nuutajarvi Notsjo, Finland, 1963, 6 x 6 In.	225.00
Vase, Bottle Shape, Amberina, Rainbow Glass Company, 12 ¾ In.	85.00
Vase, Bottle Shape, Mold Blown, Green, Rolled Lip, No. 984, 24 x 19 In.	115.00
Vase, Bottle Shape, Tapered, Green To Clear, Bengt Orup, Sweden, c.1958, 17 ½ In.	225.00
Vase, Burnt Honey, Greenwich Flint, Tom Connally, 1960s, 19 In.	195.00
Vase, Butterfly, Crystal Cased Over White, Pink, Flygsfors Coquille, 1961, 13 ¼ In.	265.00
Vase, Carnaby, Green Over White Casing, Michael Bang, Denmark, 17 In.	550.00
Vase, Cased Clear, Amber, Raised Geometrics, Riihimaki, 8 ¼ In.	145.00
Vase, Conical, Tapered, Green To Clear, Bengt Orup, Sweden, c.1958, 10 ½ In.	135.00
Vase, Fan, Crystal Cased Over White, Purple, Flygsfors Coquille, 1958, 7 ½ x 6 ¼ In.	175.00
Vase, Greenwich Flint, Blue, No. 1165, Tom Connally, Indiana Glass, 14 ½ In.	175.00
Vase, Hanging, Blue, Bulbous, Slender Neck, Side Opening, Blomberg, Sweden, 8 x 5 In.	65.00
Vase, Iridized Honey Amber, Roughed Base, Robert Barber, c.1950, 12 ¾ In.	92.00
Vase, Mold, Red, Wayne Husted, No. 6520, 15 In.	75.00
Vase, Pouch Shape, Amethyst, Winslow Anderson, c.1953, 11 In.	150.00
Vase, Rectangular, Gray, Chamfer Cut Rim, Signed, Sweden, 5 x 5 In.	75.00
Vase, Red, Blue, Lasi Oy Riihimaki, Finland, Aladin Tamara, 1970s, 9 ¾ & 7 ¾ In.	125.00
Vase, Rough Texture, Glass Buttons On Base, Viktor Berndt, Flygsfors, 7 x 5 In.	285.00
Vase, Sea Green, Flowers, Wayne Husted, c.1963, 10 x 4 In.	75.00
Vase, Smoke, Clear Horn Handles, Hand Blown, c.1960, 13 ½ In.	145.00
Vase, Smoked Gray, Straight Sides, Per Lutken, Denmark, 1962, 15 x 5 In.	395.00
Vase, Spontana, Blue, Green, Narrow Neck, Bengt Orup, Sweden, c.1967, 10 ¼ In.	175.00
Vase, Teal Exterior, Wavy Sides, Medina, 3 ½ x 3 In.	75.00
Vase, Teal Green, Oval, Holmegaard, Lutken, 9 ½ In.	145.00

GLASS-PRESSED, *see Pressed Glass category.*

GLASS-VENETIAN. Venetian glass has been made near Venice, Italy, since the thirteenth century. Thin, colored glass with applied decoration is favored, although many other types have been made. Collectors have recently become interested in the Art Deco and fifties designs. Glass was made on the Venetian island of Murano from 1291. The output dwindled in the late seventeenth century but began to flourish again in the 1850s. Some of the old techniques of glassmaking were revived, and firms today make traditional designs and original modern glass. Since 1981, the name *Murano* may be used only on glass made on Murano Island. Other pieces of Italian glass may be found in the Glass-Contemporary and Glass-Midcentury categories of this book.

Aquarium, 4 Fish In Colors Of Pink, Green, Purple & Orange, Murano, 19 x 8 In.	1120.00
Basket, Latticinio, Multicolored, Clear Handle, Murano, 9 ½ x 6 In.	117.00
Bottle, Green Stopper, Giada, Toni Zuccheri, Venini, Murano, 7 ¼ x 5 ½ In.	468.00
Bottle, Green Stopper, Giada, Toni Zuccheri, Venini, Murano, 12 x 4 In.	410.00
Bottle, Internally Decorated, Anzolo Fuga, A.V.E.M., 17 ¼ x 8 ½ In. ....*illus*	2520.00
Bottle, Stopper, Blue & Red Plaid, Ercole Barovier, c.1960, 9 In. ....*illus*	5265.00
Bottle, Stopper, Blue, Red Canes, Venini, 19 x 3 In.	780.00

G

Bottle, Stopper, Green Frosted, Label, Paolo Venini, c.1968, 14 ½ In.	1041.00
Bottle, Stopper, Multicolored, Signed, Seguso, Murano, 17 ¾ In. ....*illus*	1054.00
Bowl, Bulbous, Frosted, Blue Design, Stripes, 10 In.	146.00
Bowl, Gold Spirals, Bubbles, Candy Pieces, Murano, c.1950, 5 ½ x 4 ½ In.	146.00
Bowl, Green, Yellow, White, Recycled Glass, James Carpentar, Venini, 5 x 9 In.	780.00
Bowl, Handkerchief, Free-Form, Fazzoletto, White, 8 ¾ x 9 ¾ In.	234.00
Bowl, Leaf Shape, Venini, Signed, 1948, 2 ¾ x 7 x 6 ¾ In.	702.00
Bowl, Light Blue, Ruffled Rim, Murano, 5 x 7 ¼ In.	94.00
Bowl, Opalini Opachi, Yellow, Black Foot, Venini, Murano, c.1989, 5 x 9 ½ In.	205.00
Bowl, Round, Amethyst, Undulating Rim, Gold Sun Fish, Green Stripes, Salviati, 8 x 2 In.	173.00
Bowl, Seguso, Murano, Iridized, Amber, Reinforced Rim, Loop Handles, 4 ½ x 8 ½ In.	413.00
Bowl, Stylized Basket Weave, Purple, White, Bucket Shape, Barovier & Toso, 8 In.	1239.00
Bowl, Tortoiseshell, Murano, 4 x 9 In.	94.00
Bowl, White Opalescent, Murano, 2 ½ x 12 In.	129.00
Candelabrum, 2-Light, Applied Fruit Leaves, Murano, 18 x 13 In., Pair	600.00
Candlestick, Clear, Red Dots, Gold Flecks, Barovier, c.1950, 14 x 4 ¼ In.	176.00
Candlestick, Disc Foot, Blue Twist Column, Clear Cup, Murano, 11 In., Pair	146.00
Candlestick, Green, Yellow, Clear, Archimede Seguso, Murano, c.1950, 5 ¾ In., Pair	410.00
Candlestick, Red & Gold, Murano, 8 ½ In., Pair	293.00
Candy Dish, Red & White Laced Swirl, Cover, c.1950s, 4 x 4 In.	28.00
Chandelier, 5-Light, Glass Flowers, Stems, Amber, Topaz, c.1950, 24 x 20 In.	900.00
Charger, Black Cased, Round, 14 In.	350.00
Clamshell, Pink & Clear, Polished 2-Sided Base, Murano, 8 ¾ x 14 In.	115.00
Compote, Clear Base Tapered Base, Blue Rimmed Bowl, Murano, 6 x 8 ½ In.	76.00
Compote, Cobalt Blue, Painted Court Figures, Gold Scrolls, Clear Foot, 3 x 5 In.	41.00
Compote, Iridescent Gold, Red Baluster Stem, 10 In.	81.00
Compote, Latticinio, White & Pink Vertical Stripes, Clear Foot, 4 x 7 ¾ In.	94.00
Decanter, Amber, Tiered, Opaque Red, Black Foot, Stopper, 11 ½ In.	550.00
Decanter, Green, White Ball Stopper, Venini Style, Murano, 10 ½ x 5 ¼ In.	117.00
Decanter, Merletto, Pink, Knopped Stopper, Archimede Seguso, Murano, 9 x 3 In.	760.00
Decanter, Pink & Black, Pink Bud Shape Stopper, Murano, 11 x 5 In.	205.00
Decanter Set, Inverted Pear Shape, Band Of Enameled Diamonds, 13 Piece	2726.00
Decanter, Stopper, Bullicante, Cranberry To Gold Cased, Murano, 9 ¼ x 5 In.	322.00
Decanter, Twist Flame Stopper, Pink, Gold Spangle Trim, Swirled Spool Base, Murano, 15 In., Pair	546.00
Egg, Slag, Brass Stand, Footed, 6 In.	90.00
Ewer, Multicolored, Blown, 7 x 3 In.	47.00
Figurine, 19th Century Elegant Couple, White, Black, 11 In., Pair	234.00
Figurine, Bird, Clear Base, Open Wings, Green Neck, Head, Murano, Salviati & Co., 8 In.	94.00
Figurine, Bird, Orange, Fat, Round, Murrine Eyes, Fratelli Toso, Murano, 3 In.	275.00
Figurine, Blackamoor, Male, Female, Cornucopia Vases, Italy, 13 In., Pair	460.00
Figurine, Bull, Corroso Glass, Green, A. Barbini, 7 x 13 In., 2 Piece	1560.00
Figurine, Cat, Murano, Salviati Venezia, 8 ¾ In.	185.00
Figurine, Chicken, Translucent White, Murrine Eyes, Fratelli Toso, Murano, 6 ½ In.	250.00
Figurine, Cowgirl, Sitting On Branch, Tambourine, Multicolored, Murano, 8 x 7 ½ In.	322.00
Figurine, Dolphin, Crystal Base, Murano, 16 ½ In.	147.00
Figurine, Dolphin, White, Frosted, Murano, 10 ½ In.	110.00
Figurine, Fish, 12 ⅝ x 8 In.	118.00
Figurine, Fish, Wave, Owl, 8 x 24 In.	585.00
Figurine, Flamenco Dancers, Clear, Black, Red, Murano, 14 ½ In., Pair	380.00
Figurine, Green Parrot, Amber Branch, Murano, 1900s, 16 ½ In.	518.00
Figurine, Horse, Clear, Smoke, Signed, Murano, 8 In.	234.00
Figurine, Horse's Head, Blue, White Opaque Mane, Murano, 8 In.	243.00
Figurine, Man, Woman, Pink, Gold, Signed, C. Toso, Murano, c.1950, 13 ¾ In., Pair	293.00
Figurine, Peasant Woman, Holding Basket, Multicolored, Murano, 11 x 4 ¼ In.	123.00
Figurine, Pheasant, Bubble Inclusions, 5 ½ In., Pair	179.00
Figurine, Rooster, Multicolored, Murano, c.1960, 11 ¾ x 11 ¾ In.	322.00
Figurine, Sunset, Disc Shape, Clear, Red, Signed, Murano, 8 ½ x 9 ½ In.	88.00
Goblet, Hand Blown, Opaque Rippled Bowl, Teardrop Stem, Murano, 7 Piece	243.00
Lamp, Electric, Vistosi, Murano, Clear & Opaque, Internally Lit, 15 ½ In.	600.00
Lamp, Pink, Triangle Base, Globe Top, Venini, 7 x 10 In.	293.00
Lamp, Swollen, Spiral Shape, Clear Amber Glass, Gold Speckled Bands, Seguso, 8 x 9 In., Pair	1200.00
Lamp, Textured Glass Orbs, Applied Ruffled Band, 1950s, 16 ¼ In., Pair	999.00
Lamp, Three Cordonato Oro, Pale Pink Glass, Bulbous Base, Gold Flecked Bands, 18 x 38 In.	960.00
Lamp, Vistosi, Murano, Abstract, 17 x 13 x 9 In., Pair	3965.00
Mirror, Cracked Mirror Frame, Lattice Rods, Rosettes, Murano, 1900s, 40 x 30 In.	4320.00
Oyster Server Set, 12 Wells, Purple, Murano, 13 In.	350.00
Perfume, Flask, Gold, Pink Latticed Ribbons, Embossed Sterling Lid, Oval, 6 In.	374.00

Glass-Venetian, Bottle, Stopper, Multicolored, Signed, Seguso, Murano, 17 ¾ In. $1054.00

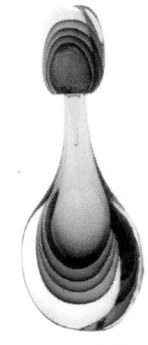

Glass-Venetian, Vase, Pink, Gold Spangles, Twisted Stopper, Stem, Swirl Base, Murano, 15 In., **Pair** $546.00

Glass-Venetian, Vase, Sommerso, Flavio Poli, Seguso, Murano, 8 ½ In. $660.00

TIP
Furs should never be stored in sealed plastic bags. They need to breathe.

Glasses, Lorgnette, 14K Yellow Gold, Sterling Silver, 4 In.
$88.00

Glasses, Lorgnette, Silver, Dragon Design, French Hallmark, 4 ¾ In.
$98.00

Glasses, Protective Goggles, Tinted, Rubber, Metal Case, 6 x 2 ¼ In.
$8.00

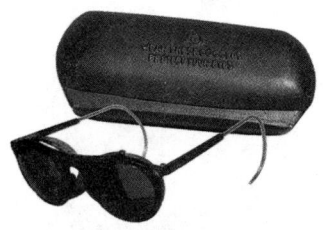

Gouda, Cruet, Tulips, House, Rust Slip, High Glaze, Incised H, Zuid, Holland, 5 In.
$219.00

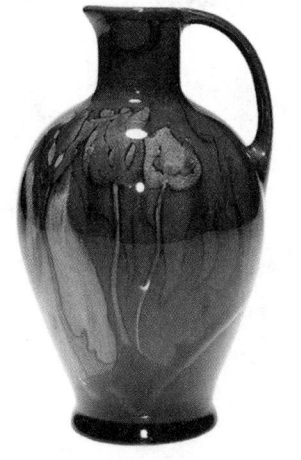

Plate, Opalescent Spiraling Circles, Coupe Shape, Barovier & Toso, 12 In.	317.00
Sconce, 2-Light, Gold Leaf, Bobeches, Urn Form Shades, 1950s, 11 In.	470.00
Sculpture, Volcano Glass, Sommerso Craters, Geometric, A. Barbini, 113 x 7 In.	900.00
Top Hat, Vetreria La Fenice, Murano, 4 x 8 ¾ In.	94.00
Vase, Abstract Swirl, Multicolored, Cylindrical, Murano, Lino Tagliapietra, 1950, 16 x 9 In.	4600.00
Vase, Aventurine Strips, Silver, Yellow Mica Flecks, Red Ground, Murano, 7 In.	2185.00
Vase, Bird & Cased Art, Murano, c.1950, 15 In.	88.00
Vase, Black Ground, Red Arches, Signed, Archimede Seguso, Murano, 9 ¾ x 5 ½ In.	761.00
Vase, Blue To Light Blue, Tower Of Pisa Style, Cylindrical, Seguso, 12 x 5 In.	300.00
Vase, Bottle Shape, Green, Black Inclusions, Bubbles, Seguso, 12 In.	540.00
Vase, Bud, Archimede Seguso, Lace Design, Yellow, 7 x 5 In.	1200.00
Vase, Bud, Green & Blue, Cased With Yellow, Murano, 1950, 10 ½ In., Pair	500.00
Vase, Bud, Green, Blue, Sommerso, Murano, c.1950, 10 ½ In, Pair	500.00
Vase, Bud, Green, Frosted Grapevine, Circular Foot, Knopped Stem, Murano, 9 ¼ In.	269.00
Vase, Bulbous, Blue Bottom, Pink Spiral Top, Flared Rim, Signed, Murano, 8 ¾ x 5 In.	70.00
Vase, Bullicante, Encased Air Bubbles, Archimede Seguso, 6 ¾ x 5 ¼ In.	205.00
Vase, Bullicante Incalmo, Cased Bubbles, White, Pink, Wing Rim, 9 ½ In.	450.00
Vase, Butterscotch Yellow, Ercolor Barovier Style, Murano, 13 ½ x 5 ½ In.	205.00
Vase, Canne Glass, Cinched, Orange, White, Clear Stripes, Gio Ponti, Venini, 11 x 5 In.	600.00
Vase, Clear, Iridescent Finish, Handle, Barovier & Toso, 1950s, 10 x 6 ½ In.	351.00
Vase, Clear Textured Sides, Signed, Luigi Vitturi, Murano, 15 ¼ x 8 ½ In.	614.00
Vase, Fan Shape, Mottled Pink, Gold Flecks, Flower Handles, Barovier & Toso, 12 In.	732.00
Vase, Fan Shape, White Opaque, Venini, Murano, 8 ¼ x 10 In.	1638.00
Vase, Fluted, Scalloped Rim, Gilt, c.1900, 24 In., Pair	468.00
Vase, Footed, Bulbous Base, Tall Slender Neck, Blue & Navy Vertical Stripes, 14 In.	129.00
Vase, Free-Form, Fazzoletto, Deep Ruffled Sides, White, Murano, 5 ½ x 7 In.	47.00
Vase, Geometric Pattern, Multicolored, Pinched Neck, 8 In.	115.00
Vase, Green, Red & White, Incalmo, Luciano Gaspari, Salviati & Co., 8 ½ In.	720.00
Vase, Green To Brown, Thick Drips From Rim, Murano, 10 x 6 ½ In.	322.00
Vase, Green To Clear, Applied Red, Green, Blue, Abstract Design, 1950s, 11 ¼ In.	411.00
Vase, Handkerchief, Black, Orange, Fulvio Bianconi, Venini, 7 x 8 In.	1080.00
Vase, Handkerchief, Clear, Blue Vertical Stripes, Murano, 6 In., Pair	146.00
Vase, Handkerchief, Fazzoletto, Pink, White, Murano, 6 ¾ x 6 ¾ In.	117.00
Vase, Handkerchief, Fazzoletto, Purple, 8 x 8 In.	117.00
Vase, Handkerchief, Fazzoletto, Turquoise, Murano, 5 ½ x 6 In.	146.00
Vase, Handkerchief, Fazzoletto, White & Pink Opaque Vertical Stripes, 7 ½ x 8 In.	99.00
Vase, Handkerchief, Yellow, 6 In.	176.00
Vase, Lobed, Green Pulegoso Glass, Murano, 10 x 6 In.	480.00
Vase, Pink, Gold Spangles, Twisted Stopper, Stem, Swirl Base, Murano, 15 In., Pair *illus*	546.00
Vase, Pulled Yellow, Green, Blue, Clear, Square, Venini, 13 x 7 ½ In.	1440.00
Vase, Red, Blue, Green, Clear Plaid Design, Fulvio Bianconi, Venini, 8 x 5 In.	4800.00
Vase, Red, Orange Swirls, Clear Glass, Applied Ruffle On Base, 11 In.	225.00
Vase, Red, Signed, Barovier & Toso, Murano, 15 ¼ x 6 In.	234.00
Vase, Ribbed, Shaded Amber, Silver Leaf Flecks, Mask Handles, Murano, c.1950, 8 In.	585.00
Vase, Shell, Pink Spiral, Archimede Seguso, Murano, 6 x 16 In.	410.00
Vase, Sommerso, Flavio Poli, Seguso, Murano, 8 ½ In. *illus*	660.00
Vase, Spiral Vertical Stripes, Cenedese, 7 ½ x 7 In.	234.00
Vase, Swirled Canes, Ocher Ground, Flat Oval, Murano, Lino Tagliapietra, 1950, 19 x 11 In.	4600.00
Vase, Swirled Celeste Blue Foot, Purple Body, Silver Aventurine, 18 In.	250.00
Vase, Tapered, Controlled Bubbles, Applied Vertical Ribs, Inscribed, 1950s, 13 In.	1116.00
Vase, Thick Wall, Submerged Green, Blue & Red Layers, Inscribed, 1950s, 13 In.	499.00
Vase, Trumpet, Cobalt Blue, Flower & Leaf Shape Metal Holder, 9 ½ In., Pair	440.00
Vase, Trumpet, Green Base, Blue Expanding Rim, Murano, 12 x 8 In.	205.00
Vase, Trumpet, Latticinio, Flaring Neck, Venini, Murano, 19 x 9 In.	380.00
Vase, Tulip, Tapered, Aventurine, Applied Colorful Trailings, 1950s, 24 In.	470.00
Vase, White Spiral Stripes, Ruffled Rim, 12 x 7 ½ In.	176.00
Vase, Yellow, Green, Blue Diagonal Stripes, Cenedese, Murano, 11 ½ x 8 ¼ In.	205.00
Vase, Yellow, Red, Blue, Green Patchwork, Fulvio Bianconi, 10 x 6 In.	1560.00
Water Set, Amethyst Pitcher, Continental Life Band, 6 Matching Goblets, Murano, 8 ½ In.	200.00

GLASSES for the eyes, or spectacles, were mentioned in a manuscript in 1289 and have been used ever since. The first eyeglasses with rigid side pieces were made in London in 1727. Bifocals were invented by Benjamin Franklin in 1785. Lorgnettes were popular in late Victorian times. Opera Glasses are listed in their own category.

Aluminum, Cat's-Eye, Floral Etching, Blue Accent, Marked, American Optical, 1950s, 5 ¾ In.	45.00
Bifocals, Round, Faceted Lens, 14K Gold Frame, 4 In.	94.00

Lorgnette, 14K Gold, Leather Case, Early 20th Century, 5 ¾ In.	270.00
Lorgnette, 14K White Gold, Sterling Silver Chain, Round Lenses, c.1920, 24 In.	130.00
Lorgnette, 14K Yellow Gold, Sterling Silver, 4 In. ....*illus*	88.00
Lorgnette, Art Nouveau, Sterling Silver, Gold Wash..................................	395.00
Lorgnette, Folded, Round, Release Button, Short Handle, 18K White Gold, 3 In.	118.00
Lorgnette, Octagonal Folded Lenses, Release Button, 14K White Gold, 4 In.	118.00
Lorgnette, Round, Column Handle, Push Button Release, 14K Gold, 4 In.	142.00
Lorgnette, Round, Folded, Square Tapered Handle, Trefoil Finial, Mark, Rose Gold, 5 In.	165.00
Lorgnette, Round, Folded, Tapered Handle, Round Finial, Yellow Gold, 5 In.	142.00
Lorgnette, Silver, Dragon Design, French Hallmark, 4 ¾ In. ....*illus*	98.00
Lorgnette, Tortoiseshell, Carved, 1920s, 7 ¾ In.	96.00
Protective Goggles, Tinted, Rubber, Metal Case, 6 x 2 ¼ In. ....*illus*	8.00
Rimless, Chinese, Tortoiseshell Temple Pads, Shagreen Case, 5 ½ & 7 In.	495.00
Spectacles, Steel Flip Top Case, c.1750..	350.00
Sunglasses, Folding, Simulated Tortoise, Green, Orange, Pierre Cardin, 1960s, 6 ¼ x 1 ¾ In.	125.00
Sunglasses, Pinco-Ney, Foldable, Gutta Percha Rim, Case, Early 1900s, 3 ½ In.	100.00
Sunglasses, Spring Frame, Hard Case, Douglas & Pittman, Atlanta, Ga., Late 1800s	88.00

GLIDDEN POTTERY worked in Alfred, New York, from 1940 to 1957. The pottery made stoneware, dinnerware, and art objects.

Casserole, Cover, Rooster, c.1950	20.00
Planter, Turquoise Matrix, Rectangular, Incised, 2 x 4 ¼ In.	15.00
Vase, Ball, Turquoise Matrix Glaze, Incised Signature, 6 ½ In.	55.00
Vase, Blue Green Tones, Green Speckled Rim, Marked, 8 In.	48.00
Vase, Turquoise Shaded To Rose, Rectangular, Marked, 8 In.	45.00

GOEBEL is the mark used by W. Goebel Porzellanfabrik of Oeslau, Germany, now Rodental, Germany. The company was founded by Franz Detleff Goebel and his son, William Goebel, In 1871. It was known as F&W Goebel. Slates, slate pencils, and marbles were made. Soon the company began making porcelain tableware and figurines. Hummel figurines were first made by Goebel in 1935 and are now being made by another company. Goebel is still in business. Old pieces marked *Goebel Hummel* are listed under Hummel in this book.

Figurine, Friar Tuck Condiment Set, Tray, Spoon, c.1960, 3 ½ In.	30.00
Figurine, Mother & Daughter, After Huldah, 8 In.	30.00

GOLDSCHEIDER was founded by Friedrich Goldscheider in Vienna in 1885. The family left Vienna in 1938, and the factory was taken over by the Germans. Goldscheider started factories in England and in Trenton, New Jersey. The New Jersey factory started in 1940 as Goldscheider-U.S.A. In 1941 it became Goldscheider-Everlast Corporation. From 1947 to 1953 it was Goldcrest Ceramics Corporation. In 1950 the Vienna plant was returned to Mr. Goldscheider, and the company continues in business. The Trenton, New Jersey, business, called Goldscheider of Vienna, imports all of the pieces.

Bust, Madonna, Wearing Peach Pink Wrap, 1940s, 4 x 1 ¾ In.	295.00
Figurine, Country Girl, Picking Up Basket, Austria, Pre 1940, 14 In.	600.00
Figurine, Deer, Mother & Child, Running, 10 x 13 In.	262.00
Figurine, Diana With Borzoi, Taking Aim, Signed Latour, c.1912, 24 In.	3500.00
Figurine, Horse, Prancing, 1950s, 4 ¼ x 14 ½ x 10 ¾ In.	300.00
Figurine, Madonna & Child, Soft Pink & Gray, Cloud Base, 16 ¼ In.	900.00
Figurine, Oriental Man Playing Instrument, Woman Dancing, c.1995, 10 ½ In., Pair............	39.00
Figurine, Trojan, Silver Gray Crackle Glaze, Brown Trim, Marked, 1930s, 10 ½ In.	550.00
Plaque, Figural Heads, Boy In Top Hat & Bowtie, Girl In Bonnet, Pair	299.00
Vanity Box, Double Horse Head Lid, 1950s, 5 ½ x 4 ¼ In.	150.00

GOLF, *see Sports category*.

GONDER CERAMIC ARTS, INC., was opened by Lawton Gonder in 1941 in Zanesville, Ohio. Gonder made high-grade pottery decorated with flambe, drip, gold crackle, and Chinese crackle glazes. The factory closed in 1957. From 1946 to 1954, Gonder also operated the Elgee Pottery, which made ceramic lamp bases.

Bowl, Centerpiece, Stylized Dolphin Form, Mottled Pink & Lavender, 12 In.	12.00
Ewer, Shaded Mauve Glaze, Angular Handle, Elongated Spout, No. H 73, 8 In.	18.00
Vase, Flared, Scalloped, Bulbous Bottom, Pink Shaded To Turquoise, Brown Accents, 6 In.	6.00

G

Gouda, Vase, 6-Sided, Painted Flowers, Handles, Paper Label, 6 ½ x 15 ½ In. $600.00

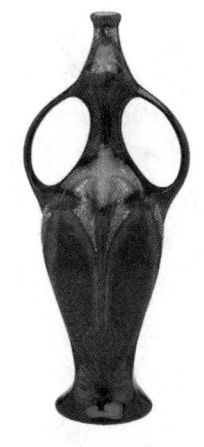

Gouda, Vase, Multicolored Leaves, Black Ground, Fluted, Footed, Marked, Bergen, 9 ⅜ In. $196.00

Greentown, Teardrop & Tassel, Relish, Blue, Beaded Rim, Indiana, 1 ½ x 4 ½ x 7 In. $259.00

Grueby, Bowl, Leaves, Carved, Applied, Green Matte Glaze, Initial R, 8 x 3 ½ In. $1200.00

Grueby, Vase, Green Matte Glaze, Leaves, Oval, 8 ¾ x 4 ½ In. $2928.00

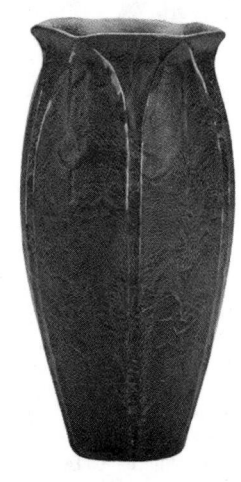

Grueby, Vase, Squat, Applied Leaves, Daffodils, Green Matte Ground, 4 ½ x 5 ½ In. $6000.00

Gundersen, Cup & Saucer, Peachblow, Matte Finish, White Applied Handle, 3 x 5 In. $69.00

Gustavsberg, Figurine, Woman, Striped Swim Suit, Lisa Larson, Sweden, Marked, 7 ¾ In. $75.00

Vase, Flared, Scalloped, Spread Foot, 2 Figural Swans, White, 8 In.	19.00
Vase, Molded Starfish, Mottled Yellow & Brown, Pink Inside, 8 In.	19.00
Vase, Ribbon Candy Form, Yellow & Green Glaze, No. 517, 11 In.	18.00
Vase, Swan Shape, Pink Mottled Glaze, No. 511, 9 In.	12.00

GOOFUS GLASS was made from about 1900 to 1920 by many American factories. It was originally painted gold, red, green, bronze, pink, purple, or other bright colors. Many pieces are found today with flaking paint, and this lowers the value.

Console, Red Iris, Gold Ground, 10 ⅝ In.	20.00
Lamp, Shade, Embossed, 8 In.	100.00
Plate, 2 Red Apples In Center, Gold, 8 ⅜ In.	30.00
Plate, Last Supper, Red & Green Robes, Jesus In Gold, Gold Ground, 10 x 7 In.	12.00
Plate, Red, Gilt Under Painted Pressed Glass Flowers & Leaves, c.1905, 10 In.	20.00
Vase, Bud, Puffy Rose, Early 1900s, 5 ⅛ In.	15.00
Vase, Cabbage Rose, Gold & Red, c.1910, 5 ⅛ In., Pair	26.00
Vase, Peacock, Gold & Black, Red Wings, 10 ½ In.	46.00

GOUDA, Holland, has been a pottery center since the seventeenth century. Two firms, the Zenith pottery, established in the eighteenth century, and the Zuid-Hollandsche pottery, made the brightly colored art pottery marked *Gouda* from 1898 to about 1964. Other factories followed. Many pieces featured Art Nouveau or Art Deco designs.

Charger, Flowers, Red, Green, 1900s, 11 In.	118.00
Cruet, Tulips, House, Rust Slip, High Glaze, Incised H, Zuid, Holland, 5 In. ....*illus*	219.00
Inkwell, Cover, Kelk Pattern, c.1900s, 3 ¾ In.	165.00
Vase, 6-Sided, Painted Flowers, Handles, Paper Label, 6 ½ x 15 ½ In. ....*illus*	600.00
Vase, Averil, Flowers, Leaves, Ivory Ground, Cylindrical, Tapered, 10 ½ In.	162.00
Vase, Multicolored Leaves, Black Ground, Fluted, Footed, Marked, Bergen, 9 ⅜ In. ....*illus*	196.00
Vase, Stylized Blossoms, Whiplashes, Arabesques, 4-Sided, 18 x 7 In.	2280.00
Vase, Stylized Flowers & Leaves, Bulbous, Flaring Neck, Multicolored, 13 In.	316.00

GRANITEWARE is an enameled tinware that has been used in the kitchen from the late nineteenth century to the present. Earlier graniteware was green or turquoise blue, with white spatters. The later ware was gray with white spatters. Reproductions are being made in all colors.

Baker, Emerald Green Swirl, Open Handle, Block Rim, 10 x 15 In.	130.00
Berry Bucket, Blue & White Swirl, Tin Lid, 4 In.	105.00 to 145.00
Bowl, Blue & White, 11 In.	10.00
Bowl, Blue & White Swirl, 12 ½ In.	17.50
Bowl, Vegetable, Brown & White Swirl, Oval, 9 ½ In.	15.00
Bread Box, Blue, Oval, Oblong, Hinge, 19 In.	22.00
Bucket, Gray Mottled, 7 In.	6.00
Butter Carrier, Brown & White Swirl, Lid, Handle, Oval	525.00
Can, Blue & White Swirl, Cream, Tin Lid	70.00
Churn, Light Blue, White, Handles, Wood Lid, 18 In.	675.00
Coffee Boiler, Blue & White Veins, Wire Bail, Block Rims, 10 x 9 ½ In.	13.00
Coffee Urn, White, Handles, 18 In., 4 Piece	400.00
Coffeepot, Blue & White Swirl, Lid, 8 ½ In.	40.00
Coffeepot, Blue Swirl, 10 In.	30.00
Coffeepot, Brown, White, Nickel Plated Copper Lid, Wood Handle, Manning & Bowman, 1889 .	36.00
Coffeepot, Yellow Flowers, White & Peach Ground, Embossed Tin Hinged Lid, 10 In.	34.00
Colander, Blue & White Swirl	7.50
Flask, Cobalt Blue	6.00
Jellyroll Pan, Brown & White Swirl, 10 In.	22.00
Kitchen Set, Rack, Sieve, Ladle, White, 17 In., 3 Piece	215.00
Milk Can, Blue Mottled, 9 ½ In.	11.00
Muffin Pan, Cobalt Blue Swirl, 8 Cup	145.00
Muffin Pan, Onyx Ware, 8 Cup	35.00
Mug, Blue, Liter	10.00
Pail, Blue & White Swirl, Paper Label	250.00
Pail, Blue, Cover, 4 In.	9.00
Pan, Blue & White, Handle, 10 In.	95.00
Pan, Sauce, Blue & White Swirl, Lid	10.00
Pie Plate, Brown & White Swirl, 10 In.	22.00
Pie Plate, Chrysolite, 9 In.	20.00
Pitcher, Blue & White Swirl, 11 In.	5.00

Pitcher, Blue Mottled	17.50
Pitcher, Water, Blue, Crimped Rim, Applied Handle, Fan Design, c.1875, 8 In.	106.00
Plate, Blue & White Swirl, 10 In.	15.00
Pudding Pan, Blue & White Swirl, 7 ½ In.	10.00
Roaster, Blue & White Swirl, Oval, 14 In.	17.00
Roaster, Blue Swirl, 16 In.	11.00
Teakettle, Gray	20.00
Teapot, Blue & White Swirl, Lid, 6 In.	45.00
Teapot, Blue, Bulbous, 5 In.	15.00
Teapot, Blue, Granite Lid, Bulbous, 4 In.	16.00
Teapot, Gray, Lid, 1 Cup	120.00
Teapot, Lid, Wood Handle, 8 In.	115.00
Tray, Relish, Blue, Rectangular, 16 x 13 In.	15.00
Washbasin, Cobalt Blue Swirl	45.00
Water Carrier, Brown & White Swirl, Lid, Bail Handle & Side Handle, 11 In.	435.00
Water Cooler, Blue & White, Lava Ware, 2 Sections	195.00

GREENTOWN glass was made by the Indiana Tumbler and Goblet Company of Greentown, Indiana, from 1894 to 1903. In 1899, the factory became part of National Glass Company. A variety of pressed glass was made. Additional pieces may be found in other categories, such as Chocolate Glass, Holly Amber, Milk Glass, and Pressed Glass.

Austrian, Wine	30.00
Bird With Berry, Dish, Cover, Bird, Teal, Basket Weave, c.1900, 4 ¾ x 4 x 5 In.	429.00
Bird With Berry, Dish, Cover, Clear, Basket Weave, c.1900, 4 ¾ x 4 x 5 In.	145.00
Bird With Berry, Dish, Cover, Teal Blue, Indiana Tumbler & Goblet Company, 4 x 4 In.	374.00
Cactus, Sugar, Cover, Red Agate, c.1900, 6 In.	212.00
Cat On Hamper, Dish, Cover, Teal Blue, c.1900, 4 ⅞ x 3 ½ x 3 ½ In.	212.00
Cord Drapery, Relish, Flattened, Amber, 1 x 6 ¼ x 10 In.	106.00
Cord Drapery, Syrup, Chocolate, c.1900, 6 ½ In.	92.00
Dewey, Creamer, Canary, 5 In.	53.00
Dewey, Cruet, Nile Green, 6 In.	1035.00
Diamond Prisms, Goblet, Clear, 5 ¾ In.	26.00
Dolphin, Dish, Cover, Red Agate, Sawtooth Rim, c.1900, 4 ⅜ x 7 In.	145.00
Hen On Nest, Dish, Cover, Clear, c.1900, 4 ½ x 4 ¼ x 5 ½ In.	212.00
Hen On Nest, Dish, Cover, Green, c.1900, 4 ½ x 4 ¼ x 5 ½ In.	92.00
Herringbone Buttress, Berry Bowl, Clear, 4 x 8 ¼ In.	66.00
Herringbone Buttress, Cake Stand, Clear, 7 x 10 ¼ In.	118.00
Herringbone Buttress, Spooner, Green, 4 ⅛ x 3 ¼ In.	66.00
Iris, Pitcher, Oval, Blue, 7 ¾ In.	250.00
Leaf Bracket, Celery Dish, 11 In.	29.00
Rabbit, Dish, Cover, Green, c.1900, 4 ¼ x 4 ¼ x 5 ½ In.	132.00
Ruffled Eye, Pitcher, Water, Amber, Raised Feet, 8 ¼ x 4 ¾ In.	79.00
Shuttle, Nappy, Red Agate, 1 ½ x 4 ¾ In.	79.00
Teardrop & Tassel, Compote, Cover, 9 x 6 ¼ In.	92.00
Teardrop & Tassel, Relish, Blue, Beaded Rim, Indiana, 1 ½ x 4 ½ x 7 In. *illus*	259.00
Wheelbarrow, Salt, Nile Green, Beaded Diamond, c.1900, 1 ⅞ x 1 ⅝ x 2 ¼ In.	397.00
Witch Head, Toothpick, Nile Green	173.00

GRUEBY FAIENCE COMPANY of Boston, Massachusetts, was incorporated in 1897 by William H. Grueby. Garden statuary, art pottery, and architectural tiles were made until 1920. The company developed a green matte glaze that was so popular it was copied by many other factories making a less expensive type of pottery. This eventually led to the financial problems of the pottery. Cuerda seca and cuenca are techniques explained in the Tile category.

Bowl, Green Matte Glaze, Carved, Applied Vertical Leaves, 8 x 3 ½ In.	1200.00
Bowl, Green Matte Glaze, Leaves, Marie Seaman, 4 ¾ x 9 ½ In.	3660.00
Bowl, Leaves, Blue, Gray Glaze, Squat, Wilhelmina Post, 2 ¼ x 2 ¾ In.	2074.00
Bowl, Leaves, Carved, Applied, Green Matte Glaze, Initial R, 8 x 3 ½ In. *illus*	1200.00
Flower Bowl, Leaves, Green Matte Glaze, Copper Insert, Marked, 9 In.	3360.00
Humidor, Cover, Green Matte Glaze, Arched Leaves, 5 ½ x 5 In.	4880.00
Paperweight, Scarab, Green Matte, 1 x 2 ½ In.	995.00
Tile, 3 Tiles, Ship At Sea, Birds, Matte Glaze, Arts & Crafts Oak Frame, 30 ½ x 13 ½ In.	6000.00
Tile, 3-Masted Ship, Square, Arts & Crafts Oak Frame, Tile Marked MD, 12 In.	2280.00
Tile, Inside Corner, Matte Glaze, Green, Gray, c.1920, 4 ¾ In., 2 Piece	30.00
Tile, Leathery Green Matte Glaze, Cuenca, Golden Tulip, Green Leaves, 6 x 6 In.	1800.00
Tile, Lily Pads, Blue Ground, Frame, 6 In. Square	1342.00

Gustavsberg, Vase, Green, Silver Clad Flowers, Rim & Base Trim, Argenta, Signed, 9 x 4 In. $205.00

Hall, Crocus, Saltshaker, Range, Handle, 4 ¾ In. $30.00

Hall, Red Poppy, Coffeepot, 8 In. $55.00

TIP
Clean the inside of a graniteware pot by filling the pot with water, adding a teaspoon of baking soda, and bringing it to a boil.

Hall, Teapot, Airflow, Chinese Green, Gold Trim
$85.00

Hall, Teapot, Lipton Tea, Light Blue
$49.00

Halloween, Game, Shooting Target, Scarecrow, Plastic, 16 In.
$59.00

Halloween, Jack-O'-Lantern, Devil, Papier-Mache, 5 ½ In.
$819.00

Tile, Medieval Monk, Playing Cello, Blue Matte, Ocher Glaze, Embossed, Frame, 6 x 6 In.	420.00
Tile, Oak Tree, Frame, Arts & Crafts, 6 In. Square	2440.00
Tile, Pines, Glazed, 6 In. Square	3660.00
Tile, Tree, Green Grass, Recessed Round, Blue Border, Stamped, Frame, 6 x 6 In.	978.00
Trivet, Tulip, Bronze Tiffany Base, Tile Signed D.C., 7 x 7 In.	2040.00
Vase, Broad, Carved, Applied Leaves, Yellow Matte Glaze, White Buds, Marked, 8 x 5 In.	8400.00
Vase, Dark Green Matte Glaze, Leaves, Shouldered, 11 ¼ x 5 ½ In.	5490.00
Vase, Frothy Green Matte Glaze, Leaves, Bulbous, 6 x 4 In.	5795.00
Vase, Green Matte Glaze, 3 Handles, Leaves, Bulbous, 9 x 7 ¼ In.	2562.00
Vase, Green Matte Glaze, Carved Leaves, Stems & Buds, 4-Sided, Marked, 7 ⅞ In.	1093.00
Vase, Green Matte Glaze, Cylindrical Neck, Bulbous, Leaves, 10 x 4 In.	1220.00
Vase, Green Matte Glaze, Embossed Blossoms, Rows Of Leaves, 13 ¼ x 8 In.	4500.00
Vase, Green Matte Glaze, Globular, Rolled Rim, Marked, 3 ¼ In.	595.00
Vase, Green Matte Glaze, Incised Leaves, Bulbous, 7 x 5 ¾ In.	1952.00
Vase, Green Matte Glaze, Leaves, Blue Iris Blossoms, 12 ½ x 8 ½ In.	5490.00
Vase, Green Matte Glaze, Leaves, Iris Blossoms, Marie Seaman, 13 ¼ x 8 ½ In.	18300.00
Vase, Green Matte Glaze, Leaves, Oval, 8 ¾ x 4 ½ In. ....*illus*	2928.00
Vase, Green Matte Glaze, Smoke Stack Form, Marie Seaman, 15 x 7 ½ In.	2806.00
Vase, Indigo, Matte Glaze, Carved, Applied Leaves, 8 x 4 In.	1140.00
Vase, Leaves, Blossoms, 23 x 8 ½ In.	18300.00
Vase, Leaves, Green Matte Glaze, Buds, Tapered, Marked, 11 ½ x 5 ½ In.	1860.00
Vase, Matte Green Glaze, Bulbous, 11 In.	1595.00
Vase, Molded Green Leaves, Yellow Flowers, Impressed, Ruth Erikson, 8 ½ In.	1955.00
Vase, Mottled Caramel Glaze, Marked, 9 ½ In.	1595.00
Vase, Shouldered, Flowered Rim, Green, Yellow Highlights, 10 ¼ In.	9775.00
Vase, Squat, Applied Leaves, Daffodils, Green Matte Ground, 4 ½ x 5 ½ In. ......*illus*	6000.00

GUNDERSEN glass was made at the Gundersen Glass Works of New Bedford, Massachusetts, from 1939 to 1952 and by its successor, Gundersen/Pairpoint, from 1952 to 1957. Gundersen Peachblow is especially famous.

Cup & Saucer, Peachblow, Matte Finish, White Applied Handle, 3 x 5 In. ....*illus*	69.00

GUSTAVSBERG ceramics factory was founded in 1827 near Stockholm, Sweden. It is best known to collectors for its twentieth-century artwares, especially Argenta, a green stoneware with silver inlay.

Gustafsberg

Figurine, Baby Seal, Paul Hoff, 5 ½ x 2 ¼ In.	75.00
Figurine, Camel, Menagerie Series, Lisa Larson, 1966-76, 4 x 4 In.	225.00
Figurine, Cat, Menagerie Series, Lisa Larson, 1966-76	495.00
Figurine, Johanna, Ungar Series, Lisa Larson, 1962-80, 5 ½ In.	200.00
Figurine, Lion, Afrika Series, Lisa Larson, c.1970, 6 In.	265.00
Figurine, Malin, Ungar Series, Lisa Larson, 1962-80, 7 In.	200.00
Figurine, Pekingese, Kennel Collection, Lisa Larson, 1972-83, 4 x 3 In.	125.00
Figurine, Spaniel, Sitting, Kennel Collection, Lisa Larson, 1972-83, 2 ½ x 2 In.	145.00
Figurine, Tabby Cat, Lilla Zoo Series, Lisa Larson, 1956-78, 4 x 3 ½ In.	175.00
Figurine, Woman, Striped Swimsuit, Lisa Larson, Sweden, Marked, 7 ¾ In. ....*illus*	75.00
Vase, Cactus Design, Orange, Gold Leaf Trim, Royal Copenhagen, Denmark, 10 x 12 In.	120.00
Vase, Green & Brown Matte Glaze, Bulbous, Berndt Friberg, 2 ¼ x 2 ¼ In.	240.00
Vase, Green, Silver Clad Flowers, Rim & Base Trim, Argenta, Signed, 9 x 4 In. ....*illus*	205.00
Vase, Squat, Tan Crystalline Glaze, Kage, 3 x 3 In.	90.00

HAEGER POTTERIES, INC., Dundee, Illinois, started making commercial artwares in 1914. Early pieces were marked with the name *Haeger* written over an *H*. About 1938, the mark *Royal Haeger* was used in honor of Royal Hickman, a designer at the factory. The firm is still making florist wares and lamp bases. See also the Royal Hickman category.

Haeger

Ashtray, Leaf Shape, Scalloped Edge, c.1950, 13 x 7 In.	18.00
Ashtray, Orange & Black Volcanic Glaze, Free-Form Shape, 8 In.	17.00
Bowl, Cosmos Blossom, Relief, Green Matte Glaze, Shaped Rim, 3 x 10 In.	53.00
Charger, Black Matte Glaze, Crackled Metallic Free-Form Design, 13 ¾ In.	207.00
Figurine, 2 Dancers, Arched, Holding Hands, Forming Circle, White Glaze, No. 6037, 15 In.	224.00
Figurine, Antelope, In Engobe, 19 x 16 In.	121.00
Figurine, Antelope, White & Gold Curdled Glaze, Royal Haeger, 15 ¾ In.	30.00
Figurine, Cat, Seated, Orange, Red Luster Glaze, 1 Green Glass Eye, Royal Haeger, 15 In., Pair.	472.00
Figurine, Panther, Speckled Orange Glaze, 12 In.	47.00
Lamp, Lamp, Rooster, Red, Planter Base, 21 ½ In.	77.00

G

Planter, Bow Shape, Green Glaze, 3 ½ x 3 In.	32.00
Planter, Flower Basket, Pink Basket, Turquoise Flowers, Fan Shape, Royal Haeger, 9 x 14 In. .	24.00
Planter, Peacock, Fanned Cutout Feathers, Pink, Blue, Green, Royal Haeger, 15 x 16 In.	43.00
Rose Bowl, Pink Drip Glaze, 4 x 3 In.	31.00
Vase, Aquatic, Relief, Mottled Turquoise, Ball Shape, Royal Haeger, 11 x 12 ½ In.	130.00
Vase, Classic Shape, Burgundy Glaze, Sterling Silver Flowers, Shaped Handles, 14 In.	106.00
Vase, Earth Wrap, Brown, Tan, Orange, Shouldered, Flared, 10 x 4 In.	40.00
Vase, Fern, Mauve Agate Glaze, 12 ¾ In.	75.00
Vase, Flared, Figural Gazelle On Base, White Glaze, Royal Haeger, 15 In., Pair	165.00
Vase, Green Foam Glaze, 8-Sided, Flared, Pedestal Base, 7 In.	43.00
Vase, Overlapping Leaves, Yellow & Green Crackle Glaze, Footed, 15 x 6 In.	118.00
Wall Planter, Mandolin, Brown Glaze, Open Front, 13 In.	60.00
Wall Pocket, Fish, Yellow, Red & Brown Accents, 16 ¾ In.	98.00

HALF-DOLL, *see Pincushion Doll category.*

HALL CHINA COMPANY started in East Liverpool, Ohio, in 1903. The firm made many types of wares. Collectors search for the Hall teapots made from the 1920s to the 1950s. The dinnerwares of the same period, especially Autumn Leaf pattern, are also popular. The Hall China Company merged with Homer Laughlin China Company in 2010. Autumn Leaf pattern dishes are listed in their own category in this book.

Crocus, Saltshaker, Range, Handle, 4 ¾ In. ....*illus*	30.00
Fairfax, Berry Bowl, 5 ¼ In.	8.00
Fairfax, Plate, Salad, 7 ⅜ In.	8.00
Fairfax, Soup, Dish, 8 In.	12.00
Heather Rose, Berry Bowl, 6 In.	8.00
Heather Rose, Bowl, Fruit, 5 ¼ In.	8.00
Heather Rose, Teacup	12.00
Orange Poppy, Sugar & Creamer	90.00
Pitcher, Matte Brown, Marked, 9 ½ In.	85.00
Red Poppy, Coffeepot, 8 In. ....*illus*	55.00
Rose Parade, Casserole, Cover, Tab Handles	45.00
Rose Parade, Sugar & Creamer, Pink Rose	200.00
Rose White, Casserole, Cover	21.00
Rose White, Jug, Sani-Grid, 5 In.	41.00
Rose White, Sugar, Open	25.00
Royal Rose, Bean Pot, Cover, 4 ¼ In.	20.00
Royal Rose, Salt & Pepper	41.00
Teapot, Airflow, Chinese Green, Gold Trim ....*illus*	85.00
Teapot, Lipton Tea, Light Blue ....*illus*	49.00
Teapot, Moderne Ivory, 6 Cup	65.00
Teapot, Parade, Yellow, Gold Acorns, Oak Leaves, 6 Cup	25.00
Tomorrow's Classic, Bowl, Cereal, 6 In.	12.00

HALLOWEEN is an ancient holiday that has changed in the last 200 years. The jack-o'-lantern, witches on broomsticks, and orange decorations seem to be twentieth-century creations. Collectors started to become serious about collecting Halloween-related items in the late 1970s. The papier-mache decorations, now replaced by plastic, and old costumes are in demand.

Button, Parade, Black Cat, Orange Ground, Pinback, 1932, ⅞ In.	158.00
Costume, Captain America, Open-Face Mask, Joe Simon, Mat, Frame, 1990s, 22 x 25 In.	1735.00
Figure, Boy Holding Pumpkin, Red Shirt, Brown Pants, Chalk, 16 In.	616.00
Figure, Puprecht Santa Devil, Protruding Tongue, 10 In.	2632.00
Game, Shooting Target, Scarecrow, Plastic, 16 In. ....*illus*	59.00
Jack-O'-Lantern, Black Cat, Papier-Mache, Cat Wearing Orange Tie, 5 ½ In.	760.00
Jack-O'-Lantern, Black Cat, Solid Composition, Cat Wearing Bowtie, 4 ¼ In.	1111.00
Jack-O'-Lantern, Black Man's Head, 4 ¼ In.	3510.00
Jack-O'-Lantern, Cat Face, Open Painted Mouth, Candle Inserts, Pressed Pulp, 1930s, 5 In. ..	650.00
Jack-O'-Lantern, Devil, Papier-Mache, 5 ½ In. ....*illus*	819.00
Jack-O'-Lantern, Double Faced, Paper Pulp, 1940s, 7 In.	450.00
Jack-O'-Lantern, Eggplant, Purple, Big Teeth, Red Nose, Bug Eyes, 4 ¾ In.	877.00
Jack-O'-Lantern, Light Set, Painted Celluloid, 2 Large, 5 Small, 1920s, 6 In.	877.00
Jack-O'-Lantern, Orange Cat On Fence, Pulp, 7 ½ In.	234.00
Jack-O'-Lantern, Painted Composition Over Papier-Mache, Wire Bail Handle, Germany, 8 In.	877.00
Jack-O'-Lantern, Papier-Mache, Lantern With Mustache, 5 In.	526.00

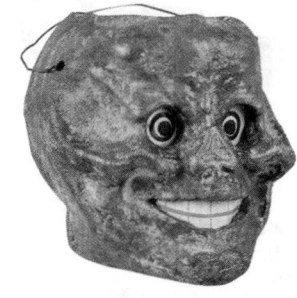

Halloween, Jack-O'-Lantern, Skull, Composition, Green, Gold Highlights, 3 ½ In.
$936.00

Halloween, Jack-O'-Lantern, Veggie Man, Driving Pickle Balloon, 6 ¼ In.
$4388.00

Halloween, Toy, Black Cat, Pop-Up Witch, Mechanical, 1930s, 4 ¼ In.
$322.00

Halloween, Toy, Jack-In-The-Box, Witch, Composition Face, Japan, c.1930, 3 In.
$468.00

Hampshire, Candlestick,
Blue Matte Glaze, Marked, 7 x 3 ⅜ In.
$81.00

Hampshire, Vase, Bud, Green,
Open Handles, 6 In.
$502.00

Handel, Humidor, Teroma,
Island Design, Chipped Ice Finish,
Signed, 8 ½ In.
$4313.00

Handel, Lamp, Arts & Crafts,
White Cased Interior, Signed, 14 x 18 In.
$690.00

Jack-O'-Lantern, Papier-Mache, Orange, Inset Eyes, Mouth, Teeth, 5 ½ In.	60.00
Jack-O'-Lantern, Papier-Mache, Orange, Inset Eyes, Smiling, No Handle, 5 ½ In.	60.00
Jack-O'-Lantern, Papier-Mache, Orange, Inset Yellow, Red, Blue Eyes, Smiling, 4 ¾ In.	70.00
Jack-O'-Lantern, Papier-Mache, Paper Insert Face Features, Bail Handle, Germany, 3 In.	240.00
Jack-O'-Lantern, Papier-Mache, Paper Insert Face Features, Bail Handle, Germany, 4 ¼ In.	295.00
Jack-O'-Lantern, Skull, Composition, Green, Gold Highlights, 3 ½ In. *illus*	936.00
Jack-O'-Lantern, Tin, Plastic, Battery Operated, Box, Japan, 5 ¾ In.	250.00
Jack-O'-Lantern, Turnip, Papier-Mache, Red, 3 In.	175.00
Jack-O'-Lantern, Veggie Man, Driving Pickle Balloon, 6 ¼ In. *illus*	4388.00
Jack-O'-Lantern, Watermelon, Solid Composition, 6 In.	1287.00
Lantern, Devil, Pulp, Paper Inserts, 6 ½ In.	409.00
Lantern, Snookums, Papier-Mache, Accordion Base, Comic Baby, Germany, 1920, 3 In.	760.00
Match Holder, Devil's Head, Striker, Cast Iron, 6 In.	295.00
Nodder, Pumpkin Man, Painted Composition, Spring Head, Germany, 6 ½ In.	351.00
Nodder, Witch, Hat, Cloak, Broom, Clockwork, c.1905, 35 In.	7500.00
Noisemaker, Pumpkin Man, Composition, Wood, Ratchet, 10 In.	1125.00
Squeaker, Devil's Head, Wood Stick, Marked, Germany, 9 In.	160.00
Squeaker, Witch's Head, Wood Stick, Germany, 8 ¼ In.	140.00
Tambourine, Black Cat, Tin Lithograph, T-Cohn, c.1940, 7 ¼ In.	32.00
Tile, Pottery, Salem Witch, Cat, On Broom, Black, White, Black Border, 6 x 6 In.	335.00
Toy, Black Cat, Pop-Up Witch, Mechanical, 1930s, 4 ¼ In. *illus*	322.00
Toy, Jack-In-The-Box, Witch, Composition Face, Japan, c.1930, 3 In. *illus*	468.00
Toy, Jack-O'-Lantern, Noisemaker, Tin Lithograph, Marked, M.B. Co., c.1920, 10 x 4 In.	24.00
Toy, Witch, Riding Broom, Balance, Wood, Japan, Box, c.1960, 9 x 6 ½ In.	75.00
Witch, Composition, Painted, Fully Dressed, Rabbit Fur Hair, Germany, 11 ½ In.	5850.00
Witch, In Pumpkin, Moves Up & Down, Composition, 36 x 26 In.	825.00

HAMPSHIRE pottery was made in Keene, New Hampshire, between 1871 and 1923. Hampshire developed a line of colored glazed wares as early as 1883, including a Royal Worcester–type pink, olive green, blue, and mahogany. Pieces are marked with the printed mark or the impressed name *Hampshire Pottery* or *J.S.T. & Co., Keene, N.H.* Many pieces were marked with city names and sold as souvenirs.

Bowl, Artichoke, Green Matte Glaze, Marked, c.1905, 3 x 4 ¾ In.	382.00
Bowl, Experimental Glaze, Keene, Signed, 1912, 4 ¾ x 3 In.	510.00
Bowl, Flower Bud Rim, Green Matte Glaze, Marked, 10 x 3 In.	431.00
Bowl, Leaves, Flower Stalks, Marked, 3 x 10 In.	345.00
Bowl, Stylized Flowers, Green Matte Glaze, c.1905, 3 x 10 In.	359.00
Bowl, Stylized Flowers, Green Matte Glaze, Marked, 2 ¾ x 9 ⅝ In.	259.00
Candlestick, Blue Matte Glaze, Marked, 7 x 3 ⅜ In. *illus*	81.00
Candlestick, Oil Lamp Shape, Green Glaze, 3 ½ In.	205.00
Ewer, Green, 6 ½ In.	300.00
Lamp, Pinecone Shade, 21 x 18 In.	7320.00
Lamp, Vase Base, Blue, Silver Mottled Ground, No. 24, 12 In.	527.00
Mug, Ale, Green, Marked, GST & Co., Keene, N.H., 5 ½ In.	185.00
Pitcher, Milk, Leaf Design Rim, Green, 7 In.	385.00
Stein, Green, 7 In.	238.00
Vase, 2 Handles, Green Matte Glaze, Marked, 4 ⅝ In.	173.00
Vase, Blue Matte Glaze, Wheel Thrown, Speckled, Incised, Early 1900s, 8 ½ In.	309.00
Vase, Broad Leaves, Green Matte Glaze, Globular, Marked, 3 ½ In.	230.00
Vase, Bud, Green, Open Handles, 6 In. *illus*	502.00
Vase, Bulbous, Raised Leaves, Green Matte Glaze, No. 123, 5 x 7 In.	510.00
Vase, Green Glaze, Bulbous, 8 ½ x 6 ½ In.	550.00
Vase, Green Mottled, 3 ½ In.	145.00
Vase, Incised Panels, Green, Shouldered, Circle M Mark, 3 In.	238.00
Vase, Shouldered, Green Matte Glaze, Mark, 4 ½ x 12 In.	575.00
Vase, Shouldered, Rolled Rim, Blue, Mottled, 3 x 6 In.	288.00
Vase, Stylized Leaves, Stemmed Open Handles, Green, 4 ½ In.	238.00
Vase, Tapered, Vertical Leaves, Buds, Yellow Matte Glaze, 4 x 6 ½ In.	660.00

HANDEL glass was made by Philip Handel working in Meriden, Connecticut, from 1885 and in New York City from 1893 to 1933. The firm made art glass and other types of lamps. Handel shades were made not only of leaded glass in a style reminiscent of Tiffany but also of reverse painted glass. Handel also made vases and other glass objects.

Candlestick, Teroma, Windmill, Shore, F. Gubisch, 8 In., Pair	1093.00
Chandelier, Teroma, Berry Branches, Etched, Enameled Globe, Amber, Bronze, 24 In.	2880.00
Chipped Ice Shade, Winter Forest Scene, Orange, 7 In.	1000.00

Humidor, Deep Red, Green, Melon Ribbed, Metal Lid, Marked, 5 x 4 In.	400.00
Humidor, Teroma, Island Design, Chipped Ice Finish, Signed, 8 ½ In. ....*illus*	4313.00
Lamp, 2-Light, Bronze Overlay, Sculpted Trees, 9 x 23 In.	900.00
Lamp, 3-Light, Gold Shade, Pastel Flowers, Scrolls, Urn Base, Design Border, Signed, 24 In. ...	5500.00
Lamp, 5-Light, Geometric Shade, Spread Foot, 31 In.	1037.00
Lamp, 6 Panels, Green & Multicolored Slag Glass, Blue Border, Signed, 16 In.	725.00
Lamp, 6 Panels, Green Slag Glass, Openwork Border, Bronze Base, Spread Foot, 16 In.	767.00
Lamp, 8 Panels, Metal Overlay, Cattails, Slag Glass, Green, Brown, Red, Spread Foot, 23 In.	4371.00
Lamp, Arts & Crafts, White Cased Interior, Signed, 14 x 18 In. ....*illus*	690.00
Lamp, Bridge, Adjustable Base, Overlaid Shade, 11 x 13 In.	1140.00
Lamp, Bronze Base, Bent, Flower Shape Shade, Metal Leading, 14 x 13 In.	840.00
Lamp, Bronze Base, Landscape, Cloth Label, Signed, 17 x 23 In.	5100.00
Lamp, Bronze, Green Pine Needle Shade, 58 x 10 In.	2640.00
Lamp, Bronze Metal, Patina, Steuben Shade, Green, Zigzag Border, 57 In.	4200.00
Lamp, Candle, Butterfly, Cylindrical, Square Base, Electrified, 9 x 3 ½ In.	825.00
Lamp, Chipped Ice Shade, Acid Textured, Butterflies, Flowers, 7 x 14 In. ....*illus*	1416.00
Lamp, Chipped Ice Shade, Apple Blossoms, Butterflies, Tripod Base, 18 x 24 In.	9488.00
Lamp, Chipped Ice Shade, Landscape, Adjustable Arm, 58 x 25 In.	2400.00
Lamp, Chipped Ice Shade, Woodland Scene, Yellow, Orange, Adjustable Base, Signed, 10 x 12 In.	1265.00
Lamp, Copper, Bronze, Slag Glass, Tropical Scene, Shade, 15 ½ x 6 In.	2806.00
Lamp, Desk, Brown Mosserine Shade, Adjustable Bronze Base, 12 x 10 ½ In. ....*illus*	1560.00
Lamp, Domed Shade, Cherry Blossoms, Branches, Molded Ribs, Strapwork, c.1917, 14 ¼ In. .	1645.00
Lamp, Domed Shade, Chipped Ice, Wooded Landscape, Bronze Base, 23 In.	6600.00
Lamp, Domed Shade, Green Mosserine, Zigzag Border, Leaf Mold Base, 3-Light, 18 x 10 In.	2300.00
Lamp, Domed Shade, Landscape, 3-Light, Signed, 23 In.	6000.00
Lamp, Domed Shade, Landscape, Birch Trees, Ribs, Copper Patina, Signed, 23 ½ x 18 In.	1860.00
Lamp, Domed Shade, Landscape, Brown, Green, Yellow, Square Bronze Base, 14 In.	3540.00
Lamp, Domed Shade, Landscape Scene, 2 Sockets, 24 x 17 ¾ In.	2726.00
Lamp, Domed Shade, Oriental Pheasant, Birds, Flowers, 3-Light, Signed, 18 x 24 In.	10350.00
Lamp, Domed Shade, Rose Blossoms, Reverse Painted, Mark, c.1919, 24 x 18 In. ....*illus*	15000.00
Lamp, Domed Shade, Trees, Shrubbery, Moon, Basket Weave Base, 14 x 7 In.	2185.00
Lamp, Domed Shade, Woodland Scene, Sunset, Clouds, 2-Light, 16 x 22 In.	1093.00
Lamp, Filigree Metal & Slag Glass, Square, 20 In.	526.00
Lamp, Forest Scene, Multicolored, 2-Light, Metal Base, Signed, 16 x 20 In.	3105.00
Lamp, Hanging, 6 Panels, Stylized Flowers, Red & Green Slag Glass, 23 x 19 ½ x 18 In.	3120.00
Lamp, Hanging, Globe, Birds, Flowers, Iridescent Orange Interior, Metal Fittings, 13 x 29 In. .	3450.00
Lamp, Hanging, Globe, Birds In Flight, Iridescent Orange, Tassel, Signed, 32 In. ....*illus*	4313.00
Lamp, Leaded Glass Shade, Caramel Slag, Bronze Base, 25 In.	300.00
Lamp, Leaded Glass Shade, Cone Shape, Green Slag, 5-Light, c.1910, 24 ½ x 30 ½ In.	3055.00
Lamp, Leaded Glass Shade, Dark, Light Green, Splayed Shape, Metal Base, Signed, 18 x 23 In.	2760.00
Lamp, Leaded Glass Shade, Flower Form, Adjustable, Bronze Metal Base, 14 x 13 In.	840.00
Lamp, Leaded Glass Shade, Tulips, Green Matte Glaze, Dogwood, Squat, 19 ½ x 16 ½ In.	4200.00
Lamp, Metal Base, Adjustable, Cylindrical Bent Glass Shade, Leaf, Berry Overlay, Marked, 9 x 23 In.	1200.00
Lamp, Metal Overlay, Bridge, Slag Glass Shade, Leaf Design, 61 In.	1200.00
Lamp, Persian Border, Flowers, Baluster Shape Base, Signed, 18 In. ....*illus*	3450.00
Lamp, Seascape, Marked, c.1913, 13 ½ In.	2750.00
Lamp, Shade, 2 Birds, Flowers, Multicolored, Teal Ground, Metal Base, Signed, 18 x 25 In.	13800.00
Lamp, Shade, 8 Panels, Oak Leaf Border, Caramel Slag Glass, Leaf Base, Paint, 18 x 25 In.	2013.00
Lamp, Shade, 8 Panels, Rose, Leaf Border, 3-Light, 8-Sided Base, 16 x 21 In.	2300.00
Lamp, Shade, 8 Panels, Slag Glass, Ivy, Painted, Metal Overlay, Copper Scroll Base, 23 x 67 In.	6600.00
Lamp, Shade, Blue Parrot, Leaves, Amber Glass, Metal Caps, Base, Signed, 15 In., Pair............	5750.00
Lamp, Shade, Dark Lake Scene, Bright Moon, Ribbed Metal Base, 7 x 14 In.	2360.00
Lamp, Shade, Flowers, Mottled Pink, Blue Ground, Leaf Decorated Metal Base, 18 x 23 In.	4313.00
Lamp, Shade, Leaf, Trellis Design, Copper Base, 18 x 20 ½ In.	2040.00
Lamp, Shade, Orange Flowers, Leaves, Yellow Ground, Tree Metal Base, Signed, 7 x 15 In.	1495.00
Lamp, Shade, Panels, Frosted, Fleur-De-Lis, Scalloped Border, 19 x 60 In. ....*illus*	2300.00
Lamp, Shade, Pine Trees, Mountains, Yellow Ground, Bent Tree Metal Base, 7 x 15 In.	2128.00
Lamp, Shade, Platinum Border, Adjustable Arm, 3-Footed, 52 In.	2460.00
Lamp, Shade, Slag Glass, Palms, Faceted Bell Shape, Candlestick Base, 16 x 6 ½ In. ....*illus*	2400.00
Lamp, Shade, Slag Glass, Pine Needle Border, Copper Base, 21 x 23 ½ In.	3000.00
Lamp, Shade, Student, Yellow Ground, Multicolored Art Deco Band, Signed, 13 ½ In.	1265.00
Lamp, Shade, White Cranes, Trees, Orange Sky, Column Metal Base, Signed, 18 x 24 In.	10350.00
Lamp, Shade, Yellow Glass, Bronze Metal, Harp, Flower Border, 10 x 28 ½ In.	4200.00
Lamp, Slag Glass Shade, Pink Roses Border, Bronzed Base, c.1917, 16 ½ x 23 In.	588.00
Lamp, White Metal, Shade, Copper, Mica, Orange, Yellow, 23 ½ x 18 ½ In.	825.00
Lantern, Glass Shade, Rivets, Hammered, Patina Socket, Chain, Arts & Crafts, 22 x 5 In.	1200.00
Sconce, Copper, Hammered, Patina, Marked, 5 ½ x 11 In., Pair..	600.00

Handel, Lamp, Chipped Ice Shade,
Acid Textured, Butterflies, Flowers,
7 x 14 In.
$1416.00

Handel, Lamp, Desk,
Brown Mosserine Shade,
Adjustable Bronze Base, 12 x 10 ½ In.
$1560.00

Handel, Lamp, Domed Shade,
Rose Blossoms, Reverse Painted,
Mark, c.1919, 24 x 18 In.
$15000.00

Handel, Lamp, Hanging, Globe, Birds In Flight, Iridescent Orange, Tassel, Signed, 32 In. $4313.00

Handel, Lamp, Persian Border, Flowers, Baluster Shape Base, Signed, 18 In. $3450.00

Shade, Greek Key, Green, Brown, White, Metal Overlay, Signed, 7 x 3 In., Pair		1035.00
Shade, Yellow Flowers, Tall Stems, Signed, Initials, RC, 4 x 9 ½ In.		780.00
Vase, Forest Scene, Green, Yellow, Orange, Brown, 8 In.		830.00

HARDWARE, *see Architectural category.*

HARKER POTTERY COMPANY of East Liverpool, Ohio, was incorporated in 1890 in East Liverpool, Ohio. The Harker family had been making pottery in the area since 1840. The company made many types of pottery but by the Civil War was making quantities of yellowware from native clays. It also made Rockingham-type brown-glazed pottery and whiteware. The plant was moved to Chester, West Virginia, in 1931. Dinnerwares were made and sold nationally. In 1971 the company was sold to Jeannette Glass Company, and all operations ceased in 1972. For more prices, go to kovels.com.

Alpine, Platter, 13 ½ In.		10.00
Amy, Salad Spoon & Fork		45.00
Bermuda, Bowl, Soup, 8 ¼ In.		3.00
Chesterton, Bowl, Vegetable, Round, Gray, 8 ¾ In.		32.00
Chesterton, Platter, Gray, 11 ¾ In.		38.00
Country Charm, Berry Bowl, 5 ¾ In.		8.00
Country Charm, Bowl, Vegetable, 8 ¾ In.		28.00
Country Charm, Plate, Dinner, 10 ¼ In.		12.00
Country Charm, Plate, Salad, 7 ¼ In.		10.00
Country Charm, Platter, 9 ½ x 11 ½ In.		22.00
Shell Pink, Cup & Saucer		15.00
Shell Pink, Saucer		5.00
Springtime, Bowl, Vegetable, 8 ¾ In.		22.00
Springtime, Cup & Saucer		12.00
Springtime, Plate, Dinner, 10 ¼ In.		12.00
Springtime, Plate, Salad, 7 ¼ In.		10.00
Springtime, Platter, 9 ½ x 11 ½ In.		22.00
Springtime, Sugar, Cover		22.00
White Clover, Ashtray, Charcoal		165.00
White Clover, Bowl, Cereal, Golden Spice		25.00
White Clover, Sugar, Cover, Charcoal		125.00
White Rose, Pie Plate, Cameo, Blue, 9 In.		22.00

HARLEQUIN dinnerware was produced by the Homer Laughlin Company from 1938 to 1964, and sold without trademark by the F. W. Woolworth Co. It has a concentric ring design like Fiesta, but the rings are separated from the rim by a plain margin. Cup handles are triangular in shape. Seven different novelty animal figurines were introduced in 1939. For more prices, go to kovels.com.

Blue, Bowl, Fruit, 5 ⅝ In.		9.00
Blue, Plate, Dinner, 10 In.		12.00
Blue, Platter, 11 In.		25.00
Chartreuse, Cup & Saucer		20.00
Chartreuse, Plate, 9 In.		12.00
Forest Green, Cup, Tea		12.00
Gray, Casserole, Cover, 9 ⅞ In.		175.00
Gray, Cup & Saucer		11.00
Gray, Eggcup, Double		42.00
Gray, Gravy Boat		20.00
Green, Plate, Deep, 8 In.		9.00
Light Green, Bowl, Fruit, 5 ⅝ In.		40.00
Light Green, Cup		15.00
Light Green, Pitcher, 22 Oz.		125.00
Light Green, Pitcher, Water, 7 ½ In.		125.00
Mauve Blue, Casserole, Cover, 9 ⅞ In.		120.00
Mauve Blue, Pitcher, Ball Shape, 7 In.		65.00
Mauve Blue, Plate, Luncheon, 9 In.		15.00
Medium Green, Bowl, Oatmeal, 36s		28.00
Medium Green, Plate, Bread & Butter, 6 ¼ In.		20.00
Medium Green, Plate, Dinner, 10 In.		15.00
Medium Green, Plate, Salad, 7 ½ In.		14.95
Red, Creamer		25.00
Red, Cup & Saucer, After Dinner		75.00
Red, Nut Cup, Basket Weave, 3 In.		40.00

H

Red, Plate, Dinner, 10 In.	15.00
Red, Salt & Pepper	70.00
Red, Teapot, 5 ½ In.	95.00
Rose, Cup & Saucer	15.00
Rose, Pitcher, 22 Oz.	85.00
Rose, Plate, Salad, 7 ½ In.	10.00
Rose, Platter, 11 In.	15.00 to 20.00
Rose, Saucer	3.00
Rose, Sugar, Cover	15.00
Rose, Teapot, 5 ½ In.	116.00
Spruce Green, Pitcher, Water, Ball Shape, 7 ½ In.	105.00
Turquoise, Bowl, Nappy, 9 In.	34.00
Turquoise, Bowl, Oatmeal, 36s	14.00
Turquoise, Bowl, Salad, 3 ½ In.	25.00
Turquoise, Creamer	10.00 to 20.00
Turquoise, Cup	8.00
Turquoise, Cup & Saucer	12.50
Turquoise, Cup, After Dinner	24.00
Turquoise, Gravy Boat	24.00
Turquoise, Nappy, 9 In.	35.00
Turquoise, Plate, Dinner, 10 In.	28.00
Turquoise, Plate, Luncheon, 9 In.	12.00
Turquoise, Plate, Salad, 7 ¼ In.	10.00
Turquoise, Platter, Oval, 13 In.	34.00
Turquoise, Saucer	2.00 to 3.00
Yellow, Casserole, Cover, 9 ⅞ In.	120.00
Yellow, Creamer, Individual	18.00
Yellow, Cup	7.50
Yellow, Cup & Saucer, After Dinner	70.00
Yellow, Pitcher, Ball Shape, 7 ½ In.	70.00
Yellow, Plate, Dinner, 10 In.	30.00
Yellow, Plate, Luncheon, 9 In.	12.00
Yellow, Plate, Salad, 7 ¼ In.	11.00
Yellow, Platter, 11 In.	28.00 to 48.00
Yellow, Soup, Dish	18.00
Yellow, Teapot	125.00

HATPIN collectors search for pins popular from 1860 to 1920. The long pin, often over four inches, was used to hold the hat in place on the hair. The tops of the pins were made of all materials, from solid gold and real gemstones to ceramics and glass. Be careful to buy original hatpins and not recent pieces made by altering old buttons.

Art Nouveau, Organic Shape, Scrolling Fleurs-De-Lis, 10K Gold, 10 ¼ x 1 ¼ In.	85.00
Bakelite, Sword, Art Deco, 1930, 6 ½ x 1 ½ In.	129.00
Ball, Open, Enameled, Red, White, Blue, 8 ¾ In.	45.00
Brass Filigree, Paste Stones, 6-Pointed Star, 11 ¾ x 1 ¾ In.	125.00
Carnival Glass, 6 Plums Design, 10 ¼ In.	125.00
Coin Cluster, 1 ¾ x 1 ¾ x 6 ½ In.	55.00
Figural, Indian Maiden Head, Sterling Silver, Beaded Headband, Feathers, 9 ½ x 1 ¾ In.	165.00
Flower Shape, Green & Clear Paste Stones, Reticulated, 2 x 4 In.	85.00
Glass, Tortoiseshell Pattern, Amber, Brown, Rhinestone Ring, 6 x 1 ½ In.	46.00
Goldtop, 14K Band, Art Noveau, Gold Pin, 14 In.	350.00
Green Blown Glass, Foil, Victorian, 11 x ¾ In.	21.00
Micro Mosaic, Multicolor Leaves, Brass Back Plate, Signed, WTR&Co., 12 x 1 ¼ In.	165.00
Peking Glass, Gilt Bronze, 19th Century, 3 In.	218.00
Porcelain, Painted, Pink Dog Roses, Gold Border, 10 ¼ x 2 ⅝ In.	80.00
Rhinestone, Cobalt Blue Glass Enamel, Gold Metal, Guilloche, Edwardian, 1 ½ In., Pair	65.00
Sterling Silver, Abalone, Oval, Germany, 2 ⅝ x ⅝ In.	19.00
Sterling Silver, Paneled Head, 6 x 1 In.	30.00

HATPIN HOLDERS were needed when hatpins were fashionable from 1860 to 1920. The large, heavy hat required special long-shanked pins to hold it in place. The hatpin holder resembles a large saltshaker, but it often has no opening at the bottom as a shaker does. Hatpin holders were made of all types of ceramics and metal. Look for other pieces under the names of specific manufacturers.

Art Nouveau, Stylized Design, 5 ¾ x 2 ½ In.	65.00
Brass, Texture, Applied Filigree, Multicolored Jewels, Marked Silvercraft, 5 x 2 ¾ In.	149.00

Handel, Lamp, Shade, Panels, Frosted, Fleur-De-Lis, Scalloped Border, 19 x 60 In.
$2300.00

Handel, Lamp, Shade, Slag Glass, Palms, Faceted Bell Shape, Candlestick Base, 16 x 6 ½ In.
$2400.00

TIP

Use a soft-bristle paintbrush to dust lampshades.

Haviland, Plate, Fish, Marine Scenes, Blue Borders, Japonesque, c.1890, 9 In., 8 Piece
$900.00

Hawkes, Vase, Trumpet Shape, Brilliant Cut, Vertical Zipper Cut, Signed, 16 ¼ In.
$377.00

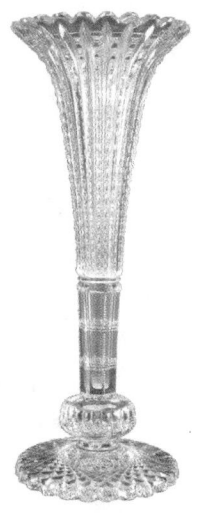

Heintz, Humidor, Applied Hunting Scene, Patina, Mark, Sterling On Bronze, 10 x 3 In.
$900.00

"Elegant" Glass

Glass collectors use the term *elegant* to refer to American hand-pressed items made from about 1925 to 1955. Even though the glassware was produced in large quantities, the "elegant" factories used higher-quality raw materials and employed skilled glassmakers. Several companies, including Heisey and Fostoria, called their glassware **American crystal.**

Cowry Shell, Turtle Shape, 4 ½ x 2 In.	65.00
Painted, Pink Roses, Leaves, Blue Ground, Gilt, Bavaria, c.1900, 4 ¾ In.	62.00
Painted, Water Scene, Swans, Blue Ground, Gold Trim, Fluted, Flared, 5 ½ In.	120.00
Pink & Blue Roses, Attached Saucer Base, Gold Trim, Marked Austria, c.1910	35.00
Pink & Red Carnations, c.1900, 4 ¾ In.	25.00
Pink, Art Nouveau Woman's Head, Gilt Highlights, Schafer & Vater, 5 ½ In.	250.00
Pink Flowers, Gold, White Ground, John H. Kanzanjian, 4 ¼ In.	41.00
Roses, Lavender, Pink, Green Ground, Scalloped Rim, Gold Filigree, 4 x 4 In.	95.00
Scenic, Cottage, Swan On Pond, Imperial Nippon, 5 ½ In.	40.00

HAVILAND china has been made in Limoges, France, since 1842. The factory was started by the Haviland Brothers of New York City. Pieces are marked *H & Co., Haviland & Co.,* or *Theodore Haviland.* It is possible to match existing sets of dishes through dealers who specialize in Haviland china. Other factories worked in the town of Limoges making a similar chinaware. These porcelains are listed in this book under Limoges.   **HAVILAND & CO.**

Bouillon, Clover	25.00
Bowl, Sandoz, Round, Fuchsia, Green Handles, Theodore Haviland, c.1910, 9 x 3 In.	2040.00
Jar, Pink, Yellow Flowers, c.1910, 9 x 9 In.	293.00
Plate, Cream & Green, Rose, Signed, 9 ¼ In.	40.00
Plate, Fish, Marine Scenes, Blue Borders, Japonesque, c.1890, 9 In., 8 Piece ....*illus*	900.00
Plate, Normandie, Cruise Ship, Limoges, 1935-39, 9 ½ In.	45.00
Plate, Salad, White, Gold Gilt Trim, Scalloped Edge, 7 ⅝ In.	22.00
Tea Set, Duck Shapes, Blue Body, White Chest, Sandoz, Signed	1440.00
Tray, White Rock Fairy, Hand Painted, Lavender, Green, Blue, Gray, Tan Ground, Gilt, 13 In. ..	395.00
Vase, Victorian Man & Woman, Garden Courting Scene, 3 Gold Handles, Green Stamp, 10 In.	690.00

HAVILAND POTTERY began in 1872, when Charles Haviland decided to make art pottery. He worked with the famous artists of the day and made pottery with slip glazed decorations. Production stopped in 1885. Haviland Pottery is marked with the letters *H & Co.* The Haviland name is better known today for its porcelain.

Jardiniere, Japonisme, Signed Maurice Bouquet, c.1880, 13 x 19 In.	6000.00
Vase, Flowers, Bird, Green, Blue, Cream, Japonisme, Signed E. Dammouse, c.1880, 13 In.	12000.00
Vase, Flowers, Multicolored, Oval, Feet, Japonisme, Signed Emile-Justin, c.1880, 5 x 12 In.	1750.00
Vase, Flowers, Pink, Bird, Japonisme, Oval, Metal Insert, Edouard Dammouse, c.1882, 12 In., 2 Piece...	12000.00
Vase, Pink Blossoms, Signed Maurice Bouquet, 13 In., c.1880, Pair	6000.00
Vase, Pink Flowers, Feet, Japonisme, Signed Jules Habert-Dys, 10 In., c.1880, Pair	6000.00
Vase, Rabbit, Brown, Mottled Blue Neck, Japonisme, Signed Coutunier, c.1880, 13 ½ In.	6000.00

HAWKES cut glass was made by T. G. Hawkes & Company of Corning, New York, founded in 1880. The firm cut glass blanks made at other glassworks until 1962. Many pieces are marked with the trademark, a trefoil ring enclosing a fleur-de-lis and two hawks. Cut glass by other manufacturers is listed under either the factory name or in the general Cut Glass category.

Bowl, 4 Oval Panels, Diamond & Blazes Flared Rim, Signed, 4 ½ x 9 ¾ In.	360.00
Bowl, American Brilliant, Signed, 10 In.	412.00
Bowl, Etched Flowers, Signed, Oval, 5 In.	130.00
Bowl, Hobstar, Crosscut Diamond, Split Strawberry Diamond & Fan, 3 x 7 In.	50.00
Bowl, Queens Pattern, 2 ¼ x 9 In.	425.00
Bowl, Salad, 8-Sided, Fruit, Hobstar Center, Underplate, 5 ½ x 12 ½ In.	9000.00
Candelabrum, Cut & Etched Stem Flowers & Leaves, 3 Well Holders, Marked, 10 x 13 In., Pair.	489.00
Carafe, Holland Pattern, Honeycomb Neck, Signed, 7 In.	100.00
Cologne Bottle, Brunswick, Signed, 5 ½ In.	400.00
Compote, Gravic Glass, Rolled Rim, Iris Pattern, Clear Blank, 7 ¼ x 6 In.	160.00
Compote, Hobstar & Fans, Prism Cuttings, Concave Stem, Marked, 8 ⅜ In.	403.00
Compote, Strawberries & Leaves, Signed, 5 x 5 In.	201.00
Decanter, Sterling Silver Top, Footed, 11 In.	146.00
Decanter, Thistle, Sterling Silver Top, 9 ½ In.	79.00
Decanter, Vintage, Sterling Silver Top, 11 In.	90.00
Dish, Apple & Hobstar Design, Signed, 6 In.	403.00
Glass, Parfait, Engraved Flowers, 6 ¾ In.	100.00
Goblet, Inverted Bell Shape, Baluster Stem, Square Foot, 6 ½ In., 6 Piece	403.00
Pitcher, Cider, Brunswick Pattern, Clear Blank, Signed, 6 ¼ In.	400.00
Pitcher, Devonshire, Triple Notched Handle, Ray Base, 12 In.	500.00
Pitcher, Fan Cut Top, Hobstar Body, Blazes & Hobstar Handle, Signed, 9 In.	770.00

Rose Bowl, Footed, Kensington, Brilliant Cut, Gorham, Signed, 10 ½ x 8 In.	16950.00
Salt Cellar, Pedestal, Optic Ribbed, Etched Flowers, Sterling Salt Spoon	55.00
Tray, Coronet, Oval, 15 x 10 ½ In.	27000.00
Tray, Devonshire, Clear Blank, Oval, 9 In.	225.00
Tray, Holland Pattern, Round, 14 ½ In.	900.00
Vase, Cinched, Chain Of Hobstar & Bull's-Eye, Hobstar Base, Signed, 12 ¼ In.	250.00
Vase, Diamond Pattern Cut Glass, Silver Base, Urn Shape, 13 ¼ In., Pair	403.00
Vase, Fan Shape, Irises & Cut Designs, 11 x 9 In.	518.00
Vase, Hobstar & Diamond, Bellflower Columns & Rim, Fluted Rim, Pedestal Base, Signed, 8 In.	430.00
Vase, Navarre, American Brilliant, Signed, 9 In.	275.00
Vase, Queen's Pattern, Trumpet, Marked, 12 In.	750.00
Vase, Queen's Pattern, Trumpet Shape, Hobstar, Faceted Knob At Base, Signed, 18 In.	1610.00
Vase, Trumpet Shape, Brilliant Cut, Vertical Zipper Cut, Signed, 16 ¼ In. ....*illus*	377.00
Vase, Trumpet, Vertical Zipper Cut, 16 ¼ In.	358.00

HEAD VASES, generally showing a woman from the shoulders up, were used by florists primarily in the 1950s and 1960s. Made in a variety of sizes and often decorated with imitation jewelry and other lifelike accessories, the vases were manufactured in Japan and the U.S.A. Less elaborate examples were made as early as the 1930s. Religious themes, babies, and animals are also common subjects. Other head vases are listed under manufacturers' names and can be located through the index in the back of this book.

Baby, Blond Curls, Blue Dress, Blue Bonnet With Applied Roses, 6 In.	65.00
Baby, Brown Curls, Blue Lace Collar & Bonnet, Artmark, 5 In.	110.00
Clown, Red Hair, Exaggerated Features, 1950s, 6 In.	55.00
Clown, Yellow Hair, Red Nose & Mouth, Bowtie, Blue Dots, Black Top Hat, 5 ¾ In.	50.00
Girl, Blond Pigtails, Gray & Black Hat With Bow, Checked Dress, 5 In.	35.00
Jackie Kennedy, Hand To Face, White Scarf, Black Gloves, Inarco, c.1964, 6 In.	96.00
Madonna & Child, Halos, Pink Glaze, Hull, 7 ½ In.	36.00
Madonna, Blond Hair, Blue Veil, 7 In.	30.00
Woman, Asian, Dark Skin, White Wide-Brimmed Hat, Hoop Earrings, Japan, 5 In.	220.00
Woman, Blond Curls, Lashes, Bonnet, Flowers, Strings Tied Under Chin, Napco, 5 ¾ In.	150.00
Woman, Blond Curls, White & Orange Bonnet, Eyes Closed, Upturned Arm, 5 ½ In.	69.00
Woman, Blond Hair, Closed Eyes, Earrings, Daisies, Green Gloved, Napcoware, 7 ½ In.	235.00
Woman, Blond Hair, Gray Hat, Black & White Bow, Hands, Relpo, 7 ½ In.	325.00
Woman, Blond Hair, Green Flattened Hat With Flowers, Napco, Old Japan, 1958	150.00
Woman, Blond Hair, Green Hat, Bow, Pearl Earrings, Napcoware, 10 ½ In.	475.00
Woman, Blond Streaked Hair, Burgundy Felt Hat, Neck Scarf, 7 In.	60.00
Woman, Blond Updo, Crown, Eyes Closed, Pearls, Inarco	290.00
Woman, Blond Updo, Hand, Red Fingernails, Pearl Earrings, Ardco, 7 ½ In.	225.00
Woman, Flapper, Looking Over Shoulder, White & Blue Bonnet, Gold Trim	25.00
Woman, Glamour Girl, Updo, White Glaze Red Lips & Dress Trim, 7 In.	75.00
Woman, Nubian, Chartreuse Glaze, Gold Basket On Head, 6 In.	36.00
Woman, Streaked Hair, Eyes Closed, Green Dress, Earrings, Napcoware, 10 In.	525.00
Woman, Streaked Hair, White Bow, Blue Cowl Neck, Pearl Earrings, Relpo, 7 In.	225.00
Woman, White Hat, Open Collar, Pearl Earrings, Necklace, Gloved Arms, Rubens, 6 In.	345.00
Woman, White High Hair, White Ruffled Collar, Pearl Earrings, Rubens, 7 In.	450.00

HEDI SCHOOP Art Creations, North Hollywood, California, started about 1945 and was working until 1954. Schoop made ceramic figurines, lamps, planters, and tablewares.

Hedi Schoop S

Dish, Butterfly, Gold, Brown & Tan Decoration, 8 In.	25.00
Figurine, Asian Man, Wide-Brimmed Hat, c.1950, 12 ½ In.	65.00
Figurine, Dancer, Burgundy Tiered Dress, Speckled Gold Trim, Pink Scarf, 12 In.	75.00
Figurine, Dutch Girl, Blond Braids, Dotted Skirt, Holding Apron, 11 ½ In.	48.00
Figurine, My Sister & I, Dutch Boy & Girl, Boy Carries Hanging Pots, 11 In., Pair	125.00
Figurine, Woman, Cobalt Blue Dress, Holding Flowered Fan, 13 In.	184.00
Figurine, Woman, Dancing, Pink & Gold Dress, 9 ½ In.	110.00
Figurine, Woman, Tiered Billowing Dress, Black & Gold, 9 In.	110.00
Planter, Abstract S-Shape, Mint Green, Speckled Gold, Ridged Edges, 14 x 6 In.	63.00
Planter, Book Lady, Bands Of Flowers On Skirt, V-Shaped Planter, c.1950, 9 In.	49.00
Planter, Horse, Pink, White Mane, Green Saddle, Looped Trim, 9 ¾ x 10 In.	60.00
Planter, Phantasy Lady, White Dress, Blue Headdress, Bustle Planter, 12 In.	105.00
Tray, Butterfly Shape, Pink Iridescent Glaze, Speckled Gold Edges, 1942, 8 In.	42.00
Trinket Box, Abstract Shape, Red Flower, Linen Weave Ground, Gold Trim, 7 x 5 In.	18.00

Heintz, Vase, Applied Flowers, Patina, Sterling On Bronze, Impressed Mark, 2 ½ x 4 In.
$240.00

Heintz, Vase, Applied Flowers, Sterling On Bronze, Impressed Mark, 3 x 6 ½ In.
$30.00

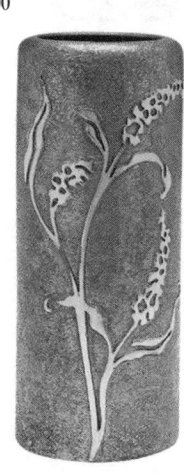

Heintz, Vase, Sterling On Bronze, Applied Organic Design, Gold Patina, Mark, 3 x 6 In.
$330.00

Heisey, Basket, Handle, 11 ½ x 7 ½ In. $395.00

Heisey, Cut Block, Sugar, Ivorina Verde, Souvenir, 2 ¾ In. $55.00

Heisey, Locket On Chain, Cruet, Ruby Stained, Gilt, Faceted Stopper, c.1900, 6 In. $3738.00

HEINTZ ART METAL SHOP used the letters *HAMS* in a diamond as a mark. Otto Heintz took over the Arts & Crafts Company in Buffalo, New York, in 1903. By 1906 it had become the Heintz Art Metal Shop. It remained in business until 1930. The company made ashtrays, bookends, boxes, bowls, desk sets, vases, trophies, and smoking sets. The best-known pieces are made of copper, brass, and bronze with silver overlay. Similar pieces were made by Smith Metal Arts and were marked *Silver Crest*. Some pieces by both companies are unmarked.

Bowl, Applied Flowers, Sterling On Bronze, Green Patina, 9 ½ x 3 ¼ In.	390.00
Bowl, Applied Organic Design, Sterling On Bronze, Green Patina, 9 ¼ x 3 ¼ In.	300.00
Bowl, Bronze, Flowers, Sterling Silver Overlay, Marked, c.1912, 8 In.	250.00
Dish, Cover, Fitted Interior, Greek Key Band	52.00
Humidor, Applied Hunting Scene, Patina, Mark, Sterling On Bronze, 10 x 3 In. ....*illus*	900.00
Lamp, Applied Flowers, Sterling, Bronze, Green Patina, 9 x 12 In.	720.00
Lamp, Applied Flowers, Sterling On Bronze, 9 x 12 In.	960.00
Lamp, Applied Geometric Design, Sterling On Bronze, Cutout Shade, Mica, 7 x 9 ½ In.	1080.00
Vase, Applied Flower, Sterling On Bronze, 2 x 6 In.	270.00
Vase, Applied Flowers, Patina, Sterling On Bronze, Impressed Mark, 2 ½ x 4 In. ....*illus*	240.00
Vase, Applied Flowers, Sterling On Bronze, Impressed Mark, 3 x 5 In.	200.00
Vase, Applied Flowers, Sterling On Bronze, Impressed Mark, 3 x 6 ½ In. ....*illus*	30.00
Vase, Applied Flowers, Sterling On Bronze, Patina, Marked, 2 ½ x 4 In.	240.00
Vase, Applied Iris, Sterling On Bronze, Rolled Rim, 11 ⅝ In.	610.00
Vase, Applied Leaf & Berries, Flared, Sterling On Bronze, Impressed Mark, 3 x 4 In.	60.00
Vase, Applied Linear Design, Leaves, Sterling On Bronze, Patina, 2 ¾ x 3 ¾ In.	330.00
Vase, Applied Palm Tree, Sterling On Bronze, Patina, Cylindrical, 2 ½ x 6 In.	450.00
Vase, Applied Rose, Sterling On Bronze, Patina, 2 ½ x 9 In.	360.00
Vase, Applied Sea Gull, Sterling On Bronze, Green Patina, Marked, 2 ½ x 3 ½ In.	210.00
Vase, Applied Sterling On Bronze, Mistletoe Design, Mark, 4 x 7 ½ In.	360.00
Vase, Applied Vine, Leaf, Sterling On Bronze, 4 x 7 ½ In.	324.00
Vase, Bud, Applied Design Of Birds, Branches, Sterling On Bronze, Marked, 4 x 11 In.	340.00
Vase, Daffodil, Sterling On Bronze, Wide Mouth, Cylindrical, 8 In.	59.00
Vase, Leaf Design, Sterling On Bronze, 5 ¼ In.	92.00
Vase, Sterling On Bronze, Applied Organic Design, Gold Patina, Mark, 3 x 6 In. ....*illus*	330.00
Vase, Thistle Design, Silver On Bronze, 5 x 12 In.	600.00

HEISEY glass was made from 1896 to 1957 in Newark, Ohio, by A. H. Heisey and Co., Inc. The Imperial Glass Company of Bellaire, Ohio, bought some of the molds and the rights to the trademark. Some Heisey patterns have been made by Imperial since 1960. After 1968, they stopped using the *H* trademark. Heisey used romantic names for colors, such as Sahara. Do not confuse color and pattern names. The Custard Glass and Ruby Glass categories may also include some Heisey pieces.

Animal, Asiatic Pheasant, Clear, Marked, c.1950, 10 ¼ In.	224.00
Animal, Horse, 2 ⅛ x 1 ½ In.	95.00
Animal, Pheasant, Asiatic, Pair	210.00
Animal, Pheasant, Ringneck	55.00
Animal, Rabbit, Paperweight	100.00
Animal, Rooster, Cocktail, Stem	150.00
Basket, Handle, 11 ½ x 7 ½ In. ....*illus*	395.00
Beaded Panel & Sunburst, Punch, Bowl, With Base	125.00
Beaded Swag, Cruet, Ruby, Scroll Design, Gold Flashed Beads, c.1900, 4 ½ In.	195.00
Beaded Swag, Nappy, Opalescent, 3 In.	20.00
Bowl, Amber Swan Handle, Crystal Flower Frog, 16 In.	675.00
Carcassone, Cordial, Sahara	20.00
Cascade, Candlestick, 3-Light	60.00
Coarse Rib, Plate, 4 In.	20.00
Cocktail Shaker, Crystal, Orchid Etch, 1940, 12 In.	225.00
Colonial, Basket, Round Handle, 7 In.	110.00
Colonial, Cup, Dessert	12.00
Colonial, Decanter, Scalloped Top	10.00
Colonial Panel, Cruet, Stopper	12.00
Colonial Star, Plate, 8 ½ In.	10.00
Crystolite, Bowl, Flared, Floral, 10 In.	45.00
Crystolite, Bowl, Gardenia, Square, 10 In.	55.00
Crystolite, Candlestick, 1-Light	40.00
Crystolite, Conserve, 2 Pt.	10.00
Crystolite, Goblet, 10 Oz.	40.00
Crystolite, Jam Jar, Ladle	35.00

Crystolite, Jelly, Spider Bottom, Handle	15.00
Crystolite, Relish, Oval, 3-Part, 13 In.	30.00
Crystolite, Salt & Pepper, Melon, Metal Lid	55.00
Crystolite, Sugar & Creamer, Round	35.00
Crystolite, Vase, Lavender, 3 In.	65.00
Cut Block, Sugar, Ivorina Verde, Souvenir, 2 ¾ In. ....illus	55.00
Diamond Point, Salt, Spoon, c.1930, 2 ½ In.	14.00
Dolphin, Bowl, Fish	235.00
Empress, Cream, Sahara	15.00
Empress, Ice Bucket, With Handle	60.00
Empress, Sugar, Individual	25.00
Fancy Loop, Nappy, Tricornered, 6 In.	15.00
Fancy Loop, Salt, Crimped, c.1897, 3 x 1 In.	19.00
Fancy Loop, Salt, Open	24.00
Fandango, Bowl, Cupped, 6 In.	30.00
Fandango, Compote, Footed, 8 In.	45.00
Flat Panel, Bowl, Grapefruit	25.00
Flat Panel, Cream & Sugar, Individual	25.00
Flat Panel, Nappy, 7 ½ In.	10.00
Frosted, Bowl, Dragons, c.1955, 14 In.	66.00
Gallagher, Jug, Rose Etch	180.00
Greek Key, Cruet, Stopper, 6 Oz.	35.00 to 50.00
Greek Key, Punch Bowl, Stand, 14 x 15 In.	374.00
Ipswich, Centerpiece, With Insert, Footed	225.00
Jack-Be-Nimble, Candlestick, Pair	28.00
Jamestown, Sherry, Barcelona Cutting	20.00
Janice, Vase, Flamingo, 4 In.	50.00
Kingfisher, Flower Frog, Flamingo	150.00
Lariat, Candlestick, 2-Light, Pair	25.00
Lariat, Cruet	30.00
Lariat, Relish, 3-Part, Oblong, 13 In.	25.00
Lariat, Relish, 3-Part, Round, 9 In.	35.00
Lariat, Sugar & Creamer, Silver Overlay	15.00
Locket On Chain, Cruet, Ruby Stained, Gilt, Faceted Stopper, c.1900, 6 In. ....illus	3738.00
Lodestar, Bowl, Crimped, 11 In.	55.00
Mercury, Candlestick, 1-Light	25.00
Narrow Flute, Relish, Sections, Handles, 9 In. ....illus	25.00
Narrow Flute, Sugar, Hotel	25.00
Narrow Flute, Sugar, Individual	25.00
Nimrod, Decanter Set, Etched, 13 & 3 ¾ In., 5 Piece	585.00
Octagon, Cheese Plate, Moongleam	20.00
Old Sandwich, Mug, Sahara, 12 Oz.	120.00
Old Williamsburg, Candelabrum, 2-Light	90.00
Old Williamsburg, Candelabrum, 3-Light, Cut Glass Prisms, c.1950, 15 In.	120.00
Old Williamsburg, Candlestick, 9 In.	25.00
Pan American, Cocktail	50.00
Paneled Cane, Nappy, 4 In.	40.00
Peerless, Molasses	10.00
Peerless, Sugar & Creamer, Individual	50.00
Peerless, Vase, 10 In.	25.00
Pineapple & Fan, Toothpick, Emerald	30.00 to 95.00
Plantation, Cake Plate, Footed	170.00
Plantation, Candleholder, 5 In.	65.00
Plantation, Champagne	60.00
Plantation, Goblet, Blown	60.00 to 70.00
Plantation, Plate, 8 In.	95.00
Prince Of Wales, Punch Cup	25.00 to 35.00
Provincial, Punch Cup	25.00
Punty Band, Saltshaker, Ruby Stained, Grandma 1901, 3 In.	40.00
Puritan, Cigarette Box, Horse Head Cover, 6 x 4 In. ....illus	85.00
Puritan, Compote, Footed, 8 ½ In.	45.00
Revere, Dish, Lemon	10.00
Ridgeleigh, Ashtray, 2 ½ In.	15.00
Ridgeleigh, Cigarette Holder	15.00
Ridgeleigh, Jelly, Handle, 6 In.	15.00
Ridgeleigh, Nut Dish, Individual	15.00
Ridgeleigh, Vase, 6 In.	30.00

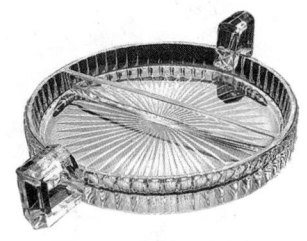

Heisey, Narrow Flute, Relish, Sections, Handles, 9 In. $25.00

Heisey, Puritan, Cigarette Box, Horse Head Cover, 6 x 4 In. $85.00

Heisey, Rose Etch, Bowl, Floral, 9 ½ In. $85.00

Heisey, Winged Scroll, Spooner, Ivorina Verde, Gold Trim, 3 ½ In. $65.00

TIP

If you live in the North and you find your gifts left out in the cold by the front door be careful. Freezing temperatures make glass and ceramics brittle. Bring the package inside, open it but do not unwrap the contents until everything is room temperature.

Holly Amber, Syrup, Golden Agate, Cover, Indiana Tumbler & Goblet Co., 6 x 2 In.
$1093.00

Ridgeleigh, Nappy, Square, 5 In. 20.00
Ring Band, Syrup, Cream, Multicolored Flowers, Gilt, Lid, c.1900, 7 ⅛ In. 264.00
Rose Etch, Bowl, Floral, 9 ½ In. .... *illus* 85.00
Sanford, Candlestick, 8 In., Pair 50.00
Saturn, Hostess Set, With Toothpick Holder 50.00
Saturn, Mayonnaise 11.00
Saturn, Mayonnaise, Metal Ring, Liner 20.00
Thumbprint & Angle, Hair Receiver, Metal Lip 15.00
Tom Thumb, Candlestick, Toy, Pair 35.00
Twist, Celery Dish, Silver Overlay, 10 In. 23.00
Twist, Nappy, Moongleam, 8 In. 25.00
Universal, Goblet 35.00
Victorian, Punch Cup 15.00
Warwick, Cornucopia, 5 In., Pair 35.00
Waverly, Butter, Cover, Seahorse Heads Finial, 5 ¼ In. 135.00
Wide Zipper, Humidor, Metal Top 60.00
Windsor, Candlestick, 7 In., Pair 45.00
Winged Scroll, Nappy, Emerald, 8 ½ In. .... 35.00 to 70.00
Winged Scroll, Spooner, Ivorina Verde, Gold Trim, 3 ½ In. .... *illus* 65.00
Winged Scroll, Table Set, Custard 110.00
Yeoman, Cruet, Moongleam, Crystal Stopper 40.00

HEREND, *see Fischer category.*

HEUBACH is the collector's name for Gebruder Heubach, a firm working in Lichten, Germany, from 1840 to 1925. It is best known for bisque dolls and doll heads, the principal products. The company also manufactured bisque figurines, including piano babies, beginning in the 1880s, and glazed figurines in the 1900s. Piano Babies are listed in their own category. Dolls are included in the Doll category under Gebruder Heubach and Heubach. Another factory, Ernst Heubach, working in Koppelsdorf, Germany, also made porcelain and dolls. These will also be found in the Doll category under Heubach Koppelsdorf.

Figurine, Baseball Player, Blue Pinstriped Jersey & Socks, White Pants, 14 ½ In. 587.00
Figurine, Basket, Brown Baby Holding Lid, 6 ½ x 5 ½ In. 266.00
Figurine, Black Boy, Dotted Baby Dress, Holding Ear Of Corn, c.1910, 4 ¾ In. 276.00
Figurine, Boy Wearing Bear Suit, 3 ½ x 4 In. 175.00
Figurine, Clown, Red Hat, Hands In Pocket, 12 ¾ In. 192.00
Figurine, Dancing Girl With Tambourine, Holding Fluted Skirt, c.1900, 15 In. 222.00
Figurine, Girl, Blond Curls, Holding Green Flowered Dress, Intaglio Eyes, 11 ½ In. 173.00
Figurine, Puppy, Wearing Bonnet & Bib, c.1910, 9 ½ In. 1348.00
Figurine, Putti, Playing Flute, Songbird, 7 x 4 ½ In. 130.00
Vase, Cows, Landscape, Puffy Clouds In Sky, Bulbous, Squat, Flared Rim, R. Mori, 5 In. 150.00
Vase, Eagle & Eaglet In Nest, Bulbous, Flared Rim, 12 In. 215.00
Vase, Riverside Landscape, Linen Ground, Tapered, c.1910, 9 In. 92.00
Vase, Urn, Blue, Oval Pink Reserve, Pate-Sur-Pate Fairy, Baluster, Flaring Handles, 7 In. 400.00

HISTORIC BLUE, *see factory names, such as Adams, Ridgway, and Staffordshire.*

HOBNAIL glass is a style of glass with bumps all over. Dozens of hobnail patterns and variants have been made. Clear, colored, and opalescent hobnail have been made and are being reproduced. Other pieces of hobnail may also be listed in the Duncan & Miller and Fenton categories.

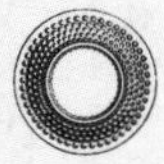

Salt, Blue, Sawtooth Rim, 14-Point Star Base, 3 ¾ x 1 1/12 In. 8.00
Toothpick, Daisy & Button, Canary Opalescence, 1885, 3 x 2 In. 65.00
Tumbler, Dew Drop, Cranberry Opalescent, Pontil, Hobbs, Brockunier & Co., c.1875, 3 ⅞ In. .. 26.00

HOLLY AMBER, or golden agate, glass was made by the Indiana Tumbler and Goblet Company of Greentown, Indiana, from January 1, 1903, to June 13, 1903. It is a pressed glass pattern featuring holly leaves in the amber-shaded glass. The glass was made with shadings that range from creamy opalescent to brown-amber.

Berry Bowl, 4 ¼ In., Pair 175.00
Butter, Cover, Paneled, Beaded, Scalloped Edge, Dome Cover, 6 In. 690.00
Butter, Dome Cover, Greentown, 7 ½ In. 1093.00
Compote, 7 ¾ x 8 In. 1041.00
Compote, Cover, 7 ½ In. 900.00
Dish, Oval, 7 In. 104.00
Mug, Applied Handle, 5 x 3 In. 460.00

Mug, Golden Agate, Patterned Body, 4 ¾ In.		529.00
Sauce, 1 ¾ x 4 ¼ In.		92.00
Sauceboat, Golden Agate, Round, Flared, Notched Edge		165.00
Syrup, Golden Agate, Cover, Indiana Tumbler & Goblet Co., 6 x 2 In. .... *illus*		1093.00
Toothpick, Bead Base, 2 ½ In.		350.00
Toothpick, Beaded Edge		257.00
Toothpick, Golden Agate, 2 ½ In.		363.00
Tumbler, 4 In.		180.00
Tumbler, Wreath, Button Pontil, 3 ⅞ In.		173.00
Vase, Pedestal, Bead Divided Bands, 6 In.		300.00

HOLT-HOWARD was an importer that started working in New York City in 1949 and moved to Stamford, Connecticut, in 1955. The company sold many types of table accessories, such as condiment jars, decanters, spoon holders, and saltshakers. The figures shown on some of its pieces had a cartoon-like quality. The company was bought out by General Housewares Corporation in 1969. Holt-Howard pieces are often marked with the name and the year or *HH* and the year stamped in black. The *HH* mark was used until 1974. There was also a black and silver label. Production of Holt-Howard ceased in 1990. Similar pieces are being made today by Grant Holt, one of the founders, and are marked *GHA*.

Angel, Feather Doll, Pink Dress, Harp, Paper Cone Body, 1950s, 7 ¾ In.		36.00
Ashtray, Christmas Tree, 1959, 4 ½ x 3 ¼ In.		9.00
Bank, Coin Kitty, Gray Cat Bobbing, 1958, 6 ½ x 5 In.		175.00
Candleholder, Angel, Bells, Christmas Red, White, Green, Gold, 1964, 4 ¼ In.		29.00
Candleholder, Angel, Gold Star, Hurricane Glass Shade, 1959, 6 x 4 In., Pair		61.00
Candleholder, Applied Rose Leaves, Petal Rim, Green, Pink, Handle, 1960		15.00
Candleholder, Boy Praying Shadow Box, 2 Candle Cups, 1959, 4 x 5 In.		22.00
Candleholder, Chimney Top, Square, Red, c.1959, 3 ½ x 3 ½ In., Pair		10.00
Candleholder, Climbers, Pixie, White, 1950s, 2 ¾ x 3 In., Pair	24.00 to 39.00	
Candleholder, Holly, Handle, 1962, 4 x 1 ¾ In., Pair		35.00
Candleholder, Santa Claus, Pair		59.00
Candy Jar, Lid, C A N D Y Spelled Out, Clip On Pop-Up Santa Inside, 6 ¼ In.		95.00
Cocktail Olives, Pixieware, c.1958, 5 In.		23.00
Condiment, Jam 'N Jelly, Spoon, Label, Pixie Ware, 1958		68.00
Condiment, Ketchup On Hat, Arm, Handles, 1959, 5 x 3 ¾ In.		32.00
Cookie Jar, Lemon Face, Yellow, Green, 6 ½ In.		55.00
Creamer, Sugar, Melon Rind, Green, Yellow, 1960		59.00
Crock, Merry Mouse, Stinky Cheese, 1958, 4 In.		20.00
Dish, Cover, Cozy Kittens, Cottage Cheese, Kissing Cats, Green, 1958, 5 x 5 In.		85.00
Dish, Tree, 3 Sections, Gold Star, 13 x 10 In.		18.00
Jar, Ketchup, Vertical Stripes, Pixie Ware, 1958, 5 ½ In.		115.00
Jar, Lid, Ketchup, Rooster Head, Red, Yellow Cream, 3 ¾ x 4 ¼ In.		63.00
Jar, Mustard, Yellow Vertical Stripes, Pixie Ware, 1958		95.00
Jar, Relish, Green Striped, Blue Face, Pixie Ware, 1959		125.00
Mug, Elf, White Beard, Red Nose, Cheeks, Handle, 1967, 2 ½ x 4 In., 4 Piece.........		58.00
Napkin Holder, Rooster, Red, Yellow, Tan, 1960, 5 ½ x 2 ½ In.		40.00
Napkin Holder, Santa Claus, 1964, 4 In.		45.00
Planter, Santa Express, 5 ¾ x 7 In.		35.00
Salt, Cat, Siamese, Pink Ribbon, 1958, 4 In.		20.00
Salt & Pepper, Blue Cat, Pink Cat, 5 In.		60.00
Salt & Pepper, Daisy Dorable, Ponytail Girls, Paper Label.....................		47.00
Salt & Pepper, Red Tomato, Green Stem, 2 ¾ x 2 In.		20.00
Salt & Pepper, Santa, Holding Present, Black Stoppers, 2 ½ In.		30.00
Salt & Pepper, Striped Bird, Gourd Shape, Green, Blue, 1960, 4 In.		41.00
Stringholder, Cozy Cat Kitten Face, Pink Plaid Bow, 1959, 5 x 5 ¼ In.		50.00

HOPALONG CASSIDY was a character in a series of twenty-eight books written by Clarence E. Milford, first published in 1907. Movies and television shows were made based on the character. The best-known actor playing Hopalong Cassidy was William Lawrence Boyd. His first movie appearance was in 1919, but the first Hopalong Cassidy film was not made until 1934. Sixty-six films were made. In 1948, William Boyd purchased the television rights to the movies, then later made fifty-two new programs. In the 1950s, Hopalong Cassidy and his horse, named Topper, were seen in comics, records, toys, and other products. Boyd died in 1972.

Alarm Clock, Round, Black, Insert, U.S. Time, Box, c.1950, 5 ½ In. .... *illus*		468.00
Booklet, Hopalong Cassidy & The Stagecoach, William Boyd, 1950, 5 x 5 In.		35.00
Cap Gun, Spurs Set, Leather Straps, Wyandotte, Box, Insert, 1950s, 8 ½ In. .... *illus*		2223.00
Clock, Marked, Copyright Wm. Boyd, Calter Products, Chicago, Ill., 1940..................		125.00
Cuff Set, Leather, Hopalong Logo, Viral Mfg. Co., Box, 6 In.		468.00

Hopalong Cassidy, Alarm Clock, Round, Black, Insert, U.S. Time, Box, c.1950, 5 ½ In.
$468.00

Hopalong Cassidy, Cap Gun, Spurs Set, Leather Straps, Wyandotte, Box, Insert, 1950s, 8 ½ In.
$2223.00

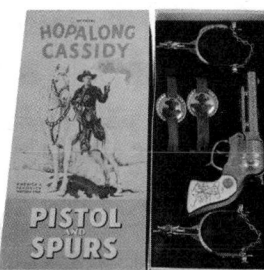

TIP
For your health and the well-being of your collection, do not smoke. The nicotine will stain fabrics, pictures, and wood.

Horn, Snuff Mull, Silver Thistle, Engraved, A Present From A Friend, Scotland, 3 x 3 In. $270.00

Howdy Doody, Toy, Band, With Bob Smith, Unique Art, 1950s, 6 ½ In. $784.00

Game, Board, Milton Bradley, c.1950, 19 x 9 ¾ In.	61.00
Game, Darts, Magnetic, Target, Stagecoach Hold Up, Box, 1950, 14 x 17 In.	89.00
Gun, Zoomerang, Red, 1950, 9 In.	210.00
Gun & Holster Set, Knife, Premium Prototype, Cardboard, 2-Sided, c.1950	345.00
Hamper, Hopalong, Horse, Metal, Lithograph, Hinged Lid, 23 In.	30.00
Hat, Bailey Of Hollywood, 100 Percent Wool, Embossed Leather Slide, 1950s, 11 x 13 In.	145.00
Lamp, Motion, Running Horses, Stagecoach, Bar 20 Ranch, Econolite, 1950s, 6 x 9 In.	348.00
Lunch Box, Hoppy On Horse, With Gun, Metal, 1954	89.00
Lunch Box, Thermos, Aladdin, Metal, Cup, Decal, 1950, 3 ¾ x 4 ¼ In.	500.00
Mask, Latex, Traveler Trading Co., Box, 1950s, 5 x 8 In.	173.00
Mug, Black Transfer, Milk Glass	11.00
Night-Light, Gun Shape, Hoppy, Glass, Molded, Aladdin, 1950s, 4 x 10 In.	316.00
Picture, Signed, Good Luck From Hoppy, Color, Premium, 8 x 10 In.	115.00
Pin, Club, Filene's, Lowe's State, Black, Red, 2 ⅛ In.	201.00
Pin, For Democracy 100 Percent, World War II, Freihofer Baking Co., c.1942, 1 ¼ In.	230.00
Pin, Hitching Post, Black & White Photo, Dark Green, Oppenheim's, 1 ¾ In.	115.00
Pin, Hopalong Cassidy Portrait, Red Ground, ⅞ In.	13.00
Pin, Portrait, Lithograph, Yellow Ground, c.1950, 1 ⅛ In.	52.00
Radio, Hopalong, Topper Rearing, Black, Arvin, c.1950, 6 ⅜ x 9 ⅝ x 5 ¼ In.	460.00
Shirt, Photos, Champ Of Hollywood, California, 1950s, Adult Medium	115.00
Tab Set, Burry's Cookies, Tin Lithograph, 2 In., 12 Piece	638.00
Wastebasket, Hoppy On Horse, Embossed, Paper Over Tin, 12 ½ x 10 ½ In.	65.00

HORN was used to make many types of boxes, furniture inlays, jewelry, and whimsies.

Beaker, Stagecoach, Horses, Driver, Engraved, Silver Mount, England, 1880, 4 x 4 In.	345.00
Cup, Ale, Ram's Horn, Wavy Pattern, Silver Rim, Engraved, Thomas Ayres, Scotland, c.1770	385.00
Cup, Coach Scene, Houses, Trees, Engraved, England, c.1800	385.00
Cup, Cover, Silver Mounts, 7 In.	176.00
Cup, Fox Hunt, Allover Engraving, England, c.1800	450.00
Figurine, Crab, Chinese, 20th Century, 1 ¾ x 4 In.	259.00
Figurine, Tree, Plants, Bird, Bone, Carved, Wood Stand, Chinese, 12 ½ x 4 ¼ In.	1058.00
Hat Rack, 10 Horns, Wood Back, 43 x 37 In.	880.00
Holder, Relief Carved, Shang Style, Chinese, 20th Century, 4 x 3 ⅛ In.	823.00
Ornament, Cherub, Viking Finial, Silver Mount, Pedestal Base, Sweden, c.1870, 16 ½ In.	920.00
Snuff Mull, Scottish Thistle Design, Engraved, Silver, Early 19th Century, 3 ¾ In.	230.00
Snuff Mull, Silver Thistle, Engraved, A Present From A Friend, Scotland, 3 x 3 In. .....*illus*	270.00
Snuff Mull, Silver, Brass Mount, Scotland, 19th Century, 3 ¾ In., 2 Piece	427.00

HOWARD PIERCE began working in Southern California in 1936. In 1945, he opened a pottery in Claremont. He moved to Joshua Tree in 1968 and continued making pottery until 1991. His contemporary-looking figurines are popular with collectors. Though most pieces are marked with his name, smaller items from his sets often were not marked.

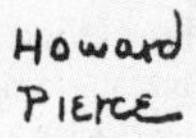

Howard Pierce

Bird, Gray & Brown High Gloss Glaze, 2 ¾ In., Pair	50.00
Figurine, African Girl, Brown Satin Glaze, Brown & White Speckled Hair, 7 ½ In.	125.00
Figurine, Bears, Brown, 6 ½-In. Mother, 2 ¾-In. Babies, 3 Piece	36.00
Figurine, Chicken, Tan, Peach Tone, 7 ½ x 5 In.	99.00
Figurine, Elephant, Trunk Up, Pink Glaze, 6 ½ In.	175.00
Figurine, Koala, On Branch, Brown Glaze, 5 ¾ In.	85.00
Figurine, Seal, Brown, 7 ¼ In.	10.00
Figurine, St. Francis Of Assisi, Holding Bird, Water Well Base, 2 Birds, 11 In.	199.00
Flower Frog, Frog Sitting On Rock, Gray, Speckled Black, 5 Holes, 5 ½ In.	150.00
Girl, Gold Glaze, Feeding Animals, Kneeling, Bowl, Open Hand, 7 In.	20.00
Nativity Set, Stylized Figures, White Glaze, 7-In. Joseph, 4-In. Mary, 3 Piece	125.00
Vase, Blue, Horizontal Ribs, Dark Blue Plaque, Raised White Deer, 4 ¼ x 4 ½ In.	99.00
Vase, Bud, Blue Glaze, 10 ½ In.	16.00
Vase, Calla Lily, Ivory Glaze, Flowing Ribbon Foot, 8 x 4 ¾ In.	198.00
Vase, Green Glaze, 4 Sides, Flared, Open Center, Palm Tree, Giraffe, 9 In.	175.00
Vase, Green Glaze, Black Specks, Open Center, Horse, Tree, 7 x 9 x 3 In.	199.00

HOWDY DOODY and Buffalo Bob were the main characters in a children's series televised from 1947 to 1960. Howdy was a redheaded puppet. The series became popular with college students in the late 1970s when Buffalo Bob began to lecture on campuses.

Bag, Washington State Delicious Apples, Plastic, 3 Lbs., 1950s	25.00
Bandage, Howdy's Face, White, Blue Graphics, Wrapping, Forest City Products, 1950s	10.00

H

Bath Mitt, Howdy As Cowboy, Sheriff, Name On Bottom, 7 x 8 In.	49.00
Bath Mitt, Howdy, Name On Bottom, 7 x 8 In.	60.00
Behavior Chart, Wall Decoration, Jolly Jumbo, Box, Cardboard, c.1949, 13 x 18 ½ In.	175.00
Book, Little Golden Book, Howdy & Clarabell On Elephant, No. 121, 1951	25.00
Can, Welch's Grape Juice Frozen Concentrate, Howdy On End, 1953, 2 x 4 In.	65.00
Catalog, Kagran, Howdy Doody Merchandising Catalog, 1955, 24 Pages............................	18.50
Christmas Card, Howdy, On Bicycle, Talking To Mr. Bluster, Red Border, 1953, 3 x 5 In.	35.00
Coloring Book, Howdy Yawning In Bed, Clarabell Under Bed, Whitman, 1956	15.00
Container, Ice Cream, Red & White Stripes, Characters On Front, 8 Oz...............................	70.00
Cookbook, Welch's Premium, Howdy & Friends, Premium, 1952, 34 Pages.........................	80.00
Cookie Jar, Howdy Doody Face, 1950s, 9 ½ In.	245.00
Doll, Howdy, Sheriff, Rubber, Chaps, Badge, Hat, 1952, 12 ¼ In.	170.00
Game, Card, Howdy's Face, Russell Mfg., 1950s..	60.00
Horn, Clarabell Clown, Plastic, Soft Rubber Head, 1950s, 7 ½ In.	150.00
Label, Howdy End Label, Wonder Enriched Bread, Color, 1950s, 2 ¾ x 2 ¾ In.	25.00
Lid, Welch's Grape Jelly, Yellow & Blue Letters, Contents, 1953	45.00
Lunch Box, Howdy, Chuck Wagon Scene, Metal, 1950s..	190.00
Marionette, Heidi Doody, Pride Products, Box, 1950s, 13 ½ In.	80.00
Marionette, Howdy Doody, Peter Puppet Playthings, Box, c.1949, 15 ¾ In.	208.00
Night-Light, Howdy's Head, Glass, Japan, 1950s	85.00
Paint Kit, 3 Unpainted Chalk Figures, Howdy, Clarabell, Indian Princess, Box, 6 ½ In.	88.00
Patch, Cloth, Embroidered, Howdy On White Ground, 1970s...	12.50
Pin, Red, White & Blue, Picture Of Howdy, Safety Club, CBS, Celluloid, 2 In.	200.00
Puppet, Buffalo Bob, Soft Vinyl Molded Head, Blue Eyes, Open Mouth, 1950s....................	120.00
Puppet, Howdy Doody, Molded Vinyl Head, Googly Eyes, Neckerchief, 1950s......................	75.00
Puppet Show, 6 Vinyl & Cloth Puppets, Box, Peter Puppet Playthings, 1950s......................	579.00
Puzzle Tray, Howdy, With Fishing Gear, Tent, Skunks, Whitman, 1953.................................	40.00
Record Album, Howdy Doody & The Air-O-Doodle, RCA Victor, 45 RPM	55.00
Ring, Flasher, Buffalo Bob, Nabisco Rice Honey's Cereal, Premium, 1950s...........................	50.00
Snow Spray, Frosty Snow Spray, Aerosol Can, 1950s	100.00
Spoon, Iced Tea, Howdy, Waist Up, Silver Plated, Kagran, 1950s, 7 In.	60.00
Toy, Acrobat, Howdy Doody, On Trapeze, Celluloid, Windup, Japan, 1950	950.00
Toy, Band, With Bob Smith, Unique Art, 1950s, 6 ½ In. ....*illus*	784.00
Wrapper, Ice Cream, Howdy Doody Deluxe Ice Cream Bar, Gehl's Farms, Foil	40.00

HULL pottery was made in Crooksville, Ohio, from 1905. Addis E. Hull bought the Acme Pottery Company and started making ceramic wares. In 1917, A. E. Hull Pottery began making art pottery as well as the commercial wares. For a short time, 1921 to 1929, the firm also sold pottery imported from Europe. The dinnerwares of the 1940s (including the Little Red Riding Hood line), the high gloss artwares of the 1950s, and the matte wares of the 1940s are all popular with collectors. The firm officially closed in March 1986.

Bank, Corky Pig, Yellow, Red & Green Design, Gold Trim, 6 x 8 In.	48.00
Bank, Razorback Pig, Mirror Brown, Light Blue Trim, Marked, Hull, U.S.A., 8 x 10 In.	40.00
Bow Knot, Basket, Pink, Green, Marked, U.S.A., 6 ½ In.	118.00
Bow Knot, Double Cornucopia, Blue, Green, 13 In.	135.00
Bow Knot, Ewer, Blue, Green, Marked, U.S.A., 5 ¾ In.	118.00
Bow Knot, Ewer, Pink, Green, B-1, Marked, U.S.A., 5 ¾ In.	118.00
Bow Knot, Jardiniere, Blue, Green, Marked, 5 ¾ In.	118.00
Bow Knot, Jardiniere, Pink, Green, Marked, U.S.A., 5 ¾ In.	78.00
Bow Knot, Vase, Double Handles, Blue Base, 10 ½ In.	178.00
Bow Knot, Vase, Green, Pink, Marked, 10 ½ In.	150.00
Bow Knot, Vase, Pink, Green, B-7, Marked, U.S.A., 5 ½ In.	68.00 to 118.00
Bow Knot, Wall Pocket, Sad Iron, Pink, Green, 6 In.	108.00
Calla Lily, Vase, Green, Pink, 13 In.	108.00
Continental, Pitcher, Mountain Blue, 12 ½ In.	165.00
Iris, Vase, Cream, Mauve, Handles, Shaped Rim, 7 In.	55.00
Little Red Riding Hood, Bank, Poppies, 7 In.	415.00
Little Red Riding Hood, Butter, Cover, Flowers, 6 ½ In.	140.00 to 298.00
Little Red Riding Hood, Butter, Cover, Poppy, 5 ½ x 6 ½ In.	140.00 to 298.00
Little Red Riding Hood, Canister, Tea, Poppies, 10 In.	420.00
Little Red Riding Hood, Cookie Jar, Closed Basket..	110.00
Little Red Riding Hood, Cookie Jar, Closed Basket, Poinsettias, 13 In.	1080.00 to 1550.00
Little Red Riding Hood, Cookie Jar, Flower Border, Open Basket, 13 In.	116.00 to 175.00
Little Red Riding Hood, Creamer, Side Pour, 5 In.	105.00
Little Red Riding Hood, Dish, Divided, Child's..	1238.00
Little Red Riding Hood, Dresser Jar, Black Trim	413.00

Hull, Little Red Riding Hood, Wall Pocket, 9 In. $200.00

H

Hull, Water Lily, Vase, Brown, Tan, Label, Marked, 9 ½ In. $81.00

TIP

When cleaning old hairbrushes backed with celluloid, do not plunge the brushes in a sink full of water. If water collects between the brush and the plastic, it will cause damage. (Never keep in direct sunlight. Celluloid, or cellulose nitrate, is flammable.)

Hutschenreuther, Figurine, Dancer, Marked, Green Mark, Tag, 11 In. $104.00

Icon, Kazan Mother Of God, Silver Gilt Repousse Riza, N. Druzhinin, Russia, c.1912, 12 x 11 In. $1800.00

Icon, Mother Of God, Painted, On Linen, Repousse, Pierced Silvered Riza, c.1900, 11 x 10 In. $295.00

Little Red Riding Hood, Jar, Cover, Marked, 9 In.	1580.00
Little Red Riding Hood, Ladle	475.00
Little Red Riding Hood, Match Holder, No. 135889, 6 In.	580.00
Little Red Riding Hood, Mustard Pot	35.00
Little Red Riding Hood, Pie Bird, Cream Glaze Under Paint, Red, Gold, 5 In.	298.00
Little Red Riding Hood, Pitcher, Milk, 8 In.	104.00
Little Red Riding Hood, Pitcher, Milk, Flowers, 7 In.	128.00
Little Red Riding Hood, Salt & Pepper, 5 In., 4 Piece	77.00
Little Red Riding Hood, Salt & Pepper, Large	38.00 to 50.00
Little Red Riding Hood, Salt & Pepper, Poinsettia, Medium	1500.00
Little Red Riding Hood, Salt & Pepper, Small	25.00
Little Red Riding Hood, Sugar & Creamer, Open, 5 In.	200.00
Little Red Riding Hood, Sugar & Creamer, Poppies	140.00
Little Red Riding Hood, Sugar, Cover, Flowers, 4 In.	360.00
Little Red Riding Hood, Sugar, Side Pour	100.00
Little Red Riding Hood, Syrup, Poppies, Spout On Head, Marked, 5 In.	198.00
Little Red Riding Hood, Teapot, Pastel Flowers, Marked, U.S.A., 8 In.	175.00 to 200.00
Little Red Riding Hood, Wall Pocket, 9 In.	*illus* 200.00
Magnolia, Vase, Marked, 8 ½ In.	125.00
Magnolia, Vase, Pink, Blue Matte, Handles, Paper Label, 15 In.	178.00
Medley, Vase, Cat, Sitting, Glaze, 11 In.	132.00
Mirror Brown, Plate, Bread & Butter, 6 ¾ In.	6.00
Mirror Brown, Plate, Dinner, 10 ½ In.	15.00
Mirror Brown, Salt & Pepper, Cork Stoppers	15.00
Mirror Brown, Sugar, Lid	15.00
Mirror Brown, Tray, Gingerbread Man, Brown Glaze, 10 In.	5.00
Planter, Elephant, Decanter, 1940s, 5 In.	85.00
Planter, Flowers, Twig Handles, 4 ½ x 11 In.	23.00
Planter, Girl Dancing, Pink Dress, 7 ½ In.	20.00
Tile, No. 2, Green, Blue, White Crystalline, 1927-32, 4 ¼ x 4 ¼ In.	55.00
Tokay, Ewer, White, 12 In.	143.00
Tokay, Vase, Pink, Green, Pedestal, 15 In.	66.00
Water Lily, Vase, Brown, Tan, Label, Marked, 9 ½ In.	*illus* 81.00
Woodland, Teapot, Yellow, Green, 7 In.	107.00
Woodland, Vase, Yellow, Green, Footed, Handles, 10 ½ In.	109.00
Woodland, Vase, Yellow, Green, Footed, Low Handles, 8 ½ In.	102.00

HUMMEL figurines, based on the drawings of the nun M.I. Hummel (Berta Hummel) were made by the W. Goebel Porzellanfabrik of Oeslau, Germany, now Rodental, Germany. They were first made in 1935. The *Crown* mark was used from 1935 to 1949. The company added the *bee* marks in 1950. The *full bee* with variations, was used from 1950 to 1959; *stylized bee,* 1957 to 1972; *three line mark,* 1964 to 1972; *last bee,* sometimes called *vee over gee,* 1972 to 1979. In 1979 the V bee symbol was removed from the mark. *U.S. Zone* was part of the mark from 1946 to 1948; *W. Germany* was part of the mark from 1960 to 1990. The Goebel, *W. Germany* mark, called the *missing bee* mark, was used from 1979 to 1990; *Goebel, Germany,* with the crown and WG, originally called the *new mark,* was used from 1991 through part of 1999. The newest version of the bee mark with the word *Goebel,* the current mark or Goebel with full bee, was adopted in 2000. A special *Year 2000* backstamp was also introduced. Porcelain figures inspired by Berta Hummel's drawings were introduced in 1997. These are marked *BH* followed by a number. They were made in the Far East, not Germany. Goebel discontinued making Hummel figurines in 2008, but they will continue to be made by Manufaktur Rodental GmbH. Other decorative items and plates that feature Hummel drawings have been made by Schmid Brothers, Inc., since 1971.

Clock, No. 442, Chapel Time, Church, Porcelain, 11 In.	380.00
Figurine, No. 6/0, Sensitive Hunter, Stylized Bee, 4 ¾ In.	77.00 to 88.00
Figurine, No. 10/1, Flower Madonna, White Over Glaze, Full Bee, 8 In.	88.00
Figurine, No. 15, Hear Ye, Hear Ye, Millennium Bee, 5 In.	30.00
Figurine, No. 18, Christ Child, Full Bee, 6 ¼ In.	161.00
Figurine, No. 20, Prayer Before Battle, Crown Mark, 4 ½ In.	41.00 to 65.00
Figurine, No. 46, Madonna, Full Bee, 10 In.	117.00
Figurine, No. 47/0, Goose Girl, Crown, 5 ¼ In.	88.00
Figurine, No. 50/0, Volunteer, New Mark, 6 ½ In.	112.00
Figurine, No. 53 Joyful, New Mark, 6 In.	41.00
Figurine, No. 63, Singing Lesson, Vee Over Gee, 2 ¾ In.	77.00
Figurine, No. 67, Doll Mother, Full Bee, 4 ¾ In.	88.00
Figurine, No. 69, Happy Pastime, New Mark, 3 ¾ In.	41.00
Figurine, No. 71, Stormy Weather, Missing Bee, 6 In.	100.00

Figurine, No. 74, Little Gardener, New Mark, 4 ½ In.	....	41.00
Figurine, No. 85/4/0, Serenade, Vee Over Gee, 3 ½ In.		53.00
Figurine, No. 86, Happiness, New Mark, 4 ½ In.		35.00
Figurine, No. 89/11, Little Cellist, Stylized Bee, 6 In.		82.00
Figurine, No. 98/0, Sister, Millennium Bee, 5 ¾ In.		41.00
Figurine, No. 112/1, Just Resting, Full Bee, 5 In.		88.00
Figurine, No. 124/0, Hello, Millennium Bee, 7 In.		41.00
Figurine, No. 130, Duet, Crown, 3-Line Mark, 5 ¼ In.		345.00
Figurine, No. 132, Star Gazer, Full Bee, 5 In.		88.00
Figurine, No. 135/0, Soloist, New Mark, 2 ¾ In.		18.00
Figurine, No. 143/0, Boots, Vee Over Gee, 5 ½ In.		53.00
Figurine, No. 175, Mother's Darling, Stylized Bee, 6 In.		70.00
Figurine, No. 199, Feeding Time, Crown Mark, 5 ½ In.		345.00
Figurine, No. 217, Boy With Toothache, Vee Over Gee, 6 In.		50.00
Figurine, No. 218/2/0, Birthday Serenade, Vee Over Gee.		35.00
Figurine, No. 238/A, Angel With Lute, New Mark, 2 ½ In.		35.00
Figurine, No. 239/B, Girl With Doll, Vee Over Gee, 3 ½ In.		41.00
Figurine, No. 240, Little Drummer, Millennium Bee, 4 ¼ In.		41.00
Figurine, No. 304, Artist, 3-Line Mark, 5 ¼ In.		47.00
Figurine, No. 309, With Loving Greetings, Missing Bee, 3 ½ In.		47.00
Figurine, No. 322, Little Pharmacist, New Mark, 6 In.		41.00
Figurine, No. 330, Baking Day, New Mark, 5 ¼ In.		59.00
Figurine, No. 347, Adventure Bound, Full Bee, 7 In.		288.00
Figurine, No. 348, Ring Around The Rosie, Three Line, 7 In.		1400.00
Figurine, No. 356, Gay Adventures, Vee Over Gee, 3 ½ In.		35.00
Figurine, No. 367, Busy Student, New Mark, 4 ¼ In.		41.00
Figurine, No. 386, On Secret Path, Missing Bee, 5 ¼ In.		59.00
Figurine, No. 408, Smiling Through, Missing Bee, 4 ¾ In.		59.00
Figurine, No. 553, Scamp, New Mark, 4 ¼ In.		35.00
Figurine, No. 2121, Soap Box Derby, Millennium Bee, 6 ½ In.		633.00
Figurine, No. 2148/B, First Mate, Millennium Bee, 4 In.		30.00
Figurine, No. 2165, Farm Days, Millennium Bee, 7 ½ In.		633.00
Plaque, No. 48/2, Madonna, Crown Mark, 5 ¾ x 4 ½ In.		385.00
Plaque, No. 93, Little Fiddler, Crown Mark, 5 x 5 ¼ In.		219.00
Plaque, No. 180, Tuneful Goodnight, Stylized Bee, 5 In.		219.00

HUTSCHENREUTHER PORCELAIN FACTORY was founded by Carolus Magnus in Hohenburg, Bavaria, in 1814. A second factory was established in Selb, Germany, in 1857. The company made fine quality porcelain dinnerwares and figurines. The mark changed through the years, but the name and the lion insignia appear in most versions. Hutschenreuther became part of the Rosenthal division of the Waterford Wedgwood Group in 2000. Rosenthal was bought by Sambonet Paderno Industries, headquartered in Orfento, Novaro, Italy, in 2009.

Berry Bowl, Favorite Pattern, White, Gold Trim	....	12.00
Coffeepot, Huntington Rose, Brown Roses, 6 Cup		85.00
Figurine, Chimney Sweep, 20th Century, 5 In.		124.00
Figurine, Dancer, Marked, Green Mark, Tag, 11 In.	*illus*	104.00
Figurine, Man, With Cape & Sword, 10 In.		289.00
Figurine, Man, With Crutch, 6 ½ In.		121.00
Group, 3 Girls Playing Ring Around The Rosie, 8 ¼ x 8 ½ In.		153.00
Group, Gute Freunde, Kneeling Nude Woman, Feeding Fawn, 9 ¾ x 12 ⅜ In.		212.00
Group, Horses, White Mare, Black Foal, Porcelain, 9 x 13 In.		146.00
Plaque, Cavalier, Horn, Woman, Hands Over Ears, Signed Wagner, Berlin, 11 x 9 In.		900.00
Plaque, Young Woman, Gesso Frame, Unna Gitana Asti, Berlin, 12 x 11 In.		850.00
Plate, Christmas, Woman, On Reindeer, Weihnachts Teller, 78, Signed Winther, Box		50.00
Plate, Wedding, No. 1, Signed Ole Winther, Box		79.00
Sugar & Creamer, White Ground, Blue Rim, Flowers, Gold Trim		10.00
Tile, Scenic, Woman, Tigers, Frame, c.1890, 9 ½ x 11 ½ In.		748.00

ICONS, special, revered pictures of Jesus, Mary, or a saint, are usually Russian or Byzantine. The small icons collected today are made of wood and tin or precious metals. Many modern copies have been made in the old style and are being sold to tourists in Russia and Europe and at shops in the United States. Rare, old icons have sold for over $50,000. Some religious statues are also included here.

Akhtuirskaya Mother Of God, Overlay, Repousse, Chased Gilt Metal Riza, 1700s, 20 x 16 In.	2280.00
Brass, Prayer Niche Shape, 4 Sections, 5 Scene Panels, Cyrillic Writing, Russia, 6 ½ x 15 ¾ In.	81.00

Icon, Our Lady Of Perpetual Help, Micro Mosaic, Gold Leaf, Label, Frame, 10 x 8 In.
$2714.00

I

Icon, St. Alexander Svirskiy, Painted, Russia, 17th Century, 12 ¼ x 10 ¼ In.
$3360.00

Icon, Tikhvin Virgin & Child, Wood, Multicolored, Enamel, Silvered Copper, 13 x 10 In.
$1440.00

Imari, Bowl, Blue, Rust, Green, Gilt, Chinese, Late 1800s, 12 In.
$510.00

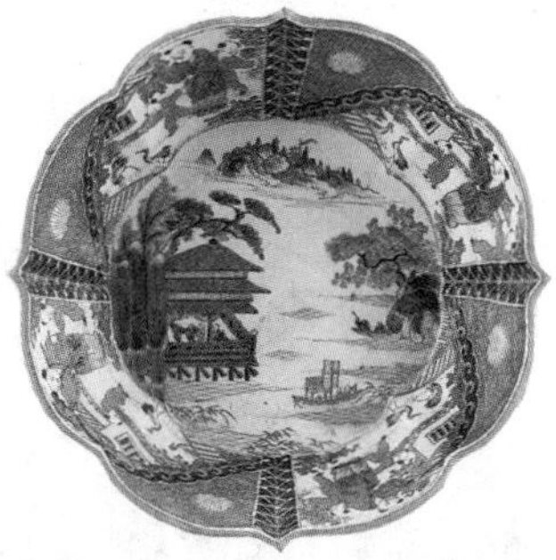

Imari, Charger, Underglaze Blue, Multicolored Enamels, Medallion, Peonies, Birds, 17 ¾ In.
$360.00

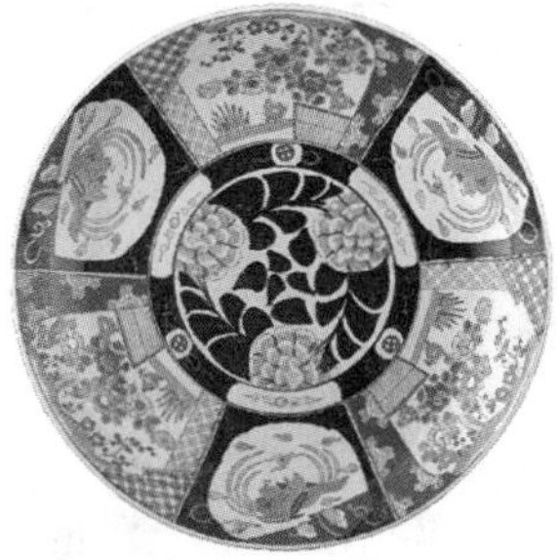

Imari, Dish, Chrysanthemum, Blue, Iron Red, Gilt, Leaves, Cartouches, 22 x 18 In.
$2271.00

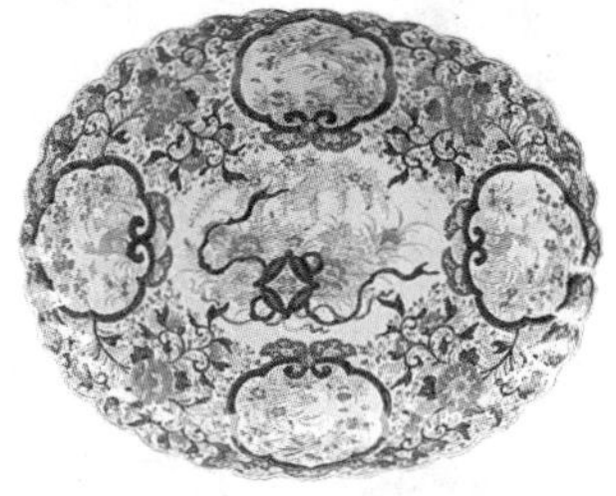

Imari, Dish, Scalloped Rim, Enameled, Gilding, Flower Medallion, Birds, 1800s, 9 ¾ In.
$120.00

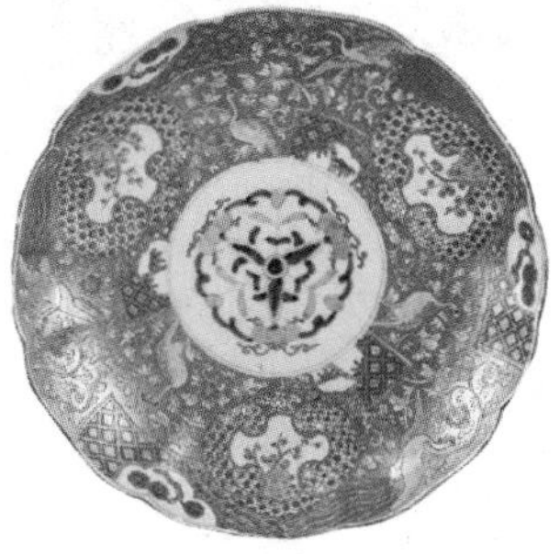

Bronze, Enameled, 4 Hinged Panels, 5 Scenes Per Panel, 19th Century, 7 x 16 In. 266.00
Christ Immanuel, Applied Gilt Metal Halo, Faux Gemstones, Metal Basma, Russia, 12 x 10 In. 4080.00
Christ, Resurrection Scenes, Giltwood, Paint, Frame, Red Velvet Mat, Greece, Russia, 14 x 18 In. 3851.00
Christ, Wood, Carved, Head, Hair, Glass Eyes, Oversize Hands, Painted, Gilt, Italy, 1800s, 19 In. 495.00
Guardian Angel, Flowers, Cloisonne, Silver, Fedor Ruckert, Moscow, c.1915, 2 ¾ x 2 In. 25620.00
Kasperov Mother Of God, Engraved Silver Gilt Riza & Halo, Moscow, c.1912, 12 x 10 In. 1020.00
Kazan Mother Of God, Silver Gilt Repousse Riza, Druzhinin, Russia, c.1912, 12 x 11 In. *illus* 1800.00
Lord Almighty, Border Overlaid, Provincial Repousse Brass Basma, 1700s, 12 x 10 In. 1440.00
Madonna & Child, Wood, Paint, Russia, 12 ½ x 11 In. 3318.00
Madonna, Enthroned, Carved Wood, 8 x 6 In. 117.00
Mother & Child, Bronze, Enamel, Russia, 4 x 3 In. 205.00
Mother Of God, Joy To All Who Sorrow, c.1800, 9 x 7 ½ In. 720.00
Mother Of God, Painted, On Linen, Repousse, Pierced Silvered Riza, c.1900, 11 x 10 In. *illus* 295.00
Nativity Of Christ, Shepherds Watching, Ornate Gilded Metal Riza, Russia, 21 x 30 In. 3120.00
Our Lady Of Perpetual Help, Micro Mosaic, Gold Leaf, Label, Frame, 10 x 8 In. *illus* 2714.00
St. Alexander Svirskiy, Painted, Russia, 17th Century, 12 ¼ x 10 ¼ In. *illus* 3360.00
St. Alexi, Silver Oklad, Painted Face, Hands, Moscow, Russia, 1896-1908, 8 ⅞ x 7 In. 878.00
St. Mitrophan Of Vornezh, Russia, 18th Century, 11 x 9 In. 900.00
St. Nicholas, Book, Christ, Madonna, Wood, Russia, 19th Century, 12 ¼ x 10 ¼ In. 633.00
St. Nicholas, Holding Open Book, Blessing With Other Hand, Gold Leaf Ground, c.1875, 13 x 11 In. 2400.00
St. Nicholas, Russia, Frame, 12 x 8 In. 660.00
St. Seraphim Of Sarov, Incised Gilt, Faux Enamel Borders, Russia, c.1902, 14 x 12 In. 2040.00
Tikhvin Virgin & Child, Wood, Multicolored, Enamel, Silvered Copper, 13 x 10 In. *illus* 1440.00
Venerable Sergiy Of Radonezh, Parents Tomb, Border Of Family Saints, Angel, 12 x 10 In. 480.00
Virgin & Child, Ukranian Catholic, c.1860, 12 ½ x 10 ½ In. 1920.00
Virgin Mary, Wood, Carved, Gessoed, Painted, 80 In. 140.00

IMARI porcelain was made in Japan and China beginning in the seventeenth century. In the eighteenth century and later, it was copied by porcelain factories in Germany, France, England, and the United States. It was especially popular in the nineteenth century and is still being made. Imari is characteristically decorated with stylized bamboo, floral, and geometric designs in orange, red, green, and blue. The name comes from the Japanese port of Imari, which exported the ware made nearby in a factory at Arita. Imari is now a general term for any pattern of this type.

Bowl, Barber, Flared Inset Rim, Scrolling Leaf & Flowers, 18th Century, 9 ⅛ x 10 ⅝ In. 1150.00
Bowl, Blue & White, Flowers, Divided Interior Panels, Flying Crane, 1 ¾ x 6 In., Pair 18.00
Bowl, Blue & White, Prunis Tree, Scalloped Rim, 4 ½ x 10 In. 35.00
Bowl, Blue, Rust, Green, Gilt, Chinese, Late 1800s, 12 In. *illus* 510.00
Bowl, Figures, Flowers, 8-Sided, Blue, White, Japan, c.1820, 9 ½ In. 294.00
Bowl, Multicolored Enamel, Gilding, Reserve Panels, Mythical Animals, 6 ½ To 9 In., 3 Piece 420.00
Bowl, Ribbed Flowers, Streamers, Brocade Blue Underglaze, Multicolored, 12 In. 660.00
Bowl, Scalloped, Garden Scenes, Blue Underglaze, Ribbed, Scalloped, 11 ¾ In. 570.00
Bowl Set, Blue, Iron Red, Enamel, Gilt, Leafy Designs, c.1890, 10 In., 8 ⅝ In., 7 ⅝ In., 3 Piece 472.00
Charger, Blue, White, Red, Flowers, Scalloped Rim, Late 1800s, 12 In. 77.00
Charger, Central Fan & Flowers, Panels Of Garden Scenes, Quatrefoil Border, 1800s, 18 ½ In. 780.00
Charger, Cranes, Birds, Butterflies, Blue, White, Orange, Japan, c.1900, 23 In. 805.00
Charger, Flower Basket Center, Scrolling Border, Lobed Rim, 17 ¾ In. 600.00
Charger, Flower Vase, Flower Panels, Phoenix, Blue, Gilt, Enamel, 18th Century, 22 In. 440.00
Charger, Hawk On Rocks, Pine Tree, Scalloped Edge, Flat Rim, Blue, White, 1800s, 18 In. 300.00
Charger, Landscape, Birds, Buddha Figure, Multicolored, Enamels, c.1900, 24 In. 588.00
Charger, Multicolored, Flowering Branches Medallion, Castles, Birds, Peonies, 18 ⅜ In. 270.00
Charger, Multicolored Designs, Gilded, Japan, c.1910, 18 In. 264.00
Charger, Scalloped Rim, Ridged Fans, Herons, Bouquet, c.1850, 18 In. 402.00
Charger, Underglaze Blue, Multicolored Enamels, Medallion, Peonies, Birds, 17 ¾ In. *illus* 360.00
Dish, Chrysanthemum, Blue, Iron Red, Gilt, Leaves, Cartouches, 22 x 18 In. *illus* 2271.00
Dish, Multicolored Enamel, Underglaze Blue, Floral Medallion, 4 Reserve Panels, 8 ¼ In., Pair. 180.00
Dish, Porcelain, Scalloped Rim, Multicolored, Enamel, Gilded, 19th Century, 12 ¼ In. 207.00
Dish, Scalloped, Central Flower Basket, Flower Panels, Blue, Multicolored, 1800s, 11 In. 180.00
Dish, Scalloped Rim, Enameled, Gilding, Flower Medallion, Birds, 1800s, 9 ¾ In. *illus* 120.00
Dish, Square Outline, Multicolored Enamels, Flowers, Phoenix Birds, Masques, 1800s, 11 x 11 In. 600.00
Jar, Cover, Flower Panels, Peonies, Blue Underglaze, Iron Red, 27 ¼ In. 420.00
Jardiniere, Gilt Bronze, Outdoor Scene, Scrolls, Flowers Mounts, 1800s, 13 x 19 In. 2938.00
Jardiniere, Outdoor Scene, Scrolling Chrysanthemums, Leaf Vines, 1800s, 13 ¼ x 18 ½ In. 2938.00
Plate, Armorial, Necklace, Pendant, Blue Underglaze, Iron Red, Pomegranates, Gourds, 11 ½ In. 2640.00
Serving Dish, Blue Underglaze, Red Blue & Green Enamel, Gilt, c.1840, 4 ¾ x 6 ½ In. 135.00
Shaving Bowl, Porcelain, Flowers, Garden Scene, 2 ¼ x 11 ¼ In., 2 Piece 259.00

Soba Cup, Landscape, Transfer, Blue & White, 3 ¼ x 2 ¾ In., Pair	100.00
Vase, Baluster, Trumpet Mouth, Reeded Body, Flowers, Marked, 1800s, 6 ½ In., Pair	518.00
Vase, Birds, Flowers, Vignettes, Scrolling Flowers Ground, Blue, Red, Pink, 1800s, 12 ½ In., Pair.	900.00
Vase, Flared Lip, Japan, 30 ¼ In.	1195.00
Vase, Reserves, Flowering Tree, Banded Rim, Base, 19th Century, 10 ½ In.	236.00
Vase, Spade Shape, Chinese Scholars, Landscape, Multicolored, Japan, c.1890, 16 In.	575.00
Vase, Temple, Figural, Flowers, Japan, 38 In.	837.00

IMPERIAL GLASS CORPORATION was founded in Bellaire, Ohio, in 1901. It became a subsidiary of Lenox, Inc., in 1973 and was sold to Arthur R. Lorch in 1981. It was sold again in 1982, and went bankrupt in 1984. In 1985, the molds and some assets were sold. The Imperial glass preferred by the collector is freehand art glass, carnival glass, slag glass, stretch glass, and other top-quality tablewares. Tablewares and animals are listed here. The others may be found in the appropriate sections.

Animal, Bunny, Milk Glass, Looking Up	24.00
Art Glass, Bowl, Freehand, Iridescent, Blue Heart & Vine, Rim, Label, 4 x 10 In. ....*illus*	604.00
Art Glass, Vase, Blue Iridescent, 8 In. ....*illus*	115.00
Art Glass, Vase, Iridescent, Colorful, Shouldered Shape, Marked, 3 ½ x 5 In.	210.00
Art Glass, Vase, Opaque Green, Marigold Interior, Freehand, 1900s, 12 In.	480.00
Candlewick, Bowl, Fruit, Ruffled, Footed, 10 In.	195.00
Candlewick, Candleholder, 3-Light, 9 ½ x 3 ½ In. ....*illus*	135.00
Candlewick, Celery Dish, 7 In.	290.00
Candlewick, Punch Set, Bowl, Underplate, Cups, 14 Piece	310.00
Candlewick, Salt & Pepper, Green	160.00
Cape Cod, Bowl, Baked Apple, 6 In.	8.00
Cape Cod, Punch Bowl, Tom & Jerry, 1948, 9 x 11 In.	225.00
Cape Cod, Relish, 3 Sections, Oval	20.00
Cape Cod, Salt & Pepper	35.00
Caramel Slag, Bowl, Lid, 5 x 2 ½ In.	30.00
Cathay, Vase, Wedding, Fu, Frosted, 7 ½ In. ....*illus*	195.00
Chroma, Goblet, Evergreen, 8 Oz. ....*illus*	29.00
Double Dutch, Plate, Rural Scene, Flora, Optic Exterior, Marigold, Iridescent, c.1912	75.00
Free Hand, Vase, Cobalt, White Heart, Vines, 10 In.	690.00
Free Hand, Vase, Cylinder Shape, Royal Blue, Hearts, Vines, 10 In.	425.00
Free Hand, Vase, Lead Luster, Butterscotch, White Looping, Pontil, Pinched Neck, c.1900, 9 ¾ In. .	212.00
Free Hand, Vase, Pearl Amethyst, Tooled Rim, Table Ring, Marked, c.1900, 6 In.	92.00
Free Hand, Vase, Shouldered, Orange, Iridescent, 6 In.	86.00
Free Hand, Vase, Tapered, Iridescent Blue, Green, Red, 8 ½ In.	144.00
Free Hand, Vase, Waisted, Orange, Iridescent, 6 ¾ In.	1035.00
Frosted Block, Dish, Pickle, Stippled, Marigold, Handles, c.1930, 6 x 3 ½ In.	65.00
Grape, Bowl, Ice Cream, No. 473, Marigold, c.1920, 9 In.	55.00
Grape, Pitcher, Grapes, Vines, Iridescent, Marigold, c.1960, 5 ½ In.	125.00
Hobnail, Water Set, Vaseline Opalescent, 9 ¼-In. Pitcher, 4 Tumblers	375.00
Homestead, Chop Plate, Rustic Scene, Smoke, c.1972, 10 In.	325.00
Lace Edge, Bowl, Blue, 9 In.	119.00
Lace Edge, Bowl, Milk Glass, 3 ½ x 6 In.	25.00
Nu-Cut, Compote, 3 ¾ x 3 ½ In.	26.00
Perfume Atomizer, Narrow, Tapered, Orange Glass, Pulled Heart & Vine, 10 In.	978.00
Pillar Flute, Compote, Amberina, 6 In. ....*illus*	48.00
Reeded, Perfume Bottle, Atomizer Lid, Spun	125.00
Reeded, Rose Bowl, Ruby, Footed	132.00
Robin, Bonbon, Blue, Handles, 7 In. ....*illus*	60.00
Robin, Water Set, Marigold, 6 Piece	125.00
Scroll Embossed, Bowl, Green, Sawtooth Edge, c.1900, 3 x 8 In.	125.00
Square, Sugar & Creamer, Ruby	24.00
Star & File, Cordial, 1 Oz. ....*illus*	25.00
Star & File, Wine Set, Octagon Stopper, Marigold, 8 Piece	135.00
Star Medallion, Plate, Iridescent, c.1925, 9 ½ In.	86.00
Twist, Candleholder, Footed, 3 In., Pair	17.00
Vintage Grape, Bowl, Milk Glass, 10 In.	35.00

INDIAN art from North and South America has attracted the collector for many years. Each tribe has its own distinctive designs and techniques. Baskets, jewelry, pottery, and leatherwork are of greatest collector interest. Eskimo art is listed under Eskimo in this book.

Awl Case, Plains, Beaded, Long Flap, Sinew, Quilled Suspensions, c.1900, 8 ½ In.	316.00
Ax, War, Pipe, Tomahawk, Missouri River, Cutout Heart, 22 ½ In.	3525.00

Imperial Glass, Art Glass, Bowl, Freehand, Iridescent, Blue Heart & Vine, Rim, Label, 4 x 10 In.
$604.00

Imperial Glass, Art Glass, Vase, Blue Iridescent, 8 In.
$115.00

Imperial Glass, Candlewick, Candleholder, 3-Light, 9 ½ x 3 ½ In.
$135.00

Imperial Glass, Cathay, Vase, Wedding, Fu, Frosted, 7 ½ In.
$195.00

Imperial Glass, Chroma, Goblet, Evergreen, 8 Oz.
$29.00

Imperial Glass, Pillar Flute, Compote, Amberina, 6 In.
$48.00

Imperial Glass, Robin, Bonbon, Blue, Handles, 7 In.
$60.00

Imperial Glass, Star & File, Cordial, 1 Oz.
$25.00

Indian, Bag, Apache, Hide, Sinew, Multicolored Beads, Tin Cones, c.1900, 5 x 4 ½ In.
$1528.00

Bag, Apache, Hide, Sinew, Multicolored Beads, Tin Cones, c.1900, 5 x 4 ½ In. .....*illus*	1528.00
Bag, Bandolier, Woodlands, Flowers, Leaves, Panel, c.1910, 17 x 13 ½ In. .....*illus*	489.00
Bag, Central Plains, Lakota, Beaded Hide, Cloth, Canvas, Multicolored Geometric, 12 ½ x 9 ½ In.	770.00
Bag, Chippewa, Beaded, Fringed, Brain Tanned, c.1930, 13 In.	180.00
Bag, Cree, Beaded, Moose Hide, Flowers, Flap, Strap, c.1970, 9 x 8 In.	345.00
Bag, Cree, Octopus, Beaded, Green, Blue, White, Yellow, Sinew, 1800s, 18 ½ In. .....*illus*	2350.00
Bag, Crow, Beaded, Lazy Stitch, Flap, Banded Design, c.1910, 8 ½ x 6 In. .....*illus*	196.00
Bag, Northern Plains, Hide, Beaded, Fringe, Ties, c.1940, 12 ½ In. .....*illus*	180.00
Bag, Plateau, Beaded, Eagle, Roses, Round, 12 ½ In.	316.00
Bag, Plateau, Beaded, Flowers, Buckskin, c.1920, 13 x 11 ½ In.	259.00
Bag, Plateau, Beaded, Horse, Butterfly, c.1925, 6 x 6 In.	546.00
Bag, Plateau, Geometric, Multicolored, 17 ½ x 12 ½ In.	563.00
Bag, Sioux, Beaded, Horsehair Cones, c.1915, 8 In.	180.00
Bag, Southern Plains, Beaded, Kiowa, Apache Buckskin, Figures, c.1940s, 15 x 6 ½ In.	559.00
Bag, Tobacco, Sioux, Beaded, Hide, Fringe, 23 In.	881.00
Bag, Yakima, Beaded, Indian In Bonnet, White Ground, Early 1900s, 11 ½ x 9 ½ In.	460.00
Bandolier, Great Lakes, Loom Beaded, Leaves, Geometric, Wool Tassels, 35 ½ In.	2607.00
Bandolier, Great Lakes, Ojibwa, Beaded, Shoulder Bag, Flowers, Early 1900s, 46 x 14 ½ In. ...	1610.00
Bandolier, Northern Plains, Beaded, Stylized Flowers, Geometric Forms, c.1925, 40 x 10 In. ..	633.00
Bandolier, Sioux, Beaded, Flags, Valero Starts, Canvas, 12 ½ x 36 In.	518.00
Basket, Apache, Bowl, Geometric, Patina, 5 x 10 ½ In.	550.00
Basket, Apache, Bowl Shape, Figural Rim, Geometric, 1900s, 8 x 3 In.	441.00
Basket, Apache, Burden, Cone Shape, Tin Cone Fringe, Butterfly Designs, c.1980, 7 x 9 In.	127.00
Basket, Apache, Coil, Geometric, 4 ¼ x 15 ½ In.	508.00
Basket, Apache, Cover, Jicarilla, Multicolored, Geometric, c.1930, 20 ½ x 14 In.	345.00
Basket, Apache, Star Center, Diamond Design, c.1900, 10 ½ In. Diam.	1045.00
Basket, Apache, Tray, Coiled, Geometric, Hide Attachment, Late 19th Century, 3 x 15 ½ In.	770.00
Basket, Burden, Apache, Tanned, Tin Cone Suspension, Hide, Cloth Bottom, 14 ½ x 15 ½ In. .	1680.00
Basket, Burden, Klickitat, Geometric Design, 13 ½ x 10 ½ In.	2467.00
Basket, Burden, Pitt River, Cone Shaped, Geometric Designs, 20 x 22 In.	3172.00
Basket, California, Bowl, Coiled, Woven, Flared, Hourglass, Diamonds, 9 ½ x 17 ½ In.	3851.00
Basket, California, Bowl, Flared, 6 Figures, Standing, Vertical Track, c.1900, 9 ¼ x 17 In.	2489.00
Basket, California, Jar, Coiled, Bottleneck Form, Hourglass, Banded, Feathers, 5 x 9 In.	2844.00
Basket, Cherokee, Cover, Oak, Brown, Red, Lock Handle, 1976 Award, Agnes Welch, 19 x 21 In.	489.00
Basket, Cherokee, Double Woven, Geometric, 2 Colors, 4 ¼ x 14 ½ x 14 ¾ In.	316.00
Basket, Cherokee, Double Woven, Square To Round, 2 Colors, Eva Bigwitch, 5 ¼ In.	81.00
Basket, Cherokee, Knitting, Oak, Red Brown, Locking Handle, R. Taylor, Qualla, 1977, 15 x 9 In.	230.00
Basket, Cherokee, Oak, Walnut, Round, 12 In.	44.00
Basket, Cherokee, River Cane, Bentwood Oak Handles, Tag, North Carolina, 14 x 11 In.	230.00
Basket, Cherokee, River Cane, Double Woven, 1970s, 6 x 9 In.	115.00
Basket, Cherokee, River Cane, Dyed Bands, Oak Handle, 13 x 16 In.	374.00
Basket, Cherokee, River Cane, Red, Brown, Diagonal Rectangles, c.1975, 14 x 19 In.	1093.00
Basket, Cherokee, River Cane, Rounded Square, Brown & Orange Diamonds, 11 In.	173.00
Basket, Cherokee, River Cane, Shopping, Browns, Lock Handle, 13 ¾ x 13 ½ x 7 ¾ In.	690.00
Basket, Cherokee, River Cane, Square To Round, Diagonal Bands, 10 ¾ x 10 In. .....*illus*	546.00
Basket, Cherokee, River Cane, Square To Round, Herringbone Design, 2 Colors, 12 ¾ In.	1380.00
Basket, Cherokee, Walnut, Red, Hinged Bentwood Handles, c.1980, 14 x 12 In.	374.00
Basket, Chitimacha, Bowl, Bear's-Ear Pattern, 4 ½ x 9 ½ x 10 In.	5079.00
Basket, Chitimacha, Bowl, Bull's-Eye Pattern, 4 ¼ x 8 x 8 In.	5079.00
Basket, Chitimacha, Bowl, Straight Plaits Between Chains, 3 x 5 x 4 In.	1434.00
Basket, Chitimacha, Bowl, Turtle Necklace Pattern, 5 x 11 x 11 ½ In.	7170.00
Basket, Chitimacha, Cover, Trinket, Double Woven, Blackbird's-Eyes Pattern, 4 x 3 x 3 In.	6871.00
Basket, Chitimacha, Cover, Trunk Shape, Double Woven, c.1922, 4 x 6 x 4 In.	8365.00
Basket, Chitimacha, Tray, Broken Plaits Pattern, 1 ¾ x 7 ¼ x 7 ¼ In.	2629.00
Basket, Choctaw, Cover, River Cane, Multicolored Bands, 2 Arched Handles, 21 In.	345.00
Basket, Choctaw, River Cane, Double Woven, Bands Of Geometric Shapes, 9 x 15 In.	230.00
Basket, Choctaw, Storage, Double Woven, Natural Fiber, Orange, Brown, Early 1900s, 7 x 8 In.	240.00
Basket, Cooking, Yokuts, Bowl, Double Rattlesnake Band, Black, Red, 5 ¾ x 12 In.	1265.00
Basket, Gathering, Pomo, c.1920, 18 In.	720.00
Basket, Hava Supai, Burden, Banded Design, c.1900, 12 x 13 In.	690.00
Basket, Hopi, Coiled, Mudhead, Kachina Heads, Late 1900s, 8 ½ x 11 In.	460.00
Basket, Hopi, Cover, Multicolored, c.1925, 7 x 11 In.	288.00
Basket, Hupa, Woven, Pedestal, Openwork, Black Designs, c.1900, 5 x 9 In.	219.00
Basket, Iroquois, Cover, Birch Bark, Etched, Moose Head, Goose, Bear, c.1925, 6 x 9 x 7 In.	575.00
Basket, Iroquois, Cover, Quilled, Birch Bark, Chief's Head, Round, c.1950, 2 ½ x 6 ½ In.	115.00
Basket, Iroquois, Cover, Quilled, Birch Bark, Flowers, Round, c.1950, 2 x 6 In.	69.00

Basket, Iroquois, Lid, Birch Bark, Quill Details, 1950s, 2 ½ x 6 ½ In. ....*illus*	115.00
Basket, Jicarilla Apache, Multicolored, Woven-In Handles, Geometric Form, c.1925, 18 x 12 In.	633.00
Basket, Klamath, Soft Weave, Rhomboid, Beige, Brown, 6 ½ x 10 In.	690.00
Basket, Klamath, Woven, Serrated Diamonds, Yellow Quill Accents, c.1910, 4 x 6 In. ....*illus*	374.00
Basket, Klickitat, Imbricated Berry, 5 ¼ In.	489.00
Basket, Maine, Woven, Yellow, Green, Orange Design, c.1890, 5 x 12 x 11 In.	761.00
Basket, Makah, Cover, Woven Grass, Oval, Whaling Scene, c.1950, 3 x 5 In.	88.00
Basket, Nez Perce, Cornhusk, Husk, Yarn, 11 ½ x 9 In.	690.00
Basket, North California, Bowl, Twined, Banded, Brown Ground, c.1900, 3 ¼ x 7 ½ In.	356.0 0
Basket, Olla, Coil, Braided Rim, Squares, 8 ¾ x 11 In.	403.00
Basket, Olla, Tohono O'Odham, Shouldered, Coiled Willow, Devil's Claw, c.1900, 13 ½ In.	235.00
Basket, Paiute, Beaded, Geometric Design, Multicolored, Julie Benjamin, 3 x 5 In.	441.00
Basket, Paiute, Beaded, Single Rod Woven, Flowing Arrow Design, Lid, c.1950, 6 x 5 ⅜ In.	518.00
Basket, Papago, Multicolored, Geometric, Figures, 16 x 14 In.	805.00
Basket, Papago, Multicolored, Repeating Geometrics, c.1950, 17 x 13 In.	316.00
Basket, Pima, Bowl, Geometric, Globular, 7 x 9 ½ In.	230.00
Basket, Pima, Figural, Flared Rim, 5 x 9 In.	235.00
Basket, Pima, Fret Design, 1920s, 11 x 5 In.	345.00
Basket, Pima, Geometrics, c.1900, 14 In.	688.00
Basket, Pima, Horsehair, Geometric, Center Star, Black, Brown, c.1980, 3 ½ In.	184.00
Basket, Pima, Man In Maze, c.1920, 4 ¾ x 17 ¾ In.	1440.00
Basket, Pima, Slant-Sided, Coiled Willow, 6 Devil's Claw Figures, Diamonds, 5 ½ x 11 In.	235.00
Basket, Pima, Straight-Sided, Flat Bottom, Cross In Box, 7 x 11 ¾ In.	230.00
Basket, Pomo, Bowl, Coiled, Flared Sides, Triangle Pattern, Feathers, Beads, 4 ⅝ x 10 ¼ In.	4148.00
Basket, Pomo, Bowl, Diagonal Zigzag, c.1900, 3 ¾ x 9 In.	356.00
Basket, Pomo, Bowl, Geometric, Woven, c.1900, 2 ¼ x 7 ¾ In.	711.00
Basket, Pomo, Single Rod, Deer Back, Clam Shell Beads, 5 x 2 In.	600.00
Basket, Quinault, Multicolored, Attached Handle, c.1925, 7 x 10 ½ In.	173.00
Basket, Saboba Reservation, California Mission, Figural, 3 ½ x 13 ¼ In.	4406.00
Basket, Santa Clara, Black Glaze, Pottery, 4 In.	96.00
Basket, Skokomish, Figural, Looped Rim, 5 ½ x 7 In.	940.00
Basket, Southwest, Seed, Coiled, Figures, Ladders, Triangles, Bulbous, Flared Neck, 27 In.	1840.00
Basket, Tlingit, Cover, Woven, Geometric Design, Rattle In, 4 ½ In. ....*illus*	761.00
Basket, Tlingit, Rattle Top, Woven, Overlapping Geometrics, c.1900, 6 x 7 In. ....*illus*	978.00
Basket, Walapai, Wide Base, Twined, Wrapped Rim, Early 1900s, 5 x 7 In.	127.00
Basket, Western Apache, Bowl, Checkered Bands, Star & Triangle Center, c.1900, 4 x 13 In.	2070.00
Basket, Woodlands, Woven, Colored Splint, 1800s, 10 x 10 x 16 In. ....*illus*	264.00
Basket, Woven, Splint, Rectangular, Bentwood Handles, Tan, Pink, Blue Splint, c.1900, 6 x 6 In.	176.00
Belt, Concha, Navajo, Hand Tooled Leather, 10 Silver Medallions, Coral Inset, 1900s, 40 ½ In.	176.00
Belt, Concha, Worked Leather, 10 Silver Medallions, Mother-Of-Pearl, Marked, 1900s, 46 In.	353.00
Belt, Navajo, 5 Conchas, 6 Butterfly Spacers, Silver, Turquoise, c.1950, 36 x 3 In. ....*illus*	863.00
Belt, Navajo, Silver & Turquoise Oval Conchas, Rectangular Buckle, c.1960, 31 ½ In.	230.00
Belt, Navajo, Silver, Scalloped Edges, Starbursts, Conchas, Butterfly Spacers, c.1950, 35 In.	708.00
Belt, Zuni, Inlay, Sterling, 29 In.	165.00
Belt Buckle, Santa Fe, Silver, Turquoise, 2 ¼ In.	135.00
Blanket, Lakota, Saddle, Beaded Panels, Multicolored, Geometric, Fringe, 31 x 78 In.	4444.00
Blanket, Navajo, Chief's, Orange, Red, Blue, Cream, Brown, Wool, c.1950, 68 x 60 In. ....*illus*	2820.00
Blanket, Navajo, Horizontal Bands, Crosses, Black, Gray, Blue, White, c.1900, 53 x 63 In.	5100.00
Blanket, Navajo, Saddle, Serrated Diamond, Indigo Stepped Device, Fringe, 33 x 25 In.	1659.00
Blanket, Navajo, Serrated Diamond, Orange, Brown, Tan, Purple, 33 x 76 In.	900.00
Bolo, Navajo, Silver, Concha Shape, Repousse, 4 ½ x 3 ½ In.	127.00
Bolo, Navajo, Turquoise, Coral Branches, Silver Leaf, Twist Work, 40 & 4 ½ x 3 In.	161.00
Bolo, Zuni, Inlay Silver, Snake Dancer, Blossom Tips, 6 x 2 In.	345.00
Bottle, Makah, Basketry, c.1920, 11 In.	240.00
Bottle, Makah, Basketry, Openwork Bands, Geometric, 10 x 4 In.	259.00
Bottle, Paiute, Basketry, Wide Mouth, Banded Design, 1900s, 8 x 6 In.	345.00
Bottle, Tlingit, Basketry Covered, Square, Cap, Openwork, c.1910, 10 x 4 In. ....*illus*	345.00
Bottle, Tlingit, Basketry, Geometric Figures, c.1875, 7 ½ x 4 x 1 ½ In.	184.00
Bow, Northern Plains, Sinew Backed, 40 In.	587.00
Bow, Pima, Stepping Design, Woven, 3 ¼ x 12 ½ In.	500.00
Bow, Plains, Parfleche & Sinew Sewn Handle, c.1900, 45 In.	240.00
Bowl, Acoma, Black, Red Geometric, L. Elwood, Signed, 8 x 6 In.	201.00
Bowl, Acoma, Pottery, Brown, Black, Geometrics, 9 x 10 ½ In.	125.00
Bowl, Apache, Basketry, 4 Armed Chevron, Geometric Panels, 24 x 4 In.	1800.00
Bowl, Apache, Basketry, Crosses, Animals, 12 In.	1100.00
Bowl, Apache, Basketry, Figural Rim, Geometric Designs, 20th Century, 8 x 3 In. ....*illus*	441.00

Indian, Bag, Bandolier, Woodlands, Flowers, Leaves, Panel, c.1910, 17 x 13 ½ In.
$489.00

Indian, Bag, Cree, Octopus, Beaded, Green, Blue, White, Yellow, Sinew, 1800s, 18 ½ In.
$2350.00

Indian, Bag, Crow, Beaded, Lazy Stitch, Flap, Banded Design, c.1910, 8 ½ x 6 In.
$196.00

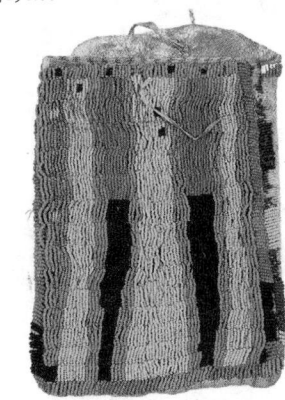

Indian, Bag, Northern Plains,
Hide, Beaded, Fringe, Ties,
c.1940, 12 ½ In.
$180.00

Indian, Basket, Cherokee, River Cane,
Square To Round, Diagonal Bands,
10 ¾ x 10 In.
$546.00

Indian, Basket, Iroquois, Lid, Birch Bark,
Quill Details, 1950s, 2 ½ x 6 ½ In.
$115.00

Indian, Basket, Klamath, Woven,
Serrated Diamonds, Yellow Quill Accents,
c.1910, 4 x 6 In.
$374.00

Bowl, Apache, Figures, 12 ½ In.	770.00
Bowl, Chippewa, Burlwood, Notched, c.1875, 5 x 15 In.	633.00
Bowl, Hopi, Wide, Black On Red, c.1975, 3 ½ x 10 In.	316.00
Bowl, Pima, Woven, Sectioned Pattern, Flared, c.1900, 4 x 15 In.	529.00
Bowl, San Ildefonso, Blackware, Feather, Maria & Santana Martinez, Signed, 5 x 6 ¾ In.	976.00
Bowl, San Ildefonso, Blackware, Silver Geometric, Squat, Maria & Julian Martinez, 3 ¼ x 6 In.	854.00
Bowl, San Ildefonso, Blue Corn, Squat, Black, Signed, 2 x 5 In.	378.00
Bowl, San Ildefonso, Polished Black, Painted Avanyu, 7 x 3 In.	178.00
Bowl, San Ildefonso, Pottery, Blackware, Geometric, Feather Devices, 3 ½ x 4 In.	948.00
Bowl, San Ildefonso, Pottery, Blackware, Maria Poveka, Signed, c.1969, 3 ½ x 11	1840.00
Bowl, San Ildefonso, Pottery, Feather Pattern, Globular, 1 ¾ x 2 ¾ In.	356.00
Bowl, Santa Clara, Black Glaze, Pottery, Southwest Designs, 4 ¼ In.	45.00
Bowl, Santa Clara, Tapered, Carved Stepped Geometric, Margaret Tafoya, Signed, 8 ¾ x 9 ½ In.	2370.00
Bowl, Santo Domingo, Terra-Cotta, Painted, Stylized Animals, Scalloped Rim, 3-Footed, 13 In.	305.00
Bowl, Zia, Effigy, Carved, Frog Figure, Tadpoles, Handle, c.1960, 6 x 7 x 8 In.	460.00
Box, Navajo, Silver, Turquoise Stone On Lid, Red Coral, c.1950, 1 ½ x 4 x 4 In.	1955.00
Box, Northwest Coast, Carved Cedar, 4 Panels, Inlaid Shell, c.1960s, 7 ½ x 11 x 16 In.	575.00
Bracelet, Navajo, Cuff, Sterling, 15 Turquoise Cabochons, c.1950, 6 ½ x 1 ¼ In.	173.00
Bracelet, Navajo, Sterling Silver, Flower, Enclosed, Marked, TP, 7 x 2 ¾ In.	115.00
Bracelet, Southwest, Cuff, Sterling Silver, Turquoise, Coral Mosaic Flowers, 2 ¼ In.	50.00
Bracelet, Zuni, Cluster, Turquoise, Sawtooth Bezel, c.1950, 7 x 3 In. ....*illus*	219.00
Bracelet, Zuni, Petit Point, Turquoise Stones, Flowers, 6 ½ In.	345.00
Buckle, Navajo, Silver, Nevada Turquoise Cabochons, c.1960, 3 ¼ x 2 ½ In.	161.00
Buckle, Navajo, Silver, Turquoise Cabochons, Stamped Edge, 3 x 2 In.	259.00
Buckle, Zuni, Sterling, Birds, Flowers, Coral, Turquoise, Jet, Abalone, c.1975, 4 x 3 In. ....*illus*	138.00
Candelabrum, Pueblo, 2-Light, Black Glaze, Incised Triangles, Dots, Santa Clara Pottery, 4 x 7 In.	118.00
Candleholder, Hopi, Red, Multicolored, Pottery, Pair, c.1930s	184.00
Cane, Eastern Sioux, Deer Foot Handle, Carved, Painted, Flowers, c.1975	546.00
Cane, Ottawa, Chief Figure, Wound Twist Staff, Carved & Burnt, c.1900, 37 In.	230.00
Canoe, Santa Clara, Black Glaze, Pottery, Southwest Designs, 7 ¼ x 2 ¾ In.	90.00
Canteen, Acoma, Multicolored, Parrot, Pottery, 6 x 6 ½ In.	288.00
Canteen, Acoma, Painted, Geometric Pattern, Black & White, 2 Handles, 8 x 7 ¾ In.	732.00
Canteen, Anasazi, Black-On-White, Bulbous, Lugs, Hatched Design, 6 x 6 In.	345.00
Canteen, Anasazi, Black-On-White, Lugs, Curvilinear, 7 ½ x 7 ¼ In.	374.00
Cap, Iroquois, Beaded, Velvet, Cloth Lined, Beaded, Flowers, c.1900, 2 ½ x 7 In.	259.00
Cape, Plateau, Beaded, Flowers, Cowry Shell, Cloth Binding, Girl's, c.1910, 10 x 15 In.	720.00
Case, Awl, Sioux, Beaded, Flap, Trade Beads, Tin Cones, Hide Fringe, 15 In.	184.00
Club, Plains, Stone Head, 28 ½ In.	499.00
Club, Woodlands, Burl, Carved Eagle Head, Painted, 18 x 4 ⅝ In.	230.00
Club, Woodlands, Burl, Carved Handle, 24 x 9 In.	161.00
Collar Tabs, Navajo, Repousse Style, Turquoise Cabochons, c.1940, 4 x ¾ In.	127.00
Cradle, Cheyenne, Cover, Hide, Quilled, Multicolored, 41 ½ In.	3525.00
Cradle, Hupa, Basketry, Open Weave, Conical Sunshade, 32 x 13 x 12 In.	374.00
Cradle, Northern Plains, Beaded, Geometric, Yellow, Blue, White, Red, Green, 1900s, 5 ½ x 2 In. ..*illus*	441.00
Cradle, Plains, Comanche, Covered, Rawhide Mounted, Brass Tack Crosses, c.1900, 15 ½ In.	2370.00
Cradle, Plains, Lakota, Rawhide, Bead, Hawk Bell Danglers, Beaded, Multicolored, 24 ½ In.	8295.00
Cradle, Sioux, Sinew Sewn Beaded, Lazy Stitch, Geometric Design, c.1900, 34 x 11 x 11 In.	4313.00
Cup, Santa Clara Pueblo, Pottery, Blackware, Carved Wind & Cloud Design, Signed, 3 ¼ x 3 In.	108.00
Dance Club, Plains, Gunstock, 24 ½ In.	1997.00
Dance Rasp, Hopi, Wooden, Noisemaker, Bird Effigy, c.1940, 15 x 3 In.	207.00
Doll, Arapaho, Male, Female, Multicolored Geometric, Tanned Hide, 12 ½ In., Pair	5700.00
Doll, Sioux, Hide, Beaded, 15 ¼ In.	1410.00
Doll, Skookum, Brown Braided Hair, Wrapped In Blanket, 13 In.	175.00
Dress, Plateau, Beaded, Hide, Fringe, Flowered Shoulders, Length 43 In., Chest 46 In.	1116.00
Dress, Plateau, Elk Hide, Hand Stitched, Fringe, Late 1900s, 47 x 45 In.	518.00
Dress, Sioux, Buckskin, Lazy Stitch, Beaded, Sinew Sewn Yoke, Fringe, c.1920, 25 x 15 In.	863.00
Dress, Sioux, Wool, Dentalium Shell Yoke, Length 52 In., Chest 56 In.	3407.00
Drum, Plains, Rawhide Faces, 17 & 24 x 29 In., 2 Piece	230.00
Drum, Pueblo, Yellow, Blue, Zigzag, 23 ¾ x 11 ¾ In.	2467.00
Drum, Tarahumera, Painted Hide, Wood Frame, Beater, c.1960s, 3 x 12 In.	52.00
Drum, Tarahumera, Rawhide, Beaters, c.1925, 21 In.	127.00
Earrings, Zuni, Needlepoint, Turquoise, Sterling Wire Style, c.1960s, 1 ⅜ x ½ In.	33.00
Envelope, Plateau, Parfleche, Red, Yellow Green, 27 x 12 In.	1645.00
Fetish, Zuni, Fox, Turquoise, 1 x 1 ½ In.	30.00
Fetish, Zuni, Frog, Coral, 1 ½ In.	60.00
Figurine, Acoma, Owl, Pottery, Black, Red, White, Eva Histia, c.1980, 8 x 9 In.	325.00

Figurine, Cochiti, Human Form, Pottery, c.1960, 8 ½ In.	259.00
Figurine, Dog, Black Glaze, Pottery, Signed Lucaria TaFoya, 3 x 6 ¼ In.	96.00
Gaming Stick, Cree, Bent Wood, Thong Laced Baskets, c.1900, 30 x 2 In., Pair	138.00
Gauntlets, Plains, Buckskin, Fringe, Silk Embroidered Flowers, Men's, Small, c.1950s	138.00
Gauntlets, Plateau, Beaded, Fringed, Multicolored, Tanned Hide, c.1920, 17 x 8 In.	660.00
Gauntlets, Plateau, Buckskin, Pictorial Beaded, Doe, Buck, Bird, 13 ½ x 6 In.	345.00
Halibut Hook, Northwest Coast, Carved, 2 Avian Forms, Cord Binding, 9 ½ In.	1185.00
Hat, Hupa, Basketry, Rhomboid Designs, c.1910, 3 ½ x 7 In. ....*illus*	489.00
Hat, Karok, Basketry, Yellow, Gold, Black Geometric, Red Ground, 3 ⅜ x 7 In.	431.00
Hat, Northwestern California, Basketry, Multicolored, 3 x 6 ¾ In.	881.00
Hat, Tlingit, Basketry, Multicolored, c.1880, 8 ½ In.	863.00
Hat, Yakima, Cornhusk, Geometrics, Cone Shape, Brown Wool, c.1950, 7 x 8 In. ......*illus*	978.00
Jacket, Cree, Hide, Embroidered, Fringe, Length 18 In., Chest 30 In.	705.00
Jacket, Sioux, Hide, Quilled, Figural, Fringe, Length 29 In., Chest 30 In.	4994.00
Jar, Acoma, Pottery, Multicolored, Black, Red, Brown Abstract, Cream Colored Slip, 9 x 11 ½ In.	948.00
Jar, Acoma, Shouldered, Black, Orange Geometric Decoration, 1900s, 6 ¼ x 6 ½ In.	118.00
Jar, Hopi, Cream Slip, Raised Corn Element, c.1970, 3 x 5 In.	662.00
Jar, Hopi, Multicolored, 6 ½ x 7 ½ In.	178.00
Jar, Isleta, Pottery, c.1900, 6 x 8 In.	353.00
Jar, Jemez, Pottery, Redware, Carved, Sgraffito, Avanyu, Feathers, 1900s, 6 x 5 ¾ In.	259.00
Jar, Jemez, Pottery, Redware, Eagle, Sgraffito, Late 1900s, 6 ½ x 4 ½ In.	230.00
Jar, Jemez, Redware, Eagle, Sgraffito, Late 1900s, 6 ½ x 4 ½ In.	230.00
Jar, Jemez, Seed, Pottery, Tanware, Swirling Fluted Melon, 4 ½ x 4 ¾ In.	127.00
Jar, Jemez, Seed, Pottery, Tanware, Swirling Fluted Melon, Late 1900s, 6 ¼ x 7 In.	230.00
Jar, Jemez, Seed, Sgraffito, Corn Harvest Basket, Feathers, Cornstalk, Egg Shape, 1 ¼ x 2 ¼ In.	259.00
Jar, Lid, Pottery, Slip, Bird Designs, Norma Ami, c.1950, 8 x 7 In. ....*illus*	460.00
Jar, Navajo, Silver, Cylindrical, Textured Band, Kokopelli Knob, c.1975, 6 x 3 ¼ In.	518.00
Jar, Pottery, San Ildefonso, Blue Corn, Blackware, Wide Shoulder, Feather, 2 x 2 ⅜ In.	259.00
Jar, San Ildefonso, Black On Black Matte, Maria Martinez, c.1975, 3 x 5 In. ....*illus*	805.00
Jar, San Ildefonso, Corn, Feather Design, Black, Gray, Clay, 6 x 5 In. ....*illus*	667.00
Jar, Santa Clara, Brownware, Raised Back Stepped, c.1978, 13 x 16 ¾ In.	805.00
Jar, Santa Clara, Red On Cream Wave, c.1970, 3 ½ x 4 In.	259.00
Jar, Santa Clara, Seed, Bears, Butterflies, Incised Bear Paw, 2 ⅛ x 2 ½ In.	345.00
Jar, Santa Clara, Seed, Blackware Olla, Turquoise Beads, Lizard, c.1977, 1 x 1 ¼ In.	181.00
Jar, Santa Clara, Seed, Redware, Turquoise Stone, Bird, Feather, Sgraffito, 1 ½ x 1 ⅝ In.	259.00
Jar, Santa Domingo, Storage, Flowers, Black, Signed R. Aguilar, 14 x 14 In.	646.00
Jar, Santo Domingo, Seed, Pottery, Geometric Designs, Baluster, 10 In.	1495.00
Jar, Shipibo, Water, Human Shape, Pottery, 7 x 15 x 11 ½ In.	316.00
Jar, Tarahumera, Water, Carved Wood, 20 x 16 ½ In.	196.00
Jar, Zia, Birds In Flight, 8 ¼ x 9 ¼ In.	705.00
Jar, Zia, Multicolored, Bird & Flower Design, c.1940, 12 ½ x 11 ½ In.	374.00
Jar, Zia, Sgraffito, Mudhead Figures, c.1975, 5 x 6 In.	316.00
Jar, Zia, Shouldered, Flowers, Double Flowing Border, c.1920, 5 ¾ x 6 ½ In.	617.00
Kachina, Hopi, Carved, Painted, Water Serpent & Mudhead, c.1975, 10 x 11 x 5 In.	127.00
Kachina, Hopi, Cottonwood Root, c.1980, 18 In.	230.00
Kachina, Hopi, Cottonwood Root, c.1980, 23 ½ In.	230.00
Kachina, Hopi, Cottonwood Root, c.1980, 24 In.	250.00
Kachina, Hopi, Cottonwood Root, Mountain Sheep Dancer, 12 x 5 In.	374.00
Kachina, Hopi, Cottonwood Root, Ogre Mana, Carved, c.1988, 5 ¾ In.	104.00
Kachina, Hopi, Hand Carved, Painted, Cottonwood Root, Mid 1900s, 16 ½ In.	259.00
Kachina, Hopi, Hand Carved, Painted Water Serpent, 17 In.	184.00
Kachina, Zuni, 1920s, 19 In.	440.00
Kachina, Zuni, Black Echo, Turquoise, Beads, c.1960, 11 In.	288.00
Knife Sheath, Gros Ventre, Beaded, Tanned Hide, Triangular	1920.00
Knife Sheath, Nez Perce, Beaded, 10 In.	2040.00
Knife Sheath, Sioux, Beaded, White, Red, Yellow, Blue Field, Tin Cone, 11 In.	3360.00
Ladle, Northeastern, Wooden, Burled, 5 ¾ In.	940.00
Ladle, Northwest Coast, Carved Horn, Incised Clan Symbols, Haliotis Shell, 15 ½ In.	1896.00
Leggings, Sioux, Wool, Cloth Binding, Blanket Strips, Metallic Beading, Man's, 27 x 2 ¾ In. ...	1080.00
Letter Opener, Navajo, Sterling Silver, Inlay, 9 In.	66.00
Mask, Cherokee, Wood Carved, c.1930, 9 ¾ In.	523.00
Mask, Hopi, Headdress For Melon Kachina, Top Knot, Thong Ties, c.1950, 22 In.	173.00
Mask, Iroquois, Cornhusk, Woven, Protruding Features, c.1910, 15 x 15 x 4 In. ....*illus*	460.00
Mask, Pacific Northwest, Eagle, Wood, Carved, 12 x 9 In.	1416.00
Mask, Pacific Northwest, Frog, Wood, Carved, 12 x 8 In.	1180.00

Indian, Basket, Tlingit, Cover, Woven, Geometric Design, Rattle In, 4 ½ In. $761.00

Indian, Basket, Tlingit, Rattle Top, Woven, Overlapping Geometrics, c.1900, 6 x 7 In. $978.00

Indian, Basket, Woodlands, Woven, Colored Splint, 1800s, 10 x 10 x 16 In. $264.00

Indian, Belt, Navajo, 5 Conchas, 6 Butterfly Spacers, Silver, Turquoise, c.1950, 36 x 3 In. $863.00

Indian, Blanket, Navajo, Chief's, Orange, Red, Blue, Cream, Brown, Wool, c.1950, 68 x 60 In. $2820.00

Indian, Bottle, Tlingit, Basketry Covered, Square, Cap, Openwork, c.1910, 10 x 4 In. $345.00

Indian, Bowl, Apache, Basketry, Figural Rim, Geometric Designs, 20th Century, 8 x 3 In. $441.00

Indian, Bracelet, Zuni, Cluster, Turquoise, Sawtooth Bezel, c.1950, 7 x 3 In. $219.00

Mask, Sioux, Horse, Santee, Quilled Lead, Flower	7500.00
Mat, Cherokee, River Cane, Walnut, Bloodroot, Serrated Diamonds, Emma Garrett, 35 x 30 In.	345.00
Mittens, Cree, Lined, Beaded Flowers, Fur Trim, c.1980s, 13 x 10 ½ In.	431.00
Moccasins, Blackfoot, Beaded, Buckskin, Multicolored, Rawhide Soles, 9 ¼ In.	179.00
Moccasins, Cheyenne, Beaded, Lazy Stitch, Geometric, Sinew Sewn, c.1890, 11 In. ....*illus*	633.00
Moccasins, Chippewa, Buckskin, 4 Hide Cuffs, Beadwork, 1900s	127.00
Moccasins, Crow, Beaded, Cornstalks, Cloth Trim, c.1870, 9 ¾ In.	660.00
Moccasins, Iroquois, Velvet Vamps & Ankle Straps, Beaded, Flowers, c.1875, 10 ½ In.	1035.00
Moccasins, Northeast, Beaded, Cloth, Hide, Flowers, 10 In.	415.00
Moccasins, Northeast, Beaded, Cloth, Hide, Multicolored Geometric Quillwork, 9 ½ In.	4740.00
Moccasins, Northern Plains, Beaded, Blue Ground, Geometric, Multicolored, Child's, 6 In.	59.00
Moccasins, Northern Plains, Metal Cut Beaded, Blue, White Arrows, Red Squares	540.00
Moccasins, Otoe, Hide, Beaded, Multicolored, c.1904	3055.00
Moccasins, Plains, Ceremonial, Beaded, c.1870, 10 In.	1100.00
Moccasins, Plateau, Buckskin, Beaded Flowers, 12 ½ x 9 ½ In.	590.00
Moccasins, Sioux, Beaded, Quilled, Multicolored, White Field, Tin Cone, 10 In.	1140.00
Moccasins, Sioux, Beaded, Red, White, Blue, c.1890, 6 In.	468.00
Moccasins, Sioux, Buckskin, Multicolored Beads, Sinew Sewn, c.1900s, 11 In. ....*illus*	717.00
Moccasins, Sioux, Cloth, Heel Fringe, Hard Soles, White Field, Blue, Red Edges, 10 ½ In.	720.00
Moccasins, Sioux, Sinew Sewn, Lazy Stitch, Beaded, Buffalo Soles, 9 ½ In.	690.00
Mukluks, Athabascan, Caribou, Sealskin, Bead Accents, Beaver Trim, c.1925, 11 In. ....*illus*	69.00
Necklace, Blackfoot, Trade Beads, Bear Claws, Beaver Wrapped, c.1975, 33 In.	575.00
Necklace, Cheyenne Style, Ceremonial, Pony Beads, Carved Wood Finger Bones, 24 In.	374.00
Necklace, Navajo, Leaf Blossom, Silver, Coral, Signed, Late 1900s, 26 ½ In. ....*illus*	353.00
Necklace, Navajo, Shell Beads, Ingot Hammered Crossed, c.1925, 27 In.	259.00
Necklace, Navajo, Silver, Kachina Pendant, Turquoise Stones, Late 1900s, 24 & 5 x 2 In.	575.00
Necklace, Navajo, Squash Blossom, Ferrous Variscite, c.1925, 34 In.	633.00
Necklace, Navajo, Squash Blossom, Naja, Beads, Leaf Stamped, Turquoise, Silver, 28 In.	690.00
Necklace, Navajo, Squash Blossom, Silver, 16 Blossoms, Sand Cast Naja, Fleur-De-Lis, 16 In.	830.00
Necklace, Navajo, Squash Blossom, Silver, Turquoise, Carinated Naja, 16 Blossoms, 1900, 4 In.	948.00
Necklace, Navajo, Squash Blossom, Sterling Pendant, Bear Claws, ½ Dollar Coins, 2 ½ x 3 In.	840.00
Necklace, Navajo, Squash Blossom, Sterling Silver, Turquoise, 3 x 3 x 26 In.	480.00
Necklace, Navajo, Sterling Silver, Disc Bead, Stamped Cones, c.1970, 18 In.	115.00
Necklace, Pueblo, Turquoise, Graduated Nuggets, c.1964, 22 In. ....*illus*	161.00
Necklace, Santo Domingo, 5 Strands, Malachite, Coral, Serpentine Bears, Shell Heshi, 28 In.	141.00
Necklace, Santo Domingo, 6 Strands, Heshi, Turquoise Nugget, Jaclas, c.1890, 30 In.	127.00
Necklace, Zuni, Fetish, Multicolored, 10 Strands, 32 In.	822.00
Necklace, Zuni, Squash Blossom, Silver, Turquoise, Needlepoint Settings, Naja, 5 ¼ In.	1896.00
Olla, Acoma, Black, Red, Lupe Concha, Signed, 9 x 8 In.	259.00
Olla, Acoma, Geometric, Hatched Leaves, Painted, Red, Black, 11 x 11 ½ In. ....*illus*	1410.00
Olla, Acoma, Multicolored, Globular, Tapered Neck, Parrots, Flowers	18700.00
Olla, Acoma, Pottery, Black On White, Spiraled Geometric, 5 x 5 ¾ In.	570.00
Olla, Anasazi, Geometric Design, 10 x 15 ½ In.	2530.00
Olla, Apache, Coiled, Stacked Diamond, Lines, High Shoulder, Late 19th Century, 14 x 12 In.	3437.00
Olla, Apache, Flared Rim, Geometric Human, Animal Figures, 19 x 14 ½ In.	1659.00
Olla, Hopi, Multicolored Geometric Designs, Patty Maho, c.1950, 10 x 7 In. ....*illus*	230.00
Olla, San Luis Potosi, Multicolored, Flowers, Black, White-On-Red, Concave, c.1920, 8 x 12 In.	127.00
Olla, Santa Clara, Multicolored, Polished & Matte Design, c.1925, 13 x 9 ½ In.	374.00
Olla, Tonto, Flared Rim, Red, Black, Cream Abstract Geometric, 10 ¼ x 13 In.	711.00
Olla, Zuni, Deer, Birds, Cream Ground, 1800s, 9 ½ x 14 In.	9400.00
Olla, Zuni, Reddish Brown, 9 x 13 In.	4406.00
Parfleche, Plains, Folded, Rawhide, Pigment Paint, 27 ½ x 17 In.	748.00
Parfleche, Sioux, Rawhide Bonnet Case, Multicolored, Geometric, 1900s, 26 ½ x 11 ½ In.	230.00
Pendant, Hopi, Eagle, Brass, Hallmarked, c.1940, 3 x 2 ½ In.	460.00
Pendant, Navajo, Sterling, Leaf & Coil, Turquoise Flower, c.1970	196.00
Pendant, Zuni Style, Butterfly, Carved Spiny Oyster, Turquoise, 2 ⅝ x 2 ½ In.	431.00
Pillow, Cree, Moose Hide, Cloth Back, Beaded Flowers, Fringe, c.1900, 21 x 20 In.	184.00
Pipe Bag, Blackfoot, Beaded Panels, Trim, Fringe, Late 1900s, 23 x 7 ½ In.	288.00
Pipe Bag, Cheyenne, Beaded, Fringe, Bar Design, 15 ½ In.	4444.00
Pipe Bag, Crow, Buffalo Hide, Multicolored Striped Panel, Fringe, 17 In.	3081.00
Pipe Bag, Plains, Beaded, 4 Fingered, Drops, Morris Bells, c.1920, 18 In.	1540.00
Pipe Bag, Plains, Beaded, Flag, Tepee, Fringe, Quilled Drop, 34 In.	3600.00
Pipe Bag, Sioux, Beaded, Quilled, Multicolored Geometric, Tanned Hide, 30 x 7 In.	1080.00
Pipe Bag, Sioux, Buckskin, 2 Color Quilled Antelope, c.1870s, 17 x 6 In.	1495.00
Pipe, Chippewa, Black Stone Bowl, Lead Inlay, Carved, Wood Stem, 22 x 3 ½ In.	431.00
Pipe, Dakota, Catlinite, Fish Stem, Incised Bird Claw, Grasping Oval Bowl, 6 ¾ In.	652.00

Pipe, Haida, Argillite, Carved Spiral Stylized Waves, 7 In.		610.00
Pipe, Lakota, Effigy, Carved Ash Stem, Catlinite Bowl, Crane Head, 26 ½ In.		4148.00
Pipe, Northwest Coast, Ivory, Hand Carved, Shark, Squid Figures, Abalone, 12 ½ x 4 x 1 In.		431.00
Pipe, Plains, Soapstone, Lead Geometric & Arrow Inlay, 19th Century, 2 ½ x 3 ½ In.		140.00
Pipe, Santee, Horse Head, Carved, Black Stone, 1970s, 4 x 7 ⅝ In.		345.00
Pipe, Sioux, Catlinite Bowl, Pewter Inlay, L Shape, c.1875, 4 ½ x 6 In.		633.00
Pitcher, Acoma, 3-Lobed, Black Design, Cream Slip, Signed, c.1960, 3 x 2 ¾ In.		230.00
Pitcher, Anasazi, Pottery, Black-On-White, Red Mesa, Small Lugs, 6 ½ x 7 ½ In.		460.00
Pitcher, Cotchti, Strap, Animal Head Spout, Painted Abstract Bird, Leaves, 8 In.		474.00
Pitcher, Picuris, Mica Flecked Clay, c.1968, 6 ¾ x 7 ½ In.		196.00
Pitcher, Southwestern, Wide Neck, 2 Spouts, White, Red, Black Geometrics, c.1900, 9 x 6 In.		605.00
Plate, Jemez, Sgraffito Redware, Corn, Stalk, Feather, 4 ½ In.		259.00
Plate, San Ildefonso, Blackware, Feather, c.1950, 14 In.		3163.00
Plate, San Ildefonso, Blackware, Feather, Maria Martinez, Signed, 11 ¾ In.		2074.00
Plate, San Ildefonso, Blackware, Pottery, Mid 1900s, 1 x 5 ¼ In.		575.00
Plate, San Ildefonso, Feather, Mid 1900s, 20 In.		6325.00
Plate, San Ildefonso, Polished, Blackware Design, Signed Marie, S.I.P., 5 In.		330.00
Plate, San Ildefonso, Pottery, Blackware, Feather Pattern, 5 ¾ In.		444.00
Pot, Mata Ortiz, Blackware, Swirl, 2 Bear Heads Handle, Hector Ortega, Mexico, c.1991, 10 x 10 In.		230.00
Pot, Santa Clara, Blackware, Raised Dog Figures, Mid 1900s, 10 x 8 ½ In.		104.00
Pot, Zuni, Olla, Deer In House, Water Bird, Late 19th Century, 6 ½ x 10 In.		2700.00
Pot, Zuni, Turquoise Encrusted, Olla, Carved Fetishes, c.1970, 5 x 7 In.		259.00
Pouch, Plains, Hide, Multicolored Bead Work, Red, Blue Cloth Trim, 10 In.		652.00
Pouch, Plains, Quilled, Red Horse Drops, c.1925, 2 ¾ x 3 ¾ In.		358.00
Purse, Iroquois, Whimsy, Lift Lid, 4 Panel Sides, Flowers, Bird, c.1930, 5 x 5 ¼ x 4 In.		106.00
Purse, Plateau, Coin, Beaded, Buckskin, Drawstring, Flowers, Bird, c.1920, 6 ¾ x 4 In.		173.00
Purse, Sioux, Hide, Beaded, Chain Handle, Clasp Closure, 10 x 7 In.		352.00
Rattle, Acoma, Black On White, Lizard, Pottery, c.1975, 6 x 2 ½ In.		127.00
Rattle, Hopi, Gourd, Wooden Handle, c.1900, 6 ¼ In.		345.00
Rattle, Northern Plains, Dew Claw, 19 In.		587.00
Rattle, Northwest Coast, Carved Raven, Painted Wood, Shaman Holding Frog, 10 ¾ In.		9480.00
Rattle, Peyote, Plains Indians, Gourd Top, Geometric Beadwork Handle, Dyed Feathers, Tassels, 16 In.		960.00
Rattle, Tsimshian, Wooden, 10 ½ x 4 ½ In.		5875.00
Robe, Cheyenne, Box & Border Painted, Buffalo Hide, c.1850, 80 x 62 In.		1045.00
Robe, Sioux, Box & Border Design, Buffalo Hide, c.1870, 72 x 99 In.		6600.00
Robe, Sioux, Buffalo Fur, Feathered Circle Paint, Quilled Rosettes, c.1950, 90 x 84 In.		805.00
Rosary Pouch, Plateau, Beaded Cross Form & Edging, c.1910, 4 In.		360.00
Rug, Navajo, 1939, 28 x 56 In.		600.00
Rug, Navajo, 2 Gray Hills, Weaving, 71 x 48 In.		470.00
Rug, Navajo, 3 Yei Figures, Wool, Multicolored, 63 x 36 In.		374.00
Rug, Navajo, 3rd Phase Chief's Revival, Diamond Pattern, Red, Brown, Cream, c.1915, 51 x 65 In.		3360.00
Rug, Navajo, 4 Corners, Diamonds, Multicolored, 1960s, 35 x 22 In.	*Illus*	69.00
Rug, Navajo, 8 Pointed Stars, Arrows, Red, Black, White, Gray Field, 79 x 46 In.		780.00
Rug, Navajo, Bird, c.1895, 38 x 56 In.		1020.00
Rug, Navajo, Chief, Stepped, Half Diamonds, Horizontal Bands, 53 x 50 In.		2880.00
Rug, Navajo, Concentric Diamonds, Brown, Gray, Orange, White, Red, Wool, c.1930, 29 x 43 In.		206.00
Rug, Navajo, Crystal, Diamonds, Multicolored, 1940s, 77 x 47 In.	*illus*	748.00
Rug, Navajo, Crystal Weaving, 60 x 42 In.		460.00
Rug, Navajo, Diamond, c.1920, 55 x 86 In.		780.00
Rug, Navajo, Diamond, Brown, Cream, c.1910, 44 x 71 In.		660.00
Rug, Navajo, Diamond, Brown, Cream, Tan, Red, Natural, Early 20th Century, 68 x 40 In.		259.00
Rug, Navajo, Diamond, Cream, Brown, Black, c.1920, 42 x 69 In.		570.00
Rug, Navajo, Diamond Stripes, c.1910, 48 x 74 In.		1680.00
Rug, Navajo, Diamonds, Brown, Tan, Cream, c.1890, 44 x 68 In.		780.00
Rug, Navajo, Diamonds, Stripes, c.1900, 55 x 96 In.		7800.00
Rug, Navajo, Feathers, Crosses, 4 Winds, Valero Stars, Fancy Edge, c.1940s, 60 x 100 In.		2588.00
Rug, Navajo, Ganado, Red, Black, Gray, White, c.1920, 59 x 82 In.		1375.00
Rug, Navajo, Geometric, 2 Center Stepped Crosses, Block Corners, White, Black, Turquoise, 40 x 71 In.		382.00
Rug, Navajo, Geometric, Brown, Gray, Cream, c.1900, 40 x 62 In.		720.00
Rug, Navajo, Geometric, Cream, Beige, 18 ¼ x 32 ¼ In.		40.00
Rug, Navajo, Geometric, Flowers, Cream Ground, 36 x 76 In.		840.00
Rug, Navajo, Geometric, Gray Field, c.1940, 48 x 82 In.		720.00
Rug, Navajo, Heather Ground, Stepped Diamond, Fylfots, 40 x 60 In.		431.00
Rug, Navajo, Homespun Wool, Concentric Stepped Crosses, Borders, 48 x 87 In.		1185.00
Rug, Navajo, Hook, Feather, White, Black On Brown, Mid 1900s, 30 x 56 In.		184.00
Rug, Navajo, Hooked, Stepped Diamond, Gray, Brown, White, Red, Black, Gray Ground, 30 x 61 In.		294.00

Indian, Buckle, Zuni, Sterling, Birds, Flowers, Coral, Turquoise, Jet, Abalone, c.1975, 4 x 3 In.
$138.00

Indian, Cradle, Northern Plains, Beaded, Geometric, Yellow, Blue, White, Red, Green, 1900s, 5 ½ x 2 In.
$441.00

Indian, Hat, Hupa, Basketry, Rhomboid Designs, c.1910, 3 ½ x 7 In.
$489.00

Indian, Hat, Yakima, Cornhusk, Geometrics, Cone Shape, Brown Wool, c.1950, 7 x 8 In.
$978.00

Indian, Jar, Lid, Pottery, Slip, Bird Designs, Norma Ami, c.1950, 8 x 7 In.
$460.00

Indian, Jar, San Ildefonso, Black On Black Matte, Maria Martinez, c.1975, 3 x 5 In.
$805.00

Indian, Jar, San Ildefonso, Corn, Feather Design, Black, Gray, Clay, 6 x 5 In.
$667.00

Cleaners

Brooms have been used in America since the Indians showed early settlers how to make them from birch sapling branches and wild grass. The carpet sweeper was invented by Anna and Melville Bissell in 1876.

Rug, Navajo, Multicolored, Geometric, c.1930, 39 x 68 In.	770.00
Rug, Navajo, Multicolored, Serrated, Stepped Diamonds, Arrows, Banded, c.1900, 66 x 38 In.	840.00
Rug, Navajo, Red, Mesa Weave, 57 x 40 In.	940.00
Rug, Navajo, Serrated Design, Cream, Brown, Gray, c.1920, 40 x 66 In.	600.00
Rug, Navajo, Serrated Diamond, c.1920, 48 x 83 In.	960.00
Rug, Navajo, Serrated Diamond Design, Tumbling Log, 60 x 45 In.	403.00
Rug, Navajo, Spider Woman Cross Center, White Serrated Diamond Medallion, 32 x 62 In.	411.00
Rug, Navajo, Spool Figure, X, 64 x 44 In.	460.00
Rug, Navajo, Stepped Central Medallion, Tan, Ivory, Red, Brown, Orange, 1930s, 61 x 38 In.	575.00
Rug, Navajo, Storm, Geometric, Multicolored, Gray Field, c.1940, 98 x 51 In.	1440.00
Rug, Navajo, Storm, Mid 1900s, 41 x 62 In.	489.00
Rug, Navajo, Teec Nos Pos, Geometric Border, Mid 1900s, 76 x 54 In.	1840.00
Rug, Navajo, Transitional Sawtooth, c.1895, 60 x 80 In.	3120.00
Rug, Navajo, Whirling Log, Wool, Cotton, c.1910, 39 x 68 In.	420.00
Rug, Navajo, White Ground, Red Bands, Homespun Wool, 72 x 48 In.	345.00
Rug, Navajo, White Ground, Repeating Diamond, 75 x 48 In.	518.00
Rug, Navajo, Yei, Cornstalk, c.1920, 46 x 56 In.	720.00
Rug, Navajo, Yei, Cream Field, c.1930, 42 x 63 In.	570.00
Rug, Navajo, Yei, Wool, Red, Blue, Green, Yellow, Black, Tan, Cornstalk Borders, 11 Figures, 35 x 62 In.	118.00
Rug, Navajo, Zigzag, Black, Brown, Red, Cream, 20th Century, 56 x 67 In.	1528.00
Rug, Navajo, Zigzag, Red, Brown, Orange, c.1940, 31 x 46 In.	480.00
Rug, Southwest, Teec Nos Pos, Woven, Geometric Designs, 8 Colors, c.1950, 102 x 54 In.	5760.00
Saddle, Visalia, Flower Tooling, Rounded Skirts, High Cantle, 1930s, 15 In.	2520.00
Saddle, Visalia, Flower Tooling, Sterling, Gold Name Plate, Inlaid Quilted, Woman's, 14 In.	2040.00
Sally Bag, Wasco, Soft Weave Basketry, Elk & Goat Figures, c.1875, 7 x 5 In.	1955.00
Sally Bag, Wasco, Woven, Human, Mythical Figures, c.1900, 4 x 4 ½ In.	978.00
Sampler, Navajo, Locomotive, Multicolored Triangles, Board Mounted, Loom, 13 ¼ x 10 ½ In.	3081.00
Sash, Eastern Woodlands, Beaded, American Flags, c.1900, 39 ½ In.	150.00
Sash, Great Lakes, Geometric Design, Stepped Sawtooth Border, 20th Century, 43 x 2 ½ In.	176.00
Scraper, Plains, Elk Horn, Patina, 13 ¼ In.	593.00
Sculpture, Toltec Chac Mol, Obsidian, Semiprecious Stones, c.1950, 4 ½ x 6 ½ x 2 ½ In.	58.00
Sheath, Knife, Sioux, Beaded, Sinew Sewn, Lazy Stitch, Tin Cone, Horsehair, 1900s, 7 x 2 ½ In.	460.00
Sheath, Plains, Beaded, Multicolored, Knife, c.1940, 10 In.	385.00
Sheath, Plains, Beaded, Tin Tinklers, 9 ½ In.	605.00
Shield, Comanche, Dance, c.1880s, 16 In.	540.00
Shirt, Great Lakes, Plaid, Loom Beaded Bib, Shoulders, Wool Tassels, c.1900, 28 In.	356.00
Shirt, Lakota, Muslin, Butterflies, Stars, Fringe	3600.00
Shirt, Northern Plains, Beaded, Quilled Geometric, Bird, Man's	6720.00
Shirt, Seminole, Multicolored, Man's, Early 1900s, 46 x 40 In. ....*illus*	3173.00
Shoes, Chippewa, Woven Grass, Trade Cloth Top, 6 ⅜ In.	144.00
Skirt, Hopi, Sash, White Ground, c.1950s, 22 x 53 & 3 ½ x 120 In.	316.00
Snowshoes, Cree, Beavertail, 2-Stave Construction, c.1900, 26 ½ x 18 ½ In.	685.00
Spoon, Crow, Goat Horn, Carved, 7 x 2 In.	178.00
Spoon, Navajo, Hand Forged, Sterling Silver, Stamped Feather, Arrow, c.1940, 3 ½ In., 6 Piece	239.00
Spoon, Northeastern, Wooden, Burled, 8 ½ In.	587.00
Spoon, Northwest Coast, Carved, Painted, Abstract Avian Head, Red Handle, 9 In.	444.00
Textile, Navajo, Regional, Serrated Diamond Design, White, Gray, Red, Black, 1900s, 45 x 64 In.	499.00
Textile, Navajo, Wool, Serrated Bands, Red, Black, Gray, White, Brown, Tan, 38 x 58 In.	294.00
Tobacco Bag, Crow, Beaded, Flower, 1880s, 5 In.	44.00
Tobacco Bag, Sioux, Beaded, Multicolored Geometric, Quilled Slats, 35 In.	1080.00
Totem Pole, Northwest Coast, Carved, Painted, V-Back, Early 1900s, 28 x 5 In. ....*illus*	4945.00
Totem Pole, Northwest Coast, Eagle, Bear, Raven, Multicolored, c.1930s, 50 In.	1680.00
Totem Pole, Northwest Coast, Haida, Carved Argillite, Flat Back, Bear, Raven, Beaver, 10 ¾ In.	711.00
Totem Pole, Northwest Coast, Haida, Concave Back, Bird, Animal Forms, 9 ¼ In.	504.00
Totem Pole, Northwest Coast, Thunderbird, Hand Carved, Painted Alder Wood, 1900s, 20 In.	219.00
Totem Pole, Northwest Coast, Wood, Carved, 3 Stylized Seated Animals, Human Mask, 23 In.	1067.00
Totem Pole, Pacific Northwest, Carved Wood, 24 x 18 In.	236.00
Tray, Apache, 5-Pointed Blossom, Floating V's, c.1910, 12 In.	540.00
Tray, Pima, Basketry, Coiled Willow, 4 Interlocking Devil's Claw Frets, Early 1900s, 17 x 5 ½ In.	499.00
Tray, Pima, Basketry, Concentric Design, 4 Panels, c.1950, 7 In.	235.00
Tunic, Tlingit, Wool, Shell Buttons, Eagle Design, Length 38 In., Chest 50 In.	1175.00
Vase, Makah, Basketry, Openwork Bands, Birds, 7 x 3 In.	150.00
Vase, San Ildefonso, Blackware, Feather Design, Signed, Maria & Santana Martinez, 5 x 7 In. *.illus*	960.00
Vase, San Ildefonso, Blackware Finish, Signed, Marie, 4 x 4 ½ In.	510.00
Vase, San Ildefonso, Blackware, Geometrics, Low Shoulder, Tapered, Signed Juanita, 3 ½ x 7 In.	120.00
Vase, San Ildefonso, Blackware, Geometrics, Low Shoulder, Tapered, Signed Marie, 6 ½ x 9 In.	520.00

Indian, Mask, Iroquois, Cornhusk, Woven, Protruding Features, c.1910, 15 x 15 x 4 In. $460.00

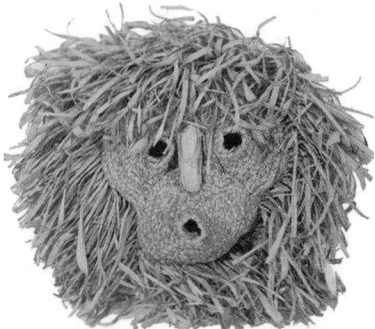

Indian, Moccasins, Cheyenne, Beaded, Lazy Stitch, Geometric, Sinew Sewn, c.1890, 11 In. $633.00

Indian, Moccasins, Sioux, Buckskin, Multicolored Beads, Sinew Sewn, c.1900s, 11 In. $717.00

Indian, Mukluks, Athabascan, Caribou, Sealskin, Bead Accents, Beaver Trim, c.1925, 11 In. $69.00

Indian, Necklace, Navajo, Leaf Blossom, Silver, Coral, Signed, Late 1900s, 26 ½ In. $353.00

Indian, Necklace, Pueblo, Turquoise, Graduated Nuggets, c.1964, 22 In. $161.00

Indian, Olla, Acoma, Geometric, Hatched Leaves, Painted, Red, Black, 11 x 11 ½ In. $1410.00

Indian, Olla, Hopi, Multicolored Geometric Designs, Patty Maho, c.1950, 10 x 7 In. $230.00

Indian, Rug, Navajo, 4 Corners, Diamonds, Multicolored, 1960s, 35 x 22 In. $69.00

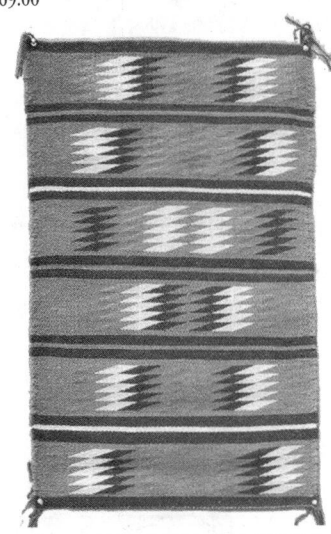

Indian, Rug, Navajo, Crystal, Diamonds, Multicolored, 1940s, 77 x 47 In. $748.00

I

367

Indian, Shirt, Seminole, Multicolored, Man's, Early 1900s, 46 x 40 In.
$3173.00

Indian, Totem Pole, Northwest Coast, Carved, Painted, V-Back, Early 1900s, 28 x 5 In.
$4945.00

Indian, Vase, San Ildefonso, Blackware, Feather Design, Signed, Maria & Santana Martinez, 5 x 7 In.
$960.00

Indian, Vase, San Ildefonso, Blackware, Incised, Camilio Tafoya, Sunflower, 10 ¾ In.
$1035.00

Indian, Vest, Eastern Plains, Buckskin, Beaded, Buttons, Girl's, c.1890, 22 In.
$288.00

Indian, Wall Pocket, Iroquois, Beaded, Fox, Flags, 1929, 8 x 6 In.
$90.00

Indian, Weaving, Navajo, Holy People, Nightway Chant, Wool, c.1950, 72 x 47 In.
$2820.00

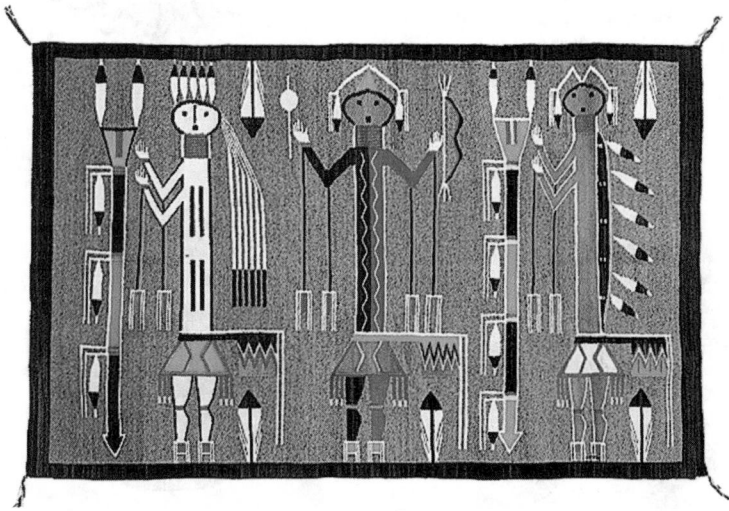

Vase, San Ildefonso, Blackware, Incised, Camilio Tafoya, Sunflower, 10 ¾ In. ....*illus*	1035.00
Vase, San Ildefonso, Bulbous, Polished Finish, Black Leather Designs, Signed Tony & Juanita, 9 x 7 In.	1080.00
Vase, San Ildefonso, Carved Avaya, Shouldered, 6 x 5 ½ In.	144.00
Vase, San Ildefonso, Polished, Blackware, Geometric, Signed Tony & Juanita, 10 x 9 In.	431.00
Vase, San Ildefonso, Round, Polished Carved Avanyu Design, 8 x 5 In.	360.00
Vase, Santa Clara, Black Glossy Glaze, Incised Matte Design, Stella Chavarria, 8 In.	1003.00
Vase, Sioux, Indian On Horseback, Shooting Arrows, Flora Huckfield, 5 ¼ x 5 ¾ In.	854.00
Vase, Wedding, Maricopa, Pottery, Redware, Black Hook, 5 ½ x 4 ½ In.	92.00
Vase, Wedding, Santa Clara, Black Glaze, Pottery, Southwest Serpent, Pottery, 9 In.	158.00
Vest, Blackfoot, Geometric, Multicolored, Blue Field, Cloth Lining, 23 x 20 In.	2040.00
Vest, Cree, Yellow Ocher, Beaded Flowers, Boy's, 12 x 12 In.	374.00
Vest, Eastern Plains, Buckskin, Beaded, Buttons, Girl's, c.1890, 22 In. ....*illus*	288.00
Vest, Plateau, Gold, Wool, Symmetrical Flower, Men's, Medium, Mid 1900s........................	374.00
Vest, Sioux, Beaded, American Flag, Geometric, Tanned Hide, Man's, 22 x 18 In.	6600.00
Vest, Sioux, Hide, Beaded, Flags, Length 18 In., Chest 38 In.	3525.00
Vest, Warm Springs, Beaded, Suede, Mountains, Pine Trees, Eagles, Men's	960.00
Violin, Apache, Carved, Painted, Arizona State Fair, 1947, 16 ½ x 2 ½ In.	259.00
Wall Pocket, Iroquois, Beaded, Fox, Flags, 1929, 8 x 6 In. ....*illus*	90.00
Wand, Dance, Sioux, Double Cow Horns, Beaded Handle, Tin Cone Tinklers, 22 ½ x 12 In.	259.00
War Club, Crow, Beaded, Sinew Sewn Handle, Grooved Red Stone Head, Late 1800s, 22 x 3 ½ In.	403.00
War Club, Plains, Rawhide Wrapped, Double Point Stone Head, c.1925, 30 x 5 In.	316.00
War Club, Sioux, Rawhide Wrapped, Double Point Stone Head, Beaded, c.1925, 23 x 6 In.	173.00
War Club, Wood, Curved, Knob End, 20 In.	1298.00
Weaving, Navajo, 5-Figure Yeibeichei, Wool, c.1960, 50 x 32 In.	403.00
Weaving, Navajo, Germantown, Floating Serrated Diamonds, Zigzag Bands, 48 x 32 ½ In.	652.00
Weaving, Navajo, Germantown, Serrated Diamonds, Red Ground, 55 x 38 In.	1541.00
Weaving, Navajo, Germantown, Serrated Diamonds, Zigzag Border, 35 ½ x 26 In.	711.00
Weaving, Navajo, Germantown, Stepped, Serrated Devices, Red Ground, 30 ½ x 20 ½ In.	1126.00
Weaving, Navajo, Holy People, Nightway Chant, Wool, c.1950, 72 x 47 In. ....*illus*	2820.00
Weaving, Navajo, Meandering Pattern, Variegated Red Ground, Indigo, 47 x 59 In.	5036.00
Weaving, Navajo, Meandering Stepped Borders, Indigo Blue, Cream Ground, 61 x 43 In.	711.00
Weaving, Navajo, Mustard Center, Serrated Borders, Black, Red, White, Mauve, 26 x 49 In., Pair.	176.00
Weaving, Navajo, Pictorial, Wool, Arrows, Feathers, Serrated Diamonds, White, Gray, 27 x 45 In. .	176.00
Weaving, Navajo, Serrated Lattice, Stripe, Cross Devices, Variegated Red Ground, 72 x 49 In. .	3081.00
Weaving, Navajo, Wool, Central Rectangle, Dancers, Fret Pattern Frame, Gray Ground, 64 x 48 In.	1067.00
Weaving, Navajo, Wool, Serrated Diamonds, Crosses, Brown, Black, Red, 39 x 61 In.	235.00
Weaving, Navajo, Wool, Serrated Diamonds, Stepped Pattern, Sawtooth Border, 85 x 62 ½ In. ..	356.00
Weaving, Navajo, Yei, Pictorial, 5 Figures, Holding Feathers, Arrows, Rainbow God, 35 x 45 In.	411.00
Weaving, Navajo, Zigzag Pattern, Black, White, Brown, Mustard Yellow, 36 x 52 In.	82.00
Whimsy, Iroquois, Bird, Hanging, Beadwork, 4 Strawberry Pincushion, 8 x 4 In.	59.00
Whimsy, Iroquois, Picture Frame, Beaded, Scalloped Top, Green Beaver, Flowers, 10 x 7 In. ...	176.00

INDIAN TREE is a china pattern that was popular during the last half of the nineteenth century. It was copied from earlier Indian textile patterns that were very similar. The pattern includes the crooked branch of a tree and a partial landscape with exotic flowers and leaves. Green, Blue, pink, and orange were the favored colors used in the design.

Bowl, Coral, Gilt, Coalport, 4 ½ x 10 In.	205.00
Cup, Johnson Brothers	5.00
Plate, Tab Handle, Salem China, 11 In.	25.00

INKSTANDS were made to be placed on a desk. They held some type of container for ink, and possibly a sander, a pen tray, a pen, a holder for pounce, and even a candle to melt the sealing wax. Inkstands date to the eighteenth century and have been made of silver, copper, ceramics, and glass. Additional inkstands may be found in these and other related categories.

Boulle Marquetry, 2 Glass Bottles, Late 19th Century, 4 x 14 ¼ In.	1342.00
Brass, Gilt Lacquered, Silvered Nickel, Mandarin, Canopy, Napoleon III, 9 ½ x 11 x 6 In.	1680.00
Bronze, 1st Empire, Brass Mounted Verde Antico Marble, Swan, Serpent, 6 x 10 In. ....*illus*	600.00
Calamander Wood, Brass Mounted, Cut Glass Bottles, Taperstick, Late 1800s, 6 ¾ x 15 In. ...	1220.00
George III, 3 Cut Glass Fitted Bottles, Silver Mounted, William Pitts, c.1785, 8 In.	549.00
Georgian Style, Pierced Gallery, Cut Glass Bottles, c.1887, 9 ¼ In.	793.00
Horse Hoof, Pewter, Horseshoe, Elf At Anvil, 2 Glass Wells, 1800s, 6 ½ In. ....*illus*	354.00
Ivory, Brass Mounted, Rosewood, Portable, Mid 19th Century, 6 ¼ x 10 In.	519.00
Lindenwood, Carved, Boar's Head, Oak Leaves, Acorns, Schwarzwald, 5 ¼ x 7 x 9 In.	960.00
Silver, 4 Paw Supports, Gadroon Border, Chased Flowers, 3 Bottles, George III, c.1810.............	2875.00
Silver, Inkwell, Sander, Box, Cut Corners, Lid, Boat Shape, Sheffield, c.1820, 3 x 9 x 3 ½ In. ...	288.00

Inkstand, Bronze, 1st Empire, Brass Mounted Verde Antico Marble, Swan, Serpent, 6 x 10 In. $600.00

Inkstand, Horse Hoof, Pewter, Horseshoe, Elf At Anvil, 2 Glass Wells, 1800s, 6 ½ In. $354.00

Inkstand, Tortoiseshell, Mother-Of-Pearl Inlay, Cut Glass Square Jar, Bone Feet, c.1900, 3 x 4 In. $480.00

Silver, Mounted Glass Bottles, Edward Edwards, c.1842, 8 ¾ In.	305.00
Silver Plate, Highlander, Kneeling, Oval, Rococo Scrolls, Victorian, 6 ¾ x 12 ¼ x 7 ¼ In.	540.00
Tortoiseshell, Mother-Of-Pearl Inlay, Cut Glass Square Jar, Bone Feet, c.1900, 3 x 4 In. *illus*	480.00
Tray, Round, Mounted Well, 2 Rings, Sand Sprinkler, Lidded Box, Pewter, England, 1700s, 6 In.	94.00
Wood, Bear, Black Forest, 7 ½ In.	595.00

INKWELLS, of course, held ink. Ready-made ink was first made about 1836 and was sold in bottles. The desk inkwell had a narrow hole so the pen would not slip inside. Inkwells were made of many materials, such as pottery, glass, pewter, and silver. Look in these categories for more listings of inkwells.

Art Deco, Brass, Crystal Ink Bottles, Monogram, 18 x 11 In.	201.00
Brass, Dolphin & Wave, Hinged Lid, 6 ½ x 8 ¼ In.	90.00
Brass, Eagle, Swivel Lid, 3 x 8 ¾ In.	60.00
Brass, Glass, Horse Hoof, LaBelle, Pen Holder, 8 In.	59.00
Brass, Pewter, Patina, Grotesque Head, Movable Eyes & Tongue, Glass Insert, 1900s, 3 x 5 In.	468.00
Brass, Silver Plate, Traveling, Footed, Screw Top, c.1770, 1 ½ x 1 ½ In.	177.00
Bronze, Boy, Dog, Pump, Grate, Broom Bottom, Pen Holder, Hinged Lid, c.1890, 6 ½ x 4 x 6 In.	220.00
Bronze, Enameled Design, 3 x 5 ½ In.	240.00
Bronze, Lion's Head, Glass Eyes, Scroll Tray, Hinged Lid, 4 ¼ In.	125.00
Bronze, Silver, Phoenix, Well In Basket, Oval Marble Base, L. Carvin, 18 x 11 In.	1588.00
Cast Brass, Ram's Head, Lift Top, 4 ½ x 6 In.	345.00
Cast Iron, Double Snail, Revolves, Glass, Pen Rack, Late 1800s, 6 ½ In.	121.00
Cast Iron, Snail, Glass, Sled Form Base, Pen Rack, Late 1800s, 4 ½ In.	96.00
Cast Metal, Devil, Frog Finial, Snail, Hinged, c.1875, 4 ¼ x 4 ⅝ x 4 ¼ In.	468.00
Cast Metal, Lion, Victorian, c.1900, 10 In.	150.00
Cast Metal, Winged Dragon, Glass, Marked, 6 ½ x 7 x 6 In.	308.00
Copper, Embossed, Shell, Hinged, Elizabeth Burton, 3 ½ x 7 In. Square	1830.00
Coventry Glass Works, Olive Green, Cylindrical, Disc Mouth, Pontil, 3 Mold, c.1830, 1 ¾ In.	179.00
Cranberry Glass, Iridescent, Multicolored, Metal Water Lilies, 2 ½ x 3 ¼ In.	374.00
Cut Glass, Geometric Diamond, Aurora Silver Plate Stand, 3 ½ In.	150.00
Glass, Amber, Squat, 24 Ribs, Swirled To Right, Sheared Mouth, Footed, c.1830, 1 ½ In.	364.00
Glass Blown, Olive Amber Keene, c.1830, 1 ½ x 2 ¼ In.	118.00
Glass, Cast Iron Base, Double Beehive, Copper Finish, Pen Rack, Late 1800s, 5 ¾ In.	60.00
Glass, Cylindrical, 2-Piece Mold, Olive Yellow, 7 Rings, Disc Mouth, Pontil, 1 ½ x 2 ⅜ In.	2070.00
Glass, Cylindrical, Sapphire Blue, 3-Piece Mold, Disc Mouth, Pontil, 1 ⅞ x 2 ⅛ In.	6325.00
Glass, Dark Olive, Blown 3-Mold, Diamond Pattern, 19th Century, 2 x 2 ¾ In.	165.00
Glass, Gilt Metal Collar, Hinged Lid, Iridescent Rose, Loetz, 3 ½ x 2 ½ In. *illus*	115.00
Glass, Iron Base, Double Snail, Pen Rack, Late 19th Century, 6 ½ In.	113.00
Glass, Iron Base, Snail, Revolves, Copper Finish, Pen Rack, Late 19th Century, 6 ¼ In.	55.00
Glass, Pitkin Type, 36 Ribs, Swirled To Right, Olive Yellow, 1 ⅞ x 2 ¾ In.	1955.00
Glass, Purple Iridescent, Threading, Pyramid Shape, Wilhelm Kralik, 3 ½ In.	230.00
Glass, Red Iridescent, Wave Pattern, Squat, Bohemia, 5 In.	345.00
Glass, Swirl Design, Iron Base, Pen Holder, 3 Fonts, Late 1800s, 10 ¾ In.	55.00
Kayserzinn, Butterfly Finial, Lobed Design, Bees, Lily Pads, Pewter, c.1910, 7 ½ x 3 ½ In.	295.00
Lead Alloy, Alligator, Tree Stump, 4 x 2 In.	234.00
Lead Alloy, Boy Scout By Tree Stump, 4 In.	205.00
Lead Alloy, Clown Head, Tin, 4 ½ In.	59.00
Lead Alloy, Elephant, Tin Well, Insert, Germany, 4 In.	59.00
Lead Alloy, Frog Playing Mandolin, Tree Trunk, 5 ½ x 2 In.	263.00
Liberty & Co., Hammered Finish, Glass Insert, Tudric, c.1905, 4 ⅜ x 3 In.	255.00
Lime Wood, Black Forest, Partridge, Oak Leaves, Glass Pots, c.1860, 4 x 12 x 8 In.	745.00
Marble, Patinated Metal, Dragon, 8 x 16 x 5 In.	374.00
Marble, Round, Hinged Brass Top, Key Wind Watch, 3 ⅛ x 4 In.	46.00
Metal, Boat, Lid, 1870	336.00
Metal, Owl, Spread Wings, White Head, Gold Feathered Body, Hinged Lid, 3 ⅞ x 9 ⅜ In.	185.00
Metal, Travel Case, Hinged, Alligator, 19th Century, 1 ¾ x 1 ½ In.	201.00
Nickel Plated, Glass, Eagle, Perched, Early 1900s, 7 ½ In.	68.00
Pewter, Art Nouveau, Woman, Flowing Hair, Hinged Lid, 6 ½ In.	48.00
Pitkin Type, 28 Ribs, Olive Yellow, Tooled Mouth, Melon Shape, 1 ⅝ x 2 ⅞ In.	7475.00
Porcelain, Bird On Nest, Snake, Chicks, Gilt, Staffordshire, c.1880, 2 ½ x 2 ¾ In.	40.00
Porcelain, Dog, Whippet, Oval Base, Staffordshire, 1800s, 7 x 7 In., Pair	294.00
Porcelain, Flowers, Lowestoft, c.1800, 2 ⅞ In.	9600.00
Porcelain, Pheasant With Nest, Staffordshire, c.1870, 5 ½ x 3 ⅜ In.	92.00
Porcelain, Phrenology Head, Bennington Pottery, Mark, F. Bridges, 5 ½ In.	1200.00
Porcelain, Punch, Seated In Chair, Painted, 4 ⅜ x 2 ¾ In.	140.00
Porcelain, Quill Holder, Hunter With Gun & Dog, Gilt, Staffordshire, c.1920, 5 ½ x 3 ⅜ In.	92.00

Porcelain, Quill Holder, Man, Seated On Rock, Staffordshire, c.1910, 4 ½ x 3 ¼ In.		65.00
Porcelain, Quill Holder, Swan, Staffordshire, c.1890, 4 ¼ x 3 ½ In.		90.00
Redware, Book Shape, 2 Pen Receivers, Incised WR, 1700s, 2 x 3 ¾ In.	*illus*	288.00
Silver Plate, Bicycle, Glass Inkwell		275.00
Silver Plate, Chased, Flowers, Leaves, Bulbous Cover, England, 19th Century, 4 ½ x 5 In.		70.00
Silver Plate, Devil With Batwings, Horns, Snake On Chest, c.1880, 11 In.		1872.00
Silver Plate, Horseshoe, Glass Insert, Early 20th Century, 3 x 5 In.		420.00
Silver Plate, Urn Shape Center Compartment, Candleholder Top, Cut Glass Pots, 5 ½ x 8 ½ In.		288.00
Soapstone, Songbirds, Prunus, Openwork, Carved, 4 In.		40.00
Spelter, c.1898, 10 x 10 ½ In.		138.00
Spelter, Glass, Building, Paris Le Sacre Coeur, Reverse Painted, Copper Finish, 1910, 8 In.		79.00
Spelter, Joan Of Arc, Holding Banner, Helmet, 2 Hinged Inkwells, Late 1800s, 15 ½ In.		210.00
Spode, Double, Blue, Gilt, Impressed Marks, 11 In.		55.00
White Metal, Camel, Resting, Saddle, Painted, Hinged Lid, 3 ¾ x 5 ¾ In.		36.00
Wood, Glass, Cabin, Tree, Double, Carved, Penholder, Black Forest, 4 ½ In.		90.00
Wood, Owl, Carved, Glass Eyes, Porcelain Pot, 4 x 2 In.		133.00
Wood, Puss In Boots, Carved, Glass Eyes, England, 19th Century, 5 x 6 x 3 ¾ In.	*illus*	177.00

INSULATORS of glass or pottery have been made for use on telegraph or telephone poles since 1844. Thousands of different styles of insulators have been made. Most common are those of clear or aqua glass; most desirable are the threadless types made from 1850 to 1870.

AM Insulator Co., Continuous Drip 134, Aqua	448.00
AM Insulator Co., Continuous Drip 145, Olive Yellow	1512.00
Brookfield No. 450, Side Wire Groove, Single Petticoat, Embossed, Yellow Green	310.00
Cable, Continuous Drip 259, Green, Amber Swirls	560.00
Cal. Electric Side Bracket, Gable Type, Cutout, 13 ½ In.	45.00 to 67.00
Cal. Electric Works, Continuous Drip, No. 120, Mold Line Over Dome, Amethyst.	504.00
Cal. Electric Works, Continuous Drip, No. 130, 3-Piece Mold, Aqua	476.00
Cal. Electric Works, Continuous Drip, No. 130, Mold Line Over Dome, Patent, Aqua	784.00
Cal. Electric Works, Continuous Drip, No. 130, Patent, Aqua, Olive Swirls, c.1870-80	6160.00
Cal. Electric Works, Continuous Drip, No. 130, Patent, Ice Blue Aqua, c.1870-80	756.00
Cal. Electric Works, Continuous Drip, No. 161, A On Dome, Drip Points, Smoky Amethyst	2464.00
Cal. Electric Works, Continuous Drip, No. 260, Pinch Groove Mold, Green Aqua	644.00
Canada, No. 010, Ice Aqua	1.00
C.D. & P.T. Co., Continuous Drip 121, Yellow Green	280.00
C.N.R., Brown Porcelain, Brown Glaze	392.00
Corning Pyrex, Made In U.S.A., 271, Carnival Glass	220.00
Diamond P, No. 010, Green	896.00
Diamond P, No. 010, Yellow, Green Vaseline	5040.00
Dominion, No. 40, Light Peach	1.00
E.C. & M. Co., Aqua, Straight Skirt	200.00
E.C. & M. Co., Continuous Drip 123, Blue Aqua, c.1878-80, 4 ¼ In.	588.00
E.C. & M. Co., Continuous Drip 123, Cobalt Blue, Round Dome, Flared Skirt, c.1873-75	6160.00
E.C. & M. Co., Continuous Drip 123, Dark Aqua, c.1873-75	1120.00
E.C. & M. Co., Continuous Drip 123, Dark Green, Aqua, c.1875-80, 4 ¾ In.	1232.00
E.C. & M. Co., Continuous Drip 123, Ink, Sapphire Blue, c.1875-78, 4 ⅛ In.	2912.00
E.C. & M. Co., Continuous Drip 123, Light Medium Aqua, c.1873-75, 4 ⅜ In.	1512.00
E.C. & M. Co., Continuous Drip 123, Olive Amber, c.1878-80, 4 In.	3136.00
E.C. & M. Co., Continuous Drip 123, Sage Green, c.1878-80, 3 ⅞ In.	2464.00
E.C. & M. Co. S.F., Continuous Drip 123, H-Mold, Aqua	280.00
E.C. & M. Co., Side Bracket, Broom Handle Type, 11 ½ In.	179.00
Fred M. Locke Victor, Tan Porcelain	134.00
Fred M. Locke Victor, U259, White, Porcelain, Flared Skirt, Pony Style	258.00
Gayner, No. 20, Blue Aqua	1.00
Hemingray, Amber Swirls	213.00
Hemingray, Blue	179.00
Hemingray, Continous Drip 162, Brilliant Orange Amber	448.00
Hemingray, Green, Amber Swirls	235.00
Hemingray, No. 9, Medium Amethyst	300.00
Hemingray, No. 16, Emerald Green	25.00
Hemingray, No. 16, Olive Green	150.00
Hemingray, No. 20, Carnival	25.00
H.G. Co., Continuous Drip, No. 145, Beehive, I Petticoat, Medium Amber	532.00
Knowles, No. 020, Cable, Green, Amber	190.00
Lynchburg, No. 90, Aqua	1.00
Lynchburg, No. 90, Green, Straw Tint	1.00

Inkwell, Gilt Metal Collar, Hinged Lid, Iridescent Rose, Loetz, 3 ½ x 2 ½ In. $115.00

Inkwell, Redware, Book Shape, 2 Pen Receivers, Incised WR, 1700s, 2 x 3 ¾ In. $288.00

Inkwell, Wood, Puss In Boots, Carved, Glass Eyes, England, 19th Century, 5 x 6 x 3 ¾ In. $177.00

Garage Sale Aftermath
We just heard of an after "garage sale" sale. If it is impossible to give the leftovers to charity, list the "after sale" on Craigslist or other free ad sources. Offer everything free. The "buyers" will cart off your unwanted items and your front lawn will be empty. We visited a ski resort where the town has a drop-off site for anything usable and unwanted. Just take what you need.

Iron, Card Holder, Pekinese, Hubley, 1 ⅜ In.
$146.00

Hatchet Souvenirs

An iron hatchet with names and dates was a popular souvenir in the late nineteenth century. Hatchets include one, 13 inches long, with President Washington's profile and the words "Washington Inaugurated President of the U.S. Apr. 30, 1789." It was probably issued in 1889 for the 100th anniversary of his inauguration. Another hatchet has Carrie Nation's profile and the relief inscription "All Nations Welcome But Carrie." It was painted blue with gold lettering and had two cast attached hangers at the top. Another had the profile of an Indian and the letters "T.O.T.E. [Totem of the Eagle]," 1909. It honored the Order of Red Men fraternal organization. The Foresters of America made an iron hatchet that had an embossed stag in a wreath on the blade and the words "Liberty, Unity, Benevolence, and Concord" on the handle.

McLaughlin, No. 16, Citrine	224.00
McLaughlin, No. 16, Emerald Green	20.00
McLaughlin, No. 16, Olive Black	20.00
Mt. Washington, Ram's Horn, Cobalt Blue	532.00
Mulford & Biddle, Continuous Drip 735, Aqua, 1866-68	476.00
National, Continuous Drip 110, Blue Aqua, Embossed Base	1344.00
Oakman MFG Co., Continuous Drip 140, Aqua	504.00
Otis Patent 1851, Copper Top, Prongs, Iron Base Bracket, Amethyst	90.00
Patent, No. 20, Pleated & Concave Skirt, Aqua	5.00
Patent, No. 20, Pleated Skirt, Leaner	2.00
Pond Style, Wooden, Zinc Cap, Wire Groove	700.00
San Francisco, Round Top, Lignum Vitae Wood	532.00
So. Ex. Co., No. 010, Embossing, Aqua	7280.00
Star, 5-Pointed	28.00
Star, No. 10, Bright Blue	2.00
Tillotson & Co., No. 020, Light Aqua, 1864-65	812.00
U-394, Brown, Porcelain	308.00
U-970, Porcelain, Threadless Egg, Tan	588.00
U-981, Elliot Pilgrim Hat, White, Porcelain	364.00
W.E. Mfg. Co., Continuous Drip 126.4, Pat. Dec. 19, 1871, Concave Mold, Blue	952.00
W.F.G., No. 10, Steel Blue, Graphite Steam	1.00
Withycombe, Grooved, Light Amethyst	420.00

IRISH BELLEEK, *see Belleek category.*

IRON is a metal that has been used by man since prehistoric times. It is a popular metal for tools and decorative items like doorstops that need as much weight as possible. Items are listed here or under other appropriate headings, such as Bookends, Doorstop, Kitchen, Match Holder, or Tool. The tool that is used for ironing clothes, an iron, is listed in the Kitchen category under Iron and Sadiron.

Ashtray, Indian, Holding Tray, Matchbox Holder, Nickel Plated, 35 In.	1957.00
Ashtray, Marked T.B. Woods Sons Co., 1975	35.00
Bird Spit, Wrought, 2 Prong Fork, Bell Shape Frame, Brass Finial, Tripod Base, Penny Feet, 27 ¾ In.	509.00
Blotter, Indian Shape, Cast, Painted, 4 ¾ In.	475.00
Book Press, Cast, 13 ½ x 19 ½ x 11 ½ In.	311.00
Bootjack, Beetle, Cast, Painted, 10 ¾ In.	25.00
Bootjack, Gun Shape, Folding, Cast, American Bulldog, 8 ¼ In.	90.00
Candlesnuffer, Scissor Form, Heart Shape Handle, 6 ¾ In.	44.00
Candlestand, Adjustable Candle Arm, Penny Feet, c.1800, 51 In.	761.00
Candlestand, Tripod Feet, 1700s, 47 x 15 In.	1495.00
Cannon, Painted, Impressed, Walter R. Flesh, 1890, 15 ½ x 33 In.	950.00
Card Holder, Pekinese, Hubley, 1 ⅜ In. ....*illus*	146.00
Cheese Curd Breaker, Hand Forged, Post Civil War	189.00
Coal Heater, Life Cover, Painted, Pierced, Scrolling Leaf, Flowers, Victorian, 29 x 10 x 10 In.	96.00
Cuspidor, Top Hat Shape, Painted Silver, Late 19th Century, 7 x 10 ½ In.	206.00
Cuspidor, Turtle, Head Raises Lid, c.1890, 6 x 12 In.	688.00
Eagle & Prey, Spread Winged Talons Open, Cast, 55 ½ In.	2056.00
Eagle, Pilot House, Spread Winged, Sphere Perch, 1800s, 8 x 14 ½ In.	176.00
Figure, Dog, Boston Terrier, Standing, Head Turned, Black & White Paint, Red Bow, 10 x 9 In.	25.00
Figure, Dog, Cocker Spaniel, Painted, Rust Colored, 3 ½ In.	95.00
Figure, Dog, Hound, Seated, Dead Fowl On Base, Black Paint, 1900s, 37 x 37 In., Pair	2185.00
Figure, Drunk Hanging On Bourbon St. Signpost, Paint, 4 In.	60.00
Figure, Drunk Man Hanging On Palm Tree, Paint, 4 In.	70.00
Figure, Dutch Boy & Girl, Kissing, 3 & 3 ¼ In., Pair	35.00
Figure, Dutch Cleanser Girl, Chasing Dirt, Cam Action, Hubley, 1932, 8 ⅝ In.	6900.00
Figure, Gamecock, Cast, 25 In.	104.00
Figure, Imperial Foo Lion, Seated, Foot On Ball, 19th Century, 10 ½ x 12 In., Pair	540.00
Figure, Striding Bull, Patinated, Cast, 41 x 65 ½ x 21 In.	4406.00
Fly Fan, Cast, Brown, Gold Paint, Fabric Paddles, Key Operated, c.1880, 30 x 50 In.	3100.00
Griddle, Hanging, Wrought, Support Arm, Circular Flat Griddle, Hook, 18th Century, 14 ½ x 11 In.	192.00
Gridiron, Riveted, 4 Legs, Flat Handle, Scrolled Rattail End, 2 ¾ x 17 x 8 In.	22.00
Herb Grinder, Boat Form, Grinding Wheel, Wood Handles, Raised Legs, 24 ½ In.	118.00
Hook, Mermaid Shape, Mounting Screw, Cast, c.1890, 4 x 7 In.	125.00
Horse Bit, Linked Snaffle, Double Interlocking Side Rings, Twisted Links, c.1800	185.00
Kettle, Cast, Copper Spigot, Bail Handle, Hook, Marked, 3 Gal.	35.00
Kettle, Round, Textured, Bud Finial, Cast, Loop Handle, Signed, Ryobunsai-Zukuri, 8 In.	143.00

Kettle, Sugar, Flared Lip, Deep Body, 19th Century, 17 x 49 In.	1175.00
Letter Opener, Indian Shape, Cast, Painted, 10 In.	350.00
Letter Rack, Owl, Pine Branches, Pinecones, Cast, Art Nouveau, 5 x 7 In.	58.00
Meat Rack, Cast, 90 ¾ In.	660.00
Ornament, Scroll, Wall, 2 Birds, Flowers, Urn, Black Paint, Cast, c.1900, 13 x 32 In.	147.00
Paperweight, Dog, Wolfhound, Reclining, Beige, White, Hubley, No. 466, 2 ½ In.	140.00
Paperweight, Duck, Dressed As Man, Atta Boy, Dark Colors, Hubley, 4 ¾ In.	395.00 to 410.00
Paperweight, Duck, The Flapper, Yellow, Grace Rayner, Hubley, 4 In.	310.00 to 322.00
Paperweight, Duck, Yellow, Orange Beak, Blue Base, 4 ¾ In.	225.00
Paperweight, Duckling, Yellow, Orange, Black Trim, Hubley, 1920s, 4 ¾ In.	335.00
Paperweight, Football Player, Kicking, Red, Brown, White, Black, Hubley, No. 133, 3 ⅜ x 1 ⅜ In.	340.00
Paperweight, Fox, Seated, Brown, White, Black, Hubley, No. 139, 2 ⅛ x 1 ⅜ In.	340.00
Paperweight, Hanging Drunk, 5 In.	50.00
Paperweight, Kitten, With Pink Bow, Hubley, 3 In. ....*illus*	146.00
Paperweight, Maine Lobster, Painted, 6 In.	575.00
Paperweight, Ski Jumper, Red, Brown, Blue, White, Hubley, No. 130, 2 ⅜ x 2 ¾ In.	250.00
Paperweight, Ski Jumper, Red, White, Blue, Hubley, 2 x 3 In.	263.00
Paperweight, Skier Girl, Standing, White, Blue, Red, Hubley, No. 132, 3 x 3 ¼ In.	175.00
Paperweight, Southern Belle, Painted, Blue & Yellow Dress, Red Hair, Bonnet, 4 ¼ In.	110.00
Placecard Holder, Dog, Pekinese, Brown, Black, Cast, Hubley	86.00
Placecard Holder, Frog, Green, Cast, Hubley	310.00
Placecard Holder, Pig, Holding Stick, Red, White, Blue, Cast, Hubley	925.00
Plaque, Roman Scenes, Horse On Parade, People, Cupid, Oval, Copper Finish, 1820s, 22 x 30 In.	495.00
Rack, Game, 4 Birds On Rail, Forged, 15 x 24 In.	468.00
Roaster, Coffee Bean, Fireplace, Wood Handle, Cylinder, Slide Lid, 45 ½ In.	62.00
Safe, Combination, Syracuse, Wheels, 26 x 16 x 18 In.	880.00
Safe, Hobnails, Wheels, Key, 32 x 22 x 19 ½ In.	2920.00
Safe, Wheels, Warth-Baum, 26 x 18 x 16 In.	550.00
Shield Buckler, Rolled Edge, Embossed Petals, Leather Grips, c.1775, 11 ⅜ In.	550.00
Shoe Scraper, Shoeshine Boy, 13 In.	100.00
Stand, Votive, Lion's Head Corners, 4 Rows Of Candleholder Cups, 40 Cranberry Glasses, 1920 .	1150.00
Steps, Carriage, Jockey Handhold, Cast, 19th Century, 54 ½ In.	1500.00
Strong Box, Dovetailed, Multicolored Flowers, c.1784, 15 x 15 x 8 In.	767.00
Teakettle, Tiller, Gooseneck Spout, Bail Swing Handle, Loop Hook, Round, 14 ¼ In.	468.00
Tie Rack, Black, Man, Leaves, 5 Hooks, Marked, 1952, 6 ¾ x 13 In.	85.00
Windmill Weight, Buffalo, 20th Century, 10 ¼ In. ....*illus*	205.00
Windmill Weight, Crescent Moon	170.00
Windmill Weight, Rooster, Stamped, Hummer, 9 x 9 ¼ In.	322.00
Windmill Weight, Rooster, White, Red, 20th Century, 20 In.	135.00

IRONSTONE china was first made in 1813. It gained its greatest popularity during the mid-nineteenth century. The heavy, durable, off-white pottery was made in white or was decorated with any of hundreds of patterns. Much flow blue pottery was made of ironstone. Some of the decorations were raised. Many pieces of ironstone are unmarked, but some English and American factories included the word *Ironstone* in their marks. Additional pieces may be listed in other categories, such as Chelsea Grape, Chelsea Sprig, Flow Blue, Gaudy Ironstone, Mason's Ironstone, Moss Rose, Staffordshire, and Tea Leaf Ironstone.

Bowl, Vegetable, Cover, Garfield Pattern, Brown Transfer, Footed, 19th Century	60.00
Cup & Saucer, Flower, Red, Blue Roses, Green Leaves, Stick Spatter, Handleless	24.00
Cup & Saucer, Flowers, Green, Yellow Roses, Red Sprigs, Stick Spatter, Handleless	60.00
Footbath, Transfer Print, Allover Flowers, Flared Rim, 2 Arched Handles, 8 x 18 In.	633.00
Pitcher & Basin, Chateau, Blue, White, 10-Sided Basin, 12-In. Pitcher	130.00
Pitcher, Mason's, Asian Ming Tree Design, Cobalt & Gild Highlights, Marked, 11 ½ In.	195.00
Pitcher, Melon Ribbed, Scalloped Rim, Johnson Brothers, Victorian, 9 In.	180.00
Pitcher, Serpent Handle, Staffordshire, 11 In.	125.00
Pitcher, Shaped Rim, Spout, Tapering Panel Body, Dragon Handle, 6 ½ In.	489.00
Plate, Flowers, Green, Purple Dot Centers, Stick Spatter, 8 ½ In.	48.00
Plate, Pansy, Purple, Green Bowtie Border, Stick Spatter, 8 ½ In.	60.00
Platter, Adams, N. Currier Transfer, Home To Thanksgiving, Flowers, Leaf Border, 15 x 19 In.	45.00
Platter, Blue Feather Edge, 19th Century, 11 ¾ x 14 ⅞ In.	28.00
Platter, Blue Feather Edge, 19th Century, Impressed Adams, 14 ⅛ x 17 ⅞ In.	23.00
Platter, G.M. & C.J. Mason, Ashworth & Bros., Asian Courtyard Scene, c.1880, 17 x 21 In.	410.00
Platter, Imari Style, Cavetto Centered, Flower Filled Vase, c.1825, 19 ¼ x 15 In.	780.00
Platter, Lakeside Pavilions, Transfer Print, Hammersley & Co., 1800s, 21 x 18 In. .... *Illus*	300.00
Platter, Well & Tree, Butterfly, Flowers, Scalloped Rim, England, c.1830, 21 x 17 In.	509.00
Punch Bowl, Transfer, White Round, Yellow Grapes, Purple & Green Leaves, 8 ½ x 17 In.	59.00
Tureen, Ashworth, Multicolored, Early 20th Century, 10 ½ x 12 In.	382.00

Iron, Paperweight, Kitten, With Pink Bow, Hubley, 3 In. $146.00

Iron, Windmill Weight, Buffalo, 20th Century, 10 ¼ In. $205.00

Ironstone, Platter, Lakeside Pavilions, Transfer Print, Hammersley & Co., 1800s, 21 x 18 In. $300.00

Ispanky, Figurine, Belle Of The Ball, Bisque, 12 ½ In. $70.00

Ivory, Figurine, Doctor's Doll, Woman, Nude, Wood Stand, Chinese, c.1900, 6 In. $353.00

Ivory, Jewelry Box, Watch Tower, Walrus, Scrolling, Hinged Door, c.1847, Russia, 10 x 6 In. $600.00

ISPANKY figurines were designed by Laszlo Ispanky, who began his American career as a designer for Cybis Porcelains. In 1966, he established his own studio in Pennington, New Jersey; since 1976, he has worked for Goebel of North America. He works in stone, wood, or metal, as well as porcelain. The first limited edition figurines were issued in 1966.

Bust, Chief Joseph, Nez Perce Indian Chief, 15 In.	600.00
Bust, David, Holding Sling & Stone, Limited Edition, 11 ½ In.	895.00
Bust, Madonna, White & Pink Veil, Limited Edition, 12 ¼ In.	175.00
Bust, Moses, White Hair, White Wrap, White Tablets, 12 ½ In.	895.00
Figurine, 2 Otters, Holding Paws, 13 In.	2400.00
Figurine, About To Gather Flowers, Girl, Holding Hat & Flowers, 9 In.	250.00
Figurine, Ballerina, On Pointe, Arms Raised, Barre	375.00
Figurine, Belle Of The Ball, Bisque, 12 ½ In. ....*illus*	70.00
Figurine, Boy Painting, Paint Spattered Overalls, Hat, Paint Can, 10 In.	350.00
Figurine, Elizabeth, Long Blond Hair, Pink Gown, Orange Flowers, 8 In.	275.00
Figurine, Moses, Holding Tablet Of Commandments, Brown Robe, Limited Edition, 15 In.	75.00
Figurine, Romance, 2 Folk Dancers, 12 x 13 In.	95.00
Vase, Seminude Woman, Long Braid, Wrap, Matte Glaze, Limited Edition, 11 In.	200.00

IVORY from the tusk of an elephant is thought by many to be the only true ivory. To most collectors, the term *ivory* also includes such natural materials as walrus, hippopotamus, or whale teeth or tusks, and some of the vegetable materials that are of similar texture and density. Other ivory items may be found in the Scrimshaw and Netsuke categories. Collectors should be aware of the recent laws limiting the buying and selling of elephant ivory and scrimshaw.

Box, Carved Bird, Flower, Panels, Fitted, Interior, Metal Handles, Chinese Export, 1800s, 3 x 4 In.	1200.00
Box, Carved, Tusk, Chrysanthemums, 4-Leaf Footed, Japan, 5 ½ In., Pair	2640.00
Brush Holder, Carved, Court Scene, Chinese, 9 ¾ In.	2390.00
Brush Holder, Carved Court Scene, Cylindrical, Openwork Foot, 4 In.	191.00
Bust, Woman, Detailed Hair, Earrings, Africa, 6 ½ In.	413.00
Canister, Tea, Oval, Hinge, Interior Lid, Finial, Silver Cartouche, c.1875, 3 ⅛ x 2 ¼ x 3 ¼ In.	270.00
Card Case, Allover Carving, Figures, Trees, 19th Century, 5 x 3 ½ In.	2928.00
Carnet De Bal, Dance Program, Louis XVI, 14K Gold, Chain, Enamel, Late 18th Century, 3 In.	1586.00
Carving, River Scene, Fruit Trees, Boats, Harvest, 20th Century, 10 x 31 ¼ In.	14688.00
Chatelaine Clip, Scrollwork, Looping, Marked, Crown, Letter R, 5 ¼ In.	675.00
Dresser Canister Set, Applied Monogram, Mushroom Cover, 5 Piece	549.00
Egg, Putti Crawling Out, Carved, Late 19th Century, 1 ¾ x 2 ½ In.	1093.00
Elephant Parade, Bridge Form, Carved, 3 Lions Attacking, Wood Base, 1900s, 20 ½ In.	960.00
Figurine, Basket Seller, Grinning Man, Signed, Japan, 8 In.	1053.00
Figurine, Birds, On Branch, Wood Stand, Late 19th Century, Chinese, 7 ⅝ In., Pair	2880.00
Figurine, Buddha, Seated, Lotus Position, Hands In Contemplation, Rosewood Base, 10 In.	560.00
Figurine, Buddha, Seated, Multicolored Beaded Necklace, Carved, Incised, Signed, 3 ½ In.	100.00
Figurine, Buddha, Smiling, Seated, Earrings, Rosewood Base, 4 ½ In.	212.00
Figurine, Corn On Cob, Carved Village Scene, Japan, 1800s, 5 ½ In.	235.00
Figurine, Cupid, Seated, Shell Form Chariot, Drawn By Swans, 4 ¾ x 5 x 3 In.	1185.00
Figurine, Diana The Huntress, Bow Set, Ivory Pedestal, 14 In.	4387.00
Figurine, Diana The Huntress, Bow, Wood Pedestal, 9 In.	1170.00
Figurine, Doctor's Doll, Nude, Lounging, Arm Supports Head, Arm At Side, Carved, 1800s, 7 In.	172.00
Figurine, Doctor's Doll, Woman, Nude, Wood Stand, Chinese, c.1900, 6 In. ....*Illus*	353.00
Figurine, Fisherman, Hand Carved, c.1900, 11 In.	293.00
Figurine, Girl, With Bundle Of Flowers, Chinese, Early, Mid 1900s, 5 ¼ x 3 In.	633.00
Figurine, Guanyin, Goddess Overturning A Carafe, Chinese, 1900s, 13 ¾ In.	1680.00
Figurine, Guanyin, On Lion's Back, Chinese, 9 In.	717.00
Figurine, Guanyin, Wood Stand, Chinese, 20 In., Pair	4112.00
Figurine, Hippopotamus, Africa, 4 In.	164.00
Figurine, Ho Tai, Laughing Buddha, Holding Fly Whisk, Chinese, 7 ¾ In.	330.00
Figurine, Immortal, Holding Peach, 11 In.	1554.00
Figurine, Koi, Multicolored, Base, Chinese, c.1950, 4 x 8 x 2 ½ In.	575.00
Figurine, Li Po, Standing, Carved Wood Base, 19th Century, 3 ½ In.	173.00
Figurine, Maiden, Holding Blossoming Prunus Branch, Wood Stand, 10 In., Pair	1041.00
Figurine, Man, Pipe, Basket, Stand, Signed, Japan, 5 ½ In.	322.00
Figurine, Man, Wearing Long Robes, Chinese, 5 ½ In.	478.00
Figurine, Man, With Birdcage, Signed, Japan, 5 In.	205.00
Figurine, Meiren, Seated, Wearing Long Robes, High Chignon, Chinese, 6 ½ In.	598.00
Figurine, Napoleon Bonaparte, Military Attire, 1800s, 9 ½ x 12 ½ In.	2233.00
Figurine, Noh Dancer, Headdress, Fan, Multicolored, Signed, Japan, 8 In.	1053.00

Figurine, Quan Am, Goddess, Seated, Lotus Flower, Arms, Prayer Position, Chinese, 1900s, 7 ¼ In.	270.00
Figurine, Schoolboy, Delivering The Word, Chinese, Early, Mid 1900s, 7 ½ x 3 ¼ In.	805.00
Figurine, Seal, Hand, Serpent, c.1870, 1 ¾ In.	385.00
Figurine, St. Margaret, Carved, Cascading Braid, Holding Book, Marble Base, c.1900, 6 ¼ In.	600.00
Figurine, Sumo Wrestler, Painted Sunburst, Facial Features, Japan, 3 In.	117.00
Figurine, Venus Awakening, Gilt Bronze, Marble Base, c.1930, 8 ⅞ In.	5639.00
Figurine, Village Merchant, Carrying Goods On Back, Incised, Signed, 4 ½ In.	120.00
Figurine, Warrior, Standing, Wearing Armor, Sword, Helmet, Chinese, 20 In.	2271.00
Figurine, Woman, Classical, Holding Bouquet, Vase At Feet, Wood Base, Continental, 7 ½ In. .	896.00
Figurine, Woman, Flower Seller, Silver Hat, Ribbons, Rock Crystal Base, Continental, 9 ⅛ In.	7110.00
Figurine, Woman, Kneeling, Africa, Mid 1900s, 11 x 2 ½ In.	196.00
Figurine, Woman, Large Headpiece, Africa, Mid 1900s, 9 ¼ x 2 In.	127.00
Figurine, Woman, Multicolored, 10 In.	264.00
Figurine, Woman, With Child, Chinese, 13 ½ In.	1814.00
Figurine, Woman, With Hoe, Wiping Brow, Chinese, c.1950, 8 x 3 x 3 In.	1380.00
Fly Whisk, Egyptian	117.00
Frame, Tortoiseshell, Applied Gold Crown, England, Early 20th Century, 8 ¾ x 6 ⅛ In.	1586.00
Glove Stretcher, 6 ½ In.	125.00
Group, 3 Entwined Figures, Rocky Ground, Oval Base, Old Patina, 13 In.	3910.00
Group, 6 Men, Cranes, Goat, Rock, Leafy Vines, Chinese, 7 In.	420.00
Group, 7 Immortals, Carved, Arched Shape, Chinese, 9 ½ In.	717.00
Group, Boat, 7 Lucky Gods, Stain, Mark, Japan, 4 In.	561.00
Group, Budai, Buddha, Children, Gifts, Carved Wood Stand, Chinese, 11 In.	1880.00
Group, Chinese Man & Woman, Carved, On Swing, Under Tree, Wood Base, 5 ½ In.	995.00
Group, Emperor & Empress, Royal Garments, Carved, Oval Wood Base, 7 ¾ In., Pair............	525.00
Group, Emperor & Empress, Standing, Carved, Scroll Carved Robes, Chinese, 1900s, 14 In., Pair .	1440.00
Group, Flowers, Bird, Chinese, 8 x 6 In.	702.00
Group, Fortune Teller, Fruitwood, 4 Figures, Tavern Scene, Haebler, Germany, 1901, 9 x 13 In.	22515.00
Group, Gazelle, Carved, Male & Female, Natural Base, Early 20th Century, 4 ½ In., Pair..........	47.00
Group, Man, Goose Tugging At Bears, Signed, 6 ¼ In.	920.00
Group, Rat, Seated, Zodiac Figures, Chinese, 4 ⅛ In.	1600.00
Group, River Scene, Carved Wood Stand, Chinese, c.1900s, 10 x 31 In.	14687.00
Group, Woman, Deer, Carved, Chinese, 5 In.	205.00
Jewelry Box, Watch Tower, Walrus, Scrolling, Hinged Door, Russia, c.1847, 10 x 6 In. ....*illus*	600.00
Knife, Library, Silver Handle, Chased, C-Scrolls, England, 1891, 18 ¾ In.	244.00
Knife, Library, Silver Mounted, c.1903, 10 ¾ & 20 ½ In., 2 Piece........................	244.00
Ladle, Walrus Ivory, Turned Handle, 2 Parts, Screw Joined, c.1860, 12 In.	382.00
Letter Opener, Mother-Of-Pearl Flowers, Inlay, Hand Painted, 8 ⅜ In.	48.00
Mirror, Dieppe Carved, Lions, Cherubs, Shields, Crest, Oval, M.S. Dinys, c.1895, 20 x 22 In.	2585.00
Mystery Ball, Carved, Sphere Above Rhinoceros, Curling Smoke, 22 Pierced Layers, c.1925, 13 In.	6000.00
Mystery Ball, Figural Garden Scene, Carved Ball Over Pedestal, 14 Layers, Finial, c.1910, 13 In.	4080.00
Plaque, Wood, 3 Strolling Chinese Women, Black & Gilt Frame, 7 ½ x 11 ½ In.	111.00
Playing Card Press, Hand Carved, c.1800, 6 In.	9500.00
Tankard, Elephant, Tigers, Silver Mounts, Art Deco, German Touchmarks, c.1920, 9 In.	16675.00
Tankard, Soldiers, Priest, Cross, Treasures, Soldier On Horseback Finial, Footed, c.1850, 14 In.	24150.00
Tankard, Soldiers, Sabine Women, Silver Mounts, Germany, c.1885, ½ Liter, 8 ¾ In.	7763.00
Tusk, Allover Carving, Asian Warrior Scenes, 11 In.	3294.00
Tusk, Carved Bone, Chinese, 36 x 6 ½ In., Pair	1170.00
Tusk, Carved Serpents, Painted Cartouches, Figure, Trees, 11 ¾ In.	1220.00
Tusk, Float, Wavy Sea Gourd Boat, 4 Female Musicians, Wood Stand, 1800s, 20 In.	1888.00
Tusk, Goddess, Man With Lute, Incised Characters On Foot, Base, Wood Stand, Asia, 6 ½ x 28 ½ In.	2990.00
Tusk, Men On Horseback Under Pine Tree, Carved, Qing Dynasty, Chinese, 27 In.	3466.00
Urn, Carved, Dragons, Flowers, Paneled, Oriental Messages, Octagonal, 9 In. ....*illus*	345.00
Vase, Warriors, Chinese, Lid, 27 In., Pair........................	2006.00
Wrist Rest, Scenic, Flowers, Plants, Woman, Children, Cutting Leaves, 5 ⅝ x 2 In.	826.00
Wrist Rest, Tusk, Scholar, Maidens, Garden Terrace, Carved, Curved, Chinese, Late 1800s, 6 ¼ In.	200.00

Ivory, Urn, Carved, Dragons, Flowers, Paneled, Oriental Messages, Octagonal, 9 In.
$345.00

Jade, Boulder, Carved, Cream, Russet Skin, Hilltop Garden, Chinese, 1900, 9 In.
$2640.00

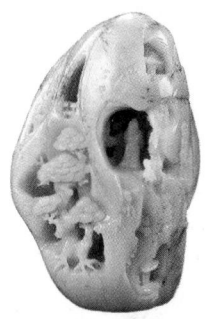

JACK-IN-THE-PULPIT vases, shaped like trumpets, resemble the wild flower named jack-in-the-pulpit. The design originated in the late Victorian years. Vases in the jack-in-the-pulpit shape were made of ceramic or glass, and the complete list of page references can be found in the index.

Vase, Amber, Embossed Rose, 7 In.	22.00
Vase, Blue Iridescent, Opalescent Pulled Feather Stem, Signed, Ableman, 15 x 9 ½ In.	375.00
Vase, Blue Opalescent, 6 ¾ In.	40.00
Vase, Blue Opalescent, Blown, 5 In.	33.00
Vase, Daisy & Fern, Opalescent, Cranberry, 11 In.	100.00

Jade, Figurine, Guanyin, Chinese, 19th Century, 14 ¾ In. $2868.00

Jade, Group, Fish Trap, Reticulated Lid, Fish, Turtles, Crabs, Shells, Wood Base, 1900s, 5 In. $600.00

Jade, Vase, Cover, Dragon & Carp, Burmese, Baluster, Carved, Wood Stand, 16 In. $3120.00

The Latest Style
Large necklaces with chains and stones are the latest style. Most are made larger by using ribbons with large bows to hold the necklace in place.

Vase, Green, Gold Highlights, Ruffled Top, 8 ½ In., Pair	112.00
Vase, Green Opalescent, Vaseline, Pontil, 7 In.	25.00
Vase, Green Shaded To Opalescent, Shaded To Cranberry, Blown, 8 In.	139.00
Vase, Opalescent Blue, Swirl Base, 7 ¾ In.	47.00
Vase, Opalescent Green To Blue, Swirl, Signed, 14 In.	167.00
Vase, Pale Green, Blue Opalescent Ruffled Rim, Late 1800s, 8 ½ In.	112.00
Vase, Pulled Feather, Pink, Green, Purple, Yellow, Signed, Vandermark, 14 In.	625.00
Vase, Purple, Ruffled Top, Blown, 4 ¾ In.	33.00

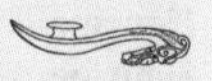

JADE is the name for two different minerals, nephrite and jadeite. Nephrite is the mineral used for most early Oriental carvings. Jade is a very tough stone that is found in many colors from dark green to pale lavender. Jade carvings are still being made in the old styles, so collectors must be careful not to be fooled by recent pieces. Jade jewelry is found in this book under Jewelry.

Belt Buckle, Dragon Shape, Carved Wood Backplate, 1800s, 3 ⅜ In.	173.00
Bottle, Snuff, Oval, Chinese, 2 ⅝ In.	250.00
Boulder, Carved, Cream, Russet Skin, Hilltop Garden, Chinese, 1900, 9 In. ....*illus*	2640.00
Bowl, Mottled Light Green, Chinese, 5 In., Pair	293.00
Bowl, Serpentine, Mottled Green, 2 x 5 In., Pair	234.00
Bowl, Spinach Green, Flared, Footed, 2 x 5 In.	575.00
Box, Cover, Bats, Relief Carved, Clouds, Cylindrical, Chinese, 1 ¼ x 2 In.	863.00
Brushpot, Carved, Scalloped Sides, Foo Dog Handles, Wood Stand, 7 ¾ In.	244.00
Brush Rest, Pale Green, Trident Form, Raised Band, 3 ¾ In.	55.00
Cup, 2 Applied Climbing Monkeys, Bat, Branches, 4 In.	460.00
Cup, Wine, Peach Shape, Splayed Leaf Handle, Chinese, c.1910, 1 ⅜ x 3 ⅛ In.	176.00
Figurine, 3 Rams, Lying, Chinese, c.1920-50, 3 ⅝ x 6 ¼ In.	1080.00
Figurine, Foo Dog, Carved, Small Foo Dog On Back, Gray, White, Wood Base, 8 x 7 In.	1037.00
Figurine, Foo Dog, Pulling Yarn, Hardwood Stand, Root Feet, 1 ⅜ x 2 ½ In.	173.00
Figurine, Guanyin, Chinese, 19th Century, 14 ¾ In. ....*illus*	2868.00
Figurine, Guanyin, Green, Chinese, 10 In.	292.00
Figurine, Hotai, Seated, Smiling Face, Mottled Celadon Green, Dish Base, 5 x 3 x 3 In.	244.00
Figurine, Salmon, Leaping, Rocky Outcrop Base, Nephrite, Signed, Sopel, 13 x 21 In.	1554.00
Group, Fish Trap, Reticulated Lid, Fish, Turtles, Crabs, Shells, Wood Base, 1900s, 5 In. ....*illus*	600.00
Incense Burner, Cover, Olive, Green, Dragon Head Handles, Paw Feet, Chinese, 6 x 6 ½ In.	240.00
Jar, Cover, Flower & Leaf Design, Spinach Green, 4 ½ x 4 In.	240.00
Knife, Carved, Tapered, Stepped Handle Knop, Maori, 20th Century, 13 ¾ In.	118.00
Lamp, Flower Form, Bird Finial, Pierced Wood Base, Japan, 5 x 4 In.	266.00
Lotus, Carved, White, Chinese, 2 ½ In.	448.00
Pendant, Disc, White, Movable Openwork Knot, Dragons Finial, Carved, Chinese, 1800s, 2 ¼ In.	1680.00
Pendant, Reticulated Butterfly, Flowers, Carved, Pale Green White, Gold Bale, c.1900, 2 ⅜ In.	420.00
Plaque, Pale Green, Dancing Figure, Flowers, Pierced & Carved, Chinese, c.1890, 3 In.	390.00
Screen, Table, Woman, Holding Basket, Carved, Wood Openwork Stand, 8 x 10 In.	427.00
Sculpture, Carved, Serpentine, Wood Base, Chinese, c.1950, 11 In.	146.00
Seal, 2 Horned, Scaled Dragons, Uncarved Square Base, White, 1800s, 3 x 2 ¾ In.	3400.00
Seal, Dragon, Chinese, 20th Century, 2 ⅞ In.	1075.00
Seal, Dragon Head, Dark Green, Jewel In Relief, Shaft, Carved, Jiaging Zhi Bao, Chinese, 4 In.	250.00
Sword, Stand, Dragon, Carved, Chinese, 13 ¾ x 5 ½ In.	878.00
Tea Set, Green, Carved, Chinese, Miniature, 8 Piece	351.00
Teapot, Translucent Green, Flying Bats, Clouds, Carved Relief, Divided Inside, Chinese, 1900s, 8 In.	1320.00
Urn, Carved, Teakwood Base, 8 In.	235.00
Urn, Cover, Carved Designs, Ring Handles, 6 ⅝ In., Pair	1980.00
Vase, Bird Shape, Spinach Green, Carved Features, Wood Spiral-Carved Stand, 10 x 8 In.	305.00
Vase, Cover, Dragon & Carp, Burmese, Baluster, Carved, Wood Stand, 16 In. ....*illus*	3120.00
Vase, Cover, Dragons, 4 Flanges, Chrysanthemum Finial, Carved, Lotus, Chinese, 10 ⅛ In.	360.00
Vase, Cover, Landscape, Pavilions, Men, Lotus Bud Finial, Celadon, c.1790, 10 ½ In.	8700.00
Vase, Domed Cover, Dragons, Mottled Green, White Burmese Jadeite, Flat Handles, Chinese, 5 ¼ In.	96.00

JAPANESE WOODBLOCK PRINTS are listed in this book in the Print category under Japanese.

JASPERWARE can be made in different ways. Some pieces are made from a solid-colored clay with applied raised designs of a contrasting colored clay. Other pieces are made entirely of one color clay with raised decorations that are glazed with a contrasting color. Additional pieces of jasperware may also be listed in the Wedgwood category or under various art potteries.

Cheese Dome, Underplate, Fern Design, Blue, 19th Century	350.00
Cheese Dome, Underplate, Figures, Animals, Trees, Blue, White, Late 1800s, 9 x 10 In.	520.00

Dish, Amorous Couple, Bronze Frame, Handles	20.00
Muffineer, Dark Blue, White Classical Women, England, 4 ½ In.	81.00 to 708.00
Pitcher, Grapevine Decoration, Blue Band, 7 In.	35.00
Teapot, Cover, Mauve, Man, Woman, Cherub, 5 In.	25.00
Vase, Green, White Cupid, Shooting Arrow At Birds, Ruffled Rim, Vine Handle, Germany	30.00

JEWELRY, whether made from gold and precious gems or plastic and colored glass, is popular with collectors. Values are determined by the intrinsic value of the stones and metal and by the skill of the craftsmen and designers. Victorian and older jewelry have been collected since the 1950s. More recent interests are Art Deco and Edwardian styles, Mexican and Danish silver jewelry, and beads of all kinds. Copies of almost all styles are being made. American Indian jewelry is listed in the Indian category. Tiffany jewelry is listed here.

Bangle, 14K Gold, 3 Rows Of Diamonds	990.00
Barrette, Art Deco, Green Rhinestone, Openwork, Mottled Green, Celluloid, c.1920, 4 In.	95.00
Belt Buckle, Filigree, Coiled Silver, Gemstones, Russia, c.1918, 7 ½ In.	480.00
Belt Buckle, Rhinestone, Blue, White, Art Deco, 4 In.	175.00
Belt, Link, Flowers, Flattened, 6 Rounded Petals, Chrome, Hook & Chain Closure, Paris, 41 In.	100.00
Bracelet, 3-Headed Dog, Diamond Eyes, Chain, Granulated Post, Etruscan Revival, 1880	2562.00
Bracelet, 8 Plaques, Mosaic, Cameo, Onyx, Carnelian, Garnet, Tiger's Eye, 14K Gold, 7 In.	748.00
Bracelet, Amethyst, Links, 14K Gold, Art Nouveau, 7 ¼ In.	830.00
Bracelet, Bakelite, Bangle, Butterscotch, 2 ½ In.	120.00
Bracelet, Bakelite, Bangle, Corn Yellow, Oval, Ridged, 1930s, 8 x ¾ In.	85.00
Bracelet, Bakelite, Rose, Carved, Green, Goldtone Rope Twist, Oval, 2 ¼ x 1 ⅝ In.	365.00
Bracelet, Bangle, 3 Diamonds, Chased Scrolls, 14K Gold, Riker, c.1900	2528.00
Bracelet, Bangle, 3 Intertwined, 18K Yellow, Rose & White Gold, 7 In.	3884.00
Bracelet, Bangle, 6 Diamond Melee, 18K Gold, Roberto Coin, 8 ¼ In.	444.00
Bracelet, Bangle, Bohemian Garnet, Rose Cut, Rose Gold Metal, c.1880, 7 ⅛ In.	650.00
Bracelet, Bangle, Diamonds, Blue Enamel, Filigree Insert, Sapphires, 14K Gold, c.1920	3910.00
Bracelet, Bangle, Flowers, 14K Gold, Etruscan Style, c.1895, 2 ½ In.	2400.00
Bracelet, Bangle, Fluted Design, Contour Fit, 14K Gold	260.00
Bracelet, Bangle, Hinged, Chased Leaves, Amethysts, 14K Gold, Alling & Co., 1906, Pair	2196.00
Bracelet, Bangle, Hinged, Graduated Beads, Sterling Silver, Gerardo Lopez, 6 ½ In.	770.00
Bracelet, Bangle, Hinged, Intarsia, Sterling Silver, Tricolor, Inset Hardstone, M. Castillo, ⅜ In.	356.00
Bracelet, Bangle, Hinged, Snake, Emerald Eyes, Diamonds, 18K White Gold, c.1930, 7 In.	1896.00
Bracelet, Bangle, Hinged, Vine, Pearl Bud, Old Mine Cut Diamond, Locket, c.1850, 6 ⅜ In.	6518.00
Bracelet, Bangle, Jade, Green, ½ In.	189.00
Bracelet, Bangle, Link, 18K Gold, Carlo Weingrill, 6 ¼ In.	1659.00
Bracelet, Bangle, Rhinestones Bands, Square, Faceted, Green, Clear, Philippe, Trifari, 1950s, 7 In.	275.00
Bracelet, Bangle, Spoked Wheel, Seed Pearl, Rose Gold Filled, Cross Over, c.1880, 7 In.	225.00
Bracelet, Bar, Black Onyx, Diamonds, Floral Spray, Gold Rope Twist, Mount, c.1860, 7 ¼ In.	1250.00
Bracelet, Baroque Pearl, Tourmaline, Sapphire, Emerald, 14K Gold, Hinged, David Rosnov, 6 In.	711.00
Bracelet, Buckle, Tassel, Turquoise Cabochons, Gold Mesh, 7 ½ In. ....*illus*	1495.00
Bracelet, Cameo, Coral, Olympian Gods, Goddesses, 14K Gold, Etruscan Revival, 7 In.	1126.00
Bracelet, Cat's-Eye, Oval Cabochons, Amber, Pewter Plaques, Links, J. Jensen, 7 ½ In.	225.00
Bracelet, Catalin, Green & Yellow Mottled, 2 ½ In.	250.00
Bracelet, Charm, Double Link, 18K Gold, 12 Charms, Deer, Wishbone, Clover, Donkey, 7 ½ In.	1725.00
Bracelet, Charm, Good Luck, 11 Charms, 18K Rose Gold, Victorian, 6 ¾ In.	2200.00
Bracelet, Charm, Link, Flowers, Amethyst, Black Enamel 14K Rose Gold	590.00
Bracelet, Citrine, 18K Gold, Marked, Paolo Costagli, 7 x 2 ⅛ In.	5975.00
Bracelet, Crepe Stone, Flexible Link, 15 Bezel Set Stones, Box Clasp, c.1880, 7 In.	110.00
Bracelet, Cuff, Applied Platinum Geometric Shapes, Diamonds, 22K Gold, R. Coppelman	1830.00
Bracelet, Cuff, Atomic, Sterling Silver, Napier, 1950s, 2 ½ In.	235.00
Bracelet, Cuff, Butterfly Design, Colored Rhinestones, Wendy Gell	30.00
Bracelet, Cuff, Crossover Cables, 4 Rows, Row Of Diamonds, 18K Gold, D. Yurman	2684.00
Bracelet, Cuff, Double Scrolling Spiral, 18K Gold, Lalaounis	1554.00
Bracelet, Cuff, Geometric Designs, Mixed Metal, Tiffany & Co., c.1970	2844.00
Bracelet, Cuff, Hinged, 3 Round Rubies, 18K Gold, Engraved	805.00
Bracelet, Cuff, Hinged, Leaves, Textured, 18K Gold, Buccellati, ¾ In.	5288.00
Bracelet, Cuff, Navajo, Leather, Dragon Fly, Silver, Turquoise	590.00
Bracelet, Cuff, Open Design, Sterling Silver, Modernist, Ed Wiener, 2 x 2 ½ In. ....*illus*	863.00
Bracelet, Cuff, Red Lizard Skin, Goldtone Metal Mount, Marked, Hermes	270.00
Bracelet, Cuff, Shagreen, Rubies, Diamonds, 18K Gold, 6 x 1 ⅝ In.	2390.00
Bracelet, Cuff, Sterling Silver, American Indian Design, Cloud & Thunder, Georg Jensen, c.1933, 6 In.	267.00
Bracelet, Cuff, Sterling Silver, Arches, Turquoise Cabochons, Tapered, Ed Weiner, c.1950	2562.00
Bracelet, Cuff, Sterling Silver, Asymmetrical, Ed Weiner, 2 ¼ x 2 ½ In.	1200.00
Bracelet, Cuff, Turquoise, Sterling Silver, 14K Gold, Andrew Redhorse Alvarez, 1 ½ In.	1290.00

Jewelry, Bracelet, Buckle, Tassel, Turquoise Cabochons, Gold Mesh, 7 ½ In.
$1495.00

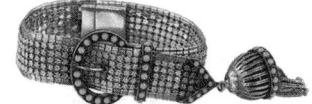

Jewelry, Bracelet, Cuff, Open Design, Sterling Silver, Modernist, Ed Wiener, 2 x 2 ½ In.
$863.00

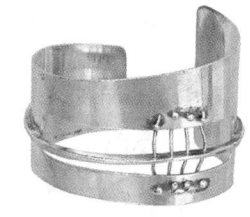

J

Jewelry, Bracelet, Elephant Skin, 18K Gold, Hinged, Hallmarks, BBY, France, 2 ¼ In.
$236.00

Jewelry, Bracelet, Snake, Coiled, Ruby, Diamonds, 14K Gold Mesh, Victorian
$891.00

Jewelry, Bracelet, Sterling Silver, Beaded & Reticulated Links, Taxco, Mexico, 7 In.
$236.00

Jewelry, Buckle, Cartouches, Dogs, Birds, Horses, 14K Yellow Gold, 2 ½ x 1 ½ In. **$587.00**

Jewelry, Chatelaine, Needle Holder, Book, Pencil, Locket, Perfume Bottle, c.1914 **$234.00**

Jewelry, Cigarette Case, Bakelite, Green, Rhinestones, 3 ⅜ x 2 ⅜ In. **$92.00**

Jewelry, Cuff Links, Squid, Beaded, 18K Gold, John Paul Miller, Potter & Mellen **$1150.00**

Bracelet, Diamonds, 6 Square Emeralds, Graduated Links, Platinum, c.1930, 6 ½ In.	2760.00
Bracelet, Diamonds, Brilliant Cut, Platinum, Elsa Peretti, 7 In.	3555.00
Bracelet, Diamonds In A Row, Platinum, Art Deco, 7 ⅛ In.	4148.00
Bracelet, Diamonds, Red Enamel, 18K Gold, Impressed Hallmarks, c.1880, 7 In.	3995.00
Bracelet, Diamonds, Sapphires, 3 Square Plaques, Tapered Ends, Silver Over Gold, 1911, 7 In.	2440.00
Bracelet, Diamonds, Sapphires, Intertwined, Strands, 18K White Gold, 7 In.	13145.00
Bracelet, Diamonds, Woven Strap, Herringbone Links, Flower Clasp, 18K Bicolor Gold, Italy, 7 In.	2133.00
Bracelet, Elephant Skin, 18K Gold, Hinged, Hallmarks, BBY, France, 2 ¼ In. .... *illus*	236.00
Bracelet, Enameled Copper Panels, White Ground, Multicolor Spatter, Rectangular, Coro, 6 ½ In.	41.00
Bracelet, Etoile, Diamond, 18K Gold, Platinum, Hinged, Tiffany & Co., 5 ⅝ In.	1067.00
Bracelet, Lapis, Octagonal, Flower Links, Wirework, 14K Gold, Arts & Crafts, 6 ⅞ In.	6518.00
Bracelet, Link, Barrel Shape, Diamond, 18K Gold, Bulgari, 7 In.	1541.00
Bracelet, Link, Cable, Black Diamonds, Yellow Sapphires, 18K Gold, 7 x ½ In.	3346.00
Bracelet, Link, Curb, Faceted 14K Gold, Bright & Matte, c.1960, 7 ½ x ¾ In.	2196.00
Bracelet, Link, Domed, Citrine, Cushion Cut, 14K Gold, Seaman Schepps, 7 x 1 In.	2489.00
Bracelet, Link, Enameled Leaves, 4 Panels, Multicolored, Germany, 7 ½ In.	115.00
Bracelet, Link, Flattened, Men's, Stainless Steel, 8 ¼ In.	135.00
Bracelet, Link, Gate, Spiral Carved Centers, Scroll Ends, 18K Gold, Italy, c.1940, 8 x 1 In.	1586.00
Bracelet, Link, Iridescent Sapphire Blue Cabochons, Blue Rhinestones, 1960s, 7 ¼ x 1 ⅝ In. .	85.00
Bracelet, Link, Navettes, Oval Black Cabochons, Juliana, 1960s, 7 x ¾ In.	65.00
Bracelet, Link, Oval, Diamonds, Platinum, c.1940, 6 ¾ In.	3437.00
Bracelet, Link, Oval, Enameled, Orange On Cobalt Blue, T Clasp, Modernist, 7 ½ In.	65.00
Bracelet, Link, Silver Bull's-Eye, Red Cabochon Stones, Bar Closure, Bent Larsen, 7 ½ In.	110.00
Bracelet, Mesh, Clear Rhinestone Panel, Butler & Wilson, 6 ¾ x 2 In.	195.00
Bracelet, Mesh, Seed Pearls, Carved Chalcedony Rings, c.1930, 6 ⅝ In.	563.00
Bracelet, Mesh, Tassel, 18K Gold, 7 ½ x 1 ⅛ In.	2390.00
Bracelet, Mosaic, Enamel, Sterling Silver, 14K Gold, Earl Pardon, 7 In.	3674.00
Bracelet, Panels, Marcasite, Silver, Coral Set Leaves, T. Fahrner, Germany, 1927, 7 In.	1342.00
Bracelet, Pearls, Rose Tone, 18K Gold, Mikimoto, 6 ¾ In.	652.00
Bracelet, Plaques, Blue Enamel, Blue & Purple Venetian Glass Bars, K. Denning, 7 In.	195.00
Bracelet, Rhinestones, Stretch Links, 1950s	89.00
Bracelet, Slide, Mesh Slide, Black Enamel, Pearl, Ball Fringe, 14K Gold, Victorian, 7 ½ In.	2800.00
Bracelet, Snake, Coiled, Ruby, Diamonds, 14K Gold Mesh, Victorian .... *illus*	891.00
Bracelet, Sterling Silver, Beaded & Reticulated Links, Taxco, Mexico, 7 In. .... *illus*	236.00
Bracelet, Sterling Silver, Fish Scale Pyramids, Spheres, H. Aguilar, Mexico, c.1950, 7 ½ In.	5795.00
Bracelet, Sterling Silver, Henning Koppel, Georg Jensen, 7 ½ In.	830.00
Bracelet, Sterling Silver, Links, Arched, Cushion Shape, Toggle Clasp, Dahlquist, Jensen, 8 In.	1342.00
Bracelet, Sterling Silver, Links, Arched, Marked, Georg Jensen, 7 In.	267.00
Bracelet, Sterling Silver, Plaques, Pearls & Doves, Georg Jensen, c.1908, 7 In.	1220.00
Bracelet, Sterling Silver, Strands Of Interlocking, Links, Bar & Circle Closure, Georg Jensen, 9 ¼ In.	444.00
Bracelet, Tennis, 2 Rows Of Diamonds, 14K Gold Links, c.1980, 7 x ¼ In.	1708.00
Bracelet, Turquoise Cabochons, Sapphires, 18K Gold, Tongue-In-Groove Clasp, 7 In.	4780.00
Bracelet, Turquoise, Diamond, 18K Gold, David Webb, 6 ¼ In.	7110.00
Bracelet, Women's Faces, Stainless Steel, 18K Gold, Kieselstein Cord, 6 ½ In., Pair	2963.00
Buckle, Cartouches, Dogs, Birds, Horses, 14K Yellow Gold, 2 ½ x 1 ½ In. .... *illus*	587.00
Buckle, Eagle Head, Enamel Eye, Clear Paste, Gilt Silver Alloy Mount, c.1900, 3 ½ In.	474.00
Charm, Carousel, Enameled Horses & Jockeys, Turns, 14K Gold, c.1955, 1 ¼ In.	732.00
Charm, Queen Of Hearts, Enamel, 14K Gold, Cartier, 1 In.	920.00
Chatelaine, Needle Holder, Book, Pencil, Locket, Perfume Bottle, c.1914 .... *illus*	234.00
Chatelaine, Silver Plate, Aide-Memoire, Scissors Sheath, Pencil, Pin Cushion, Thimble, 11 In.	1400.00
Cigarette Case, Bakelite, Green, Rhinestones, 3 ⅜ x 2 ⅜ In. .... *illus*	92.00
Cigarette Case, Book Shape, Gold, Arabesques, Incised Flowers, Sliding Lid, Asprey, 5 In.	4575.00
Cigarette Case, Geometric Moire, 18K Gold, Sapphire Push-Pin, Cartier, c.1925, 4 ½ In.	8540.00
Cigarette Case, Moire Pattern, 14K Gold, Grapevine Border, Hungary, c.1920, 4 x 3 In.	3050.00
Cigarette Case, Pin Stripes, 14K Gold, Flower Border, Hungary, c.1920, 4 x 3 ¼ In.	3050.00
Clip, Diamonds, 11 Round Brilliant Cut, 95 Single Cut, 54 Baguettes, Platinum	9735.00
Clip, Diamonds, Crossed Bands, Platinum, 18K Gold, Schlumberger, Tiffany & Co., 2 In.	1952.00
Clip, Fur, Wing Shape, Sterling Silver, Rhinestone, Marked, Eisenberg, 3 ¾ In.	981.00
Clip, Scarf, Floral Spray, Green Plastic, Blue Rhinestones, V-Shape, 1950s, 2 In.	35.00
Comb, 8 Ridged Honeycomb Balls, 5 Prongs, Gilt Metal, Victorian, 3 x 4 ¼ In.	125.00
Comb, Flowers, Engraved, 18K Gold, Victorian, Inscribed Dates, 1821-94	1053.00
Compact, Silver, Chased Decoration, Green Onyx, Houbigant, Austria, c.1920, 3 In.	497.00
Cuff Links, Bearded Man, Holding Fan, Ivory, Sterling Silver Mount, Mid 1900s, 1 ¼ In.	135.00
Cuff Links, Bud, Blossom, Trace Link Chain, 18K Gold	563.00
Cuff Links, Buddha, Ivory, Jade Ground, Gold Filled Mount, Mid 1900s, ⅞ In.	125.00
Cuff Links, Enamel, Black, Octagonal, Engraved, 14K Gold, Box, c.1880, ¾ x ½ In.	185.00

Cuff Links, Enamel, Polka Dots, Bars, 18K Gold	504.00
Cuff Links, Guilloche Enamel, Mauve, Diamond, Leafy Frame, Art Nouveau, 1 In.	854.00
Cuff Links, Half Moon, Ruby, 14K Bicolor Gold, Cartier	1126.00
Cuff Links, Hematite, Leaf Shape, 18K Gold, Schlumberger, Tiffany & Co.	1304.00
Cuff Links, Horizontal Flutes, Onyx Bar, Rectangular, 14K Gold, ¾ In.	472.00
Cuff Links, Kidney Shape, Copper, Toggle, c.1960, 1 ⅛ In.	25.00
Cuff Links, Knotted Ball, 14K Gold, J. Schlumberger, Tiffany & Co.	1150.00
Cuff Links, Lapis Lazuli, 14K Gold, Coin Edge, Box	699.00
Cuff Links, Presidential Seal, Enamel, Gold, Round	115.00
Cuff Links, Prince Of Wales, 1751	185.00
Cuff Links, Ribbed Bars, 14K Gold	533.00
Cuff Links, Ruby, 18K Gold Disc, Hallmark, Marked, ¾ In.	1995.00
Cuff Links, Sapphire Bar, Diamond Surround, Sapphire Border, Lucien Piccard	288.00
Cuff Links, Squid, Beaded, 18K Gold, John Paul Miller, Potter & Mellen ....*illus*	1150.00
Cuff Links, Sterling Silver, Cobblestone Pattern, ¾ In.	95.00
Cuff Links, Sterling Silver, Modernist, Georg Jensen, 1960s, 1 In. ....*illus*	127.00
Cuff Links, Stickpin, Animal Teeth, 8K Gold, Germany	225.00
Cuff Links, Stirrup Shape, Rubies, 18K White Gold, 1 ¼ x ¾ In.	1434.00
Cuff Links, Swirl Design, 18K Gold, Bulgari, Italy, c.1970, ½ In.	499.00
Dress Clip, Blue Rhinestone, Gold, Shield Shape, 1920s, 2 x 1 ¾ In.	95.00
Dress Clip, Chevron Shape, Sterling Silver, Opalescent Lavender Glass Stone, 1 x 1 ⅜ In.	125.00
Dress Clip, Faux Pink Moonstones, Rhodium Plated White Metal, Art Deco, 1 ¾ x 2 ¼ In.	85.00
Dress Set, Night & Day, Cuff Links, 4 Shirt Studs, Stylized Earth, Sky, Ventura	7110.00
Earrings, Alhambra, Turquoise, Quatrefoil, 18K Gold, Van Cleef & Arpels, Box	1896.00
Earrings, Art Glass, Pink Oval, Turquoise Round, Faux Pearl, Screwback, 1950s, 1 ⅛ x ⅞ In.	52.00
Earrings, Bakelite, Button, Amber, Clip-On, 1 ¼ In.	45.00
Earrings, Bakelite, Corn Yellow, Half Sphere Shape, Clip-On, 1930s, 1 x ½ In.	35.00
Earrings, Bezel Set Emerald, Pear Shape, 18K Bicolor Gold, M. Buccellati, ¾ In.	11850.00
Earrings, Black Jade, 18K Gold, Angelo Cummings, 1 x ⅞ In.	1007.00
Earrings, Cameo, Woman's Bust, Sardonyx, 12K Gold, 1 ¼ In.	995.00
Earrings, Carnelian, Round, Enameled Flowers, Twisted Rope Border, Vermeil, 1940s, 1 ⅛ In.	125.00
Earrings, Cherub, On Cloud, Pearl Wings, Halo, Sapphire Eyes, Ruser, 14K Gold, 1 ⅛ In.	444.00
Earrings, Cloisonne Enamel, Pink Roses, Leaves, Aqua Ground, Screwback, 1930s, ⅝ In.	32.00
Earrings, Copper Wire Coil, Red Enamel Ground, Copper Disc Mount, K. Denning, 1 ¼ In.	35.00
Earrings, Daisy, Diamond, Platinum, Paloma Picasso, Tiffany & Co., ⅜ In.	1304.00
Earrings, Daisy, White & Yellow, Enamel On Goldtone Metal, Accessocraft, 1 In.	15.00
Earrings, Dangle, 4 Stylized Butterfly Links, Diamonds, 14K White Gold	527.00
Earrings, Diamond, Bead Set, 20K Gold, Bulgari, ¾ In.	2489.00
Earrings, Drop Leaf, Round, 14K Gold, Pieced, Mid 1800s, 1 In.	177.00
Earrings, Drop, Ruby Heart, Round Diamond, Oval Cut Emerald, 18k Gold, A. Slater	1320.00
Earrings, Drop, Sterling Silver, George Jensen, 1 ¼ In.	385.00
Earrings, Emeralds, Diamonds, 14K White Gold, Clip-On, 1 ¾ x ¾ In.	2868.00
Earrings, Enamel, 8 Blue Teardrops, Elongated, Sterling Silver Mount, D. Andersen	85.00
Earrings, Enamel Splotches, White, Red, Brown, Gold, Copper Mount, Clip-On, K. Denning, ¾ In.	40.00
Earrings, Flower, Diamond Melee Center, 18K Gold, Tiffany & Co., ⅞ In.	444.00
Earrings, Flower, Diamonds, 18K Gold, Clip-On, Van Cleef & Arpels, 1 ½ x 1 ½ In.	3107.00
Earrings, Flower, Fuchsia Rhinestone Pave Petals, Pink Navettes, Thelma Deutsch, 2 ¼ In.	125.00
Earrings, Flower, Gold, Tiffany & Co., 1 In.	1067.00
Earrings, Flower Heads, Onyx, Diamond, 18K Gold, Van Cleef & Arpels, France, ⅞ In.	2607.00
Earrings, Flower, White, Green Leaves, Molded Plastic, Clip-On, Italy, 1950s, 1 ⅜ In.	37.00
Earrings, Garnet, 18K Gold, Marina B, ⅞ In.	1175.00
Earrings, Greek Key, Arched Square, Sterling Silver, Screwback, Mexico, 1940s, 1 x 1 In.	32.00
Earrings, Heart, Puffed, 18K Gold, Kieselstein Cord, ⅞ In.	999.00
Earrings, Hoop, Basket Weave, Goldtone, Chanel, 3 ¼ In.	119.00
Earrings, Hoop, Intertwined, Textured, 18K Gold, Clip-On, Marked, Buccellati	2629.00
Earrings, Jadeite, Carved, 14K Gold, Clip-On, 1 ¼ x 1 ¼ In.	2369.00
Earrings, Leaves, Ivy, Textured, 18K Gold, Hinged Back, 1 x ¾ In.	472.00
Earrings, Lion's Head, Diamond, Ruby, 14K Gold, 1 ½ In.	418.00
Earrings, Lion's Head, Emeralds, Rubies, Diamond Muzzle, 14k Yellow & White Gold, Clip-On	795.00
Earrings, Opal, 2 Garnets, 3-Lobed Mount, 14K Gold	86.00
Earrings, Pansy, Enamel, Blue, White, Lavender, Yellow, Dina, c.1980, 1 ¾ x 1 ¼ In.	18.00
Earrings, Pearl, 18K White Gold, Tiffany & Co.	826.00
Earrings, Pendant, Enamel, Black & White, 14K Gold, Screwbacks, Victorian, 2 In.	288.00
Earrings, Pendant, Fan Shape, Carnelian, Marcasites, Sterling Silver, Art Deco, Pendant, 1 ½ In.	195.00
Earrings, Pendant, Full Cut Diamond Melee, Platinum, Cathy Waterman, 1 ½ In.	1185.00
Earrings, Pendant, Lapis Glass Beads, Aventurine, Screwback, Art Deco, 2 ½ In.	85.00

Jewelry, Cuff Links, Sterling Silver, Modernist, Georg Jensen, 1960s, 1 In. $127.00

Jewelry, Earrings, Pendant, Moon, Arrow, Star, Seed Pearl, Victorian, 1 x ¾ In. $196.00

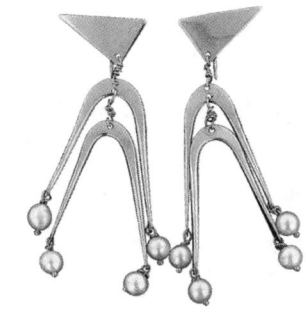

Jewelry, Earrings, Pendants, Arched, Pearls, Screwback, Modernist, Weiner, 2 ½ x ¾ In. $1765.00

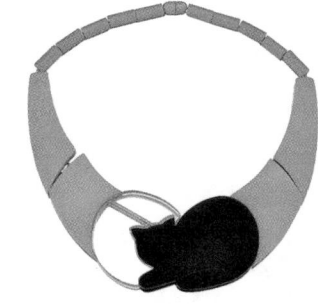

Jewelry, Necklace, Black Cat, Lucite Moon, Galalite, Isadora, France, 2 x 2 ¾ x 16 In. $403.00

J

Jewelry, Necklace, Circlet, Sterling, Hook & Loop Closure, Georg Jensen, 6 x 6 In.
$368.00

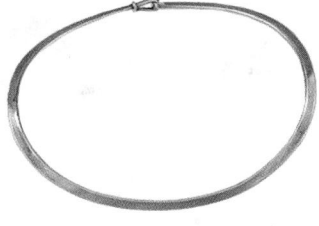

Jewelry, Necklace, Fused Glass, Link Chain, Michael & Frances, Higgins, 2 ¾ x 24 In.
$330.00

Jewelry, Necklace, Garnet Clusters, Cluster Chain, c.1900, 16 In.
$1170.00

Jewelry, Necklace, Greek Key, Sterling Silver, Marked, Antonio Belgiorno, c.1950, 16 In.
$403.00

Earrings, Pendant, Moon, Arrow, Star, Seed Pearl, Victorian, 1 x ¾ In. ....*illus*	196.00
Earrings, Pendant, Paisley, Yellow Diamond, Platinum, Cathy Waterman, ⅞ In.	1185.00
Earrings, Pendants, Arched, Pearls, Screwback, Modernist, Weiner, 2 ½ x ¾ In. ....*illus*	1765.00
Earrings, Petals, Stems, Diamonds, 18K Gold, Clip-On, Van Cleef & Arpels, 1 In.	5490.00
Earrings, Rhinestones, Green, Square, 5 Rows, Clip-On, c.1950, 1 ⅛ In.	32.00
Earrings, Rings, Open, Tapered, 2 Pearls, 14K Gold, Irena Brynner, ⅞ In.	488.00
Earrings, Sapphires, Pink, Yellow, Diamond Melee, 18K Gold, Sophia D., ⅞ In.	2726.00
Earrings, Shells, Turquoise, Mother-Of-Pearl, 14K Gold, Seaman Schepps, 1 ¼ In.	956.00
Earrings, Starburst, Rhinestone Pave, Jomaz, 1 ½ In.	190.00
Earrings, Sterling Silver, Abstract, Clip-On, Georg Jensen, 1 In.	326.00
Earrings, Tourmaline, Topaz & Sapphire Cabochons, 14K Gold, Screwback, 1 In.	667.00
Earrings, Triple Hoop, C Motif, 18K Tricolored Gold, Cartier, ⅝ In.	1007.00
Earrings, Watch, Coral Cabochons, 18K Gold, David Webb, 1 ¼ In.	1778.00
Earrings, Waterfall, Rhinestones, Rhodium Plated, Silver Tone, Clip-On, 1950s, 4 ½ x 1 ¼ In.	125.00
Earrings, Wirework, Lavender Spinels, Oval, 14K Gold, Screwback, Victorian, 1 x ½ In.	2312.00
Etui, Repousse, Scrolls, Silver, Shaped, Applied Agates, Interior Ruler, Pencil, Pick, 5 x 2 In. ...	920.00
Hatpins are listed in this book in the Hatpin category.	
Lavaliere, Diamonds, Platinum Scroll Mount, Pear-Shaped Pearl Drop, c.1920, 16 In.	1708.00
Lorgnette, Magnifying Glass, Folding, Split Handle, Ring Bail, 14K Gold, Cartier, 11 In. Open	1708.00
Money Clip, Gold Dollar	2031.00
Money Clip, Stylized Sunburst, 18K Gold, J. Schlumberger, Tiffany & Co.	863.00
Necklace & Bracelet, Link, Bamboo, Oval, Silver, Toggle Clasp, Tiffany & Co., 18-In. Necklace	1037.00
Necklace & Bracelet, Oak Leaves, Glass Cabochons, Hazel B. French, 7 ½ & 18 In.	2928.00
Necklace & Bracelet, Obsidian Cabochons, Arched Silver Links, A. Pineda, 16 & 8 In.	2318.00
Necklace & Earrings, Green Bead Clusters, Faux Pearl, Goldtone, Miriam Haskell, 2 & 16 In.	695.00
Necklace & Earrings, Pearls, Pink Beads, Clip-On, Marvella, 16 In.	120.00
Necklace & Earrings, Seed Beads, Aqua, Gold, Green, Blue, Flexible, Gold Metal, 1950s, 17 ¼ In. .	78.00
Necklace, Bracelet & Earrings, Drop, Aurora Borealis, Rhinestone Clusters, BSK, 1950s, 16 ½ & 7 ½ In.	92.00
Necklace & Pendant, Heart, Full Cut Diamond Melee, Link Chain, 18K White Gold, ¾ In.	593.00
Necklace, 3 Spirals, Suspended From Each Other, Sterling Silver, Hammered, 6 ½ In.	165.00
Necklace, 5 Graduated Heart, Round Cut Diamonds, Curved 18K White Gold Wire, 15 In.	468.00
Necklace, 14 Amphora Pendants, Arrow Shape, Beads, Persian Style, 16 In.	1725.00
Necklace, 92 Diamonds, Round Brilliant, Onyx, Tablet, 18K White Gold, Art Deco	6608.00
Necklace, 106 Pearls, Pink Tint, Single Strand, 14K Gold Clasp, Mikimoto, 30 In.	1725.00
Necklace, Akoya Pearls, 2 Strands, 14K Gold & Diamond Clasp, c.1960, 17 In.	519.00
Necklace, Akoya Pearls, Gold Spacers, Artifact Drops, Ross Coppelman, 20 In.	976.00
Necklace, Alhambra, Turquoise Quatrefoil, 18K Gold, Van Cleef & Arpels, Box	3851.00
Necklace, Amber, 5 Carved Acanthus Leaves, Tortoiseshell Link Chain, 18 In.	500.00
Necklace, Amber, Graduated Flat Square Plaques, Sterling Silver Clasp, 15 In.	165.00
Necklace, Austrian Crystal, Marquis Shape, Round, Butler & Wilson	495.00
Necklace, Baltic Amber Beads, Butterscotch, 2 Strands, 19 In.	1287.00
Necklace, Beads, Faux Amber, Graduated, 24 In.	384.00
Necklace, Beads, Glass, Millefiori, Graduated, 25 In.	71.00
Necklace, Beads, Seed, Blue Glass, Spun Glass, Enameled, c.1920, 55 In.	201.00
Necklace, Black Cat, Lucite Moon, Galalite, Isadora, France, 2 x 2 ¾ x 16 In. ....*illus*	403.00
Necklace, Book Chain, Locket, Pearl, 18K Yellow Gold, c.1875, 19 ¾ In.	1900.00
Necklace, Chain, Double Link, Beads, 15K Gold, c.1900, 60 In.	3172.00
Necklace, Choker, Angel Skin Coral, Cameo Closure, Birds, Flowers, 13 ½ In.	1500.00
Necklace, Choker, Crystal, Round, Pear, Emerald & Marquis Shape, White Beads, Butler & Wilson	595.00
Necklace, Choker, Double Scrolling Volute, Hinged Sides, 18K Gold, Lalaounis	2510.00
Necklace, Choker, Link, Textured Leaves, Graduated Tiers, Bicolor Gold, Diamonds, Cartier, 15 In.	5677.01
Necklace, Choker, Pearl, Diamonds, 4 Strands, Platinum Clasp, Raymond Yard, 12 In.	948.00
Necklace, Circlet, Sterling, Hook & Loop Closure, Georg Jensen, 6 x 6 In. ....*illus*	368.00
Necklace, Collar, Alhambra, 7 Links, Diamonds, 18K Gold, Van Cleef & Arpels, 16 ¼ In.	13035.00
Necklace, Collar, Biomorphic Form, Spheres, Wirework, Sterling Silver, Art Smith, c.1950	13420.00
Necklace, Collar, Bow Tie, Sterling Silver, Mexico, 3 ¾ x 3 In.	125.00
Necklace, Collar, Cable, Diamonds, Sterling Silver, 14K White Gold, David Yurman, 15 ½ In. .	948.00
Necklace, Collar, Hinged, Hammered Circles, Sodalite Terminals, 22K Gold, 13 ⅞ In.	3081.00
Necklace, Coral Beads, Balls, Woven, Diamonds, 18K White Gold, 16 x 1 In.	2390.00
Necklace, Coral Beads, Red, 6 Strands, Graduated, Wirework Clasp, Italy, c.1960	12810.00
Necklace, Coral Drop, Paperclip Links, 14K Gold	444.00
Necklace, Discs, Double C Logo Design, Goldtone Metal Chain, Chanel, 36 ½ In.	267.00
Necklace, Drop, Labradorite, Silver Flower Mount, Link Chain, Georg Jensen, c.1925	2196.00
Necklace, Festoon, Bow Knot, Garnets, Green Gems, Pearls, Gilt Silver, Hungary, c.1880, 17 In.	1708.00
Necklace, Fringe, Hammered & Beaded Wire, 14K Gold, B. Gabrielsen, Denmark	2806.00
Necklace, Fringe, Textured, Wheat Chain, 18K Gold, Marked, Lalaounis, 16 In.	3346.00

Necklace, Fused Glass, Link Chain, Michael & Frances, Higgins, 2 ¾ x 24 In. ....*illus*		330.00
Necklace, Garnet Clusters, Cluster Chain, c.1900, 16 In. ....*illus*		1170.00
Necklace, Glass Beads, Aventurine, Molded Rabbits, Openwork Flower, Green, Blue, 30 ½ In. .		85.00
Necklace, Greek Key, Sterling Silver, Marked, Antonio Belgiorno, c.1950, 16 In. ....*illus*		403.00
Necklace, Heart, 14K Yellow & White Gold, Diamonds, Snake Chain, c.1950, 15 ½ In.		1075.00
Necklace, Heart, Puffed, Baton Link Chain, Silver, Marked, Georg Jensen		474.00
Necklace, Indian, Cross, Oxblood Coral Cabochons, c.1964, 24 & 2 ¾ In.		115.00
Necklace, Indian, Turquoise Cabochons, Leaf Setting, Hand Wrought, c.1960, 30 In.		575.00
Necklace, Jade Beads, Graduated, Silver, Clasp Marked, Majorica, 18 In.		46.00
Necklace, Jadeite Bead, Double Strand, 14K Gold Flower Clasp, Sapphire, 18 In.		288.00
Necklace, Keshi Pearls, 120 Strands, Diamond Lion's Head Clasp, 18K Gold, 17 In.		4780.00
Necklace, Knot Design, 18K Gold, Concealed Clasp, David Webb, Marked, 15 ½ In.		5975.00
Necklace, Lariat, Onyx Stone, Silver, Braided Leather, c.1980, 40 In.		85.00
Necklace, Link, 18K Gold, Black Rhodium Finish, Box Clasp, Bulgari, 32 In.		4481.00
Necklace, Link, 18K Gold, Diamond Melee, Applied Beads, Boris LeBeau, c.1987, 17 ½ In.		7110.00
Necklace, Link, 18K Gold, Pearl, Rose, Judith Ripka, 1991, 35 In.		1422.00
Necklace, Link, Beaded, Sterling Silver, Los Castillo, Taxco, Mexico, c.1970, 15 In. ....*illus*		330.00
Necklace, Link, Discs, 2 Coral, 4 Lapis, 18K Gold, Bulgari, 32 In.		2015.00
Necklace, Link, Discs, Onyx, Pave Set Diamonds, 18K White Gold, Bulgari, 16 In.		2607.00
Necklace, Link, Flowers, Sterling Silver, Georg Jensen, Denmark, 14 ½ In. ....*illus*		2400.00
Necklace, Link, Leaves, Sterling Silver, Chrysoprase, Georg Jensen, c.1920, 16 In.		2196.00
Necklace, Link, Pewter, Dish-Shaped Drops, Purple Cabochons, J. Jensen, 16 In.		175.00
Necklace, Link, Quatrefoil, 18K White Gold, Van Cleef & Arpels		6518.00
Necklace, Link, Scored, Rectangular, 18K Gold, Marked, Wander, France, 34 In.		13035.00
Necklace, Link, Scrolls, Cherubs, 14K Gold, Seed Pearl Floret Fringe, c.1890, 18 In.		2440.00
Necklace, Link, Swags, Chain, Seed Pearls, 18K Gold, Etruscan Revival, 17 In.		2607.00
Necklace, Link, Tank Track, Buckle, 18K Rose Gold, Argentina, 16 In.		1422.00
Necklace, Link, X-Form, Polished, Ribbed, 18K Bicolor Gold, Black, Starr & Frost, 17 ¼ In.		2489.00
Necklace, Locket, Script Initials, Engraved Stars, 14K Gold Chain, c.1900, 18 ½ x 1 In.		75.00
Necklace, Lovebirds, 2 Diamonds, Sapphire Eyes, 18K Gold, c.1900, 18 ½ In.		7000.00
Necklace, Mabe Pearls, Diamonds, Textured Links, 22 & 18K Gold, Ross Coppelman, 18 In. ...		5185.00
Necklace, Mesh, 18K White Gold, Diamonds, Black Onyx Tablets, 18K Gold, 15 In.		3107.00
Necklace, Pearls, 3 Strands, Diamond Cross-Link Clasp, Schlumberger, Tiffany, 1964		2440.00
Necklace, Pearls, Cut Diamonds, 18K Gold Box Clasp, Edwardian, Tiffany & Co., 13 ⅝ In.		1541.00
Necklace, Pearls, Faceted Citrine Fringe, c.1900, 16 In.		793.00
Necklace, Pendant, Blue Teardrop Cabochon, Pewter Mount, Chain, Jensen, 3-In. Pendant		95.00
Necklace, Pendant, Chain, Wirework, Beads, Inside Compartment, c.1880, 18 In.		4880.00
Necklace, Pendant, Citrine, Marcasite, Bezel Set, Silver, Pforzheim, c.1910, 4 ¼ x 19 In.		5333.00
Necklace, Pendant, Coin, Maximinus II, Curb Link Chain, 18K Gold, Bulgari, 15 In.		2963.00
Necklace, Pendant, Heart, Open, 18K Gold, E. Peretti, Tiffany & Co., ¾-In. Pendant		826.00
Necklace, Pendant, Lapis Lazuli, Diamonds, Gold, Carrera Y Carrera		1912.00
Necklace, Pendant, Lattice Shaped, Sterling Silver, Dog Bone Chain, M. Berg, Denmark, 4 In.		500.00
Necklace, Pendant, Topaz, Square, 8-Sided Diamond Frame, 14K Gold, Chain, ¾ x ¾ In.		410.00
Necklace, Peridot, Oval, Pink Sapphires, 18K Gold, Paolo Costagli, Marked, 16 In.		8365.00
Necklace, Rose Cut Diamonds, Platinum, Edwardian, Tiffany & Co		11544.00
Necklace, Rubies, Sapphires, Emeralds, Diamond Melee, 18K Gold, Judith Ripka, 1991, 15 In.		3200.00
Necklace, Ruby, Sapphire, Emerald, Diamonds, Black Onyx, 18K Gold, Leverington, 16 In.		6572.00
Necklace, Silver, Miao Tribe, Chinese, c.1920, 16 In.		1554.00
Necklace, Sponge Coral, Beads, Diamond Melee, 18K Gold, Christopher Walling, 19 ¾ In.		1896.00
Necklace, Starburst, Turquoise Cabochons, Trace Link Chain, Silver, William Spratling, 3 ⅛ In.		948.00
Necklace, Sterling Silver, Arrow Head, Abstract Figures, Velvet Cord, A. Pineda, Mexico		9154.00
Necklace, Sterling Silver, Filigree, Blue Topaz, Marcasite, Oval Frames, Edwardian, 17 ¾ In. .		225.00
Necklace, Sterling Silver, Oval Discs, Georg Jensen, Marked, 15 ¾ In.		823.00
Necklace, Strawberry, Glass, Steuben, Gilt Chain, Box, 14 In.		360.00
Necklace, Swag Design, Baguette Diamonds, Platinum, Marked, Sophia D., 18 In.		5975.00
Necklace, Torsade, Glass Tubes, Yellow, Green, 3 Strands, Brass, Originals By Robert, 1950s, 27 In.		225.00
Necklace, Turquoise Disks, Santo Domingo, 24 In.		1762.00
Necklace, Wheat Design, 18K Gold, Lalounis, Greece, 16 In.		2509.00
Pendant, Agate, Hermes With Caduceus, Intaglio, Oval, Platinum Over Gold Mount, 3 In.		2806.00
Pendant, Alexander In Battle, Textured, 18K Gold, Van Cleef & Arpels, c.1960		7110.00
Pendant, Amethyst, Emerald, Pearl, Multicolored Enamel, Renaissance Revival, 3 ¼ In.		2726.00
Pendant, Amulet Hand, Black Jade, 18K Gold, Angela Cummings, 1 ⅞ In.		5036.00
Pendant, Aquamarine, Emerald Cut, 6 Diamonds, 14K Rose Gold, Retro, c.1950, 17 ½ In.		6995.00
Pendant, Bird, 14K Gold, Bright & Matte, Aztec Style, Eric De Kolb, c.1970, 2 ½ In.		2074.00
Pendant, Bird, Islamic Style, Etched, Stone Drop, 2 ⅝ In.		460.00
Pendant, Brass, Abstract Design, Curved Bar Links, David Yurman, c.1970s, 2 ¼ In.		1896.00

Jewelry, Necklace, Link, Beaded, Sterling Silver, Los Castillo, Taxco, Mexico, c.1970, 15 In.
$330.00

Jewelry, Necklace, Link, Flowers, Sterling Silver, Georg Jensen, Denmark, 14 ½ In.
$2400.00

Jewelry, Pendant, Chain, Art Deco, Sterling Silver, Enamel, Amethyst, Stamped, 3 ¼ In.
$546.00

Jewelry, Pendant, Edwardian, Black Opal Heart, Diamond Rim, Platinum, Seed Pearl Chain, 28 In.
$9480.00

J

Jewelry, Pendant, Hopeakuu, Moon, Silver, Tapio Wirkkala, Nilo Westerback, c.1971, 2 ½ x 28 In.
$2640.00

Jewelry, Pendant, Locket, Wreath, Blue Enamel, Seed Pearls, 14K Gold, Victorian, 1 ¼ In.
$472.00

Jewelry, Pin, Abstract, Emerald, 14K Gold, Bjorn Weckstrom, Finland, c.1935, 1 ½ x 1 ¼ In.
$949.00

Famous Artist Jewelry

In the 1960s and '70s, important jewelry was made by artists better known for their painting or sculpture, including Harry Bertoia, Georges Braque, Alexander Calder, Jean Cocteau, Salvador Dali, Max Ernst, Cleto Murari, Pablo Picasso, Man Ray, Ettore Sottsass, and Yves Tanguy. All of this jewelry is expensive, sold more as art than as wearable jewelry.

Pendant, Buddha, Burmese Jadite, Transparent, 1 ½ x 1 ½ In.	65.00
Pendant, Chain, Art Deco, Sterling Silver, Enamel, Amethyst, Stamped, 3 ¼ In. ....*illus*	546.00
Pendant, Copper, Fused Glass, Leather Strip, Abstract, C. Falkenstein, 4 ¼ x 6 In.	4575.00
Pendant, Cross, Carved Zigzags, Sun Symbol, 2 Cross Pieces, Silver, Navajo, 7 x 4 In.	767.00
Pendant, Cross, Diamonds, Rubies, Leafy Openwork Mount, c.1890, 3 ½ In.	1464.00
Pendant, Diamond, Sapphire, Pearl Drop, 18K White Gold, Edwardian, 17 In.	3000.00
Pendant, Diamonds, Emeralds, 18K White Gold, Detachable Center, Tiffany & Co., 2 x 1 In.	6274.00
Pendant, Doves, Micro Mosaic, Tesserae Border, Beads, 14K Gold, Etruscan Revival, 1 ½ In.	593.00
Pendant, Edwardian, Black Opal Heart, Diamond Rim, Platinum, Seed Pearl Chain, 28 In. ..*illus*	9480.00
Pendant, Enameled Panels, Red, Blue, Silver, Modernist Design, Meka, Denmark, 3 In.	295.00
Pendant, Eos, Scattering Light, Etruscan Revival, Eugene Fontenay, 1860, 2 ¾ In.	13648.00
Pendant, Fish Shape, Ruby Eye, Diamond Stripes, 14K Gold Body, 1 x 1 ½ In.	644.00
Pendant, Flower Drop, Diamond, Platinum, Gold, 14k White Gold Link Chain, Edwardian	8100.00
Pendant, Flower Petals, Diamonds, Center Full Cut Diamond, 10k Chain, Italy, 22 In.	823.00
Pendant, Frame Shape, Silver, Gold Streaks, Lapis Beads, Emerald Cut, 4 ½ x 3 ⅝ In.	2252.00
Pendant, Globe, Spinning, 14K Gold, 24 In.-Box Link Chain, ¾ In.	527.00
Pendant, Green Onyx, Leaf Mount, Silver, Georg Jensen, 2 In.	1185.00
Pendant, Heart, Micro Mosaic, 3 Flowers, Gold Over Brass, 10K Gold Chain, 15 x ¾ In.	45.00
Pendant, Holds Perfume, Amethyst, Diamond, Hexagonal, Hinged Lid, Krementz & Co.	2133.00
Pendant, Hopeakuu, Moon, Silver, Tapio Wirkkala, Nilo Westerback, c.1971, 2 ½ x 28 In. ..*illus*	2640.00
Pendant, Ivory, Painted, Woman, Curly Brown Hair, Purple Dress, Reverse, Birds, 2 In.	403.00
Pendant, Knot, 18K Gold, Black Enamel, Cartier, 2 ¼ In.	1007.00
Pendant, Locket, Wreath, Blue Enamel, Seed Pearls, 14K Gold, Victorian, 1 ¼ In. ....*illus*	472.00
Pendant, Mask, Moonstone, Sapphires, Enameled Gold Scroll Mount, W. Bauscher, 3 In.	2024.00
Pendant, Moonstone, Oval, Silver Mount, 4 Textured Panels, Modernist Design, 8 In.	165.00
Pendant, Mother-Of-Pearl, Freshwater Pearls, 10K Gold Mount, Arts & Crafts, 1 In.	148.00
Pendant, Pencil, Telescoping, Rose Cut Bohemian Garnets, Rose Gold, Victorian, 2 ¾ In.	425.00
Pendant, Pewter, 3 Stylized Figures, Black Ground, Rectangular, Tennesmed, Sweden, 2 In.	85.00
Pendant, Pewter, Cluster, Inset Blue Stones, Abstract Design, Lysgards, Denmark, 3 In.	100.00
Pendant, Pewter, Stylized Wheels & Spokes, Square Mount, Modernist, Tyr, Sweden, 2 In.	75.00
Pendant, Snuff Bottle, Jade, Brown, Encased Watch, Roman Numerals, Pearl Surround, 3 In.	2242.00
Pendant, Sterling Silver, Circles, Openwork, 7 Drops, Leather Cord, Marion Berg, 4 In.	400.00
Pendant, Stone, Speckled, Elongated, Silver Rectangular Openwork Mount, Tennesmed, 3 In.	95.00
Pendant, Stylized Leaves, Sterling Silver, Modernist, R. Tennesmed, Sweden, 3 ½ In.	65.00
Pendant, Tablet, Lapis, Sunburst Surround, Chain, 14K Gold, Pforzheim, c.1973, 2 ¾ In.	563.00
Pendant, Tourmaline, Heart Shape, Diamond Ribbons, Platinum Over Gold, Edwardian, 2 In.	3294.00
Pendant, Woman, Cherubs, Blue Enamel, Seed Pearls, Diamonds, Watch, Verger, c.1900, 2 In.	5490.00
Pin & Bracelet, Chrysoprase, Sterling Silver Mount, Georg Jensen, c.1940	2928.00
Pin & Bracelet, Link, Leaves, Alternating Redwood & Brown Stained, Brass, 1940s, 7 ½ & 2 ¾ In.	85.00
Pin & Earrings, African Mask, Copper, Enamel, Hammered Hair, Coiled Dangle Earrings	80.00
Pin & Earrings, Aurora Borealis, Starburst, Clip-On Earrings	85.00
Pin & Earrings, Bakelite, Turtle, Screwback, 2 ¼ & 1 ¼ In.	225.00
Pin & Earrings, Blue & Clear Rhinestones, Lisner, c.1950, 2 ½ In.	149.00
Pin & Earrings, V-Shape, Daggers, Engraved, Repousse, Rose Gold Filled, c.1870, 2 ¼ & 2 ⅜ In.	550.00
Pin & Earrings, Wing Shape, Blue Enamel, Rhinestones, Hattie Carnegie, 2 In.	159.00
Pin, 2 Birds, Flying Over Textured Cloud, Enamel, 18K Gold, Georges Braque, 2 ¾ x 2 In.	5925.00
Pin, 2 Butterflies, Leaves, Sterling Silver, Georg Jensen, 2 ⅛ In.	415.00
Pin, 2 Ducks, Sterling Silver, Marked, Georg Jensen, 2 In.	474.00
Pin, 2 Horse's Heads, Wood, Carved, Red Cord Rein Through Mouths, 4 In.	100.00
Pin, 3 Pharaoh's Heads, 18K Gold Bar, c.1880, ⅝ x 1 ⅞ In.	195.00
Pin, 4-Leaf Clover, 14K Gold, 2 ⅞ In.	127.00
Pin, 4-Leaf Clover, Pearl, Rhinestone, Gold, Vendome, 2 ¼ In.	110.00
Pin, Abstract, Emerald, 14K Gold, Bjorn Weckstrom, Finland, c.1935, 1 ½ x 1 ¼ In. ....*illus*	949.00
Pin, Abstract, Sterling Silver, 18K Gold, Donald Friedlich, c.1985, 2 ½ In.	237.00
Pin, Abstract, Sterling Silver, Fred Davis, Mexico, 2 ½ x 2 ¼ In.	1762.00
Pin, AHA, Modernist, Silver, Citrine Quartz, c.1960, 2 In.	350.00
Pin, Arrow, Ruby, 14K Gold, Scrolled Sides, Center Channel, 1 ½ In.	374.00
Pin, Bakelite, 5 Log Shapes, Red, Green, Butterscotch, 2 ½ In.	450.00
Pin, Bakelite, Dangling Cherries, 8 Carved Variegated Red Cherries, 5 Leaves, Red Bar, 3 In.	125.00
Pin, Bakelite, Horse, Prancing, Rust, Brass Studs, 3 In.	400.00
Pin, Bakelite, Horse's Head, Red, Orange Marbleized Ground, Yellow Glass Eye, Brass, 3 In.	375.00
Pin, Bakelite, Locust, 2 ½ In. ....*illus*	88.00
Pin, Bakelite, Oak Leaves, Acorn, Carved, Root Beer, 4 ¼ In.	495.00
Pin, Bakelite, Poppies, Carved, Green, 1 ½ x 2 ½ In.	225.00
Pin, Bakelite, Scottie Dog, Black, Dangles From Rope	88.00
Pin, Bakelite, Scottie Dog, Carved, Root Beer, Apple Juice, 3 In.	275.00

Pin, Bakelite, Scottie Dog, Pumpkin, 1930s, 2 In.	76.00
Pin, Bakelite, Scottie Dog, Pumpkin Color, Black Dog Collar, 2-Tone Eyes, 3 In.	75.00
Pin, Bar, 11 Sapphires, Diamonds, Platinum, Beaded, Art Deco, 3 In.	1342.00
Pin, Bar, Cameo, Double, 2 Women Facing Each Other, Brown & White, 14K Gold, 1 ½ x 1 In.	225.00
Pin, Bar, Clover Shaped Ends, Engraved, Paste Stones, Gold Over Brass, c.1890, 2 x 1 In.	95.00
Pin, Bar, Diamonds, Platinum, Pierced, Beaded, Baton Shape, c.1910, 2 ¾ x 1 In.	2440.00
Pin, Bar, Filigree, Scrolling, 14K White & Yellow Gold, Art Nouveau, c.1900, 2 ⅜ In.	150.00
Pin, Basket, Flowers, Garnet, Ruby, Sapphire Melee, Diamonds, Edwardian, 1 ¼ In.	1185.00
Pin, Bat, Multicolored Enamel, Sterling Silver, Red Stone Cabochon Eyes, Art Nouveau, 4 ½ In.	1778.00
Pin, Beetle, Micro Mosaic, Silver Mount, C-Clasp, Egyptian Revival, Early 1900s, 1 ⅛ In.	443.00
Pin, Beetle, Rubies, Diamonds, Enamel, 18K Gold, 2 ½ In.	2124.00
Pin, Bellflower, Malachite, Amber Buds & Berries, Silver, Georg Jensen, c.1920, 1 ⅝ In.	889.00
Pin, Bird, In Flight, Blue & White Enamel, Sterling Silver, Marked, J, Mexico, 1 ½ In.	70.00
Pin, Bird, Rhinestones, Red Rhinestone Eye, c.1890	110.00
Pin, Bird, Stylized, Sterling Silver, Marked, Georg Jensen, 1 ⅝ x 2 In.	178.00
Pin, Bird, Wood, Lucite, Painted, Yellow Bill, Black & White Eye, Yellow Stripe, c.1930, 4 x 2 In.	65.00
Pin, Birds, On Branch, Enamel, Multicolored, Rhinestones, Trifari, 1 ¾ x 1 ¾ In. ....*illus*	245.00
Pin, Blackamoor, Carved Onyx, Gem Set, Brocaded Coat, Aquamarine Turban, Ruby, Nardi, 2 In.	4148.00
Pin, Books In Library, Micro Mosaic, Sandstone Medallion, 14K Gold, Oval, 2 In.	150.00
Pin, Bow, Aquamarine, Emerald Cut, Diamond, 14K White Gold, 2 In.	3295.00
Pin, Bow, Citrine, 14K Gold, Cartier, Retro, 2 ¼ In.	711.00
Pin, Bow, Ribbon, European Cut Diamonds, Pearl Terminals, Edwardian, 2 ⅜ x 2 ½ In.	4148.00
Pin, Buckle, Round Rhinestones, Rhodium Plated, Marked, Boucher, 2 x ¾ In.	95.00
Pin, Buddha, Seated On Lotus, Emerald Cabochon, Diamond, Textured Gold Mount, 2 ⅝ In. .	1464.00
Pin, Butterfly, 18K Gold, Tiffany & Co., 1 ¾ In.	652.00
Pin, Butterfly, Blue Stones, Faceted Glass, Weiss, 2 x 2 In. ....*illus*	140.00
Pin, Butterfly, Diamonds, Pieced Beaded Wings, Garnet Eyes, c.1905, 2 In.	5795.00
Pin, Butterfly, Mine Cut Diamonds, Pave Set, Ruby Cabochons, Silver Over Gold, 1 ⅝ In.	5377.00
Pin, Butterfly, Pierced Jade Wings, Pearl Body, Ruby Eyes, Flexible Antennae, 2 ¼ In.	149.00
Pin, Butterfly, Rhinestones, Black & White, KJL, 2 ⅞ In.	259.00
Pin, Butterfly, Tiger's Eye, Rubies, Gold, England..........................	2151.00
Pin, Cameo, Agate, Greek Soldier, Crested Helmet, Oval Gold Wirework Mount, 1870, 2 In.	2806.00
Pin, Cameo, Carved, Young Woman, Coral Ground, 18K Gold, 1 x ¾ In.	59.00
Pin, Cameo, Shell, Woman, With Flowers, Gold Leaves At Corners, Edwardian, c.1910, 1 ½ x 2 In. .	495.00
Pin, Cameo, Woman, Red Coral, 18k Gold, Rope Turned Rim, Oval, 1 ⅜ x 1 In.	140.00
Pin, Cameo, Woman, Wearing Crown, Toga, Pearl Lined Rim, 14K Gold, 1 x 1 ¼ In.	1200.00
Pin, Cameo, Woman's Profile, Pearl Necklace, Silver Rope Twist Frame, 2 x 1 ¾ In.	115.00
Pin, Cat, With Ball, Black, Opaque, Signed, Lea Stein, 1 ¾ x 2 In.	159.00
Pin, Cat's Head, Aqua Rhinestone, Pink Eyes, Ears, Marked, Warner, 1 x 1 ¼ In.	55.00
Pin, Cat's Head, Red, Black Eyes, Ears, Signed, Lea Stein, 2 ¼ x 1 ⅞ In.	159.00
Pin, Cicada, Figural, Rounded Wings, 18k Gold, France, c.1870	1560.00
Pin, Circle, Entwined Scroll, Pierced Ribbon, 18K Gold, Retro, France, 1 ¾ In.	326.00
Pin, Circles, 4 Interlocking, 14K Gold, 1 ¼ In.	150.00
Pin, Circular Bands, 14K Gold, Tiffany & Co., 2 ¾ In.	889.00
Pin, Citrine Quartz, 2 Ruby Bars, Diamonds, 14K Rose Gold, Scrolls, Tiffany & Co., 2 In.	2300.00
Pin, Coral Branch, Looping Silver Mount, 2 In.	95.00
Pin, Coral Branch, Tahitian Pearl, 18K Gold, Marked, Tony Duquette, 4 In.	3081.00
Pin, Crown & Scepter, Gold Washed Silver, 2 ½ x 2 ¼ In.	210.00
Pin, Crown, Diamonds, Seed Pearl, J.E. Caldwell & Co., 1 ¾ In.	296.00
Pin, Daffodils, Daisies, Half Moon Shape, Celluloid, Salmon, 1930s, 1 ⅝ x 2 ⁵⁄₁₆ In.	47.00
Pin, Diamonds, Oval, Bow Knot & Swag Top, Pear Shaped Diamond Drop, c.1950, 2 In.	4575.00
Pin, Doe, Lying Down, Carved Eye & Nose, Wood, Celluloid Ears, 1940s, 2 ½ x 2 ¾ In.	95.00
Pin, Dog, Sand, House, Trees, Glass, Reverse Painted, 14K Gold Cattail Frame, c.1910, 2 In.	2196.00
Pin, Dove, Leaves, Lapis Cabochon Accents, Sterling Silver, Georg Jensen, 1 ¾ In.	533.00
Pin, Dove, Sterling Silver, Georg Jensen, 2 ⅜ In.	296.00
Pin, Dragonfly, Plique-A-Jour Enamel, Diamonds, Sapphires, Rubies, 14K Gold, 3 x 2 In.	1840.00
Pin, Enamel, 2 Birds, Orange, Modernist, Concave Rectangular Mount, M. Olivier, 2 In.	115.00
Pin, Enamel, Cloisonne, Fish, Tail Up, Blue, White, Black, Silver Mount, D. Andersen, 1 ¾ In. .	200.00
Pin, Enamel, Guilloche, Blue, Yellow, Brown, Rectangular Silver Mount, D. Andersen, 2 In.	375.00
Pin, Enamel, Triple Boomerang Form, Cobalt Blue, Silver, Marked, VB, Denmark, 2 In.	85.00
Pin, Feather, Portugal, Sterling Silver, 2 ¾ x ⅝ In.	20.00
Pin, Fez, Crescent Shape, Pave Rhinestones, Clear, Red, Green, ORA, 1950s, 1 ¾ x 1 ¾ In.	22.00
Pin, Fish, Coral, Diamond Puffer, Coral Lips, Diamond Eyes, 18K Gold, Cartier, 1 ¼ In.	4148.00
Pin, Fish, Jelly Belly, Cabochon Body, Rhinestone Eye........................	125.00
Pin, Fish, Repousse, Enameled, Speckled, Green, Yellow Gill, Originals By Robert, 1 ¾ x 1 ¾ In.	67.00
Pin, Flamingo, Standing On 1 Leg, Marked, Sterling Silver, 21 ½ In.	28.00

Jewelry, Pin, AHA, Modernist, Silver, Citrine Quartz, c.1960, 2 In.
$350.00

Jewelry, Pin, Bakelite, Locust, 2 ½ In.
$88.00

Jewelry, Pin, Birds, On Branch, Enamel, Multicolored, Rhinestones, Trifari, 1 ¾ x 1 ¾ In.
$245.00

Jewelry, Pin, Butterfly, Blue Stones, Faceted Glass, Weiss, 2 x 2 In.
$140.00

JEWELRY

Jewelry, Pin, Hummingbird, Blue Stone, Rhinestones, Trifari, 2 ½ x 2 ¼ In.
$75.00

Jewelry, Pin, Jadeite, Pearl, 18K Yellow & Pink Gold, Koi, Marked, Marsh, 2 ¼ In.
$3013.00

Jewelry, Pin, Micro Mosaic, St. Peter's Square, Black Onyx, 15K Gold, 1 ¾ In.
$661.00

Antique Jewelry

Antique jewelry is an easy item to steal and sell. Dealers and collectors must be careful to check a seller's story. Sometimes the cameo pin belongs to Mother, and Mother doesn't know it is being sold. If stolen jewelry is traced to you, the buyer, the law says you must give it back. You will not be paid for it. So buy carefully at flea markets, house sales, or Internet auctions, where pieces could come from dubious sources.

Jewelry, Pin, Mourning, Black Cameo, Portrait, Faceted Beads, Victorian, 1 ¾ x 7 In.
$178.00

Jewelry, Pin, Pomegranate Heart, Ruby, Diamond, 18K, Salvador Dali, Henryk Kaston, 4 x 2 In.
$9776.00

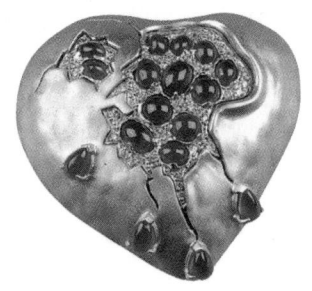

Jewelry, Pin, Retro Moderne, 14K Yellow Gold, Tapered Leaf, Pave Set Diamond Bee
$1080.00

Jewelry, Pin, Scarab, Plique-A-Jour Enamel Body, Enamel Wings, c.1900, 1 x 1 In.
$236.00

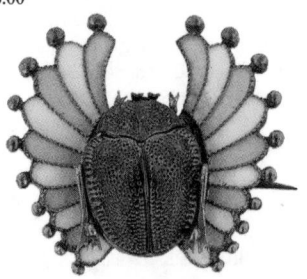

Jewelry, Pin, Shoulder, Quatrefoil, Green & Red Cabochons, Gold Chain Trim, Chanel
$720.00

Jewelry, Pin, Sterling Silver, Hammered, Agate Cabochon, Art Nouveau, Jarvie, 2 ¼ In.
$3900.00

Jewelry, Pin, Stylized Flower, Amethyst, Center, 14K Bicolor Gold, Retro, 1 ¾ In.
$207.00

Jewelry, Pin, Swallow, Diamonds, Enameled, Silver, Gold, c.1900, 4 ¼ x 2 In.
$10005.00

J

Pin, Flower & Leaf Design, Topaz, Faceted, Foil Backed, Silver Mount, 18th Century, 3 In.	3851.00
Pin, Flower Basket, Gold, Multicolored Stones, Georgian, 1 x 1 In.	468.00
Pin, Flower, Citrine, Full Cut Diamond, Rope Twist Mount, 14K Gold, Sonia Bitton, 2 ½ In.	770.00
Pin, Flower, Jadeite, Enamel, Single Cut Diamond, Platinum Mount, Art Deco, 1 ¾ In.	1778.00
Pin, Flower, Opening Bud, Emerald & Diamond Melee, 14K Gold, Tiffany & Co., 2 ⅛ In.	1896.00
Pin, Flower, Rhinestone, Gold, Schiaperelli, 2 ⅜ In.	180.00
Pin, Flower, Rose Montee Rhinestones, 5 Ridged Petals, Gold Plated, Miriam Haskell, c.1950, 1 ½ In.	245.00
Pin, Flower, Ruby, 18K Gold, Tiffany & Co., 2 ⅛ In.	563.00
Pin, Flower, Sapphires, 18K Gold, Tiffany & Co., Italy, 2 In.	1067.00
Pin, Flowers, Garnet, Diamond Shape, Victorian, 1 ¾ In.	52.00
Pin, Flowers, Glass, Purple, Green Rhinestones, Gold Plate, 1930s, 3 In.	87.00
Pin, Flowers, Green Onyx, Sterling Silver, Marked, Georg Jensen, 3 In.	1067.00
Pin, Flowers, Leaves, Sterling Silver, Malachite, Cabochon, Georg Jensen, 2 In.	593.00
Pin, Flowers, Marcasite, Red Glass, Open Flowing Vines, Silver, 1930s, 2 ⅜ x 1 ⅝ In.	115.00
Pin, Flying Goose, Bakelite, Butterscotch, Glass Eyes, 3 ¾ x 3 In.	450.00
Pin, Fox, Black & Gold, Lea Stein, 3 ½ x 2 ¼ In.	249.00
Pin, Fox, Enameled Copper, 14K Gold Oval Mount, J.W. Bailey, 1861, 2 ¾ In.	2074.00
Pin, Frog, Emerald Cabochon Eyes, 18K Gold, Retractable Bail, Marked, Webb, 1 ¾ In.	4182.00
Pin, Frog, Pave Diamonds, Emerald Melee Eyes, Platinum, McTeigue, ½ In., Pair	1422.00
Pin, Garlands & Bows In Cartouche, Diamonds, Edwardian Revival, c.1950, 2 In.	8845.00
Pin, Ginko Leaf, Gold Tone, Ted Muchling, 4 ½ x 3 In.	178.00
Pin, Grape Cluster, Pearls, Diamond Leaves, 18K Gold, Silver Mount, M. Buccellati, 1 ⅞ In.	3477.00
Pin, Green Ceramic Pillow Stone, Open Rectangular Mount, Modernist, Tennesmed, 2 ½ In.	65.00
Pin, Half Oyster Shell, Ribbed, Ruby, Diamond Melee, 14K Gold, Cartier, 1 ⅝ In.	3500.00
Pin, Hand, Woman's, Cuff, Sterling Silver, 2 ¼ In.	30.00
Pin, Heart, Bombe, Diamond Encrusted, Platinum Top, 18K Gold Mount, Edwardian, 1 In.	4740.00
Pin, Heart, Diamond Scrolls & Flowers, Pierced Platinum Over Gold, Art Deco, 2 In.	3965.00
Pin, Heart Knot, Rhinestones, Marked, Trifari, 1 ⅞ In.	135.00
Pin, Heart, Wife, Layered, Blue, White, Red, 2 ½ In.	175.00
Pin, Hummingbird, Blue Stone, Rhinestones, Trifari, 2 ½ x 2 ¼ In. ...illus	75.00
Pin, Hummingbird, Diamond Accents, Gold, Cartier, Clip-On	5676.00
Pin, Ice Rhinestone, Blue Leaves, Eisenberg, c.1970, 1 ¾ x 2 In.	145.00
Pin, Indian Chief, Diamond, Enamel, Malachite, 18K Gold, W.A. Sarmento, 2 ¾ In.	3851.00
Pin, Jabot, Diamonds, Pearl, 18K White Gold, Marked, Cartier, 3 ⅜ In.	8365.00
Pin, Jabot, Emerald, Baguette Diamonds, Ringed Baton, Art Deco, France, c.1925, 2 ½ In.	1952.00
Pin, Jacquard, Stylized Head, Enamel, Multicolored Champleve, 14K Gold	1185.00
Pin, Jade, Chinese Character, Beaded Border, 24K Gold, 1 ⅛ In.	777.00
Pin, Jadeite, Pearl, 18K Yellow & Pink Gold, Koi, Marked, Marsh, 2 ¼ In. ...illus	3013.00
Pin, Lamb, Ivy, Sterling Silver, Georg Jensen, c.1945, 2 In.	711.00
Pin, Leaf, Rhinestones, Eisenberg, 4 ½ x 1 ⅜ In.	160.00
Pin, Leaf Vein Hand, Enamel Fingernails, 18K Gold, Salvador Dali, 2 ½ In.	4740.00
Pin, Leaves, Inset Agates, Amethysts, Engraved, Silver, Round, Scotland, 3 x 2 ¼ In.	345.00
Pin, Leaves, Ribbed, Polished, Diamonds, 14K Gold, Tiffany & Co., 1 ½ In.	415.00
Pin, Leaves, Rock Crystal Plaque, Emerald, Diamond Frame, Platinum Mount, Art Deco, 1 ⅜ In.	1422.00
Pin, Leaves, Scrolling, Ruby, 14K Gold, Victorian, 1 ¼ x 2 In.	468.00
Pin, Leopard, Reclining, Diamond Eyes, Enameled Spots, 18K Gold, 2 x 1 In.	1380.00
Pin, Lily Of The Valley, Rock Crystal Buds, Nephrite, Diamond Ribbon, Austria, 1950, 4 In.	3416.00
Pin, Lion Cub, Diamonds, Emerald Eyes, Wood, 18K Gold, Van Cleef & Arpels, 1 ¾ In.	2800.00
Pin, Lion, Diamond Eyes, Ruby Nose, Textured 18K Gold, Double Pin Stem, Lalaounis, 2 In.	3585.00
Pin, Lizard, Rhinestones, Coro, 3 In.	199.00
Pin, Lobster, Claws, Pincers, Sterling Silver, 2 ¼ In.	18.00
Pin, Locket, 4-Way Frame, Enamel, Rhinestone, Coro, 2 ½ In.	95.00
Pin, Locket, Cameo, Shell, Woman In Classical Setting, Oval, 2 In.	115.00
Pin, Lotus, Plique-A-Jour Enamel, Pink Tourmaline, 18K Gold, Tiffany & Co., c.1916	10665.00
Pin, Mesoamerican Figure, Openwork, Emerald Inlaid Eyes, 18K Gold, 2 ⅝ In.	575.00
Pin, Micro Mosaic, St. Peter's Square, Black Onyx, 15K Gold, 1 ¾ In. ...illus	661.00
Pin, Miracle, Alternating Semicircles & Trapezoids, Colored Rhinestones, Scotland, 2 x 2 In.	45.00
Pin, Mourning, Black Cameo, Portrait, Faceted Beads, Victorian, 1 ¾ x 7 In. ...illus	178.00
Pin, Nymphs, Putti, Reverse Carved Glass, Onyx Back, Diamonds, Platinum, c.1925, 2 In.	2928.00
Pin, Peacock, Goldtone, Hobe	85.00
Pin, Peacock Woman, 18K Gold, Art Nouveau, P. Richard, E. Becker, France, 2 In.	2196.00
Pin, Pearl, Diamond Spray, Platinum, c.1900, 1 ¼ x 1 ¹/₁₂ In.	7934.00
Pin, Pendant, Diamonds, Platinum Over 18K Gold Mount, Edwardian, 1 ¼ x 1 ½ In.	1778.00
Pin, Pendant, Openwork Scrolls, Center Diamond, 14K Gold, Victorian, 1 In.	518.00
Pin, Persian Turquoise, Oval Cabochon, 28-Diamond Surround, 18K Gold, c.1900, 1 ¼ In.	1708.00
Pin, Pink Flamingo, Enamel, Black Dangle Legs, Rhinestone Eyes, Marked, Dancraft	65.00

Jewelry, Ring, Concave Design, Sterling Silver, Harald Nielsen, Georg Jensen
$69.00

Jewelry, Ring, Diamond, Black Onyx, Platinum, Art Deco, Size 6 ¾
$414.00

Jewelry, Ring, Love, LO Over VE, 18K Gold, Robert Indiana, Size 11
$1534.00

Jewelry, Ring, Onyx, Diamond, 14K Gold, Art Deco, Size 8 ½ In. $380.00

Jewelry, Ring, Seed Pearl, Turquoise Cabochons, 14K Gold, Engraved, Size 6 ½ $138.00

Cameo Love

Cameos, made since antiquity, are back in style again. The classical figures carved on the cameo go well with the romantic, ruffled look of today's fashions. Hard-stone cameos are best. Price is determined by the quality of the carving and the way the colored layers of the stone were used. Shell cameos were introduced in Victorian times. Today a large, decorative shell cameo is worth as much as a hard-stone example, even though they were easier to carve. Mythological scenes are the best.

Pin, Platinum, Circle, Diamonds, Double Bow, Diamond Drop, Edwardian, 1 ½ In.	3995.00
Pin, Platinum, Diamond Melee, Art Deco, 1 ½ In.	593.00
Pin, Platinum, Pear Shaped Dangling Diamonds, 2 ½ x 1 ¼ In.	2390.00
Pin, Plume, Pear-Shaped Garnets, Suspending Drops, Silver, 1700s, 7 x 3 ½ In.	6518.00
Pin, Pomegranate Heart, Ruby, Diamond, 18K, Salvador Dali, Henryk Kaston, 4 x 2 In. ...*illus*	9776.00
Pin, Poodle, Sapphire Eyes, Diamond Bowtie, 14K Gold, 1 ¾ In.	627.00
Pin, Porcelain, Mother & Child, Blue Enamel Frame, 2 x 1 ¾ In.	823.00
Pin, Portrait, Child, Blond, Blue Dress, 14K Gold Frame, 1856, 2 ⅛ x 1 ¾ In.	1126.00
Pin, Posy, Sterling Silver, Marked, Jenkins & Jenkins, Victorian, 3 ½ In.	125.00
Pin, Psyche, Matte Enamel, 18K Gold, Etruscan Revival, c.1860s, 2 ⅜ In.	4740.00
Pin, Puddle Duck, 14K Gold, Banded Agate, Tiffany & Co., 1 ¾ In.	1541.00
Pin, Purple Paste Stones, Suspending Drops, Silver Mount, 18th Century, 2 ½ In.	2726.00
Pin, Retro Moderne, 14K Yellow Gold, Tapered Leaf, Pave Set Diamond Bee *illus*	1080.00
Pin, Ribbon, Diamonds, Emeralds, Pear Shape, Round & Baguette, 1950s, 2 In.	2645.00
Pin, Ribbon Shape, Diamond, 18K Gold, Marked, Dankner, 1 ¾ x 1 ½ In.	805.00
Pin, Rose Blossoms, Coral, Diamond, 4 In.	1422.00
Pin, Rose, Carved Coral, Pearls, Diamond Melee, 18K Gold, Cartier, Signed, 2 In.	2015.00
Pin, Scarab, Plique-A-Jour Enamel Body, Enamel Wings, c.1900, 1 x 1 In. ...*illus*	236.00
Pin, Scimitar, Rose Rivoli Glass Stone, Colored Rhinestones, Gold Plated, Weiss, 4 x 1 ½ In. ...	165.00
Pin, Seahorse, Sterling Silver, Paul Lobel, 2 ⅜ In.	504.00
Pin, Semicircles, Stamped Flower, Amber, Chaton, Rhinestone, Goldtone, Scotland, 1 ⅜ In.	55.00
Pin, Shield, Bald Eagle, Star Banner, Diamonds, Rubies, Cartier, c.1923, 1 In.	7320.00
Pin, Ship On Lake, Shoreline, Diamond, Platinum, 18K Gold Mount, Art Nouveau, 1 ½ In.	2963.00
Pin, Shoulder, Quatrefoil, Green & Red Cabochons, Gold Chain Trim, Chanel ...*illus*	720.00
Pin, Smoky Rhinestone, Weiss, 2 In.	55.00
Pin, Snowman, Black Hat, Red Pipe, Yellow Broom, Plastic, Thermometer, 1940s, 2 x 1 In.	45.00
Pin, Star, 5-Point, Red Stone, Rhinestone, 3 ½ In.	185.00
Pin, Starburst, Pendant, Old Mine Cut & Rose Cut Diamonds, Platinum Topped, Edwardian, 2 In.	2726.00
Pin, Sterling Silver, Hammered, Agate Cabochon, Art Nouveau, Jarvie, 2 ¼ In. ...*illus*	3900.00
Pin, Sterling Silver, Lapis, Georg Jensen, 1 ½ x 1 ¼ In.	316.00
Pin, Strawberry, Dimpled, Molded Glass, Iridescent, Crackled Silver Foil, 2 ⅛ x 2 ⅜ In.	32.00
Pin, Stylized Aztec Serpent, Sterling Silver, William Spratling, c.1940	160.00
Pin, Stylized Butterfly, Diamonds, Pear-Shaped Diamond Drop, Chain, c.1930, 2 In.	3965.00
Pin, Stylized Flower, Amethyst, Center, 14K Bicolor Gold, Retro, 1 ¾ In. ...*illus*	207.00
Pin, Stylized Flower, Fruit Salad, Rubies, Diamonds, Sapphires, Ilias Lalaounis, 3 In.	1830.00
Pin, Stylized Leaf, Feather Shape, Inset Diamonds, Rubies, Sapphires, Emeralds, 1 ¾ x 2 ¼ In.	288.00
Pin, Stylized Snowflake, Cultured Pearl, 14K Gold, Daniel Webb	407.00
Pin, Stylized Trumpet Shape, Florentine Finish, Turquoise Beads, Marked, Sphinx, 1970s, 2 ¼ In.	39.00
Pin, Swallow, Diamonds, Enameled, Silver, Gold, c.1900, 4 ¼ x 2 In. ...*illus*	10005.00
Pin, Swan, Ruby Rhinestones, Coral Beads, Goldtone, Florentine Finish, HAR, 1 ¼ x 1 ½ In. ..	85.00
Pin, Taille Blossom, Diamonds, Enamel, Platinum, Boucheron, London, c.1950	3555.00
Pin, Thistle, Molded Blue Glass, Gilt Metal Mount, Lalique, 3 ⅛ In.	1422.00
Pin, Tortoiseshell Loops, Sterling Silver, William Spratling, 2 In.	807.00
Pin, Tussy Mussy, Silver Filigree, Painted Flowers, Brass Pin Stem, Tube Hinge, 2 ¼ x 1 ½ In. .	225.00
Pin, Violin, Bow, Enameled Wood Grain, Diamond Edges, Pearl Pegs, c.1900, 3 In.	3965.00
Pin, Watch, Lion's Head, Gold Filled, Rose Gold Curlicues, Green Stone Eyes, c.1880, ¾ x 1 ⅛ In.	185.00
Pin, Watch, Peso, Openwork, Crested Coat Of Arms Mount, 18K Gold, Paul Flato, 2 In.	2645.00
Pin, Water Lily, Plique-A-Jour Enamel, Blue, Green, Diamond, 14K Gold, Riker Bros., 1 ⅛ In. .	1422.00
Pin, Whale Shape, Spewing Ruby, Sapphire, Diamond, 14K Gold, 1 ⅜ In.	316.00
Pin, Wire Work, Undulating Border, Sterling Silver, Mother-Of-Pearl Center, 1950s, 1 ¼ In.	32.00
Pin, Wood, Aqua Stain, 2 Rows Of Discs, Brass Base, 1940s, 1 ⅝ x 7 ½ In.	68.00
Pin, Wreath, Sapphire, Diamond, 14K Gold, Platinum Leaves, Arts & Crafts, Edward Oaks	8888.00
Posy Holder, Hearts, Sterling Silver, c.1970, 2 ¼ x ¾ In.	65.00
Posy Holder, Sterling Silver, Filigree, Cornucopia Shape, Egyptian Head, Pin, Finger Ring, 3 In.	995.00
Ring & Earrings, Discs, Diamonds, Platinum, 18K Gold, Michael Zobel, Size 8, 1 ¾ In.	1896.00
Ring, 3-Stone, Diamond, 2 Rubies, 14K Gold, Marked, C. & Co., c.1910, Size 6 ½	1830.00
Ring, Aquamarine, 18K White Gold, Edwardian Style Filigree Mount, Belais, Size 6 ¼..............	259.00
Ring, Aztec Parrot, Emerald Eyes, Eric De Kolb, c.1970, Size 10 ½ In.	488.00
Ring, Bakelite, Butterscotch, Triangular, Size 7 ½	45.00
Ring, Band, 4 Cherub Masks In Relief, 14K Gold, Eric De Kolb, c.1970, Size 7 ½	1342.00
Ring, Band, Leaves, Rose Cut Diamonds, 18K Gold, Silver, M. Buccellati, Size 6	5629.00
Ring, Basket, Peridot, Diamond, 14K Gold, c.1980, Size 6	1450.00
Ring, Bear Claw, Turquoise, Coral, Sterling Silver	201.00
Ring, Blue Star Sapphire, Platinum, Men's, Size 7 ½	717.00
Ring, Cabochon, Domed, Green, Oval, Pewter Dish-Shape Mount, J. Jensen	45.00
Ring, Cat's-Eye Chrysoberyl, 2 Baguette Diamonds, Gypsy Mount, Gold, Size 7 ½....................	2684.00
Ring, Cat's-Eye, Oval Cabochon, Rectangular Pewter Mount, J. Jensen, Size 7	65.00

Ring, Citrine, Amethyst, Diamond Melee, Gold Beads, Silver, c.1930s, Size 7	830.00
Ring, Cocktail, 15 Brilliant Cut Diamonds, Various Sizes, 14K Gold, c.1950	660.00
Ring, Cocktail, Ruby, Emerald Cut, Diamonds, 14K Gold, Neiman Marcus, Size 7	805.00
Ring, Concave Design, Sterling Silver, Harald Nielsen, Georg Jensen ....*illus*	69.00
Ring, Creature, Ruby Eyes, Peridot, Heart Shape, Diamond Frame, Platinum, Edwardian, Size 2 ¾.	1778.00
Ring, Diamond, Black Onyx, Platinum, Art Deco, Size 6 ¾ ....*illus*	414.00
Ring, Diamond, Center Round Center Brilliant Cut, 9 Surrounds, Platinum, Art Deco, Size 9 ..	2360.00
Ring, Diamond, European Cut, Bezel Set, Miye For Janiye, 1974, Size 6 ½	2133.00
Ring, Diamond, Heart-Shape Emerald, Art Deco, Tiffany & Co., Size 4 ½	10073.00
Ring, Diamond, Marquise Cut, Openwork, Diamond Butterflies, Peclard, Zurich, Size 6 ½.......	15535.00
Ring, Diamond, Pave Set, Rotating, 18K White Gold, Salavetti, Size 7 ¼................................	948.00
Ring, Diamond, Prong Set, Yellow Gold, Victorian, Inscribed, Size 6	288.00
Ring, Diamond, Round Brilliant Cut, Filigree, 14K White Gold, Box, c.1930, Size 8	460.00
Ring, Diamond, Single Cut, Pear Shape Baguette, Rubies, Diamond Melee, Art Deco, Size 7	2607.00
Ring, Diamond Solitaire, Platinum, Tiffany & Co., Art Deco, Size 10	5925.00
Ring, Diamond, Stepcut, Synthetic Ruby, Platinum, Edwardian, Size 8	6750.00
Ring, Diamonds, Pierced Platinum Shield Mount, Art Deco, Size 6	8540.00
Ring, Diamonds, Platinum, Emeralds, Art Deco, Size 7 ½...	7767.00
Ring, Diamonds, Round European Cut, Platinum, Filigree Mount, Art Deco, Size 5 ½.............	14900.00
Ring, Diamonds, Rubies, Cluster, 18K Gold, c.1960, Size 8 ¾	1293.00
Ring, Diamonds, Sapphires, Double Boule Design, Van Cleef & Arpels, Box	26290.00
Ring, Diamonds, Sapphires, Shaped Oblong Mount, White Gold, Edwardian	418.00
Ring, Emerald, Diamonds, Enameled Gold Mount, c.1930...	1770.00
Ring, Eternity Band, Diamonds, Beaded Border, Platinum, 18K Gold, Tiffany & Co., Size 6	2196.00
Ring, Flowers, Filigree, Faceted Synthetic Amethyst, 18K White Gold, Edwardian, Size 8 ½.......	575.00
Ring, Garnet, Leaf, Sterling Silver, Georg Jensen, Size 7	593.00
Ring, Garnet, Oval, Faceted, 14K Gold, Victorian, Size 7 ½	245.00
Ring, Iguana, Tsavorite Garnets, Rubies, Yellow Sapphires, Diamonds, 18K Gold, Size 7	2562.00
Ring, Jadeite, Caliber-Cut Sapphires, Platinum, Art Deco, Size 4 ¾	1185.00
Ring, Love, LO Over VE, 18K Gold, Robert Indiana, Size 11 ....*illus*	1534.00
Ring, Moonstone, Cabochons, Bezel Set, Sterling Silver, Petals, Georg Jensen, Size 7 ¾............	207.00
Ring, Moonstone, Domed Oval Cabochon, Prong Set, 14K Gold, c.1940s, Size 6........................	711.00
Ring, Moonstone, Leaf, Sterling Silver, Georg Jensen, Size 8	504.00
Ring, Mourning, Rutledge Family, Diamond, Yellow Gold, Inscribed, c.1807...........................	863.00
Ring, Onyx, Diamond, 14K Gold, Art Deco, Size 8 ½ In. ....*illus*	380.00
Ring, Onyx, Single Cut Diamond Melee, Platinum, 14K Gold Mount, c.1930s, Size 5 ¾	504.00
Ring, Onyx, Sterling Silver, American Indian, Marked, Size 8 ¼	140.00
Ring, Oval Rose Quartz, Sterling Silver, Beaded Border, Art Deco, Size 7 ½.............................	55.00
Ring, Oxblood Coral Cabochon, 18-Diamond Surround, Platinum, c.1950, Size 7 ½...................	2806.00
Ring, Pearl, Bezel-Set Diamonds, Raised Stylized Flower Mount, Gold, Platinum, Art Deco	915.00
Ring, Pink Sapphire, Diamond, Cushion Cut, 14K Gold, Arts & Crafts, Edward Oaks.................	5925.00
Ring, Platinum, Engraved Flowers, 1941, Size 6 ½	711.00
Ring, Poison, Sapphire On Hinged Compartment, Rose Cut Diamonds, Cartouche Shape........	2928.00
Ring, Rhodolite Garnet, 18K Gold, Art Nouveau Style, Ben Accorso, Size 7	184.00
Ring, Sapphire, Cushion Cut, 12 Diamonds, Platinum Mount, c.1910, Size 6 ½	2440.00
Ring, Sapphire, Diamonds, 18K Gold, Platinum, Irena Brynner, Size 3 ½	2806.00
Ring, Seed Pearl, Turquoise Cabochons, 14K Gold, Engraved, Size 6 ½ ....*illus*	138.00
Ring, Snake, Scrolling Tail, Rock Crystal Head, 18K Gold, Lalaounis, Size 7 ½	1185.00
Ring, Sterling Silver, 6 Turquoise Oval Stones, Navajo Indian, Marked, Size 8 ¾....................	240.00
Ring, Sterling Silver, Applied Copper, Sam Kramer, Mushroom Mark, 1960s, ¾ In. ....*illus*	600.00
Ring, Sterling Silver, Silver Pearl, Georg Jensen, c.1940, Size 5 ¼	207.00
Ring, Stylized Bird, Free-Form Design, 18K Gold, Pearl, Irena Brynner, 2 ½ x 2 ¾ In.	2196.00
Ring, Sunburst, Oval Amber Cabochon, Pewter, J. Jensen, Size 7	65.00
Ring, Tourmaline Green, Diamond Baguette Shoulders, Tiffany & Co., c.1925, Size 8..............	3416.00
Ring, Trinity, 18K Tricolor Gold, Cartier, Size 6 ½	259.00
Ring, Turquoise, Diamond, 18K Gold, Buccellati, Size 7 ½..	7110.00
Ring, X-Shape, Pave Diamonds, Textured, 18K Gold, Schlumberger, Tiffany & Co., Size 6 ½	2196.00
Shirt Studs & Cuff Links, Cobalt Blue Stone In Gold Stylized Seed Pods, Tiffany	2185.00
Shirt Studs, Blue Enameled Ball, 14K Gold Wire Wrap, Tiffany & Co., 5 Piece	575.00
Shoe Buckles, Filigree, Oval, Cut Steel, France, 1840-80, 2 ¼ x 1 ½ In., Pair	45.00
Skirt Lifter, Ballroom Sash, Snake & Turquoise Stone, Victorian, 2 ¾ In.	325.00
Skirt Lifter, Face Design, Brass, Marked, England, Mid Victorian, 5 ¼ In.	285.00
Skirt Lifter, Hand Design, Brass, c.1880, 6 ¼ In.	285.00
Skirt Lifter, Nickel Plated, Victorian, 1884, 3 x 1 In.	165.00
Stickpin, Gathered Bow, Tied By Gold Band, Sterling, Georg Jensen, 3 ½ In.	178.00
Stickpin, Oval Disc, Embossed Nantucket Windmill, Sterling Silver, Marked, Souvenir, 2 ½ In.	225.00
Stickpin, Peridot, Square, 10K Gold, Art Nouveau, c.1900, 2 ⅜ In.	62.00

Jewelry, Ring, Sterling Silver, Applied Copper, Sam Kramer, Mushroom Mark, 1960s, ¾ In. $600.00

J

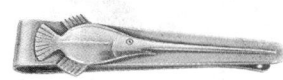

Jewelry, Tie Bar, Swordfish, Sterling Silver, Marked, Georg Jensen, 2 ¼ In. $115.00

John Rogers, Group, Weighing The Baby, 20 x 15 In. $700.00

Judaica, Spice Box, Silver Repousse, Bone Ivory, Barrel Shape, 1800s, 13 ¼ x 5 ¾ In. $633.00

Jugtown Pottery, Candlestick, Black Glaze, Impressed Mark, 13 ¾ In. $531.00

Jugtown Pottery, Jar, Red & Blue Mottled Glaze, Chinese Style, Impressed Mark, Ben Owen, 7 ½ In. $1416.00

Stickpin, Pink Garnet, Square Cut, 14K Gold, Edwardian, c.1900, 2 ⅝ In.	185.00
Tie Bar, Swordfish, Sterling Silver, Marked, Georg Jensen, 2 ¼ In. .....*illus*	115.00
Tie Clasp, Ski, 14K Yellow Gold, Marked Tiffany, Box, 2 ¾ In.	995.00
Tie Tack, Diamond, 14-Garnet Border, Gold Plated, c.1940, ½ In.	185.00
Tie Tack, Onyx, Brushed Gold, Safety Chain, c.1960, ⅜ In.	15.00
Watch Chain, Double Bar & Rope, 18K Yellow Gold, c.1880, 20 In.	2600.00
Watch Chain, Hairwork, Brunette, 14K Gold, Ends, Victorian, 14 In.	195.00
Watch Chain, Opal Cabochons, Pear Shape, Paperclip Links, 14K Gold, c.1930, 31 ½ In.	770.00
Watch Chain, Twisted Rope, Gold Filled, Swivels, Marked, S.B.C. Co., 1880-1915, 32 ¼ In.	55.00
Watch Chain, Woven Brown Hair, Corded Rope Twist, Gold Bar, Victorian, c.1870, 12 In.	110.00
Watch Pin, Circle, Arrow Head, Elongated Diamond, 14K Rose Gold, Art Nouveau, 1 1/16 In.	155.00
Watch Pin, Eagle, Diamonds, Red Enamel, 14K Gold, Krementz, c.1895, 2 x 1 In.	1200.00
Watches are listed in their own category.	
Wristwatches are listed in their own category.	

JOHN ROGERS statues were made from 1859 to 1892. The originals were bronze, but the thousands of copies made by the Rogers factory were of painted plaster. Eighty different figures were created. Similar painted plaster figures were produced by some other factories. Rights to the figures were sold in 1893, and the figures were manufactured for several more years by the Rogers Statuette Co. Never repaint a Rogers figure because this lowers the value to collectors.

Group, Council Of War, President Lincoln, General Grant, Secretary Of War Stanton, 24 In.	3990.00
Group, Fetching The Doctor, Bronze, 16 x 20 In.	1590.00
Group, One More Shot, Wounded To The Rear, 24 ½ In.	3390.00
Group, Rip Van Winkle At Home, Marked, Pat. March 14, 1871, 19 x 10 In.	1295.00
Group, School Days, Man, Monkey, 2 Children, Signed, 1877, 21 ½ In.	360.00
Group, Weighing The Baby, 20 x 15 In. .....*illus*	700.00
Group, Weighing The Baby, Mother & Baby, Doctor, Signed, 1876, 20 x 15 In.	600.00

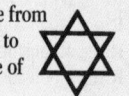

JUDAICA is any memorabilia that refers to the Jews or the Jewish religion. Interests range from newspaper clippings that mention eighteenth- and nineteenth-century Jewish Americans to religious objects, such as menorahs or spice boxes. Age, condition, and the intrinsic value of the material, as well as the historic and artistic importance, determine the value.

Box, Hudulla, Silver, Footed, 5 ½ In.	275.00
Candlestick, Shabbat, Resin, Brass, Red, Green, Gray, Matisse, Signed, Ornal Lalo, 10 In., Pair.	48.00
Clock, Moses, With Tablets, Brass, 8 In.	385.00
Menorah, Bronze, Colored Prisms, Scrolling, Converted To Lamp, c.1890, 19 x 20 In.	874.00
Menorah, Oil, Figural, Lions, Silver, 13 In.	3300.00
Menorah, Silver, Filigree, Marked, Yemeni, 12 ¾ x 10 In.	400.00
Mezuzah, Torah, Silver, 9 In.	440.00
Pitcher, Presentation, Abraham Sherwin, Footed, Sterling, c.1953, 12 In.	826.00
Spice Box, Silver Repousse, Bone Ivory, Barrel Shape, 1800s, 13 ¼ x 5 ¾ In. .....*illus*	633.00
Torah Handle Cover, Rimmonim, Octagonal, Star Of David, Taitelbaum, c.1931, 15 In.	5840.00
Torah Pointer, Yad, Silver, Faceted Handle, Clenched Hand, Inscription, Early 1900s, 10 In.	5450.00
Torah Pointer, Yad, Silver, Figural Hand, Reeded Cuff, Knopped Stem, Inscription, 10 In.	5061.00
Torah Pointer, Yad, Silver, Figural Hand, Ruff Cuff, Paneled Stem, Inscription, c.1782, 11 In.	25305.00
Torah Pointer, Yad, Silver, Silver Gilt, Figural Hand, Fluted Stem, Inscription, c.1813, 11 In.	31145.00
Torah Pointer, Yad, Silver, Square Handle, Fluted Cuff, Inscription, c.1745, 10 In.	12652.00
Torah Shield, Chain, Crown Shape, Embossed, Scrolling, Inscription, c.1800, 9 x 14 In.	16221.00
Torah Shield, Chain, Silver, Parcel Gilt, 7 Bells, Columns, Niello Work, c.1765, 11 In.	40877.00
Torah Shield, Silver, Embossed, Flowers, Leaves, Scrolls, Lions, Rosenzweig, c.1918, 11 ½ In.	3893.00
Torah Shield, Silver Gilt, Embossed Flower, Scroll, Crown, Openwork, c.1887, 14 In.	23358.00
Tray, Seder, Presentation, Repousse, Hand Raised, Sterling Silver, 13 ⅝ In.	1800.00

JUGTOWN POTTERY refers to pottery made in North Carolina as far back as the 1750s. In 1915, Juliana and Jacques Busbee set up a training and sales organization for what they named Jugtown Pottery. In 1921, they built a shop at Jugtown, North Carolina, and hired Ben Owen as a potter in 1923. The Busbees moved the village store where the pottery was sold to New York City. Juliana Busbee sold the New York store in 1926 and moved into a log cabin near the Jugtown Pottery. The pottery closed in 1959. It reopened in 1960 and is still working near Seagrove, North Carolina.

Bowl, Chinese Blue, Oval, Round Stamp Mark, c.1920-30, 4 ½ x 10 ½ In.	480.00
Bowl, White Foamy Glaze, Thumbprint Design, Marked, N.C., 1930s, 5 x 8 In.	316.00
Candlestick, Black Glaze, Impressed Mark, 13 ¾ In. .....*illus*	531.00
Jar, Lid, Runny Red, Blue Glaze, Flared Rim, Marked, V. Owens, Handles, 1989, 11 In.	431.00

J

Jar, Oval, Impressed Flowers, Orange Glaze, Textured, V. Owens, 1975, 19 In.	863.00
Jar, Red & Blue Mottled Glaze, Chinese Style, Impressed Mark, Ben Owen, 7 ½ In. ....*illus*	1416.00
Jar, Red Glaze, Celadon Base, Marked, Vernon Owens, 1989, 7 In.	403.00
Jar, Runny Cream, Blue Glaze, Incised Flowers, Handles, Marked, V. Owens, 1974, 20 In.	633.99
Jug, Bird, Incised, Handle, Signed, Vernon Owens, c.1980, 11 ¼ In.	81.00
Pitcher, Face, Winking, Ears, Speckled Olive Glaze, Spout, Stopper, V. Owens, 1992, 10 In.	460.00
Urn, Persian, Blue, Red Glaze, 16 ¼ x 11 In.	14640.00
Vase, Chinese White, Flared Rim, Marked, Master Ben Owen Potter, 7 ½ In.	130.00
Vase, Foamy White Glaze, Textured, Ben Owen, 1900s, 8 ½ In.	173.00
Vase, Red, Blue Glaze, Foamy Base, Small Mouth, Ben Owen Pottery, c.1980, 6 In.	230.00

JUKEBOXES play records. The first coin-operated phonograph was demonstrated in 1889. In 1906 the Automatic Entertainer appeared, the first coin-operated phonograph to offer several different selections of music. The first electrically powered jukebox was introduced in 1927. Collectors search for jukeboxes of all ages, especially those with flashing lights and unusual design and graphics.

Rock-Ola, Model 1428, 60 x 30 In. ....*illus*	1210.00
Rock-Ola, Series B, Imperial, Art Deco, Serial No. 30257, 52 ½ x 32 ½ x 23 In.	2980.00
Seeburg, 4 Speakers, 3 Tailfins, Holds 100 45 RPM Records, Vertical Play, 1957................	4850.00
Seeburg C, 100 Selection, 45 RPM, Oldies, 25 Cent, c.1952, 54 x 36 In.	8000.00 to 9300.00
Seeburg, Model HF100R, Detroit Deco, Select-O-Matic, 1954, 36 x 26 In. ....*illus*	1150.00
Wurlitzer 600, Plastic, Veneer, 24 Selection, 78 RPM, 25 Cent, c.1938, 54 x 33 In.	5400.00
Wurlitzer, Model 81, Mae West Stand, 57 x 23 x 19 In.	14500.00
Wurlitzer, Model 800, Keys, 59 x 38 x 28 In.	5000.00
Wurlitzer, Model 1015, 24 Selection, 78 RPM, c.1946, 59 x 33 x 24 In.	6500.00
Wurlitzer, Model 1015, Serial No. 2065569, c.1940	6123.00
Wurlitzer, Model 1080, Walnut, 24 Changer..	10350.00
Wurlitzer, Model 1800, Hi-Fidelity, SN 232378, Plays 45 RPM Records, 55 In.	660.00

KATE GREENAWAY, who was a famous illustrator of children's books, drew pictures of children in high-waisted Empire dresses. She lived from 1846 to 1901. Her designs appear on china, glass, and other pieces.

Napkin Ring, Silver Plate, Figural, Boy & Girl On Teeter-Totter...	747.00
Napkin Ring, Silver Plate, Figural, Girl, 2 Geese, With Reins, Meriden................................	5750.00
Napkin Ring, Silver Plate, Figural, Girl, Wearing Bonnet...	88.00
Plaque, Earthenware, Multicolored Enamels, Girls, Lawn Tea Party, W.H., Frame, 1800s, 18 In.	207.00
Tile, Playing Children, Dogwood Branches, Mother Goose Series, 1880s, 6 x 6 In.	245.00

KAY FINCH CERAMICS were made in Corona Del Mar, California, from 1935 to 1963. The hand-decorated pieces often depicted whimsical animals and people. Pastel colors were used.

Bowl, Shell Form, Blue, White, 3 ½ x 4 ½ In.	19.00
Bowl, Swan Form, 6 ½ x 9 x 8 In.	125.00
Candleholder, Scandie Woman, 5 ¼ In.	75.00
Figurine, Altar Boy, Kneeling, Blond, 1950s, 5 ½ In.	65.00
Figurine, Altar Boy, Kneeling, Brown Hair, 1950s, 5 ½ In.	65.00
Figurine, Angel, 1945, 3 ¾ In.	36.00
Figurine, Bird, Singing, On Stand, Pink, Gilt, 1950s, 4 x 1 ⅞ In.	195.00
Figurine, Cat, Sleeping, Cream, Aqua, Purple, 3 ½ x 3 In.	55.00
Figurine, Godey Lady, Fan, Pink, Blue, Mauve Lavender, Applied Roses, c.1940-50, 9 In.	76.00
Figurine, Kangaroo, Speckled Tan, Flower Crown, 9 x 3 ½ In.	181.00
Figurine, Mama Duck, Curlicues, 4 ½ In.	199.00
Figurine, Mr. & Mrs. Bird, Bluebird, 1930-40, Mr. Bird 4 ⅜ In., Pair	75.00
Figurine, Owl, Tootsie, Pearl Gray, Brown Eyes, Tail, Marked, 3 ¾ In.	55.00
Figurine, Peasant Boy & Girl, Brown, Yellow, Blue, Rose, Marked, 6 ¾ In., Pair	135.00
Figurine, Peep & Jeep, Ducks, White, Green, Brown, 1930-40, 4 ⅛ In., Pair	62.00
Figurine, Penguin, Pee-Wee, No. 466, 1949, 3 ¼ In.	65.00
Figurine, Squirrel, Mama & Papa, 3 ½ In., Pair..	75.00
Fountain, Mermaid, Conch Shell, Fish, Drilled Hole, 31 In. ....*illus*	945.00
Lamb, Kneeling, Pink, White, Blue Eyes, Marked, 2 x 2 ½ In.	84.00
Planter, Bassinet, Baby's First From California, Pink, Blue, Eggshell Ground, 2 ½ x 5 ¼ x 7 In.	25.00
Planter, Rabbit, Book, Our Nursery, Blue, White, Marked, 6 ½ In.	95.00
Plate, Santa Claus, 1950, 6 ½ In.	95.00

KAYSERZINN, *see Pewter category.*

Jukebox, Rock-Ola, Model 1428, 60 x 30 In. $1210.00

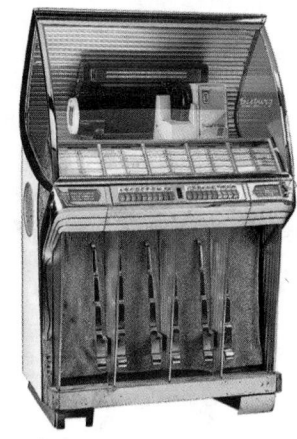

Jukebox, Seeburg, Model HF100R, Detroit Deco, Select-O-Matic, 1954, 36 x 26 In. $1150.00

Kay Finch, Fountain, Mermaid, Conch Shell, Fish, Drilled Hole, 31 In. $945.00

Kelva, Vase, Pink Flowers, Blue Mottled Ground, 2 Handles, 4-Footed, 10 In. $650.00

Kitchen, Butter Stamp, Cow, Mottled Glaze, Handle, Redware, 2 ½ x 3 ¾ In. $435.00

KELVA glassware was made by the C. F. Monroe Company of Meriden, Connecticut, about 1904. It is a pale, pastel-painted glass decorated with flowers, designs, or scenes. Kelva resembles Nakara and Wave Crest, two other glasswares made by the same company.

KELVA

Dish, Painted Flowers, Gold Trim, 6 x 4 ½ In.	255.00
Dresser Box, Bishop's Hat, Red Ground, White Lilies, C.F. Monroe, Signed, 7 In.	460.00
Dresser Box, Pivoting Mirror, Pink Wild Roses, Enamel Beading, Avocado Ground, 2 ½ In.	173.00
Humidor, Flowers, Pink, Mottled Green Ground, Inscribed, Cigars, 1870, 6 In.	380.00
Vase, Pink Flowers, Blue Mottled Ground, 2 Handles, 4-Footed, 10 In. ....*illus*	650.00

KEMPLE glass was made by John Kemple of East Palestine, Ohio, and Kenova, West Virginia, from 1945 to 1970. The glass was made from old molds. Many designs and colors were made. Kemple pieces are usually marked with a *K* on the bottom. Many milk glass pieces were made with or without the mark.

Ashtray, Milk Glass, Coal Bucket Shape, Bail Handle, 4 ¾ x 2 ¾ In.	17.00
Butter, Dome Cover, Amber, Yutec, 1960s, 5 ¼ x 7 ½ In.	22.00
Candlestick, Lace & Dewdrop, Milk Glass, 5 In.	23.00
Candlestick, Moon & Star Variant, Milk Glass, 1950s, 5 ½ In.	25.00
Compote, Cover, Milk Glass, 6 ½ x 6 In.	25.00
Compote, Milk Glass, Scalloped Edge, Hobstar, Button & Diamond Panels, 6 ½ x 6 In.	30.00
Dish, Cover, Dolphin, Fish, Blue, 4 x 7 ½ x 3 ½ In.	95.00
Dish, Cover, Rooster, Seated, Amber, Split Rib Base, 5 ½ In.	40.00
Dresser Box, Milk Glass, Scrolls, Flowers, Domed Cover, 1940s, 6 x 4 ½ In.	28.00
Figurine, Lamb, Amber, Satin, Ribbed Base, 5 ½ In.	36.00
Nut Dish, Cover, Lace & Dewdrop, Milk Glass, 1950s, 3 ¾ In.	23.00
Plate, Lacy Heart Edge, Pink Flowers, Pierced Rim, Beaded Border, 7 ⅜ In.	15.00
Toothpick Holder, Milk Glass, Pansy Flower, 3 Handles, c.1970, 2 ½ x 3 ½ In.	7.00
Toothpick Holder, Pansy Flower, Pink, Handles, Milk Glass, c.1960, 2 ½ x 3 ½ In.	7.00
Toothpick Holder, Yutec, Prescott, Regal Star, 2 ¼ x 2 In.	35.00

KENTON HILLS POTTERY in Erlanger, Kentucky, made artwares, including vases and figurines that resembled Rookwood, probably because so many of the original artists and workmen had worked at the Rookwood plant. Kenton Hills opened in 1939 and closed during World War II.

Bookends, Giraffe Head, Gunmetal Brown Crystalline Glaze, 6 ½ x 5 In.	180.00
Vase, Rose, Slope Shouldered, William Hentschel, 8 In.	650.00
Vase, Turquoise, 2 Applied Small Handles, Incised Vines, Marked, 6 ¼ In.	299.00

KEW BLAS is the name used by the Union Glass Company of Somerville, Massachusetts. The name refers to an iridescent golden glass made from the 1890s to 1924. The iridescent glass was reminiscent of the Tiffany glass of the period.

Compote, Ribbed Bowl, Base, Flared Lip, Iridescent Gold, 3 x 3 ½ In.	259.00
Nut Dish, Green Iridescence, Scalloped Rim, Inscribed Pontil, 3 In.	575.00
Tumbler, Iridescent Gold, 4 Dimples Near Base, Engraved In Pontil, 4 In.	150.00
Vase, Gold, Green Pulled Feather, White Ground, Slender, Signed, 3 x 6 In.	600.00

KEWPIES, designed by Rose O'Neill, were first pictured in the *Ladies' Home Journal*. The figures, which are similar to pixies, were a success, and Kewpie dolls and figurines started appearing in 1911. Kewpie pictures and other items soon followed. Collectors search for all items that picture the little winged people.

Candy Container, Kewpie, By Barrel, Painted, Glass, Tin	113.00
Candy Container, Kewpie, By Well, Blue Wings, Painted, Glass, No. 2862, Borgfeldt, 3 In.	68.00
Doll, Black, Side-Glancing Eyes, 25 In.	60.00
Game, Parker Bros., Scallop Shell Shape Board, 4 Plastic Dolls, Cards, c.1963, 9 x 17 In.	115.00
Sign, Kewpie, Holding Tray, C. Parker-Brawner Co., Frame, 13 ¼ x 9 In.	95.00 to 105.00
Soap, Kewpie, Box, 1917, 4 ¾ x 1 ½ In.	44.00
Wax Seal, Bronze, Initials, L.R., 2 ½ In.	295.00

KING'S ROSE, *see Soft Paste category.*

KITCHEN utensils of all types, from eggbeaters to bowls, are collected today. Handmade wooden and metal items, like ladles and apple peelers, were made in the early nineteenth century. Mass-produced pieces, like iron apple peelers and graniteware, were made in the nineteenth century. Also included in this category are utensils used for other household chores, such as laundry and cleaning. Other kitchen wares are listed under manufacturers' names or under Advertising, Iron, Tool, or Wooden.

Barware Set, Banka, Hammered, Shakers, 5 Goblets, Shot Glass	275.00

K

Basin, Copper, Brass Handle, Round, Rolled Lip, Early 1900s, 14 x 17 In.	150.00
Basket, Egg, Wire, Round, 19th Century, 12 In.	60.00
Beater Jar, Aqua, Mason Safety, Wide Mouth, Salem Glass Works, N.J., 14 ½ In.	105.00
Bin, Coffee, Tin, 18 x 28 In.	153.00
Board, Carving, Wood, End Grain, Kalmar Denmark, 12 x 17 In.	100.00
Boiler, Fish, 6 Hooks, Swivel Handle, Hanging Hole, Wrought Iron, 7 ¼ x 20 ¼ x 17 In.	283.00
Bowl, Chopping, Burl, Carved Rim, Patina, 5 ¾ x 15 ½ In.	1265.00
Bowl, Fruit, Stainless Steel, Inverted Cone Shape, Gense, Sweden, 14 x 6 In.	95.00
Bowl, Grease, Cedarwood, Frog Shape, Abalone Eyes, 4 x 11 x 5 ½ In.	4025.00
Bowl, Red, Finel Finland, 9 ½ In.	115.00
Bowl, Salad, Tapered, Dansk, IHQ, Denmark, 10 In.	145.00
Bowl, Salad, Teak, Turned, Silva, Sweden, 10 ½ x 5 In.	65.00
Bowl Set, Stainless Steel, Satin Finish, Carlo Mazzeri, Anselmo Vitale, Alessi, 8 ¼ x 6 ½ In.	115.00
Box, Salt, Hanging, Cherry, Maple, Hanging Hole, Barrel Shape, Swivel Lid, 2 ¼ In.	79.00
Broiler, Hearth, Wrought Iron, Turned Feet, Scrolled Work Handle, Rattail, 1700s, 18 x 9 In.	295.00
Broiler, Trivet, Rotates, Wrought Iron, 25 ½ In.	287.00
Bundt Pan, Copper, 19th Century, 10 ½ In.	41.00
Bundt Pan, Spiral Ribs, Pottery, Brown Glaze, 5 x 11 ½ In.	140.00
Butcher's Block, Maple, Salesman's Sample, Wolf, Sayer & Heller Co., 1890s, 3 x 3 In.	525.00
Butter Mold, look under Mold, Butter in this category.	
Butter Paddle, Maple, Carved Crook Handle, c.1750, 10 ¾ In.	705.00
Butter Stamp, 3 Flowers, Leaves, Round, Handle, Serrated Border, 4 ¼ x 4 ½ In.	154.00
Butter Stamp, 4 Hearts, Serrated Border, Carved Poplar, 4 ½ In.	302.00
Butter Stamp, Cow, Leaves, Wood, Round, Knob Handle, Carved, Serrated Border, 3 x 4 ⅛ In.	330.00
Butter Stamp, Cow, Mottled Glaze, Handle, Redware, 2 ½ x 3 ¾ In. ....*illus*	435.00
Butter Stamp, Eagle, Spread Wing, Round, Knob Handle, 3 x 4 ⅛ In.	176.00
Butter Stamp, Lollipop, Geometric 6 Point Star, Serrated Border, 9 ¼ x 4 In.	1495.00
Butter Stamp, Pineapple, Wood, 1866, 6 ½ In.	55.00
Butter Stamp, Round, Serrated Tulip & Star, Handle, Brown, Green, Orange, Redware, LB '80, 3 x 4 In.	121.00
Butter Stamp, Stylized Tulip, Serrated Border, Handle, Carved Poplar, 4 ¾ In.	467.00
Butter Stamp, Thistle, Carved Poplar, Applied Turned Handle, 4 ¼ In.	33.00
Cabbage Cutter, Walnut, Arched Top, Heart Cutout Hanger, Wright Iron Blade	302.00
Candle, Tallow, Made Of Bear Tallow Or Fat, Various Sizes, 26 Piece	1659.00
Canister, Cover, Green, Tongue & Groove Vertical Staves, 8 ¾ x 9 In.	45.00
Canister, Cover, Peaseware, Bail Handle, 19th Century, 10 ½ In. ....*illus*	1638.00
Canister, Popcorn, Farmer, Red Barrel, Old MacDonald Series, 387, Marked, Regal, 11 In.	108.00
Canister, Rosewood, Lid, Square Shoulders, Dansk, Denmark, IHQ, 1960s,	350.00
Canister, Teak, Corked Lid, Square, Rounded Corners, Denmark, 5 x 5 x 5 In.	55.00
Canister, Tidbit, Woman, Red Barrel, Old MacDonald Series, 387, Marked, Regal, 11 In.	108.00
Carafe, Glass, Gold Trim, Candle Warmer, Pyrex, Box, 8 Cup	19.00
Carving Set, Antler Handles, Abercrombie & Fitch, Box, 11 Piece	164.00
Casserole, Cover, Blue, Snowflake Design, Pyrex	19.95
Casserole, Wood, Wicker Stand, Jens Quistgaard, Dansk, 7 x 8 In.	250.00
Cauldron, Copper, Hammered, Rolled Rim, 2 Squared Handles, 9 ¾ x 21 ½ In.	118.00
Chafing Dish, Copper, Brass, Burner, Tray, Marked, Rochester, c.1904, 16 x 9 x 4 In.	175.00
Chakki, Grinding Wheel, Wood, Folk Art Pattern, Iron Handle, India, c.1800s, 7 x 8 ½ In.	165.00
Cheese Strainer, Wood, Arrow Back Spindle, White Paint	1500.00
Chopper, Steel Horse Shape, Wood Handle Grip, 6 x 11 In.	385.00
Chopping Block, Wood, Round, Ring Handle, Woodline Denmark BK, 10 ½ In.	60.00
Churn, Cedar, Ash, Red & Blue Paint, Wood Bands, 15 ½ In.	147.00
Churn, Cover, Painted Blue, Staves, Iron Bands, 34 In.	1320.00
Churn, Dasher, Slatted, Tapered, Metal Bands, Original Top, 24 x 10 ½ In.	115.00
Churn, Dasher, Yellow Pine, Blue-Gray Paint, Metal Bands, Lid, 41 In.	360.00
Churn, Dazey, 2 Qt., 12 In.	280.00
Churn, Dazey, 4 Qt., 14 In.	280.00
Churn, Dazey, No. 20, Square, Circle Mark, 16 In.	130.00
Churn, Dazey, No. 20, Square, Circle Mark, 2 Qt, 12 In.	115.00
Churn, Dazey, No. 30, Saves Labor Better Butter, Square, St. Louis, USA Mark, 13 In.	118.00
Churn, Dazey, No. 40, Square, 14 In.	82.00
Churn, Dazey, No. 60, Square, 15 In.	72.00
Churn, Dazey, No. 80, Square, 16 In.	85.00
Churn, Glass, Metal Handle, Dazey, No. 40, 14 In.	70.00
Churn, Hand Crank, Cast Iron, Wood Box, 33 x 15 x 18 In.	123.00
Churn, Lightning, No. 2, Wood, Mustard Paint, Hand Crank, c.1880	106.00
Churn, No. 2, Mustard Paint, Wood, c.1880s	110.00
Churn, Wood, Painted, Crank, Early 1900s, 35 In. ....*illus*	263.00
Clothespin, Oak, Abe Cassidy, 34 ½ In.	460.00

Kitchen, Canister, Cover, Peaseware, Bail Handle, 19th Century, 10 ½ In.
$1638.00

Kitchen, Churn, Wood, Painted, Crank, Early 1900s, 35 In.
$263.00

K

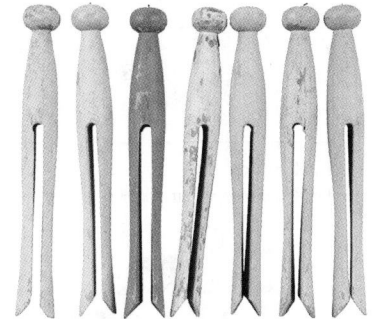

Kitchen, Clothespin, Wood, Painted, 14 In., 7 Piece
$146.00

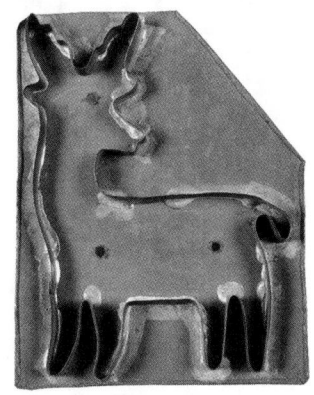

Kitchen, Cookie Cutter, Stag, Tin, Soldered, 1800s, 7 x 5 In.
$226.00

Kitchen, Gridiron, Wrought Iron, Revolving Grid, 3-Footed, N.C., 19th Century, 24 ½ In.
$403.00

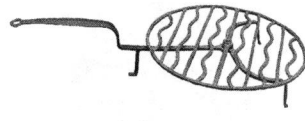

Kitchen, Laundry Agitator, Plunger, Wood, 36 In.
$88.00

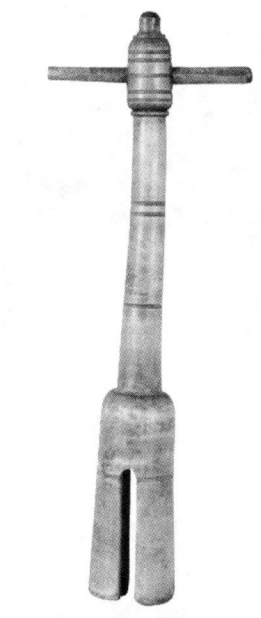

Kitchen, Laundry Bag, Printed Birdcage, Early 1900s
$117.00

Clothespin, Wood, Painted, 14 In., 7 Piece ....*illus*	146.00
Clothespin, Wood, Painted, Dressed Men, c.1900, 5 In., 5 Piece	259.00
Cocktail Pick Set, Wonder Bar, Harris Dunn, Figural Picks, Walnut, c.1939, 4 ½ In.	125.00
Cocktail Set, Chase, Blue Moon, 12-In. Shaker, 3 ½-In. Glass, 11 ¾-In. Tray, 8 Piece	506.00
Cocktail Shaker, Art Deco, Cobalt Blue, Barbell Shape, Czechoslovakia, 1930s, 13 In.	495.00
Coffee Grinders are listed in the Coffee Mill category.	
Coffee Mills are listed in their own category.	
Coffeepot, Cover, Flamestone, White Interior, Quistgaard, 13 ½ In.	135.00
Coffeepot, Enamel, Painted, Shorebird, Pewter Lid, Handle, Spout, 10 In.	395.00
Cookie Board, 12 Occupations, Rectangular, Pewter, Wood Mounted, 7 ¾ x 4 ½ In.	303.00
Cookie Board, Carved Animals, Germany, c.1890, 22 x 4 In.	135.00
Cookie Board, Walnut, Carved, Soldier, Bag, c.1880, 31 x 13 In.	353.00
Cookie Cutter, Abraham Lincoln, 19th Century, 3 x 5 ½ In.	55.00
Cookie Cutter, Begging Dog, Copper, Pennsylvania, 1800s, 10 In.	450.00
Cookie Cutter, Club, Star, Spade, Heart, Tin, 4 Piece	10.00
Cookie Cutter, Gingerbread Man, Tree, Santa With Sack, Aluminum, 1950s, 6 In, 3 Piece	40.00
Cookie Cutter, Heart & Hand, Tin, 1800s, 4 x 4 ½ In.	702.00
Cookie Cutter, Stag, Tin, Soldered, 1800s, 7 x 5 In. ....*illus*	226.00
Cookie Cutter, Tom & Jerry, Plastic, Red, Cartoon Characters, Loew's Inc., 6 Piece	17.00
Cooler, Pinstripes, Copper & Zinc Lined, Iron Handle, Rollers, c.1910, 16 ½ In.	125.00
Corn Holder, Bakelite, Butterscotch, Peg Shape, 8 Piece	125.00
Corn Holder, Red, Bakelite, Diamond Form Handles, 8 Piece	22.00
Crumber, Prayer Lady, Paper Label, Stamped, E-3350, Enesco, 8 In.	50.00
Cutlery Set, Knife & Fork, Antler Handles, 14-In. Knife, 10-In. Fork	23.00
Dough Box, Pine, Sliding Top, Tapered Shape, Splayed Legs, c.1800, 28 x 41 In.	518.00
Dough Scraper, Arched Blade, Hollow Handle, Wrought Iron, 4 x 3 ⅜ In.	88.00
Dough Scraper, Iron, Turned Brass Ferrule, Wood Handle, Stamped, P.D., 1865, 6 In.	1860.00
Dough Scraper, Iron, Turned Brass Handle, Stamped, P.D., 1865, 3 ¾ In.	1530.00
Dutch Oven, Griswold, No. 8, Glass Lid	19.50
Dutch Oven, Griswold, Wagnerware, 2 Qt.	24.00
Dutch Oven, Mi-Pet, No. 8, Lid, Western Foundry	44.00
Egg Timer Holder, Humpty-Dumpty, Cast Iron, Painted, 3 ½ In.	250.00
Flatiron, Brass, Coal, Open Back, Wood Turned Handle, Engraved Berries, 1800s	395.00
Flatiron, Knapp-Monarch, Round, Chrome, Black Handle	250.00
Fondue Fork Set, Teak, Stainless Steel, Laurids Lonborg, Denmark, 10 ½ In, 12 Pieces	40.00
Fondue Set, Enameled Steel, Chrome, Covered Orb Shape Bowl, Cathrine Holm, Norway, 11 x 8 In.	145.00
Food Chopper, Glass Jar, ¼ Cup Intervals, Chrome Lid, Yellow Metal	16.00
Fork, Toasting, Copper, Brass, Figural, Dragon Fish, c.1890, 16 ½ In.	65.00
Fork, Toasting, Iron, Wood Handle, 3 Prongs, 13 In.	20.00
Grater, Nutmeg, Tin, Walnut, Serrated Blade, 5 ¼ In.	68.00
Grater, Nutmeg, Tole, 19th Century, 5 In.	77.00
Griddle, Griswold, No. 6, Handle	275.00
Griddle, Griswold, No. 7, Rectangular	100.00
Griddle, Griswold, No. 9	65.00
Griddle, Griswold, No. 12, Bail Handle	75.00
Gridiron, Wrought Iron, Revolving Grid, 3-Footed, N.C., 19th Century, 24 ½ In. ....*illus*	403.00
Grinder, Nutmeg, Edgar Mfg., Wooden Knobs, Spring Loaded, c.1891, 5 ⅜ In.	90.00
Grinder, Nutmeg, Wood, Brass, 19th Century, 8 In.	262.00
Grinder, Spice, Wood, Painted, Metal Dome Top Opens, Square, Germany, 1960s, 2 ⅝ In.	45.00
Ice Cream Press, Cylindrical, Excelsior	140.00
Ice Cream Sandwich Maker, Mayer Mfg. Corp.	175.00
Ice Cream Sandwich Maker, Sanitary Mould Co, German Silver	605.00
Ice Cream Sandwich Maker, Square, Wood Handle, ICYPI Automatic Cone Co...............	130.00
Ice Cream Sandwich Maker, Tin	88.00
Iron, Charcoal, Cast Iron, Dragon Chimney, 9 x 4 ¼ x 9 In.	796.00
Iron, Daisy, No. 2, Central Oil & Gas Stove Co., Pat. May 16, 1893	55.00
Iron, Tailor's, Imperial	250.00
Ironing Board, Wood, Wool Homespun Cover, 1800s, 15 x 50 In.	148.00
Jar, Drippings, Delphite, Jeanette, Cover, 2 ¾ x 4 ¾ In.	165.00
Jar, Mixer, Measure, Wire Whisks, 8-Sided, Hand Crank, Cast Iron Top, Silver Co., N.Y., 12 In. .	165.00
Jar Wrench, Liberty, Metal, Spirit Of 1776, W.H. Young, Wrightsville, c.1926, 7 In.	395.00
Jigger, Big Shot, Measurement Markings, Napier	94.00
Juice Press, 13 In.	35.00
Kettle, Flat Bottom, Griswold No. 9, Bail Handle, 10 ½ In.	118.00
Kettle, Sugar, Cast Iron, Flared Lip, Deep Body, American, 1890s	1415.00
Kettle, Sugar, Flared Lip, Cast Iron, New Orleans, Mid 19th Century, 22 x 55 ½ In.	1880.00

Knife Rest, Leopard, Art Nouveau Style, Metal, Marked, Wurttembergische, 1910, 4 In.	200.00
Ladle, Flat Handle, Hanger Hook, Dome Ladle, Punched Dot Design, W.H.A. On Handle, 20 In.	22.00
Ladle, Maple, Carved, 19th Century, 11 In.	275.00
Lard Press, Cast Iron, Sheet Metal Tub & Strainer, Sensible Press N.R. Streeter & Co., N.Y.	77.00
Laundry Agitator, Figural, Hands, Cast Aluminum, 14 In.	1053.00
Laundry Agitator, Plunger, Tin, Wooden Handle, 42 In.	30.00
Laundry Agitator, Plunger, Wood, 36 In. .... *Illus*	88.00
Laundry Agitator, Wood, Metal, 36 In.	29.00
Laundry Bag, Printed Birdcage, Early 1900s ....*illus*	117.00
Laundry, Bride Stick, Carved, Diamond & Hearts, Caged Ball, Handle, Wooden, 26 In.	410.00
Laundry, Bride Stick, Fork Form, Etched Hearts, Diamonds, Stars, Wood, 1800s, 34 In.	1638.00
Laundry, Bride Stick, Wood, Painted, Mother-Of-Pearl, 28 In. ....*illus*	936.00
Lemon Squeezer, Stand, Hinged, 9 x 14 ¼ x 4 In.	99.00
Lemon Squeezer, Walnut, Nickel Plated Brass, Will & Finck, S.F., Cal., 9 ½ In.	230.00
Lemon Squeezer, Wood, c.1885	10.00
Lid, Skillet, High Domed, Griswold, No. 8	23.00
Matchholders can be found in their own category.	
Match Safes can be found in their own category.	
Measure, Handle, General Steel Wares Ltd., Qt., 6 ½ In.	23.00
Meat Hook Hanger, 4 Chains With Triple Hooks, Arched Rack, Wrought, 16 x 13 In.	176.00
Meat Skewer, George III, Hallmarks, Thomas Chawner, Londer, c.1777	700.00
Meat Slicer, Manual, Red, Wheels, US Slicing Machine Co., 1912, 35 x 28 In.	6000.00
Meat Slicer, Streamliner, Hobart Mfg. Co., Aluminum, Steel, 1940, 12 x 20 x 18 In.	600.00
Mixer, Milk Shake, Arnold, No. 15, 17 ½ In.	105.00
Mixer, Milk Shake, Gilchrist, No. 22, 17 ½ In.	92.00
Mixer, Milk Shake, Hamilton Beach, Red, Porcelain, 3 Cans, c.1950, 20 x 13 x 9 In.	400.00
Mixer, Milk Shake, Model B, 19 In.	145.00
Mixing Bowl, Glass, Ribbed, Pink, Federal, 6 ¾ In.	32.00
Mixing Bowl, Spongeware, Blue, c.1900, 6 x 11 In.	207.00
Mold, Butter, 2-Part, Fish, Leaves, Chip Carved Border, 1800s, 3 x 6 In.	415.00
Mold, Butter, 2-Part, Sheep Scene, Wood, 1800s, 5 x 6 ½ In.	207.00
Mold, Butter, Cow, Maple, Turned Handle, 5 In.	140.00
Mold, Butter, Eagle, Wood, c.1800, 3 ½ In.	411.00
Mold, Cake, Round Form With Scalloped Rim, Pumpkin Orange, Redware, 3 x 10 In.	45.00
Mold, Cake, Round, Scalloped Rim, Raised & Spiral Grooves, Pumpkin Orange Glaze, Redware, 10 In.	44.00
Mold, Cake, Scalloped Rim, Embossed Swirl Design, Yellow Slip, 10 ½ In.	5175.00
Mold, Candle, see Tinware category.	
Mold, Candy, Fish, Fruit, Geometric, Ring Handles, Brass, 9 ½ In.	45.00
Mold, Candy, Horse Head, Stone, Carved, c.1900, 5 In.	95.00
Mold, Ceramic, Fish, c.1840, 7 x 5 ¾ x 4 In.	175.00
Mold, Chocolate, 2 Hens, 8 ½ In.	65.00
Mold, Chocolate, 24 Figures, Hens On Nests, Chicks, Rabbits, 13 x 17 ¼ In.	105.00
Mold, Chocolate, Child's Head, Laughing, Copper, 2 Parts, Hinged, Marked	82.00
Mold, Chocolate, Chinese Man, Pigtail, Tin, Mark, 4 ¾ In.	110.00
Mold, Chocolate, English Bobby, Tin, Marked Vormen Fabriek, Holland, 5 ¼ In.	140.00
Mold, Chocolate, Rabbit, 11 In.	75.00
Mold, Chocolate, Rabbit, Driving Car, Tin, Heris, Marked, Germany, 7 ¼ x 7 In.	450.00
Mold, Chocolate, Rabbit, Riding Rabbit Bareback, Easter Egg, Tin, 6 ½ x 7 x 6 In.	550.00
Mold, Chocolate, Three Turkeys, 11 ½ In.	100.00
Mold, Chocolate, Tin, Black Man, Playing Saxophone, Bowler Style Hat, Germany, 1920s, 6 In.	265.00
Mold, Fish Shape, Orange Brown Interior Glaze, Arch Feet, 2 ½ x 12 In. ....*illus*	66.00
Mold, Food, Debossed Grape Interior, Manganese, Glaze, Redware, 1800s, 4 x 3 In.	115.00
Mold, Food, Turk's Head, Chain Link Design, Marked, M470, 4 In., Pair	120.00
Mold, Food, Turk's Head, Fluted Rim, Copper, 19th Century, 5 ½ x 9 In.	60.00
Mold, Grape Bunch, Redware, 19th Century, 5 ½ x 3 In.	138.00
Mold, Hearts, Spades, Diamonds, Clubs, Aluminum, Wear-Ever, 14 x 6 ½ In.	30.00
Mold, Ice Cream, 12 Removable Molds, Cast Metal, Handle, B & P, 7 ½ x 9 ¾ In.	82.00
Mold, Ice Cream, see also Pewter category.	
Mold, Jelly, Green, Scalloped Rim, Interior Center Post, Redware, Incised, Stahl, 1939, 4 ½ In.	77.00
Mold, Melon, Gray Mottled, Agate Nickel-Steel Ware, Tin Bail Cover, Ink Stamp, 8 In.	38.00
Mold, Pig Head, Relief, Cast Iron, Scalloped Edge, Handles, 8 ¾ In.	230.00
Mold, Rabbit, Cast Iron, Ges Sesch, 5 ½ In.	25.00
Mold, Rabbit, Lead, Manganese Interior, Redware, 4 ¾ x 5 ¾ In.	144.00
Mold, Rabbit, Seated, Cast Iron, 11 ½ In.	187.00
Mold, Scalloped Edge, Swirl Interior, Sponged Manganese, J. Bell, Redware, c.1860, 2 x 4 ½ In.	1150.00
Molds may also be found in the Pewter and Tinware categories.	

Kitchen, Laundry, Bride Stick, Wood, Painted, Mother-Of-Pearl, 28 In. $936.00

Kitchen, Mold, Fish Shape, Orange Brown Interior Glaze, Arch Feet, 2 ½ x 12 In. $66.00

K

TIP

Warning! Damaged enameled kitchen ware (graniteware) is being repaired by being colored then dipped in epoxy. The finished repair is difficult to detect. If the epoxy-covered piece is used for cooking the epoxy will catch on fire, burn, and smoke. If suspicious of a piece, test it with a cotton ball dipped in acetone. It will soften the epoxy.

Kitchen, Sprinkler, Bottle, Proper Lady, California Clemisons, 9 In.
$117.00

Kitchen, Stringholder, Kettle Shape, SSS For The Blood, Cast Iron, Early 1900s, 4 ½ In.
$117.00

Kitchen, Wash Board, Spiral Groove, C.W. Mott Company, 22 In.
$468.00

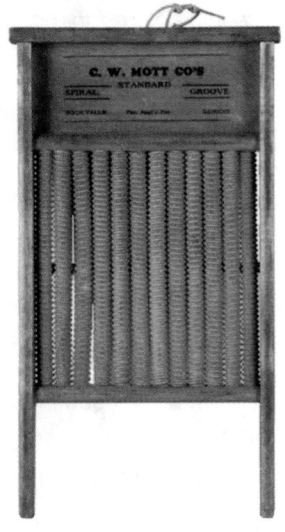

Mortar & Pestle, Iron, Early 19th Century, 6 x 5 ¾ In.	41.00
Mortar & Pestle, Iron, Inverted Bell, 2 Tiered Mortar, Brown Paint, 5 ⅝ In.	70.00
Mortar & Pestle, Poplar Log, Yellow Pine Pestle, 29 x 3 In.	115.00
Mortar & Pestle, Wood, Red Paint, Bands, 5 In.	118.00
Mortar, Iron, Griswold, c.1895, Pt.	135.00
Muffin Pan, Aluminum, Chiltonware, 11 x 7 ¾ In.	7.00
Napkin Holder, Strawberries & Vines, Ceramic, Japan.	9.00
Pan, Bake, Enamel, Burnt Orange, Handles, 13 x 10 In.	85.00
Pan, Brass, Copper Riveted Steel Handle, c.1910, 15 x 7 In.	125.00
Pan, Chicken, Griswold, No. 8, Lid.	70.00
Pan, Chicken, Griswold, No. 777, Logo On Lid, L.B.L.	77.00
Pan, Corn Bread, Griswold, No. 22	65.00
Pan, Corn Stick, Griswold No. 262, Wrought Iron, 7 Sticks, Hanging Hole, 8 ½ In.	23.00 to 75.00
Pan, Corn Stick, Griswold, No. 273-930A	19.50
Pan, Danish Cake, Griswold, No. 32	45.00
Pan, Gem, 12 Hole, New England, 13 ¼ x 7 In.	12.00
Pan, Plett, Griswold, No. 34.	50.00
Pan, Popover, Griswold, No. 10, Erie, Pa.	17.00
Pan, Roasting, Aluminum, 11 x 6 In.	25.00
Pan, Sauce, Copper, E.W. Baird Stamp, Handle, 1700s, 9 ½ In.	206.00
Pan, Sauce, Griswold, No. 412, Aluminum, Lid, No. A-412C, 2 Qt.	45.00
Pan, Sauce, Hammered, Wagner Ware, No. 3702	19.00
Pancake Set, 3 Pitchers, Batter, Syrup, Butter, Brown, Painted Fruit, Japan, 3 Piece	18.00
Pastry Wheel, Tasting Spoon, Combination, Brass, England, c.1750	295.00
Patty Bowl, Griswold, No. 72, Handle	19.00
Peel, Round Shaft, Flat Handle, Scrolled Terminal, Flat & Arched Blade, 43 ½ In.	154.00
Peel, Wrought Iron, Double Loop, Flat Blade, 7 ¾ x 7 ½ In.	79.00
Pepper Mill, Natural Beech, Lacquered, Paris, Peugeot, 19 In.	40.00
Percolator Set, Manning Bowman, Chrome, Globular, Wood Handle, 10 In.	249.00
Pie Rack, Wire, Heart Shape, 2 Tiers, Wooden Feet, 11 ½ x 12 ½ In.	45.00
Pitcher, Lucite, Rectilinear Wedge Shape, 1980s, 8 ½ x 8 In.	35.00
Plate, Chapati, Stone, Round, Footed, India, 1 ½ x 11 x 12 In.	85.00
Posnet, Pouring Spout, Straight Handle, Cast Iron, 3-Footed, 4 ¾ x 12 ¼ x 7 ¾ In.	23.00
Pot, Copper, Brass, Waisted, Tapered Cylindrical Shape, Rounded Bottom, Swing Handle, 3 x 3 In.	24.00
Pot, Copper, Jam, Brass Handles, France, 20th Century, 6 ¼ x 17 ½ In.	300.00
Pot, Frying, Aluminum, Guardian Service, 1940s, 10 x 2 In.	18.00
Pot Rack, Wrought Iron, 5 Hooks, Hearts, Scrolls Crest, c.1890, 14 x 26 In.	206.00
Pot, Sauce, Copper, Iron Handle, Dovetailed, c.1870, 18 ½ x 10 In.	195.00
Rack, Drying, Salesman's Sample, 5 In.	460.00
Rack, Roasting, Wrought Iron, Penny Feet, Adjustable, 30 In.	55.00
Reamers are listed in their own category.	
Recipe Holder, Plastic, Category Dividers, Pedestal, Yellow, 1960s	9.00
Roaster, Apple, Cast Iron, Steel, Clockjack Movement, France, 15 In.	885.00
Rolling Pin, Aluminum, Anodized, Copper Color, Plastic Handles, Queen Size, 19 In.	12.00
Rolling Pin, Glass, c.1920, 13 ¾ In.	50.00
Rolling Pin, Glass, Robin's-Egg Blue, 29 x 3 ½ In.	160.00
Rolling Pin, Glass, Spatter, Clear, Red, Blue Spots, Plaster Filled, Knob Handles, 16 In.	220.00
Rolling Pin, Glass-Blown, Green	44.00
Rolling Pin, Glass-Blown, Green, 15 In.	17.00
Rolling Pin, Maple Handles, Carved Animals, Buildings, Flowers, 18 ¾ In.	358.00
Rolling Pin, Rosewood, Whalebone Handle Tips, c.1850, 22 In.	110.00
Rolling Pin, Stoneware, Wood, Thos. Brush & Hamlin, General Merchandise, IA, 14 ½ In.	725.00
Rolling Pin, Tiger Maple, 19th Century, 10 In.	235.00
Rolling Pin, Wood, Bone Ends, Nantucket, 10 In.	95.00
Sadiron, Cast Iron, Locking Handle, Mid 1800s, 5 ½ x 6 ⅝ In.	110.00
Salad Server Set, Stainless Steel, Forged, Resin Handle, Epic, Japan, 12 ½ In.	30.00
Salad Server Set, Stainless Steel, Meridional, 11 ¼ In.	15.00
Salad Server Set, Stainless Steel, Teak Handle, 14 ¼ In.	40.00
Salad Set, Taverneau, Arthur Umanoff, Raymor, 11-In. Bowl, 12 ½ In. Servers	125.00
Salt & Pepper Shakers are listed in their own category.	
Scoop, Bird, Wood Carving, Geometrics, Hand Form Handle, 1891, 9 ½ In.	303.00
Scoop, Ice Cream, Brass, Cylindrical, Push Lever.	345.00
Scoop, Ice Cream, Cone Shape, Eureka, Nickel Plated Brass, Wood, Pat. May 1, 6, 10 ½ In.	1320.00
Scoop, Ice Cream, Cone Shape, No. 10, Erie Specialty Co.	110.00
Scoop, Ice Cream, Heart, Brass, Nickel Plated, Wood Handle, Manos Novelty Co., 1925	5000.00
Scoop, Ice Cream, Heart Shape, Brass & Nickel Plated, Wood Handle, c.1925, 11 In.	4950.00
Scoop, Ice Cream, Hollow Shank, Wood Handle, Pat'd Applied	150.00

K

Scoop, Ice Cream, Nickel Plated, Wooden Handle, Conical, Signed H.S. Greer, 9 In.	1110.00
Scoop, Ice Cream, No. 10, Wood Handle, Dover	33.00
Scoop, Ice Cream, No. 12, Boling Mfg. Co.	675.00
Scoop, Ice Cream, No. 79-6, Wood Handle, Mosihh	66.00
Scoop, Ice Cream, Peerless, Red Bakelite Handle, 1940s, 8 In.	35.00
Scoop, Ice Cream, Polar-Pak, Philadelphia Ice Cream Cone Machinery Co.	300.00
Scoop, Ice Cream, Spring Handle, Pat'd June 9 1896	450.00
Scoop, Ice Cream, Spring Loaded, Cast Iron Handle, Maximilian Bach, USA Apr 9, 1901	520.00
Scoop, Ice Cream, Swivel Bowl, Mosteller, Pat July 3 06 16	720.00
Scoop, Ice Cream, White Rapid, Metal, George C. White, Pat'd Feb. 19, 1929	5250.00
Scoop, Ice Cream, Wood Handle, Dixie Cup, Economy Pat. Apld. For	610.00
Server, Hors D'Oeuvres, Rosewood, Fish Shape, Denmark, 13 In.	85.00
Serving Bowl, Black, Pink Rim, 3-Footed, Therm-O-Bowl, USA, Proven Products, 1950s	12.00
Shaker, Basket Weave, Delphite Blue, Opaque, Jeannette, 6 In., Pair	42.00
Shaker, Salt, White Glass, Red Vertical Line Design, Hazel Atlas	45.00
Sifter, Arched Cutout Legs, Turned Handle, Blood's, 1861, 13 x 9 ¼ x 10 ¾ In.	187.00
Skillet, Colonial Breakfast, Griswold, No. 666	45.00 to 110.00
Skillet, Griswold, No. 2	395.00
Skillet, Griswold, No. 2, L.B.L. 703	330.00
Skillet, Griswold, No. 3	30.00
Skillet, Griswold, No. 3, Enameled	70.00
Skillet, Griswold, No. 3, Slant Letter	35.00
Skillet, Griswold, No. 5	40.00
Skillet, Griswold, No. 6, Chrome	40.00
Skillet, Griswold, No. 7, Smoke Ring	40.00
Skillet, Griswold, No. 8	38.00
Skillet, Griswold, No. 8, L.B.L. 704V	22.00
Skillet, Griswold, No. 8, Smoke Ring	45.00
Skillet, Griswold, No. 10	65.00
Skillet, Griswold, No. 14, 719, L.B.L.	205.00
Skillet, Griswold, No. 57, Square, S.B.L.	27.00
Skillet, Griswold, No. 768, Square	32.00
Skillet, Indian, No. 3, Wapak Hollow Ware, Cast Iron	265.00
Skillet, Lodge, No. 14, Cast Iron	30.00
Skillet, Wapak, No. 12, Smoke Ring	115.00
Skillet, Wapak, No. 3	35.00
Skillet, Wapak, No. 7, Indian Head	140.00
Skillet, Wapak, No. 9, Indian Head	150.00
Skillet, Wapak, No. 9 Nickel Plated, Indian Head	120.00
Skillet, Wrought Iron, Tapered Sides, Straight Legs, Stamped Foster, 17 ¼ x 35 x 13 In.	45.00
Skimmer, Brass, Iron, Inlay, 1773, 18 In.	120.00
Skimmer, Flat Handle, Rattail Hanger, Perforated Bowl, Wrought Iron, Brass, 18 In.	66.00
Skimmer, Star, Heart Cutout On Handle, Brass, Iron	86.00
Spatula, Round Shaft, Flat Handle, Hanger Hole, Keyhole Form Blade, 13 ⅜ In.	66.00
Spice Box, Harvard, Oval, Old Green Paint, 3 ½ x 2 ¼ In.	165.00
Spice Box, Maple, Round, 7 Spices, New England, Late 19th Century, 3 ¼ x 9 ½ In.	85.00
Spice Box, Wood, Red Paint, 5 Compartments, Herringbone Design, Scalloped, 14 ¼ In.	365.00
Spice Jar, Cream Of Tartar, Milk Glass, Dove Spice Company	18.00
Spice Tower, Mahogany, 4 Round Compartments, Silver Plated Label, 8 ¼ In.	178.00
Spoon Rack, Pine, 3 Tiers, Pierced Arch Back, Blue Paint, Initials EO, c.1800, 12 x 13 In.	2370.00
Spoon Rack, Pine, Gray Green Paint, Mortar & Pestle Compartment, c.1850, 20 x 14 In.	176.00
Spoon Rack, Poplar, Carved, Shaped Tulip Crest, Chip Carved, 3 Slotted Racks, c.1800, 23 x 9 In.	7344.00
Spoon, Stainless Steel, Quistgaard, Dansk, Odin, Germany, 9 In.	115.00
Sprinkler, Bottle, Asian Man, Green Coat, 9 In.	115.00
Sprinkler, Bottle, Dog, Poodle, Pink, 9 In.	59.00
Sprinkler, Bottle, Dutch Boy, Green Pants, Double-Breasted Button Shirt, 8 In.	88.00
Sprinkler, Bottle, Proper Lady, California Clemisons, 9 In. *illus*	117.00
Sprinkler, Bottle, Woman Hanging Laundry, Hand Painted	293.00
Sprinkler, Bottle, Woman, Polka Dot Shirt, 8 In.	59.00
Steamer Pot, Cover, Galvanized Metal, Tapered, Handles, France, 20th Century, 24 ½ x 25 In.	180.00
Stove Tools, Shovel, Tongs, Holder, Shaker, Hand Forged Steel, c.1850, 20 In.	1404.00
Stringholder, Felix The Cat, Head, Plaster, Painted, Hole In Mouth, c.1940s, 6 x 7 In.	518.00
Stringholder, Kettle Shape, SSS For The Blood, Cast Iron, Early 1900s, 4 ½ In. *illus*	117.00
Stringholder, Whiskey Barrel, Georgian, Rosewood, Gilt Brass Bands, c.1830, 4 x 3 x 3 ½ In.	320.00
Sugar, Cover, Speckled Ash, Treen, 5 ½ In.	605.00
Sugar Cutter, Hinged Handles, Leaf Spring & Close Latch, Wrought Iron, 8 ½ In.	121.00
Table, Dough, Poplar, 2-Board Top, Dovetailed Base, Storage, Mid 1800s, 28 x 41 In.	201.00

Kitchen, Washing Machine, Easy, Vacuum, Electric, Copper, 1930s, 36 In.
$59.00

K

Kitchen, Washing Machine, Superba, Wood, 31 In.
$205.00

Kitchen, Washing Machine, Trestle, Painted, 30 In.
$117.00

Kitchen, Washing Machine, Wringer, Easy, 1940s, 40 In. $59.00

Kitchen, Wringer, Wood, Ribbed Rollers, 25 In. $59.00

Kosta, Bowl, Banded, Mottled Blue, Yellow, Magenta, Marked Kosta Boda, 4 ¾ x 8 ½ In. $81.00

TIP

Clean your dishwasher regularly. Pour a cup of vinegar on the bottom shelf of an empty dishwasher. Run the wash and rinse cycles, but not the dry cycle. The vinegar will remove mineral buildups that may stain dishes later.

Taster, Round, Flat Handle, Hanger Hook, Riveted Domed Ladle, Wrought Iron, Brass, 13 ¾ In.	66.00
Teakettle, Cast Iron, Gooseneck Spout, Tilter, Swing Handle, 3-Footed, 14 ¼ In.	90.00
Teakettle, Gooseneck Spout, Cast Iron, 19th Century, 11 ½ In.	120.00
Teapot, Griswold, No. 576, Marked, 5 ¼ x 4 ½ In.	600.00
Tidbit Set, Pewter, Figural, Chef, Barrel, Vegetable Topped Hors D'Oeuvre Forks	12.50
Toaster, Scrolled, Twisted, Wrought Iron, 19th Century, 12 x 14 In.	323.00
Toaster, Tripod Base, Penny Handle, Swivel Toaster, Wrought Iron, 1800s, 8 x 17 x 12 In.	358.00
Tray, Fiberglass, Psychedelic, 1960s, 26 x 18 In.	165.00
Tray, Ice Cream, Cut Glass, Sawtooth Edge, 14 ½ x 8 x 2 In.	59.00
Trivet, see Trivet category.	
Urn, Coffee Brewing, American Duplex, Electric, 27 In.	1100.00
Waffle Iron, Green Nickel Interior, 1929, 5 ¼ x 3 ¼ In.	100.00
Waffle Iron, Heart Shape, Diamond Design, Pivot Handle, Ball Terminals, Iron, 34 In.	413.00
Waffle Iron, Wrought Iron, 27 In.	45.00
Wash Board, Blue Ribbon, Blue Enamelware, 43 In.	173.00
Wash Board, Marble, Flower Design At Top, Cutout Handle, 18 x 13 In.	527.00
Wash Board, Metal, 36 In.	146.00
Wash Board, Spiral Groove, C.W. Mott Company, 22 In. ....*illus*	468.00
Wash Board, Wooden, Horizontal Pattern, Handle, 25 In.	176.00
Wash Board, Wooden, Vertical Knob Rollers, 23 In.	1955.00
Wash Board, Wooden, Zigzag Pattern, 20 In.	117.00
Washing Machine, Diamond, Salesman's Sample, c.1875, 11 In.	2588.00
Washing Machine, Easy, Vacuum, Electric, Copper, 1930s, 36 In. ....*illus*	59.00
Washing Machine, Maytag, Electric, Model N2L, c.1950s, 44 In.	176.00
Washing Machine, Richmond's High Speed, With Wringer Attachment, Wooden, 30 In.	234.00
Washing Machine, Sunny Suds, Electric, c.1930s, 50 In.	351.00
Washing Machine, Superba, Wood, 31 In. ....*illus*	205.00
Washing Machine, Trestle, Painted, 30 In. ....*illus*	117.00
Washing Machine, Wringer, Easy, 1940s, 40 In. ....*illus*	59.00
Wringer, Bench Mounted, Crank Handle, Marked, Van Hoesen Patent Oct. 1861	77.00
Wringer, Hand Crank, Clamp, Iron, Wood, Rubber, Horse Shoe Brand, 6 ½ x 15 ½ In.	110.00
Wringer, Horseshoe Brand, 26 In.	59.00
Wringer, Wood, Ribbed Rollers, 25 In. ....*illus*	59.00

KNIFE collectors usually specialize in a single type. In the 1960s, the United States government passed a law that required knife manufacturers to mark their knives with the country of origin. This seemed to encourage the collectors, and knife collecting became an interest of a large group of people. All types of knives are collected, from top quality twentieth-century examples to old bone- or pearl-handled knives in excellent condition.

Adjustable, Walnut Handle, Bemis & Call Co., Springfield, Massachusetts	88.00
Bayonet, Steel, Horn Handle, Scabbard, Leather, Finial, 15 In.	1150.00
Bowie, Brass Eagle Head, Hand Guard, Wooden Handle, 14 ½ x 2 ¾ In.	69.00
Bowie, Clip Point Blade, Leather, Nickel Sheath, J. Rodgers & Son, c.1900, 10 ⅛ In.	5100.00
Ceremonial, Cast Bronze, Carved Steatite, Oriental, 20th Century, 14 In.	23.00
Dagger, Mahdist, Beaded Sheath, Jambiya Blade, c.1885	395.00
Dagger, Mahdist, Robust Form, Wood Grip With 3 Knots, c.1882, 8 ⅝ In.	155.00
Dagger, Pewter Hilt, Lobed Pommel, Scalloped Blade Bolster, Scrolling Leaves, c.1800, 6 ¼ In.	335.00
Dagger, Push, Bone Handle, 5 In.	4600.00
Dagger, Push, Gamblers, Spearpoint Flat Blade, 6 ½ In.	960.00
Dagger, Push, Ivory Handle, Nickel Plated Sheath, Tie Ring, 5 In.	2900.00
Dagger, Thigh Bone, Cassowary, Incised, Mounted, New Guinea, c.1920, 12 In.	950.00
Dagger, Thumb Rest, Scrolling Tendrils, Brass Chevrons, c.1800, 10 ¾ In.	275.00
Folding, Barlow, Horn Panels, Revolutionary War Period	385.00
Wood Handle, Pewter Pommel, Single Edge Iron Blade, Leather Sheath, 1800s, 12 In.	302.00

KNOWLES, TAYLOR & KNOWLES *items may be found in the KTK and Lotus Ware categories.*

KOREAN WARE, *see Sumida*

KOSTA, the oldest Swedish glass factory, was founded in 1742. During the 1920s through the 1950s, many pieces of original design were made at the factory. Kosta and Boda merged with Afors in 1964 and created the Afors Group in 1971. In 1976, the name Kosta Boda was adopted. The company merged with Orrefors in 1990 and is still working.

KOSTA

Bowl, Banded, Mottled Blue, Yellow, Magenta, Marked Kosta Boda, 4 ¾ x 8 ½ In. ....*illus*	81.00
Bowl, Can Can, Blue, Green, Red, Footed, Kosta Boda, Signed, K. Engman, 10 ⅞ x 11 In.	350.00
Decanter, Clear, Bird Shape, Head Stopper, Signed, Vicke Lindstrand, 8 x 7 In.	500.00

Decanter, Stacked Stopper, Torso Form Body, Overlapping Multiple Colors, Engraved Base, 12 In. .	316.00
Hedgehog, Etched Crystal, Vicke Lindstrand, Sweden, c.1959, 3 ½ X 2 ¼ In.	125.00
Vase, Artist Collection, Clear, Kosta Boda, 10 In.	234.00
Vase, Cylinder, Frosted Glass, Green Forest Scene, Yellow, Boda, 9 In.	250.00
Vase, Mottled Blue Glass, Black, White Striped Canes, Marked, c.1928, 7 In.	150.00
Vase, Open Minds, Woman's Face, Abstract, Signed, Ulrica Hydman-Vallien, 13 ½ x 6 ½ In.	385.00
Vase, Purple, Crystal, Tapering, 13 ½ In.	70.00
Vase, Rectangular, Mottled Blue With Black & White Striped Canes, 1928, 5 x 4 In.	150.00
Vase, Rectangular, Mottled Blue With Random Black & White Striped Canes, Marked, 1928, 7 In.	150.00

KPM refers to Berlin porcelain, but the same initials were used alone and in combination with other symbols by several German porcelain makers. They include the Konigliche Porzellan Manufaktur of Berlin, initials used in mark, 1823–1847; Meissen, 1723–1724 only; Krister Porzellan Manufaktur in Waldenburg, after 1831; Kranichfelder Porzellan Manufaktur in Kranichfeld, after 1903; and the Krister Porzellan Manufaktur in Scheibe, after 1838.

K.P.M

Basket, Reticulated, Lavender Flowers, Marked, c.1900, 9 In. ....*illus*	300.00
Bowl, Hunter & Hunted, Trees, Art Deco, 7 ½ In.	230.00
Box, Courting Couple, Cabriole Legs, Gilt, Hinge, c.1886, 12 x 21 x 10 In.	9200.00
Charger, European Ruins Scene, Labels, 19th Century, 17 In.	900.00
Compote, Interior Design, Yellow, Gilt, Reticulated, Fitted Interior, Footed, 7 x 6 In.	485.00
Creamer, Flowers, Gold Scrolled Medallions, Baluster, Footed, Stamp, 5 ½ In.	201.00
Cup & Saucer, Scenic Center, Blue Rim, 19th Century, 4 ½ In.	1287.00
Cup, Maltese Cross, Cobalt Blue, Gold Handle, Rim, Base, 4 ½ In.	146.00
Ewer, Putti Riding Dolphin, Flower Handle, Putto, 2 Rams, Scepter Mark, 8 ¾ In.	620.00
Figurine, Boy Soldier, Orange & Blue Scepter Mark, 5 In.	165.00
Figurine, Nude Woman, Ledge, Peacock, 7 ½ In.	250.00
Lithophane, Candle Stand, Seated Woman, Folded Hands, Monkey, Cast Bronze, 20 In.	325.00
Lithophane, Plaque, 2 Girls Pouring Water On Visitor, Leaded Glass, Red Border, 1890s, 11 x 9 In.	480.00
Lithophane, see also Lithophane category.	
Plaque, 8 Cherubs Frolicking On Cloud, Gilt Frame, 11 x 8 ¾ In.	1896.00
Plaque, Antigone Holding Flagon, Ornate Frame, Signed, 1890, 9 ½ x 6 ½ In.	2640.00
Plaque, Last Day Of Pompeii, Painted, Marked Glave, Gilt Florentine Frame, 13 x 8 In. ...*illus*	8190.00
Plaque, Portrait, Greek Girl, Tasseled Hat, Laurel Wreath Ivory Frame, c.1890, 6 ½ x 5 In.	4080.00
Plaque, Portrait, Young Woman, Renaissance Style, Signed, Gilt Frame, c.1890, 9 x 6 In.	3840.00
Plaque, St. Rodriquez, After Murillo, Impressed Mark, Signed, c.1890, 16 x 10 In. ....*illus*	6000.00
Plaque, Sleigh Rider, Woman, Flowers, Butterflies, Hand Painted, Enamel, 6 x 9 In.	633.00
Plaque, The New Master, Impressed, Frame, c.1800, 56 x 33 ½ In.	3163.00
Plaque, The Seafarer's Widow, Specter Mark, Frame, 7 x 10 In.	3450.00
Plaque, Theodora, Florentine Rococo Style, Giltwood Frame, Marks, 23 x 18 In. ....*illus*	17625.00
Plaque, Woman, Leaf Crown, Painted, Stamped, KPM, 6 ¾ x 5 In.	990.00
Plaque, Woman, Shawl, Wheat Field, Walnut Frame, 17 x 15 In.	4370.00
Plaque, Woman, Wheat Field, Ruth, Porcelain, Dittrich Signed, Frame, 12 x 20 In.	8625.00
Plate, Cobalt Blue, Gilt, Blue Underglaze, Royal Berlin, 9 ½ In.	354.00
Serving Dish, Woman, Undertray, Multicolored Glaze, 10 x 9 In.	120.00
Spirits Barrel, Cover, Underplate, Floral Knop, Gilt Design, 1800s, 10 x 11 ½ In., 2 Piece	173.00
Spittoon, Woman's, Flared Rim, Raised Scrolling, Gilt, Mark, 6 x 8 In. ....*illus*	35.00
Tureen, Soup, Platter, Floral & Butterfly, c.1925, 11 x 13 & 18 ½ In.	518.00
Urn, Cover, Courting Scenes, Blue Underglaze, Gold Accents, 8 x 14 In.	644.00
Vase, Dragonfly, 20th Century, 6 ½ In.	35.00
Vase, House, Barn, Trees, Marked, 15 ¼ In.	1610.00
Vase, Portrait, Gilt Swags, 3 Paw Feet, Coiling Serpents, Signed, N.C. Keisel, 19 x 8 In. ....*illus*	1495.00

KTK are the initials of the Knowles, Taylor & Knowles Company of East Liverpool, Ohio, founded by Isaac W. Knowles in 1853. The company made many types of utilitarian wares, hotel china, and dinnerwares. It made the fine bone china known as Lotus Ware from 1891 to 1896. The company merged with American Ceramic Corporation in 1928. It closed in 1934. Lotus Ware is listed in its own category in this book.

Bowl, Blue, Stylized Waves On Shoulder, Squat, Flared Rim, 2 ½ In.	46.00
Butter, Cover, Band Of Lavender Roses, Green Leaves, Tab Handles, Arched Finial	25.00
Pitcher, Blue & White Flowers, Transfer Print, Blue Sponge Border, Lobed, 4 ¼ In.	12.00
Pitcher, Ivory, 8-Sided, Bird On Branch Decal, 1930s, 5 ½ In.	19.00
Pitcher, Pink Roses, Raised Fishnet, Gold Trim, 3 x 4 ¼ In.	95.00
Planter, Art Deco, Blue, Tan, 5 ½ x 5 In. ....*illus*	85.00
Planter, Leaf, Green, Tan Drip, Rectangular, 5 x 5 ½ In.	85.00
Plate, Portrait, Milkmaid, Pittsburgh Commandery, Saratoga Springs, N.Y., 1907, 8 In.	185.00

KPM, Basket, Reticulated, Lavender Flowers, Marked, c.1900, 9 In.
$300.00

K

KPM, Plaque, Last Day Of Pompeii, Painted, Marked Glave, Gilt Florentine Frame, 13 x 8 In.
$8190.00

KPM, Plaque, St. Rodriquez, After Murillo, Impressed Mark, Signed, c.1890, 16 x 10 In.
$6000.00

KPM, Plaque, Theodora, Florentine Rococo Style, Giltwood Frame, Marks, 23 x 18 In.
$17625.00

KPM, Spittoon, Woman's, Flared Rim, Raised Scrolling, Gilt, Mark, 6 x 8 In.
$35.00

KPM, Vase, Portrait, Gilt Swags, 3 Paw Feet, Coiling Serpents, Signed, N.C. Keisel, 19 x 8 In.
$1495.00

KU KLUX KLAN items are now collected because of their historic importance. Literature, robes, and memorabilia are seen at shows and auctions. Laws passed in 1870 and 1871 caused the decline of the Klan. A second group calling itself the Ku Klux Klan emerged in 1915. There are still local groups using the name.

Card, Membership, Knights Of The Ku Klux Klan, 2-Sided, c.1917, 4 In.	39.00
Comic Book, Black Panther Fights The Klan, Marvel Comics, Feb., 1980, 36 Pages, 10 In.	10.00
Decal, Window, The Nation's Hope Stand By It, 5 ¼ In.	50.00
Figurine, Klansman, White Hood, Gown, Blood Drop Tassel, Kotie, 1923, 8 In.	229.00 to 308.00
Pamphlet, Anti-Catholic, The Pope's Secrets, Alamo Church, 1984, 11 In.	30.00
Patch, Hooded Knightrider & Horse, Flaming Cross, Embroidered Cotton, 3 ¾ In.	22.00
Patch, United Klans Of America, Embroidered Cotton, 2 ¾ In.	39.00
Patch, United Klans Of America, Embroidered, Cotton, Round, 3 In.	30.00
Patch, White Supremacy, Hooded Klansmen, Burning Crosses, 3 In.	10.00
Photo, Grand Dragon, Marching Band, Flag Bearer, Knighthawk, 6 In.	45.00
Photo, Klansmen Marching At Member's Funeral, c.1918, 5 In.	73.00
Photo, Panoramic, White Hooded Men, State Rally, Harrisburg, Pa., Sept. 7 1925, 39 In.	45.00
Photo, Washington D.C. March, Black & White, 1925, 10 In.	28.00
Pocket Mirror, Loyal Order Of KKK, La Grange, Geo., County Seat, U.S., Confederate Flag, 3 In.	50.00
Questionnaire, Imperial Wizard's, Membership Questions For Recommended Friend, 11 In.	39.00
Sheet Music, America Means The Klan, 4 Pages, 1925, 12 In.	60.00

KUTANI porcelain was made in Japan after the mid-seventeenth century. Most of the pieces found today are nineteenth-century. Collectors often use the term *Kutani* to refer to just the later, colorful pieces decorated with red, gold, and black pictures of warriors, animals, and birds.

Bowl, Cover, Painted, Quail, Bamboo Shape Handle, 5 ¾ x 8 ¼ In.	35.00
Figurine, Dog, Buddha, 6 x 8 x 4 In.	440.00
Figurine, Dove On Tree Stump, c.1900, 11 In.	150.00
Jar, 5 Panels, Flowers, Figures, Fans, Fired Gold, Octagonal, Inner & Outer Covers, 6 x 4 In.	177.00
Jar, Hand Painted, Gold Detail, c.1900, 8 x 7 In.	205.00
Lamp, 2-Light, Baluster, Women, Tables, Elephant Head Handles, Orange, c.1850, 22 In., Pair..	1058.00
Pitcher, Water, Gilt, Red Rim, Handle, Multicolored Moths, Butterflies, Webs, Celadon, 7 ½ x 6 ½ In.	118.00
Urn, Cover, Standing Figures, Red, Gilt, Inscribed, Dia Nihon Kutani-Sei, 11 ¾ In.	145.00
Vase, Baluster Shape, Handles, Vignettes, Mother & Children, Red Ground, Gilt Accents, 14 In.	104.00
Vase, Bottle Shape, Enamel, Figurines In Garden, Red Ground, Footed, c.1890, 9 ¾ In., Pair	177.00
Vase, Cover, Gold, Black, Red Enamel, Scholars, 19th Century, 15 ½ In.	533.00
Vase, Flared Neck, Vignettes, Flowering Fruit, Branches, White, Indian Red, 12 In.	52.00
Vase, Raised Peacock Feathers, Amphora, 2 Handles, 10 x 13 In.	1200.00
Vase, Rust Color, Gilt, Flowers, Scrolling, Cartouches, c.1912, 4 ½ In.	94.00

L.G. WRIGHT Glass Company of New Martinsville, West Virginia, started selling glassware in 1937. Founder "Si" Wright contracted with Ohio and West Virginia glass factories to reproduce popular pressed glass patterns, like Rose & Snow, Baltimore Pear, and Three Face, and opalescent patterns, like Daisy & Fern and Swirl. Collectors can tell the difference between the original glasswares and L.G. Wright reproductions because of colors and differences in production techniques. Some L.G. Wright items are marked with an underlined W in a circle. Items that were made from old Northwood molds have an altered Northwood mark—an angled line was added to the N to make it look like a W. Collectors refer to this mark as "the wobbly W." The L.G. Wright factory was closed and the existing molds sold in 1999.

Blue Opalescent, Pitcher, Water, Tooled Rim, Reeded Handle, 20th Century, 9 ¾ In.	106.00
Eyewinker, Goblet, Ruby, 4 ⅝ x 2 ½ In. ....*illus*	25.00
Log Cabin, Plate, Commemorative, 1971, 7 x 9 In.	60.00
Maize, Sugar Shaker, Honey Amber Overlay, Embossed Kernels, 5 ½ x 2 In. ....*illus*	145.00
Moss Rose, Plate, Swirl, Milk Glass, 8 ⅜ In.	68.00
Panel Grape, Goblet, Ruby Red, 4 In.	28.00
Panel Grape, Plate, Ruby Red, 9 ½ In.	40.00
Peach Blow, Vase, Embossed Roses, Ruffled Rim, Early 1960s, 8 ½ In.	92.00
Pitcher, Beaded, Blue Over Opalescent, Frosted Handle, Late 1940s, 5 In.	62.00
Plume, Lamp, Kerosene, Ruby, Umbrella Shade, 7 ¼ x 3 ¼ In.	79.00
Spiral Optic, Bowl, Cranberry, Double Crimped Rim, Satin, Late 1960s, 10 In.	95.00
Spiral Optic, Sugar Shaker, Blue Opalescent, Ribs, 4 ½ x 3 ½ In.	60.00
Thumbprint, Pitcher, Water, Cranberry, Tooled Rim, Tooled Handle, c.1950, 9 ½ In.	66.00
Turkey On Basket, Candy Dish, Caramel Slag Glass, 5 ½ x 4 ¾ In.	60.00

K

LACQUER is a type of varnish. Collectors are most interested in the Chinese and Japanese lacquer wares made from the Japanese varnish tree. Lacquer wares are made from wood with many coats of lacquer. Sometimes the piece is carved or decorated with ivory or metal inlay.

Box, Bento, 4 Stacked Layers, Pear Skin Gold Powder Lacquer, 11 ½ x 10 ½ In. ....*illus*	1006.00
Box, Black, Bird On Flowering Tree, Inlaid Mother-Of-Pearl, Stones, Chinese, 10 In.	4422.00
Box, Cover, Fish Shape, Tail Flipping, Red, Japan, 11 x 28 In.	518.00
Box, Mother-Of-Pearl Inlays, Round, Chinese, 2 x 11 ½ In.	234.00
Box, Red Swirl Design, Brass Rim, 4 x 10 In.	205.00
Box Set, Scenic, Women, Ethnic Dress, Black Ground, Multicolored, Russia, 4 & 3 ½ In., 3 Piece	75.00
Cigar Case, Tavern Scene Front, Hinged Lid, Initials, Russia, 5 ¼ In.	480.00
Tea Chest, Octagonal, Mother-Of-Pearl Inlay, Pewter Canister Inside, China Trade, 11 x 14 In. ...	322.00
Tray, Japanese Style, Chinoiserie, Figures, Landscape, c.1880, 28 x 22 In.	264.00
Trunk, Red, Cypress, Medallion Closure, Chinese, c.1880, 22 x 36 x 24 In.	143.00
Writing Desk, Portable, Hinged, Felt Surface, Gold Highlights, Scenic, 7 ½ x 19 ½ In.	147.00

LADY HEAD VASE, *see Head Vase*

LALIQUE glass was made by Rene Lalique in Paris, France, between the 1890s and his death in 1945. The glass was molded, pressed, and engraved in Art Nouveau and Art Deco styles. Pieces were marked with the signature *R. Lalique*. Lalique glass is still being made. Pieces made after 1945 bear the mark *Lalique*. After 1980 the registry mark was added and the mark became *Lalique ® France*. In the prices listed here, this is indicated by Lalique (R) France. Some pieces that are advertised as ring dishes or pin dishes were listed as ashtrays in the Lalique factory catalog and are listed as ashtrays here. Jewelry made by Rene Lalique is listed in the Jewelry category.

R.LALIQUE

Angel Set, Elton John, Clear, 1990s, 3 In., 3 Piece.......................................	468.00
Ashtray, Deux Colombes, Two Doves, Frosted, Stenciled R. Lalique, 2 ⅜ In.	358.00
Ashtray, Ecureuil, Squirrel, Opalescent, 4 ½ In.	385.00
Ashtray, Renard, Crouching Fox, Smoky Glass, Signed, 4 ½ x 1 ¾ In. ....*illus*	575.00
Atomizer, Art Nouveau, Bas Relief Women, Frosted Glass, Engraved Gilt Top, Mark, 5 In.	646.00
Atomizer, Molinard, Calandal, Female Nudes, Clear, Turquoise Patina, Gold Trim, Blue Ball, 4 In.	767.00
Atomizer, Molinard, Figurines Et Guirlandes, c.1930, 6 In.	644.00
Bookends, Reverie, Kneeling Female Nudes, Frosted, 8 ½ x 5 x 3 ½ In.	1830.00
Bowl, Art Deco Handles, Clear, Frosted, 5 x 2 ½ x 8 ½ In.	890.00
Bowl, Arums, Calla Lilies, Clear, Frosted, 4 x 9 ¼ x 8 ½ In.	420.00
Bowl, Asters, Opalescent, Marked, c.1937, 10 In.	720.00
Bowl, Centerpiece, Marguerites, Daisies, 3 x 14 In.	890.00
Bowl, Cremieu, Sawtooth Border, Bead Center, Molded R. Lalique, 1928, 12 In. ..... 567.00 to 1100.00
Bowl, Flora-Bella, Blue, Engraved R. Lalique, 1930, 15 ⅜ In.	5378.00
Bowl, Jaffa, Yellow Glass, Marked, c.1932, 8 ¼ In.	850.00
Bowl, Nemours, Flower Heads, Black Enamel Centers, c.1932, 4 x 10 In.	431.00
Bowl, Nemours, Flower Heads, Enameled, Clear, Frosted, c.1929, 4 x 10 In.	400.00
Bowl, Nonnettes, Love Birds, R. Lalique, France, 2 ⅛ x 8 ⅛ In.	546.00
Bowl, Oeillets, Carnations, Opalescent, Clear, Stenciled R. Lalique, 1932, 14 ⅜ In.	717.00
Bowl, Serpentine, Snakes, 15 In.	978.00
Box, Cover, Cleones, Beetles, Amber, Impressed R. Lalique, 1921, 7 In.	717.00
Box, Cover, Daphne, Molded Nude, Clear & Frosted, 2 x 3 In., Pair......................	351.00
Box, Cover, Deux Sirenes, Two Sirens, Opalescent, Molded R. Lalique, 1921, 10 In. . 2400.00 to 2629.00
Box, Cover, L'Enfant, Clear, Frosted, Nude Children Knob, Signed, 4 x 3 ¾ In.	375.00
Clock, Cinq Hirondelles, Five Cobalt Enamel Swallows, Clear, Mark, R. Lalique, 6 In.	3565.00
Clock, Inseparables, Birds On Branch, Clear, Frosted, Patina, 8-day, Engraved 4 In. 597.00 to 1680.00
Clock, Opalescent, Molded Parrots, Relief & Bronze Face, Geometric, 4 ½ x 4 ½ In.	1380.00
Compote, Nogent, 4 Sparrows, Clear, Frosted, Engraved, 3 ½ x 5 ½ In.	299.00
Decanter, Apple Shape, Clear, Frosted, Stopper, 5 x 6 In.	205.00
Decanter, Femmes Antiques, 8 Neoclassical Women, Clear, Frosted, 9 ½ x 5 ¼ x 4 In.	480.00
Figurine, Aigle, Eagle, Clear, Frosted, 9 ¼ In.	418.00
Figurine, Aigle, Eagle, Seated, Frosted, Clear, 9 ½ x 5 ¼ In.	840.00
Figurine, Ariane, Two Doves, 8 In. .... 468.00 to 717.00
Figurine, Chat Assis, Cat Seated, Frosted, 8 In.	480.00
Figurine, Chat Couche, Cat Crouching, Frosted, 3 x 9 In.	644.00
Figurine, Cheval, Horse, Rearing On Hind Legs, Frosted & Clear, 8 ½ In.	275.00
Figurine, Cheval Mistral, Horse, Raised Front Foot, 9 x 11 In.	936.00
Figurine, Cygne, Swan, Frosted, Feathers, 9 In.	1688.00
Figurine, Danseuse Bras Baisse, Dancer, Arm Down, Frosted, Signed, 9 ¼ x 4 ½ In.	240.00
Figurine, Danseuse Bras Leves, Dancer, Arm Up, Frosted, Signed, 9 ¼ x 4 ½ In.	350.00
Figurine, Deux Danseuses, Two Dancers, Frosted, 10 In.	644.00
Figurine, Elephant, Trunk Up, Frosted, Signed Lalique France, 6 x 6 x 4 In.	240.00

KTK, Planter, Art Deco, Blue, Tan, 5 ½ x 5 In.
$85.00

L.G. Wright, Eyewinker, Goblet, Ruby, 4 ⅝ x 2 ½ In.
$25.00

L.G. Wright, Maize, Sugar Shaker, Honey Amber Overlay, Embossed Kernels, 5 ½ x 2 In.
$145.00

Lacquer, Box, Bento, 4 Stacked Layers, Pear Skin Gold Powder 11 ½ x 10 ½ In.
$1006.00

Lalique, Ashtray, Renard, Crouching Fox, Smoky Glass, Signed, 4 ½ x 1 ¾ In. $575.00

Lalique, Inkwell, Biches, Does In Forest, Square, Frosted Platform, Impressed Lid, Signed, 6 x 4 In. $1093.00

Lalique, Pendant, Perfume Holder, Frosted Glass, Green Patina, Silk Cord, 2 x 1 ¼ In. $3120.00

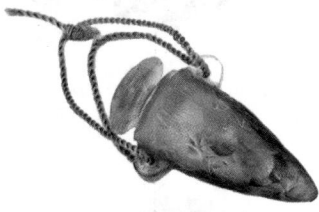

Lalique, Perfume Bottle, Dans La Nuit, Blue Matte, Box, Marked, 4 In. $176.00

Figurine, Moyenne Voilee, Veiled Woman, Opalescent, Blue Patina, Engraved 1912, 5 ⅜ In. ...	3884.00
Figurine, Nam Water Buffalo, Frosted, 8 ½ x 13 x 3 In.	620.00
Figurine, Owl, Frosted, 3 ½ In.	82.00
Figurine, Rooster, Pecking Ground, Frosted, Clear, Signed, 2 ½ x 8 In.	230.00
Figurine, Rooster, Tete De Coq, Clear, Frosted, France, 7 In.	219.00
Figurine, Seal, Canard, Duck, Topaz, Engraved R. Lalique, 1925, 2 ½ In.	567.00
Figurine, Sidonie, Turtle, Clear, Frosted, 11 In.	717.00
Figurine, Stag, Reclining, Frosted, Clear, 10 ¼ x 8 ¼ x 2 ½ In.	480.00
Figurine, Tourterelles Parement Bien, Turtledoves, Signed, 8 ¼ x 2 ½ In.	240.00
Figurine, Turtledoves, Touching Breasts, 9 x 7 ½ In.	590.00
Figurine, Zerla Panther, Black, 4 x 15 In.	760.00
Figurine, Zerla Panther, Frosted, 4 x 15 In.	760.00
Goblet, Six Figurines, 6 Maidens, Topaz, Wheel Cut, R. Lalique, 7 ¾ In.	4600.00
Hood Ornament, Chrysis, Woman, Kneeling, Flowing Hair, Frosted, 5 ½ In.	649.00
Hood Ornament, Coq Nain, Rooster, Frosted, Clear, Molded R. Lalique, 1928, 8 ⅛ In.	896.00
Hood Ornament, Faucon, Falcon, Frosted, Clear, Molded R. Lalique, 1925, 5 ⅞ In.	1195.00
Hood Ornament, Longchamp B, Horse Head, Single Mane, Molded R. Lalique, 1929, 5 ⅛ In. .	8365.00
Hood Ornament, Longchamp, Horse Head, Sept. 10, 1929, 6 ¼ x 5 ¼ In.	1020.00
Hood Ornament, Victoire, Spirit Of The Wind, Molded R. Lalique, 1928, 10 ⅜ In.	26290.00
Inkwell, Biches, Does In Forest, Square, Frosted Platform, Impressed Lid, Signed, 6 x 4 In. *illus*	1093.00
Inkwell, Myrtilles, Blueberries, Black Enamel, Mahogany Stand, Molded R. Lalique, 1924, 9 ⅛ In.	1912.00
Mirror, Hand, Deux Giseaux, Peacock Sides, Clear Grapevine Handle, Brown Patina, Signed, 7 In.	1035.00
Paperweight, Moineau Hardi, Sparrow, Head Down, Clear, Frosted, Marked, 4 x 4 ¼ In.	66.00
Pendant, Perfume Holder, Frosted Glass, Green Patina, Silk Cord, 2 x 1 ¼ In. ....*illus*	3120.00
Perfume Bottle, Ambre D'Orsay, Black Glass, Grecian Women, Frosted Figures, 5 ¼ In.	2070.00
Perfume Bottle, Black Enamel, Chrome, Frosted, Art Deco, c.1929, 4 ¾ x 2 In.	3660.00
Perfume Bottle, Blue On Blue, Art Deco Skyscraper, Signed, 11 In.	173.00
Perfume Bottle, Butterflies, Flower Stopper, Clear, Light Blue Patina, Signed, 3 x 2 In.	1725.00
Perfume Bottle, Clairefontaine, Lily Of The Valley, Signed Lalique (R) France, Box, 4 ½ x 4 x 2 In.	250.00
Perfume Bottle, Coty, Salamandres, Amber Patina, Signed, Matching Stopper, 4 In.	1610.00
Perfume Bottle, Dans La Nuit, Blue Matte, Box, Marked, 4 In. ....*illus*	176.00
Perfume Bottle, Deux Anemones, Double Flower Stopper, Signed, c.1950, 6 ½ In. ....*illus*	217.00
Perfume Bottle, Duncan, Stepped Frame, 3 Nudes, Clear, Gray, Dome Stopper, Signed, 8 In. .	1150.00
Perfume Bottle, Forvil, Les Cinq Fleurs, 1926, 7 ½ x 5 ¼ In.	2196.00
Perfume Bottle, Hirondelles, Swallows, Flat Sides, Stopper, R. Lalique, 3 ½ x 3 ⅛ In.	1610.00
Perfume Bottle, L'Elegance, Dancing Nudes, Frosted, Sepia Patina, Stopper, R. Lalique, 3 ¾ In.	2350.00
Perfume Bottle, Les Sirenes, Nudes, Frosted, Stepped Collar, Signed, 6 In.	633.00
Perfume Bottle, Lezards, Lizards, Frosted, Clear, Engraved R. Lalique, 4 ¼ In.	11950.00
Perfume Bottle, Muguet, Clear, Round, Turquoise, Lily Of The Valley, Stopper, Signed, 4 In. ..	690.00
Perfume Bottle, Nina Ricci, L'Air Du Temps, Doves, Clear Frosted, 4 x 3 In.	175.00
Perfume Bottle, Oreilles Lezards, Clear, Frosted, Etched R. Lalique, 4 x 2 ½ In.	5100.00
Perfume Bottle, Pan, Masks, Flower Garlands, Clear, Frosted, Gray Patina, Signed, Stopper, 5 In. .	2013.00
Perfume Bottle, Veolay, Niobe Violet, Birds On Branches, 1919, 4 x 3 In.	3120.00
Perfume Bottle, Worth, Cobalt Blue, Flat, Round, Moon Stopper, Signed, 5 In.	690.00
Perfume Bottle, Worth, Dans La Nuit, Cobalt Blue, Frosted Stars, Flat, Round, Moon Stopper, 10 In.	978.00
Perfume Bottle, Worth, Je Reviens, Step Shoulder, Ribs, Blue, Round Stopper, Signed, 11 In.	1150.00
Perfume Bottle, Worth, Sans Adieu, Round, Flat, Green, Stepped Stopper, Ribbon, 6 In.	978.00
Perfume Bottle, Worth, Vers Le Jour, Amber, Round Chevron Rows, Flower Stopper, Signed, 6 In. .	805.00
Perfume, Burner, Sirenes, Mermaids, Opalescent Glass, Engraved Mark, 1940s, 6 ¾ In.	1150.00
Plaque, Saint-Christophe, St. Christophe, Footed, 1943, 4 x 4 ¼ In.	420.00
Plate, Cote D'Or, Dancing Nudes, Grape Clusters, 15 ¾ In.	600.00
Plate, Cote D'Or, Dancing Nudes, Sepia Patina, Stenciled R. Lalique, 1943, 15 ¾ In.	2868.00
Plate, Ondes, Waves, Opalescent, Acid Etched, c.1935, 10 ¾ In.	720.00
Plate, Sirenes, Mermaids, Opalescent, Engraved R. Lalique, 11 In.	1673.00
Powder Box, Enfants, Dome Lid, Clear, Frosted, Signed Lalique France, Box, 3 ¼ x 4 In.	360.00
Server, Caviar, Igor, Fish Cover & Base, Clear, Frosted, 10 x 7 ½ In.	761.00
Urn, Raisins, Frosted Band, Grapes & Vines, Flared Flattened Rim, Footed, Lalique France, 14 In.	1610.00
Vase, Albert, Clear, 2 Applied Hawk Handles, 7 In.	1265.00
Vase, Arabesque, Birds & Vines, Clear & Frosted, 5 In., Pair............	320.00
Vase, Aras, Macaw, Birds & Branches, Frosted, 10 x 6 In.	895.00
Vase, Archer, Male Archers, Swooping Birds, Frosted, Oval, Signed, 10 ½ In.	1000.00
Vase, Archer, Male Archers, Swooping Birds, Maroon, Oval, Signed, 11 In.	4500.00
Vase, Armorique, Overlapping Leaves, Artichokes, Opalescent, 9 x 10 ½ In.	5400.00
Vase, Avallon, Birds & Branches, Smoky Patina, Signed, 1925, 8 In.	2800.00
Vase, Avallon, Birds, Branches, Clear, Frosted, Light Blue, 5 ½ In. .... 1553.00 to 2645.00	
Vase, Avallon, Birds, Branches, Clear Gray Patina, c.1930, 5 ¾ In.	1250.00
Vase, Avallon, Birds, Branches, Topaz, Signed, c.1925, 5 ¾ x 6 ¼ In.	475.00

L

Vase, Bacchantes, Encircling Female Nudes, Frosted, 1927, 9 ⅝ In.	1586.00 to 1645.00
Vase, Bacchus, Hiding Among Trees, Brown Patina, 7 In.	2588.00
Vase, Bagatelle, 12 Molded Birds, Leaves, Frosted, Signed, 6 ¾ x 4 ¼ In.	365.00 to 489.00
Vase, Biches, Deer, Fruit Trees, Frosted, Clear, 6 ¾ x 5 In.	439.00
Vase, Borromee, Blue, Engraved R. Lalique, 1928, 9 In.	31070.00
Vase, Ceylan, 4 Pairs Of Parakeets, Iridescent, Aqua, Signed, 9 ¼ In.	5175.00
Vase, Ceylan, 4 Pairs Of Parakeets, Opalescent, Blue Patina, Engraved R. Lalique, 1924, 9 ½ In.	4780.00
Vase, Ceylan, 4 Pairs Of Parakeets, Opalescent, Flared Rim, c.1930, 9 In.	6300.00
Vase, Chamarande, Thistle Stems, Molded Flower Handles, Frosted, 1926, 7 ¾ In.	646.00
Vase, Chardons, Thistles, 4 Corners, Stalks Of Leaves, R. Lalique, 7 ¼ In.	575.00
Vase, Corinthe, Vertical Columns, Of Protruding Leaves, Frosted, 7 ¼ In.	717.00
Vase, Courlis, Curlew, Frosted, Deep Green, Stenciled R. Lalique, 1931, 6 ¾ In.	8962.00
Vase, Dampierre, Protruding Sparrows & Vines, Clear, Frosted, Flared, Footed, 5 In.	207.00 to 468.00
Vase, Domremy, Thistles, Topaz, c.1926, 8 ¼ x 7 In.	1560.00
Vase, Druides, Mistletoe Branches, Frosted, Light Blue, Signed, 7 In.	1438.00
Vase, Druides, Mistletoe Branches, Opalescent, Green Patina, Molded R. Lalique, 1924, 7 In. ..	1314.00
Vase, Druides, Mistletoe Branches, Round, Impressed R. Lalique, 6 ¾ In. ....*illus*	1054.00
Vase, Escargot, Snail Shell Form, Clear, Engraved 1920, 8 ½ In.	3346.00
Vase, Escargot, Snail Shell Form, Frosted Opalescent, Helix Pattern, R. Lalique, 8 ¼ In.	2700.00
Vase, Espalion, Allover Ferns, Globular, R. Lalique, 6 ⅞ In.	575.00
Vase, Espalion, Allover Ferns, Opalescent, Green Patina, Impressed R. Lalique, 1927, 7 In.	896.00
Vase, Firenze, Cherubs On Panel, Sepia Patina, R. Lalique, France, 7 ⅝ In.	2875.00
Vase, Fontaines, Cascading Water, Blue, c.1912, 5 ½ In.	1287.00
Vase, Formose, Swirling Carp, Clear, Opalescent Shoulder, 6 ½ In.	2760.00
Vase, Formose, Swirling Carp, Opalescent, Blue Patina, Impressed R. Lalique, 1924, 6 ¾ In. ...	2032.00
Vase, Grignon, Stylized Wheat, Amber, 7 In.	2875.00
Vase, Gros Scarabees, Molded Beetles, Clear, Frosted, Black Patina, 11 ¾ x 10 ¼ In.	8400.00
Vase, Gui, Allover Mistletoe & Berries, Teal Green, Molded R. Lalique, 1920, 6 ¾ In.	4780.00
Vase, Ibis, Birds Amid Papyrus, Clear, Gray Patina, Flared Lip, Signed, 9 In. ....*illus*	2875.00
Vase, Ingrid, Abstract Modern Swirl, Frosted & Smooth, Signed, 1945-60, 10 In.	860.00
Vase, Languedoc, Serrated Leaf Bands, Gray, Globular, Signed, c.1929, 14 x 13 In. ....*illus*	2106.00
Vase, Lelia, Clear, Frosted, 9 ¾ x 5 In.	250.00
Vase, Malesherbes, Overlapping Medlar Leaves, Molded, Signed, R. Lalique, c.1927, 9 In.	1300.00
Vase, Marrakech, Clear To Amber, Art Deco, Signed, Lalique (R) France, c.1984, 12 x 8 x 6 ½ In.	1100.00
Vase, Meduse, Spiraling Tentacles, Flared Rim, Molded, c.1930, 4 ¾ In.	1750.00
Vase, Moissac, Overlapping Raised Leaves, 5 ½ In.	819.00
Vase, Moissac, Overlapping Raised Leaves, Molded, Frosted Golden Gray, Mark, c.1932, 5 In. ..	805.00
Vase, Moissac, Overlapping Raised Leaves, Yellow, Engraved R. Lalique, 1927, 5 In.	2151.00
Vase, Monthlery, Inverted Molded Arches, Gray, 5 ½ x 3 ½ In.	4125.00
Vase, Mortefontaine, Molded Rings, Engraved 1970, 9 ½ In.	448.00
Vase, Oursin, Sea Urchin, Frosted, Round, Clear Flared Rim, 7 ½ In.	885.00
Vase, Perruches, Parakeets, Branches, Emerald Green, Molded, c.1930, 10 x 10 ½ In.	16000.00
Vase, Pierrefonds, Yellow, Bell Shape, Thorny Handles, Signed, c.1926, 9 x 6 ¾ In. .... *illus*	4388.00
Vase, Poissons, Spiky Fish, Deep Red, Yellow, c.1921, 9 ½ x 9 ½ In.	17080.00
Vase, Poissons, Spiky Fish, White Opalescent, Green Patina, Signed, 9 In.	4600.00
Vase, Rampillon, Cabochons & Flowers, Opalescent, Signed, 5 x 4 ½ In.	780.00
Vase, Ronces, Thorny Vines, Ruby Red, R. Lalique, 1921, 9 ¼ In.	6572.00
Vase, Ronsard, Female Figures In Rose Wreath Handles, Frosted, Clear, Smoky, 8 x 8 In.	5400.00
Vase, Saint Marc, Birds On Horizontal Bands, Clear, Frosted, c.1950, 7 In.	878.00
Vase, Saint Tropez, Molded Vertical Stems & Berries, 7 In.	351.00 to 439.00
Vase, Sauge, Overlapping Sage Leaves, Stems, Clear, Frosted, Green, 10 In.	2300.00
Vase, Serpent, Molded Coiled Snake, Amber, 1924, 10 ¼ In.	47800.00
Vase, Sophora, Stylized Leaves & Vines, Bulbous, Green Patina, Signed, 10 In. ....*illus*	3278.00
Vase, Spirales, Raised Spirals, Opalescent, Stenciled R. Lalique, 1930, 6 ½ In.	2270.00
Vase, Sylvie, Bird, Clear & Frosted, 8 ⅜ In.	244.00
Vase, Terpsichore, Female Nudes, Swags, Flared, Frosted, 8 x 12 ½ In.	6600.00
Vase, Tourbillons, Molded Stylized Scrolls, Bulbous, 1900s, 8 ½ x 7 ½ In.	3738.00
Vase, Tournai, Leaf Panels, Smoky Gray, Molded R. Lalique, c.1920, 5 ⅛ In.	1400.00
Wine Cooler, Ganymede, Entwined Nudes, Engraved 9 In.	1075.00

LAMPS of every type, from the early oil-burning Betty and Phoebe lamps to the recent electric lamps with glass or beaded shades, interest collectors. Fuels used in lamps changed through the years; whale oil (1800–1840), camphene (1828), Argand (1830), lard (1833–1863), turpentine and alcohol (1840s), gas (1850–1879), kerosene (1860), and electricity (1879) are the most common. Other lamps are listed by manufacturer or type of material.

2-Light, Silver Plate, Gilt, Bouillotte, Rococo, Green Tole Shade, Adjustable, 25 In.	900.00
Aladdin, B-25, Gold Decorated China, Victorian	375.00

Lalique, Perfume Bottle, Deux Anemones, Double Flower Stopper, Signed, c.1950, 6 ½ In.
$217.00

Lalique, Vase, Druides, Mistletoe Branches, Round, Impressed R. Lalique, 6 ¾ In.
$1054.00

Lalique, Vase, Ibis, Birds Amid Papyrus, Clear, Gray Patina, Flared Lip, Signed, 9 In.
$2875.00

Lalique, Vase, Languedoc, Serrated Leaf Bands, Gray, Globular, Signed, c.1929, 14 x 13 In.
$2106.00

L

Lalique, Vase, Pierrefonds, Yellow, Bell Shape, Thorny Handles, Signed, c.1926, 9 x 6 ¾ In. $4388.00

Lalique, Vase, Sophora, Stylized Leaves & Vines, Bulbous, Green Patina, Signed, 10 In. $3278.00

Lamp, Art Nouveau, Bowl, Mermaid Handles, Glass Fruit Light, Handled Platter Base, 17 In. $374.00

TIP

Parchment lampshades can be cleaned with a cloth soaked in milk. Then wipe dry with a clean cloth.

Aladdin, B-30, White, Simplicity, Nash Burner	45.00
Aladdin, B-55, Amber Crystal	110.00
Aladdin, B-60, Alacite, Short Lincoln Drape	375.00
Aladdin, B-60, Alacite, Short Lincoln Drape, With Burner	459.00
Aladdin, B-62, Ruby Crystal, Short Lincoln Drape	375.00
Aladdin, B-75, Alacite, Tall Lincoln Drape, Postwar	75.00
Aladdin, B-77, Ruby Crystal, Tall Lincoln Drape	400.00
Aladdin, B-88, Yellow	500.00
Aladdin, B-101, Amber, Crystal, Venetian, Burner	60.00
Aladdin, B-101, Green, Venetian, Burner	12.50
Aladdin, B-105, Corinthian, Clear Font, Green Base, 6-Sided, Model B Burner, 8 In.	100.00
Aladdin, B-111, Green Moonstone, Cathedral	160.00
Aladdin, B-121, Rose Moonstone, Majestic, Gold Metal Base, Nu-Type Model B Burner, 11 ⅝ In.	190.00
Aladdin, B-126, White Rose Moonstone	160.00
Aladdin, B-610, Amber, Admiral Dewey	1500.00
Aladdin, E-205, Vogue Pedestal	850.00
Aladdin, Finial, Buckle, Alacite	60.00
Aladdin, Flat Top, Alacite Finials	65.00
Aladdin, G-18, Black Chromium, Tall Lincoln Drape	22.50
Aladdin, G-20, Alacite, Boudoir	25.00
Aladdin, G-28, Alacite, Boudoir	60.00
Aladdin, G-30, Alacite, Boudoir	30.00
Aladdin, G-163, Double Nude Glass	475.00
Aladdin, G-187, Wreath Finials	70.00
Aladdin, G-222, Alacite	40.00
Aladdin, G-228, Tall Lincoln Drape	40.00
Aladdin, G-235, Anglia Finial	45.00
Aladdin, G-237, Red, Pair	70.00
Aladdin, G-267, Moonsheaf Finial	95.00
Aladdin, G-270, Alacite, Blue	35.00
Aladdin, G-306, Tall Lincoln Drape	32.50
Aladdin, G-375, Dancing Ladies	650.00
Aladdin, Millefleur, Frosted Final	30.00
Aladdin, No. 10, Tall Lincoln Drape	35.00
Aladdin, No. 23, Short Lincoln Drape, Cobalt, Shade	100.00
Aladdin, No. 550, Swiss Scenic Shade	175.00
Aladdin, No. 1533, Whipolite Shade, 14 In.	50.00
Argand, Brass, Empire Style, Columnar, Urn Font, Reeded Handle, Frosted Glass, 20 In., Pair.	1067.00
Art Nouveau, Bowl, Mermaid Handles, Glass Fruit Light, Handled Platter Base, 17 In. ....*illus*	374.00
Astral, Column, Frosted Shade, Grapevines, Cut Glass Prisms, Blue, Marble Base, c.1850, 23 In.	323.00
Astral, Cornelius & Co., Brass Classical Woman, Frosted Shade, Marble Base, 23 In., c.1850....	382.00
Astral, Cornelius & Co., Column, Brass, Etched Frosted Shade, Marble Base, 26 In.	294.00
Astral, Cut Globe, Crystal Prisms, Brass Column, White Marble Base, Mid 1800s, 21 x 8 ½ In.	1650.00
Base, Murano, Gold Inclusion, Wood Base, Barovier & Toso, 20 x 38 In., Pair ....*illus*	1277.00
Betty, Grease, Lift Lid, Wick Spout, Hanger, 10 In.	88.00
Betty, Grease, Lift Lid, Wick Spout, Hanger, Wick Pick, 8 In.	77.00
Betty, Grease, Wrought Iron, Swivel Lid, Adjustable Arm, Round Base, 3 Feet, 16 In.	881.00
Betty, Iron, Tin, Brass, Pedestal Stand, Hinged Lid, Signed, Fhurxthal & Son, 13 In. ....*illus*	593.00
Betty, Tin, Green Paint, 9 ½ In.	110.00
Bouillotte, 1-Light, Silver Plate, Rococo, 25 In.	588.00
Bouillotte, Brass, Classical Style, 2 Round Candlecups, Intertwined Dolphins, Red Tole Shade, 18 In.	588.00
Bouillotte, Bronze, Curved Arms, Dolphins, Leafy Base, Egg-Shaped Sconce, Tole Shade, 26 In.	1185.00
Bouillotte, Electric, 2-Light, Restauration, Brass, Blue Bordered Shade, France, c.1930, 13 In.	840.00
Bouillotte, Empire Style, Bronze, 15 ½ In.	250.00
Bouillotte, Gilt Bronze, Regency, Oval Handle, Adjustable Shades, c.1820, 20 In.	1880.00
Bradley & Hubbard lamps are included in the Bradley & Hubbard category.	
Bronze, Victory Wreaths, Swan, Lyres, Acanthus, Inscription, France, 34 In. ....*illus*	477.00
Chandelier, 3 Light, Empire Revival, Gilt Bronze, Cut Glass, Cascading Curtain, 33 In.	1020.00
Chandelier, 3-Light, Barovier, Pendant, Leaf Shape Glass, 30 x 24 In.	2400.00
Chandelier, 3-Light, Candlestick, Brass Scrolls, Gargoyles, Angels, Prisms, 44 x 28 In.	525.00
Chandelier, 3-Light, Empire Style, Giltwood, Bulbous, Medallions, Griffin Arms, c.1900, 30 x 20 In. ..	2880.00
Chandelier, 3-Light, Oak, Wrought Iron, Continental, 1800s, 14 ½ x 23 In.	878.00
Chandelier, 3-Light, Tole, Red Ground, Gilt, Black Leafy Scroll, Urn Standard, 13 ½ x 16 In.	705.00
Chandelier, 4-Light, Atelier Peritot, Shell-Shaped Glass Shades, Bronze Supports, 48 x 24 In. ..	1200.00
Chandelier, 4-Light, Bronze, Loetz Shades, Enameled, Dragonflies, Oil Spot, 1800s, 40 In. ......*illus*	940.00

Chandelier, 4-Light, Fostoria, 4 Opal Shades, Gold Hearts, Green Vines, Chains, 15 x 29 In. ...	460.00
Chandelier, 4-Light, Georgian, Cut Crystal, Scrolled Arms, Beads, Pendant Drops, 43 x 31 In. ..	1035.00
Chandelier, 4-Light, Iron, 4 Lily Satin Glass Shades, Paneled, 40 x 33 In.	518.00
Chandelier, 4-Light, Louis Philippe, Urn Shape, Palmette, Flowers, Electrified, c.1850, 18 In. ...	2450.00
Chandelier, 4-Light, Wedgwood, Blue, White, Figures, Bronze Winged Griffin, Gas Keys, c.1870, 3 Ft. .	3900.00
Chandelier, 5-Light, 4 Painted Grape Globes, Large Grape Painted Globe, c.1910, 44 x 16 In. ...	1410.00
Chandelier, 5-Light, Bohemian Overlay Glass, White, Green, Painted Flowers, Gilt, c.1900, 23 In.	295.00
Chandelier, 5-Light, Brass Patina, Hinged Amber Glass Panels, Arts & Crafts, 21 x 21 x 17 In. ...	1680.00
Chandelier, 5-Light, Regency, Bag Shape, Gilt Brass, Cut Glass, Prisms, c.1910, 52 x 24 In. ...illus	2400.00
Chandelier, 6-Light, Art Moderne, Parcel Bronze, Polished Brass, Arrow Standard, 27 x 24 In. ...	960.00
Chandelier, 6-Light, Beechwood, Twist Turned Spindles, c.1900, 30 x 39 In.	780.00
Chandelier, 6-Light, Cobalt Blue, Gilt, 37 ½ x 30 ½ In.	2530.00
Chandelier, 6-Light, Flowers, Murano Opalescent Glass, Pastels, c.1950, 48 x 32 In.	2400.00
Chandelier, 6-Light, Giltwood, Stepped, Faux Candles, c.1925, 19 x 19 In., Pair......................	1560.00
Chandelier, 6-Light, Hanging Murano Glass Pieces, Tulips, Clear, Gold, Italy, 1900, 16 x 16 In. ...	1293.00
Chandelier, 6-Light, Iron, Wood, Oval Links, Glass Rondels, Faux Candles, c.1925, 42 x 19 In. ...	960.00
Chandelier, 6-Light, Italian Provincial, Pine, Wrought Iron, Sea Urchin Spines, 31 x 29 In. ...	1800.00
Chandelier, 6-Light, Louis XIV Style, Wood, Painted White, Electrified, 44 x 36 In.	1140.00
Chandelier, 6-Light, Louis XVI Style, Gilt Bronze, Cut Glass, Rock Crystal Drop Tears, 23 x 21 ½ In. .	5280.00
Chandelier, 6-Light, Nickel Plated, Reeded Stem, C-Scroll Arms, Art Deco, 30 x 30 In.	2530.00
Chandelier, 6-Light, Opalescent & Light Green, Venetian Glass, 27 In.	693.00
Chandelier, 6-Light, Fluted Torchere, Reeded Arms, Swag, Pineapple Finial, c.1900, 26 x 33 In.	2880.00
Chandelier, 6-Light, Tin, Punched, 19th Century..	904.00
Chandelier, 6-Light, Wood Hub, Iron Arms, Scalloped Candle Cups, c.1800, 27 In.	499.00
Chandelier, 7-Light, Gilt Brass, Female Masques, Coronet Form, Electric, c.1900, 24 x 16 In. ...	960.00
Chandelier, 8-Light, 4 Internal Lights, Mica Shades, Brass, Wrought Iron, 33 x 29 x 39 In. ....illus	334.00
Chandelier, 8-Light, Art Deco, Crystal, Gilt Metal, Crystal Chains, Prisms, 38 x 23 In.	1265.00
Chandelier, 8-Light, Gilt Brass, Cut Glass, Pierced Bowl, c.1900, 37 x 29 In.	3120.00
Chandelier, 8-Light, Italian Provincial, Wrought Iron, Carved Wood, Wood Drops, 48 x 47 In.	4320.00
Chandelier, 8-Light, Louis XVI Style, S-Scroll Shape, Beaded Chain, Electrified, 39 x 26 In.	1560.00
Chandelier, 8-Light, Neoclassical, Giltwood, Brass, Glass Chains, Scandinavia, 44 x 30 In.	4320.00
Chandelier, 8-Light, Neoclassical, Giltwood, Carved, Brass, Glass Chains, Pendant Drops, 44 x 30 In. ..	4080.00
Chandelier, 8-Light, Neoclassical, Parcel Gilt Brass Frame, Masques, Cut Glass, 33 x 25 In. ...	2280.00
Chandelier, 8-Light, P. Henningsen, Brass Frame, Glass Shades, Cascade Design, 28 x 30 In. ...	10800.00
Chandelier, 8-Light, Troubadour Style, Parcel Gilt, Tole, Giltwood, Wrought Iron, 35 x 28 In. ...	4800.00
Chandelier, 8-Light, Wood, Carved, Painted, Ivory & Gilt, Germany, 1800s, 21 x 20 In.	1287.00
Chandelier, 10-Light, Paavo Tynell, Brass, Painted Aluminum, Patinated Metal, 1940s, 33 x 32 In.	16250.00
Chandelier, 10-Light, V. Panton, Elliptical Abalone Shells, 3-Tier Frame, 23 x 16 In.	480.00
Chandelier, 12-Light, Datura, Lily, Gilt Brass, Opalescent Glass, France, 34 x 34 In.	2000.00
Chandelier, 12-Light, Dutch Baroque, Brass, 2 Tiers, Male Figure, Sword, 1800s, 38 x 30 In., Pair	1528.00
Chandelier, 12-Light, George IV, Prisms, Cut Glass, 37 x 31 In.	1440.00
Chandelier, 12-Light, George VI Style, Cut Glass, Bell Pendants, Mid 1900s, 31 x 28 In. ...illus	2640.00
Chandelier, 12-Light, Georgian, Inverted Bowl Form, Chains & Drops, 42 x 34 In.	478.00
Chandelier, 12-Light, Louis XV Style, Bronze, Cage Form, Glass Prisms & Drops, 36 x 27 In. ...	889.00
Chandelier, 12-Light, Louis XVI, Cut Glass, Gilt Brass, Electrified, Faux Candles, 45 x 26 In. ..	2640.00
Chandelier, 12-Light, Spanish Baroque, Wrought Iron, Crystal Chains, Drops, Orb, 36 In.	3318.00
Chandelier, 15-Light, Maria Theresa, Gilt Metal, Cut Glass, Bead Chains, Scrolling Arms, 24 x 28 In.	1680.00
Chandelier, 18-Light, 3 Tiers, Iron Arms, Blue & White Porcelain Shaft & Cups, 34 x 40 In. ...	244.00
Chandelier, 18-Light, Brass, Scrolling Arms, Disc Bobeches, Faceted Drops, Belgium, 46 x 39 In.	2585.00
Chandelier, 21-Light, Louis XVI Style, Gilt Bronze, Cut Glass Drops, Basket Shape, 57 x 32 In.	5795.00
Chandelier, 24-Light, Brass, Stepped Cupola Shape, Scrolled Arms, c.1900, 24 x 26 In.	374.00
Chandelier, Arts & Crafts, Iron, 4 Twisted Dividers, Finials, Mica Inserts, 8 x 12 In.	660.00
Chandelier, Arts & Crafts, Red & Green Slag Glass, Wrought Metal, Bead Fringe, 64 x 28 x 28 In.	546.00
Chandelier, Empire Style, Gilt Bronze, Flower, Corona, Cut Glass Shade, 24 x 19 In.	1225.00
Chandelier, Gilt, Tiered, Narrow Fronds, Curl Ends, 1960s, 17 x 22 In.	1200.00
Chandelier, Gilt Wood, Italy, 20th Century, 41 x 39 In.	2990.00
Chandelier, Leaves, Bubbles, Inverted Pyramid, Italy, 20 x 18 In.	960.00
Chandelier, Venini, Clear, Amber Prisms, 10 x 13 In., Pair.....................................	2040.00
Electric, 2-Light, Louis XV Style, Silver Plate Screen, 20th Century, 22 ⅜ x 9 ¾ In.	720.00
Electric, 6-Light, Bronze, Mythological Bust Supports, 70 In.	725.00
Electric, A. & P. Castiglioni, Gooseneck, Domed Shade, 98 ½ x 13 x 78 ½ In.	2196.00
Electric, Aluminum, 3-Light, Painted Tubular Metal, Brass, Ateliers Serge Mouille, c.1958, 83 In.	75000.00
Electric, Aluminum, Bronzed Finish, Domed Shade, Footed, Paper Label, 16 x 9 ½ In.	59.00
Electric, Aluminum, Cone Shape, Swivels, Wall Mount, 1950s, 12 x 5 In.	35.00
Electric, Amber Slag Panels, Baluster Stem, Scrolled Metal Frame, 15 ½ In., Pair	150.00

Lamp, Base, Murano, Gold Inclusion,
Wood Base, Barovier & Toso,
20 x 38 In., Pair
$1277.00

Lamp, Betty, Iron, Tin, Brass,
Pedestal Stand, Hinged Lid,
Signed, Fhurxthal & Son, 13 In.
$593.00

Lamp, Bronze, Victory Wreaths,
Swan, Lyres, Acanthus, Inscription,
France, 34 In.
$477.00

Lamp, Chandelier, 4-Light, Bronze, Loetz Shades, Enameled, Dragonflies, Oil Spot, 1800s, 40 In. $940.00

Electric, Andre Sornay, Rondins, Ebony Macassar, Linen Shades, c.1940s, 14 ¼ In., Pair	13750.00
Electric, Aquarium Block Base, 3 Fish, Seaweed, Barbini Cenedese, Murano, Shade, 12 x 11 In.	2600.00
Electric, Arco, Marble Base, Aluminum Shade, Arched Stem, Castiglioni, 3 x 30 In.	660.00
Electric, Art Deco, Brass, Ruby, Emerald Glass Jewel Shade, 3-Arm Stem, Austria, 8 x 15 In.	748.00
Electric, Art Deco, Chase, Colonel & Colonel's Lady, Light Bulb Faces, c.1910, 9 In., Pair *illus*	300.00
Electric, Art Deco, Child Carrying Lighted Baskets, Fruit Filled, Bronze, Patina, 16 x 20 In.	600.00
Electric, Art Deco, Wrought Iron, Edgar Brandt Style, c.1925, 16 In.	470.00
Electric, Art Glass, Multicolored Panes, Metal, Painted Flower Base Design, c.1930, 24 x 18 In.	263.00
Electric, Art Nouveau, Scrolling Leaves, Flickering Light Bulb, 14 x 5 In.	300.00
Electric, Arts & Crafts, Copper, Mica, Oak, Tile, Metal, 2-Light, 18 ¾ x 22 x 15 ½ In.	948.00
Electric, Arts & Crafts, Hammered Copper, Tooled, Raised Designs, Fringed Bottom Shade, 12 x 20 In.	1680.00
Electric, Arts & Crafts, Leaded Glass Shade, Pink Roses, Leaves, Twisted Iron Base, No. 114, 18 x 24 In.	6600.00
Electric, Arts & Crafts, Mica Shade, 6-Sided, Hammered 3-Sided Copper Base, 10 ½ x 9 x 15 In.	1080.00
Electric, Arts & Crafts, Oak, Green Slag Glass Panels, c.1907, 20 ⅜ In.	385.00
Electric, Arts & Crafts, Slag Glass, Acorn, Oak Leaf Overlay, Green Patina, Bronze Base, 10 x 18 ½ In.	360.00
Electric, Arts & Crafts, Wicker, Hanging, Open Weave, Oval, 18 In.	270.00
Electric, Arts & Crafts, Wrought Iron, Hammered, Gold Glass, 8 x 13 In.	240.00
Electric, Bamboo, Ecru Linen Drum Shade, Round Stepped Base, Pebbled White Finials, 70 In., Pair	660.00
Electric, Beacon, Solarclipse, Brass, Model 8505, Badger Brass Mfg. Co., 14 x 14 In.	250.00
Electric, Beaded Glass, Blue, Faceted, Frosted Fruit, Handles, Footed, Czechoslovakia, 8 x 6 In. *illus*	644.00
Electric, Bent Glass, 6 Caramel Glass Panels, Filigree Frame, Flowers, c.1920, 20 x 17 In.	900.00
Electric, Bigelow & Kennard, Pinecone Shade, 21 x 18 In.	7320.00
Electric, Bitossi, Glazed Ceramic & Wood Base, Impressed Design, Italy, 43 In., Pair	480.00
Electric, Black Deer Outlines, Yellow, White Slag Glass Panels, Metal Tree Trunk Base, 19 x 25 In.	345.00
Electric, Blue Slag Glass In Base & Shade, Spelter Openwork Mount, Domed Shade, 27 In.	458.00
Electric, Brass, Classical Style, Faceted Urn Shape, Hexagonal Plinth, Italy, Mid 1900s, 36 In.	294.00
Electric, Brass, Paneled, Allover Openwork, 8-Panel Shade, Green Slag Glass, 24 In.	366.00
Electric, Brass, Slag Glass, Early 20th Century, 33 x 18 In.	316.00
Electric, Bronze, Birds, Domed Mica Shade, Butterflies On Border, 29 In.	1037.00
Electric, Bronze, Cold-Painted, Minaret, Figures Drinking, Washing, 17 In.	13035.00
Electric, Bronze, Egyptian Merchant Under Thatched Roof, Cold Painted, Austria, 12 In.	6814.00
Electric, Bronze, Gazelle, Moon, 6-Panel Mica Shade, Yellow, Brown, Green, 18 x 10 In.	575.00
Electric, Bronze, Lighted Candle Bulbs, 58 In.	180.00
Electric, Bronze, Mosque, Minaret, Glass Window, Man Praying, Cold Painted, 29 In.	15405.00
Electric, Bronze, Nautilus Shell Shade, Aquatic Leaves, Arched Stem, Art Nouveau, 17 In.	1840.00
Electric, Bronze, Peacock, Jeweled Base, Patina, Art Nouveau, Stamped, 16 In.	395.00
Electric, Candlestick, Bronze, Renaissance Revival, Ornate, France, 10 x 22 In., Pair	1410.00
Electric, Candlestick, Giltwood, Carved, Neoclassical, Early 19th Century, 18 In.	120.00
Electric, Candlestick, Oak, Octagonal Base, Bun Feet, Drum Shade, 20 ¾ In.	240.00
Electric, Caramel Slag Glass, 8-Panel Shade, Molded Metal, Art Nouveau, Early 1900s, 23 ½ x 18 In.	288.00
Electric, Caramel Slag Panel, Filigree Overlay, Conical Shade, Metal Base, 17 x 24 In.	863.00
Electric, Ceiling, Bead Chain, Pink Forget-Me-Nots, Art Deco, c.1930s, 10 ¼ In.	145.00
Electric, Ceiling, E. Sottsass, 3-Light, Black Aluminum, Chrome Scones, 7 x 28 In.	1800.00
Electric, Ceiling, Erik Gunnar Asplund, Parachute, Painted Metal, Frosted Glass, c.1925, 20 x 50 In.	53750.00
Electric, Ceiling, Leaded Glass, Flower Design, Mahogany Base, Arts & Crafts, 17 ½ x 23 ½ In.	61.00
Electric, Ceiling, Quilted Maple, Classical Figures, Domed, Frosted Glass, Sweden, 28 x 5 In.	1140.00
Electric, Champleve, Brown Patina, Tapered Shaft, Flowering Vines, Lion's Head Feet, Japan, 56 In.	144.00
Electric, Champleve, Cherubs, Muses, Silk Shade, Signed, Collot, Sevres, 15 ¼ In., Pair	2530.00
Electric, Chapman Mfg., Native American Chief, Painted, Plaster, 18 ½ In.	90.00
Electric, Charles Et Fils, Silver Plated Steel, Corncob Sculpture, 34 x 12 In., Pair	2760.00
Electric, Charles Lotton, Multi Flora, 12-In. Ruffled Pink Flower Shade, Squat Base, 1988	2875.00
Electric, Charles Lotton, Multi Flora, Iridescent Green, Ruffled Shade, Pink Flowers, 31 In.	2990.00
Electric, Charles Schneider, Pheasant, Leaded Glass, Bronze Head, Feathers, Legs & Base, 17 x 21 In.	3450.00
Electric, Chicago Mosaic Lamp Co., Bronze Base, Leaded Glass Shade, Cherries, Leaves, 18 x 26 In.	2040.00
Electric, Chicago Mosaic Lamp Co., Pink Pansies, Leaves, White Ground, 2 Handle Base, 18 x 22 In.	978.00
Electric, Chrome, Metal X-Shape, Rectangular Cloth Shades, 1960, 9 x 35 In., Pair	270.00
Electric, Chromium, Cut Glass, Box Frame, Pendant Chains, Prism Cut, Down Lights, 13 ¾ x 16 In.	1140.00
Electric, Classique Lamp Co., Reverse Painted, Asian Landscape, Black Baluster Base, 18 x 22 In.	1668.00
Electric, Cloisonne, Court Scenes, Flowers, Multicolored, 20th Century, 28 In.	266.00
Electric, Cobbler Shop, Doors Open, Glass Windows, Amphora Mark, Austria, c.1900, 11 ¼ In.	2510.00
Electric, Cobra, Holding Gold-Speckled Red Glass Shade, Coiled Tail On Base, 60 In.	978.00
Electric, Column, Carved, Oriental Motif, Pagoda, Figures, Lit From Inside, 20 In., Pair	316.00
Electric, Consolidated Glass, Figural, Parrot, Orange, Green, Black Base, 13 ½ In.	180.00
Electric, Cordonato Ore Glass, 2-Light, White, Green, Barovier & Toso, 32 x 6 In., Pair	780.00
Electric, Cornelius & Co., 3 Graces Metal Stem, Marble Base, Etched Shade, 21 In.	323.00

Electric, Cranberry Glass, Opalescent Swirl Design, Ruffled, Bulbous Base, 14 In.	115.00
Electric, Crane In Marsh, 5-Light, Bronze, Patina, Marble Plinth, Continental, 33 In.	600.00
Electric, Curtis Jere, Chrome, Black Enamel Base, 32 x 21 In., Pair.............................	1680.00
Electric, Curtis Jere, Chrome, Stacked Cubes, Black Enamel Base, Chrome Shade, 36 x 18 In.	960.00
Electric, Cut Glass, Daisy & Button, Domed Shade, Flared Base, Chrome, Prisms, Early 1900s, 24 ½ In.	675.00
Electric, Cut Glass, Mushroom Shade, Metal Rim, Faceted Drops, Hubbell, 21 In. ....*illus*	541.00
Electric, Cut Glass, Prisms, 2-Light, Mushroom Shape Shade, c.1900, 11 x 22 In.	644.00
Electric, Cut Overlay Glass, White, Clear, Hollow Shaft, Base, Wavy Berry Design, 9 ½ In.	356.00
Electric, Danish Modern, Mahogany, Cloth Shade, 10 x 40 In. ....*illus*	90.00
Electric, Desk, Art Deco, Nickeled Brass, Shagreen, France, 12 x 9 In.	1586.00
Electric, Desk, Blue Green Cased Glass Shade, Bronzed Base, 20th Century, 18 In.	354.00
Electric, Desk, Danilo & Corrado Aroldi, Periscope, Enameled Steel, Stilnovo, Italy, c.1967, 22 In.	365.00
Electric, Desk, Pittsburgh L., B. & G. Co., Reverse Painted, Ocean, Full Moon, Metal, c.1920, 13 In. .	720.00
Electric, Desk, Polaroid, Brown Bakelite, Yellow Plastic Diffuser, Mirror Reflector, No. 112, 8 x 9 In.	120.00
Electric, Dice Base & Shade, White, Black, 1950s, 8 In.	46.00
Electric, Dorothy Thorpe, Molded Lucite, 14 x 25 ½ In. ....*illus*	600.00
Electric, Dresden Style, Flowers, Pink Ground, 1900s, 31 In.	118.00
Electric, Duffner & Kimberly, 3-Light, Brick, Hollyhock Glass Shade, Leaf Bronze Base, 20 x 25 In.	4600.00
Electric, Duffner & Kimberly, Art Nouveau, Multicolored Geometrics, Metal Base, 19 x 22 In.	3105.00
Electric, Duffner & Kimberly, Yellow Panels, Green, Pink Apron Flowers, Metal Base, 19 x 25 In.	4600.00
Electric, Dutch Windmill, Painted Glass Shade, Figural Base, Art Deco, Table	295.00
Electric, E. Brandt, Gray Marble Domed Shade, Wrought Iron Base, 14 x 6 In.	3900.00
Electric, E. Sottsass, Callimaco, Gray Cone Base, Metal Body, Yellow, Chrome, Red Cone Top, 79 In. ..	1560.00
Electric, Edgar Brandt, Wrought & Polished Metal, Alabaster Shade, c.1930, 12 ½ In.	3346.00
Electric, Enamel, Chrome, Pantonesque Flowerpot Shade, Diffuser, 22 ½ x 8 In.	155.00
Electric, Figural, Aquarium, Mermaids, Glass Bowl, Metal Base, 35 ½ In.	920.00
Electric, Figural, Eagle, Mahogany, Carved Legs, Claw Feet, 61 In.	1725.00
Electric, Figural, Girl, Flowers In Hand, Kneeling, Looking At Snail, Bronze, 15 x 10 In.	2013.00
Electric, Figural, Quick Draw McGraw, Plastic, Vinyl, Hanna-Barbera, c.1960, 22 In.	173.00
Electric, Figural, Woman, 2 Parts, Pedestal, Ivory Matte Ceramic, 38 ½ & 35 ½ In.	165.00
Electric, Flower Basket, Czechoslovakian Glass, Brass Basket, c.1930, 10 In. ....*illus*	380.00
Electric, Frank Lloyd Wright, Walnut, Spindle Base, Silk Shade, 1915, 10 ½ x 14 ½ x 64 In. ...	780.00
Electric, Fruit Basket, Walnuts, Glass, Brass Frame, 10 ¼ In.	410.00
Electric, G. Leleu, Bronze Base, Cased Repousse Dandelions, Domed Shade, Jewel Inclusions, 16 In.	2280.00
Electric, G. Nelson, Bubble, Fiberglass Over Wire, Wood Mount, Howard Miller, 1950s, 17 ½ In.	180.00
Electric, G. Sarfatti, Black Enamel, 9-Light, Adjustable, Marble Base, Arredoluce, 78 x 14 In. .	6600.00
Electric, Garlands, Flower Beading, Domed Shade, Mountain Scene, Purple, Green, c.1930, 23 In.	881.00
Electric, Garouste & Bonetti, Bronze, Sun, Moon Design, White Paper Shade, 27 x 10 In., Pair.	6000.00
Electric, George Jouve, Glazed Earthenware, Patinated Metal, Paper Shade, c.1950s, 25 ¼ In.	68500.00
Electric, George Kovacs, Chrome Plated Steel, Acrylic Shade, c.1960s, 56 x 18 ½ In.	854.00
Electric, Gilbert Watrous, White Shade, Tag, Adjustable, Heifertz Mfg., c.1951, 31 In., Pair	3063.00
Electric, Gilt Bronze Base, Grape Cluster Shape Lights, Entwining Morning Glory, Table	92.00
Electric, Gilt Enameled Porcelain, Vase Shape, 2-Light, Gilt Metal Base, Early 1900s, 27 In. ...	24.00
Electric, Gilt Metal Frame, Mica Panels, Nude Women, Glass Fruit Top, Art Deco, c.1920, 13 x 11 In. .	1715.00
Electric, Glass, 3-Light, Leaf & Flower Decoration, Pulled Feather Shade, Green Base, 19 ½ In.	115.00
Electric, Glass, Blue Mums, Multicolored Ground, Uneven Edge, Metal Tree Base, 22 x 29 In.	17250.00
Electric, Glass, Chrome, Blown, Ball Shade, 3 Bulb Posts, 1970s, 14 x 12 In.	425.00
Electric, Glass, Shade, Green, Yellow Panels, Geometric Apron, Metal Base, Wilkinson, 18 x 23 In.	4025.00
Electric, Glass, Shade, Pond Lily, Green, Purple Panels, Plants, Metal Base, Wilkinson, 16 x 22 In.	1035.00
Electric, Glass, Shade, Yellow Panels, Brick Border, Ornate Metal Base, Wilkinson, 16 x 21 In.	1770.00
Electric, Glass, Shade, Yellow, Red, Green Geometric, Brass, Wilkinson, 20 x 26 In.	2070.00
Electric, Gone With The Wind Style, Arab, White Horse, Brass Mounts, 26 In.	403.00
Electric, Gone With The Wind Style, Artichoke, Red Satin, 23 In.	500.00
Electric, Gone With The Wind Style, Cream & Burgundy, Flowers, 25 In.	150.00
Electric, Gooseneck, Jewel Shade, 16 In.	288.00
Electric, Gothic Style, Hexagonal, Caramel Glass Panels, Gold Painted Framework, 46 x 15 In., Pair	575.00
Electric, Greta Magnusson Grossman, Green, Ralph O. Smith, c.1949, 50 In.	4594.00
Electric, Hammered Copper, Mica, 2-Light, 4 Panel Shade, 21 x 16 In.	3900.00
Electric, Hammered Copper, Mica, 4 Panel Flared Shade, 4 Arms, 19 ¼ x 22 ¼ In.	4500.00
Electric, Hanging, Apothecary Show Globe, Cast Brass Canopy, Dorin Selles, c.1890, 15 In., Pair..	420.00
Electric, Hanging, Art Deco, Brass Mounts, Stepped Glass, Textured, 22 x 15 In.	329.00
Electric, Hanging, Art Nouveau, Wrought Iron, Glass Shade, Vining, 22 In.	115.00
Electric, Hanging, Arts & Crafts, 4-Light, Glass Shades, Hammered Iron, Chain, 15 x 44 In. ...	1020.00
Electric, Hanging, Arts & Crafts, 8-Sided Slag Shade, Dutch Scene, Brass Overlay, Ceiling Cap	720.00
Electric, Hanging, Arts & Crafts, Metal, Domed Shade, 4 Lanterns, Slag Glass, 19 ½ x 19 ½ x 34 In.	1140.00

Lamp, Chandelier, 5-Light, Regency,
Bag Shape, Gilt Brass, Cut Glass, Prisms,
c.1910, 52 x 24 In.
$2400.00

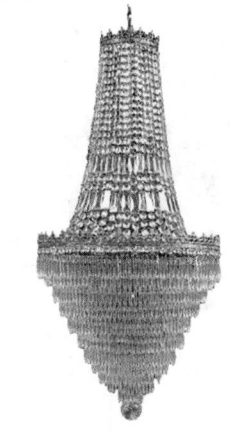

Lamp, Chandelier, 8-light,
4 Internal Lights, Mica Shades,
Brass, Wrought Iron, 33 x 29 x 39 In.
$334.00

Lamp, Chandelier, 12-Light,
George VI Style, Cut Glass, Bell Pendants,
Mid 1900s, 31 x 28 In.
$2640.00

L

Lamp, Electric, Art Deco, Chase,
Colonel & Colonel's Lady,
Light Bulb Faces, c.1910, 9 In., Pair
$300.00

Lamp, Electric, Beaded Glass, Blue,
Faceted, Frosted Fruit, Handles, Footed,
Czechoslovakia, 8 x 6 In.
$644.00

Lamp, Electric, Cut Glass,
Mushroom Shade, Metal Rim,
Faceted Drops, Hubbell, 21 In.
$541.00

Electric, Hanging, Arts & Crafts, Monk's Head, 4 Slag Glass Lanterns, Metal Overlay, 20 x 30 In.	1800.00
Electric, Hanging, Arts & Crafts, Stained Glass, 6 Caramel Curved Panels, Brass Skirt, 12 x 24 In.	360.00
Electric, Hanging, Carlo Nason, Glass, Mazzega, Italy, 15 x 18 In. ....*illus*	2400.00
Electric, Hanging, Cranberry Glass, Embossed Scrolling, Brass Fittings, Chains, c.1890, 15 In.	234.00
Electric, Hanging, Cut Glass Beads, Inverted Dome Shape, c.1900, 8 x 9 In.	236.00
Electric, Hanging, Duffner & Kimberly, Double Dome, Dichroic Leaded Glass, c.1909, 28 x 12 In. .	3525.00
Electric, Hanging, Exterior, Prairie School, Pyramid Leaded Glass Shade, Diamond Design, 11 x 27 In.	600.00
Electric, Hanging, Ezio Didone, Saucer Shape, Black Enamel, Frosted Inserts, Arteluce, 24 x 31 In.	350.00
Electric, Hanging, Gustav Stickley, 5 Staggered Copper Lanterns, Glass Shades, 75 x 55 In.	9600.00
Electric, Hanging, Noguchi, Model UF4-L10, Akari, c.1950, 75 In.	796.00
Electric, Hanging, Paul Henningsen, PH-5, Tiered Enamel Metal, Red, White, Purple, 10 x 20 In.	510.00
Electric, Hanging, Prairie School, 4-Sided Leaded Glass Shade, Flowers, Chevron, 20 In.	780.00
Electric, Hanging, Prairie School, Leaded Glass Shade, 8-Sided, Geometric Design, 24 x 54 In.	3900.00
Electric, Hanging, Stained Glass, 6 Curved Green Panels, Curved Paneled Crown, 13 x 20 In.	210.00
Electric, Hanging, Stained Glass, 8 Green & Gold Slag Glass Panels, Filigree Overlay, 13 x 20 In.	420.00
Electric, Hanging, Stained Glass, 8 Purple Slag Curved Panels, Curved Crown, 15 x 24 In.	250.00
Electric, Hanging, Stained Glass, Birds, Flowers, Green, Orange, White, Caramel, 14 x 18 In. .	210.00
Electric, Hanging, Stained Glass, Curved Glass, Crown, Green, Red, Fringe, 12 x 18 In.	540.00
Electric, Hanging, Stained Glass, Grapes, 6 Flat Panels, Multicolored, 12 x 23 In.	330.00
Electric, Hanging, Stained Glass, Molded Fruit Skirt, Curved Top Panels, Multicolored, 15 x 20 In.	180.00
Electric, Harris Strong, Walnut, Inset Tiles, 1960s, Table	1150.00
Electric, Hermes, Leather Baluster Shape Base, Brass Hardware, Leather Trimmed Shade, 29 x 12 In.	1140.00
Electric, Hermes, Leather Base, Drawer, Black Shade, 22 x 14 In.	1140.00
Electric, Hula Girl, Grass Skirt, Moves, Cast Metal, Glass Shade, Zinc, Embossed Tin Base, 20 x 8 In.	500.00
Electric, Hurel, Church, Mixed Metal, Stained Glass Windows, Doors Open, Signed, 1940, 12 x 12 In.	600.00
Electric, Iridescent Ribbed Shade, Gold, Pierced Metal Plinth Base, 11 In., Pair......................	489.00
Electric, Iron, Reticulated Shade, Geometric Cut Out Border, Slag Glass, Arts & Crafts, 11 x 11 x 17 In. .	324.00
Electric, Isamu Noguchi, 3 Graduated Shades, 20 x 15 In.	657.00
Electric, Isamu Noguchi, Bamboo, Washi Paper Shade, Iron Base, Akari, BB2 Series, 1951, 24 In.	350.00
Electric, James Mont, Wood, Carved, Suede Stitched Shade, 35 x 20 In., Pair	5400.00
Electric, Jefferson, Reverse Painted, Brass Finish Base, 2-Light, Signed, 17 x 23 In. ....*illus*	1553.00
Electric, Jefferson, Reverse Painted, Landscape, 2-Light, Bronze Base, 23 x 17 ¾ In.	1800.00
Electric, Juan Montoya, Beige Leather, Brass, White Drum Shade, 30 x ¾ x 14 In.	1159.00
Electric, L. Komulainen, Aluminum, 9-Light, Domed Shades, Amsterdam, 29 x 18 In.	2160.00
Electric, Lantern, Copper, Glazed Doors, Wrought Iron Scrolls, 17 x 44 In., Pair......................	1293.00
Electric, Lantern Shades, Pulled Green Feathers, 2-Light, Cream, Silver Swan Neck, 12 x 16 In.	748.00
Electric, L.E. Smith Co., Figural, Southern Belle, Blue Fired On Clear Glass, Opaque, c.1945...	80.00
Electric, Leaded Caramel Slag Shade, 12 Panels, Geometric, Bronzed Metal Base, c.1940, 16 x 21 In. ..	411.00
Electric, Leaded Glass, Geometric, Patinated Metal Base, Engraved Shade, 24 x 16 In.	1793.00
Electric, Leaded Glass, Honeycomb, Geometric, Poinsettias, Leaf Ground, Shade, 20 & 28 ½ In.	4312.00
Electric, Lightolier, Cone Shape Metal Base, Brass Trim, 3 Arms, Drum Shades, U.S.A., 30 ¾ In., Pair	240.00
Electric, Lily, 3-Light, Ribbed Custard, Gold, Green Shades, Ribbed, Metal Base, Lundberg, 1980, 12 In.	1035.00
Electric, Limbert, 8 Caramel Slag Panels, Hammered Copper Overlay, 23 x 25 In.	2645.00
Electric, Little Beauty, Wall, Nickel Plated, Lion's Head Arm, Green Beehive Shade, 6 ⅝ In.	129.00
Electric, Louis Poulsen, Hanging, Copper Artichoke, Late 1970s, 29 x 30 In.	7320.00
Electric, Louis XV Style, Bronze, Seated Putto, Holding Branch, Grapevines, 18 In.	267.00
Electric, Luciano Vistosi, Spiral, Glass, White, c.1972, 21 In.	1225.00
Electric, Lucite, 4 2-In. Deep Sections, Spacers, Base, 12 ¾ x 10 x 10 In.	270.00
Electric, Lucite, Brass Bands, Cylindrical, 1970s, 8 x 15 ¼ In., Pair..	480.00
Electric, Lucite, Spiral Stepped, Round Base, Linen Shade, France, 28 In. ....*illus*	270.00
Electric, M. Bellini, Chiara, Stainless Steel Sheet, White Enamel Interior, 1960s, 56 x 28 In., Pair.	2280.00
Electric, Mahogany, Leaves, Carved, Turned Base, Single Socket, 57 ½ In.	86.00
Electric, Marble, White, Woman, Swan, Water, Light Inside, Onyx Base, 18 ½ In.	708.00
Electric, Marcello Cuneo, Longobarda, Orange, Ceramic, Gabianelli, c.1966, 9 ½ In.	275.00
Electric, Maria Steinkellener, Nickel Plated Metal, Brass, c.1987, 13 In.	956.00
Electric, Mariano Fortuny, Umbrella, Black Metal Tripod Base, Domed Cotton Shade, 1907, 77 In.	1175.00
Electric, Matteo Thun, Chrome, 2 Vertical Supports, Leucos, 13 x 73 In.	600.00
Electric, Max Lauger, Ceramic, Bronze, Leaves, Green, Tonwerke, c.1900, 22 x 18 In.	3107.00
Electric, Meissen, Group, Figures, On Rocky Base, Flower Basket, 8 ¼ In.	1315.00
Electric, Meissen, Urn Shape, White Ground, Multicolored Landscape, Musicians, Gold Mounts, 14 In.	117.00
Electric, Memphis Style, Black, Yellow, 1980s, 31 ½ x 9 ½ In.	60.00
Electric, Metal Bullet Form Shade, Pierced Holes, Square Base, 13 x 8 In., Pair	460.00
Electric, Milk Glass Shade & Base, Pierced Brass Font, Flowers, 26 In.	169.00
Electric, Miller Lamp Co., Lithophane, 6 Molded Panels, Landscapes, Windmills, c.1920, 14 ¼ In.	294.00
Electric, Mining, Hand Held, Delta, 9 In.	16.95
Electric, Moet & Chandon Champagne, Figural, Ceramic, Bottle Noisemaker, 1950s, 12 In. ...	144.00

L

Electric, Multicolored Plastic Panels, Round, 20th Century, 15 In.	150.00
Electric, Mushroom Shape, Red Glass, Black Enameled Metal Base, 1960s, 10 ½ x 9 In.	270.00
Electric, Nelson Noguchi Style, Tripod, Pumpkin Shape Wire Frame, Bubble Shade, 1950s, 31 In.	190.00
Electric, Neoclassical, French Brass, Atlas, Green Tole Shade, c.1890, 25 In.	450.00
Electric, Nessen, Chrome, Black, Tubular, 35 In.	75.00
Electric, Nesso, Plastic, Mushroom Shade, Spread Foot Base, Artimeda, 9 x 12 In., Pair	144.00
Electric, Newel Post, Wood Nymph, Cattails, Patinated White Metal, Frog Base, 44 In.	2233.00
Electric, Norman Bel Geddes, Cobra, Chrome, Art Deco, Faries Mfg., c.1930, 12 ½ x 11 In.	1041.00
Electric, Nude Woman, Holding A Pinkish Glass Shade, Patina, Art Deco, 16 In.	160.00
Electric, Oak, Turned Base, White, Art Deco, c.1930, 26 x 5 x 5 In., Pair	186.00
Electric, Opaline, White, Brass Mounted, Octagonal Base, Scrolling Shield Shape, 28 ½ In.	235.00
Electric, Oval Nautilus Shell, Brass Mounted, Half Shade, Silk Cord, France, 16 x 5 ¾ x 3 In., Pair	1200.00
Electric, Paul Mayen, Chrome, Habitat Design, White Translucent Lumacryl Plastic, 1970s, 25 x 12 In.	400.00
Electric, Peacock, Glass Bead Tail, Blue, Green, Clear, Amber, White Metal, 16 ½ x 12 In.	1050.00
Electric, Pesce, Fish Design, Multicolored, 3 Black Ball Feet, c.1995, 15 x 13 In.	490.00
Electric, Pewter, Glass, Painted Shade, Osiris, Friedrich Adler, c.1901, 21 x 13 In. ....*illus*	6875.00
Electric, Piano, Wrought Iron, 4 Scrolled Feet, Paneled Shade, Pink Slag Glass, 62 x 23 In.	854.00
Electric, Pittsburgh Lamp, Brass & Glass Co., Domed Iris Shade, Bronzed Metal Base, c.1920, 22 ½ In.	940.00
Electric, Pittsburgh Lamp, Brass & Glass Co., House In Meadow, Bronze Base, Embossed, 22 x 18 In.	1255.00
Electric, Pittsburgh Lamp, Brass & Glass Co., Leaded Glass, Bronzed Base, c.1940, 18 x 23 In.	940.00
Electric, Pittsburgh Lamp, Brass & Glass Co., Reverse Painted, Autumn Leaves, 2 Handles, 22 In.	3738.00
Electric, Pittsburgh Lamp, Brass & Glass Co., Reverse Painted, Lake, Artichoke Bronze Base, 16 In.	1150.00
Electric, Porcelain De Paris, Gilt Brass, Flowers, Knife Pleat Shade, 30 ½ In.	300.00
Electric, Porcelain, Figure, Man, Woman, 18th Century Dress, Painted, Octagonal Base, 27 x 7 In., Pair	59.00
Electric, Porcelain, Souffle, Blue Glaze, Wood Base, Chinese, c.1900, 14 In.	1150.00
Electric, Poul Henningsen, Aluminum, Midcentury Modern, c.1960, 30 x 19 In., Pair	1531.00
Electric, R. Lallemant, Earthenware, Painted Ships, Countries, Stepped Wood Base, 10 x 9 In.	4800.00
Electric, R. Sonneman, Aluminum Shade, Adjustable Arm, Ball Counterweight, Swivel, 85 x 115 In.	600.00
Electric, Radio Lamp Co., Radio, Brass Over Steel, Serial No. 349654.	385.00
Electric, Rainaud, Oval Shade, 4 Painted Flower Panels, Relief Metal Base, c.1928, 20 x 24 In.	173.00
Electric, Raymor, Pottery, Glazed, Multicolored Bands, Italy, 31 In.	59.00
Electric, Reverse Painted Shade, River Landscape, Molded Metal Base, Art Nouveau, 21 ¾ x 16 In.	196.00
Electric, Royal Doulton, Figurine, Bedtime Story, Mounted As Lamp, 4 ¾ x 5 ½ In.	115.00
Electric, Silk Shade, Glass Beads, 1920s, 59 x 11 In.	200.00
Electric, Silver Overlay Shade, Base, Ruby Prisms, Art Deco, 14 In.	878.00
Electric, Slag Glass, Oak, Copper, 2 Sockets, Shoe Feet, Arts & Crafts, 19 ½ x 22 x 15 ⅜ In.	474.00
Electric, Slag Glass Shade, Bronze Tone Metal Base, 2 Sockets, Octagonal, 24 x 19 In. ....*illus*	414.00
Electric, St. George Slaying Dragon, Fruit Centerpiece, Glass, White Metal Base, 6 x 12 In.	410.00
Electric, Stefano Marcato, Donna, Frosted White Glass, Steel Base, Dimmer, Nemo, 68 In.	480.00
Electric, Stickley Brothers, 6-Sided Mica Shade, Stem, Hammered Copper Base, 18 ½ x 23 In.	4200.00
Electric, Stiffel, Pink Marble Base, 4 Brass Uprights, Marble Finial, U.S.A., 33 x 19 In.	240.00
Electric, Stilnovo, Chrome, Frosted Glass Reflector, 16 x 7 In.	780.00
Electric, Stoneware, Jug, Oval, Reeded Handle, Leaf, Cobalt Blue, c.1805, 12 In.	257.00
Electric, Student, 1-Arm, Adjustable, Center Shaft, Weighted Base, Opaque White Shade, 13 x 3 ¾ In.	152.00
Electric, Student, 2-Light, Iron Base, 22 In.	330.00
Electric, Student, Manhattan Brass Co., 2-Arm, Burners, Adjustable, Yellow Glass Shades, 29 x 20 In.	1410.00
Electric, Tapio Wirkkala, Brass, Teak, Enamel, Adjustable, 49 In.	2280.00
Electric, Tole, Copper, Octagonal, Tapering, Ocher, 34 x 6 In., Pair	1041.00
Electric, Tomasso Barbi, Brass, Leaf Shaped Reflectors, 49 x 56 In. Diam.	2562.00
Electric, Torch, Brass, Filigree Shade, Ship Finial, 72 In., Pair	1755.00
Electric, Triennale, Brass, 3 Adjustable Arms, Aluminum Shades, Arredoluce, Italy, 58 In.	2400.00
Electric, Triennale, Brass, Red, Yellow, Black Shades, Arredoluce, 67 In.	6600.00
Electric, TV, Art Deco, Patinated Metal, Marble, Nude Woman, Draped, Mid 1900s, 16 x 11 In. ...*illus*	1195.00
Electric, Urn Shape, Classical Revival, Polished Bronze, Caryatid Handles, Leaf Bands, 21 In.	411.00
Electric, V. Panton, White, Clear Glass Shade, Chrome Tulip Base, L. Poulsen, 52 x 20 In.	2220.00
Electric, Vandermark, Opal Corset Base, Mushroom Shade, Pink Hooked Feathers, Green Tips, 28 In.	650.00
Electric, Venetian Glass, Brass Base, Painted, Gold, White, Scrolling, 29 x 10 In.	35.00
Electric, Vico Magistretti, Atollo, Conical Shade, Oluce, 1977, 28 x 19 In.	420.00
Electric, Vico Magistretti, Nemea, White Lacquer Base, Chrome Shaft, Artemide, Italy, 1979, 14 x 14 In.	90.00
Electric, Victorian, Lily, After Moreau, 36 In. ....*Illus*	510.00
Electric, Viking On Ship, Copper, Mica Shade, Hand Painted, 1930s, 16 In.	575.00
Electric, Vladimir Kagan, Walnut, Sculpted, Cream String Shade, 58 x 13 ½ In.	1830.00
Electric, Walter Von Nessen, White Enameled Shades, Brushed Steel Base, 2 Arms, 1960s, 28 x 9 In.	780.00
Electric, Western Union, Metal, Black, Glass, Gold Letters, 17 x 26 In.	1293.00
Electric, Whaley & Co., Grape Shade, Leaded, Vertical Ribbed Shaft, 18 x 23 In. ....*illus*	8050.00
Electric, Whaley & Co., Tulip Shade, Bronzed Ribbed Shaft, 24 x 69 In. ....*illus*	7375.00

Lamp, Electric, Danish Modern, Mahogany, Cloth Shade, 10 x 40 In. $90.00

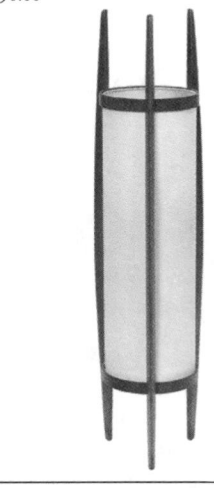

Lamp, Electric, Dorothy Thorpe, Molded Lucite, 14 x 25 ½ In. $600.00

Lamp, Electric, Flower Basket, Czechoslovakian Glass, Brass Basket, c.1930, 10 In. $380.00

L

Lamp, Electric, Hanging, Carlo Nason, Glass, Mazzega, Italy, 15 x 18 In.
$2400.00

Lamp, Electric, Pewter, Glass, Painted Shade, Osiris, Friedrich Adler, c.1901, 21 x 13 In.
$6875.00

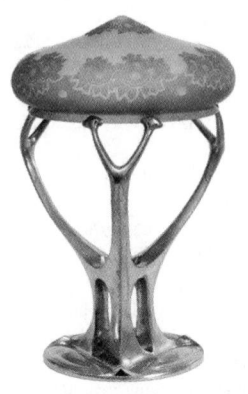

Lamp, Electric, TV, Art Deco, Patinated Metal, Marble, Nude Woman, Draped, Mid 1900s, 16 x 11 In.
$1195.00

Lamp, Electric, Jefferson, Reverse Painted, Brass Finish Base, 2-Light, Signed, 17 x 23 In.
$1553.00

Lamp, Electric, Slag Glass Shade, Bronze Tone Metal Base, 2 Sockets, Octagonal, 24 x 19 In.
$414.00

Lamp, Electric, Victorian, Lily, After Moreau, 36 In.
$510.00

Lamp, Electric, Lucite, Spiral Stepped, Round Base, Linen Shade, France, 28 In.
$270.00

Lamp, Electric, Whaley & Co., Grape Shade, Leaded, Vertical Ribbed Shaft, 18 x 23 In.
$8050.00

L

Electric, White Glass Globes, 5 Graduated Spindles, Mid 20th Century, 58 In.	115.00
Electric, White Lacquer, S-Form Support, Opaque Glass Pendant Sphere, 58 In.	173.00
Electric, Wilkinson, Leaded, Helmet Shape Shade, Intertwined Vine Base, 19 x 23 In. ....*illus*	2300.00
Electric, Winged Gold Sphinx, Berries Glass Shade, 3-Light, 2 Side Gas Arms, 24 x 21 In.	1150.00
Electric, Wood, Carved, Multicolored Finish, Woven Shade, James Mont, 44 x 21 In. ....*illus*	5490.00
Fairy, Bisque, 3 Faces, Cat, Dog, Owl, Triangular, Painted, Amber Glass Eyes, 4 x 2 ¾ In.	187.00
Fairy, Burmese, Clarke, 3 ¾ In.	152.00
Fairy, Fenton, Drape, Cased Cranberry, Opalescent, Gloss Finish, Crimped Top, 5 x 4 In.	129.00
Fairy, Fenton, Pink & White Satin, Roses, 6 ½ In., Pair	100.00
Fairy, Hanging, Filigree Gilt Metal, Faux Gem Stones, Ceramic Insert, Clarke's, 5 ½ x 13 In.	140.00
Fairy, Satin Glass, Rose, Cased, Furled Tricornered Base, 5 ½ x 2 ¾ In.	625.00
Fairy, Venetian Thread, Cranberry, Opal Satin Finish, Crimped Rim, Patterned Shade, 5 ¼ x 6 ¼ In.	644.00
Fat, Copper, Wrought Iron, Stamped, Peter Derr, 1838.	3560.00
Fat, Hanging, Double, Brass, Engraved, Filigree, Dutch, 1700s, 14 ½ In.	225.00
Fluid, 8 Ribs, Applied Handle, Double-Tube Burner, Pontil, c.1850, 4 ½ In.	195.00
Gas, Chandelier, 4-Light, French Empire, Bronze, Urn Top, Faces, Flowers, Hanging Chains, 25 In.	7660.00
Gas, Gasolier, 18-Light, Gilt Bronze, Baccarat Crystal, Flute Cut Standard, Prisms, 58 x 34 In.	12000.00
Gas, Hanging, Arts & Crafts, 6-Light, Iron, Hammered, Green, Purple Slag Glass, Burners, 25 x 17 In. .	900.00
Gone With The Wind, Electric, Painted, Flowers, Gilt Cast Iron Base, Converted, 27 In. ..*illus*	283.00
Handel lamps are included in the Handel category.	
Kerosene, 3 Tiers, Opal Cased, Yellow Fonts, Leaf Design, Ball Shades, Taplin Brown Collars, 12 In.	224.00
Kerosene, Acorn, Amber, Gold Mercury Interior, Paneled Top, 4 ¼ x 2 ¼ In.	82.00
Kerosene, Acorn, Vertical Opalescent Stripes, 4 ¼ x 2 ¼ In.	176.00
Kerosene, Amethyst, Gilt Decoration, Molded, Decorated Chimney Shade, 9 ¼ x 2 ½ In.	129.00
Kerosene, Angels, Green Umbrella Shade, 8 In.	144.00
Kerosene, Apple Blossom, White, Green, 6 ¾ In.	118.00
Kerosene, Artichoke, Opaque White, Green To Pink Stain, Patterned Shade, 8 x 2 ¾ In.	176.00
Kerosene, Baby Thumbprint Optic, Cranberry, Patterned Shade, Ruffled Rim, 9 ⅝ x 2 ⅜ In. ..	439.00
Kerosene, Banquet, Cranberry Glass Shade, Paneled Ruby Glass Font, Electrified, Late 1800s, 28 In.	118.00
Kerosene, Banquet, Molded Scroll Patterns, Medallions, Delft Transfers, 15 ¾ x 4 ½ In.	410.00
Kerosene, Banquet, Satin Glass, Green, Fruit, Silver Leaf Overlay, Umbrella Shade, 14 ½ x 4 ¼ In.	585.00
Kerosene, Beaded Drape, Frosted, Cast-Iron Base, 7 ½ In., Pair	30.00
Kerosene, Brass, Green, Purple Flowers, Hand Painted, Electrified, Gone With The Wind, 25 In.	71.00
Kerosene, Brass, Silver Handles, White Ruffled Shade, 11 In.	75.00
Kerosene, Bristol Glass, Blue, Enameled Flowers, 17 In., Pair...........................	250.00
Kerosene, Bronze, Aesthetic Movement, Turkey Feet & Legs, Turquoise Tiles, Bird's Heads, 59 In.	6325.00
Kerosene, Cat, With Umbrella, On Suitcase, Ceramic, Painted, Blue Coat, Glass Eyes, 6 ½ x 3 ¼ In.	585.00
Kerosene, Cathedral, Blue Font, Amber Base, Daisy & Button Ruffled Shade, Stand, 18 ¼ In. ...	316.00
Kerosene, Cathedral, Clear Font, Blue Base, Daisy & Button Ruffled Shade, Stand, 17 ¼ In. ...	432.00
Kerosene, Composition, Frosted, Clear, Flowers, Moon, Sun, Milk Glass Stem, 11 In.	22.00
Kerosene, Consolidated Lamp & Glass Co., Quilted Phlox, Cased Pale Green, Ball Shade, 7 In.	496.00
Kerosene, Cosmos, Paneled, Opaque White, Pink Highlights, Ball Shade, 8 ½ In.	118.00
Kerosene, Cranberry, Embossed Plume Mold, 7 ½ In.	100.00
Kerosene, Cranberry Opalescent, Clear, Ribbed, Sheldon Swirl, 6 In.	250.00
Kerosene, Cranberry Satin, Cabbage Mold, Shade, 8 ¼ In.	300.00
Kerosene, Cranberry To Clear Font, Square, Applied Base, Pressed Shell, 6-Footed, 11 x 4 ¼ In.	761.00
Kerosene, Crown Milano, Pastel Pansies, Matching Shade, Font, Brass Mounts, Base.............	2100.00
Kerosene, Cut Glass, Column, Corinthian Capital, Gilt Metal, Molded Square Base, 20 ½ In. ..	88.00
Kerosene, Cut Glass, Hobstars, Triangles, Domed Shade, Prisms, Brass Band, 17 ¼ x 8 ½ In. .	189.00
Kerosene, Cut Glass, Mushroom Shade, Silver Collar, Prisms, 12 x 20 In.	1265.00
Kerosene, Decorated Bear Face, Ceramic, Yellow Glass Eyes, Impressed, 5 ¾ x 3 ¾ In.	105.00
Kerosene, Eagle Glass & Mfg. Co., Yellow, Blue Gilt, Eagle, Ball Shade, 7 ⅜ In.	330.00
Kerosene, Elephant, Dog, Ceramic, Painted, Ivy Leaf Base, 5 ½ x 3 ½ In.	380.00
Kerosene, Etched Cut Shade, Prisms, Brass, Stepped Marble Base, c.1875, 26 x 8 In.	480.00
Kerosene, Eye Dot, Cranberry, Patterned Ball Shade, L.G. Wright Glass Co., 7 x 2 In.	152.00
Kerosene, Finger, Baby Rochester, No. 666, Footed, Nickel Finish, Saucer Base, 4 x 4 ½ In.	59.00
Kerosene, Finger, Brass Saucer Base, Pat. October 28th, 1873, 2 ⅝ x 4 ¼ In.	53.00
Kerosene, Finger, Clear, Applied Handle, Star, 2 ¼ In.	53.00
Kerosene, Finger, Cobalt Blue, Nutmeg, Brass Band, 2 ½ In.	66.00
Kerosene, Finger, Gothic Arch, White, Opalescent, 3 ⅝ In.	39.00
Kerosene, Finger, Swirled Ribs, Teal Green, Taplin Brown Collar, 3 In.	105.00
Kerosene, Firefly, Bracket, Opaque White, Embossed Font, Star, Blue Chimney Shade, 3 ½ x 6 In. .	1404.00
Kerosene, Flowers, Coralene, Blue Ground, 8 ½ x 3 ⅜ In.	250.00
Kerosene, Flowers, Geometric Design, Embossed, Taplin Brown Collar, 8 ½ In.	66.00
Kerosene, Flowers, Petals, White, Green Banding, 6 ½ x 2 ½ In.	53.00
Kerosene, Fostoria, Drape, Sylvan, Opaque White, Blue Shading, Patterned Ball Shade, 8 x 3 In.	153.00

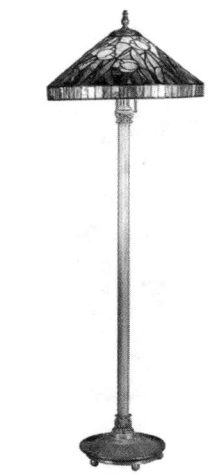

Lamp, Electric, Whaley & Co.,
Tulip Shade, Bronzed Ribbed Shaft,
24 x 69 In.
$7375.00

Lamp, Electric, Wilkinson, Leaded,
Helmet Shape Shade,
Intertwined Vine Base, 19 x 23 In.
$2300.00

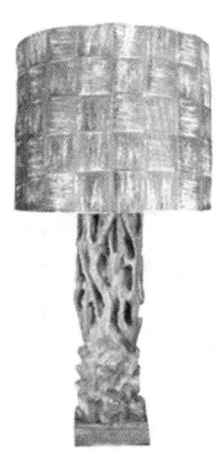

Lamp, Electric, Wood, Carved,
Multicolored Finish, Woven Shade,
James Mont, 44 x 21 In.
$5490.00

Lamp, Gone With The Wind, Electric, Painted, Flowers, Gilt Cast Iron Base, Converted, 27 In.
$283.00

Lamp, Kerosene, Gone With The Wind, Green, Brown & White Setters, Flying Ducks, 21 In.
$800.00

Lamp, Kerosene, Hanging, Opalescent Shade, Bird, Snail, On Branch, Victorian, 14 In.
$300.00

Kerosene, Gilt Brass, Melon Ribbed Opal Glass Shade, c.1875, 23 In.	420.00
Kerosene, Glow Style, Brass Cone Shape Font, Tassel Tip, Glass Tube, Burner, 19 ¾ x 3 ¼ In.	117.00
Kerosene, Gone With The Wind, Chrysanthemum, Green Ground, Electrified, Larkin, c.1895	140.00
Kerosene, Gone With The Wind, Daylilies, Green Ground, Metal Base, Handles	366.00
Kerosene, Gone With The Wind, Flowers, Electrified, 25 In.	117.00
Kerosene, Gone With The Wind, Flowers, Red-Orange Ground, Electrified, Larkin, c.1895	85.00
Kerosene, Gone With The Wind, Green, Brown & White Setters, Flying Ducks, 21 In. *illus*	800.00
Kerosene, Gone With The Wind, Painted, Pink, Red Iris, Gold, Brass, Electrified, c.1900, 25 x 10 In.	322.00
Kerosene, Gone With The Wind, Pansies, Yellow Glass, Openwork Metal Base, Duplex Burner	150.00
Kerosene, Gone With The Wind, Red Satin Glass, Bull's Eye, 26 In., Pair	525.00
Kerosene, Green, Gilded, Taplin Brown Collar, 7 ¾ x 4 In.	79.00
Kerosene, Hanging, Opalescent Shade, Bird, Snail, On Branch, Victorian, 14 In. *illus*	300.00
Kerosene, Hanging, Opaque White, Tan Ground, Pink & Blue Shading, Shells, 10 ½ In.	1989.00
Kerosene, Hanging, Prisms, Man & Woman With Parasol In Boat, Victorian, 14 In.	526.00
Kerosene, Leaf & Flowers, Satin Finish, Ball Shade, 8 ¾ x 2 ¾ In.	39.00
Kerosene, Log, Double Arm, Brass, Ribbed Shades, 11 ¾ In.	661.00
Kerosene, Marbrie Maroon Loop, Cased, Opalescent, Umbrella Shade, Ruffled Top, 9 ¾ x 2 ¾ In.	322.00
Kerosene, Milk Glass, Embossed Flowers, Painted, Pink, Blue, Yellow, Paneled Base, Ball Shade, 8 In.	46.00
Kerosene, Molded Satin Glass, Orange, Embossed, Fleur-De-Lis Pattern Ball Shade, 12 x 4 ½ In.	439.00
Kerosene, Monkey, Painted, Holding Orange, Yellow Ball, Amber Glass Eyes, 6 x 4 In.	322.00
Kerosene, Mother-Of-Pearl, Raindrop, 4-Footed, 8 ½ x 3 ⅛ In.	198.00
Kerosene, Nellie Bly, Peacock Green, Patterned Chimney Shade, Gilt Transfer, 9 x 3 In.	263.00
Kerosene, Newel Post, Figural, Diana, Bow, Dog, Leaves, 3-Light, France, 12 x 28 In.	1150.00
Kerosene, Newel Post, Figural, Don Juan, Sword, Glove, Pole, Top Pierced Font, 15 x 51 In.	1150.00
Kerosene, Northwood Glass Co., Quilted Phlox, Cased Blue, Patterned Ball Shade, 7 x 2 ½ In.	527.00
Kerosene, Northwood Glass Co., Royal Ivy, Rubina, Patterned Ball Shade, 6 x 2 In.	410.00
Kerosene, Opal, Ruby & Green Spatter, Ball Shade, 6 ½ In.	265.00
Kerosene, Opal Spatter, Pink, Patterned Shade, Applied Skirt, Ruffled Shade, 8 x 5 ½ In.	4388.00
Kerosene, Opaline Brocade, Spanish Lace, Blue, Ball Shade, 7 ¼ x 3 In.	1322.00
Kerosene, Opaque, Cream & Pink Design, Umbrella Shade, 7 ¼ In.	132.00
Kerosene, Opaque Green, Bracket, 6 ⅞ In.	53.00
Kerosene, Owl, Opaque White, Green Shading, Decorated Face, Ball Shade, 8 x 2 ¾ In.	644.00
Kerosene, Parrot, Ivy, Ceramic, Blue, Gilt, Hasag Burner, 8 ¾ x 4 ⅝ In.	322.00
Kerosene, Peacock Feather, Taplin Brown Collar, Stand, 8 ¾ In.	106.00
Kerosene, Peacock, Metal, Glass Bead Feathers, Electrified, Victorian, 16 In. *illus*	878.00
Kerosene, Peonies, Pink, Green, Yellow, Man Of The North Mask On Corners, 29 In.	480.00
Kerosene, Piano, Victorian, Brass, Ornate, 31 In.	189.00
Kerosene, Pineapple & Fan, Shepherd's Plaid, Patterned Ball Shade, Atwood Collar, 17 x 6 ¼ In.	322.00
Kerosene, Pineapple In Basket, Ball Shade, 7 ¼ In.	92.00
Kerosene, Pink, Satin, Tulip Shade, 8 ¼ In.	224.00
Kerosene, Prayer, Opaque White, Pink Shading, Angel Transfer Shade, 8 ¼ x 2 ¾ In.	105.00
Kerosene, Pressed Glass, Bellflower, Collar & Wafer Construction, 7 ⅜ x 4 ¼ In.	81.00
Kerosene, Pull Down, Cranberry Hobnail Shade, Filigree Molded Ring, Cut Glass Prisms, 33 In.	575.00
Kerosene, Queen Heart, Green, Round Base, Stand, 5 ⅜ In.	145.00
Kerosene, Raindrop, Satin Glass, Mother-Of-Pearl, Blue, Ball Shape, Crimp Top Shade, 8 x 3 ¾ In.	544.00
Kerosene, Rib Optic, Horizontal Ribs, Waisted, Patterned Ball Chimney Shade, Opalescent, 7 x 2 ½ In.	644.00
Kerosene, Rib Optic, Rose To Vaseline Opalescent, Umbrella Shade, Applied Base, 8 ½ x 3 In.	1404.00
Kerosene, Rib Optic, Umbrella Shade, Applied Base, Pressed Leaves, 5-Footed, 9 x 3 ½ In.	819.00
Kerosene, Rococo Style, Bronze Tripod Base, Onyx Font, Milk Glass Ball Shade, Late 1800s, 69 In.	900.00
Kerosene, Rubina, Patterned Umbrella Shade, Applied Base, Pressed Shell, 6-Footed, 7 ¾ x 3 ¾ In.	761.00
Kerosene, Ruby, Satin, Brass Petal Foot, 10 ¼ x 3 ¾ In.	171.00
Kerosene, Ruby, Satin, Embossed Lion Heads, 8 ¾ x 3 ¼ In.	159.00
Kerosene, Satin Glass, Cased Pink & Blue Stripes, Ruffled Top, Applied Shells, 9 x 4 In.	4388.00
Kerosene, Skeleton, Bisque, Gray, Brown, Lavender Tie, Blue Highlights, Glass Eyes, 6 ½ x 3 ¾ In.	1170.00
Kerosene, Snail, Opaque White, Red Mustard Ground, Patterned Umbrella Shade, 8 x 3 ⅜ In.	439.00
Kerosene, Spelter Figure, Opalescent Globe, Electrified, 1800s, 35 In. *illus*	330.00
Kerosene, Spider Web, Red, Satin Finish, Patterned Ball Shade, 8 x 3 ½ In.	351.00
Kerosene, Squirrel, Clear, Taplin Brown Collar, Stand, 8 ¾ In.	118.00
Kerosene, Star Tumbler, Arched Panels, Sunburst Base, Attached Handle, Hinged Lip, 8 ¼ x 6 In.	82.00
Kerosene, Student, Brass, Frosted Glass Shade, 23 ½ In.	767.00
Kerosene, Student, Single Arm, Vertical Filler Tube, Tiny Diamond Optic Umbrella Shade, 13 In.	330.00
Kerosene, Swan Shape, Blue, Opaque, Oval Base, 4 In.	106.00
Kerosene, Swirled Beads, Cased Green, Mottled Opal, Red & Brown Chimney Shade, 8 ½ x 3 In.	380.00
Kerosene, Swirled Metal Shade, Embossed, Beaded Amber Prisms, 11 ¾ In.	75.00
Kerosene, Tarentum, Heart With Thumbprint, Custard, Yellow, Enameled Flowers, c.1896, 9 x 5 ¼ In.	460.00
Kerosene, Tulip, Pink To Clear, Satin Finish, Overshot, Patterned Petal Shade, 8 ⅜ x 2 ⅝ In.	1053.00

Kerosene, Twinkle, Amethyst, Embossed Font, Stars, Ball Chimney Shade, 6 ¾ x 2 In.	152.00
Kerosene, Union, Driving, Hand Held, Dietz, 11 ½ In.	62.00
Kerosene, Vienna Bronze, Middle Eastern Figure, Cobalt Blue Honeycomb Optic Font, 10 ½ In. ...	152.00
Lard, Kettle, Tin, Saucer Base, Applied Loop Handle, Removable Reservoir, 7 x 6 In. ....*illus*	33.00
Oil, Brass, Indian, 3 Branches, Red, Blue Oil Fonts, Prisms, White Marble Base, c.1850, 25 In.	999.00
Oil, Brass, Oval Globe, Burner, Electrified, France, Mid 19th Century, 27 ½ In.	59.00
Oil, Bronze, Glass Globe, Cherub, Birds, Scrolls, Dolphin, 4-Footed, c.1910, 65 In.	652.00
Oil, Cosmos, Milk Glass, Embossed Design, Painted Flowers, 7 ½ In.	52.00
Oil, Cosmos, Opaque White, Multicolored Flowers, 8 In. ....*illus*	79.00
Oil, Cranberry, Coin Spot, Miniature, 1960s, 8 ¼ In.	75.00
Oil, Cranberry Glass Font, Milk Glass Stepped & Fluted Base, 9 ½ In.	71.00
Oil, Figural, Cobra On Plinth Base Set On Granite Base, Diffuser, Egyptian, c.1910, 14 x 13 In. .	1057.00
Oil, Flowers, Ruby Stained, Frosted, Brass Stem, Marble Base, No Burner, 9 ½ In.	77.00
Oil, Glass, Cut Overlay, White, Blue Font, Brass Column, Gray Marble Base, 1850, 13 In.	264.00
Oil, Hanging, Gimbaled, Forged Iron Rooster..	236.00
Oil, Hanging, Ribbed Blue Art Glass Shade, Crystal Patterned Font, Brass Frame, 14 In.	525.00
Oil, L.E. Smith Co., Amber Glass, Moon & Star, 1940s, 12 In.	80.00
Oil, Linen Maker's, Blown, Faceted, 8 ½ In.	69.00
Oil, Lomax, Brass Collar, Clear, c.1870, 6 ¼ x 4 ⅛ In.	65.00
Oil, Milk Glass, Embossed, Owl Shape, 8 In.	805.00
Oil, Moravian Star Shape, Tin, Worn Gold Paint, c.1850, 5 In.	1704.00
Oil, Opalescent Round Shade, Fox Chasing Duck Scene On Stem, Victorian, 23 In.	885.00
Oil, Oval Urn, 3 Cherubs, Fitted Reservoir, Electrified, Sitzendorf, Germany, 1900s, 14 In.	177.00
Oil, Paneled Decoration, Gilt Metal Pierced Base, 2-Light, Electrified, Late 1800s, 24 In.	106.00
Oil, Peg, Brass, Bulbous Cranberry Glass Font, 17 In.	95.00
Oil, Peg, Green Pressed Glass, Leaf, Swirl, Brass Collar, 19th Century, 3 ¾ In.	340.00
Oil, Ruby Flashed Font, 9 ½ In., Pair.	29.00
Oil, Solar, Classical, Brass, Baluster Shape Cut Shade, Prism Hung, Marble Plinth, c.1850, 25 ½ In. .	940.00
Oil, Solar, Cornelius & Baker, Cut Glass Globe, Tree Base, Prisms, Brass, Bronze, c.1860, 32 x 8 In.	2640.00
Oil, Solar, Cut, Blown Globe, Fluted Stem, Marble Base, Prisms, Brass, Marble, c.1850, 24 x 8 In.	660.00
Oil, Solar, Etched Glass Shade, Spherical Geometric, Patinated Bronze, c.1872, 18 ¼ x 8 ½ In.	368.00
Oil, Solar, Frosted, Cut Globe, Cobalt Edge, Tripod, Flower Base, Prisms, Brass, 25 In., Pair	3120.00
Oil, Solar, Frosted, Cut Globe, Column Stem, Prisms, Brass, Bronze, Marble Base, c.1850, 18 x 7 In.	840.00
Oil, Solar, Globe, Martha Washington, Stem, Prisms, Brass, Bronze, Marble Base, c.1850, 27 x 7 In.	1200.00
Oil, Tole, Empire Revival, Urn Form, Lion's Mask Handles, Gilt Scrolls, 12 In.	385.00
Oil, Tole, Fluted Columns, Flowers, Red Ground, c.1850, 23 In.	118.00
Oil, Vacuum Oil Company, Green Pressed Glass, Flowers, Embossed, Brass Burner, 10 ½ In.	550.00
Pairpoint lamps are in the Pairpoint category.	
Rush, Counterweight, Oak Post, Wrought Iron, 41 In.	705.00
Rush, Wood Base, Wrought Iron Top, c.1800, 42 In.	206.00
Sconce, 2-Light, Brass, Beveled Mirror Back, France, 30 x 5 ½ In., Pair	2160.00
Sconce, 2-Light, Brass, Lanterns, Hinged Glass Panels, Arts & Crafts, 11 x 8 x 10 In.	450.00
Sconce, 2-Light, Carved Parcel Gilt, Ribbon, Swag, Bows, Wheat Sheaf, Italy, 1900s, 37 In., Pair.	1725.00
Sconce, 2-Light, George IV, Cut Glass Pendants, Beads, Faceted Spear Back, 20 x 18 In., Pair ..	240.00
Sconce, 2-Light, Louis XV, Wrought Iron, Scrolled, c.1930, 10 x 11 In.	174.00
Sconce, 2-Light, Louis XVI, Leaves, Brass, Black, Gilt, 2 Faux Candles, 18 x 11 In., Pair............	1320.00
Sconce, 2-Light, S. Mouille, White Lacquered Metal, Brass, c.1954, 40 ¾ x 49 ½ x 13 ⅞ In.	50000.00
Sconce, 2-Light, Wrought Iron, Scrolled, Bobeche, c.1800, 11 x 12 In., Pair	680.00
Sconce, 3-Light, Brass, Figural Dog Mounts, Art Deco, 22 x 17 x 9 ½ In.	115.00
Sconce, 3-Light, Fontana Arte, Brass, Beveled, Smoked Glass, 18 x 9 In., Pair........................	1800.00
Sconce, 3-Light, Louis XVI, Brass, Ribbon Backplate, Electrified, 30 x 15 In., Pair....................	294.00
Sconce, 3-Light, Louis XVI Style, Gilt Metal, Scrolling, Ribbons, Cherub Heads, 20 x 11 ½ In., Pair	588.00
Sconce, 4-Light, Rose Bloom Sockets, Flowers, Drops, Crystal, Silver Leaf, France, 31 x 20 In., Pair	1320.00
Sconce, 5-Light, Cast Iron, Hands Upholding, Candelabrum Style, Pair...............................	120.00
Sconce, 6-Light, Alabaster Shade, Pendant Design, 9 x 15 In.	900.00
Sconce, Arts & Crafts, Brass, 6-Sided Slag Glass Shade, 7 x 10 x 18 In., Pair........................	2040.00
Sconce, Brass, Half Circle, Pretzel, 12 x 13 In., Pair	1920.00
Sconce, Candle, Round, Concave Back, Mirror Segments, Red Painted Tin, 17 x 15 ½ In.	237.00
Sconce, Candle, Tin, Graphic Hood, c.1910, 13 ½ x 4 x 2 ½ In.	850.00
Sconce, Clear Glass Shade, Textured, Square Chrome Mounts, 1960s, 11 x 6 In, 4 Piece	480.00
Sconce, Curtis Lighting, Golden Armor X-Ray, Mercury Glass Shade, Art Deco, 13 x 16 In.	420.00
Sconce, Dragon, Brass, Flame Shade, 24 In., Pair	403.00
Sconce, E. Barovier, Polished Brass, Glass, c.1940, 14 x 8 x 8 In., Pair...................................	2032.00
Sconce, Eagle Pediment, Gilt Metal, Arrows, Pineapple Drop Finials, Tassels, 38 In., Pair	2760.00
Sconce, E.F. Caldwell, 3-Light, Bronze, Glass, Fruit Pendant, Basket, c.1835, 11 x 24 In.	2937.00
Sconce, Etched Angel, Cut, Grape Leaves, c.1900, 8 ⅛ x 1 ⅞ In., Pair....................................	120.00

Lamp, Kerosene, Peacock, Metal, Glass Bead Feathers, Electrified, Victorian, 16 In.
$878.00

Lamp, Kerosene, Spelter Figure, Opalescent Globe, Electrified, 1800s, 35 In.
$330.00

Lamp, Lard, Kettle, Tin, Saucer Base, Applied Loop Handle, Removable Reservoir, 7 x 6 In.
$33.00

LAMP

Lamp, Oil, Cosmos, Opaque White, Multicolored Flowers, 8 In. $79.00

Lamp, Space Age, Pattyn Products, Aluminum, Brass, Bakelite Walter Von Nessen, c.1936, 19 In., Pair $9988.00

Lamp, Whale Oil, Sinumbra, Gilt Bronze, Satin Glass, Pendant Prisms, Electrified, 1800s, 19 In. $150.00

Sconce, Frank Lloyd Wright, Copper Arm, 2 Leaded Glass Panels, Pivoting, 1911, 9 ½ In.	4200.00
Sconce, Frosted Glass, V Shape Brass Frame, Art Deco, France, c.1925, 12 In., Pair..................	1200.00
Sconce, Hands Hold, Enameled, Brass, Jean Marais Style, 15 ½ x 4 x 8 ½ In., Pair....................	1037.00
Sconce, Jacques Adnet, Brass, Brown Leather Frame, Wicker Shades, 36 x 14 In., Pair	8400.00
Sconce, Metal, Orange Enamel Finish, Square, Round Opening, France, 10 x 10 In., 4 Piece ..	1080.00
Sconce, Silver Foil Glass Leaves, Wrought Iron, Gilt, Shade, France, 1975, 19 x 6 In., Pair.......	1560.00
Sconce, Sue Et Mare, Mirror Back, Embossed Metal Rim, Jean L. Bordeaux, 11 x 10 In., Pair..	1800.00
Space Age, Pattyn Products, Aluminum, Brass, Bakelite Walter Von Nessen, c.1936, 19 In., Pair ...*illus*	9988.00
Tiffany lamps are listed in the Tiffany category.	
Tiffany Style, Bronze, Domed Shade, Daffodils, 20th Century, 21 ½ In.	1292.00
Torchere, 5-Light, Blackamoor, Multicolored, Patinated Metal, Molded Base, 60 In.	1175.00
Torchere, 6-Light, Louis XV, Ormolu, Scrolls, Bacchante Heads, Blue Orb, Trefoil Base, 90 In.	28440.00
Torchere, Beaux Arts, Bronze, Ram's Heads Capitals, Round Plinth, c.1900, 79 x 22 In., Pair .	14100.00
Torchere, Classical Maidens, Bronze, Marble, Gilt, France, c.1890, 27 x 10 In.	4700.00
Whale Oil, Pewter, Double Glass Bull's Eye Lenses, 8 In.	1051.00
Whale Oil, Sinumbra, Brass, Column, Marble Plinth, Etched Shade, Prisms, Electrified, c.1800, 30 In. .	1234.00
Whale Oil, Sinumbra, Gilt Bronze, Satin Glass, Pendant Prisms, Electrified, 1800s, 19 In. ..*illus*	150.00
Whale Oil, Tin, Glass, 10 ½ In.	138.00
Whale Oil, Tin, Paint, Red, 8 x 8 In.	135.00

LAMPSHADE

Aladdin, 201-6, Opalescent White Glass, Flowers, Model 6, Bull's-Eye, 7 ¼ x 9 ¾ In.	120.00
Aladdin, 301, Chippendale, White, Satin, 7 ½ x 9 ¾ In.	45.00
Aladdin, 501-9, White Top, Clear Border, 8 x 9 ¾ In.	135.00
Aladdin, 701B, White Paint, Hobnail Apron, 7 ¾ x 9 ¾ In.	66.00
Art Glass, Green Leaves, Flowers, 20 In.	293.00
Cut Glass, Bullet Shape, Crosscut Diamond, Strawberry Diamond, Star & Fan, 8 ½ In.	50.00
Depression Glass, Lyres & Flowers, Ribs, Scalloped Rim, Stars, White, 1930s, 7 In.	225.00
Glass, Blue Pulled Feathers, Ivory Ground, Gold Trim, Fluted, Notched, 6 x 2 In., Pair..............	1010.00
Glass, Green Murano Wave Design, Flower Shape, Flared Rim, Gold Interior, 5 x 6 In.	380.00
Glass, White, Pink Pulled Feather Design, White Applied Threading, 5 x 2 In.	288.00
Leaded Glass, Dragonfly, Dome, 6 Dragonflies, Wings, Filigree, 8 ¼ x 20 In.	215.00
Leaded Glass, Wilkinson, Geometric Panels, Green, White, Orange, Metal Base, 22 x 26 In. ...	1265.00
Milk Glass, Star, Wavy Lines, 1 ⅞ x 4 In.	10.00
Plastic, Running Sheep, Red, White, Green, 6 ½ x 8 ¾ In.	20.00

LANTERNS are a special type of lighting device. They have a light source, usually a candle, totally hidden inside the walls of the lantern. Light is seen through holes or glass sections.

Baby Skater, Brass, Tin, Clear Globe, Embossed, String Burner, 4 ½ x 2 In.	585.00
Barn, Pine, Pegged Wood Frame, Glass Panels, Sliding Rod, Iron Handle, 11 ¾ In.	705.00
Brass Anchor, Seahorse Designs, Holder, 1900s, 13 x 10 In.	98.00
Brass, Tin, Clear Globe, Woodwards Patent, April 5, 1864, 9 ½ In.	450.00
Candle, Tin, ½ Round, Wire & Glass Front, 12 In.	266.00
Candle, Tin, Hanging, Box, Cylinder, Dome Sides, Hanging Holes, 11 In.	192.00
Candle, Tin, Punched, Cylinder, Cone Top, Loop Handle, Hinged Door, Hasp, 15 In.	113.00
Candle, Wood, Glass, Cotter Pin Hinged Door, Wire Bail Handle, 16 In.	303.00
Candle, Wood, Glass, Tin Dome Chimney, Wire Bail Handle, Hinged, 12 ½ x 6 ½ x 6 ½ In.	96.00
Carriage, Brass, Painted Black, England, 19th Century, 21 In., Pair.	115.00
Chinese, Pagoda Shape, Bells, Brass, 32 x 19 In.	805.00
Firefly, Cedar Wood, Glass Jar, Mid 20th Century, 9 In.	87.00
G. Stickley, Pyramid Vented, 4 Amber Glass Inserts, Chain, Ceiling Cap, 7 x 7 x 22 ½ In.	2040.00
Gas, Copper, Glazed Doors, Wrought Iron Scroll Collar, Electrified, Late 1800s, 44 x 17 In., Pair.	1293.00
Globe, Lozenge, 8 Ribs, Sheet Iron Mounts & Handle, Candle Socket, c.1860, 10 ½ In.	1725.00
Globe, Onion, 8 Ribs, Sheet Iron Mounts & Handle, Candle Socket, c.1860, 11 In.	690.00
Globe, Onion, Tin Wire Handle, Wire Guards, P & A Mfg. Co., c.1800, 12 x 9 In.	558.00
Globe, Onion, Wire Guards, Tin Font Burner, Handle, 1800s.9 ½ In.	558.00
Globe, Pear, 8 Ribs, Sheet Iron Mounts & Handle, Candle Socket, c.1855, 12 ½ In.	104.00
Hall, 3-Light, Smoke Bell Shape, Suspension Chains, Candle Style Arms, 38 x 12 ¼ In., Pair ...	575.00
Hall, Arts & Crafts, Leaf Mold Copper, Leaded Glass, Curled Straps, 18 Opaque Panels, 9 x 26 In.	2875.00
Kerosene, Tin, Loop Hanging Ring, Star Pierced Canted Top, Parker's, c.1853, 18 In. ....*illus*	283.00
Louis XVI Style, Gilt Bronze, Tapered Cylindrical Bowl, Scrolling, 30 x 16 In., Pair..................	4270.00
Oil, Brass, Sheet Metal, c.1900, 8 x 16 In.	47.00
Silver Plate, Black Enamel, Reflector, Late 19th Century, 16 ¼ In., Pair..................................	1495.00
Silver Plate, Glass, Louis XVI, 3-Light Chandelier Insert, Greek Key Fret, 20 x 9 In.	1440.00
Tin, Pierced, Allover Design, Punched Letters On Door, Ipswich, c.1825, 13 In.	750.00

L

Tin, Punched, Star, Letter R, Mid 19th Century, 13 In. ....*illus* 585.00
Tin, Star Pierced Top, Hoop Guard, Early 19th Century, 15 ½ In. 120.00
Wrought Iron, Entrance, Restauration Style, White Faux Candles, Electrified, 22 In., Pair 720.00

LE VERRE FRANCAIS is one of the many types of cameo glass made by the Schneider Glassworks in France. The glass was made by the C. Schneider factory in Epinay-sur-Seine from 1918 to 1933. It is a mottled glass, usually decorated with floral designs, and bears the incised signature *Le Verre Francais.*

Bowl, Stylized Blossoms, Mottled Cobalt Blue & Orange, Etched, 3 ½ x 8 ¾ In. 820.00
Compote, Lauriers, Yellow, Orange Ground, Purple Pedestal Foot, Rim, Signed, 10 x 4 In. 920.00
Lamp, Domed Shade, Mottled Red, Green, Frosted Ground, Bronze Wreath Base, 5 x 7 In. 2040.00
Pitcher, Kalanchoe, Amber, Blue, White, Applied Handle, Orange, Signed, 8 In. ...... 1780.00 to 2243.00
Vase, Begonia, Coupe Style, Applied Pedestal Stem, Signed, 11 In. ....*illus* 3450.00
Vase, Cameo, Leaves, 2 Applied Side Prunes, Glossy Mahogany Brown, 8 x 12 In. 1840.00
Vase, Cobalt Blue Palm Trees, Mottled White Ground, Disc Foot, Signed, 13 In. 6325.00
Vase, Crimson Cats, Footed, Bulging Collar, Cylindrical, 12 ½ In. 5175.00
Vase, Flower, Stemmed, Art Nouveau, Footed, Cylindrical, Signed, 14 In. 1725.00
Vase, Groseilles, Red, Orange Design, Yellow Ground, Red Pedestal Foot, Signed, 8 In. 1265.00
Vase, Halbrans, Blue, Brown Geese, Marsh, Yellow Mottled Ground, Flared Lip, Disc Foot, 12 In. 4025.00
Vase, Stylized Blossoms, Mottled Orange, Bulbous, Etched, Signed, Charder, 7 x 4 ½ In. 520.00
Vase, Stylized Leaves, Amethyst, Mottled Orange & Yellow, Oval, Footed, 10 x 5 In. 1600.00

LEATHER is tanned animal hide and has been used to make decorative and useful objects for centuries. Leather objects must be carefully preserved with proper humidity and oiling or the leather will deteriorate and crack. This damage cannot be repaired.

Bridle, Deer Lodge, Double Round Cheeks, Reins, Horsehair, Rosettes, Tassels, c.1915............. 4025.00
Briefcase, Nile Crocodile, Navy Blue, Lock, Expandable, 1980s, 16 x 12 ½ In. 2600.00
Bucket, Handle, Cylindrical, English Seal, England, 21 ½ In. ....*illus* 167.00
Gun Bag, Half Circle Form, Flap, Button Hasp, Stamped Arch Border, Strap, 5 ¼ x 8 In. 165.00
Humidor, Porcelain Liner, Square, c.1950 .... 358.00
Necessaire, Shagreen, 9K Gold Mounted, Monogram, Presentation Date 1876-1926, 4 ½ In. . 1586.00
Saddle, Side, Lancaster County, Tooled Tulips, Red, Yellow, Green............................... 283.00
Saddle, Western, Child, Stamped Label, Indianapolis, c.1950. .... 106.00
Writing Case, George III, Traveling, Shagreen, Gilt Metal, Book Shape, 1 x 2 ¾ In. 1220.00

LEEDS pottery was made at Leeds, Yorkshire, England, from 1774 to 1878. Most Leeds ware was not marked. Early Leeds pieces had distinctive twisted handles with a greenish glaze on part of the creamy ware. Later ware often had blue borders on the creamy pottery. A Chicago company named Leeds made many Disney-inspired figurines. They are listed in the Disneyana category.

LEEDS POTTERY.
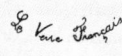

Centerpiece, Grand Platt Menage, 2 Tiers Of Shells, Dolphin Supports, Creamware, c.1785, 12 In. 1778.00
Charger, Yellow Urn, Swan's Neck Handles, Flowers, Leaf, Scalloped Feather, Edge, 14 ½ In. .. 735.00
Creamer & Sugar, Cover, Cornflower, Shell Handles, Bulbous Shape, 5& 4 In. 79.00
Creamer, Flower, Leaves, Trailing Vine, Bulbous, Soft Paste, 5 ¾ In. 220.00
Creamer, Pansy, Bulbous, Soft Paste... 44.00
Creamer, Tulip & Leaf, Bulbous, 3 ½ In. 311.00
Cup & Saucer, Blue, Yellow Flowers, Multicolored, No Handle, Soft Paste............... 88.00 to 187.00
Cup & Saucer, Central Blue Flower, Leaves, Multicolored, No Handle, Soft Paste 143.00
Cup & Saucer, Flower, Leaves, No Handle 170.00
Cup & Saucer, Flowers, Leaves, Center Blue Flower, Handleless ....*illus* 151.00
Jug, Milk, Flowers, Vine Band, Stylized Tulip, Flowers, Multicolored, 6 ¾ In. 565.00
Ladle, Blue Feather Edge, 8 In. 240.00
Pepper Pot, Blue Bands, Soft Paste, c.1790-1810, 4 ⅜ In. 110.00
Pepper Pot, Dome Top, Bulbous, Footed, Soft Paste, 4 ½ In. 143.00
Pepper Pot, White, Green Bands, Late 1700s, 4 ¼ In. 395.00
Pitcher, 2 Trailing Flowers, Buds Bands, Multicolored, Applied Loop Handle, 8 ½ In. 102.00
Pitcher, Water, Flowers, Leaves, Multicolored Banded, Bulbous, 7 In. 480.00
Planter, Bugs Bunny, With Wheel Barrow, Figural, High Glaze, Warner Bros., 1940s, 6 In. 50.00
Plate, Bird, Leaf, Embossed Green Edge, 9 In. 158.00
Plate, Flower, Leaf Multicolored, Blue Feather Edge, Soft Paste, 8 ½ In. 463.00
Plate, Flower, Leaves, Green Feather Edge, Scalloped Edge, Soft Paste, 8 In. 132.00
Plate, Flowers, Green Pansy, Scalloped Edge, Multicolored, 7 ¾ In. 311.00
Plate, Mother & Daughter, Octagonal, Blue Feathered Edge, Who Died In Days Of Infancy, 6 In. 395.00
Plate, Octagonal, Feather Edge, Eagle, Laurel Wreath, Arrow, c.1800, 6 ¾ In. 115.00
Plate, Peafowl, On Branch, Embossed Scalloped Blue Feather Edge, 10 In. 367.00
Plate, Pink Luster Anchor, Flowers, Green Border, Octagonal, c.1820 .... 92.00

Lantern, Kerosene, Tin, Loop Hanging Ring, Star Pierced Canted Top, Parker's, c.1853, 18 In. $283.00

Lantern, Tin, Punched, Star, Letter R, Mid 19th Century, 13 In. $585.00

L

Aladdins Aren't All Old

Many kerosene Aladdin lamps have been reissued since 1974. They are worth much less than old original lamps. The reissues are dated, and the metal collar may be glued on, not attached with brass threads.

Le Verre Francais, Vase, Begonia, Coupe Style, Applied Pedestal Stem, Signed, 11 In. $3450.00

Leather, Bucket, Handle, Cylindrical, English Seal, England, 21 ½ In.
$167.00

Leeds, Cup & Saucer, Flowers, Leaves, Center Blue Flower, Handleless
$151.00

Leeds, Plate, Sailing Ship, Feather Edge, Success To Die Frau Tibeta, 1700s, 9 ¾ In.
$120.00

Plate, Sailing Ship, Feather Edge, Success To Die Frau Tibeta, 1700s, 9 ¾ In. ....*illus*	120.00
Plate, White, Green Feather Edge, Scalloped Edge, Late 1700s, 8 ¼ In.	295.00
Platter, Blue Feather Edge, Embossed, c.1820, 11 ½ x 14 ½ In.	295.00
Platter, Blue Shell Edge, Embossed, c.1820, 12 x 15 ½ In.	300.00
Platter, Green Shell Edge, Embossed, c.1820, 12 ½ x 15 In.	300.00
Saucer, Bird, On Leaf Branch, Multicolored, 5 ¼ In.	90.00
Sugar, Bud, Leaf Trailing Vine, Green Buds, Brown, Tan Leaves, Soft Paste, 4 ¾ In.	55.00
Sugar, Cover, Blue & Yellow Flowers, Green Leaves, Soft Paste, 19th Century, 5 ½ In.	195.00
Sugar, Cover, Drape & Tassel, Bulbous, Drop Ring, Shell Handles, Acorn Finial, 6 ½ In.	248.00
Sugar, Cover, Flower Finial, Handles, Rectangular, Multicolored, 5 ½ In.	147.00
Sugar, Cover, Multicolored Flower & Leaf, Acorn Finial, Lion Head, Ring Handles, 5 ¼ In.	158.00
Sugar, Flowers & Leaf, Multicolored, Applied Handles, 5 ¼ In.	158.00
Teapot, Flower, Leaf, Bulbous, Beehive Finial, Blue, Tan, Green Flowers, Buds, Soft Paste, 7 In.	88.00
Teapot, Flower, Leaves, Bulbous, Beehive Finial, Blue, Tan, Green Flowers, Buds, 7 In. ......*illus*	93.00
Teapot, Flowers, Leaves, Applied Loop Handle, Squat	226.00
Teapot, Flowers, Multicolored, 4 ¼ In.	226.00
Teapot, Pansy, Squat, Bulbous, Flared Rim, Soft Paste, 4 ½ In.	121.00
Teapot, Prince, Princess Of Orange, 2-Sided Figures, Orange Tree, Bulbous, 4 ½ In.	192.00
Teapot, Tulip, Swan Finial, Shaped Handle, Paneled, 6 ¾ In.	367.00
Toddy Plate, Flowers, Leaves, Multicolored, 6 ¾ In.	1695.00
Urn, Cover, Reticulated, Creamware, 10 ¾ In., Pair	468.00

LEFTON is a mark found on pottery, porcelain, glass, and other wares imported by the Geo. Zoltan Lefton Company. The company began in 1941. George Lefton died in 1996 and the company was sold in 2001. The company mark has changed through the years, but because marks have been used for long periods of time, they are of little help in dating an object.

Bookends, Dog, Pekinese, 4 ¾ In.	22.00
Cake Topper, Bell, Clapper, Black, White, Label, c.1960	15.00
Candy Box, Lid, Roses, Pink, White, Wash Glaze, 3 Legs, Heritage Line, 5 x 5 In.	65.00
Candy Dish, Christmas, Girl In Sled, Red Bonnet, Holding Muff, 1950s, 6 x 8 In.	90.00
Coffee Set, Coffee Pot, Sugar, Creamer, Green Ground, Flowers, Green Heritage, 9 In.	125.00
Ewer, Pinecones, White Ground, Ornate Handle, 6 x 3 ½ In.	22.00
Figurine, Bird, Cardinal, Branch, Flower, Red, 6 x 5 In.	18.00
Figurine, Bloomer Girl, Ruffled Skirt, Pink, Gold, Marked, 4 In.	20.00
Figurine, Bunny, Crouching, White, 4 In.	24.00
Figurine, Girl, Bonnet, Flowers, 6 ¼ In.	24.00
Figurine, Girl, February, Purple Bouquet, White Apron, 4 ½ In.	10.00
Figurine, Spaniel, Seated, 4 ¹⁄₁₂ In.	35.00
Figurine, Woman, Blond Hair, Turquoise Straw Hat, Upturned Collar, Black Glove, 6 In.	86.00
Figurine, Woman, Blond Updo, Hat With Flattened Brim & Roses, Eyes Closed, 6 In.	50.00
Figurine, Woman, Brown Curls, Eyes Closed, Black Dress, Hat, Gloved Hand, 5 In.	75.00
Figurine, Woman, Brown Hair, Flowered Dress & Matching Hat, 6 In.	75.00
Figurine, Woman, Parasol, Bonnet, White, Gold Trim, c.1945, 6 x 3 ¾ In.	45.00
Nut Dish, Leaf Shape, Green Heritage, 1959, 7 ½ In.	20.00
Pitcher, Forget-Me-Not, Pink, Blue, Gold Handle, 4 In.	20.00
Planter, Woman, Blue Dress, Parasol, Bonnet, 8 ¼ In.	28.00
Plate, Goldfinch Birds, Yellow, Black, Red Berries, Hand Painted, 8 ¼ In.	22.00
Plate, Roses, Brown Ground, Gold Trim, Scalloped Edge	45.00
Teapot, Lid, Rose Chintz, Lavender, Pink Flowers, Gold Trim, 1970s, 6 In.	45.00
Trinket Box, Egg, Flowers, Bow, Pastels, 2 ½ x 3 In.	8.00
Trinket Box, Lid, Fan Shape, Flowers, Hand Painted, 3 ½ x 2 ½ In.	10.00
Trinket Box, Turtle, White, Violets, Gold Trim, Mark 1958, 3 ¾ x 2 ¾ In.	25.00
Vase, Dogwood Blossoms, Pink, Gold Rim, Cylinder, Paper Label, 6 ½ x 3 In.	24.00
Vase, Flowers, Multicolored, Pale Green Ground, 6 ½ In.	15.00
Wall Plaque, Cherub, Gold Wings, Clothes, c.1960, 7 ¼ In., Pair	15.00
Washbowl, Pitcher, Flowers, Leaves, Hand Painted, Gold Trim, 6 x 9 In.	25.00

LEGRAS was founded in 1864 by Auguste Legras at St. Denis, France. It is best known for cameo glass and enamel-decorated glass with Art Nouveau designs. Legras merged with Pantin in 1920 and became the Verreries et Cristalleries de St. Denis et de Pantin Reunies.

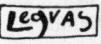

Biscuit Jar, Winter Scene, Snow Village, Woman, Cover, Handle, 7 ½ In.	725.00
Bowl, Snowy Landscape, Yellow, Gold, Brown, White, Enamel, Oval, Signed, 10 ¼ In.	400.00
Lamp, Cameo, Baluster Stem, Domed Shade, Forest Scene, Signed, 15 In. ......*illus*	575.00
Vase, 2 Lugers, Winter Scene, Enamel, Signed, Bulbous, Flared, Signed, 10 ½ x 5 In.	1500.00
Vase, 3 Cameo Enamel Garden Fountains, Water, Purple, Pink Ground, 14 ½ In., Pair	1038.00
Vase, 5 Flying Sparrows, Art Deco Band, White & Brown, Mottled, Cameo, c.1902, 21 In.	960.00

Vase, Art Deco Fountains, Tiers, Mulberry Enameled On Pale Pink, Cameo, 14 In., Pair	518.00
Vase, Blue, Yellow Mottled Shaded To Orange, Peacock Enamel, Signed, 5 ½ x 8 ½ In.	1550.00
Vase, Cone Shape, Amber Cream Ware, Multicolored Stemmed Mums, Signed, 6 In. ....*illus*	403.00
Vase, Flower, Red, Lily Pad Leaf, Fire Polished, Cameo, Signed, 3 In.	400.00
Vase, Indiana, Stylized Poppies, Textured Red & Green, Stems, Footed, Signed, c.1910, 15 In. .	3120.00
Vase, Landscape, Narrow Sides, Marked, 5 x 2 ¾ In.	750.00
Vase, Leaf Vines, Tendrils, Burgundy, White Ground, Cameo, Signed, 5 x 5 ¾ In.	350.00
Vase, Leaves, Purple, White & Yellow Ground, Genie Bottle Form, Cameo, 9 In.	280.00
Vase, Maroon Leaves, Genie Bottle Form, Cameo, 15 x 6 In.	1070.00
Vase, Opalescent Green, White Dogwood Blossoms, Pinched Waist, Cameo, Signed, 12 In., Pair	2880.00
Vase, Relief Teasel Blossoms, Leaves, Natural Colors, Cameo, Signed, 14 ¼ In.	1840.00
Vase, Sheep, Figure, Trees, Yellow, Gray, Green, Oval, Cameo, 6 In.	680.00
Vase, Snow Scene, 4-Sided, 2 In.	250.00
Vase, Stick, Burgundy Frosted Leaves, Vines, Signed Cameo, 8 In.	345.00
Vase, Stylized Flowers, Purple, Pink Ground, Cameo, Signed, 14 In.	360.00
Vase, Triangular Shape, Holly Branches, Red Berries, Orange, Green, Opal Ground, Cameo.....	575.00
Vase, Underwater Seascape, Maroon, Mustard Yellow, Opaque Matte Ground, Cameo, 14 In. ...	748.99
Vase, Winter Trees, Snow, Village, Mottled Orange Ground, Cameo, Signed, 4 ½ In.	1495.00
Vase, Yellow, Orange Ground, Blue Shoulder, Flower, Leaf Enamel Medallion, Blue Scrolls	1150.00

LENOX porcelain is well-known in the United States. Walter Scott Lenox and Jonathan Coxon Sr. founded the Ceramic Art Company in Trenton, New Jersey, in 1889. In 1906, Lenox left and started his own company called Lenox. The company makes porcelain that is similar to Irish Belleek. In 2009, after a series of mergers, Lenox became part of Clarion Capital Partners. The marks used by the firm have changed through the years, so collectors can date the ceramics. Related pieces may also be listed in the Ceramic Art Co. category.

Baking Dish, Silhouette, 15 ⅜ In.	62.00
Bowl, Cereal, Dewdrops, 6 ⅛ In.	25.00
Bowl, Cereal, Sketchbook, 6 ⅛ In.	21.00
Bowl, Cereal, Sprite, 6 ⅛ In.	11.00
Bowl, Fruit, Dewdrops, 4 ¾ In.	21.00
Bowl, Grecian, 10 ½ In.	35.00
Bowl, Vegetable, Oval, Sandflowers, 9 ⅛ In.	40.00
Bowl, Vegetable, Round, Blue Pinstripes, 9 ¾ In.	65.00
Casserole, Cover, Dewdrops, 1.25 Qt.	65.00
Casserole, Open, Sprite, 1.25 Qt.	25.00
Coffeepot, Silhouette	120.00
Creamer, Fall Bounty..	15.00
Cup & Saucer, Golden Wreath	21.00
Cup & Saucer, Imperial	25.00
Cup & Saucer, Quakertown	9.00
Cup & Saucer, Summer Spice	8.00
Gravy Boat, Dewdrops	40.00
Gravy Boat, Summer Spice	40.00
Pepper Mill, Golden Wreath..	65.00
Plate, Bread & Butter, Dewdrops, 6 ⅜ In.	6.00
Plate, Bread & Butter, Imperial, 6 ⅜ In.	10.00
Plate, Dinner, Aristocrat, 10 ¾ In.	64.00
Plate, Dinner, Autumn, 10 ½ In.	35.00
Plate, Dinner, Blue Tree, 10 ⅝ In.	41.00
Plate, Dinner, Federal Gold, 10 ⅞ In.	28.00
Plate, Dinner, Quakertown, 10 ¾ In.	12.00
Plate, Dinner, Solitaire, 10 ¾ In.	21.00
Plate, Ivory, Brown Rim & Accent, Painted Logo, G. Stickley, Marked, 9 In.	480.00
Plate, Salad, Aristocrat, 8 ⅛ In.	44.00
Plate, Salad, Blue Pinstripes, 8 ½ In.	10.00
Plate, Salad, Montclair, 8 ⅜ In.	17.00
Roaster, Oval, Sketchbook, 15 ⅛ In.	58.00
Sculpture, Gold Mask Of Tutankhamen, Headdress, Ivory Porcelain, 1978, 5 ½ x 7 In.	86.00
Soup, Dish, Fall Bounty, 6 ⅛ In.	16.00
Stein, Monk, Brown, Belleek, Pewter Lid, Thumb Tab, For Tiffany & Co., ½ Liter....................	177.00
Sugar, Cover, Dewdrops...	30.00
Sugar, Cover, Summer Spice...	20.00
Vase, Art Nouveau, Yellow, Red, Gold, Vertical Lines, White & Turquoise Ground, Tapered, 6 x 12 In.	201.00
Vase, Egrets, Marsh, Water Lilies, Oval, c.1900, 15 In.	708.00
Vase, Figurine, Child Holding Ribbon Handle, Conch Shell, Parian, 6 x 7 ½ In.	374.00
Vase, Flowers, Butterflies, Footed, 2 Handles, Marked, c.1920, 15 ¼ In.	590.00

Leeds, Teapot, Flower, Leaves, Bulbous, Beehive Finial, Blue, Tan, Green Flowers, Buds, 7 In.
$93.00

TIP
Don't keep a house key in an obvious spot in the garage.

Legras, Lamp, Cameo, Baluster Stem, Domed Shade, Forest Scene, Signed, 15 In.
$575.00

Legras, Vase, Cone Shape, Amber Cream Ware, Multicolored Stemmed Mums, Signed, 6 In.
$403.00

L

Libbey, Vase, Amberina, Optic Ribbed Urn Shape, Footed, Acid Stamp, 14 ½ In. $633.00

Lighter, Cigar, Oil Lamp, Turkish Woman, Hookah, Silver, Engraved 1858, 6 x 5 x 5 In. $1168.00

Lighter, Cigarette Case, Ronson, Art Deco, Monogram, 4 In. $59.00

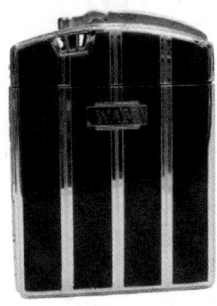

Novelty Lighters

Novelty cigarette lighters made before 1980 are exempt from a law in Louisiana that forbids the sale of newer lighters.

Vase, Parrots On Leaves, Cylindrical, c.1900, 16 In.	708.00
Vase, Young Women, Scrolled Medallions, Urn Shape, Gold Griffin Handles, Belleek, 16 In.	1035.00

LETTER OPENERS have been used since the eighteenth century. Ivory and silver were favored by the well-to-do. In the late nineteenth century, the letter opener was popular as an advertising giveaway and many were made of metal or celluloid. Brass openers with figural handles were also popular.

Alligator, Bumps, Embossed, Brass, 8 ¾ In.	15.00
Bentley Automobile, Silver, Winged B Design, Art Deco, 7 In.	400.00
Brass, Rose Quartz, Openwork, 9 In.	60.00
Cranes Feeding, Bushes, Repousse, Bronze, Mixed Metal, Cartouche, Ichiju, 1868-1911, 12 In.	275.00
Fuller Brush Man, Pink, Plastic, 7 ¼ In.	3.00
Girl In Bonnet, Brass, Patina, 8 ¼ x 1 In.	92.00
Horse Head, Brass, 1 ½ x 11 In.	45.00
Hunting Dog Head, Fish In Mouth, Bronze	55.00
Ivory, Enamel Inlay, c.1825, 10 In.	295.00
Kiddy Kloes, Brass, Marked Cinderella, 7 ½ In.	65.00
Man, E Plurbis Unum 1776, Ivory, 12 ¼ In.	285.00
Mouse On Feather, Bronze, 9 In.	80.00
Owl, Bronze	33.00
Owl, Bronzed Silver, 8 In.	42.00
Sheaves Of Wheat, Ivory, Mother-Of-Pearl, Wood, Diamond Shape	121.00
Silver Overlay Handle, Christofle, Hallmarked, 8 ¼ In.	96.00
Sword & Anchor, Circles, Swirls, 8 ¾ In.	12.00

LIBBEY Glass Company has made many types of glass since 1888, including the cut glass and tablewares that are collected today. The stemwares of the 1930s and 1940s are once again in style. The Toledo, Ohio, firm was purchased by Owens-Illinois in 1935 and is still working under the name Libbey Inc. Maize is listed in its own category.

Berry Bowl, Interlaced Hobstar & Wheat, American Brilliant, c.1900, 8 In.	210.00
Bowl, Corinthian, Cut Glass, 6 In.	100.00
Bowl, Corinthian, Lobed, Signed, 8 In.	86.00
Bowl, Fruit, Cut Glass, Etched Garlands, Scalloped Rim, Folded Pedestal Base, 8 ¼ In.	427.00
Bowl, Harvard, Hand Grip, American Brilliant, 10 In.	150.00
Bowl, Hobstar & Fan, American Brilliant, 3 ½ x 8 In.	90.00
Bowl, Hobstar, Crosscut Diamond, American Brilliant, 8 In.	25.00
Bowl, Hobstar, Cut Glass, 6-Point Star & Fan, American Brilliant, 8 In.	80.00
Bowl, Hobstar, Strawberry Diamond & Fan, Cut Glass, American Brilliant, 4 x 8 In.	70.00
Bowl, Leota, 3 ½ x 8 In.	100.00
Bowl, Low, Brilliant, Marked, 8 In.	25.00
Bowl, Low, Cut Glass, Thick Blank, American Brilliant, 10 In.	50.00
Bowl, Low, Regis, Cut Glass, American Brilliant, 9 In.	175.00
Bowl, Marcella, Cut Glass, Scalloped Edge, 9 In.	4995.00
Bowl, Prism Pattern, 8 In.	259.00
Bowl, Salad, Ripple, Diamond, Gold, 5 ¾ In.	45.00
Bowl, Senora, Cut Glass, American Brilliant, 3 ½ x 8 In.	225.00
Bowl, Senora, Cut Glass, American Brilliant, 5 ½ In.	175.00
Bowl, Spillane, Marked, 2 x 9 In.	75.00
Candlestick, Flaring Cup, Ribbed & Spiraled With Blue, Half-Twist Stems, 7 ¾ In., Pair	375.00
Champagne, Colona, Cut, Hobstar, Bulbous Stem, Signed, 4 In., 10 Piece	288.00
Decanter, Stopper, Cut Glass, Ellsmere, Bowling Pin Shape, Signed, 11 x 5 In.	1550.00
Ice Bucket, Hobstar, Nailhead Diamond, Strawberry Diamond & Fan, American Brilliant, 6 In.	150.00
Iced Tea, Ripple, Diamond, Aqua, 6 ¾ In.	18.00
Jug, Whiskey, Colonna Pattern, Stopper, 6 ½ x 7 In.	748.00
Pitcher, Geometric, Flower Design, Cut Glass, American Brilliant, 9 In.	275.00
Pitcher, Honeycomb Pattern, 8 In.	201.00
Plate, Colonna, Signed, 7 In.	100.00
Plate, Kimberly, Cut Glass, American Brilliant, Signed, 7 In.	200.00
Plate, Senora, Cut Glass, 10 ½ In.	575.00
Plate, Somerset, Signed, 7 In.	200.00
Punch Bowl, Scalloped Edge, Star Cut Pattern, Base, c.1900, 9 x 12 In.	863.00
Relish, Gem, American Brilliant, Signed, 7 In.	30.00
Tumbler, Hobstar & Notches, Cut Glass, Signed, 3 ¾ In., 11 Piece	259.00
Vase, Amberina, Optic Ribbed Urn Shape, Footed, Acid Stamp, 14 ½ In. *illus*	633.00
Vase, Bud, 3 Nude Women, Clear, Cylindrical, Marked, L, 7 In.	19.00
Vase, Chintz, Vertical Ribs, Fine Wavy Webbing, Libbey Acid Stamp, c.1900, 15 In.	480.00

Vase, Elsmere, American Cut Glass, Pinched Waist, 11 ¾ In.	400.00
Vase, Flowers, Leaves, Engraved, Trumpet Shape, Marked, 10 In.	104.00
Vase, Hobstar, Flared, Footed, Signed, 7 In.	58.00
Vase, Imperial, Cut, Hobstar Panels, Diamonds, Cylindrical, Marked, 12 In.	748.00
Vase, Lily Shape, Amberina, Round Foot, 8 In.	184.00
Vase, Parfait, Crosscut Diamond, Punty & Star, American Brilliant, 8 In.	125.00
Vase, Red Ribbing, Horizontal, Metal Rim, Tapered, 10 ½ In.	58.00
Vase, Tapered, Pink Mushroom Cap, Opalescent Interior, Marked, 10 In.	375.00
Water Set, Poppy, 6 Tumblers, 7 ¾ In.	3400.00
Wine, Kangaroo Figural Stems, Iridescent, Clear Bowl, 6 In., 6 Piece	230.00

LIGHTERS for cigarettes and cigars are collectible. Cigarettes became popular in the late nineteenth century, and with the cigarette came matches and cigarette lighters. All types of lighters are collected, from solid gold to the first of the recent disposable lighters. Most examples found were made after 1940. Some lighters may be found in the Jewelry category in this book.

Airplane, Art Deco, Chrome, c.1930	225.00
Airplane, Chrome, Hamilton, c.1950, 3 x 6 In.	50.00
Aladdin Lamp Form, Metal, Occupied Japan, 2 ½ x 4 ¼ In.	45.00
Art Deco, Teapot, Fluid, Marked Japan, c.1940	90.00
Boot, Automatic Fluid, Marked Occupied Japan, c.1940, 4 In.	125.00
Bowling Pin, White, Red, Marked, Prince Japan, 6 In.	30.00
Cannon, Fluid, Marked Japan, c.1950, 5 ½ x 2 ½ In.	80.00
Cigar, Horse, Painted, Metal, Cloth Covered Electrical Cord, Patina, 3 x 2 ¼ In.	176.00
Cigar, Oil Lamp, Turkish Woman, Hookah, Silver, Engraved 1858, 6 x 5 x 5 In. ....*illus*	1168.00
Cigar, Punch, Smoking Cigar, Brass, Hangs, 3 ¾ x 5 ½ In.	275.00
Cigarette Case, Ronson, Art Deco, Monogram, 4 In. ....*illus*	59.00
Dunhill, 14K Gold, Vertical Ribs, Flip Top, No. 1657352, 2 x 1 x ½ In.	230.00
Dunhill, Gilt Plated, Marked, Made In Switzerland, 2 ½ In. ....*illus*	64.00
Dunhill, Green, Flint & Gas, Stamped, 750	360.00
Eagle, Spread Wings, Brass, Marked, Japan, 4 In.	25.00
Evans, Art Glass, Fluid, Gold, Silver Banner Inserts, c.1950, 3 ½ x 2 ¾ In.	75.00
Horse Head, Satin Glass, Viking Glass Co., 1950-60, 4 x 3 In.	135.00
Juvenia, Art Deco, Textured Surface	499.00
Kiwi Bird, White Pot Metal, Wood Base, Marked, Japan, 3 ½ In.	35.00
Knight, Chrome Plated Metal, Music Box Base, 1950s, 8 ½ In.	165.00
Knight, Holding Sword, Figural, White Metal, Marked, Austria, 7 ¼ In.	118.00
Kool Mild Menthol Cigarettes, Chilly The Penguin, Bakelite, 1930s, 9 In.	1150.00
Marconi, Disc Discharger, Silver, Stone Base, Leather Case, c.1912, 3 ¾ In. ....*illus*	930.00
Nude, Art Deco, Leaning Against Plinth, Striker, c.1915	250.00
Pierre Cardin, Piezo, Ignition, Silver, Black, c.1970	80.00
Pioneer Mose, Toby Figure, Ceramic, Painted, Marked Japan, c.1900, 2 ½ x 2 ¼ In.	100.00
Ronson, Table, Varaflame, 3 ¾ In.	36.00
Scottish Unity, 9K Gold, c.1936	750.00
Silver, Glass, Swirl Enamel, Scrolling Design, Italy, c.1950	300.00
Tennis Ball, Silver, Marked Japan, c.1960	80.00
Tinder, Stamped, S. Cleeves, England, Late 18th Century ....*illus*	1053.00

LIGHTNING RODS AND LIGHTNING ROD BALLS are collected. The glass balls were at the center of the rod that was attached to the roof of a house or barn to avoid lightning damage.

LIGHTNING ROD

Amber Glass Ball	141.00
Amethyst Glass Ball, Star Finial	396.00
Arrow, Ruby Glass Tail Insert	339.00
Arrow, White Milk Glass Faceted Orb	113.00
Cow, Star & Wave Ball, Milk Glass	707.00
Cross Top, Light Green	112.00
Cross Top, Purple	235.00
Fisher Style, Otis, Ice Gray Straw, Pat'd 1851	420.00
Fisher Style, Otis, Pat'd 1851, Ice Green, Yellow	364.00
Hickcock's Patent, Dark Teal	62.00
Side Tab, Gray	78.00

LIGHTNING ROD BALL

Amber, 4 In.	98.00
Amethyst, 4 In.	108.00

Lighter, Dunhill, Gilt Plated, Marked, Made In Switzerland, 2 ½ In.
$64.00

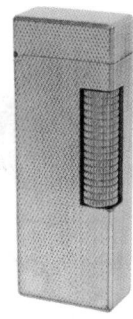

Lighter, Marconi, Disc Discharger, Silver, Stone Base, Leather Case, c.1912, 3 ¾ In.
$930.00

Lighter, Tinder, Stamped, S. Cleeves, England, Late 18th Century
$1053.00

L

TIP

Mix three parts water and one part vinegar and use the mixture to sponge off the white salt stains that form on leather shoes or boots.

Lightning Rod Ball, W.C. Shinn Mfg., Flashed Gold Interior, Metal End Caps, c.1925, 5 ⅜ In.
$431.00

Limoges, Coffeepot, Solitaire, Louis XVI, Blue, Galants Reserve, Flowers, Marked, 7 In.
$180.00

Limoges, Jardiniere, Green, Pink Roses, Gilt Lion Head Handles, Feet, 11 ½ x 14 In.
$90.00

Limoges, Plate, Poppy, Cream & Green, Gold Trim, Signed, 9 In.
$40.00

Electra, Raised Letters, Milk Glass, 4 In.	50.00
Milk Glass, 4 In.	74.00
Moon & Stars, Milk Glass, 4 ½ In.	96.00
Spratt Patent, Dark Green	123.00
W.C. Shinn Mfg., Flashed Gold Interior, Metal End Caps, c.1925, 5 ⅜ In. ....*illus*	431.00

LIMOGES porcelain has been made in Limoges, France, since the mid-nineteenth century. Fine porcelains were made by many factories, including Haviland, Ahrenfeldt, Guerin, Pouyat, Elite, and others. Modern porcelains are being made at Limoges and the word *Limoges* as part of the mark is not an indication of age. Haviland, one of the Limoges factories, is listed as a separate category in this book.

Ashtray, Colonial Couple Dancing, Garden, Gold Gilt, 4 In.	15.00
Basket, 2 Cherubs, White Ground, Rosebud Dots, Marked, Lanternier, 1891-1914, 4 In.	125.00
Bowl, Blackberries, Flowers, Footed, Gilt, T & V Limoges, 4 ½ x 10 ¼ In.	245.00
Box, Hinged, Egg Shape, Dark Blue, 6 In.	205.00
Box, Hinged, Round, Enameling, Flowers, 5 In.	102.00
Box, Lid, Porcelain, Birds, Flowers, Multicolored, Gold Ground, Gilt Mounts, Stamped, 4 x 5 In.	460.00
Cake Plate, Pansies, Purple, White, Green, Marked, T&V, 10 ¾ In.	110.00
Cake Set, Gilt Handles, Edge Band, Pastels, Platter, 6 Dessert Plates, 17 x 11 In.	285.00
Candlestick, Daisies, White, Yellow, Peach, Green Ground, Gold Trim, Signed, MLK, T&V, 5 ¾ In.	60.00
Centerpiece, Pedestal, Basket Weave Bowl, Painted Flowers, Gold Accents, 14 ½ x 11 ½ In.	230.00
Charger, Portrait, Woman, Pink Flowers, Green Border, Rose Highlights, 15 ¾ In.	400.00
Chocolate Pot, Woman, Playing Violin, Gilt, 9 ½ In.	92.00
Coffeepot, Solitaire, Louis XVI, Blue, Galants Reserve, Flowers, Marked, 7 In. ....*illus*	180.00
Cup & Saucer, Pink Roses, Gold Accents, Double Handle, Elite Works, France	190.00
Dinner Set, Pasadena Pattern, Service For 8, 46 Piece	177.00
Dish, Sweetmeat, Gilt Handle & Border, 3 Sections, 11 In.	45.00
Dresser Box, Gold Border, Maiden, Swing, Flowers, Blue Ground, Signed Tharaud, 6 x 3 In.	230.00
Dresser Box, Portrait Of A Woman, Marked, c.1900, 7 ¼ In.	236.00
Dresser Tray, Flowers, Hand Painted, Signed Sullivan, c.1900, 15 x 17 In.	146.00
Fish Set, Painted Fish Scenes, Green Ground, 23-In. Platter, 9-In. Dish, 13 Piece	770.00
Game Service, Partridge In Grass, Gilt Rope Border, Signed, Baumy, Platter, 12 Plates, 20 x 13 In.	1265.00
Jardiniere, Green, Pink Roses, Gilt Lion Head Handles, Feet, 11 ½ x 14 In. ....*illus*	90.00
Oyster Plate, 6 Wells, Blue Flowers, Gilt, Scalloped Rim, Vultury Freres, 1887-1904	699.00
Picture Frame, Yellow Flower Border, Signed, F.G. Brown, Mark, 6 ¾ x 9 ¾ In.	335.00
Pitcher, Cider, Blossoms, Berries, Gold Handle, Bernardaud, 5 ½ In.	400.00
Pitcher, Cider, Spider Web, Gold Highlights, Hand Painted, 6 ½ In.	180.00
Pitcher, Grapes On Vine, Dragon Handle, 15 In.	325.00
Pitcher, Monk, Gold, Heidrich, Signed, 9 ½ In.	375.00
Plaque, 4 Dancing Putti, White, Cobalt Ground, Oval, Bowed, Chased Metal Frame, 6 x 9 In.	173.00
Plaque, Bathing Beauty, Blue, White, Signed, 9 ¾ x 6 ⅞ In.	375.00
Plaque, Diana, Goddess Of Hunt, Gilt Rim, Signed, A. Soustre, 12 In.	495.00
Plaque, Interior, 3 Women, Desk, Signed Giraud Limoges, Giltwood Frame, 8 x 12 In.	863.00
Plaque, Monk, Sipping From Cup, Green Ground, Coronet, 9 ½ In.	80.00
Plaque, Violets, Yellow Roses, Oval, Guerin, 1900-32, 3 ¾ x 5 ⅜ In.	90.00
Plaque, Woman, Neoclassical, Wearing Wreath, Frame, c.1800s, 12 x 9 In.	1840.00
Plate, Couple Seated In Garden, Pink, Gold, Scalloped Rim, Fragonard, 4 In.	40.00
Plate, Dessert, Armorial Crest, 6 ½ In., 12 Piece	227.00
Plate, Dinner, Gilded Central Flower Basket, Superieur, 10 ¾ In., 12 Piece	840.00
Plate, Dinner, Gold Border, C. Ahrenfeldt, 10 ¼ In., 13 Piece	439.00
Plate, Dinner, Roses, Embossed, Gilt Border, 9 ¾ In., 12 Piece	657.00
Plate, Game Birds, Gold Trim, Cobalt Blue Border, 9 ½ In.	175.00
Plate, Luncheon, Flowers, 7 ¾ In., 8 Piece	69.00
Plate, Poppy, Cream & Green, Gold Trim, Signed, 9 In. ....*illus*	40.00
Plate, Service, Pink Floral, Gold Design, 9 ¾ In., 12 Piece	127.00
Plate, Woman, Flowers, Green, Blue, Guy Cahbrer, 9 ½ In.	117.00
Plate Set, Vegetation, Multicolored Fish, Late 19th Century, 9 ½ In., 12 Piece	326.00
Platter, Girl & Mother, Scalloped Gold Scrolling Rim, E. Farlaud, Signed, 13 In.	518.00
Punch Bowl, Berries, Flowers, Multicolored, Gilt, Footed, 6 x 14 In.	235.00
Punch Bowl, Grapevines, Stand, Tressemann & Vogt, c.1900, 9 x 15 In. ....*illus*	448.00
Ramekin, Underplate, Apple Blossoms, Green Leaves, Gilt, Early 1900s	76.00
Salt, Andre Giraud White, 1920s, 4 x 2 ¾ In.	13.00
Shaving Mug, Gold Flowers, Limited Edition, 1920s, 3 ½ x 5 In.	145.00
Tankard, Green, Gold Trim, Hand Painted, 15 ½ In.	365.00
Tankard, Plums, Green, Cylindrical, 14 In.	288.00
Tea Set, Artois, Floral Medallion & Border, Green Leafy Bands, Shaped Handles, 4 Piece	236.00

L

Tureen, Cover, Apple Blossoms, Pink, Green Leaves, Gilt, Early 1900s	188.00
Urn, Pastoral Scene Panel, Gold, Cobalt Blue Stripes, Handles, 11 x 14 In.	176.00
Vase, Figures In Rainstorm, Gilt Borders, 15 In.	748.00
Vase, Scenic Panels, Couple Running, Flowers, Birds, Gilt Borders, Hand Painted, 17 In.	460.00

LINDBERGH was a national hero. In 1927, Charles Lindbergh, the aviator, became the first man to make a nonstop solo flight across the Atlantic Ocean. In 1932, his son was kidnapped and murdered, and Lindbergh was again the center of public interest. He died in 1974. All types of Lindbergh memorabilia are collected.

Badge, Ribbon, Charles Lindbergh, Home State, Celluloid, c.1927, 1 ¾ In.	293.00
Bank, Bust, Lucky Lindbergh, Aviator Helmet, Metal, c.1930	84.00
Bank, Charles Lindbergh, Bust, Gold Paint, Aluminum, 6 ½ In.	25.00
Bank, Charles Lindbergh, Goggles On Neck, Bust, Painted, Lead, 5 ⅞ In.	90.00
Button, Captain Charles Lindbergh, Shield, Wings, ⅞ In.	28.00
Button, Plucky Lindy, Picture, Horseshoe, Clover, Laurel Wreath, Whitehead & Hoag, ⅞ In.	44.00
Button, Spirit Of St. Louis, Welcome Lindy, 1 ¼ In.	115.00
Button, Welcome Lindy, Whitehead & Hoag Back Paper, ⅞ In.	13.00
Candy Container, Airplane, Spirit Of St. Louis, Green Glass, Tin	605.00
Cigar Box, Lucky Lindy, Spirit Of St.Louis, 5 Cent, Wood, Paper Label, 6 x 9 ½ In.	25.00
Fan, Photo, Spirit Of St. Louis, Die Cut, Cardboard, 1927, 11 In.	60.00
Medallion, Charles Lindbergh, New York, Paris Aetatis, Bronze, Patina, 1927, 2 ¾ In.	56.00

LITHOPHANES are porcelain pictures made by casting clay in layers of various thicknesses. When a piece is held to the light, a picture of light and shadow is seen through it. Most lithophanes date from the 1825–75 period. A few are still being made. Many lithophanes sold today were originally panels for lampshades.

Lamp, Porcelain, Painted, Shade, Scenic, Women, 10 In.	130.00
Panel, Portrait, Oval, Girl, Cat, Ebonized Frame, 4 Legs, 10 x 19 ½ In.	173.00
Panel, Scenic, Bastion Falls, PPM 91, Kauterskill Glen, N.Y., 5 ⅜ x 3 ½ x 5 In.	175.00
Shadow Light, Heraldic Angel, Bisque	20.00
Shadowbox, Lamp, Children, Picking Flowers, Wood Frame, 1890s, 7 x 6 In.	100.00
Stained Glass Border, Impressed PPM, Frame, Germany, Late 1800s, 7 ¾ x 6 In.	125.00
Table, Asphaltum, Frame, Soft Metal Pedestal, Candle Sconce, c.1875, 2 In.	850.00

LIVERPOOL, England, has been the site of many pottery and porcelain factories since the eighteenth century. Color-decorated porcelains, transfer-printed earthenware, stoneware, basalt, figurines, and other wares were made. Sadler and Green made print-decorated wares from 1756. Many of the pieces were made for the American market and feature patriotic emblems, such as eagles, flags, and other special-interest motifs. Liverpool pitchers are always called Liverpool jugs by collectors.

Charger, Pagoda, Stylized Trees, Blue, White, Scalloped Feather Edge, 14 In.	288.00
Jug, 3 Medallions, Masonic Symbols, Transfer, Creamware, Baluster, 10 In.	575.00
Jug, 3-Mast Ship, Peace, Plenty & Independence, Black Transfer, 10 In.	1725.00
Jug, Ben Franklin & General Lafayette, Black Transfer, 19th Century, 5 ½ In.	200.00
Jug, Columbia, Washington's Tomb, Motto, Transfer, Creamware, Baluster, 11 In.	1610.00
Jug, George Washington, Jack On Cruise, c.1796	5600.00
Jug, George Washington & Plan Of City Of Washington, Creamware, 1880, 9 In.	2360.00
Jug, George Washington Bust, England, c.1825, 10 ¼ In.	1528.00
Jug, Jack Spritsails Frolic & Fox Hunt, Black Transfer, 10 In.	280.00
Jug, Landscape, Genre Scene, Red Transfer, Creamware, 9 In.	900.00
Jug, Major General Israel Putnam, Birds, Creamware, c.1775, 8 ¼ In.	6318.00
Jug, Man, Outstretched Arms To Woman, Cherub, Black Transfer, 2-Sided, 1780-90, 9 ½ In.	708.00
Jug, Portrait, Washington, Flag, 15 States, Success To America, Creamware, 1790s	1600.00
Jug, Ship, Flying American Flag, Washington In Glory, Creamware, Early 1800s, 9 In.	1100.00
Jug, Shipwright's Arms, Ships, c.1800, 9 ¼ In.	793.00
Jug, United States Map, Seal, Washington, Liberty, 19th Century, 10 ⅝ In.	1304.00
Jug, Washington, Chain Of 15 States, Flag, Creamware, c.1792, 10 ½ In.	2360.00
Jug, Washington Crowned With Laurels, Liberty, 15 States, 8 ½ In.	2450.00
Jug, Washington In Glory, Ship, Flag, Eagle, Monument, Mourner, Creamware, c.1830, 9 In.	1185.00
Jug, Washington, Liberty, Justice, State Banners, Black Transfer, Early 1800s, 9 ¾ In.	588.00
Mug, East View Of Liverpool Light House & Signals, Creamware, c.1830, 6 In.	474.00
Plaque, Thomas Jefferson, Black Transfer, Creamware, c.1805, 5 x 4 In.	9360.00
Plate, Storks, Birds, Blue, White, Tadpole Rim, 8 ¾ In.	210.00

Limoges, Punch Bowl, Grapevines, Stand, Tressemann & Vogt, c.1900, 9 x 15 In. $448.00

L

LLADRO

Lladro, Figurine, Flowers Of The Season, No. 1454, 11 In.
$1872.00

Lladro, Figurine, Peter Pan, No. 7529, 10 In.
$439.00

Loetz, Bowl, Art Nouveau, Footed, Flared, Blue, Iridescent, Pink Rim, Stamp, 8 In.
$403.00

Loetz, Vase, Art Nouveau, Indigo, Purple, Mounted Pewter Leaves, Stamp, 11 x 7 ½ In.
$3120.00

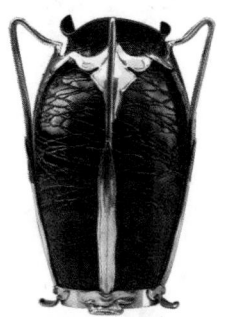

LLADRO is a Spanish porcelain. Juan, Jose, and Vicente Lladro opened a ceramics workshop in Almacera in 1951. They soon began making figurines in a distinctive, elongated style. In 1958 the factory moved to Tabernes Blanques, Spain. The company makes stoneware and porcelain figurines and vases in limited and unlimited editions. Dates given are first and last years of production.

Compote, Girl's Face, Hair Braid Handles, No. 2046, 14 In.	263.00
Figurine, 2 Horses, Fighting, No. 4597, 14 ½ In.	805.00
Figurine, Angel's Group, No. 4542, 6 ½ In.	185.00
Figurine, Beautiful Tresses, Seated Woman, Stroking Girl's Hair, No. 5757, 11 In.	176.00
Figurine, Carnival Couple, Man, Woman, No. 4882, 10 In.	410.00
Figurine, Chow Time, Kneeling Girl, Dog Bowl, Large Dog, No. 1334, 7 In.	88.00
Figurine, Cinderella, No. 4828, 9 ¾ In.	117.00
Figurine, Circus Concert, Clown, Horn, Seated Clown Playing Violin, No. 3856, 10 In.	351.00
Figurine, Court Jester, Seated Sad, No. 1405, Norman Rockwell, 9 ½ In.	205.00
Figurine, Dancing Class, Girl, Boy Cheek To Cheek, No. 5741, 7 In.	117.00
Figurine, Daydreamer, Girl, Mirror, Magazine, No. 1411, Norman Rockwell, 8 In.	351.00
Figurine, Flowers Of The Season, No. 1454, 11 In. .... *Illus*	1872.00
Figurine, Fragrant Bouquet, No. 5862, 8 In.	115.00
Figurine, Friends, 1980, 14 ¼ x 11 In.	360.00
Figurine, Girl & Basket Of Flowers, Girl, Long Dress, Pulling Basket, No. 5030, 11 In.	176.00
Figurine, Girl, Pan And Ducks, No. 5074, 6 ¾ In.	92.00
Figurine, Golfing Couple, Man, Woman Holding Clubs, No. 1453, 13 In.	117.00
Figurine, Hang On, Girl, Boy Seated On Sled, No. 5665, 6 In.	146.00
Figurine, Love Letter, Seated Boy, Writing, Dog, No. 1406, Norman Rockwell, 7 ½ In.	176.00
Figurine, Mother & Child, Nao, 15 x 8 In.	82.00
Figurine, Nature's Bounty, Girl, Holding Produce In Sack Over Shoulder, No. 1417, 11 In.	82.00
Figurine, Peter Pan, No. 7529, 10 In. .... *illus*	439.00
Figurine, Pharmacist, Seated, Bow Tie, Apron, No. 4844, 12 ½ In.	440.00
Figurine, Pick Of The Litter, Girl Seated On Doghouse, Holding Up Puppy, No. 7621, 7 In.	117.00
Figurine, Practice Makes Perfect, Band Boy, Horn, No. 1408, Norman Rockwell, 11 In.	205.00
Figurine, School Chums, Seated Black Boy, White Boy, Books, No. 5237, 9 In.	176.00
Figurine, Skier Puppet, Metal Poles, No. 4970, 7 In.	71.00
Figurine, Spring Breeze, Woman Holding Hat, Skirt Blowing, No. 4936, 13 In.	117.00
Figurine, Springtime Of 27 Man, Fixing Tie, Animals, No. 1410, Norman Rockwell, 9 In.	263.00
Figurine, Study Buddies, Boy Lying Down, Playful Dog, Books, No. 5451, 4 In.	105.00
Figurine, Summer Stock, Woman, Period Dress, Lipstick, No. 1407, Norman Rockwell, 10 In.	205.00
Figurine, Sweet Symphony, Girl, Hat, Flute, Music Stand, No. 6243, 9 In.	175.00
Figurine, Valencian Lady, No. 1304, 9 ½ In.	310.00
Figurine, Yachtsman, No. 5206, 13 ½ In.	90.00
Figurine, Young Love, Girl, Boy Seated Closely, No. 1409, Norman Rockwell, 12 In.	263.00

LOCKE ART is a trademark found on glass of the early twentieth century. Joseph Locke worked at many English and American firms. He designed and etched his own glass in Pittsburgh, Pennsylvania, starting in the 1880s. Some pieces were marked *Joe Locke,* but most were marked with the words *Locke Art.* The mark is hidden in the pattern on the glass.

Goblet, Poppies, 6 ¼ x 3 ⅛ In.	130.00
Sherbet, Poppies, 3 x 3 ½ In.	115.00

LOETZ glass was made in many varieties. Johann Loetz bought a glassworks in Austria in 1840. He died in 1848 and his widow ran the company; then in 1879, his grandson took over. Most collectors recognize the iridescent gold glass similar to Tiffany, but many other types were made. The firm closed during World War II.

Bowl, Art Nouveau, Footed, Flared, Blue, Iridescent, Pink Rim, Stamp, 8 In. ......*illus*	403.00
Bowl, Texas, Wide, Overall Striped Iridescent, Green, Yellow Flecks, 9 x 6 In.	600.00
Compote, Translucent, Iridescent Blue Foot, Leafy Cattail, 7 In.	325.00
Ewer, Green Aventurine Glass, Art Nouveau Spout, Handle, 13 ½ In.	325.00
Pitcher, Water, Carneol, Pinched Sides, Red, White Swirls, Clear Handle, Gilt Neck Border, 8 In.	190.00
Toothpick, Gold, Side Blue Punts, Iridescent	173.00
Tumbler, Green, Painted White & Lavender Flowers, Thumbprint, 5 In.	100.00
Vase, Aeolus, Applied Threading, Indented Shape, 2 ½ x 3 ½ In.	180.00
Vase, Amethyst Iridescence, Platinum Striations, Bronze Overlay, 5 In.	1035.00
Vase, Antler Handle, Gold Overlay, c.1900, 6 In.	644.00

Vase, Art Nouveau, Indigo, Purple, Mounted Pewter Leaves, Stamp, 11 x 7 ½ In. ....*illus*	3120.00
Vase, Art Nouveau, Multicolored, Silver Overlay, c.1900, 6 x 3 In.	705.00
Vase, Art Nouveau, Opaque Blue Green, Iridescent, Austria, Late 1800s, 4 ½ x 4 In.	646.00
Vase, Art Nouveau, Silver Overlay, Optic Ribbed, Cased Green Glass, 5 In.	325.00
Vase, Bulbous, Flared Rim, Yellow, Blue Threading, 3 Applied Medallions, Foot, 5 x 5 In.	1800.00
Vase, Candia Silberiris, Art Nouveau, Silver Overlay, Flower, Vining, 6 ⅝ In. ....*illus*	1265.00
Vase, Candia Silberiris Astartig, Corset Shape, Pulled Rim, Rainbow Iridescent, 3 ½ In.	150.00
Vase, Candia Silberiris Astartig, Corset Shape, Scalloped 3-Fold Rim, Rainbow Iridescent, 6 In.	374.00
Vase, Candia Silberiris, Gold Iridescent, Magenta Reflections, 9 ½ In.	115.00
Vase, Carneol, Bulbous, Marbleized Red & White, 5 ½ In.	403.00
Vase, Carneol, Swollen Shape, Geometric Band, 4 ½ x 7 In.	345.00
Vase, Cobalt Blue, Copper Foil Aventurine, Black Net Design, Neck Gold Berry Punts, 7 In.	1208.00
Vase, Cobalt Blue, Platinum Stripes, Swirls, Chalice Shape, Mottled Foot, 12 ½ In.	1495.00
Vase, Corset Shape, Deep Ruby, Iridescent, 10 In.	60.00
Vase, Diaspora, Dimpled, Blue Iridescent, Marked, 3 ¼ In.	345.00
Vase, Diaspora, Twisted Body, Tricornered Rim, Iridescent Blue, 7 ½ In. ....*illus*	489.00
Vase, Empire, Green, Linenfold, Swags, Wreaths, Flowers, Iridescent, Square, 3 ¾ In.	431.00
Vase, Enamel, Black, Wave Pattern Neck Design, 8 In.	234.00
Vase, Federzeichnung, Mother-Of-Pearl, 4-Fold Rim, Air Trapped Octopus, Browns, 6 In.	900.00
Vase, Federzeichnung, Oval, 3-Fold Rim, Brown Mother-Of-Pearl, Octopus, Gold, Signed, 5 ½ In.	2300.00
Vase, Gold, Iridescent, Cylindrical, Austria, 9 ⅞ In.	504.00
Vase, Gold, Oil Spot, Dimpled Sides, Polished Pontil, Squat	194.00
Vase, Green Glass, Creta Rusticana, Bulbous, 7 ½ In.	546.00
Vase, Green Glass, Pulled Design, Iridescent Color, Signed, 4 x 10 ½ In.	518.00
Vase, Green Iridescent, Looping Drapery, Flared Rim, Pontil, c.1910, 8 In.	90.00
Vase, Green Iridescent, Mold Blown, Ground Pontil, Early 20th Century, 7 In.	394.00
Vase, Green Iridescent, Prunts, Ruffled Top, Gold Base, Seaweed Design, 7 x 4 In., Pair	1725.00
Vase, Green Iridescent Pulled Feather Swirl, White & Blue Green Cased, No. 05700, 2 ½ x 4 ½ In.	820.00
Vase, Green, Iridescent, Stylized Rib, Flared Rim, Transparent Blue Neck, Bulbous, 1905, 13 In.	4148.00
Vase, Green, Iridescent, Wide Mouth, Swollen Cylindrical, Pulled Feathers, Teardrop, 13 ¼ In.	4444.00
Vase, Iridescent, Goblet Shape, Flared Rim, Deep Ruby, Green, 10 In.	60.00
Vase, Iridescent, Ribbed, Swirled, Early 20th Century, 6 ¾ In.	290.00
Vase, Jack-In-The-Pulpit, Green Iridescent, Blue Pulled Feather, 14 In. ....*illus*	2588.00
Vase, L. Bauer, Glass, Green, Leaves, Flowers, Pleated Sides To Flared Base, 7 In.	4183.00
Vase, Lava, Blue, Purple, Green, 3 ¾ In.	978.00
Vase, Medici Glatt, Papillon Design, Green Iridescent, Oval, Pinched Sides, 6 ½ In.	175.00
Vase, Metal Overlay, Crimped Rim, Art Nouveau Enameled Panel, Green, Red Maze, 6 ¾ In. ...	805.00
Vase, Mushroom, Marigold Iridescent, Outward Folded Rim, 8 ¼ In.	488.00
Vase, Neptune, Blue, Iridescent, 3-Fold Rim, 7 In.	460.00
Vase, Oil Spot, Enameled Peacock, Flowers, Metal Feet, Handles, Gold Highlights, 15 In.	1323.00
Vase, Orange, Purple Iridescence, Platinum Ovals, Baluster, Scalloped Rim, 5 In.	1380.00
Vase, Orpheus, Iridescent, Flared Base, Rim, Green Glass, 3 Applied Ovals, Neck Threading, 5 x 9 In. ..	840.00
Vase, Oval, Cylinder, Iridescent Blue, Oil Spot Finish, Red, Purple, Green, 6 In.	170.00
Vase, Papillon, 4-Dimpled Sides, Flared Rim, Iridescent Rim, Green, 8 In.	460.00
Vase, Papillon, Blue Iridescent, Oil Spot Design, Marked, 6 In.	1200.00
Vase, Papillon, Red, Multicolored Spatter, Iridescent, 14 In.	489.00
Vase, Phanomen, Cobalt Blue, 6 x 10 ½ In.	1920.00
Vase, Phanomen, Ruby Ground, Lady's Leg Shape, 3-Fold Rim, 12 In.	976.00
Vase, Phanomen, Ruby Ground, Pinched Sides, Elongated Neck, 9 ¾ In.	610.00
Vase, Phanomen, Tapered, Inverted Rim, Yellow Glass, Pulled Blue, Green Iridescence, 3 x 6 In.	1800.00
Vase, Pink Iridescence, Pulled Platinum Design, Signed, 6 In.	1495.00
Vase, Rusticana, Green, Flared Rim, 4 ½ x 5 In.	135.00
Vase, Shouldered, Cephalonia, Pale To Dark Green, Twisted Handles, 4 ½ x 8 In.	720.00
Vase, Shouldered, Gold Iridescent, 7 ½ In.	288.00
Vase, Silberiris, Green Iridescent, Gold Iridescent Art Deco Design, Ruby Cabochons, 7 In.	259.00
Vase, Silberiris, Iris, Stems, Leaves, Silver Rim, 9 In.	374.00
Vase, Silberiris, Silver Poppies & Leaf Blades, Gold Iridescent, Flared Rim, 6 In.	690.00
Vase, Silberis, Silver Overlay, Allover Iridescence, Shoulder Shape, 4 ½ x 8 In.	1560.00
Vase, Streifen Und Flecken, Pinched Rim, Yellow, Orange, Lines, Circles, 9 In.	2160.00
Vase, Tango, Green, Blue Threaded, Czech Acid Stamp, c.1920, 9 ½ In. ....*illus*	510.00
Vase, Tapered, Purple Glass, Applied Opal, Blue Accents, Austuhrung, 6 ¹⁄₁₂ In.	480.00
Vase, Texas Empire, Cranberry Glass, Vertical Veins, Draped Shoulder, Swags, 5 ¼ In. ......*illus*	1150.00
Vase, Texas Empire, Vertical Veins, Loops & Swags, Crimped Ruffled Rim, Shouldered, 5 ¼ In.	1150.00
Vase, Titania, Emerald Green, Silver Green Wave Design, 6-Point Star Rim, 4 x 5 ½ In.	1150.00
Vase, Tulip, Pink, Applied Blue Iridescent Leaves, Leaf Shape Base, 3 ¼ In. ....*illus*	1150.00
Vase, Yellow Iridescent, Green Threading, 3-Fold Rim, Art Nouveau, c.1900, 13 x 8 ½ In.	3500.00

Loetz, Vase, Candia Silberiris, Art Nouveau, Silver Overlay, Flower, Vining, 6 ⅝ In. $1265.00

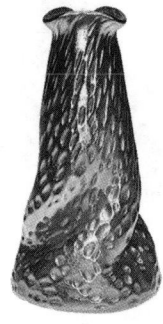

Loetz, Vase, Diaspora, Twisted Body, Tricornered Rim, Iridescent Blue, 7 ½ In. $489.00

Loetz, Vase, Jack-In-The-Pulpit, Green Iridescent, Blue Pulled Feather, 14 In. $2588.00

Loetz, Vase, Tango, Green, Blue Threaded, Czech Acid Stamp, c.1920, 9 ½ In. $510.00

L

Loetz, Vase, Texas Empire,
Cranberry Glass, Vertical Veins,
Draped Shoulder, Swags, 5 ¼ In.
$1150.00

Loetz, Vase, Tulip, Pink,
Applied Blue Iridescent Leaves,
Leaf Shape Base, 3 ¼ In.
$1150.00

Lone Ranger, Doll, Composition,
Removable Hat, Dollcraft,
c.1938, 2 x 4 ½ x 10 ½ In.
$690.00

LONE RANGER, a fictional character, was introduced on the radio in 1932. Over three thousand shows were produced before the series ended in 1954. In 1938, the first Lone Ranger movie was made. Television shows were started in 1949 and are still seen on some stations. The Lone Ranger appears on many products and was even the name of a restaurant chain for several years.

Badge, Secret Compartment, General Mills Premium, Deputy Chief, 1950s	253.00
Bread End Label Set, Merita, 2 ¾ x 2 ¾ In., 16 Piece	949.00
Button, Rodeo, Cowboy On Rearing Horse, Multicolored, 1 ¼ In.	115.00
Cap Gun, Brown Handle, Kilgore, 8 ½ In.	45.00
China Set, Red, White Milk Glass, Plate, Bowl, Cup, Saucer, 4 Piece	248.00
Cowboy Suit Box, Graphic Art, Included Hat, Late 1930s, 12 ¼ x 13 ½ In.	173.00
Doll, Composition, Removable Hat, Dollcraft, c.1938, 2 x 4 ½ x 10 ½ In. ....*illus*	690.00
Doll, Official, Composition Head, Stuffed Body, T.L.R. Co., c.1938, 15 In. ....*illus*	696.00
Double Gun Holster Set, Copper Colored Cap Guns, 12 Silver Bullets, 1950s, 9 In. ....*illus*	644.00
Figure, Accessories, Box, Hartland, 1950s, 8 ½ In.	230.00
Figure, Tonto, Horse Scout, Tag, Hartland, Box, 8 ½ In.	280.00
Game, Target, Gun, Darts, Bag, Cardboard, Marx, Box, 17 ½ In.	215.00
Game, Target, Hi-Yo Silver, Tin Lithograph, 10 Targets, 6 Bandits, Box, 16 x 27 x 1 ¾ In.	144.00
Gun & Holster Set, Double, 2 Cap Guns, Belt, Black Mask, Gabriel, Box, 18 ½ In.	205.00
Lunch Box, Lone Ranger, On Silver, Metal, 1950s	168.00
Lunch Box, Lone Ranger, Tonto, 2-Sided, Metal	100.00
Pedometer, Official T.L.R. Lone Ranger Pedometer, Aluminum	68.00
Pen, Ballpoint, Figural Bust, Metallic Blue Plastic, Everlast USA	174.00
Pin, Lee Powell, Original Motion Picture, Black & White Photo, 1938, 1 ¾ In.	230.00
Pin, Lone Ranger Every Day, Boston American, Yellow, Black, Red, ⅞ In.	39.00
Pin, Lone Ranger Every Week, Sunday Advertiser, Celluloid, 1 In.	55.00
Pin, Lone Ranger On Trigger, Black, White, Blue Accent On Pants Leg, 1 ⅜ In.	209.00
Radio, Pilot, Brown Bakelite Case, c.1947, 9 x 14 ½ In.	600.00
Ring, Atomic Bomb, Kix Cereal Premium, 1947	250.00
Shoe Brush, Wood, Oval, c.1935	18.00
Snowdome, Round Up, Figure With Lasso, Baby Steer, Plastic Base, 1940s, 2 ¾ In.	160.00
Story Puzzle, 4 Puzzles, Box, Parker Bros., c.1950, 7 x 18 In.	139.00
Toothbrush Holder, Lone Ranger & Silver, Chalkware, Painted, 1938, 4 x 3 In.	75.00

LONHUDA POTTERY COMPANY of Steubenville, Ohio, was organized in 1892 by William Long, W. H. Hunter, and Alfred Day. Brown underglaze slip-decorated pottery was made. The firm closed in 1896. The company used many marks; the earliest included the letters *LPCO*.

LONHUDA

Jug, Leaves, Berries, Green Ground, Marked, Dibowski, 7 ¼ In.	460.00
Pitcher, Spring Flowers, Yellow, Brown, Shape 815, Impressed, Shield Mark, 3 ¼ In.	89.00
Vase, Man, Herding Oxen, Brown Glaze, Pillow Shape, 4-Footed, 11 ½ x 11 In. .... 800.00 to 863.00
Vase, Pink Wild Rose, Brown, Green, Faience, No. 329, Handles, Marked, 4 ½ In.	360.00

LOTUS WARE was made by the Knowles, Taylor & Knowles Company of East Liverpool, Ohio, from 1890 to 1900. Lotus Ware, a thin porcelain that resembles Belleek, was sometimes decorated outside the factory. Other types of ceramics that were made by the Knowles, Taylor & Knowles Company are listed under KTK.

Bowl, Purple Flowers, Incised Leaves, Applied Pebbles, Cut Rim, KTK, 7 x 12 In.	900.00
Bowl, White, Applied Cherry Blossoms, Ruffled Rim, KTK, c.1900, 4 ¼ x 5 In.	750.00
Creamer, Fishnet, Flowers, Gold Trim, KTK, 4 ¼ In. ....*illus*	95.00
Jardiniere, Indents, Incised, Handles, KTK, 11 ½ x 5 In.	316.00
Jardiniere, White, Incised Leaves, Applies Pebbles, Cut Rim, KTK, 5 x 11 In.	330.00
Pitcher, Milk, Flowers, Blue Ground, Gilt, 1891-96, 4 ½ x 6 In.	550.00

LOW art tiles were made by the J. and J. G. Low Art Tile Works of Chelsea, Massachusetts, from 1877 to 1902. A variety of art and other tiles were made. Some of the tiles were made by a process called "natural," some were hand-modeled, and some were made mechanically.

J.&J.G.LOW

Box, Tile Top, Green Swirl Majolica Glaze, Wood, 1881, 4 ¼ x 4 ¼ In.	110.00
Tile, 2 Men Playing Backgammon, Woman, Baby, Dog, Green Glaze, c.1890, 4 ½ In.	250.00

LOWESTOFT was a factory in Suffolk, England, which from 1757 to 1802 made many commemorative gift pieces and small, dated, inscribed pieces of soft paste porcelain. Related items may be found in the Chinese Export category.

Jug, Sparrow Beak, Flowers, Blurry, Blue, 1765, 3 x 3 In.	520.00
Jug, Sparrow Beak, Flowers, Pink Diaper, Red Rocaille Rim Vignettes, 3 ⅔ In.	500.00

L

Teapot, Chinese Decoration, Butterflies, Flowers, Rope Twist Handle, 1700s, 5 In. ....*illus*   279.00
Teapot, Flowers, Butterflies, Rope Twist Handle, 18th Century, 5 In. 269.00

LOY-NEL-ART, *see McCoy category.*

LUNCH BOXES and lunch pails have been used to carry lunches to school or work since the nineteenth century. Today, most collectors want either early tobacco advertising boxes or children's lunch boxes made since the 1930s. These boxes are made of metal or plastic. Boxes listed here include the original Thermos bottle inside the box unless otherwise indicated. Movie, television, and cartoon characters may be found in their own categories. Tobacco tin pails and lunch boxes are listed in the Advertising category.

Addams Family, Metal, King Seeley Thermos Co., Hanna-Barbera, c.1974 ....   127.00
Agent T, King Seeley Thermos Co., 1968 ....   50.00
Annie Oakley, Metal, Aladdin Industries, 1955..   130.00
Annie Oakley, Metal, Red Vinyl Cover, Portrait Of Annie On Side, Aladdin, 1950s................   3065.00
Ballerina, Lilac With Ballerinas, Aladdin, 1960s 425.00
Banana Splits, Vinyl, Playing Band Instruments, King Seeley Thermos Co., 1960s 395.00
Barbie & Midge, Metal, Black Ground, Mattel, Canadian Thermos, c.1962 ....   115.00
Battlestar Galactica, Raised Images On Front, Aladdin, 1978 ....   120.00 to 179.00
Black Hole, Spaceship, Metal, 1979 ....   125.00
Bozo, Lion, Dome Lid, Metal, Aladdin, 1963 ....   99.00
Brave Eagle, Indians Fighting, Metal, American Thermos Co., 1957 ....   110.00
Bugs Bunny, Yosemite Sam, Vinyl, King Seeley Thermos Co., c.1971 ....*Illus*   127.00
Bullwinkle & Rocky, Red, Yellow, Vinyl, Ohio Art, 1962 ....   254.00
Cable Car, Graphics Of San Francisco Nob Hill, Trolley, Aladdin, 1962 ....   495.00
Canadian Hockey, Referee Signals, General Steel Wares, 1960s, 7 x 8 x 4 In. ....*illus*   230.00
Care Bears, Embossed Image, Aladdin, 1984..   50.00
Circus Wagon, Dome, American Thermos, 1958...   450.00
Clash Of The Titans, Pegasus Attacking Monster, King Seeley Thermos Co., 1981...............   100.00
Daniel Boone, Daniel Swinging His Musket, Indians, Aladdin, 1955....................................   250.00
Denim Diner, Dome, Blue Denim With Patchwork Dog & Flowers, Aladdin, 1975 ....   125.00
Dr. Seuss, The World Of Dr. Seuss, Cat In The Hat, Horton, Blue, Aladdin, 1970 ....   300.00
Fall Guy, Raised Graphics, Aladdin, 1981 ....   85.00
Fess Parker, Caboodle Kit, Plastic, Simulated Brown Leather, Standard Plastics, 1964...........   325.00
Flying Nun, Brunch Bag, Aladdin, 1968..   500.00
Fonz, On Motorcycle, King Seeley Thermos Co., 1976, 7 x 8 ½ x 4 In. 30.00
Fonz, Richie, Potsy, Metal, King Seeley Thermos Co., 1976...   132.00
Green Hornet, Hornet Driving Car, Punching Guy, King Seeley Thermos Co., 1976................   210.00
Grizzly Adams, Life & Times Of, Domed, Aladdin, 1977..   127.00
Gunsmoke, Matt Dillon In Gunfight, Red Plastic Cup, Aladdin, 1973.....................   115.00 to 145.00
Holly Hobbie, Friend, Flowers, Light Blue, Metal, 1981, 7 x 8 In. 45.00
James Bond Secret Agent 007, Driving, Metal, 1966 ....   66.00
Jet Patrol, Boeing B-52, Aladdin, 1957 ....   369.50
Jetsons, Dome Top, Metal, George, Judy, Jane, Elroy, Astro, Rosie, Aladdin, 1963......   348.00 to 875.00
Joe Palooka, Picnic Box, Tin, Square, Continental Can Co., 1948 ....   179.50
Kroft Supershow, Wonderbug Dune Buggy Flying Over Beach, Aladdin, 1976.....................   89.50
Laugh-In, Metal, Arte Johnson German Soldier, George Schlatter, Aladdin, 1968 ....   168.00
Lawman, Men Shooting Guns, Metal, King Seeley Thermos Co., 1961..................................   65.00
Linus The Lion-Hearted, Green, Linus In Barber Chair, Aladdin, 1965 ....   190.00
Loaf Of Bread, Dome Lid, Aladdin, 1968 ....   125.00
Looney Tunes, Bugs, Sylvester, Speedy, Elmer, Tweety, Metal, American Thermos, 1959 ....   170.00
Lost In Space, Space Craft, Robot, Cyclops, King Seeley Thermos Co., 1957 ....   288.00 to 450.00
Man From U.N.C.L.E., Jack Davis, Metal, King Seeley Thermos Co., 1966 ....*illus*   177.00
Mary Poppins, Embossed Metal, Mary Floating In Air, Aladdin, 1964 ....   200.00
Mike Mercury, Supercar Orbital Food Container, Metal, 1962 ....*illus*   221.00
Monkees, Thermos, King Seeley Thermos Co., Canada, 1967..   383.00
Monroes, Embossed Lithograph, Aladdin, 1967 ....*illus*   115.00
Munsters, Green, White Lid, 1965..   150.00
Munsters, In Munster Mobile, Metal, King Seeley Thermos Co., 1965.................................   85.00
Osmonds, Portraits Of The 5 Brothers, Close-Up Of Donny, Aladdin, 1973 ....   100.00
Pac-Man, Vinyl, Copyright By Bally, Aladdin, 1980..   79.50
Paladin, On Horse, Have Gun Will Travel, Metal, Aladdin, 1960...   130.00
Pink Panther, White Image Of Pink Panther & Inspector Clouseau, Aladdin, 1980   140.00 to 289.00
Porky's Lunch Wagon, Porky Pig, Elmer Fudd, Daffy Duck, American Thermos, 1959 ....   395.00
Raggedy Ann & Andy, Both In Blue Denim, White Handle, Vinyl, Aladdin, 1973 ....   289.00

Lone Ranger, Doll, Official, Composition Head, Stuffed Body, T.L.R. Co., c.1938, 15 In. $696.00

Lone Ranger, Double Gun Holster Set, Copper Colored Cap Guns, 12 Silver Bullets, 1950s, 9 In. $644.00

Lotus Ware, Creamer, Fishnet, Flowers, Gold Trim, KTK, 4 ¼ In. $95.00

Lowestoft, Teapot, Chinese Decoration, Butterflies, Flowers, Rope Twist Handle, 1700s, 5 In. $279.00

LUNCH BOX

Lunch Box, Bugs Bunny, Yosemite Sam, Vinyl,
King Seeley Thermos Co., c.1971
$127.00

Lunch Box, Canadian Hockey,
Referee Signals, General Steel Wares, 1960s, 7 x 8 x 4 In.
$230.00

Lunch Box, Man From U.N.C.L.E., Jack Davis, Metal,
King Seeley Thermos Co., 1966
$177.00

Lunch Box, Mike Mercury, Supercar Orbital Food Container, Metal, 1962
$221.00

Lunch Box, Monroes, Embossed Lithograph, Aladdin, 1967
$115.00

Lunch Box, Yogi Bear, Tug-O-War Contest, Vinyl,
Hanna-Barbera, Aladdin, c.1961
$371.00

Robin Hood, Shooting Bow & Arrow, Metal, Aladdin, 1956	70.00
Roy Rogers, Dale Evans, Tin Lithograph, American Thermos	71.00
Smokey The Bear, Vinyl, Smokey's Rules, Okay Industries, 1975	345.00
Snoopy, Dome, Yellow, Red Handle, Lying On Back Eating Sandwich, American Thermos, 1968	119.00
Tarzan, Tarzan Knife, Fighting Leaping Lion, Carrying Chimp, Aladdin, 1966	159.50
Twiggy, Vinyl, Portrait Image, Minnow Co., Aladdin, c.1967	173.00
Universal's Movie Monsters, Metal, Aladdin, 1979	278.00
Volkswagen Bus, Red, White, Metal, Omni Graphics, 1960s	160.00
Voyage To The Bottom Of The Sea, Metal, Aladdin, 1967	255.00
Wayne Gretzky, Plastic, Canada, Aladdin, 1980	58.00
Welcome Back Kotter, Sweathogs, Metal, Aladdin, 1976	82.00
Wild West, Stopping Train, Metal, Aladdin, 1969	128.00
Wonder Woman, Full Image Of Her On Yellow, White Handle, Yellow Cap, Aladdin, 1977	225.00
Yankee Doodles, George Washington, Crossing The Delaware, King Seeley Thermos Co., 1975	50.00
Yogi Bear, Tug-O-War Contest, Vinyl, Hanna-Barbera, Aladdin, c.1961 .... *illus*	371.00
Yosemite Sam & Bugs Bunny, Elmer Fudd, Vinyl, King Seeley Thermos Co., 1971	300.00
Zorro, Horse On Hind Legs, Fight Scene, Metal, Aladdin, 1958	80.00
Zorro, Red Sky & Border, Raised Image Of Zorro, Aladdin, 1966	179.00
LUNCH BOX THERMOS	
Blondie, King Features Syndicate, 1969	50.00
Flipper, Red Lid, 1966	45.00
NFL, Red, White & Blue Stripes, Emblem, Universal Vacuum Product, 1962-1963	30.00

LUNEVILLE, a French faience factory, was established about 1730 by Jacques Chambrette. It is best known for its fine biscuit figures and groups and for large faience dogs and lions. The early pieces were unmarked. The firm was acquired by Keller and Guerin and is still working.

Vase, Broken Pine Pattern, Brown, Cream, Footed, Cameo, Signed Muller Freres, 6 In.	1000.00
Vase, White Lilies, Art Nouveau, Carved, Stamped, c.1900, 19 In.	565.00

LUSTER glaze was meant to resemble copper, silver, or gold. The term *luster* includes any piece with some luster trim. It has been used since the sixteenth century. Some of the luster found today was made during the nineteenth century. The metallic glazes are applied on pottery. The finished color depends on the combination of the clay color and the glaze. Blue, orange, gold, and pearlized luster decorations were used by Japanese and German firms in the early 1900s. Tea Leaf pieces have their own category.

Canary Yellow, Bowl, Flower, Leaf, Twig, 2 ¾ x 5 ½ In.	237.00
Canary Yellow, Cake Plate, Flowers, Buds, Leaves, Central Flower, 8 ¼ In.	57.00
Canary Yellow, Vase, Black Band, Alternating Bell Flower, Palm Flower, Flare Top, 4 ½ In.	68.00
Canary Yellow, Waste Bowl, Rose, Scalloped Top, 3 ½ x 6 ½ In., Pair	79.00
Copper, Bowl, Yellow, Blue, Green, c.1850, 3 ½ x 6 ½ In.	225.00
Copper, Canary Yellow, Mug, Band, Multicolored Flower, Leaf, Loop Handle, 2 In.	480.00
Copper, Pitcher, Andrew Jackson, Hero Of New Orleans, Enoch Wood & Sons, 8 ½ In.	4406.00
Copper, Pitcher, Rev. John Wesley, Reverse Panel Has Clock Face, 7 In.	750.00
Copper, Pitcher, Yellow, Green Ground, Multicolored, Flowers, 8 In.	115.00
Fairyland luster is included in the Wedgwood category.	
Pink, Chamber Pot, 2 Verses, Interior Frog, 2 Handles, England, 19th Century	2600.00
Pink, Snake Overlay, Pedestal Foot, France, 10 ½ In., Pair	201.00
Sunderland luster pieces are in the Sunderland category.	
Tea Leaf luster pieces are listed in the Tea Leaf Ironstone category.	
Yellow, Plate, Award Of A Good Boy, Embossed Flower, Leaf, 6 ½ In.	136.00

LUSTRES are mantel decorations or pedestal vases with many hanging glass prisms. The name really refers to the prisms, and it is proper to refer to a single glass prism as a lustre. Either spelling, luster or lustre, is correct.

3-Light, Crystal, Long Prisms, Columnar Base, 19th Century, 20 x 14 In.	374.00
Amber Flashed, Painted Flowers, Gold Scrollwork, 8 Prisms, Czechoslovakia, 10 In., Pair	590.00
Art Glass, Pink, Enamel Strawberries, White Dot Highlights, Prisms, 15 ½ In., Pair ....*illus*	500.00
Blue Glass, Cut Bobeche, Crystal Beads & Prisms, Octagonal Base, 9 In., Pair	95.00
Blue Opaline, Painted Flowers, Applied Snake Stem, Prisms, Continental, 12 In., Pair	378.00
Bohemian Overlay Glass, White Cut To Green, Gilt, Prisms, 11 In., Pair	1298.00
Bristol Glass, Cranberry, Victorian, Crystal Prisms, 19th Century, 14 ½ In., Pair	497.00
Cased White, Cut To Green Enamel, Scallops, Alternating Portraits, Anthemion, Prisms, 15 In., Pair	3851.00
Cranberry, Gilt Enamel, White & Red Flower Swags, 17 Drop Prisms, 15 In., Pair ....*illus*	863.00
Crystal, Scalloped Bowl, Drop Prisms, Footed, Early 20th Century, Pair	115.00

Lustre, Art Glass, Pink,
Enamel Strawberries,
White Dot Highlights, Prisms,
15 ½ In., Pair
$500.00

Lustre, Cranberry, Gilt Enamel,
White & Red Flower Swags,
17 Drop Prisms, 15 In., Pair
$863.00

Maize, Syrup, Custard,
Stain, Gilt, Quadruple Plate Hinged Lid,
Scroll Handle, 6 In.
$431.00

Majolica, Bowl, Pouter Pigeon, Ribbed Interior, Blue Glaze, 3-Footed, Minton, c.1871, 12 In. $1260.00

Majolica, Cheese Keeper, Apple Blossom, Turquoise Ground, George Jones, 12 In. $1003.00

Majolica, Dish, Snake, Sardines, Shells, Palissy, GJ Mark, 1800s, 7 ½ In. $59.00

Majolica, Flagon, Minton, Late 19th Century, 13 In. $556.00

Green Glass, Gold Highlights, White Enamel, 16 Prisms, 14 In., Pair	325.00
Light Blue, Scalloped Top, Gilt, c.1850, 14 ½ x 7 ½ In., Pair	500.00
Pink Cased Glass, Urns, Flowers, Swags, Flared Ruffled Rim, Cut Glass Prisms, 14 In., Pair	1150.00
Ruby Glass, Clear Prisms, Pointy Scalloped Rim, 12 ½ In., Pair	292.00
Ruby Glass, Crystal Prisms, Scalloped Rim, 14 In., Pair	468.00
Ruby Red, Flowers, Etched, Cut, Crystal Prisms, 13 x 6 ½ In.	465.00
Ruby Red, Gold Scalloped Rim, Clear Prisms, Footed, Pair	173.00

MAIZE glass was made by W.L. Libbey & Son Company of Toledo, Ohio, after 1889. The glass resembled an ear of corn. The leaves were usually green, but some pieces were made with blue or red leaves. The kernels of corn were light yellow, white, or light green.

Butter, Cover, Custard, Brown, Green, c.1875, 6 In.	53.00
Celery Vase, Molded Ear Of Corn, Gray, Green, Yellow, 6 ½ In.	115.00
Cruet, Yellow, 7 In.	575.00
Saltshaker, Custard, Yellow & Gilt Leaves, Late 1800s, 4 In.	295.00
Sugar Shaker, Custard, Brown & Green Leaves, Lid, c.1875, 6 In.	357.00
Syrup, Custard, Stain, Gilt, Quadruple Plate Hinged Lid, Scroll Handle, 6 In. ....*illus*	431.00
Tumbler, Custard, Green, c.1875, 4 In.	92.00

MAJOLICA is a general term for any pottery glazed with an opaque tin enamel that conceals the color of the clay body. It has been made since the fourteenth century. Today's collector is most likely to find Victorian majolica. The heavy, colorful ware is rarely marked. Some famous makers include Minton; Griffen, Smith and Hill (marked *Etruscan*); and Chesapeake Pottery (marked *Avalon* or *Clifton*). Majolica made by Wedgwood is listed in the Wedgwood category.

Ashtray, Wild Rose, Rope, Cobalt Blue, Branch Handles, Oval, 15 ½ In.	150.00
Bank, Hen On Nest, 4 In.	29.00
Bank, Woman, In Green Bonnet, Painted, Glazed, Austria, c.1900, 3 ⅝ In.	748.00
Basket, Dahlia, Turquoise Weave Ground, Striped Handles, 8 x 9 In.	590.00
Bowl, 3 Clowns, Intertwined Arms, Arcaded Bowl, Eichwald, 1910, 14 In.	575.00
Bowl, Leaves, Flowers, Cobalt Blue, Lavender Interior, Pedestal, 10 In.	250.00
Bowl, Pouter Pigeon, Ribbed Interior, Blue Glaze, 3-Footed, Minton, c.1871, 12 In. ....*illus*	1260.00
Bowl, Raised Lion, Stylized Branches, Cobalt Blue Ground, Handkerchief Shape, 7 x 3 In.	53.00
Cachepot, Flowers, Wood Plank Sides, Branch & Tree Trunk Handles, Footed, 8 In.	504.00
Cachepot, Laurel Wreath, Bound Trefoil, Cartouches, Bellflowers, Ribbons, 7 ¼ x 8 ¼ In.	173.00
Charger, Green, Hare, Duck, Pigeons, Portugal, Palissy, 17 ¾ In.	1920.00
Charger, Lobster, Shells, Sandy Ground, 13 In.	120.00
Charger, Turtle, Worms, Butterflies, Frog, Lizard, Mossy Ground, Palissy, c.1870, 13 In.	2390.00
Cheese Keeper, Apple Blossom, Turquoise Ground, George Jones, 12 In. ....*illus*	1003.00
Cheese Keeper, Flower, Twig Handle, Domed Cover, 12 x 13 In.	460.00
Cheese Plate, Basket Weave & Flower Border, Blue Center	81.00
Compote, Daisy, White Ground, Etruscan, 9 In.	138.00
Compote, Satyr Masks, Winged Nude Female Handles, Garlands, Footed, c.1890, 15 In.	2880.00
Compote, Sea Creature, Multicolored Tail Support, Round Bowl, c.1900, 12 ¾ In.	147.00
Compote, Shell Shape, Green, Coral, Footed, Holdcroft, c.1880, 7 In.	385.00
Compote, Sunflowers, Pink & Yellow, Scalloped Rim, Griffen, Smith & Co., 5 x 9 In.	531.00
Creamer, Shell Form, Multicolored, Late 19th Century, 4 ½ In.	175.00
Dish, 3 Fish, Eel, Mottled Ground, Moss, Marked, Palissy, c.1870, 9 ¼ In.	657.00
Dish, Crab, Mussels, Mossy Ground, Marked, Palissy, c.1875, 8 In.	777.00
Dish, Frog, Lizard, Bugs, Worms, Butterfly, Mossy Ground, Palissy, c.1870, 9 ¾ In.	657.00
Dish, Leaf, 3 Acorns, Yellow, Green, Brown, Branch Handle, 12 In.	93.00
Dish, Leaf, 7 ½ In.	78.00
Dish, Leaf, Green, Yellow, White, 9 In.	68.00
Dish, Leaf, Yellow, White, Green, Etruscan, Impressed Mark, 9 In.	69.00
Dish, Shell, Dolphin Footed, Signed, Wedgwood	167.00
Dish, Shell, Open, Pink, Red, Blue, Green, Yellow, Brown, Grass On Base, 3-Footed, 4 x 5 In.	145.00
Dish, Snake, Sardines, Shells, Palissy, GJ Mark, 1800s, 7 ½ In. ....*illus*	59.00
Ewer, Frogs, Bugs, Butterflies, Mossy Ground, Lizard Handle, Underplate, Palissy, c.1875, 15 In.	1195.00
Figurine, Blackamoor, Multicolored, England, 19th Century, 15 In.	390.00
Figurine, Blackamoor, Outstretched Arms, Red Coats, Striped Trouser, 34 ½ In., Pair	4370.00
Flagon, Minton, Late 19th Century, 13 In. ....*illus*	556.00
Flask, Fruit, Bulbous, Cork Stopper, Handles, Painted, 12 x 6 In.	82.00
Garniture, Bianco, Neoclassical, Fruit, Leaves, Footed, Reticulated, Handles, 21 In., Pair	1440.00
Humidor, Cigar Smoker, 6 In.	177.00
Humidor, Indian Chief, 8 In.	120.00
Humidor, Pipe Smoker, 5 ¾ In.	182.00
Jar, Apothecary, Mask Head, Fruit, Scrolls, Beaker Shape, Blue Ground, Latin Words, 4 In.	2875.00

Jardiniere, 3 Satyr Heads, Flower & Fruit Garlands, Turquoise, Pink Interior, 1890s, 9 ¾ x 11 In.	940.00
Jardiniere, Boat Shape, Applied Flowers, Longchamp, 13 In.	58.00
Jardiniere, Flowers, Leaf Men, Pink, Brown, Green, Relief, 10 x 11 In.	108.00
Jardiniere, Gargoyles, Cherubs, Elephant Heads, Footed, 25 In.	602.00
Jardiniere, Lily Of The Valley, Mauve, Blue, Yellow, G. Jones, c.1861-73, 7 ¾ In., Pair	1554.00
Jardiniere, Magnolia Blossoms, Rocaille Rim, Melrose Ware, G. Jones, 11 x 13 In.	356.00
Jardiniere, Pedestal, Entwined Dragons, Green, Scalloped Rim, 36 x 13 In.	173.00
Jardiniere, Pedestal, Flowers, Birds, Purple, Green, Strap Handles, Albert Radford, 41 ½ In.	690.00
Jardiniere, Pedestal, Flowers, Green & Pink, Blue Ground, c.1900, 11 ½ x 13 ¼ In.	92.00
Match Holder, Cowboy, Standing With Rifle, Striker, 10 In.	400.00
Match Holder, Girl, Sitting On Log, Knitting, Blue Bonnet, 7 x 6 ½ In.	125.00
Match Holder, Gnome, Seated Smoking Pipe, Strike, 5 ½ x 6 In.	100.00
Match Holder, Monk, Holding Mug, Strike, 8 In.	205.00
Match Holder, Ribbed Top, Yellow, Green, Brown, 3 ¾ In.	23.00
Mirror, Tree Branches, Ivy, Birds, Lizard, Nest, Eggs, Hugo Lonitz, c.1885, 22 x 16 In.	3824.00
Oyster Plate, 6 Wells, Green Glaze, Molded Basket Weave Pattern, 9 ½ In., 3 Piece	235.00
Pedestal, Flowers, Pink, Green Ground, Blue & Green Design, Tassels, 26 ½ x 9 ½ In.	118.00
Pitcher, Bear, Seated, Goofy Face, 9 In.	111.00
Pitcher, Cherubs, Goats, Cobalt Blue, Green, Yellow, Brown, 9 ¼ In. .... *illus*	184.00
Pitcher, Corn, 5 In.	33.00
Pitcher, Corn, 6 In.	161.00
Pitcher, Daisy, Brown Wood Ground, Yellow, 6 In.	78.00
Pitcher, Fish, 12 ½ In.	222.00
Pitcher, Frog, Snake, Multicolored, 9 In.	305.00
Pitcher, Fruit Branches, Pink, Basket Weave Ground, 9 ¾ In.	236.00
Pitcher, Leaf, Yellow, Pink, Green, 6 In.	23.00
Pitcher, Lily Pad, Green, Yellow Neck, Spout, Beige, Applied Handle, 7 ⅝ x 6 ½ x 5 In.	115.00
Pitcher, Monkey Shape, Signed, Stoke On Trent, 8 In.	139.00
Pitcher, Parrot, Multicolored, 10 In.	250.00
Pitcher, Pig, As Waiter, Figural, Onnaing, 10 x 7 In.	676.00
Pitcher, Water Lilies, Blue, Green Fiddle Ferns, Brown Lily Pads, 1880, 5 ½ In.	400.00
Pitcher, Wine, Armorial, Rearing Lions, Leaves, Striped Neck & Base, Handle, 13 In.	805.00
Planter, 2 Clowns, Symbols, Violin, 11 ½ x 12 In.	75.00
Planter, Wild Mallard Duck, 7 ½ x 12 ½ In.	165.00
Plaque, Annunciation, Demilune, Multicolored, Della Robbia Style, 16 ½ x 28 ½ In.	478.00
Plate, Asparagus, Turquoise, Gold & Brown, Accents, 1850, 13 x 10 In.	105.00
Plate, Bicyclist, Green, Blue, Red, Yellow, 7 ¾ In.	366.00
Plate, Crawfish, 6 Silver Gray, Monaco, Palissy, c.1880, 11 ¼ In.	2040.00
Plate, Cupid, Carrying Net, Masks, Birds, Fan Shapes, Marked, Faenza, 1881, 10 In. .... *illus*	109.00
Plate, Fruit, Yellow Leaves, 12 In.	110.00
Plate, Green, Marked, Etruscan, Griffen, Smith & Hill, 9 In.	100.00
Plate, Lizard, Snake, Frog, On Grass, Green, Palissy, Signed, JFG, 14 In.	1300.00
Plate, Pond Lily, 4 Green Lily Pads, White Lily Center, Marked, 8 In.	75.00
Plate, Shell Shape, Mottled, 9 In., Pair	150.00
Plate, Stingray, Handle, 2 ¼ x 13 ½ x 12 In.	360.00
Plate, Strawberry, Molded Flowers, Berries, Scalloped Rim, Late 19th Century, 8 ⅝ In.	82.00
Platter, Corn, Oval, 14 In.	167.00
Platter, Fish & Pond, Ecole De Paris, Oval, Palissy, c.1880, 15 ¾ x 20 ¾ In.	2400.00
Platter, Fish, Red, Black, Gray, Stamped, Portugal, 19 ½ In.	190.00
Platter, Fish, Shellfish, Bugs, Plants, Mottled Ground, Signed, Palissy, c.1880, 19 ½ x 26 In.	5079.00
Platter, Fish, Stamped, Portugal, 19 ½ In.	206.00
Sardine Box, Duck, Fish In Mouth, Waves, Coral, George Jones .... *illus*	1121.00
Stove, Putti, Picking Grapes Around Chimney, White, Yellow, Italy, 84 In.	1035.00
Sweetmeat Stand, Man, Carrying Basket, Child, Carrying Basket, 1882, 16 x 7 ⅞ In., Pair	2520.00
Tankard, Lizard Handle & Spout, Modeled Ground, Palissy, c.1800, 5 ¾ In.	777.00
Tazza, Butterfly, Flowers, Signed Marcel Logeat, 19 x 15 In. .... *illus*	1121.00
Teapot, Chinaman, Mask, Shaped Handle, Turquoise Jacket, Green Pants, Minton, c.1875, 8 In.	460.00
Teapot, Tortoise, Mouth Spout, Tail Handle, Shell Finial, Minton, c.1876, 5 x 8 In. .... *illus*	11700.00
Tray, Eat Thy Bread With Thankfulness, 13 In. .... *illus*	263.00
Tureen, Cover, Cockerel, Red Comb, Turned Head, Multicolored, 15 x 17 In.	144.00
Tureen, Cover, Game, Lidded Basket Shape, Leaves, Multicolored, 7 x 12 ½ In. .... *illus*	719.00
Umbrella Stand, Heron, Flowers, Frog, 36 x 19 x 16 In.	500.00
Umbrella Stand, Masks, Scrolling Vines, Leaf Tips, Fruit, Shaped Rim, Green, 21 In.	178.00
Urn, 2 Birds, Head Terminal, Mottled Glaze, Applied Handles, Footed Baluster, Italy, 22 In.	378.00
Vase, Black Boy, Holding Basket Of Rolls, Tulips, Austria, 1880s, 11 ½ In.	185.00
Vase, Cylindrical, Blue & Brown Drip Glaze, Belgium, Early 20th Century, 13 ¾ In.	88.00
Vase, Dark Blue, Pink Flower Relief, Basket Weave, Square Plinth, Minton, c.1870, 7 In., Pair	830.00

Majolica, Pitcher, Cherubs, Goats, Cobalt Blue, Green, Yellow, Brown, 9 ¼ In.
$184.00

Majolica, Plate, Cupid, Carrying Net, Masks, Birds, Fan Shapes, Marked, Faenza, 1881, 10 In.
$109.00

Majolica, Sardine Box, Duck, Fish In Mouth, Waves, Coral, George Jones
$1121.00

M

Majolica, Tazza, Butterfly, Flowers, Signed Marcel Logeat, 19 x 15 In.
$1121.00

Majolica, Teapot, Tortoise, Mouth Spout, Tail Handle, Shell Finial, Minton, c.1876, 5 x 8 In.
$11700.00

Majolica, Tray, Eat Thy Bread With Thankfulness, 13 In.
$263.00

Majolica, Tureen, Cover, Game, Lidded Basket Shape, Leaves, Multicolored, 7 x 12 ½ In.
$719.00

Majolica, Vase, Flowers, Leaves, Rock Base, T.C. Brown Westhead Moore & Co., 11 In.
$3186.00

Vase, Domed Lid, Bouquets, Ribbed, Baluster Form, Lion Finial, Blue & Ocher, 24 In.	118.00
Vase, Double Stump, Bird's Nest, Songbird & Puppy, Palissy, Signed, 1850, 11 In.	900.00
Vase, Dragons, Text, Blue, Green, Twist Orange Yellow Handle, Italy, 1900s, 13 ½ In.	201.00
Vase, Fairy, Irises, Cattails, 3 Dimensional, Pastel Matte Glaze, Delphin Massier, 21 In.	2070.00
Vase, Flowers, Leaves, Rock Base, T.C. Brown Westhead Moore & Co., 11 In. ...... *illus*	3186.00
Vase, Graduated Blue Glaze, Multicolored Floral Top Edge, Green Side Handles, 8 ½ In.	127.00
Vase, Man, 1700s Attire, Base, Oval, Ring Handles, Impressed, 12 In.	176.00
Vase, Red, Amber, Brown, Handles, 7 In.	53.00
Vase, Star, Moon, Drapes, Scrolls, Elephant Handles, Brown, Germany, c.1890, 24 In.	652.00
Vase, Stork, Flowers, 35 x 15 x 16 In.	280.00
Vase, Stork, Naturalistic Base, Leaves, 20th Century, 35 x 15 In.	245.00
Vase, Stump, Serpent Raiding Bird's Nest, Lizard, Signed, Palissy, 10 ¾ In. ...... *illus*	1080.00
Vase, Three Graces, Relief, Painted Landscape, Oval, Bucklin, Wardle & Co., c.1800s, 9 In., Pair	474.00
Wall Pocket, Bellows Shape, Flowers, Scrolls, c.1900, 9 ½ x 6 ¼ In.	395.00

MALACHITE is a green stone with unusual layers or rings of darker green shades. It is often polished and used for decorative objects. Most malachite comes from Siberia or Australia.

Figurine, Hotei, Frog, Wood Base, 4 ¼ x 4 In.	250.00
Frame, Silver Trim, Easel, 3 ¼ x 2 ¾ In.	645.00
Hand Mirror, Molded, Nude On Knees, Czechoslovakia, c.1930, 7 In.	300.00
Obelisk, Pietra Dura Marble, Attached Thermometer, 15 In.	595.00
Paperweight, Africa, 3 ¼ x 3 x 1 ½ In.	145.00
Pen Rest, Napoleon III, Bronze Dore, Engraved, Serpent Handles, Footed, 13 x 3 ½ In.	395.00

MAPS of all types have been collected for centuries. The earliest known printed maps were made in 1478. The first printed street map showed London in 1559. The first road maps for use by drivers of automobiles were made in 1901. Collectors buy maps that were pages of old books, as well as the multifolded road maps popular in this century.

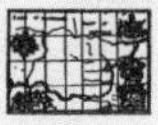

Atlas, Alameda County, California, 36 Color Maps, 70 Lithograph Views, c.1853, 17 ½ x 15 In.	858.00
Atlas, Johnson's, New Illustrated Family Atlas, Federal Census, Color Lithograph, Folio, c.1864.	919.00
Britain, Saxon Kingdoms, Vignettes, John Speed, c.1611, 20 x 15 In.	3000.00
British Isles, Homann Heirs, c.1730, 22 x 19 In.	350.00
Canada & New England, Hand Colored, James Duncan Graham, 15 x 18 In.	550.00
Canada, Labrador Coast, Thomas Jefferys, c.1770, 18 x 21 In.	150.00
Celestial, Planisphere, Cardboard, Faux Leather, Gold Lettering, J.L. Hammett Co., c.1900	275.00
Colonial Great Lakes, Lake Superior, Zatta, c.1778, 16 ½ x 12 In.	425.00
Colonial U.S. & Canada, Pierre DuVal, c.1676, 4 x 3 In.	300.00
Dakota, Wounded Knee Massacre, Cotton, Blue, White Printing, Engineer Office, c.1890, 30 x 35 In.	9400.00
England & Wales, Embroidered, Bright Colors, J. Jackson, 1781, 25 x 21 In.	450.00
Europe, Inset Climate Zone, Philippe Briet, c.1660, 19 ½ x 15 In.	300.00
Georgia, Geological Features, W.G. Bonner, Savannah, c.1849, 20 ¾ x 18 In.	316.00
Globe, Celestial, 24 Gores, Constellations, Metal Sphere, Brass Meridian, 6 x 8 ¼ In.	711.00
Globe, Celestial, Regency, Constellation, Mahogany, 1816, 18 In.	2585.00
Globe, Lunar, 12 Printed Gores, Half Meridian, Wood Base, 1959, 12 x 19 In.	533.00
Globe, Terrestrial, 12 Printed Gores, Metal Sphere, Brass Meridian, Calendar, Zodiac Signs, 32 In.	178.00
Globe, Terrestrial, Arts & Crafts, In Iron Ring, Splayed Legs, 41 In.	600.00
Globe, Terrestrial, Birch Tripod Base, Pad Feet, Red Oceans, Green Continents, Paint, 16 In.	887.00
Globe, Terrestrial, Copper Finish, Iron Stand, Paw Feet, W & AK Johnson, Scotland, 1930, 12 In.	188.00
Globe, Terrestrial, Copper, Iron Stand, Paw Feet, W & AK Johnson, Scotland, 1930s, 23 x 18 In.	185.00
Globe, Terrestrial, Ebonized Wood, Tripod Stand, 16 In.	8912.00
Globe, Terrestrial, Enamel, Gemstone Inlay, Armillary Outer Ring, Brass Stand, 12 In.	345.00
Globe, Terrestrial, Fruitwood Rim, Brass Band, Iron Base, Joslin, c.1888, 23 x 23 In.	1350.00
Globe, Terrestrial, Kittinger, Desktop, 16 x 12 In.	385.00
Globe, Terrestrial, Mahogany Stand, Brass Meridian, W.B. Annin, Joslin, Boston, 11 ½ In.	2925.00
Globe, Terrestrial, Maple, Painted Red, Green, Wood Stand, New England, 40 In.	3995.00
Globe, Terrestrial, Regency, 12 Gore, Lithograph, Stand, C.S. Hammond & Co., c.1924, 44 x 25 In.	2820.00
Globe, Terrestrial, Thomas, Paris, c.1920, 5 x 9 In.	1000.00
Globe, Terrestrial, Turned Wood Spindle Base, Marked Currents, Perigot, Paris, c.1905, 10 x 16 In.	2000.00
Globe, Terrestrial, Twig Style Cast Iron Stand.	660.00
Globe, Terrestrial, Weber Costello Co., Paper Lithograph, Copper Rotating Tripod Base, 12 In.	130.00
Globe, Terrestrial, Wood Stand, J. Forest, Paris, Early 1900s, 34 x 28 x 28 In. ...... *illus*	2478.00
Globe, Terrestrial, Wood Stand, Turns, Rotates, J. Forest, Paris, 34 x 28 x 28 In.	2415.00
Great Britain, Roads, Color, Cloth Backing, 18th Century, 29 ½ x 24 In.	325.00
Harbor New York-Staten Island & Narrows, Topographical, Goupil, 1854, 30 x 41 ½ In.	725.00
Mare Del Nord, North Sea, Black, White, 18th Century, 18 ½ x 24 ½ In.	1450.00
Middle British Colonies, Lewis Evans, Colonial, 21 x 29 In.	1880.00

M

New York, Topographical, Black & White, Mottram, 1857, 34 ½ x 56 In.		725.00
North America, Revolutionary War, Plan Of Operations Of The King's Army, 1777, 29 x 20 In.		6518.00
North Atlantic & Northern Europe, Ortelius & Marchetti, c.1598, 4 x 3 In.		200.00
Ocean Atlantique, North America, Mortier, Amsterdam, c.1700, 19 ¼ x 24 ½ In.		600.00
Orbis Terrarum, Terrestrial Map Of The World, Black & White, N. Visscher, 20 ¾ x 24 In.		3350.00
Scotland, Northern Coast Of Ireland, Nicolas Fils Sanson, c.1700, 8 x 10 ½ In.		110.00
South Carolina, Thomas P. Lockwood, Adapted For Schools & Families, c.1832, 9 ½ x 11 ¾ In.		173.00
Southeast U.S., Confederate Army Sites, F. Shallus, Copper Engraving, 1800s, 11 x 16 In.		431.00
Southwestern U.S., California & Mexico, c.1721, 7 x 9 In.		1200.00
Sweden, Baltic States, Johann Baptist Homann, 1730, 22 ½ x 19 In.		325.00
United States, Railroads, Asa Whitney, c.1846, 15 x 9 In.		150.00
United States, Aviation, Rand McNally, 1923, 40 x 26 In.		75.00
United States, British Provinces, Mexico, West Indies, Color Lithograph, Colton, c.1855, 53 x 60 In.		1348.00
United States, Topographical, Territorial Boundaries, J. Franklin Groff, c.1875, 12 ½ x 16 In.		235.00
University Of Michigan, Ann Arbor, Hardboard, Gertrude Strickler, 1901, 31 x 38 ½ In.		223.00
U.S. & Florida, Southern Section, John Melish, Sweden, 1824, 17 x 21 In.		1035.00
Virginia, Maryland, Chesapeake Bay, 18th Century, Mat, Frame, H. Moll 15 x 18 In.		382.00
Western Hemisphere, Hand Colored Map, G. Valck, Amsterdam, c.1702, 19 x 23 In.		1920.00

MARBLE collectors pay highest prices for glass and sulphide marbles. The game of marbles has been popular since the days of the ancient Romans. American children were able to buy marbles by the mid-eighteenth century. Dutch glazed clay marbles were least expensive. Glazed pottery marbles, attributed to the Bennington potteries in Vermont, were of a better quality. Marbles made of pink marble were also available by the 1830s. Glass marbles seem to have been made later. By 1880, Samuel C. Dyke of South Akron, Ohio, was making clay marbles and The National Onyx Marble Company was making marbles of onyx. The Navarre Glass Marble Company of Navarre, Ohio, and M. B. Mishler of Ravenna, Ohio, made the glass marbles. Ohio remained the center of the marble industry, and the Akron-made Akro Agate brand became nationally known. Other pieces made by Akro Agate are listed in this book in the Akro Agate category. Sulphides are glass marbles with frosted white figures in the center.

Agate, Christmas Tree, Red, Yellow, Green, Peltier, ¹³⁄₁₆ In.		250.00
Akro Agate, Assorted No. 1, Striped Onyx Slag, Box, 100 Piece		263.00
Christensen Agate Co., No. 00, Slag, Box, 100 Piece		2106.00
Christensen, Diaper Fold, Striped, Opaque, Blue Base, Orange, Yellow, ¹¹⁄₁₆ In.		819.00
Christensen, Flame, Light Blue Base, Orange Flames, Brown Accents, 2 ¹⁄₃₂ In.		644.00
Christensen, Guinea, Lavender, ⅝ In.		351.00
Christensen, Mint Green, Red, White, ⅝ In.		234.00
Clambroth, Black, White Lines, ¹⁹⁄₃₂ In.		205.00
Clambroth, Blue, White, ¹¹⁄₁₆ In.		175.00
End Of Day, Cloud, Multicolored, Single Pontil, Open Window Top, 2 ⅛ In.	*illus*	1989.00
Guinea, Machine Made, Cobalt Blue, Green, White, Black, Red, ⅝ In.		1872.00
Indian, Black Ground, Yellow, Green, White Stripes, ¹¹⁄₁₆ In.		205.00
Indian, Paneled Bands, Orange, Blue, White, Opposite Panels In Green, White, Red, ⅞ In.		117.00
Joseph's Coat, Swirl, Blue, White, Lime, Yellow, Red, 1 ¹⁵⁄₁₆ In.		2925.00
Lutz, Red Ribbon, White Bands, ⅞ In.		977.00
Onionskin, 2 Panel, Red, White, Yellow, Blue, 1 ¹⁵⁄₁₆ In.		517.00
Onionskin, Lutz, Multicolored Base, 1 ⅝ In.		4680.00
Onionskin, Mica, Orange, Yellow, Green Spots, 1 ²⁵⁄₃₂ In.		88.00
Onionskin, Multicolored, 1 ½ In.	*illus*	410.00
Peltier, Blue, Red, Green, ¾ In.		59.00
Peltier, Christmas Tree, White, Green, Red, ¹³⁄₁₆ In.		263.00
Ribbon, Lutz, Black Ground, Green, Gold Stripes, ¾ In.		59.00
Shooter, Clay, Early 1900s, 1 ½ In.		20.00
Sulphide, Bear, Walking, Encased In Air, Pontil, 1 ¾ In.		140.00
Sulphide, Boy On Rocking Horse, Blowing Horn, Pontil, 1 ⅝ In.	*illus*	936.00
Sulphide, Buzzard, Brown, White, Pontil, 1 ⅝ In.		195.00
Sulphide, Chicken, Standing, Pontil, 2 In.		200.00
Sulphide, Cow, Standing, Air Bubbles, 2 Pontils, 2 ⅛ In.		125.00
Sulphide, French Poodle, Standing, Pontil, 2 ⅛ In.		164.00
Sulphide, Hen, Painted, Green Nest, Cobalt Blue Wings, 1 ⅛ In.	*illus*	1404.00
Sulphide, Lamb, Looking Up, Pontil, 2 In.		205.00
Sulphide, Lamb, Pontil, 2 ⅛ In.		80.00
Sulphide, Lion, Standing, With Pole, Egyptian Tomb, Pontil, 2 ⅛ In.		58.00
Sulphide, Rabbit, Running, Pontil, 1 ⅞ In.		210.00
Sulphide, Sheep, Standing, Pontil, 2 ¼ In.		93.00
Swirl, Barber Pole, Solid Core, Yellow Latticinio Lines, 1 ¹³⁄₁₆ In.	*illus*	176.00
Swirl, Blue, Pink, Yellow Bands, White Core, Alternating Blue & White, Red & Yellow, 1 ¹⁵⁄₁₆ In.		165.00

Majolica, Vase, Stump, Serpent Raiding Bird's Nest, Lizard, Signed, Palissy, 10 ¾ In.
$1080.00

Map, Globe, Terrestrial, Wood Stand, J. Forest, Paris, Early 1900s, 34 x 28 x 28 In.
$2478.00

M

TIP
Cranberry juice will stain stone, so be careful if you have marble-top tables. Other liquids will stain, but cranberry juice stains are especially bad.

Marble, End Of Day, Cloud, Multicolored, Single Pontil, Open Window Top, 2 1/8 In.
$1989.00

Marble, Onionskin, Multicolored, 1 1/2 In.
$410.00

Marble, Sulphide, Boy On Rocking Horse, Blowing Horn, Pontil, 1 5/8 In.
$936.00

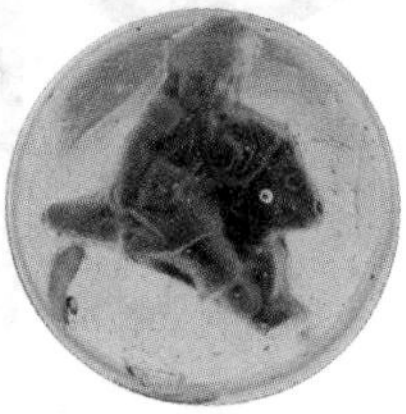

Marble, Sulphide, Hen, Painted, Green Nest, Cobalt Blue Wings, 1 1/8 In.
$1404.00

Marble, Swirl, Barber Pole, Solid Core, Yellow Latticinio Lines, 1 13/16 In.
$176.00

Swirl, Divided Ribbon, Green Base, White, Red, Blue, Yellow, 1 21/32 In. 117.00
Swirl, Peppermint, 3 Red Bands, 7/8 In. .... *illus* 263.00
Swirl, Peppermint, Green Lines Inside Blue Band, 3/4 In. 468.00
Swirl, Red, Yellow & Black Outer, White Core, 7/8 In. 38.00
Swirl, Ribbon Core, Orange, Yellow, 1 7/16 In. 322.00
Swirl, Solid Core, Tri Level, Dark Green, 2nd Stage Yellow, Red, 1 7/8 In. 7605.00
Swirl, Yellow & Red, White Core, Pontil, 1 1/4 In. 110.00
Swirl, Yellow Swirl Core, Green & Blue Outer Bands, White Borders, Pontils, 1 3/8 In. 175.00

MARBLE CARVINGS, such as large or small figurines, groups of people or animals, and architectural decorations, have been a special art form since the time of the ancient Greeks. Reproductions, especially of large Victorian groups, are being made of a mixture using marble dust. These are very difficult to detect and collectors should be careful. Other carvings are listed under Alabaster.

Bust, Caesar Augustus, Imperial Roman Style, Italian, 31 x 21 In. 1200.00
Bust, Castellana, Verso Inscribed Prof. Libero Gremigni, Italy, c.1900, 11 In. 450.00
Bust, Child, Variegated Black Marble Base, Bronze Studio Button, E. Greiner, 6 1/2 In. 422.00
Bust, Elizabethan Girl, Hair Parted In Center, Braid Over Shoulder, Italy, 20 In. 920.00
Bust, Emperor Lucius Verus, Wearing Cloak, Variegated Yellow & White, 30 In. 4025.00
Bust, Flora, A. Cipriani, Italy, 20th Century, 20 x 17 In. 1410.00
Bust, George Washington, 17 In. 3500.00
Bust, Girl, Bonnet, Grapes, Signed, Lapini, Italy, c.1890, 19 In. 1659.00
Bust, Girl, Looking Down, Hair Up, White, France, c.1890, 18 x 8 In. 384.00
Bust, Head, Happy Baby, Chester Beach, 7 1/2 x 7 In. 633.00
Bust, Lisabetta Albizzi, Polished, Grand Tour, Early 20th Century, 18 1/2 x 17 In. 6600.00
Bust, Man, 3-Tone, White, Gray, Rouge, Full Round, Neoclassical, 37 In. 1800.00
Bust, Napoleon, White, Square Plinth, Early 20th Century, 10 1/2 x 6 1/4 In. 764.00
Bust, Old Woman, Wearing Bonnet, Socle Base, 25 x 17 In. 431.00
Bust, Roman Emperor, 2-Tone White & Tan, Full Round, Neoclassical, 36 1/4 In. 1080.00
Bust, Roman Man, White, Variegated, Continental, 21 1/2 In. 1793.00
Bust, Roman, Variegated Stone Torso, c.1970, 33 1/2 In. 1020.00
Bust, Woman, Autumn, Upswept Hair, Oak Leaf Circlet, Grape Leaf Bodice, Italy, 27 1/2 In. 948.00
Bust, Woman, Bare Shoulders, Hair Back, N.F. Baker, 24 In. 1185.00
Bust, Woman, Flowers, Braided Hair, White Carrara, Puggi, Signed, 28 In. 17110.00
Bust, Woman, Hair Tied In Scarf, Fleur-De-Lis Design, G. Bossi 350.00
Bust, Woman, Italy, 19 1/2 In. 598.00
Bust, Woman, Lace Cap, Ruffled Bodice, Socle Base, A. Piazza, 25 In. 2015.00
Bust, Woman, Lace-Bordered Head Scarf, Late 19th Century, Italy, 24 In. 1830.00
Bust, Woman, Roman Style, N.F. Baker, 23 1/4 In. 4406.00
Bust, Woman, Smiling, Wearing Cloche & Scarf, Art Deco, c.1925, 16 1/2 In. 610.00
Bust, Woman, Wearing Hooded Cloak, Waisted Socle, Italy, 19th Century, 26 In. 2015.00
Bust, Woman, Wearing Lace Bonnet, Marble Socle, Pedestal, Continental, 67 1/2 In. 956.00
Bust, Young Woman, Elaborate Headdress, Socle Base, c.1900, 20 In. 299.00
Bust, Young Woman, Lace Hat, Fini C., Italy, c.1910, 15 x 7 1/2 x 9 1/2 In. 147.00
Bust, Young Woman, Socle Base, c.1890, 26 In. 442.00
Fountain, Boy Holding Dolphin, Circular, Leaf, 3 Swans, Bowl, 65 x 37 In. 4219.00
Obelisk, Multicolored Marble Inlays, Square Plinth, 52 x 11 x 11 In., Pair 2350.00
Obelisk, Neoclassical Style, Inlaid Base, 21 x 4 1/2 In., Pair 2350.00
Obelisk, Veined, Rectilinear Base, Spheres, Swedish, c.1873, 49 x 16 x 10 In. 2880.00
Pedestal, 3-Sided, Variegated Rose To Ivory, Green Borders, 46 x 18 In., Pair 805.00
Pedestal, Alabaster, Canted Corners, Ring Turned, Fluted Stem, Octagonal Base, 40 x 11 In. 294.00
Pedestal, Columnar, Aubergine, Rotating Capital, Plinth Base, 17 x 14 In. 748.00
Pedestal, Columnar, Variegated Rose To Ocher, Rotating Octagonal Top, 39 x 14 In. 460.00
Pedestal, Green, 8-Sided Base, 42 3/4 x 10 1/2 In. 200.00
Pedestal, Green, Long Top, Turned Stem, Round Foot, Italy, c.1905, 26 x 39 In. 385.00
Pedestal, Neoclassical Style, 3 Sections, Variegated, Peach, 44 1/2 x 9 1/4 x 9 1/4 In. 180.00
Pedestal, Octagonal Top, Column Base, 16 x 48 In. 144.00
Pedestal, Pink, Tapered, Bronze Capital & Masks, Square Base, 43 x 14 In. 1380.00
Pedestal, Red, Bronze Mount, Square Base, 4 Paw Feet, 19th Century, 43 x 13 x 13 In. 1708.00
Pedestal, Rouge, Fluted, Column Shape, Square Top, 12 x 12 x 40 In. 230.00
Pedestal, Square Top, Fluted, Octagonal Base, Grapes & Vines, 19th Century, 43 In. 1725.00
Pedestal, Square Top, Turned Stem, 8-Sided Base, Carrara, 41 In. 275.00
Pedestal, White & Gray Veined, Columnar, Round Top, Molded Base, 31 1/2 x 13 3/4 In. 259.00
Pedestal, White, Tapered, 3 Sections, 19 1/4 x 11 In. 173.00
Plaque, Carved Relief, Crucifixion, 12 x 12 x 2 In. 150.00
Plaque, Carved Relief, Pieta, 12 x 12 x 2 In. 150.00
Plaque, Cherubs, Roses, Gilt, Wood Frame, France, 17 x 31 In. 800.00
Plaque, Silhouette, Classical Beauty, c.1900, 16 x 13 In. 359.00

Statue, Archaic Style, Lion, Lying Down, On Elephant, Pair..	330.00
Statue, Cupid, 26 In.	441.00
Statue, Cupid, Gilt Bonze Bow & Arrow, Signed, C. Balloni, Late 1800s, 25 ½ In.	5050.00
Statue, Dog, Chihuahua, Laying, Leather Collar, Base, Italian, 10 ¾ x 17 ¼ x 7 In.	2040.00
Statue, Foo Dog, 22 x 9 x 12 In., Pair	275.00
Statue, Foo Dog, Draped Pedestal, White, Ming Style, c.1925, 21 x 8 In., Pair	330.00
Statue, Italian Carrara, Laying, Head In Hand, 11 x 21 x 10 In.	747.00
Statue, Lion, Guardian Pose, Raised Paw, Shield, Carrara, Italy, 11 x 27 In., Pair	2468.00
Statue, Lion, Seated, Gray, 19th Century, 26 In., Pair	720.00
Statue, Mother, Child, White, 32 In.	1888.00
Statue, Nude Woman, Butterfly, Base, 19th Century, 76 In.	5500.00
Statue, Rebecca At The Well, P. Gazzanti, Italy, c.1870, 7 ½ In.	3525.00
Statue, Venus De Milo, Italy, 25 x 6 ½ In.	529.00
Statue, Woman, Finger On Chin, Flower Headband On Wrist, Continental, White, 45 In.	1888.00
Statue, Woman, Leaning Against Tree Stump, Dog, Continental, 31 x 12 x 9 In.	2938.00
Statue, Woman, Seated On Bench, P.E. Fiascpi, Italy, c.1900, 12 x 12 In.	468.00
Statue, Woman, Veil, Floral Dress, White, Gray Veins, Continental, 24 ½ In.	1652.00
Urn, Cover, Green, Bronze Mount, Pierced, Scrolled, Square Base, France, 12 In.	4425.00
Urn, Napoleon III, Putto Handles, Beribboned Flower Garlands, Finial, c.1875, 28 In., Pair.....	8225.00
Woman & Swan, Marble Base, Art Deco, A. Petrilli, Italy, 20th Century, 10 In.	1913.00
Woman, Bust, Hair Up, Rose On Chest, Signed, G. Brogi, 24 In.	684.00
Woman, Robe, Roses, Signed, E. Balliglia, 8 x 37 In.	2818.00

MARBLEHEAD POTTERY was founded in 1905 by Dr. J. Hall as a rehabilitative program for the patients of a Marblehead, Massachusetts, sanitarium. Two years later it was separated from the sanitarium, it continued operations until 1936. Many of the pieces were decorated with marine motifs.

Bowl, Green Matte Ground, Stylized Trees, Arthur Baggs, 3 ½ x 6 In.	6710.00
Tile, Ship, Blue, White, Marked, 4 ¾ x 4 ¾ In.	150.00
Tile, Stylized Peacock Among Leaves, Marked, 4 ½ In.	510.00
Trivet, Ship, Blue, Beige, Brown, Marked, MP, 5 ⅛ In. Diam.	825.00
Vase, Band Of Yellow Roses, Dark Blue Ground, Mark, 3 ½ In.	1955.00
Vase, Berry Design, Blue & Brown, Green Ground, Round, HT, 4 x 3 In.	3900.00
Vase, Blue Matte Glaze, Cylindrical, 4 x 8 ½ In.	240.00
Vase, Blue Matte Glaze, Paper Label, 4 In.	161.00
Vase, Blue, Stalks, Flowers, Gray Ground, Mark, 5 ¼ In.	2760.00
Vase, Bulbous, Mottled Green, Brown & Blue Matte Glaze, Marked, 4 x 8 In.	570.00
Vase, Cylinder Shape, Green Matte Glaze, 2 ½ x 7 ½ In.	540.00
Vase, Gray Matte Glaze, Bulbous, Marked, 7 ½ x 5 ½ In.	1560.00
Vase, Stylized Flowers, Blue & Orange, Gray Ground, Round, Marked, 4 x 4 ¼ In.	7800.00
Vase, Stylized Grape, Mottled Yellow, Brown Ground, 3 ¼ x 3 ½ In.	2640.00
Vase, Tapered, Blue Matte, 5 x 8 ½ In.	600.00
Vase, Tapered, Carved Stylized Trees, Blue Matte Ground, Marked, 4 x 8 In.	2900.00
Wall Pocket, Inverted Teardrop Shape, Flared Rim, Blue Glaze, Signed, 7 x 5 In.	345.00

MARTIN BROTHERS of Middlesex, England, made Martinware, a salt-glazed stoneware, between 1873 and 1915. Many figural jugs and vases were made by the three brothers. Of special interest are the fanciful birds, usually made with removable heads. Most pieces have the incised name of the artists plus other information on the bottom.

Bird, Monk, Green, Brown, Blue, Wood Base, c.1881, Incised, 10 In.	*illus*	22151.00
Jar, Tobacco, Wally Bird, Quizzical Expression, R.W. Martin & Bros., 1887, 8 ½ In.		23700.00
Jug, Double Face, Signed Martin & Brothers..		4956.00
Tobacco Jar, Stoneware, Bird, Green Plumage, c.1913, 6 ½ x 3 ½ In.	*illus*	14400.00
Vase, 3 Animated Dragons In Blue, Brown & Ivory, Stoneware, Marked, 1898, 6 In.		3240.00

MARY GREGORY is the name used for a type of glass that is easily identified. White figures were painted on clear or colored glass as the decoration. The figures chosen were usually children at play. The first glass known as Mary Gregory was made about 1870. Similar glass is made even today. The traditional story has been that the glass was made at the Sandwich Glass works in Boston by a woman named Mary Gregory. Recent research suggests that it is possible that none was made at Sandwich. In general, all-white figures were used in the United States, tinted faces were probably used in Bohemia, France, Italy, Germany, Switzerland, and England. Children standing, not playing, were pictured after the 1950s.

Bell, Girl, Sitting On Fence, Cranberry, Clear Handle..	58.00
Bowl, Girls, Lake Scene, Prussian Blue, Optic Ribbed, Amber Feet, Rigaree Color, 8 In.	375.00

Marble, Swirl, Peppermint, 3 Red Bands, ⅞ In.
$263.00

Martin Brothers, Bird, Monk, Green, Brown, Blue, Wood Base, c.1881, Incised, 10 In.
$22151.00

Martin Brothers, Tobacco Jar, Stoneware, Bird, Green Plumage, c.1913, 6 ½ x 3 ½ In.
$14400.00

M

TIP
Never try to dry a piece of marble with a hair dryer.

Mason's Ironstone, Cruet, Pewter Lid, Imari, Pagodas, Blue, Orange, Marked, c.1880, 5 In.
$117.00

Mason's Ironstone, Tureen, Cover, Ladle, Plate, Red Transfer, Country Scene, 15 x 10 In.
$230.00

Massier, Vase, Faience, Blue Ground, Wisteria, Multicolored, Gilt, Signed, c.1890, 12 In.
$405.00

M

Butter, Domed Lid, Blue, Finial, 6 ½ In.	50.00
Cruet, Cranberry, Girl, Holding Flower, Basket, Clear Handle, Pontil, 6 ½ In.	60.00
Dresser Box, Girl, Bird, Swags, Black, Red Interior, 4-Footed, 4 In.	518.00
Jewelry Box, Cover, Boy, Juggling, Blue, Gilt Metal Trim, 4 x 4 ½ In.	150.00
Lamp, Oil, Boy, With Stick, Black Amethyst, 10 In.	110.00
Pickle Castor, Cranberry, Boy & Bird, Meriden Silver Plate Holder, 9 ¾ In.	1500.00
Tankard, Man, Horn, Flip Top, Cranberry, Clear, Enamel, Germany, 15 In.	400.00
Tumbler, Girl, White Dress, Brown Hair, Amber, Inverted Thumbprint, 3 ¾ In.	76.00
Tumbler, Iced Tea, Boy & Girl, Blue Thumbprint, 6 ¼ In., Pair	125.00
Vase, Boy, Blowing Bubbles, Amber, Pedestal, 7 In.	70.00
Vase, Children, Butterflies, Urn Shape, Optic Ribbed, 7 In., Pair	75.00
Vase, Cranberry, Gilt, Ribbed & Ruffled Rim, 10 In.	56.00
Vase, Flowers, White, Ruffled Rim, 9 x 4 In.	35.00
Vase, Girl, Feeding Birds, Red Cased, 10 In.	403.00
Vase, Green, Girl, Boy, 9 In., Pair	220.00
Vase, Ruby, Flashed, 11 x 5 In.	82.00

MASON'S IRONSTONE was made by the English pottery of Charles J. Mason after 1813. Mason, of Lane Delph, was given a patent for this improved earthenware. He usually called it *Mason's Patent Ironstone China*. It resisted chipping and breaking, so it became popular for dinnerwares and other table service dishes. Vases and other decorative pieces were also made. The ironstone was decorated with orange, blue, gold, and other colors, often in Japanese-inspired designs. The firm had financial difficulties, but the molds and the name *Mason* were used by many owners through the years, including Francis Morley, Taylor Ashworth, George L. Ashworth, and John Shaw. Mason's joined the Wedgwood group in 1973 and the name is still found on dinnerwares.

Bowl, Soup, Flowers, Scroll Border, Transfer, 19th Century, 10 ¼ In., Pair	60.00
Cruet, Pewter Lid, Imari, Pagodas, Blue, Orange, Marked, c.1880, 5 In. ....*illus*	117.00
Plate, Imari, Multicolored, c.1850, 9 In.	117.00
Platter, Willow, Blue & White, Transferware, c.1845, 23 ¼ x 18 ½ In.	388.00
Tureen, Cover, Flowers, Hand Painted, Gilt, Early 1800s, 13 In.	165.00
Tureen, Cover, Ladle, Plate, Red Transfer, Country Scene, 15 x 10 In. ....*illus*	230.00
Vase, Dragons, Blue, Yellow Ground, Gilt Trim, Mappin & Webb, 14 In.	250.00

MASSIER, a French art pottery, was made by brothers Jerome, Delphin, and Clement Massier in Vallauris and Golfe-Juan, France, in the late nineteenth and early twentieth centuries. It has an iridescent metallic luster glaze that resembles the Weller Sicardo pottery glaze. Most pieces are marked J. Massier. Massier may also be listed in the Majolica category.

J.Massier fils

Jardiniere, Butterflies, Footed, 9 ½ x 11 In.	1830.00
Jardiniere, Japanese Style, Lustered Glazes, Faceted, 4 Small Handles, 6 x 9 ½ In.	1080.00
Vase, Applied Vines, Wheat, Luster Ground, 4-Sided, Clement Massier, Golfe-Juan, 16 x 8 In. ...	3500.00
Vase, Butterflies, Iridescent Green, Blue, Peach, Luster, Marked, 7 In.	316.00
Vase, Face, Relief, Woman Handle, Red Metallic Glaze, Delphin Massier, 10 x 13 In.	2640.00
Vase, Faience, Blue Ground, Wisteria, Multicolored, Gilt, Signed, c.1890, 12 In. ....*illus*	405.00
Vase, Fairy, Irises, Cattails, Pastel Matte Glaze, Delphin Massier, Cie Vallaurius, 21 In.	2000.00
Vase, Iridescent Metallic Luster, 7 S-Shape Handles, Marked, 12 ⅜ In. ....*illus*	1725.00
Vase, Landscape Scene, Iridescent Metallic Glaze, Marked, 5 x 10 In.	1440.00
Vase, Luster, Iridescent, Metallic, Wheat Designs, Purple, Blue, Gold, 7 Handles, G. Juan, 12 In.	1725.00
Vase, Skirt Shape, Metallic Glaze, Etched Flowers, Iridescent, 7 x 9 In.	450.00
Vase, Wax-Like Drip, Iridescent Metallic Glaze, Signed, 6 ½ In.	920.00
Vase, Wheat, Iridescent Metallic Luster, 7 Handles, Signed, M. Clement Massier, 12 ⅜ In.	1650.00

MATCH HOLDERS were made to hold the large wooden matches that were used in the nineteenth and twentieth centuries for a variety of purposes. The kitchen stove and the fireplace or furnace had to be lit regularly. One type of match holder was made to hang on the wall, another was designed to be kept on a tabletop. Of special interest today are match holders that have advertisements as part of the design.

American Brewing Co., Striker, Engraved Shield, Eagle, 2 ¾ x 3 ½ In. ....*illus*	205.00
Bengal Furnaces, Bengal Tiger, Tin, H.D. Beach Co., Ohio, 3 ½ x 4 ¾ In.	468.00
Black Boy, Smiling, Minstrel, Bisque, 2 ¼ In.	73.00
Ceresota Flour, Kid Slicing Bread, Brown Pants, Barrel, 5 x 2 In.	250.00 to 321.00
Darling Mothers Worm Syrup, Grandma, 2 Children	715.00
DeLaval, Cream Separator, Die Cut, Tin Lithograph, Box, 6 ¼ x 4 In.	605.00
Dewar's White Label Scotch Whiskey, 1920s, 4 x 5 In.	110.00
Drummer Boy, Civil War Uniform, Die Cast, Cigar, Hinged Hat, 7 ½ In.	400.00
Dutch Boy Painter, Dutch Boy, Embossed, Die Cut, Tin Lithograph, 1915, 6 x 3 ½ In.	770.00

TIP

Don't soak old ceramic pieces in water for a long time. Old repairs may be loosened.

Elephant, Baby Mine, Basket On Back, Gold Trim, E.A.P.G., 3 ½ In.	118.00
Firkin, Playing Kittens, Ceramic, c.1895, 4 ½ In.	200.00
Flowers, Scrolls, Hanging, Hinged Lid, Cast Iron, 7 ½ In.	82.00
Gale Means Good, Factory, Gale Manufacturing Co., Tin, 3 ½ x 4 ¾ In. ....*illus*	263.00
Grapevines, Hanging, Cast Iron, Pat'd Mar. 12 1863, 5 ½ In.	57.00
Hunting Dog, Cast Iron, Hanging, Pat'd Mar. 12, 1863, 2 ½ x 4 In. ...	128.00
Indian, Ashtray, Striker, Cast Iron, Painted, 5 ½ x 4 ¼ In.	225.00
Lady Liberty, Columbia Flower, Die Cut, Tin, 1 ¼ x 2 ¼ x 5 ½ In. ....*illus*	293.00
Man's Head, Wide Grin, White Metal, Chicago Municipal Pier Plaque, 4 ½ x 3 In.	2970.00
Old Judson, Girl, Mom, Dad, Tin Lithograph, J.C. Stevens, 5 x 3 ½ In.	255.00
Royal Gall Remedy, Modern Surgical Treatment For Animals, Tin Lithograph, 6 x 3 x 3 In. ..	962.00
San Felice Cigars, For Gentlemen Of Good Taste, Metal, Celluloid Insert, 3 x 2 In.	143.00
Strike Anywhere, Tin, Heavy Gauge, Painted, c.1910, 6 x 3 ⅜ In. ...	165.00
Troubadour, Playing Mandolin, White Metal, 7 In.	110.00
Vulcan Plows, Blacksmith, Die Cut, Tin, 8 In.	495.00
Wild Hog, Brass Cups, Cast White Metal, c.1875, 4 ¼ In.	294.00
Woman, Arms Spread, Art Nouveau, 2 Brass Containers, Cast Iron, No. 3005, 6 x 8 In.	150.00

MATCH SAFES were designed to be carried in the pocket. Early matches were made with phosphorus and could ignite unexpectedly. The matches were safely stored in the tightly closed container. Match safes were made in sterling silver, plated silver, or other metals. The English call these "vesta boxes."

3 Dice In Window, Nickel Plated Brass, c.1920, 2 ¼ x 1 ¼ In.	145.00
3-Leaf Clover Inlay, Silver, Jade, 1 ¾ x 1 ½ In.	145.00
Anchor, Sterling Silver, Stamped F, Fairchild & Co., New York	236.00
Anheuser-Busch, Brass, Engraved, Logo, Pullman Palace Car, 3 In.	165.00
Beetle, Textured Surface, Sterling Silver, Gorham	118.00
Bowling Scene, Sterling, Hallmarks, F.S. Gilbert, Mass..............*illus*	118.00
Cat Holding Rat, Japan	206.00
Cherub, Sterling Silver, Stamped Hallmarks, Gorham, 1891	236.00
Cherubs, With Wishbone, Sterling Silver, Wm. B. Kerr & Co.	148.00
Coiled Rattlesnake, Sterling, Wm. B. Kerr & Co., N.J., c.1901 ....*illus*	1888.00
Columbus & 3 Ships, Sterling Silver, Stamped Hallmarks, R. Wallace & Sons	366.00
Cupid & Woman, Sterling Silver, Stamped Hallmarks, Gorham	177.00
Dancing Female Nudes, Scroll Border, Silver, c.1900, 2 ½ x 1 ⅝ In.	311.00
Devil's Face, Frame Of Crossed Branches, Cast Iron, 5 ½ In.	412.00
Domino Form, 5 & 3, Mother-Of-Pearl, Inscribed, Eugene, c.1890, 1 x 1 ¾ In.	300.00
Domino Form, 5 & 5, Celluloid, Inscribed, c.1930s, 1 ⅛ x 2 ¼ In.	200.00
Dr. Shoop's Lax-Ets, Only 3 Cents Per Box, Tin Lithograph, 3 x 5 In. ...	55.00
Dragon, Japan	236.00
Elephant, Lying Down, Figural, Brass, 1 ½ x 2 ½ In.	240.00
Elephant, Sterling Silver, Glass Eyes, c.1880	220.00
Engine Turned, Monogram, 9K Gold, Stamped Hallmarks, William Neale & Sons	236.00
Flowers, Scrolling, Embossed, Hinged Lid, Cast Iron, 7 In.	59.00
Flowers, Silver, 1 ¾ x 1 ¼ In.	165.00
Fox Shape, Gilt Silver, Glass Eyes, Hinged Lid, Vesta, 2 In.	580.00
Gold Dust Washing Powder, Black Twins, Logo, Metal, 3 x 1 ⅝ In.	469.00
Golfer, Sterling, Hallmark, Watrous Mfg. Co.,......................*illus*	266.00
Golfer, Woman, Sterling Silver, Monogram, 2 x 2 In. ....*illus*	165.00
Griffin, 14K Gold, Marked, K, 2 Stars, Joseph Seymour	1652.00
Hammered, Sterling Silver, Tiffany & Co., New York	236.00
Harvard Flag, Enameled, Sterling Silver, Marked 925	325.00
Heart, Spade, Diamond, Club, Enamel, Brass, c.1930s, 1 ⅛ x 1 ⅝ In. ...	85.00
Horse Hoof, Silver Plated Fittings, Marked, Royal Hussar, 1916-27, 3 In. ...	198.00
Horse, Rider, Jumping Fence, Sterling, Enamel ....*illus*	212.00
Horse, Standing, Enameled, Sterling Silver, Carter Howe.............	502.00
Horseshoe, Diamond & Ruby, 14K Gold, Marked	531.00
Hunt Scene, Embossed, Art Nouveau, Initials, 2 ½ In.	24.00
Indian Mask, Chased Repousse, Sterling, Gorham, c.1885, 2 ⅞ x 1 ¾ In. ...	956.00
Jack & Ace Of Hearts, Enamel, Sterling Silver, c.1890, 2 ¼ x 1 ¼ In. ...	1450.00
King & Ace Of Diamonds, Enamel, Sterling Silver, c.1890, 1 ¾ x 1 ¼ In. ...	1250.00
Man, Seated, Dog, Silver, Stamped Marks, Pairpoint Mfg. Co.	94.00
Mander Brothers, Founded By Charles Mander, Composition, Varnish, 1803, 1 ½ x 3 In.	30.00
Monkey, Figural, Smoking Pipe, Brass, Silver Plated, 3 In.	30.00
Monte-Carlo, Nice, France, Enamel, Silver, c.1890, 1 ¾ x 1 ¼ In.	275.00
Niello, Enameled Picture, Pont A Mousson, 1 ¾ In.	395.00

Massier, Vase, Iridescent Metallic Luster, 7 S-Shape Handles, Marked, 12 ⅜ In. $1725.00

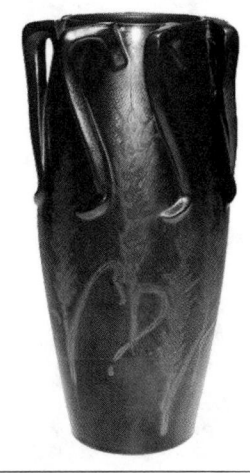

Match Holder, American Brewing Co., Striker, Engraved Shield, Eagle, 2 ¾ x 3 ½ In. $205.00

M

Match Holder, Gale Means Good, Factory, Gale Manufacturing Co., Tin, 3 ½ x 4 ¾ In. $263.00

Match Holder, Lady Liberty, **Columbia** Flower, Die Cut, Tin, 1¼ x 2¼ x 5½ In. $293.00

Match Safe, Bowling Scene, Sterling, Hallmarks, F.S. Gilbert, Mass. $118.00

Match Safe, Coiled Rattlesnake, Sterling, Wm. B. Kerr & Co., N.J., c.1901 $1888.00

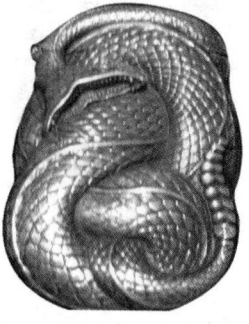

Oni Shape, Brass, Copper, Japan, 19th Century, 2 ½ x 1 ½ In.	1170.00
Owl, Brass, Glass Eyes, Gilt, c.1890, 2 ¾ In.	131.00
Owl, Figural, Brass, 2 ⅓ x 1 ⅛ In.	60.00
Owl, Flowers, Sterling Silver, Stamped Hallmarks, Simons Bro. & Co., Philadelphia	590.00
Pig, Figural, Copper, 2 In.	85.00
Playing Cards, Scorekeepers, Embossed, Silver, No. 075, R. Wallace & Sons, 1920s, 3 x 2 In.	350.00
Queen Of Hearts, Enamel, Brass, c.1890, 1 ⅝ x 1 In.	230.00
Queen Of Spades, Enamel, Brass, 1920s, 1 ¾ x 1 In.	350.00
Sailors, Brass, Engraved, Ships, Silver & Copper Inlay, F.W. Ward, 1862, 3 x 2 In.	800.00
Scroll & Flowers, Sterling Silver, Stamped Hallmarks, Webster Company	47.00
Scroll Design, Gold	177.00
Showgirl, Holding Fan, Sterling, Gorham, 1892, 2 ½ x 1 ⅝ In.	7170.00
Skull & Crossbones, Sterling, F.S. Gilbert, Mass. .... *illus*	472.00
Stag, New York No. 1, Sterling Silver, Battin & Co., New Jersey	118.00
Sword, Feather, Wreath, Copper & Silver, Gorham, 1883	319.00
Temptation Of St. Anthony, Sterling Silver, Wm. B. Kerr & Co., New Jersey	413.00
Tree Branch & Owl, Copper & Silver, Marked, Gorham.1886	307.00
Tree, Pheasant, Inlaid Mother-Of-Pearl, Gilt, Ivory, Shibayama, Japan, c.1800s, 2 ½ x 1 x ⅜ In.	450.00
Umbrella, 3 Inset Gem Stones, 14K Rose Gold, Stamped Hallmarks	319.00
Wave, Sterling Silver, Hallmarks, Gorham, R.I., c.1898 .... *illus*	295.00
Winged Foot, 14K Gold, Stamped Hallmark, Carter Howe	1180.00
Woman, Floral Setting, Sterling Silver, Battin & Co., Newark, N.J. .... *illus*	177.00
Woman, On Tiger Skin Rug, Sterling Silver, Gorham, 1908	200.00
Woman, Winged, Looking Over Cliff, Sterling Silver, Wm. B. Kerr & Co. .... *illus*	224.00
Woman, With Scarf, Portrait, Hinged, Sterling Silver	531.00

MATSU-NO-KE was a type of applied decoration for glass patented by Frederick Carder at Stevens & Williams of England in 1884. Carder started making Matsu-no-ke at Steuben in 1922.

Basket, Opalescent, Cherry Blossom, Twisted Applied Handle, 7 ½ x 3 ¾ In.	136.00
Bowl, Blue Aurene, Scalloped Rim, Branch, Handles, 13 In. .... *illus*	3335.00
Vase, Blue Cased, Footed, Rouleau Shape, Ruffled Amber Crest Rim, 9 ½ In.	66.00
Vase, Bulbous, Rolled Rim, Crimped Edges, White, Pink Cased, Fruit, Leaves, 9 ½ In.	180.00

MATT MORGAN, an English artist, was making pottery in Cincinnati, Ohio, by 1883. His pieces were decorated to resemble Moorish wares. Incised designs and colors were applied to raised panels on the pottery. Shiny or matte glazes were used. The company lasted less than two years.

Vase, Landscape, Mountains, Lake, Painted, Glazed, Oval, Signed, c.1884, 8 In. .... *illus*	800.00

McCOY pottery was made in Roseville, Ohio. Nelson McCoy and J.W. McCoy established the Nelson McCoy Sanitary and Stoneware Company in Roseville, Ohio, in 1910. The firm made art pottery after 1926. In 1933 it became the Nelson McCoy Pottery Company. Pieces marked McCoy were made by the Nelson McCoy Pottery Company. Cookie jars were made from about 1940 until December 1990, when the McCoy factory closed. Since 1991 pottery with the McCoy mark has been made by firms unrelated to the original company. Because there was a company named Brush-McCoy, there is great confusion between Brush and Nelson McCoy pieces. See Brush category for more information.

Bank, Eagle, Emigrant Industrial Savings, c.1960, 6 ½ In.	50.00
Basket, Leaves, Berries, Green, Brown, 9 ¼ x 7 In.	80.00
Bowl, Butterflies, Pink, c.1940s, 3 ¼ x 8 ½ In.	85.00
Bowl, Parading Elephants, Green, 3 x 8 In.	70.00
Caddy, Dog, Brush Tail, Blue, Black, White, For Swank, 9 In.	48.00
Cookie Jar, Chipmunk, Seated, Eating Nut, 10 ½ In.	82.00 to 135.00
Cookie Jar, Cookie Cabin, Marked, U.S.A., 7 In.	45.00 to 58.00
Cookie Jar, Indian, Feather Headdress, Made For Pontiac Motors, Marked, 11 In.	159.00
Cookie Jar, Kitten On Coal Bucket, 1983, 10 In.	130.00
Cookie Jar, Mammy, Cookies, Red Hat, Green Trim, Marked, 11 In.	24.00
Cookie Jar, Mammy, Red Hat, Yellow Dress, Marked, 9 In.	138.00
Cookie Jar, Owls, When Shadows Fall, 11 In.	69.00 to 76.00
Cookie Jar, Picnic Basket, 7 x 9 In.	85.00
Cookie Jar, Red Barn, Cow In Door, Marked, U.S.A., 10 In.	105.00
Cookie Jar, Squirrel, 1955, 11 ½ x 8 ¼ In.	165.00
Cookie Jar, Squirrel On Log, Holding Hammer, 1962, 10 ½ x 10 ¼ In.	75.00
Cookie Jar, Touring Car, Black, Cream, 11 In.	35.00
Flower Holder, Hands Of Friendship, Matte Aqua, 3 In.	85.00

M

McCOY

Match Safe, Golfer, Sterling, Hallmark, Watrous Mfg. Co., $266.00

Match Safe, Golfer, Woman, Sterling Silver, Monogram, 2 x 2 In. $165.00

Match Safe, Horse, Rider, Jumping Fence, Sterling, Enamel $212.00

Match Safe, Skull & Crossbones, Sterling, F.S. Gilbert, Mass. $472.00

Match Safe, Wave, Sterling Silver, Hallmarks, Gorham, R.I., c.1898 $295.00

Match Safe, Woman, Floral Setting, Sterling Silver, Battin & Co., Newark, N.J. $177.00

Match Safe, Woman, Winged, Looking Over Cliff, Sterling Silver, Wm. B. Kerr & Co. $224.00

Matsu-No-Ke, Bowl, Blue Aurene, Scalloped Rim, Branch, Handles, 13 In. $3335.00

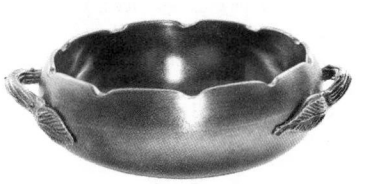

Matt Morgan, Vase, Landscape, Mountains, Lake, Painted, Glazed, Oval, Signed, c.1884, 8 In. $800.00

McCoy, Pitcher, Stoneware, Marked, 8 In. $35.00

McCoy, Tea Set, Brown Multitoned Matte Glaze, Teapot, Pitcher, Creamer, Sugar, Tray $120.00

McCoy, Wall Pocket, Rustic, 6 1/8 x 5 3/4 In. $18.00

M

McCOY

Medical, Invalid's Chair, 3 Slat Back, Rush Seat, Turned Finials, Iron Wheels, Georgia, 1800s
$374.00

Medical, Skull, Human, Clay-Adams Company, Fitted Black Case, Signed, H. Gumbert, 6 In.
$717.00

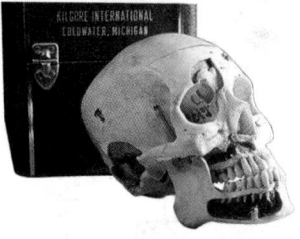

Jardiniere, Leaf & Berry, Matte White, 5 x 5 In.	55.00
Lamp, Green High Glaze, Ribbed Shade, 6 x 18 In.	324.00
Mixing Bowl, Rainbow, Burgundy Glazed, 7 In.	105.00
Pet Feeder, Yellow, Glass, 1950s, 6 ½ In.	45.00
Pitcher, Panel, Aqua, Gloss, 6 In.	55.00
Pitcher, Stoneware, Marked, 8 In. *illus*	35.00
Planter, Bird Dog, No Hunting, Marked, McCoy U.S.A., 8 ¼ x 12 ½ In.	79.00
Planter, Bookends, Bird Dog, Pheasant In Mouth, Fence, 8 ½ x 12 ½ In.	135.00
Planter, Lamb, Green, 1950s, 6 x 6 In.	45.00
Planter, Monkey Head, White Ground, Green Spectacles, Painted Eyes, Mouth, 6 ½ x 5 In.	95.00
Spoon Rest, Butterfly, Green & Yellow, 8 In.	95.00
Sprinkler, Turtle, 1950s, 5 ¼ x 10 In.	75.00
Tea Set, Brown Multitoned Matte Glaze, Teapot, Pitcher, Creamer, Sugar, Tray *illus*	120.00
Teapot, Aqua, Salada, 8 x 7 In.	50.00
Teapot, Leaves & Berries, Deep Yellow, Gloss, 1935	145.00
Vase, Bird & Cherry, Lime Green, 8 In.	55.00
Vase, Birds, Green, Footed, 8 ¼ In.	75.00
Vase, Blossoms, Cream Ground, Square, Flared Top, 7 ¾ In.	75.00
Vase, Burgundy, Gloss, 10 In.	105.00
Vase, Butterflies, Cylindrical, Pink, c.1940, 6 ¼ In.	70.00
Vase, Butterfly, Matte Aqua, 6 x 7 In.	100.00
Vase, Floraline Romanesque Swirl, Flared, Footed, 8 ¼ In.	65.00
Vase, Green Leaves With White & Pink Tulips, Wide Mouth, Marked Loy-Nel-Art, 8 In.	80.00
Vase, Leaf & Berry, Cobalt, Red Berries, 8 In.	110.00
Vase, Peacock, Aqua, Gloss, 8 In.	60.00
Vase, Red Berries, Green Leaves, Matte Yellow, 8 In.	120.00
Vase, Twist-Handle, Matte Green, 10 In.	145.00
Vase, Zig Zag, Aqua, Gloss	175.00
Wall Pocket, 3 Owls, Cutout Geometric Ground, 8 ½ x 6 ¼ In.	70.00
Wall Pocket, Bellows, Yellow, Brown, 1956, 9 ½ x 4 ¼ In.	70.00
Wall Pocket, Grape Cluster, Leaves, 7 ¼ x 6 ¼ In.	135.00
Wall Pocket, Lily, White, 7 ½ In.	90.00
Wall Pocket, Rustic, 6 ⅛ x 5 ¾ In. *illus*	18.00
Wall Pocket, Umbrella, Yellow & Green, 6 x 9 In.	70.00

McKEE is a name associated with various glass enterprises in the United States since 1836, including J. & F. McKee (1850), Bryce, McKee & Co. (1850 to 1854), McKee and Brothers (1865), and National Glass Co. (1899). In 1903, the McKee Glass Company was formed in Jeannette, Pennsylvania. It became McKee Division of the Thatcher Glass Co. in 1951 and was bought out by the Jeannette Corporation in 1961. Pressed glass, kitchenwares, and tablewares were produced. Jeannette Corporation closed in the early 1980s. Additional pieces may be included in the Custard Glass and Depression Glass categories.

Bowl, Five Flute, Chocolate, c.1925, 2 x 9 ¼ In.	66.00
Bowl, Six Flute, Chocolate, c.1900, 2 x 10 In.	39.00
Butter, Cover, Geneva, c.1900, 5 ¼ In.	159.00
Butter, Cover, Wild Rose & Bowknot, Chocolate, c.1900, 4 ¾ x 7 ½ In.	92.00
Canister, Cover, Cereal, Seville Yellow, Opaque	155.00
Creamer, Laurel, Ivory, Red Trim, Child's, 2 ½ In.	60.00
Cruet, Wild Rose & Bowknot, Chocolate, 7 In.	259.00
Goblet, Rock Crystal, Ruby, 8 Oz., 6 ½ In., 6 Piece	210.00
Nappy, Masonic, Amber Stain, Buttons, c.1875, 2 ¼ x 5 x 7 In.	26.00
Nappy, Navarre, Chocolate, c.1900, 1 ¾ x 5 In.	66.00
Plate, Bread & Butter, Rock, 1920s, 6 In.	6.00
Plate, Laurel, Scottie Dog, Jade Green, 5 ¾ In.	50.00
Smoking Set, 2 Removable Cups, Striker, Molded, Reeded Tray, c.1910, 3 ½ x 4 ¾ In.	690.00
Sugar, Laurel, Jade Green, Child's, 2 ¼ In.	70.00
Syrup, Geneva, Chocolate, 6 In.	690.00
Syrup, Sunbeam, Green, Lid, c.1875, 4 ¼ In.	264.00
Tumbler, Bottoms-Up, Custard Glass, Marked, 77725, 3 ¼ In.	70.00

MEDICAL office furniture, operating tools, microscopes, thermometers, and other paraphernalia used by doctors are included in this category. Veterinary collectibles are also included here. Medicine bottles are listed in the Bottle category. There are related collectibles listed under Dental.

Amputation Kit, 2 Saws, 3 Knives, Bistouries, Tourniquet, Autenreith, Case, 1800s, 17 In.	800.00

Apothecary Case, Mahogany, Fitted, Drawer, 16 Bottles, Supplies, Tools, Kit, c.1830, 9 x 11 In.	1160.00
Bleeder, Spring Loaded, 16 Blades	325.00
Bleeding Bowl, Pewter, Fleur-De-Lis Handle, Hallmark, France, 17th Century, 5 In.	395.00
Cabinet, Apothecary, 15 Drawers, Blue Paint, c.1890, 29 x 17 In.	473.00
Cabinet, Apothecary, 20 Drawers, White Paint	50.00
Cabinet, Apothecary, 35 Drawers, Open Grid Doors, Sides, Lacquered, 73 x 37 x 19 In.	690.00
Cabinet, Apothecary, 42 Drawers, Divided Interiors, Metal Pulls, Chinese, 46 x 33 ½ x 18 In.	374.00
Cabinet, Apothecary, 48 Drawers, Divided Interiors, Labels, Chinese, 1900s, 65 x 39 x 25 In.	575.00
Cabinet, Apothecary, Chestnut, 13 Drawers, 2 Doors, Alligatored, 21 x 21 In.	382.00
Cabinet, Apothecary, Countertop, 11 Drawers, Stenciled, England, 1800s, 19 x 18 In.	413.00
Cabinet, Apothecary, Oak, Carved, Arched Glass Doors, c.1790, 57 x 95 In.	3525.00
Cabinet, Apothecary, Pine, Beaded Edge, Dovetailed Drawers, Painted, c.1800, 36 x 45 In.	16450.00
Cabinet, Apothecary, Pine, Original Patina, c.1900, 17 x 43 In.	646.00
Cabinet, Apothecary, Pine, Poplar, Worn Green Paint, c.1890, 28 x 49 In.	764.00
Cabinet, Apothecary, Pine, Red Paint, Grain Painted, c.1840, 41 x 51 In.	558.00
Cabinet, Apothecary, Pine, Red Smoke Paint, Shelves, 50 Drawers, 1840, 72 x 44 In.	15000.00
Cabinet, Apothecary, Poplar, 143 Drawers, Black Knobs, Painted, c.1860, 58 x 83 In.	1528.00
Cabinet, Apothecary, Wood, 4 Drawers, Wood Knobs, Brass Name Plates, Mid 1800s, 16 x 17 In.	1050.00
Cabinet, Apothecary, Wood, 29 Drawers, 28 ½ x 21 x 8 ½ In.	240.00
Cabinet, Apothecary, Wood, 36 Drawers, Blue Paint, 27 x 41 x 13 In.	550.00
Cabinet, Apothecary, Wood, 45 Drawers, 21 x 31 x 7 In.	495.00
Chest, 20 Drawers, Lettering, Paint, New England, 1800s, 57 x 52 In.	859.00
Chest, Apothecary, Grain Painted, Inscribed Anna Carrie Reiley, c.1861, 13 x 6 ½ In.	750.00
Chest, Apothecary, Mahogany, 26 x 24 ¼ x 9 ¼ In.	425.00
Chest, Apothecary, Marble Top, 29 Small Drawers, 28 x 21 x 9 In.	236.00
Chest, Apothecary, Poplar, 9 Drawers, Grain Painted, c.1890, 11 x 24 In.	764.00
Chest, Pharmacy, Traveling, Mahogany, Hinged Lid, Drawer, 19th Century, 10 ½ In.	610.00
Coagulator, Mahogany, Max Wocher & Son Co.	150.00
Cupping Glass, Blown In Mold, Rolled Rim, 19th Century, 2 In.	22.00
Eye Surgeon's Kit, Leather Embossed Case, 30 Instruments, Ivory Handles, 1800s, 8 ½ x 7 In.	1116.00
Field Surgeon's Kit, Mahogany, Brass Mounts, 3 Tier Case, Instruments, c.1864, 4 x 16 In.	1440.00
Fleam, Metal, 3 Blades, Horn Handle, Marked, Butler, 5 ½ In.	250.00
Hearing Horn, Curved, Wood, 3 ¾ x 10 In.	236.00
Invalid's Chair, 3 Slat Back, Rush Seat, Turned Finials, Iron Wheels, Georgia, 1800s...... *illus*	374.00
Lancet, Bone Handle, Heart & Pistol Trademark, Jonathan Crookes	111.00
Lancet, Spring-Loaded, Brass, Engraved, D. Schierman, Cherry Wood Case, 4 In.	1995.00
Machine, Magneto-Electic, Nervous Diseases, Hinged Wood Box, Directions, Mass., 10 x 5 In.	121.00
Machine, Suppository, Archibald's, Cast Iron, Gold Paint, Stencil, Patent April, 1879, 7 x 5 In.	358.00
Medicine Spoon, Sterling Silver, Blackinton, c.1900, 6 ½ In.	110.00
Microscope, Brass, Adjustable, Accessories, Eyepieces, Slides, Mounting, France, 11 ¼ In.	805.00
Microscope, Brass, Adjustors, Lock & Key, Mahogany Case, Eyepieces, Bausch & Lomb	460.00
Model, Optometrist, Display, Male Head, Molded Zinc, Curly Hair, Stand, c.1900, 14 ½ In.	2489.00
Mortar & Pestle, Burl, Turned, 19th Century, 8 ½ In.	345.00
Mortar & Pestle, Cast Iron, Late 18th Century, 6 x 5 ¾ In.	40.00
Mortar & Pestle, Turned Maple, 1836, 5 ½ In.	360.00
Mortar & Pestle, Wreaths, Eagles, Bronze, Inscribed, Napoleon Empereur, 1802, 6 ¾ x 6 In.	480.00
Mouth Gag, Metal, Ivory Tipped, Marked, A. Broz. Graz.	200.00
Optometrist Kit, Lenses, Test Frames, Drawer, Oak, Hinged Lid, 6 ¼ x 21 x 13 In.	100.00
Optometrist Set, Glasses, Lenses, Marked, Natchet & Fils, Paris, Leather Box, c.1890, 12 x 19 In.	175.00
Phrenology Head, Porcelain, L.N. Fowler, London, 11 ½ In.	44.00
Phrenology Head, White, Earthenware, Marked, R.F. Freda, London, 11 ½ x 5 ½ In.	200.00
Phrenology Head, Wood Carving, Painted, Reverse Painted Glass Eyes, Late 1800s, 10 In.	2350.00
Pill Maker Mold, Hard Rubber, Tablet Triturate, 6 ¼ x 2 ½ In.	90.00
Pill Roller Machine, Walnut, Brass, Apothecary Pharmacy, 1800s, 16-In. Paddle, 12 x 7 ¼ In.	270.00
Pleximeter, Ivory, Hinged, Folding, 3 ½ In.	450.00
Skull, Human, Clay-Adams Company, Fitted Black Case, Signed, H. Gumbert, 6 In. .... *illus*	717.00
Sphygmometer, Marked, Down Bros., London, Late 19th Century	200.00
Splint, Walnut, Brass Screws, Hinged Knee, Handmade, 19th Century	25.00
Surgeon's Saw, Ebony Handle, Engraved, Schmidt, Newer Blade, c.1850, 14 In.	143.00
Surgical Kit, Chrome Case, Leather Suede, Pocket Book Style Case, c.1900, 6 x 3 ½ In.	450.00
Syringe, McElroy's, Gonorrhea, Male Urethral, Self-Injection, c.1872, 5 ¼ In.	195.00
Trephine, Brass, Ebony Handle, 19th Century, 4 ¾ In.	125.00
Vampire Killing Kit, Oak, Fitted Green Interior, Cross, Stake, Vials, Pistol, Box, 1900, 3 x 7 In.	999.00
Wallet, Leather, 45 3 ¼-In. Vials, Boericke & Tafel Pharmacists, 10 ½ x 4 In.	15.00
Wheelchair, Wicker, Wood Footrest, 3-Metal Wheels, 19th Century	515.00

Meissen, Figurine, Bird, Gold, Black, White Wings, Crossed Swords, c.1900, 12 ½ In.
$978.00

Meissen, Figurine, Woman, Holding Book, Gilt Highlights, Mark, c.1900, 10 In.
$282.00

M

TIP
Take off your rings and bracelets before you start to wash figurines or dishes.

Meissen, Figurine, Woman,
Selling Vegetables, Blue Underglaze,
Crossed Swords, c.1900, 5 ½ In.
$527.00

MEISSEN is a town in Germany where porcelain has been made since 1710. Any china made in the town can be called Meissen, although the famous Meissen factory made the finest porcelains of the area. The crossed swords mark of the great Meissen factory has been copied by many other firms in Germany and other parts of the world. Pieces of Meissen dinnerware in the Onion pattern are listed in their own category in this book.

Basket, Fruit, Applied Flower Handles, Blue Underglaze, 9 In., Pair	236.00
Basket, Pierced, Tree Base, Putti, Applied Flowers, Gilt, Marked, c.1910, 11 In.	260.00
Bottle, Barber, Porcelain, Cover, Baluster, Flower Spray, Paint, Gilt, c.1900, 13 In.	267.00
Bowl, 3 Shell-Form Sections, Trefoil, Blue & White, Handle, 12 x 13 In.	148.00
Bowl, Black, Gold, White, Large Center Flower, Smaller Flower Border, c.1910, 11 In.	322.00
Bowl, Fruit, Flower Bloom, Bas Relief, Gilt, 1875, 10 ¾ In., Pair	480.00
Bowl, Gilt Flowers, 11 In., Pair	345.00
Breadboard, Stylized Vine & Flowers, Open Handles, 6 x 10 In.	95.00
Cake Plate, Indian Pattern, Purple, Gold Trim, Tapered Stem, Round Foot, 4 x 13 In.	385.00
Candelabrum, 4-Light, Bud Shape Nozzles, Leaf Bobeche, Scroll Base, 1910s, 22 x 10 In., Pair	2318.00
Candelabrum, 4-Light, Flowers, Nymphs, Holding Sickle, Wheat, Rococo Style, Germany, 19 ¾ In.	1422.00
Candelabrum, 4-Light, Nymphs, Applied, Flowers, Vines, Gilt Leaves, Germany, 1800s, 19 ½ In.	1304.00
Candlestick, Figural, Man, Child, Standing Near Grapevine, 11 In.	300.00
Candlestick, Putti Holding Cornucopia, Rococo Base, 19th Century, 15 ½ In.	2300.00
Charger, Chrysanthemum Center, Flower Sprays, Gilt Rim, Blue Crossed Swords, 15 In.	120.00
Charger, Flowers, 13 ½ In.	499.00
Clock, Figural, Neptune, Bird, Flowers, Nude Figures, 29 x 12 In.	3900.00
Compote, 2 Tier, Pierced, Flowers, Figural Boy With Wreath, 15 x 11 In.	805.00
Compote, Man In Boat, Crashing Waves, Mermaids, Openwork Bowl, 28 In.	2318.00
Cup & Saucer, Demitasse, Pink Dragon, c.1910, 12 Piece	176.00
Cup & Saucer, Swan Service, Enameled Swans, Crane, Grasses	593.00
Dish, Allover Molded Flower, White, Scalloped Edge, 11 In.	71.00
Dish, Leaf Shape, Flowers, 6 ¼ x 7 ¼ In.	499.00
Dish, Leaves, Flowers, Enamel Spray, Pierced Handles, Crossed Swords Mark, 13 ¾ In.	444.00
Ewer, Birds In Flight, Juno & Zephyr, Putto, Gilt, 25 ½ In.	12547.00
Figurine, Bird, Gold, Black, White Wings, Crossed Swords, c.1900, 12 ½ In. ....*illus*	978.00
Figurine, Birds, On Branches, Flowers, Leaves, 8 ¼ x 9 In., Pair	478.00
Figurine, Boy, Holding Fish, Basket, Blue Crossed Swords Mark, 4 x 5 In.	550.00
Figurine, Boy, Holding Flower, Basket, Blue Crossed Swords Mark, 5 ½ In.	320.00
Figurine, Boy, Throwing Snowballs, Striped Pants, Green Jacket, 5 ½ In.	354.00
Figurine, Bulldog, White, Black, 3 In.	415.00
Figurine, Cherub, Blacksmith, Multicolored, Crossed Swords Mark, 1800s, 7 In.	690.00
Figurine, Cinderella, Seated, At Furnace, Crossed Swords Mark, 7 In.	2440.00
Figurine, Cupid, 2 Hearts, Blue Crossed Swords Mark, 7 ¼ In.	805.00
Figurine, Cupid, Against Tree Stump, Pink, Rose Garland, c.1900, 7 ¼ In.	597.00
Figurine, Cupid, Boy With Bird, Girl & Basket, Blue Crossed Swords, c.1850, 11 ½ In., Pair	5040.00
Figurine, Cupid, Dressed As Girl, Blue Crossed Swords Mark, 8 ¾ In.	1000.00
Figurine, Cupid, Gilt Bow, Quiver, Marble Base, Blue Crossed Swords Mark, 7 ½ In.	1000.00
Figurine, Cupid, Holding Pierced Heart, Marble Base, Blue Crossed Swords Mark, 8 In.	1100.00
Figurine, Cupid, Mending Broken Heart, Blue Crossed Swords Mark, 6 ¾ In.	1095.00
Figurine, Cupid, Nest Of Flaming Hearts, Inscribed, Blue Crossed Swords, 1800s, 5 In.	780.00
Figurine, Dog, Pug, Puppy, White, Black Markings, Blue, Gold Collar, c.1900, 6 ½ In.	1053.00
Figurine, Dog, Pug, Seated, Black, Tan, 6 ½ x 7 ¼ In.	540.00
Figurine, Gentleman Gardener, Rococo Base, c.1875, 19 ¼ In.	1955.00
Figurine, Girl, Holding Doll, Bird, Blue Crossed Swords Mark, 5 ¾ In.	840.00
Figurine, Girl, Wings, Gown, Pink, Green, Gilt, Crossed Swords Mark, 3 ½ In.	375.00
Figurine, Girl, With Tambourine, 5 In.	1135.00
Figurine, Goat, Straddling Basket Of Flowers, Oval Base, 5 ¾ In.	1116.00
Figurine, Goddess Demeter, Sheaf Of Wheat, Gilt, Blue Crossed Swords Mark, 8 In.	890.00
Figurine, Putto, Holding Broken Heart, Quiver, Arrows, Gilt, Crossed Swords Mark, 1890s, 8 In.	950.00
Figurine, Putto, Holding Masquerade Mask, Crossed Swords Mark, Late 1800s, 7 ¾ In.	550.00
Figurine, Victorian Woman, Flowered Dress, Pug Dogs, Marked, 7 x 11 In.	3220.00
Figurine, Woman, Card Player, Blue Crossed Swords Mark, 6 ¼ x 2 ¾ In.	1300.00
Figurine, Woman, Classically Dressed, Star Globe, Holding Telescope, 17 In.	2700.00
Figurine, Woman, Holding Book, Gilt Highlights, Mark, c.1900, 10 In. ....*illus*	282.00
Figurine, Woman, Holding Book, Muff, Lacework Trim, 19th Century, 7 ¾ In.	1067.00
Figurine, Woman, Holding Flower Basket, 6 x 3 In.	384.00
Figurine, Woman, Playing Harpsichord, Blue Crossed Swords Mark, 5 x 3 ½ In.	1300.00
Figurine, Woman, Selling Vegetables, Blue Underglaze, Crossed Swords, c.1900, 5 ½ In. .*illus*	527.00
Group, 2 Putti, Cannon, Gilt, G39, Blue Crossed Swords Mark, 4 ¾ x 5 x 3 In.	1600.00
Group, 4 Bacchanalian Infants, Goat, Blue Crossed Swords, Incised, c.1910, 6 ½ In.	840.00

Meissen, Group, Boy & Woman,
Gathering Bird's Eggs, Late 1800s, 7 ¾ In.
$1016.00

Group, 4 Children Dancing, Blue Crossed Swords Mark, 6 x 6 ¾ In.	1860.00
Group, Bacchus, Holding Chalice & Scepter, Maiden, Fawn, Cupid, Crossed Swords, 12 In.	2200.00
Group, Bacchus, Women With Instruments, 11 x 14 ½ In.	4888.00
Group, Boy & Girl, Grape Basket, Knapsack, Mark, Crossed Swords, c.1900, 4 In., Pair	1838.00
Group, Boy & Woman, Gathering Bird's Eggs, Late 1800s, 7 ¾ In. ....*illus*	1016.00
Group, Capture Of The Tritons, 2 Young Women, Putti, Aquatic, Blue Crossed Swords, 11 ¾ In.	2400.00
Group, Couple, In An Arbor, J. Kandler, 18th Century, 9 x 7 x 6 In.	791.00
Group, Courting Couple, Chair, Marble Base, Blue Crossed Swords, 8 ½ In.	1900.00
Group, Dancing Couple, Blue Crossed Swords, 1800s, 5 ¾ In.	1560.00
Group, Geese, Lady Holding Basket With Fish, J. Kandler, 18th Century, 6 x 6 In.	847.00
Group, Girl, Seated At Table, Flower Basket, 19th Century, 5 ½ x 4 In.	2415.00
Group, Maiden, Playing Mandolin, Dancing Cherubs, 19th Century, 7 ½ In.	1495.00
Group, Man & Woman, Oriental Style, Instruments, Multicolored, 7 ½ x 4 ½ In., Pair	1348.00
Group, Man, Reading, On Rocky Base, Dog, c.1900, 8 ½ In.	777.00
Group, Musicians, Putti, Rocks, Romantic, Blue Crossed Swords, 1800s, 14 ½ In.	4800.00
Group, Parcae, Chronos Assisting 3 Nudes, Orange Mark, 15 x 15 ½ x 6 In.	8900.00
Group, Peasant Boy & Girl, Gilt, Crossed Swords, c.1930, 6 x 5 In. ....*illus*	441.00
Group, Renaissance Cherubs, House, Multicolored, Gilt Decorated, Rococo Base, 4 ¾ In.	1175.00
Group, Silenus, On A Donkey, Porcelain, Painted, 8 ½ x 8 ½ In.	1989.00
Group, Venus, In Chariot, Cherub, Doves, Blue Crossed Swords Mark, 7 x 7 In.	1900.00
Group, Woman, Crown On Hand, Scepter, Child At Feet, Crossed Swords Mark, 1750, 6 In.	2100.00
Group, Woman, In Sedan Chair, Pug Dog, 2 Attendants, 4 ½ In.	3450.00
Jar, Lid, Flowers, Scrolls, Painted, Rococo, Gilt, Marked, c.1905, 7 In.	384.00
Jug, Bear, Seated, Holding Banner, c.1900, 10 ¼ In.	1150.00
Nodder, Pagoda, Hands & Head Move, Tongue Goes In & Out, 7 ¾ x 8 ½ In.	4100.00
Potpourri, Ormolu, Horse Drawn Chariot, Infants, Blooms, c.1800s.14 ½ x 16 ¾ In.	9200.00
Server, Shell Shape, Man With Pot, Woman Cooking, c.1800, 9 ¾ In., Pair	1314.00
Server, Woman, Holding Basket Top, Openwork Borders, Flowers, 3 Tiers, Mark, 21 In.	633.00
Sweetmeat, Woman, Reclining Over Scalloped Dish, Plinth, c.1875, 7 ¼ x 12 In.	460.00
Teapot, Angular Handle, Gilt Clover, Wreath, Leaf Finial, Forget-Me-Nots, 4 ¾ x 4 In. ...... *illus*	127.00
Teapot, Flowers, Multicolored, Gilt, Marcolini, c.1790, 4 ½ In.	240.00
Teapot, Red & Yellow Flower, Bluebells, Green Leaves, Silver Spout, 18th Century	350.00
Tureen, Basket Weave, Cartouches, Pierced & Reticulated Lid, Strawberry Finial, Spoon.........	358.00
Tureen, Cover, Spoon, Blue Flowers, Shell Handles, 8 ½ In.	148.00
Tureen, Cover, Underplate, Blue & White, Leafy Handles, Twisted Finial, 9 In.	83.00
Tureen, Flowers, White Ground, Woman Finial, 10 ½ x 13 In.	410.00
Urn, 2 Putti, Holding Floral Garlands, Pale Green Ground, Flower, Swirls, c.1920, 18 In., Pair.	374.00
Urn, Cobalt Blue, Serpent Handles, c.1900, 11 In.	460.00
Urn, Flared Lip, Scroll Handles, Gilt Campagna, c.1850, 10 ½ In., Pair	11054.00
Urn, Flowers, Gold Trim, Pedestal Foot, Twisted Snake Handles, 11 In., Pair	413.00
Urn, Lid, Harlequin, Cobalt Blue, Oval, Wreath Finial, Flowers, Snake Handle, c.1890, 11 In., Pair	3081.00
Urn, Lovers In Garden, Cobalt Ground, Snake Handles, 14 In.	518.00
Urn, Putti, Cobalt Blue, White Enameled, Figural Handles, Gilt, Crossed Swords, 6 In.	1121.00
Urn, Wreaths, Forest, Flowers, Ormolu, White, Gilt, Multicolored, c.1890, 18 In., Pair..............	1495.00
Vase, Beaker Shape, Flowers, White Ground, Gold Base, Interior, 5 In., Pair	234.00
Vase, Flowers, Asian Design, Hand Painted, Footed, Marked, c.1905, 5 In.	41.00
Vase, Garden Scene, Baluster, Gilt, Cherubs, Domed Cover, 3-Footed, 35 In.	10925.00
Vase, Snake Handles, Blue Underglaze, Pommeled Swords, Marked, 11 In.	472.00
Vase, Yellow, Couple, Playing Game, Double Snake Handle, 11 In.	1126.00

Meissen, Group, Peasant Boy & Girl, Gilt, Crossed Swords, c.1930, 6 x 5 In. $441.00

Meissen, Teapot, Angular Handle, Gilt Clover, Wreath, Leaf Finial, Forget-Me-Nots, 4 ¾ x 4 In. $127.00

M

Invest in Collectibles
If you invest in collectibles, remember the rules. Buy the best you can, buy perfect items, and care for them so they remain perfect. Provenance (written history) adds to value; so does a signature. Try to spot the trends influenced by news events, such as the death of a celebrity.

MERCURY GLASS, or silvered glass, was first made in the 1850s. It lost favor for a while but became popular again about 1910. It looks like a piece of silver.

Bowl, Grape Bunches, Vines, Leaves, Footed, 1800s, 3 ¾ x 4 ¾ x 3 ½ In.	65.00
Bowl, Hand Blown, 5 ¼ x 11 ¼ In.	60.00
Candlestick, 12 ½ x 5 ½ In.	95.00
Show Globe, Bulbous Stem, Footed, 2-Part, Late 19th Century, 11 In.	115.00
Show Globe, Lobed Stem, 1-Part Design, Footed, Late 1800s, 11 In.	115.00
Vase, Flowers, Hand Painted, Baluster Shape, Footed, 10 ⅛ In., Pair................	130.00
Vase, Victorian, Urn Form, Swirled Base, Footed, 11 ⅜ In.	130.00

MERRIMAC POTTERY Company was founded by Thomas Nickerson in Newburyport, Massachusetts, in 1902. The company made art pottery, garden pottery, and reproductions of Roman pottery. The pottery burned to the ground in 1908.

Vase, Bulbous, Raised Plant Pattern, Matte Green Glaze, Mark, Paper Label, 4 In.	3680.00
Vase, Cylindrical, Mottled Green Drip Glaze, Paper Label, 6 x 7 ½ In.	450.00

Metlox, Colorstax, Corn Holder,
Terra Cotta, 11 ¼ x 3 ½ In.
$15.00

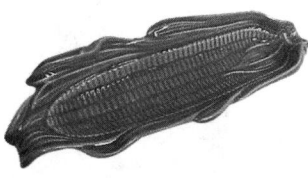

Metlox, Homestead Provincial,
Platter, 10 In.
$39.00

Metlox, Poppet, Colleen, 4 In.
$42.00

Vase, Gourd, Blue Crackle Glaze, 8 In.		3565.00
Vase, Green Matte Glaze, Lobed Opening, Stamped, Merrimac With Fish, 4 ½ x 4 In.		285.00
Vase, Oval, Frothy Yellow Matte Glaze, Stamped, Merrimac With Fish, 9 ½ x 4 ¾ In.		3200.00
Vase, Purple & Gray Crackle Luster Glaze, Marked, 5 In.		1200.00
Vase, Red Clay, Purple, Gray Luster Crackle Glaze, Marked, Paper Label, 5 In.		1150.00

METLOX POTTERIES was founded in 1927 in Manhattan Beach, California. Dinnerware was made beginning in 1931. Evan K. Shaw purchased the company in 1946 and expanded the number of patterns. Poppytrail (1946-1989) and Vernonware (1958-1980) were divisions of Metlox under E.K. Shaw's direction. The factory closed in 1989.

Autumn Berry, Creamer, 5 In.		14.00
Autumn Berry, Cup & Saucer		12.00
Autumn Berry, Plate, Dinner, 10 ¾ In.		11.00
Butterscotch, Butter, Cover, Round		24.00
Butterscotch, Plate, Dinner, 10 ⅝ In.		21.00
Butterscotch, Sugar, Cover		18.00
California Aztec, Creamer		15.00
California Aztec, Plate, Bread & Butter, 6 ½ In.		8.00
California Strawberry, Bowl, Fruit, 5 ½ In.		6.00
Colonial Heritage, Plate, Bread & Butter, 6 ⅜ In.		7.00
Colonial Heritage, Plate, Salad, 7 ½ In.		8.00
Colonial Heritage, Soup, Dish		10.00
Colorstax, Bowl, Cereal, Midnight Blue, 6 ⅜ In.		15.00
Colorstax, Corn Holder, Terra Cotta, 11 ¼ x 3 ½ In.	*illus*	15.00
Colorstax, Plate, Dinner, Lilac, 10 ¾ In.		12.00
Colorstax, Plate, Dinner, Plum, 10 ¾ In.		22.00
Colorstax, Plate, Salad, Jade, 7 ¾ In.		8.00
Cookie Jar, Cat, Yellow Hat, Bow, Noisemaker In Lid, Metlox Label		35.00
Cookie Jar, Clown, Yellow, Red, Green, 2 Labels, 13 In.		68.00
Del Rey, Bowl, Cereal, 6 ⅞ In.		14.00
Del Rey, Butter, Cover		65.00
Gold Dahlia, Saucer		3.00
Homestead Provincial, Creamer, 3 ¼ In.		12.00
Homestead Provincial, Plate, Bread & Butter, 6 ⅜ In.		6.00
Homestead Provincial, Platter, 10 In.	*illus*	39.00
Homestead Provincial, Sugar, Cover		7.00
La Mancha, Bowl, Cereal, Green, 6 ⅜ In.		10.00
La Mancha, Cup & Saucer, Gold		10.00
La Mancha, Plate, Bread & Butter, Gold, 6 ¾ In.		5.00
La Mancha, Plate, Dinner, Gold, 10 ¾ In.		15.00
La Mancha, Plate, Dinner, Green, 10 ¾ In.		13.00
La Mancha, Plate, Salad, Green, 8 ½ In.		8.00
Navajo, Plate, Dinner, 10 ½ In.		15.00
Navajo, Platter, 14 ¼ In.		36.00
Navajo, Soup, Dish, 8 In.		12.00
Pepper Tree, Compote, Divided		35.00
Pepper Tree, Cup & Saucer		10.00
Pepper Tree, Plate, Salad, 7 ½ In.		8.00
Pepper Tree, Platter, 15 In.		30.00
Poppet, Colleen, 4 In.	*illus*	42.00
Poppy Trail, Canister Set, Farm Scene, 4 Piece		45.00
Poppy Trail, Sugar & Creamer, Cover		42.00
Provincial Blue, Cup & Saucer		10.50
Provincial Blue, Plate, Bread & Butter, 6 ⅜ In.		5.00
Provincial Blue, Plate, Dinner, 10 In.		16.00
Provincial Blue, Soup, Dish, Rim, 8 ½ In.		15.00
Provincial Flower, Gravy Boat		40.00
Provincial Flower, Plate, Dinner, 10 ½ In.		18.00
Provincial Flower, Sugar, Cover		25.00
Provincial Fruit, Bowl, Fruit, 6 ¼ In.		5.00
Provincial Fruit, Bowl, Vegetable, Divided, 8 ⅝ In.		25.00
Provincial Fruit, Creamer		12.00
Provincial Fruit, Plate, Dinner, 10 ½ In.		12.00
Provincial Fruit, Salt & Pepper		15.00
Provincial Fruit, Sugar, Cover		15.00
Red Rooster, Plate, Bread & Butter, 6 ⅜ In.		6.00

Red Rooster, Plate, Dinner, 10 In.	17.00
Red Rooster, Sugar & Creamer.	28.00
Sculptured Daisy, Bowl, Cover, 6 In.	45.00
Sculptured Daisy, Plate, Bread & Butter, 6 ¼ In.	5.00
Shoreline, Bowl, Vegetable, Wet Sand, 9 In.	25.00
Shoreline, Cup & Saucer, Horizon Blue	17.00
Shoreline, Gravy Boat, Wet Sand	42.00
Springtime, Creamer.	16.00
Street Scene, Plate, Dinner, 10 ⅜ In.	16.00
Vintage Pink, Creamer.	12.00
Vintage Pink, Cup & Saucer	10.00
Vintage Pink, Plate, Dinner, 10 ½ In.	16.00
Wild Poppy, Cup & Saucer	11.00
Woodland Gold, Plate, Bread & Butter, 6 ⅜ In.	5.00

METTLACH, Germany, is a city where the Villeroy and Boch factories worked. Steins from the firm are marked with the word *Mettlach* or the castle mark. They date from about 1842. *PUG* means painted under glaze. The steins can be dated from the marks on the bottom, which include a date-number code. Other pieces may be listed in the Villeroy & Boch category.

Bowl, No. 3077, Secessionist, 4-Footed, 4 ½ x 11 In.	153.00
Cake Plate, No. 2601, Cameo, 5 ½ x 11 In.	460.00
Candleholder, Match Holder, Girl, Leaning On Tree Stump, 6 In. ....*illus*	207.00
Jardiniere, Matching Base, Vines, Flowers, Beige Ground, Petal, Scroll Border, 32 x 15 In.	1380.00
Jardiniere, Spherical, Stylized Flowers, Tripod Base, 3 ½ In. ....*illus*	124.00
Pitcher, Arts & Crafts, Line Patterns, Staple Repair, 6 ¼ In. ....*illus*	88.00
Pitcher, Stylized Leaves, Metal Overlay, Marked Orivit, No. 2541, 13 In. ....*illus*	776.00
Plaque, No. 1044-94, Cochem, PUG, 12 In. ....*illus*	127.00
Plaque, No. 1044-130, Heidelberg Schloss, Hand Painted, 12 In.	150.00
Plaque, No. 1044-172, Die Wartburg, Hand Painted, 12 In.	196.00
Plaque, No. 1044-176, Zugspitze U. Rissersee, PUG, Hand Painted, 12 In.	230.00
Plaque, No. 1044-1328, Gnome & Frog, 7 ½ In.	161.00
Plaque, No. 1044-1352, Rheinstein, PUG, 17 ½ In.	431.00
Plaque, No. 1044-1352, Stolzenfels, PUG, 17 ½ In.	403.00
Plaque, No. 1044-9031, Birds, Hand Painted, 14 In.	115.00
Plaque, No. 2112, Gnome In Tree, Signed, Schlitt, 16 In.	826.00
Plaque, No. 2149, Papageno, Etched, H. Schlitt, 16 ⅛ In.	748.00
Plaque, No. 2362, Heidelberg Castle, Etched, 17 ½ In.	546.00
Plaque, No. 2546, Woman, Flowers, Etched, 15 x 9 In.	1783.00
Plaque, No. 2549, Orchids Surround Woman's Head, Etched, 18 In.	1006.00
Plaque, No. 2770, Angels Over Town, Etched, 18 ½ In.	2990.00
Plaque, No. 7078, Phanolith, Wood Frame, 8 x 6 In.	403.00
Plaque, No. 7081, Phanolith, 10 x 8 In.	633.00
Pokal, No. 168, Drinking Scenes, Spiral Relief, Arched Panels, Verse, Figural Top, 20 In.	443.00
Pokal, No. 2522, 1 Liter, Cameo, Set On Lid.	1150.00
Punch Bowl, No. 1859, 9 Liter, Underplate, 2 Men, Etched, Lid.	920.00
Stein, No. 280, ½ Liter, Pig In A Bonnet, Hand Painted, Pewter Lid	299.00
Stein, No. 406, ½ Liter, Gaudeamus, Helmet Pewter Lid	345.00
Stein, No. 702, ½ Liter, 3 Men Dancing, PUG, Pewter Lid	161.00
Stein, No. 738, ½ Liter, Soldier On Horse, PUG, Eagle Pewter Lid	431.00
Stein, No. 980, ½ Liter, Man, With Hammer, PUG, Pewter Lid	196.00
Stein, No. 981, ½ Liter, Pug, Sculling Pewter Lid.	403.00
Stein, No. 983, ½ Liter, Falstaff, PUG, Pewter Lid	161.00
Stein, No. 993, ½ Liter, Man, Playing Drums, PUG, Pewter Lid	469.00
Stein, No. 1005, 1 Liter, Tavern Scene, Relief, Inlaid Lid	320.00
Stein, No. 1074, 1 Liter, Man, Sitting At Bar, PUG, Pewter Lid.	345.00
Stein, No. 1526, 1 Liter, Eagle, Hand Painted, Pewter Lid	207.00
Stein, No. 1570, ½ Liter, Mosaic, Inlaid Lid	403.00
Stein, No. 1725, ¼ Liter, Man & Woman, Etched, Inlaid Lid, Warth.	240.00
Stein, No. 1786, 1 Liter, St. Florian, Dragon Handle, Etched, Glazed, Pewter Lid	1282.00
Stein, No. 1786, 1 Liter, St. Florian, Extinguishing Fire, Pewter Lid	531.00
Stein, No. 1856, 1 Liter, Prussian Eagle, Horn, Etched, Pewter Lid.	1416.00
Stein, No. 1861, ½ Liter, Frederick II, Etched, Inlaid Lid.	561.00
Stein, No. 1914, ½ Liter, Man, Holding Flag, Etched, Inlaid Lid	419.00
Stein, No. 1940, 3 Liter, Keeper Of Wine Cellar, Etched, Pewter Lid	1121.00
Stein, No. 2002, 1 Liter, Munich Skyline, Verse, Etched Pewter Lid	443.00
Stein, No. 2003, ½ Liter, Troubadour, Knights, Etched, Inlaid Lid.	413.00

Mettlach, Candleholder, Match Holder, Girl, Leaning On Tree Stump, 6 In. $207.00

Mettlach, Jardiniere, Spherical, Stylized Flowers, Tripod Base, 3 ½ In. $124.00

Mettlach, Pitcher, Arts & Crafts, Line Patterns, Staple Repair, 6 ¼ In. $88.00

M

Mettlach, Pitcher, Stylized Leaves, Metal Overlay, Marked Orivit, No. 2541, 13 In. $776.00

Mettlach, Plaque, No. 1044-94, Cochem, PUG, 12 In. $127.00

Mettlach, Vase, Flowers, Ruffled Rim, Hand Engraved, No. 2571, 21 In. $690.00

M

Milk Glass, Dish, Uncle Sam Sitting On Ship Cover, 1890s, 7 x 4 ½ In. $33.00

Milk Glass, Syrup, Challinor's Forget-Me-Not, Translucent Pink, Handle, 5 ¼ In. $15.00

Stein, No. 2007, ½ Liter, Cat, Hunched, Etched, Inlaid Lid	575.00
Stein, No. 2024, ½ Liter, Etched, Coat Of Arms, Inlaid Lid	403.00
Stein, No. 2025, ½ Liter, Cherubs Carousing, Etched, Inlaid Lid	354.00
Stein, No. 2027, ½ Liter, Gambrinus, Etched, Inlaid Lid	590.00
Stein, No. 2057, 3 Liter, Etched, Inlaid Lid	196.00
Stein, No. 2082, ½ Liter, William Tell, 7 ½ In.	480.00
Stein, No. 2092, ½ Liter, Gnomes, Adjusting Clock, Etched, Pewter Lid	649.00
Stein, No. 2133, ½ Liter, Elf, Seated	670.00
Stein, No. 2181, ½ Liter, Bowling Scene, Relief, Tan, Blue, Inlaid Lid	266.00
Stein, No. 2193, 3 Liter, Man Carrying Scroll, Dog, Etruscan Style, Etched, Pewter Lid	1180.00
Stein, No. 2204, 1 Liter, Prussian Eagle, Horn, Inlaid Lid	767.00
Stein, No. 2231, ½ Liter, Men Drinking At Table, Etched, Music Box, Auld Lang Syne	374.00
Stein, No. 2235, ½ Liter, Woman Holding Glass Up, Etched, Inlaid Lid	633.00
Stein, No. 2277, ½ Liter, Burg Nurnberg, Etched, Figural Lion, Inlaid Lid	740.00
Stein, No. 2277, ⅓ Liter, Heidelberg, Etched, Pewter Lid	207.00
Stein, No. 2278, ½ Liter, Soldiers, Red, White, Relief, Pewter Lid	250.00
Stein, No. 2282, ½ Liter, Beer Cellar, 9 In.	322.00
Stein, No. 2388, ½ Liter, Pretzel, Inlaid Lid	322.00
Stein, No. 2424, 1 Liter, Town Of Wartburg, Relief, Figural Buildings On Lid	1888.00
Stein, No. 2479, ½ Liter, Hildebrand, Tan, Cameo	502.00
Stein, No. 2556, ½ Liter, Drinking Scene, Blue, White, Brown, Relief, Pewter Lid	220.00
Stein, No. 2608, 3 Liter, Cameo, Inlaid Lid	230.00
Stein, No. 2638, ½ Liter, Young Girl, Inlaid Lid, Etched	313.00
Stein, No. 2714, ½ Liter, Cameo, Inlaid Lid	661.00
Stein, No. 2717, ½ Liter, Venus Target, Landscape, Etched, Pewter Lid	1416.00
Stein, No. 2765, 1 Liter, Soldier, On Horse, Etched, Figural House, Inlaid Lid, H. Schlitt	2128.00
Stein, No. 2778, 1 Liter, Tavern Scene, Etched, Inlaid Lid, H. Schlitt	1500.00
Stein, No. 2871, 1 Liter, Cornell University, Etched, Inlaid Lid	780.00
Stein, No. 2935, 5 Liter, Inlaid Lid, Pewter Strap, Etched	604.00
Stein, No. 3034, 1 Liter, Cameo, Inlaid Lid	460.00
Stein, No. 3092, ½ Liter, Barrel Man, Etched, Schlitt	649.00
Stein, No. 3189, ½ Liter, Woman Holding Plate, Etched, Glazed, F. Ringer, Inlaid Lid	863.00
Stein, No. 3282, 5 Liter, Inlaid Lid	92.00
Stein, No. 3351, ¼ Liter, Etched, Inlaid Lid	863.00
Stein, No. 5023, 1 Liter, Eagle, Faience, Pewter Lid	2423.00
Toothpick, No. 1440, Flowers, Relief, 2 ½ In.	104.00
Vase, Flowers, Ruffled Rim, Hand Engraved, No. 2571, 21 In. ....*illus*	690.00
Vase, No. 1316, Mosaic, Bands, Beaded, Fluted, Stylized Leaves, Hearts, Squat, 3 ½ In.	106.00
Vase, No. 1875, Mosaic, Terra-Cotta Ground, 8 ½ In.	431.00
Vase, No. 1876, Mosaic, Blue, 6 ½ In.	219.00
Vase, No. 2483, Little Red Riding Hood, 4 Scenes, 13 In.	1380.00
Vase, No. 3006, Cameo, Handles, 13 In.	230.00
Wall Plaque, Nurnberg Schloss, 12 In.	120.00

MILK GLASS was named for its milky white color. It was first made in England during the 1700s. The height of its popularity in the United States was from 1870 to 1880. It is now correct to refer to some colored glass as blue milk glass, black milk glass, etc. Reproductions of milk glass are being made and sold in many stores. Related pieces may be listed in the Cosmos, Vallerysthal, and Westmoreland categories.

Apothecary Jar, Cover, 5 ¼ In., 4 Piece	105.00
Ashtray, Standing Bulldog, Amethyst Streaks, c.1900, 2 ¾ x 5 ½ In.	53.00
Bottle, Dresser, Lid, Flowers Panels, Gold Accents, 5 In., Pair	41.00
Bowl, Leaf Shape, Open Work Handle, 6 Reserves, c.1900, 8 In.	35.00
Box, Blue, Center Medallion, ¾ Woman's Profile, c.1890, 2 x 5 x 5 In.	59.00
Box, Cover, Dog Finial, Flower, Embossed, Blue, 5 x 5 In.	100.00
Box, Rapunzel, Art Deco, Cover, c.1925, 5 ¾ x 4 ½ In.	53.00
Compote, Cover, Sawtooth Design, Baluster Base, 14 x 9 In.	88.00
Compote, Grape & Leaf, Panels, High Gloss, Anchor Hocking, 5 ½ x 5 In.	12.00
Decanter, White Opaline, Genie, Smooth Base, 15 In., Pair	235.00
Dish, Cover, Bird In The Hand, Blue & Orange Stones, c.1889, 8 In.	185.00
Dish, Hen On Nest, Cover, Atterbury, Blue Head, c.1900, 7 ½ x 7 In.	111.00
Dish, Snapping Turtle, Cover, 20th Century, 3 ¾ x 6 x 10 In.	79.00
Dish, Uncle Sam Sitting On Ship Cover, 1890s, 7 x 4 ½ In. ....*illus*	33.00
Jar, Angels, Flowers, Painted, Gilt, 7 ¾ x 5 ½ In.	368.00
Jug, Applied Handle, Blob Top, Open Pontil, c.1840, 2 In.	29.00
Pitcher, Feather, Chocolate, c.1925, 8 ⅛ In.	991.00
Pitcher, Feather Design, Scalloped, Light Brown, c.1910, 8 x 4 In.	863.00

Plate, Egg, Chicken, Amethyst Head & Breast, c.1950, 6 x 11 x 12 In.	198.00
Plate, Open Rose, Flowers, Front & Back, Sculpted, 12 In.	43.00
Smoke Bell, Ruffled Edge, Red Rim	69.00
Spooner, Birch Leaf, Flint, Scalloped Rim, c.1870, 5 ½ x 3 ½ In.	40.00
Syrup, Alba, Opaque White, Flowers, Dithridge Glass, Lid, c.1900, 6 ¼ In.	165.00
Syrup, Challinor's Forget-Me-Not, Translucent Pink, Handle, 5 ¼ In. .... *illus*	15.00
Vase, Bottle Shape, Cherubs At Play, Mocha Ground, Painted, 10 In., Pair	1541.00
Vase, Flower Garlands, Blue Ribbons, Footed, 21 In.	365.00
Vase, Putti, Frolicking, Hand Painted, Gilt, Late 1800s, 14 ½ In.	60.00
Wall Plaque, A. Lincoln, Mask, Impressed, Pressed Glass, 8 In.	35.00
Water Set, Pitcher, 6 Tumblers, Wild Iris, Yellow, Pink, Blue, 9 In., 7 Piece	325.00

MINTON china has been made in the Staffordshire region of England from 1793 to the present. The firm became part of the Royal Doulton Tableware Group in 1968, but the wares continued to be marked *Minton*. In 2009 the brand was bought by KPS Capital Partners of New York and became part of WWRD Holdings. Many marks have been used. The word *England* was added in 1891. Minton majolica is listed in this book in the Majolica category.

Bowl, Stylized & Gilt Flowers, Mottled Blue Ground, c.1900, 9 In.	295.00
Cup & Saucer, Golden Diadem, Cream Ground, Gold Trim	41.00
Garden Seat, Blue & White Flowers, Pierced Hawthorn Pattern, Impressed, 1882, 19 ½ In.	588.00
Parrot, Perched On Stump, Blue, Green, Yellow Glazed Earthenware, c.1900, 8 ½ In.	148.00
Pedestal, Baluster Shape, Satyr Masks, Fruit Garlands, Cobalt Blue, Majolica, 1800s, 31 In. . *illus*	705.00
Plate, Bread & Butter, Champagne, Blue Grapes, Gold Leaves, 6 ¼ In.	12.00
Plate, Bread & Butter, Cream, Geometric Blue & Gold Band, 6 ½ In.	37.00
Plate, Gray, White Cherubs, Gold Border, Pate-Sur-Pate, England, 1918, 8 Piece, 10 ⅛ In.	6518.00
Plate, Pate-Sur-Pate, Blue Ground, White Birds, Insects, Gold Border, Signed, 8 ½ In.	518.00
Plate Set, Louis XVI, Cobalt Border, Gilded, c.1875, 9 ¾ In., 12 Piece	1080.00
Platter, Ironstone, Oval, Japanese Style Flowers, Birds, 1860, 21 x 17 In.	235.00
Stand, Walking Stick, Heron, Bulrushes, c.1876, 40 In. .... *illus*	7768.00
Vase, Bernard Moore, Flambe, Dragon, Square, Tan, Orange, Signed, c.1910, 19 In.	5925.00
Vase, Cobalt Blue, Applied Gold Handles, 1873, 23 In., Pair	468.00
Vase, Double Gourd, Applied Buttresses, Painted Flowers, Multicolored, 5 ½ x 11 In. .... *illus*	300.00
Vase, Pilgrim, Turquoise, Multicolored Flowers, Fish, Gold, Christopher Dresser, 1873, 10 In., Pair	1185.00
Vase, Rococo, Gilt, Pink Ground, Painted Birds, Bulbous, Handles, Marked, 4 x 4 In. .... *illus*	196.00
Vase, Stylized Flowers, Black, Turquoise, Yellow, Double Gourd, 2 Buttresses, Marked, 5 x 11 In.	300.00
Vase, Tree, Britannia, Africa Profiles, Leaves, Ring Handles, Blue, White, c.1885, 20 In.	2880.00
Vase, Urn Shape, Pheasant, J.E. Dean, c.1920, 5 In.	173.00

MIRRORS *are listed in the Furniture category under Mirror.*

MOCHA pottery is an English-made product that was sold in America during the early 1800s. It is a heavy pottery with pale coffee-and-cream coloring. Designs of blue, brown, green, orange, black, or white were added to the pottery and given fanciful names, such as Tree, Snail Trail, or Moss. Mocha designs are sometimes found on pearlware. A few pieces of mocha ware were made in France, the United States, and other countries.

Bowl, Earthworm, 6 ¾ In.	193.00
Bowl, Earthworm, Green Leaf, Roulette Rim Band, Rust Band, 3 ¾ x 7 ¼ In.	711.00
Bowl, Earthworm, Rust, Green Crosshatched Rim, 3 ⅛ x 6 ¼ In.	360.00
Bowl, Green Reeded Rim Band, Blue, Ocher, Brown, White, Slip Marbling, c.1800, 4 x 9 In.	1007.00
Bowl, Green Reeded Rim Band, c.1820, 3 x 6 In.	770.00
Bowl, Saucer, Child's, Seaweed, Pearlware, England, c.1820, Miniature	588.00
Bowl, Wavy White Slip, Brown Bands, 3 x 5 In.	144.00
Creamer, Cat's-Eye, Band, Applied Handle, 3 ½ In.	203.00
Jug, Cat's-Eye, Rust, Brown Bands, Blue, Brown, White Slip, Leaf Design, England, c.1890, 5 In.	770.00
Jug, Milk, Seaweed, Crisscross Band, Bulbous, Applied Handle, 6 In.	203.00
Mixing Bowl, Brown & White Stripes, Seaweed Highlights, 7 x 14 ¾ In.	248.00
Mug, Banded, Green, Red, Yellow, White Ground, Applied Leaf Molded Handle, 6 In.	1538.00
Mug, Earthworm, Blue & Cream Band, 19th Century, 5 ⅞ In.	237.00
Mug, Earthworm, Ocher Band With Blue, White & Brown, Pearlware, 1830	945.00
Mug, Green Reeded Rim Band, Brown, White, Rust Slip Marbling, Leaf Handle, Qt., 6 In.	1422.00
Mug, Seaweed, Black, Orange & Tan Band, Blue & Brown Stripes, 4 ¾ In. .... *illus*	275.00
Mug, Tree, Brown Ground Band, Lines, Handle, 5 In.	88.00
Pepper Pot, Cat's-Eye, Tan Ground, 5 ¼ In. .... *illus*	1989.00
Pepper Pot, Crosshatching, Blue Ground, Engine Turned, 4 ½ In.	265.00
Pepper Pot, Dome Top, Cylindrical, Green, Tan, Blue Checkered, 3 ¾ In.	990.00

Minton, Pedestal, Baluster Shape, Satyr Masks, Fruit Garlands, Cobalt Blue, Majolica, 1800s, 31 In.
$705.00

Minton, Stand, Walking Stick, Heron, Bulrushes, c.1876, 40 In.
$7768.00

M

Minton, Vase, Double Gourd, Applied Buttresses, Painted Flowers, Multicolored, 5 ½ x 11 In.
$300.00

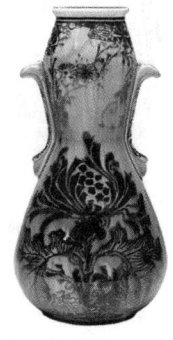

Minton, Vase, Rococo, Gilt, Pink Ground, Painted Birds, Bulbous, Handles, Marked, 4 x 4 In.
$196.00

Mocha, Mug, Seaweed, Black, Orange & Tan Band, Blue & Brown Stripes, 4 ¾ In. $275.00

Mocha, Pepper Pot, Cat's-Eye, Tan Ground, 5 ¼ In. $1989.00

Mocha, Pitcher, Cream Ground, Green, Brown, Orange Stripe, Lines, Oval, c.1820, 6 ¾ In. $4680.00

Mocha, Pitcher, Seaweed, Yellow, Brown & Cream Bands, 19th Century, 8 ½ In. $1521.00

Pepper Pot, Earthworm, Brown & Cream Stripes, Cream Ground, 4 ¼ In.	1010.00
Pitcher, Baluster, Brown, Black Band, Geometric, White, Leaf Handle, c.1800, 6 In.	1304.00
Pitcher, Cream Ground, Green, Brown, Orange Stripe, Lines, Oval, c.1820, 6 ¾ In. .... *illus*	4680.00
Pitcher, Earthworm, Bands, Black, Orange, Blue, Applied Leaf Handle, 6 x 3 In.	4840.00
Pitcher, Earthworm, Brown, Coggled Bands, 8 In.	3750.00
Pitcher, Green & Brown Stripes, Barrel Form, Oval, 6 ½ In.	5200.00
Pitcher, Green Reeded Rim Band, Brown, White, Rust Slip, Applied Leaves, Strap Handle, 3 In.	563.00
Pitcher, Seaweed, Yellow, Brown & Cream Bands, 19th Century, 8 ½ In. .... *illus*	1521.00
Tankard, Earthworm, Gray Ground, 1800s, 6 In. .... *illus*	585.00

MONMOUTH POTTERY COMPANY started working in Monmouth, Illinois, in 1892. The pottery made a variety of utilitarian wares. It became part of Western Stoneware Company in 1906. The maple leaf mark was used until 1930. If *Co.* appears as part of the mark, the piece was made before 1906.

Crock, Bristol Glaze, Albany Slip Interior, 3 Gal.	35.00
Jardiniere, Rustic, 3-Footed	60.00
Vase, Blue, 6 In.	15.00
Vase, Blue, 10 In.	15.00
Vase, Geometric Band, Tapered, Inverted Neck, Green & Blue High Glaze, Marked, 18 In.	60.00

MOORCROFT pottery was first made in Burslem, England, in 1913. William Moorcroft had managed the art pottery department for James Macintyre & Company of England from 1898 to 1913. The Moorcroft pottery continues today, although William Moorcroft died in 1945. The earlier wares are similar to the modern ones, but color and marking will help indicate the age.

Bowl, Arum Lily, Footed, 10 ¼ In.	214.00
Bowl, Cover, Undertray, Flambe, Fruit & Leaf Design, Signed, 8 ½ x 11 ¾ In.	920.00
Bowl, Grapes, Leaves, Multicolored, Cobalt Ground, England, 3 x 7 In.	374.00
Bowl, Hibiscus, Peach, Olive Ground, Stamped, 7 In.	86.00
Bowl, Pomegranates, Black Ground, Cobridge, 3 ⅜ x 8 ¾ In.	460.00
Box, Cover, Moonlit Blue Landscape, Box, 5 x 4 ¼ In.	4800.00
Candlestick, Anemone, Signed, 4 x 5 In., Pair..	263.00
Fruit Set, Pomegranate, Blue Ground, Bowl, Coupe, Integral Saucer, 10 ⅜ & 4 ½ In., 7 Piece.	1880.00
Ginger Jar, Flowers, Pink, Green Leaves, Blue Ground, Painted, 8 In.	410.00
Jar, Cover, Moonlit Blue, Stamped, 10 ¾ x 7 ¼ In.	7200.00
Jug, Flowers, Cylindrical, 2001, 9 ½ In.	181.00
Plate, Claremont, Green, 8 ½ In.	1560.00
Vase, Anemone, Signed, Emma Bossons, 8 In.	198.00
Vase, Clematis, Green Ground, Globular, 8 In.	461.00
Vase, Cornflower, Medium Blue, Signed, 15 In.	3220.00
Vase, Cornflower, Red, Ocher Ground, Stamped, 6 ½ x 3 In. .... *illus*	2520.00
Vase, Dawn Landscape, 16 In.	5370.00
Vase, Dragon, Black Ground, Blue, White, Orange, Bulbous, 7 ¾ In.	287.00
Vase, Eventide, Green, Gourd, 6 ½ x 3 ¾ In.	3000.00
Vase, Flambe, Anemone, Bulbous, 6 ¾ In.	1032.00
Vase, Flambe, Blossoms, Underglaze Mottling, 1939, 17 x 7 In.	18300.00
Vase, Flambe, Cornflower, Signed, 12 In.	2990.00
Vase, Florian, Blue Ground, Yellow Flowers, Leaves, Marked, c.1900, 7 In. .... *illus*	1638.00
Vase, Florian, Dark, Light Blue, c.1900, 6 In.	819.00
Vase, Flowers, Multicolored, Black Ground, 1983, 12 In.	527.00
Vase, Flowers, Red, Blue Ground, Leaves, Squat, Bulbous, Monogram, 7 ¾ In.	323.00
Vase, Fruit, Multicolored, Cobalt Blue Ground, Impressed, 20th Century, 9 ½ In.	565.00
Vase, Leaf & Berries, Blue Ground, Globular, 6 ¾ In.	577.00
Vase, MacIntyre, Florian, Peacock Feathers, Handles, 5 x 5 In.	1342.00
Vase, Moonlit Blue, Bulbous, 4 ¾ x 3 In.	2160.00
Vase, Red Poppies, Black Ground, Porcelain, 13 x 7 In.	585.00
Vase, Spanish, Flared Rim, Flowers, Leaves, c.1915, 12 In.	2070.00
Vase, Spring Flowers, Yellow Ground, Bulbous, 8 ¾ In.	346.00
Vase, Tudor Rose, Green, Blue, Liberty & Co., c.1905, 6 ¾ In.	995.00
Vase, Wisteria, 7 ½ In.	297.00

MORGANTOWN GLASS WORKS operated in Morgantown, West Virginia, from 1900 to 1974. Some of their wares are marked with an adhesive label that says *Old Morgantown Glass.*

Candy Jar, Clear Shaded To Amethyst, Amethyst Lid, Etched Medallions, Footed, 9 In.	83.00
Vase, Peachblow, Acid Treated, White Lined, Pressed Glass Griffin Stand, c.1885, 8 x 3 In.	235.00

MORIAGE is a special type of raised decoration used on some Japanese pottery. Sometimes pieces of clay were shaped by hand and applied to the item; sometimes the clay was squeezed from a tube in the way we apply cake frosting. One type of moriage is called Dragonware by collectors.

Ashtray, Flowers, Bird, Orange, Black Border, 5 ⅜ In.	45.00
Biscuit Jar, Monk, Drinking, Faceted, Yellow, Scrolling, 8 ½ In.	345.00
Bowl, Gray Clay, Animals, Mountains, Vines, c.1900, 2 ½ x 4 ½ In.	230.00
Fernery, Nile Scene, Sunset, Footed, Handles, c.1900, 9 ¾ In.	150.00
Figurine, Cat, Sleeping, Dark Salmon & Cobalt Blue, Flowers, Coins, Gilt, 1920s, 5 ½ x 6 ½ In.	325.00
Humidor, 5 Dogs, Border, c.1900, 6 In.	780.00
Humidor, Dragon, Nippon, 7 x 6 In.	410.00
Plate, Man In Boat, Trees, Mountains, Wire Twirled Frame, 12 In.	35.00
Tankard, Mugs, Owl, Blue Sky, Acorn & Leaf Accents, 10 ⅝ & 4 ½ In., 3 Piece .... *illus*	431.00
Vase, Birds In Flight, Scrolled Handles & Rim, c.1900, 9 In.	780.00
Vase, Dragon, Smoky Black, White, Blue, Thick Slip, Nippon, M Mark, 10 In.	345.00
Vase, Mottled Green Ground, White, Gray Dragon, Nippon, M Mark, 5 In.	150.00

MOSAIC TILE COMPANY of Zanesville, Ohio, was started by Karl Langerbeck and Herman Mueller in 1894. Many types of plain and ornamental tiles were made until 1959. The company closed in 1967. The company also made some ashtrays, bookends, and related giftwares. Most pieces are marked with the entwined MTC monogram.

Cookie Jar, Mammy, Yellow Dress, 13 In.	65.00
Rotary, Tile, Commemorative, Blue Matte Ground, White Shield, N.Y., 3 ½ In.	55.00
Tile, Border, Vine, Berries, High Relief, Curdles Cream & Blue Glaze, 4 x 6 In.	120.00
Tile, Checkerboard, Matte Blue, Textured Orange, c.1930, 2 In., Pair	50.00
Tile, Eagle, Stylized, Represents John The Evangelist, 6 In.	125.00
Tile, Fortune And The Boy, Woman Bending Over Fallen Boy, Storybook, 6 x 6 In.	173.00
Tile, Hercules & The Waggoner, Motto, Walter Crane, 6 In.	110.00
Tile, Oil Lamp, Open Book, Radiating Lines, Matte Glaze, 1950s, 6 In.	85.00
Tile, Sailing Ship On Choppy Water, Blue & White, c.1940, 4 ½ In.	35.00
Trivet, Birds, 3 Summer Tanager, Audubon Series, 4 Molded Feet, c.1960, 6 In.	10.00

MOSER glass is made by a Bohemian (Czech) glasshouse founded by Ludwig Moser in 1857. Art Nouveau-type glassware and iridescent glassware were made. The most famous Moser glass is decorated with heavy enameling in gold and bright colors. The firm, Moser Glassworks, is still working in Karlovy Vary, Czech Republic. Few pieces of Moser glass are marked.

Bowl, Amberina, Robin, Leaf, Cranberry Rim, Oval, 12 In.	805.00
Bowl, Green, Gold Enamel Flower Overlay, 3-Footed, 5 In.	175.00
Box, Amber, Tree Blossoms, Round, 3 x 6 ½ In.	125.00
Compote, Flowers, Cranberry, Gold Scrolls, 7 In.	100.00
Compote, Optic Ribbed, Raised Multicolored Hawk, Gilt Clouds, Rims, 5 ½ In.	400.00
Cordial Punch Set, Lavender, Gold Enameled Flowers, c.1900, 7 2-Inch Wines	2195.00
Cruet, Cranberry, Multicolored, Enamel, 7 In.	374.00
Cup & Saucer, Ruby, Continental Man, Gold Scrolls, 2 ½ In.	100.00
Decanter, Cranberry, Ducks, Painted, Enamel, 13 ½ In.	695.00
Decanter, Dragonfly & Flowers, Enamel, Yellow, Clear Pedestal, Handle, Stopper, 10 ½ In.	225.00
Decanter, Peachblow, Enameled Flowers, 12 In.	350.00
Decanter Set, Green Flowers, 10 & 2 ½ In., 5 Piece	148.00
Epergne, Peach Ground, Leaves, Acorn Jewels, Ruffled Compote, Horn, Signed, 11 In., 2 Piece	1955.00
Ewer, Insects, Ferns, Berries, Enamel, Cranberry Glass, 3 In.	518.00
Glass, Wine, Rhine, Flute Pattern, Petticoat Base, Lavender, Clear, Gold Trim, 7 In.	175.00
Goblet, 4-Leaf Clover, Cone Stem, Gold Scrolling, 7 In., Pair	75.00
Goblet, Acanthus Scrolling, Faceted Stem, Gilt Band, 8 ¼ In.	431.00
Goblet, Acanthus Scrolls, Overall Gilt, Gray Tracery, Multicolored, 7 In.	300.00
Goblet, Baluster, Green, Gold Scrolls, Silver Phoenix, Red, Turquoise Jewels On Stem, 8 In., Pair.	200.00
Goblet, Cherub Gilt Panels, Multicolored Flowers, Faceted Stems, 5 In.	500.00
Goblet, Cherub Panels, Multicolored Flowers, Gilt, 5 In.	259.00
Goblet, Green Baluster Stem, Grapes, Leaves, Gold Coralene, Jewel Cabochons, 8 In. .... *illus*	748.00
Goblet, Roses, Pink, Blue Flowers, Gold Leafy Stems, Silver Enameled Knop, 6 ¼ In.	518.00
Goblet, Spring Scene, Swans, Birch Tree, Enamel, 4 ¼ In., 4 Piece	978.00
Jewelry Box, Hinged Lid, Leaf, Enamel, Blue, Round, 4 x 4 In.	420.00
Juice, Enameled Flowers, Amber, Signed, 3 ¾ In.	145.00
Liquor Set, Blue Ground, Gold Detail, Green & Blue Tumblers, 10 ½-In. Decanter, 6 Piece	1062.00
Pitcher, Peacock, Butterfly, Chinese Garden, Applied Drops, Enamel, Hand Blown, c.1900, 9 In.	1117.00
Sherbet, Cranberry Bowl, Multicolored Scrolls, Peacock Eyes, Conical Foot, 4 In.	175.00

Mocha, Tankard, Earthworm, Gray Ground, 1800s, 6 In.
$585.00

Moorcroft, Vase, Cornflower, Red, Ocher Ground, Stamped, 6 ½ x 3 In.
$2520.00

Moorcroft, Vase, Florian, Blue Ground, Yellow Flowers, Leaves, Marked, c.1900, 7 In.
$1638.00

M

Moriage, Tankard, Mugs, Owl, Blue Sky, Acorn & Leaf Accents, 10 ⅝ & 4 ½ In., 3 Piece
$431.00

Moser, Goblet, Green Baluster Stem, Grapes, Leaves, Gold Coralene, Jewel Cabochons, 8 In.
$748.00

Moser, Vase, Intaglio, Vines, Flowers, Crystal Shaded To Amethyst, Gold Detail, 6 ½ In.
$460.00

The Monteith Bowl

Mr. Monteith was a Scotsman who wore a cloak with a scalloped hem. A large punch bowl with a similar scalloped edge is called a *Monteith bowl.* It is usually at least 12 inches in diameter.

Tankard, Cranberry, Bluebird Medallion, Enamel, Twist Handle, 7 ½ In.		277.00
Urn, Lid, Engraved Crystal, c.1870, 17 In.		468.00
Vase, Amber, Figures, Horses, Paneled, Flared Rim, Carved Brass Panel, Czechoslovakia, 8 ¾ In.		415.00
Vase, Amber, Paneled, Brass Central Panel, Figures, Footed, Flared, Signed, Karlsbad, 8 ¾ In.		410.00
Vase, Amber, Scalloped Ribs, Flared Rim, Footed, Josef Hoffmann, c.1923, 9 In.		4182.00
Vase, Amethyst, Etched, Faceted Baluster Shape, Gilt Panels, 10 ¼ In.		1464.00
Vase, Amethyst, Hawk Diving, 3 Ducks, Gilt Lake, Paste Enamel, Cylinder, 10 In.		2185.00
Vase, Cane Pattern, Ruby To Clear, Lacy Scrolls, Flowers, Marked, 19 ½ In.		1955.00
Vase, Clear, Green To Orange Opalescent, Padded, Intaglio Carved, 13 ¾ In.		5175.00
Vase, Cobalt Blue, Enamel, Tapered, Cylindrical, 3-Footed, Eagle Head Supports, 9 In., Pair		410.00
Vase, Cylindrical, Translucent Green, Leafy Stems, Amber Green Marquetry Flower, Signed, 7 In.		1500.00
Vase, Enamel Overlay, Flowers, Leaves, Yellow Ground, Signed, 13 x 5 In.		819.00
Vase, Green Crackle, Lily Of The Valley, Flowers, Bugs, Bulbous, Cylindrical, 7 In.		153.00
Vase, Green To Clear, Tubular, 6 ½ In.		229.00
Vase, Intaglio, Vines, Flowers, Crystal Shaded To Amethyst, Gold Detail, 6 ½ In. .... *illus*		460.00
Vase, Peach Glass, Coralene Flowers, Blue, Cased, Footed, Handles, 10 ½ In.		690.00
Vase, Pictoral Medallions, Clear, Cylindrical, Footed, Gold Scrolling Frame, 19 In.		2875.00
Vase, Roman Warriors, Faceted, Amber, Compote Shape, Signed, Moser Karlsbad, 7 ½ In.		250.00
Vase, Stick, Gold Roman Warriors Frieze, Faceted, Footed, Signed, 19 ½ In.		489.00
Vase, Underwater Scene, Clear, Applied Multicolored Aquatic Life, Cylinder, Rigaree Drips, 17 In.		863.00
Vase, Urn Shape, Optic Ribbed Cranberry, Birds, Leaves, Gilt, Footed, 19 ½ In. .... *illus*		7480.00

MOSS ROSE china was made by many firms from 1808 to 1900. It has a typical moss rose pictured as the design. The plant is not as popular now as it was in Victorian gardens, so the fuzz-covered bud is unfamiliar to most collectors. The dishes were usually decorated with pink and green flowers.

Ashtray, Round Reticulated Border, Lefton, 4 ⅛ In.		9.00

MOTHER-OF-PEARL GLASS, or pearl satin glass, was first made in the 1850s in England and in Massachusetts. It was a special type of mold-blown satin glass with air bubbles in the glass, giving it a pearlized color. It has been reproduced. Mother-of-pearl shell objects are listed under Pearl.

Biscuit Jar, Lid, Iris, Rainbow, Thumbprint, Red, Yellow, Blue Panels, Enamel, Metal, Collar, 8 In.		1898.00
Cup, Desk, Silver Banded, Paneled, Late 1800s, 3 x 3 In. .... *illus*		270.00
Finger Bowl, Underplate, Diamond Quilted, Rainbow, Red, Blue, Yellow, Stamped, 6 In.		1050.00
Lamp, Rainbow, Ribbed Base, Diamond Quilted Shade, c.1875, 15 In.		944.00
Letter Box, Inkstand, Abalone Shell, Mid 19th Century, 6 ½ x 9 In.		1830.00
Pickle Castor, Diamond Quilted, Pink To Clear, Pontil, Lid, Tongs, Frame, c.1900, 10 In.		297.00
Pitcher, Diamond Quilted, Rainbow, Oval, Pastel Blue, Red, Yellow Stripes, 8 In.		475.00
Pitcher, Herringbone, Pink, Camphor Reeded Handle, 7 ½ In. .... *illus*		144.00
Sugar & Creamer, Diamond Quilted, Pink, Camphor Hand, Ruffled Edge, 4 In.		1155.00
Tazza, Diamond Quilted, Blue, Crimped Border, Gilt, Scrolled Stand, Bird Finial, 9 x 10 In.		316.00
Vase, Diamond Quilted, Apricot, Square Rim, Pontil, c.1900, 4 ⅞ In.		92.00
Vase, Diamond Quilted, Blue, Pink Interior, Applied Green Stems, Base, 2 Lemons, 13 In.		125.00
Vase, Hobnail, Shaded Cranberry, Square Folded Rim, Sunburst, Pontil, c.1900, 5 In.		66.00
Vase, Stick, Bulbous, Peach, Blue Coralene Flowers, Green Branches, 8 In.		45.00
Violin, On Box Stand, France, 7 ½ In.		1900.00

MOTORCYCLES and motorcycle accessories of all types are being collected today. Examples can be found that date back to the early twentieth century. Toy motorcycles are listed in the Toy category.

Display, Harley-Davidson, Wicker Construction, Dual Exhaust, Turning Front End, 80 x 45 In.		345.00
Gas Tank, Harley-Davidson, Emblems, Ultra Glide Classic, 1979, 5 Gal., Pair		200.00
Harley-Davidson, Panhead, Vin. 60flh2537, 1960		9790.00
Headlamp, Old Sol, Brass, Red & Green Jewels, Hawthorne Mfg. Co., Conn., 7 ½ In.		240.00
Indian, Scout, Model R, 2 Cylinder, 55 Horsepower, 596 cc, c.1920, 54 x 32 In. .... *illus*		25850.00
Indian, Sport Scout, Vin. 641-852, 1941		14410.00
Manual, Operating Rules & Regulations, Blue Ridge Bus Lines		6.00
Mirror, Eagle Spirit, Live To Ride, Ride To Live, Pair		30.00
Pin, Indian Motorcycle, Pre World War II		100.00
Pin, Indian Motorcycle, Sport Scout, Gold Filled, c.1900		100.00
Pin, Indian Motorcycle, Whitehead & Hoag, Back Paper, Celluloid, ⅞ In.		55.00
Seat, Buddy, Harley-Davidson, Grab Rail, c.1965		150.00
Seat, Solo, Harley-Davidson, Police Style		50.00

MOVIE memorabilia of all types are collected. Animation Art, Games, Sheet Music, Toys, and some celebrity items are listed in their own section. A lobby card is 11 by 14 inches. A set of lobby cards includes seven scene cards and one title card. An American one sheet, the standard movie poster, is 27 by 41 inches. A three sheet is 40 by 81 inches. A half sheet is 22 by 28 inches. A window card, made of cardboard, is 14 by 22 inches. An insert is 14 by 36 inches. A herald is a promotional item handed out to patrons. Press books, sent to exhibitors to promote a movie, contain ads & lists of what is available for advertising, i.e., posters, lobby cards. Press kits, sent to the media, contain photos and details about the movie, i.e., stars' biographies and interviews.

Book, Punch-Out, Errol Flynn, The Sea Hawk, Cardboard, 4 Pages, 1940	610.00
Button, Freaks, Johnny Eck, Metro-Goldwyn Mayer, Celluloid, Red, Green, Black, 1 ¼ In.	863.00
Button, Peter Pan, Paramount Pictures, Ivory & Black, Pinback, 1925	36.00
Herald, In The Navy, Abbott & Costello, Andrew Sisters On Ship, 1941, 3 ½ x 7 In.	145.00
Invitation, Premiere, Gone With The Wind, Cathay Circle Theatre, 1939, 6 ½ x 10 ¼ In.	115.00
Lamp, Figural, Hollywood Movie Stars, 16 Heads, Movie Camera, 1970, 19 In.	863.00
Life Magazine, Audrey Hepburn, Nun's Story, Signed, c.1959, 10 ½ x 14 In.	173.00
Life Magazine, Fred Astaire & Ginger Rogers, Black & White, Signed, 1938, 10 ½ x 14 In.	230.00
Lobby Card, 12 Angry Men, United Artists, 1957, 11 x 14 In.	96.00
Lobby Card, 13th Hour, Lionel Barrymore, Jacquelin Gadsdon, 1927, 11 x 14 In.	173.00
Lobby Card, Alligator, Lucerna Film, Czechoslovakia, 1981, 11 ½ x 17 In.	15.00
Lobby Card, Charlie Chan At Monte Carlo, Warner Oland, Keye Luke, 1937, 11 x 14 In.	285.00
Lobby Card, Hud, Paul Newman, 1963, 11 x 14 In.	508.00
Lobby Card, Jazz Mad, Jean Hersholt, Marian Nixon, Frame, 1928, 11 x 14 In. *illus*	158.00
Lobby Card, Mad Love, Peter Lorre, MGM, 1935, 11 x 14 In.	50788.00
Lobby Card, Once Upon A Horse, Dan Rowan, Dick Martin, 1958, 11 x 14 In.	62.00
Lobby Card, Something For The Boys, Carmen Miranda, 1944, 11 x 14 In.	75.00
Lobby Card, Untamed, Joan Crawford, Ernest Torrence, 1929, 11 x 14 In.	115.00
Lobby Display, Figure, Star Wars, Yoda, Rubber, Glass Eyes, Canvas, 56 x 24 In.	1500.00
Lobby Display, Standee, 2001:A Space Odyssey, MGM, 1968, 20 x 16 In.	96.00
Magazine, Movie Weekly, Newspaper, February 17 1923, 9 ¼ x 12 ¼ In., 32 Pages	30.00
Money Clip, Stainless, Bing Crosby, Del Mar Turf Club	299.00
Photo, 2 Girls & A Sailor, June Allyson, MGM, c.1944, 10 x 13 In.	120.00
Photo, A Very Private Affair, Brigitte Bardot, MGM, 1962, 8 x 10 In.	191.00
Photo, All This & Heaven Too, Bette Davis, Warner Bros., 1940, 8 x 10 In.	156.00
Photo, Anna Christie, Greta Carbo, MGM, 1930, 8 x 10 In.	335.00
Photo, Ava Gardner, Signed, MGM, 1951, 8 x 10 In.	115.00
Photo, Black Chamber, Rosalind Russell, MGM, 1935, 8 x 10 In.	120.00
Photo, Bonnie & Clyde, Warner Bros., Seven Arts, 1967, 8 x 10 In.	28.00
Photo, Bride Of Frankenstein, Elsa Lanchester, Universal, 1935, 9 ¾ x 12 ¾ In.	4780.00
Photo, Chandu The Magician, Bela Lugosi, Fox, 1932, 7 ¾ x 9 ¾ In.	311.00
Photo, Cleopatra, Claudette Colbert, Paramount, 1934, 8 x 10 In.	598.00
Photo, Douglas Fairbanks Jr., 1928, 8 x 10 In.	368.00
Photo, Grand Hotel, Jean Hersholt, 1932, 8 x 10 In.	120.00
Photo, Greta Garbo, MGM, 1940, 8 x 10 In.	359.00
Photo, Hunchback Of Notre Dame, Lon Chaney, Universal, 1923, 7 ¾ x 9 ¾ In.	478.00
Photo, Invisible Man, Claude Rains, Universal, 1933, 8 x 10 In.	120.00
Photo, Joan Crawford, MGM, 1930s, 10 x 13 In.	1195.00
Photo, Marlene Dietrich, 1940s, 8 x 10 In.	388.00
Photo, Mary Pickford, Culver Pictures, 1935, 8 x 10 In.	120.00
Photo, Philadelphia Story, Katharine Hepburn, MGM, 1940, 8 x 10 In.	717.00
Photo, Poppy, W.C. Fields, 1936, 10 x 12 ¾ In.	179.00
Photo, Rebecca, Laurence Olivier, Joan Fontaine, United Artists, 1940, 8 x 10 In.	155.00
Photo, Reckless, Jean Harlow, MGM, 1935, 8 x 10 In.	120.00
Photo, Rita Hayworth, 1940s, 7 ½ x 9 ¼ In.	263.00
Photo, Romeo & Juliet, Leslie Howard, Norma Shearer, MGM, 1926, 11 x 14 In.	155.00
Photo, Saratoga, Clark Gable, Jean Harlow, MGM, 1937, 7 ¼ x 9 ½ In.	263.00
Photo, To Catch A Thief, Grace Kelly, Paramount, c.1955, 8 x 10 In.	167.00
Photo, Virginia Bruce, MGM, 1931, 8 x 10 In.	143.00
Photo, W.C. Fields, Signed, Paramount Pictures, 8 x 10 In.	677.00
Poster, 7 Faces Of Dr. Lao, MGM, 1964, 27 x 41 In.	30.00
Poster, 12 Angry Men, United Artists, 1957, 27 x 41 In.	69.00
Poster, 13 Ghosts, Columbia, 1960, 27 x 41 In.	50.00
Poster, 13 Ghosts, Ghost Viewer, Illusion-O Effect, Signed, William Castle, 1960, 22 x 28 In.	127.00
Poster, Adventures Of Captain Fabian, Argentina, 1951, 29 x 43 In.	35.00
Poster, Adventures Of Ichabod & Mr. Toad, Headless Horseman, 22 x 28 In.	253.00
Poster, Adventures Of Robin Hood, Warner Brothers, 1938, 27 x 41 In.	11353.00
Poster, Alfie, Michael Caine, 1966, 27 x 41 In.	17.00

Moser, Vase, Urn Shape, Optic Ribbed Cranberry, Birds, Leaves, Gilt, Footed, 19 ½ In.
$7480.00

Mother-Of-Pearl, Cup, Desk, Silver Banded, Paneled, Late 1800s, 3 x 3 In.
$270.00

Mother-Of-Pearl,Pitcher, Herringbone, Pink, Camphor Reeded Handle, 7 ½ In.
$144.00

Motorcycle, Indian, Scout, Model R, 2 Cylinder, 55 Horsepower, 596 cc, c.1920, 54 x 32 In.
$25850.00

M

Movie, Lobby Card, Jazz Mad, Jean Hersholt, Marian Nixon, Frame, 1928, 11 x 14 In. $158.00

Movie, Poster, Breakfast At Tiffany's, Audrey Hepburn, 3 Sheet, c.1961, 47 x 84 In. $2963.00

Movie, Poster, Curse Of The Undead, Eric Fleming, Kathleen Crowley, 1959, 27 x 41 In. $104.00

Poster, Baby Face, Barbara Stanwyck, Warner Brothers, 1933, 27 x 41 In.		23900.00
Poster, Baby The Rain Must Fall, Columbia, 1965, 27 x 41 In.		20.00
Poster, Barbarella, Paramount, Style A, 1968, 27 x 41 In.		179.00
Poster, Barefoot In The Park, 1967, 27 x 41 In.		38.00
Poster, Belle De Jour, Allied Artists, 1968, 27 x 41 In.		56.00
Poster, Black Rose, 20th Century Fox, 1950, 27 x 41 In.		34.00
Poster, Black Sabbath, American International, 1964, 22 x 28 In.		102.00
Poster, Blue Bird, Progress Film, Germany A2, 1977, 16 x 22 ½ In.		15.00
Poster, Body Heat, Warner Bros., 1981, 27 x 41 In.		21.00
Poster, Breakfast At Tiffany's, Audrey Hepburn, 3 Sheet, c.1961, 47 x 84 In.	*illus*	2963.00
Poster, Brenda Starr Reporter, Joan Woodbury, Serial, Columbia, 1944, 27 x 41 In.		210.00
Poster, Cabaret, Allied Artists, R-1974, 27 x 41 In.		26.00
Poster, Casablanca, Warner Brothers, France, 1942, 31 ½ x 47 In.		11950.00
Poster, Champion, Charlie Chaplin, Essanay, 1915, 27 x 41 In.		33460.00
Poster, Cinderella, Disney, Japan, R-1974, 20 ¼ x 28 ½ In.		23.00
Poster, Citizen Kane, RKO, Style B, 1941, 27 x 41 In.		47800.00
Poster, Clash Of The Titans, MGM, Australia, 1981, 27 x 40 In.		26.00
Poster, Clockwork Orange, Warner Bros., R-1982, 27 x 41 In.		28.00
Poster, Cowboy & The Senorita, Republic, Argentina, 1944, 29 x 43 In.		131.00
Poster, Creeping Unknown, United Artists, 1956, 27 x 41 In.		69.00
Poster, Curse Of The Undead, Eric Fleming, Kathleen Crowley, 1959, 27 x 41 In.	*illus*	104.00
Poster, Day Of The Dead, United Film Distribution, Japan, 1985, 20 x 29 In.		50.00
Poster, Day The Earth Stood Still, 20th Century Fox, 1951, 27 x 41 In.		10755.00
Poster, Desperadoes' Outpost, Republic, 1952, 41 x 81 In.		69.00
Poster, Desperately Seeking Susan, Madonna, Orion, 1985, 27 x 41 In.		20.00
Poster, Dinosaurus, Universal International, 1960, 22 x 28 In.		191.00
Poster, Dr. No, Sean Connery, James Bond, United Artists, Belgium, 1962, 14 x 21 In.		131.00
Poster, Dr. No, Sean Connery, James Bond, United Artists, Sweden, 1962, 28 x 39 In.		155.00
Poster, Dracula, Universal, 1931, 27 x 41 In.		310700.00
Poster, Duck Soup, Marx Bros., Frame, 20 x 16 In.		110.00
Poster, Elephant Man, Japan, 1981, 20 x 29 In.		26.00
Poster, Fiddler On The Roof, Imperial Theatre, Cardboard, 1964, 14 x 22 In.		144.00
Poster, For Those Who Think Young, United Artists, 1964, 27 x 41 In.		22.00
Poster, Forsaking All Others, Joan Crawford, Clarke Gable, Oil On Canvas, 30 x 20 In.		448.00
Poster, Freaks, MGM, 1932, 14 x 36 In.		107550.00
Poster, French Connection, 20th Century Fox, 1971, 22 x 28 In.		35.00
Poster, From Russia With Love, Sean Connery, James Bond, 1964, 27 x 41 In.		287.00
Poster, Girl Happy, Elvis Presley, MGM, 1965, 27 x 41 In.		84.00
Poster, Halloween, Compass International, 1978, 27 x 41 In.		96.00
Poster, In The Navy, Bud Abbott & Lou Costello, 1941, 14 x 36 In.		145.00
Poster, Jezabel, Warner Brothers, Italian 2, 1938, 39 x 55 In.		8126.00
Poster, Le Mans, Steve McQueen, National General, 1971, 27 x 41 In.		227.00
Poster, Mildred Pierce, Joan Crawford, Warner Brothers, Italy, 1948, 39 x 55 In.		5676.00
Poster, Raven, Universal, Style D, c.1935, 27 x 41 In.		29875.00
Poster, Sea Raiders, Serial, Chapter 10, 1941, 27 x 41 In.	*illus*	127.00
Poster, Tarzan, New York Adventure, MGM, Stiff Paper, 1942, ½ Sheet, 22 x 28 In.		201.00
Poster, Tarzan The Fearless, Buster Crabbe, Serial, Chapter 9, 1933, 26 x 41 In.	*illus*	487.00
Poster, The Doors, The Ceremony Is About To Begin, Tri-Star, 1991, 27 x 41 In.		21.00
Poster, World Without End, Vargas Art, Allied Artists, Style B, 1956, 81 x 81 In.		10755.00
Press Book, Lost Horizon, 1937, 14 x 20 In.		173.00
Prop, Time Machine, Chair, Berninghaus Hercules, Restored As Barber Chair, c.1960, 46 x 26 In.		9000.00
Sketch Art, Harvey, James Stewart, 1950		627.00
Soundtrack Album, Easy Rider, Signed, Nicholson, Fonda, Hopper, 1969, 12 x 12 In.		588.00
Wallet, Dracula-Mummy, Vinyl, Snap Closure, Universal Pictures, 1963, 3 ½ x 4 ½ In.		306.00
Window Card, Fiddler On The Roof, Cardboard, Starring Zero Mostel As Tevye, 1964, 14 x 22 In.		140.00
Window Card, Sunday In New York, Starring Jane Fonda, 1963, 22 x 14 In.		45.00
Yearbook, James Dean, Basketball Uniform, Fairmount High School, Signed, 1948		1673.00

MT. JOYE is an enameled cameo glass made in the late nineteenth and twentieth centuries by Saint-Hilaire Touvier de Varraux and Co. of Pantin, France. This same company made De Vez glass. Pieces were usually decorated with enameling. Most pieces are not marked.

Vase, Berries, Pink, Mauve, Leaves, Landscape, Green Ground, Cameo, Signed, 8 In.		805.00
Vase, Cabin, Purple, Lake, Woods, Pink, Dark Orange Ground, Cameo, Signed, 6 In.		575.00
Vase, Flowers, White, Orange, Yellow, Green Leaves, Purple, Ruffled Rim, Signed, 14 In., Pair..		1265.00
Vase, Gold Bellflowers, Red Textured Ground, Oval, 4-Fold Rim, White, Cameo, 5 In.		345.00

M

Vase, Silver Acorns, Gold Leaves, Green, Textured, Chalice Shape, Footed, Signed, 17 In. 748.00
Vase, White Flowers, Green Iridescent, Enamel, Inward Ruffled Rim, 9 ¼ In. 92.00

MT. WASHINGTON Glass Works started in 1837 in South Boston, Massachusetts. In 1870 the company moved to New Bedford, Massachusetts. Many types of art glass were made there until 1894, when the company merged with Pairpoint Manufacturing Co. Amberina, Burmese, Crown Milano, Cut Glass, Peachblow, and Royal Flemish are each listed in their own category.

Biscuit Jar, Blue Daisies, Molded Scrolling Medallions, Oval, 7 ½ In. 144.00
Biscuit Jar, Gold Flowers, Raised Berries, Ivory, Tan Satin Ground, 4 x 5 In. 201.00
Biscuit Jar, Melon Ribbed, Silver Plated Collar & Lid, Bail Handle, c.1875, 6 ½ In. 212.00
Biscuit Jar, Melon Shape, Enameled Gold Flowers, Leaves, Ivory Ground, 6 ½ x 5 In. 259.00
Biscuit Jar, Melon Shape, Green Satin Glass, Gold Water Lilies, Metal Lid, Handle, 7 x 6 In. ... 144.00
Biscuit Jar, Pink Stripes, Gold Flowers, Ivory Satin Ground, Metal Lid, Handle, 4 x 4 In. 316.00
Biscuit Jar, Stylized Gold Flowers, Berries, Ivory Ground, Metal Lid & Handle, 4 x 5 In. 201.00
Bowl, Bedford Pattern, Crimped, Wood Polished, 9 In. 60.00
Inkwell, Flowers, Leaves, Black Glass, Rectangular Panels, Metal Collar, 3 ½ In. 748.00
Jar, Cover, Flower Medallions, Gold Lattice, Scrolls, Squat, Side Handles, Finial, 9 In. 2185.00
Jar, Flowers, White, Mauve, Melon Ribbed, Green, Gold, Silver Plate Embossed Top, 6 In. 550.00
Lamp Base, Birds In Flight, Pyramids, Metal Base, Square Glass Font, 18 In. 489.00
Lamp, Cut Glass Globe, Black Lava Glass, Multicolored Shards, Metal Base, Signed, 15 In. 4026.00
Lamp, Parlor, Cherubs, Cupids, Embossed, 17 In. 210.00
Perfume Bottle, Black Ground, Colored Patches, Stopper, c.1875, 3 ¾ In. 6372.00
Saltshaker, Egg, In Blossom, White Opaque Satin Glass, c.1891 .... 125.00
Saltshaker, Fig Shape, Flowers, Multicolored, c.1875, 2 ¾ In. 39.00
Saltshaker, Pansies, Painted, Opalware, 5 Lobes, Screw Top, c.1880.. 115.00
Shade, Flowers, White, Pink, Scalloped Border, Ribbon, 3 ¼ x 7 x 4 ½ In. 1150.00
Shaker, Flowers, White Enamel, Egg Shape, Painted Leaves, Cream To Rust................... *illus* 153.00
Sugar Shaker, Dogwood Flowers, Egg Shape, Blue To White, c.1890, 4 ¼ In. 270.00
Sugar Shaker, Egg Shape, Violet Design, Pewter Top, Mark, 4 ¼ In. 450.00
Sugar Shaker, Flowers, Multicolored, Egg Shape, Opaque White, Satin, c.1875, 4 ½ In. 258.00
Sugar Shaker, White Flowers, Melon Ribbed, Stems, Embossed Metal Lid, 4 In. 316.00
Sweetmeat, Albertine, Star Pattern, White Flowers, Squat, Embossed Lid, Stamp, 6 In. 288.00
Toothpick, Hat Shape, Enamel Ferns, Flowers... 374.00
Toothpick, Oval, 3-Fold Rim, Enamel Ferns, Flowers.. 259.00
Toothpick, Oval, 5-Star Rim, Yellow Enamel Flowers 288.00
Toothpick, Red Jagged Border, Enamel Flowers, Oval 316.00
Tumbler, Albertine, Translucent White, Gilt, Pontil, Marked, c.1875, 3 ¾ In. 145.00
Vase, 4 Fish, Raised Gold Net, Napoli, Cylinderical, Translucent, Applied Handles, 8 In. 7250.00
Vase, Blue, Gold Wisteria, Canal Scene, Double Canteen Shape, Marked, 7 In. 920.00
Vase, Bulbous, Stick Neck, Flowers, 9 ½ In. 660.00
Vase, Colonial, Venetian Canal, Gondola, Gold Detail, Dolphin Handles, 15 In. .... *illus* 3910.00
Vase, Lava, Black, Multicolored Shards, Gold Outline, Oval, Reeded Handles, 5 ½ In. 4140.00
Vase, Lava, Bulbous, Flared Mouth, Multicolored, 6 ½ In. 2013.00
Vase, Lava, Dark Ground, Green, Purple, Blue, Pink, 6 In. .... *illus* 4888.00
Vase, Lava, Multicolored Shards, Gold Outline, Reeded Handles, Oval, 6 In. 4140.00
Vase, Pinched Neck, Lavender Ground, Multicolored Patches, Gilt, c.1875, 4 In. 5664.00
Vase, Pink To White Ground, Charcoal Flowers, Green Leaf, 6 In. 345.00
Vase, Reeded, Berry Prunt, 3-Footed, Pontil, c.1875, 6 ¼ In. 171.00
Vase, Stylized Flowers, Tapered Melon Ribbed Body, Ruffled Rim, 8 ½ In. 460.00

MUD FIGURES are small Chinese pottery figures made in the twentieth century. The figures usually represent workers, scholars, farmers, or merchants. Other pieces are trees, houses, and similar parts of the landscape. The figures have unglazed faces and hands but glazed clothing. They were originally made for fish tanks or planters. Mud figures were of little interest and brought low prices until the 1980s. When the prices rose, reproductions appeared.

Woman, Bearded Man, Gloss Glaze, Impressed China, Signed, 19 & 18 ½ In., Pair............*illus* 690.00

MULBERRY ware was made in the Staffordshire district of England from about 1850 to 1860. The dishes were decorated with a reddish brown transfer design, now called mulberry. Many of the patterns are similar to those used for flow blue and other Staffordshire transfer wares.

Plate, Cabinet, Winter Farm Scene, Birds, Flowers, Alcock & Co., 10 ½ In. 112.00
Plate, Calendar, God Bless Our House Throughout 1975, Alfred Meakin.................................... 12.00
Plate, Corean, 12-Sided, Podmore Walker & Co., Mid 1800s, 9 ½ In. 85.00
Plate, Episcopal Theological Seminary, Lexington Kentucky, 10 ½ In. 750.00

Movie, Poster, Sea Raiders, Serial, Chapter 10, 1941, 27 x 41 In. $127.00

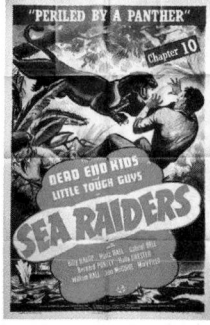

Movie, Poster, Tarzan The Fearless, Buster Crabbe, Serial, Chapter 9, 1933, 26 x 41 In. $487.00

Mt. Washington, Shaker, Flowers, White Enamel, Egg Shape, Painted Leaves, Cream To Rust $153.00

As always, the edited listings in *Kovels' Antiques & Collectibles Price Guide 2011* aren't available on any website, but readers should visit Kovels.com for information on trends, tips, reproductions, marks, old prices, and more!

M

Mt. Washington, Vase, Colonial, Venetian Canal, Gondola, Gold Detail, Dolphin Handles, 15 In. $3910.00

Mt. Washington, Vase, Lava, Dark Ground, Green, Purple, Blue, Pink, 6 In. $4888.00

Plate, Flower Border, Medallion, 10 ½ In.	55.00
Plate, Humphrey's Clock, Boy & Girl Waving At Man, Dickens, Ridgways, c.1880, 9 In.	79.00
Plate, Minerva, Roman Women, Greek Urns, Podmore Walker & Co., 7 ¾ In., Pair	195.00
Plate, Oriental, Center Transfer, Raised Relief Scroll Border, Scalloped, 8 In.	112.00
Plate, Rubens, Castles Series, Enoch Wood & Sons, Mid 1800s, 7 ½ In.	40.00
Plate, Susa, Charles Meigh & Son, Staffordshire, c.1861	62.00
Platter, Rhone Scenery, TJ&J Mayer, 13 ½ x 10 ½ In.	195.00
Platter, Washington Vase, Podmore Walker & Co., c.1859, 13 ¾ x 10 ½ In.	175.00
Relish, Mitten, Corean, Flared Ruffled Shape, Embossed Flowers, 9 x 5 ¼ In.	60.00
Spoon Holder, Romantic Staffordshire, 9 In.	95.00
Sugar, Cover, Forget-Me-Not, Girl With Dog, Ridgway & Co., Mid 1800s, 8 x 6 In.	125.00

MULLER FRERES, French for Muller Brothers, made cameo and other glass from about 1895 to 1933. Their factory was first located in Luneville, then in nearby Croismare, France. Pieces were usually marked with the company name.

Bowl, 4-Sided, Flared, 6-Sided Designs, Signed, 3 ½ x 6 ½ In.	215.00
Bowl, Pink Satin Glass, Elephant & Black Hunters In Relief, Marked, 13 In.	345.00
Lamp, Chandelier, Crystal Pearl, Fountain, c.1925, 37 x 18 In.	7768.00
Lamp, Domed Shade, Cameo Cut Landscape, Wrought Iron Base, Signed, 6 x 17 In.	2400.00
Lamp, Landscape, Trees, Apricot To Frost Ground, 3-Arm Support, Electric, 13 ¼ In.	1995.00
Shade, Globe, Peacocks, Flowers, Art Deco, 11 In.	2415.00
Vase, 5 Red Roses, Reimson Branches, Citron, Cameo, Signed, c.1910, 8 ¼ In.	1560.00
Vase, 8 Sparrows, Winter Branches, Mottled Blue, Signed, c.1910, 7 ¼ In.	1320.00
Vase, Cameo, Scenic, Marked, 6 ¼ In.	431.00
Vase, Crimson Lake Scene, Tall Trees, Shoreline, Cameo, Signed, c.1910, 13 In.	1080.00
Vase, Flowers, Green Stemmed, Oval, Cylindrical, Signed, 7 ½ In.	500.00
Vase, Geisha Girl, Lake, Green, Yellow, Earth Tones, Signed, Luneville, Cameo, 8 In.	805.00
Vase, Lake, Couple On Shore, Boat, Willow Tree, Cameo, Luneville, 8 ¼ In. ....*illus*	633.00
Vase, Red, Yellow Roses, Red Branches, Citron Ground, Cameo, Oval	1955.00
Vase, Stems, Raspberries, White Blossoms, Frosted Green, Pink, Brown, Cameo, Signed, 6 In.	4025.00
Vase, White Flecks, Tapered, Gold, Blue Mottled Bottom, 10 x 21 In.	86.00
Vase, White Flower, Mottled Yellow Leaves, Base, Blue Ground, Fluorogravure, Engraved, 5 In.	2596.00
Vase, Yellow, Dogs Hunting Boar, Mountain, Lake, Cylinder Shape, Cameo, Signed, 9 In.	1035.00

MUNCIE Clay Products Company was established by Charles Benham in Muncie, Indiana, in 1922. The company made pottery for the florist and giftshop trade. The company closed by 1939. Pieces are marked with the name *Muncie* or just with a system of numbers and letters, like *1A*.

Pitcher, Dutch, Yellow Glossy, 9 In.	400.00
Vase, Blue Drip Over Rose, Handles, 7 12 In.	325.00
Vase, Green Drip Over Mauve, Narrow Neck, c.1929, 4 In.	85.00
Vase, Green Drip Over Orange, 4 ¾ In.	85.00
Vase, Rose Glaze, Green Matte Drip, 6 ½ x 6 In.	90.00
Vase, Scalloped, Green & Lavender, 6 x 4 In.	120.00
Vase, Squat, Blue Drip Over Mauve, Marked H, c.1929, 3 ½ In.	85.00
Vase, White Matte Over Rose Glaze, Incised Mark, 6 In.	150.00

MUSIC boxes and musical instruments are listed here. Phonograph records, jukeboxes, phonographs, and sheet music are listed in other categories in this book.

Accordion, Hohner, Regina Style, c.1930, 8 ½ x 10 In.	35.00
Accordion, Tanzbar, Mechanical, Rosewood Veneered, Fretted Vents, Leather Handles, Rolls	711.00
Banjo, 4-String, Flower Decal, Grover Pat Tuning Pegs, Case	130.00
Banjo, 5-String, Fretless, Eagle Shoe Brackets, Tapered Nuts, Brass Owl In Head	400.00
Banjo, 5-String, Square Head, Ivory Tail Piece, Gut Strings	350.00
Banjo, Gibson, 4-String, Tenor, Case, 23 ¾ In.	575.00
Box, 6 Tunes, Swiss Cylinder, Internal Crank, Maple, 4 ½ x 13 x 6 ⅞ In.	360.00
Box, Brass Inlay, Banded Burlwood, Turned Melon Shape Feet, 1800s, 3 ¼ x 7 ¾ In. .... *illus*	420.00
Box, Brass, Singing Bird, Key Wind, Germany, 1 ¾ x 4 ⅛ x 2 ⅝ In.	690.00
Box, Burl Case, Swiss, 13-In. Cylinder, 8 x 24 x 12 In. .... *illus*	863.00
Box, Coin-Operated, Automated Picture, Barber Shop, 3 Dolls, 6 Bells, 8 Tunes .... *illus*	18720.00
Box, Crank, Symphonion, Cat, Automation, 6 In.	2925.00
Box, Criterion, Oak, Comb Disc, 11 ½ In.	495.00
Box, Cylinder, 3 Accessory Bells, European City, Cathedral, 8 ½ x 16 ½ x 10 In.	460.00
Box, Cylinder, Bird & Flower Image, 8 Tunes, Single Comb, Inlaid, 20 ½ x 5 ¾ In.	690.00
Box, Cylinder, Inlaid Case, 6 Bells, 8 Tunes, 13 In.	2925.00

Box, Cylinder, Inlaid Case, 12 Hidden Bells, 7 Tunes, 14 In.	1170.00
Box, Cylinder, Interchangeable, 4-6 Tunes, Inlaid Box, Zyther, 9 In.	2340.00
Box, Cylinder, Lever Wind, Mahogany, 6 Tunes, 25 x 37 x 12 In.	1422.00
Box, Cylinder, Lever Wind, Nickel Plated, Iron Bedplate, 10 Tunes, 6 ¼ In.	326.00
Box, Cylinder, Marquetry Lid, Musical Instruments, Flowers, Single Comb, 10 Tunes, Swiss, 22 In.	690.00
Box, Cylinder, Rosewood Case, Ebonized, Inlaid, Multi Tune, Swiss, c.1900, 31 In.	563.00
Box, Cylinder, Walnut, Domed Top, Applied Flowers, Panels, Internal Ratchet Wind, 29 x 16 ½ In.	2013.00
Box, Cylinder, Walnut, Inlays, Bell Strikes French Clock, 6 Tunes, Swiss, 27 x 10 In.	8050.00
Box, Cylinder, Walnut, Rosewood Grain Paint, Flowers, 6 Cylinders, 18 Tunes, 16 x 9 ½ In.	1438.00
Box, Disc, Mahogany, Dome Lid, Single Comb, 30 Discs, Regina, No. 4659, 15 ½ In.	2300.00
Box, Double Comb, Mahogany, 22 Tunes, Base, New Century, 18 ½ In.	5265.00
Box, Drums, Bells, 3 Combs, Rosewood, Flower Inlays, Legs, Handles, Swiss, 35 x 35 In.	2013.00
Box, Ebonized Rosewood, 8 Cylinders, Single Comb, Inlaid Flowers, c.1875, 7 x 22 x 10 In.	1880.00
Box, Ebony Case, Marquetry, Bow, Arrow, Single Comb, 12 Songs, Swiss, 20 In.	633.00
Box, F. Rzebitscher Musikwerk, Ebony Case, White Strapwork, Inset Glass Lid, Turned Feet, 5 x 9 In.	600.00
Box, Farm Setting, Children, Sheep, Semi Mechanical, Hand Crank, Automaton, 9 ½ x 14 In.	173.00
Box, Floor Model, Ornate Cabinet, Mahogany, Mica Decal, 22 Discs, 16 In.	8190.00
Box, Harp Form, Etched, Silver Plated, 18 x 9 x 6 In.	85.00
Box, Inlaid, Bands & Music Symbols, Ebonized Border, 13-In. Cylinder, 10 Tunes, 6 x 25 In. ...	345.00
Box, Jacot & Son, Grain Painted Rosewood, Inlaid, Label, 5 ½-In. Cylinder, 17 In.	460.00
Box, Jacot, Cylinder, Mahogany, Filigree Carved, 6 Tunes, Swiss, 31 x 8 In.	2243.00
Box, Jacot, Cylinder, Rosewood, Marquetry Inlay, Flowers, 10 Tunes, c.1890, 8 ½ x 24 In.	1200.00
Box, Kalliope, Disc, 10 Bells, 10 Discs, 17 ¼ In.	1760.00
Box, Kalliope, Tabletop, Oak Case, Inlay, 4 Bell Attachment, 7-In. Disc, 10 x 6 ½ In. ....*illus*	805.00
Box, LeCoultre, 4-Overture, Key Wind, No. 1288, 11-In. Cylinder, Walnut Case, 20 x 6 ½ In.	5750.00
Box, LeCoultre, 6-Air, Brass Comb Washers, 11-In. Cylinder, Grained Case, No. 787, 18 x 5 In.	920.00
Box, Longue Marache, Burlwood, Inlaid, 14 ½-In. Cylinder, Drawer, 1881, 15 x 46 In.	1840.00
Box, Mahogany Case, Inlaid Village Scene, Discs, Max Rettig Label, Berlin, c.1915, 7 ½ x 11 ½ In.	920.00
Box, Mermod Ideal, Soprano, Interchangeable, Ton Cards, 11-In. Cylinder, Inlay, 26 x 11 In. .	2875.00
Box, Mira, Mahogany Case, 6 ⅜-In. Comb, 16 15 ½-In. Discs, 13 x 27 x 20 In.	2070.00
Box, Music Changer, Alder Disc, Upright, Double Comb, 16 Discs, Walnut, 21 In.	1755.00
Box, Music Changer, Regina Style 9, Wood Case, 46 Discs, 15 ½ In.	1287.00
Box, Music Changer, Regina Style, Orchestral Corona, Oak, Holds 12 Discs................................	11700.00
Box, Organ, Jarome Thimbouville-Lamy, Inlays, Handles, 10 Tunes, Paris, 31 x 12 In.	3738.00
Box, Polyphon, Double Comb, Flower Inlay, 19 ⅝ In.	330.00
Box, Regina, 15 ½-In. Disc, Serpentine Mahogany Case, Stand, 15 Discs, 22 ½ In.	2760.00
Box, Regina, Bowfront, Mahogany, Plexiglas, Drawer, Carved, Upright Changer, 26 x 67 In.	16100.00
Box, Regina, Celluloid Plaques, Mahogany Case, 27 Discs, 15 ½ In.	1896.00
Box, Regina, Corona, Mahogany Case, Auto Changer, Brass Trim, 20 ¾-In. Disc, 69 In.	7313.00
Box, Regina, Corona Upright, Automatic Changer, 12 Discs, 15 ½ In., c.1900, 68 x 27 In.	9400.00
Box, Regina, Corona, Upright, Automatic Changer, Mahogany, 18 Discs, 67 x 27 In.	9400.00
Box, Regina, Disc, Double Comb, Walnut, 15 ½ In.	6250.00
Box, Regina, Double Comb, No. 71, 9 Discs, 12 In.	2340.00
Box, Regina, Mahogany, Carved, Copula Lid, Double Comb, Disc Cabinet, 32 x 25 ½ x 50 In. ..	4600.00
Box, Regina, Savings, Applied Brass Mounts, Wood, Pediment, 8 In.	2340.00
Box, Regina Style, 10 Double Combs, Brass Mounts, Mahogany, 78 Discs, 16 In.	5265.00
Box, Reginaphone, Mahogany, Serpentine Case, Side Crank, 40 Discs, 22 x 13 In.	3163.00
Box, Rosewood, Inlaid Flowers & Leaves, Ebonized Borders, 7 x 24 In.	1035.00
Box, Rosewood, Marquetry, String Inlay, 6 Tunes, Clockwork Movement, Swiss, 1835, 7 x 18 In.	920.00
Box, Shoemaker, Windup, 14 In.	410.00
Box, Singing Bird, 3 Birds In Cage, Branches, Wire Cage, Walnut Base, France, 13 x 21 In.	1150.00
Box, Singing Bird, Birdcage, 1 Piece, Round Base, 6 x 11 In.	585.00
Box, Singing Bird, Birdcage, Stand, Brass, 6 x 11 In.	351.00
Box, Singing Bird, Gilt Metal Cage, Stand, Berry Bush, Germany, 11 ¼ In. .... 299.00 to 359.00
Box, Singing Bird, Swivel Switch, Incised, Scrolled, France, 4 x 1 ½ In.	2588.00
Box, Singing Birds, Birdcage, 6-Sided Base, France..	2340.00
Box, Station Box, 2 Bell Strikers, Dancing Doll, Cylinder, Stand	83.00
Box, Stella, Mahogany, 21 15 ½-In. Discs, 25 x 21 ½ In.	976.00
Box, Sublime Harmonie, Cylinder, Fine Teeth, 8 Tunes, Bird, Flowers Inlaid Case, 38 In.	4095.00
Box, Sublime Harmonie, Cylinder, Harmony Werner, 8 Tunes, Inlaid Case, 15 In.	2925.00
Box, Swiss Chalet, Lift-Up Roof, Black Forest Style, c.1900, 10 x 14 x 7 In.	240.00
Box, Symphonion, Double Comb, Wood Case, 10 14 ½-In. Discs, c.1900 ....*illus*	2070.00
Box, Thorens, Automatic, Cherry Case, 10 4 ½-In. Discs, 4 x 10 ¾ x 6 ¼ In.	189.00
Box, Victorian, Walnut Burl, Hinged Lid, 8-Tune Cylinder, Bracket Feet, c.1880	633.00
Box, Walnut Case, Instrument Inlays, 12 Tunes, 6 Bells, Swiss, 25 x 13 In.	1035.00

Moriage

Moriage became a popular decoration on Japanese ceramics about 1900. A white clay thinned to look like toothpaste was put on the piece to make a raised decoration.

Mud Figure, Woman, Bearded Man, Gloss Glaze, Impressed China, Signed, 19 & 18 ½ In., Pair
$690.00

Muller Freres, Vase, Lake, Couple On Shore, Boat, Willow Tree, Cameo, Luneville, 8 ¼ In.
$633.00

M

Music, Box, Brass Inlay, Banded Burlwood, Turned Melon Shape Feet, 1800s, 3 ¼ x 7 ¾ In.
$420.00

451

Music, Box, Burl Case, Swiss, 13-in. Cylinder, 8 x 24 x 12 In. $863.00

Music, Box, Coin-Operated, Automated Picture, Barber Shop, 3 Dolls, 6 Bells, 8 Tunes $18720.00

Music, Box, Kalliope, Tabletop, Oak Case, Inlay, 4 Bell Attachment, 7-In. Disc, 10 x 6 ½ In. $805.00

Music, Box, Symphonion, Double Comb, Wood Case, 10 14 ½-in. Discs, c.1900 $2070.00

M

Box, Weill & Harburg, Walnut, Cylinder, Organ, Drum, Bells, Geneva, 28 x 15 In.	2300.00
Changer, Upright, Double Comb, 43 Tunes, Walnut, 15 ½ In.	2925.00
Drum, Bass, Light-Up, Hand Painted, Wood, 24 In.	118.00
Drum, Kilbourn, Eagle & Shield, Civil War, c.1865, 14 x 17 ½ In.	5850.00
Drum, Shield, Eagle, Banner, Reg. U.S. Infantry, Raymond S. Osgood, 17 ½ x 16 ½ In.	588.00
Flute, 1-Key, Pin Mounted, Metal Lined, c.1890, 24 In.	125.00
Flute, 4-Key, Blackwood, Metal Lined, 24 In.	225.00
Flute, Dark Wood, Keyless, Geo. Cloose, 24 In.	225.00
French Horn, Winter & Schoner, Linz, c.1860	1250.00
Gramophone, Berliner, Crank, Oak Arm, Turntable Clamp, 9 ½ x 15 ½ In.	9480.00
Graphophone, Columbia, Oak Case, 10-In. Arm, Hand Crank, Horn, 8 ¾ x 5 In.	474.00
Guitar, Alvarez Acoustic, Model 5045, Case, 38 In.	59.00
Guitar, Gibson, Ephiphone, 39 In.	130.00
Guitar, Nickel Plated Brass Body, 6 Strings, 2 F Holes, National Guitar, Case, 1933	3080.00
Harmonica, Hohner Marine Band, Germany, Box	5.06
Harmonica, Seydel S'hne Co., Graf Zeppelin Shape, Klingenthal, c.1930, 4 In.	84.00
Harp, Lyon & Healy, Bird's-Eye Maple, Fluted Column, Claw Feet, 7 Pedals, c.1875, 62 x 32 x 15 In.	3450.00
Harp, S & P Erand, Pedal, Gothic, 46 Strings, Green Paint, Gilt, c.1890, 35 x 70 In.	2013.00
Harpsichord, Robert Taylor, Fruitwood, Passau, 33 ½ x 50 In.	431.00
Hunting Horn, Copper, England, c.1900, 35 x 3 ¾ In.	80.00
Mandola, Gibson, No. H-2, Case, 1921	2714.00
Mandolina, Roller Organ, Mechanical Organette, Gold Stenciling, 14 x 15 ½ In. ....*illus*	605.00
Nickelodeon, Oak Case, Glass Front, 25 Cent, Western Electric, 52 x 54 In.	6500.00
Nickelodeon, Stafford, Mahogany, Stained Glass Panels, 1919	4245.00
Nickelodeon, Style 6 Orchestra, Mahogany, Nelson-Wiggins	15000.00
Orchestrion, Player Piano, Leonard, Mahogany, Glass Front, 50 Cent, 79 x 59 In.	6600.00
Organ Band, Arthur Busens Arburo, Carved, Paper Rolls, Antwerp, 8 Ft. 2 In. x 8 Ft. 7 In.	20400.00
Organ, Military Band, Wurlitzer Style, Instruments, Painted Designs, 87 x 72 In.	13800.00
Organ, Pump, J. Estep Co., Walnut, Raised Panels, Carved, Brattleboro, 1890s, 65 x 52 In.	600.00
Organ, Roller, Mechanical Orguinette Co., N.Y., Walnut Case, Paper Roll	715.00
Organ, Roller, Mechanical Orguinette Co., Walnut, Stenciled, New York	132.00
Organ, Roller, New American Musical Box, Wood Cob	303.00
Organ, Street, Mussio, Walnut, Brass Straps, Crank, Leather Strap, 23 Notes, 17 x 19 In.	3163.00
Piano, Baby Grand, Chickering, Mahogany, Bench, 37 ½ x 50 ½ x 61 In.	1815.00
Piano, Baby Grand, John Broadwood & Sons, Mahogany, Spade Feet, Casters, Bench	448.00
Piano, Baby Grand, Opus Burled Wood, Tapering Legs, Spade Feet, Bench, c.1950, 40 x 56 x 67 In.	1135.00
Piano, Baby Grand, Yamaha, Bench, Black Lacquered Case, Brass Casters, Square Legs	5310.00
Piano, Biedermeier, Figured Walnut, Line Inlay, H. Huni, Switzerland, c.1830, 72 In.	575.00
Piano, Grand, Erard, French Empire, Fruitwood, Marquetry, Bronze Mount, Paris, 93 In.	5333.00
Piano, Grand, Mahogany Case, Type A, 85 Keys, Steinway & Sons, c.1890, 72 In. ....*illus*	6038.00
Piano, Parlor Grand, Steinway, Rococo Style, Ebonized, N.Y., c.1859, 38 x 84 x 42 In. .....*illus*	588.00
Piano, Player, Starck, Mahogany, 4 Rolls, Bench, 54 x 59 x 28 In.	644.00
Piano, Player, Upright, 14 Rolls, 53 x 63 ½ x 29 In.	550.00
Piano, Upright, Burled Walnut, Zeitter & Winkelmann, 19th Century, 52 x 62 x 27 In.	777.00
Pianoforte, Hepplewhite Case, Mahogany, Inlays, J. Broadwood, England, 1700s, 34 x 64 In.	2115.00
Pianoforte, Hepplewhite, Mahogany, Coffin Shape, 61 Keys	508.00
Symphonion, Music Changer, Upright, Walnut, Double Comb, Clock, 12 In. ....*illus*	2106.00
Trumpet, Bass, Rotary Valve, Boston Musical Instrument Mfg.	2500.00
Trumpet, Martin Committee, Case, 1940s	1725.00
Trumpet, Parduba Double Cup Mouthpiece, Silvered Brass, Fitted Soft Case, 1900s, 21 In.	360.00
Violin, Bow, Lion Head Neck End, Stylized Back, Sound Holes, Key Head, 4 Strings, 23 In.	154.00
Violin, Folk Art, Pine, Carved, Black Paint Accents, Wood Case, Miniature, 16 In.	230.00
Violin, Stradivarius Type, Case, Germany, c.1875	489.00
Zither, Columbia, No. 2 ¼, Painted, U.S.A., 20 ⅛ x 13 ¼ In.	40.00
Zither, Oscar Schmidt, No. 2 Model, Eagle & Shield Decal, 1894, 13 ½ x 21 In.	79.00
Zither, Strings On Stepped Side, Hungary, 41 x 10 In.	350.00

MUSTACHE CUPS were popular from 1850 to 1900 when the large, flowing mustache was in style. A ledge of china or silver held the hair out of the liquid in the cup. This kept the mustache tidy and also kept the mustache wax from melting. Left-handed mustache cups are rare but are being reproduced.

Flowers, Painted, Tan Ground, Gold Trim & Highlights, Bavaria	50.00
Runny Olive Glaze, Alkaline Glaze, Strap Handle, Mustache Protector, 4 ½ In.	460.00

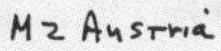

MZ AUSTRIA is the wording on a mark used by Moritz Zdekauer on porcelains made at his works in Altrolau, Austria, from 1884 to 1909. The mark was changed to MZ *Altrolau* in 1909, when the firm was purchased by C.M. Hutschenreuther. The firm operated under the name Altrolau Porcelain Factories from 1909 to 1945. It was nationalized after World War II. The pieces were decorated with lavish floral patterns and overglaze gold decoration. Full sets of dishes were made as well as vases, toilet sets, and other wares.

Bonbon, Pink Roses On Folded-In Rim, Pearl Luster Glaze, 2 Raised Handles, 7 ½ In.	78.00
Bowl, Acorns In Pods, Leaves, Lustre Glaze, Gilt, Folded-In Rim, 4 Branch Feet, 7 In.	220.00
Bowl, Stylized Pink Flowers, Green Leaves, Gold Trim, Scalloped, Footed, 4 x 10 In.	35.00
Cake Plate, Ring Of White Poppies, Gold Trim, Shaped Open Handles, 10 ½ In.	49.00
Charger, 3 Owls, In Tree, Night Sky, Snowy Ground, Black Rim, 12 ¾ In.	40.00
Creamer, Flowers, Pink, Yellow, Orange, Mint Green Border, Gold Trim, 8-Sided	40.00
Cup & Saucer, Pink Roses, Gold Leafy Rim	35.00
Fish Set, Fish, Gold Trim, Platter, Plates, Sauce Boat, Ladle, 24 Piece	275.00
Fruit Dish, Underplate, Floral Band, Gold Rim, 5-In. Plate	25.00
Pin Tray, Forget-Me-Nots, Oval, Gold Trim, 6 In.	5.00
Plate, 3 Grape Clusters, Leaves, Connecting Vine, Shaded Lilac Edge, 8 ½ In.	59.00
Plate, 4 Yellow Roses On Border, Blue Ground, 9 ½ In.	8.50
Plate, Dandelions, Gold Trim, Scalloped Border, M.G. Lohman, 1921, 8 ⅜ In.	85.00
Plate, Red Poppies, Gold Medallions Around Border, 7 In.	30.00
Sauceboat, Underplate, Pink Lustre Glaze, Gold Trim, Shaped Edges, 1936, 6 In.	45.00
Sugar, Cover, Blue Art Nouveau Secessionist Design, Shaped Rim & Handles	65.00
Tankard, Red Berries, Green Leaves, Columnar, Gold Handle, 13 In.	275.00
Tray, Dresser, Art Nouveau Flowers, Pink, White, Green Trim, Oval, Handles, 12 ¾ In.	85.00
Vase, Morning Glories, Vine, Gold Rim, 2 Open Handles, 11 In.	15.00
Vase, Purple Flowers, Green Leaves Blue Ground, Pitcher Form, Gold Handle, 8 ½ In.	65.00
Vase, Red & Yellow Roses, Green Ground, Shouldered, Buttressed Gold Handles, 7 In.	225.00

NAILSEA glass was made in the Bristol district in England from 1788 to 1873. It was made by many different factories, not just the Nailsea Glass House. Many pieces were made with loopings of either white or colored glass as decoration.

Fairy Lamp, Chartreuse, White Swirl, Ruffled Base, 6 In., 3 Piece	345.00
Flask, Clear, Pink & White Alternating Swirls, Tooled Mouth, 1870, 8 ¾ In.	160.00
Flask, Clear, Red Flashed, White Looping, Tooled Lip, Pontil, 1870-1900, 5 ¾ In.	219.00
Flask, Clear, White, Cranberry Looping, Gemel, Tooled Milk Glass Lip, 9 ¾ In.	104.00
Flask, Clear, White Looping, Applied Cobalt Blue Lip, Pontil, 1870-1900, 7 ¾ In.	104.00
Flask, Clear, White Looping, Rigaree, Tooled Mouth, Gemel, Pontil, c.1870, 8 ¾ In.	115.00
Flask, Clear, White Looping, Tooled Mouth, Gemel, Pontil, 1870-1900, 9 ¼ In.	104.00
Flask, Clear, White, Pink Broken Looping, Gemel, Red Wings, Tooled Lip, 10 ½ In.	104.00
Flask, Clear, White, Pink Looping, Gemel, Clear Swirled Lip, 10 ¼ In.	104.00
Flask, Milk Glass, Cranberry, Herring Bone, Tooled Lip, Pontil, 1870-1900, 7 In.	138.00
Flask, Milk Glass, Cranberry Looping, Gemel, Tooled Mouth, Pontil	138.00
Flask, Milk Glass, Cranberry Looping, Tooled Lip, Pontil, 1870-1900, 7 ⅜ In.	219.00
Flask, Milk Glass, Cranberry Looping, Tooled Lip, Pontil, 1870-1900, 8 ⅜ In.	230.00
Flask, Milk Glass, Red, Blue Looping, Tooled Lip, Pontil, 1870-1900, 8 ⅜ In.	316.00
Flask, Opalescent Cranberry & White Herringbone, Pontil, c.1870, 7 ¼ In. ...... *illus*	403.00
Flask, Pink, White Looping, Clear, Tooled Lip, Pontil, 1870-1900, 6 ⅞ In.	184.00
Flask, Red, Blue Swirl, Clear, Milk Glass, Tooled Lip, Pontil, 1870-1900, 7 ⅛ In.	345.00
Flask, Red Swirls Over White, Hand Blown, Late 1800s, 10 x 6 In.	120.00
Flask, Red, White Looping, Tooled Lip, Pontil, 1870-1900, 7 In.	265.00
Flask, Stopper, Red Swirls Over White, Hand Blown, Late 1800s, 8 x 4 ½ In.	270.00
Flask, White, Lavender Looping, Clear, Tooled Lip, Pontil, 1870-1900, 8 ¾ In.	144.00
Flask, Yellow, White Looping, Tooled Lip, Pontil, 1870-1900, 6 ⅛ In.	196.00
Pipe, Pink Over White Swirl, Curved, 17 In.	120.00
Rolling Pin, Glass, Burgundy & Clear Swirl, Blue & Clear Swirl, 14 In., Pair	300.00
Rolling Pin, Pink & White Wave, 18 In.	207.00

NAKARA is a trade name for a white glassware made about 1900 by the C. F. Monroe Company of Meriden, Connecticut. It was decorated in pastel colors. The glass was very similar to another glass, called Wave Crest, made by the company. The company closed in 1916. Boxes for use on a dressing table are the most commonly found Nakara pieces. The mark is not found on every piece.

Box, Collars & Cuffs, Pink Flowers, Scrolls, Blue Satin Ground, Marked, C.F. Monroe, 8 In.	1035.00
Box, Hinged Cover, Daisies, White Bead Enameling, Pink Ground, 6-Sided, 4 x 3 ½ In.	354.00

Music, Mandolina, Roller Organ, Mechanical Organette, Gold Stenciling, 14 x 15 ½ In.
$605.00

Music, Piano, Grand, Mahogany Case, Type A, 85 Keys, Steinway & Sons, c.1890, 72 In.
$6038.00

Music, Piano, Parlor Grand, Steinway, Rococo Style, Ebonized, N.Y., c.1859, 38 x 84 x 42 In.
$588.00

453

Music, Symphonion, Music Changer,
Upright, Walnut, Double Comb, Clock,
12 In.
$2106.00

Nailsea, Flask, Opalescent Cranberry
& White Herringbone, Pontil,
c.1870, 7 ¼ In.
$403.00

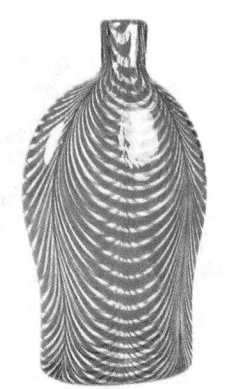

Napkin Ring, Silver Plate, Figural,
Bird On Wishbone, 3 In.
$150.00

Cigar Humidor, Blue Opaline, Pink Flowers, Verse, Cylinder Shape, Verse, C.F. Monroe, 6 In.	431.00
Dresser Box, Hinged Lid, Cherubs, Blue Ground, C.F. Monroe, Late 1800s, 3 ½ x 8 In. Diam.	600.00
Dresser Box, Pink Flowers, Green Opaline, Oval, Marked, C.F. Monroe, 4 ½ In.	173.00
Dresser Box, Pink Flowers, Purple Body, Marked, C.F. Monroe, 10 In.	978.00
Dresser Box, Pink Ground, Green Leaves, White Mums, Metal Collar, Marked, 8 In.	805.00
Humidor, The Old Sport, Bulldog, Yellow, Brown, 6 ½ In.	320.00
Jewelry Box, Burnt Orange, Original Lining, Tea Scene On Lid, Hinged, 4 In.	350.00
Jewelry Box, Round, Painted Daisies, 6 In.	950.00
Match Holder, White Scrolls, Red Ground, C.F. Monroe, 1 ½ In.	201.00
Vase, Pink Chrysanthemum, Blue Ground, Gold Ormolu Handles, Footed, Marked, 17 ½ In.	4200.00
Vase, Violets, Pale Orange, Ribbon Mold, Brass Footed, Marked, 8 ½ In.	250.00

NANKING is a type of blue-and-white porcelain made in Canton, China, since the late eighteenth century. It is very similar to Canton, which is listed under its own name in this book. Both Nanking and Canton are part of a larger group now called Chinese export porcelain. Nanking has a spear-and-post border and may have gold decoration.

Bowl, Soup, Blue, White, Gold Rim, 19th Century, 1 ¾ x 10 In.	345.00
Cider Jug, Cover, Applied Strap Handle, Foo Dog Knop, 1800s, 10 ¾ In.	2340.00
Platter, Blue & White, Lake Scene, Hexagonal Border, 14 x 18 In.	2280.00
Platter, Houses, Water, Oval, Early 1800s, 10 ½ x 13 In.	145.00
Platter, River Scene, Leafy Border, 8-Sided, 18th Century, 12 ¼ x 15 ¼ In.	145.00
Teapot, Landscape Scene, Gilt, Early 1800s, 6 x 10 In.	300.00

NAPKIN RINGS were in fashion from 1869 to about 1900. They were made of silver, porcelain, wood, and other materials. They are still being made today. The most popular rings with collectors are the silver plated figural examples. Small, realistic figures were made to hold the ring. Good and poor reproductions of the more expensive rings are now being made, and collectors must be very careful.

Bakelite, Bird, Green, Mid 1900s	75.00
Bakelite, Bunny, Green, Rod Eye	80.00
Bakelite, Duck, Black, Rod Eye, Mid 1900s	95.00
Bakelite, Elephant, Butterscotch, Mid 1900s	90.00
Silver Plate, Figural, Antelope, Standing, Ring On Back, Rogers & Bros.	176.00
Silver Plate, Figural, Bear, With Gun	321.00
Silver Plate, Figural, Big Wolf, Howling, Barbour	575.00
Silver Plate, Figural, Bird On Wishbone, 3 In. ....*illus*	150.00
Silver Plate, Figural, Birds, Blue, Engraved, James Tufts, Boston, 4 x 2 In.	55.00
Silver Plate, Figural, Boy & Begging Dog, Meriden	201.00
Silver Plate, Figural, Boy, Crawling Over American Flag, Wilcox	345.00
Silver Plate, Figural, Boy, Crawling, Stealing Bird's Eggs, Meriden Silver Plate Co.	175.00
Silver Plate, Figural, Boys, Holding Up Square, Meriden ....*illus*	51.00
Silver Plate, Figural, Cherub, Crossed Hockey Sticks, Meriden	345.00
Silver Plate, Figural, Chick, Wishbone, Good Morning, Engraved, Toronto Silver Plate, 3 x 2 In.	40.00
Silver Plate, Figural, Chicken, Standing, Meriden	402.00
Silver Plate, Figural, Cow, On Base, Marked, Rogers Smith Co., Meriden, Ct., 2 ½ x 2 ¾ In.	55.00
Silver Plate, Figural, Dog, Hall Elton & Co. ....*illus*	146.00
Silver Plate, Figural, Dog, Seated Next To Doghouse, Simpson Hall & Miller, 3 In.	300.00
Silver Plate, Figural, Eagle, Holder Between Wings, Knife Rest Base, Rogers & Smith	201.00
Silver Plate, Figural, Fawn, By Fence ....*illus*	205.00
Silver Plate, Figural, Fireman's Hat, Pairpoint	1150.00
Silver Plate, Figural, Giraffe, Under Palm Tree, Racin	2300.00
Silver Plate, Figural, Jack & Jill, Tufts.	4025.00
Silver Plate, Figural, Kangaroo, Map Of Australia, Marked, Falcon Silver Plate Co., 3 ½ x 3 In.	30.00
Silver Plate, Figural, Owl, Glass Eyes, Meriden, 3 ¼ In.	350.00
Silver Plate, Figural, Owl, Marked, F.B. Rogers Silver Co., 3 x 5 ⅛ In.	97.00
Silver Plate, Figural, Pug Dog, Glass Eyes, 3 In.	165.00
Silver Plate, Figural, Rabbit, Southington.	690.00
Silver Plate, Figural, Sailor, With Anchor, Reed & Barton	460.00
Silver Plate, Figural, Squirrel, On Branch, 3 ⅝ x 1 ¾ In.	60.00 to 120.00
Silver Plate, Winged Cherub Holding Figural Glass Vase, Meriden	288.00
Sterling Silver, Figural, Elephant, Ring On Back, Gorham, 1882, 3 x 3 In.	230.00
Sterling Silver, Flowers, Leaves, Art Nouveau	60.00
Sterling Silver, Flowers, Leaves, Enamel	66.00

NASH glass was made in Corona, New York, from about 1928 to 1931. A. Douglas Nash bought the Corona glassworks from Louis C. Tiffany in 1928 and founded the A. Douglas Nash Corporation with support from his father, Arthur J. Nash. Arthur had worked at the Webb factory in England and for the Tiffany Glassworks in Corona.

NASH

Bowl, Chartreuse, Vertical Ribs, Round, Pink Rim, 2 ¾ x 12 ¾ In.	305.00
Bowl, Chintz, Bronze Pinwheel Design, Scalloped Rim, 13 In.	850.00
Bowl, Spiral, 3 x 13 In.	293.00
Compote, Gold Iridescent, Vertical Ribs, Scalloped Rim, 6 In.	1900.00
Finger Bowl, Underplate, Chintz, Blue Opalescent, Ruffled, 6-In. Plate	35.00
Vase, Amber Iridescent, Flower Form, Stretched Ruffled Rim, Leaf Foot, 5 ½ x 6 In.	400.00
Vase, Chintz, Blue Pulled Zipper, Cylindrical, Spread Bottom, 7 ¾ In.	525.00
Vase, Gold Iridescent, Amber Highlights, Flared, Bulbous Top, Scalloped Rim, Footed, 4 In.	345.00
Vase, Grass Green Iridescent, Gold Highlights, Spherical, Inward Rolled Rim, 6 ½ x 7 In.	150.00
Vase, Stylized Leaves, Raised, Gold Iridescent, Cylindrical, Tapered, Round Foot, 5 In.	368.00

NAUTICAL antiques are listed in this category. Any of the many objects that were made or used by the seafaring trade, including ship parts, models, and tools, are included. Other pieces may be found listed under Scrimshaw.

Anchor, Brass, Double Hook, 2 Piece	131.00
Anchor, Cast Iron, 4 Hooks, Early 19th Century, 29 x 20 In.	67.00
Anchor, Wrought Iron, Early 17th Century, 7 Ft. 10 In.	600.00
Bell, Ship's, Aluminum, Mahogany Mount Board, Knotted Handle, Clanger, 23 x 6 In.	98.00
Bell, Ship's, Brass, SS New Amsterdam, Rotterdam, 1938, 7 In.	165.00
Bell, Ship's, Bronze, Rope, Bracket, 10 ½ x 7 ½ In., Pair	316.00
Bell, Ship's, Iron, Brass, 1900s, 14 x 10 In.	351.00
Bell, Ship's, Silver, Eagle Finial, Stand & Plate, 24 x 12 In.	345.00
Binnacle, Brass Case, Whale Oil Lamps, Gimbals, Negus, New York, c.1930, 34 x 13 In.	411.00
Binnacle, Brass Hood, Compass, White & Sons, Corsair, 10 x 11 In.	250.00
Binnacle, Brass Top Over Compass, Wood Base, Kelvin & Wilfried O. White, Co., 1900s, 50 In.	499.00
Binnacle, Brass, Wood, Cast Iron Balls, Compass Bonnet, Chart, Negus, N.Y., 53 x 32 In.	2100.00
Blackjack, Sailor's, Iron Cable, Rope Wrapped, 19th Century, 13 In.	311.00
Bollard, Bronze, U.S. Navy Minesweeper, 12 x 17 ½ In.	500.00
Canoe, Birch Bark, Indian, 31 ¾ In.	110.00
Canoe, Wood, 2 Caned Seats, Green Paint, Old Town Canoe, Maine, c.1900, 17 Ft.	881.00
Canoe, Wood, Canvas, Green, Padded Yoke, Paddles, Old Town Canoe Co., Me., c.1965, 16 Ft.	1896.00
Chest, Armada, Wrought Iron, Iron Bands, Handles, Lock, Germany, c.1700, 15 x 27 In. . *illus*	3744.00
Chest, Captain's, 12 Gin Bottles, Dip Molded, Amber, H.E. Drown, Dutch, c.1800, 11 ½ x 18 In.	1035.00
Chest, Sea, Pine, c.1800, 17 x 38 In.	550.00
Chronometer, Brass, Silver Dial, 2-Day, Mahogany Box, Bliss & Creighton, c.1850, 7 x 7 In.	2468.00
Chronometer, Hamilton, No. 22, 3-Tier Mahogany Box, 48-Hour Indictator, 2 ¼ In.	889.00
Clock, Chelsea, Brass Case, Black Dial, U.S. Navy, Mass., c.1900, 7 In.	353.00
Clock, Chelsea, Brass, Round, 10 In.	1150.00
Clock, Grogan & Co., Shelf, Boston, Ship's Bell, Pittsburgh, c.1900	1287.00
Clock, Schatz, Ship's Wheel, Germany, 13 In.	92.00
Clock, Seth Thomas, Ship's Bell, Wall, 1-Day, Silvered Dial, c.1920, 11 In.	201.00
Clock, Seth Thomas, Ship's, Brass, Round, 10 ¼ In.	1170.00
Clock, Seth Thomas, Ship's, Rose Brass Case, Ashton Valve Co., Mass., 10 ¾ In.	819.00
Clock, Seth Thomas, Ship's, Round, Brass, Ashcroft & Co., Stamped Dial, 8 In.	384.00
Clock, Ship's, Chelsea Clock Co., Bell, Brass, Copper, c.1957	1541.00
Clock, Ship's Deck, Brass, Mid 20th Century, 8 ¾ In.	950.00
Clock, Tide, Barometer, Brass, Mahogany, 8 ½ x 16 In.	195.00
Compass, Boat, Copper Case, Lid, Brass, Wm. Welch Mfg. Co., c.1920, 10 x 8 In.	88.00
Compass, Box, 1920s, 5 ¼ x 4 ¾ x 2 ¼ In.	150.00
Compass, Brass, 6 Glass Panes, Tapered Cone Housing, Marked, Kelvin White, Boston, 12 x 9 In.	748.00
Compass, Dry Card, Signed Label, Holland, 1800s, 9 In.	235.00
Compass, Ship's, Brass, Lionel, New York, c.1850, 9 x 10 In.	380.00
Compass, Ship's, White Case, Sestrel, England, c.1940, 10 x 7 In.	117.00
Compass, Tell-Tale, Brass, Gimbal Mount, Original Bracket, 5 ¼ x 10 In.	556.00
Compass, Whaler's Dory, Wood Case, Brass Hinges, Hook & Eye, 3 ¾ In.	650.00
Course Plotter, Teak, Numbers On Spindles, 3 Knobs, Early 1900s, 5 ½ x 13 ½ x 5 In.	195.00
Deck Bitt, Cast Iron, 3 Horns, Early 20th Century, 10 x 10 In.	66.00
Desk, Lap, Seaman's, Wood, Brass Bound, 1800s, 6 x 14 In.	173.00
Desk, Ship's Captain, Mixed Wood, Tambour Top, Lift-Up Lid, Drawer, Mid 1800s, 9 x 19 In.	980.00
Diorama, Ft. Mason, San Francisco, 4-Masted Schooner, Tugboat, 1910, 20 x 28 In.	1100.00

Napkin Ring, Silver Plate, Figural, Boys, Holding Up Square, Meriden
$51.00

Napkin Ring, Silver Plate, Figural, Dog, Hall Elton & Co.
$146.00

Napkin Ring, Silver Plate, Figural, Fawn, By Fence
$205.00

N

Nautical, Chest, Armada, Wrought Iron, Iron Bands, Handles, Lock, Germany, c.1700, 15 x 27 In.
$3744.00

TIP
Clean chrome with white vinegar or tea.

Nautical, Embroidery, Crowned Crest, Unicorn, Lion, Flags, Ship, 17 x 14 In. $234.00

Netsuke, Ivory, Cat & Toad, Applied Pigment, Signed, 1 ¼ In. $1047.00

Netsuke, Ivory, Grooming Monkeys, Applied Pigment, Painted Eyes, 2 In. $472.00

Netsuke, Wood, Fat Old Man In Red Robe, Inlaid Ivory Teeth, 1 ¼ In. $937.00

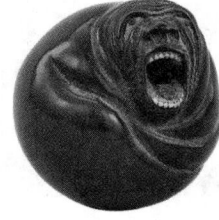

Diorama, Steamship Dundee, 2-Masted, Case, 20 x 30 ½ In.	400.00
Diving Helmet, Copper, Brass Portholes, Fittings, U.S. Navy, Morse Diving Equip., 16 x 14 In.	173.00
Embroidery, Crowned Crest, Unicorn, Lion, Flags, Ship, 17 x 14 In. ....*illus*	234.00
Figure, Old Salt, Anchor, Ship's Wheel, Boat, Green Base, Painted, Cast Iron, 8 In.	47.00
Figurehead, Viking, Wood, Carved, Painted, 45 x 15 ½ x 12 In.	600.00
Figurehead, Woman, Holding Torch, Hand On Waist, Carved, Wood, Painted, 52 In.	8050.00
Figurehead, Woman, Wearing Helmet, Red Dress, Wood, Carved, 1800s, 55 ½ x 29 In.	12000.00
Half-Model, 3-Masted Ship, Carved, Painted, Choppy Seas Base, 1800s, 17 x 24 In.	936.00
Half-Model, Side Wheeler, Pine, Teign, Vessel 55, London, 1896, 8 x 37 In.	470.00
Harpoon, Arctic, Double Flue, Cast Steel, Stamped RN, DW, 36 In.	1175.00
Harpoon, Swivel Temple Head, Conical Socket For Screw Hole, 33 ¼ In.	975.00
Harpoon, Swivel Temple Head, Forged Shaft, Medial Loop, 33 ½ In.	95.00
Harpoon, Whaling, Iron, Hand Forged, Toggle Head, Shear Tip, Painted Shaft, Late 1800s, 34 In.	1033.00
Harpoon, Whaling, Temple Style, Toggle, Rope, 1800s, 35 In.	1528.00
Hat, British Naval Officer's, Bicorn, Large Cockade On Side, Black Silk, c.1820	150.00
Ladder, Mahogany, 5 Rungs, Brass Hooks, Rubber Treads, 55 x 13 x 4 In.	350.00
Lamp, Ship's, Brass, ½ Round Pivoting Dome, Turned Stem, Round Base, 15 x 7 ¾ In.	81.00
Lance, Whaling, Stamped Cast Iron, Macy, 1800s, 57 In.	1998.00
Lantern, Copper, Brass, Clear & Colored Inner Lenses, W. Harvie, Glasgow, 25 In., Pair	633.00
Lantern, Ship's, c.1900, 14 x 16 In.	144.00
Lantern, Ship's, Copper, Brass, Wired & Mounted As Table Lamp, 18 In., Pair	1053.00
Lantern, Ship's, Oil, Copper, Brass, Glass, Handle, Marked, England, 23 ½ In.	460.00
Lantern, Ship's, Signal, Brass, Glass, 20 x 13 In., Pair	316.00
Life Ring, Cork, Canvas Cover, Dongan Hills, N.Y., Rope Handles, Early 1900s, 31 In.	170.00
Model, America's Cup Yacht, Puritan, Brass, Mahogany, Cloth, 48 x 54 ½ x 8 In.	960.00
Model, Clipper Ship, Yorkshire, Wood Stand, 20th Century, 21 x 31 In.	294.00
Model, Lifeboat, Wood, White Paint, Black Stand, c.1850, 5 x 15 In.	207.00
Model, New Hebrides Ship, Cane, Incised Decoration, c.1860, 14 ¾ In.	475.00
Model, Orion, Black Hull, 3-Masted, 2 Anchors, Cased, Late 1800s, 23 ½ x 46 In.	470.00
Model, Paddle Wheel Boat, Lily Jane, Wood, Metal, Glass, Plaster, Painted, c.1886, 18 ½ x 33 In.	2938.00
Model, Sailboat, Blue Hill, 2-Masted, 3 Canvas Sails, Wood, Painted, Railroad, String, 38 In.	165.00
Model, Sartari, Wood, 22 x 51 x 8 In.	695.00
Model, Ship, 3-Masted, Full Rigging, Painted, c.1890, 23 x 31 x 12 In.	1521.00
Model, Ship, King Of Mississippi, Paddlewheel, Wood, Painted, Case, 11 x 26 In.	130.00
Model, Ship, Robert E. Lee, Side Wheeler, Wood, Painted, 10 ½ x 26 In.	177.00
Model, Ship, USS Constitution, Wood, Painted, String Rigging, Display Case, 27 x 42 In.	266.00
Model, Steamship, SS Helen, Wood Hull, 2 Rigged Masts, Smokestack, 19 x 34 In.	146.00
Model, Tugboat, Marie, Gloucester Harbor, Shadowbox Frame, 15 ¾ x 22 ¾ In.	702.00
Model, Whaleboat, Oars, Harpoon, Keg, Rope, Wooden, Case, 3 ½ x 9 ½ In.	644.00
Octant, Samuel Emery, Brass, Inlaid Ivory, Inscribed Thomas Dodd, Ebony Case, 13 In.	702.00
Page Turner, Red Star Line, Ship, Tin Lithograph, 3 ¼ x 12 In.	610.00
Plaque, Mahogany, Brass, British Royal Navy Submarine, Crown, Dolphins, 25 x 11 In.	575.00
Pond Boat, Composition, Wood Mast, Cloth Sails, Boucher, 30 In.	1265.00
Pond Boat, Single Mast, 1880-1900, 62 x 53 In.	2000.00
Pond Boat, Single Sail, Partial Rigging, Paint, Wood, c.1975, 46 x 58 In.	235.00
Pond Boat, Wood, Brass Tiller, Rudder, Lead Keel, 5 Sails, Gaff Rigged, 87 x 74 x 10 In.	2640.00
Pond Boat, Wooden, Plank, Decking, Mast, Cloth Sails, Fully Rigged, 33 x 34 In.	173.00
Pond Yacht, Varnished Hull & Deck, Brass, Chain Plates, 5 Sails, 79 x 63 x 9 In.	1430.00
Porthole, Brass, Tempered Glass, 2 Dog Bolts, 9 In.	135.00
Porthole, Ship's, Painted Sea Gull Cover, Round, 20 In.	118.00
Propeller, British Royal Navy Ship, 4-Blade, Germany, 26 In.	135.00
Quadrant, Octant, Seaman's, Ebony, Brass, Signed Dollund, London, 1800s, 17 In.	1645.00
Sailor's Valentine, Remember Me, Double, Hinged, 2 Shell Arrangements, 10 In.	4680.00
Sailor's Valentine, Shells, Flowers, Vase, Pillars, Arches, Frame, Glass, 1886, 16 x 11 In.	1170.00
Sea Chest, Pine, Canted, Rope Handles, Footed, Early 1800s, 15 x 39 In.	1350.00
Search Light, Ship's, Brass, Gimbal Stand, Screw Down Base, 14 ½ In.	154.00
Sextant, Brass, Dovetail Box, Brass Fittings, Brandis & Sons, c.1915	177.00
Sextant, Carl Plath, Bronze, Black Enameled, Lattice Frame, Bakelite Base, c.1950, 11 x 9 ½ In.	180.00
Sextant, G. Whitbread, Silver Scale, Knob, Mirror, Telescope, Brass Box, 3 x 1 ¼ In.	237.00
Sextant, H. Lambert, Radius, Brass Scale, Sliding Arm, Thumbscrew, 11 In.	5333.00
Sextant, Rothwell, Radius, Brass Frame, Silver Scale, Index Arm Adjustable, 3 ½ In.	3081.00
Sextant, Tamaya, Radius, Iron Frame, Index Arm, Thumbscrew, Japan, 6 ½ In.	148.00
Sextant, Turnbull & Co., Brass, Silver Scale, Mirror, Sun Shades, 7 In.	1007.00
Ship In Bottle, Robin Hood, Haig & Haig, Pinch Style Bottle, 1856, 4 ½ x 8 In.	60.00
Ship Model, see Model.	
Ship Throttle, Enameled Dial, Brass Case, Joseph Harper & Son, New York, c.1900, 13 In.	353.00

Ship's Log, Thomas Walker & Son, Brass, Painted Faceplate, 7 x 3 In.	121.00
Ship's Wheel, 6 Spokes, Brass, Wood, 24 In.	175.00
Ship's Wheel, 8 Spokes, Brass, Mahogany, Early 1900s, 29 ½ In.	175.00
Ship's Wheel, 8 Spokes, Weathered, Iron Hub, Late 19th Century, 39 ½ In.	345.00
Ship's Wheel, 8 Spokes, Wood, 19th Century, 39 In.	85.00
Ship's Wheel, 8 Spokes, Wood, Brass, Inlaid Trim, Pedestal, Drake Engine Co., 34 x 36 In.	2800.00
Ship's Wheel, 8 Spokes, Wood, Chinese Characters, 38 ½ In.	350.00
Ship's Wheel, Mahogany, Satinwood, Brass Inlay, American Engineering Co., c.1900, 30 x 41 In.	795.00
Ship's Wheel, Wood, 32 In.	248.00
Spotlight, Brass, Wood & Iron Bail Handles, E & J Mfg. Co., Detroit, 9 x 11 In.	230.00
Spyglass, 3-Draw, Brass, Leather, End Cap, Black Enamel, France, 1800s, 29 x 3 ¾ In.	325.00
Spyglass, Ship's, 3-Draw Scope, Tripod, Brass, 38 x 62 In.	173.00
Spyglass, Single Draw, Octagonal, Walnut Barrel, Dust Covers, 10 In.	207.00
Spyglass, United States Navy Bureau Of Ships, Wood Case, 31 In.	1100.00
Telegraph, Brass, Double-Sided, Marked, Swan Hunter & Wigham Richardson, c.1940, 13 ¼ In.	495.00
Telegraph, Ship's, Brass, Painted Faceplate, Bendix, 38 x 10 In.	700.00
Thermometer, Deep Sea, Brass, Glass Tubes, Negretti & Zambra, Box, 15 ½ In.	178.00

NETSUKES are small ivory, wood, metal, or porcelain pieces used as toggles on the end of the cord that held a Japanese money pouch or inro. The earliest date from the sixteenth century. Many are miniature, carved works of art. This category also includes the ojime, the slide or string fastener that was used on the inro cord.

Elephant Ivory, Trick, Woman Carrying Scroll, Rotating Face, Early 1900s, 2 ½ In.	170.00
Hardwood, Dragon, Coiled, Glass Eyes, Signed, Late 19th Century, 1 ½ x 2 In.	206.00
Ivory, 2 Monkeys, Peach, 19th Century, 1 In.	711.00
Ivory, Boy, With Dog, 19th Century	176.00
Ivory, Buddha, Traveling, Carved, 2 x ½ In.	55.00
Ivory, Cat & Toad, Applied Pigment, Signed, 1 ¼ In. .... illus	1047.00
Ivory, Cricket & Tortoise, Signed, Early 1900s, 1 x 1 ¼ In.	110.00
Ivory, Figure, On Stump, Holding Sack, c.1800, 1 ⅝ In.	210.00
Ivory, Figures, In Boat, Japan, 2 In.	329.00
Ivory, Frogs, On Lily Pad, Early 1900s, 1 x 2 In.	69.00
Ivory, Grooming Monkeys, Applied Pigment, Painted Eyes, 2 In. .... illus	472.00
Ivory, Hippo, Erotic, 3 Men, Butterfly Tattoos, 2 In.	295.00
Ivory, Man, Standing, Painted, 2 x 1 In.	55.00
Ivory, Man, With Fish, 19th Century	206.00
Ivory, Monkey, Seated, Japan	82.00
Ivory, Monkey Trainer, Stained Details, Signed, 19th Century, 2 In.	441.00
Ivory, Mountain Village, 19th Century	147.00
Ivory, Ostrich Claw, 19th Century, 2 In.	1410.00
Ivory, Snake, Frog, 19th Century, 1 ¾ In.	323.00
Ivory, Wise Man, 2 Frogs, 2 In.	55.00
Mammoth Ivory, Erotic, Rabbits Mating, Onyx Eyes, Signed	200.00
Mammoth Ivory, Shrimp, Baby Shrimp, Onyx Eyes, Signed	145.00
Wood, Fat Old Man In Red Robe, Inlaid Ivory Teeth, 1 ¼ In. .... illus	937.00
Wood, Man, Hunched, Tying His Sandals, c.1915, 1 ¾ In.	90.00
Wood, Monkey & Mouse, Hand Carved, Signed, Early 1900s, 2 In.	85.00
Wood, Rat, Glass Eyes, Signed, 1800s, 1 ½ In.	4095.00

NEW MARTINSVILLE Glass Manufacturing Company was established in 1901 in New Martinsville, West Virginia. It was bought and renamed the Viking Glass Company in 1944. In 1987 Kenneth Dalzell, former president of Fostoria Glass Company, purchased the factory and renamed it Dalzell-Viking. Production ceased in 1998.

Addie, Creamer, Amethyst, 3 ¾ In.	12.50
Addie, Cup & Saucer, Amethyst	10.00
Bookend, German Shepherd, Ruby .... illus	850.00
Fancy Square, Cup & Saucer, Jade .... illus	20.00
Figurine, Bunny	24.00
Figurine, Dog, Green, Hollow Base, Sitting, c.1925, 6 In.	53.00
Moderntone, Whiskey, Cobalt Blue, 2 ¼ In.	40.00
Moondrops, Butter, Cover, Ruby	395.00
Moondrops, Butter, Metal Cover, Ruby	100.00
Moondrops, Whiskey, Cobalt Blue, 2 ¾ In.	18.50
Moondrops, Whiskey, Embossed, Ruby, 2 ¾ In.	15.00
Moondrops, Wine, Ruby, 4 ⅝ In.	20.00

New Martinsville, Bookend, German Shepherd, Ruby
$850.00

New Martinsville, Fancy Square, Cup & Saucer, Jade
$20.00

New Martinsville, Muranese, Bowl, Salmon, 10 ½ In.
$55.00

N

New Martinsville, Radiance, Candlestick, Ruby, 8 In., Pair
$245.00

TIP

Take care of horn cups, spoons, furniture, horn-handle flatware, and other vintage pieces using animal horn. Keep horn away from sunlight and heat. Rub the horn with olive or mineral oil for a shine.

Newcomb, Mug, Irises, Water, Green, Blue, Yellow Underglaze, Sara Bloom, c.1907, 5 x 6 In.
$2360.00

Newcomb, Tile, Mad Tea Party, Alice In Wonderland, Nicholson, 4 ½ x 4 ¾ In.
$3000.00

Newcomb, Vase, Drip Glaze, Baluster Shape, 4 Handles, Signed Meyer, 5 ½ In.
$720.00

Newcomb, Vase, Live Oak Trees, Moss, Squat, Henrietta Bailey, c.1932, 3 ½ x 4 In.
$1920.00

Muranese, Bowl, Salmon, 10 ½ In. .... *illus*	55.00
Muranese, Syrup, Vining Rose, Opaque Yellow Handle, Dripless Lid, c.1875, 6 In.	330.00
No.18, Dresser Set, Amber, 2 Cologne Bottles, Powder Jar, Cover, 1930s...................	55.00
Radiance, Candleholder, Double, Ice Blue...	165.00
Radiance, Candlestick, Ruby, 8 In., Pair .... *illus*	245.00

NEWCOMB POTTERY was founded at Sophie Newcomb College, New Orleans, Louisiana, in 1895. The work continued through the 1940s. Pieces of this art pottery are marked with the printed letters *NC* and often have the incised initials of the artist and potter as well. A date letter code was printed on pieces made from 1901 to 1941. Most pieces have a matte glaze and incised decoration.

Bowl, Bayou Scene, Sadie Irvine, 1917, 4 ¼ x 5 In.	3294.00
Bowl, Bulb, Freesia, Vellum Glaze, Signed, c.1919, 1 ⅜ x 7 In.	690.00
Bowl, Daffodils, Blue, Green & Yellow Underglaze, Marked, 1914, 3 x 5 In.	1175.00
Bowl, Vase, Blue Green, Stripes, Lily Pattern, High Glaze, H. Bailey Signed, 1921, 4 ¾ x 9 In. ..	138.00
Candlestick, Incised Plumbago, Blue, Green Underglaze, 1907, 6 In.	2350.00
Candlestick, Maple Wing, Blue, Green & Pink Underglaze, H. Bailey, 1919, 7 x 4 In.	1837.00
Charger, White Lilies, Green Leaves, Blue Ground, Henrietta Bailey, 1905, 13 In.	9000.00
Creamer, Milk Vine, Blue, Green, Pink, Matte Glaze, Yellow Underglaze, 3 ½ In.	823.00
Inkwell, Flowers At Base, Lid, 3 ½ In.	885.00
Jardiniere, Pear Tree Blossoms, Blue, Green, Yellow, White Slip Underglaze, 5 x 6 ⅜ In.	6756.00
Lampshade, Arts & Crafts, Brass, Hammered, Punched, 8-Sided, 2 ¾ x 6 ¼ In.	60.00
Lampshade, Brass, Pierced, Hexagonal, Dolphins, Chains, 8 In.	764.00
Mug, Buff, Yellow Flowers, Green, High Glaze, Marie De Hoa LeBlanc, 1906, 4 ½ In.	1150.00
Mug, Irises, Water, Green, Blue, Yellow Underglaze, Sara Bloom, c.1907, 5 x 6 In. .... *illus*	2360.00
Pitcher, Blue Cornflowers, Green Ground, Impressed Meyer, 2 ½ In.	1150.00
Pitcher, Juice, Everyday That I've Been Good, Harriet Joor, 1902, 6 x 7 ½ In.	6710.00
Pitcher, White Flowers, Blue Ground, Sadie Irvine, Jonathan Hunt, 1932, 3 In.	633.00
Plaque, Cypress Trees, Moss, Blue & Green Underglaze, Frame, 1930, 15 ¾ x 13 In.	10281.00
Teapot, Roses, Lid, 6 In.	4400.00
Tile, Mad Tea Party, Alice In Wonderland, Nicholson, 4 ½ x 4 ¾ In. .... *illus*	3000.00
Tile, Mary Mary Quite Contrary, Leona Fischer Nicholson, 1930s, 5 x 5 In.	1175.00
Tile, Moss Covered Oaks, Blue & Green Underglaze, Sadie Irvine, Frame, 1911, 8 x 8 In.	3819.00
Tile, Oaks, Moss, Blue, Green & Pink Underglaze, Round, Frame, 1939, 15 ⅝ In.	2937.00
Trivet, Stylized Day Lily Buds, Blue, Green & White Slip Underglaze, Round, 1908, 5 ⅝ In.	1175.00
Trivet, Trumpet Vine Blossoms, Broad Leaf, Blue & Green Underglaze, Round, c.1915, 6 In. ...	1440.00
Vase, Angel Trumpet Flower, Blue, Green, c.1905, 5 x 20 In.	1469.00
Vase, Blue & Green Underglaze, Sadie Irvine, 1939, 3 ⅛ x 3 ¾ In.	1320.00
Vase, Blue, Green, Trees & Shadows, Cylinder, High Glaze, Paper Label, 1905, 6 In.	4800.00
Vase, Bud, Daffodils, Blue, Green, Yellow Underglaze, 4 ⅝ x 2 ½ In.	764.00
Vase, Carolina Jessamine Flower, Blue, Green & Yellow, 1915, 8 In.	5875.00
Vase, Cinquefoils Branches, Green, Henrietta Bailey, 1915, 4 ¾ x 3 ½ In.	1342.00
Vase, Clematis, Blue, Green, Yellow, M. De Hoa LeBlanc, 1904, 13 In.	169200.00
Vase, Daisies, Leaves, White, Blue, Green, Tapered, Impressed Meyer, 1908, 6 ½ In.	3565.00
Vase, Drip Glaze, 4 Handles, Chinese Style, Signed, 5 ½ In.	720.00
Vase, Drip Glaze, Baluster Shape, 4 Handles, Signed Meyer, 5 ½ In. .... *illus*	720.00
Vase, Flood Scene, Blue & Green Underglaze, 1901, 6 ⅝ x 4 ½ In.	8812.00
Vase, Flowers, Blue Ground, Squat, Sadie Irvine, 1913, 2 ½ x 5 ½ In.	1295.00
Vase, Flowers, Low Form, Sadie Irvine, 5 ½ In.	960.00
Vase, Freesia Buds, Blue & Green Underglaze, Marie De Hoa LeBlanc, 1908, 9 x 3 ⅜ In.	8225.00
Vase, Geranium Band, Tapered, High Gloss, Marie De Hoa LeBlanc, c.1903, 9 ½ In.	12000.00
Vase, Ivory Crackle Glaze, Turquoise Interior, Globular, 6 In.	240.00
Vase, Jackmanii Climbing Clematis, Blue, Green, Yellow, Incised, 13 x 6 In.	169200.00
Vase, Jasmine, Leaves, Shouldered, 2, Handles, Anna Frances Simpson, 1923, 4 In.	2495.00
Vase, Landscape, Blue Ground, Shouldered, Anna Francis Simpson, 1921, 7 In.	3495.00
Vase, Landscape, Moss On Trees, Moon, Bulbous, c.1932, 6 ½ x 6 ¼ In.	4800.00
Vase, Landscape, Trees, Rose, Blue Glaze, Cylindrical, c.1915, 10 ⅝ In.	2015.00
Vase, Live Oak Trees, Moss, Squat, Henrietta Bailey, c.1932, 3 ½ x 4 In. .... *illus*	1920.00
Vase, Modernistic Swirls, Bulbous, Sadie Irvine, 1932, 6 In.	2295.00
Vase, Moon & Moss, Blue & Green Underglaze, Squat, Sadie Irvine, 1932, 3 ⅞ x 5 ¼ In.	3172.00
Vase, Moon & Moss, Blue, Green & Yellow Underglaze, Squat Baluster, S. Irvine, 1920, 4 ½ In.	2520.00
Vase, Moon & Moss, Blue, Green Underglaze, Sadie Irvine, c.1931, 2 ¼ In.	940.00
Vase, Moon & Moss, Matte Glaze, Anna Frances Simpson, 1918, 7 ¼ In.	3346.00
Vase, Moon & Pine Landscape, Blue & Green Underglaze, c.1940, 6 x 4 ⅜ In.	4200.00
Vase, Oak Grove, Incised, Handles, Blue, Green & Yellow Underglaze, S. Irvine, 1906, 3 x 4 In.	6462.00

Vase, Oak Trees, Spanish Moss, Green, Blue, Painted, Anna F. Simpson, Meyer, 1914, 10 In.	4945.00
Vase, Painted Flowers, Littlejohn, c.1904, 8 ⅝ In.	12075.00
Vase, Painted Pink Roses, Blue Matte Ground, Broad, H. Bailey, 7 x 6 In.	3120.00
Vase, Pink, Brown, Espanol Style, Impressed, Sadie Irvine, 1927, 5 In.	2875.00
Vase, Pink Flowers, Blue Ground, Painted, Squat, Henrietta Bailey, Meyer, 1920, 3 x 6 In.	1840.00
Vase, Pink Iris, Buds, Green Leaves, Matte Glaze, Marked, A. Simpson, 1927, 9 In.	6900.00
Vase, Pink Primroses, Green Rim, Blue Ground, Meyer, 5 In.	1725.00
Vase, Pink Rose, Band, Incised, Painted, Blue Glaze, Sadie Irvine, c.1922, 6 ¾ In. .... *illus*	2300.00
Vase, Plum Blossoms, Blue & Green Underglaze, Henrietta Bailey, 1923, 8 ⅝ In.	3055.00
Vase, Rice Hull, Blue, Green, Pink, Matte Glaze, S. Irvine, 1923, 3 x 5 In.	588.00
Vase, Rose, Monogram, Sadie Irvine, c.1927, 5 ¼ In. .... *illus*	2875.00
Vase, Spider Chrysanthemum Blooms, Blue Underglaze, Paneled, 1902, 8 In.	4480.00
Vase, Tulips, Carved, Bulbous, High Glaze, Leona Nicholson, 10 x 9 In.	9000.00
Vase, Vine, Blue, Pink, Green, Matte Glaze, 5 ¼ In.	2115.00
Vase, White Daffodils, Tapered, A.F. Simpson, 1921, 7 ½ x 3 ¼ In.	2040.00
Vase, Windswept Flowers, Green, Blue Ground, Henrietta Bailey, 1933, 6 In.	1380.00
Vase, Yellow Flower Clusters, Marie Ross, 7 x 6 ¾ In. .... *illus*	1800.00
Vase, Yellow Organic Band, Gourd Shape, High Glaze, Henrietta Bailey, 4 x 7 In.	7200.00

NILOAK POTTERY (Kaolin spelled backward) was made at the Hyten Brothers Pottery in Benton, Arkansas, between 1910 and 1947. Although the factory did make cast and molded wares, collectors are most interested in the marbleized art pottery line made of colored swirls of clay. It was called Mission Ware. By 1931 the company made castware, and many of these pieces were marked with the name *Hywood*.

Pitcher, Green Matte Over Brown Glaze, Foil Label, 5 In. .... *illus*	24.00
Vase, Marbleized, Brown, Blue, Cream, Rust, Round, Footed, 4 x 9 ½ In.	420.00
Vase, Mission Ware, Bulbous, 6 In.	22.00
Vase, Mission Ware, Bulbous, 9 ¼ In.	88.00
Vase, Mission Ware, Hourglass, 10 In.	77.00
Vase, Mission Ware, Multicolored, Cylindrical, Marked, Pamphlet, 4 x 9 ½ In. .... *illus*	420.00

NIPPON porcelain was made in Japan from 1891 to 1921. *Nippon* is the Japanese word for "Japan." A few firms continued to use the word *Nippon* on ceramics after 1921 as a part of the company name more than as an identification of the country of origin. More pieces marked *Nippon* will be found in the Moriage and Noritake categories.

Ashtray, Chief Joseph Portrait, Stitched Lace Border, c.1900, 5 ¼ In.	390.00
Bowl, Raspberry, Footed, 9 In.	95.00
Bowl, Scalloped Rim, Geometric, Handles, c.1910, 9 In.	94.00
Cachepot, Roses, Wavy Gold Leaf Banner, 2 Branch Handles, 4-Footed, 4 ½ x 9 In.	35.00
Celery Dish, Bird, Trees, Leaves, White, Green, Gold, Nagoya S.N.B. Lusterware, 3 ¾ x 2 ¼ In.	13.00
Cider Set, Snow Geese, Turquoise Ground, Gold Trim, Enamel, Pitcher, Mugs, 6 In.	250.00
Dresser Box, Winter Scene, Gilt Cartouche, Enameled Jewels, Footed, c.1915, 2 ¾ In.	177.00
Ewer, Roses, Textured Ground, c.1900, 10 ¾ In.	1770.00
Humidor, Collie At Sunset, c.1900, 6 In.	649.00
Humidor, Owl, On Oak Branch, c.1900, 6 ¾ In.	708.00
Jug, Birds, On Limb, Woven Wicker Base, c.1900, 9 ½ In.	1014.00
Jug, Grapes, Woven Wicker Base, c.1900, 8 In.	442.00
Jug, Melon, Ribbed, Glass Beaded Carnations, Applied Handle, Pedestal, c.1900s, 11 In.	1298.00
Pitcher, Cider, Yellow Ground, Red Rose, 6 In.	30.00
Pitcher, Fox Hunt, Horseback Riders, Hounds, Multicolored, Handle, Rim Detail, 6 In.	288.00
Plaque, Fish, Molded, Relief, Oval, c.1900, 18 ⅝ In.	660.00
Plaque, Mallard, Molded, Relief, Oval, c.1900, 18 ⅝ In.	1320.00
Plate, Collie & Terrier, Blown Out, Molded Relief, 10 ½ In.	360.00
Plate, Moose, Blown-Out, Molded Relief, 10 ½ In.	360.00
Reamer, Roses, Gold Beading, Dots, c.1900-20, 3 ¼ x 3 ½ In., 2 Piece..............................	79.00
Salt & Pepper, Orange Luster Hen, Red Head, Blue Luster Salt, Mark, c.1930, 2 ½ x 2 In.	87.00
Salt, Interior Flowers, Blue, Gold Trim, Octagonal, 3-Footed, Mark, Spoon, c.1900, 1 x 2 In. ...	15.00
Salt, Water, Mountain Interior Scene, Mark, c.1900, ¾ In.	22.00
Tankard, Beaded Flowers, c.1925, 12 In.	1652.00
Tea Strainer, Base, Cobalt Blue Trim, Flower Center, Gold Stencil Detail, 2 x 6 In. .... *illus*	60.00
Vase, Cobalt, Man On Camel, Geometric Design, Raised Gilt, 2 Handles, c.1910, 8 ½ In.	885.00
Vase, Cottage, Globular, 2 Lion's Head Handles, Paw Feet, c.1900, 8 ½ In.	540.00
Vase, Deer In Winter, Square, Handles, c.1900, 12 In.	265.00
Vase, Desert Scene, Camel & Rider, Corset Shape, Enameled, 10 ¼ In.	100.00
Vase, Egyptian Campfire Scene, Scrolled Shoulder, Bolted Pedestal, Handles, c.1900, 18 In.	944.00
Vase, Flamingos, Jeweled Floral Gilt Rim, Oval, c.1900, 12 In.	1440.00

Newcomb, Vase, Pink Rose, Band, Incised, Painted, Blue Glaze, Sadie Irvine, c.1922, 6 ¾ In. $2300.00

Newcomb, Vase, Rose, Monogram, Sadie Irvine, c.1927, 5 ¼ In. $2875.00

Newcomb, Vase, Yellow Flower Clusters, Marie Ross, 7 x 6 ¾ In. $1800.00

Niloak, Pitcher, Green Matte Over Brown Glaze, Foil Label, 5 In. $24.00

N

Niloak, Vase, Mission Ware, Multicolored, Cylindrical, Marked, Pamphlet, 4 x 9 ½ In.
$420.00

Nippon, Tea Strainer, Base, Cobalt Blue Trim, Flower Center, Gold Stencil Detail, 2 x 6 In.
$60.00

Nippon, Vase, Scenic, Field & Stream, Acorn Border, 2 Handles, 6 ½ In.
$40.00

Nodder, Candlestick, Black Man & Woman, Rococo, Bisque, Painted, Gilt, 9 ¼ In., Pair
$109.00

Vase, Flower Medallions, 2 Handles, c.1900, 9 In.	390.00
Vase, Flowering Branches, Pink Blossoms, Globular, Ruffled Lip, Green Round Foot, 6 ¼ In.	259.00
Vase, Flowers, 2 Handles, 4-Footed Base, c.1900, 10 ½ In.	2006.00
Vase, Flowers, 6-Sided, Enameled, 12 In.	51.00
Vase, Flowers, Amberina Ground, Scalloped Rim, c.1900, 8 ¼ In.	531.00
Vase, Flowers, Medallions, Cylindrical, c.1900, 17 ¾ In.	390.00
Vase, Four Geese, White, Brown, Blue Ground, Cylinder, 8 In.	316.00
Vase, Green Ground, Pink Roses, Enameled, Squat, Handles, 5 In.	50.00
Vase, Iris, 2 Handles, Marked, c.1900, 8 ½ In.	708.00
Vase, Meadow Lake Scenes, Cobalt Blue, Arched Handles, c.1900, 8 ½ In.	560.00
Vase, Mums, Red, Urn Shape, Handles, Signed, 10 In.	86.00
Vase, Outdoor Scene, Gold Pinecones, Marked, M, Wreath Stamp, 3-Footed, 10 In.	295.00
Vase, Roses, Textured Ground, Square Handles, Footed, Pinched Neck, c.1900, 8 In.	1534.00
Vase, Scenic, 14 x 6 In.	322.00
Vase, Scenic, Field & Stream, Acorn Border, 2 Handles, 6 ½ In. .... *illus*	40.00
Vase, White Ground, Multicolored Orchid Design, Gold Rim, Base, 5 x 10 In.	205.00
Vase, Wild Roses, Scalloped Rim, 20th Century, 9 In.	767.00

NODDERS, also called nodding figures or pagods, are figures with heads and hands that are attached to wires. Any slight movement causes the parts to move up and down. They were made in many countries during the eighteenth, nineteenth, and twentieth centuries. A few Art Deco designs are also known. Copies are being made. A more recent type of nodder is made of papier-mache or plastic. These often represent sports figures or comic characters. Sports nodders are listed in the Sports category.

Andy Gump, Bisque, 4 In.	750.00
Baby Skeezix, Standing, Incised, 2 ¾ In.	65.00
Betty Boop, Rubber Band Mechanism, Tin Base, 1930s, 7 ¼ In.	192.00
Black Jazz Saxophone Player, On Hassock, Bisque, Austrian, 1880s, 3 In.	56.00
Candlestick, Black Man & Woman, Rococo, Bisque, Painted, Gilt, 9 ¼ In., Pair...............*illus*	109.00

Salt & Pepper Shakers are listed in the Salt & Pepper category.

NORITAKE porcelain was made in Japan after 1904 by Nippon Toki Kaisha. The best-known Noritake pieces are marked with the *M* in a wreath for the Morimura Brothers, a New York City distributing company. This mark was used until the early 1950s. There may be some helpful price information in the Nippon category, since prices are comparable. Noritake Azalea is listed in the Azalea category in this book.

Bowl, Vegetable, Cover, Grasmere, Flowers, Urn, Blue & Black Border, Gold Trim	79.00
Compote, Man On Camel, Campfire, Gilt Scrolled Rim, Pedestal, c.1900, 8 In.	265.00
Cup & Saucer, Andrea, Gold & Gray Flowers, Gold Trim	15.00
Cup & Saucer, Homecoming, Birds & Fruit Border	10.00
Dresser Box, Magenta, Ballerina On Lid, c.1930, 4 ¼ In.	360.00
Humidor, Owl Shape, Orange & Marigold Luster, c.1900, 7 In.	240.00
Napkin Ring, Orange Luster, Harlequin Man, Blue Luster, Woman In Red Coat, Hat, 2 In., 6 Piece	595.00
Plate, Salad, Gleneden, Blue Scrolls, Tan & Blue Border, Gold Trim	12.00
Salt & Pepper, Orange Luster Hen, Red Head, Open Blue Luster Salt, Mark, c.1930, 2 ½ x 2 In.	87.00
Soup, Cream, Saucer, Alvin, Flower Sprays, Tan & Yellow Border	25.00
Sugar, Cover, Adela, Flower Sprays, Green Border	35.00
Teapot, Anaheim, Raised White Flowers, Gray Band, Platinum Trim	65.00
Vase, Basket, Roses, c.1910, 9 In.	750.00
Vase, Double, Parrot, Marked, 1930s, 7 In. ....*illus*	150.00
Vase, Flowers, Gilt Scrolls, Cobalt Blue Ground, c.1900, 12 In.	590.00
Vase, Swans, Lake, Raised Shoulder, Handles, c.1900, 10 In.	442.00

NORSE POTTERY COMPANY started in Edgerton, Wisconsin, in 1903. In 1904 the company moved to Rockford, Illinois. The company made a black pottery, which resembled early bronze relics of the Scandinavian countries. The firm went out of business in 1913.

Bowl, Figural Handles, Black Metallic Glaze, Incised Designs, Low Shape, 8 x 2 ½ In.	960.00

NORTH DAKOTA SCHOOL OF MINES was established in 1892 at the University of North Dakota. A ceramic course was included and pieces were made from the clays found in the region. Students at the university made pieces from 1909 to 1949. Although very early pieces were marked *U.N.D.*, most pieces were stamped with the full name of the university.

Figurine, Wolf, Howling, Blue Matte Glaze, 2 x 3 ¼ In. ....*illus*	510.00
Jar, Cover, Serpents, Prairie Rose, Irene Nelson, Blue Stamp, c.1943, 8 x 4 In. ....*illus*	1680.00

N

Jar, Cover, Serpents, Prairie Rose, Margaret Cable, 8 ¼ x 4 ½ In.	1708.00
Tile, Geometric, Matte Glaze, Cream, Orange, Green, 3 ⅝ x 2 ¾ In.	40.00
Tile, Painted Deer, Flowers, JT, Frame. 7 In.	360.00
Tile, Turquoise, Beige Ground, Initials, A.O.R., 4 x 2 ¾ In.	50.00
Trivet, Flower, Yellow, Green Leaves, 6-Sided, Marked, 1929, 5 In.	150.00
Vase, Buffalo, Indigo, Beige Ground, Squat, 3 x 5 In.	820.00
Vase, Embossed Flowers, Rose, Green Glaze, Incised, 3 In.	290.00
Vase, Flowers, Leaves, Beige, Blue, 5 ½ In.	420.00
Vase, Green & Brown Matte Glaze, Round, Marked, 7 x 6 In.	259.00
Vase, Green-Brown, Round, Marked, S.E.W., 7 x 6 In.	250.00
Vase, Lavender Glaze, 5 In.	300.00
Vase, Lid, Gazelles, Leaping, Indigo, Buff Ground, 1956, 10 ½ In.	880.00
Vase, Prairie Rose, Brown Glaze, Flowers, Huck SIA, 5 x 3 In. .... *illus*	420.00

NORTHWOOD glass was made by the H. Northwood Co., founded in Wheeling, West Virginia, in 1901 by Harry Northwood. He worked for the Hobbs-Brockunier and LaBelle firms in the 1880s before operating his own glass plants in Martins Ferry, Ohio, and Ellwood City and Indiana, Pennsylvania. At the Wheeling factory, Harry Northwood and his brother Carl manufactured pressed and blown tableware and novelties in many colors that are collected today as custard, opalescent, goofus, carnival, and stretch glass. Pieces made between 1905 and about 1915 may have an underlined *N* trademark. Harry Northwood died in 1919, and the plant closed in 1925.

Apple Blossom, Pitcher, Multicolored Flowers, Applied Handle, c.1875, 8 ¼ In.	118.00
Apple Blossom, Sugar Shaker, Multicolor Flowers, Lid, c.1875, 4 ½ In.	106.00
Argonaut Shell, Spooner, Custard, Gilt, Marked, c.1900, 4 ¾ In.	53.00
Beaded Cable, Bowl, Green, c.1913, 4 ½ In.	71.00
Beaded Cable, Candy Dish, Ruffled, Green, Iridescent, 3-Footed, 8 x 3 In.	45.00
Beaded Shell, Mug, Custard, Dugan, 1910, 4 x 3 In.	35.00
Blue Opalescent, Pitcher, Water, Ball Shape, Square Top, Crimps, Swirl, c.1900, 8 In.	152.00
Cherry & Cable, Goblet, Green, 1907, 6 x 3 In.	35.00
Chrysanthemum Sprig, Cruet, Blue, 7 In.	374.00
Colonial Tulip, Compote, Marigold Over Green, Scalloped Rim, c.1909, 5 ½ In.	55.00
Cranberry, Pitcher, Water, Coin Spot, Crimped Rim, Pressed Feather Handle, c.1875, 8 In.	171.00
Cranberry Spatter, Tumbler, Gold Mica Flakes, c.1875, 3 ¾ In.	145.00
Daisy & Fern, Pitcher, Water, Green, Ball Form, Short Neck, Square Crimped Top, c.1900, 9 In.	264.00
Daisy & Fern, Syrup, Opalescent, 6 In.	115.00
Daisy & Fern, Syrup, Swirl, Cranberry, Clear Handle, c.1875, 6 ¼ In.	1124.00
Daisy & Plume, Candy Dish, Ray Interior, Lime Green, 3-Footed, c.1910	600.00
Diamond Spearhead, Spooner, Vaseline Opalescent, c.1900, 4 ⅜ In.	66.00
Diamond Spearhead, Syrup, Cobalt Blue, Lid, c.1900, 5 ¼ In.	727.00
Drapery, Rose Bowl, Ice Blue, Carnival Glass, 4 In. .... *illus*	150.00
Everglade Custard Opaline, Water Set, Pitcher, 6 Tumblers, 8 In.	575.00
Fern & Feather, Custard Cup, Pink Slag, Footed, c.1900, 2 ¼ In.	106.00
Fine Cut & Roses, Candy Dish, Scalloped, Carnival Marigold, 1909, 7 x 3 ½ In.	30.00
Flower, Sugar Shaker, Opaque Turquoise Blue, c.1875, 4 ¼ In.	264.00
Geneva, Syrup, Custard, 6 In.	144.00
Good Luck, Bowl, Blue, Carnival Glass, Pie Crust Edge, 8 ¾ In. .... *illus*	240.00
Grape & Cable, Bowl, Ruffled, Green, Mark, c.1912, 5 ½ In.	50.00
Jeweled Heart, Sugar Shaker, Apple Green, Gilt, Lid, c.1900, 4 ½ In.	258.00
Leaf Mold, Cruet, Spatter, 6 ½ In.	460.00
Leaf Umbrella, Candy Dish, Cranberry, Clear Handle, Lid, c.1875, 6 ⅝ In.	727.00
Leaf Umbrella, Pitcher, Water, Yellow, Frosted, Clear Applied Handle, c.1875, 4 ½ In.	159.00
Leaf Umbrella, Sugar Shaker, c.1875, 4 ½ In.	462.00
Leaf Umbrella, Syrup, Applied Handle, 6 ⅝ In. .... *illus*	547.00
Leaf Umbrella, Toothpick Holder, Lavender, Cased, Late 1800s, 2 ½ In. .... *illus*	84.00
Lustre Flute, Bonbon, Marigold, Iridescent, Handles, Mark, c.1910, 2 ½ x 5 In.	25.00
Netted Oak, Syrup, Opaque White, Multicolor Flowers, Gilt, Handle, c.1900, 5 In.	118.00
Peacocks, Bowl, Marigold, Carnival Glass, Embossed Mark, 8 ¾ In. .... *illus*	120.00
Pleat Ribbed Pillar, Sugar Shaker, Opal & Cranberry Spatter, c.1875, 4 ¾ In.	118.00
Poinsettia, Syrup, Clear Opalescent, Pressed Leaf Handle, c.1875, 7 ¾ In.	556.00
Polka Dot, Sugar Shaker, Cranberry Opalescent, Lid, c.1900, 4 ½ In.	727.00
Pull Up, Plate, Satin Glass, Striped Blue, Yellow, Red Pulled Feathers, 8 In. .... *illus*	288.00
Quilted Phlox, Sugar Shaker, Cover, Translucent Blue, c.1900, 4 ½ In.	81.00
Quilted Phlox, Sugar Shaker, Opaque Light To Dark Pink, c.1900, 4 ¾ In.	159.00
Royal Ivy, Sugar Shaker, Rubina, c.1875, 4 ½ In.	159.00
Royal Ivy, Syrup, Rainbow Spatter, Cranberry, 7 In.	316.00
Royal Ivy, Syrup, Spatter, Applied Handle, Cover, Late 1800s, 6 ½ In. .... *illus*	546.00

Noritake, Vase, Double, Parrot, Marked, 1930s, 7 In.
$150.00

North Dakota School Of Mines, Figurine, Wolf, Howling, Blue Matte Glaze, 2 x 3 ¼ In.
$510.00

North Dakota School Of Mines, Jar, Cover, Serpents, Prairie Rose, Irene Nelson, Blue Stamp, c.1943, 8 x 4 In.
$1680.00

North Dakota School Of Mines, Vase, Prairie Rose, Brown Glaze, Flowers, Huck SIA, 5 x 3 In.
$420.00

N

Northwood, Drapery, Rose Bowl, Ice Blue, Carnival Glass, 4 In. $150.00

Northwood, Good Luck, Bowl, Blue, Carnival Glass, Pie Crust Edge, 8 ¾ In. $240.00

Northwood, Leaf Umbrella, Syrup, Applied Handle, 6 ⅝ In. $547.00

Northwood, Leaf Umbrella, Toothpick Holder, Lavender, Cased, Late 1800s, 2 ½ In. $84.00

Northwood, Peacocks, Bowl, Marigold, Carnival Glass, Embossed Mark, 8 ¾ In. $120.00

Northwood, Pull Up, Plate, Satin Glass, Striped Blue, Yellow, Red Pulled Feathers, 8 In. $288.00

Northwood, Quilted Phlox, Sugar Shaker, Cover, Translucent Blue, c.1900, 4 ½ In. $81.00

Nutcracker, Squirrel, Cast Metal, Gray Paint, Walnut Base, c.1878, 9 ½ In. $626.00

Northwood, Royal Ivy, Syrup, Spatter, Applied Handle, Cover, Late 1800s, 6 ½ In. $546.00

N

Royal Ivy, Water Set, Pitcher, 8 Tumblers, Yellow, Red Cross Design, Spatterware, 9 In.	748.00
Royal Oak, Syrup, Rubina, Leaves, Acorns, Clear Handle, Lid, c.1875, 5 ½ In.	1455.00
Rubina Swirl, Bowl, Threaded, Jewel Rose, Globular, c.1875, 5 ½ In.	53.00
Scroll, Toothpick Holder, Acanthus, Purple Slag, c.1925, 2 ½ In.	92.00
Singing Birds, Mug, Green, c.1925, 3 ½ In.	66.00
Sprig, Sugar Shaker, Paneled, Amethyst, Lid, c.1900, 4 ¾ In.	185.00
Threaded Rubina Swirl, Syrup, Jewel, Clear Handle, Lid, c.1875, 5 In.	727.00
Three Fruits, Bowl, Amethyst, Ruffled, 9 x 2 ¾ In.	86.00
Three Fruits Medallion, Bowl, Amethyst & Gold, Spatula Footed, 1915, 3 x 8 In.	150.00
Vase, Flared, Deep Fold Rim, Green, Brown, Carnival Glass, 13 ½ In.	89.00
Waterlily & Cattails, Water Cup, Marigold, c.1908, 4 x 3 In.	60.00

NUTCRACKERS of many types have been used through the centuries. At first the nutcracker was probably strong teeth or a hammer. But by the nineteenth century, many elaborate and ingenious types were made. Levers, screws, and hammer adaptations were the most popular. Because nutcrackers are still useful, they are still being made, some in the old styles.

Advertising, Potter Walnut Company, Cast Iron	50.00
Dog, Wide-Eyed, Black Spots, Cast Iron, 19th Century, 9 In.	605.00
Eagle, Aqua, Cast Iron, 8 ¼ In.	25.00
Mammy, Hair, Bandanna, Germany, c.1900	435.00
Mammy, On Tree Stump, Full Figured, 1900s, 6 ½ In.	352.00
Punch & Judy, Brass, Double-Sided, Marked, England, 5 In.	650.00
Squirrel, Cast Iron, 4 ¾ In.	25.00
Squirrel, Cast Metal, Gray Paint, Walnut Base, c.1878, 9 ½ In. ...*illus*	626.00
Squirrel, With Dog, Cast Iron, 6 In.	45.00

OCCUPIED JAPAN was printed on pottery, porcelain, toys, and other goods made during the American occupation of Japan after World War II, from 1947 to 1952. Collectors now search for these pieces. The items were made for export. Ceramic items are listed here. Toys are listed in the Toy category in this book.

Candy Dish, Painted Flowers, Gilt Scalloped Rim, Cutout Handle, 5 In., Pair	39.00
Cup & Saucer, Flower Shape, Hummingbird Handle, Forget-Me-Nots, 2 x 3 ½ In.	82.00
Figurine, Bee, Painted, 4 In.	9.00
Figurine, Boy Band, Horn, Drums, Accordion, Mandolin, 3 In., 4 Piece	79.00
Figurine, Cat Family, White, Multicolor Bows, 3 x 2 ½ In.	22.00
Figurine, Colonial Couple, Marked Mariyane, 7 ½ x 4 ½ In.	22.00
Figurine, Holstein Cow, Nursing Calf, Impressed Stamp, 4 x 6 x 3 In.	95.00
Figurine, Parlor Set, Victorian, Painted Flowers, Sofa, Chair, Piano, Miniature	59.00
Lamp, Colonial American Figures, Painted, Ruffled Shade, Mid 1940s, 10 x 4 In.	38.00
Mug Set, Dog Faces, 3 Piece	40.00
Planter, Bird & Flower, 4 x 2 ½ In., Pair	15.00
Planter, Wheelbarrow, Raised Pink & Blue Flowers, 4 ¾ x 1 ½ In.	20.00
Plate, Painted, Landscape, Lake, Lilies, Road, Signed Jushori, 6 In.	28.00
Salt & Pepper, Birds, Mama, Babies, On Tree Branch, Majolica Style, 4 x 3 In.	36.00
Salt & Pepper, Indian Couple, In Canoe, 2 & 2 ½ x 7 ½ In.	59.00
Shelf Set, Planter, 2 Candlesticks, Swan Shape, 3 Piece	40.00
Vase, Woman, Seated On Shell, 2 Cherubs, Waves Base, Painted, 8 x 5 In.	89.00

OFFICE TECHNOLOGY includes office equipment and related products, such as adding machines, calculators, and check-writing machines. Typewriters are in their own category in this book.

Calculator, Divisumma 18, ABS Plastic, Rubber, Mario Bellini, Olivetti, Yellow, 1973, 12 x 5 In...*illus*	120.00
Stock Ticker, Edison, Glass Dome, Wood Base, Plaque, 6 ½ x 8 ½ In.	294.00 to 395.00

OHR pottery was made in Biloxi, Mississippi, from 1883 to 1906 by George E. Ohr, a true eccentric. The pottery was made of very thin clay that was twisted, folded, and dented into odd, graceful shapes. Some pieces were lifelike models of hats, animal heads, or even a potato. Others were decorated with folded clay "snakes." Reproductions and reworked pieces are appearing on the market. These have been reglazed, or snakes and other embellishments have been added.

Bottle, Totemic, Sponged On Teal Blue Glaze, Amber Ground, Copperdust Striations, 7 x 3 ½ In.	4200.00
Jug, Water, Teal Green Glaze, Melt Fissures, Harry Portman, Stamped, 1896, 8 x 5 In.	1680.00
Mug, Amber Glaze, Mahogany Sponging, Angular Handle, 3 ½ x 3 In.	649.00
Mug, Puzzle, Brown, Holes In Rim, Impressed GE Ohr, Mississippi, c.1900, 3 ½ In.	1175.00

Office Technology, Calculator, Divisumma 18, ABS Plastic, Rubber, Mario Bellini, Olivetti, Yellow, 1973, 12 x 5 In.
$120.00

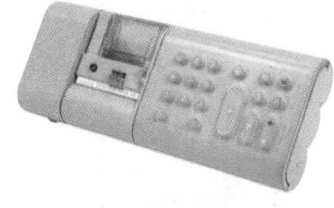

Ohr, Vase, Bulbous, Twisted, Torn Rim, Gunmetal Mottled Glaze, 4 ½ x 3 ¾ In.
$7800.00

Ohr, Vase, In-Body Twist, Raspberry Red Speckled Glaze, 4 ¼ x 3 In.
$8400.00

Ohr, Vase, White Clay, Green Mottled Matte Glaze, Squat, 3 x 3 ¾ In.
$2520.00

O

Onion, Compote, 2 Tiers,
Reticulated Borders, Blue,
Crossed Swords, Meissen, 17 x 9 ½ In.
$527.00

Onion, Compote, Basket Weave,
Reticulated, Swirl Stem, 1800s,
8 ¾ x 9 In.
$311.00

Onion, Platter, Oval, Blue,
Crossed Swords Mark, Meissen, 11 In.
$205.00

Nippon Azalea

The rarest pieces of Azalea
pattern Nippon china are said
to be the fluted square plates,
the scalloped and footed
mayonnaise, the pancake jug,
and the ashtray.

Vase, Bulbous, Flaring Rim, Mottled Brown & Red, 3 x 5 ½ In.	1265.00
Vase, Bulbous, Olive Speckled Glaze, Twist Body, Die Stamp Mark, c.1905, 4 ½ x 3 ½ In.	3055.00
Vase, Bulbous, Twisted, Torn Rim, Gunmetal Mottled Glaze, 4 ½ x 3 ¾ In. _illus_	7800.00
Vase, Gathered, Amber, Gunmetal Glaze, Flower Shape, 2 ½ x 3 ½ In.	3240.00
Vase, Gunmetal Brown, Amber Panels, 8 ¼ x 4 ½ In.	1320.00
Vase, In-Body Twist, Raspberry Red Speckled Glaze, 4 ¼ x 3 In. _illus_	8400.00
Vase, Olive Green Glaze, c.1875, 3 ⅛ x 4 ¾ In.	1292.00
Vase, Ribbed, Folded Rim, Gun Metal Brown Glaze, Stamped, 4 x 3 ¼ In.	2040.00
Vase, Sculptured, Green, Amber Mottled Glaze, Stamped, 2 ½ x 4 ¼ In.	4200.00
Vase, Speckled Gunmetal, Amber, Green Glaze, 4 ½ x 4 In.	920.00
Vase, Sponged Brown, Amber Glaze, 9 ¼ x 3 ¾ In.	1830.00
Vase, Twisted Center, Die Stamped Mark, 1901-10, 4 ½ In.	3055.00
Vase, White Clay, Green Mottled Matte Glaze, Squat, 3 x 3 ¾ In. _illus_	2520.00
Vase, White Clay, Mottled Applied Green Glaze, Flower Shape Rim, 2 ¾ x 5 In.	1920.00
Vase, White Clay, Mottled Matte Emerald Green Glaze, Squat, 3 ¼ x 4 ¾ In.	2562.00

OLD IVORY china was made by the Ohme Porcelain Works in Silesia, Germany, a factory working from 1882 to 1928. The china had an ivory matte background and was usually decorated with flowers or fruit. Dinner sets, fish sets, mustache cups, and souvenir pieces were made. Pieces were marked with a crown, the cipher OH, and the word *Silesia*. Some pieces are also marked with the words *Old Ivory*. The pattern numbers appear on the base of many pieces.

Berry Bowl, No. 41, 10 In.	205.00
Chocolate Set, No. 16, 11 Piece	475.00
Mustard, No. 15	110.00

ONION PATTERN, originally named bulb pattern, is a white ware decorated with cobalt blue or pink. Although it is commonly associated with Meissen, other companies made the pattern in the late nineteenth and the twentieth centuries. A rare type is called *red bud* because there are added red accents on the blue-and-white dishes.

Bowl, Blue & White, Meissen, Cauldon, 9 In.	85.00
Bowl, Blue & White, Square, Shaped Corners, Meissen, 10 In.	207.00
Coffee & Tea Service, Royal Copenhagen, Blue, 8 ½-In. Coffeepot, 18 Piece	153.00
Compote, 2 Tiers, Reticulated Borders, Blue, Crossed Swords, Meissen, 17 x 9 ½ In. _illus_	527.00
Compote, Basket Weave, Reticulated, Swirl Stem, 1800s, 8 ¾ x 9 In. _illus_	311.00
Compote, Blue & White, 2 Tiers, Pierced Border, Pierced Flared Top, Meissen, 17 x 9 In.	384.00
Compote, Blue & White, Floral Reserves, Lattice Pierced Border, Meissen, 9 x 9 In.	266.00
Cup & Saucer, Blue, Underglaze Blue, Crossed Swords, Meissen, 2 ⅜ In., 12 Piece	385.00
Plate, Dinner, Blue & White, Meissen, Cauldon, 9 ½ In.	95.00
Plate, Luncheon, Blue & White, Meissen, Cauldon, 8 ¼ In.	75.00
Platter, Blue, Flowers, Designs, Oval, Meissen, 20 In.	527.00
Platter, Oval, Blue & White, Blue, Underglaze Crown & Circle Mark, Meissen, c.1891, 19 x 13 In.	71.00
Platter, Oval, Blue, Crossed Swords Mark, Meissen, 11 In. _illus_	205.00
Tray, Blue Onion, Flowers, Designs, Square, Cutout Handles, 16 In.	410.00
Tureen, Blue, Meissen, 10 x 14 x 9 In.	395.00

OPALESCENT GLASS is translucent glass that has the tones of the opal gemstone. It originated in England in the 1870s and is often found in pressed glassware made in Victorian times. Opalescent glass was first made in America in 1897 at the Northwood glassworks in Indiana, Pennsylvania. Some dealers use the terms *opaline* and *opalescent* for any of these translucent wares. More opalescent pieces may be listed in Hobnail, Northwood, Pressed Glass, and other glass categories.

Alaska, Celery Dish, Vaseline, Enamel Flowers, 9 ½ In. _illus_	425.00
Alaska, Pitcher, Water, Vaseline, c.1900, 7 ¼ In. _illus_	431.00
Beatty Rib, Spooner, Blue, c.1889, 4 ¼ x 3 In.	70.00
Big Windows, Sugar Shaker, Cranberry, Lid, c.1875, 4 ¾ In.	529.00
Big Windows, Syrup, Blue, Lid, Applied Handle, c.1875, 6 ¾ In.	264.00
Bubble Lattice, Sugar Shaker, Cranberry, Lid, Buckeye Glass, c.1875, 5 In.	529.00
Bubble Lattice, Sugar Shaker, Tapered, Lid, Cranberry, c.1875, 5 In.	727.00
Christmas Snowflake, Pitcher, Ribbed, Applied Clear Handle, c.1900, 9 ¾ In.	575.00
Coinspot, Pitcher, Cranberry, Star Crimp Rim, Applied Clear Handle, c.1900, 8 ½ In.	150.00
Coinspot, Syrup, Swirl, Blue Silver Plated Top, 1880s, 6 ¼ In.	280.00
Cranberry Rim, Rippled Base, Blown, 6 In.	44.00
Daffodil, Pitcher, Tankard, White, 12 In.	748.00

Opalescent, Alaska, Celery Dish, Vaseline, Enamel Flowers, 9 ½ In.
$425.00

Opalescent, Alaska, Pitcher, Water, Vaseline, c.1900, 7 ¼ In.
$431.00

Opalescent, Daisy & Fern, Creamer, Vaseline, 5 ½ In.
$60.00

Opalescent, Daisy & Fern, Sugar Shaker, Apple Blossom Mold,
Blue, Northwood, 4 In.
$288.00

Opalescent, Vase, Blue, Tree Base, Scalloped Rim, Victorian, 6 ¼ x 3 In.
$50.00

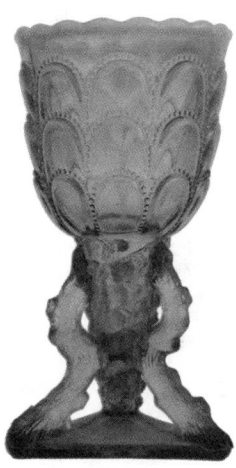

Opalescent, Windows, Syrup, Cranberry, Translucent Clambroth **Handle,**
6 ¾ In.
$575.00

O

OPALESCENT

Opera Glasses, Mother-Of-Pearl Caps, Enameled, Couple, Landscape, Lemoire, 4 x 2 ¾ In. $334.00

Opera Glasses, Mother-Of-Pearl, Gilt Metal, Hinged Handle, Premier, 4 x 2 In. $207.00

Opera Glasses, Red Guilloche Enamel, Scrolling Leaves, Flower Overlay, 18K Gold, Case, Tiffany & Co. $13035.00

Opera Glasses, Silver, Inscribed, Marked, Crescent Moon, Crown, Germany, 1800s, 7 ⅜ In. $311.00

TIP
Use paper plates between your china plates to help prevent chipping.

Daisy & Fern, Creamer, Vaseline, 5 ½ In.	*illus*	60.00
Daisy & Fern, Sugar Shaker, Apple Blossom Mold, Blue, Northwood, 4 In.	*illus*	288.00
Daisy & Fern, Syrup, Blue, 5 ½ In.		201.00
Opalescent, Toothpicks are listed in the Toothpick category.		
Opaline Brocade, Pitcher, Water, Blue Opalescent, 10 In.		259.00
Opaline Brocade, Pitcher, Water, Spanish Lace, Blue, 10 In.		374.00
Stripe, Sugar Shaker, Wide Nickel Mold, Blue, Lid, c.1875, 4 In.		297.00
Swastika, Syrup, Metal Lid, Green Dugan Glass Co., c.1910, 6 ¼ In.		4888.00
Swirl, Cruet, Cover, Blue Frosted, Cut Facet Stopper, Handle, Hobbs, Brockunier, c.1875, 6 In.		258.00
Thousand Eye, Creamer, Richard & Hartley, 5 ¾ x 4 In.		95.00
Vase, Blue, Tree Base, Scalloped Rim, Victorian, 6 ¼ x 3 In.	*illus*	50.00
Vase, Flower Form, Green, White Opalescent Petal Rim, Petal Foot, 8 In.		148.00
Vase, Molded Trees, Flowers, Gilt Leaf Base, Handles, 12 In.		345.00
Vaseline, Pitcher, Water, Swag, Brackets, Jefferson Glass, c.1900, 8 In.		171.00
Windows, Saltshaker, Sapphire, Hobbs Brockunier, c.1889, 3 ⅛ In.		70.00
Windows, Syrup, Cranberry, Translucent Clambroth Handle, 6 ¾ In.	*illus*	575.00

OPALINE, or opal glass, was made in white, green, and other colors. The glass had a matte surface and a lack of transparency. It was often gilded or painted. It was a popular mid-nineteenth-century European glassware.

Ashtray, Brass Mounts, Turquoise, c.1800, 2 ⅜ In.	84.00
Basket, Crystal, Gilt Highlights, France, 19th Century, 10 In.	176.00
Bowl, Egg Shape, Painted, Rosehips, Apple Blossoms, White Metal Mount, Handles, 13 x 18 In.	948.00
Syllabub Service, Gold Rim, Tureen With Lid, Ladle, 11 Cups	480.00
Vase, Mantel, Birds In Flight, Enamel, France, Pair	295.00
Vase, Square, Raised White Enamel Bird, Leaves, Gilt Rim, France, c.1900, 7 In., Pair	177.00

OPERA GLASSES are needed because the stage is a long way from some of the seats at a play or an opera. Mother-of-pearl was a popular decoration on many French glasses.

Ivory Case, Late 19th Century, 4 ½ x 2 ¼ x 1 ½ In.		75.00
Ivory, Gilt Bronze, J. Kollark, Dresden, 19th Century		145.00
Mother-Of-Pearl Body, Eyepieces, Paneled, Carrington Thomas & Co., 3 x 4 In.		374.00
Mother-Of-Pearl Caps, Enameled, Couple, Landscape, Lemoire, 4 x 2 ¾ In.	*illus*	334.00
Mother-Of-Pearl, Folding Handle, Paris, c.1910		237.00
Mother-Of-Pearl, Gilt Metal, Hinged handle, Premier, 4 x 2 In.	*illus*	207.00
Mother-Of-Pearl, Handle, Lemoire, Paris & H.C. Reiss, Newark, N.J., 6 In.		135.00
Mother-Of-Pearl, Marked Paris, France		44.00
Red Guilloche Enamel, Scrolling Leaves, Flower Overlay, 18K Gold, Case, Tiffany & Co..	*illus*	13035.00
Silver, French Vermeil, Rectangular, Folding, Pendant Case, Button Release, 3 In.		212.00
Silver, Inscribed, Marked, Crescent Moon, Crown, Germany, 1800s, 7 ⅜ In.	*illus*	311.00

ORPHAN ANNIE first appeared in the comics in 1924. The redheaded girl, her dog Sandy, and her friends have been on the radio and are still on the comic pages. The first movie based on the strip was produced in 1932. A Broadway musical show that opened in 1977 and a movie based on the show and produced in 1982 made Annie popular again, and many toys, dishes, and other memorabilia are being made.

Button, Portrait, Braverman's Children's Shop, Parisian Novelty, 1 ¼ In.	*illus*	95.00
Doll, Annie, Sandy, Composition Head, Green Googly Eyes, Cotton Dress, Freundlich, 1936, 12 In.		392.00
Ring, June Birthstone, Wealth, Blue Stone, Ovaltine, c.1936	*illus*	173.00
Toothbrush Holder, Annie, Sandy, Sofa, Bisque, F.A. Syn., 1930s, 3 ½ x 3 ½ In.		139.00
Toy, Annie Skipping Rope, Sandy, Tin, Cardboard Doghouse, Marx, 1935, 5 In.		819.00
Toy, Stove, Marx, c.1930, 8 ½ x 10 In.		40.00
Wristwatch, Annie Hugging Sandy, Red Vinyl Band, Box, Super Time Inc., 1980		127.00

ORREFORS Glassworks, located in the Swedish province of Smaaland, was established *Orrefors* in 1898. The company is still making glass for use on the table or as decorations. There is renewed interest in the glass made in the modern styles of the 1940s and 1950s. In 1990, the company merged with Kosta Boda. Most vases and decorative pieces are signed with the etched name Orrefors.

Bowl, Abstract, Faceted, Clear, Signed, 5 ¼ x 9 In.	145.00
Bowl, Amethyst, Stretched Bubble Design, 7 ½ In.	185.00
Bowl, Ariel, Burgundy & Clear, Radiating Stripes, Marked, 5 x 3 In.	360.00
Bowl, Black, Clear, Signed, Orrefors Gallery, Helen Krants, 4-25, 15 ¼ In.	600.00

Orphan Annie, Button, Portrait, Braverman's Children's Shop, Parisian Novelty, 1 ¼ In.
$95.00

Orphan Annie, Ring, June Birthstone, Wealth, Blue Stone, Ovaltine, c.1936
$173.00

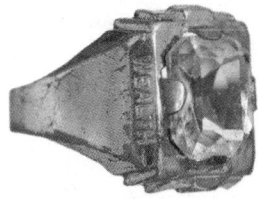

Orrefors, Vase, All Jazz, Painted, Musicians, Flared Base, Signature, 1900s, 7 x 7 In.
$932.00

Orrefors, Vase, Ariel, Woman's Portrait, Dove, Etched Edvin Ohrstrom, c.1937, 6 x 4 ¾ In.
$1409.00

Orrefors, Vase, Graal, Fish, Seaweed, Green To Clear, Flared Lip, Signed, Edvard Hald, 7 x 5 In.
$585.00

Orrefors, Vase, Kraka, Blue To Green Shading, Etched Sven Palmquist, 12 ½ x 3 ½ In.
$414.00

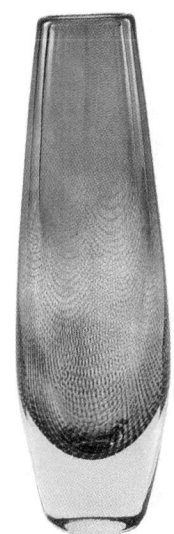

Eyeglasses
Eyeglasses did not have widespread use until the twentieth century. In England the National Health Service started giving glasses free in 1948 so more people wanted them. Designer glasses started in the 1960s. Dealers often advertise glasses as NOS. That means new old stock, glasses that were made in earlier years but never worn.

Overbeck, Vase, Brown, Shouldered, Incised Stylized Flower, Red, Green, 3 ½ x 3 ¼ In.
$6000.00

Overbeck, Vase, Incised, Stylized Horses, Yellow, Brown Matte Glaze, 3 ¾ x 2 ¾ In.
$3000.00

Owens, Mug, Transfer, Seated Indian, Headdress, Impressed Owens Utopian, 5 In.
$196.00

Owens, Vase, Brown Glaze, Fruit, Stems, Leaves, Impressed Mark, 10 x 6 ½ In.
$109.00

Bowl, Enameled Sailor's Dream Decoration, Straight-Sided, G. Cyren, 6 x 9 ½ In.	633.00
Bowl, Flared, 3 ¾ x 9 ¾ In.	30.00
Bowl, Fuga, Blue, Narrow Base, Wide Rim, Mid 20th Century, 8 In.	47.00
Bowl, Great, Round, Green, Fish, Seaweed, Marked, 9 ½ In.	259.00
Bowl, Nesting, Paneled, Notched Rim, 3 ½ x 8 ¾ In., 3 Piece	118.00
Bowl, Round, Intricate Design, Signed, Lars Hellsten, 9 In.	82.00
Candleholder, Crystal, Wide Cups, Irregular Shape, Signed, 2 ¾ x 3 ¼ In., Pair	12.00
Candlestick, Saucer Shape, 4 In., Pair	55.00
Case, Ariel, Cranberry To Clear, Marked, Olle Alberius, 7 In.	415.00
Cocktail, Prelude, Nils Landberg, c.1958, 5 ½ In, 9 Piece	71.00
Vase, All Jazz, Painted, Musicians, Flared Base, Signature, 1900s, 7 x 7 In. *illus*	932.00
Vase, Ariel, Metallic Geometric Design, Cylindrical, Marked, 3 ½ x 7 In.	1020.00
Vase, Ariel, Woman's Portrait, Dove, Etched Edvin Ohrstrom, c.1937, 6 x 4 ¾ In. *illus*	1409.00
Vase, Axe, Nils Landberg, Sommerso, 1956, 11 ½ In.	165.00
Vase, Burgundy & Clear, Swirling Stripes, Double Gourd Shape, P. Graal, Marked, 5 x 9 In.	600.00
Vase, Case Clear Over Smoke, Triangular, Nils Landberg, 1950s, 9 ½ In.	225.00
Vase, Cranberry & Clear Swirl, Opalescent Center, Round, Marked, Lars Hellsten, 6 In.	210.00
Vase, Cylindrical, Kraka, Bubbles, Blue Tint, Signed, 12 In.	431.00
Vase, Gooseneck, 2 Fold Rim, Green, White Striated Core, 11 In.	150.00
Vase, Graal, Aquarium Design, Edvard Hald, 7 In.	863.00
Vase, Graal, Fish, Seaweed, Green To Clear, Flared Lip, Signed, Edvard Hald, 7 x 5 In. *illus*	585.00
Vase, Kraka, Blue To Green Shading, Etched Sven Palmquist, 12 ½ x 3 ½ In. *illus*	414.00
Vase, Love Poem, Cranberry, Nude Couple, Engraved, Signed, Olle Alberius, 8 ½ x 3 In.	1300.00
Vase, No. 1578/4, Mist Blue, Lobed Base, 9 ⅝ In.	18.00

OVERBECK POTTERY was made by four sisters named Overbeck at a pottery in Cambridge City, Indiana. They started in 1911. They made all types of vases, each one-of-a-kind. Small, hand-modeled figurines are the most popular pieces with today's collectors. The factory continued until 1955, when the last of the four sisters died.

Brooch, Southern Belle, Blond, Pink & Blue Striped Dress, 2 In.	175.00
Figurine, Dog, Panting, White, Brown & Black Ears, Googly Eyes, Incised, 3 In.	465.00
Figurine, Farmer, Holding Watermelon, Brown Floppy Hat, Blue Pants, 5 ⅛ In.	680.00
Figurine, Farmer's Wife, Carrying Basket Of Apples, Blue Dress, White Apron, Incised, 4 ¼ In.	515.00
Figurine, George & Martha Washington, Seated, Incised, George 4 In., Martha 3 ⅜ In., Pair	2130.00
Figurine, Lady, Blue Dress, Pink Coat, Umbrella, Incised, 4 ¼ In.	230.00
Figurine, Man, Red Frock Coat, Blue Top Hat & Bowtie, Incised, 4 In.	260.00
Figurine, Southern Belle, Blue Dress, Red & Blue Spots, Blue Bonnet, Incised, 3 ⅜ In.	260.00
Figurine, Southern Belle, Striped Dress, Apron, Blue & Yellow Bonnet, Yellow Fan, Incised, 4 In.	320.00
Figurine, Southern Belle, White Dress, Blue & Pink Spots, Marked, 4 ¼ In.	230.00
Painting, Oil On Canvas, Cardinals, Chickadees, Tree, Frame, Signed, Mary Frances, 9 x 11 In.	735.00
Vase, Brown, Shouldered, Incised Stylized Flower, Red, Green, 3 ½ x 3 ¼ In. *illus*	6000.00
Vase, Incised, Stylized Horses, Yellow, Brown Matte Glaze, 3 ¾ x 2 ¾ In. *illus*	3000.00
Vase, Stylized Flowers, Red & Green, Tan Ground, Marked, 11 ⅞ In.	13500.00

OWENS POTTERY was made in Zanesville, Ohio, from 1891 to 1928. The first art pottery was made after 1896. Utopian Ware, Cyrano, Navarre, Feroza, and Henri Deux were made. Pieces were usually marked with a form of the name Owens. About 1907, the firm began to make tile and discontinued the art pottery wares.

Bowl, Aqua Verdi, Swirls, 3-Footed, 7 ⅝ In.	173.00
Creamer, White Violets, Green To Brown Ground, Incised, 5 ⅞ In.	115.00
Ewer, Utopian, 3-Footed, Brown Glaze, Orange Roses, Silver Overlay, Marked, 4 x 5 In.	920.00
Jug, Utopian, Large Cherries, Silver Overlay, 5 In.	288.00
Mug, Transfer, Seated Indian, Headdress, Impressed Owens Utopian, 5 In. *illus*	196.00
Vase, Brown Glaze, Fruit, Stems, Leaves, Impressed Mark, 10 x 6 ½ In. *illus*	109.00
Vase, Bulbous, White Ground, Green Poppies, Marked, 4 x 12 In.	150.00
Vase, Lotus, Orange Wild Rose Blossom, Impressed Utopian J.B. Owens, 9 ¼ In. *illus*	345.00
Vase, Monumental Shape, Green Matte Glaze, 9 x 11 In.	259.00
Vase, Utopian, Bud, Metallic Glaze, Handles, 12 In.	219.00
Vase, Utopian, Bulbous, Brown Glaze, Cat Portrait, 5 x 8 In.	1840.00
Vase, Utopian, Bulbous, Brown Glaze, Painted Cat, Mae Timberlake, 3 ¾ x 5 ¼ In.	1093.00
Vase, Utopian, Dog Portrait, Footed, Marked, 9 x 7 ½ In.	2300.00
Vase, Utopian, Gold & Ivory Glaze, Painted Indian Portrait, Marked, 8 x 12 In.	2530.00
Vase, Utopian, Stork, Yellow Portrait, Dark Ground, Charles Chilcote, 8 In.	259.00
Vase, Utopian, Wild Rose, Leaves, Tan, Green, Hole For Lamp, 13 In.	92.00

OYSTER PLATES were popular from the 1880s. Each course at dinner was served in a special dish. The oyster plate had indentations shaped like oysters. Usually six oysters were held on a plate. There is no greater value to a plate with more oysters, although that myth continues to haunt antiques dealers. There are other plates for shellfish, including cockle plates and whelk plates. The appropriately shaped indentations are part of the design of these dishes.

5 Wells, Flowers, Leaves, Scrolling, Musical Symbols, Gilt Rim, Haviland, 7 ¾ In., 6 Piece	189.00
5 Wells, Shell & Undersea Decoration, White Ground, Haviland, Limoges, 8 ¾ In.	225.00
6 Wells, Brown, Peach Flowers, Haviland & Co., Limoges, 1887, 8 ¼ In.	295.00
6 Wells, Lemon Well Center, Green, White, Black, Impressed, Limoges, 8 ¾ In., 6 Piece	588.00
Violets, Gilt, Limoges, 7 ½ In., 12 Piece	650.00

PADEN CITY GLASS MANUFACTURING COMPANY was established in 1916 at Paden City, West Virginia. The company made over twenty different colors of glass. The firm closed in 1951. Paden City Pottery is not listed here. Paden City Pottery may be listed in Dinnerware.

Figurine, Pheasant, Blue, 13 ½ In.	238.00
Greenbrier, Casserole, Cover, Dell Green	55.00
Greenbrier, Casserole, Cover, Green, Handles	55.00
Greenbrier, Chop Plate, Dell Green, 12 ¾ In.	62.00
Greenbrier, Plate, Dinner, Green, 9 ¼ In.	13.00
Greenbrier, Plate, Salad, Green, 7 ¼ In.	12.00
Greenbrier, Soup, Dish, Green, 6 ⅛ In.	10.00
Minion, Bowl, Fruit, 5 ½ In.	8.00
Party Line, Decanter, Pink, 9 ½ In.	125.00
Party Line, Sandwich Server, Amber, Marie Cutting, Center Handle, 10 ½ In. ....*illus*	28.00
Peacock & Wild Rose, Ice Tub, Green, Tab Handles ....*illus*	223.00
Rosalee, Plate, Dinner, 9 ⅞ In.	15.00
Spring Orchard, Cocktail Shaker, Gold Encrusted, Brass Cover, 11 In. ....*illus*	225.00
Vanity Set, 2 Perfume Bottles, Puff Box, Tray, Pink, Pre 1950	214.00
Willow, Plate, Dinner, 10 In.	9.00

PAINTINGS listed in this book are not works by major artists but rather decorative paintings on ivory, board, or glass that would be of interest to the average collector. Watercolors on paper are listed under Picture. To learn the value of an oil painting by a listed artist you must contact an expert in that area.

Miniature, Man, Blue Eyes, Wearing Light Blue Vest, Leather Case, c.1835, 3 ½ x 3 In.	474.00
Miniature, On Ivory, 2 Dutch Girls Eating Cherries, Giltwood Frame, 4 x 5 In.	488.00
Miniature, On Ivory, British Officer, Red Brocade Coat & Sash, Frame, 3 x 2 In.	1265.00
Miniature, On Ivory, Dancing Couples, Carved, Round Discs, Frame, Spain, 18 x 9 In.	88.00
Miniature, On Ivory, Madonna & Child, Frame, Italy, 20th Century, 5 In.	290.00
Miniature, On Ivory, Man, Colonel Knight Erskine, Ruffles, 1809, 3 x 2 ¼ In.	1265.00
Miniature, On Ivory, Man, Red Velvet Vest, Cornelius Durham, 1845, 4 In.	460.00
Miniature, On Ivory, Z. Boylston Of Boston, Oval Gilt Frame, 12 x 1 ½ In.	690.00
Miniature, On Porcelain, Madonna & Child, Stylized, Frame, 9 ¼ x 8 ¼ In.	290.00
Oil On Board, 2 Stacks, 3 Rigged Masts, Flags, Passengers, Frame, 23 x 37 In.	518.00
Oil On Board, Cat, Red Curtain, 1800s, 12 x 9 In.	1541.00
Oil On Board, Covered Wagon, Carl Rudolph Drafft, Signed, Titled, Frame, 1935, 15 x 20 In.	1440.00
Oil On Board, Landscape, Philadelphia City Hall, Frame, 1800s, 9 x 12 In.	1170.00
Oil On Board, Ohio Farm, Bird's-Eye Maple Frame, R. Tschudi, Ohio, c.1885, 18 x 24 In.	3290.00
Oil On Canvas, African American Girl On Porch, Looking At Landscape, P.T. Davis, 24 x 36 In.	88.00
Oil On Canvas, Asian Girl, Green Robe, Chinese School, Gilt Frame, 21 x 15 In.	13750.00
Oil On Canvas, Bird's-Eye View, Andersonville Prison, Eastlake Frame, 26 x 35 In.	17500.00
Oil On Canvas, Coastal Sunset, Alexander A. Dzigurski, Signed, Frame, c.1945, 24 x 36 In.	2280.00
Oil On Canvas, Indian Woman In Silhouette, Eagle Feather, 30 x 25 In.	460.00
Oil On Canvas, Laundress, Myron G. Barlow, 1900s, 30 x 30 In.	9400.00
Oil On Canvas, Still Life & Tomato, Signed, Greg Tienaz, c.1940, 20 x 16 In.	575.00
Oil On Canvas, Washington At Valley Forge, 1800s, 24 x 30 In.	4600.00
Oil On Canvas, Winter Scene, Gilt Gesso Frame, 18 x 24 In.	1541.00
Oil On Composite Board, Barn, Horses Eating, Landscape, Frame, c.1962, 20 ½ x 26 ½ In.	44.00
Oil On Composite Board, Children, Sheep, Landscape, Oak Frame, M.R. Wylie, 24 x 36 In.	193.00
Oil On Composite Board, Red Barn, Rolling Hillside, Oak Frame, 20th Century, 15 x 19 In.	33.00
Oil On Leather, American Indian Chief, 27 x 23 In.	472.00
Oil On Masonite, Portrait Of A Boy, Chevis, Clark, 1900s, 8 ½ x 6 ½ In.	235.00
Oil On Masonite, Summer Mist, Wray Manning, Signed, Titled, Frame, c.1950, 22 x 30 In.	600.00
Oil On Panel, Boy With Green Jacket & Book, Frame, c.1830, 13 x 10 In.	6250.00

Owens, Vase, Lotus, Orange Wild Rose Blossom, Impressed Utopian J.B. 9 ¼ In. $345.00

Paden City, Party Line, Sandwich Server, Amber, Marie Cutting, Center Handle, 10 ½ In. $28.00

Paden City, Peacock & Wild Rose, Ice Tub, Green, Tab Handles $223.00

Paden City, Spring Orchard, Cocktail Shaker, Gold Encrusted, Brass Cover, 11 In. $225.00

P

Labels Help

When trying to trace an old oil painting, look at more than the artist's signature. Valuable information comes from labels of frame makers, exhibition and auction labels, artist board marks, and even shipping labels.

Oil On Panel, Gray Tiger Cat, Portrait, Giltwood Frame, 6 x 6 In.		3200.00
Oil On Paper, Ship, Banner, Enterprise, N.Y., 10 On Sails, Frame, 9 x 11 In.		264.00
Oil On Poplar Board, Child, Seated, White Dress, Book, Frame, 26 x 22 In.	*illus*	2585.00
Oil On Slate, Winter Landscape, Wood Frame, Taped Note On Back, c.1890, 10 x 7 In.		55.00
On Ivory, Gentleman, Hair Locket On Back, Signed, T.H.E., 1805, 2 5/8 x 2 In.		1534.00
On Ivory, Girl, Blue Dress, Oval, Frame, 2 x 2 In.		1808.00
On Ivory, Girl, Crossed Arms, Brown Dress, White Collar, Oval, Signed, M. Lawrence, 3 x 2 ½ In.		173.00
On Ivory, Man, Black Coat, In Front Of Window, Drapes, Sky, ½ Portrait, Frame, 3 ½ x 3 In.		270.00
On Ivory, Woman, White Shawl, Signed, Danilux, 1771, 3 In. Diam.		1860.00
On Porcelain, Portrait Of Mme. Recamier, Giltwood Frame, 1880, 5 ¼ x 7 In.		458.00
Reverse On Glass, Christ Child, Globe, Roses, Frame, Germany, 1800s, 12 x 9 In.	*illus*	235.00
Reverse On Glass, George Slaying Dragon, Frame, 11 x 9 In.		354.00
Reverse On Glass, Portrait, Sahra, China Trade, 19th Century, 10 x 7 ½ In.	*illus*	431.00

Painting, Oil On Poplar Board, Child, Seated, White Dress, Book, Frame, 26 x 22 In. $2585.00

Painting, Reverse On Glass, Christ Child, Globe, Roses, Frame, Germany, 1800s, 12 x 9 In. $235.00

PAIRPOINT Manufacturing Company started in 1880 in New Bedford, Massachusetts. It soon joined with the glassworks nearby and made glass, silver-plated pieces, and lamps. Reverse-painted glass shades and molded shades known as "puffies" were part of the production until the 1930s. The company reorganized and changed its name several times but is still working today. Items listed here are glass or glass and metal. Silver-plated pieces are listed under Silver Plate.

Biscuit Jar, Florette, Pink Satin, Metal Rim & Handle, 6 x 6 ½ In.		173.00
Biscuit Jar, Flower Medallions, Lattice Accents, Stamped Lid, Mt. Washington, 7 In.		690.00
Biscuit Jar, Mold Blown, Translucent, Gold Scrolling Flowers, 7 ½ In.		1955.00
Biscuit Jar, Square, Enameled Flowers, Yellow Ground, Metal Lid & Handle, Marked, 5 x 6 In.		230.00
Biscuit Jar, Square, Gold Chrysanthemums, Yellow Ground, Metal Lid & Handle, 5 x 8 In.		201.00
Bowl, Console, Silver Overlay, Flambeau, Footed, Pontil, Marked, c.1900, 3 ½ x 11 In.		132.00
Bowl, Flared, Footed, Turn Down Rim, Ruby Red, 12 ½ x 3 In.		115.00
Bowl, Flared, Silver Leaf Pattern, 4 ½ x 10 In.		750.00
Candlestick, Ambero, Leaf, Vine, Yellow Ground Shade, Mahogany Base, Signed, 16 In.		575.00
Compote, Cut Glass, Floral Wreath, Brass Squared Handles, Base, Collar, Signed, 9 x 11 In., Pair.		661.00
Creamer, Footed Heart Shape, White Dove, Flowers, Rose, Pink, Bryden Peachblow, 5 In.		201.00
Dresser Box, Oval, Pink, Scrolls, Gilt Flowers, Stamped, 8 In.		275.00
Dresser Box, Yellow, Brown Flowers, Opaline Glass, Metal Rim, Base, 7 In.		374.00
Lamp, 6-Sided Shade, Flowers Design, Brass, Onyx Base, 15 In.		1025.00
Lamp, Banquet, Brass, Clear & Frosted Shade, Prisms, Square Base, Footed, 33 In.		1180.00
Lamp, Berkley Shade, Reverse Painted, Ribbed Bulbous Stem, 16 x 21 In.	*illus*	2300.00
Lamp, Candlestick Shade, Green, Burgundy, Camphor Ground, Wood Base, 20 In., Pair		1035.00
Lamp, Lilac Blossoms, Purple, Red, Butterflies, Begonia Tree Base, c.1929, 17 x 8 ½ In.		23500.00
Lamp, Nautical Scene, Sailing Ships, Birds In Flight, Clouds, Green Ground, 14 In.		1265.00
Lamp, Oil, Swedish, Candle, Opaque White, Windmill Transfer, Swirled Shade, No. 87, 6 x 5 In.		702.00
Lamp, Puffy, Apple Tree Blossoms, Bees, Tree Trunk Base, 2-Light, 12 x 25 In.		25875.00
Lamp, Puffy, Boudoir, Roses.		310.00
Lamp, Puffy, Butterflies, Flower Shade, Multicolored, c.1907, 21 In.		3510.00
Lamp, Puffy, Flower Curtain Glass Shade, Silver Base, 14 x 8 ½ In.		1159.00
Lamp, Puffy, Flower Garland Wreaths, Reverse, Green, Yellow, Rose, White, 14 x 23 In.		12650.00
Lamp, Puffy, Flower Garlands, Devonshire, Closed Top, Signed, 16 In. Diam.		12000.00
Lamp, Puffy, Marlborough, White Flowers, Lace, 4-Sided Base, 16 x 23 In.	*illus*	7475.00
Lamp, Puffy, Oxford, Flowers, Multicolored, Green Patina Metal Base, Signed, 14 x 21 In.		16100.00
Lamp, Puffy, Papillon, Green, Roses, Poppies, Reverse Painted, 14 ½ In.		4600.00
Lamp, Puffy, Papillon, Red Flowers, Butterflies, Square Platform Base, Signed, 16 x 21 In.		4600.00
Lamp, Puffy, Pink, Purple Flowers, Yellow, White Window Panes, Brass Base, 8 x 15 In.		2818.00
Lamp, Reverse Painted, Apple Green, Purple, Pink, Orange, White, Yellow, Flowers, 21 In.		5750.00
Lamp, Reverse Painted Shade, Sea Gulls, Matching Glass Base, Blue, Green, Copley, 20 x 25 In.		6250.00
Lamp, Reverse Painted, White, Green, Flower Shade, Tuscano, Ball Feet Base, 16 x 24 In.		4600.00
Lamp, Reverse Painted, Yellow Flowers, Green, Red, 3-Candle Base, Signed, 16 x 26 In.		2013.00
Lamp, Seascape, Ship Reverse Painted Shade, Metal Scroll Base, C. Durand, 16 x 22 In.		4025.00
Lamp, Woman's Face, Pink To Frosted, Flowers, Brass Base, Footed, Urn Shape, 12 & 18 In.		1725.00
Paperweight, Pedestal, Narcissus, Leaves, Windows, Pontil, 4 ¾ x 3 ⅝ In.		224.00
Perfume Bottle, Twisted Vertical Ribs, Cranberry Lines, Flower Stopper, 5 ½ In.		403.00
Pitcher, Syrup, Pink Opaline, Smith Brothers' Dandelion, 7 In.		403.00
Pitcher, Water, Savoy, Double Notched Handle, 10 ¾ In.		700.00
Plate, Mikado Pattern, 8-Sided, 8 ½ In.		70.00
Vase, Cylinder, Swirled Shape, Opal With Yellow, Purple Pansies, 17 ½ In.		100.00
Vase, Delft Decorated, Windmill, House, Limoges, 10 ¼ In.		350.00
Vase, Inverted Neck, Bulbous, 4 ¾ In., Pair		201.00
Vase, Ruby Red, Flared, Clear Globular Bubble Stem, Footed, 10 In., Pair		260.00

PAPER collectibles, including almanacs, catalogs, children's books, some greeting cards, stock certificates, and other paper ephemera, are listed here. Paper calendars are listed separately in the Calendar category. Paper items may be found in many other sections, such as Christmas and Movie.

Advertisement, Wine, Chateau Margaux, Lithograph, France, J. Michaelsen & Cie, 19 ¼ x 11 In.	294.00
Almanac, New York Clipper, Graphics Of Baseball, Track, Crew, Circus, 9 x 6 In., 64 Pages	255.00
Almanac, N.Y. Clipper, 1880, Colored Graphics On Cover, 9 x 5 ½ In., 64 Pages........................	255.00
Bank Check, Wells Fargo & Company, Frank Koff, $145.00, February 10, 1894, 3 ½ x 8 ½ In.	175.00
Birth, Baptismal Certificate, Calico Township, Penn., 1783, 15 x 11 ⅝ In.	2750.00
Birth Certificate, Ink & Watercolor, Johan Jacob Schweicker, Heart & Flower Border, 12 x 16 In. .	1053.00
Bond, State Of Louisiana, Reconstruction, 5 Dollar Value, Issue 1871, Redeemed In 1884	38.00
Book, Hood's Sarsaparilla, Pansy, Lowell, Mass., Late 19th Century	11.00
Book, Little Golden Book, Nurse Nancy, Simon & Schuster, 1952	400.00
Book, Pop-Up, Little Red Riding Hood, Blue Ribbon Books, c.1933, 6 ½ x 8 ¾ In., 16 Pages.....	139.00
Book, Pop-Up, Sleeping Beauty, Blue Ribbon Books, c.1933, 6 ½ x 8 ¾ In., 16 Pages	139.00
Book, Punch-Out, Errol Flynn, The Sea Hawk, 1940s..	610.00
Book, Wrigley's, Mother Goose, Color, Illustrated, c.1915, 4 ¼ x 6 ¼ In., 24 Pages...................	173.00
Catalog, Golden Opportunities, Coin-Operated Machines, Bradford Scale Co., 1913, 8 x 11 In.	330.00
Catalog, Henrie & Bolthoff Mfg. Co., Mining Machinery, Denver, Colo., 11 x 8 In., 62 Pages.....	221.00
Catalog, L.L. Bean, Snowshoes, Camp Gear, Bobcat, Preventing Forest Fires, Fall, 1944, 60 Pages.	24.00
Catalog, Spencer Fireworks Headquarters, Spring 1939, Featuring Buck Rogers, 40 Pages.......	145.00
Catalog, Spencer Fireworks, 1937, Featuring Buck Rogers On Cover, 40 Pages	145.00
Certificate, Land Registration, Sacramento, M. Stoddard, Embossed Seal, Oct. 1, 1862, 9 ¾ x 16 In.	184.00
Coloring Book, Alice In Wonderland, Children's Press, c.1947, 14 ¼ x 10 ½ In.	58.00
Coloring Book, Story Of Guns, 1940, Unused, Illustrations Of World War II, 64 Pages.............	45.00
Concert Book, Elton John, Color, Fan Club Membership Form, Oct. 16, 1974, 29 Pages...........	24.00
Concert Book, Johnny Mathis, Program, Feb. 14, 1964, Everett Civic Auditorium, 24 Pages	21.00
Concert Book, This Is Tom Jones, August 1, 1970, Photos, 24 Pages	17.50
Cutwork, Remember Me Myrtie, Birds, Flowers, Signed, John B. Walker, 1815-1908, 14 x 10 In.	840.00
Deed, Warranty, Shaker, Sale Of Enfield Conn., Signatures, Seals, Stamps, Dec. 3, 1898...........	321.00
Delaware Survey, John Pettigreu, Feb. 20, 1799, 13 x 16 In.	177.00
Drawing, Borden's Original Ice Plant, Woburn, Mass., Frame, 1954, 31 x 21 In.	250.00
Drawing Sampler, Graphite, Ink On Paper, Child's Ledger Book, Gilt Frame, c.1835, 13 x 8 In.	558.00
Fashion Plate, Parisian Costumes, Townsend, Hand Colored, 79 Plates, Bound, 1820s, 8 x 5 In.	306.00
Fraktur, Angel, Heart Body, Verse, Dec. 24, 1824, Watercolor, Wood Frame, 8 x 9 In.	411.00
Fraktur, Baptism, Elizabeth Hartman, Lowhill Twp., Leigh Co., Wood Frame, 1834, 19 x 16 In.	44.00
Fraktur, Baptism, Hand Drawn, Flowers, Angels, 9 Hearts, German Text, Frame, 1795, 16 x 18 In.	550.00
Fraktur, Birds, Stylized Flowers, Center Script, Hand Colored, Frame, 1792, 13 x 16 In.	2840.00
Fraktur, Birth, Baptismal Certificate, Watercolor, Feronica Risser, Frame, c.1835, 10 x 8 In. ....*illus*	3540.00
Fraktur, Birth, Christian Schlobach, Watercolor, Flowers, Basket, Text, Frame, 1870, 19 x 9 In.	294.00
Fraktur, Birth, Laid Paper, Printed, Watercolor, Border, Wood Frame, c.1803, 15 ½ x 18 ½ In.	441.00
Fraktur, Birth, Sara Hoch, Ink, Watercolor, Frame, Berks County, 1800s, 8 x 13 ¼ In. ..... *illus*	1989.00
Fraktur, Birth, Watercolor, Jemima Harlin, April 27, 1801, Swags, House, Frame, 10 x 12 In. .	1880.00
Fraktur, Bookplate, Stylized Tulip, Tree, Ink, Watercolor, Frame, c.1829, 4 ¾ x 2 ¾ In. ...*illus*	936.00
Fraktur, Horse, Flower, Made By Your Mother, February 5th 1882, Remember Me, 13 x 11 In.	385.00
Fraktur, Ink & Watercolor, Sara Hoch, Berks County, Penn., Frame, c.1810, 8 x 13 In.	1989.00
Fraktur, Printed, Hand Colored, Script, Trumpeting Angels, Frame, 1814, 11 ¾ x 14 ½ In.	380.00
Fraktur, Watercolor, Ink, German Script, Bird, Dragon, Tulip, Acorn, Leaf, 1806, 14 In. Square.	523.00
Fraktur, Watercolor, Ink, German Script, Flower Border, Rag Paper, 1771, 10 ¼ x 15 ¼ In.	248.00
Fraktur, Watercolor, Hand Drawn, Eagle, Grain Painted Frame, Lancaster Co., 1800s, 13 x 11 In.	660.00
Guide Book, Yosemite, 8 Engraved Plates, Maps, Cloth Cover, Whitney, c.1869, 9 x 6 In., 155 Pages	306.00
Gum Card Wrapper, Soldier Boys, Waxed Paper, Goudey Gum Co., 1930s, 4 x 5 In.	115.00
Indenture, Issac Davis, March 26, 1813, Duck Creek Hundred, Del., 13 x 16 In.	70.00
Indenture, Joseph Aydelott, Aug.2, 1798, Wax Seals, Signed Simon Wilson, 22 x 17 In.	118.00
Invitation, Mardi Gras, Rex Ball, History Of The World, New Orleans, c.1879 .... *illus*	1652.00
Land Grant, Delaware, Signed Robert Morris Sr., Dec.17, 1754..	531.00
Magazine Cover, Movie Story, Hedy Lamarr & John Garfield On Cover, 1942	25.00
Magazine, Field & Stream, 1975	6.00
Magazine, Life, July 14, 1947, Photo Of Elizabeth Taylor On Cover, 10 x 14 In.	175.00
Marriage Certificate, C.F. Hescock & Mary Sherman, Cutwork, J.B. Walker, c.1885, 16 x 12 In. *illus*	1872.00
Notebook Pad, The A-Team, Spiral, Photos Of Mr. T On Cover, Stuart Hall Co., 1983	24.00
Report Card, Cornelius Winkleblack, Ohio, 1866, Signed L. Biddle, Ink, Watercolor, Frame, 8 x 12 In. ..	764.00
Scroll, Gouache, Ink, Pavilions, Pagoda In Gardens, Li Tieguai, Frame, Chinese, 1700, 50 ½ x 20 In.	360.00
Scroll, Green, Gold Silk, 8 Taoist Immortals, Eating, Feeding Cranes, Japan, 1800s, 78 x 27 In., Pair	420.00
Scroll, Ink, Garden Scene, 2 Women, Eroded Rock, Shrubs, Flowering Trees, Frame, 60 x 33 ½ In.	540.00
Silhouette, Woman Gazing In Mirror, 1920, Germany, 6 ¾ x 7 ½ In.	30.00

Painting, Reverse On Glass, Portrait, Sahra, China Trade, 19th Century, 10 x 7 ½ In. $431.00

Pairpoint, Lamp, Berkley Shade, Reverse Painted, Ribbed Bulbous Stem, 16 x 21 In. $2300.00

Pairpoint, Lamp, Puffy, Marlborough, White Flowers, Lace, 4-Sided Base, 16 x 23 In. $7475.00

Paper, Fraktur, Birth, Baptismal Certificate, Watercolor, Feronica Risser, Frame, c.1835, 10 x 8 In. $3540.00

Spencerian Composition, 2 Birds, Signed, Dellie Benson, Frame, 16 x 21 ½ In.	176.00
Steamship Advertising Broadside, Frank McElroy Steam Book & Job Printer, 1862, 15 x 10 In.	115.00
Stock Certificate, Milford Steam Boat Co., Milford, Del., April 30, 1852, 8 ½ x 5 ½ In.	130.00
Stock Certificate, Northwest Equipment Co., 200 Shares, J.D. Rockefeller Signed, c.1890	1180.00
Stock Certificate, Philadelphia & Lancaster Turnpike Road, On Vellum, 1795, 7 x 9 In.	1521.00
Survey, Hand Drawn, New Castle, Delaware, Feb.1810, Dan Blaney, 17 x 20 In.	413.00
Vorschrift, Writing Specimen, Ink & Watercolor, Signed Samuel Landis, Penn., c.1815, 7 ¾ x 12 In.	380.00

PAPER DOLLS were probably inspired by the pantins, or jumping jacks, made in eighteenth-century Europe. By the 1880s, sheets of printed paper dolls and clothes were being made. The first paper doll books were made in the 1920s. Collectors prefer uncut sheets or books or boxed sets of paper dolls. Prices are about half as much if the pages have been cut.

Airline Hostess & Pilot, Merrill, 12 ¾ x 10 ¼ In., Uncut	86.00
Ann Sothern, Saalfield Publishing Co., 1943, Uncut	113.00
Bedknobs & Broomsticks, With London Village Scene, Whitman, 1971, 10 x 13 In.	45.00
Betty Grable, Punch-Out Dolls, Book, 6 Pages, c.1951, 10 ½ x 13 In., Uncut .... *illus*	173.00
Betty Grable, Whitman Publishing Company, 1946, Uncut	226.00
Beverly Hillbillies, Jed, Granny, Elly May & Jethro, Whitman, 1955, 9 x 12 In.	65.00
Buffy, Family Affair, Photo Of Anissa Jones On Back Holding Mrs. Beasley, Whitman, 1969	95.00
Buster Brown & Tige, J. Ottmann Litho Co., 6 ½ x 12-In. Envelope, c.1910 .... *illus*	424.00
Debbie Reynolds, Whitman, c.1958, 15 x 11 In., Uncut .... *illus*	230.00
Hopalong Cassidy, Bar 20 Ranch, Whitman Publishing Co., Uncut	260.00
John Wayne, 2 Dolls, 31 Costumes, Tom Tierney, Dover Publication, 1981	25.00
Lennon Sisters, Whitman Publishing Company, 1957, Uncut	136.00
Mary Martin, Saalfield Publishing Co., 1942, Uncut	170.00
Mrs. Beasley, Family Affair, Whitman, 1972, 10 x 13 In.	135.00
Nurses, CBS TV Series, Carrying Case, Whitman, 1963	65.00
Oklahoma, Simon & Schuster Publishing Co., 1956, Uncut	85.00
Old Lady Who Lived In The Shoe, Book, 8 Pages, 12 x 14 ½ In., Uncut .... *illus*	127.00
Patti Page, Samuel Lowe Publishing, 2 Statuettes, Wardrobe, 1958, Uncut	136.00
The Nurses, From 1963 CBS TV Series, 2 Dolls, 53 Outfits, Whitman, No. 1975, Case	65.00
Twiggy, 1 Doll, 50 Costumes, Pinup, Mod Fashion, Whitman, 1967	95.00

PAPERWEIGHTS must have first appeared along with paper in ancient Egypt. Today's collectors search for every type, from the very expensive French weights of the nineteenth century to the modern artist weights or advertising pieces. The glass tops of the paperweights sometimes have been nicked or scratched, and this type of damage can be removed by polishing. Some serious collectors think this type of repair is an alteration and will not buy a repolished weight; others think it is an acceptable technique of restoration that does not change the value. Baccarat paperweights are listed separately under Baccarat.

Advertising, Barr-Goodwin Lumber Co., House On Car, Orlando, Fla., 3 ½ In.	250.00
Advertising, Bates Expanded Steel Truss Co., Chicago Steel Poles, Glass, 4 x ¾ In.	60.00
Advertising, Bell Telephone, Tile, Depicts Salesman, Green, 1941-64, 4 ½ In.	75.00
Advertising, Big News In Buick, Newsiest Buick Yet, Cast Iron, Red & White, 6 In.	90.00
Advertising, C.F. Boehringer & Soehne, Factory, Manheim, Germany, 2 ¼ In x 4 In.	99.00
Advertising, Champion Blower & Forge, Cast Iron, 1900s, 3 ½ x 2 ¾ In.	115.00
Advertising, Chef, Enamel, Cast Iron, Warm Friend, Boilers, Ranges, Furnace, 3 ½ In.	187.00
Advertising, Dexter Portland Cement Co.	110.00
Advertising, Dice Game, P & W Tobacco Co., Glass, 2 ½ x 4 ¼ x 1 In.	35.00
Advertising, Dutch Boy Painter, Cast Metal, Copper Flashed, 2 x 4 x 2 In.	56.00
Advertising, Edison Phonograph, Boy Listening, National Phonograph Co.	39.00
Advertising, El Reco Gas, Man, Here's A Pal For You, White, Red, Black, Cast Iron, 3 ⅜ x 3 In.	55.00
Advertising, Figure, El Reco Gas Man, Here's A Pal For You, Cast Iron, 3 x 4 In.	59.00
Advertising, Goodyear, 15 Years Of Friendly Relations, Bronze, Medallion, 4 In.	125.00
Advertising, HMV Victor Talking Machine, Marked	88.00
Advertising, Marshalltown Western Grocers, Buildings, Glass, 1 x 4 x 2 ½ In.	50.00
Advertising, Nodome Standard Oil, Painted, Moise-K.S.F., Calif., Iron, c.1930, 5 ¼ In.	60.00
Advertising, The Dutch Boy Painter, Cast Metal, Copper Flashed, 2 x 4 In.	56.00
Advertising, Turtle & Hughes Electrical Supplies, Figural, Iron, Painted, 2 ⅜ In.	127.00
Advertising, WF Robertson Steel & Iron Co., Springfield Ohio Mfg., Tin Litho, 3 ½ In.	300.00
Air Twist, Spirals, Egg Shape, Steuben, 3 x 3 In.	236.00
Art Glass, Isle Of Wight, Gold Speckled Ground, Pansies, White, Amber, Label, 1 ⅞ In.	83.00
Ayotte, Double Pansy Bouquet, Mauve, Ladybug, No. 48, Signed, 1988, 3 ¹¹⁄₁₆ In.	1650.00

P

Paper, Fraktur, Birth, Sara Hoch, Ink, Watercolor, Frame, Berks County, 1800s, 8 x 13 ¼ In.
$1989.00

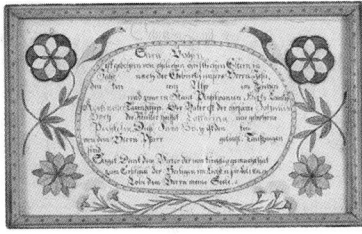

Paper, Fraktur, Bookplate, Stylized Tulip, Tree, Ink, Watercolor, Frame, c.1829, 4 ¾ x 2 ¾ In.
$936.00

Paper, Invitation, Mardi Gras, Rex Ball, History Of The World, New Orleans, c.1879
$1652.00

Paper, Marriage Certificate, C.F. Hescock & Mary Sherman, Cutwork, J.B. Walker, c.1885, 16 x 12 In.
$1872.00

Paper Doll, Betty Grable, Punch-Out Dolls, Book, 6 Pages, c.1951, 10 ½ x 13 In., Uncut
$173.00

Paper Doll, Buster Brown & Tige, J. Ottmann Litho Co., 6 ½ x 12-In. Envelope, c.1910
$424.00

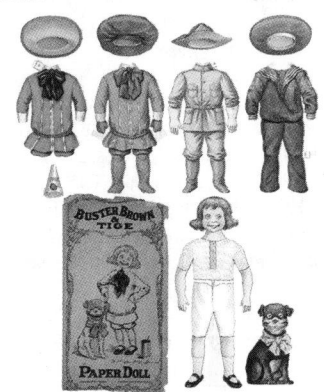

Paper Doll, Debbie Reynolds, Whitman, c.1958, 15 x 11 In., Uncut
$230.00

Paper Doll, Old Lady Who Lived In The Shoe, Book, 8 Pages, 12 x 14 ½ In., Uncut
$127.00

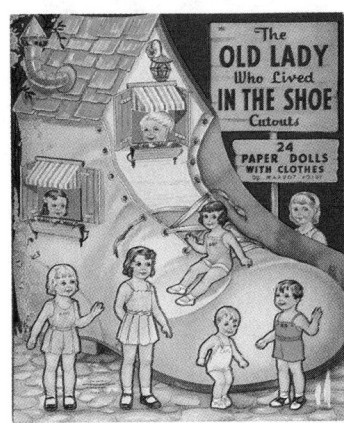

Paperweight, Ayotte, Rick, Swamp Sparrow, Mushrooms, Berries, Snowdrops, c.1988, 3 ¾ In. $1265.00

P

Ayotte, Rick, Swamp Sparrow, Mushrooms, Berries, Snowdrops, c.1988, 3 ¾ In. .... *illus*	1265.00
Ayotte, Turtle, Driftwood, Pond Lily, Signed, c.1999, 4 x 3 ½ In.	1150.00
Bacchus, Close Concentric, Pastel Colors, Basket Shape Blue, White Cogs, 3 ³⁄₁₆ In.	8500.00
Banford, Bob, Cherries, Filigree Twist Ground, Red Fruit, Green Leaves, 2 ⅞ In.	750.00
Banford, Bob, Fish, Underwater View Of Tomato Clown Fish, 3 ¼ In.	650.00
Banford, Bob, Flower Blossoms, Multicolored, Signed, 3 ½ x 2 ½ In.	345.00
Benjamin Franklin, Green High Glaze, Franklin Pottery, 1950s, 5 ⅜ x 3 ⅝ In.	85.00
Bergman, Owl, Eyes Open, Close, Bronze, Mechanical, Signed, 5 x 5 ¼ In.	1395.00
Bohemian, Hunting Dog, Faceted, Engraved, Amber Base, 2 ½ In. .... *illus*	978.00
Boyer, Harry, Red, Orange, Turquoise Swirl, Controlled Air Bubbles....................	29.00
Bronze, Bear, Standing, Raised Paw, Painted, 2 ½ In.	165.00
Buzzini, White-Rayed Wyethia, Daisies, Purple Blossoms, Signed, 1992, 3 In. .... *illus*	690.00
Clear, Geometric, Square, Steuben, 2 ½ In.	234.00
Clichy, Millefiori, Checker Pattern, White Upset Muslin Ground, 1 ⅞ x 2 ⅞ In.	711.00
Clichy, Millefiori, Rose Canes, Pink & Green Rose Cane, 3 In. .... *illus*	3738.00
Clichy, Nosegay, Pink Pastry Canes, Green Canes Surround, Upset Muslin, 2 ⅞ In.	7500.00
Clichy, Paneled Weight, Opaque Green Ground, Multicolored Radiating Canes, 3 ¼ In.	5400.00
Clichy, Swirl, Red, White Spirals, Blue Center, 2 ¾ In.	2400.00
Cranberry To Clear, 3 ¼ In.	70.00
Cut Glass, Soccer Ball, Nailhead Diamond, 2 ½ In.	225.00
Ferris, Colin, Caithness, Pagan Ritual, 4 Druids, Solstice Sunrise, 4 ¼ In.	173.00
Glass, Photograph, Rocky Glen Sanatorium, Get Well In Ohio, c.1911, 4 In.	11.00
Grubb, Randall, Lilies, White Ground, Simple Plant, Pink Blossom, 1994, 3 In.	550.00
Ipsen, Kent, Oval, Clear Glass, Bubbled Amber Veil, Opalescent Rim, Signed, 1977, 5 In.	175.00
Kaziun, Charles, Millefiori, Green, Red, White Canes, Blue Ground, Signed, 2 ¼ In.	633.00
Kaziun, Charles, Pansy Blossom, Petals, Bud, Green Leaves, Bee, 2 ⅜ In.	633.00
Labino, Cow Jumping Over Moon, Greenish Amber, 1971, 2 x 2 ½ In.	230.00
Labino, Fish, Blue Ground, 1972, 1 ⅛ x 2 ⅜ In.	196.00
Labino, Serpent, Greenish Opal Swirls Of Burgundy, Signed, 1970, 2 ⅜ x 2 ¾ In.	345.00
Labino, Smoke Crystal, Green & Ebony Splashes, 3 ½ In.	288.00
Latticinio, White Spiral Lines, Blue, Pink, Green, Blue Ribbons, 2 ⅛ In.	59.00
Lotton, Sea Green, Crimson Central Post, Turquoise Hearts, Vines, Signed, 6 In. .... 374.00 to 863.00	
Lundberg, Aquarium, Fish, Sea Life, Plants, Lucite Base, Signed, c.1993, 5 In. .... *illus*	633.00
Lundberg, Aquarium, Fish, Seaweed, Frosted, Signed, c.1991, 4 ½ In. .... *illus*	201.00
MacIntosh, A., Caithness, Space Tulip, Green, Red Encased Flower, Scotland, 5 In.	184.00
Manson, W., Ocean Encounter, Octopus, White Fish, Seashells, Signed, 3 ⅜ In.	259.00
Memorial Hall, Oval, Frosted, Pressed Intaglio Image, 1776-1876, 1 ¼ x 3 ⅛ x 5 In.	161.00
Milk Glass, Dog, Mastiff, Stepped Oval Base, c.1900, 2 x 2 ⅞ x 4 ⅛ In.	145.00
Millefiori, White Ground, Multicolored, Early 20th Century, 2 In.	58.00
Murano, Millefiori Center, Radiating White, Pink Ribbons, Lutz Case, 3 ½ In.	263.00
New England Glass Co., Millefiori Nosegay, Garlands, Concentric Rings, 2 ¼ In. .... *illus*	2875.00
Pantin, Apples, Golden, Green Leaves, Clear Ground, Lampwork, 3 In. .... *illus*	23000.00
Perthshire, Candle, Christmas Candle, White Ground, 1980, 2 ⅝ In.	350.00
Perthshire, Millefiori, Multicolored Canes, Center Flower, Cross Design, 1979, 2 ¹⁵⁄₁₆ In.	350.00
Perthshire, Multicolored Swirl, Millefiori Center, 2 ¼ In.	125.00
President Garfield Memorial, Copper Filings, 4 x 2 ½ In.	38.00
Ribbed, Flat Top, Millefiori Field, 2 ¾ In.	25.00
Sandwich, Weedflower Blossom, Red, White, Blue Petals, 2 ¾ In.	863.00
Satava, Blue Opal Cap, Golden Interior, Iridescent Veils, Lighted Wood Base, 3 In.	127.00
Satava, Richard, Moon Jellyfish, Brown Tendril, Oval, Signed, 4 ½ In.	316.00
Satava, Richard, Moon Jellyfish, Triple Veil, Gold, Blue, Green Tendrils, Signed, 8 ½ In.	1150.00
Scarab Beetle, Blue Iridescent Glass, 4 ⅞ In.	356.00
Silver, Hunting Scene, Riders, Dogs, Continental, Stamped, 3 x 4 In.	176.00
Slazar, D.P., Oval, Iridescent Gold, Raised Red Flower, Iridescent Blue Leaves, 1984, 1 In.	75.00
Smallhouse, Frog On Leaves, Yellow With Black Dots, Blue Limbs, 3 ⅛ x 3 ½ In.	259.00
Smallhouse, Frog, Sapphire Blue, Orange Base, 3 x 3 ½ In.	288.00
Smallhouse, Octopus On Moss Rock, Red, 2 ½ x 3 ½ In.	431.00
Snowdome, Children, Around Christmas Tree, Musical, Oh, Tannenbaum, 7 x 8 In.	65.00
Snowdome, Santa, Snow Covered Tree, F.B. Small World Designers, 13 x 11 In.	90.00
Snowdome, Watermelon Boy, Down In Dixie, Atlas Crystal Works, c.1940, 4 x 3 In.	85.00
St. Louis, Bouquet, Twisted, Faceted, Upright, Lampwork, Clear Ground, 3 ¼ In. .... *illus*	6325.00
St. Louis, Chrysanthemum, Pink Flower, Yellow Center, Filigree, 6-Sided Printies, 2 ⅞ In.	2400.00
St. Louis, Coronation, Sulphide, Queen Elizabeth Profile, c.1953, 2 ⅞ In.	350.00
St. Louis, Crocus, Fleurs De Lorraine, Signed SL 1988, 3 In.	575.00
St. Louis, Lion Head, Crystal, Jewel Eyes, 4 In.	374.00
St. Louis, Red & Blue Crown, Red, Blue Ribbons, Alternating Filigree Twists, 2 ½ In.	2800.00

Paperweight, Bohemian, Hunting Dog, Faceted, Engraved, Amber Base, 2 ½ In. $978.00

Paperweight, Buzzini, White-Rayed Wyethia, Daisies, Purple Blossoms, Signed, 1992, 3 In. $690.00

Paperweight, Clichy, Millefiori, Rose Canes, Pink & Green Rose Cane, 3 In. $3738.00

Paperweight, Lundberg, Aquarium, Fish, Sea Life, Plants, Lucite Base, Signed, c.1993, 5 In. $633.00

Paperweight, Lundberg, Aquarium, Fish, Seaweed, Frosted, Signed, c.1991, 4 ½ In. $201.00

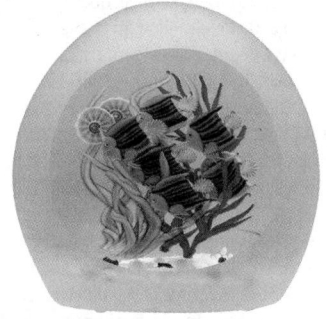

Paperweight, New England Glass Co., Millefiori Nosegay, Garlands, Concentric Rings, 2 ¼ In. $2875.00

Paperweight, Pantin, Apples, Golden, Green Leaves, Clear Ground, Lampwork, 3 In. $23000.00

Paperweight, St. Louis, Bouquet, Twisted, Faceted, Upright, Lampwork, Clear Ground, 3 ¼ In. $6325.00

Paperweight, Stankard, Paul, Summer Field Arrangement, Bouquet, Signature Cane, c.1977, 2 ¾ In. $1955.00

Paperweight, Stourbridge, Millefiori, Concentric, White, Blue, Pink Cog Cane, 3 In. $230.00

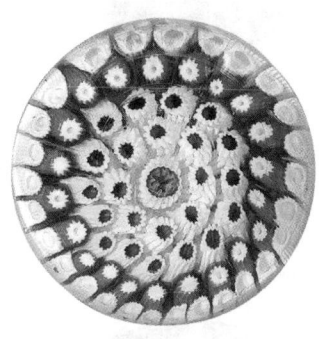

Paperweight, Ysart, Fish, White Latticinio Basket, Signed PY, Paper Label, 2 ¾ x 2 ¼ In. $518.00

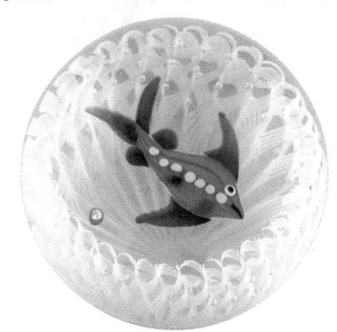

P

Papier-Mache, Milliner's Head, Woman's, Painted, Dorothee, Label, France, Early 1900s, 16 In. $646.00

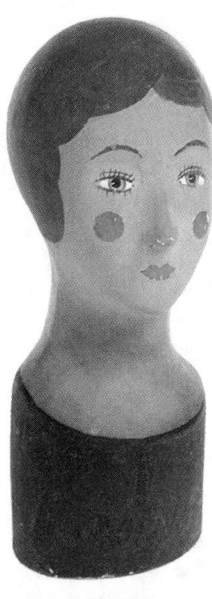

Papier-Mache, Tray, Center Reserve, Trompe L'Oeil Documents, Gilt Rim, Oval, c.1870, 24 x 29 In. $826.00

Parian, Pitcher, George Washington, Wreath, Garland, Late 19th Century, 10 ¼ In. $205.00

Stankard, Honeysuckle, Opaque Green Ground, Pink Blossoms, C.S. Kressley, 3 ¼ In.	1000.00
Stankard, Paul, Summer Field Arrangement, Bouquet, Signature Cane, c.1977, 2 ¾ In. .... *illus*	1955.00
Stourbridge, Millefiori, Concentric, White, Blue, Pink Cog Cane, 3 In. .... *illus*	230.00
Sulphide, 5-Petal Flowers, Orange, Gold Tips, Branch, 1800s, 2 ½ In.	72.00
Sulphide, 6-Petal Flower, Yellow To Orange, Green Leaves, 1800s, 2 ½ In.	72.00
Venetian Glass, Sagittarius, 4 ½ In.	17.50
Victorian Glass, Trembling Turtle, 19th Century, 3 ¼ In.	81.00
Weiss, Max, Die, Silvered Metal, Mark, c.1926, 3 ½ In.	85.00
Wendell Willkie, 1940 Campaign, Glass, 2 ¾ x 4 ½ In.	61.00
Whitefriars, Jubilee Weight, Millefiori, Blue, E.R., Queen Elizabeth, 1977, 3 ¼ In.	500.00
Ysart, Fish, White Latticinio Basket, Signed PY, Paper Label, 2 ¾ x 2 ¼ In. .... *illus*	518.00

PAPIER-MACHE is made from paper mixed with glue, chalk, and other ingredients, then molded and baked. It becomes very hard and can be painted. Boxes, trays, and furniture were made of papier-mache. Some of the nineteenth-century pieces were decorated with mother-of-pearl. Papier-mache is still being used to make small toys, figures, candy containers, boxes, and other giftwares. Furniture made of papier-mache is listed in the Furniture category.

Box, Cover, Red, Japanned, Raised Overlapping Pendants, Grape Clusters, 3 x 12 In.	115.00
Box, Inlaid Abalone, Bombe Shape, Ogee Edges, Domed Lid, Painted Harbor, 12 x 8 In.	119.00
Bust, Skeleton, Wood, Spring Loaded Jaw, Early 20th Century, 14 ¾ In.	176.00
Cigar Case, Accordion Type, Nude In A Swing, 19th Century, 5 ⅛ x 3 In.	294.00
Cigar Case, Hinged, Military Officer, White Horse, 19th Century, 5 ¼ x 3 In.	206.00
Milliner's Head, Woman's, Painted, Dorothee, Label, France, Early 1900s, 16 In. .... *illus*	646.00
Tobacco Box, Round, Lacquered, Inscribed, God Save The King, c.1760	450.00
Tray, Center Reserve, Trompe L'Oeil Documents, Gilt Rim, Oval, c.1870, 24 x 29 In. .... *illus*	826.00
Tray, Chinoiserie, Mother-Of-Pearl Inlay, Stand, 32 x 25 In.	434.00
Tray, Flowers, Dark Red Ground, c.1860, 30 ½ x 23 ½ In.	382.00
Tray, Red Ground, Gilt Butterfly Flowers, Leaves, Henry Clay, England, 1800, 26 x 20 In.	3850.00
Tree, Trunk, Silk Wrapped Wire Stems, Hardstone, Fruit Flowers, Cloisonne Base, 1900s, 12 In., Pair	633.00
Writing Box, Mother-Of-Pearl Inlay, Velvet Surface, Fitted Slots, c.1880, 4 ½ x 13 In.	147.00

PARIAN is a fine-grained, hard-paste porcelain named for the marble it resembles. It was first made in England in 1846 and gained in favor in the United States about 1860. Figures, tea sets, vases, and other items were made of Parian at many English and American factories.

Box, Bisque, Cherub Sleeping, Head On Basket Lid, Oval, 4 x 5 In.	90.00
Bust, Edward VII, Crystal Palace Union, M. Wood, 1863, 12 ½ In.	125.00
Bust, George Peabody, Veteran Of The War Of 1812, 12 In.	1075.00
Bust, Princess Alexandria, Crystal Palace Art Union, F.M. Miller, 1863, 10 In.	110.00
Bust, Princess, Elaborate Dress, Necklace, 8 In.	30.00
Bust, Shakespeare, Book Shape Base, Title Ribbon, Robinson, Leadbeater, c.1880, 14 In.	356.00
Figurine, Bounty, Woman Holding Grape Bunches, c.1870, 13 In.	365.00
Figurine, George Washington, Standing, Robes, Scroll, England, c.1840, 14 In.	1528.00
Figurine, Isaac & Rebekah, Signed, W. Beattie, 20 ½ x 14 ½ In.	5500.00
Figurine, Leda & The Swan, Schibe-Alsbach, Blue S, Crossed Lines Mark, c.1910, 14 In.	390.00
Figurine, Maiden Holding Bundle Of Hay, 11 ¼ In.	144.00
Figurine, Man, Dog, Tree Stump, 7 In.	30.00
Figurine, Queen Louisa, Light Highlights, 16 In.	125.00
Figurine, Seated Nude, Rock Ledge, Bells, Miranda, Marked Minton, 15 In.	75.00
Figurine, St. Philomena, Wearing Classical Robe & Wreath, Holding Spear, 24 In.	978.00
Figurine, Stag Deer, Antler Loss, Eating From Fruit Tree, 11 ½ x 12 In.	150.00
Figurine, Winged Angel, Holding Flower Sprays, Signed, A. Godard, 30 ½ x 10 In.	720.00
Figurine, Woman, Basket, Grapes, 16 In.	50.00
Figurine, Woman Carrying Vessels, 15 In.	100.00
Figurine, Woman, Seated, Horse Leg Stool, 13 ½ x 13 In.	300.00
Figurine, Woodpecker, Stump, 6 ½ In.	50.00
Group, 3 Children, Canoe, 2 Ducks, 6 x 8 In.	75.00
Group, Can't You Talk, Crawling Baby Boy, Dog, c.1875, 11 x 15 In.	660.00
Group, Children Lying In Bed, 4 x 9 ½ In.	75.00
Group, Christ Child, John The Baptist, Lamb, 19th Century, 10 ½ In.	144.00
Group, Mother, Child, 2 Dogs, Rocky Ground, c.1850, 12 ¾ x 9 ½ In.	230.00
Group, Woman Holding Paddle, Cherub, Wheel, 9 ¾ In.	100.00
Jug, Claret, Swiss Family Robinson, Island, Stippled Brown, Signed, T.T. & J. Mayers, 1850, 9 ½ In.	310.00
Pitcher, Frolicking Cherubs, Impressed, 1845, 6 x 10 In.	210.00
Pitcher, George Washington, Wreath, Garland, Late 19th Century, 10 ¼ In. .... *illus*	205.00
Pitcher, Thieving Birds, 1849, 9 In.	210.00

PARIS, Vieux Paris, or Old Paris, is porcelain ware that is known to have been made in Paris in the eighteenth or early nineteenth century. These porcelains have no identifying mark but can be recognized by the whiteness of the porcelain and the lines and decorations. Gold decoration is often used.

Basket, Porcelain Twig Handles, Applied Flowers, Shaped Parcel Gilt Base, c.1875, 9 x 19 In. .	420.00
Basket, Reticulated, Round, Ocher, Red Garland, White Ground, Gilt Foot, 6 ¾ x 11 In.	529.00
Bough Pot, Underplate, Portrait Reserve, Pink Ground, Gilt Trim, Mid 1800s, 7 ¾ x 6 ¾ In., Pair	184.00
Coffeepot, Animal Face Spout, Tapering Finial, Gilt Accents, Scenic, 7 ¼ In. .... *illus*	98.00
Figurine, Woman, Passing Envelope To Man, Dog, c.1930, 8 x 8 x 6 In.	262.00
Figurine, Workman, On Conch Shell, Frog, Fern, Coral, Gilt, 1800s, 8 x 9 In.	546.00
Jar, Apothecary, Latin Label, c.1890, 12 In., Pair	382.00
Teapot, Pink, Green, White, Gilt Scrolls, Mid 1800s, 10 In.	720.00
Urn, Baluster Shape, Scrolling Black Enamel Handles, Neoclassical Portrait, 18 x 11 In., Pair .	1880.00
Urn, Cover, Classical Shape, Floral Spray, Giltwork, Cartouches, c.1900, 14 In., Pair	316.00
Urn, Flowers, Multicolored, Gilt, Handles, Square Base, 15 ½ x 10 In.	675.00
Urn, Multicolored Flowers, Gilt Wheat Stalks, Mask Head Mounts, Gold Trim, 11 In., Pair	329.00
Urn, Neoclassical, Gilded, Floral Swags, Puce Ground, Square Foot, 1800s, 12 ¼ x 5 ¼ In., Pair.	2233.00
Vase, Baluster Shape, Painted Flowers, Multicolored, c.1900, 15 In., Pair........................	575.00
Vase, Bulb, Jacob Petit, Flowers, Violet Ground, Gilt, Scrolled Feet, c.1840, 9 In.	1175.00
Vase, Etruscan Style, Figures, Animals, Flowers, Orange, Black, Gilt Base Rim, Handles, 19 ½ x 9 In. ..	235.00
Vase, Fisherman, Woman, Child, Blue, Gilt, Handles, Marked, IQ, 1850s, 13 In.	240.00
Vase, Flared, Applied Flowers & Leaves, Painted Sprays, 19th Century, 12 In.	201.00
Vase, Flared, Paul, Virginie, Flowers, Leaves, Multicolored, Gilt, Bisque, c.1840, 14 In., Pair.....	823.00
Vase, Flowers, Cobalt Blue, Gold, Leaf Handles, Marked, 13 ½ x 10 In., Pair....................	520.00
Vase, Multicolored Flowers, Man, Wreath, Woman, Pen, White, Gold, Mark, 1800s, 16 In., Pair.	805.00
Vase, Reticulated Basket, Ocher, Red Garlands, White Ground, Gilt Foot, c.1850, 7 x 11 In.	529.00
Veilleuse, Turret Shape Pedestal, Gilt Base, Rustic Scenes, 3 Sections, 3 ½ x 5 In. .... *illus*	420.00

PATE-DE-VERRE is an ancient technique in which glass is made by blending and refining powdered glass of different colors into molds. The process was revived by French glassmakers, especially Galle, around the end of the nineteenth century.

Paperweight, Spread Winged Butterfly, Multicolored, Oval Base, 4 x 3 In.	3000.00
Plaque, Mythological, Goddess Releasing Angels, Henri Cros, 5 In. .... *illus*	1035.00

PATE-SUR-PATE means paste on paste. The design was made by painting layers of slip on the ceramic piece until a relief decoration was formed. The method was developed at the Sevres factory in France about 1850. It became even more famous at the English Minton factory about 1870. It has since been used by many potters to make both pottery and porcelain wares.

Plaque, Woman's White Profile, Flowers, Green, Gesso Frame, Limoges, 4 x 14 In.	518.00
Tile, Cobalt Blue Glaze, Gilt, Nymph, Cherubs, Fountain, Frame, 5 ¾ x 5 In. .... *illus*	575.00

PATENT MODELS were required as part of a patent application for a United States patent until 1880. In 1926 the stored patent models were sold as a group by the U.S. Patent Office and individual models are now appearing in the marketplace.

Chair, Swivel, Brass & Crossed Strips, H.S. Hale, December 11, 1875, 9 In.	402.00
Clothes Drier, Wooden, Folding, Iron, Schematic Drawing, N.J.M. Hock Hazelton, 6 x 7 In.	650.00
Extension Table, No. 89266, J.M. Blaisdell, April 20, 1869, 7 ½ x 5 x 5 ½ In.	460.00
Forging Machine, No. 18115, Elbridge Wheeler, Sept. 1, 1857, 14 ½ x 12 In.	5750.00
Table, Sewing Machine, No. 42318, April 12, 1864, N.D. Stoofis, 8 x 9 x 6 In.	776.00

PAUL REVERE POTTERY was made at several locations in and around Boston, Massachusetts, between 1906 and 1942. The pottery was operated as a settlement house program for teenage girls. Many pieces were signed *S.E.G.* for Saturday Evening Girls. The artists concentrated on children's dishes and tiles. Decorations were outlined in black and filled with color.

Bowl, Flared, Tan Matte Glaze, 8 ½ x 2 ½ In.	120.00
Bowl, Painted, Stylized Flowers, Blue Ground, 8 ½ x 2 ½ In.	570.00
Pitcher, Lotus Blossoms, Geese, S.E.G., T. Block, 1912, 4 ⅜ In.	600.00
Plate, Early To Bed, Early To Rise, Cuerda Seca, Roosters, S.E.G., 1909, 7 ½ In.	4800.00
Plate, House, Landscape, Blue, Green, Yellow, S.E.G., 1930, 8 ½ In.	600.00
Tile, Scenic, Hartt House Hull Street, Signed Initials F.L., 3 ¾ In. ....*illus*	1680.00
Tile, Tulips, Multicolored, S.E.G., 4 ¼ x 6 In.	14640.00
Trivet, Blue, Green, Square Design, S.E.G., Marked, 1913, 5 ¼ In.	195.00
Vase, Bulbous, Pink Matte Glaze, Marked R.B., S.E.G., c.1917, 8 ½ x 6 ½ In.	86.00
Vase, Cylindrical, Stylized Landscape, Brown, Green, Tan, Mark, S.E.G., c.1920, 3 ½ x 8 In.	489.00

Paris, Coffeepot, Animal Face Spout, Tapering Finial, Gilt Accents, Scenic, 7 ¼ In.
$98.00

Paris, Veilleuse, Turret Shape Pedestal, Gilt Base, Rustic Scenes, 3 Sections, 3 ½ x 5 In.
$420.00

Pate-De-Verre, Plaque, Mythological, Goddess Releasing Angels, Henri Cros, 5 In.
$1035.00

Pate-Sur-Pate, Tile, Cobalt Blue Glaze, Gilt, Nymph, Cherubs, Fountain, Frame, 5 ¾ x 5 In.
$575.00

P

PEACHBLOW

Paul Revere, Tile, Scenic, Hartt House Hull Street, Signed Initials F.L., 3 ¾ In.
$1680.00

Peachblow, Tumbler, Coral Glossy Glaze, Hobbs, Brockunier & Co., Late 1800s, 3 ½ In.
$230.00

Peachblow, Vase, Glossy Finish, Pontil Mark, New England Glass Co., Late 1800s, 7 ½ In.
$161.00

Pearlware, Coffeepot, Pear Shape, Domed Lid, Cobalt Blue Border, Early 1800s, 11 ½ In.
$288.00

Pearlware, Mug, Banded, Orange, Black, Blue Flowers, c.1800, 4 ¾ In.
$293.00

Pearlware, Sugar, Cover, Cream Ground, Blue, Orange, 19th Century, 5 ¼ In.
$88.00

Peking Glass, Vase, Cobalt Blue Stemmed Gingko Branch, Teak Wood Base, 9 In., Pair
$780.00

Peking Glass, Vase, White, Red Carved Overlay, Bird & Branch, 9 In., Pair
$325.00

PEACHBLOW glass was made by several factories beginning in the 1880s. New England peachblow is a one-layer glass shading from red to white. Mt. Washington peachblow shades from pink to bluish-white. Hobbs, Brockunier and Company of Wheeling, West Virginia, made Coral glass that they marketed as Peach Blow. It shades from yellow to peach and is lined with white glass. Reproductions of all types of peachblow have been made. Related pieces may be listed under Gunderson and Webb Peachblow.

Creamer, Smoothed Ribbed Body, Enameled Daisies, Leaves, New England, c.1893, 2 ½ In. ...	316.00
Creamer, Square Rim, Red, Pink, Orange Body, Amber Handle, Wheeling, 5 In.	460.00
Cruet, Amber Stopper, Handle, c.1880, 7 In.	146.00
Cruet, Bulbous, Stick Neck, Ball Stopper, c.1875, 7 In.	150.00
Pear, Wire Stem Mount, Mt. Washington, 3 ¾ In.	35.00
Pitcher, Water, Hobbs, Brockunier, Blue Opalescent, Windows Pattern, 6 In.	748.00
Pitcher, Water, Hobbs, Brockunier, Christmas Snowflake, Cranberry, 8 ½ In.	173.00
Pitcher, Water, Hobbs, Brockunier, Poinsettia, Green, 13 ½ In.	345.00
Sugar Shaker, Hobbs, Brockunier, Wheeling, 6 In.	1380.00
Toothpick, Oval, Ruffled Rim, New England..	662.00
Toothpick, Yellow Wheat Coralene, Aurora Silver Plate Holder	690.00
Tumbler, Coral Glossy Glaze, Hobbs, Brockunier & Co., Late 1800s, 3 ½ In. ....*illus*	230.00
Tumbler, Dusty Rose To Blue Gray, Pontil, Mt. Washington, c.1875, 3 ¾ In.	364.00
Vase, Bud, Glossy, 8 ½ In., Pair	690.00
Vase, Bulbous, Acid Finish, Shaded Red To Apricot, 3 ½ In.	150.00
Vase, Double Gourd, Glossy, 7 In.	633.00
Vase, Flower Branch, Pink To White, Yellow, Blue, White, Bulbous, Square Mouth, c.1890, 8 In.	335.00
Vase, Glossy Finish, Pontil Mark, New England Glass Co., Late 1800s, 7 ½ In. ....*illus*	161.00
Vase, Jack-In-The-Pulpit, Lemon Shaded To Pink, 10 ¾ In.	111.00
Vase, Morgan, Acid Finish, 5 Headed Griffin Holder, Hobbs, Brockunier, Wheeling, 10 In.	800.00
Vase, Morgan, Glossy Finish 5 Headed Griffin Holder, Hobbs, Brockunier, Wheeling, 10 In.	900.00
Vase, Morgan, Glossy, Hobbs, Brockunier, Wheeling, 8 In.	518.00
Vase, Morgan, Shouldered Form, Narrow Neck, Wood Stand, 9 In.	431.00
Vase, Pink To White Ground, Flowers, Leaves, Mt. Washington, 6 In.	345.00
Vase, Trumpet, Pink To Ivory Opalescent, Ruffled Rim, Spread Foot, 9 ½ In.	230.00
Water Set, Hobbs, Brockunier, Seaweed, Cranberry, Pitcher, 6 Tumblers, 9 In.	518.00
Water Set, Hobbs, Brockunier, Stars & Stripes, Cranberry, Tankard, 7 Tumblers, 8 ½ In.	1380.00

PEANUTS is the title of a comic strip created by cartoonist Charles M. Schulz (1922–2000). The strip, drawn by Schulz from 1950 to 2000, features a group of children, including Charlie Brown and his sister Sally, Lucy Van Pelt and her brother Linus, Peppermint Patty, and Pig Pen, and an imaginative and independent beagle named Snoopy. The Peanuts gang has also been featured in books, television shows, and a Broadway musical.

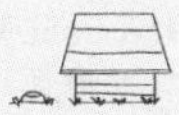

Book, Golden Celebration, Charles Schulz, Snoopy Sketch, Hardcover, 10 x 12 In., 256 Pages .	1518.00
Button, Snoopy For President, White, Red, Blue, 1960s, 1 ¾ In.	127.00
Colorforms, Snoopy's Beagle Scouts, Original Watercolor Cover, 1965, 15 x 18 In.	2018.00
Figurine, Schroeder & Lucy At Piano, Composition, 7 x 4 In.	68.00
Lunch Box, Have Lunch With Snoopy, Dome Lid, Metal, 1960s	70.00
Lunch Box, Snoopy, Comic Strip, Red Vinyl, Thermos, 1960s	45.00
Music Box, Snoopy, Figural, WWI Flying Ace, Wooden, c.1968, 4 ½ x 4 ½ In.	115.00

PEARL items listed here are made of the natural mother-of-pearl from shells. Such natural pearl has been used to decorate furniture and small utilitarian objects for centuries. The glassware known as mother-of-pearl is listed by that name. Opera glasses made with natural pearl shell are listed under Opera Glasses.

Mirror, Hand, Gold Filigree Overlay, 5 x 10 In.	176.00

PEARLWARE is an earthenware made by Josiah Wedgwood in 1779. It was copied by other potters in England. Pearlware is only slightly different in color from creamware and for many years collectors have confused the terms. Wedgwood pieces are listed in the Wedgwood category in this book. Most pearlware with mocha designs is listed under Mocha.

Pearl

Bowl, Flower Sprigs, c.1810, 4 ½ x 9 ¼ In.	410.00
Coffeepot, Pear Shape, Domed Lid, Cobalt Blue Border, Early 1800s, 11 ½ In. ....*illus*	288.00
Mug, Banded, Orange, Black, Blue Flowers, c.1800, 4 ¾ In. ....*illus*	293.00
Plaque, Oval, Raised Flower Border, Classical Figures Center, Staffordshire, c.1800, 10 In.	356.00
Platter, Blue Feather Edge, Molded Flower Borders, England, 14 x 18 & 13 x 16 In., 2 Piece....	165.00
Shaving Mug, Pink Luster, Enamel, c.1815, 6 In.	4680.00
Sugar, Cover, Blue, Pink, White, 19th Century, 5 ¼ In.	88.00

Pen & Pencil, Parker Pen 75, Cisele, Sterling Silver, Ballpoint, Case, 1960s, 5 In. $66.00

Pen & Pencil, Sheaffer, Lifetime, Sterling Silver, Ballpoint, Case, 1960s, 5 In. $33.00

Pencil Sharpener, Angell, Crank, 2 Adjustable Round Blades, Cast Iron, 4 ¾ x 6 ½ In. $1035.00

Pencil Sharpener, Chain Driven, Round Disc File, Crank Handle, Cast Iron, 3 ¾ x 5 ¼ In. $2818.00

Pencil Sharpener, Everett, Nickel Plated, Crank Handle, Dovetailed Wood Box, 4 ½ In. $920.00

P

Pepsi-Cola, Clock, With Bottle, Electric, 1960s
$527.00

Pepsi-Cola, Sign, Light-Up, Bottle
$322.00

Pepsi-Cola, Soda Dispenser, Metal, Tin, Plays Pepsi Jingle, 1940s, 19 In.
$403.00

Perfume Bottle, Silver Flowers, Green, Hinged Cap, Rampant Lion Mark, Laydown, 9 In.
$633.00

Sugar, Cover, Cream Ground, Blue, Orange, 19th Century, 5 ¼ In. .... *illus*	88.00
Tankard, Flowers, Yellow, Blue, Green, 19th Century, 6 ¼ In.	180.00

PEKING GLASS is a Chinese cameo glass first made popular in the eighteenth century. The Chinese have continued to make this layered glass in the old manner, and many new pieces are now available that could confuse the average buyer.

Bowl, Imperial Yellow, Stylized Dragons, Square, Stand, 19th Century, 2 ⅜ In., Pair	1860.00
Bowl, Mustard Yellow, Carved Birds, Flowers, Footed, 6 x 3 In.	575.00
Bowl, Pink, Flowers, Etched, Carved Stand, c.1900, 2 ⅞ x 6 ¼ In., Pair	288.00
Cup, Purple, Dragon, Facing Flaming Pearl, 4 Character Mark, 3 ⅜ In.	2900.00
Ginger Jar, Bats, Leaves, Carved, Green, White, Dome Lid, 18th Century, 4 ⅝ In.	1420.00
Ginger Jar, Lid, Blue Flowers, 2 Cranes, White Ground, 18th Century, 5 ¾ In.	1150.00
Vase, Bird On Prunus Branch, Blue, Clear, Frosted, Etched, Tapered, 14 In.	329.00
Vase, Blue, Dragon Head, Plantain Leaves, Key, Clouds, Wood Base, Marked, 5 ½ In., Pair.......	130.00
Vase, Cobalt Blue Stemmed Gingko Branch, Teak Wood Base, 9 In., Pair .... *illus*	780.00
Vase, Green Bird, Flower, Vine, White Ground, Cameo, Baluster, 11 In., Pair	397.00
Vase, Imperial Yellow, Flared Rim, 8 ⅜ In.	1150.00
Vase, Mustard Yellow, Butterfly, Flowers, Cameo, c.1900, 8 In.	270.00
Vase, Warriors, 2 Men On Horseback, Prunus Trees, Birds, Castle, Yellow, 10 ⅝ In.	384.00
Vase, White, Red Carved Overlay, Bird & Branch, 9 In., Pair .... *illus*	325.00
Vase, Yellow, Bulbous Bottom, Cylindrical Neck, Qing Dynasty, Chinese, 9 ¼ In.	167.00

PELOTON glass is a European glass with small threads of colored glass rolled onto the surface of clear or colored glass. It is sometimes called spaghetti, or shredded coconut, glass. Most pieces found today were made in the nineteenth century.

Creamer, Clear, White Canes, Applied Handle, Pontil, c.1875, 5 ⅜ In.	79.00
Vase, Fan, Impressed Flowers, Crimped Ruffle Rim, Yellow, Red, Blue Canes, Clear Foot, 4 In.	259.00

PENS replaced hand-cut quills as writing instruments in 1780, when the first steel pen point was made in England. But it was 100 years before the commercial pen was a common item. The fountain pen was invented in the 1830s but was not made in quantity until the 1880s. All types of old pens are collected. Float pens that feature small objects floating in a liquid as part of the handle are popular with collectors. Advertising pens are listed in the Advertising section of this book.

PEN

18K Gold, Vacuum Filled, Machined Design, Engraved, Initials, 4 In.	220.00
Aurora Mare, Fountain, 18K Gold Nib, Inkwell, Case, 5 ⅛ In.	527.00
Caran D'Ache, Fountain, Vermeil, Sterling, Grapevine, Lacquer, Riviera, 18K Nib, Refills, Case, 5 ⅜ In.	878.00
Eversharp, Skyline, Lever, 14K Gold Filled, Screws Together, Marked, 5 ½ In.	790.00
Michel Perchin, Fountain, Enamel, Vermeil, Sterling, Fleur-De-Lis, 18K Gold Nib, Case, 5 ½ In.	1053.00
Montblanc, Fountain, Resin, 18K Gold Dragon Clip, Ruby Eyes, Pearl Mouth, 18K Nib, Case, 5 ¼ In.	2574.00
Montblanc, Meisterstuck, Chevron Design, Bicolor 18K Gold, No. YG0123, Box, 5 ½ In.	2684.00
Montegrappa, Fountain, Resin, 18K Gold, Diamonds, 18K Gold Nib, Euro 2002, Case, 5 ½ In.	4680.00
Parker, 51, Empire State Pattern, 14K Gold Cap, Black, Vacumatic Disposable Filler, 5 ½ In. ..	900.00
Wahl, Gold Filled, Lever Fill, Screw Cap, 4 ⅞ In.	80.00
Waterman's, Fountain, Sterling Silver, Monogram, Jump Ring, 3 ⅓ In.	71.00
Waterman's, No. 452, Sterling Overlay, Lever Fill, Monogram, c.1915-33, 5 ⅜ In.	140.00

PEN & PENCIL

Parker Pen 75, Cisele, Sterling Silver, Ballpoint, Case, 1960s, 5 In. .... *illus*	66.00
Sheaffer, Lifetime, Sterling Silver, Ballpoint, Case, 1960s, 5 In. .... *illus*	33.00

PENCILS were invented, so it is said, in 1565. The eraser was not added to the pencil until 1858. The automatic pencil was invented in 1863. Collectors today want advertising pencils or automatic pencils of unusual design. Boxes and sharpeners for pencils are also collected. Advertising pencils are listed in the Advertising category. Pencil boxes are listed in the Box category.

PENCIL

Mechanical, Eversharp, 14K Gold, Skyline Model, 5 ⁵⁄₁₆ In.	120.00
Mechanical, Sterling Silver, Chatelaine, c.1890, 2-In. Sheath, 3 ½ In.	295.00

PENCIL SHARPENER

Airplane, Red, Bakelite, 1 ½ In.	50.00
Amish Buggy, Horse, Embossed, Silvertone Finish, Penn. Dutch Land, 1 ¾ x ¾ In.	40.00
Angell, Crank, 2 Adjustable Round Blades, Cast Iron, 4 ¾ x 6 ½ In. .... *illus*	1035.00
Chain Driven, Round Disc File, Crank Handle, Cast Iron, 3 ¾ x 5 ¼ In. .... *illus*	2818.00
Everett, Nickel Plated, Crank Handle, Dovetailed Wood Box, 4 ½ In. .... *illus*	920.00
Green, Vertical Disc With Sandpaper, Crank, Chelsea, Cast Iron, 6 x 6 In.	3162.00
Iduna, Adjustable, Cast Iron, Tabletop, 11 x 5 In.	575.00

P

Roneo, Mechanical, Cast Iron, Table Mount Clamp, 6 ¾ In.	290.00
Scottie, Bakelite, Green, Multicolored Spots	45.00
Uncle Sam, Cast Metal, Painted, Occupied Japan, 2 In.	101.00
U.S. Automatic Pencil Sharpener, Wood Base, 1907, 5 x 3 In.	340.00
Violin, Metal, Bronze Colored Patina, Marked Germany, 2 ½ In.	56.00

PENNSBURY POTTERY worked in Morrisville, Pennsylvania, from 1950 to 1971. Full sets of dinnerware as well as many decorative items were made. Pieces are marked with the name of the factory.

Pennsbury Pottery

Ashtray, Fairless Works, U.S. Steel, Shovel Shape, 6 ¾ x 5 ¼ In.	50.00
Bowl, Eagle, American Shield, 11 ¾ x 8 ½ In.	50.00
Creamer, Rooster, 4 In.	25.00
Mug, Fishermen, 4 ½ In.	38.00
Pitcher, Pennsylvania Dutch Style, 3 ¾ In.	20.00
Plaque, Rooster, 4 ¼ In.	25.00
Plate, Folk Art, 8 In.	25.00
Teapot, Hex & Hearts, 8 In., 32 Oz.	58.00
Tray, Heart, Lovebirds, 7 ⅜ x 5 ¼ In.	15.00
Vase, Gourd, Slick Chick, 5 In.	65.00

PEPSI-COLA, the drink and the name, was invented in 1898 but was not trademarked until 1903. The logo was changed from an elaborate script to the modern block letters in 1963. Several different logos have been used. Until 1951, the words *Pepsi* and *Cola* were separated by 2 dashes. These bottles are called "double dash." In 1951 the modern logo with a single hyphen was introduced. All types of advertising memorabilia are collected, and reproductions are being made.

Bottle, Hobbleskirt, Embossed Base, Akron, Ohio, 6 ½ Oz.	80.00
Clock, Drink Red, White, Blue, Double Bubble	375.00
Clock, Light-Up, Red, White, Blue, Glass, 15 In. Diam.	325.00
Clock, With Bottle, Electric, 1960s ....*illus*	527.00
Lunch Box, Pepsi, Red, White, Blue, Plastic, Thermos	18.00
Sign, Bigger & Better Reputation, 5 Cent, Paper, Frame, 1920-30, 12 x 30 In.	66.00
Sign, Bottle, 5 Cent, Red, White, Double, Die Cut, Tin, 1940, 29 ½ x 8 In.	1450.00
Sign, Bottle Cap, Double, Red, White, Blue, 2-Sided, Porcelain, 42 In. Diam.	1750.00
Sign, Bottle Cap, Pepsi-Cola, Red, White, Blue, Painted, Embossed, Tin, 30 In.	105.00
Sign, Bottle Cap, Pepsi-Cola, Red, White, Blue, Pressed Wood, 41 ½ x 40 ¾ In., 2 Piece	118.00
Sign, Drink Pepsi-Cola, 5 Cents, Pepsi Pete, Red, White, Blue, Embossed, Tin Litho, c.1930, 3 ½ x 21 In.	253.00
Sign, Drink Pepsi-Cola Today, Red, White, Blue, Reverse Painted, Glass, Chains, 18 x 15 ½ In.	480.00
Sign, Light-Up, Bottle ....*illus*	322.00
Sign, Pepsi Pete Cop, 5 Cent, Cardboard, 17 In.	110.00
Soda Dispenser, Metal, Tin, Plays Pepsi Jingle, 1940s, 19 In. ....*illus*	403.00
Stringholder, Join The Swing To Pepsi-Cola, Double, 5 Cent, Tin, 2-Sided, 16 x 12 In.	600.00
Thermometer, Bigger, Better, Bottle, Tin Lithograph, c.1930s, Box, 15 ½ x 6 ⅛ In.	770.00

PERFUME BOTTLES are made of cut glass, pressed glass, art glass, silver, metal, enamel, and even plastic or porcelain. Although the small bottle to hold perfume was first made before the time of ancient Egypt, it is the nineteenth- and twentieth-century examples that interest today's collector. DeVilbiss Company has made atomizers of all types since 1888 but no longer makes the perfume bottle tops so popular with collectors. These were made from 1920 to 1968. The glass bottle may be by any of many manufacturers even if the atomizer is marked *DeVilbiss.* The word *factice,* which often appears in ads, refers to store display bottles. Glass or porcelain examples may be found under the appropriate name such as Lalique, Czechoslovakia, Glass-Bohemian, etc.

Amber Glass, Enameled, Paneled Shoulders, White Flowers, Flecks, Early 1900s, 5 In.	59.00
Amethyst Glass, Recessed Panels, Stopper, 5 ¾ In.	795.00
Art Deco, Amethyst Glass, Silver Overlay, 10 In.	46.00
Art Glass, Atomizer, Tapered, Clear, Etched Leaves, Blue Base, Gold Highlights, 6 ½ In.	58.00
Black Boy, Bakelite, Big Lipped, Newsboy Cap, Holding Flowers, 1920s, 3 In.	89.00
Blown Glass, Sulphide Eagle, Paperweight Form, Stopper, Late 1800s, 7 ¼ In.	4406.00
Body Cut With Cane, Fans, Flowers, Stopper, 7 In.	460.00
Cobalt Blue, Silver Tone Glass Hinged Stopper, 3 ¾ In.	195.00
Cranberry, Flowers, Enamel, Stopper, 7 In.	125.00
Cranberry, Gold Lattice Overlay, Gold Lid Stopper, 3 In.	316.00
DeVilbiss, Atomizer, Birds, Berries, Gold Etched, Contents, Box, 9 ¾ In.	410.00
DeVilbiss, Atomizer, Blue Iridescent, Marked, 7 In.	259.00
DeVilbiss, Atomizer, Tapered, Blue Iridescent, Marked, 6 ½ In.	288.00
Emerald Green, Silver Tone Glass Hinged Stopper, 3 ¾ In.	195.00
Flattened Shape, Brass, Stopper, Flower Band, 4 In.	115.00

Perfume Bottle, Stopper, Cobalt Blue, Pillar Molded, 8 Ribs, Collared Neck, Footed, 8 ¾ x 3 ½ In.
$546.00

Peters & Reed, Vase, Shadow Ware, Pumpkin, Blue, Green Drip, Burnt Orange, 8 In.
$178.00

Pewabic, Plate, Embossed Crab, Iridescent Glaze, 9 ¼ In.
$2340.00

Pewabic, Plate, Geese In Flight, Blue, White, Black Glazes, Marked, 10 In.
$480.00

P

481

Pewabic, Vase, Bulbous, Multicolored Metallic Glaze, Marked, 3 x 3 ½ In.
$900.00

Pewter, Coffeepot, Allen Porter, Westbrook, Maine, Touchmark, c.1835, 11 ¾ In.
$380.00

Pewter, Coffeepot, Boardman & Hart, New York, Touchmark, c.1835, 11 ½ In.
$240.00

Frosted, Sunflower Stopper, Band Of Flowers, 10 In., Pair	94.00
Green Jade, Teardrop Stopper, Stevens & Williams, 6 In.	173.00
Guerlain, Paris, Bowtie Shape, Gold, Black, 2 ½ x 3 ⅓ In.	155.00
Hand Blown, Aqua, Torpedo Shape, Gold Decoration, Flowers, Vines, 1890s, 2 x ¾ In.	395.00
Harvard, Brilliant Cut, Teardrop Shape, Sterling Lid, 8 In.	316.00
Hexagonal, Enameled Glass, Cobalt Blue, Gilt Metal, Woman, Cupid	1760.00
Nailsea Type, Hinged Silver Tone Metal Stopper, Snail Shape, 5 In.	450.00
Peter Max Sun-Shine Raspberry Psychedelic, Bearded Man, 1973, Contents, 2 ½ In.	30.00
Red Glass, Glass Stopper, Gold Tone Hinged Cover, 3 ¾ In.	280.00
Rosaline, Teardrop Stopper, Stevens & Williams, 6 In.	201.00
Silver Flowers, Green, Hinged Cap, Rampant Lion Mark, Laydown, 9 In. ....*illus*	633.00
Silver Lid, Geometric Cut Glass, American Brilliant, 2 ¾ In.	210.00
Silver Lid, Overlaid Flowers, 5 In.	410.00
Stopper, Cobalt Blue, Pillar Molded, 8 Ribs, Collared Neck, Footed, 8 ¾ x 3 ½ In. ....*illus*	546.00
Swirl, Ray Base, Cut Glass, American Brilliant, 5 ½ In.	175.00
Teardrop, Green Frosted, Flowers, Flip Sterling Lid, Chain, Stevens & Williams, 3 ½ In.	1150.00
Topaz, Key Shape, Stopper, 7 In.	288.00

PETERS & REED POTTERY COMPANY of Zanesville, Ohio, was founded by John D. Peters and Adam Reed in 1897. Chromal, Landsun, Montene, Pereco, and Persian are some of the art lines that were made. The company, which became Zane Pottery in 1920 and Gonder Pottery in 1941, closed in 1957. Peters & Reed pottery was unmarked.

Bowl, Landsun, Flower Frog, 3 x 9 In.	81.00
Bowl, Zane Ware, Green Matte Glaze, Ruffled Edge, 6 ½ x 3 In.	55.00
Figurine, Cat, White, Seated, Mirror Black Glaze, Early 1900s, 10 ½ In.	176.00
Jardiniere, Green Matte Glaze, 4 Buttresses, Flowers, 12 ½ x 12 In.	259.00
Vase, Flaring Shape, Grape Designs, Green Matte Glaze, 8 ½ x 12 ½ In.	115.00
Vase, Marbleized Green Glaze, Lug Handles, c.1900, 18 In.	235.00
Vase, Shadow Ware, Pumpkin, Blue, Green Drip, Burnt Orange, 8 In. ....*illus*	178.00

PEWABIC POTTERY was founded by Mary Chase Perry Stratton in 1903 in Detroit, Michigan. The company made many types of art pottery, including pieces with matte green glaze and an iridescent crystalline glaze. The company continued working until the death of Mary Stratton in 1961. It was reactivated by Michigan State University in 1968.

PEWABIC

Bowl, Green Glaze, Brown Rim, 3 x 9 In.	472.00
Bowl, Luster Glaze, Mid 20th Century, 2 x 4 In.	293.00
Dish, Celadon Green Luster Glaze, c.1930, 1 ¾ x 3 ½ x 4 ¾ In.	175.00
Pitcher, Fish Shape, Tail Forms Handle, 14 In.	176.00
Plate, Embossed Crab, Iridescent Glaze, 9 ¼ In. ....*illus*	2340.00
Plate, Geese In Flight, Blue, White, Black Glazes, Marked, 10 In. ....*illus*	480.00
Tile, Carved Flowers, Green, Pink, Brown Ground, 3 In. Square	180.00
Tile, Little Blower, Little Girl, Blowing Out Candle, Green, 1940-60, 6 ⅛ x 3 ⅛ In.	145.00
Tile, Oak Leaf, Acorns, Red Clay Faience, Black, Gold Iridescent Luster Glaze, 5 ¾ x 5 ¾ In.	165.00
Tumbler, Blue, Footed, 6 In., 5 Piece	70.00
Vase, Blue Iridescent, Glazed, c.1920, 10 x 5 In.	644.00
Vase, Blue, Luster, Bulbous, 6 x 5 ½ In.	3538.00
Vase, Brown, Green Metallic Glaze, Hand Thrown Shape, 6 x 5 ½ In.	960.00
Vase, Brown, Green Metallic Glaze, Iridescent, Waisted, 6 x 4 ½ In.	780.00
Vase, Brown, Red Metallic Glaze, Bulbous, 6 x 10 In.	1200.00
Vase, Bulbous, Multicolored Metallic Glaze, Marked, 3 x 3 ½ In. ....*illus*	900.00
Vase, Colorful Metallic Glaze, Bulbous, Marked, 3 x 3 ½ In.	900.00
Vase, Copper Luster Glaze, Bulbous, c.1920-30, 5 ½ x 6 In.	614.00
Vase, Crackle Luster Glaze, c.1910-20, 9 x 7 ½ In.	2691.00
Vase, Luster Glaze, c.1920, 3 ½ x 3 In.	878.00
Vase, Oval, Tapered, Green Iridescent Glaze, 9 In.	1380.00
Vase, Purple, Brown Metallic Glaze, Hand Thrown Flared, 5 x 7 In.	1320.00
Vase, Purple, Green Metallic Glaze, Bulbous, Paper Label, 5 ½ x 9 ½ In.	1800.00
Vase, Russet, Mottled, Early 20th Century, 7 In.	644.00

PEWTER is a metal alloy of tin and lead. Some of the pewter made after 1840 has a slightly different composition and is called Britannia metal. This later type of pewter was worked by machine; the earlier pieces were made by hand. In the 1920s pewter came back into fashion and pieces were often marked Genuine Pewter. Eighteenth-, nineteenth-, and twentieth-century examples are listed here.

Basin, Thomas Danforth III, Reeded Rim, Interior Ring, 1807-13, 10 ¼ In.	153.00
Basin, Thos. Danforth, Reeded Rim, Interior Ring, Eagle Mark, Star Border, 1807-13, 10 In.	156.00

Basket, Handle, Flowing Design, 3-Petal Shape, 11 ¼ x 8 ¾ In.	125.00
Biscuit Jar, Tudric, 8 Turquoise, Emerald Glazed Cabochons, 4 ¾ In.	1830.00
Bowl, Fruit, Archibald Knox, Tudric, Pierced, Green Glass Liner, 4 x 9 In.	2562.00
Bowl, Kayserzinn, Grapes, Round, Handles, 11 ½ x 3 ¼ In.	235.00
Box, Biscuit, Liberty & Co., Tudric, Art Nouveau Flowers, Cylindrical, 4 ½ x 4 ½ In.	863.00
Candelabrum, Kayserzinn, Leven, 3-Light, Fledermaus, Bat Stem Support, c.1900, 12 In.	1434.00
Candlestick, Archibald Knox, Tudric, 5 ¾ x 4 ¾ In.	1342.00
Candlestick, Archibald Knox, Tudric, 9 x 6 In., Pair	2074.00
Candlestick, Cartier, Stepped Knop, Round Stepped Base, 4 ½ x 3 ½ In., Pair	83.00
Chalice, Roswell Gleason, Dorchester, Mass., Mid 19th Century, 6 In., 2 Piece	176.00
Chamberstick, Kayserzinn, Thistle Leaves, Flowers, Handle, c.1915, 9 ½ x 5 ½ In.	65.00
Chamberstick, Roswell Gleason, Baluster, Applied Scroll Handle, c.1825, 6 In., Pair...........	575.00
Charger, Burford & Green, Crested, England, c.1775, 18 In.	1740.00
Charger, Robert Baldwin-Wigan, England, Touchmark, 1690-1726, 16 ¾ In.	1800.00
Charger, Samuel Danforth, Hartford, Conn., Touchmark, 1795-1816, 13 ¼ In.	1295.00
Charger, Samuel Hamlin, Hartford, Connecticut, c.1775, 11 ½ In.	676.00
Charger, Shadow Bowl, Flared, Molded Rim, 2 ⅛ x 14 ¾ In.	187.00
Charger, Townsend & Compton, Signed, Touchmark, 14 ½ In.	110.00
Coffeepot, Allen Porter, Hinged Lid, Finial, Shaped Handle, Bulbous, Maine, c.1835, 11 ¾ In.	380.00
Coffeepot, Allen Porter, Westbrook, Maine, Touchmark, c.1835, 11 ¾ In. ....*illus*	380.00
Coffeepot, Boardman & Hart, New York, Touchmark, c.1835, 11 ½ In. ....*illus*	240.00
Coffeepot, Enamel, Berries, Flowers, Leaves, 9 ¾ In.	96.00
Coffeepot, L.L. Williams, Hinged Lid, Shaped Handle, Philadelphia, c.1840, 9 ¼ In.	88.00
Commode, Pilgrim's Hat, Deep Basin, Wide Brim, c.1775, 7 ½ In.	411.00
Compote, Woodbury & Colton, Philadelphia, c.1835, 4 ½ x 7 In.	705.00
Crumber Set, DuMont, Jugendstil, Pressed Roundels, Stars & Mountains, 9 ⅜ x 6 ¾ In.	165.00
Cup, 2 Handles, Thomas Boardman, Hartford, Connecticut, c.1840, 6 In.	120.00
Decanter, J.M. Olbrich, Lid, Long, Faceted Shape, Black, Hueck, c.1901, 13 In.	4183.00
Dish, Deep, Thomas Danforth, Philadelphia, c.1770, 13 In.	330.00
Dish, Jeheil Johnson, Reed Edge, Faint Eagle, c.1820, 13 In.	237.00
Dish, Liberty & Co., Arts & Crafts, Carved Flowers, Openwork Handles, Tudric, 11 ⅛ x 8 ½ In.	125.00
Dish, Orivit, Jugendstil, Reticulated, Tricorner, Molded Ball Feet, c.1910, 7 x 2 ½ In.	185.00
Drink Set, Kayserzinn, 2 Duck Decanters, 4 Cups, Tray, Leven, Lids, Art Nouveau, c.1900, 8-In. Tray	1673.00
Flagon, Domed Lid, Incised Rings, Applied Handle, 19th Century, 10 In.	160.00
Flagon, E. Kaufman, Lamb Finial, Hinged Lid, Philadelphia, c.1870, 16 In., Pair..........	705.00
Flagon, Hinged Lid, Mid 18th Century, 9 ¼ x 5 ½ In.	49.00
Flagon, Wine, Stegkanne, Ribbed, Pear Shape, Hexagonal Spout, Serpent Finial, 9 ¾ In.	270.00
Frame, Art Nouveau, Woman, Swirling Dress, Stylized Flowers, Leaves, 9 x 11 ¼ In.	450.00
Ladle, John Harrison Palethorp, Philadelphia, c.1830, 13 ¼ In.	59.00
Matchbox, Nekrassoff, Applied Tulip Decoration, 2 ⅜ x 1 ½ In.	35.00
Measure Set, Graduated, France, 19th Century, 7 ¼ To 2 ⅛ In., 6 Piece	294.00
Meat Dish, Cover, Bristol, Footed, Grazer, Booke & Co., 19th Century, 12 In.	110.00
Mold, Candle, 24 Tube, Pine Frame, W. Hunston, Troy, 19th Century, 17 x 20 ½ In.	1500.00
Mug, Incised Edge, Banded, Stepped Flared Base, S-Handle, Monogram, c.1875, ½ Pt., 3 In. ...	690.00
Mug, Robert Palethorp Jr., Shaped Handle, c.1820, 4 ½ x 5 ½ In.	5510.00
Mug, Tulip Shape, Curve Ball Terminal Handle, England, 19th Century, Pt........	165.00
Mustard Set, Liberty & Co., Cobalt Blue Liner, Open Salt, Hammered Finish, Tudric, c.1910 ...	185.00
Pitcher, Liberty & Co., Hammered, Enameled Design, Wicker Wrapped Handle, 6 ½ x 8 In. *illus*	720.00
Pitcher, Water, Cover, 1800s, 10 In.	176.00
Plate, Frederick Bassett, Tudor Rose Touchmark, Late 1700s, 8 ½ In.	150.00
Plate, Kayserzinn, Bees & Beehive, Vines, Leaves, c.1910, 10 x 1 In.	225.00
Plate, Lovebird Touchmark, Late 1700s, 7 ¾ In.	147.00
Plate, Nathaniel Hamlin, Charlestown, Massachusetts, c.1775, 8 In.	176.00
Pokal, Ostrich Egg, Late 1800s, 25 ½ In.	834.00
Porringer, 2 Handles, Floral Stamp, Harp Touchmark, Initials, R.G., 7 In.	55.00
Porringer, Boardman & Co., Pierced Crown Handle, Marked, 7 x 5 In.	240.00
Porringer, Crescents & Hearts, Pierced Handle, Late 18th Century, 4 ¾ In.	115.00
Porringer, Crown Handle, S G, Early 19th Century, 8 In.	260.00
Porringer, Flower Style, Pierced Handle, Late 18th Century, 8 In.	115.00
Porringer, Heart & Crescent Handle, New England, c.1775	195.00
Porringer, Nekrassoff, c.1940, 4 ¾ x 3 ½ In.	30.00
Porringer, Old English Style, Pierced Handle, Late 18th Century, 4 ¾ In.	115.00
Porringer, Samuel Hamlin, Jr., Old English Handle, Providence, R.I, c.1825, 4 ¼ In.	646.00
Rose Bowl, Liberty & Co., Tudric, Handles, Embossed Rose Hips, 6 ¼ x 12 In. ....*illus*	1920.00
Salt, Footed, Beaded Borders, Philadelphia, Late 18th Century, 2 ¼ In. ....*illus*	936.00
Sculpture, Head Of Racehorse, Signed, Casasola, 4 x 3 ½ In.	390.00

Pewter, Pitcher, Liberty & Co., Hammered, Enameled Design, Wicker Wrapped Handle, 6 ½ x 8 In.
$720.00

Pewter, Rose Bowl, Liberty & Co., Tudric, Handles, Embossed Rose Hips, 6 ¼ x 12 In.
$1920.00

Pewter, Salt, Footed, Beaded Borders, Philadelphia, Late 18th Century, 2 ¼ In.
$936.00

Pewter, Tea Set, Jean Theobald, Wood Handles, Pot, Sugar & Creamer, Tray, Wilcox
$1680.00

P

Phonograph, Amberola, Table Model 5, Mahogany
$234.00

Phonograph, Columbia, A.J., Disc, Black Bracket, Red Horn
$585.00

Phonograph, Edison, Home, Cylinder, Suitcase, C Reproducer, 14-In. Brass Horn
$322.00

Phonograph, Emerson, Model 892, Carry Case, 4-Speed, 1950s, 14 ½ x 6 ½ In.
$168.00

Sculpture, Woman, Dog, Ebonized Wood Dog, Base, 9 x 10 In.	3120.00
Spoon, Cast Initials, Pennsylvania, Mid 19th Century, 4 In.	235.00
Stuffing Spoon, Royal Arms Of England On Handle, England, c.1800, 13 In.	295.00 to 425.00
Tankard, Mason Design, Lid, c.1798	132.00
Tankard, Richard Yates, Hinged Lid, Tulip Shape, Shaped Handle, Thumblift, c.1780	895.00
Tea Set, Jean Theobald, Wood Handles, Pot, Sugar & Creamer, Tray, Wilcox ......*illus*	1680.00
Teapot, Boardman & Hart, Polish, Bulbous, Curved Spout, 8 ¾ In.	345.00
Teapot, Boardman, Gooseneck Spout, Dome Lid, Scroll Handle, Impressed, c.1835, 7 ½ In.	440.00
Teapot, Broadhead & Atkin, Floral Finial, Mark, 5 ½ In.	395.00
Teapot, D. Curtis, Gooseneck, Stamped, 11 ¾ In.	385.00
Teapot, George Richardson, Pear Shape, Boston, c.1818-28, 7 In.	323.00
Teapot, Orivit, Bird Spout, Jugendstil, Pressed Designs, Flowers, Vines, c.1900, 8 ¼ x 5 ½ In.	385.00
Teapot, Queen Anne, Pear Form, Ivory Wafer, Applied Handle, 18th Century, 6 ½ In.	135.00
Teapot, Tin, Spout, Lid, Handle, Rufus Dunham, Maine, 1837-61, 10 ¾ In.	147.00
Tray, Nekrassoff, Leaf Shape, Free-Form, c.1930, 17 ¼ x 7 In.	115.00
Tumbler, Kayserzinn, Jugendstil, Shield, Crest, Mythical Creature, 4 ½ x 3 In.	125.00
Urn, Cover, Branches, Waisted, Standing Officer Finial, 1786, 20 ½ In.	175.00
Vase, Art Deco, Shouldered Shape, Brass Patina, Gold Swirls, Bands, Handles, 21 In.	1140.00
Vase, James Powell, Tudric, Pierced, Green Glass Liners, 6 ¾ x 4 ½ In.	2196.00
Vase, Kayserzinn, Figural, Bird, Lift-Up Lid, Handle, Germany, c.1902, 6 ½ x 11 ¼ In.	780.00
Vase, Tudric, Footed Stand Shape, Hammered Flower Design, 5 ½ x 6 In.	840.00
Vase, Tudric, Stylized Flower Shape, Marked, 6 x 10 In.	900.00
Vase, Tudric, Tapered, 3 Lower Handles, Repousse Arts & Crafts Design, 5 x 10 In.	570.00
Wine Taster, Fish Decoration In Bowl, Crown Shape Handle, c.1770, 3 In.	250.00

PHOENIX GLASS Company was founded in 1880 in Pennsylvania. The firm made commercial products, such as lampshades, bottles, and glassware. Collectors today are interested in the "Sculptured Artware" made by the company from the 1930s until the mid-1950s. Some pieces of Phoenix glass are very similar to those made by the Consolidated Lamp and Glass Company. Phoenix made Reuben Blue, lavender, and yellow pieces. These colors were not used by Consolidated. In 1970 Phoenix became a division of Anchor Hocking, which was sold to the Newell Group in 1987. The factory is still working.

Ashtray, Phlox, Clear, Applied Blue Ceramic Wash, 1938, 5 ½ In.	325.00
Candy Dish, Phlox, Opaque White, Pink, Green, Cover, c.1950, 4 ¾ x 6 ¾ In.	79.00
Lamp, Electric, Green, Blue, Mushroom Shade, Scroll Supports, Carl Radke, c.1975, 20 In.	500.00
Lamp, Electric, Red, Blue Pulled Feather, 20 ½ x 12 In.	1200.00
Pitcher, Blue Opalescent, Ball Shape, Round Rim, Reeded Handle, Pontil, c.1900, 4 ¼ In.	53.00
Pitcher, Water, Mottled, Maroon & Opal, 8 Lobes, Star Shaped Rim, c.1875, 8 ½ In.	106.00
Sugar Shaker, Inverted Thumbprint, Barrel, Blue, 2-Part Cover, c.1900, 5 ¼ In.	357.00
Vase, Flying Geese, White, 11 x 10 In.	366.00
Vase, Katydid, Clear, Green Wash, Squat, c.1950, 7 ¼ x 4 x 8 ¼ In.	66.00
Vase, Star Flower, Opaque White, Blue Shading, Globular, c.1925, 7 x 3 ½ In.	66.00
Vase, Wild Geese, Opaque White, Tan Shading, c.1925, 9 ½ x 3 ¼ x 6 ½ In.	79.00

PHONOGRAPHS, invented by Thomas Edison in 1877, have been made by many firms. This category also includes other items associated with the phonograph. Jukeboxes and Records are listed in their own categories.

Amberola, Table Model 5, Mahogany ....*illus*	234.00
Cheney, Disc, Upright, Burl Walnut	248.00
Colorgraphic Company, Chicago, Twirl A Tune, Crank, Child	110.00
Columbia Style, Harmony, Inside Horn, Reproducer, Crank, Oak Case	110.00
Columbia, A.J., Disc, Black Bracket, Red Horn ....*illus*	585.00
Columbia, AT Cylinder Unit, Crank, Reproducer, Aluminum Horn	165.00
Columbia, BN Disc, Mahogany Base, Wood Horn	1170.00
Columbia, Grafonola, Mahogany Case, Floor Cabinet, Record Player, 2 Doors, 50 x 22 In.	125.00
Columbia, Graphophone, Disc, Outside Horn, Reproducer, Crank, Morning Glory Horn	77.00
Columbia, Graphophone, Model BA, Oak, Crank Handle, 1907, 30 In.	450.00
Columbia, Graphophone, Model Q, Alum Horn	175.00
Columbia, Graphophone, Morning Glory Horn, Oak Case, 1890s, 28 x 32 In.	480.00
Columbia, The Graphophone, Oak Case, Type B, 7 x 7 x 11 In.	330.00
Edison, A-150, Diamond Disc, Oxidized Copper Reproducer, Mahogany	248.00
Edison, Amberola 30, Oak Case, Cylinder	303.00
Edison, Amberola, 50 Cylinder, Oak	248.00
Edison, Amberola 75, Mahogany Case, Cylinder	330.00
Edison, Amberola 75, Oak Case, Floor Model, Cylinder	468.00

Edison, Amberola, V Cylinder, Mahogany Case	44.00
Edison, Amberola VIII, Cylinder	303.00
Edison, Amberola, Windup, Oak, 22 Cylinders, c.1900	300.00
Edison, Banner Model A, Cylinder, Conical Horn	440.00
Edison, Cylinder, 4-Latch, Automatic Reproducer, Crank	1100.00
Edison, Cylinder, 4-Latch, Shaver, Reproducer, Cover, Crank	523.00
Edison, Cylinder, C Reproducer, Crank, Brass Bell, Witch's Hat Horn	33.00
Edison, Cylinder, Fireside Model B, Reproducer, Oak Cygnet Horn	1287.00
Edison, Cylinder Maroon, Gem Model K, Reproducer, 2-Piece Horn	410.00
Edison, Diamond Model B, Reproducer	88.00
Edison, Fireside, C Reproducer, Oak Case, Horn, c.1905, 25 x 12 In.	960.00
Edison, Gem, Cylinder, C Reproducer, Black Horn & Crank	660.00
Edison, Hepplewhite, Diamond Disc, Mahogany, Fleur-De-Lis Grill	28.00
Edison, Home, Cylinder, H Reproducer, Crank, Silver Morning Glory Horn, Tulips	770.00
Edison, Home, Cylinder, Suitcase, C Reproducer, 14-In. Brass Horn .... *illus*	322.00
Edison, No. A-150, Mahogany, 44 x 20 In., Square	880.00
Edison, No. C250, Diamond Disc, Chippendale Style, Oak	83.00
Edison, Oak Case, Dome Lid, Horn, Cylinders, Containers, Decals, c.1900, 11 x 17 In.	403.00
Edison, Oak Case, Red Morning Glory Horn, Early 20th Century, 12 In.	397.00
Edison, Opera, Mahogany, Cygnet Horn	3850.00
Edison, S-19, Walnut Case, Floor Model, Diamond Disc, Crank	132.00
Edison, Serial No. S291055, Bell Marked Thomas A. Edison, Sygnet, No. 10, 11 x 12 ½ In.	770.00
Edison, Sheraton, S19, Upright, 1919, 43 x 19 ½ x 20 In.	385.00
Edison, Standard, C Reproducer, Cylinder, Brush, Crane, Cover, Crank, Morning Glory Horn	578.00
Edison, Standard Cylinder, H Reproducer, No. 10 Horn, Crank, Crane	770.00
Edison, Triumph Banner, Model A, Cylinder, Reproducer, Brass Witch's Hat Horn	1760.00
Edison, Triumph, C Reproducer, Shaver, Crank, Cylinder, Brass Bell, Witch's Hat Horn	1100.00
Edison, Triumph, Model A, Disc Type, Morning Glory Horn, c.1904, 12 x 18 In.	1840.00
Edison, Triumph, Model D, Cylinder, O Reproducer	825.00
Emerson, Model 892, Carry Case, 4-Speed, 1950s, 14 ½ x 6 ½ In. .... *illus*	168.00
Lamp, Disc, Capital Elect, Blue Shade Top, Gold Fringe, Brass Base	1170.00
McDonald, Graphophone, Model AB, Cylinders, Alum Horn	1287.00
Needles, Cutter, Alto Fibre, Box	11.00
RCA, Victrola, Electric, Table Model, 1942 Anniversary Model	99.00
Record Player, Columbia, Graphophone, Busy Bee, Cylinder, Horn, Key, c.1901, 10 x 7 ½ In.	480.00
Record Player, Quartersawn Oak, Carved, Kovell Talking Machine Co., c.1920, 42 x 36 In.	960.00
Record Player Stand, Cabinet, Mahogany, Hinged Doors, Herzog, c.1925, 38 x 18 In.	600.00
Regina, Disc Console Player, Walnut Base, 10 15 ½-In. Discs, 69 In. .... *illus*	16100.00
Reginaphone, Double-Comb, 20-In. Regina, 7 Discs, Mahogany Stand, Nickel Horn, 47 In.	7475.00
Sonora Elite, Bombay Sides, 46 x 23 In.	385.00
Sonora, Oak Case, Table Model, Disc, Reproducer, Crank	165.00
Victor, D Disc, Exhibition Reproducer, Fancy Case, Crank, Brass Bell Horn	2860.00
Victor, E, Small Brass Bell Horn	1287.00
Victor, II, Black Bell Horn, Slip In Elbow, 13 ⅝ x 6 ½ In. .... *illus*	1112.00
Victor, II, Exhibition Reproducer, Disc, 10-Panel Morning Glory Horn, Crank	880.00
Victor, IV, Disc, Mahogany Spear Tip Horn, Exhibition Reproducer, Crank	2475.00
Victor, L, Door VV-XVI, Mahogany Case, Floor Model, Exhibition Reproducer	495.00
Victor, O, Disc, Exhibition Reproducer, Yellow Horn	1989.00
Victor, R, Rigid Arm, Exhibition Reproducer, Columbia Horn	1053.00
Victor, V, Oak, Disc, Exhibition Reproducer, Crank, Brass Bell Horn	1870.00
Victor, V, Table Model, Crank, Oak, Spear Tip Horn	19.25
Victor, Victrola, Model VV-IX, Mahogany, c.1912	150.00
Victor, Victrola, No. 5, Oak, Horn, 16 x 30 In.	3450.00
Victor, Victrola, No. 6, Mahogany, Stenciled Horn, Brass Mounts, 16 x 30 In.	5750.00
Victor, Victrola, No. 50, Portable, Suitcase Model	132.00
Victor, Victrola, VV-IV, Table Model, Inside Horn & Crank	77.00
Victor, VV-1-1, Table Model, Disc, Exhibition Reproduce, Crank	99.00
Victor, VV-50, Oak, Suitcase Model, Victrola No. 2, Reproducer, Crank	187.00
Victor, VV-IV, Dancing Dan Attachment, Oak Case, Speaker, Early 1900s, 18 ½ In.	165.00
Victor, VV-XI, Mahogany Case, Floor Model, Disc	154.00
Victor, VV-XI, Mahogany, Floor Model, Tooth Bull Gear	187.00
Victor, VV-XXV Schoolhouse, Disc, Oak Horn	2750.00
Victrola, Brunswick Panatrope, Model P-2, Mahogany Cabinet, 35 x 39 In.	390.00
Victrola, IX, Tabletop, 14 x 16 x 19 In.	440.00
Victrola, Model 37577, Oak Case, Morning Glory Horn, 29 ½ In.	1150.00

Phonograph, Regina,
Disc Console Player, Walnut Base,
10 15 ½-In. Discs, 69 In.
$16100.00

Phonograph, Victor, II, Black Bell Horn,
Slip In Elbow, 13 ⅝ x 6 ½ In.
$1112.00

Phonograph Needle Case,
His Master's Voice, Nipper & Phonograph,
1 ⅜ x 1 ½ In.
$59.00

P

Photography, Ambrotype, Postmortem, Girl, Gutta-Percha Case, 3 ¾ x 3 In. $144.00

Photography, Magic Lantern, Standard, Lens, 12 Slides, Wood Case, 5 x 11 ½ x 9 In. $303.00

Victrola, Orthophonic, 8-30, Credenza Form, 1925-28, 46 ½ x 30 x 21 In.	440.00
Victrola, RCA, Suitcase Model	88.00
Westinghouse, Model H-184, Brown Plastic Case, Lift Top, Radio	66.00
W.W. Kimball, Crank, Reproducer, Floor Model	165.00
Zon-O-Phone, Champion Model, Black Paneled Horn	995.00

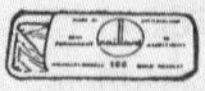

PHONOGRAPH NEEDLE CASES of tin are collected today by music and phonograph enthusiasts and advertising addicts. The tins are very small, about 2 inches across, and often have attractive graphic designs lithographed on the top and sides.

Aegir, Red, Blue, Phonograph	33.00
All-U-Need, 5 Compartments, Germany	88.00
His Master's Voice, Nipper & Phonograph, 1 ⅜ x 1 ½ In. .... *illus*	59.00
Marschall Marathon, Record, Round, Germany, Tin	28.00
Peacock, Germany, Tin	88.00
Victor, Door, 4 Sections, Tin	33.00
Village Scene, Knights With Flags, Bavaria	72.00

PHOTOGRAPHY items are listed here. The first photograph was a view from a window in France taken in 1826. The commercially successful photograph started with the daguerreotype introduced in 1839. Today all sorts of photographs and photographic equipment are collected. Albums were popular in Victorian times. Cartes de visite, popular after 1854, were mounted on 2 ½-by-4-inch cardboard. Cabinet cards were introduced in 1866. These were mounted on 4 ¼-by- 6 ½-inch cards. Stereo views are listed under Stereo Card. The cases for daguerreotypes are listed in the Gutta-Percha category. Stereoscopes are listed in their own section.

Album, Silver Print, Mines, Miners, Machinery, Black Cloth Cover, 210 Photos, c.1917, 7 x 11 In.	5513.00
Albumen Print, Northern Pacific Railroad Locomotive Trapped, Montana Landslide, 10 x 8 In.	540.00
Albumen Print, Sod Roof J.H. Ranch House, Skulls, Powder River, Wyoming, Dalgliesh	940.00
Ambrotype, 4 Kentucky Confederate Cavalrymen, Ornate Frame, 1860, ½ Plate	5275.00
Ambrotype, Abraham Lincoln, Wide Awake Marcher, Man, Banner, ⅙ Plate, c.1860	10575.00
Ambrotype, Man, Holding Opossum, Tall Hat, Ornate Metal Frame, ⅙ Plate	382.00
Ambrotype, Niagara Falls, 2 Men, Pressed Paper Case, c.1850s, Full Plate	2938.00
Ambrotype, Postmortem, Girl, Gutta-Percha Case, 3 ¾ x 3 In. .... *illus*	144.00
Ambrotype, Steven Douglas, Little Giant Club Supporter, Seated, Hat, Union Case, c.1860	8813.00
Ambrotype, Union Cavalryman, Sword, Pistol, Frame, ⅙ Plate	411.00
Ambrotype, Well Dressed Black Woman Slave, White Child On Lap, Paper Case, ⅙ Plate	2350.00
Cabinet Card, American Indian, Woman, O.S. Golf, c.1877	705.00
Cabinet Card, Apache Chief, San Juan, Studio Portrait, H. Buehman, Arizona	1645.00
Cabinet Card, Jesse James, Kansas City	2350.00
Cabinet Card, J.X. Beidler, Montana Vigilante, Imprint Keller, Montana, Autographed	4700.00
Cabinet Card, Victoria Claflin Woodhull, First Woman To Run For President	925.00
Cabinet Card, Walk A Heap, Sioux Indian, G.W. Scott, Studio Portrait, 1888	382.00
Cabinet Card, White Lake Dakota Hotel, Saloon, M.J. Trits	206.00
Camera, Canon 7, No. 801150, Ultrafast, 0.95/50 mm Lens, Selenium Meter, c.1961	652.00
Camera, Kodak 1888, Rollfilm, No. 4525, Cylindrical Shutter, Lens Cap, Embossed Case	2027.00
Camera, Kodak, Ektra, No. 4871, 1.9/50 mm, Interchangeable Lenses, c.1941	579.00
Camera, Leica IIIc, Wetzlar, No. 372621, Black Shutter Curtains, Elmar 3.5/5 cm, c.1941	174.00
Camera, Leicaflex SL2, MOT, Motor Drive, No. 1441695, Black, Body Cap, c.1975	652.00
Camera, Nikon SP, No. 6201375, Chrome, Black, Nikkor-H 2/5 cm, c.1957	724.00
Camera, Olympus-Pen F, Gold Plated, No. 127499, Reptile Skin, F. Zuiko Auto-S 1.8/38 mm, c.1963	290.00
Camera, Ontoflex, TLR, 6 x 9 cm, Rotating Back, Model B, Interchangeable, Cornu, c.1935	130.00
Camera, Rollei-Werke, 24K Gold Plated, 35 S, No. 1013, Lizard Case, Box, Manual, 60th Anniversary.	434.00
Camera, Stereo, Voigtlander, 45 x 107 mm, Changeable Magazine, Case, c.1923	246.00
Camera, Thornton & Pickard, Mahogany, Framed Bellows, Tripod, 1800s, 51 x 12 In.	351.00
Carte De Visite, Abraham Lincoln, Seated, Desk, A. Gardner, Frame, 5 x 6 In.	411.00
Carte De Visite, Wild Bill Hickok, D.D. Dare, Cheyenne, Wyoming, 1874	18800.00
Collo-Type, Norman Rockwell, Doctor & Doll, Signed, Frame, 28 x 23 In.	1955.00
Collo-Type, Norman Rockwell, Outward Bound, Signed, 35 x 29 In.	1025.00
Collo-Type, Norman Rockwell, Saying Grace, Signed, Frame, 26 ¾ x 28 In.	2030.00
Collo-Type, Norman Rockwell, Shuffletons Barber Shop, Signed, Frame, 27 ½ x 26 In.	955.00
Daguerreotype, 2 Union Soldiers, Seated, In Uniform, Metal Case, Embossed, 1960s, 4 In.	309.00
Daguerreotype, Double Union Case, Gutta-Percha, Mother & Child, c.1857, 6 ¼ x 3 ¾ In.	850.00
Daguerreotype, Draftsman, Compass, Book, Top Hat, Leather Case, ⅙ Plate	2100.00
Daguerreotype, Elderly Man, Marked, J. Gurney, Case, ½ Plate, 5 ¾ In.	750.00
Daguerreotype, Girl, Kitten, Red, Yellow Metal Frame, ⅑ Plate	881.00
Daguerreotype, Harness Maker, Straw Hat, Bench Clamp, Striped Apron, ⅙ Plate	1528.00

Daguerreotype, Man, Brother's Grave, Fence, Leather Case, Frame, Gold Rush, G. Johnson, 1852	7638.00
Daguerreotype, Man Sitting, Bandage Amputated Hand, Paper Tag, c.1852, ⅙ Plate	1750.00
Daguerreotype, Portrait, Couple, Union Case, Cupid, Wounded Stag, 1800s, ¼ Plate	140.00
Daguerreotype, Seated Child, Table, Chalk Dog, Book, ⅙ Plate, 3 ¼ x 3 ¾ In.	475.00
Daguerreotype, Thaddeus Stevens, ¼ Plate, Cased, 4 ½ In.	1200.00
Daguerreotype, Woman, Semiprofile, Seated, Brooch, ½ Plate	353.00
Ferrotype, Lincoln, Hamlin Jugate, Back-To-Back, Silver Plated Frame, 1 ¾ In.	441.00
Magic Lantern, Brass, Tin, Oil Lamp, Hand Crank, Kaleidoscope, 3 Slides, Germany, 12 In.	150.00
Magic Lantern, Oil Lamp, Black, 12 Slides, Germany, Box, 6 x 14 x 11 In.	275.00
Magic Lantern, Standard, Lens, 12 Slides, Wood Case, 5 x 11 ½ x 9 In. ....*illus*	303.00
Megalethoscope, Walnut, On Turn Leg Base, Charles Ponti, Venice, Italy, c.1870, 35 In.	1528.00
Photo Coloration Set, Wood Case, 24 Bottles, Brushes, c.1930	471.00
Photograph, Bettie Page, Cheesecake, Pinup Queen, Negligee, Candle, Signed, 8 x 10 In.	316.00
Photograph, Boy On Bicycle, In Folio, c.1920, 8 x 10 & 11 x 14 In.	28.00
Photograph, Bromide, Building, Statue, Light & Shade, A. Fassbender, 1940, 16 x 13 In.	2400.00
Photograph, Chief Joseph, Silver Print, W.M. Sawyer, 7 x 9 In.	1175.00
Photograph, Firefighting, Black Hills, Silver Gelatin Print, J.H. Grabill, 1891, 6 x 10 In.	1058.00
Photograph, Garry Winogrand, John F. Kennedy, Gelatin Silver Print, 1960, 9 x 6 In.	3750.00
Photograph, George Tice, Petit's Mobil Station, Cherry Hill, N.J., 15 x 19 In., c.1974	8750.00
Photograph, Marion Davies, Black Velvet Gown, Apeda Studios, N.Y., 13 x 10 In.	112.00
Photograph, Silver, New York Post Office, G. Platt Lynes, c.1940, 5 x 8 In.	4200.00
Photograph, Simon Cameron, Lincoln Cabinet Member, Hand Colored, Oval Frame, 12 x 14 In.	1645.00
Photograph, Stagecoach In Desert, Goldfield, Nevada, Silver Gelatin Print, 1900s, 4 x 6 In.	940.00
Photograph, Tea House, San Francisco, Monte Nagler, Signed, Frame, 19 x 15 In.	146.00
Photograph, Union Boy Squad, Caisson, Intersection, Sacramento, 1879, 9 x 12 In.	646.00
Photograph, U.S. Mail Stagecoach, Men, Horses, Arizona, Silver Gelatin Print, c.1900, 9 x 4 In.	588.00
Photograph, William Wegman, Contemplating Bust Of Man Ray, Gelatin Silver Print, 7 x 7 In.	4375.00
Photogravure, Hesquiat Root Digger, Edward Curtis, Copyright 1915, 15 ½ x 11 ½ In.	360.00
Photogravure, Old Eagle, Oto, Edward Curtis, Copyright 1927, 15 ½ x 11 ½ In.	510.00
Silver Print, Cerastium Chloraefolium, Karl Blossfeldt, Frame, Early 1900s, 11 x 8 ¼ In.	338.00
Silver Print, Physolegia Virginiana, Karl Blossfeldt, Frame, Early 1900s, 11 x 8 ¼ In.	338.00
Stereographoscope, Mixed Woods, Lacquer Finish, c.1875, 21 x 14 In.	323.00
Tintype, 2 Soldiers, Smoking Pipes, Spanish American War Era, Leather Case, ⅙ Plate	275.00
Tintype, Ohio Town, Posed People, General Store, c.1888, Full Plate	646.00
Tintype, Soldier, Girl, Case, Reverse On Glass Cover Image, Hinged Case, 3 ½ x 3 In.	316.00

PIANO BABY is a collector's term. About 1880, the well-decorated home had a shawl on the piano. Bisque figures of babies were designed to help hold the shawl in place. They range in size from 6 to 18 inches. Most of the figures were made in Germany. Reproductions are being made. Other piano babies may be listed under manufacturers' names.

Baby, Crawling, Bisque, 8 x 4 ½ In.	39.00
Baby, Crawling, Bisque, Heubach, 12 In. ....*illus*	225.00
Baby, Crawling, Black Eyes, Nude, Pouty Mouth, Enesco, Japan, c.1955, 3 x 4 In.	45.00
Baby, Crawling, Rosy Dimpled Cheeks, Brown Hair, Bisque, 9 In.	35.00
Baby, Crawling, Thumb In Mouth, Black, Bisque, 5 In.	88.00
Baby, Crawling, Thumb In Mouth, Intaglio Eyes, 5 x 3 ½ In.	150.00
Baby, Holding Cup, Dimples, Japan, c.1970, 6 In.	65.00
Baby, Holding Dog, Blue Gown, 6 ½ In.	125.00
Baby, Kneeling, 4 In.	25.00
Baby, Lying On Tummy, Holding Kitty, Intaglio Eyes, Closed Mouth, 7 In.	125.00
Baby, On Back, Holding Grapes, Bisque, Heubach, 1900s, 5 x 3 x 2 In.	33.00
Baby, On Back, Touching Left Foot, Marked, Heubach, 3 x 4 In.	260.00
Baby, On Stomach, Playing With Dog, Bisque, 7 x 2 ½ In.	120.00
Baby, Reclining, Cherries In Hand, Bisque, Goebel, Germany, 5 ½ x 3 x 2 In.	30.00
Baby, Sitting, Intaglio Eyes, Blue Eyes, Germany, 8 ½ In.	425.00
Baby, Sitting, Playing With Fingers & Toes, Hat, 6 In.	100.00
Baby, Sucking Toe, Heubach, 7 ½ x 6 ½ In.	1100.00
Boy, In Dad's Shoes, Gebruder Heubach, Germany, 10 In.	899.00
Boy, Lying Down, Hugging Ball, Blue Eyes, Bisque, 7 ½ In.	65.00
Boy, Lying On Back, Clapping Cymbals, 4 In.	50.00
Girl, Blue Bonnet, Finger To Chin, Bisque, 12 ½ In.	40.00
Girl, Crawling, Bisque, Molded Brown Hair, Dimples, 8 ½ In.	39.00
Girl, Crawling, Smiling, 10 In.	250.00
Girl, Highchair, Feeding Puppy, Bisque, 1881	225.00
Girl, Lying On Back, Clapping, Pink & White Outfit, Bisque, 6 In.	45.00
Girl, Lying On Side, Bisque, Smock, Sleep Cap, 3 ¾ In.	89.00

Piano Baby, Baby, Crawling, Bisque, Heubach, 12 In.
$225.00

Picture, Needlework, Crewel, Flower & Leaf Wreath, Shadowbox, Victorian, 20 x 20 In.
$162.00

Photos Fade
We have been receiving warnings about using digital cameras for important photos you plan to save. Ten years from now, we probably won't have the proper computers to read the CDs storing the photos, and homemade prints will not last. The solution: Have your digital photos printed professionally.

P

Picture, Needlework, Dog, Wool, Frame, Victorian, 9 x 11 In. $480.00

Girl, Lying On Side, Curly Blond Hair, Pink Bow, Bisque, c.1907, 4 In.	85.00
Girl, Lying On Tummy, Arched Head, Green Dress, Lefton, 5 x 3 ½ In.	40.00
Girl, Seated, Dachshund Dog Licking Her Face, 3 x 3 ¼ In.	41.00
Girl, Sitting, Bonnet, Blond Hair, Bisque, c.1955, 8 x 4 ½ In.	10.00
Girl, Sitting, Hand On Face, Chalkware, c.1920, 11 In.	75.00
Girl, Sitting, Holding Dog, Hat, Bisque, Germany, 4 ½ x 3 In.	50.00
Girl, Sitting, Holding Doll, Bisque, Japan, c.1960, 12 In.	65.00
Girl, Sitting, Raised Arms, Bisque, 4 ½ In.	35.00
Girl, Sitting, Reading Book, Bisque, Heubach, c.1900, 4 x 3 x 3 In.	49.00
Twins, Boy & Girl, Sitting Hands Near Mouth, Intaglio Eyes, Camille Naundot, 1940, 12 In.	599.00

PICKARD China Company was started in 1893 by Wilder Pickard. Hand-painted designs were used on china purchased from other sources. In the 1930s, the company began to make its own china wares in Chicago, Illinois. The company now makes many types of porcelains, including a successful line of limited edition collector plates.

Bowl, Pink & Yellow Flowers, Cream Ground, Gold Highlights, Footed, Signed, P.G., 10 ¼ In.	325.00
Bowl, Walled Garden Scene, Pedestal, Vellum, Signed, E. Challinor, 2 ¾ x 9 In.	350.00
Celery Dish, Italian Garden Scene, Vellum, Signed, F. Vobor, 13 ¼ In.	165.00
Charger, Lotus, White Center, Gold, Signed, 12 ¼ In.	150.00
Dish, Leaf Shape, Green, Violet, Gold Trim, Signed, H. Kevvy, 9 In.	150.00
Dish, Limoges, Poppy, Yeschek, Double Mark, 7 ¾ x 6 ¼ In.	495.00
Dresser Set, Blue Flowers, Gold Trim, White & Light Blue, Signed, Alex, 5 Piece	255.00
Mayonnaise Set, Leaf & Violets, Cream, Gold Trim, Signed, Marker, 7 In., 2 Piece	230.00
Mug, Fruit, Dark Rose Ground, Signed, V. Meek, 3 ½ In.	150.00
Pitcher, Cider, Blossom & Berry, Brown, Gold, Signed, Bitterly, 6 ¾ In.	350.00
Pitcher, Tankard, Blue Berry Bush, Gold Scrolls, Signed, J.P. France Pickard, 15 In.	1178.00
Pitcher, Water, Red Poppy, Light Green Ground, Gold, Signed, Fuchs, 10 ½ In.	1500.00
Plate, Berry & Leaf, Cream Ground, Gold Border, Signed, E. Challinor, 6 In.	30.00
Plate, Blue & Pink Flowers, Cream Center, Gold Highlights, Signed, Richler, 8 ¾ In.	100.00
Plate, Gold Serpentine & Flowers, Cream Center, Signed, E. Gibson, 8 ½ In.	75.00
Plate, Night Harvest Scene, Vellum, Signed, Alex, 8 ¼ In.	
Salt & Pepper, Gold Gilt, 3 ½ In.	10.00
Salt & Pepper, White Daisy, Silver Bands, Gold, Signed, Passoni, 3 In.	25.00
Sugar & Creamer, Fruit, Gold, Square, Signed, Vorkal	81.00
Sugar & Creamer, Night Time Ruins Scene, Vellum, Signed, E. Challinor	375.00
Vase, Courting Couple, Gold, 7 ¾ In.	150.00
Vase, Pheasant, Vellum Flower Ground, Brocaded Gold, Handles, Signed, E. Challinor, 7 ¼ In.	100.00
Vase, Pink Rose, Gold, Green, Corset Shape, Handles, Signed, Challinor, 16 In.	7010.00
Vase, White Iris, Blue Shoreline, Trees, Cylinder, Gold, Rim, Base, Signed, 10 In.	374.00

PICTURES, silhouettes, and other small decorative objects framed to hang on the wall are listed here. Sandpaper pictures are black and white charcoal drawings done on a special sanded paper. Some other types of pictures are listed in the Print and Painting categories.

Beadwork, Madonna, Black Frame, Rounded Corners, Continental, 6 x 4 In.	59.00
Beadwork, Madonna, Painted Detail, Spain, c.1900, 8 x 9 ¼ In.	56.00
Cast Plaster, Church Interior, Angels, Shell, Ebonized Wood Plaque Mount, 13 x 6 In.	173.00
Charcoal, On Paper, Portrait, Mr. George, Alligatoring To Wood Frame, 17 x 14 In.	35.00
Charcoal, White Pastel, Gray Paper, Dancing Figure, Arthur B. Davis, 13 ½ x 10 In.	431.00
Cutwork, Tomb, Willows Vignette, Maple Frame, 19th Century, 16 ¾ x 22 ¼ In.	235.00
Drawing, Calligraphy, Watercolor, Pencil, Mammoth Hog, Thomson, c.1839, 24 x 30 In.	7750.00
Drawing, Graphite, Mt. Vernon, Signed, Almira Knapp, 1800s, 10 ¾ x 5 In.	117.00
Drawing, Graphite, Trees, Edgar Alwin Payne, Signed, Frame, c.1920, 8 x 10 In.	960.00
Drawing, Pen & Ink, Laid Paper, Flowering Tree, Bird, P. Willets, Gilt Frame, c.1795, 8 ½ x 7 In.	206.00
Floral Arrangement, Wax Flowers, Oval Giltwood Shadowbox Frame, 15 x 18 In.	173.00
Hair, Wreath, Flowers, Leaves, Victorian, Oval, Walnut Frame, 40 x 35 In.	2000.00
Hair, Wreath, Heart Shape, Victorian, Oval, Walnut Frame, 20 x 17 In.	400.00
Hair, Wreath, Woven, Blond, Gray, Brown, Shadowbox Frame, c.1860, 24 x 23 In.	177.00
Hair, Wreath, Woven, Blond, Gray, Shadowbox Frame, c.1860, 18 x 18 In.	106.00
Hair, Wreath, Woven, Shadowbox Frame, c.1860, 20 x 22 In.	106.00
Hair, Wreath, Woven, White Flowers, Paper Leaves, Flags, Shadowbox Frame, 20 x 17 In.	83.00
Micro Mosaic, Venetian Scene, St. Mark's Square, Italy, 5 ¾ x 3 ⅝ In.	230.00
Needlework, Allegorical, Biblical, Elijah Visited By Angel, Gilt Frame, c.1820, 12 In.	235.00
Needlework, Appliqued, Balthazar's Feast, King David, Bible Stories, Dorothy Goss, 35 x 32 In.	4963.00
Needlework, Basket Of Flowers, Birds, Girl, Lamb, Cat, Dog, Ducks, 27 ½ x 27 ½ In.	90.00
Needlework, Crewel, Flower & Leaf Wreath, Shadowbox, Victorian, 20 x 20 In. ....*illus*	162.00

Picture, Needlework, Embroidered, Georgia,
Spread Eagle, In Banner,
Flags, Asian, c.1900, 18 x 20 In.
$374.00

Picture, Needlework, Roses, Beadwork,
Stump Work, Walnut Frame, England,
1800s, 22 x 21 In.
$293.00

Picture, On Ivory, Woman In Black,
Newark, Ohio, Frame, c.1835, 6 x 5 In.
$264.00

Picture, Petit Point, Landscape, Girl,
Straw Hat, Flowers, Oval Gilt Frame, 12 x 14 In.
$127.00

Picture, Portrait, Woman, Ivory,
Gilt Bronze Frame, Signed Drea,
3 ½ x 3 In.
$133.00

Picture, Silhouette, Busts,
Vernon Anders To Cora Mohl June,
C. Anders, Cut Paper, c.1846, 12 x 9 In.
$620.00

Beadwork Roses
Victorian beadwork picturing
roses is the highest priced. Other
flowers are less popular with
collectors.

Picture, Theorem, Bird, Perched On Flower
Garland, Woolwork, Frame, 1800s, 16 x 21 In.
$878.00

Picture, Tinsel, Flower Wreath,
Castle, Gilt Frame, c.1875, 21 x 23 In.
$2350.00

Picture, Tinsel, Reverse Painted On Glass,
Flower Wreath, Frame, c.1875, 22 x 28 In.
$59.00

Picture, Watercolor, Persian Scene,
Islamic Script, Frame, c.1750, 8 x 4 In.
$176.00

P

Pillin, Bowl, Blue Mottled Ground, Girl Holding Bird, Polia Pillin, Poland, 7 x 2 In.
$184.00

Pillin, Chalice, Fish, Painted, Multicolored, Green Ground, Footed, Signed, 7 x 8 ¼ In.
$480.00

Pillin, Vase, Bulbous, Swimming Fish, Multicolored, Incised, 6 ½ In.
$1035.00

Fake Pillin

Fakes of Pillin Pottery are not uncommon. Experts say they are being made in Texas and sold online. The forgeries have the same scene on both sides of the vase. Pillin used different scenes. Fakes are heavy, the artwork crude. The mark is painted on the bottom, not incised.

Needlework, Deer Is Slain, Multicolored, Red & Black Geometric Border, Frame, 15 x 19 In. .	200.00
Needlework, Dog, Wool, Frame, Victorian, 9 x 11 In. ....*illus*	480.00
Needlework, Embroidered, Georgia, Spread Eagle, In Banner, Flags, Asian, c.1900, 18 x 20 In. *illus*	374.00
Needlework, Embroidered, Silk, Bouquet, Ribbon, Beige, Gilt Frame, 1800s, 19 x 15 ½ In.	70.00
Needlework, Embroidered, Silk, Painted, Boy & Girl, Rock, Tree, Sheep, Dog, Frame, 16 x 20 In.	595.00
Needlework, Embroidered, Silk, Shepherdess, Carving Name Into Tree, 12 x 10 In.	288.00
Needlework, Embroidered, Wool On Linen, Urn, Flowers, Leaf Border, 1748, 28 x 23 In.	575.00
Needlework, Map, By Maria Leach, Crediton, Devonshire, Silk On Wool, Oval, England & Wales, 1808	500.00
Needlework, Mourning, Silk & Wool, Grieving Women, Urn Monument, 1856, 6 x 5 In.	1775.00
Needlework, Pastoral Scene, Ruins, Gothic Tracery, Frame, c.1900, 37 ½ x 26 ½ In.	259.00
Needlework, Pastoral Scene, Shepherd, Flock, House, Scotland, Mid 1700s, Frame, 25 x 29 In.	470.00
Needlework, Roses, Beadwork, Stump Work, Walnut Frame, England, 1800s, 22 x 21 In. ..... *illus*	293.00
Needlework, Silk, 2 Birds On Nest, Gilt Oval Wood Frame, Early 1800s, 10 ½ x 9 In.	264.00
Needlework, Silk, American Eagle, Flags, Shield, Frame, 21 x 24 In.	144.00
Needlework, Silk, Chenille, Silk Thread, Painted, Women Reading, Frame, 19 x 16 In.	288.00
Needlework, Silk, Ink, Linen, Memorial, Mrs. Submit Parker, Age 41, Frame, c.1815, 23 x 23 In.	382.00
Needlework, Silk, Metallic Thread, Servant Lifting Infant Moses, Flowers, 24 ½ x 23 ½ In.	58.00
Needlework, Tapestry Ground, Red, Blue Wool, Woman, Silk Threads, England, 30 ½ x 20 ½ In.	717.00
Needlework, Wool, Dog, Spaniel, Sitting On Pillow, Wood Frame, Victorian, 9 x 11 In.	480.00
Needlework, Yarn Work, Flower Arrangement, Glass Dome, Victorian, c.1890, 11 ½ x 6 In., Pair.	266.00
On Ivory, Woman In Black, Newark, Ohio, Frame, c.1835, 6 x 5 In. ....*illus*	264.00
Pastel, On Paper, 2 Young Brothers, Hugging, Wood Frame, 14 x 9 In.	518.00
Pen & Ink, On Paper, Dogs Chasing Deer, Frame, 1898, 11 ¼ x 13 ¼ In.	147.00
Pencil, On Paper, Still Life, Flowers, Basket, Frame, Ferdinand Brader, Mid 1800s, 23 x 27 In.	470.00
Petit Point, Landscape, Girl, Straw Hat, Flowers, Oval Gilt Frame, 12 x 14 In. ....*illus*	127.00
Picture Frames are listed in this book in the Furniture category under Frame.	
Plaster Relief, Pioneer Woman, Child, Conestoga Wagon, Signed, Bryant Baker, c.1931, 43 x 33 In.	177.00
Portrait, Woman, Ivory, Gilt Bronze Frame, Signed Drea, 3 ½ x 3 In. ....*illus*	133.00
Scroll, Watercolor, On Paper, Hope, Monument, Sacred To Religion, c.1829, 5 ¾ x 5 In.	235.00
Silhouette, 2 Boxers, Fabric Applique On Paper, May 19, 1867, Frame, 12 ½ x 14 ½ In.	558.00
Silhouette, Busts, Vernon Anders To Cora Mohl June, C. Anders, Cut Paper, c.1846, 12 x 9 In. ..*illus*	620.00
Silhouette, David Dale, Walking, Cane, Hand Colored, Etched, Cutout, Gilt Frame, 1800s, 4 x 6 In.	94.00
Silhouette, Man, Bust, High Collar, Highlights, Ebonized Frame, 1800s, 3 ¼ x 3 In.	271.00
Silhouette, Profile, Hollow Cut, Man, Woman, Watercolor, Ink, Frame, c.1820, 5 x 4 ½ In.	1410.00
Silhouette, Woman, Blue Dress, Eunice Currier, Watercolor, Black Paper, c.1835, 5 x 4 In.	385.00
Silhouette, Woman, Hollow Cut, Gilt Frame, 6 x 5 In.	118.00
Silhouette, Woman, Lace Cap, Full Cutout Portrait, Black, White, 15 x 11 In.	206.00
Silhouette, Woman, Mary Walker, Information On Sitter Verso, Frame, 1850, 3 ½ x 3 In.	153.00
Silhouette, Young Boy, Bust, Gilt Highlight, Rosewood Frame, 1800s, 4 x 3 In.	106.00
Silhouette, Young Man, Young Woman, Gilt Highlights, Maple Frame, 4 ½ In., Pair...............	165.00
Silhouette, Young Woman, Standing, Gilt Highlights, Rosewood Frame, 11 ¾ x 8 ¾ In.	319.00
Theorem, 2 Tulips, Red Vase, Watercolor, Signed, D. Ellinger, Frame, 6 ½ x 4 ½ In.	240.00
Theorem, Basket Of Fruit, Velvet, c.1830	1121.00
Theorem, Bird, Perched On Flower Garland, Woolwork, Frame, 1800s, 16 x 21 In. ....*illus*	878.00
Theorem, Watercolor, Basket Of Flowers, Gilded Frame, 4 ¼ x 5 ⅞ In.	450.00
Theorem, Watercolor, On Velvet, Bird Picking, Fruit Basket, Gilt Frame, c.1840, 12 ½ x 15 In.	1293.00
Theorem, Watercolor, On Velvet, Fruit Basket, Parrot, Butterfly, Frame, c.1820, 17 x 19 In.	2015.00
Tinsel, Flower Wreath, Castle, Gilt Frame, c.1875, 21 x 23 In. ....*illus*	2350.00
Tinsel, Reverse Painted On Glass, Flower Wreath, Frame, c.1875, 22 x 28 In. ....*illus*	59.00
Watercolor & Ink, Woman, Memorial, In Black, Memory Of Robert Spear, c.1825, 23 x 29 In.	823.00
Watercolor & Pencil, Hawk, Sponge Decorated Frame, James Abert, Late 1800s, 13 ¾ x 17 ¾ In.	617.00
Watercolor, 2 Blue Birds, On Pot, Tulip, Signed, D. Ellinger, Frame, 7 ½ x 5 ½ In.	295.00
Watercolor, African Vista, Paul Bough Travic, Signed, Frame, 1937, 10 x 14 In.	600.00
Watercolor, Exmouth, England, Titled, Richard Hayley Lever, Signed, 1905, 6 x 9 ¼ In.	1320.00
Watercolor, Girl, White Dress, Blue Sash, Round, Wood Sunburst Frame, 7 In.	201.00
Watercolor, Gouache, On Ivory, Girl In Red, Holding Flower, Frame, 2 ¾ x 2 ⅛ In.	1778.00
Watercolor, Gouache, On Ivory, Man, Red Hair, Brass Case, 2 ¾ x 2 ⅛ In.	711.00
Watercolor, Gray Duck, S. Northcote, Jr., March, 1787, 5 ½ x 11 ¾ In.	575.00
Watercolor, Heart, Roses, Verse, Remember Me, Annie B. Witmer, Frame, c.1866, 11 x 12 ½ In.	118.00
Watercolor, Lace Making, William Harris Weatherhead, Frame, Signed, 1889, 31 x 19 In.	3360.00
Watercolor, New England Street With Red Bicycle Shop, F. Chapin, Frame, c.1945, 15 x 26 In.	960.00
Watercolor, On Ivory, Col. Dudley Coleman, Gilt Brass Case, 1 ½ x 1 In.	2489.00
Watercolor, On Ivory, Man, Oval Portrait, Hinged Case, c.1840, 2 x 1 ½ In.	504.00
Watercolor, On Silk Panel, Chinese Figures, Warriors Under Ornate Gate, 83 x 35 In.	1872.00
Watercolor, Persian Scene, Islamic Script, Frame, c.1750, 8 x 4 In. ....*illus*	176.00
Watercolor, Porch, Basket, Fruit, Pumpkin, Potted Plant, Frame, 1900s, 19 x 25 In.	35.00

Watercolor, Still Life, Strawberry Baskets, Morning Glories, Embossed, Frame, 15 x 17 In.	264.00
Watercolor, Teepees Along The River, Charles S. Graham, Signed, Frame, c.1890, 13 x 25 In.	2640.00
Wax, Portrait, Admiral Duncan, Signed, J. Tassie, Frame, c.1797, 6 ¾ In.	948.00
Woolwork, Man & Woman, Hound, Linen Canvas, Mahogany Frame, Silk, 1800s, 21 x 24 In.	353.00

PIGEON FORGE POTTERY was started in Pigeon Forge, Tennessee, in 1946. Red clay found near the pottery was used to make the pieces. Molded or thrown pottery with matte glaze and slip decoration was made. The pottery closed in 2000.

Figurine, Chipmunk, D. Ferguson, 3 ¾ x 3 ¾ In.	37.00
Figurine, Owl Head, Black & Gray Volcanic Finish, 3 ½ x 3 In.	45.00
Figurine, Raccoon, Cream & Brown, D. Ferguson, 9 x 6 x 5 In.	75.00
Mug, Bear, Marked	27.00
Pitcher, Milk, Pink, Dogwood Flowers, 5 ½ In.	35.00
Planter, Dogwood Blossoms, 2 ¾ x 5 In.	19.00

PILKINGTON TILE AND POTTERY COMPANY was established in 1892 in England. The company made small pottery wares, like buttons and hatpins, but soon started decorating vases purchased from other potteries. By 1903, the company had discovered an opalescent glaze that became popular on the Lancastrian pottery line. The manufacture of pottery ended in 1937. Pilkington's Tiles Ltd. has worked from 1938 to the present.

Tile, Art Nouveau, Yellow Flowers, Green Leaves, c.1900, 6 x 6 In.	30.00
Tile, Bullfight Scene, 6 In., 3 Piece	75.00
Tile, Majolica, Flower, Caramel, c.1910, 6 x 6 In.	40.00
Tile, Majolica, Green Ground, Sky Blue Flower, Cream, c.1900, 6 x 3 In.	28.00
Tile, Mountain Lake Scene, Hand Painted, Metal Holder, D. Williams, c.1940, 8 ⅝ x 4 ¼ In.	90.00
Tile, Red & White, Floral Geometric, c.1900, 6 x 6 In.	20.00
Trivet, Souvenir, Indiana Places, Iron Skillet Shape Frame, c.1970, 4 ½ x 7 ½ In.	8.00

PILLIN pottery was made by Polia (1909–1992) and William (1910–1985) Pillin, who set up a pottery in Los Angeles in 1948. William shaped, glazed, and fired the clay, and Polia painted the pieces, often with elongated figures of women, children, flowers, birds, fish, and other animals. Pieces are marked with a stylized Pillin signature.

Bowl, Blue Mottled Ground, Girl Holding Bird, Polia Pillin, Poland, 7 x 2 In. ...... illus	184.00
Chalice, Fish, Painted, Multicolored, Green Ground, Footed, Signed, 7 x 8 ¼ In. ...... illus	480.00
Vase, Bottle, Painted, Figures, Horse, Signed, 10 ¼ x 3 ½ In.	976.00
Vase, Bulbous, Green Glaze, Small Opening, 10 x 9 In.	300.00
Vase, Bulbous, Swimming Fish, Multicolored, Incised, 6 ½ In. ...... illus	1035.00
Vase, Cylinder, 2 Women, Flowering Crab Apple Tree, Yellow Ground, Green, Orange, Signed, 7 In.	546.00
Vase, Cylindrical, Multicolored Birds, Green, Blue Horizontal, Stripe Ground, Polia Pillin, 7 In.	431.00
Vase, Horizontal Bands, Black, Gray, 3 Cubist Style Figures, Signed, 3 ¾ x 5 ¾ In. ...... illus	570.00
Vase, Woman, Playing Lute, Horse, Animal, Tree, Signed, 8 ½ x 8 In.	2100.00

PINCUSHION DOLLS are not really dolls and often were not even pincushions. Some collectors use the term "half-doll." The top half of each doll was made of porcelain. The edge of the half-doll was made with several small holes for thread, and the doll was stitched to a fabric body with a voluminous skirt. The finished figure was used to cover a hot pot of tea, powder box, pincushion, whiskbroom, or lamp. They were made in sizes from less than an inch to over 9 inches high. Most date from the early 1900s to the 1950s. Collectors often find just the porcelain doll without the fabric skirt.

Bisque Head, Mohair Wig, Flowing Velvet Dress, Germany, 1920s	177.00
Flapper, Appliqued, Felt, Royal Society Embroidery, c.1928, 8 In.	25.00
Woman, Lavender Skirt, Tatting Trim, Handmade, 6 ½ x 4 ½ In.	85.00
Woman, Mohair Wig, Velvet Dress, c.1920	175.00
Yellow Kid, Figure, Holds Basket, Cloth Covered Insert, Silver Plated, Text, 3 ½ In.	392.00

PIPES have been popular since tobacco was introduced to Europe by Sir Walter Raleigh. Carved wooden, porcelain, ivory, and glass pipes may be listed here.

Ceramic, Woman, Smoking Man's Pipe, Head Shape Bowl, Scotland, c.1800, 6 In. ...... illus	702.00
Clay, Queen Victoria, 2 ¼ In.	50.00
Meerschaum, Carved, Woman, Cuffed Wrist, Open Flowers, Leaves, Leather Case, 1800s, 4 ¼ In.	60.00
Meerschaum, Erotic Scene, Carved, 4 ½ In.	80.00
Meerschaum, Woman's Head, Cherub, Eagle, Figural, Carved	145.00
Meerschaum, Yodeler, Carved, Amber Stem, Case, Germany, Late 1800s, 8 In. ...... illus	540.00

Pillin, Vase, Horizontal Bands, Black, Gray, 3 Cubist Style Figures, Signed, 3 ¾ x 5 ¾ In.
$570.00

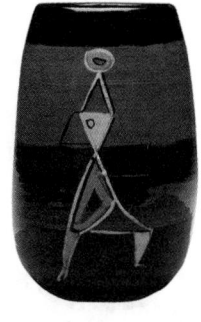

Pipe, Meerschaum, Yodeler, Carved, Amber Stem, Case, Germany, Late 1800s, 8 In.
$540.00

Pipe, Ceramic, Woman, Smoking Man's Head Shape Bowl, Scotland, c.1800, 6 In.
$702.00

Pisgah Forest, Vase, Cameo, Fiddler, Dog, Log Cabin, Mountain, Blue Ground, c.1936, 9 In.
$1298.00

Planters, Doll, Wood, Jointed, Painted, Cameo, 1930s, 8 ½ In.
$224.00

Campaign Collectibles

If you collect U.S. political memorabilia, you probably won't find anything made before William Henry Harrison's 1840 presidential campaign. That was the first presidential campaign to produce a large number of political souvenirs. Brass buttons, bandannas, and dinnerware were made picturing the log cabin and cider casks that symbolized Harrison's supposed pioneer background (he was actually born to an aristocratic Virginia family).

Porcelain, Regimental, 2. Comp, Train Bataillon Nr. 10, Hannover, 1893-94		92.00
Porcelain, Regimental, Stephan Schwager, 1909-12, 46 In.		196.00

PIRKENHAMMER is a porcelain manufactory started in 1802 by Friedrich Holke and J. G. Lilst. It was located in Bohemia, now Brezova, Czechoslovakia. The company made tablewares usually decorated with views and flowers. Lithophanes were also made. The mark of the crossed hammers is easy to remember as the Pirkenhammer symbol.

Figurine, Dog, Spaniel, Seated, Hand Painted, 19th Century, 8 ½ In.		394.00

PISGAH FOREST POTTERY was made in North Carolina beginning in 1926. The pottery was started by Walter B. Stephen, who had been making pottery in that location since 1914. The pottery continued in operation after his death in 1961. The most famous kinds of Pisgah Forest ware are the cameo type with designs made of raised glaze and the turquoise crackle glaze wares.

Cup & Saucer, Turquoise & Pink Glaze, 6 ½ & 4 ½ x 2 ½ In.		30.00
Pitcher, Wagon Train, Blue Matte Glaze, Marked, 1952, 6 In.		230.00
Teapot, Wagon Train, Green Matte Glaze, S. Longpine, Marked, 1953, 5 x 8 In.		115.00
Vase, Cream, Blue, Gray Crystal Design, Yellow Ground, Flared Rim, 5 In.		316.00
Vase, Crystalline Glaze, Tapered, Marked, c.1936, 6 ¼ In.		230.00
Vase, Fiddler, Dog, Log Cabin, Mountain, Blue Ground, c.1936, 9 In.	*illus*	1298.00
Vase, Settlers, White Crystalline Base, 16 ¼ x 7 ½ In.		2806.00

PLANTERS PEANUTS memorabilia are collected. Planters Nut and Chocolate Company was started in Wilkes-Barre, Pennsylvania, in 1906. The Mr. Peanut figure was adopted as a trademark in 1916. National advertising for Planters Peanuts started in 1918. The company was acquired by Standard Brands, Inc., in 1961. Standard Brands merged with Nabisco in 1981. Some of the Mr. Peanut jars and other memorabilia have been reproduced and, of course, new items are being made.

Bank, Mr. Peanut, Coin Slot In Hat, Red Paint, 1950s, 10 In.		1610.00
Display, Woman Aviator, My These Planters Peanuts Are Delicious, Cardboard, 1940, 2 Piece		825.00
Doll, Wood, Jointed, Painted, Cameo, 1930s, 8 ½ In.	*illus*	224.00
Figure, Mr. Peanut, Spelter, Painted, White Marble Base, 13 ¼ In.		1220.00
Goblet, Champagne, Glass, Figural Mr. Peanut Stem, 5 ¾ In., 6 Piece		519.00
Jar, Clipper, Celluloid Label, Tin Lithograph Lid, Box, 1939, 8 x 10 x 5 ¼ In.		2320.00
Jar, Counter, Mr. Peanut Shape, Pink, 12 ¾ In.		275.00
Jar, Mr. Peanut, Orange Metal Snap-On Lid, 1940s, Unused, 8 Oz.		150.00
Jar, Planters Peanut Jumbo Block, Elephant, Peanut Man, Paper, Glass, c.1930, 10 x 8 In.		523.00
Puppet, Mr. Peanut, Rubber, Beige, Black Hat & Arms, Mark, 6 In.		995.00
Sign, WBZ Radio Station, Mac 'n' Moore, Cardboard, Boston, 14 ½ x 9 In.		632.00
Tin, Salt-In-Shell, Seaside Scene, 10 Lb., c.1920, 12 ¼ x 10 ¼ In.		907.00
Toy, Mr. Peanut, Walker, Plastic, Windup, Light Blue, Box, c.1950, 8 ½ In.		495.00
Wrapper, Gum Card, Big Game Peanut Blocks, Hunted Animals, 1933, 5 ¼ x 5 ¼ In.		575.00
Wrapper, Old Fashioned Peanut Candy, Lady Smiling, 10 Oz., 5 ½ x 10 ½ In.		608.00

PLASTIC objects of all types are being collected. Some pieces are listed in other categories; gutta-percha cases are listed in the Photography category. Celluloid is in its own category.

Airplane Propeller, Bakelite, Stamped, Westinghouse, Brass Center Bushing, 95 x 8 ½ In.		600.00
Butter Dish, Clear Top, Yellow Base, Blisscraft Plastic Co., Hollywood, Calif., 7 ½ In.		15.00
Candles, Battery Operated, Guzzini, Italy, Pre 1984, 9 & 10 ½ In.		30.00
Desk Organizer, Red ABS, Round, 4 Sections, Rino Pirovano, Rexite, Italy, c.1999, 5 x 5 In.		45.00
Dish Set, Red, Yellow, Copco, 6 Plates, 6 Side Plates, 6 Bowls, 1980s		120.00
Hair Comb, Pearlized, Openwork, Birds, Flowers, Scrollwork, 10 ¾ x 9 ½ In.		59.00
Hair Comb, Tortoiseshell, Openwork, Rhinestones, 9 ¾ x 7 In.		71.00
Ice Bucket, Dome Master, Nicholas Angelakos, Colony, 1970s, 10 x 8 In.		45.00
Ice Bucket, White Bowl, Amber Smoked Base, Clear Handle, 1970s, 13 x 10 In.		35.00
Napkin Holder, Teapot Shape, Yellow, Rogers Plastic Co., 4 ½ x 6 In.		15.00
Sugar & Creamer, Lucite, Minimalist, Sculptural, 1970s, 3 x 3 ½ x 2 ¾ In.		85.00

PLATED AMBERINA was patented June 15, 1886, by Joseph Locke and made by the New England Glass Company. It is similar in color to amberina, but is characterized by a cream colored or chartreuse lining (never white) and small ridges or ribs on the outside.

Sugar Bowl, Ribbed, Amber Handles, New England, 5 In.		8625.00
Syrup, Ribbed, Tufts Silver Plate, 6 In.	*illus*	8050.00
Toothpick, Oval, New England		10925.00

P

Tumbler, Ribbed, New England, 4 In.	1495.00 to 2588.00
Tumbler, Ribbed, New England, 5 In.	1955.00

PLIQUE-A-JOUR is an enameling process. The enamel is laid between thin raised metal lines and heated. The finished piece has transparent enamel held between the thin metal wires. It is different from cloisonne because it is translucent.

Vase, Baluster Shape, Multicolored Flowers, Celadon Ground, Metal Mounts, Japan, 7 In.	189.00
Vase, Bulbous, Tapered, Flowers, Dragonfly, Multicolor Glass, Japan, 3 ½ In. .... *illus*	960.00

POLITICAL memorabilia of all types, from buttons to banners, are collected. Items related to presidential candidates are the most popular, but collectors also search for material related to state and local offices. Memorabilia related to social causes, minor political parties, and protest movements are also included here. Many reproductions have been made. A jugate is a button with photographs of both the presidential and vice presidential candidates. In this list a button is round, usually with a straight pin or metal tab to secure it to a shirt. A pin is brass, often figural, sometimes attached to a ribbon.

Arm Band, Hoover, Common Sense, Cloth, 11 ½ In.	90.00
Ashtray, Barry Goldwater, 30th Annual Youth Banquet, Glass, 5 x 5 In.	45.00
Ax, Anti Carrie Nation, All Nations Welcome Except Carrie, Woman On Blade, 10 ½ In.	80.00
Badge, Anti-Saloon League, General Officer, Prohibition, Brass Bar Pin, Medallion, 2 ¾ In.	140.00
Badge, Doorkeeper, Democratic National Convention, Blue Ribbon, 1952, 1 ⅝ x 5 In.	45.00
Badge, McKinley, Roosevelt, Whistling Eagle, Mechanical, Brass, Jugate, 1900, 1 ½ x 1 ½ In.	748.00
Ballot, Sample, State Of Virginia, Sixth Congressional District, Parties Listed, 1948, 17 x 4 In.	7.50
Bandanna, Cleveland, Stevenson, Red, 1892, 18 x 19 In.	320.00
Bandanna, Garfield, Arthur, Grand National, Red, Frame, 1880, 25 x 24 In.	182.00
Bandanna, Garfield, Arthur, Oval Portraits, Red Ground, 1880, 19 x 20 ½ In.	297.00
Bandanna, George Washington, Portrait, Effect Of Principle, Cotton, Early 1800s, 11 ¼ In. Square	2242.00
Bandanna, Harrison, Morton, Silk, Blue, White, 1888, 9 ½ x 20 ½ In.	132.00
Bandanna, Hubert H. Humphrey, Blue H Design, Green Border, Autographed, 1968, 34 In.	30.00
Bandanna, Parker, Davis, Good Government For The People, 1904, 22 x 23 In.	396.00
Bandanna, Roosevelt, Fairbanks, Flags, Stars, Red, White, Blue, Cotton, 21 ½ x 23 ½ In.	333.00
Bandanna, Tilden, Hendricks, G. Washington Portrait, 1876	7170.00
Bandanna, Zachary Taylor, Military Symbols, Red, Sepia, 1848, 30 ¾ x 26 ½ In.	7000.00
Banner, Cultural Revolution, 2 Men, Text, Chinese, 49 x 72 In.	633.00
Banner, Cultural Revolution, 2 Men Walking, Text, Chinese, 82 x 38 In.	374.00
Banner, Cultural Revolution, Mao, Flag, Text, Chinese, 30 x 35 In.	259.00
Banner, George Washington, Horse, Liberty Bell, Red, White Field, c.1885, 25 x 17 In. .... *illus*	708.00
Banner, George Washington, Horse, Text, Red, White, Blue Stripe Ground, 18 x 28 In.	488.00
Banner, Grant, Colfax, Grand National Campaign, Currier & Ives, Frame, 1868, 17 x 22 In.	467.00
Banner, Happy Days Are Here Again, Full Beer Mug, c.1932, 96 In.	799.00
Banner, Henry Clay, Grand National Whig, Currier, Frame, 1844, 15 x 20 In.	429.00
Banner, Roosevelt-Fairbanks, Frame, 1904, 30 ¼ x 43 ¼ In.	1500.00
Banner, Son In The Service, Gold Fringe, Red, White & Blue, 5 x 9 In.	35.00
Bell, Ceramic, Votes For Women, Old & Young Women, 2-Sided, Clapper, 4 In.	995.00
Belt, Blaine, Logan, Gold Cloth, Metal Buckle, B & L, 1884, 2 ½ x 3 ½ In.	110.00
Belt, Hubert Humphrey, Sun, White, Blue, Green, Plastic Discs, Metal Chain	33.00
Bobbin' Head, Jack & Jackie Kennedy, Kissing, Magnetic, 1960s, 5 In., Pair	700.00
Booklet, Carter, Byrd & Rockefeller, 8 x 11 In.	6.50
Booklet, Goldwater Vs. American Labor, The Record, The Threat	4.00
Booklet, Here Are The Humphreys, Picture Of Couple, 45 Pages, 3 x 4 In.	5.00
Booklet, Negro People & The Soviet Union, Paul Robeson, 1950, 3 ½ x 5 In.	7.50
Booklet, The Path Of Negro Liberation, Benjamin Davis, 1946, 22 Pages	12.50
Bookmark, J.F.K., L.B.J., Pennsylvania Coattails, Paper, 2 ½ x 8 ½ In.	12.00
Bookmark, W.J. Bryan, Denver Democratic Convention, Aluminum, c.1908, 2 In. .... *illus*	108.00
Bottle, Robert Kennedy, Amber Glass, Psychedelic Paper Label, Cork Stopper, c.1968, 7 ¼ In.	173.00
Bowtie, Vote Humphrey, Muskie, Donkey, Red, Clip-On, 1968	35.00
Broadside, Jefferson Davis Speaker, Hospital Benefit, Kansas City, Sept 16, 1875, 6 x 9 In.	531.00
Broadside, Lincoln Memorial, We Mourn, Our Chief Has Fallen, 18 ½ x 23 ¼ In. .... *illus*	527.00
Bubble Pipe, Uncle Sam, Child In Navy Uniform Blowing Bubbles, 1900s, 4 Pipes In Box	175.00
Bubble Pipe, Uncle Sam, Spanish American War, Bisque, Box, 1900s, 4 ¼ x 7 In.	173.00
Bucket, Fire, Stephen Douglas, Little Giant, First Pumper Responder To Chicago Fire, 1871	1750.00
Bumper Plate, I Am A Dixiecrat, Aluminum, Blue Ground, c.1948, 4 In.	190.00
Bumper Plate, Landon For President, Die Cut Metal, Erickson, Des Moines, 5 ½ x 6 ¼ In.	139.00
Bumper Sticker, Nixon For Governor, Orange, Black, 7 ½ In.	7.50
Bust, General Grant, Plaster, Painted, Bernard Dreyfuss, c.1885, 17 In. .... *illus*	294.00

Plated Amberina, Syrup, Ribbed, Tufts Silver Plate, 6 In.
$8050.00

Plique-A-Jour, Vase, Bulbous, Tapered, Flowers, Dragonfly, Multicolor Glass, Japan, 3 ½ In.
$960.00

TIP

If your collectibles are caught in muddy water from a rainstorm, flood, or just an overflowing bathtub, rinse off the dirt with a gentle stream of clean running water or put one at a time, in a water-filled container and shake gently. Do not scrub; it will embed the dirt. Use a sponge or soft cloth to blot off mud or debris.

P

Political, Banner, George Washington, Horse, Liberty Bell, Red, White Field, c.1885, 25 x 17 In.
$708.00

Political, Bookmark, W.J. Bryan, Denver Democratic Convention, Aluminum, c.1908, 2 In.
$108.00

Bust, Teddy Roosevelt, Gold Paint, Iron, A.C. Williams, c.1919, 5 In.	175.00
Button, 100 Percent Americanism Union, 1 In.	11.00
Button, A Lady For Reagan, Blue, White, 2 In.	5.00
Button, A Used Ford Is Better Than A New Carter, Red, White, Blue, 3 In.	43.00
Button, Adlai Stevenson, Candid Photo, Black & Orange, Celluloid, 1950s, 6 In.	132.00
Button, Adlai Stevenson, I'm Madly For Adlai, U.S. Presidential Campaign, Celluloid, 1952, 2 1/8 In.	3424.00
Button, Adlai Stevenson, Vote Democratic, Photo, 7/8 In.	318.00
Button, Agnew, Black, Gray, 1 In.	4.50
Button, Agnew, Eagleton, Losers Society, Official Members, 2 In.	8.50
Button, Alf Landon Flying Over Capital, Land On Washington, 1936, 1 1/4 In.	3509.00
Button, Alf Landon, Giant Sunflower, Celluloid, 1936, 3 1/2 In.	1650.00
Button, Alfred E. Smith, For President, Attached Derby Hat, 3-D, Celluloid, Ribbon, 1 1/4 In.	115.00
Button, Alfred E. Smith For President, Portrait, 1 1/4 In.	31.00
Button, Alfred E. Smith, Our Governor, Next President, N.Y., 1928, 1 3/4 In.	1815.00
Button, Alton Parker, Celluloid, 1904, 3/4 In.	148.00
Button, Alton Parker, Flags, Celluloid, Frame, 1904, 1 3/4 In.	132.00
Button, Alton Parker, Jacksonian Party, Our Candidate, 1903, 1 1/4 In.	176.00
Button, American Liberty, Al Smith, Statue Of Liberty, Celluloid, 1 1/4 In.	3194.00
Button, Andrew Pulley, Socialist, Presidential Candidate, 1980, 1 In.	5.00
Button, Ann W. Richards, Democratic Convention, Keynote Speaker, 1998, 2 In.	6.50
Button, Anti Bryan, We Want A 100 Cent Dollar, 7/8 In.	35.00
Button, Anti Goldwater, In Your Guts You Know He's Nuts, Portrait, Celluloid, 3 1/2 In.	624.00
Button, Anti Goldwater, Mushroom Cloud, What, Me Worry, 1964, 2 1/8 In.	160.00 to 259.00
Button, Anti Goldwater, Periodic Table Symbols, Urinate On Goldwater, 1964, 1 1/2 In.	30.00
Button, Anti JFK, Just For Kinfolk, Capitol Building, 3 1/2 In.	39.00
Button, Anti JFK, Member, Sons Of Business Society, Dog, Doghouse, Black, White, 1 1/2 In.	33.00
Button, Archie Bunker, For President, I'm A Dingbat, Lithograph, 1 1/4 In.	7.00
Button, Ax, Carrie Nation Temperance Symbol, Nation On Head, 3 In.	28.00
Button, Benjamin Harrison, Color, Bastien Bros., Back Paper, 1890s, 7/8 In.	120.00
Button, Benjamin Harrison, Protection, Lithograph, Raised Dome, 1892, 1 1/4 In.	201.00
Button, Bill Clinton, I'm An Arkansas Traveler, Red, Blue, 1 3/4 In.	177.00
Button, Bill Gray, 1992 Hopeful, 1 3/4 In.	3.50
Button, Blaine, Logan, Horseshoe, Brass Shell, Cardboard Photos, Jugate, 1884, 1 1/4 In.	173.00
Button, Bobby Kennedy, Red, White, 1968, 3 1/2 In.	466.00
Button, Bobby Kennedy, Yeah, Yeah, Yeah, Celluloid, 1968, 3 1/2 In.	33.00
Button, Bryan, 16 To 1 O'Clock, Baltimore Badge, Back Paper, 1 1/4 In.	446.00
Button, Bryan, Clean Streets, Honest Government, Whitehead & Hoag Back Paper, 1 1/4 In.	60.00
Button, Bryan, Dewey, Democratic Clubs, Jugate, 1900, 1 1/4 In.	34.00
Button, Bryan, Enemies Of Special Privilege, 5 Portraits, Celluloid, 1 3/4 In.	948.00
Button, Bryan, My Hobby A Winner, Child Attire, Riding Hobby Horse, Color, 1900, 2 1/8 In.	7103.00
Button, Bryan Over McKinley, Total Eclipse, Nov. 6, Color, c.1900, 1 1/2 In.	7475.00
Button, Bryan, Photo, Red, White, Blue Bands, 1908, 1 1/4 In.	50.00
Button, Bryan, Sewall, Celluloid, Jugate, 1 1/4 In.	128.00
Button, Bryan, Sewall, Cheshire Imprint, Jugate, 1896, 1 1/2 In.	389.00
Button, Bryan, Stars, Bastian Paper, Graphic, c.1908, 1 1/4 In.	173.00
Button, Bryan, Stevenson, Bow, Celluloid, Jugate, Whitehead & Hoag Back Paper, 1900, 1 1/4 In.	30.00
Button, Bryan, Stevenson, Stand By The Republic, Jugate, Rock Island, Ill., 1900, 1 1/4 In.	5676.00
Button, Bryan, Watson, Populist, Jugate, 1896, 7/8 In.	165.00
Button, Buffalo Nine, Right On, Draft Resisters, 1968, 2 1/4 In.	253.00
Button, Cajuns For Reagan, Yellow, 1980s, 1 3/4 In.	11.00
Button, Cale Boggs, Delaware, U.S. Senate, Lithograph, 3/4 In.	11.00
Button, Calvin Coolidge, Black & White Lithograph, 1 In.	20.00
Button, Carter Harrison For President, Chicago Mayor, Photograph, 1904, 1 1/4 In.	389.00
Button, Carter, I'm For Full Employment, 1976, 1 1/4 In.	5.50
Button, Carter, Mondale, Binghamton, New York, Coattail, Blue, 1980, 1 3/4 In.	443.00
Button, Carter, Mondale, Minnesota Map, 1976, 2 1/4 In.	13.00
Button, Chelsea Clinton, Asking America To Vote For Her Daddy, 2 1/4 In.	528.00
Button, Chelsea Clinton, Vote For My Daddy, Chelsea Photo, Celluloid, 1992, 2 1/4 In.	394.00
Button, Citizens For Eisenhower, Let's Back Ike, Vote For Ferguson, Coattail, 1954, 3 1/2 In.	875.00
Button, Clinton, Arkansas Governor, 1990, 3, In.	101.00
Button, Clinton, University Of Va., Young Democrats, 4 Photographs, Celluloid, Red, Blue, 3 In.	130.00
Button, Clothing, Protesting Stamp Act, Metal, 1766	8963.00
Button, Coolidge, Dawes, Jugate, 1924, 1 3/4 In.	1500.00
Button, Coolidge, Dawes, Red, White, Blue, Cello, 1924, 1 In.	30.00
Button, Cox, Peace Progress Prosperity, 1920, 3/4 In.	177.00
Button, Cox, Photo, 1920, 1 1/4 In.	288.00

P

Button, Cox, Roosevelt, Red, Blue, Coshocton Back Paper, ¾ In.	154.00
Button, Davis, Bryan, Jugate, 1924, 1 ¼ In.	8963.00
Button, Davis, Nelson, Coattail, Jugate, 1924, ⅞ In.	1554.00
Button, Debs For President, Portrait, 1912, ⅞ In.	120.00
Button, Debs, Seidel, Sepia, Jugate, 1912, ⅞ In.	218.00
Button, Debs, Seidel, Socialist Party, Oval, Sepia, 1912, 1 ⅛ In.	429.00
Button, Democrat For Nixon, Lodge, Lithograph, 1 In.	5.50
Button, Dewey, Bricker, Celluloid, 1 In.	15.00
Button, Dewey, Race To Independence, Celluloid, ⅞ In.	15.00
Button, Dianne For Mayor, Dianne Feinstein, 1978 San Francisco Race, 2 ¼ In.	157.00
Button, Dick Gregory For President, Day-Glo Pink, 1 ¼ In.	5.50
Button, Dole, Kemp, 15 Percent Tax Cut, Jugate, 1996, 3 ½ In.	11.00
Button, Don't Blame Me I Voted For Ford, Pink, Black, Blue, 2 ¼ In.	24.00
Button, Draft Dewey, White, Blue, 1 In.	17.00
Button, Drunken Sailors For Reagan, Blue, White Stars, Celluloid, 2 ¼ In.	50.00
Button, Dukakis, Boston Red Sox, Winners In 1988, Photograph, 2 ¼ In.	11.00
Button, Dukakis For President, Novello For Commissioner, Coattail, 1 ¼ In.	6.50
Button, Dump Nixon, AFL/CIO, 1 ¾ In.	5.50
Button, Eisenhower, Inaugural Committee, Working Press, 3 ½ In.	115.00
Button, Eisenhower, Woman Power For Victory, 1 ½ In. ....*illus*	139.00
Button, Eldrige Cleaver For President, 1 ¼ In.	5.50
Button, Elect Earl K. Long Governor, Louisiana, c.1955, ⅞ In.	83.00
Button, End The War Now, Anti Vietnam, April 15, 1967, Green, Blue, 2 ½ In.	40.00
Button, Eugene McCarthy, Crown Of People, Celluloid, 1968, 2 ½ In.	132.00
Button, Eugene McCarthy, Embroidery, Flowers, White Ground, 1968, 3 In.	1331.00
Button, Eugene McCarthy, Me Tarzan, Eugene, 1976, 1 In.	30.00
Button, Eugene McCarthy, Portrait, Metal Back, Bar Pin, 1968, 2 ¼ In.	221.00
Button, FDR, Carry On With Roosevelt, 1 In.	9.00
Button, FDR, For President, 1 ¼ In.	50.00
Button, FDR, Garner, Stars, Stripes, Jugate, 1 ¼ In.	23.00
Button, FDR, Photograph, Red, White, Blue Edge, 3 ½ In.	66.00
Button, FDR, Profile, Sepia, Bronx Back Paper, 1 ¾ In.	264.00
Button, FDR, Roosevelt, White, Blue Letter, Red Edge, Celluloid, 1 In.	40.00
Button, FDR, Willkie For Millionaires, Roosevelt For The Millions, Cream, Red, 1 ¼ In.	33.00
Button, Fifth Avenue Parade, Sick Of The War, Vietnam Protest, c.1968, 1 ½ In.	28.00
Button, For The Love Of Ike, Vote Republican, Red, White, Blue, Celluloid, 6 In.	47.00
Button, Ford, Dole, Celluloid, 1976, 9 In.	22.00
Button, Ford, Dole, Photograph, Jugate, 1976, 1 ¼ In.	28.00
Button, Ford, Dole, Republican, 1976, 1 In.	7.50
Button, Ford, Dole, White, Red, Black, Jugate, 2 ¼ In.	50.00
Button, Ford Family Making Us Proud Again, 1976, Picture Of Betty & Sons, 2 ¼ In.	239.00
Button, Ford, Keep A Good Guy President, Black & White, 1976, 2 ¼ In.	83.00
Button, Franklin Roosevelt, Sweeping The Depression Out, 1 ¼ In.	101.00
Button, Franklin Roosevelt, Truman, Sepia, Celluloid, 1944, 1 In.	221.00
Button, Franklin Roosevelt, Wallace, Ear Of Corn, 1940, 1 In.	6.50
Button, Fred Harris For President, Blue, White, 1976, 1 ¼ In.	4.50
Button, Frederick Douglass, Emancipation Exposition, 1913, ⅞ In. ....*illus*	281.00
Button, Freedom Ride, CORE, Civil Rights, Black, White, 1960s, 1 ¼ In.	34.00
Button, George Bush, For President, U.S. Map, Photograph, 1988, 2 ¼ In.	8.00
Button, George Bush, Texas, U.S. Senate, 1970, 1 ¼ In.	132.00
Button, George H.W. Bush, David Duke, Do The White Thing, '92, 1 ¾ In.	5.00
Button, George Wallace, Champion For States Rights, Cream, Green, 2 ¼ In.	419.00
Button, George Washington, Inaugural, Brass, 1789, 1 ⁵⁄₁₆ In.	4740.00
Button, Gerald Ford In 76, Black & White, 2 ¼ In.	66.00
Button, Get Out Of Vietnam, International Days Of Protest, Globe, Blue, Black, c.1969, 2 ¾ In.	91.00
Button, Goldwater, Glasses, Gold, 1 ½ In.	23.00
Button, Goldwater, Miller, A Choice Not An Echo, Red, White, Blue, Celluloid, Photo, 3 In.	24.00
Button, Goldwater Portrait, Blue, Gold, 1964, 1 ½ In.	7.00
Button, Gore, Ted Kennedy, Massachusetts, Coattail, 2001, 1 ¾ In.	17.00
Button, Greenwich For Nixon, Lodge, 3 In.	432.00
Button, Harding, Coolidge, Jugate, 1920, ⅞ In.	1300.00
Button, Harding, Coolidge, RWB Lithography, J.L. Lynch, ⅞ In.	30.00
Button, Harding Pacific Coast Tour, Portrait, Flags, Celluloid, 1923, 1 ¼ In.	879.00
Button, Harriman For Me, Photograph, Governer, New York, 1 ¾ In.	52.00
Button, Harriman Is The Man, Photograph, Lithograph, 1 ⅝ In.	11.00
Button, Harry S. Truman For President, Photograph, 2 ½ In.	120.00

Political, Broadside, Lincoln Memorial, We Mourn, Our Chief Has Fallen, 18 ½ x 23 ¼ In.
$527.00

Political, Bust, General Grant, Plaster, Painted, Bernard Dreyfuss, c.1885, 17 In.
$294.00

Political, Button, Eisenhower, Woman Power For Victory, 1 ½ In.
$139.00

P

Political, Button, Frederick Douglass, Emancipation Exposition, 1913, ⅞ In. $281.00

Political, Button, Hoo But Hoover, Poppy, A.G. Trimble, Back Paper, ⅞ In. $2507.00

Button, Harry S. Truman For President, Portrait, 1 ¼ In.	440.00
Button, Harry S. Truman, Our President, Portrait, 1 ½ In.	33.00
Button, Harry S. Truman, Sepia, 2 ¼ In.	66.00
Button, Harry Truman, Flags, 9 In.	510.00
Button, Harry Truman, Our President, Seated At Desk, Celluloid, 3 In.	660.00
Button, Herbert Hoover For President, Whitehead & Hoag Back Paper, ⅞ In.	30.00
Button, Herbert Hoover, Portrait, Whitehead & Hoag Back Paper, 1 In.	89.00
Button, Hillary Clinton As Wicked Witch, On Yellow Brick Road To White House, 3 In.	19.00
Button, Honest Days With Davis, Oppenheimer & Shah Back Paper, 1924, ⅞ In.	1771.00
Button, Hoo But Hoover, Poppy, A.G. Trimble, Back Paper, ⅞ In. .... *illus*	2507.00
Button, Hoover For President, Sepia, Lithograph, Green Duck, 1928, ⅞ In.	83.00
Button, Housewives For Ike, Red, White, Blue, Celluloid, 2 ½ In.	139.00
Button, Huey Long, Every Man A King, Long Back Paper, ⅝ In.	120.00
Button, Hughes Alliances, 1916, ⅞ In.	20.00
Button, Hughes, Fairbanks, Stars, Stripes, 1916, ⅞ In.	24.00
Button, Humphrey For President, Red, White, Blue Border, 1 ¾ In.	5.00
Button, Humphrey, Muskie, Eagle, Black, White, Jugate, 1968, 1 ¼ In.	26.00
Button, Humphrey, My Man, Wobble Eyes, Drawing, 1968, 3 ½ In.	167.00
Button, Huntington For Davis, Red, White, Blue, Whitehead & Hoag, 1924, 4 In.	4392.00
Button, I Am A Watergate Bug, 2 In.	10.00
Button, I Like Ike, 1 In.	11.00
Button, I Like Ike, Everybody Loves Food Mart, Celluloid, 1950s, 1 ¼ In.	254.00
Button, I Like Ike, Flasher, Pictorial Productions, 2 ½ In.	25.00
Button, I Told You So, Richard Nixon, U.S. Capitol Photo, 1960, 3 ½ In.	396.00
Button, I Want To Be A Captain Too, Anti FDR, Red, White, 1 In.	7.50
Button, I Won't Live With Jim Crow, Civil Rights Congress, Green Duck Co., 1 In.	248.00
Button, If I Were 21 I'd Vote For Bobby Kennedy, 3 ½ In.	11.00
Button, Ike & Dick, Photo, Celluloid, 3 ½ In.	35.00
Button, Ike, If We Ever Needed Him We Need Him Now, Music Notes, Blue, Gold, 1 ½ In.	23.00
Button, Jack Kennedy, USA Map, 1 In.	22.00
Button, James Cox For President, Portrait, 1920, 6 In.	7768.00
Button, James Garfield, Eagle, 4 Flags, Gilt, 1881, 1 ¼ In.	895.00
Button, Jesse Helms, Give 'Em Helms, S. Carolina, Red, White, Blue, 1 ¼ In.	11.00
Button, JFK For President, Blue, White Tab, 1 In.	12.00
Button, JFK, Young Democrat Club Of America, Photograph, White, Blue, 1 ¾ In.	33.00
Button, Jimmy Carter For President In 76, Mirror, Portrait, 2 ¼ In.	440.00
Button, Jimmy Carter In 76, Celluloid, 1 ¼ In.	6.00
Button, Joe & I For Willkie, Joe Louis Portrait, 1940, 1 ¼ In.	660.00
Button, John Davis, Clarksburg, West Virginia, 2 ¼ In.	3800.00
Button, John F. Kennedy, 1960, 3 ½ In.	2300.00
Button, John W. Davis, 1924, 4 In.	6050.00
Button, Johnson, Humphrey, Scientists, Engineers, 1 ½ In.	5.50
Button, Johnson, Portrait, Ladies For Johnson, Celluloid, 1964, 3 In.	264.00
Button, Kennedy, Our Next President, Bug Eyes, 4 In.	248.00
Button, Kennedy, Red, White, Blue, 1 ¼ In.	7.50
Button, Kentucky For Willkie, Member, Lithograph, Red, White, Blue, 1 In.	3.50
Button, Kerry, Edwards, Obama, McHugh, Mercer County Irish Americans, 2004, 1 ½ In.	30.00
Button, Kerry, Obama, Let's KO Bush, Lake County Federation Of Teachers, Illinois, 2004, 1 ⅞ In.	168.00
Button, Kerry, Obama Winning Team, Illinois Coattail, 2004, 2 ¼ In.	152.00
Button, Kucinich, Ben & Jerry Support Dennis Kucinich, 2 Men, Roses, 2 ¼ In.	91.00
Button, Kusek For Congress, Portrait, Eye Patch, Illinois, Lithograph, 1958, 1 ⅜ In.	11.00
Button, La Follette For President, Progressive Party, St. Louis Button Back Paper, 1924, ¾ In.	358.00
Button, La Follette, To Win, Photo, Sepia, Hyatt Mfg. Back Paper, 1912, ⅞ In.	484.00
Button, La Follette, Wheeler, People's Choice, 1924 Presidential Race, ⅞ In.	341.00
Button, Landon, Sunflower, Photo, Plastic, ⅞ In.	15.00
Button, LBJ, Crocodile Tears, 6 In.	372.00
Button, LBJ, Fred Harris, Lithograph, Oklahoma, Coattail, 1 In.	2.00
Button, LBJ, Let's Back Johnson For President, Photograph, 2 ¼ In.	26.00
Button, Let's All Register To Vote, Lithograph, 1 In.	3.00
Button, Let's Back Ike, Lithograph, Red, White, Blue, 4 In.	17.00
Button, Levering, Johnson, Prohibition, Jugate, Stud, 1896, ⅞ In.	607.00
Button, Levi P. Morton, New York, Celluloid, Tab, c.1895, ⅞ In.	22.00
Button, Lincoln, Albumen Photo, Under Glass, Sepia, Brass Rim, Black Onyx Stones, ⅝ In.	1000.00
Button, Lincoln, Eisenhower, Nixon, Centennial, 1st Republican Presidential Race, 1956, 1 ¼ In.	365.00
Button, Lyndon Johnson, George Miller, California Coattail, Celluloid, 1964, 2 ½ In.	244.00
Button, Make Love, Not War, Vietnam Protest, Embracing Couple, 3 In.	115.00

Button, March On Washington For Jobs & Freedom, Black, White, 1963, 2 ¼ In.	75.00
Button, Martin Luther King, Drum Major For Peace, 1992, 2 ¼ In.	28.00
Button, Martin Luther King Jr., Keep The Dream Alive, 1988, 3 In.	7.50
Button, McCain, Palin, Multicolored, Jugate, 2008, 2 ¼ In.	28.00
Button, McGovern, Hugh Carey, IVI, Coattail, Green, White, 1972, 1 ½ In.	6.00
Button, McGovern, KMA, Kiss My Ass, Yellow, Black, 1 ¾ In.	21.00
Button, McGovern, Peace Dove, Stars, 1972, 1 ½ In.	21.00
Button, McGovern, Peter Max Style, 1972, 1 ½ In.	337.00
Button, McGovern, Shriver, Green, Photographs, Jugate, 1972, 2 ¼ In.	40.00
Button, McGovern, Shriver, Stripes, Stars, Jugate, D. Russell, 1972, 3 In.	436.00
Button, McGovern, Shriver, Vote Liberal, 1972, 1 ½ In.	318.00
Button, McKinley, Dinner Bucket, Jugate, 1900, ⅞ In.	94.00
Button, McKinley, Dinner Pail Rebus, National Equipment Co., 1900, 1 ¼ In.	190.00
Button, McKinley, Eclipse, 1900, 1 ¼ In.	1800.00
Button, McKinley, Gold & Prosperity, 1896, ⅞ In.	34.00
Button, McKinley, Hobart, National Wheelmen's Club, Jugate, 1896, 1900, 1 ¼ In.	160.00
Button, McKinley, In Gold We Trust, 1896, ⅞ In.	33.00
Button, McKinley, Mechanical Flag, ⅞ In.	99.00
Button, McKinley, Money We Want, Lady Liberty Profile, ⅞ In.	107.00
Button, McKinley, National Wheelmen's Club, National Mfg., Back Paper, 1 ¼ In.	396.00
Button, McKinley, Portrait, Flag, Celluloid, 1 ¼ In.	28.00
Button, McKinley, Roosevelt, Easel Back, Celluloid, Jugate, c.1900, 4 In.	696.00
Button, McKinley, Roosevelt, Uncle Sam On Bike, Portraits In Wheel, Pacific Regalia, 1 ¼ In.	8250.00
Button, McKinley, Sepia, ⅞ In.	26.00
Button, McKinley, T.R. Roosevelt, Dinner Bucket, Prosperity, Jugate, Whitehead & Hoag, 1 ¼ In.	73.00
Button, McKinley, T.R. Roosevelt, Jugate, 1 ½ In.	12.00
Button, McKinley, T.R. Roosevelt, Jugate, Baldwin & Gleason, Back Paper, 1 ½ In.	288.00
Button, McKinley, T.R. Roosevelt, My Choice, Sepia, Jugate, 1900, 1 ¼ In.	297.00
Button, McKinley, Whitehead & Hoag Back Paper, ⅞ In.	23.00
Button, Mondale, Another Jackass Off & Running, He-Haw, Celluloid, 1984, 3 ½ In.	216.00
Button, Mondale, Ferraro, Bradley, Lithograph, 1 ½ In.	2.00
Button, Mondale Victory Party, Official Host, Stars, Bunting, Celluloid, 1984, 3 In.	330.00
Button, NAACP Membership, 1967, ⅞ In.	17.00
Button, Nixon & Spiro, Zero, 1968, Black, Orange, 1 ¾ In.	7.50
Button, Nixon, Agnew, 1968, 1 ½ In.	5.00
Button, Nixon, Agnew, Eagle, Black, White, Jugate, 1968, 1 ¼ In.	51.00
Button, Nixon, Agnew, White, Black, 2 ⅛ In.	8.00
Button, Nixon, Bagwell For Nixon, Michigan, Blue, White, Celluloid, 3 ½ In.	363.00
Button, Nixon Bugs Me, Watergate, White, Blue, 1 ¼ In.	23.00
Button, Nixon For President, Photo, Celluloid, Pinback & Easel, 6 In.	30.00
Button, Nixon, Grass Rooters For Dick, 1960, 3 ½ In.	22.00
Button, Nixon, Lodge, Experience Counts, Photographs, Jugate, 1960, 2 ½ In.	220.00
Button, Nixon, Texas, Lithograph, 1 In.	5.00
Button, Obama For Congress, Democrat, 2000	621.00
Button, Obama For State Senate, Blue, White, Celluloid, Forest Printing, Ill., 2 ¼ In.	888.00
Button, Oklahoma Needs Nixon-Agnew, Photo, Celluloid, Blue On White, 1 ½ In.	6.00
Button, Parker, Bunting, Portrait, 1904, 1 ¼ In.	257.00
Button, Parker, Davis, Celluloid, Jugate, Pulver Back Paper, 1904, 1 ¼ In.	1207.00
Button, Parker, Davis, Flag, Jugate, 1904, 1 ¼ In.	360.00
Button, Parker, Davis, Flags, Bunting, Jugate, 1 ¼ In.	448.00
Button, Parker, Davis, Lady Liberty, Jugate, ⅞ In.	120.00
Button, Parker, Davis, Lady Liberty, Whitehead & Hoag Paper, 1904, 1 ¼ In.	270.00
Button, Parker, Davis, White Elephant, Anti Teddy Roosevelt, White Elephant Paper, 1904, 1 ½ In.	533.00
Button, Parker, Flag Bunting, Pulver Back Paper, ⅞ In.	33.00
Button, Parker, Portrait, White House, Baltimore Badge Back Paper, 1904, ⅞ In.	138.00
Button, Parker, Sepia, Celluloid, Frame, 1 ¾ In.	55.00
Button, Parker, Uncle Sam's White Elephant, Red, White, Blue, 1904, 1 ½ In.	484.00
Button, Paul Wellstone, Minnesota Liberal Democrat, 2000, 1 ¾ In.	19.00
Button, Pershing For President, General's Portrait, Shapiro & Karr Back Paper, 1 ¼ In.	580.00
Button, Re-Elect Jim Ryun, U.S. Congress, Kansas, c.2000, 2 ¾ In.	111.00
Button, Reagan, Bush, Delaware County Pa., Jugate, 1984, 3 ½ In.	13.00
Button, Reagan, Bush, Mountain High, 1980, 1 ¼ In.	10.00
Button, Reagan, Cowboy Hat, Utah For Reagan, State Republican Convention, Celluloid, 1980, 3 In. .	242.00
Button, Reagan, Smiling, Photograph, 1980s, 2 ¼ In.	12.00
Button, Reagan, Tired Of Losing, Run Ron, 66, 3 In.	325.00
Button, Republicans For McGovern & Eagleton, White, Blue, 1972, ⅞ In.	17.00

Political, Button, Theodore Roosevelt, Coattail, Hand Of Cards, Trigate, c.1904, 1 ¼ In. $144.00

Political, Button, Votes For Women, Golden Sunburst, c.1915, ⅞ In. $86.00

Political, Button, Wilson, U.S.-Mexico Crisis, Salute Or I Shoot, c.1914, 1 ¼ In. $557.00

P

Political, Handkerchief,
Washington Memorial, Copper Engraved,
c.1800, 19 x 20 In.
$2106.00

Political, Nodder, Viva Castro, In Toilet,
Composition, Painted, Foil Sticker,
1960s, 5 In.
$329.00

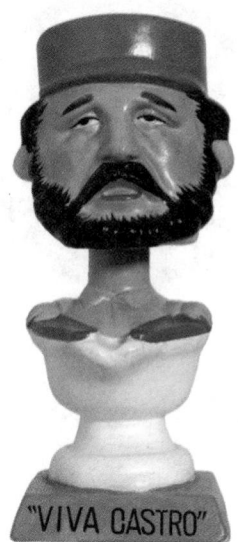

"VIVA CASTRO"

Button, Ribbon, Inauguration Day, I Like Ike & Dick, Jugate, 1957, 3 ½ In.	115.00
Button, Ribbon, Kennedy, It's Great To Be A Democrat, Red, White, 2 ¼ In.	185.00
Button, Ribbon, Kennedy, Our President, Inauguration, Berks County, Green, Cream, 2 ¼ In.	303.00
Button, Ribbon, McKinley, Photo, Flag Ribbon, Whitehead & Hoag Back Paper, 1 ¼ In.	75.00
Button, Ribbon, Wilson, Teacher, President, North Dakota Education Association, 1 ¼ In.	1026.00
Button, Robert Kennedy, Martin L. King, Black, White, 1968, 1 ½ In.	367.00
Button, Robert Kennedy, On To Chicago, Red Arrow, 1968, 1 In.	79.00
Button, Robin McGovern, George Dressed As Robin Hood, Celluloid, 1972, 4 In.	303.00
Button, Rock Against Reagan, 1983-84, 1 ¾ In.	7.50
Button, Rocky '68, Blue, White, 1 ¼ In.	5.50
Button, Rod Blagojevich, Congress, Illinois, Red, White, Blue, 1996, 1 ¾ In.	17.00
Button, Roemer Of LA, Louisana, 1992 Hopeful, 1 ¾ In.	3.50
Button, Ronald Reagan Loves Texas, Photo, Heart Shape, 2 ¾ In.	19.00
Button, Roosevelt, Fairbanks, Eagle & Shield, Jugate, 1904, 1 ¼ In.	783.00
Button, Roosevelt, Fairbanks, Home Trust, Lady Liberty, Ribbon, Yellow, Back Paper, 1904, 1 ¼ In.	726.00
Button, Roosevelt For Ex President, Anti FDR, Red, White, Blue, 1 In.	5.50
Button, Roosevelt, Garner, Black, White, Jugate, Bastian Brothers Imprint, 1932, ⅞ In.	155.00
Button, Santa, White Power, White Ground, Red, Green, 1960s, 1 ½ In.	115.00
Button, Shirley Chisolm For President, 1972, 1 ½ In.	5.00 to 17.00
Button, Sign For Stevenson, Celluloid, 1950s, 6 In.	48.00
Button, Smith, Photo, Flags, Roehn Back Paper, 1928, ⅞ In.	266.00
Button, Smith, Separate Derby Pin, Bespeckled Profile, Metal, 1928, ¾ In.	91.00
Button, South Carolina Needs Nixon-Agnew, Photo, Celluloid, Blue On White, 1 ½ In.	6.00
Button, Spiro Agnew, The Spiro Of '76?, Black, Red, ⁷⁄₁₆ In.	5.00
Button, Stevenson, Flasher, All The Way With Adlai, Image Moves, 1950s, 2 ½ In.	30.00
Button, Stevenson, For Governor, For You, 1 In.	18.00
Button, Stevenson, Kefauver, Black, White Lithograph, 1956, 1 In.	4.50
Button, Stevenson, Kennedy The Winning Team, Celluloid, 1956, 2 ¾ In.	3894.00
Button, Stevenson, Peace Progress, Prosperity, Photo, Red, White, Blue, 1 ¾ In.	174.00
Button, Stevenson, Wisconsin Map, White, Blue, 1 In.	22.00
Button, Stop The War Now, Vietnam, 3 ½ In.	17.00
Button, Suffrage Means Prohibition, Blue, Gold, ⅝ In.	775.00
Button, Support Phase III, Dump Nixon, 1 ¾ In.	6.50
Button, Taft, Bryan, March To Washington, Cartoon, 1908, 1 ¼ In., Pair	1600.00
Button, Taft, Clothiers Industry, Our Craft Is For Taft, Celluloid, Photo, 4 In.	353.00
Button, Taft, I Am For Playgrounds, Photo, Meyer Back Paper, ⅞ In.	360.00
Button, Taft, Red, White, Blue, Border, 1 In.	40.00
Button, Taft, Sherman, Celluloid, W.F. Miller Back Paper, Jugate, 1 ¼ In.	1452.00
Button, Taft, Sherman, Eagle, Bunting, Jugate, 1908, 1 ¼ In.	327.00
Button, Taft, Sherman, Red, Gold, Jugate, 1908, 1 ¼ In.	89.00
Button, Taft, Sherman, Seated Miss Liberty, Jugate	7768.00
Button, Taft, Sherman, Shield, Jugate, 1 ¼ In.	48.00
Button, Teddy Roosevelt & Robert Hitt, Our Choice, Jugate, 1904, 2 ⅛ In.	3006.00
Button, Teddy Roosevelt, 5 Aces, Stand Pat, 1 ¼ In.	275.00
Button, Teddy Roosevelt, 5 Aces, Stand Pat, ⅞ In.	320.00
Button, Teddy Roosevelt, Booker T. Washington, Equality, 1 ¼ In.	6871.00
Button, Teddy Roosevelt, Colonel, Rough Rider, National Equipment Back Paper, ⅞ In.	69.00
Button, Teddy Roosevelt, Fairbanks, Flag, Eagle, Jugate, Whitehead & Hoag, 1904, 1 ¼ In.	199.00
Button, Teddy Roosevelt, Fairbanks, Flag, Jugate, International Badge, 1904, 1 ¼ In.	1716.00
Button, Teddy Roosevelt, Fairbanks, Flag, Jugate, Pulver Back Paper, ⅞ In.	103.00
Button, Teddy Roosevelt, Fairbanks, Railroadmen's, Indianapolis, Whitehead & Hoag, 1 ¾ In.	967.00
Button, Teddy Roosevelt, Horseback, San Juan, 1904, 1 ¼ In.	806.00
Button, Teddy Roosevelt, L.A. Mantel & Tile Co., 1 ¼ In.	516.00
Button, Teddy Roosevelt, Labor Capital, Equal Protection, 1 ¼ In.	8063.00
Button, Teddy Roosevelt, Our Teddy Never Pulls Leather, Bucking Horse, 1 ¼ In.	2514.00
Button, Teddy Roosevelt, Progressive 1916 & Victory, 1 ¼ In.	3920.00
Button, Teddy Roosevelt, Rose, Ribbon Velt, Multicolored, 1 ¼ In.	160.00
Button, Teddy Roosevelt, Rose, Velt, Back Paper, ⅞ In.	1119.00
Button, Teddy Roosevelt, Rough Rider, Teddy In Uniform, Celluloid, 1900, 1 ¼ In.	477.00
Button, Teddy Roosevelt, Rough Rider Uniform, Sepia, Florsheim Back Paper, 1 ¼ In.	639.00
Button, Teddy Roosevelt, Rough Rider, Whitehead & Hoag Back Paper, 1 ¼ In.	737.00
Button, Teddy Roosevelt, Square Deal, L Square, Portrait, 1912	11950.00
Button, Teddy Roosevelt, The American, Sepia, Pilgrim Back Paper, ⅞ In.	109.00
Button, Temperance Day, Prohibition, Fountain, ⅞ In.	17.00
Button, The Beaver For President, c.1960, 1 ½ In.	7.00
Button, Theodore Roosevelt, Brown, White, 1 ¼ In.	75.00

Button, Theodore Roosevelt, Coattail, Hand Of Cards, Trigate, c.1904, 1 ¼ In. ....*illus*	144.00
Button, Theodore Roosevelt, Eagle, Shield, Whitehead & Hoag, Back Paper, 1 ¼ In.	55.00
Button, Theodore Roosevelt, Fairbanks, Lady Liberty, Jugate, Whitehead & Hoag Back Paper, 1 ¼ In. .	220.00
Button, Theodore Roosevelt, Horseback, San Juan Hill, 1904, 1 ¼ In.	330.00
Button, Theodore Roosevelt, Horseshoe, Flag, Wm. Hartman, Ohio, 1904, 1 ¼ In.	1515.00
Button, Theodore Roosevelt, Portrait, Preparedness, 1916, ⅞ In.	220.00
Button, Theodore Roosevelt, Portrait, Star Border, ⅞ In.	44.00
Button, Theodore Roosevelt, Rough Rider, Celluloid, 1900, 1 ¼ In.	477.00
Button, Theodore Roosevelt, Rough Rider Uniform, Domed, Celluloid, Tin Frame, c.1894, 1 ¼ In.	288.00
Button, Theodore Roosevelt, Rough Rider Uniform, Whitehead & Hoag Back Paper, 2 ⅛ In. ..	1667.00
Button, Theodore Roosevelt, Sepia, Celluloid, Metal Frame, No Pin, 4 In.	215.00
Button, Theodore Roosevelt, Victory, Portrait, Flags, Zig Zag Paper, ⅞ In.	107.00
Button, Theodore Roosevelt, Welcome Home From Africa, 1910, 1 ¼ In.	2200.00
Button, Thomas E. Dewey For President, Photo, Union Bug On Rim, 3 ½ In.	32.00
Button, Tom Dewey, 1 ¾ In.	8.00
Button, Truman, Barkley, Inauguration, Midwest Badge Co., Jugate, 1949, 1 ¾ In.	816.00
Button, Truman, Barkley, Jugate, 1948, ⅞ In.	445.00
Button, UAW For Kerry, 2004, 3 In.	4.00
Button, Uncle Sam Marching With Miss Liberty, c.1916, 1 ¾ In.	145.00
Button, U.S. For Ike, Philadelphia Badge Co., 9 In.	112.00
Button, Veteran For Nixon, Lodge, Celluloid, Red, White & Blue, 1960, ⅞ In.	8.00
Button, Veterans For Nixon, Lodge, Red, White, Blue, Lithograph, 1 In.	4.50
Button, Vietnam Veteran For Nixon, 2 ¼ In.	88.00
Button, Vietnam War, Indochina, Peace, Amnesty, America, Black, White, 6 In.	125.00
Button, Vote Al Gore Sr., Picture, Text, Vari-Vue Flasher, c.1950, 2 ½ In.	177.00
Button, Vote Gladly For Adlai, Blue, White, Lithograph, 1 In.	23.00
Button, Vote Republican, Nixon, Lodge, Jugate, 1960, 2 ⅛ In.	1650.00
Button, Vote Republican Today, I Like Ike, Ribbon, Yellow, 2 ¼ In., 6-In. Ribbon.	215.00
Button, Vote Truman For President, Portrait, Celluloid, 3 ½ In.	1513.00
Button, Votes For Women, Connecticut Women's Suffrage Association, CWSA, 1 ¼ In.	543.00
Button, Votes For Women, Golden Sunburst, c.1915, ⅞ In. ....*illus*	86.00
Button, Votes For Women, Green, Black, White, Gold, 1 In.	375.00
Button, Votes For Women, Woman, Bugle, Flag, 6 Stars, W.P.U., Clarion, 1 ¼ In.	875.00
Button, Votes For Women, Woman, Bugle, Flag, 11 Stars, W.P.U., Celluloid, 1 ¼ In.	841.00
Button, Wallace, LeMay, Black, White, 1 ¼ In.	5.00
Button, Walter Mondale, 2 ¼ In.	83.00
Button, We Want Roosevelt, Black & White Photograph, Philadelphia Badge Co., 3 ½ In.	360.00
Button, We Want Truman To Nominate Ike, 1948 Democratic Convention, Celluloid, 3 ½ In.	3250.00
Button, Wendell Willkie, For President, 1 ¼ In.	9.50
Button, Wendell Willkie For President, 1940, 2 ½ In.	66.00
Button, West Virginians For Bush, White, Blue, 1 ¾ In.	11.00
Button, Who Wins, The Am. Gentleman, Taft, 1 In.	50.00
Button, William Jennings Bryan, Brown Tones, 1 ¼ In.	65.00
Button, William Jennings Bryan, The People's Choice, Photos Of Former Presidents, 2 In.	2125.00
Button, William McKinley, Celluloid, 1 ¼ In.	446.00
Button, William McKinley, Colonies, Image, Celluloid, 1 ¼ In.	446.00
Button, Willkie, Bricker, License Plate Attachment, Burton, Ohio, 1944, 5 In.	50.00
Button, Willkie, Cartoon, F.D.R Out At Third Base, 1940, 1 ¼ In.	9560.00
Button, Willkie, GOP Guard Our Peace, Red, White, Blue, 1 ¼ In.	9.00
Button, Willkie, He Will, Key Symbol, 1 ¼ In.	58.00
Button, Willkie, McNary & Chemurgy, Technology, Farming, Prosperity, c.1940, 1 ½ In.	417.00
Button, Willkie, No New Deal, We Want A Square Deal, 1 ¼ In.	23.00
Button, Willkie, No! No! A Thousand Times No, Blue, White, Red Rim, 1940, 2 ¼ In.	367.00
Button, Wilson, Marshall, Flag, Shield, Jugate, c.1915, 1 ¼ In.	1222.00
Button, Wilson, Marshall, I've Paid My Dollar, Have You, Jugate, 1 ¼ In.	806.00
Button, Wilson, Photo, Bunting, 1912, 1 ¼ In.	360.00
Button, Wilson, Shield, ⅞ In.	72.00
Button, Wilson, Shield, Color, Celluloid, 1912, 1 ¾ In.	1463.00
Button, Wilson, U.S.-Mexico Crisis, Salute Or I Shoot, c.1914, 1 ¼ In. ....*illus*	557.00
Button, Woodrow Wilson, Photo, My Heart Is In The Right Place, Brass Rim, 1 ¼ In.	115.00
Button, W.Va. Prohibition, X For Ratification, Blue, White, ¾ In.	45.00
Calendar, 1961, JFK, Past Presidents, National Landmarks Surround Portrait, 10 x 17 In.	31.00
Cane, McKinley, People's Choice, Script Slogan, White Metal Grip, Silver Luster, 39 In.	125.00
Cane, Teddy Roosevelt, Figural, Copper Plate, c.1904, 34 ½ In.	333.00
Card, Adlai Stevenson For President, Charter Member, Red, White, Blue, 1956, 2 x 3 In.	10.00
Card, Anti Third Term, Elect Wendell Willkie, Reverse Blank..............	5.50

Political, Patch Box, John Q. Adams, Book Shape, Glass Covers, 1848, 1 ¾ x 2 ¾ In. $1438.00

Political, Pin, Harrison, Log Cabin, Flag, Brass Frame, Glass Cover, c.1840, ⅞ x 1 In. $2760.00

Political, Pin, McKinley, Horseshoe, He's All Right, Brass, Mechanical, c.1896, 1 In.
$259.00

Political, Pitcher, President James A. Garfield, C-Scroll Handle, 10 x 6 In.
$115.00

Card, Beware Third Termites, Elect Wendell Willkie, Anti Roosevelt, Reverse Blank	5.50
Card, Carter Mondale Staff, Green, White, Stick Back, 2 ¾ x 3 ½ In.	5.00
Card, Dinner With Ike, TV Closed Circuit, Radio, Jan.27, 1960, 2 ¼ x 3 ½ In.	5.50
Card, Eisenhower Volunteers For Northern California, Membership, 2 ⅜ x 3 ⅞ In.	11.00
Card, Garfield Assassination, Memorial, Marysville, Ohio, Furniture Company	12.00
Card, L.B.J., Ladybird, H.H.H., Rifles, We Want Gun Control, Pro Gun Ownership, 3 x 5 In.	6.50
Card, LBJ, U.S. Senate, FDR Coattail, LBJ Drawing, Red, White, Blue, 2 ⅜ x 4 In.	145.00
Card, McGovern In '72, Campaign Information On Reverse, 2 ½ x 5 ¼ In.	4.50
Card, Taft, Bryan, Washington, Jugate, 2 ½ x 4 ¼ In.	5.50
Card, Truman, Barkley, Club, Membership, 1948	20.00
Certificate, Democrat, Goodwill, Stevenson, Kefauver, Donkeys, 1956, 13 ½ In.	22.50
Change Purse, James Buchanan, Leather & Metal, Image Of Buchanan, 2 ⅜ x 3 ½ In.	2420.00
Chin Tapper, FDR, Going To Run 3rd Term, Smiling Caricature, High Relief, 2 ¾ x 3 In.	183.00
Cigar Band, Wm. Jennings Bryan, Portrait, Flowers, Multicolored, 5 ½ In.	25.00
Clicker, Nixon, Click For Dick	8.50
Clock, President McKinley, Pressed Oak Case, Ingraham, c.1905, 25 In.	540.00
Cookie Jar, Horace Greeley, Seated, Book On Lap, 10 ½ In.	4601.00
Cup & Saucer, Adams, White House, Gold Rim, La Courtille, France, c.1800, 4 x 6 In.	4406.00
Cup & Saucer, Confederate General Wade Hampton, 1877	307.00
Cup, Cover, William Jennings Bryan, People's Money, Handle, c.1896, 3 ½ x 3 ½ In.	140.00
Earrings, Ike, Photo, Ceramic, 1 ⅛ In., Pair	22.00
Envelope, Willkie Chases FDR With Sling Shot, Watch Willkie Blast That Ambition	12.50
Epaulette, Mourning, Wool, G. Washington Profile, Applied Wig, Clothes, c.1800, 14 x 10 In.	575.00
Face Mask, Jacqueline Kennedy Onassis, 1964, Full Size	45.00
Fan, Barry Goldwater, DuPage County Republicans, White, Blue, Paper, Wood, 1964, 8 ¾ In.	17.00
Fan, I Am A Nixon Fan, Wooden Stick Handle, Cardboard	7.50
Feather, Paper FDR Badge, Blue, 11 ½ In.	20.00
Ferrotype, Abe Lincoln, 1 ⅛ x 1 ⅝ In.	1199.00
Ferrotype, Garfield, Brass Shell, Top Eagle Pin, 1801, ¼ x 2 ⅛ In.	825.00
Figurine, Votes For Women, Cast Metal, Painted, 2 ¼ In.	1200.00
Flag, American, 13 Stars, Hand Sewn, U.S. Ensign No. 8, Oct. 1889, 30 x 53 In.	2530.00
Flag, American, 43 Stars, 1890-91, 50 x 69 In.	410.00
Flag, Auto Antenna, Goldwater, Red, White, Blue, Cloth, 7 x 9 ½ In.	5.50
Flag, Blaine, Logan, Silk, Red, White, Blue, 39 Stars, 17 ½ x 11 ¾ In.	1200.00
Flag, Campaign, Lincoln, Johnson, 34 Stars, 1864, 22 x 33 In.	19550.00
Flag, Eisenhower, Nixon, Elephant, Blue, White, Wooden Flagstaff, 1950s, 6 In.	22.00
Flag, Grant, Wilson, Jugate, 1872 Campaign, 7 x 12 In.	17925.00
Flag, John Breckenridge For President, Portrait, 1860, 17 x 27 In.	95600.00
Flag, Lincoln, Hamlin, Campaign, 1860, 17 x 27 In.	28680.00
Flag, Lincoln, Portrait, Stars Surround, 17 ½ x 20 In.	7170.00
Flag, William Henry Harrison, Hero Of Tippecanoe, 1840, 33 ½ x 34 In.	5500.00
Flue Cover, Al Smith, For President, Blue, Yellow, 8 In. Diam.	88.00
Flyer, McGovern, Kennedy, Stars Of Hollywood & T.V., N.Y.C. Rally, 6 x 9 In.	4.50
Funeral Wreath, Lincoln, Shadowbox Frame, Columbus, Ohio, April 29, 1865, 22 In.	3525.00
Glass, I See Things Barry's Way, Elephant's Face, Black, Gold, 6 ½ In.	7.00
Glass, Smith, Robinson, Drink-Up, Milk White, Green Image, 1928, 4 In.	533.00
Greeting Card, Tojo Weeping Over Tombstones, Interior Graves, Adolph & Mussie	24.00
Greeting Card, Vote For Lyndon B. Johnson, Man Standing At A Voting Booth	6.50
Handkerchief, Copper Engraved, Andrew Jackson, Military & Presidential Service, 23 x 24 In.	360.00
Handkerchief, Washington Memorial, Copper Engraved, c.1800, 19 x 20 In. *illus*	2106.00
Hanger, Robert F. Kennedy, RFK, Cardboard, Plastic, 13 ½ In.	55.00
Hat Band, L.B.J. For The U.S.A., Red, White, Blue, Paper, 21 In.	7.00
Hatchet, Carry Nation Prohibition Symbol, A Dry Nation, Metal, c.1905, 12 In.	55.00
Hatchet, Washington Portrait, GAR Chicago 1900, Nickel Plated, Iron, 13 In.	275.00
Helmet, Blaine, Logan, 1884 Campaign, Gilt B. & L., Plume, Fabric	2314.00
Horn, Anti Hoover, Hoover Prosperity Horn, Turn Over For Bronx Cheer Noise, 2 ½ In.	132.00
Horn, Cleveland, Stevenson, Red, White, Blue, Tin, 1892, 14 In.	400.00
Horseshoe, Garfield 1880 Campaign Symbol, Garfield Profile, Iron, 4 ½ In.	99.00
Knife, Mexican War, Gen. Z. Taylor, Horseback, Inscription On Blade, Stag Grip, 9 In.	2500.00
Label, Cigar Box, Andrew Jackson, Old Hickory, Multicolored, c.1900, 6 ½ x 8 In.	8.00
Lantern, McClellan Campaign, Portrait, Slogans, Paper Box, 1864	7170.00
Lapel Hanger, Carter, Mondale, Paper, 6 ½ In.	5.00
License Plate Attachment, Elect Landon, Uncle Sam, 1936, 5 ½ In.	132.00
License Plate Attachment, Franklin Roosevelt, Green, White, Metal, 12 In.	133.00
License Plate Attachment, From The Sidewalks Of N.Y. To The White House, Al Smith, 1928, 10 ¼ In.	152.00

P

License Plate Attachment, Goldwater, White, Red, Metal, 1964, 6 x 12 In.	30.00
License Plate Attachment, Great Race Of 68, George Wallace, Tortoise & Hare, Metal, 12 In.	51.00
License Plate Attachment, Hoover, Blue, White Letters, 14 ½ In.	85.00
License Plate Attachment, Hoover For President, Yellow, Oval, Metal, 5 ¾ In.	44.00
License Plate Attachment, I Like Ike, 1950s, 7 In.	88.00
License Plate Attachment, Ike, Yellow, Blue, Metal, 1950s, 8 In.	63.00
License Plate Attachment, La Follette For President, Green, White, Metal, 1924, 12 In.	424.00
License Plate Attachment, Landon, Knox, Yellow, Metal, 1936, 11 ½ In.	114.00
License Plate Attachment, Our Choice, Hoover & Curtis, Yellow, Metal, 15 In.	188.00
License Plate Attachment, Repeal 18th Amendment, Anti Prohibition, Orange, Blue, Metal, 10 In.	109.00
License Plate Attachment, Victory In '64, Goldwater, Yellow, Black, Metal, 12 In.	55.00
License Plate Attachment, Want Prosperity?, Repeal The 18th Amendment, Metal, 14 In.	212.00
License Plate Attachment, Willkie, Wendell With C. Wayland Brooks & Dwight Green, 1940, 9 In.	150.00
License Plate Attachment, Win With Hoover, Blue, White, 10 ¼ In.	83.00
License Plate Attachment, Win With Willkie, Red, White, Blue, Metal, 1940, 10 In.	165.00
License Plate Attachment, Win With Willkie, Reflector, Red, White, Blue, 1940, 6 ½ In.	54.00
License Reflector, Willkie, McNary, 1940, 6 In.	91.00
Light Switch Plate, Peace, Agnew, Cartoon, Mickey Mouse Ears	6.50
Magazine, Suffragist, February 5, 1916, President Woodrow Wilson On Cover, 10 x 13 ½ In.	60.00
Match Holder, Top Hat, Harrison, Glass, The Same Old Hat, He's All Right, 2 In.	66.00
Match Holder, Woman, Votes For Women Sash, A Match For Any Man Base, Ceramic, 4 In.	1264.00
Match Safe, U.S. Grant Presented To J.R. Jones, Gold, Quartz, Moss Agate Panel, 1869	13060.00
Matchbook Cover, Eisenhower For President Club, Red, White, Blue	10.00
Matchbook Cover, In Ohio We Like Ike, Red, White	6.50
Matchbook Cover, Vote The Entire Republican Ticket, 1956	5.00
Medal, George Washington, Inaugural, Bronze, 1889, 4 ½ In.	1185.00
Medal, Raised Profile, Abraham Lincoln, Bronze, Engraved, Morgan, 3 In.	165.00
Mug, Assassination, Lincoln, Garfield, Pressed Glass, Blue, c.1881, 2 ⅝ In.	425.00
Mug, Clinton, Gore, Donkey Shape, Frankoma Pottery, 1993, 4 In.	22.00
Mug, Hoover, Head Shape, Syracuse China, 6 ½ In.	83.00
Mug, James Monroe, Misspelled Munroe, Portrait, 1818	14340.00
Mug, Lincoln, Garfield Assassinations, Blue, Adams & Co., 2 ⅝ x 2 ½ In.	425.00
Newspaper, Dewey Defeats Truman, Chicago Daily Tribune, 16 x 20 In.	967.00
Newspaper, Dewey Defeats Truman, Chicago Sun Times, 16 x 20 In.	472.00
Nodder, Castro, Kissin Kuzzins, Magnetized Lips, Ceramic, c.1962, 4 ½ In.	157.00
Nodder, Khrushchev, Kissin Kuzzins, Magnetized Lips, Ceramic, c.1962, 4 ½ In.	154.00
Nodder, Viva Castro, In Toilet, Composition, Painted, Foil Sticker, 1960s, 5 In. .... *illus*	329.00
Patch Box, John Q. Adams, Book Shape, Glass Covers, 1848, 1 ¾ x 2 ¾ In. .... *illus*	1438.00
Patch, I Like Ike, Shield Shape, Cloth, Red, White, Blue, 2 ½ In.	7.00
Patch, Watergate Bug, Headphones, Tapes, Bug, Cloth, 3 x 3 ¾ In.	5.00
Pencil Box, Our Chief Commanders, Hoover, Curtis, Yellow On Blue, Lift-Off Tray, 1928, 10 x 7 In.	125.00
Pencil Clip, Charles Evans Hughes, 1916, 1 ⅜ In.	53.00
Pennant, Dwight D. Eisenhower Inauguration, White Letters On Purple Felt, 1953, 26 In.	45.00
Pennant, Harry Truman For President, Blue, White, 1948, 25 In.	109.00
Pennant, I Like Ike, White Letters On Green Felt, Gold Border, Tassels, 1952, 26 In.	60.00
Pennant, John F. Kennedy For President, Yellow Ground, Red, Blue, Felt, 1960, 23 In.	139.00
Pennant, Votes For Women, Original Stick, 24 x 9 In.	587.00
Pennant, Votes For Women, Suffragist Statue Image, 12 x 35 In.	1103.00
Photograph, JFK, Our Next President, 4 In.	297.00
Piano Cover, General MacArthur, American Hero, Green, Yellow, 7 x 35 In.	35.00
Pin Tray, Cleveland, Thurman, Ceramic, Concave, Appears As Folded Hanky, 4 ¼ x 6 ½ In.	230.00
Pin, Crossed Flags, Enameled, Clutch Back, 1 ¼ In.	18.00
Pin, Delegate, Communist Party, 1939 Convention, New York City, 2 ¼ In.	365.00
Pin, Donkey, Franklin Roosevelt On Top Bar, Plastic, 1 ¾ In.	18.00
Pin, Harrison, Log Cabin, Flag, Brass Frame, Glass Cover, c.1840, ⅞ x 1 In. .... *illus*	2760.00
Pin, James Garfield, Cardboard Portrait, Goldtone Eagle On Top, 1 ⅛ In.	896.00
Pin, McKinley, Horseshoe, He's All Right, Brass, Mechanical, c.1896, 1 In. .... *illus*	259.00
Pin, Stick, Bryan Silver Bug, Shield, 1 ¼ In.	66.00
Pin, Teddy Roosevelt Bear, Carrying Stick, Gazing At Moon	330.00
Pin, Ulysses S. Grant, 1868, Photo, Cardboard, Round Brass Frame, 1 In.	239.00
Pitcher, Log Cabin Shape, W.H. Harrison Campaign Symbol, Glass, 4 ¼ In.	238.00
Pitcher, President James A. Garfield, C-Scroll Handle, 10 x 6 In. .... *illus*	115.00
Plaque, Franklin D. Roosevelt, Our Next President, Celluloid, Bastian Bros., 1932, 4 x 6 In. ... *illus*	127.00
Plate, Fort Meigs, William Henry Harrison, Amber Glass, 8 In.	45.00
Plate, In Memoriam, Robert F. Kennedy 1925-1968, John F. Kennedy, 1917-1963, 9 In.	26.75

Political, Plaque, Franklin D. Roosevelt, Our Next President, Celluloid, Bastian Bros., 1932, 4 x 6 In.
$127.00

Political, Poster, Landon, Knox, Deeds Not Deficits, Bluetone, Jugate, 14 x 20 ½ In.
$230.00

P

Political, Ribbon, Garfield, Arthur,
Black On Cream Ground,
1880, 1 ½ x 5 ¼ In.
$279.00

Political, Ribbon, Harrison, Reid,
Victory Protection, Celluloid Picture,
J.H. Shaw, 2 x 7 In.
$153.00

Political, Statue, Dick Nixon, Plaster,
Exaggerated Head, Brass, 5 x 5 x 17 In.
$183.00

Plate, James K. Polk, White House China, Stars & Stripes Shield, Gilt Trim, 1845-1849, 9 ¾ In., Pair	3884.00
Plate, Jimmy Carter, 39th President, Bone China, 1976, 9 In.	16.75
Plate, Lincoln White House China, 9 ½ In.	8963.00
Plate, McKinley Monument, State House, Columbus, Ohio, Bone China, 1905, 6 In.	19.75
Plate, President Garfield, Portrait, c.1881, 10 In.	39.00
Plate, Republican Centennial 1854-1954, Lincoln, Eisenhower, Jugate, 10 In.	29.75
Plate, William Howard Taft For President, James Sherman, President Border, Vienna Art, 1908, 9 ½ In.	240.00
Postcard, Anti Bryan, Bryan Back To Farm, 3 Strikes & Out, Cartoon, 1908, 3 ½ x 5 ½ In.	31.00
Postcard, Democratic Rally To See President Harry S. Truman & Senator Symington	18.00
Postcard, Dewey, Bricker, Unused, Vote For These Candidates	15.00
Postcard, Franklin Delano Roosevelt, President, Color Tint	11.00
Postcard, Gov. Teddy Roosevelt, Speaking From Porch, N.Y., Sept 23, 1899, Cancelled	18.00
Postcard, I Miss Ike, Hell, I Even Miss Ol' Harry, Cartoons, Unused, 6 x 9 In.	15.00
Postcard, Parker, Davis, Uncle Sam, Handwritten Message, Jugate, 1904	85.00
Postcard, President Taft Inaugural Parade, Blue & White, March 19, 1909	7.50
Postcard, Results Of The Suffrage Victory, Woman Walking Out Door, Father Holds Baby	22.00
Postcard, Roosevelt, Taft, Wilson, Triple Flasher, Magic Moving Picture Card, 1912, 4 x 6 In.	127.00
Postcard, Roosevelt, Wilson, Taft, 3 Presidential Hats In The Ring, Photo, c.1912, 3 ½ x 5 ½ In.	115.00
Postcard, Taft In Greeley, Colorado, Oct. 2, 1908, Cancelled	7.00
Postcard, Taft, Sherman, Our Choice, Flags, Ornate Swags, Eagle, Jugate	240.00
Postcard, Taft, Walking Down Road With Group	20.00
Postcard, Taft, William Howard Taft For President, 3 ½ x 5 ½ In.	24.00
Postcard, Teddy Roosevelt, African Trip, Standing Beside Dead Lion	10.00
Postcard, The Grin Will Win, Carter, Ford Cartoons, Unused	4.00
Postcard, The Way It's Going, The New Woman, Woman Walking Out, Dad Holds 2 Babies	22.00
Postcard, Woman Carrying Sign, Vote For Women, Man Tends To Baby	25.00
Poster, Anti Alcohol, Aviator Douglas Corrigan, Just Give Me A Glass Of Water, c.1938, 9 x 11 In.	45.00
Poster, Breckenridge, Lane, Grand National Banner, Currier & Ives, 1860	23900.00
Poster, Bryan, Stevenson, Republic, Not The Empire, Linen, Jugate, c.1900, 28 ½ x 40 In.	1026.00
Poster, Edward Kennedy, U.S. Senate, He Can Do More, Portrait, 1962, 13 x 21 In.	288.00
Poster, Equal Suffrage Regardless Of Sex, Massachusetts, Socialist Party, c.1912, 17 x 21 In.	438.00
Poster, Eugene McCarthy For President, Consumer Party, 1988, 11 x 17 In.	79.00
Poster, FDR, Truman, Red Lettering, Leon Perskie, New Jersey, 1944, 11 x 15 In.	238.00
Poster, Goldwater For President, Cardboard, Blue, White, Gold, 1964, 18 x 22 In.	55.00
Poster, Hancock, 1880 Presidential Campaign, Political Symbols, Green Matte, Frame, 27 x 33 In.	881.00
Poster, Kennedy For President, Frame, 29 x 20 In.	72.00
Poster, Kennedy, Johnson, 2 Great Democrats, Paper, Nat'l. Democratic Comm., 13 x 20 ¾ In.	146.00
Poster, Landon, Knox, Deeds Not Deficits, Bluetone, Jugate, 14 x 20 ½ In. *illus*	230.00
Poster, Lincoln, Jefferson, 1864, 12 x 16 In.	5079.00
Poster, MacArthur, Gerald L.K. Smith, Tenney, Christian Nationalist Party, c.1948, 14 x 20 ½ In.	253.00
Poster, McGovern, Silk Screened, Signed, B.M. Jackson, 1972, 20 x 26 In.	115.00
Poster, McKinley, Cleveland, Bicycle, 6 Men On Bicycles, Frame, 1896, 30 ½ x 40 In.	3500.00
Poster, Roosevelt, Woodruff, 1898 New York Campaign, 28 x 34 In.	1175.00
Poster, Russian Propaganda, Collective Farming, Cyrillic Text, c.1920, 26 x 20 In.	212.00
Poster, Theodore Roosevelt, High Cost Of Living Must Come Down, 1912, 16 x 23 In.	538.00
Poster, W. McKinley, Half Profile, 1896 Campaign, Chromolithograph, 7 Ft. 10 In x 9 Ft. 8 In.	4465.00
Poster, Wilson, Peace With Honor, He Kept Us Out Of War, Photograph, c.1916, 13 x 16 In.	115.00
Program Card, Ronald Reagan Dinner, May 29, 1975	7.50
Program, Andrew Jackson Inaugural, 1829	5079.00
Program, Obama Inauguration, Jan. 20, 2009, Text, Pictures, 36 Pages	53.00
Puppet, Jimmy Carter, Vinyl Head, Cloth Body, I Am Jimmy Button, 1970	60.00
Purse, Change, James Buchanan Image, Leather, Metal, Reverse On Glass, 3 ½ x 2 In.	2420.00
Record, Let's Put Ike In The White House, Eisenhower, Frank Boulet, 10 In.	50.00
Reflector, Franklin Roosevelt, Another American For Roosevelt, 10 ¾ In.	262.00
Ribbon, Benjamin Harrison, Morton, Red, White, Blue, Centennial Inaugural, 1889, 1 ½ In.	43.00
Ribbon, Earl Warren, California GOP Convention Delegate, Gold Bear, Medal, 2 ½ In.	50.00
Ribbon, Fillmore, Donelson, Picture, Flag, 1856, 7 ¾ In.	1650.00
Ribbon, Garfield, Arthur, Black On Cream Ground, 1880, 1 ½ x 5 ¼ In. *illus*	279.00
Ribbon, George Washington Temperance Society, Silk, 1840, 4 x 7 In.	315.00
Ribbon, Harrison, Reid, Victory Protection, Celluloid Picture, J.H. Shaw, 2 x 7 In. *illus*	153.00
Ribbon, Inauguration, Philadelphia GOP Leader's Club, Badge, Tassels, c.1905, 13 In.	209.00
Ribbon, Landon, Photo, Sunflower, White Elephant, 1 ¼ In.	19.00
Ribbon, Lewis Cass, Portrait, Silk, 1848.	10755.00
Ribbon, Lincoln, Buffalo, New York, Union Minutemen, 5 ⅜ In.	2541.00
Ribbon, MacArthur Was Right, Republican Hopeful, Blue, White, Paper, 1952, 3 x 9 In.	9.50
Ribbon, McKinley, Republican Marching Club, Blue, Portrait On Face, Watch Pin, 8 In.	799.00

Ribbon, McKinley, Roosevelt As Rough Rider, War Veterans, Jugate, 1900, 3 x 9 In.	456.00
Ribbon, Michigan Equal Suffrage Association, Port Huron, 1905, 6 x 2 In.	869.00
Ribbon, Pierce, King, Jugate..	7768.00
Ribbon, Prohibition Party, St. John, Daniel, Anti Alchol Candidates, Red, Jugate, 1884, 6 In. ..	823.00
Ribbon, Truman, Inauguration, Photo, Medal, Jan. 20, 1949, 1 ¾ In.	45.00
Ribbon, Winfield Scott, Hero Of Mexican War, Portrait, Battle Scene, Text, 7 ¼ In.	605.00
Ring, Commemorative, George Washington Profile, Silver, Carved Carnelian Intaglio, Man's..	299.00
Ring, Hoover, Photo, Red, ⅝ In.	88.00
Ring, Memorial, George Washington Lock Of Hair, Yellow Gold...........................	5378.00
Sash, Vote For The Suffragettes, Suffragette Figure, Blue Felt, White Lettering, 24 ½ x 1 ½ In.	345.00
Sewing Kit, Hoover, Curtis, Red, White, Blue, Stripes, Jugate, Needles Inside, 2 ¾ x 4 ½ In.	19.00
Sheet Music, Cleveland Grand March, 6 Pages, C.D. Ditson & Co., 1884, 11 x 14 In.	47.00
Sheet Music, Prosperity, USA Recovery Song, FDR On Cover, 1934	20.00
Sheet Music, The President's Birthday Ball, Irving Berlin, 1942, 6 ½ x 10 ¾ In.	8.50
Sheet Music, There's Nothing Else But Teddy, Girl Musically Conducting Stuffed Animals.......	7.50
Sheet Music, Woodrow Wilson, March, Progressive, 6 Pages, 10 ½ x 14 In.	31.00
Shot Glass, Vote Dry, The Saloon Must Go, Woman, Ax, 1917, 2 ¼ In.	40.00
Sign, Stevenson, Sparkman, Cardboard, Nat'l. Democratic Comm., Jugate, 14 x 22 In.	145.00
Soup, Dish, Lincoln, White House, Patriotic Symbols, Purple, Haviland, Porcelain, c.1861, 9 In. .	17625.00
Statue, Dick Nixon, Plaster, Exaggerated Head, Brass, 5 x 5 x 17 In. ....*illus*	183.00
Sticker, American Party, Don't Blame Me, I Voted A.P., 3 ¾ x 7 In.	4.00
Sticker, Goldwater, Au H2O, 1964, Aluminum Back, 2 ½ x 7 In.	5.50
Stickpin, Fiske, Brooks, Prohibition Party, Porcelain, On Brass, c.1888, 1 ½ In.	242.00
Stickpin, Horace Greeley, Acts Not Words, Ferrotype, 1872, 1 ⅝ x 1 ⅜ In.	2300.00
Stickpin, Horatio Seymour, Ferrotype, Purple Insert, Brass Frame, c.1868, ⅞ In. ....*illus*	436.00
Stickpin, McKinley, Gold Bug, 1 ¼ In.	63.00
Stickpin, McKinley, Gold Bug Riding Bicycle, Original Card, 2 In.	136.00
Stickpin, Rutherford B. Hayes, Photo, Die Cut, Embossed, Cardboard, Brass Frame, 1 In.	662.00
Stud, Ax, Nixon, California, 1 Percent On Blade, ⅞ In.	14.00
Stud, Bryan, The Money We Want, Liberty's Profile, 1896, ⅞ In.	238.00
Stud, McKinley, 4-Leaf Clover, Red, White, Blue, Enamel, ¾ In.	22.00
Stud, Teddy Roosevelt, Metal Flag, 1 ¼ In.	22.00
Stud, Willkie, Dig In For Willkie, Shovel, 1 ⅜ In.	145.00
Tag, Buy War Bonds & Stamps, Made Of Pacific Tactag Fabric, Shield Shape, 3 In.	9.00
Textile, British American Stamp Act, King George, 4 Englishmen, Red, Cotton, 26 x 30 In.	13000.00
Textile, William Jennings Bryan, Head Portrait, Sepia, 38 x 46 In.	254.00
Thermometer, Hoover, White House, Skeleton Key Form, Pewter, 8 ½ In.	67.00
Thimble, Calvin Coolidge, c.1924, ⅞ In.	9.00
Ticket Stub, Andrew Johnson, Impeachment, Cardboard, May 6, 1868, Cardboard, 3 x 3 ½ In. .	170.00
Ticket, Federation Of Republican Women, Montgomery County Conference, 1957.	5.00
Ticket, Inaugural Dinner, Salute To Eisenhower, Rep. For D.C., Jan.20, 1956, 4 x 6 In.	10.00
Ticket, JFK Texas Welcome Dinner, Nov. 22, 1963, 2 ½ x 4 In.	440.00
Ticket, No Negro Suffrage, Democratic National Union, Blue Paper, c.1869, 11 x 3 In.	708.00
Tie, Ford, Whip Inflation Now, Polyester, Rivetz Of Boston..........................	23.00
Tie, Franklin Roosevelt, For President, Image, Brown, 1936.........................	91.00
Tie, Wayland Brooks, Dewey, Warren, Coattail, Elephant, GOP, Green, 1948...............	80.00
Top, William McKinley, Image, Wood, Paper, 2 ¼ In.	198.00
Torch, Campaign, Lincoln, Hamlin, Musket Form, Wood, Carved, Painted, Tin, 69 In.	600.00
Tray, McKinley, Roosevelt, Color Lithograph, Oval, 1900, 13 x 16 In.	774.00
Tray, Presentation, J. Edgar Hoover, Inscribed, Oval, Shaped Rim, Sterling Silver, 18 In.	191.00
Tureen, Lid, Log Cabin Pattern, W.H. Harrison, 1840, Wm. Adams & Sons, 6 x 8 In.	698.00
Umbrella, McKinley, Hobart, Panels, Jugate..	499.00
Voting Machine, Gray Enameled Metal, c.1980, 72 x 48 x 24 In.	60.00
Watch Fob, Bryan, Kern, Celluloid, Jugate, 1908, 1 ¼ In.	392.00
Watch Fob, Harding, Best Ever, Portrait, Mirror, Shoenberg Clothes Maker, 1 ½ In.	3484.00
Watch Fob, Roosevelt, Our Teddy For President, Bakelite, Jewels, Leather Band, 1 ½ In.	490.00
Watch Fob, Taft, Lock Shape, W.H. Lock, 1908, 1 ¾ In.	35.00
Watch Fob, Teddy Roosevelt, Horseshoe, Photo, Sepia, 1 ½ In.	89.00
Watch Fob, Wilson, Padlock Shape, Movable Brass Keyhole Cover, c.1912, 1 ⅝ In.	115.00
Watch, Lincoln Portrait, Eagle, Stem Wind, 18K Gold, Borel & Co., Pocket, c.1870............	6463.00
Whistle, Horace Greeley, Metal, 1872, 2 In.	1195.00
Window Sticker, Draft Stevenson, 4 x 8 In.	8.00
Window Sticker, Goldwater '64, Black, Gold, White, Liberty Bell Shape...............	5.00
Writing Paper, Envelope, America Needs Stevenson, 6 x 8 ½ In.	9.50
Yarn Spool, Roosevelt Silk Gimp, Picture Of Teddy, 2 ½ In.	99.00

Political, Stickpin, Horatio Seymour,
Ferrotype, Purple Insert, Brass Frame,
c.1868, ⅞ In.
$436.00

Popeye, Alarm Clock,
Lithographed Metal Case, King Features,
c.1932, 4 ½ x 3 ¾ In.
$1872.00

Popeye, Doll, Swee'pea, Muslin,
Stiffened Mask Face, Stitched Limbs,
c.1935, 14 In.
$392.00

P

503

Popeye, Thimble Theatre,
4 & 5-In. Bisque Dolls, Painted Clothes,
Box, c.1920, 9 Piece
$616.00

Popeye, Game, Popeye Menu, Marble, Tin
Lithograph, Bagatelle, Cardboard, Box,
c.1935, 14 x 23 In.
$468.00

P

POMONA glass is a clear glass with a soft amber border decorated with pale blue or rose-colored flowers and leaves. The colors are very, very pale. The background of the glass is covered with a network of fine lines. It was made from 1885 to 1888 by the New England Glass Company. First grind was made from April 1885 to June 1886. It was made by cutting a wax surface on the glass, then dipping it in acid. Second grind was a less expensive method of acid etching that was developed later.

Spooner, Cornflower Pattern, Scalloped Rim, New England, 5 In.	403.00
Toothpick, A, Enamel Flowers, Stained Square Rim, c.1875, 2 ½ x 1 ½ In.	152.00

POOLE POTTERY was founded by Jesse Carter in 1873 in Poole, England, and has operated under various names since then. The pottery operated as Carter & Co. for several years and established Carter, Stabler & Adams as a subsidiary in 1921. The company specialized in tiles, architectural ceramics, and garden ornaments. Tableware, bookends, candelabra, figures, vases, and other items have also been made. The name Poole Pottery Ltd. was taken in 1963. The company went bankrupt in 2003, but is in business today with new owners.

Bowl, Pastel Flowers, Pink Interior, 9 ½ x 2 ¾ In.	55.00
Dish, Dolphin, Swimming, Blue Water, Marked, 1953-73, 7 x 4 In.	15.00
Pin Dish, Flower Center, Dotted Edge, Marked, 4 In.	12.00
Plate, Scooped, Blue Rooster, Red & Yellow Flowers, Green Leaves, Marked, 10 In.	45.00
Vase, Cylindrical, Green Ground, Blue Abstract Leaves, Marked, 5 ½ x 5 In.	250.00
Vase, Orange, Green & Yellow Stylized Flowers, Black Outline, Footed, Marked, 8 ¾ In.	145.00
Vase, Round, Fuchsia, Art Deco, Signed, 3 ½ x 2 ¾ In.	130.00

POPEYE was introduced to the Thimble Theatre comic strip in 1929. The character became a favorite of readers. In 1932, an animated cartoon featuring Popeye was made by Paramount Studios. The cartoon series continued and became even more popular when it was shown on television starting in the 1950s. The full-length movie with Robin Williams as Popeye was made in 1980. KFS stands for King Features Syndicate, the distributor of the comic strip.

Alarm Clock, Lithographed Metal Case, King Features, c.1932, 4 ½ x 3 ¾ In. ....*illus*	1872.00
Bank, Daily Quarter, Register, Tin Lithograph, Kalon Mfg., Illustrations, c.1956, 2 ½ x 2 ½ In.	173.00
Bank, Dime Register, Red, White, Blue, 8-Sided, King Features, 1929	45.00
Bank, Mechanical, Knock-Out, Tin Lithograph, Key, Straits Mfg. Co., Box, 1935, 3 ½ x 2 In.	936.00
Bubble Set, Wooden Pipe, Soap Dish, Bakelite Pipe Attachment, No. 35, Transogram, Box	172.00
Button, Popeye The Sailor, Blue, White, ⅞ In.	13.00
Cookie Jar, Olive Oyl, Green Hat, Ruffled Collar, Marked, U.S.A., 10 In.	315.00
Cookie Jar, Printed Scene, 3-Bar Mark, McCoy, 10 ¾ In.	75.00
Costume, Hat, Mask, Pipe, Suit, Halco, Box, 1935	70.00
Cracker Box, Cardboard, Cartoon Characters All Around, Loose-Wiles Sunshine Co., 1935, 3 x 5 In.	280.00
Doll, Olive Oyl, Spring Body, Paper Sauceboat, Sign Push Me Down I Pop Up, Japan, c.1950, 7 In.	504.00
Doll, Swee'pea, Muslin, Stiffened Mask Face, Stitched Limbs, c.1935, 14 In. ....*illus*	392.00
Doll, Wood, Composition, Jointed, KFS, Jaymar, Box, 1935, 8 In.	2066.00
Doorstop, Cast Iron, Hubley, King Features, 1929, 4 In. ...... 1638.00 to 1755.00	
Doorstop, Painted, Cast Iron, Full Figure, No. 328, Hubley, Signed, 1929, 9 x 4 ⅜ In.	1700.00
Figure, Celluloid, Head Goes Up & Down, Japan, c.1935, 5 ¼ In.	448.00
Figure, Cloth Body, Molded Rubber Head, Composition Shoes, Corncob Pipe, 17 In.	820.00
Figure, Jointed, Composition, Wood, Ideal, 1935, 14 ½ In.	605.00
Figure, Jointed, Wood, Composition Head, Celluloid Hat Brim, Bag, Chein, 1932, 8 ½ In.	1182.00
Figurine, With Galleon Ship, Carnivale, Plaster, 11 x 12 In.	288.00
Game, Board, Play Hockey Fun With Popeye & Wimpy, Metal Goal, 9 ¼ x 26 ¼ x 1 ½ In.	863.00
Game, Board, Who Gets The Spinach, Cardboard, 16 Player Discs, 9 x 12 ¾ x 1 In. 150.00 to 173.00	
Game, Popeye Menu, Marble, Tin Lithograph, Bagatelle, Cardboard, Box, c.1935, 14 x 23 In. *illus*	468.00
Lamp, Popeye Leans On Lamp, Figural, Painted, White Metal, King Features, c.1935, 11 In.	118.00
Music Box, Pop Open Top, Crank, 5 ½ x 5 ½ In.	45.00
Music Set, Popeye's Big Band, Instruments, Baton, Wood, Tin, Bar Zim Toy, Box, 1933	230.00
Pail, Beach Scene, Popeye, Olive Oyl, Wimpy, Swee'pea, Jeep, Tin Lithograph, c.1930, 8 In.	702.00
Pail, Under The Sea Scene, Popeye, Olive Oyl, Wimpy, Swee'pea, Tin Lithograph, c.1930, 8 In.	936.00
Pin, Popeye, New York Evening Journal, ⅞ In.	39.00
Record Player, Dynamite Music Machine, Emerson, 4 ¼ x 12 x 9 ½ In.	48.00
Sign, Believe It Or Not, Popeye Impersonator, Bulging Forearms, Pipe, Frame, 26 x 33 ¼ In.	417.00
Sign, Popeye Guaranteed To Pop Popcorn, Popeye Punches Popcorn, Frame, 14 x 30 ¼ In.	401.00
Target, Gun, Paper Lithograph, Cardboard, Battery Operated, Box, Early 1930, 8 x 18 In. *illus*	322.00
Thermos, Boat Dock Scene, Red Lid, Tin Lithograph, Canada, c.1964, 8 In.	52.00
Thermos, Boat Dock Scene, Yellow Lid, Tin Litho, Thermos Co., Norwich, Conn., 1964, 8 In.	60.00
Thimble Theatre, 4 & 5-In. Bisque Dolls, Painted Clothes, Box, c.1920, 9 Piece ....*illus*	616.00
Thimble Theatre, Ramp Walkers, Popeye, Olive Oyl, Wimpy, Harding Products, Box, 10 x 12 In.	878.00

Toy, Handcar, Popeye, Olive Oyl, Tin Lithograph, Rubber Figures, Windup, Box, Marx, 6 In.		384.00
Toy, Marbles, Akro Agate, 6 Oxblood, 3 Green, 3 Orange, 3 Yellow Corkscrew, Bag, Box.............		1540.00
Toy, Paddle Wagon, Crew, Die Cast, Plastic Parts, No. 802, Corgi, Box, c.1967-72, 6 In.		190.00
Toy, Popeye, Boom Boom, Plays Drum, Pull Toy, Fisher-Price, No. 491, 1929-33, 9 ½ In.		400.00
Toy, Popeye, Carrying Parrot Cages, Tin, Windup, Marx, c.1935, 7 ¾ In.		255.00
Toy, Popeye, Carrying Parrot Cages, Walking, Tin Lithograph, Clockwork, Chein, 8 ½ In.		431.00
Toy, Popeye, Champ, Boxing Ring, Tin, Celluloid, Windup, Marx, Box, c.1935, 7 x 6 ½ In. . illus		1680.00
Toy, Popeye, Dances, Head Moves Up & Down, Celluloid, Windup, Japan, 8 ½ In.		79.00
Toy, Popeye, Green Hat, Wood, Composition, Jointed Body, 8 In.		130.00
Toy, Popeye, Head Bobs, Celluloid, Windup, 8 ½ In.		390.00
Toy, Popeye, Holding Ship's Wheel, Head Moves, Musical, Windup, Japan, Box, 16 In.		380.00
Toy, Popeye, Motorcycle, Removable Figure, Iron, Painted, Rubber, Hubley, c.1929, 9 In. .... illus		2106.00
Toy, Popeye, Motorcycle, Small Balancing Wheels, Red, Black, White, Cast Iron, 8 ½ In.		1872.00
Toy, Popeye, On Roof, Tin Lithograph, Windup, Marx, 9 ½ In.		403.00
Toy, Popeye, Pilot, Tin Lithograph, Windup, Marx, 1940, 7 ½ x 8 In.	360.00 to 750.00	
Toy, Popeye, Playing Basketball, Tin, Windup, Linemar....................................	820.00 to 1200.00	
Toy, Popeye, Punching Bag, Overhead, Tin Lithograph, Windup, Chein, Box, 1932, 9 ½ In.		7020.00
Toy, Popeye, Pushing Trunk, Parrot, Tin Lithograph, Windup, Marx, 8 In.		374.00
Toy, Popeye, Roller Skating, Holds Can Of Spinach, Windup, Lehmann......................		585.00
Toy, Popeye, Sparkler, Tin Lithograph, J. Chein & Co., c.1934, Box, 6 In. .... illus		1521.00
Toy, Popeye, Turn Over Tank, Windup, LineMar		295.00
Toy, Popeye, Waddler, Tin Lithograph, Windup, J. Chein & Co., Box, 6 In. .... illus		995.00
Toy, Popeye & Olive Oyl In Planes, Arm Moves Around Airport Tower, Windup, 1930s, Marx.....		1250.00
Toy, Popeye & Olive Oyl, Jiggers, Tin Litho, Windup, Louis Marx, Box, c.1936, 9 ½ In. ...... illus		2223.00
Toy, Popeye & Olive Oyl, Juggling, Tin Lithograph, Windup, Linemar, Box, 9 ½ In. .... illus		2340.00
Toy, Popeye & Olive Oyl, On Roof, Windup, Marx, 1930s...................................		1150.00
Toy, Popeye & Olive Oyl, Playing Accordion, Dancing, Tin Lithograph, Windup, 9 ½ In.		489.00
Toy, Popeye Colorforms, Popeye Cartoon Kit, Watercolor Cover, No. 117, 1957, 14 x 9 ½ In.		1516.00
Toy, Popeye Express, Wheelbarrow, Parrot, Tin Lithograph, Windup, Marx, c.1930s, 9 In.		448.00
Toy, Sailboat, Popeye On Sail, With Telescope, Wood, Metal, Cloth, 1929, 22 x 18 In.		156.00
Toy, Speedboat, Covered Deck, Pressed Steel, Clockwork, Hoge Mfg. Co., 15 In.	201.00 to 259.00	
Toy, Spinach Motorcycle, 3 Wheels, Cart, Cast Iron, Hubley, 1930s, 5 ½ In.	605.00 to 675.00	
Truck, Friction, Linemar Co., 12 In.		550.00

PORCELAIN factories that are well known are listed in this book under the factory name. This category and the two following list pieces made by the less well-known factories. Porcelain-Contemporary lists pieces made by artists working after 1975. Porcelain-Midcentury includes pieces made from the 1940s to about 1975.

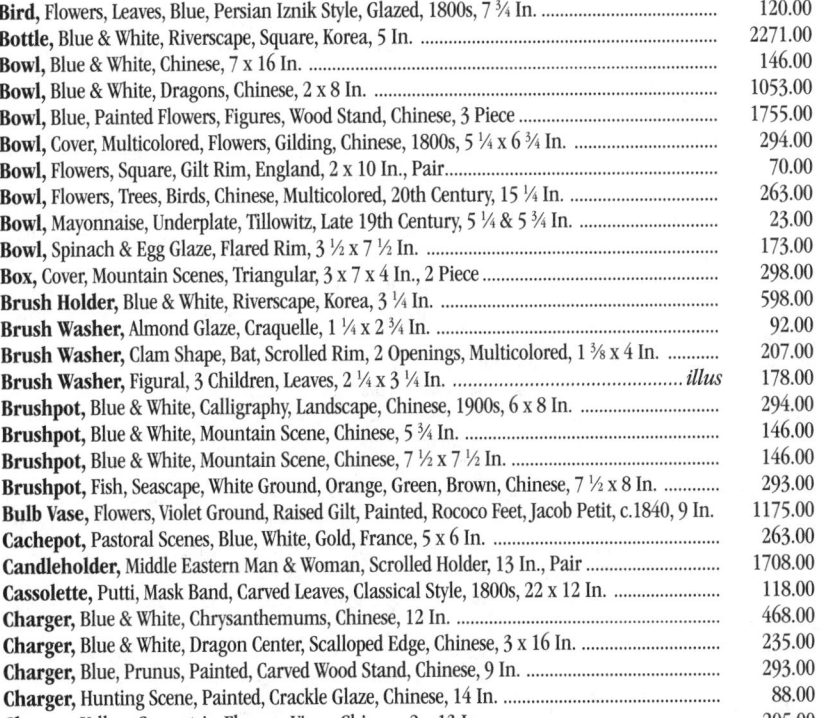

Bird, Flowers, Leaves, Blue, Persian Iznik Style, Glazed, 1800s, 7 ¾ In.	120.00
Bottle, Blue & White, Riverscape, Square, Korea, 5 In.	2271.00
Bowl, Blue & White, Chinese, 7 x 16 In.	146.00
Bowl, Blue & White, Dragons, Chinese, 2 x 8 In.	1053.00
Bowl, Blue, Painted Flowers, Figures, Wood Stand, Chinese, 3 Piece	1755.00
Bowl, Cover, Multicolored, Flowers, Gilding, Chinese, 1800s, 5 ¼ x 6 ¾ In.	294.00
Bowl, Flowers, Square, Gilt Rim, England, 2 x 10 In., Pair..............................	70.00
Bowl, Flowers, Trees, Birds, Chinese, Multicolored, 20th Century, 15 ¼ In.	263.00
Bowl, Mayonnaise, Underplate, Tillowitz, Late 19th Century, 5 ¼ & 5 ¾ In.	23.00
Bowl, Spinach & Egg Glaze, Flared Rim, 3 ½ x 7 ½ In.	173.00
Box, Cover, Mountain Scenes, Triangular, 3 x 7 x 4 In., 2 Piece	298.00
Brush Holder, Blue & White, Riverscape, Korea, 3 ¼ In.	598.00
Brush Washer, Almond Glaze, Craquelle, 1 ¼ x 2 ¾ In.	92.00
Brush Washer, Clam Shape, Bat, Scrolled Rim, 2 Openings, Multicolored, 1 ⅜ x 4 In.	207.00
Brush Washer, Figural, 3 Children, Leaves, 2 ¼ x 3 ¼ In. .... illus	178.00
Brushpot, Blue & White, Calligraphy, Landscape, Chinese, 1900s, 6 x 8 In.	294.00
Brushpot, Blue & White, Mountain Scene, Chinese, 5 ¾ In.	146.00
Brushpot, Blue & White, Mountain Scene, Chinese, 7 ½ x 7 ½ In.	146.00
Brushpot, Fish, Seascape, White Ground, Orange, Green, Brown, Chinese, 7 ½ x 8 In.	293.00
Bulb Vase, Flowers, Violet Ground, Raised Gilt, Painted, Rococo Feet, Jacob Petit, c.1840, 9 In.	1175.00
Cachepot, Pastoral Scenes, Blue, White, Gold, France, 5 x 6 In.	263.00
Candleholder, Middle Eastern Man & Woman, Scrolled Holder, 13 In., Pair	1708.00
Cassolette, Putti, Mask Band, Carved Leaves, Classical Style, 1800s, 22 x 12 In.	118.00
Charger, Blue & White, Chrysanthemums, Chinese, 12 In.	468.00
Charger, Blue & White, Dragon Center, Scalloped Edge, Chinese, 3 x 16 In.	235.00
Charger, Blue, Prunus, Painted, Carved Wood Stand, Chinese, 9 In.	293.00
Charger, Hunting Scene, Painted, Crackle Glaze, Chinese, 14 In.	88.00
Charger, Yellow, Geometric, Flowers, Vines, Chinese, 2 x 13 In.	205.00

Popeye, Target, Gun, Paper Lithograph, Cardboard, Battery Operated, Box, Early 1930s, 8 x 18 In.
$322.00

Popeye, Toy, Popeye, Champ, Boxing Ring, Tin, Celluloid, Windup, Marx, Box, c.1935, 7 x 6 ½ In.
$1680.00

Popeye, Toy, Popeye, Motorcycle, Removable Figure, Iron, Painted, Rubber, Hubley, c.1929, 9 In.
$2106.00

Popeye, Toy, Popeye & Olive Oyl, Jiggers, Tin Litho, Windup, Louis Marx, Box, c.1936, 9 ½ In.
$2223.00

P

Popeye, Toy, Popeye & Olive Oyl, Juggling, Tin Lithograph, Windup, Linemar, Box, 9 ½ In.
$2340.00

Popeye, Toy, Popeye, Sparkler, Tin Lithograph, J. Chein & Co., c.1934, Box, 6 In.
$1521.00

Popeye, Toy, Popeye, Waddler, Tin Lithograph, Windup, J. Chein & Co., Box, 6 In.
$995.00

Porcelain, Brush Washer, Figural, 3 Children, Leaves, 2 ¼ x 3 ¼ In.
$178.00

Cheese Keeper, Triangular, Painted, England, 5 ¾ x 7 In.	82.00
Chocolate Pot, Sevres Style, Gilt Flowers, Hinged Cover, Handle, 7 ½ In.	178.00
Coffeepot, Renaissance Woman's, Profile, Multicolored, Deruta, Italy, 11 In.	47.00
Compote, Figural, Putti, Flowers, C.G. Schierholtz & Son, c.1900. 17 x 11 In.	351.00
Compote, Shaped, 3 Cherub Supports, Pierced Borders, Thieme, Germany, 1900s, 6 x 10 In.	207.00
Creamer, Clover Mold, Lavender, Green, Clover Leaf Spout, 4 In.	79.00
Cup & Saucer, Wedding, White, Gilt Trim, Der Braut, Dem Brautigam, 5 ½ & 2 ½ In., Pair *illus*	85.00
Cup, Stem, Copper Inlay, Blue, White, Chinese, 3 ⅛ x 5 In.	96.00
Cuspidor, Tonquin Pattern, Bucket Design, Wicker Handle, Winkle & Co., c.1880, 15 ½ In.	115.00
Dessert Stand, Multicolored, 3 Graduated Tiers, Gilt Baluster Supports, 11 In.	470.00
Dish, Applied Lobster, Flowers, Shell Shape, Scalloped Edge, Marked F & M, 4 ¾ x 12 In.	104.00
Dish, Cover, Heart Shape, Flowers, Ribbon, Hand Painted, Marked, Leonard, Vienna, 5 ¼ x 5 ¼ In.	140.00
Dish, Cover, Landscape, Yellow Flower Finial, Rouen, France, c.1900, 5 In.	410.00
Dish, Leaf Shape, Chinese, 8 ½ In.	59.00
Dresser Box, Round, Cobalt Blue, Red Roses, Metal Fittings, 2 In.	230.00
Dresser Set, Tray, Containers, Vase, Candle Holder, Lavender, Flowers, Gilt, 9 x 9-In. Tray *illus*	155.00
Easter Egg, Painted, St. Alexandra, Cartouche, Cross, Russia, c.1880, 4 ½ In. *illus*	900.00
Ewer, Vine & Flowers, Cobalt Blue Ground, Gold Trim & Handle, Greenwood, 9 ¾ In.	1220.00
Ewer, White, Korea, 3 ¾ In.	418.00
Figure, Monkey, Eating Fruit, White Glaze, Open Work Base, Continental, 18 In.	460.00
Figurine, Aristocratic Lady, Medieval Dress, Frankenthal, Germany, 18th Century, 12 ½ In.	904.00
Figurine, Ballerina, Germany, Early 20th Century, 9 In.	205.00
Figurine, Birds, Perched On White Base, Germany, 8 ½ In., Pair	259.00
Figurine, Boy, Dog, Cat, Ludwigsburg, Germany, 18th Century, 7 x 4 In.	452.00
Figurine, Buddha, Orange Face, Multicolored Robe, Japan, 11 x 16 In.	88.00
Figurine, Catherine De Medicis, Wife Of Henri II, Blue Mark, Sitzendorf, Germany, 11 In.	360.00
Figurine, Foo Dog, Male With Ball, Female With Cub, Plinth Base, Chinese, 10 In., Pair	390.00
Figurine, Foo Dog, Painted, Wood Scroll Stand, Chinese, 9 ½ x 4 In., Pair	35.00
Figurine, Girl Pushing Sleigh, Majolica Style, 6 x 6 In.	100.00
Figurine, Hunter, Dogs, Woman, Sheep, Goats, Painted, Bisque, Germany, 13 x 14 In., Pair	118.00
Figurine, Lady In Medieval Dress, Frankenthal, Germany, 18th Century, 11 In.	1356.00
Figurine, Seminude Women, Multicolored, Germany, 12 In.	230.00
Figurine, Woman & Child, Lace, Pink & White, Gold Highlights, Germany, 8 In.	142.00
Figurine, Woman Equestrian Warrior, Holding Sword, Eschenbach, Germany, 7 In.	394.00
Figurine, Woman, Holding Wicker Basket, Flowers, Painted, c.1890, 6 ½ x 5 In.	370.00
Figurine, Woman, Pushing Cart, Voigt & Sitzendorf, Germany, 1900s, 9 In.	322.00
Figurine, Woman, Reclining, Shaubach, Germany, c.1930, 12 In.	410.00
Figurine, Woman, Seated, Blue Apron, Babushka, Russia, 5 x 3 In.	878.00
Fish Pot, Multicolored, Flowers, Chinese, 18th Century, 8 x 10 ⅝ In.	411.00
Fruit Basket, Figural, Multicolored Enamel Flowers, 4 Putti, Oval, Austria, 1800s, 13 ¼ In.	148.00
Garden Seat, Blue & White, Cash Symbols, Cobalt Blue Ground, Barrel, Slipware, 18 x 16 In.	960.00
Ginger Jar, Blue & White, Shou Characters, Scepters On Flaps, Lappets, Globular, Chinese, 8 ½ In.	210.00
Ginger Jar, Enameled, Flowers, Blue Ground, Chinese, 7 ½ x 5 ¼ In.	47.00
Goblet, Dragon, Orange White Ground, Navy Blue Details, Chinese, 3 x 4 In, Pair	468.00
Group, 3 Children, Geese, Flowers, c.1935, 6 x 9 In.	94.00
Group, White Biscuit, Roman Warrior, Woman, Child, Maid, Continental, 16 x 12 In.	540.00
Humidor, Horned Devil, 4 ½ In.	125.00
Humidor, Skull, Top Lifts, 5 In. *illus*	550.00
Jar, Cover, Blue & White, Ginger Jar Shape, Birds, Peonies, 7 ¾ In., Pair	173.00
Jar, Cover, Lotus Leaves, Blue, White, Ormolu Mounts, Raised Feet, 11 In., Pair	2640.00
Jar, Flowers, Taoist Emblems, Blue Underglaze, Bulbous, Raised Feet, Korea, 1800s, 5 x 5 ⅜ In.	881.00
Jar, Funerary, Figures, Clouds, Ribbed, Green, Blue Glaze, Chinese, 12 ½ In., Pair	300.00
Jar, Squat, Globular, Blue, White, Leaves, Flowers, Scepter Heads, Wooden Top, Chinese, 1800s, 11 In.	270.00
Jardiniere, Blue & White, Flowers, Shishi Decoration, Japan, 14 x 18 In.	115.00
Jardiniere, Pierced C-Scrolls, Boat Shape, Art Nouveau Style, Scroll Feet, 18 ½ x 27 In.	86.00
Jardiniere, Roses, Multicolored, Painted, Bronze Base, Signed, S. Kennedy, c.1897, 17 x 15 In.	1053.00
Jardiniere, Seated Figures, Trees, Text, Deep Blue Ground, Chinese, 13 x 13 In.	293.00
Jardiniere, Yellow, Branches, Blue Underglaze, Chinese, 7 x 7 x 7 In., Pair	1020.00
Jug, Milk, Birds, Perched On Flowering Stumps, Round, Cobalt Blue Rim, Austria, 5 In., Pair	115.00
Mug, Ski Scene, Children, Playing, Toboggan, Gold Luster, Early 1900s, 3 x 2 ⅞ In.	34.00
Pitcher, Cottage Landscape, Grisaille, Gilt Bands, Tucker, Philadelphia, c.1830, 9 ¼ In. *illus*	3600.00
Pitcher, Frogs, Bicycle, Boneshaker, Multicolored, c.1898, 5 ½ In.	28.00
Pitcher, Lid, Turquoise Green, Chinese, 8 x 9 In.	117.00
Planter, Blue & White, Boys Playing, Landscape, Plantain Leaves, Chinese, 19 x 20 In., Pair	660.00
Planter, Blue & White, Children, Bird, Branches, Butterflies, Japan, 22 x 31 ¾ x 22 ⅝ In.	598.00
Planter, Women, Cherubs, Marked R, 7 x 13 In.	100.00
Plaque, Flowers, Shaded Brown Ground, Gilt Rococo Frame, 15 x 15 In.	1035.00

Plaque, Leafy Branches, 4 Panels, Chinese, 23 x 8 In.	527.00
Plaque, Portrait, Ruth, Rococo, Giltwood Frame, Oval, 13 ¼ x 11 ¼ In.	8700.00
Plaque, Princess In Bath, Attended By Maid, Giltwood Frame, Germany, 11 x 9 In.	7110.00
Plaque, Woman, Hat, Flowers, Marked, H. Hohenberg, Black Forest Frame, c.1900, 3 x 2 In.	316.00
Plaque, Woman, Holding Fan, Landscape, Cartouche Shape, France, 1900s, 13 x 9 In.	118.00
Plaque, Woman, Putti, Blossoms, Cobalt Blue Border, Gold Trim, Round, Leafy Frame, c.1875, 20 In.	1292.00
Plaque, Woman, White Dress, Blue Scarf, Ornate Gold, Frame, Wagner, Germany, 4 x 6 In.	1495.00
Plaque, Woman With Peach Drape, Landscape, Gilt Highlights, Germany, 9 ⅜ x 6 ⅜ In.	1150.00
Plate, Blue & White, Chinoiserie, 8-Sided, c.1785, 9 In.	142.00
Plate, Blue & White, Fisherman Pattern, Asian Man, Boat, England, c.1775, 7 ½ In.	293.00
Plate, Cabinet, Classical Scene, Der Spiegel Der Venus, Gilt, Vienna, c.1890, 9 ⅝ In.	177.00
Plate, Cabinet, Woman's Portrait, Black & Gilt Border, Austria, c.1900, 9 ½ In.	23.00
Plate, Chantilly, Molded Basket Weave Edge, Center Flower, France, 18th Century, 9 ½ In.	115.00
Plate, Child's, Teddy Bears Playing Sports, Kidney Shape, Underwood's High Chair, 1918, 10 In.	115.00
Plate, Courting Scene, Stenciled, Gilt Scalloped Rim, E. Bourgeois Carrieres, France, 11 In., Pair	176.00
Plate, Duchess, Gilt Vines, Green Enamel Band, Atlas China Co., 10 ¾ In., 14 Piece	546.00
Plate, Kentish Rockery, Royal Albert, 6 In., 6 Piece	35.00
Plate, Portrait, Vestal Virgin, Veil, Vienna, 9 ½ In.	118.00
Plate, Rouen Pattern, Floral Bouquet, Multicolored, R. Briggs, Late 1800s, 9 ¾ In., 12 Piece	264.00
Plate, Washington D.C., Blue & White, c.1900, 10 In.	59.00
Platter, Blue & White, Canton Vignettes, Oval, Scalloped, Late 1800s, 16 ½ x 14 In.	144.00
Punch Bowl, Landscape, Multicolored, Gold, Cameo, Old Paris, France, c.1840, 7 x 8 In.	410.00
Salt, Flowers, Brown, Green, Gold, Leonard Vienna, c.1900, 1 ¾ In.	12.00
Sauce Set, Fish Shape, Charger, Blue & White, 11 Piece	410.00
Screen, Carved Wood Frame, Chinese, c.1900, 27 x 19 In.	410.00
Stamp Licker, Humpty Dumpty, Green, Yellow, Red, Cloth Wrapped Tongue, 4 ⅞ x 3 In.	60.00
Sugar, Cover, Blue Rose Transfer, Applied Flower Finial, c.1750, 5 x 4 In.	147.00
Sugar, Floral Bouquet, Scalloped Rim, Lowestoff, c.1800, 5 In.	70.00
Sugar Shaker, Cobalt Blue, Church Scene, Gilt, 2-Section Lid, c.1900, 5 ¼ In.	66.00
Teapot, Blue Transfer, New Orleans, Sailing Ships, Buildings, Acorn Finial, 11 In.	1150.00
Teapot, Flowers, Butterfly, Blue Transfer Print, Applied Finial, c.1750, 6 In.	352.00
Teapot, Violets, Ivy, Brass & Pewter Top, Victorian, 5 ½ x 8 ½ In.	86.00
Toothpick, Skull Shape	201.00
Tureen, Cover, Landscape, Flowers, Putto Finial, Meissen Style, 11 In.	239.00
Tureen, Cover, Pear Form, Painted, Leaves, Branch Handle, 3 ½ x 5 In., Pair	1495.00
Tureen, Cover, Underplate, Flowers, Iron Red, Gilt, Oval, Applied Shell Handles, England, c.1810.	118.00
Tureen, Tortoise Shape, Painted, Multicolored, Wood Stand, Chinese, 7 x 13 In.	527.00
Urn, Cover, Burgundy, Classical Scene, Viennese Style, G. Forster, Austria, 1800s, 25 In., Pair	12980.00
Urn, Cover, Courtyard Scene, Gilt, Angel Handles, Thieme, France, 1900s, 17 In., Pair	649.00
Urn, Palace, Sevres Style, Domed Cover, Oval, Flared Neck, Cherubs, 53 x 16 In., Pair	345.00
Urn, Sevres Style, Courting Couple In Reserve, U-Shape Body, Gilt Bronze Foot, 17 ½ In., Pair.	1080.00
Urn, Sevres Style, Courting Couple, Landscape, Gilt Metal Mount, Early 1900s, 27 x 12 In.	1220.00
Urn, Sevres Style, Green, Dancing Couple, Landscape, Gilt, Baluster, Bronze Mount, 26 In.	2596.00
Vase, Allegorical Female Figure, 4-Footed, Mount, Gilt, France, c.1900, 12 ½ x 7 ¼ In.	1800.00
Vase, Berries & Leaves, Vine Handles, Art Nouveau Style, 10 ½ In.	12.00
Vase, Birds In Reserves, Cobalt Blue, Quilted, Egg Shape, Footed, 8 In., Pair	115.00
Vase, Black, Seated Men, Urn Shape, Squared Handles, Germany, c.1850, 8 x 20 In., Pair	234.00
Vase, Blue & White, Bamboo, Birds, Elongated Neck, Korea, c.1900, 12 x 7 In.	499.00
Vase, Blue & White, Chinese Scene, Baluster Shape, 14 x 9 In.	235.00
Vase, Blue & White, Disc Shape, Landscape, Korea, c.1900, 10 ¾ x 9 In.	382.00
Vase, Blue & White, Dragon, Japan, 19th Century, 32 x 18 In.	643.00
Vase, Blue & White, Flowers, Korea, 8 ¾ In.	1315.00
Vase, Blue & White, Garden & Flower Scenes, Octagonal, Chinese, 9 x 8 In.	146.00
Vase, Blue & White, Oval Reserves, Fish, Seascape, Korea, c.1900, 11 x 7 ¼ In.	382.00
Vase, Blue, White Flower Ground, Orange Dragons, Chinese, 16 x 10 In.	527.00
Vase, Bottle, Kakiemon Style, Flowers, Squared, Bulbous, Elongated Neck, Japan, 11 ½ In.	570.00
Vase, Cobalt Blue Glaze, Double Gourd Shape, Chinese, 6 ½ In.	388.00
Vase, Courtyard Scene, Multicolored, Applied Handles, Chinese, 23 x 8 ½ In.	439.00
Vase, Cover, Diamond Shaped Panels, Blue Underglaze, Twin Fish, Peonies, 23 In., Pair	840.00
Vase, Cover, Double Gourd Shape, Birds, Flowers, Yellow Ground, Chinese, 18 x 9 In.	146.00
Vase, Cover, White Swirls, Blue Ground, Leduc, c.1928, 19 In.	1912.00
Vase, Domed Cover, Gilt Flame Finials, Cobalt Blue, Flowers, Germany, 18 ½ In., Pair	300.00
Vase, Dragon Head, Jacob Petit Style, 1850s, 13 x 10 In.	6200.00
Vase, Dragons Over Waves, Blue Ground, Bulbous, Long Neck, Chinese, c.1800, 8 ⅜ In.	1035.00
Vase, Fanghu, Red & Blue Flambe Glaze, Pear Shape, Lug Handles, Chinese, c.1800, 12 In.	1315.00
Vase, Figures, Animals, Orange, White Ground, Chinese, 24 x 11 In.	1120.00
Vase, Flambe, Streaked Red To Blue Glaze, 10 In., Pair	30.00

Porcelain, Cup & Saucer, Wedding, White, Gilt Trim, Der Braut, Dem Brautigam, 5 ½ & 2 ½ In., Pair
$85.00

Porcelain, Dresser Set, Tray, Containers, Vase, Candle Holder, Lavender, Flowers, Gilt, 9 x 9-In. Tray
$155.00

Porcelain, Easter Egg, Painted, St. Alexandra, Cartouche, Cross, Russia, c.1880, 4 ½ In.
$900.00

Porcelain, Humidor, Skull, Top Lifts, 5 In.
$550.00

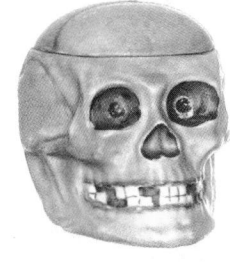

P

Porcelain, Pitcher, Cottage Landscape, Grisaille, Gilt Bands, Tucker, Philadelphia, c.1830, 9 ¼ In.
$3600.00

Porcelain-Midcentury, Dish, Malachite Pattern, Gilt, Fornasetti, c.1956, 7 x 7 In.
$173.00

Porcelain-Midcentury, Figurine, Hedi Schoop, Playing Horn, Oriental Style Costume, Art Deco, 6 x 10 ½ In.
$75.00

Vase, Flowers & Leaves, Exotic Birds, Pomegranate Handles, Seal, Chinese, 12 ¾ In.	89.00
Vase, Flowers, Multicolored, Gilt, Cobalt Blue Ground, Paris, c.1820, 22 ⅜ In.	3491.00
Vase, Fluted, Gilt, Multicolored Enamel, Flowers, Spray, 19th Century, 13 In., Pair	1304.00
Vase, Garniture, Watteau Scenes, Gilt, Rose, Free-Form Handles, 1800s, 10 x 8 ½ In., Pair	353.00
Vase, Gold Flowers, Dragon Handles, Germany, 20th Century, 14 ¼ In.	58.00
Vase, Green Crystalline Glossy Glaze, Adelaide A. Robineau, 2 In.	805.00
Vase, Harbor Scene, Baluster, Late 19th Century, 16 ¾ In.	1185.00
Vase, Hound Chasing Ducks, Relief Molded, Blue Ground, Gilt Scrolled Border, 21 In., Pair	732.00
Vase, Hummingbird, Gilded, Heinrich, 20th Century, 7 ½ In.	23.00
Vase, Incised, Painted Scenes, Applied Dragon, Dog, Asia, 8 x 16 ½ In., Pair	978.00
Vase, Ladies At Leisure, Baluster Shape, Shines, c.1937, 13 ¾ In.	529.00
Vase, Meiping, Copper Red Glaze, Baluster, Pinched Neck, Chinese, 11 ½ In.	239.00
Vase, Molded Birds, Ivory Glaze, Bulbous, Signed Boch, Louviere Belgium, c.1925, 9 In.	960.00
Vase, Moon Flask, Chinoiserie, Sang-De-Bouef Glaze, Dragon Handles, France, 1900s, 15 In.	480.00
Vase, Orange, Embossed, Everted Rim, 12 x 18 In.	526.00
Vase, Peach Bloom Underglaze, Blue, Buddhistic Lion, Cub, Bat, 8 ¾ In.	1440.00
Vase, Peacock, Pink, Orange, White Interior, Applied Handles, 14 ½ In.	176.00
Vase, Peacocks, Austrian Blank, 10 x 5 ¾ In.	610.00
Vase, Portrait, Young Girl's Profile, Red, Footed, Scroll Handles, Marked, Victoria, Austria, 9 In.	40.00
Vase, Potpourri, Cover, Romance Scenes, Grisaille, Gilt Flowers, 1900s, 10 In.	354.00
Vase, Seated Women, Painted, Magenta Ground, 2 Handles, France, c.1920, 10 x 5 In., Pair	410.00
Vase, Trumpet, Multicolored, Gilt Rim, Roulette Bands, Flowers, Paris, 6 ¼ In., Pair	294.00
Vase, Turquoise Crystalline Glaze, Adelaide Robineau, 2 ¾ x 5 In.	4800.00
Vase, White, Painted Blue Bamboo, Chinese, 7 In.	70.00
Vase, Woman, Cylindrical, Chinese, 11 x 5 In.	47.00
Vase, Yellow, Flowers, Baluster Shape, Chinese, c.1920, 6 x 12 In.	117.00
Vase, Yellow Glaze, Double Gourd Shape, Bottle Neck, Japan, 14 In.	230.00
Wash Set, Green, Painted, Flowers Inside, Grimwades, Stoke-On-Trent, 6 Piece	88.00
Water Cooler, Fox Hunt Scene, 13 ½ x 11 ½ In.	115.00
Water Dropper, Animal Shaped Finial, Bamboo Leaf, Brown Underglaze, 2 x 2 ½ In.	480.00
Water Dropper, Blue Glaze, Square, Bronze Spoon, Dragon Handle, Korea, 1800s, 1 ½ x 2 In.	588.00
Water Dropper, Boy Beating Drum, White, Blue Accents, 2 ¼ x 3 In.	460.00
Water Dropper, Dog Shape, Multicolored, San Cai Period, 3 ¼ x 3 ½ In.	230.00
Water Dropper, Seated Man, Red Cloak, Coiled Pattern, 19th Century, 1 ¾ x 2 ½ In.	150.00
Water Dropper, Turquoise Glaze, Scrolled Pattern, 2 x ½ In.	150.00
Water Pitcher, Double Gourd Shape, Foo Dog Finial, Dragon Handle, Chinese, 29 ½ In.	230.00
Water Stopper, Octopus Form, Raised Shells, Spout, Korea, 19th Century, 3 ¼ x 5 In.	538.00

PORCELAIN-CONTEMPORARY lists pieces made by artists working after 1975.

Bowl, Centerpiece, Putto With Basket, Germany, 20th Century, 7 ¼ In.	35.00
Bust, Man With Pipe, Borsato, Milan, Italy, 8 In.	117.00
Figurine, Horse, On Hind Legs, 20th Century, Gilded, 6 ½ In.	58.00
Figurine, Lady Godiva, On Horse, Armani, 13 In.	351.00
Plaque, Bisque, Couple Sitting By Branches, Continental, 20th Century, 7 ½ In.	52.00
Salt Cellar, White, Gold Trim, Spoon, Schmid, West Germany, c.1980, 2 x 2 In.	22.00
Vase, Bulbous, Double Spout, Toshiko Takaezu, 8 ½ x 7 ¾ x 5 ¼ In.	4575.00
Vase, Tapering Baluster, Flowering Plants, Crackle Ground, 34 ¼ In.	352.00

PORCELAIN-MIDCENTURY includes pieces made from the 1940s to about 1975.

Bowl, Silver Plated Rim, Hanley, England		18.00
Dish, Malachite Pattern, Gilt, Fornasetti, c.1956, 7 x 7 In.	*illus*	173.00
Figurine, Hedi Schoop, Playing Horn, Oriental Style Costume, Art Deco, 6 x 10 ½ In.	*illus*	75.00

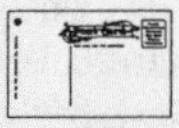

POSTCARDS were first legally permitted in Austria on October 1, 1869. The United States passed postal regulations allowing the card in 1872. Most of the picture postcards collected today date after 1910. The amount of postage can help to date a card. The rates are: 1872 (1 cent), 1917 (2 cents), 1919 (1 cent), 1925 (2 cents), 1928 (1 cent), 1952 (2 cents), 1958 (3 cents), 1963 (4 cents), 1968 (5 cents), 1971 (6 cents), 1973 (8 cents), 1975 (7 cents), 1976 (9 cents), 1978 (10 cents), March 1981 (12 cents), November 1981 (13 cents), 1985 (14 cents), 1988 (15 cents), 1991 (19 cents), 1995 (20 cents), 2001 (21 cents), 2002 (23 cents), 2006 (24 cents), 2007 (26 cents), 2008 (27 cents), 2009 (28 cents). While most postcards sell for low prices, a small number bring high prices. Some of these are listed here.

Academy Campus View, Mercersburg, Pa., C.A. Laughlin	22.00
Big Pond, South Mountain, Pa., C.A. Laughlin	20.00
Book, John Travolta, 23 Pictures, 1978, 8 ½ x 11 In.	25.00
Case Motor Cars, Advertising, Barney Oldfield, Joe Tinker, c.1910, 5 ½ x 5 ½ In.	250.00

Concert, Fleetwood Mac, Pink Floyd, The Who, Grande Ballroom, Detroit, c.1968, 4 x 7 In.	196.00
Coulee Dam, Construction, West Side, Black & White, 1930s	5.00
Creek At Wilson College, Chambersburg, Pa., C.A. Laughlin	18.00
Fruit, Color Lithograph, Alphonse Mucha, 7th Series, c.1900 ....*illus*	300.00
Girl Rector's Mechanical, Pop-Up, c.1900, 5 ½ x 3 ½ In.	45.00
Horse-Drawn Wagon, Peddler, John Meehan On Side Of Wagon, 1910............................	16.00
Indian Girl, Fringed Buckskin Skirt, Color, 1915	8.50
Interior Rocky Spring Church, Built 1794, Chambersburg, Pa., C.A. Laughlin..............	15.00
Klansmen With Largest Flag In The Nation, Black & White, 1925, 5 ½ In.	73.00
Liberty Limited Train, Uncirculated, 1940s..	8.00
Mt. Alyeska, Alaska's Year Round Resort, Chair Lift Ride, Timber Lane, 1960s	4.00
Nantucket, Martha's Vineyard, Unused, 10 ¾ x 6 ¾ In.	14.00
Petersburg, Alaska, Airplane View 1952, Unused...	6.00
RR Street, Leesburg, Pa., C.A. Laughlin...	45.00
Rudolf Valentino, Paramount Film License, 1895-1926..	14.00
San Francisco Fire 1906, Black & White, Ruins Of The Concordia Club.........................	8.50
School House, Leesburg, Pa., C.A. Laughlin	45.00
Simmons By The Falls, Tour Buses, Columbia River Highway, Oregon, 1920s................	7.50
St. Anthony's Hospital, Oklahoma City, 1940...	10.00
The Falls, Caledonia Park, C.A. Laughlin	18.00
The Roosevelt Bears Go Fishing...	10.00
Vin Fiz Bottling Float, Ideal Drink, Buffalo Bill's Wild West Show, c.1900	210.00
Vin Fiz, Rodgers In Salamanca, Men, Early Airplane, 1911...	390.00
Wright Flyer, Souvenir Of The Carmi Fair, 1913	150.00

POSTERS have informed the public about news and entertainment events since ancient times. Nineteenth-century advertising and theatrical posters and twentieth-century movie and war posters are of special interest today. The price is determined by the artist, the condition, and the rarity. Other posters may be listed under Movie, Political, and World War I and II.

2 Men On Tandem, c.1890, 22 ¼ x 16 In.	39.00
6 Day Overland California Mail Routes, Coach, Blue, Red Text, Frame, 1866, 22 x 17 In. ..	14100.00
Achille Philion, Marvelous Equilibrist & Originator, Frame, 26 ½ x 40 In.	511.00
Aix En Provence, Town Square, Clock Tower, Acid Free Linen, France, 30 x 42 In.	750.00
Alaska Klondike Gold Fields Lecture, Pink, Black, 1890s, 18 x 24 In.	499.00
Alice Soulie, Woman, Ostrich Feathers, Lithograph, Frame, France, 1926, 60 x 44 In.	575.00
Bagnoles Of Lorne, Woman & Horse, Acid Free Linen, France, 30 x 42 In.	749.00
Bal Dynamique, Lithograph, Multicolored, Rolf Stoll, Crane Howard, c.1930, 21 x 14 In. ...	3738.00
Bill Graham, Yardbirds, Doors, Ritchie Havens, Fillmore, c.1967, 14 x 21 In. ....*illus*	1012.00
Buffalo Ranch Real Wild West, Cowboys, Indians, Riverside Print Co., Frame, 23 x 57 In. ..	705.00
Children's Book Week, Go Exploring In Books, Lithograph, F. Rojankovsky, c.1959, 22 x 17 In.	264.00
Circus, Clyde Beatty & Cole Bros., World's Largest, Lion, Marshalltown, Iowa, 49 x 14 In.	190.00
Circus, Cole Bros., Tarzan Star Betty Lou Chimpanzee, ½ Sheet, c.1942, 20 ¼ x 27 ½ In.	115.00
Circus, Walter L. Main, 3 Ring, Trained Wild Animal Shows, Bengal Tiger, c.1920, 27 x 41 In.	635.00
Grateful Dead, Bill Graham Production, Black, Yellow, c.1966, 14 x 2 In.	239.00
Grateful Dead, Quicksilver Messenger Service, Hundred Dollar Bill Design, Concert, 1968	657.00
Horse Show, Girl Carrying Pull-Toy Horse, Delaware State Fair, Sept 4-8, 1922, 16 x 10 In.	95.00
Kar-Mi, Buried Alive, National PTG & ENG Co., 2 Sheet, c.1914, 80 x 40 In. ....*illus*	316.00
Kokoon, Bal Artistique, Lithograph, Multicolored, A. Leysens, Crane Howard, c.1935, 21 x 15 In.	2300.00
Lenny Bruce, The Mothers, Concert, Bill Graham, 1966, 14 x 20 In. ....*illus*	115.00
Music, Bjorn Winblad, Spil Selv, Frame, 1960s, 33 x 24 In., 3 Piece ....*illus*	702.00
Music Connection, Psychedelic, Signed Wilson, Telejockey Inc., 1970s, 23 x 29 In.	25.00
National Championship Auto Race, Los Angeles Coliseum, Color, Frame, Oct. 13, 1946, 22 x 17 In.	184.00
Pawnee Bill's Wild West & Far East Show, Chromolithograph, Red, White, Black, Frame, c.1905	2585.00
San Salvador, Multiscenic, Acid Free Linen, 30 x 42 In.	749.00
She Loves You, Yea, Yea, Yea, The Beatles Come To Town, 1964, 35 ⅛ x 48 ¼ In.	300.00
Tommy, Jimmy Dorsey Orchestra, Terrytown, Nebraska, 1953, 14 x 22 In.	388.00
Union Stock Yard, Chicago Intern'l Live Stock Expo, Frame, Signed, Tolson, c.1940, 25 x 16 ½ In.	720.00

POTLIDS are just that, lids for pots. Transfer-printed potlids had their heyday from the 1840s to the early 1900s. The English Staffordshire potteries made ceramic containers with decorative lids for bear's grease, shrimp or meat paste, cold cream, and toothpaste. Printed advertising and pictures of historical events, portraits of famous people, or scenic views were designed in black and white or color. Reproductions have been made.

Cherry Toothpaste, Patronized By The Queen, John Gosnell & Co.	23.00
English Scene, 3 Victorian Men, Sitting, 1 Leaning On Cane, Blue, Brown, Frame, 5 ½ In.	125.00

Postcard, Fruit, Color Lithograph, Alphonse Mucha, 7th Series, c.1900 $300.00

Poster, Bill Graham, Yardbirds, Doors, Ritchie Havens, Fillmore, c.1967, 14 x 21 In. $1012.00

Poster, Kar-Mi, Buried Alive, National PTG & ENG Co., 2 Sheet, c.1914, 80 x 40 In. $316.00

P

Poster, Lenny Bruce, The Mothers, Concert, Bill Graham, 1966, 14 x 20 In.
$115.00

Poster, Music, Bjorn Winblad, Spil Selv, Frame, 1960s, 33 x 24 In., 3 Piece
$702.00

Pottery, Vase, Painted, Apple Blossoms, Flared Base, Rim, Octagonal, Mark, 17 x 7 In.
$104.00

Pottery-Art, Jardiniere, Spanish Style, Birds, Flowers, Pedestal, 9 x 7 ½ In.
$35.00

Garden Scene, Couple, Man On One Knee, Offering Flowers To Woman, Frame, 6 ¼ In.	50.00
J. Bell & Co. Cold Cream, Hastings	7.00
The Rivals, Woman, 2 Men, Pratt, 4 ¼ In.	32.00
The Shrimpers, Pratt, c.1875	27.00
Village Wedding, Pratt, c.1900	18.00

POTTERY and porcelain are different. Pottery is opaque; you can't see through it. Porcelain is translucent. If you hold a porcelain dish in front of a strong light, you will see the light through the dish. Porcelain is colder to the touch. Pottery is softer and easier to break and will stain more easily because it is porous. Porcelain is thinner, lighter, and more durable. Majolica, faience, and stoneware are all pottery. Additional pieces of pottery are listed in this book in the categories Pottery-Art, Pottery-Contemporary, Pottery-Midcentury, and under the factory name. For information about pottery makers and marks, see *Kovels' Dictionary of Marks—Pottery & Porcelain: 1650–1850* and *Kovels' New Dictionary of Marks—Pottery & Porcelain: 1850 to the Present.*

Basket, Flattened Handle, Yellow, Green, Brown Drip Glaze, Cole Pottery, 5 ½ x 4 In.	22.00
Basket, Handle, Crimped Edges, Blue Glaze, Nell Cole Graves, North Carolina, c.1950, 6 x 6 In.	65.00
Bottle, Flared Rim, Oxblood Glaze, Celadon Ground, Steven Polchert, 1975, 7 x 6 ½ In.	720.00
Bottle, Pinch, Light Green High Glaze, Monticello, 1930s, 5 ¾ x 3 ¾ In.	85.00
Bowl, Blue Band, Beige, Incised, Tapered, Marked, Gobble 996, 9 x 20 In.	345.00
Bowl, Red & Blue Glaze, Incised, Tapered, Marked, Gobble 930, 6 ¾ x 14 In.	173.00
Creamer, Tan Matte Glaze Exterior, Gloss Glaze Interior, North Carolina, 3 ¼ x 4 ¼ In.	30.00
Crock, Ivory Glazed, 2 Handles, Continental, 20th Century, 12 x 9 ½ & 10 ½ In., Pair	420.00
Cup, Glazed, White, Blue Design, 2 Handles, 19th Century, 8 In.	88.00
Figurine, Bust, Woman, Multicolored, Susan Bolt, 15 x 9 In.	292.00
Figurine, Camel, Rider, 16 In.	359.00
Figurine, Cat, Playing With Spool Of Thread, Glass Eyes, Black Paint, 10 In.	1250.00
Figurine, Dog, Spaniel, Seated, Black, Glass Eyes, Jackfield, 1800s, 11 ¼ In., Pair	300.00
Figurine, Turkey, Multicolored, 1974, 12 ¼ x 13 In.	70.00
Jar, Edgefield, Oval, Lug Handles, Mottled Celadon Glaze, White, Brown Slip, 1840s, 15 In.	2990.00
Jar, Medicine, Round, Split Handle, Turquoise, Blue Glaze, A.R. Cole, 1930s, 4 ⅝ x 5 ¾ In.	115.00
Jar, Olive, Star Of David, Incised, Spain, 19th Century, 16 ½ x 15 In.	140.00
Jar, Storage, Mediterranean, Glazed, Oval, Rounded Lip, 32 ½ x 25 In.	780.00
Jar, Umbrella, Fish Shape, Multicolored, 25 x 16 In.	35.00
Jug, Brown Hold Drip High Glaze, Dark Brown Glaze Base, C.C. Cole, 4 ¾ x 4 In.	18.00
Jug, Brown, Iron Wash, Flat Handle, Tooled Neck, c.1750, 15 ¾ In.	132.00
Jug, Dark Olive Runny Alkaline Glaze, Handles, Catawba Valley, N.C., 1800s, 16 ½ In.	1035.00
Jug, Edgefield, Double Strap Handles, Wreath, 5, Brown Slip, Celadon, c.1850, 17 In.	7360.00
Jug, Edgefield, Oval, White Slip Flowers, Wreath, 1, Alkaline Glaze, 1840s, 10 In.	7130.00
Jug, Honey, Brown, Green & Gold Drip Glaze, C.C. Cole, c.1940, 6 In.	35.00
Jug, Rainbow Drip Glaze, Handle, C.C. Cole, 5 ½ x 5 In.	20.00
Jug, Rebecca, Blue, Green, Rutile Drip Glaze, Footed, 12 x 5 In.	95.00
Jug, Rebecca, Curved Handle, Wide Spout, Purple, Tan, Unglazed, N.C., 9 ½ x 4 ½ In.	55.00
Jug, Wood Stopper, Runny Olive, Glaze, Handles, Catawba Valley, N.C., c.1859, 18 ¾ In.	518.00
Loving Cup, Feet, Mythological Scene, Embossed Bronze, Handles, Le Chervr De Schlick, 6 In., Pair	150.00
Mug, Chinese Blue Double Glaze, North Carolina, 4 x 5 ½ In.	90.00
Pie Plate, Green Mottled Glaze, Ruffled Edge, J.B. Cole, 9 x 2 In.	40.00
Pitcher, Brown Matte Glaze, Drip Glaze, Handle, North Carolina, 4 ½ x 3 ¼ In.	15.00
Pitcher, Farmers Arms, Brown Transfer Decoration, Farmers Working, Dancing, 9 In.	345.00
Pitcher, Squat, Green, Brown Speckled Semimatte Glaze, North Carolina, 3 x 2 ½ In.	20.00
Pitcher, Sweeping Fuchsia Vine, Stylized Brushwork, c.1880, 9 ½ In.	1175.00
Pitcher, Washbasin, East Anglia, White, Blue Sailboats, Empire Ware	70.00
Pitcher, Wine, Korea, 19th Century, 10 x 7 In., Pair	588.00
Plaque, Bacchus, Panther, Black Basalt, High Relief, Frame, England, c.1800, 6 x 11 In.	1304.00
Plate Set, Romany, Tile, Asian Design, Turquoise & Tan Glaze, Mark, 8 ¾ In., 8 Piece	115.00
Platter, Green Glaze, Impressed, Switzerland, 18 ¾ x 10 ¼ In.	94.00
Pot, Red Glaze, Oblong, A.R. Cole, Sanford, North Carolina, c.1940, 7 ⅝ x 2 ½ In.	25.00
Pot, Turquoise Gloss Glaze, 3 Handles, A.R. Cole, North Carolina, c.1940, 4 ½ x 3 In.	40.00
Rice Jar, Cover, Cornish Ware, Blue & White Bands, Black Shield Mark, T.G. Green, 5 ½ In.	125.00
Sculpture, Covered Container, House Shape, White, Signed Jack Earl Ohio, 12 x 11 x 11 In.	4500.00
Sculpture, Figural, Man, Cap, Dog, Brown, Green, Ohio, Jack Earl, 1981, 26 In.	5100.00
Sculpture, Garbage Pail, Yellow Glaze, Victor Spinski, 16 x 13 In.	3900.00
Sign, Camark Pottery, Arkansas Shape, Melon Green Glaze, 6 ⅜ In.	345.00
Sugar Sifter, Cornish War, Blue & White Bands, White Cover, Green Shield Mark, 4 ½ In.	125.00
Syrup, Brown Drip Glaze, Tan Ground, Green, Yellow, C.C. Cole, 1940s, 6 ¼ x 3 ½ In.	30.00
Syrup, Red Glaze, Green, Yellow, Southern, 1940s, 6 x 3 ½ In.	35.00
Tobacco Jar, Bulbous, Painted Flowers, Scrolls, Burgamot, R.S., Dutch, c.1800, 10 In.	443.00

P

Umbrella Stand, Flowers, Yellow Ground, Lobed, Bands, George Jones & Sons, 1800s, 22 ½ In.	400.00
Urn, Lemon Tree Design, Italy, 20th Century, 27 ½ In.	1016.00
Urn, Red Glaze, Baluster, 2 Handles, North State Pottery, Sanford, N.C., 9 ½ In.	288.00
Vase, 4 Handles, Blue, Brown Glaze, W. Scheller & Sons, Austria, 11 ½ In.	94.00
Vase, 4-Sided, Faceted Rim, Brown Glaze, Brushed Designs, Shoji Hamada, 10 x 4 ¾ In.	3600.00
Vase, Art Nouveau, Bronze Overlay, Blue Green Iridescent Glaze, Continental, 7 ½ x 5 ¼ In.	940.00
Vase, Baluster, Multicolored, Landscape, Patterned Ground, Handles, Japan, 27 x 9 In., Pair	3525.00
Vase, Bird Shape, Beak, Wings, Tail, White, Green, Red Flowers, B. Wiinblad, Denmark, 8 x 10 In.	60.00
Vase, Bud, Bamboo, 6 ¼ x 2 ¾ In.	1220.00
Vase, Cone Shape Lid, Green Glaze, Cylindrical, Multicolored, 10 In.	119.00
Vase, Copper Red Carp, Ivory Fishnet Ground, Bulbous, Pinched Neck, Chinese, 5 In.	403.00
Vase, Figure Of Woman, White Dark Gray Ground, 15 In.	250.00
Vase, Lavaware, Acanthus Leaf, Grapes, Child & Branch Handles, Mark, W.S. & S., 11 x 9 In.	177.00
Vase, Light Green Over Green Brown Glaze, North State Pottery, North Carolina, 5 ¾ x 4 In.	35.00
Vase, Morocco, Panel Designs, c.1940, 19 x 14 In.	146.00
Vase, Native American, Orange, Yellow, Brown, 9 x 10 In.	293.00
Vase, Ocher Glaze, Painted Butterfly, Branches, Rockwork, Clouds, Bottle Shape, Chinese, 5 In.	58.00
Vase, Painted, Apple Blossoms, Flared Base, Rim, Octagonal, Mark, 17 x 7 In. ......*illus*	104.00
Vase, Round, Glazed Earthenware, Brown, c.1947, 9 ¾ In.	146.00
Vase, Silvered Metal, Flowers, 3 Flower Stem Handles, Art Nouveau, J.P. Kayser & Sohn, 27 ½ In.	708.00
Vase, Slip Decorated, Geometric Designs, Red, Brown, White, Marked, 1980s, 6 ¾ In.	58.00
Vase, Squeezebag, Butterflies, Cobalt Blue, Albert Cusick, Signed, 8 x 4 ¾ In.	3050.00
Vase, Yellow, Green, Red Gloss Glaze Bands, c.1950, 5 x 3 ¾ In.	42.00
Vase, Yellow, Green, White Gloss Drip Glaze, Handles, C.C. Cole, 4 ¾ x 3 ½ In.	15.00
Washbasin, Pitcher, Grimwades, 5 x 12 In.	94.00
Water Dropper, Seated Man, Red Cloak, Coiled Pattern, c.1870, 1 ¾ x 2 ½ In.	150.00
Water Jar, Glaze, Handles, Muldok Onggi, Korea, c.1910, 16 ½ x 7 ½ In.	588.00

POTTERY-ART Art pottery was first made in America in Cincinnati, Ohio, during the 1870s. The pieces were hand thrown and hand decorated. The art pottery tradition continued until the 1930s when studio potters began making the more artistic wares. American, English, and Continental art pottery by less well-known makers is listed here. Most makers listed in *Kovels' American Art Pottery,* such as Arequipa, Ohr, Rookwood, Roseville, and Weller, are listed in their own categories in this book. More recent pottery is listed under the name of the maker or in another pottery category.

Bowl, Art Nouveau, Handles, Purple, Gold Ginko, Clement Massier, France, c.1900, 5 In.	205.00
Bowl, Bulbous, Aqua Blue Glaze, Incised, Scheier, 9 x 5 In.	374.00
Bowl, Caramel Glaze, Cone Shape, Gertrude & Otto Natzler, c.1960, 5 x 10 In.	3081.00
Bowl, Lapis Blue Glaze, Natzler, 3 x 7 In.	1680.00
Bowl, Paneled, Rose Semimatte Glaze, 14 Panels, 2 ½ x 6 In.	45.00
Box, Oval, Beetle On Lid, Brown, Green Matte Glaze, Denbac, 2 ½ x 4 In.	240.00
Charger, Birds, Branches, Fish, Multicolored, Gilt, Montereau, Barluet & Cie., c.1875, 19 In.	1541.00
Dish, Harris Strong, Lion, Yellow Semimatte Glaze, 1950s, 10 x 4 ⅛ In.	165.00
Dish, Soap Set, Vines, Blue, White, Dallas Pottery, K. Cairns, 1881, 6 ½ In., 3 Piece	633.00
Ewer, Lily Of The Valley, Blue, Green Matte Glaze, Art Nouveau, Denver, 10 ½ In.	745.00
Figurine, K. Klaus, Serapis, Dancing Woman, Black, Gold, Blue, E. Wahliss, c.1910, 12 In.	2988.00
Figurine, Lion, White, Reclining, Bristol Glaze, Cobalt Eyes, Summit County, Ohio, Early 1900s, 10 In.	382.00
Figurine, Menacing, Staff, Standing, Oval Base, Chinese Blue, 12 In.	382.00
Jar, Lid, K. Klaus, Serapis Faience, Blue, Gold, Scroll Panel, E. Wahliss, c.1912, 22 In., Pair	17925.00
Jar, Oval, Triangular Handles, Coffee Brown Glaze, 6 x 8 ½ In.	92.00
Jardiniere, Cat, Raised Feline Faces, Bodies Around Bowl, Vance Avon Faience Co., 7 In.	345.00
Jardiniere, Mermaids, Sea Life, High Relief, Brown, Green Glaze, Vance Faience Co., 10 x 12 In.	201.00
Jardiniere, Spanish Style, Birds, Flowers, Pedestal, 9 x 7 ½ In. ......*illus*	35.00
Pitcher, Bloomfield, Yellow Matte Glaze, Embossed Mark, 5 ½ x 6 In.	70.00
Pitcher, Forked Trees, Green, Orange, Brown, Jervis Pottery, 4 In.	575.00
Pitcher, Jean Baptiste Massier, Handle Figure Of Woman, Black, Gold, c.1900, 18 In.	5378.00
Pitcher, Red, Green Semimatte Glaze, Gourd Shaped, W.J. Walley, 9 ½ x 6 In.	2520.00
Pitcher, Rose Semimatte Glaze, Incised, Zanesville, 9 In.	95.00
Planter, Art Nouveau, Flowers, Red Ground, Scalloped Rim, Inner Liner, Mark, Austria, 12 x 5 In.	144.00
Plate, Painted Abstract Decoration, Signed, Henry Varnum Poor, 1970, 9 ½ In.	366.00
Plate, Stylized Peacock, Walter I. Anderson, 8 ½ In.	2806.00
Pot, Verdantone, Embossed, Drip Glaze, Footed, Zanesville Stoneware Co., c.1920, 6 In.	120.00
Tankard, Figure Walking, Landscape, Red Sky, Multicolored, Dark High Glaze, J. Hale, 12 In.	115.00
Vase, 2 Handle Shape, Flowers, Geometric Designs, Multicolored Glaze, Art Nouveau, Mark, 4 x 8 In.	210.00
Vase, 2 Layers Glaze, Leaves, Stems, Green, Lavender, Oval, Zark, 9 x 4 In.	1464.00
Vase, 3 Twisting Handles, Blue, Brown Glaze, Crystalline, Continental, 8 x 12 In.	90.00

Pottery-Art, Vase, Asian Style, 4 Figural Handles, Oxblood Majolica Glaze, 9 x 6 ¼ In. $3900.00

Pottery-Art, Vase, Baluster, Brown-Eyed Susans, Black, Green, John Bennett, 7 x 4 ¾ In. $4800.00

Pottery-Art, Vase, Brown, Ivory Mottled, Bulbous, Signed Vivika & Otto Heino, 6 x 5 In. $360.00

Pottery-Art, Vase, Glazed, Rene Buthaud, Marked RB Underglaze, c.1925, 14 ½ In. $10625.00

Pottery-Art, Vase, Gray,
Red Mottled Drip Glaze, Bulbous,
Rhead, 2 ¼ x 3 In.
$540.00

Pottery-Art, Vase, Ivory Glaze, Incised,
French Words, Taxile Doat, c.1907, 4 x 10 In.
$4200.00

Pottery-Art, Vase, Persian Flower,
4 Openings, Multicolor, 19th Century, 8 In.
$81.00

Pottery-Art, Vase, Yellow Mottled Glaze,
Iridescent, Wishbone Mark,
Brouwer, 4 x 4 In.
$1020.00

Pottery-Contemporary, Figurine, Girl,
Bjorn Wiinblad, Copenhagen,
c.1990, 5 Ft. 1 In.
$1610.00

Pottery-Contemporary, Vase, Bauhah,
Glazed, Signed, Claude Conover, 22 x 18 In.
$6900.00

Pottery-Contemporary, Vase, Blue,
Green Drip Glaze, Signed Fantoni, Raymor,
1970s, 10 x 4 ¼ In.
$100.00

Pottery-Midcentury, Charger,
Stylized Exotic Fish, Signed,
Marc Bellaire, 13 ½ In.
$84.00

Pottery-Midcentury, Figurine, Cat,
Applied Details, Label, Signed,
Marcello Fantoni, Italy, 12 x 22 In.
$960.00

P

Vase, 5 Oval Panels, Primitive Face, Green, Brown Glaze, Edwin Scheier, 5 ½ x 7 In.	745.00
Vase, Abstract Flowers, Brown Base, Gourd Shape, Art Deco, Mougin Nancy, 8 ½ In.	244.00
Vase, Abstract Pattern, Green, Black, White, Yellow, Distel, Theodoor Nieuwenhuis, c.1915, 9 In.	7170.00
Vase, Abstract Sunflower Design, Brown Tones, Chris Lanooy, c.1907, 13 ¼ In.	1793.00
Vase, Amphora Shape, Leaves, Black, Pink, Green, Gold, 5 Handles, Marked, 12 x 5 In.	480.00
Vase, Amphora Shape, Painted Landscape, Rose Garlands, Gold Knot Neck, MPH, Mark, 5 x 10 In.	360.00
Vase, Amphora Shape, Shouldered, Raised Green Lines, Mottled Green, Red Metallic Glaze, 4 x 7 In.	390.00
Vase, Andre Delatte, Nancy Etched, Enameled, c.1920, 8 In.	1053.00
Vase, Arched Handle, Brown Tones, Abstract Design, c.1900, 12 ⅜ In.	2988.00
Vase, Art Nouveau, Double Elongated Handles, Green, Swirled Design, c.1900, 18 In.	146.00
Vase, Arts & Crafts, Embossed Raised Tulips, Green Matte Glaze, 6 ½ x 11 ½ In.	390.00
Vase, Arts & Crafts, Ribbed, Red Panels, Green Matte Glaze, Signed S. & S. W, 12 In.	1150.00
Vase, Asian Style, 4 Figural Handles, Oxblood Majolica Glaze, 9 x 6 ¼ In. .... *illus*	3900.00
Vase, Baluster, Brown-Eyed Susans, Black, Green, John Bennett, 7 x 4 ¾ In. .... *illus*	4800.00
Vase, Bird Shape, Beak, Wings, Tail, White, Green, Red Flowers, B. Wiinblad, Denmark, 8 x 10 In.	60.00
Vase, Blue Crystalline Glaze, Bulbous, Arts & Crafts, 5 ½ x 6 ½ In.	240.00
Vase, Bretby, Dark Green High Glaze, Tapered, Inverted Rim, Mark, 9 x 8 ½ In.	86.00
Vase, Bronze Mounted, Beaded Rim, Painted, Dragon Handles, Footed, Enameled, 20 In.	224.00
Vase, Brown, Gold, Fire Painted, Impressed, T. Brower, Middle Lane Pottery, 7 In.	805.00
Vase, Brown, Ivory Mottled, Bulbous, Signed Vivika & Otto Heino, 6 x 5 In. .... *illus*	360.00
Vase, Bulbous, Green, Blue, Brown Crystalline Glaze, Pierrefonds, 8 ½ In.	420.00
Vase, Bulbous Shape, Ivory, Red, Blue Matte Glaze, Mark, Dalpayrat, 9 x 11 In.	3600.00
Vase, Bulbous Shape, Painted Portrait, Pastels, Mark, 4 x 5 In.	1800.00
Vase, Bulbous, Tan Glaze, Crystalline Highlights, Laura Anderson, 5 ¼ In.	720.00
Vase, Cafe-Au-Lait Crystalline Glaze, Long Neck, Grand Feu, 12 x 4 ½ In.	3050.00
Vase, Carved Mountain, Trees, Rhead, 3 ¾ x 4 In.	1464.00
Vase, Carved, Painted, 2 Muscular Nudes, Flowers, Gray Crackle Glaze, Red Brown Ground, 11 ½ In.	1610.00
Vase, Cloud Design, Scalloped Rim, Green, Brown, Twin Handles, R. St. & K. Mark, 19 In., Pair.	460.00
Vase, Cover, Santa Barbara, Bulbous, Morning Glories, Lavender & Black Ground, 7 x 8 ½ In.	374.00
Vase, Crackle Glaze, Flowers, Green, Orange, Wood Stand, Chinese, 8 x 13 In.	88.00
Vase, Double Opening, Gunmetal Glaze, White Interior, George Jouve, France, 17 x 12 In.	7800.00
Vase, Drip High Gloss Glaze, Green, Blue, Gold, Devonmoor, 9 ½ x 6 In.	135.00
Vase, E. Wahliss, Round, Overlapping Leaves, White, Green, Orange, 3 Handles, Paul Daschel, 5 x 6 In.	1200.00
Vase, Enamel, Urn Shape, Rhead, 4 ½ x 4 ½ In.	4270.00
Vase, Floor, Bulbous, Green, Brown, Ivory Drip Glaze, Robinson Ransbottom, 13 x 17 ½ In. ...	115.00
Vase, Glazed, Rene Buthaud, Marked RB Underglaze, c.1925, 14 ½ In. .... *illus*	10625.00
Vase, Grapes, Vines, Leaves, Cream, White, W. Stephen, Nonconnah Pottery, 1914, 7 In.	1093.00
Vase, Gray, Red Mottled Drip Glaze, Bulbous, Rhead, 2 ¼ x 3 In. .... *illus*	540.00
Vase, Green, Gourd Shape, Applied Leaves, W.J. Walley, 6 ½ x 5 In.	3172.00
Vase, Green, Squat, Applied Leaves, W.J. Walley, 4 ½ x 7 ¾ In.	4270.00
Vase, Incised Poppies, Green Matte Glaze, Vance Avon Faience, 11 In.	575.00
Vase, Iridescent Blue Glaze, Embossed White Dragonfly, Austria, 5 In.	546.00
Vase, Iridescent Glaze, 4 Twisted Ribbon Handles, Austria, 10 In.	633.00
Vase, Ivory Glaze, Incised, French Words, Taxile Doat, c.1907, 4 x 10 In. .... *illus*	4200.00
Vase, Kitty Rix, Double Shape, Applied Designs, Green, Orange, Wiener Werkstatte, 9 x 8 In. ...	1140.00
Vase, Klint Style, Winged Black, Blue Beetle, Flowers, Gold, Green, White, Handles, R. St. & K, 16 In.	3335.00
Vase, Leaf Molded, Bulbous, Green Semigloss Glaze, Walley Pottery, 7 In.	1898.00
Vase, Leaves & Flowers, White Ground, Basket Design Base, Bow Shape Handles, 8 In.	12.00
Vase, Louis Lourloux, Green & Brown Mottled Matte Glaze, 4 Handles, 9 In.	230.00
Vase, Lustered Glaze, Baluster, Incised Whalebone, Theophilus A. Brouwer, 7 x 3 ¾ In.	1159.00
Vase, Microcrystalline Glaze, Bottle Shape, Grand Feu, 9 x 4 In.	4200.00
Vase, Molded Leaf, Scottish Rose, Gold, Yellow, Brown, Vance Avon Faience, c.1902, 7 In., Pair	345.00
Vase, Multicolored, Green Semigloss Ground, Modern Designs, Handles, Plateelbakkerij, Dutch, 16 In.	345.00
Vase, Multitoned Blue Matte Glaze, Slender, William Wyman, 1958, 17 ½ In.	660.00
Vase, Narrow Base, Molded Leaves, Red, Blue, Ivory Matte Glaze, Applied Metal Overlay, 4 x 3 ½ In.	450.00
Vase, Oval, White Bridge, Branches, Green Ground, N. Steven, Nonconnah, 11 In.	8740.00
Vase, Pear Shape, Iridescent Cinnamon, Bronze Frame, Wilhelm Kralic, 1900s, 27 In.	2160.00
Vase, Persian Flower, 4 Openings, Multicolor, 19th Century, 8 In. .... *illus*	81.00
Vase, Primavera, Horses, Trees, 3 Handles, Art Deco, 13 In.	878.00
Vase, Purple Gray Striations, Matte Glaze, Narrow Neck, Julie Larson, 9 ¼ x 5 ½ In.	94.00
Vase, Shouldered, Hand Tooled Leaves, Green, Brown Glaze, Impressed, Walley Pottery, 8 In. ..	2875.00
Vase, Shouldered Shaped, Multitoned Blue, Brown, Mougin, Marked, J. Wolfe, c.1900, 8 In.	480.00
Vase, Snake Rim, Whalebone, Theophilus A. Brouwer, 4 ½ x 4 ¼ In.	5795.00
Vase, Square, Stepped, Round Rim, Cubist Panels, Black, Tan, Orange, R. Lallemant, c.1925, 10 In.	2868.00
Vase, Stylized Owls, White, Orange, Yellow, Egg Shape, Chris Van Der Hoef, c.1906, 13 In.	3585.00
Vase, Stylized Trees, Blue, Ivory Glaze, Bulbous, Paul Daschel, 5 ½ x 5 ½ In.	1440.00

Pottery-Midcentury, Figurine, Cubist, Incised, Marcello Fantoni, Italy, 1950s, 9 x 18 In., Pair
$3360.00

Pottery-Midcentury, Figurine, Persephone, Rose Glaze, Cut Back To White, Waylande Gregory, 11 ⅝ In.
$1725.00

Pottery-Midcentury, Plaque, Picasso, Visage No. 157, Madoura Edition, 10 In.
$4140.00

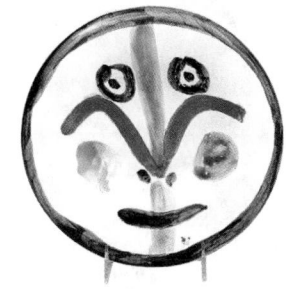

Pottery-Midcentury, Umbrella Stand, Birds, Signed Fornasetti, Milano, Italy, 10 x 23 In.
$960.00

P

Pottery-Midcentury, Vase, Balba, Glazed, Signed, Claude Conover, 21 ½ x 18 In.
$6600.00

Pottery-Midcentury, Vase, Brown Butterflies, Indigo Ground, California Faience, 5 x 5 In.
$840.00

Pottery-Midcentury, Vase, Celadon, Olive Splotches, Impressed Marks, Bernard Leach, St. Ives, 6 In.
$403.00

Pottery-Midcentury, Vase, Sgraffito, Faces, Mottled Cinnabar, Lawrence Blazey, 12 x 6 In.
$322.00

Vase, Tapered, Brown, Tan Glaze, Large Red Crystals, Signed, Adelaide Robineau, 6 ¼ In.	10800.00
Vase, Tiger Eye Crystalline Glaze, Squat, Grand Feu, 4 ½ x 7 ½ In.	3600.00
Vase, Walley, Bulbous, Flared Rim, Green Striated Glaze, 3 Handles, Signed W.J.W., 10 In.	748.00
Vase, Wardle, Brown Glaze, Painted, Docked Boats, Signed A. Eaton, 4 ½ x 10 ½ In.	86.00
Vase, Yellow Flowers, Red Berries, Green Ground, John Bennett, Signed, 9 In., Pair	9000.00
Vase, Yellow Mottled Glaze, Iridescent, Wishbone Mark, Brouwer, 4 x 4 In. *illus*	1020.00
Water Jug, Bird Shape, Picasso, Madoura, France, 9 ¼ x 8 ¾ In.	3000.00

POTTERY-CONTEMPORARY lists pieces made by artists working after 1975.

Basket, Stoneware, Hare Handle, Ken Ferguson, 14 x 12 In.	5400.00
Bowl, Common Ground, Canna Lily, Mark, Eric Olson, No. 112, 12 In.	360.00
Bowl, Gilded, Inlaid Porcelain, Thomas Hoadley, 7 x 9 In.	1680.00
Bowl, Glazed Ceramic, Incised, James Lovera, c.1980, 4 x 10 In.	2185.00
Bowl, Incised Stoneware, Blue, Brown Wavy Lines, Gustavo Perez, 5 x 7 In.	1920.00
Bowl, Jar, Lid, Red Clay, Yellow, Green Abstract Marks, Betty Woodman, 10 x 6 In.	720.00
Charger, Blue Underglaze, Enameled Iris, Patterns, Ralph Bacerra, 22 In.	1800.00
Charger, Dipped Glazes, Cream, Brown, Toshiko Takaezu, 18 In.	900.00
Charger, Musicians, Days Of Be Bop On Rim, Michael Frimkess, 1972, 14 ½ In.	2400.00
Charger, Rider On Horse, Beatrice Wood, Signed, 1 ½ x 12 ¼ In.	1586.00
Charger, Stylized Leaves, Tan & Brown Ground, Signed, E. Olson, 12 ½ In.	390.00
Charger, Woman Inside Lion, Cobalt, Gunmetal Glaze, Scheier, 12 ½ In.	1220.00
Cup, Orange, Yellow Glaze, Gilt Interior, Black Feet, Bennett Bean, 5 ½ x 5 In.	1560.00
Figurine, Girl, Bjorn Wiinblad, Copenhagen, c.1990, 5 Ft. 1 In. *illus*	1610.00
Planter, John Follis, Architectural Pottery, White Glaze, c.1955, 10 x 11 In.	270.00
Sculpture, 2 Figures, The Superior Masculine Mind, Beatrice Wood, 19 x 14 In.	2640.00
Sugar & Creamer, Tray, Organic Shape, Black Glaze, Peter Saenger, 9 x 6 x 5 In.	100.00
Vase, Abstract Figures, Dead Matte Band, Brown Speckled Ground, 9 x 9 In.	4880.00
Vase, Abstract Landscape, Blues & Browns, Wavy Neck, No. 141, Claude Renoir, 13 In.	61.00
Vase, Amber, Bulbous, Orange & White Blossoms, Leaves, Lotton, 1982, 6 ¼ In.	470.00
Vase, Bauhah, Glazed, Signed, Claude Conover, 22 x 18 In. *illus*	6900.00
Vase, Black Outlined Figures, Orange, Keith Haring, Signed, 1989, 11 In.	13200.00
Vase, Black Walnut, Squat, Ridges, Robert Ward, Canada, 5 x 12 In.	380.00
Vase, Blue, Green Drip Glaze, Signed Fantoni, Raymor, 1970s, 10 x 4 ¼ In. *illus*	100.00
Vase, Bulbous, Blue & White Drip Glaze, Signed, 20th Century, 7 ½ In.	12.00
Vase, Calla Lilies, Mottled Tan & Brown Ground, Signed, E. Olson, 2003, 5 x 9 In.	390.00
Vase, Common Ground, Bulbous, Water Lily, Eric Olson, No. 331, 8 x 8 In.	360.00
Vase, Iridescent Gold, Oval, Blue & White Blossoms, C. Lotton, 1979, 6 ¼ In.	588.00
Vase, Men Inside Fish, Turquoise, Bronze Glaze, Scheier, Signed, 12 ½ x 12 In.	2806.00
Vase, Rust, Blue Speckled Glazes, Peter Voulkos, Signed, 7 ¼ x 6 ½ In.	3995.00
Vase, Squat, Geometric, James Mac Anderson, 4 ¾ x 7 In.	2562.00
Vase, White, Silver Green Pulled Vine, Crimson Inside, Lotton, 1975, 7 ¾ In.	588.00
Vase, Women, Fish, Lavender, Eggplant, Gunmetal Dead Matte Glaze, 13 x 13 In.	4575.00
Vase, Women, Fish, Ultramarine, Bronze, Glaze, Scheier, Signed, 10 x 14 In.	3050.00

POTTERY-MIDCENTURY includes pieces made from the 1940s to about 1975.

Bottle, Green Matte Glaze, Gray Crystalline Inclusions, Rose Cabat, 6 In.	1600.00
Bowl, Asymmetrical, Gun Metal Black, Signed, Georges Jouve, 6 ¼ x 5 ½ In.	2800.00
Bowl, Bisque, Guy With A Strange Eye, Ed Eberle, 6 In.	480.00
Bowl, Black Patterned Glaze, Boat Shape, Norway, 8 x 4 ½ In.	45.00
Bowl, Blue, Incised Fish, Aluminia, Nils Thorsson, Early 1950s, 7 x 7 In.	40.00
Bowl, Fish, Multicolored Glaze, Desimone, Vietri, Italy, 9 ¼ x 5 In.	125.00
Bowl, Fish, White Interior, Blue Exterior, Sgrafo, Germany, 13 In.	85.00
Bowl, Flared, Mottled Blue & Lavender Glaze, Footed, Natzler, 7 x 3 In.	1800.00
Bowl, Incised Geometrics, Green, Brown Matte Glaze, Footed, H. McIntosh, 6 x 3 In.	1020.00
Bowl, Iridescent Glaze, Stylized Leaf Shape, Scandinavia, 7 x 5 In.	50.00
Bowl, Pink Volcanic Glaze, Signed, Beato, c.1955, 7 ½ x 13 In.	4594.00
Bowl, Red Clay, Gray Drip Glaze, Signed, Edna Arnow, 1950, 7 x 4 In.	270.00
Charger, Stylized Exotic Fish, Signed, Marc Bellaire, 13 ½ In. *illus*	84.00
Chess Piece, Figural, Queen, Desimone, Vietri, Italy, 13 In.	185.00
Compote, 3 Cherubs, Carrying Boat, Germany, c.1950, 8 x 11 In.	70.00
Compote, Incised Pear Designs, Yellow, Green, Henry Varnum Poor, 1948, 5 ½ x 9 ½ In.	3360.00
Cup, Mottled Oxblood Glaze, Melt Fissures, Natzler, 4 ¼ x 4 ¼ In.	610.00
Feelie, Beige, Yellow, Light Green, Signed, Rose Cabat, 2 ¾ In.	285.00
Feelie, Flying Saucer, Cobalt Blue, Green, Signed, Rose Cabat, 2 ⅛ In.	240.00
Feelie, Olive Gray Over Black, Signed, 384, Cabat, 3 In.	250.00
Feelie, Turquoise, Gunmetal Gray, Signed, 441, Cabat, 2 ¾ In.	210.00

Figurine, Cat, Applied Details, Label, Signed, Marcello Fantoni, Italy, 12 x 22 In.	*illus*	960.00
Figurine, Cubist, Incised, Marcello Fantoni, Italy, 1950s, 9 x 18 In., Pair	*illus*	3360.00
Figurine, Persephone, Rose Glaze, Cut Back To White, Waylande Gregory, 11 ⅝ In.	*illus*	1725.00
Figurine, Viking Dude, Denmark, 9 ½ In.		75.00
Jar, Cover, Stoneware, Signed, Vivika & Otto Heino, c.1958, 14 ½ x 9 In.		796.00
Jug, Grotesque, Runny Blue Glaze, China Teeth, Marked, Bill Flowers, N.C., 10 ½ In.		398.00
Pitcher, Gold, Brown Patch Glaze, JASBA Keramic, Germany, 1950s, 6 ½ In.		65.00
Pitcher, Light Glaze, Gray Ground, Soholm, Denmark, 7 ½ In.		65.00
Pitcher, Painted, Flowers, Fauna, Desimone, Italy, 8 ½ In.		125.00
Pitcher, Picasso, Painted Abstract Faces, Black, Orange, Terra-Cotta, 11 x 6 In.		2040.00
Pitcher, Picasso, Painted Owl, Blue, Black, Faience, Maddura, 10 x 8 In.		2520.00
Planter, Architectural, Flame Glaze, David Cressey, c.1968, 17 x 20 ½ In.		1225.00
Planter, Pig, Architectural, John Follis, Rex Goode, c.1949, 14 x 40 x 27 In.		2818.00
Planter, Textured, Signed, Victoria Littlejohn, c.1965, 7 ¾ x 13 ½ In.		613.00
Plaque, Chicken, Bennington Potteries, 15 x 11 ½ In.		75.00
Plaque, Fish, Abstract, Blue Glaze, On Tan Tile, Knabstrup, 11 ¾ x 9 ¼ In.		185.00
Plaque, Giraffe, Abstract, Blue Glaze, On Tan Tile, Knabstrup, 5 ¾ x 14 ¼ In.		185.00
Plaque, Picasso, Visage No. 157, Madoura Edition, 10 In.	*illus*	4140.00
Plate, Face With Hands, Pablo Picasso, White Earthenware, c.1956, 16 ½ In.		1470.00
Plate, Jacquline's Profile, Pablo Picasso, White Earthenware, c.1956, 16 ½ In.		6738.00
Sculpture, Head, Horizontally Elongated, Signed, 6 x 4 In.		185.00
Sculpture, Mad Scientist, Man, Beakers, Tubes, White, 1974, 11 x 12 In.		1680.00
Smoking Set, Ashtray, Cigarette Holder, Incised Blue, Signed, 5 & 2 ½ x 3 In.		35.00
Trivet, Fish, Blue Pattern, Porsgrund, c.1967, 8 x 5 ¼ In.		45.00
Umbrella Stand, Birds, Signed Fornasetti, Milano, Italy, 10 x 23 In.	*illus*	960.00
Vase, Architectural, La Mediterranea, White Matte Glaze, Spain, 1970s, 14 x 7 In.		65.00
Vase, Balba, Glazed, Signed, Claude Conover, 21 ½ x 18 In.	*illus*	6600.00
Vase, Blue Drip Lava Glaze, Black Glaze Ground, Scheurich Keramik, 1970s, 8 ¾ In.		40.00
Vase, Blue Speckled Glaze, Signed, Scheier, 9 x 7 In.		900.00
Vase, Brown Butterflies, Indigo Ground, California Faience, 5 x 5 In.	*illus*	840.00
Vase, Bulbous, Brown Over Blue Glaze, Bill Meadows, 9 ½ x 5 ¾ In.		75.00
Vase, Bulbous, Light Purple Glaze, Brown Accents, Otto Heino, 5 x 8 In.		660.00
Vase, Celadon, Olive Splotches, Impressed Marks, Bernard Leach, St. Ives, 6 In.	*illus*	403.00
Vase, Drip Glaze, Blue, Green, Brown Glaze, Textured, Yellow, Fantoni, 8 ¾ x 3 In.		225.00
Vase, Flared, Tooled, Blue Matte Glaze, Painted Clouds, E. Deutsch, 1945, 5 ¾ In.		480.00
Vase, Linie, Girl Holding A Flower, Bjorn Wiinblad, 14 ½ In.		600.00
Vase, Mottled Blue, Purple & Brown Glaze, Crystalline Accents, Heino, 5 ½ In.		360.00
Vase, Round, Mottled Blue & Brown Glaze, Vertical Ribs, V & O Heino, 4 x 3 In.		390.00
Vase, Sgraffito, Faces, Mottled Cinnabar, Lawrence Blazey, 12 x 6 In.	*illus*	322.00
Vase, Tea Bowl, Wood Fired, Cut Back Geometrics, Brown, Gray, Peter Voulkos, 6 In.		3600.00
Vase, Turquoise & Red Glazes, William Wyman, 1969, 4 x 4 ½ In.		150.00
Vase, Waisted, Rust, Drip Glaze, Fantoni, Italy, 12 In.		150.00
Woman's Head, Blended Glaze, Signed, Rudolph Mafko, c.1931, 13 ½ In.	*illus*	265.00

POWDER FLASKS AND POWDER HORNS were made to hold the gunpowder used in antique firearms. The early examples were made of horn or wood; later ones were of copper or brass.

POWDER FLASK

Brass, Embossed Guns, Leaves, Marked Hawksley & Sheffield, 9 ½ In.	*illus*	205.00
Brass, U.S., 1850		978.00
Brass, U.S., Eagle, 1832		920.00
Camel Scrotum, Penis Sheath, Embossed, Chain, Clip, Cap, Persia, c.1880, 14 x 4 In.		625.00
Pewter, Brass, 1860s		26.00

POWDER HORN

Carved, Whaling Ship, American Flag, Whale, Cornucopia, Whalebone Knob, c.1800	1600.00
Double, 3 Molded Bands, Yellow Surface, 11 ¾ In.	1112.00
Engraved, Revolutionary War, Ship, Anchor, Crown, Gun, Tomahawk, 13 ½ In.	1778.00
Engraved, Sailing Ships, Mermaid Holding Flowers, Elisha Bennett, 1772, 12 In.	1053.00
Engraved, Ships, Fish, Rifle, Inscribed, Samuel Harris, 1769, 13 ½ In.	2106.00
Engraved, Ships, Flowers, Animals, Deep Curved Body, c.1800, 13 ½ In.	1755.00
Engraved, Spread Wing Eagle, Deer, Dog, F.G. Hearn, January 4, 1848, 8 In.	176.00
Engraved Text, Women, Ships, Horses, Riders, Spout Stopper, 1821, 12 ½ In.	819.00
Etched, Animals, People, 8 ½ In.	351.00
Glass, Gray, White Looping, Applied Rings, Knop End, Pontil, c.1860, 10 In.	190.00
Horn, Domed & Gadrooned Wood End, Brass Ball Finial & Measure, 10 ½ In.	165.00
Lancaster County Type, Screw Tip, 10 ½ In. .... *illus*	322.00

Pottery-Midcentury, Woman's Head, Blended Glaze, Signed, Rudolph Mafko, c.1931, 13 ½ In.
$265.00

Powder Flask, Brass, Embossed Guns, Leaves, Marked Hawksley & Sheffield, 9 ½ In.
$205.00

Powder Horn, Lancaster County Type, Screw Tip, 10 ½ In.
$322.00

Powder Horn, York County Type, Screw Tip, Domed End Plug, Ring Turned, Leather Strap, 13 In.
$995.00

P

Pratt, Canister, Tea, Lid, Canted Corners, Relief Figures, 5 x 3 ¼ In.
$460.00

Pressed Glass, Actress, Dish, Pickle, Kate Claxton, Loves Request Is Pickles, c.1880, 9 x 5 In.
$50.00

Pressed Glass, Bull's-Eye & Wishbone, Goblet, 6 In.
$196.00

Pressed Glass, Chestnut, Tumbler, Ruby Stained, Jefferson Glass Co., 4 In.
$69.00

TIP

Pressed glass banana stands are being used today to hold rolled hand towels in a bathroom.

Map, New York, Engraved, Forts, 12 ½ In.	702.00
Pennsylvania, Screw Tip, Turned End Plug, 10 ½ In.	936.00
Pennsylvania, Screw Tip, Turned End Plug, Yellow, 11 ½ In.	2106.00
Ships, Bird, Trees, Inscribed Happy Birthday Jeremiah, June 28, 1834	5800.00
York County Type, Screw Tip, Domed End Plug, Ring Turned, Leather Strap, 13 In. ...... *illus*	995.00
York County Type, Turned Screw Tip, Chip Covered End Plugs, Patina, 13 In.	1989.00

PRATT ware means two different things. It was an early Staffordshire pottery, cream-colored with colored decorations, made by Felix Pratt during the late eighteenth century. There was also Pratt ware made with transfer designs during the mid-nineteenth century in Fenton, England. Reproductions of the transfer-printed Pratt are being made.

PRATT
FENTON

Canister, Tea, Lid, Canted Corners, Relief Figures, 5 x 3 ¼ In. ...... *illus*	460.00
Creamer, Cow, Maiden, Multicolored Enamel, 8-Sided Base, Leaf Border, c.1800, 6 In.	593.00
Creamer, Strawberry, Leaf, Helmet Form, Gadroon Border, Grape, Leaf Vine, 4 ¼ In.	88.00

PRESSED GLASS, or pattern glass, was first made in the United States in the 1820s after the invention of glass pressing machines. Hundreds of patterns of pressed glass were made in complete table settings. Although the Boston and Sandwich Works was the most famous of the pressed glass factories, there were about sixteen other factories making pressed glass from 1830 to 1850, and still more from 1850 to 1900, when pressed glass reached its greatest popularity. It is now being widely reproduced. The pattern names used in this listing are based on the information in the book *Pressed Glass in America* by John and Elizabeth Welker. There may be pieces of pressed glass listed in this book in other categories, such as Lamp, Ruby, Sandwich, and Souvenir.

1000-Eye pattern is listed here as Thousand Eye.	
ABC, Platter, Ice Cream Master, Federal Glass Co., c.1900, 5 ¾ x 4 ⅜ In.	119.00
Acanthus pattern is listed here as Ribbed Palm.	
Acme pattern is listed here as Butterfly With Spray.	
Acorn, Creamer, 3 ¼ In.	120.00
Actress, Cake Stand, Frosted, 6 ¾ x 10 In.	161.00
Actress, Dish, Pickle, Kate Claxton, Loves Request Is Pickles, c.1880, 9 x 5 In. ...... *illus*	50.00
Amberette, Celery Dish, Frosted, Amber Stain, c.1898, 4 ¼ x 10 ½ In., Pair	144.00
Amberette, Spooner, Frosted, Amber Stain, c.1898, 3 ¼ x 3 ¼ In., Pair	130.00
Amberette, Syrup, Pewter Lid, Frosted Glass, Amber Stain, c.1898, 3 x 8 In.	316.00
Arched Fleur-De-Lis, Banana Stand, Bryce Higbee, c.1898, 7 ¼ x 9 ⅞ In.	65.00
Argent, Plate, Bryce Brothers, c.1890, 8 x 6 In.	14.00
Argus, Compote, 8 x 3 ¾ In.	75.00
Ashburton, Champagne, 4 ⅞ x 2 ¾ In., Pair	184.00
Atlantic Cable, Bread Plate, Round, Handles, c.1858, 10 ½ In.	30.00
Austrian, Pitcher, Canary Vaseline, c.1900, 9 ⅛ x 5 In.	460.00
Austrian, Vase, Footed, Indiana Tumbler & Goblet Co., 10 In.	85.00
Baby Face, Goblet, Frosted Stem, 6 ¼ In.	259.00
Baby Thumbprint pattern is listed here as Dakota.	
Barred Oval, Celery Dish, Sloped Sides, Duncan & Sons, c.1892, 10 ½ x 4 ½ In.	35.00
Barred Oval, Compote, Duncan & Sons, c.1892, 7 ¼ x 7 In.	50.00
Barrel Honeycomb, see also the related pattern Honeycomb.	
Beaded Dewdrop pattern is listed here as Wisconsin.	
Beaded Grape Medallion, Goblet, Boston & Sandwich, c.1869, 6 x 3 ⅛ In.	49.00
Beaded Shell, Tumbler, Blue, Gold Trim, 3 ¾ x 2 ¾ In.	65.00
Bearded Head pattern is listed here as Viking.	
Bent Buckle pattern is listed here as New Hampshire.	
Bird in Ring pattern is listed here as Grace.	
Bird On Branch, Mug, Amber, Bryce Brothers, 1880s, 3 ⅜ x 2 ⅞ In.	43.00
Birds At Fountain, Mug, 1880s, 1 ¾ x 1 ⅞ In.	29.00
Birds, Mug, Amber, c.1880, 3 ½ x 3 ³⁄₁₆ In.	39.00
Bleeding Heart, Pitcher, Water, Boston & Sandwich, c.1875, 8 ½ x 4 ⅝ In.	325.00
Bleeding Heart, Salt, King Son & Co., Master, c.1875, 3 ½ In.	170.00
Block & Fine Cut pattern is listed here as Fine Cut & Block.	
Bouquet, Beverage Set, Stained, Rose, Green, Gilt, Pitcher, Tumblers, 8 ⅜ In., 7 Piece	150.00
Bowtie, Punch Bowl, Flat Bottom, 10 x 5 ¼ In.	190.00
Broken Column, Water Bottle, Columbia Glass Co., c.1888, 8 ½ In.	170.00
Broughton pattern is listed here as Pattee Cross.	
Bucket pattern is listed here as Oaken Bucket.	
Buckle, Goblet, Flint, Boston & Sandwich, c.1870, 6 x 3 ¼ In.	45.00
Bull's-Eye & Fan, Toothpick, U.S. Glass, Collar Base, c.1897, 3 x 2 In.	22.00
Bull's-Eye & Wishbone, Goblet, 6 In. ...... *illus*	196.00

Pressed Glass, Colorado, Butter, Domed Cover, Green, Gold Trim, Footed, 6 ¼ x 7 In.
$58.00

Pressed Glass, Colorado, Punch Cup, Green, Gold Trim, 3-Footed
$20.00

Pressed Glass, Columbia, Syrup, Lid, Amber, Vaseline, Gilt, 7 In.
$81.00

Pressed Glass, Daisy & Button, Match Holder, Umbrella Shape, Vaseline, Metal Handle, 6 ¼ In.
$518.00

Ruby Glass
Remember the singer Kate Smith? She collected ruby stained glass— and started a collecting craze in the 1950s.

Pressed Glass, Dakota, Goblet, Ruby Stained, Engraved Flowers 6 ¼ In.
$81.00

Pressed Glass, Deer & Pine Tree, Cake Stand, 6 x 9 ¼ In.
$104.00

Pressed Glass, Diamond Point, Compote, 10 ¼ x 10 ⅜ In.
$104.00

Pressed Glass, Excelsior, Compote, Cover, Double-Ringed Stem, 13 ¼ x 9 ¼ In.
$489.00

Pressed Glass, Feather, Pitcher, Milk, Patterned Foot, 8 x 4 ¼ In.
$196.00

Pressed Glass, Fine Cut & Block Variant, Ice Cream Set, Amber Stained, Tab Handle, 7 Piece
$46.00

Pressed Glass, Flying Birds, Wine, 5 ¾ In.
$104.00

Pressed Glass, Frosted Lion, Cheese Dish, 5 ¾ x 7 ¾ In.
$403.00

P

Pressed Glass, Horn Of Plenty, Jam Jar, Pontil, 5 x 2 ⅜ In.
$920.00

Pressed Glass, Horseshoe, Cheese Dish, 5 ¾ x 7 ½ In.
$259.00

Pressed Glass, Hummingbird, Pitcher, Water, Blue, 9 In.
$259.00

P

TIP

Old milk glass is slightly opalescent at the edge when held up to a strong light. New glass is not.

Butterfly & Fan pattern is listed here as Grace.

Butterfly With Spray, Mug, Bryce Higbee & Co., c.1883, 3 ½ x 3 ¼ In.	42.00
Buzz Star, Butter, Cover, c.1910	33.00
Cable, Eggcup, Boston & Sandwich, c.1860, 3 ¾ x 2 ⅝ In.	44.00

Candlewick as a pressed glass pattern is properly named Banded Raindrop. There is also a pattern called Candlewick, which has been made by Imperial Glass Corporation since 1936. It is listed in this book in the Imperial Glass category.

Cathedral, Wine, Bryce Brothers, c.1885, 4 ⅜ x 2 In., 3 Piece	36.00
Centennial, see also the related patterns Liberty Bell and Viking.	
Chestnut, Tumbler, Ruby Stained, Jefferson Glass Co., 4 In. ....*illus*	69.00
Chicks & Pugs, Mug, Bryce Brothers, c.1890, 2 x 1 ⅞ In.	70.00
Church Windows pattern is listed here as Columbia.	
Clematis & Scroll, Salt & Pepper, Blue Opaque Glass, Late 1800s	68.00
Coin Spot pattern is listed in this book in its own category.	
Colorado, Butter, Domed Cover, Green, Gold Trim, Footed, 6 ¼ x 7 In. ....*illus*	58.00
Colorado, Punch Cup, Green, Gold Trim, 3-Footed ....*illus*	20.00
Columbia, Syrup, Lid, Amber, Vaseline, Gilt, 7 In. ....*illus*	81.00
Compact pattern is listed here as Snail.	
Cordova, Creamer, Ruby Stain, Enamel Flowers, O'Hara Glass Co., 2 ¾ x 2 ¼ In.	37.00
Cosmos pattern is listed in this book as its own category.	
Cottage, Cup & Saucer, Adams & Company, c.1870, 3 x 3 In.	42.00
Crane pattern is listed here as Stork.	
Cupid & Venus, Compote, Cover, Scalloped Rim, Richards & Hartley, c.1891, 8 ½ x 8 In.	95.00
Cut Log, Wine, 3 ⅞ In.	90.00
Dahlia pattern is listed here as Square Fuchsia.	
Daisies in Oval Panels pattern is listed here as Bull's-Eye & Fan.	
Daisy & Button, Candy Dish, Gondola Railroad Car, Blue, 10, 000 Lbs., 2 ½ x 4 ¼ In.	161.00
Daisy & Button, Finger Bowl, Crossbars, Canary Yellow, c.1890, 3 x 4 ¼ In.	40.00
Daisy & Button, Match Holder, Blue, 2 Stippled Striker Surfaces, c.1880, 3 x 2 In.	45.00
Daisy & Button, Match Holder, Umbrella Shape, Vaseline, Metal Handle, 6 ¼ In. ....*illus*	518.00
Daisy & Button, Punch Cup, Amber, Bryce Bros., 4 Piece	70.00
Daisy & Button, Toothpick, Anvil Shape, Blue, U.S. Glass, c.1886, 2 x 4 In.	60.00
Daisy & Button, Tumbler, Vaseline, Hobbs, Brockunier & Co., c.1885, 4 x 2 ⅞ In.	60.00
Dakota, Goblet, Ruby Stained, Engraved Flowers 6 ¼ In. ....*illus*	81.00
Deer & Dog, Mug, Amber, U.S. Glass, c.1880, 2 ⅜ x 2 ⅝ In.	75.00
Deer & Pine Tree, Cake Stand, 6 x 9 ¼ In. ....*illus*	104.00
Deer & Pine Tree, Mug, Amber, c.1886, 2 ⅜ x 2 ⅜ In.	48.00
Diamond & Bull's-Eye Band, Pitcher, Water, Engraved Leaves, 10 ¼ In.	56.00
Diamond Panels, Spooner, Child's, 1800s, 2 ⅜ x 2 ⅛ In.	33.00
Diamond Point, Compote, 10 ¼ x 10 ⅜ In. ....*illus*	104.00
Diamond Thumbprint, Tumbler, Lemonade, Applied Handle, 3 In.	855.00
Dog Hunting, Pitcher, Water, 8 ⅝ In.	288.00
Doric pattern is listed here as Feather.	
Double Ribbon, Creamer, Bakewell Pears & Co., c.1870, 5 ½ x 3 ½ In.	29.00
Earl pattern is listed here as Spirea Band.	
Egyptian, Water Set, Pitcher, 3 Goblets, 9 ½ & 6 In.	219.00
Emerald Green Herringbone, Wine, 3 ⅞ In.	35.00
Empress, Syrup, Emerald Green, Gold Trim, Riverside Glass, c.1900, 7 In.	145.00
English Hobnail Cross pattern is listed here as Amberette.	
Etched Dakota pattern is listed here as Dakota.	
Eureka, Salt & Pepper, National Glass Co., c.1901	45.00
Excelsior, Compote, Cover, Double-Ringed Stem, 13 ¼ x 9 ¼ In. ....*illus*	489.00
Eyewinker, Saltshaker, Dalzell Gilmore & Leighton, c.1860	110.00
Fan, Relish, Aesthetic, Beaded Edge, Handle, 3-Footed, c.1890, 6 In.	38.00
Feather, Pitcher, Milk, Patterned Foot, 8 x 4 ¼ In. ....*illus*	196.00
Festoon & Grape pattern is listed here as Grape & Festoon.	
Fine Cut & Block Variant, Ice Cream Set, Amber Stained, Tab Handle, 7 Piece ....*illus*	46.00
Fine Cut & Block, Water Set, Amber Stained, 10-In. Pitcher, 7 Piece	219.00
Fine Cut & Feather pattern is listed here as Feather.	
Fine Cut & Panel, Wine, Blue, 3 ¾ In., 8 Piece	46.00
Florida pattern pieces are listed here as Sunken Primrose if made of clear glass and as Emerald Green Herringbone if made of green glass.	
Flute, Eggcup, 3 ⅛ x 2 ⅝ In.	20.00
Flying Birds, Wine, 5 ¾ In. ....*illus*	104.00
Flying Robin pattern is listed here as Hummingbird.	

Forget-Me-Not, Salt, Challinors, White Mold Blown, 1880s	28.00

Frosted Crane pattern is listed here as Frosted Stork.

Frosted Leaf, Salt, Master, c.1860, 3 x 2 ¾ In.	95.00
Frosted Lion, Cheese Dish, 5 ¾ x 7 ¾ In. .... *illus*	403.00
Frosted Lion, Goblet, 6 ½ In., 4 Piece	127.00
Frosted Lion, Syrup, Britannia Lid, Applied Handle, 7 ¼ x 4 In.	547.00
Frosted Stork, Compote, Footed, 7 ½ x 8 ¼ In.	55.00
Frosted Stork, Creamer, Lily-Of-The-Valley Sprays, Crystal Glass Co., c.1880, 6 x 3 ½ In.	65.00

Frosted patterns may also be listed under the name of the main pattern.

Fuchsia, Spooner, Scalloped Rim, c.1875, 5 In.	37.00

Garden of Eden, see the related pattern Lotus & Serpent.

Garland Drape, Goblet, Gilt Rim, 5 ¾ x 2 ⅞ In.	350.00

Good Luck pattern is listed here as Horseshoe.

Grace, Celery Vase, George Duncan & Sons, c.1880, 9 ⅛ In.	155.00

Grand Army of the Republic pattern is listed here as Historical.

Grape & Cable pattern is listed in this book in the Northwood category.

Grape & Festoon, Eggcup, c.1880, 3 ⅞ x 2 ½ In.	22.00

Grape, see the related patterns Beaded Grape Medallion and Magnet & Grape.

Hamilton, Tumbler, Whiskey, 3 x 2 ½ In.	219.00
Hamilton, Wine, 4 ⅞ In.	60.00

Hamilton With Clear Leaf pattern is listed here as Hamilton With Leaf.

Hamilton With Leaf, Dish, Sweetmeat, Leaf Covered, Wafer Construction, 6 ¾ x 6 In.	92.00
Hand, Jam Jar, O'Hara Glass Co., c.1880, 6 x 2 ¾ In.	55.00
Hawaiian Lei, Spooner, Scalloped Edge, Bryce Higbee, c.1913	16.00
Heart With Thumbprint, Ice Bucket, Tarentum Glass Co., c.1898, 5 x 5 ¾ In.	130.00
Historical, Mug, George Peabody, Blue, c.1869, 2 ½ x 2 ½ In.	95.00

Hobnail pattern is in this book as its own category.

Holly, Dish, Pickle, Greentown, 2 Handles, c.1900, 8 ⅞ x 4 In.	75.00

Honeycomb, see also the related patterns Barrel Honeycomb and Vernon Honeycomb.

Honeycomb, Cake Stand, Silver Metal Connector, 6 x 10 In.	58.00
Honeycomb, Jar, Tobacco, Cover, 13 ¼ x 4 ¾ In., Pair	518.00
Honeycomb, Punch Bowl, Wager Construction, Scalloped Rim, 11 ⅞ x 11 ¾ In.	138.00
Honeycomb, Syrup, Cover, Opaque White Flint, Applied Handle, 7 In.	546.00
Horizontal Threads, Spooner, Child's, c.1890, 2 ⅛ x 1 ¾ In.	45.00
Horn Of Plenty, Jam Jar, Pontil, 5 x 2 ⅜ In. .... *illus*	920.00
Horn Of Plenty, Salt, Oval, Master, 1 ¼ x 2 ¼ In., Pair	92.00
Horsehead Medallion, Sugar, Cover, Footed, c.1885, 8 x 5 In.	110.00
Horseshoe, Bowl, Adams & Co., c.1881, 9 ¼ x 5 ⅝ In.	43.00
Horseshoe, Cheese Dish, 5 ¾ x 7 ½ In. .... *illus*	259.00
Horseshoe, Goblet, 6 In., 4 Piece	81.00
Horseshoe, Goblet, Knob Stem, Adams & Co., c.1881, 3 ¼ In.	60.00
Hourglass, Wine, 1880s, 4 x 2 In.	18.00
Hummingbird, Pitcher, Water, Blue, 9 In. .... *illus*	259.00

Indiana Swirl pattern is listed here as Feather.

Inverted Fern, Tumbler, Water, Scalloped Rim, 3 ½ x 3 ⅛ In.	316.00
Ivy In Snow, Cake Stand, Round, c.1898, 8 x 4 ⅜ In.	80.00
Ivy In Snow, Relish, Oval, Flint Glass Co., c.1898, 6 ¾ x 4 ⅝ In.	22.00
Ivy Leaves, Cup & Saucer, 1890s, Child's, 2 ⅜ x 2 ⅝ In.	40.00
Jewel & Dewdrop, Bread Plate, Oval, U.S. Glass, c.1914, 10 ¼ x 8 In.	85.00
Jewel & Dewdrop, Cake Stand, 3 In.	65.00

Jeweled Moon & Star pattern is listed here as Moon & Star.

Kansas pattern is listed here as Jewel & Dewdrop.

Klondike pattern is listed here as Amberette.

Lacy Medallion, see the related pattern Princess Feather.

Lamb, Creamer, Child's, c.1890, 2 ⅞ x 1 ½ In.	70.00
Lamb, Mug, Blue, Child's, c.1881, 3 x 2 ¾ In.	120.00
Liberty Bell, Creamer	140.00
Liberty Bell, Mug, White Opaque, 2 x 1 ¾ In.	225.00
Lily Of The Valley, Goblet, 6 ¼ In.	145.00
Lion With Cable, Celery Vase, Handles, Richards & Hartley, 8 In.	68.00

Loops & Drops pattern is listed here as New Jersey.

Lotus & Serpent, Pitcher, Water, 8 ½ In. .... *illus*	58.00
Lotus Leaf, Bread Plate, Amber, Bryce Walker, c.1870, 10 ½ In.	48.00
Magnet & Grape, Decanter, Stopper, Frosted Leaf, Qt., 13 ½ In., Pair	207.00
Magnet & Grape, Wine, Frosted Leaf, American Shield, 6 ⅜ In.	230.00
Maine, Spooner, Paneled Stippled Flower, U.S. Glass, c.1899, 4 x 3 ¼ In.	75.00

Pressed Glass, Lotus & Serpent, Pitcher, Water, 8 ½ In.
$58.00

Pressed Glass, Moon & Star, Compote, Cover, 16 x 10 ½ In.
$196.00

Pressed Glass, Paneled Cosmos, Beverage Set, Rose Stained, Gold Trim, 8 ¾-In. Pitcher, 7 Piece
$92.00

Pressed Glass, Petticoat, Butter, Cover, Vaseline, Gold Trim, 6 x 7 ¾ In.
$104.00

P

Pressed Glass, Rebecca At The Well,
Compote, Frosted Ribbon Bowl,
12 x 10 In.
$316.00

Pressed Glass, Rose Sprig, Tray, Vaseline,
10 ½ x 10 ¾ In.
$339.00

Pressed Glass, Wildflower, Cake Basket,
Blue, Metal Handle, 5 x 7 ¾ x 10 ¾ In.
$127.00

Mardi Gras, Toothpick Holder, Duncan Glass Co., c.1898, 2 ½ x 1 ¾ In.	24.00
Mascotte, Butter, Cover, Footed, Ripley & Co., c.1874, 7 ¾ x 5 ¾ In.	70.00
McKinley, Plate, It's God's Way, Born 1843, Died 1901, Oval, 10 ½ In., Pair	18.00
Menagerie, Spooner, Amber, c.1890, 3 ½ In.	130.00
Michigan, Tumbler, U.S. Glass, c.1902, 3 ¾ x 2 ¾ In.	32.00
Monkey, Mug, Molded Handle, Valley Glass Co., c.1891, 3 ⅜ x 3 ⅛ In.	125.00
Moon & Star, Bowl, Cover, Footed, 12 x 10 ¼ In.	115.00
Moon & Star, Compote, 10 ¼ x 13 In.	127.00
Moon & Star, Compote, Cover, 16 x 10 ½ In. .... *illus*	196.00
Moon & Star, Sugar, Pontil, Acorn Finial, 6 ½ x 4 ½ In.	108.00
New Hampshire, Tumbler, U.S. Glass, c.1903, 4 x 2 ¾ In.	25.00
New Jersey, Wine, U.S. Glass Co., c.1900, 4 ¼ x 2 ½ In.	35.00
Nicotiana, Goblet, Acid Etched, 5 ¾ x 3 In.	20.00
Oaken Bucket, Pitcher, Water, Amethyst, 8 ⅛ In.	90.00
One-Thousand Eye pattern is listed here as Thousand Eye.	
Orion pattern is listed here as Cathedral.	
Owl In Horseshoe, Mug, White Opaque, Atterbury, 1880s, 3 ⅛ x 3 ⅜ In.	85.00
Palm Leaf Fan, Banana Stand, Bryce Higbee & Co., Child's, c.1904, 5 ¼ x 6 ½ In.	68.00
Paneled Cherry, Mug, 2 Panels, DC Jenkins Glass Co., c.1920	18.00
Paneled Cosmos, Beverage Set, Rose Stained, Gold Trim, 8 ¾ In. Pitcher, 7 Piece .... *illus*	92.00
Paneled Jewels, Goblet, c.1890, 6 x 3 In.	30.00
Paneled Sprig, Cake Stand, 10 Panel Top, Bryce Higbee, c.1885, 9 ½ x 6 ¾ In.	95.00
Pattee Cross, Sugar & Creamer, Amethyst, Gold Trim, c.1909, 3 ¼ x 3 ⅝ In.	19.00
Pavonia, Mug, Ruby Stained, Ripley & Co., c.1885, 4 ¼ x 2 ¾ In.	70.00
Pennsylvania, see the related pattern Hand.	
Petticoat, Butter, Cover, Vaseline, Gold Trim, 6 x 7 ¾ In. .... *illus*	104.00
Petticoat, Toothpick, Hat Shape, Riverside Glass Co., c.1899	50.00
Pillar & Bull's-Eye pattern is listed here as Thistle.	
Pinafore pattern is listed here as Actress.	
Plain Smocking pattern is listed here as Smocking.	
Pleat & Panel, Celery Vase, Bryce Brothers, c.1882, 8 In.	30.00
Pleat & Panel, Waste Bowl, c.1882, 4 ¾ In.	95.00
Plume, Pitcher, 9 ¼ In.	90.00
Pointing Dog, Mug, Bryce Brothers, 1880s, 2 ⅜ x 2 ⅝ In.	29.00
Polar Bear, Tray, Water, Frosted, Egg & Dart Border, 11 x 15 ¼ In.	113.00
Popcorn, Wine, 3 ¾ x 1 ¾ In.	35.00
Prayer Rug pattern is listed here as Horseshoe.	
Pressed Leaf, Compote, Cable Edge, Patterned Foot, McKee, 8 ¼ x 4 ⅞ In.	45.00
Princess Feather, Butter, Cover, Flint, Bakewell Pears, c.1870, 6 x 4 In.	80.00
Puritan, Pitcher, Water, Ruby Stained, Gilt Decoration, 8 ½ In.	113.00
Rabbit, Mug, Vaseline, Central Glass, 1880s, 3 ¼ x 3 In.	90.00
Rebecca At The Well, Compote, Frosted Ribbon Bowl, 12 x 10 In. .... *illus*	316.00
Reticulated Cord, Creamer, Hollow Base, c.1891, 4 ⅞ In.	23.00
Reverse Torpedo pattern is listed here as Diamond & Bull's-Eye Band.	
Ribbed Ivy, Lemonade, Handle, 2 ¾ x 2 ⅝ In.	345.00
Ribbed Ivy, Tumbler, Water, Flint, Boston & Sandwich, c.1875, 3 ½ x 3 In.	125.00
Ribbed Ivy, Whiskey, Boston & Sandwich, c.1875, 2 ¾ x 2 ½ In.	90.00
Ribbed Ivy, Whiskey, Handle, Boston & Sandwich, c.1850, 2 ⅞ In.	350.00
Ribbed Ivy, Wine, Flint, c.1875, 4 x 1 ⅞ In.	95.00
Ribbed Palm, Goblet, Flint, McKee Bros., c.1863, 6 In.	50.00
Ribbed Palm, Spooner, Flint, McKee, c.1863, 5 ¾ x 3 ½ In.	50.00
Ringed Holly, Mug, Twig Handle, c.1880, 4 ½ x 3 In.	85.00
Ripple Band pattern is listed here as Ripple.	
Rochelle pattern is listed here as Princess Feather.	
Rope Bands pattern is listed here as Argent.	
Rose In Snow, Compote, Cover, 10 x 8 In.	33.00
Rose In Snow, Mug, Blue, Bryce Brothers, Child's, 3 ⅜ x 3 ¼ In.	65.00
Rose Sprig, Cake Stand, 6 ⅜ x 9 ⅛ In.	127.00
Rose Sprig, Goblet, Amber, Campbell Jones & Co., c.1886, 5 ⅝ x 3 In.	50.00
Rose Sprig, Pitcher, Water, Blue, 9 ½ In.	219.00
Rose Sprig, Tray, Vaseline, 10 ½ x 10 ¾ In. .... *illus*	339.00
Sawtooth, Compote, Opaque White Flint, 7 ¼ x 9 ½ In.	150.00
Sawtooth, Creamer, Footed, Child's	30.00
Scroll With Flower, Bread Plate, Round, Handles, Late 1870s, 10 x 12 In.	40.00
Shell & Tassel, Bowl, Amber, Oval, 9 ¾ x 5 ½ In.	95.00
Shrine, Toothpick, Beatty-Brady Glass Co., c.1896, 2 ⅜ x 2 ¼ In.	75.00

Singing Birds, Pitcher, Water, 8 ⅝ In.	203.00
Six Panel Fine Cut, Cake Stand, Amber Stained, 7 x 10 ½ In.	56.00
Six Panel Fine Cut, Pitcher, Milk, Amber Stained, 7 ¾ In.	90.00
Smocking, Tumbler, Flint, 1850s, 3 ½ x 3 In.	90.00
Snail, Sugar, Ruby Stained, George Duncan, c.1891, 4 ⅛ x 4 In. ...	30.00
Spirea Band, Pitcher, Water, Blue, Bryce Higbee, c.1885, 9 x 5 In.	80.00
Square Fuchsia, Champagne, Portland Glass Co., c.1865, 5 x 2 ½ In.	65.00

Star & Punty pattern is listed here as Moon & Star.

Stippled Dahlia pattern is listed here as Square Fuchsia.

Stippled Paneled Flower pattern is listed here as Maine.

Stork, Sugar, Cover, Stork Finial, Oval & Bar Border, 9 In.	203.00
Sunbeam, Wine, Emerald Green, Gold Trim, McKee, c.1898, 4 ½ x 3 ¼ In.	23.00
Sunken Button, Salt & Pepper, Blue, Late 1800s, 3 In.	30.00
Swag With Brackets, Creamer, Blue, Jefferson Glass Co., 1900, 4 ½ In.	65.00
Swan, Bowl, Scallops To Rim, Oval Footed, Covered, 6 ½ x 5 In.	135.00
Swan, Mustard, Blue, Handle, 1880s, 3 ⅝ x 3 In.	60.00
Swan, Pitcher, Water, 9 ¾ In.	56.00
Swirl & Diamonds, Tray, Amber, Daisy & Button Center, 10 In.	35.00
Teardrop & Tassel, Creamer, Greentown, c.1900, 4 x 3 ½ In.	50.00
Tennessee, Tumbler, 3 ⅞ x 2 ¾ In.	115.00
Tennessee, Tumbler, Water, 4 In.	169.00
Tepee, Sauce, Ruby Stained, Folded Rim, 1 ¾ x 5 ¼ In.	46.00
Tepee, Wine, Duncan Glass, c.1896, 4 ¼ x 2 In., 4 Piece	95.00
Texas, Compote, Cover, 10 x 6 In.	214.00
Thistle, Cake Stand, Purple, Pedestal, 10 x 4 ½ In.	55.00
Thistle, Relish, Oval, Bryce McKee, c.1872, 9 x 6 In.	28.00
Thousand Eye, Toothpick, Blue, Richards & Hartley, c.1880, 2 ¼ x 2 In.	39.00
Three Face, Champagne, Hollow Stem, 4 In.	904.00

Three Graces, see also the related pattern Three Face.

Three Sisters pattern is listed here as Three Face.

Torpedo, Wine, c.1890	35.00
Tree Of Life, Celery Vase, Clear Band, Flint, Portland, c.1870, 7 x 3 ½ In.	95.00
Tree Of Life, Waste Bowl, Footed, Portland Glass Co., c.1870, 4 ⅝ x 3 In.	35.00
Tulip & Honeycomb, Bowl, Oval, Scalloped Edge, Federal Glass, c.1905, 3 ¼ x 2 ⅜ In.	77.00
Tulip With Sawtooth, Celery Vase, Scalloped Rim, Bryce Richards, c.1854, 9 ½ x 3 ¾ In.	63.00
Twist, Butter, Cover, Albany Glass Co., Child's, c.1900, 3 ½ x 2 ¾ In.	35.00
Vernon Honeycomb, Celery Vase, Amber, 8 ⅝ In., Pair	81.00
Vernon Honeycomb, Celery Vase, Blue, 8 ⅝ In., Pair	184.00
Viking, Apothecary Jar, Engraved Fern & Leaf, 3-Footed, 7 ¾ x 3 ½ In.	104.00
Waffle, Creamer, Flint, Applied Handle, Boston & Sandwich, c.1850, 6 ¼ x 7 In.	325.00
Waffle, Sugar & Creamer, Cover, Applied Handle, 6 ½ x 9 ¼ In.	173.00
Waffle, Sweetmeat, Cover, Footed, On Round Rim, 12 Scallops, 8 ¼ x 5 ¼ In.	45.00
Washington, Celery Vase, Flint, New England Glass Co., c.1869, 8 ½ x 3 ⅝ In.	225.00
Wee Branches, Mug, U.S. Glass, Child's, 1890s, 2 x 2 In.	55.00
Westmoreland, Eggcup, Gillinder Glass Co., c.1898, 4 x 2 ½ In. ...	38.00
Westward Ho, Pitcher, Water, Frosted, 9 ½ x 5 ½ In.	104.00

Whirligig pattern is listed here as Buzz Star.

Wildflower, Cake Basket, Blue, Metal Handle, 5 x 7 ¾ x 10 ¾ In. .... *illus*	127.00
Wildflower, Plate, Apple Green, 8-Sided, Adams & Co., c.1891, 9 ⅞ In.	42.00
Wildflower, Tray, Water, Apple Green, Oval, Adams & Co., 1870s, 13 x 11 In.	125.00
Willow Oak, Mug, Amber, c.1880, 3 ¾ x 3 ⅛ In.	53.00
Wisconsin, Sugar Shaker, Cover, 4 ¾ In.	81.00
Wisconsin, Wine, 4 In., 4 Piece	115.00

Wooden Pail pattern is listed here as Oaken Bucket.

Yoked Loop, Whiskey, Flint, Applied Handle, c.1850, 2 ⅞ x 3 ¼ In.	95.00

PRINT, in this listing, means any of many printed images produced on paper by one of the more common methods, such as lithography. The prints listed here are of interest primarily to the antiques collector, not the fine arts collector. Many of these prints were originally part of books. Other prints will be found in the Advertising, Currier & Ives, Movie, and Poster categories.

A Scouting Party, 1877, 13 x 18 ¾ In.	89.00
Abbot, John, Peacock Emperor Moth, Many Lobed Oak, Etching, Frame, 14 ¾ x 11 ¼ In.	1035.00
Abbot, John, Yellow-Spotted Tyger Hawk Moth, Grapes, Plate, Frame, 14 ¾ x 11 ⅜ In.	1093.00
Alden, A., Life & Age Of A Woman, Hand Colored, Linen, c.1850, 17 x 23 In.	588.00
Armington, Caroline, Gare De L'Arsenal, Paris, Signed, c.1915, 5 ⅜ x 8 ⅞ In.	173.00

Print, Audubon, Canada Jay, R. Havell, Engraved, c.1831, 26 x 20 ½ In. $3720.00

Print, Audubon, Texian Hare, J.T. Bowen, Color Lithograph, c.1848, Frame, 20 x 25 In. $1440.00

Print, Gregson, Woman, Red Dress, Long Stemmed Rose, Cosmopolitan, c.1914, 32 x 7 ½ In. $220.00

P

PRINT

Print, Icart, Autumn Grapes,
Etching, Mat, Frame,
c.1922, 29 ½ x 22 ¼ In.
$406.00

Print, Jacoulet, L'Etoile De Cobi,
Signed, Sealed, Frame, 15 ⅜ x 11 ⅝ In.
$1195.00

Print, Japanese, Kikugawa, Eizan,
Geisha, Shamisen, Woodblock, Mat,
Frame, 15 x 10 In.
$173.00

Audubon bird prints were originally issued as part of books printed from 1826 to 1854. They were issued in two sheet sizes, 26 ½ inches by 39 ½ inches and 11 inches by 7 inches. The quadrupeds were issued in 28-by-22-inch prints. Later editions of the Audubon books were done in many sizes, and reprints of the books in the original size were also made. The words *After John James Audubon* appear on all of the prints, including the originals, because the pictures were made as copies of Audubon's original oil paintings. The bird pictures have been so popular they have been copied in myriad sizes by both old and new printing methods. This list includes originals and later copies because Audubon prints of all ages are sold in antiques shops.

Audubon, American Flamingo, Color Lithograph, Frame, Ariel Press Edition, 37 ½ x 25 In. ...	920.00
Audubon, Bachman's Swamp Warbler, J.T. Bowen, Color Lithograph, Frame, 9 ¼ x 5 ¼ In.	173.00
Audubon, Black-Bellied Darter, R. Havell, Engraved, Aquatint, Frame, 1836, 38 x 25 In.	18750.00
Audubon, Blue Grosbeak, J. Bien, Chromolithograph, c.1860, 31 ¾ x 23 ¼ In.	264.00
Audubon, Canada Goose, Engraved, R. Havell, Aquatint, Frame, c.1830, 38 ½ x 25 ⅜ In.	36250.00
Audubon, Canada Jay, R. Havell, Engraved, c.1831, 26 x 20 ½ In. ....*illus*	3720.00
Audubon, Carolina Parrot, Havell, Engraved, Hand Colored, 1830, 37 x 26 In.	38513.00
Audubon, Cat Squirrel, J.T. Bowen, Lithograph, Frame, 27 ⅛ x 20 ¾ In.	1093.00
Audubon, Cerulean Warbler, Havell, Engraved, Hand Colored, c.1828, 35 x 25 In.	2728.00
Audubon, Chipping Squirrel, Hackee, J.T. Bowen, Lithograph, 26 ½ x 20 ½ In.	444.00
Audubon, Common American Swan, R. Havell, Etching, Aquatint, Frame, 1838, 25 x 37 In. ..	80500.00
Audubon, Dusty Petrel, R. Havell, Etching, Frame, c.1836, 12 ¼ x 19 ¼ In.	748.00
Audubon, Fish Hawk, R. Havell, Engraved, Aquatint, Frame, 1830, 38 ½ x 25 ½ In.	56250.00
Audubon, Frigate Pelican, R. Havell, Engraved, Aquatint, Frame, 1835, 38 x 25 In.	22500.00
Audubon, Golden Eye Duck, R. Havell, No. 69, Frame, 1836, 20 ¾ x 29 ¾ In.	4914.00
Audubon, Golden-Winged Woodpecker, Havell, Engraved, Hand Colored, 1831, 39 x 25 In.	8888.00
Audubon, Great White Heron, R. Havell, Etching, Aquatint, Frame, 1835, 24 x 38 In.	6875.00
Audubon, Hawk, J. Gould, Signed, Certificate, Frame, 1875, 28 x 36 In.	585.00
Audubon, Louisiana Heron, Havell, Engraved, Hand Colored, c.1834, 22 x 26 In.	16590.00
Audubon, Manks Shearwater, R. Havell, Engraving, Frame, c.1836, 24 ⅞ x 37 ⅝ In.	978.00
Audubon, Mexican Marmot, No. 25, Mat, 22 x 28 In.	999.00
Audubon, Passenger Pigeon, R. Havell, Color Engraving, Frame, c.1829, 25 ¾ x 20 ¾ In.	403.00
Audubon, Purple Heron, R. Havell, Engraved, Aquatint, Frame, 1835, 25 ⅜ x 37 ⅜ In.	33750.00
Audubon, Putorius Agilis, Little Nimble Weasel, J.T. Bowen, Lithograph, Frame, 22 x 28 In. ...	230.00
Audubon, Salt Water Marsh Hen, R. Havell, Engraved, Frame, 37 ¾ x 24 ⅝ In.	920.00
Audubon, Sandwich Tern, Havell, Engraved, Hand Colored, c.1835, 18 x 24 In.	1778.00
Audubon, Say's Squirrel, Hand Colored, J.T. Bowen, 1846, 20 ¾ x 26 ¾ In. .... 275.00 to 295.00
Audubon, Stanley Hawk, Havell, Etched, Aquatint, 38 x 25 ¼ In.	2703.00
Audubon, Texan Skunk, No. 11, Mat, 22 x 18 In.	5399.00
Audubon, Texian Hare, J.T. Bowen, Color Lithograph, c.1848, Frame, 20 x 25 In. ....*illus*	1440.00
Audubon, Townsend's Warbler Arctic Blue-Bird, Western Blue-Bird, Havell, 38 x 26 In.	2844.00
Audubon, Viviparus Quadrupeds Of North America, J.T. Bowen, 1844, 21 ¾ x 27 ½ In.	593.00
Audubon, Viviparus Quadrupeds Of North America, J.T. Bowen, 1846, 21 ¾ x 27 ½ In.	1778.00
Audubon, White Headed Eagle, J. Bien, Chromolithograph, c.1860, 40 x 26 ¾ In.	3819.00
Audubon, Wolverine, No. 6, Mat, 22 x 28 In.	12150.00
Audubon, Yellow-Breasted Rail, R. Havell, Engraved, Frame, c.1836, 12 x 19 In. .... 1150.00 to 1688.00
Besler, Malua Rosea Multiplex, Eichstatt & Nuremberg, Botanical, 1613, 20 x 16 In.	1185.00
Burleigh, Danbury, Connecticut, Bird's-Eye View, Lithograph, c.1884, 22 x 39 In.	1725.00
Burleigh, Mount Morris, New York, Bird's-Eye View, Lithograph, 1883, 19 x 28 In.	230.00
Burleigh, Saratoga Springs, New York, Bird's-Eye View, Lithograph, Frame, 1888, 23 x 33 In.	1150.00
Catesby, Mark, Black Squirrel, Yellow Lady's Slipper, Engraved, Frame, 13 ¾ x 10 ⅛ In.	1725.00
Catesby, Mark, Eastern Cotton Mouth, Swamp & Doghobble, Etching, Frame, 9 ½ x 13 In.	575.00
Catesby, Mark, Eastern King Snake, Coastal Doghobble, Etching, Frame, 8 ¾ x 11 ⅞ In.	690.00
Catesby, Mark, Kalmia Augustifolia, Rhododendron Maximum, Engraved, 20 x 14 In.	1035.00
Catesby, Mark, Yellow-Breasted Chat, Sessile Trillium, Etching, Frame, 13 ⅞ x 10 ⅜ In.	1150.00
Catlin, Buffalo Hunt, Surround, No. 9, Day & Haghe, 1844, Lithograph, Frame, 14 ¼ x 19 In.	770.00
Cheffetz, Asa, Pastoral, Vermont, Black & White, Signed, Frame, 4 ½ x 9 In.	104.00
Civil War, Encampment, Woman Kissing Union Soldier, Chromo, 1897, Buffalo, 28 x 49 In. ..	999.00
Colescott, Warrington, Lincoln At Ford's Theater, Multicolored, Signed, c.1973, 23 ½ x 16 ¼ In.	115.00
Curry, John Stewart, Manhunt, Titled, Numbered, Lithograph, Signed, 1934, 10 x 13 In.	840.00
Dahlgreen, Charles W., Down To The Valley, Drypoint, Signed, 8 x 9 ¾ In.	52.00
Danchin, Leon, 5 Ducks Flying, 17 x 22 In.	83.00
Dohanos, Stevan, Connecticut Yankee Farmer, Lithograph, Signed, 1935, 12 x 9 In.	540.00
Erte, Evening, Night, Morning, Day, Silkscreen, 44 x 33 ½ In.	2714.00
Erte, Gemini, Silkscreen, Frame, Signed, 20 x 25 ½ In.	1121.00
Erte, Myths Suite, Silkscreen, Frame, Signed, 30 x 21 ¾ In.	2832.00
Erte, Salome, Serigraph, Signed, 17 x 22 ½ In.	944.00
Erte, Slave, Serigraph, Frame, 33 ½ x 25 In.	885.00

JW.Audubon

P

Fraser, James Earle, View Of Esplanade Row, Engraved, Aquatint, Havell, c.1824, 11 x 17 In. ..	441.00
Gould, Hummingbirds, Aglaectis Pamela, Color Lithograph, Frame, 11 ½ x 9 ¼ In.	230.00
Gould, Richter, Hummingbird, Pied Jocobin, Lithograph, 21 ⅜ x 14 ⅛ In.	288.00
Gregson, Woman, Red Dress, Long Stemmed Rose, Cosmopolitan, c.1914, 32 x 7 ½ In. ..*illus*	220.00

Icart prints were made by Louis Icart, who worked in Paris from 1907 as an employee of a postcard company. He then started printing magazines and fashion brochures. About 1910 he created a series of etchings of fashionably dressed women and he continued to make similar etchings until he died in 1950. He is well known as a printmaker, painter, and illustrator. Original etchings are much more expensive than the later photographic copies.

Icart, Autumn Grapes, Etching, Mat, Frame, c.1922, 29 ½ x 22 ¼ In. ....*illus*	406.00
Icart, Ballerina In The Wings, Etching, c.1925, 15 ½ x 9 ½ In.	1003.00
Icart, Carmen, Etching, 1927, 20 x 13 ½ In.	500.00
Icart, Dans Les Passes, Signed, 1928, 12 x 16 ½ In.	1711.00
Icart, Departure, Etching, c.1941, 16 x 11 ¾ In.	700.00
Icart, Fair Dancer, Ballerina, Aquatint, Signed, 1939, 18 ¾ x 22 ¼ In.	900.00
Icart, Faust, Woman, By Column, Devil, Hand Colored, Signed, Frame, 20 ½ x 13 In.	2015.00
Icart, Girl In Crinoline, Hand Colored, Signed, Frame, 1937, 23 ½ x 19 ¼ In.	1640.00
Icart, Hydrangeas, Les Hortensias, Signed, Frame, 21 ¾ x 26 In.	620.00
Icart, L'Elegante A La Cigarette, Frame, 1929, 17 x 21 ½ In.	2065.00
Icart, Lovers, Hand Colored, Signed, Frame, 1930, 22 ½ x 15 ⅝ In.	1020.00
Icart, Nude Woman, Lying On Side, Signed, Frame, 19 ½ x 46 ¼ In.	3884.00
Icart, Professor, Etching, Hand Colored, Signed, Frame, 10 ½ x 8 ½ In.	480.00
Icart, Red Riding Hood, Forest Scene, Aquatint, Signed, 1927, 20 ¼ x 13 ¼ In.	1140.00
Icart, Spilled Milk, 2 Women, Kitten Lapping Spilled Milk, Aquatint, Signed, 1925, 16 x 20 ½ In.	720.00
Icart, Tosca, Woman, At Gate, Hand Colored, Signed, Frame, 20 ½ x 13 In.	1195.00
Icart, Tosca, Woman, Gown, Hat, Hand Colored, Frame, 1928, 23 x 15 In.	1100.00 to 1200.00
Icart, Visible Veins, Hand Colored, Signed, Frame, 1945, 11 x 17 In.	400.00
Icart, Wistfulness, Woman, Garden Scene, Birds, Birdbath, Aquatint, 1924, 11 ¾ x 16 ¾ In. ...	390.00
Icart, Woman At The Window, With Dog, Frame, 1929, 20 ½ x 16 In.	1947.00
Icart, Woman Dreaming, Signed, Numbered, Stamped, 1938, 16 x 19 In.	560.00
Icart, Woman With Flower Garlands, Signed, Frame, 1928, 18 ½ x 14 ¼ In.	360.00

Jacoulet prints were designed by Paul Jacoulet (1902–1960), a Frenchman who spent most of his life in Japan. He was a master of Japanese woodblock print technique. Subjects included life in Japan, the South Seas, Korea, and China. His prints were sold by subscription and issued in series. Each series had a distinctive seal, such as a sparrow or butterfly. Most Jacoulet prints are approximately 15 x 10 inches.

Jacoulet, Apres La Pluie, Tarang, Yap, 2 Men, Palm Tree, Frame, 15 ⅜ x 11 ¾ In.	1400.00
Jacoulet, Bebe Coreen En Costume De Ceremonie Seoul, Korean Baby, Frame, 15 ⅜ x 11 ¾ In.	1320.00
Jacoulet, Filles De La Brousse, Nord Celebes, 2 Women, Frame, 15 ⅜ x 11 ¾ In.	3600.00
Jacoulet, Fleurs De Soir, Truck-Toloas, Woman & Flowers, Frame, 15 ⅜ x 11 ¾ In.	1750.00
Jacoulet, Flocons De Neige, Pengyong, Coree, 3 Women, Frame, 15 ⅜ x 11 ¾ In.	1310.00
Jacoulet, Hokkan-Zan Seoul, Coree, Old Man Smoking Pipe, Frame, 15 ⅜ x 11 ¾ In.	850.00
Jacoulet, Homme De Menado Et Mangoustans, Celebes, Man's Profile, Frame, 15 ⅜ x 11 ¾ In.	840.00
Jacoulet, L'Etoile De Cobi, Signed, Sealed, Frame, 15 ⅜ x 11 ⅝ In. ....*illus*	1195.00
Jacoulet, L'Homme Accroupi, Chinois, Man, Crouching, Frame, 15 ⅜ x 11 ¾ In.	985.00
Jacoulet, La Chenille Verte, Coree, Man Watching Caterpillar, Frame, 15 ⅜ x 11 ¾ In.	910.00
Jacoulet, La Corbeille De Nefles Chinois, Figure With Fan, Frame, 15 ⅜ x 11 ¾ In.	740.00
Jacoulet, La Mariee, Seoul Corree, Woman, Elaborate Headdress, c.1948, 15 ½ x 11 ⅞ In.	403.00
Jacoulet, La Tresseuse De Paniers, Remoue, Yap, Basketweaver, Frame, 15 ⅜ x 11 ¾ In.	1210.00
Jacoulet, Le Bronze Errant Coree, Wandering Buddhist Priest, Frame, 15 ⅜ x 11 ¾ In.	315.00
Jacoulet, Le Nid, Coree, Old Man Feeding Birds, Frame, 15 ⅜ x 11 ¾ In.	920.00
Jacoulet, Le Phare De Mikomoto, Shimoda Izu, Man In Kimono, Seated, Frame, 15 ⅜ x 11 ¾ In. .	820.00
Jacoulet, Le Reveil, Saipan, Marianes, 2 Boys On Beach, Frame, 15 ⅜ x 11 ¾ In.	1970.00
Jacoulet, Le Tabouret De Porcelaine Mandochoukuo, Woman On Stool, Frame, 15 ⅜ x 11 ¾ In.	1150.00
Jacoulet, Le Tresor, Woman Holding Baby, Signed, c.1940, 15 ⅛ x 11 ¾ In.	890.00
Jacoulet, Les Papillons Tropiques, Woman, Butterflies, Flowers, Frame, 15 ⅜ x 11 ¾ In.	2400.00
Jacoulet, Les Paradisiers, Mendo, Celebes, Woman, Birds, Frame, 15 ⅜ x 11 ¾ In.	1320.00
Jacoulet, Les Repas Des Mendiants, Seoul, Coree, Beggers Eating, Frame, 15 ⅜ x 11 ¾ In.	985.00
Jacoulet, Melle Rita Sablan-Diaz, Chamorro De Guam, Mariames, Woman, Frame, 15 ⅜ x 11 ¾ In.	1100.00
Jacoulet, Sawara Fisherman, Frame, 1936, 15 ½ x 11 ¾ In.	570.00
Jacoulet, Sous Les Bananiers, Woman, Banana Tree, Tomil, Yap, Frame, 15 ⅜ x 11 ¾ In.	2840.00
Jacoulet, Une Jeune Fille De Fidji, Young Woman, Frame, 15 ⅜ x 11 ¾ In.	1650.00
Jacoulet, Vendeur De Masques, Mask Vendor, Frame, 15 ⅜ x 11 ¾ In.	850.00

Print, Japanese, Kiyoshi, Saito, Temple, Glazed, Black Wood Frame, Mat, Signed, 19 ¾ x 14 ¼ In.
$1560.00

Print, Japanese, Koryusai, Isoda, Geishas On Balcony, Woodblock, 1700s, 10 x 8 In.
$316.00

P

Print, Japanese, Utamaro, Kitagawa, Geisha, Crossing Puddle, Parasol, Mat, Frame, 19 ¼ x 9 In.
$529.00

Print, McKenney & Hall, Tah-Ro-Hon, Warrior, Lithograph, Frame, c.1838, 19 x 13 In.
$1320.00

Print, Mucha, Salome, Color Lithograph, Signed, Blind Stamp, Frame, c.1897, 13 ¼ x 9 In.
$1315.00

Print, Parrish, Daybreak, Wood Frame, c.1922, 17 ½ x 29 ½ In.
$230.00

Print, Parrish, Tree & Mountain Scene, Frame, 33 x 21 In.
$322.00

Japanese woodblock prints are listed as follows: Print, Japanese, name of artist, title or description, type, and size. Dealers use the following terms: Tate-e is a vertical composition. Yoko-e is a horizontal composition. The words Aiban (13 by 9 inches), Chuban (10 by 7 ½ inches), Hosoban (13 by 6 inches), Koban (7 by 4 inches), Nagaban (20 by 9 inches), Oban (15 by 10 inches), Shikishiban (8 by 9 inches), and Tanzaku (15 by 5 inches) denote approximate size. Modern versions of some of these prints have been made. Other woodblock prints that are not Japanese are listed under Print, Woodblock.

Japanese, Chikanobu Toyohara, Beauty With Feathered Toy, Mirror Of The Ages, c.1897, 14 x 9 In.	23.00
Japanese, Geisha Girl, Multicolored, 17 ½ x 13 ¼ In.	29.00
Japanese, Hiroshi Yoshida, Autumn In Hakkodasan, Signed, c.1929, 9 ¾ x 7 ⅜ In.	196.00
Japanese, Inland Sea, Mt. Fujiyama In Background, Woodblock, Signed, Frame, 17 x 31 In.	270.00
Japanese, Kikugawa, Eizan, Geisha, Shamisen, Woodblock, Mat, Frame, 15 x 10 In. *illus*	173.00
Japanese, Kiotsu, Tsuchiya, Wisteria At Kameido, Frame, 15 x 9 ¾ In.	144.00
Japanese, Kiyoshi, Saito, Tahiti, c.1971, 14 ⅞ x 20 ⅞ In.	920.00
Japanese, Kiyoshi, Saito, Temple, Glazed, Black Wood Frame, Mat, Signed, 19 ¾ x 14 ¼ In. *illus*	1560.00
Japanese, Koryusai, Isoda, Geishas On Balcony, Woodblock, 1700s, 10 x 8 In. *illus*	316.00
Japanese, Shiro Kasamatsu, Toriire, Multicolored, 14 ¼ x 9 ⅜ In.	127.00
Japanese, Toyokuni III, Man, Multicolored, Signed, 13 ¾ x 10 In.	69.00
Japanese, Uchida, Cherry Blossoms In Kyoto, Multicolored, Japan, 14 ½ x 9 ½ In.	35.00
Japanese, Utamaro, Kitagawa, Geisha, Crossing Puddle, Parasol, Mat, Frame, 19 ¼ x 9 In. *illus*	529.00
Kent, Rockwell, Beowulf & The Dragon, Lithograph, Signed, c.1931, 13 ½ x 9 ⅞ In.	403.00
Kimse, Marguerite, So Bad, Seated Dog, Signed, 7 ⅝ x 5 ¼ In.	311.00
Kohn, Misch, General, Colored, Signed, c.1958, 17 x 8 ¾ In.	58.00
Kuehne, Max, Harkness Tower, Signed, 13 ¼ x 9 In.	17.00
Kuhler, Otto, Roman Arch, Etching, Signed, 7 ⅝ x 5 ⅜ In.	46.00
Kuhler, Otto, Street Scene, Etching, Signed, 7 ⅝ x 5 ½ In.	150.00
Lamore, Chet, After The Harvest, Lithograph, Titled, Numbered, Signed, 1938, 10 x 14 In.	240.00
Locke, Walter R., Glorious Eucalyptus, Engraving, c.1938, 10 x 12 ⅞ In.	92.00
Locke, Walter R., On The Banks Of The Amalote, Fla., Etching, c.1936, 11 ¾ x 8 ¼ In.	69.00
Luciono, Luigi, Trees & Shadows, Signed, c.1957, 10 ⅜ x 9 In.	184.00
McKenney & Hall, Portrait, Ki-On-Twog-Ky, Lithograph, Hand Colored, c.1837, 21 ½ x 15 In.	660.00
McKenney & Hall, Tah-Ro-Hon, Warrior, Lithograph, Frame, c.1838, 19 x 13 In. *illus*	1320.00
McKenney & Hall, Tschusick, Objiway Woman, Lithograph, Hand Colored, Frame, 1836, 16 x 12 In.	270.00
McKenney & Hall, Wa-Pa-Shaw, Sioux Chief, Lithograph, Hand Colored, Frame, 14 x 10 In.	235.00
Merrill, Katherine, Rue St. Yves Chartres, Etching, Signed, c.1930, 9 ⅜ x 7 1/16 In.	115.00
Mucha, Salome, Color Lithograph, Signed, Blind Stamp, Frame, c.1897, 13 ¼ x 9 In. *illus*	1315.00
Norman Rockwell, Celebration, Offset Print, Signed, Frame, 28 ½ x 22 ½ In.	1600.00
Norman Rockwell, Main Street Stockbridge At Christmas, Signed, Frame, 9 x 28 ½ In.	1150.00
Norman Rockwell, Young Love, Offset Print, Signed, 15 ⅞ x 16 In.	345.00
Norris, Wellije & Co., Green Cove, Florida, Bird's-Eye View, Lithograph, 1885, 21 x 28 In.	1840.00

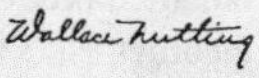

Nutting prints are now popular with collectors. Wallace Nutting is known for his pictures, furniture, and books. Nutting prints are actually hand-colored photographs issued from 1900 to 1941. There are over 10,000 different titles. Wallace Nutting furniture is listed in the Furniture category.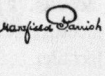

Nutting, Among October Birches, Signed, 13 x 16 In.	59.00
Nutting, Autumn Riverscape, Frame, 18 x 11 ½ In.	55.00
Nutting, Christmas Jelly, Woman, Tea Set, Parlor, Signed, 12 x 16 In.	118.00
Nutting, Connecticut Blossoms, Signed, 11 x 14 In.	95.00
Nutting, Red, White & Blue, 11 x 14 In.	89.00
Nutting, Rosa's Coming Out, Rosa On Porch With Mother, Signed, Mat, Frame, c.1920, 15 x 12 In.	2200.00
Nutting, Spring Fishing, Man Fishing In Shallow Stream, Signed, Mat, Frame, c.1920, 16 x 10 In.	2310.00

Parrish prints are wanted by collectors. Maxfield Frederick Parrish was an illustrator who lived from 1870 to 1966. He is best known as a designer of magazine covers, posters, calendars, and advertisements. His prints have been copied in recent years.

Parrish, Daybreak, Wood Frame, c.1922, 17 ½ x 29 ½ In. *illus*	230.00
Parrish, Tree & Mountain Scene, Frame, 33 x 21 In. *illus*	322.00
Peale, Titian, Wild Turkey Male & Female, Engraving, 1800s, 13 ⅝ x 10 ½ In.	1380.00
Reeves, Horse, Secretariat, Lithograph, Signed By Jockey Ron Turcotte, Frame, 23 x 26 In.	1180.00
Rice, William Seltzer, Haystack, Linocut, Frame, c.1940, 7 x 10 ½ In. *illus*	660.00
Roth, Ernest, Iron Grill Venice, Etching, Signed, c.1913, 10 ⅜ x 7 ⅞ In.	265.00
Sanchez, Emilio, Costa De Gloria, Shuttered House, Yellow Door, Lithograph, c.1975, 16 ½ x 24 In.	700.00
Sauer, Leroy, Deserted Farm, 8 ¼ x 9 ½ In.	92.00
Scofield, Levi, Cuyahoga County Soldiers & Sailors Monument, Engraving, c.1910, 28 x 22 In.	374.00
Travies, Edouard, Greater Bird Of Paradise, Lithograph, c.1857, 17 ⅛ x 13 ⅞ In.	173.00
Villion, Jacques, Le Grillon, Signed, 10 ¼ x 7 ⅜ In.	92.00

Woodblock prints that are not in the Japanese tradition are listed here. Most were made in England and the United States during the Arts and Crafts period. Japanese woodblock prints are listed under Print, Japanese.

Woodblock, Baumann, G., Indiana Red Gum Trees, Oatmeal Paper, Frame, 9 x 10 ¾ In.	9150.00
Woodblock, Baumann, G., Redwood Tree, Signed, Frame, 20 x 21 In.	6000.00
Woodblock, Bresslern-Roth, Norbertine, Finches, Pencil Signed Right, Handdruck In Left, 3 x 7 In.	1080.00
Woodblock, Brussel-Smith, Bernard, Bowery, Signed, c.1941, 6 x 4 In.	1093.00
Woodblock, De Lemos, Pedro, Cliff Dweller, Oak Frame, Signed, c.1920, 11 ⅞ x 9 In.	5625.00
Woodblock, De Lemos, Pedro, Night Reflections, Frame, c.1925, 12 x 9 In.	2160.00
Woodblock, Deer Park In Winter, Multicolored, Signed, Koyo, Japanese School, 15 ½ x 10 ⅝ In.	40.00
Woodblock, Esherick, Wharton, April Ploughing, Mat, Frame, Signed, 10 ¼ x 12 ¼ In.	4830.00
Woodblock, Fletcher, Frank Morley, California Salinas River, Signed, Frame, 1927, 13 x 17 In.	9600.00
Woodblock, Hopkins, Edna, Boies Orange Sunflower, Mat, Frame, 7 ¾ x 8 ¾ In.	18300.00
Woodblock, Hopkins, Edna, Garden Flowers, Signed, Frame, c.1915, 7 ⅞ x 9 In.	20000.00
Woodblock, Hopkins, Edna, Nicotiana, Flowers, Frame, c.1909, 10 ¾ x 7 ⅛ In.	13700.00
Woodblock, Johonnot, Ralph, Stylized Tree, Waves, Signed, Frame, 8 x 7 ½ In.	780.00
Woodblock, Lum, Bertha, Road To The Forest, Signed, 1913, 12 ½ x 7 ⅜ In.	8125.00
Woodblock, Patterson, Margaret, Morning Glories, Signed, c.1915, 9 ⅞ x 7 In.	3438.00
Woodblock, Poppies, Arts & Crafts, Frame, 5 ¾ x 15 In.	840.00
Woodblock, Rice, William, The Wave, Signed, Mat, Frame, c.1940, 5 x 7 In. .... *illus*	2196.00
Woodblock, Stickley, G., Seed Pod, No. 345, Copper, c.1905, 20 ⅛ In.	22500.00

PURINTON POTTERY COMPANY was incorporated in Wellsville, Ohio, in 1936. The company moved to Shippenville, Pennsylvania, in 1941 and made a variety of hand-painted ceramic wares. By the 1950s Purinton was making dinnerware, souvenirs, cookie jars, and florist wares. The pottery closed in 1959.

Apple & Pear, Grease Jar, 6 x 4 ½ In. .... *illus*	25.00
Apple & Pear, Sugar, 2 In.	10.00
Apple, Sugar, Cover..	9.50
Ivy, Jug, Red Blossom, 5 ½ In. .... *illus*	50.00
Petals, Honey Jug Pitcher, Sears & Roebuck Co., 1950s, 6 ½ In.	21.00
Shooting Star, Vase, 6 In.	25.00

PURSES have been recognizable since the eighteenth century, when leather and needlework purses were preferred. Beaded purses became popular in the nineteenth century, went out of style, but are again in use. Mesh purses date from the 1880s and are still being made. How to carry a handkerchief and lipstick is a problem today for every woman, including the Queen of England.

Alligator, Black, Bamboo Handles, Shoulder Strap, Coin Purse, Rudolph Knoll, 12 x 10 In.	2465.00
Alligator, Black, Clasp, Signed, Trimingham's Bermuda, c.1960	96.00
Alligator, Burgundy, Octagonal, Cord Handle, Gold Dragon, Kieselstein, 1991, 3 x 4 In.	275.00
Alligator, Gold Tone Clasp, Leather Interior, 11 x 7 x 3 In.	79.00
Alligator, Gold Tone Clasp, Leather Lined & Trimmed, 12 x 8 x 5 In.	124.00
Alligator Skin Frame, Rectangular, Button Clasp, Shoulder Strap, 13 ⅞ x 6 ⅞ x 1 ⅛ In.	360.00
Bakelite, 2 Tiers When Open, Handle, Wilaridy, c.1920, 6 ¼ x 3 x 4 ¼ In.	144.00
Bakelite, Amber, Wilaridy, c.1920, 6 ¼ x 3 x 4 ¼ In. .... *illus*	761.00
Bakelite, Basket Shape, Double Handles, Oval, Clear Lid, 10 x 7 x 4 In. .... *illus*	70.00
Bakelite, Link Strap, Hinged, Lord & Taylor, Spain, 6 x 6 x 3 In. .... *illus*	403.00
Basket, Nantucket, Friendship, Lid, Oval, Ebony Whale, Swing Handle, Jose F. Reyes, c.1950, 10 x 8 In.	2844.00
Basket, Nantucket, Friendship, Lid, Oval, Incised, Painted Pineapple, C. Betram, c.1985, 12 x 10 In.	119.00
Basket, Nantucket, Hinged, Carved Ivory Sea Gull, Ivory Latch, Swing Handle, 4 ¾ In.	1195.00
Basket, Nantucket, Lid, Oval, Carved Ivory Whale Medallion, Handle, S.G. Ibbs, c.1985, 7 x 11 In.	2252.00
Basket, Nantucket, Oval, Hinged Lid, Rawhide Strap, Swing Handle, Bone Pin, c.1950, 11 x 6 x 9 In.	230.00
Basket Weave, Gold & Silver, Box Shape, Dorset Rex, 5th Avenue, 1950s, 9 ¼ x 3 ¼ x 4 In.	150.00
Basket Weave, Gold, Diamond, Suede Interior, Mirror, Scalloped Edge, 6 ½ x 4 In.	8591.00
Beaded, Brass Plated Metal Frame, 6-Sided, Blue, Twist Handle, Satin Lining, c.1957 x 15 In.	83.00
Beaded, Flowers, Beaded Looped Fringe, Chain Handle, France, Victorian, 7 In. .... *illus*	293.00
Beaded, Flowers, Scrolling, Multicolored, Cinch Closure, Beaded Fringe, Victorian, 10 In. . *illus*	205.00
Beaded, Geometric, Orange, Blue, Yellow, Metal Swan Clasp, 1920s, 8 In.	92.00
Beaded, Mesh, Roses, Silk Lining, Loop Fringe, Chain Handle, France, 7 x 6 In.	425.00
Beaded, Peacock, Roses, Initial, Multicolored, Beaded Looped Fringe, Victorian, 11 In. ... *illus*	293.00
Beaded, Tapestry, Victorian Couple Scene, Jeweled Top, Beaded Fringe Bottom, 8 x 6 In.	351.00
Black Taffeta, Faux Amethyst, Sterling Silver Frame, Marked, Tiffany, Chain, 6 In.	1095.00
Brass, Lucite, Herringbone Cut Out, U-Shape Clasp, Faux Stones, Red Handle, Dorset Rex, 7 ½ In.	353.00
Brilliants, Leopard Print, Detachable Braid Chain, Clasp, K. Baumann, 2 ⅝ x 6 In.	840.00
Brilliants, Silver, Black, Tassels, Clasp, Mardi Gras Masque Shape, K. Baumann, 3 x 6 ½ In. ..	180.00

Print, Rice, William Seltzer, Haystack, Linocut, Frame, c.1940, 7 x 10 ½ In. $660.00

Print, Woodblock, Rice, William, The Wave, Signed, Mat, Frame, c.1940, 5 x 7 In. $2196.00

Purinton, Apple & Pear, Grease Jar, 6 x 4 ½ In. $25.00

Purinton, Ivy, Jug, Red Blossom, 5 ½ In. $50.00

P

As always, the edited listings in *Kovels' Antiques & Collectibles Price Guide 2011* aren't available on any website, but readers should visit Kovels.com for information on trends, tips, reproductions, marks, old prices, and more!

Purse, Bakelite, Amber, Wilaridy, c.1920, 6 ¼ x 3 x 4 ¼ In.
$761.00

Purse, Bakelite, Basket Shape, Double Handles, Oval, Clear Lid, 10 x 7 x 4 In.
$70.00

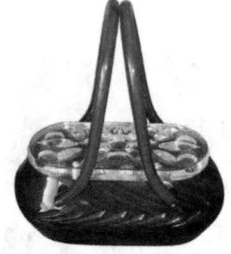

Purse, Bakelite, Link Strap, Hinged, Lord & Taylor, Spain, 6 x 6 x 3 In.
$403.00

Brilliants, Travel Stickers, Gold Braid Detachable Chain, Push Closure, K. Baumann, 4 x 7 In.	900.00
Canvas, Leather Strap & Handle, Detachable, Gold Hardware, Stamped, Louis Vuitton, 8 x 10 In.	488.00
Cluster Of Grapes, Minaudiere, Gilt Metal Strap, Comb, Mirror, Judith Leiber, 5 ½ In.	1464.00
Coin, Ivory, Flowers, Carved, Silver Frame, Accordion Divider, c.1875, 2 ¼ x 3 ½ In.	316.00
Coin, Silver, Flowers, Cherubs, Repousse, Hinged Bottom, Continental, 3 ⅜ x 2 ¾ In.	96.00
Coin, Tortoiseshell, Gold Cartouche, Accordion Pleated Moire Holders, c.1900, 3 x 2 In.	570.00
Crochet, Black, Brown Lucite Handles, Bottom, 9 ¼ x 10 x 6 In.	150.00
Crochet, White, Rosettes, Flowers, Shells, Irish, Carrickmacross Co.	175.00
Crocodile, Black, Brass Horse Head Flap & Handle, Brass Feet, Shoulder Strap, 7 x 9 In.	450.00
Crystal, Elephant, Minaudiere, Cabochon, Chain Strap, J. Leiber, 4 x 5 x 3 In.	1093.00
Crystal, Inset, Minaudiere, Clutch, Goldtone, Stuart Weitzman, 3 ¼ x 6 x 1 ¾ In.	575.00
Crystal, Pearl & Clear, Sleeping Cat, Mirror, Leather Lining, Judith Leiber, 6 x 3 In.	1200.00
Crystal, Studded, Minaudiere, Butterfly, Goldtone, Chain Strap, J. Leiber, 3 ¾ x 6 x 2 In.	805.00
Crystal, Studded, Minaudiere, Chest, Goldtone, Chain Strap, J. Leiber, 3 x 5 x 3 In.	690.00
Crystal, Studded, Minaudiere, Easter Basket, Chain Strap, J. Leiber, 6 x 4 x 2 ¾ In.	978.00
Cut Steel, Beaded Double Looped Fringe, Brass Frame, 15-In. Steel Chain, 9 ½ x 6 In.	250.00
Embossed Gold Leather, Clutch, Stones, Tiger's-Eye, Fitted Frame, Judith Leiber, 1982	480.00
Envelope, 14K Gold, Sapphire Cabochon, Engraved Flowers, Initial, Chain, 4 x 3 In. ...... *illus*	2185.00
Fabric, Clutch, Green Celluloid Button, Turquoise Fabric Liner, 10 ½ x 7 In.	15.00
Faille, Black, Pierced Silver & Gold Plaque, Birds, Flowers, Rubies, Boucheron, c.1935, 4 x 7 In.	793.00
Gilt Metal, Minaudiere, Oval, Horizontal Flutes, Braided Cord, Yves St. Laurent, 6 In.	359.00
Gold Mesh, Sapphire, England, c.1905	2390.00
Ivory Flower, Oriental, Compartment, On String, 3 ½ In.	1050.00
Jersey, Lunch Box, Harlequin Plaid, Silver Hardware, Fabric Interior, Ken Scott, 1960s, 6 x 9 In.	122.00
Leather, 2 Handles, Louis Vuitton, 13 x 10 x 4 In.	220.00
Leather, 2 Sleeves, Zippered Section, Palladium Plated Buckles, Hermes	5570.00
Leather, Absolut Vodka, Gold Medusa Heads, Bottle Top At Side, Zipper, Gianni Versace, 4 x 8 In.	336.00
Leather, Beading, Jeweled, Butterfly, Exotic Birds, Brass Frame, Tassel, 9 In.	495.00
Leather, Black, Gold Latch, Rectangular, Rich's, France, 1950s	75.00
Leather, Black, Silvertone Hardware, Shoulder Strap, Evelyne, Hermes, 15 x 14 ½ x 4 In.	1896.00
Leather, Black, White Stitching, Red Suede Interior, Strap Drop, Salvatore Ferragamo, 10 x 6 x 2 In.	102.00
Leather, Brown, Logo, Strap Drop, 12 ½ x 6 ½ In.	226.00
Leather, Brown, Woven, Barry Kieselstein, Italy	944.00
Leather, Burgundy, Adjustable Strap, Coach, 12 x 11 x 3 In.	102.00
Leather, Camel, Cream, Duffel, Strap, Coach, 13 x 13 x 6 In.	181.00
Leather, Gold Hardware, Shoulder Strap, Marked, Hermes, Paris, 1998, 12 ½ x 12 In.	1708.00
Leather, Gray, Arched Translucent Butterscotch Handles, Grosgrain Lining, Retro	65.00
Leather, Kelly, Interior Side Pockets, Lock, Key Dust Case, Hermes, Box, c.1970	14400.00
Leather, Logo Pattern, Brown, Inside Pocket, Adrienne Vittadini	80.00
Leather, Lucite, Burgundy, Gold Metal Shoulder Chain, Logo, Pierre Cardin, 1970s	210.00
Leather, Messenger Satchel, Steel Plates, Detachable Strap, Stamped, Gucci, 10 x 13 In.	275.00
Leather, Orange, Goldtone Hardware, Zipper, 2 Sleeves, Padlock, Key, Hermes	2370.00
Leather, Quilted Red, Box, Zipper Top, Leather Strap, Pockets, Stamped, Chanel, Italy, 6 x 10 In.	519.00
Leather, Shoulder Strap, Gucci, 1970s, 12 x 8 ½ In.	295.00
Leather, Tan, Clutch Envelope, Goldtone Snap Closure, Ferragamo, 10 ¼ x 7 ¾ In.	395.00
Leather, Toiletries, Brown, Blue Piping, Removable Sleeve, Hermes, 11 x 2 In.	237.00
Leather, White, Shoulder Straps, Bottega Veneta, 10 ½ x 7 In.	195.00
Lizard, Brown, Gold Tone Hinge, Coin Purse, Mirror, Strap, Judith Leiber, 5 ½ x 9 In.	410.00
Lizard, Pink, Clutch, Klarung, Strap, Judith Leiber, 5 ¾ x 8 ½ In.	395.00
Mesh, 9K Gold, Openwork Frame, 10 In.	345.00
Mesh, 14K Gold Frame, Pierced, Chased, Sapphire Cabochon Pin, Link Chain, 6 x 12 In.	4575.00
Mesh, 18K Gold, Rectangular, Oval Link Chain Handle, 4 ½ x 5 In.	5185.00
Mesh, Attached 1850 Dollar Coin, Cabochon Sapphire Clasp, 14K Yellow Gold, 2 ½ x 2 In.	975.00
Mesh, Crystal, Austrian, Minaudiere, Buddha, Goldtone, Chain Strap, 5 ½ x 4 ½ In.	978.00
Mesh, Enamel, Aztec Design, Ecru, Red, Green, Fringe, Mandalian, 7 ¾ In.	295.00
Mesh, Enamel, Chaplin, Silvertone Frame, Pinch Clasp, Whiting & Davis, 6 x 3 ¾ In. ..... *illus*	1784.00
Mesh, Enamel, Clark Gable, Gilt Metal Frame, Pinch Clasp, Whiting & Davis, 6 x 3 ¾ In. ...... *illus*	1989.00
Mesh, Enamel, Cream, Magenta, Black, Fringe, Marked, Mandalian, 7 ½ In.	350.00
Mesh, Enamel, Embossed Frame, Pinch Clasp, Chain Handle, Whiting & Davis, 1930s, 7 x 4 In. ...*illus*	117.00
Mesh, Enamel, Flowers, Chain Link Fringe, Silvertone Frame, Mandalian Mfg. .... *illus*	281.00
Mesh, Enamel, Flowers, Chain Link Fringe, Silvertone Frame, Mandalian, 8 x 4 In. .... *illus*	88.00
Mesh, Enamel, Peafowl, Hinged Frame, Mandalian Mfg. Co., 8 ¾ In.	275.00
Mesh, Flowers, Yellow, Blue, White, Orange, Stamped, Whiting & Davis	270.00
Mesh, Silver, Beaded Fringe, Stamped Hallmark, c.1920, 7 x 4 In.	210.00
Mesh, Sterling Silver, Repousse Floral Frame, Teardrop Beads, Chain Handle, 1800s, 6 In.	475.00

Purse, Beaded, Flowers, Beaded Looped Fringe, Chain Handle, France, Victorian, 7 In. $293.00

Purse, Beaded, Flowers, Scrolling, Multicolored, Cinch Closure, Beaded Fringe, Victorian, 10 In. $205.00

Purse, Beaded, Peacock, Roses, Initial, Multicolored, Beaded Looped Fringe, Victorian, 11 In. $293.00

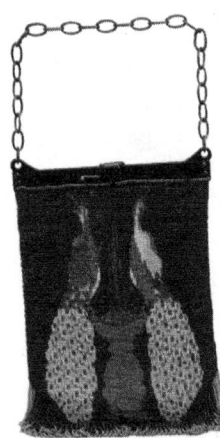

Purse, Envelope, 14K Gold, Sapphire Cabochon, Engraved Flowers, Initial, Chain, 4 x 3 In. $2185.00

Purse, Mesh, Enamel, Chaplin, Silvertone Frame, Pinch Clasp, Whiting & Davis, 6 x 3 ¾ In. $1784.00

Purse, Mesh, Enamel, Clark Gable, Gilt Metal Frame, Pinch Clasp, Whiting & Davis, 6 x 3 ¾ In. $1989.00

Purse, Mesh, Enamel, Embossed Frame, Pinch Clasp, Chain Handle, Whiting & Davis, 1930s, 7 x 4 In. $117.00

Purse, Mesh, Enamel, Flowers, Chain Link Fringe, Silvertone Frame, Mandalian Mfg. $281.00

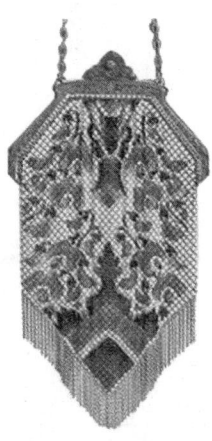

Purse, Mesh, Enamel, Flowers, Chain Link Fringe, Silvertone Frame, Mandalian, 8 x 4 In. $88.00

P

Quezal, Compote, Green Leaves, Ivory Ground, Gold Iridescent Interior, Signed, 5 x 10 In. $1610.00

Quezal, Vase, Gold Iridescent Tendrils, Green Pulled Feather, Platinum Detail, 9 ¾ In. $6325.00

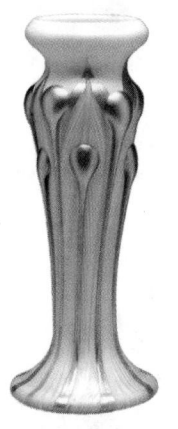

Quezal, Vase, Jack-In-The-Pulpit, Gold Iridescent, Green Hooked Feather, Signed, 8 ¾ In. $8000.00

Ostrich, White, Square, Goldtone Clasp, 8 x 7 x 2 ¼ In.	195.00
Rhinestones, Comb & Mirror, Box, Bag, Judith Leiber	472.00
Satin, Velvet, Stripes, Rhinestone Buckle Accent, Clutch, Martin Van Schaak, 1930s	118.00
Shoulder, Off White, Tan Trim, Straps, Longchamp, 11 x 8 ½ In.	175.00
Silk, Black, Beaded, Enameled, Flowers, France	300.00
Silk, Clutch, Envelope, Victorian Couple, Woodland, Deer, Multicolored, 8 ¼ x 6 ½ In.	450.00
Silk, Gemstones, Openwork Sterling Frame, Tapestry Style, 8 x 7 ½ In.	1725.00
Silk, Suede, Blue Ground, Yellow Embroidered, Butterflies, Chinese, 14 x 11 ¾ In.	210.00
Silver Gold Features, Minaudiere, Owl, Pink Crystal Eyes, Judith Leiber, 5 ½ In.	1159.00
Silver, Round, Ornate Closure Band, Victorian, 6 In.	205.00
Snakeskin, Black, Clutch, Chain Shoulder Strap, Judith Leiber, 9 x 8 ½ In.	177.00
Snakeskin, Clutch, Red, Black Enamel Closure, Black Silk Interior, Judith Leiber	502.00
Snakeskin, Pink, Gold Hardware, Cabochon Closure, Hidden Strap, Judith Leiber, 7 x 11 In.	458.00
Stewardess Bag, Navy, Foldover Flap, Adjustable Strap, Coach, 11 x 11 x 4 ¼ In.	169.00
Straw, Black Patent Leather Trim, Lined, Pierre Cardin, 9 ¼ x 7 ½ In.	183.00
Suede, Jeweled, Pleated, Hobe, Josef, c.1950s, 12 x 8 x 4 In.	275.00
Suede, Red, Bracelet Style, Red Leather Interior, Perez Sanz, Marked, 9 x 12 In.	181.00
Suede, Red, Portfolio, Braid Closure, Strap, Black Leather Interior, Perry Ellis	85.00
Tapestry, Amorous Couple, Castle Scene, 2-Sided, Jeweled Brass Frame, Chain, 8 ½ In.	1950.00
Tapestry, Petit Point, Memorial Scene, Coin Purse, Austria, 5 x 7 In.	375.00
Velvet, Black, Textured Gold Frame, Diamond Pave Push Closure, Strap, Cartier, 7 x 7 In.	4270.00
Velvet, Steel Beaded, Rust Color, Beaded Fringe, Drawstring Top, Silk Lining, Early 1900s, 7 ¾ In.	59.00
Wicker, Beaded, White Seed Beads, Flower On Front, Metal Handle, Midas Of Miami, 1950s	125.00

QUEZAL glass was made from 1901 to 1924 at the Queens, New York, company started by Martin Bach, Sr. Other glassware by other firms, such as Loetz, Steuben, and Tiffany, resembles this gold-colored iridescent glass. Martin Bach died in 1921. His son-in-law, Conrad Vahlsing, Jr., went to work at the Lustre Art Company about 1920. Bach's son, Martin Bach, Jr., worked at the Durand Art Glass division of the Vineland Flint Glass Works after 1924.

Quezal

Bowl, Gold Fishnet, White Ground, Gold, Pink Iridescent Interior, 4-Footed, Signed, 3 x 4 In.	1092.00
Candlestick, Blue, Purple, Iridescent, Inverted Trumpet Shape, Flared Lip, Signed, 10 In., Pair.	2070.00
Compote, Green, Blue, Signed, 8 In.	604.00
Compote, Green Leaves, Ivory Ground, Gold Iridescent Interior, Signed, 5 x 10 In. .... *illus*	1610.00
Lamp, Hanging, 5-Light, Hooked Feather Teardrop Shade, Ivory Ground, 30 In.	3163.00
Lamp, Hanging, Dome, Pulled White, Gold Shade, Brass Base, Signed, 7 ½ x 16 In.	3525.00
Lamp, Hanging, Pendant, Shade, Alabaster, Overall Green Pulled Feather, Gold Tipped, 10 x 6 ½ In.	900.00
Shade, Bell Shape, Ruffled, Gold Iridescent, Threading, Hearts, Vines, Green, Gold, 5 ½ x 5 In., 4 Piece	805.00
Shade, Blue Pulled Feather, Gold Iridescent, Creamy Ground, Signed, 5 ⅞ x 2 ¼ In., 5 Piece	1610.00
Shade, Blue Pulled Feather, Gold Tip, Opal Ground, Signed, 5 ½ In.	316.00
Shade, Flared, Opal Feathers Pulled Over Green, Ribs, Engraved, 5 ¼ In., 5 Piece	633.00
Shade, Gold, Iridescent Ground, Ribbed, Bell Shape, 6 In., Pair	144.00
Shade, Gold, Iridescent, Ribbed Body, Signed, 5 In., Pair	259.00
Shade, Gold Iridescent, Ribbed Gourd Shape, Signed, 4 ½ In., 4 Piece	750.00
Shade, Gold, Platinum, White Snakeskin Design, Wavy Rim, Purple Iridescent, 5 x 2 In.	230.00
Shade, Green Leaf, Platinum, Petals, Gold Vines, Ivory Ground, White Opalescent, 2 ¼ x 4 ¾ In.	2185.00
Shade, Ivory Iridescent Ground, Hooked Feather, White, Gold, 2 ¼ x 4 ½ In., Pair	115.00
Shade, Opal, Gold Heart, Vine Design, Oval, Flared Rim, Signed, 4 ½ In.	144.00
Shade, Pulled Gold Feather, Opal Glass, Bell Shape, Signed, 5 In.	115.00
Shade, Pulled Red Feather, Gold, Platinum Border, Gold Trim, Signed, 6 x 2 In.	1725.00
Shade, Pulled Red Feather, Ivory Ground, Gold Trim, Fluted, Notched, 5 x 2 In.	1518.00
Shade, Red, White Pulled Feather, Gold Ground, Signed, 5 x 2 In.	177.00
Shade, Ribbed, Cone, Gold Pulled Feathers, Iridescent Green Tip, Signed, 15 In.	1955.00
Shade, Ribbed Yellow Pulled Feathers, Green Trim, Trumpet Shape, 6 x 2 In., Pair	403.00
Shade, Snakeskin, Golden Yellow, Ivory Ground, Flared, Signed, 2 ¼ x 4 ¼ In.	345.00
Shade, Snakeskin, White Over Gold, Purple Iridescence, Scalloped Border, 2 ¼ x 4 ¼ In.	230.00
Shade, Tulip, Green Pulled Feathers, Gold Trim On Ivory, Signed, 2 ¼ x 5 In., Pair	460.00
Shade, Wave, White To Green, Gold Ground, Iridescent, Bulbous, Scalloped Border, 2 ¼ x 4 In.	518.00
Toothpick, Gold, Oval, Ribbed, Pinched Sides, Signed	489.00
Vase, Art Glass, Green, Ivory Ground, Platinum Feather, Chain, Bulbous, 6 ¼ In.	2070.00
Vase, Blue Iridescent, Green, Yellow, Orange Ground, Long Neck, Flared Rim, Bulbous, 6 x 4 In.	678.00
Vase, Blue Iridescent, Pontil, Signed, c.1900, 4 ½ x 2 ½ In.	171.00
Vase, Blue Iridescent, Stretched Ruffled Rim, 5 ⅝ In.	805.00
Vase, Blue Iridescent Tapered Oval Shape, Flared Rim, 7 In.	500.00
Vase, Bulbous Urn Shape, Opal, Gold Iridescent Coil Design, Signed, 6 ½ In.	1000.00
Vase, Burnished Gold To Gold, Art Nouveau Silver Overlay, Marked, 5 ¼ In.	1265.00

Q

Vase, Cobalt Blue, King Tut Pattern, Gold Iridescent, Marked, 6 In.	1035.00
Vase, Cylinder Shape, Flared Scalloped Rim, Opal, Gold, Green Pulled Feathers, Signed, 8 In.	3500.00
Vase, Cylinder Shape, Half Moon Rim, Opal, Green Pulled Feather, Gold Interior, 8 In.	3100.00
Vase, Egyptian Hooked Feather, Gold, Green Hearts, Purple Iridescent, Signed, 7 In.	2760.00
Vase, Flower Shape, Gold Interior, Green Pulled Feathers, Gold Accented Foot, 6 In.	1100.00
Vase, Footed Compote Shape, Opal, Green Pulled Feather Design, Gold Tipped, 5 In.	2250.00
Vase, Footed, Oval Shouldered Shape, Gold Iridescent, Coil Design, 6 In.	950.00
Vase, Gold Iridescent Tendrils, Green Pulled Feather, Platinum Detail, 9 ¾ In. .... illus	6325.00
Vase, Gold Pulled Feather Neck, Gold, Ivory Netting, Purple, Green Iridescent, Signed, 10 In.	2300.00
Vase, Gold, Purple Ground, Silver Flower Overlay, Thin Stem, Purple Iridescent, Signed, 9 ½ In.	3105.00
Vase, Green & Blue Pulled Design, Oval, Footed, Stamped, Late 1900s, 6 In.	195.00
Vase, Green, Gold Hooked Designs, Ivory Ground, Pink Iridescent, Signed, 10 In.	4025.00
Vase, Green, Ivory Pulled Feather, Pink, Purple, Gold Interior, Ruffled Flower Shape, Signed, 6 In.	1265.00
Vase, Green Pulled Feather, Gold Trim, Interior, Ruffled Trumpet Shape, 11 In.	2645.00
Vase, Iridescent Gold, Green Pulled Feather, Flower Form, 5 ¼ In.	1265.00
Vase, Iridescent Green Pulled Feather, Zigzag, Hooked Feather, Multicolored, 4 ½ In.	2645.00
Vase, Jack-In-The-Pulpit, Gold Iridescent, Footed, Signed, 9 ½ In.	1725.00
Vase, Jack-In-The-Pulpit, Gold Iridescent, Green Hooked Feather, Signed, 8 ¾ In. .... illus	8000.00
Vase, Jack-In-The-Pulpit, Gold, Rolled Face, Green, White Swirls, Gold Feathers, Signed, 7 In.	5175.00
Vase, King Tut, Urn Shape, Marigold Iridescent Gold Foot, Blue Design, Signed, 8 In.	2300.00
Vase, Long Neck, Bulbous Bottom, Blue Green, Iridescent, Signed, 1920s, 6 x 4 In.	880.00
Vase, Multicolored Agate Glass, Art Nouveau Silver Overlay, Signed, 7 In.	2530.00
Vase, Opal Body, Flared Neck, Green Iridescent Hooks, Pulled Gold Lappets, Signed, A 385, 12 In.	3600.00
Vase, Platinum Hooked Design, Purple, Blue Vines, Flared Pink, Gold Neck, 7 In.	3450.00
Vase, Purple Iridescent, Art Glass, Green Pulled Feather, Gold Ground, Footed, 11 In.	2645.00
Vase, Tapered Shape, Flared Rim, Green Iridescent, Gold Hooked Feather Design, 15 In.	2500.00
Vase, Trumpet Shape, Footed, Scalloped Rim, Opal, Pulled Feathers, Gold Chain To Rim, Signed, 7 In.	3500.00
Vase, Trumpet Shape, Wavy Rim, Opal, Green Pulled Feather Design, Gold, 8 In.	3000.00

QUILTS have been made since the seventeenth century. Early textiles were very precious and every scrap was saved to be reused. A quilt is a combination of fabrics joined to a filler and a backing by small stitched designs known as quilting. An appliqued quilt has pieces stitched to the top of a large piece of background fabric. A patchwork, or pieced, quilt is made of many small pieces stitched together. Embroidery can be added to either type.

Amish, Black Border, Red, Blue Geometric, Machine Pieced, Penn., Crib, 31 x 37 In.	470.00
Amish, Center Star, Purple, Green, Blue Ground, Mounting Bar, 40 x 40 In.	240.00
Amish, Mosaic Star, Red, Blue, Pink, Cotton, Wool, c.1910, 75 x 77 In.	353.00
Amish, Patchwork, 9 Block Variation, Wine, Lavender, White, Cotton, Early 1900s, 78 x 79 In.	1116.00
Amish, Patchwork, Postage Stamp, Purple, Black Border, Green Backing, 35 x 37 ½ In.	85.00
Amish, Triple Irish Chain, Blue & Purple, 1900s, 40 52 In.	610.00
Amish, Turquoise, Cream, Double Inside Border, Cotton, 75 x 78 In.	420.00
Appliqued, 48 Baskets, Green Ground, White Border, 98 x 75 In.	205.00
Appliqued, 48 Baskets, Pink Ground, White Border, 94 x 74 In.	210.00
Appliqued, 9 Patches, Red & Green, 8-Leaf Clover Design, White Ground, c.1850, 80 x 80 In.	575.00
Appliqued, Album, Flowers, Signatures, Louise Blessing, Elizabeth Sharp, Baltimore, 1845, 98 x 99 In.	28250.00
Appliqued, Carolina Lily, Sawtooth Inner Border, Cotton, c.1850, 91 x 78 In.	411.00
Appliqued, Circles, Blue, Pink, Red Floral, Swag Border, Cotton, Medina, Ohio, Mid 1800s, 94 x 95 In.	441.00
Appliqued, Cockscomb, Leaf & Flower Border, White, Green, Red, Late 1800s, 96 x 88 In. . illus	1404.00
Appliqued, Cockscomb, Red, Green, Flowers & Leaf Border, Late 1800s, 96 x 88 In.	1320.00
Appliqued, Floral Blocks, Yellow Sashing, Sawtooth Border, Scalloped Edge, Ohio, 80 x 98 In.	646.00
Appliqued, Flower Girl, 24 Panels, Pink Ground, 87 x 58 In.	280.00
Appliqued, Flowers, Leaves, Plumes, Red, Green, 93 x 98 In.	275.00
Appliqued, Flowers, White Ground, Rectangles, Circles, Red Contoured Binding, 86 x 71 In.	117.00
Appliqued, Flying Geese, Red, White, Early 20th Century, Crib, 46 x 35 In.	195.00
Appliqued, Flying Geese, Red, White, Multicolored, Grandma Elizabeth Phippins, 70 x 77 In.	283.00
Appliqued, Lady Of The Lake, Tester Bedpost Cut, 1884, 69 x 77 In.	610.00
Appliqued, Lone Star, Sawtooth Border, Multicolored, Blue Ground, 1800s, 88 x 95 In.	847.00
Appliqued, Patchwork, 5 Cats, Glass Eyes, Flowers, Red, Navy, Black, Wool, c.1910, 81 x 82 In.	5629.00
Appliqued, Princess Feather, 4 Squares, Flower, Red & Tan Sashing, Georgia, c.1850, 76 x 70 In.	1610.00
Appliqued, Princess Feather, Brown, Green, White Ground, 1800s, 74 x 70 In.	396.00
Appliqued, Red, Green, Rose, Pink, Yellow Print, White Ground, Diamonds, 1830s, 89 x 82 In.	410.00
Appliqued, Red Tulip, Vine, White Ground, Red Border, 79 x 88 In.	90.00
Appliqued, Rose Of Sharon, Coxcomb, Cotton, c.1850, 92 x 92 In.	881.00
Appliqued, Rose Of Sharon, Dress Prints, Pennsylvania, 1875, 92 x 92 In.	880.00
Appliqued, Rose Variation, Pink, Green, c.1900, 75 x 78 In.	210.00
Appliqued, Sawtooth Baskets, Stars, Hearts, Flowers, Red, White, c.1890, 80 x 102 In.	605.00

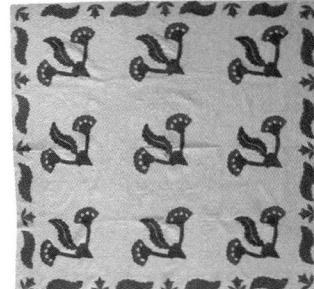

Quilt, Appliqued, Cockscomb, Leaf & Flower Border, White, Green, Red, Late 1800s, 96 x 88 In. $1404.00

Quilt, Appliqued, Star Rosette, Sawtooth Border, Mary Ann Kepler, Ohio, c.1856, 76 x 78 In. $3525.00

Quilt, Dresden Plate, Blue, White Ground, 97 x 86 In. $201.00

Quilt, Patchwork, Appliqued, Animals, Toys, 25 Block, Ohio, c.1896, 42 x 44 In. $2070.00

QUILT

Quilt, Patchwork, Drunkard's Path, Printed Cotton, Early 18th Century, 64 x 76 In.
$230.00

Quilt, Patchwork, Ocean Wave, Inscribed, To Martha From Gandmak, c.1892, 82 x 87 In.
$761.00

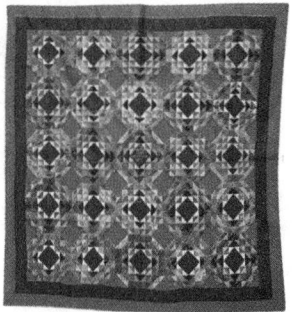

TIP

Use your computer to help repair an old quilt with a worn patch. Put the worn part of the quilt on the flatbed of a scanner (you may have to remove the scanner cover). Print it on paper. Then add a border as a seam allowance by hand. Use the picture as a pattern and cut the fabric patch.

Appliqued, Star, 25 Blue Stars, White, 71 x 77 In.	250.00
Appliqued, Star Rosette, Sawtooth Border, Mary Ann Kepler, Ohio, c.1856, 76 x 78 In. ....*illus*	3525.00
Appliqued, Striped, Red, Blue Plaids, Linsey-Woolsey, Wool, c.1800, 89 x 69 In.	206.00
Appliqued, Sunburst, Red, White, Blue Squares, Yellow Border, White Backing, c.1900, 81 x 69 In.	575.00
Appliqued, Tobacco Flags, 12 Flags, Doll Size, c.1920, 20 x 24 In.	50.00
Appliqued, Touching Star, Red, White, Late 19th Century, 90 ½ x 91 In.	700.00
Appliqued, Tulip, Red & Green On White, Swag Border, Cotton, c.1850, 78 x 70 ½ In.	382.00
Appliqued, Whig Rose, Diamonds, Cotton, 89 x 82 In.	411.00
Appliqued, Whig Rose, Red & Green, 1850s, 89 x 82 In.	250.00
Appliqued, White, Navy Border, Flowers, Red, Blue & Yellow, 1940s, Twin Size	600.00
Crazy, 25 Blocks, Flowers, Animals, Embroidered, Wool, Cotton, Silk, Virginia, 1900, 73 x 73 In.	2760.00
Crazy, Black Border, Backing, c.1900, 66 x 69 In.	351.00
Crazy, Silk, Black Velvet Border, Green Silk Backing, c.1850, 57 x 61 In.	767.00
Dresden Plate, Blue, White Ground, 97 x 86 In. ....*illus*	201.00
Friendship, Central Floral Wreath, Squares, Flowers, Stars, Birds, Navy Ground, c.1870, 91 x 79 In.	3042.00
Mennonite, Appliqued, Sunshine & Shadows, Multicolored, 1800s, 82 x 88 In.	650.00
Mennonite, Geometric, Sawtooth Border, Orange, Green, Red, 80 x 80 In.	5300.00
Mennonite, Patchwork, 8-Point Star Pattern, Pink Ground, 60 x 72 In.	106.00
Mennonite, Patchwork, Log Cabin, Blue & Yellow Border, 60 x 72 In.	177.00
Patchwork & Appliqued, Lily, White Ground, Double Sawtooth Border, 19th Century, 80 x 84 In.	345.00
Patchwork, 6 Block, 25 Patches, Circles, c.1930s, Crib, 26 x 37 In.	23.00
Patchwork, 8-Point Star, 94 x 115 In.	34.00
Patchwork, 8-Point Stars, Multicolored, Crib, 38 x 38 In.	121.00
Patchwork, 16 Block, Cross, Block Design, Printed, Blue Backing, 75 x 75 In.	79.00
Patchwork, Album, Cotton Print, Amy Stanley, Columbiana County, Ohio, c.1846, 83 x 93 In.	558.00
Patchwork, Appliqued, Animals, Toys, 25 Block, Ohio, c.1896, 42 x 44 In. ....*illus*	2070.00
Patchwork, Appliqued, Yellow Lilies, Initialed JMW, 1851, 81 x 90 In.	3975.00
Patchwork, Basket, Brown, Turquoise, Late 19th Century, 80 x 79 In.	840.00
Patchwork, Bowtie, Brown, White, Vine, Leaf, 80 x 92 In.	165.00
Patchwork, Bowtie, Cheddar, Red Border, 60 x 69 In.	136.00
Patchwork, Bowtie, Solid, Print, Yellow, Blue, Red, Cotton, Kentucky, c.1890, 77 x 67 In.	353.00
Patchwork, Broken Star, Multicolored, Prints, Cotton, c.1930, 78 x 84 In.	495.00
Patchwork, Center Square, Multicolored, Flower Backing, 82 x 82 In.	143.00
Patchwork, Center Sunburst, 25 Blocks, 1850, 88 x 89 In.	1135.00
Patchwork, Diamond, Block, Yellow, Pink, Blue Bar Border, Flower Backing, 75 x 78 In.	158.00
Patchwork, Diamond Blocks, Triangle Patches, 82 x 83 In.	385.00
Patchwork, Double Irish Chain, White Ground, Blue, c.1920, 80 x 82 In.	350.00
Patchwork, Drunkard's Path, Printed Cotton, Early 18th Century, 64 x 76 In. ....*illus*	230.00
Patchwork, Embroidered, Velvet, Burgundy Ground, 72 x 60 In.	119.00
Patchwork, Evening Star Blocks, 2-Sided, 1890s, 18 x 26 In.	35.00
Patchwork, Fan, Blue, Gray Ground, Red, Yellow Border, Flowers, c.1920, 66 x 43 In.	119.00
Patchwork, Flowers, Crescent Moon, Animals, Velvet, Taffeta, Brocade, Embroidery, 1800s, 60 x 59 In.	460.00
Patchwork, Flowers, Embroidered, Satin, Black Velvet Ground, 48 x 72 In.	598.00
Patchwork, Friendship, New Haven, Connecticut, c.1885, 92 x 91 In.	1170.00
Patchwork, Geometric, Block, Multicolored, Striped Backing, 66 x 69 In.	358.00
Patchwork, Goose Track Variation, Squares, Triangles, Black, Blue, Stars, Cotton, c.1950, 74 x 63 In.	296.00
Patchwork, Grandmother's Flower Garden, Multicolored Prints & Solids, 79 x 73 In.	176.00
Patchwork, Grandmother's Flower Garden, Newspaper Backing, 78 x 58 In.	79.00
Patchwork, Indigo Blue Glazed, 6 Woven Worsted Wool Panels, Center With Flowers, 1810, 92 x 90 In.	1185.00
Patchwork, Irish Chain, 68 ½ x 82 In.	96.00
Patchwork, Irish Chain, c.1860, 64 x 80 In.	395.00
Patchwork, Irish Chain, Nine Patch Variation, Red, White, Signed, Debora, c.1920, 62 x 78 In.	299.00
Patchwork, Irish Chain, Tan, Red, Orange Bands, White, Flowers, Lines, Feathers, 1886, 79 x 68 In. .	770.00
Patchwork, Lancaster Rose, Navy, Red Flowers, 97 x 115 In.	57.00
Patchwork, Log Cabin, Multicolored, Star, Stripe Backing, Late 19th Century, 7 ½ x 6 In.	90.00
Patchwork, Log Cabin, Orange, Brown Floral, Wood Stretcher, Crib, c.1800s, 25 ½ x 34 In.	504.00
Patchwork, Log Cabin, Triple Sashing & Borders, Cotton, c.1875, 80 x 74 In.	176.00
Patchwork, Log Cabin, United States Flag Center, 45 ½ x 64 ½ In.	59.00
Patchwork, Lone Star, Blue, White, Cotton, Feathered Wreath Quilting, Late 1800s, 74 x 78 In.	382.00
Patchwork, Mariner's Compass, Red, Green, Blue, Brown, Pink & White, 1844, 99 x 100 In. ..	660.00
Patchwork, Mariner's Compass, White Ground, Blue, Flower & Vine Quilting, Late 1800s, 76 x 86 In.	1058.00
Patchwork, Moon, Stars, 35 Circles, 10 Half Circles, Wool, Blue, Black, Brown, Frame, 77 x 48 In.	7703.00
Patchwork, Ocean Wave, Inscribed, To Martha From Gandmak, c.1892, 82 x 87 In. ....*illus*	761.00
Patchwork, Patchwork Bars, Cheddar, Lancaster Co., Crib, 40 x 42 In.	90.00
Patchwork, Pinwheel, Red Patches, White, 70 x 83 In.	68.00
Patchwork, Red, Green Flowers, White Border, Cotton, c.1850, 82 x 88 In.	470.00

Patchwork, Robbing Peter To Pay Paul, Green, White, Cotton, c.1920, 73 x 85 In.	176.00
Patchwork, Rolling Pinwheels, Yellow, Blue, Cotton, c.1920, 62 x 77 In.	176.00
Patchwork, Round The World, Cotton, ¼-In. Squares, Box, Maud Oakes, Mich., 1930s, 55 x 57 In.	588.00
Patchwork, Sampler, Friendship, Family, Lancaster County, Late 1800s, 88 x 84 In. .... *illus*	4680.00
Patchwork, Sawtooth, Red, White, Cotton, c.1900, 68 x 81 In.	441.00
Patchwork, Silk Ribbons, Cycle Race, Second Annual Race, May 30, 1893, 21 x 20 In.	61.00
Patchwork, Squares, Flowers, Blue, Purple, Diamond, Rope, Heart, Scroll, Cotton, 80 x 66 In.	385.00
Patchwork, Star, Alternating Green Square, Cotton, c.1845, 84 x 73 In.	235.00
Rectangular Panels, Embroidered Flowers, Landscapes, Satin, 1890, 48 x 74 In.	1534.00
Trapunto, Cotton White Work, 3 Sections, Urn, Flowers, Grapes, Feather, 100 x 86 In.	593.00
Wool, 2-Sided, Roman Stripes, Shades Of Red, Black, White, Gray, Brown & Blue, 1920s	975.00

QUIMPER pottery has a long history. Tin-glazed, hand-painted pottery has been made in Quimper, France, since the late seventeenth century. The earliest firm, founded in 1685 by Jean Baptiste Bousquet, was known as HB Quimper. Another firm, founded in 1772 by Francois Eloury, was known as Porquier. The third firm, founded by Guillaume Dumaine in 1778, was known as HR or Henriot Quimper. All three firms made similar pottery decorated with designs of Breton peasants and sea and flower motifs. The Eloury (Porquier) and Dumaine (Henriot) firms merged in 1913. Bousquet (HB) merged with the others in 1968. The group was sold to a United States family in 1984. The American holding company is Quimper Faience Inc., located in Stonington, Connecticut. The French firm has been called *Societe Nouvelle des Faienceries de Quimper HB Henriot* since March 1984.

Ashtray, Cross Of Lorraine, Red, Gen. Charles DeGaulle, June 12, 1949, Marked, 3 ⅞ In.	36.00
Basket, Breton Man, Walking Stick, Flowers, 4-Footed, Marked, 1922-68, 10 x 11 ½ In.	600.00
Bowl, Porridge, Cover, Woman, Handles, Marked, HB, 3 ½ x 6 ¾ In.	264.00
Butter Pat, Flower, Geometric, Yellow Rim, Marked, Henriot Quimper 198, 3 ⅓ In.	55.00
Chamberstick, Woman, Flowers, Marked, Henriot Quimper France, c.1935, 6 In.	150.00
Double Salt, Man, Woman, Blue Border, Marked, HB, 3 x 3 ¾ In.	175.00
Inkwell, Man, Playing Bagpipes, Flowers, Leaves, Pinched Edge, Signed, 3 x 5 In. .... *illus*	66.00
Jardiniere, White Ground, Multicolored Flowers, Birds, Signed, 19th Century, 13 In.	1200
Knife Rest, Flowers, Blue Sponging, 3-Sided, 3 ½ In.	56.00
Oyster Plate, 6 Wells, Man, Walking Stick, Handles, 1960-70, 9 ½ In.	125.00
Oyster Plate, 6 Wells, Red Plant, Green Leaves, Blue Rim, 9 In.	135.00
Oyster Plate, 6 Wells, Shell Form, Starfish Center, Fouillen, 1920-30, 9 In.	150.00
Oyster Plate, 7 Wells, Fish Form, c.1935-40, 10 x 8 ¾ In.	175.00
Pitcher, Breton Woman, Trees, Plants, Flowers, Blue Band, Signed, Henriot, c.1920, 8 In.	330.00
Planter, Breton Flowers, Breton Man, Marked, CB, 7 x 8 ½ In.	125.00
Plate, Breton Man, 8-Sided, Beige Ground, Brown Rim, 1940, Marked, HB, 5 ½ In.	125.00
Plate, Breton Woman, 8-Sided, Beige Ground, Brown Rim, 1940, Marked, HB, 5 ½ In.	125.00
Plate, Sailor, Song Verse, Joel Sevellec...	89.00
Platter, Fish Form, Woman, Blue, Green, Rust, Yellow, Signed, H.B., 9 x 19 ½ In.	225.00
Server, Woman, Man, Flowers, 4 Sections, Blue Sponging, 9 x 9 In.	250.00
Teapot, Petit Breton, Man, Flowers, 6 ½ x 8 ¾ In.	300.00
Tidbit, 2 Tiers, Man, Woman, Trees, Red, Blue, Green...	145.00
Wall Pocket, Breton Couple, Double Coronet, Geometrics, c.1900, 10 ½ x 7 ½ In.	475.00
Wall Pocket, Girl, Garden, Multicolored Porcelain, Breton, c.1920, 4 ½ x 3 In.	200.00
Wall Pocket, Shoe Form, Breton Woman, Flowers, Late 1800s, 9 ½ In.	325.00

RADFORD pottery was made by Alfred Radford in Broadway, Virginia; Tiffin and Zanesville, Ohio; and Clarksburg, West Virginia, from 1891 until 1912. Jasperware, Ruko, Thera, Radura, and Velvety Art Ware were made. The jasperware resembles the famous Wedgwood ware of the same name. Another pottery named Radford worked in England and is not included here.

RADURA.

Vase, Red Clay, Textured Green Finish, Applied, Portrait & Eagle Emblem, 7 In.	259.00

RADIO broadcast receiving sets were first sold in New York City in 1910. They were used to pick up the experimental broadcasts of the day. The first commercial radios were made by Westinghouse Company for listeners of the experimental shows on KDKA Pittsburgh in 1920. Collectors today are interested in all early radios, especially those made of Bakelite plastic or decorated with blue mirrors. Figural advertising radios and transistor radios are also collected.

Aircastle, Spiegel Inc., Model 891, c.1938	55.00
Automatic Radio Mfg. Co., Tom Thumb, Bicycle, Red, Mass., 1948, Portable	764.00
Baseball, Trophy, Official League, 1940s, 9 ½ x 8 ½ In.	925.00
Brunswick, Tuscany, Mahogany, Leather Top, 1947, 30 x 17 ½ In.	330.00
Crosley Ace, 3B, 1923, Tube	66.00
Crosley, Model 11-104U, Black, Plastic, c.1951, 5 ½ x 9 ½ x 6 ¼ In.	66.00

Quilt, Patchwork, Sampler, Friendship, Family, Lancaster County, Late 1800s, 88 x 84 In.
$4680.00

Quimper, Inkwell, Man, Playing Bagpipes, Flowers, Leaves, Pinched Edge, Signed, 3 x 5 In.
$66.00

Radio, Emerson, Model 400, Aristocrat, Butterscotch, Catalin, c.1940, 11 x 5 ½ x 7 In.
$960.00

R

Railroad, Bell, Locomotive, Bangor & Aroostook Brass, 24 ½ x 17 In. $1438.00

Railroad, Eggcup, Chicago, Milwaukee, St. Paul & Pacific Footed, 2 ⅜ In. $176.00

Railroad, Headlight, Locomotive, Northern Pacific, No. 1733, Pyle National, 22 ½ x 17 In. $1208.00

Railroad, Lantern, Interior, Pullman, Silver Plated, Adams & Westlake, 10 ¼ In. $920.00

Crystal Set, Philmore, Box	33.00
Dahlberg, Model 430-D, Pillow Speaker, Coin Operated, c.1955, 11 ½ x 13 In.	540.00
Dewald, Model A-501, Catalin, Harp Form, Slide Rule Dial, c.1946, 6 ½ x 9 ¾ x 5 ½ In.	600.00
Edison, Light-O-Matic, Upright, 1928	77.00
Emerson, Model 400, Aristocrat, Butterscotch, Catalin, c.1940, 11 x 5 ½ x 7 In. .... *illus*	960.00
Emerson, Model 414, AC/DC, Wood Cabinet, 1933, 7 ½ x 7 In., Table	180.00
Emerson, Model 520, Catalin, c.1946, 8 ¾ x 11 ¼ In.	110.00
Fada, Model 252, Butterscotch, Catalin, Red Knobs, 7 x 11 In.	540.00
Fada, Model 845, Ivory, Red Knobs, 1950, 6 x 10 ½ In.	480.00
General Electric, J-82, Superheterodyne, Cathedral Form, c.1932, 18 ¾ x 14 In.	79.00
General Electric, Mickey Mouse, Clock, Blue, White, 4 ½ x 10 ½ In.	60.00
Howard, Model 427F, Light Wood Cabinet, 39 x 22 In.	240.00
Magic-Tone, Model 504, Liquor Bottle Shape, Bakelite Base, 1947, 15 In.	168.00
Majestic, Charlie McCarthy, Monocle, c.1938, 7 x 6 In.	960.00
Philco, Model 20, Tapestry Grill Cloth, Bird's-Eye Maple Front, 1930, 34 x 19 In., Floor	150.00
Philco, Model 38-7, Wooden Case, 1938, Table	17.00
Philco, Model 38-10, Wooden Case, 1938, Table	132.00
Philco, Model 39-25, Wooden Case, 1939, Table	44.00
Philco, Model 48-482, AM-FM, 1947, Table	33.00
Princess Telephone Shape, AM, Hong Kong, 1960s	75.00
RCA Victor, Model 75X17, Plastic Case, Oriental Scenes, 1948, 8 x 10 In.	150.00
RCA Victor, Model C8-20, Mahogany Cabinet, 39 x 24 In., Floor	330.00
RCA Victor, R-73, Table, Tombstone Case, c.1933, 19 ½ x 14 ⅝ In.	49.00
RCA Victor, Radiola, 17, Wood, c.1927, 8 ¾ x 27 ½ In.	46.00
RCA Victor, TRK-12, Mahogany Case, Bakelite Controls, Mirror, Lid, 1939, 30 x 34 In.	10200.00
Sentinel, Model 195, Catalin, Butterscotch, 1940s, 8 x 6 ½ x 7 ½ In.	480.00
Silver Radio Co., Model Z10, Mahogany Cabinet, Bird's-Eye Maple Front, 40 x 27 In., Floor	120.00
Silvertone, Model 125, Cathedral, Mahogany, 17 x 15 In.	50.00
Transistor, Globe, Gold, Plastic, Peerless, Constellation, c.1960, 8 ½ In.	70.00
Westinghouse, H-130, Wooden Case, 1946, Table	22.00
Zenith, Model R699285, Push & Pull Switches, Waterfall Style, 1930-1940s, 25 x 29 In., Floor.	310.00
Zenith, No. 8G005YT, Trans Oceanic, 1948, Portable	17.00
Zenith, No. H500, Trans Oceanic, 1951, Portable	13.75

RAILROAD enthusiasts collect any train memorabilia. Everything is wanted, from oilcans to whole train cars. The Chessie system has a store that sells many reproductions of their old dinnerware and uniforms.

Ad, Magazine, Collier's, New Haven R.R., World War II, Jan. 9, 1943, 10 ½ x 13 ¾ In.	3.00
Ad, Magazine, Collier's, Pennsylvania Railroad, World War II, 1944, 10 ½ x 13 ¾ In.	4.00
Badge, Baltimore & Ohio Railroad Company, Celluloid, Metal, c.1930, 2 In.	28.00
Banner, Flying Scotsman Tour Of U.S.A., Cotton, Oct. 8-13, 1969, Frame	23.00
Bell, Locomotive, Bangor & Aroostook Railroad, Brass, 24 ½ x 17 In. .... *illus*	1438.00
Bell, Locomotive, Brass, Harp, Round, 28 x 16 ½ In.	1092.00
Bell, Locomotive, Brass, Northern Pacific Railroad, No. 5106, Iron Harp Base, Wood Stand, 29 In.	575.00
Bench, Back Flips Over, Changes Seat Direction, Wood, 31 ½ x 48 ½ In.	550.00
Bowl, B & O Railroad, Blue Transfer, Potomac Valley, Lamberton, 9 In., 6 Piece	354.00
Eggcup, Chicago, Milwaukee, St. Paul & Pacific Railroad, Footed, 2 ⅜ In. .... *illus*	176.00
Hat, Conductor, Amtrak Trainman	40.00
Hat, Conductor, Milwaukee	215.00
Headlight, Locomotive, Northern Pacific, No. 1733, Pyle National, 22 ½ x 17 In. .... *illus*	1208.00
Headlight, Locomotive, Northern Pacific Railroad, No. 1847, Brass Plaque, 30 x 22 x 17 In. ..	1495.00
Horn, Leslie, Typhon, No. 200, Cast Metal, 26 In.	325.00
Invitation, Opening Of Union Pacific Track, Lithograph, Illustration, c.1864, 5 ½ x 8 ¼ In. ..	337.00
Key, B & O, Caboose Door, Brass	15.00
Key, CRI & PRR, Brass, Heart Shape, Hansle Mfg. Co.	75.00
Key, Switch Lock, B & O	35.00
Lamp, Candle, Brass, NYCS, Wall Mount	100.00
Lamp, Signal, 4-Way, Adlake	113.00
Lamp, Signal, 4-Way, Handlan	158.00
Lamp, Switch, WMRR, Handlan	375.00
Lantern, Arlington, Blue & Red Lenses, 21 In.	195.00
Lantern, Burlington Route, Metal, Red Globe, Embossed	130.00
Lantern, C & O, Adlake Kero, Red Globe	150.00
Lantern, C & O, Metal, Amber Globe, Embossed	68.00
Lantern, Caboose Tail Marker, Dressel, 3 Blue Lenses, 1 Red Lens	350.00
Lantern, Dietz, XLCR, Switchman's, c.1914	250.00

Lantern, Dressel L & N, Caboose Tail Marker, Red Lens, 3 Amber Lenses	375.00
Lantern, Erie, Clear Etched Globe, Adams & Westlake Co.	100.00
Lantern, I H Railroad, Wire Wrapped, Metal Handle, Adams & Westlake, 1895, 9 ½ In.	60.00
Lantern, ICRR, Handlan	125.00
Lantern, Interior, Pullman, Silver Plated, Adams & Westlake, 10 ¼ In. ....illus	920.00
Lantern, NYCS, Adlake, Kerosene, Tin, Handle, 9 In.	58.00
Lantern, NYCS, Dietz, Red Globe, No. 999	100.00
Lantern, P & LE, Red Globe, Dressel, Arlington, N.J.	125.00
Lantern, Penn Central, Adlake Kero, Clear Globe	85.00
Lantern, Penn Central, Adlake Kero, Red Fresnel Globe	85.00
Lantern, PRR, Dressel, Rubber Coated Handle	110.00
Lantern, PRR Railroad, Etched Globe, Armspear Man'f'g Co., New York 1925	100.00
Lantern, PRR Railroad, Tail Marker, Red Lens	250.00
Lantern, Rock Island Lines, Metal, Clear Globe, Embossed	68.00
Lantern, Switch, Adlake, Non-Sweating, 2 Green, 2 Red Lenses, Handle, 17 In.	140.00
Lantern, Switch, CNR, 3 Green & 1 Red Lens, HLPM, Handle, 15 In.	130.00
Lock, B & O, Signal Dept. Cumberland Division, Brass, Key	75.00
Lock, CVRR, Yale, Patent	250.00
Lock, P & R, Brass, Yale	65.00
Lock, Switch, B & O, Key, 1969	65.00
Lock, Switch, WMRR, Brass, Heart Shape, Key	85.00
Match Holder, Striker, Plant System, Union Porcelain Works, New York, 2 ¾ In.	295.00
Paperweight, Moffat Road Colorado, Looping The Loop, Glass, 4 ¼ x 1 In.	38.00
Plate, B & O Railroad, Blue Transfer, Harper's Ferry, Lamberton, 10 ½ In., 6 Piece	189.00
Plate, B & O, Locomotive, Cast Brass, 16 ½ In. ....illus	748.00
Seat, Train Car, Double, Metal, Upholstered, Ashtray, Heywood Wakefield, 40 x 44 In.	59.00
Sign, Alamo, Missouri-Kansas-Texas, Frame, 25 x 21 In.	115.00
Sign, M-K-T Freight Station, Red, White, Porcelain, Die Cut, 41 x 48 In.	580.00
Sign, New York Central System, Metal, 30 x 48 In.	299.00
Sign, Railway Express Agency, Black, Gold, Porcelain, Flange, 12 x 72 In.	175.00
Sign, Railway Express Agency, Packages Received Here, Red, White, Porcelain, Flange, 18 x 15 In.	275.00
Step, Metal, NYC Railroad	254.00
Torch, Dovetailed Side, Wick, Marked, R. Wall, Pittsburgh	35.00
Torch, PRR	20.00
Whistle, Steam, Canadian National Railroad, Release Lever, 34 In.	1840.00

RAZORS were used in ancient Egypt and subsequently wherever shaving was in fashion. The metal razor used in America until about 1870 was made in Sheffield, England. After 1870, machine-made hollow-ground razors were made in Germany or America. Plastic or bone handles were popular. The razor was often sold in a set of seven, one for each day of the week. The set was often kept by the barber who shaved the well-to-do man each day in the shop.

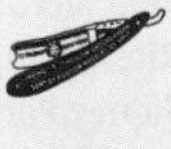

C.V. Hejestrand, Safety, For Wanamaker's, Philadelphia, 1920-30	75.00
Johan Engstrom, Celluloid, Peacock, Horn Handles Frameback, Challenge Cutlery, c.1928	105.00
Keen Kutter, Woman, Scrolls, Embossed, Aluminum, Metal, 6 ¼ x ⅞ In.	77.00
Straight, Steel, Black Boy, 9 In.	112.00
Strap, Winchester, No. 8373	95.00

REAMERS, or juice squeezers, have been known since 1767, although most of those collected today date from the twentieth century. Figural reamers are among the most prized.

Aluminum, Long Handle, 4 x 8 In.	12.00
Custard Glass, Handle, 1930-50, McKee Glass Co., 3 ¼ x 7 In.	85.00
Glass, Amber, Ribs, Federal Glass Co., 2 x 5 In.	18.00
Glass, Clear, Easleys Improved Tab Handle, 2 ¼ x 4 ½ In.	44.00
Glass, Cobalt, Blue, Crisscross, Handle, Hazel Atlas	290.00
Glass, Crystal, Crisscross, Tab Handle, Hazel Atlas	10.00
Glass, Delphite Blue, Jeannette Glass Co., 2 x 7 x 5 ½ In.	80.00
Glass, Green, Anchor Hocking, 1930-40, 2 ½ x 5 In.	25.00
Glass, Jadeite, 2-Cup Measuring Cup, Handle, Jeannette Glass Co	50.00
Glass, Jadeite, Grapefruit, 2 ¼ x 8 ½ In.	250.00
Glass, Red To Light Red, Handle, Marked, Duboe, 4 ½ In.	33.00
Glass, Sunkist, Jade, McKee, 1930s	85.00
Glass, Sunkist, Orange, McKee, Marked U.S.A., 1930s	25.00
Glass, Ultramarine, Jeannette Glass Co., 1937-38, 3 ½ x 7 ½ In. ....illus	85.00
Milk Glass, Sunkist, Handle	14.00
Plastic, Pink, Marked, Lustroware, 6 In.	8.00

Railroad, Plate, B & O, Locomotive, Cast Brass, 16 ½ In. $748.00

Reamer, Glass, Ultramarine, Jeannette Glass Co., 1937-38, 3 ½ x 7 ½ In. $85.00

Reamer, Porcelain, Figural, Duck, Green Head, Orange Feet, Beak, Japan, 3 x 6 In. $95.00

Reamer, Porcelain, Figural, Pear, Stem, Yellow Luster, Japan, 1930s, 5 x 6 In., 3 Piece $85.00

TIP
Chipped enamel "graniteware" sinks can be repaired with several coats of enamel paint. Sand between coats.

Reamer, Pottery, Delft Scene, Yellow, Blue Windmill, Sailboats, 1930s, 5 x 4 In., 2 Piece
$22.00

Red Wing, Capistrano, Gravy Boat, 6 ¼ In.
$35.00

Red Wing, Modern Lotus, Teapot, Gray, 11 In.
$75.00

Red Wing, Orleans, Sugar & Creamer, Cover
$18.00

Porcelain, Figural, Duck, Green Head, Orange Feet, Beak, Japan, 3 x 6 In. ......*illus*	95.00
Porcelain, Figural, Pear, Stem, Yellow Luster, Japan, 1930s, 5 x 6 In., 3 Piece ......*illus*	85.00
Pottery, Child's Face, Red, White, Marked, Japan, 1940s, 3 In.	165.00
Pottery, Citrus Face, Green, Stamped, Japan, 1940s, 5 ¼ In.	210.00
Pottery, Citrus Face, Orange, Stamped, Japan, 1940s, 5 ¼ In.	210.00
Pottery, Clown, Figural, Blue, Red, Yellow, Hand Painted, Marked, Mikori Ware, Red Stamp, 7 ½ In. ..	105.00
Pottery, Clown, Figural, Green, Red, Blue, Hand Painted, Marked, Japan, Red Stamp, 7 ½ In.	195.00
Pottery, Delft Scene, Yellow, Blue Windmill, Sailboats, 1930s, 5 x 4 In., 2 Piece ......*illus*	22.00
Pottery, Duck, Figural, Orange, Green, Flowers, Japan, 2 ¾ x 5 ½ In.	95.00
Pottery, Pear, Figural, Green Leaves, Dimpled, 1930s, 5 ½ In., 3 Piece	85.00
Pottery, Toucan, Figural, Hand Painted, Japan, 1930s, 2 ¾ x 5 ¾ In.	152.00
Sunkist, Jadeite Green, McKee, 3 ½ x 6 In.	30.00
Vaseline Glass, c.1920s, 5 ½ x 2 ¾ In.	28.00
Vaseline Glass, Tab Handle, Hazel Atlas, 5 ½ In.	10.00

RECORDS have changed size and shape through the years. The cylinder-shaped phonograph record for use with the early Edison models was made about 1889. Disc records were first made by 1894, the double-sided disc by 1904. High-fidelity records were first issued in 1944, the first vinyl disc in 1946, the first stereo record in 1958. The 78 RPM became the standard in 1926 but was discontinued in 1957. In 1932, the first 33 ⅓ RPM was made but was not sold commercially until 1948. In 1949, the 45 RPM was introduced. Compact discs became available in the U.S. in 1982 and many companies began phasing out the production of phonograph records.

Babe Ruth, Home Run Story	19.25
Bing Crosby, Merry Christmas, With The Andrews Sisters, 1949, Deco Album Set	55.00
Cylinder, Uncle Josh, On Bicycle, 1898-1900	72.00
Cyndi Lauper, True Colors, Vinyl, 45 RPM, 1986.	10.00
Dinah Shore, I'm Your Girl, RCA Camden, 1955	12.00
Elvis Presley, Baby Let's Play House, Sun Label, 45 RPM, 1955	500.00
Elvis Presley, Christmas Album, RCA, 1970	10.00
Elvis Presley, Money Honey, RCA Label, 45 RPM, 1956	125.00
Gene Autry, Christmas Time With Gene Autry, Mistletoe Record, 33 RPM	11.00
John Lennon, Watching The Wheels, Vinyl, 45 RPM, 1980, Geffen Records, 7 In.	20.00
Michael Jackson, Off The Wall, Vinyl, Epic Label, 1979	40.00
Michael Jackson, Thriller, Vinyl, Epic Label, 33 ⅓ RPM, 1982	65.00
Michael Jackson, We Are The World, 45 RPM, 1985	24.00
Paul McCartney, Take It Away & I'll Give You A Ring, Vinyl, Columbia, 45 RPM, 1982	14.00
Rick Springfield, Love Is Alright Tonight & Everybody's Girl, RCA Label, Vinyl, 45 RPM	11.00
Sidney Poitier, To Sir With Love, Soundtrack, 1967	10.00
South Pacific, Original Soundtrack, RCA, 1958	16.00
Swing Low, Negro Spirituals, 1940s, 78 RPM, 4 Record Album	75.00
The Beatles, In The Beginning, Vinyl, 33 ⅓ RPM Album, 1960	35.00
The Best Of Belafonte, RCA Victor, Box Set Of 10, 7 In.	35.00
The Partridge Family, Featuring David Cassidy & Shirley Jones, 33 ⅓ RPM, 1970s	81.00
The Wizard Of Oz Story Record, Narrated By Kay Lande, 33 ⅓ RPM, 1970s	13.00

RED WING POTTERY of Red Wing, Minnesota, was a firm started in 1878. The company first made utilitarian pottery, including stoneware jugs and canning jars. In the 1920s art pottery was introduced. Many dinner sets and vases were made before the company closed in 1967. Rumrill pottery made by the Red Wing Pottery for George Rumrill is listed in its own category. For more prices, go to kovels.com.

Advertising, Beater Jar, It Pays To Mix With Meier Bros., Nashua, Iowa, 4 ¾ In.	295.00
Advertising, Beater Jar, Stoneware, Blue Banded, Wesson Oil	30.00
Advertising, Crock, Butter, Meadowgold Always Good, 5 Lb.	135.00
Advertising, Jug, Banner Liquor Store, Winona, Minn., Top Shoulder, Gal.	225.00
Advertising, Jug, Mini, Brown Top, Red Wing Welcomes You	1000.00
Advertising, Stoneware, Bean Pot, Farmers Elevator, Inc., Mason City, Iowa, Lid	75.00
Advertising, Stoneware, Crock, Marigold Fancy Butter, 2 Lb.	45.00
Advertising, Stoneware, Pitcher, Jensen Merc. Co., Milltown, Wis., Saffron	225.00
Ash Receiver, Cat, Light Green	85.00
Ash Receiver, Donkey, Light Green	100.00
Ash Receiver, Elephant, Blue	155.00
Ash Receiver, Fish, Brown	285.00
Ash Receiver, Scotty Dog, Turquoise	245.00
Ashtray, Indian Maiden	375.00

R

Blue Band, Bowl, 8 In.	50.00
Blue Band, Bowl, 9 In.	50.00
Blue Band, Bowl, Saffron, 12 In.	40.00
Bob White, Cookie Jar, 2 Birds, Brown, Blue, Tan, Tab Handles, 9 In.	25.00
Bowl, Center, Deer Frog, White	15.00
Capistrano, Gravy Boat, 6 ¼ In. ....*illus*	35.00
Churn, Cover, Wing, Ski Oval	175.00
Clock, Chef, 1947, 10 In.	105.00
Crock, Molded Handles, 3 Gal.	195.00
Crock, Salt Glaze, Drop Target, 4 Gal.	125.00
Crock, Wing & Potteries Oval, 2 Gal.	25.00
Crock, Wing, Ski Oval, 20 Gal.	395.00
Cuspidor, Reground Hourglass Form, Yellow Interior Glaze, Red, Blue & Brown, 4 ½ In.	11.00
Figurine, Albany Slip Pig	700.00
Figurine, Bulldog, Brown Glaze	525.00
Figurine, Pig, Brown Glaze	105.00
Futura, Butter, Cover, Montmartre	180.00
Jar, Ball Lock, Wing & Union Oval, Lid, 5 Gal.	185.00
Jug, Albany, Beehive, 4 Gal.	145.00
Jug, Beehive, Wing & Oval, 5 Gal.	325.00
Jug, Blue Sponge, ¼ Pt.	2200.00
Jug, Shoulder, Birch Leaves, 5 Gal.	135.00
Jug, Shoulder, Wing & Oval, 5 Gal.	55.00
Modern Lotus, Teapot, Gray, 11 In. ....*illus*	75.00
Nokomis, Pitcher, Mark, 5 ½ In.	173.00
Orleans, Sugar & Creamer, Cover ....*illus*	18.00
Pitcher, Western Colonial	525.00
Pompeii, Bowl, Vegetable, 8 In. ....*illus*	18.00
Rolling Pin, Western Colonial	400.00
Rolling Pin, White Ground With Blue Flowers, Cylindrical, Softwood Handles, Marked, 15 ½ In.	275.00
RoundUp, Mug, Casual	325.00
Saffron, Casserole, Cover, Blue & Red Sponge, Tab Handles, 8 In. Diam.	82.00
Salt, Hanging, Cover, Western Colonial	275.00
Spongeware, Bowl, Brown, Blue, 10 In.	108.00
Stoneware, Bean Pot, Albany Slip, Cover	30.00
Stoneware, Beater Jar, Wesson Oil, 5 ¼ In. ....*illus*	85.00
Stoneware, Butter Pail, Blue Banded, Bail Handle, Cover	165.00
Stoneware, Churn, Butterfly, 6 Gal.	575.00
Stoneware, Churn, Leaf, 4 Gal.	265.00
Stoneware, Churn, Molded, Wing & Union Oval, Lid, 4 Gal.	175.00
Stoneware, Churn, Wing & Oval, Lid, 6 Gal.	275.00
Stoneware, Crock, Bee Sting, 3 Gal.	30.00
Stoneware, Crock, Birch Leaf, Ski Oval, 2 Gal.	25.00
Stoneware, Crock, Birch Leaf, Ski Oval, 8 Gal.	245.00
Stoneware, Crock, Birch Leaf, Union Oval, 12 Gal.	105.00
Stoneware, Crock, Butterfly, Salt Glaze, 20 Gal.	1600.00
Stoneware, Crock, Cobalt Blue Leaf, 6 Gal.	325.00
Stoneware, Crock, Double Birch Leaf, Union Oval, 20 Gal.	195.00
Stoneware, Crock, Lazy 8, 3 Gal.	125.00
Stoneware, Crock, Molded Handles, Union Oval, 6 Gal.	135.00
Stoneware, Crock, Transition, Birch Leaf, 40 Gal.	450.00
Stoneware, Crock, Wing & Oval, Bung Hole, 50 Gal.	750.00
Stoneware, Crock, Wing & Potteries Oval, Bail Handle, 5 Gal.	30.00
Stoneware, Crock, Wing & Union Oval, 30 Gal.	225.00
Stoneware, Crock, Wing & Union Oval, Bail Handle, 8 Gal.	40.00
Stoneware, Jar, Fruit, Dome Lid, Shield, ½ Gal.	3500.00
Stoneware, Jar, Fruit, Dome Lid, Shield, Gal.	8000.00
Stoneware, Jar, Refrigerator, Blue & White, Bail Handle, Lid, 3 Lb.	225.00
Stoneware, Jar, Wing, Lid, 2 Gal.	1050.00
Stoneware, Jar, Wing, Lid, 10 Lb.	950.00
Stoneware, Jug, Beehive, Gal.	10.00
Stoneware, Jug, Beehive, Rib Cage, Target, 4 Gal.	525.00
Stoneware, Jug, Beehive, Salt Glaze, Rib Cage, 4 Gal.	400.00
Stoneware, Jug, Beehive, Wing, 5 Gal.	150.00
Stoneware, Jug, Brown Top, ⅛ Pt.	105.00
Stoneware, Jug, Imperial, Beehive, Wing & Union Oval, 5 Gal.	275.00

TIP

To clean a 78 rpm record, use two soft cloths or paper towels. Spray the towels, not the record, with window cleaner. Then clean as if it were a pane of glass.

Red Wing, Pompeii, Bowl, Vegetable, 8 In. $18.00

Red Wing, Stoneware, Beater Jar, Wesson Oil, 5 ¼ In. $85.00

TIP

Store records on edge, straight up (not tipped) and in their sleeves.

R

Red Wing, Town & Country, Casserole, Cover, Peach, Lug Handle, 3 x 9 In. $115.00

Red Wing, Vase, Deer, Purple & Cream, Yellow Interior, 7 ¼ In. $65.00

Redware, Birdhouse, Cone Shape, Fluted Edge, Twisted Perch Branch, 7 ½ In. $580.00

Redware, Charger, Sgraffito, Tulip, Conrad Mumbouer, Bucks County, 13 ¼ In. $8190.00

Stoneware, Jug, Salt Glaze, Top Shoulder, Gal.	25.00
Stoneware, Jug, Shoulder, Wing & Union Oval, 3 Gal.	25.00
Stoneware, Jug, Shoulder, Wing & Union Oval, 5 Gal.	55.00
Stoneware, Mason Fruit Jar, Blue Label, ½ Gal.	200.00
Stoneware, Mason Fruit Jar, Blue Label, Gal.	850.00
Stoneware, Mason Fruit Jar, Blue Label, Qt.	275.00
Stoneware, Mason Fruit Jar, Zinc, Screw Lid, Blue Label, 7 In.	132.00
Stoneware, Water Cooler, Bee Sting, 5 Gal.	400.00
Stoneware, Water Cooler, Birch Leaf, Union Oval, 6 Gal.	450.00
Stoneware, Water Cooler, Lid, 3 Gal.	275.00
Stoneware, Water Cooler, Wing & Union Oval, 3 Gal.	165.00
Stoneware, Water Cooler, Wing & Union Oval, 5 Gal.	300.00
Stoneware, Water Cooler, Wing & Union Oval, 6 Gal.	300.00 to 475.00
Toothpick, Monk Head	155.00
Town & Country, Casserole, Cover, Peach, Lug Handle, 3 x 9 In. ...*illus*	115.00
Urn, Funerary, Brush Ware	55.00
Vase, Deer, Purple & Cream, Yellow Interior, 7 ¼ In. ...*illus*	65.00
Vase, Green, White, Handles, No. 157, 12 In.	60.00
Wall Pocket, Banjo, Copper Strings, Marked, USA, 15 In.	125.00
Water Cooler, Molded, Wing, 3 Gal.	275.00
Water Cooler, Wing & Union Oval, Lid, 2 Gal.	2500.00

REDWARE is a hard, red stoneware that originated in the late 1600s and continues to be made. The term is also used to describe any common clay pottery that is reddish in color.

Ale Mug, Black Glaze, 18th Century	195.00
Bank, Birdhouse Shape, Braided Handle, Brown & Green Glaze, Breininger, 1974, 11 x 5 In.	88.00
Bank, Chick, Worms, Impressed, Incised Detail, Round Base, April 4, 1861, 4 ¼ x 5 In.	2070.00
Bank, Cream, Green Stump, Indian Kneeling, Stump Slot, Penn., N. Fales, 1800s, 5 ½ x 5 ¾ In.	4715.00
Bank, Dog, On Hind Legs, Stump, Incised Detail, Oval Base, Penn., 1800s, 4 ⅞ x 6 ⅛ In.	1725.00
Bank, Doghouse, Dog, Incised Roof Walls, Roof Slot, Penn., 1800s, 3 x 4 ¾ In.	805.00
Bank, Girl, Book, High Back Chair, Slot In Chair, Clear Glaze, Redware Disc, Penn., 1800s, 8 x 5 In.	2300.00
Bank, Jug Shape, Handle, Mottled Green & Yellow, 1800s, 3 ¾ In.	1053.00
Bank, Long-Tailed Bird Finial, Cream Slip, Clear Lead Glaze, Oval, c.1850, 6 ½ In.	604.00
Bank, Parrot, On Stump, Yellow, Green Slip, Clear Glaze, Slot On Parrot, Penn., 10 In.	6325.00
Bank, Peach, 3 In.	66.00
Bean Pot, Brown Manganese Splotches, Bulbous, 2 Handles, 5 ½ x 8 ¾ In.	12.00
Birdhouse, Cone Shape, Fluted Edge, Twisted Perch Branch, 7 ½ In. ...*illus*	580.00
Bowl, 2 Hearts, Lines, Yellow & Green Glaze, 12 In.	90.00
Bowl, Grapes, Vines, Mottled Green Glaze, Foot Ring, 1800s, 2 x 9 In.	345.00
Bowl, Round, Mottled Green Glaze, Teal S In Center, T.S. Stahl, 1938, 5 ¾ In.	99.00
Bowl, Runny Brown Glaze, Handle Attached To Footed Base, 1800s, 5 In.	374.00
Bowl, Tin, Round Foot, 7 Wavy Cream Slip Trails, Clear Glaze, 2 ¾ x 5 ¼ In.	1093.00
Candlestick, Bird Form, Oval Base, Marked JCS, 3 ¾ x 6 ½ In.	181.00
Candlestick, Dome Base, Applied Handle, Black Splotches, Marked, JCS, 6 ¼ In.	90.00
Charger, Coggled Rim, Swirled Yellow Slip, c.1850, 13 In.	1058.00
Charger, Coggled Rim, Yellow Slip, 1800s, 11 ½ In.	353.00
Charger, Coggled Rim, Yellow Slip, 1800s, 14 In.	623.00
Charger, Coggled Rim, Yellow Slip, c.1850, 12 In.	822.00
Charger, Molded Relief Profile Of Washington, Circle Of Stars, 19th Century, 13 In.	499.00
Charger, Sgraffito, Tulip, Conrad Mumbouer, Bucks County, 13 ¼ In. ...*illus*	8190.00
Charger, Slip Flower, Orange, Yellow, c.1810, 17 ¼ In.	5382.00
Charger, Yellow Slip Horse, Sponged Manganese, Coggled Rim, Inscribed, c.1890, 12 ¾ In.	2300.00
Charger, Yellow Slip, Greg Shoomer, Ohio, 1900s, 16 ½ In.	206.00
Charger, Yellow Slip, Wavy & Straight Lines, Green Splashes, 1800s, 10 ¼ In.	644.00
Charger, Yellow Slip, Wavy Lines, 1800s, 12 In.	878.00
Colander, Green Glaze Wavy Lines, Perforated Star, Heart, Rope Handles, 6 ¼ x 10 ¼ In.	226.00
Crock, Cake, Cover, Manganese Sponging, Yellow, Handles, Impressed J. Bell, c.1840, 8 x 9 In.	4350.00
Crock, Flowers, Green Splotches, Sgraffito, Late 19th Century, 21 In.	360.00
Crock, John Bell, Waynesboro, 7 ½ x 7 In.	350.00
Crock, Orange & Green Mottled Glaze, Manganese Splotches, 1800s, 9 ¾ In. ...*illus*	263.00
Cup, Oval, Flared Rim, Applied Handle, Splashed Manganese Lead Glaze, 1800s, 3 In.	201.00
Cuspidor, Mottled Glaze, Round, Applied Handle, 3 In. ...*illus*	136.00
Dish, Copper Slip Stripes, Lead, Manganese Glaze, c.1850, ⅞ x 3 ¼ In.	86.00
Dish, Cover, Goat Form Handle, Manganese Sponge Dots, Embossed Leaf, 10 x 10 ½ x 9 ¼ In.	158.00
Dish, Loaf, Applied Wavy Yellow Slip, Coggled Rim, Oblong, c.1850, 15 ½ x 11 ¾ In.	1955.00
Dish, Loaf, Flowers, Swag, Dots Border, Coggled Rim, 8 x 17 ¼ In.	187.00

Dish, Loaf, Rectangular, Sloped, Slip Decorated, c.1819, 10 x 13 In.	711.00
Dish, Loaf, Yellow Slip, 3 Sets Of 3 Wavy Lines, Sprigs, Pa., 1800s, 11 ½ x 15 ¾ In.	819.00
Dish, Loaf, Yellow Slip, Wavy Lines, Coggled Rim, 13 ¾ x 8 ½ In.	649.00
Dish, Loaf, Yellow Wavy Slip, 19th Century, 11 ½ x 15 ¾ In.	840.00
Dish, Yellow Slip Leaves, Butterfly, c.1850, 2 x 7 ¾ In.	176.00
Duck Sander, Clay Ball Eyes, Clear Olive, Orange Ground, N. Car., c.1910, 2 ¾ x 3 ¾ In.	173.00
Fat Lamp, Green Glaze, c.1800, 3 ½ x 4 ½ In.	720.00
Figurine, Bird, Green, Splotches, James Seagraves, 4 ⅞ x 6 ½ In.	147.00
Figurine, Bird, Manganese Splotches, Orange Ground, Marked, JCS, 6 ¾ In.	79.00
Figurine, Dog Over Child, Clear Lead Glaze, Oval Base, c.1850, 4 ⅛ x 7 In.	5980.00
Figurine, Dog, Spaniel, Seated, Glazed, 5 In., Pair.	345.00
Figurine, Dog, Spaniel, Seated, Impressed John Bell, Waynesboro, 9 In.	9200.00
Figurine, Dog, Spaniel, Seated, Signed, Bishop, 19th Century, 9 ¾ In.	470.00
Figurine, Goose, Turned Head, Incised Details, 8-Sided Base, Orange, Yellow, c.1875, 2 ¾ x 3 ½ In.	4485.00
Figurine, Hen, Nest, Brown Glaze, 1800s, 3 ½ x 4 ½ In.	94.00
Figurine, Lion, Seated, Molded, Dark Brown Glaze, 9 x 10 ½ In.	147.00
Flask, Bottle Shape, Flared Spout, Streaky Lead Manganese Glaze, c.1850, 6 ¾ In.	345.00
Flask, Ring Form, Harvest, Hollow Center, Brown, 3 x 10 In.	44.00
Flowerpot, Attached Underplate, Impressed John W. Bell, Pa., 19th Century, 5 ¼ In.	240.00
Flowerpot, Cone Shape, Crimped Banding, Drip Tray, Light Brown, Black Spatter, 5 ½ In.	220.00
Flowerpot, Manganese Mottled Glazing, Pennsylvania, c.1850, 8 x 9 In. .... *illus*	117.00
Flowerpot, Tapered, Rounded Rim, Attached Saucer, Sponged, Impressed, J. Bell, 1880, 5 In. .	518.00
Flowerpot, Tree Trunk Shape, Brown Glaze, 5 In.	85.00
Goblet, Manganese Splash, Pencil Inscription, c.1860, 5 ½ In.	1860.00
Jar, Apple Butter, Oval, Daubed Manganese Glaze, Penn., c.1860, 6 In.	353.00
Jar, Black Green, Slip Decoration, Molded Rim, Handle, c.1850, 7 ¼ In.	575.00
Jar, Brown Manganese Streaked Glaze, Lug Handles, c.1810, 10 In.	444.00
Jar, Straight-Sided, Black Manganese Glaze, c.1835, 11 In.	536.00
Jar, Yellow Slip Over Olive Green Ground, Oval, c.1850, 1 ⅝ In.	201.00
Jug, Albany Slip Glaze, Ear Handle, 6 ½ In.	110.00
Jug, Batter, Oval, Tapered Spout, Orange, Green Glaze, 2-Strap Handles, c.1850, 11 In.	35.00
Jug, Face, Applied Eyes, Broken China Teeth, Brown Glaze, W.T.B. Gordy, 8 ½ In.	9430.00
Jug, Face, Grotesque, Gold Painted Eyeballs, Teeth, 6 ½ In.	10665.00
Jug, Green & Orange Glaze, Bulbous, Applied C-Shape Handle, Incised, Stahl, 1937, 8 In.	209.00
Jug, Green Speckled Glaze, Mid 1800s, 7 In.	325.00
Jug, Puzzle, Bulbous, Tube Spout, Incised, Copper, Cream Slip, c.1850, 3 ½ In.	1840.00
Jug, Reddish Brown, Mottled, Handle, Slip Decorated, c.1850, 7 ¼ In.	287.00
Jug, Ring Shape, Applied 10-Sided Spout, Mottled Glaze, 1800s, 8 ½ In.	230.00
Jug, Squat, Applied Handle, Manganese, Lead Glaze Over Yellow Orange, 1800s, 3 In.	460.00
Loaf Pan, Coggled Rim, Yellow Slip Designs, c.1850, 8 ½ x 12 ½ In.	617.00
Loaf Pan, Coggled Rim, Yellow Slip Flag Design, c.1850, 9 ½ x 14 In.	940.00
Match Holder, Hunt Dog, Rabbit, Bird, Hollowed Stump, c.1875, 2 ⅞ x 6 ¼ In.	719.00
Mug, Handle, Round, Tapered Sides, Raised Band, Orange Glaze, Black Manganese Spatter, 4 In.	88.00
Mug, Incised Line Band, Green Glaze, C-Shape Handle, Stahl Pottery, 1942, 4 ½ In.	55.00
Mug, Manganese Daubs, Applied Strap Handle, c.1850, 5 ¾ In.	117.00
Mug, Yellow Slip, Early 19th Century, 5 ¼ In.	275.00
Pie Plate, Coggled Rim, Yellow Slip Bird In Center, 19th Century, 9 In. .... 755.00 to 880.00	
Pie Plate, Coggled Rim, Yellow Slip, c.1850, +8 In.	470.00
Pie Plate, Coggled Rim, Yellow Slip, c.1850, 10 In.	499.00
Pitcher, Bulbous, Flared Collar, Applied Loop Handle, Swag, Flower Slip, 8 ¼ In. ..	154.00
Pitcher, Embossed Dog Chasing Stag, Game Scene, Mottled Glaze, 6 ¾ In.	55.00
Pitcher, Face Spout, Arms Across Body, Baluster Form, 19th Century, 7 ¼ In.	175.00
Pitcher, Figural, Baluster Form, Face Spout, 2 Arms Sloping Across Body, 1800s, 7 ¼ In.	176.00
Pitcher, Flowers, Slip, Green, Cream On Red Ground, Applied Handle, Penn., c.1830, 6 In.	189.00
Pitcher, Mottled Manganese, Coggled Wheel Decoration, Flattened Handle, 9 ½ In. .	854.00
Pitcher, Multicolored Splotch, Marked JCS, 5 ½ In.	113.00
Pitcher, Pinched Spout, Applied Loop Handle, Orange Glaze, Bulbous, 6 ½ In.	154.00
Pitcher, Presentation, Alabama, Inscribed Julia, Daphne Ala, 1904, 6 In.	322.00
Pitcher, Scratch Decoration, Copper Oxide Glaze, Tulip, Early 19th Century	29000.00
Pitcher, Seated Pig Shape, Applied Handle & Ears, Mouth Pour Spout, Orange Glaze, 9 ¾ In.	11.00
Plate, 5-Line Yellow Slip, Round, Coggled Rim, Orange & Black Spatter Ground, 8 ¼ In.	121.00
Plate, Bird, Tulips, Hearts Border, Coggled Rim, Octagonal, 19 x 18 ¾ In.	132.00
Plate, Coggled Rim, Yellow Slip, Inscribed, Sally, Round, 1800s, 2 x 9 ½ In.	5925.00
Plate, Inscribed, Pray For The Loving & The Dead, Notched Rim, 14 ½ In.	6250.00
Plate, Orange, Black Spatter, 3 Yellow Wavy 2-Line Slip, 8 ⅜ In.	77.00
Plate, Rounded Edge, Clear Interior Glaze, Impressed J. Bell, c.1880, 12 ½ In.	489.00

Redware, Crock,
Orange & Green Mottled Glaze,
Manganese Splotches, 1800s, 9 ¾ In.
$263.00

Redware, Cuspidor, Mottled Glaze,
Round, Applied Handle, 3 In.
$136.00

Redware, Flowerpot,
Manganese Mottled Glazing,
Pennsylvania, c.1850, 8 x 9 In.
$117.00

Redware, Wall Pocket, Lead, Manganese,
Copper Glaze, White Slip, Eberley,
c.1908, 6 x 4 In.
$575.00

R

Richard, Vase, Bottle Shape,
Brown Stemmed Leaves, Signed, 4 In.
$115.00

Richard, Vase, Grasshoppers, Brown,
Yellow, Austria, Early 1900s, 7 ⅜ x 4 In.
$219.00

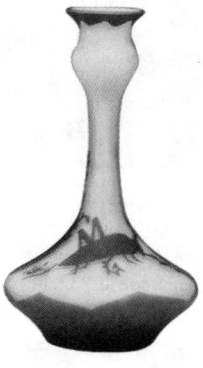

Ridgway, Platter, Turkey, Blue & White,
Ironstone, c.1900, 22 x 17 In.
$840.00

Ridgway, Tureen, Cover,
Athenaeum, Boston, Marked, 6 ½ In.
$1725.00

Plate, Sgraffito, Bird, Perched On Flower, Leaf Branch, Swag Border, Coggled Rim, 12 ⅝ In.	99.00
Plate, Sgraffito, Birds On Branch, Green Glaze, Verse Border, Stahl, 1949, 9 ⅝ In.	467.00
Pot, Brown Ring Design, 2 Handles, 3 ½ In.	83.00
Pot, Lid, Figural Snail, Dome Shape, Incised Detail, Cream Slip, Clear Glaze, Penn., 1800s, 3 In.	403.00
Pot, Tooled Bands, Mottled Surface, 19th Century, 8 In.	59.00
Puzzle Cup, Pedestal, Loop Handle, Marble Glaze, 1800s, 3 In.	210.00
Shoe, Whimsy, High Heel, Buttons, Bow, Clear Lead Glaze, c.1890, 4 ¾ x 4 ¾ In.	374.00
Stand, Sauceboat, Cylinder, Carved Dragons, Landscape, Chinese, 1800s, 24 x 9 In.	206.00
Stew Pot, Handle, 5 ½ In.	1150.00
Toddy Plate, Yellow Slip Drips, Clear Glaze, Coggled Rim, c.1850, 5 In.	316.00
Trivet, Trefoil Shape, Shaved Feet, c.1800, 5 In.	235.00
Umbrella Stand, Cylinder Shape, Relief Dragon & Cloud, Early 20th Century, 24 In.	115.00
Umbrella Stand, Tree Stump Mold, Leafy Vines, Original Paint, c.1890, 21 ½ In.	633.00
Urn, Scroll Handles, Applied Florets, Coggled Wheel Base, James Mackley, 8 In.	19890.00
Vase, Applied Flower, Brown Glaze, Bulbous, Flared & Crimped Rim, R.R. Stahl, 12/30/48, 6 In.	825.00
Vase, Incised Wavy Band, Green Glaze, Bulbous, Flared Rim, R.R. Stahl 11/10/47, 3 x 2 ¾ In.	99.00
Vase, Panels, Flower Sgraffito, Perched Bird, Flower, Bulbous, Signed Breininger, 11 ½ In.	367.00
Wall Pocket, Bird, Perched On Flower Branch, Green Glaze, Shenandoah Valley, 7 In.	6500.00
Wall Pocket, Lead, Manganese, Copper Glaze, White Slip, Eberley, c.1908, 6 x 4 In. *illus*	575.00
Whistle, Bird, Yellow, Green, Blue, Red, Brown, 19th Century, 3 In.	60.00
Whistle, Frog, Bulging Manganese Eyes, Lead, Copper Glaze, Penn., 1800s, 4 ½ In.	460.00
Whistle, Owl, Pinched Body, Tufts, Round Eyes, Brown Albany Slip, 3 ¾ In.	518.00

RICHARD was the mark used on acid-etched cameo glass vases, bowls, night-lights, and lamps made by the Austrian company Loetz after 1918. The pieces were very similar to the French cameo glasswares made by Daum, Galle, and others.

Vase, Bottle Shape, Brown Stemmed Leaves, Signed, 4 In. *illus*	115.00
Vase, Brown Pods, Leaves, Butterfly, Insect, Mottled Orange Ground, Stick, 5 In.	345.00
Vase, Butterfly, Insect, Hops On Stems, Mottled Orange Ground, 5 In.	207.00
Vase, Citron, Blue Austrian Chalet, Lake, Mountains, Signed, c.1920, 20 In.	720.00
Vase, Grasshoppers, Brown, Yellow, Austria, Early 1900s, 7 ⅜ x 4 In. *illus*	219.00
Vase, Yellow, Blue Mountains, Lake, Castle, Footed, Urn Shape, Signed, 11 In.	575.00
Vase, Yellow, Crimson Scene, Villa, Mountains, Oval, Signed, c.1920, 10 In.	840.00

RIDGWAY pottery has been made in the Staffordshire district in England since 1808 by a series of companies with the name Ridgway. The transfer-design dinner sets are the most widely known product. Other pieces of Ridgway may be listed under Flow Blue.

Pitcher, Figures, Drinking, Relief, Stamped, W. Ridgway & Co., 1835, 6 In.	40.00
Pitcher, Knights On Horses, Banded Grape Relief, 1840, 11 In.	52.00
Plate, Turkey, Flow Blue, 10 In.	40.00
Platter, Turkey, Blue & White, Ironstone, c.1900, 22 x 17 In. *illus*	840.00
Tureen, Cover, Athenaeum, Boston, Marked, 6 ½ In. *illus*	1725.00

RIVIERA dinnerware was made by the Homer Laughlin Co. of Newell, West Virginia, from 1938 to 1950. The pattern was similar in coloring and in mood to Fiesta and Harlequin. The Riviera plates and cup handles were square. For more prices, go to kovels.com.

Blue, Bowl, Dessert, 5 ¼ In.	14.00
Green, Bowl, Fruit, 5 ½ In.	14.00
Ivory, Sugar	15.00
Yellow, Tumbler	55.00

ROCKINGHAM, in the United States, is a pottery with a brown glaze that resembles tortoiseshell. It was made from 1840 to 1900 by many American potteries. Mottled brown Rockingham wares were first made in England at the Rockingham factory. Other types of ceramics were also made by the English firm. Related pieces may be listed in the Bennington category.

Coffeepot, Yellowware, Shaped Handle, Footed	290.00
Figurine, Dog, Spaniel, Seated, Brown Glaze, 1890s, 10 In.	200.00
Figurine, Dog, Spaniel, Seated, Free Standing Legs, Mid 1800s, 11 In. *illus*	264.00
Figurine, Dog, Spaniel, Seated, Incised Curly Coat, Domed Oval Base, c.1860, 11 ¾ In.	570.00
Group, Dog & Cat, Spaniel, Molded Base, Mid 19th Century, 11 ¼ & 10 ½ In.	999.00
Inhalator, Baluster Form, Vented Lid, Mottled Brown Glaze, 6 ½ x 5 In.	71.00
Pitcher, Protection To American Industry, Scattergood Hightstown, N.J., 9 In.	1840.00
Pitcher, Straight-Sided, Peacocks On Wall, Exotic Trees, c.1850, 8 ¼ In.	59.00

R

Pitcher, Toby, Grape Decorated Handle, Flat Bottom, 6 ½ In.	210.00
Tobacco Jar, Gothic Panels, Leaves, Late 1800s, 9 In.	197.00
Washboard, Mottled Glaze, Ribbed Yellowware Scrub Surface, Wood Frame, 27 x 14 In.	330.00

ROOKWOOD pottery was made in Cincinnati, Ohio, from 1880 to 1960. All of this art pottery is marked, most with the famous flame mark. The *R* is reversed and placed back to back with the letter *P.* Flames surround the letters. After 1900, a Roman numeral was added to the mark to indicate the year. The company went bankrupt in 1941. For several years various owners tried to revive the pottery, but by 1967 it was out of business. The name and some of the molds were bought by a collector in 1984. The molds were kept in his basement until 2006 when a group of investors bought them and revived the pottery. The Rookwood Pottery Co. currently makes fireplaces, tiles, and bookends in old designs and special items for limited edition vases and steins for Christmas.

Ash Receiver, Frog, Open Mouth, Green Glaze, 1951, 2 ⅞ In.	230.00
Ashtray, Crow, Black, 1957, 4 x 7 x 7 In.	230.00
Ashtray, Leaping Fish, Bronze, E.T. Hurley, ¾ x 5 ⅝ In.	633.00
Ashtray, Seal, Nubian Black Glaze, Kataro Shirayamadani, 1923, 6 ¾ x 3 In.	920.00
Bookends, Bird, Matte Green Glaze, Impressed, 1922, 6 ¼ In.	748.00
Bookends, Blackbird, Green Crystalline Matte Glaze, 1923	403.00
Bookends, Buddha, Seated, 1916, 7 ½ x 5 In.	895.00
Bookends, Couple Reading, Tan Matte Glaze, Louise Abel, 1920, 6 ⅞ In.	1035.00
Bookends, Dutch Boy & Girl, Kneeling Over Fence, Tulips, Sallie Toohey, 1928, 6 In.	805.00
Bookends, Elephant Gray, Blue Glaze, 1919, 6 x 7 In.	489.00
Bookends, Elephant, Ocher Over Brown Matte Glaze, 6 ⅜ In.	1093.00
Bookends, Elephant, Walking, Ivory Matte Glaze, 1923, 5 ½ x 5 In.	201.00
Bookends, Hippopotamus, Open Mouth, Ivory Matte Glaze, A. Conant, 1933, 4 x 6 In.	748.00
Bookends, Penguins, Blue & Tan Matte Glaze, 1924	950.00
Bookends, Rook, Green Glaze, William McDonald, 1944, 5 In.	230.00
Bookends, Rook, Leaves, Berries, Blue Matte Glaze, W. McDonald, 1928, 5 ½ x 5 ¼, Pair	288.00
Bookends, Rook, Turquoise, High Gloss Glaze, 5 ½ x 6 In.	140.00
Bookends, Rooks, Nubian Black Glaze, 1957, 5 ¼ In.	518.00
Bookends, Swan, White, Blue & Green Water Design, Sallie Toohey, 1928, 4 x 5 In.	690.00
Bowl, Bamboo, Bat Design, Tan Ground, A. Valentien, c.1882, 6 x 11 In.	345.00
Bowl, Blueberries, Leaves, 8-Sided, Footed, Signed, KJ, 9 ½ In.	325.00
Bowl, Cherry Blossoms, French Red, Sara Sax, 1917, 2 ⅜ x 9 ⅝ In.	2645.00
Bowl, Greek Key Surround, Pink, Brown Glaze, Footed, 9 In.	159.00
Bowl, Landscape, Figures, Turquoise Matte Glaze, Arthur Conant, 1918, 8 x 5 In.	86.00
Bowl, Poppy Design, Red & Green Matte Glaze, William Hentschel, 1913, 7 x 2 In.	431.00
Bowl, Porridge, Bats Flying, Oriental Grass, Gold Trim, Martin Retting, 1883, 2 x 5 In.	173.00
Bowl, Shamrocks, Incised, Painted, Green Matte Glaze, Albert Pons, 1907, 2 ⅛ In.	518.00
Bowl, Squat Globe Shape, Blue Matte Glaze, Incised Design, c.1915, 3 x 8 ¼ In.	230.00
Box, Circular, 3-Footed, Painted Flowers On Lid, Charles Todd, 1916, 2 ¼ x 4 In.	518.00
Box, Document, Dome Top, Molded, Lions, Doves, Vines, Caramel Glaze, 9 x 7 In.	705.00
Box, Rose, Leaves, Blue Ground, Round, 1922, ¾ x 3 In.	288.00
Candleholder, Fish Shape, Aventurine Glaze, Lorinda Epply, 1928, 5 In., Pair	1150.00
Candleholder, Lotus Pattern, Blue Glaze, Impressed, 1 ½ x 3 ½ In., Pair	33.00
Candleholder, Nude Figure, Peacock, Ivory Glaze, 1915, 5 x 10 ½ In.	431.00
Candlestick, Nude Woman, Long Hair, Mask, 12 ¾ In.	950.00
Candlestick, Seahorse, Bronze, Marked, E.T. Hurley, c.1916, 10 ⅝ In., Pair *illus*	2185.00
Chocolate Pot, Cover, Cameo Glaze, Pink Wild Roses, Impressed, Anna Bookprinter, c.1887 *illus*	633.00
Chocolate Pot, Orange Rose, Olive, Brown Ground, 1891, 7 ¾ In.	474.00
Chocolate Pot, Red Clay, Molded Daisies, Brown Glaze, c.1886, 6 x 10 In.	115.00
Clock, Panther, Nubian Black Glaze, 1950	460.00
Coffeepot, Owl On Branch, Bats, Cloudy Sky, Albert Valentien, 1883	978.00
Compote, Elephant Base, Scroll Handles, c.1921, 12 ¼ x 16 In.	625.00
Compote, Slip Dragon, White Madder Glaze, Earl Menzel, 1955, 5 x 6 ⅜ In.	1380.00
Corbels, Faience, Mills Restaurant, Cincinnati, c.1921, 22 x 11 ½ In.	411.00
Cruet, Portrait Of Dog, E.T. Hurley, 1900, 7 ⅞ In.	2300.00
Dish, Bird On Basin, Cream, c.1940, 5 x 7 In.	59.00
Ewer, Blossoms, Applied, Albert Valentien, c.1890, 6 x 10 In.	690.00
Ewer, Chrysanthemums, Painted, Sallie Toohey, 4 ½ x 7 In.	173.00
Ewer, Daffodils, Painted, Standard Glaze, Clara Lindeman, 1900, 4 ½ x 8 In.	489.00
Ewer, Flowers, Silver Overlay, Amelia Browne, 1893, 9 ¾ In.	3995.00
Ewer, Fuchsia, Standard Glaze, Squat, Shaped Handle, 1891, 8 In.	413.00
Ewer, Honeysuckle, Dull Finish, Albert Valentien, 1888, 12 In.	1380.00
Ewer, Leaves, Berries, Silver Overlay, Flowers, Bulbous, K. Matchette, 1894, 5 x 7 In.	3220.00
Ewer, Leaves, Blossoms, Olga Reed, 1893, 7 x 10 ½ In.	201.00

Rockingham, Figurine, Dog, Spaniel, Seated, Free Standing Legs, Mid 1800s, 11 In.
$264.00

Rookwood, Candlestick, Seahorse, Bronze, Marked, E.T. Hurley, c.1916, 10 ⅝ In., Pair
$2185.00

Rookwood, Chocolate Pot, Cover, Cameo Glaze, Pink Wild Roses, Impressed, Anna Bookprinter, c.1887
$633.00

Rookwood, Humidor, Indian, Chief Mountain Black Feet, Edith Felton, c.1900, 7 x 6 In.
$3000.00

R

ROOKWOOD

Rookwood, Jar, Cover, Pink Roses, Long Stems, Vellum Glaze, Impressed, Sara Sax, c.1917, 7 In. $3105.00

Rookwood, Match Holder, Oak Leaf, Acorn, Green, Blue & Tan Matte Glaze, Footed, c.1928 $316.00

TIP

Always test an art pottery vase before you put it on a table. Fill it with water for 24 hours and check for seepage. Our Red Wing vase was just the right shape for a special flower arrangement. But we learned the hard way that the glaze was not perfect. The water slowly leaked into the turquoise glaze and left a white salt-like deposit on the outside of the vase. It also left a white ring on the table.

Ewer, Leaves, Green, Berries, Sallie Toohey, 1892, 4 x 9 ½ In.	374.00
Ewer, Organic Design, Edward Abel, 1892, 5 ½ x 7 ½ In.	431.00
Ewer, Red Firebird, Branch, Goldstone, Standard Glaze, A. Valentien, 21 In.	9780.00
Ewer, Rose Hips, Ruffled Rim, Van Briggle, 1899, 7 ¼ In.	196.00
Ewer, Yellow Flowers, Carrie Steinle, 1892, 5 In.	425.00
Figurine, Blue Jay, Magnolia Branch, Lorinda Epply, 1934, 10 ¼ In.	4600.00
Figurine, Cat, Seated, Blue Matte Glaze, 1927, 4 ¼ x 5 In.	575.00
Figurine, Dog, Sitting, Butch, Louise Abel, 1935, 5 x 5 In.	863.00
Figurine, Frog, Black & Green Glaze, 1930, 3 ¼ x 3 In.	230.00
Flower Frog, Turtle, Cream Matte Glaze, 1927, 2 ⅞ In.	345.00
Flower Holder, Pink Flower Blossom, Yellow Base, Shirayamadani, Sax, 1927, 3 In.	259.00
Frame, Oval, Tiles, Fruit, Berries, Flowers, Mounted To Wood, 14 x 22 In.	1610.00
Frieze, Faience, Bacchus, Mills Restaurant, Cincinnati, c.1921, 19 x 25 In.	823.00 to 1175.00
Ginger Jar, Birds, Branches, Painted, Limoges, William McDonald, 1885, 5 x 4 In.	144.00
Humidor, Indian, Chief Mountain Black Feet, Edith Felton, c.1900, 7 x 6 In. *illus*	3000.00
Jar, Cover, Glazed, Pansies, Sterling Silver Lid, Monogram, Bruce Horsfall, c.1894, 5 x 3 ¼ In.	374.00
Jar, Cover, Pink Roses, Long Stems, Vellum Glaze, Impressed, Sara Sax, c.1917, 7 In. *illus*	3105.00
Jardiniere, Molded Cherries, Blue Matte Glaze, Production, 1928, 5 x 7 In.	207.00
Jardiniere, Yellow Flowers, Matthew Daly, 1886, 7 ½ In.	325.00
Jug, Japanese Style Blossoms, Enameled, White, Handle, Laura Fry, 4 In.	518.00
Jug, Stopper, Ear Of Corn, Yellow, Green, Standard Glaze, O. Reed, 1897, 10 ½ In.	690.00
Jug, Whiskey, Ears Of Corn, Bruce Horsfall, 1894, 6 ⅝ In.	1035.00
Lamp Base, Green Matte Glaze, Leaves, Berries, 1903, 14 x 6 ½ In.	3050.00
Lantern, Chinese, Painted Rabbits, Birds, M. Nichols, 1882, 8 ½ In., Pair	2300.00
Match Holder, Oak Leaf, Acorn, Green, Blue & Tan Matte Glaze, Footed, c.1928 *illus*	316.00
Mug, Clown, Scarf, Pewter, Standard Glaze, W. McDonald, 1894, 12 In.	6038.00
Mug, Flowers, Katharine Hickman, 1895, 4 ¾ In.	115.00
Mug, Portrait, Indian, Standard Glaze, 5 x 5 In.	793.00
Paperweight, Bunny, Cinnamon High Glaze, Impressed Symbol, c.1961, 3 In. *illus*	460.00
Paperweight, Cocker Spaniel, Glossy Black Glaze, 4 In.	460.00
Paperweight, Cocker Spaniel, Paw Up, Wine Madder Glaze, 1954, 4 ⅛ In.	345.00
Paperweight, Duck, Yellow & Green Glaze, Jens Jensen, 1948, 4 ⅝ In.	219.00
Paperweight, Elephant, Blue Matte, Plinth, William McDonald, 1917, 3 ¼ In.	403.00
Paperweight, Flower Basket, Multicolored, Sallie Toohey, 1929, 3 ¼ In.	288.00
Paperweight, Gazelle, Ivory Matte Glaze, Louise Abel, 1927, 4 In.	374.00
Paperweight, Goose, Double, Ivory Matte Glaze, Sallie Toohey, 1927, 4 In.	489.00
Paperweight, Monkey, Nubian Black Glaze, 1928, 3 ⅝ In.	403.00
Paperweight, Rooster, Multicolored, Plinth, 1943, 5 In.	288.00
Paperweight, Rooster, Multicolored, W. McDonald, Plinth, 1946, 4 ⅞ In.	316.00
Paperweight, Squirrel, Eating Nut, 1928	173.00
Paperweight, Z-Line Tulip, Green Matte, 1904, ¾ x 4 ¾ In.	525.00
Pencil Holder, 5-Sided, Seated Rook, Leafy Branch, Pink Matte Glaze, 1928	316.00
Pin Tray, Reclining Nude Female, Ivory Matte Glaze, A. Valentien, 1946, 1 ¾ x 4 In.	288.00
Pitcher, Carved Leaves, Red Clay, Handle, Nettie Wilson, 1883, 4 x 5 In.	259.00
Pitcher, Flowers & Leaves, 1887, 8 In.	489.00
Pitcher, Ribbed, Bats, Asian Flowers, Clouds, Red, Brown, A. Valentien, 1882, 7 In.	345.00
Pitcher, Spiders, Weaving Web, Mottled White, Gold, Stamped, ARV Signed, 9 In.	920.00
Pitcher, Standard Glaze, Flowers, Leaves, Matthew Daly, 1893, 18 x 9 In.	2440.00
Planter, Figures, In Leaves, Incised, Painted, Faience, W. Hentschel, 15 ½ x 19 In.	2875.00
Plaque, A Quiet Scene, Vellum, Lorinda Epply, Frame, 1913, 12 x 10 In.	4025.00
Plaque, Forest Lakefront Sunset, Vellum Glaze, Signed F. Rothenbusch, Frame, 1918, 9 x 5 In.	3163.00
Plaque, Landscape, Birch Trees, Vellum, E.T. Hurley, Frame, 1913, 16 x 18 In.	4600.00
Plaque, Landscape, Vellum, Elizabeth McDermott, Arts & Crafts Frame, 14 x 10 In.	3450.00
Plaque, Landscape, Vellum, Frame, Edward T. Hurley, 1921, 7 ½ x 8 ¾ In.	4575.00
Plaque, Painted Forest Scene, Vellum, Ed Diers, Frame, 8 ½ x 11 ½ In.	2875.00
Plaque, River Scene, Late Afternoon, Green Vellum Glaze, Signed, Frame, 1914, 9 x 5 ½ In.	2875.00
Plaque, Snowy Woods Landscape, Vellum, Fred Rothenbusch, Frame, 1914, 5 x 8 In.	3335.00
Plate, Crab, Berried Vine, Sage Clay, Martin Rettig, 1885, 6 ¼ In.	316.00
Plate, Crayfish, Sage Clay, William P. McDonald, 1885, 6 ¼ In.	288.00
Plate, Logo, Jens Jensen, 1934, 5 ⅞ In.	863.00
Stein, G. Washington, 1776, Blue, Iris Glaze, Pewter, McDonald, 1896, 10 In.	3220.00
Stein, Hinged Lid, Turning Eagle, Standard Glaze, Silver Plated Copper, 8 ½ x 6 In.	8400.00
Sugar & Creamer, Leaves, Berries, Butterfly Wing Handles, Perkins, 4 ½ x 3 & 6 x 4 In.	230.00
Sugar, Clovers, Lid, Worm Finial, 1923, 4 ⅜ In.	150.00
Teapot, Band Of Sailboats, Lid, Sara Sax, Marked, c.1915	1035.00
Tile, 3 Seahorses, Brown, Green, Blue, Faience, Arts & Crafts Oak Frame, 14 ½ In.	1800.00
Tile, Blue & Green Designs, Gray Ground, Copper Frame, 12 x 8 In.	489.00

Tile, Frieze, Landscape, Willow Tree, Multicolored, Faience, Arts & Crafts Frame, 3 Tiles, 45 x 17 In.	4313.00
Tile, Landscape, Trees, Mountain, Matte Glazes, Faience, Arts & Crafts Frame, 45 x 17 In.	3450.00
Tile, Landscape, Trees, Mountains, Faience, Arts & Crafts Oak Frame, Square, 12 In.	3000.00
Tile, Oak Tree, Brown, Green, Purple, Blue Ground, Faience, Arts & Crafts Frame, 14 x 14 In. . .	4200.00
Tile, Panel, 2-Stack Steamboat, Bridge, Train, 26 ½ x 32 ¼ x 16 In.	4248.00
Tile, Panel, Windmill, Dutch Boy, Faience, Mills Restaurant, c.1921, 31 x 24 In.	353.00
Tile, Rook, Blue & White, 5 ¾ x 5 ¾ In.	184.00
Tile, Stylized Flower Designs, Faience, Frame, 30 x 31 In.	2875.00
Tile, Tea, Geometric Design, White & Blue Matte Glaze, 1916, ¾ x 3 ⅝ In.	138.00
Tile, Tropical Bird, 1930, 6 x 6 In.	300.00
Tile, Windmill, Bushes, 1919, 5 ¾ x 5 ¾ In.	225.00
Tile, Woman, With Parasol, Hoopskirt, Pastel, c.1925, 6 x 6 In.	300.00
Tray, Clown, Yellow Costume, Black Pointed Hat, Marked, Sallie Toohey, c.1929 .... *illus*	219.00
Tray, Rook Perched On Oak Leaves & Corns, Brown & Red Matte Glaze, 1912, 11 x 2 In.	575.00
Tray, Rook, Wine Madder & Blue Glaze, 1942, 7 x 4 ½ In.	210.00
Tray, Seal, Dark Orange Matte Glaze, Shirayamadani, 1930, 4 In.	805.00
Trivet, Art Deco Design, 1954, 5 ¾ x 5 ¾ In.	165.00
Trivet, Flower Shape, Design, Violet, Gray Glaze, Impressed, 1957, 7 In. .... ·	46.00
Tyg, Native American Profile, Standard Glaze, J. Swing, 1900, 5 In.	863.00
Umbrella Stand, Green Matte Glaze, Carved Vertical Leaves, Faience, 14 x 26 In.	1920.00
Urn, Garden, Drip Glaze, Bisque, Wrought Iron Stand, 26 ⅛ In.	575.00
Vase, 2 Black Swans, Iris Glaze, C. Schmidt, 1905, 9 ¾ x 4 In.	6600.00
Vase, 2 Geese, Mahogany Glaze, Pinched Neck, Daly, 1891, 9 ½ In.	625.00
Vase, 2 Geese, Reeds, Tiger Eye, Mahogany Glaze, A. Sprague, 1893, 7 In.	1255.00
Vase, 2 Pink Poppies, Green Ground, Iris Glaze, C. Amelia Baker, 1903, 7 ½ In.	920.00
Vase, 3 Putti Hanging From Side, Footed, 5 In.	748.00
Vase, 4 Panels, Flowers, Butterflies, Green Tint Glaze, L. Epply, 1927, 14 In.	4140.00
Vase, 5 Birds, Branch, Standard Glaze, K. Shirayamadani, 1903, 10 ½ In.	6325.00
Vase, Abstract Irises, Matte Glaze, Cobalt Blue Ground, Jens Jensen, 1933, 5 ⅞ In.	1093.00
Vase, Antelope, Squeezebag, Mottled Brown Matte Glaze, Bulbous, 1929, 5 x 6 ½ In.	2300.00
Vase, Antique Olive Green Glaze, Bulbous, Slender Neck, Flared Rim, c.1951, 4 ½ x 10 In.	58.00
Vase, Autumn Leaves, Standard Glaze, Handles, 8 ¾ In.	326.00
Vase, Birds, Blossoms, Mark, E.T. Hurley, c.1933, 6 ½ x 4 In. .... *illus*	1200.00
Vase, Birds, Grasses, Limoges Glaze, Matt Daly, c.1885, 3 ½ x 9 In.	316.00
Vase, Black Iris, Carved, Painted, Kataro Shirayamadani, 1901, 17 ½ x 6 ½ In.	31720.00
Vase, Blossoms, Butterfat Ground, c.1922, 6 ¾ x 3 ½ In. .... *illus*	1140.00
Vase, Blossoms, Leaves, Shouldered, Jens Jensen, c.1933, 4 ½ x 8 In.	1093.00
Vase, Blue & Green Matte Glaze, Flower Glaze, Flared Shape, 1925, 7 x 5 ½ In.	144.00
Vase, Blue Crocuses, Bottle Shape, Standard Glaze, Irene Bishop, 1900, 6 In.	230.00
Vase, Blue Flowers, Stippled Ground, Bulbous, J. Jensen, 1931, 6 In.	1035.00
Vase, Blue Matte Glaze, Dragonflies, 1916, 4 x 9 In.	230.00
Vase, Blue Orchids, Green Fronds, Pink Ground, Vellum, V. Tischler, 4 ½ In.	633.00
Vase, Blue Violets, Standard Glaze, Long Neck, E. Lincoln, 1895, 6 ½ In.	259.00
Vase, Blueberries, Handle, Globular, Ed Diers, 1897, 4 ½ x 5 ½ In.	230.00
Vase, Boats, Water, Shore, Scenic Vellum, E.T. Hurley, 1912, 7 In.	3335.00
Vase, Bud, Sang De Boeuf Glaze, Bulbous, R. Menzel, 1951, 3 ¾ In.	499.00
Vase, Carnations, Carved, Painted, Albert Valentien, 1904, 5 x 12 In.	2185.00
Vase, Carp, Japanese Detail, Dull Finish, A. Valentien, 1885, 11 In.	1610.00
Vase, Catfish, Bottle Shape, Sea Green Glaze, E.T. Hurley, 1904, 8 In.	4370.00
Vase, Cavalier Portrait, Standard Glaze, S. Laurence, 1898, 8 In.	575.00
Vase, Cherries, Laura Lindeman, c.1904, 3 ½ x 7 In.	374.00
Vase, Cherry Blossom Branches, Iris Glaze, Sara Sax, c.1906, 3 ½ x 8 In.	1495.00
Vase, Cherry Blossoms, Matte Glaze, Kataro Shirayamadani, 1933, 4 x 8 In.	1380.00
Vase, Cherry Blossoms, Vellum, E.T. Hurley, 1919, 5 x 3 In.	288.00
Vase, Cherry Blossoms, Vellum Glaze, Blue, Green, Brown Ground, K. Van Horne, 1905, 4 x 7 In.	1035.00
Vase, Chick, Yellow, Standard Glaze, Flared Rim, C. Steinele, 1896, 5 ½ In.	690.00
Vase, Chrysanthemums, Painted, Standard Glaze, 2 Handles, Artus Van Briggle, 1887, 6 x 8 In.	690.00
Vase, Clematis, Dark Red, Olive Ground, Silver Overlay, 1892, 4 ¾ In.	1045.00
Vase, Clover, Iris Glaze, Applied Bronze, Sara Sax, 1905, 5 x 5 In.	1830.00
Vase, Clover, Iris Glaze, Bulbous, Caroline Steinle, 1906, 4 ½ x 4 ½ In.	633.00
Vase, Clover, Painted, Applied Silver Overlay, Flowers, Broad Shape, 5 x 5 In.	3738.00
Vase, Clover, Painted, Standard Glaze, Edith Noonan, 1904, 3 ½ x 5 ¼ In.	230.00
Vase, Comical Character, Mushrooms, Handle, Constance Baker, 1895, 5 ½ x 6 In.	805.00
Vase, Cylinder, Green To Red Base, Art Deco Arrow, Flame Mark, 9 In.	200.00
Vase, Cylinder, White Glaze, Vertical Gray Leaves, Lines, WR Mark, 1946, 7 ½ In.	300.00
Vase, Cylindrical, 4 Fish Underwater, Vellum, Edith Noonan, c.1909, 3 x 6 ¼ In.	633.00
Vase, Cylindrical, Flaring Rim, Yellow, Pink & Green Drip Glaze, 1932, 5 In.	201.00

Rookwood, Paperweight, Bunny, Cinnamon High Glaze, Impressed Symbol, c.1961, 3 In. $460.00

Rookwood, Tray, Clown, Yellow Costume, Black Pointed Hat, Marked, Sallie Toohey, c.1929 $219.00

Rookwood, Vase, Birds, Blossoms, Mark, E.T. Hurley, c.1933, 6 ½ x 4 In. $1200.00

Rookwood, Vase, Blossoms, Butterfat Ground, c.1922, 6 ¾ x 3 ½ In. $1140.00

R

Rookwood, Vase, Daffodils, White, Blue Vellum Glaze, Signed, Caroline Steinle, 6 ¾ In.
$155.00

Rookwood, Vase, Hibiscus, Matte Glaze, Oval, Clara Lindeman, c.1925, 9 ¼ x 6 In.
$976.00

Rookwood, Vase, Iris Glaze, Sax Sara, Flame Mark, c.1905, 10 x 4 ½ In.
$1586.00

TIP
Glue broken china with an invisible mending cement that is waterproof.

Vase, Cylindrical, Flower Bands, Jens Jensen, Marked, 1948, 7 ¼ In. 184.00
Vase, Cylindrical, Pink Roses, Carl Schmidt, 1910, 12 ¼ In. 2595.00
Vase, Cylindrical, Yellow, Embossed Flower Band, c.1923, 11 ½ In. 439.00
Vase, Daffodils, Leaves, Sea Green Glaze, S. Coyne, 1901, 7 In. 2070.00
Vase, Daffodils, White, Blue Vellum Glaze, Signed, Caroline Steinle, 6 ¾ In. .... *illus* 155.00
Vase, Daffodils, White, Pink & Green Ground, Shirayamadani, 1941, 7 In. 920.00
Vase, Daisies, Painted, Applied Silver Overlay, Flower, 2 x 6 In. 1725.00
Vase, Daisies, Sea Green Glaze, Constance Baker, 1904, 3 ½ x 5 ¼ In. 1150.00
Vase, Daisies, Vellum, Ed Diers, c.1926, 3 ½ x 7 In. 2070.00
Vase, Dark Blue Matte Glaze, Geometric Design, Rose Fechheimer, c.1904, 3 ¼ x 3 ¼ In. 374.00
Vase, Dogwood Blossoms, Matte Glaze, Albert Valentien, c.1901, 5 ½ x 7 In. 1725.00
Vase, Dogwood Blossoms, Pale Green, Gray, White, Sarah Sax, 8 ¾ In. 819.00
Vase, Dragonflies, Indigo, William Hentschel, 2 ½ x 5 ½ In. 1830.00
Vase, Dragonflies, Iris Glaze, Shouldered, Carl Schmidt, 1906, 3 x 9 ¼ In. 17250.00
Vase, Dutch Landscape, Painted, Vellum Glaze, Bulbous, Ed Diers, 1912, 4 x 5 ½ In. 1035.00
Vase, Dutch Landscapes, Gray Ground, Scenic Vellum, A. Conant, 1916, 9 In. 1725.00
Vase, Embossed Fruit Border, Brown Matte, Bulbous, Signed, 4 ½ In. 200.00
Vase, Fiddle Head Fern, Incised, Loretta Holtkamp, 1954, 10 In. 325.00
Vase, Fish, Iris Glaze, 4 ¼ x 4 ½ In. 1800.00
Vase, Fish, Swimming Underwater, Vellum Glaze, E.T. Hurley, 1907, 7 x 6 ½ In. 2185.00
Vase, Fish, White Blossom, Green, Blue, Vellum Glaze, Schmidt, 1925, 18 In. 4715.00
Vase, Flower Border, Handles, Lorinda Epply, 1915, 8 ¼ In. 374.00
Vase, Flower, Butterfly Design, Decorated Porcelain, H. Wilcox, 1927, 11 In. 3450.00
Vase, Flower, Standard Glaze, Signed, Edith Noonan, c.1905, 4 In. 595.00
Vase, Flower, Stems, Persian Designs, Blue, White High Glaze, Oval, 1821, 7 In. 326.00
Vase, Flowering Quince, Orange, Green, Standard Glaze, A. Valentien, 1898, 22 In. 920.00
Vase, Flowers, Flared, Porcelain Glaze, Painted, Jens Jensen, c.1944, 5 ¼ x 7 In. 288.00
Vase, Flowers, Green Tinted Glaze, Flared, 1922, 5 x 11 In. 1200.00
Vase, Flowers, Incised, Blue, Brown, Mottled Matte Glaze, 2 Handles, Sara Sax, 1912, 4 ½ In. . 153.00
Vase, Flowers, Incised, Matte Glaze, C.S.T., 1914, 10 In. 520.00
Vase, Flowers, Iris Glaze, Shouldered, Ed Diers, c.1903, 3 x 6 ¾ In. 518.00
Vase, Flowers, Leaves, Vellum, Pink, Blue Interior, K. Jones, c.1929, 7 ¾ In. 823.00
Vase, Flowers, Matte Glaze, Harles Todd, c.1919, 3 ¼ x 7 In. 259.00
Vase, Flowers, Matte Glaze, Shouldered, Katherine Jones, 1926, 3 x 5 In. 431.00
Vase, Flowers, Mottled Purple, Yellow, Blue, Red Green Stems, E.T. Hurley, 10 In. 115.00
Vase, Flowers, Painted, Incised, Gray, Katherine Van Horne, c.1911, 2 ½ x 6 ¼ In. 288.00
Vase, Flowers, Pinched Neck, Footed, Luella Perkins, 1890, 9 ½ In. 431.00
Vase, Flowers, Relief, Mottled Blue-Green Glaze, 11 ¼ In. 385.00
Vase, Flowers, Shield Pattern, Blue, Standard Glaze, A. Conant, 1919, 8 In. 650.00
Vase, Flowers, Squat, 1906, 2 ⅝ In. 316.00
Vase, Flowers, Standard Glaze, Flared, Cylindrical, Albert Valentien, 1886, 6 x 17 In. 660.00
Vase, Flowers, Stems, Vellum, Olga Geneva, 1912, 5 ⅞ In. 403.00
Vase, Flowers, Vellum, Fred Rothenbusch, c.1931, 5 ½ In. 633.00
Vase, Flowers, Vellum, Sara Sax, 1907, 5 x 6 In. 1150.00
Vase, Flowers, White, Pale Blue Ground, Glossy Glaze, KS, c.1945, 8 In. 546.00
Vase, Flowers, Wide Mouth, Arthur Conant, 1920, 8 x 9 ¾ In. 575.00
Vase, Flowers, Yellow, Green Leaves, Anna Marie Bookprinter, c.1886, 3 ½ x 8 ¼ In. 403.00
Vase, Fruit, Leaves, Yellow Vellum, Lenore Asbury, c.1926, 4 ½ x 4 ½ In. 2070.00
Vase, Geese, Mahogany Glaze, Matt Daly, 1891, 9 ½ In. 230.00
Vase, Geometric, Exotic Glazes, Elizabeth Barrett, 1928, 13 ⅛ In. 5175.00
Vase, Geometric, Green Matte Glaze, Incised, c.1902, 5 ½ x 2 ¾ In. 431.00
Vase, Goldenrod, Brown, Yellow, Sea Green, S. Coyne, 1901, 8 In. 1150.00
Vase, Grapes, Green, White, Vellum Glaze, Lorina Epply, 7 ¼ x 4 In. 1220.00
Vase, Grapes, Vines, Green, Matte Glaze, Long Neck, C. Todd, 1914, 10 In. 1265.00
Vase, Grapes, Vines, Iris Glaze, Irene Bishop, 1903, 6 ¼ In. 1840.00
Vase, Grapevines, Painted, Standard Glaze, Matt Daly, 1902, 10 x 20 In. 1093.00
Vase, Green, Silver Insert, Rose Fechheimer, 1906, 4 x 6 In. 497.00
Vase, Hanging Flowers, Rose To Cream Ground, Vellum, Lenore Asbury, 1927, 7 In. 1150.00
Vase, Harbor Scene, Iris Glaze, Painted, Flared, Sallie Coyne, 1911, 4 x 9 In. 2875.00
Vase, Hibiscus, Matte Glaze, Oval, Clara Lindeman, c.1925, 9 ¼ x 6 In. .... *illus* 976.00
Vase, Honeysuckle, Applied Silver Overlay, Emma Foertmeyer, 1892, 4 ½ x 10 ½ In. 2300.00
Vase, Horn, Daisies, Footed, Elizabeth Lincoln, 1894, 3 ⅞ x 8 ½ In. 288.00
Vase, Hydrangeas, Bottle Form, Flared Neck, Signed, Amelia B. Sprague, 1897, 12 ½ In. 690.00
Vase, Incised, Blue, Decorated Porcelain, Squat, W. Hentsche, 1915, 5 x 9 In. 460.00
Vase, Iris Glaze, Sax Sara, Flame Mark, c.1905, 10 x 4 ½ In. .... *illus* 1586.00
Vase, Irises, Blue Irises Glaze, Rose Fechheimer, 1902, 8 ¾ In. 1495.00
Vase, Irises, Trumpet Shape, Jens Jensen, 1929, 10 ⅛ In. 1035.00

Vase, Landscape, Autumn, Vellum, Sallie Coyne, 1909, 7 x 4 In.	2040.00
Vase, Landscape, Blue, Vellum Glaze, Tapered, Ed Diers, 1921, 2 ½ x 6 ¼ In.	1093.00
Vase, Landscape, Green, Vellum Glaze, Tapered, Sallie Coyne, 1920, 4 x 9 ½ In.	2645.00
Vase, Landscape, Vellum, Ed Diers, c.1924, 6 ½ In.	3738.00
Vase, Landscape, Vellum, Fred Rothenbusch, c.1937, 5 x 12 ¼ In.	2875.00
Vase, Landscape, Vellum Glaze, 1922, 5 ½ x 12 ½ In.	1200.00
Vase, Landscape, Vellum Glaze, Shouldered, Lorinda Epply, c.1913, 4 x 8 ½ In.	403.00
Vase, Leaves, 2 Dolphin Handles, Red Matte Glaze, Urn, 1947, 8 x 10 In.	518.00
Vase, Leaves, Berries, Lorinda Epply, 1915, 9 ¼ x 4 ½ In.	1464.00
Vase, Leaves, Incised, Mottled Brown, C.S. Todd, 1912, 6 ⅜ In.	633.00
Vase, Leaves, Painted, Standard Glaze, Edith Felten, 1899, 3 x 5 ½ In.	288.00
Vase, Leaves, Red Berries, Geometric Panels, Pink Ground, S. Sax, 1920, 7 In.	1778.00
Vase, Leaves, Vertical, Purple Matte Glaze, Cylindrical, c.1914, 4 x 8 ½ In.	633.00
Vase, Lilies Of The Valley, Black Iris Glaze, C. Schmidt, 1912, 11 In.	3910.00
Vase, Lotus, Pads, Peach, Green, Vellum Glaze, K. Shirayamadini, 1907, 9 In.	4600.00
Vase, Magnolia Sprig, Iris Glaze, Lenore Asbury, 1907, 8 In.	518.00
Vase, Man With Mustache, Standard Glaze, 1895, 14 ¼ x 7 ¼ In.	305.00
Vase, Maroon Matte Glaze, Tapered, Geometric Design, c.1922, 3 ¼ x 6 ¾ In.	230.00
Vase, Mistletoe, Berries, Leaves, Iris Glaze, Sara Sax, 1905, 8 ½ In.	518.00
Vase, Misty Cactus Flowers, Decorated Matte, K. Shirayamadani, 1936, 10 In.	4500.00
Vase, Misty Lake, Trees, Blue, Scenic Vellum, F. Rothenbusch, 1928, 11 In.	4025.00
Vase, Misty Landscape, Lake, Blue, Pink, Scenic Vellum, L. Asbury, 1920, 9 In.	1727.00
Vase, Mottled Blue Green Glaze, Rolled Handles, 1925, 3 ¼ x 13 ¼ In.	215.00
Vase, Multicolored Drip Glaze, Crystalline Highlights, Shouldered, c.1929, 4 x 6 ¼ In.	173.00
Vase, Mums, Elizabeth Lincoln, 1926, 16 ½ x 6 ½ In.	3172.00
Vase, Nasturtium, Standard Glaze, Anna Marie Valentien, 1898, 10 ¾ x 5 In.	549.00
Vase, Oak Leaves, Painted Matte, 1901-10, 5 ¼ x 4 ½ In.	1464.00
Vase, Orchids, Iris Glaze, Carl Schmidt, 1903, 17 ¾ x 7 In.	29280.00
Vase, Organic Design, Blue Matte Glaze, Tapered, 1904, 5 x 7 In.	480.00
Vase, Organic Design, Incised, Green Vellum, c.1905, 6 x 13 In.	510.00
Vase, Painted Dragonflies, Bulbous, Incised, Clara Lindeman, c.1906, 3 ½ x 4 ½ In.	2300.00
Vase, Painted Landscape, Fred Rothenbusch, c.1921, 3 x 7 ½ In.	1668.00
Vase, Pansies, Standard Glaze, Elizabeth Lincoln, 1901, 3 ½ x 6 ½ In.	546.00
Vase, Parrots, Jewel, Edward T. Hurley, 1927, 11 x 8 In.	2928.00
Vase, Peacock Feather, Blue, Orange, Green, Copper Rim, E. Lincoln, 1904, 6 In.	1840.00
Vase, Peacock Feathers, Pink, Light Green Matte Glaze, 1919, 5 x 9 In.	240.00
Vase, Pegasus, Tapered, Cream Glaze, Green Interior, Barrett, 1948, 12 In.	676.00
Vase, Pink & Green Matte Glaze, Vertical Leaves, Tapered, c.1914, 3 ½ x 7 In.	201.00
Vase, Pink Flowers, Vellum Glaze, Margaret McDonald, 1920, 5 ½ In.	690.00
Vase, Pink, Green, Iris Glaze, L. Asbury, c.1900, 7 In.	881.00
Vase, Poppies, Iris Glaze, Sallie Coyne, 1906, 3 ½ x 8 In.	2415.00
Vase, Poppies, White, Green Leaves, Blue, Vellum Glaze, E. Diers, 1906, 8 In.	2300.00
Vase, Poppy, Applied Silver Overlay, Bulbous, Sallie Coyne, 1898, 5 ½ x 6 In.	4600.00
Vase, Poppy, White, Green, Gray, Iris Glaze, F. Rothenbusch, 1903, 10 In.	2300.00
Vase, Porcelain Glaze, Flowers, Bulbous, Kataro Shirayamadani, c.1926, 6 ½ x 5 In.	1610.00
Vase, Purple Grape Clusters, Green Leaves, Matte Glaze, c.1911, 9 ½ x 7 In.	570.00
Vase, Purple Matte Glaze, Tapered, Painted, Incised, Hentschel, c.1915, 3 ¾ x 9 ¼ In.	1955.00
Vase, Rabbits, Mottled Brown Blue Ground, Porcelain, J. Jensen, 1934, 5 In.	4370.00
Vase, Red & Green Matte Glaze, Geometric, Round, 1906, 3 x 2 In.	253.00
Vase, Red & Green Mottled Glaze, Blue Raised Design, Tapered, Hentschel, 3 ½ x 5 ½ In.	288.00
Vase, Red Leaves, Seeds, Blue Ground, Matte Glaze, O. Geneva, 1905, 10 In.	6038.00
Vase, Red Roses, Leaves, Shouldered, Charles Todd, 1915, 6 ¼ In.	575.00
Vase, River, Rising Moon, Vellum, E.T. Hurley, c.1910, 9 x 4 ¾ In. ...... *illus*	3900.00
Vase, Rooks, Blue Matte, 5 ⅜ In.	316.00
Vase, Roses, E.T. Hurley, 1919, 9 ¼ In.	575.00
Vase, Roses, Painted Matte, Olga G. Reed, 1906, 9 x 4 In.	2196.00
Vase, Salamander, Sea Green Glaze, Tapered, Matt Daly, 1896, 3 x 6 In.	3738.00
Vase, Seahorses, Vellum, Bulbous, E.T. Hurley, 1904, 4 x 4 ½ In.	4025.00
Vase, Ship, Sea Green Glaze, Sturgis Laurence, 1903, 11 x 5 ½ In.	7320.00
Vase, Silver Vine Overlay, Gorham, Standard Glaze, A. Sprague, 1892, 13 In.	5060.00
Vase, Snowy Canadian Rockies, Scenic Vellum, C. Schmidt, 1913, 15 In.	11500.00
Vase, Southwestern, Raised Design, Figure On Burro, Tan Glaze, Impressed, 5 ½ In.	147.00
Vase, Stylized Trees, Moon, Vellum, Sallie Coyne, 1909, 9 ¼ In.	1595.00
Vase, Thistle, Iris Glaze, Fred Rothenbusch, c.1902, 3 ½ x 8 In. ...... *illus*	900.00
Vase, Thistles, Lilies, 2 Handles, Footed, Matte Glaze, 1925, 10 ½ In.	690.00
Vase, Trees, Buildings, Vellum Glaze, Fred Rothenbusch, 1930, 11 ⅞ In.	920.00

Rookwood, Vase, River, Rising Moon, Vellum, E.T. Hurley, c.1910, 9 x 4 ¾ In. $3900.00

TIP
Be careful about displaying paperweights or other heavy objects on glass shelves. With each new purchase you add more weight to the display shelf, until one day there is a crash and the shelf and weights are damaged. It may seem safe for years, but a slight jar from a slamming door may be enough to cause the glass to crack. We also add a word of warning about wall-hung shelves on metal strips: These develop "creep" and after several years may pull loose at the top and eventually collapse.

Rookwood, Vase, Thistle, Iris Glaze, Fred Rothenbusch, c.1902, 3 ½ x 8 In. $900.00

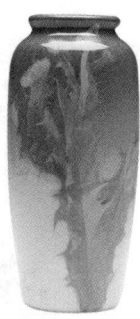

Rookwood, Vase, Venetian Harbor Scene, Vellum Glaze, Marked, Carl Schmidt, c.1922, 6 ¾ In. $2875.00

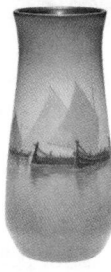

Rookwood, Vase, Weasaw Shoshone, Hopi Indian, Impressed Mark, Grace Young, c.1901, 8 ½ In. $10575.00

Vase, Trees Lining River, Blue Hills, Vellum, Sallie Coyne, 1921, 7 ¾ In.	1610.00
Vase, Trees, Vellum, E.T. Hurley, 1931, 10 ⅞ In.	2990.00
Vase, Tropical Landscape, Vellum Glaze, E.T. Hurley, 1908, 8 In.	2300.00
Vase, Trumpet Creeper, Handles, Porcelain, K. Shirayamadani, 1940, 7 In.	1150.00
Vase, Trumpet Flowers, Standard Glaze, Matt Daley, 1888, 5 x 13 In.	1610.00
Vase, Tulips, Orange, Carolyn Steinle, 1903, 8 ¾ In.	546.00
Vase, Tulips, Silver Overlay, Gorham Mark, Katharine Hickman, c.1898, 5 x 9 In.	3565.00
Vase, Turquoise & Purple, Bulbous, 1933, 4 x 4 In.	144.00
Vase, Turquoise Blue Glaze, Stylized Flowers, Lorinda Epply, c.1920, 5 x 11 ½ In.	863.00
Vase, Venetian Harbor Scene, Vellum Glaze, Marked, Carl Schmidt, c.1922, 6 ¾ In. .... *illus*	2875.00
Vase, Violets, Stretched Neck, Virginia Demarest, 1900, 5 ½ In.	288.00
Vase, Wave, Raised, Pastel Green Glaze, Impressed, 4 ¾ x 3 ½ In.	88.00
Vase, Weasaw Shoshone, Hopi Indian, Impressed Mark, Grace Young, c.1901, 8 ½ In. ..... *illus*	10575.00
Vase, White To Green, Iris Glaze, Lenore Asbury, 1911, 6 ⅛ In.	920.00
Vase, Wild Irises, Yellow, Brown, Standard Glaze, Mary Nourse, 1902, 10 In.	633.00
Vase, Wisteria, Purple, Green Black, Pink, Decorated Mat, Todd, 1919, 25 In.	3680.00
Vase, Woman In Forest, Tiger, Aerial Blue, Sallie Toohey, 1895, 8 ¾ In.	17250.00
Vase, Yellow Daisies, Blue, Decorated Matte, K. Shirayamadani, 1926, 8 In.	2645.00
Vase, Yellow Hi-Glaze, Bulbous, 4 ½ x 9 ½ In.	60.00
Vase, Yellow Orchids, Standard Glaze, Long Neck, A. Valentien, 1894, 12 ½ In.	431.00
Vase, Yellow Parrot Tulip, Green Ground, Iris Glaze, S. Sax, 1903, 11 In.	6900.00
Vase, Yellow, Wisteria, Gold, Brown, Standard Glaze, Albert Valentien, 1899, 22 In.	5060.00
Ventilator Grate, Molded, Faience, Mills Restaurant, Cincinnati, c.1921, 42 x 22 In., Pair......	1763.00
Wall Pocket, Green Over Pink Matte Glaze, 1926, 7 ⅝ In.	161.00 to 350.00

RORSTRAND was established near Stockholm, Sweden, in 1726. By the nineteenth century Rorstrand was making English-style earthenware, bone china, porcelain, ironstone china, and majolica. The company is still working. The three crown mark has been used since 1884.

Cup, Entre, Yellow, Black & White Striped Tab Handle, Carl-Harry Stalhane, 4 ¼ In.	35.00
Dessert Set, Majolica, Blue Center, Scalloped Border, Tazza, Plates, 8 Piece	800.00
Drinking Horn, Gnome Holding Horn On Back, Porcelain, Marked, 8 In.	256.00
Pitcher, Cream, Cruise Ship Stockholm, 3 Gray Crowns, White Ground, 2 x 3 In.	50.00
Plate, Christmas, 1969, Julen, Blue & White, Box.	110.00
Plate, Father's Day, 1971, Blue & White, Box, 8 ¼ In.	32.00
Plate, Maya, Green On Green, 10 ¾ In.	20.00
Plate, Mother's Day, 1971, Painted, Carl Larsson, 8 ¼ In.	27.00
Tureen, Flow Blue, Cover, c.1840, 12 x 9 ½ In.	345.00
Vase, Birds, Flowered Branches, Pink, White, Ilse Claesson, 11 x 7 In.	300.00
Vase, Globular, Black, Green, Ilse Claessen, c.1932, 4 ¾ x 4 ¾ In.	350.00
Vase, Jugendstil, Blue, White, Orange Brown, Dessin Alf Wallander, 14 x 11 In.	395.00

ROSE BOWLS were popular during the 1880s. Rose petals were kept in the open bowl to add fragrance to a room, a popular idea in a time of limited personal hygiene. The glass bowls were made with crimped tops, which kept the petals inside. Many types of Victorian art glass were made into rose bowls.

Clear, Fostoria, c.1890, 6 x 2 ⅝ In.	185.00

ROSE CANTON china is similar to Rose Mandarin and Rose Medallion, except that no people or birds are pictured in the decoration. It was made in China during the nineteenth and twentieth centuries in greens, pinks, and other colors.

Corner Bowl, Flowers, Butterflies, Gilt Highlights, 19th Century, 9 ½ In.	478.00
Vase, Pear Shape, Flared Rim, 17 ½ In., Pair	1080.00

ROSE MANDARIN china is similar to Rose Canton and Rose Medallion. If the panels in the design picture only people and not birds, it is Rose Mandarin.

Bough Pot, Petal Handles, Court Scene, 9 x 7 ½ In. ....*illus*	1380.00
Bowl, Figures In Garden, c.1770, 4 ½ x 10 In.	244.00
Bowl, Figures, Landscape, Central Peony, Aster, 9 ⅛ In.	300.00
Bowl, Leaf & Butterfly Border, Center Interior Flowers, Court Life, 5 x 1 ¼ In.	2070.00
Bowl, Melon Shaped Cartouches, Scrolling Lotus, Gilt, 4 x 10 In.	115.00
Chocolate Pot, Fruit Finial, Birds, Landscape, Rococo Shape Handle, c.1795, 7 In.	1035.00
Tureen, Chinese, 19th Century, 10 ¼ x 14 ½ In.	889.00
Urn, Baluster Shape, Flowers, Salamander Handles, c.1700s, 9 In.	288.00
Vase, Cover, Enamel, 1700s, 11 In., Pair	2040.00

ROSE MEDALLION china was made in China during the nineteenth and twentieth centuries. It is a distinctive design with four or more panels of decoration around a central medallion that includes a bird or a peony. The panels show birds and people. The background is a design of tree peonies and leaves. Pieces are colored in greens, pinks, and other colors. It is similar to Rose Canton and Rose Mandarin.

Bowl, Blue & White, Boys, Lip Rim, 4 Buddhist Panels, 8 ¼ In.	1800.00
Bowl, Figures, Flowers, Bird, Shaped Top, 4 ½ x 9 ½ In.	220.00
Bowl, Flower Spray, Birds, Cash Symbols, 5 ½ In.	180.00
Bowl, Footed, Scalloped Rim, Cream Interior, 10 x 4 ½ In.	325.00
Bowl, Landscape, Flowers, Birds, Butterflies, 4 ⅝ x 9 ½ In.	605.00
Bowl, Round, Interior, Exterior Courtyard Scenes, 12 x 5 ½ In.	738.00
Bowl, Scalloped Edge, c.1875, 1 ½ x 8 In.	264.00
Bowl, Vegetable, Cover, 10 ½ x 3 ½ In.	201.00
Candlestick, Flared Base, 7 ½ x 3 ½ In., Pair	345.00
Candlestick, Serpent, Figures, Flowers, Birds, 8 ½ In., Pair	110.00
Charger, Famille Verte, Hawk On Branch, Tree, Deer, Mappies, 8 ½ In.	800.00
Charger, Pavilion Scene, Figures, Fruit, Birds, Butterflies, 13 ½ In.	420.00
Compote, Diamond Shape, Rounded Corners, Footed, 14 In.	518.00
Dish, Hot Water, Dragon Border, Birds & Insects, c.1830, 2 ½ x 11 In.	316.00
Figure, Flowers, Foo Dog Handles, Linen Fold Top, Mid 1800s, 14 In., Pair	600.00
Flowerpot, Figural, Scrolling Flower Ground, 9 ½ In.	510.00
Fruit Basket, Stand, Pierced, Flared Rim, Oval, Chinese, 10 x 11 In. .... *illus*	1320.00
Garden, Seat, Hexagonal, 20th Century, 18 In., Pair	690.00
Jar, Cover, Butterflies, Flowers, 1800s, 18 In., Pair	2280.00
Lamp, Sleeve, Pattern, Gilt Metal Mounts, 1800s, 16 In., Pair	4800.00
Plate, Blue & White, Flowering Tree Peony, Swallows, 8 ¼ In., Pair	1020.00
Plate, Luncheon, Bird, Flowers, 4 Panels, Figural, Natural, 8 ½ In.	84.00
Platter, Oval, Sepia House, Landscape, White Ground, Blue Trim, c.1830, 15 In.	148.00
Platter, People, Flowers, Birds, Oval, 10 ⅞ x 13 ¾ In.	165.00
Platter, Round, Flowers, People Panels, 18 x 14 ½ In.	472.00
Platter, Round, Flowers, People Panels, Gold, 12 x 9 In.	148.00
Platter, Scholar At Desk, Attendants, Oval, 9 ⅛ x 12 In.	240.00
Punch Bowl, 1800s, 14 In.	1680.00
Punch Bowl, 4 Panels, Figures, Natural Scenes, 14 ⅝ In.	1320.00
Punch Bowl, 5 ¾ x 14 ½ In.	1067.00
Punch Bowl, Court Scenes, Birds, Flowers, 6 ¾ x 15 ½ In.	1150.00
Punch Bowl, Figures, Flowers, 1800s, 6 x 15 In.	1304.00
Punch Bowl, Figures, Flowers, 1800s, 7 x 17 In.	948.00
Punch Bowl, Figures, Flowers, White Diamond Diaper Ground, 1800s, 7 x 16 In.	1304.00
Punch Bowl, Figures, Landscape, Peonies, 4 ¼ x 10 ¼ In.	600.00
Punch Bowl, Paneled, Garden Scene, Flowers, Figures, 1800s, 8 x 15 In. .... *illus*	764.00
Teapot, Figures, Panels, 5 ½ x 8 ½ In.	156.00
Teapot, Squat, Shaped Handle, Dome Lid, Ball Finial, Figures, Flowers, c.1850, 8 ½ In.	546.00
Tureen, Cover, Birds, Flowers, Gilt Knop, Handles, 11 x 14 x 11 In.	1495.00
Tureen, Cover, Courtyard Scenes, Gilt Finial, 11 ½ x 9 ½ In.	177.00
Tureen, Cover, Flowers, Figures, Gold Finial, 11 x 8 In.	266.00
Tureen, Tray, Flowers, Courtyard Scenes, Gold Finial, Handles, 8 ½ x 5 ½ In.	384.00
Vase, Courtyard Scenes, Children, 1800s, 15 ½ x 6 In., Pair	1150.00
Vase, Courtyard Scenes, Gilt Handles, 9 In., Pair	472.00
Vase, Dragons, Squirrel Handles, Flower Ground, 1800, 17 ¾ In.	720.00
Vase, Floor, Famille Rose Pattern, 1800s, 24 In.	823.00
Vase, Floor, Foo Dog Handles, 17 ½ x 9 In.	400.00
Vase, Floor, Rosewood, Stand, 1900s, 47 In., Pair	470.00
Vase, Flowers, Courtyard Scenes, Urn Shape, Gilt Handles, 18 In.	413.00
Vase, Hexagonal, Panels, Late 19th Century, 13 ⅜ In.	415.00

ROSE TAPESTRY porcelain was made by the Royal Bayreuth factory of Tettau, Germany, during the late nineteenth century. The surface of the porcelain was pressed against a coarse fabric while it was still damp, and the impressions remained on the finished porcelain. It looks and feels like a textured cloth. Very skillful reproductions are being made that even include a variation of the Royal Bayreuth mark, so be careful when buying.

Bowl, Royal Bayreuth, 10 ¾ In.	320.00
Box, Cover, Pink & Yellow Flowers, Shell Shape	175.00
Cake Plate, Art Nouveau, Open Handles, 10 ½ In.	245.00

Rose Mandarin, Bough Pot, Petal Handles, Court Scene, 9 x 7 ½ In. $1380.00

R

Rose Medallion, Fruit Basket, Stand, Pierced, Flared Rim, Oval, Chinese, 10 x 11 In. $1320.00

Rose Medallion, Punch Bowl, Paneled, Garden Scene, Flowers, Figures, 1800s, 8 x 15 In. $764.00

Rosenthal, Figurine, Horse, Green Mark, Th. Karmer, 15 ¾ x 20 ¼ In. $920.00

Rosenthal, Figurine, Woman, Seated, Holding Removable Vase, Stamped, 1930s, 7 x 9 In. $420.00

Creamer, Roses, 3 ¼ In.	59.00
Cup & Saucer, Pink Roses, Flared, Waisted, Loop Handle, 2 x 4 & 5 ½ In.	29.00
Dish, Multicolored Roses, Leaf Shape, 4 ¼ x 5 In.	169.00
Dresser Tray, Green Mark, Royal Bayreuth Bavaria, 7 ¼ x 10 In.	78.00
Flowerpot, Insert, Handles, Marked, Bavaria, 2 ¾ In.	87.00
Hair Receiver, Pink, Yellow & White Roses, Footed, 2 ¾ x 4 In.	245.00
Lamp, Urn Shape, Beaded Rim, Flora & Fauna, Brass Base, Gilt, 33 In.	395.00
Nappy, Leaf Shape, Marked, Royal Bayreuth Bavaria, 4 ¾ In.	60.00
Pin Dish, Cover, Oval, No. 5, Marked, Bavaria, 2 x 4 In.	58.00
Pitcher, Pinch Spout, Yellow, Green & Brown, Image Of Woman, Royal Bayreuth, 5 In.	200.00
Pitcher, Pink, Yellow & White Roses, Gilt, 4 ¾ In.	275.00
Powder Jar, Lid, Footed, Marked, Royal Bayreuth, Bavaria, 2 ¼ x 4 In.	118.00
Toothpick, Coal Scuttle Bucket, Woman With Horse, Royal Bayreuth, 3 In.	75.00
Tray, Castle, Lake, Marked, Royal Bayreuth Bavaria, 8 x 11 In.	148.00
Vase, Cattle Scene, Royal Bayreuth, 5 In.	300.00
Vase, Lady With Muff, Royal Bayreuth, Blue Mark, 7 In.	200.00
Vase, Yellow, Pink, White Roses, 5 ¼ x 3 In.	115.00

ROSEMEADE POTTERY of Wahpeton, North Dakota, worked from 1940 to 1961. The pottery was operated by Laura A. Taylor and her husband, R.I. Hughes. The company was also known as the Wahpeton Pottery Company. Art pottery and commercial wares were made.

Candleholder, Blue, Sticker, 1 ¾ x 3 In.	82.00
Figurine, Indian Moccasins, Sticker, 1949, 3 ½ In.	65.00
Flower Frog Pick Holder, Pheasant, Figural, Gold & Yellow Green, 4 ⅝ x 4 ¾ In.	35.00
Flower Holder, Heron, White, Green Base, 1950, Original Label, 6 ¾ In.	87.00
Lamp, Pheasant, TV Light, Brown, Yellow, Green, Electric, Paper Label, 10 x 12 In.	360.00
Salt & Pepper, Bear, Brown, Original Stopper, 3 ¼ In.	77.00
Salt & Pepper, Black Cat, High Gloss, Sticker, 3 In.	89.00
Salt & Pepper, Corn, Tray, Paper Label	150.00
Salt & Pepper, Duck, Black With Orange Bill, Original Cork, 2 ½ In.	82.00
Salt & Pepper, Flamingo, Pink, 4 ½ In & 3 ¼ In.	185.00
Salt & Pepper, Greyhound, Sandy Color, Original Corks, 2 ½ In.	82.00
Salt & Pepper, Kangaroo, Yellow Brown, 1950, 3 In.	72.00
Salt & Pepper, Mice, Gray With Pink Nose, 1 ¾ x 2 In.	75.00
Salt & Pepper, Pelican, Red With Brown Beaks, 3 ½ In.	35.00
Salt & Pepper, Pheasant, Orange Color, Original Cork, 2 & 3 In.	45.00
Salt & Pepper, Pheasant, Squatting, Brown & Yellow, 5 ½ In.	99.00
Salt & Pepper, Prairie Rose, Pink With Green Leaf, 1950, 2 ½ In.	65.00
Salt & Pepper, Siamese Cat, White With Pink Accents, Original Cork, 2 ¾ In.	65.00
Salt & Pepper, Terrier, Brown & White, 3 In.	81.00
Shaker, Pheasant, Souvenir Sticker, Brown, White Tail, 3 In.	10.00
Sugar & Creamer, Corn, Stamped, 2 ½ & 3 In.	49.00
Vase, Mint Green, 3 x 4 ½ In.	68.00

ROSENTHAL porcelain was made at the factory established in Selb, Bavaria, in 1880. The factory is still making fine-quality tablewares and figurines. A series of Christmas plates was made from 1910. Other limited edition plates have been made since 1971. In 1998 Rosenthal was acquired by the Waterford Wedgwood Group. Rosenthal was bought by Sambonet Paderno Industries, headquartered in Orfento, Novaro, Italy, in 2009. Rosenthal china is still being produced in Bavaria.

MARKE
Rosenthal

Figurine, Cat, Reclining, Gray, Striped, No. 1304, Himmelstoss, 6 ½ In.	36.00
Figurine, Dog, Dachshund, Reclining, 5 ¾ x 8 ½ In.	260.00
Figurine, Dove, White, F. Heidenreich, 5 x 6 In., Pair	177.00
Figurine, Fawns, Sleeping, Black, White, c.1912, 10 In.	527.00
Figurine, Female, Nude, White Cap, Flowing Wrap, Signed, Schlipstein, 13 In.	1159.00
Figurine, Horse, Green Mark, Th. Karmer, 15 ¾ x 20 ¼ In. *illus*	920.00
Figurine, Nude Woman Riding Horse, 9 x 11 In.	95.00
Figurine, Peacock, Long Tail Feathers, Bright Blue Neck, Breast, No. 948, Handgemalt B, 5 x 9 In.	266.00
Figurine, Woman, Seated, Holding Removable Vase, Stamped, 1930s, 7 x 9 In. *illus*	420.00
Figurine, Woman, Seated, Holding Vase, White, Stamped, 1930s, 7 x 9 ½ In.	420.00
Figurine, Woman, Snake Charmer, Signed, 7 ¾ In.	173.00
Figurine, Woman, Standing, Arms Upraised, Bisque, 35 x 13 In.	205.00
Ramekin, Underplate, Dessert Plate, Painted, 5 x 1 ½ In., 6 Piece	40.00

R

Vase, 1001 Nights, Flared, Multicolored, Bjorn Wiinblad, 13 x 11 In. ....*illus*	403.00
Vase, Blue, Linnie Line, Bjorn Wiinblad, c.1972, 9 x 2 ½ In.	185.00
Vase, Flower Sprays, Enamel, Gilt, Hand Painted, Flared Rim, 11 ½ In.	200.00
Vase, Handle, Lava & Green Glaze, Jopeko Keramik, West Germany, 1970s, 5 In.	25.00
Vase, Love Story, Reclining Woman, Arundo, Bjorn Wiinblad, 4 ¾ In.	60.00
Vase, Peacocks, Luster Glaze, Black Ground, Gold Trim, M.A. Brooks, c.1910, 13 ½ In.	354.00
Vase, White, Oval, Studio Line, Signed, 4 ½ In.	25.00

ROSEVILLE POTTERY COMPANY was organized in Roseville, Ohio, in 1890. Another plant was opened in Zanesville, Ohio, in 1898. Many types of pottery were made until 1954. Early wares include Sgraffito, Olympic, and Rozane. Later lines were often made with molded decorations, especially flowers and fruit. Most pieces are marked *Roseville*. Many reproductions made in China have been offered for sale the past few years.

Apple Blossom, Basket, Blue, 8 In.	168.00
Apple Blossom, Basket, Blue, 10 In.	148.00
Apple Blossom, Candleholder, Green, 4 ¾ In., Pair	175.00
Apple Blossom, Console, Green, White Blossoms, Handles, 12 In.	176.00
Apple Blossom, Jardiniere, Blue, Marked, 8 In.	158.00
Apple Blossom, Teapot, Lid, 7 ½ In.	79.00
Apple Blossom, Teapot, Pink, 7 ¼ x 11 In.	195.00
Apple Blossom, Vase, Blue, 15 In.	260.00 to 280.00
Apple Blossom, Vase, Pink, 18 In.	375.00
Apple Blossom, Vase, Rose, 8 ¼ In.	124.00
Apple Blossom, Wall Pocket, 8 In.	125.00
Artcraft, Vase, Blue, Bulbous, 18 ¼ x 11 In.	1995.00
Artwood, Planter, Palm Tree, Gray, 9 ¼ x 12 ½ In.	375.00
Artwood, Planter, Yellow, 6 ¾ x 10 ¾ In.	120.00
Aztec, Pitcher, Blue Gray Glaze, c.1916, 8 ¼ In.	206.00
Aztec, Vase, Black, Cylindrical, 7 ¾ In.	395.00
Aztec, Vase, Ivory Ground, Squeezebag, 8 ½	595.00
Azurean, Box, Lid, Flowers, Blue Ground, 1 ¼ x 3 ½ In.	450.00
Azurean, Box, Lid, Flowers, Leaves, Blue, c.1902	345.00
Azurean, Pitcher, Blue & White, Cherry Blossoms, Marked, 7 x 8 In.	403.00
Baneda, Vase, 3-Sided, Mauve Glaze, Footed, 4 ¼ In.	316.00
Baneda, Vase, Green, Blue, Handles, Footed, 15 In.	2760.00
Baneda, Vase, Green, Blue, Handles, Marked, 7 In.	360.00
Bittersweet, Basket, Gray, Flowers, Cream, 6 ½ x 5 ¼ In.	125.00
Bittersweet, Double Cornucopia, Green, 4 ¼ x 8 ½ In.	125.00
Bittersweet, Vase, Fan Shape, Green, Handles, Marked, 8 ¼ x 7 In.	165.00
Bittersweet, Vase, Gray, Low Handles, 14 ¼ In.	235.00
Blackberry, Jardiniere, Handles, 8 ¼ x 10 ½ In.	675.00
Blackberry, Vase, Gourd, Marked, 5 ¼ In.	450.00
Blackberry, Vase, Green, Brown, Paper Label, 5 In.	288.00
Blackberry, Wall Pocket, 8 ¼ In.	995.00
Bleeding Heart, Basket, Pink, Footed, 9 ½ In.	325.00
Bleeding Heart, Console Set, Blue, Candlesticks, 16-In. Bowl, 3 Piece	155.00
Bleeding Heart, Planter, Green, Oval Handles, c.1938, 12 In.	71.00
Bleeding Heart, Vase, Blue, Scalloped Rim, 4 ¼ In.	165.00
Bleeding Heart, Vase, Flared 6-Sided Rim, 2 Reeded Buttressed Handles, 9 In.	148.00
Bleeding Heart, Vase, Pink, Globular, Handles, 6 ¼ x 8 ¼ In.	185.00
Bushberry, Basket, Green, Blue, 8 In.	118.00
Bushberry, Urn, Blue, Footed, Square Handles	71.00
Bushberry, Vase, Marked, 15 In.	375.00
Capri, Bowl, Mottled Red, Boat Shape, 2 ¾ x 9 ¼ In.	85.00
Capri, Candleholder, Cactus Green, Shell Bowl, 1 ¼ x 4 ½ In., 2 Piece	125.00
Capri, Cornucopia, Mottled Blue, 6 x 7 ½ In.	95.00
Capri, Shell, Cactus Green, 2 ¼ x 10 In.	135.00
Carnelian I, Vase, Coffee, Green Matte Glaze, Scrolled Handles, 7 ¼ In.	92.00
Carnelian I, Vase, Green, Pink, Handles, 8 ½ x 9 ½ In.	259.00
Casserole, Stoneware, Ohio	5.00
Cherry Blossom, Vase, Brown, Loop Handles, 8 ¼ x 8 ¾ In. ....*illus*	311.00
Chloron, Chamberstick, Green Matte Glaze, 2 ½ x 9 ½ In.	295.00
Chloron, Vase, Green, Stylized Branches, 11 In.	1265.00
Chloron, Wall Pocket, Green Matte Glaze, Flowers, 11 In.	395.00
Clemana, Flower Frog, Blue, Flowers, 4 ¼ In.	175.00

Rosenthal, Vase, 1001 Nights, **Flared,** Multicolored, Bjorn Wiinblad, **13 x 11 In.** $403.00

R

Roseville, Cherry Blossom, Vase, Brown, Loop Handles, 8 ¼ x 8 ¾ In. $311.00

Roseville, Fuchsia, Vase, Blue, Handles, 10 ¼ x 9 ¼ In. $173.00

Roseville, Fudji, Vase, Blue, Green, Brown Gloss Glaze, Tan Bisque Ground, Marked, 8 ¾ In. $1380.00

Clemana, Vase, Brown, Handles, 6 ¼ x 5 ¼ In.	235.00
Clematis, Bowl, Brown, Handles, 4 x 6 In.	70.00
Clematis, Candlestick, Brown, 2 x 5 In., Pair	50.00
Clematis, Ewer, Brown, 10 In.	72.00
Clematis, Planter, Green, Rectangular, Squat	83.00
Clematis, Tea Set, Flowers, Green, Raised Letters, Teapot, Creamer, Sugar, 3 Piece	170.00
Clematis, Vase, Blue, 5 In.	80.00
Clematis, Vase, Raised, Purple, Blue, Blue Green Ground, Handles, Experimental, 8 In.	1150.00
Clematis, Wall Pocket, Marked, 8 In.	275.00
Columbine, Basket, Brown, Flowers, Handle, 10 ¼ In.	225.00
Columbine, Bowl, Blue Ground, Bulbous, Angular Handles, 3 In.	148.00
Columbine, Bowl, Handles, 5 In.	73.00
Columbine, Bowl, Pink, Flowers, Handles, 6 ¼ x 9 ½ In.	100.00
Columbine, Bowl, Pink Ground, Squat, Handles, 3 x 5 ¾ In.	83.00
Columbine, Candleholder, Blue, Buttressed, 5 In., Pair	145.00
Columbine, Cornucopia, Base, Marked, 6 In.	45.00
Columbine, Vase, Blue, Handles, 10 In.	195.00
Columbine, Wall Pocket, Brown, Flowers, Swirled Bottom, 8 ½ In.	350.00
Corinthian, Bowl, 5 In.	56.00
Cosmos, Basket, Blue, Flowers, Handle, Footed, 10 x 9 ¼ In.	295.00
Cosmos, Basket, Blue, Hanging, Flowers, 5 x 7 ¼ In.	395.00
Cosmos, Bowl, Console, Blue, Flowers, Handles, 5 ¼ x 15 ½ In.	295.00
Cosmos, Jardiniere, Blue, Flowers, Handles, 3 ¾ x 4 ½ In.	150.00
Cosmos, Vase, Tan, Footed, Handles, 5 ¼ In.	95.00
Cremona, Vase, Green, Flat & Flared Rim, 12 ¼ In.	345.00
Cremona, Vase, Green, Flowers, Handles, 8 ¼ In.	215.00
Crystalis, Vase, Stick, 3 Faces, Mottled & Flowing Glaze, 15 ¼ In.	2195.00
Dahlrose, Jardiniere, Brown, White Daisy Border, 9 In.	173.00
Dahlrose, Vase, 8 In.	138.00
Dahlrose, Vase, Handles, 4 ½ x 10 ½ In.	97.00
Dahlrose, Vase, Handles, 6 In.	85.00
Dahlrose, Vase, Handles, 8 In.	73.00
Dahlrose, Vase, Pillow, 5 ½ In.	85.00
Dahlrose, Wall Pocket, Handles, 8 In.	124.00
Dawn, Bowl, Pink, Art Deco, 4 ¼ x 6 ¾ In.	185.00
Dawn, Bowl, Pink, Footed, Handles, Art Deco, 6 ½ x 10 ¾ In.	300.00
Dawn, Vase, Yellow, Art Deco, 6 ¼ x 5 ¼ In.	165.00
Dawn, Vase, Yellow, Square Base, 1937, 9 ½ In.	178.00
Della Robbia, Ewer, Brown, Carved Verse, 5 ½ In.	2395.00
Della Robbia, Pitcher, Scenes Of Roman Charioteers, Blue, Brown, Marked, 8 In.	3450.00
Della Robbia, Vase, Stylized Flowers, High Glaze, Incised, Signed, Rozane Ware, 8 In.	7200.00
Della Robbia, Vase, Stylized Trees, Celadon Green, 8 ¾ x 4 ¼ In.	1586.00
Dogwood, Basket, Hanging, Flowers, Textured, 3 ½ x 7 In.	295.00
Dogwood, Bowl, Brown, Flowers, Textured, 2 ¼ x 5 ½ In.	135.00
Dogwood, Bowl, Handles, 5 ¼ x 5 In.	125.00
Dogwood, Vase, Applied Flowers, Handles, Marked, 7 ½ x 12 ½ In.	230.00
Dogwood, Vase, Brown, Flowers, Textured, 6 ¼ x 5 ½ In.	235.00
Dogwood, Wall Pocket, Brown, Flowers, Textured, 9 ½ x 4 ½ In.	365.00
Donatello, Ashtray, 2 ¾ x 5 In.	95.00
Donatello, Bowl, 2 ¼ x 5 ¼ In.	125.00
Donatello, Compote, 5 x 6 ½ In.	125.00
Donatello, Flower Frog, 2 ¼ x 7 ½ In.	115.00
Donatello, Jardinere, Pedestal, 22 ¼ In.	384.00
Donatello, Vase, Double Bud, 4 ¼ x 7 ¾ In.	95.00
Donatello, Vase, Flared Rim, 12 ½ x 7 ¼ In.	165.00
Earlam, Vase, Blue Green Glaze, Handles, 4 ¼ x 6 ¼ In.	250.00
Earlam, Window Box, Arts & Crafts, 5 ¼ x 10 ½ In.	295.00
Egypto, Vase, Green Matte Glaze, Footed, Handles, 6 ¾ x 5 ¼ In.	465.00
Egypto, Vase, Green Matte Glaze, Scalloped Rim, Embossed Leaves, 5 ½ x 5 ¾ In.	550.00
Falline, Vase, Brown, Green Curved Design, Handles, 6 In.	230.00
Falline, Vase, Brown, Green, Handles, 6 In.	720.00
Falline, Vase, Mottled Pink, Matte Green, Handles, 6 ¼ In.	200.00
Ferella, Vase, Mottled, Handles, 9 ¼ In.	814.00
Florentine, Umbrella Stand, Footed, Marked, 10 x 18 In.	345.00
Foxglove, Basket, Blue, Marked, 12 In.	178.00
Foxglove, Basket, Green, 8 In.	148.00

Foxglove, Console, 14 In.	90.00
Foxglove, Vase, Pink, Green, Angular Handles, 6 ½ x 5 ½ In.	82.00
Freesia, Vase, Blue, Handles, Marked, 10 In.	153.00
Freesia, Vase, Low Handles, 6 ¼ In.	75.00
Fuchsia, Flowerpot, Blue, Footed, Handles	59.00
Fuchsia, Vase, Blue, Handles, 8 In.	189.00
Fuchsia, Vase, Blue, Handles, 10 ¼ x 9 ¼ In. .... *illus*	173.00
Fudji, Vase, Blue, Green, Brown Gloss Glaze, Tan Bisque Ground, Marked, 8 ¾ In. .... *illus*	1380.00
Futura, Bowl, Sandtoy, Pedestal, Buttressed, Tan & Blue Matte Glaze, 4 In. ...... *illus*	259.00
Futura, Vase, Black Flame, Dark Green, Flame Design, Stepped Neck, 10 In.	546.00
Futura, Vase, Pleated Star Shape, Pink & Green Glaze, 4 x 8 In.	259.00
Futura, Vase, Square, Handles, c.1928, 4 ½ In.	101.00
Gardenia, Basket, Hanging, Green, Flowers, Handles, Chain, 5 ½ x 8 In.	265.00
Gardenia, Bowl, Green, 5 In.	57.00
Gardenia, Ewer, Tan, Flower, 15 ½ x 5 ¼ In.	325.00
Gardenia, Vase, Cornucopia, 6 In.	34.00
Gardenia, Wall Pocket, Golden Tan, Marked, 8 ¾ In. .... *illus*	345.00
Gardenia, Wall Pocket, Green, Flowers, Fan Shape, 8 ¾ x 7 ¼ In.	215.00
Gardenia, Window Box, 6 In.	56.00
Gardenia, Window Box, Gray, Flowers, 2 ½ x 10 In.	90.00
Geometrics, Wall Pocket, Green Matte Glaze, 5 x 10 ½ In.	173.00
Imperial, Vase, Red, Bulbous, Ribbed Neck, 6 ½ x 7 In.	633.00
Imperial II, Vase, Green Matte Glaze, 4 ½ In.	288.00
Iris, Basket, Flowers, Hanging, Handles, 5 ¼ x 9 In.	225.00
Iris, Ewer, Pink, Flowers, 10 ¼ x 6 In.	245.00
Iris, Vase, Tan, 15 ½ x 9 ¾ In.	525.00
Ixia, Flowerpot, Pink, Applied Handles, Saucer, 5 ½ x 6 ½ In.	215.00
Ixia, Vase, Green, Handles, 10 ¼ x 5 In.	325.00
Jonquil, Bowl, 5 ¼ x 7 In.	245.00
Jonquil, Bowl, 7 In.	490.00
Jonquil, Vase, Bulbous, Handles, 4 ¾ x 4 ¼ In.	235.00
Jonquil, Vase, Globular, Handles, 4 ½ x 7 In.	185.00
Jonquil, Vase, Handles, 8 In.	482.00
Laurel, Vase, Green, 9 ¼ x 6 In.	450.00
Laurel, Vase, Yellow, 7 ¼ x 5 In.	275.00
Lotus, Planter, Red, 3 x 11 ¼ In.	165.00
Magnolia, Ashtray	53.00
Magnolia, Jardiniere, Handles, 4 In.	40.00
Magnolia, Vase, Footed, Handles, 9 In.	62.00
Meadow, Swans, Trees, Jardiniere, Pedestal, 26 In.	1955.00
Mock Orange, Teapot, Pink, 6 x 11 In.	150.00
Morning Glory, Lamp, Yellow, Orange Flowers, Brown Ground, 11 In.	489.00
Morning Glory, Vase, 6 ¼ In.	750.00
Morning Glory, Vase, Footed, Handles, 7 ½ x 9 ½ In.	748.00
Moss, Bowl, Footed, Handles	100.00
Mostique, Jardiniere, Stylized Flowers, 8 ½ x 7 In.	210.00
Mostique, Jardiniere, Stylized Roses, 11 ½ x 10 In.	115.00
Mostique, Vase, Flowers, Tan Textured, c.1915, 12 In.	215.00
Mostique, Vase, Spade Design, Orange, Green, Brown, 8 x 15 In.	351.00
Owl On Branches, Vase, Gray Glaze, 7 ½ x 14 In.	4600.00
Pauleo, Vase, Black Bands, Purple High Glaze, Cherries, Leaves, Squat, 6 In.	403.00
Pauleo, Vase, Cherries, Leaves, Black Bands, Purple Luster Glaze, 6 In. .... *illus*	403.00
Pauleo, Vase, Dark Red, Gold Veins, Rolled Lip, Marked, 8 ½ In.	575.00
Peony, Bowl, 3 In.	51.00
Peony, Pitcher, Yellow, 7 ½ In.	120.00
Peony, Vase, Green Ground, White Flower, Handles, 12 In.	176.00
Pine Cone, Ashtray, Green, Pinecones In Corner, Marked, 1935, 4 ¾ In.	180.00
Pine Cone, Basket, Blue, 6 In.	280.00
Pine Cone, Basket, Blue, Marked, 8 In.	288.00
Pine Cone, Basket, Brown, Branch Handle, 10 In.	260.00
Pine Cone, Basket, Brown, Footed, Marked, 10 In.	300.00
Pine Cone, Bowl, Blue, Canoe Shape, 15 In.	210.00
Pine Cone, Bowl, Green, 4 In.	79.00
Pine Cone, Candleholder, 3-Light, Blue, Marked, 5 ½ In.	190.00
Pine Cone, Candleholder, 6-Light, Brown, Marked, 5 ½ In.	275.00
Pine Cone, Dish, 3-Footed, Green, 12 In.	205.00

Roseville, Futura, Sandtoy, Bowl, Pedestal, Buttressed, Tan & Blue Matte Glaze, 4 In. $259.00

Roseville, Gardenia, Wall Pocket, Golden Tan, Marked, 8 ¾ In. $345.00

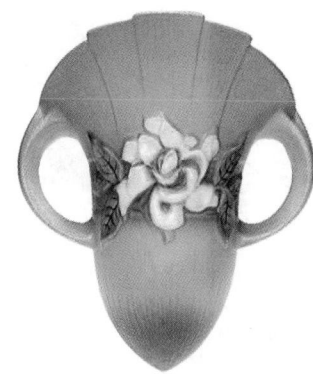

TIP
Don't store an oil painting in a damp basement or hot or cold attic.

R

Roseville, Pauleo, Vase, Cherries, Leaves, Black Bands, Purple Luster Glaze, 6 In. $403.00

Roseville, Pine Cone, Jardiniere, Brown, Twig Handles, Marked, 15 x 8 In. $270.00

Roseville, Rozane, Vase, Della Robbia, Stylized Grapes, Incised, Painted, 6 ½ In. $3910.00

R

TIP

A matte glazed pottery piece can be rubbed with olive oil, then wiped clean.

Pine Cone, Flowerpot, Blue, Paper Label, 5 In.		132.00
Pine Cone, Jardiniere, Brown, Twig Handles, Marked, 15 x 8 In. .... *illus*		270.00
Pine Cone, Pitcher, Ice Lip, Brown, Marked, 7 ½ x 8 ½ In.		195.00
Pine Cone, Planter, Brown, Hanging, 6 In.		175.00
Pine Cone, Tray, Blue Bottom, 12 In.		175.00
Pine Cone, Vase, Blue, Footed, Low Handles, 10 ¼ In.		305.00
Pine Cone, Vase, Blue, Handles, Marked, 7 In.	200.00 to 260.00	
Pine Cone, Vase, Blue, Handles, Marked, 10 In.		150.00
Pine Cone, Vase, Blue, Round, Square Foot, Low Handles, 7 In.		305.00
Pine Cone, Vase, Brown Glaze, Lower Handles, 1930s, 10 In.		220.00
Pine Cone, Vase, Brown, Marked, 7 ½ In.		610.00
Pine Cone, Vase, Bud, Blue, 7 In.		280.00
Pine Cone, Vase, Green, Brown Applied Pinecone, Footed, Handles, 15 In.		316.00
Pine Cone, Vase, High Gloss Blue, Footed, 6 In.		62.00
Pine Cone, Vase, Peach, Handles, Marked, 11 In.		230.00
Pine Cone, Wall Pocket, Double, Brown, Marked, 8 In.		360.00
Pine Cone, Water Pitcher, Ice Lip, Greens, Teardrop Form, 9 ¼ In.		113.00
Pine Cone, Window Box, Blue, 15 In.		226.00
Pine Cone, Window Box, Blue, Marked, 12 In.		215.00
Primrose, Sand Jar, 14 x 12 In.		239.00
Primrose, Vase, Footed, Handles, 7 In.		40.00
Raymor, Bowl, Vegetable, Divided, Terra Cotta, Ben Seibel		100.00
Raymor, Chop Plate, Beach Gray, Ben Seibel		100.00
Raymor, Creamer, Golden Burst, Universal, Ben Seibel		40.00
Raymor, Gravy Boat, Terra-Cotta, Ben Seibel		80.00
Raymor, Stack Server, Cover, Contemporary White, Ben Seibel		145.00
Roses, Vase, Stylized, Painted, Pillow, Ruffled Rim, 11 ½ x 9 ½ In.		518.00
Rozane Royal, Pitcher, White, Silver Rim, Handle, Base, Overlay, Violets, Tot Steele, 4 ½ In. ..		200.00
Rozane Royal, Vase, Bud, Yellow, Brown, Pansies, 7 ½ In.		104.00
Rozane Royal, Vase, Dogwood, Gray, Ivory, c.1904, 8 ¾ In.		750.00
Rozane Royal, Vase, Pillow, Green, Pink, White, J. Imlay, c.1902, 9 In.		690.00
Rozane, Mug, Blue & White Glaze, Wheat Design, Marked, Handle, 4 x 4 In.		230.00
Rozane, Vase, Binocular Form, Brown Matte Glaze, Gray Overglaze, 4 ¾ x 7 In.		135.00
Rozane, Vase, Brown, Spaniel, With Pheasant, Pillow, Handles, Signed, M. Timberlake, 11 x 9 In.		1840.00
Rozane, Vase, Della Robbia, Stylized Grapes, Incised, Painted, 6 ½ In. .... *illus*		3910.00
Rozane, Vase, Egypto, Green Glaze, Double Handles, Footed, 4 ½ x 7 In.		345.00
Rozane, Vase, Olympic, Euyclea Discovers Ulysses, Red, Black, Ivory, Handles, 10 x 11 In.		3105.00
Rozane, Vase, Pinched Neck, Flared Rim, Blue & White, Violets, Marked, 3 x 6 ½ In.		374.00
Rozane, Vase, Portrait, Man, Glossy Brown, Green Ground, A. Dunlavy, Stamped, 14 ¼ In.		550.00
Rozane, Vase, Retriever, Holding Pheasant, Brown Glaze, Pillow, Handles, Dunley, 11 x 9 In. ..		1265.00
Silhouette, Cornucopia		59.00
Silhouette, Vase, Green, Brown, 11 ½ In.		170.00
Silhouette, Vase, Nude, Aqua, Art Deco Style, Fan, 7 In.		518.00
Snowberry, Ewer, Blue, 10 In.		138.00
Snowberry, Teapot, Green, Marked, 7 x 10 In.		150.00
Snowberry, Vase, Blue, Low Handles, Marked, 12 In.		205.00
Snowberry, Vase, Floor, Green, Orange, Raised Design, Handles, 19 In.		431.00
Snowberry, Vase, Green, Footed, Handles, 18 In.		425.00
Snowberry, Vase, Pillow, 6 In.		73.00
Snowberry, Wall Pocket, Blue, Handles, Marked, IWP, 8 In.		148.00
Sponge, Pitcher & Bowl, Yellow, 15-In. Bowl		68.00
Sunflower, Vase, Globular, Handles, 6 x 4 In.		489.00
Sunflower, Vase, Handles, 9 In.		748.00
Sunflower, Vase, Leaves, Green, Tan, 5 ½ In.		460.00
Sunflower, Wall Pocket, Rolled Lip, 7 ¼ In.		649.00
Teasel, Bowl, Handles, 4 In.		23.00
Thorn Apple, Jardiniere, Brown, Yellow, 9 ¼ x 11 ½ In.		203.00
Thorn Apple, Vase, Jug, Handles, 4 In.		68.00
Topeo, Console, Green Washed Glaze, Pink Raised Design, 13 x 8 ½ In.		106.00
Trees, Vase, Tan Glaze, Stylized, Tapered, Footed, Flared Rim, 5 ½ x 11 In.		4280.00
Tuscany, Vase, Black, High Glaze, Handles, 8 In.		173.00
Vase, Creamware, Dutch Women, Child, 11 ½ In.		260.00
Velmoss, Bowl, Leaves, 2 ¼ x 10 ¾ In.		375.00
Velmoss, Vase, Gathered Waist, Leaf Edge, 11 ¾ x 7 ¼ In.		1295.00
Velmoss, Vase, Green, Brown, Yellow, Spade Leaves, 6 x 4 ½ In.		475.00
Velmoss, Vase, Raised Leaf Design, Green & Brown Matte Glaze, 4 ½ x 8 In.		546.00

Vista, Vase, Handles, 6 x 10 In.	719.99
Water Lily, Bowl, Handles, 3 In.	45.00
Water Lily, Bowl, White, Blue Ground, Handles, 4 ½ x 6 x 6 In.	82.00
White Rose, Flower Frog, 3 ½ In.	71.00
White Rose, Jardiniere, Handles, c.1940, 5 x 8 In.	50.00
White Rose, Planter, C-Shape Handles	59.00
White Rose, Vase, 4 In.	69.00
White Rose, Vase, Cornucopia, 8 In.	46.00
White Rose, Vase, Footed, Elongated Handles	112.00
White Rose, Vase, Handles, Footed, 7 In.	56.00
Wincraft, Vase, Flower Shape, Yellow Tulip, c.1940, 8 In., Pair	146.00
Windsor, Vase, Carved Stylized Flower Rim, Blue, 2 Bowed Handles, 9 ¼ In.	480.00
Wisteria, Vase, Blue, Pale Pink, Green Flowers, Leaves, 8 In.	575.00
Wisteria, Vase, Leaf, Dark Blue To Cream, Tapered, 12 ½ In.	230.00
Wisteria, Vase, Squat Jug Shape, Blue Brown, Pink & Green Flowers, Handles, 8 In.	575.00
Zephyr Lily, Basket, Blue, 10 ½ In.	113.00
Zephyr Lily, Basket, Brown, 7 In.	46.00
Zephyr Lily, Candleholder, Blue, 2 In., Pair	57.00
Zephyr Lily, Pedestal, Blue, Marked, U.S.A., 17 In.	145.00
Zephyr Lily, Vase, Baluster, Handles	77.00
Zephyr Lily, Vase, Brown, Green, White, Handles, Marked, 19 In.	345.00
Zephyr Lily, Vase, Green, Embossed, Handles, c.1946, 16 In.	1320.00
Zephyr Lily, Vase, Green, Rose, Yellow Flowers, 10 ½ In.	136.00
Zephyr Lily, Wall Pocket, Brown, c.1940, 4 x 8 ½ In.	450.00

ROWLAND & MARSELLUS COMPANY is part of a mark that appears on historical Staffordshire dating from the late nineteenth and early twentieth centuries. *Rowland & Marsellus* is the mark used by an American importing company in New York City. The company worked from 1893 to about 1937. Some of the pieces may have been made by the British Anchor Pottery Co. of Longton, England, for export to a New York firm. Many American views were made. Of special interest to collectors are the plates with rolled edges, usually blue and white.

Pitcher, Birth Of U.S.A., Presidents, Blue, White, Staffordshire, 1908, 7 x 7 In.	550.00
Plate, Bridgeport, Conn., Landmarks, Blue, White, c.1900, 10 In.	22.00
Plate, Capitol Washington DC, Blue, White, 10 In.	50.00
Plate, Commodore Paul Jones Capturing The Serapis, Sept. 1779, Blue, White	48.00
Plate, Historical Boston, Faneuil Hall, Blue, White, Rolled Rim, 10 In.	50.00
Plate, Landing Of Hendrick Hudson, Blue, White, Rolled Rim, 10 In.	150.00
Plate, Myles Standish, Blue, White, Rolled Rim, 10 In.	175.00
Plate, Plymouth Rock, Blue, White, Rolled Rim, 10 In.	75.00
Plate, Teddy Roosevelt, Blue, White, 8 Scenes, 10 In.	265.00
Plate, View Of Denver, Blue, White, 6 Scenes, 10 In.	110.00
Plate, William Shakespeare, Blue, White, Rolled Rim, 10 In.	145.00

ROY ROGERS was born in 1911 in Cincinnati, Ohio. In the 1930s, he made a living as a singer; in 1935, his group started work at a Los Angeles radio station. He appeared in his first movie in 1937. From 1952 to 1957, he made 101 television shows. The other stars in the show were his wife, Dale Evans, his horse, Trigger, and his dog, Bullet. Roy Rogers memorabilia, including items from the Roy Rogers restaurants, are collected.

Button, Attached Holster, Gun, Until We Meet Again, Roy Photo, Silver Lettering, 1 ¾ In.	66.00
Button, Dale Evans, Portrait, Hat, Color, Celluloid, 1 ¾ In.	19.00
Button, Roy Rogers, Portrait, 1930s, 1 ¼ In.	86.00
Button, Roy Rogers, Portrait, Hat, Color, Celluloid, 1 ¾ In.	21.00
Button, Souvenir Roy Rogers, Rearing Horse, Rider, Color, Celluloid, 1 ¾ In.	36.00
Cap Gun, Brown Handle, Kilgore, 9 ½ In.	45.00
Cap Gun, Brown Handle, Schmidt, 10 ½ In.	90.00
Clock, Alarm, Roy & Trigger, Insert, Ingraham, Box, 1950s, 3 ½ x 3 ½ In.	351.00
Game, 2 Ring Toss, 4 Horseshoes, Tin Lithograph, Ohio Art, 1950s	55.00
Gloves, Leather, Fringe, Cuffs, c.1950, Size 5	155.00
Gun, Cap, Tuck-A-Way	94.00
Hat, Dale Evans, Queen Of The West, Wool, Size Medium, 1950s *illus*	117.00
Holster Set, Double, 2 Cap Guns, Box, 10 ½ In.	995.00
Lamp, Graphic Shade, White Trigger, Fence Rail, Elasto Mfg., 1950s, 8 ½ x 9 In.	230.00
Lamp, Roy, Riding Trigger, Waving, Molded Hat, Guns, Hartland, 22 In. *illus*	410.00
Lunch Box, Roy Rogers & Dale Evans, Double Bar Ranch, Thermos, 1953, 8 ½ In.	253.00
Lunch Box, Roy Rogers Saddlebag, Trigger, Thermos, Metal, 8 In.	345.00

Roy Rogers, Hat, Dale Evans, Queen Of The West, Wool, Size Medium, 1950s
$117.00

Roy Rogers, Lamp, Roy, Riding Trigger, Waving, Molded Hat, Guns, Hartland, 22 In.
$410.00

TIP
Brush fur in the direction it grows. If brushed the other way, the hairs will break off.

R

Royal Bayreuth, Mug, Elk, Antler Handle, Blue Mark, 5 ¾ In. $75.00

Royal Bayreuth, Wall Pocket, Red Clown, Blue Mark, 5 In. $170.00

Royal Bonn, Vase, Persian Style, Round Body, Stamped, 8 ¼ In. $118.00

Magazine Cover, Movie Life, With Dale Evans, 1948	35.00
Nodder, Roy, Hand On Gun At Hip, Box, 3 x 3 In.	206.00
Pants, Denim, Autograph, Cotton, Waist 26, Inseam 28, Holster Shape Label, 1950s, Size 12	253.00
Puppet, Gabby Hayes, Rubber Head, White Beard, Blue Upturned Hat, c.1949	200.00
Puzzle, Roy Roping Calf, Frame Tray Inlay, Whitman, 1950s, 15 x 11 ½ In.	63.00
Sign, Trigger, Cardboard, Certificate, Hartland, Original Package, c.1960, 7 x 11 ½ In.	221.00
Stamp, Branding Iron Form, Metal, 7 x 2 In. Diam.	35.00
Sweater, Virgin Wool, Parker Boyswear	94.00
Wristwatch, Roy Rogers, Gold, Leather Straps, Box, 5 ¼ In.	278.00

ROYAL BAYREUTH is the name of a factory that was founded in Tettau, Bavaria, in 1794. It has continued to modern times. The marks have changed through the years. A stylized crest, the name *Royal Bayreuth,* and the word *Bavaria* appear in slightly different forms from 1870 to about 1919. Later dishes may include the words *U.S. Zone,* the year of the issue, or the word *Germany* instead of *Bavaria.* Related pieces may be found listed in the Rose Tapestry, Sand Babies, Snow Babies, and Sunbonnet Babies categories.

Ashtray, Eagle, Handle Head, Green Mark, 5 ½ In.	150.00
Basket, White Rose, White Ground, 5 ¼ In.	25.00
Bowl, Cavalier Tavern Scene, Blue Mark, 10 ½ In.	275.00
Bowl, Maiden, Basket Of Flowers, Scalloped Rim, Gilt, Marked, 10 ½ In.	120.00
Cake Plate, Little Jack Horner, Cutout Handles, Bavaria, 10 ½ In.	138.00
Cake Plate, Polar Bear Scene, Handles, 10 ½ In.	1700.00
Candleholder, Clown, Seated, Holding Gray Hat, Orange Suit, 3 x 6 In.	138.00
Candleholder, Girl, Victorian Dress, Puppy, 2 Fingerholes, Painted, 3 ½ In., Pair	995.00
Candleholder, Little Jack Horner Rhyme, Blue Mark, 5 In.	230.00
Candleholder, Red Clown, 3 ½ x 6 In.	75.00
Charger, Hunter Shooting Game, Marked, c.1900, 11 ¼ In.	354.00
Chocolate Pot, Poppy, Red, Green Base, Handle, Blue Mark, 8 ½ In.	725.00
Creamer, Cat, Black, Seated, Marked, Royal Bayreuth Bavaria, 4 ½ In.	128.00
Creamer, Devil & Cards, 3 ¾ In.	197.00
Creamer, Dog, Poodle, Gray, Marked, Royal Bayreuth Bavaria, 4 ½ In.	128.00
Creamer, Eagle, Marked, Royal Bayreuth Bavaria, 3 ½ In.	140.00
Creamer, Fish Head, Gray, White, Marked, Royal Bayreuth Bavaria, 4 In.	98.00
Creamer, Lemon, Marked, Royal Bayreuth Bavaria, 4 In.	98.00
Creamer, Monk, Brown, Yellow, Marked, Royal Bayreuth & Deponiert, 4 In.	182.00
Creamer, Orange, Marked, Royal Bayreuth Bavaria, 4 In.	108.00
Creamer, Pansy, Purple, Green, Marked, Royal Bayreuth Bavaria, 3 ½ In.	88.00
Creamer, Pig, Seated, Gray, Marked, Royal Bayreuth Bavaria, 4 In.	158.00
Creamer, Seal, Gray, Marked, Royal Bayreuth Bavaria, 4 In.	148.00
Creamer, Stylized Parrot, Pierced Border, Blue Mark, 3 ¼ In.	50.00
Creamer, Water Buffalo, Black, Red, Marked, Royal Bayreuth Bavaria, 4 ¾ In.	118.00
Cup, Demitasse, Devil & Dice, 2 ¼ In.	175.00
Ewer, Nymph Sitting On Rock, Green, Handle, 8 ½ In.	325.00
Humidor, Man With Pipe, Marked, 7 In.	725.00
Match Holder, Clown, Red Outfit, White, Marked, Royal Bayreuth Bavaria, 5 In.	248.00
Mug, Elk, Antler Handle, Blue Mark, 5 ¾ In. .... *illus*	75.00
Mug, Little Boy Blue, 3 In.	80.00
Pitcher, Devil & Cards, Orange Lucifer Hugs Face Playing Cards, 5 In.	173.00
Pitcher, Fox Hunt, Green Ground, 8 ½ In.	65.00
Pitcher, Jack & The Beanstalk, 4 ¼ In.	175.00
Pitcher, Lemon, Blue Mark, 6 ½ In.	350.00
Pitcher, Sailboat, Gray, Brown, 4 ¼ In.	75.00
Pitcher, Saint Bernard Head, 3 In.	100.00
Pitcher, Standing Eagle, c.1900, 4 ½ In.	118.00
Salt & Pepper, Corn, Yellow, Green, 2 ¾ In.	300.00
Shoe, Man's, Brown, Black Stitching, Blue Mark, 5 In.	1600.00
Stein, Devil & Cards, 4 ½ In.	300.00
Toothpick, Yellow Rose, 2 ¼ In.	110.00
Tray, Fisherman, Trees, Birds, Scalloped Rim, Royal Bayreuth Bavaria, 8 x 11 In.	130.00
Tray, Relish, Rose Tapestry, Handles, 8 In.	100.00
Vase, Hummingbird, Pierced Border, 4 Handles, 7 ¾ In.	250.00
Vase, Nymph Sitting On Bench, Green, 6 ½ x 5 In.	400.00
Vase, Nymph Sitting On Rock, Cobalt Blue, 4 ½ In.	375.00
Vase, Nymph Sitting On Rock, Cobalt Blue Bands, Iridescent & Gold Stencils, Bulbous, 5 x 5 In.	400.00
Vase, Nymph Sitting On Rock, Green, Reticulated Rim, 7 ½ In. .... 330.00 to 375.00
Vase, Polar Bear, 4 ½ In.	650.00

Vase, Polar Bear, 5 ½ In.	1000.00
Vase, Polar Bear, 6 ¼ In.	1200.00
Vase, Waterfall & Cottage, Pierced, 2 Handles, Blue Mark, 8 ¼ In.	350.00
Wall Pocket, Chimpanzee, Black, White, Gray, 5 ¼ In.	350.00
Wall Pocket, Man Cutting Hay, c.1900, 8 ¾ In.	354.00
Wall Pocket, Red Clown, Blue Mark, 5 In. .... *illus*	170.00

ROYAL BONN is the nineteenth- and twentieth-century trade name used by Franz Anton Mehlem, who had a pottery in Bonn, Germany, from 1836 to 1931. Porcelain and earthenware were made. The factory was purchased by Villeroy & Boch in 1921 and closed in 1931. Many marks were used, most including the name Bonn, the initials FM, and a crown. Royal Bonn made many clock cases and they are listed in the Clock category.

Clock, Ansonia, Blue & White, Flowers, 10 In.	127.00
Clock, Ansonia, La Charny, 8-Day Time & Strike, Porcelain Dial, c.1905, 11 ½ In.	253.00
Clock, Ansonia, La Marm, Green, Flowers, Open Escapement, 2 x 14 In.	400.00
Clock, Ansonia, La Nord, 8-Day Time, Strike, Signed, Wood Base, c.1900, 12 x 14 In.	353.00
Clock, Ansonia, Scrolled Shape, Painted Flowers, Gold Trim, 15 x 9 In.	58.00
Dish, Bonbon, Red Flowers, Gilt, 4-Footed, Handles, 6 ½ In.	150.00
Dish, Cheese, Cover, Orchids, Impressed Mark, 6 x 7 ½ In.	59.00
Ewer, Flowers, Cream Ground, 1900s, 8 ¾ In.	67.00
Ewer, Portrait Of Young Woman, Marked, c.1900, 14 ½ In.	294.00
Letter Holder, Dutch Farm Scene, White With Blue, Rococo Style, 7 ¾ x 4 ½ In.	300.00
Plate, Dutch Pattern, Allover Floral, Rust & Green, c.1890	250.00
Punch Bowl, Flowers, Garlands, Blue, White, Footed, 9 ¼ x 17 In.	360.00
Urn, Cover, Gold Pineapple Finial, Cobalt Blue, Pink, Yellow Roses, 38 In.	2588.00
Vase, 2 Handles, Seminude Woman Looking At Pond, Marked, c.1900, 10 ¼ In.	708.00
Vase, Bird, Gold Overlay & Sun, Fall Leaves, 6 In.	245.00
Vase, Flowers, Hand Painted, Gilt, Large & Small Handle, Late 1800s, 8 ½ In.	135.00
Vase, Green Ground, Yellow Rose, Brass Frame, Handles, 19 ¼ In.	425.00
Vase, Maiden, On Brick Wall, 4-Leaf Clover Band, Gilt, Signed, 19 In.	720.00
Vase, Persian Style, Round Body, Stamped, 8 ¼ In. .... *illus*	118.00
Vase, Pinched Neck, Ruffled Rim, Roses, Scrolling Handles, c.1900, 15 ¼ In.	354.00
Vase, Portrait, Art Nouveau, Young Woman, Signed, H. Wicharz, 7 ¾ In.	59.00
Vase, Rose Design, Dark Green, 10 In.	175.00
Vase, Round Body, Persian Style Design, Blue, Iron Red, Taupe, Marked, 8 ¼ In.	118.00
Vase, Tapered, 2 Handles, Gilded Top & Base, Nature Scenes, 19th Century, 13 In.	79.00

ROYAL COPENHAGEN porcelain and pottery have been made in Denmark since 1775. The Christmas plate series started in 1908. The figurines with pale blue and gray glazes have remained popular in this century and are still being made. Many other old and new style porcelains are made today.

Bowl, Faience, Yellow, Black Abstract Design, 6 ¾ x 6 ¾ In.	55.00
Bowl, Flora Danica, Pierced Sides, Jagged Rim, Flowers, Multicolored, Handles, 4 x 9 In.	2530.00
Compote, Blue, White, Fluted, Open Lace, 5 ¾ In.	263.00
Compote, Flora Danica, 3-Sided Plate, Blue Flower Center, Trumpet Foot, Gilt, 1900s, 5 x 9 In.	1007.00
Custard Cup, Saucer, Flora Danica, Blue Triple Wave Mark, 3 x 4 In. .... *illus*	702.00
Dessert Service, Flora Danica, Cake Plate, Sauce Dish, 8 ¾ & 9 ¾ In., 14 Piece	6756.00
Figurine, 2 Children With Dog, Marked, Initial, G.E., 5 ½ x 6 In.	95.00
Figurine, 2 Females, 1 Nude, 1 In Exotic Dress With Fan, Shaped Base, 9 In.	837.00
Figurine, Boy With Umbrellas, 7 In.	54.00
Figurine, Crane, Openwork Reeds, Leaves, 11 ¼ & 10 ¾ In., Pair	384.00
Figurine, Danish Girl, Seated, Green Dress, White Apron, Red Hair, 5 In.	117.00
Figurine, Elephant, Raised Trunk, Brown & Black Glaze, Mottled, Marked, 3 ½ In.	115.00
Figurine, Falcon, Underglaze Blue Wave Marks, 15 ½ In. .... *illus*	598.00
Figurine, Foal, Lying Down, Brown, Tan & Black Glaze, Mottled, Kyhn, 6 ⅜ In.	115.00
Figurine, Girl Knitting, 6 In.	58.00
Figurine, Girl With Goose, 9 In.	47.00
Figurine, Goat, Seated, 1940, 11 ¼ In.	237.00
Figurine, Pan, On Goat, Glazed, Marked, 8 ¼ In.	325.00
Figurine, Pheasant, 8 x 12 In.	240.00
Figurine, Polar Bear, Looking Down, 5 ¾ x 8 In.	255.00
Figurine, Polar Bear, Mouth Open, 12 ¾ In.	340.00
Figurine, Polar Bear, On Hind Legs, 12 ¾ In.	359.00
Figurine, Snowy Owl, Green Molded Leaf Base, 15 ½ In.	598.00
Group, Polar Bear, Seal, 9 x 14 ¼ In.	777.00

Royal Copenhagen, Custard Cup, Saucer, Flora Danica, Blue Triple Wave Mark, 3 x 4 In. $702.00

Royal Copenhagen, Figurine, Falcon, Underglaze Blue Wave Marks, 15 ½ In. $598.00

TIP

Have your paintings "re-keyed" if the canvas seems to be loose. There are small wooden wedges or "keys" at the back of the frame that stretch the canvas. Have a professional framer do the job.

R

Royal Copley, Wall Vase, Boy & Girl, Marked, 6 ¼ In., Pair
$24.00

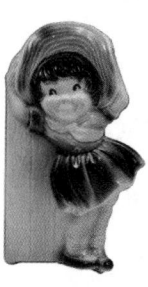

Royal Crown, Dish, Imari, Cobalt, Iron Red, Flowers, Gilt, Hexagonal, Mark, 9 x 9 In.
$63.00

Royal Crown, Figurine, Man & Woman Holding Baskets, Vegetables, Flowers, Gilt, 8 & 7 ¾ In., Pair
$357.00

Royal Doulton, Animal, Mallard, HN 807, 1923-77, 2 ¼ In.
$40.00

Jar, Flower, Blue, White, Putti Finial, Hand Painted, 11 ½ In.	153.00
Plaque, Blue Fish, Brown Clay, Marked, 7 ⅝ x 11 ⅝ In.	288.00
Plate, Christmas, Angel, Praying At Christmas Rose Bush, 1945	148.00
Plate, Christmas, Bird, Eating Berries, Stone Bench, 1919	48.00
Plate, Christmas, Mother & Child, 1908	5490.00
Plate, Christmas, Old Couple Holding Hands, Christmas Tree, 1912, 7 In.	72.00
Plate, Mother, Child, Cradle, Danish Text, c.1907, 7 ¾ In.	325.00
Plate, Mother's Day, Bird & Family, 1975	48.00
Plate, Mother's Day, Daughter Handing Flowers To Mother, 1973	38.00
Plate, Mother's Day, Doe & Fawns, 1975	69.00
Plate, Mother's Day, Eskimo Family, Dogs, 1974, 6 In.	18.00 to 30.00
Plate, Mother's Day, Mother Holding Child's Hand, Cat & Kitten, 1971, 6 In.	9.50
Plate, Mother's Day, Oriental Mother, 5 Children, 1972	38.00
Platter, Flora Danica, Cinched Rectangle Shape, Grass Plant Center, Gilt, 1900s, 12 In.	770.00
Sugar, Cover, Flowers, Multicolored, Rose Finial, Gilt, 3 ½ In.	89.00
Teapot, Flowers, Leaves, Mask Spout, Reticulated Lid, Blue, White, 8 ¾ In.	155.00
Tureen, Underplate, Blue, Fluted, Half Lace, 14 & 17 In.	380.00
Vase, Bird & Flowers, Mark, 4 ½ In.	17.00
Vase, Blue & White, Lattice Pattern, Scalloped Base, Denmark, 4 x 3 In.	117.00
Vase, Blue, Black, Mottled, Faiance, J. Gerber, c.1950, 14 In.	205.00
Vase, Boat, In Harbor, City Skyline, Signed, Marked, 12 In.	280.00
Vase, Branch, Blackberries, Blossoms, Marked, 9 In.	57.00
Vase, Owl, 8 In.	111.00

ROYAL COPLEY china was made by the Spaulding China Company of Sebring, Ohio, from 1939 to 1960. The figural planters and the small figurines, especially those with Art Deco designs, are of great collector interest.

Wall Vase, Boy & Girl, Marked, 6 ¼ In., Pair .... *illus*	24.00

ROYAL CROWN DERBY COMPANY, LTD., is a name used on porcelain beginning in 1890. There is a complex family tree that includes the Derby, Crown Derby, and Royal Crown Derby porcelains. The Royal Crown Derby mark includes the name and a crown. The words *Made in England* were used after 1921. The company is now privately owned.

Bowl, Centerpiece, Old Imari, No. 1128, 11 In.	563.00
Bowl, Old Imari, 8-Sided, No. 1128, 4 x 9 ½ In.	375.00
Bowl, Old Imari, Fluted Rim, Footed, Handles, No. 1128	495.00
Creamer, Sugar, Lid, Duesbury, Fluted, Blue Underglaze, Gilt, c.1775, 5 x 5 In.	235.00
Cup & Saucer, Demitasse, Cobalt Blue, Gilt, White Ground, 12 Piece	138.00
Dish, 3 Sections, Red & White Flowers, Cobalt Blue Ground, Gilt, 10 ½ In.	290.00
Dish, Cover, Chrysanthemum, Crown Finial, Abbeydale, 7 ½ x 8 ½ In.	465.00
Dish, Imari, Cobalt, Iron Red, Flowers, Gilt, Hexagonal, Mark, 9 x 9 In. .... *illus*	63.00
Figurine, Man & Woman Holding Baskets, Vegetables, Flowers, Gilt, 8 & 7 ¾ In., Pair .... *illus*	357.00
Goblet, Old Imari, 4 ¾ In.	82.00
Ladle, Imari	230.00
Paperweight, Friesian Cow, Boxed	81.00
Platter, Japan Pattern, Blue, Red, Gilt, c.1820, 23 x 17 ½ In.	999.00
Server, Lid, Undertray, Blue Flowers, White Ground, Gold Trim, 8 x 7 In.	70.00
Teapot, Fluted, Gilt, Painted Overglaze, Flowers, Gold Finial, c.1800, 7 x 9 In.	176.00
Tray, Old Imari, Oval, No. 1128, 13 In.	225.00
Vase, Ruby Ground, Gilded Flowers, Lid, 1891, 7 ½ x 4 ¼ In.	450.00

ROYAL DOULTON is the name used on Doulton and Company pottery made from 1902 to the present. Doulton and Company of England was founded in 1853. Pieces made before 1902 are listed in this book under Doulton. Royal Doulton collectors search for the out-of-production figurines, character jugs, vases, and series wares. Some vases and animal figurines were made with a special red glaze called flambe. Sung and Chang glazed pieces are rare. The multicolored glaze is very thick and looks as if it were dropped on the clay. In 2005 Royal Doulton was acquired by the Waterford Wedgwood Group, which was bought by KPS Capital Partners of New York in 2009 and became part of WWRD Holdings.

Animal, Dog, Bulldog, HN 1074, White, 1932-85, 3 ¼ In.	74.00
Animal, Dog, Bulldog Puppy, K 2, 1931-77, 2 In.	24.00
Animal, Dog, Cairn Terrier, HN 1035, 1931-85, 3 ¼ In.	73.00
Animal, Dog, Cocker Spaniel, Pheasant In Mouth, HN 1138, 1937-85, 5 ½ In.	58.00
Animal, Duck, Mallard, Drake, HN 807, 1923-77, 2 ¼ In. ....*illus*	40.00

R

Animal, Rabbits, Black & White, HN 969, 1928-46, 3 ½ In.	359.00
Ashtray, Marston, Thompson & Evershed Ltd., Art Deco, c.1925, 4 x 4 In.	20.00

Royal Doulton character jugs depict the head and shoulders of the subject. They are made in four sizes: large, 5 ¼ to 7 inches; small, 3 ¼ to 4 inches; miniature, 2 ¼ to 2 ½ inches; and tiny, 1 ¼ inches. Toby jugs portray a seated, full figure.

Character Jug, Arriet, D 6208, 1947-60, Large	57.00
Character Jug, Arry, D 6207, 1947-60, Large	57.00
Character Jug, Auld Mac, D 5823, 1937-86, Large	95.00
Character Jug, Bahamas Policeman, D 6912, 1992, Large	115.00
Character Jug, Beefeater, D 56202, 1947-53, Large	56.00
Character Jug, Cavalier With Goatee, D 6114, 1940-50, Large	1750.00
Character Jug, Churchill, D 6170, 1940-41, Large	1400.00
Character Jug, Clown, White Hair, D 6322, 1951-55, Large	442.00
Character Jug, Confucius, Flambe, D 7003, 1995, 7 ½ In.	140.00
Character Jug, Falstaff, D 6287, 1950-95, Large	40.00
Character Jug, Farmer John, D 5789, Small	*illus* 50.00
Character Jug, Fortune Teller, D 6497, 1959-67, Large	198.00
Character Jug, Fortune Teller, D 6503, 1959-67, Small	74.00
Character Jug, George Tinworth, D 7000, 1995-96, Small	33.00
Character Jug, Gondolier, D 6589, 1964-69, 8 In.	104.00 to 179.00
Character Jug, Granny, D 5521, 1935-41, Large	3501.00
Character Jug, Henry V, D6671, 1982-84, Large	66.00
Character, Jug, Henry VIII, D 6642, 1975-2000, Large	150.00
Character Jug, Jesse Owens, D7019, c.1996, Large	135.00
Character Jug, Lobster Man, D 6617, 1968-91, Large	85.00
Character Jug, Mae West, D 6688, 1983-86, Large	41.00 to 73.00
Character Jug, Mephistopheles, D 5758, 1940, 3 ¼ In.	354.00
Character Jug, Neptune, D 6548, 1961-91, Large	110.00
Character Jug, Old Charley, D 5420, 1934-83, Large	100.00
Character, Jug, Old Salt, D 6551, 1961-2001, Large	150.00
Character Jug, Paddy, D 5768, 1937-60, Small	33.00
Character Jug, Pearly Boy, Blue, 1947, Large	1263.00 to 3501.00
Character Jug, Pearly Boy, Brown, Small	621.00
Character Jug, Pearly Girl, 1946, Large	2918.00
Character Jug, Pharaoh, Flambe, D 7028, 1996, 7 ½ In.	253.00
Character Jug, Robin Hood, D 6527, 1960-92, Large	118.00
Character Jug, Sam Johnson, D 6289, 1950-60, Large	40.00
Character Jug, Santa Claus, D 6675, Reindeer Handle, 1982, Large	66.00
Character Jug, Santa Claus, D 6690, Sack Of Toys Handle, 1983, Large	66.00
Character Jug, Smuggler, D 6616, 1968-81, Large	200.00
Character Jug, Snake Charmer, D 6912, 1992, Large	115.00
Character Jug, The Mikado, D 6501, 1959-69, Large	179.00
Character, Jug, The Poacher, D 6429, 1955-95, Large	100.00
Character Jug, Town Crier, D 6895, 1991-94, Large	58.00
Character Jug, Viking, D 6496, 1959-75, Large	49.00 to 58.00
Character Jug, William Shakespeare, D 6933, 2 Handles, 1992, Large	107.00
Character Jug, Yeoman Of The Guard, D 6883, Limited Edition, 1990, Large	259.00
Charger, Dickens, Tony Weller, 13 ½ In.	*illus* 55.00
Figurine, A Good Catch, HN 2258, 1966-86, 7 ¼ In.	73.00
Figurine, Abdullah, HN 2104, 1953-62, 6 In.	173.00
Figurine, Adrienne, HN 2304, 1964-91, 7 ½ In.	*illus* 100.00
Figurine, Afternoon Tea, HN 1747, 1935-82, 5 ¾ In.	200.00
Figurine, Aileen, HN 1645, 1934-38, 6 ¼ In.	600.00
Figurine, Aileen, HN 1664, 1938, 6 In.	978.00
Figurine, All Aboard, HN 2940, 1982-86, 9 ¼ In.	114.00
Figurine, Antoinette, HN 2326, 1967-79, 6 ¼ In.	70.00
Figurine, Autumn Breezes, HN 1911, 1939-76, 7 ½ In.	58.00 to 132.00
Figurine, Autumn Breezes, HN 2147, 1955-71, 7 ½ In.	69.00
Figurine, Babie, HN 1679, 1935-92, 4 ¾ In.	23.00
Figurine, Baby Bunting, HN 2108, 1953-59, 5 ¼ In.	80.00
Figurine, Balloon Seller, HN 1315, 1928-98, 7 ½ In.	146.00
Figurine, Barbara, HN 2962, 1982-84, 8 In.	70.00
Figurine, Bedtime, HN 1978, 1945-97, 5 ¾ In.	29.00
Figurine, Blacksmith, HN 2240, 1960-83, 6 ¾ In.	46.00
Figurine, Blithe Morning, HN 2021, 1949-71, 7 ½ In.	*illus* 215.00

Royal Doulton, Character Jug, Farmer John, D 5789, Small
$50.00

Royal Doulton, Charger, Dickens, Tony Weller, 13 ½ In.
$55.00

Bunnykins

Bunnykins children's dishes have been popular—and in production—since Royal Doulton introduced them in 1934. The bunny characters on the dishes were based on drawings by Sister Barbara Vernon, a nun whose father was manager of the famous Royal Doulton Pottery in Stoke-on-Trent, England. The success of Bunnykins dishes led to the introduction of six Bunnykins earthenware figurines in 1939. Production of the figurines stopped during World War II. It started up again in 1972. Royal Doulton has made more than 250 Bunnykins figurines. Some were commissioned for special events, such as the 1984 Summer Olympics (Olympic Bunnykins, DB28), or made in limited editions for collectors. The figurines are still being made.

R

ROYAL DOULTON

Royal Doulton, Figurine, Adrienne, HN 2304, 1964-91, 7 ½ In. $100.00

Royal Doulton, Figurine, Blithe Morning, HN 2021, 1949-71, 7 ½ In. $215.00

Royal Doulton, Figurine, Fox, Curled, Red Glaze, c.1920, 1 ¾ In. $300.00

Royal Doulton, Figurine, Huckleberry Finn, HN 2927, 1982-85, 7 In. $259.00

Figurine, Blithe Morning, HN 2065, 71950-73, 7 ¼ In.	69.00
Figurine, Blossom, HN 1667, 1934-49, 6 ¾ In.	1093.00
Figurine, Bluebeard, HN 1528, 1932-49, 11 ½ In.	546.00
Figurine, Bonnie Lassie, HN 1626, 1934-53, 5 ¼ In.	288.00
Figurine, Bride, HN 1600, 1933-49, 8 ¾ In.	633.00
Figurine, Bride, HN 2166, 1955, 8 In.	120.00
Figurine, Broken Lance, HN 2041, 1949-75, 8 ¾ In.	228.00
Figurine, Bunnykins, Basketball, DB 262	33.00
Figurine, Bunnykins, Daisie, Bunnykins, DB 7, 1972-83, 3 ½ In.	49.00
Figurine, Bunnykins, Daytrip, DB 260, Box, 3 ½ In.	66.00
Figurine, Bunnykins, Farmer, D 6003, 1939-40, 7 ½ In.	1285.00
Figurine, Bunnykins, Goalkeeper, DB 122, Box, 1991, 4 ½ In.	363.00
Figurine, Bunnykins, Touchdown, DB 98, 1990, 3 ½ In.	313.00
Figurine, Camille, HN 1586, 1933-49, 6 ½ In.	299.00
Figurine, Carpenter, HN 2678, 1986-92, 8 In.	130.00
Figurine, Carpet Seller, HN 1464, 1929, 9 ¼ In.	115.00
Figurine, Carpet Seller, HN 2776, 1990-95, 9 In.	184.00
Figurine, Cavalier, HN 2716, 1976-82, 9 ¾ In.	46.00
Figurine, Cellist, HN 2226, 1960-67, 8 In.	115.00
Figurine, Charlotte, HN 2421, 1972-86, 6 ½ In.	69.00
Figurine, China Repairer, HN 2943, 1982-88, 6 ¾ In.	58.00
Figurine, Choir Boy, HN 2141, 1954-75, 4 ¾	29.00
Figurine, Christmas Time, HN 2110, 1953-67, 6 ½ In.	46.00
Figurine, Cleopatra, HN 2868, 1979, 7 ¼ In.	920.00
Figurine, Clothilde, HN 1599, 1933-49, 7 ¼ In.	403.00
Figurine, Collinette, HN 1999, 1947-49, 7 ¼ In.	161.00
Figurine, Columbine, HN 2738, 1982, 12 ½ In.	460.00
Figurine, Confucious, Flambe, HN 3314, 1990-95, 9 In.	115.00
Figurine, Country Maid, HN 3163, 1988-91, 8 ¼ In.	138.00
Figurine, Court Jester, HN 3335, 1990, 4 In.	86.00
Figurine, Cup Of Tea, HN 2322, 1964-83, 7 In.	59.00 to 65.00
Figurine, Curly Knob, HN 1627, 1934-49, 6 In.	460.00
Figurine, Daydreams, HN 1731, 1935-92, 5 ¾ In.	81.00
Figurine, Dorcas, HN 1558, 1933-52, 6 ¾ In.	184.00
Figurine, Drummer Boy, HN 2679, 1976-81, 8 ½ In.	127.00
Figurine, Easter Day, HN 2039, 1949-69, 7 ¼ In.	127.00 to 165.00
Figurine, Eastern Grace, Flambe, HN 3683, 1995, 12 ½ In.	207.00
Figurine, Elfreda, HN 2078, 1951-55, 7 ¼ In.	374.00
Figurine, Ellen Terry, HN 3826, 1996, 9 In.	81.00
Figurine, Elyse, HN 2429, 1972-95, 5 ¾ In.	52.00
Figurine, Ermine Coat, HN 1981, 1945-67, 6 ¾ In.	89.00 to 195.00
Figurine, Fiddler, HN 2171, 1956-62, 8 ¾ In.	633.00
Figurine, Fiona, HN 1924, 1925-33, 5 ¾ In.	805.00
Figurine, Flora, HN 2349, 1966-73, 7 ¾ In.	77.00 to 114.00
Figurine, Flower Seller's, Children, HN 1206, 1926-49, 8 ¼ In.	805.00
Figurine, Flower Seller's, Children, HN 1342, 1929-93, 8 In.	219.00
Figurine, Foaming Quart., HN 2162, 1955-92, 6 In.	106.00
Figurine, Folly, HN 1750, 1936-49, 8 ½ In.	1380.00
Figurine, Forgot-Me-Not, HN 1813, 1937-49, 6 In.	104.00
Figurine, Fortune Teller, HN 2159, 1955-67, 6 ½ In.	173.00 to 264.00
Figurine, Forty Winks, HN 1974, 1945-73, 6 ¾ In.	58.00
Figurine, Fox, Curled, Red Glaze, c.1920, 1 ¾ In. ....*illus*	300.00
Figurine, Frangcon, HN 1720, 1935-49, 7 ½ In.	1840.00
Figurine, Geisha, Flambe, HN 3229, 1989, 9 ½ In.	150.00
Figurine, Genevieve, HN 1962, 1941-75, 7 ½ In.	82.00
Figurine, Genie, HN 2989, 1983-90, 9 ¾ In.	99.00
Figurine, Georgiana, HN 2093, 1952-55, 8 ¼ In.	978.00
Figurine, Good King Wenceslas, HN 2118, 1953-76, 8 ½ In.	98.00 to 138.00
Figurine, Hinged Parasol, HN 1578, 1933-49, 6 ½ In.	450.00 to 805.00
Figurine, Honey, HN 1910, 1939-49, 6 ¾ In.	495.00
Figurine, Hornpipe, 1955-62, 9 ¼ In.	489.00
Figurine, Huckleberry Finn, HN 2927, 1982-85, 7 In. ....*illus*	259.00
Figurine, Ibrihim, HN 2095, 1952-55, 7 ¾ In.	138.00
Figurine, Jack Point, HN 2080, 1952, 16 ¼ In.	978.00
Figurine, Jasmine, HN 1862, 1939-49, 7 ¼ In.	1150.00
Figurine, Jester, HN 2016, 1949-97, 10 In.	100.00 to 150.00
Figurine, Jolly Sailor, HN 2172, 1956-65, 6 ½ In.	460.00

Figurine, Katie Hardcastle, HN 1719, 1935-49, 8 In.	518.00
Figurine, Lady April, HN 1958, 1940-59, 7 In.	92.00 to 205.00
Figurine, Lady Farye, HN 1265, 1928-38, 5 ¼ In.	374.00
Figurine, Laird, HN 2361, 1969-2001, 8 In.	92.00
Figurine, Land Girl, HN 4361, 2001, 8 ¾ In.	294.00
Figurine, Lesley, HN 2410, 1986-90, 8 In.	52.00
Figurine, Lilac Time, HN 2137, 1954-69, 7 ¼ In.	89.00
Figurine, Linda, HN 2758, 1984-88, 7 ¾ In.	59.00
Figurine, Little Bridesmaid, HN 1433, 1930-51, 5 ¼ In.	92.00
Figurine, Lizana, HN 1756, 1936-49, 8 ½ In.	748.00
Figurine, Lobster Man, HN 2317, 1964-94, 7 ¼ In.	81.00
Figurine, Loretta, HN 2337, 1966-81, 7 ¾ In.	46.00
Figurine, Lunchtime, HN 2485, 1973-81, 8 In.	89.00
Figurine, Margery, HN 1413, 1930-49, 10 ¾ In.	190.00
Figurine, Marjorie, HN 2788, 5 In. ....*illus*	100.00
Figurine, Mask Seller, HN 2103, 1953-95, 8 ½ In.	89.00 to 92.00
Figurine, Masquerade, Man, HN 636, 1924-36, 6 ¾ In.	978.00
Figurine, Masquerade, Woman, HN 637, 1924-38, 6 ¾ In.	978.00
Figurine, Maureen, Woman, HN 1770, 1936-59, 7 ½ In.	146.00
Figurine, Meditation, HN 2330, 1971-83, 5 ¾ In.	70.00
Figurine, Mendicant, HN 1365, 1929-69, 8 ¼ In.	69.00 to 81.00
Figurine, Michele, HN2234, 1967-93, 7 In.	82.00
Figurine, Miranda, HN 3037, 1987-90, 8 ½ In.	92.00
Figurine, Mirror, HN 1852, 1938-49, 7 ½ In.	2530.00
Figurine, Miss Demure, HN 1402, 1930-75, 7 ½ In.	81.00
Figurine, Moon Dancer, HN 3181, 1988-90, 11 ¾ In.	81.00
Figurine, Moor, HN 4646, 2005, 10 ½ In.	288.00
Figurine, Moorish Minstrel, HN 34, 1913-38, 13 ½ In.	2233.00
Figurine, My Love, HN 2339, 1969-96, 6 ¼ In.	118.00 to 120.00
Figurine, Napoleon, HN 3429, 1992, 11 ½ In.	621.00
Figurine, Nicola, HN 2804, Box, 1987, 7 In.	52.00 to 120.00
Figurine, Ninette, HN 2379, 1971-97, 7 ½	32.00
Figurine, Noelle, HN 2179, 1957-67, 6 ¾ In.	210.00 to 242.00
Figurine, Odds & Ends, HN 1844, 1938-49, 7 ¾ In.	1380.00
Figurine, Old Balloon Seller, HN 1315, 1929-78, 7 ½ In.	69.00 to 86.00
Figurine, Old Lavender Seller, HN 1492, 1932-49, 6 In.	460.00
Figurine, Omar Khayyam, HN 2247, 1965-83, 6 In.	69.00 to 117.00
Figurine, Orange Lady, HN 1759, 1936-75, 8 ¾ In.	81.00
Figurine, Orange Lady, HN 1953, 1940-75, 8 ½ In.	106.00
Figurine, Organ Grinder, HN 2173, 1956-65, 8 ¾ In.	575.00
Figurine, Paisley Shawl, HN 1987, 1946-59, 8 ¼ In.	69.00
Figurine, Pamela, HN 1469, 1931-37, 7 ½ In.	1035.00
Figurine, Pamela, HN 3223, 1989, 7 In.	118.00 to 120.00
Figurine, Parson's Daughter, HN 564, 1923-49, 9 ½ In.	299.00
Figurine, Patchwork Quilt, HN 1984, 1945-59, 6 In.	140.00
Figurine, Pauline, HN 2441, 1984-89, 5 In.	90.00 to 95.00
Figurine, Phyllis, HN 1420, 1930-49, 9 In.	633.00
Figurine, Piper, HN 2907, 1980-92, 8 In.	81.00
Figurine, Polka, HN 2156, 1955-69, 8 In.	70.00
Figurine, Potter, HN 1493, 1932-92, 7 In. ....*illus*	196.00
Figurine, Professor, HN 2281, 1965-81, 7 ¼ In.	69.00
Figurine, Puppetmaker, HN 2253, 1962-73, 8 In.	150.00
Figurine, Rag Doll, HN 2142, 1954-75, 4 ¾ In.	12.00
Figurine, Rag Doll Seller, HN 2944, 1983-95, 7 In.	106.00 to 115.00
Figurine, Railway Sleeper, HN 4418, 2001, 7 In.	114.00
Figurine, Ritz Bell Boy, HN 2772, 1989-93, 8 In.	81.00
Figurine, Robin Hood, HN 2773, 1985-90, 8 In.	89.00
Figurine, Romany Sue, HN 1757, 1936-49, 9 ½ In.	1265.00
Figurine, Rose, HN 1368, 1930-95, 4 ½ In.	23.00
Figurine, Rosebud, HN 1581, 1933-38, 3 In.	460.00
Figurine, Rosina, HN 1358, 1929-37, 5 ¾ In.	311.00
Figurine, Rowena, HN 2077, 1951-55, 7 ½ In.	173.00
Figurine, Royal Governor's Cook, HN 2233, 1958-81, 6 In.	138.00
Figurine, Sabbath Morn, HN 1982, 1945-59, 7 ¼ In.	81.00
Figurine, Sailor, HN 4632, 2004, 8 ¼ In.	92.00
Figurine, Sailor's Holiday, HN 2442, 1972-79, 6 ¼ In.	115.00
Figurine, Samurai Warrior, Flambe, HN 3402, 1992, 9 In.	180.00

Royal Doulton, Figurine, Marjorie, HN 2788, 5 In. $100.00

Royal Doulton, Figurine, Potter, HN 1493, 1932-92, 7 In. $196.00

Royal Doulton, Figurine, Top O' The Hill, Red, HN 1834, 1937-2010, 7 In. $375.00

R

Royal Doulton, Vase, Babes In Woods, Spring, Woman & Girl, Basket, In Meadow, 16 ¾ In. $2000.00

Royal Doulton, Vase, Flambe, Castle, Meadow, Trees, Daisies, Marked, Logo, Charles Noke, 7 ¾ In.
$259.00

Royal Doulton, Vase, Stoneware, Painted, Blue, Yellow, Grapes, Flowers, 6 x 5 ½ In.
$46.00

Royal Doulton, Wall Mask, Jester, c.1937, 11 In.
$150.00

Royal Dux, Figurine, Elephant, Trunk Up, Green To Brown Matte Glaze, c.1900, 13 x 16 In.
$368.00

Figurine, Seafarer, HN 2455, 1972-76, 8 ½ In.	122.00
Figurine, Shepherd, HN 1975, 1945-75, 8 ½ In.	92.00
Figurine, Shore Leave, HN 2254, 1965-79, 7 ½ In.	110.00
Figurine, Silks & Ribbons, HN 2017, 1949-2001, 6 In.	81.00
Figurine, Sir Henry Doulton, HN 3891, 1997, 8 ¾ In.	65.00
Figurine, Sleepyhead, HN 2114, 1953-55, 5 In.	1610.00
Figurine, Songs Of The Sea, HN 2729, 1982-91, 7 In.	124.00
Figurine, Sophistication, HN 3059, 1987, 11 ½ In.	58.00
Figurine, Sorcerer, HN 4252, 2000-2002, 9 ¼ In.	219.00
Figurine, Spring Flowers, HN 1807, 1937-59, 7 ¼ In.	104.00
Figurine, Spring Morning, HN 1922, 1940-73, 7 ½ In.	210.00
Figurine, St. George, HN 2051, 1950-85, 7 ½ In.	184.00
Figurine, Summer, HN 2086, 1952-59, 7 ½ In.	110.00
Figurine, Summer's Day, HN 2181, 1957-62, 5 ¾ In.	82.00
Figurine, Sunday Morning, HN 2184, 1963-69, 7 ½ In.	74.00
Figurine, Sweet & Fair, HN 1864, 1938-49, 7 ½ In.	1840.00
Figurine, Sweet & Twenty, HN 1549, 1933-49, 6 In.	460.00 to 690.00
Figurine, Taking Things Easy, HN 2680, 1987-96, 6 ¾ In.	282.00
Figurine, Teatime, HN 2255, 1972-95, 7 In.	71.00
Figurine, This Little Pig, No. 1793, 1936-95, 4 In.	110.00
Figurine, Tinsmith, HN 2146, 1962-67, 6 ½ In.	92.00 to 163.00
Figurine, Top O' The Hill, Red, HN 1834, 1937-2010, 7 In. ...*illus*	375.00
Figurine, Tuppence A Bag, HN 2320, 1968-95, 5 ½ In.	106.00
Figurine, Vera, HN 1729, 1935-40, 4 ¼ In.	345.00
Figurine, Veronica, HN 1517, 1932-51, 8 In.	115.00
Figurine, Victorian Christmas, HN 4675, Box, 2004, 8 ¼ In.	82.00
Figurine, Victorian Lady, HN 727, 1925-38, 7 ½ In.	334.00
Figurine, Victorian Lady, HN 728, 1925-52, 7 ¾ In.	173.00
Figurine, Victorian Lady, HN 1345, 1929-49, 7 ¾ In.	220.00 to 230.00
Figurine, Votes For Women, HN 2816, 1978-81, 9 ¾ In.	161.00
Figurine, Wizard, HN 2877, 1979, 9 ¾ In.	92.00
Figurine, Yeoman Of The Guard, HN 2122, 1954-59, 5 ¾ In.	489.00
Figurine, Young Love, HN 2735, 1975-90, 10 In.	81.00
Figurine, Young Widow, HN 1399, 1930, 8 In.	2415.00
Figurine, Yum-Yum, HN 2899, 1980-85, 10 ¾ In.	276.00
Ginger Jar, Cover, Flambe, Trees, Road, Building, 9 In.	388.00
Humidor, Coaching Days, 3 ¼ x 4 ¾ In.	138.00
Jar, Life In The Forest Of Sherwood, D 3751, 5 ½ In.	150.00
Pitcher, Arabian Nights, 7 ¾ In.	150.00
Pitcher, Compleat Angler, Izaak Walton, St. Dunstan's Church, Mark, 7 ½ In.	171.00
Plaque, Babes In Woods, Woman Crossing Bridge In Snowstorm, 14 x 10 ¾ In.	675.00
Plate, Birds, Chinoiserie, Blue Wrigglework Border, Gold Dots, c.1914, 10 In., 12 Piece	1896.00
Plate, Falstaff & Dame Quickly, I Warrant Thee, Nobody Hears, 10 ½ In.	40.00
Plate, The Parson, 10 ½ In.	60.00
Tea Set, Monks, Teapot, Open Sugar, Creamer, Mark, 5 ¼ & 3 & 3 In.	295.00
Toby Jug, Huntsman, D 6320, 1950-91, 6 ¾ In.	144.00
Toby Jug, Winston Churchill, D 6171, 1941-91, 8 In.	110.00
Vase, Babes In Woods, Girl & Boy, Looking At Tree, Fluted Rim, Oval, 13 x 6 ½ In.	775.00
Vase, Babes In Woods, Spring, Woman & Girl, Basket, In Meadow, 16 ¾ In. ...*illus*	2000.00
Vase, Bird & Butterfly Design, Black Ground, 12 ⅜ In.	60.00
Vase, Flambe, Castle, Meadow, Trees, Daisies, Marked, Logo, Charles Noke, 7 ¾ In. ...*illus*	259.00
Vase, Flambe, Red, Black, Small Opening, 17 In.	920.00
Vase, Incised Decoration, Band, Bird, Leaves, Blue Base, Harry Simeon, c.1920, 15 ¼ In.	705.00
Vase, Stoneware, Painted, Blue, Yellow, Grapes, Flowers, 6 x 5 ½ In. ...*illus*	46.00
Vase, Sung Glaze, Browns, Bottle Shape, C.J. Noke, Fred Moore, c.1920, 6 In., Pair	504.00
Vase, Sung Glaze, Melon Lobed, Short Neck, Charles Noke, Bulbous, c.1935, 6 ½ In.	920.00
Vase, Woman & Girl, White, 8 ¾ In.	360.00
Wall Mask, Jester, c.1937, 11 In. ...*illus*	150.00

ROYAL DUX is the more common name for the Duxer Porzellanmanufaktur, which was founded by E. Eichler in Dux, Bohemia (now Duchov, Czech Republic), in 1860. By the turn of the century, the firm specialized in porcelain statuary and busts of Art Nouveau–style maidens, large porcelain figures, and ornate vases with three-dimensional figures climbing on the sides. The firm is still in business.

Centerpiece, 2 Maidens, Shell, Wave, Lily Pads, Gilt, Black, Signed, 12 x 16 In.	805.00
Centerpiece, Figural, 3 Graces, Maiden Around Tree, Stamped, 20 ¾ In.	353.00

Figurine, Elephant, Tan, Black, High Gloss, Inscribed, Signed, 8 In.	65.00
Figurine, Elephant, Trunk Up, Green To Brown Matte Glaze, c.1900, 13 x 16 In. ....*illus*	368.00
Figurine, Nude Woman, Art Deco Style, 10 In.	398.00
Figurine, Parrot, On Stump, 15 In.	120.00
Figurine, Polar Bear, Pink Triangle Mark, c.1950, 14 x 13 ½ In. ....*illus*	265.00
Figurine, Seal, Gray, High Gloss, Impressed, Cobalt Blue 5, Signed, 7 ½ In.	65.00
Figurine, Seal, Matte Black, Embossed, Incised, Signed, 7 ½ In.	65.00
Figurine, Woman, Basket On Head, Vase At Feet, Marked, 18 In. ....*illus*	250.00
Figurine, Woman, Blue Dress, White Blouse, Hands Holding Hat, Gilt, 9 In.	60.00
Figurine, Woman, Leaning Back, Rectangular Base, Bisque, Marked, 10 x 12 In. ....*illus*	104.00
Group, Farmer, Wife, Child, Rock, Axe, 22 In.	384.00
Group, Man, Holding Fruit, Woman, Carrying Vase, Enamel, 17 ½ In., Pair	889.00
Group, Pierrot & Pierette, 16 In.	499.00
Group, Woman, Dog, Art Deco, 14 ½ In.	235.00
Group, Woman In Carriage, 2 Attendants, Stamped, Raised Pink Triangle, 13 In.	1450.00
Jardiniere, Oblong, Scalloped Rim, Resting Nymph, Daisies, Flowers, Pearl Iridescence, 10 x 18 In.	385.00
Statue, Woman, Peering Into Pond, Purple Iris, Applied Red Diamond, 12 In.	259.00
Statue, Woman, Sitting On Rock, Holding Foot, Mark, 22 In.	690.00
Vase, Bulbous, Flared Rim, Sculpted & Applied Dragons & Waves, Marked, 8 x 13 In.	374.00
Vase, Moose Profile, Pinecones, Flowers, 2 Roundels, Handles, Marked, 16 ½ In.	160.00
Vase, White, Flowers, Leaves, Bulbous Stick, Gold Pierced Handles, 19 In., Pair	403.00

ROYAL FLEMISH glass was made during the late 1880s in New Bedford, Massachusetts, by the Mt. Washington Glass Works. It is a colored satin glass decorated with dark colors and raised gold designs. The glass was patented in 1894. It was supposed to resemble stained glass windows.

Biscuit Jar, Gold & Silver Coins, Multicolored, Silver Plate Cover, 9 ½ In. ....*illus*	3450.00
Biscuit Jar, Stars, Roman Coins, Pairpoint Lid, Collar, Handle, 8 In.	2588.00
Bisquit Jar, Rectangular, Silver, Amber Thistle, Leaves, Embossed Lid, 8 In.	2013.00
Creamer, Roses, Raised Gold Veins, Reed Handle, Paper Label, 2 In.	575.00
Creamer, Square, Painted, Pink & Yellow Wild Roses, 2 In. ....*illus*	978.00
Ewer, Coat Of Arms, Cherubs, Flowers, Applied Handle, Stopper, 19 ½ In.	10350.00
Vase, Hedge, Rose, Bull's-Eye, Raised Gold Panels, Prunts, Flowers, 9 In.	3163.00
Vase, Multicolor, Narrow Neck, Label, c.1865, 11 In. ....*illus*	2760.00
Vase, Reed Handles, Violets, Frosted, Globular, Marked, 5 ⅞ In.	1093.00
Vase, Roman Coins, Trifold Rim, Gold, Amethyst Scrolling, Bulbous, Squat, 8 In.	3738.00
Vase, Roman Coins, Trifold Rim, Gold, Amethyst Scrolling, Bulbous, Squat, 13 ½ In.	4313.00
Vase, Violet Sprigs, Reed Handles, Scrolled Shoulders, Gold, 6 In. ....*illus*	1093.00

ROYAL HICKMAN designed pottery, glass, silver, aluminum, furniture, lamps, and other items. From 1938 to 1944 and again from the 1950s to 1969, he worked for Haeger Potteries. Mr. Hickman operated his own pottery in Tampa, Florida, during the 1940s. He moved to California and worked for Vernon Potteries. During the last years of his life he lived in Guadalajara, Mexico, and continued designing for Royal Haeger. Pieces made in his pottery listed here are marked *Royal Hickman* or *Hickman*.

Cigarette Box, Cube, Figural Whale Finial, Persian Gray Glaze, 7 x 4 In.	48.00
Dish, Leaf, Aluminum, Bruce Fox, Signed, 15 x 11 In.	75.00
Planter, Green Glaze, Bowl On Pedestal, Marked, 1948, 10 ¾ In.	77.00
Planter, White Glaze Over Brown Glaze, Applied Mocha Base, Round, Marked, 8 In.	125.00
Vase, Applied Fish & Knobs To Simulate Air Bubbles, Blue Green, Signed, 20 In.	575.00
Vase, Double Shell, Mauve Agate Glaze, Cream Glaze Inside, Marked, 6 ½ In.	48.00
Vase, Leaf, Retro, Mauve Agate, Embossed, Incised Mark, 12 ½ x 5 In.	65.00
Vase, Petty Crystal Glaze, Bulbous, Marked, 8 In.	175.00
Vase, Petty Crystal Glaze Over Turquoise, Marked, 4 ½ In.	55.00
Vase, Rose & Blue, Bulbous, Bottleneck Top, Petty Glaze, Marked, 11 In.	150.00
Vase Set, Swan, Blue & Mauve Agate Glaze, Facing Left To Right, Marked, 8 ½ In., Pair	120.00

ROYAL NYMPHENBURG is the modern name for the Nymphenburg porcelain factory, which was established at Neudeck-ob-der-Au, Germany, in 1753 and moved to Nymphenburg in 1761. The company is still in existence. Marks include a checkered shield topped by a crown, a crowned *CT* with the year, and a contemporary shield mark on reproductions of eighteenth-century porcelain.

Casserole, Cover, Flowers, Lemon Finial, Gilt, Handles, 5 ½ x 10 ¾ In.	265.00
Figurine, Bacchanalian Bust, Pedestal, Multicolored Glaze, 6 In.	90.00
Figurine, Hummingbird, Flower, Multicolored Glaze, 7 In.	101.00

Royal Dux, Figurine, Polar Bear, Pink Triangle Mark, c.1950, 14 x 13 ½ In. $265.00

Royal Dux, Figurine, Woman, Basket On Head, Vase At Feet, Marked, 18 In. $250.00

Royal Dux, Figurine, Woman, Leaning Back, Rectangular Base, Bisque, Marked, 10 x 12 In. $104.00

R

Royal Flemish, Biscuit Jar, Gold & Silver Coins, Multicolored, Silver Plate Cover, 9 ½ In. $3450.00

Royal Flemish, Creamer, Square, Painted, Pink & Yellow Wild Roses, 2 In. $978.00

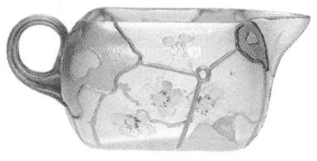

Royal Flemish, Vase, Multicolor, Narrow Neck, Label, c.1865, 11 In. $2760.00

Royal Flemish, Vase, Violet Sprigs, Reed Handles, Scrolled Shoulders, Gold, 6 In. $1093.00

Royal Worcester, Jar, Potpourri, Gilt, Fruit, Bulbous, Signed, John Freeman, 9 ½ In., Pair $3738.00

Figurine, Rearing Horse, c.1900, 11 In.	527.00
Figurine, Woman Attacked By Dog, Green & Purple Dress, 9 x 6 In.	266.00
Group, Stag, Hounds, White Glaze, 20th Century, 4 In.	225.00
Vase, Painted, Parrots, Gilded, 20th Century, Bulbous, 17 ¼ In.	956.00

ROYAL WORCESTER is a name used by collectors. Worcester porcelains were made in Worcester, England, from about 1751. The firm went through many different periods and name changes. It became the Worcester Royal Porcelain Company, Ltd., in 1862. Today collectors call the porcelains made after 1862 "Royal Worcester." In 1976, the firm merged with W.T. Copeland to become Royal Worcester Spode. The company was bought by the Portmeirion Group in 2009. Some early products of the factory are listed under Worcester.

Biscuit Box, Cover, Flower Painted, Reeded, Cylinder Shape, c.1890, 7 ¼ x 5 ½ In.	58.00
Biscuit Jar, Cover, Gray & Brown Flowers, Branches, c.1889, 7 In.	465.00
Bowl, Elephant, Cream, Gold Highlights, Footed, 5 x 7 ¾ In.	362.00
Bowl, Fruit, 4 x 11 In.	351.00
Bowl, Molded Flower Border, Multicolored Enamel Flowers, 1909, 9 In.	415.00
Bust, Maiden, Green Dress, Gilt, 12 In.	275.00
Candlestick, Flower Bud, Frog-On-Leaf Base, Gilt, Marked, 1889, 4 ½ x 4 In.	77.00
Eggcup, Coddled Eggs, Chrome Top, c.1960, 3 ⅜ In., Pair	40.00
Ewer, Butterflies, Gold Leaf, Applied Dragon Handle, 9 In.	65.00
Ewer, Cream, Wild Flowers, Bamboo Handle, 8 In.	50.00
Ewer, Double Snake Handle, Multicolored Enamel Flowers, c.1902, 12 ½ In.	267.00
Figurine, Birds, Lesser Whitethroat, Wild Rose, D. Doughty, c.1964, 9 In., 10 In., Pair	889.00
Figurine, Blue Birds, Male, Female, Tree Branch, D. Doughty, c.1936, 9 In., 10 In., Pair	356.00
Figurine, Boy, Holding Basket, 7 ½ In.	75.00
Figurine, Cerulean Warbler, Maple, Male, Female, D. Doughty, c.1965, 8 ½ In., Pair	295.00
Figurine, Fish, Blue Angel Fish, Seascape, R. Van Ruyckevelt, 1900s, 12 In.	652.00
Figurine, Grandmother's Dress, 6 ½ In.	125.00
Figurine, Horse, Palomino, Oval Wood Base, D. Lindner, 7 ¾ In.	488.00
Figurine, Kingfisher, Bird Flying Branches, D. Doughty, Fitted Wood Base, c.1964, 12 In.	711.00
Figurine, Magnolia Warbler, White Flower, Dorothy Doughty, 1950, 14 x 14 ½ x 11 In., Pair	9450.00
Figurine, Man, Hand On Hip, Shorts, Hat, Holding Bowl, Mark, 17 ½ In.	374.00
Figurine, Mockingbird, Pink Flowers, Dorothy Doughty, 11 ½ In., Pair	2200.00
Figurine, Mountain Bluebirds, Dorothy Doughty, 9 ¼ x 10 ¼ In., Pair	575.00
Figurine, Nijinsky, Race Horse, Oval Wood Base, D. Lindner, 10 ¾ In.	610.00
Figurine, Robin, Branch, Mushroom, Leaves, Dorothy Doughty, 1964, 6 ¾ In.	865.00
Figurine, Surprised Bather, White, Gilt, Thomas Brock, 10 ⅜ In.	565.00
Figurine, Swordfish, 12 ½ x 16 In.	351.00
Figurine, Water Carrier, Man In Turban, Long Cloak, Holding Amphora, 8 ⅝ In.	415.00
Group, Fish, Spanish Hog Fish, Sergeant Major, Seascape, R. Van Ruyckevelt, 1900s, 11 In.	770.00
Jar, Potpourri, Gilt, Fruit, Bulbous, Signed, John Freeman, 9 ½ In., Pair ....*illus*	3738.00
Jar, Potpourri, Relief Decoration, Purple Flowers, Gold Trim & Handles, 16 In.	3965.00
Pitcher, Elephant Head, Trunk Handle, Banded, Gilt, Flowers, Cream Ground, c.1887, 5 In.	130.00
Pitcher, Flowers, Cream Ground, 5 In. ....*illus*	100.00
Plaque, Mother & Child, White Silhouette, Beige Ground, Frame, 14 x 9 In.	176.00
Plate, Botanical, Gilt, Cobalt Blue Band, 9 In., 12 Piece	2070.00
Plate, Chantilly, Sterling Silver Rim, 11 In.	146.00
Plate, Ernest Barker, Floral Center, Red & Gold Scrolled Rim, c.1925, 10 ½ In., 6 Piece	702.00
Plate, Fish, Textured Cream Ground, Fish, Underwater Plants, 9 ¼ In., 8 Piece	264.00
Plate, Flowered Border, 10 ½ In.	17.70
Plate, Painted, Green Ground Rims, Leaf, Oval Medallions, c.1929, 10 ½ In., Pair	1778.00
Urn, Cover, Highland Cattle, Gilt, Handles, Signed, John Stinton, c.1825, 14 ½ In.	5500.00
Urn, Flowers, Raised, Green, Gilt, Handles, Base, 7 ¼ In.	265.00
Vase, Art Nouveau, Lobed Body, Blue Ground, Multicolored, Gilt, Tree, Birds, c.1915, 10 In.	825.00
Vase, Birds, Globular, 2 Shaped & Buttressed Handles, 17 In.	708.00
Vase, Blue Jays, Enameled, Gold Leaves, Moon, 2 Handles, Bulbous, 6 ½ x 11 In.	460.00
Vase, Flowers, Pink, Green Leaves, Gilt, Dragon Handle, 9 x 5 ½ In.	350.00
Vase, Leaves, Ivory, Gilt, 6 ¾ In.	204.00
Vase, Lighthouse, Dolphin Head Handles, 2-Tone Gilt, c.1890, 18 In.	2832.00
Vase, Multicolored, Gilt Enamel Leaves, Bottle Shape, Dolphin Handle, 1892, 7 ¼ In.	178.00
Vase, Pink & Yellow Roses, Cream & Green Panels, Gold Stencil, Pedestal, 10 ½ In.	450.00
Vase, Purple Thistles, Applied Gold Accents, Double Handles, Meet, 6 x 7 ½ In.	316.00
Vase, Purple Thistles, Wild Flowers, Enameled, Applied Dragon Handle, 5 x 9 In.	546.00
Vase, Swan, Supports Basket Weave Vase, 1890, 7 ¼ In.	474.00
Vase, Trumpet, Pate-Sur-Pate, Pink Ground, White Slip, Gilt Border, Grainger, 8 In.	593.00

R

Royal Worcester, Pitcher, Flowers, Cream Ground, 5 In.
$100.00

Roycroft, Andirons, Twists, Curlicues, Joined By Chain, 27 ½ x 13 x 20 In.
$1560.00

Roycroft, Candelabrum, 6-Light, Bronze, Linear, Scrolled Feet, Stamped, 15 ½ In.
$341.00

Roycroft, Lamp, Copper, Hammered, Domed Shade, Early 20th Century, 16 In.
$1440.00

Roycroft, Platter, Geometric, Red, Green, Handles, Orb Logo, Buffalo Pottery, 11 ½ In.
$1080.00

RRP, Cookie Jar, Cow Jumped Over The Moon, Marked, R.R.P. Co., 10 In.
$118.00

RRP, Vase, Tionesta, Label, Marked, 8 In.
$29.00

RS Prussia, Bowl, Iris Mold, Green & White, Poppy, Gold Highlights, 10 ½ In.
$175.00

RS Prussia, Bowl, Pink & Yellow, Poppy, 10 ½ In.
$125.00

RS Prussia, Cake Plate, Steeple, Bronze, Iridescent Border, Wildflowers, Handles, 10 ½ In.
$140.00

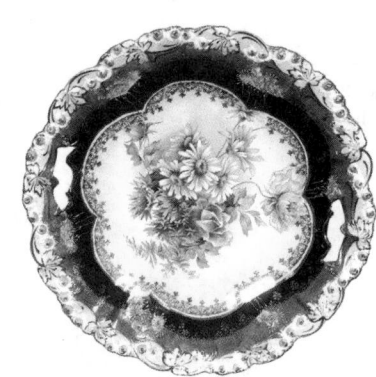

R

RS Prussia, Celery Dish, Carnation Mold, White & Lavender Satin, Pink Rose, 13 In. $75.00

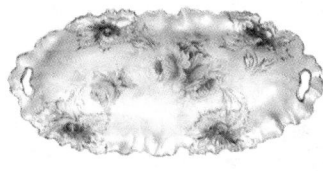

RS Prussia, Chocolate Pot, Carnation Mold, Woman, Summer Season, 10 In. $1600.00

RS Prussia, Muffineer, White, Tan Satin, Pink Rose, Handles, Skirted, 4 ¾ In. $110.00

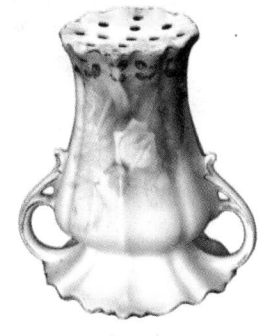

RS Prussia, Pitcher, Bowtie Mold, White, Pink Ribbon, Pink Flowers, 5 In. $180.00

Vase, Wild Flowers, Enameled, 2 Spouts, Handle, Gold, 6 x 9 ½ In.	230.00
Vase, Wild Flowers, Enameled, Elongated Neck, Bulbous, Gold, 5 ½ x 12 ¾ In.	345.00
Vase, Wild Flowers, Enameled, Shoulder Form, Gold, Handle, 6 ½ x 9 In.	144.00
Whistle, Dog Head, Brown, White, c.1900, 1 ¾ In.	379.00

ROYCROFT products were made by the Roycrofter community of East Aurora, New York, in the late nineteenth and early twentieth centuries. The community was founded by Elbert Hubbard, famous philosopher, writer, and artist. The workshops owned by the community made furniture, metalware, leatherwork, embroidery, and jewelry. A printshop produced many signs, books, and the magazines that promoted the sayings of Elbert Hubbard. Furniture by the Roycroft community is listed in the Furniture category.

Andirons, Cast Iron, Seahorse, W.W. Denslow, 9 ½ x 19 In.	14400.00
Andirons, Twists, Curlicues, Joined By Chain, 27 ½ x 13 x 20 In. .... *illus*	1560.00
Bench, Ali Baba, Slab Side, Split Log Support, Lower Stretcher, 42 x 19 ½ In.	3120.00
Bookends, Copper, Hammered, Border Design, Flowers, Signed, 5 In.	300.00
Bookends, Copper, Hammered, Large Tooled Poppies, Impressed, 5 x 5 ½ In.	570.00
Bookrack, Arched Ends, Signed With Orb, Wooden, 18 x 6 x 4 ½ In.	780.00
Bowl, Copper, Hammered, Protruding Feet, 10 ½ In.	575.00
Bowl Set, Round, Copper, Hammered, Tooled Designs, 5 In., 6 Piece	240.00
Candelabrum, 6-Light, Bronze, Linear, Scrolled Feet, Stamped, 15 ½ In. .... *illus*	341.00
Humidor, Round, Copper, Hammered, Patina, Marked, 4 x 5 In.	450.00
Inkwell, Copper, Hammered, Cut Glass Insert, 4 ½ x 4 ½ In.	145.00
Jug, Brown, Handle, Signed, 5 In.	32.00
Lamp, Copper, Hammered, Domed Shade, Early 20th Century, 16 In. .... *illus*	1440.00
Lamp, Hammered Base, Shade, Tooled Designs, Mica Shade Lining, 7 x 14 In.	1560.00
Lamp, Hanging, Copper, Hammered, 3 Chains, Up Lighter, Signed, 17 x 26 In.	18000.00
Plate, Copper, Hammered, Repousse Dot Pattern, Round, Patina, Marked, 8 In.	390.00
Platter, Geometric, Red, Green, Handles, Orb Logo, Buffalo Pottery, 11 ½ In. .... *illus*	1080.00
Tray, Copper, Hammered, Applied Handles, Marked, 15 In.	420.00
Tray, Copper, Hammered, Applied Handles, Marked, 19 In.	390.00
Vase, American Beauty, Copper, Hammered, Marked, 3 ½ x 7 In.	1080.00
Vase, American Beauty, Copper, Hammered, Monument Shape, 8 x 21 In.	3120.00
Vase, Copper, Hammered, 4 Handles, 4 Silver Squares, Patina, 8 x 4 ¼ In.	4800.00
Vase, Copper, Hammered, Crimped Rim, Tooled Flowers, 3 ½ x 9 ½ In.	840.00
Vase, Copper, Hammered, Cylindrical, Riveted, Flared Base, Orb & Cross Mark, 10 x 6 In.	1220.00
Vase, Copper, Hammered, Heavy Gauge, Tapered, Patina, 4 x 8 In.	1140.00
Vase, Copper, Hammered, Rivets, Bulbous, Flared Rim, Marked, 18 ½ In.	2640.00
Vase, Copper, Hammered, Shouldered, Original Patina, 5 x 5 In.	540.00
Vase, Copper, Hammered, Squat, Marked, 6 ½ x 4 ½ In.	390.00
Vase, Copper, Hammered, Tooled Designs, Green Enamel, Patina, Flared Cylindrical, 3 x 3 In.	720.00

ROZENBURG worked at The Hague, Holland, from 1890 to 1914. The most important pieces were earthenware made in the early twentieth century with pale-colored Art Nouveau designs.

Chocolate Pot, Domed Lid, Flowers, Leaves, Eggshell Porcelain, c.1900, 10 In.	6195.00
Cup & Saucer, Lilies, Leaves, Octagonal, Eggshell Porcelain	885.00
Cup & Saucer, Poppy, Leaves, Octagonal, Eggshell Porcelain, 5 ¼ In.	1003.00
Pitcher, Fuchsia, Spider On Web, Eggshell Porcelain, c.1900, 10 In.	7965.00
Tile, Peasant, Medieval Farm, Oak Frame, Signed, 1892, 25 x 18 ½ In, 12 Piece	1320.00
Vase, Bird, Wings Spread, Green Scrolling Leaves, Bulbous, Eggshell, 1904, 6 ½ In.	4780.00
Vase, Crab, Yellow Flowers, Green Leaves, Eggshell, S. Schellink, 1900, 10 ¾ In.	3585.00
Vase, Flowers, Pastel, White Ground, Eggshell, Arched Handle, Narrow Mouth, 1899, 8 In.	2629.00
Vase, Painted Butterflies, Flowers, Marked, c.1902, 2 x 5 In.	1560.00
Vase, Village Scene, Flowers, Brown, Green, Footed, Handles, 7 ⅝ In.	360.00

RRP, or RRP Roseville, is the mark used by the firm of Robinson-Ransbottom. It is not a mark of the more famous Roseville Pottery. The Ransbottom brothers started a pottery in 1900 in Ironspot, Ohio. In 1920, they merged with the Robinson Clay Product Company of Akron, Ohio, to become Robinson-Ransbottom. The factory is still working.

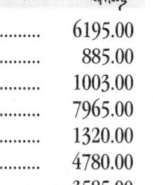

Cookie Jar, Chef, Holding Bowl, Spoon, Gold Trim, 11 In.	140.00
Cookie Jar, Cow Jumped Over The Moon, Marked, R.R.P. Co., 10 In. .... *illus*	118.00
Cookie Jar, Dutch Boy, No. 423, Marked, RRP Co., 12 In.	74.00
Cookie Jar, Sheriff Pig, Gold Trim, 12 In.	60.00
Cookie Jar, Sheriff Pig, Yellow Hat, Marked, RRP Co., 11 In.	68.00
Vase, Tionesta, Label, Marked, 8 In. .... *illus*	29.00
Vase, Yellow Rose, Skirted, 2 Handles, Dark Green, Yellow, 11 In.	80.00

RS GERMANY is part of the wording in marks used by the Tillowitz, Germany, factory of Reinhold Schlegelmilch from 1914 until about 1945. The porcelain was sold decorated and undecorated. The Schlegelmilch families made porcelains marked in many ways. See also ES Germany, RS Poland, RS Prussia, RS Silesia, RS Suhl, and RS Tillowitz.

Creamer, Sugar, Bird Of Paradise	100.00
Pitcher, Milk, White Blossoms, Green Mark, 8 In.	33.00
Toothpick, 3 Handles	60.00
Tray, Bird Of Paradise, Hummingbird, Rectangular, 16 In.	325.00

RS POLAND (German) is a mark used by the Reinhold Schlegelmilch factory at Tillowitz from about 1946 to 1956. After 1956, the factory made porcelain marked *PT Poland*. This is one of many of the RS marks used. See also ES Germany, RS Germany, RS Prussia, RS Silesia, RS Suhl, and RS Tillowitz.

Bowl, Mayonnaise, Underplate, Hydrangea, White, Footed	175.00
Hatpin Holder, White Rose, Pearlized, Gold Trim, Signed, 5 In.	81.00
Vase, Chinese Pheasants, Woodland Scene, Bulbous, Flared Rim, 4 ½ x 4 In.	275.00
Vase, Flowers, Handle, Red Mark, 7 ¾ In.	61.00
Vase, Ostrich, Leaf Silhouette, Brown Ground, 5 In.	30.00
Vase, Pink Poppies, Buds, White Ground, Marked, 7 In.	24.00
Vase, White Rose, Brown Ground, Cobalt Blue Border, Gilt Detail, Handles, 8 In.	113.00

RS PRUSSIA appears in several marks used on porcelain before 1917. Reinhold Schlegelmilch started his porcelain works in Suhl, Germany, in 1869. See also ES Germany, RS Germany, RS Poland, RS Silesia, RS Suhl, and RS Tillowitz.

Bowl, Autumn Portrait, c.1900, 10 ½ In.	527.00
Bowl, Carnation Mold, Pink, Green, White Satin, Pink Poppy, Gold Detail, 15 ½ In.	2200.00
Bowl, Flowers, Peacock Blue Border, Gold Trim, Molded Scroll & Flower Rim, 10 In.	148.00
Bowl, Fruit, Painted, Pink Flower Center, Blue & Gilt Scalloped Edge, c.1900, 9 ¾ In.	47.00
Bowl, Fruit, Pink Roses, Molded Edge, c.1910, 10 In.	83.00
Bowl, Iris Mold, Green & White, Poppy, Gold Highlights, 10 ½ In. ....*illus*	175.00
Bowl, Masted Ship, c.1900, 10 ½ In.	351.00
Bowl, Pink & Yellow, Poppy, 10 ½ In. ....*illus*	125.00
Bowl, Portrait Medallion, c.1900, 1 In.	527.00
Bowl, Portrait, Woman, Red Mark, 10 In.	167.00
Bowl, Recamier Portrait, Late 19th Century, 11¾ In.	995.00
Bowl, Teardrop Shape, Hidden Image Pattern, Green, Pink Highlights, 11 ¾ In.	800.00
Cake Plate, Point & Clover Mold, Scattered Flowers, Gold Trim, Handles, 11 In.	150.00
Cake Plate, Steeple, Bronze, Iridescent Border, Wildflowers, Handles, 10 ½ In. ....*illus*	140.00
Cake Plate, Swans, Swimming, Molded Floral Rim, c.1900, 9 ½ In.	354.00
Celery Dish, Carnation Mold, White & Lavender Satin, Pink Rose, 13 In. ....*illus*	75.00
Chocolate Pot, Carnation Mold, Woman, Summer Season, 10 In. ....*illus*	1600.00
Chocolate Pot, Woman, Green, Yellow Ground, Gold, Lid, 6 ½ x 10 In.	920.00
Ewer, Scenic, Summer Season, Green Ground, Pedestal, Handle, 7 ¾ In.	850.00
Hair Receiver, Pink & White Flowers, Green & Gold Border, Square, 3 ¼ x 1 ¾ In.	299.00
Muffineer, White, Tan Satin, Pink Rose, Handles, Skirted, 4 ¾ In. ....*illus*	110.00
Pitcher, Bowtie Mold, White, Pink Ribbon, Pink Flowers, 5 In. ....*illus*	180.00
Pitcher, Stipple, Yellow & Green, Pink & Yellow Rose Design, 13 ¼ In.	300.00
Pitcher, Tankard, Fruit, Red, Green Wreath Mark, 13 In.	201.00
Plate, Flower, Gold Border, Marked, 8 ¾ In.	55.00
Plate, Gold Band, White & Purple Azaleas, Marked, 8 ⅜ In.	125.00
Plate, Icicle Mold, Pink Ground, Hanging Basket, 8 ½ In. ....*illus*	100.00
Sugar Basket, Flowers, Multicolored, Gilt, Footed, Tillowitz, Silesia, Marked, 3 ⅝ x 5 x 4 In.	70.00
Tankard, Carnation Mold, Yellow & Pink, Roses, 11 In.	350.00
Tea Tile, Scenic, Schooner, Luster Glaze, 7 In.	700.00
Teapot, Clover & Jewel Mold, Dice Thrower Scene ....*illus*	900.00
Tray, Dresser, Poppy Mold, Iridescent Border, Flowers, Saxe Altenburg, 11 In. ....*illus*	100.00
Vase, Flower Shape, Flowers, Enamel, Gilt, Scalloped Edge, 9 ¼ In.	195.00

RS SILESIA appears on porcelain made at the Reinhold Schlegelmilch factory in Tillowitz, Germany, from the 1920s to the 1940s. The Schlegelmilch families made porcelains marked in many ways. See also ES Germany, RS Germany, RS Poland, RS Prussia, RS Suhl, and RS Tillowitz.

Creamer, White, Squat, Angular Handle	13.00
Dish, White Flowers, Orange Luster Ground, 4 Lobes, 2 Handles	48.00

RS Prussia, Plate, Icicle Mold, Pink Ground, Hanging Basket, 8 ½ In. $100.00

RS Prussia, Teapot, Clover & Jewel Mold, Dice Thrower Scene $900.00

RS Prussia, Tray, Dresser, Poppy Mold, Iridescent Border, Flowers, Saxe Altenburg, 11 In. $100.00

Rubina, Bowl, Shells & Ribs, 3 Shell Feet, Floral Prunt, Hobbs, 4 x 8 ¾ In. $219.00

R

Rubina, Pitcher, Water, Coin Spot, Oval, Square Mouth, Twisted Rope Handle, 8 In. $316.00

Rubina Verde, Pitcher, Water, Dew Drop, Opalescent, Transparent Canary, Handle, 8 In. $184.00

Rubina Verde, Pitcher, Water, Dew Drop, Vaseline Handle, 1880, 8 ½ In. $460.00

Ruby Glass, Banana Boat, Delaware, Flashed, 4 x 11 ½ In. $50.00

Sugar & Creamer, Morning Glories, Straight Sides, Angular Handles	25.00
Tray, Poppies, Red & White, Butterflies, Violet Ground, Oval, Open Handles, 14 x 5 In.	96.00

RS SUHL is a mark used by the Reinhold Schlegelmilch factory in Suhl, Germany, between 1900 and 1917. The Schlegelmilch families made porcelains in many places. See also ES Germany, RS Germany, RS Poland, RS Prussia, RS Silesia, and RS Tillowitz.

Figurine, Shoe, Flowers, Gold Trim, Scalloped Rim, 3 ¼ x 7 In.	38.00
Hatpin Holder, Pink Flowers, White Shaded To Blue Ground, Fluted, Flared, 5 In.	149.00
Plate, Classical Women In Garden, Green & Gold Bands, Gold Scrolling, 10 In.	120.00
Vase, Castle, Kobenhaven, Fired-On Gold, Gold Dots, Shouldered, 4 ½ In.	450.00
Vase, Melon Eaters, Mountain Landscape, Bulbous, Pinched Neck, Flared Rim, 5 In.	675.00

RS TILLOWITZ was marked on porcelain by the Reinhold Schlegelmilch factory at Tillowitz from the 1920s to the 1940s. Table services and ornamental pieces were made. See also ES Germany, RS Germany, RS Poland, RS Prussia, RS Silesia, and RS Suhl.

Biscuit Jar, Cover, Blue Iris, Gold Leaves, Bulbous, Ribbon Handles, 7 ¾ In.	499.00
Cake Plate, Rose, Bud, Leaves, Beige & Brown Ground, Cutout Handles, 9 ¾ In.	129.00
Chocolate Pot, Apple Blossoms, Gold Trim, 9 ¾ In.	225.00
Plate, Parrots, White Flowers, Blue Ground, 3 Open Handles, 8 In.	185.00
Powder Jar, Cover, Melon Eaters, Round, 4 x 3 In.	350.00

RUBINA is a glassware that shades from red to clear. It was first made by George Duncan and Sons of Pittsburgh, Pennsylvania, about 1885. This coloring was used on many types of glassware. The pressed glass patterns of Royal Ivy and Royal Oak are listed under Northwood.

Bowl, Shells & Ribs, 3 Shell Feet, Floral Prunt, Hobbs, 4 x 8 ¾ In.	*illus*	219.00
Pitcher Set, Coin Spot, 4 Side Prunt Hooks, 4 Matching Cordials, 7 ½ In.		1400.00
Pitcher, Water, Coin Spot, Oval, Square Mouth, Twisted Rope Handle, 8 In.	*illus*	316.00
Pitcher, Water, Swirled, Wide Ribbed, Reeded Handle, Pontil, c.1875, 9 ¼ In.		145.00
Syrup, Coin Spot, Opalescent, 6 In.		173.00

RUBINA VERDE is a Victorian glassware that was shaded from red to green. It was first made by Hobbs, Brockunier and Company of Wheeling, West Virginia, about 1890.

Cruet, Hobnail Pattern, 7 ½ In.		1035.00
Pitcher, Water, Dew Drop, Opalescent, Transparent Canary, Handle, 8 In.	*illus*	184.00
Pitcher, Water, Dew Drop, Vaseline Handle, 1880, 8 ½ In.	*illus*	460.00

RUBY GLASS is the dark red color of a ruby, the precious gemstone. It was a popular Victorian color that never went completely out of style. The glass was shaped by many different processes to make many different types of ruby glass. There was a revival of interest in the 1940s when modern-shaped ruby table glassware became fashionable. Sometimes the red color is added to clear glass by a process called flashing or staining. Flashed glass is clear glass dipped in a colored glass, then pressed or cut. Stained glass has color painted on a clear glass. Then it is refired so the stain fuses with the glass. Pieces of glass colored in this way are indicated by the word *stained* in the description. Related items may be found in other categories, such as Cranberry Glass, Pressed Glass, and Souvenir.

Banana Boat, Delaware, Flashed, 4 x 11 ½ In.	*illus*	50.00
Goblet, Cut To Clear, 7 In., 6 Piece		94.00

RUDOLSTADT was a faience factory in the Thuringia region of Germany from 1720 to about 1791. In 1854, Ernst Bohne began working in the area. From about 1887 to 1918, the New York and Rudolstadt Pottery made decorated porcelain marked with the RW and crown familiar to collectors. This porcelain was imported by Lewis Straus and Sons of New York, which later became Nathan Straus and Sons. The word *Royal* was included in their import mark. Collectors often call it "Royal Rudolstadt." Most pieces found today were made in the late nineteenth or early twentieth century. Additional pieces may be listed in the Kewpie category.

Celery Tray, Yellow, White, Cream Ground, 12 x 5 In.	65.00
Figurine, Art Deco, Woman Dancer, Bare Breasted, Karl Ens, 6 ½ In.	56.00
Vase, Teardrop Shape, Floral Handles, Painted Flowers, Cream Ground, 11 ½ In.	17.00 to 29.00

RUGS have been used in the American home since the seventeenth century. The oriental rug of that time was often used on a table, not on the floor. Rag rugs, hooked rugs, and braided rugs were made by housewives from scraps of material. American Indian rugs are listed in the Indian category.

Afshar, Geometric Flowers, Sawtooth Spandrels, Red, Multiple Borders, c.1920, 4 Ft. 5 In. x 8 Ft. 2 In.		620.00
Art Deco, Flower Medallion, Lilies Of The Valley, Pink, Gold, Green, Flowers, 8 x 11 Ft.	*illus*	780.00

Art Deco, Geometric, Blue, Gray, Wool, France, 1930s, 6 Ft. 5 In. x 9 Ft. 7 In. 2124.00
Art Deco, Geometric, Burgundy Field, Red, Yellow, White, 8 Ft. 6 In. x 12 Ft. .... *illus* 1200.00
Arts & Crafts, Bird, Multicolored, 3 Ft. x 4 Ft. 9 In. 180.00
Arts & Crafts, Gavin Morton, Runner, 10 Ft. 6 In. x 3 Ft. 610.00
Arts & Crafts, Geometric, Multicolored, Rust Border, Initials, 2 Ft. 8 In. x 4 Ft. .... *illus* 780.00
Aubusson, Needlework, Center Wreath, Tan Field, Shaped Egg & Dart Border, 17 Ft. x 20 Ft. 5750.00
Bakhtiari, Blue Spandrels, Red & Blue Round, 4 Ft. 7 In x 6 Ft. 6 In. 235.00
Bakhtiari, Flower Medallions, Blue, Black, Salmon, Blue Borders, 2 Ft. 11 In. x 17 Ft. 1 In. ... 1980.00
Beluch, Stylized Animal, Flowers, 7 Medallions, Indigo, Ivory, Borders, 2 Ft. 10 In. x 5 Ft. 2 In. 266.00
Bidjar, Center Medallion, 2 Pendants, Red Field, Multicolored, Geometric, Flower Border, 4 x 7 Ft. 805.00
Bidjar, Flower, Red Field, Central Medallion, Persian, c.1920, 3 Ft. 6 In. x 5 Ft. 1 In. 450.00
Bidjar, Repeating Lattice & Flowers, Blue Ground, Ivory Field Borders, Runner, 3 Ft. 5 In. x 17 Ft. 1093.00
Bokhara, Octagonal Guls, Blue, Red, Red Field, Geometric Borders, Afgan, 8 Ft. 9 In. x 10 Ft. 8 In. 173.00
Caucasian, 4 Medallions, Geometric, Animals, Salmon Field, 5 Ft. 1 In. x 11 Ft. 6 In. 1840.00
Caucasian, Geometric, Yellow Field, Ivory Border, c.1890, 5 Ft. 7 In. x 4 Ft. 2 In. 2808.00
Caucasian, Prayer, Diagonal Bands, Geometric Shapes, Blue, Ivory, 2 Ft. 11 In. x 4 Ft. 9 In. ... 978.00
Caucasian, Repeating Geometric, Navy Field, Multiple Borders, c.1910, 7 Ft. 8 In. x 3 Ft. 5 In. 468.00
Caucasian, Soumak, 3 Indigo Medallions, Brick Field, Borders, c.1900, 6 Ft. 10 In. x 9 Ft. 9 In. 2040.00
Chinese, Art Deco, Flowers, Navy Border, c.1930, 8 Ft. 8 In. x 11 Ft. .... *illus* 780.00
Chinese, Art Deco, Flowers, Navy Field, c.1920, 10 Ft. x 13 Ft. 6 In. 2520.00
Chinese, Courting Scene, Oriental Story, Multicolored, 2 Ft. x 2 Ft. 9 In. 715.00
Chinese, Flower & Coin Design, Blue Ground, Mid 1900s, 8 Ft. 11 In. x 11 Ft. 7 In. .... *illus* 805.00
Chinese, Flowers, Dark Blue Ground, Silk Thread, 5 Ft. 9 In. x 6 Ft. 385.00
Chinese, Pillar, Figure Under Tasseled Canopy, Flowers, Yellow Ground, 7 Ft. 9 In. x 3 Ft. 431.00
Geometric, Brown Shades, Rectangular, France, c.1960s, 11 Ft. 3 In. x 6 Ft. 7 In. 837.00
Geometric, Curves, Rectangles, Taupe, Gray, Chocolate, Gold, B. Joel, 4 Ft. x 6 Ft. 10 In. 6095.00
Geometric, Gray Ground, Red & Beige, Jack Larsen, 1980s, 8 Ft. x 7 Ft. 7 In. 3308.00
Geometric, Multicolored, Black Ground, Early 20th Century, 3 x 6 Ft. 200.00
Hamadan, Geometric Flowers, Pink Ground, Turquoise Border, Runner, 6 Ft. x 3 Ft. 6 In. 295.00
Hamadan, Geometric, White Ground, Red Border, 3 Ft. x 3 Ft. 9 In. 176.00
Hamadan, Serrated Diamond, Pendants, Allover Beige Designs, 3 Ft. x 3 Ft. 8 In. 288.00
Heriz, Center Lobed Medallion, Red Ground, Ivory, Blue, Mid 19th Century, 8 Ft. 9 In. x 6 Ft. 6 In. 1250.00
Heriz, Cross Medallion, Brick Red Ground, Blue & Green Bands, 7 Ft. 10 In. x 11 Ft. 1093.00
Heriz, Flower, Center Medallion, c.1940, 6 Ft. 7 In. x 8 Ft. 3 In. 450.00
Heriz, Flowers, Central Medallion, Red Field, Persian, c.1920, 6 Ft. 8 In. x 9 Ft. 4 In. 1140.00
Heriz, Ivory Ground, Red Medallion, c.1940s, 8 Ft. 8 In. x 12 Ft. 3525.00
Heriz, Medallion, Rose Field, Ivory Spandrels, Blue & Ivory Guard Border, 8 Ft. 9 In. x 12 Ft.... 2185.00
Heriz, Medallion, Salmon Field, 9 Ft. 6 In. x 12 Ft. .... *illus* 1265.00
Hooked, Bears, Drinking, Flowers, Red Border, Wool, c.1890, 24 x 44 In. .... *illus* 5148.00
Hooked, Beaver, On Log, Red & Black Ground, Maple Leaf Corners, 21 x 38 In. 155.00
Hooked, Birds, In Tree Tops, French Words, Canada, c.1930, 25 x 41 In. .... *illus* 259.00
Hooked, Black Panther, On Tree, Flowers, Burlap, 24 x 41 ½ In. 34.00
Hooked, Branding Emblems, Diamond Blocks, Octagon Borders, Wool, Burlap, c.1940, 38 x 59 In. ... 588.00
Hooked, Cat & Kittens, Multicolored, Wool, Burlap, Late 19th Century, 32 x 53 In. 235.00
Hooked, Cat, Dog, Flowers, Brick Wall, Cotton, Wool, Frame, 29 x 48 In. 504.00
Hooked, Cat, Reclining, Scrolled Border, Floral Corners, Cloth, Burlap, 38 x 23 In. 77.00
Hooked, Cats, Arched Backs, Stars, Moon, Multicolored, Burlap, 16 x 26 In. 45.00
Hooked, Civil War Uniforms, Blue, Tan, Red, 30 x 15 In. 117.00
Hooked, Diamonds, Triangles, Undulating Lines, Multicolored, Wool, Burlap, 23 x 38 In. 295.00
Hooked, Dog, Lying Down, Dogs At Corners, Black, Beige, Ivory, Brown Tones, c.1900, 32 x 39 In. 410.00
Hooked, Dog, Lying Down, Patchwork Ground, c.1928, 29 x 55 In. .... *illus* 497.00
Hooked, Dog, Reclining, Yellow, Double Yellow Border, Early 1900s, 27 x 42 In. 350.00
Hooked, Fireplace Scene, Spinning Wheel, Black Kettle, Beige, Black Border, 1930, 38 x 56 In. .. 285.00
Hooked, Flowerpot, Diamond Shaped Panels, Hearts & Scrolls, 68 x 39 In. 1195.00
Hooked, Flowerpot, Striated Ground, Hexagon Border, Wool, Burlap, 45 x 36 In. .... *illus* 881.00
Hooked, Flowers, Birds, Multicolored, 96 x 48 In. 2300.00
Hooked, Flowers, Green Ground, Wool, Burlap, c.1930, 19 x 30 In. 150.00
Hooked, Flowers, Leaf Border, c.1900, 74 x 49 In. 518.00
Hooked, Flowers, Multicolored, Black Border, Round, 1800s, 31 In. 110.00
Hooked, Flowers, Shirred, Zigzag Borders, Wool, Wood Frame, 1800s, 31 x 44 In. 10073.00
Hooked, Flowers, Star Center, Brown, Green, Red, Scroll Border, c.1900, 49 x 62 In. 705.00
Hooked, Flowers, Striped Pot, Multicolored, Blue, Black Borders, Wool, Burlap, c.1900, 35 x 44 In. 411.00
Hooked, Flowers, Urn, Floral Border, Oval, Signed, Bea Nagle, c.1950, 29 x 39 In. 235.00
Hooked, Flowers, Vines, Wool, Burlap, Early 20th Century, 65 x 35 In. 59.00
Hooked, Garden Lattice, Floral Vines, Wool, Burlap, Runner, c.1940, 27 x 90 In. 795.00
Hooked, Geometric, 1923 In Center, Black, Brown, Tan, Wood Frame, 27 x 52 In. 173.00

Rug, Art Deco, Flower Medallion,
Lilies Of The Valley, Pink, Gold, Green,
Flowers, 8 x 11 Ft.
$780.00

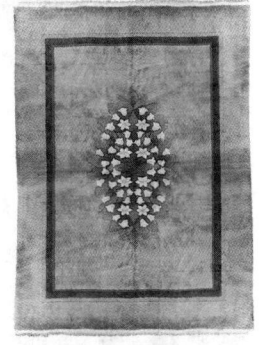

Rug, Art Deco, Geometric,
Burgundy Field, Red, Yellow, White,
8 Ft. 6 In. x 12 Ft.
$1200.00

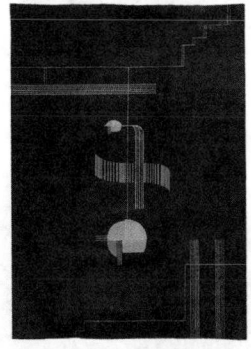

Rug, Arts & Crafts, Geometric,
Multicolored, Rust Border, Initials,
2 Ft. 8 In. x 4 Ft.
$780.00

R

TIP
*Always keep a rug
on a pad. It will
wear out sooner on
a bare floor.*

Rug, Chinese, Art Deco, Flowers, Navy Border, c.1930, 8 Ft. 8 In. x 11 Ft. $780.00

Rug, Chinese, Flower & Coin Design, Blue Ground, Mid 1900s, 8 Ft. 11 In. x 11 Ft. 7 In. $805.00

Rug, Heriz, Medallion, Salmon Field, 9 Ft. 6 In. x 12 Ft. $1265.00

Rug, Hooked, Bears, Drinking, Flowers, Red Border, Wool, c.1890, 24 x 44 In. $5148.00

Rug, Hooked, Birds, In Tree Tops, French Words, Canada, c.1930, 25 x 41 In. $259.00

Rug, Hooked, Dog, Lying Down, Patchwork Ground, c.1928, 29 x 55 In. $497.00

Rug, Hooked, Flowerpot, Striated Ground, Hexagon Border, Wool, Burlap, 45 x 36 In. $881.00

Rug, Hooked, Grenfell, Polar Bear, Kayak, 1910, 26 x 40 In. $761.00

Rug, Hooked, Halley's Comet, Black, Beige, Red, c.1910, 40 x 36 In. $403.00

TIP

There is a modern safe way to hang an antique Oriental rug on the wall. Put a strip of 2-inch-wide Velcro on a strip of wood. Mount the wood on the wall. Hang the rug directly on the Velcro. The rug will stay in place and can be pulled loose to be cleaned.

R

Hooked, Geometric, Multicolored, Burlap, 34 x 53 In.	34.00
Hooked, Grenfell, Multicolored, Man, Snow Shoes, Gun, Backpack, 10 ¾ x 8 In.	190.00
Hooked, Grenfell, Polar Bear, Kayak, 1910, 26 x 40 In. ....*illus*	761.00
Hooked, Halley's Comet, Black, Beige, Red, c.1910, 40 x 36 In. ....*illus*	403.00
Hooked, Heart, Ruffled Border, Heart In Hands, Flowers, Leaves, Wool, Burlap, c.1900, 21 x 35 In.	382.00
Hooked, House, In Roundel, Fruit Trees, Blossom Border, 48 x 45 In.	489.00
Hooked, Lion, Cotton & Wool, 1920s, 27 x 32 In.	440.00
Hooked, Owl, Branch, Circle, Random Field, Black, Red Edge, Multicolored Corners, Wool, 29 x 49 In.	178.00
Hooked, Pink & Red Flowers, Brown Scrolling, Beige Ground, 1897, 14 x 61 In.	472.00
Hooked, Red, Plates, Cups & Saucer, Tea & Coffeepots, Rag, Wool, Burlap, 36 x 87 In.	310.00
Hooked, Roses, Daisies, Morning Glories, Green Ground, Scalloped, Oval, c.1940, 30 x 41 In. .	350.00
Hooked, Running Horse, Wavy Border, White, Dark Ground, Wool, Burlap, c.1900, 21 x 40 In.	588.00
Hooked, Scottie Dog, Pink Bow, Gray Ground, Wool, Burlap, 1920, 36 x 23 In.	350.00
Hooked, Ship, Ocean Scene, Black Border, Wool, Burlap, c.1900, 30 x 52 In.	176.00
Hooked, Snow Scene, Trees, Cottage, Mountains, Brown Border, 36 x 29 In.	275.00
Hooked, Spotted Dog, Blue & Brown, Black Field, Stylized Blue Heart Corners, 1910, 19 x 35 In.	460.00
Hooked, Swan, White, Green, Blue, Signed, W, 28 x 49 In.	392.00
Hooked, Teddy Bears, Alphabet Border, Multicolored, Signed, Mc G, 29 x 54 In.	138.00
Hooked, The Team, Horses, Wool, Burlap, Salome Stoltzfus, Amish, c.1930, 25 x 44 In. ...*illus*	575.00
Hooked, Tiger, Stylized Profile, Blue & Cream Triangle Border, 36 x 24 In.	173.00
Hooked, Wedding Band, Gray, Pink, Black Border, 1800s, 25 x 38 ½ In.	88.00
Hooked, Yellow Dog, Multiple Borders, c.1915, 27 x 42 In.	351.00
Isfahan, Blue Field, Stylized Floral Tree, Navy Border, c.1910, 7 Ft. 9 In. x 4 Ft. 10 In.	702.00
Karaja, 3 Medallions, Flowers, Indigo Crab Border, Red Field, Borders, c.1930, 4 Ft. 9 In. x 6 Ft.	708.00
Karastan, Geometric, Multicolored, Navy Field, Runner, 2 Ft. 6 In. x 12 Ft.	180.00
Kashan, Floral Medallion, Indigo Spandrels, Multiple Borders, Ivory Field, Vines, c.1930, 9 x 12 Ft.	2596.00
Kashan, Flower, Red Field, c.1920, 9 Ft. 4 In. x 13 Ft.	1200.00
Kashan, Flowers, c.1945, 8 Ft. 9 In. x 12 Ft. 5 In.	587.00
Kashan, Flowers, Indigo Field, Red, Ivory Medallion, Vase & Flower Border, 4 Ft. 3 In. x 6 Ft. 7 In. .	2006.00
Kashan, Red Medallion, Olive Ground, Floral Decoration, c.1900, 14 Ft. x 9 Ft. 7 In.	9360.00
Kazak, 3 Medallions, Blue Field, Multiple Borders, c.1910, 7 Ft. x 3 Ft. 7 In.	644.00
Kazak, 3 Medallions, Blue Ground, Red, 3 Color Border, Early 19th Century, 8 Ft. 5 In. x 5 Ft. 3 In.	575.00
Kazak, 5 Interlocking Diamonds, Hook Borders, Ivory, Blue, Red, 3 Ft. 10 In. x 7 Ft.......	748.00
Kazak, Diamonds, Hook Borders, Sawtooth Minor Borders, 3 Ft. 6 In. x 7 Ft. 1 In. ....*illus*	1093.00
Kazak, Geometric, Animal, Flowers, 4 Medallions, Blue, Ivory, Red Ground, 4 Ft. 8 In. x 7 Ft. 11 In.	1380.00
Kerman, Meditation, Mihrab, Tree, Hanging Fruit, Burgundy Field, 5 Ft. 10 In. x 3 Ft. 9 In. ...	115.00
Kerman, Multicolored Flowers, Medallion, Navy Blue Field, 6 Ft. x 9 Ft. 1 In.	506.00
Kerman, Tiered Floral Medallions, Branches, Rose Ground, Shaped Border, 4 Ft. x 6 Ft. 8 In. .	316.00
Kermanshah, Flower, Center Medallion, c.1920, 4 x 12 Ft...........................	480.00
Khorasan, Flowers, Medallion, Red, Herati Border, Ivory & Blue Border, 4 Ft. 5 In. x 6 Ft. 6 In.	354.00
Kuba, Navy Ground, Geometric, Tan Border, c.1910, 3 Ft. 3 In. x 5 Ft. 3 In. ....*illus*	633.00
Kurdish, Center Medallion, Navy Field, c.1930, 2 Ft. x 5 Ft. 6 In. ....*illus*	390.00
Kurdish, Geometric, Tan Field, Multiple Borders, Wool, c.1915, 3 Ft. 4 In. x 8 Ft. 5 In.	1121.00
Lillihan, Flowers, Red Field, Indigo Border, Heriz Khaki Gold Borders, c.1920, 3 Ft. 5 In. x 4 Ft. 9 In.	738.00
Lillihan, Vase & Flowers, Red Field, Multiple Borders, c.1950, 2 Ft. 7 In. x 9 Ft. 7 In.	944.00
Malayer, Center Panel, Flowers, Scattered Boteh, Brown Field, Multicolored, 4 Ft. 4 In. x 6 Ft. 2 In.	633.00
Mohtasham, Kashan, Central Medallion, Floral Background, c.1900, 6 Ft. 2 In. x 4 Ft. 5 In. ..	2574.00
Multicolored, Dotted Border, Oval, Edward Fields, c.1958, 6 Ft. 10 In. x 8 Ft. 9 In.	1080.00
Nain, Medallion, Ivory & Blue Spandrels, Tan & Navy Borders, Silk Inlay, 6 Ft. 4 In. x 9 Ft. 6 In.	944.00
Needlework, 12 Square Panels, Flowers, Geometrics, Rose Border, 5 Ft. 2 In. x 6 Ft. 5 In.	863.00
Persian, 5 Medallions, Red Field, Runner, 3 Ft. 6 In. x 9 Ft. 5 In.	415.00
Persian, Blue Ground, Red & Ivory Borders, c.1900, 3 Ft. 5 In. x 6 Ft.	352.00
Persian, Central Medallion, Ivory Field, Multiple Borders, Silk, c.1900, 6 Ft. 7 In. x 4 Ft. 1 In.	380.00
Persian, Cobalt Blue Ground, Trellis Overlay, 3 Guard Borders, 23 Ft. 6 In. x 11 Ft. 10 In.	2300.00
Persian, Northwest, Flowers, Tan Field, Blue Border, c.1930, 9 x 12 Ft..................	1440.00
Portuguese, Flowers, Beige Field, Green Border, c.1960, 10 Ft. x 13 Ft. 8 In.	115.00
Prayer, Purple, Salmon Mihrab, Stepped, Olive Ground, Turkey, 3 Ft. 1 In. x 5 Ft. 2 In. ...*illus*	690.00
Sarouk, Allover Flowers, Red Field, Indigo Border, Multiple Guard Borders, c.1940, 3 Ft. 6 In. x 5 Ft.	797.00
Sarouk, Allover Stylized Flowers, Wine Ground, Hand Woven, c.1930, 16 x 10 Ft.....................	3840.00
Sarouk, Allover Vase & Flowers, Herati & Guard Borders, Tan Field, 8 Ft. 10 In. x 11 Ft. 7 In. .	1652.00
Sarouk, Flowers, Geometric Medallion, Indigo Field, Multiple Borders, c.1915, 3 Ft. 8 In. x 5 Ft. 3 In.	1180.00
Sarouk, Flowers, Red Field, Navy Border, c.1920, 7 Ft. 9 In. x 5 Ft........................	995.00
Sarouk, Multicolored, Flower Sprays, Burgundy Field, 1950s, 8 Ft. 10 In. x 12 Ft.	1013.00
Sarouk, Red Ground, Navy Border, Persia, c.1930, 8 Ft. 11 In. x 17 Ft. 1 In.	2832.00
Sarouk, Repeating Flowers, Burgundy Field, 1920s, 12 Ft. 6 In. x 21 Ft. 7 In.	2990.00
Sculpted, Stylized Veined Leaves, Tan Ground, M. Weinrib, 9 Ft. x 10 Ft. 10 In.	748.00

Rug, Hooked, The Team, Horses, Wool, Burlap, Salome Stoltzfus, Amish, c.1930, 25 x 44 In.
$575.00

Rug, Kazak, Diamonds, Hook Borders, Sawtooth Minor Borders, 3 Ft. 6 In. x 7 Ft. 1 In.
$1093.00

Rug, Kuba, Navy Ground, Geometric, Tan Border, c.1910, 3 Ft. 3 In. x 5 Ft. 3 In.
$633.00

R

Rug, Kurdish, Center Medallion, Navy Field, c.1930, 2 Ft. x 5 Ft. 6 In. $390.00

Rug, Prayer, Purple, Salmon Mihrab, Stepped, Olive Ground, Turkey, 3 Ft. 1 In. x 5 Ft. 2 In. $690.00

Rug, Shiraz, Pendant Medallions, Red & Brown Field, 3 Ft. 8 In. x 5 Ft. $633.00

Serab, 3 Serrated Diamonds, 6-Sided Cartouches, Beige Ground, Runner, 3 Ft. 5 In. x 14 Ft.	575.00
Serab, 6 Medallions, Beige, Ivory Field, Runner, 3 Ft. x 10 Ft. 10 In.	230.00
Serab, Geometric, Red, Blue, 3 Ft. 7 In. x 5 Ft. 8 In.	353.00
Serapi, Blue Petal Medallion, Red Field, Ivory Ground, 8 Ft. x 14 Ft. 1 In.	575.00
Serapi, Brick Red Medallion, Pendants, Green, Pink, Ivory Field, 8 x 10 Ft.	1840.00
Shag, Red Squares, Cotton, 3 Ft. x 6 Ft. 9 In.	225.00
Shiraz, 2 Amber Medallions, Blue Ground, Quadrupeds, Bipeds, 6 Ft. 11 In. x 9 Ft. 7 In.	690.00
Shiraz, Pendant Medallions, Red & Brown Field, 3 Ft. 8 In. x 5 Ft. *illus*	633.00
Shirvan, 3 Medallions, Cobalt Blue Ground, Geometric Borders, c.1900, 6 x 3 Ft.	2160.00
Shirvan, Medallion, Red Field, Geometric Border, c.1920, 5 Ft. 4 In. x 11 Ft. 10 In.	1342.00
Soumak, 3 Blue Hexagons, Rose Ground, Sawtooth & Guard Border, 7 Ft. 9 In. x 9 Ft.	1380.00
Sumac, Flowers, Green, Gray Field, c.1950, 10 x 10 In. *illus*	1020.00
Tabriz, Lobed Medallion, Teal, Ivory Border, Teal Floral Border, Red Borders, 8 Ft. 2 In. x 11 Ft. 5 In.	1534.00
Tabriz, Multicolored, Flowers, Medallion, Navy Blue Field, Medallion Border, 11 x 16 Ft.	2813.00
Tekke, Allover Guls, Geometric, Red Field, Multiple Borders, c.1950, 4 Ft. 2 In. x 6 Ft. 4 In.	295.00
Tekke, Red Field, Multiple Geometric Borders, 3 Gul Rows, 3 Ft. 4 In. x 3 Ft. 11 In.	148.00
Tibetan, Dragon Design, Coral, Cream, Black Ground, Wool, 5 Ft. 11 In. x 4 Ft.	173.00
Turkoman, Blue Field, Red Border, 22 x 22 In.	90.00
Turkoman, Diamonds, Burgundy Field, c.1940, 5 Ft. 10 In. x 8 Ft. 1 In.	1220.00
Turkoman, Geometric, Multicolored, Border, 3 Ft. 2 In. x 3 Ft. 10 In.	480.00
Veramin, Allover Flowers, Ivory Field, Gray & Orange Samovar Borders, 6 Ft. 5 In. x 6 Ft. 5 In.	708.00
William Morris, Geometric, Flowers, Beige, Red, Green Border, Wool, Arts & Crafts, 8 x 10 Ft.	708.00
Wool, Crewel, Central Medallion, Flowers, Black Ground, Allover Flowers, 5 Ft. 9 In. x 4 Ft.	237.00
Wool, Geometric, Multicolored, Beige Ground, 4 Ft. 2 In. x 2 Ft. 9 In.	4183.00
Wool, Gray, White, Pierre Cardin, Signed, 8 Ft. 2 In. x 8 Ft. 2 In.	1708.00
Wool, Purple, Brown, Taupe Ground, Pierre Cardin, Signed, 10 Ft. 9 In. x 6 Ft. 9 In.	1830.00
Wool, Red, Tan, 2 Stylized Trees, Squares In Border, Geometric, Austria, 1920s, 11 Ft. x 8 Ft. 6 In.	5975.00

RUMRILL POTTERY was designed by George Rumrill of Little Rock, Arkansas. From 1933 to 1938, it was produced by the Red Wing Pottery of Red Wing, Minnesota. In January 1938, production was transferred to the Shawnee Pottery in Zanesville, Ohio. It was moved again in December of 1938 to Florence Pottery Company in Mt. Gilead, Ohio, where Rumrill ware continued to be manufactured until the pottery burned in 1941. It was then produced by Gonder Ceramic Arts in South Zanesville until early 1943.

RumRill

Bowl, Lobed, Cream Exterior, Green Interior, Grecian Handles, 1930s, 15 x 8 In.	40.00
Jug, Blue Gray, Stopper *illus*	72.00
Pitcher, Ball Jug, Dutch Blue, Blue White Stipple, 7 ¾ In.	25.00
Pitcher, Pot Kettle, Green, 6 ½ x 8 In.	25.00
Planter, Aqua, Wide Cream Lip, Handles, Footed, Red Wing, c.1936, 6 ½ x 5 ¼ In.	10.00
Vase, Art Deco Fan Shape, Pale Pink, Scroll Handles, 11 ½ In.	50.00
Vase, Dutch Blue Stipple, Footed, 6 ½ x 4 In.	55.00
Vase, Flared Stylized Leaves, Blue, Shawnee, 1938, 6 x 13 In.	30.00
Vase, Green, Brown, 2-Petal Flared Mouth, 9 x 6 ¼ In.	20.00
Vase, Green, Lavender, Matte Glaze, Curled Handles, 5 In.	39.00
Vase, Light Green, Petal Flared Mouth, Mt. Gilead, Ohio, c.1940, 8 In.	10.00

RUSKIN is a British art pottery of the twentieth century. The Ruskin Pottery was started by William Howson Taylor, and his name was used as the mark until about 1899. The factory, at West Smethwick, Birmingham, England, stopped making new pieces in 1933 but continued to glaze and sell the remaining wares until 1935. The art pottery is noted for its exceptional glazes.

RUSKIN POTTERY WEST SMETHWICK

Lamp, Cylindrical, Orange Iridescent Glaze, Reticulated Top, Metal Base, 10 In.	144.00
Vase, Cylindrical, Orange & Gold Iridescent Glaze, Mottled, Marked, 10 In.	58.00
Vase, Tapered, Orange Luster Glaze, Yellow, Green, Blue, Impressed, 4 x 9 In.	420.00

RUSSEL WRIGHT designed dinnerwares in modern shapes for many companies. Iroquois China Company, Harker China Company, Steubenville Pottery, and Justin Tharaud and Sons made dishes marked *Russel Wright.* The Steubenville wares, first made in 1938, are the most common today. Wright was a designer of domestic and industrial wares, including furniture, aluminum, radios, interiors, and glassware. Dinnerwares and other pieces by Wright are listed here. For more prices, go to kovels.com.

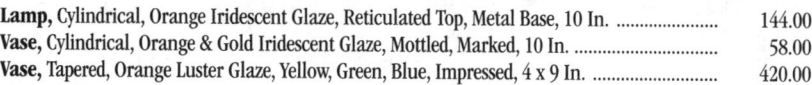

Russel Wright MFG. BY STEUBENVILLE

Aluminum, Ice Bucket, Rattan Loop Handle	300.00
Aluminum, Torchere, Shade, Flared, Wrapped Wire Trim, 65 In., Pair	270.00
Aluminum, Tumbler, 6 Piece	400.00
American Modern, Bowl, Fruit, Lug, Coral	12.00

R

American Modern, Bowl, Salad, Black Chutney, 8 In.	125.00
American Modern, Creamer, Coral	10.00
American Modern, Cup & Saucer, Coral	8.00
American Modern, Cup, Chartreuse, 2 x 3 In.	12.00
American Modern, Dish, Celery, Granite Gray, 13 In.	40.00
American Modern, Gravy Boat, Underplate, Coral	32.00
American Modern, Ice Box Jar, Cover, Bean Brown	500.00
American Modern, Plate, Bread & Butter, Coral, 6 ⅛ In.	5.00
American Modern, Plate, Dinner, Coral, 10 In.	9.00
American Modern, Plate, Dinner, White, 10 In.	25.00
American Modern, Plate, Salad, Cantaloupe, 8 In.	45.00
American Modern, Sugar & Creamer, Cover, Glacier Blue	125.00
Grass, Bowl, Knowles, Justin Tharaud, 6 ¼ x 2 ½ In. ....*illus*	40.00
Iroquois Casual, Bowl, Cereal, Oyster, 5 In.	25.00
Iroquois Casual, Bowl, Fruit, Nutmeg Brown, 5 ½ In.	35.00
Iroquois Casual, Bowl, Fruit, Ripe Apricot, 5 ½ In.	15.00
Iroquois Casual, Bowl, Gumbo, Cantaloupe	160.00
Iroquois Casual, Bowl, Salad, Lemon Yellow, Raindrop, 10 In.	120.00
Iroquois Casual, Bowl, Vegetable, Lemon Yellow, Raindrop, 8 In.	75.00
Iroquois Casual, Butter, Cover, Nutmeg Brown	85.00
Iroquois Casual, Carafe, Nutmeg, 10 ¼ In. ....*illus*	325.00
Iroquois Casual, Casserole, Cover, Lettuce Green, 2 Qt.	150.00
Iroquois Casual, Cup & Saucer, Ice Blue	10.00
Iroquois Casual, Gravy, Fast-Stand, Ripe Apricot	125.00
Iroquois Casual, Pitcher, Cover, Lettuce Green, 1 ½ Qt.	500.00
Iroquois Casual, Plate, Dinner, Ice Blue, 10 ⅛ In.	12.00
Iroquois Casual, Plate, Salad, White, Raindrop, 7 In.	30.00
Iroquois Casual, Salt & Pepper, Stacking, Aqua	875.00
Iroquois Casual, Saucer, Ice Blue	2.00
Iroquois Casual, Soup, Cover, Sugar White, Raindrop	75.00
Iroquois Casual, Teapot, Sugar White	199.00
Oceana, Bowl, Starfish, Marked, 13 ½ In.	1200.00

SABINO glass was made in the 1920s and 1930s in Paris, France. Founded by Marius-Ernest Sabino (1878–1961), the firm was noted for Art Deco lamps, vases, figurines, and animals in clear, colored, and opalescent glass. Production stopped during World War II but resumed in the 1960s with the manufacture of nude figurines and small opalescent glass animals. Pieces made in recent years are a slightly different color and can be recognized. Only vintage pieces are listed here.

Sabino France

Bottle, 5 Nudes, Standing, Iridescent, Teardrop Shape, Acorn Stopper, 6 ½ In.	472.00
Bowl, Blue Opalescent, Blossoms & Berries, 3 Leafy Feet, 8 In.	120.00
Figurine, Fish, Opalescent, Clear Blue Fins, Wavy Stepped Base, 4 ¾ In.	61.00
Figurine, Gazelle, Leaping, Opalescent, Round Base, 6 ½ x 5 In.	176.00
Figurine, Isadora, Nude Woman, Dancing, Flowing Scarves, Opalescent, 9 ½ In.	424.00
Figurine, Isadora, Woman, Opalescent, 9 ½ x 6 ½ In.	410.00
Perfume Bottle, Leaves & Berries, Amber, Opalescent, Egg Shape, Squat Stopper, 4 In.	36.00
Plate, Birds, Blue, Opalescent, 9 ¾ In.	272.00
Vase, Eucalyptus, Clear & Opalescent, Shouldered, Rolled Rim, 6 ½ x 4 In.	300.00
Vase, Ferns, Bulbous, Pinched, Flared, 9 x 6 In.	580.00
Vase, Fish, Overlapping, Opalescent, Flared, Square Foot, 5 ¼ x 5 In.	400.00
Vase, Green, Satin, Vertical Ribs, Bulbous, Pinched, Flattened Rim, 5 ½ In.	275.00
Vase, La Danse, Dancing Female Nudes, Blue Opalescent, c.1929, 14 In.	793.00
Vase, Ovals & Pearls, Opalescent, Flared, Cylindrical Foot, 6 x 5 In.	440.00

SALOPIAN ware was made by the Caughley factory of England during the eighteenth century. The early pieces were blue and white with some colored decorations. Another ware referred to as Salopian is a late-nineteenth-century tableware decorated with color transfers.

Salopian

Creamer, Asian Figures, Pagodas, Landscape, Helmet Form, Footed, 6 In.	55.00
Cup & Saucer, Double Bird, Multicolored Flowers, Honeycomb Ground	90.00
Cup & Saucer, Flower, Leaves, Acorn, Greek Key Border, Multicolored	113.00
Cup & Saucer, Milking Scene, Multicolored Flower Border	136.00
Cup & Saucer, Pagoda, Stream, Boat, Village, Multicolored Transfer, Handleless	88.00
Cup & Saucer, Stag, Cottage, Multicolored Flower Border	102.00
Cup & Saucer, Stag, Cottage Scene, Village Border, Handleless, Child's	254.00
Cup & Saucer, Stag, Sheep Herding, Castle, Multicolored Flower Band	68.00
Plate, Stag, Multicolored Border, 7 ¼ In.	73.00
Teapot, Stag, Cottage, Landscape, Flowers & Leaf Border, 5 ¼ In. ....*illus*	116.00

Rug, Sumac, Flowers, Green, Gray Field, c.1950, 10 x 10 In.
$1020.00

Rumrill, Jug, Blue Gray, Stopper
$72.00

Russel Wright, Grass, Bowl, Knowles, Justin Tharaud, 6 ¼ x 2 ½ In.
$40.00

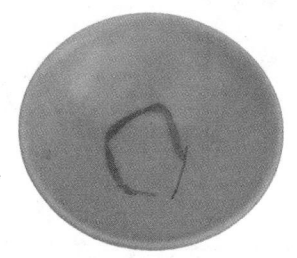

Russel Wright, Iroquois Casual, Carafe, Nutmeg, 10 ¼ In.
$325.00

S

Salopian, Teapot, Stag, Cottage, Landscape, Flowers & Leaf Border, 5 ¼ In. $116.00

Salt & Pepper, Bear, Hugger, Van Tellingen, 3 ½ In. $25.00

Salt & Pepper, Mary & Her Little Lamb, Hugger, Van Tellingen $59.00

Salt & Pepper, Milk Glass, Roses, c.1900, 3 x 2 ½ In. $12.00

New Use For Old Salts

Old salt and pepper shakers without tops can be used as small flower vases.

SALT AND PEPPER SHAKERS in matched sets were first used in the nineteenth century. Collectors are primarily interested in figural examples made after World War I. Huggers are pairs of shakers that appear to embrace each other. Many salt and pepper shakers are listed in other categories and can be located through the index at the back of this book.

Aunt Jemima & Uncle Mose, Red, White, Black, Yellow, F & F, 3 ½ In.	55.00
Bag, Lamb's Wool, Old MacDonald Series, 384, Marked, Regal	79.00
Bakelite, Half Circle, Round Base, Butterscotch	95.00
Bear, Hugger, Van Tellingen, 3 ½ In. .....*illus*	25.00
Black Chef & Mammy, Salty & Peppy, Painted, Pearl China Co., 8 In.	34.00
Bullet Shape, Plastic Stoppers, Silver Plate, Reed & Barton, 3 In.	55.00
Color Craft, Aluminum, Copper Color, Black Plastic Lid, 3 ⅛ In.	15.00
Cook, Man, Woman, Yellow & Black Glaze, Salty & Peppy	68.00
Corn, Majolica	44.00
Cut Glass, Nailhead Diamond, Strawberry Diamond & Fan, Sterling Tops, 4 In.	75.00
Dutch Girl, Holding Flower, Red Hat, Yellow Hair, Shoes, 4 ¼ In.	58.00
Laurel & Hardy, Ceramic, Glazed, Hardy In Admiral Hat, 1950s, 4 ½ In.	173.00
Lennie Lennox, Composition, Marked, Juan Products, Columbus, OH, 1950, 5 In.	73.00
Mary & Her Little Lamb, Hugger, Van Tellingen .....*illus*	59.00
Milk Glass, Roses, c.1900, 3 x 2 ½ In. .....*illus*	12.00
Modernist, Tapered, Glass Beads, Cohr Co., Denmark, 1950s, 4 ½ x 4 In.	250.00
Mushroom, Bakelite, Green, Apple Juice	75.00
Peppermill, Wood, Natural Nissen, 5 ½ In.	135.00
Round, Stainless Steel, Concave Top, Sweden, 1 ¾ x 1 ½ In.	35.00
Teddy Bear, Marked, Otagiri, Japan, 1983, 3 ¾ In.	10.00
Totem, Seal, Walrus, Polar Bear, Ivory, Carved, 2 ½ In.	175.00
White, Flowers, Schwab Gmund Coat Of Arms, 2 In.	20.00
Wood, Lauffer, Dan Droz Designs, 1875, 6 In.	85.00

SALT GLAZE has a grayish white surface with a texture like an orange peel. It is a method of decoration that has been used since the eighteenth century. Salt-glazed pieces are still being made.

Crock, Butter, Eagle, Bail Handle	300.00
Teapot, Cobalt Blue Highlights, Late 18th Century, 4 ¾ In.	890.00

SAMPLERS were made in America from the early 1700s. The best examples were made from 1790 to 1840. Long, narrow samplers are usually older than square ones. Early samplers just had stitching or alphabets. The later examples had numerals, borders, and pictorial decorations. Those with mottoes are mid-Victorian. A revival of interest in the 1930s produced simpler samplers, usually with mottoes.

ABCDE

Alphabet, Adam & Eve, Jane Wanless, April 12, 1843, Frame, 19 x 18 In. .....*illus*	351.00
Alphabet, Birds, Trees, Unicorn, Lion, Elizabeth Webb, 1846, Silk, Wool, England, 13 ½ x 14 In.	323.00
Alphabet, Darning, Flower Vases, Anno, WB, MK, 1851, 14 x 12 In.	320.00
Alphabet, House, Cows, Trees, Lydia Visscher, Age 8 Years, 1830, Silk, Linen, Frame, 19 x 18 In.	3643.00
Alphabet, House, Strawberry Border, Adeline Patterson, Age 13, c.1833, Frame, 18 ½ x 17 In.	764.00
Alphabet, House, Trees, Birds, Dr. Watts' Children Hymn, 1826, Linen, Frame, 16 x 13 In.	295.00
Alphabet, Larson Family, Susanna Larson, Frame, 1758, 10 ¼ x 7 ¾ In.	553.00
Alphabet, Mary A. Jeruld, 1855, Silk, Cotton, Brown Tan, Frame, Ind., 13 x 14 In.	411.00
Alphabet, Mary Ann Twitchell, Silk, Linen, Frame, c.1819, 8 x 10 In.	235.00
Alphabet, Needlework On Cotton, Numbers, House, Tree, Vine Border, 1889, Frame, 11 x 12 In.	413.00
Alphabet, Number, Verse, Araminta Heser, In The 12th Year Of Her Age, AD 1841, 19 x 17 In.	4000.00
Alphabet, Numbers, Birds, Dogs, Trees, Buildings, Lillie May Waygood, 1894, 16 x 12 In.	120.00
Alphabet, Numbers, Crown, Florets, Blue, Gold, Frame, 10 ½ x 14 ½ In.	143.00
Alphabet, Numbers, Crowns, Animals, Birds, Wreath, Monogram, BM, 1878, Frame, 26 x 23 In.	290.00
Alphabet, Numbers, Flower Bands, Eliza Meserole, Age 16 Years, 1819, Silk, Linen, 19 x 23 In.	1058.00
Alphabet, Numbers, House, Trees, Family, Dog, Horse, Vine Border, Poem, 1835, Frame, 24 x 23 In.	523.00
Alphabet, Numbers, Mary Patterson, Frame, Early 1800s, 10 ¼ x 8 In.	120.00
Alphabet, Numbers, Poem, Urns, Birds, Butterflies, Dogs, Mary Wood, 1809, Frame, 15 x 12 In.	267.00
Alphabet, Numbers, Rose, Crown, Well, Insect, Gazebo, Multicolored, 1971, Frame, 13 x 14 In.	121.00
Alphabet, Numbers, Verse, Angelina Wallace, 1837, Silk On Linen, Frame, 17 x 16 In.	1050.00
Alphabet, Numbers, Verse, Elizabeth K. Hunt, Age 12, Frame, N.H., c.1825, 17 x 16 In.	2115.00
Alphabet, Numbers, Verse, House, Trees, Flowers, Mary Medges, 1839, Frame, 17 x 13 In.	770.00
Alphabet, Numbers, Verse, Mary Kopfer, AE, 1805, Frame, 18 ½ x 19 ½ In.	250.00
Alphabet, Numbers, Verse, Susan Colemore, Aged 10, Silk, Wool, Frame, 17 x 17 ½ In.	265.00
Alphabet, Numbers, Verse, Zigzag Border, Zelphia Merrill, 1827, Silk On Linen, 10 x 8 In.	510.00
Alphabet, Stitch Samples, Flowers, Fruits, Sarah F. Belcher, 1827, Silk, Linen, Mass., 18 x 19 In.	1410.00
Alphabet, Verse, 6-Line, Bird, Flower, Ann Bailey, Flower Vine Border, Silk On Linen, 17 x 13 In.	460.00

S

Alphabet, Verse, Animals, Flowers, Susanna Chapman, 1790, Silk, Wool, Frame, 15 x 15 In. ..	411.00
Alphabet, Verse, Figures, Dog, Birds, House, Lucenia Bradley Aged 11, Frame, 1800s, 15 x 20 In.	395.00
Alphabet, Verse, Floral Vine, Leah Catherine Stymets, Silk, Canvas, Frame, c.1846, 15 x 18 In.	235.00
Alphabet, Verse, Lancaster, Ohio, 1811, Frame, 13 x 8 In.	850.00
Alphabet, Verse, Laurel Wreath, Strawberry Border, Silk Threads, Linen Ground, 17 ¾ x 16 ¼ In.	896.00
Alphabet, Verse, Mary Adams, 1882, Frame, 14 x 12 In.	200.00
Alphabet, Verse, Mary Dobson Did This Work In The Twelfth Year Of Her Age 1733, 16 In.	5035.00
Alphabet, Verse, Sarah Riley, Bethel, Clermont County, Silk On Linen, Frame, c.1841, 18 x 18 In. .	1175.00
Alphabet, Verse, St. Paul's Cathedral, Eliza James, Flowers, Fruit, Silk On Linen, 16 ½ x 12 ½ In.	805.00
Alphabet, Verse, Strawberry Border, Rachel Aston, 1786, Silk On Linen, 16 ½ x 11 In.	3800.00
Alphabet, Verse, Vines, Frances Crowells, Tenth Year Of Her Age, Nov. 26 1824, 15 x 18 In.	805.00
Alphabets, Bluebird, W Basket, Birds, Flowers, Savers Family, Silk, Linen, c.1830, 13 x 20 In. .	470.00
Alphabets, Flower Basket, Birds, Trees, Evelina Gilman, Age 12 Years, 1835, Silk, Linen, 16 x 17 In. .	9400.00
Alphabets, Flowers, Figures, Dogs, Castle, Linen, Frame, Dutch, c.1871, 20 ½ In.	1265.00
Alphabets, Numbers, Jerusha Bartlett, 1806, Silk, Linen, Mass., Frame, 15 ½ x 22 In.	617.00
Alphabets, Numbers, Ship, English Flag, Ales Jump, Aged 12 Years, 1798, Linen, Frame, 17 x 14 In. .	605.00
Alphabets, Numbers, Verse, Dolly Brown, 1819, Silk, Linen, Frame, New York, 17 ½ x 17 In. ..	206.00
Alphabets, Numbers, Verse, Fruit Baskets, Silk Threads, Linen Ground, Frame, 12 ½ x 13 In.	239.00
Alphabets, Numbers, Verse, Mary King Gilkey, Plymouth County, c.1812, 8 ½ x 15 ¼ In.	294.00
Alphabets, Silk, Linen, Signed, M. Sinclair, c.1830, 9 ½ x 11 ¾ In. ....*illus*	235.00
Alphabets, Trees, Flowers, Animals, Jannet Sinclair, Aged 8, 1818, Silk On Linen, Frame, 24 x 23 In. ..	1645.00
Alphabets, Verse, Hearts, Eliza'h McCarthy, Silk Threads, 1780, 20 x 9 In.	475.00
Animal, Black Figure, Seated Female, Anne Singleton, 20 ¼ x 22 ¾ In.	575.00
Basket, Butterflies, Flowers, Verse, Ribbon, Maria Miller, Age 12 Years, 1836, Silk, Linen, 24 x 25 In.	999.00
Birds, Flowers, Urn, Catharine Rebecca Oldis, Aged 13 Years, 1834, Frame, 17 In.	339.00
Church, Birds, Butterflies, Leaves, Beaded, Embroidered, Frame, 1874, 14 ½ x 17 ½ In.	2500.00
Courting Scene, Man, Woman, Fountain, Fowl, Beast, Buildings, 1900s, Frame, 16 x 19 In. ..	1430.00
Family Record, Alphabet, Tombs, Weeping Willows, Benton, Scranton, Frame, 1830s, 17 x 19 In. .	1410.00
Flower Vine Border, Verse, Lions, Birds, Basket Of Fruit, Shepherds, Frame, 16 x 12 In.	236.00
Flowerpots, Brick Home, Pine Trees, Strawberry Border, Harriet Arnold, 1828, 17 x 16 In.	15600.00
Flowers, Leaves, Acorns, Band Pattern, Multicolored, Sarah Baker, Silk Thread, 1664, 32 x 7 In. ...	9480.00
House, Flowers, Baskets, Vines, Elizabeth Eaton, Silk, Wool, Frame, c.1820, 23 x 20 In.	499.00
Mary Dobson, Did This Work In The Twelfth Year Of Her Age, 1733, 16 In.	5035.00
Memorial, Tomb, Angels, Poem, Vines, Lincoen Sharples Booth, 1873, Cotton, Frame, 17 x 27 In. ...	198.00
Potted Flowers, Brick Home, Pine Trees, Vine Border, 1828, Silk On Linen, 17 x 15 ¾ In.	15210.00
Quaker, Flower & Leaf Vine, Birds, Elizabeth Mitchell, 1828, Silk On Linen, Frame, 17 x 19 In.	881.00
Repeating Medallions, Crowns, 1781, Silk On Linen, England, 13 ½ x 10 ¾ In.	435.00
Roll Up, Embroidery Eagle, Flower, Heart, Black, Red, Gold, Wool, Silk, 5 Pockets, 1836, 5 x 29 In.	2370.00
Spotted Deer, Dog, White Swan Flapping Wings, Lawn, Pond, Ann Brown, 1788, 12 x 15 In. ..	2115.00
Trees, Flowers, Mary Ann Gardner, 9 Partners Boarding School, New York, c.1834, 20 x 23 In.	881.00
Verse, 6-Line, 2 Peacocks, Sarah Kinston, Aged 7, 1818, Silk On Linen, 12 x 15 In.	550.00
Verse, Adam & Eve, Sun, Moon, Figures, Flowers, Mary Bagshaw, 1793, Silk, Linen, 22 x 17 In.	1185.00
Verse, Alphabet, House, Fence, Trees, Virginia Miles, 1844, Silk On Linen, Frame, 16 x 17 In. ..	18400.00
Verse, Alphabets, Numbers, 1835, Silk & Wool On Linen, Frame, 17 x 17 ¼ In.	21850.00
Verse, Alphabets, Numbers, Strawberry Vine Border, Silk On Linen, 19 ½ x 17 In.	10925.00
Verse, Birds, Flower Basket, Border, Cat, Silk On Linen, 11 ¼ x 13 ¾ In.	1046.00
Verse, Building, Cherubs, Sophia Marshill Work 1844, Frame, 23 In.	283.00
Verse, Building, Flowers, Woman, Mary Morris, 1820, Silk, Linen, Frame, 16 x 16 In.	411.00
Verse, Flower Basket, Pasture, Sarah Ann Gibbons, 1834, Silk On Linen, 17 x 17 ½ In.	48875.00
Verse, Flowers, Shields, Elizabeth Robinson, 1824, Silk, Linen, Frame, 17 x 19 In.	529.00
Verse, Hannah Riley's Work, 1828, Dukinfield Chapel, Silk On Linen, Frame, 16 x 16 In.	936.00
Verse, House, Bricks, Birds, Stylized Feather Border, Wool, 13 ½ x 12 In.	805.00
Verse, House, Fence, Potted Flowers, Elizabeth Francis, 1833, Aged 11 Years, 19 x 12 In.	633.00
Verse, House, Fence, Trees, Elizabeth Kinsey, Silk, On Linen, Frame, c.1840, 22 x 18 In. ...*illus*	764.00
Verse, House, Flowers, Trees, Ellen Rhodes Finished This Work Dec. 1845, Frame, 24 In.	339.00
Verse, House, Trees, Flowers, Doves, Ellen Baxter Aged 10 Years, 1836, 17 x 12 In.	403.00
Verse, Religious, Pastoral Scene, Silk On Wool, Frame, 18 ½ x 21 ½ In.	558.00
Verse, Silk On Linen, Fabric Backing, Frame, 1806, 16 x 12 In.	431.00
Village, Lake, School, Children, Animals, Wool Thread, Giltwood Frame, c.1885, 25 x 26 In. ..	1067.00

Sampler, Alphabet, Adam & Eve, Jane Wanless, April 12, 1843, Frame, 19 x 18 In.
$351.00

Sampler, Alphabets, Silk, Linen, Signed, M. Sinclair, c.1830, 9 ½ x 11 ¾ In.
$235.00

Sampler, Verse, House, Fence, Trees, Elizabeth Kinsey, Silk, On Linen, Frame, c.1840, 22 x 18 In.
$764.00

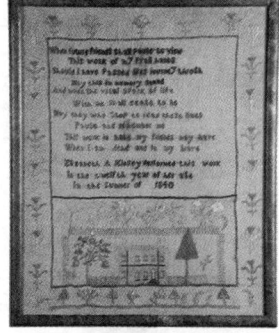

TIP
Mint, rosemary, lavender, and thyme will repel moths. Hang bunches of the herbs near stored textiles.

SAMSON and Company, a French firm specializing in the reproduction of collectible wares of many countries and periods, was founded in Paris in the early nineteenth century. Chelsea, Meissen, Famille Verte, and Chinese Export porcelain are some of the wares that have been reproduced by the company. The firm uses a variety of marks on the reproductions. It is still in operation.

Bowl, Ormolu Mounted, Multicolored Enamel, Rose Famille Palette, Bronze Base, 8 ¾ x 7 In.	1293.00

Sandwich Glass, Candlestick, Petal, Columnar, Translucent Chartreuse, 6-Petal Socket, 9 ¼ In.
$489.00

Sandwich Glass, Cologne, Star & Punty, Canary Yellow, Hexagonal, 7 x 3 In.
$219.00

Sandwich Glass, Pomade Jar, Figural, Chained Bear, Opaque Black, 4 ⅝ x 2 In.
$633.00

SANDWICH GLASS is any of the myriad types of glass made by the Boston and Sandwich Glass Works in Sandwich, Massachusetts, between 1825 and 1888. It is often very difficult to be sure whether a piece was really made at the Sandwich factory because so many types were made there and similar pieces were made at other glass factories. Additional pieces may be listed under Pressed Glass and in related categories.

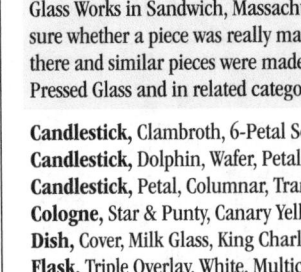

Candlestick, Clambroth, 6-Petal Socket, Dolphin On Base, c.1850, 10 ½ In.	230.00
Candlestick, Dolphin, Wafer, Petal Socket, Green, 9 x 4 x 4 ½ In., Pair	117.00
Candlestick, Petal, Columnar, Translucent Chartreuse, 6-Petal Socket, 9 ¼ In. .... *illus*	489.00
Cologne, Star & Punty, Canary Yellow, Hexagonal, 7 x 3 In. .... *illus*	219.00
Dish, Cover, Milk Glass, King Charles Spaniel Finial, 4 ¾ In.	1125.00
Flask, Triple Overlay, White, Multicolored Swirls, Paperweight Technique, 7 In.	1323.00
Lamp, Fluid, Pressed Ring Punty, Baroque Milk Glass Base, Brass Connector, 1860s, 10 ½ In.	250.00
Lamp, Fluid, Star & Punty, Flint, Hexagonal Base, c.1850, 9 x 4 In.	195.00
Lamp, Whale Oil, Blown Font, Lacy Acanthus Leaf Base, c.1835, 6 ¼ In., Pair	294.00
Paperweight, Millefiori Flowers, Lampwork Leaves, 2-Swirl Cushion, c.1865, 1 ½ x 2 In.	267.00
Pomade Jar, Figural Bear, Milk Glass, c.1890, 5 ¼ In.	1250.00
Pomade Jar, Figural, Chained Bear, Opaque Black, 4 ⅝ x 2 In. .... *illus*	633.00
Salt, Cranberry, Barrel, Threaded Ground Mouth, Lid, c.1880, 2 ½ In.	95.00
Salt, Gaines, Milk Glass, Fiery Opalescent, Looped Sides, Fluted Lip, 2 ¼ In.	115.00
Salt, Round, Floral Pressed, Mottled Opaque, Silver Swirls, Scalloped Foot, 2 x 3 In. .... *illus*	2185.00
Spoon Holder, Cable, Blue, Hexagonal, Fan Scallop Rim, Gilt, 5 ¾ In. .... *illus*	518.00
Vase, Blue, 8 Icicles Rim To Base, 8 In.	460.00
Vase, Deep Rose Amethyst, Paneled, Footed, Mid 19th Century, 10 ¼ In.	2800.00
Vase, Tulip, Amethyst, 8-Paneled Top, Bottom, c.1850, 10 In., Pair	2015.00
Vase, Tulip, Puce Amethyst, Paneled, Footed, Mid 19th Century, 10 In., Pair	3000.00
Vase, Tulip, Violet Amethyst, Panel, Footed, Mid 19th Century, 9 ¾ In.	1800.00
Wine, Bellflower, Knob Stem, 4 x 1 ⅝ In.	140.00

SARREGUEMINES is the name of a French town that is used as part of a china mark. Utzschneider and Company, a porcelain factory, made ceramics in Sarreguemines, Lorraine, France, from about 1775. Transfer-printed wares and majolica were made in the nineteenth century. The nineteenth-century pieces, most often found today, usually have colorful transfer-printed decorations showing peasants in local costumes.

Dish, Underplate, Cover, Cabbage Shape	67.00
Plaque, Tradesmen, Scribe, Potter, Transfer Print, Shell Edge, 11 In., Pair	89.00
Tray, Majolica, Strawberries & Blossoms, Rectangular, Notched Corners, 10 x 12 In.	236.00

SASCHA BRASTOFF made decorative accessories, ceramics, enamels on copper, and plastics of his own design. He headed a factory, Sascha Brastoff of California, Inc., in West Los Angeles, from 1953 until about 1973. He died in 1993. Pieces signed with the signature *Sascha Brastoff* were his work and are the most expensive. Other pieces marked *Sascha B.* or with a stamped mark were made by others in his company. Pieces made by Matt Adams after he left the factory are listed here with his name.

Bowl, Oval, Abstract, Blue, Green, Signed, 7 ¼ x 5 ¾ In.	55.00
Bowl, Rectangular, Abstract, Blue, Green, Signed, 6 ½ x 6 ½ In.	55.00
Bowl Set, Copper, Vineyard Scene, 11 ¼, 6 ½, 5 ¾ & 5 ¼ In.	55.00
Pitcher & Bowl, White, Gold & Silver Horses, 10 ½ & 7 ½ In.	255.00
Vase, Organic Shape, Multicolored, Gilt, Signed, 11 ¼ In. .... *illus*	63.00

SATIN GLASS is a late-nineteenth-century art glass. It has a dull finish that is caused by hydrofluoric acid vapor treatment. Satin glass was made in many colors and sometimes has applied decorations. Satin glass is also listed by factory name, such as Webb, or in the Mother-of-Pearl category in this book.

Basket, Pink, Leaves, Acorn Feet, Frosted, Tall Handle, 14 In.	150.00
Bowl, Flower Branches, Diamond Design, Pink, Lobed, Ruffled Rim, Cased Ivory, c.1890, 4 ¾ x 10 In.	550.00
Bowl, Vertical Ribbon, Silver Collar, Red, White Interior, Brass Holder, 10 In.	118.00
Butter, Pink Shell Pattern, Gold Branches, Crystal, Silver Tray, 8 In.	127.00
Dome, Pink, Enamel Flowers, Finial, c.1870, 5 x 4 ½ In.	23.00
Ewer, Pink, Bulbous, Camphor Handle, Stemmed Flowers, 8 ½ In.	50.00
Humidor, Blue, Cover, Boar, 8 ½ In.	66.00
Rose Bowl, Blue, Herringbone, 3 ¾ In.	185.00
Vase, Enamel Branch Design, Pink, 8 In.	100.00
Vase, Flowers, Leaves, Pink & Caramel Ground, Ruffled Rim, Late 1800s, 6 ¾ In.	59.00

Vase, Honeycomb, White Shaded To Blue, Urn Form, Folded-Up Ruffled Rim, 9 In.	118.00
Vase, Pink, Swirled Ribs, Applied Molded Handles, c.1900, 10 x 5 In. ....*illus*	104.00
Vase, Raspberry, Herringbone, Threading, Leaf, Stem Handles, 7 In.	1150.00
Vase, Seaweed Design, Applied Jewels, Ruffled Rim, Blue, Pontil Mark, 5 x 4 In.	127.00

SATSUMA is a Japanese pottery with a distinctive creamy beige crackled glaze. Most of the pieces were decorated with blue, red, green, orange, or gold. Almost all Satsuma found today was made after 1860, especially during the Meiji Period, 1868–1912. During World War I, Americans could not buy undecorated European porcelains. Women who liked to make hand-painted porcelains at home began to decorate plain Satsuma. These pieces are known today as "American Satsuma."

Bottle, Women, Applied Twisted Dragons, 6 ⅔ In., Pair	350.00
Bowl, 4 Women, Flowers, Birds, Imperial Kiln Mark, c.1890, 11 In.	58.00
Bowl, Butterflies, Wisteria, Chrysanthemums, Gilt Mark, Early 1900s, 4 x 4 ½ In. ....*illus*	3680.00
Bowl, Fox Spirits, Bugs, Floral Interior, Boys, Insects Flower Bands Exterior, c.1900, 3 x 5 In. .	14900.00
Bowl, Lobbed, Enamel, Gilt, Flowers, Alternating Panels, Blue Ground, c.1912, 4 ¾ x 10 ½ In.	764.00
Bowl, Swirling Crane Design Interior, Flowers, Leaves Exterior, c.1900, 2 x 4 ½ In.	4600.00
Bowl, Tree, Birds, Scalloped Gold Rim, Signed, 1800s, 3 x 8 ⅜ In.	316.00
Box, Cover, Kogo, Allover Flowers, Gold Spirals, Arabesques, Teardrop Shape, 3 In.	649.00
Box, Square, Panels, Krako Boys Playing, Square Lid, 4-Footed, Ryozan, 2 x 1 ¾ In.	944.00
Box, Women & Children In Landscape, Iris, Peonies, Square, Cut Corners, Ryozan, 3 In.	649.00
Censer, Chrysanthemums & Kikyo, Cloud Collar, Shimazu Crest, 3-Footed, Signed, Koyama, 4 In.	510.00
Censer, Openwork, Gilt Basket Weave Bamboo Ground, Gilt Mark, c.1900, 6 In. ....*illus*	8050.00
Censer, Women, Landscape, Round, 3-Footed, Signed, 3 In.	365.00
Cup, Cover, Figures Tumbling, Reclining, Signed, 1800s, 4 ¾ x 2 ¾ In., Pair	173.00
Flask, Pilgrim, Noblemen, Lion, Enamel, Gilt, Mark, c.1900, 18 In.	294.00
Jar, Cover, Asian Vase Theme, Crest Mark, 1912-25, 10 ½ In. ....*illus*	8050.00
Koro, Cover, 3 Foo Dog Head Feet, Handles, Foo Dog Finial, Figures, Brocade Ground, 17 ½ In.	540.00
Koro, Figures In Reserves, Black Ground, Round, Dragon, 2 Shaped Handles, c.1900, 11 In. ..	1416.00
Plate, Seated Lohan, Children, Lion, c.1900, 7 ¾ In.	288.00
Tea Caddy, Cover, Figures, Landscape, 3-Sided, Footed, Signed, 5 ½ In.	2700.00
Tea Caddy, Cover, Figures, Landscape, Scroll Handles, Flask Shape, Signed, 5 In.	4010.00
Tea Caddy, Ginger Jar Shape, Figures In Reserves, Military Men, Sages, Kitayama, 6 In.	1298.00
Tea Caddy, Kingfisher On Branch, Ducks, Blue Ground, Cylindrical, Kinkozan, 6 x 5 In.	3245.00
Teapot, Gilt, Multicolored Enamel, Deities, Rosewood Stand, Signed, 3 ½ x 5 In. ....*illus*	150.00
Tray, Round, White Egrets, Flowering Blossoms, Mt. Fuji, 20th Century, 18 In.	413.00
Urn, Flowers, Leaves, Multicolored, Raised Gilt, Mounted As Lamp, 14 ¼ In., Pair	88.00
Vase, 2 Panels, Shogun With Generals, Figures, Street Scenes, Egg Shape, Kinkozan, 4 In.	708.00
Vase, 3 Panels, Multicolored Flowers, Cream Ground, 7 In.	104.00
Vase, 4 Reserves, Men In Landscape, Ceremonial Objects, Flat Shoulder, Kozan, 5 ¼ In.	1770.00
Vase, 6 Overlapping Panels, Daily Scenes, Flower & Tapestry Ground, Baluster, Kozan, 5 In. ...	2242.00
Vase, Baluster Shape, Applied Ring & Tassel Gilt, Painted Flora, Fauna, c.1880, 12 ¼ In.	950.00
Vase, Baluster Shape, Scenic, Birds, Blooming Branches, Bamboo, Yellow Ground, 9 In., Pair .	115.00
Vase, Birds, Leaves, White Ground, Brocaded Flowers On Neck, Yokohama Imura, 5 In.	354.00
Vase, Ducks, Crane, Stylized Leaves, Bulbous, Flared Rim & Base, Lion Mask Handles, 9 In.	944.00
Vase, Figures, 2 Panels, Cobalt Blue Ground, Gilt, 12 In.	1250.00
Vase, Figures Marching, White Ground, Flowers On Shoulder, Gold Bands, Kinkozan, 5 In.	1416.00
Vase, Figures, Shaped & Overlapping Panels, Landscapes, Cylindrical, 4 ½ In., Pair	1416.00
Vase, Flowers, Dark Blue Ground, Gilt, Tapered, 5 In.	175.00
Vase, Men, Women, Gardens, Tapered Square, Short Neck, Kinkozan, 5 In.	944.00
Vase, Mt. Fuji, Hanging Wisteria, Birds, 4-Sided, Signed, 6 In.	175.00
Vase, Oval, Boys Playing, Court Officials, Base, c.1900, 9 ¼ In.	115.00
Vase, Painted, Peacocks, Flowering Landscapes, Gilt Highlights, 12 In.	12.00
Vase, Panel, Figures, Birds & Flowers, Squat Base, Elongated Neck, 5 In., Pair	443.00
Vase, Peacock, Birds, Rooster, Chickens, Gold Trim, Egg Shape, Flared Rim, Kinkozan, 14 In.	8260.00
Vase, Peonies, Brocade Shoulder, Gold, Baluster, Wooden 3-Footed Stand, Taizan, 5 In., Pair...	443.00
Vase, Rectangular Reserves, Women, Flowers, Brocaded Flowers, Kozan, 4 ¾ In.	384.00
Vase, Roosters, Chickens, Wisteria, Basket Weave Band, Gilt, Hexagonal, 3 ⅝ x 2 In. ....*illus*	667.00
Vase, Scenic Mountain Garden, Oval, Shouldered, 20th Century, 8 ¼ In.	88.00
Vase, Scenic Panels, Gilt, Signed, Japan, c.1910, 8 In. ....*illus*	1800.00
Vase, Sloped Shoulder, Mountain Landscape, Hand Painted, Gold, H. Hontani, 15 x 7 In.	702.00
Vase, Women, Children, Landscape, Greek Key Borders, Bell Shape, Shozan, 3 In., Pair	767.00
Vase, Women In Garden, Cobalt Blue Ground, Gold Flowers, Shouldered, Kinkozan, 9 In.	885.00
Vase, Women Outdoors, Flowers, Double Gourd Shape, Gold Brocade, 5 ½ In.	1298.00
Wedding Cup, Cover, Figures, Gilt Ground, Inside Painted With Poems, Marked, 5 x 3 In., Pair.	207.00

Sandwich Glass, Salt, Round, Floral Pressed, Mottled Opaque, Silver Swirls, Scalloped Foot, 2 x 3 In. $2185.00

Sandwich Glass, Spoon Holder, Cable, Blue, Hexagonal, Fan Scallop Rim, Gilt, 5 ¾ In. $518.00

Sascha Brastoff, Vase, Organic Shape, Multicolored, Gilt, Signed, 11 ¼ In. $63.00

Satin Glass, Vase, Pink, Swirled Ribs, Applied Molded Handles, c.1900, 10 x 5 In. $104.00

S

Satsuma, Bowl, Butterflies, Wisteria, Chrysanthemums, Gilt Mark, Early 1900s, 4 x 4 ½ In. $3680.00

Satsuma, Censer, Openwork, Gilt Basket Weave Bamboo Ground, Gilt Mark, c.1900, 6 In. $8050.00

Satsuma, Jar, Cover, Asian Vase Theme, Crest Mark, 1912-25, 10 ½ In. $8050.00

Satsuma, Teapot, Gilt, Multicolored Enamel, Deities, Rosewood Stand, Signed, 3 ½ x 5 In. $150.00

SCALES have been made to weigh everything from babies to gold. Collectors search for all types. Most popular are small gold dust scales and special grocery scales.

Analytical Balance, Brass Post, 2 Pans, Mahogany Case, Marked, Towers, c.1910, 18 x 16 In.	235.00
Analytical Balance, Wood, Glass Cabinet, Drawers, c.1920, 8 x 16 ½ x 17 In.	723.00
Balance, Brass, Victorian, Iron Base, 1800s, 45 x 35 In.	585.00
Balance, Brass, Wedgwood Blue & White, Jasperware Plaques, Classical Scenes, Victorian, 3 x 8 ¼ In.	239.00
Balance, Bronze Arm, Pan, Walnut Case, France, 20th Century, 17 ½ x 16 ½ In. .... *illus*	570.00
Balance, Degrave & Co., Brass, London, 22 x 21 x 9 In.	115.00
Balance, Howe, Cast Iron, Painted Red, 8 x 18 In.	47.00
Balance, Iron Base, Brass Pans, Gem No. 5, Weighs To 5 Oz. .... *illus*	138.00
Balance, Iron Base, Brass Rail, Pan, Weighs To 8 Lb., Howe-Rutland, Vt., c.1867 .... *illus*	110.00
Balance, Iron, Brass, Painted Black, 7 x 16 In.	59.00
Balance, Metinel, Brass Pans, France, 1930s, 23 x 10 In.	235.00
Balance, Red Paint, Tole Tray, Cast Iron, 19th Century, 11 In.	55.00
Balance, Voland & Sons, New Rochelle, N.Y., Wood Case, 20 ¼ x 21 In.	115.00
Balance, W & T Avery Makers, Iron, Brass, Harp Top, Marked, Birmingham, 33 ½ In.	75.00
Candy, Blue, Weights, Graniteware, 7 x 12 x 7 In.	330.00
Candy, Toledo, Enamel, Brass Pan, 15 In.	130.00
Columbia, 1 Cent, Key, 71 x 18 ½ x 27 ½ In.	385.00
Jockey, Chatillon Dial, Oak Chair, Caned Seat, Tripod Frame, Early 1900s, 17 x 104 In.	600.00
Penny, Mills Novelty Co., Coin-Operated, Art Deco, 47 x 24 x 12 In.	196.00
Penny, RC Cola, Royal Crown, Best By Taste Test, 44 x 13 x 21 In.	5010.00
Postage, Brass, Mahogany, Desktop, c.1900, 10 x ¼ x 4 ¾ In.	450.00
Postage, Brass, Oak Base, 3 Weights, 3 ½ x 7 x 4 In.	140.00
Postage, Letter Rates, Weights, Brass, Wood, 3 ½ x 7 x 3 ¾ In.	150.00
Weighing, Brass, No. 4, Scoop, Marked, 6 x 12 ½ x 7 In.	330.00
Weighing, Honest Weight Plaque, Penny, Lollipop Penny Scales	266.00
Weighing, Horoscope, 1 Cent, Coin-Operated, Red Enamel, American Steel, 53 In.	940.00
Weighing, Postal, Winged Maiden On Dolphin, Cast Brass & Porcelain, 5 ½ x 7 x 3 In.	257.00
Weighing, Scrolls, Bull, Figural, Up To 28 Lb., Southend, Croyden, 26 x 13 x 23 In.	1210.00
Weighing, Toledo, 3 Lb., Green, Brass Trim	440.00
Weighing, Walla-Walla Chewing Gum, National Store Specialty Co., c.1910, 10 ½ x 12 In.	2400.00
Weighing, Watling, Style 1 Guessing Scale, Coin-Operated, Oak Case, c.1902, 67 x 18 In.	4200.00
Weighing, Wrigley's Spearmint Pepsin Gum, Brass, Painted Metal, Embossed, 7 ¾ x 10 In.	852.00
Wells Fargo, Howe 60 Lb., c.1890, 22 x 18 x 13 In.	1800.00

SCHAFER & VATER, makers of small ceramic items, are best known for their amusing figurals. The factory was located in Volkstedt-Rudolstadt, Germany, from 1890 to 1962. Some pieces are marked with the crown and *R* mark, but many are unmarked.

Bottle, Figural, Man, Use It Daily, You'll Live Gaily, Blue, White, Top Hat Stopper, 7 In.	41.00
Bottle, Key Shape, Black Matte Glaze, 11 ½ In.	105.00
Bottle, Pretzel Shape, Brown, Speckled Salt, c.1905, 5 ½ x 3 ½ In.	130.00
Box, Cover, Raised & Figural Sphinx, Pink, White, 4 ¼ In.	71.00
Candy Dish, 2 Sections, Pink Jasper, White Classical Figures, Center Handle, 8 In.	48.00
Figurine, Bear, Beehive, Germany, 4 ¼ In.	150.00
Hatpin Holder, Egyptian Style, Gray, Woman's Mask, Sphinx, Tapered, 5 In.	212.00
Hatpin Holder, Woman's Face At Opening Of Tent, Fan Headdress, Tapered Top, 5 In.	118.00
Nodder, Cigar Boy, Derby Hat, And Dad Said, Be A Man, 4 In.	215.00
Pitcher, Bear In Plaid Overcoat, Muff, Green Glaze, Square Handle, 3 ¾ In.	234.00
Tea Set, Mad Hatter, Cream, Pink, Figural Character Handles & Finials, 7 Piece	1440.00

SCHNEIDER GLASSWORKS was founded in 1917 at Epinay-sur-Seine, France, by Charles and Ernest Schneider. Art glass was made between 1917 and 1930. The company still produces clear crystal glass. See also the Le Verre Francais category.

Bowl, Purple To Mottled Lavender, Purple Stem, France, 7 ¾ In.	296.00
Lamp, Mushroom Form, Mottled Yellow, Brown, Purple, Butterfly Finial, 13 ½ In., Pair	1150.00
Lamp, Red, Maroon Swirled Pointed Shade, Base, Forged Iron Collar, 7 x 12 In.	767.00
Vase, Mottled Blue, Ribbed, Footed Majorelle Bronze Holder, 12 ½ In.	518.00
Vase, Mottled Orange, Amethyst, Bubbles, Footed, Signed, 9 In.	431.00
Vase, Mottled Yellow, Optic Ribbed Red Bowl, Crimson Waves, Footed Coupe, 8 In.	1380.00
Vase, Mottled Yellow, Orange, Purple, Flared Rim, Footed, Signed, c.1920, 11 ¾ In.	1640.00
Vase, Red Mottled Design, Amber Body, Art Deco, Signed, 13 In.	885.00

SCIENTIFIC INSTRUMENTS of all kinds are included in this category. Other categories such as Barometer, Binoculars, Dental, Medical, Nautical, and Thermometer may also price scientific apparatus.

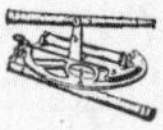

Altimeter, Surveyor's, Wallace & Teirman, Round Scale, Wood Case, 4 x 6 ½ In.	210.00
Anemometer, Hot Air Balloon Wind Meter, Casartelli, c.1880	82.00
Calipers, Wrought Iron, Stamped GWE 18181, 24 In.	59.00
Compass, Brass, Binnacle, Helmet Cover, Viewing Ports, Weighted Balls, 18 In.	1422.00
Compass, Lorkin, Brass Gimbal, Frame, Stop Lever, Box, 2 ¾ In.	326.00
Compass, Surveyor's, Augustus Platt, Brass, 2 Spirit Levels, Case, Mark, c.1875, 17 In.	705.00
Compass, Surveyor's, Foster & Company, Brass, 2 Spirit Levels, Box, c.1870, 14 ½ In.	764.00
Compass, Surveyor's, W. & L.E. Gurley, Brass, Silvered Dial, 13 x 10 In.	588.00
Galvanic Stimulator, Full Label	25.00
Microscope, Bausch & Lomb, Brass, Black Lacquer, c.1929, 14 In.	210.00
Microscope, Bausch & Lomb, Rochester, Cast Brass, Mahogany Case, 12 In.	230.00
Microscope, Binocular, Bausch & Lomb, Enameled, Case, 10 In. ....*illus*	360.00
Microscope, Binocular, Bausch & Lomb, Mahogany Case, c.1927, 11 x 7 ½ In.	360.00
Microscope, Monocular, Brass, Black Enamel, Student's, Victorian, 9 ½ In.	240.00
Microscope, Monocular, R & J Beck, Model 22, Brass, Iron, Enameled, c.1925, 12 ½ In. ..*illus*	540.00
Microscope, Stieren, Mahogany Case, c.1880	275.00
Microscope, W. Lawley & Son, Adjustable Stage, Case, 15 In. ....*illus*	345.00
Navigation Course Plotting Set, Hoades & Son, 8 Tools, Case, 1890s, 6 ¾ In.	865.00
Protractor, Graduated, Double Scale, Brass, Fitted Case, H.H.L.D., 12 In.	77.00
Quadrant Trigonometer, Benton, Whitely, Surveyor's Sight Vanes, c.1850, 13 In.	3290.00
Slide Rule, Barron & Harding, Brass, Boxwood, W. Hartlepool, England	88.00
Slide Rule, Dring & Fage, Brass, Boxwood, London England	38.00
Slide Rule, Stanley, Boxwood, German Silver, Great Turnstile, London	159.00
Spyglass, Cord Wrapped, Brass, Single Draw, 20 In.	178.00
Surveyor's Chain, Galvanized, Brass Handles & Tags, 100 Ft.	77.00
Telescope, 2 Section, Leather Over Brass, 1860s	150.00
Telescope, Abercrombie & Fitch, William Stanton, Brass, 1950s, 73 x 36 In.	1850.00
Telescope, Bate, Wood, Brass, London, c.1870, 36 In.	176.00
Telescope, Brass, Mahogany Tripod, 20th Century, 57 x 39 ½ In.	200.00
Telescope, Carl Zeiss, Double Eyepiece, Case, 18 x 10 In.	350.00
Telescope, Refracting, Brass, 10 ½ In.	1778.00
Theodolite, Surveyor's, Brass, Case, c.1890, 13 In.	294.00
Transit, Surveying, 8-In. Side Focus, Mountain Transit, Wooden Case	632.00
Vernier Compass, Surveyor's, R. Patton, Levels, Sight Vanes, Metals, c.1820, 16 In.	1410.00

SCRIMSHAW is bone or ivory or whale's teeth carved by sailors and others for entertainment during the sailing-ship days. Some scrimshaw was carved as early as 1800. There are modern scrimshanders making pieces today on bone, ivory, or plastic. Other pieces may be found in the Ivory and Nautical categories.

Basket, Knitting, Wood, Pierced Bone Ribs, Circles, Star, Inlaid Base, c.1850, 6 x 10 In.	12760.00
Basket, Oval, Pine Base, Overlapping Circles, Swing Handle, c.1850, 3 x 5 x 7 In.	13920.00
Belt Buckle, Ivory, Nude Women, Dragon, Signed, Bob Hergert, 2 ½ x 3 In.	750.00
Binoculars, Multicolored Eagle, Banner, Captain D.A. Taft, c.1861, 4 ⅛ In. ....*illus*	1093.00
Box, Mahogany, Panbone, Engraved Eagle, House, Animals, Flowers, Oval, Lid, c.1850, 3 x 6 In.	1778.00
Box, Slide Lid, Whalebone, 29 Dominoes, c.1860, 1 x 5 In.	646.00
Box, Slide Lid, Whalebone, Dovetailed, Pinned, c.1860, 1 x 3 In.	764.00
Busk, Whalebone, American Eagle Engraved Side, 5 People Engraved Flip Side, c.1890, 13 In.	563.00
Busk, Whalebone, Pink, Green Ink Flowers, Vines, Diamonds, Signed Ellis, c.1850, 14 In.	1410.00
Busk, Whalebone, Women In Spanish Attire, Inscribed, 1800s, 13 In.	558.00
Busk, Woman's, Russian Architecture, Carved, Inked, c.1900, 13 In.	353.00
Cane, Whalebone, Ivory, Brass, Turned, Polished, c.1850, 37 In.	1175.00
Cane, Whalebone, Turk's Head Knot, Black Ink Fill, Sperm Whales, Waves, 1800s, 35 ¼ In.	495.00
Chamberstick, Split Whale Teeth Shape, Whalebone, Ivory, 1800s, 3 x 6 In., Pair	881.00
Cribbage Board, Ivory, Walrus Tusk, Mounted Seals, Carved, 15 In.	160.00
Dipper, Coconut Shell, Whale Ivory Handle, Baleen, Ebony, Mahogany, c.1850, 17 x 5 In.	1400.00
Dipper, Whalebone, Coconut, Mahogany, Union Shield, Branches, Sun, Text, c.1860, 13 In.	470.00
Ditty Box, Vine Flowers, Trees, Ships, Lapped, Baleen, 3 x 7 In.	940.00
Knife, Seal & Duck Designs, Albert Berry, Box, 7 ½ In.	480.00
Letter Opener, Walrus Ivory, Handle Carved As Walrus Head, 1800s, 14 In.	176.00
Naval Battle Scene, 3-Masted Warship, 2 Other Ships Firing Canons, c.1870, 13 ½ In.	2350.00
Panbone, Return Of The Whaler Orion 1849, Man, Ship, Lighthouse, 3 ¼ x 5 ¼ In.	499.00
Penholder, Arctic Wolf, 7 ½ x 5 In.	92.00

Satsuma, Vase, Roosters, Chickens, Wisteria, Basket Weave Band, Gilt, Hexagonal, 3 ⅝ x 2 In.
$667.00

Satsuma, Vase, Scenic Panels, Gilt, Signed, Japan, c.1910, 8 In.
$1800.00

Scale, Balance, Bronze Arm, Pan, Walnut Case, France, 20th Century, 17 ½ x 16 ½ In.
$570.00

Scale, Balance, Iron Base, Brass Pans, Gem No. 5, Weighs To 5 Oz.
$138.00

S

Scale, Balance, Iron Base, Brass Rail, Pan, Weighs To 8 Lb., Howe-Rutland, Vt., c.1867
$110.00

Scientific Instrument, Microscope, Binocular, Bausch & Lomb, Enameled, Case, 10 In.
$360.00

Scientific Instrument, Microscope, Monocular, R & J Beck, Model 22, Brass, Iron, Enameled, c.1925, 12 ½ In.
$540.00

Scientific Instrument, Microscope, W. Lawley & Son, Adjustable Stage, Case, 15 In.
$345.00

Pickwick, Bell Shape, Incised, Ink Designs, Whale Ivory, c.1850, 2 In.	1175.00
Pickwick, Bell Shape, Turnings On Wick, Whale Ivory, 3 In.	470.00
Pie Crimper, Baleen Band, Ivory, Fluting Wheel, Pistol Shape, c.1860, 6 ½ In.	588.00
Pie Crimper, Star, Diamond, Cut Out, Coggle Wheels, Ivory, 8 In.	565.00
Pie Crimper, Whale Ivory, Pierced, Fluted Wheel, 5 In.	1763.00
Pie Crimper, Whale Ivory, Serpent Form, 19th Century, 7 x 2 ¾ In.	900.00
Pulley, Double Block, Whalebone, Pinned Construction, 1800s, 4 In., Pair	1116.00
Rolling Pin, Mahogany, Whalebone, Baleen, Sailor Made, 1800s, 13 In.	294.00
Sewing Basket, Whalebone, Picket Fence Design, Brass Tacks, 4 x 6 In.	5875.00
Spool Caddy, Whale Ivory, Abalone, Tortoiseshell, Rueben Chase, Nantucket, 1838, 5 ½ In.	12760.00
Swift, Whalebone, Ivory, Turned Ivory Yarn Cup, Blue Ribbons, c.1850, 23 x 20 In.	764.00
Tusk, 5 Sailing Ships, 20th Century, 22 ¼ In.	690.00
Tusk, Ivory, 3 Whaling Ships, Black Ink Wash, Signed Kathy, 13 ¾ In. ....*illus*	930.00
Whale's Tooth, 4 Ships, Man Sleeping On Table, Flowers, 19th Century, 6 ⅝ In.	1875.00
Whale's Tooth, 8 Rigged Tall Ships, c.1860, 5 In.	823.00
Whale's Tooth, Barque Narwhal Ship, Engraved, England, 1843, 7 In.	1645.00
Whale's Tooth, Boy, Dog, Squirrel, Portrait Of Isadora, Engraved, Inked, c.1845, 5 ½ In.	8225.00
Whale's Tooth, Flowers, Love, American Sailing Ship, Inked, Multicolored, c.1800s, 4 In.	499.00
Whale's Tooth, Full Length Portrait Of Woman, c.1845, 8 In.	999.00
Whale's Tooth, Indian, On Horse, 5 In.	6325.00
Whale's Tooth, Lady Justice, Barrel, Ship, Family Addition, Leaves, 7 In. ....*illus*	1998.00
Whale's Tooth, Lady Liberty, Laurel Garland, Shield, c.1875, 5 ¼ In.	1150.00
Whale's Tooth, Masonic Arch, House, American Flag, Mary Gorden, 1800s, 5 In.	940.00
Whale's Tooth, Mermaid, Carved, 8 ½ In.	3575.00
Whale's Tooth, Native American Figures, Horse & Rider, Eagle, Flag, 1813, 3 In.	1380.00
Whale's Tooth, Romantic Couple, Tree, 1800s, 7 In.	734.00
Whale's Tooth, Ship, Inscribed, Star Of India, 2 Women Holding Parasols, 7 ¾ In.	720.00
Whale's Tooth, Ship, Lady, Parasol, c.1850, 5 In.	588.00
Whale's Tooth, Tudor Woman's Portrait, Plumed Hat, Sawtooth Border, c.1840, 6 ½ In.	7638.00
Whale's Tooth, Urn, Sunburst, Leaves, Mother-Of-Pearl, Engraved, 19th Century, 7 x 2 In.	2640.00
Whale's Tooth, Whale & Mermaid, Inscribed Love Ladies N.J., 1800s, 3 ¼ In.	2574.00
Whale's Tooth, Whale Ship, 2 Whaleboats, Crew, Dead Whale, 7 ⅝ In., Pair	9480.00
Whale's Tooth, Whaling Scene, American Ship, Engraved, Inked, Multicolored, 6 ½ In.	15275.00
Whale's Tooth, Woman, Birds, Hearts, c.1850, 7 In.	470.00
Whale's Tooth, Woman, Day, Evening Attire, Multicolored, Engraved, 6 In.	1175.00
Whale's Tooth, Woman, Leaning On Pedestal Portrait, Pin Pricked, c.1860, 5 ½ In.	558.00
Whale's Tooth, Woman, Patriotic Slogan, Building, Flag, c.1840, 6 In.	705.00

SEBASTIAN MINIATURES were first made by Prescott W. Baston in 1938 in Marblehead, Massachusetts. More than 400 different designs have been made and collectors search for the out-of-production models. The mark may say *Copr. P.W. Baston U.S.A.*, or *P. W. Baston, U.S.A.*, or *Prescott W. Baston*. Sometimes a paper label was used.

America Remembers, Family Reads Aloud, 2 ½ In.	16.00
Baby Buggy Of 1850, Box	16.00
Candy Store, 1947	8.00
Captain John Smith, 3 In.	59.00
Cleopatra, Queen Of Egypt, c.1955, 3 In.	250.00
Colonial Glass Blower, 1957, 3 ¼ x 3 In.	23.00
Colonial Kitchen, Box	14.00
Corner Drug Store, Box	18.00
Cranberry Picker, 1950	25.00
Dame Van Winkle, Box	10.00
Dickens Cottage, Box	30.00
Doctor, Box	18.00
Emmett Kelley Clown, Box	30.00
Farmer, Box	15.00
First Kite, Father & Son, Box, 1981, 3 ¼ In.	13.00
Games In Springtime, 1953	12.00
Girl At Desk, Boy At Desk, Box, Pair	26.00
Lobsterman, Box	18.00
Masonic Water Tower, Charlton, Massachusetts, 1986	10.00
Old Salt, Fisherman, Yellow	19.00
Pilgrim Couple, Box	16.00
Pocahontas, 2 ½ In.	80.00
Ride To The Hounds, Child On Rocking Horse, 4 In.	28.00
Rip Van Winkle, 3 In.	22.00

Self-Portrait, Man Lounging, 1981, 3 ¾ x 4 ½ In.	29.00
Shawmut, Indian Chief, 1964	45.00
Shoemaker, Box	20.00
Sidewalk Days, Boy, Box	25.00
Sidewalk Days, Girl, Box	26.00
Switching The Freight, Boy, Toy Railroad, 1955, 2 ½ x 4 In.	40.00
Uncle Sam, Whiskey Barrel, 1967, 4 ¼ In.	24.00

SEVRES porcelain has been made in Sevres, France, since 1769. Many copies of the famous ware have been made. The name originally referred to the works of the Royal Porcelain factory. The name now includes any of the wares made in the town of Sevres, France. The entwined lines with a center letter used as the mark is one of the most forged marks in antiques. Be very careful to identify Sevres by quality, not just by mark.

Bowl, 4 Women, Bisque, Paw Footed, Gilt Bronze Mounts, 18 x 17 x 10 ½ In.	489.00
Bowl, Children Playing, 2 Handles, 4 Lobed Feet, Gilt, Pink, 13 x 8 x 8 In.	173.00
Bowl, Louis XVI Style, Base, Putti & Flower Garlands, Gilt Bronze, c.1800, 19 In.	11162.00
Bowl, Priests, Soldiers, Dead Farmer, Cobalt, Gilt Flower Rim, Handles, 12 x 5 In.	460.00
Box, Stationary, Courting Scene, Flowers, Oval Plaque, Gilt, Bronze, 4 ½ x 6 ¾ In.	1130.00
Bust, Girl, Cobalt Blue Glaze, Gilt Trim, c.1922, 8 ¾ In.	237.00
Bust, Napoleon, 11 ½ x 5 x 4 In.	790.00
Cake Stand, Mottled Blue Leafy Border, Gilt Leaf Tip Edge, Anthemion Legs, Disc Base, 9 In. .	770.00
Centerpiece, 3 Standing Women, Dressed, Gilt Highlights, Marked, 1800s, 18 ½ In. .... *illus*	2806.00
Charger, Fruit, Flowers, 4 Kidney Shape Vignettes, Cobalt Blue Ground, 18 In., Pair	9200.00
Clock, Flowers, Blue & Gold, Scrolled Form & Feet, 19th Century, 9 ½ In.	580.00
Figurine, Napoleonic Officer, Marked, 15 In.	508.00
Ice Cream Cooler, Cover, Footed, Gilt, Marked, c.1900, 10 x 8 In. .... *illus*	357.00
Pedestal, Porcelain, Shaped Top, Scrolled Corners, Cartouches, Molded Plinth, 46 x 13 In., Pair.	489.00
Plaque, Men At Table, Period Attire, Ornate Surround, Hand Painted, c.1900, 25 x 13 In.	546.00
Plate, Dessert, Louis-Philippe, Woman Portrait, Gilt Flowers, Fond Ivoire, 1837, 9 In.	180.00
Plate, Dinner, White, Gold, First Empire, Putto, 9 ⅞ In., 12 Piece	3360.00
Plate, Gilt Ivy Border, Kelly Green Band, Gilt Rondelle, Cupid's Labors, 9 ¾ In., 12 Piece	173.00
Plate, Portrait, Woman, Jeweled Headdress, Looking Left, Gilt Enameled Border, S. Roy, 10 In. .	460.00
Sucrier, Cover, Paneled, Bouquets, Gold Gilt Knot Handles, Finial, c.1820, 5 x 4 In. .... *illus*	147.00
Teapot, Napoleonic, Portraits, Laurel Wreath, Bird's-Head Spout, Painted, Gilt, 1810, 6 ¾ In. ..*illus*	690.00
Urn, Baluster, Seated Maiden, Pineapple Finial, Marked, c.1875, 14 In.	633.00
Urn, Cobalt Blue, Gilt Designs, Multicolored Panels, Bronze, Signed, 27 ½ In. .... *illus*	1898.00
Urn, Country Landscape, Scenic Panels, Cobalt Blue Ground, Ormolu Mounted, 26 ½ In.	748.00
Urn, Courting Scene, Pink Glaze, Gold Highlights, Brass Foot Base, Handles, 9 ½ In., Pair	374.00
Urn, Cover, Couple Dancing, Handles, 19th Century, 56 In.	14850.00
Urn, Cover, Couple, Pastoral Landscape, Seascape, Cobalt Blue, Ormolu Mounts, c.1885, 18 In.	1638.00
Urn, Cover, Flower, Ormolu Mounts, 8 In., Pair	431.00
Urn, Cover, Painted Pastoral Scene, Bronze Mounts, Swivel Base, 1800s, 12 x 30 In.	4888.00
Urn, Cover, Woman, Playing Harp, Cherub, Hand Painted, Bronze Mounts, Handles, 17 In.	965.00
Urn, Draped Lioness Skin, Potpourri, Handles, Marked, 19th Century, 13 x 9 In.	3600.00
Urn, Gilt Bronze Mounts, Landscapes, Courting Figures, Lucot, c.1890, 21 In.	999.00
Urn, Stand, Kneeling Satyr, Maiden, Attendant Pouring Water, Bagpipes, Flowers, Blue, 10 In.	489.00
Vase, Baluster Shape, Cobalt Blue Mottled Glaze, Gilt Metal Rims, c.1900, 8 ½ In., Pair	207.00
Vase, Bleu Celeste, Baluster, Birds, Flowers, 19th Century, 23 ½ In., Pair	2350.00
Vase, Cobalt Blue, Woman's Head Medallion, Ormolu, Bronze Band, M.P., 15 In., Pair	950.00
Vase, Landscape Cartouches, Bleu Celeste, Bronze Lappet Rim, Mask Handles, 10 In., Pair	2726.00
Vase, Ormolu Mounts, Turquoise Glaze, c.1900, 4 ¾ In.	58.00
Vase, Pierced Arabesques, Gilt Edges, Flared & Flattened Rim, Blue Foot, 10 In., Pair	10925.00
Vase, Pink Bellflowers, Green Leaves, Flared, Footed, White Ground, c.1930, 11 ½ In.	1912.00

SEWER TILE figures were made by workers at the sewer tile and pipe factories in the Ohio area during the late nineteenth and early twentieth centuries. Figurines, small vases, and cemetery vases were favored. Often the finished vase was a piece of the original pipe with added decorations and markings. All types of sewer tile work are now considered folk art by collectors.

Bust, Aviator, World War I, White Porcelain Eyes, Teeth, Early 1900s, 13 x 16 In.	940.00
Figure, Baseball, Ohio, Early 20th Century, 2 ½ In.	235.00
Figure, Brick, Molded Lion Head, Painted, Tuscarawas County, Ohio, Early 1900s, 5 x 5 In., Pair	235.00
Figure, Camel, Signed, Bill Miller 12B, 20th Century, 11 In.	176.00
Figure, Dog, Flat Head, Seated, Tooled Collar, Ohio, Early 1900s, 10 ½ In.	764.00
Figure, Dog, Gold Paint, J.W. Moore, Uhrichsville, Ohio, 11 In.	88.00
Figure, Dog, Seated, Tooled Collar, Ohio, Early 20th Century, 11 ½ In. .... *illus*	323.00

Scrimshaw, Binoculars, Multicolored Eagle, Banner, Captain D.A. Taft, c.1861, 4 ⅛ In. $1093.00

Scrimshaw, Tusk, Ivory, 3 Whaling Ships, Black Ink Wash, Signed Kathy, 13 ¾ In. $930.00

Scrimshaw, Whale's Tooth, Lady Justice, Barrel, Ship, Family Addition, Leaves, 7 In. $1998.00

Sevres, Centerpiece, 3 Standing Women, Dressed, Gilt Highlights, Marked, 1800s, 18 ½ In. $2806.00

S

Sevres, Ice Cream Cooler, Cover, Footed, Gilt, Marked, c.1900, 10 x 8 In. $357.00

Sevres, Sucrier, Cover, Paneled, Bouquets, Gold Gilt Knot Handles, Finial, c.1820, 5 x 4 In. $147.00

Sevres, Teapot, Napoleonic, Portraits, Laurel Wreath, Bird's-Head Spout, Painted, Gilt, 1810, 6 ¾ In. $690.00

Sevres, Urn, Cobalt Blue, Gilt Designs, Multicolored Panels, Bronze, Signed, 27 ½ In. $1898.00

Figure, Dog, Seated, Unglazed, Walter Smith, Superior Clay Corp., Uhrichsville, Ohio, 10 ¾ In.	59.00
Figure, Dog, Spaniel, Lying Down, Ohio, Late 19th Century, 5 x 8 In.	695.00
Figure, Dog, Spaniel, Seated, Octagonal Base, Mark, Ohio, Early 1900s, 10 ¾ In.	118.00
Figure, Horse, Free-Standing Legs, Inscribed, D. Krapp, 1957, 7 ½ In.	118.00
Figure, Man, Wearing Liberty Cap, 10 In.	370.00
Figure, Man's Face, 4 x 4 x 4 In.	110.00
Figure, Owls, Eagle, Laurel Branches, Arrows, Stump, 11 x 9 ½ In. ....*illus*	161.00
Plaque, Deer Head, Molded, Smith, Superior Clay, Ohio, Mid 1900s, 9 In., Pair ......*illus*	323.00
Umbrella Stand, Tree Bark Decoration, 26 In.	135.00

SEWING equipment of all types is collected, from sewing birds that held the cloth to tape measures, needle books, and old wooden spools. Sewing machines are included here. Needlework pictures are listed in the Picture category.

Basket, Pine Needles, Cotton Thread Flowers, Pink, Yellow, Green, Round, 3 ¼ x 1 ½ In.	47.00
Basket, Red & White, Woven Plastic, Wire Frame, Handle, 1960s, 6 ½ x 9 ½ In.	32.00
Basket, Wicker, Figural, Auto, Hood Opens, Needles, Yarn, Lanterns, Canvas Top, Germany	2300.00
Basket, Wicker, Woven, Coiled Rattan, Victorian, 28 In. ....*illus*	72.00
Basket, Woven Straw, Natural & Green, Loop Clasp Handle, Blue Satin Lined, Puff Top, 12 x 8 In.	20.00
Bird, Brass Clamp, 3 In.	71.00
Bird, Iron, Stylized, c.1850, 5 In.	150.00
Bird, Painted, Heart Shape Thumbscrew, England, Cast Iron, c.1790, 5 ½ In.	355.00
Bobbin Box, Georgian, Papier-Mache, Metal Hinge, Oval, c.1830, 3 x 1 x 1 ½ In.	50.00
Bobbin Winder, Oak, Bobbin Basket, Shaped Peg Legs, c.1800, 40 x 40 In.	58.00
Bobbin Winder, Oak, Mixed Woods, Wrought Nail Construction, 1700s, 48 x 53 In.	69.00
Box, 2 Tiers, Folk Art, Pincushion, Drawer, Scalloped & Pierced Shelf, 1800s, 9 x 10 x 7 In.	1725.00
Box, Chinoiserie, Lacquered, Octagonal, Drawer, Lift Top, Landscape, Brass Handles, 14 In.	127.00
Box, Ivory, Panels, Incised, Pierced, Vine Scrolls, Hinged Lid, Russia, c.1836, 12 x 10 In.	2880.00
Box, Kingwood, Ivory, Ebony & Wood Inlays, Geometric Borders, 1800s, 4 x 12 x 8 In.	385.00
Box, Mahogany, Cloth Pincushion Top, Dovetailed Drawer, Bone Pull, 4 ½ x 3 ¾ x 6 In.	121.00
Box, Painted, Red Scrolling Vines, Landscape, Hinged, Sloped Edges, Ball Feet, 5 x 9 In.	1850.00
Box, Tole, Black, Tulips, Leaves, Round, 10 In.	20.00
Box, Tortoiseshell, Hinged Lid, Satin Interior, Compartments, Ivory Feet, 4 x 8 x 6 ½ In.	418.00
Box, Victorian, Mother-Of-Pearl, Abalone Shell, Fitted, Mid 19th Century, 5 ½ x 13 In.	3660.00
Box, Walnut, Inlay, 2 Lacquered Bird Panels, Brass Handle, c.1890, 11 x 17 In.	275.00
Box, Wood, 6 Trays, 4-Footed, Handle, Stamped, Stromenn Bruk, 23 x 20 x 11 In.	265.00
Box, Wood, Japanned, Painted, Courtyard Scene, Early 1900s, 10 In.	35.00
Box, Wood, Mother-Of-Pearl, Drawer, Victorian, 6 x 9 ½ x 7 In.	60.00
Cabinet, Flying Birds, Black Lacquer, Fitted Interior, 2 Supports, Gilt, Japanned, c.1880, 24 x 26 In.	560.00
Cabinet, Spool, Maple, Paneled Decoration, 4-Drawer, c.1875, 30 x 17 x 18 In.	590.00
Cabinet, Spool, see also the Advertising category under Cabinet, Spool.	
Clamp, Cast Iron, Painted, c.1840, 4 ¼ In.	335.00
Clamp, Dolphin Shape, Nickel Plated Bronze, Silvertone, c.1850, 5 x 7 In.	1375.00
Clamp, Hemming, Ivory, C-Clamp, Yellow Pincushion, 6 In.	275.00
Cuff Holder Clip, Spring Action Swivel, Metal, Marked, Wizard, Pat. 1889, 1902, 1903, 2 ½ In.	8.00
Darner, Glove, Sterling Silver, Twist Design, c.1915, 4 ¼ In.	165.00
Darning Egg, Champleve Handle, Enameled, Blue Ground, c.1900, 5 ½ x 3 In.	195.00
Darning Egg, Ebony, Egg Shape, Sterling Silver Handle, Chased, Scrolled, 6 ¾ In., Pair	142.00
Darning Egg, Turned Handle, Painted Wood, 6 ½ In.	12.50
Dressmaker's Square, J.F. Wingate, Boston, Mass., Patent May 21, 1878	44.00
Etui, Satinwood, Grain Painted, Mirrored Interior Top, Mother-Of-Pearl Implements, 3 x 8 x 5 In.	288.00
Lacemaker's Lamp, Hollow Baluster Stem, Cork & Pewter Burner, c.1850, 8 ½ In.	287.00
Machine, Barlow & Son, Pat. April 18, 1871	880.00
Machine, Buttonholer, Singer, Touch & Sew, No. 161829, 20 Templates	25.00
Machine, Little Comfort, Smith & Egge, Early 20th Century, 7 x 6 x 3 In.	375.00
Mannequin, White Ribbed Jersey Cotton, Child, Size 6, 24 ¼ In.	150.00
Needle Case, Georgian, Ivory, Cylindrical, Turned, Acorn Finials, c.1800, 3 ¼ In.	175.00
Needle Case, Gold, Embossed, France, c.1870	1200.00
Needle Case, Hand Crafted, Wooden, Marked, Essence Derose, Bulgaria, 3 ¼ In.	18.00
Needle Case, Mauchline, Copal Sycamore, Burns Cottage Transfer, c.1890, 3 ½ x 2 In.	191.00
Needle Case, Walnut On Leaf, Brass, Avery, c.1873, 6 x 6 x 3 In.	295.00
Pattern, Butterick No. 6091, Belted Dress & Cap, Uncut, 1965, Size 42 Bust	15.00
Pattern, McCall's, No. 582, Babushka Cap, Belt, c.1937, Unused	40.00
Pin Safe, McLean, Tartan, 19th Century, 1 ⅜ In.	195.00
Pincushion Dolls are listed in their own category.	
Pincushion, Bulldog, Cushion Top Barrel, Painted Spelter, c.1900, 2 ½ x 2 In.	395.00
Pincushion, Glass Base, Cloth Strawberry Top, c.1900, 10 ¼ In.	264.00

Pincushion, Heart Shape, Embossed Flowers, Red Cushion, Aluminum, 2 ¼ x 2 In.	53.00
Pincushion, Horse Hoof, Silver Plated Fittings, Marked, Rowland Ward, 167 Piccadilly, 4 In. .	115.00
Pincushion, Peacock, White Marble Base, 19th Century, 4 x 2 ½ In.	500.00
Pincushion, White & Green Flowers, Red Ground, Ship, Parrot, Continental, 1835	285.00
Scissor Case, Oval Form, Floral Beadwork, Felt & Cloth, 9 x 3 ½ In.	44.00
Scissors, Needleworking, Brass, Steel, Marked, 17th Century, 4 In.	165.00
Spool Cabinets are listed here or in the Advertising category under Cabinet, Spool.	
Spool Knave, Silver, Hanging, MacKay & Chisholm, Edinburgh, c.1876, 6 ¼ In.	875.00
Stand, Marquetry Inlay, Lyre Supports, Fabric Bag, Late 1700s, 29 ½ x 20 x 14 In.	2620.00
Stand, Walnut, Tiger Maple, Cherry, Pincushion, 3-Tier Spool Pedestal, c.1890, 17 x 11 In. *illus*	283.00
Tailor's Dummy, Muslin, Tripod Wood Stand, France, Size 6, 49 In.	660.00
Tape Measure, Basket Of Fruit, Painted, Celluloid, 1 ¾ x 1 ¼ In.	75.00
Tape Measure, Bell, Mauchline, Copal Varnished Sycamore, Transfer, Scotland, c.1880, 2 In.	127.00
Tape Measure, Carved Vegetable, Ivory Knob, Late 19th Century, 2 x 1 In.	95.00
Tape Measure, Flower Basket, Painted, Celluloid, Japan, 1 ¾ x 1 ½ In.	135.00
Tape Measure, Lydia Pinkham's, Round Metal Tape, 1 ⅜ In.	121.00
Tape Measure, Oval, Pink Rose, Pale Green Leaves, Celluloid, Germany, 1 ¾ In.	125.00
Tape Measure, Paper, Marked, Haband Co., Paterson New Jersey, 50 In.	9.00
Tape Measure, Pig, In Boot, Painted, Celluloid, Japan, 2 ¼ In.	110.00
Tape Measure, Sailing Ship, Painted, Celluloid, Germany, 2 ½ x 2 ¼ In.	85.00
Tatting Shuttle, Art Deco, Sterling Silver, Marked, Nassbaum & Hunold, 2 ⅞ In.	145.00
Thimble Case, Egg Shape, Yew, Carved, Painted, Victorian, 2 ¼ In.	84.00
Thimble Holder, Doll Shoes, Silk, Vellum Toe, Tan Sole, 1700s, 1 ½ In., Pair..................	295.00
Thimble Holder, Egg Shape, Enameled, Cobalt Blue Ground, Gold Trim, Cherubs, Women, 1 ¼ In. .	900.00
Thimble, Gold, Engraved E, Chased Scroll Rim, Size 8, ¾ In.	165.00
Thimble, Gold, Engraved Leaf Border, 2 In.	250.00
Thimble, Pewter, Flowers, Relief, Maker's Mark, 1 In.	13.00
Thread, Spool, Forest Green, 3 ½ In.	15.00
Thread Box, Mauchlinware, Tartanware, John Rogers Group Emblem, c.1850, 4 x 3 In.	375.00
Thread Dispenser, Wooden Box, Inlaid Sliding Lid, Regency Period, c.1815, 8 ½ x 2 ½ In.	325.00
Thread Winder, Sterling Silver Repousse, Monogram, Marked, 2 x 1 ⅛ In.	250.00
Threader, Automatic, Original Box, Instructions, Witch, West Germany, c.1954..................	15.00
Travel Kit, Gold Case, Clasp, Thread, Buttons, Measuring Tape, Scissors, c.1960, 2 ½ x 3 ½ In.	10.00
Winding Clamp, Ivory, c.1800, 5 ½ In.	450.00
Yarn Reel, Yellow Pine, 2 Reels, Tripod Base, American, c.1800, 53 x 18 x 15 In. .... *illus*	69.00
Yarn Winder, Maple, Pine, Painted, Finial, 5 Legs, 41 x 27 In.	90.00

SHAKER items are characterized by simplicity, functionalism, and orderliness. There were many Shaker communities in America from the eighteenth century to the present day. The religious order made furniture, small wooden pieces, and packaged medicines, herbs, and jellies to sell to "outsiders." Other useful objects were made for use by members of the community. Shaker furniture is listed in this book in the Furniture category.

Abacus, Cherry Frame, Steel, Red, White, Blue Beads, Turned Handle, c.1865, 15 x 12 In.	1765.00
Apple Peeler, Pine, Ash, Maple, Mechanical, 14 In.	118.00
Auger, Wood, Red Wash Stain, 25 x 29 In.	330.00
Basket, 3-Finger, Maple, Tacks, Swing Handle, Cloth Lining, Sabbathday, Maine, 8 In.	176.00
Basket, 4-Finger, Copper Tacks, Swing Handle, Pink Cloth Lining, 4 x 11 In.	235.00
Basket, Apple, 2 Bands, Ash Slats, Hoop Handle, Label, Sabbathday, Maine, Bushel	644.00
Basket, Apple, Splint, Ash, Marked, ACW, 19th Century, 12 x 15 In.	175.00
Basket, Black Ash Splint, Square To Round Shape, Loop Handle, Harvard, c.1870, 8 x 16 In. ..	644.00
Basket, Feather, Lid, Splint, Ash, Maple, 19th Century, 24 In.	145.00
Basket, Feather, Lid, Splint, Handle, 19th Century, 18 In.	145.00
Basket, Gathering, Black Ash, Carved Hoop Handle, Cat's Head Base, c.1850, 13 x 14 In.	702.00
Basket, Gathering, Maple, Ash, Carved Handle, Arched Bottom, Signed, Will Thornton, 12 x 16 In.	200.00
Basket, Sewing, Round, 8 Interior Baskets, Handles, Black Ash Splint, 1870, 7 x 19 In.	761.00
Bootjack, Maple, Wall Mount, 19th Century, 19 ½ In. .... 106.00 to 115.00	
Bowl, Pine, Beveled Rim, Finger Hold, Yellow Paint, c.1850, 6 x 19 In.	819.00
Bowl, Pine, Oval, Carved Finger Grip, Red Finish, 3 ½ x 19 ½ In.	468.00
Box, 2-Finger, Oval, Lid, Copper Tacks, Maple, Pine, Red Paint, 1 ¾ x 4 ⅝ In.	4973.00
Box, 2-Finger, Oval, Lid, Maple, Pine, Yellow Paint, c.1835, 1 ¼ x 3 ½ In.	3042.00
Box, 2-Finger, Oval, Lid, Pine, Maple, Blue Paint, c.1815, 1 ½ x 3 ⅝ In.	3978.00
Box, 2-Finger, Oval, Lid, Yellow, Harvard, 1800s, 3 In.	294.00
Box, 2-Finger, Oval, Maple, Pine, Multicolored Flower Lid, Paint, Mt. Lebanon, c.1900, 2 ¾ x 6 In.	526.00
Box, 3-Finger, Oval, Lid, Green Paint, 3 ⅜ x 9 x 6 ¼ In.	468.00
Box, 3-Finger, Oval, Lid, Maple, Pine, Copper Tacks, Varnish, c.1840, 5 x 13 In.	761.00
Box, 3-Finger, Oval, Lid, Pine, Maple, Blue Paint, c.1830, 1 ¾ x 5 In.	760.00

Sewer Tile, Figure, Dog, Seated, Tooled Collar, Ohio, Early 20th Century, 11 ½ In.
$323.00

Sewer Tile, Figure, Owls, Eagle, Laurel Branches, Arrows, Stump, 11 x 9 ½ In.
$161.00

Sewer Tile, Plaque, Deer Head, Molded, Smith, Superior Clay, Ohio, Mid 1900s, 9 In., Pair
$323.00

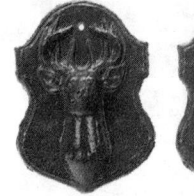

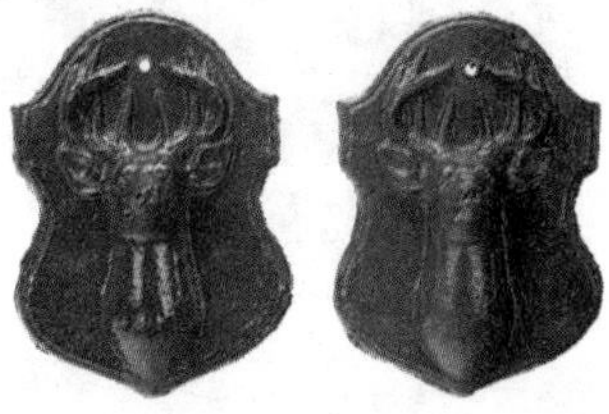

TIP
If a bottle stopper is stuck, try using Liquid Wrench, an oil found at the hardware store, to loosen it.

S

Sewing, Basket, Wicker, Woven, Coiled Rattan, Victorian, 28 In. **$72.00**

Sewing, Stand, Walnut, Tiger Maple, Cherry, Pin Cushion, 3-Tier Spool Pedestal, c.1890, 17 x 11 In. **$283.00**

Box, 3-Finger, Oval, Lid, Yellow Paint, 2 ¾ x 7 x 4 ¾ In.	523.00
Box, 3-Finger, Oval, Maple, Pine, Yellow Finish, Hoop Handle, Mt. Lebanon, c.1830, 10 x 15 In.	8775.00
Box, 4-Finger, Horse & Carriage On Lid, Flower Band, Painted, Oval, c.1830, 5 ½ x 13 ½ In. ...	1200.00
Box, 4-Finger, Oval, Lid, Copper Tacks, Maple, Pine, Salmon Red Paint, 6 x 13 ¼ In.	4680.00
Box, 4-Finger, Oval, Lid, Maple, Pine, Copper Tacks, Marked, Natural Finish, 5 ½ x 13 In.	1287.00
Box, 4-Finger, Oval, Maple, Pine, Cherry, Copper Tacks, 2 ⅛ x 5 ⅜ In.	4388.00
Box, Beekeeper, Lid, Pine, Inset Screws, Interior Carrier, Screen, Tube, Green, c.1885, 8 x 14 In.	644.00
Box, Lid, 3-Finger, Oval, White Pine Bottom, Green, 1875, 5 x 9 In.	860.00
Box, Lid, Cherry, Pine, 2-Hinge, Red Varnish, 8 Compartments, N.Y., c.1840, 3 x 13 In.	1580.00
Box, Lid, Pine, Forged Hinges, Dovetailed, Leather Strap Handles, Orange Finish, 13 x 24 In. ..	702.00
Box, Lid, Poplar, Fitted Interior, Iron Handles, Red Paint, Conn., c.1850, 16 x 32 In.	819.00
Box, Lid, Red Leather Hinge, Poplar, Yellow Varnish, Canterbury, c.1850, 2 ¾ x 8 In.	2106.00
Box, Pine, Dovetail Construction, 19th Century, 5 ½ x 8 x 6 In.	295.00
Box, Pine, Lettered Lunch, Hickory Handle, Red Paint, Harvard, c.1825, 10 x 16 In.	2223.00
Box, Sewing, 3-Finger, Oval, Sabbathday, Maine, 6 x 8 x 5 In.	295.00
Box, Spit, 3-Finger, Oval, Maple, Pine, Black 6 Stenciled, Yellow Ground Paint, 3 ¾ x 9 In.	3627.00
Box, Storage, Oval, Lid, Mount Lebanon, c.1869, 5 ¾ x 13 ½ x 9 ¾ In.	1725.00
Box, Swallowtail Fingers, Copper Tacks, 19th Century, 5 ½ x 13 ¼ In.	411.00
Box, Swallowtail Fingers, Copper Tacks, c.1800, 3 ½ x 9 ½ In.	470.00
Box, Walnut, Varnished Wood Strips, Lid, Hinged Spiral Molding, T. Fisher, Enfield, c.1890, 5 x 10 In.	761.00
Bucket, Lid, Pine, 2 Iron Bands, Birch Hand Hold, Bail Handle, Blue Paint, c.1850, 15 x 12 In.	702.00
Bucket, Lid, Pine, Black Metal Bands, Wire Bail, Turned Handle, Cherry Finish, 9 ½ x 7 In.	819.00
Bucket, Lid, Pine, Iron Band, Stamped, N.F. Shakers, Enfield, N.H., 10 x 13 In.	643.00
Bucket, Lid, Tin, Yellow Label, Shaker's Applesauce N.F., Mt. Lebanon, N.Y., c.1880, 7 x 6 In. ...	761.00
Bucket, Pine, Red Paint, 2 Metal Bands, Signed, 14 In.	240.00
Bucket, Pine, Steel Hanging Tab, Yellow, Red Paint, 10 x 12 In.	234.00
Bucket, Pine, Wire Bail, Pine Handle, Blue Exterior, Red Interior, 16 x 12 In.	1053.00
Bucket, Sugar, Lid, Salmon Paint, Wrought Iron Straps, Bail Handle, 1800s, 11 In.	295.00
Cabinet, Seed Saver, Pine, Hanging, 10 Drawers, 19th Century, 22 x 20 In.	1770.00
Cane, Hardwood, Varnish, Block Print Carved F.W. Evans, Mt. Lebanon, c.1880, 33 In.	1755.00
Cheese Press, Pine, Pulley System, Carved Handle, Trestle Feet, Blue Paint, c.1840, 49 x 29 In.	468.00
Chest, Tool, Lid, 38 Tools, New Lebanon, N.Y., c.1830, 16 x 42 In.	1763.00
Churn, Dasher, Blue Paint, 26 In.	200.00
Cloak, Child's, Hood, White, Dorothy Label, Shadow Box Frame, Canterbury, 32 x 22 In.	1053.00
Clothes Press, Poplar, Pine, Molded Cornice, Blind Paneled Door, 3 Drawers, c.1830, 89 x 34 In.	6463.00
Desk, Slanted Top, Box, Side Bottle Drawer, Butternut, Pine, Mt. Lebanon, c.1840, 5 x 20 In. ..	3978.00
Dipper, Maple, Copper Nails, 19th Century, 9 In.	118.00
Dipper, Wood, Copper Nails, c.1870, 4 ½ In.	875.00
Drying Rack, Pine, 3 Rails, Shoe Feet, Mortised, Stamped Addison Illsley, c.1875, 37 x 25 In.	470.00
Drying Rack, Walnut, 3 Bars, 2 Vertical Supports, Trestle Feet, Varnish, c.1850, 36 x 26 In.	1170.00
Food Chopper, Mechanical, Cast Iron, Tin, Pine, Gears, Pump Blade, Green Paint, Base, 6 x 16 In.	702.00
Foot Warmer, Sliding Lid, Walnut, Diamond Shaped Holes, 2 Tin Coal Holders, c.1850, 6 x 15 In.	702.00
Grain Shovel, Birch, 1-Board, Carved, Hancock, 36 In.	1872.00
Hanger, Shawl, Wood, 51 In.	110.00
Hat, Brother's, Black Beaver, Black Silk Bow, Hand Sewn Interior Band, 4 ½ x 11 In.	761.00
Knitty Knotty, Maple, Carved, 19th Century, 18 ½ In.	670.00
Knitty Knotty, Maple, Carved, Wood Peg Construction, 19th Century, 17 ½ In.	220.00
Measure, Builder's, Maple, Lapped Seam, Hand Stamped Numbers, 7 ½ x 36 In.	1053.00
Mold, Church Candle, Tole, 19th Century, 16 ½ In.	177.00
Neckerchief, Sister's, Purple Silk, Kentucky Raised Silk Worms Tag, c.1850, 33 ½ In.	2105.00
Nutcracker, Maple, Turned, 19th Century, 11 In.	115.00
Pattern, Fly-Wheel, Wood, 24 In.	176.00
Peeler, Apple, Pine, Ash, Maple, Mechanical, 14 In.	110.00
Peg Board, Harness, Pine, Oak, 4 11-In. Pegs, 4 6-In. Pegs, Beveled, Red Stain, 90 In.	1755.00
Peg Board, Pine, Turned Cherry Pegs, Pumpkin Stain, 13 Ft. 2 In. x 3 In.	1872.00
Pen Wipe Doll, Glazed Clay, Felt, Silk Ribbon, Gray, Tan, Red Felt Dress, 2 ½ In.	263.00
Quilt Rack, Pine, Bifold, 19th Century, 60 In.	266.00
Rug Beater, Maple Handle, Late 19th Century, 24 In.	160.00
Rug, Yarn, Woven, Twisted, Red, Gray, Green, White, Runner, N.Y., c.1850, 21 Ft. 3 In. x 2 Ft. 10 In.	585.00
Rule, Maple, Hand Stamped, Blackened Numbers, 1857, 12 In.	819.00
Seed Box, Lid, Pine, Exterior, Interior Labels, Fitted, Red Paint, Mt. Lebanon, 4 x 24 In.	2925.00
Seed Box, Pine, Shaker Choice Vegetable Seeds, Paper Label, N.Y., 22 x 9 In.	995.00
Seed Sifter, Butternut, Arched Lifting Handle, Screen Bottom, Pail Guide Open End, 4 x 31 In.	234.00
Sewing Kit, Leather, Interior Embroidered Pincushion, Compartments, 3 ¾ In.	250.00
Sewing Kit, Linen, Hand Painted Interior, Flowers, Scissors, Needles, Silver Thimble, 4 x 2 ½ In.	275.00
Shovel, Applewood, Grain, Carved, 19th Century, 36 In.	275.00
Skimmer, Wrought Iron, Metal Handle, 19th Century, 41 x 19 In.	71.00

S

Stepladder, Pine, 2-Rod Folding Mechanism, Cross Brace Back, Gray Paint, N.Y., 5 x 22 In. ...	644.00
Stringholder, Fitted Lid, Cherry, Walnut, Maple Strips, Center Hole, Varnish, 3 ½ x 4 ½ In.	410.00
Swift, Cherry, Poplar, Adjustable Arms, Table Clamp, Yellow Stain, Hancock, c.1860, 27 In. ...	702.00
Tailor's Measure, Maple, Hanging String, Paper Label, 36 In. ...	2340.00
Thread Holder, Clover Shape, Black Leather, Red Trim & Ties, 3 Thread Spools, 2 ¼ In. ...	200.00
Toast Holder, 4 Tines, Wood Handle, 16 In. ...	150.00
Washtub, Pine, 3-Finger, Staves, Cut Handles, Gray Paint, 27 In. ...	936.00
Washtub, Pine, Iron Bands, Copper Handles, Red, Cream, c.1835, 24 x 25 In. ...	527.00
Whisk, Twisted Wire, Maple Handle, Carved, 19th Century, 14 In. ...	195.00
Wood Box, Fireplace, Pine, Hinged Lid, High Turned Legs, Yellow Finish, Maine, c.1840, 31 x 26 In.	6143.00
Yarn Swift, Mid 1800s, 22 x 5 In. ...	185.00
Yarn Winder, Maple, Ash, 6-Arm, Chip Carving, 19th Century, 39 In. ...	300.00
Yarn Winder, Maple, Birch, 4 Arms, Carved Gear Wheel, Splayed Legs, Red Paint, c.1830 ...	1170.00

SHAVING MUGS were popular from 1860 to 1900. Many types were made, including occupational mugs featuring pictures of men's jobs. There were scuttle mugs, silver-plated mugs, glass-lined mugs, and others.

Coal Wagon, Driver, Horse, H.H. Cope, 3 ½ In. ...	560.00
Fraternal, 2 Boots, Hand Holding Mat, Masonic Symbol, Gilt, L.K. Niagaw ...	240.00
Fraternal, B. Of L.E. Railroad Engineer's, J.O. Shakelford, Limoges ...	485.00
Fraternal, Civil War, Sons Of Veterans, Gilt, Porcelain, G.C. Stickney ...	176.00
Fraternal, Knights Of Pythias, Orchid, J.A. Perry, Full Black Wrap, 3 ¾ In. ...	138.00
Fraternal, Railroad Trainmen, Gilt, Limoges, Porcelain, B.A. Tucker ...	294.00
Frog, Smoking Pipe, Holding Umbrella, Gilt, R. Malloy ...	323.00
Man Shooting Ducks, R.B. Miller, 4 In. ...	238.00
Mr. & Mrs. Garfield, Ivy, Laurel Leaves, Milk Glass, Ring Handle, c.1875, 2 x 3 x 5 In. ...	118.00
Occupational, Accountant, At Desk, D.G. Yorke, Gilt, Limoges ...	325.00
Occupational, Baker, Lester C. Sterner, Gilt, 3 ½ In. ...	220.00
Occupational, Baker, Zebler, Bakery Oven, CFH, GDM, Marked, 3 ¾ In. ...	201.00
Occupational, Barber, Scissors, Razor, Striped Pole, Gilt, John A. Hellmeth, Limoges ...	420.00
Occupational, Bartender, Serving Men At Bar, Gilt, Harrison Holmes, Porcelain ...	235.00
Occupational, Blacksmith, Changing Horseshoe In Stable, Gilt, W.F. Shade, Limoges ...	153.00
Occupational, Blacksmith, Shoeing Horse, A.F. Cain, 4 In. ...	633.00
Occupational, Blacksmith, Shoeing Horse, Christ Pederson, Gold Rim, 3 ¾ In. ...	190.00
Occupational, Bricklayer, New Jersey Bricklayer Working, F. Dastram, 3 ¾ In. ...	690.00
Occupational, Butcher, Meat Cleaver, Gilt, C.M. Hodges, 4 In. ...	345.00
Occupational, Butcher, Preparing Meat For Woman, Gilt, James H. Smith, Limoges ...	499.00
Occupational, Butcher, Steer's Head, Leafy Branches, Marked D & C, France, 3 ¾ In. ...	170.00
Occupational, Butcher, Steer's Head, Tools, James D. Wooley, 4 In. ...	115.00
Occupational, Carpenter, Carpentry Tools, F.C. Tasler, 4 In. ...	144.00
Occupational, Carpenter, Sawing Board, Gilt, Paul Boehm, Porcelain ...	353.00
Occupational, Carpenter, Tools, Gilt, F.D. Van Brunt, 3 ¾ In. ...	196.00
Occupational, Chariot Racing Scene, Chas. Benson, Gilt, Limoges ...	425.00
Occupational, Coal Wagon, W.M. Ergermuth, Gilt, Limoges ...	600.00
Occupational, Cobbler, On Bench, W.M.F. Meier, Gilt ...	100.00
Occupational, Delivery Truck, 2 Men, W.P. Allen, Gilt, Germany ...	1500.00
Occupational, Delivery Wagon, Stoll's Home Made Bread Co., France, 3 ¾ In. ...	489.00
Occupational, Denture Set, Gilt, Dr. E.R. Boston, Porcelain ...	206.00
Occupational, Doctor, Skeleton, In Graduation Cap, Smoking Pipe, Dr. J. Frank Gordner ...	881.00
Occupational, Engineer, Steaming Locomotive, J.O. Shackleford, Gilt, Porcelain ...	529.00
Occupational, Express Wagon, G. Webster, Vienna, Austria, 3 ½ In. ...	160.00
Occupational, Farmer, Milking Cow, Danny Heins, Germany, 3 ¾ In. ...	287.00
Occupational, Farmer, Picture Frame, Flower Border, Gilt, A.B. Dickerson ...	71.00
Occupational, Fire Hose Wagon, Dog, G.C. Chandler, Marked, CFH, GDM ...	700.00
Occupational, Fireman's Crest, Ax, Ladder, Helmet, Gilt, Geo. C. Dewald, Porcelain ...	353.00
Occupational, Firemen, Horse Drawn Fire Engine, Blue Monochrome Wrap ...	112.00
Occupational, Fisherman, In Rain Hats, Pipes, Geo. McGuffin, Gilt, Porcelain ...	71.00
Occupational, Fisherman, With Fishing Rod, John Bogart, Gilt, Porcelain ...	823.00
Occupational, Gambling, Gilt, Arnold Rothstein, Marked Limoges, 3 ¾ In. .... *illus*	690.00
Occupational, Grain Mill Operator, Gilt, Ryan Jackson, Marked, Germany ...	2900.00
Occupational, Great Lakes Pleasure Boat Captain, John Inglese, Gilt ...	1175.00
Occupational, Grocery Wagon, Albert Redick, Gilt, Marked, Germany, 1⅓9 ...	400.00
Occupational, Harness Maker, Derge Mott, Gilt, Porcelain ...	270.00
Occupational, Horse Drawn Dairy Wagon, Gilt, Chas. Wilkelm, Limoges ...	376.00
Occupational, Horse Head, Black Letters, Porcelain, A.E. Deschambault ...	36.00
Occupational, Hotel Clerk, Geo. Greene, Gilt, Austria ...	325.00

Sewing, Yarn Reel, Yellow Pine, 2 Reels, Tripod Base, American, c.1800, 53 x 18 x 15 In.
$69.00

Shaving Mug, Occupational, Gambling, Gilt, Arnold Rothstein, Marked Limoges, 3 ¾ In.
$690.00

S

Shaving Mug, Occupational,
Loom Machine, Signed Limoges,
3 ½ In.
$410.00

Shaving Mug, Occupational, Oil Wells,
Gilt, D.K. Burns, Marked Limoges France,
3 ¾ In.
$460.00

Shaving Mug, Occupational, Plasterer,
Gilt, James Hafenna, Marked France,
3 ¾ In.
$518.00

Shaving Mug, Occupational,
Undertaker, Harry Miller, Limoges, 3 ½ In.
$439.00

Occupational, Housepainter, Scaling Ladder, Bucket, Gilt, G. Morrison		646.00
Occupational, Hunter, 3 Deer Running		118.00
Occupational, Hunter, 3 Pheasants, Hound Pointing, Gilt, Vali		206.00
Occupational, Hunters, Shooting At Ducks, Dog, Retrieving Duck, Gilt, G.L. Baun		118.00
Occupational, Ice Wagon, B. Forester, Gilt, Limoges		220.00
Occupational, Ice Wagon, Man, J.B. Worth Jr., Gilt, Limoges		275.00
Occupational, Loom Machine, Signed Limoges, 3 ½ In.	*illus*	410.00
Occupational, Mail Carrier, Letter In Hand, Gilt, H.F. Seip, Porcelain		588.00
Occupational, Man, Auctioneer, With Steer, Gilt, W.L. Parker, Porcelain		235.00
Occupational, Man, Dog, Driving Horse Drawn Buggy, Gilt, Walter Rohner, Porcelain		558.00
Occupational, Man, Driving 3 People In Horse Drawn Buggy, Gilt, Porcelain		264.00
Occupational, Man, Driving Flatbed Stake Wagon, Gilt, John Warburon, Porcelain		118.00
Occupational, Man, Driving Grocery Wagon, Porcelain		470.00
Occupational, Man, Driving Horse Drawn Baker's Wagon, John Selzer, Limoges		558.00
Occupational, Man, Driving Horse Drawn Buggy, Flowers, Magenta Wrap, A.J. Rogers		176.00
Occupational, Man, Driving Horse Drawn Ice Wagon, Gilt, J.B. Worth Jr., Porcelain.		317.00
Occupational, Man, Raised Ax To Slaughter Steer, Gilt, A. Irwin, Porcelain		176.00
Occupational, Man, Standing Beside, Horse Drawn Ice Wagon, Porcelain		235.00
Occupational, Men, Driving Delivery Truck, Gilt, W.O. Allen, Porcelain		1763.00
Occupational, Men, On Handcart, Gilt, Otto Senf, Signed E.E. Koken, Porcelain		588.00
Occupational, Men Playing Billiards, Gilt, C.B. Stephenson, Porcelain		558.00
Occupational, Merchant, Showing Box To Woman, Gilt, J.C. Dobbs, Procelain		270.00
Occupational, Oil Derrick, Green Plain, Porcelain		353.00
Occupational, Oil Wells, Gilt, D.K. Burns, Marked Limoges France, 3 ¾ In.	*illus*	460.00
Occupational, Paper Hanger, Gilt, Z.C. Perkins, Austria		500.00
Occupational, Plasterer, Gilt, James Hafenna, Marked France, 3 ¾ In.	*illus*	518.00
Occupational, Police Badge, Silver Gilt, W.S. Hawley, Porcelain		1292.00
Occupational, Printer, Gilt, Martin Egrich, Marked Limoges France, 3 ¾ In.		230.00
Occupational, Railroad Engineer, Locomotive, Gilt, C.H. Jacobus		100.00
Occupational, Rifle, Fishing Pole, Satchel, Gilt, Geo. M. Ross		475.00
Occupational, Shoe Salesman, Woman Seated, Gilt, Chas. Lowenthal, Porcelain		176.00
Occupational, Side Wheel & Sail Steamer, Capt. Samuel Waters, Marked, 3779		850.00
Occupational, Soldier, Military Base, C.G. Stoney, 21st Conn. Infantry, Limoges		800.00
Occupational, Steam Mechanic, Pink Wrap, Gilt, M.C. Boucher		750.00
Occupational, Steam Tractor, O.C. McCune, 3 ⅝ In.		1725.00
Occupational, Steamboat, Samuel Waters, Gilt, Porcelain		940.00
Occupational, Stone Cutter, Chiseling Stone, Gilt, M.B. Chambers, Limoges		199.00
Occupational, Street Car Operator, In Front Of Building, Gilt, Porcelain		235.00
Occupational, Tailor, Man, Being Fitted, Gilt, E.F. Hunzicker, Porcelain		235.00
Occupational, Tailor, N.E. Wilson, Tailor Showing Customer Fabric, 4 In.		201.00
Occupational, Teamster, Driving Stake Bed Wagon, T.A. McConnell, Pabst & Kobler		159.00
Occupational, Telegraph, Gilt, D.W. Clemens, Porcelain		705.00
Occupational, Telegraph Operator, D.W. Clemens, Gilt		475.00
Occupational, Telephone Linesman, J.C. Wharton, Gilt, Limoges		800.00
Occupational, Tinsmith, Man Standing, R.W. Folsom, Gilt		150.00
Occupational, Tinsmith, Working With Mallet, Flower Border, Emil G. Decker		217.00
Occupational, Train Engineer's, Locomotive, Frank B. Cameron, Gilt		50.00
Occupational, Turner, At Wood Lathe, Wood Shavings On Floor, Gilt, Porcelain		411.00
Occupational, Undertaker, Harry Miller, Limoges, 3 ½ In.	*illus*	439.00
Occupational, Wallpaper Hanger, On Ladder, Gilt, A.D. Klein, Porcelain		120.00
Occupational, Watchmaker, Pocket Watch, Gilt, G.O. Warren, Porcelain		176.00
Owl & Man, D.C. Freeborn, Gilt, Halloween Theme, 3 ½ In.		518.00
Owl & Moon Scene, N.C. Baley, Gold Rim, 3 ½ In.		160.00
Snow Covered Cabin, Woods, Smoking Chimney, Gilt, Geo. S. Biggs, Limoges		180.00
Stallions, White, Black, George Batche, 3 ¾ In.		55.00

SHAWNEE POTTERY was started in Zanesville, Ohio, in 1937. The company made vases, novelty ware, flowerpots, planters, lamps, and cookie jars. Three dinnerware lines were made: Corn, Lobster Ware, and Valencia (a solid color line). White Corn pattern utility pieces were made in 1945. Corn King was made from 1946 to 1954; Corn Queen, with darker green leaves and lighter colored corn, from 1954 to 1961. Shawnee produced pottery for George Rumrill during the late 1930s. The company closed in 1961.

Shawnee
USA

Cookie Jar, Bank, Smiley Pig, Green Neckerchief, Butterscotch Brown Bottom, Marked, 10 In.		295.00
Cookie Jar, Dutch Girl, Jill, Blue Skirt, 12 In.		68.00
Cookie Jar, Dutch Girl, Jill, Painted, Tulip, Marked U.S.A., 12 In.	*illus*	236.00
Cookie Jar, Dutch Girl, Jill, Tulip, Cookie On Shoulder, Marked, U.S.A., 12 In.		238.00

S

Cookie Jar, Jumbo Elephant, Flowers, Gold, 11 In.	89.00
Cookie Jar, Muggsy, Blue Bow, Gold, Marked, U.S.A., 11 In.	170.00
Cookie Jar, Muggsy, Painted, Gold Highlights, Marked U.S.A., 11 In. ....*illus*	177.00
Cookie Jar, Owl, Winking, Gold, Cold Painted, 11 ½ In.	69.00
Cookie Jar, Puss 'N Boots, Gold & Orange Tulip, Gold Design, Marked, U.S.A., 10 In.	190.00
Cookie Jar, Puss 'N Boots, Red Bow, Gold, Marked, 10 In. .... 121.00 to	199.00
Cookie Jar, Puss 'N Boots, Roses, Gold Design, Marked, U.S.A., 10 In. ...... 140.00 to	200.00
Cookie Jar, Smiley Pig, Flowers, Yellow Neckerchief, Marked, U.S.A., 11 In.	238.00
Cookie Jar, Smiley Pig, Shamrocks, Gold & Green Neckerchief, Marked, U.S.A., 11 In.	420.00
Cookie Jar, Smiley Pig, Tulips, Red Neckerchief, Marked, U.S.A., 11 In.	140.00
Cookie Jar, Winnie Pig, Blue Collar, Gold, Marked, Patented Winnie U.S.A., 11 In. . 225.00 to	295.00
Cookie Jar, Winnie Pig, Green Collar, 11 In. ....*illus*	225.00
Cookie Jar, Winnie Pig, Peach Collar, Marked, U.S.A., 11 In. .... 130.00 to	153.00
Figurine, Parrot, 3 ½ In.	32.00
Mixing Bowl, Corn King, 6 ½ In.	35.00
Pitcher, Bo Peep, Flowers, Gold, Marked, 8 ¼ In.	78.00
Pitcher, Chanticleer, Flowers, Gold Design, Marked, U.S.A., 8 In.	235.00
Planter, Doe In Shadowbox, Yellow, Green, 9 In. ....*illus*	30.00
Salt & Pepper, Owl, Blue Eyes, 3 In.	22.00
Shaker, Smiley & Winnie, Heart, 5 In.	58.00
Vase, Bamboo, 6 In.	29.00
Vase, White Matte, Impressed Mark, 1930s, 8 In.	48.00
Wall Pocket, Teapot, Yellow Apple, Green Leaves, Maroon Spout, c.1940, 6 ½ x 3 In.	30.00
Wall Pocket, Wheat, 5 In.	35.00

SHEARWATER POTTERY is a family business started by Mr. and Mrs. G.W. Anderson, Sr., and their three sons. The local Ocean Springs, Mississippi, clays were used to make the wares in the 1930s. The company is still in business.

Bowl, Lavender, Flared Rim, Peter Anderson, c.1935, 3 ⅜ x 6 ⅛ In.	420.00
Figure, Chesty Horse, Green Glaze, Walter Inglis Anderson, c.1935, 14 x 14 In. ....*illus*	5520.00
Figure, Pirate With Sword, Walter Inglis Anderson, c.1945, 8 In. ....*illus*	120.00
Figurine, Elephant, Antique Green Glazed, Cast, James Anderson, c.1965, 7 In.	600.00
Lamp Base, Antique Green Glazed, c.1927-29, 6 ¼ In.	720.00
Lamp Base, Pelican, Antique Green, Walter Anderson, c.1930, 13 ¼ x 7 ¼ In.	1800.00
Vase, Bronze & White Enameled, Peter Anderson, c.1928, 4 ¼ x 5 ½ In.	720.00
Vase, Deco, 14 Dancing Figures, Grapevines, Bulbous, Gray Metallic Glaze, Signed, 10 x 9 In.	3335.00
Vase, Footed, Double Glazed, Blue Rain, Flaring Beaker Form, c.1975, 8 x 4 ½ In.	450.00
Vase, Green, Lobed Form, Peter Anderson, c.1940, 4 ¼ x 5 ½ In.	1680.00
Vase, Pelicans, Mottled Blue & Turquoise Glaze, 7 x 6 In.	6600.00

SHEET MUSIC from the past centuries is now collected. The favorites are examples with covers featuring artistic or historic pictures. Early sheet music covers were lithographed, but by the 1900s photographic reproductions were used. The early music was larger than more recent sheets, and you must watch out for examples that were trimmed to fit in a twentieth-century piano bench.

American, 39 Bound Pieces, Woodcuts, H. Hoster, Sacramento, Calif., 1870s, 13 ½ x 10 ½ In.	276.00
Baby It's Cold Outside, From Neptune's Daughter, Esther Williams, 1948, 9 x 12 In.	10.00
Burning Of Rome, E.T. Paull, City Burning Scene, c.1903...................................	5.90
If I Were A Big Victrola...	88.00
Millionaires, March 2-Step, Baseball Team, D.C. Henninger, c.1908, 14 x 10 ½ In.	187.00
Put Another Nickel In, Music, Music, Music, Carmen Cavallaro, 1950........................	13.00
Snowbird, Indian Reminiscences, American Indian, Early 1900s...........................	4.32
Sophie Tucker, I'm Doing What I Am Doing For Love	11.00

SHELLEY first appeared on English ceramics about 1912. The Foley China Works started in England in 1860. Joseph Ball Shelley joined the company in 1862 and became a partner in 1872. Percy Shelley joined the firm in 1881. The company went through a series of name changes and in 1910 the then Foley China Company became Shelley China. In 1929 it became Shelley Potteries. The company was acquired in 1966 by Allied English Potteries, then merged with the Doulton group in 1971. The name Shelley was put into use again in 1980. A trio is the name for a cup, saucer, and cake plate set.

Bowl, Centerpiece, Orange Red Deco Ground, Cranes, White, Yellow.......................	110.00
Candy Dish, Rose Chintz, Dainty Shape, Pink Shell Tab Handles, 5 ½ In.	128.00
Cup & Saucer, Bubble Floral, Ripon Shape, Gold Trim, 1965	168.00
Cup & Saucer, Green Daisy, 1960s...	182.00
Cup & Saucer, Maytime, Chintz, Green Trim..	125.00

Shawnee, Cookie Jar, Dutch Girl, Jill, Painted, Tulip, Marked U.S.A., 12 In.
$236.00

Shawnee, Cookie Jar, Muggsy, Painted, Gold Highlights, Marked U.S.A., 11 In.
$177.00

Shawnee, Cookie Jar, Winnie Pig, Green Collar, 11 In.
$225.00

Shawnee, Planter, Doe In Shadowbox, Yellow, Green, 9 In.
$30.00

Shearwater, Figure, Chesty Horse, Green Glaze, Walter Inglis Anderson, c.1935, 14 x 14 In.
$5520.00

Shearwater, Figure, Pirate With Sword, Walter Inglis Anderson, c.1945, 8 In.
$120.00

Shelley, Cup & Saucer, Yellow Charm, Demitasse
$165.00

Cup & Saucer, Melody		188.00
Cup & Saucer, Melody, Chintz, Crested, Gold Trim, c.1940		188.00
Cup & Saucer, Pansy		178.00
Cup & Saucer, Sheraton		55.00
Cup & Saucer, Summer Glory		148.00 to 168.00
Cup & Saucer, Wild Anemone		55.00
Cup & Saucer, Yellow Charm, Demitasse	*illus*	165.00
Jam Jar, Cover, Melody		113.00
Plate, Luncheon, Primrose, 8 In.		90.00
Toast Rack, Maytime, 7 x 2 ½ In.		300.00
Trio, Primrose		105.00
Vase, Violets, Urn Shape, Leaves, Marked, 4 ½ In.		53.00

SHIRLEY TEMPLE, the famous movie star, was born in 1928. She made her first movie in 1932. Thousands of items picturing Shirley have been and still are being made. Shirley Temple dolls were first made in 1934 by Ideal Toy Company. Millions of Shirley Temple cobalt blue glass dishes were made by Hazel Atlas Glass Company and U.S. Glass Company from 1934 to 1942. They were given away as premiums for Wheaties and Bisquick. A bowl, mug, and pitcher were made as a breakfast set. Some pieces were decorated with the picture of a very young Shirley, others used a picture of Shirley in her 1936 Captain January costume. Although collectors refer to a cobalt creamer, it is actually the 4 ½-inch-high milk pitcher from the breakfast set. Many of these items are being reproduced today.

Button, Profile, Wood, Medium		30.00
Doll, Baby, White Dress, Bonnet, Ideal, c.1935, 19 In.		616.00
Doll, Composition, Blond Mohair Wig, Dimples, Smiling, Dress Tag, c.1930s, 27 In.		322.00
Doll, Composition, Blue Organdy Little Colonel Outfit, Box, c.1935, 20 In.	*illus*	672.00
Doll, Composition, Green Sleep Eyes, Painted Face, Red Dress, Box, Ideal, c.1935, 16 In.		504.00
Doll, Composition, Metal Eyes, Blond Mohair, Jointed, Ideal, 13 In.		148.00
Doll, Composition, Open Mouth, Metal Eyes, Leatherette Shoes, Socks, 18 In.		326.00
Doll, Composition, Sleep Eyes, Open Mouth, Cowgirl Costume, Ideal, 12 In.		2070.00
Doll, Composition, Sleep Eyes, Yellow Curly Top Dress, c.1935, 18 In.	*illus*	560.00
Doll, Composition, Socket Head, Mohair Wig, Pink Starburst Pleated Dress, Ideal, c.1935, 20 In.		672.00
Doll, Composition, Wig, Original Clothing, Ideal, 18 In.		195.00
Doll, Ideal, Yellow Party Dress, Brown Sleep Eyes, Open Mouth, Blond Wig, c.1960, 17 In.		140.00
Doll, Little Colonel, Composition, Green Sleep Eyes, Open Mouth, Madame Alexander, c.1935, 20 In.		896.00
Doll, Our Little Girl, Composition, Socket Head, Green Sleep Eyes, Open Mouth, Ideal, c.1935, 18 In.		560.00
Lobby Card, Dimples, 1936, 17 x 14 In.		320.00
Mug, Blue, 6 Oz., 3 ¾ In.		55.00

SILVER DEPOSIT glass was first made during the late nineteenth century. Solid sterling silver is applied to the glass by a chemical method so that a cutout design of silver metal appears against a clear or colored glass. It is sometimes called silver overlay.

Decanter, Black Glass, Ribbed Stopper, Geishas, Flowers, 9 ¾ In.	*illus*	184.00
Decanter, Cranberry & Green Glass, Silver Overlay, Alvin Co., Early 1900s, 12 ½ In., Pair		1708.00
Decanter, Overlay, Cranberry Glass, Bulbous, Slender Neck, Stopper, c.1900, 10 In.		1800.00
Decanter, Overlay, Emerald Glass, Squat Lobed, Goffered Rim, c.1900, 10 In.		1680.00
Vase, Art Nouveau, Silver Overlay, Flower Pattern, Glass, Early 20th Century, 8 In.		69.00
Vase, Green Glass, Silver Overlay, Alvin Co., Early 20th Century, 6 ½ In.		1830.00
Vase, Tapered, Green Glass, Silver Flower, Marked Alvin, 6 ½ In.		480.00

SILVER FLATWARE includes many of the current and out-of-production silver and silver-plated flatware patterns made in the past eighty years. Other silver is listed under Silver-American, Silver-English, etc. Most silver flatware sets that are missing a few pieces can be completed through the help of one of the many silver matching services listed on our website, www.kovels.com.

SILVER FLATWARE PLATED

Adam, Dinner Fork, Oneida Community, 1917		9.00
Adam, Dinner Knife, Oneida Community, 1917		9.00
Adam, Lemon Fork, Oneida Community, 1917		25.00
Adam, Salad Fork, Oneida Community, 1917		9.00
Adam, Soup Spoon, Oneida Community, 1917		11.00
Adam, Teaspoon, Oneida Community, 1917		5.50
Anniversary, Dinner Fork, Rogers Bros., 1923		9.00
Anniversary, Dinner Knife, Rogers Bros., 1923		10.00
Anniversary, Gravy Ladle, Rogers Bros.		24.00

Anniversary, Iced Tea Spoon, Rogers Bros.	10.00
Anniversary, Teaspoon, Rogers Bros.	7.00
Avon, Soup Ladle, Rogers Bros.	99.00
Beethoven, Serving Fork, Oneida Community	20.00
Berkshire, Oyster Ladle, Rogers Bros.	87.00
Berkshire, Serving Spoon, Rogers Bros.	20.00
Bridal Wreath, Dinner Fork, Tudor Plate, Oneida Community	8.50
Bridal Wreath, Dinner Knife, Tudor Plate, Oneida Community	8.50
Bridal Wreath, Dinner Teaspoon, Tudor Plate, Oneida Community	5.00
Bridal Wreath, Salad Fork, Tudor Plate, Oneida Community	8.50
Bridal Wreath, Serving Spoon, Tudor Plate, Oneida Community	17.00
Danish Princess, Dinner Knife, Holmes & Edwards	13.00
Danish Princess, Fork, Holmes & Edwards	11.00
Danish Princess, Salad Fork, Holmes & Edwards	10.00 to 13.00
Danish Princess, Serving Spoon, Holmes & Edwards	16.00 to 20.00
Danish Princess, Soup Spoon, Holmes & Edwards	11.00
Danish Princess, Sugar Spoon, Holmes & Edwards	9.00
First Love, Dinner Fork, Rogers Bros.	15.00
King Cedric, Butter Knife, Oneida Community	8.00
King Cedric, Jelly Server, Oneida Community	8.00
King Cedric, Salad Fork, Oneida Community	10.00
King Cedric, Serving Spoon, Oneida Community	16.00
King Cedric, Sugar Spoon, Oneida Community	8.00
Lady Fair, Butter Knife, Wm. Rogers	7.00
Lady Fair, Cocktail Fork, Wm. Rogers	6.00
Lady Fair, Serving Fork, Wm. Rogers	14.00
Leyland, Pickle Fork, Rogers, 1910	19.00
Magnolia, Butter Knife, Rogers Bros., 1951	9.00
Magnolia, Dinner Knife, Rogers Bros., 1951	9.00
Old Colony, Pickle Fork, Floral Handle, Engraved 1847 Rogers Bros., 6 In.	25.00
Plymouth, Serving Fork, Plymouth Silver Co., 1897	35.00
South Seas, Dinner Fork, Community, 1955	15.00
South Seas, Dinner Knife, Community, 1955	14.00
South Seas, Salad Fork, Community, 1955	11.00
South Seas, Serving Spoon, Pierced, Community, 1955	25.00
South Seas, Soup Spoon, Community, 1955	9.00
South Seas, Sugar Spoon, Community, 1955	6.50
Valley Rose, Cold Meat Fork, Wm. Rogers Oneida	22.00
Valley Rose, Serving Spoon, Pierced, Wm. Rogers Oneida	19.00

SILVER FLATWARE STERLING

Acanthus, Pie Server, c.1917, 8 ⅞ In.	300.00
Acorn, Cake Server, Georg Jensen, 1940s, 10 ½ In.	535.00
American Beauty, Sardine Fork, George W. Shiebler	110.00
Athenia, Meat Fork, Charles Wendell	49.00
Bird, Serving Spoon, Wendt	130.00
Blossoms, Spoon, Georg Jensen, 8 ¼ In.	435.00
Burgundy, Butter Knife, Reed & Barton, 8 Piece	292.00
Buttercup, Serving Fork, Gorham	125.00
Buttercup, Teaspoon, Gorham	34.00
Cactus, Fish Set, Engraved Fish, Georg Jensen, 1915-19, 9 In., 2 Piece	535.00
Cactus, Ladle, Georg Jensen, 1940s, 11 ½ In.	850.00
Calla Lily, Serving Set, Stamped Peer Smed .... *illus*	660.00
Candlelight, Dinner Fork, Towle	24.00
Candlelight, Dinner Knife, Towle	30.00
Canterbury, Serving Spoon, Towle, 1893	189.00
Chantilly, Olive Fork, Gorham	48.00
Chateau Rose, Salad Fork, Alvin, 1940, 6 ½ In., 8 Piece	150.00
Contempora, Carving Set, Eliel Saarinen, Stamped, Dominick & Haff .... *illus*	120.00
Craftsman, Butter Spreader, Towle	12.00
Craftsman, Dinner Fork, Towle, 1923	23.00
Craftsman, Dinner Knife, Towle, 1923	32.00
Craftsman, Salad Fork, Towle, 1923	28.00
Craftsman, Teaspoon, Towle, 1923	11.00
Cupid, Teaspoon, Dominick & Haff	28.00
D'Orleans, Dinner Knife, Towle	36.00
Devonshire, Dinner Knife, International	15.00

Shirley Temple, Doll, Composition, Blue Organdy Little Colonel Outfit, Box, c.1935, 20 In.
$672.00

Shirley Temple, Doll, Composition, Sleep Eyes, Yellow Curly Top Dress, c.1935, 18 In.
$560.00

Silver Deposit, Decanter, Black Glass, Ribbed Stopper, Geishas, Flowers, 9 ¾ In.
$184.00

S

Silver Flatware Sterling, Calla Lily, Serving Set, Stamped Peer Smed
$660.00

Silver Flatware Sterling, Contempora, Carving Set, Eliel Saarinen, Stamped, Dominick & Haff
$120.00

Silver Flatware Sterling, Fish Serving Set, Pierced, Engraved, Carved Bone Handles, Victorian, 2 Piece
$63.00

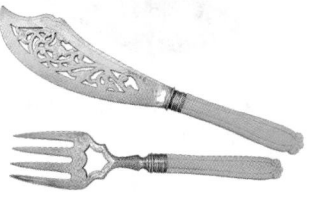

Diamond, Butter Knife, George W. Shiebler	64.00
Diamond, Carving Set, Gio Ponti, Reed & Barton, 2 Piece	510.00
Dorothy Vernon, Bouillon Spoon, Monogram, Whiting, 5 In.	39.00
Duke Of York, Teaspoon, Whiting	18.00
Etruscan, Carving Set, Fork, Knife, Gorham, c.1923, 2 Piece	150.00
Fiddle & Thread, Spoon, Strainer, Stephen Adams, London, 1807, 12 In.	690.00
Fish Serving Set, Pierced, Engraved, Carved Bone Handles, Victorian, 2 piece .... *illus*	63.00
Flower Lane, Lemon Fork, Heirloom, Oneida	15.00
Forget-Me-Not, Demitasse Spoon, Gold Wash, Silk Lined Box, 1895, 12 Piece	106.00
Fuchsia, Spoon, Georg Jensen, 1940s, 10 ¼ In.	850.00
Gossamer Engraved, Dinner Knife, Gorham	20.00
Grand Victorian, Dinner Knife, Wallace	35.00
Heraldic, Punch Ladle, Elliptical Bowl, Engraved Initials, Whiting, c.1880, 13 In.	294.00
Ivy, Ladle, Oval Gilt Bowl, Whiting, 13 In.	201.00
Kensington, Tea Strainer, Gorham	60.00
King Richard, Butter Knife, Towle	45.00
Lafayette, Bonbon Spoon, Towle, 1898	95.00
Lancaster, Ice Cream Fork, Gorham, c.1897, 12 Piece	480.00
Landers No. 2, Bonbon Spoon, Baker Manchester, 1900	35.00
Landers No. 2, Olive Fork, Baker Manchester, 1900	30.00
Landers No. 2, Serving Fork, Baker Manchester, 1900	36.00
Lily, Cake Server, Monogram, Whiting, 10 In.	50.00
Lily, Fish Slice, Monogram, Whiting, 9 ¾ In.	240.00
Lily, Seafood Fork, Whiting, Pair	92.00
Lily, Serving Fork, Monogram, Whiting, 7 ⅝ In.	60.00
Lily, Serving Set, Fork & Spoon, Whiting, c.1910	295.00
Lily, Serving Spoon, Scoop, Monogram, Whiting, 7 ½ In.	121.00
Louis XV, Butter Knife, Birks	90.00
Majestic, Butter Spreader, Alvin, c.1900, 12 Piece	263.00
Marcell, Pie Server, International	145.00
Marrow Scoop, Samuel Kirk, Baltimore, c.1850, 7 ¾ In.	410.00
Medallion, Fish Slice, Engraved, Gorham, c.1864, 12 In.	176.00
Melbourne, Youth Knife, Oneida	9.50
Monticello, Butter Knife, Lunt	60.00
Mount Vernon, Olive Fork, Lunt	15.00
Mount Vernon, Pickle Fork, Lunt	15.00
Old Fiddle, Soup Spoon, Gorham	45.00
Orchid, Youth Fork, International	15.00
Oval Twist, Salad Servers, Whiting, 9 ½ In., Pair	131.00
Pierced Trianon, Salad Servers, Gilt, Dominick & Haff, c.1885, 11 ¾ & 13 ½ In.	1560.00
Poppy, Dinner Fork, Gorham, 1902	59.00
Prelude, Butter Knife, International	24.00
Prelude, Dinner Fork, International	48.00
Prelude, Knife, International	54.00
Prelude, Oyster Fork, International	38.00
Prelude, Salad Fork, International	36.00
Repousse, Berry Spoon, S. Kirk & Son, 5 In.	48.00
Rosalind New, Cold Meat Fork, International	35.00
Rose Marie, Dinner Knife, Gorham	18.00
Scroll, Salad Set, Georg Jensen, 1940s, 9 In., 2 Piece	850.00
Silver Rose, Dinner Knife, Oneida	20.00
Silver Rose, Salad Fork, Oneida	24.00
Silver Wheat, Dinner Knife, Reed & Barton	25.00
Stanton Hall, Butter Knife, Heirloom, Oneida	95.00
Strasbourg, Butter Knife, Gorham	28.00
Strasbourg, Carving Set, Gorham, 2 Piece	125.00
Strasbourg, Dinner Knife, Gorham	34.00
Strasbourg, Youth Fork, Gorham	45.00
Sulgrave, Serving Fork, Gorham	110.00
Trajan, Butter Spreader, Reed & Barton	46.00
Trajan, Fruit Spoon, Reed & Barton	38.00
Trumbull, Dinner Fork, International	98.00
Trumbull, Lettuce Spoon, International	98.00
Versailles, Cheese Scoop, Gorham, c.1888, 8 ¼ In.	300.00
Versailles, Serving Spoon, Monogram, Marked, Gorham, 12 ½ In. .... *illus*	391.00
Violet, Cold Meat Fork, Monogram, R. Wallace & Sons, 8 ⅜ In. .... *illus*	75.00

Violet, Salad Fork, Wallace, c.1904, 6 Piece	94.00
Virginiana, Butter Knife, Gorham	175.00

SILVER PLATE is not solid silver. It is a ware made of a metal, such as nickel or copper, Ⓔ Ⓟ Ⓝ Ⓢ that is covered with a thin coating of silver. The letters *EPNS* are often found on American and English silver-plated wares. *Sheffield* is a term with two meanings. Sometimes it refers to sterling silver made in the town of Sheffield, England. Sometimes it refers to an old form of plated silver.

Bacon Server, Rectangular, Gadroon, Lid, Handle Spout, Old Sheffield, c.1830, 5 x 12 In.	230.00
Bacon Warmer, Neoclassical, Ivory Handle, Elkington & Co., England, c.1889, 13 In. .... *illus*	403.00
Basket, Centerpiece, Meriden Co., 19th Century	94.00
Bowl, Centerpiece, Scroll Arms, Flowers, Cut Glass Bowl, Diamonds, Scalloped, 10 In.	173.00
Bowl, Centerpiece, Standing Deer Under Palm Tree, Holds Bowl, Spain, 16 x 11 In.	518.00
Bowl, J. Hoffmann, Brass, Spiral Flute, Hand Wrought, Wiener Werkstatte, c.1924, 4 In.	1793.00
Bowl, Repousse Flowers, Horse Head Handles, Wilcox Silver Co., c.1900, 8 x 17 In.	546.00
Box, Embossed Figures, c.1910, 6 x 8 x 5 ¾ In.	176.00
Box, Stamp, WMF, Pinecone, Needles, Mark, Art Nouveau, 5 x 1 In.	180.00
Box, Tobacco, Cover, Tomb Of Washington, Woman, Child, Engraved, Oval, 1 x 3 In.	374.00
Box, Tortoiseshell, Ivory Inlay, Victorian, Mid 19th Century, 2 ¾ x 9 ½ In.	1708.00
Cake Basket, Regency, Gadrooning, Palmettes, Swing Handle, Sheffield, 7 x 11 In. .... *illus*	180.00
Candlestick, Figural, Flamingo, Leafy Bobeche Held In Mouth, 7 x 15 In., Pair	460.00
Candy Tazza, J. Hoffmann, Brass, Spiral Flute, Wiener Werkstatte, c.1924, 3 In.	2032.00
Card Tray, Sculpted Wing, Verse, Speed Away, Derby Silver, c.1880, 5 ½ In. .... *illus*	330.00
Casserole, Round, Domed Top, Scroll Border, Handle & Feet, Matthew Boulton, 12 In.	230.00
Centerpiece, Turkey, Removable Head, Tail, Boat Shaped Tray, 3 Pad Feet	104.00
Chafing Dish, Cover, Mid 1800s, England, 13 ¼ x 10 In.	176.00
Champagne Flute, India, 9 x 3 In., 24 Piece	293.00
Cheese Scoop, El Dorado, Gorham, 8 ½ In.	58.00
Cocktail Shaker, Boston Lighthouse Shape, Marks, Meriden Silver Plate Co., c.1820, 14 In. ..	2070.00
Cocktail Shaker, Lid, Lighthouse Shape, Cylindrical, Tapering, 14 In.	1440.00
Cocktail Shaker, Lighthouse Shape, Lid, J.T. & Company, Sheffield, 14 In.	1880.00
Cocktail Shaker, Penguin, Napier, Meriden, Conn., 1900s, 12 ½ In.	1076.00
Cocktail Shaker, Relief Design, Windmills, Houses, Cork, Holland, 1920s, 11 ¼ In.	375.00
Cocktail Shaker, Rooster, Hammered, Wallace Brothers, Wallingford, Conn., 1900s, 14 ½ In.	3346.00
Cocktail Shaker, Skyscraper, Cap, Bernard Rice's Sons Inc., N.Y., c.1930, 11 In.	2271.00
Cocktail Shaker, Zeppelin, Art Deco, 3 Pieces, Center Section Strainer, 12 In.	510.00
Coffee Set, Pot, Creamer, Sugar, Tray, Wood Handles, Arts & Crafts, 8 ½ In.	191.00
Coffee Urn, Victorian, Engraved Flower, Lion Finial, Batwing Handles, 18 ½ In.	89.00
Coffee Urn, W.W. Harrison, Sheffield, c.1900, 23 In.	702.00
Coffeepot, Pear Shape, Hinged Lid, Wood Handle & Finial, M. Boulton, 6 In.	403.00
Coffeepot, Pod & Leaf Finial, Acanthus Spout, Scroll Handle, Shaped Feet, c.1800, 9 In.	106.00
Coffeepot, Urn Form, Hinged Lid, Acorn Finial, Wood Handle, 12 ⅞ In.	66.00
Compote, Art Nouveau, Oval, Molded, Chased, Leaf Handles, Quatrefoil Base, 18 ½ x 21 In. ...	345.00
Compote, French Style, Crystal Bowl, Etched, Cherubs, Scrolling Feet, 16 x 10 ½ In., Pair	489.00
Compote, Scalloped, Oval Shape Basin, Scrolling Handles, Supports, 18 ½ x 21 ¼ In., Pair	230.00
Condiment Set, Middle Eastern Man, Shoulder Pole, 2 Glass Barrels, Figural, 6 ⅜ In.	136.00
Condiment Set, Scroll Dragon, Engraved Flowers, Simpson Hall & Miller, 4 Inserts, 9 In.	40.00
Cover, Meat, Oval Stepped Center, Flowers, Scroll Handle, England, c.1830, 11 x 20 In.	4043.00
Creamer, Helmet Form, Square Base, Monogram M/B/B. To L.H.D., 1923, 7 ¼ In.	132.00
Decanter Set, Georgian, Hinged Handle, Shaped Frame, Ball Feet, 3 Crystal Bottles, 12 x 12 In.	173.00
Dessert Set, Aesthetic, Monogram, Quadruple Plated, Reed & Barton, 4 Piece	295.00
Dish, Entree, Incurved Sides, Gadroon Border, Handles, 5 x 8 x 7 In., Pair	360.00
Dish, Entree, Scroll & Shell Border, Platform Base, Burner, c.1900, 10 x 20 x 14 In.	259.00
Epergne, Victorian, Triangular Base, 5 Glass Vases, Scrolls, Sphinx, Leaves, c.1875, 24 x 9 In.	1200.00
Etui, Beaker Shape, Fitted Interior, Utensils, Ivory Handles, Leather Case, France, 6 In.	633.00
Fish Serving Set, Ivory, Engraved Floral Scrolls, Arabesques, Case, Late 1800s, 18 Piece	420.00
Fish Serving Set, Knife, Fork, Beaded Handle, Dixon & Sons, c.1865, 12 ½ x 10 In.	82.00
Fish Serving Set, Rococo, King's Shape Handle, Scrollwork, 14 & 10 In., Pair .... *illus*	120.00
Flask, Fish, Art Nouveau, Raised Design, Lid Is Collapsible Cup, Meriden, 6 In.	201.00
Fruit Bowl, D. Peche, Brass, Horizontal Bands, Wiener Werkstatte, c.1919, 6 In.	5378.00
Ice Water Stand, Porcelain Liner, Aesthetic, Reed & Barton, 19 x 10 ½ In. ...... *illus*	282.00
Incense Burner, Urn Shape, Ibis, Dragon Handles, Chinese, 29 x 16 In.	1755.00
Jug, Beer, Hinged Lid, Hand Hammered, Bohrnabbm, Nachfolger, Germany, c.1905, 8 x 6 In. .	47.00
Jug, Hot Water, WMF, c.1909, 8 ½ x 3 ½ In.	90.00
Kettle, Hot Water, Stand, Hinged Lid, Incised Leaves, Atkin Brothers, 16 In. ...... *illus*	161.00
Kettle, Stand, Lion Masks, Victorian, c.1875, 19 ½ In. ...... *illus*	316.00

Silver Flatware Sterling, Versailles, Serving Spoon, Monogram, Marked, Gorham, 12 ½ In.
$391.00

Silver Flatware Sterling, Violet, Cold Meat Fork, Monogram, R. Wallace & Sons, 8 ⅜ In.
$75.00

Silver Plate, Bacon Warmer, Neoclassical, Ivory Handle, Elkington & Co., England, c.1889, 13 In.
$403.00

Silver Plate, Cake Basket, Regency, Gadrooning, Palmettes, Swing Handle, Sheffield, 7 x 11 In.
$180.00

As always, the edited listings in *Kovels' Antiques & Collectibles Price Guide 2011* aren't available on any website, but readers should visit Kovels.com for information on trends, tips, reproductions, marks, old prices, and more!

S

SILVER PLATE

Silver Plate, Card Tray, Sculpted Wing, Verse, Speed Away, Derby Silver, c.1880, 5 ½ In.
$330.00

Silver Plate, Fish Serving Set, Rococo, King's Shape Handle, Scrollwork, 14 & 10 In., Pair
$120.00

Silver Plate, Ice Water Stand, Porcelain Liner, Aesthetic, Reed & Barton, 19 x 10 ½ In.
$282.00

Silver Plate, Kettle, Hot Water, Stand, Hinged Lid, Incised Leaves, Atkin Brothers, 16 In.
$161.00

Kettle, Stand, Scrolls, Flowers, Finial, c.1900, 16 x 12 In.	374.00
Ladle, Potosi Silver Co., Mark, Late 19th Century, 13 In.	71.00
Meat Dish, Embossed Flowers, Stand, Gadroon Border, Leaf Feet, Lid, 15 x 26 In.	1586.00
Mirror, Pressed Frame, Scrolling Leaf Design, Oval, Beveled, 25 x 18 In., Pair	201.00
Mirror, Tapered Columnar Supports, Acanthus Finials, Bun Feet, c.1800, 16 x 13 In.	411.00
Muffin Warmer, Engraved Butterfly, Bird, Fern, Cylindrical, Panels Rotate, 6 ¾ x 8 ¾ In.	1750.00
Nut Dish, Base Frame, Wheels, Putti, Squirrel Finial, Middletown Plate Co., 11 x 13 In.	805.00
Pitcher, Lid, Embossed Bird, Flower, Porcelain Lining, Wilcox, 13 In.	150.00
Pitcher Set, Water, Goblet, Pitcher, Stand, Pairpoint, 4 ⅞ & 13 ⅜ & 19 ¼ In.	450.00
Pitcher Set, Water, Stand, Goblets, Aesthetic, Liner, Reed & Barton, 18 x 15 In. .... *illus*	265.00
Pitcher, Sheffield, Paul Revere Silver Co., Boston, 9 ½ In.	59.00
Pitcher, Water, Arctic Exploration, Depicting Elisha Kent Kane, c.1861, 11 ¼ In.	705.00
Plateau, 4 Mirror Sections, Openwork Sides, Swag Detail, 60 ½ x 22 In.	5980.00
Plateau, Mirror, Round, Scrolls, Vines, Grape Edge, Creswick & Co. Mark, Eng., c.1875, 4 x 16 In.	863.00
Plateau, Mirror, Water Lily Border, 21 In.	350.00
Plateau, Reeded Border, 3 Section Cartouche Mirrors, Risler & Vachette, France, 41 x 20 In.	2300.00
Platter, Sheffield, Gadroon Rim, Engraved Anchor Cipher, 12 ⅛ In., 12 Piece	1293.00
Punch Bowl, Cherub Mask, Chased, Embossed Flowers, Victorian, England, 1893, 10 x 6 In.	948.00
Punch Bowl, Pierced, Scalloped Base, Round Stepped Base, 5 x 10 ¼ In., Pair	345.00
Punch Bowl, Scalloped Rim, Decorated, Grape Clusters, Round Pedestal, 10 ¼ x 14 ¼ In.	86.00
Punch Bowl, Scalloped Rim, Grapevine Design, Pedestal Base, 10 x 14 ½ In., Pair	345.00
Roast Cover & Platter, Fluted, Applied Leaf Handle, Armorial Crest, Sheffield, 16 x 11 & 18 In.	127.00
Salt, Art Deco Swirls, Face, Cobalt Glass Insert, Spoon, 1 ½ x 2 ½ In.	45.00
Salt, Blue Liner, Round, Japan, 1 In.	15.00
Salt, Etched Flowers, Round, Ellis-Barker, c.1920, 1 ½ In.	17.00
Salt Set, 2 Salts, 2 Spoons, Case, Redfield & Rice, Inscribed, New York, 1800s	468.00
Salver, Dolphin Footed, Shell Shape, Engraved Lion, Early 1800s, 10 In.	225.00
Serving Dish, Cover, Removable Handle, Marked Elkington & Co., 11 ¾ In.	295.00
Spoon Holder, 24 Slots, Revolving, Bailey Kettell & Chapman, 9 ½ x 7 ½ In. .... *illus*	540.00
Spoon, Souvenir, see Souvenir category.	
Spoon Warmer, Aladdin's Lamp Shape, Marked Wilson & Gill, Victorian, 8 ¾ In.	295.00
Spoon Warmer, Helmet Form, 5 x 6 ½ In.	210.00
Spoon Warmer, Keg Form, Scroll Legs, 6 x 6 In.	360.00
Spoon Warmer, Nautilus Shape, Continental, 7 ½ x 5 ¼ In., Pair	431.00
Sugar & Creamer, Cover, Beaded Band, Swan Head & Shell Handles, Monogram, 8 & 6 In.	495.00
Sugar, Cover, Embossed, Applied Flowers, Footed, Aurora SP Co., Victorian, 6 In.	46.00
Tazza, 3 Griffin Supports, Glass Bowl, Tripod Paw Feet, 13 x 14 In.	201.00
Tazza, Hammered, Applied Shapes To Foot, J. Despres, 3 x 15 In.	5100.00
Tea & Coffee Set, Sheridan Silver Co., c.1960, 4 Piece	58.00
Tea & Coffee Set, Towle, 5 Piece	176.00
Tea Caddy, Hinged Flame Shape Finial Top, Engraved Crest, England, 1800s, 6 x 6 In.	236.00
Tea Set, Coffeepot, Cream, Sugar, Tray, Wood Handles, Art Deco, Tray 14 x 20 In.	1200.00
Tea Set, Tray, Teapot, Sugar, Creamer, W.M. Rogers, Early 1900s, 4 Piece	29.00
Tea Set, Tray, Teapot, Sugar, Creamer, Wood Handles, Suzuyo, Art Deco	2640.00
Tea Urn, Sheffield, Adam, Square Base, 4 Ball Supports, Applied Shell Mounted, 27 In.	1093.00
Teapot, Flowers, Leaves, F.B. Rogers, 1950s, 9 ¾ In.	45.00
Teapot, Melon Form, Scroll Handle, Ruffled Rim & Foot, 8 x 11 In.	115.00
Tray, Chariot Scene, Flowers, Engraved, Half Moon Shape, 33 ½ x 18 In.	300.00
Tray, Edwardian, Octagonal, Vine Reticulation, Flower Chasing, Ball Feet, 4 x 24 x 16 In.	1116.00
Tray, Engraved, Scrolled Handles, 27 ½ x 18 ½ In.	495.00
Tray, Faux Shell, Oval, Pierced & Shaped Gallery, Turned Feet, 4 ½ x 26 In.	575.00
Tray, Footed, Applied Grapevine Border, Acanthus Handles, Gorham, 29 x 18 In.	374.00
Tray, Gallery, Serpentine Shape, Handles, Reticulated, Chased, 25 x 16 In. .... *illus*	299.00
Tray, Grape & Vine Design, Handles, Monogram, 30 In. .... *illus*	316.00
Tray, Leaf Rim, Engraved Leaf Design, Raised Rim, c.1900, 31 In.	92.00
Tray, Leaf Scroll Rim, Reeded Handles, Scroll Feet, 29 x 18 ½ In.	214.00
Tray, Lids, 4 Sections, Lamp, Fish Finials, Wood Interior, Handles, England, c.1900, 3 x 14 In.	316.00
Tray, Neoclassical, Scalloped, Pierced, Gadroon Band, Winged Hairy Paw Feet, 25 x 16 In.	1093.00
Tray, Oval, Pierced, Garland, Shagreen, Starburst Pattern, Ball Feet, 5 x 26 x 17 In.	690.00
Tray, Rectangular, Grape, Vines, Handles, Jas. Dixon & Son, Old Sheffield, c.1850, 39 x 25 In.	5060.00
Tray, Round, Scroll, Shell, Flowers, Feet, Elkington, 1901, 12 ½ In.	863.00
Tray, Tortoiseshell, England, 4 x 25 ½ x 15 ¾ In.	863.00
Tray, Wilcox, Double Handles, Footed, 26 ½ x 17 In.	58.00
Tureen, Breakfast, Revolving, Reeded, Hinged Dome Cover, Oval, 1800s, 9 ½ x 14 In.	230.00
Tureen, Cover, Oval, Deer Finial & Handles, Hoof Feet, Rogers Smith & Co., 10 x 14 In.	403.00
Tureen, Greek Key Design, Stag Heads, Figural Stag, Hoof Feet, Ladle, Stamped, Gill, 13 x 14 In.	600.00

Tureen, Oval, Shield, Shell & Scroll Border, Leafy Handle & Feet, Sheffield, 6 x 8 In. 403.00
Tureen, Sauce, Lid, Lion, Ring Handle, Paw Feet, Ellis-Barker Silver Co., 1900s, 7 x 6 ½ In., Pair. 489.00
Tureen, Soup, Chased Crest, Gadroon Borders, Paw Feet, Oval, 10 x 15 ½ In. ....*illus* 1195.00
Tureen, Soup, Urn Shape, Finial, Gadroon Border, Reeded Handles, England, 1900s, 11 x 15 In. 288.00
Urn, Classical Revival, Glass, Bead, Leaf Tip, Acanthus Ear Handles, Trumpet Foot, 11 ⅜ In. .. 107.00
Urn, Hot Water, Georgian, Lid, Ball Finial, Column Legs, Leaves, Gadroons, 17 x 14 In. 518.00
Urn, Hot Water, Neoclassical Style, Reeded Posts, Paw Feet, Stepped Base, Spout, 18 In. 518.00
Urn, Hot Water, Squat, Domed Lid, Floral Rim & Finial, Scroll Pedestal Base, 15 In. 115.00
Urn, Hot Water, Trophy Shape, Crest, 4 Paw Legs, Ball Feet, Gorham, 15 In. ....*illus* 173.00
Vase, Rococo Style, Fluted, Cupid Handles, 18 In. 878.00
Vase, Stork Feet, Derby, Removable Inserts, 11 In. 250.00
Vase, Trumpet, Ram's Head Masks, Handles, England, Edward VII, 16 ¾ In., Pair 296.00
Vase, Victorian, Eagle, 3 Trees Supporting Glass, James Dixon, c.1875, 16 ½ x 6 ¾ In. 300.00
Waiter, Oval, Applied Leafy Handles, Scalloped Gadroon Edge, Prospect Silver Co., c.1900 .... 34.50
Waiter, Tortoiseshell, Round, Chased Gallery, Shaped Handles, Sunburst Pattern, 4 ½ x 21 In. ... 690.00
Watering Can, Embossed Flowers, Wilcox, 7 x 10 In. ....*illus* 450.00
Wedding Cup, Woman Holding Up Cup, Gold Washed, Swivels, Continental, 7 In. 65.00
Wine Bottle Holder, Hammered, Dragonfly, Meriden Britannia, 11 x 6 ½ In. ....*illus* 288.00
Wine Coaster, Regency Style, Cast Acanthus, Flowers, Hardwood Base, 2 ¼ x 7 ¼ In., Pair...... 294.00
Wine Cooler, Etched Glass, Flared Basin, Leaves, Fruit Clusters, 10 ½ x 10 In., Pair 345.00
Wine Cooler, Flowers, Stepped Base, 9 ½ x 8 ½ In., Pair... 201.00
Wine Cooler, Regency Style, Acanthus Design, Mask Handles, 10 x 10 ½ In., Pair 1410.00
Wine Cooler, Repousse Design, Bacchus, English, c.1907, 7 ¾ In. 1320.00
Wine Cooler, Rococo Style, Urn Shape, 11 x 9 In., Pair 673.00
Wine Cooler, Ruffled Rim, Base, Applied Grapes, Leaves, Handles, Eng., c.1890, 12 x 10 In., Pair. 3450.00
Wine Cooler, Scroll Handles, Sheffield, 19th Century, 10 In. 644.00
Wine Cooling Bowl, Repousse, Banding, Domed Foot, 5 Bottle Receptacles, 11 x 16 In. 1200.00
Wine Funnel, Campana Shape, Strainer, Late 1800s, 6 x 3 ¾ In. ....*illus* 109.00
Wine Trolley, Cannon Shape, 12 In., Pair.. 646.00

SILVER-AMERICAN. American silver is listed here. Coin and sterling silver are included. Most of the sterling silver listed in this book is subdivided by country. There are also other pieces of silver and silver plate listed under special categories, such as Candelabrum, Napkin Ring, Silver Flatware, Silver Plate, Silver-Sterling, and Tiffany Silver. For information about makers and marks, see *Kovels' American Silver Marks: 1650 to the Present.*

Ashtray, Indian Chief, Full Headdress, Unger, 4 ½ x 4 In. 600.00
Ashtray, Inscribed Harvard University, Stieff, c.1962 .... 75.00
Basket, Castle Pattern, Ruffled Border, Flowers, Birds, Loring Andrews & Co., 5 x 7 In. 978.00
Basket, Centerpiece, R. Wallace & Sons, 8 x 9 In. 293.00
Basket, Filigree, Ivy Pierced Frame, Cobalt Blue Glass Liner, Bailey & Co., 5 x 3 ½ In. 374.00
Basket, Flower, Tapered, Faceted, Pierced Handle, Watson, 19 In. 359.00
Basket, Fruit, Repousse, Fruits & Flowers, A.E. Warner, c.1860, 11 ⅞ In. 1287.00
Basket, Openwork, 3 Loop Handles, Mark, Gorham, c.1914, 13 ¼ In. ....*illus* 546.00
Basket, Oval, Applied C-Scrolls, Rocaille, Chased, Embossed, Coin, 1846-61, 4 ¾ In. 1896.00
Basket, Pedestal, Rope Border & Handle, William Gale & Son, 6 ¾ x 6 ½ In. 345.00
Basket, Repousse Fruit & Game, Oval, E.F. Caldwell & Co., N.Y., c.1885, 10 x 8 In. 975.00
Basket, Silver Gilt Cover, Engraved Flowers, Handle, Whiting, 13 ¼ x 11 ½ In. 600.00
Bell, Alice In Wonderland, Arms Form Twisted Arch, Dali, Franklin Mint, Box, 7 In. 266.00
Bill Clip, Indian Chief, Full Headdress, Unger, 2 ¾ x 2 ½ In. 1200.00
Bit, Conchas, Cheeks, Slobber Bar, G.S. Garcia Co., Elko, Nev, c.1912 .... 1380.00
Bonbon, Grape Leaves, Conjoined Bunch Of Grapes, Vine Tendril Handle, Watson, 11 In. 207.00
Bonbon, Heart Shape, Cluster Of Fruit & Vegetables, Watson, 8 ¾ In., Pair........................ 299.00
Bonbon, Repousse Fruit, Flowers, Dome Cover, S. Kirk & Sons, c.1868, 6 ½ In. 956.00
Bowl, 3 Open Mask Supports, Squared Feet, Gorham, 1870, 15 In. 5312.00
Bowl, Beaded Edge, Monogram, Etched Shield, John David, c.1790, 4 ¾ x 6 ¼ In. 1920.00
Bowl, Beaded Leaf, Openwork Stem, Marked, 5 ½ In. 165.00
Bowl, Cattails, Leaves, George Shiebler, 1902, 2 ¼ x 5 In. 320.00
Bowl, Center, Pierced, Flowers, Swags, Etched, American Sterling, Patent 1909, 3 x 12 In. 531.00
Bowl, Chased Tulips, Stylized Leaves, Stamped, 6 x 12 In. 7200.00
Bowl, Cover, Vegetable, Raised Fruit Garland, Ribbons, 4 Feet, Gorham, 1887, 9 x 8 In. 2196.00
Bowl, Deep, Rectangular, Monogram, Marked, Randahl, 6 ¾ x 2 In. 330.00
Bowl, Eliel Saarinen, Pedestal Foot, Sterling, c.1929, 3 x 11 In. 74500.00
Bowl, Footed, 5 ½ x 10 ½ In. 175.00
Bowl, Footed, Cone Shape, 3-Footed, Arts & Crafts, 4 ⅝ x 6 ½ In. 385.00
Bowl, Footed, Double Swell Navette, Ram's Head Handles, Tuttle, 1900s, 5 ¼ x 8 ¼ In. 147.00
Bowl, Footed, Oval, Lobed Calyx, Federal Coin, 5 ½ x 6 ¾ x 5 ¼ In. 240.00

Silver Plate, Kettle, Stand, Lion Masks, Victorian, c.1875, 19 ½ In.
$316.00

Silver Plate, Pitcher Set, Water, Stand, Goblets, Aesthetic, Liner, Reed & Barton, 18 x 15 In.
$265.00

Silver Plate, Spoon Holder, 24 Slots, Revolving, Bailey Kettell & Chapman, 9 ½ x 7 ½ In.
$540.00

Silver Plate, Tray, Gallery, Serpentine Shape, Handles, Reticulated, Chased, 25 x 16 In.
$299.00

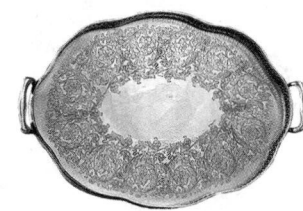

S

Silver Plate, Tray, Grape & Vine Design, Handles, Monogram, 30 In.
$316.00

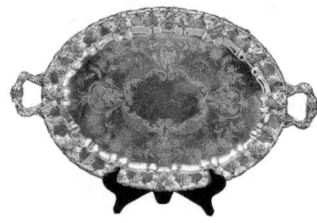

Silver Plate, Tureen, Soup, Chased Crest, Gadroon Borders, Paw Feet, Oval, 10 x 15 ½ In.
$1195.00

Silver Plate, Urn, Hot Water, Trophy Shape, Crest, 4 Paw Legs, Ball Feet, Gorham, 15 In.
$173.00

Silver Plate, Watering Can, Embossed Flowers, Wilcox, 7 x 10 In.
$450.00

Bowl, Gadroon Border, Shell & Flower Decoration, Ellmore Silver Co., 3 x 15 ¼ In.	345.00
Bowl, Grape Leaf Form, Upward C Handle, Redlich, c.1900, 8 ¼ In.	460.00
Bowl, Grapes, Vines, Repousse, Oval, 4 Toed Feet, Frank M. Smith, 17 In.	5938.00
Bowl, Greek Key Border, Arabesque Rim, Coin, Clark & Biddle, c.1880, 6 x 6 In.	201.00
Bowl, Leamington Pattern, Ribbed Border, Engraved Initial P, Gorham, 8 In.	148.00
Bowl, Molded Acanthus Rim, Foot, Chased, Gorham, Early 1900s, 8 ¾ In.	281.00
Bowl, Monogram, Mark, Watson Co., Early 20th Century, 11 ½ In.	354.00
Bowl, Openwork Border, Flower, Swags, Dominick & Haff, 2 ½ x 11 ¼ In.	633.00
Bowl, Oval, Footed, Rolled Handles, c.1875	6100.00
Bowl, Oval, Gadroon Rim, Kent Pattern, Fisher, 10 ½ In., Pair	354.00
Bowl, Oval, Scalloped, Flowers, Dominick & Haff, 9 ½ In., Pair	288.00
Bowl, Piecework, Applied Flower Rim, Pierced Design, Mark, Towle, c.1925, 3 x 11 In.	294.00
Bowl, Round, Openwork Scroll, Poppy Border, Whiting, c.1900, 11 In.	374.00
Bowl, Satyr Design, Oak Leaf Ribbon, Gorham, 1925, 13 In.	1159.00
Bowl, Spherical, Footed, Melon Ball Finial, Dolphin, E. Magnussen, Gorham, 6 In.	8540.00
Bowl, Square, Rounded Corners, Marked, Erickson Sterling, 1 ½ x 6 ½ In.	83.00
Bowl, Stepped Foot, Applied Rim, Monogram, W. Carrington & Co., c.1850, 3 ¼ x 6 In.	1725.00
Bowl, Thistle, Leaves, Wavy Cartouche, 4-Footed, Curls, Whiting, c.1885, 11 In.	8750.00
Bowl, Vegetable, Chased Leaves, Acanthus, Bailey Banks & Biddle, 13 In., Pair	881.00
Bowl, Vegetable, Cover, Scenic Decoration, Acorn Finial, S. Kirk & Son, 8 ¾ In.	2440.00
Bread Bowl, Chased, Embossed Leaves, Oval, C-Scroll Rim, 13 ⅜ x 10 ⅛ In.	563.00
Butter, Cover, Floral Finial, Chased Dome, S. Kirk & Son, c.1860, 6 ½ x 6 In.	1840.00
Buttonhook, Glove, Art Nouveau, H & H Sterling, 3 ¼ In.	22.00
Cake Basket, Oval, Spreading Foot, Pierced Border, Victor Siedman, 6 ¾ x 11 ¼ In.	478.00
Cake Basket, Oval, Twisted Handle, Monogram, c.1785	8125.00
Candelabra are listed in the Candelabrum category.	
Candlesticks are listed in their own category.	
Cann, Cup, Engraved, Abraham Carlisle, Inscribed, IR To IR, Philadelphia, c.1785, 5 ½ In.	5148.00
Cann, Cup, Shaped Handle, Low Foot, Revere, 5 In.	15000.00
Card Case, Albert Coles, c.1875, 3 ½ In.	250.00
Card Holder, Peacock Form, Fan Holder, c.1930, Gorham & Durgin, 4 x 9 In., Pair	1076.00
Centerpiece, Sleigh, Ice Skater, Stepped Base, Art Nouveau, Whiting, c.1875, 6 x 19 In.	9400.00
Cheese Scoop, Gold Washed, Enameled Scroll Handle, R. Blackinton, 7 In. *illus*	58.00
Chocolate Pot, Gooseneck, Scroll Handle, Gorham, 10 x 6 ½ In.	260.00
Cigar Lamp, Figurine, Dragon, Ball, Horn Tail, Shreve, Crump & Low, 5 x 4 In.	1840.00
Cigarette Case, Men In Car, Woman, Dog, Amethyst Button, Blackinton, c.1890, 3 In. Sq.	896.00
Cigarette Case, Mermaid & Lobster In Sea, 2 Swing Arms, Wm. B. Kerr, c.1890, 3 x 2 In.	1673.00
Cigarette Case, Reclining Female Nude, Clouds, Light Rays, Unger Bros., c.1900, 3 x 2 In.	1195.00
Claret Jug, Cut Glass Body, Sterling Collar, Spout, Handle, Gorham, 12 In.	24000.00
Cocktail Pitcher, Braided, Beaded Scroll Handle, Zimmermann, N.Y., c.1920, 10 In.	10755.00
Cocktail Shaker, Cylindrical, Stepped Ring Base, 13 ¾ In.	920.00
Cocktail Shaker, Marked Reed & Barton, 5 ¼ In.	245.00
Coffee Server, U.S. Navy, Reed & Barton, Wood Handle, 11 In.	77.00
Coffee Set, After Dinner, Hampton Court, Gilt Wash Interior, Reed & Barton, 10 In.	368.00
Coffee Set, Fruit & Flowers, Coffeepot, Sugar, Pitcher, Loring Andrews, c.1910	1763.00
Coffee Urn, 2 Handles, Leaf Molded Spout, Repousse Summer Flower, J.E. Caldwell, 17 In.	2875.00
Coffeepot, Domed Lid, Oval, Engraved Acanthus, Leaf Tip Base, Coin, 1853-55, 10 In.	533.00
Coffeepot, Shell Foot, Watson, 12 ½ In.	260.00
Comb, Pineapple & Thistles, Coin, 1820-40	200.00
Compote, Art Deco, Gorham, 26 Oz., Pair	720.00
Compote, Crystal, Ruffled Edge, Flower, Pierced, 8 In.	153.00
Compote, Flower Repousse, Pedestal Base, Monogram, S. Kirk & Sons, c.1900, 7 x 9 In., Pair	1093.00
Compote, Folded Lobes, Marked, Randahl, 5 x 4 ¼ In. *illus*	120.00
Compote, Japonesque, Hammered, Applied Mixed Metal Leaves, Gorham, 14 In.	22500.00
Compote, Lid, Flowers, Filigree, Beaded Borders, Handles, Bailey & Co., 1853, 8 x 7 ½ In.	690.00
Cordial Set, Tray, Randahl, 3 & 7 ½ In., 9 Piece	263.00
Cream Jug, Classical Style, Footed, Elongated Handle, c.1790, 7 ¾ In.	234.00
Cream Jug, Pear Shaped, Chased Repouse Strawberries, Foot Ring, Hinged, c.1850, 6 In.	4320.00
Creamer, 4-Footed, Scalloped Rim, Philip Syng Jr., Philadelphia, c.1755, 3 ½ In.	4680.00
Creamer, Beaded Rim, Engraved Flowers, John McMullin, c.1795, 5 ¼ In.	468.00
Creamer, Beaded Rim, Pedestal Base, c.1770, 4 ½ In.	117.00
Creamer, Embossed, Chased Flowers, Birds, Scrolled Reserves, Shell Feet, 6 In.	805.00
Creamer, Gadroon Calyx, Arched Strap Handle, 6 ¼ x 5 ½ x 3 ⅜ In.	300.00
Creamer, Helmet Shape, Loop Handle, Beaded Rims, Trumpet Foot, Coin, c.1775, 6 ⅞ In.	326.00
Creamer, Helmet Shape, Round Pedestal, Strap Handle, Engraved Designs, c.1790, 7 In.	474.00
Creamer, Helmet Shape, Square Pedestal, Reeded Handle, T.K. Emery, Boston, c.1805, 7 In.	504.00
Creamer, Helmet Spout, Monogram, Marked S. Kirk, 5 ¼ x 5 ¾ In. *illus*	431.00

S

Creamer, Lid, Sugar, Cover, Repousse, Coin, Cincinnati, c.1850, 9 In.	1763.00
Creamer, Pear Shape, Scroll Handle, 3-Footed, Coin, c.1730, 4 ½ In.	1126.00
Creamer, Sugar, Monogram, Square C Handles, International, 4 ½, 3 ¾ In.	59.00
Cup, Flower & Wheat Bands, Scroll Handle, Marked, G.B. & N., 1820s, 4 ¾ In.	205.00
Cup, Inscribed, Gorham & Co., Providence, Rhode Island, c.1860, 4 In.	176.00
Cup, Stemmed, Allan Adler, Mid 20th Century, 5 ½ In.	207.00
Decanter, Stopper, Signed, Black, Starr & Frost, 10 ¼ In.	106.00
Dipper, Floral Repousse, Engraved Bowl, Beaded Rim, Inscribed, c.1850, 14 ¾ In.	3220.00
Dish, Embossed Flower Rim, Engraved Initials, S. Kirk & Son, 10 In.	165.00
Dish, Sweetmeat, Swans, On Crowns, Boat Shape, Gorham, 1869, 7 ¾ x 4 In.	207.00
Dresser Jar, Cupid, Flowers, Cut Glass Base, Star & Hobnail, Gorham, 3 x 5 In.	86.00
Ewer, Repousse, Trumpet Foot, Chased, Embossed Flowers, A.G. Schultz & Co., 14 ¼ In.	2844.00
Ewer, Wine, Lead Banding, Scroll Handle, Coin, C. Bard, c.1840, 12 In.	1763.00
Fish Server, Fiddle & Thread Handle, Round Fins, 1825, 11 ½ In.	920.00
Fish Server, Shell Tip Handle, Openwork Blade, Coin, 12 In.	460.00
Fish Serving Set, Aesthetic, 4-Tine Fork, Knife, Flowers, Scrolls, 2 Piece, 9 ¾ & 11 ⅝ In.	720.00
Fish Slice, Engraved Fish, Reticulated Stars, Fiddle Handle, 12 In.	1434.00
Flask, Hammered, Engraved, Monogram, TJC, Dec. 20 1928, Pt.	69.00
Flask, Oblong, Repousse Scroll Design, Gorham, 5 ¾ In.	248.00
Frame, Double, Lions, Shield, Crown, Oval, Easel, 9 x 9 In.	915.00
Fruit Bowl, Cherry, Strawberry, Blackberry, Gorham, 2 ½ x 10 ½ In.	207.00
Fruit Knife, Embossed Design, 2 Blades, Gorham, Ladies, 2 ⅜ In.	125.00
Goblet, Flared, Footed, A.G. Schultz & Co., Mid 20th Century, 6 ½ In., 12 Piece	885.00
Goblet, Flared Rim, Spread Foot, Reed & Barton, 6 ½ In., 12 Piece	1380.00
Goblet, Frank W. Smith Silver Co., Mid 20th Century, 6 ¼ In., 12 Piece	671.00
Grooming Set, Hammered, Arts & Crafts, Lebolt, 3 Piece	295.00
Hoof Pick, Presentation, Decorative, 5 In.	395.00
Humidor, Glass Melon Base, Prism Pattern, Silver Lid, Floral Impressed, 6 In.	115.00
Iced Tea Spoon, Starr, 12 Piece	147.00
Jam Jar, Drum Shape, Red Glass Liner, Ladle, R. Blackinton & Co., c.1920, 3 ¼ In.	495.00
Jar, Cover, Native American Chief, Crystal, Wilcox, 5 ¼ In.	418.00
Jardiniere, 4 Seasons, Square, 4 Folded Up Feet, Friedel Pasadena, c.1915, 10 In.	11875.00
Jelly Server, Fork, Stamped, Allan Adler, 7 ⅝ & 6 ¼ In., 2 Piece .... *illus*	92.00
Jelly Server, Pressed Glass, Pineapple Shape, Spoon, Gorham, 1930s, 5 ½ In.	365.00
Jewel Casket, Embossed Rococo Scroll & Flower Band, Hinged, Gorham, 2 ¾ x 7 In.	780.00
Jug, Hot Milk, Cylindrical, Ear Handle, Hammered, Arts & Crafts, 4 ½ In.	178.00
Julep Cup, Banded Lip, Base, Coin, Sharrard, Kentucky, c.1855, 3 In.	2115.00
Julep Cup, Inscribed, E&D Kinsey, Kentucky, c.1861, 3 ½ x 3 In. .... *illus*	1035.00
Julep Cup, Intaglio Impressed Mark, Inscription, John McMullin, 3 ¼ In.	823.00
Julep Cup, Pear Shape, Double Rim, Inscribed, Marked, Wilson & Klein, c.1845, 3 ¼ In.	2990.00
Julep Cup, Rim, Banded Foot, Monogram, Coin, Ohio, c.1836, 4 In., Pair	646.00
Julep Cup, Rolled Rim & Foot, Bailey, Banks & Biddle, Phila., 4 In., 4 Piece	671.00
Julep Cup, Slightly Tapered, Reeded, Molded Rim, Manchester Silver Co., 3 ¾ In., 8 Piece	974.00
Julep Cup, Tapered, Beaded Rim, Monogram N, Coin, S. Wilmot, c.1850, 4 x 3 In.	1725.00
Julep Cup, Tapered, Molded Rim, Foot, Coin, Cincinnati, A. Palmer, c.1850, 3 ½ In.	881.00
Julep Cup, Tapered, Reeded Border, Marked, E&D, c.1850, 3 ½ x 3 In.	990.00
Julep Cup, Trees, Lexington, KY, 20th Century, 3 ¾ In.	235.00
Kettle, Hot Water, Stand, Seville, No. 76210, Towle, 14 x 9 x 7 In.	1265.00
Kettle, Stand, Oval, Reeded Base, Shell Feet, Burner, Gorham, 1894, 12 In.	830.00
Kettle, Swag, Bud & Acanthus, Dominick & Haff, 11 ¼ In.	748.00
Ladle, Coin, J. Rafel, New Orleans, c.1850, 12 In.	382.00
Ladle, Fiddle Handle, Shaped Bowl, Marked RR, Philadelphia, c.1800, 11 ¾ In.	259.00
Ladle, Fiddle Handle, Tip Front, Gilded Bowl, c.1845, 13 ¼ In.	395.00
Ladle, Flower Embossed Handle, Monogram Phoenix, Black, Ball & Co., 7 ¼ In.	72.00
Ladle, Hand Wrought, Applied Monogram, Kalo, Marked, 12 In.	450.00
Ladle, Monogram, J. Lockwood, New York, 1799-1838, 8 ¼ In.	350.00
Ladle, Round Bowl, Monogram, Gorham, 11 In.	173.00
Ladle, Starr & Marcus, NYC, c.1880, 14 x 1 ½ x 4 In.	360.00
Ladle, Tip Front, Fiddle Handle, Coin, Mark, New York, 13 In.	144.00
Ladle, Turn Down Fiddle Handle, Oval Bowl, Coin, T & H, North Carolina, 12 In.	1495.00
Ladle, Twist Handle, Engraved Designs, Duhme & Co., Ohio, c.1850, 11 ½ In.	235.00
Lemon Fork, 3 Splayed Tines, Reticulated Terminus, Whiting, c.1920, 5 In.	38.00
Letter Holder, Openwork Scrolls, Howard Sterling Co., c.1900, 6 x 8 ½ In.	1380.00
Letter Opener, Gold Woman's Head Handle, Geo. W. Shiebler & Co., 2 ¼ x 11 In.	575.00
Letter Opener, Horse Head, Celluloid, Mark, 10 ¼ In.	395.00
Mirror, Flowers, Scrolls, Felt Holder, Towle, Box, 3 ¼ In.	50.00

Silver Plate, Wine Bottle Holder, Hammered, Dragonfly, Meriden Britannia, 11 x 6 ½ In. $288.00

Silver Plate, Wine Funnel, Campana Shape, Strainer, Late 1800s, 6 x 3 ¾ In. $109.00

Silver-American, Basket, Openwork, 3 Loop Handles, Mark, Gorham, c.1914, 13 ¼ In. $546.00

Silver-American, Cheese Scoop, Gold Washed, Enameled Scroll Handle, R. Blackinton, 7 In. $58.00

S

591

Silver-American, Compote,
Folded Lobes, Marked, Randahl,
5 x 4 ¼ In.
$120.00

Silver-American, Creamer,
Helmet Spout, Monogram,
Marked S. Kirk, 5 ¼ x 5 ¾ In.
$431.00

Silver-American, Jelly Server, Fork,
Stamped, Allan Adler, 7 ⅝ & 6 ¼ In.,
2 Piece
$92.00

Silver-American, Julep Cup, Inscribed,
E&D Kinsey, Kentucky, c.1861, 3 ½ x 3 In.
$1035.00

Muffineer, Footed, Baluster Shape, Gorham, Providence, Rhode Island, 7 In.	207.00
Muffineer, Urn Form, Whiting Mfg., 1915, 8 ¼ In.	142.00
Mug, Beaded, Ribbed Ear Handle, Fan Rim, Bead, Leaf Tip Base, Gorham, 1883, 3 ⅛ In.	178.00
Mug, Child's, Chased Flowers, Engraved, Gilt Inside, Simons Bro. & Co., 2 ¾ In.	118.00
Mug, Cylindrical, Chased, Embossed, Rocaille Rim, Vine, Coin, Boston, 1852, 3 ¾ In.	207.00
Mug, Fruiting Grapevine, Acanthus Scroll Handle, Trumpet Foot, Coin, 1853, 5 ⅛ In.	267.00
Mug, Presentation, Hammered, Jarvie, 1911, Stamped, 3 ½ x 4 ½ In.	6710.00
Mug, Round Body, Flower Handle, Gorham, 1892, 3 x 4 x 2 ½ In.	92.00
Mug, Square Handle, Bead Border, Engraved Names, Hearts, Garlands, Georgia, 3 x 4 In.	1035.00
Mug, Trophy, Repousse Scroll, Scroll Handle, Inscribed, Georgia, 1851, 4 ½ In.	3680.00
Mustard Pot, Inverted Pear Shape, Leaf & Dart Calyx, Beaded Rim, 1870s, 4 x 2 In.	480.00
Napkin Rings are listed in their own category.	
Picture Frame, Art Deco Style, Engraved Letters, Black, Starr & Frost	330.00
Pie Server, Leaf, Berry, Twist Handle, Openwork, Coin, 11 ¼ In.	1093.00
Pie Server, Pierced, Flowers, Birds, Incised, Squire & Lander, N.Y., c.1840, 10 ½ In.	189.00
Pitcher, Bulbous, Squat, Elongated Spout, Shaped Handle, International, 7 In.	207.00
Pitcher, Cocktail, R. Blackinton & Co., 9 In.	234.00
Pitcher, Flowers, Scrolls, Repousse, Squat, Footed, Dominick & Haff, 1903, 11 In.	3750.00
Pitcher, Globular Body, Vine & Berry Bands, Openwork Handle, Dominick & Haff, 6 In.	940.00
Pitcher, Gorham, 20th Century, 10 In.	705.00
Pitcher, Hand Chased, Flowers, Footed, Amston Silver Co., Inc., Conn., 10 In.	413.00
Pitcher, Helmet Shape, Monogram, Wm. B. Durgin, 8 In.	295.00
Pitcher, Inverted Pear Shape, Scrolling Handle, Hammered, A.G. Schultz, c.1920, 10 In.	1495.00
Pitcher, Iris, Bulbous Base & Neck, Martele, Shaped Foot, Gorham, 1906, 16 In.	37500.00
Pitcher, Pear Shape, Bands, Applied Beaded Foot & Handle, Scroll Rim, c.1860, 13 In.	3819.00
Pitcher, Repousse, Birds, Insects, Flowers, Kirk & Son, c.1953, 13 In.	4212.00
Pitcher, Scroll Handle, Coin, Bailey Kettell & Chapman, c.1856, 12 In.	468.00
Pitcher, Urn Form, S-Scroll Handle, Helmet Spout, Marked, Krider & Biddle, c.1865, 11 In.	3910.00
Pitcher, Water, Arrow Leaf Border, Acanthus Handle, John Curry, c.1825, 11 ¼ In.	2160.00
Pitcher, Water, Baluster, Scroll & Flower Decoration, Monogram, c.1950, 15 ½ In.	1610.00
Pitcher, Water, Chased Flowers, Coin, New Orleans, c.1855, 11 In.	1998.00
Pitcher, Water, Chased Morning Glories, Grapevine, New Orleans, c.1855, 11 In.	1998.00
Pitcher, Water, Footed, Baluster, Gadroon Rim, Durham Silver Co., c.1950, 9 ½ In.	472.00
Pitcher, Water, Helmet Shape Spout, Monogram, New England, 10 In.	690.00
Pitcher, Water, Kent Pattern, No. 1521, Fisher Silversmith, Inc., 9 In.	384.00
Pitcher, Water, Paneled Body, Engraved Scroll, Flowers, Dominick & Haff, 9 ½ In.	748.00
Pitcher, Water, Paneled, Reeded Border, Scroll Handle, Footed, 10 In.	575.00
Pitcher, Water, Paneled, Scroll & Acanthus Border & Handle, Reed & Barton, 12 In.	575.00
Pitcher, Water, Pattern No. 122, Monogram, Preisner Silver Co., 9 ¼ In.	531.00
Pitcher, Water, Raised Flowers, Tobacco Leaves, Ram's Head Handle, Gorham, 1859, 12 In.	5185.00
Pitcher, Water, Royal Danish Pattern, International Silver Co., 8 ½ In.	259.00
Pitcher, Water, Shells, Chased, Round, Cylindrical Neck, Whiting, 1880, 7 In.	17500.00
Pitcher, Water, Urn Shape, Square Handle, Gorham, 1918, 10 x 10 In.	489.00
Pitcher, Water, Washington Pattern, R. Wallace & Sons, c.1913, 9 In.	388.00
Plate, Butter, Shaped Edge, Scrolls, Monogram Center, Whiting, 6 In., 12 Piece	263.00
Plate Set, Pierced, Cast Flower Border, Gorham, Stamped, 11 In., 11 Piece	4800.00
Porringer, Carmel, Arts & Crafts, Hammered Handle, Applied Band, c.1912, 4 ¼ In.	112.00
Porringer, Engraved, Thomas Coverly, c.1755, 5 ¼ In.	1058.00
Porringer, John Coney, Boston, c.1700, 2 x 8 In.	12870.00
Porringer, Marked, Thomas Shields, Philadelphia	2223.00
Porringer, Marquand, Georgia, Mid 1800s, 1 ¾ x 7 ¾ In. .... *illus*	4025.00
Punch Bowl, Bulbous, Flared Rim, Hexagon, Grape Leaf, Gorham, c.1905, 6 x 16 In.	3360.00
Punch Bowl, Flared Rim, Applied Leaves, Chased, Pierced, Gorham, 1905, 6 x 17 In.	2280.00
Punch Bowl, Grapes & Vines, Undulating Rim, Footed, Dominick & Haff, 17 In.	8125.00
Salt, Arts & Crafts, Porter Blanchard, Urn Shape, c.1910, 2 ½ x 4 ¼ In.	188.00
Salt, Flared, Scalloped Rim, Footed, 2 Spoons, Myer Myers, N.Y., c.1765, 4 In., Pair	62500.00
Saltshaker, Repousse, Kirk & Sons, 4 ½ In., Pair	130.00
Salver, Card, Husk Swag Rim, Monogram, Pad Feet, Gorham, 1869, 9 In.	178.00
Serving Bowl, Chased, Embossed Leaves, Monogram, 1903-24, 13 In.	444.00
Serving Bowl, Hammered, Arts & Crafts, Jenkins & Jenkins, 9 ½ In.	267.00
Serving Spoon, Fork, Calla Lily, Stamped Peer Smed	671.00
Slicer, Angel Food Cake, Repousse Handle, Marked, S. Kirk & Son, 10 ¾ In. .... *illus*	75.00
Soup Ladle, Fiddle Handle, Coin, 13 ¼ In.	1175.00
Spoon, Black Boy Sitting On Wall, Filigreed Edges, 1900s, 5 ¼ In.	134.00
Spoon, Preserve, Bird's Nest Handle, Scalloped Bowl, Gilt, Gorham, 9 In. .... *illus*	1840.00
Spoon, Scalloped Shell, Initials, AL, Marked, JE, 18th Century, Coin, 4 ¾ In.	300.00

Stamp Box, Filigree, Flowers, Ferns, Shiebler, Marked, 2 In.	385.00
Sugar & Creamer, Cover, Castle Pattern, Flowers, Birds, Repousse, Footed, Loring Andrews, 7 & 6 In.	920.00
Sugar & Creamer, Oval, Hand Wrought, Marked, Randahl, 5 x 2 ½-In. Creamer	330.00
Sugar, Anthemion, Paneled Body, Navette Form Lid, Urn Finial, c.1800, 7 In.	956.00
Sugar, Cover, Lobes, Flowers, Finial, Scroll Handles, Coin, Baldwin Gardiner, c.1825, 10 x 10 In.	748.00
Sugar, Cover, Urn Form, Liberty Browne, Baltimore, c.1800, 10 ½ In.	2106.00
Sugar, Oval, Lobed & Dart Body, Flower Finial, Coin, W. Thomason, 8 ¾ x 9 ¾ In. ....*illus*	345.00
Sugar Tongs, Fiddle Thread, Rectangular, Engraved Script, Hyde & Goodrich, 1850, 7 In.	400.00
Tablespoon, Leafy Scrolls, Coin, Late 18th, Early 19th Century, 8 In.	119.00
Tablespoon, Monogram, F & G, Boston, Philadelphia, 1810-15, 8 ¾ In.	85.00
Tankard, Stepped Top, Tapered Sides, Scroll Thumbpiece, 5-Ring Base, Coin, N.Y., c.1760, 8 x 8 In.	2300.00
Tea & Coffee Set, Coffeepot, Teapot, Waste Bowl, Creamer, Strawberry Finial, Coin, 4 Piece	8813.00
Tea & Coffee Set, Engraved Swag & Line, Mark, William Durgin, c.1900, 5 Piece	1180.00
Tea & Coffee Set, John Prip, Reed & Barton, 5 Piece	1109.00
Tea & Coffee Set, Prelude Pattern, International Silver, 4 Piece	1180.00
Tea & Coffee Set, Puritan, Gorham, 1951, 8 ½-In. Teapot, 6 Piece	3245.00
Tea & Coffee Set, Scrolled Cartouches, Beaded Foot, Frank M. Whiting, 5 Piece	6250.00
Tea & Coffee Set, Square Form, Floral Repousse, Stippled Ground, S. Kirk & Son, 7 Piece	9760.00
Tea & Coffee Set, Urn Shape, Scroll Rim, Scroll Feet, Gorham, 20th Century, 5 Piece	881.00
Tea Caddy, Cover, Mixed Metal, Fruit Shape, Stippled, Branch Knop, c.1881, 4 x 4 ⅛ In.	2440.00
Tea Set, Gadroon Lobes, C-Scroll Handle, Acanthus Finials, Coin, 1837-50, 8 In. Teapot	1640.00
Tea Set, Ivory Collars, Art Nouveau Flowers, R. Wallace & Sons, Marked, 4 Piece	805.00
Tea Set, Kettle, Stand, Teapot, Sugar, Creamer, Waste Bowl, M.F. Hamilton & Son	1830.00
Tea Set, Pear Shape, Shells, Scrolls, Gorham, 1960, 9 ½-In. Teapot, 5 Piece	1495.00
Tea Set, Urn Form Body, C-Scroll Handles, Marked, c.1830, 9 ½-In. Teapot, 3 Piece	3910.00
Tea Set, Urn Shape, Acanthus, C-Scroll Handle, Frank Whiting, 11-In. Teapot, 4 Piece	863.00
Teapot, Flowers, Repousse, Animal Head Spout, Andrew Warner, Baltimore, c.1825, 7 In.	2340.00
Teapot, Hinged Lid, Ivory Connectors, Repousse Leaves, Flowers, S. Kirk & Sons, 7 In.	460.00
Teapot, Lid, Acorn Finial, Squat, Lobed, c.1814, 5 In.	3081.00
Teapot, Square Lobes, Spout, A. Jacobi Co., Baltimore, 8 ½ In.	260.00
Thread Dispenser, Repousse Scroll, Inscribed, Shiebler, N.Y., c.1890, 1 ⅝ x 1 ⅛ In.	177.00
Tongs, Fiddle Handles, Oval Terminals, Coin, T & H, North Carolina, 6 In.	1495.00
Tray, Aesthetic, Handles, Monogram, Engraved, Chased, Reed & Barton, 32 & 20 ½ In.	236.00
Tray, Beading, Handles, Flowers, Animals, Haddock, Lincoln, & Foss, Coin, c.1855, 25 x 16 In.	2530.00
Tray, Dresser, Indian Chief, Full Headdress, Unger, 6 In. Diam.	600.00
Tray, Francis I, Scalloped, Reed & Barton, 1949, 12 In.	288.00
Tray, Hammered, Octagonal, Monogram, Dominick & Haff, N.Y., 12 x 7 ¾ In.	177.00
Tray, Openwork Scroll & Flower Border, Ring Foot, Caldwell & Co., c.1875, 11 ⅜ In.	690.00
Tray, Oval, Leaf & Bead Border, Coin, 14 x 10 In.	2644.00
Tray, Oval, Rocquille Border, William B. Durgin Co., c.1900, 20 x 14 In.	1037.00
Tray, Oval, Tree, Well, Scalloped Rim, 2 x 18 In.	1035.00
Tray, Puritan Pattern, Oval, Threaded Rim, Pierced Handles, Gorham, 1951, 24 In.	4130.00
Tray, Rectangular, Cut Corners, Stepped Rim, Handles, Gorham, c.1940, 30 In.	10000.00
Tray, Windsor, Reed & Barton, c.1950, 18 In.	702.00
Tray, Windsor, Square, Scalloped, Monogram, Reed & Barton, 1949, 14 x 14 In.	489.00
Trophy, Old Newbury Crafters, Inscribed, c.1903, 14 x 12 In.	761.00
Tureen, Flared Foot, Applied Cherubs, Ring Handles, D Finial, Gorham, 1872, 12 In.	3125.00
Tureen, Leaves, Tassels, Shaped Upswept Handles, Lion Finial, Gorham, 16 In.	5312.00
Vase, Castle Pattern, Vines, Leaves, Buildings, Footed, Loring Andrews, Ohio, 13 In.	2300.00
Vase, Curving Neck, Applied Leaf Scrolls, Cherub Heads, Mauser, c.1900, 8 ½ In.	274.00
Vase, Flared Rim, Footed, Fisher, 8 ½ In.	34.00
Vase, Flower & Scroll Edge, Reeded Shoulder, Baluster, Footed, Gorham, 1907, 12 ½ In.	2070.00
Vase, Flowers, Shaped Handle, Rim & Foot, Martele, Gorham, 1904, 15 In.	43750.00
Vase, Trumpet, Openwork Flowers, Swag Border, Pedestal, Marcus & Co., c.1925, 18 In.	2185.00
Vase, Tulip Shape, Pierced Outturned Rim, Vermeil, Acorn Finial, c.1895, 12 In.	748.00
Vase, Urn Shape, Applied Roses, Leaves, Shaped Upswept Handles, Gorham, 26 In.	11875.00
Wine Coaster, Maker's Mark G.P., c.1820, 1 ¾ x 5 In.	410.00
Wine Coaster, Shaped Floral Rim, Athenic, Art Nouveau, Gorham, 7 In.	173.00
Wine Ewer, Classical, Leaf Banding, Leaf Scroll Handle, Coin, Conrad Bard, 12 In.	1763.00
Youth Set, Knife, Fork, Spoon, Engraved, Case, Marked, 5 ½ To 6 ½ In. ....*illus*	178.00

SILVER-AUSTRIAN

Case, Enameled Nude Woman On Balcony, Hinged Lid, Gilt Wash Inside, 4 In.	978.00
Dish, Shell Shape, Chased, Folded Handle, Cartouche Medallion, 1897, 9 In.	259.00
Plate, Round, Applied Rim, Bachruch A. Succ., Early 20th Century, 7 ¾ In., Pair	184.00
Sauceboat, Undertray, Pedestal, Applied Scroll Handle, Reeded Rim, 6 x 9 ½ In.	173.00
Tea Caddy, c.1900, 5 ½ x 5 ½ In.	385.00

Silver-American, Porringer, Marquand, Georgia, Mid 1800s, 1 ¾ x 7 ¾ In. $4025.00

Silver-American, Slicer, Angel Food Cake, Repousse Handle, Marked, S. Kirk & Son, 10 ¾ In. $75.00

Silver-American, Spoon, Preserve, Bird's Nest Handle, Scalloped Bowl, Gilt, Gorham, 9 In. $1840.00

Silver-American, Sugar, Oval, Lobed & Dart Body, Flower Finial, Coin, W. Thomason, 8 ¾ x 9 ¾ In. $345.00

S

Silver-American, Youth Set, Knife, Fork, Spoon, Engraved, Case, Marked, 5 ½ To 6 ½ In.
$178.00

Silver-Austro-Hungarian, Basket, Neoclassical, 4 Pierced Feet, Glass, 12 x 18 ¾ In.
$834.00

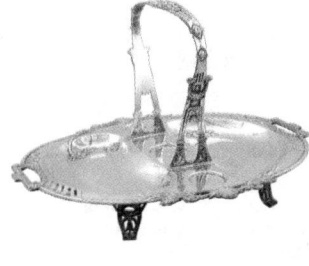

Silver-Austro-Hungarian, Teapot, Art Nouveau, Hinged, Bone Insulators, Marked, 5 x 10 In.
$357.00

Silver-Chinese, Cup, 2 Dragon Handles, Repousse, Gilt Interior, Marked Wing Chun, 7 ¼ In.
$1725.00

SILVER-AUSTRO-HUNGARIAN
Basket, Neoclassical, 4 Pierced Feet, Glass, 12 x 18 ¾ In. .... *illus* 834.00
Teapot, Art Nouveau, Hinged, Bone Insulators, Marked, 5 x 10 In. .... *illus* 357.00

SILVER-BELGIAN
Ladle, Oval Bowl & Handle, Monogram, c.1815, 14 ¼ In. 173.00

SILVER-CANADIAN
Cigar Case, Engraved Falcon, Bracket Feet, Drop Handles, c.1920, 10 x 6 In. 1830.00
Compote, Shell Shape, Grape Clusters, Hammered, Bud Handle, Poul Petersen, 8 In. 1098.00
Presentation Cup, Coach & Horse, Flared & Folded Up Rim, Repousse, Ellis, 1905, 14 In. 5625.00

SILVER-CHINESE
Bowl, Chased, Repousse, Chrysanthemums, Marked Yuchang, Chinese Export, 8 ½ In. 1111.00
Cigarette Case, Chased, Embossed Branches, Bamboo, Prunus Blossoms, 3 ¼ In. 207.00
Cup, 2 Dragon Handles, Repousse, Gilt Interior, Marked Wing Chun, 7 ¼ In. .... *illus* 1725.00
Cup, Dragon, Hand Chased, Bamboo Style Handle, Early 1900s, 3 ⅜ In. .... *illus* 437.00
Egg Set, Chased, Repousse, Scenes, 4 Cups, Stand, 4 Spoons, Marked, c.1900, 7 In. 1053.00
Tea Set, Melon Shape, Kettle, On Stand, Teapot, Sugar, Cream Pot, Marked, 5 Piece 1755.00
Vase, Iris, Wisteria, Enameled Accents, Baluster, c.1900, 8 ½ In. 13750.00

SILVER-CONTINENTAL
Candle Stand, Pierced Bowl, Beaded Rim, Ball & Claw Feet, Hallmarked, 12 In. 265.00
Candy Dish, Boat Shape, Footed, Chased Flowers, Gilt, Handles, 5 x 9 In. 177.00
Caviar Coupe, Hinged Top, 12 Spoons On Holders, Crystal Dish, Ball Feet 960.00
Cigarette Case, Enameled Cover, 2 Bare Breasted Women Fencing, 3 ¼ x 3 ½ In. 3450.00
Crumb Pan & Brush, France, 19th Century, 2 Piece 255.00
Figurine, Bird, 7 x 5 ⅞ In. 185.00
Humidor, Silver Mounted, Amber, Ruby Flashed, Early 1900s, 7 ¾ In. 610.00
Jug, Hot Water, Beaded Bands, Short Spout, Handle, Reeded, Bulbous, 9 ¾ In. 711.00
Ladle, Fiddle Handle, Hallmarked, 19th Century, 13 ½ x 4 ¼ In. 115.00
Platter, Round, Scalloped Rim, Neoclassical Chased Relief Border, 1900s, 15 In. 413.00
Salt, Master, Flower Ribbon, Medallion, Ram's Head Mounts, Liner, Footed, 2 ½ x 4 In., Pair... 72.00
Server, 3 Sections, Center Handle, Openwork, Marked, 7 ½ x 12 ½ x 12 In. 380.00
Tea Set, Hammered, Rosewood Handles, ACC, Crown Mark, c.1925, 5 Piece................. 881.00
Urn, Cover, Pierced, Scrolls, Ram's Head Handles, Blue Glass Liner, 18 In., Pair 4140.00
Wine Coaster, Gilt, Round, Pierced Scrolling, Anthemion, 2 ¾ x 5 In., Pair............... 687.00

SILVER-DANISH
Bell Push, Stylized Flower Bud, Ivory Button, Leaf Tip, Beaded, Georg Jensen, 2 ¾ In. 385.00
Bell, Scroll Finial, Johan Rohde, c.1930, 3 In. 205.00
Bowl, Blossom, Hammered Surface, 1945, Georg Jensen, 3 x 7 ½ In. 1955.00
Bowl, Cone Shape, Circular Foot, Marked, Georg Jensen, 2 ½ x 5 In. 326.00
Bowl, Flared, Openwork Pedestal, Georg Jensen, c.1920, 6 x 7 ¾ In. .... *illus* 2473.00
Bowl, Flared Rim, Stepped Foot, No. 430, Georg Jensen, 1910, 4 x 9 ½ In. 3100.00
Bowl, Footed, Berry & Leaf, Hammered, Flared Rim, Georg Jensen, 4 ⅜ x 5 ¾ In. 770.00
Bowl, Footed, Georg Jensen, 3 ⅛ x 5 In. 177.00
Bowl, Footed, Signed, Georg Jensen, 4 x 8 In. 275.00
Bowl, Georg Jensen, No. 197C, Stamped Mark, c.1916, 8 x 10 In. .... *illus* 6875.00
Bowl, Leaf & Berry Stem, Georg Jensen, 7 ¾ x 10 In. 5382.00
Bowl, Leaves, Buds, Stepped Rim, Georg Jensen, 5 ⅛ In. 326.00
Bowl, Openwork Berry & Leaf Stem, George Jensen, 1945, 4 ½ x 4 ½ In. 575.00
Cheese Set, Scalloped Design, Knife, 2 Forks, Georg Jensen, Marked, 6 In., 3 Piece 1140.00
Cocktail Shaker, Art Deco, C.C. Hermann, 22 Oz. 730.00
Coffee Set, Blossom, Covered Sugar, Creamer, Ivory Handles, Georg Jensen............ 2252.00 to 4148.00
Compote, Grape, Footed, Spiral Stem, G. Jensen, c.1950, 7 ½ In., Pair.................. 7050.00
Compote, Hammered, 8-Sided Bowl, Rope Rim, Berries, Vine, Signed, SJ Skreijh, 5 x 4 ¾ In. . 515.00
Creamer, Crowned, Beaded Oval, Paw Feet, Ivory Handle, Georg Jensen, 2 ⅛ In. 326.00
Creamer, Georg Jensen, c.1925 .... 597.00
Dish, 6-Holes, IHJ, Dansk, 4 In. 75.00
Dish, Pedestal, Lanyard Wrapped Handles, 6 x 3 In. 85.00
Gravy Boat, Stand, 9 In., 2 Piece 230.00
Ladle, Leaves, Georg Jensen, 7 ¾ In. 260.00
Pitcher, Swollen Cylindrical, Johan Rohde, Georg Jensen, 7 ¼ In. 2489.00
Salad Spoon, Georg Jensen, 12 ¾ In. 95.00
Salt & Pepper, Spherical, Stepped Foot, Etchings, Georg Jensen, 1945, 1 ⅞ In. 356.00
Sauceboat, Ebony Handle, Beaded Oval, Georg Jensen, 3 ⅜ In. 1778.00
Sauceboat, Ivory Mounted Handle, Impressed, c.1950, 9 In. 382.00
Serving Bowl, Domed Lid, Berry Finial, Leaves, Flower Buds, Georg Jensen, 1926, 9 In. 2844.00
Snuffer Tongs, Acanthus, Georg Jensen, 1910-25, 6 ¼ In. 725.00

S

Sugar & Creamer, Cover, Pyramid, Curled Handle, Georg Jensen, 2 ⅞ & 3 ⅛ In.	1185.00
Sugar Spoon, Curved Under Handle, Leaf Terminal, Georg Jensen, 5 ¼ In. .... *illus*	207.00
Sugar Tongs, Georg Jensen, Marked Copenhagen, 10 ½ x 3 ½ In.	500.00
Sugar, Round Base, Georg Jensen, Marked, Copenhagen, 15 x 2 ½ In.	1100.00
Tankard, Flowers, Leaves, Scrolls, 19th Century, 14 Oz.	428.00
Tea & Coffee Set, Blossom, Georg Jensen, 1940s, 8-In. Coffeepot, 5 Piece	18000.00
Tea & Coffee Set, Blossom, Ivory Handles, Georg Jensen, c.1905, 4 Piece	9375.00
Tea & Coffee Set, Blossom, Ivory Handles, Georg Jensen, c.1950, 5 Piece	17625.00
Tea & Coffee Set, Coffeepot, Teapot, Sugar, Creamer, Tray, Ebony Handles, Georg Jensen, c.1965 .	9200.00
Tongs, Acorn, Sterling, Georg Jensen, 7 ¼ In.	850.00
Tray, Presentation, Oval, Ebony Handles, Reeding, Curlicue, Georg Jensen, 20 ¾ In.	5333.00

SILVER-DUTCH

Castor, Rooster Form, Domed Oval Base, Glass Eyes, c.1910, 7 ¾ In., Pair	1007.00
Serving Spoon, Pierced Twist Stem, Ship Finial, Engraved, c.1900, 13 In.	88.00
Urn, Cover, Neoclassical, Reticulated, Cobalt Blue Glass Liner, 1900s, 10 ¾ In., Pair	3050.00

SILVER-ENGLISH. English sterling silver is marked with a series of four or five small hallmarks. The standing lion mark is the most commonly seen sterling quality mark. The other marks indicate the city of origin, the maker, and the year of manufacture. These dates can be verified in many good books on silver.

Baby Cup, Reeded, Laurel Leaves, Wreath Medallion, Monogram, George III, 2 ½ In.	161.00
Bacon Server, Sheffield, Matthew Boulton, c.1800, 3 ½ x 13 ¼ In. .... *illus*	345.00
Basket, Cutwork Sides, Applied Grape, Vine, 1810, 6 ½ x 8 ¾ x 7 In.	575.00
Basket, Flowers, Gadroon Rim, Swing Handle, Thos. Jenkinson, 1824, 11 ½ In.	890.00
Basket, George III, Round Wirework, Grapes, Vines, Smith, London, 1810, 10 x 13 In.	5750.00
Basket, Husk Borders, Reeded Rim, Swing Handle, Boat Shape, George III, 12 ⅞ In.	711.00
Basket, Oval, Coin & Scroll Openwork, Rope Borders, 1770, 10 x 12 x 10 In.	1150.00
Basket, Oval, Pierced, Engraved, Bead Foot, Swing Handle, Old Sheffield, c.1765, 6 In.	470.00
Basket, Oval, Reeded Bowl, Gadroon Border, H. Matthews, 1984, 9 x 11 In.	633.00
Basket, Sweetmeat, Pierced, Bright Cut, Hester Bateman, 1786, 6 ¾ In.	881.00
Berry Spoon, Chased Fruit, Mark, Thomas Wallis, c.1831, Pair	115.00
Bottle, Nursing, Tapered Cylindrical Shape, George III, c.1810, 6 In.	1293.00
Bowl, Elongated Handles, Turquoise Accent, C.R. Ashbee, Marcus & Co., 4 x 13 In.	6710.00
Bowl, Glass, Mounted, Intaglio Carved, Flowers, Leaves, Flared Rim, c.1901, 7 ½ x 9 In.	4880.00
Bowl, Leafy Swirls, Art Nouveau Style, J. Deakin & Son, 1911, 7 x 11 In.	805.00
Bowl, Reeded, Ribbons, James Deakin & Son, Sheffield, 1897, 6 x 10 In.	863.00
Bowl, Scalloped Rim, Horned Angel Handles, Acanthus & Scroll Repousse, 1883, 11 x 9 In.	633.00
Caddy Spoon, Bright Cut Handle, Oval Reserve, Shell Bowl, H. Bateman, 1786, 3 In.	323.00
Caddy Spoon, Filigree, Engraved Greek Key, J. Wilmore, c.1809, 3 ¼ x 1 ½ In. .... *illus*	460.00
Caddy Spoon, Round, Acorn Engraved Bowl, Square Handle, Ledsam & Vale, 1821, 3 In.	144.00
Caddy Spoon, Shell Bowl, Gadroon Border, 2 ½ In.	374.00
Cake Basket, Crest Center, Pierced, Loop Handle, Oval, 1751, 10 ½ x 12 ¾ In.	2200.00
Cake Basket, Oval Body, Stippled, Beaded Handle, George III, c.1785, 11 x 13 x 10 In.	2185.00
Cake Basket, Plate Wire, Handle, Old Sheffield, 7 ½ x 8 ¾ In.	235.00
Cake Basket, Swing Handle, Lily Of The Valley, Foot, Reeded, George III, c.1817, 11 x 13 In.	2115.00
Cake Basket, Wheat Sheaf Rim, Woven Sides, JS & S, Sheffield, 1783-84, 7 ¾ x 12 In.	4446.00
Cake Slice, Filigree Server, Hallmarked London, c.1759	780.00
Candelabra are listed in the Candelabrum category.	
Candle Snuffer, Regency, Crest, R. Eames & E. Barnard Mark, 1813, 7 In.	411.00
Candlesticks are listed in their own category.	
Card Case, Lattice Design, Scalloped Edge, Woman's, Victorian, 2 ½ x 3 ½ In.	165.00
Casserole, Cushion Cover, Fluted Rim, Bird Finial, Richard Cooke, 1803, 11 In., Pair	5313.00
Casserole, Rectangle, Rounded, Gadroon Border, Shell Handle, Paul Storr, 12 In.	4140.00
Castor, Baluster Shape, Abraham Buteux, c.1726, 6 ¼ In., Pair	1159.00
Castor, Victorian, Baluster Shape, Engraved, Charles Boyton, c.1885, 8 ½ In., Pair	732.00
Chalice, Bright Cut, Chased Bands, Rose Crest, Motto, George III, c.1787, 7 ½ In.	1150.00
Cheese Scoop, Ivory Handle, George III, Samuel Pemberton, c.1812, 6 ¾ In.	117.00
Cigar Case, Engraved Decoration, Inscribed, Robert Mitchell, c.1875, 5 ¼ In.	173.00
Cigar Case, Raised & Chased Hunting Landscape, Crest, Birmingham, 1846, 4 ¾ In.	671.00
Cigarette Case, Engine Turned Design, Inscribed, Birmingham, c.1950, 4 ½ x 3 ⅜ In.	115.00
Claret Jug, Bright Cut, Fans, Scrolls, Rose Ribbons, Flared Foot, J. Barnard, 12 In.	1220.00
Claret Jug, Glass Parakeet Shape, Silver Head & Mounts, London, c.1881, 13 ½ In.	1194.00
Claret Jug, Urn Form, Finial, Trumpet Foot, Rims, Fruitwood Handle, George III, 1790, 12 In.	385.00
Coffee Set, Pear Shape, Cut Card Work Leaves, Crichton Bros., c.1920, 5 Piece	3172.00
Coffeepot, Baluster, Gadroon Body, Scroll Wooden Handle, George II, 1740, 8 ¼ In.	1495.00
Coffeepot, Baluster Shape, Spiral Fluted Body, Flowers, Shells, Swags, George III, 12 In.	3450.00

Silver-Chinese, Cup, Dragon, Hand Chased, Bamboo Style Handle, Early 1900s, 3 ⅜ In.
$437.00

Silver-Danish, Bowl, Flared, Openwork Pedestal, Georg Jensen, c.1920, 6 x 7 ¾ In.
$2473.00

Silver-Danish, Bowl, Georg Jensen, No. 197C, Stamped Mark, c.1916, 8 x 10 In.
$6875.00

Silver-Danish, Sugar Spoon, Curved Under Handle, Leaf Terminal, Georg Jensen, 5 ¼ In.
$207.00

S

TIP
Don't have old Sheffield silver replated. You can replate wares that were originally electroplated.

Silver-English, Bacon Server, Sheffield, Matthew Boulton, c.1800, 3 ½ x 13 ¼ In. $345.00

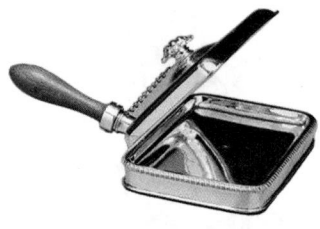

Silver-English, Caddy Spoon, Filigree, Engraved Greek Key, J. Wilmore, c.1809, 3 ¼ x 1 ½ In. $460.00

Silver-English, Goblet, Coconut Shape, Geometric Designs, Georgian, 7 x 4 ¾ In. $690.00

Silver-English, Goblet, George III, Coconut, Carved, Monogram, c.1799, 6 x 4 In. $633.00

Item	Price
Coffeepot, Fluted Oval, Urn Finial, Flowers, Wood Handle, J. Robins, London, 1796, 12 x 10 In.	1035.00
Coffeepot, Lighthouse, Fruitwood Handle, Edward Yorke, George I, 1714, 10 ¼ In.	2489.00
Coffeepot, Oval, Waisted Neck, Gooseneck Spout, Wood Handle, Urn Finial, c.1787, 13 In.	5760.00
Coffeepot, Pear Shape, Domed Lid, Wood Scroll Handle, Hester Bateman, 1781, 12 In.	1725.00
Coffeepot, Pear Shape, Raised Floral Garlands, Domed Lid, B. Gignac, 1765, 10 In.	1586.00
Coffeepot, Scrolled Ebony Handle, Duck's Head Spout, Acorn Finial, Georgian, 9 ½ In.	460.00
Cover, Meat, Entwined Acanthus Leaf Handle, Stepped Dome, 1800s, 9 x 16 In.	201.00
Cream Jug, Helmet Shape, Square Base, Upswept Handle, Hester Bateman, George III, 5 In.	1840.00
Creamer, Domed Foot, Pear Shape, Chased, Embossed Flowers, George III, 1764, 3 ¼ In.	237.00
Creamer, Helmet Shape, Beaded, S-Handle, Hester Bateman, 1786, 5 ½ In.	353.00
Creamer, Helmet Shape, Squared Handle, Engraved Leaf Border, 1800, 4 In.	201.00
Cruet Set, 8 Bottles & Containers, Stand, R. & S. Henell, 1804-05, 10 x 14 In.	351.00
Cruet Stand, 5-Part Base, Scroll, Shell Feet, Central Stem, Loop Handle, 9 ⅞ In.	385.00
Cup, Art Nouveau Design, Engraved Letters	210.00
Cup, Caudle, Lid, Applied Girdle, Handle, Coat Of Arms, George I, 1721, 6 ⅛ x 6 ¼ In.	1126.00
Cup, Caudle, Scrolls, c.1705-06, 4 ¾ In.	5000.00
Cup, Handles, Monogram, George II, 1749, 2 ½ In.	359.00
Cup, Loop Handles, Chased, Embossed Girdle, Reeded, Fluted, George III, 1763, 4 ¾ In.	504.00
Dessert Spoon Set, Oval Downturned Handle, P. & A. Bateman, 1798, 6 Piece	575.00
Dish Cross, Burrage Davenport, London, George III, 10 ¼ In.	1600.00
Dish Cross, Shell Feet, Dish Supports, London, c.1790, 3 x 14 In.	1610.00
Dish Ring, Pierced, Chased, Grapes, Birds, Fish, Figures, Cobalt Blue Glass Liner, 7 x 8 In.	2300.00
Dish, Entree, Cover, Warming Stand, William IV, Cast Lion Handle, 7 ¾ x 12 ¼ In., Pair	1708.00
Dish, Sweetmeat, Rocaille Scrolls, Leaves, Flower Heads, Victorian, 1891, 8 ⅞ In.	148.00
Dish, Sweetmeat, Trumpet Foot, Handles, Lion Masks, George V, 1919, 3 ¼ x 5 ⅛ In., Pair	178.00
Dresser Bottle, Glass, Silver Mounted, Globular, Green & Clear, c.1901, 5 ½ In., Pair	1342.00
Dresser Box, Lid, Couple In Carriage, Oval, Edward VII, 1903, 2 x 5 ¾ In.	326.00
Egg Cruet, Gold Interior, Spoons, Marked, GS & WF, 1813, 7 x 9 In.	3200.00
Epergne, 3 Arms, Hexagonal, Notched Standard, Basket, Bowl, c.1912, 11 ¾ x 15 In.	2196.00
Epergne, Acanthus, Shells, Scroll Arms, Walker & Hall, Late 19th Century, 18 ¼ In.	3981.00
Ewer, Wine, Engraved Flower & Scroll, Cartouche, Rampant Lion, Motto, 13 In.	805.00
Fish Slice, Engraved, Pierced, Peter & Jonathan Bateman, c.1790, 11 ¾ In.	881.00
Fish Slice, Pierced, Iris Engraved, Hester Bateman, 1788, 11 ½ In.	411.00
Frame, Heart Shape, Rococo Style, Repousse, Pierced, London, 1898, 19 x 15 In.	560.00
Goblet, Coconut Shape, Geometric Designs, Georgian, 7 x 4 ¾ In. ....*illus*	690.00
Goblet, Fluted, Repousse Band, Scrolls Flowers, P. & W. Bateman, 1814, 7 In.	690.00
Goblet, George III, Coconut, Carved, Monogram, c.1799, 6 x 4 In. ....*illus*	633.00
Goblet, Gold Wash Interior, Trumpet Foot, John Schofield, George III, 6 ¼ In., Pair	1422.00
Goblet, Reeded Rim, Stepped Pedestal Base, Lion Crest, M. Boulton, 1774, 6 In.	1093.00
Hot Water Pot, Lid, Ball Finial, Spreading Foot, Ivory Handle, George II, 1740, 6 In.	770.00
Jigger, Thimble, Blue Enamel Letters, Just A Thimbleful, G. Unite, 1898, 3 In.	403.00
Jug, Hot Water, Oval, Wriggle Work, Floral Scroll Band, George III, 6 x 5 ¼ In., Pair	4800.00
Jug, Milk, Serpentine Scroll Handle, Dome Foot, Oval, George II, 1734, 5 ½ In.	652.00
Kettle, Stand, Ivory Handle, D. Whyte, W. Holmes, c.1764, 19 In. ....*illus*	5208.00
Label, Port, Crescent Shape, P. & J. Bateman, 1791, 4 In.	575.00
Ladle, Crest, Engraved, George Smith, William Fearn, George III, 12 ½ In.	178.00
Ladle, Old English, James Nasmyth, Hallmarked, George III, 14 ½ In.	295.00
Ladle, Onslow, Ribbed Bowl, Engraved, Shell, Flowers, Crest, Mark, c.1763, 15 In.	230.00
Ladle, Twisted Handle, Oval Bowl, Fruit, Flower Chased, Embossed, 1758, 15 In.	148.00
Lamp, Cigar, Wire, Ball Frame, Ball Support Handle, J.B., London, 1911, 3 x 6 In.	230.00
Mirror, Shaped, Pierced, Raised Scrolls, W. Comyn & Sons, 1902, 27 x 32 In.	1342.00
Mote Spoon, Engraved P, c.1720	425.00
Muffin Warmer, Hammered, Guild Of Handicraft, C.R. Ashbee, 9 ½ x 6 In. ....*illus*	2400.00
Mug, Ale, Engraved Initials & Date 1790, Qt.	325.00
Mug, Baluster Shape, Repousse Military Scenes, A.B. Savory & Sons, 1861, 6 In.	978.00
Mug, Barrel Form, Peter & William Bateman, c.1811, 2 ⅞ In.	315.00
Mug, Cut Glass, Ear Handle, Domed Foot, Scrolling Hops, Vines, Victorian, 1867, 5 ⅛ In.	296.00
Mug, Incised Lines, Ear Handle, Coat Of Arms, Queen Anne, 1702, 3 ⅜ In.	830.00
Mug, Leaf Topped, Serpentine Handle, Domed Foot, Pear Shape, George III, 1862, 5 In.	652.00
Mug, Leaf Wreath, Monogram, Baluster, Serpentine Handle, George III, 1771, 5 ⅜ In., Pair	1304.00
Mug, Scrolled Handle, Monogram, Touchmark, R.L., 18th Century, 3 ¾ In.	506.00
Mug, Serpentine Handle, Flared Foot, Engraved Leaves, C-Scrolls, George II, 1746, 4 In.	385.00
Mustard Pot, Cover, Shell Form Thumbpiece, Handle, George III, 1809, 3 ½ In.	237.00
Mustard Pot, Oval, Ear Handle, Cobalt Blue Glass Liner, William IV, 1837, 3 In.	207.00
Napkin Rings are listed in their own category.	
Nutmeg Grater, Melon Shape, Chased Scrolling, Hilliard & Thomason, c.1853, 1 ½ In.	1380.00
Page Turner, Thos. Northcote, George III, c.1783, 10 In.	322.00

Pepperette, Oval Body, Falcon Crest, Domed Lid, Regency, c.1804, 3 ⅝ x 2 In., Pair	450.00
Plate, Dinner, Shaped Border, Engraved, George II, c.1744, 9 ½ In., 12 Piece	14640.00
Plate, Scalloped, Gadroon Borders, 1754, 9 ½ In., 5 Piece	2185.00
Porringer, Beaded Border, George II, 5 ½ In.	374.00
Porringer, Charles II, Flared, Flowers, Leaves, Handles, London, 1680, 3 ¼ x 3 ¾ In.	978.00
Porringer, Flared Rim, Scroll Handle, Acanthus, Bellflowers, Charles II, 1680	850.00
Punch Bowl, Trumpet Foot, Ribbed, Gold Wash Interior, W. Kingdon, George III, 9 ¾ In.	4444.00
Punch Strainer, Oval, Rim Hook, Reeded Rim, 17th/18th Century, 4 ½ In.	267.00
Ring Box, Repousse, Angels, Holds 6 Rings, 4 ¾ x 1 ¾ In.	595.00
Salt Set, Cased, Wilson & Sharp, 1919, 4 Piece	223.00
Saltshaker, Urn Shape, Reeded Border, Pedestal, P. & W. Bateman, George III, 6 In.	403.00
Salt, 3 Horned Mask Supports, Cloven Feet, Gold Wash Interior, 3 x 3 ¼ In., 4 Piece	1265.00
Salt, Urn Shape, Fluted Corners, Angular Handle, George III, c.1790, 3 ½ x 5 In., 6 Piece	1220.00
Salver, Card, Scalloped Sides, Reed Pierced Edge, Beaded Rim, Edward VII, 1902, 8 ⅝ In.	178.00
Salver, Coat Of Arms, Gadroon Edge, Ball & Claw Feet, Marked, R.R., 18 In.	1750.00
Salver, Double Beaded, Seedpod Border, 3 Ball & Claw Feet, H. Bateman, 1786, 12 In.	3819.00
Salver, Edwardian, Shell Capped Shape Rim, Bands, c.1928, 12 ¼ In.	1093.00
Salver, Footed, Reeded Edge, Engraved Family Crest, John Hutson, George III, 14 In.	1840.00
Salver, George III, Beaded Edge, Swag, Rosette Border, Ball & Claw Feet, 1817-18, 15 In.	1763.00
Salver, Hanover Style, Chippendale Rim, Scroll Feet, Asprey & Co., 14 ½ In.	1200.00
Salver, Molded Ogee, Shell Rim, Hoof Feet, Henry Morris, George II, 1742, 13 ¾ In.	1303.00
Salver, Oval, Crest, Wm. Bennett Mark, 1803, 9 ½ x 7 In.	206.00
Salver, Round, Beaded, Scroll Feet, Swag & Ribbon Cartouche, Monogram, George III, 7 In.	633.00
Salver, Shaped Beaded Edge, 4 Ball & Claw Feet, J. Cotton, T. Head, George III, 15 In.	1776.00
Salver, Shaped Border, Scrolls, Shells, 3 Scroll Feet, c.1765, 10 In.	353.00
Sauceboat, 3-Footed, Acanthus Terminals, Scroll Handle, George V, c.1934, 3 ¾ In.	227.00
Sauceboat, Beaded Border, Flying Scroll Handle, 3-Footed, George III, 4 ½ x 7 ½ In.	717.00
Sauceboat, Family Crest, Motto, 1844, 5 x 9 ½ In.	470.00
Sauceboat, Stand, Edwardian, Chester, 1910-11, 7 In.	293.00
Sauceboat, Tripod, Georgian Style, Flying Scroll Handle, Victorian, c.1845, 8 ⅜ In.	610.00
Serving Spoon, Gold Wash Bowl, Silver Lobster On Mother-Of-Pearl Handle, Pair	2640.00
Stamp Scale, Weighted Base, Mark, Levi & Salaman, Birmingham, 1900, 3 In.	130.00
Sugar & Creamer, Engraved, Peter, Ann, Wm. Bateman, 1802, 4 In.	529.00
Sugar & Creamer, Vine, Swing Handle, Trumpet Foot, J. Denzilow, George III, 5 ⅜ In.	563.00
Sugar Basket, Oval, Bright Cut, Hester Bateman, 1785, 3 ½ x 5 ½ In.	764.00
Sugar Basket, Oval, Pierced Latticework, Swag & Patera Band, George III, 4 ¼ x 4 In.	1680.00
Sugar Basket, Wirework, Cobalt Blue Glass Liner, Chased Swags, George III, c.1778, 7 In.	671.00
Sugar Castor, Pear Shape, Rose & Thorn, Hammered, Footed, Ramsden & Carr, 7 In.	3965.00
Sugar Shaker, Urn Shape, Dome Lid, Reeded Foot, Peter & William Bateman, 1808, 4 In.	646.00
Sugar Tongs, Harlequin Figure Handle, Serpent Ring Handles, 1865, 4 ¾ In.	288.00
Sugar Tongs, Monogram, George IV, c.1827, 5 ½ In.	120.00
Sugar, Openwork, 2 Classical Scenes, 2 Handles, Cobalt Liner, Nathan & Hayes, 1896, 5 In.	236.00
Tankard, Scrolled Thumbpiece & Handle, Hinged Cover, Carrington & Co., 7 In.	1037.00
Tankard, Tapered, Flared Rim, S Scroll Handle, P. & W. Bateman, 1806, 5 In.	460.00
Tazza, Pierced, Chased Rococo Border & Foot, Howard & Co., 5 x 13 In.	1830.00
Tea & Coffee Set, Creamer, Sugar, Clovers, Roses, Pear Shape, Victorian, 4 Piece	948.00
Tea Caddy, Oval, Reeded, Beaded, Flower Finial, George III, 1776, 4 ¾ x 5 x 4 In.	2185.00
Tea Caddy, Scrolling Trim, Flower Handles, Marked London, George III, 1781, Pair	2760.00
Tea Caddy, Tapering Sides, Wood Finial, Flower & Shield Cartouche, 1866, 4 x 3 x 2 In.	575.00
Tea Caddy, Tiered Lid, Chased, Embossed, George II, 1741, 3 ½ x 3 ⅝ In.	948.00
Tea Infuser, Spoon Shape, Victorian, 8 In.	29.00
Tea Set, Pot, Creamer, Sugar, Georgian Style Salver, 1906, 14 ⅜ In., 4 Piece	830.00
Tea Set, Ribbed, Chased Flowers, Leaves, Leaf Feet, Mermaid, Dolphin Handles, 4 Piece	1725.00
Tea Urn, Lid, Chased, Embossed, Urn Form Finial, Ivory Handle, George III, 1771, 22 In.	2370.00
Teapot, Cartouche Shape, Mark, B.M., London, George III, 1782, 4 ¾ x 9 ½ In. ... *illus*	403.00
Teapot, Domed Lid, Oval, Squat, Chased, Embossed, Flower Band, Finial, William IV, 6 ¼ In.	593.00
Teapot, Gadroon, 4 Ball Feet, Flower Finial, Bird Holding Wheat, c.1789, 6 ½ x 12 In.	403.00
Teapot, George III, Banded, Faceted Handle, Spout, Finial, Ball Feet, c.1807, 5 x 11 In. ...*illus*	458.00
Teapot, Neoclassical, Helmet Shaped, Chased Wreaths, Leaf Borders, 5 ½ In.	889.00
Teapot, Oval, Turned Wood Handle, Engraving, Crest, London, George III, 1783, 5 In.	266.00
Teapot, Round, Wooden Finial & Handle, Tapered Spout, Swag Handle, George III, 8 In.	748.00
Teapot, Warming Stand, Oval, Wood Handle, Mappin & Webb, Sheffield, 1909, 12 In.	531.00
Teapot, Wood Handle, Richard Morton & Co., c.1773, 4 ¾ In.	3050.00
Toast Rack, Acanthus Leaf Feet, Marked, JE In Oval, Victorian, 4 ¾ x 6 In.	413.00
Toast Rack, Oval, 5 Racks, Scroll Feet, Ram's Head Handles, George III, 1775, 10 In.	1464.00
Toast Rack, Oval Wirework Dividers, Finial Handle, Victorian, 1840-41, 5 ⅛ x 3 ¾ In.	1200.00
Tray, Applied Roses, Openwork Fleur-De-Lis Border, E. Hutton, 1892, 9 ½ In.	460.00

Silver-English, Kettle, Stand, Ivory Handle, D. Whyte, W. Holmes, c.1764, 19 In.
$5208.00

Silver-English, Muffin Warmer, Hammered, Guild Of Handicraft, C.R. Ashbee, 9 ½ x 6 In.
$2400.00

Silver-English, Teapot, Cartouche Shape, Mark, B.M., London, George III, 1782, 4 ¾ x 9 ½ In.
$403.00

Silver-English, Teapot, George III, Banded, Faceted Handle, Spout, Finial, Ball Feet, c.1807, 5 ¾ x 11 In.
$458.00

S

Silver-English, Tray, Reeded Border, Incised, Armorial Crest, Loop Handles, c.1817, 26 In.
$3720.00

Silver-English, Tureen, Sauce, Oval, Beaded Border, Scroll, Leaves, H.C., Birmingham, c.1865, 6 x 10 In.
$1035.00

Silver-French, Cigarette Case, Sapphire Clasp, Ribbed, Marked, C.C. Gumps, c.1920, 4 x 3 In.
$468.00

Silver-French, Sauceboat, Leaf Handle, Attached Underplate, Marks, Late 1800s, 5 x 11 In.
$575.00

Tray, Engraved, Shell & Scroll Border, Footed, J. & A. Savory, London, 1844, 14 In.	863.00
Tray, Gadroon Border, 2 Handles, 29 ½ x 17 ½ In.	2702.00
Tray, Gadroon Rim, Engraved Armorial, Charles II, 1674-75, 12 ⅜ In.	2083.00
Tray, Oval, Engraved, Central Ribbon & Swag Cartouche, Monogram, 1791, 7 x 5 In.	575.00
Tray, Oval, Stepped Sides, Gadroon Border, Crest With Dog, Paul Storr, 1798, 13 In.	1610.00
Tray, Raised Rim, Sunburst Pattern Of Faux Tortoiseshell, Handles, 4 x 20 In.	403.00
Tray, Reeded Border, Incised, Armorial Crest, Loop Handles, c.1817, 26 In. *illus*	3720.00
Tray, Reeded Rim & Handles, Scroll Border, George III, 1795	3400.00
Tray, Round, Reeded Border, Vines, Ribbon Feet, Hunt & Roskell, 1867, 12 In.	978.00
Tray, Round, Shell & Leaf Border, 4 Lion's Paw Feet, Sheffield, c.1920, 21 In.	2562.00
Tumbler, Armorial Emblem, Presentation Inscription, George II, c.1727, 2 ⅝ In.	4575.00
Tureen, Cover, Oval Bombe Shape, Eagle Handles, Leafy Feet, Wm. Elliot, Regency, 12 x 20 In.	25960.00
Tureen, Engraved Crest, Gadroon Border, Paw Feet, c.1815-16 In., 8 ½ In.	4800.00
Tureen, Sauce, Cover, George III, Handles, Oval, Wakelin & Taylor, c.1778, 9 ½ In.	915.00
Tureen, Sauce, Domed Lid, Oval, 2 Handles, Paw Feet, Gadroon Rim, Sheffield, 6 x 8 In., Pair.	767.00
Tureen, Sauce, Oval, Beaded Border, Scroll, Leaves, H.C., Birmingham, c.1865, 6 x 10 In. *illus*	1035.00
Tureen, Soup, Gadroon Edge, Scroll Handles, Paw Feet, Sheffield, 10 ½ x 16 In.	588.00
Vase, Portland, Handles, Chased, Figures, Gods, John Samuel Hunt, London, 1846, 12 ½ In.	20700.00
Waiter, Hanover Style, Round, Pad Feet, Crichton Brothers, George V, 10 ½ In.	420.00
Whitefish Server, W. Eley, London, c.1805, 11 ½ In.	2050.00
Wine Coaster, Inset Medallion, Beaded Rim, Turned Wood Base, c.1825, 2 x 7 In.	1500.00
Wine Coaster, Shaped From Liquor Tags, Wood Base, Mark, c.1806, 6 x 3 ¾ In., 6 Piece	3450.00
Wine Cooler, Lion, Glass Liner, Handles, George III, 1810-11, 4 In.	980.00
Wine Ewer, Banded, Flared Neck, Masque Spout, Martin & Hall, Victorian, c.1876, 9 In.	1093.00
Wine Funnel, Bombe Form, Beaded Rim, H. Bateman, George III, 5 In.	830.00
Wine Funnel, Bombe Form, Gadroon Rim, George IV, 5 ¼ In.	715.00
Wine Funnel, Reeded Neck, Oval, Engraved Rose Crest, George III, c.1804, 6 x 3 In.	1610.00
Wine Funnel, Stag's Head, Beaded Rim, George III, 4 ½ In.	565.00

SILVER-FRENCH

Beaker, Flat Chased, Shells, Shields, Leaves, Flower Heads, J. Debrie, 4 ½ In.	1287.00
Chalice, Gilt Metal, Hammered Cup, Beaded & Chased Flower Stem, Dome Base, 9 ½ In.	1265.00
Cigarette Case, Flower Heads, Leaf Ground, Gilt, Signed, G. Sandoz, 3 ¼ x 2 In.	1829.00
Cigarette Case, Sapphire Clasp, Ribbed, Marked, C.C. Gumps, c.1920, 4 x 3 In. *illus*	468.00
Coffee Set, Demitasse, Coffeepot, Sugar, Creamer, Lid, Minerva Mark, Boulinger, Paris, c.1910.	590.00
Coffeepot, Acanthus Scroll Handle, Chased, Embossed, C-Scroll, Rocaille, Odiot, 9 ½ In.	1422.00
Compote, Glass, Fluted, Hemispherical, Gadroon & Shell Rim, c.1900, 6 ¼ In., Pair	1080.00
Decanter, Silver Mounted, Cobalt Blue Overlay Cut To Clear, Early 1900s, 12 In., Pair	915.00
Fork Set, Vermeil, 3 Tines, Marked, Fitted Case, c.1900, 5 ½ In., 12 Piece	260.00
Hot Water Urn, Burner, Bellied Shape, Scrolling Leaves, Cartouche, c.1900, 16 In.	1800.00
Kettle, Dolphin Spout, Dragon Terminal, Flowers, Shell, Scroll Base, Odiot, c.1830, 17 x 12 In.	4830.00
Magnifying Glass, Domed Glass, Horse Head Handle, Marked, Hermes, 2 ¼ x 5 ½ x 3 In.	1345.00
Oyster Fork, 3 Tines, Carved Ivory Handle, Hippolyte Thomas, 5 ¾ In., 12 Piece	345.00
Pitcher, Mask Design, Stamped, E. Hugo, c.1890, 14 In.	1080.00
Plate, Round, Applied Ribbon Bound Reeded Border, Engraved Armorial Crest, 10 ½ In.	288.00
Platter, Canted Rectangular, Molded Rim, Monogram, Art Deco, 13 ¼ x 23 ½ In.	2640.00
Platter, Gadroon Rim, Coat Of Arms, 19th Century, Odiot, 12 In.	504.00
Sauceboat, Leaf Handle, Attached Underplate, Marks, Late 1800s, 5 x 11 In. *illus*	575.00
Serving Fork, Flower Design, Crest On Handle, Hallmarked	96.00
Snuff Mull, Horn, Jeweled, Spread Wing Eagle, Suspension Chain, Early 1900s, 13 ½ In.	1586.00
Sugar Tongs, Grapevines, Fox Heads, Clawed Paw Feet, 1800, 6 ¼ In.	71.00
Tea & Coffee Set, Coffeepot, Teapot, Sugar, Creamer, Tray, Puiforcat, c.1900, 25-In. Tray	13145.00
Tea & Coffee Set, Oval Tray, Gallery, Chased, Swirled Lobes, Early 1900s, 4 Piece	1342.00
Teapot, Rococo, Globular, Artichoke Finial, Scroll Handle, Amelie Cardeilhac, 7 In.	1763.00
Tray, Rococo, Applied Rocaille Border, Putti Masks, Crest, Turquet, c.1850, 34 x 24 In.	5520.00
Tray, Rounded Corners, Bellflower Border, c.1850, 7 ⅝ x 6 ⅜ In.	863.00
Urn, Pear Form, Gold Washed Interior, Scroll Feet, Handles, Signed, Linzeler, 9 x 8 In.	650.00
Wine Taster, Round, Chased, Engraved Handle, Inscription, Late 1800s, 2 ½ In.	69.00

SILVER-GERMAN

Asparagus Server, Modernist, Fluted Blade, Karl Gross, c.1915, 9 ¼ In. *illus*	240.00
Biscuit Box, Putti Finial, 3 Gilt Lined Compartments, Hoof Feet, 9 ½ In. *illus*	3510.00
Bowl, Center, Circular Foot, Swirling Lobe Form, Late 19th Century, 7 ½ x 10 ¼ In.	837.00
Bowl, Creamer, Sugar, A. Mayer, c.1900, 3 In.	205.00
Bowl, Footed, Scalloped, Bands, Lobed, Gold Wash, 20th Century, 4 ½ In.	394.00
Bowl, Fruit, Quartrefoil, Upswept Lobes, Gadroon, Leaf, Berry Banding, 3 x 10 In.	600.00
Chalice, Presentation, Repousse, Twisted Stem, Inscribed, S.I. Herman, Vermabluns, 1903, 8 In.	360.00
Chocolate Pot, Allover Scrolling Leaves, Masque Head Spout, 4 Ball & Claw Feet, 8 ½ In.	418.00

S

Claret, Hinged Cover, Spiral Cut, Baluster Form, Flower, C-Scroll Handle, 13 ½ In., Pair.........	1195.00
Compote, Square Base, Scalloped Bowl, 8 x 5 x 5 ½ In.	322.00
Cream Jug, Rococo Style, Silver Gilt Cover, 3 Scroll Feet, Early 20th Century, 6 In.	159.00
Creamer, Helmet Shape, Elongated Handle, 8 Oz., 9 ¼ In.	239.00
Cup, Gilt, 3 Ball Feet, Marks, Cologne, Late 1800s, 2 ¾ x 2 ¾ In. ....*illus*	1035.00
Dish, Chased Flowers, Bouquet Center, Impressed, Adam Manns & Sohn, 9 In.	118.00
Ewer, Cut Glass, Baluster Body, Star, Beam, Hinged Finial Lid, Handles, 1900s, 12 In.	259.00
Ewer, Wine, 4 Lobe Glass Body, Bands, Silver Top, Handle, Finial Lid, Gunther, 1800s, 12 In. ..	307.00
Flagon, Cut Glass, Chased Grape, Vining, Mark, 9 In.	58.00
Goblet, Neptune Riding Dolphin, Open Latticework, 6 In., Pair..	878.00
Jar, Condiment, Blue Glass Liner, Spoon, Rams Head Feet, Pinecone Finial, 1890s, 4 In.	165.00
Ladle, Gilt Helmet Bowl, Shell Design, Turned Wood Handle, 17th Century, 15 In.	201.00
Planter, Art Nouveau, c.1900, 8 x 18 In.	3159.00
Sauceboat, Footed, Handles, Impressed, 1900s, 6 x 8 In.	130.00
Scoop, Tavern Scene, 5 In.	101.00
Sugar & Creamer, Square, Dancing & Tavern Scenes, Scroll Feet & Handle, 4 In.	690.00
Sugar, Bird In Grapevine, Clear Glass Liner, Gilt Bowl, Oval, 5 In., Pair......................................	956.00
Sugar, Rococo Revival, Rocaille Cartouches, Flower Heads, Sy & Wagner, 6 ⅝ In.	237.00
Tankard, Castle Scene, 31 ½ In.	1800.00
Tea Strainer, Black Bakelite Handle, 3 ½ In.	39.00
Tray, Dresser, Oval, Scroll, Flowers, Lobed Rim, 12 ⅜ In.	356.00
Tureen, Cover, Ebonized Wood, Marked, c.1925, 18 ¾ In.	8125.00
Vase, Art Nouveau, Chased, Embossed, Poppy Flower, Wheat Stems, 12 ¾ In.	7007.00
Vase, Bottle Shape, Applied Putti, Flower Round, Signed, Wilkens & Sohn, 1906, 14 In.	2242.00
Vase, Flared Rim, Acanthus, Scroll & Flower Decoration, Inset Coins, c.1875................................	500.00
Vase, Urn Shape, Pedestal, Leaves, Swags, Birds, Repousse Openwork, c.1875, 14 In.	448.00
Wedding Cup, Woman, Holding Cup, Scrolls, Flowers, Masks, 10 x 3 ¼ x 4 ⅞ In.	1920.00
Wine Coaster, Hunting Dog, Early 20th Century, 5 In.	410.00

SILVER-INDIAN

Bowl, Chased, Embossed Deities, Lion Head Pedestals, Double Wall, Footed, 6 ¼ x 7 In.	3674.00

SILVER-IRISH

Basket, Sweetmeat, Leaves, Oval Swing Handle, 4-Footed, c.1750, 6 ½ In.	1500.00
Coffeepot, Hinged Flat Dome Cover, Tapered Body, c.1723, 9 x 7 ¾ In.	4880.00
Coffeepot, Pear Shape, Wood Handle, Acorn Finial, M.W., Dublin, George III, 9 In.	690.00
Creamer, Paw Feet, Engraved Flowers, Dublin, c.1815, 5 x 6 ¼ In. ....*illus*	374.00
Cup, Coconut, Silver Mount, Footed, c.1725, 4 ¼ In.	390.00
Cup, Diamond, Flower, Amethyst, Quartz, Lion, 4 ¼ x 3 ¼ In.	1020.00
Dish Ring, Chased Musicians, Farmers, Houses, Wakely & Wheeler, 1924, 4 In., Pair	976.00
Goblet, Geometric Band, Dublin, 1808, 6 ½ In. Pair...	5100.00
Mug, Barrel Shape, Strap Handle, 1813, 3 ¾ In.	489.00
Platter, Gadroon Border, Engraved Armorial, c.1808, 16 ½ x 22 ¼ In.	6000.00
Salver, Scroll Design, Crown Monogram, 4-Footed, Thomas Bolton, Dublin, 1728, 6 ⅛ In.	8500.00
Snuffer Tray, Scalloped Rim, Oval, Matthew West, Dublin, c.1790, 7 ¼ In.	365.00
Sugar Basket, Bust, Boy, Crest, Fish Scale Ground, Swing Handle, George III, c.1770, 3 ⅜ In.	593.00
Teapot, Barrel Shape, Engraved Design, Ebony Finial, Wood Handle, Michael Homer, c.1785, 4 ⅜ In. .	1310.00
Tureen, Leaf Handles, Oval, Pedestal Foot, Dome Lid, Dublin, George III, 1802.......................	8250.00

SILVER-ITALIAN

Asparagus Tongs, Anacapri, Buccellati, 1900s, 10 In.	294.00
Bowl, Cover, Onyx, Carved Rim, Base, 20th Century, 6 ½ In.	113.00
Candlestick, Gold Wash, Rose Quartz Stem, Garland, 9 ¼ In.	158.00
Centerpiece, Milano, Footed, Handles, Mid 20th Century, 9 x 18 In.	1404.00
Decanter Set, Crystal, Etched, 12 x 5 ½ In., 3 Piece...	322.00
Figurine, Group, Birds, On Branch, 20th Century, 6 ¼ In.	460.00
Frame, Enamel, Oval Opening, Applied Swag, 4 x 3 In. ....*illus*	316.00
Pillbox, Grapes & Flowers, Figures, Repousse, Hinged Lid, 1 ¼ x 1 ⅜ x ½ In.	36.00
Sculpture, Owl On Leaf, Signed, M. Buccellati, 5 In.	978.00
Table Service, Shaped Border, Banded Rim, Platter, Charger, Plate, 19 To 5 In., 37 Piece	5795.00

SILVER-JAPANESE

Bowl, Iris, Repousse, Early 20th Century, 2 ½ x 5 In.	585.00
Figurine, Elephant, 6 x 10 x 5 In.	2040.00
Loving Cup, Handles, Chased Flowers, Hallmarks, 9 ¾ In.	3350.00
Planter, Iris, Raised, Stippled, Footed, Art Nouveau, Samurai Shokai, 5 x 8 In.	4130.00
Tea Urn, Ivory, Carved, Rice Growing, Enameled Silver Base, Top, c.1888, 7 In. ....*illus*	2880.00
Teapot, Tete-A-Tete, Cranes In Flight, Oval, Spherical Finial, Swing Handle, 4 ¾ In.	119.00
Vase, Figures, Landscape, Flowering Vines, Bamboo, Hexagonal, 7 ½ In., Pair........................	356.00
Water Dropper, Leaf Shape, Veins, Stem, Turquoise, Coral & White Beads, 1 ¾ In.	259.00

Silver-German, Asparagus Server, Modernist, Fluted Blade, Karl Gross, c.1915, 9 ¼ In.
$240.00

Silver-German, Biscuit Box, Putti Finial, 3 Gilt Lined Compartments, Hoof Feet, 9 ½ In.
$3510.00

Silver-German, Cup, Gilt, 3 Ball Feet, Marks, Cologne, Late 1800s, 2 ¾ x 2 ¾ In.
$1035.00

Silver-Irish, Creamer, Paw Feet, Engraved Flowers, Dublin, c.1815, 5 x 6 ¼ In.
$374.00

S

Silver-Italian, Frame, Enamel, Oval Opening, Applied Swag, 4 x 3 In. $316.00

Silver-Japanese, Tea Urn, Ivory, Carved, Rice Growing, Enameled Silver Base, Top, c.1888, 7 In. $2880.00

Silver-Mexican, Child's Set, Fork, Knife, Aztec, Hector Aguilar, 3 ⅝ & 4 In. $300.00

Silver-Mexican, Pitcher, Water, Juventino Lopez Reyes, 10 ¾ x 6 ¾ In. $489.00

SILVER-MEXICAN

Basket, Open Braided, Base, Double Rope Twist Handle, 8 x 10 ¾ In.	150.00
Bowl, 4 Griffin Feet, Lobed Sides, Applied S-Scroll Rim, Round, Tapered, 17 ¼ x 5 In.	444.00
Bread Tray, Chippendale Style, Leaves & Scrolling, Mid 1900s	253.00
Child's Set, Fork, Knife, Aztec, Hector Aguilar, 3 ⅝ & 4 In. *illus*	300.00
Dish, Shell Shape, Scrolling Grapevines, 3-Footed, Sanborns, 3 x 9 ¾ In.	299.00
Goblet Set, Oval, Baluster Stem, Domed Foot, 7 x 3 ⅛ In., 12 Piece	1684.00
Iced Tea Spoon, Leaf Design, Marked, Mexico Sterling, 8 In., 12 Piece	240.00
Ladle, Silver, Double Spout, Wood Handle	47.00
Pitcher, Carved Wood Handle, William Spratling, 7 x 9 In.	1320.00
Pitcher, Round, Arched Handle Connecting 2 Spouts, Tane, 8 ½ x 8 ¼ In.	748.00
Pitcher, Sangria, 4 Lobed Sides, Interior Strainer, Spratling, 1940, 7 ½ In.	4770.00
Pitcher, Tall Lip, Marked, Taxco, Hector Aguilar, 9 In.	1010.00
Pitcher, Tapered, Strap Handle, William Spratling, Marked, c.1959, 5 In.	225.00
Pitcher, Water, Juventino Lopez Reyes, 10 ¾ x 6 ¾ In. *illus*	489.00
Platter, Paneled Rim, Scalloped Edge, Marked Sanborn, Mexico, 38 Oz.	540.00
Stirrers, Sipping, Spoon Shape, Taxco, 7 ½ In., 8 Piece	288.00
Straw Set, Leaf Terminals, 8 ¼ In., 12 Piece	59.00
Tea Set, Melon Rib, Teapot, Covered Sugar, Creamer, Tray, 4 Piece	2040.00
Tea Set, Sugar & Creamer, Tray, 3 Piece	295.00
Teapot, Chased, Flowers, Leaves, Scroll Handle, 8 ½ In.	499.00
Teapot, Wood Handle, Marked, Spratling, 14 Oz.	565.00
Tongs, Serving, Vegetable, Signed, 925 Mexico Silver, Juvento Lopez Reyes, 10 ¼ In.	96.00
Tray, Embossed Flowers & Panel Border, Oval, Cut-Out Handles, 20 In.	670.00
Tray, Rounded Rectangular, Applied Scroll Edge, Handles, 15 ½ x 25 ½ In.	1320.00
Tray, Ruffled Edge, Chased Flower Center, Casa Prieto, 7 ¼ In.	69.00

SILVER-NORWEGIAN

Bowl, Scroll, Creature, Pierced Rim, Pedestal, c.1900, 11 x 12 In.	1380.00
Serving Spoon, 9 ½ In., 2 Piece	234.00
Spoon Set, Guilloche Enamel, Multicolored, David Anderson, 4 In., 6 Piece *illus*	288.00

SILVER-PERSIAN

Cigarette Case, Blue & White Enameled Design, Gold Wash, Hallmark, 4 x 3 ¼ In.	142.00

SILVER-PERUVIAN

Pitcher, Cylindrical, Footed, 10 x 4 In.	275.00
Pitcher, Flower Handle, Signed, Oata E Sterling, Camusso, 5 x 6 ½ In.	170.00
Tea & Coffee Set, Sugar, Creamer, Oval, Flowerhead Roundels, 1900s, 6 Piece	889.00

SILVER-PORTUGUESE

Kettle, Hot Water, Stand, 16 x 8 In.	1763.00

SILVER-RUSSIAN. Russian silver is marked with the Cyrillic, or Russian, alphabet. The numbers 84, 88, or 91 indicate the silver content. Russian silver may be higher or lower than sterling standard. Other marks indicate maker, assayer, or city of manufacture. Many pieces of silver made in Russia are decorated with enamel. Faberge pieces are listed in their own category.

Beaker, Gold Wash, Conical, Multicolored, Geometric Enameling, 1883, 6 ¾ In.	8295.00
Bowl, Flower Stems, Enamel, Garnet, 1896-1908, 2 x 3 ⅛ In.	4148.00
Box, Gilt Interior, Scrolls, Town Scene, 1858, ¾ x 2 ¾ x 1 ¾ In.	230.00
Change Purse, Black Niello Enameling, Basket Design, Nikoli Koulikoff, c.1811, 3 x 2 In.	354.00
Cheroot Case, Niello Work, Engraved, Cartouche, Assayer A. Romanov, c.1889, 3 ½ x 2 In.	750.00
Cigarette Case, 3 Bogatyr & Bogatyr Warrior, Hinged Lid, Cabochon Thumbpiece, 4 In.	720.00
Cigarette Case, Enameled Nautical Flags, Charms, Crest, Hallmarks, c.1905, 3 In.	2400.00
Cigarette Case, Enameled, Polar Bears Walking, Winter Landscape, Teal Ground, 4 ¼ In.	2963.00
Cigarette Case, Engraved, Enameled Flowers, Mark, Nikoli Koulikoff, c.1881, 4 x 2 ⅜ In.	384.00
Cigarette Case, Samorodok, Textured, Red Thumbpiece, Faux Diamond, Cyrillic Mark, 4 ½ In.	420.00
Cigarette Case, Woodsman, Bear, Hinged Lid, Hallmark, Moscow, 1908-17, 4 ¼ In.	1080.00
Creamer, Flowers, Leaves, Multicolored, Enamel, Jewel Inlays, Gilt Interior, 1891, 3 x 3 x 5 ½ In.	2750.00
Cup, Coronation Blood Cup, Enamel Over Copper, Tsar Nicholas II, 1896, 4 x 3 ¾ In.	702.00
Cup, Tea, Enameled, Cobalt Blue, Red, Turquoise, Scrolled Panels, 2 In.	1432.00
Demitasse Spoon, Rose Handle, Late 19th Century, 4 ½ In., Pair	50.00
Dish, Round, Hand Chased, Flowers, Mark, E. Blumberg, c.1861, 5 ½ In.	118.00
Egg, Blue Basse Taille Enamel, Stone Set, Pearl Finial, Husk Swags, Stand, 5 In.	1778.00
Egg, Enamel, Pink Birds, Flowers, Blue Waves, Stamped, Marked, 3 ½ In.	660.00
Figurine, Boy & Dog, Napping, Green Marble Base, 1896, 5 x 3 ½ In.	889.00
Fish Slice, Gold Wash Blade, Nephrite Handle, Engraved, Marked, 10 ⅜ In. *illus*	92.00
Flute, Enameled, Trumpet Bowl, Flowers, Man, Holding Beaker, 6 ¼ In., Pair	1659.00
Frame, Tea Glass, 2 Figures In Troika, Handle, Demilune Rim, 1902, 4 ⅜ In.	711.00

S

Knife, Paper, Enamel, Stone, Gold Wash, Green Jade Blade, 9 ¼ In.	830.00
Kovsh, Cloisonne, Oval, 3 ¼ x 7 ¼ x 3 ⅝ In.	5185.00
Kovsh, Enamel, Flowers, Beads, Gilt Finish, c.1910, 2 x 4 In.	460.00
Kovsh, Fan, Crosscut Glass, Warrior In Helmet, Tapered Handle, 13 ½ x 8 ¼ In.	2726.00
Ladle, Enamel, St. Petersburg Kokoshnik Mark, 1896-1903, 7 In.	355.00
Mug, Urn Shape, Gilt Interior, Hollow Scroll Handle, Pedestal, 1849, 5 ¼ In.	345.00
Salt, Enamel, Blue, Red, Black Flower Design, Gilt Spoon	175.00
Salt, Enamel, Gilt, White, Multicolored, 3 Ball Feet, Sterling Spoon	250.00
Salt, Rococo Style, Footed, Hallmark, 1849, 2 x 4 In.	330.00
Saucer, Enameled, Flowers, Green, Burgundy Ground, Marked, M.C., c.1912, 4 ¼ In.	1020.00
Stuffing Spoon, Fiddle, Shell Stem, Monogram, 1845, 12 ½ In.	119.00
Sugar Basket, Enamel, Swing Handle, Roundels, Rope Twist Border, 1882, 5 In.	1185.00
Sugar, Sides Chased With Basket Weave, Marked, Vilnius, c.1905, 2 ¾ In.	150.00
Teapot, Gadroon Band, Wood Handle, Finial, Karpinsky, c.1823, 4 ¾ x 9 In. .... *illus*	431.00
Tray, Reeded Edge, Eagle Ribbon Border, Looped Handles, Bubrovin, 1829, 23 x 15 In.	3172.00

SILVER-SCOTTISH

Coffeepot, Wood Handle, Reeded, Marked, Thistle, George III, c.1818, 10 In. .... *illus*	439.00
Jug, Hot Water, Chased Decoration, Engraved Crest, Victorian, c.1845, 13 ¼ In.	1342.00
Sauceboat, Gadroon Rim, Shell Feet, 1753-54, 7 x 9 In.	175.00 to 510.00
Snuff Mull, Horn, Silver Mounted, Inscribed Thomas Crabb, Late 1700s, 3 ½ In.	397.00
Snuff Mull, Horn, Silver Mounted, Monogram, 19th Century, 3 ¼ In.	397.00
Tea Set, Chinoiserie, Chased, Embossed, Figural Cartouches, Teapot, Creamer, Sugar	2070.00
Tea Set, Pot, Creamer, Sugar, Oval, Beaded Edges, George Edward & Sons, 5 ¼ In.	368.00
Toddy Ladle, Engraved, Armorial Crest, Patrick Robertson, 1770	450.00

SILVER-SPANISH

Reliquary, Reticulated Pendant, Porcelain Sacred Heart Plaque, Early 1800s, 3 x 2 In.	58.00

SILVER-STERLING. Sterling silver is made with 925 parts silver out of 1,000 parts of metal. The word *sterling* is a quality guarantee used in the United States after about 1860. The word was used much earlier in England and Ireland. Pieces listed here are not identified by country. Other pieces of sterling quality silver are listed under Silver-American, Silver-English, etc.

Basket, Acorn & Leaf Repousse Decoration, Swing Handle, c.1875, 6 x 5 x 4 In.	374.00
Basket, Openwork Scrolls, Shell Feet, Flower & Scroll Border, 1900s, 9 x 9 x 9 In.	518.00
Bottle Holder, Open Work, Double Hinged Top, 14 Oz.	840.00
Bowl, Bicentennial Scenes, 24K Gold Interior, Franklin Mint, 7 x 14 In.	2760.00
Bowl, Center, Scalloped, Scrolling Leaves, Applied Wide Rim, Pedestal Base, 5 x 10 ¾ In.	403.00
Bowl, Fruit, Georgian Style, Shaped Rim, Engraved Design, 16 Oz.	330.00
Bowl, Round, Heather Matthews, 10 ½ In.	177.00
Bowl, Scalloped Flower Garland Rim, 2 ¼ x 10 ¼ In.	360.00
Bread Tray, Rounded Rectangular, Embossed Flowers, 9 x 12 ½ In.	330.00
Brush, Clothes, Flat, Scrolling Monogram	95.00
Cake Knife, Lily, Gorham Mark, 12 ½ In.	50.00
Candelabra are listed in the Candelabrum category.	
Candlesticks are listed in their own category.	
Cigar Holder, 3 Sections, Hinged, Engraved, Vine Pattern, Monogram, 5 x 2 ⅓ In. .... *illus*	121.00
Cigarette Case, Woman On A Bee, Enamel, Gorham, 3 ¼ x 2 ½ In. .... *illus*	1652.00
Coat Brush, Repousse, Flower Handle, Continental, 1900s, 7 x 3 ½ In. .... *illus*	81.00
Cordial Set, Footed, Glass Insert, Cutout Cage, Marked, 3 In., 6 Piece	125.00
Dish, Art Nouveau, Nude Woman In Shell, Oval	300.00
Dresser Set, Hairbrush, Mirror, Gadroon, Floral & Leaf Design, 2 Piece	46.00
Flask, Screw Cap, Etching, Civil War	150.00
Goblet, Water, Inverted Bell Form Bowl, Raised On Trumpet Foot, 6 ¾ In., 8 Piece	1080.00
Knife & Fork Set, Mother-Of-Pearl Handles, Fitted Box, c.1865, 7 ¼ & 6 In., 12 Piece	205.00
Meat Holder, Oval Handle, Leaf Design, c.1835, 9 ½ In. .... *illus*	322.00
Mirror, Repousse, Flowers & Birds, Tabletop	900.00
Muffineer, Gadroon Border, Footed, 6 ½ In.	156.00
Mug, Handle, Engraved, Bird, On Branch, Leaves, Berries, Hallmark, 1877, 4 x 2 ½ In.	440.00
Napkin Rings are listed in their own category.	
Pepperette, Hammered Sterling, Ruskin Glazed, Grapevine, 1900, 2 ¼ x 1 ¾ In.	1708.00
Picks, Ear Of Corn Handles, Pasteboard Case, 3 & 8 x 3 ½ In., 12 Piece	660.00
Pill Box, Fleur-De-Lis Shape, Praying Priest, Marked, 1 ½ In.	86.00
Pitcher, Arts & Crafts, Hammered, Scrolling, Randahl, 8 x 6 In. .... *illus*	426.00
Pitcher, Overlay, Emerald Glass, Cylindrical, Grapevines, Clusters, c.1900, 10 In.	1800.00
Pitcher, Water, Stag Handle, c.1910, 7 In.	700.00
Plate, Bread & Butter, Molded Rim, Script Monogram, 6 ½ x 6 ⅜ In., 12 Piece	411.00
Punch Bowl & Underplate, Poppies, Hemispherical, 1930s, 7 ½ x 10 ½ In.	1920.00

Silver-Norwegian, Spoon Set, Guilloche Enamel, Multicolored, David Anderson, 4 In., 6 Piece
$288.00

Silver-Russian, Fish Slice, Gold Wash Blade, Nephrite Handle, Engraved, Marked, 10 ⅜ In.
$92.00

Silver-Russian, Teapot, Gadroon Band, Wood Handle, Finial, Karpinsky, c.1823, 4 ¾ x 9 In.
$431.00

Silver-Scottish, Coffeepot, Wood Handle, Reeded, Marked, Thistle, George III, c.1818, 10 In.
$439.00

Bad Company
Never put silverware and stainless-steel flatware in the dishwasher basket together. The stainless can damage the silver.

S

Silver-Sterling, Cigar Holder, 3 Sections, Hinged, Engraved, Vine Pattern, Monogram, 5 x 2 ⅓ In.
$121.00

Silver-Sterling, Cigarette Case, Woman On A Bee, Enamel, Gorham, 3 ¼ x 2 ½ In.
$1652.00

Silver-Sterling, Coat Brush, Repousse, Flower Handle, Continental, 1900s, 7 x 3 ½ In.
$81.00

Silver-Sterling, Meat Holder, Oval Handle, Leaf Design, c.1835, 9 ½ In.
$322.00

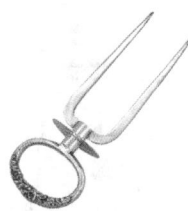

Spoon, Demitasse, Twist Handle, 4 In.	20.00
Spoon, Enamel & Gold Plate, J. Tostrop, Norway, Box, c.1978, 5 ¾ In.	125.00
Spoon, Souvenir, see Souvenir category.	
Sugar Castor, Baluster Shape, Molded Foot, Pierced Dome Cover, Monogram, 7 In.	176.00
Tazza, Leaf Relief Edge, Pierced Rim, Monogram, Gorham, 7 x 4 In. .... *illus*	190.00
Tea & Coffee Set, Martel, Silver Plate Tray, c.1930, 5 Piece	936.00
Tea Set, Coffeepot, Teapot, Tilt Stand, Creamer, Sugar, Waste Bowl, 5 Piece	1093.00
Tea Strainer, Clover Decoration, Monogram, 7 ½ In.	633.00
Teaspoon & Sugar Tong Set, Spiraled Stem, Apostle End, Cased, 1880s, 10 x 7 In., 13 Piece..	300.00
Tray, Flower, Leaf Repousse, Round, 12 In.	826.00
Vanity Set, Flowers, Leaves, Brush, Mirror, 2 Piece	20.00
Vase, Bud, Cylinder, Overlay Design, c.1880, 7 In.	82.00
Vase, Trophy, Poppy Openwork Neck, Rim & Base, Inscribed, Art Nouveau, 1936, 20 ½ In.	2875.00
Vase, Trumpet, Griffin Mark, c.1915, 16 In.	705.00
Wedding Cup, Woman Base, Skirt Forms Cup, Arms Hold Swinging Cup, 4 ½ In.	316.00

SILVER-SWEDISH
Tureen, Cover, Sauce, Scrolled Handle, Feet, Ladle, c.1943-44, 8 ½ In., Pair	1175.00

SILVER-SWISS
Holy Oil Container, Cylindrical, Hinged Lid, Cross Finial, 17th Century, 2 ¾ In.	354.00

SILVER-THAI
Plaque, Marching Figures, Trees, Pagodas, Horses, Frame, Early 1900s, 13 x 10 In.	495.00

SILVER-TURKISH
Belt Buckle, 3-Part, Linen, Wirework Filigree, Palm Bud, Glass Cabochons, 3 x 9 In.	830.00

SINCLAIRE cut glass was made by H.P. Sinclaire and Company of Corning, New York, between 1904 and 1929. He cut glass made at other factories until 1920. Pieces were made of crystal as well as amber, blue, green, or ruby glass. Only a small percentage of Sinclaire glass is marked with the *S* in a wreath.

Bowl, Assyrian, Marked, 5 x 10 In.	3600.00
Bowl, Queens Pattern, 10 In.	600.00
Bowl, Rolled Rim, Leaves & Flowers, 3 ½ x 8 In.	300.00
Bowl, Rose, Diamond Point Cut Body, Punty Highlights, American Brilliant, 5 ½ In.	225.00
Dish, Pickle, Engraved, Insert, 7 ½ In.	600.00
Punch Bowl, Hobstar Chain, Vintage Panels, Vine Decor, 14 x 15 In., 2 Piece	7000.00
Teapot, Engraved Flowers, Marked, 5 ¼ x 8 ½ In.	900.00
Vase, Crystal Design, Greek Key, Laurel Wreath, Urn Form, Footed, Signed, c.1910, 15 In.	180.00
Vase, Rose Pattern, Pinched Neck, Signed, 10 x 8 ½ In.	489.00
Vase, Tazza Shape, Vintage Design, Signed, 6 ½ x 10 In.	3500.00

SLAG GLASS resembles a marble cake. It can be streaked with different colors. There were many types made from about 1880. Caramel slag is the incorrect name for chocolate glass. Pink slag was an American product made by Harry Bastow and Thomas E.A. Dugan at Indiana, Pennsylvania, about 1900. Purple and blue slag were made in American and English factories in the 1880s. Red slag is a very late Victorian and twentieth-century glass. Other colors are known but are of less importance to the collector. New versions of chocolate glass and colored slag glass are being made.

Caramel Slag is listed in the Imperial Glass category.

Pink, Cruet, Inverted Fan & Feather, Dugan, 6 ½ In.	403.00
Purple, Candy Dish, Nesting Hen, 9 In.	22.00
Purple, Vase, Challinor, 9 x 5 ½ In.	245.00

SLEEPY EYE collectors look for anything bearing the image of the nineteenth-century Indian chief with the drooping eyelid. The Sleepy Eye Milling Co., Sleepy Eye, Minnesota, used his portrait in advertising from 1883 to 1921. It offered many premiums, including stoneware and pottery steins, crocks, bowls, mugs, and pitchers, all decorated with the famous profile of the Indian. The popular pottery was made by Western Stoneware, Weir Pottery Company, and other companies long after the flour mill went out of business in 1921. Reproductions of the pitchers are being made today. The original pitchers came in only five sizes: 4 inches, 5 ¼ inches, 6 ½ inches, 8 inches, and 9 inches. The Sleepy Eye image was also used by companies unrelated to the flour mill.

Blotter, Sleepy Eye Flour	37.00
Bowl, Indian, Stoneware, 4 x 6 ½ In. .... *illus*	410.00
Creamer, Indian, Teepee, Stoneware, Diamond Mark, Monmouth Stoneware Co., 4 In.	80.00
Letter Head,	55.00 to 70.00
Mug, Indian, Teepee, Brown Glaze, Western Stoneware, Maple Leaf Mark, 5 ½ In.	95.00
Mug, Indian, Teepee, Stoneware, Diamond Mark, Monmouth Stoneware Co., 4 ½ In.	98.00

Pitcher, Indian, Standing, Blue Stoneware, 8 In.	300.00
Pitcher, Indian, Teepee, Stoneware, Diamond Mark, Monmouth Stoneware Co., 9 In.	180.00
Pitcher, Yellow Ground, Blue Indian, Handle, Monmouth, 9 In. .... *illus*	189.00
Postcard, Indian In Canoe	30.00
Salt, Indian, Teepee, Stoneware, Weir Stoneware Co., 6 ¼ In.	238.00
Sign, Sleepy Eye Meritorious Flour, Indian, Tin Lithograph, Self-Framed, 24 x 20 In.	2650.00
Sign, That Sleepy Eye Flour, Indian, Tin Over Cardboard, 19 x 14 ¼ In.	1500.00
Stein, Indian, Teepee, Stoneware, Incised S, Weir Stoneware Co., 8 In.	260.00
Vase, Indian, Teepee, Stoneware, Incised O, Weir Stoneware Co., 9 In.	305.00
Vase, Indian, Teepee, Stoneware, Incised W, Weir Stoneware Co., 9 In.	165.00

SMITH BROTHERS glass was made after 1878. Alfred and Harry Smith had worked for the Mt. Washington Glass Company in New Bedford, Massachusetts, for seven years before going into their own shop. They made many pieces with enamel decoration.

Smith Bros. Co.

Biscuit Jar, Crabs, Shells, Plants, Gold, Swirled, Rectangle, Gold Lid, Handle, 8 In.	460.00
Biscuit Jar, Melon Shape, Leaves & Acorns, Metal Lid & Handle, 7 x 5 In.	316.00
Biscuit Jar, Satin Ribbed Body, Gold Birds, Bamboo, Embossed Metal, Lid, Mark, 7 In.	425.00
Biscuit Jar, Swirled Rib, Translucent White, Satin Finish, Pansies, Gilt, 8 ¾ In. .... *illus*	230.00
Bowl, 6-Lobed, Gilt Flowers, Cream Ground, c.1875, 2 ⅜ x 3 ¾ In.	66.00
Cologne Bottle, Melon Ribbed, Russet, Ivy, Embossed Lid, Rampant Lion Stamp, 5 In.	230.00
Perfume Bottle, Atomizer, Melon Ribs, Red Flowers, Stems, Stamp, 5 In.	173.00
Sugar & Creamer, Blue Pansy, Cream Ground, Silver Cover, Fittings, 3 ½ x 3 ½ In.	288.00
Sugar Shaker, Ribbed Pillar Shape, Yellow Daisies, 6 In.	144.00
Syrup, Melon, Opaque White, Yellow Ground, Gilt Flowers, Handle, 5 ¾ In. .... *illus*	184.00
Toothpick, Columned Ribs	125.00
Vase, Purple Iris, Cream Ground, Shouldered, Pinched, Lion Mark, 5 In.	144.00
Vase, Water Lily, Mottled Yellow, Globe Shape, Mark, 4 ¼ In.	230.00

SNOW BABIES, made from bisque and spattered with glitter sand, were first manufactured in 1864 by Hertwig and Company of Thuringia. Other German and Japanese companies copied the Hertwig designs. Originally, Snow Babies were made of candy and used as Christmas decorations. There are also Snow Babies tablewares made by Royal Bayreuth. Copies of the small Snow Babies figurines are being made today and a line called "Snowbabies" was introduced by Department 56 in 1987. Don't confuse these with the original Snow Babies.

Figurine, Mama, Twins In Sled Buggy, 2 ¼ In.	365.00

SNUFFBOXES held snuff. Taking snuff was popular long before cigarettes became available. The gentleman or lady would take a small pinch of the ground tobacco or snuff in the fingers, then sniff it and sneeze. Snuffboxes were made of many materials, including gold, silver, enameled metal, and wood. Most snuffboxes date from the late eighteenth or early nineteenth centuries.

18K Gold, Blue Guilloche & White Enamel Borders, France, 1762, 3 ½ In.	3050.00
18K Gold, Engine-Turned, George III, England, 1803, 3 In.	2806.00
Brass, Copper, Man & Woman Playing Bagpipes, Scotland, c.1760	295.00
Brass, Dutch, Man Rocking Cradle, Round, 1782	385.00
Deer Hoof, Silver Mounts, Monogram, Scotland, c.1800, 3 In.	365.00
Enamel, Scenic, Country Manor, Folly, Gibbet, Gilt Metal Mounts, 18th Century, 2 ½ In.	288.00
George Washington, Papier-Mache, Portrait In Clouds	839.00
George Washington, Wooden, 1797, 3 ¼ In.	3000.00
Gold, Engine Turned Lid, Chased Fox & Grape Border, Hungary, c.1880, 3 x 2 In.	3172.00
Gutta-Percha, Shell Medallion Under Glass, Napoleon Standing, 3 ½ In.	525.00
Horn, Boot, Carved, Hinged Lid, Silver Fittings, Scrolls, 1880s, 4 ¾ In.	400.00
Horn, Boot, Silver Monogrammed Lid, Italy, c.1830, 2 ¾ In.	325.00
Ivory, Tortoiseshell, Scenic, Tall Ship Off Harbor, Figures, Temple, 3 ¼ In.	1037.00
Micro Mosaic, Enamel, Cranberry Glass, Classical Ruins, Hinged Lid, 1 x 2 ½ In. .... *illus*	851.00
Papier-Mache, Black, Hinged Lid, Oval, Mid 19th Century, 3 ¼ x 2 ¼ In.	85.00
Papier-Mache, Bust Portrait, Gen. Zach. Taylor, Inscriptions, c.1848, 3 ¼ In.	585.00
Papier-Mache, Landing Of Lafayette, Leaf, Berry Border, 3 ⅜ In.	385.00
Pewter, Hinged, Winged Wheel Logo, 3 ½ x 1 ¾ x 1 In.	44.00
Porcelain, Cherubs, Horse, Town Harbor, Trunk Form, Danish, 1893, 1 ½ In.	95.00
Silver, Amorous Couple, Pond, Enameled Inset, Oval, Engraved, 3 ¼ x 2 ½ In.	403.00
Silver, City Square, Buildings, Statue, War Trophies, Russia, 3 In.	296.00
Silver, Crow, Gold Washed Interior, Hinged, Incised, Tooled, Dutch, 3 x 1 ¾ In. .... *illus*	178.00
Silver, Farmer, Cows, Tree, Repousse, Oval, 1 ¾ x 2 In.	82.00
Silver, Fish Scale Ground, Gold Washed Interior, Chinese, 2 ⅜ In.	119.00
Silver Guilloche, Enameled, Gilt, Flowers, Tooled Dots, Hallmarked, ¾ x 1 ¾ In. .... *illus*	155.00
Silver, Hunt Scene, Engraved, c.1850-60, 2 ¾ In.	80.00

Silver-Sterling, Pitcher, Arts & Crafts, Hammered, Scrolling, Randahl, 8 x 6 In. $426.00

Silver-Sterling, Tazza, Leaf Relief Edge, Pierced Rim, Monogram, Gorham, 7 x 4 In. $190.00

Sleepy Eye, Bowl, Indian, Stoneware, 4 x 6 ½ In. $410.00

Sleepy Eye, Pitcher, Yellow Ground, Blue Indian, Handle, Monmouth, 9 In. $189.00

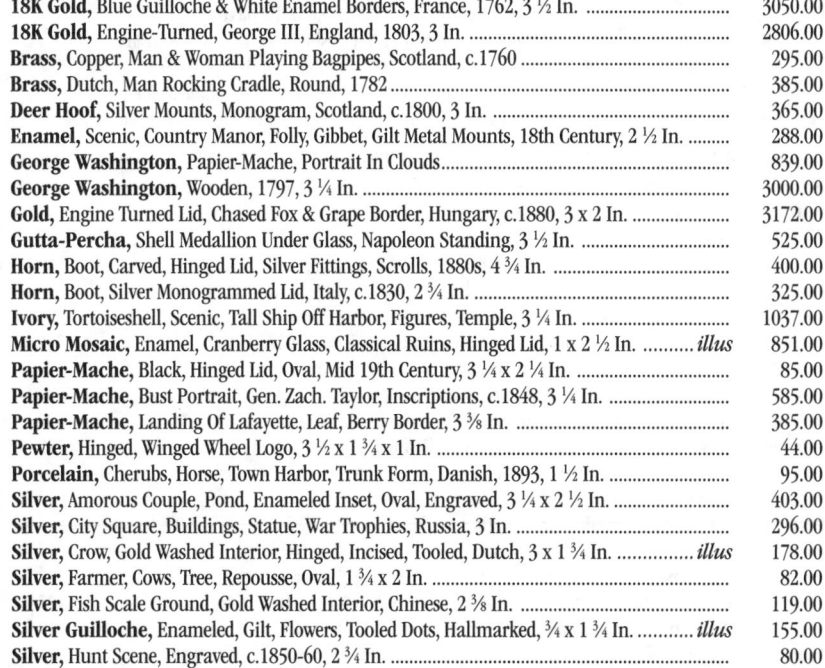

S

Smith Brothers, Biscuit Jar, Swirled Rib, Translucent White, Satin Finish, Pansies, Gilt, 8 ¾ In.
$230.00

Smith Brothers, Syrup, Melon, Opaque White, Yellow Ground, Gilt Flowers, Handle, 5 ¾ In.
$184.00

Snuffbox, Micro Mosaic, Enamel, Cranberry Glass, Classical Ruins, Hinged Lid, 1 x 2 ½ In.
$851.00

Snuffbox, Silver, Crow, Gold Washed Interior, Hinged, Incised, Tooled, Dutch, 3 x 1 ¾ In.
$178.00

TIP

Save your travel souvenirs: the giftshop snowdomes, glasses, keychains, and postcards. They can form the start of a collection.

Silver, Lid, Gold Wash, Engraved Basket Weave, George III, 1802, 3 ⅛ In.	237.00
Silver, Lines, Inscribed, Dated, 1826, 3 x 1 ¾ In.	72.00
Tole, Horseshoe, Hinged, Painted, Applied Silver Bust, Early 1700s, 3 ½ In. .... *illus*	531.00
Tole, Mottled Paint, Applied Silver Bust Of Queen, Horseshoe Shape, Hinged, 4 In.	546.00
Tortoiseshell, Gold Pique, Flowers, Pierced Border, Louis XVI, Silver, Late 1700s, 3 ⅛ In.	1342.00
Wood, Shoe, Huntsman, Hounds, Fox, Carved, Gold Piquet, 1836, 4 ½ In.	936.00

SOAPSTONE is a mineral that was used for foot warmers or griddles because of its heat-retaining properties. Soapstone was carved into figurines and bowls in many countries in the nineteenth and twentieth centuries. Most of the soapstone seen today is from China or Japan. It is still being carved in the old styles.

Block Stamp, Red, Dragon Top, Chinese, 5 x 2 In.	468.00
Bookends, Foo Dog, Pedestal Base, Chinese, Late 19th Century, 9 x 3 In.	144.00
Bowl, Translucent, Mottled, Flared, Chinese, 1 ¾ x 3 ⅞ In., Pair	58.00
Carving, Group, Lohan, Qilin, Late Qing Dynasty, Chinese, 8 In.	777.00
Carving, Pagoda In Mountain Landscape, Figures On Bridge, Chinese, 8 ¼ In.	956.00
Figurine, 2 Women, Facing, 20 x 21 x 4 ½ In.	633.00
Figurine, Bamboo Bird Temple, Carved, 13 ½ x 6 ½ In.	88.00
Figurine, Eve & Serpent, Carved, Signed, William Cross, 8 ½ x 7 ½ x 3 In.	250.00
Figurine, Fat Matilda, Carved, Signed, William Cross, 21 ½ x 9 In.	220.00
Figurine, Joseph, Carved, Signed, William Cross, 8 x 5 ½ x 4 In.	220.00
Figurine, Longevity, Man, Children, Carved, Chinese, 5 In.	120.00
Figurine, Moses, Carved, Signed, William Cross, 11 ½ x 7 x 7 In.	220.00
Figurine, Seal With Cub, 11 x 24 In.	2357.00
Seal, Chilong, Recumbent, Honey Color, Boulder Form, Inscribed, Wu San Ba, Chinese, 1 ¼ In.	1360.00
Stamp, Amber, Carved, Mountain Scene, 2 Buddhas, Egg Shape, Chinese, 3 In.	266.00
Vase, Red, Carved Flowers, Chinese, 6 ¼ In.	83.00

SOFT PASTE is a name for a type of pottery. Although it looks very much like porcelain, it is a chemically different material. Most of the soft-paste wares were made in the early nineteenth century. Other pieces may be listed under Gaudy Dutch or Leeds.

Cup & Saucer, Pink Basket Of Strawberries, Queen's Rose, Handleless	339.00
Plate, King's Rose, Queen's Rose, Vine Border, 6 ¾ In.	85.00
Plate, King's Rose, Solid Border, 10 In.	85.00
Platter, Well & Tree, Figures, Black, White, c.1770, 15 ¾ x 20 ¼ In.	375.00
Soup, Dish, King's Rose, Enamel, Pink Luster Banded Border, 10 ¼ In. .... *illus*	22.00
Teapot, Peafowl On Branch, Blue Banding, 7 In.	374.00
Vase, Derby, Urn Form, Fruit, 2 Scrolling Handle, Mask Terminals, Footed, c.1810, 9 In.	118.00

SOUVENIRS of a trip–what could be more fun? Our ancestors enjoyed the same thing, and souvenirs were made for almost every location. Most of the souvenir pottery and porcelain pieces of the nineteenth century were made in England or Germany, even if the picture showed a North American scene. In the twentieth century, the souvenir china business seems to have gone to the manufacturers in Japan, Taiwan, Hong Kong, England, and America. Another popular souvenir item is the souvenir spoon, made of sterling or silver plate. These are usually made in the country pictured on the spoon. Related pieces may be found in the Coronation and World's Fair categories.

Booklet, Bridal Veil Lumbering Co., 14 Photographic Plates, Black Cloth, 1890s, 7 x 11 In., 14 Pages.	429.00
Button, New Orleans, Mardi Gras, Color, Woman With Black Eye Mask, c.1912, 2 ⅛ In.	1055.00
Button, Spanish Civil War, Medical Bureau, Donate To Save A Life, c.1910, ⅞ In.	45.00
Button, Treasury Dept, Junior Commando, 1 In.	3.50
Dish, St. Lawrence Seaway Opening, Porcelain, 1959, 5 In.	30.00
Flag, 1932 Olympiad, Los Angeles, Ca., Red, White, Black, Silk, July 30-August 14, 10 ½ In.	30.00
Fork, State Of Washington, State Seal, Mt. Rainier, Pickax, Shovel, Engraved, 7-14-12	35.00
Pennant, Harvard Boston Aero Meet, Planes, Lighthouse, Red, Felt, 1910, 23 In.	335.00
Pin, Mardi Gras, Consus, Shakespeare & His Creations, T. Hausman & Sons, 1901	529.00
Pin, Mardi Gras, Elves Of Oberon, Satan Dethroned, 1912	646.00
Pin, Mardi Gras, Krewe Of Proteus, Frantz & Opitz, 1896	1293.00
Pin, Mardi Gras, Krewe Of Proteus, Sterling Silver, Enamel, 1922	588.00
Pin, Mardi Gras, Twelfth Night Revelers, Sterling Silver, Enamel, Early 20th Century	764.00
Pipe, Glass, Hand Painted Flowers, Hershey Park	20.00
Plate, 225th Anniversary, Trindle Spring Lutheran Church, Mechanicsburg, 1765-1990, 10 In.	4.00
Plate, 34th President Dwight D Eisenhower, W.S. George Co., 1953, 10 In.	15.00
Plate, America's First Family, President & Mrs. Dwight D. Eisenhower, 9 In.	6.00
Plate, Calendar, Compliments Of Peter Wold, Pool Room & Livery, 1910, 7 ¼ In.	125.00
Plate, Civil War Centennial Commission, 16th President A. Lincoln, 10 In.	19.00
Plate, Compliments Of Lonesome Pine Antiques, RT. 16, Mercersburg, Pa., 1969, 9 In.	14.00

Plate, Fort Frederick Bicentennial, 1756-1956, 10 In.	9.00
Plate, Hagerstown 200th Anniversary, Antietam, South Mountain Centennial, 10 In.	14.00
Plate, Heidelberg United Church Of Christ, Marian, Pa., 10 In.	10.00
Plate, Hotel Saga In Reykavik, Iceland, Marked Bing & Grondahl, 3 ¼ In., Pair	45.00
Plate, Irwinton, Mercersburg, Pa., 10 ¼ In.	12.00
Plate, Irwinton Mills, Mercersburg, Penna., Hurricane Agnes Flood, 6-23-1972, 10 In.	10.00
Plate, J.R. Dudley, Route 2, Mercersburg, Pa., 1965, 10 In.	10.00
Plate, Macedonia United Brethren Church Greencastle, Penna., Built-1882, 10 In.	10.00
Plate, McConnellsburg, Pa. 175th Anniversary, 1786-1961, 10 In.	8.00
Plate, Meckley Store, Where Your Dollars Have More Cents, Upton, Penna., 7 In.	12.00
Plate, Mercersburg Bicentennial Memorial 1750-1950, 10 In.	5.00
Plate, Merry Xmas Art Bar, Mercersburg, Pa., 1964, 10 In.	14.00
Plate, Minneapolis, MN, Historical Scenes, Blue, New England Furniture Co., 10 In.	52.00
Plate, National Apple Museum, Biglerville, Pa., 9 ¼ In.	10.00
Plate, Old Log Church, Protestant Methodist Church, Blairs Valley Penna., 1844-1972, 9 In.	14.00
Plate, Pleasant Hill United Brethren In Christ Church, Coseytown, Penna., 1899-1970, 10 In.	10.00
Plate, Red Bridge, Franklin County, Mercersburg, Penna., 10 ¼ In.	10.00
Plate, Robert E. Lee 1807-1870, General In Chief Of All Confederate Armies, 10 In.	24.00
Plate, Salem United Brethren In Christ Church, R.D. 2, Chambersburg, Pa., 10 In.	10.00
Plate, Samoset Hotel, Rockland, Maine, 10-Sided, Reticulated Border, Germany, 8 In.	287.00
Plate, Shenandoah Caverns, Virginia, Cardross Castle, 9 ¼ In.	10.00
Plate, Souvenir Of Tuscarora Summit Inn, McConnellsburg, Pa., 9 ⅜ In.	100.00
Plate, The Diamond In 1893, Mercersburg, Pa., 10 In.	10.00
Plate, The Fordway Program In Action, Black Glass, 1939, 10 In.	18.00
Plate, U.S. Bicentennial, Fort Loudon, Pa., 1776-1976, 10 In.	10.00
Plate, Washington County's Last Trolly, Washington County, Md., 9 ¾ In.	14.00
Plate, Waynesboro, Pa., Sesquicentennial, 1818-1968, 10 In.	14.00
Plate, William O. Shuman, Shows Martins Mill Bridge, August 7-12, 1977, 10 In.	16.00
Plate, Windsor, Canada, Indian Chief, Turquoise Ground, 7 ¼ In. ....*illus*	50.00
Program, Souvenir, Woodstock, 3 Days Of Peace & Music, 1969, 12 x 9 In., 52 Pages	649.00
Salt & Pepper, Coney Island, Photos Of Luna Park, 1900s, 2 ¼ In.	75.00
Saltshaker, Winnipeg, Canada, Pressed Glass, Button Arch, Ruby, 3 In., Pair	70.00
Spoon, Demitasse, Salem Witch, Sterling Silver, Daniel Low, Marked, 4 ¼ In.	115.00
Spoon, Palm Beach, Sterling Silver, Engraved Bowl, Grinning Black Boy On Handle, 4 In.	135.00
Textile, 1936 Berlin Olympics, Flags Of Nations, Browns, Blacks, Red, 28 x 28 In.	190.00
Tip Tray, Russel IA., Dog, Pointer, Black, White, Outdoor Scene Border, Tin, 3 ⅜ x 5 In.	147.00
Watch Fob, Stone Mountain, Woven Hair, Double Strand, Brass, Pinback, c.1929	120.00

SPATTER GLASS is a multicolored glass made from many small pieces of different colored glass. It is sometimes called End-of-Day glass. It is still being made.

Cheese Dome, Amber, Opal, Cranberry, Silver Plated, Finial, c.1900, 5 ½ x 6 ¾ In.	106.00
Pitcher, Cased, Multicolored, Swirled, Ribbed, Square Rim, Reeded Handle, Pontil, c.1900, 6 In.	127.00
Pitcher, Water, Optic, Cranberry, Opal, Bulbous, Square Crimped Rim, 3 Spouts, c.1900, 8 In.	66.00
Pitcher, Water, Ribbed, Multicolored, Round Rim, Reeded Handle, c.1900, 7 ½ In.	132.00
Pitcher, Water, Ribbed Swirl, Multicolored, Round Rim, Reeded Handle, Pontil, c.1900, 7 ½ In.	132.00
Pitcher, Water, Tortoiseshell Glass, Red, Gray, Opal, Square Crimped, Turned Rim, c.1900, 10 In.	66.00
Pitcher, Water, Vertical Panels, Cream, Tortoiseshell Glass, Brown, Swirled Rib Body, c.1875, 9 In.	330.00
Sugar Shaker, Cased, Pink & White, Ring Neck, c.1883, 5 In.	175.00
Sugar Shaker, Ring Neck, Cranberry & White Opaque, Lid, Late 1800s, 4 ¾ In. ....*illus*	81.00

SPATTERWARE and spongeware are terms that have changed in meaning in recent years, causing much confusion for collectors. Some say that *spatterware* is the term used by Americans, *sponged ware* or *spongeware* by the English. Spatterware is creamware or soft paste dinnerware decorated with colored spatter designs. The earliest pieces were made in the late eighteenth century, but most of the spatterware found today was made from about 1800 to 1850. Early spatterware was made in the Staffordshire district of England for sale in America. Collectors also use the word *spatterware* to refer to kitchen crockery with added spatter made in America during the late nineteenth and early twentieth centuries. Spongeware is very similar to spatterware in appearance. Designs were applied to ceramics by daubing the color on with a sponge or cloth. Many collectors do not differentiate between spongeware and spatterware and use the name interchageably. Modern pottery is being made to resemble old spongeware, but careful examination will show it is new.

Bowl, Purple, Blue Rainbow, Rectangular, 8 ½ In.	209.00
Charger, Rabbitware, 4 Rabbit Panels, Stick Spatter, Virginia Rose, 12 ⅞ In.	536.00
Charger, Rabbitware, Rabbits & Frog, Stick Spatter, Virginia Rose, 12 ⅞ In.	895.00
Charger, Rabbitware, Rabbits Running, Stick Spatter, Virginia Rose, 12 ½ In.	895.00
Coffeepot, Dahlia, Blue, Red Flower, Green Sprigs, 9 ½ In.	339.00

Snuffbox, Silver Guilloche, Enameled, Gilt, Flowers, Tooled Dots, Hallmarked, ¾ x 1 ¾ In.
$155.00

Snuffbox, Tole, Horseshoe, Hinged, Painted, Applied Silver Bust, Early 1700s, 3 ½ In.
$531.00

Soft Paste, Soup, Dish, King's Rose, Enamel, Pink Luster Banded Border, 10 ¼ In.
$22.00

Souvenir, Plate, Windsor, Canada, Indian Chief, Turquoise Ground, 7 ¼ In.
$50.00

S

SPATTERWARE

Spatter Glass, Sugar Shaker, Ring Neck, Cranberry & White Opaque, Lid, Late 1800s, 4 ¾ In.
$81.00

Spatterware, Cup & Saucer, Blue & Yellow Rainbow, 19th Century
$878.00

Spatterware, Cup & Saucer, Schoolhouse, Blue, 19th Century
$936.00

Spatterware, Cup, Balls, Green, Handleless, Child's
$522.00

Creamer, Castle, Blue, Gray, Brown, Red Fort, Green Trees, Shaped Handle, 5 ½ In.	124.00
Creamer, Peafowl, Blue, Red Green Sponge Spatter, Bulbous, 3 ½ In.	791.00
Creamer, Rainbow, Red, Green, Black, Yellow, Applied Loop Handle, Bulbous, 3 ½ In.	9605.00
Creamer, Red, Blue, Green, Bulbous, 4 ½ In.	990.00
Creamer, Rose, Rainbow, Red, Green, 4 In.	360.00
Creamer, Tree, Purple, 2-Sided, Helmet Shape, 4 ½ In.	226.00
Cup & Saucer, Blue & Yellow Rainbow, 19th Century .... *illus*	878.00
Cup & Saucer, Blue, Green, Red Stripes, Plaid, Handleless	1100.00
Cup & Saucer, Half Moon, Star, Red, Green, Yellow, Blue, Handleless	3955.00
Cup & Saucer, Peafowl, Dark Brown To Black Spatter, Blue, Red, Green, Handleless	1582.00
Cup & Saucer, Peafowl, Handleless, Blue Spatter	357.00
Cup & Saucer, Peafowl, Purple, Green, Red, Green, Handleless	715.00
Cup & Saucer, Rainbow, Blue & Yellow, 1800s	878.00
Cup & Saucer, Red, 2 Men In Raft, Handleless	8250.00
Cup & Saucer, Red Rooster, Purple, Yellow, Blue, Handleless	170.00
Cup & Saucer, Rose, Red, Green Spatter, Handleless	141.00
Cup & Saucer, Schoolhouse, Blue, 19th Century .... *illus*	936.00
Cup & Saucer, Thistle, Blue, Red Flower, Green Leaves, Handleless	316.00
Cup & Saucer, Yellow, Red Rainbow, Handleless	825.00
Cup, Balls, Green, Handleless, Child's .... *illus*	522.00
Cup, Green, Christmas Balls, Handleless, Child's	495.00
Cup, Schoolhouse, Blue Spatter, Yellow Roof, Brown Ground, Tree	79.00
Egg, Rainbow, Bird, Olive Branch, George Mowbray, c.1800, 2 ½ In.	822.00
Mug, Flowers, Rabbits, Applied Handles, c.1850, 5 ½ In.	646.00
Mug, Flowers, Rabbits, Frogs, Applied Handles, c.1850, 5 ½ In.	705.00
Mug, Rabbitware, Cricket, Stick Spatter, Virginia Rose, 4 ½ In.	2800.00
Mug, Rabbitware, Frog, Stick Spatter, Virginia Rose, 5 ⅜ In.	2510.00
Mug, Rabbitware, Rabbit Running, Stick Spatter, Virginia Rose, 5 ⅜ In.	2510.00
Mug, Rabbitware, Rabbits In Meadow, Stick Spatter, Virginia Rose, 5 ⅜ In.	515.00
Pitcher & Washbowl, Rainbow, Red, Blue, Paneled	660.00
Pitcher, Blue Sponge, c.1900, 10 In.	95.00
Pitcher, Blue, White, Band, 8 In.	230.00
Pitcher, Rabbitware, Golf, Stick Spatter, Virginia Rose, 8 ½ In.	8400.00
Pitcher, Rainbow, Red, Blue, Green, Horizontal Bands, Bulbous, 4 ½ In. .... *illus*	1044.00
Plate, Blue, Purple Sponge Spatter, 9 ½ In.	283.00
Plate, Blue School House, 8 ⅛ In.	3510.00
Plate, Bull's Eye, Rainbow, Purple, Brown, 9 ½ In. .... *illus*	986.00
Plate, Castle, Brown, Scalloped Edge, 8 In.	198.00
Plate, Crisscross, Rainbow, Red, Blue Spatter, Paneled, 7 ½ In.	283.00
Plate, Lily Of The Valley, Purple, 1830, 9 ½ In.	940.00
Plate, Lily Of The Valley, Purple, c.1800, 9 ½ In.	59.00
Plate, Loop, Yellow, Red, Blue, Green, 8 ¼ In.	2372.00
Plate, Peafowl, Green, Spatter Field, Blue, Yellow, Red, Scalloped Edge, 7 ¾ In.	254.00
Plate, Rabbitware, Croquet, Stick Spatter, Virginia Rose, 9 ¼ In.	1970.00
Plate, Schoolhouse, Blue Border, Early 1800s, 9 ½ In. .... *illus*	881.00
Plate, Schoolhouse, Green, 19th Century, 10 ¼ In. .... *illus*	556.00
Plate, Schoolhouse, Green Spatter, 1800s, 10 ¼ In.	556.00
Plate, Schoolhouse, Red, Blue, Yellow Roof, Brown Ground, Tree, 8 ½ In.	537.00
Plate, Soup, Peafowl, Red Spatter, Blue, Green, 9 In.	339.00
Plate, Soup, Thistle, Red, Green, Yellow Border, Paneled, 9 ¾ In.	11200.00
Plate, Tulip, Blue, Green Rainbow, Paneled, 8 ½ In.	5775.00
Plate, Tulip, Purple, Blue, Green Leaves, 8 ¾ In.	165.00
Plate, Tulip, Red Spatter, Blue, Red Flower, Green Leaves, Black Stem, Paneled, 8 ½ In.	113.00
Platter, 5-Color Rainbow, 19th Century, 13 x 15 ¼ In. .... *illus*	39780.00
Platter, Octagonal, Bull's-Eye, c.1800, 12 ½ In.	734.00
Platter, Rabbitware, Rabbits & Frog, Stick Spatter, Virginia Rose, Oval, 14 ⅝ In.	1200.00
Spatter Glass, Teapot, Brown, Metal Lid, 7 In.	12.00
Sugar, Cover, Peafowl, Green, 2-Sided, Blue, Green, Red, 4 ¾ In.	73.00 to 88.00
Sugar, Cover, Peafowl, Red Spatter, Blue, Yellow, Green, 4 ½ In.	198.00
Sugar, Cover, Rainbow, Red, Blue, Spatter, 4 ½ In.	57.00
Sugar, Cover, Thistle, Red Spatter, Yellow Flower, Black Leaves, Stem, 4 ¾ In.	283.00
Sugar, Cover, Tulip, Red, Blue, Green Leaves, Bulbous	176.00
Sugar, Cover, Tulip, Red, Green Leaves, 5 ¾ In.	99.00
Sugar, Cover, Windmill, Blue, 19th Century, 5 In. .... *illus*	2106.00
Sugar, Rooster, Purple, 2-Sided, Yellow, Blue, Red, 4 ½ In.	136.00
Toothpick, Leaf Umbrella, Cranberry	55.00
Waste Bowl, Fort, Blue, 19th Century, 3 ½ x 6 ¾ In.	174.00

S

SPELTER is a synonym for a zinc alloy. Figurines, candlesticks, and other pieces were made of spelter and given a bronze or painted finish. The metal has been used since about the 1860s to make statues, tablewares, and lamps that resemble bronze. Spelter is soft and breaks easily. To test for spelter, scratch the base of the piece. Bronze is solid; spelter will show a silvery scratch.

Calling Card Holder, Nubian Man, Feathered Headdress, Brass Plated, 20th Century, 17 In. ..	602.00
Candleholder, Woman & Butterfly, 2-Flower Holders, Art Nouveau, 13 In.	140.00
Cigarette Holder, Dog, Dachshund, Hanging Brass Ashtray In Mouth, Painted, 14 In.	140.00
Garniture Set, Figural Clock, Putto, Harp, Woman, 2 Ornate Urns, 18 x 10 In., 3 Piece..........	322.00
Lamp, Lion, Tree Supporting Red Paper Shade, 22 In.	575.00
Lamp, Woman, Czech Glass Shade, Flowers, Leaves, Bronze Verde, Germany, 24 x 8 In.	2100.00
Lamp, Woman, Upraised Arms, Under Leafy Branch, L'Autonne, E. Dorvais, Paris, 24 In., Pair.	460.00
Plaque, Woman's Bust, Hat, Flower Locket, Stylized Flower Rim, Signed, D. Lenoir, 23 ¾ In. ..	346.00
Sculpture, Bust, Mozart, Painted, 11 In.	40.00
Sculpture, Bust, Pushkin, Poet, Writer, Russia, c.1890, 12 In.	390.00
Sculpture, Conquistador, Holding Flag, 19th Century, 6 ½ In.	3650.00
Sculpture, Dancing Couple, White Patina, Barefoot Maiden, Boy With Tambourine, 35 In.	237.00
Sculpture, Dog, German Shepherd, Molded Onyx Base, 1930s, 7 In.	60.00
Sculpture, Dog, Pointer, Pointing, Oval Stepped Base, 7 x 12 In.	83.00
Sculpture, Galatea, Nymph, Leaves, Brown & Green Patina, Round Base, 29 In.	889.00
Sculpture, George Washington, Holding Scroll, Standing By Stump, Bronze Patinated, 22 In. .	575.00
Sculpture, Maiden, Seated, Birds In Hand, Impressed, Fozety, 22 In.	135.00
Sculpture, Tower, White, Removable Lid, Marble Base, Italy, 20 In.	725.00
Sculpture, Woman, Seated, Isoprene Head, Hands, Gilding, Art Deco, c.1920, 10 x 15 In. *illus*	468.00
Tobacco Jar, Dog, Seated, Open Mouth, Painted, Copper Finish, 5 In.	88.00
Vase, Flower Form, 7 x 6 In.	70.00

SPINNING WHEELS in the corner have been symbols of earlier times for the past 100 years. Although spinning wheels date back to medieval days, the ones found today are rarely more than 200 years old. Because the style of the spinning wheel changed very little, it is often impossible to place an exact date on a wheel.

Blue Paint, Bobbin, Treadle, Alfred Andresen & Co., 36 In.	165.00
Carved, Turned Spindles, Giraffe Head Finial, 39 x 31 In. .... *illus*	236.00
Castle, Mixed Wood, Painted, Ring Turning, Penn., 55 In. .... *illus*	986.00
Oak, 25 In.	190.00
Oak, Maple, Flax Wheel, c.1800, 32 x 33 In.	81.00
Turned Wood, Spindle Tripod Base, 45 In.	176.00

SPODE pottery, porcelain, and bone china were made by the Stoke-on-Trent factory of England founded by Josiah Spode about 1770. The firm became Copeland and Garrett from 1833 to 1847, then W.T. Copeland or W.T. Copeland and Sons until 1976. It then became Royal Worcester Spode Ltd. The company was bought by the Portmeirion Group in 2009. The word *Spode* appears on many pieces made by the factories. Most collectors include all the wares under the more familiar name of Spode. Porcelains are listed in this book by the name that appears on the piece. Related pieces may be listed under Copeland, Copeland Spode, and Royal Worcester.

SPODE
Stone-China

Dish, Cover, Chelsea Pattern, 8 ¾ In.	47.00
Jar, Potpourri, Cover, Blue & White, Tower Pattern, Octagonal Body, Flame Shape Finial, 15 ½ In.	127.00
Pitcher, Marble, Blue Transferware, White Blossoming Flowers, Cracked Ice, 1821, 9 ½ In.	83.00
Plate, Luncheon, Alden Pattern, 9 ⅛ In., 14 Piece	69.00
Platter, Blue & White, Transferware, Leaf, Berry, Medallions, Urns, Classical Scenes, 20 ½ x 16 In.	299.00
Platter, Blue Willow, Octagonal, Mark, c.1910, 21 x 16 In. .... *illus*	115.00
Platter, Castle Pattern, Marked, c.1850, 19 x 14 In.	113.00
Urn, Cover, Cobalt Blue, Flowers, Fish Scale Overlay, 8-Sided, Tapered, Eagle, 22 In., Pair........	13800.00

SPORTS equipment, sporting goods, brochures, and related items are listed here. Items are listed by sport. Other categories of interest are Bicycle, Card, Fishing, Sword, Toy, and Trap. Kentucky Derby glasses are listed in the Decorated Tumblers category.

Auto Racing, Pennant, Vanderbilt Cup Grand Prize, Santa Monica, Calif., Felt, 1914, 30 In. ..	820.00
Baseball, Ball, Autographed, 1947 Brooklyn Dodgers, 28 Signatures........................	649.00
Baseball, Ball, Autographed, Babe Ruth..........................	5310.00
Baseball, Ball, Autographed, Babe Ruth, c.1936........................	4113.00
Baseball, Ball, Autographed, Detroit Tigers, 1968........................	649.00
Baseball, Ball, Autographed, Mickey Cochrane........................	5015.00
Baseball, Ball, Autographed, Mickey Mantle, 536 Home Runs........................	1410.00

Spatterware, Pitcher, Rainbow, Red, Blue, Green, Horizontal Bands, Bulbous, 4 ½ In. $1044.00

Spatterware, Plate, Bull's-Eye, Rainbow, Purple, Brown, 9 ½ In. $986.00

Spatterware, Plate, Schoolhouse, Blue Border, Early 1800s, 9 ½ In. $881.00

Spatterware, Plate, Schoolhouse, Green, 19th Century, 10 ¼ In. $556.00

S

Spatterware, Platter, 5-Color Rainbow, 19th Century, 13 x 15 ¼ In. $39780.00

Spatterware, Sugar, Cover, Windmill, Blue, 19th Century, 5 In. $2106.00

Spelter, Sculpture, Woman, Seated, Isoprene Head, Hands, Gilding, Art Deco, c.1920, 10 x 15 In. $468.00

Spinning Wheel, Carved, Turned Spindles, Giraffe Head Finial, 39 x 31 In. $236.00

Baseball, Ball, Autographed, Mickey Mantle, Letter Of Authenticity	780.00
Baseball, Ball, Autographed, N.Y. Yankees, 1951	3051.00
Baseball, Ball, Autographed, Tris Speaker	8260.00
Baseball, Ball, Autographed, Wilbert Robinson, 1927	2937.00
Baseball, Ball, Autographed, Thurman Munson	9000.00
Baseball, Bank, Pittsburgh Pirates, Mascot, Stanford Pottery, 3 x 3 x 7 ½ In. .... *illus*	158.00
Baseball, Bat, Autographed, Jackie Robinson, Louisville Slugger, 1950-56	30000.00
Baseball, Blanket, Ty Cobb, At Bat, Tobacco Premium, Felt, White Ground	236.00
Baseball, Bowl, Dapper Dan Award, Bob Gibson, Post Gazette, Engraved Bowl, 1973, 12 In.	385.00
Baseball, Box, Glove Display, Joe Cronin Model, 1930s, 8 ¾ x 9 ½ x 3 ⅞ In.	296.00
Baseball, Button, 1957 World Series, New York Yankees, Milwaukee Braves, Celluloid, 1 ¾ In.	33.00
Baseball, Button, Baltimore Orioles, Bird, Baseball, Orange, Black, Celluloid	15.00
Baseball, Button, Cleveland Indians, American League Champs, Indian Profile, Cream, Red, 1 ¾ In.	20.00
Baseball, Button, Frank Howard Fan Club, Frank At Bat, Shades Of Blue, 1970, 2 ¼ In.	145.00
Baseball, Button, Joe Black, Brooklyn Dodgers, Portrait, Celluloid, 1 ¾ In.	23.00
Baseball, Button, Joe Hauser Day, Baltimore Orioles, Black, White, 1930, ⅞ In.	207.00
Baseball, Button, Lou Boudreau Day, Cleveland Indians, Oct. 28, 1948, 1 ½ In.	210.00
Baseball, Button, Pittsburg Pirates, N.L. Champions, 18 Faces, c.1909, 2 ¼ In. .... *illus*	1404.00
Baseball, Button, St. Louis Browns, American League Champions, Celluloid, 1944, 2 ¼ In.	61.00
Baseball, Button, St. Louis Cardinals, I'm Supporting The Cardinals, Red, White, Celluloid	15.00
Baseball, Cap, Autographed, Mickey Mantle, New York Yankees, Game Used, 1968	7637.00
Baseball, Cap, Autographed, Roberto Clemente, Game Used, New Era, 1966	12000.00
Baseball, Cap, Joe DiMaggio, Cloth Tag, 1940s	135.00
Baseball, Catcher's Equipment, Mask, Protector, Kneepads, Mitt, Stand, 1900s, 26 x 52 In.	2370.00
Baseball, Check, Ty Cobb, Signed, 1930	940.00
Baseball, Cigar Box, New York Giants, 1926, 9 x 7 In.	82.00
Baseball, Figure, Roger Maris, Plastic, Hartland, Box, c.1960 .... *illus*	1067.00
Baseball, Figurine, Player & Ball, National League World Tour, 1913-14, 6 In.	444.00
Baseball, Game, Home Run Babe, Batter, Mechanical, Tin Lithograph, Selrite, 1920s, 7 In.	425.00
Baseball, Glove, First Baseman's, Double-Buckle, Spalding, c.1912, 9 In. .... *illus*	326.00
Baseball, Glove, Bob Gibson, Rawlings, Game Used	9000.00
Baseball, Glove, Bob Gibson, Rawlings, Mickey Mantle Model, Practice Used	1185.00
Baseball, Glove, J.R. Richard, Houston Astros, Game Used, c.1979	593.00
Baseball, Hat, Joe DiMaggio, Irving L. Lewis & Sons, 1940s	145.00
Baseball, Jersey, Autographed, Mickey Mantle	1778.00
Baseball, Jersey, Bob Gibson, St. Louis Cardinals Spring Training Coach, Game Used, 1998.....	415.00
Baseball, Jersey, Cleon Jones, New York Mets, Road, Game Used, 1972	248.00
Baseball, Jersey, Dick Allen, Chicago White Sox, Game Worn, 1972	563.00
Baseball, Jersey, Greg Maddux, Atlanta Braves, Road, Game Used, 2001	1659.00
Baseball, Jersey, Nolan Ryan, Houston Astros, Road, Game Used, 1985	266.00
Baseball, Jersey, Tony Taylor, Philadelphia Phillies, Flannel, Pinstripes, Game Used	213.00
Baseball, Model Kit, Babe Ruth, Greatest Moments In Aurora, Box, Sealed, 9 x 14 In.	448.00
Baseball, Nodder, Baltimore Orioles, Mascot, Composition, Label, c.1961, 6 ½ In. .... *illus*	145.00
Baseball, Nodder, Roberto Clemente, Pittsburgh Pirates, c.1962, 6 In. .... *illus*	819.00
Baseball, Pen & Pencil Set, Wooden, Bill Dickey, Facsimile Signature, Atlantic Oil Co., 1930s, 6 In.	145.00
Baseball, Pennant, Boston Braves, N.L., Red, White, Blue Felt Letters, Frame, 1914, 32 In.	1600.00
Baseball, Pennant, George Burns Day, N.Y. Giants, Silk Screen, Utica, N.Y., June 14, 1914, 28 In. .. *illus*	538.00
Baseball, Pennant, Lou Brock, 3000 Hits, Red, Felt, 29 ½ In.	70.00
Baseball, Pin, Congratulations, Jackie Robinson, Brooklyn Dodgers, c.1947, 1 ¼ In. ...... *illus*	443.00
Baseball, Pin, Malarkey, Oakland P.C.L., Whitehead & Hoag, 1910s, 1 In. .... *illus*	415.00
Baseball, Pin, NY News, Say Hey, Willie Mays, Mets, 3 In.	58.00
Baseball, Plaque, Hall Of Fame, Bob Gibson, St. Louis Cardinals, 1981, 17 x 21 In.	1896.00
Baseball, Plaque, Pitcher Of The Year Award, Bob Gibson, 1970, 18 x 5 In.	563.00
Baseball, Poster, Lou Gehrig, Knot Hole League Of America, Goudey, 1934, 9 x 20 In.	28800.00
Baseball, Press Pin, 1939 World Series, New York Yankees, Enamel, Metal .... *illus*	598.00
Baseball, Program, 1927 World Series, Game 2, New York At Pittsburgh	4720.00
Baseball, Program, Baltimore Base Ball Club, October 7-8, 1895	2520.00
Baseball, Ring, Bob Gibson, Hall Of Fame, 10K Yellow Gold, 1981, Size 10 ½	30000.00
Baseball, Ring, New York Giants, 1922 World's Series, Size 11 ¼	58750.00
Baseball, Scorer, Umpire, Photo Of Babe Ruth, Boston Braves Cap, 1935, 1 ¾ In.	224.00
Baseball, Seat, Yankee Stadium, Autographed, Joe Torre, Phil Rizzuto, 1999, Pair	1003.00
Baseball, Stadium Seat, Wood, Iron, Numbers Stenciled, Blue Paint, 29 x 44 In., Pair	3081.00
Baseball, Sweater, Bill Hoffer, Baltimore Orioles, Navy Blue, Red Border, c.1895	24000.00
Baseball, Toy, N.Y. Yankees Catcher, Windup, Celluloid, Box, 1940s, 5 ½ In.	142.00
Baseball, Tray, St. Louis Cardinals, World Champions, Given To Bob Gibson, 2006, 12 ¾ In. ..	830.00
Baseball, Trophy, Earl Smith Award, Bob Gibson, 1981, 19 ¼ In.	237.00

Baseball, Tumbler, Baltimore Colts, Team Roster, 1964, 6 In., 8 Piece....................	175.00
Baseball, Uniform, Ted Williams, Washington Senators, Game Used, 1969, Size 40	10200.00
Baseball, Watch, Bob Gibson, Old Timer Game, 1986	830.00
Baseball, Watch Fob, Napoleon Lajoie, Celluloid, Portrait, 1908........................	822.00
Baseball, Watch Fob, N.Y. Yankees, 1923 World Championship, Gold Baseball........................	5310.00
Baseball, Wiffle Balls, Mantle & Mays, Champions Choice, Box, 1963, 3 x 9 x 3 In.	144.00
Basketball, Ball, Autographed, Chicago Bulls, Jordan's Rookie Year, 16 Signatures, 1984	1541.00
Basketball, Ball, Autographed, Michael Jordan	444.00
Basketball, Jacket, Pants, Michael Jordan, Warm Up, Chicago Bulls, 1990-91	4740.00
Basketball, Jersey, Autographed, Larry Bird	295.00
Basketball, Sneakers, Autographed, LeBron James, UDA Nike, Size 15	563.00
Basketball, Uniform, Shaquille O'Neal, Orlando Magic, 1994-95, Game Used........................	770.00
Boxing, Button, Joe Louis, Celluloid, Photo, Ribbon, Boxing Glove On Chain, 1 ¾ In.	85.00
Boxing, Button, Muhammad Ali, Float Like A Butterfly, Sting Like A Bee, Celluloid, 1978, ⅞ In.	44.00
Boxing, Button, Muhammad Ali, Signature, Float Like A Butterfly, Tan Ground, 2 ¼ In.	296.00
Boxing, Gloves, Autographed, Mike Tyson, Red, Everlast, Display Case	295.00
Football, Ball, Autographed, 1986 New York Giants, 44 Signatures, Display Case	496.00
Football, Ball, Autographed, Green Bay Packers, 44 Signatures, 1968	1007.00
Football, Ball, Autographed, Green Bay Packers, 45 Signatures, 1962	1659.00
Football, Ball, Super Bowl XI, Oakland Raiders Vs. Minn. Vikings, Game Used, 1977 .... *illus*	717.00
Football, Button, Army Navy Foot-Ball Game, Chicago, 1926, 2 ¼ In.	138.00
Football, Button, Cleveland Browns, Brownie, Orange, Black, White, Celluloid, 1 ¾ In.	28.00
Football, Button, Rose Bowl, Ohio State Buckeyes, Oval, Celluloid, 1985, 2 ¾ In.	13.00
Football, Helmet, Autographed, Joe Willie Namath, Wood & Glass Display Case	425.00
Football, Helmet, Autographed, Phil Simms, Wood & Glass Display Case.....................	236.00
Football, Helmet, Jack Youngblood, Los Angeles Rams, Yellow & Black, Game Used.................	610.00
Football, Helmet, Suspension, Bob Griese, Miami Dolphins, c.1970 .... *illus*	1778.00
Football, License Plate, Tennessee National Championship, 1951, Pair.....................	83.00
Football, Matchbook, Baltimore Colts, Maryland Match Co., c.1948 .... *illus*	474.00
Football, Nodder, Cincinnati Bengal, 1968........................	89.00
Football, Nodder, Detroit Lion, Blue Jersey, 1968	89.00
Football, Pennant, Los Angeles Rams, Team Photo, c.1960, 29 ½ x 4 ¾ In.	115.00
Football, Program, 3rd Annual All-Star Pro-Bowl Game, Jan. 10, 1953........................	200.00
Football, Program, 6th Annual All-Star Pro-Bowl, Frank Gifford On Cover, Jan. 15, 1956	200.00
Football, Program, Baltimore Colts At Minnesota Vikings, Unitas, Tarkenton, 11/14/65...........	38.00
Football, Program, Boston Patriots At Oakland Raiders, Oct. 6, 1968	49.50
Football, Program, Buffalo Bills At Oakland Raiders, Oct. 19, 1969........................	49.50
Football, Program, Chicago Cardinals At San Francisco 49ers, Charlie Trippi, Aug. 21, 1954...	35.00
Football, Program, Chicago Cardinals Vs. New York Giants, Don Heinrich, Oct. 17, 1954........	85.00
Football, Program, Dallas Cowboys At Minnesota Vikings, Don Meredith, Oct. 20, 1968	45.00
Football, Program, Detroit Lions At Chicago Bears, Oct. 22, 1961	21.00
Football, Program, Detroit Lions At Minnesota Vikings, Nov. 24, 1963........................	35.00
Football, Program, Los Angeles Rams At Minnesota Vikings, Gabriel Vs. Tarkenton, Oct. 16, 1966.	40.00
Football, Program, Los Angeles Rams At San Francisco 49ers, Nov. 30, 1952........................	35.00
Football, Program, Los Angeles Rams At San Francisco 49ers, Oct. 4, 1963........................	8.00
Football, Program, Los Angeles Rams At San Francisco 49ers, Oct. 5, 1958........................	21.00
Football, Program, Los Angeles Rams Vs. New York Giants, Elroy Hirsch, Aug. 8, 1954	60.00
Football, Program, New York Giants At Minnesota Vikings, Oct. 9, 1965........................	35.00
Football, Program, New York Giants At Minnesota Vikings, Tarkenton, Sept. 6, 1969........................	35.00
Football, Program, New York Giants At San Francisco 49ers, Aug. 19, 1962........................	28.00
Football, Program, Philadelphia Eagles At Chicago Cardinals, Oct. 25, 1953........................	35.00
Football, Program, Philadelphia Eagles At Chicago Cardinals, Oct. 3, 1954........................	30.00
Football, Program, Pittsburgh Steelers At Minnesota Vikings, Oct. 18, 1964	35.00
Football, Program, Pittsburgh Steelers At Oakland Raiders, Divisional Playoff, Dec. 22, 1973 .	5.00
Football, Program, San Francisco 49ers At Los Angeles Rams, Sept. 10, 1954........................	30.00
Football, Program, San Francisco 49ers At Minnesota Vikings, Sept. 23, 1963........................	38.00
Football, Program, Washington Redskins At Pittsburgh Steelers, Nov. 29, 1953........................	40.00
Football, Program, Washington Redskins Vs. Baltimore, 58 Pages, Aug. 3, 1966	28.00
Football, Washington Redskins Fact Book & Record 1988, Spiral Bound, Team Photo	15.00
Golf, Ball Holder, Ostrich Leather, Marker, Tees........................	125.00
Golf, Ball, Leather, Bird Feather, Hand Sewn, 1 ¾ In. .... *illus*	263.00
Golf, Ball, Scotch Feather Style, Stamped 7 Morris, Display Case, 19th Century	144.00
Golf, Owl Golf Balls, Red Ground, Owls, Cardboard Box, 3 Original Balls, 5 x 2 In.	303.00
Golf, Putter, Orvis 33, Bamboo Shaft, Leather Wrapped Handle, Stamp, 26 ½ In.	71.00
Hockey, Jersey, Autographed, Mark Messier, N.Y. Rangers, Stanley Cup Patch, 1994..................	224.00
Hockey, Jersey, Autographed, Wayne Gretzky, N.Y. Rangers................................	566.00

Spinning Wheel, Castle, Mixed Wood, Painted, Ring Turning, Penn., 55 In. $986.00

Spode, Platter, Blue Willow, Octagonal, Mark, c.1910, 21 x 16 In. $115.00

Sports, Baseball, Bank, Pittsburgh Pirates, Mascot, Stanford Pottery, 3 x 3 x 7 ½ In. $158.00

S

TIP
Postage stamps, produce seals, or other gummed paper pieces that have stuck together can be separated with this simple trick: put them in a freezer overnight. The glue will loosen.

Sports, Baseball, Button,
Pittsburg Pirates, N.L. Champions,
18 Faces, c.1909, 2 ¼ In.
$1404.00

Sports, Baseball, Figure, Roger Maris, Plastic,
Hartland, Box, c.1960
$1067.00

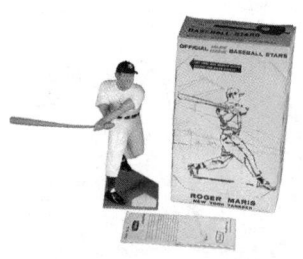

Sports, Baseball, Glove, First Baseman's,
Double-Buckle, Spalding, c.1912, 9 In.
$326.00

Sports, Baseball, Nodder, Baltimore Orioles,
Mascot, Composition, Label, c.1961, 6 ½ In.
$145.00

Sports, Baseball, Nodder,
Roberto Clemente, Pittsburgh Pirates,
c.1962, 6 In.
$819.00

Sports, Baseball, Pennant, George Burns Day,
N.Y. Giants, Silk Screen, Utica, N.Y.,
June 14, 1914, 28 In.
$538.00

Sports, Baseball, Pin, Congratulations, Jackie
Robinson, Brooklyn Dodgers, c.1947, 1 ¼ In.
$443.00

Sports, Baseball, Pin, Malarkey,
Oakland P.C.L., Whitehead & Hoag,
1910s, 1 In.
$415.00

Sports, Baseball, Press Pin, 1939 World Series,
New York Yankees, Enamel, Metal
$598.00

Sports, Football, Ball, Super Bowl XI, Oakland
Raiders Vs. Minn. Vikings, Game Used, 1977
$717.00

Sports, Football, Helmet, Suspension, Bob
Griese, Miami Dolphins, c.1970
$1778.00

Determining Baseball Card Value

Condition. Newer cards must be
in near-perfect condition to have
any value. Older cards in less-
than-perfect condition sell, but
the highest prices are for those in
excellent condition.

Unopened packs of cards sell
better than opened packs.

Topps has been making sets of
baseball cards since 1951. The
1952 Topps set is one of the most
valuable and is worth more than
$150,000.

S

Horse Racing, Cup, Mint Julep, Silver, Willie Shoemaker, Candy Spots, Horseshoe, 1963	2360.00
Horse Racing, Ice Bucket Trophy, Willie Shoemaker, Cicada, Sterling Silver, 1961, 10 In.	1298.00
Horse Racing, Tray Trophy, Belmont, Willie Shoemaker, Sword Dancer, Silver, 1959, 11 In. ...	1888.00
Horseback Riding, Tack & Saddle Tree, Chestnut, Finials, Chamfered Post, Arms, 92 ½ In. ...	353.00
Hunting, Box, Winchester Leader Shot Shell, Bird In Flight, 4 x 2 ½ x 4 In.	672.00
Hunting, Display, Peter's Victor Shot Shell Pop, 2 Hunting Dogs, Rifle, Shells, 26 x 20 In.	1344.00
Hunting, Duck Call, Duck Head, Feathered Texture, Glass Eyes, Tom Condo, 5 ½ In.	130.00
Hunting, Duck Call, Wood, Metal, Muchlistein, St. Paul, Minn., c.1932, 6 ½ In.	236.00
Hunting, License, California, 1916, Cast Lead Grizzly Bear, 2 ¾ x 1 ⅜ In.	125.00
Hunting, Pin, Dead Shot Smokeless Powder, Celluloid, ⅞ In.	45.00
Pool, Cue Holder, Base Rotates, Holds 10 Cues, Bronze, Brunswick, 61 In.	266.00
Pool, Cue Rack, Mahogany, Holds 8 Sticks, 3 Spool Feet, 8 Ball Handle, 29 ½ x 15 In.	550.00
Pool, Cue Rack, Mixed Wood, Round, Grape Cluster Finial, Center Pole, Spindles, 1800s, 62 x 20 In. ..	546.00
Pool, Cue Rack, Wood, 12 Holders, Brunswick, 55 x 28 In.	195.00
Pool, Table, Mahogany Frame, Gilded Cast-Iron Lion's-Head Base, Brunswick Monarch	23000.00
Skating, Ice Skates, No. 12, Metal, Winchester	25.00
Skating, Roller Skates, Wood Body, Rollers, Leather Bindings, Vineyard, c.1882, 10 ½ In.	235.00
Skiing, Skis, Oak, Varnished, Red Paint, Rubber Pad Boot Rest, 2 Straps, Child's, 1930s, 53 In. ...	70.00
Snowshoes, Cedar, Bentwood, Thong, c.1890, Child's, 26 x 5 ½ In. .... *illus*	69.00
Tennis, Tobacco Premium, Leather, Woman Holding Tennis & Racquet, Ball, Fringe, 9 In., c.1910 *illus*	448.00

STAFFORDSHIRE, England, has been a district making pottery and porcelain since the 1700s. Hundreds of kilns are still working in the area. Thousands of types of pottery and porcelain have been made in the many factories that worked and still work in the area. Some of the most famous factories have been listed separately, such as Adams, Davenport, Ridgway, Rowland & Marsellus, Royal Doulton, Royal Worcester, Spode, Wedgwood, and others. Some Staffordshire pieces are listed under categories like Fairing, Flow Blue, Mulberry, Shaving Mug, etc.

Bowl, Building, River, Leaves, Sepia Transfer, Scalloped Rim, Handles, Footed, 6 x 11 In.	395.00
Bowl, Caledonia, Black Transfer, Scalloped Edge, Scenic Border, 11 In.	88.00
Bowl, Earthworm, Beige Field, Blue Band, First Half 19th Century, 2 ½ x 4 ½ In.	173.00
Bowl, Fruit, Battle Of Monterey, Black Transfer, Texian Campaigne, J.B., 14 In.	1404.00
Bowl, Officers, Soldiers In Retreat, Purple Transfer, Texian Campaigne, A. Shaw, 13 In.	1989.00
Bowl, Red Border, Gray Ship Center, Ship Caroline, 1800, 5 x 10 In.	146.00
Bowl, Transfer, Blue, Octagon Church, Boston, Historic, Rose, Leaves, Handles, 11 In.	3105.00
Bowl, Vegetable, Alpine Amusement, Blue, White, Marked, Davenport, 3 In.	200.00
Bowl, Vegetable, Blue Transfer, Flower Border, Castle, People, 2 ½ x 9 x 7 In.	424.00
Bowl, Vegetable, Cover, Battle Of A Bridge, Brown Transfer, Texian Campaigne, J.B., 12 In.	1638.00
Casserole, Hen On Nest, Basket, Multicolored, Feathers, c.1910, 7 ½ x 9 In.	81.00
Chamber Set, Gloria Pattern, Blue & White, Dudson, Wilcox & Till, 1910, 17-In. Bowl	236.00
Coffeepot, Dome Top, Drape, Flower, Leaves, Multicolored....................................	495.00
Coffeepot, Strawberry, Pink Roses, Oval, 10 ¾ In.	960.00
Creamer, Flower, Bud, Vine	44.00
Creamer, Pagoda Helmet, Lake, Figures, Blue Transfer, 5 ¼ In.	110.00
Cup & Saucer, Battle Of Chapultepec, Purple Transfer, Texian Campaigne, J.B.	1053.00
Cup & Saucer, Lady Of The Lake, Copper Luster Band, Blue Transfer	33.00
Cup & Saucer, Mt. Vernon, Black Transfer, 12 Piece..	154.00
Cup & Saucer, Water Girl, Girl At Well, Seated Dog, Marked Clews	88.00
Cup & Saucer, Woodsman, Purple Transfer, Handleless	55.00
Dish, Cover, Bedfords Essex, Blue, White, c.1825	220.00
Figurine, Alas Poor Yorick, 11 In.	368.00
Figurine, Bedd Gelert, Dog Saves Boy From Snake, Mid 1800s, 6 & 6 ½ In., Pair..................	531.00
Figurine, Bocage Deer, Painted, c.1825, 6 In., Pair...	322.00
Figurine, Canary, Yellow, Green, c.1820, 2 In.	105.00
Figurine, Dandy Couple, Bocage Background, Flowers, Multicolored, 6 ½ x 3 ½ In. .... *illus*	541.00
Figurine, Dog, Black Pottery, 1800s, 14 In., Pair	480.00
Figurine, Dog, Dalmatian, Sitting, Oval Base, 4 ½ In., Pair...................................	518.00
Figurine, Dog, Hound, On Cushion, Brown, Cream, Green, Ralph Wood, 1790, 7 In., Pair	6000.00
Figurine, Dog, Poodle, Standing, Basket In Mouth, Late 19th Century, 11 ½ x 10 ½ In.	374.00
Figurine, Dog, Pug, Brown To Tan Mottled Glaze, Glass Eyes, Gilt, 12 x 9 ½ In. .... *illus*	236.00
Figurine, Dog, Spaniel, 5 ½ In., Pair	86.00
Figurine, Dog, Spaniel, Dark Brown Glaze, Yellow Ground, Round Base, 16 ¾ In., Pair..........	1840.00
Figurine, Dog, Spaniel, Gold Collar & Highlights, Early 1900s, 12 ½ In., Pair	110.00
Figurine, Dog, Spaniel, Orange & Ivory Matte Glaze, 10 x 13 In., Pair	115.00
Figurine, Dog, Spaniel, Seated, Glass Eyes, Gilded, 19th Century, 14 In.	113.00
Figurine, Dog, Spaniel, Seated, Glazed Stoneware, White, Gilt, 1800s, 9 In., Pair	236.00
Figurine, Dog, Spaniel, Seated, Red Patches, White, Gilt, 1800s, 9 In., Pair...................	354.00

Sports, Football, Matchbook, Baltimore Colts, Maryland Match Co., c.1948
$474.00

Sports, Golf, Ball, Leather, Bird Feather, Hand Sewn, 1 ¾ In.
$263.00

Sports, Snowshoes, Cedar, Bentwood, Thong, c.1890, Child's, 26 x 5 ½ In.
$69.00

Sports, Tennis, Tobacco Premium, Leather, Woman Holding Tennis & Racquet, Ball, Fringe, 9 In., c.1910
$448.00

S

611

STAFFORDSHIRE

Staffordshire, Figurine, Dandy Couple, Bocage Background, Flowers, Multicolored, 6 ½ x 3 ½ In. **$541.00**

Staffordshire, Figurine, Dog, Pug, Brown To Tan Mottled Glaze, Glass Eyes, Gilt, 12 x 9 ½ In. **$236.00**

Staffordshire, Figurine, Wallace, Painted, Flatback, Victorian, 16 x 8 In. **$127.00**

Figurine, Eng & Chang, World's First Siamese Twins, 3 ½ In.	78.00
Figurine, Hawk, Perched On Stump, Salt Glaze, Blue, White, c.1750, 6 In.	7110.00
Figurine, Hen On Nest, Multicolored, 19th Century, 6 ¾ x 7 ½ x 5 ½ In.	57.00
Figurine, Hen On Nest, Multicolored, 19th Century, 7 ¼ x 9 ½ x 7 ¼ In.	90.00
Figurine, Hen On Nest, Multicolored, 19th Century, 8 x 9 ¾ x 7 In.	124.00
Figurine, Hen On Nest, Multicolored, 19th Century, 8 ¼ x 9 ¼ x 6 ⅝ In.	311.00
Figurine, Hen On Nest, Multicolored, 19th Century, 8 ½ x 11 x 7 ¾ In.	283.00
Figurine, Lion, Standing, Brown, Glass Eyes, Base, c.1900, Pair, 11 x 13 In.	323.00
Figurine, Lion, Tongue Out, Paw On Globe, Green Glaze, Marble Base, 9 In., Pair	2300.00
Figurine, Louis Napoleon, Standing, Military Uniform, Holding Hat, 1800s, 16 ½ In.	200.00
Figurine, Man, Woman, Riding Goats, Multicolored, 20th Century, 7 In., Pair	127.00
Figurine, Squirrel, Seated, Eating Nut, Green, Yellow, Brown, Cream Ground, c.1770, 7 ¼ In.	7605.00
Figurine, Swan, Yellow, Brown, Green, Cream, c.1790, 4 ½ In.	1200.00
Figurine, Wallace, Painted, Flatback, Victorian, 16 x 8 In. *illus*	127.00
Figurine, Woman, Riding Side Saddle, On Galloping Horse, 19th Century, 7 ½ In.	50.00
Group, Bird, Young Bird, Perched On Stump, Rockwork Base, Snail, 8 In.	4313.00
Group, Dr. Syntax Playing Cards, 2 Players, Brick Arch, Grapevine, 6 In.	1150.00
Group, Friendship, Boys, Tree, Dog, Multicolored Enamel, Walton Bocage, c.1820, 7 In.	504.00
Group, Man On Horse, Drawing Sword, Marbelized Base, Pink Rope Twist, 12 In.	1840.00
Group, Milkmaid, Sheep, Blue, Yellow, Brown, Cream, 6 ¼ In.	1900.00
Group, Vicar & Moses, Vicar Asleep On Pulpit, Moses Reading, 9 ¾ In.	489.00
Jug, Brig, Stormy Seas, When The First Sea Struck Her, The Second, c.1800, 9 ³⁄₁₆ In.	10530.00
Jug, Cavalier, Seated, Hat Cover, 19th Century, 10 In.	131.00
Jug, Girl At Well, Holding Pitcher, Dog, Landscape, Bulbous, Blue Transfer, 6 ¼ In.	254.00
Jug, Lord Nelson, Multicolored Glaze, Gilt, 19th Century, 10 In.	115.00
Jug, Milk, Cover, Solid Agateware, Pear Shape, Brown, Tan, Gray, Green, c.1760, 6 In.	356.00
Jug, Portrait, Thomas Jefferson, Great Seal Of United States, 10 ¹⁄₁₆ In.	9360.00
Jug, Portraits, Oliver H. Perry, Z.M. Pike, Pink Luster, Black Transfer, c.1816, 8 In.	9360.00
Mug, Boy, Riding Horse, Girl Playing Hoop, Transfer, Child's, 2 ¾ In.	99.00
Mug, Frog, Flowers, Verse, George Wrightson Died, Aged 20 Months, 1825, 6 In.	207.00
Mug, Stag, Deer In Stream, Cottage, Village, Castle Scene, Shaped Handle, 5 ¼ In.	203.00
Pitcher, Blue, Erie Canal, 9 ½ In.	1170.00
Pitcher, Hounds Chasing Stag, Relief, Full Frog Interior, W.D. Watts, 1800s, 9 In.	770.00
Pitcher, Landing Of General Lafayette At Castle Garden, Blue, Clews, 1818-34, 8 ½ In.	1783.00
Pitcher, Wash Basin, Water Girl, Flower Border, Clews, 1818-34, Pitcher 10 In., Bowl 13 In.	920.00
Pitcher, Water, Flowers, Leaves, Bulbous, Scrolled Handle, 10 In.	110.00
Pitcher, Water, Persian Palace, Green, Red Transfer, Bulbous, 8 In.	330.00
Pitcher, Water, Shell, Flower, Bulbous, Shaped Handle, 8 In.	79.00
Pitcher, Welcome LaFayette, Nation's Guest, Dark Blue, Clews, 6 ½ In.	1700.00
Plaque, Apollo In Garden, Temple, Enamel, Transfer, Frame, Metal, c.1770, 3 x 3 ¾ In.	345.00
Plate, 3 Figures Washing Clothes, Landscape, Blue Transfer, 9 ¼ In.	424.00
Plate, 15 States, America & Independence, Blue & White, Clews, c.1820, 10 ½ In.	495.00
Plate, Abbey, Red & White Transfer, George Jones & Sons, c.1890, 10 ½ In.	65.00
Plate, Aesthetic, Bamboo, Blue, c.1875, 10 ½ In.	50.00
Plate, Alphabet, Clock Face, 52 Weeks, Blue & White, c.1887, 7 ⅝ In.	200.00
Plate, America & Independence, Swags Of 15 States, Blue Transfer, Clews, 10 In.	345.00
Plate, Ancient Greece, Scalloped Edge, Black Transfer, 9 ½ In.	44.00
Plate, Bank Of U.S., Eagle & Flower Border, Blue, c.1800, 10 ¼ In.	352.00
Plate, Boston State House, Cows, Trees, Blue Transfer, 10 ¼ In.	275.00
Plate, Caledonia, Green, Red Transfer, Scalloped Edge, 9 ½ In.	165.00
Plate, City Hall, New York, Blue Transfer, 9 ¾ In.	358.00
Plate, Columbia, Eagle Of The Republic, Washington's Tomb, 10 In.	690.00
Plate, Commodore MacDonnough's Victory, Shell, Flower Border, 10 In.	192.00
Plate, Cottage View, Pastoral, Boating Scene, 6 ¾ In.	143.00
Plate, Dinner, Flowers, Blue, 1802-28, 10 In., Pair	201.00
Plate, Don Quixote & Sancho Panza, Blue Transfer, 9 In., 6 Piece	440.00
Plate, Don Quixote & Shepherdesses, Blue Transfer, 9 In.	99.00
Plate, Dr. Syntax Reading, Flower, Leaf Border, Blue Transfer, Clews, 9 In.	136.00
Plate, Eagle, Blue Transfer, Podmore Walker & Sons, 1850s, 8 ¾ In.	75.00
Plate, Flowers, Leaf Border, Man, Camel, 3 Pyramids, Blue Transfer, 8 ½ In.	28.00
Plate, Gilpins Mills On The Brandywine Creek, Blue, 9 ¼ In.	439.00
Plate, Historic Carolina, Urn, Birds, Boats, Buildings, Red, 8 In., Pair	259.00
Plate, Hope, Seated On Shore, Gazing At Sailing Ship, Transfer, 9 ½ In.	115.00
Plate, Landing Of General LaFayette, Blue Transfer, Impressed Clews, c.1830, 9 In.	345.00 to 382.00
Plate, Old City Gate, St. Augustine, Gold Rim, Blue Transfer, 8 ¾ In.	90.00
Plate, Peace & Plenty, Blue & White, Clews, 10 ¼ In. *illus*	439.00

Plate, Peace & Plenty, Blue, 1818-36, 9 In.		270.00
Plate, Regent, Multicolored Transfer, Bates Gildea & Walker, c.1880, 9 In.		35.00
Plate, Scalloped Edge, 2 Story Structure, Blue Transfer, 8 In.		330.00
Plate, Soup, City Of Albany, Blue Transfer, 9 ¼ In.		303.00
Plate, Soup, Landing Of Lafayette, Flower Border, Clews, 8 ⅝ In.		192.00
Plate, Soup, Romantic View, Castle Ruin Scene, 10 In.		65.00
Plate, Soup, Valentine From Wilkie's Design, Flower Border, Clews, 7 ⅝ In.		68.00
Plate, Soup, Villa In Regents Park, Blue Transfer, 10 In.		88.00
Plate, South Carolina Arms, Palmetto Tree, Thomas Mayer, 7 ¼ In.	*illus*	1380.00
Plate, States, Scalloped Edge, 3-Story Building, Observatory, Clews, 10 ¾ In.		283.00
Plate, Strawberries Basket, Queen's Rose, Flower Vine Border, 7 In.		113.00
Plate, Table Lock Niagara, Shell, Leaf Border, Blue Transfer, 10 In.		254.00
Plate, Thomas, Flower Border, Black Transfer, 19th Century, 5 In.		60.00
Plate, University Building, 6 Sections, Scalloped Edge, Blue Transfer, 8 ¾ In.		237.00
Plate, Woman Walking In Forest, Basket, The Pride Of The Village, Impressed, 5 ¼ In.		65.00
Platter, Albion, Blue Transfer, Impressed Crown, 13 ⅝ x 16 ⅝ In.		57.00
Platter, Asian Scene, Zebra, Blue Transfer, Rogers, 1800s, 15 In.		117.00
Platter, Battle Of Resaca De La Palma, Blue, Texian Campaigne, J.B., 17 In.		1638.00
Platter, Cape Coast Castle, Gold Coast Africa, Wood & Sons, 16 ½ In.		1140.00
Platter, Castle, Bridge, Vignette Pattern, Wood Stand, Queen Anne Legs, 19 ¾ x 16 x 19 ½ In.		920.00
Platter, Figural Landscape, Trajan's Column, Blue & White, c.1840, 17 x 12 ½ In.		196.00
Platter, Florentine Villas, Blue, White, Scalloped Rim, Marked, Jackson Warranted, 14 x 18 In.		120.00
Platter, Georgia Arms, 3 Females, Wisdom, Justice, Moderation, Seacoast, Blue, 13 In.		5520.00
Platter, Goddesses, Sailing Ships, North Carolina, Blue, T. Mayer, 15 In.		2190.00
Platter, Hoboken, House, Figures, Sheep, 12 ½ In.		230.00
Platter, House, States, American Independence Figures, Blue, Clews, c.1825, 14 x 17 In.		1058.00
Platter, Kent, Blue Transfer, Swinerton, 15 ½ x 11 ¾ In.		75.00
Platter, Oriental Scenery, Blue, White, Transfer, Stamped, Mayer, 19 In.		220.00
Platter, Pennsylvania Treaty, Blue & White, 13 ¾ x 17 In.	*illus*	497.00
Platter, View Of New York City, Governor's Island, 20 ½ In.		5200.00
Platter, Winter View Of Pittsfield, Mass., Dark Blue, Flower Border, 15 x 12 In.		520.00
Sauceboat, White Enamel Salt Glaze, Basket Weave, Scrolls, Multicolored, 6 ½ In.		830.00
Soup, Dish, DeFete, Gray Transfer, Knight Elkin & Co., c.1846, 10 ¼ In.		65.00
Sugar & Creamer, Blue Transfer, Asian Scenes, Flowers, Blossom Finial, Clews, c.1820, 6 In.		207.00
Sugar, Cover, Applied Scroll Shell Handles, Seashell, Flowers, Scroll Border, 7 In.		147.00
Sugar, Cover, Pastoral Scene, Sheep, Blue Transfer, 6 In.		66.00
Sugar, Dome Cover, Woman Feeding Chicken, Village Scene, Drop Ring Handles, 7 In.		79.00
Tea Container, Green Glaze, Rectangular, Rope Framed Panels, Dots, Stars, c.1750, 45 In.		1067.00
Teapot, Cover, Globe Shape, Crabstock Handle, White, Multicolored Flowers, 4 In.		178.00
Teapot, Cover, Globe Shape, Leaf Mold Spout, Entwined Handle, Flowers, c.1765, 4 In.		593.00
Teapot, Cover, Lead Glaze Cauliflower, Globe Shape, Cream Flowers, Leaves, 1700s, 4 In.		474.00
Teapot, Cover, Salt Glaze, Lobed, Reeded Handle, Houses, Sheep, Cows, c.1760, 5 In.		1659.00
Teapot, Cover, Salt Glaze, Pecan Shell, Molded Serpent Spout, 3 Claw Feet, c.1775, 4 In.		1304.00
Teapot, Cover, Solid Agate, Globe Shape, Lion Mask, Paw Feet, Blue, Brown, Tan, c.1760, 5 In.		830.00
Teapot, Cover, Stoneware, Salt Glaze, Houses, Flowers, Orange, Green, Paw Feet, c.1755, 4 In.		1304.00
Teapot, Flower, Vase Design, Blue Transfer, 7 In.		99.00
Teapot, Little Old Lady, Purple Skirt, Red & Green Cape, Bonnet, 8 In.		47.00
Teapot, Officer & Men At Rest, Campfire, Purple Transfer, Texian Campaigne, J.B., 7 In.		1989.00
Teapot, Virginia Church, Boy Fishing, Floral Borders, Blue, 7 ¾ In.		690.00
Teapot, Washington Standing, Monument, Beehive Finial, Blue, 12 ¾ In.		4830.00
Tile, Purple Iris, 19th Century, 14 x 14 In.		82.00
Toby Jugs are listed in their own category.		
Toddy Plate, Christmas Eve, Blue Transfer, Clews, 6 ¾ In.		170.00
Toddy Plate, Commodore MacDonnough's Victory, Blue Transfer, 6 ½ In.		136.00
Toddy Plate, Transferware, Cabins, c.1819, 5 In.		117.00
Tureen, Cover, Exchange Charleston, Bank Savannah, c.1825, 7 ¼ x 8 ½ In.	*illus*	4830.00
Tureen, Cover, Stand, Battle Of Buena Vista, Blue, White, Texian Campaigne, J.B., 7 x 8 In.		3803.00
Tureen, Cover, Stand, Battle, Resaca De La Palma, Blue, White, Texian Campaigne, J.B., 13 x 14 In.		11115.00
Tureen, Soup, Cover, Tray, Ladle, Views Of The Hudson, Blue, c.1818-46		14950.00
Vase, Cow Form, Standing By Tree Trunk, Grass, Ferns, 10 x 18 In.		2300.00
Vase, Spill, Boy With Dogs, Sitting Under Tree, 6 ½ In.		275.00
Vase, Spill, Lamb, Multicolored, 19th Century, 4 ⅞ x 4 ¼ In., Pair		136.00
Waste Bowl, Hunt Scene, 2 Men Loading Guns, 2 Dogs, Bird, Flower Border, 9 ¾ In.		147.00
Waste Bowl, Hunt Scene, Dog Chasing Stag, Flower, Blue Transfer, 3 ¼ x 6 ¼ In.		113.00
Waste Bowl, Lafayette At Tomb Of Franklin, Flower Border, Blue Transfer, 3 ¼ x 6 ¼ In.		311.00

Staffordshire, Plate, Peace & Plenty, Blue & White, Clews, 10 ¼ In.
$439.00

Staffordshire, Plate, South Carolina Arms, Palmetto Tree, Thomas Mayer, 7 ¼ In.
$1380.00

Staffordshire, Platter, Pennsylvania Treaty, Blue & White, 13 ¾ x 17 In.
$497.00

Staffordshire, Tureen, Cover, Exchange Charleston, Bank Savannah, c.1825, 7 ¼ x 8 ½ In.
$4830.00

S

Stangl, Bird, Bluebirds, Double, No. 3276D, Oval, 7 ¾ In. $40.00

Stangl, Bird, Chickadees, Double, No. 3581D, 8 ¾ x 5 ½ In. $58.00

Stangl, Wig Stand, Woman, Short Red Hair, Incised, 15 In. $322.00

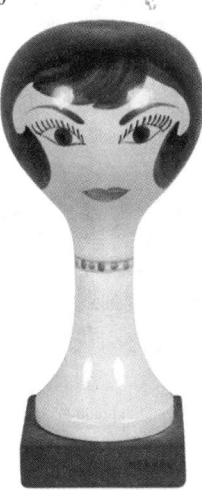

A Confusing Mark

Another way around the law: A town in the Philippines changed its name to Zuni so it can mark the Indian-style jewelry it makes "Made in Zuni." The mark could fool people into thinking the jewelry was made by Zuni Indians.

STANGL POTTERY traces its history back to the Fulper Pottery of New Jersey. In 1910, Johann Martin Stangl started working at Fulper. He left to work at Haeger Pottery from 1915 to 1920. Stangl returned to Fulper Pottery in 1920, became president in 1926, and changed the company name to Stangl Pottery in 1929. Stangl acquired the firm in 1930. The pottery is known for dinnerware and a line of bird figurines. Martin Stangl died in 1972 and the pottery was sold to Frank Wheaton, Jr., of Wheaton Industries. Production continued until 1978, when Pfaltzgraff Pottery purchased the right to the Stangl trademark and the remaining inventory was liquidated. A single bird figurine is identified by a number. Figurines made up of two birds are identified by a number followed by the letter *D* indicating Double.

Bird, Blue Jay, Leaf, No. 3716, Marked, 10 In.	490.00
Bird, Bluebirds, Double, No. 3276D, Oval, 7 ¾ In. .... *illus*	40.00
Bird, Bunting, Painted, 4 ½ x 6 In.	125.00
Bird, Chickadees, Double, No. 3581D, 8 ¾ x 5 ½ In. .... *illus*	58.00
Bird, Cockatoo, No. 3405, Impressed Mark, 6 ¼ In.	69.00
Bird, Duck, Quacking, No. 3250, Marked Stangl F, 3 ⅝ In.	40.00
Bird, Fish Hawk, No. 3459, Impressed Mark, 10 x 11 In.	4500.00
Bird, Painted Bunting, No. 3452.	43.00
Bird, Parakeets, Double, No. 3582D, 7 In.	180.00
Bird, Penguin, No. 3274, 6 In.	480.00
Bird, Red-Headed Woodpecker, Double, No. 3729D, Marked, 8 In.	3000.00
Bird, Rooster, No. 3425, 16 In.	1320.00
Bird, Rooster, No. 3435, 16 In.	8400.00
Bird, Vermilion Flycatcher, No. 3923, Marked, 5 ¾ In.	2760.00
Bird, Yellow Warbler, No. 3820	67.00
Elephant, Black, Trunk Raised, 5 In.	60.00
Fruit & Flowers, Gravy Boat, Underplate, Brown Interior	27.00
Plate, Little Quackers, White Ground, Blue Center, Yellow Ducks, Kiddieware, Marked, 9 In. ...	140.00
Wig Stand, Woman, Short Brown Hair, 15 In.	275.00
Wig Stand, Woman, Short Red Hair, Incised, 15 In. .... *illus*	322.00

STAR TREK AND STAR WARS collectibles are included here. The original *Star Trek* television series ran from 1966 through 1969. The series spawned an animated TV series, three TV sequels, and a TV prequel. The first Star Trek movie was released in 1979 and ten others followed, the most recent in 2009. The movie *Star Wars* opened in 1977. Sequels were released in 1980 and 1983; prequels in 1999, 2002, and 2005. Other science fiction and fantasy collectibles can be found under Batman, Buck Rogers, Captain Marvel, Flash Gordon, Movie, Superman, and Toy.

STAR TREK

Beer Stein, 3D Sculptures, Engraving, Chekov Image, 5 ½ x 4 ¼ In.	30.00
Board Game, Ideal, c.1967, 10 x 20 In.	55.00
Book, Star Fleet Technical Manual, 20th Anniversary, Franz Joseph, Del Rey, c.1986	20.00
Card, Teeny Bopper, Spock, McCoy, No. 23, Leaf, c.1967 .... *illus*	1422.00
Comic Book, Volume 4, Golden Press, Racine, Wisconsin, c.1977, 6 ½ x 10 ¼ In.	19.00
Doll, Mr. Spock, Posable, Packaging, Mego, c.1974, 8 In.	150.00
Game, Board, Cards, Discs, Die, Ideal, Unused, c.1967, 10 x 19 ½ In. .... *illus*	115.00
Ornament, Klingon Bird Of Prey, Packaging, Keepsake, Hallmark, c.1994	29.00
Ornament, Mr. Spock, Box, Keepsake, Hallmark, c.1996, 2 ½ In.	18.00
Ornament, Shuttlecraft Galileo, Lights Up, Mr. Spock's Voice, Keepsake, Hallmark, c.1992	25.00
Ornament, Vulcan Command Ship, Lights Up, Keepsake, Hallmark, C.2004	24.00
Plate, Beam Us Down Scotty, Hamilton, Box, c.1983, 8 ¾ In.	55.00
Plate, Spock, 23K Gold Rim, No. 2013J, Hamilton, Box, c.1991, 8 ¾ In.	75.00
Plate, USS Enterprise NCC 1701, 23 K Gold Rim, Hamilton, c.1983, 10 ¼ In.	110.00
Puzzle, Kirk, Bones, Chekov, Scotty, Whitman Western, Paramount, c.1978, 200 Piece	26.00
Sketch, Costume, Mixed Media, Star Trek: The Motion Picture, c.1978, 11 x 17 In.	950.00
View-Master, Mr. Spock's Time Trek, No. B555, Paramount, c.1974, 3 Reel Set	15.00

STAR WARS

Figure, Boba Fett, Box, Kenner, 13 In.	200.00
Figure, IG-88, Bounty Hunter, Empire Strikes Back, On Card, 4 ½ In.	30.00
Figure, Luke Skywalker, Return Of The Jedi, Blister Card, Lucasfilm, 1983, 3 ¾ In.	127.00
Figure, Power Droid, No. 39090, On Card, Kenner, 3 In.	72.00
Figure, Storm Trooper, Posable, Laser Rifle, Box, Kenner, c.1979, 12 In. .... *illus*	345.00
Lobby Display, Yoda, Pepsi-Cola Promotion, Plastic Base, Rubber, Canvas, 56 x 24 In.	1800.00
Lunch Box, Airship, Droids, 2-Sided, Metal, Thermos, 1977	150.00
Puppet, Yoda, Full-Bodied, Molded Vinyl With Silky White Hair, Kenner, 1980	90.00
Wristwatch, Darth Vader, Holographic Dial, Third Dimension Arts, c.1990, 1 ¼ In.	115.00
Wristwatch, Plastic Case, Vinyl Straps, Bradley Time, Chromed Face 1 ⅛ In., c.1977 ...... *illus*	345.00

STEINS have been used by beer and ale drinkers for over 500 years. They have been made of ivory, porcelain, stoneware, faience, silver, pewter, wood, or glass in sizes up to nine gallons. Although some were made by Mettlach, Meissen, Capo-di-Monte, and other famous factories, most were made by less important German potteries. The words *Geschutz* or *Musterschutz* on a stein are the German words for "patented" or "registered design," not company names. Steins are still being made in the old styles. Lithophane steins may be found in the Lithophane category.

Anheuser-Busch, Tavern Scene, Cermarte, 1976, 8 In.		45.00
Brew House, 1st Landmark Series, Ceramarte, 7 ½ In.		25.00
Budweiser, Hofbrau Style, Barley, Hops, Relief, 1996, 6 ½ In.		28.00
Budweiser, Holiday, Ceramarte, 1985, 6 ½ In.		20.00
Budweiser, Holiday, Ceramarte, 1986, 6 ½ In.		20.00
Budweiser, Holiday, Ceramarte, 1987, 6 ½ In.		20.00
Character, Artillery Shell, Stoneware, Pewter & Brass Lid, Marked, J. Reinemann, ½ Liter		368.00
Character, Bismarck, Porcelain Inlaid Lid, Porcelain, ½ Liter	431.00 to	978.00
Character, Bowling Pin, Pottery, Marked, Schierholz, ½ Liter		92.00
Character, Cat On Book, Porcelain, E. Bohne & Sohne, ½ Liter		2013.00
Character, Cat, With Hangover, Porcelain, Inlaid Lid, Marked, Musterschutz, Schierholz, ½ Liter		345.00
Character, Cat With Seltzer Bottle, Pottery, ½ Liter		431.00
Character, Cavalier, Stoneware, 1 ½ Liter		276.00
Character, Clown, Hanke, Porcelain, ½ Liter		140.00
Character, Drunk Monkey, Porcelain, Inlaid Lid, Musterschutz, Schierholz, ½ Liter.	196.00 to	219.00
Character, Dutch Man & Women, Pottery, Marked C.F., 1 Liter		201.00
Character, East Berlin City Hall, Porcelain, ½ Liter		719.00
Character, Frauenkirche Tower, Purple Salt Glaze, Stoneware, Pewter Strap, Marked, T.W., 1 Liter		150.00
Character, Gentleman Rabbit, Porcelain, Marked, Musterschutz, Schierholz, ½ Liter		2415.00
Character, Hops Lady, Leaves In Hair, Prosit, Pottery, Musterschutz, Schierholz, ½ Liter		184.00
Character, Monk, Molded Body, Incised Design, Reinhold Hanke, 1880s, ½ Liter		197.00
Character, Monk, Porcelain, Lithophane, Inlaid Lid, ½ Liter		127.00
Character, Monk, Pottery, ¼ Liter		127.00
Character, Monkey With Apple, Porcelain, Marked, E. Bohne & Sohne, ½ Liter		2990.00
Character, Monkey With Banjo, Pottery, ½ Liter		127.00
Character, Monkey With Boot, Pottery, ½ Liter		431.00
Character, Munich Child, Black Robe, Pottery, Porcelain Inlaid Lid, Marked, ½ Liter		253.00
Character, Munich Child, On Barrel, Porcelain, ½ Liter	150.00 to	242.00
Character, Munich Child, On Barrel, Porcelain, Musterschutz, Schierholz, ½ Liter	690.00 to	891.00
Character, Nurnberger Trichter, Porcelain, Lithophane, Marked, Musterschutz, Schierholz, ½ Liter..		403.00
Character, Owl, Inlaid Lid, Porcelain, E. Bohne & Sohne, ½ Liter		1610.00
Character, Owl, Pottery, Inlaid Lid, Marked, ½ Liter		161.00
Character, Sad Radish, Porcelain, Marked, Musterschutz, Schierholz, ⅓ Liter		127.00
Character, Sailor, Hamburg Ship's Name On Cap, Pottery, Music Box, Marked, Germany, ½ Liter.		518.00
Character, Sleepy Hunter, Porcelain, G. Bauer, ½ Liter		920.00
Character, Smiling Woman, Porcelain, Marked, Musterschutz, Schierholz, ½ Liter		1955.00
Character, Snake & Apple, Porcelain, Inlaid Lid, ½ Liter		920.00
Character, Soldier, Porcelain, Musterschutz, ½ Liter		834.00
Character, Stoneware, Brewer, Hauber & Reuther, Inlaid Lid, ½ In.		403.00
Character, Stoneware, Clown, ½ Liter		518.00
Character, Stoneware, Iron Maiden, ½ Liter		276.00
Character, Stoneware, Knight, Marked F & M, Inlaid Lid, ½ Liter	161.00 to	345.00
Character, Stoneware, Owl, Inlaid Lid, ½ Liter	242.00 to	435.00
Character, Stoneware, Woman On Stump, Inlaid Lid, ½ Liter		357.00
Faience, Bird With Flower, Pewter Lid, Foot Ring, 1700s, 1 Liter, 9 ½ In.		1495.00
Faience, Child Under Tree, Grasshopper, Pewter Lid & Footring, c.1700s, 1 Liter, 8 In.		403.00
Faience, Flower, Pewter Lid & Footring, Thuringen, 1783, 1 Liter, 10 In.		690.00
Faience, Fox, Pewter Lid, Footring & Vertical Handle Strap, c.1775, 1 Liter, 10 In.		978.00
Faience, Man Fishing, Pewter Lid & Footring, Bayreuth, c.1750, 1 Liter, 9 In.		920.00
Faience, Man Walking, Gmunden, Pewter Lid & Footring, c.1775, 1 Liter, 10 In.		1006.00
Faience, Religious Scene, Pewter Lid, Loebersdorf, c.1775, 1 Liter, 10 In.		1265.00
Faience, Woman With Butterfly Net, Pewter Lid, Foot Ring, c.1800, 1 ¼ Liter, 10 ½ In.		575.00
Fosters Lager, Westminster Stoneware, 5 ⅛ In.		18.00
Fountain Dispenser, Anheuser-Busch, Marked Patented December 5th, 1919, 10 In.		489.00
Glass, Blown, Blue & White On Clear, Inlaid Lid, c.1850, ½ Liter		891.00
Glass, Blown, Clear, Coat Of Arms, Enameled, Ostrich, Horseshoes, Pewter Lid, ¼ Liter		138.00
Glass, Blown, Clear, Cut, Engraved, Mercury Pewter Lid, Anchor Thumblift, Mid 1800s, ½ Liter.		265.00
Glass, Blown, Clear, Fluted, Carved Antler, Dog, Pewter Lid, ½ Liter		253.00
Glass, Blown, Clear, Fluted, Coin In Bottom, 1 Crona 1848, Pewter Lid, ½ Liter		150.00
Glass, Blown, Clear, Green Prunts, Pewter Lid, Cat Finial, ½ Liter		138.00

Star Trek, Card, Teeny Bopper, Spock, McCoy, No. 23, Leaf, c.1967
$1422.00

Star Trek, Game, Board, Cards, Discs, Die, Ideal, Unused, c.1967, 10 x 19 ½ In.
$115.00

Star Wars, Figure, Storm Trooper, Posable, Laser Rifle, Box, Kenner, c.1979, 12 In.
$345.00

Star Wars, Wristwatch, Plastic Case, Vinyl Straps, Bradley Time, Chromed Face 1 ⅛ In., c.1977
$345.00

S

Stein, Regimental, Inft. Regt.,
Nr. 135, Diedenhofen, Hillebrand,
1912-14, 11 ½ In.
$210.00

Stein, Regimental, Roster,
Eagle Thumbprint, Gren. Regt., Nr. 109,
Karlsruhe, Sotzel, 1911-13, 12 In.
$210.00

Stein, Regimental, Roster,
Eagle Thumbprint, Inft. Regt., Nr. 81,
Frankfurt, Appel, 1902-04, 11 In.
$180.00

Glass, Blown, Clear, Red Overlay, Double Porcelain Inlaid Lid, c.1860, ½ Liter	403.00
Glass, Blown, Clear, Red Staining, Spa, Engraved, Mid 1800s, 2 Liter	196.00
Glass, Blown, Clear, White & Pink Enamel Overlay, Inlaid Lid, 2 Liter	253.00
Glass, Blown, Clear, White Interior, Purple Overlay, Gilded, Inlaid Lid, c.1850, ½ Liter	1783.00
Glass, Blown, Coat Of Arms, Blue & White On Clear, Porcelain Inlaid Lid, c.1850, ¾ Liter, 6 In.	2530.00
Glass, Blown, Coat-Of-Arms, Amber, Pewter Lid, ½ Liter	115.00
Glass, Blown, Cobalt Blue, Hand Painted Flower, Liebe, Pewter Lid, 1800, ½ Liter	288.00
Glass, Blown, Cranberry, Pewter Lid, Base, ½ Liter	138.00
Glass, Blown, Defregger Style Scene, Transfer & Enameled, Pewter Lid & Base Ring, 1921, 1 Liter	546.00
Glass, Blown, Faceted, Castle, Hand Painted, Porcelain Inlaid Lid, c.1870, ½ Liter	115.00
Glass, Blown, Green Opaline, Inlaid Lid, c.1870, ½ Liter	345.00
Glass, Blown, Hunter, Dog, Deer, Clear To Purple, Pewter Lid, c.1875, ½ Liter	690.00
Glass, Blown, Knight, Pale Green, Hand Painted, V. Hauten, Pewter Lid, 1 ½ Liter	403.00
Glass, Blown, Man With Beer Stein, Pipe, White, Blue Cased, Cut Porcelain Inlaid Lid, ½ Liter	219.00
Glass, Blown, Mary Gregory Style, Child, Inlaid Lid, Thumbprint, Blue, ¼ Liter	150.00
Glass, Blown, Milk Glass, Dead Fox, Enameled, Pewter Lid, c.1775, 1 Liter	690.00
Glass, Blown, Milk Glass, Father With Child, Enameled, Pewter Lid & Base Ring, 1 Liter, 10 In.	1265.00
Glass, Blown, Milk Glass, Flowers, Enameled, Pewter Lid & Footring, c.1800, 1 Liter	518.00
Glass, Blown, Orange, Thumbprint, Pewter Overlay, Pewter Lid, 3 Liter, 15 In.	460.00
Glass, Blown, Pink & White On Clear, Silver Lid, ½ Liter	1035.00
Glass, Blown, Red Clear Overlay, Cut, Porcelain Inlaid Lid, Hand Painted, ½ Liter	253.00
Glass, Blown, Red Inlaid Lid, Red Flashed, Enameled, ¼ Liter	150.00
Glass, Blown, Red, Pewter Overlay, Pewter Lid, ½ Liter	345.00
Glass, Blown, Stag In Forest, Antler Finial, Thumbprint, Pewter Lid, ½ Liter	460.00
Glass, Blown, Stag, Ruby Flashed, Faceted, Wheel Engraved, Glass Inlaid Lid, c.1860, 1 Liter	920.00
Glass, Blown, Stags, Yellow Flashed, Faceted, Wheel Engraved, Glass Inlaid Lid, c.1870, ½ Liter	978.00
Glass, Blown, White On Ruby, Bird, Flowers, Hand Painted, Silver Lid, c.1850, ½ Liter	5635.00
Glass, Clear, Applied Green Glass Stripping, Florals & Leaf, Metal Lid, 3 Liter	138.00
Glass, Clear, Fluted, Engraved Florals & Baskets, Pewter Lid, Mid 1800s, ½ Liter	253.00
Glass, Frog & Mushrooms, Enameled, Pewter Lid, ½ Liter	230.00
Glass, Pressed, Clear, 3 Relief Cats, Inlaid Lid, Katzenjammer, Mid 1800s, ½ Liter	219.00
Glass, Pressed, Fireman's Helmet, Clear, Glass Inlaid Lid, ⅓ Liter	219.00
Leavenworth Brewery, Stoneware, 4 ½ In.	18.00
Little Kings-Cream Ale, Bear Claw, Ceramic, 5 ⅜ In.	25.00
Michelob, Since 1896, Black, Cream Ground, Logo, Ceramic, c.1969, 4 ½ In.	12.00
Michelob, Summer Olympics, Los Angeles, Ceramarte, 1982, 7 ½ In.	50.00
Military, Deutschland Uber Alles In Der Welt, ½ Liter	403.00
Military, Einigkeit Macht Stark, Stoneware, Pewter Lid, Impressed Eagles, ½ Liter	121.00
Military, Glass, Relief Iron Cross, Pewter Lid, 1914, ½ Liter	242.00
Military, Stoneware, Pewter Lid, Eagle ½ In.	230.00
Mug, Silver, Relief Figures, Late 1900s, 2 Liter, 9 In.	690.00
Musician Playing Horn, Palm Trees, Tin, Glazed, Pewter Lid, Germany, 8 In.	1067.00
Occupational, Bierbrauerei, Brewer, Transfer, Enamel, Pewter Lid, 1 Liter	311.00
Occupational, Brick Maker, Pewter Lid, Transfer, Enameled, ½ Liter	690.00
Occupational, Dairy Worker, Transfer, Enameled, Pewter Lid, ½ Liter	748.00
Occupational, Electrician, Porcelain, Transfer, Enameled, Pewter Lid, ½ Liter	719.00
Occupational, Fuhrmann, Coachman, Wagon, Tuttlinger, Transfer, Enamel, 1922, Pewter Lid, ½ Liter.	299.00
Occupational, Kaminkehere, Chimneysweep, Transfer, Enamel, Pewter Lid, ½ Liter	374.00
Occupational, Knitter, Pewter Lid, Red Cross Scene, Transfer, Enameled, ½ Liter	776.00
Occupational, Landmann, Farmer, Prism Lid, School Building, ½ Liter	92.00
Occupational, Papermaker, Papier-Mache, Transfer, Enamel, Pewter Lid, ½ Liter	978.00
Occupational, Postal Delivery, Porcelain, Pewter Lid, Lithophane, Transfer, Enameled, ½ Liter.	374.00
Occupational, Rudolf Gampe, Electric Lamps, Flat Metal Lid, Strap Handle, 1923, ½ Liter	173.00
Occupational, Saddle Maker, Transfer, Enameled, Porcelain, Pewter Lid, ½ Liter	311.00
Olympia, Pilsen Brewing Co., Glass, Pewter Handle, Lid, Porcelain Insert, 7 x 5 In.	88.00
Pewter, Quilted, Footed, Late 1800s, 2 Liter, 13 ¾ In.	115.00
Pewter, Lid, Figural Thumb Pull, Scrolls, Leaves, Facial Medallions, Continental, 8 In.	118.00
Porcelain, Blue & White, Lid, Hand Painted Birds, Flowers, ½ Liter	161.00
Porcelain, Capo-Di-Monte, Battle Scene, Hand Painted, Inlaid Lid, 1 Liter	196.00 to 489.00
Porcelain, Capo-Di-Monte, Inlaid Lid, Nude Figures, Hand Painted, 1 Liter, 10 ¾ In.	690.00
Porcelain, Inlaid Lid, Blue & White Lithophane, ½ Liter	92.00
Porcelain, Man Under Tree, Hand Painted, Silver Base & Lid, Thuringen, c.1800s, ¼ Liter, 6 In.	1150.00
Porcelain, Meissen, Hunting Scene, Porcelain Lid, Hand Painted, Strawberry Finial, c.1800s, ¾ Liter	8050.00
Porcelain, Monk, Copper, Silver Lid, Transfer, ½ Liter	288.00
Porcelain, Monk, Hand Painted, Inlaid Lid, ½ Liter, 6 In.	2415.00
Porcelain, Tapestry, Pewter Lid, Etched, Hauber & Reuther, ½ Liter	150.00

Porcelain, White Ground, Flowers, Relief, Hand Painted, Inlaid Lid, Nymphenburg, ½ Liter ...	1725.00
Pottery, Couple Dancing, Etched, Hauber & Reuther, Pewter Lid, ½ Liter...................................	161.00
Pottery, Eagle, State Coat Of Arms, Pewter Lid, Relief, ⅓ Liter	1150.00
Pottery, Gnome, King Drinking Beer, Pewter Thumb Rest, Lid, Germany, Late 1800s, 6 ½ In. .	153.00
Pottery, Gnome Musicians, Inlaid Lid, 3 Liter..	334.00
Pottery, Monkeys, Relief, Inlaid Lid, ½ Liter..	219.00
Regimental, 3 Batt., Feld Artl. Regt. Nr. 30, Rastatt, 1906-08, ½ Liter	207.00
Regimental, 5 Batt., Feld Artl. Regt. Nr. 10, 1912-13, ½ Liter..	690.00
Regimental, 7 Comp. Inft. Regt. Nr. 109, 1904-1906, Griffin Thumblift, ½ Liter	377.00
Regimental, 9 Comp. Inft. Regt. Nr. 111., Rastatt, Porcelain, 2 Scenes, Griffin Thumblift, ½ Liter	173.00
Regimental, Comp. Inft. Regt. Nr. 87, Mainz, 2-Sided Scenes, Roster, 1901-03, ½ Liter.............	184.00
Regimental, Inft. Regt., Nr. 135, Diedenhofen, Hillebrand, 1912-14, 11 ½ In. ....*illus*	210.00
Regimental, Naval Sailor, Pewter Lid, Porcelain, ½ Liter, 9 ½ In.	173.00
Regimental, Pionier, Nr. 10, Minden, 1910-11, ½ Liter..	1035.00
Regimental, Regt. 122, Weingarten, Glass, Porcelain Inlay, 1892, ½ Liter	173.00
Regimental, Regt. Nr. 4, Metz, Porcelain, 2 Scenes, Flower Thumblift, ½ Liter, 1896-98, 9 ½ In. ..	253.00
Regimental, Regt. Nr. 10, Ingolstadt, Porcelain, 3 Scenes, Lion Thumblift, 1903-04, ½ Liter...	546.00
Regimental, Regt. Nr. 19, Erfurt, Porcelain, 4 Scenes, Wreath Thumblift, 1895-97, ½ Liter	328.00
Regimental, Roster, 1 Batt., Feld Artl. Regt. Nr. 65, Ludwigsburg, 4 Scenes, Thumblift, ½ Liter	288.00
Regimental, Roster, 1 Comp, Bayr, Inft. Regt. NR. 8, Metz.4 Scenes, Thumblift, 1908-10, ½ Liter	242.00
Regimental, Roster, 7 Battr., Feld Artl Regt. Nr. 8, Koln, 1893-95, Wreath Thumblift, ½ Liter.......	403.00
Regimental, Roster, 9 Comp., Inft. Regt. Nr. 29, Trier, 2 Scenes, 1911-13, ½ Liter....................	518.00
Regimental, Roster, 81st Frankfurt Infantry, Lithophane, Eagle Thumb Rest, c.1903, 11 ¼ In. ...	180.00
Regimental, Roster, 109th Grenadier, Eagle Thumb Rest, Lithophane, Karlsruhe, c.1912, 12 In.	210.00
Regimental, Roster, Eagle Thumbprint, Gren. Regt., Nr. 109, Karlsruhe, Sotzel, 1911-13, 12 In. *illus*	210.00
Regimental, Roster, Eagle Thumbprint, Inft. Regt., Nr. 81, Frankfurt, Appel, 1902-04, 11 In. ..*illus*	180.00
Regimental, Roster, Mainz, 12 Comp., Inft. Regt. Nr. 117, 2 Scenes, Porcelain, ½ Liter	230.00
Regimental, Roster, Regt. Nr. 3, Coblenz, Porcelain, 2 Scenes, Eagle Thumblift, 1900-02, ½ Liter	920.00
Regimental, Roster, Regt. Nr. 8, Metz, Porcelain, 4 Scenes, Gargoyle Thumblift, 1906-08, ½ Liter	196.00
Regimental, Roster, Regt. Nr. 12, Neu-Ulm, 4 Scenes, Lion Thumblift, 1904-06, ½ Liter, 11 In. .	345.00
Regimental, Roster, Regt. Nr. 13, Dresden, 2 Scenes, Saxon Thumblift, ½ Liter, 1899-1901......	1380.00
Regimental, Roster, Regt. Nr. 13, Ingolstadt, 4 Sides, Lion Thumblift, ½ Liter, 1899-1901........	253.00
Regimental, Roster, Regt. Nr. 18, Landau, Lion Thumblift, 1902-04, ½ Liter, 11 In.	328.00
Regimental, Roster, Regt. Nr. 23, Darmstadt, 2 Scenes, Lion Thumblift, 1898-1901, ½ Liter....	276.00
Regimental, Roster, Regt. Nr. 30, Rastatt, Scenes, Griffin Thumblift, 1906-08, ½ Liter 207.00 to 633.00	
Regimental, Roster, Regt. Nr. 79, Hildesheim, Glass, Faceted, Gargoyle Thumblift, ½ Liter......	518.00
Regimental, Roster, Regt. Nr. 109, Karlsruhe, Griffin Thumblift, 1904-06, ½ Liter, 10 ¾ In. ...	377.00
Regimental, Roster, Regt. Nr. 110, Mannheim, Porcelain, Thumblift, 1890-93, ½ Liter, 9 In. .	92.00
Regimental, Roster, Regt. Nr. 112, Mulhausen, 2 Scenes, Griffin Thumblift, 1894-96, ½ Liter .	288.00
Regimental, Roster, Saarburg, 2 Reit. Battr.1., Field Artl. Regt. Nr. 15, Pottery, 1 Liter, 15 ¼ In.	288.00
Regimental, Roster, Speyer, 2 Comp., Bayr, Pionier Batl. Nr. 2, 2 Scenes, 1900-02, ½ Liter.......	374.00
Regimental, Roster, Strassburg, 6 Battr., Field Artl. Regt. Nr. 51, 2 Scenes, Porcelain, 1902-04, ½ Liter	385.00
Regimental, Roster, Strassburg, 6 Comp., Inft. Regt. Nr. 126, 2 Scenes, Porcelain, 1894-96, ½ Liter	184.00
Stables, 2nd Landmark Series, Ceramarte, 7 ½ In.	25.00
Stoneware, Bar Scene, Etched, Hauber & Reuther, Pewter Lid, ½ Liter	276.00
Stoneware, Bartmannkrug, Relief Dark Cobalt Blue, Pewter Lid, 1 ½ Liter, 9 In.	127.00
Stoneware, Bird, Incised, Blue Salt Glaze, Pewter Lid, Westerwald, c.1775, ½ Liter, 8 In.	546.00
Stoneware, Blue, Purple Salt Glaze, Pewter Lid, Mid 1700s, ¾ Liter.......................................	230.00
Stoneware, Coat Of Arms, Relief, Hand Painted, White Glaze, Relief Pewter Lid, 3 Liter	345.00
Stoneware, Daniel, 4 Panels, Color Glazes, Pewter Lid, 1 ¼ Liter..	1208.00
Stoneware, Deer Head, Hand Painted, Fox Thumblift, Saltzer Rehbock, Pewter Lid, ½ Liter....	299.00
Stoneware, Deutscher Michel, Man Smoking Pipe, Germany, 10 In. ....*illus*	94.00
Stoneware, High Wheel Bicycle, No. 982, Strap, Pewter Lid, ½ Liter	115.00
Stoneware, Hikers On Mountain, Transfer, Enamel, Pewter Lid, 1 Liter	242.00
Stoneware, Jester, Transfer, Enameled, Pewter Lid, 2 Liter..	207.00
Stoneware, Marked 701, Enameled, Hammered Pewter Lid, 2 Liter	1208.00
Stoneware, Marked 2428, Brown Glaze, Pewter Lid, 3 Liter...	161.00
Stoneware, Night Watchman, Hand Painted, Relief Pewter Lid, 1 Liter.....................................	207.00
Stoneware, Outdoor Fight Scene, Blue, Germany, 13 In.	238.00
Stoneware, Relief, Hand Painted, Creussen, Hanns Stenbach, Pewter Base & Lid, c.1750, 1 Liter .	834.00
Stoneware, Target Shooting, Transfer, Enameled, F. Ringer, Pewter Lid, 1 Liter	311.00
Stoneware, Third Reich, Swastika, Relief Helmet, Pewter Lid, ½ In. .... 345.00 to 443.00	
Stoneware, Westerwald, Hand Engraved, Flowers, Pewter Lid, c.1800, 1 Liter, 6 ½ In.	299.00
Summer Olympics, Barcelona, Ceramarte, 1992, 5 ½ In.	18.00
Third Reich, 2 Horse Heads, In Horseshoe, Helmet With Swastika, Stoneware, ½ Liter............	115.00
Third Reich, Komp. Korps-Nachr, Abtlg, 47, 1938, 5 Liter	230.00

Stein, Stoneware, Deutscher Michel, Man Smoking Pipe, Germany, 10 In. $94.00

Steuben Glassware
Steuben's glassware included Cluthra, Cintra, Verre de Soie, and other styles hand-made in a variety of colors. Aurene, an iridescent glass, remains the most popular of its early products. Aurene was often combined with Calcite (white) or Ivrene (ivory) opaque glass and hand-tooled to make swirled and feath-ered designs.

S

Stereoscope, Kis-Me Gum, Chicle Co., 5 Views, Tin, 1 ¼ x 4 ¼ x 3 ¼ In. $351.00

Steuben, Bowl, Acid Cutback, Green To Alabaster, Flowers, Medallion, 10 ⅛ x 3 ¾ In. $1495.00

Steuben, Bowl, Jade, Transparent Blue, 3 ¾ x 9 ¾ In. $518.00

Steuben, Candlestick, Oriental Poppy, Pink, White Bobeche, Opalescent White Stem, 6 In. $2875.00

Third Reich, Roster, Pottery, Pewter Lid, Wren Thumblift, 1 Liter	403.00
Third Reich, Soldier With Rifle, Porcelain, Pewter Lid, ½ Liter	403.00
Third Reich, Stoneware, Pewter Lid, Helmet Finial, ½ Liter	334.00
Third Reich, Wetzlar, Lahn, Pottery, Metal Lid, ½ Liter	374.00
Woman In Garden, Tin, Glazed, Pewter Lid, Coin, Dorotheenthal, Germany, 7 In.	533.00
Wood, Black Forest, Carved Grapevines, Hinged Chicken, Leaf Lid, Handle, 1 Liter	2013.00
Wood, Burl, Handle, Lid, Carved Animals, 1 Liter, 8 ¼ In.	518.00
Wood, Burl, Lid, 3-Footed, Lion Thumblift, 1 Liter, 9 ¾ In.	716.00
Wood, Tavern Scene, Carved, Footed, Dog Finial, 1905, ½ Liter, 10 ½ In.	920.00

STEREO CARDS that were made for stereoscope viewers became popular after 1840. Two almost identical pictures were mounted on a stiff cardboard backing so that, when viewed through a stereoscope, a three-dimensional picture could be seen. Value is determined by maker and by subject. These cards were made in quantity through the 1930s.

Abraham Lincoln Memorial, c.1865, 3 ¼ x 6 ¾ In.	10.00
Bucksport, Maine, 1881, H. Young	39.00
Eiffel Tower & Entrance To Exposition, Paris, 1876, 3 ½ x 7 In.	40.00
Farming In Wisconsin, Reclaiming Swamp Land, Keystone	12.00
Farmington, Maine, Canning Factory	79.00
Indian Leader, Mahatma Gandhi, Keystone	45.00
Jerusalem, The Wall Of Wailing, Frank M. Good, London	39.00
Largest Stationary Engine In The World Columbian Exposition, 1876, 3 ¼ x 7 In.	65.00
Les Theatres De Paris, Faust Dieu Pardon, Tissue	60.00
Les Theatres De Paris, Faust Le Duel, Tissue	45.00
Lincoln Statue, U.S. Capital, 1866	35.00
Madison Square Garden At Night, Man Speaking On Stage, Flags	6.00
New York Railroad Bridge, Treadwell Collection	24.00
Old North Church, North End, Copps Hill, Boston, Keystone, 1900s	30.00
Picturesque Camp, Teepees, Water Scene, Popular Series	10.00
Playing Rainstorm On Mamma's Parlor Carpet, R.Y. Young, 1897	8.00
Pleasant St. Baptist Church, W.G.C. Kimball	39.00
Police Headquarters, Cleveland, Ohio, Alfred Campbell, 1896	49.00
Rangeley, Maine Hotel, Moore	99.00
Round Up Sherman Ranch, Geneseo, Lansas, Keystone	15.00
Stolen Sweets, No. 84, Griffith & Griffith	7.00
Transport Saratoga Carrying Troops To Santiago De Cuba, Strohmer & Wyman, 1898	24.00
Troop B Third U.S. Cavalry As Infantry For Cuban Invasion, Strohmeyer & Wyman, 1898	24.00
Watkins Pacific Coast, San Francisco, U.S. Mint	99.00
Yellowstone Park, Old Faithful Geyser, Keystone	20.00
Young Cattle Queens, Girls On Horseback, Roundup, Montana	18.00
Zeppelin Flying Over German Town, Keystone	28.00

STEREOSCOPES were used for viewing stereo cards. The hand viewer was invented by Oliver Wendell Holmes, although more complicated table models were used before his was produced in 1859. Do not confuse the stereoscope with the stereopticon, a magic lantern that used glass slides.

Brewster Style, Burl Wood, Brass, Focusable Oculars, c.1865	145.00
Brewster Style, Painted Black, Color Detail, Marble, Applied Tin Figure, 18 In.	2172.00
Educa, Unis France, Table Viewer, Vertical Transport, Sliding Box, 15 Plates, 18 In.	362.00
Kis-Me Gum, Chicle Co., 5 Views, Tin, 1 ¼ x 4 ¼ x 3 ¼ In. ....*illus*	351.00
Underwood & Underwood, Aluminum, Wood, Pat. 1901, 12 ¾ In.	60.00
Unis France, Table Viewer, Mahogany, Rack & Pinion Focus, 140 Slides, Early 1900s	406.00
Vistascope, Griffith & Griffith, Burl, Walnut, Standing, Viewing Card, c.1896, 12 In.	395.00

STEUBEN glass was made at the Steuben Glass Works of Corning, New York. The factory, founded by Frederick Carder and T.G. Hawkes, Sr., was purchased by the Corning Glass Company. Corning continued to make glass called Steuben. Many types of art glass were made at Steuben. The firm is still making exceptional quality glass but it is clear, modern-style glass. Additional pieces may be found in the Aurene, Cluthra, and Perfume Bottle categories.

Ashtray, Clear, 1967, 7 In.	17.70
Ashtray, Ivory, Applied Mirror Black Leaf Handle, 5 In.	550.00
Basket, Calcite, Gold Aurene Interior & Handle, 4 x 5 In.	374.00
Bookends, Horse Heads, Marked, 5 In.	431.00
Bottle, Astringent, Orchid, Amethyst, Opalescent Stripes, Petal Stopper, Metal Collar, 5 ½ In.	2588.00
Bowl, 4 Scroll Feet, Signed, 10 ½ In.	150.00

S

Bowl,	Acid Cutback, Green To Alabaster, Flowers, Medallion, 10 ⅛ x 3 ¾ In. .... *illus*	1495.00
Bowl,	Art Glass, Iridescent Gold, Ruffled Rim, 3 x 6 In.	69.00
Bowl,	Blue Jade, Factory Acid Stamp, 5 x 3 In.	400.00
Bowl,	Calcite, Double Bulbous, Gold, 11 ¼ In.	316.00
Bowl,	Calcite, Gold Aurene Interior, Iridescent, Flared Flat Rim, 14 x 1 ¼ In.	230.00
Bowl,	Cinnamon Gold Ruby, Applied Blue Pears, Footed, Flaring, 11 ¼ x 6 In.	173.00
Bowl,	Clear, Underplate, Opalescent, Ruffled Rim, Translucent Ruby, Threading, 6 In.	60.00
Bowl,	Cobalt Blue, Blue Iridescent, c.1900, 3 x 14 ½ In.	501.00
Bowl,	Dark Amethyst, Optic Spiral Design, 4 ½ In.	50.00
Bowl,	Flared Rim, Rosaline, White Opalescent Foot, 12 x 4 In.	201.00
Bowl,	Flared Rim, Yellow, 10 x 3 ½ In.	201.00
Bowl,	Footed, Low, John Dreves, Signed, c.1942, 10 ½ In.	360.00
Bowl,	Gold Calcite, Flared Rim, 3 ¼ In.	259.00
Bowl,	Green Jade, Inverted Rim, 12 In.	200.00
Bowl,	Iridescent Green, Etched Stylized Flowers, Zigzag Border, 1923-27, 4 ½ x 11 ½ In.	1659.00
Bowl,	Ivory, Art Deco Design, 4 ½ In.	90.00
Bowl,	Jade, Alabaster, Footed, Early 20th Century, 5 In., 12 Piece	1170.00
Bowl,	Jade, Transparent Blue, 3 ¾ x 9 ¾ In. .... *illus*	518.00
Bowl,	Jadette, Art Glass, 1 ¾ x 10 In.	323.00
Bowl,	Lattice, Topaz Ribbed, Flemish Blue Accents, Swirled Prouts, 6 In.	375.00
Bowl,	Latticework, Topaz, Blue, 3 x 6 In.	518.00
Bowl,	Leaf Form Stem, Footed, 8 ¼ In.	145.00
Bowl,	Oval, Clear, Marked, 7 x 2 ½ In.	29.00
Bowl,	Pedestal, Amethyst, Ribbed, Connecting Clear Wafer, 6 In.	225.00
Bowl,	Prunted Base, Donald Pollard, c.1956, 6 ⅞ x 9 In.	330.00
Bowl,	Ribbed, Cobalt Blue, 7 x 4 In.	259.00
Bowl,	Rosaline, Alabaster Foot, 5 x 12 In.	354.00
Bowl,	Rosaline, Oval, Inverted Rolled Rim, 8 ½ In.	100.00
Bowl,	Rosaline, Pedestal, 4 ¼ x 7 ½ In.	150.00
Bowl,	Teardrop, 7 x 8 In.	351.00
Bowl,	Threaded, Ruffled Rim, Early 20th Century, 5 In., 6 Piece	293.00
Bowl,	Yellow Jade, Rolled Rim, 11 In.	2500.00
Candleholder,	3-Lobed Base, Signed, 2 ½ x 5 In., Pair	96.00
Candlestick,	2-Light, Ivory, Saucer Foot, Ribbed Stem, Petal, 10 ¼ In.	978.00
Candlestick,	Amethyst Swirl Cups, Base, Clear Half Twist Stem, 10 In.	400.00
Candlestick,	Cintra, Light Blue, Flanged Rim, 6 ½ x 6 In.	316.00
Candlestick,	Clear, Baluster Form, Round Foot, Signed, 10 In., Pair	490.00
Candlestick,	Coiled Shape, Round Base, 8 ½ In., Pair	230.00
Candlestick,	Green Jade, Alabaster Stem, Tiered Base, 10 In.	460.00
Candlestick,	Oriental Poppy, Pink, White Bobeche, Opalescent White Stem, 6 In. .... *illus*	2875.00
Candlestick,	Rosaline, Alabaster Standard, 10 In., Pair	550.00
Candlestick,	Venetian, Transparent Yellow, c.1910, 10 In., Pair	390.00
Candy Dish,	Cover, Amber, Optic Ribbed, Body, Pomona Green Foot, Finial, 10 In.	316.00
Champagne,	Strawberry Mansion, 8 Piece, 4 ½ In.	1404.00
Charger Set,	Pomona Green, Acid Cut Flower Swags, Charger 14 In., 4 Matching Plates, 9 In.	200.00
Compote,	Bristol, Yellow, Etched Fruit Design, Pedestal, Signed, 5 ¾ x 12 In.	351.00
Compote,	Calcite Exterior, Gold Aurene Interior, Pedestal, 4 x 4 In.	120.00
Compote,	Calcite, Ribbed, Flared Rim, Gold Aurene Interior, 6 x 3 In.	288.00
Compote,	Celeste Blue Matsu-No-Ke Rim, Ribbed, Clear, Stem Wrap, 6 In.	325.00
Compote,	Celeste Blue, Ribbed Bowl, Flared Swirled Base, 6 x 8 In.	403.00
Compote,	Cone Foot, Ribbed, Celeste Blue, Amethyst Threading, 8 In.	525.00
Compote,	Cover, Finial, Acid Cutback, Green Jade, Goblet Shape, 9 ½ In.	300.00
Compote,	Cover, Topaz Jar, Celeste Blue Twist Finial, 7 In.	275.00
Compote,	Empire, Blue Over Clear, Clear Stem, Foot, Signed, 7 x 4 ¼ In.	2875.00
Compote,	Gold Aurene, Calcite, Trumpet Shape, Footed, 5 In.	250.00
Compote,	Green Jade, Cone Shape, Alabaster Foot, Grapes, Vines, Fleur-De-Lis, Acid Cutback, 12 In.	450.00
Compote,	Green Jade, Footed, 13 ½ In.	125.00
Compote,	Optic Diamond Rosa, Cone Form, Pomona Green Swirled Base, c.1920, 12 In.	660.00
Compote,	Rosaline, Alabaster Foot, 8 In.	175.00
Compote,	Roseline, Alabaster, Twist Stem, 7 In.	225.00
Compote,	Twisted Rope Stem, Yellow Iridescent, 9 x 9 In.	546.00
Console,	Alabaster, Glass, Green Jade, Flower Heads, Medallions, Acid Cut, 11 In.	1035.00
Console Set,	Aquamarine, Blue Lip Wrap, 2 Candlesticks, 10-In. Center Bowl, 10 In.	550.00
Console Set,	Pedestal Bowl, Candlestick, Green, Amber Glass, 5 x 12 & 12 x 6 In., 3 Piece	1093.00
Console Set,	Rosaline, Petal Rims, 2 Compotes, 8-In. Center Bowl, 13 In.	1400.00
Cruet,	Amber, Green Stopper, Blue Handle, c.1900, 9 In.	234.00

Steuben, Figurine, Gazelle, Crystal, Signed, 6 ¾ In.
$460.00

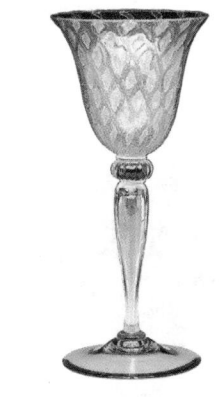

Steuben, Goblet, Silverina, Canary Yellow, Faceted Stem, Yellow Foot, 9 ½ In.
$1652.00

Steuben, Jar, Cover, Acid Cutback, Green Cut To Alabaster, Medallion, Flowers, 6 In.
$2430.00

S

Steuben, Lamp, Art Deco, Kneeling Woman, Cast Lead Glass, Grape Clusters, 9 ¼ x 66 In. $4715.00

Steuben, Lamp, Segar Bronze, Male Nudes Base, Aurene Orb With Cage, c.1925, 10 x 27 In. $4800.00

Steuben, Lamp, Torchere, Oriental Poppy, Applied Iridescent Threading, Brass Finish, 68 In. $5750.00

Decanter, Bulbous, Green, Silver Overlay, Grapes & Leaves, Stopper, 6 x 10 In.	600.00 to 620.00
Dipper, Rosaline, Applied Alabaster Handle, 2 x 4 In.	250.00
Dish, Apple Shape, Blown-Out Stem, 8 ½ In.	35.00
Dish, Tapered, Clear, Rams Head Cover, Marked, 5 ½ x 7 In.	259.00
Figurine, Armadillo, 5 ⅛ In.	234.00
Figurine, Bear, 2 ½ In.	88.00
Figurine, Beaver, 3 x 5 ½ In.	176.00
Figurine, Beaver, 4 x 9 ½ In.	585.00
Figurine, Beaver, Red Garnet Eyes, 6 ¼ In.	527.00
Figurine, Beaver, Red Garnet Eyes, 9 In.	410.00
Figurine, Bull, Frosted, Matte Finish, 5 In.	920.00
Figurine, Caterpillar, 6 ½ x 9 x 7 In.	920.00
Figurine, Christmas Tree, Inverted Cone, Bubbles, 5 x 3 ½ In.	176.00
Figurine, Dolphin, 5 x 9 In.	265.00
Figurine, Eagle, Spread Wings, Clear, 4 ½ x 3 ¾ In.	200.00
Figurine, Elephant, 6 ½ In.	351.00
Figurine, Fox, Clear, Marked, c.1950, 3 ½ In.	66.00
Figurine, Frog, 2 x 4 In.	234.00
Figurine, Gazelle, Crystal, Signed, 6 ¾ In. .... *illus*	460.00
Figurine, Goose, In Flight, Clear, 9 ¾ x 10 In.	340.00
Figurine, Hippopotamus, 4 x 9 In.	761.00
Figurine, Horse, Head Down, Marked, 7 ¼ x 9 ¼ x 2 ½ In.	460.00
Figurine, Koala, 8 x 7 In.	878.00
Figurine, Monkey, 6 ¼ In.	351.00
Figurine, Monkey, Hand Cooler, 3 In.	205.00
Figurine, Owl, 5 ½ In.	263.00
Figurine, Panther, Attacking Snake, Clear, Carder Cire, Impressed F. Carder 1938, 8 x 6 In.	9200.00
Figurine, Penguin, 6 ½ In.	322.00
Figurine, Pheasant, Clear, Cut Glass, 12 In.	700.00
Figurine, Pheasants, Cut Crystal, c.1932, 6 x 12 ½ In., Pair	995.00
Figurine, Porcupine, Clear, 3 x 5 In.	175.00
Figurine, Porpoise, 12 In.	644.00
Figurine, Puppy Love Hand Cooler, 2 x 3 In.	146.00
Figurine, Roman Cat, 2 x 5 In.	117.00
Figurine, Rooster, 10 In.	585.00
Figurine, Seahorse, 7 In.	585.00
Figurine, Shore Bird, 3 x 8 In.	205.00
Figurine, Snail, 2 ½ In.	41.00
Figurine, Snail, Hand Cooler, 3 In.	205.00
Figurine, Swan, Curved Neck, 4 ½ x 6 ½ In.	205.00
Figurine, Trout, With Fly, Clear	996.00
Figurine, Turtle, 2 ½ In.	77.00
Figurine, Walrus, 4 ½ x 7 ½ In.	351.00
Figurine, Walrus, Clear, 7 ½ In.	310.00
Figurine, Wild Dove, 8 ½ In.	323.00
Finger Bowl, Underplate, Amethyst, Optic Ribbed, Signed, 6 In.	100.00
Finger Bowl, Underplate, Gold Calcite, 2 ½ x 6 In.	300.00
Flower Frog, 2 Tiers, 8 Bud Holders, 4 In.	115.00
Flower Frog, Water Bearer, Amethyst, 4 x 9 In.	1150.00
Flower Frog, Water Bearer, Pomona Green, 4 x 9 In.	1495.00
Goblet, Baluster, Teardrop Stem, 6 ½ In., 7 Piece	585.00
Goblet, Grenadine, Cranberry, Clear Knotted Stem, 4 x 5 In., 7 Piece	403.00
Goblet, Oriental Jade, Green Swirl, Twist Stem Base, 8 In.	475.00
Goblet, Oriental Jade, Green Swirled, Opalescent, Twist Stem Base, 8 In.	1610.00
Goblet, Rosalene, Pink, Hourglass Shape, Opalescent Base, 5 In., 8 Piece	690.00
Goblet, Selenium Red, Intaglio Cut, Signed F. Carder, 6 In.	175.00
Goblet, Silverina, Canary Yellow, Faceted Stem, Yellow Foot, 9 ½ In. .... *illus*	1652.00
Goblet, Strawberry Mansion, 6 In., 8 Piece	1989.00
Goblet, Tangerine Swirl Body, Blue Base, Trumpet Shape, 6 ½ In.	98.00
Goblet, Water, Floral, Ruby Cut To Clear, Signed, 10 In., 12 Piece	4370.00
Goblet, Wine, Grenadine, Cranberry, Clear Knotted Stem, 3 ½ x 8 In., 8 Piece	1093.00
Jar, Cover, Acid Cutback, Green Cut To Alabaster, Medallion, Flowers, 6 In. .... *illus*	2430.00
Jar, Cover, Amethyst, Footed Optic Ribbed, Swirled, Topaz Finial, 10 In.	200.00
Lamp, Acid Cut, Urn Shape, 2 Applied Handles, Purple Trees, 3 Birds, Lake, 13 In.	2900.00
Lamp, Alabaster, Purple Grapes, Acid Cutback, Alabaster Stems, Metal Base, 35 In.	2300.00
Lamp, Art Deco, Kneeling Woman, Cast Lead Glass, Grape Clusters, 9 ¼ x 66 In. .... *illus*	4715.00

Lamp Base, Gold Pegasus In Motion, Clouds, Art Deco Style Suns, Citron, Gold Aurene, 31 ½ In.	1035.00
Lamp Base, Rose Quartz, Applied Clear Leaves, Flowers, Handles, Bottle Form, 11 ½ In.	1150.00
Lamp, Brass, Column, Square Base, 2-Light, 2 Gold Aurene Shades, Steuben	350.00
Lamp, Chandelier, 3-Light, Oval, Rams, Leaves, Gold Aurene Pulled Feather Opal Shades, 30 In.	1000.00
Lamp, Gold Aurene Helmet Shade, Green Heart, Vines, Millefiori, Roycroft Trim, 17 In.	9200.00
Lamp, Green Jade, Applied Handles, Brass Fittings, Flared Black Shade, 26 In.	2300.00
Lamp, Green Jade, Stems, Mums, Acid Cutback, Shouldered, Leaf Metal Base, 20 In.	690.00
Lamp, Green Pulled Feathers, Gold Aurene Topped, Crimped, Cone Base, Domed Shade, 14 In.	2300.00
Lamp, Segar Bronze, Male Nudes Base, Aurene Orb With Cage, c.1925, 10 x 27 In. .... *illus*	4800.00
Lamp, Torchere, Oriental Poppy, Applied Iridescent Threading, Brass Finish, 68 In. .... *illus*	5750.00
Lamp, Urns, 4-Sided, Ginko Flowers, Acid Cutback, Gold Aurene, Double Swan Metal Base, 26 In.	1000.00
Lamp, Yellow, Acid Cut Glass, Gilt Bronze, 4 Socket, Floral Finial, Shade, 19 x 38 In. .... *illus*	719.00
Lampshade, Dish, Cylindrical, Clear, Twisted Lid, 3 ¾ x 5 In.	115.00
Lemonade, Jade, Alabaster Handles, Ribbed, Marked, 6 In., 6 Piece	330.00
Luminary, Ball Shape, Bubbles, Metal Base, Light, 4 ½ In.	748.00
Olive Dish, Curved Handle, 5 In., 2 Piece	176.00
Paperweight, Ballerina, Engraved	351.00
Paperweight, Cane Twist, 3 ½ In.	205.00
Paperweight, Crown Form, 4 ¼ In.	101.00
Paperweight, Eagle, Clear, Marked, 4 ½ In.	259.00
Paperweight, Pear Shape, Crystal, Cutout Section, Gilt Metal Partridge, Marked, 5 ¾ In.	885.00
Perfume Atomizer, Cylindrical, Flat Base, Gold Aurene, Gold Bulb, 8 ½ In.	201.00
Perfume Atomizer, Cylindrical, Flat Base, Green, Pulled Design, Gold Bulb, 7 ¼ In.	575.00
Perfume Bottle, Amethyst Glass, Melon Shape, Stopper, 6 ¼ In.	144.00
Perfume Bottle, Atomic Cloud, Gold Aurene, Stopper, 4 In.	2300.00
Perfume Bottle, Atomizer, Bulbous, Gold Aurene, Gold Bulb, 8 ¼ In.	546.00
Perfume Bottle, Atomizer, Gold Aurene, Metal Neck, Jewel Finial, 10 In.	400.00
Perfume Bottle, Blue Aurene, Stopper, Marked, 7 ½ In.	920.00
Perfume Bottle, Blue Stopper, Tapered, Spiral Amethyst Glass, Clear Base, 9 ½ In.	690.00
Perfume Bottle, Fig Shape, Green Jade, Stopper, 4 ¼ In.	184.00
Perfume Bottle, Fig Shape, Ivory Color, Mirror Black Stopper, 4 ⅜ In.	633.00
Perfume Bottle, Gold Aurene, Stopper, 5 ½ In.	259.00
Perfume Bottle, Gold Aurene, Stopper, 7 In.	633.00
Perfume Bottle, Gold Aurene, Tapered, Teardrop Stopper, Early 1900s, 8 In.	585.00
Perfume Bottle, Green, Etched Grapevine, Amber Foot & Stopper, Elongated Tip, 4 x 12 In. ..	770.00
Perfume Bottle, Melon Shape, Ruby, Red Flame Stopper, 3 ½ In.	144.00
Perfume Bottle, Pink, Cerise Ruby Threading, Stopper, 3 ½ In.	201.00
Perfume Bottle, Pomona Green, Stopper, 6 ¾ In.	230.00
Perfume Bottle, Rosaline, Alabaster Stopper & Base, Embossed Fleur-De-Lis Logo, 7 ⅞ In.	173.00
Perfume Bottle, Rosaline, Footed, Cylinder, Alabaster Teardrop Stopper, 10 In.	375.00
Perfume Bottle, Tapered, Bristol Yellow, Stopper, 7 ½ In.	201.00
Perfume Bottle, Tapered, Purple Glass, Blue Stopper, Foot, 7 ¾ In.	489.00
Perfume Bottle, Tapered, Spiraled Amethyst, Blue Stopper, 9 ½ In.	690.00
Perfume Bottle, Verre De Soie, Applied Green Threading, Green Flame Stopper, 4 In.	316.00
Perfume Bottle, Verre De Soie, Blue Flat Stopper, 7 ¾ In.	460.00
Perfume Bottle, Verre De Soie, Pink Flame Stopper, 3 ½ In.	460.00
Pitcher, Clear, 10 ⅞ In.	112.00
Pitcher, Translucent, Gold Ruby Threading, 7 In.	85.00
Plaque, Black F.D.R., Mule, Graduation Attire, Four More Years, Purple, F. Carder, Frame, 21 x 20 In.	5175.00
Plate, Rouge Flambe, Opaque Red, 8 ½ In.	700.00
Plate, Scrolled Handle, Signed, 8 In.	118.00
Plate, Vanderbilt, Black Glass, Engraved Poussin, c.1928, 11 In.	9775.00
Salt Cellar, Pedestal, Amethyst, Sterling Salt Spoon	275.00
Salt Cellar, Pedestal, Jade Green, Sterling Salt Spoon	360.00
Salt Cellar, Pedestal, Topaz, Sterling Salt Spoon	450.00
Sauce Dish, Underplate, Amethyst	300.00
Sculpture, Abstract Geometric, 4 x 4 x 4 In.	527.00
Sculpture, Geometric Star, 5 In.	205.00
Sculpture, Lighted, 2 Etched Male Nudes, Water Bearers, Green Enamel, Frederick Carder, 12 x 13 In.	3240.00
Sculpture, Star Stream, 5 ½ In.	410.00
Serving Dish, Curved Handle, 10 In.	176.00
Shade, Acid Cut, Cone Shape, Opal, 3 Aurene Medallions, Swags, Silver Fleur-De-Lis, 5 ½ In., Pair	350.00
Shade, Dome, Butterscotch, Intarsia Border, 2 ¼ x 7 In.	1725.00
Shade, Gas, Ivrene, Iridescent, Etched Flowers, 4 ½ In.	100.00
Shade, Gold Aurene, Ribbed, Helmet Shape, Purple Iridescence, 11 In.	1150.00
Shade, Torchere, Moss Agate, Scalloped, Mottled, Green, Yellow, Gold Flakes, 8 ½ In.	800.00

Steuben, Lamp, Yellow, Acid Cut Glass, Gilt Bronze, 4 Socket, Floral Finial, Shade, 19 x 38 In.
$719.00

Steuben, Vase, Acid Cutback, Shelton, Cone Shape, Flemish Blue Cased, 11 In.
$3680.00

Steuben, Vase, Green Cluthra, Bubbling, 10 In.
$805.00

S

Steuben, Vase, Grotesque, Topaz, Signed, 5½ x 12 In. $288.00

Steuben, Vase, Moss Agate, Flared Rim, Blue Mottled, Silver Aventurine, Footed, 12 In. $6090.00

Steuben, Vase, Selenium Red, Footed, Pedestal, Ribbed, Signed, 14 In. $1955.00

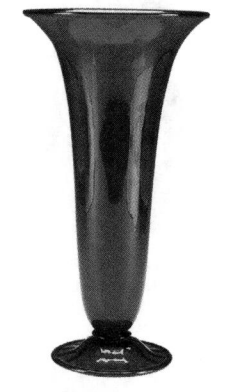

Stevens & Williams, Vase, Morning Glories, Champagne Satin Glass, Cameo Glass, 11 In. $1955.00

Sherbet, Underplate, Gold Ruby, Bouquet, 8-In. Plate, 3 x 5-In. Cup	500.00
Tazza, Cintra, Blue, Amethyst, 7 x 7 In.	1380.00
Torchere, Moss Agate, Scalloped, Amber Ground, Swirls, Crackled, Twisted Shaft, 65 In., Pair.	6900.00
Vase, 3-Prong, Triangle Rim, Footed, Ivory, 10 In.	425.00
Vase, Abstract, Tilted Form, Clear, 6½ x 6 In.	144.00
Vase, Acid Cutback, Art Deco, Flowers, Fauna, Black On White, 6½ In.	1610.00
Vase, Acid Cutback, Black Mirror Deco, Leaves, Berries, White Textured Ground, 8 In.	575.00
Vase, Acid Cutback, Boothbay, Rosa, Pomona Green Leave, Shouldered, 14 In.	5750.00
Vase, Acid Cutback, Chrysanthemum, Green Jade, Bordered Collar, 7 In.	1600.00
Vase, Acid Cutback, Dragon, Jade Over Alabaster, Scrolls, Oval, Shouldered, 10 In.	1380.00
Vase, Acid Cutback, Oriental Tree, Green Cut To Alabaster, Stylized Clouds, 7 x 7½ In.	575.00
Vase, Acid Cutback, Oriental Tree, Green To Alabaster, Clouds, 7 x 7½ In.	575.00
Vase, Acid Cutback, Peking, Plum Jade, Bulbous Base, Smokestack Neck, 12 In.	5000.00
Vase, Acid Cutback, Rose, Rosaline, Alabaster, Cone Shape, 12 In.	1050.00
Vase, Acid Cutback, Shelton, Cone Shape, Flemish Blue Cased, 11 In. .... *illus*	3680.00
Vase, Alabaster, Optic Ribbed Shade Shape, 5 In.	75.00
Vase, Amber, Stump, 3-Prong Bud, Oval Base, 6 In.	460.00
Vase, Amber, Swags, Prisms, Beaded Band, Cone Shape, 9 In.	173.00
Vase, Amethyst Glass, Tapered, Ribbed, Applied Green Handles, 4 x 10 In.	316.00
Vase, Asian Medallions, Etched, Flowers, Leaves, Scroll Ground, Amethyst, 8 In.	3200.00
Vase, Black Mirror, Acid Etched Roman Women, Swags, Medallions, 9 In.	1265.00
Vase, Blue Jade, Acid Stamp, 6 In.	1050.00
Vase, Blue Jade, Ribs, Cylinder, Ribs, 8½ In.	2070.00
Vase, Bowl, Deep Red, Low Hat Shape, Rim, 13 In.	403.00
Vase, Bristol Yellow, Footed Trumpet, Ribbed, 10 In.	300.00
Vase, Bud, Clear, Footed, 8¼ In.	100.00
Vase, Bulbous, Calcite, 8½ In.	400.00
Vase, Calcite, Blue Aurene, Footed, Fluted Top, Signed, 12 In.	1150.00
Vase, Calcite, Flared, Gold Aurene Interior, 5 x 4 In.	173.00
Vase, Calcite, Gold Aurene Interior, Iridescent, Footed, 5 x 4 In.	259.00
Vase, Calcite, Signed, 6¼ x 8½ In.	250.00
Vase, Calcite, White, Flared, 5 x 5 In.	125.00 to 205.00
Vase, Celeste Blue Handle, Shell Design, Matsu-No-Ke, Clear Glass, 4½ x 6 In.	710.00
Vase, Celeste Blue, Ribbing, Applied Handles, Rope Rings, 8 In.	460.00
Vase, Clear, 3-Prong Bud, Oval Foot, Art Deco, Signed, 10 In.	115.00
Vase, Clear Shading To Green, Free-Form, Footed, 9 In.	201.00
Vase, Cornucopia, Clear, 7½ x 5½ In., Pair	144.00
Vase, Fan, Alabaster, Rosaline, 8½ In.	288.00
Vase, Fan, Black To White Cluthra, Saucer Foot, Clear Wafer, 8 In.	805.00
Vase, Fan, Green Jade, White Circular Foot, 10 x 9 In.	403.00
Vase, Flaring, Ribbed, Blue Aurene, Signed, 5 x 5¾ In.	374.00
Vase, Florentia, Footed, Pink To Coral, 6 x 7 In.	2875.00
Vase, Green Cluthra, Bubbling, 10 In. .... *illus*	805.00
Vase, Green Jade, Bucket Shape, Alabaster Rings, Signed, 6½ In.	173.00
Vase, Green Jade, Bulbous, Rolled Collar, 8½ In.	115.00
Vase, Green Jade, Cylinder, Flared Rim, Twist Decor, 10 In.	325.00
Vase, Green Jade, Cylinder, Swirled, 7 In.	175.00
Vase, Green Jade, Diagonal Twist Design, 5½ In.	100.00
Vase, Green Jade, Oval, Shouldered, Alabaster M Handles, 10 In.	700.00
Vase, Grotesque, Fan, Cranberry To Clear, Footed, Signed, 11¼ In.	200.00
Vase, Grotesque, Topaz, Signed, 5½ x 12 In. .... *illus*	288.00
Vase, Handkerchief, Royal Blue, Clear, Ruffled, Oblong, 12 x 6 In.	431.00
Vase, Ivory, Black Glass, c.1930, 9 In.	702.00
Vase, Ivory, Conical, 6 In.	180.00
Vase, Ivrene, Footed Trumpet Shape, Spreading Scalloped Rim, 10½ In.	200.00
Vase, Jade Green, Alabaster Foot, Urn Form, Marked, Fleur-De-Lis, c.1915, 8 In.	420.00
Vase, Jadette, Art Glass, 3 x 6¾ In.	206.00
Vase, Lavender Stripes, Amber, Bowling Pin Shape, Signed, 15½ In.	25.00
Vase, Lotus, Flared, Applied Fins, G. Thompson, Etched, 14 x 7⅝ In.	649.00
Vase, Matsu-No-Ke, 2 Applied Topaz Handles, Rim, 8 In.	431.00
Vase, Ming Trees, Clouds, Acid Cut, Globular, 6⅞ In.	1150.00
Vase, Mirror Black, 3-Triangle Prong Bud, Oval Foot, Art Deco, Signed 10 In.	633.00
Vase, Mirror Black, Cylinder, Footed, Gold Paper Label, 8 In.	575.00
Vase, Mirror Black, Fan Shape, Footed, Ribs, 6 In.	748.00
Vase, Moss Agate, Flared Rim, Blue Mottled, Silver Aventurine, Footed, 12 In. .... *illus*	6090.00
Vase, Oriental Jade, Shouldered, Green Pastel, Ribs, 6 In.	2000.00

Vase, Oriental Poppy, Flared Rim, Pink & White Vertical Stripes, Footed, 6 In.	1035.00
Vase, Plum Jade, Bulbous, 7 ¼ x 8 In.	1725.00
Vase, Plum Jade, Flower Medallions, Scrolling Background, 3 ¾ x 8 In.	2415.00
Vase, Pomona Green, Topaz Glass, Double Handle, 5 x 15 ¼ In.	230.00
Vase, Pulled Feather, Threaded, Gray, Blue, Red, Flared Rim, Footed, Marked, 9 x 7 In.	1060.00
Vase, Red, Oval, Swirled Shape, Footed, 7 In.	300.00
Vase, Rosaline, Tapered, White Foot, 2 ½ x 18 In.	575.00
Vase, Rosaline, Urn Shape, Alabaster Foot, 6 In.	120.00
Vase, Rose Cintra, Ruffled Rim, Flared Body, 8 In.	1400.00
Vase, Scroll, Engraved Cats, 6 In.	936.00
Vase, Selenium Red, Footed Cornucopia, Scalloped Rim, 10 In.	325.00
Vase, Selenium Red, Footed, Pedestal, Ribbed, Signed, 14 In. ....*illus*	1955.00
Vase, Silverina, Amethyst, Silver Optic Diamonds, Urn Shape, Footed, 7 In.	805.00
Vase, Silverina, Bowl, Blue, Diamond Quilted, Silver Flecks, 5 x 10 In.	748.00
Vase, Silverina, Diamond Pattern, Trapped Air Bubbles, 8 In.	403.00
Vase, Stump, Green Jade, Three Prongs, 6 In.	325.00
Vase, Tapered Cylinder Shape, Aquamarine, 10 In.	100.00
Vase, Topaz, Crackled, Applied Lion Masks, Rectangular, 5 ¾ x 8 ¾ In.	259.00
Vase, Triangular, Ribbed, Selenium Ruby, 8 ⅛ In.	259.00
Vase, Trumpet Shape, 6 Snail Scrolled Feet, 10 In.	170.00
Vase, Tulip Shape, Dark Blue Shaded To Clear, Acid Etched Signature, Early 1900s, 9 ½ In.	230.00
Vase, Twisted Top, Cylindrical, Clear, Round, 3 ¾ x 5 In.	115.00
Vase, Whirlpool, 10 ¾ In.	329.00
Vase, Yellow, Green Edging, Ribbed, Bristol, 7 In.	234.00
Vase, Yellow Jade, Shouldered, 9 ¾ In.	1035.00
Wine, Dark Lavender Bowl & Base, Light Blue Stem, Signed, 5 ¾ In.	232.00
Wine, Green Opaque Bowl, White Opaque Base, 5 In.	53.00
Wine, Strawberry Mansion, 5 In., 8 Piece	1521.00 to 1638.00

STEVENGRAPHS are woven pictures made like fancy ribbons. They were manufactured by Thomas Stevens of Coventry, England, and became popular in 1862. Most are marked *Woven in silk by Thomas Stevens* or were mounted on a cardboard that tells the story of the Stevengraph. Other similar ribbon pictures have been made in England and Germany.

Drummer's Day, Cincinnati, Woven Silk, Sept. 15 1888, Frame, 2 ½ x 7 ¾ In.	88.00
Washington Temperance Benevolent Society, Silk Ribbon, c.1842, 3 ⅛ x 7 ½ In.	316.00

STEVENS & WILLIAMS of Stourbridge, England, made many types of glass, including layered, etched, cameo, and art glass, between the 1830s and 1930s. Some pieces are signed *S & W*. Many pieces are decorated with flowers, leaves, and other designs based on nature.

Bowl, Swirled, Ruffled Rim, Frosted Lip, Peach, Green, White, 7 x 9 In.	575.00
Cruet, Rosaline, Bulbous Shape, Ball Stopper, 6 ½ In.	130.00
Vase, Amber, Cascading Honeysuckle Branch, Ring Collar, Bulbous, Cameo, 5 In.	2185.00
Vase, Flowers, Applied Vaseline Stems, Bulbous, 6-Prong Foot, 6 In.	69.00
Vase, Morning Glories, Champagne Satin Glass, Cameo Glass, 11 In. ....*illus*	1955.00
Vase, Mother-Of-Pearl, Cinched Waist, Caramel Stripes, Gilt Branches, Footed, 3 ½ In.	259.00
Vase, Mother-Of-Pearl, Pompeiian Swirl, Reverse Amberina, 6 ¾ In. ....*illus*	748.00
Vase, Pink Cased, Opal, Applied Acorns, Rigaree Feet, 8 In., Pair	175.00
Vase, Striated Amber Base, Top Rings, Leaves, Bulbous, White Crackle, Cameo, 7 In.	1800.00

STIEGEL TYPE glass is listed here. It is almost impossible to be sure a piece was actually made by Stiegel, so the knowing collector refers to this glass as "Stiegel type." Henry William Stiegel, a colorful immigrant to the colonies, started his first factory in Pennsylvania in 1763. He remained in business until 1774. Glassware was made in a style popular in Europe at that time and was similar to the glass of many other makers. It was made of clear or colored glass and was decorated with enamel colors, mold blown designs, or etching.

Bottle, Clear, Flower Urn, Squiggle Lines, Enamel, 6 ½ In.	360.00
Bottle, Clear, Flowers, Leaves, Enamel, Pewter Collar, Screw Cap, 7 ¼ In.	295.00
Bowl, Cobalt Blue, Footed, Flint, 3 In.	240.00
Cologne Bottle, Cobalt Blue, Raised Neck Band, Reeded Body, Flint, 5 ⅝ In.	143.00
Creamer, 16 Ribs, Cobalt Blue, Applied Foot, Handle, Early 1800s, 5 In. ....*illus*	936.00
Creamer, 16 Ribs, Cobalt Blue, Applied Foot, Handle, Late 18th Century, 4 ½ In.	440.00
Cup, Flip, Tulip, Leaf, Copper Wheel Engraved, 5 ¼ In.	253.00
Glass, Flip, Blown, Clear, Wheel Engraved Basket, Flowers, Leaves, Teardrop Finial, 11 In.	356.00
Master Salt, Cobalt Blue, Footed, Flint, 3 In.	240.00

Stevens & Williams, Vase, Mother-Of-Pearl, Pompeiian Swirl, Reverse Amberina, 6 ¾ In. $748.00

Stiegel Type, Creamer, 16 Ribs, Cobalt Blue, Applied Foot, Handle, Early 1800s, 5 In. $936.00

S

Stone, Sculpture, Conch Shell, Carved, 3 Graces, White, Mottled Brown Oval, 8 ½ x 6 ½ In.
$354.00

Stoneware, Bowl, Lug Handles, Alkaline Glaze, Landrum-Stork, Edgefield, c.1850, 5 x 15 In.
$1955.00

Stoneware, Charger, Cowboy, Lasso, Incised, Signed, Waylande Gregory, 18 In.
$1200.00

Stoneware, Crock, Cover, Blue Slip, Flower Band, Molded Rim, Ear Handles, 6 x 8 In.
$377.00

Salt, 12 Diamond Pattern Over Flute, Amethyst, Applied Petal Foot, 1820s, 3 ⅛ In.	2800.00
Salt, 12 Diamond Pattern Over Flute, Cobalt Blue, Applied Petal Foot, 3 ⅜ In.	1200.00
Tumbler, Clear, Enamel Bird, Flower, 3 ½ In.	68.00
Tumbler, Flip, Engraved, Copper Wheel, Flower In Vase, Flint, Pontil, 1700s, 7 ¼ In.	302.00

STONE includes those articles made of stones, coral, shells, and some other natural materials not listed elsewhere in this book. Micro mosaics (small decorative designs made by setting pieces of stone into a pattern), urns, vases, and other pieces made of natural stone are listed here. Stoneware is pottery and is listed in the Stoneware category. Alabaster, Jade, Malachite, Marble, and Soapstone are in their own categories.

Book, Alabaster, Marble, Slate, Early 20th Century, 3 To 4 ¼ In., 5 Piece	382.00
Bust, Child, Laughing, Carved, Signed, Brooks, 14 ¼ In.	250.00
Bust, Head, Sandstone, Signed E. Reed, Ohio, c.1976, 6 In.	294.00
Bust, Indian Chief, Sandstone, Signed E. Reed, Ohio, c.1970, 6 In.	176.00
Compote, Lapis, Quartz, Engraved Metal Inlay, Applied Handles, Oval, Footed, c.1900, 3 ⅝ x 6 ½ In.	1175.00
Figure, Bear, Agate, Seated, Carved, Open Mouth, Green Stone Eyes, 2 ½ x 2 In.	805.00
Figure, Buddhist Lions, Gray, Mirrored Images, Round, Chinese, 14 In., Pair	173.00
Figure, Couple Embracing, Eskimo Carved, Canada, 12 x 7 x 37 In.	117.00
Figure, Dragon, Carved, Green, Chinese, 10 ½ x 8 ¼ In., Pair	468.00
Figure, Eagle, Green Hardstone, Black Veining, Removable Head, Wood Stand, 1900s, 6 x 8 In., Pair	173.00
Figure, Figure Bending Over Another, Marianna Pineda, 1970s, 19 ¼ In.	356.00
Figure, Flowers, Carved, Polished, Diamond Set Stamens, Rock Crystal Bowl, 11 ½ x 7 ½ In.	5520.00
Figure, Foo Dog, Carved, 12 x 5 x 7 ¼ In., Pair	165.00
Figure, Pig, Agate, Full Figure, Carved, Red Stone Eyes, Pasteboard Case, 1 x 2 ½ In.	230.00
Figure, Pipe Figure, Sandstone, Signed E. Reed, Ohio, c.1978, 51 In.	999.00
Figure, Polar Bear, Resting, Eskimo Carved, 3 ½ x 5 x 11 In.	470.00
Figure, Rabbit, Agate, Seated, Red Stone Eyes, Wood Case, 2 x 1 ½ In.	230.00
Figure, Woman, Gong, Pale Green, Wood Stand, Chinese, c.1920, 7 ½ In.	173.00
Figure, Woman, Rose Quartz, Holding Fan, Spray, Robes, Ribbons, Chinese, 10 ½ x 12 In.	374.00
Garniture, Seashell, Napoleon III, Tree Shape Gilt Bronze Standard, 8-Sided Base, 6 ½ In., Pair	1560.00
Group, 2 Squirrels, Owl Peering From Within, Sandstone, Signed E, Reed, Ohio, c.1975, 15 In.	881.00
Lamp, Soapstone, Flowering Prunus, 4 Sections, Art Deco, 56 In.	652.00
Masque, Putto, Wing Frame, Louis XIV Style, Cast, France, 18 x 10 In.	570.00
Parlor Dome, Coral, Napoleon III, Arched, Cylindrical Glass, Wood Base, Lacquered, 12 ½ In.	360.00
Sculpture, Buddha, Standing, Multicolored, Double Lotus Pedestal, 48 ½ x 62 In.	1175.00
Sculpture, Conch Shell, Carved, 3 Graces, White, Mottled Brown Oval, 8 ½ x 6 ½ In. ...... *illus*	354.00
Sculpture, Lion, Reclining, Molded, Cambridge, N.Y., c.1900, 36 In., Pair	2495.00
Sculpture, Lohan, Standing, Downcast Eyes, Hands Steepled, Clasped, 1900s, 53 ½ In., Pair	805.00
Sphinx, Crouched, Cast, Pedestal Base, 53 x 55 In., Pair	3525.00
Urn, Cover, Serpentine, Onion Green, Baluster, Flower Handles, Elephant Heads, Chinese, 7 ¾ In.	150.00
Urn, Cover, Serpentine, Spinach Green, Baluster, Ring Handles, Dog Head Holders, Chinese, 6 ½ In.	480.00
Vase, Malachite, Ingrid, Green, Nudes, Grapevines, Schlevogt, 5 In.	86.00
Water Trough, French Provincial, Carved, Pedestal, Square Vase Shape Section, 36 x 25 In.	1560.00
Wine Pot, Lid, Agate, Mughal Style, Translucent Tan, Amber, Rings, Chinese, 1800s, 4 ¾ In.	2400.00

STONEWARE is a coarse, glazed, and fired potter's ceramic that is used to make crocks, jugs, bowls, etc. It is often decorated with cobalt blue decorations. In the nineteenth and early twentieth centuries, potters often decorated crocks with blue numbers indicating the size of the container. A *2* meant 2 gallons. Stoneware is still being made. American stoneware is listed here.

Bank, Tanware, Burgundy, Glazed Designs, New Geneva, c.1850, 5 ¼ In.	1293.00
Bank, Whimsical, Blue, Incised, Barberton Ohio Earma L. Cox, Dec 25 1908, 4 ½ In.	5875.00
Barrel, Blue Banded, Bail Handle, 1 ½ Pt.	50.00
Barrel, Cover, Rope-Like Handle, Brown Glaze, c.1880, 28 In.	652.00
Batter Bowl, Blue Slip Decoration, Molded Rim, Pinched Spout, 4 x 9 In.	102.00
Batter Bowl, Flower Sprays, Leaf Slip Decoration, Pinched Spout, Gal., 5 x 11 In.	68.00
Bean Pot, Black Glaze, Rope Handles, 12 In.	5.00
Bean Pot, Brown, Tan, E. Swasey & Co., Portland, Me., 2 ¼ In.	225.00
Bean Pot, Cover, Orange Red Lead Glaze, c.1930-40s, 7 ¼ In.	121.00
Beater Jar, Blue Band, When Beating Think Of Eating From Farmer's Store, 5 ⅛ In.	132.00
Beater Jar, Cash Groceries, Blue Band, Where Quality Sells, 5 In.	128.00
Bowl, Blue Drip Glaze, Earthenware, Glen Lukens, Signed, 2 ¼ x 6 In.	655.00
Bowl, Brown Glaze, Geometric Wax Relief, Clyde Burt, 3 x 9 In.	390.00
Bowl, Ceramic, Glaze, Richard Devore, 3 x 10 ½ In.	2440.00
Bowl, Chicken, Olive, Alkaline Glaze, Signed, John Meaders, 6 ½ x 9 In.	5170.00
Bowl, Footed, Laura Anderson, 1976, 12 x 5 In.	900.00

Bowl, Lug Handles, Alkaline Glaze, Landrum-Stork, Edgefield, c.1850, 5 x 15 In. .... *illus*	1955.00
Bowl, Milk, Spitting Tulip, Applied Ear Handles, F.H. Cowden, 2 Gal., 6 ½ x 12 ½ In.	339.00
Bowl, Ribbed, Brown Glaze, 7 In.	5.00
Bowl, Shoulder, Macomb Stoneware Co., 8 In.	15.00
Bowl, Shoulder, Strainer Holes, 9 In.	115.00
Bowl, Yellow, Red, Blue, Black, Metallic Glaze, Kastrup, Denmark, 13 ¼ x 2 ½ In.	90.00
Bust, Olive, Aqua Albany Slip Glaze, Incised Hair, Eyelash, Clay Eyes, M.R. Rogers, 11 In.	523.00
Cake Pan, Cover, Blue Flower Banding, Crescent Handles, 6 x 8 ½ In.	165.00
Candelabra, Glossy Blackened Raku Type, Gunmetal Finish, 10 ½ In.	55.00
Canister, Cover, Applied Grapes, Leaves, Blue, Green, Georgia, Lanier Meaders, 1900s, 7 In.	1495.00
Canteen, Blue Daubs, Molded Leaves, Loop Handles, Salt Glaze, c.1880, 3 ¾ x 3 In.	299.00
Casserole, Cover, Ribs, Blue Stenciled Design, 5 x 9 In.	38.00
Chamber Pitcher & Basin, Roses, Blue Trim, 15-In. Bowl, 11-In. Pitcher	105.00
Chamberstick, Forest Green Glaze, Groove Top Handles, 1950-60s, 6 ¼ In.	55.00
Charger, Cowboy, Lasso, Incised, Signed, Waylande Gregory, 18 In. ....*illus*	1200.00
Chicken Waterer, Blue Tulip, 2-Sided, 1800, 11 ¾ In.	556.00
Chicken Waterer, Dark Brown Glaze, Base Pocket, Wire Bail, Incised 2, c.1900, 15 ½ In.	316.00
Chicken Waterer, Salt Glaze, Speckled Gray, Open Base Pocket, 1800s, 11 In.	115.00
Churn, 2-Color Swirl, Lug Handles, Signed, Wayne Hewell	210.00
Churn, 3 Blue Bands, Bristol Glaze, 2 Handles, 6 Gal., c.1885, 18 In.	3220.00
Churn, Applied Lunette Handle, Blue Floral Swag, 19th Century, 14 ½ In.	765.00
Churn, Bird On Branch, Applied Ear Handles, 14 ⅞ x 8 ¼ In.	132.00
Churn, Blue 6, Stripes, Applied Handles, c.1860, 16 In.	118.00
Churn, Blue Design, Speckled Bird Perched On Branch, 1885, 5 Gal.	2232.00
Churn, Blue Flowers, Impressed Number 4, c.1885, 20 In.	323.00
Churn, Blue Script, 333 Springfield County Ohio, c.1855, 15 In.	1028.00
Churn, Blue Speckled Bird Perched On Leafy Branch, 1870s, 5 Gal.	2250.00
Churn, Blue Splashes, Oval, Applied Handles, P. Rodenbough, Ohio, c.1890, 16 In.	264.00
Churn, Brown, Solomon Bell, Strasburg, Va.	300.00
Churn, Cobalt Blue Stripes, Crown, Ear Handles, 17 In.	18.00
Churn, Cover, Blue Leaves, Cylinder Shape, Lug Handles, Wood Dasher, c.1850, 4 ½ In.	460.00
Churn, Cover, Flowers, Dasher, 6 Gal., 19 In.	750.00
Churn, Cover, Salt Glaze, Masonic Emblem, Oval Top Handles, Thumb Pressed Ends, 18 In. ..	1265.00
Churn, Flowers, Molded Handles, 30 Gal., 23 In.	350.00
Churn, J.M. Pruden, Squiggle Line Blue Slip, Molded Rim, Ear Handles, 2 Gal., 12 In.	170.00
Churn, Lug, Olive Alkaline Glaze, Strap Handles, Wiley Meaders, Georgia, 18 In.	575.00
Crock, 2 Birds On Branch, Blue, Salt Glaze, Kendall & Whitney, Me., 5 Gal., 12 In.	1070.00
Crock, 2-Tone, Nalder & Collyer's Brewery Co. Ltd., Croydon 5110, 4 Gal.	125.00
Crock, Beaded Circle, Blue, Letters, No. 3, Monmouth Pottery Co., Monmouth, Il., 10 In.	109.00
Crock, Bird On Branch, Blue, Salt Glaze, Minnesota Stoneware Co., 2 Gal.	2380.00
Crock, Bird, Pecking Chicken, Applied Ear Handles, 2 Gal., 9 ¾ x 10 ¼ In.	495.00
Crock, Black Design, Tab Handles, Impressed, Fulper Brothers, 9 In.	82.00
Crock, Blue Band, Incised Fish, 19th Century, 8 In.	625.00
Crock, Blue, F.H. Cowden, Gal.	50.00
Crock, Blue, Flower, Tab Handles, Impressed, A.K. Ballard, Vt., 11 x 11 ½ In.	136.00
Crock, Blue, Signed, T.F. Reppert, Greensboro, Pa., 19th Century, 2 Gal., 10 In.	240.00
Crock, Blue Tulips, Oval, 2 Handles, Impressed Label, c.1850, 20 In.	822.00
Crock, Bluebird, Blue, N.A. White & Son, Utica, N.Y., 6 Gal., 13 ½ x 14 In.	595.00
Crock, Branches, Blue, Handles, 8 In.	189.00
Crock, Brown, Handle, Cowden, Gal.	45.00
Crock, Chicken Pecking Corn, Blue, Tab Handles, 3 Gal.	500.00
Crock, Cover, Blue Slip, Flower Band, Molded Rim, Ear Handles, 6 x 8 In. ....*illus*	377.00
Crock, Cover, Boston Baked Beans, Blue, Salt Glaze, 19th Century, 7 In.	240.00
Crock, Cover, Butter, Blue, White, Bail Handle, 3 Lb.	75.00
Crock, Cover, Flower Spray, Flat Molded Rim, Ear Handles, Swiggle Line, 6 x 8 ¼ In.	358.00
Crock, Cover, Oak Leaves, Blue, Crescent Handles, Stamped 2, 2 Gal., 10 x 10 In.	302.00
Crock, Design On Shoulder, Blue, 12 Gal., 10 In.	105.00
Crock, Ear Handles, Bulbous, M. Tyler, Gal., 9 ½ In.	45.00
Crock, Flemish Blue Geometric Designs, Applied Handle, Bulbous, 6 ½ x 5 ¾ In.	22.00
Crock, Flower & Sprig Band, Blue, Crescent Handles, 9 ½ x 8 In.	495.00
Crock, Flower, Blue, 19th Century, 6 Gal., 14 In.	228.00
Crock, Flower, Blue, 19th Century, 8 ¼ In.	480.00
Crock, Flower, Blue, Applied Handles, FB Norton & Co., Mass., c.1850, 10 In.	294.00
Crock, Flower, Blue, Cylindrical, Rolled Rim, C.L. & A.K. Ballard, Vt., 2 Gal.	201.00
Crock, Flower, Blue, E. White & Co., Binghamton, 1800s, 13 In.	360.00
Crock, Flower, Blue, Impressed, D.P. Shenfelder, Reading, Pa., 1800s, 1 ½ Gal.	234.00

Stoneware, Crock, Man's Portrait, Hat, A.O. Whittemore, Havana, N.Y., 7 x 8 In. $3795.00

Stoneware, Crock, Salt Glaze, Blue Flower, 19th Century, 6 Gal., 14 In. $228.00

Stoneware, Crock, Tapered, Rounded Rim, Strap Handles, Cheever Meaders, c.1940, 1 ½ In. $1093.00

Stoneware, Figurine, Bird, Blue Comb & Feathers, Arie Meaders, Georgia, 8 ¼ In. $6440.00

S

Stoneware, Figurine, Rooster,
Olive Runny Alkaline Glaze,
Edwin Meaders, Georgia, 1924, 14½ In.
$1725.00

Stoneware, Flowerpot, Drip Tray, Flower,
Slip Decoration, Pinched Edge Rim,
5 x 6 In.
$638.00

Stoneware, Jug, Face,
Olive Mottled Alkaline Glaze, Rock Teeth,
Lanier Meaders, 10 In.
$1955.00

Crock, Flower, Blue, Molded Rim, Ear Handles, M. Woodruff, 7 ½ In.	79.00
Crock, Flower, Blue, N. Eberhardt, Toronto, Ont. Mark, c.1870, ½ Gal., 8 x 9 ¾ In.	349.00
Crock, Flower, Blue, Rolled Rim, 2 Ear Handles, Seymour Bros., Hartford, 3 Gal.	95.00
Crock, Flower, Blue, Tab Handles, C.L. & A.K. Ballard, Burlington, Vt., 2 Gal., 9 In.	203.00
Crock, Flower, Blue, Tab Handles, Seymour Bros., Hartford, Ct., 3 Gal., 10 ¼ x 12 In.	95.00
Crock, Flower, Blue, Tab Handles, Stamped J. Burger, Rochester, 1800s, 3 Gal.	175.00
Crock, Flower, Leaves, Bulbous, Ear Handles, Molded Rim, Blue, 4 Gal., 15 ¼ In.	495.00
Crock, Flower Spray, 3 Flowers Along Rim, Blue, 12 In.	1912.00
Crock, Flowers, Blue 3, M. Woodruff, Cortland, New York, 3 Gal., 11 In.	283.00
Crock, Flowers, Blue, Impressed, 2 Gal., 9 In.	385.00
Crock, Flowers, Blue, Leaves, Tab Handles, 19th Century, 3 Gal., 14 ½ In.	345.00
Crock, Flowers, Blue, Signed, Hamilton & Jones, Greensboro, 5 Gal., 13 ¼ In.	250.00
Crock, Flowers, Blue, Stamped, Twilley & Bennett, Sharptown, Md., 9 In.	825.00
Crock, Flowers, Blue, Tab Handles, 12 ½ In.	150.00
Crock, Flowers, Blue, Tab Handles, 19th Century, 4 Gal., 12 In.	79.00
Crock, Flowers, P. Herman, Gal.	210.00
Crock, Green, Brown Slip Glaze, Handles, J. Fisher, Lyons, N.Y., 1 ½ Gal.	95.00
Crock, Heinz Peach Butter, White, Wire Bail, Wood Handle, 5 ¼ x 5 In.	1072.00
Crock, Horse, Blue, Stamped W.H. Wheaton, Danielsonville, Conn., c.1875, 10 In.	1955.00
Crock, J.H. Dipple, Lewistown, Pa., Gal.	56.00
Crock, J.M. Hickerson, Strasburg, Va., Gal.	225.00
Crock, Leaves, Blue, Handles, Burger & Co., Rochester, N.Y., 2 Gal.	265.00
Crock, Macomb Stoneware, Macomb, Ill., 5 Gal.	105.00
Crock, Man's Portrait, Hat, A.O. Whittemore, Havana, N.Y., 7 x 8 In. .... *illus*	3795.00
Crock, Monarch Pickle, Cobalt Blue Letters, Squat, Glass & Wire Hinged Lid, 14 In.	118.00
Crock, Montpelier, Iowa, Blue, Salt Glaze, 4 Gal.	118.00
Crock, Mottled Blue, ½ Gal.	48.00
Crock, Onondaga Cottage Cheese, Cobalt Blue Letters, Straight-Sided, 9 ½ In.	47.00
Crock, Profile Of Man, Hat, Neckerchief, Blue, Bulbous, 13 x 8 In.	1210.00
Crock, Salt Glaze, 2 Handles, 9 In.	605.00
Crock, Salt Glaze, Blue Flower, 19th Century, 6 Gal., 14 In. .... *illus*	228.00
Crock, Salt Glaze, Fort Dodge, 1997, 4 Gal.	40.00
Crock, Salt Glaze, Macomb Stoneware Co., 6 Gal.	75.00
Crock, Script, Blue, Oval, Impressed I.M. Mead, Ohio, c.1855, 12 x 10 In.	734.00
Crock, Spitting Tulip, Closed Tulip, Blue, Ear Handles, Cowden & Wilcox, 12 In.	79.00
Crock, Stencil, Blue, James Benjamin, Cincinnati, Ohio, 2 Gal.	177.00
Crock, Stenciled Flower, Blue, T.F. Repert, Greensboro, Pa., 2, 2 Gal., 11 ½ x 8 In.	143.00
Crock, Stylized Flower, Blue, Bosworth, Hartford, 2 Ear Handles, 3 Gal, 10 In.	148.00
Crock, Stylized Flower, Blue, Bulbous, Flared Neck, 2 Ear Handles, 12 In.	148.00
Crock, Swags, Blue, Squared Rim, Stamped Solomn Bell, c.1875, Gal., 9 In.	288.00
Crock, Tapered Body, Olive Glaze, Strap Handles, Cheever Meaders, c.1940, 10 ½ In.	1093.00
Crock, Tapered, Rounded Rim, Strap Handles, Cheever Meaders, c.1940, 1 ½ In. .... *illus*	1093.00
Crock, Tulip, Blue, Bulbous, Cowden & Wilcox, 1 ½ Gal., 8 ½ x 9 In.	158.00
Crock, Tulip, Blue, Bulbous, Crescent Handle, Sam Irvine, Newville, 14 ¾ x 10 In.	209.00
Crock, Tulip, Blue, Lug Handles, Whites, Utica, N.Y., 7 ½ x 8 ½ In.	110.00
Crock, Tulip, Flowers, Leaf, Blue Decoration, Molded Lip, Ear Handles, Bulbous, 10 x 9 In.	124.00
Crock, W. Hart & Co., Mark, Gal.	149.00
Cup, Runny Olive Alkaline Glaze, Strap Handle, 3 ¼ In.	978.00
Cuspidor, Blue, Concave Sides, Molded Base, Round, 4 x 7 In.	51.00
Cuspidor, Blue, Impressed Cowden & Wilcox, Harrisburg, 3 ¾ x 6 ½ In.	360.00
Cuspidor, Blue Vines, Cylinder, Baltimore, c.1850, 2 ¼ x 4 ⅛ In.	1840.00
Figurine, Abraham Lincoln, Black Copper Luster Suit, Hat, 2 Birds On Podium, 9 ½ In.	1045.00
Figurine, Bird, Blue Comb & Feathers, Arie Meaders, Georgia, 8 ¼ In. .... *illus*	6440.00
Figurine, Chicken, Salt Glaze, Blue, Fly Ash, c.1990s, 5 x 7 In.	55.00
Figurine, Devil Torso, Snake, Glossy Olive Variation Glaze, Horns, Red Tongue, 24 In.	463.00
Figurine, Dog, Spaniel, George Bagnall, Buff Colored, Freestanding Front Legs, Incised Eyes, 9 ¾ In.	940.00
Figurine, Dog, Spaniel, Seated, Black Paint, Earl 20th Century, 12 ¾ In.	206.00
Figurine, Donkey, Orange, Black Lead Glaze, Raised Ears, Mane, Tail, 4 ½ In.	44.00
Figurine, Man, Seated With Chicken, Glossy Blue, Blue Green Feldspathic Glaze, 11 In.	132.00
Figurine, Romeo & Juliet, Hands Heart To Juliet, Multicolored, 9 x 6 ½ In.	990.00
Figurine, Rooster, Blue Glaze, Marked, Edwin Meaders, 15 ½ In.	1093.00
Figurine, Rooster, Matte & Glossy Green Glaze, Stamped, R Armfield, 10 ¾ In.	316.00
Figurine, Rooster, Olive Runny Alkaline Glaze, Edwin Meaders, Georgia, 1924, 14 ½ In. . *illus*	1725.00
Figurine, Witch, Riding Broom, Orange, Black, Detailed Face, 5 In.	77.00
Flagon, 4 Steins, Blue Design, Pewter Thumbpiece, 16 & 6 In., 5 Piece	410.00

Flask, Blue Clock Design, Flat Sides, Incised Border, N.Y., c.1840, 6 ¼ In.	3450.00
Flask, Boot Shape, Brown Rockingham Glaze, Earthenware, 6 ½ x 7 ¼ In.	143.00
Flask, Brushed Blue Tulips, Side Blue Leaves, 8 Flat Sides, c.1835, 7 In.	2760.00
Flowerpot, Blue, Flowers, 2-Sided, Underplate, 19th Century, 7 In.	275.00
Flowerpot, Drip Tray, Flower, Leaf Slip, Pinched Rim, 5 ½ x 6 ⅜ In.	605.00
Flowerpot, Drip Tray, Flower, Leaf Slip, Pinched Rim, 6 x 6 ½ In.	463.00
Flowerpot, Drip Tray, Flower, Slip Decoration, Pinched Edge Rim, 5 x 6 In. .... *illus*	638.00
Ice Cooler, Cover, Flemish, Whites, Utica..	300.00
Jam Pot, With A Caveat, Dancing Golliwog, Seedless Bramble Label, Harley's, c.1920, 5 In.	225.00
Jar, 3 Blue Swags, Square Rim, RCR Mark, Phil., c.1875, ½ Gal., 7 In.	374.00
Jar, 3-Leaf, Blue, Peter Herman, Baltimore, c.1860, 1 ½ Gal.	250.00
Jar, 3-Part Totemic, Val Cushing, Signed, 1985, 32 x 11 In.	1464.00
Jar, Apothecary, Glossy Yellow, Black Red Lead Glaze, Ribbing, Split Handle, 8 In.	165.00
Jar, Blue Bird, Oval, Lug Handles, c.1950, 12 ½ In.	83.00
Jar, Blue, Cylinder Form, Molded Rim, Leaf Banded, 9 ¼ x 5 ⅝ In.	154.00
Jar, Blue Design, Oval, Lug Handles, 3, P.H. Smith, Ohio, Mid 1800s, 12 In.	294.00
Jar, Blue Design, Oval, Ribbed Lug Handles, 5, Phila., Early 1900s, 16 In.	470.00
Jar, Blue Leaf, Flower, Tapered Sides, Wide Mouth, Maryland, c.1835, 3 Gal., 13 In.	593.00
Jar, Blue Squiggly Lines, Oval, American, 19th Century, 13 ¾ In.	115.00
Jar, Brown Alkaline Glaze, Lug Handles, 4 Hash Marks, Edgefield, c.1850, 14 In.	863.00
Jar, Brown, Cowden & Wilcox, 6 ½ In.	45.00
Jar, Canning, Gray, Blue Leaves, 11 In.	330.00
Jar, Canning, Gray, Muted Blue Leaves, Incised 1 ½, 11 ¼ In.	280.00
Jar, Canning, Light Brown, ½ Gal.	85.00
Jar, Canning, Tomato, Blue Banded, Molded Rim, 8 ½ In.	1695.00
Jar, Cover, Blue Band, Barrel Form, 9 ¾ In.	124.00
Jar, Cover, Brown, Violet Blue Crystalline Glaze, Allover Crystals, Medallion, 7 ¼ In.	88.00
Jar, Cover, Ledge, Salt Glaze, Flare Neck, Angled Rim, Shoulder Fly, 11 ¼ In.	523.00
Jar, Cover, Raised Grapes & Leaves, Green Alkaline Glaze, Arie Meaders, 7 ½ In.	2185.00
Jar, Glossy Earthy Olive, Brown Alkaline Glaze, 2 Lug Handles, Glass Melts, 14 ½ In.	413.00
Jar, Glossy Olive, Alkaline Glaze, Oval Top Handle, 13 ½ In.	550.00
Jar, Grape, Alkaline Glaze, Leaves, Vines, Marked Lanier Meaders, 12 In.	2415.00
Jar, Heinz Tomato Preserves, Standard Quality, Clamp & Lid, 8 x 4 In.	1045.00
Jar, Horizontal Stripes, 2, Pennsylvania, 2 Gal., 9 ½ In.	374.00
Jar, Man, Woman Picking Cotton, High Gloss Olive Crush Glaze, c.1993, 10 ½ In.	715.00
Jar, Oval, Flared, Alkaline Glaze, Stamped J.F.S., N. Car., c.1875, ½ Gal., 9 ½ In.	1035.00
Jar, Oval, Flat Rim, Mottled Brown, Red Alkaline Glaze, I. Craven, Georgia, c.1785, 7 ½ In.	115.00
Jar, Oval, Impressed, Cyrus Felton, c.1820, 17 In.	444.00
Jar, Palatine Pottery, Blue Pear, Molded Lip, 8 ¼ In.	876.00
Jar, S. Purdy, Portage Co. Ohio, Blue Design, Molded Handles, 2 Gal., 11 ¾ In.	145.00
Jar, Salt Glaze, Orange, Oval Top Handles, Thumb Pressed Ends, Flat Rim, 15 x 40 In.	4290.00
Jar, Salt Glaze, Rolled Rim, Impressed, Miller & Davison, Strausberg, Va., 8 ¼ In.	240.00
Jar, Salt Glaze, Rolled Rim, Oval, Yellow Dragons, Brown Ground, c.1890, 27 x 22 In.	230.00
Jar, Salt Glaze, Semioval, Square Rim, Neck Ring, 10 ½ In., 5 ⅝-In. Neck Ring........	3450.00
Jar, Satin Olive Alkaline Glaze, Roll Rim, Oval Handles, Bulbous, 13 ½ x 39 In.	303.00
Jar, Speckled Olive Glaze, 2 Hash Marks, Large Lug Handles, Edgefield, c.1850, 13 In.	1150.00
Jar, Stag Hunters, Blue Glaze, No. 6, 6 x 9 In.	168.00
Jar, Woman, Hoop Skirt, Umbrella, Handles, Glossy Olive Crush Glass Glaze, c.1993, 13 In.	385.00
Jug, 2 Faces, Crying Eye, Smiling Eye, Jerry Brown, 10 ½ In.	240.00
Jug, 2 Strap Handles, Mottled Brown Alkaline Glaze, Impressed HN, 15 ¼ In.	489.00
Jug, 3 Faces, Glossy Olive Mottled Glaze, 3 Loop Handles, Clay Eyes, 9 ¼ In.	160.00
Jug, Alkaline Glaze, 2 Strap Handles, 16 ¾ In.	575.00
Jug, Alkaline Glaze, Double Strap Handles, Mottled Brown, Green Glaze, 17 ¼ In.	345.00
Jug, B.B. Craig, Runny Dark Glaze, Handles, Stamped, 16 In.	259.00
Jug, Beehive, Salt Glaze, Blue Decoration, 3 Gal..	145.00
Jug, Bellarmine, Tiger Mottled, Oval, Bearded Face Mask, Pinwheel, Crest Heart, c.1660, 8 In.	728.00
Jug, Bird, Blue, Applied Handle, JA & CW Underwood, NY, c.1850, 15 In.	353.00
Jug, Bird, Blue, Scrolling, Binghamton, 11 In.	200.00
Jug, Blue Design, Impressed, S. Purdy, 3 Gal., Late 1800s, 16 In.	95.00
Jug, Blue Inscribed 1848, 2 Gal., 11 ½ In.	296.00
Jug, Blue, Leaf, Bulbous, Clark & Fox, 2 Gal., 13 In.	220.00
Jug, Blue Letters, Peter O'Toole, Clinton, Ma., 2 Gal., 14 In.	236.00
Jug, Blue Letters, P.J. Wallace, Albany, N.Y., Ottman Bros., 2 Gal., 14 In.	148.00
Jug, Blue, No. 3, E. S. & B., New Brighton, Pa., 14 ¼ In.	115.00
Jug, Blue, Oval, Applied Handle, Impressed I.M. Mead, Ohio, c.1855, 11 In.	206.00
Jug, Blue, Peter O'Toole, Clinton, Mass., 2 Gal., 14 In.	255.00

Stoneware, Jug, Salt Glaze, Blue Double Tulips, Cowden & Wilcox, Embossed, 1800s, 13 ¼ In. $330.00

Stoneware, Jug, Salt Glaze, Flower, Dohlen, Charleston, 19th Century, 2 Gal., 13 ¾ In. $2300.00

Stoneware, Pitcher, Albany Slip Glaze, Jos. L. Friedman & Co., Paducah, Ky., 8 ¾ In. $230.00

As always, the edited listings in *Kovels' Antiques & Collectibles Price Guide 2011* aren't available on any website, but readers should visit Kovels.com for information on trends, tips, reproductions, marks, old prices, and more!

S

Stoneware, Teapot, Salt Glaze,
Blue Highlights, England,
Late 18th Century, 4 ¾ In.
$878.00

Stoneware, Water Cooler, Blue Flower,
Wells & Richards, Reading Berks Co.,
13 In.
$11115.00

Jug, Blue, P.J. Wallace, 100 Madison Ave., Albany, N.Y., Ottman Bros., 2 Gal., 14 In.	155.00
Jug, Blue, R. Heller, Newark, N.J., 11 In.	55.00
Jug, Blue Streaks, Thick Spout, Applied Strap Handle, c.1875, 4 ⅜ In.	489.00
Jug, Blue, Tulip, Handle, Oval, Ohio, c.1850, 14 ½ In.	823.00
Jug, Brown Glaze, F.H. Cowden, Handles	95.00
Jug, Brown Mottled, Olive Alkaline Glaze, T.J. Averett, 1875, 9 ¾ In.	489.00
Jug, Deer, Leaves, Blue, Brown Glaze, Neuhol, Signed, 7 In.	58.00
Jug, Devil, Incised Eyebrows, Mustache, Broken China Teeth, B.B. Craig, N.C., 11 In.	920.00
Jug, Face, 2 Handles, Signed, Joe Reinhardt, 14 In.	300.00
Jug, Face, Alkaline Glaze, Blue Overlay, China Plate Teeth, Stamped, BB Craig, 6 ¾ In.	600.00
Jug, Face, Devil, Broken China Teeth, White Horns, Red Lips, Brown, Arden, N.C., 18 In.	460.00
Jug, Face, Devil, Chocolate Albany Slip Glaze, E. Miller, 9 ⅜ In.	99.00
Jug, Face, Devil, Glossy Olive, Alkaline Glaze, Double Face, Handles, W.T. McLennan, 9 ¾ In.	99.00
Jug, Face, Devil, Snake, Albert Hodge, 13 In.	480.00
Jug, Face, Double, Happiness, Weeping Eyes, Clay Teeth, Lead Glaze, Multicolored, 10 In.	550.00
Jug, Face, Drippy Alkaline Glaze, Upper Row Clay Teeth, Signed, Lanier Meaders, 9 In.	920.00
Jug, Face, Glossy Lead Glaze, Blue Green Over Orange, Yellow Eyes, Glaze Dripping, 8 ¾ In.	495.00
Jug, Face, Ivory, Dark Caramel Glaze, Flowing Hair, Grape, Leaf, Biblical Verse, 2 Handles, 7 In.	303.00
Jug, Face, Molded, Insects Crawling, Brown Glaze, White Teeth, Jackson Pottery, 9 x 6 In.	209.00
Jug, Face, Mottled, Olive Alkaline Glaze, Ceramic Teeth, Base, Lanier Meaders, 9 In.	1150.00
Jug, Face, Olive, Alkaline Glaze, White Clay Teeth, Eyes, Lanier Meaders, 1980, 8 ⅜ In.	1100.00
Jug, Face, Olive Mottled Alkaline Glaze, Rock Teeth, Lanier Meaders, 10 In. .... *illus*	1955.00
Jug, Face, Salt Glaze, Face Accents, Brown Teeth, Inserted Pupils, Double Dip Handle, 9 ¾ In.	55.00
Jug, Face, Salt Glaze, Goatee, Mustache, Eyebrows, China Teeth, c.1993, 10 ¼ In.	88.00
Jug, Face, Satin Gloss Alkaline Streaked Glaze, Eyebrows, Mustache, China Teeth, 6 In.	61.00
Jug, Face, Snake & Frog, Motto, Brown Glaze, White Teeth, Jackson Pottery, 9 x 5 ½ In.	121.00
Jug, Face, Snake Handle, Lizard, Sculpted Face, Incised Hair, Beard, Marie Rogers, 10 ¾ In.	248.00
Jug, Face, Snake, Signed, Joe Reinhardt, 1995, 14 In.	300.00
Jug, Face, Teeth, Glazed Eyes, Runny Olive Glaze, Handles, B.B. Craig, N. Carolina, c.1970, 12 In.	546.00
Jug, Flower, Blue, Handle, R. Mugler & Co. Buffalo, N.Y., 2 Gal.	644.00
Jug, Flower, Blue, Impressed, White & Wood, Binghamton, 2 Gal., 13 ¾ In.	195.00
Jug, Flower, Blue, Impressed, White & Wood Binghamton, N.Y., 1800s, 2 Gal.	205.00
Jug, Flower, Blue, Oval, Applied Handle, I. Seymour, Troy, Factory, 3, 17 x 11 In., 3 Gal.	413.00
Jug, Flower Bouquet, Blue, Cowden & Wilcox, Harrisburg, Pa., 18 In., 5 Gal.	385.00
Jug, Flowers, Blue, Applied Handles, J. Stadden, Ohio, c.1850, 14 ½ In.	881.00
Jug, Flowers, Blue, Cowden & Wilcox, Harrisburg, Pa., 2 Gal., 13 ½ In.	1500.00
Jug, Flowers, Blue, Leaves, Nichols & Boynton, Burlington, Vt., 1800s, 3 Gal.	185.00
Jug, Flowers, Blue, No. 3, Handle, 15 In.	263.00
Jug, Flowers, Blue, Spout, J.S. Taft & Co., Keene, N.H., 2 Gal., 13 In.	270.00
Jug, Flowers, Leaf Blue Slip Decoration, 13 In.	136.00
Jug, Glossy Caramel Feldspathic Glaze, Snake, Don Craig, c.1993, 13 In.	193.00
Jug, Glossy Feldspathic Glaze, Brown, Caramel Swirlware, China Teeth, Eyes, 11 ¾ In.	463.00
Jug, Glossy Olive Alkaline Glaze, Handle, Tooled Neck, Roll Rim, Oval Handles, 9 ¾ In.	3300.00
Jug, Glossy Olive Variation Alkaline, Salt Glaze, Handle, 23 x 57 In.	523.00
Jug, Glossy Variation Crush Glass Glaze, Handle, White Clay Slip, c.1993, 11 In.	463.00
Jug, Goodale Stedman, Applied Handle, Gal., 12 In.	102.00
Jug, Gray, Peter Herman Stoneware, Baltimore, c.1860, 2 Gal., 15 In.	150.00
Jug, Green Alkaline Glaze, Handle, Stamped D.S. 6, N. Car., c.1840, 6 Gal., 17 ½ In.	10005.00
Jug, Green Alkaline Glaze, Oval, Handles, Stamped J.S. Nash, c.1850, 16 ½ In.	10925.00
Jug, Heinz Pure Cider Vinegar, Paper Label, 9 x 6 ½ In.	242.00
Jug, Honey Glaze, Applied Snake Breaking Through Side, O. Norris, S.C., 13 In.	288.00
Jug, Incised Birds, Blue, Impressed, Hartford, 19th Century, 12 In.	4300.00
Jug, Incised Lines, Designs, Applied Deer, Branch Handle, Albany Glaze Interior, c.1890, 8 In.	705.00
Jug, Leaf Blue Slip Decorated, Applied Handle, S. Hart, 1 ½ Gal., 10 ¼ In.	113.00
Jug, Leaf, Blue, Straight Sides, Impressed, F.C. Norton, Mass., c.1865, 4 Gal., 17 In.	148.00
Jug, Mark Hawthorn Pottery Co., Hawthorn, Pa., Gal.	45.00
Jug, Milk, Indoor & Outdoor Scenes, Blue Glaze, 7 In.	95.00
Jug, Mottled Brown Alkaline Glaze, Strap Handle, Impressed HN, c.1880, 11 ½ In.	403.00
Jug, Mottled Runny Olive Alkaline Glaze, 3 Incised Lines, c.1920, 16 In.	305.00
Jug, New York Liquor Stores, Brown Cone Top, A. Vogel, Danbury, Conn., ½ Gal., 9 In.	78.00
Jug, Orchid, Blue, Oval, Handle, Stamped, White's Utica, N.Y., 17 x 10 In., 3 Gal.	248.00
Jug, Oval, Applied Handle, Incised Tulips, Blue, Early 1800s, 12 In.	500.00
Jug, Oval, Applied Strap Handle, Albany Slip Glaze, Signed W.C. Robertson, Georgia, 16 In.	1955.00
Jug, Oval, Applied Strap Handle, Blue Accent, J. Bennace, J.A. Sutherland, 14 ½ In.	323.00
Jug, Oval, Brown Glaze, Lug Handles, Dave, Slave Potter Mark, Edgefield, 1851, 16 In.	19550.00
Jug, Oval, Celadon Glaze, Brown Slip Design, Edgefield, South Carolina, c.1850, 13 In.	2070.00

Jug, Oval, Double Handles, Applied Strap Handles, Blue, 5, Late 1800s, 18 ½ In.	206.00
Jug, Oval, Stamped 1, Incised Fish, Strap Handle, c.1800, 11 ½ In.	587.00
Jug, Oval, Strap Handle, Mottled Olive Brown Glaze, Marked WB, Becham, Georgia, 12 In.	1725.00
Jug, Pigeon On Branch, Blue, Salt Glaze, No. 5, 19 In.	920.00
Jug, Ring, Dark Reddish Brown Glaze, Georgia, 1900, 13 ½ In.	2300.00
Jug, Robinson Clay Products, John P Thompson, ½ Gal.	30.00
Jug, Salt Glaze, 3 Groove Wide Handles, Neck Rim, Shoulder Fly Ash, 4 In.	2640.00
Jug, Salt Glaze, Blue Double Tulips, Cowden & Wilcox, Embossed, 1800s, 13 ¼ In. .... *illus*	330.00
Jug, Salt Glaze, Flower, Dohlen, Charleston, 19th Century, 2 Gal., 13 ¾ In. .... *illus*	2300.00
Jug, Salt Glaze, Handle, Incised Shoulder Lines, Square Rim, 8 ¼ In.	4290.00
Jug, Salt Glaze, Orange Peel, Fly Ash Meltings, Roll Rim, Top Handle, c.1840s, Craven, 18 In. .	2200.00
Jug, Shield, Blue, Brown Spout, McCoy Pottery, 2 Gal.	50.00
Jug, Square Handle, Pat' Oct. 3rd., Gal.	80.00
Jug, Squatty, 2 Applied Handles, Olive Glaze, Stamped CJB, Georgia, c.1880, 14 ½ In.	5060.00
Jug, Strap Handle, Blue Flowers, Impressed Label, Woodruff, Cortland, 17 ½ In.	235.00
Jug, Strap Handle, Mottled Brown Olive Alkaline Glaze, Marked, TJA, Georgia, 9 ¾ In.	489.00
Jug, Tapered Top, Alkaline Glaze, Marked, T In Handle, Timmerman, 1880s, 11 ⅜ In.	863.00
Jug, Tulip, Blue, Applied C-Shaped Handle, D.P. Shenfelder, Reading, Pa., 9 ½ In., 2 Gal.	330.00
Jug, Tulip, Double, Blue Slip, Applied Handle, 3 Gal., 15 ½ In.	264.00
Jug, Wavy Line Flower, Blue, Applied Handle, N.A. White & Son, 11 In.	248.00
Keg, Glossy Clear Crush Glass Glaze, Gray, White Swirl Pattern, 4 ⅝ In.	248.00
Mug, Flaccus Bros., Gray, Blue, Handle, Wheeling, W. Va., 4 ¼ In.	225.00
Mug, Lucky Strike, Blond Woman, Seated, Western Stoneware, 3 ¾ x 5 ¼ In.	35.00
Mug, Paulaner, Gold Letters, Germany, 5 ¼ In.	20.00
Mug, Shoulder, Base Blue Band, Narrow Opening, Oval, c.1850, 7 ⅝ In.	150.00
Peacock, Mike Hanning, 14 x 17 x 5 In.	300.00
Pig, Olive, Rust Albany Slip Glaze, Pearl Eye, Curly Tail, Snout, M. Rogers, c.1980s, 4 x 6 ¾ In.	55.00
Piggy Bank, Glossy Olive, Crush Coca-Cola Glaze, Pop Eye, c.1979, 6 In.	358.00
Pipe, Coiled Serpent Form, Brown Salt Glaze, Early 1800s, 10 ½ In.	1450.00
Pitcher, Albany Slip Glaze, Jos. L. Friedman & Co., Paducah, Ky., 8 ¾ In. .... *illus*	230.00
Pitcher, Blue Design, Impressed, Gilson & Co., 19th Century, 10 ¼ In.	1700.00
Pitcher, Blue Design, Incised, 2, 10 In.	150.00
Pitcher, Blue Glaze, Mark, Owen Batchelder, North Carolina, 1920s, 5 In.	633.00
Pitcher, Blue Tulip, Leaf, Oval, Stamped Cowden & Wilcox, c.1865, 8 In.	1208.00
Pitcher, Clover, Oval, Strap Handle, Baltimore, c.1870, 2 ¾ In.	4255.00
Pitcher, Flowerpot Shape, Brown Drip Metallic Glaze, Handle, c.1890, 5 In.	1093.00
Pitcher, Flowers, Applied Handle, Incised C.D., c.1850, 9 In.	1880.00
Pitcher, Flowers, Blue, 19th Century, 3 Gal., 14 ¾ In.	678.00
Pitcher, Flowers, Tanware, Burgundy, Applied Handle, New Geneva, c.1850, 9 In.	646.00
Pitcher, Forest Green Lead Glaze, Coggle Wheel Shoulder, 13 ½ In.	77.00
Pitcher, Glossy Aqua Olive Crush Glass Glaze, Grape Cluster, Leaves, Branch, 7 ¼ In.	132.00
Pitcher, Green Crystalline Glaze, Silver Flower Armature Overlay, Du Bigot, 9 x 5 ½ In.	1952.00
Pitcher, Hunting Scene, Deer, Blue & White, 6 ½ x 5 In.	132.00
Pitcher, Incised Tree, Albany Glazed, 1891, 9 x 4 ⅝ In.	2415.00
Pitcher, Men In Tavern, Man With Raised Mug Sitting On Keg, Flowers, Marked, 8 In.	44.00
Pitcher, Milk, Stencil, Slip Decorated, James Hamilton, 8 In.	424.00
Pitcher, Pastel Matte Blue Glaze, Wagon Scene Cameo, Potter Seated At Wheel, 3 ¾ In.	193.00
Pitcher, Rock Island Lumber Co., West Branch, Iowa, Sponge Brown & Green	60.00
Pitcher, Salt Glaze, 3-Groove Wide Handle, 9 ¾ In.	1980.00
Pitcher, Slip Design, Light Brown Alkaline Glaze, Edgefield, 11 In.	978.00
Pitcher, Speckled Salt Glaze, Ribbon Handle, J.D. Craven, N.C., c.1885, 12 ¾ In.	288.00
Pitcher, Spirit Of 76, Fife & Drum Players, Flag, Blue & White, 8 ½ x 6 In.	99.00
Pitcher, Tapered, Applied Strap, Handle, Mottled Brown Glaze, 10 In.	430.00
Pitcher, Water, 2-Tone Glaze, Applied Handle, Pinched Spout, 9 ¼ In.	237.00
Pitcher, Water, Arts & Crafts Style, Copper Skin, Rivets, 10 In.	196.00
Plate, Concentric Green Circles, Bristol Glaze, Timmerman, Incised Marks, 1880s, 7 ¼ In.	700.00
Plate, Dogwood Blossom, Glass Crush Glaze, Sandy, Green Leaves, Brown Branch, 9 In.	275.00
Pot, Flower Design, Blue, Marked, R.C.R./Phil., 6 In.	2691.00
Pot, Harley's English Jam, Dancing Golliwog, Seedless Bramble Label, 1920, 5 ¼ In.	225.00
Rooster, Camel, Glaze, Red Comb, Waddle, Eye, Edwin Meaders, 16 ½ In.	5500.00
Rooster, Glossy Olive Glaze, Snake, Open Mouth, Fangs, Tongue, Eyes, 17 ¼ In.	440.00
Soap Dish, Blue & White Spatter, Blue Bands, 6 In. Diam.	48.00
Strawberry Jar, Unglazed, Incised Signature On Base, Lanier Meaders, 16 In.	92.00
Teapot, Salt Glaze, Blue Highlights, England, Late 18th Century, 4 ¾ In. .... *illus*	878.00
Vase, Abstract, Verdigris Glaze, C. Gustin, Signed, 1986, 19 x 11 ½ In.	1464.00
Vase, Albany Slip Glaze, River Scene, Grassy Field, House, Handles, J. Meaders, 7 In.	303.00

Store, Change Maker, 5 Slots, Johnson Fare Box Co., Pat. 1465509, Chicago, 10 x 3 ¾ In. $35.00

Store, Clothing Rack, Circular, Cast Iron, Revolving Top, 60 x 32 In. $165.00

S

Store, Strawholder, San-L, Glass, Metal Top, Lancaster, c.1917, 12 In. $146.00

Stove, Box, Cast Iron, Scrolled Leaves, Paw Feet, Pleis, Foening & Thudium, 20 x 22 x 11 In. $147.00

Stove, Conowingo Furnace, Iron, Flower & Sawtooth Panels, 33 x 13 x 25 In. $754.00

Vase, Bottle, Flattened, Rectangular, Kaki Glaze, Japan, c.1965, 8 ½ In.	1912.00
Vase, Caanhal, Double Gourd, Claude Conover, c.1970, 18 ¾ In.	20000.00
Vase, Ceramic, Glaze, Richard Devore, 7 ½ x 8 ½ In.	3538.00
Vase, Cinem, Painted Horizontal Bands, Beige, Claude Conover, c.1970, 21 ⅝ In.	9375.00
Vase, Gilau, Vertical Stripes, Plastic Liner, Claude Conover, c.1970, 17 ½ In.	7500.00
Vase, Glossy Clear Glaze, Yellow, Cream, 2 Handles, 9 ⅛ In.	44.00
Vase, Glossy Milk Color Clear Glaze, Dogwood Blossom Flute Top, 9 In.	39.00
Vase, Green Glaze Bands, Incised Peony Decoration, c.1920, 16 ½ In.	71.00
Vase, High Gloss Clear Glaze, Multicolored, Cream, Bulbous, 5 ¼ In.	385.00
Vase, Landscape, Leaves, Salt Glaze, 3 Twisted Handles, S. Frackelton, 1903, 6 x 5 ¼ In.	7800.00
Vase, Multicolored Drip, Butter Colored Lead Glaze, Bulbous, 5 ¾ In.	77.00
Vase, Painted, Bulbous, Narrow Opening, Claude Conover, c.1970, 18 ¼ In.	7500.00
Vase, Rust, Emerald, Turquoise Lead Glaze, 2 Groove Top Handles, 1950-60s, 5 ¾ In.	44.00
Vase, Shoulder, Glossy Chrome Red Lead Glaze, Dark Drools, Crystals, 1929-35, 10 In.	385.00
Vase, Vertical Lines, Brown, Tan, Brown Ground, Bulbous, Clyde Burt, c.1975, 13 x 14 In.	1440.00
Water Cooler, 2-Tone Brown Glaze, Brass Spigot, Barrel Shape, England, 1800s, 24 In.	264.00
Water Cooler, Alkaline Glaze, Shaped Rim, Lug Handles, Medium Olive Glaze, 19 ¾ In.	230.00
Water Cooler, Beehive, 10 Gal., 20 In.	120.00
Water Cooler, Blue, Flower, Leaf, Spigot, Applied Ear Handles, 13 x 7 ¾ In.	248.00
Water Cooler, Blue Flower, Wells & Richards, Reading Berks Co., 13 In. .... *illus*	11115.00
Water Cooler, Blue, Flowers, Leaves, Applied Ear Handles, 15 ½ x 8 In.	1017.00
Water Cooler, Blue Flowers, Round, Flat Rim, Crescent Handles, Baltimore, Md., 14 x 10 In.	2530.00
Water Cooler, Keg Shape, Incised Rings, Double Flower, c.1875, 6 Gal., 15 In.	411.00
Water Cooler, Oval Top, Impressed Birds, 2, Blue, Applied Handles, Mass., 12 ¼ In.	1528.00
Water Cooler, Rachel At The Well, Textured Blue Ground, Oval Reserve, Brass Spigot, 16 In.	230.00
Water Cooler, Rebecca At The Well, 2-Tone Blue Glaze, Metal Spigot, 11-In. Base	195.00
Water Cooler, Rebecca At The Well, 2-Tone Blue Glaze, Metal Spigot, 13-In. Base	295.00
Whimsy, Mother, 6 Ducklings, Painted, Signed, William Perry, Ohio, Early 1900s, 7 In.	1175.00

STORE fixtures, cases, cutters, and other items that have no advertising as part of the decoration are listed here. Most items found in an old store are listed in the Advertising category in this book.

Burglar Alarm, Porcelain Plague, Copper Case, O.B. McClintock Co., Minn., 23 x 14 In.	472.00
Bust, Display Bust, Millinery, Girl, Wax, Blue Glass Eyes, Blond Wig, 10 In.	702.00
Cabinet, Baker's Display, 1800s, 22 ½ x 22 ½ In.	200.00
Cabinet, Cigar, Cast-Iron Indian, Miller Cubrul & Peters Cigars, c.1875, 25 ½ In.	1998.00
Cabinet, Drugstore, Corner, Quartersawn Oak, Curved Glass, 2 Panel Doors, 1880s, 9 Ft.	2400.00
Cabinet, Humidor, Oak, Cigar, Icebox, Cedar Lined, 3 Doors, 51 x 47 x 39 In.	5200.00
Cabinet, Ribbon, Round, Revolving, Oak, Iron Base, Brass Knobs, David Lochner, c.1912, 44 x 29 In.	1320.00
Case, Display, Hat, Oak, Double Curved Front, Perfection Brand, Mar. 21 1903, 41 x 56 x 23 In.	4680.00
Case, Display, Nickel Plated Metal, Curved Glass, Drop Down Back Door, 13 x 24 In.	177.00
Case, Display, Oak, 2 Paneled Doors, 47 Drawers, Shelf, c.1900, 112 x 128 x 34 In.	1952.00
Case, For Canes, Umbrellas, Oak, Shelf, Curved Glass, 25 x 19 x 47 In.	1520.00
Case, Mahogany Glass, Drop Mirror Doors, Cabriole Legs, Paw Feet, 99 x 42 In., 5 Piece	9200.00
Change Maker, 5 Slots, Johnson Fare Box Co., Pat. 1465509, Chicago, 10 x 3 ¾ In. .... *illus*	35.00
Cheese Cutter, Computing Cheese Cutter Co., Success Model, Maroon Paint, c.1904, 19 x 11 In.	600.00
Cigar Cutter, Full Weight, Figural Weight, Cast Iron, Gumpart Bros., 5 x 5 In.	231.00
Clothing Rack, Circular, Cast Iron, Revolving Top, 60 x 32 In. .... *illus*	165.00
Coffee Grinders are listed in their own category.	
Counter, Walko Tablets, 10 Boxes, Cardboard, Walker Remedy Co., Iowa, 8 x 8 In.	55.00
Counter, Wood, 3-Board, 32 x 70 x 24 In.	880.00
Counterfeit Coin Detector, Nickeled Ricker, Walnut Base, Signed, J.T. McNally, c.1879	368.00
Dispenser, Bromo-Seltzer, Blue Bottle, Blue Painted Metal Base, Marble, 16 In.	330.00
Dispenser, Cigarette, Woman's Face, Scarf, Painted, Composition Wood, Mechanical, 7 ½ x 7 In.	255.00
Dispenser, Counter, Glass, Clear & Clambroth, Metal Top & Spigot, 14 In.	106.00
Display, 2 Glass Doors, 2 Shelves, Nickeled Corners, JNO Phillips, 48 x 43 In.	690.00
Display, 3 Sections, Double Steeple, Curved Glass, Chromed, 72 x 42 In.	1955.00
Display Case, Obelisk Shape, Leather, Gold Tooling, Leaves, Glass Shelves, 1900s, 73 In., Pair.	1067.00
Display Case, Stand, Mahogany, Arched Top, 3 Drawers, Tapered Legs, c.1920, 68 x 30 In.	431.00
Display, Pinup Woman, In Swimsuit, Composition, Painted, 35 ½ In.	100.00
Display, Shoe, Wood, Turned Pedestal, Pair Leather High-Top Button Shoes On Top, 15 In.	94.00
Figure, Uncle Sam, Stars & Stripes, Painted, Red, White, Blue, Wood, 80 In.	810.00
Jar, Cocain Mur., Lug, Apothecary, Wt. & Co., 5 In.	1155.00
Jar, Codein. Crvs., Lug, Apothecary, Wt. & Co., 5 In.	275.00
Lighter, Cigar, Elephant, Multicolored, Iron, Drop-In Font, Handles, Swirls, 12 x 3 ½ In.	1404.00
Lighter, Cigar, Floor Model, Oak Cabinet, Carved, Marble Base, Brass, Bronze Dragon, 82 x 18 In.	9000.00

Lighter, Cigar, Midland Jump Start, Model No. 111859, Wood, 14 ¾ x 7 ¼ In.	330.00
Mannequin Bust, Woman, Blond, Stamped, Lamourel Mannequin, NYC, 16 x 16 In.	77.00
Mannequin, Bridal Store, Composition, Jointed Arms, Ivory Satin Gown, Veil, c.1940, 22 In. .	150.00
Mannequin, Carved Head, Glass Eyes, Articulated Arms, Tapered Base, 19th Century, 38 ½ In.	999.00
Mannequin, Man, Composition, Standing, Vintage Tweed Suit, Black Felt Hat, 73 In.	840.00
Mannequin, Man, Golfer, Swinging Golf Club, Knickers, Shirt, Composition, 71 In.	1700.00
Mannequin, Man, Vintage Golf Clothes, Tan Checked Knickers, White Shirt, 71 In.	1560.00
Mannequin, Woman, Composition, Standing, Vintage Clothing, Black Hat, 71 In.	1080.00
Mannequin, Woman, Papier-Mache, Cast Iron Shoes, No Arms, Early 1800s, 44 In.	315.00
Mannequin, Young Girl, Composition, Seated, Beige Vintage Outfit, Straw Hat, 23 In.	480.00
Money Changer, Embossed, Feb. 25 1890, 11 ¼ In.	250.00
Postcard Carousel, Walnut, Footed, 45 x 17 In.	2750.00
Rack, 11 Wire Baskets, 40 x 50 x 26 In.	1100.00
Rack, Hat & Coat, Brass, Salesman's Sample, 15 ½ In.	165.00
Rack, Revolves, 4-Footed, 73 ½ In.	440.00
Register Store Receipt Box, Hinged, National, Brass Plated, 1900s, 6 ¾ x 6 In.	175.00
Sharpener, Razor Blade, Knife, Wheel Form, Sponge, 17 x 16 In.	250.00
Shirt Collar Display, Greek Key Design, Hanging, 12 Arrow Collars, 50 x 12 ½ x 7 ½ In.	330.00
Shoeshine Stand, Double, Theo Koch Co., Quartersawn Oak, Pink Marble, Brass, c.1916, 59 x 53 In.	3300.00
Show Globe, Brass Pierced Wall Mount, Oval Clear Globe, Brass Crown Top, 28 In.	2415.00
Show Globe, Milk Glass, Stopper, Pedestal Base, 15 x 4 In.	440.00
Showcase, Double Tower, Center Step Back Steeple, Walnut, Claes & Lehnbeuter, 1890s, 54 x 59 In.	4800.00
Showcase, Floor, Lighted, 2 Glass Sliding Doors, 3 Adjustable Glass Shelves, 82 x 49 x 18 In. .	270.00
Showcase, Floor Model, Oak, 2 Graduated Shelves, Scrolled Nickel Brackets, 42 x 72 In.	540.00
Showcase, Silver Tower, Wood Frame, Nickeled Tin, Curved Glass Front, Shelves, 15 x 11 x 12 In. .	3163.00
Sign, Anchor, Wood, Dark Blue-Green Paint, Hanging Bracket, Late 19th Century, 53 x 40 In.	1560.00
Sign, Bait & Tackle, Lure, Red, Yellow, Wood, 36 In.	530.00
Sign, Barber's, Scissors, Figural, Wrought Iron Bracket, 17 ¼ In.	770.00
Sign, Boot, Painted, Zinc, 20 In.	1700.00
Sign, Bull Head, Red Paint, Zinc, 19th Century, 12 In.	565.00
Sign, Butcher, Green, Sheet Iron, Steer, Butcher Tools, 1800s, 27 x 35 In.	470.00
Sign, Butcher, Pig, Painted, Carved, c.1900, 19 x 32 In.	390.00
Sign, Cobbler, Shoe, Leather, c.1900, 13 ½ x 23 In.	200.00
Sign, Coffee Shop, Coffeepot, 5 Cent A Cup, Painted, Tin, 24 x 24 In.	385.00
Sign, Cup, Saucer, Spoon In Cup, Cast Iron, Green Paint, Stand, c.1910, 6 x In.	830.00
Sign, Decoy Carving Workshop, Plywood, 2-Sided, White, Gray, 1900s, 20 x 75 In.	374.00
Sign, Double Barrel Shotgun, Hand Carved, Wood, 18 In.	6000.00
Sign, Dr. Bertha Anthony, Tin, 19th Century..	20.00
Sign, Fish, Red Paint, Sheet Metal, 12 x 32 In.	440.00
Sign, Furs Remodeled, Red, Gold, Reverse Glass, Frame, 8 x 38 In.	240.00
Sign, Glasses, Red & Blue Lenses, Glass, Cast Iron, 8 ½ x 17 ½ In.	187.00
Sign, Grape Cluster, Painted, Figural, 24 x 11 In.	1870.00
Sign, Haberdasher, Red, 20 x 19 ½ In.	440.00
Sign, Key Shape, Giltwood & Tin, Continental, 1800s, 32 In.	1200.00
Sign, Livery, Horse Head, Molded Zinc, Open Mouth, Flowing Mane, 1800s, 22 x 14 In.	1880.00
Sign, Millinery, Stovepipe Hat, Painted, Tin, Bracket, 28 x 23 In.	500.00
Sign, Mortar & Pestle, Figural, Painted, Wood, Bracket, 20 x 11 In.	1980.00
Sign, Optician, Glasses, Red & Blue Lenses, Figural, 12 x 27 ½ In.	770.00
Sign, Pawn Shop, 3 Balls, Bracket, Painted, 36 x 42 In.	280.00
Sign, Pipe, Brown, White, Black, 36 In.	280.00
Sign, Plumber, Spigot, Painted, Wood, Bracket, 18 In.	1700.00
Sign, Pocket Watch, Jeweler, 17 x 11 ½ In.	250.00
Sign, Pot, In Fire, Wood, Wrought Iron, 36 x 35 In.	395.00
Sign, Saw, Wood, Gold Paint, 57 In.	311.00
Sign, Shoe Repair, Boot, Painted, Wood, 36 In.	240.00
Sign, Shoemaker, Shoe, Full Figure, Painted, Wood, Bracket, 20 In.	600.00
Sign, Silversmith, White, Black, Painted, Wood, 13 ¼ x 31 ½ In.	85.00
Sign, Skate Sharpening, Tin, 2-Sided, Rectangular, Painted White, Red Letters, c.1935, 16 x 4 In.	85.00
Sign, Skeleton Key, Giltwood, Tin, Continental, 19th Century, 32 In.	1200.00
Sign, Spigot, Plug, Wood, 46 In.	360.00
Sign, Tailor, Scissors, Painted, Wood, Forged Iron, 18 x 48 ½ In.	620.00
Sign, Umbrella, Sold & Repaired, Figural, Painted, Brass, 12 x 32 In.	765.00
Stool, Shoeshine, Black Paint, Cast Iron, Walnut Seat, 33 In.	88.00
Strawholder, Glass, Purple, Lid, Straws, 14 In.	230.00
Strawholder, Green, Pressed Glass, Flared Metal Base, Metal Lid, Lift-Up Rod, 12 x 4 ⅝ In.	330.00
Strawholder, San-L, Glass, Metal Top, Lancaster, c.1917, 12 In. ....*illus*	146.00

Stove, Round, Oak, Model E18, Footrest, Embossed Scrolling, 56 In.
$400.00

S

Sumida, Vase, Multicolor Gloss Drip Glaze, Applied Glazed Monkeys, c.1890, 29 In.
$11500.00

Sumida, Vase, Pinched Body, Rim, Red Biscuit, Glazed Figures, Peach Of Immortality, 8 ½ In., Pair
$360.00

Sunbonnet Baby, Hair Receiver, Monday, Hanging Clothes, 4 ½ In.
$176.00

Sunbonnet Baby, Pitcher, Tuesday, Ironing
$176.00

Stringholder, Beehive Form, 4 ½ x 6 ½ In.		99.00
Stringholder, Beehive Form, Cast Iron, 6 ¼ x 7 ⅜ In.		45.00
Stringholder, Cast Iron, Wood, Pat. March, 1841, 10 x 6 ¼ In.		200.00
Stringholder, Nickel Plated, Cast Iron, Footed Base, 1880s, 15 x 9 In.		390.00
Table, Soda Fountain, Cast Iron Feet, Glass Display Top, 4 Chairs, Triangular Shape Seat, 24 x 36 In.		900.00
Tobacco Cutter, Benham & Griffin, Cast Iron, 6 x 16 ½ In.		113.00
Tobacco Cutter, Brown & Williamson, No. 2, Black, Cast Iron, 6 ½ x 17 In.		59.00
Tobacco Cutter, F.J. Sorg, Wood Base, 10 x 20 In.		99.00
Tobacco Cutter, Haas Baruch & Co., 16 In.		130.00
Tobacco Cutter, Iron, Maple, Butternut, Trotting Horse, 19th Century, 13 ¼ In.		323.00
Tobacco Cutter, Sylvester Bros. Co., Pat. 1914, Seattle, Wash., 8 ¼ x 15 ½ In.		125.00
Tobacco Cutter, Wood, Rope Twist Brass Handle, 12 x 6 In.		130.00
Tobacco Cutter, Wrought Iron, Tin, Wood Case, 39 In.		248.00
Wrapping Paper Holder, Keen Kutter, 2 Tiers, Embossed Iron Feet, Logo, 28 x 25 In.		270.00

STOVES have been used in America for heating since the eighteenth century and for cooking since the nineteenth century. Most types of wood, coal, gas, kerosene, and even some electric stoves are collected.

Box, Cast Iron, Scrolled Leaves, Paw Feet, Pleis, Foening & Thudium, 20 x 22 x 11 In.	*illus*	147.00
Classical, Iron, Hipped Pediment, Eagle Finial, Cabriole Legs, c.1844, 52 x 32 In.		1763.00
Conowingo Furnace, Iron, Flower & Sawtooth Panels, 33 x 13 x 25 In.	*illus*	754.00
Dumb, George Washington, Lady Liberty, Multicolored, Painted, c.1843, 48 ¾ In., Pair		22600.00
Iron, Zoar Foundry, Tuscarawas County, Ohio, Mid 1800s, 25 In.		118.00
Laundry, 6 Flat Irons, Delmas & F. Co., 21 ½ In.		2750.00
Parlor, Gothic Revival, Castle, Cincinnati, Ohio, Cast Iron, Pat. 1853, 45 ½ x 31 In.		2400.00
Parlor, Green, Porcelain, 25 x 18 x 14 In.		392.00
Parlor, Sea Serpents, Scrolls, Cast Iron, Nickel, Lakeside Foundry Co., Chicago, 30 x 63 In.		1898.00
Round, Oak, Model E18, Footrest, Embossed Scrolling, 56 In.	*illus*	400.00
Twilight Franklin, Iron, Tiles, Scrolls, Leaves, 3-Footed, Cribben, Sexton & Co., 36 x 22 In.		600.00
Wood, Shaker, Iron, Wood Handle, Cast Iron Door, Damper, Penny Feet, c.1830, 17 x 36 In.		468.00

STRETCH GLASS is named for the strange stretch marks in the glass. It was made by many glass companies in the United States from about 1900 to the 1920s. It is iridescent. Most American stretch glass is molded; most European pieces are blown and may have a pontil mark.

Bowl, Centerpiece, Dolphins, Ice Green, 10 ½ In.	95.00
Compote, Dolphins, Ice Blue, 6 ½ In.	55.00

SUMIDA is a Japanese pottery that was made from about 1895 to 1941. Pieces are usually everyday objects–vases, jardinieres, bowls, teapots, and decorative tiles. Most pieces have a very heavy orange-red, blue, brown, black, green, purple, or off-white glaze, with raised three-dimensional figures as decorations. The unglazed part is painted red, green, black, or orange. Sumida is sometimes mistakenly called *Sumida gawa*, but true Sumida gawa is a softer pottery made in the early 1800s.

Bowl, Applied Blossoms & Branches, Coiled Base, 7 x 7 In.		375.00
Dish, Condiment, Applied Geisha On Rim, Red, Black, Japan, c.1925, 3 x 4 In.		96.00
Vase, 2 Men, Woman, Handing Peach To Boy, Japan, 8 ½ In., Pair		360.00
Vase, Boys, 9 ½ x 5 In.		300.00
Vase, Multicolor Gloss Drip Glaze, Applied Glazed Monkeys, c.1890, 29 In.	*illus*	11500.00
Vase, Pinched Body, Rim, Red Biscuit, Glazed Figures, Peach Of Immortality, 8 ½ In., Pair	*illus*	360.00
Vase, Stick, Olive Green, 3 Applied Male Figures, 9 x 4 ½ In.		1062.00

SUNBONNET BABIES were introduced in 1900 in the book *The Sunbonnet Babies*. The stories were by Eulalie Osgood Grover, illustrated by Bertha Corbett. The children's faces were completely hidden by the sunbonnets. The children had been pictured in black and white before this time, but the color pictures in the book were immediately successful. The Royal Bayreuth China Company made a full line of children's dishes decorated with the Sunbonnet Babies. Some Sunbonnet Babies plates have been reproduced, but are clearly marked.

Candlestick, Girls Ironing, Back Shield, Handle, 5 In.		205.00
Hair Receiver, Monday, Hanging Clothes, 4 ½ In.	*illus*	176.00
Hair Receiver, Sweeping Lid, Scrubbing Base, Royal Bayreuth Bavaria, 3 x 4 In.		160.00
Pitcher, Tuesday, Ironing	*illus*	176.00
Plate, Monday, Hanging Clothes, 9 ½ In.		59.00
Plate, Wednesday, Mending, Marked, Royal Bayreuth Bavaria, 6 In.		87.00
Sugar & Creamer, Sunday, Fishing, Signed, Royal Bayreuth		77.00

Teapot, Tuesday, Ironing, 4 ½ In.	176.00
Tray, Monday, Washing, Marked, Royal Bayreuth Bavaria, 7 x 9 ½ In.	88.00

SUNDERLAND luster is a name given to a special type of pink luster made by Leeds, Newcastle, and other English firms during the nineteenth century. The luster glaze is metallic and glossy and appears to have bubbles in it. Other pieces of luster are listed in the Luster category.

Bowl, Gadener's Arms, Sailors Farewell, Verse, Purple Luster, Black Transfer, c.1865, 9 In.	468.00
Butter Pot, Cover, Wear Iron Bridge, Verse, Black Transfer, c.1825, 5 ½ In.	702.00
Chamber Pot, 6-Line Verse, Pink Luster Borders, Man, Frog, 6 x 12 In. ....*illus*	1872.00
Jug, Sailor's Farewell, Verse, Mariners Compass, Black Transfer, c.1850, 7 In.	468.00
Pitcher, Bridge, Sailor's Poem, Black Transfer, Inscribed, To John & Elizabeth Cillock, 1796, 8 In.	230.00
Pitcher, Farmer's Arms, Cast Iron Bridge, Verse, c.1850, 7 In.	176.00
Pitcher, Frigate, Motto, Crimean Memorial, Pink Lustre, 9 x 8 In. ....*illus*	288.00
Pitcher, Pink Luster, Bridge, c.1850, 9 ¼ In.	323.00
Pitcher, Ships, c.1850, 8 ½ In.	264.00

SUPERMAN was created by two seventeen-year-olds in 1938. The first issue of Action comics had the strip. Superman remains popular and became the hero of a radio show in 1940, cartoons in the 1940s, a television series, and several major movies.

Badge, Junior Defense League, Premium, Holding Flag, Multicolored, c.1941, 1 ⅛ In.	144.00
Brush Set, Wood Handle, Decal, Monarch Brush Co., Box, c.1940, 4 ¼ x 7 In.	633.00
Certificate Of Merit, Superman, Hands On Hips, Lines For Name, Age, 8 ½ x 11 In.	612.00
Doll, Jointed, Wood, Composition, Decals, Ideal, c.1940, 12 ½ In. ....*illus*	644.00
Figure, More Powerful, Holding Back Oncoming Train, Cast Metal, 8 ½ In.	173.00
Figure, To The Rescue, Rises Through Clouds, Carries Lois Lane, Cast Metal, 7 ¼ In.	115.00
Play Suit, Cotton, Red, Blue, Plastic Buttons, Funtime Playwear, c.1950, 11 x 17 In., 3 Piece	173.00
Record Player, Model SP-19, Plastic, Cardboard Lithograph, De Jay Corp.	45.00
Ring, Action, Superman Leaping, Name Below, Variety Base, 1966	253.00
Socks, Screen Printed Design, Figure Flying Over Skyline, Child's, c.1949, 12 In.	144.00
Thermos, Superman Flying Toward Large Robot, Universal, 1954	1650.00
Ticket, Complimentary Admission, Macy's Toyland, Stamped, 1940, 2 ½ x 5 In.	417.00
Toy, Rollover Plane, Tin Lithograph, Silver Plane, Marx, Box, c.1940, 6 x 5 ½ In. ....*illus*	1755.00
Toy, Turnover Tank, Tin Lithograph, Windup, Linemar, 2 ½ x 4 In.	180.00
Watch, Pocket, 1940s	485.00

SUSIE COOPER began as a designer in 1925 working for the English firm A.E. Gray & Company. In 1932 she formed Susie Cooper Pottery, Ltd. In 1950 it became Susie Cooper China, Ltd., and the company made china and earthenware. In 1966 it was acquired by Josiah Wedgwood & Sons, Ltd. The name Susie Cooper appears with the company names on many pieces of ceramics.

Chop Plate, Endon, 8 ¾ In.	48.00
Cup & Saucer, Endon	38.00
Muffineer, Cover, Dusty Rose, Beige, 1930s, 4 x 8 ¾ In.	40.00
Plate, Dinner, Endon	68.00
Plate, Salad, 8 In.	20.00
Plate, Stylized Flowers, Multicolored, Yellow Border, Marked, 9 In.	38.00
Platter, Dresden Spray, Pink Border, Oval, 9 ¼ x 12 In.	32.00
Platter, Lilies, Rust, Green, Cream Ground, Oval, 10 ½ x 12 In.	27.00
Teapot, Corinthian, Blue Flowers, White Ground, 3 ⅞ In., 3 Cup	55.00

SWANKYSWIGS are small drinking glasses. In 1933, the Kraft Food Company began to market cheese spreads in these decorated, reusable glass tumblers. They were discontinued from 1941 to 1946, then made again from 1947 to 1958. Then plain glasses were used for most of the cheese, although a few special decorated Swankyswigs have been made since that time. For more prices, go to kovels.com.

Antique, Blue, 3 ¾ In.	7.00
Antique, Red, 3 ¾ In.	7.00

SWORDS of all types that are of interest to collectors are listed here. The military dress sword with elaborate handle is probably the most wanted. A *tsuba* is a hand guard fitted to a Japanese sword between the handle and the blade. Be sure to display swords in a safe way, out of reach of children.

Artillery, Brass, 5-Ball Hilt, Eaglehead Pommel, Bone Grip, Scabbard, c.1820, 33 ⅝ In.	1380.00
Artillery Officer's, Imperial German, Sheath	1150.00

Sunderland, Chamber Pot, 6-Line Verse, Pink Luster Borders, Man, Frog, 6 x 12 In. $1872.00

Sunderland, Pitcher, Frigate, Motto, Crimean Memorial, Pink Lustre, 9 x 8 In. $288.00

Superman, Doll, Jointed, Wood, Composition, Decals, Ideal, c.1940, 12 ½ In. $644.00

Superman, Toy, Rollover Plane, Tin Lithograph, Silver Plane, Marx, Box, c.1940, 6 x 5 ½ In. $1755.00

Sword, Saber, Gilt Hilt, Leather, Gilt Shield, Engraved, Wire Wrap, Schutzen Corp., 1800s, 37 In. $588.00

Syracuse, Lady Louise, Creamer $22.00

Syracuse, Rose Marie, Plate, Salad, 7 In. $15.00

Bayonet, Trowel, Chillingworth Design, c.1873, 14 ½ In.	144.00
British Officer's, Gilt Brass Hilt, Modeled Lion Head, c.1803, 32 ¾ In.	1350.00
Cavalry Officer, Scrolling Leaves On Guard & Pommel Ring, 1860	1275.00
Foot Officer's, Lion's Head, Leather Grip, Divided Guard, c.1780, 31 ¼ In.	3220.00
Gentleman's, Triangular Steel Blade, Oval Guard, Silver Wire Grip, Copper Ribbon, 29 ¾ x 36 In.	777.00
German, Imperial, NCO, Curved Blade Marked Puma, c.1900, 31 ⅝ In.	325.00
Hollow Wedge Blade, Fluted Iron Guard, Engraved, Ebony Grip, Iron Oval Studs, c.1770, 15 In.	465.00
Hunting, Brass Mounted, Steel Blade, Scrolling Leaves, Hunting Scene, Ivory Grip, 20 ½ x 26 In.	717.00
Iron Hilt, Pommel & Grip Set With Studs, Matching Knuckle Bow, c.1800	1050.00
Japanese, Hand Forged, Shirasaya, 27 In.	1080.00
Japanese, Katana, Wrapped Handle, Brass Flowers, Scabbard, Japan, c.1940, 25 In.	1112.00
Militia, Helmet Pommel, Pearl Plaque Grip, Eagle Counterguard, c.1840, 37 In.	546.00
Philippine, Short, Brass Guard & Base, Ivory Inlaid Black Horn Grip, Pre 1902, 13 In.	550.00
Presentation, Engraved, Blued Straight Blade, Gilt Brass Scabbard, Whalebone Grips	1304.00
Saber, Calvary, Brass Guard, Sharkskin Grip, Steel Scabbard, Mark, Mid 1800s, 40 ¾ In.	470.00
Saber, Cavalry, David J. Millard, Clayville, Leather Grip, Brass Guard, Civil War, c.1860, 40 ½ In.	588.00
Saber, Cavalry, Leather Grip, Copper Wire Wrap, Curved Blade, 40 In.	610.00
Saber, Cavalry, Leather Grip, Wristbreaker No. 1840	360.00
Saber, Gilt Hilt, Leather, Gilt Shield, Engraved, Wire Wrap, Schutzen Corp., 1800s, 37 In. *illus*	588.00
Saber, Infantry, Eaglehead Pommel, Bone Grip, Scabbard, c.1808, 33 ¼ In.	1150.00
Saber, Infantry, Silvered Brass, Eagle Langet, Bone Grip, Trophy Of Arms, c.1820, 35 ⅞ In.	4313.00
Shark's Tooth, Wood Haft, Fish Belly Grip, Thumb Rest, c.1788, 24 In.	675.00
Swordfish Bill, American Eagle, Battleship, Mermaid Handle, Folk Art, c.1900, 35 In.	176.00
Swordfish Bill, Eagle Clutching Flags, Shield, Seascape, Vine Border, c.1908, 37 In.	345.00

SYRACUSE is a trademark used by the Onondaga Pottery of Syracuse, New York. The company was established in 1871. The name became the Syracuse China Company in 1966. Syracuse China closed in 2009. It was known for fine dinnerware and restaurant china.

SYRACUSE China

Alpine, Plate, Dinner, 10 ⅝ In.	12.00
Coralbel, Platter, Oval, 12 In.	30.00
Dogwood, Ash Tray, Railroad	13.00
Greenwood, Bowl, Vegetable	24.00
Greenwood, Platter, Serving, Oval, 14 In.	24.00
Highland, Plate, Salad, c.1952, 7 In.	4.00
Lady Louise, Creamer *illus*	22.00
Lilac Rose, Platter, Gold Trim, 12 x 8 In.	40.00
Marlene, Berry Bowl, 5 ¼ In.	12.00
Marlene, Plate, Bread & Butter, 6 ¼ In.	10.00
Marlene, Plate, Dinner, 9 ¾ In.	26.00
Minuet, Cup & Saucer, Tea	7.00
Montana State Seal, Sugar, 1960	10.00
Old Harlem, Plate, Salad, Vintage OPCo, 8 In.	16.00
Old Ivory, Bowl, Vegetable, Cover, Round	33.00
Old Ivory, Bowl, Vegetable, Oval, 9 ⅞ In.	28.00
Old Ivory, Gravy Boat, Underplate, Pat. SY40	28.00
Orleans, Plate, Dinner, c.1920, 9 ¾ In.	10.00
Pine Cone, Bowl, Cereal, Adobe Ware	10.00
Pine Cone, Sugar Bowl, Cover	58.00
Puritan, Plate	20.00
Rose Marie, Bowl, Vegetable, Cover	95.00
Rose Marie, Plate, Salad, 7 In. *illus*	15.00
Rose Marie, Serving, Bowl	10.00
Selma, Bowl, Fruit	8.00
Sharon, Creamer, Gold Trim	19.00
Shelledge, Platter, Vogue, Oval, 1950, 13 x 10 In.	45.00
Sherwood, Sugar, Cover, 5 ¾ In.	17.00
St. Elmo, Bowl, Cereal	6.00
Stansberry, Sugar, c.1960	20.00
Strawberry Hill, Plate, Side, 8 In.	6.00
Suzanne, Plate, Bread & Butter	5.00
Windswept, Cup, Coffee	8.00
Windswept, Creamer	12.00
Windswept, Platter, Serving, 8 In.	8.00
Wintergreen, Serving, Bowl, 1973, 10 In.	15.00
Woodbine, Cup & Saucer	12.00
Woodbine, Plate, Dinner, 10 ⅛ In.	12.00
Woodbine, Plate, Dinner, c.1965, 10 In.	7.50
Woodbine, Plate, Salad, 8 ⅛ In.	10.00

S

TEA CADDY is the name for a small box made to hold tea leaves. In the eighteenth century, tea was very expensive and it was stored under lock and key. The first tea caddies were made with locks. By the nineteenth century, tea was more plentiful and the tea caddy was larger. Often there were two sections, one for green tea, one for black tea.

Brass Mounted, Silver Inlaid, Tortoiseshell, Coffin Shape, Regency, 8 ¼ x 11 ¼ In.	4880.00
Brass, Lion Mask Shape, Bun Feet, Hinged Lid, Tin Interior, Ring Handles, England, 6 x 8 In.	325.00
Brass, Octagonal, Domed Lid, Hammered, Arts & Crafts, Engraved, c.1900, 4 ¾ x 4 ¼ In.	385.00
Brass, Tooled Swag, Geometric, Oval, Finial, 5 ¾ x 3 ¾ x 2 ⅝ In.	248.00
Burl Veneer, Domed Lid, 19th Century, 5 ½ x 6 ¾ In.	140.00
Burl Walnut, Coffin Shape, Hinged Lid, Disc Feet, 19th Century, 6 ½ x 11 x 5 ½ In.	173.00
Burl Wood, Boxwood Stringing, Shell Inlay, Key, c.1790, 5 ½ In.	550.00
Cherry, Patera Inlay, Ball Finial, Hepplewhite, c.1800, 4 ¼ x 4 ½ In.	295.00
Copper, Mahogany, Flared, Tiered Lid, Silver, Mother-Of-Pearl Scoop, England, c.1900, 7 In.	237.00
Coromandel, Brass Inlay, Moire Interior, 2 Porcelain Bottles, France, 5 x 8 In.	178.00
Fruitwood Panels, Fiddleback Mahogany Strung, Cherubs, c.1700, 3 ¼ x 3 ⅝ In.	650.00
Fruitwood, Apple Shape, Hinged, Stem Finial, George III, England, 5 ½ In.	610.00
Fruitwood, Apple Shape, Stem, Lock, c.1800, 5 ¾ In.	3055.00
Fruitwood, Pear Shape, Steel Escutcheon, George III, c.1780, 7 In.	6250.00
Georgian, Rosewood, Metal, Pearl Inlay, Hinged Lid, 8 x 5 In. *illus*	299.00
Hardwood, Hinged Lid, Brass Swing Handles, Chinese, 19th Century, 11 x 19 x 9 ½ In.	178.00
Inlaid Satinwood, Flowers, Hinged Lid, Regency, c.1800, 5 x 8 In.	550.00
Inlaid Shell, Canted Corners, Lidded Interior, Flowers, Filigree, Regency Style, 5 ⅜ x 4 ⅝ In.	633.00
Ivory Inlaid Tortoiseshell, Mid 1800s, 4 x 5 In.	1586.00
Ivory, Tortoiseshell, Faceted Oval, George III, Late 18th Century, 4 ¾ x 4 ¼ In.	4575.00
Ivory, Tortoiseshell, Gold Pique-Inlaid, Facetted Oval, George III, Late 1700s, 5 x 4 ¼ In.	5490.00
Lacquer, Hinged Lid, Handwritten Labels, Pewter Canisters, Chinese Export, 5 x 11 In.	840.00
Mahogany Inlay, Hinged Lid, Center Shell Cartouche, Divided Interior, 4 ½ x 5 x 4 In.	345.00
Mahogany, Boulle Marquetry, Silver Inlay, Hinged Lid, Napoleon III, 4 ½ x 8 x 4 In.	495.00
Mahogany, Central Mixing Bowl, 2 Tea Boxes, 19th Century, 6 x 12 x 6 In.	200.00
Mahogany, Checkerboard Inlay, Brass Escutcheon, Handle, England, 11 ½ In.	356.00
Mahogany, Coffin Shape, Compartments, Flattened Bun Feet, Regency, c.1800, 7 x 14 x 8 In.	230.00
Mahogany, Coffin Shape, Tapered Lid, Turned Feet, England, Early 1800s, 12 In.	135.00
Mahogany, Coffin Shape, Turned Feet, 2 Compartments, 5 ½ x 7 ½ x 4 ½ In.	320.00
Mahogany, Concave Stepped Lid, Inlaid Veneer, Brass Handle, George III, 9 ½ In.	474.00
Mahogany, Ebony String Inlay, Drawer, Brass Handle, 4 x 7 x 4 ½ In.	350.00
Mahogany, Fan Inlay, 2 Canisters, Leather Lining, George III, 6 ¾ x 13 ¾ In. *illus*	518.00
Mahogany, Floral Inlay, Early 1900s, 5 ½ x 7 ⅛ x 4 In. *illus*	978.00
Mahogany, Hepplewhite, Early 19th Century, 5 x 11 In.	135.00
Mahogany, Inlaid Bands, Brass Mounts, Bail Handle, 3 Canisters, 7 ¾ x 4 ¾ In.	460.00
Mahogany, Inlaid Shells In Oval Reserves, Ivory Escutcheon, George III, 5 x 7 ½ In.	345.00
Mahogany, Lift Top, Handle, 2 Foil Lined Wells, Mixing Bowl, 11 x 6 x 6 In.	267.00
Mahogany, Oak, Fitted Interior, Bun Feet, Lion Head Handles, Regency, Silver Spoon, 6 x 12 In.	411.00
Mahogany, Plum Pudding, Apple Shape, Ivory Stem, 5 ½ x 4 ¾ In.	260.00
Mahogany, Regency, Coffin Shape, Hinged Lid, 2 Fitted Interiors With Lids, 5 x 9 In.	266.00
Mahogany, Ring Handles, Brass Feet, Inlaid Kite Escutcheon, 19th Century, 6 x 9 x 6 In.	403.00
Mahogany, Satinwood Inlaid, Swing Handles, George III, c.1800, 4 x 4 x 4 In., Pair	1075.00
Mahogany, Satinwood Inlay, Ring Handles, 3 Interior Compartments, c.1840, 7 x 13 In.	625.00
Mahogany, Satinwood, Oval Shell Inlays, Stringing, Federal, England, c.1810, 6 x 12 In.	881.00
Mahogany, String Inlay, England, 19th Century, 7 In.	121.00
Mahogany, Twist Banded, Brass, c.1875, 6 x 7 x 4 ½ In.	540.00
Mother-Of-Pearl, Abalone, Mid 19th Century, 5 x 8 In. 1952.00 to	2928.00
Porcelain, Bird Of Paradise, Flowers, Gilt Trim, Red & White, Imperial, Russia, 1914, 3 In.	1020.00
Porcelain, Ribbed, Sloping Shoulders, Landscape Medallions, Gilt, c.1775, 4 ½ In.	117.00
Quillwork, Hexagonal, Rolled Paper Panels, Barber Pole Borders, c.1800, 5 x 7 In. *illus*	1521.00
Regency, Tortoiseshell, Bone, Mother-Of-Pearl, 2 Sections, 8-Sided, c.1890, 6 x 6 In. *illus*	466.00
Rosewood Veneer, England, 19th Century, 7 ½ x 12 In.	180.00
Satinwood, Conch Shell Patera Top, String & Band Inlays, George III, Oval, 5 ½ x 6 In.	720.00
Scrolled Paper, Hexagonal, Zebra Stripe Inlaid Banding, Quillwork, Silver Knop, c.1790	3500.00
Silver Plate, Cover, Serpentine Shape, Engraved Flowers, Swags, Urn Finial, 5 ½ x 6 In.	115.00
Silver Plate, Locomotive Shape, Heating Unit, Griffin Spout, c.1925, 16 x 14 In. *illus*	1638.00
Silver Plate, Musician, Flowers, Village, Repousse, Hallmark, Dutch, 4 x 2 ½ In.	48.00
Silver, Ivory Inlaid Tortoiseshell, George III, Coffin Shape, 6 ½ x 6 ½ In.	4270.00
Silver, Ivory Inlaid Tortoiseshell, Ivory Ball Feet, William IV, Bombe Shape, 6 ¼ x 7 In.	4575.00
Silver, Ivory Inlaid Tortoiseshell, Monogrammed Tablet, 6 ¾ x 8 ½ In.	5185.00
Silver, Ivory Inlaid Tortoiseshell, Silver Tablet, Escutcheon, Victorian, 6 x 8 In.	5490.00
Silver, Oval, Scrolling, Flags, Hinged, Finial, George III, 5 x 4 ¾ In.	6600.00

Tea Caddy, Georgian, Rosewood, Metal, Pearl Inlay, Hinged Lid, 8 x 5 In. $299.00

Tea Caddy, Mahogany, Fan Inlay, 2 Canisters, Leather Lining, George III, 6 ¾ x 13 ¾ In. $518.00

Tea Caddy, Mahogany, Floral Inlay, Early 1900s, 5 ½ x 7 ⅛ x 4 In. $978.00

Tea Caddy, Quillwork, Hexagonal, Rolled Paper Panels, Barber Pole Borders, c.1800, 5 x 7 In. $1521.00

T

Tea Caddy, Regency, Tortoiseshell, Bone, Mother-Of-Pearl, 2 Sections, 8-Sided, c.1890, 6 x 6 In. $466.00

Tea Caddy, Silver Plate, Locomotive Shape, Heating Unit, Griffin Spout, c.1925, 16 x 14 In. $1638.00

Tea Caddy, Tortoiseshell, Mother-Of-Pearl, Bone, Brass, 2 Compartments, 1800s, 4 ¾ x 7 ¾ In. $2160.00

Silver, Reverse Pear Shape, Embossed, Shell Finial, Samuel Taylor, George II, 5 ¾ In.	3250.00
Silver, Shield Form, Fluted Bottom, Ball Feet, Netherlands, 1818, 4 x 4 ½ x 2 ½ In.	805.00
Sterling Silver, Oval, Bulbous, Fluted, Ball Feet, George III, J. Foskett, London, 1808, 6 In.	978.00
Tortoiseshell, Bone Grips, Sterling Plaque, England, c.1825, 4 ⅜ x 6 ¾ x 3 ¾ In.	1080.00
Tortoiseshell, Foil Interior, Silver Plated Bail, c.1825, 5 x 8 x 5 In.	1265.00
Tortoiseshell, Hinged Lid, Silver Inlay, Compartments, Ivory Ball Feet, 5 ½ x 6 ½ x 4 ¼ In.	1793.00
Tortoiseshell, Hinged Lid, Single Shell Lid Inside, Pewter Line String Inlay, c.1820, 4 x 4 ½ In.	1750.00
Tortoiseshell, Mother-Of-Pearl, Bone, Brass, 2 Compartments, 1800s, 4 ¾ x 7 ¾ In. ...... *illus*	2160.00
Tortoiseshell, Mother-Of-Pearl, Bow Front, Hinged Lid, Flared Base, 1800s, 5 x 8 x 5 In.	2415.00
Tortoiseshell, Mother-Of-Pearl, Inlaid, Mid 19th Century, 5 ½ x 8 In.	3660.00
Tortoiseshell, Mother-Of-Pearl, Mid 19th Century, 4 ½ x 6 ½ In.	1708.00
Tortoiseshell, Mother-Of-Pearl, Silver Inlay, Bone Grips, Spherical Feet, c.1850, 6 x 7 x 4 In.	1680.00
Victorian Style, Shell, Mother-Of-Pearl, Coffin Shape, Coffered Lid, 6 ¼ x 7 ¼ In.	633.00
Winter Troika Scene Top, Rounded Corners, Hinged, Marked, Vishniakov, 10 x 5 In.	330.00

TEA LEAF IRONSTONE dishes are named for their decorations. There was a superstition that it was lucky if a whole tea leaf unfolded at the bottom of your cup. This idea was translated into the pattern of dishes known as "tea leaf." By 1850 at least twelve English factories were making this pattern, and by the 1870s it was a popular pattern in many countries. The tea leaf was always a luster glaze on early wares, although now some pieces are made with a brown tea leaf. There are many variations of tea leaf designs, such as Teaberry, Pepper Leaf, and Gold Leaf. The designs were used on many different white ironstone shapes, such as Bamboo, Lily of the Valley, Empress, and Cumbow.

Baker, Alfred Meakin, 8 x 6 In.	25.00
Baker, Anthony Shaw, 10 In.	20.00
Baker, Lily Of The Valley, Oval, Anthony Shaw, 11 ½ In.	170.00
Baker, Oval, Alfred Meakin, 9 ⅝ x 7 In.	10.00
Basin, Anthony Shaw, 14 ½ In.	130.00
Brush Vase, Bamboo, Alfred Meakin, 5 In.	60.00
Cake Plate, Hexagonal, Pierced Handles, Anthony Shaw, 12 x 9 In.	50.00
Creamer, Bamboo, Alfred Meakin, 6 ¼ In.	50.00
Creamer, Cable Shape, H. Burgess, 5 ½ In.	50.00
Dish, Handles, Alfred Meakin, 9 ⅝ x 4 ¾ In.	55.00
Dish, Pickle, Bamboo, Alfred Meakin, 8 x 4 ½ In.	40.00
Dish, Pickle, Cable Shape, Anthony Shaw	5.00 to 30.00
Dish, Pickle, DeSoto Shape, Anthony Shaw	200.00
Dish, Pickle, Handles, Alfred Meakin, 9 ⅝ x 4 ¾ In.	55.00
Dish, Pickle, Lily Of The Valley, Anthony Shaw	40.00
Gravy Boat, Fish Hook, Alfred Meakin, 3 ½ In.	35.00
Mug, Anthony Shaw, 3 ⅞ In.	190.00
Mug, Fish Hook, Alfred Meakin	40.00
Mug, Johnson Brothers	110.00
Pitcher, Chelsea, Alfred Meakin, 8 In.	160.00
Pitcher, Empress Shape, William Adams & Sons, 6 ½ In.	65.00
Pitcher, Fish Hook, Alfred Meakin, 8 In.	70.00
Pitcher, Lions Head, Mellor Taylor, 8 ¼ In.	30.00
Plate, Chinese Shape, Anthony Shaw, 9 In.	5.00
Plate, Hanging Leaves, Anthony Shaw, 9 In.	10.00
Platter, Oval, Anthony Shaw, 15 In.	7.00
Platter, Oval, Anthony Shaw, 17 In.	3.00
Sugar, Basket Weave, Anthony Shaw, Lid, 6 ⅝ In.	35.00
Sugar, Cable Shape, Anthony Shaw, Lid	5.00
Sugar, Cable Shape, H. Burgess, Lid	30.00
Sugar, Cable Shape, T. Furnival, Lid	30.00
Teapot, Fish Hook, Alfred Meakin, Lid, 9 In.	40.00
Teapot, Lily Of The Valley, Anthony Shaw, Lid	40.00
Tureen, Vegetable, Scroll, Alfred Meakin, Lid, 7 x 10 In.	15.00

TECO is the mark used on the art pottery line made by the American Terra Cotta and Ceramic Company of Terra Cotta and Chicago, Illinois. The company was an offshoot of the firm founded by William D. Gates in 1881. The Teco line was first made in 1885 but was not sold commercially until 1902. It continued in production until 1922. Over 500 designs were made in a variety of colors, shapes, and glazes. The company closed in 1930.

Bookends, Girl Reading Book, Terra-Cotta, 5 x 6 In.	425.00
Bowl, Low, Incised Design, Green Matte Glaze, Marked, 8 ½ x 3 In.	720.00
Bowl, No. 80, Green Matte Glaze, Low Shape, 7 x 2 ½ In.	480.00

Candleholder, Blue Matte Glaze, Handle, W.D. Gates, Impressed Mark, 5 x 2 ½ In., Pair	420.00
Case, Oval, Flared Rim, Gray Matte Glaze, 6 ¾ In.	550.00
Jardiniere, Matte Green Glaze, Applied Details, 21 ½ x 12 In.	1560.00
Jardiniere, Sculpted Lobes, Green Matte Glaze, Gray Highlights, Hugh Garden, Marked, 8 x 4 In.	900.00
Pitcher, Bulbous, Green Matte Glaze, W.D. Gates, 3 x 5 In.	840.00
Pitcher, Green Matte Glaze, Whiplash Handle, 9 ¼ x 5 In. ....*illus*	1200.00
Urn, Low, Broad Form, Mottled Cream High Glaze, 20 x 9 In., Pair	1560.00
Vase, 2 Buttress, Yellow, 6 ½ In.	65.00
Vase, 4 Buttress, Brown Matte Glaze, 10 ½ In.	110.00
Vase, Aqua Matte Glaze, Flared Bottom, Marked, 7 x 5 ½ In.	65.00
Vase, Buttressed, Orange Matte Glaze, 7 In.	125.00
Vase, Double Gourd, 4 Handles, Brown, 13 In.	185.00
Vase, Globular, 3-Footed, White, 8 In.	85.00
Vase, Green, Charcoal Matte Glaze, Angular Handles, W.D. Gates, Impressed Mark, 4 ½ x 5 ½ In.	1150.00
Vase, Green Matte Glaze, 3 Handles, Cylindrical, 11 x 5 In.	1220.00
Vase, Green Matte Glaze, 4 Handles, Impressed, William Dodd, 4 ½ x 12 In.	780.00
Vase, Green Matte Glaze, Buttressed, 15 x 7 ½ In.	17080.00
Vase, Green Matte Glaze, Buttressed, Stamped, 7 ¼ x 3 ¼ In.	2928.00
Vase, Green Matte Glaze, Spherical, Label, Stamp, 4 ¼ x 4 ½ In.	366.00
Vase, No. 60, Green Matte, Tapered, Raised Flowers, Gates & Albert, Marked, 4 ½ x 9 In.	780.00
Vase, No. 60B, Adventurine Glaze, Shouldered, Tapered, 4 x 8 In.	840.00
Vase, No. 115, Green Matte Glaze, 3-Footed, 7 x 9 In.	1920.00
Vase, No. 126, Green Matte Glaze, Charcoal Highlights, Broad Shape, Marked, 5 x 3 ½ In.	900.00
Vase, No. 197, Bulbous, Lobed, Flared Neck, Scalloped, Green Matte Glaze, 8 x 10 In.	1440.00
Vase, No. 257, 2 Twisted Handles, Green Matte Glaze, Signed, 11 ½ In.	2640.00
Vase, No. 336, 3-Sided, Brown Matte Glaze, Marked, 4 x 7 In.	633.00
Vase, No. 417, Green Matte Glaze, 2 x 5 In.	1680.00
Vase, No. 447A, 2 Buttressed Handles, Green Matte Glaze, 2 ½ x 6 ½ In.	863.00
Vase, Organic Tulip Shape, Green Glaze, Charcoal Highlights, Fernand Moureau, 5 x 12 In. ....*illus*	2040.00
Vase, Oval, Aqua Matte Glaze, Ribbed Rim, 17 ½ In.	195.00
Vase, Pagoda, Brown Matte Glaze, Squared Handles, 9 x 7 In.	95.00
Vase, Rolled Rim, Green, 16 In.	110.00
Vase, Sleek, 4 Integral Handles, Impressed, 11 In.	8050.00

Teco, Pitcher, Green Matte Glaze, Whiplash Handle, 9 ¼ x 5 In. $1200.00

Teco, Vase, Organic Tulip Shape, Green Glaze, Charcoal Highlights, Fernand Moureau, 5 x 12 In. $2040.00

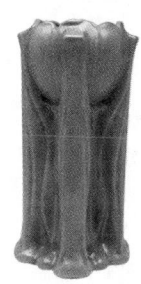

Telephone, Candlestick, Accordion, Wall Mount $275.00

TEDDY BEARS were named for a president of the United States. The first teddy bear was a cuddly toy said to be inspired by a hunting trip made by Teddy Roosevelt in 1902. Morris and Rose Michtom started selling their stuffed bears as "teddy bears" and the name stayed. The Michtoms founded the Ideal Novelty and Toy Company. The German version of the teddy bear was made about the same time by the Steiff Company. There are many types of teddy bears and all are collected. The old ones are being reproduced. Other bears are listed in the Toy section.

Chad Valley, Swivel Head, Jointed, Glass Eyes, Tag Under Arm, 10 In.	57.00
Cotton, Gold, Plush, Jointed, Paw Pads, Black Stitched Yarn Nose, 29 In.	403.00
Gold Mohair, Triangular Head, Side-Set, Shoebutton Eyes, Felt Nose, 10 In.	296.00
Mohair, Beige, Jointed Head, Limbs, Muzzle Humps, Glass Eyes, c.1900, 18 In.	201.00
Mohair, Beige, Jointed, Shoebutton Eyes, Felt Paw Pads, 12 ½ In.	489.00
Mohair, Gold, Jointed, Red Jewel Eyes, Straw Filled, Humpback, 20 ½ In.	195.00
Mohair, Golden, Jointed, Swivel Neck, Glass Eyes, 11 In.	51.00
Mohair, Jointed, Humpback, Red Felt Hat, Swivel Neck, Straw Filled, 23 In.	62.00
Mohair, Light Brown, Swivel Neck, Jointed, Crochet Dress, Glass Eyes, 20 In.	17.00
Mohair, Tan, Swivel Head, Jointed, Glass Eyes, 12 ½ In.	57.00
Squeaker, Growler, Mohair, Gold, Jointed, Swivel Neck, Glass Eyes, 18 ½ In.	57.00
Squeaker, Growler, Mohair, Pink, Swivel Head, Jointed, Glass Eyes, 8 In.	102.00
Squeaker, Growler, White, Swivel Neck, Jointed Limbs, Button Nose, Glass Eyes, 19 In.	113.00
Steiff, Blond, Mohair, Jointed Arms & Legs, Felt Pads, c.1907, 17 In.	180.00
Steiff, Growler, Stitched Nose, Mouth, Jointed, Felt Paw Pads, Glass Eyes, 15 In.	403.00
Steiff, Mohair, Apricot, Sewn Nose, Humpback, Button Eyes, Germany, c.1900, 12 In.	2340.00
Steiff, Mohair, Blond, Embroidered Nose, Mouth, Claws, Jointed, Shoebutton Eyes, 12 In.	593.00
Steiff, Mohair, Blond, Embroidered Nose, Mouth, Claws, Jointed, Shoebutton Eyes, c.1905	1541.00
Steiff, Mohair, Embroidered Nose, Mouth, Claws, Jointed, Shoebutton Eyes, c.1905, 15 In.	2252.00
Steiff, Mohair, Gold, Embroidered Nose, Claws, Oval Body, Steel Eyes, c.1905, 20 In.	2250.00
Steiff, Mohair, Jointed, Sewn Nose, Felt Pads, Ear Button, 8 In.	920.00
Steiff, Mohair, Jointed, Shaved Snout, Felt Pads, Shoebutton Eyes, c.1910, 19 ½ In.	1035.00
Steiff, Mohair, Swivel Head, Tag On Arm, Blue Collar, Bell, Glass Eyes, 18 ½ In.	424.00
Steiff, On Wheels, Embroidered Nose, Mouth, Shoebutton Eyes, Cast Iron Wheels, c.1905, 9 In.	830.00
Steiff, Santa, Friend Of Christmas, In Sleigh, Reindeer, 1989, 9 x 7 In.	225.00
Steiff, White, Brown Nose, Tag In Ear, 5 ½ In.	934.00

TIP

If an old teddy bear needs washing, do it very carefully. First vacuum the fur, then mix water and liquid detergent and brush the detergent through the fur. Dry with a towel, then a hair dryer on low. Let dry completely, comb with a dog comb.

T

Telephone, Sign, Local, Long-Distance, 2-Sided, Porcelain, Flange, 11 x 11 In. $173.00

Teplitz, Bust, Daphne, Ernst Wahliss, Stamped, Amphora, 28 ½ x 17 ½ In. $9150.00

Teplitz, Figurine, Woman, Stylish Pose, Amphora, Red Stamp, Crown, Art Nouveau, 25 x 8 In. $1098.00

Steiff, White, Pink Nose, Tag In Ear, 5 ½ In.	550.00
Tan, Swivel, Jointed, 15 In.	34.00

TELEPHONES are wanted by collectors if the phones are old enough or unusual enough. The first telephone may have been made in Havana, Cuba, in 1849, but it was not patented. The first publicly demonstrated phone was used in Frankfurt, Germany, in 1860. The phone made by Alexander Graham Bell was shown at the Centennial Exhibition in Philadelphia in 1876, but it was not until 1877 that the first private phones were installed. Collectors today want all types of old phones, phone parts, and advertising. Even recent figural phones are popular.

American Bell Telephone, Operator Switchboard, Oak, Chair, Pat. 1892, 50 x 23 x 28 In.	1500.00
Bensabott, Art Nouveau, Silver Base, Brass Dial, Headset, Chicago, 7 In.	600.00
Call Box, Western Union, Cobalt Blue, Porcelain, 3 ½ x 6 x 2 In.	44.00
Candlestick, Accordion, Wall Mount .... *illus*	275.00
Gray Telephone, Pay Station Co., Hartford, Bell Candlestick, 12 In.	413.00
Heinz Ketchup, Full Bottle, Twist-Off Cap, Paper Label, 8 ½ In.	60.00
Rotary Dial, Trimline, Orange, 1970s	75.00
Sign, American Telephone & Telegraph Co., Blue, White, Porcelain, 12 ¼ x 17 ¼ In.	330.00
Sign, Local, Long-Distance, 2-Sided, Porcelain, Flange, 11 x 11 In. *illus*	173.00
Sign, Public Telephone, Bell System, Blue, White, Porcelain, Flange, 18 x 18 In.	82.00
Sign, Public Telephone, Cobalt Blue, Enameled, 2-Sided, 13 x 11 In.	101.00
Sign, Western Union Telegraph & Cable Office, Blue, White, Flange, 12 x 24 In.	170.00
Snoopy, Woodstock, Rotary, 1976-79, 13 ½ x 9 ½ x 8 ½ In.	250.00
Stowaway, Oiled Walnut Box, Push Button, Retractable Cord, 1970s, 11 x 5 x 6 In.	200.00
Stromberg-Carlson, Black, Model No. 1248, Metal Case, 1940s	172.00
Wall, Alexander Graham Bell, Metal, Early 20th Century, 9 x 9 x 7 In.	83.00
Wall, Chicago Telephone Supply, Oak Case, Crank, Bells, 24 In.	175.00
Wall, Monarch, Oak, Double Box, No. L225700, 32 x 9 ½ In.	140.00
Wall, Oak, Double Box, Stromberg-Carlson, Monarch Telephone Co., c.1894, 32 x 12 In.	300.00
Western Electric, Candlestick, Brass, Expanding Wall Bracket, c.1915, 11 In.	480.00
Western Electric, Candlestick, Key, 1904	495.00
Western Electric, Wall, No. 323W, Oak, 20 ½ x 9 ½ In.	110.00

TEPLITZ refers to art pottery manufactured by a number of companies in the Teplitz-Turn area of Bohemia during the late nineteenth and early twentieth centuries. Two of these companies were the Alexandra Works founded by Ernst Wahliss, and The Amphora Porcelain Works, run by Riessner, Stellmacher, and Kessel.

Basket, 4 Handles, Gres-Bijou, Amphora, 10 x 10 ¾ In.	2196.00
Bowl, Flowers, Raised Gilt, Reticulated Handles & Rim, Red Backstamp, c.1900, 17 In.	1080.00
Bust, Daphne, Ernst Wahliss, Stamped, Amphora, 28 ½ x 17 ½ In. *illus*	9150.00
Bust, Maiden, Ondine, Olive Green & Ivory, Carmine Luster, Gold Accents, Marked, Amphora, 14 In.	1920.00
Bust, Woman, Eyes Half Closed, Choker, Amphora, Riessner, Stellmacher & Kessel, 15 x 8 In.	1037.00
Bust, Woman, Flower Hat, Ernst Wahliss, Amphora, 28 ½ x 17 ½ In.	9150.00
Bust, Woman, Golden Bronze, Ernst Wahliss, Amphora, 8 ½ x 7 ½ In.	488.00
Bust, Woman, Large Collar, Eyes Closed, RStK, Amphora, 18 x 15 In.	1037.00
Bust, Woman, Poppies, Riessner, Stellmacher & Kessel, 16 x 10 ½ In.	915.00
Bust, Woman, Upswept Curly Hair, Low Decolletage Gown, 17 x 16 In.	4500.00
Bust, Woman, Victorian Attire, Red Hair, Green Hat, Corset, 15 x 17 In.	1783.00
Candlestick, Hosta, Green, Blue, Rose, Tan, Handle, RStK, Amphora, 11 In.	1035.00
Candlestick, Jewels, Blue, Gold Flowers, Handle, Imperial Amphora Stamp, 9 In.	374.00
Compote, Gres-Bijou, Chestnuts, Jeweled Rim, Green, Gold Overlay, Impressed, Amphora, 12 In.	1495.00
Ewer, Porcelain, Yellow, Enameled Flowers, Gilt, Printed Mark, c.1900, 8 In.	135.00
Figurine, Boy At Well, 6 ½ In.	58.00
Figurine, Girl, Classical Dress, Holding Vase With Flowers, Amphora, 12 ⅞ In.	115.00
Figurine, Madonna & Child, Standing, Flowing Robes, Amphora, 23 In.	189.00
Figurine, Maiden, Holding Basket & Pail, Amphora, 17 In.	520.00
Figurine, Monkey, Gray & Ivory High Glaze, Marked, Amphora, 8 x 9 ½ In.	960.00
Figurine, Peasant Woman, Collecting Water, Gold Accents, Amphora, Elvir Otto, 11 x 24 In.	900.00
Figurine, Woman Astronomer, Enameled, Gilded, Marked, c.1900, 10 In.	309.00
Figurine, Woman, Dancing With Veil, Amphora, 19 ¼ x 16 In.	4575.00
Figurine, Woman, Posing, Hand On Hip, Amphora, Art Nouveau, 25 x 8 In.	1098.00
Figurine, Woman, Stylish Pose, Amphora, Red Stamp, Crown, Art Nouveau, 25 x 8 In. *illus*	1098.00
Figurine, Woman, Water Lily Platter, Ernst Wahliss, Amphora, c.1897, 4 ½ x 13 In.	976.00
Jardiniere, 2 Winged Cherubs, Basket Weave Form, Blossoms, Amphora, c.1910, 13 In.	510.00
Jug, Macintosh Roses, Red, Green, Gold, Gray, 2 Spouts, Handles, Paul Dachsel Stamp, 6 In.	546.00
Pitcher, Insects, Roses, Amphora, Riessner, Stellmacher & Kessel, 7 ¾ x 5 ¼ In.	1708.00

T

Planter, Jeweled Flowers, Sweeping Handles, Impressed, Amphora, 6 x 11 In.	345.00
Teapot, Jeweled, 3-Prong Handle, Marked, Amphora, 6 In.	575.00
Urn, Handles, Gres-Bijou, Riessner & Kessel, Amphora, 17 x 12 ½ In.	2562.00
Vase, 4 Buttresses, Blue Luster Glaze, Applied Grapes, Amphora, 15 In.	127.00
Vase, 4 Handles, Yellow Roses, Mottled, Marked, Amphora, 10 x 16 In.	86.00
Vase, 5-Spout, Flower, Handles, Amphora, 1905, 13 In.	475.00
Vase, Applied Daughter Of The Rhine, Gres-Bijou, Amphora, Marked, 16 x 13 In.	9600.00
Vase, Applied Dragon, Marked, Eduard Stellmacher, Amphora, c.1900, 13 x 17 In. .... *illus*	8400.00
Vase, Applied Grape Clusters, Vines, Cobalt & Carmine, Marked, Edda Series, c.1902, 8 x 11 In.	600.00
Vase, Applied Red & Gold Raindrops, Carved, 3 Central Handles, P. Dachsel, Amphora, 7 In. ...	390.00
Vase, Art Nouveau, Duck With Flowers, Multicolored, Marked, c.1905, 3 ¾ x 4 In.	104.00
Vase, Art Nouveau, Flowers, Handles, Paul Dachsel, Amphora, 7 ¼ In.	460.00
Vase, Art Nouveau, Squeezebag, Female Warrior, Eagle Helmet, Marked, 12 x 7 In. .... *illus*	7200.00
Vase, Birds, Multicolored, Handles, Amphora, 7 In.	90.00
Vase, Blossoms & Leaves, Enameled Dots, Gold Trim, Secessionist, Paul Dachsel, 14 In.	2074.00
Vase, Blossoms, Stylized Lotus Leaves, Stems Twisted Handles, Blue Ground, 9 ¾ x 5 ¼ In.	2880.00
Vase, Blue Enameled Flowers, Spider Webs, Foaming Rim, Sea Serpent Handles, c.1900, 13 ¼ In.	510.00
Vase, Blue, Gold Linear Decoration, Squat, Amphora, c.1900, 4 ½ x 8 ½ In.	1080.00
Vase, Blue Matte, Gold Highlights, Riessner, Stellmacher & Kessel, Amphora, Handles, 5 In. ...	748.00
Vase, Brown, Trees, Seahorse Handles, Riessner, Stellmacher & Kessel, Amphora, 11 ¼ x 7 ¼ In.	2440.00
Vase, Butterflies, Gres-Bijou, Amphora, Stamped, Red R. St. & K., 1899, 9 ¼ x 8 In.	2318.00
Vase, Butterflies, Gres-Bijou, Riessner & Kessel, Amphora, 1899-1900, 7 ¾ x 4 ¾ In.	1830.00
Vase, Confetti, Mottled Red, Black Matte Glaze, Gold Trim, Ribbing, Amphora, 7 In.	633.00
Vase, Dark Brown, Green Lizard, Edward Stellmacher, Amphora, 15 ½ x 9 In.	9760.00
Vase, Double Gourd, Multicolored, Carved, 4 Central Handles, Amphora, 5 x 8 In.	720.00
Vase, Double Gourd Shape, 5 Spouts, Painted, Amphora, c.1907, 8 x 12 ½ In. .... *illus*	450.00
Vase, Double Handled, Leaves, Berries, Blue, Red Matte Glaze, Amphora, 9 ½ x 16 ½ In.	600.00
Vase, Double Handled Shape, Leaves, Berries, Blue, Red Matte Glaze, Amphora, 9 ½ x 16 ½ In.	600.00
Vase, Drape On Wrapped Neck, Crab, Amphora, Marked, 10 x 22 In.	7200.00
Vase, Flowers, Multicolored, Gilt, Amphora, Marked, 9 ¼ x 4 ¼ In.	180.00
Vase, Flowers, Stems, Cabochons, Amphora, Marigold, 13 ¾ x 8 In.	854.00
Vase, Forest Scent, Gold Handle & Rim, Bulbous, Amphora, c.1900, 6 In.	300.00
Vase, Gold Macintosh Roses, Luster Glaze Base, Marked, Riessner, Stellmacher & Kessel, 15 In. ..	1610.00
Vase, Gourd Shape, Enameled Wisteria, Blue, Gold, Green, Paul Dachsel, 7 In.	403.00
Vase, Green & Gold Decorations, Bulbous, Amphora, c.1907, 15 x 8 In.	510.00
Vase, Green Matte Glaze, Applied Poppies, Vine Handles, Shaped Rim, Amphora, 20 ¾ In.	183.00
Vase, Green Pine Tree Trunks, Carved & Applied Pine Cones, Bulbous, Marked, Amphora, 15 ½ In.	4200.00
Vase, Gres-Bijou, Enamel Cabochons, Cloisonne, c.1920, 4 x 8 In.	150.00
Vase, Gres-Bijou, Mushrooms, Landscape, Amphora, Dachsel, c.1906, 11 x 7 In.	2440.00
Vase, Handle, Bulbous, Trees, Mushrooms, Iridescent Highlights, Paul Dachsel, Amphora, 6 x 6 In.	978.00
Vase, Leaves, 4 Handles, Amphora, Paul Dachsel, c.1911, 12 ¾ x 7 In.	3294.00
Vase, Leaves, 4 Handles, Amphora, Riessner, Stellmacher & Kessel, 16 x 6 ½ In.	3660.00
Vase, Luster, Fired On Gold, 3 Raven Handles, Impressed Imperial Amphora, 9 In.	690.00
Vase, Mushrooms, Landscape, Handle, Amphora, Dachsel, c.1906, 6 ½ x 5 ½ In.	1464.00
Vase, Nude Woman, Cobalt Blue, Gold Accents, Art Nouveau, Amphora, 22 ½ x 14 In.	2700.00
Vase, Owl, 2 Handles, Amphora, 5 ½ In.	45.00
Vase, Painted Portrait, Flowers, Pale Yellow To Purple Iridescence, Amphora, 4 ½ x 6 In.	1080.00
Vase, Parrot, Incised, Carved, Painted, Amphora, 1900s, 18 In.	570.00
Vase, Peasants, Landscape, Amphora, c.1909, 18 ¼ x 10 In.	2074.00
Vase, Petunias, Pink & White, Green Leaf Ground, West's Terraline, Amphora, 15 In.	167.00
Vase, Poppies, Enameled, Gres-Bijou, RStK, Glaze, Amphora, 17 x 8 ¾ In.	1342.00
Vase, Secessionist Ball, Oval, Slip Trailed Roses, Purple, Green, Brown, Paul Dachsel, Amphora, 9 In. .	1610.00
Vase, Slip Painted, Wild Roses, Multitoned Green Ground, Handle, Marked, Amphora, 15 In. ..	120.00
Vase, Spider Web, Insects, Red Cabochon Jewel, Gold Trim, RStK, 8 In.	1003.00
Vase, Stag, Forest, Relief, Earth Tones, 12 ¾ In.	795.00
Vase, Summer Queen, Queen Profile, Multicolored, Gold Overlay, RStK, 6 In.	4025.00
Vase, Swan, Cloud Background, Blue Roses, Dachsel, Amphora, c.1900, 6 ¾ In.	598.00
Vase, Teardrop, Handle Within Handle, Amphora, Paul Dachsel, 10 x 6 ½ In.	4575.00
Vase, Thistles, Green, Brown Mottled Matte Glaze, Gold, 2 Handles, Paul Dachsel, Amphora, 7 In.	863.00
Vase, Thistles, Handles, Amphora, Riessner, Stellemacher & Kessel, c.1902, 20 x 8 ¼ In., Pair..	1708.00
Vase, Tree, Mottled Green Matte Glaze, Gold, Paul Dachsel, 9 In.	2300.00
Vase, Twisted Shape, Amphora, c.1900, 7 ½ x 5 In.	1440.00
Vase, Volateria Style, Carmine & Bronze Luster, 3 Ibis Handles, Marked, Amphora, 7 x 9 In. ...	390.00
Vase, White Tiger, Stylized Flowers, Yellow, Brown, RStK, Amphora, 11 In.	805.00
Vase, Woman, Crowned, Gres-Bijou, Amphora, 6 ¼ x 4 In.	2684.00
Vase, Woman, Crowned, Gres-Bijou, Amphora, 9 ¼ x 4 ½ In.	5185.00

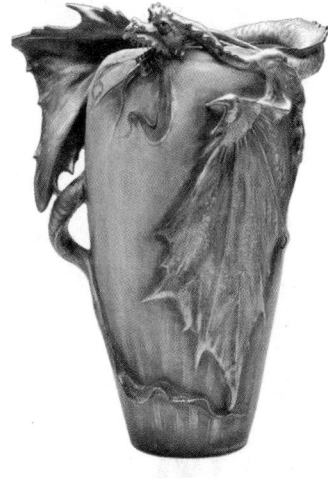

Teplitz, Vase, Applied Dragon, Marked, Eduard Stellmacher, Amphora, c.1900, 13 x 17 In.
$8400.00

Teplitz, Vase, Art Nouveau, Squeezebag, Female Warrior, Eagle Helmet, Marked, 12 x 7 In.
$7200.00

Teplitz, Vase, Double Gourd Shape, 5 Spouts, Painted, Amphora, c.1907, 8 x 12 ½ In.
$450.00

Terra-Cotta, Figurine,
Sacred Heart Of Jesus, Signed,
P. Marioni, 1900s, 27 In.
$480.00

Textile, Blanket, Camp, Red, White,
Geometric, Running Horses, 75 x 70 In.
$127.00

Vase, Woman, Crowned, Jeweled Flowers, Amphora, 1899-1900, 13 x 6 In.	5490.00
Vase, Woman, Posing, Bats On Rim, 2 Handles, Ernst Wahliss, Amphora, 16 x 8 In.	915.00
Wine, Wright Iron Stand, Rene Herbst, Amphora, c.1927, 12 ¾ In.	1553.00

TERRA-COTTA is a special type of pottery. It ranges from pale orange to dark reddish-brown in color. The color comes from the clay, which is fired but not always glazed in the finished piece.

Bowl, French Provincial, Ocher Glaze, Flared, 2 Handles, Pouring Spout, 9 x 21 ½ In.	588.00
Bust, Crying Baby, 4 x 4 x 4 In.	316.00
Bust, Goethe, Bronzed Patina, c.1870, 19 In.	147.00
Bust, Julius Caesar, Blue Cloak, Glazed, Gold Highlights, Italy, 34 In.	460.00
Bust, Young Girl, Long Hair, Painted, Chester Beach, 12 In.	575.00
Bust, Young Woman, Curly Hair, Eyes Glancing Left, Chester Beach, 1923, 16 In.	978.00
Dish, French Provincial, Round, Molded Lip, Partial Glaze, 2 ½ x 12 In.	180.00
Figurine, Asian Man & Woman, Holding Birds & Cages, 13 ¼ In., Pair	403.00
Figurine, Bull, Standing, Tilted Head, Black & Brown Slip Cover, Chinese, 13 ½ x 17 In.	180.00
Figurine, Children, Linking Arms, Holding Flowers, Ebonized Wood Base, Signed, 14 x 20 In.	71.00
Figurine, Griffin, Winged, Raised Head, Seated, c.1910, 28 x 19 x 17 In.	4320.00
Figurine, Horse, Tang Style, Brown, Braided Yellow, Green Mane, Glaze, Chinese, 15 x 15 In., Pair	173.00
Figurine, Lion, Glancing Backward, Stylized Mane, England, Late 1800s, 31 x 23 In.	1410.00
Figurine, Lion, Recumbent, Mouth Fountain Opening, Base, France, 1800s, 26 x 16 In., Pair	460.00
Figurine, Lion, Stylized Mane, Turned Backward, England, c.1880, 31 x 23 In., Pair	1410.00
Figurine, Monkey, White Glaze, Smoking Pipe, Playing Saxophone, 16 In., Pair	690.00
Figurine, Sacred Heart Of Jesus, Signed, P. Marioni, 1900s, 27 In. ....*illus*	480.00
Figurine, Venus, After Antonio Canova, Continental, 46 x 12 In.	881.00
Figurine, Woman, Classical Toga, Holding Cup, Ewer, Hebe, After Canova, Oval Base, 40 In.	296.00
Humidor, Log Shape, Dapper Man, Seated, Painted, Impressed, Austria, 1800s, 6 x 8 In.	720.00
Jardiniere, Arts & Crafts, Green Crackle Glaze, Oval, Galloway, Philadelphia, 16 x 21 In.	646.00
Jardiniere, Dragon Motif, Short Legs, Chinese, 14 ½ x 20 In.	115.00
Jardiniere, Oval, Rope Twist Handles, Mediterranean, 33 x 23 In.	550.00
Jardiniere, Reading Lesson, 2 Girls, Reading, Figural, 23 x 19 In.	450.00
Ornament, Louis XVI Style, Fruit & Flower Filled Vase, Melon Ribbed, 24 x 12 In., Pair	1200.00
Plaque, Baby Bacchus Head, Grape Clusters, Leaves, 4 x 3 ½ In., 15 Piece	650.00
Plaque, Gypsy Woman, Tambourine, Holly Border, Painted Scene, Mark, Austria, 12 ⅛ In.	142.00
Sculpture, Boy, With Tambourine, Monkey, Square Base, 34 x 12 In.	1060.00
Sculpture, Seminude Woman, Feeding Deer, Signed, G. Bom, 12 x 23 In.	750.00
Tile, Fish, High Relief, 7 ½ x 7 ½ In.	52.00
Tobacco Jar, Man In Cigar Bundle, Czechoslovakia, 9 In.	69.00
Urn, Classical, Grapevine, 2 Handles, Ribbed Base On Waisted Standard, Lid, 35 x In., Pair	1020.00
Urn, Louis XVI, Conservatory, Handles, Bas-Relief Masques, Medallions, 44 x 25 ½ In.	2280.00
Urn, Louis XVI Style, Fluted, 2 Handles, Square Slab Base, Cannele Cover, 24 In., Pair	840.00
Urn, Mythological Figures, Water, Mountains, Scroll Handles, Footed, 34 In.	3400.00
Urn, Red Flambe Glaze, Applied Berries, Cicada, Fold Rim, Gilt Bronze Mounts, 34 In.	1445.00
Vase, Arabesque, Iron Stand, Navarre, Spain, 19th Century, 42 x 16 x 18 In.	600.00
Vessel, Drinking, Rolled Rim, Iran, 9 x 4 In.	41.00

TEXTILES listed here include many types of printed fabrics and table and household linens. Some other textiles will be found under Clothing, Coverlet, Rug, Quilt, etc.

Bandanna, Centennial, 1776-1876, Memorial Hall Art Gallery, Blue Star Border	125.00
Banner, White Ground, Red Star, Cloth Gold Fringe, 5 x 9 In.	55.00
Bedspread, Chenille, Peacock, Brown, Green, Yellow & Pink, 1950s, 93 x 110 In.	398.00
Bedspread, Crewel Embroidered, Linen, Flowers, Leaves, Fruit, Center Design, 79 x 49 In.	948.00
Blanket, Buggy, Glass Eye Tiger, Stroock, 46 x 60 In.	83.00
Blanket, Camp, Red, White, Geometric, Running Horses, 75 x 70 In. ....*illus*	127.00
Bolster, Linen, Blue & White Checked, Cloth Tape Ties, 63 x 21 In.	99.00
Cover, Cushion, Crewel, Round, 23 In.	11.00
Cover, Paisley, Beige Center Block, 63 x 121 In.	68.00
Curtain, Battle Of Buena Vista, Roller Print, Pleated Tops, Lined, 1847, 90 x 75-In. Panels, 6 Piece	1170.00
Doily, Battenburg Lace, 12 In. Diam.	22.00
Doily, Battenburg Lace, Ecru, c.1890, 11 In. Diam.	24.00
Doily, Pinwheel, 9 ⅛ In. Diam.	10.00
Drapes, Cotton, Western Design, Cream Ground, Horses, Cowboys, Indians, 1940s, 54 In.	275.00
Embroidery, Garden Scene, Gold Mesh, Chinese, Frame, 31 x 21 In.	761.00
Embroidery, Laughing Twins, Men, Birds, Orange Ground, Silk, H. Erxian, 1800s, 31 x 31 In.	403.00
Embroidery, Peafowl On Branch, Flower, Scroll Borders, Silk Chenille, Gauze, 14 x 12 ¾ In.	690.00
Fabric, 100 Children, Terrace, Stylized Dragons, Phoenixes, Cloud Scrolls, Chinese, Frame, 80 x 29 In.	460.00

T

Fabric, Silk, Scalamandre, Patrick Barry, Turquoise On Pearl, Italy, 1970s, 26 Yds. x 50 In.	2300.00
Flag, 22 Stars, Hand Stitched, 35 x 58 In.	6380.00
Flag, American, 13 Stars, 3-2-3-2-3 Pattern, U.S. Navy, 1864-76	7500.00
Flag, American, 13 Stars, Appliqued, Cotton, Wool, Single-Ply Thread, 1850, 40 x 68 In. .. *illus*	2703.00
Flag, American, 13 Stars, Cotton, Wool, Hand Sewn, Civil War, 38 x 58 In.	9400.00
Flag, American, 13 Stars, Eagle, Shield, Text, Hand Painted, Blood Stripe, Wool, c.1865...........	11750.00
Flag, American, 20 Stars, Double Appliqued, Hand Sewn, Cotton, 17 ½ x 29 In.	1293.00
Flag, American, 31 Stars, Worsted Wool, Machine, Hand Sewn, c.1850, 58 x 107 In.	2820.00
Flag, American, 32 Stars, Wool, Cotton, Geo. H. Gould, c.1859, 8 Ft. 2 In. x 11 Ft.	940.00
Flag, American, 32 Stars, Wool, Cotton, Georgie K.S. Soule, c.1859, 9 x 15 Ft.	1140.00
Flag, American, 34 Stars, Cotton, Hand Sewn, c.1861, 48 x 67 In.	4113.00
Flag, American, 34 Stars, Cotton, Wool, Linen, Civil War, 56 x 104 In.	2468.00
Flag, American, 36 Stars, Central Star, Hand, Machine Sewn, c.1885, 85 x 90 In.	6600.00
Flag, American, 48 Stars, Embroidered Stars, Sewn Stripes, Shadowbox Frame, 73 x 57 ½ In.	448.00
Flag, Centennial, Wool, Printed, Machine Sewn, c.1876, 42 x 45 ½ In.	1880.00
Flag, U.S. Presidential Seal, Embroidered, Navy Ground, Shadowbox Frame, 73 x 57 ½ In.	1912.00
Gauntlet, Leather, Beads, Eagle, Olive Branch, Tan, Gold, Blue, Rose, Pony, Express Rider, 13 In., Pair	1528.00
Hammock, Cotton, Red, Blue, Yellow, Black, Signed Alexander Calder, 125 x 60 In. .... *illus*	2640.00
Linen, Drawn Work, Geometric Center & Corner Designs, 1930s, 34 x 32 In.	9.00
Napkin Set, Cocktail, Art Deco, Maroon & White, 5 x 7 In., 8 Piece	95.00
Needlework, Crewel, Wool, Linen, Flowering Tree, Borders, Wood Frame, 1700s, 72 x 19 In. ..	420.00
Needlework, Embroidered, Silk, Shepherdess, Carving Name Into Tree, 12 x 10 In.	288.00
Panel, Embroidered, Multicolored Silk, Metallic Threads, Armorial Crest, 36 x 37 In.	568.00
Panel, Embroidered, St. Bernard At Prayer, Palm Trees, Chenille, Metal Threads, 26 x 30 ¼ In. ..	600.00
Panel, Ship, Red, Gold, Signed, Mariano Fortuny, Early 20th Century, 38 x 20 In.	220.00
Panel, Tapestry, Napoleon III Style, Floral Bouquet, On Pedestal, 50 x 74 In., 3 Piece.............	3360.00
Panel, Woven, Tan Ground, Phoenix Birds, Clouds, Trees, Foo Dogs, Frame, Chinese, 64 x 23 In., Pair	2596.00
Piano Scarf, Needlework, Flowers, Red, Pink, Blue, Green, Lavender, Fringe, 64 x 64 In.	150.00
Piano Scarf, Silk, Embroidered Flowers, 1900s, 17-In. Fringe, 44 x 46 In.	350.00
Pillow Cover, Arabian Men, On Horseback, 22 x 22 In.	60.00
Pillow Cover, Farm Couple, Offering Thanks, 22 ½ x 22 ½ In.	65.00
Pillow Cover, Indian Chief, Full Headdress, 1906, Frame, 23 x 23 In.	395.00
Pillow Cover, Indian Woman, Side View, Frame, 23 x 23 In.	200.00
Pillow Cover, Patchwork, Necktie Design, Multicolored Triangles, 24 x 24 In.	11.00
Pillow Cover, Roll, Cotton, Lace Corners, 1930s, 15 x 15 In.	8.00
Pillow Cover, She's My Idol, She's My Queen, Man Smoking, 22 x 22 In.	200.00
Pillow Cover, Silk Screen, Hollywood Bowl, Brown Derby, NBC Studios, 1950s......................	100.00
Pillow Cover, U.S. Army, Mother & Dad Poem, Fringe, Square, 1940s, 16 In.	22.00
Pillow Cover, Woman, Standing At Fountain, 20 x 25 In.	175.00
Pillow, Needlepoint, Aubusson Style, Fringe, 19th Century Panel, 18 x 18 In., Pair.................	345.00
Remnant, Toile De Jouy, George Washington, Iron Red, Cream, Cotton, c.1785, 21 x 30 In.	840.00
Runner, Tea Cart Tray, Knitted Leaf Trim, 1900s, 14 x 20 In.	105.00
Table Mat, Felt, Twill, Cotton, Appliqued Cat Playing With Ball Of Yarn, 1845, 33 x 34 In.	380.00
Table Mat, Hooked Center, Knotted & Braided Border, New England, c.1900, 20 x 42 In.	350.00
Table Runner, Arts & Crafts, Embroidered, Multicolored, Butterfly, Geometric, Lace, 16 x 60 In. . *illus*	570.00
Table Runner, Damask, Tulip Hem, 2-In. Hems, 96 In.	210.00
Table Runner, Pennies, Graduated Cloth Discs, Brown & White Ground, 38 x 19 In.	412.00
Table Runner, Wool, Cotton, Lozenge Shaped Muslin Ground, Appliqued Peonies, c.1875, 59 x 34 In.	382.00
Table Scarf, Arts & Crafts, Embroidered, Flowers, Linen, 33 In. .... *illus*	330.00
Tablecloth, Cotton, Crochet, 86 x 102 In.	110.00
Tablecloth, Lace, Embroidered Linen, Cream Ground, Italy, c.1930, 98 x 61 In.	354.00
Tablecloth, Linen, Drawn Thread Work, Daffodil Filet Lace Drop, Square, 25 x 25 In.	175.00
Tablecloth, Linen, Lace, Cutwork, Embroidered, Square, 44 x 44 In.	145.00
Tablecloth, Napkins, Cotton, Blue & White Flower Appliques, 96 x 62 In., 13 Piece.................	250.00
Tapestry, 4 Reserves, Animals, Urns, Flowers, Birds, Black Ground, 18th Century, 53 x 51 In. .	565.00
Tapestry, Dog, Embroidered, Flower & Leaf Border, c.1890, 70 x 70 In.	402.00
Tapestry, Draped Garden Vase, Pedestal, Peacock, Musical Still Life, 6 x 7 ½ In.	3360.00
Tapestry, French Colonial Scene, Nubian Woman, Porters, Animals, c.1860, 81 x 93 In.	3120.00
Tapestry, French Renaissance Style, Hunting Scene, Wooded Landscape, c.1900, 77 x 79 In. ..	1920.00
Tapestry, Hunt Scene, Deer, Birds, Dogs, Forest, Brown, Green, Blue, 17 Ft. 3 In. x 7 Ft. 6 In. ..	245.00
Tapestry, Hunter, Dogs, France, Early 20th Century, 76 x 70 In.	316.00
Tapestry, Napoleon III Style, Country Scene, Farmers Smoking, c.1900, 77 x 48 In.	1150.00
Tapestry, Pastoral, Birds, Wooded Landscape, c.1890, 25 x 35 In.	630.00
Tapestry, Pastoral, Ducks, Ducklings, Barrel, Pond, c.1890, 25 x 35 In.	630.00
Tapestry, Unicorn, Birds, Botanical Theme, Silk, Burlwood Frame, England, 6 x 10 In.	176.00
Tapestry, Wool, Foot Soldiers, Battlefield, Swiss Flag, France, 18th Century, 115 x 88 In.	4740.00

Textile, Flag, American, 13 Stars, Appliqued, Cotton, Wool, Single-Ply Thread, 1850, 40 x 68 In.
$2703.00

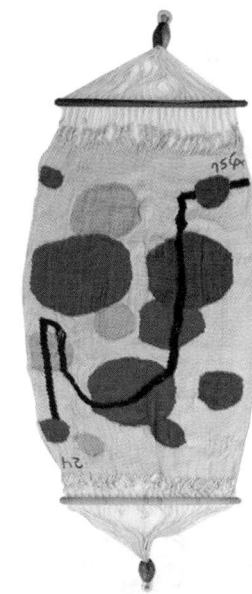

Textile, Hammock, Cotton, Red, Blue, Yellow, Black, Signed Alexander Calder, 125 x 60 In.
$2640.00

TIP

Don't send out your antique white linen or cotton items to be dry-cleaned. The chemicals will yellow the fabric. Hand wash them in soap, non-chlorine bleach, and tepid water. Be sure to rinse until all soap is removed.

T

Textile, Table Runner, Arts & Crafts, Embroidered, Multicolored, Butterfly, Geometric, Lace, 16 x 60 In.
$570.00

Textile, Table Scarf, Arts & Crafts, Embroidered, Flowers, Linen, 33 In.
$330.00

Thermometer, Farmers' Milk, Wax Milk Carton, Tin, 14 ¾ x 5 ¾ In.
$146.00

Tapestry, Wool, Landscape, Trees, Crane, Temple, Bridge, 17th-18th Century, 94 x 72 ½ In.	7110.00
Towel, Guest Damask, Greek Key Edge, Pulled Work, Blue Embroidered, Filet Inset, 23 x 45 In.	105.00
Towel, Show, Embroidered, Elizabeth H. Longenecker, Pennsylvania, 1840, 60 x 17 ½ In.	1053.00
Towel, Show, Flower Vases, Wool On Linen, Signed, Mary Kurtz, 1846, 52 x 16 In.	550.00
Wall Hanging, Musical Instruments, Screen Print, Linen, Black, Red, Gold, Top, Supports, 17 x 43 In.	30.00
Wallet, Wool, Double Folding, Irish Stitch, Zigzag Diamond Pattern, Green, Red, Yellow, 1786.	4445.00

THERMOMETER is a name that comes from the Greek word for heat. The thermometer was invented in 1731 to measure the temperature of either water or air. All kinds of thermometers are collected, but those with advertising messages are the most popular.

7Up, Bottle, Go Navigate, Green, White, Red, Porcelain, 15 x 6 In.	110.00
7Up, Ca Ravigote, Bottle, Agreeable A Tous, White, Red, Green, Canada, 15 In.	59.00
A.B.C. Refrigeration, Metal, 4 Digit Phone Number, 11 In.	15.00
Alligator Baby, Bakelite Insert, Brown, Germany, 6 ½ In.	170.00
Baby's Guardian, Baby Within Milk Bottle, Celluloid Over Tin, 8 x 3 In.	132.00
Baltimore Tank & Tower Co., Celluloid, 6 ¼ x 2 In.	80.00
Bath, Dr. Forbes, Testrite, Wood & Glass, 12 In.	15.00
Bireley's Orange Soda, Enamel, Rolled Edge, Tin, 10 x 26 x ¼ In.	112.00
Black Forest, Linden Wood, Hunter, Late 1800s, 7 ½ In.	207.00
Born Well Drilling, Minnesota, Red Lettering, White Ground, Pressed Steel Body, 13 ¼ In.	10.00
Bronze, Putto, Sitting Atop Satyr's Shoulders, Vining, Pedestal, Step Base, 8 ¾ In.	895.00
Delco Energizer Batteries, White, Tin, 39 x 8 ¼ In.	36.00
Dr Pepper, Frosty Cold, Red, White, 1958, 25 ¾ x 10 In.	140.00
Dr Pepper, Hot Or Cold, Red, White, Tin, 16 x 6 ½ In.	175.00
Drink The Wright Root Beer, Metal, It's Energized, 1940s, 7 x 27 In.	115.00
Eagle Pencil Co., Pencil, 75th Anniversary, Wood, Rubber Eraser, 14 ¼ x 1 ¼ In.	580.00
Esso Atlas Anti-Freeze, Red, White, Blue, Dial, Aluminum, Glass, 17 x 17 In.	275.00
Ex-Lax, Chocolate Laxative, Porcelain, Multicolored, 1950s, 4 x 6 In.	512.00
Farmers' Milk, Wax Milk Carton, Tin, 14 ¾ x 5 ¾ In. .... *illus*	146.00
Fatima Cigarettes, Porcelain, 27 x 7 In. .... *illus*	88.00
Figural, Pharaoh, Egyptian Revival, Bronze, Holding Shield, Signed Freres, 3 x 10 In.	748.00
Ft. Myers Florida, Flamingo & Palm Tree, Round, Wooden, 1960s, 4 ¾ In.	16.00
Hires Root Beer, Bottle, Tin, 28 ¾ x 7 ¾ In.	310.00
Hooker Bros. Ice Cream, Taste Tells Why, Children, White, Black, Wood, 14 x 4 In.	550.00
Jack Frost Co., Tacoma, Washington, Indoor, Outdoor, 1940s, 11 ½ x 3 In.	20.00
John Deere, Nothing Runs Like A Deere, Yellow, Green & Black Lettering, 1960s, 13 In.	22.00
John E. Dohner Marble & Granite Works, 12 In.	100.00
Keep Regular With Ex-Lax, The Chocolate Laxative, Wood, 9 x 2 In.	121.00
Ken-L-Biskit, Diet Of Champions, Round, 12 In.	21.00
Magic Chips, Deep Fat Frying, Enamel, Wood	30.00
Mail Pouch Tobacco, Treat Yourself, Black, Yellow, White Porcelain, 39 x 8 In. ... 250.00 to 580.00	
Malto-Hopo For Nervousness, Indigestion, Fatigue, Wood, Paint, 12 x 3 In.	440.00
Meat, Box, Ohio Thermometer Co., Springfield, Ohio	4.00
Moxie, Girl With Bottle, Glass, Frank Archer, 9 ½ x 12 In.	1430.00
M.W. Powell Roofing & Paving, Wood, Yellow Paint, Mercury On Top & Bottom, 12 In.	80.00
Neuweiler Beer & Ale, Tin Lithograph Dial, Aluminum, Glass Dome, 1960s, 12-In. Diam	115.00
Obelisk Shape, Marble, Brass, Grand Tour, 1800s, 12 In.	920.00
Orange-Crush, Bottle, Feel Fresh, Carbonated Beverage, Masonite, 1943, 16 x 4 ½ In. ... *illus*	1265.00
Park & Pollards Lay Or Bust Poultry Feed, Yellow, Red, Black, Porcelain, 27 x 7 In.	3198.00
Perfection Seeds, Geo. P. Sexauer & Son, Yellow, Black, Porcelain, 27 x 7 In.	180.00
Peter's Shoes, Solid Leather, We'll Put Together, Blue, White, Yellow, Porcelain, 19 ¼ x 6 In.	715.00
Prestone Anti-Freeze, White, Red, Blue, Porcelain, 36 ½ x 9 ¼ In.	195.00
Pureoxia Ginger Ale, For Sale Here, Wood, 21 x 8 ¾ In.	550.00
Reymond's Bread Mirror, 8 x 18 In.	94.00
Rolls-Royce, 1933 Classic Phantom Model, Stamped Metal, Silvery Finish, 8 ¼ In.	25.00
Royal Crown Cola, Red, Yellow, 25 ½ x 10 In.	110.00
Salem Cigarettes, Refreshes Your Taste, Triangular Shape, Round Thermometer, Tin, 9 x 9 In.	25.00
Sauer's Vanilla Flavoring, Box Shape, Wood, c.1918, 8 x 3 ¾ In.	480.00
Star Cleaners, Art Deco, Black & White, Massillon, Ohio, c.1940, 9 ½ x 3 ½ In.	50.00
Stephenson Union Suits, Red, White, 39 x 8 In.	195.00
Sunbeam Bread, Round, c.1957, 12 In. .... *illus*	527.00
Tin, We Recommend Trophy Motor Oil, Red Arrow, 1930s, 7 x 27 In.	345.00
Traveling, Victorian, Sterling Silver, Signed, Black Starr & Frost, 4 ½ In.	95.00
Tums For The Tummy, Tin Lithograph, Box, 9 x 4 In.	187.00
Valentine's Valspar Enamel Paints, Red, White, Blue, Porcelain, 1915, 72 ½ x 17 In.	2750.00
Vess Soda, People, Billion Bubble Beverages, All Your Favorite Flavors, Chalkware, c.1945, 16 x 12 In.	198.00

We Recommend Trophy Motor Oil, 1930s, 7 x 27 In.	345.00
Williams Jersey Cream Toilet Soap, Cow's Head, Children, Glass, Brass Frame, 14 x 3 In. ...	82.00
Winchester, Shotgun Shell Shape, Gun Shell Display, 1960s, 26 ½ In.	94.00
Winston Cigarettes, How Good It Is, Yellow, Cigarette Package Image, 13 ½ x 5 In.	75.00

TIFFANY is a name that appears on items made by Louis Comfort Tiffany, the American glass designer who worked from about 1879 to 1933. His work included iridescent glass, Art Nouveau styles of design, and original contemporary styles. He was also noted for stained glass windows, unusual lamps, bronze work, pottery, and silver. Other types of Tiffany are listed under Tiffany Glass, Tiffany Gold, Tiffany Pottery, or Tiffany Silver. The famous Tiffany lamps are listed in this section. Tiffany jewelry is listed in the Jewelry and Wristwatch categories. Some Tiffany Studio desk sets have matching clocks. They are listed here. Clocks made by Tiffany & Co. are listed in the Clock category. Reproductions of some types of Tiffany are being made.

Louis C. Tiffany

Ashtray, Ribbed Handles, Bronze, Round, 4 x 1 In.	150.00
Ashtray Set, Nesting, Graduate, Bronze, 4 ½ In.	350.00
Blotter Ends, Adam, Bronze, Gold Patina, Stamped, c.1910, 12 ¼ In.	295.00
Blotter Ends, Zodiac, Bronze, Dore, 12 ⅛ In.	140.00
Blotter, Hand, Abalone, Bronze, Gold Dore, 5 ¾ x 2 ¾ In.	650.00
Bookends, Graduate, Bronze, Gold Dore...	1500.00
Bookends, Landscape, Bronze, Gold Dore, Stamped, c.1900, 4 ½ In.	836.00
Bookends, Leaves, Peacock, Urns, Cross, Bronze, 6 x 4 ½ In.	2000.00
Bookends, Pine Needle, Bronze, Caramel Glass, Signed, No. 1024, 6 x 6 In.	1140.00
Bookends, Pine Needle, Bronze, Gold Dore, Caramel Glass, Sliding, Adjustable, 6 x 14 ¼ In. ..	1725.00
Bookrack, Bronze, Abalone Discs In Flower & Leaf Design Pattern, Adjustable, 6 x 20 In.	7500.00
Bowl, Copper, Hexagonal, Marked, c.1910, 2 ½ x 4 ½ In.	146.00
Bowl, Plique-A-Jour, Flower Border, Stamped, 3 x 1 ¼ In. ....*illus*	2185.00
Box, Bronze, Flowering Trees, 3 x 6 x 3 ¾ In.	345.00
Box, Desk, Spider Web, Gold Toned Metal, Slag, Ball Feet, 7 x 4 In. ....*illus*	380.00
Box, Gambler's, Mother-Of-Pearl Chips, Burl Walnut Case, 4 ½ x 8 x 8 In.	1700.00
Box, Grapevine, Bronze, Glass, 4 Round Feet, 8 x 2 ½ In.	1610.00
Box, Hinged Cover, Bronze, 8 Gold Favrile Panels, Signed, 6 In.	3000.00
Box, Hinged Cover, Chinese Pattern, Bronze, Line, Curve, Gold Dore, 8 x 5 x 3 In.	3000.00
Box, Hinged Cover, Half Moons, Ribs, Bronze Border, Feet, Hexagonal, Favrile, 6 x 2 In.	4500.00
Box, Jewelry, Hinged Cover, Bronze, 4 Footed, Velvet Liners, 8 x 3 ¾ x 3 In.	4000.00
Box, Lid, Bronze, Gold Dore, Geometric, Signed Tiffany Studios, 5 x 2 In.	420.00
Box, Stamp, Hinged Cover, Abalone, Bronze, 3 Tray, 2 ¼ x 1 ½ In.	850.00
Box, Stamp, Hinged Cover, Venetian, Sculptured Minks, 3 Sections, 2 ½ x 4 ¾ x 3 ¼ In. ...	750.00
Box, Stamp, Pine Needle, Green Slag Glass, Brass Dore Metal Overlay, c.1920, 4 x 2 ¼ In.	411.00
Box, Twine, Pine Needle, Bronze, Brown Patina, Green Glass, 6-Sided, Signed, 3 x 4 In.	2300.00
Box, Utility, Pine Needle, Bronze, Carmel Glass, Beading, c.1920, 1 ⅝ x 4 ¼ x 3 ¼ In.	620.00
Box, Zodiac, Bronze, 1 x 5 ¼ x 3 ½ In.	195.00
Calendar Frame, Grapevine, Gilt Bronze, Reticulated Design, Green Favrile Glass, 4 ¾ x 3 ½ In.	176.00
Calendar Frame, Pine Needle, Gilt Bronze, Caramel Slag Glass, 6 x 7 In.	431.00
Candelabrum, 2-Light, Bronze, Blown Out Green Glass, Cabochons, Stamped, 12 ½ x 10 In.	3240.00
Candelabrum, 3-Light, Patinated Bronze, Favrile Glass Shades, c.1910, 17 ¾ In.	7500.00
Candelabrum, 4-Light, Bronze, Blown-Out Glass Bobeches, Jeweled, Favrile, c.1900, 11 ¾ In. ..	2988.00
Candelabrum, 4-Light, Oval Base, Stick Body, Holds Snuffer, Bronze, Marked, 15 x 14 In.	7500.00
Candelabrum, 4-Light, Patinated Bronze, Favrile Glass, Jeweled, c.1910, 12 ½ In.	8750.00
Candelabrum, 6-Light, Patinated Bronze, Favrile Glass, 15 ⅛ In.	8750.00
Candlestick, Bamboo Pattern, Gold Washed Silver, Stepped Foot, 4 x 3 In., Pair.	403.00
Candlestick, Blown-Out Green Glass, Bead Bobeche, Thin Stem, Round Base, Signed, 25 In. .	5750.00
Candlestick, Bronze, 2 Cups, Center Bud, Oval Foot, Signed, 9 In.	1840.00
Candlestick, Bronze, Blown Green Favrile Glass Cup, Patina, Impressed Logo, 17 ¾ In.	4200.00
Candlestick, Bronze, Blown Green Favrile Glass Top Inserts, Signed, 6 x 18 In.	4200.00
Candlestick, Bronze, Blown Green Glass Top Shade, Metal Overlay, 6 x 21 In.	1140.00
Candlestick, Bronze, Blown-Out Glass Bobeche, Favrile Glass, Stamped, c.1900, 16 In.	1434.00
Candlestick, Bronze, Cobra Style, Rectangular Base, Green Glass, 7 ½ In.	5000.00
Candlestick, Byzantine, Jade Shaft, Chased Silver Knop & Tripod Base, 1900, 11 In., Pair.......	22500.00
Candlestick, Cat's Paw, Bronze, 4 Legs, Green Pulled Feather Cups, Signed, 10 ½ In., Pair...	2990.00
Candlestick, Dog Paw, Bronze, Pair...	1900.00
Candlestick, Gilt Bronze, Flattened Nozzle, Glass Balls, Tripod Stem, Ball Feet, 9 In., Pair.......	2990.00
Candlestick, Gilt Bronze, Stick Stem, Stamped, c.1900, 20 ½ In., Pair...................	2032.00
Candlestick, Queen Anne's Lace, Blown Green Glass Cup, Bronze, Marked, 8 ½ x 18 In.	4500.00
Candlestick, Rowfant Club, Green Mottled Matte Glaze, Cowan, c.1925, 9 In. ....*illus*	1294.00
Candlestick, Vase Shape Socket, Removable Bobeche, 3-Footed, Ball Feet, Bronze Dore, 8 ¾ In., Pair.	2100.00
Canister, Bronze, Gold Dore, Relief Sailboat, Cover, 3 ½ In.	450.00

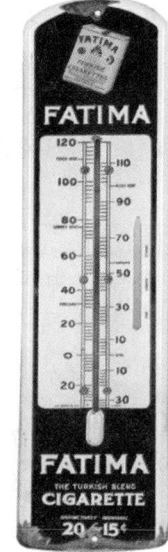

Thermometer, Fatima Cigarettes, Porcelain, 27 x 7 In.
$88.00

Thermometer, Orange-Crush, Bottle, Feel Fresh, Carbonated Beverage, Masonite, 1943, 16 x 4 ½ In.
$1250.00

Thermometer, Sunbeam Bread, Round, c.1957, 12 In.
$527.00

T

Tiffany, Bowl, Plique-A-Jour, Flower Border, Stamped, 3 x 1 ¼ In. $2185.00

Tiffany, Box, Desk, Spider Web, Gold Toned Metal, Slag, Ball Feet, 7 x 4 In. $380.00

Tiffany, Candlestick, Rowfant Club, Green Mottled Matte Glaze, Cowan, c.1925, 9 In. $1294.00

Catalog, Tiffany Studios 1900, Yellow Cloth Cover, 6 x 4 ½ In., 45 Pages	1100.00
Chandelier, Dogwood, Leaded Glass, Patinated Bronze Shade, c.1905, 68 ½ x 28 ¾ In.	290500.00
Chandelier, Patinated Bronze, 4 Iridized Gold Favrile Shades, Acorn Finial, 47 ½ In.	16500.00
Cigar Tray, Bronze, Indian Pattern, Patina, Signed, Tiffany Studio, N.Y., 3 ½ x 4 ½ In.	270.00
Clock, Acanthus Pattern, Bronze, Gold Dore, Top Knob, Scrolls, Signed Face, Boston, 11 x 8 In.	2300.00
Clock, Desk, Zodiac, Gilt Bronze, Octagonal, Stamped, c.1900, 4 ¼ In.	1434.00
Clock, Pine Needle, Brown Patina, Beveled Glass Panel, 6 x 3 ¼ x 4 ½ In. ....*illus*	8625.00
Compote, Bronze, Gold Dore, Signed, Tiffany Studios, 8 x 3 In.	240.00
Compote, Bronze, Gold Dore, Sunburst Line Design, 3 ½ In.	550.00
Desk Set, Bookmark Pattern, Gilt Bronze, Stamped, c.1900, 7 ⅝ In., 10 Piece	3346.00
Desk Set, Marble, Black, Sterling Silver Mounted, c.1950, 13-In. Inkstand, 7 Piece	5000.00
Desk Set, Ninth Century Pattern, Gilt Bronze, Favrile Glass Cabochons, c.1905, 16 Piece	37500.00
Frame, Bronze, Abalone Discs, Gold Dore Patina, Signed, 7 x 9 In. ...... 3600.00 to 6500.00
Frame, Bronze, American Indian Pattern, Signed, 8 x 6 In.	1320.00
Frame, Bronze, Arms & Armor Border, Easel, Signed, 10 x 12 In.	5500.00
Frame, Bronze, Polished, Laurel Wreaths, Acanthus, Rampant Lion, Unicorn, 27 x 16 In.	4113.00
Frame, Double, Pine Needle, Bronze, Green, White Glass, Hinged, 12 ¼ x 14 ½ In.	9000.00
Frame, Grapevine, Bronze, Glass, Easel Style, Gold Dore, Oval Opening, 12 x 14 In.	4500.00
Frame, Grapevine, Bronze, Green & White Glass, Beaded Edge, Signed, 6 ½ x 7 ½ In.	2640.00
Frame, Grapevine, Green Slag Glass, Beaded Sides, Oval Center, Patina, Stamped, 10 x 8 In.	3850.00
Frame, Grapevine Pattern, Bronze, Amber Slag Glass, Easel Style, Marked, 12 x 14 In.	4500.00
Frame, Ninth Century Pattern, Animals, Symbols, Blue, Green Jewels, Signed, 7 x 9 In.	5750.00
Frame, Pine Needle, Bronze, Chocolate Brown Patina, Green Glass, Beading, 14 x 12 ½ In.	9600.00
Frame, Pine Needle, Bronze, Green, Brown Patina, Beading, 6 x 4 In.	1265.00
Frame, Pine Needle, Bronze, Patina, Green & White Glass, Signed, 12 ½ x 14 ½ In.	3600.00
Frame, Venetian, Bronze, Ermine Base, Dull Gold Ground, Signed, 6 x 7 In.	1380.00
Frame, Venetian, Flowers, Ermine Border, Gold Over Bronze, Signed, 7 x 6 In.	1610.00
Frame, Venetian, Gold Dore, 14K Gold Plate, Minks, 9 x 12 In.	4500.00
Frame, Zodiac, Bronze, Original Patina, Signed, 7 x 8 In.	1200.00
Frame, Zodiac, Bronze, Signed, 7 x 8 In.	1320.00
Frame, Zodiac, Entwined Line, Bronze, Gold Dore, 9 x 11 In.	3000.00
Glass, Goblet, Optic Ribbed Foot, Clear Stem, Pale Green Bowl, Favrile, Signed, 8 In.	400.00
Glass, Goblet, Twist Stem, Gold Favrile, Signed, 5 ½ In., Pair	400.00
Humidor, Cigar, Geometric Designs, Red Enamel, Wood Lining, Signed, 6 x 4 In.	1495.00
Humidor, Cover, Grapevine, Gold, Green Glass, 6 ½ In.	4130.00
Humidor, Green Favrile Glass, Gold Designs, Bronze Lid, Gold Dore, Signed, 5 x 7 In. .....*illus*	3000.00
Inkstand, Clear, Favrile Glass, Patinated Bronze, c.1905, 3 ¾ x 6 ¾ In.	12500.00
Inkstand, Crab, Clear Glass Inkwell, Patinated Bronze, c.1905, 4 x 8 x 7 In.	33750.00
Inkstand, Double, Turtleback Tile, Oak, 2 Inkwells, Gilt Bronze, 7 x 12 x 4 ⅝ In.	18750.00
Inkwell, Adam, Bronze, Gold Dore, Oval, c.1920, 2 ¾ x 4 In.	390.00
Inkwell, Adam, Oval, Hinged Cover, Bronze, Sunburst, Ribbed & Flower Body, 4 x 3 x 2 In.	750.00
Inkwell, Blue, Pink Enamel, Gold Ground, Glass Inserts, 4 Bun Feet, Signed, 4 In.	2645.00
Inkwell, Bookmark Pattern, Bronze, Gold Dore, Glass Insert, c.1920, 2 ⅝ In.	600.00
Inkwell, Bookmark Pattern, Hinged Cover, Bronze, Gold Dore, Square, Diagonal Corners, 3 x 3 x 2 In.	750.00
Inkwell, Bronze, Blue Iridescent Glass Scarab, Hinged Lid, Flower Bulb Shape, 4 x 5 ½ In.	5300.00
Inkwell, Bronze, Glass, 3 ½ x 3 In.	650.00
Inkwell, Chinese Pattern, Bronze, Stamped Tiffany Studio, c.1900, 4 ¾ In.	598.00
Inkwell, Double, Venetian, Bronze, Gold Dore, Treasure Chest Style, 5 x 3 x 2 In.	1500.00
Inkwell, Graduate, Hinged Cover, Bronze, 4 x 4 x 2 In.	550.00
Inkwell, Grapevine, Bronze, Ball Feet, Beaded Edge, 4 x 3 In.	950.00
Inkwell, Grapevine, Bronze Beading, Glass Insert, Slag Glass, Square 3 ½ In.	950.00
Inkwell, Heraldic, Green, Enamel, Silver Shield, Canister Shape, 3 x 3 In.	3500.00
Inkwell, Hinged Cover, Abalone, Bronze, Octagon, 3 ½ x 3 ½ x 3 ½ In.	850.00
Inkwell, Hinged Cover, Green Blown-Out Glass, Glass Liner, Stamp, 4 x 6 ½ In. ....*illus*	7800.00
Inkwell, Pine Needle, Bronze, Green Slag Glass, Ball Feet, Beaded, 4 x 4 In. ...... 403.00 to 950.00
Inkwell, Venetian, Bronze, Panels, Ermine Base, Glass Insert, Signed, 2 x 3 In. ....*illus*	863.00
Inkwell, Zodiac, Bronze, 4 In.	1000.00
Jar, Gold Iridescent, Rose & Blue Highlights, Silver, Top Rim, Cover & Handle, 3 ½ x 2 In.	2000.00
Jewelry Box, Grapevine, Bronze, Green Slag Glass, Beaded Edge, Signed, 9 x 6 x 3 In.	4500.00
Jewelry Box, Italian Renaissance Pattern, Gilt Bronze, c.1900, 8 ⅛ In.	1434.00
Key, Clock, Nautical	130.00
Lamp Base, 3-Arm, Bronze, Bulbous Grecian Urn Base, Square Foot, 19 In.	4888.00
Lamp Base, Blue Favrile, Gold Hardware, Wristed Stem, Electrified, Acorn Pull, 12 In.	575.00
Lamp Base, Desk, Harp Style, Gold Dore, Inverted Saucer Base, 17 In.	1610.00
Lamp, 2-Light, Bronze Indian Base, Open Work Cap, Gold Dore, Linenfold Shade, 1923, 18 x 26 In.	19200.00
Lamp, 2-Light, Cylindrical Standard, 4 Spade Feet, Marked, 61 In.	1423.00

Lamp, 2-Light, Pink, Yellow Flowers, Blue Ground, Metal Base, 19 x 12 In.	23000.00
Lamp, 3-Light, Acorn Shade, Bronze Vase Base, Inlaid Turtleback Glass Tiles, 24 x 16 In.	28060.00
Lamp, 3-Light, Blue, Green Brick, White, Red Dragonflies, Bronze Base, 16 x 23 In.	40250.00
Lamp, 3-Light, Bronze, Base, Leaves, Damascene Shade, Iridescent, 6 ¾ & 13 In.	6043.00
Lamp, 3-Light, Daffodil Shade, Bronze Base, 24 x 20 In.	42700.00
Lamp, 3-Light, Leaded Geometric, Mottled Shade, Bronze 4-Footed Base, Mark, 18 x 23 In.	14400.00
Lamp, 6 Yellow Dragonflies, Green Wings, Red Eyes, Glass, Bronze Base, 20 x 26 In.	80500.00
Lamp, 6-Light, Green Shades, Telescopic Bronze Base, Bulbous Foot, 19 In.	13225.00
Lamp, 6-Light, Linenfold Shade, Bronze Base...	17700.00
Lamp, 6-Light, Tulip Shade, Tree Trunk Base, c.1924, 22 x 10 In.	14688.00
Lamp, Abalone, Gilt Bronze, Adjustable Shade, Caramel Slag Glass, 9 In.	3900.00
Lamp, Acorn, Art Nouveau, Bronze, Green, Cream & Gold, c.1900, 21 ½ x 16 In.	9000.00
Lamp, Adjustable Bronze Base, Ribbed Foot, Abalone Shell Shade, Signed, 8 x 13 In.	10200.00
Lamp, Adjustable, Weighted Stem, Quezal Gold Ribbed Shade, 10 In.	3240.00
Lamp, Apple Blossom, Pink, Green Flowers, Leaves, Bronze, Adjustable Base, 12 x 16 In.	42500.00
Lamp, Blue, Green Damascene Shade, Wavy Iridescent, Bronze Urn Base, Signed, 7 x 3 ½ In.	8050.00
Lamp, Bronze, Glass Shade, Leaf Design, 15 In.	6000.00
Lamp, Bronze, Gold Dore, Gold Favrile Glass Shade, 9 x 13 ½ In.	3000.00
Lamp, Bronze, Gold Dore, Spread Foot, Red Paint Accents, Domed Metal Shade, 13 ½ In.	1610.00
Lamp, Bronze, Harp Base, Favrile Shade, Green Pulled Feather Design, Signed, 9 x 12 In.	3900.00
Lamp, Bronze Harp, Frame, Linenfold Glass Shade, Signed, 1942, 14 In.	7000.00
Lamp, Candle, Bronze, Iridescent Jewels, Gold Favrile Shade, Signed, 22 ½ In., Pair	28800.00
Lamp, Candle, Gold Favrile Twist Stem, Crimped Favrile Onion Skin Shade, 17 In.	2600.00
Lamp, Candle, Gold Honeycomb Shade, Green Feathers, Opal Insert, Twisted Base, 13 In.	1150.00
Lamp, Candle, Iridescent, Favrile Glass, Engraved L.C.T., c.1900, 12 In.	2091.00
Lamp, Candle, Twist Stem Base, Gold Favrile Crimped Shade, Signed, 15 In.	1400.00
Lamp, Clematis, Rippled, Mottled, Cat's Paw Base, Applied Tag, 18 ½ x 24 In. .... *illus*	69000.00
Lamp, Colonial, Blown Out, Bronze Base, Converted Oil Font, 20 ½ x 16 In.	26840.00
Lamp, Colonial Shade, Mottled Yellow Panels, Mauve Inserts, Metal Trumpet Base, 16 x 24 In.	20700.00
Lamp, Domed Shade, Turtleback Tiles, Adjustable, Iridescent, Zodiac Base, 10 x 14 ½ In.	18000.00
Lamp, Double Student, Favrile Glass, Patinated Bronze Shade, c.1910, 29 ½ & 10 ⅛ In.	6250.00
Lamp, Dragonfly, Leaded Glass, Favrile, Telescopic Base, Finial, c.1910, 26 ¼ x 20 ¼ In.	194500.00
Lamp, Floor, Weight-Balance, Etched, Gold Cream Iridescent Shade, 5-Footed, Favrile, 8 x 6 In.	12000.00
Lamp, Gilt Bronze, Etched Domed Shade, Harp Form, Marked, c.1910, 17 ½ In.	1920.00
Lamp, Glass, Intaglio Carved Green Vines, Gold Favrile, Matching Base, Signed, 8 x 16 In.	7763.00
Lamp, Gold, Twisted Candlestick, Ruffled Shade, Gold Pierced Top, 12 In.	1610.00
Lamp, Green, Blue, Yellow Leaf, Vine Shade, Wide Reddish Bronze Base, Signed, 20 x 30 In. ...	24000.00
Lamp, Green Curtain Glass Shade, Bronze Tripod, 55 x 12 In.	7320.00
Lamp, Green Linenfold Shade, Bronze Frame, Matching Cap, 8-Sided Dore Base, 19 x 24 In. .	23000.00
Lamp, Green Tiles, Acorn Row, Yellow, Blue, White, Bronze Base, Signed, 20 x 29 In.	16100.00
Lamp, Harp, Square Iridescent Glass Shade, Bronze Base, Signed, L.C.T., 8 x 11 In.	2013.00
Lamp, Harp, Tripod, Handel Shade, Reverse Painted, Flower Band, Bronze Collar, 54 ¾ x 10 In.	3600.00
Lamp, Laburnum, Leaded Glass, Patinated Bronze Shade, Skeleton Base, c.1905, 30 x 22 In. .	422500.00
Lamp, Library, Base, 3-Light, Bronze, Vented Cap, 13 x 7 ½ In.	3600.00
Lamp, Lily, 3-Light, Gold Favrile, Ribbed Shades, 3-Column Base, Gold Dore Finish, 13 In.	2300.00
Lamp, Lily, 3-Light, Gold Lily Shades, Round Bronze Base, Signed L.T.C., 9 ½ x 13 In.	5750.00
Lamp, Lily, 3-Light, Gold Quezal Shades, Bronze Base, Signed, 13 ½ In.	2530.00
Lamp, Lily, 6-Light, Favrile Lily Shades, Bronze Base, Marked, 10 x 22 In.	10200.00
Lamp, Lily, 7-Light, Gold Iridescent, Flared Rims, Bronze Lily Pad Base, Signed, 21 x 15 In. ...	13225.00
Lamp, Lily, 12-Light, Gold Favrile, Lily Shades, Gold Lily Pad Base, Signed, 17 In.	31625.00
Lamp, Lily, 12-Light, Gold Favrile Lily Shades, Iridescent, Bronze Lily Pad Base, Signed, 21 In.	37375.00
Lamp, Lily, 18-Light, Favrile Glass, Patinated Bronze Base, c.1902, 20 ⅛ In.	158500.00
Lamp, Linenfold 9-Panel Shade, Gold Dore, Ribbed Base, Signed, 1949, 7 x 18 In.	5750.00
Lamp, Mesh Ground, Applied Rose, Blue, Purple Beads, Gold Platform Base, 17 x 23 In.	4600.00
Lamp, Multicolored Daffodil Shade, Twisted Vine, Bronze Base, Signed, 20 x 26 In.	50600.00
Lamp, Murano Favrile Shade, Green, White, Harp Metal Base, Signed, 7 x 18 In.	5750.00
Lamp, Nautilus Shell Shade, c.1910, 12 In.	4800.00
Lamp, Night-Light, Candlestick, Mesh Shade, Blue Flower, Green Leaf, Arm Supports, 12 In. ..	978.00
Lamp, Oak Leaf & Acorn Shade, Leaded Glass, Bronze, Green Patina, 26 x 18 In.	36000.00
Lamp, Oil, Gilt Bronze, Stamped The Twilight, Molded, Favrile, c.1900, 10 ¼ In.	1793.00
Lamp, Persian, Favrile Shade, 14 ¼ x 7 In.	3660.00
Lamp, Piano, Weight-Balance, 2-Arched Top Arms, 5 Leg Base, Patina, 15 x 31 In.	4600.00
Lamp, Pomegranate, Green, White, Yellow, Patinated Bronze Base, c.1900, 19 ½ x 16 In.	10575.00
Lamp, Poppy, Leaded Glass, Patinated Bronze Base, c.1905, 22 ⅝ x 16 ¾ In.	104500.00
Lamp, Queen Anne's Lace, Bronze, No Shade, 13 In.	1800.00

Tiffany, Clock, Pine Needle,
Brown Patina, Beveled Glass Panel,
6 x 3 ¼ x 4 ½ In.
$8625.00

Tiffany, Humidor, Green Favrile **Glass,**
Gold Designs, Bronze Lid, Rim, **Gold Dore,**
Signed, 5 x 7 ½ In.
$3000.00

Tiffany, Inkwell, Hinged Cover,
Green Blown-Out Glass, Glass Liner,
Stamp, 4 x 6 ½ In.
$7800.00

T

Tiffany, Inkwell, Venetian, Bronze, Panels, Ermine Base, Glass Insert, Signed, 2 x 3 In.
$863.00

Tiffany, Lamp, Clematis, Rippled, Mottled, Cat's Paw Base, Applied Tag, 18 ½ x 24 In.
$69000.00

Tiffany, Lamp, Zodiac, Bronze, Green, Cylinder Shape Shade, Signed, 9 ¾ x 11 In.
$2875.00

Tiffany Glass, Bowl, Center, Green Iridescent Leaf & Vine, Gold Iridescent, 13 In.
$920.00

Lamp, Ribbed Green Damascene Shade, Iridescent Purple, Pink, Yellow, 7 & 14 12 In.		10350.00
Lamp, Salamander, Claw Feet, Telescopic Base, Leaded Glass, Bronze Shade, 31 x 27 ½ In.		362500.00
Lamp, Slag Glass, Stepped Feet, Triangular Shaped Base, Mottled Green, Teal, Emblems, 18 ¼ In.		8365.00
Lamp, Spanish Dore, Art Nouveau Designs, Signed, 14 In.		8625.00
Lamp, Student, 2-Light, Gold Iridescent, Flared, Ribbed Shades, Bronze Base, Signed, 19 In.		2645.00
Lamp, Student, Double, Green Linenfold Shades, 19 ½ In.		10200.00
Lamp, Student, Twisted Moorish, Shades, Flower, Petals, Gold Favrile, 10 x 29 ½ In.		7188.00
Lamp, Turtleback, Blue, Purple, Green, Pink Iridescent, Bronze, Jewel Base, 14 In.		16675.00
Lamp, Vine Shade, Yellow, Green, Signed		14950.00
Lamp, Weight-Balance, Gold Shade, Art Nouveau, Signed, 7 x 15 In.		3680.00
Lamp, Weight-Balance, Turtleback Tiles, Shade, Dragonflies, Insect, Favrile, c.1905, 28 x 10 In.		18750.00
Lamp, Wild Rose, Leaded Glass, Patinated Bronze Shade, c.1910, 21 ¾ x 16 In.		46875.00
Lamp, Zodiac, Bronze, Green, Cylinder Shape Shade, Signed, 9 ¾ x 11 In.	*illus*	2875.00
Lamp, Zodiac, Linenfold, Harp Arm, Early 1900s, 17 x 10 In.		9750.00
Letter Holder, Zodiac, Bronze, Patina, Signed, 9 ½ x 6 ¼ In.		420.00
Letter Opener, Bookmark Pattern, Bronze, Gold Dore, 10 ½ In.		950.00
Letter Opener, Grapevine, Bronze, Green Glass Handle, 9 ½ In.		950.00
Letter Opener, Grapevine, Bronze, White Glass, Gold Patina, Stamped, c.1920, 9 ⅛ In.		460.00
Letter Opener, Ninth Century Pattern, Bronze, Gold Dore, 10 In.		950.00
Letter Opener, Pine Needle, Bronze, 7 In.		950.00
Letter Opener, Venetian, Bronze, Gold Dore, 10 ½ In.		950.00
Letter Rack, Abalone, Bronze, Leaf, Line, 2 Sections		1500.00
Letter Rack, Grapevine, 2 Sections, Bronze, Slag Glass, 10 x 6 ½ x 2 ½ In.		1500.00
Letter Rack, Pine Needle, Bronze, Caramel Glass, Signed, 10 x 6 In.		600.00
Letter Rack, Pine Needle, Bronze, Green Slag Glass, 2 Compartments, 10 x 6 x 2 ¼ In.		1500.00
Letter Rack, Venetian, Bronze, Gold Dore, 10 x 6 x 2 ¾ In.	1725.00 to	2000.00
Letter Rack, Venetian, Bronze, Sculptured Minks, 2 Compartments, 10 x 6 x 2 In.		2000.00
Loving Cup, Gold Iridescent, Green Leaf, Trailing Vine, 3 Handles, Favrile, 5 x 3 ¼ x 3 In.		2200.00
Magnifying Glass, Abalone, Iridescent Discs, Bronze, Gold Dore, Signed, 4 x 8 ¾ In.		2000.00
Match Safe, Zodiac, Bronze, Gold Dore, Entwined Line Design, Signed, 2 x 13 x ¾ In.		450.00
Medallion, Eagle, Liberty Bell, Gold Iridescent, 1918, 2 ¾ In.		1500.00
Mirror, Grapevine, Bronze, Amber Slag Glass, Bevel Edge, Handle, 7 ½ x 11 ½ In.		2500.00
Paper Clip, Grapevine, Bronze, Green Glass, 2 ½ x 3 ¼ In.		650.00
Paper Clip, Zodiac, Bronze, Gold Dore, Entwined Line Design, 2 ½ x 4 In.		550.00
Paper Rack, Grapevine, Bronze, White, Green Striated Glass, Signed, 13 x 8 In.		2300.00
Paper Rack, Zodiac, 2 Tiers, Bronze, Green Patina, Tiffany Studios, 6 x 10 In.		850.00
Paperweight, 4 Sections, Cabochon Green Stone, 2 ¼ x 4 ¼ In.		889.00
Paperweight, Lioness, Crouching, Bronze, 4 In.		633.00
Paperweight, Lioness, Reclining, Bronze, Green, Brown Patina, 5 In.		805.00
Paperweight, Pine Needle, Bronze, Green Slag Glass, Curved Spindle, 7 ½ In.		1500.00
Paperweight, Venetian, Bronze, Gold Dore, 2 ½ x 4 ¼ x ¾ In.		2500.00
Paperweight, Venetian, Bronze, Minks, High Relief, Ornate, Signed, 2 x 4 x ¾ In.		2500.00
Pen Brush, Abalone, Bronze, Octagon, 2 ¼ x 2 ¼ In.		650.00
Pen Brush, Venetian, Bronze, Gold Dore, Octagon, Square 2 ¾ x 2 ½ In.		850.00
Pen Tray, Byzantine Pattern, Bronze, Beading, Green Glass Inserts, Tiffany Studios, 9 In.		600.00
Pen Tray, Grapevine, Green Glass, Bronze Edge, 4 Ball Feet, 9 ½ x 3 ½ x ¾ In.		550.00
Pen Tray, Zodiac, Bronze, Patina, 9 ½ x 3 In.		120.00
Pen Wipe, Ninth Century Pattern, Marked, c.1910, 2 x 2 ¾ In.		2100.00
Pen Wipe, Pine Needle, 2 Layer Chamois Petals, Bronze Center, Signed, 5 In.		2875.00
Pin Tray, Ninth Century Pattern, Stamped, c.1920, 2 x 4 x 2 In.		1050.00
Planter, Geometric Design, Bronze, Liner, Signed, 8 ½ x 2 ½ In.		750.00
Postage Scale, Pine Needle, Bronze, Green Glass Panels, 1806-09, 7 x 5 In.		4773.00
Postage Scale, Venetian, Bronze, Gold Dore, 1 ¾ x 3 x 3 ¼ In.		2500.00
Powder Box, Cover, Grapevine, Silver, White Striated Yellow Glass, Signed, 5 x 4 In.		5750.00
Powder Box, Hinged Lid, Favrile Glass, Bronze, Dore Edge, Round, Signed, 4 ¼ x 1 ¾ In.		3000.00
Shade, Metal, Domed Grapevine Pattern, Frosted Cranberry Glass Liner, Stamped, 6 In., 4 Piece.		1200.00
Shade, Round, Raised Swirled Ribs, Gold, Cream Favrile Glass, Signed, 7 In.		5400.00
Smoking Stand, Bronze, Engraved 4561, c.1900, 27 ¼ In.		836.00
Tazza, Bronze, Green, Footed, Dore Finish, Pink Enamel Handles, Tiffany Furnace, 13 In.		900.00
Thermometer, Pine Needle, Bronze, Green Slag Glass, Beaded, 8 ½ x 4 In.		3500.00
Thermometer, Venetian, Easel, Gold Dore, Sculptured Minks, 8 x 4 In.		3000.00
Tray, Bronze, Bird Of Paradise Enameled Center, 8 In. Round		3000.00
Tray, Coin, Brass Bronze, Woman Carrying Water, Man Fishing, Marked, 9 In.		90.00
Tray, Intaglio Cut, Enameled Blossoms, Emerald Green Border, Cut Leaves, Vines, 6 In.		2500.00
Tureen, Cover, Satyrs, Cherubs, Animals, Gilt Trim, Gourd Knop, Mask Head Stand, 11 x 18 In.		2760.00
Urn, Bronze, Oval Cauldron, Masks, Scrolls, Ribbons, Sea Creature Handles, Gilt, 18 x 21 In.		3220.00

Vase, Bud, Mushrooms, Copper, Enameled, 4 x 3 In.	18300.00
Vase, Tel El Amarna, Iridescent Swag, Blue Ground, 8 ¼ x 8 In.	6785.00
Vase, Trumpet, Metal, Gold Iridescent, Green Heart, Vines, Artichoke Bronze Base, 15 In.	1265.00

TIFFANY GLASS

Bowl & Underplate, Iridescent Blue, Gold & Pink, Marked, 2 ½-In. Bowl, 6-In. Plate	430.00
Bowl, 10 Ribs, Scalloped Rim, Green, Gold Iridescent Favrile Interior, Signed, c.1895, 2 ¾ In.	1900.00
Bowl, Blue Favrile, Rippled Rim, Signed LCT	450.00
Bowl, Center, Bronze, Favrile Glass, c.1920, 5 x 12 In.	4095.00
Bowl, Center, Flower Frog, Iridescent, Favrile, Engraved, c.1910, 10 ¼ In.	1195.00
Bowl, Center, Footed, Peacock Blue, Favrile Blue, 11 ½ In.	3000.00
Bowl, Center, Green Iridescent Leaf & Vine, Gold Iridescent, 13 In. .... *illus*	920.00
Bowl, Center, Ribbed, Scalloped, Gold Favrile, 3 x 7 ½ In.	173.00
Bowl, Clear, Wave, 4 ¾ x 7 ¾ In.	115.00
Bowl, Flared, Ruffled Rim, Gold Iridescent, Pink, Platinum Highlights, Signed, 10 In.	767.00
Bowl, Flower Frog, Leaf, Vine Design, Blue Favrile, 2 x 5 In.	1440.00
Bowl, Flower Frog, Peacock Blue, 2-Tier Flower Frog, 9-In. Bowl	2390.00
Bowl, Footed, Gold Iridescent, 3 Shell Feet, Ribs, Curls, Iridescent, Favrile, 2 ½ In.	2500.00
Bowl, Gold Favrile, Flared Rim, 2 ½ x 6 ¼ In.	144.00
Bowl, Gold Favrile, Pink, Purple Highlights, Signed, 5 x 4 In.	805.00
Bowl, Gold, Inverted Rim, Pulled Feather Design, Prunt Handles, Signed, c.1902, 2 ½ In.	1300.00
Bowl, Gold Iridescent, Shell Feet, Favrile, Signed, 2 ½ In.	2500.00
Bowl, Iridescent Gold, Carved Butterfly Intaglio, L.C.T. Favrile, 1925, 2 x 6 In.	1150.00
Bowl, Sterling Collar, Fruit & Scroll, Marked, 3 ½ x 11 ½ In.	2300.00
Bowl, Yellow Pastel, Spiral Rays, Flared Rim, Favrile, Inscribed, 1900s, 7 ¼ In.	300.00
Bowl, Yellow, Wide Rim, Footed, Signed, L.C.T., 2 ⅛ x 4 ⅞ In.	385.00
Box, Hexagon, Curved Half Moons, Ribbed & Raised, Footed, Favrile, 6 x 2 In.	4500.00
Candlestick, Favrile, Green Pastel, Flower Petal Socle, White Plinth, Round Foot, 4 x 4 In.	345.00
Candlestick, Gold Iridescent, Ribbed, Wide Flange, Pair, 7 x 4 ¼ x 3 ½ In.	1000.00
Candlestick, Ruffled Top, Gold Iridescent, Footed, Favrile, Marked, 3 ¾ In., Pair	720.00
Compote, Blue Favrile, Green, Purple Highlights, Stretched Edge, 1921, 6 x 6 In.	1035.00
Compote, Blue Favrile, Pigtail Prunts, Signed, 3 ½ In. .... *illus*	518.00
Compote, Blue Iridescent, Rounded, Ribbed, 2-Tier Body, Scalloped Top, Signed, 6 In.	2500.00
Compote, Flower Shape, Pulled Leaves, Green, Ruffled Rim, Signed, Favrile, 5 ½ In.	1265.00
Compote, Gold Iridescent, Intaglio Cut, Leaf, Vine, Favrile, 4 ½ x 5 ½ x 2 ¾ In.	2200.00
Compote, Intaglio Cut, Green, Ruffled, White, Iridescent, Butterfly, 3 ¾ x 6 In.	1495.00
Compote, Iridescent, Diamond Pattern, 2 ¼ In.	950.00
Compote, Opalescent, Green Pastel, Stretched Rim, Circular Foot, Signed, 8 ¼ In.	533.00
Compote, Optic Ribbed Foot, Amber Stem, Orange Bowl, Gold Favrile, Signed, 11 In.	1750.00
Compote, Pink Pastel Iridescent, Stretch Edge, Gold Underside, Signed, 8 x 2 ½ In.	1500.00
Compote, Rolled Yellow Rim, Leaf Center, Clear Stem, Iridescent Saucer Foot, Signed, 7 x 7 In.	1438.00
Compote, White Net Design, White Opalescent, Seafoam Green Rim, Signed, 3 x 5 In., Pair	1035.00
Compote, Yellow, Leaf Pattern Bowl, Rope Spiral Stem, White Ribbed Base, 7 x 7 ½ In.	1150.00
Decanter Set, Stopper, Bulbous, Flared Rim, Gold Favrile, 6 Wine, 7 Piece	2530.00
Decanter, Stopper, Bulbous, Gold Iridescent, Double Neck Bands, Gold Paper Label, 12 In.	700.00
Decanter, Stopper, Double Bulbous, Gold Translucent, Applied Tadpoles, c.1889, 12 In.	1600.00
Decanter, Stopper, Iridescent, Gold To Deep Purple, Bulbous Stick, Signed, Favrile, 9 ½ In.	978.00
Flower Frog, Iridescent, 5 Lily Pads, Tendrils, Gold Favrile, c.1916, 14 In.	1035.00
Goblet, Aqua, Scalloped Rim, Clear Reeded Stem, L.C.T. Favrile, 8 ½ In, Pair	1035.00
Goblet, Blue, White Stylized Leaves, Spiral Turned Stem, Footed, Favrile, c.1925, 7 ¾ In.	499.00
Goblet, Champagne, Gold, Signed, Favrile, 6 ¼ In.	115.00
Goblet, Green Translucent Stem, Pink, Baluster, Signed, Favrile, 10 ½ In.	978.00
Goblet, Intaglio Cut, Gold Favrile, Grapes, Leaf Band, Signed, 6 In.	275.00
Goblet, Optic Ribbed, Gold Favrile, Signed, 7 In.	325.00
Goblet, Pastel Pink Bowl, Green Melon, Teardrop Stem, L.C.T. Favrile, 7 In.	748.00
Jar, Gold Iridescent, Cover, Knob Handle, Favrile, Signed, 7 ½ In.	2000.00
Jar, Gold Iridescent, Cover, Knob Handle, Sunburst Design, Silver & Blue Highlights, 7 In.	2000.00
Jug, Claret, Clear, Hobstar, Palmettes, Diamond Cuts, Silver Mount, 13 ¾ In.	5000.00
Loving Cup, 3 Handles, Favrile, Engraved, c.1915, 6 In.	1315.00
Loving Cup, Gold Iridescent, Green Leaf & Vine, Applied Handles, Signed, 5 In.	220.00
Nut Dish, Flared Rim, Blue Favrile, Inscribed, 2 In.	500.00
Nut Dish, Gold Favrile, Handles, Inscribed, Sterling Salt Spoon, 1 x 3 In.	275.00
Nut Dish, Gold Favrile, Signed, 3 In.	421.00
Nut Dish, Opalescent Pastel Green, Favrile, Stretch Border, Inscribed, 3 x 2 In.	750.00
Nut Dish, Pastel Blue, Stretch Border To Pearl, Flared Rim, Signed, 3 x 1 In.	625.00
Ornament, Gold Iridescent, Ball Shape, Favrile, 2 In.	325.00
Pendant, Dragonfly, Jeweled Eyes, Brown Body, Green Wings, Bronze Chain, 10 In.	6325.00

Tiffany Glass, Compote, Blue Favrile, Pigtail Prunts, Signed, 3 ½ In. $518.00

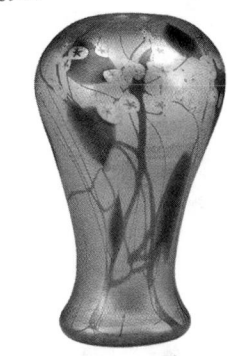

Tiffany Glass, Vase, Cabinet, Millefiori, Bulbous, Shouldered, Gold Favrile, Signed, 4 ¾ In. $3335.00

Tiffany Glass, Vase, Cabinet, Snakeskin, Bulbous, Blue, Purple Iridescent, 3 ½ In. $885.00

Tiffany Glass, Vase, Cameo, Clambroth Iridescent Ground, Carved Flowers, Signed, 6 In. $11500.00

T

Tiffany Glass, Vase, Flower Shape, Ruffled Top, Green Pulled Feather, Bulb Stem, 15 In.
$12075.00

Tiffany Glass, Vase, Gold Pulled Feather, Platinum Accents, Signed, 9 ¾ In.
$3163.00

Tiffany Glass, Vase, Pastel, Green, Inverted Saucer Foot, Vertically Ribbed Bowl, 7 ¼ In.
$1955.00

Tiffany Glass, Vase, Red Favrile, Squat, Bulbous, Hooked Feather, Signed, Paper Label, 3 In.
$6785.00

Perfume Bottle, Agate, Silver Lid With Chain, Favrile, Signed, 3 In.	7700.00
Pitcher, Leaf, Vine Design, Gold Favrile, Signed, c.1909, 6 ½ In.	2300.00
Pitcher, Water, Gold Iridescent, Corset Shape, Engraved Vintage, Favrile, 8 ½ In.	2700.00
Plate, Aqua, Pinwheel Pattern, Scalloped Edge, L.C. Tiffany Favrile, 11 In., Pair	633.00
Plate, White Pulled Feathers, Blue Pastel, Scalloped Rim, Signed, Favrile, 10 ½ In.	920.00
Powder Box, Round, Hinged, Bronze Edge, Gold Iridescent, Signed, 4 x 1 ¾ In.	3000.00
Punch Cup, Blue, Gold Iridized, Handle, Favrile, Inscribed 2 x 3 In.	425.00
Salt, 8 Pigtails, Gold Favrile, Inscribed L.C.T., Sterling Salt Spoon, 3 x 1 In.	225.00
Salt, Gold Aurene, Ruffled Rim, Footed, 3 ½ In.	518.00
Salt, Gold Favrile, c.1910, 3 In.	293.00
Salt, Gold Iridescent, Purple, Platinum, 4 Pulled Prunts, 2 ½ In.	2243.00
Salt, Gold Iridescent, Ruffled Edge, Mark, 2 ½ In.	350.00
Salt, Golden, Magenta & Blue Iridescent, 10 Ridges, Engraved Mark, ⅞ x 1 ⅝ In.	489.00
Salt, Pigtail, Gold Favrile, Signed, 1 In.	173.00
Salt, Pressed Design, Gold Favrile, Sterling Cobra Shape Spoon, 2 x 3 In.	800.00
Salt, Pulled Pigtails, Magentas, Purples, Blue Iridescent, Gold Ground, 1 ¼ In.	518.00
Seal, 4 Scarabs, Purple Iridescent, Gold, Favrile, 1 ¾ In.	431.00
Shade, Arabian, Green Zipper Design, 3 Top Gold Prunts, Signed, 7 x 6 ¾ In.	3105.00
Shade, Bell, Green Pulled Feather, Platinum, Gold Border, Ivory Ground, 4 x 6 In.	1840.00
Shade, Damascene Pattern, Gold Iridescent, Favrile, Signed, 10 ½ x 5 ½ In.	9600.00
Shade, Domed, Beige Pulled, Green Ground, Favrile, 7 In.	1521.00
Shade, Geometric, Wavy Rows, Seafoam, Deep Green, Signed, 16 In.	7475.00
Shade, Gold Iridescent, Cone Form, Favrile, Signed, 6 ½ In.	360.00
Shade, Green, Cream, Flowers, Green Brickwork Borders, Label, 9 ½ x 22 ¾ In.	46000.00
Shade, Lily, Rum To Light, White Opalescent, Yellow, Orange Ribbing Interior, 5 ⅛ x 3 In.	1437.00
Shade, Murano, Gold Favrile, Pink, Purple Iridescent, Ribbed, Signed, 10 In.	6490.00
Shade, Tyler Scroll, Mottled Translucent Green, Yellow, Cream, Bronze Rim, 18 In.	17250.00
Shade, Whirling Leaf, Mottled Green, Yellow, Signed, 18 x 4 In.	14950.00
Sherbet, Green Rim, Pulled White Design, Clear, White, Stem, Foot, 7 x 7 In.	345.00
Tazza, Iridescent Gold, Blue, Mark, 11 In.	978.00
Tile, Turtleback, Blue, Purple, Amber Iridescent, Glass Mosaics, Bronze Frame, 12 x 10 In.	1035.00
Toothpick Holder, Gold Aurene, Round Body, Pushed In Areas, Marked, 2 In.	177.00
Tumbler, Paperweight, Barrel Shape, Translucent Crystal, Green Leaves, Yellow Flowers, 5 In.	3500.00
Underplate, Pink, Purple Iridescent, Gold Ruffled, Stretched Rim, Signed, 7 In.	230.00
Vase, 5 Fold Flared Top, Round Body, Short Stem, Gold Iridescent, Signed, 4 In.	1800.00
Vase, Agate, Ribbed, Gold, Favrile, Engraved, c.1900, 6 ⅜ In.	3346.00
Vase, Aurene, Applied Scroll Tripod Base, Signed, L.C.T., 5 x 3 ½ In.	780.00
Vase, Blue, Black Iridescent, Swollen Shape, Favrile, c.1898-1900, 6 ⅜ In.	11250.00
Vase, Blue, Bucket Shape, Handles, Favrile, Signed, 1907, 1 ¾ In.	403.00
Vase, Blue Iridescent, Bulbous Body, Favrile, Signed, 9 ½ In.	805.00
Vase, Blue Iridescent, Silver Tones, Ribbed, Urn Shape, Favrile, Signed, 7 In.	978.00
Vase, Bud, Blue, Ribbed, Favrile, 6 ¾ x 2 ¾ In.	1560.00
Vase, Bud, Enamel, Green, Gold, Blue Iridescent, Bronze, Gold Dore, Favrile, 13 In., 2 Piece	1800.00
Vase, Bud, Flower Shape, Amber To Green, Leaves, Favrile, 9 ¼ x 2 ¾ In.	2806.00
Vase, Bulbous, Blue Favrile Glass, Iridescent, Handles, Signed L.C.T., 2 x 2 In.	960.00
Vase, Bulbous, Pulled Iridescent, Yellow Favrile, Signed L.C.T., 2 x 3 In.	960.00
Vase, Bulbous, Ribbed Shape, Gold Favrile, Iridescent, Signed L.C.T., 3 x 4 In.	720.00
Vase, Bulbous, Tulip Shape, Favrile, Green Base, Tan Pulled Swirls, Signed, 13 In.	805.00
Vase, Burgundy Iridescent, Squat, Wide Neck, Favrile, c.1903-04, 4 ¼ In.	17500.00
Vase, Cabinet, Beehive Bottle Shape, Gold Favrile, Signed, 2 ¼ In.	288.00
Vase, Cabinet, Black, Squat, Oval, Silver Damascene Design, Signed, c.1900, 2 In.	1400.00
Vase, Cabinet, Bulbous Shape, Aqua, Turquoise Lines Of Lily Pads, Favrile, Signed, 3 ½ In.	1850.00
Vase, Cabinet, Millefiori, Bulbous, Shouldered, Gold Favrile, Signed, 4 ¾ In. *illus*	3335.00
Vase, Cabinet, Oval Ribbed Body, Iridescent Blue, Green, Signed, c.1897, 2 In.	600.00
Vase, Cabinet, Snakeskin, Bulbous, Blue, Purple Iridescent, 3 ½ In. *illus*	885.00
Vase, Cameo, Clambroth Iridescent Ground, Carved Flowers, Signed, 6 In. *illus*	11500.00
Vase, Cypriot, Blue, Purple Ground, Platinum, c.1915, 4 ¼ In.	9775.00
Vase, Cypriote, Gold, 7 ¼ x 3 ¾ In.	2400.00
Vase, Double Gourd Shape, Blue Favrile, Signed, 2 x 3 In.	1080.00
Vase, Egyptian, Gold Favrile, Pedestal Base, Pulled Handles, 2 In., Pair.	746.00
Vase, Egyptian, Iridescent Purple, Green, Blue, Pulled Platinum Feather, Signed, 4 In.	2530.00
Vase, Elongated Thumbprint, Sapphire Blue To Purple, Black, Blue Favrile, 5 In.	1553.00
Vase, Favrile, Pinched Rim, Ribbed, Tapered, Circular, 7 ⅜ In.	830.00
Vase, Flower Shape, Gold Favrile, Blue, Pink, Yellow Iridescent, Signed, 6 x 11 In.	2160.00
Vase, Flower Shape, Gold Favrile, Peach Accents, Signed, 5 x 9 ¾ In.	324.00
Vase, Flower Shape, Gold Favrile, Pulled Green Leaves, White, Signed, 6 x 4 ½ In.	1020.00

Vase, Flower Shape, Gold Iridescent, 5 Fold Flare Out, Favrile, 5 x 2 ½ In.	1800.00
Vase, Flower Shape, Gold Iridescent, Favrile, c.1897-99, 12 ¼ In.	10000.00
Vase, Flower Shape, Gold Iridescent, Favrile, c.1910, 12 ¾ In.	8125.00
Vase, Flower Shape, Gold Iridescent, Favrile, Signed, 3 x 7 In.	1080.00
Vase, Flower Shape, Gold Iridescent, Ribbed Foot, Body, Ruffled Rim, c.1912, 12 ½ In.	2013.00
Vase, Flower Shape, Gold, Ribbed, Favrile, 8 ¾ x 3 In.	1200.00
Vase, Flower Shape, Green, Orange, Favrile, c.1898-1900, 11 ⅜ In.	20000.00
Vase, Flower Shape, Green, Orange, Favrile, c.1903-04, 11 ¾ In.	11250.00
Vase, Flower Shape, Green Pulled Feather, Orange Iridescent Foot, Favrile, 19 ½ In.	15000.00
Vase, Flower Shape, Green Pulled Feathers, Cream Ground, Gold Stem, Base, c.1903, 5 In.	3450.00
Vase, Flower Shape, Green Pulled Feathers, Iridescent Clambroth Ground, 10 ¾ In.	9260.00
Vase, Flower Shape, Green, White Pulled Feather, Allover Iridescent, Favrile, 5 x 10 ½ In.	7800.00
Vase, Flower Shape, Ribbed, Iridescent, Gold, Favrile, 11 ¼ In.	1725.00
Vase, Flower Shape, Ruffled Top, Green Pulled Feather, Bulb Stem, 15 In. .... *illus*	12075.00
Vase, Glass, Metal, Trumpet, Green Pulled Feather Design, Bronze Base, Signed, 15 In.	1150.00
Vase, Gold, 8 Pigtail Prunts, Oval, Shouldered, Oval, Favrile, Signed, c.1917, 3 ¾ In.	633.00
Vase, Gold, Faceted, Favrile, 2 ½ In.	900.00
Vase, Gold Favrile, Green Leaf, Vine, 3 ½ x 6 ½ In.	2400.00
Vase, Gold Favrile, Iridescent, Applied Rim, 10 ⅜ In.	1007.00
Vase, Gold Favrile, Long Neck, Green, Leaf, Vine, Signed L.C. Tiffany, 4 x 6 In.	1800.00
Vase, Gold Favrile, Swirls, Lines, 5 x 6 In.	1560.00
Vase, Gold, Intaglio Cut Green Hearts, Vines, Bulbous, Favrile, Signed, c.1917, 9 In.	4600.00
Vase, Gold Iridescent, 8 Ribs, Flared Central Collar, Favrile, Etched L.C.T. 2 ¼ In.	460.00
Vase, Gold Iridescent, Bulbous Onion, Slender Stem, Green Pulled Leaf, 14 In.	20700.00
Vase, Gold Iridescent, Green Heart Shape Leaves, Vines, Cameo, Favrile, 9 In.	3200.00
Vase, Gold Iridescent, Raised Twists, Gathered Neck, Signed, Favrile, 6 ½ x 3 In.	2500.00
Vase, Gold Iridescent, Slender, Bulbous, Ribs, Favrile, Engraved, c.1915, 12 In.	1195.00
Vase, Gold Iridescent, Translucent Amber, Bulbous To Opaque Gold Mouth, 8 ½ In.	10350.00
Vase, Gold Pulled Feather, Platinum Accents, Signed, 9 ¾ In. .... *illus*	3163.00
Vase, Gold, Pinched Trellis, Favrile, 3 ¾ x 4 In.	1920.00
Vase, Gold, White Iridescent Ground, Green Pulled Feather, Bronze Base, Signed, 12 In.	2013.00
Vase, Green & White Pastel, Footed, Iridescent, Veining, Favrile, Signed, 4 ¼ x 3 ½ In.	240.00
Vase, Green Ivy Leaves, Vines, Iridescent Gold, Magenta Halo, Favrile, 2 ½ x 3 ½ In.	1380.00
Vase, Green Pulled Feather, Gold, Optic Ribbed, Knopped, Opal Ruffled Rim Top, 11 In.	6900.00
Vase, Iridescent, Green Waves, White Shoulder & Neck, Favrile, Label, Signed L.C.T., 2 ¾ In. ...	1200.00
Vase, Iridescent Pulled Feather Design, Green, Gold, Signed, 19 x 10 In.	4000.00
Vase, Iridescent, Slender Neck, Soft Ribs, Engraved, c.1915, 11 ½ In.	1016.00
Vase, Jack-In-The-Pulpit, Favrile, c.1905, Engraved, 9 ⅞ In.	5313.00
Vase, Jack-In-The-Pulpit, Gold Favrile, Ruffled Face, Signed, 20 x 10 In.	3220.00
Vase, Jack-In-The-Pulpit, Gold Iridescent, 14 In.	4700.00
Vase, Jack-In-The-Pulpit, Gold Iridescent, Favrile, c.1911-12, 20 ⅛ x 10 ½ In.	23750.00
Vase, Jack-In-The-Pulpit, Gold, Purple, Green Iridescent, Scalloped Face, Signed, 18 In.	17250.00
Vase, Jack-In-The-Pulpit, Multicolored Iridescent, c.1907-10, 18 x 9 ⅞ In.	86500.00
Vase, King Tut Design, Platinum Iridescent, Bulbous, Signed, 5 In.	3163.00
Vase, Lava, Tapered, Drip Rim, Amber Ground, Mottled Brown, Favrile, Mark, 6 In.	2070.00
Vase, Lily, Green Pulled Feathers, Ivory Ground, Iridescent, Signed, 1915, 6 In.	1150.00
Vase, Lily Pad, Green, Yellow, White, Purple, Bulbous, Favrile, 6 In.	11100.00
Vase, Opaque Blue, Opalescence, Shouldered, Black Foot, Favrile, Signed, c.1910, 6 In.	2358.00
Vase, Optic Ribbed Shape, Green Pulled Feathers, Gold Tips, Favrile, Signed, c.1910, 10 In.	4250.00
Vase, Pastel, Green, Inverted Saucer Foot, Vertically Ribbed Bowl, 7 ¼ In. .... *illus*	1955.00
Vase, Peacock, Iridescent, Bulbous Top, Narrow Mouth, Engraved, c.1900, 8 ⅜ In.	5378.00
Vase, Platinum Iridescent, Blue Pulled Designs, Favrile, Signed L.C.T., 3 ½ x 3 ½ In.	1440.00
Vase, Pulled Clambroth Feather, Green Trim, Gold Favrile, Iridescent, 5 ⅞ In.	1438.00
Vase, Pulled Feather, Cream, Green, Long Stem, Wide Flat Rim, Signed, 12 In.	7590.00
Vase, Pulled Feather, Gold Iridescent, Trumpet, Bronze, Dore Base, Favrile, Marked, 11 ½ In. .	3200.00
Vase, Pulled Feather, Green, White, Iridescent, 4 In.	1020.00
Vase, Pulled Feathers, Green, Gold, Oval Shouldered Form, Favrile, 1 ½ In.	1208.00
Vase, Pulled Tadpole, Bulbous, Applied Glass, Gold Favrile, c.1894, 10 ½ In.	2300.00
Vase, Purple, Blue, Iridescent Gold Feathers, Squat, Shouldered, Favrile, c.1926, 6 ¼ In.	6875.00
Vase, Purple, Platinum, Purple Iridescent, Green, Blue Ribbon, Bulbous, Signed, 8 In.	6900.00
Vase, Red Favrile, Squat, Bulbous, Hooked Feather, Signed, Paper Label, 3 In. .... *illus*	6785.00
Vase, Red, Pink Nasturtium, Green Leaves, Pink Opalescence, Favrile, Mark, 5 In.	2300.00
Vase, Ribbed Iridescent Red, Purple, Gold, Tapered Oval, Cinched Neck, Favrile, c.1910, 5 In. .	1400.00
Vase, Round, Green Vines, Red, Gold Ground, L.C.T. Favrile, 2 In.	863.00

Tiffany Glass, Vase, Tel El Amarna, Egyptian Shape, Green, Applied Blue Collar, c.1919, 8 In. $7245.00

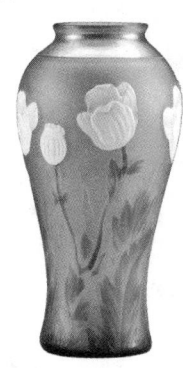

Tiffany Glass, Vase, White Padded Poppies, Iridescent Shouldered Rim, Signed, 11 In. $37375.00

Tiffany Gold, Spoon Set, Marquise, Demitasse, Monogram, Paulding Farnham, c.1902, 4 ½ In., 4 Piece $3120.00

T

Tiffany Pottery, Vase, Cabbage Shape, Mottled Matte Glaze, Incised LCT, 8 ½ x 8 In. $48000.00

Tiffany Silver, Baby Rattle, Whistle, Mother-Of-Pearl, Repousse, Bells, 4 In. $311.00

Tiffany Silver, Basket, Sterling, Reticulated, Flared, Applied Ribbon Bows, Swags, 1 ¾ x 4 In. $213.00

Tiffany Silver, Bowl, Center, Gilt Metal, Filigree, Openwork, c.1920, 14 In. $5313.00

Vase, Ruffled Edge, Pulled Green Feathers, White Ground, Gold Interior, 4 x 5 In.	230.00
Vase, Slender, Gold Favrile, Pink Iridescent, 3 x 8 In.	840.00
Vase, Spherical, Green Pulled Feathers, Opal Ground, Favrile, Marked, c.1900, 4 In.	2124.00
Vase, Spherical, Red Iridized, Blue Undulating Waves, Favrile, Marked, c.1900, 2 ¾ In.	5192.00
Vase, Squat, Oval, Iridescent Green, Swirled White Bands, Signed, 4 In.	850.00
Vase, Squat Urn Shape, Applied Scroll Handles, Blue Favrile, 1916, 4 ½ In.	2457.00
Vase, Star Shape, Gold Favrile, Pulled Feather, 6 x 3 ½ In.	1200.00
Vase, Swirled Iridescent Gold & Green, Rolled Rim, Etched Within Pontil, 1892	4370.00
Vase, Tel El Amarna, Egyptian Shape, Green, Applied Blue Collar, c.1919, 8 In. ...... *illus*	7245.00
Vase, Trumpet, Blue, Ribbed, Saucer Foot, c.1916, 10 ¼ In.	1668.00
Vase, Trumpet, Gold Iridescent, Green Heart, Vines, Bronze Base, 12 In.	1495.00
Vase, Trumpet, Green Pulled Feathers, Gold Favrile, Signed, 8 In.	863.00
Vase, Tulip Blossom, Green, Gold Ribbed, Opalescent, Favrile, 6 In.	600.00
Vase, Turquoise Iridescent, Pale Blue Interior, Wafer Pontil, c.1910, 7 In.	1100.00
Vase, Urn Form, Footed, Flared Rolled Rim, Blue Favrile, Signed, c.1916, 10 In.	1320.00
Vase, White Padded Poppies, Iridescent Shouldered Rim, Signed, 11 In. .... *illus*	37375.00

TIFFANY GOLD

Cigarette Case, 14K Gold, Monogram, MJL, 3 x 2 In.	1300.00
Cigarette Case, Strapped Pinstripe Design, Sapphire Stripe, c.1938, 3 ½ In.	2928.00
Clock, 14K Gold, Woven Pattern, Malachite Base, c.1930	2540.00
Desk Set, Engraved Pinstripe Design, Art Deco Style, 14K Gold, 8 Piece	8540.00
Purse, Edwardian, Yellow, Mesh, Square, Smoky Quartz, Fringe, 1 ⅞ Square, 4 ½ In.	2390.00
Spoon Set, Marquise, Demitasse, Monogram, Paulding Farnham, c.1902, 4 ½ In., 4 Piece ... *illus*	3120.00

TIFFANY POTTERY

Vase, Cabbage Shape, Mottled Matte Glaze, Incised LCT, 8 ½ x 8 In. .... *illus*	48000.00
Vase, White Matte, Cherry Blossoms, Green Glazed Interior, Signed, 7 In.	2200.00

TIFFANY SILVER

Baby Rattle, Whistle, Mother-Of-Pearl, Repousse, Bells, 4 In. .... *illus*	311.00
Basket, Pierced Design, Oval, 4 Scrolling Feet, 7 ½ In.	395.00
Basket, Sterling, Reticulated, Flared, Applied Ribbon Bows, Swags, 1 ¾ x 4 In. ...... *illus*	213.00
Berry Spoon, Olympian, c.1878, 8 ¼ In.	470.00
Berry Spoon, Olympian, Kidney Shaped Bowl, 1897, 9 ¼ In.	385.00
Bowl, 6-Sided, 8 ½ In.	475.00
Bowl, Center, Chrysanthemum, c.1886	15000.00
Bowl, Center, Flared, Flattened Knop, Hammered Foot, c.1925, 9 x 14 In.	5000.00
Bowl, Center, Folded Out Rim, Rope & Scroll Border, Openwork Frog, 13 In.	1725.00
Bowl, Center, Folded Out Rim, Scrolls, Flowers, c.1915, 15 In.	5625.00
Bowl, Center, Gilt Metal, Filigree, Openwork, c.1920, 14 In. .... *illus*	5313.00
Bowl, Center, Gold Washed, Fluted Rim, Stag Head Handles, Trumpet Foot, 1865, 9 x 12 In.	4148.00
Bowl, Center, Rolled Edge, Scrolls, Repousse Band, Paw Feet, Marked, c.1883, 5 ¼ x 11 In.	2420.00
Bowl, Center, Spot Hammered, Flared, Ribbed, Scalloped Edge, 1921, 4 x 15 In.	2684.00
Bowl, Footed, Flowers, Conforming Stepped Foot, Marked, 3 ¼ x 8 ¾ In.	431.00
Bowl, Fruit, Ogee Molded Sides, Reeded Rim, Low Foot, 9 ⅛ In.	444.00
Bowl, Fruit, Round, Reeded Bands, Script Monogram, c.1914, 1 ¾ x 9 In.	353.00
Bowl, Leaf & Dart Border, Drake Head Handle, Hoof Feet, 4 x 7 x 6 In.	403.00
Bowl, Octagonal, Marked, 2 ¼ x 9 In.	288.00
Bowl, Reeded Rim, Monogrammed DDG, 2 ¾ x 7 ⅞ In.	345.00
Bowl, Reeded, Stepped & Scalloped Border, 9 ¾ In.	288.00
Bowl, Repousse Band Of Flowers, Gold Washed Interior, Bulbous, Monogram, 5 In.	236.00
Bowl, Rose, Repousse, Scalloped Rim, 12 In.	600.00
Bowl, Scalloped Border, Marked, 4 ½ x 10 In.	748.00
Bowl, Scalloped Rim, Footed, Monogram, 3 ½ x 9 In.	748.00
Butter Knife Set, Marked, c.1920, 5 ¾ In., 9 Piece	360.00
Cake Plate, Flower Form, Scalloped Rim, Lobed, Rolled Rim, Arts & Crafts, 9 In.	593.00
Cake Stand, Round, Scalloped Edge, Applied Shell & Scroll Border, 2 x 12 ½ In.	1920.00
Candlestick, Georgian, Paneled, Marked, c.1915, 6 ½ In.	2070.00
Candlestick, Stepped Base, Monogram, 7 ¾ In., Pair .... *illus*	374.00
Candlestick, Teardrop Shape, Monogram C.L.K., Signed, 5 x 10 In., Pair	748.00
Castor Set, 3 Clear Glass Bottles, Marked, 1860-1865, 8 ½ In.	2250.00
Chalice, Chased, Repousse, Panel Reserve, c.1910, 6 x 3 ½ In. .... *illus*	414.00
Check Cutter, c.1870, 11 In.	2151.00
Child's Set, Flowers, Plate, Cup, Napkin Ring, Fork, Knife, Spoon, 8-In. Plate, 7 Piece	3125.00
Cigar Box, Chased Strapwork Bands, Art Deco Leaves, Monogram, c.1930, 14 In.	62500.00
Cigar Tray, Match Holder Top, Swag & Acanthus Border, Monogram, 3 x 4 In.	173.00
Clock, Dresser, Guilloche Enamel, Translucent Rose Overlay, Easel, Marked, c.1900, 3 ¼ In.	1200.00

Cocktail Shaker, Reeded Border, Monogram, 9 ½ x 7 ¼ In. ....*illus*	690.00
Cocktail Shaker, Tapered, Reeded, Silver Plate, 11 In.	201.00
Coffee Set, After Dinner, Urn Shape, Footed, Oval Tray, c.1930, 26-In. Tray, 5 Piece...............	6875.00
Coffee Set, Faceted, 8-Sided Foot, Wood Handle, Finial, c.1910, 15-In. Tray, 4 Piece...............	2562.00
Coffeepot, Marquise, Monogram, Marked, c.1930, 9 ½ In.	540.00
Coffeepot, Olympian, Lighthouse Shape, Renaissance Design, 9 In. ....*illus*	2990.00
Compote, Acanthus & Scroll Design, Marked, Monogram, 2 x 8 ½ In.	546.00
Compote, Flared Sides, 4 Band Post, Marked, 2 x 6 In.	403.00
Compote, Openwork Flowers, Shells & Scrolls, Marked, 4 x 9 In.	1035.00
Crumber, Plated, Engraved Flower Sprigs, Monogram, 13 ½ In. ....*illus*	92.00
Cup, Flowers, Butterfly, Marked, 3 In.	333.00
Cup, Stirrup, Stag's Head, c.1900, 6 In.	1098.00
Dish, Oval, Divided, Reeded Border, 1 ½ x 8 ½ x 11 In.	374.00
Ewer, Flowers, Repousse, Short Spout, Oval, Spreading Foot, Ear Handle, 1875-91, 12 In.	4444.00
Figurine, Tiger Trainer With Hoop, Enamel, 3 ¼ In.	1600.00
Flacon, Floral Repousse, 5 In.	987.00
Flask, Engraved, Monogram, Flower Edge, Silver Chain ....*illus*	276.00
Flask, Hammered, 2 Boxing Bears, Stamped, 3 ½ x 3 In.	2183.00
Fork & Spoon, Olympian, 9 ½-In. Spoon, 8 ½-In. Fork...	350.00
Grapefruit Spoon, Atlantis, 4 Piece..	165.00
Gravy Boat, Scroll Handle, 3-Footed, 4 x 7 x 3 In.	295.00
Hairbrush, Floral Repousse, 8 ¾ In.	110.00
Ice Bowl, Hammered, Flared Foot, Removable Drainer, 1875-91, 5 ⅛ x 7 In.	563.00
Ice Bucket, Wood Grained Staves, Hoops, Handles, John C. Moore, c.1850, 10 In.	4388.00
Ice Cream Slice, Gold Washed, Monogrammed Handle, 1884-91, 11 ⅜ In.	385.00
Ice Tongs, St. James, Claw Foot Blade, 1902-07, 5 ¾ In.	504.00
Jug, Cream, Monogram, Acanthus, Oval, 4 In. ....*illus*	132.00
Ladle, Cream, English King, 1885, 7 ¼ In.	510.00
Ladle, Lily Of The Valley, Gold Washed Bowl, 13 In.	720.00
Ladle, North Wind Face Mount Handle, 7 In.	175.00
Ladle, Soup, Persian Pattern, 1872, 11 In.	1440.00
Ladle, Soup, Scrolling Vine Tomato Handle, Embossed, 1800s, 12 In.	840.00
Loving Cup, Stepped Base, Acanthus Caps, Scroll Handles, Mark, c.1940, 11 x 6 In.	690.00
Mug, Child's, Beaded Rim, Leaf Tip Foot Rim, Lambrequins, Ear Handle, 1865-70, 2 ⅞ In.	207.00
Mug, Presentation, Leaftip Band, Angular Handle, 1931, 2 ¾ In.	119.00
Mug, Repousse, Inscribed, Tiffany & Co., 3 ¼ In.	644.00
Mustard Pot, Clear Glass Liner, Ladle, Marked, 1865-69, 3 ½ In.	1195.00
Pie Server, Etched Flowers, Pointed Blade, Monogram, 1880-91, 10 ⅝ In.	504.00
Pitcher, Butterfly, Dandelion, Japanese Style..	9300.00
Pitcher, Raised Bands, Cherubs, Flowers, Bulbous, Cylindrical Neck, c.1900, 8 In.	5312.00
Pitcher, Water, Repousse Flowers, Allover C-Scroll Handle, c.1895, 10 In.	2988.00
Pitcher, Water, Urn Shape, Chased Leaves, Squared Upswept Handle, c.1880, 17 In.	7500.00
Pitcher, Water, Winthrop, Monogram, c.1909, 9 ¼ x 8 ½ In.	1440.00
Plate, c.1892-1902, 6 ½ In., Pair..	1170.00
Plate, c.1892-1902, 15 In., Pair...	528.00
Platter, Etched Elongated Flower Tendrils, Budding Blossoms, Round, 1907, 13 ¼ In.	1126.00
Platter, Leaf Scrolls, Flower Heads, Round, 1907, 13 In.	889.00
Porringer, Openwork Tab Handle, c.1945, 2 x 8 In.	403.00
Punch Ladle, 15 In.	351.00
Salad Set, St. James, Spoon, Fork, Gilt Bowl, Monogram, 10 In, 2 Piece	489.00
Salt & Pepper, Domed Lid, Flared Foot, Chased, Embossed Leaves, 1875-91, 3 ⅞ In., Pair.......	119.00
Salver, Card, Suspending Lotus Lappets, Leaf Scroll, 1907, 8 In.	296.00
Salver, Chased Putti, Pan, Scrolls, Leaves, Oval, Greek Key Border, c.1860, 12 x 9 In.	610.00
Salver, Footed, 10 ¾ In.	200.00
Salver, Pilgrim, Engraved, Flower & Fruit Border, Square, Rounded Corners, 11 In.	5625.00
Salver, Shells, Rocaille, C-Scroll Rim, 1902-07, 13 ⅞ In.	1778.00
Sauceboat, Floral Repousse, Gadroon, Cast Floral Handle, 5 ¾ x 2 ½ In. ....*illus*	414.00
Sauceboat, Oval, Loop Handle, Ram's Head, Leaves, Gadroon Rim, 1865-70, 8 ½ x 6 In.	1778.00
Serving Fork, Indian Pattern, Medicine Dance Terminal, Enamel, c.1884, 9 ¼ In.	10157.00
Serving Fork, V-Shape, 2 Tines, Chrysanthemum Pattern, Tiffany & Co., Pat. 1880, 7 ½ In. ..	345.00
Serving Scoop, Grape Vine, Scalloped Edge, Monogram, 1872-91, 9 ⅜ In.	563.00
Serving Spoon, Chrysanthemum, Vermeil Shell Bowl, 8 ¼ In.	236.00
Spoon, Sorbet, Wave Edge Pattern, 1884, Monogram, 5 ¼ In., 8 Piece...............................	660.00
Sugar & Creamer, Footed Helmet Form, Arched Handle, 6 ½ x 3 ½ In.	2070.00
Sugar & Creamer, Repousse, Chased, Embossed Flowers, Leaves, 2 ¼ In.	770.00
Sugar Sifter, Pierced Shell Bowl, Leaves, Ram's Head Handle, Edward Moore, 7 In.	1464.00

Tiffany Silver, Candlestick, Stepped Base, Monogram, 7 ¾ In., Pair
$374.00

Tiffany Silver, Chalice, Chased, Repousse, Panel Reserve, c.1910, 6 x 3 ½ In.
$414.00

Tiffany Silver, Cocktail Shaker, Reeded Border, Monogram, 9 ½ x 7 ¼ In.
$690.00

Tiffany Silver, Coffeepot, Olympian, Lighthouse Shape, Renaissance Design, 9 In.
$2990.00

T

Tiffany Silver, Crumber, Plated, Engraved Flower Sprigs, Monogram, 13 ½ In.
$92.00

Tiffany Silver, Flask, Engraved, Monogram, Flower Edge Border, Silver Chain
$276.00

Tiffany Silver, Jug, Cream, Monogram, Acanthus, Oval, 4 In.
$132.00

Tiffany Silver, Sauceboat, Floral Repousse, Gadroon, Cast Floral Handle, 5 ¾ x 2 ½ In.
$414.00

TIP
Never steam-clean an old Oriental rug. It will remove the natural lanolin in the wool. Wash the rug with mild soap and water.

Tazza, Flowering Vine Rim, Trumpet Foot, Paw Feet, Rose Sprays, 3 ¼ x 9 In., Pair	1304.00
Tazza, Incised Arched Panels & Leaves, Flared Foot, c.1915, 3 ½ x 9 ½ In.	915.00
Tea & Coffee Set, Acanthus Rims, Loop Handles, 4 Piece	4444.00
Tea & Coffee Set, Chased Band, Squat Ball Shape, Edward C. Moore, 8 Piece	12500.00
Tea Caddy, Chased & Fluted Bands, Flower Basket, Scrolls, c.1885, 4 ⅜ In.	7500.00
Tea Caddy, Diamonds, Greek Key Border, Square Bail Handle, 2 Hinged Lids, 6 In.	8125.00
Tea Caddy, Japanesque, Birds On Branch, Ball Finial, Stepped Border, c.1876, 5 In.	8125.00
Thimble Holder, Acorn Form, Gold Wash Top, Monogram, D.F.S., 1 ½ In.	84.00
Tongs, Sterling, Palmette, 1947, 7 In.	450.00
Tray, Oval, Stepped & Flaring Rim, c.1959, 15 x 19 ¼ In.	1912.00
Tray, Presentation, Scalloped Edge, Reed Clark, NY Coffee & Sugar Exchange	480.00
Trophy, Chalice Shape, Mounted Side Stag Heads, 1872, 7 x 9 ½ In.	1610.00
Tumbler, Flared Rim, Stepped Ring Base, Monogram, 3 ¼ In.	115.00
Tureen, Cover, Oval, Pedestal Foot, Square Base, Bead Trim, 11 ½ x 14 ¾ In.	3346.00
Tureen, Cover, Wavy Band, Shaped Handles, Footed, c.1890, 15 In.	6250.00
Tureen, Domed Cover, Artichoke Finial, Loop Handles, Tiered, 1870-75, 12 ½ x 10 ½ In.	3318.00
Vase, Incised Curls, Shouldered, Curled Handles, Stepped Foot, 1905, 18 In., Pair	15000.00
Vase, Japanesque, Hammered, Butterfly, Leaves, Bottle Shape, c.1875, 8 In.	7500.00
Vase, Japanesque, Hammered, Mixed Metal Dragonfly, Branches, c.1875, 8 In.	6250.00
Vase, Trumpet, Geometric Floral Engraving, Pedestal Base, 1910, 10 In.	720.00
Vase, Trumpet, Spot Hammered, Ribbed, Scalloped Edge, c.1920, 9 x 8 In.	2196.00
Vermouth Applicator, Oil Can Form, Tapered Neck, Molded Base, 3 ¾ In.	225.00
Walking Stick Handle, L-Shape, Inscribed 584 Fifth Ave., c.1902	102.00
Waste Bowl, Leaf Repousse, Round Base, 4-Footed, Marked *illus*	224.00
Wine Funnel, Gadroon Borders, Monogram, Marked, 5 ¾ x 3 ½ In.	863.00

TIFFIN Glass Company of Tiffin, Ohio, was a subsidiary of the United States Glass Co. of Pittsburgh, Pennsylvania, in 1892. The U.S. Glass Co. went bankrupt in 1963, and the Tiffin plant employees purchased the building and the inventory. They continued running it from 1963 to 1966, when it was sold to Continental Can Company. In 1969, it was sold to Interpace, and in 1980, it was closed. The black satin glass, made from 1923 to 1926, and the stemware of the last twenty years are the best-known products.

Candlestick, Ruby Flashed Cup & Base, 8 ½ In. *illus*	45.00
Dresser Set, Pink Satin, Swirl Pattern, Tray, Covered Box, 2 Perfumes, Paper Labels, 10 In.	58.00
Fishbowl, Blue, Green Dolphin Base, 10 ½ x 9 In. *illus*	375.00
Flanders, Decanter, Yellow, Cut Clear Stopper, Footed *illus*	495.00
June Night, Plate, Luncheon, 8 In. *illus*	15.00
Palm Beach, Creamer, Milk Glass, 4 ½ In.	25.00
Palm Beach, Nappy, Milk Glass	23.00
Persian Pheasant, Console, Pale Pink, 13 In.	125.00
Sign, Vaseline Glass, Embossed United States Glass, 4 In.	44.00

TILES have been used in most countries of the world as a sturdy building material for floors, roofs, fireplace surrounds, and surface toppings. The cuerda seca (dry cord) technique of decoration uses a greasy pigment to separate different glaze colors during firing. In cuenca (raised line) decorated tiles, the design is impressed, leaving ridges that separate the glaze colors. Many of the American tiles are listed in this book under the factory name.

Aqua, Daisies, Glass, c.1880, 5 x 4 In.	115.00
Art Nouveau, Green Majolica Glaze, Raised, Brown Recesses, 6 x 6 In.	35.00
Art Nouveau, Woman, Dancing, Green Dress, Long Hair, Cuenca, Frame, Carl Luber, 14 ½ x 4 ¾ In.	3240.00
Art Nouveau, Woman, Looking Into Landscape, Medieval Ruins, Carl Luber, 14 ¼ x 4 ¾ In.	3600.00
Art Nouveau, Woman, Looking Into Night Sky, Cuenca, Carl Luber, 14 ¼ x 4 ¾ In.	2520.00
Art, Nouveau, Woman, Picking Flowers, Carl Luber, 11 x 6 ½ In.	1200.00
Art Nouveau, Woman, Picking Grapes, Frame, Cuenca, Carl Luber, 6 ½ x 11 In.	2880.00
Art Nouveau, Woman, With Flower Basket, Cuenca, Carl Luber, 11 x 6 ½ In.	1200.00
Arts & Crafts, Boy, Picking Flowers, Oak Frame, Signed, M. Wintemote, 16 x 16 In.	86.00
Bird, Goat, Brown, Blue, Green, Magenta, Enameled, 7 ¾ In.	495.00
Bird, Raised Beak, Open Flower, Earth Tones, Burnished, Tonala, Mexico, 1920s, 4 ½ x 4 ½ In.	165.00
Bird, Stylized, Green Matte Glaze, Press Molded, c.1910, 2 ¾ x 2 ¾ In.	85.00
Blue Matte Glaze, Empire, J.B. Owens Pottery, c.1929, 4 x 4 In.	38.00
Bluebirds, On Pine Tree Branches, Painted, Signed, E. Thorne, National Tile Co., c.1907, 6 x 6 In.	125.00
Canterbury Tales, Parson's Tale, Packard & Ord, 1950s, 4 x 4 In.	65.00
Canterbury Tales, Wife Of Bath, Packard & Ord, 1950s, 4 x 4 In.	65.00
Cat, Stylized, Black, Turquoise, Chartreuse, Wax Resist, Giers, 1940s, 9 x 9 In.	85.00
Centaur Of Nuremberg, Green Glaze, Moravian, c.1920, 4 x 4 In.	115.00

Christmas Carol, Bob Cratchit, Tiny Tim, Packard & Ord, 1950s, 4 x 4 In. 65.00
Confederate States, Soldier, On Horse, Wheeling Tile Company, Round, 1862, 6 In. 35.00
Courtyard Scene, White, Blues, Brown, Cuerda Seca, Frame, Signed, 8 x 3 In. 35.00
Dog, Crow, Dog House, Majolica, Raised Round Edge, Glazed, Blue, Green, Brown, c.1890....... 225.00
Don Quixote, Man, Woman, Serving Soldier, Cuerda Seca, Spain, c.1940, 5 ⅜ x 5 ⅜ In. 60.00
Dutch Country Scene, Road, Canal, Homes, Windmills, H. Utrecht, c.1890, 24 x 30 In., 20 Piece 960.00
Fleur-De-Lis, Yellow Ground, Dark Blue Border, Flint Tile Co., 6 In. 68.00
Flower Swags, Bowknots, Neoclassical, Terracotta, Stamped, Jabez Thompson, 10 x 24 In., 8 Piece 2280.00
Flower, Leaves, Hand Painted, Anton Lang, Germany, c.1913, 4 ¾ x 4 ¾ In. 75.00
Flowers, Earth Tones, Burnished, Tonala, Mexico, 1920s, 4 ½ x 4 ½ In. 135.00
Flowers, Gold, Brown, Iridescent Luster Glaze, Maw & Co., c.1900, 6 x 6 In., 4 Piece.............. 800.00
Flowers, Matte, Semimatte Glaze, Blue, Brown, Kraftile, c.1930, 4 ¼ x 4 ¼ In., 4 Piece......... 280.00
Geometric, Multicolored, Faience, Incised, Mueller Tile Co., c.1920, 6 x 6 In. 25.00
Giraffe & Squirrel, Mustard Yellow, Incised, D. Williamson, c.1944, 3 ¾ x 3 ¾ In. 40.00
Girl, With Blanket, Pink Glaze, Intaglio, Self Frame, Hemixem, Belgium, c.1900 .... 285.00
Goat, Horned, Round, Wood Frame, Gold Glossy Glaze, Turquoise Ground, c.1935, 6 In. 120.00
Goose Girl, White Clay, Blue Matte Glaze, Moravian, c.1920, 6 x 6 In. 240.00
Harris Strong, Clock, Wall, Battery, Walnut, Blue & Green Tiles, Mosaic Decoration, 11 x 42 In. 850.00
Highland Sheep, Brown On White Transfer, William Wise, Hayes Mfg., c.1890, 6 x 6 In. 165.00
Horse, Plastic, Frame, Arthur Osborne, Signed, 12 ½ x 7 ¾ In. 1586.00
Horse, Rider, Blue Majolica Glaze, Minton Hollins, c.1880, 8 x 8 In. 285.00
Lincoln, Bust, Circular, Gunmetal Glaze, Eljer, 9 In. 150.00
Man, Woman, Multicolored Enamel, 7 x 14 In., Pair 770.00
Man, Woman, On Horse, Bird, Sunflower, Multicolored Glaze, 1960s, 13 ¼ x 13 ¼ In. 300.00
Mayflower, Buff Semimatte Glaze, Blue Recesses, Moravian, c.1974, 3 ¾ x 3 ¾ In. 20.00
Mosaic Tile Co., Art Nouveau, Flowers, Majolica, Transfer Print, Hand Colored, Iridescent, c.1910 90.00
Mother & Child, Along Canal, Windmill, Frame, Holland, 6 x 6 In. 58.00
Mother, 2 Children, Thatched Cottage, Stream, Painted, Oak Frame, 12 x 8 In. 237.00
Mountain, Man, On Burro, Church, Gray, Brown, Turquoise, Signed, Frame, 8 x 3 ¾ In. 35.00
Oliver Twist, Bill Sykes, Packard & Ord, 1950s, 4 x 4 In. 65.00
Peacock, Male Display, Cream Ground, Majolica, c.1930, 6 x 6 In. 155.00
Pig, Flowers, Border Tile, Pastel Glossy Glaze, Belgium, c.1900, 6 x 3 In. 60.00
Pink & White, Transfer Print, Geometric, Minton Hollins, c.1880, 6 x 6 In. 15.00
Plaque, 2 Toucans, Iron Frame, Scrollwork, Catalina, 28 ¾ x 21 In. 6100.00
Shield, Cartouche, Banner, Coarse Buff Clay, Blue, Green, Claycraft, 1920s, 3 ¾ x 1 ¾ In. 45.00
Shore Scene, Multicolored, Houses, Trees, Distant Water, Pardee, Early 1900s, 4 ½ x 4 ½ In. . 518.00
Squirrel, Tan, Blue Glaze, Iron Stand, Moravian, c.1975, 4 x 4 In. 45.00
Stove, Acanthus Leaves, Blue Green Majolica Glaze, Round, High Relief, Bolt Hole, c.1880, 3 In. 40.00
Stove, Portrait, Woman, Gold Majolica Glaze, c.1880, 4 ¼ x 4 ¼ In. 110.00
Stove, Putti, Blue Green Majolica Glaze, Oval, High Relief, c.1890, 8 x 4 ¾ In. 270.00
Stove, Rose, Gold Majolica Glaze, Round, High Relief, c.1880, 3 In. 115.00
Stove, Stylized Flowers, Green Stippled Glaze, c.1890, 7 ¾ x 8 ½ In. 160.00
White, Blue, Aqua, Majolica, Press Molded, Fujimiyaki Tile Works, Japan, c.1900, 6 x 6 In. 15.00
Zodiac, Aries, Ram, Blue Ground, Unglazed Red Clay, Moravian, c.1920, 4 x 2 ¾ In. 75.00

TINWARE containers for household use have been made in America since the seventeenth century. The first tin utensils were brought from Europe, but by 1798, tin plate was imported and local tinsmiths made the wares. Painted tin is called tole and is listed separately. Some tin kitchen items may be found listed under Kitchen. The lithographed tin containers used to hold food and tobacco are listed in the Advertising category under Tin.

Basket Of Flowers, Footed, Oval Glass Dome, c.1891, 5 ¼ x 8 ½ In. .... *illus* 2468.00
Bread Basket, Leaves, Berries Border, Red Ground, 2 ¾ x 7 ½ x 12 ¾ In. 385.00
Bread Basket, Red Blossom, Yellow, Green, Oval, Cutout Handles, 4 x 8 ¼ x 14 In. 474.00
Can, Oil, Embossed, 5-Point Star Pattern, Brass. 192.00
Candlesnuffer, Cone Shape, Handle, c.1860, 2 ¼ In. 79.00
Candle Box, Hinged Lid, Hasp, Cylinder, Domed Ends, 2 Wire Hangers, 6 ¼ x 13 ¼ In. 176.00
Chest, Dome Top, Flowers, Leaves, Brass Handles, Clasp, 10 ¾ x 12 ¾ x 10 ¼ In. 248.00
Coffeepot, Cone Shape, Flared Base, C-Shaped Handle, Hinged Lid, Brass Finial, 9 ¼ In. 357.00
Coffeepot, Ear Handle, Continental Pat. By S. Culver, Miller Cronise & Co., 1858, 20 x 13 x 9 In. 1090.00
Coffeepot, Molded, Pewter Finial, 11 In. 147.00
Coffeepot, Red, Gooseneck Spout, Brass Finial, Flowers, Leaves, Hinged Lid, 10 ¼ In. 6518.00
Coffeepot, Wrigglework, Flag, Eagle On Vine, Snake, Sword, Brass Finial, c.1800, 9 In. 17625.00
Coffeepot, Wrigglework, Peafowl, In Tree, Eagle, Flag, Serpent Handle, Late 1700s, 12 In. .. *illus* 4446.00
Hearing Horn, Lapped, Soldered Joints, c.1900, 18 In. .... *illus* 136.00
Horse Medicine Cure, Newton Horse Remedy Co., Yellow, Race Horse Graphic, c.1906, 7 ¼ In. 155.00
Ladle, Candle, 6 Pouring Spouts, Applied Tubular Handle, 3 ⅝ x 12 x 8 In. .... *illus* 523.00

Tiffany Silver, Waste Bowl, Leaf Repousse, Round Base, 4-Footed, Marked
$224.00

Tiffin, Candlestick, Ruby Flashed Cup & Base, 8 ½ In.
$45.00

Tiffin, Fishbowl, Blue, Green Dolphin Base, 10 ½ x 9 In.
$375.00

Tiffin, Flanders, Decanter, Yellow, Cut Clear Stopper, Footed
$495.00

A Dollar, 12 Dozen
A 19th-century tinsmith made 12 dozen nutmeg graters in a 12-hour work day for a dollar wage. He worked six days a week.

TINWARE

Tiffin, June Night, Plate, Luncheon, 8 In.
$15.00

Tinware, Basket Of Flowers, Footed,
Oval Glass Dome, c.1891, 5 ¼ x 8 ½ In.
$2468.00

Tinware, Coffeepot, Wrigglework, Peafowl,
In Tree, Eagle, Flag, Serpent Handle,
Late 1700s, 12 In.
$4446.00

Tinware, Hearing Horn, Lapped,
Soldered Joints, c.1900, 18 In.
$136.00

Trash to Treasure
Pierced-tin wall shrines for saints
were made from tin cans left
behind by soldiers in New Mexico
and nearby areas during the 1840s
and 1850s.

Tinware, Ladle, Candle, 6 Pouring Spouts,
Applied Tubular Handle, 3 ⅝ x 12 x 8 In.
$523.00

Tinware, Mold, Candle, 7 Tube,
Round, 19th Century, 9 x 7 In.
$293.00

Tinware, Mold, Candle, 8 Tube,
Arched Legs, Applied Loop Handle,
13 x 6 ½ In.
$367.00

Tinware, Mug, Punched Star,
Heart Handle, 19th Century, 4 ¼ In.
$117.00

Tinware, Squirrel Cage, House Shape, Domed Roof, Spoked Wheel, Wood Base, 16 x 32 x 11 In.
$468.00

T

Map Case, Cylindrical, 19th Century, 16 ½ In.	30.00
Mold, Candle, Tube, Shaker, 19th Century, 16 ½ In.	165.00
Mold, Candle, 6 Tube, C-Shape Handle, 6 ¼ x 4 x 4 In.	311.00
Mold, Candle, 7 Tube, Round, 19th Century, 9 x 7 In. ....*illus*	293.00
Mold, Candle, 8 Tube, Arched Legs, Applied Loop Handle, 13 x 6 ½ In. ....*illus*	367.00
Mold, Candle, 10 Tube, 19th Century, 11 In.	66.00
Mold, Candle, 12 Tube	33.00
Mold, Candle, 36 Tube, 1800s, 11 x 7 ¾ In.	88.00
Mold, Candle, 36 Tube, Handles, 19th Century, 11 x 7 ¾ In.	100.00
Mug, Punched Star, Heart Handle, 19th Century, 4 ¼ In. ....*illus*	117.00
Oven, Reflector, Hinged Lid, Hasp, Handles, Feet, Hanging Hooks, 11 ½ x 13 ½ x 7 ¼ In.	154.00
Pitcher, Syrup, Cone Shape, Hinged Lid, Rolled Finger Pull, 4 x 3 In.	121.00
Plaque, Lusitania, Full Port View, Lithograph, Serpentine Border, Marked, Cunard Line, 38 In.	956.00
Sconce, Wall, Sunburst, Mirror, Beaded Border, Arched Arm, Candle Holder, 13 ¼ x 7 ¼ In. ...	176.00
Squirrel Cage, House Shape, Domed Roof, Spoked Wheel, Wood Base, 16 x 32 x 11 In. ..*illus*	468.00
Squirrel Cage, House Shape, Turret, Flag, Cylindrical Runner Wheel, 11 x 19 x 10 In.	148.00
Squirrel Cage, Pine Base, Gable House, Glass Pane Windows, Punched Designs, 17 x 30 In. ..	558.00

TOBACCO JAR collectors search for those made in odd shapes and colors. Because tobacco needs special conditions of humidity and air, it has been stored in special containers since the eighteenth century.

Dog With Cigar Box, Terra-Cotta, 5 ½ In.	276.00
Housewife, Terra-Cotta, Germany, 11 ½ In.	345.00
Humidor, Curly Maple, Lacquered, Hinged Lid, Dunhill, France, 1900s, 3 ½ In.	94.00
Soldier, Terra-Cotta, 12 ½ In.	518.00

TOBY JUG is the name of a very special form of pitcher. It is shaped like the full figure of a man or woman. A pitcher that shows just the top half of a person is not correctly called a toby. More examples of toby jugs can be found under Royal Doulton and other factory names.

Man, Blue Coat, Holding Pitcher, Pearlware, Staffordshire, c.1790, 10 In. ....*illus*	2106.00
Man, Seated, Blue Transfer Jacket, Outstretched Arms, Staffordshire, 1890s, 7 ¼ In.	175.00
Man, Seated, Holding Lantern, Late 18th Century, 9 ¼ In.	385.00
Man, Seated, Holding Pitcher, Blue Jacket, Yellow Pants, Staffordshire, 1830s, 9 ½ In.	243.00
Man, Seated, Legs Crossed, Outstretched Arms, Staffordshire, 1890s, 8 In.	175.00
Man, Seated, Mug, Spongeware Coat, Pratt Style, Staffordshire, 1800s, 9 In. ....*illus*	353.00
Man, Standing, Holding Pitcher, Pipe, Pink Vest, Staffordshire, 1850s, 11 In.	175.00
Man, TR On Belt, Book Marked Africa, Elephant Head & Trunk Handle, Lenox, 8 In.	1750.00

TOLE is painted tin. It is sometimes called *japanned ware, pontypool,* or *toleware.* Most nineteenth-century tole is painted with an orange-red or black background and multicolored decorations. Many recent versions of toleware are made and sold. Related items may be listed in the Tinware category.

Baking Pan, Tulips, Black, Yellow, Rickrack Trim, Ekco, No. 2, 8 x 4 x 2 In.	12.00
Bottle Capper, Maple, Metal, Wall Mount, Adjustable Platform, c.1900 ....*illus*	138.00
Bowl, Center, Black, Gold Leaves, Boat Shape, Notched Edge, Handles, 9 x 13 In.	115.00
Bowl, Cheese, Black Paint, Stenciled Flowers, c.1850.14 In.	264.00
Box, Cutlery, Fruit, Red, Yellow, Green Leaves, Cutout Heart Handle, 19th Century, 12 x 8 In. ..	7700.00
Box, Document, Black Ground, Leaves, Flowers, c.1825, 5 x 8 In. ....*illus*	588.00
Box, Document, Domed Lid, Blue Stenciled Flowers, Green Ground, Bail Handle, c.1850, 7 x 10 In.	646.00
Box, Document, Domed Lid, Peaches, Flowers, Wire Handle, Tin Hasp, c.1865, 9 ½ x 5 x 6 In.	117.00
Box, Document, Domed Lid, Stenciled Flowers, Mustard Ground, Wire Bail Handle, 6 ¼ In. ...	235.00
Box, Document, Domed Lid, Swag, Flower, Leaf, Black Japanned, 5 ½ x 8 ¾ x 5 In.	124.00
Box, Document, Fruit, Flowers, Berry & Leaf Border, Loop Handle, c.1825, 5 ¾ x 9 In.	862.00
Box, Document, Hinged Lid, Flowers, Black Japanned, Wire Handle, 4 ½ x 8 ¼ x 4 In.	124.00
Box, Document, Lily Of The Valley, Flat Top, Handle, c.1820, 3 ¾ x 6 x 3 In.	3995.00
Box, Document, Red Ground, Red, White, Blue, Brass Ball Handle, c.1820, 6 x 12 In.	705.00
Box, Flowers, c.1830, 4 ½ x 3 In.	100.00
Box, Flowers, Divider, Squared Handle, Oval, c.1800, 6 ¼ x 12 ¼ x 8 ½ In.	8225.00
Box, Flowers, Red, Green, Gold, Round, c.1915, 4 x 6 In.	118.00
Box, Knives & Forks, Handle, 13 x 9 In.	55.00
Bread Tray, Flowers, Japanned, Arched Ends, Wire Rim, Rectangular, 2 ⅝ x 12 ⅝ x 8 In.	88.00
Bucket, Lid, Black, Leaves, Bail Handle, 5 ¼ In.	20.00
Cachepot, Scroll & Cartouche, Red Ground, Paneled Balustrade Shape, 13 ¼ x 8 In., Pair......	86.00
Candlestick, Tin, Candlesocket Base, Lighting Tube, Red, c.1850, 11 In., Pair	764.00
Canister, Black, Gold Landscape Scene, Hinged, Side Handles, 1700s, 10 x 11 In.	263.00

Toby Jug, Man, Blue Coat, Holding Pitcher, Pearlware, Staffordshire, c.1790, 10 In. $2106.00

Toby Jug, Man, Seated, Mug, Spongeware Coat, Pratt Style, Staffordshire, 1800s, 9 In. $353.00

Toby Jugs

The Toby jug shaped like a seated man was named for Toby Philpot, a notorious drinker mentioned in a song written in 1761. Toby jugs were popular from 1776 to 1825, but many later versions have been made.

T

Tole, Bottle Capper, Maple, Metal, **Wall Mount,** Adjustable Platform, c.1900 $138.00

Tole, Box, Document, Black Ground, **Leaves,** Flowers, c.1825, 5 x 8 In. $588.00

Tole, Coffeepot, Gooseneck Spout, Domed Lid, Brass Finial, Flowers, Japanned, 10 x 6 In. $1392.00

Canister, Coffee, Black Ground, Gilt Stencil, Figures, Palm Trees, Scrolls, c.1900, 22 x 19 In.	207.00
Canister, Crosshatched Flowers, Leaves, White Band, Japanned, Round, Lid, c.1800, 5 ¾ x 7 In.	147.00
Canister, Lamp Mount, Tea Scenes, Chinoiserie, Olive, c.1850, 12 x 19 In., Pair	2233.00
Canister Set, Yellow, Flower Designs, Hand Painted, Lids, Ransurg, 7 Piece	79.00
Coal Scuttle, Black, Flowers, Red Interior, Red, Green, Yellow, Wood Handle, c.1935, 7 ½ In.	40.00
Coaster, Rooster Center, Gold, Black Ground, 3 In., 8 Piece	10.00
Coffeepot, Domed Lid, Gooseneck Spout, Brass Finial, C-Shape Handle, 10 ½ x 6 ⅜ In.	1320.00
Coffeepot, Flowers, Fruit, Japanned Ground, 19th Century, 8 ½ In.	176.00
Coffeepot, Flowers, Green Ground, Side Spout, 2 Handles, 1850s, 12 In.	2458.00
Coffeepot, Flowers, Oak Leaf Borders, Red Ground, Gooseneck Spout, Mid 1800s, 11 In.	350.00
Coffeepot, Gooseneck Spout, Applied Handle, Light House Shape, Signed, Nancy Hulling, 10 ¾ In.	28.00
Coffeepot, Gooseneck Spout, Domed Lid, Brass Finial, Flowers, Japanned, 10 x 6 In. *illus*	1392.00
Coffeepot, Red Flowers, Japanned Ground, Brass Finial, c.1850, 10 ½ In.	499.00
Cutlery Box, Red, Yellow, Green, Leaf & Fruit, Heart Cutout Handle, 1800s, 12 ⅜ x 8 In. *illus*	7605.00
Egg Server, Black, Gold Painted Woman, Tree, Applied Gold Handles, 1700s, 9 In.	322.00
Flour Shaker, Flowers, Leaves, Handle, 3 ½ In.	40.00
Foot Tub, Figures, Buildings, Landscape, Handles, 1800, 7 ⅜ x 9 x 13 In.	85.00
Jardiniere, Harbor Scene Reserve, Green Ground, Gilt, 1800s, 4 ¼ x 10 ½ In.	235.00
Kettle, Stand, Black, Gold Painted Woman, Landscape Scene, 19 In.	146.00
Match Safe, Red & Gold Flowers, c.1890, 3 ¼ x 2 ½ In.	125.00
Pail, Flower Band, Japanned, Bail Handle, 4 ¾ x 6 ½ In.	323.00
Pail, Lid, Tulips, Fruit, Twisted Rope, Japanned Ground, Wire Bail Swing Handle, 4 ¾ x 7 In.	192.00
Pitcher, Yellow & Orange Flowers, Black Ground, Pt., 4 ½ In.	15.00
Planter, Boat Shape, Swan's Head, Scalloped Rim, Painted, Gilt, 7 x 13 x 5 In. *illus*	581.00
Plaque, Flowers, Green Ground, Round, 1970, 10 ½ In.	10.00
Sconce, Green Paint, Gold Trim, Alcove Under Tapering Roof, 27 In.	230.00
Silent Butler, Incised Mark, Plymouth Tole, 1960s, 10 ¼ x 5 ¾ In.	35.00
Tea Caddy, Bow Front, Sloped Lid, Chinoiserie, C. Oolong, Paint, Philadelphia, c.1850, 14 x 18 In.	384.00
Tea Caddy, Knob, Olive Green, Red Flower, Leaves, Door Opens Downward, c.1940, 5 ¾ x 6 In.	38.00
Tea Caddy, Lobed Shape, Amber Applied Metal Paw Feet, c.1850, 4 ½ In.	323.00
Tea Caddy, Red, Leaves, Japanned Ground, c.1800, 7 ¾ In.	206.00
Tea Canister, Chinoiserie, Mounted As Lamp, 20 x 33 In., Pair	299.00
Teapot, Apple, Pear, Grape, Mustard Yellow, 1940, 8 ½ x 8 ½ In.	45.00
Tray & Coaster Set, Red Pink, Roses & Leaves, 11-In. Tray, 3-In. Coasters, 8 Piece	47.00
Tray, Butterfly, Fruit Basket, Flowers, Cutout Handles, Early 19th Century, 21 ½ x 30 In.	110.00
Tray, Flower Spray, Sprigs, Saffron Ground, Oval, Pierced Gallery, Handles, 29 x 21 In.	690.00
Tray, Flowers, Gold, Black Ground, Cutout Handles, 19th Century, 21 x 28 ¾ In.	300.00
Tray, Flowers, Japanned Ground, Octagonal, 6 x 9 In.	588.00
Tray, Flowers, Multicolored, Yellow Ground, 19th Century, 19 ½ In. Diam.	90.00
Tray, Flowers, Pink, White, Yellow, 8-Sided, Cutout Edge Design & Handles, 22 x 16 In.	65.00
Tray, Grand Turk, Capt. Holten, J. Breed Of The Privateer, Oval, 22 x 27 ½ In.	339.00
Tray, On Stand, Black, Gilt, Grapes, Leaves, Pierced Rim, Faux Bamboo Stand, 26 x 18 x 22 In.	2750.00
Tray, Painted Flowers, Yellow Ground, Round, 19th Century, 19 ½ In.	94.00
Tray, Pear, Apple, Lemon, Alligatored Black Paint, 6 In.	145.00
Tray, Pear, Grapes, Leaves, Black Ground, Nash Co., c.1940, 15 ½ In.	45.00
Tray, Red Ground, Gilt Leaf Border, Scenic Landscape, Tin, Oval, c.1840, 30 x 22 ½ In.	1950.00
Tray, Rooster, Red & Gold, Black Ground, Wall Hanger, Round, 12 In.	12.00
Tray, Seated Italian, Woman, Landscape, Flower, Oval, Molded Rim, France, c.1885, 23 x 30 In.	267.00
Tray, Stripes, Octagonal, c.1800, 8 ¾ x 12 ½ In.	2702.00
Tray, Stylized Flower Basket & Blossoms, Leaves, Black Ground, Shaped Rim, 23 x 29 In.	89.00
Tray, Table, Apple, Gilt Gold & Green Flowers, Yellow Ground, 14 x 9 In.	302.00
Tray, Victorian, Exotic Bird In Garden, 30 ¼ In. *illus*	248.00
Tray, White Border, Flowers, Buds, Red, Japanned Ground, c.1840, 8 x 12 ¾ In.	264.00
Urn, Chestnut, Red, Gold, Black Flowers, Lion's Head Handles, c.1800, 13 In., Pair	1200.00 to 1880.00
Urn, Landscape Panels, Swan Handles, Gilt, Black Paint, White Metal, France, 1800s, 9 In., Pair	793.00
Wall Pocket, Flowers, Butterflies, 8 In., Pair	18.50
Wine Measure, Orange Paint, Early 1800s, 25 x 22 In.	550.00

TOM MIX was born in 1880 and died in 1940. He was the hero of over 100 silent movies from 1910 to 1929, and 25 sound films from 1929 to 1935. There was a Ralston Tom Mix radio show from 1933 to 1950, but the original Tom Mix was not in the show. Tom Mix comics were published from 1942 to 1953.

Bracelet, Charm, Brass Link, 4 Charms, 6-Gun, Steer Head, Tom, Tony, 7 In.	1044.00
Button, I Am A Member Of The Tom Mix Wildwest Club, Photo, 1934	1163.00
Hat, Stetson, Felt, Box, Size 7 ⅛ *illus*	193.00
Poster, Tom Mix Circus, No. 228, Stone Lithograph, 3 Sheet, c.1935, 80 x 41 In.	375.00

Ring, Tom Mix Deputy, Shield & Star, 14K White Gold, Premium, 1933	1896.00
Telescope, Bird Call, Plastic Bullet Shape, Box, Insert, c.1950..	115.00
Toy, Wagon, Big Six Circus & Wild West, 2 Horses, Driver, Wood, Cast Iron, 7 x 17 In.	605.00

TOOLS of all sorts are listed here, but most are related to industry. Other tools may be found listed under Iron, Kitchen, Tinware, and Wooden.

Adze, Bowl, 7 ¼-in. Edge, Wood Handle, France .... *illus*	385.00
Adze, Carpenter's, Handwrought, 4 ½ In.	22.00
Adze, Chair Maker's, Curved Blade..	33.00
Adze, Wooden Handle, 9-In. Edge...	132.00
Angle Divider Bevel, Patent, Frank H. Coe, Bronton, New Jersey.......................................	467.00
Anvil, Cast Iron, Painted, 3 ¾ x 8 x 3 In.	55.00
Ax, Chisel, Sun With Rays, Face Touchmark, 18 In.	230.00
Ax, Double Bit, Kretschmer-Treadway Co., 34 In.	193.00
Ax, Double Bit, Mann Edge Tool Company, Embossed Logo, Sheath	302.00
Ax, Embossed, Dana, Boston, Massachusetts..	357.00
Ax, Felling, Bearded, Applied Poll & Edge, 7 ½ In.	55.00
Ax, Goosewing, 19th Century, 25 In. .... *illus*	88.00
Ax, Goosewing, Applied Edge, Wallbecher, Handle, 7 ½-In. Head, 12 ½-In. Edge	275.00
Ax, Goosewing, Sanders, Offset Handle...	60.00
Ax, Jelco, John E. Larrabee, Amsterdam, New York, Embossed...	132.00
Ax, Marking, Strap Type, Poll Stamps, 8-Point Star, Replaced Handle	50.00
Backsaw, Brass Back, Split Nuts, Spear & Jackson, 10-In. Blade......................................	50.00
Bark Spud, Blacksmith Made, 24 In.	32.00
Bench, Cobbler's, Pine, Drawer, 40 x 16 x 17 In. .... *illus*	322.00
Bench, Cobbler's, Walnut, Drawer, 19th Century, 19 x 41 In.	60.00
Bevel, Patent November 5, 1867, L.D. Howard, St. Johnsbury, Vermont	192.00
Bit, Countersink Auger, Melvin Jincks, Dansville, New York, Patent April 2, 1867	55.00
Book Press, Double Dolphin Pattern, Iron	286.00
Book Press, Georgian, Oak, c.1790, 47 x 27 In.	570.00
Book Press, Georgian, Oak, Late 1700s, 47 x 27 In.	520.00
Book Press, Iron Thread, Brass Handle, 19th Century, 17 In.	85.00
Book Press, Wooden Screws & Nuts .... 66.00 to 200.00	
Boot Pulls, Ivory Handle, Steel Hook, 3 ¼ x 8 In., Pair..	85.00
Bootjack, Hardwood, Blue Paint, Early 20th Century, 24 ½ In.	147.00
Boring, Bone Tee Handle, Handwrought, 18 In.	385.00
Box, Miter, Goodell Pratt Co., No. 1285, Greenfield, Mass., Paper Label	77.00
Brace, Bit, D. Flather, Solly Works, Sheffield, England	220.00
Brace, Coffinmaker's, T.B. & Co., 7 ½ In.	44.00
Brace, Corner Ratchet, Stanley, No. 984, Rosewood Handle..	187.00
Brace, J. Holley Patent May 14, 1907..	9900.00
Brace, Wooden, Brass Chuck, Lignum Head, Beech Body, Wm. Kent, Sheffield.......................	66.00
Broadax, Goosewing, Wrought Iron, Wood Handle, 22 In. .... *illus*	55.00
Buggy Whip Holder, Cast Iron, Embossed, Black Paint, Hanging, Cooley, c.1868, 17 In.	210.00
Bullet Mold, Buck Shot, Marked 24, 1860s	25.00
Cabinet, Bolt, 8-Sided, 80 Pie Shape Drawers, Porcelain Knobs, Stenciled .... *illus*	880.00
Cabinet, Bolt, Wood, 6-Sided, Square Base, 12 Drawers, Rotates, 67 x 30 ½ In.	1100.00
Caliper, Log, Wheel, Brass & Wooden Jaws, Steel Tips...	633.00
Caliper, Mermaid Shape, Cast Iron, Signed, A.H.A., Ontario, 1850s, 5 ¼ In.	657.00
Caliper, Outside, 30 In., Pair...	99.00
Caliper, Rolling Wheel Log, F.M. Greenleaf, Belmont, Massachusetts	962.00
Candlesnuffer, Wick Cutter, Steel, Mechanical, Springs Co., c.1840, 7 In.	115.00
Carrier, Pine, Painted, Cutout Handle, 2 Hinged Lids, 1800s, 18 x 12 ½ In.	702.00
Chalk Line, Carved Wood, Bear, Honey Pot Shape, Side Score Marks, Black Paint, Stand, 6 x 11 In.	1422.00
Chamfer Shave, Adjustable, Complete With Stops, Birmingham Plane Mfg. Co. Pat..............	253.00
Chest, Carpenter's, Tools, Square Cut Nails, Rope Handles, Brass Hinges, Lock, c.1850, 36 x 16 In.	1650.00
Chest, Oak, Finger Joint, Drawers, Gerstner, Dayton, Ohio...	286.00
Chest, Oak, Fold-Down Lid, Drawer, Lift-Out Tray, Hammacher, Schlemmer & Co., 22 x 12 x 6 In.	148.00
Chest, Pine, Walnut, 2 Tills In Top Lid, 5 Trays, Saw Till, Dovetailed.................................	198.00
Chest, Stanley, No. 902, Oak...	198.00
Chest, Walnut, Poplar, Dovetailed Interior Tray, Delaware County, Ohio, Mid 1800s, 10 ½ x 35 In.	264.00
Chest, Woodworker's, Oak..	275.00
Chisel, Marked PRR, 8 ½ In.	5.00
Chisel Set, Stanley, No. 20, Hickory Handle, ¼ In., 1 In., 1 ½ In., 3 Piece	264.00
Clapboard Gauge, Brass, Mahogany Infill, Nester's Patent December 31, 1867.....................	55.00
Clapboard Gauge, Solid Iron, Peter Moberg Patent September 13, 1887.............................	66.00

Tole, Cutlery Box, Red, Yellow, Green, Leaf & Fruit, Heart Cutout Handle, 1800s, 12 ⅜ x 8 In.
$7605.00

Tole, Planter, Boat Shape, Swan's Head, Scalloped Rim, Painted, Gilt, 7 x 13 x 5 In.
$581.00

Tole, Tray, Victorian, Exotic Bird In Garden, 30 ¼ In.
$248.00

Tom Mix, Hat, Stetson, Felt, Box, Size 7 ⅛
$193.00

T

TOOL

Tool, Adze, Bowl, 7 ¼-in. Edge, Wood Handle, France
$385.00

Tool, Ax, Goosewing, 19th Century, 25 In.
$88.00

Tool, Bench, Cobbler's, Pine, Drawer, 40 x 16 x 17 In.
$322.00

Combination, Lathe & Jigsaw, Foot Powered, Jig Saw Attachment, Star Brand	330.00
Combination, Level, Square, Rule, Brass, Proportional Scales, 18th Century, 7 ½ x ¾ In.	262.00
Combination, Odd Jobs, Stanley, No. 1, Miter, Try Square, Depth Gauge, Level, Scribe, 4 In. .. *illus*	242.00
Countersink, P.W. Company, Adjustable, Patent January 23, 1877	55.00
Crown Molder, Chestnut, 6 x 26 In.	236.00
Crown Molder, Ogee & Bevel, Handle, Gardiner & Murdock, Boston, Box, 3 ½-In. Wide	160.00
Drafting Set, Fitted Case, Conversion Tables, Stanley, London, 6 x 14 In.	77.00
Drawing Knife, Wooden Handles	12.50
Drill, Bench, Hand, Millers Falls No. 5, Mounted On Frame	385.00
Drill, Breast, Oak, Brass, Iron, Key Lock Chuck	143.00
Drill, Flywheel, Brass Bar & Wheel, Boxwood Handles, 14-In. Shaft, 17 In.	440.00
Drill, Hand, Red & Gold Striping, Cast Iron, 19th Century, Box	385.00
Flax Cutter, Beechwood, Pine, Iron Fittings, Continental, 1800s, 27 x 26 In.	206.00 to 220.00
Gauge, Chisel, Stanley, No. 96, Patent April 10, 1888	220.00
Gauge, Marking, Knurled Fixing Screw, Brass	159.00
Gauge, Panel Marking, Mahogany, Twin Carved Eagles, Orange Glass Eyes, 12 In.	2530.00
Grain Cradle, Primitive, Decal, 14 Finger, Mixed Hardwoods, Seymour Mfg., 56 x 44 In.	240.00
Hammer Ax, Wrought Iron, Wooden Handle, Stamped, R. Adams, 10 ¾ In.	66.00
Hammer, Claw, Hand Forged, Octagonal Poll, 7 ½ In.	143.00
Hammer, Claw, Maydole, No. 12	550.00
Hammer, Cobbler's, 4-Jaw Chuck, Hammerhold Awl Bit, Letche, Peter's Patent Jan. 22, 1878 ..	302.00
Hammer, Double Claw, Pat. Nov. 4, 1902, 12 ¾ In.	303.00
Hammer, Metal Working, Hexdall Implement Co., Elburn, Illinois, Box	154.00
Hammer, Napping, Marked, Morone, 1 ¼ Lbs.	26.00
Hatchet, Double Bevel, Underhill Edge Tool Co., Nashua, New Hampshire	66.00
Hatchet, Plumb, Etched, Fayette R. Plumb, Philadelphia, Pennsylvania	198.00
Hay Fork, Wood, 3 Tines, 19th Century	110.00
Inclinometer, Black & Copper Color, Chrome Plated Rails, Acme Level, Toledo, Oh., 28 In. ...	468.00
Inclinometer, Davis Level & Tool Co., Springfield, Mass., Patent September 17, 1867	154.00
Inclinometer, Iron Mantel Clock Style, Melick Clinometer Co. Patented Dec. 3, 1889	605.00
Inclinometer, Japanning, Davis Level & Tool Co., 7 In.	248.00
Inclinometer, L.L. Davis, Springfield, Mass., Pat. Sept. 17, 1867, 12 In.	3630.00
Iron, Bookbinder's, Spine Forming, Cast Iron	247.00
Jack, Wagon, Green Paint, 19th Century, 31 x 37 In.	60.00
Jigsaw, Treadle, Cast Iron, Overhead Rocker Drive, J.W. Penney & Sons, Dirigo, Maine	2640.00
Ladder, Tin, 4 Steps, Folding, Wood, Salesman's Sample, Stamped, 9 ½ x 3 In.	550.00
Level Stand, Adjustable, Mount On Mahogany Base, Stanley, 9 In.	2090.00
Level, Bench, Cast Iron, Brass Top Plate, Gray Instrument Co., Queen Instruments, Pa., 18 In.	132.00
Level, Bench, Cast Iron, Brass Top Plate, Green Japanning, 7 ½ In.	335.00
Level, Bit & Square, Stanley, No. 44, Box	83.00
Level, Brass, Wood, C.S. Co., Pine Meadow, Conn., 28 ⅛ In.	22.00
Level, Bull's-Eye, Brass Case, Bevel Glass Top, R. Merrill & Sons, N.Y., 2 ⅞ In.	60.00
Level, Davis & Cook Pretzel, Cast Iron Open Framework, Japanned, Patented, 24 In. ...... *illus*	523.00
Level, No. 125, Rosewood, Brass, Tower & Lyon, New York, New York, 26 In.	247.00
Level, Pocket, L.L. Davis 38, Brass, Japanning, 4 ¾ In.	94.00
Level, Stanley, No. 36G, Grooved Bottom, Box	110.00
Level, Surveyor, Sighting, Brass, Green Patina, Wood Case, W & LE Gurley, 15 In.	302.00
Mane Singe, Brass, Copper, Eagle Decoration, 5 x 4 In.	265.00
Mold, Rubber Gloves, Metal, Black Painted Wooden Base, 12 x 4 ½ x ⅜ In.	80.00
Monkey Wrench, Marked, B & O RR, 12 In.	15.00
Padlock, Cast Iron, Heart Escutcheon, Key, 19th Century, 11 ¼ In. .... *illus*	644.00
Padlock, Cavalry, 7th Army Swords, Brass, Iron, Keys, 19th Century, 4 x 2 ¾ x 1 ¼ In.	235.00
Padlock, Iron, Heart Escutcheon, Key, 19th Century, 11 ¼ In.	644.00
Padlock, R&E, Embossed, Diana The Huntress, Flowers, Keystone Shape, 3 In. .... *illus*	920.00
Padlock, Whitlock, Key, Brass, 1 ½ x 1 ½ In., Pair	45.00
Pipe Kiln, Wrought Iron, Cylinder, 3 Rings, Stretcher Supports, Handle, Arch Legs, 11 x 18 x 10 In. .	181.00
Plane Set, Dado, Stanley, No. 39, Cast Iron, Set Of 8	1458.00
Plane, Bead Molding, Left-Hand, L. Gardner, Green St., Boston	88.00
Plane, Bed Rock, Jointer, Stanley, No. 607	132.00
Plane, Bed Rock, Stanley, No. 605, Type 6, Bed Rock Cap, Later Blade, Japanning	88.00
Plane, Beech Plow, Applewood Arms & Nuts, No. 96 ½, Ohio Tool Co., Columbus, Ohio	104.00
Plane, Bench, Bed Rock, Thomas Lie-Nielson, No. 2, Cast Bronze, 7 In.	176.00
Plane, Bench, Rabbet, Stanley, No. 10 ½, 1950s	198.00
Plane, Bench, Stanley, No. 2, Second Sweet Heart, Box, Script Logo Label	743.00
Plane, Bench, Stanley, Siegley STS, No. 4 ½C, Corrugated, Tapered Iron	121.00
Plane, Block, Stanley, No. 15 ½, Tail Handle, Rosewood Knob, 7 In.	209.00

Plane, Block, Stanley, No. 62, c.1910	302.00
Plane, Block, Stanley, No. 131, Double End	159.00
Plane, Body Block, Stanley, No. A18, Patent February 18, 1913, Aluminum	220.00
Plane, Bone, Boxwood, Carved, Woman, Hair, Hat, Ebony Plugs, 4 ¼ In. ....*illus*	1540.00
Plane, Bullnose Block, Stanley, No. 101 ½, Marked Cutter, Japanning	330.00 to 341.00
Plane, Butcher Block, Stanley, No. 64, Vee Logo, Japanning	1155.00
Plane, Cabinet Scraper, Stanley, No. 212, Adjustable, Japanned Finish	1238.00
Plane, Cabinetmaker's Block, Stanley, No. 9, Japanning, c.1890	1045.00
Plane, Cam Lock Cap, Stewart Spiers, Ayr, Scotland, Screw Adjust, 6 ½ In.	2090.00
Plane, Carriage Maker's Bench Rabbet, Stanley, No. 10	154.00
Plane, Chamfer Spoke, Stanley, No. 65	143.00
Plane, Chamfer, Stanley, No. 72, Adjustable	275.00 to 385.00
Plane, Chute Board, James W. Hall, c.1890	250.00
Plane, Combination Match, Stanley, No. 147, ⅝ In.	297.00
Plane, Combination, Type 11, Stanley, No. 45, Box	275.00
Plane, Corebox, Stanley, No. 56, Cast Iron, Patent March 23, 1909	632.00
Plane, Corner Rounding, Stanley, No. 144, ½ In.	176.00
Plane, Crown Molding, L. Little, Boston, Mass., Round & Ogee Shape, Birch, 1700s	1870.00
Plane, Crown Molding, Yellow Birch, Ogee Cutting Profile, James Transitt Stamp, 1700s	440.00
Plane, Dado, Stanley, No. 39 ½, Sweet Heart	115.00
Plane, Dado, Stanley, No. 239, c.1910	605.00
Plane, Double Iron Cornice, D.P. Sanborn, Littleton, N.H., 4 ¼ x 15 In.	2200.00
Plane, Dovetail, Stanley, No. 444, 4 Cutters, Wooden Case, No Lid	468.00
Plane, Edge Trimming, Stanley, No. 95, Japanned	77.00
Plane, Fiberboard, Stanley, No. 193	82.00
Plane, Fore, Stanley, No. 28	71.00
Plane, Gage Iron, Stanley, No. G4, Box	880.00
Plane, Infill, Rosewood, Dovetailed, Gunmetal Keeper, Moulson Iron, 11 ½ In.	1210.00
Plane, Jointer, Carved Designs, Inscribed, Continental, 1836	440.00
Plane, Jointer, Stanley, No. 8, Cast Iron, c.1920s	154.00
Plane, Low Angle, Bronze Body, W.C. Scott, Cincinnati, Ohio, c.1886	1650.00
Plane, Low Angle Jack, Stanley, No. 62, Sweet Heart, Japanned	220.00
Plane, Molding, A. Inglis, Delhi, New York, Double Iron, A Handle	412.00
Plane, Molding, Left Hand Cut, 18th Century	33.00
Plane, Norris, No. 54, Buck & Ryan, London, Original Cutting Iron, c.1824	2640.00
Plane, Open Throat, No. 67 Router, Millers Falls Company, Box	66.00
Plane, Plow, 4 Ivory Tips, Ebony, Boxwood Arms, Screw Arm, A. Howland & Co., No. 100	1072.00
Plane, Plow, Jonathan Ballou, Yellow Birch, Imprinted, Jon Ballou, Rhode Island, c.1850	4950.00
Plane, Plow, Rosewood, Boxwood Arms & Nuts, Whalebone, Marked G. Davis	1320.00
Plane, Plow, Rosewood, E.W. Carpenter's, Patent Improved Arms, Lancaster	688.00
Plane, Plow, Screw Arm, E. Danbury, New Brunswick, Beech, Boxwood, Ivory	633.00
Plane, Plow, Yellow Birch, Joseph Fuller, Providence, Rhode Island	907.00
Plane, Rabbet, Bull Nose, Bronze, Edward Preston & Sons, Birmingham, England	275.00
Plane, Rabbet, Stanley, No. 10 ¼, Tilt-Handle, c.1920	770.00
Plane, Rabbet, Stanley, No. 10 ½, c.1930s	143.00
Plane, Rabbet, Stanley, No. 289, Skew Blade	198.00
Plane, Rabbet, Weatherstrip, Stanley, No. 378, Box	198.00
Plane, Rosewood Infill Shoulder, Norris, London, England, No. 20	825.00
Plane, Router, Stanley, No. 71, Open Throat, Box	137.00
Plane, Sash Molding, Handle, Boxwood Arms & Nuts, Arrowmammet Works, No. 194	143.00
Plane, Scraper, Stanley, No. 212, Adjustable	1237.00
Plane, Smoothing, Bed Rock, Stanley, No. 602C, Wedge Lever Casting, Stanley R & L Co., 7 In.	1540.00
Plane, Smoothing, Fulton Tool Company, No. 2, 7 In.	143.00
Plane, Smoothing, Low Angle, Stanley, No. 164, Sweet Heart, Japanned	2090.00
Plane, Smoothing, Nooris Type, No. A-6, Steel & Bronze, Karl Holtey	3740.00
Plane, Smoothing, Stanley, No. 3, Type 2	154.00
Plane, Smoothing, Stanley, No. 4, Type 2	143.00
Plane, Sole Jack, Removable, Mahogany Top & Knob, c.1880	159.00
Plane, Stanley, No. 45, 5 ½ x 9 In. ....*illus*	77.00
Plane, Stanley, No. 50, Bronze Cast, Miniature, 4 In.	121.00
Plane, Swing Fence Match, Stanley, No. 49, Nickel Plated	110.00
Plane, Tongue & Groove, Stanley, No. 148, Cast Iron, Nickel Plated, Box	132.00
Plane, Transitional, Carpenter's, Wood, 14 x 2 ½ x 6 In.	90.00
Plane, Transitional, Stanley, No. 24, 9 In.	220.00
Plane, Wood, Carved, Man Reading Book, Painted, 16 In. ....*illus*	303.00
Plow, Salesman's Sample, Oak, Brass, Steel, Engraved, J. Woody, Mt. Vernon, Ind., c.1900, 12 In.	1351.00

Tool, Broadax, Goosewing, Wrought Iron, Wood Handle, 22 In.
$55.00

Tool, Cabinet, Bolt, 8-sided, 80 Pie Shape Drawers, Porcelain Knobs, Stenciled
$880.00

Tool, Combination, Odd Jobs, Stanley, No. 1, Miter, Try Square, Depth Gauge, Level, Scribe, 4 In.
$242.00

Tool, Level, Davis & Cook Pretzel, Cast Iron Open Framework, Japanned, Patented, 24 In.
$523.00

Tool, Padlock, Cast Iron, Heart Escutcheon, Key, 19th Century, 11 ¼ In. $644.00

Tool, Padlock, R&E, Embossed, Diana The Huntress, Flowers, Keystone Shape, 3 In. $920.00

Tool, Plane, Bone, Boxwood, Carved, Woman, Hair, Hat, Ebony Plugs, 4 ¼ In. $1540.00

Tool, Plane, Stanley, No. 45, 5 ½ x 9 In. $77.00

Plumb Bob Set, S In Shield Mark, Steel Tips, Sizes, 1, 2, 4, 6 & 7, 5 Piece	132.00
Plumb Bob, Brass, 14 Lbs.	495.00
Plumb Bob, Ivory, Brass	357.00
Plumb Bob, Turnip Shape, Knurled Cap	82.00
Press, Tobacco Leaf, Wood, Adjustable Rollers, Kagoshima Region, 1800s, 14 ½ x 16 In.	495.00
Radiator, Salesman's Sample, Cast Iron, Green Paint, 11 x 11 In.	1007.00
Rake, Cranberry, Wood	85.00
Rake, Wood Handle, c.1960, 16 In.	12.00
Repair Kit, Machinist, Pliers, Oiler, Thread, Screwdrivers, Sand Paper, Leather Case, 8 x 5 In.	41.00
Router, Old Woman's Tooth, ¼-In. Cutting Edge, Alex Mathieson & Sons, Glasgow, Scotland	44.00
Rule, 2-Fold, Stephen & Co., No. 35 ½ Caliper, Ivory, German Silver	143.00
Rule, 4-Fold, Boxwood, Rabone, England, 36 In.	136.00
Rule, 4-Fold, E.A. Stearns & Co., No. 57, Ivory, German Silver	154.00
Rule, 4-Fold, E.M. Chapin, No. 57, Ivory, German Silver, Pine Meadow, Connecticut, 12 In.	93.00
Rule, 4-Fold, Imperial Dip, I. Long, Brass Joints, 48 In.	55.00
Rule, 4-Fold, Stanley, No. 40 Caliper, Ivory, Silver Bound, Yellow, Germany, 12 In. .... *illus*	220.00
Rule, 4-Fold, Stanley, No. 86, Ivory, German Silver, 2 Ft.	495.00
Rule, 4-Fold, Stanley, No. 95, Ivory, German Silver Bound, 2 Ft.	1430.00
Rule, 6-Fold, Stephens & Co., Riverton, Conn., 6-In. Segments, 3 Ft.	3630.00
Rule, Boxwood, Stanley, No. 23, Button Caliper	522.00
Rule, Desk, Daniel Webster Clegg, San Francisco, California, Patent September 10, 1867	176.00
Rule, Folding, Boxwood, Brass, J. Rathbone & Sons, c.1930-90, 8 Ft.	4180.00
Rule, Folding, German Silver, Ivory, Level, Bevel, No. 38, Stephens Patent, Jan. 12, 1858, 12 In.	6160.00
Rule, Hatter's, Boxwood, Brass, Sliding Scale, Caliper Slide, J.B. Mast Co., New York, N.Y.	154.00
Rule, Log Measure, A.B. Eaton, 1868	44.00
Safety Ax, No. 5, Marble, 1898 Patent, c.1913, 4 ½-In. Head, 9 ¼-In. Handle	106.00
Sand Mold Pounder, Maple, Double Ended, 19th Century, 14 In.	165.00
Saw, Crosscut, 8-Point, E.C. Atkins & Co., Indianapolis, Ind., No. 401, Rosewood	198.00
Saw, Crosscut, 9-Point Finish, Henry Disston & Sons, No. 16, Applewood Handle, 20 In.	143.00
Saw, Crosscut, Acme, No. 120, Ten-Point	137.00
Saw, Crosscut, Marked Great American H. Disston, c.1885, 70 x 18 In.	115.00
Saw, Dovetail, H. Disston & Sons, Philadelphia, Pennsylvania, No. 68, 6 In.	132.00
Saw, Dovetail, Henry Disston & Sons, Philadelphia, USA, 7 ½-In. Blade	99.00
Saw, Dovetail, Richardson Brothers, Newark, New Jersey, 8 In.	154.00
Saw, Frame, Pit Type, Chestnut, Tiller Handle, Mortise & Pegged Construction, 40 In.	154.00
Saw, Miter, H. Disston & Sons, No. 4, 30 In.	66.00
Saw, Rip, 5 ½ Point, Carved Applewood, Hammacher Schlemmer & Co., N.Y., 21 In.	110.00
Saw, Rip, H. Disston & Sons, No. 16, 6 Point, 26 In.	154.00
Saw, Stair, Beechwood, Henry Disston & Sons, Philadelphia, 10 In.	83.00
Saw, Stair, Chip Carved, Squirrel Image Along Sides, 11-In. Blade, 16 In.	99.00
Saw, Tenon, Henry Disston & Sons, Philadelphia, Pa., No. 4, 12 In.	231.00
Saw, Tenon, James Turner, Philadelphia, Pa., Steel Back, c.1850, 14 In.	231.00
Scissor Sharpener, Charles L. Emery, Biddeford, Maine, Pat. May 24, 1881	55.00
Scissors, Iron, 19th Century, 16 x 5 In.	110.00
Scissors, Iron, England, 18th Century, c.1760	145.00
Scraper, Stanley, No. 12 ¾, Rosewood Sole, 32 Teeth Per In.	1320.00
Scraper, Stanley, No. 282, Wood, Sweet Heart, Instructions, Box	77.00
Shoe Last, Anvil, Brass, 2 In. .... *illus*	17.00
Shovel, Cranberry, Wood, 40 In.	195.00
Shovel, Mahogany, Stirrup Handle, Round Shaft, Scoop, 36 x 11 In.	147.00
Slick, Carpenter's, Provost & Williams, Newark, New Jersey, Oak Handle, 3 In.	110.00
Slick, T-Handle, H.H. Date, Galt, Ontario	110.00
Snip, Metal Cutting, A. Rominger, Wood, Adjustable, Gutenberg, Germany	22.00
Splitter, Leather, Aiken's, Patent, March 12, 1823, Franklin, New Hampshire	77.00
Spoke Shave, C.H. Weston, Cast Iron, Yarmouth, Maine, Patent June 1, 1858	159.00
Spoke Shave, Stanley, No. 151 R, Round Sole, Sweet Heart, Japanning, Marked	358.00
Sprayer, Brass, Copper Tank, Blizzard Continuous Sprayer, D.B. Smith & Company, N.Y.	35.00
Square, Lap Joint, Mahogany, Mortised Arched Corner Brace, Ogee Ends, 11 x 22 In.	154.00
Square, Rosewood Handle, George Wheatcroft, Newark, New Jersey, 18 In.	154.00
Square, Try, Stanley, No. 12, Vee Logo, 2 In.	132.00
Sugar Devil, Cast Iron, Double Auger, Wooden Handle, Pat. July 1873	83.00
Tape Measure, Stanley, No. 7506	231.00
Torch, W.M.R.R., Western Maryland, 33-In. Wooden Handle	65.00
Trowel, W.H. Hunt & Sons Brades Co., England, 19th Century, 54 In.	990.00
Vise, Emertt's, No. 82 Articulated, c.1891, 21 x 7 In.	153.00
Washer, Steam, Copper, Tin Lid, Cone Top Vent, Wood Finial, Handles, Howell, 21 ½ x 27 ½ x 14 In.	79.00

T

Wheat Thresher, Wood, Marble Chips, Galicia, Spain, 19th Century......	2500.00
Wheelbarrow, Wood, Iron, Removable Sides, Forge Strap Wheel, Blue Paint, N.Y., 1850, 28 x 71 In.	527.00
Wheelbarrow, Wood, Red & Blue Paint, Spoke Wheel, Iron Rim, 12 ½ x 42 x 17 In.	490.00
Yoke, Oxen, Wood, 19th Century......	85.00

TOOTHBRUSH HOLDERS were part of every bowl and pitcher set in the late nineteenth century. Most were oblong covered dishes. About 1920, manufacturers started to make children's toothbrush holders shaped like animals or cartoon characters. A few modern toothbrush holders are still being made.

Bear, Painted, Gold, White, Blue, Germany, 3 In.	110.00
Bonzo, Marked, Japan, 1940s, 5 ½ In.	45.00
Boy Playing Flute, Hand Painted, Lusterware Base, Japan, 4 ¼ x 2 ¾ In.	85.00
Dog, Down On Front Paws, Hind End Up, Ceramic, 1960s, 4 ½ x 2 In.	20.00
Donkey, Incised, Japan, c.1950, 6 ¼ In.	125.00
Duck, Painted, Trico Nagoya Japan, 3 x 2 14 x 4 ½ In.	85.00
Dutch Girl, Chalkware, Wall Plaque, Miller Studio, c.1964, 4 ¼ x 1 ¾ x 6 ¾ In.	125.00
Dutch Girl, Lusterware, Toothpaste Holder, Japan......	95.00
Girl, Washing Boy's Face, Japan, 3 x 2 ½ x 5 ¾ In.	110.00
Iron, Enameled, Aqua Blue, Wall Mount, c.1930s, 4 x 4 ¼ In.	145.00
Ironstone, Center Handle, Tonquin, E.M. & Co.	67.00
Pink Panther, Pottery, 3 Slots, Marked, 1970s, 4 ½ In.	35.00
Pirate, Ceramic, Arms Form 2 Holes, Japan, 5 x 3 ½ In.	85.00
Porcelain, Applied Gold Design, 4 Open Slots, 4 In.	10.00
Rocky The Flying Squirrel, Ceramic, Painted, P.A.T. Ward, c.1960, 5 In. ......illus	196.00
Skippy, Bisque, 6 In.	145.00
Skunk, Victoria Ceramics, Paper Label, 4 ½ x 3 ¾ In.	39.00
Turtle, Wearing Hat, Painted, 5 ½ x 3 ¼ x 2 ½ In.	50.00

TOOTHPICK HOLDERS are sometimes called *toothpicks* by collectors. The variously shaped containers used to hold small wooden toothpicks are made of glass, china, or metal. Most of the toothpick holders are made of Victorian pressed glass. Additional items may be found in other categories, such as Bisque, Silver Plate, Slag Glass, etc.

Banded Portland, Clear, Gold Accents, United States Glass Co., c.1901, 2 x 2 In.	38.00
Bellaire, No. 505, Amber, Octagon, Mark Imperial, 1960, 2 ½ x 2 ½ In.	12.00
Blue Moon & Stars, Scallop Base, Blue Iridescent, 2 ½ x 2 In.	12.00
Bow Knot, Opal, Wheeling, The Stogie City, 2 x 2 In.	13.00
Cased Pink, Multicolored Flowers, Tooled Rim, Pontil, c.1875, 2 x 2 ⅜ In.	39.00
Cat, On Back, On Pillow, Daisy & Button, Blue, 3 ½ In.	140.00
Cut Glass, Ball Shaped, Russian Pattern, Star Cut Buttons, 3 Ball Feet, 3 In.	200.00
Delaware, Emerald Green & Gold Design......	80.00
Field Scene, Cobalt Blue, Gold Stencil, Handles, 1 ½ In.	150.00
Fig Mold, Opal......	400.00
Figural, Birds In Eggshell......	35.00
Figural, Boy Standing Near Chimney, Blue & White, Bisque, 5 In.	100.00
Figural, Corn With Husks, Milk Glass, Painted, c.1900, 2 x 2 In.	26.00
Figural, Daisy, Clear & Button......	35.00
Figural, Devil, Footed......	75.00
Figural, Gnome, Holding Seashell, Bisque, 4 ½ In.	125.00
Georgia, Pear Green Opaque With Gold Trim......	25.00
Green, Gilt, Croesus, 2 ¾ In.	125.00
Man's Head, Black, Milk Glass, Painted, 3 ¼ In.	295.00
Michigan, Clear & Blue Enamel Design......	95.00
New Hampshire, Clear & Ruby Stain With Decoration	130.00
Pennsylvania, Emerald Green......	70.00
Portland, Clear & Cold Flash	35.00
Rib Optic, Rose To Clear Opalescent, Square Top, Pontil, c.1875, 3 In.	118.00
Rose Amber Diamond Optic, Pontil, Square Rim, c.1875, 2 ½ In.	171.00
Scalloped Panel, Clear, United States Glass Co., c.1896, 3 x 2 In.	40.00
State Of New York, Emerald Green, Gold Trim......	55.00
Tacoma Ruby, Stained, Greensburg Glass, c.1875, 2 ½ In.	39.00
Vermont, Ivory With Enamel Design......	60.00
Virginia, Clear & Rose Stain	50.00
Washington, Clear & Ruby Stain......	70.00
Washington, Custard & Gold......	70.00
Wisconsin, Clear......	25.00

Tool, Plane, Wood, Carved, Man Reading Book, Painted, 16 In.
$303.00

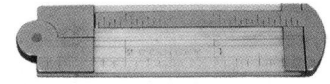

Tool, Rule, 4-Fold, Stanley, No. 40 Caliper, Ivory, Silver Bound, Yellow, Germany, 12 In.
$220.00

Tool, Shoe Last, Anvil, Brass, 2 In.
$17.00

Toothbrush Holder, Rocky The Flying Squirrel, Ceramic, Painted, P.A.T. Ward, c.1960, 5 In.
$196.00

Tortoiseshell, Box, String, Cover, Silver, Gadrooned Bands, London, c.1888, 5 In. $546.00

Toy, Airplane, Kilgore TAT, Rubber Tires, Nickel Plated Disc Tires, 13 ½ In. $8625.00

Toy, Alley Oop, Club, Standing, Resin Blend, Painted, Flocking, Box, R.W. Kerr Co., 5 In. $1898.00

TORQUAY is the name given to ceramics by several potteries working near Torquay, England, from 1870 until 1962. Until about 1900, the potteries used local red clay to make classical-style art pottery vases and figurines. Then they turned to making souvenir wares. Items were dipped in colored slip and decorated with painted slip and sgraffito designs. They often had mottoes or proverbs, and scenes of cottages, ships, birds, or flowers. The Scandy design was a symmetrical arrangement of brushstrokes and spots done in colored slips. Potteries included Watcombe Pottery (1870–1962); Torquay Terra-Cotta Company (1875–1905); Aller Vale (1881–1924); Torquay Pottery (1908–1940); and Longpark (1883–1957).

TORQUAY

Candlestick, Terra-Cotta, Geometric Band, Spread Foot, Aesthetic, 7 ¾ In., Pair	115.00
Creamer, House, Landscape, Motto, Green, Brown, Handle, 2 ¼ In.	68.00
Cup & Saucer, Cottage Design, Tree & Motto, Royal Watcombe, c.1960	74.00
Dog Dish, From Dalry, Ilka Dog Has His Day, c.1915, 5 x 5 ½ In.	68.00
Eggcup, Seagull Design, Blue Ground, Pedestal, Attached Saucer, c.1925, 3 ½ In.	78.00
Figurine, Cat, Toothache, White, 3 ½ In.	45.00
Jam Jar, Lid, Cottage, Plate & Spoon, Motto, I Improve Everything, 4 ¾-In. Plate	68.00
Loving Cup, Give Every Man Thy Ear But Few Thy Tongue, 2 Handles, 4 ¼ In.	60.00
Plate, Motto, There's Gladness In Remembrance, House, Trees, 6 In.	19.00
Sugar & Creamer, Cottage, Still Waters Run Deep, c.1930	128.00
Syrup, Pigeon Blood Red, Clear Handle, c.1900, 6 In.	171.00
Syrup, Pigeon Blood Red, Squat, Attached Silver Plated Lid, c.1900, 6 In.	330.00
Teapot, Burns Cottage, Alloway, 3 ½ x 6 In.	135.00

TORTOISESHELL is the shell of the tortoise. It has been used as inlay and to make small decorative objects since the seventeenth century. Some species of tortoise are now on the endangered species list, and old or new objects made from these shells cannot be sold legally.

Box, Anglo-Indian, Veneer, Applied Details, Hinged, Octagonal Lid, Paw Feet, c.1880, 6 x 6 In.	975.00
Box, Decorated Silver Hinge Mounts, 2 ¼ x 1 x 5 In.	500.00
Box, String, Cover, Silver, Gadrooned Bands, London, c.1888, 5 In. ....*illus*	546.00
Cigarette Box, Rectangular, Hinged Lid, 3 ¼ x 5 x 4 In.	448.00
Dresser Box, Edwardian, Banded, Nickel-Silver Stringing, Bone, Velvet, c.1900, 2 x 2 x 3 In.	2400.00
Dresser Box, Silver Thumbpiece, Pique Monogram, c.1900, 2 x 6 x 3 ½ In.	570.00
Etui, Scent Bottle, Silver, Hinged Cover, 2 ½ In.	2600.00
Etui, Silver Flower Basket, Vines, Tapered, 5 Implements, 3 ½ In.	633.00
Frame, Bronze Dore Accent Corners, Italy, 19th Century, 8 x 12 In.	375.00
Glove Stretcher, Gold Monogram, Victorian, 8 In.	200.00
Hair Comb, Gold & Stone Mountings, 2 x 3 ½ In.	100.00
Necessaire, George III, Gilt, Garlands, Tapered Oval Outline, Paneled, 3 In.	2196.00
Necessaire, George III, Silver, Tapered Oval, Inlaid, Festoons, Swags, c.1789, 3 In.	1220.00
Page Turner, Sterling Silver, Chased Handle, Ferns, Scrolls, Hallmark, 15 ¾ In.	147.00
Pillbox, Edwardian, Domed Lid, c.1900, 2 ½ x 2 ½ In.	300.00
Powder Box, Gold Initial, Round, 3 ⅝ x 2 ¼ In.	395.00
Sewing Case, Rectangular, Canted Corners, Silver Plaque, 3 ¾ x 2 In.	805.00
Shell, Polished, 19th Century, 18 x 17 In.	896.00
Trinket Box, Domed Lid, Polished Bone Bun Feet, England, 1 ½ x 3 x 2 In.	300.00
Writing Case, George III, Traveling, Gold Inlaid, Flowers, Bloodstone Seal, 1 ½ x 2 ½ In.	1220.00
Writing Case, George III, Traveling, Silver, Domed Cover, 2 Bottles, 2 x 2 ¾ In.	1586.00
Writing Case, George III, Traveling, Silver, Drop Handle, Strapwork, 1780s, 1 ¾ x 2 ¾ In.	2745.00
Writing Case, Silver, Shield Shape, Cut Glass Bottle, Folding Pen, Late 1700s, 2 ¾ In.	488.00

TOY collectors have special clubs, magazines, and shows. Toys are designed to entice children, and today they have attracted new interest among adults who are still children at heart. All types of toys are collected. Tin toys, iron toys, battery-operated toys, and many others are collected by specialists. Dolls, Games, Teddy Bears, and Bicycles are listed in their own categories. Other toys may be found under company or celebrity names.

2 Minstrels, Plays Music, Tin Lithograph, Cloth Clothing, Windup, Gunthermann, 9 In.	1888.00
Acrobat, 2 Figures, On Steps, Wood, 10 ½ x 9 ½ In.	330.00
Acrobat, 2 Movable Figures, Poles, Stairs, Wood, Papier-Mache Head, Cloth Clothes, 10 x 11 In.	351.00
Acrobat Marvel, Metal, Windup, U.S.A., 1930s, 13 In.	225.00
Acrobatic, Aerial, Propeller Spins, Man Does Tricks, Tin, Guntermann, c.1920, 7 In.	1323.00
Action Figure, Barbarino, John Travolta, Welcome Back Kotter, Jointed, Mattel, 1976, 9 In.	30.00
Action Figure, Big Jim, Press Back For Karate Chops, Mattel, 1971, 10 In.	15.00
Action Figure, Epstein, Welcome Back Kotter, Jointed, Mattel, 1976, 9 In.	24.50
Action Figure, Horshack, Welcome Back Kotter, Jointed, Mattel, 1976, 9 In.	24.00
Action Figure, Mr. Kotter, Gabe Kaplan, Welcome Back Kotter, Jointed, Mattel, 1976, 9 In.	24.00
Action Figure, Washington, Welcome Back Kotter, Jointed, 1976, Mattel, 9 In.	24.00

Admiral Peary, Tin, Cloth Dressed Figure, Driving Windup Sleigh, Martin, 8 In.	8050.00
Airplane Tower, Einfalt, Tin, 5 ¾ In.	204.00
Airplane, Airmail AP, Tin, Windup, Girard, U.S.A., 1930s, 8 ½ In.	245.00
Airplane, America, Silver, Cast Iron, Hubley, 17 In.	2633.00
Airplane, Biplane, Whistle, Clicks When Spinning, France, Penny Toy, 4 ⅞ In.	50.00
Airplane, Bomber, 4 Prop, Black, Gold, Tin, Plastic, Windup, Marx, 13 ½ x 18 In.	80.00
Airplane, Cargo, Plastic, Gray, Swadar, Box, c.1952	150.00
Airplane, Dagwood's Solo Flight, Marx, Box, 1935	850.00
Airplane, Fighter, Blue, Gray, Metal, Wood Wheels, Marx, 4 ¼ x 16 In.	285.00
Airplane, Flying Fortress 2095, 4 Prop, Red, Silver, Tin, Windup, Marx, 13 ½ x 18 In. ...	170.00
Airplane, Giro, Blue, Rubber Wheels, Cast Iron, 3 In.	140.00
Airplane, Giro, Red Paint, Cast Iron, Rubber Tires, Hubley, 3 ½ x 4 ½ In.	305.00
Airplane, Jet Fighter, Blue, Gray, Red, Plastic, Metal, Friction, Marx, 3 ¾ x 15 In.	60.00
Airplane, Jupiter Rocket, Tin, Masuya, Japan, 1950s, 9 In.	175.00
Airplane, Kilgore TAT, Rubber Tires, Nickel Plated Disc Tires, 13 ½ In. ....*illus*	8625.00
Airplane, Lindy, Monoplane, Blue, Hubley, 4 ¼ In.	250.00
Airplane, Lindy, Monoplane, Silver, Hubley, 4 ¾ In.	150.00
Airplane, Loop The Loop, Marx, Box, 7 ½ In.	270.00
Airplane, Metal Wheels, Wood, Multicolored, Propeller, 6-In. Wingspan....................	45.00
Airplane, Monoplane, Bremen, Green Nickeled Wheels, Propeller, Passengers, Hubley........	1500.00
Airplane, Police Patrol, Tin, Friction, Japan, 1950s, 14-In. Wingspan.....................	95.00
Airplane, Pressed Steel, Wood Steering Handle, Rubber Tires, Disc Wheels, 24-In. Wingspan...	1150.00
Airplane, Propeller, Windup, Prewar Japan, 6 ½ In.	385.00
Airplane, Rollover, Windup, Built-In Key, Tin Lithograph, Marx, 1930s, 5 x 6 In.	253.00
Airplane, Satellite Space, Tin, Windup, West Germany, Box, 8 x 8 In.	75.00
Airplane, Sea Horse, Iron, Green, Yellow, Wheel Covers, Kilgore, 13 ½-In. Wingspan......	1093.00
Airplane, Seaplane, Nickel Plated Propellers, Tri Motor, Yellow, Blue, Pull, Hubley, 13 In.	5462.00
Airplane, Stratoliner, Pan American Airways, Marx, c.1950, 22 In.	24.00
Airplane, Super Sabre Jet, Tin, Bombs, Korean War, Japan, 9 In.	175.00
Airplane, Taxi, Steel, Propeller, Rubber Tires, Clockwork, Kingsbury, Box, 12-In. Wingspan....	805.00
Airplane, Tin, Friction, Strato, 1950s, 18 In.	175.00
Airplane, Tin Litho, Painted, Red & Yellow Wings, Yellow Body, Pilot, 15 ½ x 12 In.	350.00
Airplane, U.S. Army Bomber, Pilot, Green, Tin Windup, Marx, 13 ¼ x 18 In.	139.00
Airplane, U.S.A. Copper Airplane, Windup, Marx, 18-In. Wingspan	225.00
Airplane, USAF, Tin, Friction, Japan, 1950s, 19 In.	225.00
Airplane, UX-166, Star In Circle, Red Paint, Cast Iron, Nickel Plated, 5 ⅞ x 6 ¼ In.	200.00
Airplane, Wooden, Seat, Painted, Spring, Metal Propeller, 17 x 27 x 15 In.	58.00
Airship, Aluminum, Propeller, Windup, Embossed, Strauss, Box, 10 In.	345.00
Airship, Wire Frame, Fabric Covered, Tin Lithograph, Gondola, Cabin, Clockwork, 12 In.	1265.00
Alabama Coon Jigger, Dances On Box, Windup, Lehmann, 1910................................	550.00
Alley Oop, Club, Standing, Resin Blend, Painted, Flocking, Box, R.W. Kerr Co., 5 In. ....*illus*	1898.00
Ambulance, Dodge, Tin, Friction, Japan, 1950	95.00
Ambulance, Driver, Blue, Red Wheels, Bell Rings, Tin Lithograph, Windup, 8 In.	330.00
Ambulance, Red Cross, Driver, Nurse, Stretchers, Electric Lamps, Rubber Tires, 1912, 16 In. ..	5175.00
Ambulance, Red Cross, Driver, Tin Litho, Red, Black, Emblems, Windup, Box, c.1920, 7 ½ In.	2070.00
Ambulance, Red Cross, Pressed Steel, Gray, Lincoln, 14 In.	985.00
Ambulance, Tin, Original Tin Litho Driver, Bell, Blue, Red Paint, Windup, 8 In.	351.00
Amos 'n' Andy, Amos, Walking, Stationery Eyes, Windup, Andrew Brown, 1930	850.00
Amos 'n' Andy, Andy, Walking, Moving Eyes, Windup, Marx, 1930s...................... 475.00 to 750.00	
Amos 'n' Andy, Andy, Walking, Stationery Eyes, Windup, Marx	850.00
Amos 'n' Andy, Sparkler, Squeeze Mechanism, Sparks Amos' Eyes, 1930s....................	460.00
Amos 'n' Andy, Sparkler, Squeeze, Sparks Glass Eyes, 1930s	560.00
Amos 'n' Andy, Walker, Moving Eyes, Marx, Box, c.1930, 11 In., Pair ....*illus*	3218.00
Amusement Park, Tin, Windup, Figures, Gondola Cars, Painted, Japanned, Moko, Germany, 12 In.	1765.00
Amusement Ride, Octopus, Tin Lithograph, Battery Operated, Japan ....*illus*	351.00
Amusement Ride, Roller Cars, Ramp, Figures, Tin Litho, Clockwork, Sports Land, 6 x 6 In. ..	489.00
Aquaman, Mego Figure, Bend 'n Flex, Kresge Card, NPP Inc., c.1972, 5 x 9 ¾ In.	173.00
Army Rocket, Tin, Friction, Japan, 1950s, 10 In.	95.00
Arnold Speedboat, Windup, Germany, 1950s, 9 ½ In.	225.00
Arnold The Acrobat, Motorcycle, Tin, Windup, c.1950, 11 ¼ x 8 ⅞ In.	690.00
Astronaut, Moon, Tin, Raises Arm Holding Gun, Firing Noise, Daiya, c.1955, 9 In.	4294.00
Atomic Boat, X-90, Tin, Crank Operation, Blade Propeller, Robot Driver, Japan, 14 In.	814.00
Atomic Rocket, Tin, Propeller, Masudaya, Box, 7 ½ In.	333.00
Atomic Spaceship XX-2, Tin, Plastic, Spark, Rubber Nosecone, Nomura, Box, 13 In.	198.00
Baby Bear, Sleeping, Mixed Material, 6 Actions, Battery Operated, Linemar, 9 In.	250.00
Baby Buggy, Victorian, Wood, Iron Fittings, Adjustable Leather & Silk Sunshade....................	950.00

Toy, Amos 'n' Andy, Walker, Moving Eyes, Marx, Box, c.1930, 11 In., Pair
$3218.00

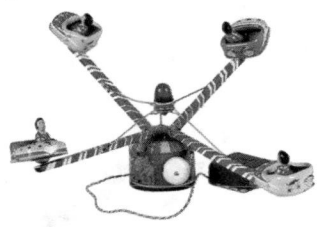

Toy, Amusement Ride, Octopus, Tin Lithograph, Battery Operated, Japan
$351.00

Toy, Ballerina, Parasol, Dangling Balls, Rotating, Bells, Windup, Kuramochi, 1930s, 13 In.
$607.00

T

Toy, Bell, Are You A Buffalo, Iron Base, Gong Bell Toy Co., c.1890, 5 ½ In.
$6325.00

Toy, Bicycle, Black Man Rider, Wood Stick, Penny Farthing, Push Toy, c.1895, 35 x 15 In.
$311.00

TIP

If you want to use your old sled, yet keep it in the best possible condition as a collectible, coat it with a liquid furniture wax, then buff it, then a few days later coat it with paste furniture wax. Even the metal can be waxed after you remove the rust—and the waxing should make the sled slide even faster.

Baby In Carriage, Tin Lithograph, Penny Toy, Fischer, Germany, 3 ¼ In. ... 5463.00
Baby, Creeping, Silk, Bonnet, Clockwork Movement, Ives, Box, 11 ½ In. ... 173.00
Baking Set, Glasbake, Our Betty Jane, Box, 1950s, 15 ½ x 17 ½ In. ... 144.00
Bale Master, Green, Aluminum, No. 9829, Oliver Corp., Box, 10 ¾ In. ... 358.00
Ball, Canvas, Painted, Red, White, Blue, 4 ½ In. ... 316.00
Ballerina, Parasol, Dangling Balls, Rotating, Bells, Windup, Kuramochi, 1930s, 13 In. ... *illus* 607.00
Barber, Shakes, Rubs In Hair Tonic On Customer, Dressed, Tin, Wire Windup, 8 In. ... 4025.00
Barney Google, Riding Sparkplug, Tin Litho, Windup, Nifty, c.1925, 7 In. ... 672.00 to 950.00
Barrel Roller, Man Rolls Barrels, Walks, Tin, Partially Dressed, Martin, 7 ½ In. ... 2875.00
Bear Wagon, Overland Circus, Driver, 2 Horses, Rider, Painted, Cast Iron, Kenton, 14 In. ... 530.00
Bear, Blacksmith, Mixed Material, 6 Actions, Battery Operated, 9 In. ... 225.00
Bear, Golfer, Mechanical, Tin Lithograph, Built-In Key, Windup, Box, 1950s, 4 x 5 In. ... 139.00
Bear, Growling, Head Turns, Jaw Moves, Windup, 1800s, 4 x 8 In. ... 862.00
Bear, Hungry, Rabbit Fur & Blood Dripping From Mouth, Claws, Windup, Ives, 1800s, 4 x 8 In. 863.00
Bear, Playing Cymbal, Mechanical Windup, German Emo, Box, 1950s ... 325.00
Bear, Reading, Cubby, Windup, Japan ... 120.00
Bear, Stuffed With Rags, Lamb's Wool, Black, Brown Nose, Crazy Quilt Vest, 1940s, 23 In. ... 395.00
Bears are also listed in the Teddy Bears category.
Bed, Doll's, Sheraton, Four-Poster, Tiger Maple, 1800s, 15 ½ x 9 ¾ x 14 ½ In. ... 702.00
Bed, Doll's, Victorian, Painted, Cast Iron, Scroll, Latticework, 7 ¾ x 14 x 8 In. ... 148.00
Bell Chimes, Saratoga, Child Rides Horse, Pulls Wagon, Tall Bell, Iron, J. & E. Stevens, 11 In. 144.00
Bell Push, On Stick, 1910 ... 225.00
Bell, Are You A Buffalo, Iron Base, Gong Bell Toy Co., c.1890, 5 ½ In. ... *illus* 6325.00
Bicycle, Black Man Rider, Wood Stick, Penny Farthing, Push Toy, c.1895, 35 x 15 In. ... *illus* 311.00
Bicycle, Men, Tin, Windup, Bicycle Rolls, Bell Rings, Painted, Germany, 7 In. ... 4095.00
Bicycle, Riders, 2 Big Wheels, Circle Base, Painted, Tin, Windup, Germany, 9 In. ... 1910.00
Bicycles, 2 Cyclists Rotate Base, Tin, Windup, Painted, Germany, 9 In. ... 1989.00
Bicycles that are large enough to ride are listed in their own category.
Bicyclists, Tandem, 2 Tin Figures, Ornate Wheels, Bell Hubs, Clockwork, Gunthermann, 8 In. 173.00
Bicyclists, Tandem, 2 Tin Riders, Circle, Articulated Legs, Bicycle, Clockwork, France, 8 In. ... 748.00
Big Ben, Hand Carved, Working Clock, Wood, c.1920, 36 In. ... 402.00
Bill Bailey, Coming Home, Walks, Lamppost, Cane, Tin, Windup, M & K, Germany, 1904, 7 In. 1200.00
Binoculars, Tom Corbett, Aluminum, Red Eye Pieces, Decals, Herold Mfg. Co., 5 In. ... 173.00
Bird, In Cage, Yellow Bird, Chirps, Hanger, Windup, Japan, 8 In. ... 150.00 to 195.00
Bird, Singing, Cage, Windup, Germany, 3 ½ In. ... 112.00
Bison, Fur, Hide Covered, Harness, Glass Eyes, Nose Chain, Cast Wheels, Pull Toy, 15 In. ... 173.00
Black Mammy, Pull Toy, Jay Mar Products, U.S.A., 1930, 3 ½ In. ... 56.00
Black Man, Dances On Box, Crank, Germany Penny Toy, Distler ... 350.00
Black Man, Woman Dancing, Tin, Windup, Gunthermann, 6 ¼ In. ... 4025.00
Blimp, Pony, Blue, Kenton, 5 ½ In. ... 295.00
Blinky The Circus Clown, Walker, Eyes Light, Battery Operated, Box ... 175.00
Block Set, Alphabets, 2 Sets Of Numbers, Wooden, Carved, Box, I. Dierdorff, 4 x 14 x 6 In. ... 495.00
Boat, 2 Boys, In Boats, Rowing, Wood, Papier-Mache, Painted, Pull Toy, 5 ½ x 8 In. ... 1970.00
Boat, Aircraft Carrier, Battery Operated, Marx, 1950s ... 395.00
Boat, Battleship, Cast Iron, Multicolored, Gun Turrets, Masts, Wilkens Kearsarge, 14 In. ... 1035.00
Boat, Battleship, Gray, Black, Masts, Flags, Fleischmann, 21 In. ... 3800.00
Boat, Battleship, Gray, Flag, Spoked Wheels, Tootsietoy, 2 ½ In. ... 135.00
Boat, Battleship, New York, Lithographed Paper, Wooden Guns, Porthole, Bliss, 28 In. ... 173.00
Boat, Big Wood, Flying Yankee, Windup, U.S.A., 1920, 18 In. ... 575.00
Boat, Bremen Travel Agency, Enameled Tin, Lighting, Portholes, Stand, Marklin, 38 In. ... 7475.00
Boat, Cannon, Gray, Decal, Clockwork, Turns 180 Degrees, Germany, 19 In. ... 1035.00
Boat, Excursion, M-1024, Sun Roof, Tin, Crank, Japan, 1950s, 10 In. ... 145.00
Boat, Ferry, Union, Flat Platform, Removable Stack, Paddle Wheel, Bing, Germany, 16 In. ... 920.00
Boat, Launch, Brass, Neptune Steam Propeller, Boiler, Ives, Box, c.1890s, 11 In. ... 1265.00
Boat, Liner, Tin, Clockwork, 2 Masts, Stacks, Lifeboats, Fleischmann, Germany, c.1936, 12 In. 748.00
Boat, Luxury Liner, Friction, Tin, Marx, U.S.A., 14 ½ In. ... 145.00
Boat, Mighty Atom Speedboat, Moves Forward In Water, Tada, Japan, Box, 7 In. ... 518.00
Boat, Ocean Liner, Queen Janie, 2 Masts, 3 Deck Superstructure, 3 Stacks, 21 In. ... 1150.00
Boat, Ocean Queen, Crank Friction, Japan, 10 In. ... 295.00
Boat, Putt Putt, Metal, Windup, Box, U.S.A., 1930s, 5 In. ... 75.00
Boat, Racing, Diamond, Battery Operated, Japan, 1950, 8 ½ In. ... 195.00
Boat, Reed Ocean Wave, Paper On Wood, Sails, Cargo, Sailors, Anchor, 36 In. ... 805.00
Boat, Riverboat, Green Hull, Pilot's Cabin, Figure At Helm, Penny Toy, Meier, Germany, 4 ⅝ In. 575.00
Boat, Rowboat, Wooden, Black, 3 Oarsmen, c.1922, 18 ½ In. ... 748.00
Boat, Sailboat, Ladders, Flywheel, Spokes, Tin Litho, Fischer, Penny Toy, Germany, 4 ½ In. ... 345.00
Boat, Sailboat, Sailor, White, Red, Hipp-Hipp, Tin, Windup, Marked, Hans Ebrel, 9 In. ... 605.00

Boat, Scull, Tin, Painted, 2 Figures Rowing, Penny Toy, Germany, 6 ½ In.	920.00
Boat, Shore Patrol, Guns, Battery Operated, Japan, 1950s, 8 ½ In.	145.00
Boat, Speed, Remote, Japan, c.1950, 11 In.	225.00
Boat, Speedboat, Boucher, Live Steam, Compressed Air Cylinder, Mahogany, Brass, 48 In.	3450.00
Boat, Speedboat, Driver, Static, Red, Cast Iron, Hubley, 10 In.	4100.00
Boat, Speedboat, Driver, Wheels, Motor, White, Red, Silver, Partial Decals, Iron, Hubley, 10 In.	4388.00
Boat, Speedboat, Helmsman, Hand On Throttle, Mounted Engine, Iron, Green, Hubley, 10 In.	431.00
Boat, Speedboat, Iron, Passengers, Motor Tender, Painted Blue, Gold Striping, Hubley, 14 In. .	8625.00
Boat, Speedboat, Meccano Metal, Windup, Hornby, England, Box, 1930s, 12 ½ In.	675.00
Boat, Speedboat, Metal, Battery Operated, Japan, 1950s, 12 In.	145.00
Boat, Speedboat, Outboard Motor, Cast Iron, 2 Rubber Tires, Hubley, 4 ¾ In.	450.00
Boat, Speedboat, Passenger, Wheels, Green Paint, 45 ½ In.	176.00
Boat, Speedboat, Tin, Battery Operated, Japan, 1950s, 10 ½ In.	225.00
Boat, Speedboat, Tin, Faded Red, Green Paint, Lindstrom, 7 ¾ In.	47.00
Boat, Speedboat, Tin, Windup, Arnold, Compo Driver, Germany, 1950s, 10 In.	175.00
Boat, Speedboat, Twin Screw, Lights, Metal Trim, Black, Red, Wood, Ito, Japan, 18 In.	450.00
Boat, Speedboat, Windup, Lindstrom, 14 In.	175.00
Boat, Spring Wound Motor, Figures, Tin, Lionel, Stand, c.1935, 17 In.	383.00
Boat, Steamboat, Canopy, Bell, Stack, Pilot's Station, Tin Litho, Pull Toy, Orobr, c.1915, 10 In.	1840.00
Boat, Steamship, Tin Lithograph, Clockwork, Flag, 8 ¼ In.	605.00
Boat, Torpedo, Tin, Battery Operated, Japan, Box, 1950s, 11 In.	175.00
Boat, Tugboat, Tin, Sound, Smoke, Marusan, Box, 13 ½ In.	185.00
Boat, Warship, Clockwork, Bing, Germany, c.1909-12, 19 In.	805.00
Boat, Water Boat, Driver, Front Propeller Spins, Pontoons, Tin Lithograph, Windup, 9 In.	890.00
Bobbin' Head, Beetle Bailey, Zero, King Features Syndicate Copyright, 1960s, 7 ½ In.	151.00
Bombo The Monkey, Swings From Palm Tree, Tin, Windup, Unique Art, Box	70.00
Boxers, Knockout Champs, Move Around Metal Ring, Celluloid, Windup, Marx, Box, 1930s....	650.00
Boy, Clown Suit, Drumming, Windup, Box, 12 ¼ In.	204.00
Boy, Diavolo Top, Painted, Tin, Dressed, Raises Hands, Balances Diavolo, Windup, 7 In.	3738.00
Boy, Drummer, Drum Stand, Celluloid, Tin Lithograph, Windup, 10 ½ In.	431.00
Boy, Drumming Sailor, Windup, Japan, Box, 11 In.	187.00
Boy, Girl Dance Tango, Tin, Windup, Back, Forth Action, Gunthermann, Box, 7 In.	2587.00
Boy, Holding Sister's Hand, Dutch Style Clothing, Felt Faces, Arms, Windup, Bing, 9 ½ In.	259.00
Boy, In Car, Goggles, Tin Lithograph, Modern Toys, c.1935, 6 ¼ In.	1760.00
Boy, Kicking Ball, Spins Around Base, Tin, Celluloid, Painted, Germany, 12 In.	815.00
Boy, On Sled, Painted, Tin, Windup, Marked, JHL, Germany, 6 ½ In.	560.00
Boy, On Sled, Tin, Painted, Windup, Hess, Germany, c.1915, 7 In. ....*illus*	334.00
Boy, On Stilts, Walker, Painted, Tin, Windup, Germany, 9 In.	1100.00
Boy, Playing Ball With Cat, Tin, Windup, Pulls String, Cat Bats Ball, Gunthermann, 10 In.	1380.00
Boy, Riding Tricycle, Bisque Head, Molded Hair, Clockwork, 1800s, 16 ½ x 15 In. ....*illus*	4388.00
Boy, Spinning Weights, Painted, Tin, Windup, Germany, 8 In.	600.00
Boy, Stick Horse, Celluloid, Tin Lithograph, Japan, Box, 7 ½ In.	518.00
Boy, Walks Dog, Nods Head, Tin, Windup, Gunthermann, 6 ½ In.	2588.00
Boy, Weights, Tin, Windup, Arms Spin Weight Pins, Painted, Germany, 8 In.	644.00
Bridge, Buses, Cars On Bridge, Tin Lithograph, Clockwork, Marx, Box, 24 In.	863.00
Bridge, George Washington, Tin Lithograph, Greyhound Bus, Clockwork, 25 In.	1150.00
Bridge, Pedestrian, Open Stairs, Hand Operated Signals, Bing, 16 x 13 In.	518.00
Bugs Bunny, Molded White Vinyl, Holding Cane & Straw Hat, 1970s, 3 In.	18.00
Building, Fireman At Pump, Climbs Ladder, Clockwork, Wood Building, 19 ½ In.	518.00
Bulldozer Blade, Green, Aluminum, John Deere, Box, 2 x 6 ¼ x 5 ¼ In.	150.00
Bulldozer, Caterpillar, Tin, Driver, Doepke	350.00
Bulldozer, Tin, Driver, Lighted Eyes, Battery Operated, Yoshiya, Box, 7 In.	282.00
Bullwinkle Magic Color Kit, Gold Medal Flour Premium, 1962, 5 ½ x 7 ½ In., 8 Pages	195.00
Bus, 7 Figures On Top, Green, Red, White Tires, Kenton, 1927, 12 In.	3360.00
Bus, Chicago World's Fair, Iron, Closed Cab, Passenger Trailer, Box, 1933, 7 ½ In.	546.00
Bus, Coach, Cast Aluminum, Blue, White Roof, Embossed, Rubber Tires, 19 ½ In.	4600.00
Bus, Coast To Coast, Driver, Green, Cast Iron, 10 In.	500.00
Bus, Coast To Coast, Greyhound, Packard, Lights, Steering Handle, Keystone, 1930s, 32 In.	5750.00
Bus, Coast To Coast, Light Blue, Embossed, Nickel Wheels, Cast Iron, 13 In.	1030.00
Bus, Double-Decker, 4 Passengers, Green, Cast Iron, Arcade, 3 ½ x 8 In.	495.00
Bus, Double-Decker, Driver, Yellow Coach, Cast Iron, Bench Seating, Arcade, c.1920, 13 ½ In. .	1265.00
Bus, Double-Decker, Green, Cast Iron, Rubber Tires, Arcade, 8 In.	320.00
Bus, Double-Decker, Green, Nickeled Grille, Passengers, Arcade, 1940, 8 In.	500.00
Bus, Double-Decker, Iron, Green, Bench Seating, Rear Stairs, Rubber Tires, Arcade, 7 ½ In. ...	288.00
Bus, Double-Decker, Kenton City, Figures, Stairway, Rubber Tires, 10 In.	1150.00
Bus, Double-Decker, Lithograph, Painted Tin, Windup, Rear Staircase, Lehmann, 8 In.	863.00

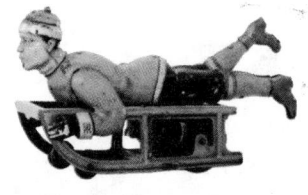

Toy, Boy, On Sled, Tin, Painted, **Windup,** Hess, Germany, c.1915, 7 In. $334.00

Toy, Boy, Riding Tricycle, Bisque **Head,** Molded Hair, Clockwork, 1800s, 16 ½ x 15 In. $4388.00

Souvenir Mug

A souvenir mug is decorated or shaped to remind you of a location or event.

T

Toy, Bus, Double-Decker, Painted, Cast Iron, Disc Wheels, Kenton, 6 In. $878.00

Toy, Bus, Mack 6, 3 Colors, Nickel Plated Bumper, Rubber Tires, Arcade, 13 In. $8625.00

Toy, Calliope, Royal Circus, Deluxe, Plumed Horses, Embossed, Hubley, Box, c.1915, 16 In. $23085

Toy, Candlestick, Doll's, Pressed Glass, 3 x 2 In., Pair $50.00

Bus, Double-Decker, Nickel Passengers, Green, Cast Iron, Rubber Tires, Arcade, 8 In.	340.00
Bus, Double-Decker, Painted, Cast Iron, Disc Wheels, Kenton, 6 In. .... *illus*	878.00
Bus, Double-Decker, Red, Green, Cast Iron, Kenton, 9 ¾ In.	445.00
Bus, Double-Decker, Tin, 6 Wheels, Electric Lights, Driver, Clockwork, Gunthermann, 20 ½ In.	1840.00
Bus, Double-Decker, Windup, Penny Toy, Distler, 4 ½ In.	204.00
Bus, Double-Decker, Yellow Coach, Dual Rear Wheels, Rubber Tires, Arcade, 13 ½ In.	920.00
Bus, Driver, Electric Lights, Tin Lithograph, Clockwork, Distler, c.1920, 15 ½ In.	3738.00
Bus, Driver, White, Green, Cast Iron, Grille, Nickel Disc Wheels, Spares, Arcade, c.1928, 13 In.	4600.00
Bus, Express, Wolverine, U.S.A., 1950s, 14 In.	195.00
Bus, Fageol Coach, Green, Cast Iron, Rubber Tires, Arcade, 8 In.	256.00
Bus, George Fischer, 5 ⅞ In.	413.00
Bus, Green, Red, Kenton, 10 In.	850.00
Bus, Greyhound, Century Of Progress, Chicago, Painted, Iron, Arcade, 1933, 8 In., 2 Piece	115.00
Bus, Greyhound, Century Of Progress, Driver, GMC Tractor, 1933, 7 ½ In.	235.00
Bus, Greyhound, Century Of Progress, Driver, GMC Tractor, 1933, 11 ½ In.	325.00
Bus, Greyhound, Iron, Blue, White, Nickel Grille, Rubber Tires, Arcade, Box, c.1937, 8 ¾ In.	920.00
Bus, Greyhound, Pressed Steel, Blue, White, Battery Lights, Clockwork, Buddy L, 16 ½ In.	345.00
Bus, Greyhound, Steel, Rubber Tires, Clockwork, Lights, Grille, Kingsbury, c.1938, 16 In.	748.00
Bus, Greyhound, World's Fair, Cast Iron, 1939, 7 In.	195.00
Bus, Hercules, Tin Lithograph, Orange, Blue, Red, Bench Seating, Chien, c.1928, 18 In.	1725.00
Bus, Honeymooners, Jackie Gleason, Tin Litho, Star Passengers, Wolverine, Box, 13 ½ In.	711.00
Bus, Interstate, Upper Deck, Driver, Stairs, Clockwork, Metal Wheels, Tin, Strauss, Box, 10 In.	805.00
Bus, Jackie Gleason, Wolverine, U.S.A., 1950s, 14 In.	475.00
Bus, Junior, Tin Lithograph, Windup, Chein, 9 In.	288.00
Bus, Mack 6, 3 Colors, Nickel Plated Bumper, Rubber Tires, Arcade, 13 In. .... *illus*	8625.00
Bus, Open Door, Table, Chair, Tin, Friction, Japan, 1950s, 11 ½ In.	145.00
Bus, Passenger, Kingsbury, Steel, Clockwork, Rubber Tires, License, c.1925, 16 In.	4313.00
Bus, Raised Roof, Emblazoned White On Grill, Disc Wheels, Blue, Arcade, 13 In.	5175.00
Bus, Red, Passenger Silhouettes, Tin Lithograph, Holland, 21 In.	1150.00
Bus, Red, Plastic, Schuco, 1960s, 3 ½ In.	75.00
Bus, Robocon, Rolls Forward, Friction Motor, Masudaya, Japan, Box, 16 In.	805.00
Bus, Stairway, Tin Lithograph, Clockwork, Lehmann, Box, 8 ¼ In.	3163.00
Bus, Steel, Blue, Red Band, Radiator, Black Fenders, Clockwork, Bench, Kingsbury, 1928, 16 In.	2070.00
Bus, Steel, Dual Rear Tires, Doors Open, Buddy L, 28 ½ In.	6325.00
Bus, Steel, Painted Green, Spares, Running Boards, Nickel Lights, Bumper, Buddy L, 28 In.	489.00
Bus, Tin, Windup, Portugal, 9 ½ In.	120.00
Bus, Touring, Tippco, Tin Lithograph, Clockwork, Removable Top, Driver, c.1920, 17 In.	4600.00
Buttercup & Spareribs, Tin Lithograph, Pull Toy, Motion, Nifty Co., c.1920, 7 ½ In.	633.00
Button, Daredevil, Official Member Superhero Club, Cello, Marvel Comics, 3 ½ In.	201.00
Cab, Horse Drawn, Fischer, c.1910, 4 ¾ In.	292.00
Cackling Hen, White, Legs & Wings Go Up & Down, Pull Toy, 1958, 8 ½ x 10 In.	85.00
Cake Walker, Hanging Dancing Figure, Wooden Stage, J.M. Cromwell, c.1879, 9 ¾ In.	403.00
Calculator, Boy, Chalkboard, Tin Litho, Clockwork, Tipp & Co., Germany, c.1925, 7 ½ In.	460.00
Calliope, Overland Circus, Driver, 2 Horses, Riders, Painted, Cast Iron, Kenton, 15 In.	200.00
Calliope, Royal Circus, Deluxe, Plumed Horses, Embossed, Hubley, Box, c.1915, 16 In. ..... *illus*	23085.00
Camel, Painted Eyes, Schoenhut	250.00
Camel, Painted Wood, Jointed, Closed Mouth, Leather Ear, Glass Eyes, Schoenhut, 8 In.	254.00
Camera, Bugs Bunny, Figural, Bugs Reclining, Reads Eh Doc Smile, By Helm, 1976, 5 In.	20.00
Candlestick, Doll's, Pressed Glass, 3 x 2 In., Pair .... *illus*	50.00
Cannon, Iron Wheels, Soft Wood Caisson, 1900s, 38 In.	823.00
Cannon, Metal, Tippco, Germany, 1930s, 6 In.	225.00
Canoe, Wood, Ribbed Interior, Green, Old Town Canoe, Sample, c.1900, 48 x 9 In.	18400.00
Cap Bomb, Abraham Lincoln, Nickel Plated, Cast Iron, 1 ½ In.	120.00
Cap Bomb, Admiral Dewey, Cast Iron, 1 ¾ In.	140.00
Cap Bomb, Andrew Jackson, Nickel Finish, Cast Iron, 1 ¾ In.	125.00
Cap Bomb, Bulldog, Pistol, Japanned Finish, Cast Iron, Pat. June 21, 1887, 4 In.	310.00
Cap Bomb, Deadshot, Powder Barrel Form, Cast Iron, 1 x 1 ¼ In.	75.00
Cap Bomb, Elephant, Firecracker, Cast Iron, Ives, c.1900, 3 ¾ x 2 ½ In.	92.00
Cap Bomb, George Washington, Nickel Finish, Cast Iron, 1 ½ In.	112.00
Cap Bomb, Niggerhead, Cast Iron, Pat. Mar. 22, 1887, 4 ½ In.	555.00
Cap Bomb, Pickaninny, Nickel Finish, Cast Iron, Ives, 2 ½ In.	210.00
Cap Bomb, Yellow Kid, Nickel Finish, Cast Iron, 1 ½ x 1 ½ In.	60.00
Cap Cane, Eagle Handle, Wood, Cast Iron, c.1900, 32 In.	115.00
Cap Gun, 6 Shot, Flowers, Cast Iron, Stevens, Pat'd U.S.A., Jan. 22., 1895, 6 ¾ In.	255.00
Cap Gun, Atom Disintegrator, Hubley, 7 ¼ In.	350.00

Cap Gun, Bronco, 6-Shooter Action, Kilgore, Box, 10 In.	135.00
Cap Gun, Buffalo Bill, Cast Iron, Marked, S, Kenton, c.1925, 11 ⅜ In.	118.00
Cap Gun, Bullet Loading Fanner 50, 8 Bullets, Mattel, Box, 10 In.	263.00
Cap Gun, Captain America, Plastic, Original Bag, 5 In. ....*illus*	59.00
Cap Gun, Daisy, Die Cast, Single Shot, Silver Finish, Plastic Stag Grips, 8 ½ In.	135.00
Cap Gun, Duck, Figural, Cast Iron, 4 ½ x 3 ¾ In.	550.00
Cap Gun, Lightning Express, Locomotive, Cast Iron, Kenton, c.1900, 4 ½ In.	360.00
Cap Gun, Magazine, Cast Iron, Nickel Plated, Pat'd April 26, 1892, 7 ¼ In.	275.00
Cap Gun, Mule & Clown, Mule Kicks Clown In Butt, Cast Iron, 5 x 5 ½ In.	232.00
Cap Gun, Presto, Kilgore, Box, 5 ½ In.	80.00
Cap Gun, Private Eye, Circle K, Badge, Kilgore, Box..	80.00
Cap Gun, Punch & Judy, Cast Iron, 6 x 5 ½ In.	358.00
Cap Gun, Red Ranger, Jeweled & Embossed Leather Holster, 8 ½ In.	55.00
Cap Gun, Red Ranger Jr., Automatic Repeater, Wyandotte, Box, 8 In.	115.00
Cap Gun, Sea Serpent Form, Cast Iron, J. & E. Stevens, c.1890, 4 In.	465.00
Cap Gun, Sheriff, Engraved, Wyandotte, Box, 8 In.	80.00
Cap Gun, Shoot The Hat, Man Puts Hat On Seated Man, Cast Iron, 4 ½ x 4 ¾ In. ...	330.00
Cap Gun, Stallion 45, Nichols, 12 In.	45.00
Cap Gun, The Forty Five, Cast Iron, Made In U.S.A., National, c.1928, 11 In.	118.00
Cap Gun, The Sheriff, White Handle, Stevens, 9 In.	35.00
Cap Gun, Victor, Cast Iron, 5 ½ In.	130.00
Cap Gun, Western, 250 Shot Repeater, Hubley, On Card, 8 In.	115.00
Cap Gun, Wild Bill Hickok 44, Leslie-Henry, 11 In.	56.00
Cap Gun, Wild West, Cast Iron, Kenton, c.1926, 10 ½ In.	240.00
Capitol Hill Racer, Box, U.S.A., 1930s, 18 In.	195.00
Car, 3 Wheels, Driver, Long Bonnet, Tin Litho, Clockwork, Germany, Fisher, 6 In.	1093.00
Car, Andy Gump, 348 Deluxe, Painted Multicolor, Iron, Arcade, 7 In. ....*illus*	878.00
Car, Andy Gump, Cast, 1920s, 3 ½ In.	110.00
Car, Armored, Canon, Penny Toy, Distler, Germany..	285.00
Car, Armored, Pressed Steel, Cast Spokes, Lanterns, Clockwork, France, Pre 1940, 13 In.	575.00
Car, Austin, Coupe, Blue, Nickeled Wheels, A.C. Williams, 3 ¾ In.	275.00
Car, Austin Healey, Blue, Japan, Box, 8 ½ In.	295.00
Car, Austin Healey, Yellow, Dinky Toys, 1857, 3 ½ In.	55.00
Car, BMW, Turbo, Steering Mechanism, Battery Operated, Schuco, 13 In.	295.00
Car, Boat Tail Roadster, Windup, Penny Toy, 4 ½ In.	275.00
Car, Buick, Coupe, Tin, Friction, Germany, 1950s, 13 In.	295.00
Car, Buick, Coupe, Tin, Friction, Hub Caps, Japan, 1954, 10 ½ In.	295.00
Car, Buick, Sedan, La Sabre, Blue, Tin Lithograph, Friction, Box, 1961, 16 In.	863.00
Car, Cadillac, Convertible, Doors, Hood, Trunk Open, Plastic, Die Cast, Battery, Schuco, 12 In.	225.00
Car, Cadillac, Convertible, Tin, Friction, White, Red Interior, Bandai, Japan, 1959, 11 In.	345.00
Car, Cadillac, Fat, Tin, Friction, Japan, 1954, 9 ½ In.	175.00
Car, Cadillac, Head Lights, Horn, Battery Operated, Korea, 1960s, 13 In.	175.00
Car, Cadillac, Sedan, Red, Rubber Tires, Friction, Seating, Yonezawa, Japan, Box, 22 In.	254.00
Car, Cadillac, Stunt, Rolls Over, Battery Operated, Japan, Box, 11 In.	175.00
Car, Cadillac, Tin, Battery Operated, Headlights, Japan, 1954, 9 In.	95.00
Car, Cadillac, Tin, Painted, Battery Operated, Numura, Japan, 1950s, 13 ½ In.	345.00
Car, Chevrolet, Coupe, Gray, Black, Arcade, 1928, 8 In.	1500.00
Car, Chevrolet, Coupe, Painted Iron, Nickel Wheels, Mounted Spare, Arcade, 8 In.	920.00
Car, Chevrolet, LaSalle, Blue, Battery Headlights, Steel, All Metal Prod. Co., 15 In.	405.00
Car, Chevrolet, LaSalle, Sedan, Convertible, Tan, Green, Die Cast, Tootsietoy, 1934, 4 ½ In.	285.00
Car, Chevrolet, Red, Yellow Top, License No. LM-200, Friction, Linemar, 1955, 3 x 11 In.	880.00
Car, Chevrolet, Sedan, 2 Doors, Gray, Black Roof, White, Friction, Box, 1954, 11 In.	259.00
Car, Chevrolet, Sedan, 2 Doors, Red, Yellow, White Stripe, Nickel Plated, Friction, 1954, 11 ¼ In.	6900.00
Car, Chevrolet, Sedan, Painted, Iron Wheels, Mounted Spare Arcade, 8 In.	863.00
Car, Chevrolet, Tin, Friction, Japan, 1963, 11 In.	175.00
Car, Chitty Chitty Bang Bang, Die Cast, Corgi, Box, 1968..................................	220.00
Car, Chrysler, Airflow, Green Paint, Rubber Tires, Cast Iron, Hubley, 6 In.	89.00
Car, Chrysler, Airflow, Salmon Paint, Rubber Tires, Cast Iron, Hubley, 4 ½ In.	110.00
Car, Chrysler, Airflow, Tan Paint, Rubber Tires, Cast Iron, Hubley, 6 In.	105.00
Car, Chrysler, Coupe, Airflow, 1935, Cast Iron, Battery Operated, Hubley, Box, 7 In.	460.00
Car, Chrysler, Imperial, Cream Seating, Nickel Finish, Ashi Toys, Japan, 1962, 15 In.	2070.00
Car, Chrysler, Newport, Sedan, Yellow, Orange, Chrome, Rubber Tires, Friction, 1957, 14 In. ...	6900.00
Car, Chrysler, Sedan, Airflow, 1934, Cast Iron, Battery Operated, Hubley, 8 ½ In.	259.00
Car, Chrysler, Sedan, Green, Hubley, 6 ½ In.	450.00
Car, Chrysler, Town Car, Airflow, Cast Iron, Battery Operated, Hubley, 1935, 7 ½ In.	288.00
Car, Circus Parade, Bear, Makes Noise, Goes Up, Down, Japan, 1960s...................	110.00

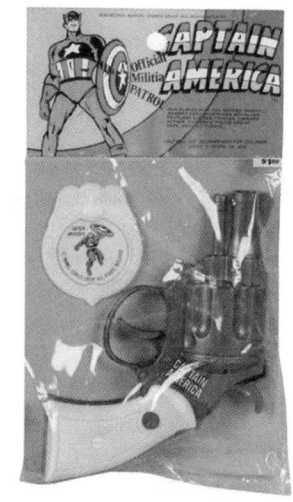

Toy, Cap Gun, Captain America, Plastic, Original Bag, 5 In.
$59.00

Toy, Car, Andy Gump, 348 Deluxe, Painted Multicolor, Iron, Arcade, 7 In.
$878.00

Toy, Car, Crazy, Uncle Wiggily,
Tin Lithograph, Head Turns, c.1935, 8 In.
$1792.00

Car, Circus, Tin, Windup, 5 In.	175.00
Car, Citroen, B6, Coupe, Gray, Running Boards, Electric Lights, Spare, Clockwork, 16 In.	1035.00
Car, Convertible, Red Tin Lithograph, Deco Style, 17 In.	635.00
Car, Convertible, Take-Apart, Yellow, Black, Rubber Tires, Cast Iron, Hubley, 6 In.	530.00
Car, Convertible, Tin, Friction, Linemar, 1950s, 8 ½ In.	375.00
Car, Corvette, Coupe, Cougar, Battery Operated, Japan, 15 In.	295.00
Car, Corvette, Friction, Tin Lithograph, Orange, Bandai, 1950s, 8 In.	115.00
Car, Corvette, Tin, Battery Operated, Stop & Go, Japan, 8 ½ In.	175.00
Car, Coupe, Blue, Pressed Steel, Plastic Top, Pop Up Lights, Buddy L, 1968-69, 9 In.	250.00
Car, Coupe, Canvas Top, Driver, Electric Lights, Nickel Bumpers, Gunthermann, c.1930s, 15 In.	6900.00
Car, Coupe, Driver, Green, Nickel, Cast Iron, Hubley, 9 In.	840.00
Car, Coupe, Driver, Tin Litho, Luggage, Spare Wheel, Head Lights, Distler, c.1930, 16 In.	2875.00
Car, Coupe, Ingap, Tin Lithograph, Red, Spare Tire, Driver, Clockwork Driven, Box, 13 ½ In.	4025.00
Car, Coupe, Painted Steel, Fly Wheel Mechanism, Schieble, 18 In.	259.00
Car, Coupe, Red, Pressed Steel, Rubber Wheels, Windup, 1940s, 5 ½ In.	45.00
Car, Coupe, Red, Pressed Steel, Tin, Rubber, Wyandotte, 9 In.	105.00
Car, Coupe, Red, White Rubber Tires, Hubley, 1930s, 4 ½ In.	110.00
Car, Coupe, Rumble Seat, Blue, Electric Headlights, Clockwork, Kingsbury, 12 ¾ In.	720.00
Car, Coupe, Spare Wheel On Side, White, Orange, Green, Rubber Wheels, Die Cast, 4 In.	118.00
Car, Coupe, Steel, Blue, Tan Roof, Rumble Seat, Headlights, Kingsbury, c.1931, 12 In.	5175.00
Car, Crash Car, Indian, Blue Driver, Red, Cast Iron, 11 ½ In.	1500.00
Car, Crazy, Removable Suitcase, Tin, Windup, Marx, 1920s	750.00
Car, Crazy, Uncle Wiggily, Tin Lithograph, Head Turns, c.1935, 8 In. ....*illus*	1792.00
Car, Crown, Wings, Red, Yellow, Black, Embossed, 5 ½ x 9 In.	232.00
Car, Delivery, Tin Lithograph, 3 Wheels, Driver, Rear Door Opens, Hoge, Box, 10 In.	4312.00
Car, Edsel, Station Wagon, Tin, Friction, Gray, Yellow, White, Nomura, 1958, 11 In.	600.00
Car, Electric Motor, Battery, Removable Seat, Wood, Spokes, Ohlmacher, Box, 10 In.	1380.00
Car, Electric, Tiller, Painted Wood, Metal Axle, Battery Storage, Rubber Tires, 10 In.	2875.00
Car, Ferrari, Speed Demon, Battery Operated, Driver, Japan, Box, 1960, 11 In.	375.00
Car, Fiat, Coupe, Electric Light, Tin Litho, Tan, Orange, Blue, Driver, Clockwork, Ingap, 7 In.	3153.00
Car, Fire Chief, No. 1, Red, Tin Lithograph, Friction, Battery Operated, Marx, 11 ¼ In.	115.00
Car, Fire Department, Lupor, Box, 1950, 10 ½ In.	175.00
Car, Fire, Metal, Battery Operated, Japan, 1950s, 9 ½ In.	295.00
Car, Flattop Cab, Rubber Tires & Spare, Arcade, 1929, 8 ½ In.	2500.00
Car, Flywheel Drive, Driver, Penny Toy, 4 ¼ In.	132.00
Car, Flywheel Drive, Issmayer, Driver, Penny Toy, 4 ¼ In.	132.00
Car, Ford, Battery Operated, Plays Music, London Bridge, Japan, 1955, 8 ½ In.	195.00
Car, Ford, Convertible, 1940, Red, Gold, Silver, Tootsietoy, 5 ½ In.	150.00
Car, Ford, Convertible, Blue, Tin Lithograph, Rubber Tires, Steering Wheel, 1956, 11 In.	1150.00
Car, Ford, Convertible, Tin, Friction, Driver, Dog Makes Noise, Japan, 1955, 7 ½ In.	225.00
Car, Ford, Convertible, Tin, Friction, Japan, c.1962, 8 In.	145.00
Car, Ford, Coupe, Blue Roof, Tin, Friction, Rubber Tires, Hood Open, Fan, Japan, Box, 10 ¾ In.	460.00
Car, Ford, Dog, Happy Pup, Tin, Japan, 1962, 18 In.	245.00
Car, Ford, Fairlane 500, Convertible, Red, Black Fins, Friction, Japan, Box, 1957, 12 In.	1265.00
Car, Ford, Fairlane, Driver, Passenger, Tin, Japan, 12 In.	9605.00
Car, Ford, Fairlane, Tin, Friction, Japan, 1985, 8 In.	120.00
Car, Ford, G Men, Battery Operated, Japan, 1954, 10 In.	145.00
Car, Ford, Model A, Coupe, Orange, Striping, Spoke Wheels, Rumble Seat, Arcade, c.1930, 6 ½ In.	633.00
Car, Ford, Model A, Green, Black, Litho Wheels, Upton, 6 ½ In.	265.00
Car, Ford, Model A, Sedan, 2 Door, Nickeled Spoke Wheels, Arcade, 6 ½ In.	900.00
Car, Ford, Model T, Coupe, Blue Nickeled Spoke Wheels, Kilgore, 5 In.	350.00
Car, Ford, Model T, Coupe, Gray, Nickeled Wheels, Driver, Kilgore, 6 ½ In.	375.00
Car, Ford, Model T, Roadmaster, Driver, Bing	690.00
Car, Ford, Ranchero, Red, Black, Fairlane, Tin Litho, Tailgate, Bandai, Japan, 1957, 11 ⅝ In.	1093.00
Car, Ford, Sedan, Painted Tin Lithograph, Driver, Windup, Bing, 6 ¼ In.	316.00
Car, Ford, Sedan, Painted Tin, Windup, 2 Opening Rear Doors, Orbor, 6 In.	288.00
Car, Ford, Taurus, Battery Operated, Remote, Japan, 8 ½ In.	95.00
Car, Ford, Thunderbird, Battery Operated, Japan, 1960	225.00
Car, Ford, Tin, Friction, Japan, Box, 1958, 8 ½ In.	195.00
Car, Garage, Embossed Roof, Fischer, 5 In., Penny	121.00
Car, Green Hornet, 3 Missile Launchers, Die Cast, Corgi, Box, 1966, 6 In.	275.00
Car, Hot Rod, Battery Operated, 10 In.	295.00
Car, Hot Rod, Tin, Friction, Moving Piston, Japan, 1963, 9 In.	225.00
Car, Humphrey Mobile, Joe Palooka, Windup, Wyandotte, 1940s	425.00
Car, Humphrey Mobile, Metal, Windup, Wyandotte, 9 In.	345.00
Car, Humphrey Mobile, Windup, Wyandott, Box, 1940s	650.00

Car, Jaguar, Tin, Friction, Green Top, Yellow, Japan, 1950s, 10 In.	175.00
Car, Jaguar, XK-120, Light Blue, Doepke, 18 In.	425.00
Car, Just Married, Bride & Groom, Battery Operated, Japan, 1950s, 10 ½ In.	45.00
Car, Kaiser, Green Enamel, Aluminum, Wheels, Bumper, Grill, Steering Wheel	1495.00
Car, Kingsbury, Sedan, Red, Black, Gold, Rumble Seat, 5 x 13 x 5 In.	275.00
Car, Limousine, Carl Bubb, Windup, Driver, 1920s, 11 In.	1050.00
Car, Limousine, Delage, Maroon, Running Boards, Grill, Clockwork, France, c.1930, 13 In.	1380.00
Car, Limousine, Driver, Green, 4 Suitcases, Beveled Windows, Tin, Windup, Carette, 16 In.	6200.00
Car, Limousine, Driver, Green, Doors, Windows, Lamps, Roof Rack, Tires, Carette, 12 In.	2588.00
Car, Limousine, Driver, Green, Tin Litho, Padded Doors, Celluloid Windows, Hess, c.1920, 10 In.	5463.00
Car, Limousine, Driver, Spoke Wheels, Rubber Tires, Clockwork, Gunthermann, 1910, 10 In.	1840.00
Car, Limousine, Driver, Tin Litho, Green, Yellow, Clockwork, Bing, Germany, c.1920, 10 In.	2070.00
Car, Limousine, Driver, Tin Litho, Lanterns, Head Lamps, Doors Open, Clockwork, 10 In.	1380.00
Car, Limousine, Jep Delage, Green, Red Stripes, Side Lamp, Clockwork, France, 13 In.	1495.00
Car, Limousine, Passenger Peering From Roof, Tin Litho, Germany, c.1930s, 5 ½ In.	1093.00
Car, Limousine, Tin Lithograph, Brown, Blue, Cream, Windup, Burnett, England, 1930, 7 ¾ In.	805.00
Car, Lincoln, Futura, Plastic Bubble Roof, Friction, Tin, Japan, Box, 11 In.	5750.00
Car, Lincoln, Hardtop, 4 Door, Celluloid Windshield, Friction, Ichiko, Japan, Box, 17 In.	2588.00
Car, Lincoln, Sedan, Bronze, White, Chrome Plated, Rubber Tires, Friction, Box, 1954, 12 In.	2070.00
Car, Lincoln, Sedan, Zephyr, House Trailer, Iron, Red, Silver, Rubber Tires, Hubley, 9 In.	805.00
Car, Machinery, Orange, Green, American Flyer, 1928-33	225.00
Car, Man From U.N.C.L.E., Die Cast, Corgi, Box, 1966	250.00
Car, Man With Horn, Tut-Tut, Lehmann, 1903	860.00
Car, Mercedes-Benz, 350SL, Battery Operated, Metallic Blue, Schuco, Box, 12 In.	225.00
Car, Mercedes-Benz, Automatic Jack Friction, SSS/Shioji/Cragstan, 12 In. ...... *illus*	127.00
Car, Mercedes-Benz, Metallic Blue, Friction, Cragstan, Japan, 8 In.	77.00
Car, Mercury, 1910 Model, Blue, Schuco, Box, 7 In.	155.00
Car, Mercury, Sedan, Bank, Stamp Dispenser, Maroon, Straights Mfg., 1939, 5 In.	115.00
Car, Mercury, Solido, Plastic Roof, Windup, c.1955, 4 ½ In.	185.00
Car, Metal, Windup, Headlights, England, 15 In.	295.00
Car, MG, Japan, Box, 1954, 10 ½ In.	395.00
Car, Military, Coupe, Army Staff, Steel, Tin Litho, Soldier, Gun, Marx, Box, 1930s, 14 In.	3738.00
Car, Milton Berle, Windup, Marx, Box	435.00
Car, Monkeemobile, Red, Figures, Die Cast, Box, 1968-72, 6 In.	220.00
Car, Mustang, James Bond, Red, Die Cast, Corgi, Box, c.1972, 6 In.	185.00
Car, Nash, S.W., Tin, Friction, Japan, 1950s, 9 ½ In.	110.00
Car, Old Jalopy, Driver, Tin Lithograph, Windup, Marx, Box, 7 In.	275.00
Car, Open Touring, Eberl, Tin Lithograph, Windup, Driver, 14 In.	920.00
Car, Orange, Black, Trim, Cast Iron, 6 In.	1872.00
Car, Packard, Coupe, Brown, Running Boards, Doors Open, Windows, Vinyl, 1925, 69 In.	6900.00
Car, Packard, Driver, Blue, Black, Doors & Hood Open, Cast Iron, Hubley, 11 ½ In.	4100.00
Car, Packard, Sedan, Pressed Steel, Roof, Windshield, Radiator, Bumper, Pull Toy, 28 In.	4600.00
Car, Phaeton, Tin Litho, Red, Top Down, Driver, Disc Wheels, Clockwork, Germany, 6 In.	460.00
Car, Pierce Arrow, Sedan, Cast Iron, Arcade, 1935, 7 In.	980.00
Car, Plymouth, Sedan, Roof, Cast Iron, Red, Nickel Grill, Rubber Tires, 4 In.	1265.00
Car, Plymouth, Station Wagon, Tin, Friction, Japan, 1950s, 8 In.	95.00
Car, Police, Chevrolet, Battery Operated, 2 Policemen, Japan, 14 ½ In.	225.00
Car, Police, Highway Patrol, Guns Out Windows, Tin Lithograph, Friction, Japan, 6 In.	115.00
Car, Police, Impala, Tin, 2 Policemen, Battery Operated, Japan, 1964, 14 ½ In.	245.00
Car, Police, Lupor, Tin, Windup, U.S.A., 1950, 7 ½ In.	145.00
Car, Police, Mercedes-Benz, Battery Operated, 2 Tone, Siren, Flashing Light, Schuco, 1970, 10 In.	245.00
Car, Police, Siren, Green, Black, Marx, 8 In.	750.00
Car, Police, Tin, Battery Operated, Japan, 1 Box, 1960s, 5 In.	375.00
Car, Pontiac, Sedan, Metal, Plastic, Windup, 1952, 7 ½ In.	95.00
Car, Racing, Astro, 2 Speeds, Lights, Battery Operated, Japan, 1950s, 12 In.	475.00
Car, Racing, Atom Race Car, Tin, Friction, Rubber Tires, Japan, Box, 16 In. ...... *illus*	2925.00
Car, Racing, Battery Operated, Japan, T.P.S., 1969	150.00
Car, Racing, Bear Cat, Tin, Windup, Marx, 1930s, 7 In.	125.00
Car, Racing, Boy Driver, Red, Yellow, Celluloid, Tin, Windup, Japan, c.1930, 5 x 7 ¾ In.	1150.00
Car, Racing, Driver, Blue, Tin Litho, Bird, Clockwork, Disc Wheels, Spain, Paya, 13 In.	1093.00
Car, Racing, Driver, Bob Cat, Tin, France, 1920s, 8 In.	245.00
Car, Racing, Driver, Bullet-Nose, Nickel, Rubber Tires, Arcade, 1930s, 10 In. ...... *illus*	17825.00
Car, Racing, Driver, Golden Arrow, Painted Steel, Rubber Tires, Kingsbury, 19 In.	403.00
Car, Racing, Driver, Green, Exhaust Pipe, Dial, Swift, c.1920s, 11 In.	1093.00
Car, Racing, Driver, Iron, Rubber Tires, Aluminum, Silver, Red, Black, 9 ½ In.	644.00
Car, Racing, Driver, No. 3, Red, Silver, Rubber Tires, Sun Rubber Co., 6 ¾ In.	55.00

Toy, Car, Mercedes-Benz, Automatic Jack Friction, SSS/Shioji/Cragstan, 12 In. $127.00

Toy, Car, Racing, Atom Race Car, Tin, Friction, Rubber Tires, Japan, Box, 16 In. $2925.00

Toy, Car, Racing, Driver, Bullet-Nose, Nickel, Rubber Tires, Arcade, 1930s, 10 In. $17825.00

Toy, Car, Uncle Wiggily, Joke, Tin Litho, Windup, Japan, Box, c.1938, 4 ¾ In. $1989.00

T

Car, Racing, Driver, No. 5, Red, Silver, Rubber Tires, Aluminum, Cast Iron, 9 ½ In.		605.00
Car, Racing, Driver, No. 5, Yellow, Red, Cast Iron, Hubley, 9 In.		605.00
Car, Racing, Driver, No. 7, Demon, Tin, Japan		225.00
Car, Racing, Driver, No. 410, Metal, Windup, England, 1940s, 10 ½ In.		195.00
Car, Racing, Driver, Pistons, Silver, Red, 12 Cylinder, Rubber Tires, Cast Iron, Hubley		725.00
Car, Racing, Driver, Pistons, Yellow, Red, Nickel Wheels, Cast Iron, Hubley, 8 ¾ In.		1080.00
Car, Racing, Driver, Red, Working Lights, Rubber Tires, Cast Iron, Hubley, 6 ¼ In.		495.00
Car, Racing, Driver, Red, Yellow, No. 6, Tin, Windup, Ingap, Italy, 6 ½ In.		1000.00
Car, Racing, Driver, Sparks, Tin Lithograph, Graphics, Marx, 8 ½ In.		345.00
Car, Racing, Driver, Tin Lithograph, Wind Breaker Tail Fin, Siren, Japan, Box, 11 ½ In.		978.00
Car, Racing, Driver, Tin, Spoke Wheels, Penny Toy, Germany, 4 ¼ In.		2875.00
Car, Racing, Driver, Tin, Yellow, Exhaust Pipe, Fenders, Wind Fin, Gunthermann, c.1930, 18 In.		3450.00
Car, Racing, Driver, Yellow, Iron, Front Grill, Electric Lights, Hood Opens, Hubley, 9 In.		5175.00
Car, Racing, Falcon, Red, Metal, Friction, Marx, 5 x 19 ½ In.		115.00
Car, Racing, Golden Racer, Tin, Friction, Japan, 1950s, 11 In.		120.00
Car, Racing, Green, Black, Yellow, Strauss, 8 ¼ In.		250.00
Car, Racing, Green, Doepke, 1955, 15 In.		325.00
Car, Racing, Mercedes-Benz CIII, Doors Open, Windup, Orange Body, Schuco, 5 In.		150.00
Car, Racing, Metal, Windup, Germany, 1950s, 9 In.		195.00
Car, Racing, Metal, Windup, Japan, c.1950, 4 In., Pair		55.00
Car, Racing, No. 3, Tin, Push, 7 ½ In.		295.00
Car, Racing, No. 5, Blue, Red, Tin, Windup, Marx, 1950, 5 In.		120.00
Car, Racing, No. 7, Red, Yellow, Marx, 1950s, 5 In.		95.00
Car, Racing, Oh Boy, Tin, Decals, Embossed Exhaust Pipes, Kiddies Metal Toys, 18 In.		259.00
Car, Racing, Open Wheel, Red, Silver, Auburn, 1930s, 10 ½ In.		60.00
Car, Racing, Plastic, Red, Pagco, Instructions, Box, 11 In.		250.00
Car, Racing, Plastic, Windup, Marx, Box, 1950s		110.00
Car, Racing, Porsche 911R, Monte Carlo Rally, Plastic, Yellow, Battery, Schuco, 10 ½ In.		199.00
Car, Racing, Red Flash, Red, Yellow, Driver, Strauss, 9 ½ In.		295.00
Car, Racing, Speed King, Yellow, Red, Orange, Marx, Box, 16 In.		765.00
Car, Racing, Stewart, Cast Iron, Red, Walker, c.1920, 5 ½ In.		200.00
Car, Racing, Thimble Drome, Prop Rod, Blue, Aluminum, Rubber Tires, Champion, Box, 10 In.		185.00
Car, Racing, Thimble Drome, Red, Metal, Rubber Tires, Roy Cox, Champion, Box, 10 In.		510.00
Car, Racing, Tin, Friction, Japan, 1950s, 9 In.		225.00
Car, Racing, Tin, Friction, Linemar, Japan, 1950s, 10 In.		175.00
Car, Racing, Tin Litho, Green, Driver, Gold Spoke Wheels, Ingap, Penny Toy, Italy, 6 In.		1840.00
Car, Racing, Tin Litho, Multicolored Wheels, Graphics, Exhaust Pipes, Japan, Prewar, 13 In.		2875.00
Car, Racing, Tin, Windup, Lupor, 11 ½ In.		145.00
Car, Racing, Tin, Windup, Marx, 1950s, 13 In.		295.00
Car, Racing, Tin, Windup, U.S. Zone, Germany, 9 ½ In.		125.00
Car, Racing, Yellow, Red, Green, Driver, Strauss, 9 ½ In.		250.00
Car, Racing, Zephyr, Green, Black, Wood Wheels, Windup, Wyandotte, Box, 9 ¾ In.		675.00
Car, Radio 4012, Convertible, White, Metal, Music Box, Schuco, Box, 6 ¼ In.		300.00
Car, Renault, Coupe, Tin Lithograph, Green, Clockwork Driven, France, c.1930, 11 ½ In.		1495.00
Car, Renault, Sedan, Tin Litho, 3 Green Combo, Driver, Luggage, Spare Tire, Battery, 15 In.		1725.00
Car, Reo, Coupe, Pressed Steel, Tan, Green, Orange, Marx, Windup, 1932, 14 In.		685.00
Car, Reo, Rumble Seat, Rubber Tires, Gray, Red Striping, Driver, Arcade, 9 In.		6325.00
Car, Roadster, Black, Red Wheels, Flivver, Buddy L, 1925, 11 In.		625.00
Car, Roadster, Fire Chief, Steel, Red, Disc Wheels, Bell, Motor Driven, Kingsbury, 1927, 12 In.		1725.00
Car, Roadster, Green, Paint, Steel, Fly Wheel Mechanism, Inset Wheels, Schieble, 18 In.		259.00
Car, Roadster, Orange, Metal Masters, 1938, 7 In.		50.00
Car, Roadster, Pressed Steel, Turner, 1928 Parkard, Nickel-Plated Headlights, 18 In.		500.00
Car, Roadster, Red, Blue, Painted Steel, Fly Wheel Mechanism, Rubber Tires, Schieble, 17 In.		173.00
Car, Roadster, Red, Tan, Painted Steel, Fly Wheel Mechanism, Schieble, 18 In.		173.00
Car, Roadster, Red, Yellow, Nonpareil, 10 In.		195.00
Car, Roadster, Rumble Seat, Tin Litho, Woman Driver, Wheel, Clockwork, Tippco, 12 In.		4313.00
Car, Roadster, Steam, Mamod, England, Box, 15 ½ In.		180.00
Car, Roadster, Tin Litho, Orange, Blue Roof, Luggage Rack, Clockwork, Marx, 11 In.		460.00
Car, Rocking, Dashboard, Wood, Green, Red Tulips, Rockers, American, c.1920, 29 In.		326.00
Car, Saloon, Tin Lithograph, Driver, Red, Brown, Tan, Bing, 9 ¼ In.		415.00
Car, Sedan, 2 Door, Die Cast, Orange, Black, 4 ½ In.		175.00
Car, Sedan, 4 Door, Orange, Yellow, Tin Litho, Disc Wheels, Driver, Clockwork, Tippco, 9 In.		2185.00
Car, Sedan, Airflow, 4 Door, Red, Corrugated Grille, Tin Disc Wheels, c.1934, 7 In.		518.00
Car, Sedan, Blue, Black, Cast Iron, Kenton, 6 ½ In.		365.00
Car, Sedan, Blue, Red, Die Cast, Rubber Tires, Marked, No. 1895963, 6 In.		105.00
Car, Sedan, Brennabor, Red, Blue, Tin Lithograph, Lehmann, Germany, 7 In.		2875.00

Car, Sedan, Chad Valley, Clockwork, Disc Wheels, White, Blue, England, Box, 1930s, 9 In.	1093.00
Car, Sedan, Driver, Green Paint, No. 1615, Cast Iron, Metal Wheels, 5 In.	180.00
Car, Sedan, Driver, Orange Paint, No. 1438, Cast Iron, Metal Wheels, 5 ¾ In.	300.00
Car, Sedan, Driver, Orange, Spare Tire, Cast Iron, Hubley, 6 ¼ In.	1800.00
Car, Sedan, Driver, V Front Grille, Headlights, Cord Wheels, Tin Litho, Clockwork, Box, 13 In.	1265.00
Car, Sedan, Gray, Red, Litho Wheels, Distler, Germany, 1930s, 14 ½ In.	1575.00
Car, Sedan, Lana, Yellow, Blue Roof, Fenders, Tin Lithograph, Clockwork, Lehmann, 7 In.	2300.00
Car, Sedan, Man Standing, Paper, Wood Die Cut, Mounted, Display, Birchcraft, 9 In.	805.00
Car, Sedan, Silver Arrow, Red, Cast Iron, Nickel Plated, Arcade, 7 In.	210.00
Car, Sedan, Steel, Blue, Nickel Plated Grille, Rubber Tires, Spare, Cor-Cor, 1932, 20 In.	920.00
Car, Sedan, Tin, Windup, England, 1940s, 11 In.	245.00
Car, Sedan, Trailer, Cast Iron, Red, Silver, A.C. Williams, c.1937, 12 In.	1495.00
Car, Sedan, White, Red Headlights, Tin Litho, Clockwork, Orobr, Germany, c.1920s, 8 In.	1035.00
Car, Sedan, Windup, Chein, 1930s, 7 In.	295.00
Car, Sedan, Windup, Lehmann, 1927, 5 ½ In.	385.00
Car, Soap Box Derby, Fiberglass, Steel Wheels, Hand Built, Blue, 1960s, 17 ½ x 79 In.	360.00
Car, Space Patrol, Astronaut, Lighted Gun, Antenna Spins, Tin, Nomura, Box, 9 ¾ In.	1718.00
Car, Sports, Tin, Friction, Driver, Japan, 1950s, 7 ½ In.	120.00
Car, Structo Roadster, Pressed Steel, Clockwork Motor, Decal, Yellow, c.1920, 6 x 16 In.	720.00
Car, Studebaker, Avanti, Metal Friction, Gold, Japan, 8 ½ In.	295.00
Car, Studebaker, Commander Starline, Coupe, Green, England, 1953	85.00
Car, Studebaker, Coupe, Champion, Starlight, Black, 1952	75.00
Car, Studebaker, Red, Silver, Plastic, Metal, Windup, 2 ½ x 8 In.	78.00
Car, Studebaker, Roadster, Red, Hubley, 7 In.	395.00
Car, Televi Jeep, 2 Boxers Fighting, Metal, Japan, Box, 7 In.	175.00
Car, Tin, Battery Operated, Head & Taillights, Japan, Box, 1959, 11 In.	295.00
Car, Tin Lithograph, Child Riding, Clockwork, Issmayer, 5 ½ In.	3163.00
Car, Tin Lithograph, Red, Black, Spoke Wheels, Clockwork, Lehmann, Box, 7 In.	2875.00
Car, Tin, Push, Windup, Wolverine, U.S.A., 13 In.	245.00
Car, Touring, 2 Seat, Stripes, Rubber Tires, Spoke Wheels, Clockwork, Bing, 1910, 8 In.	5750.00
Car, Touring, 4 Seats, Windshield, Lamps, Hand Brake, Clockwork, Red, Carette, 1912, 13 In.	3450.00
Car, Touring, Chauffeur, Woman, Movable Arms, Cast Iron, Kenton, 9 In.	775.00
Car, Touring, Cream, Fold Down Windshield, Side Brake, Clockwork, 1920s, 7 In.	6900.00
Car, Touring, De Dion, Tin, 2 Seater, Cast Head Lamp, Spoke Wheels, Clockwork, Bing, 6 In.	4600.00
Car, Touring, Driver, Red, Yellow, Metal Spoked Wheels, Cast Iron, 9 In.	310.00
Car, Touring, Driver, Woman, Blue, Red, Horn, Gold Stencil, Iron, Jones & Bixler, 10 In.	480.00
Car, Touring, Fold Down Top, Open Doors, Driver, Passengers, Clockwork, France, 22 In.	748.00
Car, Touring, Lamps, Rubber Tires, Spoke Wheels, Tin Litho, Clockwork, Gunthermann, 6 In.	1495.00
Car, Touring, Lincoln, Green, Cast Iron, A.C. Williams, 6 ¾ In.	720.00
Car, Touring, Open, Chauffeur, Woman, Movable Arms, Cast Iron, 9 In.	775.00
Car, Touring, Packard, Cast Iron, Doors, Hood Open, Blue, Black Paint, Hubley 11 ½ In.	4388.00
Car, Touring, Phaeton, 4 Seater, Orange, Yellow, Brass Lamp, Lanterns, Bing, 12 ½ In.	489.00
Car, Touring, Wood, Tin, Driver, Yellow Iron, Spoke Wheels, Arcade, 8 ¾ In.	288.00
Car, Toyota, 2000 GT, Tin, Friction, Japan, 1960s, 14 In.	295.00
Car, Trailer, Lincoln, Roamer, Green, Die Cast, Door Moves, Tootsietoy, 4 In.	665.00
Car, Uncle Walt, Driver, Figure, Tootsietoy, 1932, 3 In.	350.00
Car, Uncle Wiggily, Joke, Tin Litho, Windup, Japan, Box, c.1938, 4 ¾ In. ...... *illus*	1989.00
Car, Volkswagen, Tin, Battery Operated, Lights, Motor Sounds, Japan, 15 In.	295.00
Car, Volkswagon, Beach Bomb, Brown, Surf Board, Flowers, Hot Wheels, 1969, 2 ½ In.	348.00
Car, Wrecker, Service, Blue, Hubley, 4 ¾ In.	275.00
Cards, Three Little Pigs, Who's Afraid Of The Big Bad Wolf, Delarue, 1930s	100.00
Carnival Swing Ride, 3 Boat Gondolas, Figures In It, Germany, 1920s, 11 In.	465.00
Carnival Swing Ride, 4 Riders, Tin, Windup, Key, 10 ½ In.	660.00
Carousel, Horse Race, Tin Windup, 10 x 6 ½ In.	385.00
Carousel, Wyandotte, 1930s, 6 In.	175.00
Carriage, Baby, Wax, Moving Arms, Legs, Pull Toy, 9 In.	201.00
Carriage, Doll's, Cream Tin, Folding Hood, Wooden Handle, Spoke Wheels, Marklin, 9 In.	3081.00
Carriage, Doll's, Painted, Wood, Blue, Spoke Wheels, Sun Shade, 28 ½ In.	207.00
Carriage, Doll's, Victorian, Wicker, Fringed Top, 32 In.	72.00
Carriage, Doll's, Wicker Rattan, Reversible Canvas Canopy, Wire, Wood Handle, 5 In.	237.00
Carriage, Surrey, 2 Seats, Figure, Black Horse, Red Wheels, Cast Iron, Shimer, 9 In.	410.00
Carrier, Army Tank, Tin, Friction, Japan, Box, 1950s, 9 In.	175.00
Cart, Carpenter, Coal, Wood, Driver, Horse, 1880s, 12 ½ In.	950.00
Cart, Goat Drawn, Yellow Kid, Tin, Pressed Steel, Nickeled Spoke Wheels, Kenton, 7 In.	863.00
Cart, Gold Goat Pulling Cart, Meier, Penny Toy, 5 ⅜ In.	633.00
Cart, Mail, Figure, Flywheel, Friction, Spoke Wheels, Tin Lithograph, Germany, 4 In.	575.00

Toy, Castle, Domed Towers, Wood, Composition, Germany, 15 x 21 x 17 In. $263.00

Toy, Cat, Felix, Black, White, Red, Steiff Button In Ear, c.1927, 9 ½ In. $4888.00

Toy, Cat, Felix, On Scooter, Mechanical, Tin Lithograph, Germany, 1920s, 6 In. $1120.00

Toy, Cat, Felix, Wood, Jointed, Performo, Pat Sullivan, Penn., 1926-1928, 6 ½ In. $293.00

Toy, Dancing Children, Bisque Head, Painted, Tin Bodies, Windup, 6 In. $205.00

Toy, Digger, Panama, Mack Chassis, Simulated Caterpillar Treads, Hubley, 9 In. $22415.00

Cart, Mule Drawn, Comic Driver, Nodder, Cast Iron, Kenton, 6 In.	146.00
Cart, Trip-Trapp, 2 Boys, Tin Litho, Windup, Push, Pull Handle, Hans Eberl, Germany, 7 In.	2633.00
Cart, Woman Pushing Cart, 2 Boys On Top, Tin, Japanned, Windup, Germany, 8 In.	3218.00
Cash Register, American Flyer, Black, Key, Coins, Chicago, Ill., 9 x 9 In.	120.00
Cash Register, Champion, Black, Gold, Metal, 3 ½ x 3 ½ In.	45.00
Cash Register, Little Folks, Nursery Rhyme, Tin Litho, Spring Drawer, 1920s, 3 x 3 ¾ In.	127.00
Castle, Domed Towers, Wood, Composition, Germany, 15 x 21 x 17 In. .... *illus*	263.00
Cat, Felix, Black, White, Red, Steiff Button In Ear, c.1927, 9 ½ In. .... *illus*	4888.00
Cat, Felix, Cast Iron, Painted, Walking, 2 ⅝ In.	173.00
Cat, Felix, On Scooter, Mechanical, Tin Lithograph, Germany, 1920s, 6 In. .... *illus*	1120.00
Cat, Felix, Sparkler, Metal, Mechanical, Big Smile, Copyright By Pat Sullivan, 1930s	330.00
Cat, Felix, Walker, Windup, Germany, 1920s	575.00
Cat, Felix, Wood, Jointed, Performo, Pat Sullivan, Penn., 1926-28, 6 ½ In. .... *illus*	293.00
Cat, Pushing Mouse In Chair, Tin, Windup, Gunthermann, 6 In.	1725.00
Chair, Doll's, Rod-Back Windsor, Original Green Paint, Pennsylvania, 1800s, 13 ¼ In.	497.00
Chair, Sedan, 2 Chinese Men, Carry Chair, Lehmann, Germany, 7 ¼ In.	2300.00
Chaise Longue, Doll's, Pine Frame, Cream, Yellow Flowers, Upholstered, 15 ½ x 30 In.	148.00
Chariot, 3 Horses, White Driver, Black Horses, Cast Iron, Hubley, 10 ½ In.	205.00
Chariot, Horse, Clown Driver, Gold, Red Wheels, Cast Iron, 5 In.	29.00
Charleston Trio, Black Musicians, Dog, Windup, Marx, Box, 1921	950.00
Charleston Trio, Tin Lithograph, Louis Marx & Co., 8 ½ x 5 x 3 In.	360.00
Chick, Walker, Wood, Lead Feet, Cardboard, Glass Eyes, Composition, Windup, Germany, 7 In.	120.00
Chicken, Egg Laying, Lays Marble Egg, Tin, Push Down, Wyandotte, 7 x 8 In.	95.00
Chicken Snatcher, Dog Biting Man, Windup, Marx, 1920s	1250.00
Child, In Walker, Papier-Mache, Jointed, Germany, c.1860, 4 In.	770.00
Children On Rocker, Tin, Windup, Rocks Back & Forth, Gunthermann, 9 x 6 In.	1840.00
Chinese Man, With Parasol, Tin Lithograph, Penny Toy, Distler, Germany, c.1920s, 3 ½ In.	575.00
Chinese, Pulls Jitney, Tin, Composition, Windup, Les Jouets, 6 ¾ In.	374.00
Classroom, Welcome Back Kotter, Fold-Out Vinyl Case, Mattel	145.00
Clown & Duck, Tin, Windup, 6 ½ x 10 ½ In.	660.00
Clown Orchestra, Dressed, Tin, Figure, 5 Piano Keys, Rings, V.B. & Cie, 10 In.	1035.00
Clown, Artist, Cam Operated, Tin Lithograph, Phillip Vielmetter, Early 1900s, 4 ¾ In.	2530.00
Clown, Balancing Ball, Walker, Tin, Cloth, Windup, Box, 10 ½ In.	160.00
Clown, Base Player, Composition Head, Plays Base Fiddle, Seated On Drum, Cloth, Staudt, 12 In.	3163.00
Clown, Car, Peter, Windup, Tin, Lehmann, 1920s	2250.00
Clown, Cat, Plays Clarinet, Nods, Tail Holds Music, Wags, Gunthermann, 8 ½ & 8 In.	2185.00
Clown, Circus, Aerial Tightrope, Tin, Windup, Cragstan, Japan, Box, 8 ½ In.	125.00
Clown, Clockwork Mechanical, Bisque Head, Glass Eyes, Mohair Wig, Poodle, 9 x 11 In.	878.00
Clown, Crawling, Tin Lithograph, Windup, Gunthermann, 6 x 8 In.	520.00
Clown, Dancing With Poodle, Lever, Mechanical, Embossed, Meier, 3 ½ In.	1870.00
Clown, Fiddler, Tin, Cloth, Felt, Windup, Schuco, 4 ½ In.	215.00
Clown, Juggler, Ball Spins, Riding Horse, Wheeled Platform, Windup, c.1900, 12 In.	950.00
Clown, Juggler, Riding Horse, Painted Tin, Windup, 11 In.	690.00
Clown, Mandolin Player, Celluloid Head, Seated On Drum, Plays Mandolin, Staudt, 10 ½ In.	1495.00
Clown, Oak-Hytex Toy Balloons, Plastic, 15 ½ In.	118.00
Clown, On Cart, Celluloid, Prewar, 1930s, 11 In.	375.00
Clown, Playing Drum, Painted, Lithograph, Windup, 6 ¼ In.	489.00
Clown, Plays Metal Harp, Cloth Dressed, Composition Head, Tin, Drum, Staudt, 11 In.	4025.00
Clown, Plays Violin, Bisque Head, Cloth Dressed, Tin Base, Staudt, 15 In.	1725.00
Clown, Plays Zither, Seated On Painted Tin Bench, Cloth Dressed, Staudt, 12 In.	2012.00
Clown, Propeller On Nose, Multicolored, Tin, Windup, J. Chein, 7 ¾ In.	195.00
Clown, Pulling Mules Tail, Painted, Celluloid, Windup, Japan	46.00
Clown, Spins Forward On Wheels, Arms Move, Painted, Tin, Windup, Germany, 7 In.	495.00
Clown, Stands On Head, Pushes Up, Splits Legs, Twirls, Tin, Dressed, Windup, Martin, 7 In.	4025.00
Clown, Tom Twist, Waddles, Stand On Head, Windup, Strauss, 1920s	485.00
Clown, Top Hat, Red Coat, Winds Up By Revolving Arms Over Head, Tin, Germany, 7 In.	240.00
Clown, Tumbling, Celluloid, Tin, Cloth, Windup, Japan, 6 ¼ In.	110.00
Clown, Walking Drummer, Moves Head, Japan, Box, 1950s, 11 In.	105.00
Clown, Wire Walker, Painted, Tin, Cloth, Windup, Germany, 8 In.	385.00
Clown, Wire Walker, Tin, Windup, Poles, Wire, Base Set, Tattered Suit, Germany, 8 In.	410.00
Clowns, On Elephant, Celluloid, Japan, c.1935, 7 In.	275.00
Clowns, Performing, Form Tricycle, Stunt, Red, Green, Gold, Penny Toy, Germany, 3 In.	1093.00
Coach, Touring, Goat Drawn, Wicker, Upholstered, Tin, Spokes, Clockwork, 25 In.	7475.00
Coal Hopper, Elevator Tipple, Buckets, Steel, Wood Base, Kelmet Big Boy, c.1926, 23 In.	575.00
Colorforms, Curious George, Watercolor Cover, No. 611, 1978, 12 x 8 In.	633.00
Colorforms, Sesame Street Ernie & Bert Puppetforms Theater, 1973, 10 x 16 In.	1516.00

Combine, Grain Master, Slik-Toy, Green, Aluminum, Oliver Corp., Box, 11 ¼ In.		390.00
Construction Set, Auto Assembly Parts, Meccano, No. 1, England, Box, 1930s		748.00
Construction Set, Auto Builder, No. 12, Painted Steel, Windup, Iron Wheels, Structo, 16 In. ..		633.00
Construction Set, Motor Car, Windup Model Car, Meccano, Box, 15 In.		316.00
Construction Set, Tractor Builder No. 11, Painted Steel, Windup, Structo, Box, 15 ½ In.		1495.00
Container, Tin, Commemorative, European Flight, 1934, 7 In.		150.00
Contractor Set, Truck, 3 Trailers, Painted Die Cast, 4 Piece, Tootsietoy, Box, 12 In. .	259.00 to	316.00
Cosmic Ray Gun, Dan Dare, Plastic, Battery Operated, Palitoy, c.1950s, 6 In.		225.00
Cow, Brown, White, Mohair, Script Button, Steiff, 6 ½ x 10 In.		92.00
Cow, Hide Covered, Head Turns, Moos, Wood Platform, 14 In.		69.00
Cow, Jumped Over Moon, Elsie, Painted, Pull Toy, Wood Commodities Corp., 10 In.		118.00
Cow, Walker, Moves Head, Moos, Wags Tail, Batter, Rosko Toy, Box, 7 x 13 ½ In.		115.00
Cow, Wood, Felt, Pull Toy, Glass Eyes, Horns, Wheeled Base, c.1885, 8 x 4 In.		470.00
Cowboy, Bret Maverick, Horse, Plastic, Molded, Painted, Hartland, Box, 9 In.		295.00
Cowboy, Gallop, Jumps, Cart, Pulled By Zebra, Windup, Lehmann, 1954		350.00
Cowboy, With Gun, Clicker, Tin, Mechanical, Japan, 3 ¾ In.		95.00
Cradle, Doll, Butternut, Poplar, c.1890, 25 In.		88.00
Cradle, Doll, Poplar, Dovetailed, Cut Nails, 19th Century, 7 x 26 ½ x 8 ½ In.		58.00
Crane, 4 Wheels, Crank Operated, O Gauge, 3 ¼ x 5 In.		1380.00
Crane, Bucket, Pressed Steel, Buddy L, 21 x 43 In.		2070.00
Crapshooter, Man, Holding Money, Tin, Battery Operated, Cragstan, Box..............		124.00
Creeping Baby, Cast Iron, Crawls Along Floor As Pulled, Ives, 6 ½ In.		374.00
Crib, Doll Shape, Bakelite, String Cord, Multicolored, 5 ¾ In.		153.00
Cruiser, Tin, Crank, Japan, 1950, 9 In.		120.00
Cycle, Parcel Post Delivery, Driver, Spoke Wheels, Rubber Tires, Hubley, 9 ½ In.		748.00
Cyclist, Boy, Tricycle, Windup, Paint, Metal, Unique Art, 1940s, 8 ¾ In.		431.00
Cymbal Player, Head Turns, Plastic, Painted, Cloth Uniform, Fur Hat, Windup, 10 In.		71.00
Dancing Children, Bisque Head, Painted, Tin Bodies, Windup, 6 In. ....*illus*		205.00
Dancing Dan, Black Dancer, Bell U.S.A., Box, 14 In.		224.00
Dancing Sailor, Waddles Side To Side, Windup, Tin Lithograph, Lehmann, 1903, 7 In.		795.00
Deer, Brown, Composition, Germany, Box, 5 Piece..................................		45.00
Delivery Cart, Driver, Tin Lithograph, Windup, Cardboard Arms, Legs, Marx, 9 ½ In.		489.00
Derrick, Cast Iron, Swivels, Hand Lever, Buddy L, 20 ½ In.		374.00
Derrick, Mask & Boom On Base, Clamshell Grab Bucket, Buddy L, c.1921-24, 24 In.		1150.00
Desk, Writing, Doll's, Walnut, Hinged, Stained, Gold Stenciled, 2 x 6 ⅛ x 4 ⅜ In.		237.00
Digger, Panama, Mack Chassis, Simulated Caterpillar Treads, Hubley, 9 In. ....*illus*		22415.00
Diner, Silver Streak Diner, Silver, Red, White, 31 ½ In.		460.00
Dirigible, Tin Lithograph, Gondolas, Propeller, Clockwork, Germany, 16 ¼ In.		1265.00
Dirigible, Whistle, French, Penny Toy, 4 ⅞ In.		138.00
Disc Harrow, Brass, Wood, Steel, Formed Seat, Spring Levers, Sample, 13 x 11 In.		7475.00
Diver, Cellulose Acetate, Painted, Saxon, U.K., Box, 6 ¼ x 2 ¼ In.		250.00
Dog On Platform, Wheels, Penny Toy, 3 ½ In.		44.00
Dog, Boston Terrier, Nodding Head, Papier-Mache, Wooden Wheels, Pull Toy, 14 In.		1126.00
Dog, Bulldog, Pull Toy, Chain Growler, Glass Eyes, Painted, Composition, 18 In.		460.00
Dog, Cat In Chimney, Clicker, Tin, Mechanical, Germany, 2 ¾ In.		330.00
Dog, Chasing Cat, Dog House, Celluloid, Tin, Windup, Japan, 3 In.		173.00
Dog, Cloth, Swivel Neck, Collar, Glass Eyes, c.1900, 10 In.		29.00
Dog, Collie, Standing, Germany Tyrolean Outfit, Steiff, 9 In.		60.00
Dog, Doberman, Pip-Squeak, Papier-Mache, Mouth Opens, Tail Wags, 10 ¼ In.		1185.00
Dog, Flippo, Metal, Windup, Linemar, Japan....................................		95.00
Dog, German Shepherd, Stuffed, Steiff, Mid 1900s, 28 In.		260.00
Dog, Growler, Composition, Glass Eye, Wood Caster, Pull Toy, Paris, c.1900, 15 x 18 In.		3120.00
Dog, Rabbits, Pip-Squeak, Papier-Mache, 3 Eggs, Ears Wiggles, 20th Century, 7 ½ In.		2963.00
Dog, Schafer-Hund, Tag On Collar, Steiff, 7 In.		890.00
Dog, Wee Scottie, Metal, Windup, Marx, 5 ¼ In.		110.00
Dog, White Fur, Glass Eyes, Barks When Cord Is Pulled, Squeak, Germany, 9 In.		260.00
Dollhouse Furniture, Bedroom Set, Walnut, Strombecker, 4 Piece......................		100.00
Dollhouse Furniture, Cathedral Table Radio, Walnut, Knobs & Speakers, Strombecker, ¾ x 1 ¼ In.		12.00
Dollhouse Furniture, Desk, Slant Lid, Cross Stretcher, Silver, 1800s, 2 ¼ x 2 ¼ x 1 ½ In.		165.00
Dollhouse Furniture, Highchair, Crib, Armchair, 2 Pot Chairs, Cast Iron, Arcade.................		119.00
Dollhouse Furniture, Piano, Wood, Strombecker, 1930		14.00
Dollhouse Furniture, Secretary Bookcase, Continental, Silver, 19th Century, 3 ½ x 2 ¾ In. ..		275.00
Dollhouse Furniture, Table, 2 Arm Chairs, Stained Wood, Tea Set.		58.00
Dollhouse Furniture, Table, Tulipwood, Napoleon III, Brass, 6 ¾ x 6 x 4 In.		830.00
Dollhouse Furniture, Wall Telephone, Mahogany Stained Wood, 4 ½ In.		95.00
Dollhouse, 2 Rooms, 2 Chimneys, Paper On Wood, Gottschalk, 16 x 10 x 7 In.		546.00

Toy, Dollhouse, 3 Story, 6 Rooms, Balconies, Electrified, Gottschalk, 38 x 31 x 19 In. $2530.00

The Cricket

On the night of June 5, 1944, 17,000 British and American paratroopers and glider troops landed in Normandy to capture or destroy bridges, cut communication wires, take out gun emplacements, and create confusion. It was dark, and the men's faces were blackened. How to communicate? Flashlights would have given away their location. Someone came up with the idea of giving every soldier a child's cricket—a toy made of thin metal that, when squeezed, clicked. If a soldier saw a figure, he clicked once. The response was two clicks. No response and you shot. Reproductions of "Le Criquet" are for sale in museums in Normandy.

Toy, Drum, Uncle Wiggily, Parade, Tin Lithograph, Fred A. Wish, c.1924, 6 x 8 In. $468.00

Toy, Easter On Parade, Bell, Windup, Celluloid, Tin, Mitsushima, Box, 1940s, 4 x 8 In. $221.00

Dollhouse, 2 Story, 4 Rooms, Paper On Wood, Hinged, Gottschalk, 24 x 20 x 10 In.	1380.00
Dollhouse, 2 Story, 5 Rooms, Wood, White, Green, Top Lifts, 1900s, 33 x 26 In.	690.00
Dollhouse, 2 Story, 5 Rooms, Wraparound Porch, Banister, Windows, 25 x 26 x 16 In.	136.00
Dollhouse, 3 Story, 6 Rooms, Balconies, Electrified, Gottschalk, 38 x 31 x 19 In. .... *illus*	2530.00
Dollhouse, 4 Rooms, White, Black, Gold Trim, Shingles, F.A.O. Schwarz, 1897, 24 x 34 In.	2870.00
Dollhouse, Bedroom, White & Gold Flowers, Bed, Piano, Rocker, Table, Vanity, Spielwaren, Germany	115.00
Dollhouse, Bungalow, Shingle Roof Lifts, Porch, Fence, Steps Detachable, 17 x 22 x 12 In.	920.00
Dollhouse, Shaker Meeting House, Mt. Lebanon, Wood, Furniture, Dolls, c.1950, 34 x 61 In. .	1053.00
Dollhouse, Wallpaper, Doors, Windows, Shingles, Brown Paint, c.1859, 36 x 36 In.	499.00
Dolls are listed in their own category.	
Dolphin, Tail Flips, Tin, Wood, Glass Eyes, Windup, France, 15 In.	385.00
Dolphin, Windup, Tin Body, American Flag, Tail, Fins Move, France, 15 In.	410.00
Donkey, Cart, 2 Passengers, Flywheel, Gold Wash Wheel, Tin Litho, Germany, 8 In.	760.00
Donkey, Cart, 2 Riders, Painted, Tin Lithograph, Windup, Germany, 8 In.	725.00
Donkey, Cart, Clown, Umbrella, Celluloid, Windup, Built-In Key, Japan, 1930s, 9 x 8 In.	173.00
Donkey, Gray, White, Black, Button In Ear, Steiff, 21 x 22 x 9 ½ In.	375.00
Dottie The Driver, Convertible Car, Tin, Plastic, Windup, Box, 6 ¾ In. .... 145.00 to 245.00
Double Irish Mail, Tin, Windup, 2 Men Pull Toy, Handles, Painted, Germany, 9 In.	1755.00
Double Plow, 2 Knife Blades, Orange, Black, Morgrette Constructeur, Sample, 14 x 8 In.	2300.00
Dr. Doodle, No. 477, Pull Toy, Fisher-Price, c.1940	47.00
Dracula, Tin, Vinyl, Windup, Mike Toy, Japan, Universal Studios, 8 ¾ In.	39.00
Dragline, Yellow, Black, No. 415, Tonka, Box, 16 ¾ In.	240.00
Dragster, Tin, Friction, Front Motor, Japan, 1950s, 9 In.	195.00
Dresser, Doll's, Eastlake, Woods, 4 Drawers, Mirror, White Flowers, c.1900, 26 x 17 In.	118.00
Drinking Monkey, Windup, Linemar, Japan, Box, 6 In.	175.00
Drum Major, No. 27, Green Drumsticks, Wolverine, 1950, 13 ½ In.	55.00
Drum Major, Soldier Figure, Windup, Tin Lithograph, Wolverine, 13 ½ In.	225.00
Drum Major, Tin Lithograph, Windup, Chein, Box, 9 In.	201.00
Drum, Barney Google, Tin Litho, Barney On Sparkplug, Other Scenes, 1923, 7 x 11 In.	643.00
Drum, George Washington Dancer, Tin Lithograph Drum, Clockwork, 1874, 9 ½ In.	374.00
Drum, Uncle Wiggily, Parade, Tin Lithograph, Fred A. Wish, c.1924, 6 x 8 In. .... *illus*	468.00
Drum, Wood, Eagle Decal, Heavy Paper Heads, Cord Stringing, 9 In.	71.00
Drum, Wood Veneer, Embossed Rims, Battleships, Armored Cruiser, 10 In.	259.00
Drummer Boy, Tin Lithograph, Windup, Chein, Box, 9 In.	130.00
Drummer, Celluloid, Windup, Japan, 1930s, 10 ½ In.	209.00
Drummer, Mechanical, Windup, Marx, 1930s, 9 In.	195.00
Drummer, Tin, Celluloid, Umbrella, Prewar, Japanese, 9 ½ In.	138.00
Drunkard, Staggers, Bottle, Cup To Mouth, Dressed, Tin, Lead, Wire, Martin, 8 In.	632.00
Drunkard, Tin, Cloth Clothing, Windup, Made In France, 1900, 8 In.	595.00
Dry Sink, Pine, 2 Doors, Drawer, 18 x 8 In.	1100.00
Dry Sink, Wood, Drawer, 2 Doors, Cutouts, Fitted Interior, c.1890, 20 x 24 In.	527.00
Duck, Bill, Legs Move, Green, Brown, Red, Pull Toy, Cast Iron, Hubley, 9 ½ In.	468.00
Duck, Bill Opens & Closes, Legs Move, Painted, Cast Iron, Pull Toy, Hubley, 9 ½ In.	480.00
Duck, Head Bobs, Bill Opens Closes, Wood, Painted, 3 Wheels, Pull Toy, 4 In.	275.00
Duck, Hillclimber, Green, Red, 8 x 8 ½ In.	220.00
Duck, Iron, Waddles, Mouth Opens, Rubber Tire, Pull Toy, Hubley, c.1930, 9 ⅜ In.	2300.00
Duck, Pecking, Flowered Shawl, Tin, Windup, Unique Art, 9 ½ In.	62.00
Duck, Push Pull, Head Bobs Up & Down, Wood, Cardboard, Painted, Lithograph, 9 In.	36.00
Dune Buggy, Oh Happy Days, Battery Operated, Schuco, Box, 9 In.	195.00
Dutch Girl, Carrying Stick & Old Dutch Cleanser, Arms Move, Iron, Hubley, 9 In.	2700.00
Earth Hauler, Steel, Painted, Orange, Doepke Scale Model, Box, 1950s, 27 ½ In.	460.00
Earthman, Tin, Raises Arms, Gun Lights & Sounds, Nomura, c.1955, 9 In.	927.00
Easter Bunny, Pull Toy, Cart, Rabbit Roost, Tin Lithograph, Chein, 1950s, 4 x 11 x 7 ½ In. ...	158.00
Easter On Parade, Bell, Windup, Celluloid, Tin, Mitsushima, Box, 1940s, 4 x 8 In. .... *illus*	221.00
Elephant, Canvas Saddle, Nailed To Wooden Wheel Platform, Pull Toy, 15 x 13 In.	115.00
Elephant, Circus, Kuromachi, Celluloid, Box, 1930s, 9 ¾ In.	605.00
Elephant, Composition, Pull Toy, 1940s, 12 In.	75.00
Elephant, Jumbo, Painted, Tin, Windup, Germany, 3 ½ In.	68.00
Elephant, Musical, Head Moves, Blue Wheels, Pull Toy, Fisher-Price, 1948, 12 x 8 In.	175.00
Elephant, Smokes Pipe, Walker, Tin, Windup, Marusan, Box, 9 ½ In.	65.00
Elephant, Walker, Hide Cover, Clockwork, On & Off Switch, Decamps, France, 10 x 15 In.	495.00
Elmer Fudd, Wiggle, Red Plastic Base, Windup, Waves Hand, By Centau, 1950, 2 ½ In.	60.00
Erector Set, Big Girder, Case, A.C. Gilbert, 1927	1500.00
Erector Set, Chemistry Outfit For Boys, Set 1, A.C. Gilbert, 1920s....................................	79.00
Erector Set, Father, Son, Bridge On Box, A.C. Gilbert, 10 x 18 In. .... *illus*	59.00
Erector Set, Hudson Locomotive, Set A, A.C. Gilbert, 1931..	2200.00

Erector Set, No. 4, Case, A.C. Gilbert, 1915....................................	415.00
Erector Set, No. 6, Mysto, Case, A.C. Gilbert, 1914.............................	1000.00
Erector Set, No. 7, Case, A.C. Gilbert, 1915....................................	821.00
Erector Set, No. 7, Steam Shovel, Wood Box, A.C. Gilbert, 1928.................	125.00
Erector Set, No. 7 ½, Case, A.C. Gilbert, 1926.................................	4350.00
Erector Set, No. 7 ½, Red Box, A.C. Gilbert, 3 x 18 ¼ x 10 In.	165.00
Erector Set, No. 8, Case, A.C. Gilbert, 1925....................................	1440.00
Erector Set, No. 8, Zeppelin, Canvas, Manual, Wood Box, A.C. Gilbert, 11 x 26 In.	1650.00
Erector Set, No. 10, 9 Drawers, Wood, A.C. Gilbert, 1928......................	10500.00
Erector Set, No. 44, Case, A.C. Gilbert, 1918-19..............................	1250.00
Farm Cart, 2 Wheels, Platform, Nickel Plated Bed, Dumps, Salesman Sample, 11 x 7 In.	2300.00
Farm Set, 3 Figures, 5 Animals, Composition, C.C. Milano, Box	145.00
Ferdinand The Bull, Tin, Windup, Tail Spins, Moves In Circles, Marx, Box, 1938............	450.00
Ferris Wheel, Merry-Go-Round, Musical, Moving, Paper, Reed, Box, c.1943........	115.00
Ferris Wheel, Metal, Windup, Box, U.S.A., 16 In.	295.00
Figure, Pongo Pongo, Tin, Windup, Japan, 10 In.	125.00
Fire Pumper, Driver, 3 Horses, Painted, Cast Iron, 19th Century, 29 In.	523.00
Fire Pumper, Driver, Fireman, Painted, Cast Iron, No. 1837, Kenton, 12 In.	600.00
Fire Pumper, Driver, Red, Cast Iron, A.C. Williams, 5 In.	150.00
Fire Pumper, Horse Drawn, Cast Iron, Harris, 20 In.	480.00
Fire Pumper, Horses, Firemen, Hubley No. 10, c.1910, 21 In.	2100.00
Fire Pumper, Kingsbury, Pressed Steel, Boiler, Hose Supports, Disc Wheels, Tires, 22 In.	316.00
Fire Pumper, Ladder, 2 Horses, Bench Seating, Boiler, 3 Ladders, Spoked Wheels, 36 In.	230.00
Fire Pumper, Metal Disc Wheels, Yellow Hubs, Nickel Firemen, Tools, Red Paint, Iron, 13 In. ...	819.00
Fire Pumper, Painted Cast Iron, Rubber Tires, Metal Spoke Wheels, Hubley, 11 In.	230.00
Fire Pumper, Painted, Open Frame, Clockwork, Bing, Germany, c.1910, 10 ¼ In.	2588.00
Fire Pumper, Pressed Steel, Red, Vertical Boiler, Motor, Dual Cylinders, Kingsbury, 22 In.	863.00
Fire Pumper, Stationary Driver, Red, Gold Wheels, Cast Iron, 6 ¼ In.	105.00
Fire Pumper, Steel, Painted, Clockwork, Open Frame, Boiler, Kingsbury, c.1911, 9 In.	259.00
Fire Pumper, Tin, Friction, Red, Black, Gold, Japan, Modern Toys, 1950s, 9 In.	85.00
Fire Station, No. 8, Red, Black, Fire Bell, Cast Iron, Dent...................	490.00
Fire Truck, 2 Ladders, Tin Lithograph, Steel, Wyandotte, 19 In.	118.00
Fire Truck, Hook & Ladder, Driver, Decals, Hubley, c.1929, 9 ½ In.	975.00
Fire Truck, Hose, Figures, Clockwork, Headlights, Spare Tire, Delahaye, Box, c.1900, 15 In. ...	2070.00
Fire Truck, Ladder, Aerial, Electric Lights, Bing, Germany, 20 ½ In.	1150.00
Fire Truck, Ladder, Aerial, Mack, Aluminum Ladders, Red, Smith, Miller, 1952, 36 In.	495.00
Fire Truck, Ladder, Cast Iron, Driver, Fireman, Red, A.C. Williams, 5 ¼ In.	150.00
Fire Truck, Ladder, Cast Iron, Red, Nickel Hose Reel, Rubber Tires, Disc Wheels, 16 In.	144.00
Fire Truck, Ladder, Clockwork, Firemen, Open Frame, Tippco, Germany, c.1930s, 20 In.	2300.00
Fire Truck, Ladder, Clockwork, Trestle Tower, Figures, Gunthermann, Germany, c.1900, 15 In. ...	2588.00
Fire Truck, Ladder, Iron, Open Frame, Figure, Skoglund & Olsen, Sweden, Seto, 16 In.	690.00
Fire Truck, Ladder, Los Angeles Fire Department, Smith-Miller, 26 In.	290.00
Fire Truck, Ladder, Pressed Steel, Hose, Bell Rings, Keith Lowe, England, 1930s.........	295.00
Fire Truck, Ladder, Windup, Bakelite Cab, Tin Tanker, Germany, 8 ½ In.	195.00
Fire Truck, Ladders, Open Cab, Hand Crank Hose Reel, Red, Buddy L, c.1930s, 26 In.	711.00
Fire Truck, Nickel Plated Wheels, Driver, Pressed Steel Ladders, Red, Arcade, 21 In.	1725.00
Fire Truck, No. 5, Red, Metal, Tonka, 17 x 6 ½ In.	120.00
Fire Truck, Search Light, Doepke...	1050.00
Fire Truck, Steam Pumper, Nickeled Boiler, Hubley, 5 In.	250.00
Fire Truck, Water Tower, No. 9, Red, LaFrance, 12 x 32 ½ x 9 In.	135.00
Fire Truck, Water Tower, Steel, Open Cab, Brass Bell, Horn, Keystone, U.S.A., 1925, 30 In.	2070.00
Fire Truck, Windup, Metal, Germany, 1930s, 14 In.	375.00
Fire Wagon, Driver, 3 Horses, Hose Reel, Hubley, 1915, 14 In.	995.00
Fire Wagon, Fire Chief, Driver, 2 Horses, Hubley, 19 In.	1295.00
Fire Wagon, Fire Chief, Horse, Painted, Cast Iron, Ives, 14 ½ In.	1900.00
Fire Wagon, Hook & Ladder, 2 Firemen, 2 Horses, 1893, 21 In.	1295.00
Fire Wagon, Hook & Ladder, 2 Firemen, Horses, Bell, Ladders, Hubley, 1910, 24 In.	825.00
Fire Wagon, Hook & Ladder, 2 Riders, Horses, Bell, Folding Seats, Hubley, 1910, 32 In.	2200.00
Fire Wagon, Hook & Ladder, Firemen, 2 Horses, Bell, Pratt & Letchworth, 1885, 28 In.	2095.00
Fire Wagon, Ladder, 2 Firemen, 2 Horses, Ives, 1893, 21 In.	1295.00
Fire Wagon, Ladders, Figures, 3 Horses, Dent Front, Nickel Plate, Cast Iron, Harris, 30 In.	702.00
Fire Wagon, Ladders, Red Figures, 3 Black Horses, Cast Iron, Kenton, 19 In.	176.00
Fire Wagon, Patrol, 5 Firemen, 3 Horses, Kenton, 1911, 12 ¾ In.	895.00
Fire Wagon, Pulled By A Pair Of Horses, Horsehair Tails, c.1880, 8 ½ x 20 In.	605.00
Firefighters Watercart, Iron, Painted, Fireman, Wheels Move, 9 ½ x 2 ½ In.	50.00
Fireman, Climbing Ladder, Tin Lithograph, Windup, Plastic, Marx, Box, 21 ½ In.	173.00

Toy, Erector Set, Father, Son,
Bridge On Box, A.C. Gilbert, 10 x 18 In.
$59.00

Topps Baseball Cards
Baseball cards from the 1952 Topps set did not sell well back when they were issued. The high numbers from 311 to 407 came out late, probably in smaller quantities. Many were dumped by the company. So today the cards are hard to find and sell well even in poor condition. No. 320, Brooklyn Dodgers pitcher John Rutherford, is the hardest to find in mint condition. High numbers from other sets also can be scarce and expensive.

T

Toy, Football Place Kicker, Cast Iron, Painted, c.1925, 8 In. $547.00

Toy, Grand Central Station, Windup Trains, Die Cut Tin, Katz, Box, 1920s, 16 In. $2243.00

Toy, Grasshopper, Clicker, Legs Move Up & Down, Cast Iron, Pull Toy, 12 In. $293.00

Toy, Grasshopper, Metal, Pull Toy, 12 In. $518.00

Fish, Rattle, Copper, England, 10 In.	234.00
Fisherman, Pond, Tin, Windup, Arm Moves, Green, Red, Yellow, Painted, Germany, 4 In.	527.00
Flintstones, Bedrock Express Playset, Plastic, Hanna-Barbera, Marx, Box, c.1962, 23 x 27 In.	180.00
Flintstones, Dino The Dinosaur, Hopping, Windup, Tin Litho, Built-In Key, Marx, 1962, 3 In.	173.00
Flying Bird, Paper Wings, Lehmann, 1920	1200.00
Flying Man, Tin, Swinging Car, Mouth Opens & Closes, Flag, Yoneya, Box, 11 In.	299.00
Flying Saucer, Astro 8, Tin, Celluloid Windows, Dome, Marubishi, 7 ½ In.	209.00
Flying Saucer, Cat Driver, Mystery Action, Illuminated Scenes Rotate, Nomura, Japan, 9 In.	316.00
Flying Saucer, Martian, Tin, Sparks, Spinning Pilot, Celluloid Dome, Nomura, Box, 6 In.	441.00
Flying Saucer, Terre Mars W-902, Tin, Push, France, c.1950	169.00
Flying Saucer, Z-106, Tin, Litho Crew, Masudaya, 5 ½ In.	333.00
Football Place Kicker, Cast Iron, Painted, c.1925, 8 In. .... *illus*	547.00
Fork Lift, Lionel No. 264, Box, c.1958	595.00
Fort & Trading Post, Superior Metal, T. Cohn, N.Y., Box, c.1953, 8 ½ x 24 In.	179.00
Fox The Magician, Tin, Windup, Box, 1950s, 6 ¼ In.	135.00
Foxy Grandpa, On Rollers, Tin, Windup, Does Splits, Raises Arms, Gunthermann, 8 In.	1265.00
Foxy Grandpa, Roly Poly, Papier-Mache, 1900s, 9 ½ In.	450.00
Frankenstein, Aurora, 1964, 19 ¼ In.	523.00
Frankenstein, Mechanical, Tin, Plastic, Stepover Motion, Arms Move, Marx, c.1963, 5 In.	301.00
Friendship 7, Friction Capsule, Tin Litho, Plastic Window, Keiichi, Japan, c.1962, 4 In.	115.00
Games are listed in their own category.	
Garage, Racing Car, Driver, Litho, Opening Doors, Shingle Roof, Windup, Lehmann, 6 In.	1150.00
Garage, Wood, Painted Cream, Red Roof, 5 Opening Doors, Overland, 17 ½ In.	431.00
Gas Pump, Crank, Red, Cast Iron, A.C. Williams, 6 ⅜ In.	195.00
Gas Pump, Green, Red Trimmed, Glass Globe, Side Lever, Wooden Handle, Rebb, 10 In.	863.00
Gas Pump, Iron, Red, Front Dial, Globe, Rope Hose, Metal Handle, Arcade, c.1930, 6 In.	489.00
Gas Pump, Iron, Red, Orange, Embossed Globe, Rope Hose, Kilgore, Box, 6 In.	1610.00
Gas Pump, Red, Gold Paint, Cast Iron, Arcade, 4 ⅜ In.	165.00
Gas Pump, Red, Logos, Spoke Wheels, Glass Side Doors, Bottle Storage, Door, 6 In.	2300.00
Gas Pump, Tin, Crank, 1930s, 7 ½ In.	195.00
Gas Station, Quick Start, Car Wound At Gas Pump, Tin, Push Button, Japan, 4 x 9 x 5 In.	150.00
Gas Station, Race Car, Penny Toy, Germany, Prewar	195.00
Gas Station, Red, Green Wheels, Chein, 8 In.	395.00
Gas Station, Tin, Marx, 1930s, 9 ½ In.	175.00
Gee Wiz Race, No. 40, Tin Lithograph, Windup, Wolverine, Box, 6 ¼ x 16 In.	22.00
George The Drummer Boy, Tin, Windup, Plays Drum, Eyes Move, Marx, 9 In.	35.00
George The Drummer Boy, Tin, Windup, Plays Drum, Eyes Move, Marx, Box, 9 In.	165.00
G.I. Joe, Action Sailor, Navy Manual, Club Membership, Insignia Sheet, 1964, 12 In.	173.00
G.I. Joe, Jeep, Tin Lithograph, Windup, Unique Art, 6 ½ In.	77.00
G.I. Joe, K-9 Pups, Tin, Windup, Unique Art, 9 In.	68.00
Girl, At Well Pump, Tin Clocker, Tin Spiral Simulate Water, Gunthermann, 9 ¾ In.	1840.00
Girl, Chickens, Head Scarf, Mechanical, Tin Litho, Windup, T.P.S., Japan, Box, 3 x 5 In.	285.00
Girl, Dog, On Bicycle, Bisque Head, Glass Eyes, Wig, Clockwork, Rubber Tires, 9 x 10 In.	144.00
Girl, Mechanical, Blue Eyes, Wig, Wheeled Platform, Mirror, Clockwork, France, 12 ½ In.	403.00
Girl, Roller Skating, Celluloid, Windup, 8 In.	275.00
Girl, Seated In Highchair, Lithograph Of 2 Goats, Table Folds, Penny Toy, 3 ¾ In.	316.00
Girl, Waves Whip, Chases Goat, Nods Head, Tin, Windup, Gunthermann, 7 In.	1495.00
Girls, Tennis, Tin, Windup, Celluloid Ball Moves, Arms Move, Germany, 10 In.	1872.00
Gly-Da-Jet Set, 2 Planes, Abbo, Box, 7 ¾ x 12 ⅜ In.	60.00
Gnome, Feeding Parrot, Embossed, Tin Lithograph, Penny Toy, 4 ¼ In.	403.00
Go-About, Man, Boy, Chasing In Circle, Tin, Windup, Marked, SGW, Germany, 5 In.	1404.00
Go-Kart, Super Kun, Moves Forward, Engine Noise, Nomura, Japan, Box, 10 In.	1265.00
Godzilla, Against Mothra, Windup, Blue Tin, Swings Arms, Box, 5 x 8 In.	144.00
Golden Bear, Windup, Plush, Celluloid, Helmet, Football, Metal Feet, Box, 1950s, 6 In.	201.00
Gondola, Man, With Pole, Tin, Windup, Germany, 6 In.	1650.00
Goodtime Charlie, Hat, Horn, Tin, Windup, Box, 10 ½ In.	82.00
Goose, Nodding, Lithograph, Windup, Marx, 1924, 6 In.	75.00
Grader, Adams Motor, Steel, Painted, Doepke Scale Model, Box, 1950s, 26 In.	345.00
Grader, Slik-Toy, Yellow, Aluminum, Rubber Tires, Lansing, Box, 3 ½ x 9 ½ In.	164.00
Grand Central Station, Windup Trains, Die Cut Tin, Katz, Box, 1920s, 16 In. .... *illus*	2243.00
Grasshopper, Aluminum Leg, Green, Clicker Noise, Antennas, Hubley, 11 In.	1380.00
Grasshopper, Clicker, Legs Move Up & Down, Cast Iron, Pull Toy, 12 In. .... *illus*	293.00
Grasshopper, Green, Cast Iron, Nickel Cast Legs, Hubley, 4 ¼ In.	546.00
Grasshopper, Metal, Pull Toy, 12 In. .... *illus*	518.00
Grasshopper, Pull Toy, 2 Front Wheels, Painted, Cast Iron, Hubley, 13 In.	380.00
Grocery Shop, Pet's, Oak, Shelves, Counter, Sign, Canned Goods, Scales, 24 x 15 x 12 In.	144.00

T

Gun & Holster Set, Double, Western Boy, Box, 10 ¼ x 10 ¼ In. ....*illus*	200.00
Gun, Alley Sloper, Gun Game, Pistol, Ammo, Milton Bradley, Box, 1907	295.00
Gun, Big Bill Cap Pistol, Raised Lettering On Grip, Kilgore, 1920s, 5 ½ In.	45.00
Gun, Colt 455, Sparkling Gun, Tin Lithograph, Japan, By K.O., 1950s, 5 ¼ In.	70.00
Gun, Flintlock, Hubley, Box	35.00
Gun, G-Man, Automatic, Sparkler, Marx, Box, 4 In. ....*illus*	117.00
Gun, Jesko, Rubber Bank Disc Shooting Pistol, 10 Discs, Sekiden Chem. Ind., Co., 5 In. ...	33.00
Gun, Luger, Miniature Cap Gun, Black, Tin Grips, Hong Kong, 1960s, By Victory, 2 ½ In.	18.00
Gun, Space, Red, Plastic, Battery Operated, Remco, 9 In.	33.00
Gun, Tom Corbett, Space Cadet, Marx, Box, 1950s, 10 In. ....*illus*	585.00
Gunfighter, Dan Troop, Plastic, Molded, Painted, Hartland, Box, 7 ¾ In.	384.00
Gunfighter, Johnny McKay, Plastic, Molded, Painted, Hartland, Box, 7 ¾ In.	413.00
Gunfighter, Paladin, Plastic, Molded, Painted, Hartland, Box, 7 ¾ In.	384.00
Gunfighter, Wyatt Earp, Plastic, Molded, Painted, Hartland, Box, 7 ¾ In.	236.00
Ham & Sam, Minstrel Team, Tin Lithograph, Windup, Strauss, 7 x 6 ½ x 3 In.	605.00
Handcar, 2 Riders, Windup, 1930s, 6 In.	225.00
Handcar, Blue, Red Cast Iron Wheels, Decals, Doepke, 1957, 30 In.	400.00
Handcar, Clowns, Hoky & Poky, Tin, Windup, Box, 5 ½ x 6 ¼ In.	225.00
Handcar, Moon Mullins & Kayo, Tin Lithograph, Windup, Marx, 1930s	295.00 to 530.00
Handcar, Moon Mullins & Kayo, Windup, Marx, Box, 1930s	750.00
Handcar, Wood Body, Wheels, Iron Straps, Multicolored Paint, c.1890, 22 ½ x 62 In.	385.00
Hansom Cab, Horse Drawn Tin, Windup, Cab Rolls, Rubber Tires, Germany, 12 In.	995.00
Happy Hooligan, Cloth, Jointed, Wood, Schoenhut, 8 ½ In.	633.00
Happy Hooligan, Dances On Drum, Windup, Kiddies Metal Toy Co., 1930s....................	1075.00
Happy Hooligan, Walker, Green, White, Red, Tin Litho, Windup, Chein, c.1930, 6 ¼ In.	180.00
Happy Skating Bunny, Tin, Windup, T.P.S., Box, 6 ¾ In.	255.00
Harold Lloyd, Walker, Funny Face, Tin Windup, Marx, 10 ¾ In.	325.00
Harold Lloyd, Walks With Cane, Windup, Box, 1930s..	750.00
Hay Rake, C.M. Clinton Model Maker, Ithaca, N.Y., Wood, Brass, Sample, 15 x 14 In.	7760.00
Hay Rake, Driver, Horse Drawn, Tin, Wire, Cast Iron, Wilkins, 9 In. ....*illus*	1725.00
Helicopter, Air Force, Tin, Friction, Japan, 1950s, 10 ½ In.	75.00
Helicopter, Red, Yellow, Woodette, Box, 4 ¾ x 10 In.	70.00
Helmet, Satellite Explorer, Aluminum, Plastic Face Plate, Mirro, Box, 9 ¼ x 9 ¾ In.	244.00
Helmet, Weird-Ohs, Plastic, Exhaust Piping, Visor, Chin Strap, Box, c.1964, 10 x 10 In.	304.00
Hen On Nest, Tin Lithograph, Windup, Baldwin, 5 ½ In.	59.00
Henry, Celluloid, Riding 4 Wheel Tin Cart, Pulled By Goose	1250.00
Henry, Eating Ice Cream, Tin Lithograph, Windup, Linemar, 5 ¾ In.	590.00
Henry, On Elephant Trunk, Friend, Celluloid, Tin, Moves, Windup, Borgfeldt, 1930s, 8 In.	448.00
Henry, Riding 4 Wheel Tin Cart, Goose, Celluloid, Windup...	1450.00
Hey-Hey The Chicken Snatcher, Black Man, Tin Lithograph, Windup, Marx, 8 In.	780.00
Hippopotamus, Painted Eyes, Schoenhut..	250.00
Hobby Kit, Genuine Leather, Crestcraft, Box, 10 x 16 ¾ In.	22.00
Hobbyhorse, Carved, Applied Mane, Tail, Studded Saddle, Metal Stirrups, 37 x 33 x 8 In.	239.00
Hobbyhorse, Molded Birch, Blue Trim, Burned Signature, Creative Playthings, 1960s, 25 In. ...	360.00
Hoisting Tower, Buckets, Telescoping Chutes, Pressed Steel, Buddy L, c.1928-31, 29 In.	1725.00
Honeymoon Express, Tin Lithograph, Windup, Marx, Box, 9 ½ In.	120.00 to 150.00
Horn, Carrot, Figural, Blue, Pressed Paper, Germany, 8 ½ x 2 ¼ In.	12.00
Horn, Salamander, Figural, Blue, Pressed Paper, c.1930, 9 ½ x 2 ½ In.	30.00
Horse & Buggy, Driver, Doctor's, Painted, Cast Iron, Wilkins, 1890	410.00
Horse & Carriage, Driver, Hide Covered, Bisque, Glass Eyes, Mohair, Windup, France, 1800s, 14 In.	500.00
Horse & Cart, 2 Horses, Bell, Cast Iron, Steel, Nickel Plated, Gong Bell Mfg., 11 In.	238.00
Horse & Cart, Tin, Windup, Rolls On Front Wheel, Painted, Germany, 8 In.	468.00
Horse & Chariot, Invictus, Tin, Windup, Italy, 1922, 15 In.	660.00
Horse & Covered Wagon, Driver, La Maraiche, T & M, Paris, France, 8 In.	2750.00
Horse & Jockey, Tin, Hull & Stafford, Pull Toy, c.1870..	1125.00
Horse & Sleigh, Woman, 2 Black Horses, Green Sleigh, Cast Iron, Hubley, 14 ¾ In.	600.00
Horse & Van, Driver, Tin, Yellow, Red, Composition Driver, Push Toy, Germany, 12 In.	819.00
Horse & Van, Driver, Yellow, Red Wheels, Tin, Push Toy, Germany, 12 In.	795.00
Horse & Wagon, 2 Dray Horses, Driver, Kenton, 15 In.	325.00
Horse & Wagon, 2 Horses, Brake, Seats, 6 Figures, Spoke Wheels, Iron, Hubley, 18 In.	575.00
Horse & Wagon, 2 Horses, Riders, Passengers, Kenton Band, 1930s, 14 In.	895.00
Horse & Wagon, 2 Horses, Tin Litho, Trolley Body, Die Cut Figures, Hutzler's, 20 ½ In.	230.00
Horse & Wagon, 2 Wheel Cart, Carved Wood, Tin Wheel Guards, 8 x 11 x 11 In.	259.00
Horse & Wagon, 4 Horses, Brake, Black, Orange, 7 Figures, Pratt & Letchworth, 27 In.	460.00
Horse & Wagon, American Ice Company, Wooden, Pull Toy, Handle, Jacrin, 29 In.	575.00
Horse & Wagon, Barrel, White Denton Horse, Barrels, Cast Iron, Tin, Wilkins, 15 In.	146.00

Toy, Gun & Holster Set, Double,
Western Boy, Box, 10 ¼ x 10 ¼ In.
$200.00

Toy, Gun, G-Man, Automatic, Sparkler,
Marx, Box, 4 In.
$117.00

Toy, Gun, Tom Corbett, Space Cadet,
Marx, Box, 1950s, 10 In.
$585.00

Toy, Hay Rake, Driver, Horse Drawn, Tin,
Wire, Cast Iron, Wilkins, 9 In.
$1725.00

T

Toy, Krazy Kat, Express Train, Oil, Moving Head, Cloth Ears, Tin Litho, Chein, c.1932, 12 In.
$1112.00

Toy, Maggie & Jiggs, Squeeze, Tin Lithograph, U-Shape Handle, 1920s, 8 In.
$784.00

Bobbin'-head Fakes
Bobbin'-head sports dolls have been faked. The only real gold-base college football doll is Wisconsin; the others are fakes. There are also fake basketball dolls for Indiana, Kentucky, and perhaps others.

Horse & Wagon, Black Driver, On Green Log, Painted, Iron, Signed, Kenton, 14 ¾ In.	852.00
Horse & Wagon, Carved Wood, 13 Wood Barrels, 29 In.	288.00
Horse & Wagon, Delivery, Red, Cast Iron, Harris, 15 ¼ In.	104.00
Horse & Wagon, Dray, 5 Barrels, Figure, Cast Iron, Tin, Wilkins, 11 In.	146.00
Horse & Wagon, Driver, 2 White Horses, Confectionary, Tin, Painted, 1890s, 14 In.	3000.00
Horse & Wagon, Driver, Coal, Wood, Harris, 1903, 12 ¼ In.	775.00
Horse & Wagon, Driver, Tin, Painted, Embossed, CR, France, 8 In.	495.00
Horse & Wagon, Dump, Contractor, Driver, Arcade, 14 In.	550.00
Horse & Wagon, Dump, Driver, Cast Iron, Bench Seating, Spoke Wheels, Arcade, 14 In.	288.00
Horse & Wagon, Dump, Kenton, 10 In.	275.00
Horse & Wagon, Fancy Goods & Toys, Tin, Stencils, Fallows Of Philadelphia, 23 In.	12500.00
Horse & Wagon, Flags, Tailgate, Driver, Paint, Litho, Tin, Charles Rosingal, France, 8 In.	527.00
Horse & Wagon, Ice Delivery, Yellow Spoke Wheels, Removable Tailgate, Hubley, 15 In.	230.00
Horse & Wagon, Milk, Borden's, Driver, 4 Glass Bottles, Wood Carrier, Richtoy	500.00
Horse & Wagon, Milk, White, Cast Iron, Open Doors, Kenton, 12 ½ In.	104.00
Horse & Wagon, Milk, Wood Milk Crate, Bottles, Borden's, Tin Lithograph, Wood, 17 In.	374.00
Horse & Wagon, Polar Ice, Painted, No Driver, Cast Iron, Ives	780.00
Horse & Wagon, River, 3 Horses, Wood, Painted, Signed, Rich Toy Co., 1920s, 35 In.	319.00
Horse & Wagon, Tin, Cast Iron, Spoke Wheels, Hull & Stafford, c.1880, 16 In.	1610.00
Horse Racing, 3 Horses & Riders, Bell, Tin, Windup, Japan	110.00
Horse, Black, Cloth, Leather, Wood Platform, Pull Toy, 28 In.	600.00
Horse, Gliding, Painted, Wood, Glass Eyes, Horsehair Mane, Tail, Tack, Saddle, 36 ½ In.	178.00
Horse, Gliding, Wood, Carved, Painted, Saddle, Stirrups, Bridle, Horsehair Mane, 41 x 48 In.	896.00
Horse, Gong Bell, Wood, Metal, Front Wheels Are Bells, 15 x 17 In.	55.00
Horse, Horse Hair, Wood Hooves, Glass Eyes, Platform Base, Wheels, 32 x 32 In.	236.00
Horse, Mechanical, Bucking Motion, Wood, Carved Saddle, c.1940, 56 x 68 In.	3525.00
Horse, Platform, Tin, Soldiers, Horses Move Up & Down, Pull Toy, August, 1886, 9 In.	1287.00
Horse, Prancing, Black Paint, Cast Iron, Arcade	25.00
Horse, Riding, 2 Wheels, Wood, Carved, Painted, 40 In.	140.00
Horse, Riding, Mobo, Pressed Steel, Leather Reins, Painted, 31 x 26 In.	240.00
Horse, Rocking, Carved, Oilcloth Saddle, Joined Rockers, Hair, c.1850, 24 x 43 In.	294.00
Horse, Rocking, Dapple Gray, Leather Ears, Vinyl Seat, Plastic Eyes, 32 x 16 x 29 In.	150.00
Horse, Rocking, Doll's, Composition, Leather Saddle, Iron Bases, 4 Wheels, 27 x 25 In.	345.00
Horse, Rocking, Double Silhouette, Painted Saddle, Straw Filled Seat, 23 x 40 x 14 In.	102.00
Horse, Rocking, Jockey, Meier, Penny Toy, 3 ¼ In.	149.00
Horse, Rocking, Mixed Woods, Carved, Mounted, Dappled Paint, c.1920, 25 x 34 In.	294.00
Horse, Rocking, Painted White, Metal Swing Supports, Platform, 31 x 44 x 15 In.	147.00
Horse, Rocking, Straw Filled, Mohair, Germany, c.1900, 27 In.	147.00
Horse, Rocking, Wood & Masonite, Red Body, Lack Saddle, Spring Form, 1940s, 34 In.	135.00
Horse, Rocking, Wood, Carved, Painted, Dappled, Horsehair Tail, Glass Eyes, 28 x 42 In.	207.00
Horse, Rocking, Wood, Carved, White, Black, Gold Paint, Red Support, c.1905, 30 x 33 In.	441.00
Horse, Sparkplug, Race, Barney Google's, Tan Flannel, Beige Horse Blanket, 10 ¼ In.	475.00
Horse, Swinging, Wood, Horsehair Mane, Cast Iron, J.A. Crandall, 45 In.	230.00
Horse, Wood, Paint, Pull Toy, c.1910	1096.00
Horses, Platform, 2 Brown, 2 White Horses, Moves, Pull Toy, Fallows, 1886, 9 In.	1210.00
Hose Reel, Iron, Tin, Lions, Liberty Shield, Pull Toy, George W. Brown & Co., 11 In.	48875.00
Hot Air Balloon, Global, Tin Litho, Gondolas, Figures, String, Lehmann, Box, c.1899, 6 In.	4888.00
House, Carpenter Engine, Iron Doors, Bell Tower, Canvas Roof, 26 x 18 x 10 In.	460.00
House Trailer, Aluminum, Removable Roof, Plastic, Wood, Fabric, Smith-Miller, Box, 26 In.	403.00
Humphrey Mobile, Driver, Tin Lithograph, Windup, Wyandotte, 1940s, 7 ¼ In.	288.00
Humpty Dumpty, Rolling & Rocking Action, Pull Toy, Fisher-Price, 1971, 7 x 5 In.	45.00
Hupmobile, Sedan, Orrill Motor Co., Paper On Wood, c.1926, 5 In.	150.00
Ice Box, Quartersawn, Wood, Galvanized Shelves, Salesman's Sample, 16 x 11 x 9 In.	2750.00
Ice Box, White Paint, Iron, Fake Ice Block, Alaska, Salesman's Sample, 11 x 9 x 6 In.	485.00
Ice Cutting Machine, Double Flywheel, Belt Driven Motor, G.B. Gruman, 17 ¼ x 8 In.	7130.00
Indian, Brave Eagle, White Cloud Horse, Plastic, Molded, Painted, Hartland, Box, 8 ½ In.	354.00
Jack-In-The-Box, Bell Hop, Cloth Outfit, Nadine Wenden, 10 ¾ In.	104.00
James Bond, Attache Case, Secret Agent 007, Plastic, Glidrose, c.1965, 11 x 17 In.	759.00
Jazzbo Jim, Dances On Roof, Tin Lithograph, Windup, Unique Art, 1921, 10 In.	380.00
Jazzbo Jim, Fiddler On The Roof, Tin, Windup, Unique Art Mfg. Co.	300.00
Jazzbo Jim, Strumming Banjo, Dancing On Roof, Tin Litho, Unique Art, 1920s	1200.00
Jeep, Army, Olive, Composition Tires, Die Cast, Tootsietoy, 1947, 4 ¾ In.	95.00
Jeep, Jumping, Marx, Box, 4 ⅜ x 5 ½ In.	145.00
Jeep, Police, Policeman, Arm Moves Gun, Lights Up, Tin, Dayia, Japan, 1950s, 9 ½ In.	275.00
Jeep, Trailer, Willys, Green, Pressed Steel, Canvas, Marked, Lumar, Marx, Box, 18 In.	195.00
Jeep, Willys, Headlights, Trailer, Red & Blue, Box, 1948, 12 In.	500.00

Jeep, Windup, Marx, 6 In.	175.00
Jenny The Balking Mule, Tin Lithograph, Windup, Strauss, Box, 6 x 9 ¼ In.	275.00
JFK, Rocking Chair, Happy Days Are Here Again Music Box, Kamar, c.1963, 11 In.	748.00
Jigger, Dances On Paddle, Wood, Jointed Shoulders, Hip, Knees, 8 ¾ In.	533.00
Jigger, Man, Top Hat, Painted, Tin, 16 In.	82.00
Jiggs, Cloth, Metal Ball Jointed Arms, Legs, Composition Head, Hands, Feet, Bucherer, 7 In.	316.00
Joe Penner & His Duck Goo Goo, Tin Litho, Windup, Louis Marx Co., Box, 8 ½ In.	1053.00
Jungle Trio, Monkeys, Elephant, Instruments, Tin Litho, Battery Operated, Linemar, Box, 8 In.	502.00
Kaleidoscope, Tin Litho, Paper Scope, Space Scenes, Okabe-Occupied Japan, Box, 9 In.	802.00
Kiddy Cyclist, Boy On Tricycle, Tin, Windup, Unique Art, 1940-60, 8 ¾ In.	77.00
Kiddy Cyclist, Boy Riding Tricycle, Tin, Windup, Unique Art, Box	120.00
King Kong, Windup, Gray, Black, Marx, 7 ½ In.	375.00
Kitten, With Ball, Painted, Tin, Wood, Push Down Tail, 4 ¾ x 7 ½ In.	38.00
Knockout Champs, Boxers, Celluloid, Tin Litho, Boxing Ring, Windup, Marx, 7 In.	345.00
Krazy Kat, Express Train, Oil, Moving Head, Cloth Ears, Tin Litho, Chein, c.1932, 12 In. . *illus*	1112.00
Krazy Kat, On Scooter, Tin Lithograph, Windup, Chein, 1932, 6 In.	820.00
Kriter, Dizzy Donkey, Pop-Up, Gray, Paddle, 4 Strings, Fisher-Price, 1930s, 11 x 5 In.	65.00
L'Entraineur Skiff, Tin Lithograph, Partially Dressed Driver, Windup, FV, Box, 7 In.	5175.00
Land Sea Air Super Battle Set, Punch Out, Homefront, Electric Corp., 1943, 181 Piece	139.00
Le Charcutier, Cloth Dressed, Tin, Wire Figure, Windup, Martin Butcher, Box, 8 In.	6325.00
Li'l Abner Dogpatch Band, Windup, Unique Art, Box, c.1945	487.00 to 675.00
Lighthouse, Moat Base, Boat Circles, Embossed, Germany, 15 x 15 In.	173.00
Limousine, Carette, Tin Plate, Glass Windows, Rear Doors Open, Hand Brake, 15 ½ x 9 In.	1035.00
Limousine, Front Crank Clockwork, Glass Windows, Rubber Tires, c.1907, 22 ½ In.	80500.00
Limousine, Moko Tin, Driver, Windup, 9 ½ In.	805.00
Limousine, Tin Lithograph, Windup, Penny Toy, Fischer, c.1925, 4 ½ In.	1495.00
Little People, Drive-In Movie, Yellow Car, Black Male, 1990, 12 ½ x 8 ½ In.	70.00
Little Red Riding Hood, Walks, Wolf Nods Head, Tin, Windup, Gunthermann, 6 ¾ In.	2300.00
Louis Armstrong, Playing Trumpet, Windup, Tin, 1950s	395.00
Machine Gun, Clip, Bullets, Tin, Box, c.1950, 20 ½ In.	49.00
Machine Gun, Ra-Ta-Ta-Tat, Cast Iron, Nickel Plated, Kilgore, c.1935, 5 In.	85.00
Maggie & Jiggs, Squeeze, Tin Lithograph, U-Shape Handle, 1920s, 8 In. *illus*	784.00
Maggie & Jiggs, Tin, Windup, Germany, 1924, 7 In.	498.00
Magician, Lowers Lid, Raises Wand, Man's Head Appears, Tin, Windup, Gunthermann, 6 ½ In.	4888.00
Mail Car, Irish, 2 Riders, Tin Lithograph, Windup, Animated, Bing, 11 In.	2300.00
Man, Bowling, Tin, Lever, Marbles Roll On Arm, Thrown By Pushed Lever, Martin, 8 In.	1380.00
Man, Butter & Eggs, Man Holds Duck, Tin Lithograph, Windup, Marx, 7 ¾ In.	505.00
Man, Fishing, Arm Moves Up & Down, Tin, Painted, Windup, Germany, 4 In.	495.00
Man, Grinding Wheel, Tin Lithograph, Steam Accessory, Bing, 4 ½ x 5 ½ In.	173.00
Man, On Roller Skates, Tin, Cloth Dressed, Gold Letters, Martin, 8 In.	6325.00
Man, On Wire, Twirls Ball, Tin, Windup, Gunthermann, 9 In.	4025.00
Man, Planer, Planes Curl Of Wood, Tin, Wire, Cloth Dressed, Martin, 6 In.	3450.00
Man, Pulling Hay Cart, Painted, Tin Lithograph, Windup, Germany, 8 In.	395.00
Man, Pushing Cart, Bag, Accessories, Blue, Stenciled, Tin, Windup, Germany, 8 In.	790.00
Man, Rowboat, Wheels, Tin, Windup, Sailors Arms, Oars Move Up, Down, Germany, 6 In.	1755.00
Man, Shoots Pool, Windup, c.1900, 8 In.	750.00
Manure Spreader, Oliver Superior, Rubber Tires, Iron, Arcade, Box, 1940, 10 In.	1840.00
Marine, Wiggles, Tin Lithograph, Windup, J. Chein, 5 ¼ In.	130.00
Marionette Theater, Windup, Celluloid, Prewar, Japan, 1930s, 11 In.	725.00
Marionette Theater, Windup, Celluloid, Tin Lithograph, Japan, Box, 9 ½ In.	518.00
Mask, Monkey, Cotton, Velvet, Metal, Mechanical Mouth, Black, Red, Stand, 11 x 6 In.	830.00
Men Sawing, Tin, Electric Powered, Martin, 9 ½ In.	3450.00
Merry-Go-Round, 5 Horses, 5 Swan Chariots, Tin Litho, Windup, Bell Rings, Chein, 11 In.	230.00
Merry-Go-Round, Cars, Airplanes, Drivers, Tin Litho, Canopy, Clockwork, HMN, Germany, 13 In.	5750.00
Merry-Go-Round, Tin Figures Riding Horses, In Gondolas, Canopy Top, 18 x 18 In.	374.00
Merry-Go-Round, Tin, Windup, Germany, 4 ½ In.	121.00
Merrymakers Band, 4 Mice, Piano, Tin Lithograph, Marx, c.1925, 9 In.	470.00
Merrymakers Band, Windup, Marx, 1920s	1100.00
Military Figure, Cloth & Composition, Painted Face, Base, Germany, c.1910, 6 In.	805.00
Milkman, Painted Wood, Jointed Arms, Legs, Cloth, Schoenhut, 7 ½ In.	343.00
Minstrel, Black, Men Play Banjo, Tap Tambourine, Tin, Windup, Gunthermann, 8 In.	1265.00
Miss Friday, The Typist, Tin Lithograph, Windup, Box, 7 ¾ x 8 ½ In.	135.00
Missile Launcher, Chevy Truck Cab, Bump & Go Action, Lights, Nomura, 11 ½ In.	323.00
Monkey, Acrobat, Composition Head, Wooden Body, Windup, Dressed, 7 ½ In.	489.00
Monkey, Acrobat, Rocks, Balancing On Rod, Tin, Cloth Dressed, Martin, 6 In.	4025.00
Monkey, Climbing, Penny Toy, Distler, 6 ⅝ In.	132.00

Toy, Motorcycle, Delivery, Say It With Flowers, Clockwork, Cast Iron, 10 In. $63250.00

Fisher-Price

Fisher-Price toys were made of wood from 1931 to 1950. Some plastic was used in the 1950s. By 1964 the toys were almost entirely plastic.

T

Dating Teddy Bears

Early teddy bears had boot-button eyes used before World War I, glass eyes beginning in the 1920s, and plastic eyes and noses since the 1950s. After World War II, teddy bears had shorter arms and flatter faces.

Toy, Movie Camera, Tripod, Wood, Metal, Schoenhut Co., Box, c.1915, 10 In.
$205.00

Toy, Ostrich & Cart, Black Man Driver, Africa On Side, Tin, Flywheel, Lehmann, 7 In.
$351.00

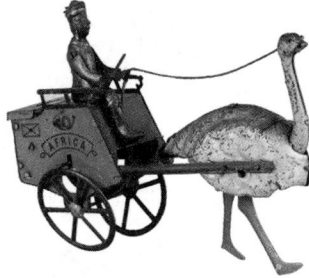

Teddy Bear Paws

Early teddy bears had felt or cotton paws. Later ones had paws of velvet, plush, or leather. By the 1970s, the paws were Ultrasuede.

Monkey, Cloth Dressed, Cast Iron, Legs Creep As Pulled, Ives, 9 In.	633.00
Monkey, On Cycle, Trick, Push Wood Stick, Ives, 1880	1250.00
Monkey, Riding Tricycle, Cast Iron, Peddles, Pull Toy, String, Hubley, 6 ½ In.	4889.00
Monkey, Sitting, Mohair, Long Arms & Tail, Jointed Neck, Steiff, Germany, 1940s, 12 In.	58.00
Monkey, Tumbling, Voice, Mouth Opens, Mohair, Felt, Schuco, c.1920, 8 ¾ In.	240.00
Moon Creature, Tin, Opens Mouth, Noise, Rubber Antenna, Litho Jet Packs, Marx, Box, 5 ¾ In.	322.00
Moon Doctor, Tin, Plastic, Litho Gears, Glasses, Daiya, Box, 7 In.	633.00
Moonbase, Playset, Instructions, Marx, Box, 22 ½ x 31 ¼ In.	215.00
Motorcycle, 3 Wheel, Tin Lithograph, Driver, Graphics, Kellerman, Penny Toy, Germany, 3 ¾ In.	978.00
Motorcycle, Delivery, Say It With Flowers, Clockwork, Cast Iron, 10 In. *illus*	63250.00
Motorcycle, Driver, Cast Iron, Hubley, 1930s, 4 ½ In.	120.00
Motorcycle, Driver, Red, Black, Rubber Tires, Cast Iron, Hubley, 4 In.	120.00
Motorcycle, Driver, Stops, Dismounts, Remounts, Drives Away, Arnold Mac, Box, 7 ¾ In.	1035.00
Motorcycle, Driver, Tin Lithograph, Windup, Technofix, Box, 7 In.	403.00
Motorcycle, Driver, Wagon, Speed Boy 4, Powered Head, Taillights, Windup, 1930s	259.00
Motorcycle, Harley-Davidson, Driver, Orange, Cast Iron, Rubber Tires, Hubley, 6 ¼ In.	295.00
Motorcycle, Harley-Davidson, Painted, Tin, Friction, TN Japan, 1959, 9 In.	180.00
Motorcycle, Harley-Davidson, Piston Movement, Japan, 8 ½ In.	275.00
Motorcycle, Harley-Davidson, Policeman, Sidecar, Iron, Rubber Tires, Hubley, 5 ¼ In.	170.00
Motorcycle, Harley-Davidson, Red, Twin Headlights, Rider, Hubley, 6 ½ In.	500.00
Motorcycle, Parcel Post, Blue Driver, Green, Cast Iron, 9 ½ In.	2010.00
Motorcycle, Police, Sidecar, Rubber Tires, Spoke Wheels, Clockwork, Hubley, c.1932, 8 ¾ In.	4313.00
Motorcycle, Police, Siren, Rider, Marx, Box, c.1938, 8 In.	750.00
Motorcycle, Policeman, Blue Paint, Cast Iron, Rubber Tires, Champion, 7 In.	350.00
Motorcycle, Policeman, Blue, Yellow Wheels, Cast Iron, 6 In.	585.00
Motorcycle, Policeman, Cast Iron, Blue Paint, White Rubber Tires, Champion, 7 In.	266.00
Motorcycle, Policeman, Red, Siren, Tin Lithograph, Clockwork, Marx, Box, 8 ¼ In.	460.00
Motorcycle, Policeman, Sidecar, Moves In Circle, Tin Lithograph, Windup, Marx, 8 In.	410.00
Motorcycle, Policeman, Sidecar, Police Siren Squad, Tin, Windup, Marx, 8 ½ In.	480.00
Motorcycle, Rider, Tin, Windup, Arnold M.C., Germany, 1950s, 7 ½ In.	395.00
Motorcycle, Rider, Tin, Windup, Marx, 1950s, 8 In.	195.00
Motorcycle, Rider, Tin, Windup, U.S. Zone, Germany, 7 In.	295.00
Motorcycle, Sidecar, Driver, Passenger, Battery Headlight, Red, Black, Cast Iron, Hubley, 9 In.	936.00
Motorcycle, Sidecar, Driver, Passenger, Iron, Cylinders, Handle Bars, Hubley, Late 1920s, 8 In.	805.00
Motorcycle, Sidecar, Driver, Passenger, Shield, Indian, Red, Cast Iron, 8 ½ In.	1530.00
Motorcycle, Sidecar, Driver, Woman, Tin Lithograph, Greppert & Kelch, 1920s, 6 In.	3450.00
Motorcycle, Sidecar, Red, Blue, 2 Riders, Hubley, 4 In.	250.00
Motorcycle, Soldier, Camouflaged, Gun, Tin Lithograph, Clockwork, 8 ½ In.	518.00
Motorcycle, Space Patrol, Tin, Rubber Tire, Vinyl Rider, License Plate, Usagiya, Box, 8 In.	1469.00
Motorcycle, U.S. Air Mail, Blue Driver, Red, Cast Iron, Hubley, 9 In.	1300.00
Motorcycle, Venus, Tin, Friction, Japan, 1950, 8 ½ In.	295.00
Movie Camera, Tripod, Wood, Metal, Schoenhut Co., Box, c.1915, 10 In. *illus*	205.00
Mower, Sickle Bar, Jones, Cast Brass, Raised Seat, Salesman's Sample, 19 x 8 ½ In.	5750.00
Mr. Big Head, Celluloid, Windup, Paper Label, Japan, 9 In.	440.00
Mule & Cart, Driver, Yellow, Red, Green, Cast Iron, 10 In.	100.00
Mule & Coal Wagon, Driver, Painted, Cast Iron, Kenton, 13 ¾ In.	365.00
Mule, Bell Ringer, Painted, Cast Iron	495.00
Musical Birdcage, Mechanical, France, 11 ½ In.	316.00
Musical Dancers, 3 Couples, Bisque, Painted, Windup, Wood Base, 11 ½ In.	805.00
Musical Trio, Tin, Crank Operated, Violist, Violinist, Harp, Bing, 9 ½ In.	2875.00
Musician, Plays Drum, Eyes Move, Windup, Marx, 1930s, 9 In.	145.00
Musicians, 3 Black Men On Bench, Tin, Windup, Violinist, Viola, Guitar, Germany, 10 In.	4025.00
Musicians, 3 Cats, Tin, Windup, Clarinet, Drum, Trombone, Gunthermann, 11 x 9 In.	3738.00
Musicians, 3 Clowns, On Bench, Instruments, Tin, Hand Crank, Gunthermann, 9 ½ In.	2185.00
Noah's Ark, Noah & His Wife, 30 Animals, 26 x 15 In.	1092.00
Old Dutch Cleanser Girl, Stick, Can, 4 Wheels, Movable Arms, Iron, Hubley, 9 In.	2633.00
Old Woman In Shoe, Red, Blue, Yellow, Renwal, Box	69.00
Omnibus, Bing, Clockwork, Rubber Tires, c.1920, 11 ½ In.	13800.00
Omnibus, London & Bath, Steel, Wood, Steam Motor, Steam Gauges, 1940s, 22 x 12 In.	1092.00
Orange Seller, Tin Figure, Pushing Orange Cart, Cloth Dressed, Windup, Martin, 7 In.	3450.00
Organ Grinder, Monkey, Cranks Street Organ, Monkey Twirls Hat, Tin, Gunthermann, 9 In.	3738.00
Organ Grinder, Monkey Hops, Tin Lithograph, Windup, Distler, 8 In.	1035.00
Ostrich & Cart, Black Man Driver, Africa On Side, Tin, Flywheel, Lehmann, 7 In. *illus*	351.00
Ostrich, Nifty Rudy, Tin, Flapping Beak, Litho & Painted, Windup, 1920s, 8 ½ In.	690.00
Ostrich, Painted Wood, Open Mouth, Painted Feathers, Glass Eyes, Schoenhut, 8 In.	805.00
Our Gang, Club House Playset, Mego, Plastic, 8 ½ x 11 x 10 ½ In.	115.00

Owl, Molded Rubber, Paint, c.1950, 17 In.	237.00
Paddy & Pig, Man Riding Pig, Blanket, Saddle, Clockwork, Lehmann, Germany, 5 ⅝ In.	1265.00
Paddy, Riding Pig, Tin, Painted, Windup, Lehmann, Germany, c.1900, 6 In. .... *illus*	1276.00
Pail, Duck Pond, Duck Driving Truck, Tin Lithograph, Chein, 8 x 8 In.	209.00
Paladin, Rearing White Horse, Accessories, Hartland, 1959-1963, 8 ½ In.	148.00
Parrots, Feeding, Embossed, Tin Lithograph, Meier, Penny Toy, 3 ¾ In.	230.00
Peacock, Ebo, Walker, Blue, Red, Green, Tin Lithograph, Germany, 10 In. .... 234.00 to 385.00	
Peacock, Tail Fans, Walker, Tin Lithograph, Windup, Marked, B&S, Germany, 9 In.	460.00
Peacock, Walker, Tin Lithograph, Windup, Japan, 1950s, 5 ¼ x 7 ¾ In.	175.00
Pedal Car, Airplane, Gendron Air King, Hand Built, Bob Olsen, Steel, 1938, 26 x 50 In.	2280.00
Pedal Car, Airplane, Nazi Swastikas, Yellow	1980.00
Pedal Car, Airplane, Orange, Black Wings, Spirit Of America, Tires, Steelcraft, 52 In.	3163.00
Pedal Car, Airplane, Steel, Silver, Red, Army Decals, Murray Pursuit, 1950s, 26 x 46 In.	2400.00
Pedal Car, Airport Jet Service, Rubber Tires, Ringing Bell, 32 In. .... *illus*	805.00
Pedal Car, Ambulance, Van Style, Pressed Steel, Oval Windows, Rear Door Opens, 60 In.	1725.00
Pedal Car, Auburn Skippy Custom Boattail, Gilmore Speedway Special, Olsen, 1932, 22 x 44 In.	1680.00
Pedal Car, Boat, Jolly Roger, White, Red, Motor, Murray, 1950s	880.00
Pedal Car, Chrysler, Blue, Pressed Steel, Steelcraft, c.1941, 19 x 26 In.	840.00
Pedal Car, Dump Truck, Jetliner, Yellow, Red Hubcaps, BMC	290.00
Pedal Car, Fire Truck, Hook & Ladder, Bell, Red, BMC, 1950s	330.00
Pedal Car, Ford, Mustang, Luggage Rack, Red, White	495.00
Pedal Car, Ford, Mustang, Steel, Red, c.1965, 19 x 38 In.	540.00
Pedal Car, Ford, Roadster, Convertible, Fiberglass, Upholstered, Green, 1932, 22 x 50 In.	1080.00
Pedal Car, Ford, Roadster, Light, Dark Blue, American National, 1935, 46 In.	1725.00
Pedal Car, Garton, Spin-A-Roo, Steel, Red, White, Sheboygan, Wisc., 24 x 48 In.	450.00
Pedal Car, Good Humor Ice Cream, Chain Driven, Red, White, Blue, 1970s	1100.00
Pedal Car, Hudson, Red, Yellow, American National Pedal Car, Toledo, OH, 1932, 48 In.	12000.00
Pedal Car, Mercedes-Benz, Silver, Red Interior, 1980s, 12 x 24 In.	660.00
Pedal Car, Mobo Pony Express Surrey, Pressed Steel, Multicolored, 21 x 33 In.	360.00
Pedal Car, Murray, Champion, Blue, 1950s, 21 x 15 x 36 In.	220.00
Pedal Car, Nash, Mustard, Windshield, Disc Wheels, Sidway Toplift, 35 In.	2300.00
Pedal Car, National Pierce, American, c.1920, 52 In.	3163.00
Pedal Car, Packard, Fenders, Footboards, Horn, Lights, Rumble Seat, Gendron, 1925, 60 In.	5750.00
Pedal Car, Packard, Shovel Nose, Pressed Steel, Maroon, American National, c.1930, 50 In.	5750.00
Pedal Car, Pierce Arrow, Purple, White, Steelcraft, 1934, 42 In.	2070.00
Pedal Car, Pressed Steel, Red, Hand Rails, Rear Platform, Ladders, 43 In.	230.00
Pedal Car, Pressed Steel, Wood Body, Butterfly Fenders, Keystone, 42 In.	5750.00
Pedal Car, Roadster, Yellow, Nickeling, Spare On Trunk, National Apperson, c.1920, 50 In.	4600.00
Pedal Car, Skippy, Red, Steel Craft, 1935, 45 In.	1210.00
Pedal Car, Station Wagon, Woody, Black, Garton Toy Co.	1650.00
Pedal Car, Tandem, 2 Children Pedal, Silver, Maroon, American National, 1936, 64 In.	2070.00
Pedal Car, Tow Truck, Blue, Pressed Steel, 1920s, 50 In.	920.00
Pedal Car, Tractor, Ford, Cast Aluminum	28.00
Pedal Car, Tractor, Orange, Black, White, 2 Ton, Murray	115.00
Pedal Car, Truck, Rapid Transit, Stake Bed, Green, 28 x 66 x 23 In.	1980.00
Pedal Car, Vauxall, Wood, Fenders, Driver's Door Opens, Triang, 1932	50.00
Pedal Cart, Horse, 3 Wheels, Spain, 61 In.	395.00
Pedal Cart, Horse Figure, Handle, Wrought Iron, Wood, Paint, c.1890, 20 x 20 ½ In.	101.00
Phaeton, Open, Lithographed, Clockwork, Figures, Germany, 1910s, 9 ½ In.	62100.00
Piano Player, Violinist, Perform, Tin, Crank Operated, Bing, 9 ½ In.	1955.00
Piano, Angels Playing Instruments, Flags, Wood, Bliss, 17 x 12 In. .... 250.00 to 263.00	
Piano, Grand, Bench, Cast Iron, Detailed, Blue, Pink, Music Stand Folds Down, Arcade, 5 In.	460.00
Piano, Musical, Mechanical, Window For Player Piano, Black Wood, 5 ¼ x 5 ¾ In.	863.00
Piano, Upright, Stenciling, Schoenhut, c.1900, 23 x 24 In.	88.00
Pig, Push Pull, Stuffed Body, Shoebutton Eyes, Velvet Nose, Iron Axles & Wheels	239.00
Pig, Walker, On Wheels, Clockwork, On-Off Switch, Decamps, France, 9 In.	293.00
Pigeon, Head Moves, Bellows, White, Green, Tin, Windup, Germany, 8 In.	92.00
Pillbox Emplacement, Rotating, Landscaped Mound, Fires Caps, Lineol, 18 x 18 x 7 In.	1380.00
Pirate, Mechanical, Yone, Tin Lithograph, Made In Japan, 6 ¾ In.	150.00
Planet Gun, Dan Dare, Plastic, 3 Shockproof Spinning Wheels, Box, 4 ½ In.	125.00
Plantation Cart, Black Driver, Painted, Cast Iron, Ives, 10 ½ In.	935.00
Play Golf, Windup, Strauss, Box, 12 In.	480.00
Play House Set, Tin, Sink, Stove, Ice Box, Cabinet, Paper Litho, Hoge, Box, 11 x 11 In.	1265.00
Play Suit, Annie Oakley, Cowgirl, Herman Iskin & Co., Autographed, Box, Size 12 .... *illus*	176.00
Plow, Oak, Brass, Steel, Curved Handles, J.L. Robinson, Concord, N.H., Sample, 17 x 6 In.	3450.00
Plow, Oliver, Arcade, Red, Nickel Wheels, 1940, 6 ¼ In.	250.00

Toy, Paddy, Riding Pig, Tin, Painted, Windup, Lehmann, Germany, c.1900, 6 In. $1276.00

Toy, Pedal Car, Airport Jet Service, Rubber Tires, Ringing Bell, 32 In. $805.00

Toy, Play Suit, Annie Oakley, Cowgirl, Herman Iskin & Co., Autographed, Box, Size 12 $176.00

Toy, Rabbit, Velveteen, Button Eyes, Cotton Dress, Apron, Madame Alexander, 12 In.
$702.00

Toy, Rabbit, Walking, Fur Covered, Applied Glass Eyes, Felt Dress, Wicker Basket, Clockwork, 6 In.
$633.00

Toy, Road Roller, Driver, Cast Iron, Nickel Plating, Hubley
$234.00

Police Patch, Embroidered, Red On Orange, Reads Security, Fisher-Price Toys, 1950s, 3 x 4 In.	75.00
Pond, Tin, Wood Branch Railings, Steps, Benches, Bridge, Germany, 22 x 16 x 15 In.	230.00
Pool Player, Man At Pool Table, Preparing To Shoot, Kellermann, Penny Toy, 4 In.	805.00
Pool Player, Tin Lithograph, Shooting Action, Penny Toy, 4 In.	104.00
Pool Player, Tin, Windup, Germany, 4 ⅜ x 6 ⅛ In.	320.00
Pool Table, Stick, Marble Balls, Tin, 4 x 17 x 11 ½ In.	70.00
Porky Pig, Twirls Umbrella, Raises Arm, Holds Top Hat, Windup, Marx, Box, 1939	50.00 to 142.00
Porter, Black, Red Cap, Walking, Tin Lithograph, Windup, Marx, 8 ½ In.	420.00 to 675.00
Porter, Pushes Baggage Cart, Dog Jumps Out Of Trunk, Windup, Strauss, 1920s	850.00
Porter, Pushing Cart, Penny Toy, 3 In.	176.00
Presidents Of United States, Figures, Washington To Eisenhower, Box, 1950s, 17 x 17 In.	612.00
Punch, Rides 3 Wheeler, Tin, Composition, Pedals, 10 ½ In.	9488.00
Punch, Squeak, Hand Held On Stick, Bells, Papier-Mache Head, Germany, 1900s, 14 In.	805.00
Rabbit, Brown, Painted, Tin, Windup, Germany, 7 In.	110.00
Rabbit, Bunny On Donkey, Ears Move, Celluloid, Windup, Prewar Japan, 1935, 5 ¾ In.	268.00
Rabbit, Hops, Tin Lithograph, Windup, Felt Ears, Key, c.1950s, 3 ½ In.	115.00
Rabbit, In Cabbage, Clockwork, Peers Out, Ears Twitch, Chops Food, Austria, 9 In.	2875.00
Rabbit, Mohair, Wheels, Honey Color, Amber Glass Eyes, Pull Toy, Steiff Button, 1930s, 9 In.	890.00
Rabbit, Playing Violin, Ears Move, Celluloid, Windup, Prewar Japan, 9 ⅜ In.	271.00
Rabbit, Pulling Cart, Japan, 9 ¼ In.	385.00
Rabbit, Seated, Cream, Tan Mohair, Amber Glass Eyes, Unjointed, Steiff, 4 ½ In.	71.00
Rabbit, Velveteen, Button Eyes, Cotton Dress, Apron, Madame Alexander, 12 In. ......*illus*	702.00
Rabbit, Walking, Fur Covered, Applied Glass Eyes, Felt Dress, Wicker Basket, Clockwork, 6 In. .*illus*	633.00
Radar Station, Tin, Lights, Noise, Antenna, Masudaya, Box, 7 ½ In.	418.00
Radio, Car, Maroon, 6 In.	395.00
Rapid Transit Trolley, Lionel Lionelville No. 60, 1960s	175.00
Rat, Top Hat, Rubber, Cloth, Seven Arts Inc., R. Dakin & Co., 1970, 8 In.	19.00
Rattle, Fish, Copper, Red Eyes, Articulated, England, 10 In.	240.00
Rattle, Mickey Mouse, Wire Tail, Celluloid, Japan, 1930s, 3 ⅞ In.	110.00
Record Player, Tin, Rodeo Scene, Magnetic Motor Corp.	150.00
Riding Push-Pull Lever Operated, Steel, Green, Child's, 22 x 32 In.	180.00
Road Grader, Ny-Lint, Pressed Steel, 1950s, 6 x 17 In.	126.00
Road Roller, Driver, Cast Iron, Nickel Plating, Hubley ......*illus*	234.00
Road Roller, Driver, Orange, Nickel Wheels, Front Roller, Hubley, c.1930, 8 In.	1150.00
Road Roller, Live Steam, Brass, Steel, Johnson Bar, Flywheel, Chain Drive, 1910, 19 x 14 In.	2300.00
Road Roller, Steel, Canopy, Spoke Wheels, Steam Cylinders, Flywheel, Buddy L, c.1930, 20 In.	2588.00
Robot, Astro Boy, Lights Up, Stop & Go, Chest Door Opens, Battery, Tin, Japan, 12 In.	518.00
Robot, Astronaut, Apollo 2000X, Plastic, Tin Face, Chest, Leg, Tin, Windup, Box, 5 In.	297.00
Robot, Astronaut, Plastic, Windup, Moves Arms, Box, 5 ½ In.	153.00
Robot, Astronaut, Razer, Sparks, Tin, Windup, NASA Logo, Noguchi, Box, 6 ¼ In.	848.00
Robot, Astronaut, Vinyl, Click Noise, Tin, Windup, Shudo, Mitsuhashi, Box, 5 ¼ In.	904.00
Robot, Atomic Man, Tin, Shuffles, Occupied Japan, 5 In.	1254.00
Robot, Atomic, Plastic, Clicking, Head, Arms Turn, Tin, Windup, Yonezawa, 6 ¼ In.	588.00
Robot, Blink-A-Gear, Walker, Arms Swing, Eyes Blink, Tin, Plastic, Battery, Taiyo, Box, 14 In.	3955.00
Robot, Car R-3, Tin, Firing Gun, Noise, Robot Driver, Box, 8 ¼ In.	2938.00
Robot, Conehead, Tin, Sparking Head, Rubber Ears & Head, Yonezawa, c.1957, 8 ½ In.	2147.00
Robot, Garon, Tin, Walks, Raises Arms, Lights Up, Remote Control, Osaka Toy, Japan, Box, 7 In.	316.00
Robot, Ground Zero, Granzer, Windup, Tin Lithograph, Vinyl Head, Box, 1970s, 9 In. ......*illus*	190.00
Robot, Jupiter, Walker, Arms Swing, Brain Spins, Battery Remote, Yonezawa, Box, 13 In.	16950.00
Robot, Lavender, Tin, Battery Operated, Nonstop Action, Lights, Masudaya, Box, 15 In.	8193.00
Robot, Lilliput, Shuffles, Spiked Feet, Tin, Windup, Japan, Box, c.1939, 6 ½ In.	3164.00
Robot, Martin, The Martian, 6 Legs Octopus Like, Tin, Windup, Walks, Japan, 7 In.	4803.00
Robot, Mechanical, Hard Plastic, Tin Lithograph, Battery, Box, Late 1960s, 6 ½ x 12 In.	209.00
Robot, Mechanical, Sparking, Bronze, Pink, White, Black, Tin Litho, Windup, Box, 5 In.	1130.00
Robot, Mego Man, Red Face, Tin, Windup, Wheels Turn, Mouth Opens, Box, 7 In.	531.00
Robot, Mego Man, Silver Face, Tin, Windup, Wheels, Mouth Opens, Bell, Yoneya, Box, 7 In.	576.00
Robot, Moon Astronaut, Walks, Shoots, Tin Lithograph, Windup, Daiya, Box, 9 In.	2832.00
Robot, Moon Man 001, Plastic, Chrome, Battery, Head Turns, Hong Kong, Box, 6 In.	514.00
Robot, Mr. Atomic, Tin, Battery, Mystery Action, Whistling Sound, Yonezawa, Box, 9 In.	7345.00
Robot, Mr. Rembrandt, Plastic, Draws Pinwheel Pictures, Ideal, Box, 7 In.	169.00
Robot, Mr. Robot Jr., Tin, Plastic, Battery Operated, Walks, Swing Arms, Bandai, 4 ¼ In.	401.00
Robot, Mr. Smash, Plastic, Windup, Arms Move, Mouth Opens, Close, Box, 7 ½ In.	119.00
Robot, Polka Dot, Blue, Chrome Strip On Head, Tin, Windup, S.Y., Japan, 4 In.	391.00
Robot, Polka Dot, Silver, Tin, Windup, S.Y., Japan, Box, 4 In.	305.00
Robot, Radicon, Tin, Wireless Remote, Arms Move, Eyes Flash, Masudaya, Box, 15 In.	16950.00
Robot, Ranger, Gray, Plastic, Moving Feet, Head, Box, 4 ¾ In.	441.00

T

Robot, Robby, Black, Walker, Dome Lights, Pistons, Antennae, Tin, Battery, Nomura, Box, 12 In. 6780.00

Robot, Robert The Robot, Hard Plastic, Eyes Lights, Ideal, Box, 1950s, 7 x 8 ½ In. .... *illus* 173.00

Robot, S Astronaut, Tin, Battery Operated Remote Control, Lighted Helmet, Nomura, 7 ½ In. 5424.00

Robot, Space Patrol, Vinyl Head, Tin, Plastic, Windup, Walks, Tomiyama, 5 ¼ In. 735.00

Robot, Space Trooper, Black, Remote Control, Tin, Moves, Red Lights, Head Turns, Box, 6 In. 2882.00

Robot, Spaceman, Mechanical, Walking, Tin, Plastic, Windup, Moves Arms, Tomiyama, Box, 6 In. 542.00

Robot, Spaceman, Take Apart, Plastic, Helmet Holds Ray Gun, Renwal, 5 In. 203.00

Robot, Spaceman, Television, Tin, Windup, Shuffles, Antenna, Screen, Alps, Box, 7 In. 255.00

Robot, Super, Green, Plastic, Tin, Windup, Box, 6 ¼ In. 254.00

Robot, Super Space, Tin, Silver Body, Opening Chest, Walks, Shoots, Horikawa, Japan, 16 In. . 805.00

Robot, T-281 Tetsujin, Tin, Windup, Light Blue, Box, Japan, 7 ½ In. 201.00

Robot, Take Apart, Plastic, Gears, Windup, Movable Arms, Lincoln International, Box, 7 In. .. 735.00

Robot, Target, Turns After Hit, Guns, Darts, Tin, Battery, Masudaya, Box, 15 In. 10170.00

Robot, Telephone, Tin, Plastic, Windup, Walker, Sparks, Dial, Bell, Yonezawa, Box, 9 In. 7345.00

Robot, Tin, Walking, Eyes Light-Up, Battery Operated, Linemar, 1950s, 6 ½ In. .... *illus* 1035.00

Robot, Train, Tin, Battery, Nonstop Action, Whistle Noise, Arms Swing, Masudaya, Box, 15 In. 9323.00

Robot, War Boat R-7, Tin, Crank, Spring Loaded Gun, Rockets, Robot Driver, Box, 12 In. 7910.00

Rocket, Jeep, Tin, Lithograph, On Sides, Masudaya, Box, 1950s, 6 ¼ In. 282.00

Rocket, Mercury, Tin, Rubber Wheels, Spark Movement, Daiya, 10 In. 1921.00

Rocket Racer, Driver, Tin Lithograph, Windup, 16 ½ In. 375.00

Rocket Ride, Mechanical, Tin Lithograph, Windup, Chein, Box, 1950s, 11 ½ x 19 In. 633.00

Rocky Mountain Express-Way Cable Train, Mechanical, S&E, Japan, 15 x 7 In. 108.00

Rodeo Joe, Tin, Windup, Unique Art, 9 x 7 In. .... 210.00 to 330.00

Roller Coaster, Giant Dip Ride, Coney Island, Tin, Airplanes, Tower, Clockwork, Box, 13 x 17 In. 104.00

Roller Skater, Motor, Celluloid, Windup, 5 ⅝ In. 66.00

Rolling Bunny Basket, Wooden Handle, 4 Wheels, Pull Toy, Fisher-Price, 1954, 7 ¾ In. 99.00

Roly Poly, Clown, Yellow, Green, Red Hat, Musical, Painted, Papier-Mache, 10 In. 175.00

Rooster, Composition, Painted, Squeak, c.1885, 7 ¾ In. 117.00

Rooster, On Platform, Painted, Tin, Pull Toy 700.00

Round Race Jet No. 1, Tin, Rubber Track, Chrome Trim, Asahi Toy, Box, 5 ½ In. 271.00

Safari Wagon, Expedition Kilimandscharo, Mercedes-Benz, Battery Operated, Schuco, 12 In. 295.00

Sailor, Walker, Tin, Cloth, Windup, Lehmann, 7 ½ In. 720.00

Salamander, Flywheel, Germany, Penny Toy, 7 ¼ In. 72.00

Sam, City Gardener, Tools, Plastic, Tin, Windup, Marx, Box. 350.00

Sambo Special 7-11, Pull, Wood, Painted, Metal Wheels, Marked, Barry Mfg., 16 In. 1125.00

Sand Loader, Nickel Plated Chain, Scoop Bucket, Driver, Arcade, 8 ½ In. .... *illus* 2530.00

Sand Screener, Pressed Steel, Buddy L, 1927-30, 29 x 21 In. 863.00

Satellite, Circles Earth, Tin, Plastic, Sputnik 2, Laika The Dog, Germany, Box, 4 ¼ In. 124.00

Satellite X-107, Tin, Lights, Suspended Astronaut, Masudaya, Box, 7 ¾ In. 508.00

Scale, Dayton, Blue, Cast Iron, Nickel Plated, 4 ½ In. 68.00

Scooter, 2 Riders, Tin, Friction, Technofix, Germany, 1950s, 6 ½ In. 395.00

Scooter, Black Steel, Rubber Mat, Hand Pump, Red Steel Frame, Buddy L, 36 x 25 In. 4600.00

Scooter, Centrifugal Rear Wheel, Wood Platform, Ingo, c.1932, 41 x 66 In. 300.00

Scooter, Ice Cream, Windup, U.S.A. Courtland, Tin, 1948. .... 375.00

Scooter, Postman Driver, Plastic, Friction, Telsada, Box, 5 In. 74.00

Scooter, Red, Wood, Steelcraft. 250.00

Scooter, Super Sonda Scooter, Steel, Silver, Red, c.1957, 27 x 40 In. 1140.00

Scooter, Tin, Friction, Japan, 1950, 9 In. 295.00

Scotsman, Playing Bagpipes, On Stump, Painted, Tin, Windup, Germany, 11 In. .. 234.00 to 600.00

Scotsman, Tin Lithograph, Windup, Germany, 6 In. 260.00

Sea Lion, Windup, Lehmann, Box, Early 1900s, 7 In. .... *illus* 460.00

Seeder, Split Front Wheel, Plow Blade Back Wheel, Tole Hopper, U.S.A. Planet Jr., 28 x 15 In. . 690.00

Seesaw, Gibbs, Tin, Painted, Swivel Shaft Seats, Japanned Finish, 1920s, 14 ½ x 12 In. 144.00

Seesaw, Tin, Cloth, Celluloid, Boy & Girl, Umbrella, Windup, 10 In. 523.00

Service Station, Cars, Gas Pump, Ramp, Work Benches, Tin Litho, Kibri, Clockwork, 18 x 12 In. 5175.00

Service Station, Overhang Covers, Drive Up Area, Pump, Tin Litho, Box, 6 x 5 ½ In. 575.00

Sewing Machine, Singer, No. 221-1, Attachments, Instructions. 148.00

Sewing Machine, Stitchwell, Cast Iron, Wooden Box, 8 x 6 In. 88.00

Sheep, Composition Face, Wooden Legs, Base, Pull Toy, 12 In. 819.00

Sheep, Glass Eyes, Bell, Dresden Collar, Pull Toy, 10 x 12 In. 1380.00

Sign Set, 5 Road Signs, Red Gas Pump, Square, Iron, Arcade, Box, 1934, 7 x 17 In. 2875.00

Sign, Street, School Zone, Safety Sal, Girl, Holding Sign, Die Cast, Phone Number, 7 ½ In. 748.00

Singing Bird, A Musical Novelty, Tin Lithograph, Windup, Kohler, Box, 8 In. 79.00

Ski Jumper, Wood, Board Ski Jump, Spring Action, Flagpoles, Flags, Schoenhut, Box, 26 In. .. 201.00

Ski Skates, F.D. Peters Co., Patented 1928, Box 30.00

Ski Troops, No. 2017, Britains, Box, 4 Piece. 350.00

Toy, Robot, Ground Zero, Granzer, Windup, Tin Lithograph, Vinyl Head, Box, 1970s, 9 In.
$190.00

Toy, Robot, Robert The Robot, Hard Plastic, Eyes Lights, Ideal, Box, 1950s, 7 x 8 ½ In.
$173.00

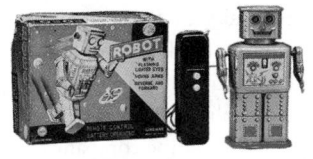

Toy, Robot, Tin, Walking, Eyes Light-Up, Battery Operated, Linemar, 1950s, 6 ½ In.
$1035.00

Toy, Sand Loader, Nickel Plated Chain, Scoop Bucket, Driver, Arcade, 8 ½ In.
$2530.00

T

Toy, Sea Lion, Windup, Lehmann, Box, Early 1900s, 7 In.
$460.00

Toy, Skittles Set, Mother Bunny Carries 7 Babies On Her Back, 1870s
$6900.00

Slinky

Slinky was created by Richard James. With the help of his wife, Betty, he first sold some in 1945. It cost $1. The toy was a huge success and so was the company, James Industries. In 1960, Richard decided to leave Betty and their six kids and the rest of his old life and go to Bolivia to join a religious cult. He also took a lot of the company's money. Betty, then 42, saved James Industries by making tough financial decisions and clever additions to the line of Slinky toys. There is a Junior Slinky, plastic Slinky, Slinky dog, Slinky glasses, and more. The James family sold the business to Poof Products, Inc., in 1998.

Skittles Set, Bobbies, Uniforms, Helmets, Wooden Bases, Parade Rest, 10 In., 7 Piece	345.00
Skittles Set, House Staff, Prosperous Couple, Maid, Butlers, House Attendants, 14 In., 8 Piece.	144.00
Skittles Set, Indian, Carrying Weapons, Painted, Warfare Outfits, 9 ½ In., 9 Piece.	173.00
Skittles Set, Mother Bunny Carries 7 Babies On Her Back, 1870s .... *illus*	6900.00
Sled, Dog, Iditarod, Wood, Salesman's Sample, 3 ½ x 17 x 3 In.	285.00
Sled, Doll's, Flowers, Red, Green, Painted, Wood, Iron Runners, 7 ¼ x 14 ¼ In.	670.00
Sled, Doll's, Horse Pulling Chariot, Painted, Wood, Iron Runners, 7 ¾ x 25 In.	980.00
Sled, Doll's, Mountain Scene, Painted, Wood, Iron Runners, 5 ¼ x 15 In.	220.00
Sled, Doll's, Yellow, Red Flowers, Painted, Wood, Iron Runners, 4 ¼ x 15 In.	890.00
Sled, Flexy Racer, Child's	77.00
Sled, Flexy Racer, No. 300, Slatted Oak Seat, Steel Suspension, Wheels, c.1938, 8 x 48 In.	30.00
Sled, King Of The Hills, Landscape, Volcanoes, Pine, Metal Rails, Late 1800s, 34 x 18 In.	230.00
Sled, Stencil, Painted Bird & Flowers, Wood Seat, Frame, Metal Runners, 14 x 37 In.	330.00
Sled, Swan Heads, Red Painted Surface, Wooden, 38 In.	345.00
Sleigh, 1 Horse, Red, Black Button Tufted Leather, John Gutelius & Sons, 1880s, 66 x 42 In.	4200.00
Sleigh, Green Chaise, Purple Woman Passenger, 2 Black Horses, Cast Iron, Hubley, 15 In.	351.00
Sleigh, Old Paint, Wrought Iron Runners, Wood, 47 In.	47.00
Sleigh, Painted, Upholstered Seat, Metal Runners, Raised Push Handle, Wood, 36 x 43 In.	71.00
Sleigh, Push, Painted, Bent Wood Handle, Wood Runners, Stencils, c.1890, 30 x 52 In.	450.00
Smitty Scooter, Hinged Arms, Glides, Pumps, Tin Lithograph, Windup, Marx, 1920s, 8 In.	1008.00
Snoopy Sniffer Dog, Black, White, Spring Tail, Felt Ears, Pull Toy, Fisher-Price, 1940s, 16 In.	95.00
Soldier Set, Barclay Dime Store, Marching Band, Cast Metal, Plated Metal Hats, 26 Piece	345.00
Soldier Set, No. 20, Royal Company, Archers, Queen's Scottish Bodyguard, Britains, Box, 13 Piece	465.00
Soldier Set, No. 39, Royal Horse Artillery, Gun, Team, Galloping Escort, Britains, Box, 14 ¾ In.	288.00
Soldier Set, No. 78, Royal Navy Bluejackets, Slotted Base Card, Britains, Box 15 In., 8 Piece	403.00
Soldier Set, No. 110, Devonshire Regiment, Britains, Box, 1901, 15 In., 8 Piece	748.00
Soldier Set, No. 133, Russian Infantry, Tie Card, Britains, 1904, Label Box, 15 In, 8 Piece	633.00
Soldier Set, No. 241, Chinese Infantry, Tie Card, Britains, Box, 14 ¾ In., 8 Piece	288.00
Soldier Set, No. 267, U.S. Army Cavalry & Infantry, Britains, Box, 11 Piece	120.00
Soldier Set, No. 1621, Indian Army, 3rd Battalion Sikhs Regiment, Britains, Box, 15 In., 8 Piece.	345.00
Soldier Set, No. 1893, Indian Army Service Corps, Britains, Box, 7 Piece	145.00
Soldier Set, No. 2056, Union Cavalry, Britains, Box, 5 Piece	120.00
Soldier Set, No. 2059, Union Infantry, Britains, Box, 7 Piece	69.00
Soldier Set, No. 9435, Highland Piper Band, Black Watch, Musical Figures, Britains, Box 14 ¾ In.	546.00
Soldier Set, WWI, Camp Scene, Tent, Vehicle, Lead, 14 Piece	139.00
Soldier, Take-A-Part, Red, Blue, Yellow, Black, Doepke, 1957, 9 In.	75.00
Space Capsule, Astronauts, Mystery Action, Battery Operated, Tin Litho, 1960s, 4 x 6 In.	145.00
Space Capsule, Mercury, Astronaut Spins, Tin, Beep Noise, Horikawa, Box, 9 In.	260.00
Space Commander Ship, X-15, Tin, Dome, Spark Movement, Yoshiya, Box, 5 ½ In.	1525.00
Space Dog, Sparks, Wobbles, Ears Flap, Tin Lithograph, Windup, K.O., Box, 5 x 7 ½ In.	325.00
Space Dog, Tin, Waddling, Mouth Opens & Closes, Lights, Flying Saucer, Yoshiya, Box, 7 In.	5396.00
Space Elephant, Tin, Waddling, Ears, Trunk & Tusks Move, Red, Yoshiya, 9 In.	476.00
Space Explorer, Tin, Battery Operated, Japan, 1950s	125.00
Space Gun, Strato, Cast Metal, 9 Cap Repeater, 50 Shot Roll, Futuristic Products, c.1955, 9 In.	259.00
Space Pistol, Flashing Light, Noise, Tin, Plastic, Battery Operated, Japan, Box, 7 In.	180.00
Space Tank, Looping, Tin, Lighted Dome, Firing Noise, Flips Over, Daiya, Box, 8 In.	203.00
Spaceman, Cap't. Astro, Plastic, Tin, Windup, Moving Arms, Box, 5 In.	107.00
Sparking Eye Blackface, Archie, Tin, Pull Toy, Ronson Toys, c.1924, 9 In.	246.00
Squirt Gun, Black, Pressed Steel, Model No. 41, Wyandotte Toys, 1930s, 7 In.	30.00
Squirt Gun, Flash Gordon, Blue Plastic, Marx, 1950s, 7 In.	885.00
Stagecoach, Doors Open, Celluloid Windows, Wire, Gold Leaf Trim, Wooden, 1940s, 17 In.	748.00
Station, Roof, Awning, Amber Glass Panels, Tin Lithograph, Schoenner, c.1890, 14 x 10 x 8 In.	5175.00
Steam Engine, Doll, Cast Iron, Tin, Brass, 12 In.	144.00
Steam Roller, Driver, Reverse Action, Tin, Battery Operated, Japan, 1950s, 11 x 7 x 4 In.	79.00
Steam Shovel, Corrugated Roof, Vertical Boiler, Cylinders, 4 Wheels, Buddy L, 1929, 27 In.	2185.00
Steam Shovel, Ride-On, Boom, Wood Handles, Pressed Steel, Keystone, c.1925, 21 In.	201.00
Stove, Abendroth Bros., Uncle Sam, Shelf, Glass Door, Skillets, Cast Iron, N.Y., 14 x 24 In.	1900.00
Stove, Beauty Range, Cast Iron, Nickel, 18 x 15 ½ x 6 ½ In.	660.00
Stove, Buck's Brilliant, 19 x 20 x 12 In.	2640.00
Stove, Charter Oak, No. 103, Blue Enamel, Nickel, Pat. June 14, 1867, 19 x 14 x 12 In.	1010.00
Stove, Cookware, Baking Pan, Cast Iron, 13 x 14 x 6 ½ In.	356.00
Stove, Crescent, Birds, Flowers, Cherubs, Cast Iron, Nickel Plated, 17 x 12 ½ x 7 In.	480.00
Stove, Dainty, Cast Iron, Cover Plates, Accessories, 8 In.	263.00
Stove, Eagle, No. 1394, Painted, Cast Iron, 5 ⅝ x 6 ¼ In.	165.00
Stove, Eclipse, Cast Iron, Nickel Plated, 16 x 20 x 8 ½ In.	1000.00
Stove, Electric, Utensils, Cream, Green, Porcelain, Lionel, 33 x 26 In.	1638.00

T

Stove, Engman-Matthew, Cast Iron, Nickel Trim, Side Shelf, 30 x 18 In.	1800.00
Stove, Favorite, Fry & Sauce Pan, Blue, Cast Iron, Tin, 7 ¼ x 5 ¾ In.	180.00
Stove, Favorite Stoves & Ranges, Blue, Gold, Piqua, Ohio, 30 x 20 x 11 In.	2650.00
Stove, Home Comfort, Wrought Iron Range, Co., Granite, St. Louis, 24 x 23 In.	3500.00
Stove, Iron, 3-Footed, Internal Grate, No. 9, 2 Fire Bricks, Geometrics, Flowers, 23 In.	275.00
Stove, Karr Range, Blue Speckled, Enamel, 21 x 13 ½ x 9 In.	1350.00
Stove, Little Willie, Cast Iron, Painted, Philadelphia, 14 In.	177.00
Stove, Pot Belly, Relief Flower Pattern, Finial, Iron, Isinglass Doors, Sample, 20 x 8 In.	4600.00
Stove, Pots & Pans, Painted, Cast Iron, Crescent, Child's ....*illus*	59.00
Stove, Range, Green, White, Porcelain, Electric, Utensils, Lionel, 33 x 25 ½ x 12 In.	1540.00
Stove, Red & Black Enamel, Gold Plated, 24 x 12 ½ x 8 ¼ In.	1980.00
Stove, Rival, Cast Iron, Nickel Plated, J. & E. Stevens Co., Patent 1895, 14 x 13 x 7 In.	890.00
Stove, Royal, Cast Iron, Accessories, Marked, 9 x 6 In.	88.00
Stove, Royal, Nickel Plated, Cover Plates, 2 Side Panel Shelves, 15 In.	955.00
Stove, Spark, Marked In Raised Letters, Cast Iron, c.1880, 14 In.	249.00
Stove, Steel Stovepipe, Ash Bin, Coal Scuttle, Frying Pan, Wash Boiler, Iron, 23 x 19 x 11 In. ..	593.00
Stove, The Great Majestic Junior, Cast Iron, Nickel, 31 x 24 In.	2200.00
Street Lamp, Cast Iron, Blue, Glass Globe, Nickeled Top, Frame, Bing, Germany, 7 ¾ In.	633.00
Streetcar, Pressed Steel, Windup, 1920, Kingsbury, 9 In.	325.00
Structo Pile-Driver, Pressed Steel, c.1920s, 10 x 13 In.	575.00
Submarine, Enameled Tin, Windup, Marklin, 22 In.	4313.00
Suffragette, Behind Podium, Wood Base, Cloth Dress, Clockwork, c.1880s, 10 In.	4600.00
Sunny Monday Washing Set, Iron, Box, Parker Bros., Early 1900s, 9 x 13 In. ....*illus*	527.00
Sunshine Animal Crackers, Elephant, Stuffed, Cloth, Cardboard Base, 7 x 5 ½ x 2 In.	358.00
Surrey, 2 Horses, Figures, Green, Red, Aluminum, Stanley, Box, 12 In.	88.00
Surrey, Doll's, Fringe, Orange Paint, Leather Upholstery, 26 ½ x 36 x 13 In.	173.00
Suzy, Bouncing Ball, Metal, Windup, Japan, 1950s...............	95.00
Sweeping Katinka, Windup, Lindstrom Co., Box, 1930s...............	385.00
Table, Banquet, 3 Different Tops, Salesman's Sample, 7 ½ x 18 In.	360.00
Taco Bell Chihuahua, Plush, Talking, 1990, 6 In.	15.00
Tailspin Tabby, Kriter, Black & Yellow, Leatherette Ears, Pop-Up, Fisher-Price, 6 ½ In.	75.00
Tank, Army, Camouflage, Rubber Tracks, Shoot Balls, Iron, Arcade, Box, c.1930, 8 In.	1150.00
Tank, Camouflage, Tin Lithograph, Windup, Rubber Tracks, 5 x 9 ¾ In.	315.00
Tank, Cannon, Solido, 6 ½ In.	85.00
Tank, Gray, Plastic, Tin, Windup, Marx, Box, c.1950, 6 In.	100.00
Tank, Metal, Windup, France, 1950s, 10 ½ In.	275.00
Tank, Metal, Windup, Marx, 1930s, 9 In.	225.00
Tank, Olive, Treads, Plastic, Tin, Windup, Marx, Box, 6 In.	95.00
Tank, Painted, Cast Iron, Arcade, 8 In. ....*illus*	322.00
Tank, Pompom, Tin, Guns Move, Light, Noise, Battery, Suzuki & Edwards, Box, 12 In.	384.00
Tank, Pressed Steel, Clockwork, Structo, c.1918, 12 In. ....*illus*	351.00
Tank, Rollover, Tin Lithograph, Windup, Marx, 4 ½ In.	75.00
Tank, U.S. Tank Division, Sparks, Recoiling Cannon, Marx, Box, 6 x 9 ½ In.	198.00
Tarzan, Tarzan Yell, Loincloth, Knife, Tin, Vinyl, Copyright, Marusan, c.1966, 13 In.	678.00
Taxi, Amos 'n' Andy, Lithograph Tin, Windup, Marx, Box, 8 In. .... 275.00 to 632.00	
Taxi, Black, Red Wheels, Cast Iron, 6 ¾ In.	390.00
Taxi, Brown, White, Disc Wheels, Driver, Cast Iron, Arcade, c.1923, 9 In.	1380.00
Taxi, Buick, Electric Lights, Rubber Tires, Tin Lithograph, Battery Operated, Box, 1950, 8 In. .	316.00
Taxi, Cadillac, Hubley, 1941...............	250.00
Taxi, Checker, Driver, No. 69, Tin Litho, Black Roof, Disc Wheels, Clockwork, Strauss, 8 In.	863.00
Taxi, Checker, Driver, Yellow, Black, Cast Iron, Embossed Sign, Arcade, 1932...............	4888.00
Taxi, Checker, Yellow, Green, Windup, No. 4000, Cortland, Box, 2 ½ x 7 In.	200.00
Taxi, DeSoto, Plastic, Windup, Sky View, Yellow, Red, Marx, 1946-68, 10 In.	195.00
Taxi, Driver, Electric Light, Hand Brake On Side, Tin Litho, Clockwork, Germany, c.1930s, 8 ½ In.	1150.00
Taxi, Driver, Orange, Luggage Rack, Rubber Tires, Cast Iron, Hubley, 8 ¼ In.	240.00
Taxi, Driver, Red, Tin Lithograph, Clockwork, Germany, c.1910, 7 In.	495.00
Taxi, Driver, Striped Panel, Tarp Cover, Meter, Lanterns, Tin Litho, Germany, Fisher, 1920s......	4888.00
Taxi, Driver, Yell-O-Taxi, Orange, Black, Tin Lithograph, Windup, Strauss, Box, 7 ½ In.	144.00
Taxi, Driver, Yellow, Cast Iron, Hubley, 5 ¾ In.	120.00
Taxi, Orange, Black, Saloon Style, Spoke Wheels, Tin Litho, Clockwork, Driver, Bing, c.1920s, 11 In.	2010.00
Taxi, Red Top, Arcade, 8 In.	1250.00
Taxi, Renault, Brown, Luggage Rack, Lanterns, Tin Litho, Rossignol, France, 1920, 6 In.	2875.00
Taxi, Yellow & Black Paint, Cast Iron, No. 1495, Kenton, 6 ½ In.	480.00
Taxi, Yellow, Black, Metal, Rubber Tires, Hubley, 2 ⅜ x 7 In.	50.00
Taxi, Yellow Cab, Double Stripe, No. 3, Rubber Tires, Arcade, 5 In.	1850.00
Taxi, Yellow Cab, Driver, Cast Iron, Arcade, 7 ¾ In.	650.00

Toy, Stove, Pots & Pans, Painted, Cast Iron, Crescent, Child's
$59.00

Toy, Sunny Monday Washing Set, Iron, Box, Parker Bros., Early 1900s, 9 x 13 In.
$527.00

Toy, Tank, Painted, Cast Iron, Arcade, 8 In.
$322.00

Toy, Tank, Pressed Steel, Clockwork, Structo, c.1918, 12 In.
$351.00

T

Toy, Tractor, Driver, Cast Iron,
Rubber Tires, Arcade, 7 In.
$322.00

Tractor Toys
The first tractor was built
by J. I. Case in 1892, so no
tractor toys were made before
that date.

Taxi, Yellow Cab, Driver, No. 1327, License Plate 543, Painted, Cast Iron, Arcade, 4 x 8 In.	740.00
Taxi, Yellow Cab, No. 3, Arcade, 5 In.	1200.00
Taxi, Yellow, Driver, Cast Iron, Arcade, 7 ¾ In.	650.00
Tea Chest, 2 Chinese Men Carrying Box, Flywheel, Tin Litho, Lehmann, Germany, 7 ½	1495.00
Tea Set, Kittens, Tin Lithograph, Ohio Art, Box, 7 ¾ x 4 ¾ In.	80.00 to 92.00
Teddy Bears are listed in the Teddy Bear category.	
Terraplane, Light Blue, Rubber Tires, Cast Iron, Hubley	600.00
Thresher, Deering, Iron, Stacker, Spoke Wheels, Bundle Apron, McCormick, Box, c.1930, 9 In.	920.00
Tidy Tim, Walks & Pushes Trash Barrel, Tin Lithograph, Windup, 1933, 8 x 8 In.	750.00
Tiger, Painted, Jointed, Open Mouth, Glass Eyes, Ball Neck, Leather, Schoenhut, 7 ½ In.	575.00
Tombo, Alabama Coon Jigger, Windup, Strauss, 1918	550.00
Tool Chest, Boys Union, No. 50B, Wood, Paper Label, 3 ½ x 11 ¾ x 5 ¾ In.	92.00
Tool Chest, Wood, Decal, Tool Tray, Buddy L, c.1927, 24 In.	259.00
Toonerville Trolley, Cast Iron, Red, Marked, Dent, Box, 6 In.	1755.00
Toonerville Trolley, Penny Toy, 2 In.	220.00
Toonerville Trolley, Tin Lithograph, Windup, Germany, Fontaine Fox, 1922, 6 ¾ In.	309.00
Toonerville Trolley, Windup, Nifty Co., Germany, 1922	485.00
Top, Doll Shape, Painted, Cloth, Bisque Head, Arms, Tin Body, Toupie, Brevette, 3 x 2 In.	300.00
Top, Flying, Archimedes, Mars, Aerial Flyer, Lehmann, 1906	125.00
Top, Tam-Tam, Rod & Finger Slide, No. 677, Tin Lithograph, Lehmann, 1910, 9 ½ x 3 In.	145.00
Topcat, TV-Tinikins Set, Plastic, Painted, Hanna-Barbera, Marx, Individual Boxes, 7 Piece	115.00
Tractor Train, World's Fair, Iron, 3 Coach Cars, Tin, Driver, Box, 1939, 15 ¾ In.	920.00
Tractor, Airport, Trailers, Red, Green, Yellow, Doepke, 1955, 26 In.	225.00
Tractor, Allis-Chalmers, Trailer, Red, Green, 7 In.	225.00
Tractor, Arcade, McCormick-Deering Farmall Regulator, 1929, 6 In.	550.00
Tractor, Avery, Green, Red Spoke Wheels, Cast Iron, Arcade, c.1920s, 4 ½ In.	403.00
Tractor, Caterpillar, Driver, Yellow, Rubber Tires, Cast Iron, Arcade, 8 In.	960.00
Tractor, Cultivator, Red, Silver, Cast Aluminum, Hubley, 9 In.	69.00
Tractor, Dairy Tanker, Pressed Steel, 1920s, 33 In.	5100.00
Tractor, Driver, Cast Iron, Rubber Tires, Arcade, 7 In. *illus*	322.00
Tractor, Driver, Caterpillar, Exposed Engine, Steel Trends, Box, 8 In. *illus*	2013.00
Tractor, Driver, Caterpillar, Green, Metal, Cast Iron, 9 In.	775.00
Tractor, Driver, Fordson, Red Wheels, White Body, Cast Iron, Arcade, 6 In.	146.00
Tractor, Driver, Fordson, Silver, Red Wheels, Cast Iron, Arcade, 6 In.	150.00
Tractor, Driver, John Deere, No. 3730, Nickel Plated, Iron, Rubber Tires, Decal, Arcade, Box, 7 In.	2300.00
Tractor, Driver, Nickel Plated, Rubber Tracks, Cast Iron, Arcade, 1941, 7 ½ In.	850.00
Tractor, Driver, Orange, Cast Iron, Extended Steering Wheel, Spoke Wheels, Kilgore, 6 In.	748.00
Tractor, Driver, Wagon, Red, White, Lever For Dump Bed, Cast Iron, Arcade, 18 In.	500.00
Tractor, Fordson, Red, Tootsietoy, 5 In.	125.00
Tractor, International Diesel, Driver, Red, Rubber Tires, Cast Iron, Arcade	840.00
Tractor, Orange Plastic, Case, Box, c.1950, 8 ½ In.	485.00
Tractor, Plow, Yellow, Red, Litho Wheels, Marx, 14 In.	350.00
Tractor, Roller, Driver, Green, Star, Chains, Huber	360.00
Tractor, Trac, Driver, Red, Cast Iron, Metal, Arcade, 7 ½ In.	480.00
Tractor, Trailer, Dump, Red, Green, Allis-Chalmers, Arcade, 8 In.	250.00
Tractor, Wagon, Driver, Dump Bed Side Lever, Red, White, Cast Iron, Arcade, 18 In.	527.00
Trailer, Milk, Painted Die Cast, Tootsietoy, Box 13 ¼ In., 4 Piece	345.00
Trailer, Roamer, Green, Die Cast, Tin, Sliding Door, Tootsietoy, 4 ½ In.	435.00
Train Accessory, Gateman, Lionel, Automatic, 45N, 153C Track Contactor, Box, Postwar	57.00
Train Accessory, Hillcraft Ind., Skyway, Trestle Bridge, Red Steel, Box	23.00
Train Accessory, Lumber Loader, Lionel, No. 364, Instruction Sheet, Box, Postwar	57.00
Train Accessory, Platform, Painted Tin, 2 Sided Seats, 8 Posts, Marklin, 10 ½ x 7 ¼ In.	978.00
Train Accessory, Roundhouse, G Scale Layout, Mounted On Door, 79 x 18 x 36 In.	182.00
Train Accessory, Station, Bing, Ticket Office, Canopy, Brickwork, Dome Roof, Germany, 19 ½ In.	173.00
Train Accessory, Station, Bing, Tin Litho, Canopies, Removable Roof, Windup Bell, c.1902, 16 x 10 In.	1955.00
Train Accessory, Station, Marklin, Telegraph Office, Painted Tin, Pierced Roof, 10 ½ x 10 In.	2070.00
Train Accessory, Station, Marx, Electric, Tin, Gate, Pickup, Stake Bed, Box, 10 x 13 ½ In.	575.00
Train Accessory, Station, Montclair, Painted, Wooden, Carved, Paper Litho, 1910, 15 x 10 In.	575.00
Train Accessory, Station, Painted Steel, Clock Tower, Green Roofs, Double Doors, 9 ⅝ x 15 x 6 ⅝ In.	296.00
Train Accessory, Switch Tower, Lionel No. 445, Box, c.1955	225.00
Train Accessory, Tunnel, Marx, Houses, Hills, Roads, Tin Lithograph, 7 x 11 x 9 In.	40.00
Train Car, American Flyer, Caboose, 1928-36	225.00
Train Car, American Flyer, Cattle Car, Green, 1928-36	275.00
Train Car, Bing, Boxcar, Cudahy Refer, Old Dutch Cleanser, Side Doors, Tin Litho, 1 Gauge, 9 In.	316.00
Train Car, Buddy L, Engine, Tender, 1 Track, 1929, 48 In.	2495.00
Train Car, Buddy L, Zephyr, Pressed Steel, Red, White, Electric Headlight, Box, 30 In.	3163.00

Train Car, Excelsior, Locomotive, Painted, Stenciled Tin, Windup, Cast Iron Wheels, 14 In.	6325.00
Train Car, Ives, Locomotive, Tin, Die Cast Bell, Cast Iron, Spoke Wheels, 1870, 10 ½ In.	288.00
Train Car, Ives, Mail Car, No. 332, Peacock Body, Orange Inserts, Green Roof, Decals	91.00
Train Car, Lionel, Diesel, No. GP9, Boston & Maine, Postwar	194.00
Train Car, Lionel, Diesel Unit, 218 Santa Fe Alco A, Postwar	34.00
Train Car, Lionel, Engine, No. 38, New York Central Lines, Standard Gauge, c.1935, 11 In.	146.00
Train Car, Lionel, Locomotive, No. 2026, 10 In.	72.00
Train Car, Lionel, Pullman, No. 1766, Terra-Cotta, Maroon Roof, Standard Gauge, Box	428.00
Train Car, Lionel, Pullman, No. 2533, Silver Cloud	180.00
Train Car, Lionel, Pullman, No. 2534, Silver Bluff, 1952-60	180.00
Train Car, Lionel, Snowplow, No. 53, Rio Grande, Postwar..	91.00
Train Car, Lionelville, Rapid Transit Trolley, 60, Yellow, Red, Blue Lettering, 2-Piece Bumper..	80.00
Train Car, Locomotive, Fulgruex HO, SBBCE6-8, Crocodile, Electric, Box	805.00
Train Car, Locomotive, Tender, S-Scale, Brass, K-4 Pennsy 462, Sam Hongsa, Korea, c.1987 ...	518.00
Train Car, Locomotive, Tin, Painted, Clockwork, Cast Iron, Spoke Wheels, 10 ½ In.	374.00
Train Car, Locomotive, Triang, Puff, Puff, Rider, Decals, England, 1950s, 18 In.	95.00
Train Car, Marklin, Fidelitas, Clowns, Germany, c.1909, 37 ½ In.	103500.00
Train Car, Sunny Andy, Tin Lithograph, Wood Wheels, 1920s....................................	275.00
Train Car, Williams, Conrail Diesel, No. E-60, Cab No. CR960, Blue, White Lettering	57.00
Train Set, American Flyer, Tin Lithograph, Cast Metal Windup, Box, O Gauge, 4 Piece..........	267.00
Train Set, Bing, Lithographed, Iron Locomotive, Tin Tender, 3 Passengers, Clockwork, 1920s.	316.00
Train Set, Buddy L, 5 Cars, Diesel Engine, 12 Curved Tracks, 1929, 5 Ft. Diam......................	1650.00
Train Set, Engine, Tender, Box Car, 2 Passenger, Figures, Label, Box, 5 Piece....................	6325.00
Train Set, Exploration, Tin, Locomotive, Blinking Lights, Tracks, 3 Cars, Sankei, Box, 21 In. .	1921.00
Train Set, Fleischmann, Locomotive No. 4375, 5 Passengers, 5160 & 5162, HO, Boxes.........	920.00
Train Set, Issmayer, Locomotive, Tender, Baggage, Passenger, Floor, 24 In., 6 Piece...............	690.00
Train Set, Issmayer, Locomotive, Tender, Passenger Cars, Painted Tin Lithograph, 4 Piece......	1955.00
Train Set, Ives, No. 3257, Greyhound, Orange, O Gauge, Prewar....................................	403.00
Train Set, Jones & Bixler, Locomotive, Passenger, Painted Cast Iron, 48 In.	173.00
Train Set, Lionel, Locomotive, Pullman, Baggage, Observation Cars, 13 In.	5175.00
Train Set, Lionel, New York Central, Diesel Engine, Passenger Cars, 7 Piece	295.00
Train Set, Lionel, No. 628, Northern Pacific Diesel Switcher Engine, 4 Cars, 5 Piece	285.00
Train Set, Lionel, No. 11715, 90th Anniversary, Individual Boxes, Set Box......................	114.00
Train Set, Lionel, Soo Line, Diesel Engine, Hopper, Refrigerator Car, Caboose, 6 Piece	236.00
Train Set, Marklin, Model No. 3015, Crocodile, HO, Box, 1970s...................................	690.00
Train Set, Nabisco, Locomotive, 5 Freight Cars, Electric, 0-27 Gauge, Box......................	32.00
Train Set, Pratt & Letchworth, Engine, 2 Gondolas, 2 Standing Men, 1890s, 4 Piece.............	950.00
Train Set, Scratch-Built, Engine, 3 Cars, Wood, Paint, c.1900, 5 x 9 In.	4740.00
Train Set, Stafford Liner, Steel, Aluminum Wheels, 1940s, 25 In., 3 Piece......................	75.00
Train Set, Union Station, Tin Lithograph, Windup, Art Deco, Box, 20 x 15 In.	92.00
Train Set, United Scale HO, Locomotive, Tender, C&O 284, Kawaguchi, Japan, Box, 1960s......	288.00
Train Set, Zephyr Union Pacific, Cast Aluminum, Electric, General, 2 Piece.....................	863.00
Train, Handcar, Figures, Holding Handles, Clockwork, Germany, 5 In.	748.00
Train, Pull, Wolverine, 19 In., 2 Piece..	195.00
Train, Sparky The Locomotive, Tin Lithograph, Friction, Modern Toys, 4 x 14 In.	120.00
Train, Steam, Locomotive, Tender, Eleanor Phillips, Iron, Metal, Brass, 58 In. .... *illus*	6900.00
Train, Tin Locomotive, Tender, Red, Green, Blue, Penny Toy, 7 ½ In., 3 Piece......................	633.00
Train, Transcontinental Railroad Express, Marusan, Japan, Box, 5 ½ x 17 In.	150.00
Trick Pony, Bell Ringer, Cast Iron, c.1900, 7 ½ In.	950.00
Tricycle, Child, Metal, Windup, 1930s, 9 In.	195.00
Trip-Trapp, 2 Boys, Sailor Suits, Painted, Tin Lithograph, Windup, Marked, HEN, 7 In.	2500.00
Trolley, Brass, Black Tin Roof, Embossed, 4 Trucks, Open Platforms, Carlisle & Finch, 13 In. .	4313.00
Trolley, Broadway, Lithograph, U.S.A. Chein, 1930s, 8 ½ In.	195.00
Trolley, Lionel, Standard Gauge 3, 1908...	4400.00
Trolley, Metal, Friction, Germany, 1950s, 11 In.	175.00
Trolley, Orange, Stenciled, Clockwork, Lever Control, Bell, Kingsbury, c.1920, 14 In.	805.00
Trolley, Tin, Friction, Ichiko, Japan, 1960s, 14 In.	95.00 to 145.00
Trolley, Tin, Friction, Madison, Japan, 10 ½ In.	275.00
Trolley, White, Red Stripes, Tin Lithograph, Friction, Marked, S.G., c.1950, 12 In.	82.00
Truck Set, Milk, Domaco, Stake, Van Trailers, Coal, Wrecker, Dairy, Delivery, Tootsietoy, Box...	978.00
Truck, 3 Wheel, Tin Windup, Rider, Marx, U.S.A., 10 In.	395.00
Truck, Army, Steel, Canvas Cover, Battery Searchlight, Keystone, 1941, 26 ½ In.	518.00
Truck, Artillery, Pressed Steel, Tan, Cannon, Disc Wheels, Motor Driven, Kingsbury, 1921, 12 In.	805.00
Truck, Auto Express, Black Driver, Red, Yellow Wheels, Embossed, Cast Iron, Kenton, 9 In.	1420.00
Truck, Battery Operated, Tippco, Germany, 1930s, 5 In.	195.00

Toy Trains

The easiest trains to sell are the O gauge trains of the 1950s, not the larger trains of earlier years.

Tractor, Driver, Caterpillar, Exposed Engine, Steel Trends, Box, 8 In.
$2013.00

Toy, Train, Steam, Locomotive, Tender, Eleanor Phillips, Iron, Metal, Brass, 58 In. **$6900.00**

Toy, Truck, Cement Mixer, Mack, **Revolves,** Iron, Nickel Plate, Hubley, 7 ½ In. **$12650.00**

Truck, Bell Telephone, Accessories, Red, Hubley, 10 In.	1100.00
Truck, Bell Telephone, Ford, Olive, Die Cast, Tools, Trailer, Hubley, 1949, 9 ¼ In.	225.00
Truck, Bell Telephone, Green, Rubber Tires, Cast Iron, Hubley, 4 In.	295.00
Truck, Bell Telephone, No. 2011, Green, Red, Ladder, Pole Diggers, Cast Iron, Hubley, 16 In.	535.00
Truck, Bell Telephone, Red, Cast Iron, Pole Carrier, Auger, Shovels, Boom, Hubley, 9 In.	1840.00
Truck, Bell Telephone, Tools, Ladders, Green, Hubley, 8 ¼ In.	635.00
Truck, Bell Telephone, Trailer, Auger, Tools, Log, Olive Green, Cast Iron, Hubley, 9 In.	293.00
Truck, Bell Telephone, Wood Stake, Canvas Cover, Green, Smith-Miller, 19 In.	265.00
Truck, Bucket Loader, Green, Doepke, 1954, 22 In.	295.00
Truck, Buckeye Ditch Digger, Nickel Plated Chain Drive, Green, Red, Iron, Kenton, c.1930, 9 In.	234.00
Truck, Calliope, Circus, Orange, Ornate, Cast Iron, Figures, Kenton, c.1920s, 9 In.	920.00
Truck, Car Carrier, 3 Cars On Trailer, Red, Light Blue, Cast Iron, Hubley, 13 In.	830.00
Truck, Car Carrier, 3 Cars, Red, Blue, Green, A.C. Williams, Box, 12 In.	920.00
Truck, Car Carrier, Plymouth, Iron, Steel, 3 Cars, Truck, Nickel Grille, Arcade, 19 In.	633.00
Truck, Cattle, Nodder Cows, Tin, Friction, Japan, 1950s, 8 ½ In.	110.00
Truck, Cement Mixer, Green Water Tank, Drum Rollers, Hand Shovel, Buddy L, 1927	4650.00
Truck, Cement Mixer, Iron, Red, Drum, Side Lever, Spoke Wheels, Vindex, Box, 6 In.	8050.00
Truck, Cement Mixer, Jaeger, Silver, Red, Green, Kenton, 6 ½ In.	500.00
Truck, Cement Mixer, Mack, Revolves, Iron, Nickel Plate, Hubley, 7 ½ In. .... *illus*	12650.00
Truck, Cement Mixer, No. 32, Steel, Rotating Drum, Folding Chute, Buddy L, c.1920, 8 In.	173.00
Truck, Cement Mixer, Pressed Steel, Buddy L, 16 x 15 x 18 In.	1900.00
Truck, Cement Mixer, Wonder, Red, Nickeled Drum & Wheels, Hubley	175.00
Truck, Cement Mixer, Yellow, Black, Doepke, 1947, 15 In.	225.00
Truck, Cement, Tin, Friction, Japan, 1950s, 12 In.	175.00
Truck, Chemical, Ladder, Red, Kilgore, 7 ½ In.	350.00
Truck, Chemical, Steel, Red, Packard, Open Cab, Tank, Hose Reel, Bell, Keystone, 27 ½ In.	288.00
Truck, Chevrolet, Pickup, Ranch, Tin, Friction, Japan, 1960, 10 In.	155.00
Truck, Circus, 2 Piece, Pressed Steel, England, 1950s, 24 In.	475.00
Truck, Coal, Coke, Blue, Yellow, Renwal, c.1948, 8 In.	125.00
Truck, Coal, Coke, Red, Yellow, Plastic, Renwal, 11 In.	450.00
Truck, Coal, Lift, Blue, Rubber Tires, Arcade, 10 In.	3500.00
Truck, Coal, Mack, Driver, Red Paint, Cast Iron, No. 244, Arcade, 4 ¾ x 10 ½ In.	620.00
Truck, Coal, Red, Blue, Black Steel Wheels, Marx, c.1947, 21 In.	395.00
Truck, Coal, Red, Blue, Black Tin Wheels, Marx, c.1947, 21 In.	325.00
Truck, Coal, Tin Lithograph, Coal Chute, Hercules, 19 ½ In.	748.00
Truck, Cola, Plastic, Windup, Marx, 1950s, 7 ½ In.	95.00
Truck, Courtland Grade A Milk, Tin Lithograph, Plastic Cab Roof, Windup, Box, 12 ½ In.	316.00
Truck, Crane, Red, Green, Roberts, 1950s, 18 In.	150.00
Truck, Dairy Delivery, Cream, Red, Marx, 10 ½ In.	400.00
Truck, Delivery, Barrels, Blue, White, 132.5, Smith-Miller, 14 ¼ In.	180.00
Truck, Delivery, Divco Truck, Dugans Bakers, Tin, Friction, Japan, 1950, 7 ½ In.	295.00
Truck, Delivery, Kraft, Variety Of Cheese, Yellow, Metal, Smith-Miller, 7 ¼ x 13 ½ In.	560.00
Truck, Delivery, Merchants, Driver, Yellow, Red, Embossed, Spoke Wheels, Cast Iron, 6 In.	410.00
Truck, Delivery, Milk, Borden's, Cast Iron, Nickel Grille, Spoke Wheels, Hubley, 8 In.	518.00
Truck, Delivery, Open Bench Cab, Driver, Spokes, Clockwork, Germany, c.1920, 8 ¼ In.	863.00
Truck, Delivery, Panel, Arcade, Green, Nickeled Side Mount, 1925, 8 ¼ In.	2500.00
Truck, Delivery, Railway Express, Green, Cast Iron, No. 2054, 3 x 5 In.	210.00
Truck, Delivery, RCA Panel, Friction, Red, Timpo, England, 1950s, 4 In.	365.00
Truck, Delivery, Tin Litho, Driver, Chain, Spoke Wheels, Penny Toy, Meier, Germany, 3 ¼ In.	345.00
Truck, Delivery, Tin Litho, Enclosed, Yellow, Black, Driver, Clockwork, Hans Eberl, 7 ½ In.	4888.00
Truck, Delivery Van, Berlin Store, Tin Lithograph, Yellow, Black, Stake, Hans Eberl, 7 In.	4313.00
Truck, Delivery Van, Driver, Roof, Running Boards, Clockwork, Karl Bub, c.1931, 14 In.	1840.00
Truck, Delivery Van, Driver, Tin Litho, Doors Open, Roof Rack, Clockwork, Tippco, 9 ½ In.	5463.00
Truck, Delivery Van, Wrigley's Gum, Removable Roof, Rubber, Headlights, Buddy L, 26 In.	4312.00
Truck, Dump, Blue, Red, Nickeled Wheels, Kilgore, 6 In.	250.00
Truck, Dump, Chester, Horse, Driver, Cast Iron, Arcade, 7 ½ In.	205.00
Truck, Dump, Electric Lights, Wyandotte	225.00
Truck, Dump, Ford, Green, Red, Die Cast, Hubley, Box, 1940s, 9 ½ In.	185.00
Truck, Dump, Ford, Red, Green, Nickeled Wheels, Arcade, 1930, 6 In.	300.00
Truck, Dump, Giant Const Co., Yellow, Blue, Red, Wyandotte, 1950, 20 In.	110.00
Truck, Dump, High Lift, Semi-Trailer, Silver, Red, Black, Kingsbury, 17 In.	400.00
Truck, Dump, Hydraulic, Bronze, Yellow, Structo, 18 In.	55.00
Truck, Dump, Hydraulic, Pressed Steel, Painted, Pneumatic Tilt, Lever, Steers, Buddy L, 24 In.	189.00
Truck, Dump, International, Rubber Tires, Disc Hubs, Arcade, 10 ½ In. .... *illus*	4600.00
Truck, Dump, Lumar Construction Co., Red, Orange, Tin, Marx, Box, 12 ¼ In.	35.00
Truck, Dump, Mack, Driver, Iron, Blue, Decal, Hoist, Cast Spoke Wheels, Arcade, 1928, 12 In.	863.00

T

Truck, Dump, Mack, Iron, Green, Nickel Tilt Lever, Clockwork, Hubley, c.1930s, 10 In.		6325.00
Truck, Dump, Mack Jr., Pressed Steel, Steering Seat, Battery Operated, Steelcraft, 25 In.		895.00
Truck, Dump, Mack, Tin, Friction, Japan, 1950s, 5 ½ In.		95.00
Truck, Dump, Metal, Windup, 6 Wheels, Red, England, 1950s		195.00
Truck, Dump, Penny Toy, Fischer, 4 ⅜ In.		88.00
Truck, Dump, Red, Blue, Cast Iron, Disc Yellow Wheels, Hoist Bar, Lever, Dent, 11 In.		920.00
Truck, Dump, Red, Cast Iron, Hubley, 6 ¾ In.		1860.00
Truck, Dump, Ride 'Em, Green, Red, Keystone, c.1930s, 25 In.		210.00
Truck, Dump, Sand & Gravel, Blue Diamond, Orange, Mack, Smith-Miller, 18 ¾ In.		240.00
Truck, Dump, Sand, Stainless Steel Cab, White Bed, 109, Smith-Miller, 11 ½ In.		115.00
Truck, Dump, Scissor, Coal, Mack, Nickel Plate Wheels, Arcade, 10 In.	*illus*	3450.00
Truck, Dump, Sit-On, Pressed Steel, Painted, Buddy L, 19 ½ In.		189.00
Truck, Dump, Stop & Go, Tin, Windup, Japan, 1950, 9 In.		95.00
Truck, Dump, Wooldridge Bottom, Yellow, Doepke, 1946, 25 In.		200.00
Truck, Dump, Yellow, Arcade, 1923, 10 ¾ In.		400.00
Truck, Dump, Yellow, Doepke, 1946, 25 In.		200.00
Truck, Dumpster, Green, White, 1953, 22 In.		225.00
Truck, Easter Bunny Truck, Pressed Steel, U.S.A. Marx, 5 ½ In.		145.00
Truck, Express, Friction, Japan, 1950s, 10 In.		145.00
Truck, Ferris Wheel, Japan, Box, 1950s, 8 ½ In.		275.00
Truck, Ferris Wheel, Tin, Friction, Japan, 1950s, 8 ½ In.		145.00
Truck, Ferris Wheel, Tin Litho, Battery Operated, TN, Japan, Box, 11 x 9 In.	*illus*	1380.00
Truck, First Prize Ham, Steel, Art Deco Style Hood, White, Decals, Metalcraft, Box, 13 In.		144.00
Truck, Ford, 1953 Model, Die Cast, Hubley, Green, 6 ½ In.		165.00
Truck, Ford, Canopy Overland Express, Marx, 1958, 15 ½ In.		375.00
Truck, Ford, Model T, Pickup, Black, Spoke Wheels, Pressed Steel, Buddy L, 7 x 12 In.		720.00
Truck, Ford, Model T, Stake, Blue, Nickeled Wheels, Arcade, 7 In.		650.00
Truck, Ford, Pickup, Blue, Embossed Bed, Hubcaps, Tin Litho, Friction, Bandai, 1955, 12 In.		546.00
Truck, Ford, Stake Body, Red, Nickel Plated Wheels, Driver, Arcade, 9 In.		2185.00
Truck, Freight, Yellow, Blue, Red, Litho Wheels, Marx, Box, 17 ½ In.		400.00
Truck, Good Flavor Ice Cream, Japan, 1950s, 7 In.		325.00
Truck, Grader, Yellow, Doepke, 1949, 26 In.		195.00
Truck, Heinz Pickle, Pressed Steel, Painted White, Battery Operated, Box, 12 In.		173.00
Truck, Ice, Mack Bulldog, Blue Nickeled Wheels, End Gate, Ice, Tongs, Arcade, 8 ½ In.		750.00
Truck, Ice, Red & White Black Wood Wheels, Marx, c.1940, 11 ¼ In.		250.00
Truck, Ice, Studebaker, Arcade, Blue Gold Trim, 6 ¾ In.		650.00
Truck, Ice Cream, Ford, Tin, Friction, Japan, 1950s, 8 In.		145.00
Truck, Ice Cream, Howard Johnson's, 26 Flavors, White, Marx, Box		240.00
Truck, International Stake, Red & Green, Arcade, 1931, 11 ½ In.		1750.00
Truck, Livestock, 2 Cows, Green, Yellow, Die Cast, Plastic, Berlict, Box		285.00
Truck, Log, 1955 Model Studebaker, Die Cast, Box, 6 ½ In.		165.00
Truck, Log, Die Cast, Flat Bed, Log Supports, Kiddie Toy, Hubley, Box, 6 ½ In.		259.00
Truck, Log, Ford, Orange, Hubley, Box, 9 ¼ In.		225.00
Truck, Log, Tin, Pressed Steel, Lithograph, Wyandotte, 25 In.		94.00
Truck, Lumber, Black, Red Stakes, Pressed Steel, Buddy L, 1920s, 24 In.		3960.00
Truck, Mack, Red, Pressed Steel, Early 1900s, 22 ½ In.		175.00
Truck, Mail, Royal Mail Canada, Dodge, Tin, Friction, Japan, 1950s, 9 In.		95.00
Truck, Mail, U.S. Mail, Pressed Steel, Black, Green, Rear Door, Disc Wheels, Keystone, 26 In.		115.00
Truck, Metal, Battery Operated, 3 Actions, Side Dump, Back, Forward, Japan, 1950s, 12 In.		195.00
Truck, Milk, Borden's, Spoked Nickel Plated Wheels, Grill, Hubley, 7 ½ In.	*illus*	6613.00
Truck, Milk, Borden's, Tin Litho, Logo, Gray Fenders, Wooden Hood, Yellow Roof, Bottles, 13 ½ In.		259.00
Truck, Milk, Cream, Orange, Rubber Tires, Cast Iron, Hubley, 3 ½ In.		400.00
Truck, Milk, Mack, Wood, Arcade, Green, Driver, 13 ½ In.		4715.00
Truck, Morton Salt, Tin, Semi, Blue, Yellow, Friction, Rear Doors, Box, 12 ½ In.		525.00
Truck, Motor Express, Red, Green Plastic, Hubley, 1953, 12 ¼ In.		135.00
Truck, Motor Express, Red, Green, Plastic, Tilt Cab, 3 Opening Doors		135.00
Truck, Motor Express, Red, Green, Rubber Tires, Cast Iron, Hubley, 7 ½ In.		260.00
Truck, Moving Van, 7 Brothers, Pressed Steel, Building Pictures, Rubber Tires, Disc Wheels, 29 In.		1725.00
Truck, Moving Van, Driver, Blue, Embossed White, Cast Iron, Rubber Tires, Arcade, c.1929, 13 In.		4025.00
Truck, Navy Livestock, Red, Steel, Tonka, 25 In.		105.00
Truck, Packard, Pressed Steel, Rubber Tires, Disc Wheels, Keystone, 1926, 26 ¼ In.		1725.00
Truck, Pickup, Blue, Tonka, 1955, 13 In.		125.00
Truck, Plumbing Service, Take-A-Part, Red, Yellow, Blue, Revell, Box		240.00
Truck, Pontiac Steam Pumper, Arcade, 4 ½ In.		125.00
Truck, Pressed Steel, Marx, 1930s, 9 ½ In.		145.00
Truck, Railway Express, Rubber Tires, Green, Cast Iron, Hubley, 5 In.		410.00

Toy, Truck, Dump, International, Rubber Tires, Disc Hubs, Arcade, 10 ½ In.
$4600.00

Toy, Truck, Dump, Scissor, Coal, Mack, Nickel Plate Wheels, Arcade, 10 In.
$3450.00

Toy, Truck, Ferris Wheel, Tin Litho, Battery Operated, TN, Japan, Box, 11 x 9 In.
$1380.00

Toy, Truck, Milk, Borden's, Spoked Nickel Plated Wheels, Grill, Hubley, 7 ½ In.
$6613.00

T

Toy, Truck, Tow, Mack, Weaver Boom, Enameled Cast Iron, Arcade, 10 ½ In. $8913.00

Truck, Sanitary, Blue, White, Tonka, 1969, 16 In.	110.00
Truck, Scraper, Red, Doepke, 1951, 29 In.	275.00
Truck, Searchlight, Camouflaged, Matching Soldiers, Clockwork, Hausser, c.1936, 12 In.	1035.00
Truck, Searchlight, Hollywood Film-Ad, Red, Generator, 18 ½ In.	500.00
Truck, Semi-Trailer, Cattle, Pressed Steel, Painted, Tonka, 22 In.	177.00
Truck, Semi-Trailer, Diesel, Oliver, Die Cast, Green, Ertl, Box, 1993, 9 In.	60.00
Truck, Semi-Trailer, Keystone Express, Red, Yellow, Friction, 5 x 20 In.	195.00
Truck, Semi-Trailer, Tootsietoy, c.1950, Box	275.00
Truck, Shovel, Green, Red, Hubley, 8 ½ In.	575.00
Truck, Sit-N-Ride, Pressed Steel, Painted, Railroad Transfer, Buddy L, 23 In.	354.00
Truck, Soda, Tin, Friction, Japan, 1950, 7 ½ In.	110.00
Truck, Speedster, Steel, Red, Yellow, Open Frame, Removable Seat, Buddy L, Box, 1930s, 20 In.	1265.00
Truck, Stake, 5-Ton, Green, 8 Barrels, Rear Gate, Cast Iron, Hubley, 16 ½ In.	1050.00
Truck, Stake, Driver, Tin Litho, Red, Blue, Removable Stakes, Pull Toy, Marx, 11 ¾ In.	805.00
Truck, Stake, Green, Arcade, 7 In.	300.00
Truck, Stake, Green, Orange, Headlights, Wyandotte, 1930s, 10 In.	175.00
Truck, Stake, International, Green, Cast Iron, Arcade, 1936, 11 ⅞ In.	700.00
Truck, Stake, Orange, Motor Driven, Brake Lever, Clockwork, Kingsbury, 1926, 25 In.	4025.00
Truck, Stake, Painted Cast Iron, Rubber Tires, Iron Spoke Wheels, Arcade, 11 ½ In.	546.00
Truck, Stake, Red, Cast Iron, Rubber Wheels, 7 ¼ In.	136.00
Truck, Stake, Red Paint, Gold Wheels, Cast Iron, Marked, Champion, Geneva, Oh., 7 ⅝ In.	290.00
Truck, Stake, Red, Silver Wheels, Cast Iron, 4 ½ In.	240.00
Truck, Stake, Red, Wood Bed, Smith-Miller, 14 ¼ In.	240.00
Truck, Stake, Teamsters Union, Red, Smith-Miller, 18 ½ In.	360.00
Truck, Stake, Tin, Friction, Japan, 1950s, 8 In.	65.00
Truck, Stake, Tin, Windup, Courtland, 1950s, 8 In.	95.00
Truck, Stake, White, Decals, Marx, 1941, 14 In.	130.00
Truck, Steam Shovel, Green Cab, Corrugated Roof, Bucket, Crank, Steelcraft, 1925, 21 In.	1725.00
Truck, Sturditoy Coal Co., Pressed Steel, Painted, Orange, Black Fenders, 11 x 26 In.	840.00
Truck, Tanker, Black Body, Green Tank, Red Chassis, Brass Spigot, Decals, Buddy L, 25 In.	1265.00
Truck, Tanker, Gas & Oil, Red, Kenton, 7 ¼ In.	575.00
Truck, Tanker, Gasoline, Blue, 4 Wheels, Screw Top, O Gauge, Bing, 3 ¼ In.	201.00
Truck, Tanker, Gasoline, Blue, Green, Renwal, c.1948, 8 In.	125.00
Truck, Tanker, Gasoline, Gray, 4 Wheels, Screw Top, O Gauge, Bing, 3 ¼ In.	115.00
Truck, Tanker, Gasoline, Orange, Nickeled, Spoke Wheels, Hubley, 5 In.	250.00
Truck, Tanker, Gasoline, Orange, Rubber Tires, Cast Iron, Hubley, 4 ½ In.	260.00
Truck, Tanker, Gasoline, Shell & Mobil, Japan, 8 ½ In., 2 Piece	245.00
Truck, Tanker, Gasoline, Steel, Blue, 3 Nickeled Fill Caps, Spoke Wheels, Oil Cans, 29 In.	978.00
Truck, Tanker, Gasoline, Tin, Friction, Japan, 13 ½ In.	325.00
Truck, Tanker, GMC Mobilgas, Aluminum, Pressed Steel, Hoses, Smith-Miller, 21 In.	201.00
Truck, Tanker, Mack, Bulldog, Orange, Hubley, 4 ½ In.	175.00
Truck, Tanker, Mobilgas, Wood, Metal, Painted Red, Smith-Miller, 6 x 36 In.	351.00
Truck, Tanker, Oil, Driver, Tin Lithograph, C Mack Cab, 3 Fill Caps, Windup, Marx, 12 In.	460.00
Truck, Tanker, Shell, Red, Black, Green, Clockwork, Driver, Bing, Germany, c.1920s, 10 In.	2875.00
Truck, Tanker, Texaco, Cast Iron, Red, White Rubber Tires, Kenton, 12 In.	1675.00
Truck, Tanker, Texaco, Red, Decals, Buddy L, 1959, 23 In.	95.00
Truck, Tanker, Texaco, Red, Plastic Grill, Steel, Buddy L, 24 In.	131.00
Truck, Telephone, Ohio Bell, Red, Cas Iron, Hubley, 17 ¾ In.	700.00
Truck, Terreplane Steam Pumper, Hubley, Nickel Grille & Boiler	325.00
Truck, Texaco, Mack AC Bulldog Flatbed, 19 Die Cast Banks, 1:32 Scale, Box, c.1918	210.00
Truck, Tow, AA, 24 Hr. Service, White, Red, Steel, Tonka, 14 In.	118.00
Truck, Tow, Die Cast, Rubber Tires, Orange, Black, Factory Tag, Barclay, c.1940, 3 In., 2 Piece.	165.00
Truck, Tow, Ford, Model A, Arcade, 12 In.	650.00
Truck, Tow, Ford, Tonka, 1957	225.00
Truck, Tow, Green, Yellow, Cast Iron, Nickel Hoist, Lever, Spoke Wheels, Kilgore, c.1931, 12 ½ In.	2070.00
Truck, Tow, Light, 1950, 17 In.	225.00
Truck, Tow, Mack, Weaver Boom, Enameled Cast Iron, Arcade, 10 ½ In. .... *illus*	8913.00
Truck, Tow, National Auto Club, White, Smith-Miller, 17 In.	600.00
Truck, Tow, Pressed Steel, Lincoln, Canada, 1951, 14 In.	135.00
Truck, Tow, Red, Blue, Nickeled Grill, Rubber Tires, Champion	1000.00
Truck, Tow, Red, Cast Boom, Open, Nickel Winch, Rubber Tires, Champion, Box, 7 ¾ In.	345.00
Truck, Tow, Red, Iron, Boom, Hoist, Wire Chain, Hook, Driver, Disc Wheels, Arcade, 1920s, 12 In.	3163.00
Truck, Tow, Red, Yellow, Steel, Blue Grill, Wood Wheels, Wyandotte, 21 In.	164.00
Truck, Tow, White, Cast Iron, Boom, Rubber Tires, Disc Wheels, Seto, Sweden, 9 ⅝ In.	1093.00
Truck, Tow, Winch Hoist, Red, Gold Wheels, Cast Iron, Arcade, 5 ½ In.	153.00
Truck, Trans-Continental Freighter, Red, Wood Sides, Painted, Smith-Miller, 23 ½ In.	115.00

Truck, Transcon Lines, Cab, Double Trailer, Tin Lithograph, Box, 1960s, 8 x 11 In.	115.00
Truck, Trash Compactor, Yellow, Red, Ideal, 6 ½ In.	125.00
Truck, U.S. Army, Bulldog, Open Cab, Steel, Olive Drab, Disc Wheels, 1925, 26 In.	4888.00
Truck, Water, Packard, Red, Bell, Siren, Keystone, 30 In.	1900.00
Truck, Water Tower, Bell, Siren, Rubber Tires, Decals, Red, Steel, Keystone, 30 In.	1989.00
Truck, Water Tower, LaFrance, Red, Yellow, 1926, Tootsietoy, 3 ½ In.	125.00
Truck, Water Tower, Steel, Red, Nickeled Trestle, Aluminum Wheels, Buddy L, 38 In.	431.00
Truck, White, Dump, Driver, Cast Iron, Dual Rear Tires, Disc Wheels, Box, Arcade, 11 In.	575.00
Truck, Windup, Tippco, 2 Passengers, Prewar Germany, 1930, 10 In.	575.00
Truck, Wrigley's Spearmint Gum, Green, Metal, Double Back Doors, Buddy L, 7 x 14 ½ In.	176.00
Truck, Wyandotte Truck Lines, Blue, Red, Metal, 7 ¾ x 24 In.	280.00
Truck, Wyandotte Truck Lines, Red, Green, 8 x 24 In.	82.00
Tunnel, Lincoln, 6 Vehicles In Tunnel, Clockwork, City Skyline, Country View, Unique, 24 In.	431.00
Turkey, Bellows Make Sound, Painted, Tin, Windup, Germany, 4 In.	263.00
Turkey, Rolls, Bellows, Stationary Wings, Painted, Tin, Windup, Germany, 4 In.	275.00
Ukulele, Aloha, White, Plastic, Instructions, 1927-28, 20 ½ In.	22.00
Uncle Sam, Tin Lithograph, Figure, Bicycle, Spoke Wheels, American Flyer, Box, 8 ¼ In.	144.00
Uncle Tom, Walks, Lead Head, Cast Hands, Shoes, Clockwork Mechanism, Ives, Box, 9 ¾ In. .	115.00
Uncle Wiggily, Driving Car, Windup, Distler, Germany	3500.00
Union Station, Mystery Action, Automatic Toy Co., Tin Litho, 3 Sections, Box, 1950s, 14 x 20 In.	259.00
U.S. Air Force Jet Plane Base, Super Sabre FW-707 Jet, Tin Lithograph, Japan, 7 ½ x 11 In.	245.00
Van, 7UP, Tin, Friction, Japan, 1950s, 8 ½ In.	275.00
Van, Delivery, Green, Grill, Rear Door, Nickel Disc Wheels, Spare Tires, Arcade, 1929, 8 In.	2185.00
Van, Delivery, LeVitan, Tin Litho, Electric Lights, Doors Open, Latil, France, c.1930s, 16 In.	6325.00
Van, Delivery, Sunshine Biscuits, Decals, Metalcraft..	1350.00
Van, Freeman's Dairy, Red & Black, Rubber Tires, Dent, 5 ¾ In.	1200.00
Van, Mail, Red, Tin Litho, Driver, Clockwork, Roof Rack, Lehmann, Germany, c.1930, 7 In.	3163.00
Van, Mail, Tin Litho, Red, Open Doors, Clockwork, Lehmann, Germany, Box, 7 ½ In.	5750.00
Van, Postal, Wiking VW, Yellow, Plastic, Black Trim, Driver, Box, c.1960, 4 ¼ In.	325.00
Van, White, Blue, Friction, Rear Doors, Daya, Japan, Box, 1959, 8 In.	295.00
Velocipede, Woman, Rides Bicycle, Hollow Head, Cloth Outfit, Clockwork, England, 8 In.	3163.00
View-Master Case, Victorian, Walnut, 50 Revolving Cards, Turning Knobs, 12 x 19 In.	950.00
Violinist Plays, Dancers Twirl, Tin, Crank Operated, Bing, 6 ¾ In.	748.00
Waffle Iron, No. 8, Iron, Wood Handle Grips, Original Box, 7 x 7 In.	75.00
Wagon, Airflow, Red, White Stripes, Headlights, Art Deco, American Juvenile Vehicle Co.	450.00
Wagon, Auto Wheel Coaster, Ash, Iron, Hand Brake, 8-Spoke Wheels, c.1900, 41 In.	325.00
Wagon, Beer, Budweiser, Wood, Carved Horses, Driver, Barrels & Wheels, 17 In.	561.00
Wagon, Circus, Blue Cage, Black Horses, Driver, Bear, Cast Iron, 9 In.	146.00
Wagon, Circus Calliope, Orange Chassis, 4 Black Horses, Cast Iron, 25 In.	936.00
Wagon, Circus Monkey, Paper Litho Over Wood, Gibbs Mfg. Co., Canton, Ohio, c.1910, 13 In. .	578.00
Wagon, Circus, Overland, 2 Horses, Riders, Painted, Cast Iron, Kenton, 6 x 14 In.	180.00
Wagon, Circus, Overland, Band 9 Riders, Cast Iron, Kenton..	585.00
Wagon, Circus, Overland, Band, Driver, 2 Horses, 4 Men, Painted, Cast Iron, Kenton, 15 ½ In.	380.00
Wagon, Circus, Overland, Calliope, Painted Cast Iron, Driver, 2 Figures, Kenton, 14 In.	173.00
Wagon, Circus, Overland, Calliope, Painted Orange, Gilt Trim, 9 In. ....*illus*	1725.00
Wagon, Circus, Overland, Driver, 2 Horses, Painted, Cast Iron, Kenton, 14 ½ In.	530.00
Wagon, Circus, Overland, Figures, Horses, Reins, Chains, Kenton....................................	600.00
Wagon, Circus, Overland, Red Cage, 3 Figures, Polar Bear, Cast Iron, Kenton, 14 In.	1170.00
Wagon, Circus, Royal Circus, Blue Cage, Black Horses, Driver, Polar Bear, Cast Iron, 9 In.	351.00
Wagon, Circus, Royal Circus, Blue Cage, Black Horses, Driver, Polar Bear, Cast Iron, 12 In.	468.00
Wagon, Circus, Royal Circus Calliope, Blue, Gold Chassis, Black Horses, 16 In.	410.00
Wagon, Circus, Royal Circus Farmer, Horses, Driver, Iron, Steel, Aluminum, Hubley, 16 In.	3738.00
Wagon, Circus, Royal Circus, Green Mirror Van, Black Horses, Plumes, Iron, Hubley, 16 In.	3510.00
Wagon, Circus, Royal Circus, Orange Cage, Gold Horses, Driver, Rhino, Cast Iron, 12 ½ In.	351.00
Wagon, Circus, Royal Circus, Red Cage, 2 Side Gates, Driver, 4 White Horses, 2 Lions, 23 In. ..	936.00
Wagon, Circus, Royal Circus, Red Cage, Black Horses, Driver, Lion, Cast Iron, 12 In.	410.00
Wagon, Circus, Royal Circus, Red Cage, Horses, Driver, Bears, Iron, Hubley, 15 In.	1112.00
Wagon, Circus, Royal Circus, White Cage, White Horses, Driver, 2 Giraffes, 16 In.	410.00
Wagon, Circus, Tan Cage, White Horses, Driver, Lion, Paint Wear, Cast Iron, 12 ½ In.	382.00
Wagon, Coaster Express, Wood, Hand Brakes, 1900, 47 ½ In.	290.00
Wagon, Covered, 2 Black Horses, Cast Iron, Hubley, 15 In.	644.00
Wagon, Covered, Pressed Steel, Cloth, 2 Wood Horses, Paper Litho, Iron Wheels, Gibbs, 18 In.	863.00
Wagon, DeSoto, Steel, Painted Rubber Tires, Decals, Disc Wheels, Pull Toy, Handle, 20 ½ In. ..	288.00
Wagon, Express Flyer, Iron, Orange, Nickel Disc Wheels, Handle, Embossed, Kilgore, 7 In.	259.00
Wagon, Farm, Green, Red Wheels, Bench Seat, Weber, Salesman's Sample, 17 x 9 In.	4887.00
Wagon, Farm, Green, Red Wheels, Yellow Pinstripes, Raised Bench Seat, Brake, 17 x 10 In.	2243.00

Toy, Wagon, Circus, Overland, Calliope, Painted Orange, Gilt Trim, 9 In. $1725.00

Toy, Windmill, Rockford, Sheet Metal, Derrick Style Base, Hand Lever, 15 x 32 In. $7475.00

T

Tramp, Frame, Tiered,
Acorn Terminals Applied Rosettes,
Leaves, 12 x 11 In.
$174.00

Trench, Lamp,
75 mm Artillery Shell Base, Copper Plate,
Glass Globe, c.1918, 7 ½ x 23 In.
$127.00

Wagon, Farm, Ox Drawn, Driver, Cast Iron, Kenton, 16 In.	205.00
Wagon, Ice, 2 Horses, Cast Iron, Painted, Gold Letters ICE, Hubley, 12 In.	189.00
Wagon, Jenny, Bulking Mule, Tin, Windup, Strauss, Box	450.00
Wagon, Log, 2 Oxen, Driver, Hubley, 1915, 15 ½ In.	1050.00
Wagon, Log, Ox Drawn, Cast Iron, Black Driver, Kenton, c.1885, 16 In.	450.00
Wagon, Log, Oxen, Driver, Hubley, 1906, 6 ½ In.	1200.00
Wagon, Monkey Cage, Revolving, Hubley, Horses, U.S.A., c.1920s, 16 In.	97750.00
Wagon, Mule Drawn, Farm, Welker Crosby, 1885, 11 In.	1295.00
Wagon, Painted, Green, Red Wheels, Handle, Yellow, White Trim, Raised Seat, 39 x 27 In.	1265.00
Wagon, Pioneer Racer, Green, Red, Pressed Steel, 34 In.	150.00
Wagon, Radio Flyer, White, World's Fair, Rubber Tires, Decals, 1939, 7 In.	120.00
Wagon, Royal Band, 4 White Horses, Band Figures, Cast Iron, Hubley, 22 In.	1112.00
Wagon, Sand & Gravel, Driver, 2 Horses, Cast Iron, Kenton, 15 In.	375.00
Wagon, Wood Body, Wheels, Victory Special, 32 In.	142.00
Walkie-Talkie Set, Space Patrol, Space-A-Phones, Ralston Premium, Box, 1950s, 4 ¾ x 7 In.	230.00
Walking Tiger, Tin Lithograph, Windup, Marx, Box, 8 In.	79.00
Waltzer, Man, Woman Dancing, Twirling, Tin, Windup, Gunthermann, 8 In.	1265.00
Waltzing Couple, Windup, Multicolored, Late 1800s Dress, Issamayer, 8 In.	2070.00
Washer & Ringer, Wood, Metal, Rotapex, Electric, Salesman's Sample, 27 x 11 x 14 In.	2600.00
Washer, Copper, Paramount Steam Washer Co., Salesman's Sample, Pat Aug., 11, 1825, 8 In.	390.00
Washer, Doll Clothes, Wood, Metal Bands, Salesman's Sample, 8 x 6 ⅛ In.	275.00
Washing Machine, Busy Betty, Pressed Steel, Wringer, Agitator, Nickeled Lid, Hog, 10 In.	259.00
Washing Machine, Wringer, Wood, Iron, Metal, Salesman's Sample, c.1900, 17 x 10 In.	1500.00
Washtub, Doll's, With Mangle, Banded Wood, Horseshoe Brand, 9 In.	175.00
Water Elevator, Buckets, Water Platform, Water Wheel, Steam Pulleys, Carette, 9 x 15 In.	144.00
Whistle, Fish, Yellow, Green, Brown, Pressed Paper, 8 x 4 ⅛ In.	120.00
Whistle, Fish, Yellow, Green, Pressed Paper, Papier-Mache, c.1920, 10 x 3 In.	120.00
Whistle, Tap Dancer Performs When Whistle Blown, Penny Toy, 4 ⅝ In.	4888.00
Whistling Spooky Kooky Tree, Tin, Arms, Eyes, Mouth, Battery Operated, Marx, Box, 14 ½ In.	633.00
Whoopee Car, Cowboy Driver, Cows On Wheels, Tin, Windup, Marx, 6 ½ x 8 In.	360.00
Windmill, Rockford, Sheet Metal, Derrick Style Base, Hand Lever, 15 x 32 In. .... *illus*	7475.00
Windmill, Sampson, Brass Blades, Stover Mfg. Co. Of Freeport, Sample, 23 x 35 In.	4025.00
Windmill, Wood Base & Blades, Monitor Mfg. Co., Auburn, Ind., Case, 14 ½ x 26 In.	6325.00
Winking Pig, Tin, Windup, J. Chein, 4 ½ In.	65.00
Winky-Blinky Fire Truck, 3 Wooden Firemen's Heads, Bell, Clapper, Fisher-Price, 1954, 12 In.	125.00
Woman Pianist, Cloth Dress, Plays Piano, Tin, Wire, Windup, Martin, 5 In.	1495.00
Woman, Balancing Stack Of Dishes, Cloth Dress, Tin Litho, Martin Madelon, Box, 6 In.	6325.00
Woman, Oriental, Rolls Forward, Spins Fan, Painted, Tin, Windup, Germany, 8 In.	4750.00
Woman, Pushing Baby In Carriage, Tin, Windup, Cast Nickel, Plated, Gunthermann, 8 In.	5175.00
Woman, Pushing Boys In Cart, Blue Dress, Painted, Tin, Windup, Germany, 8 In.	3100.00
Woman, Pushing Goose In Cart, Tin, Clocker, Goose Flaps Wings, Gunthermann, 8 In.	1380.00
Woodpecker, Clicker, Tin, Mechanical, 4 In.	140.00
Zebra Cart, Man, Driving Cart, Zebra Kicks, Clockwork, Lehmann, Germany, 7 ¼ In.	489.00
Zeppelin, Atlantic Records, Led Zeppelin, Inflatable, Silver, Red, c.1970, 21 x 23 In.	173.00
Zeppelin, Tin, Painted, 1920-30, 7 x 31 In.	145.00
Zigzag, Black Man & White Man In Cart, Clockwork, Lehmann, 1920s, 5 In.	747.00
Zilotone, Tin Lithograph, Windup, Clown Taps Tunes, 6 Discs, 7 ½ In.	489.00
Zippo Climbing Monkey, Tin Lithograph, Pull Toy, Strings, Marx, c.1930, 9 ½ In.	70.00
Zorro, Horse, Plastic, Molded, Painted, Marx, Box, 10 ½ In.	443.00

TRAMP ART is a form of folk art made since the Civil War. It is usually made from chip-carved cigar boxes. Examples range from small boxes and picture frames to full-sized pieces of furniture.

Box, Chip Carved, Pincushion Top, Drawer, Footed, 5 ½ x 7 In.	169.00
Box, Desk, Hinged Lid Pulls Forward, 19th Century, 13 In.	55.00
Box, Gesso Painted Lid, Treasure Chest Style, Dome, Loop Handles, 9 ¾ x 8 x 12 In.	132.00
Box, Hearts, Squares, Crescents, Heart Shaped Mirror, 1898, 6 ½ x 9 x 6 In.	550.00
Box, Hinged Lid, Brass Hook, Eye Clasp, Signed, 6 x 6 x 12 In.	66.00
Box, Slide Lid, Multicolored Rooster Finial, Green Painted Base, Daniel Strawser, Jr., 6 ½ In.	113.00
Clock, Fretwork, Riverboat, Side Wheeler, 1-Day, c.1900, 12 In.	46.00
Cross, With Jesus, Ladder, Porcelain, White Metal, Late 19th Century, 26 ¾ In.	285.00
Cupboard, Hanging, Mixed Woods, Alligatored Varnish, c.1910, 27 x 22 ½ In.	323.00
Frame, Applied Horns, Engraved To & My, Black, White Matador Photo, c.1900, 15 x 13 In.	2115.00
Frame, Beveled Mirror, Geometric Pattern, Serrated Tiers, Black & Gold Paint, 23 x 20 In.	176.00
Frame, Geometric, Applied Serrated Edged Tiers, 20 x 17 ½ In.	11.00
Frame, Geometric, Serrated, Edged Tiers, Black & Gold Paint, 26 x 21 In.	55.00

T

Frame, Hearts, Cone Shapes, Pyramids, Chip Carved Rows, Signed, c.1910, 19 x 15 In.	225.00
Frame, Mixed Woods, Applied Shields, Flags, Red, White, Blue, Penn., c.1925, 24 x 20 In.	1469.00
Frame, Softwood, Cross Corner, Tree Branch Carving, Early 1900s, 22 x 28 In.	264.00
Frame, Stepped Chip Carved Mullions, Applied Hearts, Vines, c.1900, 24 x 22 In.	948.00
Frame, Tiered, Acorn Terminals Applied Rosettes, Leaves, 12 x 11 In. ....*illus*	174.00
Frame, Wood, Crown Of Thorns, President Harding Print, c.1900, 14 x 11 ½ In.	235.00
Frame, Wood, Gold Paint, Reverse Painting, 1st Church Of Christ, Boston, 26 x 49 In.	353.00
Frame, Wood, Gold Painted Highlights, Early 20th Century, 23 x 27 In.	676.00
Mirror, Chip Carved, Hearts, Numbers, Geometric Shapes, c.1910, 29 ½ x 30 In.	474.00
Sugar Bowl, Lid, Turned, Carved, Green Paint, Late 19th Century, 4 ½ In.	499.00

TRAPS for animals may be handmade. One of the most unusual is the mousetrap made so that when the mouse entered the trap, it was hit on the head with a mallet. Other traps were commercially manufactured and often are marked with the name of the manufacturer. Many traps were designed to be as humane as possible, and they would trap the live animal so it could be released in the woods.

Bear, No. 6, 43 ½ In.	990.00
Fly, Blown Glass, Green, Cork Top, 6 ½ In.	55.00
Fly, Blown Glass, Green, Stopper, Footed, 8 In.	110.00
Fly, Cobalt Blue, Blown Glass, Footed, 7 In.	55.00
Mouse, Hollowed Out Log, Wire, Wood, Steel Door, 8 ½ In.	104.00
Squirrel, Schoolhouse Shape, Flag, Tin, 19th Century, 11 x 19 x 10 In.	150.00

TRENCH ART is a form of folk art made by soldiers. Metal casings from bullets and mortar shells were cut and decorated to form useful objects, such as vases.

Lamp, 75 mm Artillery Shell Base, Copper Plate, Glass Globe, c.1918, 7 ½ x 23 In. ....*illus*	127.00
Lighter, Bomb Casing, Brass, Early 1900s, 3 ¾ In.	135.00
Lighter, Bomb, Brass, World War I, 3 ½ x ⅞ In.	126.00
Lighter, Bomb, World War I, Brass, Case, 1 x 3 ¾ In.	127.00
Lighter, Brass, Shell Casing, Flick Lighter In Pull-Out Base, 2 ¾ x ⅝ In.	62.00
Shell, Eagle Design, 7 ½-In. Military Round, Inactive, 10 In.	89.00
Tray, Propeller Plane, German Writing, World War II, Nazi, 9 ¼ x 9 ¼ In.	71.00
Vase, Artillery Shell, Brass, Copper Plating, Hand Hammered, 8 In.	85.00
Vase, Brass Shell Casing, Dragon Design, Wooden Base, Handles, 12 In., Pair	250.00
Vase, Brass Shell Casing, Holly Design, World War I, 13 ¾ In., Pair..........	435.00
Vase, Hand Hammered, Solid Brass, Copper Plating, 8 x 1 ¾ In.	85.00
Whiskey, Brass Shells, World War II, 1 ¾ x 1 ⅜ In., 6 Piece..........	200.00

TRIVETS are now used to hold hot dishes. Most trivets of the late nineteenth and early twentieth centuries were made to hold hot irons. Iron or brass reproductions are being made of many of the old styles.

Aluminum, Pierced, Expandable, Red Plastic Feet, 7 ¾ x 12 In.	8.50
Brass, Filigree Top, Victorian, 4 Turned Legs, Marked, JC & S, 9 ¼ In.	82.00
Brass, Footman, George III, Iron, Late 18th Century, 13 x 14 In., Pair..........	610.00
Brass, Footman, Slotted, Perforated, 4 Turned Legs, 7 ½ x 20 ¼ x 12 In.	34.00
Brass, Openwork, Cast Iron Legs, Wood Handle, Incised, No. 4, 14 In.	425.00
Brass, Pierced, Double Footman, England, 19th Century, 16 ½ x 24 ¼ In.	610.00
Bronze, Tile, Glazed Earthenware, Patinated, Label, c.1905, 1 ½ x 5 x 5 In.	5000.00
Cast Iron, Flowers, Cold Paint, 3 Peg Feet, RSW Group, England, 1970s, 6 ¾-In. Diam.	18.00
Cast Iron, Flowers, Orange, Yellow, Green, Ceramic Tile Insert, Footed, Japan, 4 ¼ x 4 ¼ In. ..	15.00
Cast Iron, Openwork, 3-Sided, Handle, 3-Footed..........	12.00
Cast Iron, Tassel & Grain Design, Virginia Metalcrafters Inc. Symbol, 1930s, 8 ¾ x 5 In.	36.00
Cast Iron, Tile Insert, Dewberry, Japan, 9 ¾ x 5 In.	13.00
Cast Iron, White Enamel Paint, Partridges In Flight, Hunting Dog, 1950-60s, 9 ½ x 6 In.	58.00
Ceramic, Bird & Grape Design, Pfaltzgraff, Marked, USA 615, 7 ½ x 7 ½ In.	20.00
Copper, Hammered, Pinecones, Terra-Cotta Tile, Arts & Crafts, 6 x 6 In.	35.00
Enamel, On Copper, Ceramic Tile, Metal Caddy, Round, Wheeling, 6 In.	65.00
Forged Iron, Heart Shape, Open Center, 3-Footed, New England, 1700s, 5 x 5 x 2 In.	350.00
Iron, Hearth, c.1800, 10 ½ x 17 In.	119.00
Iron, Wood Handle Grip, Arched Legs, Flat Feet, 14 x 15 ½ x 15 ½ In.	34.00
Marblehead, Kidney Shape, Olive Green Glaze, Marked, 8 ¼ In.	69.00
Porcelain, Fired Gold, Tile, Signed, Patsy, 6 ½ In.	12.00
Silver Plate, Butterfly Shape, Imported, Made In Italy, 1960s, 7 x 11 In.	22.00
Stand, Iron, Wrought, Wood Handle, Arched Legs, Scroll Ends, 11 ¾ x 15 ½ In.	107.00

Trivet, Wrought Iron, Heart Shape, Heart Cutout, Copper Peg Legs, 1 ½ x 11 In. $399.00

Trivet, Wrought Iron, Heart Shape, Pinprick Inscribed Anne Thomas, c.1825 $390.00

Trivet, Wrought Iron, Round, 3-Footed, 5 ½ x 8 ¾ In. $93.00

Trunk, Louis Vuitton, Suitcase, No. 113072, 17 x 24 x 7 In. $920.00

Trunk, Louis Vuitton, Trunk, No. 848726, 18 x 32 x 15 In. $6900.00

> ### TIP
>
> *To remove the musty smell from an old trunk, try some of the commercial products found in hardware stores. Several new types claim to remove odors by filtering the air.*

Tile, Canadian Grain, 4 Varieties, Beige, Marked, Made In Italy, 6 In.	7.50
Tile, Metal Frame, Mountie, On Horseback, Handles, Square, Canada, 6 In.	5.00
Wood, 2-Tone, Star Shape, Trapezoid Shape Sections, West Germany, 7 ½ In., Pair	25.00
Wrought Iron, 3 Legs, Handle, Hanging Hold, 6 x 15 In.	88.00
Wrought Iron, Heart Shape, Heart Cutout, Copper Peg Legs, 1 ½ x 11 In. .....*illus*	399.00
Wrought Iron, Heart Shape, Pinprick Inscribed Anne Thomas, c.1825 .....*illus*	390.00
Wrought Iron, Revolves, Curled Rat's Tail Handle End, Round, 11 ¾ x 28 ¼ In.	121.00
Wrought Iron, Round, 3-Footed, 5 ½ x 8 ¾ In. .....*illus*	93.00
Wrought Iron, Sadiron, Pierced, Hudson Valley, 19th Century, 10 In.	170.00
Wrought Iron, Triangle, Ram's Horn Grid, 3 Arched Legs, 5 ¾ x 12 x 12 In.	154.00
Wrought Iron, Triangle, Twisted Bars, Flat Penny Feet, 2 ¼ x 9 x 9 In.	55.00
Wrought Iron, Turned Handle, Pad Feet, Wavy Crosspieces, c.1850, 10 In.	45.00

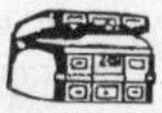

TRUNKS of many types were made. The nineteenth-century sea chest was often handmade of unpainted wood. Brass-fitted camphorwood chests were brought back from the Orient. Leather-covered trunks were popular from the late eighteenth to mid-nineteenth centuries. By 1895, trunks were covered with canvas or decorated sheet metal. Embossed metal coverings were used from 1870 to 1910. By 1925, trunks were covered with vulcanized fiber or undecorated metal. Suitcases are listed here.

Bamboo, Woven Sides, Top, Metal Hardware, Key, Characters, Asia, 23 ½ x 17 x 21 ½ In.	86.00
Camphor, Hinged Lid, Brass Bound, Brass Handles, c.1850, 13 x 30 x 16 In.	345.00
Camphor, Medallion Closure, Chinese, c.1900, 18 x 37 x 19 In.	717.00
Crocodile Leather, Train Case, Brass Hardware, Mirror, Key Holder, Jewelry Box, 1940s, 10 x 14 In.	294.00
Deer Hide, Nailhead Trim, Key, c.1850, 9 ¼ x 15 ¼ x 10 In.	425.00
Dome Top, Elm, Burl Wood, Fruitwood, Inlaid Panels, Bun Feet, Mid 1800s, 44 x 22 In.	2640.00
Dome Top, Grain Painted, Brass Bail, Cape Cod, 1800s, 9 x 10 In.	385.00
Dome Top, Pine, Iron Strap, Interior Monogram A I S, 1800s, 22 x 46 In.	325.00
Dome Top, Wrought Iron Straps, Multicolored Flowers, Names, Painted, Inside Till, 21 x 39 In.	264.00
Grain, Lift Top, Drawer For Shiftings, Paint Decorated, c.1820, 61 In.	1850.00
Gucci, Attache Case, Leather, Metal Mounts, Combination Locks, Italy, 13 ¼ x 17 ⅝ x 4 In.	472.00
Immigrant's, Pine, Dovetailed, Wrought Iron Handles & Straps, Norway, 25 x 17 x 15 In.	450.00
Lacquered, Black, 8 Immortals, Crossing Sea, Gilt, 14 ⅛ x 31 ⅛ x 19 ⅝ In.	149.00
Leather, Brass, Flower Border & Panels, Blue Ground, Handles, c.1850, 15 ½ x 35 x 17 In.	690.00
Louis Vuitton, Brass, Leather, Yellow & Green Striped Paint, c.1925, 30 x 44 x 21 In.	19717.00
Louis Vuitton, Damier, Oak Barred, Treated Canvas, Late 1800s, 17 x 24 x 20 ¼ In.	1200.00
Louis Vuitton, Leather, Wood, Locks, Fitted Interior, c.1985, 20 ½ x 43 ½ x 22 In.	7080.00
Louis Vuitton, Steamer, 35 ½ x 21 x 23 In.	7930.00
Louis Vuitton, Steamer, Leather Straps, No. 759760, 19 ½ x 36 x 15 ½ In.	3960.00
Louis Vuitton, Steamer, Leather, Wood, Brass, 25 ½ x 25 ½ x 25 In.	5310.00
Louis Vuitton, Suitcase, No. 113072, 17 x 24 x 7 In. .....*illus*	920.00
Louis Vuitton, Suitcase, Removable Compartment, 9 x 30 x 20 In.	550.00
Louis Vuitton, Trunk, No. 848726, 18 x 32 x 15 In. .....*illus*	6900.00
Louis Vuitton, Wardrobe, Leather, Lock Plate, Brass, Travel & Hotel Labels, c.1885, 23 x 21 x 44 In.	2520.00
Louis Vuitton, Wardrobe, Monogram, Canvas Covering, 43 x 22 x 22 In. .....*illus*	8913.00
Oak, Iron Bands, Strapwork, 22 x 30 18 In.	58.00
Oriental, Ebony, Pearl Inlay, Classic Scene, 18 x 32 In.	160.00
Packer, Wells Fargo, Wood, Metal Corners, Strapping, Iron Hardware	2160.00
Pine, Iron Strap Work, Paint, Plain Interior, 19 x 43 In.	35.00
Portmanteau, Molded Top, Bottom Hanging Hooks, Brass Tack Front, England, 16 x 50 In.	236.00
Ship's, Faux Grain, Painted, Metal Mounted, 20 x 30 ¾ x 17 ½ In.	657.00
Shipping, Dome Top, Wood, Dovetailed, Black Paint, Calligraphy Address, 27 x 13 x 14 ¾ In.	6500.00
Shipping, Pine, Walnut, Minton Tile, Lift Lid, Reeded Corners, c.1875, 22 x 51 x 24 In.	1220.00
Steamer, Goyard, c.1900, France, 22 ½ x 31 ½ In.	1912.00
Steamer, Hump Back, Wood Slats, Leather Handles, Metal Fittings, c.1900, 22 x 32 In.	117.00
Travel Case, Alligator, Tan, Brushes, Manicure Set, Vanity Mirror, Tray, Monogram, 11 x 9 ½ In.	595.00
Travel, Leather Over Wood, Iron Hardware, Continental, 1749, 21 x 15 In.	2675.00
Walnut, Leaf & Scroll Carved Panels, Plinth Base, Shaped Foot, Continental, 25 x 57 In.	299.00
Wood, Dome Top, Poplar, Grained Finish, c.1850, 12 x 26 In.	118.00

TUTHILL Cut Glass Company of Middletown, New York, worked from 1902 to 1923. Of special interest are the finely cut pieces of stemware and tableware.

Compote, Rolled Rim, Vintage, Signed, 4 ¼ x 8 In.	450.00
Perfume Bottle, Tapered, Etched Berries & Leaves, Faceted Stopper, Signed, 9 ½ In.	345.00
Pitcher, Etched Wild Rose, Handle, Signed, 13 ½ In.	403.00
Pitcher, Milk, Rosaceae, 5 In.	375.00

T

Vase, Etched Grapes & Leaves, Notched Edges, 4-Sided, Signed, 12 In. 489.00
Vase, Ruffled Rim, Columns Of Diamond Shaped Miters, Stars, c.1900, 9 In. 530.00

TYPEWRITER collectors divide typewriters into two main classifications: the index machine, which has a pointer and a dial for letter selection, and the keyboard machine, most commonly seen today. The first successful typewriter was made by Sholes and Glidden in 1874.

Lambert, Quartersawn Oak Case, Original Manual, c.1902, 7 ½ x 12 In. 1200.00
Olympia, Deluxe, Manual, Portable, Carrying Case, 1960s.. 125.00
Remington, Quiet-Riter, Portable, 1953 .... 125.00
Royal, Apollo 10, Electric, Portable, Carrying Case, 1970s.. 90.00
Royal Jubiliee, Model 12, Electric, Portable, Carrying Case, 1970s.. 125.00
Royal, Model 890, Portable, Carrying Case, 1960s 105.00
Smith-Corona, Glaxie, Blue, Manual, Carrying Case, 1970s.. 165.00
Smith-Corona, Skyriter, Portable, 1954, 11 x 12 In. 120.00
Smith-Corona, Sterling, Green Key Buttons, Portable, Carrying Case, 1949............................ 125.00
Underwood, Model 319, Portable, Carrying Case, 1963.. 95.00
Underwood, Standard, Portable, Carrying Case, 1929... 265.00
Wards, Signature 300, Manual, Carrying Case 95.00
Webster, XL 500, Sky Blue, Manual, Portable, Carrying Case, 1960s 98.00

TYPEWRITER RIBBON TINS are now being collected. The lithographed tin containers have been used since the 1870s. Most popular with collectors are tins with pictorial graphics.

Allied, Sea Gull Flying Over Ocean, Gray, Black, White, Round, 2 ½ In. 30.00
Bellaire, White, Black & Gold Graphics, Slip-On Lid, Round, Burroughs, 2 ⅝ In. 14.00
Bucki Typewriter Ribbons & Carbon Paper, Cleveland, Buck Deer 125.00
Burroughs Addressograph, Art Nouveau, Black & Gold, Early 1900s, 1 ⅝ x 2 In. 24.00
Burroughs, Silver, Orange, Brown, Round, 2 ½ In. 12.00
Butterfly & Trees, Oriental Style, Orange Ground, Slip-On Lid, Codo Mfg., 2 ½ In. 28.00
Challenge, Knight In Armor, Green, Silver, Underwood, Black, 2 ¼ x 2 ¼ In. 30.00
Elk, Black Silhouette, Yellow Ground, Round, Miller-Bryant-Pierce, 2 ½ In. 20.00
Elk, Blue, Yellow, White, Underwood, Miller-Bryant-Pierce Co., 2 ⅝ In. 16.00
Fine Service, Airplane, Cream, Blue, Underwood Black & Red Med., 2 x 2 In. 18.00
Five O'Clock, Gold, White, Secretary Powdering Nose, Round, 2 ½ In. 30.00
Government Brand, Tan, Black, Round, Mittag & Volger, c.1940, 2 ½ In. 24.00
Keelox Better Brands, Cream, Gold, Slip On Cover, Round, 2 ½ In. 14.00
Madame Butterfly, Black, White, Red Ground, Round, Miller-Bryant-Pierce, 2 ½ In. 24.00
Manifold Supplies, Panama Canal Image, Orange, Multicolored, 2 ⅝ x 2 ⅝ In. 19.00
Old Town, Blue, White Medallion, Red Band, 2 ⅛ x 2 ⅛ In. 14.00
Park Avenue, Blue, Silver Lettering, Slip-On Lid, Round, Royal Typewriter, 2 ½ In. 22.00
Pinnacle, Underwood, Medium Black Record, Columbia Ribbon & Carbon Mfg.................... 24.00
Secretarial, Gold, Black, White, Round, Smith-Corona, 2 ½ In. 20.00
Silver Craft, Silver Wreath, Black Ground, Round, Carter's, 2 ½ In. 28.00

UHL POTTERY was made in Evansville, Indiana, in 1854. The pottery moved to Huntingburg, Indiana, in 1908. Stoneware and glazed pottery were made until the mid-1940s.

Jug, Baseball, Ohio Port Wine Paper Label 55.00
Jug, Merry Christmas, 1939 .... 150.00
Vase, Taper, Blue, White Interior, c.1930, 9 ½ In. 53.00

UMBRELLA collectors like rain or shine. The first known umbrella was owned by King Louis XIII of France in 1637. The earliest umbrellas were sunshades, not designed to be used in the rain. The umbrella was embellished and redesigned many times. In 1852, the fluted steel rib style was developed and it has remained the most useful style.

Bakelite Handle, Blue & Red Design, Black Ground, Curved Handle, 24 In. 60.00
Bakelite Handle, Burgundy, Stars, 22 ½ In. 25.00
Carved Handle, Dog Head, Airedale, Malacan Shaft, c.1920, 32 ½ In. 300.00
Celluloid Handle, Black, Multicolored Stripes At Top, 25 In. 43.00
Gold Filled Handle, L-Shape, Leafy Designs, Metal Frame, Black Cloth, 35 ½ In. 44.00
Gold Filled Handle, Mother-Of-Pearl, Black, 35 In. 225.00
Gold Handle, Mother-Of-Pearl, Ornate Design, Black Replaced Material & Spines, 1800s, 33 In. . 265.00
Ivory Handle, Carved, Silk Embroidered, Dragon Design, c.1900... 850.00
Lucite Handle, Black Painted Wood Section, Plaid, c.1940, 31 ½ In. 31.00
Oval Handle & Tip, Ivory, Oriental, Child & Adults In Robes, Blue Cloth Hood, 31 ¼ In. 55.00
Parasol, Cotton Lace, Ruffles, Victorian Style, 19 In. 43.00
Parasol, Ivory Handle, Carved, Inlaid Mother-Of-Pearl, Silk... 100.00

Trunk, Louis Vuitton, Wardrobe, Monogram, Canvas Covering, 43 x 22 x 22 In. $8913.00

U
V

Vallerysthal, Vase, Cameo, Cylindrical, Textured, Green, Purple Iris, Incised, France, 12 In. $575.00

Vallerysthal, Vase, Rambling Rose, Cameo, Enameled, Parcel Gilt, c.1920, 6 x 10 In. $576.00

Van Briggle, Bowl, Flower Frog, Mulberry, Marked, c.1915, 8 ½ In. $92.00

Van Briggle, Flower Frog, Swan, 1920s, 4 x 2 ⅝ In. $35.00

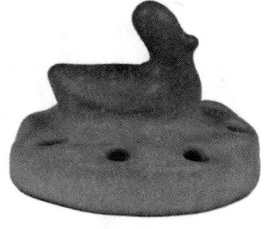

Parasol, Ivory Paneled Handle, 3 Layered Cloth, Black Lace Exterior Hood, 24 x 24 In.	66.00
Parasol, Linen & Lace, Knotty Wood Handle, Tassel, Victorian, 37 In.	395.00
Parasol, Silk, Lace, Victorian	245.00
Pearl Inlaid Handle, Flowers, Cloth Top, Gold, 8 In.	146.00

UNION PORCELAIN WORKS was established at Greenpoint, New York, in 1848 by Charles Cartlidge. The company went through a series of ownership changes and finally closed in the early 1900s. The company made a fine quality white porcelain that was often decorated in clear, bright colors.

Oyster Plate, Late 1800s, 8 ½ In.	250.00

VAL ST. LAMBERT Cristalleries of Belgium was founded by Messieurs Kemlin and Lelievre in 1825. The company is still in operation. All types of table glassware and decorative glassware have been made. Pieces are often decorated with cut designs.

Ashtrays, Nesting, 3 Different Sizes, 7 In., 6 ¼ In., 5 In., 3 Piece	45.00
Candlestick, Paneled Sides, 2 Faceted Knops, 6-Sided Foot, 9 ½ In., Pair	115.00
Coaster, Wine, Fruits, 6 In.	45.00
Figurine, Monkey, Acid Etched, Marked, 6 ½ In.	22.00
Knife Rest, Double, Curved Bar, Horn Like Ends, c.1910, 4 ¼ In.	48.00
Paperweight, Alligator Etching, Label, 4 ½ x 3 ½ In.	50.00
Paperweight, Frog, Clear, Signed, 4 x 3 In.	49.00
Pitcher, Milk, Applied Handle, Diamond Cut Pattern, 5 ¾ In.	65.00
Pitcher, Water, 7 ³⁄₁₆ In.	45.00
Vase, Campagna Form, Raised Square Base, 7 ¼ x 6 ¾ In.	395.00
Vase, Cobalt Blue Cut To Clear, Paneled, Ovals, Clear Square Foot, 12 In.	115.00
Vase, Trumpet, Crosscut Diamond, Star & Fan, Red To Clear, 14 In.	400.00
Vase, Trumpet, Strawberry Diamond, Star & Fan Motif, Trumpet, Green To Clear, 8 In.	250.00
Wine, Green To Clear, c.1800, 7 Piece	350.00
Wine, Vaseline Cut To Clear, Teardrop Stem, Hobstar & File, 5 In.	125.00

VALLERYSTHAL GLASSWORKS was founded in 1836 in Lorraine, France. In 1854, the firm became Klenglin et Cie. It made table and decorative glass, opaline, cameo, and art glass. A line of covered, pressed glass animal dishes was made in the nineteenth century. The firm is still working.

Box, Cover, Dog On Steamer Rug, Opaque Blue, c.1900, 4 ⅞ x 3 ¾ x 4 ¾ In.	79.00
Breakfast Set, Hen-On-Nest Serving Dish, 7 In., Tray, 10 x 11 In., 6 Chick Eggcups	230.00
Dish, Cover, Setter Lying Down, Opaque Blue, Rifle, Game Bag, c.1900, 5 x 4 x 6 In.	118.00
Vase, Cameo, Cylindrical, Textured, Green, Purple Iris, Incised, France, 12 In. ...... *illus*	575.00
Vase, Cylinder, Green, Intaglio Pond Scene, Enameled Insects, 2 Cameos, Signed Leaf, 14 In.	700.00
Vase, Dark Green, Intaglio Cut Lily Pond, Gilt Leaves, Insects, Cameo, Signed, 14 In.	1035.00
Vase, Rambling Rose, Cameo, Enameled, Parcel Gilt, c.1920, 6 x 10 In. .... *illus*	576.00

VAN BRIGGLE POTTERY was started by Artus Van Briggle in Colorado Springs, Colorado, after 1901. Van Briggle had been a decorator at Rookwood Pottery of Cincinnati, Ohio. He died in 1904 and his wife took over managing the pottery. The wares usually had modeled relief decorations and a soft, dull glaze. The pottery is still working and still making some of the original designs.

Bookends, Mountain Craig Peacocks, 1920s, 4 ¾ x 5 ½ In.	325.00
Bowl, Dogwood, Squat, 1905, 4 ¾ x 7 ½ In.	2074.00
Bowl, Flower Frog, Mulberry, Marked, c.1915, 8 ½ In. .... *illus*	92.00
Bowl, Green Matte Glaze, Frothy, Leaves, 1907, 4 ¼ x 5 ¾ In.	1830.00
Bowl, Green Matte Glaze, Maple Leaves, 1906, 6 x 12 In.	1830.00
Bowl, Lily, Turquoise, 6 In.	35.00
Bowl, Mermaid & Fish, Turquoise, 14 In.	235.00
Chamberstick, Maroon & Blue Matte Glaze, c.1915, 5 ½ x 5 In.	210.00
Figurine, Woman With Shell Bowl, Turquoise	125.00
Flower Frog, Swan, 1920s, 4 x 2 ⅝ In. .... *illus*	35.00
Lamp Base, Indian Head, Mountain Craig Brown, 1914, 12 ¼ x 5 ½ In.	2074.00
Lamp Base, Red, Green, Bulbous, 1905, 13 x 4 ¼ In.	1952.00
Lamp, Indian Maiden Holding Pot, Butterfly Shade, Turquoise	170.00
Planter, Conch Shell, Mulberry, 9 In.	35.00
Planter, Conch Shell, Mulberry, 12 In.	35.00
Planter, Conch Shell, Mulberry, 16 In.	40.00
Planter, Shell Shape, 9 x 5 In.	55.00
Planter, Swirl Leaf, Mulberry, 5 In.	60.00
Tankard, Green Matte Glaze, 1907, 6 ½ In.	295.00

Tile, Indigo Stellar's Jay, Oak Branch, Cuenca, 6 x 6 In. .... *illus*	1920.00
Tile, Red Parrot On Branch, Cuenca, 6 x 6 In.	1320.00
Tray, Mermaid, Purple, 10 ½ In.	95.00
Vase, 2 Handles, Flowers, Blue & Green Matte, c.1930, 7 x 9 In.	173.00
Vase, 2 Handles, Leaves, Blue & Green Matte, Marked, c.1930, 6 ½ x 7 In.	86.00
Vase, 2 Lower Handles, Iris, Blue & Green Matte, c.1930, 7 x 14 In.	86.00
Vase, 3 Butterfly Decorated Panels, Mulberry Glaze, Mark, 1917, 3 In.	388.00
Vase, 3-Headed Indian, Purple, 12 In.	285.00
Vase, Bud, 3 Holes, Pink..........	35.00
Vase, Bulbous, Maroon & Blue Matte Glaze, Spade Designs, Handles, c.1920, 7 x 6 ½ In.	86.00
Vase, Bulbous, Stylized Poppies, Brown Matte Glaze, Incised, Marked, 1906, 7 x 8 In.	2280.00
Vase, Cone Flowers, Globular, Blue & Green Matte Glaze, Marked, c.1930, 8 x 9 In.	316.00
Vase, Daffodils, Swirling Leaves, Green To Teal Glaze, Bulbous, 10 x 4 In.	1920.00
Vase, Daffodils, Turquoise, 9 ½ In.	82.00
Vase, Daffodils, Yellow Matte Glaze, Blue Overspray, 10 ¼ In.	1895.00
Vase, Dragonflies, Blue & Green Matte Glaze, c.1930, 3 x 7 In.	201.00
Vase, Dragonflies, Gray, Blue Matte Glaze, Brown Body, Mark, c.1906, 4 In.	1035.00
Vase, Embossed Leaves, Green Over Brown Matte Glaze, Marked, 3 ⅞ In.	460.00
Vase, Flared Shape, Raised Flower Design, Maroon, Blue Matte Glaze, No. 21, c.1920, 8 x 16 In.	510.00
Vase, Flared Shape, Yucca Plant, Blue & Green Matte Glaze, Marked, c.1930, 5 x 14 In.	230.00
Vase, Flower, Maroon, Blue Matte Glaze, Double Handle, c.1930, 7 ½ x 9 ¼ In.	300.00
Vase, Flower Shape, Blue To Green Glaze, Incised Monogram, 3 ¾ In.	47.00
Vase, Flowers, Maroon Glaze, Signed, c.1930, 12 ½ In.	720.00
Vase, Flowers, Turquoise, 5 In.	40.00
Vase, Frosted Mottled Cream Matte Glaze, Flared Rim, 1906, 9 ½ In.	1695.00
Vase, Globular, Blue Matte Glaze, Crocus, Marked, 1907, 2 ½ x 2 ¾ In.	365.00
Vase, Green Matte, Purple Glaze, Raised Decoration, 1907-12, 10 In.	717.00
Vase, Leaves, Red, Brown Matte Glaze, 1903, 15 ½ x 4 ½ In.	3538.00
Vase, Lorelei, Turquoise, Anna Mark, Colo. Springs, 10 ½ In.	250.00
Vase, Lotus Leaf, Blue, Bulbous, 9 x 4 In.	165.00
Vase, Maroon Matte Glaze, Rolled Rim, c.1906, 3 ¼ In.	403.00
Vase, Molded Leaves, Green Matte Glaze, Red Brown Body, Mark, c.1910, 6 In.	920.00
Vase, Molded Leaves, Handles, Maroon & Blue Matte Glaze, c.1918, 4 x 10 In.	300.00
Vase, Mottled Green, Red Matte, 2 Handles, 1903, 7 ½ x 6 In.	1440.00
Vase, Mulberry, Dark Maroon Matte Glaze, Mark, 1918, 2 ½ In.	345.00
Vase, Pinecone, Blue, 3 x 6 In.	110.00
Vase, Poppy Pods, Green & Brown Matte Glaze, c.1906, 4 ½ x 4 ½ In.	2160.00
Vase, Poppy Pods, Green Matte Glaze, 7 x 3 ½ In.	915.00
Vase, Poppy Pods, Lime Green Glaze, 1902, 9 x 6 In.	5795.00
Vase, Raised Pinecones, Needles, Green, Brown Matte Glaze, Round, 1914, 10 x 5 In.	960.00
Vase, Red, Green, Pods, Leaves, 1907, 16 x 11 In.	4270.00
Vase, Shouldered, Incised Poppy Pod Design, Maroon, Blue Matte Glaze, c.1930, 3 ½ x 3 ½ In.	330.00
Vase, Shouldered, Waisted Shape, Incised Vertical Leaves, Maroon, Blue Matte Glaze, 5 x 8 In.	210.00
Vase, Stylized Flower, Brown, Green Matte Glaze, c.1930, 4 ½ x 9 ½ In.	300.00
Vase, Stylized Leaf, Mottled Matte Glaze, 1915, 6 ½ In.	546.00
Vase, Stylized Leaves, Mulberry, 6 ¾ In.	1495.00
Vase, Teal, Light Green Glaze, Frothy Amber, Quatrefoils, 11 ¼ x 4 ½ In.	1220.00
Vase, Three Graces, Purple, 17 In.	225.00
Vase, Tulips, Red, Brown Glaze, Oval, 14 In.	3360.00
Vase, Vertical Leaves, Blue Matte Glaze, c.1907, 6 ½ x 3 ½ In. .... *illus*	1440.00

VASA MURRHINA is the name of a glassware made by the Vasa Murrhina Art Glass Company of Sandwich, Massachusetts, about 1884. The glassware was transparent and was embedded with small pieces of colored glass and metallic flakes. The mica flakes were coated with silver, gold, copper, or nickel. Some of the pieces were cased. The same type of glass was made in England. Collectors often confuse Vasa Murrhina glass with aventurine, spatter, or spangle glass. There is uncertainty about what actually was made by the Vasa Murrhina factory. Related pieces may be listed under Spangle Glass.

Vase, Blue, Spangled, Pinched Sides, 6 In. .... *illus*	20.00

VASELINE GLASS is a greenish-yellow glassware resembling petroleum jelly. Pressed glass of the 1870s was often made of vaseline-colored glass. Some vaseline glass is still being made in old and new styles. Additional pieces of vaseline glass may also be listed under Pressed Glass in this book.

Aquarium, Wrought Iron Base, Underneath Bulb, c.1910, 42 x 16 In. .... *illus*	715.00
Ashtray, Hat Form, Bent Rim, 3 ¼ x 2 ¾ In.	10.00

Van Briggle, Tile, Indigo Stellar's Jay, Oak Branch, Cuenca, 6 x 6 In. $1920.00

Van Briggle, Vase, Vertical Leaves, Blue Matte Glaze, c.1907, 6 ½ x 3 ½ In. $1440.00

Vasa Murrhina, Vase, Blue, Spangled, Pinched Sides, 6 In. $20.00

Pattern Numbers

The pattern numbers on Van Briggle pottery can help date a piece. Numbers below 899 were used before 1912. AA alone was used before 1920, AA-USA was used from 1922 to 1929.

U
V

Vaseline Glass, Aquarium,
Wrought Iron Base, Underneath Bulb,
c.1910, 42 x 16 In.
$715.00

Vaseline Glass, Epergne, Yellow,
Ruffled Trumpets, Opalescent Edge,
Convex Base, 17 x 11 In.
$201.00

Basket, Satin Finish, Candlewick Edge, 6 x 4 ¾ In.	95.00
Bowl, Daisy & Button, Silver Plate Holder, E.G. Webster & Bros., c.1900, 8 ½ x 10 In.	495.00
Bowl, Diamond Pattern, 7 ⅛ In.	25.00
Bowl, Folded Square, Enamel Highlights, Opalescent, 9 In.	450.00
Bowl, Spangle, Ruffled Edge, Hobbs, 9 In.	235.00
Cake Stand, Pedestal, 12 In.	75.00
Candlestick, Petal & Loop Pattern, c.1860, 7 In.	345.00
Candy Dish, Nesting Hen, Cover, 6 x 8 In.	19.25
Celery Dish, Alaska Pattern, Enameled Flowers, Opalescence, 9 ½ In.	425.00
Compote, Dolphin Stem, Yellow, 12-Sided Base, c.1900, 8 ½ In.	171.00
Compote, Hobnail & Fan, Shaded To White, Ruffled Rim, Flared Foot, 8 x 11 In.	83.00
Epergne, Ruffled Bowl, Rimmed By 4 Green Yellow Vases, c.1900, 18 In.	443.00
Epergne, Yellow, Ruffled Trumpets, Opalescent Edge, Convex Base, 17 x 11 In. ......*illus*	201.00
Fishbowl, Bulbous Center, c.1925, 7 ½ In.	625.00
Ice Bucket, Ribbed, 5 ½ In.	125.00
Pitcher, Water, Windows, Tricorner Crimped Rim, Feather Handle, Pontil, c.1875, 9 In.	463.00
Plate, Scalloped Edge, 10 In.	33.00
Relish, Banner Pattern, 5 x 7 In.	38.00
Salt & Pepper, Alaska Pattern, Opalescent, 3 In.	110.00
Shade, Opalescent, Teardrop Form, 8 ⅞ x 3 In.	56.00
Toothpick, Daisy & Button, Hat Shape, 1885, 3 x 3 In.	35.00
Toothpick, Opalescent, Ribbed Spiral, 2 ⅜ In.	179.00
Vase, 3 Trees & Branches On Base, Ruffled Rim, 7 In.	155.00
Vase, Art Deco, Fluted Vertical Panels, Pad Base, Raised Polka Dots, 5 ¾ In.	83.00
Vase, Jack-In-The-Pulpit, 13 In.	249.00
Vase, Mary Dugan, Opalescent, 6 ¼ In.	45.00
Vase, Rigaree, Footed, 6 In.	235.00
Vase, Victorian, Clear, Bulbous, Green Ruffled Expanded Rim, 19th Century, 7 In.	60.00
Water Set, Alaska Pattern, Opalescent, Pitcher, 8 In., 6 Tumblers	700.00
Water Set, Bulbous, Columnar Top, Pitcher, 6 Glasses, 9 ½ In. & 5 ⅜ In., 7 Piece	795.00

VERLYS glass was made in Rouen, France, by the Societe Holophane Francais, a company that started in 1920. It was made in Newark, Ohio, from 1935 to 1951. The art glass is either blown or molded. The American glass is signed with a diamond-point-scratched name, but the French pieces are marked with a molded signature. The designs resemble those used by Lalique. *Verlys*

Bowl, Cupids & Hearts, Etched & Frosted, 6 In.	145.00
Bowl, Flower, Signed, 11 ¾ In.	82.00
Bowl, Pinecone, Smokey Topaz, 3 Pinecone Feet, 6 ¼ In.	175.00
Charger, Birds, Frosted, 11 ½ In.	106.00
Dish, Duck Perched On Edge, Oval, Silky Acid Finish, Signed, c.1930, 3 ¾ x 4 In.	105.00
Dish, Matte Finish Flowers, Handles, Viktor Schreckengost, 6 In. ......*illus*	69.00
Jardiniere, Bouquets, Frosted, Molded, Signed, 3 ¾ x 9 ¼ In.	60.00
Vase, Frosted, Inverted Textured Polka Dots, Footed, Mid 20th Century, 7 In.	205.00
Vase, Lovebird, Frosted & Clear, Signed, 6 ½ x 2 ¾ In.	110.00

VERNON KILNS was the name used by Vernon Potteries, Ltd. The company, which started in 1931 in Vernon, California, made dinnerware and figurines until it went out of business in 1958. The molds were bought by Metlox, which continued to make some patterns. Collectors search for the brightly colored dinnerware and the pieces designed by Rockwell Kent, Walt Disney, and Don Blanding. For more prices, go to kovels.com. *VERNON MONTECITO*

Brown Eyed Susan, Chop Plate, 12 ¼ In.	20.00
Brown Eyed Susan, Lazy Susan, Center Handle, 10 ¾ In.	30.00
Casual California, Tumbler, Mahogany Brown, 5 ⅜ In.	30.00
Chintz, Bowl, Vegetable, 9 In.	35.00
Chintz, Cup & Saucer, After Dinner ......*illus*	36.00
Chintz, Plate, Salad, Marked, 7 ½ In.	15.00
Commemorative Plate, American Presidents, Washington To Eisenhower, Plate No. 2, 10 ½ In.	22.00
Commemorative Plate, General MacArthur Victory, Morse Code & V Border, 10 ½ In.	25.00
Country Cousins, Cup & Saucer	9.95
Cup & Saucer, Mount Vernon, Scenic America, Demitasse, 2 In.	18.00
Dolores, Plate, Dinner, 10 ½ In.	12.00
Dolores, Plate, Hand Painted, c.1945, 10 ½ In.	12.00
Dolores, Teapot ......*illus*	125.00
Early California, Cup & Saucer, Turquoise, 1937	12.50
Early California, Cup & Saucer, Yellow	12.50
Early California, Plate, Dinner, Blue, 10 ½ In.	15.00

Early California, Plate, Dinner, Orange, Rim Ring, 10 ½ In.	8.00
Early California, Plate, Dinner, Pink, 10 ½ In.	15.00
Figurine, Anne Shirley, Sculpted By Janic Pettee, c.1940, 11 In.	750.00
Gingham, Sauceboat .... *illus*	10.00
Gingham, Vegetable, Open, Green & Yellow, 8 ⅞ In.	25.00
Homespun, Pitcher, Green, Rust, Yellow, Plaid, Montecito Shape, 5 In.	37.00
Homespun, Platter, 10 In.	23.00
May Flower, Cup, Red, Blue, Yellow Flowers, 2 ½ In.	6.00
May Flower, Plate, Bread, 6 ½ In.	15.00
May Flower, Plate, Dinner, Embossed Edge, Bright Flowers, Marked, 9 ½ In.	10.00
Modern California, Platter, Pistachio, c.1940, 12 ¼ In.	18.00
Monterey, Plate, Dinner, 9 ½ In.	15.00
Monterey, Plate, Luncheon, 8 ½ In.	13.00
Monterey, Salt & Pepper	20.00
Monterey, Sugar & Creamer	20.00
Organdie, Chop Plate, Brown & Yellow Plaid, 12 In.	10.00
Organdie, Cup, Brown & Yellow Plaid	5.00
Organdie, Plate, Salad, Brown & Yellow Plaid, 7 ½ In.	5.50
Poppy Trail, Plate, Dinner, Yellow, Aqua, Gray, Metlox, 10 In.	9.00
Raffia, Butter, Cover	35.00
Raffia, Jug, Shades Of Green & Brown Swatches, San Marino Shape, 6 ½ In.	23.00
Sherwood, Bowl, Vegetable, Divided, 9 ¾ x 8 ⅞ In.	12.50
Sherwood, Gravy Boat	20.00
Sherwood, Plate, Dinner, 10 In.	10.00
Sherwood, Relish, 3-Section, Ink Mark, 12 ⅞ x 7 ⅛ In.	25.00
Sierra Madre, Platter, 2-Tone, White, Broad Blue Trim, 12 ¼ In.	12.00
Souvenir, Coaster, State Of Texas, Cattle Brands Border, 4 ½ In.	16.00
Souvenir, Plate, Chicago Landmarks, Blue & White, 10 ⅜ In.	35.00
Souvenir, Plate, Church Of The Immaculate Conception, 12 Churches, 10 ⅜ In.	20.00
Souvenir, Plate, Colorado Springs, Red & White, 10 ⅜ In.	35.00
Souvenir, Plate, New Orleans, Blue, Scenes From Historic New Orleans, 1930s	33.00
Souvenir, Plate, Our West, 1st Edition, 7 Scenes, Maroon Glaze, Floral Rim, 1942	48.00
Souvenir, Plate, Vermont, Freeman's Oath 1777 On Back, Marked, 10 ⅜ In.	25.00
Tam O'Shanter, Cup & Saucer, Plaid	10.00
Tweed, Chicken Pie Dish, Lid, Blue & Yellow, Individual, c.1953, 4 In.	42.00
Tweed, Chop Plate, Blue & Yellow, 12 ¼ In.	35.00

VERRE DE SOIE glass was first made by Frederick Carder at the Steuben Glass Works from about 1905 to 1930. It is an iridescent glass of soft white or very, very pale green. The name means "glass of silk," and it does resemble silk. Other factories have made verre de soie, and some of the English examples were made of different colors. Verre de soie is an art glass and is not related to the iridescent, pressed, white carnival glass mistakenly called by its name. Related pieces may be found in the Steuben category.

Bowl, Fan Shape, Ruffled Rim, Pedestal Base, Steuben, 13 x 9 x 7 In.	397.00
Bowl, Steuben, 10 x 4 In.	150.00
Candlestick, Blue, Diamond Quilting, Applied Reeding Above Base, Steuben, 4 x 5 In., Pair.	316.00
Compote, Lily Pad Foot, Green Stems, Root Base, 5 x 6 ½ In., Pair	316.00
Compote, Low Foot, Rose DuBarry Rim, Steuben, 8 ½ In.	100.00
Goblet, Wine, Stem Pink Melon Connectors, Teardrop Baluster, Steuben, 4 x 5 In.	431.00
Perfume Bottle, Onion Stopper, Double Pulled, Pink, Purple, C. Lotton, 1989, 6 In.	259.00
Salt Cellar, Pedestal, Sterling Silver Salt Spoon	75.00
Shade, White Etched Flowers, Blue Thread Rim, Blue Ground, Steuben, 4 x 2 In.	633.00
Tray, Loop Handle, Jade Green, Steuben, 6 In.	144.00
Tumble Up, Steuben, 7 In.	250.00
Vase, Applied Green Rigaree, 3 ¾ In.	110.00
Vase, Applied Splashed Gold Glass, Vandermark, 1981, 6 In.	127.00
Vase, Baluster Shape, Blown, Paper Label, Steuben, 6 ⅛ In.	546.00
Vase, Bud, Footed Flower Shape, Steuben, 10 In.	225.00
Vase, Cylinder Shape, Scalloped Rim, Steuben, Signed F. Carder, 8 In.	400.00
Vase, Egyptian Form, Bulbous Shoulder, Flared Rim, Steuben, 10 In.	201.00
Vase, Green, Threaded, Flared Rim, Cylindrical, 7 ½ In.	810.00
Vase, Iridescent, Cylindrical, Flared, Steuben, 10 ½ In.	144.00
Vase, King Tut, Purple, Oval Shouldered, Iridescent Swirl, Charles Lotton, 1982, 9 In.	700.00
Vase, Neoblue, Multi Flora, Leaves, Pink, Green, Gold, C. Lotton, 1988, 10 In.	920.00
Vase, Neoblue, White Flowers, Green Split Leaves, Blue Ground, C. Lotton, 1986, 6 In.	489.00
Vase, Pale Green, Darker Green Rim, Footed, Steuben, c.1920, 7 In.	351.00

Verlys, Dish, Matte Finish Flowers, Handles, Viktor Schreckengost, 6 In. $69.00

Vernon Kilns, Chintz, Cup & Saucer, After Dinner $36.00

Vernon Kilns, Dolores, Teapot $125.00

Vernon Kilns, Gingham, Sauceboat $10.00

U
V

699

Volkstedt, Figurine, Hussar, Horse, 1930s, 13 x 9 ½ In. $138.00

Volkstedt, Figurine, Parrot, On Tree Stump, Cherries, Multicolor, Gilt, 4 In. $253.00

Watch, Avalon, Rectangular, Copper Tone Dial, 14K Gold, Retro, Lapel Pin, ¾ x 2 In. $86.00

Vase, Pinched Waist, Light Blue Jade Threading, Cabochons, c.1920, 11 In.	510.00
Vase, Ribbed Body, Scalloped Rim, Steuben, 8 ½ In.	150.00
Vase, Ruffled Rim, Clear Stem, Fluted Body, Steuben, 5 In.	125.00

VIENNA ART plates are round metal serving trays produced at the turn of the century. The designs, copied from Royal Vienna porcelain plates, usually featured a portrait of a woman encircled by a wide, ornate border. Many were used as advertising or promotional items and were produced in Coshocton, Ohio, by J. F. Meeks Tuscarora Advertising Co. and H.D. Beach's Standard Advertising Co.

Plate, Topless Woman, Green Ground, Gilt Rim, 1905, 10 In.	85.00
Plate, Woman, Blond, Red & Gilt Rim, 1907, 9 ½ In.	120.00
Plate, Woman, Green Ground, Blue Rim, 1907, 9 ½ In.	120.00
Plate, Woman, Holding Flower Basket, Green Ground, Gilt Rim, 10 In.	95.00
Plate, Woman, Pink Dress, Green & Gilt Rim, 9 ½ In.	55.00
Plate, Woman, Topless, Compliments Of American Sheet & Tin Plate Co., 10 In.	200.00

VILLEROY & BOCH POTTERY of Mettlach was founded in 1836. The firm made many types of wares, including the famous Mettlach steins. Collectors can be confused because although Villeroy & Boch made most of its pieces in the city of Mettlach, Germany, the company also had factories in other locations. The dating code impressed on the bottom of most pieces makes it possible to determine the age of the piece. Additional items, including steins and earthenware pieces marked with the famous castle mark or the word *Mettlach*, may be found in the Mettlach category.

Bowl, Vegetable, Collage, Round, Straight-Sided, 8 ¼ In.	42.00
Candlestick, Red & White Transfer, 4 ½ In., Pair	65.00
Charger, Hand Decorated, Flower Border, German Motto, 15 ½ In.	100.00
Coffeepot, Lid, Geranium, Yellow Flowers, Green Leaves, 5 Cup	65.00
Coffeepot, Piedmont Primavera Pattern, Mint Green, Sticker, 8 ½ In.	50.00
Creamer, Collage, 2 ⅝ In.	14.00
Cup & Saucer, Ascoli	12.00
Cup & Saucer, Black Beaulieu	6.00
Napkin Ring, Sienna, Salmon Orange Marble Color, 1-In. Wide, 4 Piece	52.00
Pedestal, Summer Flowers, Brown Ground, Ebonized Wood Stand, 42 x 21 In.	288.00
Plate, Dinner, Rimmed, Castell, 10 ½ In.	12.00
Plate, Divided, Nautical Theme, Cobalt Blue, White, Marked, c.1950, 10 ⅞ In.	50.00
Plate, Dreams Of Katharina, Katharina Receives A Promise Of Love, Heinrich, 8 ⅜ In.	28.00
Plate, Heidelberg Castle, 12 In.	139.00
Plate, Salad, Rusticana, Red, 8 In.	16.00
Plate, Saxony, Flow Blue, 9 ½ In., 8 Piece	30.00
Tile, Floor, Encaustic, Geometric, Matte Glaze, c.1880, 6 ⅝ x 6 ⅝ In., 4 Piece	225.00
Tureen, Soup, Cover, Piedmont Primavera, Mint Green, Apple Finial, 2 Qt., 10 In.	60.00
Vase, Bud, Sponged Blue Glaze, Black Squares, Red Broken Lines, c.1910, 6 ⅝ In.	75.00
Vase, Multicolored Flowers, Yellow Mottled Ground, 12 In.	58.00
Vase, Twisting, 4-Sided, Green Glaze, Stylized Designs, Marked, 6 x 12 In.	144.00

VOLKMAR POTTERY was made by Charles Volkmar of New York from 1879 to about 1911. He was associated with several firms, including the Volkmar Ceramic Company, Volkmar and Cory, and Charles Volkmar and Son. He was hired by Durant Kilns of Bedford Village, New York, in 1910 to oversee production. Volkmar bought the business and after 1930 only the Volkmar name was used as a mark. Volkmar had been a painter, and his designs often look like oil paintings drawn on pottery.

Vase, Pansies, Yellow, Brown, Bulbous, Cylindrical Neck, 5 ½ In.	375.00

VOLKSTEDT was a soft-paste porcelain factory started in 1760 by Georg Heinrich Macheleid at Volkstedt, Thuringia. Volkstedt-Rudolstadt was a porcelain factory started at Volkstedt-Rudolstadt by Beyer and Bock in 1890. Most pieces seen in shops today are from the later factory.

Bowl, Heavy Gilt On Cream Ground, Ram Heads Handles, c.1920, 12 x 6 ½ In.	595.00
Box, Cover, Footed, Pastel Blue Cloud, Green Tree Branch, c.1920, 4 ¼ x 3 In.	225.00
Bust, Young Girl, Scarf Around Neck, Marked, c.1875, 5 ½ In.	210.00
Candlestick, Cherub Children, Perched, c.1915, 13 In., Pair	750.00
Figurine, Cherub Sitting On Shoe, Meissen Lace, c.1880, 4 ¼ In.	185.00
Figurine, Girl & Boy, Girl Picking Grapes, Boy Holding Grapes, 4 ½ In., Pair	150.00
Figurine, Hussar, Horse, 1930s, 13 x 9 ½ In. .... *illus*	138.00
Figurine, Napoleon, Signed, c.1890, 11 In.	385.00
Figurine, Parrot, On Tree Stump, Cherries, Multicolor, Gilt, 4 In. ...... *illus*	253.00
Vase, Bouquet, Flower Sprigs On White, Snake Handles, Marked, c.1910, 8 ½ x 9 In.	695.00

WADE pottery is made by the Wade Group of Potteries started in 1810 near Burslem, England. Several potteries merged to become George Wade & Son, Ltd. early in the twentieth century, and other potteries have been added through the years. The best-known Wade pieces are the small figurines given away with Red Rose Tea and other promotional items. The Disney figures are listed in this book in the Disneyana category.

Ashtray, Red Fox, Green 3-Leaf Clover Border, Ireland, 4 x 4 In.	22.00
Bank, Lyons Tetley Brew Gaffer, White Coat, Long Brown Hair, Glasses, 5 ½ In.	155.00
Bank, Maxwell Pig Nat West, Pig, Tie, Blue Pants, Bank Premium, c.1986, 6 ¾ In.	165.00
Candy Dish, Cottage Flowers, Stamp, 6 ½ x 1 ½ In.	25.00
Creamer, Ridges, Green, Ireland, 3 In.	16.00
Dresser Box, Multicolored, Fly Fisherman, Shamrocks, Blue Green, 2 ¾ x 5 In.	45.00
Figurine, Boy, Drum, Soldier Nursery Rhyme Series, 1950s, 3 In.	250.00
Figurine, Bunny Rabbit, Laughing, Heath Green, 6 ¼ In.	65.00
Figurine, Dog, Airedale Terrier, Underglaze, c.1930, 7 In.	396.00
Figurine, Fireside Friend, Seated Blonde Girl, Pink Robe, Hugging Dog, Wood Base	44.00
Figurine, Gingerbread Man, Red Rose Tea Premium, No. 224, England, 1 ½ In.	10.00
Figurine, Horse, Palomino, 1950s	150.00
Figurine, Leprechaun, Cottage, Base, 5 ½ In.	71.00
Figurine, Togetherness, Blond Girl, Hugging English Sheepdog, Wood Base	47.00
Mug, Hearth Scene, Woman, Cat, Ireland, 4 ¼ In.	16.00
Mug, Hunter, Dog, Green, Blue Base, Ireland, 3 In.	14.00
Mug, Jaunting Cart Scene, Green, Blue Base, Ireland, 3 In.	15.00
Pipe Stand, Red Dog, Green Dish, 5 x 3 In.	49.00
Pitcher, Green Ground, Blue, Yellow Flowers, Flaxman Ware, c.1940, 9 x 7 In.	35.00
Pitcher, Harvestware, Luster, 5 In.	76.00
Sugar & Creamer, Bramble, Berries, Twigs, Yellow Ground, England, 3 ½ x 4 In.	28.00
Teapot, T. Potts China Shop, c.1955, 6 ½ x 7 In.	29.00
Toothpick, Ducks, Green, Blue Ground, Handle, Ireland, 2 x 1 ¾ In.	20.00
Trinket Tray, Squirrel Whimsie-Land Tray, England, c.1987, 4 ½ x 4 In.	55.00
Vase, Art Deco, Drip Blue, Orange, Green Yellow, Orcadia Line, 6 x 4 In.	95.00
Vase, Green Glaze, Orange Flowers, Incised Hallmark, Gaelic Phrase, 7 In.	53.00
Whimsey, Old King Cole, 1 ⅜ In.	9.00

WALL POCKETS were popular in the 1930s. They were made by many American and European factories. Glass, pottery, porcelain, majolica, chalkware, and metal wall pockets can be found in many fanciful shapes.

5 Flying Cranes, Pine Tree, Banko Earthenware, Japan, c.1950, 7 x 7 In.	195.00
Art Deco Design, Green Bronze Glaze, Leigh Art Ware, Paper Label, Sebring, c.1930	275.00
Bird's-Eye Maple, Scalloped Front, Sides, 3 ½ x 10 In.	411.00
Brown, White Speckled, Coral Flowers, Gold Leaves, Japan, 7 ½ x 3 ½ In.	30.00
Daisy & Button, Amber, 8 ¼ x 2 ½ In.	85.00
Face, Signed, Walter Fleming, 7 In.	90.00
King Elephant, Amber Pressed Glass, King Glass, c.1890, 5 x 5 In.	58.00
Shield Shape, Pebbled Flowers, Brass, Jewel Inserts, 5 x 5 In.	95.00

WALRATH was a potter who worked in New York City; Rochester, New York; and at the Newcomb Pottery in New Orleans, Louisiana. Frederick Walrath died in 1920. The piece listed here is from his Rochester period.

Vase, Brown & Tan Organic Design, Gray Ground, Broad Shape, 5 ¼ x 4 ¾ In.	2760.00

WARWICK china was made in Wheeling, West Virginia, in a pottery working from 1887 to 1951. Many pieces were made with hand painted or decal decorations. The most familiar Warwick has a shaded brown background. The name *Warwick* is part of the mark; sometimes the mysterious word *IOGA* is also included.

Bowl, Cereal, Sunflower, 6 In.	8.00
Chop Plate, Regency, Gold Trim, Tab Handles, 10 ¾ In.	35.00
Pitcher, Blackfoot Indian Chief, 13 In.	431.00
Planter, Woman, Blue Dress, Flower In Hair, Pink Ground, Gilt, Ball Feet, Handles, 8 x 8 x 4 In.	170.00
Vase, Verona, Poinsettias, Red, Handles, Marked, c.1880, 11 ¾ In.	180.00

WATCH pockets held the pocket watch that was important in Victorian times because it was not until World War I that the wristwatch was used. All types of watches are collected: silver, gold, or plated. Watches are listed here by company name or by style. Wristwatches are a separate category.

18K Gold, 3 Color Engraved Gold Dial, Applied Florets, Key Wind, Engraved, Pocket, 2 In.	764.00

Watch, Cherries, Twig, Stems, Aluminum, Painted, Lapel Pin, 1950s, 2 ½ x 1 ¼ In. $92.00

Watch, Elgin, Porcelain Dial, 3-Color 14K Gold, Peacock, Cartouche, 1890s, Pocket, 1 ½ In. $604.00

Watch, Hamilton, Gambling, Card Face Design, c.1900, 2 ¼ In. $110.00

W

Watch, Hamilton, Open Face,
Porcelain Dial, 17 Jewel, Engraved,
c.1916, 2 In.
$69.00

Watch, Illinois Railroad,
Bunn Special Movement, 60-Hour,
10K Gold Filled, 21 Jewel, 2 In.
$293.00

Watch, J. Calame Robert, Enameled,
Portrait, 18K Yellow Gold, Swiss,
1800s, 1 ½ In.
$1754.00

18K Rose Gold, Sweep Second Hand, Tiffany, Pocket, c.1900	956.00
18K Yellow Gold, Blue Enamel, Roses, Leaves, Bow, Diamonds, 18 Jewel, Pendant, Woman's, c.1910	2031.00
Avalon, Rectangular, Copper Tone Dial, 14K Gold, Retro, Lapel Pin, ¾ x 2 In. .... *illus*	86.00
Boucheron, Fluted Dial, Bezel, Windup, 17 Jewel, 18K Gold, Woman's	1422.00
Bucherer, Silvertone Metal Dial, Baton Numerals, Windup, 18K Gold, Woman's	889.00
Buttonhole, Silver Case, Embossed, Bern, Switzerland, 19th Century	2200.00
Cartier, 18K Yellow Gold, Arabic Numbers, Sub Sections, c.1930, Pocket	597.00
Cartier, Open Face, Roman Numeral, 24-Hour Scale, Pocket	2133.00
C.H. Meylan, 18K Yellow Gold, Open Face, 20 Jewel, Arabic Numbers, c.1905, Pocket	986.00
Cherries, Twig, Stems, Aluminum, Painted, Lapel Pin, 1950s, 2 ½ x 1 ¼ In. .... *illus*	92.00
Courvoisier & Co., Gold, Enamel, Flowers, Lady With Lute, Key Wind, 13 Jewel, c.1850	6572.00
Cylinder Escapement, Key Wind, Engraved Case, Dial, Yellow Gold, France, Pocket, 1 ⅝ In.	316.00
Derrick, Pierced Edges, Roman Numerals, Chimes, c.1817, Pocket	4780.00
Double Headed Eagle, Enameled Blue, Black, Gold Hands, Silver Chain, Russia, Pocket	5593.00
Duhme Bros. & Co, Woman's, Engraved 14K Gold Case, 17 Jewel, 1901, 1 ¾ In.	235.00
E. Howard Watch Co., 14K Yellow Gold, 23 Jewel, Jurgensen Lips, c.1908, Pocket	1553.00
Elgin, 14K Gold Scrolls, Swirls, Initial, Arabic Numbers, 15 Jewel, c.1889, Pocket	2031.00
Elgin, 15 Jewel, Yellow Gold Case, Amethyst Set Crown, Porcelain, Chain, Pocket	281.00
Elgin, 18K Multicolored Gold, Flowers, Heron, Cattail, Pocket, Roman Numerals, c.1878	3107.00
Elgin, Gold Plate, Chain, Enamel Face, Pocket	117.00
Elgin, Hunting Case, 14K Gold, Woman's, Early 20th Century, Pocket, 1 ⅛ In.	259.00
Elgin, Hunting Case, Roman Numerals, Enamel Dial, 14K Yellow Gold, Engraved Accents, Chain	474.00
Elgin, Multicolored Gold, Flowers, Leaves, Woman's, Pocket, c.1903	418.00
Elgin, Porcelain Dial, 3 Color 14K Gold, Peacock, Cartouche, 1890s, Pocket, 1 ½ In. .... *illus*	604.00
Gold, Enameled, Bird Fending Off Snake, Engraved, Gold Filigree, 14K Gold, c.1895, 1 ½ In.	441.00
Gray's Of Belfast, 18K Gold Case, Enamel Dial, Gold Hands, Key Wind, 1820s, Pocket, 2 ½ In.	1410.00
Gublin, Twenty Dollar 1903 Liberty Coin Case, Roman Numerals, 18 Jewel, c.1950, Pocket	1673.00
Guilloche, Enameled, Silvered Flowers, c.1900, 1 ¼ In.	106.00
Hamilton, 14K Gold, 4 Colors Of Gold, Horse Heads, Flowers, 21 Jewel, Signed, c.1918, Pocket	3884.00
Hamilton, 17 Jewel, Lever Set, Double Sunk Dial, Pocket, 2 ¾ In.	150.00
Hamilton, Gambling, Card Face Design, c.1900, 2 ¼ In. .... *illus*	110.00
Hamilton, Open Face, Porcelain Dial, 17 Jewel, Engraved, c.1916, 2 In. .... *illus*	69.00
H.L. Matile, Chronometer, 18K Yellow Gold, 20 Jewel, Signed, 1880s, Pocket	4481.00
Illinois Railroad, Bunn Special Movement, 60-Hour, 10K Gold Filled, 21 Jewel, 2 In. ..... *illus*	293.00
Illinois Watch Co., 7 Jewel, 14K Gold, Birds, Flowers, Woman's, 1 ½ In.	322.00
J. Calame Robert, Enameled, Portrait, 18K Yellow Gold, Swiss, 1800s, 1 ½ In. .... *illus*	1754.00
J. Laforge Besancon, 18K Gold, Enameled Diamonds, Marked, Lapel Pin, 1 x 2 ½ In. ..... *illus*	863.00
James Murray, Hunting Case, White Enamel Dial, Key Wind, c.1870, Pocket, 1 ¾ In.	441.00
John Forrest, Hunting Case, Key Wind, Engraved, White Enamel Dial, 1840s, Pocket, 2 ¼ In.	529.00
John Forrest, Sterling Silver, Engraved Dial, Lever Escapement, Key Wind, c.1898, Pocket, 2 ½ In.	294.00
Ladybug Form, 18K Gold, Blue Enamel Wings, Diamonds, Ruby Eyes, 18 Jewel, c.1915	4182.00
LeCoultre, Hunting Case, Jeweled Movement, Roman Numerals, 18K Gold	711.00
Lighter, Dunhill, Sterling, 15 Jewel, Arabic Dial, c.1928	1255.00
Longines, Sterling Silver, Enamel Dial, Arabic Numbers, Alarm, c.1910, Pocket	478.00
Lucerne, Chain Tassel, 14K Chain, Repousse Rose, Swiss, 1 ⅜ In.	285.00
Omega, 21 Jewel, Canadian Dial, Swiss, Early 20th Century, 2 In.	210.00
Patek Philippe, 18K Gold, Gilt Metal Dial, 18 Jewel, Chain, James Allen & Co., c.1910, Pocket	575.00
Patek Philippe, 18K Gold, Split Second Chronograph, Pocket	7110.00
Patek Philippe, Baton Link Chain, 18K Gold, Enamel, Pendant, Edwardian, Woman's, 22 In.	3792.00
Patek Philippe, Enamel, Gold, Sub Seconds, 18 Jewel, Wolf's Tooth, c.1925, Pocket	3585.00
Patek Philippe, Goldtone Dial, Arabic, Dart Numerals, 18K Gold, c.1960	7229.00
Patek Philippe, Silvertone Dial, 18 Jewel, Open Face, Pocket	3437.00
Paul Ditisheim, Platinum, Roman Numerals, Blue Steel Hands, Oval, Monogram, c.1915, Pocket	2390.00
Platinum, Diamond, Onyx, Engraved, White Gold Link Chain, Art Deco, Pendant, 23 In.	2370.00
Robert Stoddart, 18K Gold, Roman Chapter Ring, Chain Fusee Movement, 1860s, Pocket, 2 ¼ In.	558.00
Swiss, 18K Gold, Key Wind, Key Set, Cylinder Escapement, Swiss Bar, c.1900, Pocket, 1 ¾ In.	588.00
Swiss, 18K Yellow Gold, 28 Jewel, Repeater, Roman Numbers, c.1890, Pocket	2509.00
Swiss, 18K Yellow Gold, Repeater, Monogram, Arabic Numbers, 32 Jewel, c.1895, Pocket	1792.00
Swiss, Enamel & Pearl, Doves, Flowers, Pearl Edges, Roman Numerals, c.1835, Pocket	3884.00
Swiss, Gold, Enamel, Couple On Lawn, Roman Numerals, 10 Jewel, Pendant, Woman's, c.1890	1075.00
Swiss, Hunting Case, 18K Rose Gold, Leaves, Flower Vases, Doves, 31 Jewel, c.1890, Pocket	6572.00
Swiss, Moon Phase Calendar, Gun Metal, Roman Dial, c.1890, Pocket	657.00
Thos. Russell, 18K Gold, Engine Turned Case, Gold Hands, Chain Fusee, c.1866, Pocket, 2 In.	441.00
Tiffany & Co., 18K Yellow Gold, Jeweled Movement, Pocket, c.1908	2587.00
Tiffany & Co., 18K Yellow Gold, Split Second, Sub Seconds, Arabic Numbers, c.1888, Pocket	2629.00
Tiffany & Co., Platinum, Spade Hands, Roman Numerals, Diamonds, c.1925, Pocket	1912.00

Tiffany & Co., Repeater, 8-Day, 15 Jewel, Gilt Metal Case, White Enamel Open Face, 3 ½ In. .. 805.00
Tiffany & Co., Rose Cut Diamonds, Enamel, 18K Gold, Pendant, Edwardian, Woman's, 2 ¾ In. 1778.00
Tiffany & Co., Violet Enamel, Sunburst Ground, Diamond Frame, Silver Chain, c.1910.......... 1314.00
Vacheron & Constantin, 18K Hunting Case, Flowers, 13 Jewel, Key Wind, c.1875................. 896.00
Vacheron & Constantin, 18K Rose Gold, Stepped Bezel, 18 Jewel, c.1930, Pocket................. 2151.00
Waltham, Appleton Tracy & Co., 17 Jewel, Marked, 2 ¼ In. 76.00
Waltham, Box Hinge, Multicolored Gold, Buck In Flower Field, Woman's, c.1892, Pocket....... 538.00
Waltham, Hunting Case, 14K Gold, 10 Jewel, Engraved, 1890, 2 In. 878.00
Waltham, Hunting Case, 14K Gold, Box Hinge, Stem Wind, Lever Set, Marked, c.1875, Pocket, 2 In. 705.00
Waltham, Hunting Case, 14K Gold, Sunken Second Dial, c.1900, 1 ¾ In. 420.00
Waltham, Hunting Case, 3 Color, 14K Gold, Engraved Stag & Flowers, c.1913, Pocket, 1 ¾ In. 4700.00
Waltham, Hunting Case, Damascened Movement, Diamond Cut Crescent, 14K Gold, Chain.... 504.00
Waltham, Hunting Case, Enamel Dial, 14K Gold, Pocket... 296.00
Waltham, Hunting Case, Enamel Dial, Nickel Movement, Leaf Turned Case, 14K Gold, Pocket. 474.00
Waltham, Hunting Case, Metal Dial, Arabic Numerals Japanesque Designs, Mixed Metal........ 267.00
Waltham, Seaside, Gilt Movement, 14K Yellow Gold Case, Porcelain Dial, Woman's............... 180.00
Waltham, Sterling Silver, Stem Wind, Chain, c.1917, Pocket... 1553.00

WATCH FOBS were worn on watch chains. They were popular during Victorian times and after. Many styles, especially advertising designs, are still made today.

Agate, 10K Rose Gold, c.1875... 110.00
Albert, George III Guinea, Gold Chain, T-Bar, c.1885, 10 In. 1912.00
Art Nouveau, Grosgrain Ribbon, Black, Fringe, Script Initials, 6 ½ x 1 ⅕ In. 78.00
Bulldog Tobacco, Metal, Celluloid, 1 ¾ x 1 ⅝ In. 275.00
Cameo, Green, Goldtone Frame, ⅝ In. 20.00
Classical Warrior, 14K Yellow Gold, Bloodstone Intaglio, Chased Mount, 2 In. 504.00
Crown Shape, Gold & Colored Gemstones, c.1860.. 422.00
Gold Filled Mesh, Circle Of Pearls Around Opal, 4 ¾-In. Chain, 4 ¼-In. Fob......................... 75.00
King Motor Car Co., King The Car Of No Regrets, Silvered Brass, 1 ¾ In. 115.00
Monogram Seal, CVS, Sterling Silver, Openwork Bell Shape, 1 ¼ In. 175.00
National Sportsman, Raised Moose, Marked Geo, Mtta, O., 1 ½ In. 25.00
One Cent Coin, Gold Filled Frame, 1 ¼ x 1 ½ In. 74.00
Open Pierced Fob, 2 Sections Attached To Bars, Fine Link Chains, Gold Finish, 5 In. 35.00
Schoolmasters Club, Sterling Silver & 10K Gold Fob, Golf Clubs, 1950, 20 In. 139.00
Ship's Compass Within Ship's Wheel, Black Grosgrain Ribbon.. 55.00
Vin Fiz, Printed Medallion, Sports Time Clock, c.1910, 2 In. .... *illus* 270.00

WATERFORD type glass resembles the famous glass made from 1783 to 1851 in the Waterford Glass Works in Ireland. It is a clear glass that was often decorated by cutting. Modern glass is being made again in Waterford, Ireland, and is marketed under the name Waterford. Waterford merged with Wedgwood in 1986 to form the Waterford Wedgwood Group. Most Waterford Wedgwood assets were bought by KPS Capital Partners of New York in 2009 and became part of WWRD Holdings.

Biscuit Jar, Cover, Crystal, 6 x 8 In. 146.00
Bowl, Boat Shape, Diamond Cut Sides, Mark, 9 x 13 In. .... *illus* 690.00
Bowl, Boat Shape, Pedestal Base, Marked, 9 x 13 x 6 In. 253.00
Bowl, Crystal, Red, White, 7 ½ In. 264.00
Bowl, Footed, Ciarfa, Acid Etched Signature & Seahorse, 3 ½ In. 210.00
Bowl, Footed, Marked, Late 20th Century, 5 ½ x 11 ¼ In. 71.00
Bowl, Padova, Box, 8 In. 150.00
Bowl, Star Burst Design, Cut Diamond Design Around Sides, 2 x 4 ½ In. 50.00
Bowl, Turn Over Rim, Lemon Squeezer Base, c.1800, 9 x 10 ¼ In. 805.00
Brandy Snifter, Lismore, 5 ¼ In., 8 Piece.. 202.00
Clock, Desk, Quartz, 2 ½ x 3 In. 69.00
Cordial, Alana, Signed, 3 ⅜ In., 6 Piece.. 120.00
Decanter, Ship's, Sterling Silver Label Wine, 10 ¼ In. 56.00
Decanter, Stopper, Eleana, Crystal, 11 ½ In. 146.00
Decanter, Stopper, Lismore, Marked, 9 ½ In. 59.00
Decanter, Stopper, Maureen, Marked, 13 In. 59.00
Globe, Cut Glass, Chrome & Glass Base, 11 x 7 In. 315.00
Honey Pot, Diamond Cut, Lid Has Aperture For Spoon, 5 x 3 ¼ In. 145.00
Lamp, Table, Cross Hatch, Scalloped Shade, 14 & 21 In. 788.00
Paperweight, Flower, Etched Mark, 3 ½ x 1 ¼ In. 95.00
Trinket Box, Oval, Etched Bottom, Foil Label, 2 x 3 In. 90.00

Watch, J. Laforge Besancon, 18K Gold, Enameled Diamonds, Marked, Lapel Pin, 1 x 2 ½ In. $863.00

Watch Fob, Vin Fiz, Printed Medallion, Sports Time Clock, c.1910, 2 In. $270.00

Waterford, Bowl, Boat Shape, Diamond Cut Sides, Mark, 9 x 13 In. $690.00

W

Watt, Greenbriar, Salt & Pepper,
White Drip, 4 In.
$81.00

Watt, Rooster, Bowl, Cover,
Marked Oven Ware USA 67, 5½ x 8 In.
$83.00

Watt, Starflower, Mixing Bowl,
4-Petal, No. 6, 6 x 3¼ In.
$17.00

Watt Apple

Apple is the most popular Watt pattern. It is sometimes called Red Apple. Dinnerware sets and kitchenware were made beginning in 1952. The company burned to the ground in 1965. There are several variations within the Apple pattern, including 2-leaf, 3-leaf, Reduced Apple (looks like a red heart), Open Apple (shows the core), and Double Apple. There are some price differences between the pattern variations.

Tumbler, Low Ball, Lismore, 3 ½ In., Pair	468.00
Vase, Posy, Etched Mark, Foil Label, 4 ¼ In.	90.00

WATT family members bought the Globe pottery of Crooksville, Ohio, in 1922. They made pottery mixing bowls and tableware of the type made by Globe. In 1935 they changed the production and made the pieces with the freehand decorations that are popular with collectors today. Apple, Starflower, Rooster, Tulip, and Autumn Foliage are the best-known patterns. Pansy, also called Rio Rose, was the earliest pattern. Apple, the most popular pattern, can be dated from the leaves. Originally, the apples had three leaves; after 1958 two leaves were used. The plant closed in 1965. For more prices, go to kovels.com.

Apple, Bowl, Spaghetti, Green Band, No. 44	25.00
Apple, Casserole, Cover	75.00
Apple, Casserole, Cover, No. 2 & 48	75.00
Apple, Cookie Jar	35.00
Apple, Cookie Jar, Cover	250.00
Apple, Mug, No. 121	65.00
Apple, Mug, Padberg Machinery 1965, Lexington, Oregon	500.00
Apple, Pie Plate, Ft. Atkinson, Iowa	35.00
Apple, Pitcher, 2-Leaf, No. 16	50.00
Apple, Plate, Dinner, Lewisville, Minn.	170.00
Apple, Salt & Pepper, Hourglass Shape	75.00
Apple, Sugar, Cover, Handles, Cambridge Lumber Co., Cambridge, Iowa, 4 ¾ In.	354.00
Apple, Tumbler Slant Side, No. 56	3400.00
Bands, Bowl, Spaghetti, Brown, No. 44	60.00
Bands, Grease Jar, Brown, No. 01	15.00
Bands, Jar, Cover, Goodies, Red, Green, Marked, Oven Ware, U.S.A., 9 In.	59.00
Brownstone, Bowl, Ribbed, Green, No. 5	40.00
Brownstone, Grease Jar, Green, Lid, No. 01	55.00
Brownstone, Pitcher, Green, No. 16	60.00
Cherry, Bowl, No. 5	15.00
Cherry, Cookie Jar, No. 21	325.00
Christmas, Creamer, Merry Christmas 1957, The Watt Pottery Co.	3600.00
Corn Row, Pitcher, Pink	35.00
Custard Cup, Turquoise, Marked	22.00
Double Apple, Bowl, Salad, No. 73	45.00
Double Apple, Creamer, No. 62	250.00
Double Apple, Pitcher, No. 15	275.00
Dutch Tulip, Pitcher, No. 15	105.00
Dutch Tulip, Pitcher, No. 16	105.00
Eagle, Canister, Lid, No. 72	225.00
Eagle, Churn, Bail Handle, 4 Gal.	110.00
Eagle, Crock, Brown Top, 6 Gal.	95.00
Esmond, Canister Set, Coffee, Sugar, Tea, Flour, Wood Base & Lid, 4 Sections, No. 32, 10 ¼ In.	44.00
Esmond, Cookie Jar, Apple, Pear, Cookies, Wood Lid, No. 34, 7 In.	64.00
Greenbriar, Salt & Pepper, White Drip, 4 In. *illus*	81.00
Kitch-N-Queen, Bowl, No. 14	45.00
Leaf Apple, Bowl, Spaghetti	105.00
Moon & Stars, Bowl, Green, 3 ½ In.	75.00
Moon & Stars, Custard Cup, Tan	10.00
Moonflower, Berry Bowl, Black, No. 22	60.00
Moonflower, Cup & Saucer, Black, No. 40 & 41	65.00
Moonflower, Plate, Black, No. 42	60.00
Morning Glory, Creamer, Quilted, Ivory	70.00
Morning Glory, Creamer, Quilted, Yellow	220.00
Morning Glory, Creamer, Quilted, Yellow, No. 97	220.00
Morning Glory, Sugar, Quilted, Ivory	140.00
Morning Glory, Sugar, Quilted, Yellow	425.00
Morning Glory, Sugar, Quilted, Yellow, No. 98	425.00
Nassau, Salt & Pepper	30.00
Orchard Ware, Carafe	7.50
Orchard Ware, Pitcher, Greenbriar, No. 17	65.00
Pansy, Bowl, Cross-Hatch	40.00
Pansy, Bowl, Cross-Hatch, No. 4	40.00
Pansy, Bowl, Cut-Leaf, 5 In.	10.00
Pansy, Cookie Jar, Cross-Hatch	175.00
Pansy, Cookie Jar, Cross-Hatch, No. 21	175.00

Pansy, Creamer, No. 35	550.00
Pansy, Nappy, Open, No. 7	20.00
Pansy, Pitcher, Cross-Hatch, No. 16	375.00
Pansy, Pitcher, No. 15	95.00
Pansy, Plate, Cut-Leaf, No. 28	12.50
Pansy, Plate, Snack, Bullseye	15.00
Punch Bowl, Christmas, 1998	50.00
Rio Rose, see Pansy	
Rooster, Bowl, Cover, Marked Oven Ware USA 67, 5 ½ x 8 In. .... *illus*	83.00
Rooster, Bowl, Cover, No. 67, Marked, Circle, Oven Ware, 5 ½ x 8 In.	79.00
Rooster, Bowl, No. 68	35.00
Rooster, Creamer, White Glaze, No. 62	350.00
Rooster, Ice Bucket, Lid, 6 ½ In.	89.00
Rooster, Mixing Bowl, No. 63	75.00
Rooster, Pitcher, Refrigerator	185.00
Rooster, Salt & Pepper, Barrel, No. 45 & 46	275.00
Rooster, Shaker, Hourglass Shape, Lance's Grade A Dairy Products, Sac City, 4 ½ In.	258.00
Rooster, Sugar, Lance's Grade A Dairy Products, Sac City, Handles, 4 ¼ In.	172.00
Silhouette, Pitcher	95.00
Starflower, Bowl, 4-Petal, No. 04	17.50
Starflower, Bowl, Spaghetti, 4-Petal, White Flower, Blue Ground, No. 39	45.00
Starflower, Grease Jar, No. 47	155.00
Starflower, Mixing Bowl, 4-Petal, No. 6, 6 x 3 ¼ In. .... *illus*	17.00
Starflower, Pitcher, Compliments Of Danube Creamery & Produce, Christmas 1954	120.00
Starflower, Pitcher, No. 17	50.00
Starflower, Salt & Pepper, Barrel, No. 45 & 46	45.00
Starflower, Sugar, Renville, Minn.	135.00
Tear Drop, Baker, Rectangular	45.00
Tear Drop, Baker, Square, Lid, No. 84	225.00
Tear Drop, Creamer, No. 62	200.00
Tear Drop, Pitcher, Refrigerator	140.00
Tomah, Creamer, No. 62	125.00
Tulip, Cookie Jar	325.00
Tulip, Creamer, No. 62, 4 ½ In.	70.00 to 85.00
Tulip, Pitcher, Ice Lip	45.00
Tulip, Plate, Dinner, Divided	400.00
Westwood, Casserole, Cover	5.00
Woodgrain, Pitcher	7.50

WAVE CREST glass is an opaque white glassware manufactured by the Pairpoint Manufacturing Company of New Bedford, Massachusetts, and some French factories. It was decorated by the C.F. Monroe Company of Meriden, Connecticut. The glass was painted in pastel colors and decorated with flowers. The name Wave Crest was used after 1898.

WAVE CREST
WARE

Atomizer, Painted Yellow & Orange Flowers, 5 In.	650.00
Biscuit Jar, Blue Blossoms, Branches, Bail Handle, Cover, c.1900, 4 x 7 ½ In.	293.00
Biscuit Jar, Egg Crate Mold, Pink & Blue Flowers, Square, Silver Plated Cover, 8 In. .... *illus*	180.00
Biscuit Jar, Fern, Silver Lid, Bail Handle	78.00
Biscuit Jar, Flowers, Enameled, Silver Plated Handle, Cover, 6 ½ In.	215.00
Biscuit Jar, Green, Painted Flowers, Barrel Shape, Silver Plated Cover, Bear Finial, 6 In.	295.00
Biscuit Jar, Morning Glories, Blue, 8 ½ In.	125.00
Box, Egg Crate Mold, Square, Banner Mark, 3 ¼ In.	125.00
Box, Floral Cut Top, Miter Ribbed Base, Silver Plate, Octagon, 4 ½ x 6 ½ In.	595.00
Box, Hinged, Landscape, Red Flowers, 4 Gold Feet, 6 ¾ x 6 In.	288.00
Box, Mirror, Green Ground, Painted, Cover, Black Mark, 6 x 3 ¾ In.	750.00
Cologne Bottle, Painted Pink Flowers, Ball Stopper, 5 ¾ In.	295.00
Dresser Box, Blue, White Panels, Daisies, Metal Collar, Footed, Egg Crate Shape, C.F. Monroe, 6 In.	575.00
Dresser Box, Cherubs Playing Harp, Round, c.1875, 5 ½ In.	240.00
Dresser Box, Daisies, Helmschmied Swirl, 6 In.	175.00
Dresser Box, Glass, Knobby Surface, Metal Feet, Painted Flowers, Lined, 6 x 4 ½ x 5 In.	440.00
Dresser Box, Multicolored, Flowers, Raised Rococo Pattern, Round, c.1900, 3 x 4 In.	159.00
Dresser Box, Orange, Green Flowers, Helmschmied Swirl, Blue Opaline, C.F. Monroe, 6 In. ...	345.00
Dresser Box, Oval, Blue Flowers, Original Lining, Key, Signed, 5 ½ In.	250.00
Dresser Box, Pink Roses, Blue Opaline, Metal Stand, Key, Signed, C.F. Monroe, 8 In.	633.00
Dresser Box, Round, Swirl, Yellow, Pink Flowers, 4 x 6 ½ In.	225.00
Dresser Box, Shell Shape, Blue, Pink Flowers, Stamped Red Banner Mark, 3 In.	100.00
Dresser Box, Swirl, c.1875, 5 ½ In.	188.00

Wave Crest, Biscuit Jar, Egg Crate Mold, Pink & Blue Flowers, Square, Silver Plated Cover, 8 In.
$180.00

Wave Crest, Dresser Box, Swirl Mold, White, Blue Flowers, Pink Band, Round, 3 ½ x 5 In.
$300.00

Wave Crest, Dresser Box, White, Pink, Blue Flowers, Swirl Mold, Round, Hinged, 4 ½ x 6 In.
$175.00

Wave Crest, Dresser Box, Woman In Field, Lining, Round, Hinged, 2 ½ x 5 ½ In.
$150.00

W

Wave Crest, Jardiniere,
Cherubs On Rim, Blue Flowers,
10 x 7 ¾ In.
$385.00

Weapon, Brass Knuckle Duster,
Sharp Points, 4 x 3 In.
$690.00

The Howard Johnson Weather Vanes

The Howard Johnson weather vanes used on top of the company's orange-roofed buildings sent a message. The silhouette of the pieman and the boy meant the building was a restaurant. A lantern indicated an inn. A combination of pieman, boy, and lantern advertised an inn with a typical full-service restaurant, clam rolls, its specialty, and 28 flavors of ice cream.

Dresser Box, Swirl Mold, White, Blue Flowers, Pink Band, Round, 3 ½ x 5 In. .... *illus*	300.00
Dresser Box, White, Pink, Blue Flowers, Swirl Mold, Round, Hinged, 4 ½ x 6 In. .... *illus*	175.00
Dresser Box, Woman In Field, Lining, Round, Hinged, 2 ½ x 5 ½ In. .... *illus*	150.00
Fernery, Blue Mums, Pink & White, Mauve, Egg Crate Mold, Insert, Banner Mark, 6 ½ In.	175.00
Fernery, Painted Blue Daisies, Red Banner Mark, 5 ½ In.	575.00
Fernery, Pink, Opal Glass, Blue Flowers, Gold Rim, Stamped, 8 In.	170.00
Humidor, Cylinder Shape, Blue Daisies, Metal Foot, 2 Handle Rim, 4 In.	270.00
Jardiniere, Cherubs On Rim, Blue Flowers, 10 x 7 ¾ In. .... *illus*	385.00
Jewelry Box, Hinged, Round, Blue, White, Flowers, Rope Mold, Enamel, Cover, Banner Mark, 5 x 8 In.	475.00
Jewelry Box, Pink Rose, Pink & White Ground, Shell Mold, Hinged Cover, Banner Mark, 4 In.	255.00
Jewelry Box, Pink Zinnia, Emerald Green, Zinnia Mold, Hinged Cover, Stamp Mark, 5 In.	200.00
Jewelry Box, Venice Scene, Cream, Hinged Cover, Marked, Signed, 4 ½ In.	212.00
Napkin Ring, Painted Blue Flowers, Silver Removable Rims, c.1886, 2 In.	425.00
Photo Holder, Embossed, Pink, Forget-Me-Nots, Red Banner Mark, 6 ½ x 3 ½ In.	600.00
Pin Dish, Egg Crate, Gold Trim, Handles, Blue Forget-Me-Not, 1 ¼ x 3 In.	295.00
Pin Tray, Bisque, Enameled Flowers, Mark, 1 x 3 In.	295.00
Plate, Cherub, Blossom, Fairy, 8 In.	154.00
Salt & Pepper, Necklace, White Ground, Painted Flowers, 3 In.	99.00
Shaker, Erie Twist, Pink & White, Raised Flowers, Leaves, 2 ½ In.	99.00
Sugar & Creamer, Painted, Pink Flowers, White To Blue Ground..	225.00
Sugar & Creamer, Peach Ground, Bird & Blue Flowers, Silver Plated Cover........................	100.00
Sugar & Creamer, Woman's Portrait, Gold Enameled, Stylized Flowers, Gold Rim, Cover, 4 x 3 In.	115.00
Sugar Shaker, Purple, Green Flowers, Helmschmied Swirl, Blue Opaline, 3 In.	230.00
Syrup, Draped Column, Opalware, Tan Skirt, Flowers, Metal Handle, c.1875, 6 ⅛ In.	118.00
Toothpick, Beaded Edge, Enameled Flowers, Ormolu Mounted, Stamped, 2 ½ In.	200.00
Tray, Shell Shape, Flower Sprays, 3 In., Pair.	80.00
Vase, Glass, Cylinder, Blue, Woman, Cherubs In Cameo, Scroll Metal Handles, Base, Rim, 18 In.	5500.00
Vase, Ormolu Mount, Elongated Neck, Flower Bouquet, 8 In.	184.00
Vase, Painted Pink Daisies, Green To White Ground, Gilt Handles, Black Mark, 9 ¼ In.	650.00
Vase, Pink Flowers, Green, White Opal Glass, Metal Handles, Footed, C.F. Monroe, 13 In.	1610.00
Vase, Pink Thistle, Cream Ground, Fancy Scroll Mold, Gilt, Banner Mark, 10 In.	275.00
Vase, Pink, White, Green, Blue Flowers, Dolphin Feet, Swirl Mold, Stamp Mark, 12 In.	350.00
Vase, Urn Shape, Brown, Green, Enameled White Flowers, Metal Handles, 4-Footed, Marked, 11 In.	2100.00

WEAPONS listed here include instruments of combat other than guns, knives, rifles, or swords. Firearms are not listed in this book. Knives and Swords are listed in their own categories.

Ax, Horseman's, Iron Head, Crescent Form Blade, Krishna Playing Flute Blade, 18th Century..	650.00
Battle-Ax, Indo-Persian, All Steel, Leaf Panel, c.1780-1800...	485.00
Battle-Ax, Iron Trade Head, Pierced Open Side Bar Cage, First Half Of 19th Century.............	1050.00
Battle-Ax, Persian, All Steel, Tubular Haft With Mushroom Form Butt, c.1800, 25 In.	525.00
Battle-Ax, Zulu, Wood Shaft, Iron Crescent Blade, c.1870, 33 ¼ In.	675.00
Brass Knuckle Duster, Sharp Points, 4 x 3 In. .... *illus*	690.00
Dagger, Sudanese, Leaf Shape Blade, Leather Scabbard, c.1850, 6 ⅛ In.	255.00
Mace, Dervish Ritual, Carved Wood, Crocodile Nile Skin Sheath, 1880s...........................	1250.00
Musket Ball, France, c.1800	30.00

WEATHER VANES were used in seventeenth-century Boston. The direction of the wind was an indication of coming weather, important to the seafaring and farming communities. By the mid-nineteenth century, commercial weather vanes were made of metal. Today's collectors often consider weather vanes to be examples of folk art, even though they may not have been handmade.

Arrows, Crossed, Center Spear, Directionals, Zinc, Iron, 60 ½ x 26 In.	235.00
Banner, Directionals, Wrought Bronze, Sheet Copper, Verdigris, c.1905, 68 x 26 In.	1185.00
Banner, Dragon Head, Tin, 1839, 5 x 7 In.	410.00
Banner, Lyre, Arrow, Copper, Wood, Verdigris, Black, 33 In. x 8 Ft. 11 In.	11850.00
Bull, Copper, 127 x 24 In.	6820.00
Canada Goose, Flying, Pine, Carved, Painted, A.E. Crowell, Mass., c.1920, 13 In.	23750.00
Chef, Boy, Dog, Howard Johnson's, Cast Aluminum, 30 x 48 In.	1130.00
Cock, Green Paint, Pierced Eye, Tail Feathers, Sheet Iron, Iron Pole, 1800s, 14 x 28 In.	1422.00
Cow, Full Body, Molded Copper, Cast Zinc, Verdigris, c.1890, 21 x 33 ½ In.	9480.00
Cow, Full Body, Molded Copper, Copper Rod, Verdigris, c.1890, 23 x 36 ½ In.	14220.00
Cow, Molded Copper, Gilt, Copper Rod, Verdigris, c.1920, 16 ½ x 26 ½ In.	3555.00
Cow, Molded Sheet Copper, Copper Rod, Verdigris, Late 19th Century, 16 x 27 In.	5925.00
Cow, Standing, Horns, Copper, Cushing, c.1880, 26 In.	7425.00
Dog, Setter, Full Body, Sheet Copper, Copper Rod, Molded, Gilt, c.1910, 16 x 33 In.	8295.00

Dog, Setter, Pointing, Copper, Repousse Ears, Green & Gold Paint, 15 x 35 In.	8125.00
Eagle, Full Body, Globe, Directionals, Copper, Verdigris Patina, Early 1900s, 42 x 32 In.	323.00
Eagle, Full Body, Spread Wings, Ball, Copper, Gilded, 21 x 22 In.	585.00
Eagle, Full Body, Spread Wings, Copper, Gilt, 13 x 14 ½ In.	350.00
Eagle, Spread Wings, Arrow, Directionals, Copper, Older Regilt, c.1908, 26 ½ In.	881.00
Eagle, Spread Wings, Gold Gilt, Directional Letters, Mounted On Block, 20 x 21 In.	288.00
Eagle, Spread Wings, On Ball, Directionals, 19 x 20 In.	311.00
Fish, Sheet Copper, Silver Paint, Molded, Black Stand, c.1910, 10 ½ x 30 In.	5036.00
Fox, Running, Patina, 12 x 32 In.	3503.00
Game Cock, Cushing Type, 28 ½ x 26 In.	4068.00
Goat, Full Body, Iron, Painted Red, 26 ½ x 31 ½ In. ...... *illus*	580.00
Grasshopper, Copper, 13 x 31 ½ In.	4400.00
Grasshopper, Copper, Verdigris Patina, 9 x 16 In.	707.00
Grasshopper, Etched, Sheet Iron, 9 x 18 In.	339.00
Haley's Comet, Copper, Iron, Zinc, Directional, On Pine Board, c.1915, 19 x 18 In.	750.00
Haying, Horse Pulling Wagon, 3 Figures, Dog, Copper, 19 x 24 In.	330.00
Horse & Jockey, Gilt, Copper, 19 x 31 In.	8475.00
Horse & Sulky, Copper, Driver, Gilded, c.1875, 17 x 35 ½ In.	4025.00
Horse & Sulky, Verdigris, 20 x 39 In.	7910.00
Horse, Cast Iron, Rochester Iron Works, 19th Century, 27 x 39 In.	18645.00
Horse, Jockey, Full Body, Cast Iron, Copper, 18 x 30 In.	7110.00
Horse, Prancing, Cast Iron, Directionals, Rochester N.H. Iron Works, 1800s, 27 x 39 In.	18645.00
Horse, Prancing, Sheet Iron, c.1900, 37 x 19 In.	1494.00
Horse, Racing, Zinc Jockey, Copper, Gilt, Painted, 18 x 30 In.	10000.00
Horse, Rider, House, Flag, Wood, Sheet Metal, 28 x 44 In.	595.00
Horse, Running, Copper, Directionals, Stamped, J, Harris & Co., 34 ½ In.	1200.00
Horse, Running, Copper, Full Body, Directionals, Post, 19th Century, 20 x 29 In.	2950.00
Horse, Running, Copper, Gilt, 19 ¼ x 27 In.	1320.00
Horse, Running, Copper, Gilt, Molded, Directionals, Ball, 20 x 29 In.	1875.00
Horse, Running, Copper, Harris & Co., c.1900, 14 x 28 ½ In.	1265.00
Horse, Running, Copper, Molded, Gilded, Patina, Harris & Co., 17 x 33 In.	7500.00
Horse, Running, Copper, Zinc Head, Mounted On Board, 34 x 22 In.	1495.00
Horse, Running, Cutout Silhouette, Sheet Iron, Gold Paint, Stand, Iowa, c.1890, 33 In.	382.00
Horse, Running, Flowing Mane, Tail, Sheet Iron, Hand Forged, 1800s, 25 x 45 In.	605.00
Horse, Running, Flowing Tail, Copper, Zinc Head, c.1885, 18 ½ In.	6800.00
Horse, Running, Full Body, Cast Head, New England, 1800s, 15 x 24 In. ...... *illus*	2223.00
Horse, Running, Molded Copper, Cast Brass, Cast Bronze Head, Copper Rod, 20 x 33 In.	593.00
Horse, Running, Molded Copper, Zinc, A.L. Jewell & Co., Mass., 16 x 28 In.	7500.00
Horse, Running, On Directionals, Copper, Verdigris, Base, c.1890, 35 In.	646.00
Horse, Running, Sheet Copper, Molded, Copper Rod, Stand, Verdigris, 1890, 16 x 29 In.	3437.00
Horse, Running, Sheet Iron, Patina, c.1880, 41 x 25 In.	2200.00
Horse, Running, Sulky, Jockey, Hollow Body, Copper, 16 ¾ x 35 In.	577.00
Horse, Running, Swelled Body, Cast Iron Head, New England, 1800s, 15 x 24 In.	2223.00
Horse, Running, White Paint, Directional, 58 x 28 In.	175.00
Horse, Running, White, Patina, Copper, Cast Iron, Directionals, 48 x 44 In.	1800.00
Horse, Sheet Iron, 3 Layers, Worn Silver Paint, c.1890, 16 x 32 In.	353.00
Horse, Trotting, Blackhawk, Copper, Base, c.1880, 20 x 40 In.	2600.00
Horse, Trotting, Blackhawk, Full Body, Zinc Ears, Gilt Copper, Rod, 19 ¾ x 26 ¼ In.	3318.00
Horse, Trotting, White & Black Paint, Sheet Metal, 22 x 40 In.	339.00
Horse, Walking, Cast Iron, Rochester Iron Works, 27 x 39 In.	18645.00
Horse, Walking, Copper, Iron, 32 In.	6710.00
Horse, Walking, Full Body, Copper, Iron, 32 In.	6710.00
Indian, Holding Tomahawk, Bow, Sheet Zinc, 46 In.	5850.00
Indian, On Charging Horse, Silhouette, Sheet Iron, c.1900, 25 x 36 In.	2467.00
Indian, Shooting Bow & Arrow, 2 Dogs, Sheet Tin, 71 ¼ In.	312.00
Indian, Shooting Bow & Arrow, Copper, Verdigris, 20th Century, 27 In.	236.00
Indian, With Bow & Arrow, Copper, 20th Century, 27 In.	240.00
Ketch, Wood & Tin, Multiple Jibs, Main Sail, 35 ¾ x 36 In.	410.00
Lady Liberty, Copper, Patina, 23 In.	2260.00
Locomotive, Steam, Engineer, Sheet Iron, 20 ½ x 46 In.	1093.00
Pig, Flattened Full Body, Copper, Stand, 11 ⅛ x 13 ¼ In.	6418.00
Plow, Copper, Cut, J.W. Fiske & Co., New York, c.1893, 38 x 62 In.	4375.00
Ram, Hollow Body, Copper, Gilt, Bullet Holes, 22 x 28 In.	6250.00
Rooster, Cast Metal, Gilt, 25 ½ x 26 ¼ In.	6050.00
Rooster, Copper, 19th Century, 28 ½ In.	1100.00
Rooster, Copper, Stamped Sheet Tail, Green Patina, Gilt, Red Traces, Base, c.1870, 21 In.	999.00

Weather Vane, Goat, Full Body, Iron, Painted Red, 26 ½ x 31 ½ In.
$580.00

Weather Vane, Horse, Running, Full Body, Cast Head, New England, 1800s, 15 x 24 In.
$2223.00

Weather Vane, Rooster, Sheet Metal, 19th Century, 28 In.
$633.00

As always, the edited listings in *Kovels' Antiques & Collectibles Price Guide 2011* aren't available on any website, but readers should visit Kovels.com for information on trends, tips, reproductions, marks, old prices, and more!

W

Webb, Goblet, Alexandrite, Optic Diamond, Amber Foot To Fuchsia & Blue Rim, 4 ½ In. $1610.00

Webb, Vase, Blue, Bulbous, Buds, Leaves, Double White Bands, Cameo, Mark, 10 ½ In. $2588.00

Webb, Vase, Blue To White Satin Glass, Enamel Leaves, Flowers, Ruffled Rim, Signed, 13 x 4 In., Pair $380.00

Rooster, Crowing, Cutout Silhouette, Red Paint, Sheet Metal, 1900s, 28 x 23 In.	176.00
Rooster, Crowing, Zinc, 19th Century, 19 ¾ x 23 ¼ x 7 ¾ In.	429.00
Rooster, Crowing, Zinc, 2 Molded Formed Parts, Ball & Claw Bottom, 1900s, 23 x 18 In.	248.00
Rooster, Directional Arrow, Red, Yellow, Black Paint, Cardinal Top, 1800s, 14 ½ In.	560.00
Rooster, Directionals, Arrow, Multicolored, Painted, Iron, 4-Footed Base, 29 x 17 In.	293.00
Rooster, Flattened Full Body, Arrow, Molded Sheet Copper, Cast Iron Tip, c.1940, 22 x 23 In.	563.00
Rooster, Full Body, Sheet Iron, Iron Pole, 36 x 24 In.	1175.00
Rooster, Gilt Copper, Mounted On Copper Rod, Stand, c.1920, 18 In.	504.00
Rooster, Iron, White Paint, 18 x 14 In.	565.00
Rooster, Molded Copper, Zinc Legs, c.1880, 19 x 14 In.	4800.00
Rooster, Molded Gilded Sheet Copper, Zinc Feet, Stand, New York, 32 x 38 In.	8295.00
Rooster, On Arrow, Flat, Applied Comb, Copper, Zinc Head, c.1880, 26 In.	9650.00
Rooster, Sheet Copper, Wood Base, 24 In.	124.00
Rooster, Sheet Iron, Iron Rod, Wood Base, 49 In.	170.00
Rooster, Sheet Metal, 19th Century, 28 In. .... *illus*	633.00
Rooster, Standing, Copper, Light Green Patina, Mounted On Wood Stand, 24 x 18 In.	2040.00
Rooster, Tin, c.1900, 20 x 19 In.	4083.00
Rooster, White, Lead, 20th Century, 22 ½ In.	175.00
Sailboat, Double Sail, 30 x 30 In.	118.00
Ship, Copper, Stand, Late 19th Century, 24 x 23 In.	550.00
Stag, Leaping, Copper, 27 In.	322.00
Stag, Leaping, Copper, Gilt, 23 x 27 In.	6780.00
Stag, Leaping, Directionals, Copper, Brass, Disc Base, 16 x 11 In.	234.00
Steer, Copper, Soldered, 19 ½ x 32 In.	330.00
Swan Perched On Mermaid's Back, Cut & Painted Tin, 19th Century	777.00
Viking Longboard, Dragon Head & Tail On Keel, Copper, 1920, 22 x 24 In.	5035.00
Whale, Molded Copper, Globe, Bronze Directionals, c.1950, 19 x 37 In.	889.00

WEBB glass was made by Thomas Webb & Sons of Ambelcot, England. Many types of art and cameo glass were made by them during the Victorian era. Production ceased by 1991 and the factory was demolished in 1995. Webb Burmese and Webb Peachblow are special colored glasswares of the Victorian era. They are listed at the end of this section. Glassware that is not Burmese or Peachblow is included here.

Webb

Biscuit Jar, Mother-Of-Pearl, Metal Lid, Oval, Yellow, Vertical Ribs, 8 In.	225.00
Bowl, Blue, Transparent, Protrusions On Bottom, Folded Up Sides, 4 x 10 ½ In.	59.00
Bowl Set, Oval, Cased Yellow, Gold Gingko Branches, Insects, Bowl, 9 In., 2 Serving Spoons, 11 In.	625.00
Cologne Bottle, Swan's Head, Laydown, White Cut To Blue, Screw-On Carved Cap, 9 ¼ In.	9775.00
Ewer, Yellow, Gilt Flowers, Pink Interior, Amber Handle, 7 ¼ x 4 ½ In.	175.00
Goblet, Alexandrite, Optic Diamond, Amber Foot To Fuchsia & Blue Rim, 4 ½ In. .... *illus*	1610.00
Jar, Potpourri, Mother-Of-Pearl, Blue Moire, Branches, Red Collar, Gold Flowers, Metal, 8 In.	1265.00
Perfume Bottle, Cameo, White Flowers, Cranberry Ground, Metal Hinged Top, 4 In.	3450.00
Perfume Bottle, Cased Yellow Satin Glass, Red Flowers, Butterfly, Round, Sterling Top, 6 In.	920.00
Perfume Bottle, Laydown, Citron, Carved Flower, Fauna, Cameo, 7 In.	1437.00
Perfume Bottle, Oval, Tree Bark, Dragon, Metal Leaf Embossed Flip Lid, Cameo, 5 In.	2100.00
Perfume Bottle, Red, Round, Flowers, Leaves, Butterfly, Bulbous Cap, 6 ½ In.	1725.00
Perfume Bottle, Rouge, White, Pink Iridescent Ground, Flowers, Butterfly, 6 ½ In.	3163.00
Perfume Bottle, Stopper, Prussian Blue, Sunflowers, Greek Key, Phillips & London, 4 In.	4500.00
Perfume Bottle, Teardrop, Citron, Stemmed Branch, Sterling Twist-Off Lid, 4 In.	1035.00
Perfume Bottle, Teardrop, Flower Branch, Cream To Umber, 4 ¼ In.	374.00
Rose Bowl, Cased Caramel Glass, Gilt Branches, Butterfly, 2 ½ In.	288.00
Vase, 2 Handles, Ribbed, Purple & Black, Gold Leaves & Butterflies, 5 ½ x 7 In.	978.00
Vase, 5-Ball, Leaf, Vine, Butterfly, Deep Rouge, Applied Feet, Cameo, 2 x 12 In.	1265.00
Vase, Acid Cutback, Robin's-Egg Blue Ground, Leaf, Berry, Bulbous, Cameo, 2 ¾ In.	1725.00
Vase, Allover Bell Shape Flower, Leaves, 2 Butterflies, Bulbous, Red, Cameo, 6 ½ In.	4600.00
Vase, Berry, Flower Sprigs, Opaque Ground, Blue, Flint Layer, Cylinder Neck, 3 ½ In.	500.00
Vase, Birds, Butterflies, Flowers, Blue, Red, Green, 4 Layers, Acid Stamped, 5 ½ In.	8500.00
Vase, Birds Flying, Perched, Bamboo Shoots, Cameo, 9 In.	15525.00
Vase, Blue, Bulbous, Buds, Leaves, Double White Bands, Cameo, Mark, 10 ½ In. .... *illus*	2588.00
Vase, Blue To White Satin Glass, Enamel Leaves, Flowers, Ruffled Rim, Signed, 13 x 4 In., Pair .. *illus*	380.00
Vase, Brown, White Acorns, Branches, Bulbous Stick Shape, Triple Carved Zigzag Rim, 9 In.	6038.00
Vase, Bulbous, Long Neck, Blue & White, Apple Blossoms, 15 ¾ In.	230.00
Vase, Citron, Cameo, England, 4 ½ In.	633.00
Vase, Citron, Flower, Fauna, Butterfly, White Over Red, Cameo, Signed, 8 ¼ In.	6900.00
Vase, Coraline, Footed, Pink Satin, Beaded Flowers, Leaves, 5 x 3 ½ In.	230.00
Vase, Double Gourd, Yellow Over Red, Amber, Elephant Handles, 6 ¼ In.	173.00
Vase, Flower Blossoms, Enamel, Yellow Satin, 13 In., Pair	270.00

Vase, Flowers, Stems, Leaves, Butterfly, White Over Gray, Yellow Ground, Cameo, 5 ½ In.	2588.00
Vase, Glass, Enamel, White, Blue, Red, Yellow Vining, 8 x 3 ½ In.	94.00
Vase, Green Tulip, Clear, Textured Ground, Inverted Hat Shape, Cameo, 6 ½ x 8 ½ In.	374.00
Vase, Insects, Butterfly, Red Ground, White Flowers, Bulbous Stick, Cameo, 13 ½ In.	6038.00
Vase, Intaglio Bird, Flowers, Tapered Cylinder, Rose Opal Liner, 10 In.	1500.00
Vase, Ivory Ground, Brown Branches, 6-Sided Rim, Oval, Stamp, 4 In.	1093.00
Vase, Leafy Flowers, Buds, Butterflies, Red, Shouldered, Cameo, 8 ½ In.	1700.00
Vase, Leaves, Fruit, White, Purple, Blue Ground, Cameo, 8 ¾ In.	4600.00
Vase, Narcissus, Citron Body, Spring Flowers, Fern Fronds, Cameo, 4 ½ In.	748.00
Vase, Prussian Blue, 2 Lily Blooms, Leafy Stem, Butterfly On Reverse, Cameo, c.1890, 8 In.	3120.00
Vase, Red To White Flowers Cut To Citron, Expanded Body, 3 x 2 In.	300.00
Vase, Smokestack Rim, Cascading Honeysuckle, Arrow Point Border, English Cameo, 3 ½ In.	1610.00
Vase, Swag & Tassel, Bellflowers, Tapered Oval, Footed, Marked, 12 ¼ In.	690.00
Vase, White Birds, Flowers, Branches, Rose Ground, 4 In.	3738.00
Vase, White Dahlia, Citron Ground, Cameo, Mark, 5 In. .... illus	863.00
Vase, White, Flower, Leaf, Citron Ground, White Bands, Cameo, 8 ½ In.	173.00
Vase, White Flowers, Butterfly, Rose Background, Double Band White Neck, 8 In.	2588.00
Vase, White Fruit, Branches, Citron Ground, Chevron Border, Cameo, Signed, 6 In.	805.00
Vase, White Fuchsia Flowers, Buds, Leaves, Flying Insect, Cameo, 10 ¼ In.	3737.00
Vase, White Over Red, Frosted Ground, White To Red Hobnails, Cameo, 7 In.	2300.00
Vase, Yellow, Butterfly, Vines, Triple Collar Ting, Cameo Glass, 6 In.	1380.00

WEBB BURMESE is a shaded Victorian glass made by Thomas Webb & Sons of Stourbridge, England, from 1886. Pieces are shades of pink to yellow.

Creamer, Red Dogwood Branch, Oval, Scalloped Rim, 1 ¾ In.	259.00
Epergne, Domed Satin Shades, Clarke Bases, Ruffled Rim Vases, 11 In. .... illus	2300.00
Fairy Lamp, Domed Satin Shade, Double Mark Clarke Holder, 5 In.	144.00
Fairy Lamp, Epergne, 3 Bud Vases, Clarke Bases, Candle Inserts...................................	3800.00
Saltshaker, Rose, Yellow, Metal Top, Finial, Cylinder Shape, 2 ½ In.	374.00
Sweetmeat Jar, Red Butterfly, Red Branch, Cylinder, Metal Lid, Stamp, 5 In.	690.00
Vase, Bulbous, Square Top, Satin, 3 ⅞ In.	425.00
Vase, Lilac, 7-Point Star Rim, Shading Light Blue To Rose, Oak Leaves, Acorns, 3 In.	403.00
Vase, Morning Glory Blossom Shape, Ribbed, Scalloped, 5 x 3 In. .... illus	633.00
Vase, Octagonal Rim, Flowers & Buds On Branch, 3 In.	92.00
Vase, Pink, Yellow, 4-Sided, 2 Handles, 7 ½ In.	374.00
Vase, Red Berries, Fall Leaves, Ruffled Rim, Footed, 4 In.	259.00

WEBB PEACHBLOW is a shaded Victorian glass made by Thomas Webb & Sons of Stourbridge, England, from 1885.

Bowl, Underplate, Ruffled Rim, Cased Red, Gold Butterfly, Branch, 6 In. .... illus	1150.00
Fairy Lamp, Epergne, Gold Holder, 2 Pyramid Shades, Flower Holder, Hawthorn Blossoms, 8 In.	2185.00
Jam Jar, Silver Plated Mounts, Spoon, Raised Flowers, 5 ¼ In.	450.00
Perfume Bottle, Flowers, Butterfly, Oval, Glass Case, 4 ¼ In.	748.00
Perfume Bottle, Rose, Teardrop, Cased Glass, Gilt Branch, Gold Washed Twist Lid, 4 In.	546.00
Sweetmeat, Silver Plated Lid, Bail Handle, Gilded Base, 3 ½ x 4 ¼ In.	450.00
Vase, Cylinder, Trifold Rim, Blue Interior, 5 In.	60.00
Vase, Hobnail, Ruffled Edge, Amber Petal Feet, 6 In.	200.00
Vase, Stick, Amber, Rose, Gold Gingko Branches, Butterfly, 15 In.	633.00
Vase, Stick, Gold Enameled Flowers, Propeller Mark, c.1880, 8 ⅞ In.	425.00

WEDGWOOD, one of the world's most successful potteries, was founded by Josiah Wedgwood, who was considered a cripple by his brother and was forbidden to work at the family business. The pottery was established in England in 1759. A large variety of wares has been made, including the well-known jasperware, basalt, creamware, and even a limited amount of porcelain. There are two kinds of jasperware. One is made from two colors of clay, the other is made from one color of clay with a color dip to create the contrast in design. In 1986 Wedgwood and Waterford Crystal merged to form the Waterford Wedgwood Group. Most Waterford Wedgwood assets were bought by KPS Capital Partners of New York in 2009 and became part of WWRD Holdings. Some manufacturing will be transferred to Germany, Indonesia, and Slovakia. Other Wedgwood pieces may be listed under Flow Blue, Majolica, Tea Leaf Ironstone, or in other porcelain categories.

WEDGWOOD

Ashtray, Space Odyssey, Issued With Kubrick's 2001 A Space Odyssey......................................	85.00
Biscuit Box, Jasperware, Figures, Blue, Silver Lid & Base, 3 Ball Feet, 6 In.	150.00
Bough Pot, Cover, D-Shape, Floral Festoons, 3 Wells, Green Glaze, Gilt Traces, c.1785, 5 In. ...	3851.00
Bough Pot, Cover, Jasperware, Pale Blue, Pierced Cover, Classical Figures, Urns, c.1790, 6 In.	948.00
Bouquetiere, Cover, White Terra-Cotta, Pierced Strapwork, Iron Red Matte, c.1785, 11 In.	3437.00

Webb, Vase, White Dahlia, Citron Ground, Cameo, Mark, 5 In. $863.00

Webb Burmese, Epergne, Domed Satin Shades, Clarke Bases, Ruffled Rim Vases, 11 In. $2300.00

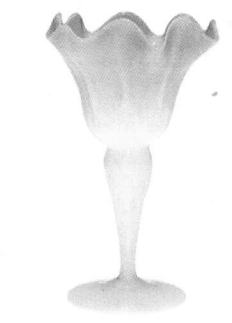

Webb Burmese, Vase, Morning Glory Blossom Shape, Ribbed, Scalloped, 5 x 3 In. $633.00

Webb Peachblow, Bowl, Underplate, Ruffled Rim, Cased Red, Gold Butterfly, Branch, 6 In. $1150.00

W

Wedgwood, Jar, Jasperware, Lavender, Floral Swags, Ram's Heads, Cartouches, Reeded, 3 In. $144.00

Wedgwood, Salt, Figural, Man, Seated, Black Hat, Holding Basket, Majolica, 7 ¾ In. $236.00

Wedgwood Daisy Had A Temper Tantrum

The Wedgwood company had financial problems in 1930 and had to fire many employees. Reports say that Daisy Makeig-Jones, the designer of Wedgwood's Fairyland Luster, was so infuriated when she was fired in 1931 she broke every piece that was still in her studio. Josiah Wedgwood V found her an uncooperative artist who had become eccentric and dictatorial and often did not meet work deadlines. Daisy retired to live a stormy life with her mother and sisters. She died in 1945.

W

Bowl, Black Basalt, Engine Turned, Faceted Sides, Keith Murray, 9 ½ In.	830.00
Bowl, Black Basalt, Footed, 9 In.	41.00
Bowl, Cane Glaze, Flared, Engine Turned Bands At Rim, Keith Murray, 6 ⅝ In.	948.00
Bowl, Fairyland Luster, Butterflies, Mottled Amber Ground, 8-Sided, 3 ⅝ x 7 In.	748.00
Bowl, Fairyland Luster, Dana, 8-Sided, Bead Border, Pixies, Toadstool, Frogs, c.1920, 5 In.	1659.00
Bowl, Fairyland Luster, Elves, Playing Among Trees, Birds, Gilt Trees, 8 ¾ x 5 ½ In.	9200.00
Bowl, Fairyland Luster, Moorish, 8-Sided, Smoke Ribbons, c.1920, 8 In.	2133.00 to 8050.00
Bowl, Fairyland Luster, Willow, 8-Sided, Coral, Sponge Red, Willow Interior, c.1920, 8 In.	1304.00
Bowl, Fairyland Luster, Woodland Bridge Imperial, Picnic, River Interior, c.1920, 8 In.	4740.00
Bowl, Footed, Tricolored Dice, Impressed, 1978	313.00
Bowl, Fruit, Black Tonquin, 10 In.	74.00
Bowl, Jasperware, Blue, Navette, Textured, White Arabesques, Flowers, 2 Handles, 9 In.	3555.00
Bowl, Jasperware, Dark Blue, Silver Plated Rim, Horses, Men, c.1880, 9 In.	117.00
Bowl, Luster, Butterfly, Gold Butterflies On Exterior, c.1925, 2 x 3 ¾ In.	255.00
Bowl, Luster, Hummingbird, Gold Highlights, Marked, c.1925, 1 ¼ x 3 ¾ In.	255.00
Bowl, Luster, Turtle, Gold Highlights, Marked, c.1925, 1 ¼ x 3 ¾ In.	255.00
Bowl, Orange, Black Basalt, Applied Rim Border, Alternating Trellis & Flowers, 9 In.	1067.00
Bowl, Pedestal, Black, Raised Classical Design, 6 ¼ x 6 ½ In.	75.00
Bowl, Poplar Trees, Sky, Elves, Bell Branch, Mother-Of-Pearl Interior, c.1920, 9 In.	3200.00
Bowl, Queen's Ware, Centenary Transfers, Relief Portraits, 1845-1945, Footed, 12 In.	237.00
Box, Cover, Celadon, Stylized Relief Nude With Lyre, Dog, Tree, Erling Olsen, 5 In.	296.00
Box, Mahogany, Oval Cut Steel Frame, Jasper Mounts, White Classical Figures, 2 x 4 In.	119.00
Bulb Pot, Jasperware, Blue, Repeating White Leaves, Festoons, Handles, 4-Cup Insert, 10 In.	13035.00
Bust, Havelock, Carrara, Round Base, c.1858, 15 In.	948.00
Bust, Isaac Newton, Black Basalt, Impressed, 1800s, 9 In.	267.00
Bust, Mercury Gazing To Left, Basalt, 19th Century, 17 ¾ In.	1410.00
Bust, Robert Burns, Black, Basalt, c.1840, 7 ½ x 6 In.	1425.00
Bust, Shakespeare, Carrara, Mounted Base, Shakespeare Memorial Bust, c.1864, 12 In.	711.00
Candlestick, Creamware, Raised Light Blue Classical Decoration, 7 ¾ In., Pair	69.00
Candlestick, Dolphin, Upturned Tail, Flower Cup, Pink Glaze, c.1870, 9 ½ In., Pair	652.00
Candlestick, Jasper Dip, Dark Blue, Applied White Classical Figures, c.1890, 7 In.	148.00
Candlestick, Jasperware, Cobalt Blue Ground, Classical Design, Spreading Foot, 7 In., Pair	353.00
Candlestick, Moonlight Luster, Column Shape, Square Plinth, Gilt Trim, c.1800, 8 In., Pair	563.00
Charger, Woman, Portrait, Daisy Border, Marked, 13 ¾ In.	58.00
Cheese Dish, Cover, Argenta Majolica, Leaves, Blossoms, Yellow, Green, c.1870, 9 In.	444.00
Cheese Dish, Cover, Jasperware, Blue, White Oak Leaf Band, Figures, 11 In.	415.00
Cheese Dish, Cover, Marsden Art Ware, Slip Flowers, Leaves, Buff Ground, c.1885, 11 In.	889.00
Cheese Dish, Cover, Scrolls, Flowers, Mottled Blue Ground, c.1900, 7 In.	590.00
Coffee Cup, Saucer, Rosso Antico, Egyptian, Hieroglyphic Bands, Impressed, c.1800, 5 In.	1659.00
Compote, Nautilus Shell, Pearlware, Pink Enamel, Impressed Mark, c.1870, 8 In.	770.00
Compote, Pearlware, 3-Footed, Figures, Urns, Landscape, E. Lessore, c.1865, 9 In.	533.00
Cruet Set, Queen's Ware, Oval Tray, 2 Cups, 2 Covered Ewers, Black Enamel, c.1800, 11 In.	948.00
Curd Mold, Pearlware, 3 Tiers, Oval, Pierced Body, c.1800, 9 In.	563.00
Decanter, Cobalt Glass Medallion, Cameo Plaque, 9 ½ x 6 ¾ In.	118.00
Dish, Ceiling, Jasperware, Black, Round, Applied White Relief, Cherubs, Flowers, c.1890, 13 In.	1126.00
Epergne, Queen's Ware, Fluted, Pineapple Finial, Goat Masks, 6 Baskets, c.1900, 18 In.	3851.00
Figurine, Black Basalt, Diana, Seated On Free-Form Base, 9 In.	2370.00
Figurine, Pearlware, Shepherd, Shepherdess, Lambs, Multicolored Enamel, c.1820, 8 In., Pair.	1776.00
Figurine, Venus, Crouching, Nude, Black Basalt, Stepped Base, Brass Stand, 1800s, 15 In.	1896.00
Fish Set, Creamware, Fish, Griffin, Vases, Letters, 12 Plates, Serving Platter, c.1860, 9 In., 13 Piece	974.00
Flask, Pearlware, Blue Flowers, Leaves, Beadwork, Gilt Trace, c.1780, 6 In.	2252.00
Food Warmer, Pearlware, Pierced Base, Handles, Insert Bowl, Cover, Cup, c.1790, 11 In.	944.00
Frame, Double, Ormolu, 2 Inset Blue Medallions, White Classical Relief, c.1890, 6 In.	267.00
Garniture Set, Black Basalt, Tripod Censer, Pierced, Sphinx, 3 Piece	3220.00
Humidor, Oval, Dancing Maidens, 6 In.	68.00
Inkstand, Jasper Dip, Dark Blue, Bellflowers, Grapevine, Gilt Bronze Mount, 4 In.	830.00
Inkstand, Jasperware, Blue, Oval, Scalloped, Top Fitted Well, Applied Leaves, c.1790, 6 In.	1185.00
Jar, Jasperware, Lavender, Floral Swags, Ram's Heads, Cartouches, Reeded, 3 In. *illus*	144.00
Jardiniere, Blue Ground White Classical Figures, 7 ¼ In.	403.00
Jardiniere, Figures, Ram's Head Masks, Grapevine Swags, Blue, c.1900, 9 x 10 In.	179.00
Jardiniere, Jasperware, Blue, White Classical Figures, Leaf, Vine Banding, 10 ½ In.	366.00
Jelly Mold Core, Cover, Pearlware, Wedge Shape, Enameled Flowers & Festoons, 7 In.	1422.00
Jelly Mold Core, Queen's Ware, Enameled Flowers, 9 ½ In.	1185.00
Jelly Mold Core, Queen's Ware, Wedge Shape, Enameled Flowers, 5 ¼ In.	1304.00
Jug, Black Basalt, Central Band, Bacchanalian Boys Relief, Handle, c.1790, 7 In.	711.00
Jug, Black Basalt, Split Loop Handles, c.1810, 6 In.	107.00

Jug, Jasper Dip, Brown, White Relief Classical Figures, Grapevine, 5 In.	652.00
Jug, Milk, Jasperware, Figures, Lid, Handle, 6 ½ In.	135.00
Jug, Rosso Anitco, Club Shape, Black Relief Bacchanalian Boys, Vine, 7 In.	1007.00
Jug, Tall, Kenlock Ware, Black Basalt, Dragons, Foo Dogs, Insects, Multicolored, 1800s, 8 In. ..	237.00
Jug, White Stoneware, Blue Ground Collar, Children Playing, Texture Glaze, 1800s, 6 In.	326.00
Lamp, Oil, Jasper Dip, Drum Shape, Underplate, Gilt Brass Fitted, Classical Relief, c.1880, 5 In.	1896.00
Medallion, Bust, Embossed, Round, Ebony Frame, 2 ½ In.	300.00
Medallion, Jasper Dip, Green, Black, 8-Sided, White Classical Relief, c.1790, 3 In.	652.00
Medallion, Portrait, Jasperware, Black, Audrey Wedgwood Portrait, Oval, 1900s, 5 In.	178.00
Medallion, Portrait, Basalt, Washington, Franklin, Wedgwood & Bentley, c.1776, 2 In., Pair ...	3200.00
Perfume Bottle, Jasperware, Light Blue, Relief Portraits Of King & Queen, 2 In.	593.00
Philadelphia Bowl, American Liberty Design, 13 x 5 ½ In.	99.00
Pin, Blue Jasper Dip, Oval, Applied White Classical Figures, Gold Frame, 2 In.	326.00
Pin, Fairyland Luster, Oval, Silver Mounted, Pagoda Landscape, c.1920, 2 In.	652.00
Pitcher, Brown & Cobalt Blue Drip Glaze, Ribbed Band, Handle, Impressed, 7 ½ In.	11.00
Pitcher, Flowers, Multicolored, Black, Basalt, 6 ½ In.	165.00
Plaque, 7 Ages Of Man, Jasper Dip, Applied White Relief, Frame, c.1880, 10 x 26 In.	4148.00
Plaque, Achilles, Homer, Jasper Dip, Walls Of Troy White Relief, Rectangle, Frame, 6 x 15 In. .	593.00
Plaque, Black Basalt, Oval, Fluted Border, Bacchanalian Boys, Self-Framed, 1700s, 8 x 10 In.	1778.00
Plaque, Black Basalt, Oval, Satyr, Child, Molded, 1900s, 10 x 12 In.	119.00
Plaque, Dancing Hours, Jasperware, Dark Blue, White Classical Figures, Shaped, 4 x 10 In. ...	1126.00
Plaque, Jasper Dip, Green, White Relief Cupid, Psyche, Arrow, c.1850, 10 x 14 In.	1067.00
Plaque, Jasperware, Blue, 2 White Relief Bacchanalian Boys, Oval, c.1900, 5 ½ In.	356.00
Plaque, Jasperware, Woman Of Day, Woman Of Night, Green, White, 9 In., Pair	90.00
Plaque, King George III, Jasperware, Blue, Wedgwood & Bentley, c.1777, 2 In.	593.00
Plaque, Oliver Wendell Holmes, Jasper Dip, Dark Blue, Oval, c.1890, 5 x 7 In.	178.00
Plaque, Shakespeare, Jasperware, Blue Oval, Frame, Wedgwood & Bentley, 4 In.	1126.00
Plaque, Silhouette, Abraham Lincoln, Jasperware, Blue, Oval, 4 x 3 In.	58.00
Plate Set, Majolica, Grapes, Leaves, Multicolored, Impressed, 9 In., 8 Piece..........	489.00
Plate Set, Majolica Leaf, Green, Scalloped Edge, 7 ⅞ In., 8 Piece	235.00
Plate, Columbia, 11 In., Pair.	69.00
Plate, Dinner, Green Boar's Head, Border, Gilt Rims, 12 Piece	359.00
Plate, Fairyland Luster, Imps, Bridge, Bird, Multicolored, Wide Gold Rim, Signed, 11 In.	6900.00
Plate, Fairyland Luster, Imps On Bridge, Bird Flying, Canoe Floating, Signed, 19 ½ In.	4600.00
Plate, Fish, Cream Ground, Brown, Turquoise, Rose, Marked, 1870s, 8 ¾ In., 6 Piece........	1800.00
Plate, Ivanhoe, Urfried Relating Her Story To Cedric, Blue, 8 ⅝ In.	33.00
Plate, Rosso Antico, Egyptian, Orange, Black Relief, Hieroglyphics Border, 1800s, 8 In.	830.00
Plate, Salad, Bone China, Silver Luster Leaves, Bell Flowers, Flower Heads, 8 In., 12 Piece.......	538.00
Plate, Service, Queen's Ware, Husk, Rose, Flower Garlands, c.1770, 10 In.	1067.00
Plate, Shell, Pearlware, Putti, Trellis, Vines, Grapes, c.1877, 9 In.	107.00
Plate, Young Man, Beach, Griffin, Dolphin, Phoenix Border, 10 In.	60.00
Platter, Blue & White, Cattle In Stream, Transfer, c.1906	767.00
Platter, Queen's Ware, Frog Service, Oval, Black Enville Landscape, c.1774, 12 In.	54510.00
Platter, Seine, Blue, 14 In.	89.00
Roundel, Majolica, Trembley Landscape, Yellow, Dark Blue, Gray, c.1876, 13 In.	296.00
Rum Pot, Cover, Black Basalt, Engine-Turned, Lobed Bail Handle, Sybil Finial, 8 ½ In.	1007.00
Salt Cellar, Creamware, 2 Basket, Basket Weave Design, Impressed, 4 x 5 In.	260.00
Salt Dip, Jasperware, Green, Lilac, White, Festoons, Leaves, Silver Plated Rims, c.1890, 2 In., Pair.	2015.00
Salt, Figural, Man, Seated, Black Hat, Holding Basket, Majolica, 7 ¾ In. .... *illus*	236.00
Salt, Pearlware, Dolphin Shape, Shell Shape Bowl, John Bell, c.1850, 5 In., Pair............	444.00
Sconce, 5-Light, Jasper, Ormolu Mounts, Light Blue Medallions, White Relief, 34 In., Pair	5036.00
Shadowbox, Cameo, 5 ½ In.	165.00
Sugar & Creamer, Black Basalt, 3 x 2 & 2 ¾ x 2 ½ In.	70.00
Sugar, Cover, Jasper Dip, Tricolored, Green, Lilac, White Medallions, Festoons, Ram's Heads ...	889.00
Tea & Coffee Service, Black Basalt, Geometric Diagonal Hatched Band, 23 Piece................	59.00
Tea Set, Jasperware, Blue, White Classical Figures, 4-In. Teapot, 3 Piece........	71.00
Teapot, Cover, Jasper Dip, Crimson, White Relief Figures, 4 ¾ In.	593.00
Teapot, Cover, Jasperware, Blue, White Relief Designs, Domestic Employment, Footed, 6 In. ...	563.00
Teapot, Cover, Victorian Ware, Cream, Heavy Gilt, Green Relief Festoons, 4 In.	4740.00
Teapot, Drabware, Woven Handle, Late 1800s, 6 In.	385.00
Tile, Black Knight & Friar Tuck, Blue Transfer, White Ground, c.1880, 6 x 6 In.	125.00
Tile, Ram, Blue Transfer Print, Fresco Heads Series, c.1880, 6 x 6 In.	135.00
Tile, Snipe, Guarding Eggs, Transfer Print, Fresco Head Series, c.1880, 6 x 6 In.	150.00
Tray, Black Basalt, Encaustic Decorated, Oval, White, Red Enamel Border, c.1785, 12 In.	504.00
Tray, Fairyland Luster, Garden Of Paradise Lily, Mother-Of-Pearl Sky, c.1920, 11 In.	2963.00
Tray, Luster Lily, Gold Wave Design, Orange, Gray, Green, Mother-Of-Pearl Interior, c.1920, 8 In.	267.00

Wedgwood, Vase, Fairyland Luster, Daventry, Signed, 10 ½ In.
$2875.00

TIP

Don't be confused by Wedgwood marks. Josiah Wedgwood, the famous English maker, never used his initial in a mark. He used just the company name. Ironstone marked "J Wedgwood" was made by John Wedge Wood, a potter working in Burslem (1841–1844) and Tunstall (1845–1860) in the Staffordshire district. If you look closely, you can see a small gap or a dot between "Wedg" and "Wood." "Wedgwood" also appears on pieces by Podmore, Walker & Co., Ralph Wedgwood, and other companies with some family rights to the name "Wedgwood." And there is also a company using the mark "Wedgewood."

W

Weller, Cameo, Vase, Blue, Handles,
7 ½ x 9 In.
$58.00

Weller, Coppertone, Frog,
Waterlily Shape Bowl, Marked,
Green Slip M, 2 ½ x 4 ¼ In.
$207.00

Weller, Dickens Ware, Mug,
Mr. Pickwick, Incised, 5 ⅝ In.
$104.00

W

Urn, Chocolate, Raised Classical Design, Angular Handles, 12 In.	70.00
Urn, Cover, Black Basalt, Flowers, Multicolored Enamel, Upturned Scroll Handles, 10 In.	563.00
Urn, Cover, Jasperware, Blue, Apotheosis Of Virgil, 1910, 10 x 19 In.	5850.00
Urn, Green, Jasperware, 2 Handles, Cover, Box, 13 In.	363.00
Urn, Lavender Ground, Classical Figures, Swags, Tassels, Ram's Head Handles, 12 In.	748.00
Vase, Agate Ware, Bacchus Head Handles, Gilt, Wedgwood & Bentley, c.1775, 8 In.	711.00
Vase, Aura Basalt, Gold Slip Leaves, c.1885, 10 In.	444.00
Vase, Black Basalt, Engine Turned Bands, Flared, Footed, Keith Murray, c.1940, 8 In.	830.00
Vase, Black Basalt, Gold, Multicolored Flowers, Satyr Masks, Handles, c.1850, 8 In.	1126.00
Vase, Black Basalt, Iron Red, White Classical Figures, Leaves, Fret Border, c.1800, 9 In.	2252.00
Vase, Black Basalt, Iron Red, White, Classical Figures, Loop Handles, c.1810, 10 In.	3081.00
Vase, Blue Ground, Classical Figures, Shouldered, 2 Handles, 10 In.	403.00
Vase, Borghese, Cover, Blue Jasper, White Classical Figures, Gadroon, Handles, 18 In.	8888.00
Vase, Columns, Swags, Acanthus Trim, Gilt Ground, Brown Rim, Stamped, c.1891, 5 In.	1530.00
Vase, Cover, Black Basalt, Festoons, Applied Leaves, Upturned Handles, c.1775, 15 In.	3081.00
Vase, Cover, Black Basalt, Iron Red Finial, Laocoon, Looped Handles, c.1800, 15 In.	11850.00
Vase, Cover, Jasper Dip, Black, Apotheosis Of Homer, Snake Handles, Pegasus, 24 In.	10665.00
Vase, Cover, Jasper Dip, Black Pierced Cover, Classical Relief, Handles, 1800s, 13 In.	1185.00
Vase, Cover, Jasper Dip, Black, White Relief Figures, Zodiac Border, Plinth, 10 In.	1541.00
Vase, Cover, Jasper Dip, Lilac, Trophy Shape, Medallion, Goat Mask Handles, 6 In.	2133.00
Vase, Cover, Jasper Dip, Lilac, White Relief Classical Figures, Leafy Bands, Plinth, 9 In.	1778.00
Vase, Cover, Jasper Dip, Tricolored, Leaves, Lions' Masks, 3 Buttressed Legs, 8 In.	4148.00
Vase, Cover, Jasperware, Black, Muse Medallion, Festoons, Upturned Handles, 1900s, 12 In.	770.00
Vase, Cover, Majolica, Multicolored Enamel, Bacchus Head Handles, c.1872, 13 In., Pair	1659.00
Vase, Cover, Majolica, Woman, Blue, White, Scroll Flower Handles, Pastels, c.1870, 11 In., Pair	1422.00
Vase, Cover, Potpourri, Yellow Jasper Dip, Pierced Cover, Black Relief Flowers, c.1930, 8 In.	889.00
Vase, Duck Egg Blue Slip, Globular, Concentric Bands, Keith Murray, c.1940, 6 In.	711.00
Vase, Fairyland Luster, Butterfly, Woman On Branch, Flowers, Leaves, 9 ½ In.	5462.00
Vase, Fairyland Luster, Candlemas, Black, Blue Ground, c.1920, 8 In.	2252.00
Vase, Fairyland Luster, Daventry, Signed, 10 ½ In. ....*illus*	118.00
Vase, Fairyland Luster, Gold Highlights, Firbolgs, Trees, Dark Blue Ground, Signed, 8 In.	4025.00
Vase, Fairyland Luster, Rainbow, Goats Drinking, Butterfly, Woman, 7 ½ In.	2760.00
Vase, Fairyland Luster, Vertical Pillar, Panels, Birds, Stairways, Fairies, 11 ⅞ In.	12650.00
Vase, Flared Rim, Blue Ground, Gold Dragon, Blue, Green Border, 9 In.	173.00
Vase, Green Slip, Squat, Concentric Circles To Shoulder, Keith Murray, 6 ⅝ In.	1126.00
Vase, Jasper Dip, Green, Classical Medallions, Flowers, Ram's Head, c.1850, 11 In.	415.00
Vase, Jasperware, Figures, Leaf Border, Blue, White, Cylindrical, 6 In., Pair	150.00
Vase, Jasperware, Light Blue, Flowers, Medallions, Masks, Paws, 1800s, 7 In.	948.00
Vase, Pearlware, Bottle Shape, Multicolored, Putti, Landscapes, Lizards, E. Lessore, c.1879, 9 In.	711.00
Vase, Pearlware, Red Enamel Trim, Red Putti Transfer, Mermaid Handles, c.1875, 13 In.	770.00
Vase, Portland, Jasper Dip, Dark Blue, Applied Classical Figures, 1800s, 10 In.	1659.00
Vase, Portland, Jasperware, Blue Tinted White, Classical Figures, Handles, c.1862, 10 In.	3200.00
Vase, Portrait, Black, White Jasper Dip, Portraits, Festoons, Borders, c.1860, 7 In.	770.00
Wine Cooler, Terra-Cotta, Classical Relief, 1800s, 10 In., Pair	1007.00

WELLER pottery was first made in 1872 in Fultonham, Ohio. The firm moved to Zanesville, Ohio, in 1882. Artwares were introduced in 1893. Hundreds of lines of pottery were produced, including Louwelsa, Eocean, Dickens Ware, and Sicardo, before the pottery closed in 1948.

LOUWELSA
WELLER

Ardsley, Bowl, Cattail, Flower Frog, Green, Bowl 12 In., Frog 5 ½ In.	219.00
Ardsley, Umbrella Stand, Cattails, White Water Lilies, Stamp, 20 In.	518.00
Ardsley, Vase, Bud, Purple Iris, Plant Shape, Mark, 7 In.	127.00
Art Nouveau, Jardiniere, Flowers, Handles, Pedestal, 41 ¾ In.	1495.00
Art Nouveau, Pincushion, Star Shape, 2 ½ x 5 In.	295.00
Athens, Vase, Mythological Scenes, Green & Brown Matte Glaze, 7 x 15 In.	633.00
Aurelian, Jardiniere, Footed, Flowers, 12 In.	565.00
Aurelian, Lamp, Oil, Footed, Triangle Shape, Flowers, 7 In.	85.00
Aurelian, Mug, Brown Glaze, Ear Of Corn, Silver Overlay, 1889, 4 ½ x 6 In.	1265.00
Aurelian, Mug, Signed, c.1900, 6 In.	176.00
Aurelian, Pedestal, Irises, 27 In.	230.00
Aurelian, Vase, Bulbous, Brown Glaze, Geraniums, Marked, 8 x 11 In.	863.00
Aurelian, Vase, Twist Form, Fuchsia, Charles Fouts, Marked, 11 ½ In.	575.00
Baldin, Vase, Bulbous, Branch Handles, Brown, Monogram, c.1930, 9 In.	247.00
Besline, Candleholder, Flowers, Orange, 10 ¾ In.	100.00
Besline, Vase, Swollen Form, Etched Leaves & Berries, Orange Ground, 7 In.	86.00
Blue Ware, Lamp Vase, Classical Women, Ivory, Dark Blue Ground, Multicolored Flowers, Fruit.	431.00
Bowl, Blue & Teal Mottled Drip Glaze, Rounded Sides, Stamped, 2 ¾ x 8 In.	22.00

Breton, Jardiniere, Green Matte, 4 ¼ x 5 ¼ In.	95.00
Brighton, Figurine, Parrot, Perched, Spread Wings, Marked, 13 In.	978.00
Brighton, Flower Frog, Kingfisher, 9 In.	395.00
Bronze Ware, Lamp, Ceramic, Wood Body, Mica, Brass Shade, Mark, 18 In.	863.00
Burnt Wood, Vase, Egyptian Scene, 7 ¼ In.	360.00
Camelot, Jardiniere, 9 ¼ x 10 In.	395.00
Camelot, Vase, Bulbous, 6 ¼ In.	295.00
Cameo Jewel, Vase, Incised, House, Plants, Lavender, Green, Gray, Rudolph Lorber, 16 ½ In. .	2990.00
Cameo, Vase, Blue, Handles, 7 ½ x 9 In. ....*illus*	58.00
Coppertone, Bowl, Frog, Water Lilies, 15 ½ x 3 ½ In.	633.00
Coppertone, Candlestick, Green, Mottled Brown Marks, 3 In., Pair	173.00
Coppertone, Figure, Frog, Hole In Mouth, 5 ¾ x 7 In.	695.00
Coppertone, Frog, Waterlily Shape Bowl, Marked, Green Slip M, 2 ½ x 4 ¼ In. ....*illus*	207.00
Coppertone, Vase, 2 Frogs, Climbing Up Sides Of Vessel, 7 ½ In.	978.00
Coppertone, Vase, Applied Fish & Lily Pad, Marked, 8 x 8 In.	690.00
Coppertone, Vase, Bud, 2 Fish, Green Fish Standing, Yellow Opens Mouth, 8 In.	1093.00
Coppertone, Vase, Bud, Fish, Rising From Lotus Blossom, Dark Green, 8 In.	1610.00
Coppertone, Vase, Water Lily, Frog, Marked, 4 ½ x 3 ½ In.	259.00
Delta, Vase, Iris Blossom, Dark Blue Slip, Blue, Green Ground, c.1900, 10 In.	207.00
Dickens Ware, Humidor, Irishman, Incised Mark, 7 x 6 ½ In.	290.00
Dickens Ware II, Pitcher, Fish, Swirled Blue Glaze, E.L. Pickens..................	920.00
Dickens Ware II, Pitcher, Sgraffito, Fish, Water, 5 In.	184.00
Dickens Ware II, Tankard, Conquistador Portrait, John Herold, 12 In.	316.00
Dickens Ware II, Vase, Green Ground, Woman, Trees, Flowers, Basket, 13 In.	920.00
Dickens Ware II, Vase, Pillow, 2 Hunting Dogs, E.L. Pickens, 10 x 10 In.	1150.00
Dickens Ware, Lamp, Bird On Branch, Ed Abel, 20 ¾ In.	395.00
Dickens Ware, Lamp, Oil, Birds In Grass, 9 ½ In.	1295.00
Dickens Ware, Mug, 2 Handles, Butterflies, 5 In.	250.00
Dickens Ware, Mug, 2 Yellow Butterflies On Dark Brown Ground, Marked, 4 ⅝ In.	115.00
Dickens Ware, Mug, Mr. Pickwick, Incised, 5 ⅝ In. ....*illus*	104.00
Dickens Ware, Mug, Stag, Etched, Marked, 562, 5 ½ In.	120.00
Dickens Ware, Tankard, 3 Ducks, Dolphin Handle, 12 ⅞ In.	403.00
Dickens Ware, Vase, American Indian, 2 Spears, Crimped Top, 4 ½ x 8 ½ In.	480.00
Dickens Ware, Vase, Colonial Women, Flower Garden, Trees, 14 ⅞ In.	1380.00
Dickens Ware, Vase, Flattened, 4-Footed, Deer, Forest, Marked, 7 ½ x 7 In.	316.00
Dickens Ware, Vase, Gladiator Holding Shield & Sword, 2 Handles, Impressed, 7 ⅛ In.	104.00
Dickens Ware, Vase, Indian Chief, Marked, 8 ½ In.	207.00
Dickens Ware, Vase, Oval, Cavalier, Blue Shawl, Marked, 3 x 8 In.	86.00
Dickens Ware, Vase, Pillow Form, 4-Footed, Daring Fox, E.L. Pickens, 6 x 5 In.	575.00
Dickens Ware, Vase, Shouldered, Native American In Headdress, Marked, 6 x 13 In.	345.00
Dickens Ware, Vase, Trees, Water, Indian Men, Canoe, Blankets, Oars, C.B. Upjohn, 13 In.	1035.00
Dickens Ware, Vessel, Handle, Profile Of Young Boy, Turquoise Ground, 4 ½ x 5 In.	485.00
Dish, Figural, Female, Cover, Rose Garlands, Marked, 5 x 7 In.	173.00
Eocean Rose, Vase, Shouldered, Dogwood Blossoms, Marked, 4 x 9 ½ In.	805.00
Eocean, Mug, Cat Portrait, E. Blake, 5 x 5 In.	690.00
Eocean, Vase, Blue Columbine, 8 ⅜ In.	184.00
Eocean, Vase, Cylindrical, Bull Dog, Marked, 3 x 10 In.	1035.00
Eocean, Vase, Red, Pink Clover, Long Stems, Dark Green To Light Base, Incised, 8 In.	288.00
Eocean, Vase, Shouldered, Pansies, Lavender, Yellow, Gray, Marked, 4 x 10 In.	374.00
Eocean, Vase, Storks, Chilcote, 6 ½ x 10 ½ In.	2070.00
Eocean, Vase, Trumpet, White & Lavender Carnations, 10 ½ In.	288.00
Eocean, Vase, Woodbine, Gray Green Ground, 7 ¼ In.	345.00
Etched Matte, Vase, Green, Woman, Blown Hair, Molded Leaves To Rim, Handles, 5 ½ In.	375.00
Etna, Vase, 3 Flowers, Cylindrical, 8 ¾ In.	235.00
Etna, Vase, Cluster Of Flowers, Looped & Open Handles, Marked, 5 x 9 In.	185.00
Etna, Vase, Grapes On Vine, Shouldered, Marked...................................	374.00
Experimental, Vase, Cylindrical, Green Oak Leaves, Acorns, Yellow Crackle Ground, 10 In. ...	805.00
Fairfield, Bowl, Cherubs, 5 x 8 ¾ In.	100.00
Fairfield, Jardiniere, Tinted Ivory, Playful Cherubs, 5 ¾ In.	80.00
Figure, Hen, Bug Eyed, Nest, Chicks, Multicolored, 8 In.	1495.00
Figure, Rooster, Harbinger Of Dawn, Impressed, Multicolored, 9 In.	1035.00
Flemish, Pedestal, Parrot, Blue, c.1900, 21 ¾ In.	150.00
Floretta, Vase, 2 Handles, Squat, Grape Cluster, 7 ½ In.	68.00
Floretta, Vase, Cylindrical, Bulbous Bottom, Lavender Poppies, Marked, 3 x 8 In.	144.00
Flower Frog, Boy Fishing, 6 ½ In.	225.00
Flower Frog, Brighton, Kingfisher, On Tangled Roots, Impressed, 5 ¾ In.	330.00

Weller, Gloria, Vase, Flowers, Leaves,
No. G-14, 6 ⅝ In.
$23.00

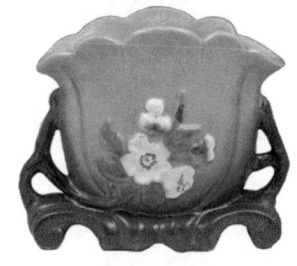

Weller, Jap Birdimal, Vase, Geisha,
White Vase On Tray, Clouds, Impressed,
9 ¼ In.
$2300.00

Weller, Louwelsa, Ewer, Trefoil,
Open Rose, 4 ½ In.
$75.00

Weller, Muskota, Flower Holder,
Frog, 4 ⅝ In.
$161.00

W

Weller, Orris, Vase, Daffodil, Brown & Green Glaze, 10 In. $196.00

Weller, Sicardo, Vase, Bulbous, Flowers, Metallic Glaze, Impressed 30, 3 x 9 In. $1560.00

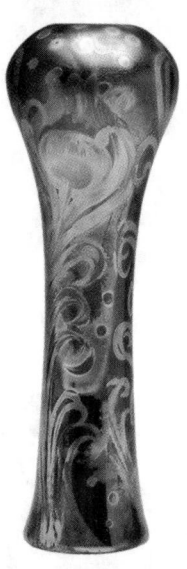

W

Forest, Jardiniere, Marked, 4 ½ In.	150.00
Forest, Planter, Pastoral Landscape, Marked, Rudolph Lorber, 10 In.	1200.00
Forest, Vase, Flared, 8 In.	82.00
Fru Russet, Vase, Irises, Mottled Green, Brown Glaze, 6 In.	1035.00
Fudzi, Vase, Cylinder, Incised, Colored Leaves, Berries, Gloss Glaze, Bisque Ground, 7 In.	748.00
Garden Ware, Chicken, Hen, Marked, 12 ¼ x 10 In.	2495.00
Garden Ware, Dog, Terrier, Seated, 12 In.	1695.00
Glendale, Candlestick, Yellow Bird, Egg Filled Nest, Berry Tree, Marked, 5 In.	220.00
Glendale, Vase, Brown Bird, On Forest Floor, Marked, 5 In.	230.00
Glendale, Vase, Bulbous Bottom, Bird, 6 x 11 In.	633.00
Glendale, Vase, Double Bud, Bluebird On Nest, Raspberries, Dragonfly, Marked, 7 ¼ In.	315.00
Glendale, Wall Pocket, Birds On Branch, 7 ¼ x 7 In.	425.00
Glendale, Wall Pocket, Mother, 3 Baby Birds In Nest, Marked, 12 In.	470.00
Gloria, Vase, Flowers, Leaves, No. G-14, 6 ⅝ In. ....*illus*	23.00
Hudson, Jardiniere, Pale Pink Tulips, 9 x 11 In.	138.00
Hudson, Vase, Blue, Band Of Forget-Me-Nots, Impressed Mark, 7 ¼ In.	161.00
Hudson, Vase, Blue Flowers, Green Ground, Claude Leffler, Impressed, 12 In.	196.00
Hudson, Vase, Blueberries, 22 In.	1150.00
Hudson, Vase, Bulbous, Pink Lilacs, Sarah Timberlake, Marked, 10 ½ In.	978.00
Hudson, Vase, Cherry Blossoms, Multicolored, Sara McLaughlin, 7 In.	196.00
Hudson, Vase, Cylindrical, Lilacs, Pillsbury, Marked, 4 x 13 In.	748.00
Hudson, Vase, Early 20th Century, 9 In.	293.00
Hudson, Vase, Flared Rim, Cherries, Pink Ground, 11 In.	325.00
Hudson, Vase, Flowers, 6 ½ x 11 ¾ In.	316.00
Hudson, Vase, Flowers, Yellow Ground, 11 In.	375.00
Hudson, Vase, Green Ground, White, Blue Iris, L. Morris, 9 In.	431.00
Hudson, Vase, Handles, Light Green, Daisies, Square Handles, Mae Timberlake, 6 In.	288.00
Hudson, Vase, Hollyhocks, Pillsbury, 12 In.	978.00
Hudson, Vase, Iris, Blue Ground, Impressed, Signed, Sarah Reid McLaughlin, 15 ½ In.	883.00
Hudson, Vase, Iris, Cylinder, Blue, Yellow, Green, Mae Timberlake, 8 In.	978.00
Hudson, Vase, Iris, Dorothy England, Marked, 8 ½ In.	460.00
Hudson, Vase, Iris, Flowers, Pale Green, Brown, Yellow, Stamp, 15 In.	633.00
Hudson, Vase, Iris, Green, Blue, Indianapolis Kappa Gamma Sorority, Hester Pillsbury, c.1930.	207.00
Hudson, Vase, Irises, Hester Pillsbury, 3 x 6 In.	259.00
Hudson, Vase, Lilacs, Pillsbury, 13 ¼ In.	825.00
Hudson, Vase, Pale Blueberries, Green Leaves, Yellow Ground, Hester Pillsbury, 6 In.	633.00
Hudson, Vase, Shouldered, Roses, Marked, 6 ½ x 13 ½ In.	144.00
Hudson, Vase, Urn Shape, Nasturtium, White, Orange, Green, Blue, Footed, Mae Timberlake, 9 In.	978.00
Hudson, Vase, White Iris Flowers, Gray On Green, Impressed, 11 ¼ In.	575.00
Hudson, Vase, Yellow Nasturtiums, Green Leaves, Black Outline, Signed, 9 ⅜ In.	230.00
Hudson, Vase, Yellow Poppies, Stems, Pillsbury, Marked, 13 ⅛ In.	690.00
Jap Birdimal, Pitcher, Geisha, Trees, Blue Ground, 6 x 11 In.	920.00
Jap Birdimal, Vase, Black Spider, Web, Green Ground, Black Lines, Rhead Faience, 4 In.	1150.00
Jap Birdimal, Vase, Geisha, White Vase On Tray, Clouds, Impressed, 9 ¼ In. ....*illus*	2300.00
Jap Birdimal, Vase, Japanese Man, Dragonfly, Butterflies, Mark, 6 In.	1150.00
Jap Birdimal, Vase, Tube Lining, Japanese Man, Cloudy Skies, Rhead Faience, 6 In.	805.00
Jardiniere, Footed, Vertical Overlapping Leaves, Green Matte Glaze, 9 ½ x 8 In.	173.00
Jardiniere, Green Matte, Corn, Husk, Molded, Crystalline Matte Green, 8 x 9 In.	173.00
Jardiniere, Red Apples, Branches, Matching Tree Trunk Pedestal, Stamp, 38 In.	1725.00
Jewel, Pedestal, Cameo Design, 10 x 20 ¼ In.	144.00
Kenova, Vase, Raised Flowers, Rare Blue Ground, Green, Orange, 8 In.	690.00
Klyro, Basket, Circle, Incised Mark, 9 In.	105.00
Klyro, Basket, Flowers, Yellow Ground, Footed, 6 x 5 ¾ In.	150.00
L'Art Nouveau, Umbrella Stand, Dragon, Shells, 9 x 24 In.	489.00
L'Art Nouveau, Umbrella Stand, Pheasant, Grapes, 11 x 22 In.	690.00
L'Art Nouveau, Vase, 4 Upper Buttresses, Raised Grape & Flower Designs, Marked, 6 ½ x 12 In.	259.00
LaSa, Vase, Cylindrical, Flaring Foot, Metallic Glaze, Landscape, 6 x 12 In.	288.00
LaSa, Vase, Palm Trees, Tropical Landscape, Marked, 12 ½ In.	403.00
LaSa, Vase, Trees By Lake, Evening Sky, Marked, 11 In., Pair	546.00
Louella, Vase, Ribbed, Marked, 4 ¾ x 6 In.	100.00
Louwelsa, Ewer, Trefoil, Open Rose, 4 ½ In. ....*illus*	75.00
Louwelsa, Humidor, Native American, Brown Glaze, Leffler, 6 x 7 In.	1840.00
Louwelsa, Jardiniere, Ruffled Edge, Iris, 7 ½ In.	90.00
Louwelsa, Jug, Brown, Yellow, Green, Seed Corn Ear, High Handle, Impressed, 5 ½ In.	127.00
Louwelsa, Jug, Whiskey, Wheat, Silver Overlay, 6 ½ In.	288.00
Louwelsa, Lamp, Round Mark, Brass Burner, 9 ½ In.	345.00

Louwelsa, Pitcher, Molded Shell Design, Fish, Pillsbury, Marked, 11 ¼ In.	690.00
Louwelsa, Tankard, Native American Portrait, Handle, Levi Burgess, Marked, 12 ⅝ In.	690.00
Louwelsa, Vase, American Indian Portrait, Impressed, 7 x 6 ¾ In.	1500.00
Louwelsa, Vase, Berries, Blue, Marked, 5 ⅜ In.	415.00
Louwelsa, Vase, Blue Grapes, Olive Ground, Signed M. Lybarger, c.1900, 11 ½ In.	764.00
Louwelsa, Vase, Brown Glaze, Painted Flowers, Applied Silver Overlay, Impressed Mark, 3 x 10 In.	1725.00
Louwelsa, Vase, Bulbous, Leaves, Marked, 7 In.	68.00
Louwelsa, Vase, Cylindrical, Orange Poppy Blossoms, Bud, Incised, 8 ½ In.	161.00
Louwelsa, Vase, Daisies, Blue, 8 In.	518.00
Louwelsa, Vase, Finger Hole, Squat, Marked, 3 In.	45.00
Louwelsa, Vase, Flared Rim, Bull Dog Portrait, L. Blake, 6 x 6 In.	920.00
Louwelsa, Vase, Honeysuckle Flowers, Blue, Impressed, 7 In.	518.00
Louwelsa, Vase, Narrow Neck, Brown, Green Yellow, Portrait, Hat, Man, 12 In.	403.00
Louwelsa, Vase, Nasturtiums, Blue, 11 ⅝ In.	1610.00
Louwelsa, Vase, Nasturtiums, Red, Yellow, Green, M. Lybarger, 16 In.	184.00
Louwelsa, Vase, Pale Dandelions, Blue, 2 In.	403.00
Louwelsa, Vase, Pale Dogwood Flowers, Deep Blue, 10 In.	518.00
Louwelsa, Vase, Pansies, Brown, Orange, Colored Ground, 1896-1924, 8 ½ In.	267.00
Louwelsa, Vase, Poppies, Blue, Cylindrical, Marked, 6 ½ In.	403.00
Louwelsa, Vase, Red, Woodbine, Rectangular, Pillsbury, 10 In.	1840.00
Louwelsa, Vase, Yellow Rose, Red Rose, Impressed 7, 8 ¼ In.	115.00
Mammy, Bowl, Batter, Figural Handle, 5 ½ x 11 In.	235.00
Marvo, Umbrella Stand, 24 In.	403.00
Minerva, Vase, Orange Oak Leaves, Acorns, Brown Ground, Impressed, 7 In.	2990.00
Muskota, Bowl, Sculpted Birds, Spread Wings, Gray & Green Glaze, Marked, 8 x 7 In.	201.00
Muskota, Figurine, Kneeling Woman, 6 x 5 ½ In.	325.00
Muskota, Flower Holder, Frog, 4 ⅝ In. .... *illus*	161.00
Orris, Vase, Daffodil, Brown & Green Glaze, 10 In. .... *illus*	196.00
Patra, Vase, Lobed, 3-Footed, Flared Rim, 10 ½ In.	225.00
Planter, Green Matte Glaze, Sheep, Flower Design, 6 ½ x 10 ½ In.	495.00
Roma, Jardiniere, Pedestal, 1906-17, 29 x 12 ½ In., Pair	470.00
Roma, Vase, 4-Sided, Pinecones, Needles, Marked, 5 ½ x 10 In.	259.00
Roma, Wall Pocket, Flowers, 10 ½ In.	135.00
Sabrinian, Ewer, Seahorse Handle, Shells, 10 ½ In.	345.00
Sabrinian, Ewer, Shell, Seascape, Seahorse Handles, Mark, c.1930, 9 ½ In.	207.00
Sabrinian, Vase, c.1920, 7 In., Pair	176.00
Sicardo, Jardiniere, Butterfly, Branches, Marked, 8 In.	2530.00
Sicardo, Vase, Bud, Snowflakes, Iridescent Gold, Purple, 4 In.	431.00
Sicardo, Vase, Bulbous, Flowers, Metallic Glaze, Impressed 30, 3 x 9 In. .... *illus*	1560.00
Sicardo, Vase, Bulbous, Ribbed, Flowers, Purple & Green Metallic Glaze, Marked, 5 x 7 In.	720.00
Sicardo, Vase, Daisies, Metallic Luster, Purple, Peach, Green, Upright Handles, 3 In.	173.00
Sicardo, Vase, Exotic Flowers, 4 In.	288.00
Sicardo, Vase, Holly Leaves, Berries, Green, Blue Metallic Glaze, Signed, 5 In.	374.00
Sicardo, Vase, Holly, Metallic Glaze, Broad Shape, 5 x 5 In.	420.00
Sicardo, Vase, Metallic Color Flowers, Marked, 9 In.	575.00
Sicardo, Vase, Narrow, Shouldered, Metallic Glaze, Organic Designs, Signed, 3 ½ x 10 In.	920.00
Sicardo, Vase, Nasturtium, 3-Dimensional, Green, Red, Purple Glaze, 11 In.	7480.00
Sicardo, Vase, Nasturtium, Cylindrical, Signed, 16 ¾ x 4 ½ In.	2074.00
Sicardo, Vase, Ribbed, Etched Flower Design, Metallic Glaze, 2 Handles, Marked, 5 ½ x 6 ½ In.	1800.00
Sicardo, Vase, Scalloped, Daisies, Maroon, Blue, Green, Gold, Handles, Jacques Sicard, 6 x 8 In.	690.00
Sicardo, Vase, Shamrocks, Flowing Design, Purple Ground, 6 ¾ In.	1095.00
Sicardo, Vase, Sorrel Plants, Red, Green, Molded, Painted, Signed J. Sicard, 4 ½ In.	345.00
Sicardo, Vase, Stylized Flowers, Green, Purple, 5 In.	184.00
Sicardo, Vase, Sunflowers, Multicolored Metallic Glaze, 7 ½ x 15 ½ In.	2875.00
Sicardo, Vase, Tulips, 2 Handles, 9 x 9 ½ In.	3416.00
Silvertone, Basket, Flower, Multicolored, Branch Handle, Signed, 8 ½ x 7 In.	235.00
Silvertone, Candleholder, Dolphin Stem, Half Kin Stamp, 6 ½ In., Pair	159.00
Silvertone, Vase, Pink Red Poppies, Lavender Ground, Fluted Mouth, Askew Handles, 8 In. ...	230.00
Umbrella Stand, Birds, Squirrels, Ducks, Faience, Frederick H. Rhead, 22 x 15 In.	4575.00
Umbrella Stand, Clinton Ivory, Molded Renaissance Designs, c.1920, 20 x 11 In.	323.00
Umbrella Stand, Ivory., 24 In.	165.00
Umbrella Stand, Storks, Ducks, Leaves, Flowers, Rhead Faience, Signed, 22 x 15 In. ...... *illus*	4500.00
Vase, Bud, Matte Green, 6-Sided, 11 In.	403.00
Vase, Geisha, Rhead Faience, Signed, 10 ½ x 4 ½ In. .... *illus*	732.00
Vase, Sporting Dog, Marked, Hunter Arms Co. First Prize Class A, Signed, Mae Timberlake, 13 In.	2300.00
Velvetone, Vase, Ruffled Rim, Yellow & Mauve Glaze, 7 In.	125.00

The Sicard Secret

Jacques Sicard, who worked with Clement Massier in Golfe-Juan, France, was hired in 1901 by Samuel Weller because Sicard knew how to create a metallic luster glaze. Weller Pottery was selling Sicard's work, known as Sicardo ware, by 1902. But Sicard was suspicious and worried that Weller would try to steal his glaze techniques, so he worked in secret at the Weller plant. No visitors, no explanations of how he created the Sicardo pieces. When he left in 1907, he took his secret with him and Weller could no longer make the luster glazed pottery.

Weller, Umbrella Stand, Storks, Ducks, Leaves, Flowers, Rhead Faience, Signed, 22 x 15 In. $4500.00

Weller, Vase, Geisha, Rhead Faience, Signed, 10 ½ x 4 ½ In. $732.00

Weller, Warwick, Vase, Branch Handles, 10 ¼ In.
$69.00

Weller, White & Decorated, Vase, Warbler, Hawthorn Branch, Marked, 8 ½ In.
$978.00

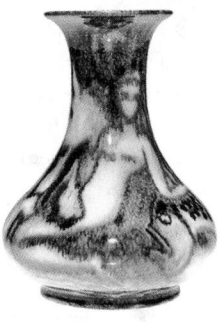

Weller, Wild Rose, Basket, Brown, Green, 5 ¾ In.
$29.00

Weller, Woodcraft, Vase, Brown Slip, 6 ½ In.
$75.00

Warwick, Vase, Branch Handles, 10 ¼ In.	*illus*	69.00
White & Decorated, Vase, Warbler, Hawthorn Branch, Marked, 8 ½ In.	*illus*	978.00
White Rose, Vase, Blue Ground, Petal Shape Foot, Reticulated Handles, Incised, 6 ½ x 5 In.		94.00
Wild Rose, Basket, Brown, Green, 5 ¾ In.	*illus*	29.00
Woodcraft, Bowl, Squirrel, Marked, 5 ⅛ In.		259.00
Woodcraft, Vase, Brown Slip, 6 ½ In.	*illus*	75.00
Woodcraft, Vase, Chalice Form, Tree, Handles Base, 9 ¼ In.		260.00
Woodcraft, Vase, Owl In Tree, 15 ½ In.		1586.00
Woodcraft, Vase, Trunk Shape, Apples, Leaves, Branches, Semimatte Glaze, 1920-33, 9 ½ In.		155.00
Woodcraft, Wall Pocket, Plums, 9 In.		215.00
Woodcraft, Wall Pocket, Squirrel, 10 In.		102.00
Zona, Pitcher, Kingfisher, On Perch, Aged Tree, Marked, 8 ⅜ In.		205.00

WEMYSS Wemyss ware was first made in 1882 by Robert Heron, the owner of Fife Pottery in Kirkaldy, Scotland. Large colorful flowers, hearts, and other symbols were hand painted on figurines, inkstands, jardinieres, candlesticks, buttons, pots, and other items. Fife Pottery closed in 1932. The molds and designs were used by a series of potteries until 1957. In 1985 the Wemyss name and designs were obtained by Griselda Hill. The Wemyss Ware trademark was registered in 1994. Modern Wemyss Ware in old styles is still being made.

Figurine, Cat, Smiling, Pink Cabbage Roses, Glass Eyes, Marked, Nekola Pinxt, 13 In.	3210.00

WESTMORELAND GLASS was made by the Westmoreland Glass Company of Grapeville, Pennsylvania, from 1890 to 1984. The company made clear and colored glass of many varieties, such as milk glass, pressed glass, and slag glass.

Anchor & Yacht, Plate, Milk Glass, 1950s, 7 ⅜ In.		25.00
Animal, Dish, Cat On Basket, Cover, Amethyst, 4 In.	*illus*	55.00
Animal, Dish, Camel Cover, Caramel Slag, 5 ½ x 6 ½ In.	*illus*	71.00
Animal, Dish, Cover, Cat Finial, Green Glass Eyes, Milk Glass, Mark, 8 In.		185.00
Animal, Dish, Hen On Nest Cover, Milk Glass, Blue Head, 4 ½ In.	*illus*	22.00
Animal, Dish, Rabbit Cover, On Fence, Pink Ears & Mouth, Rectangular, 5 In.		45.00
Animal, Dish, Rooster Cover, Basket Design Base, Milk Glass, 7 x 6 ¼ In.		30.00
Ball & Swirl, Basket, Split Handle, Light Amber, 3 ¾ x 5 In.		20.00
Beaded Edge, Bowl, Teddy Cuddles, Milk Glass, Child's, 4 ⅝ In.		75.00
Beaded Edge, Torte Plate, Zodiac Symbols, 14 ½ In.		175.00
Beaded Grape, Box, Cover, Square, Milk Glass, WG Monogram, 5 ¼ x 3 ½ In.		25.00
Beaded Grape, Plate, Salad, Milk Glass, 8 ¼ In.		34.00
Blue Mist, Box, Duck Cover, Oval, Embossed Mark, 8 x 6 x 5 In.		70.00
Box, Lamb Cover, Blue, Fence Pattern Around Box, 5 In.		120.00
Deer Etch, Pitcher, Cover, Pink, Gold, 1930s		160.00
Della Robbia, Candy Dish, Cover, Milk Glass		45.00
Della Robbia, Torte Plate, 1930s, 14 In.		85.00
Doric, Candleholder, Milk Glass, 4 ½ In., Pair		22.00
Doric, Compote, Candy, Green Mist, Pedestal, Crimp Ruffle Bowl, 5 x 5 ¼ In.		35.00
Doric, Compote, Milk Glass, Hand Stretched Lacy Edge, 11 x 7 In.		30.00
English Hobnail, Candy Dish, Cover, Ruby		25.00
English Hobnail, Console Set, Bowl, 2 Candlesticks, Milk Glass, 12 x 10-In. Bowl		55.00
English Hobnail, Cruet, Milk Glass, 5 In.		20.00
English Hobnail, Vase, Jack-In-The-Pulpit Shape, Purple Opalescent, 7 ½ In.		22.00
Figurine, Owl, On Books, Almond Color, Rhinestone Eyes, 3 ½ In.		20.00
Figurine, Robin On Twig Nest, Soft Blue, 6 ¾ In.		129.00
Figurine, Rooster, Standing, Milk Glass, 8 ¾ In.		40.00
Grapes & Vines, Dish, Candy, Milk Glass, Covered		22.00
Holly Sprig, Basket, Handle, Crystal Mist, Marked, 6 ½ In.		27.00
Lacy Daisy, Dish, Rows Of Crisscross Buttons, Clear, 2 ½ In.		13.00
Lotus, Candlestick, Milk Glass, 6 In., Pair		40.00
Lotus, Compote, Footed, Orange, Yellow Highlights, Marked, 6 x 3 ½ In.		35.00
Old Quilt, Compote, Flared Rim, Milk Glass, 5 ¾ x 7 ½ In.		26.00
Old Quilt, Pitcher, Juice, Milk Glass, 7 ¼ In.		24.00
Old Quilt, Pitcher, Syrup, Milk Glass, 3 ½ In.		33.00
Old Quilt, Sugar & Creamer, Milk Glass, 1950s, 3 ⅝ In.		30.00
Paneled Grape, Basket, Split Handle, Oval, Milk Glass, 6 ½ x 3 ⅞ In.		40.00
Paneled Grape, Bowl, Belled, Milk Glass, 3 ½ x 9 ½ In.		55.00
Paneled Grape, Candy Dish, Milk Glass, Marked, 5 x 4 ¾ In.		36.00
Paneled Grape, Cheese Dish, Cover, Milk Glass, 5 ⅛ x 4 ⅝ In.		22.00
Paneled Grape, Cruet, Milk Glass, 4 ¾ In.		22.00
Paneled Grape, Cruet, Milk Glass, Pontil, 5 In.		25.00
Paneled Grape, Decanter, Wine, Golden Sunset, Stopper, 12 ½ In.		95.00

Paneled Grape, Dresser Set, Milk Glass, Roses & Bows, 4 Piece	*illus*	400.00
Paneled Grape, Puff Box, Cover, Milk Glass, c.1960		25.00
Paneled Grape, Sugar & Creamer, Covered Sugar, Milk Glass, 1950s		50.00
Purple Slag, Toothpick, Owl, 2 ½ In.		35.00
Roses & Bows, Vase, Bud, Flung, Slender, Milk Glass, Label, 10 ½ In.		28.00
Roses & Bows, Vase, Bud, Milk Glass, 1950s, 11 In.		40.00
Roses & Bows, Vase, Bud, Milk Glass, 9 ⅝ In.		23.00
Roses & Bows, Vase, Bud, Swung, Paneled Grape, Milk Glass, 8 ¾ In.		25.00
Roses & Bows, Wedding Bowl, Cover, Milk Glass, 9 ½ In.		90.00
Sawtooth, Compote, Open, Blue, Embossed Mark, 8 ¾ x 11 ¾ In.		138.00
Scrolled Spray, Creamer, Cover, Blue Milk Glass, 6 ¼ In.	*illus*	12.00
Swan & Rushes, Sugar & Creamer, Cover, Green	*illus*	45.00
Swan, Toothpick, Milk Glass, 2 ⅜ In.		30.00
Two Seventy, Compote, Scalloped, Base, Iridescent Green, c.1908, 6 x 2 ¼ In.		100.00
Wakefield, Compote, Red & Clear, 7 In.		40.00
Waterford, Compote, Ruby Flash, 10 In.	*illus*	110.00

WHEATLEY POTTERY was established in 1880. Thomas J. Wheatley had worked in Cincinnati, Ohio, with the founders of the art pottery movement, including M. Louise McLaughlin of the Rookwood Pottery. Wheatley Pottery was purchased by the Cambridge Tile Manufacturing Company in 1927.

Fountain, Dolphin, Curled Tail, Open Mouth, Old Red Paint, Incised 7-10-31		219.00
Jardiniere, Mottled Green Matte Glaze, 4-Footed, Round, 7 x 7 In.		510.00 to 780.00
Lamp Base, Green Semimatte Glaze, Bulbous, Decorated Shade, 24 ½ x 20 In.	*illus*	840.00
Plate, Painted, Incised, Lilies, c.1880, 11 In.		1200.00
Tile, 4 Conjoined Circles, Green & Brown Matte Glaze, c.1925, 4 ¼ x 4 ¼ In.		300.00
Tile, Fleur-De-Lis, Gray & Peach Matte Glaze, Raised Outline, c.1915, 6 ⅛ x 6 ⅛ In.		345.00
Tile, Geometric, Salmon, Green, Matte Glaze, c.1910, 4 x 4 In.		195.00
Umbrella Stand, Panel, Seminude Woman, Hexagonal, Marked, Monogram, 21 ½ In.	*illus*	431.00
Vase, Embossed Grapes, Multicolored Thick Matte Glaze, Green Ground, 10 In.		1380.00
Vase, Leaf Mold, Green Matte Glaze, 11 ½ In.		1783.00
Vase, Thistles, Applied, Green Matte Glaze, 11 In.		1700.00
Wall Pocket, Green Matte Glaze, Grape Design, High Relief, 5 x 11 In.		288.00

WHEELING POTTERY COMPANY of Wheeling, West Virginia, worked from 1879 to about 1923. The firm went through a number of mergers and name changes during that time. Pottery, semiporcelain, artware, and sanitary wares were made.

Creamer, Peachblow, Amberina Handle, 3 In.	316.00
Tumbler, Peachblow, Cherry Red Shading To Custard Yellow, 3 ½ In.	115.00
Tumbler, Peachblow, Red To Beige, 3 ⅝ In.	173.00
Vase, Peachblow, Morgan, Seated Resin Griffin Holder, 7 ⅞ In.	1035.00
Vase, Peachblow, Red Shading To Custard Yellow, Marked, 4 ¼ In.	288.00

WILLETS MANUFACTURING COMPANY of Trenton, New Jersey, began work in 1879. The company made belleek in the late 1880s and 1890s in shapes similar to those used by the Irish Belleek factory. It stopped working about 1912. A variety of marks were used, all including the name *Willets*.

Chalice, Trophy, Monk, Smoking Cigar, Pistakee Yacht Club, Signed, Belleek, c.1902, 11 ¼ In.	365.00
Mug, Elk Scene, Gold Trim, c.1907, 5 ¾ In.	50.00
Nut Dish Set, Master, 6 Shell Bowls, Silver Overlay, Footed, Black Willets Mark, c.1900, 7 Piece	447.00
Pitcher, Grapes & Vines, Green, Yellow, Orange Ground, Marked, 6 In.	40.00
Salt Dip, White Ground, Blue Enamel, Gold Garland, Gold Interior, Ruffled Rim, 6 Piece	130.00
Salt Set, Master Salt, 8 Individual Salts, Gold Trim, Green Willets Mark, 9 Piece	305.00
Urn, Theatrical Scenes, Ruffled Rim, 2 Handles, c.1900, 10 ½ In.	501.00
Vase, 7 Song Birds, Leaves, Bulbous, Signed, Belleek, 13 In.	776.00
Vase, Oval, Catalia Orchid, Leaves, c.1900, 18 In.	295.00
Vase, Poppy, Footed, Belleek, Pair	585.00
Vase, Squat, Roses, Marked, Belleek, 5 ¾ x 7 In.	975.00

WILLOW pattern has been made in England since 1780. The pattern has been copied by factories in many countries, including Germany, Japan, and the United States. It is still being made. Willow was named for a pattern that pictures a bridge, birds, willow trees, and a Chinese landscape. Most pieces are blue and white.

Bowl, Cereal, 6 ¾ In.	10.00
Bowl, Cereal, Scio, 6 ⅝ In.	8.00

Westmoreland, Animal, Dish, Cat On Basket, Cover, Amethyst, 4 In. $55.00

Westmoreland, Animal, Dish, Camel, Cover, Caramel Slag, 5 ½ x 6 ½ In. $71.00

Westmoreland, Animal, Dish, Hen On Nest Cover, Milk Glass, Blue Head, 4 ½ In. $22.00

Westmoreland, Paneled Grape, Dresser Set, Milk Glass, Roses & Bows, 4 Piece $400.00

Westmoreland, Scrolled Spray, Creamer, Cover, Blue Milk Glass, 6 ¼ In. $12.00

Westmoreland, Swan & Rushes, Sugar & Creamer, Cover, Green $45.00

Westmoreland, Waterford, Compote, Ruby Flash, 10 In. $110.00

Wheatley, Lamp Base, Green Semimatte Glaze, Bulbous, Decorated Shade, 24 ½ x 20 In. $840.00

Bowl, Vegetable, Pink, Royal China, 9 In.	22.00
Bowl, Vegetable, Royal China, 10 ¼ In.	15.00
Bowl, Water, House, Trees, Bat Printed, 11 In.	150.00
Creamer, Royal China	12.00
Cruet Set, Oil & Vinegar, Handle, 5 ¾ In., Pair	139.00
Cup & Saucer, No Decal In Cup, Johnson Brothers	12.00
Cup, Angled Handle, 2 ¼ In.	15.00
Cup, Marked, Churchill, England, 2 ¾ In.	8.95
Gravy Boat, Allerton's Ltd., 7 ¾ In. ....*illus*	60.00
Mug, Bottom Marked USA, 3 ½ In.	16.00
Plate, Bread & Butter, Johnson Brothers, 6 ⅛ In.	8.00
Plate, Dinner, Back Stamped, Royal China, 10 In.	12.50
Plate, Dinner, Royal China, 9 In.	12.50
Plate, Dinner, Transfer, Johnson Brothers	22.00
Plate, Luncheon, Stamped USA, 7 ¼ In.	9.50
Plate, Salad, Johnson Brothers, 7 ¾ In.	12.00
Platter, Blue Transfer, c.1830, 19 In.	500.00
Platter, Grooved, Late 1800s, 14 ½ x 19 In.	650.00
Platter, Pink, Japan, 8 x 10 ¼ In. ....*illus*	53.00
Salt & Pepper, Blue Willow Top, Teak Wood Base, Cork Stoppers	23.00
Saucer, Japan, 6 In.	4.00
Sugar, Cover, Royal China Co., 3 ¾ In. ....*illus*	15.00
Teapot, Crosshatch Handle, Lid, 6 ¾ In.	75.00
Tureen, Cover, Pink, Churchill England	60.00

WINDOW glass that was stained and beveled was popular for houses during the late nineteenth and early twentieth centuries. The old windows became popular with collectors in the 1970s; today, old and new examples are seen.

Leaded, 2 Parrots & Aquarium, Blue Striation, 2-Layer Plated Aquarium, 26 x 45 In.	16100.00
Leaded, American Arts & Crafts, Wood Frame, Red Inserts, c.1910, 44 x 18 In., Pair	760.00
Leaded, Opalescent Bull's-Eye Jewel, Leaf, Vine, Ribbed Glass, Textured, 12 ½ x 37 In.	748.00
Leaded, Panel, Cathedral Shaped Center, Orange, Green Mottled, Maroon, 14 x 25 ¾ In.	86.00
Leaded, Panel, Frank Lloyd Wright Style, Balloons & Confetti, 34 x 18 & 21 x 7 In., 2 Piece	675.00
Leaded, Pink Center Flower, Purple Flowers, Eastlake, Frame, 1800s, 3 x 4 Ft.	1020.00
Leaded, Red Flowers On Vine, Caramel Panes, Amber, Frame, 53 x 24 In.	145.00
Leaded, Screen, American Art Deco, Wood Frame, c.1920, 74 x 21 In., Pair	819.00
Leaded, Stained, Cornucopia, Faceted, Rippled, c.1910, 27 x 25 In. ....*illus*	819.00
Leaded, Stained, Flower, Leaves, Frame, 68 x 25 In.	201.00
Leaded, Stained, Resurrected Christ, c.1880, 52 x 24 In.	1003.00
Leaded, Stained, Sacred Heart, Cabochon Border, 19th Century, 19 ¼ x 12 ¼ In.	450.00
Leaded, Walnut, Tudor, 18 Amber Stained Panels, Rosettes, c.1900, 66 x 23 In., Pair	210.00
Panel, Clear, Fleur-De-Lis, Scrolls, 8 ½ x 48 In.	448.00
Stained, Arch, Multicolored, Panels, Ripple Glass, Frame, 94 x 37 ½ In.	400.00
Stained, Art Nouveau Style, Clear Diamonds, Yellow Border, Flower Spray, 18 x 27 In.	209.00
Stained, Arts & Crafts, Grapevine, Oak Frame, 11 ¼ x 45 ¼ In., Pair	1920.00
Stained, Crowned Merchant's Symbol, 1700s, 7 x 5 In.	325.00
Stained, Design, Watercolor, Wisconsin Art Glass Co., Mat, Frame, c.1908, 21 x 7 In.	88.00
Stained, Flowers, Blue, Red, Ocher Panels, Frame, 24 ¼ x 49 In.	269.00
Stained, Geometric Design, Early 20th Century, 17 ½ x 55 In.	130.00
Stained, Hand Painted Cherubs, France, c.1900, 36 ½ x 28 In.	24.00
Stained, Jeweled, Center Medallion, Early 20th Century, 85 x 37 In.	354.00
Stained, Josiah Gilbert, Daniel, In Lion's Den, Painted, Mid 1900s, 11 x 35 In.	748.00
Stained, Man, Woman Kissing, Gustav Klimt Style, Frame, 59 ½ x 36 In.	4270.00
Stained, Painted, Roses, Leaves, Mid 20th Century, 17 x 27 In.	489.00
Stained, Red, Blue, Amber, Geometric Circles, 33 x 24 In.	269.00
Stained, Tiffany Style, Grape Arbor, Frame, 42 ½ x 41 ½ In. ....*illus*	5700.00
Stained, Transom, Arched, Slag Glass, Jewel, Early 1900s, 16 x 32 In.	142.00

WOOD CARVINGS and wooden pieces are listed separately in this book. Many of the wood carvings are figurines or statues. There are also wooden pieces found in other categories, such as Kitchen.

3 Fish, Rocks, 9 x 41 In.	105.00
3 Owls, On Knotted Log, Brown & Gold Paint, Turned Wood Base, 14 ½ x 7 ½ In.	2300.00
Abstract, Driftwood, Stump, Yellow, Red, Black, c.1980s, 17 ½ In.	44.00
Adam & Eve, White Pine, Red Black Wash, Detail Facial Features, 8 ½ x 13 In., Pair	110.00

African Man, Facial Details, Knife Carved Hair, Black....................	55.00
Alligator, Vertical Line, White Painted Teeth, Red Mouth, Glass Eye, 4 x 20 ½ In.	88.00
Angel, Altar, Oak, High Relief, Cascading Hair, Flat Back, c.1920, 6 Ft., Pair...........	1200.00
Angel, Holding Banner, Oak, Silver Leaf, Germany, 1800s, 9 x 15 In.	390.00
Angel, Kneeling, Stained Oak, Outspread Wings, c.1800, 17 ¼ x 33 x 4 In.	1200.00
Angel, Multicolored, Gilt, Standing, Spain, 18th Century, 20 x 11 ¼ In., Pair	4700.00
Angel, Plaster, Painted, Gilt Scroll, Playing Harp, Guitar, 14 In., Pair............	450.00
Angel, Spread Wings, 9 x 17 In.	130.00
Antelope, On Rock Pile, Black Forest, 7 x 5 In.	284.00
Apostle, Seated, Book, Lamb, Polychrome, Gold, Gesso, c.1800, 34 x ½ In.	11258.00
Arm, Spread Hand, Old Paint, c.1800s, 8 ½ x 13 In.	830.00
Artist Model, Ball Joints, Stand, 1800s, 30 ½ In.	1896.00
Ashtray, Black Forest, Bear, Early 1900s, 3 ½ x 3 ½ In.	185.00
Ashtray, Totem Pole, Painted, Adirondack, 1930s, 29 In.	193.00
Atlas, Supports Blue Globe, Tapering, Stepped Base, Dutch, 16 ¼ In.	533.00
Bacchus With Grapes, Chalice, P. Vinotti, 20th Century, Italy, 67 In.	3713.00
Bag Stamp, Oval, Pegged & Nailed, Relief Carved 1840, Compass Wheels, 1 ½ x 7 ⅝ In.	248.00
Ball & Chain, Whimsy, 1-Piece Carving, Rectangular Links, Free Floating Balls, 6 ½ Ft.........	143.00
Basket, Burl, Gnarled Handle, Tree Trunk Stand, 10 ¼ In.	1000.00
Bavarian Boy, Feeding Fawn, Stained, 20th Century, Germany, 15 In.	56.00
Bear, Cub At Side, Cub On Shoulder, Frog On Ground, Black Forest, 20 In.	1725.00
Bear, Glass Eyes, Black Forest, Brienz, Switzerland, 17 ½ x 13 ½ In.	3565.00
Bear, On Stump, Incised Fur, Teepee, Signed, R. Crowe, Cherokee, N.C., 3 ½ x 6 In.	99.00
Bear, Seated, Cross-Legged, Open Mouth, Black Forest, 10 ¾ In.	575.00
Bear, Standing, Mouth Open, Base, Black Forest, 14 ½ x 6 In.	535.00
Bird, Open Wings, Perched On Rockwork, Red Stained Pedestal, 30 x 20 In.	9775.00
Bird, Preening, Green Mound, Multicolored, Signed, D&DS, 1992, 8 ¾ In.	147.00
Bird, Red-Breasted Robin, Singing, Standing In Open Red Flower, Pine, 12 In., Pair.............	20000.00
Bird, Robin, Wire Legs, Applied Wings, Feather Lines, Tack Eyes, c.1935, 8 x 4 ½ In.	125.00
Bison, Brass Horns, Hagenauer Wein, Mid 20th Century, 12 In.	431.00
Blackamoor, Coat, Vest, Bowtie............................	2260.00
Bowl, Blue Gray Paint, Turned, Patina, 6 ½ x 19 ½ In.	862.00
Bowl, Burl, Turned, Patina, 3 x 11 ¾ In.	1265.00
Bowl, Formed From Hollowed Out Log, Beech, 19th Century, 12 x 37 ½ x 23 ½ In.	805.00
Bowl, Maple, Turned, Figured, 19th Century, 20 ½ In. Diam.	260.00
Bowl, Pipe, Cupped Hand Shape, c.1890, 2 In.	444.00
Bowl, Turned, Red Paint, 19th Century, 22 In. Diam................	226.00
Box, Black Forest, Carved, Bear, On Log, Late 1800s, 6 ¾ x 3 ½ In.	650.00
Boy, On St. Bernard Rescue Dog, Linden Wood, Black Forest, c.1900, 16 x 14 In.	2645.00
Brushpot, Bamboo, Carved Figural Scenes, Chinese, 5 x 6 In.	468.00
Buddha, Gilt, India, c.1935, 82 x 32 In.	761.00
Burled Slab, Rosewood Stand, Organic Shape, Chinese, c.1900, 17 ¾ x 12 In.	153.00
Busk, Pine, Heart Design, c.1830, 12 ½ In.	147.00
Busk, Ships, Heart, Pinwheel, Celtic Designs, 1700s, 14 In.	705.00
Bust, Bacchus, Stained, Germany, 9 ¼ In.	101.00
Bust, Benjamin Franklin, Walnut, Shaped Base, 18 In.	1380.00
Bust, Old Man Thinking, Walnut, c.1900, 7 ¾ In. .... *illus*	270.00
Canada Goose, Flying Position, Tin Wings, 29 x 33 In.	1693.00
Canada Goose, Hardwood, Original Paint, Glass Eye, 1900s, 10 x 26 In.	823.00
Cardinal, On Nest, Poplar, Detailed, Signed, C. Stringfield, 5 ¼ x 8 ¼ In.	77.00
Cat Head, Black, Red, White, Yellow, 10 ½ x 9 In.	310.00
Cat, Cedar Rail Fence, Paint, Quebec, c.1940, 8 x 16 In.	498.00
Cat, Lying Down, Multicolored, Donna Long, 1988, 6 ¼ In.	66.00
Checker Players, Checkerboard, Walnut, Detailed Features, 8 ¼ x 7 ¼ x 12 In.	99.00
Cherubs, On Dolphin, Signed, Ricardo Merino, 1908, 15 ¾ In., Pair.	545.00
Chinese Figure, Sitting On Basket, Under Tree, Boxwood, 8 ½ In.	172.00
Church Spire, Pine, Telescoping, Hearts, Top Cross, 31 ½ In.	711.00
Container, Turned, Lid, Vinegar Sponged Design, 6 ¾ x 6 ½ In.	1116.00
Cowboy, Yellow Pine, Detailed Clothing, Face, Signed, JMS, 17 ¼ In.	215.00
Crab, Base, Mahogany, Early 20th Century, 21 ¼ x 17 In.	605.00
Creche Figure, Angel, Cloth, Painted, Neapolitan, 1820s, 12 In.	465.00
Creche Figure, Man, Seated, Holding Walking Stick, Cloth, Painted, 18th Century, 17 In.	595.00
Creche Figure, Man, Standing, Wearing Turban, Cloth, Painted, 18th Century, 10 In.	2675.00
Creche Figure, Old Woman, Arm Out, Cloth, Painted, 18th Century, 18 In.	185.00
Creche Figure, Spanish Colonial, Multicolored, 1800s, 3 To 7 ½ In., 7 Piece........................	441.00
Creche Figure, Woman, Seated, Porcelain Head, Cloth, Painted, 18th Century, 12 In.	388.00

Wheatley, Umbrella Stand, Panel, Seminude Woman, Hexagonal, Marked, Monogram, 21 ½ In.
$431.00

Willow, Gravy Boat, Allerton's Ltd., 7 ¾ In.
$60.00

Willow, Platter, Pink, Japan, 8 x 10 ¼ In.
$53.00

Willow, Sugar, Cover, Royal China Co., 3 ¾ In.
$15.00

WOOD CARVING

Window, Leaded, Stained, Cornucopia, Faceted, Rippled, c.1910, 27 x 25 In. $819.00

Window, Stained, Tiffany Style, Grape Arbor, Frame, 42 ½ x 41 ½ In. $5700.00

Wood Carving, Bust, Old Man Thinking, Walnut, c.1900, 7 ¾ In. $270.00

Wood Carving, Putto, On Sphere, Baroque, Gilt, Austro-Germany, 20 x 9 In. $390.00

Creche Figure, Woman, Standing, Cloth, Painted, Neapolitan, 18th Century, 21 In.	595.00
Crest, Regency Style, Giltwood, Carved, Floral Spray, Scallop Shell, 7 x 17 In.	510.00
Cresting, Neoclassical, Giltwood, Stylized Leaf, Scrolls, France, Late 1800s, 9 x 9 In.	480.00
Crucifix, Corpus Set On Cross, Vines, Rocky Base, Black Forest, c.1880, 30 ¼ In.	1080.00
Cup, Libation, Magnolia & Cherry Blossoms, Metal Liner, Chinese, 3 ¼ In.	175.00
Deer, Head Bent, Antlers In Branch, Germany, 20th Century, 15 ½ In.	46.00
Deer, Lying Down, Brass Antlers, Hagenauer Wein, Mid 20th Century, 16 In.	748.00
Deer, Stained, Germany, 20th Century, 10 ¼ In.	23.00
Devil Head, Wall Hanging, Blue Eyes, Red Lips, Horns, Signed, Jim Lewis, c.1991, 14 ½ In.	66.00
Diorama, Sailing Ship, Wire Rigging, Painted, Shadowbox Frame, 23 x 32 In.	470.00
Dog, Glass Eyes, Black Forest, c.1900, 8 In.	690.00
Dog, Green Surface, Late 19th Century, 16 ½ In.	4446.00
Dog, Walnut, Terrier On Hind Legs, Paws On Shield, Platform Base, 6 x 17 In.	575.00
Dragon, Foo Dog, Ivory Claws, Teeth, Teak Stand, 8 x 12 In.	60.00
Dragon, Mouth Open, Painted Details, Gold Trim, Southeast Asia, 28 x 80 In.	460.00
Duck, On Flint Rock Base, Green, Yellow, Varnish, 3 x 4 In.	22.00
Duck, Preening Posture, Glass Eye, Wire Legs, Paint, 17 ½ In.	173.00
Eagle, Bellamy Style, 20th Century, 29 In.	115.00
Eagle, Figurehead, Gilded, Wood Plinth, c.1890, 22 In.	2133.00
Eagle, Hardwood, Perched On Rocks, Spread Winged, Gilt, 16 ½ x 38 ½ In.	969.00
Eagle, Holding Banner, Bellamy Style, 29 In.	118.00
Eagle, Multicolored, Stretched Neck, Signed, June & Walter Gottshall, 18 ¼ In.	509.00
Eagle, On Pedestal, Spread Wings, Painted, 50 ½ In.	207.00
Eagle, On Stand, Spread Wings, Plinth, Gilt, c.1900, 17 ½ In.	575.00
Eagle, On Stump, Chain Saw Carved, Tooled Feathered Surface, Glass Eyes, 43 ½ x 21 In.	209.00
Eagle, Pedestal, Standing On Orb, Lectern Shelf, Mahogany, Paint, c.1890, 44 x 32 In.	1896.00
Eagle, Pine, Laminated, Charleston, Spread Wings, 54 In.	633.00
Eagle, Pine, Spread Wings, Banner, Don't Give Up The Ship, Red, White, Blue, 45 ½ In.	9987.00
Eagle, Spread Wings, c.1860, 68 In.	7800.00
Eagle, Spread Wings, Cannon, Balls, Arrows, Gilt, 1800s, 8 x 18 In.	4740.00
Eagle, Spread Wings, Holding Arrows, Flag Badge, Gilt, Painted, 17 x 44 In.	1870.00
Eagle, Spread Wings, Multicolored, Green Base, Strawser, 13 x 19 In.	187.00
Eagle, Spread Wings, Multicolored, Green Mound, Gottshall, Signed, 10 In.	226.00
Eagle, Spread Wings, On Ball, Hooked Beak, Metal Rod, Cross Base, 28 x 18 x 23 In.	1495.00
Eagle, Spread Wings, Talons, Gilt, 10 ½ x 36 In.	2185.00
Egret, Walnut, Varnished, Signed, c.1970-80s, 15 ½ In.	44.00
Elephant, Ivory Tusks, Toes, c.1900, 11 x 14 x 6 In.	178.00
Elk, Walking, Glass Eyes, Rocks, Black Forest, 14 ½ x 17 In.	863.00
Filipino Princess, c.1975, 62 In.	59.00
Finial, Neoclassical, Vase Shape, Painted White, Fitted As Lamp Base, 11 x 5 ¼ In., Pair	660.00
Finial, Newel Post, White Cut, Cobalt Blue Glass, Brass Collar, c.1850, 6 ¼ In., Pair	206.00
Fish, 2 Brook Trout, Plaque, Painted, 12 x 28 In.	1380.00
Fish, Bass, Plaque, Painted, Signed, 12 x 28 In.	1265.00
Fish, Brook Trout, Plaque, Birchbark, Maine Shape, Painted, Signed, 34 x 21 ½ In.	4083.00
Fish, Char, Plaque, Painted, Signed, 15 x 33 In.	2818.00
Fish, Perch, Plaque, Painted, Signed, 9 ½ x 15 In.	1380.00
Fish, Pickerel, Plaque, Painted, Signed, 8 x 22 In.	1495.00
Fish, Salmon, Tandem Streamer Fly In Mouth, Maine State Plaque, Signed, 28 x 18 In.	4313.00
Fisherman, Bamboo, Chinese, 7 In.	2390.00
Flower Bouquet, Hardwood, 2 Flowers, Leaves, Bloom, c.1900, 11 ½ In.	33.00
Foo Dog, Standing, Painted, Pedestal Base, Chinese, Early 1900s, 17 ½ x 9 ½ In.	115.00
Frame, Easel Back, Softwood, Chip Carved, Early 20th Century, 12 ½ x 8 ½ In.	294.00
Frog, Teak, Paint Eyes, 1 x 2 In., Pair	65.00
God Of Longevity, Dog, 6 In.	529.00
Holy Basin, Louis XV Style, Walnut, Shell, Acanthus, Porcelain Basin, c.1860, 15 x 10 In.	845.00
Horse Head, Softwood, Glass Eyes, 20th Century, 22 In.	1410.00
Horse, Caparisoned, White Painted, North Indian, 19 x 28 x 8 In.	1800.00
Horse, Gesso Paint, Glass Eyes, Leather Ears, Horsehair Mane, Tail, c.1900, 22 ½ x 27 In.	207.00
Horse, Jockey On Horse, Painted, Stand, Marked, 1890-1910, 13 In.	1093.00
Horse, Spotted, Sleigh, Driver, Passenger, Original Paint, 25 In.	13500.00
Humidor, Bamboo, Relief, Chinese, Early 20th Century, 6 ½ In.	60.00
Humidor, Owl, Feathers, Glass Eyes, Base, Late 19th Century, 13 In.	1610.00
Humidor, Snake In Skull, Frog Finial, 6 ½ In.	245.00
Hunter, Dog, Duet, White Pine, Painted, c.1990, 8 In.	44.00
Huntsman, Pipe, Gun, Dog, Stained, 20th Century, Germany, 16 ¾ In.	169.00
Immortals, Attendants, On Cloud Plinth, Chinese, 12 ¼ In.	227.00

Intertwined Shapes, Burled Wood, Dark, High Gloss Finish, c.1950, 16 x 28 In.	780.00
Japanese Merchant, Seated 10 In.	82.00
Jardiniere, Pedestal, Tripod Base, Late 1800s, 41 x 27 In.	1975.00
King David, Nude, Slingshot Over Shoulder, Walnut, 86 ½ x 27 ½ x 14 ½ In.	500.00
Knot Of Abundance, Giltwood, Carved, Pomegranates, Leaf Scroll Terminal, 8 ½ x 52 In.	600.00
Last Supper, 20th Century, 7 x 15 In.	472.00
Lion, Reclining, France, 19th Century, 10 ½ In.	235.00
Lohan, Standing On Rock, Smiling, Opens Gourd, Glass Eyes, Chinese, 43 x 16 x 13 In.	690.00
Longhorn Bull, White Pine, Detailed Hooves, Features, 4 ½ x 5 ½ In.	66.00
Looking Glass Crest, Baroque Style, Pine, Cartouche Shape, Flowers, Gilding, 13 x 25 In.	570.00
Lumberjack, Button Eyes, Leather Nose, Bear Hair Beard, Stand, 1800s, 11 In.	4740.00
Man, Afro-American, Watermelon, Overalls, White Beard, Hair, c.1970-80, 8 ¾ In.	88.00
Man, In Boot, Red Cap, Collared Boot, Multicolored, 10 ¾ In.	68.00
Man, Poplar, Blue Shirt, Green Hat, Bowtie, Painted, c.1900, 10 ½ In.	88.00
Man, Poplar, Yellow Shirt, Black Hat, Bowtie, Signed, J.B. Bailey, c.1900, 11 ½ In.	110.00
Man, Reclining, Black Paint, Gilt Highlights, Red Block, Plastic Plinth, 6 x 17 In.	236.00
Man, Tribal, Congo, 12 ½ x 4 In.	518.00
Man, White Pine, Detailed, 7 In.	22.00
Mask, Distorted Shaman Face, Black, White Halves, Congo, 13 x 8 In.	3360.00
Mask, Helmet, Painted, Bulbous Head, Anteater, Glass Eyes, Raffia Collar, Zaire, 23 In.	240.00
Mask, Mendi, Helmut, Sowowui, Dome Form, Fiber, Rope Collar, Sierra Leone, 35 ½ In.	600.00
Mask, Oak, Gilded, Putto, Wind Mantled, Germany, 10 ½ x 5 ½ In.	360.00
Mask, Yaruba Masquerade, Painted, Downcast Eyes, Carved Beads, Nigeria, 14 In.	300.00
Michael The Archangel, Painted, Spanish Colonial, 15 In.	478.00
Millner's Model, Jointed Arms, Painted, Slatted Base, France, Early 1800s, 35 ½ In.	2115.00
Model, Pine, Artist, Arm, Hand, Stand, c.1800s, 18 In.	1422.00
Mold, Snowman Carrying Firewood, 15 ½ x 9 x 8 In.	450.00
Monk, Saint, Robes, Mounted Metal Nimbus, Gesso, Black, Gold Paint, c.1800, 21 In.	652.00
Mountain Goat, Black Forest, Late 1800s, 17 ¾ x 10 In.	1150.00
Nude Woman, Leaning Backwards, Jose Pinal, Tiered Base, Dark Wood, Mexico, 24 In.	600.00
Ornament, Eagle, Painted Black, Spread Wings, Turned Head, 1800s, 10 x 22 In., Pair	259.00
Ornament, Scrolls, Fish Head Terminals, Gilt Trim, Oak, 18 In., Pair	345.00
Owl, Black Forest, c.1830, 20 x 10 In.	2600.00
Owl, Cat's-Eye Marble Eyes, Base, Paint, 1900s, 11 In.	206.00
Owl, Head, 6 In.	295.00
Owl, On Stump, Maple, Patina, Signed, Wm. H. Crowe, Cherokee, N.C., 4 ½ In.	55.00
Owl, Painted, 18 In.	226.00
Paddle, Grain, 19th Century, 43 x 11 In.	30.00
Panel, Hunter With Stag, Walnut, Late 1800s, 8 ½ x 11 In.	403.00
Panel, Launch Of 3-Masted Schooner, Factory, Richard S. Spofford, 12 x 47 In.	6250.00
Panel, Napoleon III, Boiserie, Flowers, Bas-Relief, Gilded, White Paint, 30 x 9 ½ In.	1080.00
Panel, Supra Porta, Louis XVI, Beechwood, Napoleon III, Painted, 17 x 49 In.	960.00
Panel, Supra Porta, Louis XVI, Center Scroll Mantled Vase, Rondels, 28 x 39 In., Pair	4320.00
Peacock, Painted, Red, Black Tail, Blue, Gold, 6 x 7 ¾ In.	77.00
Penguin, Whimsical, Charles Hart, c.1925, 5 ½ In.	1121.00
Picture, Buck & Doe In Woods, Lake, Vernon-Salem Mass., Frame, c.1880, 17 x 18 In.	1400.00
Pig, Grooved Feet, Painted, 13 x 22 x 12 In.	978.00
Pig, Seated, Multicolored, Black Spots, Signed, June & Walter, 4 ½ In.	113.00
Pig, Standing, Softwood, Brown, Ohio, Early 20th Century, 7 x 13 ½ In.	176.00
Piglet, White Pine, 2 ½ x 5 In.	22.00
Pine Tree, 1 Side With Bark, Chainsaw Carved, Oak, Sternal, 78 In.	275.00
Plaque, 2 Cherubs With Horn, Ricardo Merino, 1908, 11 ½ x 13 In.	201.00
Plaque, Angel, Winged Figure, Holding Urn, Costa Rica, 19 ½ In.	59.00
Plaque, Cherub's Head, Wings, Fruitwood, 17 ½ In.	385.00
Plaque, Eagle, American Flag, U.S. Shield, c.1950, 16 x 53 In.	5175.00
Plaque, Eagle, Banner, Don't Give Up The Ship, Attributed J. Bellamy, 1836-1914, 9 x 26 In.	51750.00
Plaque, Eagle, Banner, Wood, Carved, Gilded, Red, Blue, Artistic Carving Co., c.1950, 16 x 46 In.	3851.00
Plaque, Eagle, Blue Banner, Live & Let Live, Shield, Gilt, c.1945, 25 x 72 In.	5925.00
Plaque, Eagle, Draped Flags, Banner, E. Plurbis Unum, Gilt, Red, White, Blue, Signed, 25 x 42 In.	3450.00
Plaque, Eagle, Pine, Shield, Banner, Don't Give Up The Ship, Painted, c.1910, 10 x 29 In.	3081.00
Plaque, Eagle, Spread Wings, Shield, Canon, c.1900, 23 x 41 In.	4740.00
Plaque, Fish & Fauna, 12 x 43 ½ In.	85.00
Plaque, Giltwood, Rococo Style, Putti Heads, Stylized Cloud, Austro-German, 8 ½ x 11 In.	570.00
Plaque, Hunting, Oak, 3-D Hunting Dog Head, Pond Scene, 67 x 31 In.	4600.00
Plaque, Man On Horseback, D.P. Kurtz, c.1800, 5 x 8 In.	207.00
Plaque, Provincial, Mounted Turk, Austrian Officer, Multicolored, Oval, c.1807, 15 x 13 In.	600.00

Wood Carving, Shelf Bracket, Boar's Head, Fox's Head, Scrolls, Schwarzwald, 9 ¾ x 7 In., Pair
$420.00

Wood Carving, Squirrel, Red, Eating Nut, Wilhelm Schimmel, Penn., 4 In.
$25740.00

Wood Carving, Tiger, Bone Teeth, Glass Eyes, 8 x 8 to 9 x 8 In., 3 Piece
$46.00

Wooden, Bowl, Burl, Carved Ends, Cutout Handles, Stained, 1800s, 9 ¼ In.
$382.00

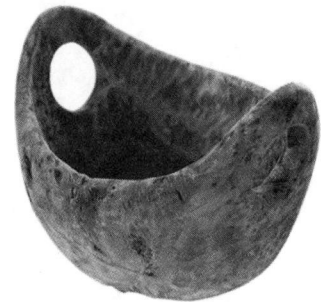

Wooden, Cheese Tray, Mahogany, 19th Century, 8 ½ x 18 In. $439.00

Wooden, Tray, Burlwood, Glossy Finish, 2 Handles, 17 x 11 In. $207.00

Wooden, Wine Rack, Oak, Brass, Beveled Edge, Drawer, Bun Feet, Holds 6, 1800s, 14 x 16 In. $527.00

Pocketwatch Holder, Falcon, On Rocks, Branch Hook, 6 ½ x 4 In.	255.00
Policeman, Poplar, Painted, Detailed Features, Movable Arms, c.1990, 8 In.	110.00
Propeller, Airplane, c.1918, 6 Ft.	299.00
Putto Head, Pine, Singing, Winged, Austro-Bavarian, c.1775, 30 x 28 x 13 In.	2040.00
Putto, On Sphere, Baroque, Gilt, Austro-Germany, 20 x 9 In. .... *illus*	390.00
Quail, Walnut Base, Painted, Marked, 10 ¾ In.	288.00
Rabbit Hunter, Antler Skis, Glass Eyes, Lindenwood, Germany, c.1875, 10 ½ In.	840.00
Rabbit, White, Pink Costume Jewelry Eyes, J. Lemire, Quebec, 19 x 13 ½ In.	523.00
Rattlesnake, Diamond Shape Head, Rattler, Glass Eyes, Signed, Tony Dills, 1900s, 13 ½ In.	44.00
Raven, Octagonal Base, Strawser, Signed, 1977, 12 In.	158.00
Rooster, Multicolored, Schimmel Type, Signed, DS, 1982, 11 In.	124.00
Rooster, Painted, Wilhelm Schimmel Style, 22 In.	767.00
Rooster, Pine, 12 In.	4680.00
Rooster, Pine, Aaron Mountz, 12 In.	4800.00
Rooster, Tin Comb, Tail, Multicolored, Foutz, 20 ½ In.	132.00
Santo, Madonna, Folded Hands, Multicolored, Spain, 18th Century, 10 ¾ In.	113.00
Scroll Pot, Rootwood, Natural Openings, Chinese, 1900s, 17 In.	460.00
Seal, Black Forest, Bear, Early 1900s, 4 ¼ x 5 ½ In.	195.00
Seaman, Bearded, White Pine, Blue Coat, Brown Pants, Black Hat, Shoes, 5 ¾ In.	33.00
Shade, Hans-Agne Jakobsson, Round, Thin Wood Strips, Signed, Sweden, 19 x 17 In.	270.00
Sheep, Glass Eyes, Leather Ears, Paint, Schoenhut, Philadelphia, 1820s, 5 ½ x 8 In.	1304.00
Shelf Bracket, Boar's Head, Fox's Head, Scrolls, Schwarzwald, 9 ¾ x 7 In., Pair .... *illus*	420.00
Shield, American Flag, Stars & Stripes, Red, White, Blue, 31 x 23 In.	236.00 to 240.00
Shorebird, Running Dowitcher, Virginia, c.1900, 8 In.	238.00
Soldier, Royal Guard, Teak, Oak, Furry Hat, Head, Conical Base, Denmark, 6 In.	55.00
Sphinx, Crouching, Raised Wings, Empire Style, Mahogany, 37 In., Pair	5807.00
Squirrel, Red, Eating Nut, Wilhelm Schimmel, Penn., 4 In. .... *illus*	25740.00
Squirrel, Running, Hardwood, Gray Overpaint, 20th Century, 14 ½ In.	118.00
St. Anthony, Painted, Spanish Colonial, 10 In.	418.00
St. Michael, Ecclesiastic Figure, Wearing Gilt Circlet, Gesso, Painted, Italy, 43 In.	2252.00
Stag, Trophy Antlers, 19th Century, 50 x 55 In.	4500.00
Statue, Bishop, Wearing Miter, Vestment, Pine, Stained, 32 In.	1896.00
Statue, Male Saint, Long Beard, Flowing Robe, Hands Crossed At Wrists, 33 In.	1304.00
Statue, Man, Playing Cavaquinho, Multicolored, Continental, 48 x 15 In.	529.00
Stick, Ruyi, Carved Pomegranates, Vines, Chinese, 13 In.	410.00
Swan, Glass Eyes, Original Paint, White, Black, Frank Finney, 15 x 30 In.	2115.00
Swan, Whistling, Signed Harnham, Paint, Glass Eye, 1900s, 7 x 16 In.	88.00
Tantalus, 2 Bears, Holding Tree Stump, Walnut, Decanter, Cordials, Black Forest, 16 x 13 In.	3100.00
Tantalus Set, 2 Doors, Goat Head, Leaf Mullions, Glassware, Black Forest, 14 x 15 In.	690.00
The Mexican, Signed, Andy Anderson, c.1950, 9 ½ In.	1200.00
Tiger, Bone Teeth, Glass Eyes, 8 x 8 To 9 x 8 In., 3 Piece .... *illus*	46.00
Trencher, Salmon Paint, 20 In.	195.00
Turtle, Painted, Yellow Daubs, Red Eyes, Late 19th Century, 3 x 8 ½ In.	3525.00
Vase, Rosewood, Narrow Base, Wide Top, 1980s, 18 ½ x 9 In.	2760.00
Virgin Mary, On Cloud, Moon, Cherub, 19th Century, 13 ½ In.	264.00
Virgin Mary, Painted, Glass Eyes, Spanish Colonial, 18 ¾ In.	777.00
Waiter, Formal Attire, Painted, 1920s, 59 In.	8500.00
Whale, Flat-Sided, Voorhees, Signed, 1950s, 12 In.	3450.00
Whirligig, Applied Metal Stars, Wood Propeller, Paint, Stand, 11 x 17 In.	415.00
William Penn, Walnut, Full Body, Gold Paint, Rev. Robert S. Grier, 1853 12 ½ In.	7703.00
Woman Dancer, Mahogany, Art Deco, J.J., Adnet, Signed, 13 ½ x 6 In.	10370.00
Woman, Child, Henry More, c.1940, 3 ½ x 12 ½ In.	510.00
Woman, Pipe, Wash Board, Basin, Mark, Edsel Martin, 9 ½ In.	690.00
Woman, Saint, Colonial, Ivory Eyes, Tunic, Red Slippers, Spain, 1800s, 43 In.	474.00
Woman, Squat Legs, Round Buttocks, Bulging Belly, Spherical Breasts, Mali, 43 ½ In.	780.00
Woodpecker, Cockatoo, On Wooded Perches, Glass Bell Dome, 22 ¾ In.	173.00
Yoke, Oxen, Red Paint, 19th Century, 38 In.	110.00

WOODEN wares were used in all parts of the home. Wood was used for many containers and tools. Small wooden pieces are called treenware in England, but the term *woodenware* is more common in the United States. Additional pieces may be found in the Advertising, Kitchen, and Tool categories.

Bag Holder, Softwood, Graduated Shelves, Painted Red, Black Stenciled, 16 x 15 x 8 ¼ In.	593.00
Barrel, Ice Cream, Bucket Shape, Iron Handles, Straps, Incised, 18 x 26 In.	70.00
Barrel, Oval, Wood Banding, Open Handle, 27 ½ In.	259.00
Basket Tree, Pine Branch, 3-Footed Base, c.1900, 60 ½ In.	4411.00

Book Slide, Walnut, Fox & Hare, 19th Century, 6 ½ x 22 In.	612.00
Bowl, Ale, White Flowers, Blue Scrolls, Red Interior, Blue Border, Green, Norway, 1868, 3 x 9 In.	835.00
Bowl, Ash Burl, Flared Cone Shape, c.1800, 3 ¾ x 9 ½ In.	1116.00
Bowl, Ash Burl, Footed, Beaded Rim, 19th Century, 14 In.	1880.00
Bowl, Ash Burl, Late 18th Century, 6 ½ x 16 In.	2938.00
Bowl, Ash Burl, Oblong, Carved Handles, 19th Century, 7 x 15 ¼ In.	5875.00
Bowl, Ash Burl, Oval, c.1800, 7 x 21 In.	2703.00
Bowl, Ash Burl, Thick Sides, Square Cut Handholds, 10 x 24 x 23 In.	12500.00
Bowl, Burl, 3 Painted Plaster Fruit, c.1900, 4 x 10 In.	356.00
Bowl, Burl, Carved Ends, Cutout Handles, Stained, 1800s, 9 ¼ In. .... *illus*	382.00
Bowl, Burl, Incised Decorations, 1800s, 4 x 11 ½ In.	382.00
Bowl, Burl, New England, 19th Century, 3 x 9 In.	115.00
Bowl, Burl, Round, c.1800, 5 x 12 In.	940.00
Bowl, Burl, Spout, Gouged Exterior, Smooth Interior, 1800s, 5 x 11 In.	176.00
Bowl, Cherry, Tage Frid, 6 x 4 In.	60.00
Bowl, Cypress Knee, Polished, Free-Form, 20 ½ x 55 ¼ x 45 ½ In.	960.00
Bowl, Green Paint, 19th Century, 21 In.	495.00
Bowl, Knotted Pine, Ron Kent, 7 ½ x 7 In.	854.00
Bowl, Laminated, Orange, Red, Paavo Asikainen, Finland, 7 ½ x 6 In.	55.00
Bowl, Mahogany, Half Turnings, c.1890, 6 x 8 In.	382.00
Bowl, Maple Burl, Turned Molded Rim, Late 18th Century, 5 ¼ x 14 ¾ In.	2300.00
Bowl, Maple, Pinwheels, Tulips, 19th Century, 7 ¾ In.	117.00
Bowl, Maple, Turned, 19th Century, 11 In.	30.00
Bowl, Nesting, Turned, Red Wash, 11 ½ To 21 In., 4 Piece.....................	1888.00
Bowl, Oblong, Blue Interior, c.1800, 7 x 24 In.	1234.00
Bowl, Pistachio, Bob Stocksdale, 1988, 5 x 10 ¾ In.	1098.00
Bowl, Poplar, Collared Rim, 19th Century, 31 In.	499.00
Bowl, Rice, 10 x 28 x 29 In.	1093.00
Bowl, Salad, Stainless Steel Band, Jens Quistgaard, 11 In.	225.00
Bowl, Softwood, Red Paint, 19th Century, 23 ¾ x 9 ¼ In.	441.00
Bowl, Spalted Maple, Mark Lindquist, 1976, 6 x 9 In.	900.00
Bowl, Staved Teak, 2 Sections, Dansk IHQ, Denmark, 13 x 9 In.	45.00
Bowl, Staved Teak, Round, Oval Opening, Ducks Logo, Jens Quistgaard, Dansk, 12 x 5 In.	155.00
Bowl, Teak, Hand Carved, Handles, Scandinavian, 15 x 9 ½ In.	225.00
Bowl, Teak, Laur Jensen, Denmark, 13 x 7 ½ In.	105.00
Bowl, Teak, Oval, Quistgaard, Dansk, 14 x 9 In.	150.00
Bowl, Tiger Maple, c.1810, 19 ½ In.	1450.00
Bowl, Treen, 1800s, 7 ½ In.	889.00
Bowl, Treen, 19th Century, 3 ¼ x 12 ½ In.	115.00
Bowl, Treen, Maple, Oblong, Light Blue Paint, 1800s, 22 In.	588.00
Bowl, Treen, Turned, Blue Paint, 1800s, 4 ½ x 13 In.	3318.00
Bowl, Trencher, Blue Gray Paint, 18th Century, 20 In.	177.00
Bowl, Trencher, Oval, 18th Century, 23 ½ In.	177.00
Bowl, Turned, Light Blue Paint, 1800s, 3 x 8 In.	3437.00
Bowl, Turned, Red Paint, 1800s, 5 x 13 In.	1067.00
Bowl, Turned, Waxed, Continental, 19th Century, 6 ½ x 14 ½ In.	300.00
Bowl, Viking, Teak, Jens Quistgaard, Dansk, 10 x 10 In.	175.00
Brush Holder, Inlaid, Rabbit, Flowering Prunus Branch, Chinese, 5 ½ In.	239.00
Brush Holder, Zitan Wood, Painted Calligraphy Decoration, Straight Sides, Chinese, 7 In.	837.00
Brush Washer, Ebonized, Carved Dragon Handles, Applied Jade Emblem, 7 ½ x 7 In.	270.00
Brushpot, Zitan Wood, Chinese, 20th Century, 7 ¼ x 6 ⅛ In.	411.00
Bucket, Georgian, Mahogany Plate, Brass Bands, Swing Handle, Cylindrical, 17 In.	2015.00
Bucket, Kindling, Mahogany, Copper Banded, Coat-Of-Arms, Brass, Rope Handle, 13 x 16 In.	300.00
Bucket, Lehnware, Oak, Stave, 3 Bands, Turned Lid, Grain Vines, Penn., c.1840, 9 ½ In.	1880.00
Bucket, Peat, Mahogany, Brass Bands, Bail Handle, Ireland, 26 ½ In., Pair	6169.00
Bucket, Peat, Mahogany, Brass Bands, Metal Liner, Plinth, Turned Feet, 15 x 14 In.	529.00
Bucket, Peat, Regency, Mahogany, Brass Bands, Swing Handle, 13 In.	1659.00
Bucket, Pine, Painted Red, 14 In.	236.00
Bucket, Pine, Single Finger Bands, Iron Tacks, Swing Handle, Blue, c.1860, 10 x 10 In.	264.00
Bucket, Pine, Stave Construction, Bands, Escutcheons, Bail Handle, Lid, c.1875, 7 x 9 In.	1057.00
Bucket, Softwood, Splayed Vertical Staves, Metal Band, Wire Bail Handle, 10 ½ In.	305.00
Bucket, Strawberry, Oval, Twig Bands, Heart Shape Cutout Handles, Multicolored, 7 x 14 In. .	1528.00
Bucket, Sugar, Finger Bands, Copper Tacks, Bentwood Swing Handle, Blue, Murdock, 12 In. ..	529.00
Bucket, Sugar, Pine, Finger Bands, Iron Tacks, Swing Handle, Blue, 10 x 10 In.	529.00
Bucket, Sugar, Softwood, Finger Bands, Copper Tacks, Swing Handle, Black Paint, c.1890, 10 x 10 In.	235.00
Bucket, Sugar, Stave Construction, Green Paint, c.1875, 12 x 12 In.	499.00

Blind Earl Pattern

One of the famous 18th century patterns made by the Worcester pottery in England is called "Blind Earl." The pattern was first made about 1750 and has been copied many times. It was named Blind Earl for the Earl of Coventry, who lost his sight in a riding accident. It is said that he ordered dishes with a raised design of rosebuds, leaves, and butterflies so he could feel where the food was placed.

Worcester, Creamer, Double Walled, Islamic Style, Lavender Script, Chamberlaine, 4 In.
$330.00

Worcester, Serving Dish, Armorial, Pink Border, Gilt Rim, Footed, c.1840, 10 x 12 In.
$293.00

Worcester, Vase, Shell, Lizards, Seashells, Snails, 8 ½ In., Pair
$575.00

Worcester, Vase, Warwick, Enameled, Cobalt Blue, Handles, Wheel Mark, 7 x 8 In.
$960.00

World War I, Badge, Volunteers, Poultry Show, Ribbon, 1917, 4 ½ x 2 ½ In.
$345.00

World War I, Button, Victory Garden, Army Of The Furrows, Do It Now, c.1917, 1 In.
$198.00

Bucket, Teak, Lid, Plastic Liner, Skjode Skjern, Denmark, 11 In.	105.00
Bucket, Walnut, Flared, Turned Bands, Brass Mounts, 11 x 10 ¾ In.	58.00
Cage, Cricket, Bamboo, Ru Yi, Pierced, 4-Lobe Base, Jade Bead, Tassel, Chinese, 3 ¾ In.	550.00
Canteen, Blue Paint, Round, c.1800, 9 In.	250.00
Canteen, Painted, Flowers, Round Turned Beads, 4-Footed, 2 x 10 ½ In.	324.00
Card Carrier, Carved, Victorian, Clarke Bros & Co., 8 x 6 x 8 In.	77.00
Carrier, Bentwood, Lapped Seams, Blue Paint, Bail Handle, Late 1800s, 6 x 11 ¾ In.	441.00
Charger, Burl, Cherry Stain, 19 ½ In.	823.00
Cheese Coaster, Mahogany, Brass Casters, George III, c.1775, 7 x 16 x 8 In.	478.00
Cheese Tray, Mahogany, 19th Century, 8 ½ x 18 In. .....*illus*	439.00
Coffee Set, Teak, 6 Sculptural Cup, Glass Inserts, Tray, Denmark, 1960s, 11 x 8 In.	175.00
Coffin, Walnut, Cutout For Head Viewing, 12 x 52 In.	575.00
Compote, Pine, Treenware, Green, Black Over Mustard Yellow, c.1880, 8 ½ x 10 In.	705.00
Cradle, Cherry, Dovetailed, Scrolled Edges, Cutout Heart Handles, Mid 1800s, 24 x 45 In.	71.00
Cup, Cover, Edwardian, Brass Handles, Mahogany, Ringed Lion Masques, 12 x 5 In.	540.00
Cup, Cover, Poplar, Strawberry Design, Saffron, Salmon Ground, Lehnware, 4 x 2 ¼ In.	413.00
Cup, Cover, Poplar, Thistle Design, Saffron, Salmon Ground, Lehnware, 4 ¼ x 2 ¼ In.	880.00
Cup, Maple, Saffron, Joseph Lehn, c.1890, 4 ¾ In.	235.00
Dressing Case, Victorian, Calamander, Silver Fitted Interior, Mid 1800s, 3 ½ x 12 ½ In.	1342.00
Dummy Board, Robin Hood, Painted, Early 20th Century, 59 In.	269.00
Firkin, Cover, Paint, Handle, 1800s, 13 x 14 In.	235.00
Firkin, Cover, Softwood, Vertical Staves, Metal Bands, Peg Mounts, 7 ½ x 8 ½ In.	68.00
Firkin, Green Paint, Handle, 9 In.	660.00
Firkin, Softwood, Tongue & Groove Staves, Wire Bail Handle, New England, 6 ¼ In.	170.00
Firkin, Stave, Lap Hoop Construction, Blue Paint, 14 In.	1126.00
Glove Stretcher, Dog's Head Carved At Each End, Glass Eyes, 1880, 8 In.	175.00
Hopper, Pine, c.1850, 40 x 30 x 17 In.	47.00
Hourglass, Red Tartanware, Treen, Red Sand, Victorian, 6 ⅜ In.	326.00
Hourglass, Sheesham Wood, Turned, Blown Glass, Red Indian Sand, Gama Co., 7 ¼ In.	570.00
Humidor, Doghouse, Hinged Lid, Metal Dog Figure, Tin Lined, 19th Century, 13 In.	147.00
Ice Bucket, Cover, Black Plastic Liner, Damsk, IHQ, Denmark, 9 x 5 In.	75.00
Ice Bucket, Cover, Teak, Staved, Jens Quistgaard, Dansk, 14 In.	155.00
Ice Bucket, Teak, Cover, Plastic Liner, Skjode Skjern, Denmark, 14 ¾ x 9 In.	75.00
Ice Bucket, Teak, Cover, Staved, Plastic Liner, Jens Quistgaard, Dansk, 13 x 8 In.	105.00
Jar, Lid, Maple, Turned, Mustard Paint, 6 ½ x 6 ¼ In.	823.00
Jug, Ocher Grain, Painted, 1800s, 8 ½ In.	2808.00
Keg, Olive, Carved, Wrought Iron Bands, 10 In.	110.00
Lazy Susan, Georgian, Mahogany, 9 Carved Circles, England, c.1800, 5 x 22 In.	633.00
Lazy Susan, Mahogany, Turned, Round, Pedestal Base, 4 ½ x 16 In.	179.00
Log Cabin, Model, Porch, Stacked Log Fireplace, 15 ½ x 24 x 15 ½ In.	345.00
Man, Artist Model, Jointed, 36 In.	785.00
Pipe Rack, Folding, Painted, 7 Pipe Slots, England, c.1920, 6 ¼ x 18 ¾ In.	150.00
Pitcher, Oil, Carved, Boat Shape, 4 Circle Rows, Animal Head Spout, Indian, 12 ½ In.	24.00
Plate, 18th Century, 7 ¾ In.	310.00
Porridge Container, Lid, Multicolored, Norway, c.1868, 10 In.	180.00
Shoes, Dutch, c.1700	265.00
Shoeshine Stand, Lift Top Box, Black, Green Paint, c.1935, 15 x 18 In.	144.00
Stein, Burl, Carved Flowers, 3-Footed, Lid, Norway, c.1875, ½ Liter, 7 In.	518.00
Tankard, Birch Burl, Lion Thumbpiece, Bas Relief Lid, Lion Feet, c.1800, 9 In.	420.00
Tankard, Burl, Lid, Animals, Lion Thumblift, Norway, c.1775, Liter, 8 ½ In.	920.00
Tray, Bamboo, Leaf Shape, Inlaid Birds, Chinese, 12 x 9 In.	86.00
Tray, Burlwood, Glossy Finish, 2 Handles, 17 x 11 In. .....*illus*	207.00
Tray, Chestnut, Splayed Side, Cut Out Handles, Pegged Construction, 3 x 22 x 14 ½ In.	226.00
Tray, George III, Mahogany, Inlaid Urn Medallion, Brass Handles, c.1800, 25 In.	388.00
Tray, Georgian, Mahogany, Barber Pole Inlaid Rim, Round, c.1800, 9 In.	264.00
Tray, Pine, Beveled Corners, Green Paint, Cutout Handles, 3 ½ x 26 x 17 ½ In.	115.00
Tray, Pine, Tole Painted, Flowers, Green Ground, 19th Century, 27 x 17 In.	556.00
Tray, Rosewood, Knife Edge, Jens Quistgaard, Dansk, Denmark, 1960s, 20 x 16 ½ In.	575.00
Tray, Rosewood, Long Handle, Brazil, 6 x 24 In, Pair	525.00
Tray, Rosewood, Molded Ply, Scandinavian, 1960s, 20 x 11 In.	55.00
Tray, Teak, Glass, Impressed Mark, Arne Base, Denmark, c.1970, 6 x 13 In.	85.00
Tray, Teak, Jens Quistgaard, Dansk IHQ, Denmark, 22 x 16 In.	165.00
Tray, Tiger Maple, Bird's-Eye Maple, Center Handle, c.1820	350.00
Trencher, Blue Gray Paint, 19th Century, 20 In.	175.00
Trencher, Maple, Red Paint, c.1803, 22 In.	310.00
Trencher, Oval, 18th Century, 23 ½ In.	175.00

Trencher, Poplar, Oval, Shaped Handles, Gray Paint, 1800s, 6 x 16 In.	911.00
Trencher, Red Paint, Impressed, Kristi N. Soleval, 17 In.	420.00
Trencher, Tiger Maple, 9 In.	390.00
Tub, Pine, Laced Bentwood Bands, Cutout Handles, Red Paint, c.1830, 22 x 25 In.	118.00
Vase, Burl Maple, Red Leaf, Flared, Bruce Mitchell, 8 ½ x 8 In.	259.00
Vase, Kero, Painted, Flared, Diagonals, Geometric, Nazca Style, 19th Century, 3 ½ In.	316.00
Wine Cask, Wood Stand, Wrought Iron Hoops, Spigot, 1920s, 9 ½ x 6 ½ In.	395.00
Wine Rack, Bent Rosewood & Birch, Sweden, 15 x 11 ½ x 7 In.	245.00
Wine Rack, Oak, Brass, Beveled Edge, Drawer, Bun Feet, Holds 6, 1800s, 14 x 16 In. .... *illus*	527.00
Yard Ball Set, Burlwood, 4 ½-In. Ball, 6 ¾ x 22 x 5 ¾-In. Tray, 5 Piece....................	160.00

WORCESTER porcelains were made in Worcester, England, from 1751. The firm went through many name changes and eventually, in 1862, became The Royal Worcester Porcelain Company Ltd. Collectors often refer to Dr. Wall, Barr, Flight, and other names that indicate time periods or artists at the factory. It became part of Royal Worcester Spode Ltd. in 1976. The company was bought by the Portmeirion Group in 2009. Related pieces may be found in the Royal Worcester category.

Bulb Jar, Panels, Grazing Sheep, White, Gold, Demilune Shape, c.1810, 5 In., Pair................	2600.00
Card Tray, Open Basket, Handle, Shells, Coral, Flower Bouquet, Rectangular, Flat, 6 ¾ In.	504.00
Creamer, Double Walled, Islamic Style, Lavender Script, Chamberlaine, 4 In. .... *illus*	330.00
Pitcher, Cabbage Leaf, Mask, Flowers, Blue, White Ground, c.1780, 9 In.	259.00
Plate, Porcelain, Green, White, Gold, Flight, Barr & Barr, c.1813-40, 8 In.	94.00
Serving Dish, Armorial, Pink Border, Gilt Rim, Footed, c.1840, 10 x 12 In. .... *illus*	293.00
Tureen, Cover, Undertray, Armorial, Gilt, Lion Over Motto, Chamberlain, 8 x 8 In., 5 Piece	288.00
Urn, Cover, Paneled, Figures In Landscapes, Bird Shape Finials, 1760s, 14 ½ In.	374.00
Vase, Flowers, Leaves, Gilt, Bottle Shape, 12 ½ In.	72.00
Vase, Shell, Lizards, Seashells, Snails, 8 ½ In., Pair .... *illus*	575.00
Vase, Warwick, Enameled, Cobalt Blue, Handles, Wheel Mark, 7 x 8 In. .... *illus*	960.00
Wall Pocket, Cornucopia, Blue Flowers, Landscape, c.1770, 8 ½ In., Pair.......................	1755.00

WORLD WAR I and World War II souvenirs are collected today. Be careful not to store anything that includes live ammunition. Your local police will tell you how to dispose of the explosives. See also Sword and Trench Art.

WORLD WAR I

Badge, Volunteers, Poultry Show, Ribbon, 1917, 4 ½ x 2 ½ In. .... *illus*	345.00
Buckle, Medical, Cast Brass, Applied Silver Letters, MD, 2 ½ In.	71.00
Button, Victory Garden, Army Of The Furrows, Do It Now, c.1917, 1 In. .... *illus*	198.00
Buzzerphone, Type EE1-A, Signal Corps, U.S.A., c.1918, 7 x 10 In.	210.00
Calendar, Enlistment Campaign, Cardboard, Metal, 23 x 14 In.	295.00
Cartridge Case, Leather, Holds 20 Cartridges, Embossed, Rock Island Arsenal, 5 x 6 In.	145.00
Helmet, Adrian, Leather Liner, France, c.1915, 5 ½ In.	35.00
Map Carrier, Canvas, Mounted France Map, Cloth Backing, Strap, U.S. Army 29th Eng., c.1918.	83.00
Patch, Army Rank Chevron, 1st Class Infantry, Wool, Crossed Rifles, 2 ½ In.	50.00
Postcard, Soldier, Cannon, Shield, Slogans, Red, White, Blue, c.1914..............................	7.00
Poster, Food Will Win The War, U.S. Food Admin., Lithograph, c.1917, 29 ½ x 19 ½ In.	115.00
Poster, I Want You For The Navy, Recruiting, Woman In Uniform, Paper, Frame, 43 x 28 In. ..	1015.00
Poster, Red Cross, Nurse, Globe, Join The Greatest Mother, Lithograph, 30 x 20 In.	41.00
Poster, Red Cross, Nurse, Greatest Mother In The World, Lithograph, 42 x 28 In.	59.00
Relief Effort, France Needs Food, Send 50 Cents, Chicken & Egg, Cardboard, 2 ½ x 5 In.	115.00
Sheet Music, Gen. Pershing's Grand March..	5.90
Sheet Music, Hurrah For The Liberty Boys Hurrah, Marching Band Cover............................	1.18
Uniform, German Naval, Jacket, Blue Wool, 30 Brass Buttons, Emblem, Size Medium............	865.00

WORLD WAR II

Ad, Magazine, Collier's, Boeing Flying Fortress, 1943, 10 ½ x 13 ¾ In.	3.00
Armband, U.S. Army Air Force, Air Craft Warning Service, Observer, Blue, Gold.....................	10.00
Bracelet, Red, White, Blue God Bless America, Brass Chain, 7 In.	65.00
Button, Harvest For Victory, Double Duty, Couple Holding Fruit Basket, ⅞ In. .... *illus*	168.00
Button, Kilroy, Buy War Bonds, 1 ¼ In.	4.50
Button, Photo, Sailor, Color Tinted, Brass Pin, Celluloid, 2 ¾ In. .... *illus*	75.00
Flag, Nazi, Hitler Youth, 2-Sided, Red & White Stripes, Black Swastika, 46 x 67 In.	354.00
Flag, Nazi, Red, White, Black Emblem, Stamped Border, 94 x 58 In.	301.00
Glass, Remember Pearl Harbor, Clear, Red & White To Blue Design, Dec. 7, 1941, Pair...........	40.00
Gloves, Army, Green, Wool, Size Medium..	8.99
Hat, American Legion, Dunkirk, N.Y., Post 1344, Wool, Size 7 ⅛ In.	18.00
Helmet, Airman's, Luftwaffe, Leather, Wool, Ear & Throat Phones, Germany, c.1940 .... *illus*	439.00
Helmet, German, Artillery, Combat...	580.00

World War II, Button, Harvest For Victory, Double Duty, Couple Holding Fruit Basket, ⅞ In. $168.00

World War II, Button, Photo, Sailor, Color Tinted, Brass Pin, Celluloid, 2 ¾ In. $75.00

World War II, Helmet, Airman's, Luftwaffe, Leather, Wool, Ear & Throat Phones, Germany, c.1940 $439.00

TIP
Never move an object that might explode. Call the local police bomb squad. Many accidents are caused by old souvenir hand grenades and firearms.

W

World War II, Pin,
I'm Looking For Kilroy, Yellow, Red,
Celluloid, 2 ¼ In.
$211.00

World's Fair, Badge, 1933,
Chicago, Century Of Progress,
Silvered Brass, 2 ¼ In.
$184.00

World's Fair, Banner, 1939,
New York, N.T.G's Congress Of Beauty,
Felt, 24 x 33 In.
$285.00

War Souvenirs

War souvenirs can be dangerous, so if you find or are given a bullet casing, grenade, or any other supposedly safe bit of memorabilia from an armed conflict, have it checked by your local police or fire department. Souvenirs of past wars that have been stored in a hot attic are very unstable and could blow up.

Helmet, German, M35, Police Decals, Swastika Shield, Eagle, Laurel, Liner Size 56		115.00
Helmet, German, M40, Kriegsmarine, Decal, Leather Liner, Chin Strap		259.00
Helmet, German, M40, Luftwaffe, Decal		425.00
Helmet, German, M42, Civil Defense, Police, Decals, Liner, Chin Strap		173.00
Helmet, German, M42, Luftwaffe, Combat		316.00
License Topper, War Worker, Cleveland Tow Motor, Reflective, Yellow, Black, Red, 4 ½ x 11 In.		288.00
Magazine Cover, Star Weekly, Toronto, August 1, 1942, Soldier & Sailor, 11 x 15 In.		12.00
Needlework, Four Freedoms, Jan. 6, 1941, Crossed Flags, Multicolored, Frame, 10 x 13 In.		250.00
Pamphlet, U.S. Army Indoctrination, Number 21-13, War Department August 10, 1944		10.00
Pin, Army, Navy, White, Blue Ribbon, E, Laurel Wreath, Marked, 2 ¼ In.		9.00
Pin, Artillery, German, 2 ½ In.		75.00
Pin, Husband In The Service, 1 ¼ In.		10.00
Pin, I'm Looking For Kilroy, Yellow, Red, Celluloid, 2 ¼ In.	*illus*	211.00
Pin, Son In The Service, 1 ¼ In.		10.00
Pin, Sweetheart, Seabees Mascot, Sterling Silver, Blue Enamel Ground, Marked, 2 In.		45.00
Pin, To Hell With Hitler, Celluloid, White Ground, Black Lettering, 3 ½ In.		115.00
Postcard, I'm All Out For Victory		10.00
Postcard, Unused, A Royal Flush, Uncle Sam Flushing Axis Down Commode		5.50
Poster, Grow Your Own, Can Your Own, Lithograph, U.S. Government, c.1943, 22 ½ x 16 In.		104.00
Poster, Help Harvest, Join U.S. Crop Corps, War Food Administration, 1943, 20 x 28 In.		115.00
Poster, Hitler Falling Into Mud, Chariot, Mules, Cyrillic Text, Black, Brown, Russia, 1943, 29 x 22 In.		472.00
Poster, Join The U.S. Cadet Nurse Corps, Frame, 24 x 19 In.		165.00
Poster, Roosevelt, Churchill, United For Victory, Patriotic Symbols, 16 x 21 In.		101.00
Sailor Suit, U.S. Navy, Top & Bottom, Dark Blue, 1943, Size Small		175.00
Scarf, U.S. Navy, Cream Color, Stitched Emblem, 31 x 30 In.		65.00
Sign, With The U.S. Army, 2 Stars, Silver Sparkle Letters, Cardboard, 7 x 11 In.		25.00
Socks, U.S. Navy, Wool Knit, Stenciled Logano, 1943, 18 In., Pair		20.00
Utility Bag, U.S. Navy, Pull String, American Red Cross New York, 1943, 10 x 13 In.		18.00
Vest, Ammo, Khaki, Size 38-40, 1942		16.00

WORLD'S FAIR souvenirs from all of the fairs are collected. The first fair was the Great Exhibition of 1851 in London. Some other important exhibitions and fairs include Philadelphia, 1876 (Centennial); Chicago, 1893 (World's Columbian); Buffalo, 1901 (Pan-American); St. Louis, 1904 (Louisiana Purchase); Portland, 1905 (Lewis & Clark Centennial Exposition); San Francisco, 1915 (Panama-Pacific); Philadelphia, 1926 (Sesquicentennial); Chicago, 1933 (Century of Progress); Cleveland, 1936 (Great Lakes); San Francisco, 1939 (Golden Gate International); New York, 1939 (World of Tomorrow); Seattle, 1962 (Century 21); New York, 1964; Montreal, 1967; Knoxville (Energy Turns the World) 1982; New Orleans, 1984; Tsukuba, Japan, 1985; Vancouver, Canada, 1986; Brisbane, Australia, 1988; Seville, Spain, 1992; Genoa, Italy, 1992; Seoul, South Korea, 1993; Lisbon, Portugal, 1998; Hanover, Germany, 2000; and Aichi, Japan, 2005. Memorabilia of fairs include directories, pictures, fabrics, ceramics, etc. Memorabilia from other similar celebrations may be listed in the souvenir category.

Apron, 1939, New York, Cotton, Trylon & Perisphere, 40 x 62 In.		175.00
Badge, 1933, Chicago, Century Of Progress, Silvered Brass, 2 ¼ In.	*illus*	184.00
Bank, 1939, New York, Trylon & Perisphere, Tin, 12 ¼ In.		105.00
Banner, 1939, New York, N.T.G's Congress Of Beauty, Felt, 24 x 33 In.	*illus*	285.00
Button, 1904, St. Louis, Kansas, Pinback, Sunflower, Celluloid, 2 In.		30.00
Button, 1905, Portland, Lewis & Clark Centennial Exposition, Color, Logo, 1 ½ In.		115.00
Button, 1907, Norfolk, Jamestown Exposition, Multicolored, Celluloid, 2 ⅛ In.		348.00
Button, 1909, Seattle, Alaskan Yukon Pacific Exposition, Pinback, 500, 000 Portland, 1 In.		55.00
Button, 1909, Seattle, Alaskan Yukon Pacific Exposition, Pinback, You'll Like Tacoma, 1 In.		16.00
Button, 1933, Chicago, Century Of Progress, Pinback, Hello Simoniz, Celluloid, Red, Yellow, 1 In.		24.00
Button, 1933, Chicago, I Was There, Green, Red, White, ¾ In.		21.00
Button, 1933, Chicago, I'm From Chicago, Century Of Progress, Green Duck Co., Celluloid, 1 ¼ In.		10.00
Button, 1939, New York, The Dawn Of A New Day, Celluloid, 1 ¾ In.		39.00
Button, 1940, New York, General Electric Philadelphia, Blue, Gold, 1 ¾ In.		24.00
Button, 1940, New York, Puerto Rico, Map, Flag, Whitehead & Hoag Paper, 1 ½ In.		17.00
Cane Seat, 1939, New York, Decal Variation, Wood, Tripod Seat, Kan-O-Seat, 35 x 9 In.		173.00
Chair, Rocking, 1892, Chicago, Columbian Exposition, Lion Arms, Indian Crest, Italy, 18 x 43 In.		7344.00
Cup & Saucer, 1893, Chicago, Sunflower, Libbey Glass		35.00
Cup & Saucer, 1939, New York, Zodiac, Capital & Labor Exhibit, Aqua, Fiestaware, 4 x 6 In.		218.00
Earrings, 1962, Seattle, Space Needle, Box		80.00
Fan, 1904, St. Louis Expo, New Home Sewing Machine Co., 8 x 9 In.	*illus*	86.00
Figurine, 1904, St. Louis, Hat, Thomas Jefferson, Black & White Transfer, Cascade Gardens, 3 In.		65.00
Handkerchief, 1909, Seattle, Alaskan Yukon Pacific Exposition, White & Black, 17 In.		80.00
Key, 1933, Chicago, 8 ½ In.		34.00

w

License Plate, 1964, New York, Pressed Steel, 6 x 12 In.		365.00
Mug, 1876, Philadelphia, Centennial Exhibition, E Pluribus Unum, 5 x 2 ½ In.		99.00
Padlock, 1904, St. Louis, Steel, Brass, Portraits Of Indian & Jefferson, 3 ½ In.		275.00
Paperweight, 1893, Chicago, Columbian Exposition, US Glass Co., 4 ¼ x 2 ⅝ In.		110.00
Photograph, 1893, Chicago, Cold Storage House Fire, Silver Plate Frame, 5 x 5 ½ In.		60.00
Photograph Book, 1893, Chicago, Shepp's, Blue Cover, 9 x 11 In., 528 Pages		115.00
Pin, 1933, Chicago, Century Of Progress, Red Paint, Employees, Serial Number, 2 ¼ In.		201.00
Plaque, 1904, St. Louis, McKinley, Raised Silhouette, Weller, 4 ½ In.		100.00
Plaque, 1964, New York, Wood Grained Ceramic, 4 ¾ x 7 In.		29.00
Plate, 1893, Chicago, Horticulture, Pink & White, Wedgwood, 8 In.		60.00
Plate, 1893, Chicago, Santa Maria Ship, White, Opaque Glass, 7 ¾ In.		863.00
Plate, 1904, St. Louis, Palace Of Electricity, Multicolored Transfer, 8 ½ In.		53.00
Plate, 1904, St. Louis, Palace Of Manufacturers, Blue Border, Carlsbad, 7 ½ In.		100.00
Plate, 1904, St. Louis, Shield, Washington, Jefferson, Lafayette, Napoleon, Flag, 6 ½ In.		89.00
Plate, 1982, Knoxville, Tennessee		6.00
Poster, 1893, Columbian Expo, Libbey Factory, Blue Ridge Household Chemicals, 21 x 29 In.		920.00
Ribbon, 1893, Chicago, Columbian Expo, Silk, Multicolored, 7 ¼ x 2 ½ In.		90.00
Ribbon, 1905, Portland, Lewis & Clark Exposition, Image Of Dr. John McLoughlin, 2 x 8 In.		40.00
Scarf, 1909, Seattle, Alaskan Yukon Pacific Exposition, White, Pink & Blue, 17 In.		75.00
Scarf, 1964, New York, Unisphere, U.S. Steel, Square, 26 In.		85.00
Skull, 1904, St. Louis, Louisiana Purchase, Red Clay, Running Boy Weller, 1 ½ In.		575.00
Souvenir Card, 1893, Chicago, Columbian Exhibition, Oswego Corn Starch Factory, 6 x 8 In.		12.00
Spoon, 1933, Chicago		20.00
Spoon, 1933, Chicago, Silver Plate, Green Duck Co., 6 In., Pair		20.00
Stein, 1904, St. Louis, Relief Images, Cascade, Buildings, Germany, ½ Liter, 6 In.		77.00
Stein, 1904, St. Louis, Relief Images, Palace Of Liberal Arts, Blue, White, ¼ Liter		41.00
Tip Tray, 1904, St. Louis, Antikamnia Pharmacy, 3 ¼ x 4 ¾ In.		275.00
Toothpick Holder, 1893, Chicago, Columbian Coin, Frosted, Footed		85.00

WPA is the abbreviation for Works Progress Administration, a program created by executive order in 1935 to provide jobs for millions of unemployed Americans. Artists were hired to create murals, paintings, drawings, and sculptures for public buildings. Pieces are marked WPA and may have the artist's name on them.

Panel, Plaster, Architectural, Tools In Relief, Wood Mount, New Jersey, 24 In.		900.00
Print, Woven Paper, Nude Study, Edward Hagedorn, Signed, 11 x 15 In.		195.00
Tag, Brass, W.P.A. 7733		15.00

WRISTWATCHES came into use during World War I. Wristwatches are listed here by manufacturer or as advertising or character watches. Wristwatches may also be listed in other categories. Pocket watches are listed in the Watch category.

Arts & Crafts, Bracelet, Platinum, Flowers, Leaves, Windup, Edward Oaks, 6 ¾ In.		9776.00
Audemars Piguet, Diamond, Emerald, Platinum, Woman's, Art Deco, c.1930	*illus*	2160.00
Baum & Mercier, Oval Black Dial, Baton Numerals, 18K Gold Paver Band		805.00
Bertolucci, Pulchra, Gold Bezel, Stainless, Luminous, 6 Jewel, 18K Gold Links		597.00
Blancpain, 14K Rose Gold, Rubies, Diamonds, 17 Jewel, Signed, Woman's, 1940s, 6 ¾ In.		597.00
Bracelet, 18K White Gold, Sapphire, Diamond, Bezel Set, France, Woman's, c.1930s, 7 ¾ In.		2489.00
Breitling, Stainless, Date, Luminous, Leather Band, c.1809		2031.00
Bulgari, Stainless Steel, Black Dial, Abstract, Arabic Numeral, 18K Gold, 6 ⅛ In.		948.00
Cartier, 18K Gold, White Dial, Roman Numerals, Automatic, Leather Strap, 22 x 32 In.		5333.00
Cartier, 18K White Gold, Diamond Melee, Double C, Alligator Strap, Deployant Buckle, Woman's		2133.00
Cartier, White Dial, Square, Roman Numerals, 17 Jewel, Leather Strap, 14K Gold, c.1950		474.00
Character, Raggedy Ann, Red Leatherette Band, Bobbs-Merrill Co., 1971, 5 ½ In.		175.00
Character, Rudolph The Red Nosed Reindeer, Silver Luster, Vinyl, Case, Ingraham, 1940s, 5 ¾ In.		444.00
Corum, 1893 Ten Dollar Liberty Gold Coin, Reeded Rim, Diamond Crown, c.1980		1852.00
Croton, Platinum, Diamonds, Black Silk Band, Woman's		1320.00
Des Cartes Onsa, 17 Jewel, Mesh Link Band, Oval Bezel, Woman's, 6 ½ In.		288.00
Diamonds, Platinum, Ollendorf, Swiss, Woman's, c.1930, 6 ½ In.		173.00
Ebel, 18K Yellow Gold, Pink Mother-Of-Pearl, Roman Numeral, 2-Tone Band		777.00
Eddie Boiner, Flip Top, Black Band, Quartz		240.00
Gruen, 14K Yellow Gold, Stepped Bezel, 17 Jewel, Leather, 1930s		1016.00
Hamilton, 10K Gold, Lizard Band, c.1930		310.00
Hamilton, 14K White Gold, Diamond Bezel, 17 Jewel, Woman's, 1940s, 6 In.		358.00
Hamilton, 14K Yellow Gold, Piping, Roman Numerals, 17 Jewel, Leather, c.1937		1075.00
Hamilton, Gold Filled, Dome Crystal, Rectangular, Leather Band, 1940s		140.00
Hamilton, Manual, 19 Jewel, 14K Yellow Gold Case		141.00

World's Fair, Fan, 1904, St. Louis Expo, New Home Sewing Machine Co., 8 x 9 In. $86.00

Wristwatch, Audemars Piguet, Diamond, Emerald, Platinum, Woman's, Art Deco, c.1930 $2160.00

Wristwatch, Vacheron Constantin, Patrimony, Grand Taille, 18K Gold Case, Leather Strap
$5520.00

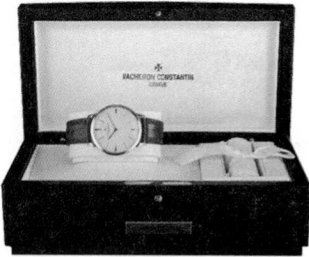

Zsolnay, Jardiniere, Leaf Buttresses, Lustered Glaze, c.1900, 6 ½ x 8 In.
$6000.00

Zsolnay, Vase, Brown, Tan, Mottled Glaze, Incised Flowers, Eosin Glaze, 6 x 8 In.
$840.00

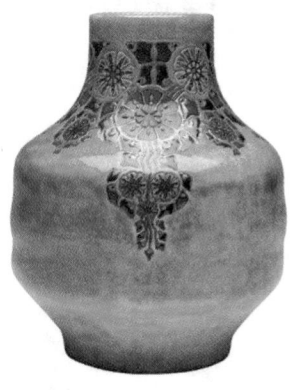

Hamilton, Platinum, 65 Diamonds, 17 Jewel, Manual Wind	575.00
Hamilton, Platinum, Diamond Dial, 19 Jewel, Lizard, White Metal, c.1940	1912.00
Hamilton, Ventura, 14K Yellow Gold, Gold & Black Toned Leather, c.1957	2629.00
Hamilton, Whitney, 17 Jewel, Shadow Numerals, Leather Band, c.1932, 1 ¼ x 1 ¼ In.	425.00
Hermes, Bangle, Hinged, Stainless Steel, Enamel, Helios In Chariot, Black Ground, 6 ¾ x 2 ½ In.	444.00
Hot Wheels, Chrome Metal Case, Vinyl Band, Plastic Case, c.1971	253.00
International Watch Co., 14K Yellow Gold, 17 Jewel, Lizard Band, c.1950	777.00
LeCoultre, 14K Yellow Gold, Octagon Bezel, Roman Numerals, 17 Jewel, Leather, 1960s	478.00
LeCoultre, Memovox Alarm, 10K Gold Filled, 17 Jewel, Alligator Band, c.1950	508.00
Longines, Diamond Bezel Surround, 18K Gold, Gray, Green Enamel, Wreaths, Woman's, 7 In.	2990.00
Longines, Gold Filled, Rectangular, Black Leather Band, 1950s	190.00
Movado, Platinum, Diamond, 17 Jewel	1093.00
Neiman Marcus, 14K Gold, 17 Jewel, 8 Diamonds, Lusina Watch, Swiss, Woman's	920.00
Omega, 14K Yellow Gold, Constellation Automatic, Date, Leather Band, c.1958	1075.00
Omega, 14K Yellow Gold, Mosaic Opal, Scalloped Bezel, Dauphine Hands, 7 In., c.1975	2151.00
Omega, 17 Jewel, No. 300, Rectangular, Leather Band, c.1944	325.00
Omega, Aviator, Stainless, Airplane Logo, 17 Jewel, Steel Link, c.1972	1912.00
Omega, Constellation Chronometer, Date, Stainless, 24 Jewel, 1960s	1195.00
Omega, Constellation, Quartz, 18K Yellow Gold, Black Leather, c.1973	3000.00
Omega, Moon, 17 Jewel, Steel, Deployant Clasp, c.1970	1314.00
Omega, Seamaster, 14K Gold, Leather Band	720.00
Overton, Art Deco, Diamond, Ruby, 14K Yellow Gold Basket Weave Band, 7 In.	2300.00
Patek Philippe, 18K Yellow Gold, 18 Jewel, Signed, Woman's, 1950s, 6 ½ In.	1314.00
Patek Philippe, Blue Dial, Bark Textured Case & Bracelet, 18K White Gold, 7 ¼ In.	2151.00
Patek Philippe, Ivorytone Metal Dial, Baton Numerals, 20 Jewel, 18K Gold, Woman's, 6 ¼ In.	1009.00
Platinum, Diamond, Bezel, Lugs Set, Tiffany & Co., Art Deco	2370.00
Protex, Platinum, Diamond, Arabic Numerals, Woven Silk Strap, Art Deco, Woman's	388.00
Rolex, 17 Jewel, 14K Yellow Gold, Diamonds, Woman's, c.1970	836.00
Rolex, 18K Yellow Gold, Alpha Hands, 18 Jewel, Integral Band, Woman's, c.1960	896.00
Rolex, 18K Yellow Gold, Date, Sapphire Crystal, Pearlmaster, Link Band, Woman's	2400.00
Rolex, Bubbleback, 18K Gold, Bezel, Box, c.1945	12000.00
Rolex, Bubbleback, 18K Yellow Gold, Dauphine Hands, Leather Band, c.1950	2390.00
Rolex, Oyster Perpetual Datejust, Jubilee Dial, Bracelet, Diamond Numeral, Automatic	2370.00
Rolex, Stainless Steel, Oyster, 17 Jewel, Riveted Steel Link Band, c.1949	1075.00
Rolex, Stainless Steel, Oyster, Chronograph, 3 Metal Dials, Goldtone Dart, 17 Jewel	17775.00
Rolex, Stainless Steel, Oyster, Perpetual, 25 Jewel, Foldover Link Band, c.1950	1015.00
Speedmaster, Stainless, 17 Jewel, Steel Link Band, c.1974	956.00
Tiffany & Co., 14K Yellow Gold, Diamond, Rectangular Case, Stick Markers, Woman's, 6 ½ In.	1673.00
Tiffany & Co., Silvertone Dial, Arabic Numerals, Platinum, Diamonds, Art Deco, Woman's	3555.00
Vacheron Constantin, 18K Gold, Silvered Dial, Roman Numerals, Leather Band	2185.00
Vacheron Constantin, Patrimony, Grand Taille, 18K Gold Case, Leather Strap .... *illus*	5520.00
Vulcain, Art Deco, Sterling Silver, Brushed Chrome Face, Black Leather Snakeskin Band, 9 In.	173.00

YELLOWWARE is a heavy earthenware made of a yellowish clay. It varies in color from light yellow to orange-yellow. Many nineteenth- and twentieth-century kitchen bowls and jugs were made of yellowware. It was made in England and in the United States. Another form of pottery that is sometimes classed as yellowware is listed in this book in the Mocha category.

Beater Jar, Green & Brown Sponge	45.00
Bowl, Blue, 11 In.	45.00
Bowl, Brown & White Bands, 5 In.	17.50
Bowl, Green & Brown Glaze, Beehive Shape, Ohio, 19th Century, 8 In.	125.00
Bowl, Rolled Lip, Rockingham Glaze, 7 ¾ x 4 In.	195.00
Cup & Saucer, Yellow Glaze, 2 x 3 ⅝ In. & 5 ¾ In.	22.00
Figurine, Dog, Spaniel, Mottled, Brown Glaze, c.1850, 9 ¾ In.	201.00
Figurine, Lion, Reclining, Incised Mane, Rockingham, Manganese Glaze, Oval Base, 8 x 15 x 9 In.	995.00
Figurine, Spaniel, Rockingham Glaze, East Liverpool, Ohio, c.1860, 10 In.	385.00
Figurine, Spaniel, Rockingham Glaze, Separate Front Legs, 9 ½ In.	411.00
Flask, Basket Weave, Rockingham Glaze, C.C. Thompson, Ohio, 1890-1915, 6 In.	195.00
Mixing Bowl, Brown & White Banding, 7 ½ x 16 ½ In.	110.00
Mixing Bowl, Wide Band At Top, 5 ½ In.	80.00
Mold, Cake, Turk's Head, Sponged, 7 ¼ x 2 ¾ In.	145.00
Mold, Corn, 6 x 4 ½ x 3 In.	145.00
Mold, Jelly, Round, Round Panels, Interior Yellow Glaze, 1 ⅜ x 2 ¾ In.	33.00
Mustard Pot, Cover, Green Seaweed, Applied Handle, Finial On Lid, 2 ¼ x 3 ⅛ In.	358.00
Nappy, Brown, Caramel, Flared Sides, Rockingham Glaze, c.1900, 2 ¾ In.	150.00

Pitcher, Barrel Form, Applied Handle, Green Glaze, 8 x 5 In. 165.00
Planter, Pear Shape, 3 ½ x 2 In. 40.00

ZANE Pottery was founded in 1921 by Adam Reed and Harry McClelland in South Zanesville, Ohio, at the old Peters and Reed Building. Zane pottery is very similar to Peters and Reed pottery, but it is usually marked. The factory was sold in 1941 to Lawton Gonder.

Flowerpot, Hanging, Ivory & Yellow, Ink Mark, Zane Ware, 5 x 8 ⅝ In. 185.00
Vase, Ivory & Yellow, Trunk Appearance, Leaves At Top Section, Ink Mark, Zane Ware, 8 In. 150.00
Vase, Watery Matte Green, Dripped Over Dark Matte Green, Impressed Mark, 8 ¾ In. 375.00

ZANESVILLE Art Pottery was founded in 1900 by David Schmidt in Zanesville, Ohio. The firm made faience umbrella stands, jardinieres, and pedestals. The company closed in 1962. Many pieces are marked with just the words *La Moro*.
LA MORO

Bean Pot, Cover, Cornflower Blue, Incised, 3 x 2 ½ In. 45.00
Bowl, Dog, Brown, 2 x 6 In. 36.00
Candlestick, Glass Rose, Hooked Handle, 1926 .... 95.00
Jardiniere, Blue, 5 ¾ x 6 ¾ In. 75.00
Planter, Duck, Runny Green Glaze Over Yellow, 5 ½ x 4 In. 45.00
Planter, Semigloss Green Glaze, ZSC, c.1950, 5 x 6 In. 34.00
Teapot, Rose, 7 ½ In. 100.00
Vase, Bud, Long Neck, Pedestal Base, Aqua, 6 x 3 ½ In. 30.00
Vase, Creamy Matte Glaze, 9 ½ x 5 In. 35.00
Vase, Flared Geometric Shape, Gloss Rose, 6 In. 40.00
Vase, Flared Shell Shape, High Gloss Pink, Low Handles, 5 In. 60.00
Vase, Flat, Stubby Handles, Glaze Drips, Skips, Seacrest Green, 6 x 5 In. 35.00
Vase, Green Gloss Glaze, Triangular, 4 x 5 In. 35.00
Vase, High Neptune, Heart Shape Opening, Blue, Brown, 4 In. 75.00
Vase, Raised Flower Design, Aqua Gloss, 8 ½ x 4 ¾ In. 77.00
Vase, Ruffled Rim, Aqua, Runny Glaze, 8 x 3 ¼ In. 75.00
Vase, Shell Shape, White, 7 ½ In. 60.00

ZSOLNAY pottery was made in Hungary after 1853 and was characterized by Persian, Art Nouveau, or Hungarian motifs. A series of new Zsolnay figurines with green-gold luster finish is available in many shops today. Early Zsolnay was not marked, but by 1878 the tower trademark was used.

Bowl, Flowers, Blue, White, Gilt, Crimped Border, Late 19th Century, 8 In. 84.00
Bowl, Red & Gray Iridescent Glaze, Hammered Design, Marked, 7 ½ In. 690.00
Box, Cover, Round, Iridescent, Carved Egyptian Style Figures, After 1925 .... 395.00
Figurine, Genie Flambe, R. Tabbenor, 9 ¾ In. 196.00
Figurine, Goat Boy, Iridescent, Signed, 9 x 7 In. 300.00
Jar, Cover, Persian, 5-Church Medallion, 11 x 5 ¼ In. 1464.00
Jardiniere, Leaf Buttresses, Lustered Glaze, c.1900, 6 ½ x 8 In. ....*illus* 6000.00
Pitcher, Flowers, Leaves, Yellow, Brown, Handle, Blue Mark, 1880, 12 In. 2000.00
Pitcher, Iridescent Green To Gold, Impressed Mark, 9 ¾ In. 805.00
Tile, Green Eosin Glaze, Raised, Molded, Pyrogranite, 9 ⅛ x 9 ⅛ In. 490.00
Urn, Green Marbleized Gold Glaze, Footed, Dimpled, Serpent Handles, 1930, 12 ¾ x 9 ½ In. .. 960.00
Vase, 2 Handles, Iridescent Blue Glaze, Marked, 6 ¾ In. 834.00
Vase, Allegory Of The Flood, Figures Reach To Maiden, Metallic Green, c.1900, 25 In. 10800.00
Vase, Brown, Tan, Mottled Glaze, Incised Flowers, Eosin Glaze, 6 x 8 In. ....*illus* 840.00
Vase, Building, Boat, Landscape, Marked, 12 ⅜ In. 4600.00
Vase, Cornucopia, Cream Peach, Yellow Flowers, Enamel, Gilt, Mark, 1900s, 9 In. 115.00
Vase, Crocuses, Swirled Ground, Cylindrical Faience, 1886, 13 ½ x 5 ½ In. 3600.00
Vase, Osiris, Art Deco, Ceramic, Red, Green Flowers, Pewter Mount, Handles, 9 x 16 In. 2280.00
Vase, Red & Green Eosin Glazes, Cutout Openwork Base, 3 Handles, Marked, 5 x 9 ½ In. 9600.00
Vase, Red Flowers, Turquoise, Marked, 2 ½ x 3 In. 1800.00
Vase, Reticulated Top Section, Yellow Flowers, 2 Handles, Footed, c.1900, 8 In. 650.00
Vase, Shouldered, Red Flowers, Marked, 2 ½ x 3 In. ....*illus* 1800.00
Vase, Tree, Rocks, Sailboat, Red Iridescent, Gold Glaze, Oval, Marked, 5 ¼ x 3 In. 2150.00

Zsolnay, Vase, Shouldered, Red Flowers, Marked, 2 ½ x 3 In. $1800.00

Never Too Much Shopping
Have a bad day? Psychologists have proven that shopping is one way to combat depression. Cheer up. Rummage through some antiques for sale. You can even stay at home and look via your computer. Collecting can make you happy.

INDEX

This index is computer-generated, making it as complete and accurate as possible. References in uppercase type are category listings. Those in lowercase letters refer to additional pages where pieces can be found. There is also an internal cross-referencing system used in the main part of the book, so if you look for a Kewpie doll in the Doll category, you will be told it is in its own category. There is additional information at the end of many paragraphs about where to find prices of pieces similar to yours.

PICTURE CREDITS
Allard Auctions 51, 361-368, 611,
  640
Arabia 27
Aspire Auctions 28, 35, 37, 50,
  55-57, 80-81, 88, 90, 93-96, 108,
  110, 113-115, 124, 127, 136,
  138, 146-148, 157, 160, 168-
  169, 172, 201, 212, 215, 224,
  234-235, 262, 272, 277, 291,
  298-300, 302, 304, 316, 321,
  333, 335, 338-339, 354, 366,
  371, 377-382, 384-388, 396,
  398-399, 403, 405-406, 408,
  416, 427-428, 432, 437, 439,
  443, 456, 460, 464, 466-468,
  477, 489-490, 500, 506-510,
  512-516, 522-523, 527, 547,
  550, 554, 558-560, 573-575,
  578-579, 585, 587-595, 601-605,
  609, 612, 621, 633, 635-636,
  644, 650-653, 657, 664, 692,
  695, 698-702, 710, 721-723
Belhorn Auction Services 2, 98,
  164, 234, 340, 344, 355-356,
  435, 459, 481, 548, 554, 557,
  561, 614, 696, 704, 712-713, 716
Bertoia Auctions 112, 136-137,
  202, 209-210, 682, 684
Bonhams 429, 431
Brown Auction Services 2, 658-661
Brunk Auctions 16, 29, 46-47,
  50-51, 58, 86-89, 94-95, 97, 108,
  110, 115, 132, 140, 146-147,
  160-161, 172, 178, 186, 213,
  215, 222-224, 236-240, 243-
  247, 249-255, 257-272, 274,
  276-277, 279, 281, 283-285,
  291-294, 301-302, 304-315,
  318, 320-321, 324, 327, 362,
  368-369, 371, 385, 388, 392,
  436, 456, 471, 478, 489, 491-
  492, 494, 514, 530, 537-538,
  545, 566-568, 574, 576-577,
  581, 590-594, 596-600, 605,
  613, 622, 624-627, 633, 635,
  651, 655, 662, 694, 703
Cincinnati Art Galleries 1, 25, 99,
  104, 106, 150, 164, 173-174, 235,
  334, 337-338, 375, 389, 421-422,
  433, 446, 450-451, 459, 468-469,
  480, 490, 513, 539-542, 544,
  548-550, 558, 560, 621, 623, 709,
  712-714, 716, 719
Collect.com 527
Conestoga Auction Co. 39, 46-47,
  137, 162, 169, 220, 227-228,
  328, 348, 390-391, 393, 403,
  410-415, 444, 462, 487, 522,
  531, 536-537, 570, 580, 605-
  607, 609, 624, 626, 630, 654,
  656, 659, 692-693, 707